HISTORY
OF
HUMANITY

History of Humanity

Volume I   *Prehistory and the Beginnings of Civilization*

ISBN 92-3-102810-3 (UNESCO)
ISBN 0-415-09305-8 (Routledge)

Volume II   *From the Third Millenium to the Seventh Century BC*

ISBN 92-3-102811-1 (UNESCO)
ISBN 0-415-09306-6 (Routledge)

Volume III   *From the Seventh Century BC to the Seventh Century AD*

ISBN 92-3-102812-X (UNESCO)
ISBN 0-415-09307-4 (Routledge)

Volume IV   *From the Seventh to the Sixteenth Century*

ISBN 92-3-102813-8 (UNESCO)
ISBN 0-415-09308-2 (Routledge)

Volume V   *From the Sixteenth to the Eighteenth Century*

ISBN 92-3-102814-6 (UNESCO)
ISBN 0-415-09309-0 (Routledge)

Volume VI   *The Nineteenth Century*

ISBN 92-3-102815-4 (UNESCO)
ISBN 0-415-09310-4 (Routledge)

Volume VII   *The Twentieth Century*

ISBN 92-3-102816-2 (UNESCO)
ISBN 0-415-09311-2 (Routledge)

In memory of Paulo E. de Berrêdo Carneiro,
President of the first International Commission
for a Scientific and Cultural History of Mankind
as well as of the present Commission, 1979–82.

HISTORY OF HUMANITY

Volume I
Prehistory and the Beginnings of Civilization

EDITED BY

S. J. De Laet

CO-EDITED BY

A. H. Dani
J. L. Lorenzo
R. B. Nunoo

First published in 1994
by the United Nations Educational, Scientific and Cultural Organization
7 Place de Fontenoy, 75352 Paris 07 SP
and
Routledge
11 New Fetter Lane, London EC4P 4EE

Simultaneously published in the USA and Canada
by Routledge
a division of Routledge, Chapman and Hall, Inc.
29 West 35th Street, New York, NY 10001

© UNESCO 1994

Typeset by Selwood Systems, Midsomer Norton
Printed in Great Britain by Clay Ltd, St Ives plc

∞ Printed on acid-free paper

Index compiled by Indexing Specialists
202 Church Road, Hove, East Sussex BN3 2DJ

Authors are responsible for the choice and the presentation
of the facts contained in this book and for the opinions
expressed therein, which are not necessarily those
of UNESCO and do not commit the Organization.

The designations employed and the presentation of material
throughout this publication do not imply the expression of
any opinion whatsoever on the part of UNESCO concerning
the legal status of any country, territory, city or area or of
its authorities, or concerning the delimitation of its frontiers
or boundaries.

The International Commission for the History of the Scientific
and Cultural Development of Mankind bears intellectual
and scientific responsibility for the preparation of
this new edition.

Generic names containing the word 'man' (e.g. Peking Man)
should be understood to refer to both sexes of the species.

British Library Cataloguing in Publication Data
A catalogue record for this book is available on request

Library of Congress Cataloging in Publication Data
A catalogue record for this book is available on request

ISBN 92-3-102810-3 (UNESCO)
ISBN 0-415-09305-8 (Routledge)

PREFACE

Federico Mayor
Director-General of UNESCO

'Our civilization is the first to have for its past the past of the world, our history is the first to be world history.'[1] As we approach the year 2000, the phenomenon described over fifty years ago by Jan Huizinga becomes an ever more sensible reality. In a bounded and increasingly interconnected world, we necessarily find ourselves a part of that emerging global civilization that constitutes the matrix of our collective destinies.

The years immediately following the Dutch historian's assertion were indeed to illustrate, and in the most horrific manner, the interdependence of the world community. The planet on which millions of humans wished for nothing more than to live in peace and well-being presented the unnatural spectacle of a world at war. Land, sea and air routes were patrolled day and night by armadas venting fury on all that was most precious and vital to the inhabitants. The dreadful hurt that the populations sustained, physically and morally, dispelled *in perpetuum* a number of illusions and faced humanity with a stark choice – that of being, in the words of Albert Einstein, 'one or none'.

Thenceforth the grave danger attendant on inter-racial, and consequently inter-cultural, ignorance was conspicuous to thinking minds. A flawed consciousness of our common humanity must be incompatible with the survival of a world armed with knowledge of such awesome potential. Clearly the only course of action, the only way forward lay in building bridges between peoples, in forging a resilient awareness of the unity inherent in human diversity.

Such was the background to UNESCO's decision in 1947 to produce a truly universal work of international co-operation that would provide 'a wider understanding of the scientific and cultural aspects of the history of mankind and of the mutual interdependence of peoples and cultures and of their contributions to the common heritage'.[2] That initiative, which was one of UNESCO's earliest projects, sprang from the Organization's fundamental priciples and was widely acclaimed, although not a few saw in it a Sisyphean undertaking at which past attempts had signally failed.

Three years later, in 1950, the first International Commission for a History of the Scientific and Cultural Development of Mankind began the task of fashioning a history that – in the words of René Maheu – would 'present to man the sum total of his memories as a coherent whole'. As the distinguished international team of collaborators took shape and as the first results of its work began to appear in the Commission's review the *Journal of World History*, it became clear that new ground was being broken in pursuit of this ambitious goal. When some fifteen years later the first edition began to appear in six languages, the reception accorded to the work confirmed – some inevitable reservations apart – the success of this 'first attempt to compose a universal history of the human mind from the varying standpoints of memory and thought that characterize the different contemporary cultures'.

The compilers of the first edition of the *History of Mankind* were conscious that all historiography is 'work in progress', that in the continuous flux of history nothing is fixed, neither facts nor interpretations. In 1969, Paulo de Berrêdo Carneiro declared: 'The day will come when what we have written . . . will, in its turn, have to be replaced. I like to think that our successors will attend to this, and that a revised edition of the work we have begun may be published at the dawn of a new millennium.'

That day is now with us. The General Conference of UNESCO decided in 1978 that the work should be revised, and two years later the Second International Commission met to formulate its aims.

Much has changed since the publication of the first edition. In recent years, the historical sciences have been enriched by contributions from many disciplines, giving rise to new methods of investigation and bringing to light new facts, particularly in the realm of 'prehistory'. At the same time, a heightened awareness of cultural identity has intensified the demand for a corresponding decentralization of historical viewpoints and interpretaions. UNESCO has both heeded and nurtured this trend by undertaking a series of regional histories, one of which – *The General History of Africa* – is on the point of completion while others are in active preparation. Finally, history itself has moved on, altering in the process the perspectives from which the past is viewed.

For all these reasons and to take account of some valid criticisms of the original version, it was decided that the new edition to be called simply the *History of Humanity*, should not be merely a revision, but rather a radical recasting

---

1 HUIZINGA, J. 1936. A Definition of the Concept of History. In: KLIBANSKY, R.; PATON, H. J. (eds), *Philosophy and History*. Oxford. p. 8.
2 UNESCO. 1947. *General Conference; Second Session*. Paris. Resolution 5.7.

of its predecessor. Its goal – to provide an account of the history of humanity in terms of its varied cultural and scientific achievements – remains unchanged, but the view it offers of its subject is – it is hoped – more detailed, more diverse and broader in scope.

Ten years after the launching of the project, it is my privilege to present this new *History* which has built upon and extended the pioneering work of those dedicated scholars responsible for the first edition. I should like to express my admiration and deep gratitude to the members of the Second International Commission and to the some 450 distinguished specialists from all geocultural backgrounds who have contributed to this historic undertaking. Readers will, I feel sure, make known their own views in the years to come. In committing this work to their scrutiny, the International Commission – and, through it, UNESCO – is taking the final step in the task entrusted to it by the community of Member States represented at the General Conference. Each of us, I am sure, stands to benefit from this concerted testimony to our common past and act of faith in our shared future.

CONTENTS

FOREWORD

Among the great tasks assigned to UNESCO by the Constitution is the duty to promote and encourage mutual knowledge and understanding throughout the world. While many of the divergencies which divide people date from a distant past, an analysis of their historical antecedents discloses links which draw them nearer to one another, brings to light their contributions to a common patrimony of humanity, reveals the ebb and flow of cultural exchanges and emphasizes their increasing tendency to become integrated into an international community.

This is how Paulo E. de Berrêdo Carneiro, President of the International Commission (1952–69), expressed himself in the opening paragraph of the Preface to the *History of the Scientific and Cultural Development of Mankind* in 1963. Today, it would be difficult to say anything about humanity's 'increasing tendency to become integrated into an international community', unless an attempt is made to assess the outcome of this 'tendency' as reflected in the state of the world since. Today, few events remain local. Information on any minor or major occurrence is communicated to almost everyone immediately and an action undertaken in one part of the world inevitably has its repercussions on the others. Those who experience fully this 'planetarization' sense the 'integration' of all human beings into an international community less as a 'tendency' than as a *fait accompli*. But what about the subordinates who are more or less associated or the vast excluded majority of people? These others, put the question in completely different terms. What they seem to ask is: can a 'common patrimony of humanity' be achieved solely through an integration based on scientific and technical developments? What then can we do to ensure an equal access to such means for all when the more fundamental task of reducing existing differences in the very standards of living lags far behind?

The idea of writing a history of the development of humankind was first put forward by Julian Huxley, the Executive Secretary of the Preparatory Commission of UNESCO. In 1946 Huxley wrote that 'the chief task before the Humanities today would seem to be to help in constructing a history of the development of the human mind, notably in its highest cultural achievements'. He underscored the major role that historians would play in the realization of what he called a 'gigantic enterprise'. Huxley later outlined a project which was to be submitted to the future UNESCO.

In 1950, in accordance with a resolution passed by the General Conference of UNESCO, an International Commission was set up and the publication of a *History of the Scientific and Cultural Development of Mankind* in six volumes was approved. The first volume appeared in 1963.

What was this 'gigantic enterprise', conceived by Huxley worth? Critics received the volumes more often badly than well. They did not question the data included. What they objected to mainly were the criteria of the selection of data and the interpretations offered. Yet a closer look at these criticisms revealed that, skilled as they were at pointing out certain flaws and misconceptions, these commentators hardly ever came up with concrete suggestions that would lead to any improvement of the work in the future. On the whole, however, we were left with the impression that, notwithstanding its shortcomings, a very large number of readers found the work commendable, particularly as a first step towards the achievement of an 'essential task'.

No elucidation, rational or otherwise, of the origins or the evolution of human beings can be offered once and for all, as if by divine revelation. Writing a history of the development of humankind necessarily constitutes a work that one has to return to over and over again. Nearly thirty years passed by before UNESCO decided to take up once more a work that could by no means be regarded as finished. Requested by the new Member States, a recasting of the first edition deserved the wholehearted support of all those who helped establish the Organization. The changes which have taken place over these last thirty years rendered necessary and amply justified a revision and revaluation of history, and the members of the International Commission were the first to acknowledge such a need. There were, of course, other and more imperative reasons. Two of these should be pointed out here.

The first concerns the developments in the area of research methodology since the 1960s. Over the last three decades historical knowledge has increased considerably and has turned from factual history to greater interest in anthropological research. Although they still remain far from being fully capable of answering all the questions that we ask today – or for that matter the more serious of those posed thirty years ago – the added insight that present studies offer us deserves to be transmitted to a larger public. The second, and perhaps less obvious, reason springs from the very role that the writing of history can, and is meant to, play in increasing our level of awareness. A writing or, as in the present case, a rewriting of the history of human scientific and cultural evolution signifies not only taking stock of the new data available but also helping one and all in evaluating and assessing the various implications, positive and also negative, of all the changes. Justifying science in the name of all its benefits and advantages amounts to refusing to accept the damaging effects it can have. We have gradually accustomed ourselves to the presence of many latent nuclear volcanoes without compensating for the technological risks. Not enough has been done to counterbalance the excessive monetary investments needed to build up such arsenals with sufficient funds to help confront the problems and miseries afflicting one section of humanity and which is on the way to becoming a danger for the other. Technological development has also begun seriously to endanger animal and plant life on this planet. Factors such as these plead for greater vigilance.

Universal histories and histories of the world abound. So many have already been published and continue to be published that one could question the need to bring out yet another one. No doubt many readers will be surprised at this venture. Each in his own way will of course judge this work better or worse than another of its kind. There is however one major difference. Other works of history enjoy a certain freedom that has in a sense been denied to the present one. They are free to choose themes, periods and regions that suit best the demands of a particular readership and a specific conception of history. Such works can thereby claim a certain cohesion of the elements introduced; a cohesion which also helps establish a certain uniformity of expression and style. The present work is founded on an entirely different principle: a maximum of diversity. This diversity proves to be, on the one hand, so great that it is difficult to stop it from becoming disparate and, on the other, not great enough to allow for a convenient regrouping of elements into types. The fault lies not in the venture itself nor in those who took up the task. It lies mainly in the present state of historical knowledge. The analytic nature of historical research today blocks the way to synthesis, to the kind of approach required in the writing of a history that can be considered truly universal.

This work can serve only as a history of the world and not as a universal history. This, of course, is already a great deal. We should not count on the diffusion of a universalism, which is the subject of reflection by a very small, privileged minority, as long as all cultures are not equally represented and historians from all parts of the world are not endowed with the same means and cannot claim the same status, social and otherwise.

Not claiming to attain the unattainable does not, however, mean renunciation. The roads to universalism are full of bends and curves. But, they all lead to the same destination: one history for one united world. Since this history could not reach the highest common factor, it had to tend towards the lowest common multiple. And in this respect, the present work has not failed in its mission.

In 1950 we opted in three days for a plan that would take thirteen years to complete. With a view to ensuring a unity of style and presentation, we decided that each of the six volumes would be written by a single author. Such ideas had to be abandoned. Some thirty years later, the New Commission decided to take more time over the distribution of the work to be done among seven and not six volumes, each well co-ordinated with the other and allowing free play to as many authors as would be necessary to cover a maximum of domains. The selection of the criteria on which the new history would be based first led to a detailed examination of the comments made by the readers of the first edition. After many debates and discussions, all agreed that it would not do simply to juxtapose a series of regional histories one after the other. Then one of the two possible solutions had to be chosen: dividing history either into themes or into periods and analysing each according to themes and regions. The first option – an idea that had already been put forward before 1948 – would perhaps have helped bring out in a more significant manner the factors which render manifest the common destiny of mankind. But the present state of historical research, which in most cases and owing to an ever-increasing acquisition of skills, proceeds in the form of temporal as well as regional specializations, constituted a real obstacle to the realization of such a scheme. It was therefore decided that each of the seven volumes would be devoted to a single period and would contain a thematic and a regional section.

Yielding to the constraints imposed by the state of knowledge and research today does not, however, solve all probable problems. Let us take a look at the issue point by point.

The idea of splitting up into periods a past that the mission of all historians is to revive as an organic whole pleased no one. But, taking everything into consideration, had the objective been to separate one cultural component from another or, for example, the physical from the cultural or the religious from the profane, this surgery would have turned literally into a vivisection. Opting for the lesser evil, the Commission thus decided to work on chronological sections. This, at least, allowed for the preservation of a certain unity within each group.

Already in the 1950s it had become evident that the form of periodization upheld by the European tradition loses its signification when applied to the other parts of the world. Terms such as 'Antiquity', 'the Middle Ages' or 'modern times' do not correspond to much in so far as Asia is concerned, and perhaps even less for what concerns Africa. Admittedly we continue using such words for the sake of convenience. We cannot totally discard them, but we should try at least not to trust them fully.

The importance of each period is measured more in terms of what humankind has contributed to each than in terms of a duration defined by astronomy. The 'Grand Discoveries' of the sixteenth and the seventeenth centuries led to some spectacular changes in the history of the world. A sudden growth of ideas and of commercial capitalism accompanied by or resulting from military conquests gave rise to migrations that brought about the creation of a new map of the world and new conceptions of humanity's destiny. This moment marks a turning point that we have ever since sensed as an acceleration of history. It was, therefore, decided that three volumes of the present work would be devoted to the period succeeding these significant changes and transformations as against only four which would cover the entire preceding period, starting from the origins of humankind and leading up to the sixteenth century. The Commission also decided to devote more and more pages to the more and more recent years. The fifth volume thus covers three centuries; the sixth, one and a half; and the seventh only about seventy-five years.

A word of caution is, however, necessary. We often make use of a concept of progress that is based on the quantitative and not the qualitative value of what has been achieved. Manufactured goods, consumer items and exchanges, whether they concern concrete objects or ideas, can be more or less quantified. But, as we do not possess any means of measuring happiness or well-being, we cannot infer therefrom that the quantitative and the qualitative values of this progress are the same, particularly in so far as the world in general is concerned. This notion of progress should not, moreover, hinder a proper appraisal of all that was contributed to history by our ancestors, to whom we owe our existence and our way of living.

Great care was taken to avoid putting an undue emphasis on what could be considered as being only the European landmarks of history. The years 1789 and 1914, although highly significant in the history of Europe, served only nominally as points of reference. It was understood that, depending on the case, the ethnocentrism implied by these dates would be reduced as much as necessary through a proper and adequate treatment of the issues preceding or following them. Similarly, to avoid falling into the traps of Western traditionalism, it was considered necessary to cease using the Christianization of the Roman Empire as a mark of the end of the Ancient World and the beginning of the Middle Ages and, therefore, to include the first years of the Hegira in the third volume, which covers the period from 700 BC to AD 700, the middle of which comes before the beginning of the era acknowledged – belatedly – also by the Muslims.

The Commission's choice does not conflict very much with the Chinese system of dating, because around the same epoch the same phenomenon appeared in both the east and west of Eurasia: the awakening of tribes in these Central Steppes who until then had been restricted to a disorderly, Brownian form of movement of particular groups, henceforth united together and set off to conquer the largest empire that the world has ever known. Events such as this draw our attention to the advantages of following a calendar determined not according to the permanent aspects of the planets but according to the variations of climate. Indeed, the Mongols would not have reached such a high degree of power had the climate not favoured the humidification of the pasture lands which nourished their horses. However, it will be a good while before we have available a calendar based on climatic variations. We still lack information on some vital factors: the evaluation of harvests, the extension or the regression of lacustrine and forest areas, phytographical analyses, etc. Only when we have obtained such necessary data can we think of establishing a new type of periodization that can be verified through metereological calculations extrapolating and applying to the past our present conjectures about the influence of solar explosions on the atmosphere.

The period to be treated in the fourth volume was therefore set by the end of Volume III (the seventh century) and the beginning (the sixteenth century) of Volume V. Volumes I and II have been devoted to the many thousands of years constituting the origins of humanity. The richness of the new data at our disposal made it necessary to treat separately the period spreading from the third millennium to the beginning of the seventh century before our era.

This division into seven volumes, dictated by a combination of factors ranging from the abstract to the practical – amongst the latter, being that of ensuring the more or less equal size of the volumes – is more or less in keeping with historical facts. Beyond all specific differences, five principal stages can be recorded in human evolution: the use of material tools accompanied by the emergence of cultures destined to be full of meaning for a long time to come; the moulding of a geo-politics or a geo-culture signalled by the appearance of major works of all kinds, all of which were to be of lasting value; partitive convulsions that forced in advance the distinction of cultural identities through the play of mutual influences; conceptions resulting from a closed human universe whose planetary course lies within a limitless space; the intensification of centres of development under the pressure of a capitalism that has become industrial and an industry that is becoming scientific – phenomena which push to the outskirts the excess of constraints from which the thus privileged zones escape. The seventh volume will thus deal with the issue of these new currents and the tidal waves that they provoke; facets that lead to the birth of a new type of polarization and as a result of which traditional cultures fall into abeyance.

Such bird's-eye views as those offered here are not misleading because they are crude; they seem questionable because they escape our sight when we keep ourselves too close to the ordinary facts. And it is in this that we mainly confront the limitations of our methods of research. No one is unaware of the difficulties that continue to affect all attempts to provide a synthetic view of humankind's common destiny. There is no answer to these difficulties from which the present subdivision of each volume into themes and regions suffers; into themes to bring out what all human beings share in common; into regions to mark the diversities.

In each volume, the thematic parts should have been the easiest to work out. Several problems were, however, encountered. In order to ensure that the cultures that benefit from the spectacular development that we witness today be no longer favoured beyond measure, it was considered necessary to reduce the importance granted to theoretical innovations and their applications and therefore to refrain from using scientific discoveries as chronological pointers. Had this not been the case, the distribution of themes would have been a simple matter. It would have sufficed to begin with a survey of the scientific and technical knowledge acquired over a given period of time and then retrace the causes in their sequential order.

Now, from the moment when it becomes necessary for history to tone down the privileges conferred on some by the process of evolution – and, more particularly, to question a system of values rooted in an overly univocal notion of progress – it also becomes necessary to standardize the distribution of themes by including more 'ordinary' references, for example, by starting with a description of the physical and natural conditions in order to arrive at the scientific through the demographic and the cultural. This not only increased the uniformity of the volumes but also offered the major advantage of emphasizing the ways of living. Whatever they are, these must first satisfy the basic physiological needs – a vital minimum dictated by the instincts of survival and rendered partially relative by the differences of climate. Each culture responds to this in its own manner and according as much to its natural environment as to the habits that it inherits. Certain acquired needs are then added to this vital minimum – superfluous needs turned into necessary ones and established in varying degrees according to the social hierarchies and geohistorical differences. Moreover, as human beings are not only biological but also thinking and feeling entities, each material culture is accompanied by a culture that can be called 'spiritual' in the widest sense of the term and that also varies according to the situations already mentioned. Finally, even though the conditions are not identical, material culture and spiritual culture are interrelated.

This enunciation of the common grounds on which all human lives are established stands to reason and would seem evident to any lay person. It could also, however, lead us to think that it is easy to find historians ready to develop each theme. The present state of historical knowledge proves that it is not so and, as always, for the same reason. Insignificant as this problem may be, the solution lies in turning one's back on analytical methods and adopting an approach that would be one of synthesis.

Undoubtedly, current research and investigations help us in our evaluation of material and spiritual cultures, but separately. We are completely ignorant about the interconnections between the two. Where does this notorious deficiency come from? Two main reasons can be put forward.

The first concerns the elaboration of a global history. Indeed, when it comes to local or regional histories, each confined to a particular epoch, the data that we possess help us either to deal with some of the problems or to contribute by offering some information. But when one or the other problem needs to be looked at from a global point of view, then we confront a major difficulty: which elements of the data available should be included in an inventory of an absolutely common heritage? In other words, what advances made at one place or the other, or at one point of time or another, effectively contributed to what can be called 'general progress'? The workshops of historians can boast of few if any historians at all who specialize in the evaluation of 'generalities'! When the need for one arises, then it has to be admitted that the courageous few who have undertaken such a task suffered from the absence of sufficient information and were compelled to work in conditions that rendered their merits highly eminent but curbed considerably their influence.

This first reason leads to the second, the absence of criteria that would make it possible to distinguish effectively the subjective from the objective as much in the work accomplished as in the reputations won. Here we touch upon an issue that is too important to dismiss without fuller attention.

The studies on primitive or savage societies, particularly those conducted over the last fifty years, carried anthropology to a high degree of what must be called the 'intelligence' of cultures. Indeed, in these societies, myth plays a fundamental role. It legitimizes matrimonial and social behaviour as well as customs and ways of living – the way one eats, dresses and organizes one's life inside and outside one's own dwelling. In an even more significant manner, it legitimizes humankind's spiritual behaviour as much in times of war as in peace. This global aspect of myth itself leads us to the heights from which, at one glance, we can view not only the various behaviours as a whole, but also, and as a result, the very logic that sustains them.

Historical evolution disperses myth, without however abolishing the mythological function. It provokes the growth of branches and favours ramifications. What had been thanks to myth, at one and the same time, religion and literature, moral and political, art and technique, breaks up later into more and more subdivided areas of knowledge; differentiations that led namely to the belief that the logic of myth or of the sacred is gainsaid by that of science. 'Science': this word which obstructs more than all others what we term historical intelligence. In the original sense of the word, science means knowledge, with no distinction implied between knowledge and know-how. Today this same word has taken on such a specific meaning that for a vast majority

of the most highly informed minds, science denotes truth, as against the falsity of myth. Yet, many eminent scholars acknowledge that this 'truth' contains a part of myth and that it is indeed thanks to this that methods and knowledge advance. It is by working within the mythological that we reduce the part of myths, something of which always survives in the very heart of science.

The barriers that have been most resolutely built against the 'intelligence' of history have their sources in the gradual formation of separate enclaves of investigation. Social, economic, political, literary history and so on: each domain follows its own path and rarely meets the other, or never enough to allow for the establishment of criteria common to all that could constitute the basis for a truly universal history of scientific and cultural developments. The worst form of such separations can be found in the cosmic distance that has been introduced between the history of religion and that of science, and this, in spite of some highly remarkable, though rare, attempts to make them move towards each other via the social and the philosophical. No significant results should be expected until the gaps between ordinary language and scientific language are bridged, particularly when the latter makes use of mathematical terms so fully exploited by the initiated few and so little accessible to the secular mass.

This brings us back to the question of the limitations of this edition referred to earlier: limitations concerning the basic logical presuppositions on which a truly universal history of humankind should be founded. It is only on the basis of certain common features that one culture can comprehend something that is part of another culture and that the people of today can understand a little of what lies in the past. But then, given the present state of our knowledge and the manner in which the basic logical presuppositions are handled, our history will remain beyond the reach of the general public, however enlightened, for which it is intended.

None the less, a certain merit – perhaps less significant than hoped for – makes this second edition worthy of our attention. By eliminating the notion that the cultures rendered marginal by 'progress' represent groups of people 'without history', the study of cultures wherein myth is dispersed among all kinds of domains could only gain from the experience of those whose lives are, even today, steeped in a mythology that they all consider fundamental. We have not as yet reached our goal, but the step taken marks a sure improvement in terms of our understanding of history. And, as the readers will themselves find out, it is this aspect of the thematic part of each volume that makes this work truly exceptional.

We now come to the question of the treatment of regions in each volume. To begin with, let us look at a major ambiguity which threatened the very conception of these sections. An example will suffice. To which region does Newton belong? To Cambridge? England? Europe? The West? The world? There is no doubt that the universality of his law of gravitation makes him a part of the common heritage of humanity. Yet, undoubtedly this law discovered by a particular man, at a particular place and point of time, would seem to have miraculously descended from the skies, if we did not take into account the facts of the discovery, the circumstances leading to it and the manner in which the law was adopted by all. Should we have then talked about Newton in one way in the thematic chapter and in another in the regional? Although the difficulties involved in solving such a problem are great, they turn out to be less so when confronted with yet another problem that would have resulted from any attempt to merge the two parts into one: for, in that case, the question would have been, which one? A fusion of all into the regional would, to a great extent, have simplified the task, given that we are dealing with specializations in different fields. But it would have led to the very unpleasant need to emphasize the merits of one culture at the cost of the others. A fusion of all into the thematic? In that case, Newton's law would have been stripped of its socio-cultural characteristics and this would have led to some kind of sanctification of the 'genius'. Needless to say, what has been noted as regards Newton applies to all thinkers, discoverers and to all that humankind has created.

Some readers will perhaps regret the fact that this history, whose dominant note is certainly transcultural, does not succeed better in overcoming certain problems resulting from habits and preconceived notions. We all talk about Asia, Africa and Europe. Originally, these were names given to Greek nymphs and were used to distinguish the three principal, cardinal points of the world perceived by the Mediterranean navigators: the south, the east and the north, respectively. To these seafarers the west was nothing but a vast indecipherable stretch, presumably a part of the legendary Atlantis. As for the continent of America, its name was curiously given to it by a cartographer who, while outlining a map of this continent, used the information supplied to him by Amerigo Vespucci – thus depriving Christopher Columbus of the recognition he deserved. In the case of the nymphs as well as in that of the cartographer, we can no longer distinguish the subjective from the objective. What was in fact a very subjective decision in the first place now appears to be very objective because it is commonly accepted by everyone. We cannot change something that has been so firmly established over the years, but the often very serious problems and disadvantages that result from the ethnocentrism implied by such customs need to be pointed out.

Depending on the epochs, Egypt is at times best understood when considered as African and at others when its civilization is regarded as having acquired much of its significance from a dual Nile–Euphrates identity. Similarly, instead of remaining Mediterranean, southern Europe became continental when the centre of gravity of exchanges and developments shifted to the Atlantic. China constitutes another example. This Middle Kingdom felt the effects of the existence of other continental regions when its Great Wall no longer protected it from the conquerors it tried later to assimilate, or when it yielded, perhaps for too long a period, to the attacks of the seamen and naval forces coming from the other end of the world, that is, from Europe.

Geographical perspectives change from one era to the other. But it is difficult to incorporate such changes and align them with the periodization adopted for a work on history. Those responsible for planning the seven volumes had to devise the ways and means of solving such problems. At times they had to have recourse to certain subterfuges so as to prevent the periodization from turning into some kind of a jigsaw puzzle and requiring a frequent arrangement and rearrangement. This entailed, however, the risks of introducing certain anachronisms.

Such risks are in no way negligible. To a modern mind, for example, the commerce or the conquests in ancient times across the deserts of Sinai appear as manifestations of the hostilities existing between Africa and Asia. This distinction between the two continents becomes nonsensical when applied to the period when Egypt did not see itself as African nor Assyria as Asian. Each region thought of itself first as constituting in itself the whole universe or as representing in itself the whole universe as defined by its own gods. We must be aware of the dangers of accepting such ideas, which still survive in the unconscious, affect our conscious minds, and foster notions of rights and privileges detrimental to the development of universalism.

The need to determine the number of pages to be devoted to each 'continent' arose from certain customs that, although anachronic, generate at times very strong emotions and influence our decisions. It also arose from the fact that the distrust of ethnocentrism expressed itself in terms that were very ethnocentric. Including Cro–Magnon man in an inventory of 'European' sites amounts to attributing to him a label that contradicts all that was felt in times when existence could not be conceived of except in terms very different from those related to our planetary territoriality. Similarly, the concept of Africa was itself foreign to the African empires or kingdoms, each constituting for each a world in itself and, at the same time, a world which belongs to all. The readers will themselves correct such imperfections, which have resulted from a need to adopt a pragmatic approach.

Applying modern notions of geography to any period of the past relieves us of the dizziness felt when we look down into the immense depths of time, yet it is in these depths that cultural but also natural interactions, direct or indirect, multiplied: a swarming mass much too indecipherable to allow for the delineation of linear ancestry. It is, therefore, better to avoid distinguishing overmuch our distant common ancestors. Physical evolution leads perhaps to the formation of races. But as the human species can be known through its customs, faculties and cerebral activities, this privilege common to all reduces practically to nothing the particularisms that some not always disinterested viewpoints defined formerly as racial.

The human species cannot really be differentiated except as ethnic groups and through customs that defy any simplistic typology. A strong capacity for adaptation, peculiar to humans, enables them to invent a practically limitless number of solutions to the problems posed by all kinds of environments, and even more so by circumstances that the smallest events modify and great events transform altogether. In this lies the most amazing aspect of history: the infinite variety of answers that each individual or collectivity finds to the questions put to it by destiny. The more history accelerates its pace and becomes more specific, the more our destiny becomes enigmatic. This is because every human being is a human being and no single one resembles another.

The end of the colonialisms that believed or claimed themselves to be the civilizers of this world led to the birth of many new nations and many new Member States of international organizations. 'New' in what sense? The establishment of a 'New World Order' is bound to remain a Utopian idea as long as history has not explained how a local body of historical cultures finally engendered what it has over the centuries referred to as 'civilization'; a word full of contradictions. Intended as universal and respectful to other cultures, this civilization turned out to be materialist and destroyed many cultures as a result of the superiority that it attributed to its own system of laws and rights. Two heavy tasks thus face historians: acknowledging the universalism that lies hidden beneath all particularisms and agreeing among themselves on what should be made generally known in this respect.

An elucidation of the past requires personal as well as

collective efforts. This two-fold process should therefore have found spontaneous expression in a work meant to aid the advancement of knowledge. The Commission recommended therefore that, in addition to the thematic and regional parts, a third part be added that would have comprised specific supplements on details that needed developing, problems that needed solving, and finally an exposition of different and opposing opinions on interpretations in dispute. This project met with overwhelming difficulties and some explanation is called for!

This international history, which had been conceived as a result of dialogues and discussions, would evidently have gained considerably from an exposition of the differences in interpretation in their proper dimensions. It would have been more lively and instructive and have given readers more food for thought. Unfortunately, the dispersion of authors to be included and chosen from the whole world demanded means and time that we did not have. The Editors, who already had a heavy task, could not have undertaken this extra work without assistance, in particular from committees specifically chosen and brought together in the light of the subjects to be discussed. Taking into account the costs of travel and accommodation, the already high cost of the operation would have almost doubled. No doubt a day will come when, debates on themes and regions being easier than they are now, it will be possible to expound history as it is revealed by a confrontation of knowledge and viewpoints on particular questions concerning all humanity.

Until the state of knowledge and of historical research in the world has reached this convergent point, we are obliged to give up the idea of showing the divergences that future workshops of historians will have to face. We have, however provided notes at the end of articles, which have been written so as to ensure maximum diversity and the broadest possible participation. A certain arbitrariness persists, of course. But this will remain unavoidable as long as the excesses that analyses lead to are not minimized through the elaboration of syntheses based on criteria derived from irrefutable logical presuppositions – presuppositions that help establish universal certitudes. Let us not forget, however, that innovations originate only within the gaps of certitude.

One of the merits of this work lies in that it has succeeded in enlisting the collaboration of a very large number of people, representing a large number of regions and cultures. The Commission also encouraged the formation of local working groups responsible for obtaining and organizing the data to be included in the various chapters. This present work marks perhaps only the beginning of such collective efforts. Nevertheless, it permits us to anticipate satisfactory results. Knowing oneself well in order to make oneself better known constitutes a major contribution to mutual understanding. In this respect, historical research resembles an awareness of unconscious phenomena. It brings into the daylight what in the nocturnal depths of individual or collective existences gives them life, so to say, in spite of themselves or against their will.

This publication will no doubt give rise to many criticisms. If these turn out to be harsh, they will justify the project, whose main objective is to arouse us from our dogmatic slumber. Historical events take care of this much more efficiently, but at a much higher price.

Charles Morazé
Former President of the International Commission

GENERAL INTRODUCTION

Societies are making greater demands than ever on history, but urgent as they might be, these demands by various groups are not altogether straightforward. Some societies look to historians to define their identity, to buttress the development of their specific characteristics or even to present and analyse the past as confirming a founding myth. Conversely, other societies, influenced both by the *Annales* school of historiography and by the geographical, chronological and thematic enlargement of history, aspire to the building of bridges, the ending of self-isolation and the smoothing out of the lack of continuity that is characteristic of the short term.

In 1946 those attending the meeting of the first Preparatory Commission of UNESCO agreed that it was part of the fundamental mission of the United Nations Educational, Scientific and Cultural Organization to lay the foundations for a collective memory of humanity and of all its parts, spread all over the world and expressing themselves in every civilization. The International Scientific Commission came into being four years later with the apparently gigantic task of drafting a *History of the Scientific and Cultural Development of Mankind*. Publication of the six volumes began in 1963, marking the successful conclusion of an international endeavour without parallel, but not without risks. Success with the general public was immediate and lasting, notwithstanding the reservations expressed by the critics, who often found certain choices disconcerting but were not consistent in the choices and interpretations they proposed as alternatives.

For its time – not the time of its publication but that of its long preparation – the first edition of the *History of the Scientific and Cultural Development of Mankind* must be seen as a daring achievement, having a number of faults inherent in the very nature of historical knowledge but opening up new avenues and encouraging further progress along them.

In 1978, the General Conference of UNESCO decided to embark on a new and completely revised edition of the *History of the Scientific and Cultural Development of Mankind* because it realized that the considerable development of historiography, the improvement of what are called its auxiliary sciences and its growing links with the social sciences had combined with an extraordinary acceleration of day-to-day history. What it did not know, however, was that the pace of this acceleration would continue to increase until it brought profound changes to the face of the world.

It scarcely needs saying that the task laid upon the International Scientific Commission, under the chairmanship of the late Paulo de Berrêdo Carneiro and then of my eminent predecessor, Professor Charles Morazé, was both enormous and difficult.

First of all, international teams had to be formed, as balanced as possible, and co-operation and dialogue organized between the different views of the major collective stages in the lives of people, but without disregarding the cultural identity of human groups.

Next, attention had to be given to changes in chronological scale by attempting a scientific reconstruction of the successive stages of the peopling of our planet, including the spread of animal populations. This was the goal pursued and largely attained by the authors of the present volume.

Lastly, steps had to be taken to ensure that traditional methods of historical research, based on written sources, were used side by side with new critical methods adapted to the use of oral sources and contributions from archaeology, in Africa for the most part.

To quote what Professor Jean Devisse said at a symposium in Nice in 1986 on 'Being a historian today': 'If we accept that the history of other people has something to teach us, there can be no infallible model, no immutable methodological certainty: listening to each other can lead to a genuine universal history.'

Although historians must be guided by a desire for intellectual honesty, they depend on their own views of things, with the result that history is the science most vulnerable to ideologies. The fall of the Berlin Wall a few weeks after I assumed office symbolized the end of a particularly burdensome ideological division. It certainly makes the work of the International Scientific Commission easier whenever it has to come to grips with the past–present dialectic from which history cannot escape.

In a way, the impact of ideologies will also be lessened by the fact that the Chief Editors of each volume have sought the invaluable co-operation not only of experienced historians but also of renowned specialists in disciplines such as law, art, philosophy, literature, oral traditions, the natural sciences, medicine, anthropology, mathematics and economics. In any event, this interdisciplinarity, which helps dissipate error, is undoubtedly one of the major improvements of this second edition of the *History of Humanity*, over the previous edition.

Another problem faced was that of periodization. It was out of the question systematically to adopt the periodization long in use in European history, i.e. Antiquity, the Middle Ages, modern times, because it is now being extensively called into question and also, above all, because it would have led to a Eurocentric view of world history, a view whose absurdity is now quite obvious. The seven volumes are thus arranged in the following chronological order:

Volume I   Prehistory and the beginnings of civilization
Volume II   From the third millennium to the seventh century BC
Volume III From the seventh century BC to the seventh century AD
Volume IV From the seventh to the sixteenth century
Volume V   From the sixteenth to the eighteenth century
Volume VI The nineteenth century
Volume VII The twentieth century.

It must be stated at once that this somewhat surgical distribution is in no way absolute or binding. It will in no way prevent the overlapping that there must be at the turn of each century if breaks in continuity and the resulting errors of perspective are to be avoided. Indeed, it has been said that we are already in the twenty-first century!

In his preface, Professor Charles Morazé has clearly described and explained the structure of each of the volumes, with a thematic chapter, a regional chapter and annexes. This structure, too, may be modified so as not to upset the complementarity of the pieces of a mosaic that must retain its significance.

When the International Scientific Commission, the Chief Editors of the volumes and the very large number of contributors have completed their work – and this will be in the near future – they will be able to adopt as their motto the frequently quoted saying of the philosopher Etienne Gilson:

We do not study history to get rid of it but to save from nothingness all the past which, without history, would vanish into the void. We study history so that what, without it, would not even be the past any more, may be reborn to life in this unique present outside which nothing exists.

This present will be all the more unique because history will have shown itself to be, not an instrument for legitimizing exacerbated forms of nationalism, but an instrument, ever more effective because ever more perfectible, for ensuring mutual respect, solidarity and the scientific and cultural interdependence of humanity.

Georges-Henri Dumont
President of the International Commission

THE INTERNATIONAL COMMISSION

for the New Edition of the History of the Scientific and Cultural Development of Mankind

President: G.-H. Dumont (Belgium)

Members of the International Commission:

I. A. Abu-Lughod (United States of America)
A. R. Al-Ansary (Saudi Arabia)
J. Bony (Côte d'Ivoire)
E. K. Brathwaite (Barbados)
G. Carrera Damas (Venezuela)
A. H. Dani (Pakistan)
D. Denoon (Australia)
M. Garašanin (Serbia)
T. Haga (Japan)
F. Iglesias (Brazil)
H. Inalcik (Turkey)
S. Kartodirdjo (Indonesia)
J. Ki-Zerbo (Burkina Faso)
C. Martinez Shaw (Spain)
E. Mendelsohn (United States of America)

E. M'Bokolo (Zaire)
K. N'Keita (Ghana)
T. Obenga (Congo)
B. A. Ogot (Kenya)
Pang-Pu (China)
W. Sauerlander (Germany)
B. Schroeder-Gudehus (Ms) (Canada)
R. Thapar (Ms) (India)
I. D. Thiam (Senegal)
K. V. Thomas (United Kingdom)
S. L. Tikhvinsky (Russian Federation)
N. Todorov (Bulgaria)
E. Weinberg (Argentina)
M. Yardeni (Ms) (Israel)
E. Zurcher (the Netherlands)

Bureau of the International Commission:

A. R. Al-Ansary (Saudi Arabia)
E. K. Brathwaite (Barbados)
G. Carrera Damas (Venezuela)
A. H. Dani (Pakistan)
E. Mendelsohn (United States of America)

R. Thapar (Ms) (India)
I. D. Thiam (Senegal)
K. V. Thomas (United Kingdom)
S. L. Tikhvinsky (Russian Federation)
N. Todorov (Bulgaria)

Honorary Members:

S. A. Al-Ali (Iraq)
P. J. Riis (Denmark)
T. Yamamoto (Japan)

Former Presidents:

P. E. B. Carneiro (Brazil) (deceased)
C. Moraźe (France)

Former Members:

E. Condurachi (Romania) (deceased)
G. Daws (Australia)
C. A. Diop (Senegal) (deceased)
A. A. Kamel (Egypt) (deceased)
M. Kably (Morocco)
H. Nakamura (Japan)
J. Prawer (Israel) (deceased)
S. Zavala (Mexico)

xvii

HISTORY OF HUMANITY
IN SEVEN VOLUMES

LIST OF FIGURES

LIST OF MAPS

LIST OF PLATES

LIST OF TABLES

THE AUTHORS

Alexeev, Valeriy P. (Russian Federation); spec. physical anthropology, ethnology and prehistoric archaeology; Director, Institute of Archaeology, Russian Academy of Sciences. Member, Russian Academy of Sciences.

An Zhimin (China); spec. Neolithic archaeology of China; Chief, Section I (Neolithic) and Deputy Director, Archaeology Institute of the Chinese Academy of Social Sciences.

Bandi, Hans-Georg (Switzerland); spec. Palaeolithic art and archaeology; Curator and Deputy Director, History Museum of Bern, Secretary-General, *Schweizerisch-Lichtensteinische Stiftung für archäologische Forschungen im Ausland.*

Bartstra, Gert-Jan (the Netherlands); spec. Pleistocene and Palaeolithic archaeology in South-East Asia; Professor, Biologisch-archaeologisch Instituut, Universiteit, Groningen.

Bar-Yosef, Ofer (Israel); spec. Middle Eastern Palaeolithic and Neolithic; Professor, Department of Anthropology, Peabody Museum, Harvard University, Cambridge, Massachusetts.

Bökönyi, Sandor (Hungary); spec. palaeozoology; Director, Hungarian National Museum.

Bryan, Alan L. (Canada); spec. American prehistory; Professor, University of Alberta.

Chavaillon, Jean François Henri (France); spec. geology and prehistory, especially in Greece, the Sahara, Ethiopia and the Republic of Djibouti; Director, Laboratoire de Recherches sur l'Afrique orientale, Centre National de la Recherche Scientifique (CNRS).

Clark, John Desmond (United Kingdom); spec. prehistory of Africa, Western Asia and India; Professor, University of California at Berkeley. Member, British Academy and of the American Academy of Arts and Sciences.

Close, Angela E. (United Kingdom); spec. prehistory of North Africa and the European Palaeolithic; Visiting Associate Professor of Anthropology and Research Associate, Southern Methodist University in Dallas, Texas.

Coppens, Yves (France); spec. palaeoanthropology and prehistory (especially of Africa); Professor, Collège de France (Chair of Palaeoanthropology and Prehistory). Member, French Academy of Sciences (Institut de France).

Dani, Ahmad Hasan (Pakistan); spec. archaeology; Professor, University of Islamabad; Director, Centre for the Study of Central Asian Civilizations. Member of many national and international academic bodies.

De Laet, Sigfried Jan (Belgium); spec. Roman history, European archaeology and prehistory; Editor, *History of Humanity,* Vol. I (1994). Member of the Royal Academy of Sciences, Letters and Fine Arts of Belgium.

Derevyanko, Anatoly P. (Russian Federation); spec. prehistory of Siberia. Corresponding member of the Russian Academy of Sciences.

Doumas, Christos (Greece); spec. archaeology of the Aegean world; Supervisor, Antiquities in various regions of Greece; Director, Antiquities at the Ministry of Culture; Professor, University of Athens.

Flood, Josephine M. (Australia); spec. cultural heritage of the Aborigines; Principal Conservation Officer, Australian Heritage Commission in Canberra.

Garašanin, Milutin (former Yugoslavia); spec. prehistory (Neolithic and Bronze Age) of the Balkans; Senior Researcher, Archaeological Institute in Belgrade; Professor of Archaeology, University of Belgrade. Member, Serbian Academy of Sciences and Arts and of the Academy of Sciences and Arts of Bosnia and Herzegovina.

Geraads, Denis (France); spec. vertebrate and human palaeontology; researcher, CNRS; Professor, Laboratoire de Paléontologie des Vertébrés et de Paléontologie Humaine, Université Pierre et Marie Curie.

Giot, Pierre-Roland (France); spec. geology, archaeology and anthropology of Brittany; Professor, University of Rennes, in charge of the Armorican Anthropology, Prehistory, Protohistory and Quaternary Laboratory.

Guilaine, Jean (France); spec. Mediterranean Neolithic; Director of Research, CNRS; Director of Neolithization and Early Rural Societies, École des Hautes Études en Sciences sociales; Inspector-General of Archaeology.

Harlan, Jack R. (United States); spec. archaeobotany; Professor Emeritus.

Heredia, Osvaldo Raimundo (Argentina), deceased 1989; spec. archaeology of South America.

Hours, Francis, SJ (France) deceased 1987; spec. Palaeolithic archaeology of western Asia.

Hutterer, Karl Leopold (Austria); spec. archaeology and anthropology of Hawaii, the Philippines and Australia; Lecturer, Bryn Mawr College, University of Hawaii, University of San Carlos (Cebu City); Director of Burke Museum, University of Washington, Seattle, Washington.

Jelinek, Arthur J. (United States); spec. prehistoric archaeology of western Asia; Professor, University of Arizona at Tucson.

Jia Lanpo (formerly known as Chia L. P.) (China); spec. palaeoanthropology; Professor, Shaanxi University and Xiamen University; Professor, Institute of Vertebrate Palaeontology and Palaeoanthropology, Academia Sinica in Beijing. Member, Chinese Academy of Sciences (Academia Sinica).

Joshi, Ramchandra V. (India); spec. natural sciences as applied to archaeology, prehistoric archaeology of the coastal areas of India; Professor of Archaeology, Deccan College, Postgraduate and Research Institute.

Kaelas, Lili (Sweden); spec. European Neolithic, megaliths, post-glacial rock art; Guest Professor, Universities of Gothenburg and Olso and the University of California (Los Angeles). Member, Göteborgs Kungl. Vetenskaps och Vitterhets Samhälle (Royal Society of Arts and Sciences in Gothenburg).

Klima, Bohuslav (Czech Republic); spec. Upper Palaeolithic in Central Europe; Director, Archaeological Institute of the Czechoslovak Academy of Sciences in Brno.

Krzyzaniak, Lech (Poland); spec. Egyptology (especially prehistoric); Director, Archaeological Museum at Poznan.

Lorenzo, José Luis (Mexico); spec. prehistory of Central America; Chief, Department of Prehistory, Department for pre-Columbian Monuments, Department of the School of Restoration and Museology at INAH; Chief, Latin American Regional Centre for the Preservation and Restoration of Cultural Property (Unesco); Chairman, Archaeological Council, Instituto Nacional de Antropología e Historia (INAH).

Lumbreras Salcedo, Luis Guillermo (Peru); spec. Pre-Columbian archaeology of the Andean region; Professor, Universidad Nacional Mayor de San Marcos in Lima.

Lüning, Jens (Germany); spec. Neolithic in Central Europe; Professor, University of Frankfurt am Main.

Masry, Abdullah Hassan (Saudi Arabia); spec. archaeology; Assistant Deputy Minister for Antiquities and Museum Affairs of Saudi Arabia; Editor-in-Chief of *Atlal*, Journal of Saudi Arabian Archaeology.

Mellaart, James (United Kingdom); spec. archaeology of western Asia and in particular of Anatolia; Professor, Institute of Archaeology, University of London. Member, British Academy.

Merpert, Nikolai J. (Russian Federation); spec. Neolithic and Bronze Age in the European part of the post-Soviet republics; Professor, Chief of Neolithic and Bronze Age Section at the Institute of Archaeology of the Russian Academy of Sciences.

Núñez Atencio, Lautaro (Chile); spec. prehistoric archaeology of the southern part of South America; Professor and co-founder of the Institute of Archaeological Research at the Northern University in Atacama. Member, Chilean Academy of Social Sciences.

Nunoo, Richard B. (Ghana); spec. archaeology of Sub-Saharan Africa; formerly Director of National Museums and Monuments of Ghana in Accra.

Otte, Marcel (Belgium); spec. European Upper Palaeolithic; Professor, University of Liège.

Phillipson, David W. (United Kingdom); spec. archaeology of East and Southern Africa; Curator, Archaeology and Anthropology Museum, University of Cambridge.

Sanoja Obediente, Mario (Venezuela); spec. archaeology and anthropology of the northern part of South America; Research Fellow, Smithsonian Institution, United States National Museum in Washington, DC. Member, National Academy of History, Venezuela.

Schild, Romuald (Poland); spec. archaeology of north and East Africa; Director-General of the Polish Academy of Sciences, Institute of the History of Material Culture.

Shepherd, Robert (United Kingdom); spec. history of mining during prehistoric and Roman times; mining engineer.

Solheim, Wilhelm G., II (United States); spec. prehistory of South-East Asia; Director, Centre for South-East Asia, University of Hawaii at Manoa.

Valoch, Karel (Czech Republic); spec. Upper Palaeolithic of Central Europe; Curator, Anthropology Institute of the Moravian Museum in Brno. Member, Czechoslovak Academy of Sciences.

Vandermeersch, Bernard (France); spec. archaeology and physical anthropology of the Middle Palaeolithic; Research Assistant, CNRS; Senior Assistant, University of Paris VI; Professor, University of Bordeaux I; Director of Studies, École Française des Hautes Études.

Villa, Paola (Italy); spec. Lower Palaeolithic archaeology; Research Assistant and Lecturer, University of California of Berkeley; Visiting lecturer, Universities of Colorado, California at Santa Cruz and San Diego and Wyoming; Research Associate, University of Colorado at Boulder.

Wendorf, Fred (United States); spec. prehistory of Africa; Henderson-Morrison Professor, Department of Anthropology, Southern Methodist University at Dallas.

Wu Rukang (formerly known as Woo, Ju-Kang) (China); spec. palaeoanthropology of China; Research Professor, Institute of Vertebrate Palaeontology and Palaeoanthropology, Academia Sinica in Beijing. Member, Chinese Academy of Sciences (Academia Sinica).

ACKNOWLEDGEMENTS

The UNESCO International Commission, the authors and the publishers wish to thank all those who have kindly given permission for the reproduction of the plates in this book.

The UNESCO Secretariat wishes to express its heartfelt thanks to Ms Iris Bettembourg, former Head of Publications Unit, Sector for Culture and Communication, UNESCO, who generously accepted to edit the English version of the manuscript.

The Chief Editor, on his own behalf, wishes to pay tribute to the support received from Professor Paulo E. Benêdo Carneiro and, after his death in 1982, from Messrs Charles Morazé and Georges-Henri Dumont, Presidents of the International Commission, from his Co-Editors, Ahmad H. Dani, José L. Lorenzo and Richard B. Nunoo, from all the authors of chapters, from the members of the Working Group and of the Reading Committee, and finally from all the members of the Secretariat of the venture in Paris.

UNESCO also wishes to express its gratitude to the Islamic Call Society for its generous financial assistance to this project.

INTRODUCTION

Sigfried J. De Laet

GENESIS OF THE VOLUME

In 1979, when plans for a new edition of the *History of Humanity* were taking shape, Professor Paulo E. de Berrêdo Carneiro, President of the International Commission for a History of the Scientific and Cultural Development of Mankind, asked me, as a consultant, to write a critical analysis of the first edition in so far as prehistory was concerned. This report (De Laet, 1979) was distributed among the members of the Commission. I was then invited to attend, as an observer, the first meeting of the Commission in September 1980. The members, on the basis of the reports of some sixty consultants, considered that a revision of the first edition, as initially planned, would be difficult to carry out and that it would be preferable to set about preparing an entirely new edition in which *all* cultures would have their rightful place.

I was entrusted by the Commission with organizing a Prehistory Working Group to determine the place to be given in the work as a whole to the preliterate peoples. This group, made up of Pedro Carrasco (Mexico), Ahmad H. Dani (Pakistan), the late Cheikh Anta Diop (Senegal), Joachim Herrmann (Germany), José L. Lorenzo (Mexico), Richard B. Nunoo (Ghana), Wilhelm G. Solheim II (United States of America) and the late Xia Nai (China) met twice – on 29 and 30 April 1981 and from 16 to 18 November 1981. It dealt first with the methodological problems involved in the study of the periods before writing.

Since in the meantime the Commission's Bureau, meeting in Oxford on 25 and 26 September 1981, had dealt with the division of the work into periods and had set the chronological limits of the different volumes of the new edition, the second meeting of the Working Group was devoted to drawing up a fairly detailed plan for Volume I and a list of those colleagues who might be invited to contribute one or more chapters to this volume. Two criteria were adopted in their selection – as wide a geographical distribution as possible and, above all, competence. In January 1983 the plan and the list were submitted first to the Bureau and then to the Commission and approved. I was appointed Chief Editor of Volume I, assisted by three Co-Editors – A. H. Dani for Asia, R. B. Nunoo for Africa and J. L. Lorenzo for America. Since that time this editorial committee has met on several occasions. The authors listed were approached (there were very few refusals) and I asked them to prepare a fairly detailed outline of the chapters they had agreed to write, bearing in mind certain guidelines laid down by the Commission concerning the main themes to be emphasized. From these outlines I was able to frame a fairly detailed plan of Volume I and submit it for comments and criticism to the Bureau at

its meeting in September 1984. The authors, who number fifty-three including the working group and the editorial committee and who come from thirty-one different nations, were asked to send in the first drafts of their texts by the end of 1985. These texts were then submitted first to the members of the Commission and all the authors of Volume I, and later to a Reading Committee, made up of the Chief Editor, the Co-Editors, Lili Kaelas (Sweden), Joachim Herrmann (Germany) and Luis G. Lumbreras Salcedo (Peru), which met from 12 to 23 January and from 9 to 20 March 1987. Any comments and criticisms were then submitted to the authors to assist them in preparing their definitive texts. It should be stressed that no pressure was exerted to obtain any considerable alterations in the chapters. In cases in which opinions differed, the members of the editorial committee drafted a brief note on the subject. Owing to unavoidable circumstances, the International Commission was in possession of all texts only by mid-1988. It was thus impossible to take new data into account after that date.

PREHISTORY

The duration of the period before the invention of writing

This first volume of the new edition of the *History of Humanity* covers a period extending from the appearance of the first being in the hominid family that can be classified in the genus *Homo* up to the invention of writing and the advent of the first states, some 5,000 years ago. This 'prehistoric' period lasted from 2 to 3 million years. It is so enormously long that few people can imagine it; however, two comparisons may help the reader to visualize this idea.

First, if the $2\frac{1}{2}$ million years or so that have elapsed since the appearance of *Homo habilis* were represented by a line of a total length of 5 kilometres, each year would count as less than 2 millimetres. The period before writing would represent 4,990 metres, whereas the whole of the so-called 'historical' periods (those for which we possess written sources) would be reduced to the last 10 metres. The beginning of the Christian era would be indicated 4 metres from the terminal point and the discovery of America by Columbus only 1 metre from the same terminal point.

Second, the total duration of the existence of humankind might also be compared to a 24-hour day, *Homo habilis* first appearing when the day was only 1 second old and each century corresponding to 3.456 seconds. The invention of writing and the beginnings of the first states would then be situated less than 3 minutes before midnight and Columbus's first voyage to America just over 17 seconds before the end of the day.

'Prehistory': an erroneous but well-established term

This enormously long period before the invention of writing is commonly referred to as 'prehistory'. Widespread as it is in practically all languages, this term is basically erroneous. Strictly speaking, it rejects as history about 99.8 per cent of the total existence of humanity and reduces 'history proper' (that based on written sources) to 0.2 per cent of that existence. Moreover, the term is resented as pejorative by the populations who adopted writing only quite recently and who think, with good reason, that their own past is as much 'historical' as that of populations which became literate much earlier.

This 'prehistoric' period witnessed the birth, childhood and adolescence of humankind. It takes us from anthropogenesis right up to the invention of writing, the birth of the first towns, the first states, the rise of the class society which was for millennia to be a feature of the period of 'history proper'. It witnessed the slow elaboration of the basic characteristics of human civilization, and without a knowledge of which most of the outstanding features of contemporary cultures would remain incomprehensible.

The term 'prehistory' was coined in the nineteenth century, originally to indicate the period during which humans were the contemporaries of animals now extinct, the remains of which were found by geologists and palaeontologists in very old geological deposits. This indicated that humans had appeared much earlier than the six millennia granted them up to that time by the Biblical chronology (see pp. 640–1). The adjective 'antediluvian' ('before the Deluge') was used for a short time to designate the same period. On the other hand, the meaning of 'prehistory' was extended to all periods before the knowledge of writing, thus including the remains of much more recent periods. Many of the latter had for a long time attracted the attention of 'antiquaries', sometimes even from a historical viewpoint (see further). Historians, however, showed no interest in those periods for which written sources were lacking, and indeed for a very long time prehistorians and historians had little or no contact. Times have changed, however, and since the period between the two world wars, these contacts have become gradually more frequent, as a consequence of the evolution of both disciplines: on the one hand, great strides have been made in the study of prehistoric times, and on the other hand, the concept of history itself has changed radically since the *École des Annales*. According to L. Fèbvre (1953, p. 428), history in the fullest sense is concerned with *'everything which, belonging to man, depends on man, serves man, expresses man, indicates the presence, activity, tastes and manners of man'*. Now, when Fèbvre wrote these lines, the goals of history in this broad sense had already been pursued for many years by the best of the prehistorians. This parallel trend obviously facilitated the integration of the study of so-called prehistoric periods into the general framework of the history of humankind (De Laet, 1978, p. 228; 1985, pp. 149ff.).

So the term 'prehistory' is inadequate. One could perhaps think to replace it by 'protohistory' (i.e. the very first history), but this term is already well established in current usage to indicate, in the history of a people or of a region, the period during which the people or the region's inhab-itants were still illiterate but during which they were written about in the texts of neighbouring peoples who were more advanced and already literate (e.g. the Celtic tribes, still illiterate but mentioned by Greek and Latin historians). Sometimes the term 'protohistoric' is also used for populations who used writing but whose language is still not understood (e.g. the Etruscans). However this may be, the terms 'prehistory' and 'protohistory' are so deeply rooted that they have become practically ineradicable and any attempt to replace them would be unrealistic.

The diachronic development of cultures and the problems involved in the division of prehistoric times into periods

An important preliminary remark is called for here. This volume does not cover the whole of the times before writing, but only the period during which all peoples without exception were still at this stage. The first systems of writing were invented in Egypt and Mesopotamia some five millennia ago, but the other regions of the globe remained at the prehistoric stage for a long time after that. For instance, writing was unknown in China until a thousand years or so after it was invented in Egypt; written documents do not appear in Crete until the end of the second millennium before the Christian era; in Western Europe history based on written sources began only just before the Christian era, and in Eastern and Northern Europe a thousand years later. Then again, in many parts of Africa, Asia, America and Oceania written sources do not go back further than the period of colonization. Thus, peoples without writing will often figure in the ensuing volumes of this *History of Humanity*.

This non-synchronous development of the different cultural stages poses major problems in regard to synchronization. Ought one to adopt a diachronic division into periods, based on the different cultural stages, or to give preference to a purely chronological division into periods? The Bureau of the International Commission decided on the latter course, after serious consideration of the problem. The terminal dates selected for each volume mark events of prime importance in the history of large parts of the globe; very often, however, these same events passed unnoticed in other regions. So in the 'regional' chapters a regionally significant date more or less contemporary with the terminal date of the volume had often to be selected, with a large measure of flexibility. Volume I, for instance, includes Europe up to two or three centuries after the general terminal date. Within this same volume, the division into periods posed considerable problems. C. J. Thomsen's 'three-age' system (see p. 4), with its traditional subdivisions as adopted in Europe (Early, Middle and Late Palaeolithic, Mesolithic or Final Palaeolithic, Early, Middle and Late Neolithic, Copper or Eneolithic, Early, Middle and Late Bronze Ages, the first Iron Age or Hallstatt period, the second Iron Age or La Tène period), representing both stages in technological development and socio-economic stages, is inapplicable to many other regions, simply because some of these stages are absent, or because some of their characteristics are very different, or because the chronological order is not the same. For instance, in Japan ceramic vessels (the appearance of which elsewhere is regarded as one of the characteristics of the Neolithic) were made much earlier than anywhere else, around 12,500 years ago and hence well within the Upper Palaeolithic, whereas agriculture was introduced very late, around 2,500 years ago, almost contemporaneously with metalworking, both bronze and iron. Using the European period divisions, the Neolithic, Bronze and Iron Ages would begin almost simultaneously! It was therefore essential to establish different divisions for other regions, including sub-Saharan Africa and America. For this Volume I it was essential to work out a division into periods that would be valid, or at least acceptable, for the whole of the globe. It was proposed that the volume be divided into two major parts, the division being marked by the beginnings of food production – an event which unquestionably constitutes one of the main cultural breaks with the past in the history of humankind.

The first part, which corresponds to the period of anthropogenesis and the traditional 'Palaeolithic', still covers more than 99 per cent of the total duration of human history. So it in turn, had, of necessity, to be divided into periods. Rather than base these subdivisions on purely archaeological criteria, in some cases questionable, as was often done in the past, it seemed preferable to adopt a classification borrowed from human palaeontology and to take as the main stages the appearance of the different species and subspecies of the genus *Homo* that have succeeded one another in the course of time. After an introductory chapter on anthropogenesis, three broad subdivisions would deal respectively with the period of *Homo habilis* and *Homo erectus*, the period of *Homo sapiens neanderthalensis* and his contemporaries, and the period of *Homo sapiens sapiens* up to the beginnings of food production.

It should be mentioned here that, with the aim of presenting all periods of history according to a basically similar outline plan, the Commission decided that each broad subdivision of the work would comprise one or more thematic chapters presented as 'overviews' (in which the general features of the period dealt with would be brought out clearly and emphasis laid on the major scientific and cultural themes selected) and a series of 'regional' chapters (in which the period under review would be examined on a more regional plane and emphasis laid on the characteristics of the different cultures peculiar to a region). The regional chapters would necessarily reflect analytical research, whereas the 'overviews' would endeavour to present a comprehensive survey of that analytical research.

The second part of the volume would take the reader from the beginnings of food production up to the birth of the first states or, if the reader prefers, from the 'Neolithic revolution' to the 'urban revolution'. (These two terms, coined originally by the great Australian-born prehistorian V. Gordon Childe, are now in general use, even if, taken literally, they are somewhat questionable, see Chapter 36.) This second part, too, would contain chapters presented as 'overviews', and many regional chapters. It should be emphasized here that the beginnings of food production do not go back everywhere to the same period, and that in certain regions they occur well after the terminal date of the volume; these regions would be dealt with in the first part of the volume up to 5,000 years ago and would, in the second part, be merely mentioned with a cross-reference to the first part.

SOIL ARCHIVES

The lay person may wonder how the history of this remote period can be known in the absence of written sources. Luckily, we have other sources preserved in what may in general be called *soil archives*, which we have gradually

managed to decode. These archives are made up of all the traces that the men and women of the past have left in the soil: on the one hand, their bones, on the other, the products of their activities. The former are the subject of study of human palaeontology (a term often replaced by palaeoanthropology) and the latter that of prehistoric archaeology. These two disciplines can be likened to the two scales of a balance, 'bearing as they do the two essential sources of our information, the bones and the stones, the body and the spirit, biology and culture' (Coppens, 1984, p. 9).

Soil archives hold even greater riches, however, for they contain much information about the natural environment in which prehistoric humanity lived and also information that enables us to establish a chronology (both relative and absolute) for prehistory and to date past cultures.

THE ORIGINS AND DEVELOPMENT OF THE PREHISTORIC SCIENCES

In this short survey of the development of prehistory, we can distinguish several periods:

1 A formative phase, which can be divided into two periods:
   A From the beginnings to 1859
   B From 1859 to 1918.
2 A transitional phase (1918–45).
3 The current phase (since the end of the Second World War).

The formative phase

From the beginnings to 1859

To understand current research trends in prehistory, it is worth recalling that they are the outcome of the aggregation of the gradual merging of the aims of a number of earlier approaches and often differ greatly.

First, a few words must be said about *classical archaeology* because of its strong influence on prehistoric archaeology. It was born in Europe at the time of the Renaissance and Humanism, and was then devoted essentially to the study of the monumental and artistic vestiges of Greek and Roman antiquity, to which those of Egyptian and Western Asiatic antiquity were added later. This approach, which makes classical archaeology almost synonymous with the history of antique art, was still broadly represented in the nineteenth century and during the first half of the twentieth. Even today, although the two disciplines are clearly differentiated in regard to both aims and methods, they are still confused to some extent, especially by the general public. Classical archaeology, limited at first to the search for ruins of monuments and art works, experienced a rebirth in the eighteenth century with the excavation of Herculaneum (begun in 1719) and of Pompeii (begun in 1748). The names of Anne-Claude de Caylus in France and Johann Joachim Winckelmann in Germany remain associated with this period, which also marked the beginnings of *active* archaeology, the searching by means of excavation for further material vestiges of the civilizations of the past. Another important date was 1798, the year of Napoleon's expedition to Egypt. The future emperor took with him a team of scholars whose ten-volume report marks the real beginnings of Egyptology. This increased interest in Pharaonic antiquities resulted in some wild excavations, mainly for the benefit of a few important

European museums. In 1885, therefore, the Khedive set up the Antiquities Service and strictly regulated excavations. In Mesopotamia, archaeology began at about the same time as it did in Egypt. There, too, pillaging unfortunately occurred and, for want of adequate legislation, continued much longer than it had in Egypt.

Second, one of the oldest roots of the study of prehistory is to be sought in the activities of *antiquaries* – a term originally synonymous with archaeologists. Indeed, the tradition of antiquarianism is almost as old as classical archaeology, with which it was closely connected. The antiquaries were active mainly in European countries in which vestiges of classical antiquity are rare. Like the classical archaeologists, they first devoted themselves to the description and study of ancient monuments in their own regions. Many of these monuments – megalithic tombs, sanctuaries, fortifications and the like – dated back to prehistoric times. Legends were often attached to them: the megalithic tombs were supposed to have been built by the Devil or by giants. Alternatively, the objects found were attributed to natural causes: polished axes made of flint were regarded as 'thunder-stones' caused by lightning striking the ground. Thanks to the antiquaries, these remains began to be attributed to the peoples who had inhabited the region in pre-Roman times and who were known by name to the historians of antiquity – Gauls, Ancient Britons, Germans, Goths and so on. Among these antiquaries might be mentioned John Leland and William Camden in the sixteenth century, John Aubrey in the seventeenth and William Stukeley in the eighteenth century in Britain and, in France, Bernard de Montfaucon, Anne-Claude de Caylus and Theophile Corret de la Tour d'Auvergne in the eighteenth century. It was in Scandinavia, however, that antiquaries, protected by the royal houses of Sweden and Denmark, exerted a decisive influence on the progress of prehistoric studies. Gustav II Adolphus, King of Sweden from 1611 to 1632, established a post of *Antiquarius Regni* (today *Riksantikvar*), whose task it was to draw up an inventory of the country's archaeological monuments and ensure their protection. It was in Sweden too that, in 1662, under the reign of Karl XI, the first chair of 'national' archaeology, occupied by a *Professor antiquitatum*, was established, at the University of Uppsala. (It was not until 1818 that the second chair was to be established, at the University of Leyden in the Netherlands). Four years later, in 1666, the King of Sweden promulgated the very first law on the protection of archaeological monuments and sites. Mention should also be made of Ole Worm (1558–1654) in Denmark, who drew up an inventory of his country's archaeological monuments, wrote a history of Denmark in which he tried to combine written sources and archaeological data, and assembled a considerable archaeological collection, later incorporated in the royal collections and finally, in 1844, in the Museum of Nordic Antiquities in Copenhagen. Following the example of Sweden, Denmark established the post of State Antiquary in 1684. It was also on the Swedish model that Tsar Peter the Great (1672–1725) promulgated a decree obliging everybody who discovered antiquities to deliver them to the Archaeological Service, specially created for that purpose.

The first excavations that can be described as scientific were begun in Denmark around the middle of the eighteenth century; they were those of the megalithic tomb of Jaegerpris, undertaken in 1744 by Erik Pontopiddan and the future King Frederik V, then still Crown Prince. The only scientific excavation made before that time was that of another megalithic tomb at Cocherel in France in 1685.

Another great Danish achievement was the founding of the Museum of Nordic Antiquities in Copenhagen under the impetus of Rasmus Nyerup. Its construction was decided on in 1807 and it was inaugurated in 1819. To organize the display of the collections Christian J. Thomsen, appointed Keeper, worked out his famous chronological scheme, the three-age system. He postulated that weapons and tools had first been made of stone, later of bronze and finally of iron, hence the 'Stone Age', 'Bronze Age' and 'Iron Age'. A similar theory had already been put forward by the Latin poet Lucretius, in the first century before the Christian era, but on purely theoretical grounds, while Thomsen founded his system on precise observation. During the nineteenth century, museums organized on the same lines as the Copenhagen museum were founded in a number of other countries.

The influence of the antiquaries was strengthened by the setting up all over Europe of learned societies concerned with archaeology, though not exclusively. Most of them date back to the seventeenth century: the Accademia dei Lincei (Rome, 1603), the Royal Society (London, 1663) or the Académie des Inscriptions et Belles-Lettres (Paris, 1663). The first society concerned exclusively with archaeology was the Society of Antiquaries of London, founded in 1718, which received its royal charter in 1751.

The best of these antiquaries contributed greatly to the development of scientific methods, both in digging techniques and in dating and interpreting the remains of the past. They played a considerable part in setting up the great museums, in working out regulations governing excavations and legislation to protect monuments and sites and in organizing university courses in national archaeology alongside those in classical archaeology.

Third, another no less important root of present-day prehistoric research was the studies made by geologists and palaeontologists who, mainly from the eighteenth century onwards, took an interest in the human remains – artefacts and fossil bones – which they found in the course of their research in certain geological strata. As early as 1797, at Hoxne, Suffolk, in Britain, John Frere discovered a few artefacts, later recognized as Acheulian handaxes, at the base of an undisturbed layer of gravel at a depth of more than 2.7 metres, along with bones of extinct animal species. He concluded that humans had been the contemporaries of extinct animal species and that their appearance on earth went back much further than the six millennia generally accepted on the basis of biblical chronology.

Around the same time, similar discoveries were made in Germany, Austria, France and Belgium, and all those who made them came to the same conclusions as Frere. These conclusions were contested not only by those who adhered to the biblical chronology, but also by many geologists and palaeontologists influenced by Georges Cuvier in France and William Buckland in Britain. Cuvier had rejected Jean Baptiste Lamarck's transformism, launched his own catastrophist theories and denied the possibility of the existence of fossil humans. Many years elapsed before the discoveries referred to here were given full recognition.

During the second quarter of the nineteenth century, the prehistorian Jacques Boucher de Crèvecoeur de Perthes undertook research in the quarries and gravels of the banks of the Somme in France, where he discovered many artefacts of the Lower Palaeolithic, again associated with bones of fossil animals. His publications were at first greeted with scepticism in learned circles, until two eminent members of the Royal Society of London, Joseph Prestwich and John

Evans, did him justice in a paper submitted to the Society in 1859.

Four years later, the geologist Charles Lyell published his work *The Geological Evidence for the Antiquity of Man* and obtained definitive recognition for the theories put forward by Boucher de Perthes and his precursors concerning the great antiquity of humankind. Besides, the time was ripe for this veering of opinion. In 1857, in the Neanderthal valley in Germany, the skull and various bones of a fossil human were found which were to give the Neanderthalers their name. This discovery led to epic discussions among palae-ontologists, but finally demonstrated the existence in the genus *Homo* of the fossil subspecies *Homo sapiens nean-derthalensis*, quite different from the present-day *Homo sapiens sapiens*.

The year 1859 saw the vindication of Boucher de Perthes and also the publication of Charles Darwin's famous work, *The Origin of Species by Means of Natural Selection or the Preservation of Favoured Races in the Struggle for Life*. Four years later Thomas H. Huxley extended the Darwinian theories to the evolution of human beings. It can therefore be stated that it was around 1859 that prehistoric research, especially into the earliest periods, was accepted as a scientific disci-pline.

The influence of the geologists was instrumental too in developing stratigraphic excavations and in the recognition of their importance in the establishment of a relative chron-ology. For instance, shortly before the middle of the nine-teenth century Jens A. Worsaae undertook excavations of this kind in Denmark in collaboration with geologists to test the validity of C. J. Thomsen's three-age system. Thus began the collaboration between archaeologists and specialists in the natural sciences – a collaboration now so common that it is regarded as one of the major characteristics of prehistoric research.

Fourth, to understand current research in prehistory one must also take into account the relationships between archae-ology and anthropology. The latter term is rather ambiguous and requires clarification.

In French, the word *'anthropologie'* on its own means biological or physical anthropology, the discipline that studies the anatomical and biological characteristics of the different human groups and their evolution. When it deals more particularly with prehistoric humans, this *'anthro-pologie'* (then often called human palaeontology or palaeo-anthropology) is closely connected with prehistory. In the English-speaking world, and especially in the United States, 'anthropology' corresponds to what is known in French as *'anthropologie culturelle et sociale'*: it studies the human groups which in modern times (from the eighteenth to the twen-tieth centuries) were still without writing and formed fairly small units possessed of a relatively simple technology, and it attempts by means of field studies to analyse their cultural and social structures (Freedman, 1978). In the United States, anthropologists of this school at a very early stage included prehistory in their field of research. There are historical reasons for this. The discovery of the New World in 1492 brought the Europeans into contact with tribes still living at a prehistoric stage: most of them, unacquainted with the use of metals, were using stone weapons and implements. At this time there was uncertainty whether the stone objects already found in Europe were in fact the products of human activity. With a knowledge of the American artefacts, certain scholars such as Michele Mercati were able to interpret the European finds correctly as early as the sixteenth century and to attribute them to former populations whose cultural

stage must have been comparable to that of these American tribes.

One of the problems raised by the existence of the Amer-indians was that of their origin. According to the theories put forward in this connection, they were descendants of the Egyptians, of the Phoenicians, of the Canaanites, of the Lost Tribes of Israel, or of the inhabitants of the submerged continent, Atlantis. To these supposed ancestors were attri-buted the most impressive pre-Columbian monuments, such as the great mounds in the Middle West. However, some more sober-minded antiquaries thought that the builders of these mounds were none other than the ancestors of the contemporary indigenous inhabitants. Thomas Jefferson (who was to become the third President of the United States) undertook the excavation of one of these mounds in 1784. Although he was unable to prove this theory, his excavation was, owing to the techniques he employed and the accuracy of his observations, almost a century ahead of any field research carried out previously. Jefferson was also the first to detect the possibilities of dendrochronology.

The links gradually established between earlier and con-temporary populations in America led American anthro-pologists quite naturally to include the study of prehistoric populations, in the first place those of the New World, within the purview of anthropology. According to the auth-ority of this school, *Current Anthropology*, that discipline should encompass not only cultural and social anthropology, but also physical anthropology, prehistory, archaeology, linguistics, folklore and ethnology – and the list is by no means exhaustive. It should be noted that anthropologists very soon described the human groups studied as 'primitive' without realizing how derogatory were this epithet and the condescending attitude it implied, which the people it was applied to were justified in resenting. The term has now generally been abandoned. Anthropology may be compared to sociology, and anthropologists often describe themselves as the sociologists of societies without writing. The aims pursued by anthropology are therefore quite different from those of the prehistoric sciences as conceived in the present work. However, there have obviously been contacts between the two disciplines (see pp. 9–10).

From 1859 to 1918

The period 1859–63 marked a decisive stage in prehistoric research. The second part of the formative phase, up to the First World War, can be dealt with more briefly.

The important advances already made were the rejection of the biblical chronology for the antiquity of man and the almost universal acceptance of the 'three-age' system. Between 1865 and 1875 several other divisions into periods of prehistory were proposed which were built on socio-economic models. They had much more influence on anthropologists than on prehistorians. The most influential one was presented in 1865 by Sven Nilsson, whose theses were taken over by Edward Tylor in Britain and by Lewis H. Morgan in the United States. Morgan (1877) dis-tinguished seven phases, which he called 'ethnic periods', in the development of civilization:

1 Lower Savagery, from anthropogenesis to the discovery of fire;
2 Middle Savagery, from the discovery of fire to the dis-covery of the bow and arrow;
3 Upper Savagery, from the discovery of the bow and arrow to the discovery of pottery;

4 Lower Barbarism, from the discovery of pottery to the domestication of animals;

5 Middle Barbarism, from the domestication of animals to the smelting of iron ore;

6 Upper Barbarism, from the discovery of iron to the invention of a phonetic alphabet;

7 Civilization, from writing and the alphabet onwards.

Morgan's scheme had a considerable influence on Friedrich Engels and for a long time formed the basis of the Marxist conception of prehistory.

Darwinian evolution had been extended to the cultural field, and the nineteenth century saw the beginning of the controversy between evolutionism and diffusionism, which has gone on until our own time. As early as 1866, the need was felt for an organization to promote international collaboration. In that year an International Palaeo-ethnological Congress was held in Neuchâtel, Switzerland, and in the following year the International Congress of Prehistoric Anthropology and Archaeology was founded, which was the predecessor of the present International Union of Prehistoric and Protohistoric Sciences (De Laet, 1971). Many of the excavations undertaken during this period leave much to be desired from the technical standpoint, but a few pioneers whose excavations deserve admiration must be mentioned. The names of Thomas Jefferson and Jens J. Worsaae were quoted earlier; to these might be added those of Giuseppe Fiorelli (Pompeii), Ernst Curtius (Olympia), William M. Flinders Petrie (Egypt), Augustus H. Pitt-Rivers (in Britain) and the Reichslimeskommission (systematic excavations on the fortified frontier of the Roman Empire in upper Germany and Rhaetia). All these excavations brought out the importance of stratigraphy in the establishment of a relative chronology and the division into periods of the sites excavated. The need for an absolute chronology as well was already being increasingly felt. Thomas Jefferson had sensed the possibilities of dendrochronology. It was first successfully applied in 1901 by A. E. Douglass to date the pre-Columbian dwelling-site of Pueblo Bonito in Arizona. In the same year, A. Penck and E. Brückner, by distinguishing four glacial periods in the Pleistocene, provided a geological framework for the relative chronology of the Palaeolithic. In Sweden, Gerard de Geer worked out an absolute chronology for the last twelve millennia in northern Europe on the basis of an analysis of varved clays. During the winter of 1853–4, Ferdinand Keller discovered the first lake villages in Switzerland, and obtained the collaboration of specialists in various natural sciences, thus giving great importance to the study of the natural environment. Finally, the discovery in France and Spain of rock paintings and carvings dating back to the Upper Palaeolithic and the bringing to light in Europe, Asia and America of vestiges of brilliant vanished prehistoric civilizations had a tremendous effect on the interest of the general public in prehistory.

Transitional phase (the period between the two world wars)

During this transitional phase, archaeology still suffered from a series of childhood diseases, in particular, its undisciplined empiricism, a lack of scientific accuracy in its research and analytical methods, and the subjectiveness of its interpretations. In addition, prehistoric archaeology had to take up the challenge of the racist theories of the Kossinna school,

which claimed to provide a scientific basis for Hitler's imperialism.

Fortunately, this phase also has many positive aspects. Archaeological research was no longer generally limited to Europe, Egypt, western Asia and some regions in America (United States, Mexico, Peru). It was gradually extended to the other regions of the globe, and archaeology became world-wide. Archaeological prospecting by means of aerial photography made great strides. Excavation techniques developed with the new three-dimensional methods worked out by a few outstanding archaeologists such as Sir Mortimer Wheeler in Britain and Albert E. van Giffen in the Netherlands. Whereas during the formative phase the main aim was to find objects – artefacts – in this transitional phase it was realized that the soil could yield much more important archaeological finds – different structures, traces of soil discoloration due to the rotting of remains of organic material, and so on. To unearth and record such data, highly sophisticated techniques, in some cases almost as delicate as those used in surgery, had to be developed. Determining the circumstances in which the archaeological material had been buried in the soil – 'contextual evidence' – became one of the aims of field research. In addition, geographical, environmental and ecological approaches assumed increasing importance in the interpretation of archaeological data. The whole purpose of prehistoric archaeology changed. The exclusive interest in artefacts, implements, pottery and art works gave way to an interest in the very people who had left these remains in the soil, their way of life, their economic and social organization and their beliefs.

In this connection, three sentences from Mortimer Wheeler might be quoted: 'the archaeologist is not digging up *things*, he is digging up *people*'. 'In a simple direct sense, archaeology is a science that must be lived, must be "seasoned with humanity".' 'Dead archaeology is the driest dust that blows' (Wheeler, 1954, pp. v, 2).

Current phase (since the end of the Second World War)

Current trends in prehistoric archaeology can be summed up briefly as follows.

1 An ever-increasing reliance on the natural sciences, which have supplied new means of absolute dating, especially in regard to the most remote periods of the history of humankind, and have pushed back the beginnings of that history to two and a half or three million years ago. The natural sciences are also providing us with a more and more accurate picture of the environment in which people lived in the past and the evolution of that environment.

2 A growing interest in the epistemology, theory and methodology of archaeology. This interest is due, to some extent at least, to the stronger influence exerted by the anthropology of the English-speaking world and the 'new archaeology' beyond the frontiers of the United States.

3 The stepping up of prehistoric research, not only in Europe (including the former USSR and its successors), in the United States and China, but also in other regions of the world, in the young nations that became independent after the Second World War in particular. There it is now practised more often than not by scientists who are nationals of the countries concerned and it is closely bound up with the investigation of their past history, their cultural identity and their 'authenticity'.

4 Simultaneously with this geographical extension, inter-

national exchanges have become more frequent, with countless congresses, colloquia and symposia devoted to prehistory. Thus, the various ideological, philosophical and methodological trends in the interpretation of archaeological data are now better known and discussed outside the areas in which they arose.

REVIEW OF THE MAIN PREHISTORIC SCIENCES AND THEIR SUPPORTING DISCIPLINES

Archaeology

The terms 'prehistory' and 'archaeology' are frequently confused. It should be borne in mind, however, that while prehistory is a period of the history of humanity for which there are no written sources, archaeology is a method of research: it studies the past, taking as its basis the examination of the material remains left by the people of the past. Archaeology is the main but not the sole discipline that can inform us about prehistory. What is more, archaeology is not limited to the prehistoric period; it can inform us about all periods of the past, even the most recent. For instance, 'industrial archaeology' deals mainly with the material remains of the nineteenth century. Here of course we shall confine ourselves to prehistoric archaeology. We propose to review briefly the various phases in archaeological work and to note the different supporting disciplines to which recourse is made during each of these phases.

Archaeological prospection

Today archaeologists are no longer content with registering and excavating vestiges of the past that have remained visible on the surface of the soil or have been brought to light accidentally as a result of cultivation of the land, public works or erosion. A whole series of methods of active prospection have been developed, by means of which deposits hidden in the ground or imperceptible to the ordinary observer can be detected. The need for such methods arose *inter alia* from the risk of destruction of a great many sites, some extending over vast regions, owing to industrialization, the building of new highways, hydro-electric dams, and so on, and the desire to save as much as possible of these vestiges, which belong to our cultural heritage. Among the chief methods of prospection might be mentioned:

1 Aerial photography, often combined with photogrammetry, which records the slightest change in the level of the ground surface, otherwise practically imperceptible, often due to the traces of foundations hidden in the ground or ditches filled in (shadow sites). It also records differences in the colouring of the soil (soil marks) or the development vegetation (crop marks), which are often due to buried archaeological remains. Electronic manipulation of aerial photographs can often sharpen their colour contrasts and facilitate their interpretation. It must be stressed, however, that aerial photography as a method of prospection gives results only in open landscapes and not in forested areas. It is not impossible that, in the not-too-distant future, photographs taken by satellite (remote sensing) may also be used in archaeology.

2 Underwater prospection to detect wrecks of ships or submerged sites. Highly sophisticated equipment has been developed for this purpose (underwater television cameras, bathyscaphes, etc.).

3 Magnetic detection of metal objects, ovens, hearths, filled-in pits and wells, foundations, tombs, and so on, by means of equipment such as proton or caesium magnetometers, proton gradiometers, etc.

4 Detection of electrical anomalies in the subsoil caused by the presence of foundations (which reduce conductivity) or filled-in pits (which increase conductivity) by means of potentiometers designed to measure the resistivity of the subsoil.

5 Prospection by acoustic or seismic methods using instruments that register vibratory phenomena obtained by reflection, refraction or resonance following the sounding of the site or variable-frequency Hertzian wave transmission.

6 Chemical analysis of soils, especially the measurement of phosphate and potassium contents, makes it possible to detect soils on which humanity has left its mark (former dwelling sites).

Excavations

At one time excavations were limited to the unearthing of a monument or to looking for works of art or other objects for display. Today's archaeologist endeavours to reconstitute all aspects of the cultures of the past in so far as material remains allow. The aim is to find out how prehistoric people lived, how they reacted to their natural environment, what the bases of their economy were, what kind of social organization they had, how they behaved as individuals. The field worker's task is therefore to obtain from the soil as much information as possible for this purpose. This means not only recovering all the objects down to the tiniest flakes of flint, but also registering the slightest traces of features such as discolorations of the soil caused by objects and structures made of perishable organic materials, of which only the 'ghosts' remain.

As the same site may have been occupied repeatedly over a long time, the archaeological level to which each vestige belongs, the artefacts and structures to be correlated, must be determined with precision. The remains of different periods are usually found in their stratigraphical order, but very often the levels have been mixed up and overlap, and sophisticated techniques are required to sort them out. In addition, various samples must be taken for radiocarbon dating, palynological or chemical analyses and the like. As any excavation entails destroying the site to a greater or lesser extent, since the upper layers must be removed to uncover the lower levels and the objects found are of course taken out of their context, it is absolutely essential to record carefully (as far as practical possibilities and circumstances allow) the three-dimensional position of each vestige, each object and each feature, and their relationship to the different archaeological and geological levels. This is done by means of written notes, very accurate scale drawings of plans and sections, photographs, impressions – taken with latex, for instance – typical profiles taken by means of cellulose-based films, the Cartesian data method, etc.

In theory an excavation and its recording should be carried out with such precision that ideally the deposit can be reconstituted as it was before the excavation. The 'ethnographical' excavations developed by the French prehistorian André Leroi-Gourhan are typical of what can be done with current techniques. Modern excavations therefore demand of the archaeologist practical knowledge of the natural and the exact sciences and the ability to use specialized instruments and to make very complicated calculations. Geometry, trigonometry and logarithms are sometimes necessary.

Unfortunately, not all the excavations undertaken today come up to these exacting standards. However, casual or unauthorized excavations are clearly on the wane. Most field research today falls into one of the following categories.

First, rescue and salvage excavations undertaken on sites where deposits are at risk. In some countries it is laid down by law that any site on which a factory or a road is to be built must first be prospected by archaeologists. The latter are provided with the time and funds required to excavate the site should it prove to contain archaeological material. Such excavations have been carried out on occasion on an international basis under the auspices of UNESCO, as, for instance, in upper Egypt and Sudan when the new Aswan Dam was to be built.

Second, excavations undertaken to enhance a country's monumental heritage, to increase the number and attractiveness of its tourist sites, and thus contribute to its overall economy. This economic aim does not necessarily affect the scientific value of the research, which shows the authorities that archaeology can be worthwhile as a means of increasing national revenue.

The third category, scientifically the most important, comprises 'thematic excavations' undertaken on carefully selected sites for the purpose of obtaining fresh data likely to contribute to the solving of major cultural or historical problems. Such excavations are usually on a large scale, and a dwelling-site or a whole area may be entirely excavated (settlement excavations and area excavations). Such research is almost always multidisciplinary and is often international – as, for instance, that undertaken in southern and eastern Africa to solve the problem of anthropogenesis and in western Asia to investigate the origins of stock-raising and agriculture.

Description and classification of archaeological material

Radical changes have occurred in the methodology of the descriptive analysis and classification of archaeological material since the Second World War. Formerly, there was a total lack of discipline, in some respects anarchy, in regard to both the typology of artefacts and the definition of taxonomies: artefacts were named by virtue of mere external resemblance to nineteenth-century tools, terms were used loosely, typological differentiation was not taken very far and terms with a number of different meanings were employed. For some forty years now there has been a strong reaction against this. In an attempt at systematization and classification very strict taxonomic rules are applied, often much like those observed in biology, palaeoanthropology and other natural sciences. The elements on which the typology is based, the form and dimensions of the artefacts, are determined accurately and objectively (with the help of graphs, diagrams, histograms, scalograms, etc.). The raw material used to make the artefact is also determined (by petrography, spectral analysis, neutron activation analysis, etc., and by its colour – colorimetry). Considerable efforts have been made, too, to standardize terminology. Furthermore, in the classification of archaeological material increasing recourse is made to quantification – the development of different systems of quantitative and dimensional statistics and typological tables to determine taxonomic units and their subdivisions (cultures, industries, etc.). The use of computers and the development of data banks for the drawing up of typologies and the classification of material – especially when the latter abounds – are becoming common. These new methods, in which complex codes and symbols are often used, demand a knowledge of mathematics, statistics and data processing that most archaeologists do not possess, so they have to collaborate closely with mathematicians and, above all, computer programmers.

This veritable revolution in methodology also has its drawbacks, which it would be vain to deny. The efforts to standardize the nomenclature, to work out new typologies and new taxonomic methods, made in an uncoordinated fashion, sometimes result in still greater confusion, and even controversies (see pp. 9–10).

Restoration and conservation problems. Laboratory methods

When one is excavating, it is not enough to extricate the vestiges of the past. They must also be preserved as far as possible, for they are a part of the cultural and artistic heritage of humankind. Such vestiges have very often been damaged by time and by the surrounding earth and, after removal from the soil, are subjected to atmospheric, biological, physical and chemical agents. Great progress has been made over the past few decades in their conservation. In this connection, a distinction must be drawn between monumental or artistic vestiges preserved *in situ* and objects kept in museums.

In so far as monuments are concerned, spectacular but rather unscientific reconstructions such as those of the French architect Viollet-le-Duc seem fortunately to be a thing of the past. The main problems are, on the one hand, the consolidation and preservation of monumental ruins and, on the other, the protection of ancient monuments and works of art from the onslaughts of time. The increasing atmospheric pollution in highly industrialized zones constitutes a serious threat to many prehistoric, antique or medieval monuments – one has only to think of the Parthenon in Athens and the monumental vestiges of ancient Rome. Elsewhere, ruins that were buried for a long time and are now exposed in the open air are subject to other destructive agents. The ruins of Mohenjodaro in Pakistan, which for millennia were protected by the earth, are now threatened by rising groundwater, by corrosion caused by the salt contained in that water and by the flooding of the Indus. As for the rock paintings at Lascaux in France, discovered in 1940, the stream of visitors to the cave once it was opened to the public very soon upset the precarious climatological and biological equilibrium of the site and led to a proliferation of colonies of algae that were very difficult to eradicate. Then there is the problem that arises when great monuments can no longer be kept *in situ* and have to be moved, of which the famous temple of Abu Simbel, on a site that was to be submerged when the Aswan Dam was built, is a striking example.

As for the objects found in the course of excavation, conservation work must begin on the site in some cases – for instance, when they are made of organic materials. Objects made of metal, glass, ceramics, etc., must also undergo special treatment with a view to their preservation and restoration. Specialized laboratories attached to the big museums or set up as independent scientific units have developed highly perfected methods for this purpose.

It might be mentioned that in respect of restoration and conservation, international solidarity is strong and is seen at work in various organizations, such as the International Council of Museums (ICOM), the International Council of Museums and Sites (ICOMOS) and the International Centre for Conservation in Rome (ICCROM), some of which collaborate with UNESCO. It will be recalled that UNESCO has itself launched a number of campaigns to save prestigious monuments and sites – the Parthenon, the ruins of Angkor and Mohenjodaro, the temples of Abu Simbel and of Philae, for instance – which have met with great success as a result of international scientific and financial collaboration.

Archaeologists and laboratory workers collaborate too in determining the origins of artefacts found in the course of excavation, as also the origins of the raw materials of which they were made. This can provide clues to trade relations, routes and the spread of technical skills. Some of the natural sciences play an important part in this research – chemistry, microchemistry, spectrography, petrography and so on.

Although a knowledge of the specific purpose served by the various categories of structures and artefacts (implements, weapons, etc.) is part of archaeology it is a rather special part because in the case of artefacts, recourse is made increasingly to laboratory analysis such as chemistry, petrography, metallography and X-ray examination, as well as to practical experiments involving the use of copies and the reconstruction of working methods and parallels supplied by ethnology or by the tools and manufacturing methods in use before the industrial revolution. The use of such comparisons calls for great caution, however. Until quite recently little progress had been made in this direction: for instance, although the techniques employed in making flint artefacts were well known, practically nothing was known about the purposes they actually served. It was only in 1964 that the Soviet archaeologist S. A. Semenov led the way with his trace studies of the flint industry. As a result of this 'micro-wear analysis', involving examination under a microscope of the traces of wear left on flint implements, it was possible to determine the raw material (wood, bone, skin, meat, etc.) that had been worked using these artefacts and thus the purpose that they served.

Clearly, the advances made so far in archaeometry (the whole of the laboratory methods applied to archaeology) are merely the first steps, and great hopes can be entertained for the future.

Anthropology

Physical anthropology

Physical anthropology and its close relations with prehistoric archaeology were mentioned earlier, and we here revert to it only briefly. It will be recalled that the object of palaeoanthropology is to study fossil human remains from the most remote times and to try to retrace the stages of anthropogenesis. To do this it has recourse not only to palaeontology and comparative anatomy but also to molecular biology and even to the ethology of the great apes (gorilla, chimpanzee and orang-utan). Physical anthropology is also concerned with more recent times. So when an archaeologist excavates a necropolis, he or she is well advised to call immediately on the collaboration of an anthropologist, who will provide much information of a demographic nature – the age, sex and stature, of the dead, their life expectancy, the proportion of men to women and of different age groups, and so on. Examination of the bones

may also reveal traces of fractures and wounds, tumours and bone lesions resulting from afflictions that struck people in the past, such as rickets, dental decay, scurvy, various forms of rheumatism, gout, syphilis, smallpox, malaria, poliomyelitis, leprosy and sleeping sickness. Mention should also be made of traces of the earliest attempts at medicine, nearly always combined with magical practices, for instance the reduction of fractures or trepanations performed in Neolithic times with stone instruments *in vivo* on patients, of whom some survived. For both archaeology and anthropology, *palaeopathology* has become a valuable supporting science (Wells, 1964; Janssens, 1970). It might be added that the study of cremated bones can yield information similar to that obtained from studies of uncremated ones.

Genetics attempts to give some idea of the biological relationship of present-day groupings of physical types and the way in which they diverged in the course of prehistory. Using the studies of the mutations in DNA (the desoxyribonucleic acids present in cell nuclei and carrying the genetic characteristics), *Biogenetics* has launched rather revolutionary theories concerning the evolution of the phyletic line of the Homininae and the first *Homo* (Chapters 1 and 2). Closely linked with genetics, *historical haematology*, by studying the blood and certain particularities or anomalies in its composition, can sometimes shed light on history. One example will suffice here. In 1955 an original blood group was discovered in the red blood cells of a tribe living in Venezuela – the Diego. It is now known that this 'Diego group' is to be found in the blood of many Amerindian tribes and also in that of populations of eastern Asia. A blood study thus confirms the reality of the long route followed by an Asian population when it peopled America in Upper Palaeolithic times (Bernard, 1983).

Cultural and social anthropology – ethnology

Anthropology in American usage – an ensemble of diverse disciplines including prehistory – was discussed earlier. Conceived in this way, it is above all a comparative social science with nomothetic tendencies, that is, it seeks recurrences that might reveal the laws governing human behaviour in society. Prehistory, as understood in the present work, is a historical discipline, and history – like many other human sciences – is not nomothetic, but idiographic. According to American conceptions, only the nomothetic sciences deserve the appellation 'science', the human sciences not being sciences (since, in contrast to the natural sciences, they are not governed by laws) but 'humanities' or 'humanistic studies'. The old conception of a unilinear progressive evolution of human civilization had a nomothetic aspect. Long since abandoned in Europe, it is still upheld by some adherents of this anthropological school of thought: it is still found, for instance, in an American textbook on archaeology by G. Willey and P. Phillips (1958). These authors argue that archaeology and prehistory should turn resolutely away from the aims and methods of history (which is seen in a very narrow sense as the recording of the facts of the past with the interest centred on events – a definition few historians would agree with today) and, on the contrary, should deal with prehistoric societies in exactly the same way as ethnologists study the cultures of peoples without writing in our own time. In their view such societies should be classified according to their degree of cultural, economic and social development, regardless of considerations of space and time (the expression 'timeless and spaceless' recurs constantly) and the causes of their stages of development should be sought outside any chronological and geographical context. Those very complex causes should then be examined to see whether any of them reappear, in which case the recurrences should be studied with the ultimate purpose of inferring the laws that determined similar social and economic situations in various periods and in regions far away from one another. Willey and Phillips, therefore, by eliminating time and space from their research, adopt a non-historical attitude and their approach is purely sociological. Not every cultural anthropologist shares this attitude. For instance, the best known of them, Claude Lévi-Strauss (1967, p. 23), writes:

> Scorning the historical dimension [of anthropology] on the pretext that we have insufficient means to evaluate it, except approximately, will result in our being satisfied with an impoverished sociology, in which phenomena are set loose, as it were, from their foundations.

Notwithstanding these disputes, cultural and social anthropology and ethnology have undoubtedly exerted an influence on the interpretation of prehistoric cultures, mainly by providing certain models of interpretation. A number of general works, on the Stone Age for instance, still include chapters on present-day peoples with 'Palaeolithic' and 'Neolithic' technology. In this connection considerable caution must, however, be exercised.

The environmental sciences

No excavations of a high standard can now afford to neglect the systematic collection of all the data that can provide information on the natural environment, the biotope in which lived the people whose remains are being brought to light. The environment had a tremendous influence on the everyday lives of the peoples of the past, whether they were Palaeolithic hunters or medieval peasants. It was mentioned earlier that studies of the environment began in the middle of the nineteenth century, and interest in it has been increasing ever since. Today some members of the 'new archaeology' school think they are the first to have discovered the importance of the environment, and even believe in a sort of environmental determinism. This neglects the fact that of all living creatures human beings have the greatest capacity to adapt to the most diverse habitats and that their behaviour is by no means strictly determined by their environment, although they will make the best of its potential, as far as they can. What is more, right from the beginnings of food production they have gradually managed to adapt that environment to their needs.

The environment itself has been determined substantially by two factors, the nature of the soil and the climate, which have in turn determined the flora and fauna, the primary sources of subsistence for prehistoric peoples. A great many disciplines are concerned with the study of that environment and its evolution, but only the main ones can be enumerated here.

The geological disciplines

Among these are the geology of the Tertiary, Pleistocene and Holocene periods, including core-sampling of the sea-bed, the study of glaciers and moraines, the geology of rivers, the sedimentation of caves, the study of deposits of diatoms and pedology, to which might be added geomorphology, orogeny, tectonics and, more generally, palaeogeography and palaeoclimatology.

Since 1901, the year of Penck and Brückner's publication on the glacial periods, the contribution of geology (allied with other disciplines such as palaeobotany and nuclear physics) to a better knowledge of the palaeoclimate has grown to be tremendously important. For instance, the study of the moraines of Scandinavia, Siberia and Alaska, which indicate the advance and retreat of the ice-sheets, has made it possible to fill out our knowledge of the succession of glacial and interglacial periods, their stages, interstadia, fluctuations, oscillations and so on. Considerable ground was gained in the 1940s when it was found that seawater contains two different stable oxygen isotopes, oxygen-16 and oxygen-18, the proportions of which vary from year to year according to the temperature of the water: the higher the temperature, the higher the proportion of oxygen-18. Even slight variations in temperature produce *measurable* differences in the proportions of the two isotopes. An important practical application was effected in the 1960s when the ice-sheet some 1,400 metres thick covering Greenland was explored in depth by core-sampling. The annual levels of the snow (which had turned into ice) over the past 8,300 years could be ascertained, and hence the slightest variations in climate over that long period, though only for the northern hemisphere of course. In the case of earlier periods, the annual levels of which were no longer discernible, complicated and less reliable calculations were required. More recently it was discovered that the same fluctuations between the two oxygen isotopes exist in the shells of foraminifera covering the sea-bed. By means of core-sampling of sea-bed deposits, which can reach great depths, going back to very remote times, it has been possible to establish a long sequence of warmer and cooler periods and correlate this with the data of land geology. The approximate duration of each of these stages could thus be calculated and dated closely enough by radiometric methods using radiocarbon and protactinium–thorium (see pp. 11–12).

Orogeny, tectonics and palaeogeography also supply prehistory with important data. The role which Y. Coppens (1983) attributes to the collapse of the Rift Valley in eastern Africa in anthropogenesis might be mentioned as an example. At the time of the last glaciation the advance or retreat of the glaciers of Alaska barred or allowed the access of human beings to America (Chapter 29). The rise in the sea-level following the melting of the thick ice-cap at the end of the Pleistocene and the beginning of the Holocene, accompanied by considerable isostatic movements, transformed the human environment, causing, for instance, the collapse of the land bridge between Britain and the European continent, the emergence of the North Sea and the Baltic and the remodelling of shorelines.

Palaeobotany

This discipline, which studies the vegetation of former times and its evolution, is based partly on palynology (the study of pollens) and partly on the study of macroscopic remains of plants (usually collected in the course of excavation by flotation). A related discipline is palaeoethnobotany, which studies the influence of the plant environment on the behaviour of prehistoric peoples, and, conversely, their influence on the vegetation. A particular aspect of these studies concerns the domestication of plants (Chapter 37).

The method most commonly employed is undoubtedly palynology. Under favourable circumstances, when the pollen grains have not been destroyed by unsuitable soils, the plant environment even of Palaeolithic sites can be reconstructed in this way. It has, however, been used mainly for more recent sites, those of the Holocene. The subdivision of the Holocene into a number of climatic periods – Pre-Boreal, Boreal, Atlantic, Sub-Boreal, Sub-Atlantic – is based largely on the findings of palynology, which can thus serve as a relative dating method, especially in countries such as Denmark, the Netherlands, France and the United Kingdom, where pollen analyses are numerous enough to establish with sufficient accuracy the evolution of the plant environment in a particular region.

Another discipline based on the remains of plants and one that is above all a dating method, dendrochronology, can also provide information on the climate, for the thickness of each ring of annual growth on a tree depends on the temperature and the degree of humidity prevailing in the year in which the age-ring was formed.

Palaeozoology

Palaeozoology and animal palaeontology ('animal' in the widest sense) – provide information about the fauna of a particular region at a particular period and also on the evolution of that fauna. A special branch of these disciplines deals with the domestication of animals (Chapter 38). Palaeozoology yields valuable information on the way of life and diet of hunters, stock-rearers and fisherfolk of the past.

In many cases the faunas in particular regions are characteristic of particular periods and can thus also serve as a means of dating. In addition, the palaeontological variability of certain animal species can help in the establishment of a relative chronology. For instance, the variability of ancestors of the pig (before it was domesticated, of course) in eastern Africa helped in the relative dating of certain levels in which the fossil bones of hominids were also found.

Palaeozoology is not concerned solely with the remains of the megafauna: those of minute animals – like some rodents, insects and molluscs – can also yield useful information. For instance, malacology – the study of the shells of molluscs, especially snails, some of which live in the open, others in forests, some preferring a dry climate, others a damp one – can help determine the climate of the period during which the level in which the shells were found was formed.

Dating methods

The prehistorian's need for dating systems has already been stressed. For a long time prehistorians had to be content with a relative chronology (one determining the time-sequence of the different cultures of which traces have been found), because they were unable to establish a chronometric date, i.e. one expressed in figures. Since the end of the Second World War a whole series of increasingly reliable chronometric dating methods have been developed, thanks mainly to the progress of laboratory techniques, and they have revolutionized the absolute dating of prehistoric times.

Relative chronology

Here the method that makes use of typological evolution has been perfected owing to greater strictness and objectivity in the drawing up of typologies and classifications of archaeological material. Similarly, the stratigraphic method has benefited from the great progress made in excavation techniques, in some cases making it possible to establish a 'microstratigraphy'. The 'closed find' or 'closed association' method and the drawing up of synchronisms have been applied more widely and more strictly. Among methods known in theory before 1939 and since applied in practice might be mentioned the relative dating of bones from the same site by their fluorine, nitrogen and uranium contents – a method that exposed the notorious Piltdown forgery in the United Kingdom. Relative dates can be obtained for obsidian artefacts from the same site by measuring the thickness of their layers of hydration. Certain attempts to base relative dating on the statistical evaluation of archaeological remains should also be mentioned. In addition, a number of environmental sciences referred to here, such as the geology of glaciers, the geology of the sea-bed, palynology, as well as the variability of certain animal species, make it possible to situate a geological layer or an archaeological level in a particular climatic phase and thus provide the elements of a relative dating.

Chronometric chronology

This term is used rather than 'absolute chronology', because most of the methods it involves provide dates that can be expressed in figures, but they are usually approximate or contain a margin of error. Reliable dates expressed in calendar years are the exception. However, considering the tremendous length of prehistoric times, even an approximation to within a few centuries is highly satisfactory – especially for the earliest periods.

Among the chronometric dating methods developed long ago, De Geer's analysis of clay varves might be mentioned *pro memoria*. Though it has not been entirely abandoned, its field of application is geographically very limited and it is generally regarded as not very reliable. As for the theory developed by M. Milankovitch (1930), who worked out a curve of variations in the intensity of solar radiation and correlated it with the curve of the alternation of glacial periods and warmer intervals, in the belief that such a curve could be dated in an absolute way, it seems to have been abandoned entirely, at least by archaeologists.

Here we refer only to the methods most commonly used today.

Dendrochronology The beginnings and the first practical applications of this method of dating based on the number of annual growth rings on trees and the variations in thickness of those rings due to the influence of the climate were mentioned earlier. Regarding the limits of dendrochronology, it should be mentioned that some species of trees are very sensitive to these climatic variations, others less so or not at all. Further, the data concerning a given region cannot automatically be transferred to another one with a different microclimate. However, dendrochronology is used increasingly because it now enables the dating of wood samples going back as far as eight millennia. Moreover, it became tremendously important when it was found that it could be used to check reliably the accuracy of other dating methods, in particular radiocarbon dating (see further).

Radiocarbon dating (carbon-14 or ^{14}C dating) When in 1949 the American physicist W. F. Libby presented the method of absolute dating by the measurement of carbon-14, he brought about a major revolution in archaeology. This method, hailed over-enthusiastically by a large proportion of archaeologists but rejected by some, has undeniably provided prehistoric archaeology with a sound chronological basis, even if when checked against dendrochronology it has been shown to require correction and calibration. There are a number of carbon isotopes, including carbon-12, which is stable, and carbon-14, which is radioactive. Carbon-14 is formed in the upper layers of the ionosphere as a result of the cosmic irradiation of atmospheric nitrogen. All living things – plants, animals, human beings – contain a fixed proportion of carbon-12 and carbon-14. The latter gradually breaks down spontaneously and changes back to nitrogen-14, but its concentration in a living organism remains constant, for it is reintroduced through exchanges with the environment. These exchanges cease with death and the proportion of carbon-14 decreases at a steady rate: after 5,730 years (originally calculated to be 5,568 years) only half of the carbon-14 is still present (hence the expression 'a half-life of 5,730 years'); after another period of 5,730 years only a quarter of the original carbon-14 remains, and so on. By rather intricate laboratory methods, it is possible to determine the ratio between carbon-14 and carbon-12 present in the sample (charcoal, bone, wood or other organic materials) and thus to calculate the date of the death of the organism from which the sample originates. According to a convention between all the laboratories, all radiocarbon dates are given 'BP' (before present); the dates are calculated with 1950 as the reference year (1949 being '1 BP'). To translate the given dates into dates in the Christian era, one has to substract 1,950 from the date given by the laboratory. More and more archaeologists give their radiocarbon dates in years BP. However, to avoid boring calculations which could only give the reader the illusion that radiocarbon dates are real calendar-years, and taking into account the many uncertainties still existing about the strict accuracy of radiocarbon dates, all the dates given in this volume are to be considered as approximations and are expressed by periphrases mostly employing round figures such as 'about 5,000 years ago'.

From the very beginning there have been some misunderstandings between physicists and many archaeologists. The laboratories always give their radiocarbon dates with a standard deviation (or a margin of error), written as the Greek letter sigma (σ), and too many archaeologists believe that the real calendar-date falls between the limits of the standard deviation. If for instance a date is given as '4550 $\pm$ 200 BP', they believe that the real date falls between 2800 and 2400 BC; they are not aware that there is only a probability of 68 per cent that the real date falls within the limits of the standard deviation. Other archaeologists forget sometimes that radiocarbon dating measures the time that has elapsed since the death of the organism from which the sample derives, but that there may also have been a lapse of time, of variable duration, between the death of this organic material and the moment when it was used by human beings (and the latter of course is the date the archaeologist wishes to know). Carbon-14 dates can also be distorted by many other factors: samples taken in bad conditions or badly preserved, samples contaminated by different factors, etc. Actually, a single carbon-14 date is not entirely reliable: to have a sufficient security margin to date a site, a culture, or a cultural phase we need a cluster of convergent dates.

Since radiocarbon dating was first introduced, discrepancies have been observed. One major postulate of the method, the constant intensity of cosmic radiation, has proved to be erroneous: when results obtained with carbon were compared with those obtained by dendrochronology, it was found that the two dating curves gradually diverged to the extent of about a millennium towards 8,250 years ago (the earliest date obtainable using dendrochronology), the carbon dates being too recent. A more accurate figure was

calculated for the half-life – 5,730 years instead of 5,568 – but this has provoked some difficulties, as already many thousands of carbon dates had been published on the basis of the half-life of 5,568 years. Efforts were therefore concentrated on working out numerous calibration tables (between the carbon-14 dates on the basis of the 5,568 years' half-life and the dendrochronological dates), though none has met with the unanimous approval of nuclear physicists. The most recent calibration tables (published in the periodical *Radiocarbon*, Vol. 24, No. 2, 1982, and Vol. 28, No. 2, 1986) do not present any more important divergences. It is of course evident that even with calibrated dates, one has to take into account the standard deviation σ and there are still only two chances in three that the real date falls between the limits of the standard deviation.

Despite its drawbacks, the radiocarbon method is accurate enough for the period going back to about 40,000 years ago (although it can scarcely be used to establish a very detailed chronology). While theoretically the method can be used for dates going back as far as about 80,000 years ago, it becomes much less accurate for materials of such great ages because the quantities of carbon-14 surviving in them are very small.

A new technique using the AMS (accelerator mass spectrometry) is still in the experimental stage. This is based on measuring the concentration of carbon-14 directly rather than calculating it by measuring its rate of decay. The technique will have the two-fold advantage of requiring less material (samples need contain no more than 10 milligrams of carbon) and of being able to date an even more distant past.

Potassium–argon (K–Ar) dating This method too is based on radioactivity. Eruptive rocks issuing from the volcanic magma contain a radioactive isotope of potassium (potassium-40) at the time of their cooling. This isotope decays, 89.52 per cent changing into a calcium isotope (calcium-40) and 10.48 per cent into an argon isotope (argon-40). The age of rock can be gauged by determining the proportions of potassium and argon it contains. The half-life of potassium-40 is 1.25×10^9 years, i.e. 1,250 million years. With this method dates can be obtained for the 5,000 million years of the earth's existence, although not for periods less than 100,000 years ago. In archaeology and anthropology this method has made it possible to date those fossil hominid levels in eastern Africa that are situated stratigraphically between layers of volcanic origin.

Palaeomagnetism The polarity of the earth's magnetic field varies slightly from year to year, whence the divergence between the geographic pole and the magnetic pole. In the course of the earth's history, however, it has quite often happened that this polarity has been completely reversed, the magnetic field then being directed southwards. Four such major reversals have occurred over the past 5 million years – the Brunhes, Matuyama, Gauss and Gilbert reversals – not to mention some minor episodes. Both eruptive rocks and the ferromagnetic particles contained in marine sediments retain the magnetic direction of the period when the rocks and sediments were formed, as if it were fossilized. Examination of the sea-bed by means of core sampling has made it possible to establish the stratigraphy of these reversals of polarity, which have been dated using methods based on radioactivity. As the reversals were the same all over the globe, volcanic or sediment levels dating back to the same magnetic phase can be dated by correlation with already well-dated levels. Note that for the duration of the magnetic reversals the earth lost its magnetic protection from cosmic radiations, which may have affected the climate and fauna.

Thermoluminescence (TL) This method is used mainly for dating objects made of baked clay. The soil, including the clay from which pottery is made, contains many natural isotopes, mainly of uranium, thorium, potassium and rubidium, which irradiate certain minerals, such as quartz, causing displacement of electrons which accumulate in 'traps' (or defects in the crystal lattice) at a regular rate. When such minerals are heated the accumulated energy is liberated at 320 °C or more in the form of light. Once they have cooled, such minerals again accumulate energy, owing to irradiation. For instance, a piece of pottery during firing releases the energy accumulated in the quartz it contains, but as soon as it has cooled down the quartz again starts to accumulate energy. When potsherds are heated, the energy is liberated once more with the emission of light. The intensity of this light depends on the quantity of energy accumulated. The light can be measured by means of very complex laboratory processes, and the rate of accumulation of energy ascertained, and thus the time that has elapsed since the pottery was baked can be calculated. This method, which, incidentally, can be applied also to flints that have been subjected to fire, will in all likelihood become one of the most reliable for dating prehistoric cultures already familiar with the making of pottery.

Other dating methods There are a number of other methods which, for lack of space, we cannot go into here. They are methods that in archaeology have a restricted field of application, are unreliable, or are still in the experimental stage.

Among the methods based on radioactive decay are uranium–helium (U–He) dating, uranium–thorium (U–Th) dating, uranium–protactinium (U–Pa) dating, protactinium–thorium (Pa–Th) dating (which has been used for dating the stratified levels of the sea-bed), rubidium–strontium (Rb–Sn) dating (which is used mainly for dating the earth's oldest rocks and which was also used for dating the fragments of rock brought back from the moon), the study of the imbalances in the uranium family, and lastly dating by counting fission tracks (used for the dating of minerals containing the uranium isotope U-238, including zircon, titanite, monazite and apatite, or fragments of volcanic glass, such as obsidian, and pumice-stone). Direct datation by non-destructive gamma-ray spectrometry is quite recent. The 'racemization' of amino acids, for dating fossil bones, though still at the experimental stage, seems from the start to be too delicate and too uncertain to come into regular use soon. Lastly might be mentioned electron spin resonance (ESR) dating, which is still being developed.

PROBLEMS OF INTERPRETATION IN PREHISTORIC ARCHAEOLOGY

The classification of archaeological material has already been discussed. It must be reverted to here in so far as the *taxonomic grouping* of such material is concerned. During the formative period, under the influence of geological stratification and evolutionary theories in the natural sciences, archaeologists believed in the unilinear progressive evolution of human culture, so they employed *reference fossils* in order to attribute archaeological remains to some stage or other of that evol-ution. The continual increase in the amount of material and the geographical extension of prehistoric archaeology soon revealed through numerous specific cases the fallacious character of this theory. So, following the example of precursors such as H. Schliemann and R. Pumpelly, they began to group archaeological remains in *cultures* – a term employed in practically all languages. (In French the term *civilisations* was preferred, but it is tending to give way to *cultures*.) This term is borrowed from ethnology, which distinguishes 'material culture', 'moral culture' and 'mental culture'. Ethnologists, using geographical and statistical distribution, also determined 'cultural areas' (*Kulturkreise*). As early as the beginning of the twentieth century, the *archaeological* concepts of 'culture', 'cultural area' and 'cultural level' were developed in Germany, but G. Kossinna and his disciples gave these concepts ethnic, linguistic and racial significance. In the United Kingdom, V. Gordon Childe, who enjoyed tremendous influence all over Europe from about 1925 until his death in 1957, adopted these concepts while rejecting Kossinna's interpretation.

Already in 1929 Childe (in his book *The Danube in Prehistory*, pp. v–vi) had given the following definition of an archaeological culture:

> We find certain types of remains – pots, implements, ornaments, burial rites, house forms – constantly recurring together. Such a complex of regularly associated traits we shall term a 'cultural group' or just a 'culture'. We assume that such a complex is the material expression of what would today be called a 'people'.

In this last sentence, the word 'people' today has too precise a connotation, which we hesitate to project into the remote prehistoric times. If it is replaced by the much broader and vaguer term of 'human group', the definition given by Childe (a culture being the sum of the artefacts – tools, weapons and ornaments – and structures – dwellings, tombs, fortifications and so on – regularly encountered together and associated with a particular way of life, shown by plans of the dwellings, funeral customs, social and economic organization, at a particular period and in a particular region) is still generally accepted today as the basic taxonomic unit. The progress of prehistoric research has, however, made it necessary to broaden this definition, by putting the stress on other facets of prehistoric cultures. On the one hand, prehistorians insist on the very conservative character of prehistoric communities, where traditional and ancestral conceptions and ideas prescribe and regulate the norms that have to be respected as much in the manufacture of artefacts and ornaments as in the construction of dwellings and in the practice of the rituals connected with every important event (such as birth and death) in the life of the community. On the other hand, prehistorians are also aware that every culture is the result of the adaptation of a community to its natural environment. A culture can thus be considered as the archaeological reflection of a human group with its own economic system, its social structures, its religious concept and its dynamics. However, this is an ideal definition; in practice the criteria employed for identifying a culture are often still subjective and indefinite and they vary depending on the school to which the investigator belongs, his or her ideology, and the methods adopted. So despite its unilateral character the 'reference fossil' is only too often still given a role out of proportion to its real value. Different cultures may be found occurring in the same region at different times, or at the same time over different areas, or even simultaneously in the same region.

The concept of culture still constitutes the basis on which problems of interpretation are approached. In some cases it is fairly easy to define the different cultures. This is so mainly in the case of periods in which relatively small, stable and sedentary human communities lived apart, any contacts being sporadic. In the case of other periods, such as the Palaeolithic, on the contrary, relatively few categories of artefacts (basically, the stone and bone industry) were available until quite recently and, in addition, typological evolution was extremely slow, with the result that the same assemblages are to be found over a vast area. These archaeological remains were grouped not in cultures but in *assemblages*, subdivided in turn into *industrial complexes, industries, phases* and *archaeological horizons*. Advances in excavation techniques have led in recent years, however, to the discovery of other categories of archaeological information, such as the structure of dwellings, tombs, plastic representations and the like, so that in these cases too there is now some justification for referring to cultures. The transition from the concept of industry to that of culture gives rise to a number of problems, however (Otte, 1985). It is more difficult to establish well-defined cultures in the case of less sedentary populations, when the different human groups come in contact with one another more frequently and individuals pass from one to another more easily: here we have cultural complexes, the transition from one group to another being gradual and it being almost impossible to draw clear cultural boundaries. So far as the remains of more highly evolved human communities, such as the Scythians or the Celts, are concerned, trade exchanges with other populations, deep-seated social differences, links arising from the interdependence of different tribes and so on, break up the homogeneity of the relevant archaeological material and render the delimitation of archaeological cultures hazardous. This also brings into relief the illusory character of the racial, linguistic, ethnic or political interpretations sometimes put forward in the case of certain cultures (De Laet, 1957, pp. 76–92).

So much for the problem of the limitations on the interpretation of archaeological sources; the question now is what positive contributions these sources can make. Here of course the ideological approaches of prehistorians using the sources and the philosophies of the schools to which they belong must be taken into account. These differing attitudes are seldom encountered in field research, but they will permeate the interpretations that are put forward of the archaeological data. To discuss these different schools and trends is beyond the scope of this introduction. The authors who have collaborated in this volume obviously belong to different trends, and it goes without saying that they have been given complete freedom of interpretation and have not been subjected to the slightest pressure in this connection.

A few words must be said, however, about 'new archaeology' on account of the influence it exerts on many young prehistorians and its opposition to a 'historical' interpretation of prehistoric cultures. In this it follows the trends of American anthropology (see pp. 9–10), in which it has its origins, moreover. It was launched by K. C. Chang (1967) and S. R. and L. R. Binford (1968) and made known in Europe by D. L. Clarke (1968). In fact, this 'new' archaeology was not so new as all that and its main features were already to be found in many earlier studies. However, the adherents of the new trend claimed the right to question everything established in archaeology before the Binfords. 'New archaeology' manifestly has some positive aspects. A typical feature is the interest taken by 'new' archaeologists in the epistemology, theory and methodology of archaeology. Every year new essays are published in this field, which might be described as 'theoretical archaeology' (Klejn, 1977). The authors of these essays seldom have many practical experiences of excavation; their theories, elaborated far from the everyday realities of archaeology, hardly ever stand up to the test of practical application. The chief aim of 'new archaeology' is to explain and elucidate cultural process and evolutionary change in culture, the term 'culture' being taken in its ethnological sense and hence covering moral and mental culture as well as material culture. Archaeology should therefore broaden its scope and study these non-material aspects too. For this purpose it should have recourse to ethnological paradigms and extrapolate from the data supplied by ethnology. We have already expressed our misgivings about taking ethnological comparisons too far. According to the 'new' archaeologists, not only is this initial aim possible to attain, but the explanation of cultural process could lead to the discovery of the laws of cultural dynamics and even the laws governing human behaviour in general.

The adherents of 'new archaeology' severely criticized the old methods of classifying archaeological material as a means to attain these aims and developed a new typology involving numerical classification of archaeological data and computer processing. The next stage was the development of *models* in an attempt to solve specific problems and to exercise strict control over a working hypothesis. The use of models in archaeology was not new, either. The concept of a *model*, borrowed from sociology, indicates in the first place the basic postulates determining the archaeologist's logical reasoning. When, for instance, cultural changes in a particular region are explained by migrations or when an ethnic interpretation of archaeological cultures is put forward, specific models are being employed. In the narrower sense, a model is a mechanism that can be expressed in a mathematical or quasi-mathematical formula and that serves as a support for the leading idea behind an archaeological investigation. Such models, which are also used in cultural anthropology, are heuristic schemata, working hypotheses, rather than veritable theories. The only innovation in 'new archaeology' is that models are used more systematically than they were before. However, the use of models is not in itself without risk. Some archaeologists, instead of trying to find out whether or not the model they have developed is contradicted by the archaeological facts, have no hesitation about 'forcing' the facts to make them conform to the model at any cost. Even when the model leads to positive results and seems to confirm the hypothesis, it would be mistaken to conclude that the model is correct: there is no reason why another hypothesis based on the same material should not also be proved correct. However, the greater the number of basic data and the greater the number of variables integrated in the model, the more chance there is that the positive result can be accepted as correct.

It remains for us to enumerate the broad aspects on which archaeological findings can shed light. Four or five can be distinguished, as follows:

1 All remains concerning production, means of production and the economy: tools or implements, evidence relating to agriculture and stock-rearing, traces of buildings (dwellings, barns, workshops), mines, quarries, bridges, tracks, dykes, testimonies of barter or trade with other communities.

2 The many remains that relate to everyday needs, such as food and clothing, domestic utensils, etc.

3 Objects designed to meet both material and spiritual and/or aesthetic needs. These are the objects serving a particular purpose that are also decorated (items of clothing, belts, buckles, decorated pottery, etc.). There are also objects that might be regarded as symbols of prestige or rank (e.g., ceremonial axes, objects made of materials imported from distant lands or of precious materials). The importance of decorated objects also resides in the fact that the decoration is often traditional and plays a big part in the attribution of such remains to a particular culture.

4 All the material remains reflecting spiritual and/or religious conception: funeral customs and structures, cult representations and symbols, places of worship, etc.

5 Items indicating social organization (an aspect of prehistoric cultures increasingly stressed today). Social structures go hand in hand with production and the means of production (group 1 above) and are often reflected in remains which fall into group 3 or group 4 as well. However, there are many other remains that provide direct information on social structure – differences in the size of dwellings and in the opulence of their furnishings (in some centres the 'palace' of the chief stands out clearly, set on a hill and defended by a rampart isolating it from the other dwellings); differences in the richness of the funeral furnishings of tombs in the same necropolis; 'princely' tombs; remains of engineering works (fortifications, irrigation and drainage systems) that could have been carried out only under the direction of a 'chief', etc.

All these remains have to be 'decoded' of course, and it is here that the ideology of the archaeologist who does the decoding often asserts itself.

Finally, there is the question of the precise nature of a prehistoric culture. It has been seen that any racial interpretation is to be rejected, that an ethnic interpretation does not correspond to any reality, for no one could assign a precise meaning to an 'ethnic group' in prehistoric times, and that, although a culture may correspond to a linguistic area, many examples demonstrate that this was not always the case; and the same can be said of political interpretations.

The following definition is put forward: A prehistoric culture consists of all the remains of a human community (the vaguest possible term is intentionally used here) that has common technological, economic, social, religious and aesthetic traditions; such a culture very often also reflects the optimum adaptation of that community to its natural environment. Many of these cultures lasted over several centuries and with the advances made in dating methods they can be studied diachronically and their internal evolution followed; they can also be compared with contemporary cultures extending over different areas. Whereas formerly efforts were concentrated on the static description of the contents of these cultures a dynamic stage has now been reached with the interest shifted to research into the reasons and the modalities of this evolution; an interest is taken not only in the particular nature of the cultures, but also, and above all, in *why* and *how* they acquired the characteristics that constitute their originality, and also *why* they have features different from those of contemporary or neighbouring cultures.

BIBLIOGRAPHY

As a result of the rapid development of prehistory, its methods and its supporting disciplines, as well as of the numerous new archaeological discoveries occurring practically every year, most of the syntheses and works on archaeological methodology are quickly outdated. Therefore we have included in this bibliography only the most important books published since 1960, with the exception of a few of the previous contributions of basic value or which represent an important step in the history of prehistoric archaeology or which have strongly influenced the development and the contemporary conceptions in prehistoric research.

ADAM, J. P. 1975. *L'Archéologie devant l'imposture*. Paris.

ATKINSON, R. J. C. 1946. *Field Archaeology*. London.

BARISANO, E.; BARTHOLOME, E.; BARCOLONGO, B. 1984. *Télédétection et archéologie*. Paris, CNRS.

BARKER, P. 1977. *The Techniques of Archaeological Excavations*. London.

BERNAL, I. 1980. *A History of Mexican Archaeology*. London.

BERNARD, J. 1983. *Le Sang et l'histoire*. Paris.

BIBBY, G. 1957. *The Testimony of the Spade*. New York.

BINFORD, L. R. 1962. Archaeology as Anthropology. *Am. Antiq.*, Vol. 28.

—— 1972. *An Archaeological Perspective*. New York/London.

—— 1983. *In Pursuit of the Past: Decoding the Archaeological Record*. London.

BINFORD, S. R.; BINFORD, L. R. (eds) 1968. *New Perspectives in Archaeology*. Chicago.

BORILLO, M. (ed.) 1978. *Archéologie et calcul*. Paris, CNRS.

BORILLO, M.; GARDIN, J.-C. 1974. *Les Banques de données archéologiques*. Paris, CNRS.

BORILLO, M.; GUENOCHE, A.; VEGA, W. F. DE LA. 1977. *Raisonnement et méthodes mathématiques en archéologie*. Paris, CNRS.

BRAIDWOOD, R. J. 1984. *Prehistoric Men*. Chicago.

BROMLEY, Y. V.; PERSIC, A. I.; TOKAREV, S. A. 1972. *Problemy etnografii i antropologii v svete neucnogo nasledija F. Engelsa* [Ethnographical and Anthropological Problems in the Light of F. Engels's Scientific Heritage]. Moscow.

BROTHWELL, D. 1962. *Digging Up Bones*. London.

BROTHWELL, D.; HIGGS, E. S. (eds) 1970. *Science in Archaeology: A Survey of Progress and Research*. 2nd edn. London.

BUSHNELL, G. H. S. 1965. *Ancient Arts of America*. London.

CERAM, C. W. 1971. *The First American: A Study of North American Archaeology*. New York.

CHAMPION, T. et al. 1984. *Prehistoric Europe*. London.

CHANG, K. C. 1967. *Rethinking Archaeology*. New York.

—— (ed.) 1968. *Settlement Archaeology*. Palo Alto.

CHAPLIN, R. E. 1971. *The Study of Animal Bones from Archaeological Sites*. London.

CHILDE, V. G. 1929. *The Danube in Prehistory*. Oxford.

—— 1942. *What Happened in History*. Harmondsworth.

—— 1957. *The Dawn of European Civilization*. 5th edn. London.

—— 1958. *The Prehistory of European Society*. Harmondsworth.

CLARK, J. D. 1970. *The Prehistory of Africa*. London.

—— 1983. From the Earliest Times to c.500 BC. In: CLARKE, J. D. (ed.) *The Cambridge History of Africa*. Cambridge. Vol. 1.

CLARK, J. G. D. 1952. *Prehistoric Europe: The Economic Basis*. London.

—— 1957. *Archaeology and Society: Reconstructing the Prehistoric Past*. 2nd edn. London.

—— 1977. *World Prehistory in New Perspective*. 3rd edn. Cambridge.

CLARKE, D. L. 1968. *Analytical Archaeology*. London. (2nd edn 1978.)

—— (ed.) 1972. *Models in Archaeology*. London.

COLES, J. 1972. *Field Archaeology in Britain*. London.

—— 1979. *Experimental Archaeology*. London.

COLES, J. M.; HIGGS, E. S. 1969. *The Archaeology of Early Man*. London.

COLES, J. M.; SIMPSON, D. A. (ed.) 1968. *Studies in Ancient Europe: Essays Presented to Stuart Piggott*. Leicester.

COPPENS, Y. 1983. *Le Singe, l'Afrique et l'homme*. Paris.
—— 1984. *Paléoanthropologie et préhistoire: leçon inaugurale*. Paris, Collège de France.
CORNWELL, I. W. 1958. *Soils for the Archaeologist*. London.
DANIEL, G. E. 1975. *A Hundred and Fifty Years of Archaeology*. London.
—— 1981. *A Short History of Archaeology*. London.
—— (ed.) 1981. *Towards a History of Archaeology*. London.
DANIEL, G. E.; CHIPPINDALE, C. (eds) 1989. *The Pastmasters. Eleven Modern Pioneers of Archaeology*. London.
DANIEL, G. E.; RENFREW, C. 1988. *The Idea of Prehistory*. 2nd edn. Edinburgh.
DECHELETTE, J. 1908–14. *Manuel d'archéologie préhistorique, celtique et gallo-romaine*. Paris. 4 vols.
DEETZ, J. (ed.) 1971. *Man's Imprint from the Past: Readings in the Methods of Archaeology*. Boston.
DE LAET, S. J. 1957. *Archaeology and its Problems*. London.
—— 1963. Review of J. Hawkes and L. Woolley, Prehistory and the Beginnings of Civilization. *Antiquity*, Vol. 36, No. 148, pp. 322–7.
—— 1971. Un Siècle de collaboration dans le domaine des sciences préhistoriques et protohistoriques: du Congrès de Neuchâtel (août 1866) au Congrès de Prague (août 1966). In: CONGRÈS INTERNATIONAL DES SCIENCES PREHISTORIQUES ET PROTOHISTORIQUES, 7, Prague, 1966. *Actes* (Prague), Vol. 2, pp. 1423–39.
—— 1978. Archaeology and Prehistory. In: HAVET, J. (ed.), *Main Trends of Research in the Social and Human Sciences*. Paris, UNESCO. Vol. 1, Part 2, pp. 177–226.
—— 1979. *Rapport à la commission internationale pour une histoire du développement scientifique et culturel de l'humanité sur les parties concernant la préhistoire dans la première édition de cet ouvrage*. Paris, UNESCO. (Mimeo.)
—— 1985. Archéologie et histoire. In: CONGRÈS INTERNATIONAL DES SCIENCES HISTORIQUES, 16, Stuttgart, 25 août–1 sept. 1985. *Rapports*, Vol. I: *Grands thèmes – méthodologie*. Stuttgart. pp. 149–79.
DENNELL, R. 1983. *European Economic Prehistory*. London.
DIMBLEBY, G. W. 1967. *Plants and Archaeology*. London.
DORAN, J. E.; HODSON, F. R. 1975. *Mathematics and Computers in Archaeology*. Edinburgh.
ECKSTEIN, D.; BAILLIE, M. G. L.; EFFER, H. 1984. *Dendrochronological Dating*. Strasburg, European Science Foundation. (Handb. Archaeol., 2.)
ELIADE, M. 1976. *Histoire des croyances et des idées religieuses: I – De l'âge de la pierre aux mystères d'Eleusis*. Paris.
EVANS, J. G. 1978. *An Introduction to Environmental Archaeology*. London.
FAGAN, B. M. 1974. *Men of the Earth: An Introduction to World Prehistory*. Boston.
—— 1978. *Quest for the Past: Great Discoveries in Archaeology*. Reading, Mass.
—— 1985. *The Adventure of Archaeology*. Washington, DC.
FÈBVRE, L. 1953. *Combats pour l'histoire*. Paris.
FILIP, J. 1966–9. *Enzyklopädisches Handbuch zur Ur- und Frühgeschichte Europas – Manuel encyclopédique de préhistoire et de protohistoire européennes*. Prague. 2 vols.
FREEDMAN, M. 1978. Social and Cultural Anthropology. In: HAVET, J. (ed.), *Main Trends of Research in the Social and Human Sciences*. Paris, UNESCO. Vol. 1, Part 2, pp. 2–176.
GARDIN, J. C. (ed.) 1969. *Archéologie et calculateurs: problèmes sémiologiques et mathématiques*. Paris, CNRS.
—— 1979. *Une Archéologie théorique*. Paris.
GEER, R. DE. 1912. A Geochronology of the Last 12,000 Years. In: CONGRÈS GÉOLOGIQUE INTERNATIONAL, Stockholm. *Acta*. pp. 24–253.
GREIG, J. 1989. *Archaeobotany*. Strasburg, European Science Foundation. (Handb. Achaeol., 4.)
HAWKES, C. F. C. 1954. Archaeological Theory and Method: Some Suggestions from the Old World. *Am. Anthropol.*, Vol. 56, No. 2, pp. 155–68.
HAWKES, J.; WOOLLEY, L. 1963. Prehistory and the Beginnings of Civilization. In: UNESCO. *History of Mankind*. Paris. Vol. 1.

HEIZER, R. F.; GRAHAM, J. A. 1967. *A Guide to Field Methods in Archaeology: Approaches to the Anthropology of the Dead*. Palo Alto.
HEIZER, R. F.; SHERBURNE, F. C. (eds) 1960. *The Application of Quantitative Methods in Archaeology*. New York.
HERRMANN, J. (ed.) 1977. *Archäologie als Geschichtswissenschaft: Studien und Untersuchungen*. Berlin.
HERRMANN, J.; SELLNOW, I. (eds) 1982. *Produktivkräfte und Gesellschaftsformationen in vorkapitalistischer Zeit*. Berlin.
HIGGS, E. S. (ed.) 1972. *Papers in Economic Prehistory*. Cambridge.
—— (ed.) 1975. *Palaeoeconomy*. Cambridge.
HODGES, H. 1976. *Technology in the Ancient World*. London.
HODSON, F. R.; KENDALL, D. G.; TAUTU, P. (eds) 1971. *Mathematics in the Archaeological and Historical Sciences*. Edinburgh.
HOLE, F.; HEIZER, R. F. 1965. *An Introduction to Prehistoric Archeology*. New York.
HROUDA, B. (ed.) 1978. *Methoden der Archäologie: Eine Einführung in ihre naturwissenschaftlichen Techniken*. Munich.
JAMES, E. O. 1957. *Prehistoric Religion: A Study in Prehistoric Archeology*. New York.
JANKUHN, H.; WENSKUS, R. (eds) 1979. *Geschichtswissenschaft und Archäologie: Untersuchungen zur Siedlungs-, Wirtschafts- und Kirchengeschichte*. Sigmaringen.
JANSSENS, P. A. 1970. *Palaeopathology: Diseases and Injuries of Prehistoric Man*. London.
JAZDZEWSKI, K. 1984. *Urgeschichte Mitteleuropas*. Wroclaw/Warsaw.
JENNINGS, J. D.; NORBECK, E. (eds) 1984. *Prehistoric Man in the New World*. Chicago.
KLEJN, L. S. 1977. Panorama of Theoretical Archaeology. *Curr. Anthropol.*, Vol. 18, No. 1, pp. 1–42.
KLINDT-JENSEN, O. 1975. *A History of Scandinavian Archaeology*. London.
KOSSINNA, G. 1912. *Die deutsche Vorgeschichte: Eine hervorragende nationale Wissenschaft*. Leipzig.
LEROI-GOURHAN, A. 1943–5. *Évolution et technique*. Paris. 2 vols.
—— 1964–5. *Le Geste et la parole*. Paris. 2 vols.
—— 1965. *Préhistoire de l'art occidental*. Paris.
—— 1966. *Les Religions de la préhistoire*. Paris.
LÉVI-STRAUSS, C. 1963. *Structural Anthropology*. New York.
—— 1967. *The Scope of Anthropology*. London.
LÜNING, J. 1972. Zum Kulturbegriff im Neolithikum. *Prähist. Z.*, Vol. 47, pp. 145–73.
MCBURNEY, C. B. M. 1960. *The Stone Age of Northern Africa*. Cambridge.
MEGGERS, B. J. (ed.) 1968. *Anthropological Archaeology in the Americas*. Washington.
MILANKOVITCH, M. 1930. Mathematische Klimalehre und astronomische Theorie der Klimaschwankungen. *Handbuch der Klimatologie. I(A)*. Berlin.
MOBERG, C. A. 1976. *Introduction à l'archéologie*. Paris.
MOOK, W. G.; WATERBOLK, H. T. 1985. *Radiocarbon Dating*. Strasburg, European Science Foundation. (Handb. Archaeol., 3.)
MORGAN, L. H. 1877. *Ancient Society*. Chicago.
MÜLLER-KARPE, H. 1966–75. *Handbuch der Vorgeschichte*. Munich. 9 vols.
Natural Science in Archaeology in Denmark, Finland, Iceland, Norway and Sweden. 1978. Copenhagen.
NILSSON, S. 1888. *The Primitive Inhabitants of Scandinavia*. London. (Orig. Swedish edn pub. 1865.)
OAKLEY, K. P. 1961. *Man, the Tool-Maker*. 5th edn. London.
OTTE, M. (ed.) 1985. *La Signification culturelle des industries lithiques*. Liège. (Actes du Colloque de Liège du 3 au 7 Oct. 1984.)
PENNIMAN, T. K. 1952. *A Hundred Years of Anthropology*. 2nd edn. London.
PHILLIPS, P. 1980. *The Prehistory of Europe*. London.
PIGGOTT, S. 1965. *Ancient Europe*. Edinburgh.
PLENDERLEITH, H. L. 1956. *The Conservation of Antiquities and Works of Art*. Oxford.
PYDDOKE, E. (ed.) 1963. *The Scientist and Archaeology*. London.
RENFREW, C. (ed.) 1973. *The Explanation of Culture Change: Models in Prehistory*. London.
—— 1973. *Before Civilization*. London.
—— 1979. *Problems in European Prehistory*. Edinburgh.

RENFREW, J. M. 1973. *Palaeobotany: The Prehistoric Food Plants of the Near East and Europe*. London.

SABLOFF, J. A.; LAMBERG-KARLOWSKY, C. C. 1978. *Ancient Civilization and Trade*. Albuquerque. (Proceedings of the Research Seminar in Archaeology and Related Subjects.)

SAHLINS, M. D. 1972. *Stone Age Economics*. London.

SCOLLAR, I. 1970. *Einführung in neue Methoden der archäologischen Prospektion*. Düsseldorf.

SEMENOV, S. A. 1964. *Prehistoric Technology*. London/New York.

SIEVEKING, G. DE G.; LONGWORTH, I. H.; WILDON, K. E. (eds) 1976. *Problems in Economic and Social Archaeology*. London.

SINGER, C.; HOLMYARD, E. J.; HALL, A. R. (eds) 1954. *A History of Technology*. Oxford. 5 vols.

STJERNQVIST, B. 1967. *Models of Commercial Diffusion in Prehistoric Times*. Lund.

TITE, M. S. 1973. *Methods of Physical Examination in Archaeology*. London.

TRIGGER, B. C. 1968. *Beyond History: The Methods of Prehistory*. New York.

VERHAEGHE, F. 1979. *Archaeology, Natural Science and Technology: The European Situation*. Strasburg, European Science Foundation. 3 vols.

WAGNER, G. A.; AITKEN, M. J.; MEJDAHL, V. 1983. *Thermoluminescence Dating*. Strasburg, European Science Foundation. (Handb. Archaeol., 1.)

WATSON, P. J.; LE BLANC, S. A.; REDMAN, C. L. (eds) 1971. *Explanation in Archaeology: An Explicitly Scientific Approach*. New York.

WELLS, C. 1964. *Bones, Bodies and Disease*. London.

WHEELER, M. 1954. *Archaeology from the Earth*. Oxford.

WHITEHOUSE, D.; WHITEHOUSE, R. 1975. *Archaeological Atlas of the World*. London.

WILLEY, G. S. 1966–71. *An Introduction to American Archeology*. Englewood Cliffs. 2 vols.

WILLEY, G. S.; PHILLIPS, P. 1958. *Methods and Theory in American Archeology*. Chicago.

WILLEY, G. R.; SABLOFF, J. A. 1980. *A History of American Archaeology*. 2nd edn. London.

WILSON, D. 1975. *Science and Archaeology*. Harmondsworth.

WOOLLEY, L. 1937. *Digging up the Past*. Harmondsworth.

ZIVANIVIC, S. 1982. *Ancient Diseases*. London.

Part I

FROM ANTHROPOGENESIS TO THE BEGINNINGS OF FOOD PRODUCTION

A: Anthropogenesis and the period of *Homo habilis* and *Homo erectus*

CONTENTS

1

ANTHROPOGENESIS

An overview

Yves Coppens and Denis Geraads

THE MAJOR GROUPS OF PRIMATES

Having diverged from the branch of the great apes of Africa no more than a few million years ago, the human line itself has only a brief geological history. For upwards of 60 million years the human saga merges with that of the other primates, which, like most of the major groups of mammals, take root deep in the Secondary era, the age of the reptiles.

At the end of the Cretaceous period, 70 million years ago, the dinosaurs and their relatives, which still reigned supreme on land and ocean, occupied most of the ecological niches with the notable exception of those that today occupied by small animals, the rodents and insectivores. The first mammals, which emerged during the Triassic (190 million years ago) from a very ancient line of reptiles, evolved, with some success, to fill the gap.

Among these as yet undifferentiated types of shrew, the most ancient primate, *Purgatorius ceratops*, was recognized in North America, on the basis of a single tooth. The identification was no easy matter, since most primates were very conservative in their dentition and the recognition of their distinguishing features naturally becomes more difficult the further back one goes.

The 'crisis' of the Cretaceous–Tertiary transition of 65 million years ago, which had such disastrous consequences for the dinosaurs and many other reptiles, benefited the primates and many other mammals. From the very beginning of the Palaeocene the remains of *Purgatorius* become more abundant, showing it to be the only primate still in possession of a complete dentition: 3 incisors, 1 canine, 4 premolars and 3 molars on each half-jaw, a total of 44 teeth.

Purgatorius heralds the vast group of Plesiadapiformes, called after *Plesiadapis*, of the Cernay site near Reims in France. Here the bone features that define the primates can be observed: principally the structure of the auditory region (where the petrous portion is formed from a single petrosal bone) and peculiarities of the carotid circulation in that area. Their dentition testifies to adaptation to a great variety of diets, which shows that from the dawn of the Tertiary these primates underwent evolutionary diversification that enabled them to exploit all the resources of the arboreal environment, which subsequent primates were to leave only rarely.

At the end of the Palaeocene, 55 million years ago, the Plesiadapiformes gave way to the Adapiformes (called after *Adapis* from the gypsum of Montmartre, which the great French palaeontologist Cuvier had discovered and named in 1821). Like their predecessors they are unknown outside Laurasia, the vast continent that then included North America and Eurasia apart from the Indian subcontinent, and was separated from the southern continents (Gondwanaland) by Tethys, a sea of which the Mediterranean is a vestige. The Adapiformes have eye sockets closed to the rear by a bony bar, and an opposable thumb – a vital asset for moving through forest. They died out at the end of the Eocene, and may have been the ancestors of the lemurians of Madagascar and the lorises of south Asia and Africa whose history, especially as regards the time of their arrival in Africa, is almost completely unknown. Only a few years ago all these primitive primates were classed as prosimians along with the tarsier, a small animal of the Celebes (Sulawesi) and the Philippines with a long tarsus and enormous eyes, as opposed to the simians or apes and monkeys, which were more evolved. In fact these 'prosimians' share only primitive characteristics which are not enough to establish a classification that reflects phylogenesis, just as the term 'invertebrates' means simply 'not vertebrates' and implies no close relationship between the branches. On the other hand, the group consisting of the tarsier, the related Eocene fossil specimens (Omomyidae) and the simians (which include humans) may be defined by many evolved characteristics and certainly constitute a natural group comprising all the descendants of a common ancestor. Most of the distinctive features of this group, called Haplorhini, derive from improvement in vision at the expense of the sense of smell, connected mainly with the transition to diurnal life. The lemur has a long muzzle and a nose like a dog's. The Haplorhini do not have that type of nose and the muzzle containing enormous olfactory mucous membranes becomes considerably smaller, as does the corresponding part of the brain (the rhinencephalon). The eye sockets, however, by this time completely enclosed at the rear, are now at the front of the head, to enlarge the field of stereoscopic vision; a fovea forms on the retina, at the centre of the field of vision, where eyesight is considerably better. Finally, the brain enters a new phase in the increase in size and complexity that characterizes the primates, which is a clear sign of the intensification of their social life.

The Simiiformes or simians (monkeys, apes and humans) are not greatly dissimilar from the Tarsiiformes, and opinions vary as to the relationship between the two groups. The most probable hypothesis is that of the derivation of the simians from the Tarsiiformes in conjunction with a dispersal towards the south, since the first simians appear more or less simultaneously in Africa and South America, some 35 million years ago.

In spite of the hopes of the Argentinian palaeontologist Ameghino, who held a Patagonian fossil simian to be the ancestor of humans, there can be no doubt that the monkeys of South America, the Platyrrhini, are not part of human history. They remained primitive in their auditory area and in the retention of three molars on either side of both rows of teeth, and they acquired a prehensile tail that is not to be found among the apes of the Old World. Their origin is a much-disputed problem. Some consider them to be direct descendants of the North American Omomyidae, whereas for others (one of the foremost being the French palae-ontologist R. Hoffstetter, who described *Branisella*, the most ancient platyrrhine known) they are descendants of the African simians. Both hypotheses assume the crossing of a large stretch of water, since palaeogeographical recon-structions show clearly that South America at that time was an island. It is known, however, that the great tropical rivers sometimes carry out to sea vast tangles of trees that could have provided sufficient food for a small troop of monkeys (and a number of rodents that pose a similar problem) for the ten days or so that the crossing would have taken. Reconstruction of ocean currents would seem to indicate that the east–west passage, which was shorter than in our day since Africa and South America were not then so far apart, would have been easier than the route from the north, but the problem cannot be considered solved.

CATARRHINI AND HOMINOID PRIMATES

If we return now to the Old World, where all the subsequent history of our ancestry unfolds, our attention is held by the very important site of Fayum near Cairo in Egypt. Many fossils have been extracted from that site since the beginning of this century, providing precious information on ancient representatives of very diverse groups of mammals, par-ticularly Proboscidians and related orders, and Primates. Around 1920 the German palaeontologist Max Schlosser made a description, on the basis of teeth and fragments of mandibles some 30 million years old that still had three premolars in each half-jaw, of two genera, *Parapithecus* and *Apidium*, which are perhaps not yet very far from the common ancestor of the Platyrrhini of the New World and the Catarrhini of the Old World, despite some features that distinguish them from our ancestry. A slightly more ancient level provided the single mandible of the genus *Oligopithecus*, so called by E. Simons, who has been excavating the sites of Egypt since 1961. For the first time in the history of the primates the dentition resembles our own and that of the Old World apes and monkeys: the first premolar (P 2 since P 1 disappears with the Plesiadapiformes) is no longer there, and there remain only two premolars (P 3 and P 4) in each half-jaw. None the less, we cannot with certainty place *Oligopithecus* at the start of the branch that leads to the later Catarrhini.

All the apes considered below have, at one time or another, been believed to be ancestors of humans, and for many of them the matter has yet to be decided. The causes of this diversity of opinion are many. The first has to do with what can only be described as emotional factors, which move the

researcher who has discovered or studied a fossil to make it 'the Missing Link', refusing to assign it to a lateral branch, a phenomenon which reassures us that 'the scientist remains accessible to human emotion'. The second cause of dis-agreement is the condition of the remains, which are often far from complete: a species that could be compared to humans on the basis of its teeth might be relegated to a more distant position when its entire skeleton becomes known. The other reasons are bound up in evolution itself, which is not regular, directional or guided. The complexity of a phyletic 'tree' is in fact much greater than the classic image of an actual tree suggests: we must, rather, imagine a bush that ramifies from its base, with each branch representing only one species. Each group is defined by evolved charac-teristics proper to the ancestral species, which persist, barring reverse evolution, in the descendants. The phenomena of parallel evolution in different lines and of reversion (return to a state quite similar to the primitive condition) are so common, however, that it is often very difficult to determine the sense of evolution of the features and to disentangle the branches, as we shall see later.

Several types of primitive catarrhines from Fayum have been described, but it is possible, given intra-generic varia-bility and sexual dimorphism, that a single form, *Proplio-pithecus*, is involved. Among the males at least, the canines are fairly strong, the dental arches widen only slightly towards the rear, and the pair consisting of the upper canine and third lower premolar have a cutting function and grind together like a pair of scissors. The females, on the other hand, have less robust canines and the P 3 is not so different from the P 4, being shorter and less 'canine'. The skull, which is well known through *Propliopithecus zeuxis*, is more rounded than that of the Adapiformes and the muzzle is shorter. But while the total morphological pattern of this genus heralds the subsequent Catarrhines fairly clearly, it is difficult to discern in it traits that foreshadow the Old World monkeys, the Cercopithecoids (baboons, macaques, cer-copithecids, colobus, langurs and so on, which are remark-able for their tubercular molars arranged in pairs), or the great apes (gibbon, orang-utan, gorilla, chimpanzee, humans). This kind of problem recurs more than once, and no doubt it is better to try to solve it than to bring together all the forms of uncertain affinities in a mixed group without evolutionary meaning.

Pliopithecus, the first ape to leave Africa after the continent collided with Eurasia, was found in the 17-million-year-old Miocene layers of Sansan in Gers, France, by Edouard Lartet in 1837. Although much more recent, it differs so little from its Fayum predecessor that some palaeontologists put both in the same family. No doubt this was an incursion without sequel to the north of the Tethys Sea, since in the first half of the Miocene period the history of humankind and related groups seems decidedly African.

The first discovery of one of these hominoid primates, *Dryopithecus*, however, was made not in Africa but in the French Pyrenees, by E. Lartet in 1856. Consisting for the most part of a mandible and a fragment of humerus, it was long considered the ancestor of the great apes (formerly called pongids) until it was realized that the history of those hominoid primates was not reducible to a simple great ape/human dichotomy. It was only in 1948 that Mary Leakey, to whom palaeoanthropology owes many another discovery besides, unearthed in Kenya the well-preserved face of the African equivalent of the *Dryopithecus* and dubbed it *Proconsul* after a famous chimpanzee in London Zoo called Consul; since then many other names have been added to the inventory of fossils from the beginning of the East African Miocene: *Dendropithecus, Rangwapithecus* and *Limnopithecus* are only the most important. It would seem that the hominoid primates, which today are represented by only a few species (gibbon, orang-utan, chimpanzee and gorilla) enjoyed in the Miocene (20–10 million years ago) a diversification comparable to that of the small, tailed monkeys (cercopithecoids) today. As many as ten species may have been in existence at the same time in a single region (Kenya), forming a considerable part of the animal biomass. Their dimensions, diet and way of life probably ran the gamut exploited today by their cercopithecoid cousins.

Before turning to the hominids proper we should say a few words about two 'evolutionary dead-ends', *Oreopithecus* and *Gigantopithecus,* which were once the object of furious debate among specialists. *Oreopithecus*, whose many remains were found in the lignite mines of Tuscany in Italy (Plate 1) and described by the Swiss palaeontologist Hurzeler, is some 8 million years old. It is astonishingly similar to humans in many ways, but most researchers today see the similarities only as convergences. The incisors are straight (not forward-sloping as in the great apes), the canines are small, the first lower premolar resembles the second, the face is small, the brain relatively voluminous, and the pelvis is flared and not elongated as in all the apes; on the other hand a number of dental traits show that *Oreopithecus* is really very far removed from us: its dentition calls to mind both *Apidium,* a parapithecid of Fayum with a central turbercle on the molars, and the Cercopithecoids, in that the upper teeth resemble the lower. Perhaps it was its arboreal way of life, like that of the gibbon whose long arms it has, that led to the alterations in the proportions of its skull and pelvis, but in any case it is clear that these modifications are independent of those found in humans.

Equally amazing is the *Gigantopithecus* both in the appearance it must have had and in the circumstances of its discovery. It was among the teeth of fossil mammals sold by the apothecaries of Hong Kong for grinding and ingesting as a cure for various ills, that the Dutchman G. H. R. von Koenigswald, another great figure in palaeoanthropology, recognized in 1935 three teeth of a gigantic primate. It transpired that they came from caves in China containing fauna from the beginning of the Pleistocene (around 1 million years ago), but in spite of the determined searching of von Koenigswald, it was not until 1956 that an entire jaw, soon followed by two others, was discovered by a Chinese peasant. The skull and skeleton, however, have not been discovered. What remains is enough to show that *Gigantopithecus* is beyond doubt the largest primate that ever existed, easily surpassing the largest of the gorillas, with a weight of over 300 kg; although no one nowadays would share the view that it was the origin of the human line, an opinion expressed in his book *Apes, Giants and Men* by the Austrian anthropologist F. Weidenreich (to whom we return on p. 32), it is still interesting to compare the dentition of *Gigantopithecus* with that of certain hominids. It is remarkable for the length of its grinding part which, though it is usually limited to molars and the last premolar, extends in this case to the canine, which is very small; so, too, are the incisors, which cannot have played an important role in the catching of food. This disproportion between grinding teeth and front teeth is, as we shall see, very reminiscent of *Australopithecus robustus*; it bespeaks adaptation to a diet based on hard vegetation (roots, seeds and the like), best exemplified today by the gelada baboon of the high plains of Ethiopia, one of the most earth-bound of all primates, and one that also has

small incisors and canines. Like this baboon, the *Gigantopithecus* must have spent long hours feeding, moving in sizeable groups to keep predators at bay: in spite of its great size, an isolated individual which had neither natural means of defence nor (as far as we know) weapons and tools must have been easy prey for the many carnivores, which is probably why its remains were accumulated in caves.

THE HOMINIDAE

It was towards the end of the nineteenth century that British geologists discovered in the Miocene sediments of the Siwalik hills on the southern slopes of the Himalayas the first fossil primate of that region, followed by several other specimens in the early years of this century. In 1931 the American palaeontologist Lewis compared this fossil to a human jaw and called it *Ramapithecus*, but his work gained recognition only after the Kenyan discoveries of Louis Leakey, husband of Mary and, like her, one of the foremost palaeoanthropologists in eastern Africa. In 1960 Leakey found in the deposits of Fort Ternan (4 million years old) some fragments of jaw which he named *Kenyapithecus* and described as a human ancestor, claiming even that it had been capable of using basalt pebbles whose natural cutting edge could have served in such operations as the breaking of bones. This revelation was greeted with the greatest of scepticism in scientific circles, but at least it served to renew interest in these primates of the end of the Miocene. Many other discoveries have since been made, in Kenya, in the Siwalik hills of India and Pakistan, and also in China, Turkey, Greece and central Europe. Until only a few years ago they were divided into two groups, *Ramapithecus* and *Sivapithecus*, the former seeming closer to human ancestry than the latter. However, the distinction between these groups, which were often discovered in the same regions or even at the same sites, was not always clear. Examination of the lower jaw, the least rare piece of diagnostic evidence, allowed *Ramapithecus* to be identified by its smaller size, a lower and relatively thicker mandibular body, a more upright symphysis, a less powerful canine and a lower and broader P 3. The discovery in 1973 in a Greek Upper Miocene deposit (10 million years old) of a representative of the same group, named *Ouranopithecus*, proved what a number of researchers already suspected: that *Ramapithecus* was simply the female of *Sivapithecus*. The marked sexual dimorphism of the several *Ouranopithecus* jaws was evinced in the same traits that distinguished *Ramapithecus* from *Sivapithecus*. The place of the *Ramapithecus–Sivapithecus–Ouranopithecus* group (and related forms) in the hominoid phyletic tree cannot be elucidated without reference to recent advances in biology.

In the past the orang-utan of South-East Asia was placed together with the gorilla and chimpanzees of the African tropical forests, in the family of Pongidae, characterized by adaptation to arboreal locomotion, a powerful masticating system with enlarged front teeth, and many traits that are primitive in comparison with their advancement in humans: small brain, non- upright body, opposable big toe and so on. But for at least the last twenty years biologists have been trying to establish a phyletic tree based not on anatomy but on chromosomes and proteins; and this is quite different from the classic model.

In chromosomes, alternating light and dark bands of various widths can be shown which are sufficiently specific to enable a segment of a line to be pinpointed even if it undergoes inversion, or translocation in another chromosome. This permits us to establish the history of events that have taken place in the karyotype of several similar species and thus the phyletic tree of those species.

Immunological analysis of proteins can show the distance between species, even if they are far apart, as long as a very common protein (such as haemoglobin) is available for examination. The sequences of amino acids that compose them can be directly examined also, to find the order of substitutions, each of which corresponds to a mutation allowing transition from one haemoglobin to another. This latter method is more troublesome in that it involves the identification of many sequences of complex proteins, but it allows us not only to assess a resemblance but also to establish the succession of dichotomies.

All recent research proves beyond cavil that in the group consisting of the great apes and humans, it was the orang-utan that separated first. The African great apes are therefore closer relatives of humans than the orang-utan, and until what was probably a fairly recent date (perhaps only 5 million years ago), human history was bound up with that of the chimpanzee and the gorilla. These apes certainly do not, as was once thought, represent the end-product of an evolution that was radically different from the human; today they can even be included in the subfamily of Hominini. Thus the term 'pongid' no longer has any phyletic meaning unless it is restricted to the orang-utan (*Pongo*, type of the Pongidae subfamily).

Where do the *Sivapithecus* and related forms fit into this Hominini–Pongidae dichotomy? Most authorities would probably have continued to class them with the Hominini had it not been for the almost simultaneous discovery in Turkey and Pakistan of more complete remains, including the face. To the surprise of all concerned, the face of the *Sivapithecus* was much more similar to the orang-utan than to the African great apes or to humans (concave profile, no fold of flesh above the eye-socket, eyes close together and so on). This does not imply that all the hominoid primates of the close of the Miocene were pongids, but if the conclusion is correct then the line of Hominini, between *Kenyapithecus* 14 million years ago and the earliest *Australopithecus* 10 million years later, is marked by only a few fragmentary fossils. How can we account for this dearth?

The most likely explanations are ecological and geographical. The diffusion of hominoid primates of the *Sivapithecus* group seems to be linked to the expansion of open spaces, wooded savannah which spread progressively to a great part of Eurasia at the end of the Miocene. The dentition of these apes testifies to adaptation to abrasive vegetation such as roots, seeds or grasses rather than leaves or fruit, the dental enamel is thick and the eruption of the molars is often retarded, to prolong their usefulness. Such an environment is much more propitious to fossilization than more heavily afforested areas and, with few exceptions, forest soils are too acid for the preservation of bones. It is therefore no surprise that hardly any remains have been found of the ancestors of humans and the African great apes, which lived in a forest environment. Moreover, like the chimpanzee and the gorilla, all the Hominini more than 1.5 million years old are exclusively African, and it may be considered that since its separation from the Pongidae (orang-utan and *Sivapithecus*) this line is solely African. Sites dating from between 5 and 10 million years ago are much more rare and poor in Africa than those of the same age in Eurasia: this difference alone could well explain the apparent abundance of Pongidae as compared with Hominini.

As we have learned, this last subfamily in its turn divides,

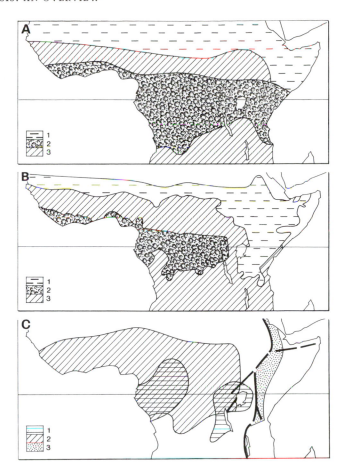

Map 1 A – Intertropical Africa during the Upper Miocene: 1, open environment; 2, forest; 3, savannah. B – Intertropical Africa today showing the shrinkage of the forest on the west side of the Rift Valley: 1, open environment; 2, forest; 3, savannah. C – Distribution of the Panidae (gorillas and chimpanzees) west of the Rift and of the hominians (australopithecines and early *Homo*) east of the Rift: 1, gorillas; 2, chimpanzees; 3, hominians.

at a date biologists and palaeontologists have set at 5 to 6 million years ago, into the African great apes or Panidae (a name formed from *Pan troglodytes*, the chimpanzee) and humans or hominians, which includes only two genera: *Australopithecus* and *Homo*. Here we find the same problem as with the previous dichotomy: whereas the history of the hominians is relatively well known, that of the Panidae is not illustrated by even a single fossil. Here again we may, as Yves Coppens has suggested, invoke an 'eco-geographical' explanation: the group of primitive Hominini, which was spread over a sizeable region of East Africa, was split by the great trench of the Rift Valley, that immense gash that runs from the Red Sea to Tanzania and separates eastern Africa, where open spaces predominate, from the more humid and afforested central and western parts of the continent. The eastern Hominini (or hominians) therefore adapted then, like the *Sivapithecus*, to an open environment (their dental adaptations are analogous): these were the proto-*Australopithecus*. The western Hominini (or Panidae), on the other hand, chose a domicile in the tropical forests, where they still live (Map 1). Deposits there are sadly rare, and the likelihood of finding ape fossils there is very small.

This hypothesis, suggesting that new species are formed as a result of the isolation of a territory, is supported by the observation that even in the more afforested sites of eastern Africa no fossil remains of chimpanzee or gorilla have yet been discovered, whereas the pre-*Australopithecus* is fairly well represented.

Many problems in this remote history of humankind await solution, and we have not dwelt on them because the hypotheses advanced are not very satisfactory: what we need are not hypotheses that are constantly being challenged, but fossils, fossils and more fossils!

BIBLIOGRAPHY

CIOCHON, R. L.; CORRUCCINI, R.S. (eds) 1983. *New Interpretations of Ape and Human Ancestry.* New York.

CLARKE, R. 1980. *Naissance de l'homme.* Paris.

COLLINS, D. 1978. *The Human Evolution: From Ape to Artist.* Oxford.

COPPENS, Y. 1983. *Le Singe, l'Afrique et l'homme.* Paris.

—— 1984. Hominoïdes, hominidés et hommes. *Vie Sci., C. R. Acad. Sci.* (Paris), Sér. Gén., Vol. 1, No. 5, pp. 459–86.

COPPENS, Y. et al. (eds) 1976. *Earliest Man and Environments in the Lake Rudolf Basin.* Chicago.

DELSON, E. (ed.) 1985. *Ancestors: The Hard Evidence.* New York.

DORST, J. (ed.) 1985. *Histoire des êtres vivants.* Paris.

GERAADS, D. 1982. Paléobiogéographie de l'Afrique du Nord depuis le Miocène terminal d'après les grands mammifères. *Géobios* (Lyons), Mém. spéc., 6, pp. 473–81.

—— 1984. Découverte d'un Hominidé fossile dans le Pléistocène de la République de Djibouti. *C. R. Acad. Sci.* (Paris), Vol. 299, No. 15, pp. 1097–1100. (In collaboration with L. de Bonis, G. Guérin, A. Haga, J.-J. Jaeger and S. Sen.)

—— 1985a. La faune des gisements de Melka-Kunturé (Ethiopie). *L'Environnement des Hominidés au Plio-Pléistocène.* Paris, Fondation Singer-Polignac. Vol. 12, pp. 165–74.

—— 1985b. Contribution des vertébrés à l'histoire de la Téthys et des continents péritéthysiens. *Bull. Soc. Géol. Fr.* (Paris), Sér. 8, Vol. 1, No. 5, pp. 781–6. (In collaboration with L. de Bonis et al.)

—— 1987. The Pleistocene Hominide Site of Ternifine, Algeria: New Results. *Quat. Res.*, Vol. 15, pp. 380–6. (In collaboration with J. J. Hublin et al.)

GOWLETT, J. A. J. 1985. *L'Invention de la civilization.* Paris.

JOHANSON, D. C.; EDEY, M. A. 1982. *Lucy: The Beginnings of Mankind.* London.

KORTLANDT, A. 1972. *New Perspectives on Ape and Human Evolution.* Amsterdam.

LEAKEY, R. E. 1981. *La Naissance de l'homme.* Paris.

LEAKEY, R. E.; LEWIN, R. 1977. *Origins: What New Discoveries Reveal about the Emergence of our Species and its Possible Future.* London. (French trans. 1985. *Les Origines de l'homme.* Paris.)

LE GROS CLARK, W. E. 1955. *The Fossil Evidence for Human Evolution.* Chicago.

LUCKETT, W. P.; SZALAY. F. S. (eds) 1975. *Phylogeny of the Primates: A Multidisciplinary Approach.* New York.

MARLIAC, M.; MARLIAC, A. 1979. *La Préhistoire.* Paris.

MUSÉE DE L'HOMME. 1976. *Origine de l'homme.* Paris.

—— 1981. *Les Premiers Habitants de l'Europe: 1.500.000–100.000 ans.* Paris.

NOTEN, F. VAN (ed.) 1981. *De evolutie van de mens: de speurtocht naar ontbrekende schakels* [The Evolution of Men: The Search for the Missing Link]. Maastricht.

SMITH, F. H.; SPENCER, F. (eds) 1984. *The Origins of Modern Humans.* New York.

SUSANNE, C. 1984. *Sur les traces des premiers hommes.* Brussels.

SZALAY, F. S.; DELSON, E. 1979. *Evolutionary History of the Primates.* New York.

WOOD, B.; MARTIN, L.; ANDREWS, P. (eds) 1986. *Major Topics in Primate and Human Evolution.* Cambridge.

2

THE PERIOD OF *HOMO HABILIS* AND
HOMO ERECTUS

An overview

Yves Coppens and Denis Geraads

Our history for the entire second half of the Miocene, between 14 and 5 million years ago, is marked by only a few, very incomplete fossils, all of which come from Kenya. The main ones are a half-jaw from the Samburu hills (of 8.5 million years ago), a tooth from Lukeino (6 million years ago) and a half-jaw from Lothagan (5.5 million years ago). Are these few fossils still part of the common branch of the great apes and hominians, or had the branch already bifurcated by then? It is difficult to decide, although we do know that it is at the presumed date of that separation that the candidates for our ancestry begin to be a little less shy of showing themselves. Between 4 and 2 million years ago all were African and belonged to the group of *Australopithecus*, in the broad sense, the name deriving from the discovery of the first of them at the southern end of the continent. The first genuine humans, of the genus *Homo*, appeared 2 million years ago, and some of them soon left the land of their ancestors to spread fairly quickly across the Old World. The Americas and Australia were not populated until much later, a few tens of thousands of years ago.

Thus it would seem that, from the time of the first Catarrhini of Fayum in Egypt, which were perhaps already hominoids, the history of the human species unfolded almost entirely in Africa, although, as we shall see, it is only in the last few decades at most that scientists have become aware of the almost exclusive role of the 'Dark Continent'.

THE AUSTRALOPITHECINES

It was the French geologist Maurice Taieb who, while researching his thesis on the Awash valley in Ethiopia, discovered in 1971 the deposits of Hadar, in the Afar depression. In an environment which today is sub-desert beyond the river forest, erosion makes deep ravines in the Pliocene clays, sandstones and sands of lake and river origin which are interrupted by basalt flows and layers of ash deposited beneath the water. Whatever animal fossils are contained in the sediments are gradually exposed, and remain exposed for some time before being destroyed in their turn by erosion and severe climatic conditions. Taieb discovered thousands of fossils littering the ground over tens of square kilometres; hippopotamuses, proboscideans, antelope, giraffe, rhi-

noceros, equids and crocodiles formed the bulk of the biomass. The first hominians were discovered there in 1972 by the international mission co-directed by M. Taieb, D. C. Johanson and Y. Coppens. First of all a knee, then some jaws and then, at locality 162, a skeleton, which was called 'Lucy' after a Beatles song, soon created a sensation among the international scientific community and the general public. Lucy (Plate 2) is the most ancient hominian skeleton known, at almost 3 million years of age, and yet is very well preserved, almost 40 per cent complete: most of the bones are there, right and left. It is the morphology of the pelvis which, as in our species, is dissimilar to the male pelvis, that shows the skeleton is of a female.

Many other human remains, older than Lucy for the most part, have been found at Hadar (notably the 'family' of locality 333), making this region one of the world's richest in fossil hominians.

While one discovery followed another at Afar, others 1,500 km to the south confirmed and complemented them. At the Laetoli site in northern Tanzania, Mary Leakey (already mentioned in connection with *Proconsul* in Chapter 1) was unearthing fauna a little more ancient than that of Hadar and from a more open environment, which yet contained a very similar hominian. In 1976 she brought to light the surface of a layer of ash that had hardened rapidly after its deposition in a humid environment and which contained several sets of animal footprints, including those of two creatures that were certainly bipeds, of different sizes, and which perhaps had been walking together. Over and above this moving evocation of a few seconds in the life of our remote ancestors those footprints establish beyond doubt that bipedality had been acquired 3.8 million years ago. This feature of hominization (which happened in stages) therefore preceded in time those which were generally seen as more noble: toolmaking and brain growth.

At that date dentition remained generalized and still resembled that of such creatures as *Ouranopithecus*, of 10 million years ago. It was indeed the absence of derived (evolved) traits proper to *Australopithecus*, which came later, that gave rise to the initial thought that the Afar fossils were of the genus *Homo*. The dental arches, while not parallel and U-shaped like those of the great apes, diverge only slightly; the incisors are broad and proclivous, the upper ones being separated from the canines by narrow gaps (diastemata) and the lower canines are still larger. The skull is known only in part, but the cranial capacity is still small (of the order of 400 cc), the brow ridge is absent and the face is prognathous – all of which suggest a state only slightly evolved from the primitive state of the Hominini. The conjunction of features associated with upright stance, on the other hand, shows that that first revolution in hominization had already taken place. There is hardly a single bone in the skeleton whose anatomy is not affected to a greater or lesser degree by that realignment of the entire frame. A double arch reinforces the cohesion of the foot, now an essential organ of propulsion. The big toe loses all opposability and takes up a position parallel to the other toes (as it was already tending to do in the eastern gorilla, an earthbound ape); the foot now supports most of the body's weight. The lower half of the body lengthens considerably but Lucy still has arms that are long in relation to her legs. The femur, which is vertical in the ape, is angled obliquely downwards and inwards in Lucy's case, in such a way that the head is on the same vertical line as the tibial articulation; the body weight is thus transferred directly, avoiding the imbalance that makes the circus chimpanzee hop from one leg to the other. This reorientation results from the broadening of the pelvis, which is perhaps the most remarkable of the transformations of the skeleton: whereas in the apes it is narrow and elongated, here it broadens into a basin, supports the intestines, offers better purchase for the buttock muscles that extend the legs and, during childbirth, allows the bulky head of the child to pass through. The spinal column acquires a double curve with posterior concavities, at the lumbar and cervical regions, whose effect is to place the main articulations between head, trunk and lower limbs on one vertical axis (examination of the surfaces of the joints of Lucy's vertebrae shows that she had already acquired this double curve). The skull, too, is recast, although it is not always easy to determine the role played by each of the components of 'hominization'. The change in position of the occipital foramen, which is now underneath the cranium, is related to the change to upright posture, though it is not directly linked with bipedalism, since we find a similar position in the tarsier, which holds on to tree-trunks in a vertical position; it must also have something to do with the expansion of the hemispheres of the brain. Finally, the forelimbs are freed of their locomotive function, the neck and pectoral girdle become lighter, and the hands can be devoted exclusively to prehension which is both strong and delicate, thanks in part to the strength of the thumb, which can be opposed to the other fingers together and separately. This radical improvement in the working of the hand is a prerequisite for the making of tools, although subsequently it must have improved with use, and manual dexterity has probably never ceased to increase.

Some near-complete hominian hands have been unearthed at Hadar: they do not have the articular abutments that enabled the great apes to walk on the back of the folded second phalanx of the knuckles, although since Lucy's forelimbs are still long and since her knee has the capacity for only slight rotational movements, it has been assumed that she was still capable of taking to the trees when the need arose. It should nevertheless be noted that even the chimpanzee, which is better adapted to arboreal locomotion, descends to the ground when threatened.

It would therefore seem that in the steps towards hominization bipedalism succeeded adaptation to an open environment (which entailed adaptation to a diet based on hard and abrasive vegetation) and preceded toolmaking and the considerable increase in brain size. The belief that the *Ramapithecus–Sivapithecus* group were our ancestors was for a long time encouraged by the fact that, like the first australopithecines, they had accomplished the first step: their thick dental enamel, robust jugal teeth and strong canines are simply adaptations to the same open environment, although they probably remained quadrupeds. What, then, made the proto-*Australopithecus* become a biped? Of the many hypotheses advanced, no single one can account for the phenomenon, although there again improvement with use must have rapidly reinforced the nascent trend towards the upright stance. Freeing the hands for carrying food is necessary only in the context of hunting, which is hardly a likely activity of hominians who had neither natural nor artificial weapons. Transporting young, on the other hand, must have been a necessity: incapable of moving on their own before reaching a considerable size, they must have been unable to achieve a sufficiently firm grip on a mother with sparse hair. Another theory, which has been fashionable of late, would explain bipedalism by the greater endurance in walking and running it conferred on hunting hominians: their survival would thus have been attributable to their ability to pursue a quarry for hours or even days.

Yet the most passionately debated problem concerning these primitive australopithecines is that of their relations to those that succeeded them. The Americans D. Johanson and T. White and the Frenchman Y. Coppens have given the specimens from Afar and Laetoli the name of a single species, *Australopithecus afarensis*, although that specific identification of the two populations is not universally accepted. The Laetoli site is older than the Hadar sites and an evolutionary difference between the two populations is likely. Some researchers, however, consider it to be of the same kind as that which separates *A. afarensis* of Hadar from the most recent form from southern Africa, so that there is no need to make a distinction: *A. afarensis* would thus be simply a sub-species of *Australopithecus africanus*. For Y. Coppens, however, *A. afarensis* evinces on the one hand features that are more primitive than those of subsequent australopithecines, which is why he would describe it as a 'pre-australopithecine', and on the other hand distinctive evolved features (autapomorphs) that distinguish it from its direct forebears. (This is a good illustration of the difficulty of discovering ancestral forms, forms without distinguishing features that relegate them to a lateral branch.) For other researchers, *A. afarensis* is the ancestor of *Australopithecus* alone, because the genus *Homo* had already branched off at that point, without its remains having been discovered, unless, that is, they were actually among material which was wrongly bracketed together with *Australopithecus afarensis*! Close anatomical study of certain elements of the skeleton point to the coexistence of two species, one considerably more 'modern' than the other. It should be remembered that all these differences of opinion are on matters of detail: in general all specialists agree that *A. afarensis* is close to the line of the other australopithecines, both gracile and robust.

Although the latter succeed *A. afarensis* in time, they have been known to us for considerably longer, since it was in 1924 that R. B. Young, a geologist at the University of Witwatersrand, noticed a strange paperweight on the desk of an engineer working at the Taung mines in South Africa; the anatomist Raymond Dart later identified it as the skull of a young primate of an unknown species which he named *Australopithecus africanus*. Dart thought it an intermediary between human and ape, although considerably closer to us than to the ape. It was not the first time that a human fossil had been discovered, but compared with the Taung skull, the Neanderthal or even *Pithecanthropus* skulls seemed much more akin to ours, and Dart's find was treated with the utmost scepticism. This missing link was decidedly too similar to the apes, in whose favourite continent it had been found. It was not until 1936, when R. Broom discovered in the South African deposit of Sterkfontein a skull which today is held to be the adult form of *Australopithecus africanus* (then called *Plesianthropus*) that specialists began to realize that it was in Africa that our roots were to be unearthed. In 1938 the same R. Broom discovered in another South African cave, Kromdraai, a second type of australopithecine, which was named *Paranthropus robustus*. One find followed another in the 1950s, and even today australopithecines are occasionally discovered in those South African deposits, which also contain many remains of fauna. But the broken animal bones which R. Dart saw as evidence of a human-made industry and called 'osteodontokeratic' are probably no more than the leftovers of carnivores' meals.

The disadvantage of the South African caves is that they can be dated only in relative terms, by reference to the fauna they contain. This is why Mary Leakey's discovery of the *Zinjanthropus* in 1959 at the Olduvai site in Tanzania came as a bombshell. The *Zinjanthropus* itself, a skull in excellent condition, is not greatly dissimilar to the South African robust form, but Leakey put its age at 1.75 million years, which was much older than the boldest minds could then have imagined. That dating, obtained from basalt at the base of the sedimentary series of Olduvai, launched potassium–argon radiometric dating and shifted palaeoanthropologists' main focus of attention to East Africa. In the years that followed, Louis and Mary Leakey were to make Olduvai a model field of research where many specialists from a variety of disciplines worked together to retrace not only the anatomy of fossil hominians but also their evolution in time, their way of life, and their geographical, animal and vegetable environment.

Soon afterwards Camille Arambourg, Professor at the Muséum National d'Histoire Naturelle, a palaeontologist and pioneer of French palaeoanthropology in East Africa, with Y. Coppens led an international team in the lower valley of the river Omo in Ethiopia (north of the Lake Turkana basin) where he had collected fossils many years earlier. On Arambourg's death in 1969, Y. Coppens took over leadership of the French side, and each year a large team went to Omo until political obstacles prevented access. During that time, several volcanic and sedimentary series, of which the Shungura formation is the most important, provided tens of thousands of animal fossils and hundreds of hominian remains, most of which belonged to the robust australopithecines. Above all, the long and well-calibrated chronological sequence it contains (extending from 3 to 0.8 million years ago) makes the Omo valley an unparalleled frame of reference for dating the first chapters of human history.

A sedimentary series of comparable age is at present being excavated by the team of Richard Leakey in Kenya, on the eastern shore of Lake Turkana, a few dozen kilometres from the Omo settlement. It is this region that has provided the most complete specimens of primitive African hominians, namely robust australopithecine, *Homo habilis* and *Homo erectus*.

A number of other East African sites have yielded australopithecines, and although none is comparable to the above sites, we should mention Lake Natron in Tanzania,

next to Olduvai, which held a fine lower jaw of a robust australopithecine, and Melka Kunturé in Ethiopia, with a child's lower jaw.

For the moment, therefore, no australopithecine from outside East and southern Africa is known, although it should be remembered that the deposits in central and northwest Africa that are likely to provide any have not been explored so thoroughly.

The chronological scope of *Australopithecus* has not been determined with any great precision, although the majority of specimens are from around 2 million years ago. Some are surely older, but it is not always easy to distinguish them from *Australopithecus afarensis*; others are much more recent and it has even been thought the Taung skull was no older than 0.8 million years, although, as we have already said, the dating of South African sites is very difficult; in East Africa, *Australopithecus robustus* seems to have died out around 1.2 million years ago (Lake Natron, site Garba IV at Melka Kunturé).

A number of researchers maintained for a long time that the gracile australopithecine (*Australopithecus africanus*) was simply the female form of the robust specimen (called *A. robustus* and *A. crassidens* in South Africa and *A. boisei* in East Africa), but if this was the case then male and female would have neither the same geographical distribution (*A. africanus* is rare if not absent in East Africa) nor the same time span (since *A. africanus* disappeared around 2 million years ago, considerably before the robust form). Furthermore, the true female of the robust form is known from one well-preserved half-skull from east Turkana (KNM–ER 732) and there is no doubt that it is different from *A. africanus*, notwithstanding certain superficial similarities, and the existence of two distinct types is today acknowledged by all specialists (Plate 3).

The features of these australopithecines can be divided into three categories: those which are still primitive and by which they are hardly distinguishable from the apes; those which, in contrast, put them close to the genus *Homo*; and those which are peculiar to the australopithecines themselves. In the first category we must place the low skull capacity, which amounts to only 500 cc or so, which is similar to that of the great apes, whereas in Modern humans it is around 1,400 cc. Even if we relate this volume to body weight, the brain of the australopithecine is hardly greater than that of the chimpanzee. One result of this small brain size is that instead of being globular, as in humans, the skull is still hardly bulging: there is no forehead, since the frontal bone is horizontal (in the robust form) or only slightly angled upwards (in the slender form). Seen from the rear, the maximal width of the skull is at the base, and the parietal bones converge towards the top (a 'tent-shaped' skull), whereas in our species the lateral parts of the skull are parallel or even slightly divergent towards the top, which is the place of maximal width ('house-shaped' skull). Primitive, too, are the prognathism (jaws in advance of the cranium) which goes with the absence of a chin, the lack of a prominent nose and the presence of a strongly marked brow ridge which is constant in all hominians with the exception of Modern humans, yet whose function is not clear (protection of the orbits? strengthening of the facial architecture?).

The similarities to genuine humans (of the genus *Homo*) are many and fundamental. As we have seen in the case of Lucy, bipedalism has been achieved, even though the mechanism is probably rather different, as the long and compressed femur, among other features, indicates.

The skull is now well known from a number of specimens. The principal difference from that of the great apes is in the relative proportions of the face and the cranium. The muzzle becomes smaller and is placed not in front of but below the cranium, which seems to fan out around a centre situated in the vicinity of the pituitary gland (pituitary fossa). Further forward, the frontal part tends to cover the orbits. Further back, the development of the cortical associative areas creates an 'occipital balance' that pushes the zone of insertion of the nape muscles under the skull. Obviously, this shift cannot be dissociated from the changes arising from bipedalism, which also brings forward the occipital foramen, where the spinal cord passes. Bipedalism and cerebral expansion therefore lead to complete reorganization of the skull's architecture, which thereafter undergoes only minor adjustments.

Finally, among the foremost of the traits peculiar to *Australopithecus* is adaptation to a diet based on hard vegetation, which is reminiscent of *Gigantopithecus* and the group of *Sivapithecus*. This specialization, which is clear in the gracile form, is even more obvious in the robust form. Incisors and canines are reduced to make way for premolars and molars which are so developed that they have earned *Zinjanthropus* the nickname 'Nutcracker Man'. The strength of the masticatory system is confirmed by the weight of the jaw (which is sometimes comparable to that of the earliest *Gigantopithecus*!) and especially by the extraordinary development of the temporal muscles. In the male of the robust form, those muscles are so well developed that they result in the formation of a sagittal crest in the middle of the skull, along the line where right and left muscles join. Lower down at the front the muscular fibres splay the zygomatic arches and push the cheekbones forward, giving the face a very distinctive flat or even concave profile. The slender form must have been less narrowly specialized, although it is unlikely that it was carnivorous, as has sometimes been supposed.

What picture, then, can we form of these *Australopithecus*, with fossils which give only partial testimony? It is agreed that they were between 1.3 and 1.5 m in height, but their weight varies from one type to another, between a minimum of 30 kg for the gracile form and a maximum of 100 kg for the robust form. We know almost nothing of their appearance, since body hair and skin colour are not preserved in sediments and only more or less likely suppositions can be made. A reconstruction of the living *Australopithecus* can be attempted by putting sets of muscles on the skeleton, then the internal organs, then the skin, but the arbitrary element increases to such an extent that the final result might look like a chimpanzee or a palaeoanthropologist, depending on the goodwill of the artist!

The problem of toolmaking among the australopithecines has not yet been completely solved. At Omo, J. Chavaillon has found small splinters of quartzite from 3 million years ago, that is before the appearance of *A. boisei* (whose oldest specimen, a very fine skull from west Turkana of 2.5 million years ago, was discovered in 1986). Some specialists, such as R. Leakey, think that these first industries are the work of a *Homo* that has not yet been discovered, which, as we shall see on pp. 32–4, is a reasonable speculation. At a later date, around 2 million years ago, industries become more abundant; the basic tool is the pebble, from which a small number of flakes are removed to form a point or an uneven cutting edge (this is called a chopper or flaked pebble). This industry was defined at Olduvai and for this reason is known as Oldowan; its author, unfortunately, is not always known with any degree of certainty, but the genus *Homo*, present at that time, is a better candidate than *Australopithecus*.

Australopithecines are not associated with a structured 'living floor' such as we encounter later, and we imagine them more readily in small groups, leading an itinerant life like that of the baboons, for example, devoting most of the day to the search for food.

The ecological relations between the species are still more obscure. The gracile form coexists only rarely with the robust, and it would seem that they were mutually exclusive, which could imply either a great similarity in ecological niches (with one species chasing the other away) or a difference so great that the two species never met in the same environment (and hence the same sediment). In view of their anatomical similarities, the former hypothesis is clearly the more likely.

The main problem, which is often posed by the frequent coexistence of *Homo* and the *Australopithecus boisei* in East Africa, is that of the relations between the two species. Many authors see the latter simply as game for the true humans, the hunters and sole makers of the Oldowan industries. Until recently that view was faced with the serious objection that the ancestors of the australopithecines, 3 million years ago, made tools, so that *Zinjanthropus* and his brothers would have had to have lost that aptitude – a most unlikely hypothesis in view of the enormous selective advantage the ability must have conferred. As we shall see, that objection has now been resolved by the recent discovery at west Turkana of a robust skull of 2.5 million years ago.

None of these questions, interesting as they are, has caused anything like as much discussion and disagreement among dozens of specialists the world over as has been provoked by the problem of the phyletic links between these primitive hominians. The abundance of literature on the subject, and the passion that often surrounds it, lead on occasion to a certain lack of rigour, so that the formulation of a reasoned opinion is no easy task. We now attempt such a formulation, bearing in mind that a new discovery could well call any evolutionary scenario into question.

We should recall in the first place that history has advanced in a succession of dichotomies; it has not burgeoned like a nebulous cauliflower. With each evolutionary event (speciation), at least one of the lines acquires new features that enable us to define a monophyletic group. For example the 'hominian' branch of the dichotomy between the Panidae (the African great apes) and the hominians is characterized by bipedalism, reduction of the canine/P 3 complex, a certain increase in the volume of the brain and so on. Within this group, the set comprising gracile and robust *Australopithecus* and *Homo* displays, in skull and dentition alone, more than fifty features that are evolved in comparison with *A. afarensis*! It could be admitted that a few might have appeared separately in both *Australopithecus* and *Homo*, but certainly not fifty, and there is thus no doubt that that set constitutes a natural group, to which *Australopithecus afarensis* does not belong. Since the latter species too possesses a number of evolved characteristics of its own, the conclusion that *A. afarensis* on the one hand and the rest of the hominians on the other form two branches of one dichotomy (these are known as brother groups) is inevitable. Such is the hypothesis advanced in 1980 by Y. Coppens, who had already described *Australopithecus afarensis* as a pre-*Australopithecus*.

If we now turn to the group comprising *Australopithecus sensu stricto* and *Homo*, we find in the australopithecines, especially in their masticatory system, adaptations which are clearly evolved, although here it is more difficult to be sure that the tendency for the grinding teeth to grow at the expense of incisors and canines does not typify the entire group, including the ancestors of humans, from the outset.

In other words, we do not know whether *Australopithecus sensu stricto* and *Homo* form two groups that were separate from their origin, or if *Homo* might have derived from a gracile australopithecine that was as yet only slightly specialized. The fossils seem to argue against the former hypothesis, in that the appearance of *Australopithecus*, as far as we can tell at present, preceded that of *Homo* by a long way (whereas two sibling groups would obviously appear at the same time). The recent discovery of a skull of *Australopithecus boisei* from 2.5 million years ago forces us to set further back in the past the time at which the gracile and robust australopithecines diverged, and to relegate still further (to at least 3 million years ago) the preceding dichotomy which may have separated either the australopithecines from *Homo*, or robust *Australopithecus* (which would then be known as *Paranthropus*) from the group comprising *Australopithecus gracilis* and *Homo* (in which case we should concede that the features of the *Australopithecus* had undergone reversion in *Homo*). Consensus has not yet been reached on this matter, but the discovery of skull KNM-WT 17000 in any event enables us to restrict the making and use of tools to the non-robust branch, without the need to suppose that that capacity was lost in the *Australopithecus boisei*.

HOMO HABILIS

It was in 1960 – only a year after the astonishing revelation of *Zinjanthropus* – that Louis Leakey discovered at Olduvai a number of skull fragments, a mandible and an almost complete foot which had belonged to a hominian that was different from the australopithecines and which he and his colleagues P. Tobias and J. Napier named *Homo habilis* in 1964. It goes without saying that if the announcement of the age of *Zinjanthropus* evoked some scepticism, the proposal of the existence of a true human at the same period was to arouse passionate debates that lasted almost twenty years. It is indeed only in the last few years that *Homo habilis* has been recognized by the entire scientific community, after a series of discoveries in eastern and southern Africa.

First at Olduvai, skull OH 24, which is fairly well preserved, also dates to around 2 million years ago. In Ethiopia, at Omo and Melka Kunturé, a number of fragments could correspond to a more recent *Homo habilis*, but the finest East African pieces come from the east of Lake Turkana, which, as we have seen, had also contained australopithecines and, as we shall see on p. 33, *Homo erectus*. The most famous specimen is the skull prosaically baptized KNM-ER 1470, which is almost complete, although it was toothless and had to be reconstructed from many fragments. Its age was estimated at first to be 2.6 million years, since it comes from a level situated beneath the KBS tuff, for which radiometric methods (potassium–argon) had given that date, but palaeontologists, considering the degree of evolution of the mammal fauna in comparison with that of the neighbouring deposits of the Omo, considered it to be more recent. New absolute datings were then made until results the palaeontologists could agree with were obtained; the age accepted nowadays for skull 1470 is slightly less than 2 million years. Another skull from east Turkana, KNM-ER 1813, comes from above the KBS tuff and is therefore somewhat more recent. *Homo habilis* was present in South Africa also around the same time: skull STW 53 from the Sterkfontein deposit is very similar to skull OH 24 of Olduvai.

What are the traits that enable us to recognize in this 'Handy Man' a species so close to our own that it can be

included in the same genus? In the first place, the cranial capacity is greater than even the most voluminous of the australopithecines: in skull KNM-ER 1470 it is approximately 775 cc, slightly over half the capacity in our species, but for a body weight that cannot have been greater than 40 kg; in comparison with *Australopithecus* the cranium is wider in relation to the face and the forehead is more upright. The masticatory system, on the other hand, is less powerful; there is never sign of a sagittal crest, the zygomatic arches are narrower, the cheekbones are not so far forward and the lower jaw is less heavy; the disproportion between the grinding teeth (premolars and molars) and front teeth is less marked. *Homo habilis* was no longer content with an exclusively vegetable diet and must at times have supplemented this with animal prey or carrion.

It must, be acknowledged, however, that whereas in East Africa it is fairly easy to highlight the presence of *Homo habilis*, since the most frequently encountered hominian is the very distinctive *Australopithecus boisei*, in South Africa it is not so easily distinguished from *Australopithecus africanus*, from which it may derive. *Homo habilis* has similar skull proportions and, like *A. africanus*, brow ridges, a prognathous face, and a cranium that is broader at the base than at the parietal level; it is probable that the two species were similar in appearance.

The essential difference is cultural: in *Homo habilis* humankind reached a new evolutionary level which was to influence the whole of its subsequent development. The evidence of that cultural revolution comes mainly from eastern Africa. Flake tools, choppers and chopping tools are the most frequently preserved objects, although there can be no doubt that bone and especially wood must have played an important or even essential role. The preservation of the latter, unfortunately, is mostly a matter of chance, and it is less easy than in the case of stone objects to be sure of intentional fabrication or retouch.

Stone, bone and wooden tools, however, are only one facet of the cultural life of these first humans, even though they are the most tangible, the most measurable. Several eastern African sites in Ethiopia, Kenya and Tanzania have given us an image of their daily life that is moving and instructive, if still somewhat lacking in clarity. The DK I site at Olduvai and Gomboré I at Melka Kunturé are the most famous. These are riverside living floors where *Homo habilis* made permanent settlements. A circle of large stones at Olduvai and a raised emplacement at Melka Kunturé suggest a first organizing of space which prefigures the partitioning of dwelling space we find with *Homo erectus*. The ground is strewn with waste flakes, abandoned tools and split bones. A breakdown of the anatomical elements of the species represented shows that only certain parts of the hunted beasts or of corpses disputed with other scavengers were brought back to camp; the large animals were torn to pieces where they had died (examples of such butchery sites, too, are known); hippopotamus, antelope, zebra and giraffe were the commonest prey. Yet the animal component of the diet must be overrepresented, since vegetable remains do not preserve nearly so well.

Evidence of intense social and family life, with complex relations inside the group, has led to the suggestion that a language was used which was more elaborate than that of the apes, even if it was far from having the complexity of our own. Anatomical study of the production of sounds and their cerebral control can provide an answer to this question of the mastery of articulated language by *Homo habilis*.

On the inner surface of the cranium the bone shows traces

of the encephalon in the form of tracks of blood vessels and convexities – attenuated by the meninges – corresponding to convolutions of the brain. In this way, to an extent, we can deduce from endocranial morphology the development of the different areas of the brain, knowing that in humans of the Modern type they correspond to particular functions. In the inferior frontal convolution the French physician Broca in the last century showed the importance of an area that has since been known as Broca's area, the lesion of which provokes aphasia: from this he deduced that it played a central role in articulated language. This convolution was found on the endocranial cast of skull KNM-ER 1470: it would seem that *Homo habilis* possessed the intellectual aptitude for a certain form of complex language.

The production of phonemes and their rapid association to form words entails also the power to form and co-ordinate through the interplay of palate, tongue and lips, sounds produced by the vocal chords. In humans of the Modern type, the palate is deep, the tongue mobile and the larynx low: this arrangement leaves the bucco-pharyngeal cavity enough space for ample and complex movements. In the apes, the palate is shallow, the tongue less mobile because the chin recedes and the larynx is high, so that certain processes of the base of the skull have a different orientation. These bone arrangements are to be found in *Homo habilis* and would seem to indicate that the latter, like apes, had a bucco-pharyngeal cavity that was not large enough for the emission of articulated sounds.

Anatomy therefore gives an ambiguous answer to the question of language. The brain would seem to precede in evolution the organ it commands – always assuming, of course, that Broca's area had the same function then as it has now.

HOMO ERECTUS

Although *Homo erectus* succeeded *Homo habilis*, the former species is much older historically, since it was discovered at the end of the nineteenth century. By then a number of Neanderthalers had already been discovered, but they had passed unnoticed or, worse, been taken for idiots ... or Cossacks! (See Chapter 9, p. 100.) Naturalists in those days were passionately debating the theory of evolution, and the search for the 'missing link' was the order of the day. It was with a mind full of such modern evolutionary ideas that the Dutch doctor E. Dubois set off for the East Indies in 1890 with the firm intention of discovering the 'ape-man' predicted by theory. In Sumatra, he heard tell of finds made on the neighbouring island of Java, so he went there and on the banks of the Solo river unearthed a jaw and a skull-cap which had strong brow ridges, a low, receding forehead and a robust occipital torus (see Plate 13). Soon afterwards he exhumed in almost the same place a femur in perfect condition (notwithstanding a pronounced exostosis, an ossification due to the tearing of muscle). The *Pithecanthropus erectus* or 'upright ape-man' thus was born in 1891 and immediately prompted criticism. Most 'scientists' then saw the creature as no more than a kind of giant gibbon, all the less worthy of their interest in coming from an exotic land. At that time, in fact, and until the discovery of the Taung *Australopithecus* in 1924, all known human fossils were from western Europe: Neanderthal, Cro-Magnon or ... Piltdown. This last 'discovery' of 1912, recognized as false in 1953, shows what the anthropologists of the beginning of the century expected: a human skull associated with simian

teeth; the (still unidentified) perpetrator of the fraud had put together with sediments and genuine fossils a fragment of the skull of a recent *Homo sapiens* and the jaw of an orang-utan with filed teeth. Obviously in such a context, Dubois's discovery, which associated the opposite features, would not have been well received. Research in Java was not resumed until 1930, firstly under the palaeoanthropologist G. H. R. von Koenigswald and then under Indonesian geologists. Many human fossils have now been discovered on that island. Although they are still referred to colloquially as *Pithecanthropus*, the term *Pithecanthropus* is no longer used scientifically, since it is considered that the differences from *Homo* are specific rather than general. Several human types have been described in Java, and in the past different chronological periods were attributed to them since it was thought that the most ancient of them (the Modjokerto child) was 1.9 million years old and therefore a contemporary of *Homo habilis*. Of late, however, the absolute dating and estimates based on the evolution of fauna have been called into question, and it would seem that none is older than 700,000 to 800,000 years at most: this makes the coexistence of several types of humans very unlikely, and what we have is probably a single, highly variable species. The animal environment of the Java *Pithecanthropus* hardly differs from that of the continent, since the fauna, like humans, was able to cross dry land to Java at a time when the level of the oceans dropped because of glaciation. This drop, estimated at 50 to 100 m, is similar to the depth of the straits that separate Java from the continent. The fauna is that of a hot, humid and predominantly afforested environment. It is therefore not surprising that the array of stone tools is poor and crude in comparison with those of Europe and Africa: wood, lianas, fibres and bamboo must have provided most of the requisite materials for the making of shelters, traps, weapons, tools and so on, and of course none of these have remained.

In China, the first teeth of *Homo erectus*, known under the name of *Sinanthropus*, were bought like those of the *Gigantopithecus* as 'dragon's teeth' from apothecaries in Hong Kong. Regular excavations began in 1921 in the caves of Zhoukoudian (Choukoutien), near Beijing (Peking), from which they came. The first tooth discovered on site was found in 1927, followed by skull-caps, some more fragmentary remains of faces, teeth and some bones from the postcranial skeleton. All these pieces were magisterially studied, drawn and cast by the Austrian anthropologist F. Weidenreich, but they all disappeared in 1941 during the Second World War.

F. Weidenreich and G. H. R. von Koenigswald soon realized that profound similarities united the fossils of Java and China, despite the difference in age (the Zhoukoudian site, which is difficult to date, is probably not more than 500,000 years old). Such a geographical range for a single evolutionary grade of human, which was called Archanthropine, was soon to be confirmed by other finds – the *Telanthropus* of Swartkrans in South Africa, the *Atlanthropus* of Ternifine in Algeria, discovered by C. Arambourg and Hoffstetter in 1954–6, and discoveries in Europe, where *Homo erectus* specimens are nevertheless not very common.

Soon afterwards *Homo erectus* was to begin to descend into time. Other Chinese fossils (of Yuanmou (Yüan-mou) and Lantian) are older than those of Zhoukoudian, but once again it is in East Africa that the records in this field were to be broken most often. At Olduvai in 1969 Leakey discovered the crown of a skull of *Homo erectus*, named OH 9, in a level more recent than those which had contained *Homo habilis* and *Zinjanthropus*, but still more than 1 million years old.

In 1975 an almost complete skull, KNM-ER 3733, was exhumed from levels dated at 1.5 million years (Okoté tuff, Koobi Fora): it is indubitably more developed, especially in its cranial capacity, than the *Homo habilis* that preceded it in the same sedimentary series, although that continuity shows both that the filiation of the two species is beyond doubt and that the boundary between them is somewhat arbitrary. Finally, and very recently, the sedimentary series of the west of Lake Turkana have provided the skeleton of an adolescent, KNM-WT 15000, which is also more than 1.5 million years old. In the interim other sites in eastern and north Africa have provided more recent specimens of *Homo erectus*. Examples include Bodo and Melka Kunturé in Ethiopia and a variety of sites on the coast of Morocco, the most important of which is Salé in Rabat.

In Europe the most ancient human remains (mandibles from Mauer in Germany and Montmaurin in France) are scarcely 500,000 years old, although in the deposit at Chilhac in the Massif Central C. Guth discovered a number of flaked pebbles that testify to human presence in France at least 1.5 million years ago.[1] *Homo erectus* is therefore the first member of the human line to have left the African continent, which had been the scene of all its history from 30 million years ago.

The anatomical characteristics of the Archanthropines are to a large extent inherited from *Homo habilis*. The face is still voluminous, chinless but with a more prominent nose; robust brow ridges separate the face from a slightly rising forehead. The cranial capacity, which is rather variable, is sometimes hardly superior to that of *Homo habilis*, but it reaches 1,100 cc in certain *Sinanthropus* specimens, which is similar in size to the smallest modern brains (the brain of Anatole France was no larger). The shape of the cranium, however, is still primitive, the maximal width being at the base, behind the apertures for the ears. Although the teeth are still large, their proportions are the same as our own, and skull KNM-ER 3733, which is 1.5 million years old, already has a back molar that is slightly smaller than the second. The reduced masticatory muscles no longer push the cheekbones forward, and a depression appears between these bones and the nasal aperture.

The most remarkable features of the skull of these *Homo erectus* are its robustness and its tendency to be burdened with bony superstructures. In certain African forms (skulls from Bodo in Ethiopia and Broken Hill in Zambia) and Indonesian specimens (*Pithecanthropus* VIII) the face is bulky and massive, and the brow ridges are extremely thick, much heavier than in any other hominid. Above the point of entry of the nape muscles a supra-occipital ridge forms that has a bulge behind the ear apertures, accentuating the 'tent-like' shape of the skull. At the same time the cranial walls become much thicker, and can even exceed 10 mm. The function of this massiveness of the skull, unparalleled among even the most robust of the australopithecines, is unknown to us. It is somewhat reminiscent of the effects of certain modern endocrinal imbalances, although it would be difficult to explain in terms of pathology the traits of a species that was spread over all the Old World for more than 1 million years.

This robustness is equally marked in the rest of the skeleton, which is morphologically similar to our own, as is demonstrated by the uncertainty over the true identity of the original femur found by Dubois: although the pithecanthropic nature of the crown of the skull is not in doubt, some researchers believe that the femur belonged to a *Homo sapiens*. For a long time it was thought that the *Homo erectus* was small in stature, but skeleton KNM-WT 15000, after reconstruction, indicated a height of 1.68 m, in an individual that was not fully grown!

On the cultural level, it is generally admitted that *Homo erectus* equals Acheulean, which is more or less true, although some find it too much of a simplification. It would seem in particular that the earliest *Homo erectus* still belonged to the Oldowan culture: the transition to the Acheulean, marked by a diversification of tools, changes in the way of life, the structuring of the habitat and probably the use of fire, appears to occur a short time after the *Homo habilis* → *Homo erectus* speciation. The Acheulean (Plate 4) still made much use of the Oldowan type of pebble-tool, but was typified by the appearance of a new tool, the handaxe, which was to last until very recent times. It is a large tool (averaging 20 cm in length) made from pebble, flint or flake; it is flattish and usually elliptical, ovoid or almond-shaped. The handaxe is found all over Africa but is rarer in east Asia, where for a long time it was thought to be absent. The cleaver is a variety of handaxe with a broad, straight transverse edge; it is rarely found outside Africa. Another remarkable tool is the bola, made by hammering a polyhedral rock. A well-shaped bola, such as those excavated by J. Chavaillon at Melka Kunturé, can seem perfectly spherical until the calliper rule shows a 1 or 2 mm difference between two diameters! However, the nature of the varieties of tools encountered in a prehistoric deposit depends not only on the cultural tradition of the one who fashioned them, but also to a large extent on the uses to which they were to be put and on the nature of the material used. The features of the material, be it obsidian, basalt, flint, quartzite sandstone or calcareous stone, introduce constraints (ease of cutting, solidity and so on) that have a strong influence on the result obtained. The term Acheulean therefore embraces many varied industries, among which it is difficult to establish classifications and recognize filiations.

It is also with the Acheulean that we find the first indications of the construction of shelters, external protections against predators or bad weather. At the same time, the living space begins to be subdivided into distinct areas where one can, without being too adventurous, identify a workshop or sometimes a hearth. The domestication of fire seems to mark the beginning of the Acheulean; it has been shown at the Escale site in France, which is almost 1 million years old, and perhaps also at Chesowanja in Kenya, which dates from 1.4 million years ago. Nevertheless it would perhaps be incorrect to think that fire revolutionized the daily life of the first *Homo erectus*, who did not cast metals, fire ceramics or cook food, at least not in any systematic way, and who did not need to warm themselves. It was only in recent periods of the Acheulean that it took on what might be seen as an essential role, in view of the severe climatic conditions then prevailing in Eurasia.

Whereas the transition from *Homo habilis* to *Homo erectus* poses hardly any problems for palaeoanthropologists, the evolution of *Homo erectus* and transition to *Homo sapiens* is the object of one of the great current debates.

As we shall see, the line between *H. erectus* and *H. sapiens* is very difficult to draw, and this makes us ask whether the evolution from the first *Homo habilis* down to ourselves is gradual, with arbitrary limits between species, or if on the contrary each transition really corresponds to a rapid phase of evolution, since *Homo erectus* in fact remained stable for 1 million years. The two hypotheses correspond to competing theories on the rhythm of evolution – phyletic gradualism (regular evolution) and punctuated equilibrium (rapid evolution followed by periods of stasis) respectively. In order to choose the appropriate model we require a quantifiable feature, and cranial capacity fits the bill. Cerebral volume seems to increase through time within the single species of *H. erectus*, and this would seem to confirm the idea of gradual evolution, yet the aggregate of uncertainties concerning the measured value and geological age of the fossils is such that it is easy to demonstrate the inverse (evolution slight or absent from 1.5 to 0.5 million years ago). In any case, it is clear that the evolution of a single characteristic does not necessarily apply to the rest of the organism. In fact it does not seem possible to treat *Homo erectus* as a unit which was homogeneous (panmixic) in a given period, and regional continuities of various durations and degrees of distinctiveness have been known to science for a long time.

The first and undoubtedly the best-established regional line leading from *Homo erectus* to *Homo sapiens* is European. In this case, however, it certainly did not come down to us, because it ended in an evolutionary cul-de-sac some 30,000 years ago with the Neanderthalers. Until a few years ago scientists thought they could recognize alongside these pre-Neanderthalers representatives of another line that was part of our ancestry. In fact, as J. J. Hublin has shown, that 'line' was founded on very fragmentary fossils (such as the all too famous Fontéchevade skull-cap) or on better-preserved pieces such as the Steinheim cranium or the Swanscombe skull fragments whose supposedly *sapiens* traits were really no more than primitive features that had not yet become 'Neanderthalized'. The principal relics of these first Europeans are: the mandible from Mauer near Heidelberg, the most ancient in Europe, discovered in a gravel pit in 1907; the jawbone from Montmaurin in Haute Garonne, the oldest in France; the Tautavel Man of the eastern Pyrenees, represented by a skull, several mandibles and a number of bones of the skeleton; the human from the Petralona cave in Greece, discovered resting on a stalagmitic table by speleologists; the Swanscombe and Steinheim remains of Britain and Germany, respectively (mentioned above); the human remains of Biache-Saint-Vaast in the Pas-de-Calais in France, recently discovered in the course of extension work on a steel mill, and a number of other parietal and frontal bones and mandibles. All these pieces have in varying degrees features that herald the Neanderthalers, but the difficulties in dating all these sites militate against detailed analysis of the ways in which this line evolved.

In Java, in levels containing the 'Ngandong' fauna, which are more recent than those associated with *Pithecanthropus*, a number of skull-caps have been exhumed which resemble those of the *Homo erectus* that had previously lived at the same place, but with greater cranial capacity, approaching that of Modern humans. These Ngandong remains are near-perfect morphological intermediaries between *Pithecanthropus* and the Modern type of human in that part of the world: those of Wadjak in Java and of Kow Swamp in Australia, which are approximately 20,000 years old. Despite their recent date, these crania actually retained vestiges of the brow ridge, sloping forehead and thick bones, traits found even in contemporary Australian aborigines and more generally in all the original peoples of Oceania.

The same phenomenon is to be encountered in China. From the *Sinanthropus* of Zhoukoudian to the present 'Mon-goloid' peoples by way of the human remains of the upper cave of Zhoukoudian (Upper Palaeolithic) we find certain morphological traits – 'spade-shaped' incisors and prominent cheekbones – that suggest a phyletic continuity in east Asia.

Eastern and southern Africa too had late *Homo erectus*, of the order of 100,000 to 200,000 years old; these are evolved in their voluminous cranium; which tends to broaden in the parietal region giving a rather high cranial capacity. The face, however, where it is known (Bodo in Ethiopia, Broken Hill in Zambia) is hyper-Archanthropic in its massivity and in the heaviness of the brow-ridge. At Omo in levels of comparable age (much more recent than those that yielded *Australopithecus*) skull-caps were discovered that are much more '*sapiens*' than the others; this is not at all surprising if this was a population where evolution was in full swing and where not all individuals acquired the same evolved traits simultaneously. In that part of Africa, however, there is as yet no evidence of a persistent morphological feature that bespeaks continuity of local evolution.

In north-west Africa the idea of evolution *in situ* of an endemic line extending from the *Atlanthropus* of Ternifine to humans of the Modern type, of the Iberomaurusian, by way of many remains from the Moroccan coast (at Salé, Thomas Quarry, Sidi Abderrahman and Rabat) has often been proposed and perhaps should not be rejected; it is based mainly on the large size of human teeth in that region, as well as on some indications – which are not really very convincing – of some biogeographical isolation of north-west Africa during the Middle Pleistocene.

How, then, was *Homo erectus* transformed into *Homo sapiens*? Is it conceivable that in three or four regions of the Old World groups or subspecies of *Homo erectus* existed which all evolved by augmentation of brain size and a thinning of the skull towards a *sapiens* stage?

In other words, do the major human groups, Australoid, Mongoloid, Negroid and Caucasoid, which we distinguish in accordance with certain biological criteria, have their roots within the species of *Homo erectus* or, on, the contrary, if there is a biological reality in the grouping, are we dealing with a recent diversification stemming from a well-established *Homo sapiens*?

The truth is probably somewhere in between. The homogeneity of contemporary humanity scarcely accords with the theory of polycentric evolution, but the indications of local evolution are too numerous to ignore. No doubt the flow of genes between populations has never been completely interrupted, and the role of the genome of the regional groups must vary in accordance with the intensity of exchanges between neighbouring groups.

NOTE

1 On Chilhac, however, see Paola Villa in Chapter 4 (p. 44) – Ed.

BIBLIOGRAPHY

See Chapter 1.

3

AFRICA

during the Lower Palaeolithic and the first settlements

Jean Chavaillon

The invention of the first tools is a landmark in the physical and psychological development of hominids. The techniques used and the function of the objects made are closely related to activities performed in the Palaeolithic camps and to the first signs of social organization and culture. The oldest skeletal remains of the genus *Homo* date back more than 3 million years, even though none have yet been discovered in association with worked tools. The earliest evidence of an organized toolkit was found in the deposits at Hadar[1] in the Awash valley and at Shungura in the lower Omo valley,[2] both in Ethiopia. It can be considered, although not asserted, that the reasoned, widespread, use of stone or bone tools coincided with a particular stage in the physical, social and psychological development of hominians, whether the species belonged to the genus *Homo* or the genus *Australopithecus*.

Palaeontology is a scientific discipline which contributes to our understanding of the evolution of humans as physical beings: on the basis of anatomical features of bones or teeth, a palaeontologist can chronologically place hominian skeletal fragments with some degree of accuracy. The prehistorian, however, adds another dimension to this shared area of research: the search for, discovery and study of early Palaeolithic camps, with their stone tools, animal remains and often discernible internal structure, make it possible to imagine what might have been the social life of these first beings, to whom we are related by a long chain of technological and cultural progress.

Stone tools are indisputable evidence of the presence of humans, as convincing as a fragment of hominid skull. They are usually in good condition, as they survive better than human skeletal remains, animal bones and teeth, or evidence of the organization of a camp site, which such an ordinary event as a river bursting its banks could wipe out for ever. A stone tool may not be found in its original position, but if it has not been broken or damaged it may still be of great interest in providing information about manufacturing techniques and its repeated use. A tool is also unmistakable evidence of the presence of humans, at least as far as worked objects are concerned, whether in bone or stone, because no other animal, not even an ape, can shape a chopper or chip a handaxe or, above all, transmit such technological knowledge to its descendants.

THE FIRST TOOLS

What is a tool? 'A human-made object used to perform manual work.' Prehistorians and archaeologists can but approve this lexicographical definition. The word 'human-made' should be stressed, however, because it clearly distinguishes the unworked implement, a pebble or piece of wood that human and ape alike can use, from the shaped tool made with a specific purpose in mind and whose function would be to scrape, cut or break. The adjective 'human-made' confers on the tool a social value, and it plays an increasingly demanding and pervasive role in human life, to such an extent that as the technology of artificial intelligence advances one may wonder whether the roles are not far from being inverted. Are we still able to control our tools, and if so, will we always be able to do so?

Since the beginning of the Palaeolithic period, however, some natural, unworked objects found in occupation levels, together with bones and chipped tools, must simply have been used as they were. These objects are also called tools or weapons by virtue of the use to which they were put, or of their human-intended purpose. The social context is related to the technical operation.

Individualism is the rule among chimpanzees, despite a certain degree of community organization. The chimpanzee occupies a different nightly nook each evening, fighting over it with other chimpanzees. Its activities consist of cracking nuts, an individual operation undertaken more by the females, which feed more on nuts, the males living off the products of hunting. The techniques they use are interesting. In Gabon, for instance, the chimpanzee collects a dozen or so *Cola edulis* nuts and puts them near a root or a large piece of stone, a sort of anvil lying on the ground.[3] The ape places a nut in a depression in the tree-root or stone, a sort of cup mark often produced by previous operations. The nut thus held in the depression is crushed with a manual striker which performs the function of a wooden or stone hammer.

The first worked tools are definitely associated with dwelling areas: the temporary settlement at Omo, the base camps of a group at Olduvai[4] in Tanzania and at Melka Kunturé in Ethiopia.[5] The worked stone tool is most often associated with settlement structures and thus indicates community activities. Various tools have been found at these base camps, which date from 1.8 to 1.6 million years ago: choppers or chopping-tools made from pebbles more or less simply worked to obtain a cutting edge. These objects sometimes serve a dual purpose: the stone cores or pieces that have provided flakes then themselves become cutting tools. Objects have also been found that were used to scrape roots, and skins or to break up bones and grain. There are also rough, untrimmed flakes that would make good knives to cut tendons or meat. Finally there are many natural stones which bear signs of blows: these are hammerstones, some of which still show the position of the cup mark. The implements found on these sites recall those used by present-day chimpanzees. It could be that the Oldowan cup-marked stones were used in the same way as the chimpanzee uses its stones, because food gathering must have been one of the chief activities. It may also be that these are hand-held strikers, often used on the same side.

So the basic point seems to be that between the *Kenyapithecus* discovered by Louis Leakey at Fort Ternan (Andrews and Walker, 1976) in Kenya, whose stone equipment is similar to that found in the ecological niches of today's chimpanzees, and the present day there is a gap of 14 million years for the chimpanzees to close!

Present-day chimpanzees use stones whose hollows or cup marks hold the nut, which is then crushed with another stone. This action and this implement are the most efficient, technically speaking, used by this animal; however, far earlier, the Oldowan humans of Gomboré I (1.7 million years ago)[6] and of Omo 123 at Shungura (2.0 million years ago) carried out an identical operation using the same implement. But the Oldowan hollowed stones, if they were used for this purpose, were technically the simplest and most ordinary implements in the repertoire compared with the scrapers, choppers and flake-tools used by these populations. Thus the same tool and the same action do not occupy the same rank in the technological hierarchy of a present-day ape and of a hominid of 2 million years ago: they represent the most complex manoeuvre executed by the ape and the least complicated one carried out by the hominid.

In the most remote times, whether at Hadar (2.6 million years ago) or at Omo-Shungura (2.3 million and 2 million years ago),[7] shaped objects were already being made, associated with flakes that were either waste from the manufacture of choppers or else deliberately produced for use as knives. This leads to the conclusion that techniques were already comparatively far advanced 2.6 million years ago. It may also be considered that these objects were not the first tools ever produced. But the theory according to which a chopper produced by removing a single flake would be the oldest tool, and that toolmaking gradually became more technically complicated with the use of alternate and biface chipping, may not correspond to reality!

Thus, in camps such as those at Olduvai (Bed I) and Melka Kunturé (Gomboré IB), the association of technically advanced tools with distinctly primitive pieces clearly shows the difficulty of building up a technological hierarchy. Even a few rare bifaces, or rather pieces that take their place, called 'proto-bifaces', appear from the most remote periods. Naturally some objects are representative of specific periods and cultures, for example, the choppers and chopping tools for the Oldowan,[8] the biface handaxes and cleavers for the Acheulean, flake implements for the Middle Stone Age[9] and miniaturization resulting in geometric microliths for the Late Stone Age.[10]

Any increase in the varieties of tools must have been accompanied by an increase in the kinds of manual operations required both to produce and to use the tools. Control of the brain over the hand improved, the hand executing increasingly precise movements, often related to an increasingly complex series of operations. The hand is the intermediary between the brain and the object, whether this is a shaped tool, a stone, a branch or prey. The hand plays the same role as a predatory animal's teeth. Despite the undisputed technical ability that the chimpanzee shows when it goes after termites with a straw, it was the brain's ability to control, and its increasing complexity during Palaeolithic times, that triggered human technological progress. This evolution was made possible by bipedal carriage, which freed the front limbs. The ability to pick up an object, transport it over long distances with hands that were now free, and use it to best advantage in the light of its shape and the requirements of the task foreseen, was a crucial development. Very soon humans were able to use both hands at the same time, either in exactly the same way, as when transporting a heavy stone or prey, or else in different, complementary actions, as when shaping a tool, when one hand had to hold the workpiece while the other struck it with a hammerstone or pounder. The same situation occurred when the human-made tool was put to use: one hand to hold the branch or bone to be broken or the piece of skin to be scraped while the other held the chopper or the scraper. The co-ordination of movements here was no longer synchronous but complementary.

Technical equipment consists of things collected, used or shaped by human beings. Thus account also has to be taken of the unworked pebbles or pieces of stone often discovered at Early Palaeolithic sites in Africa, even when they show no sign of blows or shaping. These stones, picked up by humans either to make a shelter or to be used as raw material for tools or hammerstones, are considered to be archaeological objects, even if of less significance, since they had been deliberately imported. Examples are found in the Olduvai, Melka Kunturé and Karari deposits,[11] among others.

These pounders, pieces of stone and pebbles bearing marks of blows, were used, although not themselves shaped. They may be hand-held hammerstones, large pieces of stone placed on the ground and used as anvils, or else stones in which a depression varying in size and depth had been hollowed out by continuous use of the same side of the pebble to pound or to hold a nut.

This category can also include numerous pebbles, most of them broken in the course of their use as a temporary hammer. Of poor-quality stone, they would often be shattered by the blow. In the same way, certain pebbles, with more or less flat, parallel sides, could have been used to support an object to be crushed. The reverberation of the blow often broke the supporting pebble. These broken stones are particularly numerous and are mixed with tools from pre-Acheulean sites (2.0 million to 1.4 million years ago).

'Knapping' is a word used to describe the removal of one or more fragments or flakes from a piece of material called a core, while 'debitage' is the word used for the waste material. The techniques used to separate flakes and blades from a core were improved during Palaeolithic times. The kinds of cores evolved from the simplest one, the unipolar core from which a single flake or two contiguous flakes were removed, to the most complex one, the Levallois core, which, after rather complicated preparation, made it possible to obtain a flake or a blade of predetermined size and shape.

The first cores are sometimes taken for pebble-tools; these pieces of stone, at first cores, were often used as such or later themselves worked as tools: this is the case with some choppers and other pieces, polyhedral in shape and volume, such as the 'faceted balls'.

Flakes are found in all sizes. The very first flakes removed from a core kept part of their natural outside surface, called the cortex – the 'apple skin' – and these are very numerous at the oldest sites. But this archaism is often tempered by association with more elaborate pieces. It should also be understood that the use of these rough flakes, showing no trace of previous trimming of the cores with or without traces of the cortex, can be regarded as evidence of technological and cultural archaism. This is often misleading, however, because a good knife should be judged by its blade, by the angle of its cutting edge: the retouch is sometimes only a resharpening, the repair of a nicked tool. Nevertheless, retouching was often a deliberate modification of the cutting edge: the knife then became a side-scraper or a tool with notched or serrated edges. During the Acheulean period, the numerous flake-tools, and the variety of sizes, kinds and hence functions, even included the most typical objects of this culture, the handaxe and the cleaver. The latter was still made on a flake, the flaked side having been more or less heavily retouched. Handaxes were often shaped from large flakes, and this feature became widespread towards the end of the Acheulean culture, for example in the north-western Sahara or the high plateaux of eastern Africa.[12]

OLDOWAN OR PRE-ACHEULEAN IMPLEMENTS

Oldowan or pre-Acheulean implements (Plate 4) are usually rather varied, but the most typical piece is no doubt a kind of chopper whose edge was formed by removing flakes from one of the sides of a flat or egg-shaped river-worn pebble or even an ordinary pebble. The cutting edge could be one of the ends, one or other of the side edges, or a part of the periphery. One of the methods most frequently used to study these tools is that recommended by H. L. Movius, who directed attention to the technology used, regardless of the configuration of the cutting edge. If the piece was shaped by removing one, two or more flakes from the same side of the pebble it is known as a 'chopper', while if the facets are on both sides it is called a 'chopping-tool'. P. Biberson (1967) retained these subdivisions in his classification of pebble-tools but preferred the terms 'unidirectionally faceted' pebbles (choppers) or 'bidirectionally faceted' tools. Mary Leakey (1971) and J. and N. Chavaillon (1981) adopt a more functional approach, regarding the uniface or biface criterion as of secondary interest. Special attention is given to the form of the cutting edge and particularly to its position on the edge of the pebble. Thus the term 'chopper' is used for both uniface and biface tools. There are therefore, for example, lateral choppers, distal (or end) choppers, also called 'transverse' by Collinat (1975), point choppers, chopper-chisels, whose cutting edge takes in the breadth of the pebble, and choppers with a peripheral cutting edge. The latter, sometimes called 'discoid' by English-speaking prehistorians, are thought to be the predecessors of the biface. The cutting edge of the Oldowan choppers has an 80° to 100° angle, whereas the Acheulean choppers usually have a 70° to 80° angle. The cutting edge may be straight or sinuous. The cutting edge on the main plane of the object may also be convex, concave, straight, and so on.

From the Oldowan period on, the choppers that provided the flakes must have been cores themselves before being used as tools. During the Oldowan period, however, and even more during the Acheulean period, the choice of raw material and the shape and size of the potential chopper were uppermost in the minds of the humans who picked up a piece of stone or pebble. The idea of the kind of tool must have arisen at the sight of certain pebbles or stones with useful shapes and edges. In the Oldowan occupation levels the chopper was used for everything: to cut, crush, break, sever, and so on. The variety of shapes of the cutting edge and the great variety of sizes and weights indicate that these tools must have been intended for different activities.

One tool that is perhaps even more typical than the chopper seems to be the pebble scraper and scraping-plane. Large numbers of these are found at the Oldowan and Developed Oldowan sites at Melka Kunturé and elsewhere, where they are sometimes classified in the polyhedron category. Often large and heavy, these objects have one flat or concave side, either natural or artificial, from which the perpendicular removal of several small, contiguous or overlapping flakes gave a sharp, sturdy edge with an angle close to 90°. The term 'scraper' or 'plane' certainly implies an assumption about their function, which is obviously quite different from that of projectiles, strikers or choppers, bringing to mind a kind of tool intended for removing bark from branches, scraping roots and perhaps, even in the Oldowan period, for scraping skins. These tools, more sophisticated technically and more specialized in their function than the choppers, contribute to a better understanding of the activities of the first hominids. In the Acheulean settlements the fact that flake scrapers were widespread meant that there were fewer heavy, cumbersome tools, except, however, for some scraping-planes which can have up to three intersecting working surfaces on the same piece (double and triple scraping-planes).

Although choppers and scraping-planes are typical of this culture, it should not be forgotten that there are other objects made from pebbles, tools with notched or serrated edges, or pieces with several facets – polyhedrons – which look like balls or parallelepipeds, or have an edge more suitable for crushing and breaking than for cutting. Neither should the flake-tools be disregarded. The crude flake, without any prior retouching, must have been used as a knife, for example. Several small transverse scrapers have been found at Gomboré I, an Oldowan deposit at Melka Kunturé (1.7 million years old) (Plate 5). But as early as the Developed Oldowan period, scrapers were already numerous at the same site in Garba IV (1.4 million years old) (Plate 6), associated with different kinds of tools, all made from flakes. By now the first true handaxes and cleavers had appeared and humankind was on the threshold of a technical and cultural transformation.

Pebble industries also exist in the Maghreb. There are the Saharan tools from the Guir Saoura valley and the Ougarta mountains, from the Salé plateau in Morocco, and later tools from the Sidi Abderrahman deposit (Biberson, 1961), near Casablanca, or the Aïn Hanech deposit (Arambourg, 1949; Sahnouni, 1985) in Algeria.

Pebble cultures also exist in Angola and South Africa. R. Dart identified a culture in the caves at Sterkfontein, Swartkrans and Makapansgat which only used bone, teeth or horn for tools.[13]

ACHEULEAN IMPLEMENTS

Acheulean implements are very varied, the most typical being handaxes, cleavers and bola stones. Handaxes, common in Palaeolithic deposits, have been known by various names since their discovery in the Somme valley in France. They are usually referred to as 'bifaces', because the cutting edge is formed either wholly or partly by chipping from both sides. The working end may be the point, but more often it is one or other of the sides, sharpened by much delicate retouch. In the ancient Palaeolithic deposits in Africa the blank used to make a handaxe was usually a piece of stone or a pebble, continuing the chipping technique used to make biface choppers which had a peripheral cutting edge. What distinguishes them from the choppers, however, is their axial symmetry. Starting in the Middle Acheulean period in Africa, the blank from which the handaxe was made could also be a large flake, a trend which became predominant during the Upper Acheulean period. Some handaxes are squat, roughly chipped and often pointed (known as lanceolate handaxes). They are typical of the ancient Acheulean period, and also of the developed Acheulean period along the sea-shores of north Africa, the river-banks of South Africa, or the dried-up beds of the Saharan wadis. Flat handaxes were usually made on flakes and could be heart-shaped, oval or elliptical. Handaxes made on flakes are more representative of the Middle and Upper Acheulean cultures in Kenya, Ethiopia or Tanzania, or else of the Late Acheulean period in Djibouti, Egypt or the north-west Sahara. The handaxe could be used as a knife or scraper, depending on its shape, size and volume, and whether it was hand-held or hafted, which requires axial symmetry; it could be used both as a tool and as a weapon.

The cleaver is typical of the African Acheulean, although it is also found in Spain, France and India. This is a large flake which has a straight cutting edge at one end, shows no signs of retouch and is sometimes convex or with an obtuse angle, obtained simply by removal of the flake from the core. The cleaver is a fragile tool, which explains why its cutting edge is always nicked or broken. It could not be resharpened without changing its original function; its length of service must therefore have been short. It is difficult to imagine a tool of this kind being used to lop off branches, but it could have been used to butcher animals, dismember carcasses, or remove the bark from branches. The cleaver is a tool which changed very little. It was refined and improved, but remained the same technically from the Oldowan period up to the Late and Final stages of the Acheulean period (1.4 million to 0.2 million years ago). At the end of this period a cleaver known as the 'Tachenghit' cleaver was produced in the north-west Sahara by a series of rather complex operations, but the geographical distribution of this tool is very limited. In another deposit, the Garba I site at Melka Kunturé (Plates 7 and 8), the sides of the cleaver had been trimmed to form sharp, straight edges sufficiently resistant to make extremely efficient, large scrapers, which was a way of recycling these tools whose first period of service had been so brief.

The third implement that is typical of the Acheulean period in Africa is known, rightly or wrongly, as the 'bola' stone. This developed from a more or less spherical polyhedron, a faceted ball that was transformed into an almost perfect sphere by pecking the sides or crushing the edges. These items are called bola stones after the balls tied together by a rope which are hurled at the legs of cattle in the Argentinian pampas. They differ from them, however, in volume and weight, so that they are more like a *pétanque* ball, and it is not known whether they were really part of a net made of skin and bark. Even if they were not used as projectiles for capturing antelopes and horses, there must have been some reason for their presence in encampments;

they must have played some role in daily, domestic life, perhaps for pounding or striking. The bola stones, often found in Middle and Upper Acheulean settlements, have recently been discovered in association with tools on a site in the Republic of Djibouti where *Elephas recki* were dismembered (the Borogali site near As Eyla).

Although handaxes, cleavers and bola stones are typical of the Acheulean period, this culture also made considerable progress in the working of small flake-tools. The variety of small flake-tools (mostly obsidian) of outstanding technical quality dating from the Middle Acheulean period (0.9 million years ago at Melka Kunturé) that were discovered at the Garba XII (Plate 9) and Gomboré II localities makes one wonder what would have happened had these same tools been collected on the surface: they might perhaps have been dated to 50,000 to 100,000 years ago, instead of 1 million years ago! There are end-scrapers, gravers and a great number of side-scrapers, as well as small borers, knives and many notched and serrated tools. Significantly, these tools are associated with handaxes, cleavers and some remains of a *Homo erectus* skeleton.

It is not until the Middle Stone Age, about 180,000 years ago, according to the information supplied by Fred Wendorf and his team during their excavations at Lake Ziway, situated to the south of Melka Kunturé in Ethiopia, that the geographical spread of these flake pieces suggests a kind of standardization.

We have thus seen that whereas some tools – the choppers, handaxes and cleavers – were predominant for a time, flake-tools went on being produced. It is possible that since the first tools were simply pebbles, their use as hammers sent flakes flying off. These fragments, which would have had a sharp, cutting edge, may then have been noticed and put to use by the first craftspeople. Long before they were reproduced by deliberately chipping them from a prepared piece of stone – a core – these by-products of the use of pebbles may simply have been put into service as hammerstones or crushers. No doubt the first knife was a flake chipped off by accident.

Two million years ago, at Shungura, the very small quartz flakes at the Omo 84, Omo 123 and other sites were perhaps the by-product of the preparation of a chopper, such as the one at Omo 71, which was not found at the site, no doubt because it was intended for hunting. Some of these fragments, however, are flakes which were deliberately removed from a core. Some of the cores have been found with them; their small size suggests that they were flaked until they were exhausted to ensure that the maximum use was made of these small quartz pebbles, which were such a scarce raw material. Some flakes bear marks of scaling, which suggests that they may have been used. Others, admittedly exceptions, have been found which had been perfunctorily retouched for use as end-scrapers, notched tools or knives. These implements are so small (1–4 cm) that they may have been made to cut up meat (although no fragments of bone have been discovered with them) or else to scrape roots or remove bark from branches. The fact there are only australopithecine fossils near these camps, and the possibility of vegetarian use, leads to speculation that these small flakes could be the work of hominians belonging to the genus *Australopithecus* (Chavaillon, 1982, p. 76; Coppens, 1983, p. 92). Omo 123 was a stopping place for hunters or nomads: it was also a temporary camp, a stone-tool workshop, a place for working or resting. The specialization of living sites did not appear until several thousand years later. This was only the dawn of organized society.

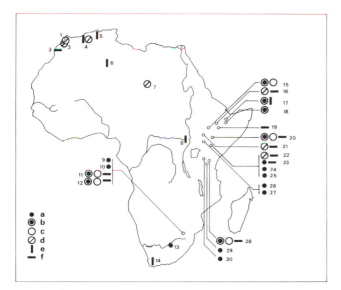

Map 2 Africa – major archaeological deposits and hominian sites from the Pliocene and the Lower Pleistocene: a, *Australopithecus*; b, *Homo habilis* + *Australopithecus*; c, *Homo habilis*; d, *Homo erectus*; e, deposits; f, deposits + settlements. 1, Salé; 2, Rabat; 3, Sidi Abderrahman; 4, Ternifine; 5, Ain Hanech; 6, Oued Guir/Oued Saoura; 7, Yayo; 8, Kaguera; 9, Makapansgat; 10, Kromdraai; 11, Sterkfontein; 12, Swartkrans; 13, Taung; 14, Stellenbosch; 15, Omo; 16, Melka Kunturé; 17, Hadar/Afar; 18, Middle Awash/Bodo; 19, Gadeb; 20, Koobi-Fora; 21, West Turkana; 22, Kapthurin; 23, Chesowanja; 24, Chemeron; 25, Lukeino; 26, Kanapoi; 27, Lothagam; 28, Olduvai; 29, Laetoli; 30, Natron.

LOCATION OF THE MAIN DEPOSITS (Map 2)

The Early Palaeolithic, pre-Acheulean or Acheulean sites were always close to water: a spring, an artesian well, a river or a lake. This is the basic requirement both in the Sahara and in the high plateaux of East Africa. These were open-air settlements, camps on river banks, beaches or ancient terraces, or, exceptionally, sheltered settlements or settlements in caves such as those at Sterkfontein, Swartkrans or Makapansgat in South Africa. The last form of dwelling was frequent in the Middle Palaeolithic period. The choice of location for a camp is as significant as that for a farm or a village: it is a guide to the preoccupations of the populations concerned since it required positive selection of various features. The criteria were certainly not the same in the Middle Stone Age or in the Neolithic Age as in the Early Palaeolithic period. In some deposits in eastern Africa, including both Olduvai and Melka Kunturé, an evolution in the choice of camp sites is discernible. In Europe climatic conditions are very influential in this choice. A camp was always located near a river or spring, but, unlike the African camps, was often established in a rock shelter or in a deep cave as protection against cold and attacks from wild animals. In Africa, the climatic conditions varied between dry and damp. Open-air settlements were all subject to the risk of unwelcome attention from predators; but the inhabitants must also have been wary of the seasonal flooding of rivers overflowing their banks. Fortunately for archaeologists, flooding would also preserve Palaeolithic occupation levels, as the silt and mud which inundated the settlement trapped the objects used in the camp and the kitchen middens in their original position as effectively as the collapse of a cave roof often did.

The first camps, which were pre-Acheulean, were totally dependent on the natural environment: a water hole, a quarry or a river bed of pebbles, a hunting or fishing place. There had to be water close at hand, at least for long-term camps. In fact the sites where large animals, such as hippopotamus or elephant, were dismembered were often near a water hole, marsh or river, but could also have been on the spot where the hunted animal had come to the end of its strength, perhaps on the plateau or in the savannah. So this spot, sometimes a great distance from the base camp, became a temporary camping site, a stopping place where hunters settled for few days. This kind of camp, determined by the movements of animals, was not structured, whereas the base camp, the long-term settlement (inhabited for several months or even several years) must have been chosen because it offered better facilities, the location of the temporary camp being dictated by the dying animal.

The main camp of the family or group was situated close to a river, on a bank or on a beach. Water was necessary, as were the presence of animals that came to drink and also raw materials, the stones or pebbles to make tools and weapons. (Structures, possibly defensive, are described on p. 41.) These camps could be situated on the seashore, as was the Obock deposit at Djibouti and the Sidi Abderrahman deposit in Morocco; on the banks of a river, such as in the Oued Guir and the Oued Saoura valleys in the Algerian Sahara, the Stellenbosch valley in South Africa, the Nile valley in Sudan and Egypt, the Bangui valley, the Congo valley, and so on; or on the shores of a lake, as in Olduvai Gorge in Tanzania, Lake Turkuna (Koobi Fora) in Kenya, Lake Langano in Ethiopia, and the dried lakes at As Eyla in Djibouti and Tihodaïne in the Sahara.

Without going into the stratigraphy of the main deposits, the African features of the Early Palaeolithic deposits should be made clear. The archaeological levels and the settlements that have been discovered are often spread out over a distance of several kilometres. At Olduvai, for example, areas of occupation can be seen along the full length of the present gorges, that is over a total of 50 kilometres. And in terms of depth from the surface down, archaeological strata can be identified at various levels down to a depth of as much as 90 metres. At Melka Kunturé the deposit extends over 60 kilometres along the banks of the Awash on either side of the river bed. Although the visible thickness of the alluvial deposits rarely exceeds 30 metres, that of the various geological deposits, embedded one in another (usually formed after a hollowing period due to fluvial erosion) can reach a depth of as much as 50 metres. Finally, in the Omo valley and in the Hadar and Bodo regions (Clark et al., 1984), the Ethiopian deposits have a very high sedimentary rate and are spread over a considerable area. Settlements near the seashore, springs or even some river or lake terraces are certainly more limited in size, but they still cover several thousand square metres.

When the geological deposits reach a depth of 20 or 30 metres or more, it is clear that the archaeological strata do not succeed one another continuously but are separated by 'sterile' geological levels, that is levels with no remains of animals or stone artefacts. These geological levels are nevertheless important because they are often the best markers. One example is the volcanic ash usually redeposited in the bed of a river or the bottom of a lake, called a tuff. It is very useful because it corresponds to an extremely short period of time, the moment an eruption occurred in a very precise spot. The petrographic composition of tuff makes it very amenable to the application of dating techniques and it also makes an excellent separation between two sedimentary complexes, for example in the lower Omo valley, Lake Turkana, the Olduvai Gorge, Melka Kunturé and so on. The same is true of the marine dunes of the Mediterranean and Atlantic shores and the fossil dunes that have often invaded the dry beds of Saharan wadis. All these make good marker levels because they possess clearly defined petrographic features, often specific to each stratum or formation. For example, two ash tuffs may appear alike in the field, but laboratory analysis can reveal that their petrographic composition is different. Layers of fluvial sand and gravel and lacustrine clay (former banks of a river or lake) are not always as helpful, although it is these layers that most often contain the occupational levels.

So on what bedrock, or ground, did the hominians establish their camps? The petrographic composition varies. At Olduvai, Melka Kunturé and other sites, it has been observed that the Oldowan populations, those who preceded the makers of handaxes, seemed to prefer the banks of rivers and lakes where the ground was clay and not very sandy, no doubt with a more or less thick plant cover, depending on the climatic conditions. The Acheulean people, on the contrary, preferred to settle in the sandy bed of an intermittent waterway, a small, seasonal stream that was often the tributary of a river. Such camps were set back from the main waterway, no doubt in a slightly raised position, so as not to be disturbed by seasonal floods. This is the case at Olorgesailie (Isaac, 1977) in Kenya, and Melka Kunturé (Garba I, III, XII) and Gadeb (Clark and Kurashina, 1976) in Ethiopia. The topographic conditions are similar in the Algerian Sahara. In the Ougarta mountains the Acheulean people preferred to establish their camps and stone-working sites in the dry and stony beds of small wadis, tributaries of the Oued Saoura. They were thus not affected by the violent floods of the river, and the raw material they needed to make their tools was close to hand.

In fact this distinction between grassy banks and sandy beaches as camp sites has often been observed by prehistorians, and seems to be a feature of certain regions of Africa. Over and above the preference for a certain kind of ground – clay bank or sandy beach – it also indicates a change in inherited traditions, in the approach to the organization of camps, and in the behaviour of their occupants. In this area as in many others there was an evolution from the Oldowan way of life to that of the Acheuleans. The latter were no longer bound by certain constraints. The Oldowans were tied to the pebbly beach or the river, but whereas the Acheuleans still needed to be near a watering place the main camp could be at some distance from the source of raw material. This has been observed at Garba I and at Melka Kunturé. The exceptionally large number of handaxes and cleavers found at these two sites (300,000 to 400,000 years old) had been made elsewhere. Before then, during the Middle Acheulean period, at Gomboré II (850,000 years old), humans had still used the pebbles from the beach on which they had settled, but from this period on, the large handaxes and cleavers, although less numerous than at the Garba site, were not made in the settlement itself.

The camps were not all the same. A distinction should be drawn between a cave settlement and an open-air site, and between deposits discovered and surveyed by the prehistorian that were found beneath ground level and those found on the surface. Deposits where objects have remained on the surface of the ground, such as those in the Sahara, are not without interest, but the information they yield is limited. Bones are not preserved and the layout of the pieces on the ground has for thousands of years been subject to

external influences before being discovered by prehistorians or, sadly, pillaged by collectors of flint tools. Settlements (*in situ*) discovered below the present surface are much more reliable, but a distinction should be drawn between those that have not been disturbed, remaining the same as when the inhabitants left them, and those which have been more or less disrupted. Flooding is the most common problem. The gradual covering over of a settlement with mud from a river or lake may be an advantage. This is true of Gomboré I at Melka Kunturé. If submergence was only temporary and the settlement stratum was subjected to alternative flooding and exposure, the archaeological pieces would undergo phenomena such as chemical decomposition or erosion by sand and water. In some exceptional cases, the site may have undergone the tilting pressure of the earth after tectonic movements (for instance the Omo deposits in Ethiopia) or else may have been divided by a small fault crossing the site, a break connected with the collapse or elevation of one of the sections (such as the Olorgesailie deposits in Kenya). Finally, objects may have been carried off by a river and redeposited elsewhere together with pebbles, sand and clay (the *meksem* deposits of the Ougarta mountains in the Sahara), or disturbed by artesian water (the Ternifine deposit in Algeria).

The prehistorian must be able to specify whether the site was a place set aside for some particular activity or else a base camp, a fixed, long-term main camp, the kind which supplies the most information for archaeologists (bones, tools, organization of the site, shelters and the like). Continuous occupation over a long period or annual return to the same spot makes a deposit much more interesting, but also makes its interpretation more difficult and often ambiguous. Successive occupations give a mix of tools and debris from earlier and later dwelling strata, for example a place where stone was worked may be superimposed on one which had previously been used as a butchery site.

Sites occupied on a short-term basis are often the most interesting, for example the sites where animals were dismembered. This activity could take as much as fifteen days for a large animal. The oldest known site of this kind is the FLK N6 of Bed I at Olduvai, where the carcass of an elephant was cut up (1.8 million years ago). Other examples are those of Koobi Fora and Olorgesailie (Kenya) and Gomboré II (Ethiopia), all sites where hippopotami were killed, and also that of Barogali, near As Eyla in the Republic of Djibouti, where the remains of *Elephas recki* have been discovered together with stone tools (choppers, bola stones and flakes).

These camps, briefly but intensively inhabited, correspond to the one- or two-day halts of hunters and nomads. The sites of Omo 71 and Omo 57 in Ethiopia are such places. Finally, stone-working sites should also be mentioned, where a large number of flakes and fragments are mixed with broken pebbles, hammerstones, cores and pieces of stone. In ancient, pre-Acheulean times, these various activities were carried out mostly at the main site. During the Acheulean period, special activity sites increased in number and were distinct from one another: butchering sites, stone-working sites and so on.

Attempting to understand the organization of a dwelling level means attempting to understand the way of life of the hominians who lived along the banks of the Awash or of the lake at Olduvai, or on the coastal beaches of Morocco. Not all deposits lend themselves to this reconstruction of the past, although in Africa much evidence has been discovered of the most ancient cultures. This evidence, however, only reflects certain aspects of life in society: hunting and butchering, shelters, limits of the settlement, and fire.

One of the chief activities of Palaeolithic people must have been finding food, in other words hunting and gathering. The gathering of plants must have been a daily activity. Roots, grains and fruit were probably collected, but although hammerstones may have been used for cracking nuts, crushers for breaking up plant structures and notched tools or scrapers for removing bark, we have no concrete evidence of this. These tools must also have been used for other purposes.

Even though hunting involved the capture and slaughter of animals, the gathering of carrion, whether or not in competition with other animals, must have been quite common, particularly among the ancient populations. When the carcass was too cumbersome it was torn up and consumed on the spot, hence the butchery sites, especially common for hippopotamus and elephant, whether carrion or the produce of the hunt. Quarters of meat were often carried to the base camp: antelope, horse, elephant and hippopotamus are well represented. But there must also have been rodents, birds and other creatures, and so the remains of a variety of animals, from the largest to the smallest, are found in the camp sites. Some deposits such as those at Olduvai and Melka Kunturé contain an abundance of animal remains. The presence of inedible anatomical pieces is more puzzling, however. More than 120 antelope horns have been discovered at the Garba IV site at Melka Kunturé (Plate 6). It seems clear that a large number of horns were specially taken there, but why? Perhaps they were used to build a shelter.

In the same way, hippopotamus canines, often sharpened, could have been used as picks. The degree to which bones were broken up, at first limited, gradually evolved, with a larger number of splinters being produced. Long bones, without being completely broken, were split lengthways to extract the marrow. This has been observed at the Garba IV site of the Developed Oldowan period. Carcasses must have been divided up with many sharp-edged flake-tools, some trimmed, some not. Preparation of the cutting edge transformed other flakes into side-scrapers, end-scrapers, burins, notched tools and other tool types. All these implements were used for a variety of activities, including scraping bone and skin.

The boundaries of the settlements are not easy to identify. To do so, the remains of a structure have to be discovered or the real limits of the dwelling area have to be identified. The outer limits have been found in some sites. At Melka Kunturé (Gomboré I) the boundary is not clear-cut, being indicated by a gradual reduction in the number of artefacts found. This is reminiscent of the area surrounding the dwellings in some villages in the savannah today, which leads to the conclusion that there were probably no fences or barriers.

The internal limits are very different from this gradual petering out on the periphery. There are areas more or less devoid of bones and artefacts, measuring from 1 to 8 square metres, and usually oval in shape, although sometimes circular. There is a layer of pebbles, similar to a pavement, around these clear spaces, or sometimes a ridge perhaps caused by the collapse of a structure (Olduvai). This is evidence of artificial boundaries, that is of an obstacle, a hut, shelter or hedge. The pebbles found there are thought to have been brought along to consolidate the structure – the stones placed at the base of the Olduvai hut, for example – or else to wedge the branches which supported the construction, as in the Acheulean shelter at Melka Kunturé.

This stone ridge, however, could also have been produced after the construction of a shelter against which discarded stones and tools may have piled up (Barbetti et al., 1980; Clark et al., 1984).

The large spaces could correspond to huts or shelters, although a roof would not be essential in Africa. The small areas of 1 to 2 square metres are more intriguing. This kind of formation is often associated with the presence of large stones and is more often a feature of the Oldowan settlements.

In Europe, especially during the cold periods, shelter and fire were complementary. Fire was used for heating and also as protection from an occasionally hostile environment. It was doubtless different in the temperate to warm climate of Africa. Fire was first used to keep away predatory animals, to protect the group. Subsequently it offered numerous advantages: it could be used to harden wood, split rocks, cook food, especially plants, and so on.

The oldest traces of fire are found in Africa, in Kenya and Ethiopia. The two sites, Chesowanja and Bodo, are similar. The former is 1.4 million years old. Slabs of burnt clay have been found there, but neither ashes nor hearth stones. The slabs could certainly be considered as the work of a bush fire, one of those unintentional conflagrations so common in these regions. The prehistorians who have studied these sites believe that a slowly burning tree-trunk could have produced this burnt area of limited dimensions. If this is correct then there would have been two stages in the conquest of fire: first what can be called the 'maintained' fire, 'captured' during a bush fire and carefully tended to keep it alive; a domesticated fire, perhaps, but not yet human-made. This state of affairs must have lasted a very long time until finally true hearths were constructed. Fire was then available where and when it was wanted.

Current evidence seems to indicate that the inhabitants of Eurasia had these first hearths earlier. It should be borne in mind, however, that in Africa not only is the climate milder, less cold, but also that the remains are of open-air settlements, which have either been exposed to the elements for thousands of years (in the Sahara, for instance), or been flooded. This certainly makes the preservation of ashes difficult. The scarcity of burnt bones and stones, as well as the appearance only later of unusual hollows dug in the ground, which could, very cautiously, be identified as ancient hearths (the settlement of the Final Acheulean period at Garba III), leads to the conclusion that the first convincing proof of the real conquest of fire dates from about 500,000 years ago.

At the end of the Acheulean age humans had already conquered all the ancient world. Already in possession of a certain amount of technical and economic knowledge, they were ready to adapt to the specific environment of the region in which they then found themselves. This was the point of departure for the plethora of cultures which suddenly sprang up in the various countries of Eurasia and Africa.

NOTES

1 Hadar is a major palaeontological deposit in Ethiopia, located in the Afar region, in the lower Awash valley, between Addis Ababa and Djibouti. It was discovered by M. Taieb and explored by an international mission led by M. Taieb, Y. Coppens, D. Johanson and J. Kalb. Apart from vertebrate fauna dating back 2 to 4 million years, the team found hominian remains of the genera *Homo* and *Australopithecus*, includ-

ing *A. afarensis* (Lucy). The lithic industries found *in situ* are rare; some would appear to date back 2.6 million years (Roche and Tiercelin, 1977; J. Harris, 1978), while the others are Acheulean.

2 The Lower Omo valley deposits are situated in Ethiopia along the border with Kenya and Sudan. They occupy an area several kilometres wide and 100 kilometres in length. Discovered by the Bourg de Bozas mission in 1901, they were explored in 1933 by C. Arambourg, and from 1967 to 1976 by an international team led by C. Arambourg, Y. Coppens and Clark Howell. There are 100 metres of sedimentary, lacustrine and volcanic deposits (1 million to 4 million years old). Finds include a variety of vertebrate fauna, over 400 fragments of hominian skeletons (*Australopithecus* and *Homo*) and several prehistoric sites *in situ*.

3 Boesch and Boesch (1983), ethologists, studied the behaviour of chimpanzees in the forests of Gabon, examining in particular their use of unworked tools to break nuts.

4 Olduvai is a major deposit in the north of Tanzania. The alluvial deposits of former Lake Olduvai contain the remains of fauna and stone objects in their original position. The earliest areas to have been occupied date back 1.8 million years. Louis and Mary Leakey found some hominian remains including those of *Homo habilis* and an *Australopithecus*, *Zinjanthropus boisei*, together with a great number of tools from the pre-Acheulean and Acheulean cultures, areas for dismembering elephants and the site of a structure now considered to be the earliest-known dwelling (a circle of stones)

5 On the banks of the Awash, 50 km from Addis Ababa, the deposit at Melka Kunturé presents a remarkable succession of archaeological levels, the earliest of which could date back 1.7 million years. Under the auspices of the Ministry of Culture in Addis Ababa, J. Chavaillon and his team conducted excavations of the floors of pre-Acheulean and Acheulean dwellings. Remains were found of fauna and hominids, as were numerous tools and the sites of huts or shelters and butchering areas (Plates 5–9).

6 Gomboré I is one of the sites at Melka Kunturé (n. 5); it has an abundance of pre-Acheulean (Oldowan) tools (Plate 5). Twelve thousand artefacts have been listed, together with the remains of fauna and hominids: the humerus of a *Homo erectus*. The site contained an empty area which J. and N. Chavaillon felt must have been the site of a dwelling.

7 The deposits at Shungura in the lower Omo valley have yielded many fragments and flakes, mostly of quartz, discovered *in situ* by J. Chavaillon (Omo 57, 71, 84 and 123) and by V. Merrick (FtJi 1 and FtJi 2). The very small cores and flakes, only some of which have been used or retouched, are the remains of a camp or toolmaking area where hominians settled in the old valley of the Omo. Only the Omo 71 site, excavated by J. Chavaillon, was a lakeside habitat (Chavaillon, 1976; Merrick and Merrick, 1976).

8 The Oldowan industry preceded the Acheulean. It has pebble-tools (choppers, chopping-tools and polyhedrons) together with flakes. The areas inhabited were southern and eastern Africa. The eponymous deposit is in the Olduvai Gorge in Tanzania (n. 4): Bed I (Oldowan s.s.) and Bed II (Developed Oldowan A, B, C) levels (Leakey, 1971).

9 The term Middle Stone Age (MSA) is an umbrella term for various cultures corresponding to the Middle Palaeolithic and the beginning of the Late Palaeolithic in Europe. There are many flake-tools; a reduction can be observed in the dimension of tools inherited from the Acheulean Period, such as the handaxe.

10 The Late Stone Age (LSA) corresponds to the end of the Late Palaeolithic, the Epi-Palaeolithic of the Maghreb and the beginning of the Neolithic. The tools were miniaturized and fashioned from flakes, blades and lamellae with geometric microliths and sometimes ceramics.

11 At Koobi Fora, east of Lake Turkana in Kenya, Richard Leakey's team described a succession of levels distributed among two formations separated by a volcanic tuff referred to as KBS. The upper formation, called Karari, includes fourteen sites which yielded 15,000 artefacts belonging to the Developed Oldowan of 1.4 to 1.3 million years ago (Harris and Isaac, 1976; Harris, 1978).

12 Evidence of the developed and final stage of the Acheulean culture in the north-western Sahara is provided by many deposits in the Saoura valley and the Ougarta mountains (Anchal, Tabelbala).

13 R. Dart's 'osteodontokeratic' industry is no longer accepted by most archaeologists, who see in it no more than the leftovers of predators' meals (see Y. Coppens and D. Geraads, Chapter 2) – Ed.

BIBLIOGRAPHY

ALIMEN, H. 1955. *Préhistoire de l'Afrique*. Paris.

ALIMEN, H.; ZUATE Y ZUBER, J. (ed.) 1979. *L'Évolution de l'Acheuléen au Sahara nord-occidental*. Paris, CNRS.

ANDREWS, P.; WALKER, A. 1976. The Primate and Other Fauna from Fort Ternan, Kenya. In: ISAAC, G. L.; MCCOWN, E. (eds), *Human Origins: Louis Leakey and the East African Evidence*. Menlo Park, Calif. pp. 279–304.

ARAMBOURG, C. 1949. Sur la présence dans le Villafranchien d'Algérie de vestiges éventuels d'industrie humaine. *C. R. Acad. Sci.* (Paris), Vol. 229, pp. 66–7.

BALOUT, L. 1955. *Préhistoire de l'Afrique du Nord: Essai de chronologie*. Paris.

BARBETTI, M. et al. 1980. Palaeomagnetism and the Search for Very Ancient Fire Places in Africa. *Anthropologie* (Brno), Vol. 18, No. 2/3, pp. 299–304.

BIBERSON, P. 1961. *Le Paléolithique inférieur du Maroc atlantique*. Rabat. (Publ. Serv. Antiq. Maroc, 17.)

—— 1967. *Fiches typologiques africaines – 2ème cahier*, fiches 33–64: *Galets aménagés du Maghreb et du Sahara*. Paris, Muséum d'Histoire Naturelle de Paris.

BOESCH, C.; BOESCH, H. 1983. Optimization of Nut-cracking with Natural Hammers by Wild Chimpanzees. *Behaviour* (Leiden), pp. 265–86.

CHAVAILLON, J. 1976. Evidence for the Technical Practices of Early Pleistocene Hominids. In: COPPENS, Y. et al. (eds), *Earliest Man and Environments in the Lake Rudolf Basin*. Chicago. pp. 565–73.

—— 1982. L'Outil et les débuts de la grande aventure humaine. *Archeologia* (Paris), No. 60, pp. 70–86.

CHAVAILLON, J.; CHAVAILLON, N. 1981. Galets aménagés et nucleus du Paléolithique inférieur. *Préhistoire africaine. Mélanges offerts au Doyen Lionel Balout* (Paris), No. 6, pp. 283–92.

CHAVAILLON, J. et al. 1979. From Oldowan to the Middle Stone Age at Melka-Kunturé (Ethiopia): Understanding Cultural Changes. *Quaternaria* (Rome), Vol. 21, pp. 87–114.

CHAVAILLON, J. et al. 1985. Découverte d'un site de dépeçage à *Elephas recki* en République de Djibouti. *C. R. Acad. Sci.* (Paris), Vol. 23, p. 12.

CLARK, J. D. 1982. From the Earliest Times to *c.*500 BC. In: CLARK, J. D. (ed.), *The Cambridge History of Africa*. Cambridge. Vol. 1.

CLARK, J. D. et al. 1984. Palaeoanthropological Discoveries in the Middle Awash Valley, Ethiopia. *Nature* (London), Vol. 307, pp. 423–8.

CLARK, J. D.; KURASHINA, H. 1976. New Plio-Pleistocene Archaeological Occurrences from the Plain of Gadeb, Upper Webi Shebele Basin Ethiopia, and a Statistical Comparison of the Gadeb Sites with Other Early Stone Age Assemblages. In: CONGRÉS UISSP, 9, Nice, 1976. *Colloque V*, pp. 158–216.

COLLINAT, G. 1975. *Les Industries archaïques sur galets des terrasses quaternaires de la plaine du Roussillon (France)*. Marseille. (Trav. Lab. Paléontol. Hum. Préhist., Cent. St Charles, 1.)

CONGRÈS PANAFRICAIN DE PRÉHISTOIRE ET D'ÉTUDE DU QUATERNAIRE. *Actes*.

COPPENS, Y. 1983. *Le Singe, l'Afrique et l'homme*. Paris.

HARRIS, J. W. K. 1978. *The Karari Industry: Its Place in East African Prehistory*. Berkeley.

HARRIS, J. W. K.; ISAAC, G. L. 1976. The Karari Industry: Early

Pleistocene Archaeological Evidence from the Terrain East of Lake Turkana, Kenya. *Nature* (London), Vol. 262, pp. 102–7.

HOURS, F. 1982. *Les Civilizations du Paléolithique.* Paris. (Que sais-je, 2057.)

ISAAC, G. L. 1977. *Olorgesailie: Archaeological Studies of a Middle Pleistocene Lake Basin in Kenya.* Chicago.

LEAKEY, M. D. 1971. *Olduvai Gorge: Excavation in Bed I and Bed II – 1960–1963.* Cambridge.

MERRICK, H. V.; MERRICK, J. P. S. 1976. Archaeological Occurrences of Earlier Pleistocene Age, from the Shungura Formation. In: COPPENS, Y. et al. (eds), *Earliest Man and Environments in the Lake Rudolf Basin.* Chicago. pp. 574–84.

PERLES, C. 1977. *Préhistoire du feu.* Paris.

PIPERNO, M.; BULGARELLI-PIPERNO, G. M. 1974–5. First Approach to Ecological and Cultural Significance of the Early Palaeolithic Occupation Site of Garba IV at Melka-Kunturé (Ethiopia). *Quaternaria* (Rome), Vol. 18, pp. 347–82.

Préhistoire africaine. Mélanges offerts au Doyen Lionel Balout. 1981. Paris.

ROCHE H.; TIERCELIN, J. J. 1977. Découverte d'une industrie lithique ancienne *in situ* dans la formation d'Hadar, Afar central, Ethiopie. *C. R. Acad. Sci.* (Paris), Vol. 284, pp. 1871–4.

SAHNOUNI, M. 1985. Reconnaissance d'une chaîne opératoire expliquant l'obtention des formes polyèdriques et subsphériques dans l'industrie sur galets du gisement villafranchien de l'Ain Hanech, Sétif, Algérie orientale. *C. R. Acad. Sci.* (Paris), Vol. 301, pp. 355–8.

VAUFREY, R. 1955. *Préhistoire de l'Afrique.* Vol. 1: *Le Maghreb.* Paris.

—— 1969. *Préhistoire de l'Afrique.* Vol. 2: *Au nord et à l'est de la grande forêt.* Paris.

4

EUROPE

Lower and Middle Pleistocene archaeology

Paola Villa

This chapter deals with the early phases of human settlement in Europe; it covers a time span that extends back from the end of the Middle Pleistocene, about 125,000 years ago, to the age of the earliest documented evidence of human presence in Europe, that is nearly 1 million years ago.

Present knowledge of this very long period of time is based on three major sources of information:

1 the actual skeletal remains of early humans;
2 the tools and equipment they used, the evidence of their camping sites and their food refuse;
3 palaeoenvironmental data, i.e. evidence about contemporary plant and animal communities, and about the climate and environment to which prehistoric people adapted.

The study of the fossil bones of early Europeans has been presented in Chapter 2. The archaeological record of Lower and Middle Pleistocene times, i.e. the study of the material products and traces of early human behaviour and the environment in which these people lived, is the subject of this chapter.

The time span and the geographical range of this review is very broad; its scope demands integration of a very large number of archaeological facts, reported in a wide variety of national languages. To be sure, Lower and Middle Pleistocene human sites are rare or not preserved at all in various regions of northern Europe. In western and central Europe, however, the long tradition of archaeological research has produced a wealth of detailed information about specific sites and regions; this review cannot do justice to such regional or site-specific accounts. Here we will focus on those general questions that guide and define archaeological research in this time period.

Whether or not they are explicitly stated, the questions that most accounts of Pleistocene prehistory in Europe try to answer are as follows.

1 How old is human occupation in Europe?
2 Are there sites in all kinds of environments?
3 What do we know about subsistence activities and early human life-styles?
4 How were stone tools used and for what kind of tasks?
5 What were the technical abilities of prehistoric people? Do we observe changes through time and space in techniques or artefact forms? In other words, how variable was material culture? How stable and how distinctive were early cultural systems?

At the present stage of research, answers to these questions are still tentative. In assessing the evidence we must bear in mind that the archaeological record is an accumulation of detailed observations whose meaning is not self-evident. Thus we must first outline what kind of evidence is available to recognize and reconstruct prehistoric behaviour, and how we use it to develop interpretations.

The archaeology of very early ages involves at least two lines of research. First, we must know what constitutes unambiguous evidence of human presence in the archaeological record, and what criteria we should use to diagnose correctly the traces of human activities. Second, we must know how old those traces are and what degree of certainty we can assign to our age estimates.

THE NATURE OF THE EVIDENCE

The evidence sought by archaeologists for the presence of humans and for their activities can be provided by the following materials:

1 stone or bone artefacts;
2 animal bones that show traces of human butchering activities, such as cut marks made by stone tools or breakage to extract marrow; in other words, bones that represent human food refuse;
3 fireplaces or other habitation features.

Correct and unambiguous identification of these materials may not always be as simple as it may seem. Artefacts and features that have regular, repetitive shapes and are in good state of preservation are easy to recognize. But when preservation is poor and observations are few – as is often the case for the record of early ages – problems may arise. This is because different causes may have similar or overlapping effects. For instance, impact scars on stones naturally broken in a stream, on a talus or by frost may resemble stone-knapping scars on casual, simple or unfinished implements; animal bones may be scarred and broken in rather similar ways by man or by carnivores; trampling or sedimentary abrasion may cause polish or linear marks on bones that might easily be taken as diagnostic of human butchering or tool use; rodent burrows may simulate postholes and appear as evidence of hut foundations; brush-fires will leave behind clumps of baked, reddened earth or spreads of charcoal particles which may resemble fireplace traces (Brain, 1981; Binford, 1981; Isaac, 1984, p. 36).

Analogous problems of identification and interpretation may arise in assessing the significance of prehistoric sites. Sites are the basic working units of archaeology. They may be simple find spots of just a few, isolated implements, or concentrations in a well-defined area of artefacts, bones and features. Sites of the first kind are very numerous, but they tell us little beyond the fact that certain human artefacts are present in a certain region. If the occurrence cannot be dated with certainty – as may be the case of surface finds – the information is essentially worthless. Sites of the second type are generally stratified and are uncovered by excavation. Under certain conditions, these sites can provide the evidence we seek on habitat preferences, subsistence activities and use of local resources and information on contemporary plant and animal communities.

Any Palaeolithic stratified site is formed of archaeological materials scattered through geological deposits accumulated by natural agencies. To interpret the data provided by a site excavation, we must be able to separate the effects of the behaviour of the prehistoric people from the effects of geomorphological processes and of animal activities that have changed the site content or the site location at the time of deposition or after the site was buried. Geological processes and biological agents can create, destroy or transform sites. For example, a site may be formed as a mixed assemblage of bones and a few stones that accumulated slowly on the surface of an ancient lake beach or floodplain soil during a period of little sediment deposition. A concentration of stone artefacts in a stream channel probably represents materials derived from one or several locations on an adjacent river-bank where hominids actually flaked stones. Avian and mammalian predators may accumulate bones in localities that may also have been favoured by hominids. The significance of these sites for reconstructions of early hominid behaviour is limited by our ability to: (1) distinguish between human food refuse and natural bone accumulation; (2) reconstruct the local palaeotopography and physical environment; and (3) estimate the length of time the site was actually used by hominids.

In archaeology, techniques and methods of data collecting and analysis are heavily dependent on contributions from other disciplines, especially the environmental sciences. Since the 1960s major advances in dating, in reconstructing palaeoenvironments and in recovery techniques have been made through the application of methods used in other disciplines. These technical developments have led archaeologists to rethink their own general research procedures, i.e. the way archaeologists advance arguments and interpret past human activities. There is increasing demand for high-quality data and for verifiable explanations. To escape ambiguity a lot of effort has gone into improving techniques of observation and developing detailed knowledge of the complex processes by which archaeological sites are formed and preserved. For example, we have increased our ability to distinguish human from other agencies of bone modification by using light or scanning electron microscopy, through replicating experiments and with observations of bone breakage by humans and animals in natural and ethnographic situations (Shipman, 1981; Binford, 1981; Haynes, 1983). Observations of recent environments and experiments have been carried out the better to understand the interplay of geological factors and human activities at

archaeological sites (Gifford and Behrensmeyer, 1977; Villa and Courtin, 1983; Schick, 1984). Unfortunately the application of these techniques and approaches to early European materials is not as common as one might wish.

In contrast to the African situation, where a few sites are well known and have been explored and analysed in depth, Europe offers plenty of findings that are only partly or superficially known. Several factors are responsible for this unsatisfactory state of affairs; perhaps the single most important one is the historical development of prehistoric research in Europe.

Relative chronology and classification of stone tools have been the major concern of prehistoric archaeology since its beginning. Much of the evidence about plants and animals was collected for the purpose of dating, not to build pictures of environmental resources. Geological investigations served the purpose of placing an occurrence in a palaeoclimatic sequence; the emphasis was on palaeoclimatic interpretations of sediments. Topics such as site size, local palaeotopography, sources of raw materials, processes of artefact accumulation and dispersal in the soil, information on rates of sedimentation or the intensity of occupation, in brief the kinds of data necessary to support behavioural interpretations, were neglected or presented in a cursory and superficial way which defied independent assessment. Much of the evidence has been collected following research goals and procedures quite different from those advocated today.

When interpreting the record in terms of social behaviour, archaeologists have often opted for the easy or familiar explanations, without taking into account factors independent of human activities or possible differences in behaviour between modern humans and early hominids due to evolutionary changes. They tended to read back from the present, searching for similarities between the life-style of early hominids and modern hunter-gatherers. Studies of stone tools were carried out for the purpose of defining ethnic groups, of identifying long-term cultural traditions and patterns of ethnic diversity, thus describing the Stone Age like a segment of the historical record. In both cases archaeologists have been extending back into Lower and Middle Pleistocene times a pattern of behaviour known from much later times. In both cases, new evidence is overthrowing assumptions about the social and cultural behaviour of our early ancestors.

In conclusion, there are essentially two sources of potential controversy for studies of early human culture and life-style: (1) claims about the human origin of artefacts and features may have been accepted on the basis of vague, insufficient evidence; (2) familiar patterns of behaviour may have been superimposed on equivocal evidence, interpreting behaviour perhaps quite unlike our own as being fully human.

Our viewpoint is that we need to adopt a critical attitude to our materials. We need not accept as implements stone or bone pieces so crude as to raise legitimate doubts about their human manufacture. Behavioural reconstructions must be based on published data, allowing for meaningful discussion of alternative explanations. The burden is on the excavator to make a credible case.

DATING (Tables 1 and 2)

Absolute dating methods applicable to Lower and Middle Pleistocene occurrences have been developed in the past thirty years. The most reliable is the potassium–argon (K–Ar) method for dating volcanic ash or lava horizons in

Table 1 Absolute dating of some Lower and Middle Pleistocene sites in Europe.

Site	Dating method	Years (BP)	Comments
Soleihac (France)	Palaeomagnetism	Jaramillo event 900,000 to 970,000	Dates archaeological level with fauna and artefacts.
Isernia (Italy)	K–Ar	736,000 ± 40,000	Dates upper archaeological level. Supported by two K–Ar dates for overlying levels.
Fontana Ranuccio (Italy)	K–Ar	458,000 ± 5700	Dates layer 10 with fauna and bifaces.
Swanscombe (UK)	U–Th	$326,000 \begin{array}{c} +99,000 \\ -54,000 \end{array}$	Dates bone from upper Middle Gravel with bifaces.
Clacton (UK)	U–Th	$245,000 \begin{array}{c} +35,000 \\ -25,000 \end{array}$	Dates bone in gravel with Clactonian artefacts.
Terra Amata (France)	TL	214,000 244,000	Dates burnt flint in level P2 (beach). Dates burnt flint in level M4g (below the beach). Combined as 230,000 + 40,000 by the laboratory.
Bilzingsleben (Germany)	U–Th	$228,000 \begin{array}{c} +17,000 \\ -12,000 \end{array}$	Dates travertine layer with hominid and artefacts (this date appears to be too young).
Pontnewydd (UK)	U–Th TL	180,000 ± 20,000 200,000 ± 25,000	Dates Lower Breccia with Acheulean industry. Dates burnt flint and human tooth below.
La Chaise (France)	U–Th	151,000 ± 15,000	Abri Bourgeois–Delauney: dates base of travertine layer 11 and encased or immediately underlying hominid remains of Neanderthal affinities.
		$245,000 \begin{array}{c} +42,000 \\ -28,000 \end{array}$	Abri Suard: dates travertine layer 53. Tools and hominid remains intermediate between *Homo erectus* and Neanderthaler are found above.
Biache-Saint-Vaast (France)	TL	175,000 ± 13,000	Dates burnt flints from layer with hominid skull.

Source: Modified after Dennel, 1983. Data from Aitken et al., 1984; Blackwell et al., 1983; Biddittu et al., 1979; Coltorti et al., 1982; Green et al., 1981; Harmon et al., 1980; Szabo and Collins, 1975; Soperintendenza Archaeologica del Molise, 1983; Thouveny and Bonifay, 1984; Villa, 1983, p. 35.

sequences of strata including archaeological deposits. The method has been extensively used to date Plio-Pleistocene deposits in eastern Africa. Up to the present time, however, only two European sites have been directly dated by this method: Isernia and Fontana Ranuccio, both of which are in central Italy (Table 1). The small number of occurrences that have been dated by this method is due to the fact that during Pleistocene times there have been in Europe only three major areas of intensive volcanism: Italy, the Massif Central in France and the middle Rhine region in Germany. In the two latter regions early archaeological occurrences are rare and the K–Ar method has been used mainly to date Plio-Pleistocene faunal assemblages (Massif Central) and terrace deposits (Rhine).

The palaeomagnetic timescale is based on a sequence of episodes of normal and reversed polarity in the earth's magnetic field (Table 2). Magnetic reversals occurred repeatedly in the geologic past and were synchronous over the whole world; the ages at which they occurred can be established by measuring the polarity of lavas dated by the K–Ar method. Like volcanic rocks, sediments can also acquire imprinting corresponding to the polarity of the earth's magnetic field at the time of deposition. Sequences of terrestrial sediments can be matched to the palaeomagnetic timescale to date deposits to a certain time interval. However, proper matching requires several measurements in a long sequence. Furthermore, known polarity episodes may last for a very long span of time. Thus palaeomagnetism would seem to have limited application in Europe where the majority of sites date to the Brunhes epoch of normal polarity (0.7 ± 0.05 million years ago). However, a few sites are as old or older than the Matuyama–Brunhes reversal. For example, the Soleihac deposits in the Massif Central preserve a succession of four polarity zones; the archaeological layer lies in the

time range of the Jaramillo event (Table 1). The Matuyama–Brunhes boundary has also been identified in the excavated sequence at Stránská Skála (near Brno, Czech Republic), a cave and colluvial fan site which has yielded early faunas and some chert 'artefacts', the human origin of which is in doubt (Kukla, 1975; Svoboda, 1984).

Short episodes of reversed polarity (about 10,000 years in duration) apparently occurred during the Brunhes epoch. One such occurrence is the Blake event, dated to between 117,000 and 104,000 years ago. Research on these short-lived events is continuing, in order to determine whether they reflect global changes in the earth's magnetic field or are only local anomalies (Kukla and Nakagawa, 1977). The use of such markers can greatly benefit Middle Pleistocene chronology.

An important use of the magnetic polarity timescale is in combination with the palaeoclimatic record of deep-sea cores, based on changes in oxygen isotope ratios. Geomagnetic reversals located in deep-sea sediments provide a time line against which the oxygen isotope record can be plotted. Since isotopic variations reflect past changes in ocean water temperatures and global ice volume, periods of glaciation and deglaciation, which occurred repeatedly in the Pleistocene, can thus be dated (Table 2).

Other methods, such as the uranium–thorium (U–Th) dating of travertine and bone, the thermoluminescence (TL) dating of burnt flint, the electron spin resonance (ESR) and the amino-acid racemization dating of shell, bone and teeth, are valuable because they can be applied to a variety of materials and are especially useful for the time range beyond 40,000 years, that is the upper limit of the conventional radiocarbon-dating method. However, these methods yield results which are not always reliable; the dates they provide

Table 2 Oxygen isotope record of Pacific core Y28–238 and palaeomagnetic time scale. The Olduvai normal polarity event dated 1.89 to 1.67 million years (m.y.) is not shown; the bottom part of the horizontal scale between 1.0 and 1.8 m.y. is not proportional to time. Most authors set the beginning of the Pleistocene at 1.8 or at 1.6 m.y. at the top of the Olduvai event.

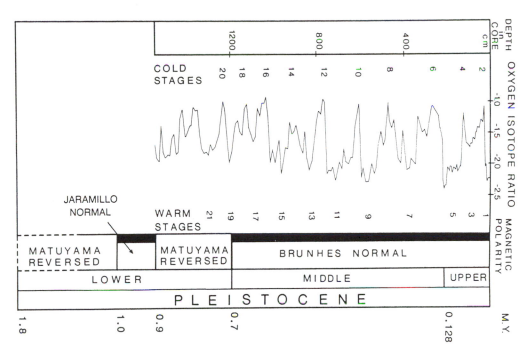

Source: Adapted from Cook et al., 1982.

should be considered as approximate age estimates, unless cross-checks are provided by multiple dates of the same stratigraphic sequence.

CLIMATIC CHANGES AND CORRELATIONS (Table 2)

Given the scarcity of radiometric dates for Early and Middle Pleistocene times, age estimates of most archaeological sites are still based on the classical chrono-stratigraphic framework of the Pleistocene, worked out since the nineteenth century by Quaternary geologists.

For periods earlier than the Quaternary, correlation and relative dating of local rock sequences are provided by the palaeontological method, that is, the use of fossils for the characterization of successive intervals of geologic time. However, this approach (called biostratigraphy) loses resolution when applied to periods of time too short for significant organic evolution. In terms of Earth's history the Quaternary is certainly very brief, while the timespan of many species is too long to allow more than a very general time placement of faunal assemblages. Moreover, faunal changes are not necessarily synchronous events across wide areas, while geographical barriers and climatic changes complicate the picture of evolutionary changes. On the other hand, climatic changes have happened much more rapidly than organic evolution in the Pleistocene. For these reasons, early Quaternary geologists have relied on the evidence of multiple glaciations in the Pleistocene to work out palaeoclimatic sequences based on alternations of glacial and interglacial deposits in areas affected by ice advances.

The classic Alpine sequence, including four glacial and three interglacial stages, was presented in 1909 by Penck and Brückner; it was based on the recognition and correlation of deposits of outwash gravels left behind by the retreat of four successive glaciations along some tributaries of the Danube in southern Germany, at the northern margin of the Alpine glaciers. The scheme was quickly transferred to other parts of the continent and similar sequences were established in northern Europe (northern Germany and the Netherlands) and Britain using a variety of indicators of past climatic oscillations (such as end moraines, pollen diagrams and deposits left by marine transgressions). Further study led to the recognition of brief intervals of warmer climate (interstadials) within a major glaciation, thus dividing each glacial unit into two or more stages.

The Pleistocene glaciers of the Alps were of much smaller size than the huge Scandinavian ice-sheet of northern Europe and there was considerable distance between the Alpine and the Scandinavian ice-sheets even at the time of maximum ice advance, so that the exact correlation of the Alpine and north-west European glacial stages always remained a matter of some doubt. Nevertheless, the fourfold Alpine system quickly achieved the position of a general scheme thought valid for the whole world (Nilsson, 1983). Correlation between sites and across regions was done by fitting a local sequence of strata with cold or warm indicators into the standard reference timescale, generally the Alpine or the north-west European sequence.

The shortcomings of the classical framework have been pointed out since the 1960s and have led to important changes in the standard reference scale for the Quaternary.

Difficulties in the correlation of Quaternary deposits arise from two facts: (1) strata show sequences of repetitive events (glacials or interglacials); (2) one interglacial (or glacial) deposit is likely to contain an assemblage of fossils similar to those in a younger or older deposit.

Given the repetitive nature of climatic changes, glacial and interglacial stages can be recognized only by downward counting in continuous long sequences, starting from the present and going back through time. However, continuous long sequences on land are not common; areas directly affected by glacial advances often provide incomplete sequences, because later ice advances tend to destroy or disturb earlier deposits. In general, terrestrial sequences are truncated and discontinuous. But counting from the top makes no allowance for gaps in the record. When matching one sequence with another, non-recognition of a single glacial or interglacial event in one of the sequences will throw correlation out of step.

Very long palaeoclimatic records such as those investigated by Shackleton and Opdyke (1976) in deep-sea cores, as well as loess profiles from Austria, the Czech Republic and Slovakia, dated through the application of the polarity timescale, indicate at least seventeen glacial–interglacial cycles within the last 1.6 million years, many more than those recognized in the traditional framework; eight of these glaciations are of Brunhes age (Table 2; Kukla, 1975; Fink and Kukla, 1977; Shackleton, 1975; Shackleton and Opdyke, 1976). The deep-sea record also indicates that Northern Hemisphere glaciations had already occurred in Pliocene times. A major change in the scale and tempo of glaciations took place about 0.8 million years ago, and these Middle and Upper Pleistocene cycles were probably responsible for the ice-sheet advances represented in terrestrial sediments. Thus the Alpine and north-west European sequences keep only an incomplete record of the later part of the Quaternary.

The major results and implications of these recent studies are as follows.

1 Deep-sea cores provide a climato-stratigraphic framework of global significance and the basis for a standard sub-division of Pleistocene time.
2 Truncated terrestrial sequences should be fitted into the oxygen isotope record only by using absolute dates or specific time horizons (such as magnetic zones).
3 Correlations between land-based sequences and oxygen isotope stages are secure only for the Upper Pleistocene (Würm–Weichsel and Eemian); older stages (Riss or Saale, Mindel, etc.) are free-floating in time.
4 The older chronological framework should not be used in interregional correlations. Use of the same stage-name for occurrences in different regions in the absence of stratigraphic markers or absolute dates can lead to serious miscorrelations and should be discontinued.
5 The Pleistocene was a period of almost constant climatic change. Ice volume increased periodically every 90,000 or 100,000 years. The sawtooth shape of the climatic curve indicates that deglaciations occurred much faster than glacial expansion. Many smaller fluctuations are superimposed on the dominant 100,000-year cycle; climatically stable phases would seem to be very short, rarely lasting more than 10,000 years, and many climatic changes were quite abrupt. Changes in mean yearly temperatures in the order of 5 to 10 °C have been suggested in some areas (Roberts, 1984; Flohn, 1979; Liu Zechun, 1985; Ruddiman and McIntyre, 1982).

In sum, it is clear that our knowledge of Pleistocene stratigraphy and climates has been revolutionized by oxygen isotope analysis, radiometric dating and palaeomagnetic stratigraphy. However, the difficult process of correlating an excellent marine record with the traditional land-based sequences has only begun, and our knowledge of Middle Pleistocene chronology is still quite unsatisfactory. There are huge portions of time past that are not known in any area and there are too many problems in correlating sites from one area to another to build a general picture of what was happening at any particular time.

THE EARLIEST SITES (Map 3 and Table 1)

European archaeologists have a longstanding concern with the question of the antiquity of human occupation in Europe. In recent years the search for the oldest traces of human presence on this continent has been sharpened by a new awareness of the great antiquity of human culture and by comparisons of the archaeological record in Europe with the African record. In East Africa stone-tool making – considered by archaeologists the most visible and direct evidence of a human way of life – is securely dated to 2 million years and may be as old as 2.5 or 2.7 million years. In contrast, the archaeological record in Europe appears to be much younger and to cover a much shorter span of time, starting at about 1 million years ago.

There are a few claims for occurrences older than 1 million years. At Chilhac III (in the Massif Central, France) recent excavations have yielded a few putative implements made on basalt, metamorphic rocks and quartz (Guth and Chavaillon, 1985). According to Guth, the fauna is similar to that found at Chilhac II, a nearby exclusively palaeontological site dated to 1.9 million years ago by a lava flow (missing at Chilhac III).

The implements have been found in several layers of sandy gravels (B3, G and K), alternating with layers of sandy clays. Some of the implements and the fauna from the sandy gravels are abraded; only fauna has been found in the sandy clays, where it is in good state of preservation and unabraded. With the exception of layer B3 which is horizontal and rests disconformably on the lower series of layers, most layers are steeply inclined (up to 45°) and appear to be soliflucted slope deposits. According to a recent interpretation (Texier, 1985), the fine-grained layers (clays and volcanic ashes) were originally deposited in a lake bottom, but later eroded, transported by gravity, mixed with colluvial elements and redeposited. If the stratigraphic interpretation is correct, the implements may not be contemporaneous with the fauna found in the sandy gravels and in the sandy clays. Chilhac III has been described as the oldest occurrence of human implements anywhere in Europe, but the age and the human manufacture of the artefacts need to be verified. To date we should consider the case as unproved.

Several other occurrences throughout southern and central Europe are said to be of Lower Pleistocene or early Middle Pleistocene age. These occurrences generally fall into one of two categories.

1 The occurrence is represented by a few crude artefacts found in caves or karst infillings, and at open-air sites, either in association with a fauna of known age or in stratigraphic situations indicating an early age. Vallonet and Escale in France, Sandalja I in Croatia and Monte Peglia in Italy are cave sites (de Lumley, 1976a, 1976b; Bonifay et al., 1976b; Malez, 1976; Piperno, 1972). Open-air examples are find spots of isolated pieces on the high terraces of the Spanish Meseta or at localities associated with palaeomagnetic events in the Rhine Basin (Santoja, 1982/4; Santonja and Perez-Gonzalez, 1984; Bosinski, 1986).

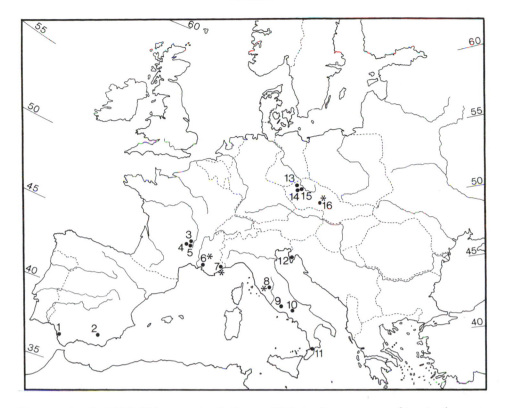

Map 3 Location of Lower and early Middle Pleistocene sites in Europe. With the clear exception of Isernia, the great age or the significance of many of these occurrences is a matter of doubt (see text); *, caves or karst. 1, Al Aculadero; 2, Cullar de Baza; 3, Soleihac; 4, Chilhac; 5, Sainzelles; 6, Escale*; 7, Vallonnet*; 8, Monte Peglia*; 9, Arce and Fontana Liri; 10, Isernia; 11, Casella di Maida; 12, Sandalja*; 13, Bečov; 14, Praha-Suchdol; 15, Přezletice; 16, Stránská Skála*.

2 The occurrence consists of many well-made artefacts of undoubted human manufacture. However, there is no associated fauna nor a continuous stratigraphic sequence and the site is dated in one of two ways: (a) by fitting the local stratigraphic sequence into the classic climato-stratigraphic timescale of the Pleistocene, generally the Alpine sequence; (b) by a judgment about the primitive or archaic aspect of the tools. Examples of occurrences of this kind are El Aculadero in Spain, Casella di Maida, Arce and Fontana Liri in Italy, the Roussillon terraces in France, and a number of other surface sites in southern and central Europe, too numerous to be listed (Bordes and Thibault, 1973; Gambassini and Ronchitelli, 1982; Villa, 1983, p. 13).

The dating of type 2 sites is an open question. As already discussed (p. 48), the Alpine sequence is a floating sequence that should not be used in interregional correlations. By giving different sites the same age label (such as Günz or Günz–Mindel or other stage name) we impose some semblance of order on a confusing abundance of occurrences, but in reality we are simply masking our ignorance of chronology.

Dating on the basis of typology or style is a valid method if applied to artefacts produced by shops or schools with established craft traditions (for example, Greek vases, Etruscan bronze mirrors, and so on); the method loses precision when used for dating early stone tools made with simple, expedient techniques and heavily influenced by the characteristics of the raw material. For example, archaic-looking, simple artefacts are quite common at the site of Terra Amata in Nice in southern France, which is dated to the younger part of the Middle Pleistocene. Thus dating by typology can entail an error of hundreds of thousand years, especially if the dated artefacts represent only a partial sample of the total artefact inventory in use at the time.

The age of the type 1 sites is better documented, though there may be a wide margin of uncertainty: Vallonnet and Monte Peglia can fall on either side of the Matuyama–Brunhes boundary; Sandalja's fauna is said to be 1.5 million years old (Valoch, 1976), but late elements suggest a more cautious attitude and a later date should be adopted (Malez, 1976). The evidence of human activities is meagre. There are five stone artefacts at Monte Peglia, two at Sandalja (where a putative hominid incisor has also been found), eleven but possibly more at Vallonnet and similar low numbers at Escale and the Spanish or German find spots. It is sometimes claimed that the animal bones found at the cave sites represent human food refuse, though little empirical evidence has been published in support of this idea. Criteria such as butchering marks made with stone tools or bone breakage to extract marrow can be used to infer human butchering activities, but they have not been reported. It is tacitly assumed that those early people inhabited the caves and carried their stone tools inside. However, bones and stones may also accumulate in caves and fissures through the action of bone-collecting carnivores, gravity and slope wash. These natural processes have acted in the geologic past to produce many sites with exclusively palaeontological materials (e.g. Kurten and Anderson, 1980, pp. 10–36). It does not seem prudent nor scientifically valid to see human activities as the cause of any kind of material evidence observed by archaeologists if natural causes have not been eliminated. In the absence of detailed analyses these claims should be regarded as possibly valid but unconfirmed. For the same reasons we must leave undecided a number of other claims, such as the occurrence of bones broken by humans

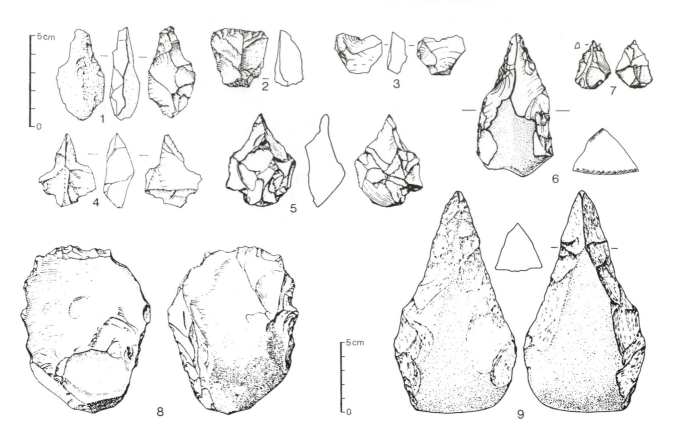

Figure 1 Stone tools, Isernia (Italy) (1–4), Ambrona (Spain) (5–7), Pech de l'Azé II (France) (8). 1, denticulate scraper, flint; 2, transverse scraper, flint; 3, notched piece, flint; 4, awl, flint; 5–7, awls, quartzite; 8, flake cleaver, flint; 9, biface, quartzite. (After C. Peretto, F. C. Howell, F. Bordes and C. Thibault.)

at the site of Sainzelles (dated to between 1.6 and 1.3 million years; Thouveny and Bonifay, 1984) and of human-made fire at the Escale cave (Bonifay et al., 1976*b*).

The site of Soleihac (France) is dated by palaeomagnetism to about 0.9 million years; it is at present the oldest dated occurrence of artefacts in Europe. The number of artefacts (on flint and basalt) is not very large, but excavations are continuing. It is not yet clear whether the occurrence is fully *in situ* and undisturbed, since some of the artefacts have rolled edges, indicating some water disturbance. Published evidence for a human-made wall, 20 m long, built with basalt blocks, is still too tenuous and must be considered as unconfirmed (Bonifay et al., 1976; Thouveny and Bonifay, 1984).

In contrast to the previous occurrences, the site of Isernia, discovered in 1978, combines several ideal conditions: (1) it is reliably dated (Table 1); (2) it has yielded thousands of stone artefacts (Fig. 1) and a very rich faunal assemblage in their original environment of deposition; (3) it has been excavated using very meticulous recovery techniques over a relatively large surface (to date, more than 200 m²).

This archaeological site was located on marshy ground, in the vicinity of a stream. The first archaeological horizon was deposited on an ancient land surface formed on top of emerged lacustrine travertine; it was covered by sterile overbank deposits (muds) over which a second horizon was found. The time interval separating the two episodes cannot be measured but could be very short, perhaps in the order of one or just a few seasons. Laterally the fluviatile muds lens out and two archaeological horizons merge on to the same ancient travertine surface. Burial of the site closely followed the time of the occupation and was due to rapid

deposition of a debris flow consisting of volcanic materials, erupted by a nearby volcano, and fluviatile sediments. The volcanic materials have been dated by potassium–argon to about 730,000 years ago. The flow that buried the archaeological materials may have moved some pieces to some distance from their original position (some large bones show preferred orientation), but the lack of edge abrasion on the flint artefacts and the occurrence of conjoinable bone fragments rather close to each other suggest only minor rearrangement of material at the time of burial. According to the excavators, water transport played no role in the accumulation of the bones and stones.

The upper archaeological horizon has yielded a spectacular high-density concentration of artefacts and disarticulated and broken animal bones, mainly remains of large mammals (bison, rhinoceros and elephant, in order of frequency) and much fewer remains of hippos and medium-sized ungulates. The only carnivore represented at the site is the bear, which is, however, less common than the large ungulates (Coltori et al., 1982; various authors in Soprintendenza Archeologica del Molise, 1983).

Because natural deaths and predator kills are common near water sources, accumulation of animal bones at these locales are not unexpected. On the other hand, the stone artefacts, made on raw materials available on the spot, are clear evidence that hominids repeatedly visited Isernia's muddy flats and river-banks. The usual inference would be that humans were the main agent of accumulation of the bones of large and medium-sized mammals. Preliminary accounts adopt this perspective, and describe Isernia as a residential site occupied at periodic intervals by a human group that lived by hunting both large and medium-sized mammals. Animal bones at the site, with the exception of the few micro-mammals, bird and fish remains, reflect human predation; the animals were killed near the site and transported there for consumption (Soprintendenza Archeologica del Molise, 1983, pp. 77, 102).

This is obviously a preliminary hypothesis; however, in view of its implications for reconstructing early subsistence patterns, this hypothesis must be carefully examined before it can be made final and incorporated in accounts of European prehistory. For this reason, we anticipate here a discussion of hominid hunting, summarized in the section on subsistence patterns (see p. 54).

As pointed out by C. K. Brain, L. R. Binford and others, the problem with a hunting hypothesis is that it neglects other possible agents or processes of bone accumulation and breakage, and it stems from a preconception about the importance of hunting in human evolution.

It is a basic theory of archaeology that the hunting and gathering way of life was the natural condition of humankind before the invention of agriculture. Like the camp sites of modern hunter-gatherers, archaeological sites are aggregations of artefacts and animal bones. Based on this resemblance, it seems plausible or even necessary to deduce that those collections of bones and stones are the remains of camp sites where early hunters lived in groups with complex social relations, sharing food and common tasks. With the exception of animal foods considered not fit for human consumption, difficult to catch or giving only a low yield for each catch, animal bones are seen as direct evidence of human hunting patterns and diet.

It is true that if one looks at certain features such as size or presence of bones and stone, all archaeological sites look alike, from 2 million years ago down to the very end of the Pleistocene (Isaac, 1975, p. 886). Thus a hunting way of life, a key distinction between hominids and non-human primates, appeared to go back to the very beginning of humankind. The hunting model was favoured by many writers and is explicitly or implicitly incorporated in all analyses of European Lower and Middle Pleistocene sites where stones and bones are found together (Bouchud, 1976; de Lumley, 1969a, 1969b; Mourer-Chauviré and Renault-Miskovsky, 1980; Kretzoi and Vértes, 1965; Freeman, 1975; Lioubin and Barychnikov, 1984). Increased attention to modern processes of bone accumulation, modification and destruction has provided important information about a variety of taphonomic processes by which archaeological sites may be formed. It has been shown by many workers (e.g. Binford, 1981, 1984; Brain, 1981; Bunn, 1982; Potts, 1986; Shipman, 1983) that faunal assemblages at early sites may often be the result of a complex series of events that took place over several years, before rapid burial.

Systematic hunting is only one of the possible explanations for dense aggregates of bones and stones. Palaeontological assemblages of non-human origin in fine-grained sediments provide partial analogues to the Isernia situation; some show large quantities of disarticulated, broken and carnivore-damaged bones belonging to two or three different species of animals that died naturally at the site in episodes of individual and mass deaths.

We must envisage the possibility that the Isernia site was created by several agents, including perhaps natural deaths of water-dependent animals and scavenging by hominids using stone tools. Bone breakage for marrow by humans is indicated at the site (Soprintendenza Archeologica del Molise, p. 99, Fig. 8). This certainly proves that humans performed butchery, but it provides no evidence relevant to actual hunting. The evidence, as it stands now, is ambiguous. The Isernia bones may represent the scavenging of naturally occurring carcasses as well as the active hunting of live prey. One may doubt whether those early humans possessed the technology or the weaponry (such as stone-tipped spears or fire for game drives) necessary to bring down such large mammals. Charcoal has not been found at Isernia; wood is present and this means that charcoal would be preserved, if present (M. Cremaschi, personal communication). To date, projectile points have not been identified at sites older than the Upper Pleistocene.

At the last-interglacial site of Lehringen in Germany a wooden thrusting spear with a simple pointed end was found between the ribs of an elephant in swamp deposits, together with a number of flakes presumably used in butchering the animal (Oakley et al., 1977). This suggests that it is possible to kill a large animal with a very thick hide, such as the elephant, using a simple pointed spear; perhaps the animal had been mired. The Isernia hominids possessed the simple stone tools needed to fashion the point of a spear. Still, this possibility must be demonstrated, not assumed: Lehringen is about 600,000 years younger than Isernia; also, the presence of many animals of different species at the latter site indicates a more complex situation.

It has been suggested that systematic hunting of large mammals and co-operative hunting of gregarious animals appear in the European Middle Pleistocene and might actually be coincident with the appearance of Homo erectus. In fact, there is no solid proof of big-game hunting from any European site before the end of the Middle Pleistocene. The site of Isernia offers a unique opportunity to test ideas about the practice of systematic hunting and to monitor the effectiveness of methods recently developed to unravel the various processes that influence bone accumulations at early sites. The very meticulous excavation techniques have generated high-quality data on patterns of associations, sedimentary features, microtopography and conjoinable bones. The artefacts are made mostly of flint, which is the only material yet to yield significant results in microwear studies. In comparison with African sites such as Olduvai, the faunal assemblage shows lower taxonomic diversity and the predominance of a single species (the bison), an intriguing fact which could be due to hunting but is also not inconsistent with a hypothesis of mass mortality as a contributing, partial agent of deposition.

In-depth analysis of different taphonomic processes that may have acted at Isernia is clearly needed before a single explanation can be retained; we can strengthen the case for hunting only by disproving alternative hypotheses. Analyses of bone-weathering stages, of body-parts frequencies, of cut marks and breakage patterns, and comparisons with palaeontological assemblages of non-human origin will provide the basis for a well-defined scenario. This work is now under way; there is no doubt that the adoption of a taphonomic viewpoint by the Isernia team will produce important data for understanding early subsistence patterns.

HOMINID OCCUPATION OF EUROPE (Maps 3 and 4)

Tempo and routes of migration

The oldest confirmed traces of human presence in Europe are dated to about 1 million years ago; they fall within the

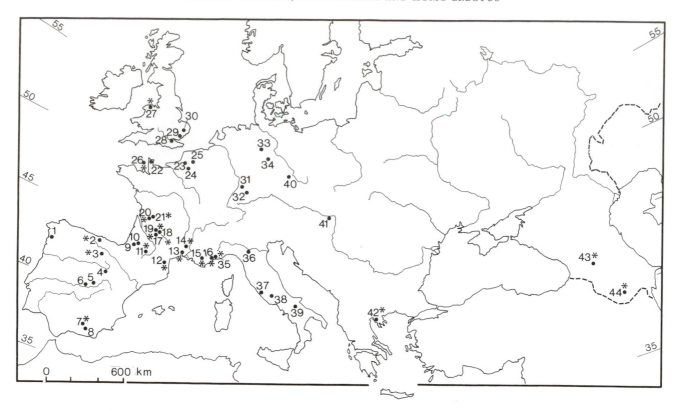

Map 4 Location of major Middle Pleistocene sites in Europe; * cave sites. 1, Budino; 2, Cueva del Castillo*; 3. Atapuerca*; 4, Torralba and Ambrona; 5, Aridos; 6, Pinedo; 7, Cueva Hora*; 8, Solana del Zamborino; 9, Bouheben; 10, Nantet; 11, Montmaurin*; 12, Arago*; 13, Lunel Viel*; 14, Orgnac*; 15, Baume Bonne*; 16, Terra Amata and Lazaret*; 17, Combe Grenal*; 18, Pech de l'Azé II*; 19, La Micoque*; 20, La Chaise*; 21, Fontéchevade*; 22, Port Pignot; 23, Abbeville; 24, Cagny and Saint-Acheul; 25, Biache-Saint-Vaast; 26, La Cotte de Saint-Brelade*; 27, Pontnewydd*; 28, Swanscombe; 29, Clacton-on-Sea; 30, Hoxne; 31, Mauer; 32, Steinheim; 33, Salzgitter-Lebenstedt; 34, Bilzingsleben; 35, Grotta del Principe*; 36, Ghiardo Cave*; 37, Torre in Pietra, Castel di Guido and Malagrotta; 38, Fontana Ranuccio; 39, Venosa; 40, Bečov; 41, Vértesszöllös; 42, Petralona*; 43, Kudaro I and II*; 44, Azikh*.

time span of *Homo erectus*, who appeared in Africa about 1.6 million years ago (Delson, 1985). The European fossil record is relatively abundant for the later phases of the Middle Pleistocene, after 0.5 million years, but provides no well-dated human remains for the earlier periods; thus the fossil record contributes little to a debate about the timing and the mode of human settlement in Europe. The only significant fact is the lack of any hominid remains older than or as old as the first African *Homo erectus*. The late dates of the earliest sites (cf. previous section) and the absence of an independently evolving line of humankind before *Homo erectus* indicate clearly that human presence in Europe was the result of radiation from tropical to temperate countries, presumably from Africa or Asia.

Radiation and dispersal over wide areas are characteristics of evolutionary history. The history of land mammals, in particular, is marked by brief periods of intercontinental dispersals. A major faunal replacement occurs in Europe at the end of the Lower Pleistocene. During that time some cold species (reindeer, woolly rhinoceros) migrated into Europe probably from central Asia. Other immigrants are the heavy rhinoceros (*Dicerorhinus mercki*) and the true horses. Changes are seen in the bovides with the appearance of large forms of *Bison* and *Bos*, in the micromammals, in the cervid fauna, and in the carnivores, with the first appearance of *Canis lupus* (the wolf), *Crocuta crocuta* (the spotted hyena), *Panthera leo* (the lion) and *Panthera pardus* (the leopard); according to Turner, some of the carnivore species may have migrated from Africa (Azzaroli, 1983; Turner, 1984). The result of this faunal revolution was the emergence of a new

assemblage of megafauna which survived with only minor changes until the end of the Pleistocene.

Hominid radiation into temperate Eurasia seems to be part of this major faunal shift, which apparently involved the northern dispersal of many large African carnivores. According to Azzaroli, this faunal replacement was, at least in part, correlated with climatic changes recorded in the deep-sea sediments as oxygen isotope stage 22 (about 0.8 million years). This cold interval marks the intensification of glacial–interglacial cycles and the beginning of the continental ice ages. Lowering of the sea-level during glacial episodes may have favoured continental connections and faunal migrations over long distances. The timing and the routes of European colonization by early hominids are none the less quite uncertain.

Two probable routes of migration into Europe are: (1) from Africa across the Straits of Gibraltar; and (2) from Asia, across the Dardanelles or the Bosphorus. Both routes offer relatively easy passage, especially at times of low sea-level, during glacial advances. With a drop in sea-level of 120–130 m (corresponding to the sea lowering during the last glacial maximum) the Dardanelles and the Bosphorus would have been dry; in contrast, the Straits of Gilbraltar (present minimum width is 11 km) would have still required a sea crossing of about 8 km (assuming that present sea-floor depth can be extrapolated into Pleistocene times; Van Andel and Shackleton, 1982; Shackleton et al., 1984).

Lower and early Middle Pleistocene sites are known from the Maghreb (Aïn Hanech, Sidi Abderrahman, Ternifine), but no Spanish sites are securely dated to the Lower Pleistocene. Plio-Pleistocene faunal relations between northern Africa and Europe were close but there is no proof of direct faunal exchanges across the Straits of Gibraltar (Jaeger, 1975). No Middle Pleistocene sites have been reported from Turkey, though handaxes have been recorded on the shores of the Bosphorus (Singer and Wymer, 1978); there is only one confirmed Middle Pleistocene occurrence in northern Greece (the hominid cranium from Petralona in the Chalcidice peninsula). In brief, the available evidence is not strong enough to argue for the primacy of one route over the other.

Two routes that are generally considered unlikely are: (1) across the Strait of Sicily between Tunisia and Sicily; and (2) the land route from Asia across Ukraine, along the north coast of the Black Sea.

The Strait of Sicily route, from Cap Bon to south of Marsala, requires crossing about 60 km of deep water before reaching land through the Adventure Bank, which would be exposed by a fall of 120 m in sea-level. There are several islands in between, but the voyage is complex enough to require a deliberate group of people on a buoyant canoe or raft. The total distance now is 140 km (US Defense Mapping Agency, 1971). Claims of Middle Pleistocene and even older traces of human presence in southern Sicily (Bianchini, 1973; Soprintendenza Speciale del Museo Pigorini, 1984, p. 126) are questionable and provide no support for the hypothesis of a Sicilian route. The peopling of Sicily (the oldest confirmed evidence is of Upper Palaeolithic age) is more likely to be the result of movement from mainland Italy across the Strait of Messina, which is only 3 km wide.

Given the present sea-floor depth, the Strait of Messina would become a dry land bridge at sea-level minus 90 m (Shackleton et al., 1984). In the Middle Pleistocene, however, sea-floor depth was probably quite different: we know that the Calabrian coast in this area has been raised by about 100 m since Late Pleistocene times (Ascenzi and Segre, 1971). Even so, a sea crossing of 3 km does not seem formidable and the absence of human settlement in Sicily is certainly surprising.

There are no traces of human settlement in Sardinia and Corsica before the Holocene (*contra* Sondaar et al., 1984). Again, assuming a drop in sea-level of 120 m, it is possible to walk from the Italian coast to the island of Capraia in the Tuscan archipelago; from there to Corsica the sea to be crossed is 15 km wide. Shallows would then permit land passage to Sardinia. If the absence of Pleistocene archaeological sites in all these islands is real and not the result of inadequate survey, it would seem that Middle Pleistocene hominids had very limited sea-voyage capabilities or very little incentive (perhaps no population pressure?). Migration of continental faunas into Sardinia, possibly through a temporary land bridge, appears to have taken place no later than the Early–Middle Pleistocene boundary (Azzaroli, 1981); at this time hominids may have been present only sporadically in Italy. The peopling of Britain did not require the use of sea-going craft since a lowering of the sea-level to minus 50 m would have connected the British Isles to the mainland (Scott, 1984, Fig. 9.1).

The possibility of a northern land route from Asia into Europe is generally ignored because, according to present knowledge, early hominids could not deal with severe and prolonged winters. Middle Pleistocene sites are found on the southern slopes of the Greater Caucasus (the Kudaro I and Tsona cave sites, in Southern Ossetia) and more to the south in Azerbaidjan (Azykh cave), but only Upper Pleistocene sites have been reported from Ukraine (Lioubin

and Barychnikov, 1984; Dolukhanov, 1982; cf. also Davis et al., 1980).

Some sites in the Czech Republic, dated to the Lower–Middle Pleistocene boundary, might indicate early expansion into northerly latitudes, if the human manufacture of the artefacts (at Přezletice and Stránská Skála) or their great age (at Bečov I and Praha-Suchdol) could be confirmed. At Přezletice a molar tooth fragment considered human by Fejfar (1969, 1976) has been attributed to bear by Vlcek (1978). In fact, the evidence of early human presence at these sites is open to doubt (Svoboda, 1984). In England the earliest sites fall in the time range 500,000 to 150,000 years (Roe, 1981, p. 301). In Germany the hominid jaw from Mauer (near Heidelberg) may be older, that is, of early Middle Pleistocene age; unfortunately no absolute dates are available from this site (Brunnacker, 1975; Cook et al., 1982).

Three observations, as follow, must be considered in summarizing present knowledge about the mode of human dispersal in Europe.

1 Securely dated sites are confined to southern Europe. Very few sites are known even after the Matuyama–Brunhes polarity change.

2 There is surprisingly little evidence of the use of fire at very early sites in southern Europe, including some where preservation of burnt bones or burnt stones, if not charcoal, might be expected (such as Vallonnet, Isernia, or Arago Cave, which has an estimated age of about 450,000; de Lumley et al., 1984). Good evidence of fire is provided by sites like Vértesszöllös in Hungary (two concentrations of burnt bone), Bilzingsleben in Germany (burnt flints and traces of charcoal), Terra Amata in France (two or three concentrations of charcoal, and burnt stones) and Pontnewydd in Wales (burnt flints). All these sites are younger than 0.5 million years, with Pontnewydd being much younger than that date, while Vértesszöllös and Bilzingsleben may be as old as (or possibly even older than) 350,000 years.

3 During the Middle Pleistocene human dispersal within north-west and north-central Europe is apparently restricted to milder climatic episodes. In central Europe, northern France and England, sites dated to periods of glacial advances are very rare (Svoboda, 1984; Roe, 1981, p. 279; Scott, 1984; Tuffreau et al., 1982b; Valoch, 1984).

Thus the data at present available suggest the following.

1 Human settlement in Europe was the result of a very slow process which started about 1 million years ago, half a million years after the first appearance of *Homo erectus* in eastern Africa. Until 0.5 million years ago, Europe appears to have been inhabited rather sparsely.

2 Human expansion was controlled by climatic factors, among others. Areas were alternatively settled and abandoned in response to climatic changes. Adaptations to periglacial conditions and to tundra or cold steppe landscapes supporting mammoths and reindeer may have begun in the later part of the Middle Pleistocene (cf. the sites of Salzgitter-Lebenstedt and Rheindahlen in northern Germany, and La Cotte de Saint-Brelade in the Channel Islands, occupied during the Riss glaciation; Bosinski, 1982; Scott, 1980). However, the site of Biache-Saint-Vaast in northern France, also dated to the end of the Middle Pleistocene, was abandoned during cold oscillations (Tuffreau et al., 1982a).

3 It is possible, though by no means certain, that the use of fire played little or no role in the early phases of human

dispersal in southern Europe. The lack of fire may have contributed to the slow rate of dispersal; however, this is only a speculation. Evidence of fire from more northern sites, dated well within the Middle Pleistocene, suggests that fire was instrumental in favouring human expansion into cold regions, north of the Mediterranean zone.

The northern boundary of human occupation in Europe appears to coincide roughly with the southern limit of the last glaciation, about 54° N in England and 52° N in Wales, eastern Germany and Poland. Sites are found as far north as the North Sea coast in Germany and just south of latitude 51° N in the Czech Republic. This pattern is clearly the result of the destruction and reworking of sediments by the repeated advances of the Scandinavian ice-sheet. However, Roe argues convincingly that in England the pattern of site distribution is not truncated but simply peters out, suggesting that even at times of warmer climates man rarely left southern and eastern England. Sporadic penetration of the area beyond the southern ice limit is indicated by Pontnewydd, a site in Wales, north of 53°. The colonization of Ireland, the northern European plain east of the Oder and the Scandinavian countries was accomplished after the last deglaciation, in late Würm and Holocene times (Map 4).

It is generally believed that the greatest challenge to hominid expansion was the intense seasonal variability of the temperate zone, and consequently the short growing season, the scarcity of vegetable resources and differences in the structure and distribution of animal resources, compared with the African savannah environment. However, we lack a specific understanding of the ecological problems faced by early hominids because there have been no detailed studies of the various sets of plants and animals living in any region in the past. We need information on the density and distribution of potential prey or plant foods, their seasonal variation, the equipment or level of effort needed to procure them and the size and organization of human groups. We are just beginning to explore these lines of research; it will take years before we can hope to provide a cohesive account of the processes of human adaptations to the extra-tropical environments of Europe. The task is difficult because the record is sparse and many Pleistocene plant and animal communities appear to have no modern equivalents.

Site location, habitation structures and big-game hunting

In the second part of the Middle Pleistocene, roughly after 0.5 million years ago, sites become much more abundant (Map 4), but we still lack a great deal of information about them, a major cause of uncertainty being their unsatisfactory chronology. The most frequent site location is near water sources (on lake shores or along river valleys) or, less frequently, in caves. It is reasonable to think that water proximity and shelter were two major determinants of site choice; we should caution, however, that these are also prime areas for the preservation of deposited sediments and fossils.

Simple hearths have been found at several sites, for instance Terra Amata, Port Pignot and Lunel Viel in France and Vértesszöllös in Hungary. At other sites (Swanscombe and Hoxne in England, Torralba in Spain) carbonaceous lumps or pieces of undoubted charcoal have been found; it is not clear whether they represent the residue of human-made hearths or of possibly natural grass fires. Only a few microscopic bits of charcoal have been found at Aridos 1,

an elephant-butchering site near Madrid, Spain (Santoja et al., 1980, p. 72). Other sites have yielded no traces of fire at all. Non-preservation of charcoal and ashes due to leaching is partly responsible for the meagre evidence; it is also possible that fire was less commonly used than in later periods and that many of the sites we know were not sleeping or cooking places but locations where only a limited range of activities was carried out. This would certainly apply to sites such as Aridos. Traces of fire are instead more common at sites dated to the end of the Middle Pleistocene: Lazaret, Pech de l'Azé II, Orgnac, and Biache-Saint-Vaast in France, La Cotte de Saint-Brelade in the Channel Islands and Pontnewydd in Wales. Accumulations of charcoal and fireplaces are a normal occurrence at late Würm sites.

There is little evidence on habitation structures such as huts or tents. This frustrating aspect of the record and the fact that the data are ambiguous in their interpretation have misled some archaeologists into replacing solid inference with speculation. The putative shelters reported from the site of Terra Amata are an example of attractively simple scenarios based on rather premature assessments of incomplete data.

Terra Amata is found in the city of Nice (south-eastern France) at an elevation of 26 m above sea-level; at the time of the prehistoric occupation the site was located on the sea-shore, near the delta of a river. Traces of oval huts, 7 to 15 m long, built with stakes and branches and braced by a ring of stone have been reported, one in each of the twenty-one superimposed excavation levels. Distinct areas for working raw materials and for cooking were recognized in each of the huts. According to the excavator's reconstruction, huts were rebuilt and fires were rekindled on the same spot, suggesting that the same group of people returned to the site, year after year. The camps corresponded to twenty-one brief seasonal halts made in the spring (de Lumley, 1967, 1969a, 1975, 1976b).

The stable organization of internal space in the huts and the planning involved in returning to the same locality always at the same season are considered normal behaviour among modern hunter-gatherers. The implication is that modern patterns of behaviour were already present in the Middle Pleistocene, some hundred thousands of years ago.

Unfortunately the evidence from the site is quite ambiguous. Traces of possible postholes were found in the upper levels but there were only two to four in each of the levels. No traces of postholes were found in the lower levels. Only one distribution plan has been published (de Lumley, 1975, Fig. 6). Moreover, the study of conjoined stone fragments indicates some vertical displacement of pieces, misunderstood contacts between adjacent excavation levels and excessive subdivision of the deposits into levels that were not stratigraphically isolated. It is clear that the published stratigraphic interpretation of the site with its twenty-one occupation episodes and clear-cut scenarios is in need of a cautious revision. More detailed studies of artefact localizations, and of the distribution patterns of stone blocks and their position relative to postholes, must be carried out before we can conclude that people lived in huts with distinct activity areas and a hearth at the centre, and that the same pattern of habitation existed throughout the repeated occupation of the site. Until better evidence is provided, interpretations about the length of stay, the season of occupation or the number of occupation episodes should be seen as tentative (Villa, 1976, 1982, 1983). Similar uncertainties attach to the interpretation of several bits of ochre, which have encouraged speculations about the aesthetic sense of primitive people (Edwards and Clinnick, 1980), even though evidence that these colourants have been transported or manipulated by early humans has not been presented. Thus we are left with a strong feeling of uncertainty about these interpretations.

Bone assemblages from archaeological sites always include a variety of species that can be assigned to several size categories. Thus it is generally believed that Middle Pleistocene people were unspecialized hunters using a broad spectrum of resources with a versatile technology capable of effectively taking animals of small to very large body size. As indicated already in the discussion of the Isernia occurrence, the hunting model has been and still is accepted unconditionally by many archaeologists. Recent taphonomic studies of bone assemblages from Arago cave and from Torralba and Ambrona (Moigne, 1983; Shipman and Rose, 1983) suggest that the popular notion of Middle Pleistocene hominids as active hunters of very large game (elephants at Torralba, rhinos, bisons and horses at Arago) may be incorrect: scavenging may have played a larger role than has previously been believed (see also Santoja et al., 1980, pp. 323–5).

There is, however, exciting evidence for the use of natural traps to drive and kill large animals at La Cotte de Saint-Brelade, a site dated to the end of the Middle Pleistocene (Scott, 1980). The cultural deposits have been found in a gully, below a rocky outcrop, forming a natural trap. Two levels (layers 3 and 6) contain impressive bone concentrations, representing the remains of several mammoths and rhinos (at least nine mammoths and two rhinos in layer 3, eight mammoths and three rhinos in layer 6). The bones have cut-marks from dismembering and filleting (Binford, 1981, p. 287).

A shift to a greater role for hunting and the development of techniques to increase success in the hunt may have taken place towards the end of the Middle Pleistocene. At this time we also observe an increase in the number of sites and greater sophistication in lithic technology, suggesting a significant acceleration in the complexity of cultural systems.

STONE TOOLS (Figs 1 and 2)

Terminology, function, technical features and time trends

The stone tools found at Lower and Middle Pleistocene sites fall into two major categories: (1) flakes, i.e. pieces detached from a larger block or cobble; and (2) flaked pieces, i.e. stones from which flakes have been detached (Isaac, 1984).

The lighter forms, that is the flakes, could be used as they were for tasks that require sharp edges; alternatively one or more edges were retouched to make a stronger, steeper edge, to obtain a desired edge outline, or to facilitate holding of the tool in the hand. Many of the smaller flakes that often have fragile edges were probably never used and are the by-product of the manufacture of the flaked pieces.

In traditional classifications only retouched pieces or elaborate flake forms (like the Levallois flakes) are considered tools because only these are clearly designed for use. However, microwear analysis has shown that simple unretouched flakes were used for a variety of tasks, in particular for meat cutting. Similar tasks were accomplished with retouched or unretouched pieces, but pieces with a re-touched and steep edge were preferred for wood or hide scraping (Keeley, 1977).

The main flake-tool forms are side-scrapers, denticulates and thick pointed forms (i.e. awls, Tayac points, and so on). Palaeolithic archaeologists use these terms with the understanding that tool names do not necessarily imply function and that unretouched flakes may also have been used as implements.

The second category, i.e. the flaked pieces, show a variable range of shapes; in traditional classifications some of the forms are considered tools (for instance core-tools, such as handaxes, choppers, core-scrapers, polyhedrons), while others (cores) are considered simply to be the by-product of flake manufacture. Again, microwear analysis runs against traditional notions. The analysis of twenty-two flint choppers found at the English site of Clacton showed that twenty had not been used at all and were just a source of flakes. Experimental knapping also shows that many chopper forms are produced unintentionally during replicative production for flakes and do not represent specific designs, as previously believed (Toth, 1985). The two choppers that exhibited wear patterns had been used for wood adzing (Keeley, 1977). Other possible uses for choppers include breaking bone for marrow extraction.

Throughout most of this period, from the earliest sites until the later part of the Middle Pleistocene, lithic technology appears relatively stable and there is only limited innovation in either tool forms or technical procedures (with the exception of the appearance of the Levallois technique, described on p. 56). Flaking was done with a hammerstone or on an anvil stone. Trimming by thin, spreading flakes (i.e. using a soft stone or an antler) is present but less common. There are no elaborate flaking patterns; flaking was simple, forceful and most often opportunistic, and the knapper took maximum advantage of the natural shape of the blank. Among the tool types there are only few elaborate forms, and the range of acceptable shapes may be quite large. There is no good evidence of hafting.

The majority of artefacts found at sites were made of locally available raw materials; often the range of raw materials used was very wide (for instance at Arago; Wilson, 1986). However, certain kinds of raw materials were clearly favoured and were transported over some distance, perhaps as much as 80 km from the source (Tavoso, 1978). Similar examples of long-distance transport have been reported in African industries (Clark, 1975, p. 628). There is clear evidence of selectivity in raw material use: siliceous rocks that produce sharp, tough edges (such as chert and quartz) were preferred for small tools, while larger, heavier implements could be made of softer raw material (limestone) (Fig. 2) or raw material that produces a robust, if coarse and less regular, edge (quartzite). This pattern of selectivity is already present at Isernia and can be observed in most Middle Pleistocene industries (for instance Arago, Terra Amata; Villa, 1983; Lebel, 1984); it actually appears at the very beginning of stone-toolmaking, in Oldowan industries (Leakey, 1971).

In the later part of the Middle Pleistocene, stone industries are consistently more refined. They are characterized by the habitual use of the soft hammer to produce thin, regular flakes. Flaking patterns are more elaborate and controlled; there is increased care in artefact manufacture, as indicated by less variable shapes and regular, continuous retouch along the working edge. During this time the stone-toolmakers often used the Levallois technique, a special flaking strategy based on more or less careful shaping of the core for

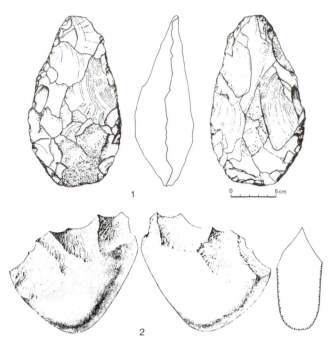

Figure 2 Limestone tools: 1, limestone biface, Ambrona (Spain); 2, limestone chopper, Terra Amata (France). (After F. C. Howell and H. de Lumley.)

The handaxes

Of all early stone tools, the handaxes, also called bifaces (Figs 1 and 2), have attracted most attention from prehistorians. They appear for the first time in Africa, in assemblages dated to between 1.5 and 1 million years, at Olduvai, Koobi Fora and Melka Kunturé. In Europe many Middle Pleistocene assemblages include bifaces but others do not (the same pattern can be observed in Africa). This absence has often been interpreted to mean that the makers of the assemblages without bifaces belonged to a different group of people.

In some cases it is possible to suggest other reasons for this absence: the size of the available raw material was too small or the assemblage represents only a limited sampling of the total artefacts in use at the time. Activity variation is, of course, a simple and more comprehensive alternative. It is, however, difficult to prove directly because handaxes and other heavy tools are often made of raw materials (quartzite, basalt, limestone) (Fig. 2) that do not preserve use-wear traces. The few flint handaxes that have been analysed by Keeley were used for animal butchery, but the wide variety of shapes suggests that bifaces may also have been used for other tasks (a biface-like implement at Hoxne was used as a wood wedge). The fact that in broadly contemporaneous assemblages bifaces occur in extremely variable proportions (some assemblages contain hundreds, others just a few or one only) suggests that bifaces are not a stable cultural feature, making the activity variation hypothesis more likely (Villa, 1983).

Though handaxes are rare or absent in East Asia (Watanabe, 1985), no clear geographic pattern appears in Europe, where they are found all over the areas occupied by Middle Pleistocene people, from Spain to Slovakia and from Southern Italy to England. Their widespread distribution suggests that handaxes were an important part of the technical equipment of early humans and a very general kind of tool, one that could be adopted over much of the world by very different groups of people and thus very similar to other generalized technological elements of later times, such as table forks, the Levallois technique, the bow and arrow, the plough, or the making of pottery.

Since some of the earliest European assemblages do not contain handaxes but only choppers and various flake forms (such as Isernia and El Aculadero; Querol and Santoja, 1983) it is often suggested that the continent was settled first by people who were not handaxe makers, later followed by another wave of handaxe-making people; the two tool traditions would have persisted side by side. This poses a curious problem, because (1) handaxes appear in Africa half a million years before the earliest dated European site, and (2) it is generally believed that human presence in Europe is ultimately the result of migrations from Africa, whether directly across the Straits of Gibraltar or from western Asia. In western Asia handaxes are found at the site of Ubeidiya, which is certainly older than 0.7 million years (Bar Yosef, 1984). If we accept the idea that the habit of making handaxes arrived late into Europe, the time lag between Europe and Africa–western Asia seems inexplicable. It is, of course, entirely possible that the repertoire of the earliest stone craftspeople in Europe did include handaxes but that the sample of early sites is simply too small (since not all patterns of behaviour are represented at all sites). Little progress can be made on this question until there are more and better-dated early sites and the function of handaxes is better understood.

producing flakes (or points or blades) of a predetermined form, requiring little or no modification before use. This technique appears for the first time in Middle Pleistocene assemblages younger than 0.5 million years, but it becomes dominant only towards the end of the period (Tuffreau, 1982, 1986).

The stone industries of late Middle Pleistocene times are in many ways indistinguishable from Mousterian industries of Upper Pleistocene age, a fact that is increasingly recognized. This technological continuity across the Middle–Upper Pleistocene boundary is paralleled by a continuum in human evolution: the earliest fossils of Neanderthal aspect, or, more precisely, with some of the traits found in the classic Neanderthals of the last glaciation, also appear during later Middle Pleistocene times (for instance at Biache-Saint-Vaast or La Chaise; Tuffreau, 1979; Stringer et al., 1984; Stringer, 1985).

Interestingly, the shift between earlier and later Middle Pleistocene industries is much less dramatic than the clear-cut changes from the Mousterian to the Upper Palaeolithic during the last glaciation. While it is certainly possible to contrast earlier and later Middle Pleistocene industries (such as Isernia, El Aculadero, Pinedo, Arago, Vértesszöllös, Ambrona, Clacton or Terra Amata on the one hand, and Biache-Saint-Vaast, La Chaise, Combe Grenal or Lazaret on the other) in terms of refinement and standardization, higher number of specific tool forms and more complex flaking techniques, we also see lines of continuity between the two groups of industries. This can be seen in the continuing use of handaxes, in the beginning of the Levallois technique in earlier industries and in the fact that all the main flake-tool forms are found in both types of industries. Given the uncertainties in dating and the low number of significant sites, it is not known whether the observed differences were the result of gradual, progressive elaboration through time or were due to a step-like period of accelerated changes, nor do we know if there was synchronism between regions (Bosinski, 1982, pp. 323–9).

Assemblage variability and Middle Pleistocene cultures

In the interpretation of stone artefacts European archaeology has long been dominated by a particular school of thought, that is the cultural historical school. The primary goal of this school has been the definition of chronological relationships between different cultures. Stone tool types and assemblages are seen as cultural markers and can be used to identify cultural groups. Similarities of tool types are due to the fact that their makers belong to the same culture; vice versa, differences in tool types indicate different cultures. In other words, cultures (or more exactly, tool traditions) are the taxonomic units of archaeology. The historical succession of different cultural traditions and different populations in various countries can be established through stratigraphy (or absolute dating) and the analysis of similarities and differences.

According to this point of view, different cultures were already present in the Lower and Middle Pleistocene; these early cultures are the forerunners of more complex cultural traditions that appear in the Upper Pleistocene. Acheulean, Clactonian, Evenosian, Tayacian or Taubachian are names given to stone industries judged to be separate cultural units. They are characterized by certain tool types: handaxes identify Acheulean assemblages, choppers and flakes with large butts are found in Clactonian assemblages, very small tools and the lack of handaxes characterize the Taubachian and so on. These stone industries are found to have very widespread distributions and to form long-term cultural traditions that continued for hundreds of thousands of years. For instance, assemblages referred to the Taubachian (also called Tautavelian or Budian) are found in central and eastern Europe (Vértesszöllös in Hungary, Bilzingsleben and other sites in Germany and the Czech Republic), in southern France (Arago, Lunel Viel, Aldène) and even Italy (Isernia). This tool tradition begins in the early Middle Pleistocene (Isernia), continues in the late Riss (Baume Bonne) and reaches the last interglacial (Tata, Kůlna and so on; Bordes, 1968; Collins, 1969; de Lumley, 1975, 1976b; de Lumley et al., 1979; Svoboda, 1984; Valoch, 1984).

An approach to ordering based on the analysis of similarities is common to all natural sciences (for instance palaeontology). The kind and extent of similarities provide the primary data in any historical discipline; clearly the basic interpretative framework of archaeology must rest on this kind of data. However, opposition and unhappiness with the cultural–historical approach rise from its dogmatic and restrictive scope. European archaeologists have allowed a strong *a priori* view to direct their inquiry into a single path, searching only for evidence of cultural connections, rigidly excluding other causes of similarities or differences and ignoring other kinds of data (Villa, 1978, 1981, 1983).

It is now generally acknowledged that Lower and Middle Pleistocene stone tools (with the exception of those dating to the later part of the period) were made by simple and expedient techniques and that their morphology was influenced by the characteristics of the raw material and by the circumstances and duration of use.

Recent studies of stone tools focus on various aspects of function and technology: analysis of use–wear to understand activities conducted at sites, identification of sources of raw material and distance of transport, study of the intensity of use and patterns of discard, experimental replication and use of artefacts, and study of the technical skills of the makers

and the attainment of certain thresholds in technical know-how (e.g. Keeley, 1977; Villa, 1978, 1981, 1983; Toth, 1982, 1985). It is clear that stone tools can provide information on site function, subsistence patterns and temporal changes in cognitive or technical skills. These studies have also shown that assemblage variability may stem from a variety of causes, of which cultural tradition and affiliation is only one. Part of the variation in Middle Pleistocene assemblages can probably be explained by differences in activities and differences in the size, shape and flaking quality of the available raw materials. Another determinant of tool size and morphology is the intensity of use and reshaping which reduces the size of the tool and increases the number of working edges. Interestingly, the microlithic tools found in Taubachian assemblages are often characterized by a high degree of modification and a high number of working edges (Valoch, 1984, p. 204).

Traditional interpretations of early tool assemblages were based on the presupposition that early societies were not radically different from modern hunting and gathering societies and that regional specialization existed. There are undoubtedly important differences in the forms of assemblages but there is no clear pattern of geographic variability – not at least within Europe. As many people have observed, far-away assemblages can be very similar to each other, while differences exist between essentially contemporaneous assemblages in the same region. This pattern of similarities across broad regions occurring together with a pattern of variability within regions is often interpreted as the expression of small bands of humans that possessed a fairly simple and generalized equipment and were experimenting with a wide variety of different foods and materials, rather than regularly and consistently selecting only certain kinds of resources and developing adaptations specific to the diverse environments they were inhabiting (Clark, 1975). Since population density was probably quite low, it is reasonable to think that there existed isolated groups that developed distinct craft practices; these may be reflected in particular knapping techniques, particular choices of raw materials or tool forms. These aspects of variation and others expressing activity differences and raw material constraints should be seen against a background of simple technical abilities and a limited tool repertoire shared by all groups.

We have noted that assemblages dated to the later part of the Middle Pleistocene show a definite increase in artefact elaboration and increased care in artefact manufacture. This is often taken as a sign that the technological diversification and economic specialization that characterize modern human cultures were beginning to appear. There is no consensus of opinion in this matter, however, since other prehistorians argue that Mousterian industries also lack the clear regional differences, evidence of rapid innovation behaviour and tight articulation between technology and environment that characterize the Upper Palaeolithic (Jelinek, 1977, p. 28, 1982, p. 1375; Bosinski and Jelinek, in Ronen, 1982; Trinkaus, 1986).

BONE AND WOODEN ARTEFACTS

Very few wooden artefacts from this time period have survived. The best studied and the oldest yet to be found is the broken end of a wooden spear found in 1911 at Clacton-on-Sea, in England, a locality dated to the Hoxnian interglacial, and the type locality of the Clactonian industry. This implement has a long, tapered end and a robust shaft, strongly suggesting that it was used as a thrusting or stabbing spear. Microscopic analysis showed that the point was shaped with stone tools that have left characteristic sets of striations. Use of fire for working wood is well known ethnographically but in this case fire was not used (Oakley et al., 1977).

According to L. Keeley (1977), microwear analyses of stone tools from Clacton, Hoxne and Swanscombe have shown that flakes, often unretouched, and choppers had been used on wood for a variety of tasks: planning, adzing, sawing, boring and wedging. Evidence for the use of stone tools to make wooden implements (such as spears, stakes, digging sticks or containers) may actually be very old: three tools used for scraping and sawing wood have been identified by Keeley and Toth (1981) in Oldowan assemblages from Koobi Fora, dated to 1.5 million years.

An interesting aspect of early industries is the use of bone to make flaked tools similar to those made of stone. During the Upper Palaeolithic bone, antler and ivory were extensively worked with a variety of techniques (grooving, sawing, drilling and polishing) to make projectile points, harpoons, spear-throwers, eyed needles and jewellery. The basic method of work in earlier times was percussion flaking only. Since well-shaped implements are very rare, positive identification of a bone tool has proved very difficult (Clark, 1977).

Similarities between carnivore breakage of bone, human breakage for marrow extraction and deliberate flaking for toolmaking have thrown considerable doubt on the reality of early bone tools (Brain, 1981; Binford, 1981; Freeman, 1983). Recently, however, elaborate bone bifaces have been found at a number of Italian sites: Castel di Guido (Plate 10; Radmilli, 1984, 1985), Malagrotta and Fontana Ranuccio; their regular shape and high degree of modification are undeniable proof of human manufacture and confirm what some people had always maintained, that early humans flaked bone by direct percussion and made tools comparable to the scrapers, awls or bifaces made of stone. Still, the great majority of bone or ivory 'tools' found at early sites show a very low degree of modification and flaking, so that problems of identification always arise. The most promising diagnostic criteria appear to be those based on wear traces, crushing damage to the working edge and traces left by the stone tools used to fashion the bone piece; experiments and microscopic analyses are the main lines of approach. Although bone or ivory tools (including points) have been described from many sites (such as Ambrona, Bilzingsleben, Salzgitter-Lebenstedt; Howell and Freeman, 1983), there is no doubt that stone was the preferred raw material. Bone is an excellent material for making pointed or spatulate tools; but when cutting or scraping edges are needed, stone is certainly better suited than bone. Thus it is often argued that bone was selected for chopping or scraping only because it was more readily to hand (Clark, 1977).

Bones modified by utilization or limited flaking have been reported from Olduvai (Leakey, 1971) and, more recently, from Sterkfontein and Swartkrans, where a total of twenty-five to thirty bone points have been recovered in recent excavations. Duplicating experiments and microscopic analyses suggest that they were used as digging-sticks, thus pushing the beginning of bone tools back to 1.5 million years ago (Brain, 1985).

ACKNOWLEDGEMENTS

I wish to thank Antonio M. Radmilli for providing a photograph of Castel di Guido. I am very grateful to S. J. De Laet for his constant encouragement and to Joachim Herrmann for very valuable critical comments. Any errors that may survive in the text are my own.

BIBLIOGRAPHY

ANDEL, T. H. VAN; SHACKLETON, J. C. 1982. Late Paleolithic and Mesolithic Coastlines of Greece and the Aegean. *J. Field Archaeol.*, Vol. 9, pp. 445–54.

ASCENZI, A.; SEGRE, A. G. 1971. A New Neanderthal Child Mandible from an Upper Pleistocene Site in Southern Italy. *Nature* (London), Vol. 233, pp. 280–3.

AZZAROLI, A. 1981. Cainozoic Mammals and the Biogeography of the Island of Sardinia, Western Mediterranean. *Paleogeogr. Paleoclimatol. Palaeoecol.* (Amsterdam), Vol. 36, pp. 107–11.

—— 1983. Quaternary Mammals and the 'End-Villafranchian' Dispersal Event: A Turning Point in the History of Eurasia. *Palaeogeogr. Palaeoclimatol. Palaeoecol.* (Amsterdam), Vol. 44, pp. 117–39.

BAR-YOSEF, O. 1984. Near East. In: BAR-YOSEF, O. et al. (eds), *Neue Forschungen zur Altsteinzeit.* Munich. Vol. 4, pp. 233–98.

BIANCHINI, G. 1973. Gli hacheraux nella Sicilia sud occidentale. [Cleavers in Southwest Sicily]. In: RIUNIONE SCIENTIFICA DELL' ISTITUTO ITALIANO DI PREISTORIA E PROTOSTORIA, 15, Florence. *Atti.* pp. 11–25.

BIDDITTU, I. et al. 1979. Anagni, a K–Ar Dated Lower and Middle Pleistocene Site, Central Italy – Preliminary Report. *Quaternaria* (Rome), Vol. 21, pp. 53–71.

BINFORD, L. R. 1972. Contemporary Model Building: Paradigms and the Current State of Palaeolithic Research. In: CLARKE, D. L. (ed.), *Models in Archaeology.* London. pp. 109–66.

—— 1981. *Bones: Ancient Men and Modern Myths.* New York.

—— 1982. Comments to Randall White's Paper. *Curr. Anthropol.*, Vol. 23, pp. 177–81.

—— 1983. *In Pursuit of the Past.* New York.

—— 1984. *Faunal Remains from Klasies River Mouth.* New York.

BLACKWELL, B.; SCHWARCZ, H. P.; DEBENATH, A. 1983. Absolute Dating of Hominids and Palaeolithic Artifacts of the Cave of La Chaise-de-Vouthon (Charente), France. *J. Archaeol. Sci.*, Vol. 10, pp. 493–513.

BONIFAY, E. et al. 1976a. Soleihac (Blanzac, Haute Loire), nouveau site préhistorique du début du Pleistocène moyen. *Bull. Soc. Préhist. Fr., Etud. Trav.*, Vol. 73, pp. 293–304.

—— 1976b. Grotte de l'Escale. In: LUMLEY, H. DE (ed.), *Livret-guide de l'excursion C2, Provence et Languedoc méditerranéen.* Nice. pp. 50–6. (IXth UISPP Congress, Nice.)

BORDES, F. 1968. *The Old Stone Age.* London.

BORDES, F.; THIBAULT, C. 1973. Thoughts on the Initial Adaptation of Hominids to European Glacial Climates. *Quat. Res.*, Vol. 8, pp. 115–27.

BOSINSKI, G. 1982. The Transition Lower/Middle Palaeolithic in Northwestern Germany. In: RONEN, A. (ed.), *The Transition from Lower to Middle Palaeolithic and the Origin of Modern Man.* Oxford. pp. 165–73. (BAR Int. Ser., 151.)

—— 1986. Chronostratigraphie du Paléolithique inférieur et moyen en Rhénanie. *Bull. Assoc. Fr. Étude Quat.*, Vol. 26, Suppl., pp. 15–34.

BOUCHUD, J. 1976. La Chasse. In: LUMLEY, H. DE (ed.), *La Préhistoire française.* Paris, CNRS. Vol. I, Part I, pp. 688–96.

BRAIN, C. K. 1981. *The Hunters or the Hunted?* Chicago.

—— 1985. Cultural and Taphonomic Comparisons of Hominids from Swartkrans and Sterkfontein. In: DELSON, E. (ed.), *Ancestors: The Hard Evidence.* New York. pp. 72–5.

BRUNNACKER, K. 1975. The Mid-Pleistocene of the Rhine Basin. In: BUTZER, K. W.; ISAAC, G. L. (eds), *After the Australopithecines*. The Hague. pp. 198–324.

BUNN, H. 1982. *Meat Eating and Human Evolution*. Berkeley. (Ph.D. Dissertation, University of California.)

CLARK, J. D. 1975. A Comparison of Late Acheulian Industries of Africa and the Middle East. In: BUTZER, K. W.; ISAAC, G. L. (eds), *After the Australopithecines*. The Hague. pp. 605–60.

—— 1977. Bone Tools of the Earlier Pleistocene. *Eretz-Isr.* (Jerusalem), Vol. 13, pp. 23–27.

COLLINS, D. M. 1969. Culture Traditions and Environment of Early Man. *Curr. Anthropol.*, Vol. 10, pp. 267–316.

COLTORTI, M. et al. 1982. Reversed Magnetic Polarity at an Early Lower Paleolithic Site in Central Italy. *Nature* (London), Vol. 300, pp. 173–6.

COOK, J. et al. 1982. A Review of the Chronology of the European Middle Pleistocene Record. *Yearb. Phys. Anthropol.*, Vol. 25, pp. 19–66.

DAVIS, R. S.; RANOV, R. A.; DODONOV, A. E. 1980. Early Man in Soviet Central Asia. *Sci. Am.*, Vol. 243, pp. 130–7.

DELSON, E. 1985. Palaeobiology and Age of African *Homo erectus*. *Nature* (London), Vol. 316, pp. 762–3.

DENNELL, R. 1983. *European Economic Prehistory*. London.

DOLUKHANOV, P. M. 1982. Upper Pleistocene and Holocene Cultures of the Russian Plain and Caucasus: Ecology, Economy and Settlement. *Advances in World Archaeology*, Vol. 1, pp. 323–58.

EDWARDS, S. W.; CLINNICK, R. W. 1980. Keeping the Lower Palaeolithic in Perspective. *Man* (London), Vol. 15, pp. 381–2.

FEJFAR, O. 1969. Human Remains from the Early Pleistocene in Czechoslovakia. *Curr. Anthropol.*, Vol. 10, pp. 170–3.

—— 1976. Recent Research at Prezletice. *Curr. Anthropol.*, Vol. 17, pp. 343 ff.

FINK, J.; KUKLA, G. J. 1977. Pleistocene Climates in Central Europe: At Least 17 Interglacials After the Olduvai Event. *Quat. Res.*, Vol. 7, pp. 363–71.

FLOHN, H. 1979. On Time-Scales and Causes of Abrupt Palaeo-climatic Events. *Quat. Res.*, Vol. 12, No. 1, pp. 135–49.

FREEMAN, L. G. 1975. Acheulian Sites and Stratigraphy in Iberia and the Maghreb. In: BUTZER, K. W.; ISAAC, G. L. (eds), *After the Australopithecines*. The Hague. pp. 661–774.

—— 1983. More on the Mousterian: Flaked Bone from Cueva Morín. *Curr. Anthropol.*, Vol. 24, pp. 366–76.

GAMBASSINI, P.; RONCHITELLI, A. 1982. L'industria arcaica su ciottolo di Casella di Maida [Early Pebble Tools from Casella di Maida]. *Riv. Sci. Preistor.* (Florence), Vol. 37, Nos. 1–2, pp. 3–30.

GENESTE, J. M. 1985. *Analyse lithique d'industries moustériennes du Périgord: une approche technologique du comportement des groupes humains du Paléolithique moyen*. Bordeaux. (Doct. thesis, Université de Bordeaux 1.)

GIFFORD, D. P. 1984. Ethnographic Analogues for Interpreting Modified Bones: The View from East Africa. In: INTERNATIONAL BONE MODIFICATION CONFERENCE, *Proceedings*. Carson City, Nev.

GIFFORD, D. P.; BEHRENSMEYER, A. K. 1977. Observed Formation and Burial of a Recent Human Occupation Site in Kenya. *Quat. Res.*, Vol. 8, pp. 245–66.

GREEN, H. S. et al. 1981. Pontnewydd Cave in Wales: A New Middle Pleistocene Hominid Site. *Nature* (London), Vol. 294, pp. 707–13.

GUTH, C.; CHAVAILLON, J. 1985. Découverte en 1984 de nouveaux outils paléolithiques à Chilhac III (Haute-Loire). *Bull. Soc. Préhist. Fr.*, Vol. 82, No. 2, pp. 56–64.

HARMON, R. S.; GLAZEK, J.; NOWAK, K. 1980. ^{230}Th/^{234}U Dating of Travertine from the Bilzingsleben Archaeological Site. *Nature* (London), Vol. 284, pp. 132–5.

HAYNES, G. 1983. Frequencies of Spiral and Green Bone Fractures on Ungulate Limb Bones in Modern Surface Assemblages. *Am. Antiq.*, Vol. 48, pp. 102–14.

HOWELL, F. C.; FREEMAN, L. G. 1983. Ivory Points from the Earlier Acheulian of the Spanish Meseta. In: *Homenaje al Prof. Martin Almagro Basch*. Madrid, Ministerio de Cultura. pp. 41–62.

ISAAC, G. L. 1975. Sorting out the Muddle in the Middle. In: BUTZER, K. W.; ISAAC, G. L. (eds), *After the Australopithecines*. The Hague. pp. 875–88.

—— 1984. The Archaeology of Human Origins: Studies of the Lower Pleistocene in East Africa 1971–1981. In: WENDORF, F.; CLOSE, A. (eds), *Advances in World Archaeology*. Vol. 3, pp. 1–87.

JAEGER, J. J. 1975. The Mammalian Faunas and Hominid Fossils of the Middle Pleistocene of the Maghreb. In: BUTZER, K. W.; ISAAC, G. L. (eds), *After the Australopithecines*. The Hague. pp. 399–418.

JELINEK, A. J. 1977. The Lower Palaeolithic: Current Evidence and Interpretations. *Annu. Rev. Anthropol.*, Vol. 6, pp. 11–32.

—— 1982. The Tabun Cave and Paleolithic Man in the Levant. *Science* (Washington), Vol. 216, pp. 1369–75.

KEELEY, L. H. 1977. *Experimental Determination of Stone Tool Uses*. Chicago.

KEELEY, L. H.; TOTH, N. 1981. Microwear Polishes on Early Stone Tools from Koobi Fora, Kenya. *Nature* (London), Vol. 293, pp. 464–5.

KRETZOI, M.; VÉRTES, L. 1965. Upper Biharian (Intermindel) Pebble-Industry Occupation Site in Western Hungary. *Curr. Anthropol.*, Vol. 6, pp. 74–87.

KUKLA, G. J. 1975. Loess Stratigraphy of Central Europe. In: BUTZER, K. W.; ISAAC, G. L. (eds), *After the Australopithecines*. The Hague. pp. 99–188.

KUKLA, G. J.; NAKAGAWA, H. 1977. Late-Cenozoic Magneto-stratigraphy. *Quat. Res.*, Vol. 3, pp. 283–93.

KURTEN, B.; ANDERSON, E. 1980. *Pleistocene Mammals of North America*. New York.

LEAKEY, M. D. 1971. *Olduvai Gorge: Excavations in Beds I and II, 1960–1963*. Cambridge.

LEBEL, S. 1984. *La Caune de l'Arago: étude des assemblages lithique d'une grotte du Pleistocène Moyen*. Paris. (Thesis for 3rd cycle, Université de Paris.)

LIOUBIN, V. P.; BARYCHNIKOV, G. F. 1984. L'Activité de chasse des plus anciens habitants du Caucase. *Anthropologie* (Paris), Vol. 88, pp. 221–9.

LIU ZECHUN. 1985. Sequence of Sediments at Locality 1 in Zhou-koudian and Correlation with Loess Stratigraphy in Northern China and with the Chronology of Deep-Sea Cores. *Quat. Res.*, Vol. 23, pp. 139–53.

LUMLEY, H. DE. 1967. Découverte d'habitats de l'Acheuléen ancien dans des dépôts mindéliens sur le site de Terra Amata (Nice, Alpes-Maritimes). *C. R. Acad. Sci.* (Paris), Ser. D, Vol. 264, pp. 801–4.

—— 1969a. A Paleolithic Camp at Nice. *Sci. Am.*, Vol. 220, pp. 42–50.

—— (ed.) 1969b. Une cabane acheuléenne dans la grotte du Lazaret. Paris. (Mém. Soc. Préhist. Fr., 7.)

—— 1975. Cultural Evolution in France in its Palaeoecological Setting during the Middle Pleistocene. In: BUTZER, K. W.; ISAAC, G. L. (eds), *After the Australopithecines*. The Hague. pp. 745–808.

—— 1976a. Les Civilizations du Paléolithique inférieur en Provence. In: LUMLEY, H. DE (ed.), *La Préhistoire française*. Paris, CNRS. Vol. 1, Part 2, pp. 819–51.

—— 1976b. Les Premières Industries humaines en Provence. In: LUMLEY, H. DE (ed.), *La Préhistoire française*. Paris, CNRS. Vol. 1, Part 2, pp. 756–65.

LUMLEY, H. DE et al. 1979. Les Industries lithiques de l'homme de Tautavel. *Doss. Archéol.*, Vol. 36, pp. 60–9.

LUMLEY, H. DE et al. 1984. Stratigraphie du remplissage Pleistocène moyen de la Caume de l'Arago: étude de huit carottages effectués de 1981 à 1983. *Anthropologie* (Paris), Vol. 88, pp. 5–18.

MALEZ, M. 1976. Excavation of the Villafranchian Site Sandalja I near Pula (Yugoslavia). In: VALOCH, K. (ed.), *Les Premières Industries de l'Europe*. Nice. pp. 104–23. (IXth UISPP Congress, Nice. Colloque VIII.)

MOIGNE, A.-M. 1983. *Taphonomie des faunes quaternaires de la Caume de l'Arago, Tautavel*. Paris. (Thesis for 2nd cycle, Université de Paris 6.)

MOURER-CHAUVIRÉ, C.; RENAULT-MISKOVSKY, J. 1980. Le Paléo-environnement des chasseurs de Terra Amata (Nice) au Pleistocène moyen: La Flore et la faune de grands mammifères. *Geobios* (Lyons), Vol. 13, pp. 279–87.

NILSSON, T. 1983. *The Pleistocene*. Boston.

OAKLEY, K. P. et al. 1977. A Reappraisal of the Clacton Spearpoint. *Proc. Prehist. Soc.*, Vol. 43, pp. 13–30.

PIPERNO, M. 1972. The Monte Peglia Lithic Industry. *Quaternaria* (Rome), Vol. 16, pp. 53–65.

POTTS, R. 1986. Temporal Span of Bone Accumulations at Olduvai Gorge and Implications for Early Hominid Foraging Behavior. *Paleobiology* (Jacksonville, NY), Vol. 12, pp. 25–31.

QUEROL, M. A.; SANTOJA, M. 1983. *El yacimiento de cantos trabajados de el Aculadero*. Madrid.

RADMILLI, A. M. 1984. Quinta campagna di scavo nella stazione del Paleolitico Inferiore a Castel di Guido presso Roma. *Atti Soc. Tosana Sci. Nat., Pisa Mem.*, Vol. 91, pp. 369–75.

—— 1985. Scavi nel giacimento del Paleolitico Inferiore di Castel di Guido presso Roma. In: SOPRINTENDENZA ARCHAEOLOGICA DI ROMA. *Preistoria e Protostoria nel territorio di Roma*. Rome. pp. 75–85.

ROBERTS, N. 1984. Pleistocene Environments in Time and Space. In: FOLEY, R. (ed.), *Hominid Evolution and Community Ecology*. New York. pp. 25–53.

ROE, D. A. 1981. *The Lower and Middle Palaeolithic Periods in Britain*. London.

RONEN, A. (ed.) 1982. *The Transition from Lower to Middle Paleolithic and the Origin of Modern Man*. Oxford. (BAR Int. Ser., 151.)

RUDDIMAN, W. R.; MCINTYRE, A. 1982. Severity and Speed of Northern Hemisphere Glaciation Pulses: The Limiting Case? *Bull. Geol. Soc. Am.* (Rochester, NY), Vol. 93, pp. 1273–9.

SANTOJA, M. 1982/4. Situación actual de la investigación del Paleolítico inferior en la cuenca media del Duero. *Portugalia* (Lisbon), Vol. 4/5, pp. 27–35.

SANTOJA, M.; LOPES MARTINEZ, N.; PEREZ-GONZALEZ, A. 1980. *Ocupaciones achelenses en el valle del Jarama*. Madrid.

SANTOJA, M.; PEREZ-GONZALEZ, A. 1984. *Las industrias paleolíticas de la Maya I en su ambito regional*. Madrid.

SCHICK, K. D. 1984. *Processes of Paleolithic Site Formation*. Berkeley. (Ph.D. dissertation, University of California.)

SCOTT, K. 1980. Two Hunting Episodes of Middle Paleolithic Age at La Cotte de Saint-Brelade, Jersey (Channel Islands). *World Archaeol.*, Vol. 12, pp. 137–52.

—— 1984. Hunter-Gatherers and Large Mammals in Glacial Britain. In: FOLEY, R. (ed.), *Hominid Evolution and Community Ecology*. New York. pp. 219–36.

SHACKLETON, J. V.; ANDEL, T. H. VAN; RUNNELS, C. N. 1984. Coastal Palaeogeography of the Central and Western Mediterranean during the Last 125,000 years and its Archaeological Implications. *J. Field Archaeol.*, Vol. 11, pp. 307–14.

SHACKLETON, N. J. 1975. The Stratigraphic Record of Deep-Sea Cores and its Implications for the Assessment of Glacials, Interglacials, Stadials and Interstadials in the Mid-Pleistocene. In: BUTZER, K. W.; ISAAC, G. L. (eds), *After the Australopithecines*. The Hague. pp. 1–24.

SHACKLETON, N. J.; OPDYKE, N. D. 1976. Oxygen-Isotope and Paleomagnetic Stratigraphy of Pacific Core V28–239: Late Pliocene to Latest Pleistocene. *Mem. Geol. Soc. Am.*, Vol. 145, pp. 449–64.

SHIPMAN, P. 1981. Applications of Scanning Electron Microscopy to Taphonomic Problems. In: CANTWELL, A. M.; GRIFFIN, J. B.; ROTHSCHILD, N. (eds), *The Research Potential of Anthropological Museum Collections*. New York. pp. 357–85. (Ann. NY Acad. Sci., 376.)

—— 1983. Early Hominid Lifestyle: Hunting and Gathering or Foraging and Scavenging? In: CLUTTON-BROCK, J.; GRIGSON, C. (eds), *Animals and Archaeology: Hunters and their Prey*. Oxford. pp. 51–62. (BAR Int. Ser.)

SHIPMAN, P.; ROSE, J. 1983. Evidence of Butchery and Hominid Activities at Torralba and Ambrona: An Evaluation using Microscopic Techniques. *J. Archaeol. Sci.*, Vol. 10, pp. 465–74.

SINGER, R.; WYMER, J. J. 1978. A Hand-Axe from Northwest Iran: The Question of Human Movement between Africa and Asia in the Lower Paleolithic Period. In: FREEMAN, L. G. (ed.), *Views of the Past*. The Hague. pp. 13–28.

SONDAAR, P. Y. et al. 1984. First Report of a Palaeolithic Culture in Sardinia. In: WALDREN, W. L. et al. (eds), *Early Settlements in the Western Mediterranean Islands and the Peripheral Areas*. Oxford. pp. 29–47. (BAR Int. Ser.)

SOPRINTENDENZA ARCHEOLOGICA DEL MOLISE. 1983. *Isernia la Pineta*. Bologna.

SOPRINTENDENZA SPECIALE DEL MUSEO PIGORINI. 1984. *I primi abitanti d'Europa*. Rome.

STRINGER, C. B. 1985. Middle Pleistocene Hominid Variability and the Origin of Late Pleistocene Humans. In: DELSON, E. (ed.), *Ancestors: The Hard Evidence*. New York. pp. 289–95.

STRINGER, C. B.; HUBLIN, J. J.; VANDERMEERSCH, B. 1984. The Origin of Anatomically Modern Humans in Western Europe. In: SMITH, F. H.; SPENCER, F. (eds), *The Origin of Modern Humans: A World Survey of the Fossil Evidence*. New York. pp. 51–135.

SVOBODA, J. 1984. Cadre chronologique et tendances évolutives du Paléolithique tchécoslovaque: essai de synthèse. *Anthropologie* (Paris), Vol. 88, pp. 169–72.

SZABO, B. J.; COLLINS, D. 1975. Ages of Fossil Bones from British Interglacial Sites. *Nature* (London), Vol. 254, pp. 680–1.

TAVOSO, A. 1978. *Le Paléolithique inférieur et moyen du Haut Languedoc*. Marseille. (Doct. thesis, Université de Provence.)

TEXIER, P. J. 1985. Chilhac III: un gisement paléontologique villafranchien soliflué? *Bull. Soc. Préhist. Fr.*, Vol. 82, pp. 68–70.

THOUVENY, N.; BONIFAY, E. 1984. New Chronological Data on European Plio-Pleistocene Faunas and Hominid Occupation Sites. *Nature* (London), Vol. 308, pp. 355–8.

TOTH, N. P. 1982. *The Stone Technology of Early Hominids at Koobi Fora: An Experimental Approach*. Berkeley. (Ph.D. dissertation, University of California.)

—— 1985. The Oldowan Reassessed: A Close Look at Early Stone Artifacts. *J. Archaeol. Sci.*, Vol. 12, pp. 101–20.

TRINKAUS, E. 1986. The Neanderthals and Modern Human Origins. *Ann. Rev. Anthropol.*, Vol. 15, pp. 193–218.

TUFFREAU, A. 1979. Les Débuts du Paléolithique moyen dans la France septentrionale. *Bull. Soc. Préhist. Fr.*, Vol. 76, pp. 140–2.

—— 1982. The Transition Lower/Middle Palaeolithic in Northern France. In: RONEN, A. (ed.), *The Transition from Lower to Middle Palaeolithic and the Origin of Modern Man*. Oxford. pp. 137–49. (BAR Int. Ser.)

TUFFREAU, A. et al. 1982a. Stratigraphie et environnement de la séquence archéologique de Biache-Saint-Vaast (Pas-de-Calais). *Bull. Assoc. Fr. Étude Quat.* (Paris), Vol. 19, pp. 57–61.

—— 1982b. Stratigraphie et environnement des industries acheuléennes de la moyenne terrasse du bassin de la Somme (région d'Amiens). *Bull. Assoc. Fr. Étude Quat.* (Paris), Vol. 19, pp. 73–82.

—— 1986. Les Niveaux acheuléens de la moyenne terrasse du bassin de la Somme à Cagny-l'Epinette (Somme). *Anthropologie* (Paris), Vol. 90, pp. 9–27.

TURNER, A. 1984. Hominids and Fellow Travellers: Human Migration into High Latitudes as Part of a Large Mammal Community. In: FOLEY, R. (ed.), *Hominid Evolution and Community Ecology*. New York. pp. 193–218.

US DEFENSE MAPPING AGENCY. 1971. *Mediterranean Sea, Bathymetric Map*. Washington, DC.

VALOCH, K. 1976. Aperçu des premières industries en Europe. In: VALOCH, K. (ed.), *Les Premières Industries de l'Europe*. Nice. pp. 178–83. (IXth Congress, Nice. Colloque VIII.)

—— 1984. Le Taubachien, sa géochronologie, paléoécologie et paléoethnologie. *Anthropologie* (Paris), Vol. 88, pp. 193–208.

VILLA, P. 1976. Sols et niveaux d'habitat du paléolithique inférieur en Europe et au Proche Orient. *Quaternaria* (Rome), Vol. 19, pp. 107–34.

—— 1978. *The Stone Artifact Assemblage from Terra Amata: A Contribution to the Comparative Study of Acheulian Industries in South-Western Europe*. (Ph.D. dissertation, University of California, Berkeley.)

—— 1981. Matières premières et provinces culturelles dans l'Acheuléen français. *Quaternaria* (Rome), Vol. 23, pp. 19–35.

—— 1982. Conjoinable Pieces and Site Formation Processes. *Am. Antiq.*, Vol. 47, pp. 276–90.

—— 1983. *Terra Amata and the Middle Pleistocene Archaeological Record of Southern France*. Berkeley/Los Angeles.

VILLA, P.; COURTIN, J. 1983. The Interpretation of Stratified Sites: A View from Underground. *J. Archaeol. Sci.*, Vol. 10, pp. 267–81.

VLCEK, E. 1978. Diagnosis of a Fragment of the 'Hominid' Molar from Přezletice, Czechoslovakia. *Curr. Anthropol.*, Vol. 19, pp. 145–6.

WATANABE, H. 1985. The Chopper–Chopping Tool Complex of Eastern Asia: An Ethnoarchaeological–Ecological Reexamination. *J. Anthropol. Archaeol.* (New York), Vol. 4, pp. 1–18.

WILSON, L. 1986. *Archéopétrographie des industries du Paléolithique inférieur de la Caume de l'Arago (Tautavel, France): identification et provenance des roches*. Paris. (Thesis for 3rd cycle, Université de Paris 6.)

5

WESTERN ASIA

in the period of *Homo habilis* and *Homo erectus*

Francis Hours, SJ

Whereas in Africa we have tools going back more than 2 million years, an absolutely reliable chronology based on material laid down by near-permanent volcanic activity, and long archaeological sequences that facilitate the fairly detailed reconstruction of the development of toolmaking, western Asia seems to be much less promising at first.

By 'western Asia' we mean modern Iran, Iraq, Turkey, Syria, Lebanon and Israel, together with the countries constituting the Arabian peninsula. These territories cover several clearly distinct and major geographical regions. Behind the Mediterranean shore, the African Rift is continued by the Wadi Araba, the Dead Sea, the Jordan valley, the Litani, the Lebanese Beqa'a, the Orontes (Asi) and the Kara Su in the Turkish Taurus mountains (Toros Daglari). Framed by its two raised eastern and western borders, this complex tectonic accident constitutes a barrier to western climatic influences and is partly responsible for the eastern deserts. However, it also provides an access route and one that has facilitated the settlement of the Levant. By contrast, the mountainous arc constituted by the Taurus and Zagros ranges was an obstacle difficult to surmount during the beginnings of prehistory: the Anatolian and Iranian plateaux to its rear were not populated during the period that concerns us here. Moreover, intense aggradation of the Euphrates and Tigris valleys has blanketed everything south of Baghdad, and we can say nothing about what happened here during the Early and Middle Pleistocene. But there is evidence that the central part of these valleys was inhabited, from the edge of the mountains up to the emergence of two rivers in Upper Mesopotamia.

In western Asia, the period that concerns us here and which ends with the appearance of *Homo sapiens neanderthalensis* about 100,000 years ago has yielded hardly any radiocarbon dates or human fossils. It is therefore impossible to fit the prehistoric industries discovered there into any but a relative chronology, based essentially on the succession of climatic events as laid down in stratigraphy and geomorphology (Perrot, 1968; Gilead, 1969; Hours et al. 1973; Tomsky, 1982).

THE CHRONO-STRATIGRAPHIC FRAMEWORK (Table 3)

The essential chrono-stratigraphic data are provided by the marine levels that P. Sanlaville has defined on the Lebanese coast (Sanlaville, 1977). The many ancient shore-lines reflect multiple fluctuations in sea-level that fit into five successions, including the present shore-line. The associated deposits have been numbered Qm 0, Qm I, Qm II, Qm III, and Qm IV (meaning marine Quaternary 0, I, II, III and IV) and have been given local names (Sanlaville, 1981). Qm 0 relates to the Holocene complex and does not concern us here.

Qm I is very important: it provides an anchor point for the entire series. The associated interglacial has left several shore-lines, one of which contains an abundance of *Strombus bubonius* (Lmk), gastropod shells nowadays found in the hot waters of the Senegalese coast. Uranium–thorium dating of these shells has provided one of the rare dates we have for the Levantine Palaeolithic; on several occasions, their age has been put at about 90,000 years (Stearns and Thurber, 1965; Arlette Leroi-Gourhan, 1980).

Qm I is the local manifestation of the Tyrrhenian interglacial, here represented by four fluctuations in two main phases: the Enfehan and the Naamian. The Enfehan, the older of the two, corresponds to period 7 of oxygen–isotope chronology (Opdyke and Shackleton, 1976), that is, to the period from 250,000 to 200,000 years ago, and is said to be separated from the Naamian by period 6 (200,000–130,000 years ago) representing a glacial. The Naamian with its strombi marks the beginning of the relatively complex temperate/warm episode of period 5. The emergence of the Middle Palaeolithic proper coincides with the middle of period 5. Within this pattern, one is led to admit a very long period of continental deposits for Qf II, which is rather puzzling.

A marine regression corresponds to the first part of the penultimate glaciation (periods 8–12) and was preceded by an important transgression (Qm II) known as the Jbaylian after the modern name – Jbayl – of ancient Byblos. The Jbaylian comes in two transgressive movements (periods 13 and 15 of Opdyke and Shackleton) separated by a regression reflecting a small glacial fluctuation (period 14).

A more important regression separates the Jbaylian shores from another, older marine level. It corresponds to a glacial complex (periods 22 to 16) that left fluvial deposits in which it was possible to detect the Matuyama–Brunhes reversal of the earth's magnetic polarity (approximately 730,000 years ago).

The oldest shore-line containing prehistoric implements

Table 3 Western Asia: chronological table (oceanic phases, geological formations, archaeological sites and industries).

Epoch	Oceanic phases 1000A	Curve	No.	Formations		Sites	Industries	
Holocene							Neolithic	
Pleistocene — Upper	10		1					
	25		2	Jraimakiyeh	Qf I	Ksar Akil Al-Wad	Upper Palaeolithic	
			3	Esh Shir b		Tabun B		Levalloiso-Mousterian
	75		4	Esh Shir a		Tabun C / Tabun D / Naahmeh	Middle Palaeolithic	
	90		5	Naamian	Qm I	Hummal (Ia) / Adlun	Transitional	Blade industries
	115							Final Jabrudian Acheulean
	130		6			Hummal (Ib) / Yabrud / Zutiyeh		
	195							
			7	Enfehan		Ma'ayan Baruch / Gharmashi (IB)		Late Acheulean
Pleistocene — Middle	250		8	Ain Abu Jamaa	Qf II	Ain Abu Jamaa / Rudo / Jraibiyate / Bireh		Late Acheulean
	280		9					
	310		10					
	350							
	390		11					
	450		12					
			13	Jbaylian II	Qm II	Offshore bar / Khellaleh / Wadi Aabet / Ras Beirut (Ia)		
			14	Jbaylian I				
			15					Lower Palaeolithic (Middle Acheulean)
	590		16	Arbain	Qf III (Latamneh)	Berzin	Lower Palaeolithic	
	650		17	Miramil		Latamneh (floor) / Evron I (quarry) / Jisr B. Ya'qub		
			18					
			19					
			20					
	750		21					
			22	Sharia		Jubb Jannin		
	850		23	Zaqrunian III	Qm III	Burj Qinnarit		Lower Palaeolithic (Early Acheulean)
			24	Zaqrunian II		Shaikh Muhammad		
			25	Zaqrunian I		Jabal Idriss		
	1000		26	Sitt Markho	Qf IV (Ubaidiya)	Sitt Markho / Khaattab		
Pleistocene — Lower			27					
			28					
			29					
			30					
			31					

Curve sources: (Ruddiman et al., 1980); (Shackleton and Opdyke, 1976) is well represented at Zaqrun on the Lebanese coast. The Zaqrunian seems to have been subjected to three fluctuations by a transgressive sea (periods 23, 24 and 25).

During regressions – resulting from world-wide glaciation during which water is stored in solid form instead of feeding the seas – western Asia as a whole had a humid climate which gave the rivers enough power to move considerable masses of sediment. These were deposited in terraces whose succession we can specify both along small coastal rivers (the Nahr Al-Kabir in northern Syria) and also on such important rivers as the Orontes and the middle Euphrates. Even small permanent rivers in the interior, for instance the Zarqa in Jordan, still bear witness to these climatic fluctuations. Like the marine Quaternary, the continental Quaternary gave rise to a complex, the various formations of which can be fitted into four main phases (Besançon, 1981).

The first, Qf I, corresponds to the last pluvio-glacial period and is sharply subdivided on the Nahr Al-Kabir at Esh-Shir and Jraimakiyeh (Syria). It is important on the Zarqa in Jordan, near Khirbet es Samra, where the deposits contain Middle and Upper Palaeolithic remains. Qf I falls outside the scope of this chapter. The second phase (Qf II) is visible along all the Levantine rivers (the Zarqa in Jordan, the Abu Ali in Lebanon, the Nahr Al-Kabir in Syria) and also the Euphrates and the Orontes. Exceptionally well preserved on the Euphrates, it has been named after the locality where it is most prominent, namely Ain Abu Jamaa. It contains deposits the most highly evolved elements of which are Late Acheulean.

The preceding formation (Qf III) was extremely important and covers a considerable time interval. Along such major rivers as the Euphrates, and even along the Litani and the Jordan to the south of the central trough, it has been completely dislodged by Qf II. But in the north of the Levant, on the Nahr Al-Kabir and the Orontes it has stood up well to erosion. Thick terraces bear witness to its presence; they contain Middle Acheulean deposits, including the Latamneh occupation floor. It has accordingly been called the 'Latamneh Formation'. It combines different facies, and corresponds to periods 22 to 16 of the oxygen isotope chronology of Opdyke and Shackleton (1976).

Traces of old continental deposits (Qf IV) are extremely rare. At one point, however, at Sitt Markho on the Nahr Al-Kabir, they are clearly visible and have accordingly been named after this site. Stratigraphic and geomorphological arguments suggest that they must be anterior to the Matuyama–Brunhes magnetic polarity reversal and that the Acheulean remains contained in them must be of Early Acheulean origin.

By way of an exception, on a point along the Syrian coast, close to the mouth of the Nahr Al-Kabir near Latakia, marine and continental deposits have been sandwiched together so as to allow the construction of a reliable sequence (Table 3), which provides a framework for the study of the Levantine Lower Palaeolithic.

THE EARLY LOWER PALAEOLITHIC
(Map 5 and Fig. 3)

It is with the early Lower Palaeolithic that we must start our prehistory of western Asia, for we have no solid evidence of the presence of *Homo habilis* during an early, pre-Acheulean, Palaeolithic. True, industries without bifacial handaxes have been found (Ariai and Thibault, 1975–7; Hours and San-laville, 1972), or are thought to have been found (Stekelis,

1966; Stekelis et al., 1969), and these industries have been more or less deliberately correlated with the earlier chopper-tool tradition. In fact, geologically dated evidence makes them of late Lower Pleistocene provenance, taking us to a period when *Homo erectus* and the Acheulean had long been established in Africa and when the Early Palaeolithic had already disappeared.

The early deposits of the greatest importance, thanks to the number of levels and artefacts involved, are those at Ubeidiya (Goren, 1981, where can be found the complete bibliography), south of Lake Tiberias. Here four formations, each containing several strata, have been identified. They are alternately marshy and pluviatile, have been named Li, Fi, Lu, and Fu and have been fitted into two cycles. The whole complex is anterior to the Matuyama/Brunhes reversal of the earth's magnetic polarity, older than the 'Yarmuk Basalt', which goes back 650,000 years, but more recent than the 'Cover Basalt', dating back 2 million years. The site is a difficult one because the strata have been scrambled by particularly vigorous neotectonic activity, so that the various borings are difficult to reconcile. It seems likely that the site was occupied, no doubt intermittently, during a long time interval. The succession of four sedimentary formations, implying major climatic changes, cannot have been a brief process. The fauna, which has been studied globally and not level by level (Bar-Yosef and Tchernov, 1972; a new analysis of the Ubeidiya fauna was made in 1986) gives the same impression.

The first archaeologists to explore the site gave concrete expression to this interpretation by their classification of the implements they found. They thought they could distinguish a pre-Acheulean phase, namely an Israel variant of Oldowan II culture (IVO II), followed by a primitive Acheulean phase which they called Abbevillian – an Israel variant of Abbevillian culture (IVA) (Stekelis, 1966). Today, archaeologists prefer to stress the homogeneity of the various assemblages found in the numerous strata and to assign them to a single tradition (Goren, 1981). The implements include bifaces, trihedrons and tetrahedrons, choppers, and massive planes and large scrapers, polyhedrons and spheroids as well as light-duty tools made on flakes (Fig. 3). The African affinities of this typology are very clear and the Ubeidiyan assemblages are now attributed to an Early Acheulean said to fall within the Oldowan tradition. The state of preservation and the patina suggest that certain levels must have been authentic habitation floors. Humans seem to have lived on the shores of the old Lake Ubeidiya, searching for the raw materials – basalt, flint and limestone – needed to fashion certain implements in the preferred way (all the spheroids were made of limestone) and, among other activities, hunting big game. All this fits in well with what we know about *Homo erectus* and, in any case, with the suggested date of 1 million years ago. Because of its stratigraphic position and age, the presence of occupation floors and the profusion and variety of its implements, the Ubeidiya assemblage is unique in western Asia.

Elsewhere, sites that might go back to the Acheulean are very rare. One of the most interesting, though incomparably less important than Ubeidiya, is Sitt Markho on the Syrian coast, at the mouth of the Nahr Al-Kabir, near Latakia (Copeland and Hours, 1979). Packed into a fluviatile terrace perched 110 m above the present course of the river, there was found a rather sparse assemblage of ninety artefacts, including seventeen implements which in turn included three bifaces, two hatchets and seven choppers (Fig. 3). The stratigraphic position of the formation, older than the

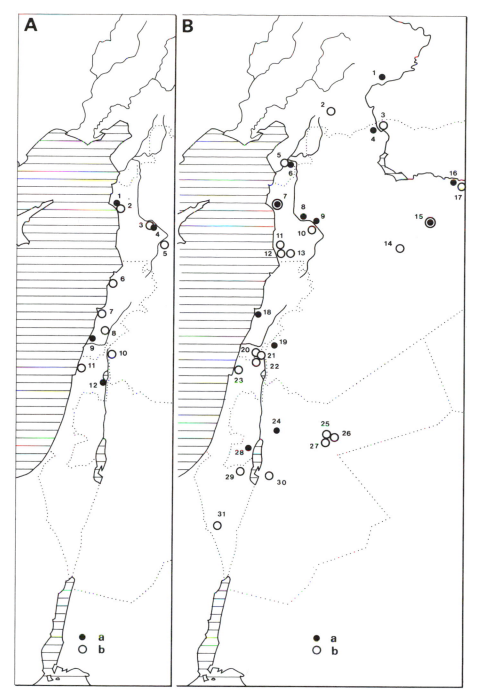

Map 5 Western Asia – A, Early and Middle Lower Palaeolithic sites: a, Early Acheulean; b, Middle Acheulean. 1, Sitt Markho; 2, Khellaleh; 3, Latamneh; 4, Khattab; 5, Rastan; 6, Wadi Aabet; 7, Ras Beyrut; 8, Jubb Jannin; 9, Burj Qinnarit; 10, Jisr banat Ya'qub; 11, Evron; 12, Ubeidiya. B, Late Lower Palaeolithic sites: a, Late Acheulean; b, Advanced Late Acheulean, 1, Sehremuz; 2, Duluk; 3, Tellik; 4, Sajur; 5, Altinozu; 6, Altindereh; 7, Rudo; 8, Aacharneh; 9, Jraibiyat; 10, Gharmashi Ib; 11, Ard Hamed; 12, Muqaa Al-Hami; 13, Q. Yahmur; 14, Duara; 15, Al-Kowm; 16, Ain Abu Jamaa; 17, Abu Chahri; 18, Ras Beyrut; 19, Birket Ram; 20, Mudawwara; 21, Ma'ayan Baruch; 22, Nahal Dishon; 23, Evron; 24, Bireh; 25, O. Rattama; 26, O. Uweinid; 27, O. Kharaneh; 28, Umm Qatafa; 29, Yatir; 30, Fjaje; 31, Ramad Matred.

Middle Pleistocene of Latamneh, probably makes it contemporary with Ubeidiya. Though not very ample, the assemblage seems clearly Acheulean, more particularly of Early Acheulean origin.

Along the Orontes, in the same geomorphological situation, several sites – Meharde, Khattab and Al-Farshe – have yielded flakes and choppers going back to the same early stage of the Lower Palaeolithic (Besançon et al., 1978). There are no bifaces, but the dispersion of the sites and the rarity of the artefacts are such that we can say little more about the subject.

The marine regression that caused the accumulation of the Sitt Markho terrace was followed by the so-called Zaqrunian transgression (Table 3), whose beaches yielded several dispersed assemblages which, because of their position, must also be attributed to an early Lower Palaeolithic, but one that is later than that of Ubeidiya and Sitt Markho. On the mouth of the Nahr Al-Kabir; the sites of Sheikh Muhammad, Fidio and Jabal Idriss (Copeland and Hours, 1979) have yielded Early Acheulean artefacts including less lanceolate and somewhat larger bifaces, their shapes still thick but tending to the oval or the almond-shaped – the beginning

65

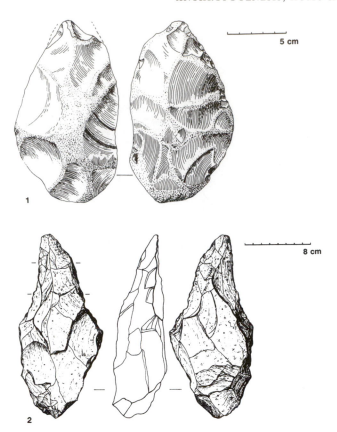

Figure 3 Early Acheulean artefacts. 1, Sitt Markho (Syria); 2, Ubeidiya (Israel).

of a tradition that would last until the end of the Lower Palaeolithic.

Whereas the Nahr Al-Kabir assemblages unquestionably belong to an Acheulean phase, the seventeen artefacts discovered at Burj Qinnarit, a little north of Saïda in Lebanon, are very difficult to classify (Hours and Sanlaville, 1972). This assemblage was located on a contemporary beach, and was therefore associated with the same Zaqrunian transgression (this belongs to the last phase of this transgression, Zaqrunian III). A large anvil, two cores and two choppers have been found in an exceptionally good state of preservation with very little weathering, blunted but not rolled. This is no doubt because they were quickly embedded in a matrix of fine sand which became consolidated soon afterwards. Here, too, there were no bifaces, but we can say little more. We can, however, draw some cautious conclusions about that early phase of the Lower Palaeolithic in the Levant, as follows.

1 It provides us with the first signs of a human presence in the region. Geomorphological studies based on the identification of various series of marine and continental deposits and the dating of basalt flows, together with palaeomagnetic measurements allow us to postulate that this presence dates back more than 730,000 years. On the other hand, the typology of the assemblages, and especially those at Ubeidiya, does not entitle us to go back more than 1.3 million years.

2 Reliable data are few and far between. If our calculations are correct, some 6,500 artefacts have been examined at Ubeidiya, 220 in the sites on the Nahr Al-Kabir, some thirty along the middle Orontes and seventeen on the Lebanese coast. Most of these assemblages contain bifaces, but some do not. There is therefore a possibility that the

Early Acheulean may not have been the only culture in the Levant at that time, but it would be rash to insist on this point and it is wiser not to pronounce on the significance of the difference between the facies. Even in Africa, the relationship between the Early Acheulean and the Developed Oldowan, if the latter did indeed exist, has not been explained satisfactorily, although the material is vastly more ample and distributed over much more homogeneous sites. In the Levant, we can do no more than ask questions.

3 So far, no evidence of an early Lower Palaeolithic has been discovered in the Levant outside the Mediterranean fossil beaches or along the rivers following the outlines of the Rift – the Jordan and the Orontes – but then the erosive power of the Euphrates has effaced all remains from that period. One might postulate that the early Lower Palaeolithic coincided with the departure from Africa of *Homo erectus*, the first human with a large brain and capable of adapting to new climates, people who went out to conquer the Old World by wisely following the great natural channels of communication, never losing contact with the favourable environment of permanently irrigated valleys.

THE MIDDLE LOWER PALAEOLITHIC (Map 5)

Several criteria enable us to isolate that phase of the Lower Palaeolithic to which we refer as the middle. In geological respects it corresponds to the first part of the Middle Pleistocene, which began with the Matuyama–Brunhes reversal of the earth's magnetic polarity. This is reflected in the relief by marine and continental formations built up during the antepenultimate pluvial (Qf III: Latamneh formation) and the ensuing transgression (Qm II: Jbaylian beaches). All the assemblages contained in these formations must therefore be assigned to the middle Lower Palaeolithic. In typological respects, and in comparison to the previous phase, these assemblages have a larger percentage of bifaces, fewer choppers and a more elaborate flaking technique culminating in the appearance of Levallois flakes, though these are still rather primitive. Some geologically well-dated deposits of this time have been found to contain relatively abundant assemblages without bifaces. This suggests the possibility of an industry differing from the Acheulean, and that is why we merely speak of a middle Lower Palaeolithic which obviously includes the Middle Acheulean.

The Levantine Rift

Desmond Clark was the first to mention the Middle Acheulean in the Levant in connection with Latamneh (Clark, 1966). For some 40 km along the Orontes, from where the road from Damascus to Aleppo crosses the river at Rastan, between Homs and Hama, to the point where the Orontes turns west to enter the plain of Ghab, massive terraces flank the river. Their geomorphological position puts them in the Middle Pleistocene, and the faunal remains corroborate this attribution (Hooijer, 1961/2; van Liere and Hooijer, 1961/2). Most of these formations have disintegrated in the rest of western Asia, but here they have been remarkably well preserved, which explains why the term 'Latamneh Formation' is used to refer to a strip running from the Euphrates to northern Jordan.

During the major works needed to construct a modern road network, numerous quarries had to be opened up and the erosion that continuously whittles down the cliffs on the banks of the Orontes has made further cuts. All in all, along the middle Orontes, sixteen deposits whose geological characteristics are clearly those of the Latamneh formation have yielded 855 artefacts including 183 tools, about a third of which were bifaces and picks. Moreover, in 1961, W. van Liere discovered an occupation floor in the top of the terrace which was excavated in 1964 and 1965 (Clark, 1966) and which yielded 2,825 artefacts including 394 implements. As in Ubeidiya, the formation as a whole undoubtedly covers a long time interval, long enough in any case to have spanned the transition from evolved mastodon to early elephant. The typology of all the Latamneh assemblages can be said to be fairly homogeneous and their state of preservation strikingly similar. The edges of the artefacts have admittedly been blunted, but there are no rolled pieces. The patina is a consistent dark maroon with small brilliant patches in places.

The Latamneh occupation floor has the usual structure of a Middle Acheulean stratum, as we know it from Africa. Pebbles and larger stones have been heaped on a surface of alluvial clay, possibly to serve as light shelter. The tools are scattered and their distribution suggests some division of labour. Unfortunately, no fauna has been found in this stratum; the animals preserved in the rest of the formation (elephant, Equidae, giraffe, camel) suggest hunting concentrated on the large mammals frequenting the forest gallery along the banks of the Orontes or crossing the steppes in search of river water.

At the beginning of the 1960s, W. van Liere, having ascertained the variety within the 'members' of the Latamneh formation and having come across, at Rastan, what later proved to be a substantial assemblage without bifaces (153 artefacts, 28 implements), suggested the possible existence of a pre-Acheulean phase (van Liere and Hooijer, 1961/2). Following the work of P. Sanlaville (Besançon et al., 1978), it now seems likely that the Latamneh formation, including the Rastan site, constitutes an entity that does not go back to much earlier than the Middle Pleistocene. Nevertheless, the Rastan assemblage shows that a population may have lived in the same environment as the Latamneh Acheuleans, possibly in a different manner, and used a set of implements that did not include bifacial handaxes. The full significance of Rastan remains unclear and poses a classic problem: do different toolkits reflect cultural differences or are they different implements for different types of work?

The Middle Acheulean of the Latamneh facies, to use Desmond Clark's terminology, occurs further south in Lebanon, still in the Levantine Rift: on the banks of the Litani, in the central Beqa'a at Jubb Jannin (Besançon et al., 1982). The assemblage found there is not *in situ* but results from the break-up of old conglomerates. It is highly concentrated and undoubtedly represents the remains of a vast and repeatedly adapted habitat. The published material comprises 1,700 artefacts including 978 implements. Approximately one-third of the collection has still to be examined and the collection is far from complete as it is. This means that the published proportions do not fully reflect the true state of affairs and that – as with so many Acheulean deposits – the Latamneh occupation floor being the exception, we must content ourselves with a purely qualitative impression of the typology and with just a few quantitative hints. This is true of nearly every Acheulean deposit in any part of the world. With its lanceolate bifaces, its trihedrons, its polyhedrons, spheroids and choppers, the Jubb Jannin assemblage closely resembles that of Latamneh. The number of trihedrons and polyhedrons suggests, if anything, that Jubb Jannin belongs to an earlier phase than that of the Latamneh floor. Moreover, the state of preservation of the Jubb Jannin and Latamneh artefacts and their respective patinas, probably due to the influence of the same hygromorphic environment, are identical. From the middle Orontes to the Beqa'a, from Latamneh to Jubb Jannin, we thus find the same Middle Acheulean facies.

Another deposit has been described further south in the Syro-Palestinian Rift. This is an assemblage on the banks of the Jordan, near the 'Bridge of Jacob's Daughters'. The first publication (Stekelis, 1960) seems to have been the only one based on a direct examination of the material; the rest (Perrot, 1968; Gilead, 1969) rely largely on the conclusions of the first. The assemblage is not very large (less than 100 artefacts) and seems selective (77 implements). Geological and geomorphological considerations suggest that the layers containing implements must be of Middle Pleistocene origin and that the assemblage as a whole, perhaps representing several phases, must date back to the Middle Acheulean. The latter has highly characteristic features: a large proportion of cleavers and the singular use of basalt as a raw material. In all probability, therefore, the 'Bridge of Jacob's Daughters' (*Jisr banat Ya'qub* or *Gesher benot Ya'agov* in Arabic and Hebrew respectively) does not belong to the same tradition as Latamneh and Jubb Jannin, but nevertheless also bears witness to the fact that the Rift was inhabited during the Middle Pleistocene.

The Mediterranean coast

Continental geomorphology merely provides the prehistorian with a discontinuous succession, because it only records the periods during which the fluvial terraces were built up. In contrast, as we mentioned earlier, the interspersion of marine with fluvial deposits at the mouth of the Nahr Al-Kabir enables us to arrive at a much more detailed sequence for the lower Middle Palaeolithic, here fully represented by the Acheulean (Copeland and Hours, 1979). The Berzin terrace, the equivalent of the Latamneh formation, contains a mass of material so heavy that a donkey had to be hired for its transport: 248 artefacts including 70 implements, 48 bifaces and 2 picks among them. Most of the bifaces were oval (51 per cent) or almond-shaped (26 per cent). The two picks were irregular and do not resemble those found in the Orontes sites. The Berzin facies is manifestly different from those at Latamneh and Jubb Jannin.

The same impression is given by the assemblages discovered near the village of Khellale directly below later fossil beaches attributable to the Jbaylian transgression. Three distinct points have yielded 480 artefacts including 172 implements, 106 bifaces and 4 picks among them. Here too the majority of the bifaces are oval (38 per cent) or almond-shaped (28 per cent).

The shore-lines of the Jbaylian transgression have also left Acheulean deposits on two sites along the Lebanese coast: at the outfall of the Wadi Aabet above the village of Batrun (Fleisch et al., 1969) and on the slopes of the Ras Beirut limestone massif south of Beirut (Fleisch, 1956, 1962). The two assemblages are of modest size but reflect the same tendency as those from Nahr Al-Kabir, with almond-shaped or oval bifaces and an absence of picks.

However, yet another, much more profuse and somewhat less enigmatic, assemblage has been discovered at Ras Beirut. At the end of the Jbaylian transgression, the sea left behind a pebble beach, the coastal strip described by H. Fleisch (1956, 1962). Mixed in with the pebbles is a rolled assemblage with the same porcelain-white patina as the beach pebbles. There are no bifaces but several choppers. The flakes are thick and rather long, with smooth butts. Some 2,000 of them have been found and this number suggests the possible existence of a non-Acheulean industry dating back to the middle Lower Palaeolithic.

Further south, still along the coast, the site of Evron, between Tyre and Haifa, lies on an old shore-line that seems to be contemporary with the last-mentioned site, though it is difficult to make stratigraphic correlations between the northern and central Levant. A sandstone quarry where there used to be dunes has revealed an ancient floor containing Acheulean remains. The most recent study (Ronen and Amiel, 1974; Ronen and Prausnitz, 1979) assigns it to the Middle Acheulean and refers explicitly to Latamneh. From the descriptions it is impossible to tell whether Evron belongs to the Latamneh or the Berzin facies.

Finally, the first traces of human penetration into the interior have recently been discovered (Hours, 1981b). On the banks of the Euphrates in Syria, at Shnine near the confluence of the Belikh, and also elsewhere – in Al-Kowm in the desert of Palmyra and at Dauqara on the banks of the Zarqa in Jordan – erosion has left disintegrated terraces. Their geomorphological position suggests contemporaneity with the Latamneh Formation. They contain rare flakes that may have to be assigned to the middle Lower Palaeolithic. The state of preservation and the patina do not contradict that possibility. In view of the small number of items, the absence of bifaces is of no significance.

The picture of the middle Lower Palaeolithic in western Asia we have briefly outlined raises a number of questions. Our account has been based exclusively on assemblages found *in situ* and in deposits whose geomorphological position is clearly established. Excavations have been few and far between and those allowing palaeoethnological investigations have been fewer still: the only one we can quote is that by Desmond Clark at Latamneh. That means that we cannot shore up our conclusions with other than chronological data, whose anchoring point, the Matuyama–Brunhes reversal of the earth's magnetic polarity, has been determined for this region in an indirect and rather loose way.

In general, the novel aspect of the middle Lower Palaeolithic was its tentative emergence east of the Syro-Palestinian Rift. It would therefore seem that *Homo erectus* dared now and then to venture far from the familiar and safe parts along the coast and in the central depression. True, during the 350,000 or so years that the Latamneh regression and the Jbaylian transgression lasted (an interval corresponding to Opdyke and Shackleton's phases 22 to 13) the climate could have changed enough and on several occasions to render the Jordano-Syrian steppes more hospitable and to allow the passage of small groups. But even if the assemblages are more numerous and more abundant than they were during the early Lower Palaeolithic and even if we detect more highly frequented centres such as the bend of the Orontes at Latamneh, Ras Beirut or the mouth of the Nahr Al-Kabir on the coast, the population of western Asia does not yet seem to have been very dense.

All in all, this phase of the middle Lower Palaeolithic marks a technical advance (Hours, 1981b). Chipping techniques were improved and choppers, instruments designed to split by crushing rather than by cutting, gradually made way for bifaces, thinner and more suitable for this type of work. Small tools multiplied and became diversified. At Latamneh, the only site whose plan we know, there was a clear organization of the available space which the absence of faunal remains prevents us from defining very precisely, but which nevertheless reflects some division of labour.

The typological difference between the coastal industries and those of the central rift suggest the separate development of two facies, perhaps constituting two cultural provinces, one using trihedral and polyhedral picks and the other shorter, oval or almond-shaped bifaces. Here we would then have a first sign of the possible existence of autonomous cultural groups in the region.

There remains the problem of the distinct life-style reflected by the existence of relatively abundant assemblages without bifaces: Rastan on the Orontes and in the coastal strip of Ras Beirut. Statistically, the absence of bifaces in these two cases seems significant and, especially at Ras Beirut, the similarities with the Clactonian of England are suggestive, but that is all we can say.

THE LATE LOWER PALAEOLITHIC
(Map 5 and Fig. 4)

The situation in western Asia changed during the Late Acheulean. We define that period with chronological criteria the material expressions of which are transformations of the landscape by climatic changes (the Qf II formations). Especially along the Euphrates and the Nahr Al-Kabir, around the *sebkhas* of the big oases such as Palmyra and Al-Kowm, or even along such interior rivers as the Wadi Zarqa, archaeologists have come across terraces dating back to the penultimate pluvial complex and containing implements.

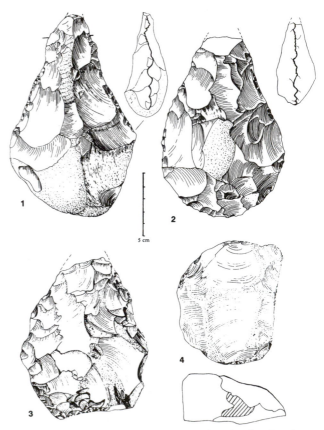

Figure 4 Late Acheulean artefacts: 1–2, Nahr Al-Kabir (Syria); 3–4, Bireh (Jordan).

Chronologically, they must be assigned to the late Lower Palaeolithic and most often to the Acheulean, because assemblages not containing bifaces are the exception. In contrast to the Latamneh occupation floor, we do not know of any western Asian occupation floors conserved *in situ* and dating back to this phase of the Lower Palaeolithic. However, the number of deposits is so large that we cannot even try to mention them all. By confining ourselves to sites in a certain geological position, we may be ignoring assemblages that should have been included, the more so since, as we shall show below, there is a large number of apparently more advanced Acheulean surface assemblages that might date back to the same phase as the assemblages in the fluvial formations. To make quite sure, however, and also for typological reasons, it seems preferable to distinguish between 'Late Acheulean' assemblages found *in situ* in the fluvial terraces of the penultimate fluvial complex (Qf II) (Table 3 and Map 5) and 'advanced Late Acheulean' assemblages found on the surface, provided, of course, that the typology allows this distinction.

The Late Acheulean

This phase was first described during the geomorphological study of the Nahr Al-Kabir (Copeland and Hours, 1979; cf. the evolution of vocabulary from Hours, 1975, adopted by Tomsky, 1982, to Hours, 1981*b*, adopted by Muhesen, 1985). Beneath the fluvial formation at Berzin (Qf III) and its beach deposits at Khellale (Qm II) there are other, highly characteristic, fluvial terraces (Qf II) near the village of Rudo but also further downstream, for instance at Swayat, or on the southern bank at Dahr Al-Ayani (Sanlaville, 1979). All in all this formation has yielded 600 artefacts, including 170 tools. The majority (70 per cent) are bifaces, oval or almond-shaped (Fig. 4); the number of lanceolate implements has decreased and picks have virtually disappeared. Choppers account for no more than 10 per cent of the implements, while the proportion of light tools has increased (15 per cent). The typological characteristics of the bifaces and their dimensions admittedly suggest that there has been some development since the production of the Berzin assemblages but, though the geomorphological position suggests a Late Acheulean provenance, the shapes are still relatively primitive.

On the Orontes the situation is more difficult to assess, because the formations are not terraced, as they are on the Nahr Al-Kabir, but interlock. The typological characteristics of the Middle and Late Acheulean assemblages are sometimes very alike here, and it is not surprising that the first investigators (Modderman, 1964; van Liere, 1966) should have failed to distinguish this phase. It occurs downstream from Latamneh at Jraibiyat, where 350 artefacts including 150 implements have been found at three different points, and at the entrance of the Ghab at Aasharne where 450 artefacts and 80 tools have come from the formation broken by a canal. The same typological tendencies as prevail on the Nahr Al-Kabir can be found here: moreover, the relative position of the terraces and the way they interlock seem to have encouraged intermixtures, and the proportion of picks at Aasharne is reminiscent of the Middle Acheulean. It might well be that the Jraibiyat terraces are partly reshaped Latamneh terraces, incorporating material that was included in the latter.

The situation seems to be somewhat similar on the Euphrates (Besançon and Sanlaville, 1981). The penultimate pluvial began with an erosive phase that emptied the valley,

leaving behind nothing but shreds of the old formations. Next there was an accumulation of thick deposits contemporary with those at Jraibiyat on the Orontes, and visible near Ragga and especially round Abu Jamaa for tens of kilometres. In some twenty sites, close on 1,500 artefacts have been collected including 112 tools, 69 bifaces among them. The proportion of picks is an astonishing 30 per cent in some places. The differences from Rudo on the Nahr Al-Kabir are obvious and can only be explained by the assumption that the Euphrates reshaped old formations when building up those at Abu Jamaa, incorporating in the new the artefacts contained in the old. This is probably what happened with the assemblage recently discovered in a terrace flanking the Euphrates a little downstream from the border between Syria and Iraq and marking one of the extreme points reached by the advance of the Acheulean towards the east.

The same conditions prevail along the Sajur (Besançon and Sanlaville, 1985), a small western tributary of the Euphrates south of the Turkish border. Here the terraces also date back to the end of the Middle Pleistocene. They are not very profuse but have yielded 777 artefacts including 109 tools. The proportion of trihedral picks is comparable to that of the deposits along the middle Euphrates and the same hypothesis can be put forward to explain this fact.

It seems likely that some Turkish deposits, and particularly that at Altindere on the banks of a stream feeding Lake Amik near Antakya (Antioch) fall into a similar category (Senyurek, 1961). That can also be said of Barda Balka near Chemchemal in the Kirkuk region of Iraq (Braidwood and Howe, 1960) where an assemblage was removed from a fluvial terrace. The industry at Barda Balka resembles that of Rudo; there is an absence of trihedral picks. The surroundings, moreover, contain several similar sites, barely mentioned and whose name is not even known. Here we have a centre of the Late Acheulean tradition that clearly reflects the Acheulean's eastward thrust at the time under consideration.

On the Lebanese coast, it is again Ras Beirut that has provided the essential data (Fleisch, 1962). Several points have produced Acheulean assemblages with more or less almond-shaped bifaces, reflecting familiarity with the Levallois tradition. These assemblages are not very large but they are well situated from the geological point of view. During the regression caused by the penultimate glacial complex, the rocky floor at Ras Beirut became eroded and the regression lasted long enough for dissolution pockets to form in the limestone substratum and to fill with clay. In the course of canal work, several assemblages were discovered: Ras Beirut III and IV (Copeland and Wescombe, 1965), contemporary with other assemblages in the various Qf II formations.

In the southern Levant several sites have been mentioned (Goren, 1981) that might belong to the same context. The details are scarce and views differ, but the upper level of the deposit at the 'Bridge of Jacob's Daughters' on the Jordan, if there are indeed two levels in that deposit, and the site at Ruhama Swamp in the Negev should perhaps be taken into account. Two deposits in the Golan are particularly interesting: those at Jubbata and at Birket Ram (Goren-Inbar, 1985). The Birket Ram deposit is embedded in a layer of clay between two basalt flows that have been dated back 230,000 and 800,000 years respectively. The age attributed to the assemblage at Birket Ram is approximately 300,000 years, which corresponds to Opdyke and Shackleton's phase 9 and takes us to the middle of the penultimate pluvio-glacial complex. The assemblage is clearly of Late Acheulean origin, with an abundance of small tools reflecting familiarity with the Levallois technique. Jubbata is an open-air site not far from Birket Ram and the two assemblages have strong typological similarities. This justifies the inclusion of Jubbata here.

Further south, on the banks of the Zarqa in Jordan, residual terraces near the village of Bireh have yielded a small assemblage whose geomorphological characteristics allow us to attribute it to the same epoch (Fig. 4; Besançon et al., 1984; Besançon and Hours, 1985). This is further evidence of the advance of the Late Acheulean into the interior.

The Late Acheulean we have been describing marks an important stage in the development of the Lower Palaeolithic in the Levant. To begin with, it is relatively well dated. With the exception of Jubbata, all the sites we have mentioned are geologically *in situ*, in fluvial formations of the Qf II. All the assemblages were therefore made during the penultimate fluvio-glacial complex and probably during its first half. If we use a chronology based on changes in the ratio of oxygen isotopes in ocean-bed deposits, then the Late Acheulean in western Asia could have lasted from 450,000 to 250,000 years ago, that is, from Opdyke and Shackleton's phase 12 to phase 8. This seems to agree with modern conclusions about Africa and Europe.

The Late Acheulean marked a real technical advance: bifaces became less bulky and were better made, while light implements were diversified and became more numerous, and Levallois flaking established itself. In some regions the types of implement used in the Middle Acheulean persisted, but this is possibly due to remodelling. Moreover, some assemblages have not been mentioned here because they are meagre and scattered and contain few tools and no bifaces. This does not seem to justify the view that what we have here is a tradition differing from the Acheulean and comparable to the Tayacian in Western Europe.

Finally, for the first time, we detect a fairly constant human presence east of the Levantine Rift. The surroundings of Barda Balka in Iraq, the middle Syrian Euphrates, and the Zarqa in Jordan bear the marks of a veritable Acheulean penetration. What we have here are not just a few scattered tools nor some rare and isolated sites. It looks rather as if these regions were occupied, and repeatedly so, by substantial groups of human beings. Nevertheless, the lines of penetration remained unchanged: the coast, the Rift and the permanent rivers.

The advanced Late Acheulean (Map 5)

Another aspect of the Late Acheulean assumes a distinct form in Western Asia. In typological respects, the industries seem more advanced: nearly all the bifaces have been worked and retouched with a soft hammer to produce straight cutting edges, often on bevelled bases. Small tools became standardized and we can now look them up in the type lists drawn up for the Middle Palaeolithic. In that sense we can speak of an advanced Late Acheulean (Muhesen, 1985). Moreover, the assemblages were almost invariably found on the surface, unlike the less-advanced preceding assemblages that we have called Late Acheulean, and which are nearly always geologically *in situ*. The surface deposits were admittedly open to the possibility of later contamination and the presence of Levallois flakes in particular should be interpreted with caution. However, their situation suggests that they came later than the Qf II terraces, during a relatively non-humid interstadial that could well correspond to Opdyke and Shackleton's period 7. Lastly, the advanced Late Acheulean is scattered throughout western Asia and the associated sites are sometimes very profuse.

Its presence has been recorded near the Syro-Turkish border, at such sites as Kartal and Duluk in the Antakya (Antioch) and Gazantiep regions (Kökten, 1947). While we have no more than brief references to these sites, the number of artefacts in them seems to be considerable. Further east, assemblages have been listed as far away as the neighbourhood of Eski Mosul (Inizan, 1985) on the left bank of the Tigris in northern Iraq.

Along the Middle Euphrates, all the sites lie on the surface of terraces of various ages and not in the valley or in formations from the penultimate pluvial complex. They are found either on top of very old formations, as at Tellik on the left bank, near the Turkish border, or near the mouths of small tributaries as in the Wadi Abu Shahri, where the deposits have not suffered the devastating effects of the draining of the Euphrates at the beginning of the pluvial.

In the Nahr Al-Kabir zone on the north Mediterranean coast of Syria, an advanced Late Acheulean tradition can be found in surface deposits at Jabal Idriss, but similar assemblages have also been retrieved from formations dating back to the last pluvial, at Jbariun, Rudo and Swayat (Copeland and Hours, 1979). The possibility of mixtures cannot be ignored, but nevertheless the assemblages differ from those assigned to the Late Acheulean both in the quality of the implements and also in their proportion: altogether there were 395 artefacts including 67 implements, 31 bifaces amongst them. The latter were mostly almond-shaped or oval. Scrapers predominated among the small tools. The redistributed position of these assemblages when fitted into the long series of the Acheulean finds along the Nahr Al-Kabir is interesting. They bear witness to temporary pauses (for the number of artefacts is small) after the formation of the Rudo terrace (because they are not included in it) and before the accumulation of the deposits at Esh-Shir (which date back to the last pluvial and contain Middle Palaeolithic remains).

East of Palmyra, to the rear of the escarpment holding the Duara cave, an assemblage with fine almond-shaped bifaces bears witness to the penetration of the advanced Late Acheulean into the Syrian desert (Akazawa, 1979). Because it is a surface deposit, without geomorphological links, the site itself cannot be dated, but the typological characteristics of the tools are explicit enough.

The valley of the Middle Orontes is more significant. Several surface stations, including some that are difficult to interpret, have made it possible to register the presence of a Late Acheulean that was undoubtedly advanced, both beside the loop of the Orontes near Latamneh and also a little upriver south of the Wadi Gharmashi (Muhesen, 1985). By chance one deposit has been preserved whose geological position is conclusive. Here, the left bank of the Orontes is flanked by powerful formations dating back to the Middle Pleistocene and containing the Latamneh occupation floor (Qf III) in particular. At some points, formations dating back to the following pluvial (Qf II) have been deposited, and these are interlocked at Jraibiyat. At Gharmashi no Qf II deposits have survived, the Orontes having swept them out during a still-active meander. However, it was possible to show that the Latamneh formation has been worn away here, together with the marly substratum on which it rested. It was on this peneplane that the Acheuleans settled and their habitat became sealed under a red colluvium containing

Middle Palaeolithic remains. Prospecting and digging have been proceeding for several years.

A series of borings using the classic sampling method (random stratified sampling) has made it possible, first of all, to determine the extent of the site and to localize two points at which the density of the artefacts seemed greater than elsewhere. Altogether, an area measuring 270 m² has since been cleared. In it were recovered 2,129 artefacts including 399 tools, 140 bifaces, 38 choppers and 61 scrapers amongst them. On the typological plane, there is a remarkable decrease in heavy tools, which account for no more than 7 per cent of the whole assemblage, whereas the proportion of light tools has risen to 48 per cent, bifaces and choppers making up the rest.

Most important of all, these results could be mapped and made the subject of an interpretative spatial analysis (Muhesen, 1985). The deposit is fully in line with what we know about the Acheulean. Several large stones have been found here and there. There are marked concentrations indicating a chipping area and probably two flaking areas. Unfortunately, as at Latamneh, the fauna has not been preserved. Gharmashi is, together with this site, one of two deposits in Western Asia to give us some indications of the Acheulean, in this case the advanced Acheulean, way of life. We can easily imagine a group of fifteen or so individuals camping on the banks of the Orontes, the river flowing below them, but at a higher level than it does today, and surveying a promising valley. But while Gharmashi is the most complete and best-preserved site from that epoch, it was possible to discover traces of five or six other encampments in the vicinity – the Orontes was certainly very much frequented in the last part of the penultimate fluvio-glacial complex.

Another privileged spot seems to have been the outlet on the Syrian coast of the Homs Gap between Tartus and the Lebanese border (Muhesen, 1985). Here, half a dozen sites are ranged round two large rivers that helped to build the coastal plain: the Nahr Al-Abrash and the southern Nahr Al-Kabir. Some of these sites have been known for a long time, for instance Qalaat Yahmur, while others such as Ard Hamed, Muqaa Al-Hami and Jdeideh were identified recently. What we know is certainly incomplete. It nevertheless suggests that these highly individualized deposits represent ancient camps, no doubt disrupted but nevertheless still recognizable.

Finds, scattered but abundant, in the southern Beqa'a in Lebanon (Besançon and Hours, 1971) relate to the same epoch. The site is interesting: it too lies at the outlet of a strategic passage. In this case it is the Kamed el Loz Gap joining the Litani and the Beqa'a to the upper Jordan valley. As we mentioned earlier, erosion seems to have been very pronounced here and the assemblages have been displaced, with the result that it is impossible to reconstruct the precise organization of the occupation zone.

Upper Galilee, by contrast, provides a fairly well-preserved and structured cultural complex, which allows us to examine the mode of occupation of a region during that epoch by considering points of passage, the nature of the terrain, the places from which raw materials were obtained and the distribution of the water resources. The region is hilly, adequately irrigated and would still be woody today were it not for human intervention. It is clear that the occupation of the valleys in the Lebanese part of Upper Galilee, around Ain Ibl, on limestone terrain where the water drains away quickly (Bovier-Lapierre, 1909; Fleisch, 1951, 1954; Copeland and Wescombe, 1965) has been rather fleeting and

involved small nomadic groups. Here the assemblages are meagre and largely confined to Mudawwara and Tibnin. In the Nahal Dishon valley, futher south (Ronen et al., 1974), the basalt retains rainwater better and the occupation, which was denser, seemed more sedentary. The exceptionally rich deposit at Ma'ayan Baruch (Stekelis and Gilead, 1966) suggests that this site might have been the centre of a fairly large zone – the thousands of bifaces amassed there have no equal outside such large African sites (which are, moreover, contemporary with the Ma'ayan Baruch finds) as Kalambo Falls, Olorgesailie or Garba I at Melka Kunturé.

Further south, no cultural complexes of equal importance or as easy to interpret have been found. In contrast, there are numerous points bearing witness to a Late Acheulean presence: the plain of Rephaim Beqa'a near Jerusalem (Arensburg and Bar-Yosef, 1963, 1967), the surface layer of the terraces at Zarqa in Jordan, from Khirbet es Samra (also on basalt) to the Bireh Heights (Besançon et al., 1984; Besançon and Hours, 1985), and the banks of Wadi Kharane, Wadi Rattama and Wadi Uweinid and similar wadis (Rollefson, 1984) which drain what meagre rain falls in the desert towards the Azraq oasis. The Fjaje heights and the environs of Kerak (Rollefson, 1981) might well lend themselves to spatial analyses of the kind made at Nahal Dishon, because they apparently contain an abundance of very widely scattered material.

On the coast, the surface deposit at Evron Zenat might lie on the same horizon (Prausnitz, 1969; Gilead and Ronen, 1977). In any case, the southern Levant seems to have been less densely populated or less frequently traversed. One of the rare sites mentioned here is Kissufim, near the coast, whose stratigraphical position needs to be clarified.

THE END OF THE ACHEULEAN

From the first manifestations of human presence, and despite some signs of industries without bifaces, the entire prehistory of western Asia has been dominated by the Acheulean. Its development has been retraced and though the industry found at Ma'ayan Baruch or Khirbet es Samra does not resemble that of Sitt Markho or of Ubeidiya, these changes have been gradual and relatively smooth. That is why many authors have distinguished between an early Middle Acheulean and a late Middle Acheulean (Hours, 1975; Tomsky, 1982) and why some describe as Middle Acheulean what we have called the Late Acheulean (Rollefson, 1984). Then, with the humid period corresponding to the end of the penultimate glacial, there began a complex phase of multiple changes which culminated in the Middle Palaeolithic (Hours, 1979). In terms of the theory of evolution we might say that a phase of broken equilibrium had followed a long static period.

Side by side with the Acheulean tradition, continued by what is often called the Final Acheulean, we observe the appearance of new facies retaining the characteristic bifaces but adding new shapes distinct from those of the classic Acheulean. These are industries with small bifaces, as found in the north of Syria, or with thick, angled or transverse, scrapers, as found in the central Levant, or surprising new blade industries, prior to the Middle Palaeolithic proper. All this happened in a relatively short period and according to a badly established succession. What we have here, moreover, is a series of partly contemporary industries. Three series of datings place one of these episodes at about 150,000 years.

The Final Acheulean (Fig. 5)

In the central Levant, from Jabrud (Yabrud) and Al-Kowm in Syria to Azraq in Jordan and from Tabun to Umm Qatafa in Israel, excavations, either at the edge of springs (Al-Kowm: Nadawiyeh I; Azraq; Lion Spring and C Spring) or in caves (Jabrud I, level 23; Tabun F and Umm Qatafa D 2 and E) have brought to light indisputably Acheulean assemblages that stratigraphic investigations place very late in the sequence and that sedimentology tends to place in a humid period (Fig. 5). The cave excavations are important because they have helped to define famous sequences (Neuville, 1931 and 1934; Garrod and Bate, 1937; Rust, 1951), but they were undertaken half a century ago and have never been resumed at these levels or checked. Moreover the material has been analysed somewhat cursorily.

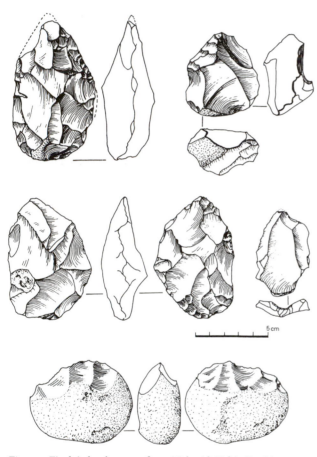

Figure 5 Final Acheulean artefacts: Nahr Al-Kabir (Syria).

Tabun for one has yielded a very advanced Acheulean industry with thin, oval or even circular bifaces made entirely by flat retouch. Umm Qatafa has been likened to Tabun F and Jabrud is known only from some drawings and a description by F. Bordes. By contrast, the Azraq springs, though the results have not yet been published, look more promising. L. Harding has given us a picturesque account of the discovery in 1957 of an assemblage, deposited beside an old spring and now covered with more than a metre of sediment, even though the spring itself is still active: to clean it, workers standing waist-deep in water scraped the bottom with baskets that came up full of bifaces. The work, which was begun as part of a study for an irrigation project, has recently been resumed and two or three springs have yielded thousands of pieces and hundreds of oval or almond-shaped bifaces. They are not very thin but were obviously fashioned with care, the two faces having large flat facets. The patina is generally

dark – black, brown or deep olive – and the bloom is surprising. Some shiny pieces and scrapers from Jabrud suggest the need for further stratigraphic analysis. All we know seems to indicate that these highly advanced Acheuleans had access to a gravel bed, the result of a run-off at a time when the floor of the Azraq depression was lower than it is today.

The offshoots of the Acheulean (Map 6 and Fig. 6)

The assemblages found in the central Levant – at Jabrud, Duara, Al-Kowm, Tabun, Umm Qatafa and Azraq, though advanced, are still strictly in the Acheulean tradition. Other assemblages, by contrast, contain innovations and pave the way for unprecedented industries. In other words, the movement that would culminate in the Middle Palaeolithic had started. A first expression of this transformation seems confined to the northern Levant and manifests itself with different nuances at different places: the Nahr Al-Kabir, the Orontes, the Euphrates, Al-Kowm. It has moreover been given several different names.

The Samukian (Copeland and Hours, 1979) was first identified in connection with an assemblage discovered on the old Pliocene coastline at Mshairfet es Samuk. The raw material was provided by small pebbles and the dimensions of the implements reflect this fact. They are small, thick, almond-shaped bifaces measuring less than 7 cm accompanied by small choppers and by cores and flakes that reflect the use of Levallois flaking. Their state of preservation is excellent; the greenish-yellow patina often has a bloom. The same facies has been discovered in six other places the most important of which are the fossil beach at Fidio and the Qf II terraces flanking the Nahr Al-Arab, all of which provides a *terminus a quo* for dating. These miniature bifaces, accompanied by small choppers and by a wealth of Levallois flakes, no longer constitute an Acheulean tradition as we normally understand it.

Something similar happened along the middle Orontes, where surface assemblages have been found in contact with flint-bearing limestone outcrops. Here, too, small bifaces are an important part of the toolkit. They are accompanied by small, more or less leaf-shaped, pieces and also by Levallois flakes. In general, the artefacts are considerably weathered and the grey patina often has a rugose appearance. The number of pieces is often considerable and allows valuable statistical conclusions. The two most important points are in the vicinity of Latamneh, at Tahun Semaan and Tulul Defai. The substitution of small bifaces for the Samukian miniature choppers has seemed to justify a new name (Besançon et al., 1978) and this facies is accordingly described as the Defaian. On the middle Euphrates, at the confluence of the Balikh near Ragga, small bifaces are accompanied by very thin Levallois flakes and small quartz choppers (Besançon et al., 1980).

The Al-Kowm basin has produced similar assemblages at two points (Hours, 1981a). On the edge of the fossil spring at Nadawiyeh I, small bifaces occupy the upper levels of a site containing classic Late Acheulean implements at the bottom. Not far away, on the edge of the Wadi Qdeir, the small bifaces are accompanied by bifacial pieces. The bifaces are either oval or almond-shaped, but in this case they are not accompanied by Levallois flakes, which distinguishes the industries of Al-Kowm from the Samukian of the Nahr Al-Kabir and the Defaian of the Orontes. By contrast, level 12 of shelter 1 at Jabrud resembles the last two: its industry includes small bifaces, and F. Bordes has

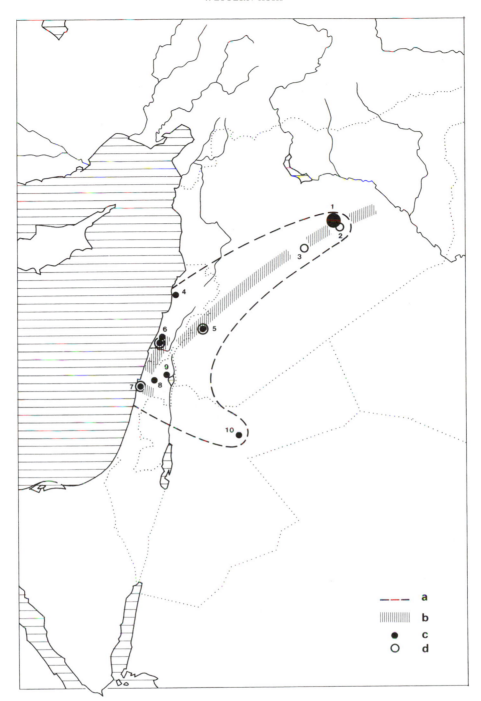

Map 6 Western Asia – The transition from the Lower to the Middle Palaeolithic: a, area of the Jabrudian culture; b, the Palmyrenian ridge; c, Jabrudian sites; d, blade industries. 1, Al-Kowm (nine sites); 2, Hummal; 3, Duara (?); 4, Maslukh; 5, Jabrud; 6, Adlun; 7, Tabun; 8, Ain Musa; 9, Zuttiyeh; 10, Azraq (C spring).

given this level a Levallois index of 15 (Rust, 1951; Bordes, 1955).

Though facies with miniature bifaces tend to be concentrated in northern Lebanon, they are not confined to that region – level D 1 of Umm Qatafa no doubt falls in the same category. R. Neuville (1931) has noted the presence here of 'minuscule' bifaces and of certain tools resembling our small biface pieces.

It is not easy to put a precise date on these industries derived from the Acheulean, for they are generally found in surface stations. Nevertheless, their typology suggests a recent age and those sites which contain strata (Umm Qatafa, Jabrud, Nadawiyeh) confirm that they represent the climax of the Acheulean series, Jabrud showing moreover that the

Middle Palaeolithic proper emerged almost immediately above. This accordingly places us in a transitional period, almost synchronous with the Jabrudian.

The Jabrudian (Map 6 and Fig. 6)

At the end of the Lower Palaeolithic in western Asia the Jabrudian held a particularly important place. It was, first of all, a tradition peculiar to the Levant and has, moreover, been the subject of long and heated discussions about its nature and chronological position. Now that the latter has been fixed by some ten datings, the Jabrudian has become all the more interesting. Last but not least, it is the only tradition associated, during the period under review, with a

73

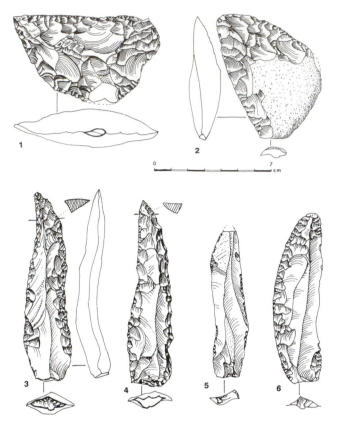

Figure 6 Transitional industries: Al-Kowm (Syria). 1–3, Jabrudian; 3–6. Hummalian.

human fossil in a fairly well-established stratigraphic position.

The Jabrudian was identified by A. Rust following his excavations, from 1930 to 1933, of a series of hollow rock shelters in the cliffs of the Wadi Skifta near the small town of Jabrud (Yabrud) in central Syria (Rust, 1951). It is characterized by the absence or near-absence of blades and the presence of trimmed, mainly transverse or angled, scrapers made of thick flakes with a plain striking platform (Fig. 6), reminiscent of the Mousterian industry of the La Quina facies of the French Middle Acheulean. In the course of his excavations, Rust distinguished between levels with and without bifaces. It is not certain whether this distinction is of real importance. The results of the excavations af Jabrud were not published until 1951. This explains why the Jabrudian was not well known before that date, and why some of the material discovered at Tabun and Al-Zuttiyeh in Palestine had to be reclassified.

Since then the Jabrudian has been identified in seventeen sites scattered across the central Levant, nine of them in the oasis of Al-Kowm (Copeland and Hours, 1983). These sites do not seem linked to any particular ecological zone: Tabun (Israel), Adlun and Maslukh (Lebanon) are coastal caves, Zuttiyeh, Ayin Mussa (Israel) and Jabrud (Syria) are located on the hills at the southern end of the Fertile Crescent, while Azraq (Jordan) and Al-Kowm with its nine deposits (Syria) are dry-steppe oases on the edge of the desert. The industries were deposited in caves and under shelters (six sites) or in the open beside springs (eleven sites). Some of the deposits also contain faunal remains, mostly of large animals but occasionally also of medium-sized herbivores. Depending on the ecological niche, they range from hippopotamus, elephant or rhinoceros to camel and horse, or from wild boar to goat, fallow-deer or roe-deer. In the

dry zone, gazelle has been recorded. This suggests non-specialized collective hunting, highly adapted to the terrain.

The human remains found at Mugharet Al-Zuttiyeh (Gisis and Bar Yosef, 1974) show that the Jabrudian people belonged to an advanced form of *Homo erectus*, described as pre-*sapiens* by some authors. The datings obtained by several methods (uranium and thermoluminescence) at Zuttiyeh and Al-Kowm indicate that they lived some 150,000 years ago (Schwarcz et al., 1979, 1980; Hennig and Hours, 1982). This agrees with the sedimentological findings and takes us, with the Final Acheulean of the springs at Azraq, to a humid period which agrees fairly well with Opdyke and Shackleton's phase 6.

Blade industries

At some sites the Jabrudian is associated with a blade industry. The relations between the two are not clear because the implements vary from deposit to deposit. However, so far these blade industries have never been discovered in isolation.

It was Rust once again who was the first to mention the inclusion in the complex marking the end of the Acheulean of lamellar flake assemblages which he described as 'pre-Aurignacian' (Rust, 1951). This name was badly chosen because it suggests a link with the Upper Palaeolithic based on some unspecified and undiscovered extension of the pre-Aurignacian for tens of thousands of years. Moreover, in about 1940 the attempts to achieve greater typological accuracy had not yet borne all their fruit and the name 'Aurignacian' was still being applied to anything that smacked of the Upper Palaeolithic. The pre-Aurignacian of Jabrud also contains burins and graters, but is nevertheless separated from the Aurignacian by the full time-depth of the Middle Palaeolithic. Nevertheless, attempts have recently been made (Bakdach, 1982), despite the stratigraphic problem, to treat it as a first manifestation of the Upper Palaeolithic.

The identification by Rust of an original blade industry prior to the emergence of the Middle Palaeolithic, and as part of the complex marking the end of the Lower Palaeolithic, persuaded D. Garrod to revise her interpretation of layer E at Tabun (Garrod, 1956) and to look for equivalent assemblages elsewhere. This was the basis of her excavations at Adlun (Roe, 1983) on the Lebanese coast, where she has described a Jabrudian and a blade industry in a stratigraphic position similar to the pre-Aurignacian but with a slightly different typology. She gave it a new name: the Amudian (Garrod and Kirkbride, 1961; Garrod, 1970).

Since then, work in the oasis of Al-Kowm has led to the discovery, in wells at Hummal, above the Jabrudian and below the Middle Palaeolithic, of an industry of the same type, but nevertheless original; traces of it have since been found near other springs: large blades with smooth butts and pointed by scalar retouch (Fig. 6). Depending on typological considerations we can give them various names: double side-scrapers, Mousterian points or San Remo points (Copeland, 1985). This type of assemblage characteristic of the Al-Kowm oasis has been called Hummalian (Hours, 1982). The pieces are mostly covered with a patina and a gloss owing to the action of the spring water (by whatever process), something that makes them look unlike any other blade tools.

At four distinct points, Mount Carmel, the Adlun caves, Jabrud and the springs of Al-Kowm, assemblages including blades therefore exist in equivalent stratigraphic positions, which puts them at the junction of the Lower and the

Middle Palaeolithic (Map 6). A. Jelinek, who has resumed excavation at Tabun, believes that the Jabrudian and the blade industries are part of the same 'Wadi Mughara' tradition (Jelinek, 1981), which is a surprising interpretation. Calculation of the length/breadth indices have been offered as corroboration, but not very convincingly.

In any case, these assemblages pose a problem and not merely because of their unusual typology. They consist of tools intended for delicate work and calling for less strenuous effort than did the Acheulean bifaces or the Jabrudian scrapers. Perhaps the geographical distribution of the various complexes will help to resolve the problems raised here. The Jabrudian is found throughout the central Levant, along the coast no less than in the interior, which reflects an ability to live in very diverse ecological zones and, as far as we can tell, to exploit a very varied faunal environment. By contrast, the blade industries, not very profuse it is true, range from Mount Carmel on the Mediterranean coast to Al-Kowm in the Syrian steppes, and run through Jabrud along the line of heights sometimes called the Palmyrian Dorsal. Without the destruction wreaked by humans, these hills would still be covered with a light forest of oak and pistachio trees, a biotope in which wild graminaceous plants developed. Perhaps the blade industries, whether pre-Aurignacian, Amudian or Hummalian, bear witness to human adaptation to that type of crop by the development of implements made to cut not very resistant material.

CONCLUSION

The complex closing the Lower Palaeolithic (the Final Acheulean, the Acheulean offshoots, the Jabrudian and the blade industries) gave rise throughout western Asia to Levallois flake assemblages, the beginnings of which date back some 90,000 years (Stearns and Thurber, 1965; Leroi-Gourhan, 1980; Hennig and Hours, 1982). They mark the advent of the Middle Palaeolithic. Neanderthal people would be associated with them.

In western Asia, as we saw, the stages of human development corresponding to the presence of *Homo erectus* cannot be determined with those absolute dating methods available for Africa. On the other hand, the geomorphological framework has been carefully analysed and provides a detailed relative chronology based on objective criteria. This enables us to specify that throughout the Acheulean – Early, Middle and Late – the typology of the implements evolved gradually while the way of life remained substantially unchanged. We have to wait for the emergence of the various facies marking the end of the Acheulean to witness profound and rapid transformations.

In this review of western Asia during the epoch of *Homo erectus* we have confined ourselves to the Levant: Lebanon, Syria and Israel. Practically nothing is known about what archaeological material dating from this period can be found in Turkey, Iraq, Iran and the Arabian peninsula. More careful prospecting and more substantial publications may well give us some idea of the development of the Acheulean in these regions, but at present we know nothing about it. The reader will have noticed that the industries are not evenly distributed in the Levant and that human occupation does not seem to have been uniform. Apart from a general movement culminating in the colonization of the interior from the Late Acheulean onwards, southern Lebanon seems to have been less densely populated than the central and northern parts.

The relatively late appearance of the Acheulean in western Asia, and then as a fully fledged industry, without any signs of trial and error at the start, suggests that it was introduced from outside, western Asia serving as a bridge between Africa and Eurasia during the settlement of the Old World. Given its position at the crossroads of three continents, this conclusion is, moreover, not at all surprising. But its role was not confined to mediation. The Acheulean experienced an original and autochthonous development in this part of the world, particularly pronounced at the end with the advent of the advanced Late Acheulean and of all the Middle Palaeolithic transitional industries.

In those ancient times, though it was not the cradle of the Acheulean, western Asia played an essential part in the evolution of humankind.

BIBLIOGRAPHY

AKAZAWA, T. 1979. Flint Factory Sites in Palmyra Basin. In: HANIHARA, K.; AKAZAWA, T. (eds), *Paleolithic Site of Douara Cave and Paleogeography of Palmyra Basin in Syria*. Tokyo. pp. 159–200. (Univ. Mus., Univ. Tokyo Bull., 16.)

ARENSBURG, B.; BAR-YOSEF, O. 1963. Emeq Rephaim (fouilles de 1962). *Mi-Tekufat ha-Even* (Jerusalem), Vol. 4/5, pp. 1–16.

—— 1967. Yacimiento paleolítico en el valle de Refaim, Jerusalem, Israel. *Ampurias* (Barcelona), Vol. 29, pp. 117–33.

ARIAI, A.; THIBAULT, C. 1975–7. Nouvelles Précisions à propos de l'outillage paléolithique ancien sur galets du Khorassan (Iran). *Paléorient*, Vol. 3, pp. 101–8.

BAKDACH, J. 1982. *Das Jungpaläolithikum von Jabrud in Syrien*. Cologne. (Doct. dissertation, Universität Köln.)

BAR-YOSEF, O.; TCHERNOV, E. 1972. *On the Palaeo-ecological History of the Site of Ubeidiya*. Jerusalem, Israel Academy of Sciences and Humanities.

BESANÇON, J. 1981. Chronologie du Pleistocène au Levant. Synthèse. In: CAUVIN, J.; SANLAVILLE, P. (eds), *Préhistoire du Levant*. Paris, CNRS. pp. 145–53.

BESANÇON, J.; COPELAND, L.; HOURS, F. 1982. L'Acheuléen moyen de Joubb Jannine (Liban). *Paléorient*, Vol. 8, pp. 11–36.

BESANÇON, J.; HOURS, F. 1971. Préhistoire et géomorphologie: les Formes du relief et les dépôts quaternaires de la région de Joubb Jannine (Beqaa méridionale, Liban) II. *Hannon* (Beirut), Vol. 6, pp. 29–135.

—— 1985. Prehistory and Geomorphology in Northern Jordan, a Preliminary Outline. *Studies in the History and Archaeology of Jordan*, Vol. 2, pp. 56–66.

BESANÇON, J.; SANLAVILLE, P. 1981. Aperçu géomorphologique sur la vallée de l'Euphrate syrien. *Paléorient*, Vol. 7, pp. 5–18.

—— 1985. Le Milieu géographique. In: SANLAVILLE, P. (ed.), *Holocene Settlement in North Syria*. Oxford. pp. 7–40. (BAR Int. Ser., 238.)

BESANÇON, J. et al. 1978. The Paleolithic Sequence in Quaternary Formations of the Orontes River Valley, Northern Syria: A Preliminary Report. *Bull. Inst. Archaeol.* (London), Vol. 15, pp. 149–70.

—— 1980. Géomorphologie et préhistoire de la vallée moyenne de l'Euphrate: essai de chronologie du Pléistocène et du Paleolithique de Syrie. *C. R. Acad. Sci.* (Paris), Ser. D, Vol. 290, pp. 162–70.

—— 1984. The Lower and Middle Paleolithic in the Upper Zarqa/Khirbet Samra Area of Northern Jordan, 1982–1983 Survey Results. *Annu. Dep. Antiq. Jordan*, Vol. 28, pp. 91–142.

BORDES, F. 1955. Le Paléolithique inférieur et moyen de Jabrud (Syrie), et la question du Pré-Aurignacien. *Anthropologie* (Paris), Vol. 59, pp. 486–507.

BOVIER-LAPIERRE, P. 1909. Stations paléolithiques du Balad Bechara. *Mélanges Fac. Orient.* (Beirut), Vol. 4, pp. 207 ff.

BRAIDWOOD, R.; HOWE, B. 1960. *Prehistoric Investigations in Iraqi Kurdistan.* Chicago, Oriental Institute of the University of Chicago.

CAUVIN, J.; SANLAVILLE, P. (eds) 1981. *Préhistoire du Levant.* Paris, CNRS.

CLARK, J. D. 1966. The Middle Acheulian Occupation Site at Latamné. *Ann. Archéol. Arab. Syr.* (Damascus), Vol. 16, pp. 31–74.

COPELAND, L. 1985. The Pointed Tools of Hummal Ia (El Kowm, Syria). *Cahi. Euphrate* (Paris), Vol. 4, pp. 177–89.

COPELAND, L.; HOURS, F. 1979. Le Paléolithique du Nahr el Kebir. pp. 21–38.

—— 1983. Le Yabroudien d'El Kowm (Syrie) et sa place dans le Paléolithique du Levant. *Paléorient,* Vol. 9, pp. 21–38.

COPELAND, L.; WESCOMBE, P. J. 1965. Inventory of Stone Age Sites in Lebanon I. *Mélanges Univ. St-Joseph,* Vol. 41, pp. 34–175.

—— 1966. Inventory of Stone Age Sites in Lebanon II. *Mélanges Univ. St-Joseph,* Vol. 42, pp. 1–174.

FLEISCH, H. 1951. Préhistoire au Liban en 1950. *Bull. Soc. Préhist. Fr.,* Vol. 48, pp. 26 ff.

—— 1954. Nouvelles Stations préhistoriques au Liban. *Bull. Soc. Préhist. Fr.,* Vol. 51, pp. 564 ff.

—— 1956. Dépôts préhistoriques de la côte libanaise et leur place dans la chronologie basée sur le Quaternaire marin. *Quaternaria* (Rome), Vol. 3, pp. 101–32.

—— 1962. La Côte libanaise au Pléistocène ancien et moderne. *Quaternaria* (Rome), Vol. 6, pp. 497–524.

FLEISCH, H.; REMIRO, J.; SANLAVILLE, P. 1969. Gisements prehistoriques découverts dans la région de Batroun. *Mélanges Univ. St-Joseph,* Vol. 45, pp. 1–28.

GARROD, D. A. E. 1956. Acheuléo-Jabroudien et 'Pré-Aurignacien' de la grotte de Taboun (Mont Carmel): étude stratigraphique et chronologique. *Quaternaria* (Rome), Vol. 3, pp. 39–59.

—— 1970. Pre-Aurignacian and Amudian. A Comparative Study of the Earliest Blade Industries of the Near East. *Fundamenta* (Festschrift Rust), Vol. 42, No. 1, pp. 224–9.

GARROD, D. A. E.; BATE, D. M. A. 1937. *The Stone Age of Mount Carmel I: Excavations at the Wady al Maghara.* Oxford.

GARROD, D. A. E.; KIRKBRIDE, D. 1961. Excavations of Abri Zumoffen, a Paleolithic Rock Shelter near Adlun, South Lebanon, 1958. *Bull. Mus. Beyrouth,* Vol. 16, pp. 7–46.

GILEAD, D. 1969. *Early Paleolithic Cultures in Israel and the Near East.* Jerusalem. (Ph.D. dissertation, University of Jerusalem.)

GILEAD, D.; RONEN, A. 1977. Acheulian Industries from Evron on the Western Galilee Coastal Plain. *Eretz-Isr.* (Jerusalem), Vol. 13, pp. 56–86.

GISIS, I.; BAR-YOSEF, O. 1974. New Excavations in Zuttiyeh Cave, Wadi Amud, Israel. *Paléorient,* Vol. 2, pp. 175–80.

GOREN, N. 1981. *The Lithic Assemblages of the Site of Ubeidiya, Jordan Valley.* Jerusalem. (Ph.D. dissertation.)

GOREN-INBAR, N. 1985. The Lithic Assemblage of the Bereket Ram Acheulean Site, Golan Heights. *Paléorient,* Vol. 11, pp. 7–28.

HANIHARA, K.; AKAZAWA, T. (eds) 1979. *Paleolithic Site of Douara Cave and Paleogeography of Pamyra Basin in Syria.* Tokyo. (Univ. Mus., Univ. Tokyo Bull., 16.)

HENNING, G. J.; HOURS, F. 1982. Dates pour le passage entre l'Acheuléen et le Paléolithique moyen à El Kowm (Syrie). *Paléorient,* Vol. 8, pp. 81–4.

HOOIJER, D. 1961–2. Middle Pleistocene Mammals from Latamne, Orontes Valley. *Ann. Archéol. Arab. Syr.,* Vol. 11/12, pp. 117–32.

HOURS, F. 1975. The Lower Paleolithic of Lebanon and Syria. In: WENDORF, F.; MARKS, A. (eds), *Problems in Prehistory: North Africa and Levant.* Dallas. pp. 249–71.

—— 1979. La Fin de l'Acheuléen en Syrie du nord, note preliminaire. *Paléorient,* Vol. 5, pp. 9–16.

—— 1981a. Le Paléolithique d'El Kowm, rapport préliminaire. *Paléorient,* Vol. 7, No. 1, pp. 33–55.

—— 1981b. Le Paléolithique inférieur de la Syrie et du Liban, le point de la question en 1980. In: CAUVIN, J.; SANLAVILLE, P. (eds), *Préhistoire du Levant.* Paris, CNRS. pp. 165–83.

—— 1982. Une nouvelle industrie en Syrie entre l'Acheuléen supérieur et le Levalloiso-Moustérien. *Archéologie du Levant* (Recueil Roger Saidah), pp. 33–46.

HOURS, F.; COPELAND, L.; AURENCHE, O. 1973. Les Industries paleolithiques du Proche-Orient, essai de corrélation. *Anthropol.* (Paris), Vol. 77, pp. 229–80.

HOURS, F.; SANLAVILLE, P. 1972. Découverte de silex taillés dans une plage située à +95 m à Borj Qinnarit (Liban). *C. R. Acad. Sci.* (Paris), Ser. D, Vol. 275, pp. 2219–21.

INIZAN, M. L. 1985. Des Indices acheuléens sur le bord du Tigre dans le nord de l'Iraq. *Paléorient,* Vol. 11, No. 1, pp. 101–2.

JELINEK, A. 1981. The Middle Paleolithic in the Southern Levant, from the Perspective of Tabum Cave. In: CAUVIN, J.; SANLAVILLE, P. (eds), *Préhistoire du Levant.* Paris, CNRS. pp. 265–85.

KÖKTEN, K. 1947. 1946 yili Tarih-öncesi arastirmalari, Antalya, Diarbakir, Urfa, Gaziantep cevreleri [The Exploration Campaign of 1946 in the Regions of Anatolia, Diarbahir, Urfa and Gaziantep]. *Belleten, Soc. turq. hist.* (Ankara), Vol. 11, No. 43, pp. 431–72.

LEROI-GOURHAN, ARLETTE. 1980. Les Analyses polliniques au Moyen-Orient. *Paléorient,* Vol. 6, pp. 79–91.

LIERE, W. J. VAN. 1966. The Pleistocene and Stone Age of the Orontes River (Syria). *Ann. Archéol. Arab. Syr.* (Damascus), Vol. 16, No. 2, pp. 7–30.

LIERE, W. J. VAN; HOOIJER, D. 1961–2. A Paleo-Orontes Level with Archidiskodon Meridionalis (Nesti) at Hama. *Ann. Archéol. Arab. Syr.* (Damascus), Vol. 11/12, pp. 165–73.

MODDERMAN, P. 1964. On a Survey of Paleolithic Sites near Hama. *Ann. Archéol. Arab. Syr.* (Damascus), Vol. 14, pp. 51–66.

MUHESEN, S. 1985. *L'Acheuléen évolué de Syrie.* Oxford. (BAR Int. Ser., 248.)

NEUVILLE, R. 1931. L'Acheuléen supérieur de la grotte d'Oumn Qatafa. *Anthropologie* (Paris), Vol. 41, pp. 13–51, 249–63.

—— 1934. Le Préhistorique de Palestine. *Rev. Biblique* (Paris), Vol. 43, pp. 237–59.

OPDYKE, N. D.; SHACKLETON, N. J. 1976. Oxygen Isotope and Paleomagnetic Stratigraphy of Pacific Core V 28–239, Late Pliocene to Latest Pleistocene. *Geol. Soc. Am. Mem.,* Vol. 145, pp. 449–64.

PERROT, J. 1968. La Préhistoire palestinienne. *Dictionnaire de la Bible.* Paris. Vol. 8 (Suppl.), cols. 286–446.

PRAUSNITZ, M. W. 1969. The Sequence of Early to Middle Palaeolithic Flint Industries along the Galilean Littoral. *Isr. Exploration J.* (Jerusalem), Vol. 19, pp. 129–36.

ROE, D. A. (ed.) 1983. *Adlun in the Stone Age: The Excavations of D. A. E. Garrod in the Lebanon, 1958–1963.* Oxford. (BAR Int. Ser., 159.)

ROLLEFSON, G. O. 1981. The Late Acheulean Site at Fjaje, Wadi el-Bustan, Southern Jordan. *Paléorient,* Vol. 7, No. 1, pp. 5–21.

—— 1984. A Middle Acheulian Surface Site from Wadi Uweinid, Eastern Jordan. *Paléorient,* Vol. 10, No. 1, pp. 127–34.

RONEN, A. et al. 1974. Notes on the Pleistocene Geology and Prehistory of the Central Dishon Valley, Upper Galilee, Israel. *Quartär,* Vol. 25, pp. 13–23.

RONEN, A.; AMIEL, A. 1974. The Evron Quarry: A Contribution to the Quaternary Stratigraphy of the Coastal Plain of Israel. *Paléorient,* Vol. 2, pp. 167–73.

RONEN, A.; PRAUSNITZ, M. W. 1979. Excavations at a Palaeolithic Hunters' site in the Evron Quarry. *Qadmoniot,* Vol. 12, pp. 51–3. (In Hebrew.)

RUST, A. 1951. *Die Höhlenfunde von Jabrud (Syrien).* Neumünster.

SANLAVILLE, P. 1977. *Étude géomorphologique de la région littorale du Liban.* Beirut. 2 vols.

—— 1979. Étude géomorphologique de la basse vallée du Nahr el Kebir. In: SANLAVILLE, P. (ed.), *Quaternaire et préhistoire du Nahr el Kebir septentrional.* Lyons. pp. 7–28.

—— (ed.) 1979. *Quaternaire et préhistoire du Nahr el Kebir septentrional.* Lyons.

—— 1981. Stratigraphie et chronologique du Quaternaire marin du Levant. In: CAUVIN, J.; SANLAVILLE, P. (eds), *Préhistoire du Levant.* Paris, CNRS. pp. 21–31.

—— (ed.) 1985. *Holocene Settlement in North Syria.* Oxford. (BAR Int. Ser., 238.)

SCHWARCZ, H. et al. 1979. Uranium Series Dating of Travertine from Archaeological Sites, Nahal Zin, Israel. *Nature* (London), Vol. 277, pp. 558–60.

SCHWARCZ, H.; GOLDBERG, P.; BLACKWELL, B. 1980. Uranium Series Dating of Archaeological Sites in Israel. *J. Earth Sci.* (Leeds), Vol. 29, pp. 157–65.

SENYUREK, M. 1961. The Upper Acheulean Industry of Altindere. *Belleten, Soc. turq. hist.* (Ankara), Vol. 25, pp. 149–98.

STEARNS, C. E.; THURBER, D. L. 1965. Th^{230}/U^{234} Dates of the Late Pleistocene Marine Fossils from Mediterranean and Marrocan Littorals. *Quaternaria* (Rome), Vol. 7, pp. 29–42.

STEKELIS, M. 1960. The Paleolithic Deposits of Jisr Banat Yakub. *Bull. Res. Counc. Isr.*, Vol. 9, G, pp. 61–87.

—— 1966. *Archaeological Excavations at Ubeidiya, 1960–1963.* Jerusalem.

STEKELIS, M.; BAR-YOSEF, O.; SCHICK, T. 1969. *Archaeological Excavations at Ubeidiya, 1964–1966.* Jerusalem, Israel Academy of Sciences and Humanities.

STEKELIS, M.; GILEAD, D. 1966. Ma'ayan Baruch, a Lower Paleolithic Site in Upper Galilee. *Mi-Tekufat ha-Even* (Jerusalem), Vol. 8, pp. 1–23.

TOMSKY, J. 1982. *Das Altpaläolithikum im Vorderen Orient.* Wiesbaden.

WENDORF, F.; MARKS, A. (eds) 1975. *Problems in Prehistory: North Africa and the Levant.* Dallas.

YALÇINKAYA, I. 1981. Le Paléolithique inférieur de Turquie. In: CAUVIN, J.; SANLAVILLE, P. (eds), *Préhistoire du Levant.* Paris, CNRS. pp. 207–18.

6

SOUTHERN ASIA

in the period of *Homo habilis* and *Homo erectus*

Ramchandra V. Joshi

The south Asian region comprising eastern parts of Iran, Afghanistan, Pakistan, India, Nepal, Bhutan, Myanmar (formerly Burma) and Sri Lanka forms a geographical unit that roughly occupies a position with the Euro-African region and Iran to the west, central Asia (the southern part of the former USSR and Tibet) to the north and Indonesia to the east. It falls approximately within latitudes 38° N and 5° S and between longitudes 60° and 100° E. Physiographically each of these parts has its own identity and within its boundaries a varied landscape pattern can be distinguished. The climatic characteristics of each of the sub-units of this landmass are different, although broadly the region falls within the tropical and subtropical belts with a predominantly monsoon climate in the Indian subcontinent and the pattern of natural vegetation varying from arid to semi-arid in the north to steppe and some semi-tropical forest to the south.

In tracing cultural evolution in South Asia during Stone Age times some limitations must be taken into consideration. Until very recently no physical remains of prehistoric humans belonging to the Pleistocene had been found anywhere in any part of South Asia. However, at the end of 1982 a nearly complete skull of *Homo erectus* was discovered at Hathnora, in the middle valley of the Narmada (Madhya Pradesh, India). The stratigraphy and the surrounding vertebrate fauna, with *Stegodon ganesa* and an archaic form of *Elephas hysudricus*, make it possible to date the site to the end of the Middle Pleistocene. This fossil skull seems to be connected with a Lower Palaeolithic industry, with handaxes and numerous cleavers (H. de Lumley and Sonakia, 1985; M.-A. de Lumley and Sonakia, 1985). Such a discovery was to be expected sooner or later, as during the trek from Africa to China and Indonesia, *Homo erectus* quite unavoidably had to cross the Indian subcontinent. Other biological evidence is available only in limited occurrence of fossils of contemporary fauna: no plant material has been found at any of the prehistoric sites. To obtain a comprehensive picture of the life-ways of the prehistoric communities it is essential to have data from excavated primary sites of Palaeolithic cultures, but the evidence available for this purpose is too meagre to be of any use.

The lithic artefacts of different stages of Palaeolithic cultures therefore are at present the chief material for the study of all aspects of the cultural development of the early human inhabitants of south Asia. Recent palaeo-environmental studies in these regions, particularly in India and Pakistan and lately in Afghanistan, have yielded substantial information to supplement these Palaeolithic typological studies.

Evidence of Lower Palaeolithic (*Homo erectus*) culture in south Asia has been found only in Pakistan, India and Myanmar. It has not yet been traced in Bhutan, Bangladesh or Sri Lanka, while its occurrence has not yet been confirmed in Afghanistan. The Palaeolithic artefacts from India and Pakistan show close similarities, but the material from Myanmar is somewhat different. There appear to be two traditions of Lower Palaeolithic cultures in India and Pakistan: (1) Soan type dominated by pebble-tools, and (2) handaxe industries (Acheulean). No stratigraphic evidence is so far available to indicate that the pebble-tools (chopper–chopping complex) represent the earliest lithic cultures. The Lower Palaeolithic tools of Myanmar are made on fossil wood which has given certain special features to the tool types although basically they may be placed in the chopper– chopping-tool tradition. Broadly the pebble tool-forms occur in mountainous regions while in the Indian peninsular region they become part of the Acheulean and are inseparable from it. The handaxe group shows a definite correspondence with those of Africa and Europe, while the pebble-tool tradition has parallels in the central Asian region (and also possibly in China). In the almost complete absence of physical remains of early humans it cannot be said with certainty whether these two traditions of Palaeolithic cultures represent two different human groups. South Asia might have functioned as a sort of corridor for early human movements from and to the west as well as to the east.

To gain a better appreciation of Lower Palaeolithic material *vis-à-vis* the contemporary environment it is necessary to review the occurrences of this culture on a subregional basis.

AFGHANISTAN

The possible extent of the Palaeolithic in Afghanistan is not yet fully understood. While undertaking such investigations it is necessary to take into consideration the prehistoric studies that have been carried out in the adjoining geographical regions of south-west, central and south Asia.

The history of Palaeolithic studies in Afghanistan can be traced back over three decades to 1951 when Carleton S. Coon made the first discoveries (Allchin and Hammond, 1978) at Kara Kamar. Later in 1959 Louis B. Dupree discovered several Palaeolithic sites in northern Afghanistan, some of which he later excavated such as the rock shelter Dara-i-kur in Badakhshan and sites near the town of Aq Kupruk. Thereafter exploratory work on the Palaeolithic continued, with a contribution by Dupree, south of the Hindu Kush which yielded in 1974 Middle Palaeolithic and

possibly Lower Palaeolithic tools on ancient lake beaches; these findings are reviewed by Davis (1978).

Although no definite Lower Palaeolithic remains have yet been found in Afghanistan proper, these have been located in the adjoining regions of the Tadjikistan in association with a loessic deposit and composed of chopper–chopping industries like those of the Soan culture in Pakistan.

PAKISTAN (Map 7)

Although a few stray finds of palaeoliths were known from the Pakistan area it should be admitted that the work of de Terra and his party initiated the systematic studies of palaeoenvironment and lithic cultures of the Quaternary in the Indo-Pakistan region. The sequence of Upper Siwalik and post-Siwalik deposits and the terraces on the Soan river and the Palaeolithic artefacts found by Terra and Paterson

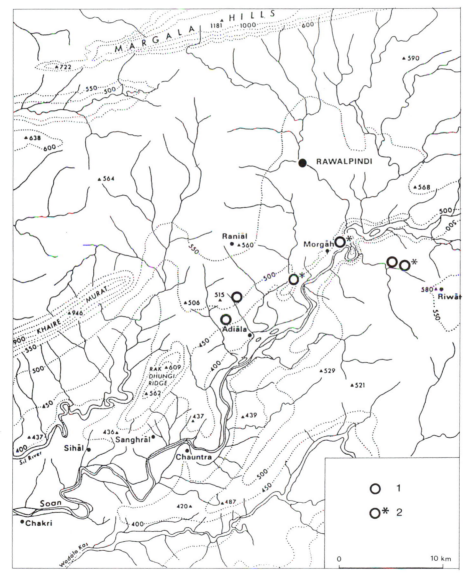

Map 7 The Soan valley and the location of Palaeolithic sites in Pakistan: 1, sites already mentioned by de Terra and Paterson (1939); 2, sites discovered since 1939. (After H. Rendell, 1981; Courtesy Cambridge University Press.)

(1939) laid the foundation for Stone Age studies in Pakistan and India. Fresh information on these aspects with respect to the Indian region are considered in the section about Palaeolithic studies in India.

The Potwar plateau is of special importance for Palaeolithic studies in Pakistan, owing to its geographical situation between western Asia and the Indian subcontinent. It is bounded by the Indus in the west, the Jhelum and the Poonch rivers to the east, the Pir Panjal foothills in the north and the Salt range in the south. It has a well-preserved geostratigraphic record in the Siwalik formations, beginning with the Miocene, and great potential in its Upper Pleistocene landscape for studying Late Palaeolithic events.

Owing to lack of systematic exploration there is a dearth of evidence for the presence of early humans in the Pliocene and the Lower Pleistocene. The Palaeolithic material from this region, comprising chopper–chopping industries and the associated flake component, seems to be of Middle Pleistocene age.

While establishing the Quaternary climatic and archaeological sequence, de Terra and Paterson (1939) followed the then current view of the existence of four major glacial episodes in Europe and tried to apply the same to the Potwar region of Pakistan. Significantly, Porter (1970) has also noted only three main glacial phases in the Swat area. Now, however, this is not tenable, because from the study of ocean sediments it has been proved that there were at least seventeen major glaciations in the last 1.7 million years.

Since Rendell's review (1981) of the Pleistocene sequence in the Soan valley it is now certain that the Alpine Quaternary glacial sequence cannot be applied to the Potwar region. Rendell has also observed that the Palaeolithic sites of the middle Soan valley are associated with Siwalik conglomerates rather than with de Terra's Boulder Conglomerate of second glacial and subsequent terraces.

The modified relative chronology of the Siwalik and Pleistocene deposits of the middle Soan valley would be as follows: Pinjor beds (Soan formation, about 2.5 million years ago) followed by the Upper Siwalik conglomerates (1.9 million years ago) which were subjected to uplift, folding and erosion. Over these rest the Lei Conglomerate complex (valley fill) and loess deposits. Subsequent erosion and warping (about 40,000 years ago) was followed by further loess deposition.

Paterson and Drummond (1962) had divided the entire collection from the Soan into three typological categories, pebble-tools, cores and flakes. The artefacts made on pebbles were further classified as follows:

(1) flat-based: pebbles split, then unifacially worked;
(2) oblates: pebbles not split, unifacially worked;
(3) nucleates: pebbles not split, bifacially worked.

They further made three divisions of the Palaeolithic artefacts which suggest evolutionary trends:

1 Middle Pleistocene Soan subdivided into (a) the Pre-Soan, (b) the Lower Soan and (c) the Middle Soan. The tool types of these groups are mostly large flakes of quartzite and include a variable proportion of pebble-tools, some of which are quite heavy;
2 Upper Pleistocene Soan, subdivisible into Upper Soan A and Upper Soan B. The tool composition is almost the same as in 1, with some tools of smaller size;
3 Final Pleistocene Soan, which also comprises pebble-tools and a few heavily rolled tools of the handaxe industry, found in the Soan Valley near Rawalpindi, Chauntra and

in the Indus Valley near Attock. However, the relationship of the successive Soan terraces and the Palaeolithic artefacts found over them has not yet been clearly understood.

Dennell (1981) has laid stress on the evaluation of the physical forms of mankind in the Pliocene and Pleistocene of the Potwar Plateau as well as of the artefactual material associated with them. As in other south Asian regions, no remains of the earliest type of hominid have been discovered in Pakistan. Another important aspect of Palaeolithic studies in the Potwar region is the flake industry found invariably in all the localities. This flake industry needs further examination to assess its position in the Asian flake-tool tradition as a whole. The most recent contribution by Rendell and Dennell (1985) is the dating of the Lower Palaeolithic artefacts from northern Pakistan. During exploration in 1983 they found three Acheulean-type handaxes *in situ* in Upper Siwalik contexts which have been dated between 700,000 and 400,000 years ago on the basis of palaeomagnetic and fission-track evidence.

B. Allchin (1981a) had also noted a rolled Acheulean handaxe on a gravel ridge. However, no handaxe was found associated with the Lei conglomerate sequence.

INDIA (Map 8)

Sites yielding Lower Palaeolithic artefacts (Fig. 7) occur in almost all parts of India and in varied geographical situations. They are found in the foothills of the Himalayas which have semi-temperate climatic characteristics, in desert or semi-arid regions like Rajasthan and Saurashtra, in forested and hilly regions in eastern India, in coastal areas, on river terraces in peninsular plateau regions, near natural rock exposures, rock shelters and in association with detrital laterite gravels. Prehistoric humans thus seem to have adapted themselves to all kinds of land forms, despite their regional differences, within the basically monsoonal climate of India.

Explorations for Stone Age material in India using a geomorphological approach were initiated by de Terra and Paterson when they systematically surveyed the Soan valley in the Potwar region (now in Pakistan) and the Kashmir valley.

While working in these areas de Terra and Paterson briefly examined Stone Age sites situated on the Narmada river in central India and on the Kortalayar river near Madras in south India. The terraces and gravel deposits in association with which lithic artefacts were found in these areas, which lie far away from the Quaternary glacial region or sub-Himalayas, were then explained by adopting the same four-fold sequence of glacial and interglacial episodes worked out by de Terra and Paterson, the boulder conglomerate horizon of the Narmada river being equated with the boulder conglomerates of the distant Potwar region. Lal (1956) employed the same sequence of glacial geomorphological events in the Kangra region of Himachal Pradesh to correlate the pebble industries of the Kangra valley with the high-level terraces on the Banganga river of that region. Sankalia's (1974) discovery of Stone Age artefacts near Pahlgaum in the Kashmir Valley again raised the problem of Quaternary glaciation in that valley. All these attempts by prehistorians were made in the hope of understanding the palaeoenvironment and chronology of the local Palaeolithic cultures: these had been reconstructed in western countries on the basis of the Quaternary Alpine glacial sequences in

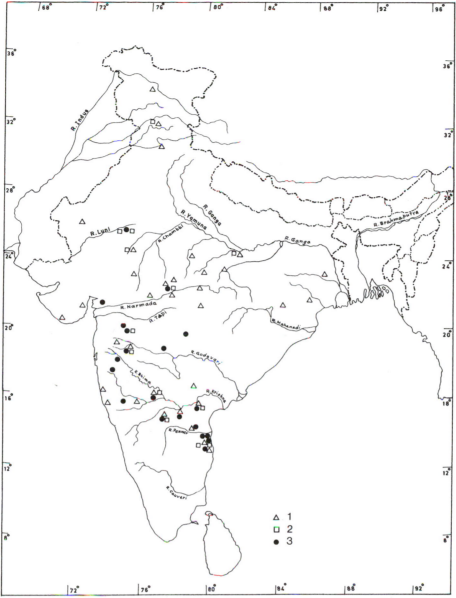

Map 8 Location of major Palaeolithic sites in India: 1, Lower Palaeolithic; 2, Middle Palaeolithic; 3, Upper Palaeolithic. (After K. Paddayya.)

Europe and the sequence of pluvial episodes in non-glaciated areas like Africa.

The recent geomorphological survey of the Liddar valley (Joshi et al., 1974) in Kashmir shows that there is no evidence consistent with such a four-fold Alpine glacial sequence in this area and the boulder-beds, screes, alluvial cones and, in places, clay and sand beds are generally the result of fluvial action, doubtless intensified by heavy monsoonal precipitation, the steep valley gradients and contemporary tectonic activity. In the Swat valley in Pakistan, Porter (1970) has traced three glaciations originating at altitudes of about 4,000 metres or more and terminating at altitudes as low as approximately 2,000 metres. Thus there is correspondence in the history of Quaternary glaciation in these two adjacent regions.

Lal (1956) had observed five high-level terraces on the Banganga river (Kangra valley), a tributary of the Beas in Himachal Pradesh, respectively at 183 m, 125 m, 50 m, 30 m and 10 m above the present river bed. Following similar terraces on the Soan, Lal had identified them as evidence of a succession in tune with the glacial sequence, but later

examination (Joshi et al., 1974) showed that these terraces are developed on fluvio-glacial cone and fan deposits composed of boulders, cobbles, sands and clays and that they are not connected with the Quaternary glacial sequence.

It is interesting to note that the Palaeolithic artefacts in this area occur on terraces and not within terrace deposits; these terraces are therefore of little value in establishing the chronology of Lower Palaeolithic cultures.

The problem of correlating glacial and interglacial stages in the Himalayas with the pluvial and interpluvial stages in the foothill zone is exceedingly complex. The actual number of Quaternary glaciations in the Himalayas is not known; this creates problems in interpreting their significance in Indian prehistory in palaeoenvironmental studies and chronology.

It appears that Pleistocene cold periods were rather dry episodes in the Indian monsoonal climatic region; this contrasts with the pluvials that occurred during these periods in some African and European areas (Joshi, 1970).

In peninsular India the problems are of a different nature. Stone Age artefacts in this region occur in association with

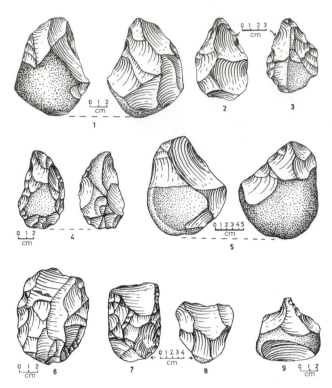

Figure 7 Lower Palaeolithic artefacts (India). 1 and 5, choppers; 2–4 and 6, handaxes; 7–8, cleavers; 9, borer.

sediments exposed in river sections or overbank deposits, in rock shelters at a higher altitude, away from the present river beds, associated with aeolian deposits and in other such situations.

In the upland region of the Deccan, peninsular Indian Quaternary deposits are mostly fluvial and are often found in river sections. Recently, geo-archaeological studies of several major river systems in Peninsular India have thrown considerable light on the behaviour of these streams in the vicinity of which prehistoric humans had located their camps or settlements. It appears that intensive fluvial erosion occurred from the late Middle Pleistocene to about 50,000 years ago. This is possibly due to tectonic movements and a small increase in rainfall implying a change in the climate. However, climatic changes during the Quaternary were not drastic and prehistoric humans could adapt themselves to such minor environmental changes, as can be observed even at the present day in this monsoonal climatic region (Rajaguru and Kale, 1985).

Indian coastal areas have also yielded Lower Palaeolithic cultures. In this respect coastal Saurashtra and Gujarat, which are situated close to climatically sensitive areas like Rajasthan, have proved very useful in understanding changing environments during Quaternary times as well as providing data on changes in sea-level and coastline. Two marine transgressions have been identified from the occurrence of marine deposits like miliolites, the first at the beginning of late Middle Pleistocene about 170,000 years ago and the second around 30,000 years ago. The Quaternary sea-level changes have also been recorded all along the west and east coasts. On the east coast the Lower Palaeolithic Acheulean sequence has been worked out on the basis of such sea-level changes.

A very large tract of north-west India in the Thar desert falls within an arid or semi-arid climatic zone. Even these areas have been found to possess Lower Palaeolithic Acheulean sites associated with sand dunes.

Animal fossils of the Lower Pleistocene period occur in

the Lower Karewa lake beds in Kashmir and in the Pinjor beds of the Upper Siwaliks, but so far no Stone Age tool has been found in the context of these geological formations. The largest number of Stone Age sites occurs in the Indian Peninsular region and a few of these localities, particularly the sites in the valleys of the Narmada, Godavari, Krishna and so on, have yielded rich faunas in fluvial deposits which could be dated from late Middle Pleistocene to early Upper Pleistocene (Badam, 1979). The most common animal types are *Sus namadicus*, *Elephas hysudricus*, *Equus namadicus*, *Bos namadicus*, *Stegodon insignisganesa*, *Cervus* sp. and the like. This fauna indicates an environment of savannah grassland interspersed with swamps. It may be mentioned here that Lower Palaeolithic artefacts occur in the same area where these animal fossils are found. But so far they have not been found together in the same horizon at undisturbed primary sites.

There is yet an unsolved problem of the placement of the Plio-Pleistocene boundary in north-west India in the Siwalik formations; this has some significance in studies of the evolution of fossil vertebrates in India.

Despite the progress made over the last two decades we have not been able to build up a complete pollen stratigraphy for the Quaternary period in India (Mittre et al., 1985). The Middle Pleistocene formations to which belong some of the earliest Stone Age cultures have so far yielded no pollen. Pollen evidence has been traced in the Upper Pleistocene, covering a period from about 130,000 to 10,000 years ago, but it can provide little information as far as the Lower Palaeolithic cultures are concerned.

Early hominid remains are extremely rare in south Asia. Fossils of *Ramapithecus* found in the Siwalik area were thought to be hominid but now are considered to belong to an ancestor of the orang-utan. The recent discovery of a skull-cap of *Homo erectus narmadiensis* from the Narmada river in central India is of importance in the study of the evolution of physical forms of humankind in the Indian subcontinent. As already mentioned, the Narmada skull represents the only physical remains of *Homo erectus* (the maker of the earliest Palaeolithic artefacts) found so far anywhere in South Asia. This fossil was found associated with Late Acheulean tools.

A large complex of open-air Acheulean sites was excavated by Paddayya (1982) in the Hunsgi Valley in Karnataka. At this locality a group of occupation or camping sites was found. An interesting feature of the Acheulean industry here is the employment of limestone as principal raw material, and although some assemblages display advanced Acheulean features the industry essentially belongs to the Early Acheulean tradition. Some social aspects in the form of extensive and in places even repeated occupation reveal that the Stone Age population practised only a localized or restricted type of nomadism, mostly dependent on the seasonal availability of food and water resources (Paddayya, 1984).

The subsistence pattern of Lower Palaeolithic populations cannot be firmly established. No excavated site has yielded faunal or pollen material associated with the lithic artefacts. The faunas occurring in river valleys contain a large number of remains of cattle. Like the Lower Palaeolithic populations of Europe and Africa, the practitioners of this culture in India must have been hunters and food gatherers.

The technology of the Lower Palaeolithic of India does not differ from what has been experimentally demonstrated to have been used in Europe or Africa. The typology by and large is also the same: common tool types include varieties of handaxes, cleavers, choppers, scrapers and points. While choppers are made on cores, pebbles, lumps of rock or thick flakes, flakes and large blades have been used for making other types of implements, depending on the locally available types of stone (and, therefore, on local geology). The most common rock types are quartzites, sandstones, basalt (Deccan Trap), chert, vein quartz, limestone and occasionally even metamorphic rocks and granite. Depending upon the texture of the rock material, the resultant tool has a coarser or finer appearance.

The Soan culture was once thought to belong to the chopper–chopping tool complex of South-East Asia (Movius, 1948). Pebble industries comparable to the Soan of Pakistan have been found in Himachal Pradesh in the valleys of the Beas-Banganga (Kangra), Sirsa, Markanda and other rivers on the high-level river terraces.

There are two opinions on the position of the Soan industry and its counterparts met with in Himachal Pradesh, which geographically belong to the sub-Himalayan region. One view is that the Soan and allied exclusive pebble industries constitute a culture or tradition quite different from the Lower Palaeolithic of the rest of India, which comprises handaxes and cleavers. According to the proponents of this view the Soan type indicates adaptation to a hilly region, while the other with its dominant Acheulean handaxe and cleaver component reflects occupation of ecological settings like river valleys, plateaux and plains (Mohopatra, 1985). According to the other view, both the pebble-based chopper group (Soan type) and the handaxe and cleaver group are part and parcel of a single Lower Palaeolithic handaxe cultural complex and thus its adherents do not support the idea of cultural dichotomy during the Lower Palaeolithic phase.

In a large country like India which has a diversity of geographical settings coupled with variations in the available raw material there are bound to be differences in the proportions of various tool types in the assemblages at different sites. The Indian Lower Palaeolithic culture is exclusively Acheulean in character. There is as yet no indisputable stratigraphic evidence of the existence of a pre-handaxe (pre-Acheulean) substratum comprising exclusively pebble industries like Oldowan in Africa. Attempts are being made to identify subdivisions of the Acheulean culture stratigraphically, but as yet without success. For this purpose excavations at primary sites were recently carried out in the Bhimbetka rock shelter area, Hunsgi in the Krishna valley and Attirampakkam and Vadamadurai sites near Madras and some are in progress in the Narmada valley. At one stage it was thought that the presence of cleavers in certain Lower Palaeolithic collections reflected well-wooded country and a moist climate, but the study of all the known excavated and explored sites showed that this was not the case. Rather, the dominance of cleavers over handaxes in a collection rather represents an advanced Acheulean cultural stage (Joshi, 1970). Flake-blades and blades occur at Stone Age sites in fairly large numbers and this also is an indication of the evolved character of the Acheulean assemblage.

MYANMAR

Systematic prehistoric investigations were initiated in Myanmar in 1937–8 in the Irrawaddy valley of Upper Myanmar, when a new Lower Palaeolithic (Anyathian) cultural development belonging to the Middle Pleistocene was recognized (Movius, 1948). On typological grounds, the Zhoukoudian (China), Pacitan (Patjitan) (South Java) and Soan (Pakistan) cultures are related to each other and as a group they form a new culture complex of the Lower Palaeolithic.

A series of river terraces in the Irrawaddy valley on which were found Palaeolithic artefacts seem to have been formed during Pleistocene pluvial and interpluvial periods; these are comparable to the sequence worked out by de Terra and Paterson for the Potwar plateau in Pakistan.

The Anyathian (Lower Palaeolithic) culture of Myanmar is devoid of handaxes and the implements of this culture were mostly found in the Dry Zone of the Irrawaddy valley of Upper Myanmar. These tools cannot be precisely dated. Three phases of the Anyathian culture have been distinguished on typological grounds. The chief raw material is fossil wood; this is difficult to work by controlled flaking, with the result that most of the implements formed are tabular 'end' implements of the adze or chopper variety. Sometimes silicified tuff and quartzite are also used as raw material.

The components of Anyathian culture are handadzes, chopper–chopping tools, cores and flake-tools. The Early Anyathian comprises cruder forms, while the Late Anyathian of Myanmar is more advanced although the tool types remain the same.

The Anyathian culture represents one industry within the chopper–chopping tool complex of the south and east Asian region. The flake element in this culture requires fresh investigation to establish its significance in the flake tradition of south and east Asia.

In the words of Movius,

the most important single conclusion to be drawn from the implications of the new archaeological material brought to light ... in Southern and Eastern Asia is that this area cannot be considered in any sense 'progressive' from a cultural point of view ... the archaeological, or palaeoethnological, material very definitely indicates that as early as Lower Palaeolithic times Southern and Eastern Asia as a whole was a region of cultural retardation. Therefore, it seems very unlikely that this vast area could ever have played a vital and dynamic role in early human evolution.

(Movius, 1948, p. 364)

No recent information on the Palaeolithic culture in Myanmar has come forth, and so no assessment of early cultural development can be made. As the artefacts have come from surface sites and since no excavations of primary sites in this country have yet been undertaken it is not possible to state anything about the life-ways of the early inhabitants of Myanmar.

SRI LANKA

Sarasin has observed that there was no evidence of a Lower Palaeolithic culture in Sri Lanka. The absence of the Acheulean in Sri Lanka, although it is quite prolific on the Madras coast of India, is explained by the suggestion that perhaps during the Lower Palaeolithic times this island was not connected to the mainland of India.

The Ratanpura gem-bearing gravels have yielded fragments of fossil vertebrates and lithic artefacts which on the basis of radiometric dating seem to represent material of two periods, partly of the Upper Pleistocene and partly of the early Holocene. On palaeontological evidence the Ratanpura fauna, when compared with that from peninsular India, can be dated to 125,000 to 80,000 years ago (Deraniyagala, 1985).

BIBLIOGRAPHY

ALLCHIN, B. 1973. Blade and Burin Industries of West Pakistan and Western India. *South Asian Archaeology.* New Jersey. pp. 39–50. (Reprinted 1981.)

—— 1981*a*. The Palaeolithic of the Potwar Plateau, Panjab, Pakistan: A Fresh Approach. *Paléorient*, Vol. 7, No. 1, pp. 123–33.

—— (ed.) 1981*b*. *South Asian Archaeology: International Conference Proceedings.* Cambridge.

ALLCHIN, B.; ALLCHIN, F. R. 1968. *The Birth of Indian Civilization in India and Pakistan before 500 BC.* Baltimore.

—— 1982. *The Rise of Civilization in India and Pakistan.* Cambridge.

ALLCHIN, B.; GOUDIE, A.; HEDGE, K. 1978. *The Prehistory and Palaeogeography of the Great Indian Desert.* London.

ALLCHIN, F. R.; CHAKRABARTI, D. K. *A Source-book of Indian Archaeology.* New Delhi. Vol. 1.

ALLCHIN, F. R.; HAMMOND, N. (eds) 1978. *The Archaeology of Afghanistan.* London.

BADAM, G. L. 1979. *Pleistocene Fauna of India with Special Reference to Siwaliks.* Poona.

BADAM, G. L.; GANJOO, R. K.; RAJAGURU, S. N. 1986. Evaluation of Fossil Hominid – the Maker of Late Acheulian Tools at Hatnora, Madhya Pradesh, India. *Curr. Sci.* (Bangalore), Vol. 55, No. 3, pp. 143–5.

BANERJEE, N. R. 1969. Discovery of Remains of Prehistoric Man in Nepal. *Anc. Nepal* (Kathmandu), No. 6.

BOWLBY, S. R. 1978. The Geographical Background. In: ALLCHIN, F. R.; HAMMOND, N. (eds), *The Archaeology of Afghanistan.* London. pp. 9–36.

CORVINUS, G. 1985. Prehistoric Discoveries in the Foothills of the Himalayas in Nepal. *Anc. Nepal* (Kathmandu), Nos. 86–8, pp. 7–12.

DANI, A. H. 1964. Sanghao Cave Excavations. *Anc. Pak.* (Peshawar), Vol. 1, pp. 1–50.

DAVIS, R. S. 1978. The Palaeolithic. In: ALLCHIN, F. R.; HAMMOND, N. (eds), *The Archaeology of Afghanistan.* London. pp. 37–70.

DENNELL, R. W. 1981. The Importance of the Potwar Plateau, Pakistan, to Studies of Early Man. In: ALLCHIN, B. (ed.), *South Asian Archaeology: International Conference Proceedings.* Cambridge. pp. 10–19.

DENNELL, R. W.; RENDELL, H.; HAILWOOD, E. 1988. Early Toolmaking in Asia: Two-Million-Year Artefacts in Pakistan. *Antiq.*, Vol. 62, No. 234, pp. 98–106.

DEO, S. B.; PADDAYYA, K. (eds) 1985. *Recent Advances in Indian Archaeology.* Poona.

DERANIYAGALA, S. U. 1980. Prehistoric Research in Sri Lanka, 1885–1980. In: *P. E. P. Deraniyagala Commemoration Volume.* pp. 152–207.

—— 1985. The Prehistory of Sri Lanka: An Outline. In: SOUTH ASIAN ARCHAEOLOGICAL CONGRESS, *Proceedings.* New Delhi.

DE TERRA, H.; PATERSON, T. T. 1939. *Studies on the Ice Age in India and Associated Human Cultures.* Washington, Carnegie Institute. (Publications, 499.)

DIXIT, K. N. (ed.) 1985. *Archaeological Perspectives of India since Independence.* New Delhi.

GUPTA, S. P. 1979. *Archaeology of Soviet Central Asia and the Indian Borderlands.* Delhi. Vol. 1.

GUZDER, S. 1980. *Quaternary Environment and Stone Age Cultures of the Konkan, Coastal Maharashtra, India.* Poona.

IKAWA-SMITH, F. (ed.) 1978. *Early Palaeolithic in South and East Asia.* The Hague/Paris.

JACOBSON, J. 1979. Recent Development in South Asian Prehistory and Protohistory. *Annu. Rev. Anthropol.*, Vol. 8, pp. 467–502.

—— 1986. *Studies in the Archaeology of India and Pakistan.* Oxford/New Delhi.

JOSHI, R. V. 1961. Stone Age Industries of the Damoh Area. *Anc. India*, Vol. 17, pp. 5–36.

—— 1966*a*. Middle Stone Age in India. In: CONGRESSO INTERNATIONALE DI SCIENZE PREISTORICE E PROTOSTORICE, 6. *Atti.* pp. 276–80.

—— 1966*b*. Prehistoric Exploration in Kathmandu Valley, Nepal. *Anc. India*, Vol. 22, pp. 75–82.

—— 1970. The Characteristics of the Pleistocene Climatic Events in Indian Sub-Continent: A Land of Monsoon Climate. *Indian Antiq.*, Vol. 4, Nos. 1–4, pp. 53–63.

—— 1973. Significance of Cleavers in Indian Acheulian Industries. *Archaeo-civilization*, No. 7/8, pp. 39–46.

—— 1978. *Stone Age Cultures of Central India (A Report on the Excavations of Rockshelters at Adamgarh, Central India).* Poona.

JOSHI, R. V. et al. 1974. Quaternary Glaciation and Palaeolithic Sites in the Liddar Valley (Jammu-Kashmir). *World Archaeol.*, Vol. 5, pp. 369–79.

LAL, B. B. 1956. Palaeoliths from the Beas and Banganga Valleys, Punjab. *Anc. India*, Vol. 12, pp. 58–92.

LUMLEY, H. DE; SONAKIA, A. 1985. Contexte stratigraphique et archéologique de l'homme de la Narmada, Hathnora, Madhya Pradesh, Inde. *Anthropologie* (Paris), Vol. 89, pp. 3–12.

LUMLEY, M. A.; SONAKIA, A. 1985. Première Découverte d'un *Homo erectus* sur le continent indien à Hathnora, dans la vallée moyenne de la Narmada. *Anthropologie* (Paris), Vol. 89, pp. 13–61.

MARATHE, A. R. 1981. *Geoarchaeology of the Hiran Valley, Saurashtra, India.* Poona.

MISRA, V. N. 1978. The Acheulian Industry of Rock Shelter III F-23 at Bhimbetka, Central India. *Indo-Pac. Prehist. Assoc. Bull.*, Vol. 1, pp. 130–71.

—— 1987. Evolution of the Landscape and Human Adaptation in the Thar Desert. (Presidential Address to Archaeological Section, Indian Science Congress.)

MISRA, V. N.; MATE, M. S. (eds) 1965. *Indian Prehistory: 1964.* Poona.

MITTRE, V. et al. 1985. Pollen Stratigraphy of India. In: DIXIT, K. N. (ed.), *Archaeological Perspectives of India since Independence.* New Delhi. pp. 115–22.

MOHOPATRA, G. C. 1985. The Lower Palaeolithic in India. In: DIXIT, K. N. (ed.), *Archaeological Perspectives of India since Independence.* New Delhi. pp. 1–8.

MOVIUS, H. L. 1944. Early Man and Pleistocene Stratigraphy in Southern and Eastern Asia. *Pap. Peabody Mus. Am. Archaeol. Ethnol.*, Vol. 19, pp. 1–125.

—— 1948. The Lower Palaeolithic Cultures of Southern and Eastern Asia. *Trans. Am. Philos. Soc.* (Philadelphia, Pa.), NS, Vol. 38, Part 4, pp. 364–76.

MURTY, M. L. K. 1985. Upper Palaeolithic Culture in India. In: DIXIT, K. N. (ed.), *Archaeological Perspectives of India since Independence.* New Delhi. pp. 16–25.

OHRI, V. C. (ed.) 1979. *Prehistory of Himachal Pradesh, Some Latest Findings.* Simla, State Museum.

PADDAYYA, K. 1982. *Acheulian Culture of the Hunsgi Valley (Peninsular India): A Settlement System Perspective.* Poona.

—— 1984. India. In: BAR-YOSEF, O. et al. (eds), *Neue Forschungen zur Altsteinzeit.* Munich. pp. 345–403.

PATERSON, T. T.; DRUMMOND, H. J. H. 1962. *Soan: The Palaeolithic of Pakistan.* Karachi, Dept. of Archaeology, Gov. of Pakistan.

PORTER, S. C. 1970. Quaternary Glacial Record in Swat Kohistan, West Pakistan. *Bull. Geol. Soc. Am.* (Rochester, NY), Vol. 81, pp. 1421–46.

RAJAGURU, S. N. 1973. Late Pleistocene Climatic Changes in Western India. In: AGRAWAL, D. P.; GHOSH, A. (eds), *Radiocarbon and Indian Archaeology.* Bombay. pp. 80–7.

RAJAGURU, S. N. et al. 1980. The Terminal Pleistocene Microlithic Industry of Inamgaon, Maharashtra. *Bull. Deccan Coll. Res. Inst.* (Poona), Vol. 40, pp. 150–9.

RAJAGURU, S. N.; KALE, V. S. 1985. Changes in the Fluvial Regime of Western Maharashtra Upland Rivers during Late Quaternary *J. Geol. Soc. India*, Vol. 26, No. 1, pp. 16–27.

RENDELL, H. 1981. The Pleistocene Sequence in the Soan Valley,

Northern Pakistan. In: ALLCHIN, B. (ed.), *South Asian Archaeology: International Conference Proceedings*. Cambridge. p. 7.

RENDELL, H.; DENNELL, R. W. 1985. Dated Lower Paleolithic Artefacts from Northern Pakistan. *Curr. Anthropol.*, Vol. 26, No. 3, p. 39.

SALIM, M. 1986. *The Middle Stone Age Cultures of Northern Pakistan.* Islamabad.

SANKALIA, H. D. 1974. *Prehistory and Protohistory of India and Pakistan.* Poona.

SAXENA, M. N. 1982. The Himalayan Uplift, Antecedent Drainage and the Elusive Fossil-Man in the North-Western India. *Recent Res. Geol.*, Vol. 8, pp. 139–52.

SCHWARTZBERG, J. E. (ed.) 1978. *A Historical Atlas of South Asia.* Chicago/London.

THAPAR, B. K. 1985. *Recent Archaeological Discoveries in India.* Paris/Tokyo, UNESCO/Centre for East Asian Cultural Studies.

7

CHINA

in the period of *Homo habilis* and *Homo erectus*

Wu Rukang and Jia Lanpo

Up to the present, no trace of *Homo habilis* has been found in China.

China has been world famous in palaeoanthropology since the discovery of the skull-cap of a variety of *Homo erectus* known as 'Peking Man'. It was found in 1929 by Pei Wen-zhong at the cave site of Zhoukoudian (Choukoutien), near Beijing (Peking) in north China. Systematic excavations have been under way at this site since 1927 but were interrupted for twelve years during the Sino-Japanese war. These produced a rich variety of finds, ranging from five fairly complete skull-caps (four adult and one juvenile), about 150 teeth and many limb bone fragments, to a large number of stone implements and, of particular importance, evidence of the use of fire. In 1949, excavation of the site was resumed and one more skull-cap of Peking Man (Plate 11), stone implements, ashes from fires and animal fossils were unearthed.

From 1977 to 1980 a multidisciplinary study of the site was carried out. The thirteen layers of deposits from the top to the lowest layer of the cave were dated by different methods such as fission track, uranium–thorium series, palaeomagnetism and thermoluminiscence. The results showed that the uppermost layers date to 230,000 years ago, the tenth layer to 460,000 years ago and the lowest layer to more than 700,000 years ago. The formation and development of the cave, the division of the geological strata and the palaeoclimate of the period of these early humans were then studied in detail (Wu et al., 1985).

The skull vault of Peking Man is thick and flattened. The forehead is receding. The widest part of the skull lies near the external auditory meatus. The supraorbital tori at the front and the transverse occipital torus at the back are well developed. A sagittal ridge is present on the top of the skull. The mandible or lower jaw bone is robust. The teeth are big and the occlusal surfaces of the molars have complicated wrinkles. The limb bones are similar to those of humans of the Modern type, but have thicker walls and a smaller marrow cavity. The five adult skulls (i.e. excluding the juvenile one) so far found have cranial capacities ranging from 1,015 to 1,225 cc, with an average of 1,088 cc. The sexual differences are marked, the males being more robust than the females.

The characteristic features of these individuals constitute the model of Peking Man not only in China but also in Asia (Plate 11).

More than 100,000 stone artefacts were found in the Zhoukoudian cave. These already display the use of different techniques to make flakes from different raw materials. Most numerous are bipolar flakes of vein quartz. The stone implements consist of a complex of types, such as different types of choppers, scrapers, gravers, points and drills (Fig. 8). Recently, Pei and Zhang (1985) published a monograph on the detailed study of these artefacts. They concluded that they showed a general tendency from the lowest (eleventh) layer to the uppermost layers to become gradually smaller and more sophisticated, having fewer choppers and chopping tools and more points, especially small ones, and also more awls and gravers; similarly, the simple percussion method of the early stage became less important and was gradually replaced by the retouch and prepared core flaking. In general the culture of Peking Man seems to be transitional from the earlier Donggutuo culture to the later Xujiayao culture.

The results of pollen analysis in the Zhoukoudian area suggest that Peking Man lived in the climate of an interglacial period that was not much different from that of northern China today (Kong et al., 1985). The vegetation consisted of temperate deciduous forests and steppes on the plains and in the valleys and coniferous forests on the mountains.

In the deposits in the cave are quantities of charred seeds

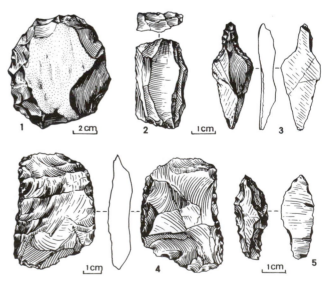

Figure 8 Artefacts, Zhoukoudian (China): 1, dicoidal chopper; 2, bipolar core; 3, awl; 4, scraper; 5, point.

of the Chinese hackberry, which evidently served as food. The analysis of pollen in the deposits gives evidence of other plants, such as walnut, hazelnut, pine, elm and rambler rose. The fruits and seeds of those species must also be considered candidates for inclusion in the cave dwellers' diet.

The Peking Man population was evidently able to compete successfully with large carnivores as hunters. An abundance of fossil bones of mammals of various sizes found in the cave indicates that they not only hunted small game but were also capable of killing large animals. The large quantity of fossils belonging to at least 3,000 individual deer of two species, the thick-jaw bone deer (*Megaloceros pachyosteus*) and the sika deer (*Pseudaxis grayi*), could be regarded as an indication that deer were the commonest prey. It can be inferred, therefore, that these people are more likely to have been living in a group when they began to hunt deer. Furthermore, thousands of fossils of prey species found in the cave suggest that these primitive hunters may have preferred to bring prey back to the cave and share meat with others. It is also possible to speculate that the hunting behaviour may have caused or contributed to the sexual division of labour within the group: the pattern of male hunters and female gatherers, which is common in hunting and gathering societies today, may have already been established. In addition, the consistent progress in lithic technology throughout a period lasting for more than 200,000 years suggests that the earliest practice of education may have taken place in the Zhoukoudian cave. Toolmaking techniques, like modern science and technology, must have been conveyed from the old to the young, from generation to generation (Wu and Lin, 1983).

Other major sites bearing *Homo erectus* fossils include one in Yuanmou (Yüan-mou) County, Yunnan Province, two in Lantian County, Shaanxi Province, one in Nanzhao County, Henan Province, and sites in Yunxian and Yunxi Counties in Hubei Province.

The *Homo erectus* specimen in Yuanmou consists of only two teeth (upper central incisors). Its date is controversial. Palaeomagnetic dating has given the age as 1.7 million years (Li et al., 1976) or 1.63 to 1.64 million years (Cheng et al., 1977). But recently Liu and Ding (1983) pointed out that the age of the Yuanmou remains might be no more than 0.7 million years and is possibly 0.5 to 0.6 million years. Pope (1984) also put forward the opinion that its age might be less than 1 million years.

The Lantian *Homo erectus* is represented by a mandible unearthed at Chenjiawo of Lantian County, Shaanxi Province, and a cranium at Gongwanling in the same county. The Lantian cranium is large with heavy supraorbital tori, the lateral parts of which apparently extend further sidewards than those of the Zhoukoudian skulls. The cranial wall is extraordinarily thick. The cranial capacity is only about 780 cc. Thus the Lantian skull seems to be more primitive than those found at Zhoukoudian.

A few stone implements were unearthed in Lantian. Representative of this culture is the thick and heavy point, probably indicating a link with the Xihoudu culture.

In 1980 a new find of a fairly complete skull of *Homo erectus* was made in Hexian County, Anhui Province, southeast China. Judging from the morphological features, it seems that the Hexian *Homo erectus* corresponds to the late, northern Zhoukoudian *Homo erectus* (Plate 12).

Only isolated teeth of *Homo erectus* were found in other sites. Many sites of this period yield only stone artefacts and no *Homo erectus* fossils. Of these, the important ones are Xihoudu and Xiaochangliang, Donggutuo and Kehe, and Guanyindong.

The Xihoudu site is located in Ruicheng County, Shaanxi Province. The artefacts include cores, flakes, chopper–chopping tools and heavy trihedral points. The faunal remains suggest a cooler and somewhat drier climate than at present. Preliminary palaeomagnetic dating gives an age of about 1.8 million years (Jia, 1985).

The Xiaochangliang site lies in the lacustrine deposits of the Nihewan Formation in Yangyuan County, Hebei Province. The artefacts are of small size and include cores, flakes, various forms of small scrapers and choppers. Associated with the stone implements are teeth of *Hipparion* sp. which would make the tools earlier than those of Peking Man.

Of special interest is the Donggutuo site near Xiaochangliang, found in the greyish-green silt layer of the lower part of the Nihewan Formation. The lithic artefacts include cores, flakes and stone implements, all of small size, made of pyroclastics, cherts and agates. Interestingly, the techniques used to retouch points and scrapers are similar to those of Peking Man. Palaeomagnetic dating gives it an age of 1 million years.

The Kehe culture is composed of stone artefacts of the transitional type from the Xihoudu culture to the Dingoun culture.

Guanyindong is situated in Qianxi County, Guizhou Province. Most of the tools were fabricated on direct percussion flakes, although a few implements were made by the anvil technique. Four types are recognized, choppers, scrapers, points and gravers. Most of them were trimmed on one side only and are quite similar to those of north China (Li and Wen, 1978). As the margins of most tools are relatively blunt with edge angles generally exceeding 80°, they seem to be parallel to the later stage of the Peking Man culture (Jia et al., 1982).

The Guanyindong culture gives evidence of a new cultural tradition in south China, similar in some respects to contemporary traditions in north China but differing in many respects. Judging from the data available at present, it seems that its localized characteristics and the complexity of its cultural overlaps are more marked than in the cultures of north China. In many sites of south China, the retouching techniques are simpler than those of north China, and in some sites of later periods, the techniques may even be less advanced than in the early ones.

All the above indicate that *Homo erectus* was widely distributed over the vast area of China and that there is great potential for discovering more *Homo erectus* fossils and related material in the future.

The wealth of *Homo erectus* fossils accumulated in China has provided reliable evidence to reveal a picture of human development in the area. It is interesting to note that certain morphological details of the Chinese *Homo erectus* show specific characteristics. For instance, without exception, every upper incisor from every locality including Zhoukoudian, Yuanmou, Yunxian and Hexian, is shovel-shaped. Such incisors occur at a very high frequency in the Mongoloids. Other features which may be regarded as close to the Mongoloids are the pronounced frontal orientation of the malar bones of the faces of Peking Man and the congenital absence of the third molars on both sides of the Lantian mandible. It can therefore be said that regional continuity of hominid evolution has existed in China and that certain morphological features of the Mongoloids had become established as early as the *Homo erectus* stage of evolution.

BIBLIOGRAPHY

CHENG, G. L.; LI, S. L.; LIN, J. L. 1977. Discussion on the Age of *Homo erectus yuanmouensis* and the Event of Early Matuyama. *Sci. Geol. Sin.*, No. 1, pp. 34–43.

JIA LANPO. 1985. China's Earliest Palaeolithic Assemblages. In: WU RUKANG; OLSEN, J. W. (eds), *Palaeoanthropology and Palaeolithic Archaeology in the People's Republic of China.* Orlando. Vol. 8, pp. 135–45.

JIA LANPO; WEI QI; CHEN CHUN. 1982. (Lower Palaeolithic in China). *Kokogaku Zasshi* (Archaeol. J.), Vol. 206, pp. 36–41.

KONG ZHAOCHEN et al. 1985. [Vegetational and Climatic Changes since Paleogene at Zhoukoudian and its Adjacent Regions.] In:

WU RUKANG et al. [*Multi-disciplinary Study of the Peking Man Site at Zhoukoudian.*] Beijing. pp. 119–54.

LI P. et al. 1976. Preliminary Study of the Age of Yuanmou Man by Paleomagnetic Technique. *Sci. Sin.*, No. 6, pp. 579–91.

LI YANXINA; WEN BENHENG. 1978. [The Discovery and Significance of the Guanyindon Palaeolithic Culture, Qianxi, Guizhou.] In: CHINESE ACADEMY OF SCIENCES. Institute of Vertebrate Palaeontology and Palaeoanthropology. *Collected Papers of Palaeoanthropology.* Beijing, Science Press. pp. 77–93.

LIU T. S.; DING M. L. 1983. Discussion of the Age of 'Yuanmou Man'. *Acta Anthropol. Sin.*, Vol. 2, No. 1, pp. 40–8.

PEI WENZHONG; ZHANG SENSHUI. 1985. A Study on the Lithic Artifacts of *Sinanthropus. Palaeontol. Sin.*, NS D, No. 168.

POPE, G. G.; CRONIN, J. E. 1984. The Asian Hominidae. *J. Hum. Evol.*, Vol. 13, No. 5, pp. 377–96.

WU RUKANG et al. 1985. [*Multi-disciplinary Study of the Peking Man Site at Zhoukoudian.*] Beijing.

WU RUKANG; LIN SHENGLONG. 1983. Peking Man. *Sci. Am.*, Vol. 248, No. 6, pp. 78–86.

8

INDONESIA

in the period of *Homo habilis* and *Homo erectus*

Gert-Jan Bartstra

It may be assumed that *Homo erectus* evolved on the grassy plains of Upper Pliocene and Basal Pleistocene East Africa some 1.5 million years ago, and from there began to wander throughout the Old World, reaching Indonesia after rather a long trek. This area provided an especially favourable niche, notably in central Java, where *Homo erectus* continued to live for hundreds of thousands of years, isolated by water barriers in the south and east, and by unattractive tropical rain forests to the north and west (Map 9).

Consequently, with regard to Indonesia (or in a geographical sense, island South-East Asia) during the period of *Homo habilis* and *Homo erectus*, an assumption can be made: one is concerned only with the species *Homo erectus* in central Java. For it is from the central part of the island of Java alone that finds of fossil hominids are known. On the basis of the distribution of such finds, it might even be conjectured that *Homo erectus* never lived in, for instance, Sumatra, Borneo or Sulawesi (Celebes).

The quest for the traces of *Homo erectus* is closely inter-woven with geological and geomorphological research. In this respect central Java is not an easy terrain. It has become a landscape dominated by cultural elements, with towns and villages, roads and fields to be found everywhere. In addition to this, the many volcanoes have spread a carpet of ash over the land. Exposures of Pleistocene deposits (in which one can expect the remains of *Homo erectus*) are not easy to find, and in fact they occur mostly where there has been downcutting action by rivers. But in spite of all this, central Java is an important region in the search for our ancestors – not least because that search actually began there.

EUGENE DUBOIS AND *PITHECANTHROPUS ERECTUS*

At the world exhibition in Paris in 1900, displayed in one of the pavilions was a remarkable statue that drew a great deal of attention. There stood a reconstruction of the 'missing

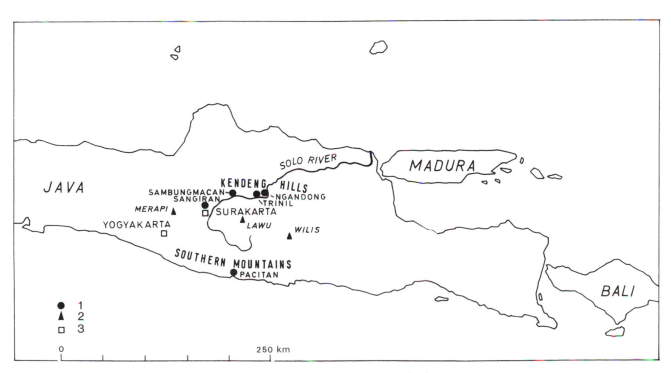

Map 9 Central and east Java: 1, location of sites mentioned in the text; 2, location of some volcanoes; 3, towns.

link,' the creature intermediate between ape and human, of which a skull-cap and a thigh-bone had been excavated in distant Java. The finder, Eugène Dubois, a Dutch physician, had also made the reconstruction, as scrupulously as possible, basing himself on the dimensions of skull-cap and thigh-bone. The low cranial capacity and the heavy brow ridges seemed indicative of a very primitive ancestor, but the shape of the femur showed that walking had nevertheless been upright.

Dubois's discovery of the 'ape-man' has become legendary. His medical studies had brought him into contact with the numerous disputes concerning Darwin's theory of evolution that occurred in the second half of the last century. Were humans really descended from the animal kingdom? Was it possible to draw a continuous line from ape to human? These all remained theoretical questions, for there were no fossils. The only human fossils known at that time were those of the Neanderthalers, the Ice-Age cave-dwellers, and opinions were divided even about these. But if one believed in primitive ancestors, one could see that the Neanderthalers were not the missing link, for their anatomical features were clearly too advanced.

Dubois took it upon himself to find a true intermediate fossil form, and he therefore set off for a region that he thought promising: Indonesia. He arrived there in 1887. At first he dug in vain in caves on Sumatra; but when he moved to Java and found rich fossil-bearing deposits there he decided to start excavating systematically. He did so along the Solo river near the village of Trinil in central Java.

In 1891, among numerous remains of an extinct vertebrate fauna, a heavily corroded skull-cap came to light (Plate 13). A thigh-bone followed a year later; it was in a better state of preservation, and was found 15 m away from the skull-cap. Dubois was convinced that the two fossils belonged together, and he described them as *Pithecanthropus erectus*, the upright-walking 'ape-man' of Java (Dubois, 1894).

The name *Pithecanthropus* is now outdated, although it is still used with affection by some research workers (especially those working in Java). In international scientific literature the remains from Trinil are now described as *Homo erectus erectus*. For the old *Pithecanthropus* is now regarded as representative of the species *Homo erectus*, which had a wide distribution over the whole of the Old World.

THE TRINIL SECTION

Dubois was initially of the opinion that the fossils he had excavated from the rich bone-bearing bed at Trinil dated from the Pleistocene. He later changed his mind on this point, however, and spoke of Pliocene fossiliferous river-laid tuffs (Dubois, 1908). This volte-face was based on palaeontological evidence (a closer study of the fossil fauna revealed to Dubois many elements that appeared archaic to him), but was also a result of geological arguments (at that time no one believed in folded or tilted Pleistocene deposits on Java).

The stratigraphical details of the local section at Trinil were extensively investigated for the first time by members of the Selenka expedition, who carried out research in Trinil from 1906 to 1908 in the hope of finding more remains of *Homo erectus*. This hope was not realized, but as a result of the expedition the geology of the landscape around Trinil became much better known (Elbert, 1908; Carthaus, 1911; Dozy, 1911). Some decades later, while a detailed geological mapping of the island of Java was being done, data from other places became available, and subsequently an attempt was made to fit the Trinil sequence within an overall view of the geology of central and east Java (Duyfjes, 1936). This general picture was rapidly accepted by those active in the field of research on early Java Man (von Koenigswald, 1939), and thereafter it also became incorporated in palaeoanthropological textbooks. It must now be concluded, however, that this process happened all too quickly, so that erroneous ideas about the geology of central and east Java (erroneous because the observations made were still too few and too widely spaced) have now become rather firmly enshrined in the literature, and are consequently difficult to eradicate. The most recent research on the fossil localities of Java shows a return to devoting attention to the local section alone, without drawing directly any wide-ranging conclusions. The banks of the Solo near Trinil, where the remains of *Homo erectus* were found, are eminently suitable for such a limited geological study, because a stratigraphical sequence is present from the Pliocene into the Holocene.

The lowermost sediments that are visible at Trinil consist of limestone and marl (a mixture of limestone and clay). These sediments indicate that this part of Java was still sea during Pliocene. From a geological viewpoint Java is indeed a very young island; the gradual regression of the sea is evident (in the upper part of the marine unit) in lenses of sandy marl, which contain many molluscs. This sediment was probably laid down in tranquil lagoons.

The marine unit is covered at Trinil by a volcanic mud stream, a lahar, that is associated with the (now extinct) Wilis volcano. This Wilis lahar can serve as a guide-horizon that is easy to trace in the field because of its remarkable composition of angular and sub-angular volcanic pebbles, cobbles, and even boulders (hence the name volcanic boulder breccia) in a matrix of sandy tuff. The deposition of such a breccia is catastrophic: several metres can be deposited in a few hours. The catastrophe concerned took place some time in the Lower Pleistocene, more than 1 million years ago.

A much longer period of time was involved in the deposition of the tuffaceous layers that are to be found around Trinil on top of the lahar. These are river-laid (i.e. fluviatile) deposits, with characteristic features, the most important of which are the distinct rounding of the components (sand grains, pebbles) and the cross-stratification (a kind of herring-bone-patterned structure). It was these fluviatile deposits at Trinil that yielded the remains of *Homo erectus*. Yet these deposits can by no means be considered as one unit. In fact there are two fluviatile units with a distinct disconformity in between: the lower river-laid unit, dating from the Middle Pleistocene (in the literature often referred to as Kabuh beds or Kabuh formation), and the upper river-laid unit, dating from the Upper Pleistocene and the Holocene, which can be directly associated with the present-day Solo river.

RIVER TERRACES

Rivers deposit material (in the form of channel load and overbank deposits), but eventually they carry it away again. There exists a certain equilibrium; only if that is disturbed is there a possibility that, once deposited, sand and gravel will remain locally preserved, and become as it were 'fossil' deposits (relict deposits). Such a disturbance of the equilibrium can occur if the river begins to cut down or incise as a result of a tectonic upheaval of the surrounding land (crust movements). But a disturbance can also result from fluctuations in sea-level (eustatic movements). During the Pleistocene both of these factors played their part on Java (Ollier, 1985) and consequently along the Solo: for example, patches of 'fossil' sand and gravel are to be found in many places. In hilly regions (in the Kendeng hills along the transverse Solo valley) such patches of sand and gravel can be discovered on the valley slopes, where they occur in the form of terraces: the highest-lying terrace remnants were deposited first and are therefore the oldest.

Frequent attention has been devoted to the Solo terraces in central Java (ter Haar, 1934; de Terra, 1943; Sartono, 1976), for in so far as they can be classified in a clear system at distinct levels on the valley slope they play a role in the relative dating of fossil hominid bones and prehistoric artefacts. Rivers were in fact the pathways of early humans. It was there that they found the water they needed and the game they hunted, as well as the pebbles they needed for their tools. Hence the traces of early humans are to be found in those 'fossil' sand and gravel-banks that now lie on the valley slope in the form of terraces.

Difficulties arise, however, with the interpretation of old river-laid deposits outside the hilly regions of central Java, namely in the lowland plains through which the Solo also flows, and where stream erosion has been for the most part lateral rather than vertical. Directly along the borders of the hilly regions one is confronted with a terrace intersection: 'fossil' stream deposits that elsewhere along the river lie high up the valley slope and are therefore called 'high terrace' are present in the border region buried actually below more recent sediments, the 'low terrace'. The existence of such plunging terraces along the Solo river in central Java has been pointed out previously (Lehmann, 1936; van Bemmelen, 1949), but nowhere have they been studied in detail. Yet it is important to realize that such a terrace intersection may be present in the meander of the Solo river at Trinil; a meander which is situated in the transitional area between the Kendeng hills and lowland plain of central Java. This would mean that on top of the Middle Pleistocene sands and gravels (the lower river-laid unit, deposited by pre-Solo rivers: the Kabuh beds) lie accumulated the Upper Pleistocene and Holocene sediments (the upper river-laid unit: the terrace deposits) in such a way that the 'high terrace' lies below the 'low terrace'.

THE TRINIL BONES

The existence of a terrace intersection near Trinil might have consequences for the interpretation of the *Homo erectus* remains from that locality. Dubois was convinced that the skull-cap and thigh-bone belonged to the same species, although they were found 15 m apart, while the question of whether the remains also came from one particular individual resolved itself when later on more femora were discovered among the fossil fauna material from Trinil.

Concerning these femora from Trinil, it has been speculated on a number of occasions that they may in fact represent two hominids. For example, G. H. R. von Koenigswald the well-known palaeontologist who devoted himself to the search for early human remains on Java, once stated that the femur from Trinil is morphologically too long to go together with such a primitive skull (von Koenigswald, 1933). Others have argued that the femur in every aspect resembles the thigh-bone of *Homo sapiens* so closely that it cannot have belonged to *Homo erectus* (Day and Molleson, 1973).

Meanwhile fluorine analysis has been carried out on the material from Trinil. Bones that lie buried take up fluorine from groundwater. In this way it is possible to determine the relative association of different bones, that is, whether they have all been in contact with the groundwater for the same length of time. The skull-cap and the first thigh-bone found at Trinil turned out to have a corresponding fluorine percentage, from which it was concluded that they are equally old (Bergman and Kartsten, 1952). But a fluorine analysis carried out on fossil material from elsewhere along the Solo gave curious results. Bones from the upper river-laid unit (the site of Ngandong) were found to contain almost the same percentage as bones from the lower river-laid unit at Trinil (Day and Molleson, 1973). Seen stratigraphically this is impossible, and thus new research is necessary, which is being carried out at time of writing (Day, 1984; Matsu'ura, 1984).

Unfortunately, in the Solo meander near Trinil where Dubois found the fossils it is no longer possible to collect any good samples: successive expeditions have dug away all the fossiliferous sediments. But in the river-bank it is still possible to study a stratigraphical profile, and here it is conspicuous that a remnant of the upper river-laid unit (the terrace deposits) is still present. The Solo meander at Trinil is a typical ingrown meander, and before Dubois began to dig there the terrace deposits close to the river must have been much thicker. Should new research in the laboratory indicate that the femur must be dissociated from the skull-cap, then it is possible to find a stratigraphical explanation for this.

However, the fact that a skull-cap of an early hominid was found in Trinil remains of course indisputable. In this connection, another site in central Java has become even more important.

SANGIRAN

About 60 km to the west of Trinil lies Sangiran, and at the present time this is the most prolific site of fossil hominid material in the whole of South-East Asia. In 1937 a *Homo erectus* skull was found there for the first time (von Koenigswald, 1938), and this find turned out to be the beginning of a long series of interesting discoveries. So far the site of Sangiran has yielded remains of more than forty hominids, not only of *Homo erectus* (the former *Pithecanthropus*), but also of the somewhat mysterious *Meganthropus palaeojavanicus* (and whether the latter is merely a variant of *Homo erectus* still remains a matter of discussion; Day, 1984). No fossil hominid femora have been found at Sangiran.

From a geological viewpoint Sangiran is quite unique: Pliocene and Pleistocene sediments have been pushed upwards, and are now exposed as a result of erosion. Therefore, research workers often refer to the dome of Sangiran. The finds of hominid remains prompted a great deal of detailed geological research and subsequently inevitable comparisons with the situation in Trinil (van Bemmelen, 1949). As has been pointed out, objections can be raised against such comparisons.

The Wilis lahar at Trinil, which overlies the marine deposits at this locality, literally created a threshold between the volcanic zone of central Java and the then rudimentary Kendeng hills. The result of this was that the region to the west of this threshold was cut off from the sea in the east (west Java was already land: Java emerged from the sea from west to east). In the region around Sangiran there thus originated in the Lower Pleistocene a large freshwater basin, and in this basin were formed the black clays that are now the most conspicuous deposits within the dome. So when the name Pucangan is used to refer to the Trinil lahar (as is often done in the literature; it was formerly Putjangan), it is somewhat rash to use the same term to refer to the black clays of Sangiran (as one can often read). For apart from completely different conditions of deposition, the lahar of Trinil is definitely older than the clay of Sangiran.

There is more justification for using the name Kabuh for both the fluviatile complex that is to be found in Sangiran on top of the black clay and the lower river-laid unit in Trinil. For these sands and gravels are in both cases the detritus of the anticlines of central Java (the Kendeng hills and Southern Mountains) that rose in the Middle Pleistocene; and thus they are one and the same synorogenic formation. These Kabuh beds are the parent layers of the greater part of the hominid remains that have been found in central Java.

Just as in Trinil, in Sangiran the interpretation of the top part of the stratigraphic section gives the most problems. Generally this top part is referred to as the Notopuro beds (the boundary with the underlying Kabuh beds remaining rather vague), but this designation is too comprehensive. In central Java the term Notopuro must be restricted to those deposits that can be associated with the very first activity of the Lawu volcano. The Lawu, situated immediately west of the Wilis, became active long after the Wilis became extinct, and therefore the various volcanic deposits can be readily identified in the field. What is frequently called Notopuro in Sangiran, however, is in fact river-laid sediment that can be associated with the drainage pattern of the present-day rivers (Bartstra, 1985).

THE VERTEBRATE CHRONOLOGY

Since the days when the first hominid remains were found in central Java there has always been the problem of dating the different deposits. Up to a point it was possible to use molluscs for this purpose, but for the younger periods this was a hazardous undertaking. So when von Koenigswald began his research on early humans in Java he attempted to use vertebrate fossils for establishing ages (von Koenigswald, 1934).

The starting point for von Koenigswald was the large collection of fossil vertebrates that had been collected at Trinil by Dubois and later by the Selenka expedition. Von Koenigswald called this the Trinil fauna; and he placed it in the Middle Pleistocene. Further down the Solo, near the village of Ngandong, fossil vertebrates were found too, but in deposits that from a geological viewpoint must be younger than those of Trinil (upper river-laid unit versus lower river-laid unit). Von Koenigswald called this second fauna along the Solo the Ngandong fauna, placed in the Upper Pleistocene. Subsequently, in east Java a locality became known with fossil vertebrates (Cosijn, 1932a, 1932b) that according to von Koenigswald had to be older than Ngandong or Trinil: this became known as the Jetis fauna (formerly the Djetis fauna), situated in the Lower Pleistocene. Finally there existed a few fossil localities on the border of central and west Java where von Koenigswald also established a classification: the Cisande (formerly Tji Sande) fauna, the Cijulang (formerly Tji Djoelang) fauna and the Kaliglagah fauna respectively, all Pliocene (von Koenigswald, 1935).

Von Koenigswald's scheme has been criticized. For example, Hooijer has stated and still maintains that in defining the various faunas too much emphasis has been laid on archaic elements and too little regard has been taken of invading new species. Hence Hooijer's pronouncement: no fauna can be older than its youngest components. However, the chronological order of the faunas (Cisande, Cijulang, Kaliglagah, Jetis, Trinil and Ngandong) has never been contested by Hooijer, because this appeared to be firmly anchored in stratigraphical observations (Hooijer, 1952, 1956, 1957).

The most recent criticism of von Koenigswald's scheme does indeed concern the chronological order of the faunas: it is said (mainly with reference to the Jetis fauna) that it is not clear from which deposits the fossils actually originate, and research-workers in the field are accused of circular reasoning (de Vos et al., 1982; Sondaar, 1984). A new scheme is presented (with Trinil as the oldest Pleistocene fauna, discarding the Jetis fauna and adding the so-called Kedungbrubus fauna). This newest scheme has evoked criticism in turn: with regard to the stratigraphical arguments put forward (Bartstra, 1983; Sartono, 1983), with regard to the faunal lists (Hooijer, 1983; Hooijer and Kurtén, 1984), and with regard to the conclusions (Groves, 1985; Heaney, 1985). Most scholars agree, however, that the classic vertebrate sequence at least needs some revision (Braches and Shutler, 1983, 1984; Shutler and Braches, 1985).

RADIOMETRIC AGES

It will be clear that the dating of sediments with the aid of fossils involves many pitfalls and limitations. For example, it is evident that in Trinil, Sangiran and elsewhere, ages have very often been established on the basis of reworked fossils that actually belong in older deposits. Ultimately a method using fossils can never give an absolute date; at most it can indicate the relative age of one deposit compared with another. Therefore one might well ask whether the laboratory techniques for radiometric age determination that have been developed and refined during the past decades could possibly establish a chronometric framework for central Java, within which the finds of fossil hominid remains can reliably be placed.

Potassium–argon (K–Ar) analysis of volcanic deposits, one of the best-known dating techniques, was first applied to samples from Java in the 1960s, and the results gave only then for the first time an idea of the kind of absolute time spans within which terms like Ngandong, Trinil and Jetis should be placed (Zähringer, 1963; Zähringer and Gentner, 1963; von Koenigswald, 1968; Stross, 1971). Since then a lot of K–Ar data have become available, although because of differing ages for what look like the same deposits they have obscured rather than elucidated the overall picture of the Javanese Pliocene and Pleistocene (Orchiston and Siesser, 1982; Hutterer, 1983; Sartono, 1985). One reason for the difficulties (in addition to purely technical problems to which samples from Java seem to give rise) lies in the reworking of the datable constituents; this is in fact the same problem that one comes up against with fossils. For example, K–Ar datings of the Kabuh beds in central Java are based on an analysis of the volcanic constituents therein. But it is still questionable whether there was much volcanic activity in central Java at the time when these beds were formed (in the Middle Pleistocene interval between the extinction of the Wilis volcano and the onset of the Lawu volcanism). If this was not the case, and the Kabuh beds are merely a synorogenic formation built up out of the erosion products of the anticlines of Java (in which at least the Southern mountains contain much Neogene volcanic material), then it will be clear that K–Ar data of these Middle Pleistocene river-laid sediments must be interpreted with due caution.

Much progress has been made with the application of palaeomagnetic research on Java that got under way at the beginning of the 1980s (Yokoyama et al., 1980; Sémah et al., 1981/2; Sémah, 1982). Palaeomagnetic determinations in themselves can never provide an absolute age, but by means of comparison with other dating methods and cross-references to palaeomagnetic series from elsewhere it is possible to establish a tentative chronology for a particular region. In central Java too the boundaries between the different subdivisions of the Pleistocene should in any case be linked to palaeomagnetic boundaries. The notorious Pliocene–Pleistocene boundary (for many years a matter of contention among palaeontologists) must now be put at the beginning of the Olduvai event, a minor geomagnetic marker, 1.8 million years ago. The boundary between Lower Pleistocene and Middle Pleistocene lies at 0.69 million years ago, at the beginning of the Brunhes (normal) epoch; and the boundary between Middle and Upper Pleistocene lies at 0.125 million years ago, at the beginning of the Blake (reversed) event.

An interpretation of palaeomagnetic samples from central Java has shown that the Kabuh beds in Sangiran (and thus also the lower river-laid unit in Trinil) for the greater part belong in the Brunhes normal epoch (Sémah, 1984). This means that most of the *Homo erectus* finds from Java are younger than 700,000 years. This conclusion has also been reached by others (Matsu'ura, 1982; Pope, 1984). As for hominid fossils that allegedly come from older layers (from the black clays of Sangiran), it appears that in many cases their precise origin is uncertain.

THE HANDAXES OF PACITAN

The problem of stone implements that could be ascribed to *Homo erectus* on Java came into the limelight in 1935, when on the south coast of the island, not far from the small town of Pacitan (formerly Patjitan), handaxes were found (von Koenigswald, 1936). At that time such implements were considered to be the very symbol of the Old Stone Age or Palaeolithic, and consequently this typological argument was used to ascribe the artefacts to *Homo erectus*. Besides, there was also a palaeontological argument: in fissures in limestone hills close to the site, fossil remains of vertebrates were found that were correlated with the Middle Pleistocene Trinil fauna (von Koenigswald, 1939).

The artefacts from Pacitan were later closely studied by Movius. He observed that true handaxes actually form only a small part of the entire tool assemblage, and moreover that they appear to have been manufactured by means of a technique completely different from that used for the hand-axes ('limandes') from the western part of the Old World. According to Movius the most characteristic core-tools from this 'Pacitanian' (formerly 'Patjitanian') assemblage are the unifacial and bifacial choppers; and he therefore classified this assemblage within his well-known chopper–chopping-tool complex in the Far East. Yet Movius remained convinced of a correlation between these tools and *Homo erectus* (Movius, 1948).

However, it has gradually become clear that archaic and primitive-looking stone artefacts are not necessarily old; rather, they are the expression of a certain activity (hunting sites versus habitation sites), or form the reflection of a particular function (functionalism versus evolutionism). The typological argument may never be used for dating artefacts, and especially in South-East Asia great caution is necessary in interpreting so-called primitive stone tool assemblages (Hutterer, 1976, 1977). As it happens, the 'Pacitanian' assemblage, considered from a purely technological point of view, is not primitive at all, but consists of a wide range of rather sophisticated core- and flake-tools (van Heekeren, 1955; Soejono, 1961; Mulvaney, 1970)

Also, the palaeontological argument that was once put forward to date the tools is of no value: the fissure deposits cannot be associated in any way with the implementiferous sediments, and therefore the fossils may under no circumstances be used for dating the implements. It has long been known that the 'Pacitanian' occurs *in situ* in terrace sediments along a small river (Teilhard de Chardin, 1938). So far it has not been possible to date these sediments by radiometric means (there are no datable constituents), but a geomorphological analysis of the surrounding landscape suggests that these terrace sediments originated in the last phases of the Pleistocene (Bartstra, 1984). The handaxes and other implements from Pacitan thus date from a time when *Homo erectus* had long disappeared from Java.

THE TOOLS OF *HOMO ERECTUS*

Directly related to the question of the tools of *Homo erectus* is the problem of the reconstruction of the former environment of the Javanese hominids, for obviously the tool assemblage is to a certain extent a reflection of what the environment could offer. (Social and cultural factors have to be disregarded, as the reconstruction of these for the first phases of prehistory remains pure speculation.) As far as the palaeoenvironment is concerned, there are two opinions to be found in the literature: *Homo erectus* either was adapted to an open woodland terrain, or else was already adapted to living in the tropical rain forests (Hutterer, 1985; Pope, 1984, 1985). In either case it is conceivable that Java Man possessed an assortment of stone tools; but also (especially in the latter case, as far as ethnological comparisons with contemporary situations can be of any use) many of their tools could have been made out of perishable material, such as wood (the lignic model). Such tools would now have disappeared completely, and their absence today could give the impression that on Java *Homo erectus* possessed hardly any implements.

Notwithstanding Pope's arguments, if one considers the finds that have been made so far then an adaptation to rainforests is not evident. In Borneo, Sumatra and west Java, regions that most probably were densely forested also in the Pleistocene, traces of *Homo erectus* have never been found. As far as Borneo and Sumatra are concerned (countries that are not easily accessible for fieldwork precisely because of the forests) it could be argued that insufficient research has been done so far; but for west Java this argument can no longer be upheld. Central Java, a region that *Homo erectus* must have reached via the now drowned river systems between Sumatra, Borneo and Java, has also had rain forests, but then locally and not during the entire Pleistocene. The animal species in the various Javanese fossil faunas often indicate open woodland: the many deer and antelope, for example (*Axis lydekkeri* and *Duboisia santeng*), and *Bubalus palaeokerabau*, the last with a horn-core span measuring sometimes as much as 1.5 m (Hooijer, 1958).

The picture outlined above fits in with the development of the stone tools in the Palaeolithic of Java that is evident from finds made in recent years. As stated, the 'Pacitanian' tool assemblage cannot be associated with *Homo erectus*: there is no evidence that the large core-tools from south Java date from before the last phases of the Pleistocene, say from before 50,000 years ago. It may well be that this 'Pacitanian' can be correlated with the first representatives of *Homo sapiens* in Indonesia, who indeed entered the rain forests. Large core-tools have also been found in the now heavily forested regions of Sumatra and south-east Borneo (Kalimantan), apparently associated with geologically recent alluvial deposits. Such core tools have also been found across the deep-water barriers to the east of Java, on for example the Lesser Sunda islands (Nusa Tenggara) and on Halmaheira.

The true tools of *Homo erectus* of Java must be sought in the small, inconspicuous stone implements that have occasionally been found in the higher-lying terrace sediments of the Solo river, dating from around 100,000 to 50,000 years ago, and thus to be associated with late *Homo erectus* groups. The same sort of small cores and flakes have been found in Upper Pleistocene sediments in Sangiran, that most prolific locality of fossil hominid bones in central Java. Up to now, these artefacts have not yet been found there in undeniable Middle Pleistocene deposits dating from before 125,000 years ago. However, it seems a mere matter of time before such finds will be reported.

BIBLIOGRAPHY

BARTSTRA, G.-J. 1983. The Vertebrate-Bearing Deposits of Kedung-brudus and Trinil, Java. Indonesia. *Geol. Mijnb.* (Dordrecht), Vol. 62, pp. 329–36.

—— 1984. Dating the Pacitanian: Some Thoughts. *CFS, Cour. Forsch.inst. Senckenb.* (Frankfurt/Main), Vol. 69, pp. 253–8.

—— 1985. Sangiran, the Stone Implements of Ngebung, and the Paleolithic of Java. *Mod. Quat. Res. SEAsia*, Vol. 9, pp. 99–113.

BEMMELEN, R. W. VAN. 1949. *The Geology of Indonesia* (Gen. geol. 1A). The Hague.

BERGMAN, R. A. M.; KARTSTEN, P. 1952. The Fluorine Content of *Pithecanthropus* and of other Specimens from the Trinil Fauna. *Proc. K. Ned. Akad. Wet.* (Amsterdam), Vol. 55, pp. 150–2.

BRACHES, F.; SHUTLER, R., JR. 1983. Early Vertebrates and the Theory of the Emergence of Java. *SEAsian Stud. Newsl.*, Vol. 13, pp. 1–2.

—— 1984. Early Vertebrates and the Theory of the Emergence of Java. *SEAsian Stud. Newsl.*, Vol. 16, pp. 1–2.

CARTHAUS, E. 1911. Zur Geologie von Java, insbesondere des Aus-grabungsgebietes. In: SELENKA, M. L.; BLANCKENHORN, M. (eds), *Die Pithecanthropus-Schichten auf Java*. Leipzig. pp. 1–33.

COSIJN, J. 1932a. Voorloopige mededeeling omtrent het voor-komen van fossiele beenderen in het heuvelterrein ten Noorden van Djetis en Perning (Midden-Java) [Provisional Com-munication about the Existence of Fossil Bones in the Hilly Grounds North of Djetis and Perning (Middle Java)]. *Verh. Geol. Mijnbouwkd. Genoot., Geol. Ser.*, Vol. 19, pp. 113–9.

—— 1932b. Tweede mededeeling over het voorkomen van fossiele beederen in het heuvelterrein ten Noorden van Djetis en Perning (Java) [Second communication concerning the Existence of Fossil Bones in the Hilly Grounds North of Djetis and Perning (Middle Java)]. *Verh. Geol. Mijnbouwkd. Genoot., Geol. Ser.*, Vol. 9, pp. 135–48.

DAY, M. H. 1984. *Guide to Fossil Man*. 3rd rev. edn. London.

—— 1984. The Postcranial Remains of *Homo erectus* from Africa, Asia and possibly Europe. *CFS, Cour. Forsch.inst. Senckenb.* (Frankfurt/Main), Vol. 69, pp. 113–21.

DAY, M. H.; MOLLESON, T. I. 1973. The Trinil Femora. In: DAY, M. H. (ed.), *Human Evolution*. London. pp. 127–54.

DOZY, C. M. 1911. Bemerkungen zur Stratigraphie der Sedimente in der Triniler Gegend. In: SELENKA, M. L.; BLANCKENHORN, M. (eds), *Die Pithecanthropus-Schichten auf Java*. Leipzig. pp. 34–6.

DUBOIS, E. 1894. *Pithecanthropus erectus: eine menschenähnliche Über-gangsform aus Java*. Batavia.

—— 1908. Das geologische Alter der Kendeng- oder Trinil-fauna. *Tijdschr. K. Ned. Aardrijkskd. Gen.* (Amsterdam), Vol. 25, pp. 1235–70.

DUYFJES, J. 1936. Zur Geologie und Stratigraphie des Ken-denggebietes zwischen Trinil und Soerabaja (Java). *De Ing. Ned.-Indië, Mijnb.; Geol., de Mijningenieur*, Vol. 3, No. 4, pp. 136–49.

ELBERT, J. 1908. Über das Alter der Kending-Schichten mit *Pithecan-thropus erectus* Dubois. *Neues Jahrb. Mineral. Geol. Paläontol.* (Stuttgart), Vol. 25, pp. 648–62.

GROVES, C. P. 1985. Plio-Pleistocene Mammals in Island Southeast Asia. *Mod. Quat. Res. SEAsia*, Vol. 9, pp. 43–54.

HAAR, C. TER. 1934. Homo-Soloënsis. *De Ing. in Ned.-Indië, Mijnb. Geol., de Mijningenieur*, Vol. 1, No. 4, pp. 51–7.

HEANEY, L. R. 1985. Zoogeographic Evidence for Middle and Late Pleistocene Landbridges to the Philippine Islands. *Mod. Quat. Res. SEAsia*, Vol. 9, pp. 137–43.

HEEKEREN, H. R. VAN. 1955. New Investigations on the Lower Palaeolithic Patjitan Culture in Java. *Berita Dinas Purbakala*, Vol. 1, pp. 1–12.

HOOIJER, D. A. 1952. Fossil Mammals and the Plio-Pleistocene Boundary in Java. *Proc. K. Ned. Akad. Wet.* (Amsterdam), Vol. 55, pp. 436–43.

—— 1956. The Lower Boundary of the Pleistocene in Java and the Age of *Pithecanthropus*. *Quaternaria* (Rome), Vol. 3, pp. 5–10.

—— 1957. The Correlation of Fossil Mammalian Faunas and the Plio-Pleistocene Boundary in Java. *Proc. K. Ned. Akad. Wet.* (Amsterdam), Vol. 60, pp. 1–10.

—— 1958. Fossil Bovidae from the Malay Archipelago and the Punjab. *Zool. Verhand.* (Leiden), Vol. 38, pp. 1–112.

—— 1983. Remarks upon the Dubois Collection of Fossil Mammals from Trinil and Kedungbrubus in Java. *Geol. Mijnb.* (Dordrecht), Vol. 62, pp. 337–8.

HOOIJER, D. A.; KURTÉN, B. 1984. Trinil and Kedungbrubus: The Pithecanthropus-bearing Fossil Faunas of Java and their Relative Age. *Ann. Zool. Fennici*, Vol. 21, pp. 135–41.

HUTTERER, K. L. 1976. An Evolutionary Approach to the Southeast Asian Cultural Sequence. *Curr. Anthropol.*, Vol. 17, pp. 1–23.

—— 1977. Reinterpreting the Southeast Asian Palaeolithic. In: ALLEN, J.; GOLSON, J.; JONES, R. (eds), *Sunda and Sahul, Prehistoric Studies in Southeast Asia, Melanesia and Australia*. London/New York. pp. 31–77.

—— 1983. Absolute Dates for the Hominid-bearing Deposits in Java: An Overview. *Asian Perspect.*, Vol. 2.

—— 1985. The Pleistocene Archaeology of Southeast Asia in Regional Context. *Mod. Quat. Res. SEAsia*, Vol. 9, pp. 1–23.

KOENIGSWALD, G. H. R. VON. 1933. Ein neuer Urmensch aus dem Diluvium Javas. *Cent. b. Mineral. Geol. Paläontol.*, Vol. 1, pp. 29–42.

—— 1934. Zur Stratigraphie des javanischen Pleistocän. *De Ing. in Ned. Indië, Mijnb. Geol., de mijningenieur*, Vol. 1, No. 11, pp. 185–200.

—— 1935. Die fossilen Säugetierfaunen Javas. *Proc. K. Ned. Akad. Wet.* (Amsterdam), Vol. 38, pp. 188–98.

—— 1936. Early Palaeolithic Stone Implements from Java. *Bull. Raffles Mus.*, Singapore, Vol. 1, pp. 52–60.

—— 1938. Ein neuer *Pithecanthropus*-Schädel. *Proc. K. Ned. Akad. Wet.* (Amsterdam), Vol. 41, pp. 185–92.

—— 1939. Das Pleistocän Javas. *Quatär* (Berlin), Vol. 2, pp. 28–53.

—— 1968. Das absolute Alter des *Pithecanthropus erectus* Dubois. In: KURTH, G. (ed.), *Evolution und Hominization*. Stuttgart. pp. 195–203.

LEHMANN, H. 1936. Morphologische Studien auf Java. *Geogr. Abh.* (Leipzig), Vol. 3, No. 9, pp. 1–114.

MATSU'URA, S. 1982. A Chronological Framing for the Sangiran Hominids. *Bull. Nat. Sc. Mus.* (Tokyo), Ser. D, Vol. 8, pp. 1–53.

—— 1984. *The Debatable Contemporaneity of the Trinil Femora with Pithecanthropus Skull 1, Reconsidered through Chemical Analyses.*

Tokyo. (Communication at the 38th Joint Meeting of the Anthropol. Soc. Nippon and Jap. Soc. Ethnol.)

MOVIUS, H. L. 1948. The Lower Palaeolithic Cultures of Southern and Eastern Asia. *Trans. Am. Phil. Soc.* (Philadelphia, Pa.), Vol. 38, pp. 329–420.

MULVANEY, D. J. 1970. The Patjitanian Industry: Some Observations. *Mankind*, Vol. 7, pp. 184–7.

OLLIER, C. D. 1985. The Geological Background to Prehistory in Island Southeast Asia. *Mod. Quat. Res. SEAsia*, Vol. 2, pp. 1–21.

ORCHISTON, D. W.; SIESSER, W. G. 1982. Chronostratigraphy of the Plio-Pleistocene Fossil Hominids of Java. *Mod. Quat. Res. SEAsia*, Vol. 7, pp. 131–49.

POPE, G. G. 1984. The Antiquity and Paleoenvironment of the Asian Hominidae. In: ORR WHYTE, R. (ed.), *The Evolution of the East Asian Environment*. Hong Kong. Vol. 2, pp. 822–47.

—— 1985. Taxonomy, Dating and Paleoenvironment: The Paleoecology of the Early Far Eastern Hominids. *Mod. Quat. Res. SEAsia*, Vol. 9, pp. 65–80.

SARTONO, S. 1976. Genesis of the Solo Terraces. *Mod. Quat. Res. SEAsia*, Vol. 2, pp. 1–21.

—— 1983. Re-evaluation on Vertebrate Stratigraphy of Java: A Rectification. *Bul. Jurusan Geologi*, Vol. 12, pp. 7–8.

—— 1985. Datings of Pleistocene Man of Java. *Mod. Quat. Res. SEAsia*, Vol. 9, pp. 115–25.

SÉMAH, F. 1982. Pliocene and Pleistocene Geomagnetic Reversals Recorded in the Gemolong and Sangiran Domes (Central Java). *Mod. Quat. Res. SEAsia*, Vol. 7, pp. 151–64.

—— 1984. The Sangiran Dome in the Javanese Plio-Pleistocene Chronology. *CFS, Cour. Forsch.inst. Senckenb.* (Frankfurt/Main), Vol. 69, pp. 245–52.

SÉMAH, F. et al. 1981/2. L'Âge et l'environnement des *Homo erectus* de Java: nouveaux résultats paléomagnétiques et palynologiques. *Anthropologie* (Paris), Vol. 85/6, pp. 509–16.

SHUTLER R., JR.; BRANCHES, F. 1985. Problems in Paradise: The Pleistocene of Java Revisited. *Mod. Quat. Res. SE Asia*, Vol. 9, pp. 87–97.

SOEJONO, R. P. 1961. Kebudajaan Patjitan. *Publikasi Mipi*, Vol. 2, pp. 234–41.

SONDAAR, P. Y. 1984. Faunal Evolution and the Mammalian Biostratigraphy of Java. *CFS, Cour. Forsch.inst. Senckenb.* (Frankfurt/Main), Vol. 69, pp. 219–35.

STROSS, F. H. 1971. Applications of the Physical Sciences to Archaeology. *Science* (Washington), Vol. 171, pp. 831 ff.

TEILHARD DE CHARDIN, P. 1938. Deuxième notes sur la paléontologie humaine en Asie méridionale. *Anthropologie* (Paris), Vol. 48, pp. 452–6.

TERRA, H. DE. 1943. Pleistocene Geology and Early Man in Java. *Trans. Am. Phil. Soc.* (Philadelphia, Pa.), NS, Vol. 32, pp. 437–64.

VOS, J. DE et al. 1982. The Fauna from Trinil, Type Locality of *Homo erectus*: A Reinterpretation. *Geol. Mijnb.* (Dordrecht), Vol. 61, pp. 207–11.

YOKOYAMA, T. et al. 1980. Preliminary Report on Palaeomagnetism of the Plio-Pleistocene Series in Sangiran and Trinil Areas, Central Java, Indonesia. *Physical Geol. Indon. Island Arcs.*, Kyoto, pp. 88–96.

ZÄHRINGER, J. 1963. K–Ar Measurements of Tektites. In: SYMPOSIUM OF RADIOACTIVE DATINGS, *Proceedings*. Vienna. pp. 289–305.

ZÄHRINGER, J.; GENTNER, W. 1963. Radiogenic and Atmospheric Argon Content of Tektites. *Nature* (London), Vol. 199, pp. 583 ff.

B: The period of *Homo sapiens neanderthalensis* and contemporaries

CONTENTS

9

PHYSICAL ANTHROPOLOGY OF THE NEANDERTHALERS AND THEIR CONTEMPORARIES

An overview

Bernard Vandermeersch

Neanderthalers unquestionably constitute the best-known population of fossil humans among all the forms preceding present humanity.[1] This is for three reasons:

1 they were the first fossil humans different from us to be discovered;
2 we know them through the remains of several hundred individuals, from a large number of deposits;
3 they have been the subject of a very large number of publications and continue to be the object of intense research.

To give the reader a fuller picture of their importance and of the role they played in our understanding of the course of human evolution, we must begin with a brief historical account. The Neanderthal concept has, in fact, experienced many changes since the first discovery, in 1856, in the Neander valley near Düsseldorf (Germany) of a member of that group. The skeletal remains, a skull-cap (Plate 14) and some postcranial elements, were found by workers extracting limestone from a cave and were removed by Johann Carl Fuhlrott, a teacher from Elberfeld, who recognized their antiquity, or more precisely their contemporaneity with mammoths.

This discovery gave rise to keen controversies: the skull was said to have come from a modern human and its special features were attributed to pathological factors. It was not until after 1863, thanks particularly to the English naturalist Thomas H. Huxley, that the idea of a representative of an extinct human population different from ours gradually took root. In 1864, W. King first applied the specific name of *Homo neanderthalensis* to this find. In 1886, two skulls of the same type were found at Spy (Belgium), this time in association with stone implements and a partly extinct fauna. Following this discovery, it was no longer possible to doubt the existence of 'Neanderthal Man'.

At the end of the nineteenth and the beginning of the twentieth century, discoveries of human fossils became more and more frequent, especially in Europe. As a result, Europe assumed an exceptional position in the study of human evolution and the Neanderthalers were considered to be the most important link in this chain.

From 1920 onwards, fossils were brought to light in western Asia (Mugharet Al-Zuttiyeh), in sub-Saharan Africa (Broken Hill) and in Asia (Solo) whose morphology turned out to be more or less similar to that of European Neanderthalers, which strengthened the belief that the general characteristics of this fossil group might have been present in greater or lesser numbers and in more or less marked form throughout the Old World. The term *Palaeoanthropus*, coined in 1916 by Eliot Smith, made it possible to combine all these finds by ignoring the differences. Being of later date than those of *Homo erectus* from Java, these fossils seemed to mark a new stage in human evolution. This suggested the idea of evolutionary phases during which the whole of humankind passed through a succession of stages each with its own skeletal architecture and characteristics. 'Neanderthal Man' was said to have represented one of these phases.

In 1933, the discovery of ancient human remains in Palestine was to upset this evolutionary scheme. Some of these were either likened to those of Modern humans or else considered to be crosses between the latter and Neanderthalers. In both cases, it meant accepting the contemporaneity of the two populations during the Middle Palaeolithic, at least in certain regions, which ran counter to the phase concept. Moreover, the possibility of crosses between the two meant that the remains represented subspecies rather than separate species, namely *Homo sapiens sapiens* and *Homo sapiens neanderthalensis*.

In about 1950 there were further developments. A better understanding of the significance of the various characteristics and a more rigorous approach to the study of fossils made it possible to come to closer grips with the Neanderthal problem and to bring out clearly what Neanderthalers had inherited from earlier forms and what they shared with *Homo sapiens sapiens*.

Today the Neanderthalers are seen as a collection of populations sharing many morphological characteristics, having the same skeletal architecture and having lived in

Europe and western Asia during the first part of the Upper Pleistocene.

THE NEANDERTHALERS (Map 10)

Though we have discovered several hundred individuals, we know them mostly from very fragmentary remains: all in all, we have some ten skulls and, thanks to the existence of burial places, several complete skeletons. The morphological evolution of this group was concluded at the beginning of the Würm glaciation, so the classic fossils date back to the first half of the last glaciation.

The European population

European Neanderthalers were relatively short (1.65 m) and had a very robust bone structure.

It is their skull which has the most marked specific characteristics. The face and brain-pan are very elongated and very large, but very shallow. The occipital region is drawn back and is not as low as it is in Modern humans.

The cranial capacity varies from 1,250 to 1,680 cc, with a mean of 1,450 cc, which is almost comparable to the Modern mean. Seen laterally, the brain-pan has a strongly developed supraorbital ridge. At the back, the frontal recedes and the dome of the skull is low. The occipital region has a marked general curvature, accentuated by a projection of the rearmost part of the skull to form a sort of 'bun'. Seen from the top, this projection sticks out on either side of the cerebral part of the frontal: the maximum width is found between the parietals, as in Modern humans, but very much to the back, and the zygomatic arches also overlap the cerebral cavity. Seen from the back, it has an ovoid shape with a large horizontal axis. The occipital has a bony protuberance which unusually splits in the median region to give rise to two lips round a small depression, the suprainiac fossa.

Here we cannot possibly enter into all the anatomical particulars of the cranium. However, the bones of which it is constituted, and especially the temporal, do have many special features.

The Neanderthal face, too, is highly characteristic. The suborbital region is flattened and lacks the canine fossa found in Modern skulls. Moreover, the malar bone is not curved but recedes. In other words, Neanderthalers had no cheekbone. This set of traits gave them what has been called, rather insultingly, a snout. It should be added that the very large mandible lacks a chin and carries a robust set of teeth, larger than our own.

While the postcranial skeleton does not differ, in its general structure, from that of Modern humans, it, too, has a number of peculiarities. Here we shall consider only the most striking. In the Modern skeleton, the lateral border of the scapula generally has a ridge running between a dorsal and a ventral groove. In the Neanderthaler that ridge has been shifted, the dorsal groove being much more prominent and the ventral one greatly reduced or absent. Howell (1978) correlates this with a much stronger development of one of the brachial muscles, providing better control of certain movements, particularly those associated with the act of throwing.

The bones of the forearm are very curved to produce a vast interosseous space, probably linked with powerful muscles. The bicipital tuberosity lies a little further away from the head of the radius than it does in Modern humans, thus lending greater power to the biceps.

The pelvis shows, among other characteristics, a curvature of the anteroinferior iliac spine and forward-lying iliac crest. Above all, the superior ramus of the pubis is elongated and thin. Trinkaus (1976) has suggested that this feature, which produces a larger pelvic canal, might have eased parturition, the Neanderthal new-born perhaps having had a larger head than a Modern new-born, possibly as the result of a longer gestation period. However, we know too little about the biology or infant morphology of these populations – the few skeletons that have been discovered are incomplete, crushed and deformed – to accept that view.

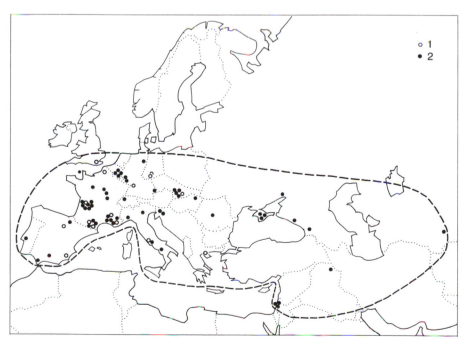

Map 10 Neanderthaler distribution. The Neanderthalers occupied central and southern Europe and part of western Asia, and spread beyond the Caspian Sea. 1, discoveries of the pre-Neanderthalers; 2, the principal discoveries of 'classic' Neanderthalers from the first stages (Würm I and II) of the last glaciation.

Among the bones of the leg, the Neanderthal femur is the most characteristic. Its diaphysis is rounded and not slightly flattened transversely as is the Modern one, nor is its posterior face pilastered. Moreover, it has a very pronounced anterior convexity and massive extremities.

In other parts of the skeleton, the various characteristics taken in isolation do not differ from those found in Modern humans, though they are often combined in a different way.

Variability in European Neanderthalers

The general characteristics we have been describing can be found, more or less prominently, in all European Neanderthalers. The individual differences are small and everything we know bears witness to the homogeneity of this population throughout Europe. It is exceptional, perhaps even unique, for a population to remain morphologically so stable over such a wide area and for such a long time, the more so as the density of that population was bound to be very low and as Europe boasts natural geographical barriers that must have been very difficult to cross, at least during cold periods. All in all, the circumstances would thus have favoured the isolation of fairly insignificant groups, that is, accentuated the differences between these groups. Since this did not happen, we must assume that exchanges of genes between European Neanderthal populations must have been frequent enough to offset these diversifying tendencies.

These comments should, however, be treated with caution. In effect, the variability of a population cannot be determined except by the application of statistical methods to adequate samples. In the event, despite the large number of individuals represented by the skeletal remains, we have no more than a small number of data on each characteristic: just five skulls containing both the cerebral region and the face. Despite these restrictions, we can nevertheless say that, as new finds come to light, they impose few if any changes on our picture of the variation of characteristics, which is, in nearly every case, narrower than that of modern populations with as wide a geographical distribution. Thus the average height of eight Neanderthalers considered to have been of the male sex is 1.65 m, with a range from 1.60 to 1.71 m. These Neanderthalers come from France, Spain, Belgium, Germany and the former USSR (Heim, 1983).

Such small metrical and morphological variations are an original feature of *Homo sapiens neanderthalis*.

The distribution of European Neanderthalers

All European Neanderthalers discovered with stone implements were associated with a Mousterian tradition. The few pieces whose archaeological environment is unknown are, for the most part, the result of very old and fortuitous finds, and it seems more than likely that the tools in them failed to attract the attention of the diggers. This is, for instance, what happened with the skeleton discovered in the Neander valley and with the skull from Gibraltar. However, when the associated industry is known, we find that the percentage of human remains associated with each Mousterian facies is very variable. In south-western France, for instance, most of the skeletal parts have come from Mousterian levels of the Charentian type, especially in the most important sites: La Quina, La Chapelle-aux-Saints (Plate 15), La Ferrassie, Le Regourdou, Marillac and so on. Next comes the Typical Mousterian to which we must probably attribute the adolescent from Le Moustier and the young child from Roc de Marsal. As for the Denticulate

Mousterian and the Mousterian of Acheulean Tradition, they have yielded few human remains. Perhaps the child from Châteauneuf-sur-Charente may be attributed to the former and – with great caution – the skull of the child from Pech de l'Azé to the second. This difference in the representation of human remains in the various technological facies of the Mousterian must certainly be attributed to the relative abundance of these facies; in southwestern France, the Charentian is much more widespread than the other industries.

The chronological distribution, too, is very uneven. Almost all the remains date back to Würm II; those which can be assigned to the beginning of the last glaciation are few and far between. Mention must, however, be made of the skeleton from Regourdou (Dordogne, France) and it would also seem that some of the many remains from Krapina (Slovenia) come from that period. This imbalance in the chronological distribution of the remains of European Neanderthalers is mainly due to the fact that Würm I deposits have been less well preserved than those of Würm II.

In Europe, all the Neanderthal remains discovered to date come from the southern or central part of the continent. The northern regions were rarely, if at all, frequented by these people. The countries involved are Belgium, the Czech Republic and Slovakia, France, Germany, Hungary, Italy, Jersey (UK), Portugal, Spain, Switzerland, the former USSR and former Yugoslavia.

In this vast area, we note zones of greater density: southwestern France, Moravia, Crimea and so on. The strongest concentration of finds is undoubtedly in south-west France (Charente and Dordogne). These are karstic regions abounding with caves and rock shelters in which human remains were particularly well preserved. The geographical distribution of these remains is therefore no indication of the original distribution of the Neanderthal population. In some regions, however, the number of individuals discovered, when considered in association with the importance of certain Mousterian layers, does reflect greater human density owing to favourable climatic and ecological factors.

Let us add, in conclusion, that some deposits have played a very important role in our knowledge of the Neanderthalers, either because of the discovery in them of near-complete skeletons (La Ferrassie, La Chapelle-aux-Saints and La Quina in France), or because they have yielded complete skulls (Monte Circeo, Italy) (Plate 16), or again because of the large number of individuals contained in them (La Quina; Krapina in Slovenia).

Neanderthalers in western and central Asia

Neanderthalers have also been found in western and central Asia where, once again, they are closely bound up with the distribution of the Mousterian tradition. Their presence has been recorded in Israel (Tabun, Amud (Plate 17), Kebara), in Iraq (Shanidar) and in Uzbekistan (Teshik-Tash) (Plate 18) through the remains of seventeen individuals, at least six of whom are represented by important parts of the skeleton.

Although they have the same general morphology as European Neanderthalers, the western Asian representatives differ significantly in a number of characteristics. To begin with, their cranial vault is more elevated and its height falls into the contemporary range of variation. The occipital region is more regularly rounded and less recessive and the occipital protuberance is less prominent. The temporal region approaches that of Modern humans and though the Neanderthal facial characteristics are still present they are so in attenuated form. These Neanderthalers are also taller than their European counterparts.

'Distance functions' computed to compare European and western Asian Neanderthalers with a reference population of the Modern type show that western Asian Neanderthalers held an intermediate position but were closer to European Neanderthalers than to Modern humans (Table 4).

Table 4 Distance functions based on nine cranial measurements comparing two western Asian and two European Neanderthalers with the Tarofalt (Morocco) series taken as a Modern morphological standard.

Taforalt	0.0
Amud I	4.2009
Shanidar I	4.7730
La Ferrassie I	6.1014
La Chapelle-aux-Saints	7.3899

The western Asian fossils, too, are very homogeneous; the skulls from Amud and Shanidar, although found almost 1,000 km apart, have many similarities. We may take it that the population in that region was as homogeneous as that of Europe and we can speak of 'eastern Neanderthalers' as a biological unit.

We must still explain the formation of these populations, and the history of the Neanderthal line culminating in these two series, the European and the western Asian, enables us to put forward a hypothesis.

Neanderthal origins – the pre-Neanderthalers

As we have seen, it is possible to draw up a list of specific Neanderthal characteristics, reflecting a morphological, and probably also a biomechanical and physiological, process of specialization responsible for the originality of this fossil group. We have tried to define that group with the help of fossils from the last glaciation in which it was brought to its conclusion. However, that did not happen suddenly, but came at the end of a long evolution whose milestones mark out the Neanderthal line.

The characteristics of that line do not, by definition, appear in older, contemporary or later lines. To reconstruct it we must therefore make certain that the characteristics we consider are not shared with other groups and look for the oldest fossils with them. The further back we go, the greater the difficulties become, because Neanderthaler morphology was built up bit by bit: the various characteristics appeared gradually and were not very pronounced at the outset. Moreover, at a particular moment, one characteristic might appear in one group and be absent in another. If we also recall the incomplete state of many of the fossils, that, say, the back of a skull may be without any Neanderthal features while the face may have had them, we see how hard it often is to arrive at the correct interpretation.

A line, when it first becomes distinct, is like a shrub, each of its twigs a subpopulation whose contacts with the exterior are less intense than its internal exchanges. It enjoys a relative degree of evolutionary independence and it takes time for the derived characteristics to be interchanged between the constituents of the whole and for the population to grow homogeneous.

The examination of pre-Würm fossils shows that, to this day, all those with Neanderthal characteristics have come from Europe; outside that continent there are no human remains of which we can say that they belonged to a pre-Neanderthaler.

At what moment, then, did the first signs of Neanderthal morphology appear? It is difficult to put a definite date to it, but in any case more than 300,000 years ago. The Tautavel skull (eastern Pyrenees, France) (Plate 19), which is the oldest, has an expanded suborbital region which heralds that of the Würm forms. The Steinheim skull (Germany), whose age is not clear but which is perhaps as old as the Tautavel, has occipital relief reminiscent of the classic Neanderthal type. By contrast, its suborbital region is concave and recalls that of *Sinanthropus*. These two fossils may well be an illustration of 'mosaic' evolution: the characteristics appear at different times in the different groups.

The face of the Petralona skull (Greece), whose age is unfortunately unknown, also has characteristics of the Neanderthal type, and so does the back of the Swanscombe skull (Britain) (Plate 20).

However, these fossils, which are amongst the oldest discovered in Europe, have retained many archaic characteristics, which shows that they are still very close to the stock from which they have sprung. Now, that stock could only have been an archaic *Homo sapiens* population. In fact, if the Neanderthalers constituted a subspecies, the process of subspeciation that led to their individuation could only have involved part of a single species. If the base of their line went back to *Homo erectus*, then we should have to refer to them as *Homo erectus neanderthalensis*.

We have no certain knowledge of archaic *Homo sapiens* in Europe, but it is possible that the occipital from Vértesszöllös (Hungary) might be evidence of one.

This first stage, marked by the emergence of Neanderthal characteristics, coincides roughly with the beginning of the Riss. The fossils concerned are sometimes difficult to identify. They correspond to a period of morphological instability marked by great variability.

The next stage extended from the middle Riss to the beginning of the Würm, and corresponds to the definite establishment of the general architectural features. All fossils from that period are already Neanderthalers. The stage begins with the back of the skull from Biache-Saint-Vaast (France), which forges a link between the morphology of the first representatives of the line – such as the Swanscombe individual (Plate 20) – and that of classic Neanderthalers. It is followed, at the end of the Riss, by numerous pieces from the Suard at La Chaise cave (Charente, France) and the Salzgitterlebenstedt occipital (Germany). From the Riss–Würm interglacial we can mention the Ehringsdorf skull (Germany), those from Saccopastore (Italy) and the many bones from the Bougeois-Delaunay cave at La Chaise and from the Krapina cave. From the middle of the Riss onwards, the fossil evidence becomes relatively abundant, so much so that we cannot list it here in full.

Neanderthal history can therefore be divided into three periods. The first, which we put roughly at between 400,000 and 250,000 years ago, corresponds to the appearance of the main characteristics of the line; the second continues until 100,000 years ago and saw the organization of these characteristics into the Neanderthal architecture. The third, a period of general stability, ended some 35,000 years ago with the disappearance of the line.

It was probably towards the end of the second period that the Neanderthalers, who by then occupied all Europe, spread out into western Asia. S. Condemi (1985) has demonstrated that western Asian Neanderthalers bore a closer resemblance to those from the European Riss–Würm than they did to those from the Würm.

The extinction of the Neanderthalers

For a long time it was believed that Neanderthalers disappeared with the Mousterian, during the last glacial period. In Europe as in western Asia, they were replaced by humans of the Modern type (*Homo sapiens sapiens*). Their disappearance must have been sudden and many anthropologists believe that they played no part in the establishment of present-day humanity. This view of Neanderthalers as a marginal branch in the evolution of humanity needs to be thoroughly re-examined.

The western Asian discoveries have proved that Neanderthal and Modern humans were contemporaries in that region during the Middle Palaeolithic (Vandermeersch, 1981*b*), and cross-breeding between the two has been considered a possibility for a long time (Dobzhansky, 1944; Thoma, 1962). More recently, the discovery at Saint-Césare (Charente-Maritime, France) of a Neanderthal skeleton (Plate 21) in a Châtelperronian layer has made it clear that, in western Europe at least, some Neanderthal groups survived the Mousterian (Levêque and Vandermeersch, 1980). They were contemporaries of the first European Aurignacians (*Homo sapiens sapiens*) and though we lack proof, it seems likely that they had contacts – amicable or violent, we cannot tell which – with each other.

We do not know the causes (or the cause) of the extinction of the Neanderthalers. No hypothesis advanced so far is satisfactory. We can only register the following facts:

1 in western Asia they disappeared at the end of the Mousterian, after a long period of 'cohabitation' with *Homo sapiens sapiens*;
2 in western Europe they disappeared soon after the arrival of the first Aurignacian *Homo sapiens sapiens*.

What is certain is that their disappearance was not as sudden as was believed until very recently, but took several millennia. Quite possibly some groups were absorbed by populations of the Modern type. In other words, we cannot completely exclude them from our ancestry; perhaps they contributed a small share to the gene pool of Modern humankind.

Though the Neanderthalers are of great interest to anthropologists, both for historical reasons and also because of their many peculiarities, they were nevertheless, in their day, no more than part of the population of the Old World. In Asia, in western Asia and in Africa there also lived completely different populations whose morphology was generally closer to that of Modern humans.

THE CONTEMPORARIES OF THE NEANDERTHALERS

Asia

Neanderthalers managed to advance to central Asia, as we know from the skull of a child found at Teshik Tash in Uzbekistan (Plate 18), but they stopped there. Asia as a whole was inhabited by other populations. We know very little about them because we have only a few fossils to go by. One of the most important of these is a skull discovered at Dali (Shaanxi, China) in 1978 (Plate 22). Though its age has not been determined accurately, the palaeontological and stratigraphic evidence suggests that it is of the order of 200,000 years. At that time, Neanderthal morphology was nearly fully fledged in Europe. The Dali skull is quite different. Of small capacity (just over 1,100 cc) it vaguely recalls those archaic forms of *Homo* we call *Homo erectus*, but it is shorter, with a slightly higher vault, a rounder occipital region and a small and more prognathous face. Wu Xin-Zhi (1981) considers it part of *Homo sapiens*, but as a form transitional between the *erectus* morphology of the remains of Zhoukoudian *Sinanthropus* and the morphology of *sapiens* in the strict sense. In that case, there would have been a regional evolution towards *Homo sapiens*.

Part of the skull discovered at Maba (Guangdong Province, China) (Plate 23) in 1958 is an important signpost of that evolution towards Modern humans. The skull may date back some 100,000 years, in which case it would have been contemporaneous with the first typical Neanderthalers. However, it differs from them in the profile of its cranial vault, the arrangement of the nasal bones and the shape of the orbits. Even so, it still had archaic characteristics – pronounced supraorbital ridges and a narrow anterior frontal region – which make it very remote from the morphology of Modern humans. Hence, if its assumed age should be confirmed, we should have proof that this type of morphology appeared late in continental Asia.

In South-East Asia, the skull-caps from Solo (Ngandong, Java) (Plate 24), whose age is unfortunately not known, might have been contemporary with one stage in the evolution of the Neanderthal line. They still have many characteristics of the *Homo erectus* from Java, but in 1943 Weidenreich drew attention to the possible phylogenetic relationship between the Ngandong population and modern Australians. More recently, Larnach and MacIntosh (1974) have compared eighteen Ngandong characteristics with Australian, European and Asian series. Of the twelve characteristics present in the modern series, nine have their greatest frequency among the Australians. The interval separating the fossil from the modern form is very long, however, and any possible relationship between them still needs to be underpinned. However, it is not impossible that South-East Asia should have followed an independent path towards Modern humans.

Parallel with the evolution of the Neanderthal line in Europe, Asia would then have experienced two evolutions leading to the Modern type (Wolpoff, Wu and Thorne, 1984), one in China following the Zhoukoudian (Choukoutien)–Dali–Mapa–Mongoloid series, the other in South-East Asia with the '*Pithecanthropus*'–Ngandong–proto-Australoid series.

Western Asia

As we saw, the Neanderthalers probably reached western Asia shortly before the Last Glaciation. There they came upon an autochthonous population, the oldest known relic of which is the Galilee skull (Israel). For a long time, its owner was considered to have been more or less contemporary with European Neanderthalers of the Würm and morphologically very close to them (Turville-Petre, 1927; Keith, 1927), but the recent work of I. Gisis and O. Bar-Yosef (1974) has demonstrated an appreciably greater age. Moreover, though the Galilee skull shares certain archaic characteristics, such as the pronounced supraorbital ridges, with Neanderthalers, it has no specific Neanderthal features (Vandermeersch, 1981*b*). The straightened frontal and the facial morphology enable us to consider it to belong to *Homo sapiens* in the strict sense.

The Mousterian levels of the Qafzeh and Skhul caves (Israel) have yielded the remains of more than twenty individuals, several of them represented by complete skeletons. Most have a very modern morphology, which enables us to treat them unhesitatingly as *Homo sapiens sapiens*: a raised cranial vault, a straightened frontal, a rounded occipital region, reduced superstructures, thinner walls, a smaller face, a protruding chin and so on. Some, nevertheless, present archaic 'residual' characteristics in the occipital, the temporal or the frontal regions. But these are rare and dispersed among various individuals.

The comparative analysis of these fossils (Table 5), and especially of those from Qafzeh (Plate 25), has shown that they have numerous similarities with Cro-Magnon Man (Vandermeersch, 1981a). This is particularly obvious in the shape of the orbits, which are rectangular and elongated, their major axis inclined downwards and outwards. One can consider them as the eastern population of European Cro-Magnon Man, whence their name of proto-Cro-Magnon (Howell, 1957).

Table 5 Distance functions based on the measurements of nine characteristics, showing the proximity of the Skhul and Qafzeh fossils to Cro-Magnon remains and their remoteness from those of Neanderthalers.

Cro-Magnon	Taforalt	0.0
Proto-Cro-Magnon	Qafzeh 9	0.9481
	Skhul V	1.0066
Cro-Magnon	Předmostí III	1.3575
Proto-Cro-Magnon	Qafzeh 6	1.5120
	Skhul IV	2.5503
Neanderthalers	Shanidar I	4.7730
	La Chapelle-aux-Saints	7.3899

It is possible that these proto-Cro-Magnons were of local origin and that they were derived from the population represented by the Galilean skull, but we cannot be certain. But no matter what their origin, there is no doubt that, during the Middle Palaeolithic and contemporaneously with Neanderthalers, western Asia contained a population heralding the emergence of the Cro-Magnons at the beginning of the European (Aurignacian) Upper Palaeolithic. This western Asian population may well have provided the rootstock of the second group. In that case, at the very end of the Middle Palaeolithic and throughout the early Upper Palaeolithic, the northern Mediterranean must have witnessed a migration of people from the east to the west.

North Africa

The situation in north Africa is much less clear. The Salé skull (Morocco) has been dated to 200,000 years ago (Jaeger, 1981) and is generally placed among *Homo erectus*. At that time, the Neanderthal line was already firmly established in Europe.

Later, the Djebel Irhoud skulls were discovered in Morocco in association with Mousterian implements, and we may take it that they belonged to contemporaries of classic European Neanderthalers. However, they had none of the specific characteristics of that group. They combined some archaic features with numerous modern ones: morphology of the face, chin, curvature of the occipital region and so on. J. J. Hublin and A. M. Tillier (1981) consider them as *Homo sapiens sapiens*.

The more recent Aterian fossils from Temara and Dar es Soltan (Morocco) date back to between 28,000 and 22,000 years ago; according to D. Ferembach (1976) they could have derived, by local evolution, from Mousterian populations of the Irhoud type. In that case, north Africa would have witnessed an evolution completely independent from that of the European Neanderthal line, and ranging from late *Homo erectus* (Salé) to the Upper Palaeolithic human (Dar es Soltan), passing through the ancient *Homo sapiens sapiens* of Djebel Irhoud.

East Africa

Discoveries in East Africa have multiplied these last few years, radically changing our ideas about the ancient population of that region. Unfortunately, most of the new finds are of uncertain date.

The Broken Hill skull (Zambia) (Plate 26) discovered in 1921 was for a long time likened to those of Neanderthalers, whose contemporary it was thought to have been. Analyses of the archaeological and palaeontological evidence in the light of recent advances have, however, shown that this fossil is probably older than it had been thought to be; it possibly goes back to more than 130,000 years ago (Rightmire, 1984). It has many archaic morphological characteristics − thick cranial vault, robust superstructures, maximum width at the base of the skull and so on − all of which place it among *Homo erectus*. However the cranial capacity − *c.*1,200 cc − was fairly high, the occipital was more rounded than in *Homo erectus* and the base of the skull was of the Modern type. Many authors have accordingly concluded that the skull came from a very archaic form of *Homo sapiens*, not yet very distant from *erectus* stock from which its owner had sprung. Other archaic *Homo sapiens* forms have since been brought to light, for instance at Ngaloba (Tanzania), and corroborate this interpretation.

The Kibish formation in the Omo valley (Ethiopia) has yielded two skulls, whose age may be of the order of 100,000 years: their capacity is 1,450 cc. Skull no. 1 (Plate 27) is very modern, while no. 2 has characteristics of the *erectus* type, especially in the occipital region. Despite these differences, the two skulls are usually treated as belonging to a single group, possibly corresponding to an African subspecies of *Homo sapiens*.

East African fossils suggest the local evolution, perhaps belatedly, of *erectus* morphological features towards *sapiens* characteristics. But that transformation might have been rapid, and if the age of the Omo subjects should be confirmed, skull no. 1 would be one of the first skulls of the Modern type.

South Africa

In South Africa the chronological problems recur with late Middle Pleistocene and early Upper Pleistocene fossils discovered in that region. The Florisbad skull cap, discovered by chance in 1932, is more than 40,000 years old, but we do not know its precise age. It has numerous archaic characteristics (thickness of cranial wall, pronounced brow-ridges) reminiscent of Broken Hill. But the absence of proper tori, the shape of the malar and the span of the anterior frontal are modern characteristics. F. C. Howell (1978) has combined it with the Omo skulls in a subspecies of *Homo sapiens*.

Other South African fossils, from the Border Cave (Plate 28) in Natal and those from Klasies River Mouth near the Cape of Good Hope, have very modern characteristics and are supposed to be more than 60,000 years old. It is therefore possible that the essential features of modern morphology were acquired very long ago in that region, but this supposition needs to be confirmed by precise datings.

In sub-Saharan Africa, *Homo erectus* remains continue until well after the Neanderthal line became individualized in Europe. Then they evolved rapidly and what chronological indications we have suggest that the modern morphology is of great antiquity in that region.

CONCLUSIONS

It is possible to draw several conclusions from this brief account of the Neanderthal line from the fossils of their contemporaries in other regions.

1 The Neanderthalers were without any doubt the best-known human branch during the period corresponding to the end of the Middle Pleistocene and the beginnings of the Upper Pleistocene, by virtue of both the number of fossils discovered so far and the large quantity of chronological data that has been accumulated, although these data are still far from adequate.

2 Their evolution is reflected in a form of specialization that profoundly transformed the original population, with the result that the most recent fossils of the line are morphologically more remote from Modern humans than were the first representatives.

3 In other regions of the Old World, the Modern form emerged before the extinction of the Neanderthalers, more than 50,000 years ago in western Asia and perhaps more than 100,000 years ago in sub-Saharan Africa.

4 The settlement of Europe in the Upper Palaeolithic was largely the result of migrations, which may have led to the disappearance of the Neanderthal line.

NOTE

1 As already emphasized by Paola Villa (see Chapter 4), the transition from the period of *Homo erectus* to the period of the first *Homo sapiens* (be it the Neanderthaler in Europe and in western Asia or another *Homo sapiens* elsewhere) is not clear-cut, archaeologically, anthropologically or geologically: it was a gradual transition. Many archaeologists see the entire Acheulean complex, including the cluster of industries derived from the final stage of this complex, as part of the Lower Palaeolithic; for others, however, the invention of the Levallois technique coincides with the beginnings of the Middle Palaeolithic. Anthropologists often have difficulty in assuming with some degree of certainty that a human skull belongs either to an advanced *Homo erectus* or to a pre-Neanderthaler. From the geological point of view, many specialists draw the line between the two periods in the second part of the Middle Pleistocene or at the beginning of the penultimate glaciation; others, however, are more inclined to put it at the middle or even at the end of this glaciation. All advance good arguments in favour of their own theses. The present volume is not of course the right place to argue the divergent opinions. Each collaborator has expressed his or her own opinion, as the reader will note from the contradictions and overlappings between the chapters concerning the end of the period of *Homo erectus* and the beginning of that of the first pre-sapiens – Ed.

BIBLIOGRAPHY

CONDEMI, S. 1985. *Les Hommes fossiles de Saccopastore (Italie) et leurs relations phylogénétiques.* Bordeaux. (Thesis, Université de Bordeaux 1.)

DOBZHANSKY, J. 1944. On Species and Races of Living and Fossil Man. *Am. J. Anthropol.* (Boston), Vol. 2, pp. 251–6.

FEREMBACH, D. 1976. Les Restes humains de la grotte de Dar-es-Soltane 2 (Maroc) campagne 1975. *Bull. Mém. Soc. Anthropol.* (Paris), Ser. 13, Vol. 3, pp. 183–93.

GISIS, I.; BAR-YOSEF, O. 1974. New Excavations in Zuttiyeh Cave. *Paléorient*, Vol. 2, pp. 175–80.

HEIM, J.-L. 1983. Les Variations du squelette post-crânien des hommes de Neandertal suivant le sexe. *Anthropologie* (Paris), Vol. 87, No. 1, pp. 5–26.

HOWELL, F. C. 1957. The Evolutionary Significance of Variation Varieties of 'Neanderthal' Man. *Quart. Rev. Biol.* (Baltimore), Vol. 32, No. 4, pp. 330–47.

—— 1978. Hominidae. In: MAGLIO, V. J.; COOKE, H. B. S. (eds), *Evolution of African Mammals.* Cambridge, Mass. pp. 154–248.

HUBLIN, J.-J.; TILLIER, A.-M. 1981. The Mousterian Juvenile Mandible from Irhoud (Morocco): A Phylogenetic Interpretation. In: STRINGER, C. B.; TAYLOR, E.; FRANCIS, L. (eds), *Aspects of Human Evolution.* London. pp. 167–85.

JAEGER, J.-J. 1981. Les Hommes fossiles du Pléistocène moyen du Maghreb dans leur cadre géologique, chronologique, et paléoécologique. In: SIGMON, B. A.; CYBULSKI, J. S. (eds), Homo erectus: *Papers in Honor of Davidson Black.* Toronto. pp. 158–87.

KEITH, A. 1927. *A Report on the Galilee Skull.* London, British School of Archaeology in Jerusalem.

LARNACH, S. L.; MACINTOSH, N. W. G. 1974. A Comparative Study of Solo and Australian Aboriginal Crania. In: ELKIN, A. P.; MACINTOSH, N. W. G. (eds), *Grafton Elliot Smith: The Man and his Work.* Sydney. pp. 95–102.

LÉVÊQUE, F.; VANDERMEERSCH, B. 1980. Découverte de restes humains dans un niveau castelperronien à Saint-Césaire (Charente-Maritime). *C. R. Acad. Sci.* (Paris), Ser. D, Vol. 291, pp. 187–9.

RIGHTMIRE, G. P. 1984. *Homo sapiens* in Sub-Sahara Africa. In: SMITH, F. H.; SPENCER, F. (eds), *The Origins of Modern Man.* New York. pp. 295–325.

THOMA, A. 1962. Le Déploiement évolutif de l'*Homo sapiens.* *Anthropol. Hung.* (Budapest), Vol. 5, No. 1/2.

TRINKAUS, E. 1976. The Morphology of the European and Southwest Asian Neanderthal Pubic Bones. *Am. J. Phys. Anthropol.* (New York), Vol. 44, pp. 95–104.

TURVILLE-PETRE, F. A. J. 1927. *Researches in Prehistoric Galilee (1925–1926).* London, British School of Archaeology in Jerusalem.

VANDERMEERSCH, B. 1981a. *Les Hommes fossiles de Qafzeh (Israël).* Paris, CNRS.

—— 1981b. Les Premiers *Homo sapiens* au Proche-Orient. In: FEREMBACH, D. (ed.), *Les Processus de l'hominisation.* Paris. pp. 97–100. (Colloques Internationaux du CNRS, 599.)

WOLPOFF, M. H.; WU, X.; THORNE, A. L. 1984. Modern *Homo sapiens* Origins: A General Theory of Hominid Evolution Involving the Fossil Evidence from East Asia. In: SMITH, F. M.; SPENCER, F. (eds), *The Origins of Modern Humans.* New York. pp. 411–83.

WU XIN ZHI. 1981. A Well Preserved Cranium of an Archaic Type of Early *Homo sapiens* from Dali, China. *Sci. Sin.* (Beijing), Vol. 24, No. 4, pp. 530–41.

10

ARCHAEOLOGY OF THE NEANDERTHALERS AND THEIR CONTEMPORARIES

An overview

Karel Valoch

ECOLOGY

Palaeoanthropians peopled almost all the Ancient World for approximately 150,000 to 200,000 years. During this period, there were many climatic variations and these had repercussions on human behaviour. Chronologically this period comprises the penultimate glacial stage (variously called Riss, Saale, Woltstonian, Dnieper and Moskva), the last interglacial age (PK III, Riss/Würm, Eem, Ipswichian, Mikulino) and the first half of the last glacial stage (Würm, Weichsel, Devensian, Valdai). During the glacial periods themselves temperatures were not consistently very low and they were modulated by minor oscillations that were more temperate (interstadials). The penultimate glacial period also saw one considerable increase in temperature (PK IV, Treene, Kärlich, Odincovo). During the first half of the last glacial period three or four temperate oscillations occurred, of which the last was the most intense and heralded the very low temperatures that followed.

During the glacial periods the high mountain glaciers spread and reached much lower altitudes. In addition, the Scandinavian glacier became several hundreds of metres thicker, and covered much of Europe east of the Rhine. During the Saale glaciation, this glacier reached Magdeburg, the source of the Oder in Moravia and the region around Moscow. During the Weichsel glaciation this glacier stretched as far south as Berlin and into northern Poland. This extension of the glaciers can also be seen in northern Asia. On the other hand, during the more temperate phases the glaciers retreated towards the north and only affected mountain tops.

Human occupation was limited by changing ecological conditions in central and eastern Europe, the southern part of western Europe and the southern regions of northern Asia. In Mediterranean Europe and the other subtropical and tropical regions, climatic changes took the form of an alternation of humid (pluvial) periods with arid (interpluvial) ones.

The territory of the Palaeoanthropians was considerably more extensive than that of *Homo erectus*. In the tropical zone, apart from the savannah and the steppes, they occupied virgin forest and the valleys of permanent or intermittent watercourses. In the high mountains, for example, the Alps and the Caucasus, caves were inhabited up to an altitude of 2,000 metres, as were the high plateaux of the Pamirs. Human beings almost reached the Arctic circle in the northern Urals. This territorial extension took place in propitious periods: the settlement of arid regions during pluvial periods, the occupation of islands during glacials (due to lowering of the sea-level) and that of mountains during temperate periods (due to withdrawal of the glaciers). So humans displayed their great capacity for adaptation to the most varied of natural conditions.

For the first time humans occupied the temperate zones of Europe and the southern regions of northern Asia. During a glacial period, *Homo erectus*, who was contemporary with the first great glacial period (Mindel, Elster, Anglian, Oka) and who came up from the Mediterranean and subtropical zone, had only reached these areas during the temperate interglacial periods. During glacial periods the environment consisted of steppe and tundra with permanently frozen soil. Climatic changes were reflected in the vegetation and fauna. The interglacial forests were replaced by grassy steppes, forest-steppes and even arctic tundra. The warm-climate fauna (elephants, rhinoceros, Cervidae, Bovidae and various wild beasts) alternated with steppe fauna (horses, various rodents) and boreal fauna (especially mammoths, woolly rhinoceros, reindeer, gluttons, and so on).

MATERIAL CULTURE

The Palaeoanthropian period of prehistory is contemporaneous with that of the Middle Palaeolithic, which can be divided into three phases:

1 the early phase during the penultimate glacial period (240/200,000 to 120,000 years ago);
2 the middle phase during the last interglacial period (120,000 to 100,000 years ago);

3 the late phase during the first half of the last glacial stage (100,000 to 40,000 years ago).

The material culture of the Middle Palaeolithic can be distinguished from that of the Lower Palaeolithic by its greater heterogeneity and regional variation. During this period the first cultural traditions began to form, based on types of tools that were already to a large extent standardized. During the Middle Palaeolithic, innovations emerged within different cultural groups. This study is based exclusively on stone tools, which form the absolute majority of all archaeological items. The most characteristic feature of the Middle Palaeolithic is the predominance of flaked tools in contrast to the bifaces and worked pebbles that dominated the Lower Palaeolithic. But even in this respect there are considerable regional differences on the three continents.

One of the technical developments that distinguish the tool-making industry of the Middle Palaeolithic from those that preceded it is the predominance of the Levallois technique, by which flakes were obtained from a prepared core. The term 'Levallois flaking' comes from Levallois-Perret (Hauts-de-Seine), a suburb of Paris, where this type of flake-tool was first discovered. This technique was widely used in Europe, in Africa and in certain parts of Asia. It required a large quantity of good-quality raw material. Its ingenuity lay in the fact that skilful trimming of the core made it possible to predetermine the form of the flake. Before obtaining the desired artefact, however, as many as several dozen preliminary flakes had to be detached, and these in general were not used as tools.

The Levallois core is discoid or oval, and most frequently flattened. Its upper surface has facets formed by centripetal flaking and roughly resembles a tortoise's shell with its divisions. The lower surface is sometimes worked. At one end of the core can be seen a surface prepared to receive the blow which detached the flake, generally consisting of small facets. The Levallois flakes, oval or rounded in shape, flat, most often have a faceted butt and the upper end shows traces of centripetal flaking. The Levallois point, triangular in form, with edges in the form of an upside-down 'Y' on the upper face, is a special type of point requiring special preparation of the cores (Bordes, 1950a, pp. 21–2). In the recent phase of the Middle Palaeolithic, discoid and oval cores are replaced by prismatic cores from which blades and narrow points can be produced.

In Europe, as on the other continents, the technique called Mousterian (from the site of Le Moustier in the Dordogne, France) is found alongside the Levallois technique. Mousterian cores also have an approximately discoid or spherical shape and have had flakes removed on two or more sides. Their preparation is less elaborate and does not allow the form of the flake to be predetermined. Sometimes the flakes are taken, with the help of a hammerstone or anvil stone, from untrimmed blocks, and they then have a smooth or cortical butt.

There is a great deal of regional variation in collections of tools and hence in tool-making industries, which allows us to distinguish one archaeological culture from another. The industries of Europe and of the eastern Mediterranean show the greatest variety of types of tools. To these can be linked the very similar industries of central Asia, while those of the Maghreb, of East Africa and especially sub-Saharan Africa, of the Indian subcontinent and east and South-East Asia, evolved in their own ways.

In Europe, two technical traditions coexisted throughout the Middle Palaeolithic. The first, derived from the African Lower Palaeolithic, used bifacial production. Both sides of the block of raw material (in later periods a thick flake) were chipped at until the desired shape was achieved: spear-shaped, almond-shaped, triangular, oval or heart-shaped. The oldest bifaces have a sinuous edge. Later, the cutting edge was straight and sharper. In the earliest periods the part which served for gripping was thick and not worked. Later the longitudinal profile of the biface handaxes was as smooth and regular as that of a lens. Their perfect crafting and symmetry made the bifaces among the most beautiful stone tools of the Palaeolithic period. The cleaver is a type of biface whose end is not pointed but forms a more or less sharp transversal cutting edge (Bordes, 1961, 1979). Although the bifaces are characteristic and remarkable, they represent only a fraction of the total number of tools. Flake-tools dominate throughout. The Acheulean and Micoquian industries and those derived from them belong to this tradition.

The second technical tradition is composed exclusively of flake-tools, the most important being scrapers of various kinds, points, and notched and denticulate tools. A flake of which one or more edges have been heavily retouched is called a 'side-scraper'. According to the parts that have been worked and the form of the tool, different types can be identified: side-scrapers that are straight, double, concave, convex, convergent or transverse, and so on. Points are tools that are triangular, subtriangular and sometimes diamond-shaped, with tapering ends shaped by considerable retouch. Notches are made on the edge of a flake by repeated retouch; their depth and width are very variable. Sometimes they are very small. The denticulated tools have, on one or more non-adjacent edges, a series of notches that are contiguous or almost contiguous (Bordes, 1961, 1979). In Europe, the eastern Mediterranean, the Caucasus and central Asia, the industries of this technical tradition can be grouped together to form the Mousterian complex. The Levallois technique appears in the Acheulean and in certain industries of the Mousterian complex.

The typological composition of toolkits apparently varies according to the traditions of the various populations. That means that the different groups of tools would seem to correspond to the ethnic groups that made them. On the basis of this supposition a classification of the cultural groups of the Palaeolithic in terms of typological and technical differences has been advanced.

At the beginning of the 1950s, a list of sixty-three types was drawn up for the Middle Palaeolithic, giving precise technical and morphological definitions, and a statistical method was devised that allows the data used to classify the material of each collection to be expressed numerically and graphically, and the results to be compared. This has enabled us to create a scheme for the various cultural facies of the Mousterian complex and the biface complex, and to determine their typological and technical characteristics (Bordes, 1950a, 1950b, 1953a, 1953b, 1954, 1961). These lists and the associated statistical methods (the Bordes system) based on the French industries, have been applied successively throughout Europe, in the Levant and in central Asia, and have undoubtedly contributed to a deeper understanding of the Middle Palaeolithic.

Objections have been raised against this cultural interpretation of the differences in the stone-tool industries and an alternative interpretation offered according to which all tools have to be seen in terms of a function: the tools found in a dwelling-place necessarily differ from those found in tool-production site or in a temporary encampment for hunters

(Binford and Binford, 1966). However, many archaeological discoveries bear witness to the fact that cultural traditions play the decisive role in the typological and technical profile of the stone-tool industries (Bordes and Sonneville-Bordes, 1970; Mellars, 1970; Oliva, 1983). Workshops, located near the source of the stone used – in which the cores and the unfinished partially worked products are generally plentiful, while finished tools are relatively rare – constitute a special case.

In Africa, the Acheulean, a culture characterized by handaxes, the whole surface of which had been beautifully shaped, developed throughout the lower and middle phases of the Middle Palaeolithic. In the upper phase, we see a pattern of evolution in the north of the continent (the Mediterranean region including the Sahara, Ethiopia and Somalia) that differs from that in the sub-Saharan region.

In north Africa, a flake-tool industry using the Levallois technique (Acheulo-Levalloisian) emerged with few bifaces. In the Maghreb, a flake-tool industry using a very specific type of Levallois technique (Aterian) is distinguished by the number of pedunculate tools (in particular pedunculate points) that it produced. The Aterian continues almost without change beyond the Middle Palaeolithic up to 20,000 years ago, and so replaces the lower and middle phases of the European Upper Palaeolithic. It is to be found sporadically west of the Nile valley in Egypt and in the Sudan. In Ethiopia and in Somalia, the Levalloisian without bifaces is still close to the Acheulo-Levalloisian (Clark, 1972). In the Nile valley the tradition of the Levallois technique continues until the appearance of industries of the Upper Palaeolithic (Khormusan, Halfan, 22,000 to 17,000 years ago) and late Palaeolithic (Sebilian, 15,000 to 11,000 years ago; Wendorf, 1968). In Ethiopia and in South Africa this technical tradition survived in the biface industries (Stillbay, Pietersburg) until the Upper Palaeolithic (40,000 to 20,000 years ago; Wendorf and Schild, 1974).

In sub-Saharan Africa the Acheulean lasted for a very long time. It produced handaxes, cleavers, numerous flake-tools and also archaic pebble-tools (choppers, chopping tools). Towards 60,000, a new culture, the Sangoan, grew out of the Acheulean in the savannahs and virgin tropical forests. It consisted, besides the handaxes and cleavers, of axes and did not use the Levallois technique. In the forests of central and west Africa the Sangoan evolved during the Upper Palaeolithic towards industries (Tshitolian, Lupemban) that gradually replaced bifaces by leaf-shaped points, and by ever more numerous axes (Clark, 1970).

On the vast continent of Asia the evolution of the Middle Palaeolithic is even more varied. In the older phase, in western Asia, the Acheulean – the most important industry – is represented by two facies: one of them, widespread along the coast, has a high percentage of Levallois elements (cores, flakes, points), while the other, situated in inland areas, shows few Levallois elements. During the middle phase, the Acheulean spread from Egypt to Anatolia.

About 150,000 years ago, the first non-biface industry, which did not use the Levallois technique (the Jabrudian) appeared in the Levant. Canted side-scrapers and transverse side-scrapers, heavily retouched, are typical of this industry. Later a flake industry using the Levallois technique and lacking bifaces (Levalloiso-Mousterian) developed throughout western Asia. Moreover, in the caves of the mountain chain of the Zagros (northern Iraq) we find a facies with a small proportion of Levallois elements, recalling that of the European Mousterian.

To the north, the Acheulean spread to the caves of the Great Caucasus and was replaced during the recent phase by the Mousterian complex. This is made up of at least three typologically different facies: the Typical Mousterian, the Charentian and the Denticulate Mousterian. Sometimes even points with bifacial retouching appeared (Ljubin, 1984). Several typological facies can also be found in the Mousterian complex of central Asia and Kazakhstan, where the influences of western Asia and of the Indian subcontinent meet (pebble-tools of Soan type) (Ranov and Nesmeyanov, 1973).

In the Lower Palaeolithic the Acheulean spread to India where, as in Africa, it lasted until almost the end of the Middle Palaeolithic. Only a little more than 40,000 years ago do flake-tool industries appear that vaguely resemble the European Mousterian. At the same time, small handaxes, cleavers and choppers were used (Sankalia, 1974). Over vast areas to the north of Pakistan and India, to the south of Iran, in Myanmar (formerly Burma), Thailand and perhaps even elsewhere during the Middle Palaeolithic, industries producing the pebble-tools of the Lower Palaeolithic existed, with choppers, chopping-tools and cleavers.

In Java the Sangiran industry, probably worked by the Ngandong people, corresponds to the Middle Palaeolithic (Sartono, 1980). In China also the flake industries can be placed in the Middle Palaeolithic; they apparently link with the local Lower Palaeolithic. They contain carefully retouched scrapers, discoid cores, choppers and sometimes even points with bifacial retouch. Several of these industries have been discovered in conjunction with human remains (Atlas, 1980). The first traces of human activity in the Japanese island of Honshu, brought to light by a number of excavations north of Tokyo, go back 120,000 years. Along with the scrapers and points, pebble-tools appear at first, followed by handaxes or biface points. These industries continue into the Upper Palaeolithic (Ikawa-Smith, 1978).

If we examine the general evolution of the Middle Palaeolithic, we can distinguish several industrial complexes that are probably linked to the different environments. The first is represented by the Asian pebble-tools industries (Soan, Anyathian, Tampanian, Ladizian and so on), which continue without change in some places from the Lower Palaeolithic until later periods (for example the Hoabinhian in Thailand lasts until the beginning of the Neolithic).[1] They are partly the result of an adaptation to a tropical environment. We also find the ancient traditions of pebble-tools in the Middle Palaeolithic of southern Siberia, central Asia and of east Asia, where they influenced even the Upper Palaeolithic (Mongolia). In other regions, such as China and Java, the pebble industries develop little by little into flake industries.

The second complex involves handaxe industries from the Acheulean and its derivatives: the Middle Palaeolithic in Africa, India, western Asia, part of western Europe and the Caucasus. In the sub-Saharan tropical forests, Acheulean handaxes and cleavers evolved into axes and points that are still found at the end of the Pleistocene. In both cases, in principle this simply meant the extension of the typological base of the Lower Palaeolithic, the changes being relatively minor.

Flake-tool industries based on the Levallois technique form the third complex. New cultural groups are seen to emerge in Europe, the eastern Mediterranean, the Caucasus and central Asia, which have little in common with the Lower Palaeolithic which preceded them. They feature a great variety of types of tool and the creation of facies which spread into distinct regions.

At the end of the Middle Palaeolithic and during the

transition towards the Upper Palaeolithic (the period of *Homo sapiens sapiens*) there is considerable variation from one region to another. Sometimes the characteristics of the Middle Palaeolithic (Levallois flaking) or even of the Lower Palaeolithic (pebble-tools) are maintained, as has already been mentioned.

At other times, on the contrary, the techniques and typologies of the Upper Palaeolithic emerge, which is very interesting. These cases are not numerous and are concentrated in Europe, the eastern Mediterranean and South Africa.

At the beginning of the recent phase of the Middle Palaeolithic, perhaps about 80,000 years ago or more, industries appeared which technically and typologically belong to the Upper Palaeolithic, but incontestably date from the Middle Palaeolithic. Up to now, these industries have been found in three sites that are fairly far apart, and they differ from one another in some of the types of tools represented. They are the pre-Aurignacian (shelter I at Jabrud, Syria), the Amudian (the Zumoffen shelter in Lebanon) and the Libyan pre-Aurignacian (cave at Haua Fteah in Cyrenaica) (Rust, 1950; Copeland, 1975; McBurney, 1967). Recently Mousterian industries have been found in northern Europe with blade facies that are reminiscent in their typology and technique of the Upper Palaeolithic. The isolated discovery of an industry that appears to be Upper Palaeolithic at Howieson's Poort in South Africa has been dated as belonging to the same period (Clark, 1982). Unfortunately, none of these sites have revealed any human remains, so it is not clear to what human type these precursors of the Upper Palaeolithic should be related; nor do we know what happened to them during the terminal phase of the Middle Palaeolithic.

In a few cases we can see the gradual transition from a Middle Palaeolithic industry to one of the Upper Palaeolithic, and sometimes the persistence of Middle Palaeolithic traditions in a new cultural environment. Such phenomena at present are known only in Europe and in the Levant.

In south-west France there is probably a direct genetic relationship between a facies of the Mousterian of Acheulean tradition (MTA B) and the subsequent Châtelperronian (Perigordian I) (Bordes, 1958). However, the discovery of a typical Neanderthal skeleton in the Châtelperronian at Saint-Césaire (Plate 21) is surprising (Lévêque and Vandermeersch, 1981). In central Europe the Micoquian is the most important culture of the recent phase of the Middle Palaeolithic. It does not use the Levallois technique and it contains many small bifaces. In its final phase we find leaf-points that are perfectly evolved from bifaces. In our present state of knowledge we may assume that the Szeletian, a culture of the beginning of the Upper Palaeolithic in the eastern part of central Europe, is the result of the meeting of Micoquian Neanderthalers and the modern *sapiens* of the Aurignacian. In fact, alongside elements of the Micoquian tradition (leaf-points, side-scrapers), the Szeletian contains Aurignacian types. In this region the leaf-points continue into the middle phase of the Upper Palaeolithic (Pavlovian) and give us reason to think that the Szeletian is one of the sources of the Pavlovian.

In the Levant the gradual transition from the Levalloiso-Mousterian to the Upper Paleolithic can be seen in two facies of somewhat different typology, but both using the Levallois technique. This technique continues to be used to make tools in the Upper Palaeolithic. The two sites are the Ksar Akil shelter in Lebanon and the open-air site at Boker

Tachtit in the Negev desert of Israel. At Ksar Akil, in the midst of this industry, an upper jaw of Neanderthal type has been discovered, and Boker Tachtit has been radiocarbon dated to betweeen 43,000 and 45,000 years (Copeland, 1975; Marks and Kaufman, 1983). It is interesting to note that at Brno-Bohunice in the Czech Republic an industry that typologically and technically resembles that of Boker Tachtit has been discovered and also dates from 43,000 to 40,000 years BP (Valoch, 1976). However, while Boker Tachtit fits into a continuous tradition of Levalloiso-Mousterian, Levalloisian industries are very rare in central Europe during the Middle Palaeolithic.

Datings of European and Levantine sites, which are the most numerous, make it clear that the Middle Palaeolithic did not end at the same time everywhere. In France and Spain the radiocarbon dates indicate 35,000 years ago for the Typical Mousterian, and the oldest industries of the Upper Palaeolithic are younger than 35,000 years. In central Europe and the Levant, the transition between the two periods seems to have taken place more than 40,000 years ago. In south-east and central Europe the Aurignacian, the first culture whose technique is purely Upper Palaeolithic, appears more than 40,000 years ago: this is represented at the cave of Bacho Kiro in Bulgaria, around 43,000 years ago (Kozlowski et al., 1982) the cave of Istallöskö in Hungary, around 44,000 years ago (Gàbori-Csánk, 1970), and the open-air site of Vedrovice II in the Czech Republic, of similar date according to its stratigraphic position (Valoch et al., 1985). The industries of the Middle Palaeolithic that led to the emergence of the Aurignacian are not yet sufficiently well known.

This summary of the evolution of the Middle Palaeolithic is based only on the lithic industries, of which we have the most abundant evidence. They are undoubtedly not the only components of the material culture of the Palaeoanthropians. However, tools of bone and antler are very rare and not very typical. Clubs made of antler indeed appear in several places in different periods. Pieces of bone and ribs (Lebenstedt, Germany) are often pointed, the thick flakes being retouched in the same way as stone tools. For the most part, bone tools are worked and occasionally used and, in the Middle Palaeolithic, there are no clearly distinguishable types yet. The so-called bone tools that come from Alpine caves in Switzerland, Germany and Austria (the *'protolithische Knochenkultur'*), published earlier, are now considered to be the result of mechanical processes in caves inhabited by bears. They were not in any case, the work of humans (Feustel, 1969).

Weapons and tools made of wood were probably very common, but practically none have survived. We must assume that sharpened sticks were used in food collection to dig up bulbs and roots and expose small animals. To carry the gathered food, bags or other recipients would be needed, made of skin and perhaps even of bark. Wood would be very suitable, for natural pieces would require little working. In the Acheulean of Kalambo Falls in Zimbabwe, for example, a wooden club has been discovered. At Florisbad (South Africa), together with stone tools of the Middle Stone Age and human bones, a wooden rod was found which may have served as a spear. The best evidence for the existence of wooden spears is a pole 2.5 m long made of yew, with its point fire-hardened. This was found at Lehringen (Germany) (Fig. 9) together with bones of *Elephas antiquus* and Levallois flakes. Pachyderms could be hunted with such weapons, as long as the hunter came close enough to bury the spear in the belly of the animal.

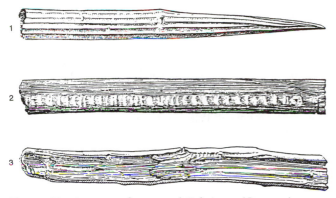

Figure 9 Hunting spear of yew wood, Lehringen (Germany). 1, the top part carefully sharpened and hardened in fire; 2, the stock with traces of scraping; 3, the bottom part. (After K. H. Jacob-Friesen, in Bosinski, 1985.)

LIFE-STYLE

The Palaeoanthropians, like *Homo erectus*, were hunter-gatherers. They hunted herds of herbivores and pachyderms in groups, probably with weapons made of wood (spears and javelins). Meat supplies were more reliable at that time. But edible plants and small animals none the less formed an essential part of their diet. At the time of the greatest geographical spread of the cave bear, in the first half of the Würm glacial stage, the Neanderthalers – especially those who lived in caves in the Alps and the Caucasus – even hunted these dangerous omnivores. One can see, in the later phase, a degree of specialization in the hunting of the different herbivores, apparently linked with the environment. In the Kůlna cave (Moravia) a great many reindeer and mammoth remains have been found; in the Bockstein cave (Germany) horses; in the open-air site at Erd near Budapest (Hungary) cave bears; in the Hortus cave (southern France) goats; in the Shanidar cave (Iraq) wild sheep; in central Asia, in the caves of Teshik-Tash (Uzbekistan) wild goats (*Capra siberica*); at Aman Kutan, Asian mountain sheep (*Ovis orientalis*) and at Obi Rachmat wild goats and deer; on the open-air site of Kuturbulak (Kazakhstan) horses and elephants. The first evidence of river fishing relates to this period, as also fishing for turtles and sea fishing. Seventy-five per cent of the 26,000 bones found in the Kudaro cave in the Great Caucasus belong to salmon. At Ogzi-Kitchik in Kazakhstan, 13,600 bones out of a total of 15,000 are the remains of steppe turtles. In the cave at the Klasies River Mouth site (South Africa) great quantities of sea-shells and penguin and dolphin bones have been found. The same is true of the cave of Haua Fteah in Cyrenaica. During the interglacial period in central Europe, elephant and rhinoceros were the most commonly hunted animals (Ehringsdorf, Germany; Taubach, Germany) but horses, Bovidae and Cervidae (Kůlna cave) have also been found.

The hunting of the bigger animals was organized in groups. The chosen animal, often a young one, was probably separated from the herd before being brought down (mammoth of the Kůlna cave). The hunters took advantage of any favourable configuration of the terrain: watering places, gorges or the narrow mouths of valleys. We should not assume that traps were laid or dug at this time. Wooden spears were useful in hunting large animals at close quarters (Fig. 9). Javelins were used more to fell swift-moving animals that lived in packs. In both cases the points were hardened by fire or by fixing a stone tip to the shaft.

The acquisition and possibly the distribution of stone for the production of tools constitutes a key element in Palaeolithic organization. In the Middle Palaeolithic encampments were most frequently situated close to sources of this raw material, so that industry dealt almost exclusively with one type of material. But more detailed studies, concerning for example Moravia and southern Germany, show that alongside the local dominant raw material there is always a small quantity of tools, or just a few isolated artefacts, made of stone obtained from some distance away (up to 100 km). Such artefacts can be seen as 'specimens' of different rocks, for their usefulness, given their very small number, is almost nil, even if the stone is of very good quality. The problem is to know how they were obtained. Were they pieces picked up by chance during hunting expeditions, or were they gifts, or objects exchanged at meetings with other groups?

Most interesting in this respect are the industries of the Taubachian interglacial, which used the most varied rocks, or at least different types of flint, collected in the form of pebbles or flint nodules in the moraines. Stone from at least 60 km away was also used (Kůlna cave).

There are far more encampments in the Middle Palaeolithic than during the period of *Homo erectus*. Caves that had already been inhabited by *Homo erectus* were sought out again by the Palaeoanthropians. As evidence of human occupation is better preserved in caves than in open-air sites, almost all the human remains discovered so far have been found in caves. Even if many encampments have been destroyed in the course of the millennia by natural processes, we have now found a fairly large number in the vast areas without caves. If they have not been disturbed, it is the open-air encampments that provide most clues to the life of Palaeolithic humans. In the caves and rock shelters people were protected by a natural roof, whereas in the open they had to build one.

Shelters were built from the period of *Homo erectus* onwards, and we may assume that it is one of the most ancient forms of human adaptation to the environment. Most frequently the dwellings were oval or circular in shape, recalling tents, with a superstructure of wood and a covering of skins. Inside there was generally a hearth. Apparently these settlements appeared whenever climatic conditions made it impossible to live out of doors; in the tropics only windbreaks were erected. But archaeologists have been able to identify these constructions only when traces have been left in the earth. Mostly these are stones or animal bones spread around the hut, thus indicating its shape.

The camp discovered at Molodova I, on the banks of the Dniester, and dated to more than 44,000 years ago, is the only one that presents several different types of dwelling structure (Chapter 12). On its surface of almost 1,200 m² there are eleven small concentrations of bones, circular or oval in form, with hearths and numerous artefacts; they are considered to have been inhabited over a short period. A bigger structure, of mammoth bones, measuring 10 by 7 m, containing several hearths, appears to be a long-term dwelling: a *yaranga* (Chernysh, 1982). A slightly dug-out structure, surrounded by stone, covering 13 m², and containing a hearth, was discovered at Bečov (Bohemia) and dates from the early Middle Palaeolithic. It is one of the best-preserved dwelling structures of the Middle Palaeolithic (Fridrich, 1982).

Like the open-air sites, several caves have revealed structures indicating that their interiors were divided, and that only the zones marked out were inhabited. In the cave of Lazaret (Nice, France), a niche measuring 11 by 3.5 m was surrounded by a low stone wall which supported a wooden construction with an awning. The niche itself was divided by a partition into two unequal parts with two separate entrances. The bigger one contained two hearths, with a litter near to them. A smaller litter was found in the other part, near the low stone wall. The two litters were made of algae covered with skins; small sea-shells were found there, together with bones of the extremities of well-furred animals (lynx, wolf, fox, panther). This cave dwelling, the most interesting yet found, dates back approximately 130,000 years (de Lumley, 1969).

Hearths are often found in the encampments of Palaeoanthropians and we may assume that they were capable of making fire. Traces of pyrites found in certain caves bear witness to this. The hearths vary in form, being most often primitive, made on the ground without a clear boundary. Hearths outlined, at least partially, by stones are also fairly numerous (Orgnac III in the south of France). Other hearths were paved, the fire being made on a stone paving (Pech de l'Azé I, south-west France). Hearths protected by drystone walls are rare (Rigabe cave, south of France) (Perlès, 1977; Wymer, 1982).

Archaeological discoveries have also thrown light on some aspects of social life. As hunting developed, an initial division of labour according to sex probably occurred already during the period of *Homo erectus*. Hunting required greater physical exertion and became the domain of the men, while the women specialized in gathering and in taking care of the children. The society of the Palaeoanthropians was one in which men hunted and the women collected food. On the basis of ethnological comparisons we assume that a group of twenty-five to thirty people was the most stable social unit and the smallest community capable of providing enough food for all its members. This would not exclude the possibility of several groups joining forces temporarily to tap specific sources of supply (for instance, passing herds of animals) or the dividing up of a basic group.

The dwelling structures that have remained could not, for the most part, shelter more than a limited number of people. In the hut of the Lazaret cave (35 m² in surface area), about ten people could comfortably lie down around the two hearths. The same is true of the huts of identical size at Molodova I. The small Bečov hut, of about 15 m², could only shelter a couple and their close relations. From the Middle to the Upper Palaeolithic the encampment probably consisted of a number of huts. Certain caves were inhabited by humans for tens of millennia – not permanently, but on a cyclical or seasonal basis according to the activities engaged in: hunting, gathering, extraction of raw materials and so on.

In the Middle Palaeolithic, regional groups developed independently, forming the many cultural traditions that are identified by the typology and the technology of the tools. This evolution involves different population groups occupying the same distinct territory, which gave rise to specific cultures. Changes appearing in the material domain would be matched by changes in the spiritual. This would explain the great variability of the lithic industries of the Middle Palaeolithic.

Relationships between the members of the same group were probably characterized by great concern, and the bonds of affection that must have been formed can be glimpsed when a person was wounded. In fact, certain Neanderthal remains show traces of wounds, sometimes perfectly healed (for example, Shanidar skeletons 1 and 2, Neanderthal skeleton) (Trinkaus, 1983). This implies that the other members of the group must have looked after injured persons during their convalescence, and even up to their deaths if they sustained handicaps preventing them, for example, from hunting or moving about. This indicates a high degree of social consciousness and solidarity on the part of the Neanderthalers.

We can only hazard guesses as to the social organization of local groups of Palaeoanthropians. If we assume that humans of the Modern type (*Homo sapiens sapiens*) lived in family groups from the beginning then we should place the emergence of this form of organization in the preceding period. It is probable that the first stages of family groupings existed in the late Middle Palaeolithic, having gradually taken shape during preceding periods.

INDICATIONS OF SPIRITUAL CULTURE

Burials provide the most important archaeological evidence for our knowledge of the spiritual life of prehistoric humans. But people have not always treated their dead in such a way that their remains have been conserved until our day. We find only the remains of those who were buried immediately and so did not become the prey of animals or of the elements.

The custom of burying the dead appears for the first time among the Neanderthalers during the late Middle Palaeolithic, that is from 100,000 to 40,000 years ago. Even though older human remains have been discovered, these have always been bones which had been covered by natural deposits and so accidentally preserved from disintegration.

How did the Palaeoanthropians treat their dead during the early and middle phases of the Middle Palaeolithic? We know nothing of this. Perhaps they were indifferent to their fate, and left them to the animals or to the elements. Or perhaps, showing the first signs of concern for the dead, they placed the remains in special places, still however without protecting them from the elements. It is certain that burial was practised for the first time in the history of humanity in the late Middle Palaeolithic.

In Europe, Africa and Asia, we know of about fifty individuals, buried in twenty sites (Harrold, 1980; Wymer, 1982). If we consider the length of time (about 50,000 years) and the geographical area (the whole of the Ancient World) involved, we have some idea of the exceptional nature of these cases. Even so, the skeletons are seldom preserved in their entirety, for we must consider as a burial the discovery of several bones of the same individual in the same place; unless they were buried immediately their preservation would not have been possible. The question whether only a few persons were interred with reverence remains unanswered. We would expect these to be first of all persons of high social rank, who were to be honoured. But more than a third (eighteen) of those buried are children, and five or seven others, women. Among the children are included foetuses, new-born babies (La Ferrassie, south-west France) and a young child (less than 2 years old; Staroselye in the Crimea). Did these child burials reflect the love and feelings of their parents? We should then conclude that the links binding fathers and mothers within the Neanderthal families were strong. But this is only speculation, and we are bound to admit our ignorance on this point. This is equally true of the following period, that of *Homo sapiens sapiens*. Summing up, it is clear that in general no special measures were taken to protect the dead, and that the bodies were completely destroyed. It is only in exceptional cases that we find isolated skulls, mandibles or even fragments of long bones.

Despite the small number of Neanderthal burials, we can none the less identify various funeral rites. The dead were placed in natural hollows (La Ferrassie), or in shallow trenches dug to a depth of 40 cm (the Moustier child, La Chapelle-aux-Saints, La Ferrassie, Roc de Marsal, Spy, Es Skhul, Kiik-koba, Border Cave). Over the burial place a mound was raised (La Ferrassie, Combe Grenal) or stones were piled up (Regourdou, La Ferrassie). In some cases the dead simply lay on the floor of the dwelling (El Tabun, Kafzeh, Amud, Staroselye) (Wymer, 1982).

The organization of the 'cemetery' at La Ferrassie is particularly interesting. The man (no. 1) and the woman (no. 2) were lying in trenches in the western part of the main shelter. The man's head was surrounded by three flat stones. To the east of these burial places, in two depressions, were a child of about 10 years (no. 3) and a full-term foetus or a new-born child (no. 4), with a new-born child of 12 or 15 days (no. 4 bis). A little further away were nine mounds, grouped in threes. Under the mound nearest to the rock face, in a depression, was buried a foetus of about 7 months (no. 5). Three splendid tools had been carefully laid on the body. And even nearer to the rock face, in a disturbed zone, the remains of another child of 23 months (no. 8) have been discovered. In the eastern part of the shelter, five depressions were filled exclusively with deposits of the Mousterian epoch; but a sixth trench contained a child of about 3 years (no. 6). Over its body lay three magnificent flint tools: one point and two scrapers. The grave was partially covered by a triangular limestone slab, showing on its lower surface a sort of cup mark surrounded by small cup marks in groups of two or four (Bergounioux, 1958; Heim, 1984). The ensemble seems to indicate the burial of a single family: the parents and their children. However, the true relations between these people will never be known. The 'cemetery' of La Ferrassie belongs to the final phase of the Middle Palaeolithic and is perhaps less than 40,000 years old.

The position of the dead varies, in those cases when it can be determined. Most frequently the bodies are tightly flexed (fourteen examples), the woman of La Ferrassie, for example, having been tied in this position before rigor mortis set in. There are fewer slightly flexed remains (four cases) and only one case of burial in a full-length position. Only in a few cases has it been possible to identify grave goods: in other words stone tools (seven cases), animal bones (seven cases) and other unworked articles deposited as funerary gifts (eight cases) (Harrold, 1980). In the cave at Teshik-Tash in Uzbekistan the body of a boy of 8 or 9 years was found in the centre of a circle made of five pairs of goat horns (Okladnikov, 1949). An unusual funeral rite can be assumed for the burial no. 4 at the Shanidar cave. Pollen has been found there of flowers that do not grow near the cave, so it is thought that the tomb was covered with flowers brought from distant regions. This seems to have been the earliest burial with flower offerings to have been found so far (Solecki, 1971).

In view of the variety of funeral practices and their wide geographical spread, it can be assumed that these rites had first been used in an earlier period: the Middle or even early Middle Palaeolithic.

The quite exceptional discovery of a skull deliberately deposited in the Quattari cave of Monte Circeo in central Italy (Plate 16) should be seen in the context of funeral rites. In this cave, sedimentation does not date back to the early stages of Würm, and the ground was inundated only periodically. On the ground lay a Neanderthal skull, surrounded by a crown of stones. There was a hole in one of the occipital bones and the foramen magnum, artificially enlarged, very probably to extract the brain, which may be an indication of the existence of (ritual?) cannibalism, was facing upwards.[2] Nearby, three groups of ox and deer bones were found (Blanc, 1942, 1958).

The discovery of the front section, probably deliberately cut, of a pre-Neanderthaler in the Caume de l'Arago cave at Tautavel (southern France) (Plate 19), raises the interesting possibility of the manipulation of a human skull. Lumley and Lumley (1979) wonder if a facial mask had not been made from it, which would make the Tautavel skull a unique piece of evidence of ritual practices during the early Middle Palaeolithic. The bodies of the dead were manipulated in different ways, as the notches on the bones of Neanderthalers in the Krapina shelter indicate (Ullrich, 1978).

The frequent discovery of isolated mandibles of Neanderthalers, but also of humans of the Modern type and even of *Homo erectus*, even gave rise to the belief in a 'mandible cult' (Bergounioux, 1958). A comparative survey was made of the proportional representation of the different parts of skeletons (teeth, mandibles, jaw-bones and long bones) of wolves and hyenas which had died a natural death in the caves (Arcy-sur-Cure excavations in France), of Modern foxes that had died in their holes, as well as of some European Neanderthalers. The results are so similar that it must be concluded that the great number of human mandibles that have been preserved is the result of natural processes of decomposition, when the deceased were not deliberately buried (Leroi-Gourhan, 1964a).

The existence of a 'bear cult' among Neanderthalers has also been suggested. In several alpine caves (especially at Drachenloch, in Switzerland) the skulls and long bones of bears have been found at the foot of the walls and between stones, their position giving the impression of an intentional deposit, or of the construction of a sort of 'stone casket' (Bächler, 1940). Though no photographs of these 'caskets' exist, only drawings, the hypothesis of a 'bear cult' was generally accepted; soon, identical discoveries were reported in the caves of Germany, Hungary, France, former Yugoslavia and even, recently, in the Caucasus. One of the most recent discoveries of 'bear burials' was in the Regourdou Cave (south-west France) where the 'casket' was covered by a stone slab weighing about 850 kg! All the caves where these skulls and deposits have been discovered had been inhabited by bears. Dissenting views were therefore expressed, suggesting that what had been seen as evidence of human intervention could be the result of natural processes (Koby, 1953; Leroi-Gourhan, 1964a, 1964b). The concentration of skulls along the walls and between the stones could thus be the result of other bears moving the remains as they continued to shuffle about in their lairs. The piling up of earth and stones above these concentrations is due to the slow but continuous erosion of the ceiling and the walls of the caves. These criticisms have been confirmed by a detailed study of Bächler's drawings, which show them to be lacking in authenticity, and by the fact that everything found in the other caves, even at Regourdou, can be explained by natural phenomena (Jéquier, 1975). None of the discoveries made in the Caucasus caves would contradict this interpretation. The so-called 'bear cult' of the Neanderthalers is therefore probably a myth, born of a romantic interpretation of perfectly natural processes in caves used by bears.

A whole series of other phenomena is linked to religious feelings or at least to aesthetic awareness. Stone tools have been found that clearly demonstrate a feeling for beauty: symmetrical bifaces, scrapers or points, intensively retouched to achieve a regular symmetrical shape which adds little if anything to the functional efficiency of the tool. In the same way, the collection of colorants from the Lower Palaeolithic onwards is an indication of this aesthetic sense. We find traces of it at Bečov I (Bohemia) for the early Middle Palaeolithic and for later periods in many other places. The colorant was probably used to dye the body and perhaps also objects made of wood, bone or skin. In the late Middle Palaeolithic colorants were used in funeral ceremonies (Wreschner, 1976; Marshack, 1981).

In the same way, the use of unusual rocks or stones of attractive colours for making tools has been observed from the Lower Palaeolithic and beyond. Sometimes it has been possible to show that 'useless' objects have been brought into dwellings: for example, two fossils in the Mousterian of Arcy-sur-Cure. All of this bears witness to the natural curiosity of human beings, their desire to experiment and their attentive observation of nature.

Pendants (bones or pierced teeth), necklaces and amulets are worn for the first time during the late Middle Palaeolithic (Quina shelter, France, cave at Pech de l'Azé II, France). The small cup marks engraved on the stone covering grave no. 6 at La Ferrassie probably had a symbolic meaning.

The Middle Palaeolithic, and especially the late Middle Palaeolithic, must have seen the beginnings of art, which in the Upper Palaeolithic is already very elaborate and varied. Bones have been found from the Lower Palaeolithic with symmetric rows of notches (Stránská Skála, Cromerian; Bilsingsleben, Holstein interglacial). In the Middle Palaeolithic, grooves appear on bones which are not due to the dismemberment of the carcass or to the cutting away of meat and tendons (caves at Bacho Kiro and Kůlna, open-air site at Molodova I). On the soft cortex of stone tools, ridging appears for the first time (Tagliente shelter, cave at Isturitz). The Bovidae rib engraved with a curved line from the Acheulean of Pech de l'Azé II (Fig. 10) (beginning of the early Middle Palaeolithic) is considered to be the first example of decorative art (Bordes, 1971; Marshack, 1977).

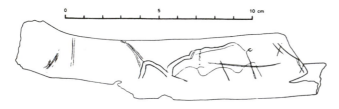

Figure 10 Engraving on an ox rib, Pech de l'Azé (France). (After F. Bordes, in Marshack, 1977.)

At Bečov I (Bohemia) a piece of worked quartzite has been found in a dwelling dating from a temperate phase of the Riss glaciation (about 200,000 years ago), and is considered to be a human-made work (Fridrich, 1982). At Tata (north-west Hungary) a palaeogene fossil (*Nummulitus perforatus*) has been discovered, on the circular surface of which was engraved a neat cross, and a small polished plaque, which came from a mammoth molar and shows traces of red colouring (cf. the Australian thundersticks) (Vértes, 1964; Marshack, 1977).

Among the tangle of engraved lines and cup marks on the mammoth's shoulder-blade found at Molodova I (Fig. 11), A. P. Chernysh distinguished a horned animal and perhaps even a female symbol. The stratum containing the dwelling structure is dated as more than 44,000 years old (Chernysh, 1982).

In conclusion, we can assume that the Palaeoanthropians

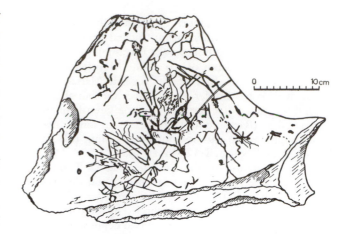

Figure 11 Engraved lines on a mammoth shoulder-blade in Mousterian level 2, Molodova I, Dniester Basin. (After Chernysh, 1982.)

had some sense of symbolism, and that the marks engraved on bones and stones, apart from any aesthetic significance, could have had the aim of communicating or of recording. But they are very far from what could strictly be described as art. The object found at Bečov and the engraving from Molodova are isolated cases for the time being, and their interpretation is not without reservations. So the beginnings of art in the Middle Palaeolithic have not yet been demonstrated beyond doubt, and it must be accepted that art appears for certain only with the Modern humans of the Upper Palaeolithic.[3]

The culture of the European Neanderthalers and pre-Neanderthalers is thus fairly varied and relatively well developed. In the recent phase, Neanderthal burials are accompanied by various ceremonies and cults, whose object is humanity itself. This implies a degree of familiarity with symbols, and probably also the capacity for communicative notation. All this, like the building of dwellings, hunting in groups and the social structure, imply oral communication with a vocabulary well stocked with abstract concepts, the result of an ability to think in symbols.

One of the most interesting problems in the evolution of humans and their culture is the transition from Palaeo-anthropians to humans of the Modern type (*Homo sapiens sapiens*) and from the Middle to the Upper Palaeolithic. It appears that the Palaeoanthropian population was, from the morphological viewpoint, highly differentiated probably much more than can be imagined from the small number of remains discovered up to the present time. We do not yet know the people who were responsible for the majority of the industries of the Middle Palaeolithic. No doubt local groups existed, some of them evolving until the succeeding state was attained, others stagnating and gradually disappearing. There were also some crossings between members of different groups.

It is the same for archaeological cultures. The origin in the Middle Palaeolithic of several cultures of the Upper Palaeolithic is proved (Ksar Akil, Boker Tachtit, Szeletian, Châtelperronian); for others (Bohunice, Aurignacian, Ulluzian), it is only assumed or totally unknown.

In other regions of the Ancient World (sub-Saharan Africa, South-East Asia, China) there are no Upper Palaeo-lithic industries comparable to those of Europe, and the ancient industries survived without any great modification. In north Asia, industries that are close to those of Europe developed, but they include many tools of archaic type. In the Indian subcontinent and in Japan, specific industries appear in which many technical and typological features differ from those of Europe. Environment was undoubtedly a decisive factor in the evolution and the modification of tools, and in the development of all the material culture of these regions. Incontestably, the polymorph Palaeo-anthropian population gave birth to the varied and poly-morph population of *Homo sapiens sapiens*.

NOTES

1 The idea that these Asian pebble-tool industries continued without change in some places from the Lower Palaeolithic until later periods needs revision in the light of extensive research done by the British team in the Soan region, the discovery of Mousterian type tools in the Sanghao Cave by A. H. Dani, and the identification of Upper Palaeolithic industries by B. Allchin – Co-Ed. A. H. Dani.
2 The circumstances of the discovery of the Monte Circeo skull and the advanced hypotheses (intentional enlargement of the foramen magnum; cannibalism) were generally accepted but have however been recently contested – Ed.
3 For a different opinion, see Chapter 13 – Ed.

BIBLIOGRAPHY

Atlas of Primitive Man in China. 1980. Beijing.

BÄCHLER, E. 1940. *Das alpine Paläolithikum der Schweiz im Wildkirchli, Drachenloch und Wildenmannsliloch*. Basle.

BERGOUNIOUX, F. M. 1958. Spiritualité de l'homme de Néanderthal. In: KOENIGSWALD, G. H. R. VON (ed.), *Hundert Jahre Neanderthaler 1856–1956*. Cologne/Graz. pp. 151–66.

BINFORD, L.; BINFORD, S. 1966. A Preliminary Analysis of Functional Variability in the Mousterian of Levallois Fazies. *Am. Anthropol.* (Washington, DC), Vol. 68, No. 2, pp. 238–95.

BLANC, A. C. 1942. I Paleantropi di Saccopastore e del Circeo. *Quartär*, Vol. 4, pp. 1–37.

—— 1958. Torre in Pietra, Saccopastore: On the Position of the Mousterian in the Pleistocene Sequence of the Rome Area. In: KOENIGSWALD, G. H. R. VON (ed.), *Hundert Jahre Neanderthaler 1856–1956*. Cologne/Graz. pp. 167–74.

BORDES, F. 1950a. Principes d'une méthode d'étude des techniques de débitage et de la typologie du Paléolithique ancien et moyen. *Anthropologie* (Paris), Vol. 54, pp. 19–34.

—— 1950b. L'Évolution buissonnante des industries en Europa occidentale: considération théorique sur le Paléo-lithique ancien et moyen. *Anthropologie* (Paris), Vol. 54, pp. 393–420.

—— 1953a. Levalloisien et Moustérien. *Bull. Soc. Préhist. Fr.*, Vol. 50, pp. 226–34.

—— 1953b. Essai de classification des industries moustériennes. *Bull. Soc. Préhist. Fr.*, Vol. 50, pp. 457–66.

—— 1954. *Les Limons quaternaires du bassin de la Seine*. Paris. (Inst. Paléontol. Hum. Mém. 26.)

—— 1958. Le Passage du Paléolithique moyen au Paléo-lithique supérieur. In: KOENIGSWALD, G. H. R. VON (ed.), *Hundert Jahre Neanderthaler 1856–1956*. Cologne/Graz. pp. 175–81.

—— 1961. *Typologie du Paléolithique ancien et moyen I/II*. 1st edn. Bordeaux, Université de Bordeaux. (Mem., 1.) 3rd edn 1979. Paris, CNRS.

—— 1971. Informations archéologiques: circonscription d'Aqui-taine. *Gallia, Préhist.* (Paris), Vol. 13, pp. 458–511.

BORDES, F.; SONNEVILLE-BORDES, D. DE. 1970. The Significance of Variability in Paleolithic Assemblages. *World Archaeol.*, Vol. 2, No. 1, pp. 61–73.

BOSINSKI, G. 1985. *Der Neanderthaler und seine Zeit*. Cologne.

CHERNYSH, A. P. 1982. *Molodova I: Unique Mousterian Settlement on the Middle Dniester Region*. Moscow.

CLARK, J. D. 1970. *The Prehistory of Africa*. London.

—— 1972. *The Prehistoric Cultures of the Horn of Africa*. 2nd edn. New York.

—— 1982. The Transition from Lower to Middle Paleo-lithic in the African Continent. In: RONEN, A. (ed.), *The Transition from Lower to Middle Paleolithic and the Origin of Modern Man*. Oxford. pp. 235–55. (BAR. Int. Ser., 151.)

COPELAND, L. 1975. The Middle and Upper Paleolithic of Lebanon and Syria. In: WENDORF, F.; MARKS, A. E. (eds), *Problems in Prehistory: North Africa and the Levant*. Dallas. pp. 317–50.

FEUSTEL, R. 1969. Zur Problematik der 'Protolithischen Knochenkultur' und der 'Osteodontokeratic Culture'. *Alt-Thüring*. (Weimar), Vol. 10, pp. 7–67.

FRIDRICH, J. 1982. *Middle Palaeolithic Settlement of Bohemia*. Prague.

GABORI-CSANK, V. 1970. Dates of the Hungarian Palaeolithikum. *Acta Archaeol. Acad. Sci. Hung.* (Budapest), Vol. 22, pp. 3–11.

HARROLD, F. B. 1980. A Comparative Analysis of Eurasian Palaeo-lithic Burials. *World Archaeol.*, Vol. 2, No. 2, pp. 195–211.

HEIM, J.-L. 1984. Les Squelettes moustériens de la Ferrassie. In: DELPORTE, H. (ed.), *Le Grand Abri de la Ferrassie*. Paris, Institut de Paléontologie Humaine. pp. 249–71. (Étud. Quat., 7.)

IKAWA-SMITH, F. 1978. The History of Early Palaeolithic Research in Japan. In: IKAWA-SMITH, F. (ed.), *Early Palaeolithic in South-East Asia*. The Hague. pp. 247–56.

JEQUIER, J.-P. 1975. *Le Moustérien alpin*. Yverdon. (Eburo-dunum, 2.)

KOBY, F. E. 1953. Modifications que les ours des cavernes ont fait subir à leur habitat. In: CONGRÈS INTERNATIONAL DE SPÉLÉOLOGIE, 1. *Actes*, Vol. 4, Sect. 4, pp. 15–26.

KOZLOWSKI, J. K. et al. 1982. Upper Palaeolithic Assemblages. In: KOZLOWSKI, J. K. (ed.), *Excavation in the Bacho-Kiro Cave (Bulgaria), Final Report*. Warsaw. pp. 119–67.

LEROI-GOURHAN, A. 1964a. *Le Geste et la parole*. Paris.

—— 1964b. *Les Religions de la préhistoire*. Paris.

LÉVÊQUE, F.; VANDERMEERSCH, B. 1981. Le Néanderthalien de Saint-Césaire. *Recherche* (Paris), Vol. 12, No. 119, pp. 242–4.

LJUBIN, V. P. 1984. Rannij paleolit Kavkaza [Early Palaéolithic of the Caucasus]. In: BORISKOVSKI, P. I. (ed.), *Paleolit SSSR*. Moscow. pp. 35–93.

LUMLEY, H. DE. 1969. *Une cabane acheuléenne dans la grotte du Lazaret/Nice*. Paris. (Mém. Soc. Préhist. Fr., 7.)

LUMLEY, H. DE; LUMLEY, M. A. DE. 1979. L'Homme de Tautavel. *Doss. Archéol.* (Dijon), Vol. 36.

MCBURNEY, C. B. M. 1967. *The Haua Fteah (Cyrenaica) and the Stone Age of the Southeast Mediterranean*. Cambridge.

MARKS, A. E.; KAUFMAN, D. 1983. Boker Tachtit: The Artifacts. In: MARKS, A. E. (ed.), *Prehistory and Palaeoenvironments in the Central Negev, Israel*. Dallas. Vol. 3, Part 3, pp. 69–125.

MARSHACK, A. 1977. The Meander as a System: The Analysis and Recognition of Iconographic Units in Upper Palaeolithic Compositions. In: UCKO, P. J. (ed.), *Form in Indigenous Art*. Canberra, Australian Institute of Aboriginal Studies. pp. 268–317.

—— 1981. Palaeolithic Ochre and the Early Uses of Color and Symbols. *Curr. Anthropol.*, Vol. 22, pp. 188–91.

MELLARS, P. 1970. Some Comments on the Notion of Functional Variability in Stone-tool Assemblages. *World Archaeol.*, Vol. 2, No. 1, pp. 74–89.

OKLADNIKOV, A. P. 1949. Issledovania must'erskoi stoianki i pog-rebenijaa neandertalca v grote Tesik-Tas, Juznyi Uzbekistan [The Investigation of the Mousterian Site and Neanderthal Burial in the Teshik-Tash Cave, South Uzbekistan]. In: NESTOURKH, M. F. (ed.), *Tesik-Tas, Paleoliticeskij celovek*. Moscow. pp. 7–85.

OLIVA, M. 1983. Kulturtraditionen, Besiedlung, Stabilität und Umwelteinfluss im älteren und mittleren Paläolithikum. *Ethnogr.-Archäol. Z.* (Berlin), Vol. 24, pp. 551–7.

PERLES, C. 1977. *Préhistoire du feu*. Paris.

RANOV, V. A.; NESMEYANOV, S. A. 1973. *Paleolit i stratigrafija antro-pogena Srednei Azii* [Palaeolithic and Stratigraphy of the Anthro-pogene Period in central Asia]. Dushanbe.

RUST, A. 1950. *Die Höhlenfunde von Jabrud (Syrien)*. Neumünster.

SANKALIA, H. D. 1974. *The Prehistory and Protohistory of India and Pakistan.* Poona.

SARTONO, S. 1980. *Homo erectus ngandongensis:* The Possible Maker of the 'Sangiran flakes'. *Anthropologie* (Brno), Vol. 18, Nos. 2–3, pp. 121–31.

SOLECKI, R. S. 1971. *Shanidar: The First Flower People.* New York.

TRINKAUS, E. 1983. *The Shanidar Neanderthals.* New York/London.

ULLRICH, H. 1978. Kannibalismus und Leichenzertückelung beim Neanderthaler. In: MALEZ, M. (ed.), *Krapinski pracovjek i evolucija hominida.* Zagreb. pp. 293–318.

VALOCH, K. 1976. *Die altsteinzeitliche Fundstelle in Brno-Bohunice.* Prague. (Stud. Archeol. úst. CSAV Brne, 4.)

VALOCH, K. et al. 1985. Das Frühaurignacien von Vedrovice II und Kuparovice I in Südmähren. *Anthropozoikum* (Prague), Vol. 16, pp. 107–203.

VERTES, L. (ed.) 1964. *Tata: eine mittelpaläolithische Travertin-Siedlung in Ungarn.* Budapest. (Archaeol. Hung., NS, Vol. 43.)

WENDORF, F. (ed.) 1968. *The Prehistory of Nubia I/II.* Dallas.

WENDORF, F.; SCHILD, R. 1974. *A Middle Stone Age Sequence from the Central Rift Valley, Ethiopia.* Warsaw.

WRESCHNER, E. E. 1976. The Red Hunters: Further Thoughts on the Evolution of Speech. *Curr. Anthropol.*, Vol. 17, pp. 717–19.

WYMER, J. 1982. *The Palaeolithic Age.* London.

11

AFRICA

in the period of *Homo sapiens neanderthalensis* and contemporaries

Fred Wendorf, Angela E. Close and Romuald Schild

Although we have considerable knowledge of the later periods of prehistory throughout the continent of Africa, information concerning the earlier periods is much rarer and tends to be concentrated in certain favoured regions. This is a reflection more of historical accident than of prehistoric fact, but has, nevertheless, a profound effect upon our approach to the subject. For the period during which the Neanderthalers flourished in Europe and western Asia, our knowledge of African prehistory comes almost entirely from three main areas: northern Africa (including the Sahara), Africa south of about latitude 10° S, and eastern Africa. This chapter is therefore organized into three main sections, corresponding to these regions. Even between these favoured areas, there are marked differences in the quality and quantity of information available, largely reflecting the interests of modern archaeologists. While there would have been a certain geographical logic to proceeding from northern through eastern to southern Africa, we have chosen to deal with both northern and southern Africa before the east. This allows us to present the two better-known regions first, and to work from them to the less well known. The least-known areas, central Africa and western Africa south of the Sahara, are briefly considered in the section dealing with southern Africa.

NORTHERN AFRICA

In northern Africa, the period of the Neanderthalers corresponds quite closely to the archaeological period called the Middle Palaeolithic. Sites assigned to the Middle Palaeolithic have been reported from throughout the region. They occur in the northern Sahel, throughout the Sahara and along the Nile valley and the Mediterranean and Atlantic coasts (Map 11). Middle Palaeolithic artefacts have been observed on the Red Sea coast but have not been systematically studied or described.

Inevitably, the history of research into the Middle Palaeolithic of this vast region is somewhat uneven, partly because of the distribution of modern archaeologists and partly because of the nature of the prehistoric record itself. Thus, earlier researches into the Middle Palaeolithic tended to be concentrated on the cave sequences of French-speaking north-western Africa, while the most recent work has been devoted to open-air sites in the desert. There are, of course, exceptions to this, but it has meant that there is, in general, considerable variability in the types and quality of information available to us from different areas.

Hominid types

Several fossil hominids are relevant to the Lower and Middle Palaeolithic of northern Africa. They seem to fall into two groups. The earlier and more primitive group includes the finds at Rabat, Sidi Abderrahman, Salé and Témara in Morocco (Saban, 1975; Arambourg and Biberson, 1956; Jaeger, 1975; Vallois and Roche, 1958) and Ternifine in Algeria (Arambourg, 1955). Many of these were initially classified as *Homo erectus*, but more recently taxonomists have tended to place them in the earliest grades of archaic *Homo sapiens* (Stringer et al., 1979; Trinkaus, 1982). Where they are associated with cultural material (Sidi Adberrahman, Témara and Ternifine) it is always Acheulean.

The second group, somewhat later in age and apparently anatomically more evolved, includes the human skeletal material from the Haua Fteah in Cyrenaican Libya (Tobias, in McBurney, 1967) and from the Mugharet el 'Aliya and Jebel Irhoud in Morocco (Ennouchi, 1962). All of the hominids in this second group were associated with Middle Palaeolithic industries and the hominids themselves have usually been identified as Neanderthalers. This assignment is no longer accepted (Trinkaus, 1982); it is now evident that they were morphologically distinct from the European and western Asian Neanderthals, although they were contemporaneous with them and equivalent to them in evolutionary grade.

The skeletal material in both groups is exceedingly fragmentary and no specimen appears to have been an intentional burial. Only the Salé and Jebel Irhoud specimens are reasonably complete crania, but they are widely separated in time so that it is not possible to determine if they represent stages in the evolution of a single population. However, as we shall see below, there is good evidence to suggest cultural continuity in northern Africa from the Lower to the Middle

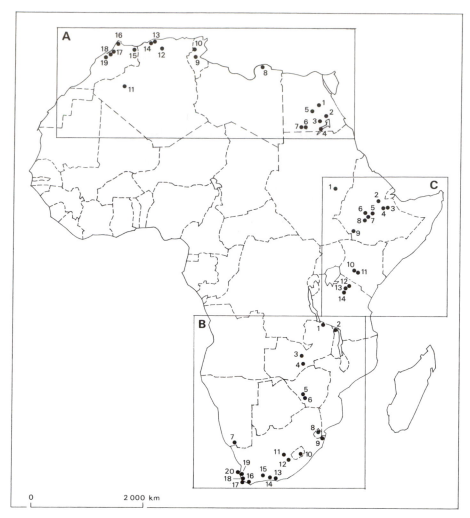

Map 11 Africa during the Middle Stone Age: principal sites mentioned in the text – A, northern Africa: 1, Nazlet Khater; 2, Wadi Kubbaniya; 3, Dungul oasis; 4, site 440; site 1017; 5, Kharga oasis; 6, Bir Tarfawi; 7, Bir Sahara basin; 8, Haua Fteah; 9, El Guettar; 10, Ain Metherchem; 11, Wadi Saoura; 12, Retaimia; 13, Karouba; 14, Ternifine; 15, Taforalt; 16, Mugharet el 'Aliya; 17, Dar es Soltan, Rabat, Grotte des Contrebandiers; 18, Sidi Abderrahman, Témara, Salé; 19, Jebel Irhoud. B, southern Africa: 1, Kalambo Falls; 2, Mwanganda; 3, Broken Hill (Kabwe); 4, Leopard's Hill; 5, Banbata, Pomongwe; 6, Tshangula; 7, Apollo 11; 8, Lion Cavern; 9, Border Cave; 10, Sehonghong; 11, Orangia; 12, Zeekoegat 27; 13, Klasies River Mouth; 14, Nelson Bay Cave; 15, Boomplaas; 16, Die Kelders; 17, Skildergat; 18, Duinefontein 2; 19, Elandsfontein; 20, Hoedjies Punt, Sea Harvest. C, eastern Africa: 1, Singa; 2, Bodo; 3, Porc Epic; 4, Afdem; 5, Koné; 6, Melka Kunturé; 7, Kulkuletti; 8, Gademotta; 9, Lower Omo valley; 10, Gamble's Caves; 11, Malawa Gorge; 12, Apis Rock; 13, Olduvai Gorge; 14, Laetoli.

Palaeolithic and corresponding continuity in population seems most likely.

Problems of classification

The Middle Palaeolithic of northern Africa is traditionally divided into two major entities, the Mousterian and the Aterian. A third variant, the Khormusan, is known only from the Nile valley between the First and Second Cataracts.

The Aterian is peculiar to northern Africa and differs from the Mousterian of south-western Asia and Europe (and, indeed, also from the Mousterian of northern Africa) principally in the presence of bifacial foliates and pedunculates (or tanged pieces). These may be extremely rare in some Aterian assemblages (for example, Site BT-14 at Bir Tarfawi in western Egypt (Wendorf and Schild, 1980, pp. 49–80). The Aterian is sometimes thought to rely more heavily on the Levallois technique than does the Mousterian, and to have generally more elongated debitage (Tixier, 1967, p. 795). However, at least some of the 'Levalloiso-Mousterian' industries from Kharga oasis and the Nile valley

(Caton-Thompson, 1946*b*, 1952) are very rich in Levallois, and there is not enough detailed information from the Middle Palaeolithic of northern Africa as a whole to determine the validity of the hypothesized difference in debitage shape. The Aterian, like other variants of the Middle Palaeolithic, is essentially a flake industry, characterized by varying frequencies of Levallois technology, and a tool kit consisting primarily of various kinds of side-scrapers and denticulates, and occasional Upper Palaeolithic-type tools, such as burins and end-scrapers.

The traditional classification of the Middle Palaeolithic of northern Africa will be significantly modified here. We regard all of the Middle Palaeolithic from west of the Egyptian oases as one entity, the Aterian; the distribution of the true Mousterian in northern Africa was limited to the Nile valley and the Egyptian oases. This change is proposed because the so-called Mousterian sites in the Maghreb are very rare, and because their distribution is not continuous with that of the Mousterian in the Nile valley to the east. Tixier (1967) noted only eight sites in the Maghreb that he would classify as Mousterian, located in Tunisia, northern

Algeria and northern Morocco, and several of these (such as El Guettar (Gruet, 1954) and Aïn Metherchem in Tunisia (Dalloni, 1955, p. 427)) also contained a few typical Aterian artefacts, even in their lowest levels. The Middle Palaeolithic in the Haua Fteah, which McBurney called Levalloiso-Mousterian, also contained pedunculates and foliates. We prefer to regard the western occurrences that have been called Mousterian as representing the lower extreme in the frequency curve of pedunculates and foliates, and believe that a coherent Mousterian can be seen only in the eastern part of northern Africa, where there are numerous sites lacking these characteristic types.

By regarding all of the Middle Palaeolithic of north-western Africa as Aterian, we avoid the temptation to view the Mousterian and Aterian as representing two very large, self-conscious, social groups, as they almost certainly do not. Instead, it seems more likely that the variations in the frequencies of pedunculates and foliates reflect functions or activities which are not yet well understood.

Chronology

The details of the transition from the Lower Palaeolithic to the Middle Palaeolithic are not well known in northern Africa. As elsewhere in Africa, the Late and Final Acheulean are characterized by relatively small and finely made bifaces, and by increasing frequencies of Levallois technology and flake-tools, often indistinguishable from those of the Middle Palaeolithic. The similarities in the flake-tools of these later Acheulean complexes, which may even include some of the tanged pieces characteristic of the Middle Palaeolithic (as at Cap Chatelier, Morocco; see Biberson, 1961, p. 367), strongly support a continuity in northern Africa from the Acheulean into the Middle Palaeolithic. In terms of typology, the difference between the two is really only the absence of handaxes in the Middle Palaeolithic.

There is, however, remarkably little evidence for a transition from the Lower to the Middle Palaeolithic. Instead, over much of northern Africa a major period of aridity, which is indicated by lower water-tables, deflation and dune migration, separates the latest Final Acheulean from the earliest Middle Palaeolithic. The topographic changes during this arid interval were of such magnitude that direct superposition of Middle and late Lower Palaeolithic occupations is extremely rare.

One site with such direct superposition is the Haua Fteah (McBurney, 1967), where the pre-Aurignacian in the lowest excavated levels is directly followed by several metres of Middle Palaeolithic occupations. The pre-Aurignacian has a high frequency of blades in the debitage, together with numerous burins and occasional end-scrapers in the retouched tools, and is similar to the pre-Aurignacian complexes in western Asia. The latter are now called Amudian and are regarded as a facies of the Late Acheulean (Jelinek, 1982). The Haua Fteah pre-Aurignacian is based on a relatively small sample from limited excavations; however, the collection does include several bifaces and biface-trimming flakes (McBurney, 1967, pp. 76–90), which would suggest that it too might be regarded as a facies or a special functional variant of the Acheulean. The pre-Aurignacian at the Haua Fteah was dated to between 70,000 and 80,000 years ago, by oxygen isotope and sedimentary evidence and by extrapolation from the long series of carbon-14 dates available for the younger levels of the site. While this age estimate seemed reasonable at the time of publication (the end of the Acheulean at Kalambo Falls was then believed to date to about

60,000 years ago (Clark, 1969)), recent evidence from elsewhere in Africa suggests that this is much too young, if the pre-Aurignacian is indeed a facies of a Lower Palaeolithic industry (see p. 131).

The stratigraphic position of the earliest Middle Palaeolithic in northern Africa is not firmly established or dated. A complex sequence has been proposed by Biberson (1961) for the Atlantic coast of Morocco, where the earliest Middle Palaeolithic has been placed in deposits of the Ouljian transgression of the last interglacial. This has been dated by U–Th to from 75,000 to 95,000 years ago, while the preceding Harounian transgression, associated with Late Acheulean, is dated to between 125,000 and 145,000 years ago (Biberson, 1970). As will be seen below, there is, again, a serious conflict between these age estimates from northern Africa and other age determinations for the onset of the Middle Stone Age in eastern and southern Africa.

The Aterian, which comprises most of the material known from this period in northern Africa, has been viewed as a very late Middle Palaeolithic for three reasons. First, it was believed that there was a direct relationship between the bifacial foliates of the Aterian and those of the Upper Palaeolithic Solutrean in Spain, so that the two must have been chronologically quite close (Caton-Thompson, 1964a; Howe, 1967, pp. 170–8). Second, some of the tanged pieces seemed to resemble the stemmed projectile points that occur in Neolithic sites in the Sahara, and therefore might reasonably be ancestral prototypes (Antoine, 1950; Balout, 1955). Third, several of the cave sequences in the Maghreb showed the Aterian directly overlain by Late Pleistocene backed bladelet assemblages (the Iberomaurusian), and the latter, until recently, were not known to be older than 14,000 years.

This view of a relatively late age has been perpetuated by finite carbon-14 dates for the Aterian ranging from about 47,000 years ago at the Haua Fteah (McBurney, 1967) to almost 12,000 years ago at Grotte des Contrebandiers (Délibrias et al., 1982), and by a tendency to treat the lower limits of infinite dates as if they were finite (Camps, 1974, p. 35). However, many of the finite dates have been run on materials of dubious reliability, such as carbonates or shells, as for example at Taforalt in Morocco where the finite Aterian dates of about 20,000 years ago are attributed to the difficulty of cleaning the snail shells on which they were run (Délibrias et al., 1982). The same problem was experienced at Bir Sahara Basin and Bir Tarfawi in western Egypt (Wendorf and Schild, 1980, pp. 29, 35). In addition, several of the finite dates are from uncertain archaeological contexts, such as those from Grotte des Contrebandiers, where it is known that pits had been dug in the Aterian layers by the Iberomaurusian occupants of the cave (Roche, 1976).

The least questionable carbon-14 dates for the Aterian are infinite, such as those from Dar es Soltan, Morocco (Ruhlmann, 1951) and Wadi Saoura, Algeria (Chavaillon, 1964), or very old, such as those from the Haua Fteah. This suggests that the Aterian lies essentially beyond the range of carbon-14 dating. The high antiquity of the Aterian is further supported by its association with beaches of the last interglacial at several localities in Algeria (Alimen, 1957, pp. 42–4; Roubet, 1969). The Middle Palaeolithic Aterian had therefore begun before the end of the last interglacial in northern Africa; and this is the oldest dated Middle Palaeolithic in this part of the continent. The discovery of a tanged Aterian point in a Late Acheulean context indicates that its origins are local and probably earlier than the last interglacial. There is, as yet, no direct evidence for such an age, but it would be consistent with the evidence that the Middle

Stone Age of eastern and southern Africa became established before the end of the Middle Pleistocene (see pp. 124–5, 131).

The dating of the end of the Aterian is equally unclear. It was replaced by an Upper Palaeolithic-type industry at the Haua Fteah by about 40,000 years ago (McBurney, 1967), and there are at least five absolute radiocarbon dates for the Aterian, in addition to the one of about 47,000 years ago from Haua Fteah, layer XXXIII, noted on p. 119. These include a second date from Haua Fteah (layer XXVIII) of about 43,000 years ago, two dates from the upper Aterian layer at Taforalt of 32,000 to 34,000 years ago (Roche, 1970–1), and two dates of about 32,000 years ago from Aïn Maarouf (Morocco) (Choubert et al., 1967, p. 435; Hébrard, 1970). It is possible that the Aterian may, in places, have survived down to almost 30,000 years ago. There is no evidence for its continued existence after that date. This leaves a disconcerting hiatus in the prehistoric record of north-western Africa in particular, where the late Pleistocene backed bladelet industry (Iberomaurusian) that followed the Aterian seems to have appeared not much before about 20,000 years ago (Close, 1980, 1984).

The chronological relationship of the Aterian and the Mousterian has not been established, although the distributions of the two entities overlap in the Nile valley between the first and second cataracts and in the Egyptian oases. In the eastern Sahara, however, there is some evidence that, locally, the Mousterian might have preceded the Aterian (Wendorf and Schild, 1980). In the Bir Sahara Basin, several levels of Mousterian occupation occur in the lower of two fossil lakes, while the Aterian in the neighbouring depression of Bir Tarfawi is associated with a single lake, which is believed to correspond to the upper lake at the Bir Sahara Basin. In addition, the most recent site at Bir Sahara (BS-1) yielded a single, poorly defined pedunculate on a Levallois point, so that, in accordance with the scheme proposed here, this assemblage should be classified as Aterian. That the Mousterian should precede the Aterian in the eastern Sahara does not necessarily mean that it was also earlier than the last interglacial Aterian of the Maghreb; the ages of these industries at Bir Sahara Basin and Bir Tarfawi lie beyond the range of carbon-14 dating, but are otherwise unknown.

After the disappearance of the Aterian-associated lake at Bir Tarfawi there followed a long period of extreme aridity, when the water-table fell to a level at least as low as that of today and spring activity ceased. The first evidence we have for any human or other animal presence in the area after the Aterian dates from the beginning of the Holocene, around 10,000 years ago.

Along the Nile, there is no direct stratigraphic evidence pertaining to the relationship between the Mousterian and the Aterian-related sites. A Mousterian site in situ is known from the mouth of Wadi Kubbaniya near Aswan, embedded in Nile silts of a small embayment (Wendorf et al., 1986). This episode of Nile valley filling has been dated by thermoluminescence to 89,000 ± 18,000 years ago (Gd-TL33), on a sample from a horizon slightly above the Mousterian site. It is regarded as a late Mousterian occurrence because there is earlier Mousterian rolled in wadi gravels stratigraphically well below these early Nile silts. The relationship between the Middle Palaeolithic silts at Wadi Kubbaniya near Aswan, Egypt, and the Debeira-Jer silts at Wadi Halfa, Sudan, discussed below, is not clear. The most economical explanation is that they represent the same episode of aggradation. In this case, the Khormusan would probably postdate

the Mousterian, but the age of the latter relative to the Aterian in the Nile valley remains obscure.

The Khormusan industry of the Nile valley (Marks, 1968b) was regarded originally as Late Palaeolithic, because of its burins and because of two erroneous radiocarbon dates. However, additional carbon-14 dates have since been obtained and some of the earlier samples have been recounted. The new dates for the Khormusan are all infinite (Wendorf et al., 1979).

The stratigraphic relationship between the Khormusan and the Aterian sites in the valley has not been firmly established, although it seems likely that the Aterian-related Site 440, in Nubia, precedes the Khormusan occupation of the same area. Two stratified assemblages of Middle Palaeolithic aspect occur at Site 440 in a lens of aeolian sand between two layers of Nile silt. It is most likely that this represents the basal portion of the so-called Debeira-Jer Formation, higher levels of which contain sites of the Khormusan industry, both here (Site 1017) and at several other localities near Wadi Halfa. The two assemblages at Site 440 include one bifacial foliate and are similar in general typological structure to the Aterian of Bir Tarfawi (see p. 121).

Because of this stratigraphic relationship and because the Khormusan occurs only in the Nile valley, it might represent an occupation that occurred during the period of extreme aridity that followed the Aterian in the eastern Sahara (Wendorf and Schild, 1980).

There are no finite radiocarbon dates for any Middle Palaeolithic sites in the Nile valley. However, a terminus ante quem for the Middle Palaeolithic may be provided by the series of dates of about 35,000 to 30,000 years ago for an Upper Palaeolithic blade industry from Nazlet Khater in Egypt (Vermeersch et al., 1982, 1984).

The Aterian

Aterian sites are numerous in northern Africa. They occur from northern Niger, Mali and Mauritania, throughout the Sahara to the Atlantic and Mediterranean coasts of Morocco, Algeria and Tunisia, and from there eastward to the Bir Tarfawi, Kharga and Dungul Oases (Caton-Thompson, 1946a; Tixier, 1967; Tillet, 1983). Aterian or Aterian-related sites also occur in the Nile valley from just north of Aswan (Singleton and Close, 1978) to the Third Cataract (see references in Wendorf and Schild, 1976), and possibly as far south as Khartoum (Arkell, 1949; Carlson, 1967).

There is considerable variation in the Aterian assemblages across northern Africa, and some have suggested that this variation has chronological or regional significance (Antoine, 1950; Ruhlmann, 1952; Balout, 1955; Dalloni, 1955; Tixier, 1967). There are localities, such as Dar es-Soltan (Ruhlmann, 1951), Mugharet el 'Aliya (Howe, 1967) and Taforalt (Roche, 1969) in Morocco, Karouba (Roubet, 1969) in Algeria and Sidi Mansour in Tunisia (Alimen, 1957, p. 41), where different Aterian assemblages occur stratified one above the other. Unfortunately, there are no consistent typological or technological trends within these occurrences. For example, at Taforalt, pedunculates, bifacial foliates and end-scrapers increase and then decline in frequency from the lower to the upper Aterian; at Dar es-Soltan, end-scrapers increase in frequency from the lower to the upper Aterian and there is also a minor increase in pedunculates; at Mugharet el 'Aliya, the value of end-scrapers does not change, but there is a dramatic increase in the percentage of bifacial foliates in the upper Aterian (data summarized in

Ferring, 1975, p. 116). It may also be observed that part of the basis for the recognition of a 'Mousterian' in north-western Africa is that the lowest Middle Palaeolithic in several sites, such as Sidi Mansour and Taforalt, lacked pedunculates and bifacial foliates and was overlain by assemblages including these types. However, none of the assemblages lacking them can be shown to be earlier than the pedunculates and foliates associated with the raised beaches of the last interglacial. According to Balout (1955, p. 311), the latter assemblages are mostly made on quartzite and are heavier and not as well made as the later Aterian, which is made on flint. Therefore the increasing refinement of the tool through time may confidently be ascribed to differences in the quality of the raw material. It seems highly likely that some changes did occur during the Aterian in north-western Africa, particularly if it survived until 30,000 years ago. However, until more absolute dates or other means of correlation and more precise environmental data are available, it will be difficult to separate the chronological trends from those that relate to activity or raw materials.

The Aterian in the Egyptian Sahara also displays considerable variability. In a modification of the Bordes system (1961) (Chapter 10), two taxonomic units have been defined at Bir Tarfawi (Wendorf and Schild, 1980). Most of the Aterian sites here have high frequencies of denticulates and have been classified as Denticulate Aterian. One assemblage, however, consists primarily of side-scrapers and Mousterian points and is called Typical Aterian. Both bifacial foliates and pedunculates are rare in all of these Tarfawi sites. At only one site has a specific toolkit been identified for the Aterian, where butchered rhinoceros, buffalo and Pleistocene camels were associated with a lithic tool assemblage composed mostly of various kinds of denticulates.

The Aterian from the spring-vents at Kharga is very different from that at Bir Tarfawi. The Kharga assemblages have a high frequency of Levallois technology, contain numerous retouched Levallois points, including distinctive specimens with thinned butts, and are dominated by tanged pieces or bifacial foliates.

Several Middle Palaeolithic assemblages have been described from along the Nile in northern Sudan, in the vicinity of the Second Cataract and southward from there to the Third Cataract, which have strong Levallois components, bifacial foliates and occasional pedunculates (Guichard and Guichard, 1965; Chmielewski, 1968). These have been compared with both the Middle Stone Age of eastern Africa and the Aterian. The sites appear to be workshops, exploiting outcrops of quartzitic sandstone, and they include foliates that are obviously unfinished or were broken during manufacture. The finished specimens are elegant, elongated and very finely made, and cannot be distinguished from typical Aterian bifacial foliates. None of the sites has yielded fauna and none of them can be related to the Nilotic sedimentary sequence.

The two stratified Aterian-related assemblages from Site 440 in the Second Cataract, near Wadi Halfa, are possibly related to these workshop localities. They are made on quartzitic sandstone and Precambrian rock, and are characterized by a low Levallois index and a heavy emphasis on denticulates. They are similar in this respect to the Aterian at Bir Tarfawi.

Since Aterian occurrences date from at least the last interglacial down perhaps to as late as 30,000 years ago, some chronological variation within the complex would be expected. Thus far, however, it has remained undetectable. We might also expect regional variation within the Aterian.

As a possible example, barbed or shouldered, tanged points (Moroccan points) seem to be more frequent in north-western Africa, and Aterian assemblages rich in denticulates seem to be characteristic of parts of north-eastern Africa. In general, however, the Aterian from the eastern edge of the continent is remarkably similar to that from the western edge.

The Mousterian

The Mousterian, as the term is used here, occurs in northern Africa only as far south as the Second Cataract and as far west as the Bir Sahara Basin. Numerous Middle Palaeolithic localities, often rich in Levallois components but lacking pedunculates and bifacial foliates, have been observed in the Nile valley or northern Sudan and Egypt (Sandford and Arkell, 1939; Caton-Thompson, 1946b; Marks, 1968a; Hester and Hoebler, 1969; Vermeersch et al., 1982), and westward into the Sahara at Kharga oasis and Bir Sahara Basin (Caton-Thompson, 1952; Wendorf and Schild, 1980; Schild and Wendorf, 1981). These occurrences have been variously referred to as Levalloisian and Mousterian.

Most of the Mousterian sites in the Nile valley consist of isolated artefacts found in Nile silts or assemblages of derived material from stream gravels. The only intact living-surface known is at the mouth of Wadi Kubbaniya near Aswan, where a cluster of lithic artefacts, mostly of quartz and consisting of a few Levallois cores and flakes, side-scrapers and denticulates, occurred embedded in Nile silts of a small embayment (Wendorf et al., 1986).

The Mousterian sites near Wadi Halfa, Sudan, are located on the tops of inselbergs or on pediment slopes, where they are sometimes buried in a red soil of unknown age. Two groups have been defined, a Denticulate Mousterian and a Nubian Mousterian, of which the latter includes a type A without bifaces and type B with bifaces (Marks, 1968a). This subdivision has been questioned (Wendorf and Schild, 1980, p. 251), because the only two known sites of type B were on the surface and the bifaces, indistinguishable from Late Acheulean types, may be admixtures. Nubian Mousterian sites have variable Levallois indices, numerous side-scrapers, occasional Upper Palaeolithic-type tools and low frequencies of denticulates.

Some of the best data on the Mousterian in northern Africa are from a series of sites in the Bir Sahara basin, a small, irregular, deflational concavity excavated into an enormous plain of consolidated aeolian sand, predating the Late Acheulean which occurs on its surface (Schild and Wendorf, 1981). Several other deflational basins occur in the area, the most prominent of which is Bir Tarfawi, located 11 km to the east. The Middle Palaeolithic sequence begins at Bir Sahara Basin with a dune containing very wind-eroded artefacts of Middle Palaeolithic aspect, deposited before the end of dune migration. This is followed by a series of lacustrine and near-shore sediments in which four sequential Mousterian levels of occurrences were recorded. Numerous fossil spring-vents exposed by modern deflation on the floor of the depression, as well as the absence of a peripheral drainage net, strongly suggest that the lakes were fed by springs rather than local rainfall.

The four Mousterian horizons at the Bir Sahara Basin display no indications of unidirectional change through time. With one exception (see p. 122), all of the Bir Sahara assemblages may be classified as Denticulate Mousterian. They are characterized by extremely heavy emphasis on denticulates, low to medium frequencies of side-scrapers, very few Upper

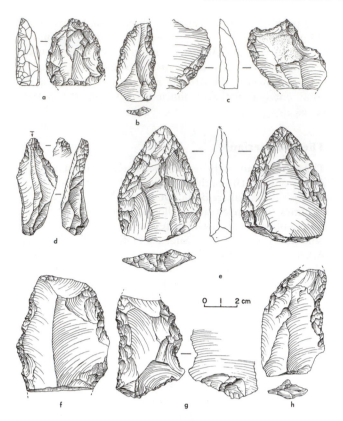

Figure 12 Mousterian artefacts, Bir Sahara site 13 (Egypt): a and h, side scrapers; b, f and g, denticulates; c, bec; d, borer; e, Mousterian point. (After Wendorf and Schild, 1980.)

Palaeolithic-type tools and few blades (Fig. 12). There are no handaxes or bifacial foliates. The importance of the Levallois technique is variable: the oldest site in the group (BS-11) has few Levallois pieces, while the slightly later site BS-13 is strongly Levallois. This variation in importance of Levallois is related more to the position of each assemblage within the sequence of stages in the working of the raw material than to any cultural factors (see p. 123). The most recent site in the basin, BS-1, is viewed as Aterian because of the presence of one atypical pedunculate; it is, however, discussed here with the Mousterian proper. The debitage and tools from BS-1 are very small in size, even though the artefacts in the succeeding Aterian at Bir Tarfawi are comparable to those of the earlier Mousterian. BS-1 also has a much higher Levallois typological index than the older Mousterian assemblages.

The several Middle Palaeolithic settlements at Bir Sahara Basin clearly reflect a complex exploitation of the lithic raw material. Site BS-11, a low-density scatter adjacent to the shore, contained high frequencies of initial core-preparation debris and of flakes for the preparation of Levallois cores, but few Levallois pieces (flakes, blades, points or cores). This is seen as a temporary stop where a number of Levallois cores were shaped, prepared and then taken elsewhere.

Site BS-13, on the other hand, a similar low-density scatter adjacent to the shore, had few of the elements associated with initial or advanced core-preparation and more emphasis on finished Levallois pieces and retouched tools. In this instance, Levallois pieces were brought to the site already made, were used there and were then abandoned.

The most recent site in the group, the Aterian locality at BS-1, had low values for the initial core-preparation group, many Levallois preparation flakes, very few Levallois cores

but many Levallois flakes. This is believed to have been a site where cores that had been roughly prepared elsewhere (the nearest outcrops of quartzitic sandstone are about 25 km to the east) were finally prepared, partially exploited and then taken elsewhere.

A meaningful comparison of these Mousterian occurrences at Bir Sahara with the 'Levalloisian' from Kharga is extemely difficult, because of the limited sample-sizes in the latter group. There are very few retouched tools and these seem to be mostly scrapers and retouched Levallois flakes and points. Besides the Levalloisian and the Aterian, Caton-Thompson (1952) recognized two other taxonomic entities in the spring-vents, wadis and mud-pans in and around the Kharga depression. These are the Levalloiso-Khargan and Khargan, which she believed to fall in time between the Levalloisian and the Aterian. They are essentially Mousterian, and are distinguished by the small size of the artefacts and by the apparently random presence of steep and semi-steep, slightly denticulated retouch. A similar phenomenon has been reported from the Dungul area, about 200 km south-east of Kharga (Hester and Hoebler, 1969), but is unknown elsewhere. McBurney (1960, pp. 155–8) has suggested that these 'tools' may result from natural retouching of blanks.

The Khormusan

The third Middle Palaeolithic entity in northern Africa, the Khormusan, is known from several sites in the area of the Second Cataract, in the Nile valley of northern Sudan. The lithic industry in these sites is almost entirely on flakes of either quartzitic sandstone or Nile chert, both of which are locally available, and the Levallois technique was commonly

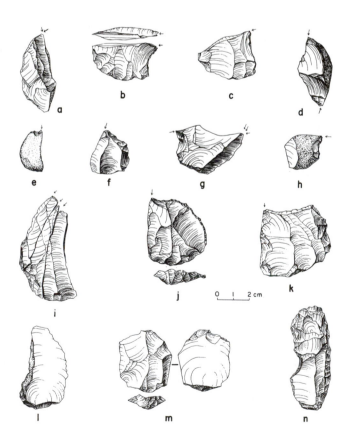

Figure 13 Khormusian artefacts, site 1017 (Nubia). a–k, burins; l, naturally backed knife; m, Levallois flake; n, notch. (After Marks, 1968.)

employed. The retouched tools include a preponderance of burins and side-scrapers (Marks, 1968b) (Fig. 13).

Although Khormusan sites occur embedded in silts of the Debeira-Jer aggradation, the stratigraphic evidence for a developmental sequence within the industry is dubious, because of the marked seasonal fluctuations in the level of the Nile. Little is known about the size and structure of Khormusan settlements. They seem to have been near-shore occupations, however, and most of them appear to have been repeatedly occupied.

Subsistence

Almost all of the evidence we have concerning subsistence in the Middle Palaeolithic of northern Africa is from Aterian sites. Very little is available for the Mousterian or the Khormusan. Aterian settlements occur in caves, along fossil beaches of the Mediterranean, in dunes above the beaches, along fossil stream courses, with deflated spring-vents and associated with fossil lake and playa sediments. In the Sahara, as would be expected, Aterian sites are invariably associated with evidence of a nearby source of water and with geological evidence of much greater moisture than today. The limited pollen data indicate the presence of more trees in the Maghreb, mostly cedar and cypress (van Campo and Coque, 1960). No Aterian site has yielded any plant remains, and grinding stones or other evidence of plant processing are not known. We have thus no information on this aspect of the diet and can only presume that plants were exploited.

The abundant faunal remains associated with some of the Aterian sites suggest a rich environment, particularly in north-western Africa where some thirty-seven different species have been reported from Aterian sites. These include elephant, rhinoceros, horse and ass or zebra, hippopotamus, pig, wart-hog, wild cattle, hartebeest, buffalo, six varieties of gazelle, hyena, giant camel and Barbary sheep. There is very little information available on the frequencies of these animals in the sites, so we are unable to determine if any of the Aterian groups specialized in particular kinds of animals, although Dalloni (1955, p. 422) has noted that most of the fauna from Retaïmia in Algeria are horse and wild cattle. There are no data available at all on the frequencies and condition of different body-parts of the various species represented. In northern Africa, therefore, any speculation as to the roles of hunting and scavenging, such as may be made in southern Africa (see pp. 127–8), is absolutely premature.

The fauna associated with the Aterian in the eastern Sahara is not as rich as that in the Maghreb sites, but includes white rhino, buffalo, giant camel, ass, dama and red-fronted gazelles and an unidentified medium-sized antelope. There is no evidence to suggest specialization in any particular species. This fauna implies a luxuriant savannah-type environment, which was moister than that near Lake Chad today and considerably moister than is indicated for even the wettest phase of the Holocene in the eastern Sahara. We have assumed (but not really demonstrated) that these large animals were hunted. The clusters of Aterian artefacts associated with the remains of animals are sure evidence that the animals were butchered (Plate 29); since it was primarily the major meat-bearing bones that were removed from the butchery sites, leaving mostly the heads and lower limb-bones (Gautier, 1980, p. 324), it seems most likely that the humans were, in this case, the primary hunters, rather than scavengers. This hypothesis remains, however, to be tested further.

From Cyrenaican Libya there is also the tantalizing suggestion that marine resources were being systematically exploited, for the first time, by the pre-Aurignacian and later the Aterian people in the Haua Fteah. McBurney (1967, p. 54) recovered masses of shells of edible marine molluscs in the Middle Palaeolithic levels at that site. In fact, the shells were so abundant that molluscs must have been a significant portion of the diet. Similar evidence has not been reported from other localities in northern Africa, but a comparable, or rather more intense, exploitation of marine resources is known to have begun in southern Africa by this period or slightly earlier (see p. 127).

Evidence from the Aterian-related sites in the Nile valley is much more limited, but the associated faunas at Site 440 in Nubia are of particular interest. The lower level is dominated by wild cattle, with rare ass, hippopotamus and gazelle. Except for one fragmentary scapula, all of the identifiable cattle remains are head-parts (especially teeth) or lower limb-bones (Gautier, 1968, table 2). The bones have not been examined for traces of gnawing by carnivores, but this distribution of body-parts is consistent with the hypothesis that the Nilotic Aterian groups tended to obtain their beef by scavenging after other predators. The fauna from the upper level of Site 440 was composed predominantly of Nile catfish. This is one of the oldest known examples of intensive exploitation of freshwater fish and complements the evidence from Cyrenaica (and from southern Africa) for use of marine resources. There is no indication of the methods used to obtain the catfish, but they need not have been conceptually or technologically very sophisticated.

The only evidence for subsistence practices during the Khormusan is from this same area, where nearby Khormusan sites have yielded abundant faunal remains, again almost all wild cattle. In the Khormusan collections, however, teeth and foot-bones are relatively much more rare, and there are significant numbers of prime meat-bearing bones (long bones, pelves and ribs; Gautier, 1968, table 2). This suggests that the regular hunting of wild cattle had begun to be undertaken by human groups before the end of the Middle Palaeolithic. Comparable indications of the development of more aggressive techniques for obtaining meat have been surmised by Binford (1984) for the Middle Stone Age (MSA) of southern Africa.

Evidence is even more limited from the Mousterian. No faunal remains have been found associated with Mousterian sites in the Nile valley, and the total from Kharga consists of one equine tooth (Caton-Thompson, 1952). The faunal remains from Mousterian sites in the Bir Sahara Basin are essentially similar to those of the Aterian, but less numerous. Most are white rhino, with some giant camel and buffalo; wild ass, wart-hog and antelope are very rare (Gautier, 1980). The paucity, relative to the Aterian, of faunal remains in the Mousterian sites may be merely a reflection of their not having been specialized butchery areas.

Other cultural activities

There is no evidence for houses or other occupied structures in the Middle Palaeolithic of northern Africa. Fire was undoubtedly used and controlled – many of the cave sequences contain major ash-layers – but even constructed hearths seem to be extremely rare.

There is some evidence for either long-distance movement by Middle Palaeolithic groups, or an extensive network of contacts between groups. Almost all of the Mousterian and Aterian artefacts at Bir Sahara Basin are made on quartzitic sandstone, which was available from outcrops about 25 km away, but there are also a few pieces of Eocene flint, for which the nearest source is over 200 km to the east. This could indicate either traffic in raw materials or the mobility of human groups at this period and the distance they covered. Unfortunately, we have no basis on which to prefer either of these hypotheses to the other.

Evidence for non-utilitarian activities in the Middle Palaeolithic of northern Africa is extremely rare. A fragment of a bone flute was found in the pre-Aurignacian levels of the Haua Fteah (McBurney, 1967, p. 90), and there is no reason to think that comparable objects would have been beyond the capabilities of later inhabitants of the region, but we lack any direct evidence for them. Ochre occurs in Aterian sites and ground haematite in all of the Khormusan sites, but their use remains almost entirely conjectural, as it does indeed elsewhere in Africa (see pp. 129, 132). The apparent absence of colouring material from the Mousterian may be in part because sites of this industry are not deeply stratified. There is a suggestion that ochre may have been deliberately used to colour two of the retouched tools from El Guettar (Tunisia) (Gruet, 1954, p. 32). The purpose of this is obscure and the practice not overwhelmingly common; it is of interest in the Maghreb, however, in that the colouring of retouched tools is well known among much later, Epipalaeolithic, groups.

El Guettar did yield the best evidence for symbolic behaviour in the constructed heap of stone balls (Gruet, 1954, pp. 67–77). The site had some 7 m of Middle Palaeolithic deposits around a spring, and the stone heap was found near the base of the sequence, built on a flat surface by the edge of the spring pool. The heap was conical, with a basal diameter of about 130 cm and a height of about 70 cm, and was built of about sixty balls, almost all of them of limestone, which were graded from large (18 cm in diameter), rather roughly shaped ones at the base to small (4.5 cm in diameter), perfectly shaped ones at the top. The interior of the cone was filled with a mass of bones and flaked stone artefacts (approximately 2,000 of the latter, including a typical tanged point). The bones and artefacts seemed to have been simply gathered up from the surrounding surface (they do not differ overall from those found elsewhere in the excavation), but some care was taken to reserve the finest artefacts for the upper part of the fill. At the base of the interior of the heap were two thin plaques of a non-local limestone.

The detectable method and consistency in the construction of the heap suggest that it was built on one occasion, rather than over a period of time. That the heap stood undisturbed thereafter until it became buried indicates that it was not just a convenient way of storing stone balls. The excavator believed that it represented an offering to the *genius loci* of the spring. Practical explanations have not been forthcoming and we too are brought to conclude that its purpose must have been symbolic.

SOUTHERN AFRICA

The second region of the African continent for which we have significant information about the period of the Neanderthalers is southern Africa, particularly south of about 10° S. The region thus includes all or parts of Malawi, Zambia, Zaire, Angola, Mozambique, Zimbabwe, Botswana, Namibia, South Africa, Lesotho and Swaziland. Unfortunately, research coverage has been very uneven thus far, so that very little work has been done in Angola, Bot-

swana and Mozambique, and most of the available data are from Zimbabwe and, above all, South Africa (Map 11).

The period of the Neanderthalers in this region corresponds quite closely to the Middle Stone Age (MSA). Attempts have been made to remove this term from current use (Bishop and Clark, 1967, pp. 896–7) since it has unwarranted cultural connotations, but it is still very widely used as a convenient shorthand and will be so used here. There is no implication of any kind of social or cultural unity among the various occurrences included within the MSA.

Hominid types

No true Neanderthalers are known from sub-Saharan Africa. The Late Acheulean, which preceded the MSA, seems to have been the work of an archaic form of *Homo sapiens*, which is sometimes regarded as a separate subspecies called *H. s. rhodesiensis*. This form is known from Zambia (Broken Hill, or Kabwe) (Plate 26) and South Africa (at several localities, of which Elandsfontein (Cape) is probably the best dated) and seems to date from the later part of the Middle Pleistocene (Rightmire, 1984, pp. 160–2). It is not clear whether or not it was ancestral to the Modern form of hominid (*H. s. sapiens*) but it does at least indicate the presence of the species in southern Africa before the MSA.

Very few remains of hominids can be definitely, or even very probably, associated with the MSA, and those few tend to be fragmentary. The best of the older MSA remains are from Klasies River Mouth, on the Cape coast, and Border Cave, on the border of Swaziland (Plate 28). Most of the Klasies River Mouth hominid fossils are from the earlier parts of the MSA sequence. The fossils are very fragmentary and of different degrees of robusticity, but at least some of them, including the earliest, are considered to be fully modern *Homo sapiens sapiens* (Singer and Wymer, 1982, pp. 139–49). They are probably more than 100,000 years old (see p. 125). Border Cave has yielded remains of at least four individuals, including an infant burial, which were probably, but not definitely, associated with the MSA (Klein, 1983). They are all anatomically Modern, although they are, again, somewhat robust (Rightmire, 1984, pp. 164–5). The earliest of them, if correctly provenanced, dates to about 115,000 years ago.

Both of these groups of fossils appear to have been contemporary with the Neanderthalers of Europe, and are among the earliest fossils of the modern human type from anywhere in the world. This means either that *H. s. sapiens* originated in sub-Saharan Africa, or, if not, was certainly not tardy in arriving there. Furthermore, rather specific similarities have been seen between these MSA remains and modern Khoi and San populations (Rightmire, 1979, 1984), implying that these might be very ancient inhabitants of southern Africa.

Chronological range

Although the Acheulean was long thought to have survived very late in sub-Saharan African and the MSA to have been contemporaneous with the European Upper Palaeolithic (Clark, 1970, pp. 247, 252), it now appears likely that the Earlier Stone Age (including the Acheulean) was essentially over by about 200,000 years ago. A uranium-series date of 174,000 ± 20,000 years ago from Rooidam (near Kimberley, South Africa) provides a useful *terminus ante quem* (Szabo and Butzer, 1979).

Lithostratigraphic and sedimentological studies of Border

Cave indicate that the long MSA sequence there begins in the later Middle Pleistocene, at the beginning of the Penultimate Glacial; an absolute age of about 195,000 years is suggested for the base of the sequence (Butzer et al., 1978). The open-air site of Duinefontein 1 (Cape) yielded a rather generalized MSA assemblage (Klein, 1976), associated with an archaic fauna, all of which is believed to predate the last interglacial near-shore dunes (Butzer et al., 1978, p. 335), and thus may be of an age comparable to that of Border Cave. At least in parts of southern Africa, therefore, the MSA seems to have been established by 200,000 years ago. This is very early, but not impossibly so, in light of the comparable dates for MSA occurrences in Ethiopia noted below, and the presence of MSA occurrences in the Middle Pleistocene at Laetoli in Tanzania (Day et al., 1980). The MSA is very firmly dated from the beginning of the Upper Pleistocene onwards at the deeply stratified cave sites on the southern Cape coast, such as Klasies River Mouth, where the earliest MSA rested on and in regressional deposits from the earliest (± 7 m) last interglacial beach, and where oxygen isotope analyses indicate an age of 125,000 to 130,000 years for the beginning of the sequence (Shackleton, 1982).

The date of the end of the MSA is not clear, but is not likely to have been synchronous over the whole of southern Africa (nor, indeed, was the beginning of the MSA). The earliest Late Pleistocene, microlithic, Later Stone Age assemblages are from Border Cave, where they are dated to about 38,000 years ago (Butzer et al., 1978). Other non-MSA occurrences (not all of them described) are known from before 20,000 years ago at several sites in South Africa (Deacon, 1984), from Sehonghong in Lesotho (Carter and Vogel, 1974), from Leopard's Hill Cave in Zambia (Miller, 1971) and possibly from Zimbabwe at some 'Tshangula' sites (Cooke, 1971), although these last may be mixed (Volman, 1984, p. 210). The stratified cave sequences frequently show a significant break in occupation (sometimes for tens of millennia) between the MSA and the Later Stone Age, a situation coincident with and reminiscent of that in northern Africa. Microlithic stone tools become very widespread in southern Africa after 20,000 years ago, in the Nachikufan of Zambia (Miller, 1971), the Tshangula of Zimbabwe and the Robberg industry to the south.

The shift away from MSA-type industries in southern Africa had therefore begun shortly after 40,000 years ago, but, overall, there was a great deal of variability in the timing of the shift. MSA-like traits remain in the Zimbabwe Tshangula down to about 12,000 years ago, while the MSA seems to have ended in the southern Cape by about 30,000 years ago and to have survived for several millennia later in Namibia (Wendt, 1976) and Lesotho (Carter and Vogel, 1974).

Stone artefacts

In so far as the MSA is defined at all, it is on the basis of stone artefacts, the MSA being characterized by the presence of tools such as denticulates, scrapers and points made on flakes and blades. In fact, however, the only major difference that can be detected with any consistency between the later Early Stone Age assemblages and the earliest MSA assemblages is that the latter do not include large, bifacial cutting-tools, such as handaxes and cleavers. Flake-tools were already known in the Acheulean and those of the early MSA showed little or no improvement over them. Methods of manufacture had improved and become more standardized by the end of the MSA, but the beginning of it did not mark

a radical departure from its predecessors (Volman, 1984).

Some regional and chronological variation can be seen in the MSA of southern Africa. It was undoubtedly more varied than the preceding Earlier Stone Age (Klein, 1983; Volman, 1984), indicating, perhaps, more specific adaptations, but actual patterns of variability are difficult to define. The clustering of studied MSA sites within certain favoured research areas makes it difficult to recognize an overall pattern of regional variability and impossible to discern chronological patterning within the less-favoured areas. In addition to the low number of studied MSA assemblages as a whole, the earlier ones in particular include very low frequencies of formal retouched tools, making characterization of them a hazardous and imprecise undertaking.

Some chronological patterning is evident, however, in the southernmost part of the region, where a relatively large number of MSA sites have been excavated, including deeply stratified cave sites. The best-known of the latter is the series of caves and rock-shelters at Klasies River Mouth on the Tzitzikama coast (Singer and Wymer, 1982), which has yielded a long MSA sequence beginning early in the last interglacial. Klasies River Mouth does not, therefore, include the very earliest MSA and few descriptions are available for the initial period. Assemblages are reported to consist of small, often wide, flakes, of which a very small percentage were retouched into tools, principally denticulates and a few scrapers; there are no retouched points (Volman, 1984).

The early MSA from Klasies River Mouth (i.e. MSA I and II of Singer and Wymer, 1982) made use of local quartzite beach-pebbles as raw material and is characterized by the production of large, elongated flakes or flake-blades (so called because they are at least twice as long as they are wide, and so have the proportions of blades, but were not punch-struck) from single and opposed platform cores. The flakes tend to become rather smaller through time. Retouched tools are more common and more varied than in the Middle Pleistocene assemblages, and include denticulates (becoming rarer through time), retouched points (being replaced by simple, pointed flake-blades through time), scrapers, utilized flakes and rare, but typical, burins. There was a slight increase in the use of non-local raw materials, but they remain unimportant. Very rare tanged artefacts also occur both here (Singer and Wymer, 1982, fig. 5.10, pp. 19–20) and elsewhere (Volman, 1984, fig. 9, p. 6) and suggest the use of composite tools. The later MSA of Klasies River Mouth (i.e. MSA III and IV of Singer and Wymer, 1982) is less rich but seems to continue the same trends seen in the earlier part of the sequence. Non-local stone is used rather more frequently, and backed flakes and small, unifacial points have been added to the repertoire, but the range of retouched tools is otherwise little different from that of the earlier MSA (Fig. 14). The end of the MSA sequence at Klasies River Mouth is estimated to date to either around 65,000 years ago (Butzer, 1978) or less than 30,000 years ago (Shackleton, 1982).

The most remarkable aspect of the Klasies River Mouth sequence is the insertion, into the middle of the otherwise homogeneous MSA, of a completely different industry, called Howieson's Poort. It occurs stratified between the earlier and the later MSA assemblages, or between MSA II and MSA III of Singer and Wymer. Local quartzite was largely replaced by non-local, fine-grained rocks, such as silcrete, indurated shale, quartz and chalcedony, which seem to have been imported from some distance. These were used for the production of small, or even microlithic, flakes and flake-blades. The most distinctive and original of the rela-

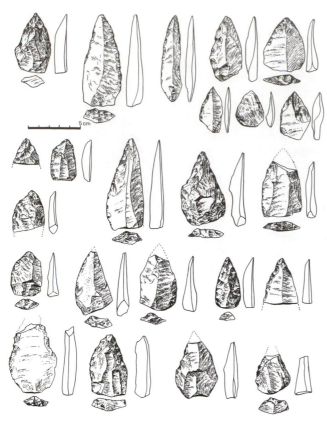

Figure 14 Worked stone points, later Middle Stone Age, Klasies River Mouth (South Africa). (After Singer and Wymer, 1982.)

tively numerous retouched tools are backed types, including crescents, trapezes, triangles and backed points. There are also scaled pieces (unknown in the rest of the Klasies River Mouth MSA sequence), rounded end-scrapers, strangulated blades and burins, but almost no denticulates (Singer and Wymer, 1982, pp. 87–106). Largely by analogy with similar backed pieces from the Later Stone Age, several scholars have suggested that the crescents and triangles of Howieson's Poort may have been hafted in mastic (Klein, 1977, p. 120; Singer and Wymer, 1982, p. 112; Volman, 1984, p. 207). There is, as yet, no direct evidence of this, but the suggestion is intriguing and would indicate the use of such a technology much earlier than had been supposed. The Howieson's Poort levels of Klasies River Mouth also yielded one finely worked, polished bone point. Other organic artefacts are known from the MSA (such as the ground suid tusks from Border Cave), but they are very rare at this period throughout the world and the example from Klasies River Mouth is an unusually good one (Singer and Wymer, 1982, fig. 8.1).

The intrusion of the Howieson's Poort industry at Klasies River Mouth is not an isolated phenomenon. The industry occurs elsewhere stratified within or below MSA sequences at sites such as Border Cave, Mossel Bay, Boomplaas, Skildergat, Montagu Cave, Nelson Bay Cave and Apollo 11. Its dating, however, is rather more controversial and depends primarily upon estimates from Border Cave and Klasies River Mouth. Butzer (1978; Butzer et al., 1978) gives the Howieson's Poort at both sites an approximate age of 80,000 to 95,000 years ago, whereas Shackleton (1982) estimates its age at Klasies River Mouth to be about 30,000 to 50,000 years. The longer chronology seems to be generally favoured (Singer and Wymer, 1982; Volman, 1984), but implies the manufacture of a semi-microlithic, backed blade industry in

southern Africa over 40,000 years earlier than anywhere else in the world.

The meaning of the Howieson's Poort episode is even more obscure. Its sudden intrusion into static MSA sequences and its radical difference from both what went before it and what came after it might suggest movement of population. This hypothesis cannot be tested, however, until we have a detailed knowledge of the distribution of Howieson's Poort in both space and time. It has also been fashionable for some time to regard such changes in lithic industries as responses to profound environmental change, but it will be difficult to assess this possibility for the Howieson's Poort industry until it can be rather more firmly dated and can be correlated with some particular episode of environmental change. In any case and whatever the significance of Howieson's Poort, it is extremely curious that people reverted afterwards to doing essentially the same as they had been doing beforehand.

The MSA north of southernmost Africa is less well known, but appears to be rather different. Sites in South Africa north of the Orange river and in Zimbabwe have been assigned to the Bambata complex (Sampson, 1974) and differ from those to the south in their higher frequencies of retouched points, side- or end-scrapers and scaled pieces. Bambata MSA sites may also include grinding stones. These are commonly viewed as having been used for grinding ochre, but such a use would not preclude the grinding of plant foods. Indigenous peoples of the American south-west frequently used the same stones for processing both food and pigment.

The dating of the Bambata MSA is insecure. There are no hints of its inception in the Middle Pleistocene, but, by analogy with MSA industries to both the north and the south, it is likely to have begun by the early Upper Pleistocene. The best carbon-14 dates for it are infinite (Sampson, 1974, pp. 206–8). It had certainly ended by 20,000 years ago and possibly considerably earlier, but the data are ambiguous. Within this rather ill-defined time span, patterned chronological change seems non-existent. The sequence from Bambata Cave in Zimbabwe has been cited to indicate increasing refinement through time (Volman, 1984, p. 210), a suggestion that should be treated with caution in view of the biased nature of the samples (originally selected and subsequently dispersed) and the tendency of archaeologists to expect such things. The sequences from the nearby sites of Pomongwe and Tshangula show no consistent pattern of chronological change (Sampson, 1974).

The MSA in Equatorial Africa, to the north of the Zambezi, consists, at least in part, of a little-known complex called the Lupemban. Lupemban sites are known from Angola, Zaire, Zambia, Malawi and Uganda and possibly into Tanzania and western Kenya. The poorly known Middle Stone Age of western Africa, south of the Sahara, seems to have been something similar. Lupemban sites tend to be confined to the Equatorial region of higher rainfall, although (disputed) claims occur as far afield as the Transvaal. Mwanganda, in northern Malawi, is the only site known that might be an undisturbed Lupemban occurrence *in situ* (Clark and Haynes, 1970). It was certainly *in situ* but not necessarily Lupemban, and its specialized nature (an elephant butchery site) restricts the range of information that can be obtained from it. All other Lupemban sites are, at best, geologically but not archaeologically *in situ*, many of them are mixed or were selectively collected, and some are isolated surface finds (Sampson, 1974, pp. 221–30). The age of the Lupemban is, therefore, essentially unknown. Mwanganda is regarded as late Middle Pleistocene or early Upper Pleistocene, which, if it is indeed Lupemban, would indicate an antiquity comparable to that of other MSA variants. The various carbon-14 dates for the complex tend to fall a little before 30,000 years ago, which again would suggest a chronological range similar to the MSA elsewhere (Clark, 1974, pp. 78–9).

The inadequacy of the Lupemban collections means that the complex cannot yet be completely described. However, it obviously differs from the MSA elsewhere in Africa in the presence of heavy-duty picks and core-axes, gouges, core-scrapers, handaxes and the large exquisitely made, bifacial leaf-points. The occurrence of these types of artefacts combined with the location of the Lupemban in the Equatorial forest zone have led to the suggestion that these may be woodworking tools and that the complex represents an adaptation to the forest environment. Until sites are discovered that are archaeologically *in situ*, this remains no more than a suggestion, but the possibility that this might represent a reponse to Upper Pleistocene development of forest is provocative.

Subsistence

It is very likely that plant foods played an important, and perhaps even dominant, role in the diet of the MSA people of southern Africa. However, as almost always for such remote periods of antiquity (and as usual even for much later periods), there is no direct evidence of this. The grinding stones present in some of the MSA sites are suggestive, but any remains of the plants themselves have long since perished.

Our knowledge of MSA subsistence in southern Africa depends upon collections of animal bones recovered from archaeological sites. At many open-air sites the bones have been destroyed by natural processes (a notable exception to this is the butchery site at Mwanganda mentioned on p. 126), and they are not preserved even in some of the cave sites in rock other than limestone. Recent years, however, have seen the detailed study and publication of large collections and long sequences of faunal remains from several sites in southern Africa, so that our knowledge of this period is incomparably richer than it was as lately as 1970. (See references to various publications by Klein in Klein, 1984.) The data from Klasies River Mouth, again, are crucial, but there is also considerable additional information available from other cave sites, such as Die Kelders (Cape) and Border Cave, and even from favoured open-air sites, such as Sea Harvest and Hoedjies Punt (western Cape).

Perhaps the most exciting aspect of the information now available from the MSA of southern Africa is the evidence it provides for the earliest systematic use of marine resources anywhere in the world. This dates from the beginning of the last interglacial at Klasies River Mouth, and can be traced through into the early Last Glacial both there and at other sites (Sea Harvest, Hoedjies Punt, Die Kelders) along the Cape coast (Klein, 1974, 1979). The evidence consists of the remains of fish, shellfish, penguins, flying seabirds, seals, dolphins and even whales. The use of marine resources was an important part of the subsistence economy at several MSA sites along the coast, but this use seems, essentially, to have been no more than an extension of normal gathering and hunting practices to the shore and near-shore zones.

The marine resources commonly used in the MSA were molluscs, seals and penguins. The molluscs could have been collected at low tide from the intertidal zone, or with a minimum of wading. The shells collected tend to be larger than those collected in the same areas during the Later Stone Age, perhaps suggesting that MSA shellfish collecting was less intensive and thus placed less stress on the local shellfish populations (Klein, 1979). Cape fur seals are abundant throughout the MSA sequence at Klasies River Mouth and elsewhere and were evidently a significant part of the MSA diet. It has been suggested that, when the climate became colder after the initial MSA, they may also have been used for their fur at Klasies River Mouth (Singer and Wymer, 1982, p. 208). Clothing must surely have long since been invented elsewhere in the world to permit human occupation of northern latitudes during glacial periods, so knowledge of it during the last interglacial in southern Africa would not be surprising; it is, however, purely conjectural. While dead seals might have been scavenged from the beaches, the awkwardness of the living animals on land would make them easy and relatively safe to hunt with nothing more than clubs or spears. The frequency with which they were taken suggests some active hunting. Penguins may have been scavenged from the beach, or, as flightless birds, could have been hunted with a simple hunting technology. Since they are today an island-breeding species (Avery and Siegfried, 1980), the former seems likely.

Those marine animals which can be hunted only with a rather sophisticated technology are rare in the MSA sequences. The flying seabirds, fish, dolphins and whales are so uncommon that they could easily represent no more than the scavenging of chance carcasses washed up on the beach. There is no evidence, direct or indirect, for a knowledge of boats during the MSA, nor for the smaller apparatus of fishing, such as hooks, gorges or sinkers. The use of marine resources by MSA groups therefore seems to represent only an extension of terrestrial hunting and gathering practices to the sea-shore, rather than the exploitation of an entirely novel ecological zone. Nevertheless, this use during the MSA was extensive and long-term, thus contrasting markedly with the Earlier Stone Age when marine resources were almost ignored. Data from the Haua Fteah in Libya (McBurney, 1967) show that marine molluscs, at least, were also collected at the other end of the African continent during the last interglacial (in the pre-Aurignacian levels as well as the Middle Palaeolithic), suggesting that that period may have witnessed the first steps towards true exploitation of the sea. Such exploitation appears fully developed around much of the world after the Last Glacial; it is unfortunate that the sites documenting the intervening stages of development, having been occupied as coastal sites, are now drowned beneath the high sea-level of the modern interglacial.

The terrestrial mammals of importance in the MSA faunal collections are bovids of various sizes. The relative frequencies of the species, and of the anatomical parts and mortality curves by which different species are represented, particularly at Klasies River Mouth, have been the basis for considerable speculation concerning the ways in which MSA groups obtained their meat (Binford, 1984; Klein, 1974, 1975, 1982).

Klein has interpreted his data on MSA faunal assemblages as indicating that the MSA people were not such accomplished or daring hunters as were those of the Later Stone Age. Very large animals (pachyderms) or very dangerous ones (big cats) were generally avoided in the MSA; small bovids were extensively hunted; suids, which can be very aggressive, were not much hunted; and, of the large bovids, the docile eland was frequently hunted, while the short-tempered Cape buffalo and the extinct giant buffalo (by analogy, probably short-tempered) were generally hunted as very young or even new-born animals. A certain amount of scavenging after predators, particularly for the larger animals, is not excluded.

Using some of the same faunal collections (the MSA from Klasies River Mouth), Binford (1984) has taken Klein's conclusion of the relative ineffectiveness of MSA hunters to even greater lengths. Both agree that small bovids were hunted, or at least killed, by MSA people, as were also the very young of the buffalo species. Klein had observed that the larger adult bovids were represented by a more limited range of body-parts than the smaller species, and attributed this to the *schlepp* effect: i.e. to the butchering of animals in the field, so that only certain parts of the body need be carried back to the camp. Binford has pointed out that the parts represented, principally heads and lower limbs, while yielding some marrow or soft tissue, are among the least productive in the body and that the prime meat-bearing bones of adult large bovids, which are above all the upper limbs, were not generally brought back to Klasies River Mouth. He concludes that MSA groups did not obtain large bovids by hunting them but by scavenging after non-human hunters, or even after non-human scavengers, so that the most desirable parts of the carcass had already been devoured, and that the importance of scavenged remains at Klasies River Mouth arises from the local source of water, where humans could scavenge during the day what had been killed the previous night.

Both Klein and Binford argue elegantly and persuasively against the traditional view of the Palaeolithic Mighty Hunter. Scavenging is now widely accepted as having been an important source of meat for hominids during the Lower Pleistocene (Binford, 1981; Isaac, 1984). It is also practised by recent hunting societies and may therefore be expected in the Upper Pleistocene. Klein sees MSA hunters as having been ineffective compared with their Later Stone Age successors, while Binford sees MSA hunting as essentially a sort of gathering in which MSA people would kill small animals when they happened upon them, but did not deliberately 'hunt' them: 'there is nothing in the data from Klasies River Mouth to suggest technologically aided hunting, or even tactical hunting' (Binford, 1984, p. 200). However, the presence of tanged or basally thinned points in the MSA suggests hafting as spearheads, a basic and useful technological aid, while tactical hunting is strongly indicated by this period elsewhere in the world, in particular elephant kills at Torralba-Ambrona (Spain) and the reindeer and horse kills of Mousterian Europe.

Site modification and site types

Water being the single most vital element needed to sustain human life, it is not surprising that the location of most MSA sites in southern Africa seems to have been determined by the availability of water. Sites occur by springs, streams, rivers and lakes. Many are open-air sites, generally occupied only briefly, but some, particularly in caves since they provide an obvious focus for occupation, were reoccupied many times over tens of millennia. Most consist simply of accumulations of stone artefacts and, if factors permit their preservation, of faunal remains. Definite and clear hearths are widely known, indicating that humans not only used fire (as they had since at least half a million years ago at Zhoukoudian (Choukoutien), in China) but also had full control over it. Apart from these, architectural features, or site modifications, are very rare and are best recognized at open-air sites.

Traces of a possible structure were found at Zeekoegat 27,

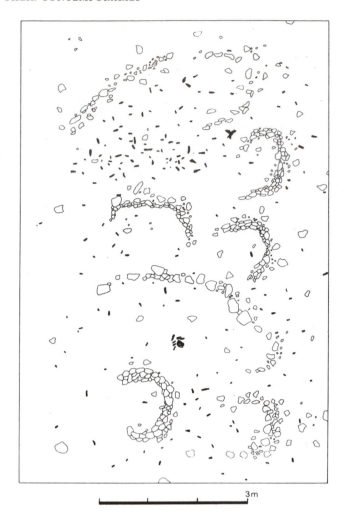

Figure 15 Plan of Middle Stone Age stone structures, Orangia I (South Africa). (After Sampson, 1974.)

an open-air site in the Orange river valley. Here there was a scatter of blocks of stone, with artefacts among them, over a circular area about 11 m in diameter. Sampson (1968, p. 63) has interpreted these as the base of a thorn-bush enclosure (windbreak), or, more likely, as anchors for the guy-ropes of a low skin tent. The latter interpretation is more consistent with the clustering of artefacts among the blocks than is the former. A cluster of seven smaller structures was found at Orangia I in the same area (Fig. 15) (Sampson, 1968, pp. 24–7; 1974, p. 169). Five of the structures are small (up to 1.5 m in diameter), semicircular walls of cobbles lining the windward sides of shallow depressions excavated in the ground; they are relatively free of artefacts and may have been sleeping hollows. The other two are larger (about 4 m long) arcs of stones, enclosing areas with clusters and heaps of artefacts; they may have been the bases of daytime windbreaks.

Apart from briefly occupied sites such as Orangia I, well-preserved MSA sites are very variable and are frequently assigned to types such as quarry sites, butchery sites and base camps. Numbers of quarry sites were found in the Orange River area (Sampson, 1968), consisting of very dense accumulations of artefacts at outcrops of indurated shale and often at long distances from water. Butchery sites normally consist of the dismembered remains of one (Mwanganda: Clark and Haynes, 1970) or a few (Duinefontein 2: Klein, 1976) animals, associated with a usually low number of stone artefacts: animals may or may not have been killed by those who butchered them. The term 'base camp', or home base, is frequently applied to those sites which show signs of considerable occupation, and especially to the deeply stratified cave sites, which were occupied over long periods of time (Singer and Wymer, 1982; Klein, 1977). It is implied that this was a base for a human group at which sleeping, food consumption, protection of the weak (young, sick or aged) and most social life took place (Binford, 1984, p. 198). The implications of 'central place foraging' are very similar and perhaps the most important of these implications, and the most obvious in the archaeological record, is that food was brought back to this place by members of the group to be shared.

Again on the basis of his examination of the Klasies River Mouth fauna, Binford (1984) suggests that food sharing, or provisioning, cannot be warranted for the MSA of southern Africa. Dealing only with the bovid fauna, he believes that the parts of the large bovids were brought back only for processing (soaking, hammering, scraping and so forth), and that neither they nor the comparatively complete smaller bovids would have yielded enough meat to be worth sharing among a large group. It is also suggested that there was no real sharing ethic among MSA inhabitants of Klasies River Mouth, since the prime parts of the smaller bovids (the upper hind limbs) were often not brought back and may have been consumed in the field. Against that, one considers that modern hunter-gatherers eat food even as they collect it to be taken back to their base for sharing and that the rest of the smaller bovid carcasses were taken back to Klasies River Mouth for *some* reason: since upper hind limbs could be eaten in the field, it was not for processing. It is further suggested that there was no intention to share among a large group, since there is no evidence that large amounts of meat were brought in at one time. However, not only is it not necessary that a commensal group be numerous, but Binford regards larger animals as beyond the capabilities of MSA hunters in any case. We therefore consider that provisioning is not shown not to have occurred but remains a very likely practice for such recent hominids as those of the last interglacial.

Binford further considers the concept of a base camp, or of central place foraging, to be inapplicable as long as humans were unable to modify the natural milieu by constructing their own shelters and controlling fire (1984, pp. 261–4). Since we have seen that both of these skills were practised in the MSA of southern Africa, his arguments against the base-camp-cum-provisioning model of MSA life lose some of their force.

Other cultural activities

Evidence for any MSA activities other than the strictly utilitarian is extremely limited. We can be sure that some kinds of social systems and probably belief systems existed, but such things leave notoriously poor traces in the archaeological record of earlier prehistory.

The possible MSA burial of an infant at Border Cave is the best evidence at present known for a belief system. It may, further, have been associated with a perforated shell imported from the coast, suggesting both the concept of grave goods and the long-distance transport of objects. Unfortunately, the provenances of the burial and the shell are not so firmly established as might be wished, but similar practices are known for the Neanderthalers of northern latitudes, so that their occurrence in southern Africa is surprising only in its rarity.

The most common evidence for symbolic, or non-utilitarian, behaviour at MSA sites is pieces of colouring material, ochre or haematite, often ground or rubbed and even, in the case of an ochre crayon from Klasies River Mouth, drilled (Singer and Wymer, 1982, p. 117). No trace of MSA parietal art has ever been found, although it was searched for with particular care at Klasies River Mouth, in a sealed cave (1C) with very suitable rock walls (Singer and Wymer, 1982, p. 25). Pigment is common in many sites, however, and must therefore have been applied to perishable surfaces, very probably to human skin. The exceptional site in this respect is the Apollo 11 cave, in Namibia, which yielded seven fragments of painted stone slabs from the top of the MSA sequence quite securely dated between 27,500 and 25,500 years ago (Wendt, 1976) (see Fig. 42). The paintings include unrecognizable, possibly composite, animals. They show no great technical mastery, but are by far the oldest dated examples of art known from the African continent, and are not much younger than the oldest art of the European Upper Palaeolithic.

The importance of colouring materials to some MSA groups is indicated by the occurrence of an MSA specularite mine at Lion Cavern in Swaziland (Beaumont, 1973). The specularite was mined from the base of a haematite cliff high on Lion Peak, and the lower deposits covering the floor of the working included many MSA artefacts, including specularite-stained mining-tools. Because of perturbation of the deposits by later miners, the MSA cannot be carbon-14 dated, but there is no reason to think it younger than the MSA elsewhere in southern Africa. Lion Cavern is therefore likely to represent the earliest mining activity yet known.

EASTERN AFRICA

Eastern Africa is the third region of the continent for which there is available a noteworthy amount of information concerning the period of the Neanderthals and their contemporaries. Eastern Africa here includes southern Sudan, Ethiopia, Somalia, Kenya, Uganda, Rwanda, Burundi and Tanzania (Map 11). Within this region, the archaeological period we are considering is, again, called the Middle Stone Age, or MSA. Unfortunately, however, neither the quantity nor the quality of information from eastern Africa is as high as that from northern or southern Africa. While some research was carried out into this period in the earlier years of modern archaeology, recent work in the area has concentrated primarily on the earliest periods of human prehistory, avoiding those sites with MSA 'overburden'. There is also considerable geographical variation in the availability of good information concerning this period. Although most of the region has received at least some study, almost all our best information today comes from Ethiopia.

Hominid types

The archaic *Homo sapiens* from Bodo in Ethiopia dates to the earlier part of the Middle Pleistocene and was responsible for at least some of the later Lower Palaeolithic remains found in eastern Africa (Conroy et al., 1978). The same is probably true of the archaic *Homo sapiens* specimens from Lake Eyasi in Tanzania, although the associated artefacts have been compared with MSA (Leakey et al., 1972, p. 334). In any case, as in southern Africa (see p. 124), *Homo sapiens* was present in eastern Africa before the period of the MSA.

The remains of three or perhaps four humans date from the period of the eastern African MSA, all of them *H. sapiens*. Only the Singa skull from Sudan is in doubt, because of the difficulty of dating it. The Ngaloba Beds, at Laetoli in Tanzania, yielded a fairly complete skull of a late archaic *H. sapiens*, which has been compared with that from Jebel Irhoud in Morocco (Day et al., 1980). The estimated age of the skull is 120,000 ± 30,000 years, and MSA artefacts occurred nearby, although they were not directly associated. Two other fossils were found in the Kibish formation of the lower Omo valley in south-western Ethiopia. They are geological contemporaries, with an estimated age of about 130,000 years (Butzer et al., 1969), and were associated with otherwise undiagnostic MSA artefacts. One of them, Omo-Kibish 2, is a somewhat archaic *H. sapiens*, while Omo-Kibish 1 (Plate 27) is, anatomically, modern *H. sapiens sapiens*.

Three of these fossils are of the same evolutionary grade as the European Neanderthalers, their contemporaries, but they are morphologically quite distinct (Trinkaus, 1982). The fourth, Omo-Kibish 2, appears to be a very early Modern form of human. This is surprising but not unique; *H. sapiens sapiens* of at least as early a date are reported from southern Africa (see p. 124).

Chronological range

Later phases of the Lower Palaeolithic Acheulean, which preceded the MSA in eastern Africa, have a uranium-series age of about 260,000 years at Isimila in Tanzania (Howell et al., 1972). A similarly late phase at Lake Baringo in northern Kenya lay over a tuff with a series of potassium–argon dates, of which the youngest and uppermost is 230,000 years old (Bishop, 1972, table 1; Leakey et al., 1969). These dates are concordant with the estimated date of about 200,000 years ago for the end of the Acheulean in southern Africa.

The key sequence for the dating of the early MSA in eastern Africa is from Lake Ziway in the central Rift Valley of Ethiopia (Wendorf and Schild, 1974). Two localities, one named Kulkuletti and the other Gademotta, were studied. They are about 2 km apart and both lie on the upper slopes of a ridge. This ridge is a remnant of a collapsed, but formerly very large, caldera on the western side of Lake Ziway, and it stands some 320 m above the level of the modern lake. Several obsidian outcrops occur in the area, particularly at Kulkuletti. Kulkuletti and Gademotta have similar sediments, which are mostly accumulations of volcanic ash. Several episodes of weathering and soil development are evident in the sediments, as well as a few thin beds of unaltered volcanic ash. The ash lenses and soils provide the best means of correlating the sequences from each locality. Some of the soils are believed to represent intervals when the slopes of the ridge were stabilized by vegetation; others are more complex and also record periods of relative aridity. There are indications that ephemeral ponds existed on the ridge in the vicinity of the sites during at least part of the period of occupation, and beach sands just below one of the sites (Eth-72-1) lie at least 150 m above the modern lake level; this suggests that the ridge may have been a promontory in a large lake at that time. The complete Pleistocene section at Gademotta is 30 m thick and archaeological material occurs in the upper 10 m. The Quaternary sediments on the ridge apparently accumulated slowly, and this, together with the numerous and complex soils preserved in them, indicates that a considerable span of time is represented in the sequence.

The earliest evidence for occupation in the Gademotta area consisted of a cultural layer with several small, finely made handaxes of Final Acheulean aspect in the base of thick brown soil. On top of this soil was the first MSA occupation, site Eth-72-8B. A colluvium, a weak brown soil and a bed of cemented ash separate this from the next occupation, Eth-72-7B. This is then overlain by two more colluvia, separated by a thin bed of cemented ash, and another weak brown soil with a third MSA horizon at the base, Eth-72-6. The brown soil was truncated by erosion and covered by a layer of bedded, cemented ash with a crust of calcium carbonate. Above this is another layer of colluvium followed by a vertisol, which sometimes crushed the artefacts of the latest MSA settlement in this section, Eth-72-5. An adjacent channel fill, which could not be precisely related to this sequence but probably goes with the earliest MSA occupation, yielded the only fauna recovered. This included bones of a zebra, a hippopotamus and two large antelopes, probably a wildebeest and a hartebeest.

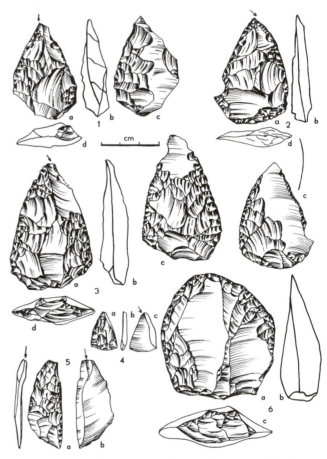

Figure 16 Middle Stone Age artefacts, site Eth-72-1 (Ethiopia). 1–3, bifacial points; 4–5, resharpening spalls; 6, end-scraper. (After Wendorf and Schild, 1974.)

On the basis of similarities in the soils and ash-layers, the sequence at the nearby area of Kulkuletti has been correlated with the upper part of the Gademotta section. Site Eth-72-1 (Fig. 16) is considered to be earlier than Eth-72-7, and Eth-72-9 was probably occupied after Eth-72-6.

There are three potassium–argon age determinations on sanidine crystals for this section. The oldest is a previously unreported date of 235,000 ± 5,000 years ago, on a sample from the cemented ash layer overlying site Eth-72-8B at Gademotta. The second sample gave a date of 181,000 ± 6,000 years ago and was from an ash layer below site Eth-72-1 at Kulkuletti. This ash had been correlated with the ash layer at Gademotta, which yielded the new date of 235,000 years ago (Wendorf and Schild, 1974). This correlation now seems unlikely in view of the discrepancy between these two dates. The third sample came from an ash layer between sites Eth-72-1 and Eth-72-9 at Kulkuletti, which is correlated with the ash layer above site Eth-72-6 at Gademotta, and gave an age of 149,000 ± 12,000 years ago.

Although these dates place the beginning of the MSA 100,000 to 150,000 years earlier than would the estimated date for the pre-Aurignacian in northern Africa (see p. 119), they are consistent with the stratigraphic and pedological evidence that a long period of time is represented in the Gademotta and Kulkuletti sequence. The sanidine crystals were regarded by the laboratory as excellent material for this dating technique and there was no indication that they had been redeposited. The dates are also supported by at least one other potassium–argon date of 240,000 years ago for an MSA site at Malawa Gorge in Kenya (Evernden and Curtis, 1965, p. 358), and by the lithostratigraphic age estimates from several MSA sites in southern Africa (see pp. 124–5). It seems unlikely that the Middle Palaeolithic, or Middle Stone Age, began 100,000 years later in northern Africa than it did in eastern and southern Africa, but this problem can be solved only by additional dating.

The end of the MSA in eastern Africa is even less well dated than in northern or southern Africa. Leakey and others (1972) have suggested an age of about 50,000 years for the indeterminate MSA from the Ndutu beds at Olduvai Gorge, but other dates, such as the obsidian hydration dates of around 61,000 and 78,000 years ago from Porc Epic in Ethiopia (Clark et al., 1984), must be regarded as minima. Unfortunately, the appearance of the Later Stone Age industries is equally poorly dated. At site GvJm 46, at Lukenya Hill in Kenya, a microlithic backed bladelet industry is now dated to at least 21,000 years ago, and overlies a considerable thickness of deposit containing an undescribed, but non-MSA, industry (Miller, 1979). This is consistent with the evidence from further south in Africa (see p. 125), and the MSA of eastern Africa may eventually be found to have continued down to about 30,000 years ago.

Stone artefacts

The MSA of eastern Africa is an industry of flakes and blades. The Levallois technique, which had become important in the later phases of the Acheulean, was commonly practised in some areas, such as the Horn (Clark, 1954) and Uganda (O'Brien, 1939), but tended to be less frequent toward the south. Formal retouched tools are often extremely rare, many assemblages consisting of unretouched flakes, especially Levallois flakes. However, when retouched tools are present, the characteristic forms are various unifacially and bifacially retouched points, usually subtriangular or leaf-shaped and, in the case of the unifacial pieces, grading into classic Mousterian points. There are also varieties of side-scrapers, which are less formal but may resemble the points rather closely, occasional backed flakes and informal burins, and some notches and denticulates. (The last were unusually numerous at Kone, in the southwestern corner of the Afar Rift, where they make up almost half of all retouched tools (Clark et al., 1984).)

Essentially similar assemblages are known right down the eastern part of the continent, extending as far west as Uganda where they overlap with the Lupemban, and have been called 'Stillbay'. The occurrences grouped under that name, however, have nothing in common except the use of flat surface retouch (Anthony, 1972), and the term is culturally and archaeologically meaningless.

As in northern and southern Africa, the principal and consistent difference between the later Acheulean and the MSA in eastern Africa is that the latter lacks large, bifacial cutting tools. In the Final Acheulean of Garba III at Melka Kunturé the Levallois technique was used, large bifacial tools are rare and there are many flake-tools, including the unifacial and bifacial points typical of the MSA (Chavaillon et al., 1979). Like the pedunculate in the Acheulean at Cap Chatelier, this may indicate the origin of the MSA in the local Acheulean. It is unfortunate that there seem to be no MSA living-sites at Melka Kunturé and that any MSA in situ there is extremely rare (Hours, 1976).

The only stratigraphically controlled, variable, MSA sequence reported from a recent excavation in eastern Africa is from the sites at Lake Ziway (Wendorf and Schild, 1974). The lithic assemblages from these sites are generally similar to each other, with low to moderate Levallois indices and a tool group consisting primarily of side-scrapers, Mousterian points, Mousterian-like points with scaled, invasive retouch and bifacial points. There are significant variations through time in the frequencies of the main tool-types, with side-scrapers first becoming more numerous and then declining in frequency. The importance of side-scrapers (other than convergent) varies inversely with the values for Mousterian points, convergent side-scrapers and bifacial points. However, on the basis of studies of use-wear, of resharpening practices (some of the resharpening spalls could be fitted back on to the tools from which they had been struck) and of the complete lack of impact fractures or other evidence that the points were used as projectiles or for stabbing, all of these varieties of tools seem to have been used for cutting. This implies that fluctuations in the relative frequencies of the tool classes do not indicate changes in activity or function, as they are so commonly interpreted elsewhere, but something more like a purely random drift in cultural preference. This hypothesis seems to be supported in the Lake Ziway sequence, and would merit testing at other MSA and Middle Palaeolithic sites.

Other indicated changes in the toolkit mostly concern very minor tool types, which, with the sole exception of the numerous ogival-based pieces at site Eth-72-5, are rare, or occur only sporadically in the sequence, or only at one site. It is variations such as these that could well be functional.

The only developmentally important change in the Lake Ziway sequence was in technology. Blade-cores with typically Upper Palaeolithic preparation and blades that were struck with a punch, rather than with a hammer, appear in the middle of the sequence at site Eth-72-6, and these techniques continued to be used thereafter. Tools of Upper Palaeolithic type, are infrequent throughout the sequence, however, except at site Eth-72-5, the latest site, where they are more common. There was also a decline in the size of artefacts at Eth-72-5, but, since this is the latest site, it was not possible to determine if this marked the beginning of a consistent trend in the local MSA, or if it was merely idiosyncratic.

The MSA sequence from the cave of Porc Epic in eastern, central Ethiopia is likely to represent a considerably shorter span of time than that of Lake Ziway. The excavators would place the sequence early in the Last Glacial (Clark et al., 1984), but the available dates are minima and it is therefore essentially undated. Several layers of MSA occupation were found sealed under a dripstone, and there are reported to be no changes in the industry through time. The assemblages have therefore been described as a single unit; most of the retouched tools are unifacial or bifacial points and various side-scrapers. Several concentrations of fire-cracked chert were found in the cave, suggesting the possibility of attempts to heat-treat the material prior to flaking it. This technique is normally found only in much later prehistoric industries and, if attempted at Porc Epic, was evidently not mastered.

Other MSA sequences in eastern Africa are from much older excavations and seem to be generally unreliable. Of some passing interest is the sequence from Gamble's Caves in Kenya (Leakey, 1931, pp. 90–171), where an industry with backed pieces and crescents may have occurred below a possible MSA assemblage. Unfortunately, the overlying MSA is very poor, and the backed pieces were supposedly associated with fine microliths and pottery. The site has obviously been much disturbed, and would be disregarded were it not for a similar occurrence, at Apis Rock in Tanzania, of backed pieces and end-scrapers reported to be underneath a 'Stillbay' MSA (Leakey, 1936, p. 62). The finds at these sites can be no more than suggestive of a phenomenon similar to the Howieson's Poort intrusion into the MSA of southern Africa, but such may also have taken place in parts of eastern Africa.

Subsistence

Almost nothing is known about subsistence practices in the MSA of eastern Africa. Any faunal materials from earlier excavations seem to be unreported and there was almost no fauna preserved in the Lake Ziway sites. A considerable amount of bone was found at Porc Epic, but almost all of that so far studied was so fragmentary and burned as to be unidentifiable. Small bovids, pig and zebra are reported (Clark et al., 1984). The excavators of the site, which is located near the top of a hill and is difficult of access, suppose that it overlooked the game migration routes and was occupied by specialized groups of hunters. This would accord with the large number of points (15 per cent) which have thinned bases and could well have been hafted. The faunal evidence to support this is not yet forthcoming, but teeth, at least, remain recognizable as such no matter how broken, and the bones are said to include very few head parts (Clark et al., 1984, p. 63). If the occupants of the cave were not bringing in animal heads, then they may indeed have been hunting rather than scavenging. This, in turn, would support the attribution of the sequence to the later part of the MSA.

Site types

The possibility that Porc Epic may have been a hunting station has been mentioned. The only other pertinent evidence available is from the sites of the Lake Ziway area, which have yielded some very interesting data on activities, site functions and the treatment of lithic raw material (Wendorf and Schild, 1974). All of the localities are regarded as living-sites; they all have relatively high frequencies of finished tools, many of which had been extensively used and often resharpened, sometimes more than once. Workshop-related activities were also carried out at the same sites, to varying degrees.

One of the sites at Gademotta, Eth-72-8B, had a shallow, saucer-like, artificial basin, which is thought to have been a hut floor. There were no clearly distinct activity areas within the basin, although there were two clusters of points. The presence of a hut floor and a high proportion of finished tools among the artefacts indicate that this was primarily a living site, and the large quantity of all artefacts indicates that occupation, or reoccupation, took place over a considerable period of time. Despite the proximity of the obsidian outcrops at Kulkuletti, workshop-related activities seem to have been unimportant at this site, since there were relatively few primary flakes or preparation flakes for Levallois cores, and relatively little Levallois debitage. The Levallois core-preparation flakes were also significantly thinner than at other sites, suggesting that only the final stages of preparation were being carried out here, which again indicates the relative unimportance of workshop activities at Eth-72-8B.

The later sites in the Gademotta sequence all yielded slightly higher values for Levallois core-preparation flakes, and one of them (Eth-72-6) had several small clusters of workshop debris. These are thought to have been living-sites, where the main tasks were normal subsistence activities, but where some of the locally available obsidian was processed. No Levallois cores were found at site Eth-72-7B, suggesting that the obsidian worked here was for later use elsewhere.

The two localities at Kulkuletti, Eth-72-1 and Eth-72-9, show a greater emphasis on workshop activity. The horizontal distributions of artefacts in both include numerous small clusters of workshop debris, with high frequencies of initial core-preparation flakes and of Levallois core-preparation flakes. Other areas of both sites, apart from these clusters of workshop debris, yielded relatively high frequencies of finished tools. This is interpreted as indicating occupation by groups who came to replenish their supplies of raw material and prepared numerous Levallois cores to be taken elsewhere; at the same time, they seem to have carried on their everyday, non-workshop, domestic tasks and subsistence activities. This suggests that we are dealing here not with special task-groups but with undivided groups of normal social composition. This is a very different social response from the highly specialized nature of the task-groups apparent at later prehistoric quarries in Africa and Europe.

Other cultural activities

The evidence from Porc Epic casts light on two other aspects of MSA behaviour. The first is raw material usage. Almost all of the stone artefacts were made on local chert, but some of them (6 per cent) were made on a good-quality, exotic obsidian. The source of this obsidian is not precisely known, but it has been suggested that it may have come from the Afdem area of the southern Afar, some 100 km to the west (Clark et al., 1984). If so, then, as in northern and southern Africa, we have evidence in the MSA either for the movement of groups over long distances to obtain preferred materials or else for extensive networks of social contacts and the passage of goods through those networks.

The second notable feature of Porc Epic is the very large quantity of colouring material found there, scattered throughout the MSA layers. The material was of several varieties – red and yellow ochre, red haematite and specularite – and much of it showed signs of rubbing or striations (Clark et al., 1984). Most of it had been subjected to heat, leading the excavators to suggest that this may have been a deliberate method of creating different colours. Since most of the stones and bones from the cave had also been burned, this remains speculative. Again, the MSA groups were much concerned with colouring something, although what that was is not known. One curiosity was the cast of an ammonite that had been completely (and naturally) replaced by pigment; one wonders if its MSA finders also considered it curious.

CONCLUSIONS

During the period of *H. sapiens neanderthalensis* in Europe and western Asia, Africa was occupied by very heterogeneous populations of *H. sapiens*, none of whom were morphologically Neanderthal. Most of them were of an evolutionary grade equivalent to that of the Neanderthals to the north, but some very early Upper Pleistocene fossils from southern and eastern Africa have been described as anatomically Modern. Unfortunately, the Upper Pleistocene human remains from Africa are few and fragmentary, so that it is difficult to establish their precise relationship to Modern humans, but the suggestion has been made that *H. sapiens sapiens* evolved in eastern and southern Africa in the late Middle Pleistocene, and spread from there throughout Africa and on into Asia and Europe (Bräuer, 1984). This remains yet to be demonstrated.

Whatever the evolutionary status of African groups during this period, there are some indications that their behaviour may not have been fully Modern. More regional variation in stone tools is apparent than for earlier periods, but stone-working throughout the period often seems to have been static, or even stagnant. In parts of Africa, at least, we may be dealing with a period some 200,000 years long, but can see almost no change taking place within it. This is very different from human behaviour during the last 30,000 to 40,000 years. There are also indications that human beings were not yet fully competent game hunters, that they did not become so until late in the period, and that much of their meat was obtained by scavenging. There is even some suggestion of rather basic differences from humans of the Modern type in social and territorial organization; these also, however, remain to be demonstrated.

Despite the lack of evidence for it, we can be sure that the African contemporaries of the Neanderthalers had social systems of some kind, and the almost ubiquitous occurrence of pigment in their sites implies symbolic behaviour. More concrete evidence of this is supplied by the enigmatic structure of stone balls built on the edge of a Tunisian spring pool. Even art was known in Africa almost as early as anywhere else. Africa may eventually prove not only to have been the cradle of humankind, but also to have been the cradle of Modern humankind.

BIBLIOGRAPHY

ALIMEN, H. 1957. *The Prehistory of Africa*. London.
ANTHONY, B. 1972. The Stillbay Question. In: HUGOT, H. J. (ed.), *VIᵉ Congrès Panafricain de Préhistoire, Dakar 1967*. Chambéry. pp. 80–2.
ANTOINE, M. 1950. Notes de préhistoire marocaine XIX: L'Atérien du Maroc atlantique, sa place dans la chronologie nord-africaine. *Bull. Soc. Préhist. Maroc* (Rabat), pp. 5–47.
ARAMBOURG, C. 1955. A Recent Discovery in Human Paleontology: Atlanthropus of Ternifine (Algeria). *Am. J. Phys. Anthropol.* (New York), Vol. 13, pp. 191–201.
ARAMBOURG, C.; BIBERSON, P. 1956. The Fossil Human Remains from the Paleolithic Site of Sidi Abderrahman (Morocco). *Am. J. Phys. Anthropol.* (New York), Vol. 14, pp. 467–90.
ARKELL, A. J. 1949. *Old Stone Age in the Anglo-Egyptian Sudan*. Khartoum.

AVERY, G.; SIEGFRIED, W. R. 1980. Food Gatherers along South Africa's Seashore. *Oceans*, Vol. 4, pp. 32–7.
BALOUT, L. 1955. *Préhistoire de l'Afrique du Nord: essai de chronologie*. Paris.
BEAUMONT, P. B. 1973. The Ancient Pigment Mines of Southern Africa. *S. Afr. J. Sci.* (Cape Town), Vol. 69, pp. 140–6.
BIBERSON, P. 1961. *Le Paléolithique inférieur du Maroc Atlantique*. Rabat. (Publ. Serv. Antiq. Maroc, 17.)
—— 1970. Index Cards on the Marine and Continental Cycles of the Moroccan Quaternary. *Quaternaria* (Rome), Vol. 13, pp. 1–76.
BINFORD, L. R. 1981. *Bones: Ancient Men and Modern Myths*. New York/London.
—— 1984. *Faunal Remains from Klasies River Mouth*. Orlando.
BISHOP, W. W. 1972. Stratigraphic Succession 'Versus' Calibration in East Africa. In: BISHOP, W. W.; MILLER, J. A. (eds), *Calibration of Hominid Evolution*. Edinburgh. pp. 219–46.
BISHOP, W. W.; CLARK, J. D. (eds) 1967. *Background to Evolution in Africa*. Chicago.
BORDES, F. 1961. *Typologie du Paléolithique ancien et moyen*. Bordeaux. 2 vols. (3rd edn 1979, Paris.)
BRÄUER, G. 1984. The 'Afro-European sapiens-hypothesis', and Hominid Evolution in East Asia during the Late Middle and Upper Pleistocene. *CFS, Cour. Forsch. inst. Senckenb.* (Frankfurt/Main), Vol. 69, pp. 145–65.
BUTZER, K. W. 1978. Sediment Stratigraphy of Middle Stone Age Sequence at Klasies River Mouth. *S. Afr. Archaeol. Bull.* (Claremont), Vol. 33, pp. 141–51.
BUTZER, K. W.; BEAUMONT, P.; VOGEL, J. C. 1978. Lithostratigraphy of Border Cave, KwaZulu, South Africa: A Middle Stone Age Sequence Beginning c.195,000 BP. *J. Archaeol. Sci.*, Vol. 5, pp. 317–41.
BUTZER, K. W.; BROWN, F. H.; THURBER, D. L. 1969. Horizontal Sediments of the Lower Omo Valley: The Kibish Formation. *Quaternaria* (Rome), Vol. 11, pp. 15–30.
CAMPO, M. VAN; COQUE, R. 1960. Palynologie et géomorphologie dans le Sud Tunisien. *Pollen et Spores* (Paris), Vol. 2, pp. 275–84.
CAMPS, G. 1974. *Les Civilisations préhistoriques de l'Afrique du Nord et du Sahara*. Paris.
CARLSON, R. L. 1967. Excavations at Khor Abu Anga and at Sites in Nubia. *Curr. Anthropol.*, Vol. 8, p. 352.
CARTER, P. L.; VOGEL, J. C. 1974. The Dating of Industrial Assemblages from Stratified Sites in Eastern Lesotho. *Man* (London), Vol. 9, pp. 557–70.
CATON-THOMPSON, G. 1946a. *The Aterian Industry: Its Place and Significance in the Palaeolithic World*. London.
—— 1946b. The Levalloisian Industries of Egypt. *Proc. Prehist. Soc.*, Vol. 12, pp. 57–120.
—— 1952. *Kharga Oasis in Prehistory*. London.
CHAVAILLON, J. 1964. *Étude stratigraphique des formations quaternaires du Sahara Nord-Occidental (Colomb-Béchar à Réggane)*. Paris, CNRS.
CHAVAILLON, J. et al. 1979. From the Oldowan to the Middle Stone Age at Melka Kunturé (Ethiopia): Understanding Cultural Changes. *Quaternaria* (Rome), Vol. 21, pp. 87–114.
CHMIELEWSKI, W. 1968. Early and Middle Paleolithic Sites Near Arkin, Sudan. In: WENDORF, F. (ed.), *The Prehistory of Nubia*. Dallas. pp. 110–47.
CHOUBERT, G.; FAURE-MURET, A.; MAARLEVELD, G. C. 1967. Nouvelles Dates isotopiques du Quaternaire marocain et leur signification. *C. R. Acad. Sci. Paris*, Vol. 264, pp. 434–7.
CLARK, J. D. 1954. *The Prehistoric Cultures of the Horn of Africa*. Cambridge.
—— 1969. *Kalambo Falls Prehistoric Site I*. Cambridge.
—— 1970. *The Prehistory of Africa*. London.
—— 1974. *Kalambo Falls Prehistoric Site II*. Cambridge.
CLARK, J. D.; HAYNES, C. V. 1970. An Elephant Butchery Site at Mwanganda's Village, Karonga, Malawi, and its Relevance for Palaeolithic Archaeology. *World Archaeol.*, Vol. 1, pp. 390–411.
CLARK, J. D. et al. 1984. A Middle Stone Age Occupation Site at Porc Epic cave, Dire Dawa (East-Central Ethiopia). *Afr. Archaeol. Rev.* (Cambridge), Vol. 2, pp. 37–71.

CLOSE, A. E. 1980. Current Research and Recent Radio-carbon Dates from Northern Africa. *J. Afr. Hist.* (London/New York), Vol. 21, pp. 145–67.

—— 1984. Current Research and Recent Radiocarbon Dates from Northern Africa, II. *J. Afr. Hist.* (London/New York), Vol. 25, pp. 1–24.

CONROY, G. C. et al. 1978. Newly Discovered Fossil Hominid Skull from the Afar Depression, Ethiopia. *Nature* (London), Vol. 275, pp. 67–70.

COOKE, C. K. 1971. Excavations at Zombepata Cave, Sipolilo District, Mashonaland, Rhodesia. *S. Afr. Archaeol. Bull.* (Claremont), Vol. 26, pp. 104–26.

DALLONI, M. 1955. La Station moustérienne de Retaimia près d'Inkermann (Algérie). In: BALOUT, L. (ed.), *Actes du Congrès Panafricain de Préhistoire, IIe session, Alger, 1952.* Paris. pp. 419–27.

DAY, M. H.; LEAKEY, M. D.; MAGORI, C. 1980. A New Hominid Fossil Skull (L.H.18) from the Ngaloba Beds, Laetoli, Northern Tanzania. *Nature* (London), Vol. 284, pp. 55–6.

DEACON, J. 1984. Later Stone Age People and their Descendants in Southern Africa. In: KLEIN, R. G. (ed.), *Southern African Prehistory and Palaeoenvironments.* Rotterdam. pp. 221–328.

DELIBRIAS, G.; GUILLIER, M. T.; LABEYRIE, J. 1982. Gif Natural Radiocarbon Measurements, IX. *Radiocarbon* (New Haven), Vol. 24, pp. 291–343.

ENNOUCHI, E. 1962. Un crâne d'homme ancien au Jebel Irhoud (Maroc). *C. R. Acad. Sci. Paris*, Vol. 254, pp. 4330–2.

EVERNDEN, J. F.; CURTIS, G. H. 1965. The Potassium–Argon Dating of Late Cenozoic Rocks in East Africa and Italy. *Curr. Anthropol.*, Vol. 6, pp. 343–64.

FERRING, C. R. 1975. The Aterian in North African Prehistory. In: WENDORF, F.; MARKS, A. E. (eds), *Problems in Prehistory: North Africa and the Levant.* Dallas. pp. 113–26.

GAUTIER, A. 1968. Mammalian Remains of the Northern Sudan and Southern Egypt. In: WENDORF, F. (ed.), *The Prehistory of Nubia.* Dallas. pp. 80–99.

—— 1980. Contributions to the Archaeozoology of Egypt. In: WENDORF, F.; SCHILD, R. (eds), *Prehistory of the Eastern Sahara.* New York. pp. 317–44.

GRUET, M. 1954. Le Gisement moustérien d'El-Guettar. *Karthago* (Paris), Vol. 5, pp. 1–79.

GUICHARD, J.; GUICHARD, G. 1965. The Early and Middle Paleolithic of Nubia: A Preliminary Report. In: WENDORF, F. (ed.), *Contributions to the Prehistory of Nubia.* Dallas. pp. 57–166.

HÉBRARD, L. 1970. Fichier des âges absolus du Quaternaire d'Afrique au nord de l'Equateur. *Assoc. Sénégal. Étude Quat. Ouest Afr.* (Dakar), Vol. 26, pp. 39–56.

HESTER, J. J.; HOEBLER, P. M. 1969. *Prehistoric Settlement Patterns in the Libyan Desert.* Salt Lake City.

HOURS, F. 1976. Le Middle Stone Age de Melka Kunturé. In: ABEBE, B.; CHAVAILLON, J.; SUTTON, J. E. G. (eds), *Actes du VII Congrès Panafricain de Préhistoire et de l'Étude du Quarternaire.* Addis Ababa. pp. 99–104.

HOWE, B. 1967. *The Palaeolithic of Tangier, Morocco: Excavations at Cape Ashakar, 1939–1947.* Cambridge, Mass.

HOWELL, F. C. et al. 1972. Uranium-Series Dating of Bone from the Isimila Prehistoric Site. *Nature* (London), Vol. 237, pp. 51–2.

ISAAC, G. L. 1984. The Archaeology of Human Origins: Studies of the Lower Pleistocene in East Africa 1971–1981. In: WENDORF, F.; CLOSE, A. E. (eds), *Advances in World Archaeology.* Orlando. Vol. 3, pp. 1–87.

JAEGER, J. J. 1975. The Mammalian Faunas and Hominid Fossils of the Middle Pleistocene of the Maghreb. In: BUTZER, K. W.; ISAAC, G. L. (eds), *After the Australopithecines.* The Hague. pp. 399–418.

JELINEK, A. J. 1982. The Tabun Cave and Paleolithic Man in the Levant. *Science* (Washington), Vol. 216, pp. 1369–75.

KLEIN, R. G. 1974. Environment and Subsistence of Prehistoric Man in the Southern Cape Province, South Africa. *World Archaeol.*, Vol. 5, pp. 249–84.

—— 1975. Middle Stone Age Man–Animal Relationships in Southern Africa: Evidence from Die Kelders and Klasies River Mouth. *Science* (Washington), Vol. 190, pp. 265–7.

—— 1976. A Preliminary Report on the 'Middle Stone Age' Open-Air Site of Duinefontein 2 (Melkbosstrand, South-Western Cape Province, South Africa). *S. Afr. Archaeol. Bull.* (Claremont), Vol. 31, pp. 12–20.

—— 1977. The Ecology of Early Man in Southern Africa. *Science* (Washington), Vol. 197, pp. 115–26.

—— 1979. Stone Age Exploitation of Animals in Southern Africa. *Am. Sci.* (New Haven), Vol. 67, pp. 151–60.

—— 1982. Age (Mortality) Profiles as a Means of Distinguishing Hunted Species from Scavenged Ones in Stone Age Archaeological Sites. *Paleobiol.* (Jacksonville), Vol. 8, pp. 151–8.

—— 1983. The Stone Age Prehistory of Southern Africa. *Annu. Rev. Anthropol.*, Vol. 12, pp. 25–48.

—— (ed.) 1984. *Southern African Prehistory and Palaeoenvironments.* Rotterdam.

LEAKEY, L. S. B. 1931. *The Stone Age Cultures of Kenya Colony.* Cambridge.

—— 1936. *Stone Age Africa.* Oxford.

LEAKEY, M. D. et al. 1969. An Acheulian Industry and Hominid Mandible, Lake Baringo, Kenya. *Proc. Prehist. Soc.* (Cambridge), Vol. 35, pp. 48–76.

—— 1972. Stratigraphy, Archaeology and Age of the Ndutu and Naisiusiu Beds, Olduvai Gorge, Tanzania. *World Archaeol.*, Vol. 3, pp. 328–41.

MCBURNEY, C. B. M. 1960. *The Stone Age of Northern Africa.* Harmondsworth.

—— 1967. *The Haua Fteah (Cyrenaïca) and the Stone Age of the Southeast Mediterranean.* Cambridge.

MARKS, A. E. 1968a. The Mousterian Industries of Nubia. In: WENDORF, F. (ed.), *The Prehistory of Nubia.* Dallas. pp. 194–314.

—— 1968b. The Khormusan: An Upper Pleistocene Industry in Sudanese Nubia. In: WENDORF, F. (ed.), *The Prehistory of Nubia.* Dallas. pp. 315–91.

MILLER, S. F. 1971. The Age of the Nachikufan Industries in Zambia. *S. Afr. Archaeol. Bull.* (Claremont), Vol. 26, pp. 143–6.

—— 1979. Lukenya Hill, GvJm 46, Excavation Report. *Nyame Akuma* (Calgary), Vol. 14, pp. 31–4.

O'BRIEN, T. P. 1939. *The Prehistory of Uganda Protectorate.* Cambridge.

RIGHTMIRE, G. P. 1979. Implications of Border Cave Skeletal Remains for Later Pleistocene Human Evolution. *Curr. Anthropol.*, Vol. 20, pp. 23–35.

—— 1984. The Fossil Evidence for Hominid Evolution in Southern Africa. In: KLEIN, R. G. (ed.), *Southern African Prehistory and Palaeoenvironments.* Rotterdam. pp. 147–68.

ROCHE, J. 1969. Les Industries paléolithiques de la grotte de Taforalt (Maroc oriental): méthodes d'études; evolution technique et typologique. *Quaternaria* (Rome), Vol. 11, pp. 89–100.

—— 1970–1. La Grotte de Taforalt (Maroc oriental). *Bull. Soc. Hist. Nat. Maroc* (Rabat), Vol. 3, pp. 7–14.

—— 1976. Cadre chronologique de l'Epipaléolithique marocain. In: CONGRÈS UISPP, 9, NICE. *Colloque II.* pp. 153–67.

ROUBET, F. E. 1969. Le Niveau atérien dans la stratigraphie côtière à l'Ouest d'Alger. In: ZINDEREN BAKKER, E. M.; COETZEE, J. A. (eds), *Palaeoecology of Africa.* Rotterdam. Vol. 4, pp. 124–9.

RUHLMANN, A. 1951. *La Grotte préhistorique de Dar es-Soltan.* Paris.

—— 1952. The Moroccan Aterian and its Sub-divisions. In: LEAKEY, L. S. B.; COLE, S. (eds), *Proceedings of the Pan-African Congress on Prehistory, 1947.* New York. pp. 210–22.

SABAN, R. 1975. Les Restes humains de Rabat (Kébibat). *Ann. Paléontol. (Vertébr.)* (Paris), Vol. 61, pp. 153–207.

SAMPSON, C. G. 1968. The Middle Stone Age Industries of the Orange River Scheme area. *Mem. Natl. Mus.* (Bloemfontein), Vol. 4, pp. 1–111.

—— 1974. The Stone Age Archaeology of Southern Africa. New York.

SANDFORD, K. S.; ARKELL, W. J. 1939. *Paleolithic Man and the Nile Valley in Lower Egypt.* Chicago.

SCHILD, R.; WENDORF, F. 1981. *The Prehistory of an Egyptian Oasis.* Wroclaw.

SHACKLETON, N. J. 1982. Stratigraphy and Chronology of the KRM Deposits: Oxygen Isotope Evidence. In: SINGER, R.; WYMER, J.

(eds), *The Middle Stone Age at Klasies River Mouth in South Africa*. Chicago. pp. 194–9.

SINGER, R.; WYMER, J. (eds) 1982. *The Middle Stone Age at Klasies River Mouth in South Africa*. Chicago.

SINGLETON, W. L.; CLOSE, A. E. 1978. Report of Site E-78-11. In: WENDORF, F.; SCHILD, R.; CLOSE, A. E. (eds), *Loaves and Fishes: The Prehistory of Wadi Kubbaniya*. Dallas. pp. 229-37.

STRINGER, C. B.; HOWELL, F. C.; MELENTIS, J. K. 1979. The Significance of the Fossil Hominid Skull from Petralona, Greece. *J. Archaeol. Sci.* (London/New York), Vol. 6, pp. 235–53.

SZABO, B. J.; BUTZER, K. W. 1979. Uranium-Series Dating of Lacustrine Limestones from Pan Deposits with a Final Acheulian Assemblage at Rooidam, Kimberley District, South Africa. *Quat. Res.* (New York), Vol. 11, pp. 257–60.

TILLET, T. 1983. *Le Paléolithique du Basin Tchadien Septentrional (Niger-Tchad)*. Paris.

TIXIER, J. 1967. Procédés d'analyse et questions de terminologie concernant l'étude des ensembles industriels du Paléolithique récent et de l'Epipaléolithique dans l'Afrique du Nord-Ouest. In: BISHOP, W. W.; CLARK, J. D. (eds), *Background to Evolution in Africa*. Chicago. pp. 771–820.

TRINKAUS, E. 1982. Evolutionary Continuity among Archaic *Homo sapiens*. In: RONEN, A. (ed.), *The Transition from Lower to Middle Palaeolithic and the Origin of Modern Man*. Oxford. pp. 301–14. (BAR Int. Ser., 5.)

VALLOIS, H. V.; ROCHE, J. 1958. La Mandibule acheuléene de Témara, Maroc. *C. R. Acad. Sciences Paris,* Ser. D, Vol. 246, pp. 3113–16.

VERMEERSCH, P. M. et al. 1982. Blade Technology in the Egyptian Nile Valley: Some New Evidence. *Science* (Washington), Vol. 216, pp. 626–8.

—— 1984. 33,000 Year Old Chert Mining Site and Related *Homo* in the Egyptian Nile Valley. *Nature* (London), Vol. 309, pp. 342–4.

VOLMAN, T. P. 1984. Early Prehistory of Southern Africa. In: KLEIN, R. G. (ed.), *Southern African Prehistory and Palaeoenvironments*. Rotterdam. pp. 169–220.

WENDORF, F.; SCHILD, R. 1974. *A Middle Stone Age Sequence from the Central Rift Valley, Ethiopia*. Wroclaw.

—— 1976. The Middle Paleolithic of Northeastern Africa: New Data and Concepts. In: CONGRÈS UISPP, 9, NICE. *Colloque III.* pp. 8–34.

—— 1980. *Prehistory of the Eastern Sahara*. New York.

WENDORF, F.; SCHILD, R.; CLOSE, A. E. (eds) 1986. *The Prehistory Wadi Kubbaniya Human Skeleton*. Vol. 1: *The Wadi Kubbaiya Skeleton: A Late Paleolithic Burial from Southern Egypt*. Dallas.

WENDORF, F.; SCHILD, R.; HAAS, H. 1979. A New Radiocarbon Chronology for Prehistoric Sites in Nubia. *J. Field Archaeol.*, Vol. 6, pp. 219–23.

WENDT, W. E. 1976. 'Art mobilier' from the Apollo 11 Cave, South West Africa: Africa's Oldest Dated Works of Art. *S. Afr. Archaeol. Bull.* (Claremont), Vol. 31, pp. 5–11.

12

EUROPE
(EXCLUDING THE FORMER USSR)

in the period of *Homo sapiens neanderthalensis* and
contemporaries

Karel Valoch

In the cultural scheme of the Old Stone Age devised by the French archaeologist G. de Mortillet towards 1870, the Mousterian was considered to mark the half-way stage in the Palaeolithic of Europe (de Mortillet and de Mortillet, 1900). The name Mousterian comes from the shelter at Le Moustier, an important site on the right bank of the Vézère (Dordogne, France). This view, which made the Middle Palaeolithic a short period of about 40,000 years, and the typical culture of the Neanderthal hominids the Mousterian, was current until quite recently.

The beginning of the Middle Palaeolithic certainly does not mark a break in cultural evolution but is more a conventional dividing line, based on the state of our present knowledge. None the less, the industries of the Lower Palaeolithic, dating from the preceding interglacial period (variously known as Mindel–Riss, Holstein, Hoxnian or Lichvino), are much less differentiated, lacking many of the features that appear in the industries of the Riss glaciation.

It was on the basis of these Lower Palaeolithic complexes that the different cultural traditions of the Middle Palaeolithic began to emerge, at the beginning of the penultimate glaciation. Although this development was probably conditioned to some extent by ecological changes brought about by the beginning of the glaciation, the development in material culture is essentially due to the development of human manual and psychological capacities, and of his intellect, at the time when the *Homo erectus* population was changing into a *Homo sapiens* population in the broad sense of the term.

ECOLOGY

The first *sapiens* groups began to spread over Europe approximately at the time of the penultimate glaciation, when the Scandinavian glacier gradually covered the greater part of Germany and Poland, and the mountain glaciers expanded down to much lower altitudes. It was the first time that human populations had dared to settle in periglacial regions, where climatic conditions were very much influenced by the proximity of the glaciers. The fauna of these periglacial regions was boreal, represented by mammoth, woolly rhinoceros, reindeer and other animals that today are extinct or live in cold steppes or in arctic regions. The vegetation was poor, being a typical steppe or tundra flora.

This penultimate glaciation, which lasted for about 100,000 years, was interrupted by one or two well-marked warmer periods during which the glaciers retreated towards the north or to the higher mountains. During these interstadials, of which it is still not possible to determine the duration, animals adapted to warmer conditions and living in southern Europe returned to the boreal zone, where woods also began to grow again.

The middle phase of the Middle Palaeolithic coincides with the last interglacial period, during which climatic conditions and vegetation in Europe were comparable to those of today, although the average temperature was a few degrees higher. The fauna was characterized by animals that live in woods or in temperate steppes, for instance the wood elephant, the steppe rhinoceros and herds of wild bovines, Cervidae and horses.

The late phase of the Middle Palaeolithic falls within the first half of the last glaciation. The transition from the interglacial to the glaciation was marked by a gradual worsening of the climate, as a result of a new advance of the glaciers in Scandinavia and in the mountainous regions. In the temperate zone of western and central Europe, the boreal fauna returned and the vegetation readjusted to periglacial conditions. However, the cold climate did not reach its peak at the time: the coldest phase of the last glaciation occurred only during its second half, at a time when Europe was already inhabited by *Homo sapiens sapiens*, Modern human beings.

THE MATERIAL CULTURE OF THE MIDDLE PALAEOLITHIC

Stone was still the most frequently used raw material for making artefacts. As their production was very easy and the quantity of raw material was more important than its quality (this is confirmed by experiments made by many archaeologists), every dwelling site has yielded hundreds or even thousands of them. Stone is practically imperishable, and stone and flint implements are still found even when a whole site has been destroyed. Throughout the Middle Palaeolithic, the most important stone implements were side-scrapers and retouched flakes of different shapes which, as shown by microwear analysis, were mostly used as knives and sometimes provided with wooden, bone or antler handles. Next in importance to side-scrapers are numerous points with carefully retouched converging edges. These points were undoubtedly attached to wooden shafts: such spears were important hunting weapons. In some industries there are also many implements the side of which has an intentionally retouched notch or series of smaller notches, the so-called 'denticulates'. The exact function of these notched artefacts and denticulates is still unknown. Bifaces, already present in the industries of the Lower Palaeolithic, still survive, but now they are more carefully retouched, thinner, and almond- or heart-shaped. Along with these basic types of implements, the Middle Palaeolithic industries include many other tools, but generally in small quantities; some of them (scrapers, burins, borers) already foreshadow Upper Palaeolithic implements.

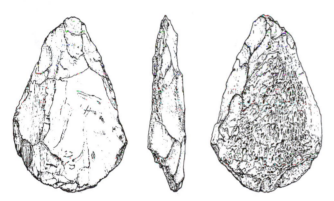

Figure 17 Ivory handaxe, Rhede (Germany). (After Tromnau, 1983.)

Artefacts made of organic material decay much more readily and are therefore preserved only in favourable conditions. Middle Palaeolithic tools of bone or antler are rare and too exceptional to allow a typological classification. In some cases one can observe some wear traces which can give some indication of the function of such implements. Bone and ivory artefacts are often found isolated or in very small numbers (Fig. 17), and it happens not infrequently that they are not even mentioned in the publications. Artefacts of reindeer or deer antler are more frequently found. They are mostly considered to have been used as clubs; some may also have been the handles of stone tools. Flakes of thick bone have sometimes been retouched in the same way as flint implements, but even so a standardized typology seems not to have existed; their retouched sides are rather similar to those of the side-scrapers. Ribs of animals sometimes have a rounded or sharpened end. In some cases the end or the sides of bone flakes are polished. The only bone artefacts which in some industries are more numerous are tools for trimming the sides of stone implements by percussion or by pressure-flaking. Those of the La Quina industry were carefully studied (Martin, 1907–10). Bones often show chance traces of butchering activities. They were also used as a support to facilitate the cutting of skins or sinews. In this way traces on bones can reveal many and various human activities (Martin, 1907–10; Binford, 1981).

Wooden weapons and tools have certainly played an important role in the hunting and gathering of food; evidence of their existence, however, is very scarce. The spear from Lehringen (Germany) (Fig. 9) has already been mentioned (Chapter 10); a fragment of a sharp-pointed stick, 29 cm long, has been found at Königsaue (Germany) (Mania and Toepfer, 1973); the site of Krapina (Slovenia) has yielded a small stake with a burnt end, which had probably been used to poke the fire (Oakley, 1958).

Many lithic implements had to be hafted. A remarkable proof of this was discovered at Königsaue: two small blocks of resin which had been used to fasten the edge of a tool to its haft. On one of them, the impression of four small flake scars made by the flat retouching of a bifacial tool were still visible. The resin casing had probably been glued in a bone or wooden handle (Mania and Toepfer, 1973).

The lithic industry represents the most important and in some cases the only category of archaeological remains of this period; it is therefore on this foundation that archaeologists have built up a system of cultures. On the basis of manifold technological and morphological criteria they not only have established differences between industries from different sites, but have also delimited groups of industries with very similar features (Figs 18–21). These technological and typological complexes have then been considered to represent archaeological cultures. Their names are derived from those of important sites.

The different cultural traditions, each recognizable by different technical and typological features, developed along parallel lines and, in principle, independently both of the ecological conditions and of the activities engaged in. It does

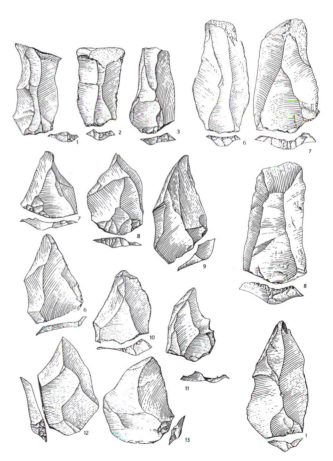

Figure 18 Lamellar flakes and Levallois points, Königsaue (Germany). (After Mania and Toepfer, 1973.)

seem that the lithic industries, which are an element of material culture much influenced by tradition, reflect ethnic differences between their creators.[1]

In Europe we see very great differentiation between various industries in the Middle Palaeolithic, and the creation of a great many cultural traditions, groups and facies. At the beginning of the 1950s, the Mousterian-type industries were defined and clearly differentiated on the basis of technical and typological criteria with the help of statistical indexes. The technical criteria are the presence or absence of the Levallois (prepared-core) technique, the faceting of the butt of the flake artefacts and the type of secondary trimming. Typological criteria are essentially the percentage of side-scrapers, denticulates and other types of tool (Bordes, 1950a, 1950b, 1953b, 1954). The chronological relationship between the different types of industry has been deduced from stratigraphical data, and a model has been created to illustrate the 'branching' evolution (évolution buissonnante) of the Mousterian complex during the first half of the Würm glaciation.

The differentiation between the material remains began approximately 200,000 years ago, with the appearance of the very heterogeneous group of the first *Homo sapiens* (pre-Neanderthal, pre-*sapiens*) (Chapter 9). It may be connected with the fact that these people began to fabricate tools of various shapes for various activities; these tool shapes were gradually standardized and became part of the cultural traditions of the different groups. A very important technological innovation, connected with the very beginnings of the Middle Palaeolithic, was the invention of the Levallois technique (Chapter 10), which allowed a series of flakes of predetermined form to be obtained from a prepared core. These flakes could easily be trimmed to make side-scrapers and points.

During the first phase of the Middle Palaeolithic, the

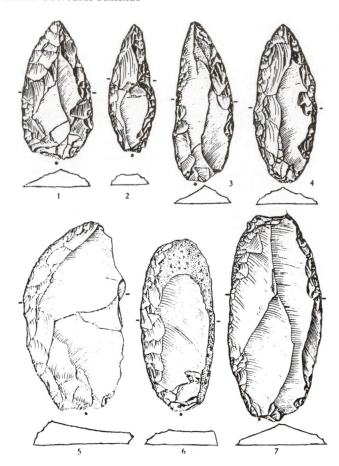

Figure 20 Charentian of La Ferrassie type, La Ferrassie (France). 1–4, points; 5–6, side-scrapers; 7, double side-scraper. (After Bosinski, 1985.)

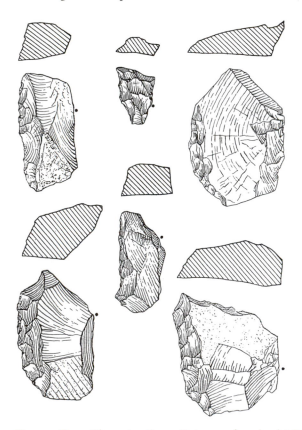

Figure 19 Proto-Charentian, Proto-Quina: artefacts, level 6, Bečov (former Czechoslovakia). (After Fridrich, 1982.)

biface was still a very important tool, especially in western Europe and Italy. It is typical of the Acheulean, which spread no further than the western part of central Europe (Bohemia). Further to the east and south-east, bifaces are found only sporadically in various cultural complexes. In the Acheulean sites, bifaces are often found together with flake-tools obtained by the Levallois technique. Alongside this very heterogeneous complex of biface industries, an equally heterogeneous complex of industries without bifaces spread all over Europe. One of these industries is the Tayacian, widespread in Mediterranean France and in Liguria (Italy). It is characterized by the small size of the tools, generally trimmed from pebbles of different kinds of stone. The Acheulean and the Tayacian are a continuation of the evolution of the Lower Palaeolithic, and the Tayacian resembles the microchopper complex of the Holstein interglacial. The 'proto-Pontinian' (or 'pre-Mousterian') industry from the area around Rome is slightly different from the Tayacian; here also the tools are made on small pebbles.

It is during this first phase of the Middle Palaeolithic that one can place the beginning of the 'branching' differentiation of the Mousterian complex, which was to reach its full development during the late phase. It began with the differentiation between the cultures that adopted the Levallois technique of preparing a core for the production of flakes, and those without knowledge of this technique. In this way, separate industries were born, each with a specific typological toolkit. The number of known sites is as yet not very great, but they are spread all over Europe, from southern England, through western and southern Europe where they

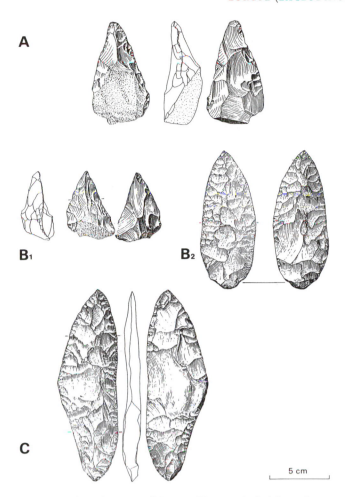

A

B₁

B₂

C

5 cm

Figure 21 Micoquian, central Europe (Germany). A, Micoquian handaxe, Bocksteinschmiede; B1, Small handaxe (*Fäustel*), Königsaue; B2, Leaf-shaped handaxe (*Faustkeilblatt*), Königsaue; C, Handaxe-knife (*Faustkeilmesser*), Königsaue. (After Wetsel and Bosinski, 1969, and Mania and Toepfer, 1973.)

During this last interglacial one finds in central Europe a specific group of microlithic industries, with tools made of small pebbles without the Levallois technique (the Taubachian). Typologically these industries are very close to the Tayacian of the preceding period, but it is still unclear if they are also genetically related. From an ecological point of view it is interesting to note that, with the exception of a single camping site (the Kůlna cave in Moravia), all the Taubachian sites are situated near to mineral sources. They are now covered by layers, sometimes very thick, of travertine, formed by the sedimentation of chalk water. Travertines are wonderful preservers not only of stone objects, but also of bones, mollusc shells and plant remains, giving us a great deal of information on the natural environment.

But in fact we possess far less evidence of this middle phase of the Middle Palaeolithic, because during this warm and humid period, pedogenesis, weathering and erosion affected both open sites and shallow caves, destroying archaeological evidence. In the caves there was also much less sedimentation than during the glaciations, so fewer objects have been preserved in this way.

We are better informed about the late phase of the Middle Palaeolithic, because a fair number of encampments of this period have been preserved in nearly all the countries of Europe. This phase also saw the full development of the 'branching' evolution of the lithic industries. This evolution has been brought to light with the help of statistical indexes, in Périgord, the Paris area and the Mediterranean region in France (Bordes, 1950b, 1953b, 1954; Bordes and Bourgon, 1951; Bourgon, 1957; de Lumley, 1969, 1971). It seems that the Neanderthal population was more numerous and Europe more densely inhabited than during the previous phases. The whole Mousterian complex has been divided up into tool types on the basis of technical and typological criteria. By collating the distribution and quantitative representation of these tool types, F. Bordes has proposed four groups of industries, each subdivided into subgroups and facies (Bordes, 1957, 1961).

From the point of view of the subsequent evolution, the most important group is the Mousterian of Acheulean tradition, which has bifaces and carries on the Acheulean of the previous phases. It is spread over western Europe (including England) but absent in central and in southwestern Europe. It seems probable that one of its facies gave birth to the Châtelperronian, the oldest industry of the Upper Palaeolithic in western Europe, but still created by the Neanderthalers (such as represented by the Saint-Césaire human; Chapter 9).

The Typical Mousterian, with many points and side-scrapers, is also spread over western Europe, but appears sporadically even in other regions.

The two remaining groups, the Denticulate Mousterian and the Charentian, are spread all over Europe, including the former USSR, but their greatest typological diversity can be observed in western Europe. The first is characterized by a high percentage of denticulates and of notched tools, the second by a high proportion of finely retouched side-scrapers, mostly of the convex or transverse varieties. The Charentian has two subgroups, the Quina facies, without the Levallois technique and the Ferrassie facies with this technique (Fig. 20).

Of the other Mousterian groups, one must mention the 'blade facies of the Mousterian', which is known only from a few sites; with its special technology for the production of narrow blades, it is a forerunner of the later Upper Palaeolithic.

are relatively numerous, to the Balkans and central Europe. These sites are, however, more numerous than those of *Homo erectus* from the late phase of the Lower Palaeolithic. It seems that the population of the first *Homo sapiens* (in the broad sense) was larger and spread over wider regions than the former population of *Homo erectus*. It would not be very wise, however, to claim a direct connection between the number of known sites and the density of the population of a given period, because one should never forget that the older the sites are, the more of them have been destroyed, erased by natural agents.

The evolution begun during the penultimate glaciation continued throughout the last interglacial (130,000–100,000 years ago). The Acheulean complex with bifaces entered its last phase. Its territory was only slightly enlarged in the north European plain. Towards the end of the interglacial, the biface tradition was revived in central Europe, in a new culture, the Micoquian (Fig. 21), which, however, reached its full development only during the late phase of the Middle Palaeolithic. Western Europe saw the development of different groups of the Mousterian complex, without bifaces and with or without Levallois flaking. These groups originated during the previous interglacial phase. The mild climate made it possible for humans to inhabit (or at least to visit periodically) some Alpine caves at high altitude (Repolust in Austria, Drachenloch in Switzerland), which, during the glaciation, had been covered by ice and snow.

In central and eastern Europe the most important culture of the early Würm is the Micoquian (Fig. 21), which originated at the end of the last interglacial. It is present in many sites of Germany, all over the Balkans and in Ukraine, is frequent in Crimea and has even been found as far as near Volgograd on the Volga. Like the Mousterian of Acheulean tradition, it is characterized by bifaces of various types but also by other specific artefacts such as knives with bifacial flat retouch and leaf-shaped points which are actually small, thin, carefully trimmed bifaces; these were used not only as knives but also as spearheads, and their importance as efficient weapons became even greater in the succeeding cultures of the Upper Palaeolithic.

The first half of the last glaciation thus saw a rapid 'branching' of the Mousterian. This development, however, was only the peak of a long evolution which had already begun, together with the development of the Neanderthalers, during the penultimate glaciation. During this whole period some cultures showed an extraordinary vitality (for instance the biface cultures), others disappeared either during the Middle Palaeolithic without leaving any offshoot (for instance the Taubachian) or at its end, and did not contribute to the formation of the subsequent cultures of Modern humans.

The causes of the birth and the existence of so many cultures, each with various facies, of the Neanderthalers still remain unclear. It is certain that not only in south-western France, where F. Bordes first pointed out this fact, but also throughout Europe, different types of cultures existed simultaneously in the same region. Three hypotheses have been advanced to explain this situation.

According to the first, the different technological and typological groups would represent different evolutionary phases of a single culture (Mellars, 1969). This theory is based on some important sites in south-western Europe, where there is an identical stratigraphic sequence of different Mousterian facies. In other sites, however, the sequence is different, and it does not support the claimed evolution.

The second theory is founded on the contention that the Neanderthalers had rather differentiated tools and that therefore each type of tool was used for a well-defined activity. The whole range of tools found on a site would reflect specific activities on the site at a given moment (Binford and Binford, 1966; Freeman, 1966). Microwear analysis of the tools and modern experiments with these tools have proved, however, that the shape of a tool does not depend directly on its function, that the same type of tool could be used for different activities and, vice versa, that the same activity could be performed with tools of different types. It is therefore very doubtful that the technological and typological characteristics of a given set of tools would depend only on a given function. Besides, it seems indubitable that all the activities necessary for the daily life of a community of hunters, women and children took place in every encampment, even if it was inhabited only for a short time. Sites that were used only for a single specialized activity (such as workshops for the production of lithic tools or camping sites occupied only during seasonal hunting) were, during the Middle Palaeolithic, extremely rare.

According to the third theory (actually the oldest one, but later improved under the influence of the other two hypotheses), the techniques of production of lithic artefacts, their function and their types were part of the cultural traditions of particular human communities. This meant that groups with different traditions could live side by side in a relatively small territory, and that these traditions were transmitted from generation to generation, evolving very slowly during the long period of the Middle Palaeolithic. The same theory of cultural traditions could also explain the relations between different periods of the Palaeolithic, especially the transition from the Middle to the Upper Palaeolithic. Many aspects, however, still remain hard to understand, for instance why and how some cultures spread over the whole of Europe while others remained limited to a smaller territory.

GENERAL CONSIDERATIONS

There are in principle two major typological and technical trends in the evolution of the Middle Palaeolithic in Europe. The technical differences depend on whether or not the Levallois technique was used for the preparation and the flaking of cores. There is thus a phylum of industries using Levallois flaking and another of industries with little or no Levallois flaking. From the typological point of view the distinction is between the phylum of industries with bifaces and that without bifaces. The former consists of the Acheulean complex and its derivatives, including the Micoquian in central Europe, and similar industries in eastern Europe (southern Ukraine, Crimea, Volgograd). The phylum of industries without bifaces is made up of several groups and facies defined in terms of technical and typological criteria. A number of these industries already emerge at the beginning of the Middle Palaeolithic, during the early phase of the Riss glaciation.

Different groups and facies existed side by side, especially during the recent phase, within relatively small areas, and one must not be surprised at the influence and the cultural diffusion of certain types (bifaces, leaf-shaped points) and their further development into new local variants. We see this phenomenon particularly in western Europe, which was more densely populated.

Towards the middle of the Würm, about 40,000 or 35,000 years ago, the industries of the Upper Palaeolithic appeared throughout Europe, and *Homo sapiens neanderthalensis* gave way to Modern humans, *Homo sapiens sapiens*. We find very few convincing traces, in the Middle Palaeolithic, of any trend which could have led to the blade industries of the Upper Palaeolithic. The Mousterian 'blade facies' industries of Rheindalen (Germany), Seclin (France) and Rocourt (Belgium) are too early: several tens of thousands of years were to pass before the beginning of the Upper Palaeolithic. But there were very similar industries in France. These were the blade Mousterian of Fontmaure and the Levallois facies blade Mousterian of the Maras shelter (layer 3–2), these two industries containing many Upper Palaeolithic types. Type B of the Mousterian of Acheulean Tradition with backed knives has been considered the forerunner of the Châtelperronian, the oldest industry of the Upper Palaeolithic in western Europe, although it emerged more than 35,000 years later (Bordes, 1958, 1972). Now there are doubts regarding the continuity of the two cultures, although the bones of a typical Neanderthaler have been found in the Châtelperronian of Saint-Césaire in France (Levêque and Vandermeersch, 1981). In central Europe the late Micoquian and the Aurignacian together gave rise to a new culture with leaf points: the Szeletian. In central and in south-eastern Europe, the beginnings of the Upper Palaeolithic are dated to more than 40,000 years ago (Valoch, 1984b).

VARIOUS ACTIVITIES OF THE PALAEOANTHROPIANS

Hunting techniques, and their division into specialized branches, have already been mentioned (Chapter 10). However, the discovery of hunting sites is exceptional. At Lehringen (Germany), *Elephas antiquus* had been hunted into a marsh, where it became bogged down. It was then transfixed by a wooden spear, which remained stuck between the ribs of the partly preserved skeleton. Nearby, fifteen scattered Levallois flakes were discovered, which had probably been used as knives to cut up the skin and the meat. Lehringen is a typical 'kill-site' with the trap, the death-dealing weapon and the tools that would subsequently be necessary, doubtless purpose-made on the spot.

Evidence of a non-utilitarian behaviour among the Palaeoanthropians or of 'spirituality' is very rare, but so convincing that there can be no doubt of their psychic maturity. The Neanderthalers used mineral dyes: manganese dioxide, red and yellow ochre (Pech de l'Azé, La Ferrassie, L'Ermitage, La Quina – four French sites). The blocks of colouring matter have often been scraped or sharpened. At Kůlna, in layer 7c, a small slab of red slate scratched on one side has even been discovered and, in layer 7a, a block of light-grey limestone chalk, also scratched.

The engravings of Pech de l'Azé (Fig. 10) and Tata (Hungary) are well enough known (Chapter 10). A flat, black pebble with two incised parallel lines comes from Erd (Hungary). On bones at La Quina, besides many accidental marks, intentionally carved marks are also found, sometimes forming groups of parallel incisions but also, it seems, simple figures (Kůlna, layer 7c).

All the engravings from the Middle Palaeolithic consist of lines which, in rare cases, perhaps form abstract figures. Although they have undoubtedly played a role in the development of the spiritual life of the Neanderthalers, they can scarcely be considered as the beginning of artistic creativity. According to some authors some figurative representations did already exist (a representation of an animal at Molodova I on the Dniester (Fig. 11); an anthropomorphic sculpture at Bečov in Bohemia (Chapter 10), but they are entirely isolated, and are not even proved. Some specialists also doubt whether the engraving on a rib at Pech de l'Azé was actually intentional.

One of the most important pieces of evidence on the level of spiritual and social life reached by the Neanderthalers is given by the burials that appear during the recent phase of the Middle Palaeolithic (Chapter 10). They provide clear indications that there already existed well-developed customs and ceremonies, which probably originated during previous phases. However, the number of interments discovered certainly bears no relation to the actual number of people living at a given camp site. This means that the dead were only exceptionally buried in such a way that their bones have been preserved until our day. This remark is true not only of the Neanderthalers, but also of humans of the Modern type, of the Upper Palaeolithic, a period that has also only very exceptionally yielded burials. These Upper Palaeolithic interments are certainly more numerous than those of the Middle Palaeolithic, but as the population throughout Europe was certainly much denser than during the Middle Palaeolithic these burials represent only a very small percentage of the actual population. In both cases the explanation of this fact is to be looked for in the spiritual realm, in the customs and ceremonies concerning the treatment of the deceased.

All these new data allow us to deduce that the Neanderthaler had reached a much higher psychic level than was thought not so very long ago. The existence of burial rituals testifies to some social relations within human groups and to the general consciousness of death. For the very first time human beings were aware of the fact that their life was limited. All this involves an already quite developed capacity of abstract thought and the possibility of expressing it in words and of communicating it to others.

On the other hand, one should be very cautious about the so-called proofs of bear worship and of other cults so often mentioned in the literature. Their rejection would contribute to a more objective view on the Neanderthalers who lived more than 40,000 years ago and who had already reached a remarkable intellectual level.

The organization of the encampments gives us more idea of their life-style. It is, however, exceptional to find an interior space as detailed in structure as that of the Lazaret cave (Nice, France) (Chapter 10). Most often, caves seem to have been used as hunting halts, with a hearth, animal bones and some tools. Less often, we find an encampment with a living floor that has, in addition to the hearth, an artificial structure in stone or a concentration of animal bones. The dwelling floor of La Caune de l'Arago (France) is covered with scattered stones and animal bones, among which stone tools and a skull have been found. The site of La Cotte de Saint-Brelade (Jersey) has yielded two heaps of mammoth and rhinoceros bones, mostly of young animals. The Reindeer and Hyena caves at Arcy-sur-Cure and the cave of L'Hortus offer a good deal of information on the recent phase. At Combe-Grenal (France) a hole for a pointed stake 27 cm long has been found, probably having formed part of the construction of a hut. Cabins seem to have been built in the cave of the Verrerie (Macassargues), at Combe-Capelle and at Baume des Peyzards (France), where they were marked by a line of large blocks (de Lumley and Boone, 1976; Scott, 1980).

Of the open sites, part of a living floor with the remains of bones has been discovered at Ariendorf and a larger surface at Bianche-Saint-Vaast (France) and Casal de Pazzi (Italy), all in Rissian deposits (Bosinski, 1985; Tuffreau, 1978b; Anzidei, 1984). The late phase is represented by different dwelling structures in several sites found in central and in south-east Europe. At Erd (Hungary) several dwelling areas have been discovered: in levels b and c, heaps of bone with a hearth in the centre; in level d, a hearth with blocks of burned calcite. At Ripiceni-Izvor (Romania), Mousterian level III, there were three structures: first, a heap of thirty mammoth tusks, thirty-six molars, other bones and some very large stones (9.6 by 4.3 m); next, big flint blocks and tools concentrated in a shallow depression 3.1 by 2.7 m; and finally, a pit 0.6 m deep and 0.75 m in diameter, with fragments of mammoth bones, in the centre of a concentration of blocks and tools over an area 3.6 by 2.5 m. The subjacent level I revealed a hearth with scattered charcoal and bones, some burned, some not. At Remeta-Somos II (Romania) a workshop has been discovered covering an area of 1.3 by 1.0 m with a depth of 0.5 m, containing 102 flakes and three cores; 2.5 m away there is a slightly hollowed out fireplace (Gábori-Csánk, 1968; Paunescu, 1965; Bitiri, 1972). Although these observations are fragmentary, they allow us none the less to conclude that the people of the Middle Palaeolithic built fixed encampments with huts or tents. Along with these there were also hunting or temporary camps.

BIBLIOGRAPHY

ANZIDEI, A. P. 1984. Casal de 'Pazzi, Lazio. In: SOPRINTENDENZA SPECIALE DEL MUSEO PIGORINI. *I Primi abitanti d'Europa*. Rome. pp. 202–7.

ARCA, M. et al. 1984. Sa Pedrosa-Pantallinu, Sardegna. In: SOPRINTENDENZA SPECIALE DEL MUSEO PIGORINI. *I Primi abitanti d'Europa*. Rome. pp. 190–3.

BASLER, D. (ed.) 1975. *Crvena Stijena*. Niksic.

—— 1979. Nalazista paleolitickog i mezolitickog doba u Bosni i Hercegovini [Findings of the Palaeolithic and the Mesolithic Period in Bosnia-Herzegovina]. In: BASLER, D. (ed.), *Praistorija jugoslavenskich zemalja: I – Paleolitsko i mezolitsko doba*. Sarajevo. pp. 313–55.

BAUMANN, W.; MANIA, D. 1983. *Die paläolithischen Neufunde von Markkleeberg bei Leipzig*. Berlin.

BIDDITTU, I.; SEGRE, A. G.; PIPERNO, M. 1984. Torre in Pietra, Lazio. In: SOPRINTENDENZA SPECIALE DEL MUSEO PIGORINI. *I Primi abitanti d'Europa*. Rome. pp. 168–73.

BINFORD, L. R. 1981. *Bones: Ancient Men and Modern Myths*. New York/London.

BINFORD, L. R.; BINFORD, S. R. 1966. A Preliminary Analysis of Functional Variability in the Mousterian of Levallois Facies. *Am. Anthropol.* (Washington), Vol. 68, No. 2, Part 1, pp. 508–12.

BITIRI, M. 1967. Paläolithische Blattspitzen in Rumänien. *Quartär* (Bonn), Vol. 18, pp. 139–55.

—— 1972. *Paleoliticul in Tara Oaşului*. Bucureşti.

BLANC, A. C. 1942. I Paleantropi di Saccopastore e del Circeo. *Quartär* (Bonn), Vol. 4, pp. 1–37.

BORDES, F. 1950a. Principes d'une méthode d'étude des techniques de débitage et de la typologie du Paléolithique ancien et moyen. *Anthropologie* (Paris), Vol. 54, pp. 19–34.

—— 1950b. L'Évolution buissonnante des industries en Europe occidentale: considération théorique sur le Paléolithique ancien et moyen. *Anthropologie* (Paris), Vol. 54, pp. 393–420.

—— 1953a. Levalloisien et Moustérien. *Bull. Soc. Préhist. Fr.*, Vol. 50, pp. 226–34.

—— 1953b. Essai de classification des industries moustériennes. *Bull. Soc. Préhist. Fr.*, Vol. 50, pp. 457–66.

—— 1954. *Les Limons quaternaires du bassin de la Seine*. Paris.

—— 1957. La Classification du Moustérien: état actuel. In: *LEXIQUE Stratigraphique International* (Paris). Vol. 1, fasc. 4b, pp. 73–7.

—— 1958. Le Passage du Paléolithique moyen au Paléolithique supérieur. In: KOENIGSWALD, G. H. R. VON (ed.), *Hundert Jahre Neanderthaler 1856–1956*. Cologne/Graz. pp. 175–81.

—— 1961. Mousterian Cultures in France. *Science* (Washington), Vol. 134, No. 3482, pp. 803–10.

—— 1972. *A Tale of Two Caves*. New York.

BORDES, F.; BOURGON, M. 1951. Le Complexe Moustérien: Moustériens, Levalloisien et Tayacien. *Anthropologie* (Paris), Vol. 55, pp. 1–23.

BOSINSKI, G. 1967. *Die mittelpaläolithischen Funde im westlichen Mitteleuropa*. Cologne/Graz.

—— 1970. Bemerkungen zu der Grabung D. Peyronys in La Micoque. In: SCHWABEDISSEN, H. (ed.), *Frühe Menschheit und Umwelt*. Cologne/Graz. Vol. 1, pp. 52–6.

—— 1984. Chronostratigraphie du Paléolithique inférieur et moyen en Rhénanie. In: CONGRÈS PRÉHISTORIQUE DE FRANCE, 22, Lille. *Colloque*. 12 pp.

—— 1985. *Der Neanderthaler und seine Zeit*. Cologne.

BOSINSKI, G.; BRUNNACKER, K.; TURNER, E. 1983. Ein Siedlungsbefund des frühen Mittelpaläolithikums von Ariendorf, Kr. Neuwied. *Archäol. Korresp.*, Vol. 13, pp. 157–69.

BOURGON, M. 1957. *Les Industries moustériennens et pré-moustériennes en Périgord*. Paris.

BRODAR, M.; OSOLE, F. 1979. Nalazišta paleolitskog i mezolitskog doba u Sloveniji [Findings of the Palaeolithic and Mesolithic Period in Slovenia]. In: BASLER, D. (ed.), *Praistorija jugoslavenskich zemalja*, Vol. I: *Paleolitsko i mezolitsko doba*. Sarajevo. pp. 135–94.

BRUNNACKER, K. et al. 1983. Radiometrische Untersuchungen zur Datierung mitteleuropäischer Travertinvorkommen. *Ethnogr.-Archäol. Z.* (Berlin), Vol. 24, No. 2, pp. 217–66.

CAHEN, D. 1984. Paléolithique inférieur et moyen en Belgique. In: CAHEN, D.; HAESAERTS, P. (eds), *Peuples chasseurs de la Belgique préhistorique dans leur cadre naturel*. Brussels. pp. 133–55.

CALLOW, O. 1984. The Saalian Industries of La Cotte de Saint Brelade, Jersey. In: CONGRÈS PRÉHISTORIQUE DE FRANCE, 22, Lille. *Colloque*. 34 pp.

CHAVAILLON, J.; CHAVAILLON, S.; HOURS, F. 1967. Industries paleolithiques de l'Élide: I – Région d'Amelias. *Bull. Corresp. Hell.* (Paris), Vol. 91, pp. 151–99.

—— 1969. Industries paléolithiques de l'Élide: II – Région du Kastron. *Bull. Corresp. Hell.* (Paris), Vol. 93, pp. 97–149.

CHMIELEWSKI, W. 1975. Paleolit środkwoy i górny [Middle and Upper Palaeolithic]. In: CHMIELEWSKI, W.; HENSEL, W. (eds), *Prahistoria ziem Polskich: T.I Paleolit i mezolit*. Wroclaw/Warsaw. pp. 9–158.

CLARK, J. D. 1982. The Transition from Lower to Middle Palaeolithic in the African Continent. In: RONEN, A. (ed.), *The Transition from Lower to Middle Palaeolithic and the Origin of Modern Man*. Oxford. pp. 235–55. (BAR Int. Ser., 151.)

COMBIER, J. 1967. *Le Paléolithique de l'Ardèche*. Bordeaux.

DAKARIS, S. I.; HIGGS, E. S.; HEY, R. W. 1964. The Climate, Environment and Industries of Stone Age Greece: Part I. *Proc. Prehist. Soc.*, Vol. 30, pp. 199–244.

DEBENATH, A. 1976. Les Civilisations du Paléolithique inférieur en Charente. In: LUMLEY, H. de (ed.), *La Préhistoire française*. Paris, CNRS. T. 1, Vol. 2, pp. 929–35.

DESBROSSE, R.; KOZLOWSKI, J. K., ZUATE Y ZUBER, J. 1976. Prondniks de France et d'Europe Centrale. *Anthropologie* (Paris), Vol. 80, pp. 431–48.

FARIZY, C.; TUFFREAU, A. 1984. Industries et cultures du Paléolithique moyen récent dans la moitié nord de la France. In: CONGRÈS PRÉHISTORIQUE DE FRANCE, 22, Lille. *Colloque*. 12 pp.

FEUSTEL, R. 1983. Zur zeitlichen und kulturellen Stellung des Palaeolithikums von Weimar-Ehringsdorf. *Alt-Thüring.* (Weimar), Vol. 19, pp. 16–42.

FREEMAN, L. G. 1966. The Nature of Mousterian Facies in Cantabrian Spain. *Am. Anthropol.* (Washington), Vol. 68, pp. 230–7 (special issue).

FREUND, G. 1968. Mikrolithen aus dem Mittelpaläolithikum der Sesselfelsgrotte im unteren Altmühltal. Ldkr. Kelheim. *Quartär* (Bonn), Vol. 19, pp. 133–54.

—— 1975. Zum Stand der Ausgrabungen in der Sesselfelsgrotte im unteren Altmühltal. In: AUSGRABUNGEN IN DEUTSCHLAND. 2nd edn. Mainz. pp. 25–41. (Monogr. Röm.-Germ. Zent. mus. Forsch.inst. Vor-Frühgesch, 1.)

—— 1978. Zum Paläolithikum aus der Höhlenruine von Hunas in der nördl. Fränkischen Alb. *Archäol. Korresp.b.*, Vol. 8, pp. 259–63.

FRIDRICH, J. 1980. Bečov IV, District of Most: An Acheulian Site in Bohemia. In: JELINEK, J. (ed.), *Homo erectus and his Time*. Brno, Moravské Museum, Vol. 1, pp. 291–8. (*Anthropologie* (Brno), Vol. 18, Nos. 2–3.)

—— 1982. *Middle Palaeolithic Settlement of Bohemia*. Prague.

GÁBORI, M. 1976. *Les Civilisations du Paléolithique moyen entre les Alpes et l'Oural*. Budapest.

GÁBORI-CSÁNK, V. 1968. *La Station du Paléolithique moyen d'Erd, Hongrie*. Budapest.

GHOSH, A. K. 1982. Pebble-Core and Flake Elements: Process of Transmutation and the Factors Thereof – a Case Study of the Transition from Lower to Middle Palaeolithic in India. In: RONEN A. (ed.), *The Transition from Lower to Middle Palaeolithic and the Origin of Modern Man*. Oxford. pp. 265–82. (BAR Int. Ser., 151.)

GIOT, P.-R.; MONNIER, J.-L. 1976. Les Civilisations du Paléolithique inférieur en Armorique. In: LUMLEY, H. DE (ed.), *La Préhistoire française*. Paris, CNRS. T. 1, Vol. 2, pp. 944–6.

GLADILIN, V. N. 1982. Stratigrafia paleolita Zakarpatia [The Palaeolithic Stratigraphy of Transcarpathia]. In: INQUA CONGRESS, 11. Moscow. *Tèzisy dokladov III*. pp. 96–7.

GONZALES ECHEGARAY, J. et al. 1971. *Cueva Morin: Excavaciones 1966–1968*. Santander.

—— 1980. *El yacimiento de la cueva de 'El Pendo'*. Madrid.

GUICHARD, G. 1976. Les Civilisations du Paléolithique inférieur en Périgord. In: LUMLEY, H. DE (ed.), *La Préhistoire française*. Paris. CNRS, T. 1, Vol. 2, pp. 909–28.

GÜNTHER, K. 1964. *Die altsteinzeitlichen Funde der Balver Höhle*. Münster.

HAESAERTS, P.; CIRAKOVA, S. 1979. Le Paléolithique moyen à pointes foliacées de Mousselievo (Bulgaria). In: KOZLOWSKI, J. K. (ed.), *Middle and Early Upper Palaeolithic in the Balkans*. Cracow. pp. 65–76.

HIGGS, E. S. 1968. The Stone Industries of Greece. In: BORDES, F. (ed.), *La Préhistoire: problèmes et tendances*. Paris, CNRS. pp. 223–35.

HIGGS, E. S.; VITA-FINZI, C. 1966. The Climate, Environment and Industries of Stone Age Greece, Part II. *Proc. Prehist. Soc.*, Vol. 32, pp. 1–19.

HOLM, J. 1984. Recent Acheulean Discoveries in Denmark. In: CONGRÈS PRÉHISTORIQUE DE FRANCE, 22, Lille. *Colloque*. 12 pp.

IVANOVA, S. 1979. Cultural Differentiation in the Middle Palaeolithic on the Balkan Peninsula. In: KOZLOWSKI, J. K. (ed.), *Middle and Early Upper Palaeolithic in the Balkans*. Cracow. pp. 13–33.

JACOB-FRIESEN, K. H. 1949. *Die Altsteinzeitfunde aus dem Leinetal bei Hannover*. Hildesheim.

JEQUIER, J.-P. 1975. *Le Moustérien alpin*. Yverdon.

LAVILLE, H.; RIGAUD, J.-P.; SACKETT, J. 1980. *Rock Shelters of the Périgord*. New York.

LEONARDI, P.; BROGLIO, A. 1962. *Le Paléolithique de la Vénétie*. Ferrara.

LEROI-GOURHAN, A.; SOMME, J.; TUFFREAU, A. 1978. Weichselien et Paléolithique moyen de Seclin (Melantois, nord de la France). *Bull. Assoc. Fr. Étud. Quat.* (Paris), Vol. 15, pp. 69–80.

LÉVÊQUE, F.; VANDERMEERSCH, B. 1981. Le Néanderthalien de Saint-Césaire. *Recherche* (Paris), Vol. 12, No. 119, pp. 242–4.

LUMLEY, H. DE. 1969. *Le Paléolithique inférieur et moyen du midi Méditerranéen dans son cadre géologique*. Paris. Vol. 1.

—— 1971. *Le Paléolithique inférieur et moyen du midi Méditerranéen dans son cadre géologique*. Paris. Vol. 2.

—— 1976a. Les Civilisations du Paléolithique inférieur en Provence. In: LUMLEY, H. DE (ed.), *La Préhistoire française*. Paris, CNRS. T. 1, Vol. 2, pp. 819–51.

—— 1976b. Les Civilisations du Paléolithique inférieur en Languedoc méditerranéen et en Roussillon. In: LUMLEY, H. DE (ed.), *La Préhistoire française*. Paris, CNRS. T. 1, Vol. 2, pp. 852–71.

LUMLEY, H. DE; BOONE, Y. 1976a. Les Structures d'habitat au Paléolithique inférieur. In: LUMLEY, H. DE (ed.), *La Préhistoire française*. Paris, CNRS. T. 1, Vol. 1, pp. 625–43.

—— 1976b. Les Structures d'habitat au Paléolithique moyen. In: LUMLEY, H. DE (ed.), *La Préhistoire française*. Paris, CNRS. T. 1, Vol. 1, pp. 644–55.

LUTTROPP, A.; BOSINSKI, G. 1971. *Der altsteinzeitliche Fundplatz Reutersruh bei Ziegenhain in Hessen*. Cologne/Vienna.

MALEZ, M. 1970. The Palaeolithic Culture of Krapina in the Light of New Research. In: MALEZ, M. (ed.), *Krapina 1899–1969*. Zagreb. pp. 57–129.

—— 1979. Nalazista paleolitskog i mezolitskog doba u Hrvatskoj [Findings of the Palaeolithic and Mesolithic Period in Croatia]. In: BASLER, D. (ed.), *Praistorija jugoslavenskich zemalja*. Saravejo. Vol. 1, pp. 227–95.

MANIA, D.; TOEPFER, V. 1973. *Königsaue: Gliederung, Ökologie und mittelpaläolithische Funde der letzten Eiszeit*. Berlin.

MARTIN, H. 1907–10. *Recherche sur l'évolution du Moustérien dans le gisement de la Quina (Charente): industrie osseuse*. Paris. Vol. 1.

MELLARS, P. A. 1969. The Chronology of Mousterian Industries in the Perigord Region. *Proc. Prehist. Soc.*, Vol. 35, pp. 134–71.

MONNIER, J.-L. 1984. Chronostratigraphie et facies culturels du Paléolithique inférieur et moyen en Bretagne: comparaison avec les régions loessiques. In: CONGRÈS PRÉHISTORIQUE DE FRANCE, 22, Lille. *Colloque*. 24 pp.

MORTILLET, G. DE; MORTILLET, A. DE. 1900. *Le Préhistorique: origine et antiquité de l'homme*. Paris.

OAKLEY, P. 1958. Use of Fire by Neanderthal Man and his Precursors. In: KOENIGSWALD, G. H. R. VON (ed.), *Hundert Jahre Neanderthaler 1856–1956*. Cologne/Graz. pp. 267–9.

OBERMAIER, H. 1925. *El hombre fósil*. Madrid.

PAUNESCU, A. 1965. Sur la succession des habitats Paléolithiques et postpaléolithiques de Ripiceni-Izvor. *Dacia*, Vol. 9, pp. 5–31.

PIPERNO, M.; SEGRE, A. G. 1984. Saccopastore, Lazio. In: SOPRINTENDENZA SPECIALE DEL MUSEO PIGORINI. *I Primi abitanti d'Europa*. Rome. pp. 207–9.

PRASLOV, N. D. 1984. Rannij paleolit Russkoi ravniny y Kryma [Early Palaeolithic of the Russian Plain and the Crimea]. In: BORISKOVSKI, P. I. (ed.), *Paleolit SSSR*. Moscow. pp. 94–134.

RADMILLI, A. M. 1977. *Storia dell'Abruzzo dalle origini all'età del bronzo*. Pisa.

—— 1984. Madonna del Fredo, Abruzzo. In: SOPRINTENDENZA SPECIALE DEL MUSEO PIGORINI. *I Primi abitanti d'Europa*. Rome. pp. 129–41.

ROE, D. A. 1981. *The Lower and Middle Palaeolithic Periods in Britain*. London.

RONEN, A. (ed.) 1982. *The Transition from the Lower to Middle Palaeolithic and the Origin of Modern Man*. Oxford. (BAR Int. Ser., 151.)

SCHWABEDISSEN, H. 1970. Zur Verbreitung der Faustkeile in Mitteleuropa. In: SCHWABEDISSEN, H. (ed.), *Frühe Menschheit und Umwelt*. Cologne/Graz. Vol. 1, pp. 90–7.

SCOTT, K. 1980. Two Hunting Episodes of Middle Palaeolithic Age at La Cotte de Saint Brelade, Jersey (Channel Islands). *World Archaeol.*, Vol. 12, No. 2, pp. 137–52.

TASCHINI, M. 1967. Il 'Protopontiniano' rissiano di Sedia del Diavolo e di Monte delle Gioie (Roma). *Quaternaria* (Rome), Vol. 9, pp. 301–19.

THIBAULT, C. 1976. Les Civilisations du Paléolithique inférieur dans le sud-ouest (Pays Basque, Landes, Gironde). In: LUMLEY, H. DE (ed.), *La Préhistoire française*. Paris, CNRS. T. 1, Vol. 2, pp. 905–8.

THIEME, H. 1978. Rheindahlen (Mönchengladbach). In: VEIL, S. (ed.), *Alt- und mittelsteinzeitliche Fundplätze des Rheinlandes*. Cologne. pp. 56–69.

TOEPFER, V. 1958. Steingeräte und Palökologie der mittelpaläolithischen Fundstelle Rabutz bei Halle (Saale). *Jahresschr. mitteldt. Vorgesch.* (Berlin), Vol. 41/2, pp. 140–77.

—— 1981. Das Acheuléen auf dem Boden der DDR. In: JELINEK, J. (ed.), *Homo erectus and his Time*. Brno. Vol. 2, pp. 55–77. (*Anthropologie* (Brno), Vol. 19, No. 1.)

TROMNAU, G. 1983. Ein Mammutknochen-Faustkeil aus Rhede, Kr. Borken (Westfalen). *Archäol. Korresp.b.*, Vol. 13, No. 3, pp. 287–9.

TUFFREAU, A. 1976. Les Civilisations du Paléolithique inférieur dans la région parisienne et en Normandie. In: LUMLEY, H. DE (ed.), *La Préhistoire française*. Paris, CNRS. T. 1, Vol. 2, pp. 947–55.

—— 1978a. Le Paléolithique dans le nord de la France (Nord-Pas-de-Calais). *Bull. Assoc. Fr. Étud. Quat.* (Paris), Vol. 15, pp. 15–25.

—— 1978b. Les Fouilles du gisement Paléolithique de Biache-Saint-Vaast (Pas-de-Calais): années 1976 et 1977 – premiers résultats. *Bull. Assoc. Fr. Étud. Quat.* (Paris), Vol. 15, pp. 46–55.

—— 1979. Recherches récents sur le Paléolithique inférieur et moyen de la France septentrionale. *Bull. Soc. R. Belge Anthropol. Préhist.* (Brussels), Vol. 90, pp. 161–77.

—— 1981. L'Acheuléen dans la France septentrionale. *Anthropologie* (Brno), Vol. 19, No. 2, pp. 171–83.

ULRIX-CLOSSET, M. 1975. *Le Paléolithique moyen dans le bassin mosan en Belgique*. Wetteren.

VALOCH, K. 1967. Le Paléolithique moyen en Tchécoslovaquie. *Anthropologie* (Paris), Vol. 17, pp. 135–43.

—— 1968a. Evolution of the Palaeolithic in Central and Eastern Europe. *Curr. Anthropol.*, Vol. 9, No. 5, pp. 351–91.

—— 1968b. Gisement du Pléistocène supérieur à Mamaia sur la côte de la Mer Noire. In: BORDES, F. (ed.), *La Préhistoire: problèmes et tendances*. Paris, CNRS. pp. 465–72.

—— 1970. Early Middle Palaeolithic (Stratum 14) in the Kůlna Cave near Sloup in the Moravian Karst. *World Archaeol.*, Vol. 2, pp. 28–38.

—— 1984a. Le Taubachien, sa géochronologie, paléoécologie et paléoethnologie. *Anthropologie* (Paris), Vol. 88, pp. 193–208.

—— 1984b. Transition du Paléolithique moyen au Paléolithique supérieur dans l'Europe centrale et orientale. In: FORTA, J. (ed.), *Scripta praehistorica Francisco Jorda oblata*. Salamanca. pp. 439–67.

VERTES, L. (ed.) 1964. *Tata: eine mittelpaläolithische Travertin-Siedlung in Ungarn*. Budapest.

VILLEVERDE BONILLA, V. 1984. *La Cova Negra de Xátiva y el Musteriense de la región central del Mediterráneo español*. Valencia.

WETZEL, R.; BOSINSKI, G. 1969. *Die Bocksteinschmiede im Lonetal (Markung Rammingen, Kreis Ulm) I/II*. Stuttgart.

NOTE

1 This ethnic interpretation of cultures based solely on the features of the lithic industries is controversial. See Chapter 4 – Ed.

13

THE TERRITORY OF THE FORMER USSR

during the Middle Palaeolithic

Valeriy P. Alexeev

The Mousterian remains from the Riss–Würm interglacial in the former USSR are isolated sites on the east European plain, located at Khotilevo on the Desna (Zavernyaev, 1978) and Sukhaya Mechetka on the Volga (Zamyatnin, 1961). In both cases there is fairly clear bedding in deposits of the Riss–Würm interglacial and fauna that testifies to an increase in temperature. All the other sites, whether in caves or in the open – and upwards of six hundred of them have been discovered to date – are from the beginning of the Würm era. On the east European plain that era was characterized by a cold and harsh climate, and in Crimea and the Caucasus it was colder than at present, although this had little effect on central Asia and southern Siberia, where the Mousterian finds are concentrated.

Data on human remains from Mousterian sites are as yet fragmentary and relate almost exclusively to Crimea, the Caucasus and central Asia; no bone relics of the bearers of the Mousterian culture have yet been documented from the vast territory of Siberia. The literature indicates that one molar from the fourth Mousterian horizon of Rozhok I by the Sea of Azov belonged to a human of the Modern type (Praslov, 1968), but that is the only such find in the whole of the east European plain. The geographical distribution of these palaeoanthropological finds is very uneven (Map 12), and states of preservation differ greatly: as well as remains that make for a fairly detailed morphological profile and taxonomy, there are individual fragments which add little to our knowledge of territorial variants in the morphology of Mousterian humans.

The progressive traits observed in the form of the tooth from the Rozhok I site, mentioned above, should not prompt a diagnostic reassessment: the differences between the crowns of teeth in the Upper Palaeolithic and the late Mousterian are not very marked, and it is difficult to draw definite conclusions on the basis of one tooth.

The palaeoanthropological finds in Crimea provide far more information. These were made during the excavations of Kiik-Koba cave in 1924 by G. A. Bonch-Osmolovski (1940) and of Zaskalnaya V and typologically similar Zaskalnaya VI by Y. G. Kolosov (1979) over a number of years from 1970. The bones of an adult hand and foot are described in two monographs by Bonch-Osmolovski (1941, 1954), and the fragmentary skeleton of a child of between 6 and 8 months has been described by E. Vlcek (1976). X-ray examination has shown that the adult skeleton was that of a

woman of around 35 years of age (Rohlin, 1965). It is interesting that even the infant of less than a year showed Neanderthaloid features.

Apart from the massiveness of the skeleton the most salient distinctive feature of the woman from Kiik-Koba is the unusual form of the first articulation of the metacarpal bone, from which the thumb leads off at an angle to the other fingers. Bonch-Osmolovski draws attention to the fact that a number of divergences – albeit minor ones – from the saddle-like forms that typify humans of the Modern type feature also in the metacarpal bones of French Neanderthalers, and he advances the hypothesis that Neanderthalers in general had limited opposability of the thumbs. Subsequent research has shown that the opposability of the thumb depends not only on the articulation but also on the development of the corresponding musculature, which may have compensated for the insufficient structure of the first articulation of the metacarpal bone (Semenov, 1950). On the basis of examination of the stone inventory of Kiik-Koba cave, the same author argues persuasively that the Kiik-Koba Neanderthalers were right-handed.

The massive form of the skeleton, which the Kiik-Koba Neanderthaler has in common with other Neanderthal forms in Europe, has been explained as an adaptation connected with reorganization of locomotion during anthropogenesis (Alexeev, 1960). The breadth of hands and feet are linked by a high morpho-physiological correlation. At a time when the human race was beginning to walk upright, the breadth of the foot in relation to other features must have had an adaptive significance. Given the direct morpho-physiological correlation, the width of the hand, which did not have a similar adaptive significance, increased also, and this led to the development in Neanderthalers of powerful and very broad hands, which were not found in earlier hominids.

A number of individuals were found at Zaskalnaya V and Zaskalnaya VI, but unfortunately they were pre-adolescent and little more than the bones of the hands remain. This makes taxonomy very difficult, because the growth pattern in the dimensions of hands has not been properly studied in Modern peoples, much less in Neanderthalers. Nevertheless, we may assert that with few exceptions the people who lived at Zaskalnaya V and VI were close in terms of morphology to the people of Kiik-Koba (Yakimov and Haritonov, 1979; Danilova, 1983).

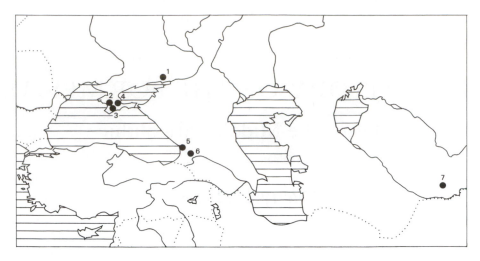

Map 12 Location of the Mousterian sites in the former USSR where palaeoanthropological remains have been found: 1, Rozhok I; 2, Kiik-Koba; 3, Starosel'e; 4, Zaskal'naya V and VI; 5, Akhshtyr; 6, Sakazhia; 7, Teshik-Tash.

A. A. Formozov (1958) made an exceptionally interesting palaeoanthropological find in 1953 in a cave at Staroselye. Unfortunately the child's skeleton that was discovered has not been described in full, and the literature provides a description of the skull only (Roginski, 1954). It is the skull of a child whose age was estimated by Roginski at approximately one and a half years. American palaeoanthropologists from Philadelphia University who worked with the original consider this to be a low estimate, and hold that the child was actually 2 to 4 years old, but unfortunately they do not publish the arguments that led them to revise the estimate for the age of the Staroselye find. The author of the original description considered the remains to be those of a typical Modern human with a number of primitive features, and he noted its similarity to the infant skull from the famous Skhul cave in Israel. It was not so much this diagnosis as the exceptional significance of finding a Modern skull in a Mousterian layer that attracted the close attention of Western European and Soviet scholars, who from various morphogenetic stances and different taxonomic points of view expressed their opinions on the place of the Staroselye skull in the evolution of hominids.

Roginski's original diagnosis was upheld by nine eminent authorities in palaeoanthopology (Y. P. Yakimov, M. M. Gerasimov, H. Ulrich, F. Clark Howell, V. V. Bunak, A. Thoma, C. Coon, M. F. Uryson and S. I. Uspenski, (surveyed in Alexeev, 1976). This traditional opinion is opposed by only two diagnoses from equally eminent authorities: H. Gross (1956) suggests that the Staroselye find comprises the bones of a Neanderthaler, while G. F. Debetz (1956) considers on the contrary that the skull of the Staroselye infant had no primitive features and is to be attributed without reservation to the Modern type.

Consideration of the change in physical proportions from childhood to adulthood with the aid of a table showing increase in size from childhood to adulthood in the Modern human afforded futher evidence for the taxonomic diagnosis of the Staroselye find (Alexeev, 1976). This procedure indicates that the 'adult' dimensions of the Staroselye skull are very small, while their proportions are typically modern. In the Upper Palaeolithic series it occupies an extreme position even among the skulls of women, so that we may conclude that this skull belonged to a female child. This is not sufficient, however, to explain its small dimensions. Hypertrophy in the frontal and occipital parts of the skull

suggests the effects of some kind of cerebral pathology such as hydrocephalus. If we take the age of the child to have been 2 to 4 years, as the American specialists suggest, on the basis of the unusual order of eruption of the teeth, then the 'adult' dimensions become even smaller, and the suggestion of pathology gains additional support.

The discovery of a Modern skull in a Mousterian layer is important in the context of the origin of Modern humans. Formozov has shown the similarity of the Kiik-Koba and Staroselye industries in one important matter: the presence in both of bifacially retouched tools. This means that the later site of Staroselye may be linked directly with the earlier site in the cave at Kiik-Koba. It thus becomes highly probable that there is a genetic continuity between the peoples who left the two monuments. This genetic succession, in turn, shows that Crimea was part of the area in which *Homo sapiens* developed.

The Caucasian palaeoanthropological finds are less significant than those in Crimea. They are from caves in Sakaziya and Akhstir. The former provided the fragment of an upper jaw and a separate molar (Nioradze et al., 1978) and the latter a single molar (Vekilova and Zubov, 1972). In neither case does the material lend itself to accurate determination of its morphological affinities. Georgian anthropologists analysing the finds at Sakaziya have tried to show that alongside the typically Neanderthal features there are Modern traits; in particular they interpret the relative narrowness of the piriform opening as a sign of similarity with Palestinian forms. However, most of the Palestinian Neanderthalers from Skhul and Qafzeh were actually broadnosed (Vandermeersch, 1981). It is therefore more prudent to assume that the fragments from Sakaziya were those of a Neanderthaler, and not to ascribe to the individual any modern traits.

The isolated molar from the Akhstir cave evinced a combination of archaic and Modern morphological features, with the latter predominating. It is likely that it belonged to a human of the Modern type. Although tentative, this diagnosis is important in that it allows us to include the Caucasus in the zone in which Modern humans developed; it is an area where previously, in the period of Mousterian culture, people with Modern traits had appeared.

For the sake of completeness we should mention the discovery of fragments of skull at the Erevan I site (Aslanyan et al., 1979), although the stratigraphic position of the find is far from clear, and the bones are so Modern in form that we have every reason to doubt the validity of this find.

Turning to the territory of central Asia, we should mention the pre-adolescent skeleton found by A. P. Oklad-nikov in 1938 in the Teshik-Tash cave, Uzbekistan (Plate 18). The skull was described by Debetz (1940), and the long bones and other fragments of the skeleton by N. A. Sinelnikov and M. A. Gremyatski (1949). X-ray examination shows that the skeleton belonged to a child of about 9 years of age (Rohlin, 1949). Of course, the taxonomy of a pre-adolescent is incomparably more difficult to establish than that of an adult. This particular case provoked a debate which has yet to be settled. The conclusion of the original diagnosis, by Debetz, was that the Teshik-Tash boy (for the sex of the find was established as male) belonged to the same classic type of European Neanderthaler as the French finds at La Chapelle-aux-Saints and La Ferrassie I. A second, more detailed, description by M. A. Gremyatski (1949) took a neutral position with regard to the skull's taxonomy, neither supporting the original diagnosis by Debetz nor coming out definitely against it.

In the interval between 1940 and 1949 there appeared an article by F. Weidenreich (1945) and a polemic reply by Debetz (1947). Weidenreich expressed grave doubts about the correctness of comparing the Teshik-Tash skull with French Classic Neanderthalers; he noted a number of pro-gressive traits in its morphology and opined that it was closer to the more advanced forms of the Neanderthal group, such as those found at Ehringsdorf (Germany). Debetz carefully examined Weidenreich's morphological arguments and did not concur with them, but stood by his original conclusion. However, study of the endocrane of the Teshik-Tash boy has also shown many progressive traits (Bunak, 1951). The reconstruction by M. M. Gerasimov (1955, 1964) of the external appearance of the Teshik-Tash boy, on the basis of independent morphological research, is a further argument in favour of regarding him as a progressive form. For this reason the vast majority of those who have written on the subject in recent years consider the Teshik-Tash boy to be a representative not of the Classic type of Neanderthaler but of the progressive type (for a review of the literature, see Alexeev, 1973). It should be noted also that Debetz (1956) subsequently adopted this view.

A later attempt to make a more precise taxonomy of this find used the procedure mentioned above for calculating 'adult' dimensions on the basis of a scale showing the tran-sition from child to adult dimensions in Modern humans. It fully confirmed the presence of significant differences from the Classic Neanderthalers of France and a certain similarity with the progressive forms of the Skhul type. The 'adult' dimensions of the Teshik-Tash boy proved to be minimal in comparison with all the other Neanderthalers, apart from the Steinheim skull, which was therefore deemed to be that of a woman. A. Thoma (1964) argued that the Teshik-Tash form belonged to the evolutionary branch that led to modern Mongoloids, but based his argument only on the form and sagittal contour of the cranium, which is not peculiar to Mongoloids. For this reason, his theory did not become widely accepted. At the same time the structural features of the facial skeleton, which actually are racially specific, show that in breadth of nose and a degree of prognathism the Teshik-Tash skull is similar to the skull of Skhul V. Taken in conjunction with the progressive features the skulls have in common, this similarity permits us to affirm that the territory of the southern regions of central Asia came into the vast eastern Mediterranean zone in which

Modern humans developed and which, given the above data about the morphology of Crimean and Caucasian finds, included also the Caucasus and the southern regions of the European parts of the former USSR.

The sites we have discussed provided all the human bone remains of the Mousterian period discovered in the former USSR. As we noted at the beginning of this section, the number of Mousterian sites with cultural remains is many times larger, although it is not yet enough to permit us to claim full knowledge of the Mousterian era in the former USSR. A great lacuna in our knowledge results from uneven study of different areas. The overwhelming majority of Mousterian sites are concentrated in Crimea and the Cauc-asus, while enormous areas of the east European plain, central Asia and Siberia are still 'blanks', and this is not because there were no Mousterian people within those areas: palaeo-geographical data indicate that they were quite suitable for settlement.

In spite of the abundance of sites, interpretation of Mous-terian culture in the former USSR is rendered still more difficult by the insuperable problem of a number of factors that complicate stratigraphic analysis. Groups of remains are separated by great distances, sites in the plain are in totally different geological situations to cave sites, and, in spite of the large number of studies made in Quaternary geology, palaeontology of the Quaternary period and archaeological taphonomy, any attempts at synchronization remain highly tentative. For these reasons the exposition of a group of remains from different periods is possible only within the confines of limited areas, and the dynamic tendencies deter-mined here and there in changes in the technology of stone inventories have a strictly local significance.

A review of all the Mousterian sites of European Russia and Ukraine was published by N. D. Praslov (1984). He rightly singles out the sites of the Crimean peninsula as the leading ones in that territory, since the vast majority of them were long-term settlements with thick cultural deposits and they may have been the source of many groups of settlements on the east European plain, which was settled from the south as well as from the west. All the data available at present on the nature of the very incomplete and fragmentary remains from the Acheulean era in eastern Europe indicate that the southern route was predominant. This is why Praslov's summary describes the territorial groups of sites primarily in comparison with Crimean ones. Of course, the proposed scheme of territorial differentiation is not definitive, since many regions do not feature in it, yet it does confer a certain order on the territorial variations observed in techniques for working stone and in the forms of the stone inventory.

The scheme identifies six groups: in Crimea (which Praslov calls the Belogorsk zone after the town of Belogorsk, near which very rich sites were found in the foothills), on the banks of the Volga, the shores of the Azov Sea, the banks of the Desna and two zones along the Dniester. Before embarking on their description, we must note that these are all open-air settlements, with the exception of Crimean ones, where only one site – Zaskalnaya – is in the open, the rest being caves. The northernmost Mousterian sites on the east European plain are at a latitude of 52° N. These include not only sites that were inhabited for various lengths of time, but also workshops, which are distinguished by a marked preponderance of unretouched artefacts – flakes and cores.

The richest and most interesting sites in Crimea are Zaskalnaya V and Zaskalnaya VI (Kolosov, 1977, 1979), men-tioned above, the Chokurtsha caves (Ernst, 1934), the Voltshii cave (Bader, 1939), Kiik-Koba (Bonch-Osmolovski, 1940)

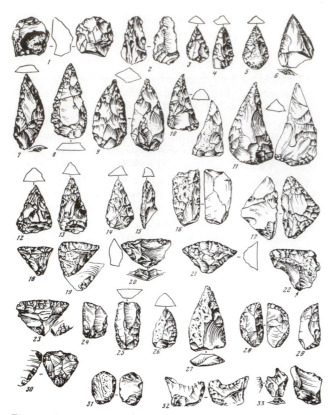

Figure 22 Mousterian artefacts, Kiik–Koba cave, Crimea.

and Staroselye (Formozov, 1958), which we have discussed in connection with the discovery of human bones of the Mousterian era. Bonch-Osmolovski, who discovered it, held the cave site of Shaïtan-Koba to be unique (it also harboured a rich assortment of stone tools), but modern evaluation, with the benefit of a greater array of data, enables us to place it in a group along with other sites. Praslov finds good typological grounds for such a grouping.

The Crimean sites share two typological features in the inventory, one of which is practically ubiquitous, while the other is to be found at all sites except Shaïtan-Koba. The former feature is the significant quantity of bifaces (Fig. 22): 40 per cent of all tools found at Zaskalnaya V and Zaskalnaya VI were bifacially retouched; in Chokurtsha, 24 per cent; in Kiik-Koba, 14 per cent; and in Staroselye, 12 per cent. Bifaces were found also in Shaïtan-Koba and Voltshii caves, but their quantity in relation to the total was not calculated. These sites are not of the same period in either chronological or typological terms; the inventory of Kiik-Koba, for example, would seem to be much more archaic than the Staroselye industry. And yet Formozov pointed out the direct continuity from one site to the other, astutely noting the presence of bifacially retouched forms and some minor details in the morphology of the tools. The establishment of continuity is particularly important in this case, because, as we have seen, osseous remains of people of either sex, different ages and dissimilar anatomy were excavated from these caves. The archaeological material fills gaps in the palaeoanthropological data and permits us to postulate a genetic link between the archaic and progressive forms of the hominids excavated.

The other feature that typifies the morphological inventory of the Crimean sites is the paucity of cores. Shaïtan-Koba is the only exception. The caves with Mousterian industries were near outcrops of good, laminated flint,

requiring no special preparation, which explains the rarity of cores in the inventory. There were no such outcrops of layered flint near Shaïtan-Koba, so its inhabitants had to split flint nodules in order to obtain blanks for secondary working. The significant quantity of cores, of course, sets this site apart from the others.

The Volga group is represented by the site of Sukhaya Mechetka, mentioned at the beginning of this section. It is situated on the right bank of the Volga on the outskirts of the city of Volgograd and was excavated by S. N. Zamyatnin (1961) in 1952 and 1954. The area excavated was 650 m², although the director of the excavation considered that the actual area of the settlement was twice as great. The excavated part of the site has a definite topography: there are traces of hearths and concentrations of tools. Within the excavated part of the site 1,000 objects were collected, although only 5 per cent of them are implements. As in Crimea, these included a significant proportion of bifacial forms (about 10 per cent of all the tools), although there is a local speciality: many angular and triangular scrapers, retouched on one side only (Fig. 23). This peculiarity, the size and richness of the site and its special geographical situation (it is the easternmost of the major sites in eastern Europe) put it in a group of its own.

Apart from the site of Rozhok I, which, as we have noted, contained a single human tooth (Praslov, 1968), the Azov Sea group includes a series of sites which are different in some details of the stone inventory but still have a certain typological and perhaps even genetic unity. Rozhok I is the key site among them because it has many layers and a rich inventory that changes little from one layer to the next – an indication that it was not inhabited for very long. The original feature in the inventory of this site, setting this entire group of sites somewhat apart, is the presence, in a typical Mousterian industry with scrapers and awls, of certain forms of a later, perhaps even Upper Palaeolithic, kind. Praslov

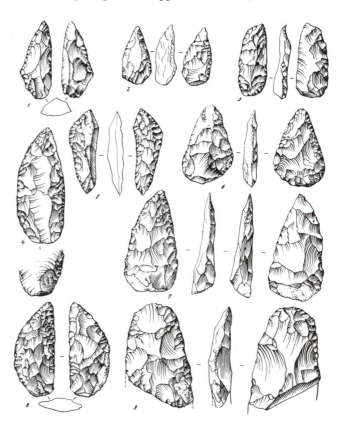

Figure 23 Mousterian artefacts, Sukhaya Mechetka, Volga Basin.

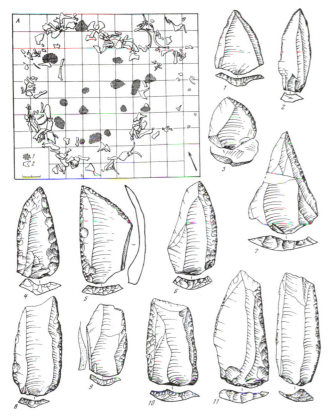

Figure 24 Mousterian culture, Molodova I, Dniester Basin. Ground plan of a dwelling: 1, Fireplaces; 2, Mammoth bones. Stone industry.

sees the end-scrapers and punches with clear-cut points as examples of such tools. Although, as we have noted, morphological diagnosis on the basis of a single molar cannot be definite, the modern appearance of the tooth would seem to fit in with the appearance of progressive forms of technology in the industry of this local group of Mousterian sites.

The Desna group, like the Volga group, consists of a single site – Khotilevo, mentioned earlier in this section (Zavernyaev, 1978). As we have observed, judging from the stratigraphy of the sites, this group, together with the Volga groups, dates to the end of the Riss–Würm interglacial, which means that it is older than the other groups. Khotilevo has no well-defined cultural layer and consists of a workshop, which contained tens of thousands of artefacts, less than 1 per cent of which are tools. The first examination turned up asymmetric cores, including many with one large platform, formed by splitting off a flake. This is the Levallois tradition, and the tools include bifaces, leaf-shaped points and knives of more or less regular shape. Perhaps the most unusual are stemmed tools that are faintly reminiscent of Folsom points from Palaeolithic sites in North America, and could almost be described as the typological prototypes of those tools. Praslov (1984) rightly considers that there is nothing similar to the Khotilevo complex among the other sites in eastern Europe, and holds that one must look to sites in western Ukraine and Germany for analogies. If this supposition proves correct, it will be possible to conclude that at the end of the Riss–Würm interglacial a group of Mousterian people moved east from central Europe to the Desna basin.

Unlike the other groups the two Dniester groups do not stand in contrast one to the other, but differ only in the typology of the stone inventory. One of these groups comprises sites around the village of Molodova on the Dniester,

of which the multi-layered sites of Molodova I and Molodova V have the largest and richest inventories (Chernysh, 1965). The Levallois technique predominates in this inventory and bifaces are completely absent (Fig. 24). The tools are mostly blades, and most of the scrapers are side-scrapers. The entire complex is referred to in the literature as the Molodova Mousterian culture (Praslov, 1968; Anisyutkin, 1971).

The nearby remains of the other Dniester group are not nearly so rich, and although there are sites with many layers, the cultural layers are poorly defined, with a weaker inventory and almost total lack of fauna (Anisyutkin, 1971; Ketraru, 1973). This group is typified by bifacially retouched tools and by a large quantity of notches and denticulates. On this basis N. K. Anisyutkin set this complex apart as a Mousterian culture in its own right and named it after the most important site – Stinka. N. D. Praslov (1984) expressed doubt about the correctness of this distinction, but it is in any case a special group of sites that is different from the groups described above, and, what is most important, it differs considerably from the Molodova group.

Now that we have completed our review of the territorial groupings of Mousterian sites in the east European plain and Crimea, it should be noted that they provide unique information in two areas. The remains of shelters were found at Molodova sites I and V (Chernysh, 1965). The remains of the dwelling at Molodova I are better preserved and were excavated by A. P. Chernysh in 1958–9 (Fig. 25). The main construction material was mammoth bone: the people used skulls, scapulae, pelves, long bones, tusks and lower jawbones. The shelter measures 10 by 7 m. That area contained fifteen hearths, and groups of tools. This find is important not only because it demonstrates the building ability of Neanderthal people and considerably enhances our estimation of their technical achievements and the level of their mental development; the size of the dwelling and the large number of hearths also show that the Neanderthalers lived in groups several dozen strong consisting of several families.

Figure 25 Reconstruction of a dwelling, Molodova I, Dniester Basin. (After Chernysh.)

Another unique find was made in the Mousterian layer of the Pronyatin site in Ukraine (Sitnik, 1983). A piece of bone with the image of an animal carved on one side was discovered (Fig. 26). It would be difficult to exaggerate the value of this very stylized sketch, which demonstrates that symbolic thinking and artistic ability were already developed in Neanderthalers to the point where they were capable of depicting images from the world around them. The great variety of graven images from the Upper Palaeolithic would

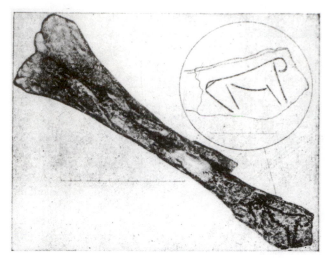

Figure 26 Drawing of an animal on a bone, Mousterian level, Pronyatin site (Ukraine).

seem to find their source in this object, which takes the prehistory of the figurative art of ancient peoples back to Mousterian times.

Turning to the territory of the Caucasus, we should note that the geology of this mountainous area offered the possibility of using volcanic rock (basalt and obsidian) as well as flint. This factor, along with the exceptional variety of the Mousterian industry, makes it difficult to compare far-flung sites to determine their typological similarities and genetic connections.

The Mousterian sites fall into two categories: open-air sites, in a number of northern locations in the northern Caucasus and on the Black Sea coast, many of which have no cultural layer and consist of assemblages on the surface, and sites in rock shelters and deep caves. The latter sites have produced a wealth of fauna, study of which permits us to reconstruct the climatic regime of the Mousterian era and to have an idea of the kinds of large mammals that were hunted by Mousterian people. Unlike the previous Acheulean epoch, when the main quarry was the cave bear, the Mousterians hunted ungulates – red deer, mountain goat, elk, horse and wild ass. To hunt these animals with the weapons available required great skill and knowledge of their habits and behaviour. Organized hunts were probably very common. Alongside these principal objects of the hunt, mountain turkey and red wolf were found – signs of a cold climate (Vereshchagin, 1959).

A full summary of the data on Mousterian remains in the Caucasus has been compiled by V. P. Lyubin (1977, 1984). That summary, which is based both on a survey of the abundant literature on the subject and on a great deal of original material, brings together all the information gathered to date. The isolation of local variants of Mousterian culture in the Caucasus is rendered difficult by the typological diversity of the inventory and by the scattering of similar types of tools. It is clear, nevertheless, that the Gubs archaeological culture in the western part of the northern Caucasus, named after the site at Gubs, may be identified with reasonable certainty (Autlev, 1964, 1973). The sites of that culture have a number of rather rare features in their inventory: prismatic, Levallois and radial techniques for the removal of flakes, small tools and an intriguing wealth of scratchers and scrapers. However, complexes of this distinctive type, which occur in a group of sites, are not to be found in such clear form in other parts of the Caucasus, and

the identification of genetically linked local variants in other areas is extremely difficult and will require even more research.

It is evidently for such reasons that V. P. Lyubin eschews the identification of archaeological cultures, preferring to write about lines of development that, strictly speaking, should be termed technological traditions. They bring together not only neighbouring sites but also sites that are comparatively far from one another, because they evince some common skills which form the basis of the technology and in some cases go back to general prototypes, mutual influence between the cultures, some sharing of their historical fate and so on. Lyubin identifies three such technological traditions: Mousterian proper, Denticulate Mousterian and Charentian. The first two are represented by dozens of sites in the northern Caucasus and in Transcaucasia (Fig. 27). They are not unusual and need no special description, since they resemble corresponding sites in western Europe. The technological tradition that Lyubin designates as Charentian is represented by only one site: Tsopi in central Georgia (Grigolia, 1963). This tradition produced very short and broad spalls from primary flaking, as well as large quantities of side-scrapers of the Quina type.

The skulls of cave bears were found in a number of cave sites in the Caucasus in situations relative to the other finds that lead us to conclude that their presence is not coincidental (for a list of the relevant sites, see Lyubin, 1984). Many researchers regard these observations as evidence of a bear cult among the Mousterian people of the Caucasus. Lyubin approaches the matter more cautiously, correctly observing that further evidence and verification is needed, and yet the data must not be ignored, especially if we recall the famous Swiss caves which also have heaps of cave bear skulls. In the light of these western European analogies it seems probable

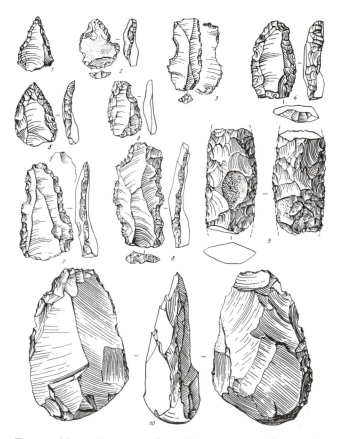

Figure 27 Mousterian stone industry, Transcaucasia, with examples of tooth-shaped secondary flaking. (After V. P. Lyubin.)

that there was a bear cult in the Caucasus in Mousterian times.

In central Asia we meet with both open-air and cave sites, whereas in southern Siberia we find only cave sites (Abramova, 1984). It is true that in the territory of Tuva there are Mousterian sites in the open in two places, but all the flint material is on the surface and it is therefore not stratified. The faunal remains in the central Asian sites allow us to differentiate them in terms of animals hunted: in the plain it was horse, onager, aurochs and elephant (it is not clear of which species) and in the mountains, mountain goat, brown bear and red deer. Among the faunal remains in the Ust-Kan cave in the Altai (Rudenko, 1960) mountain goat is replaced by mountain sheep.

Considering only the sites with a well-defined cultural layer and fauna, we may follow V. A. Ranov (Ranov and Nesneyanov, 1973) in distinguishing four groups of sites in Mousterian central Asia, each with its own technological tradition: Levalloisian, Levalloiso-Mousterian, Mousterian proper and Moustier-Soan. They are scattered, and not one of them occupies a continuous area. The most famous of all the central Asian sites is Teshik-Tash (see p. 147) with its Mousterian grave, known to western European readers through the publications of H. Movius (1953) and F. Bordes (1955). This cave provided a more or less typical Mousterian inventory. The first three technological traditions need no special description, since they correspond to typical industries of western Europe and western Asia. The Moustier-Soan tradition is represented by a few sites that had evidently been displaced (Ranov, 1965; Ranov and Nesneyanov, 1973). The principal distinguishing feature of the sites in this group is the presence in a Mousterian inventory of a large number of pebble-tools.

It is well known that four pairs of mountain goat horns lay around the skeleton of the Teshik-Tash boy. A. P. Okladnikov (1940, 1949) saw in this the beginning of a sun cult, but there would seem to be no serious grounds for such an assertion. At the same time it is clear that there is an element of deliberate arrangement in this burial, which points to some special rites connected with the burial of the dead.

It remains to make a few observations on the Mousterian sites of Siberia. Apart from the Ust-Kan cave, mention should be made of the Dvuglaska cave in Khakasia (Abramova, 1981) and the Mousterian finds on the high terraces of the Angara River (Medvedev, 1975). The finds on the Angara have no stratified cultural deposit, while the Ust-Kan site (Anisyutkin and Astahov, 1970) and the Dvuglaska site have a Levalloisian technological tradition in stone tools. This, of course, is only the most general preliminary of outlines of the Mousterian era in Siberia. At present, A. P. Derevyanko is leading excavations of several caves in the Altai with multi-layered stratigraphy, at Strashnaya, Denisovskaya and Sibiryachikha, and also open sites along the Selimdzhe river, a left-bank tributary of the Amur. These have furnished a vast amount of material from the Mousterian era – blanks, tools and fauna – but the data have not yet been published.

BIBLIOGRAPHY

ABRAMOVA, S. A. 1981. Must'erskij grot Dvuglaska v Hakasii [Mousterian cave at Dvouglaska in Khakasia]. *Kratk. soobšč. Inst. Arheol.* (Moscow), Vol. 165, pp. 73–82.

—— 1984. Rannij paleolit aziatskoj čhasti SSSR [Early Paleolithic of the Asiatic Part of the USSR]. In: BORISKOVSKI, P. I. (ed.), *Paleolit SSSR*. Moscow. pp. 135–60.

ALEXEEV, V. P. 1960. Nekotorye voprosy razvitija kisti v processe antropogeneza [Some Questions Concerning the Development of the Hand in the Process of Anthropogenesis]. In: LEVIN, M. G. (ed.), *Antropologičeskij sbornik II*. Moscow. pp. 100–14.

—— 1973. Položenie tešik-tašskoj nahodki v sisteme gominid [Position of the Teshik-Tash Find in the Hominid System]. In: LEBEDINSKAYA, G. V.; RABINOVICH, M. G. (eds), *Antropologičeskaja rekonstruktsija i problemy paleoetnografii*. Moscow. pp. 100–14.

—— 1976. Position of the Staroselye Find in the Hominid System. *J. Hum. Evol.* (London), Vol. 5, pp. 413–21.

ANISYUTKIN, N. K.; ASTAHOV, S. N. 1970. K voprosu o drevnejših pamjatnikah Altaja [A Question Concerning the Most Ancient Archeological Sites of Altai]. In: LARISHCHEV, V. E. (ed.), *Sibir' i ee sosedi v drevnosti*. Novosibirsk.

—— 1971. *Must'je Pruto-Dnestrovskogo meždureč'ja* [The Mousterian Culture of Prut and Dniester Intervalley]. Moscow.

ASLANYAN, A. T. et al. 1979. Otkrytie čerepa drevnego čeloveka v Erevane [A Discovery of the Skull of Ancient Man in Erevan]. *Vopr. antropol.* (Moscow), Vol. 60, pp. 38–51.

AUTLEV, P. U. 1964. Gubskaja paleolitičeskaja stojanka [Gubskaya Paleolithic Site]. *Sov. arheol.* (Moscow), No. 4, pp. 172–6.

—— 1973. Must'erskaja stojanka v Gubskom navese I [Mousterian Site in Gubskaya Cave I]. In: *Kavkaz i Vostočnaja Evropa v drevnosti*. Moscow. pp. 19–25.

BADER, O. N. 1939. Krupnejšaja must'jerskaja stojanka u Voltč'ego grota v Krymu [The Largest Mousterian Site at Voltchi Cave in Crimea]. *Vest. drevn. ist.* (Moscow), Vol. 1, pp. 258–63.

BONCH-OSMOLOVSKI, G. A. 1940. *Grot Kiik-Koba* [Kiik-Koba Cave]. Moscow/Leningrad.

—— 1941. *Kist' iskopaemogo čeloveka iz grota Kiik-Koba* [A Hand of Fossil Man from Kiik-Koba Cave]. Moscow/Leningrad.

—— 1954. *Skelet stopy i goleni iskopaemogo čeloveka iz grota Kiik-Koba* [Skeleton of the Foot and Shank of Fossil Man from Kiik-Koba Cave]. Moscow/Leningrad.

BORDES, F. 1955. L'Industrie moustérienne de Teshik-Tash: affinités et âge probable. *Anthropologie* (Paris), Vol. 59, p. 354.

BUNAK, V. V. 1951. Muljaž mozgovoj polosti paleolitičeskogo detskogo čerepa iz grota Tešik-Taš, Uzbekistan [An Endocranial Cast of Paleolithic Juvenile Skull from Teshik-Tash, Uzbekistan]. *Sb. Muz. antropol. etnogr.* (Moscow/Leningrad), Vol. 23, pp. 417–79.

CHERNYSH, A. P. 1965. Rannij i srednij paleolit Pridnestrov'ja [Lower and Middle Paleolithic of Dniester Valley]. Moscow.

DANILOVA, E. I. 1983. Antropologičeskaja haracteristika kostnyh ostatkov neandertal'skih detej iz III kul'turnogo sloja must'erskoj stojanki Zaskal'naja VI (Krym) [Anthropological Characteristics of the Skeletal Remains of the Neanderthal Children from the Third Cultural Layer of the Mousterian Site of Zaskalnaya VI in Crimea]. *Vopr. antropol.* (Moscow), Vol. 71, pp. 72–87.

DEBETZ, G. F. 1940. Ob antropologičeskih osobennostjah čelovečeskogo skeleta iz peščeri Tešik-Taš [On Anthropological Peculiarities of a Human Skeleton from Teshik-Tash Cave]. *Tr. Uzb. Fil. Akad. Nauk SSSR* (Tashkent), Ser. 1, Vol. 1, pp. 46–68.

—— 1947. O položenii paleolitičeskogo rebenka iz peščery Tešik-Taš v sisteme iskopaemyh form čeloveka [On the Position of Palaeolithic Child from Teshik-Tash Cave in the Hominid System]. Moscow.

DEBETZ, G. F. 1956. Sovremennoe sostojanie paleoantropologičeskih issledovanij v SSSR [Modern State of Palaeoanthropological Investigation in the USSR]. In: *Tezisi dokladov na sessii otdelenija istoričeskih nauk i plenume Instituta istorii material'noj kul'tury v 1955 godu*. Leningrad. pp. 22–3.

ERNST, H. A. 1934. Četvertičnaya stojanka v peščere u derevni Čukurtsa v Krymu [Pleistocene Site in the Cave by the Village of Chukurtsha in the Crimea]. In: *Troudy II meždunarodnoj konferencii associacii po izučeniju četvertičnogo perioda Evropy*. Leningrad. Vol. 5, pp. 184–206.

FORMOZOV, A. A. 1958. *Peščernaja stojanka Starosel'e i ee mesto v paleolite* [Cave Site Staroselye and its Place in the Paleolithic]. Moscow.

GERASIMOV, M. M. 1955. *Vosstanovlenie lica po čerepu (sovremennyj i iskopaemyj čelovek)* [Reconstruction of a Face on the Basis of a Skull]. Moscow.

—— 1964. *Ljudi kamennogo veka* [The People of the Stone Age]. Moscow.

GREMYATSKI, M. A. 1949. Čerep rebenka neandertalca iz grota Tešik-Taš, Južnyj Uzbekistan [Skull of a Neanderthal Child from Teshik-Tash Cave in Southern Uzbekistan]. In: NESTURKH, M. F. (ed.), *Tešik-Taš: paleolitičeskij čelovek*. Moscow. pp. 137–82.

GRIGOLIA, G. K. 1963. *Paleolit Kvemo-Kartli (pogrebennaja peščera copi I)* [Palaeolithic of Kvemo-Kartli (Buried Cave Tsopi I)]. Tbilisi.

GROSS, H. 1956. Die Umwelt des Neanderthalers. In: *Der Neanderthaler und seine Umwelt*. Bonn. pp. 123–46.

KETRARU, N. A. 1973. *Pamjatniki epohi paleolita i mezolita: arheologičeskaja karta Moldavskoj SSR* [The Monuments of the Palaeolithic and Mesolithic Epochs: Archaeological Map of Moldavian SSR]. Kishinev.

KOLOSOV, Y. G. 1977. *Belaja balka* [White Gorge]. Simferopol.

—— 1979. Akkajskie must'erskie stojanki i nekotorye itogi Ih issledovanija [Akkaj Mousterian Sites and Some Results of their Investigation]. In: *Issledovanija po paleolitu v Krymu*. Kiev. pp. 132–54.

KOLOSOV, Y. G. et al. 1978. Stojanki Zaskal'naja V i Zaskal'naja VI [The Sites Zaskalnaya V and VI]. In: *Arheol. Paleogeogr.* (Moscow), Vol. 84, pp. 37–42.

LYUBIN, V. P. 1977. *Must'erskie kul'turi Kavkaza* [Mousterian Cultures of the Caucasus]. Moscow.

—— 1984. Rannij paleolit Kavkaza [Early Palaeolithic of the Caucasus]. In: BORISKOVSKI, P. I. (ed.), *Paleolit SSSR*. Moscow. pp. 45–93.

MEDVEDEV, G. I. 1975. Mestonahoždenija rannego paleolita v južnom Priangar'e [Early Palaeolithic Sites in Southern Angara Valley]. In: *Drevnjaja istorija narodov juga Vostocnoj Sibiri*. Irkutsk.

MOVIUS, H. 1953. The Mousterian Cave of Teshik-Tash, Southeastern Uzbekistan, Central Asia. *Bull. Am. Sch. Prehist. Res.* (Harvard, Mass.), Vol. 17, pp. 11–71.

NIORADZE, M. G. et al. 1978. Peščera Sakaziya [The Cave Sakaziya]. *Arheol. paleogeogr.* (Moscow), Vol. 84, pp. 26–9.

OKLADNIKOV, A. P. 1940. Issledovanie paleolitičeskoj stojanki Tešik-Taš [The Investigation of the Teshik-Tash Site]. *Tr. Uzb. Fil. Akad. Nauk SSSR* (Tashkent), Vol. 1, pp. 3–45.

—— 1949. Issledovanie must'erskoj stojanki i pogrebenija neandertalca v grote Tešik-Taš [The Investigation of the Mousterian Site and Neanderthal Burial in the Teshik-Tash Cave]. In: NESTOURKH, M. F. (ed.), *Tešik-Taš: paleolitičeskij čelovek*. Moscow. pp. 7–85.

PRASLOV, N. D. 1968. *Rannij paleolit severo-vostočnogo Priazov'ja i nižnego Dona* [Early Palaeolithic of the North-Eastern Azov Valley and Lower Don]. Leningrad.

—— 1984. Rannij paleolit Russkoj ravniny i Kryma [Early Palaeolithic of the Russian Plain and the Crimea]. In: BORISKOVSKI, P. I. (ed.), *Paleolit SSSR*. Moscow. pp. 94–134.

RANOV, D. A. 1965. *Kamennyj vek Tajikistana* [Stone Age of Tajikistan]. Dushanbe.

RANOV, D. A.; NESNEYANOV, S. A. 1973. *Paleolit i stratigrafija antropogena Srednej Azii* [Palaeolithic and Stratigraphy of the Anthropogen Period in Central Asia]. Dushanbe.

ROGINSKI, Y. Y. 1954. Morfologičeskie osobennosti cěrepa rebenka iz pozdnemust'erskogo sloja peščeri Starosel'e [Morphological Features of a Child's Skull from the Late Mousterian Layer of Staroselye Cave]. *Sov. Etnogr.* (Leningrad), Vol. 1, pp. 27–39.

ROHLIN, D. G. 1949. Nekotorye dannye rentgenologičeskogo issledovanija detskogo skeleta iz grota Tešik-Taš, Južnyj Uzbekistan [Some Results of the Roentgenological Investigation of a Child's Skeleton from Teshik-Tash Cave, Southern Uzbekistan]. In: NESTOURKH, M. F. (ed.), *Tešik-Taš: paleolitičeskij čelovek*. Moscow. pp. 109–21.

—— 1965. *Bolezni drevnih ljudej (kosti ljudej različnyh epoh-normalnye i patologičeskie izmenenija)* [Diseases of Ancient Peoples: Normal and Pathologically Changed Human Bones of Different Times]. Moscow/Leningrad.

RUDENKO, S. I. 1960. Ust'-Kanskaja peščernaja paleolitičeskaja stojanka [Palaeolithic Site in Ust-Kan Cave]. In: *Paleolit i neolit*. Moscow/Leningrad. Vol. 4, pp. 104–25.

SEMENOV, S. A. 1950. O protivopostavlenii bolšogo palca ruki neandertalca [On the Opposition of the Thumb in Neanderthal Man]. *Kratk. soobšč. Inst. Etnogr.* (Moscow), Vol. 11, pp. 76–82.

SINELNIKOV, N. A.; GREMYATSKI, M. A. 1949. Kosti skeleta rebenka-neandertalca iz grota Tešik-Taš, Juznyj Uzbekistan [Skeletal Bones of a Neanderthal Child from Teshik-Tash Cave]. In: NESTOURKH, M. F. (ed.), *Tešik-Taš: paleolitičeskij čelovek*. Moscow. pp. 123–35.

SITNIK, A. S. 1983. Gravirovannyj risunok na kosti s must'erskoj stojanki pod Ternopolem [Engraved Drawing on the Bone from the Mousterian Site at Ternopol]. In: VASILYEVSKI, R. S. (ed.), *Plastika i risunki drevnih kul'tur*. Novosibirsk. pp. 39–46.

THOMA, A. 1964. Entstehung der Mongoliden. *Homo* (Göttingen), Vol. 15, Nos. 1–2, pp. 1–22.

VANDERMEERSCH, B. 1981. *Les Hommes fossiles de Qafzeh (Israel)*. Paris.

VEKILOVA, E. A.; ZUBOV, A. A. 1972. Antropologičeskie ostatki iz must'erskih sloev Ahstirskoj peščeri [Anthropological Remains from Mousterian Layers of Ahstir Cave]. *Kratk. soobšč. Inst. Arheol.* (Moscow), No. 131, pp. 61–4.

VERESHCHAGIN, N. K. 1959. *Mlekopitajusčie Kavkaza: istorija formirovanija fauny* [Mammals of the Caucasus: A History of the Fauna Formation]. Moscow/Leningrad.

VLCEK, E. 1976. Remains of a Neanderthal Child from Kiik-Koba in the Crimea. *Acta Facult. Rerum Nat. Univ. Comenia. Anthropol.* (Bratislava), Vol. 22, pp. 194–202.

WEIDENREICH, F. 1945. The Palaeolithic Child from the Teshik-Tash Cave in Southern Uzbekistan (Central Asia). *Am. J. Phys. Anthropol.* (New York), NS, Vol. 3, No. 2, pp. 151–62.

YAKIMOV, V. P.; HARITONOV, V. M. 1979. K probleme krymskih neandertalcev [On the Problem of Crimean Neanderthals]. In: *Issledovanija po paleolitu v Krymu*. Kiev. pp. 191–201.

ZAMYATNIN, S. N. 1961. Stalingradskaja paleolitičeskaja stojanka. *Kratkie soobšč. Inst. Arheol.*, Moscow, Vol. 82, pp. 5–36.

ZAVERNYAEV, F. M. 1978. *Hotilevskoe paleolitičeskoe mestonahozdenie* [Hotilevo Palaeolithic Site]. Leningrad.

14

WESTERN ASIA
during the Middle Palaeolithic

Arthur J. Jelinek

THE SIGNIFICANCE OF THE MIDDLE PALAEOLITHIC IN HUMAN DEVELOPMENT

'Middle Palaeolithic' is a term traditionally used in prehistory to refer to cultural remains left by small groups of hunter-gatherers in the early Late Pleistocene, prior to the appearance about 35,000 years ago of a greater diversity of stone tools and evidence of more complex cultural activities associated with anatomically modern *Homo sapiens sapiens*. Throughout the Middle Palaeolithic the evidence of cultural behaviour is very largely confined to the products and by-products of the manufacture of chipped stone tools. In Europe and western Asia the bones of *Homo sapiens neanderthalensis* are found associated with Middle Palaeolithic stone tools. These industries typically have an abundance of tools made by chipping the edges of simple flint flakes or of flakes made by the Levallois technique of core preparation. This special technique is evidence of an ability to conceptualize a complex succession of actions. It was used to shape a piece of flint into a plano-convex core from which flakes of predetermined form could be struck. The technique takes its name from Levallois-Perret, a suburb of Paris, where it was first described. Its presence, as well as the presence of bifacial handaxes (the 'hallmark' of the western Lower Palaeolithic) in some Middle Palaeolithic industries, is strong evidence for technological continuity between the Lower and Middle Palaeolithic in the western Old World. In fact, as our knowledge of late Middle Pleistocene and Lower Palaeolithic cultures has expanded, an increasing number of features traditionally considered characteristic of the Middle Palaeolithic have been found in this earlier period, and a firm boundary between the Lower and Middle Palaeolithic near the boundary of the Middle and Late Pleistocene geological periods has become more difficult to define on the basis of industrial criteria. It is thus reasonable to see the Middle Paleolithic as a final development in the long, slow evolution of the Lower Palaeolithic cultures of the Middle Pleistocene.

This continuity should not obscure the distinctive nature of typical Middle Palaeolithic cultures as opposed to those of the Lower Palaeolithic. There are clearer repeated patterns of association of distinctive kinds of tools in the Middle Palaeolithic. The cultural meaning of these patterns continues to be the subject of controversy, especially for the western European industries. Apart from its possible social significance, this clearer patterning probably reflects more complex conceptual behaviour than is seen in earlier cultures. Beyond the stone tools, we have glimpses of these higher conceptual developments in such features as the repeated instances of deliberate burial of the dead in the later Middle Palaeolithic, as opposed to a total absence of such evidence in the Lower Palaeolithic.

The major historical importance of the Middle Palaeolithic, then, lies in its developmental position at the end of a very long Lower Palaeolithic sequence that is characterized by only small changes over many hundreds of thousands of years, and directly preceding the highly innovative and more rapidly changing cultures of the Upper Palaeolithic. The major questions that we address in our study of this phase of cultural history concern the significance of the distinctive patterns that we see in the stone tools and other archaeological remains, and the relationships of these patterns to the first appearance of people like those in present-day human populations. For historical reasons, our most detailed current knowledge of the Middle Palaeolithic is derived from archaeological research in western Europe and in western Asia; this chapter treats the evidence from the latter region.

THE ENVIRONMENTAL BACKGROUND

Two major regions of western Asia have yielded the vast majority of our evidence of Middle Palaeolithic cultures and the people who left this evidence: the Levant at the eastern end of the Mediterranean, and the margins and lower elevations of the Zagros Mountains in western Iran and northern Iraq. There are significant environmental contrasts between the two regions at present, and there is every reason to believe that similar contrasts prevailed in the past. These contrasts are due primarily to the proximity of the Mediterranean Sea to the Levant and to the more continental situation and higher elevations of the Zagros region.

Present information shows that, during the period when Middle Palaeolithic peoples inhabited western Asia (around 125,000 to 40,000 years ago), environmental conditions in that region passed through several major episodes of change and probably were never precisely the same as they are today. In general, during peak periods of advance of the continental glaciers in the northern hemisphere, temperatures were lower than at present. It is likely that, during colder intervals, present plant and animal communities that correspond to differences in elevation were forced down to lower altitudes. Along the Mediterranean coast, episodes of lower sea-level (and therefore the exposure of more extensive coastal plains) resulted from the conservation of moisture within the ice masses during periods of maximum growth of the glaciers. These periods of glacial growth and retreat have been reconstructed from evidence in deep-sea sediments that contain a generally uninterrupted record of global climatic change. When this record can be correlated with the less complete information preserved on the continents it helps us better to understand and interpret cultural and environmental evidence from particular archaeological sites. However, this global evidence is largely a reflection of changes in temperature. Since we know that rainfall and wind patterns varied regionally to some unknown degree, our knowledge of the precise environmental challenges that faced Middle Palaeolithic peoples remains somewhat limited.

THE BASIC LEVANTINE SEQUENCE

Two major time periods can be distinguished for Middle Palaeolithic stone tool industries in the Levant. The earlier includes varying relative quantities of handaxes and large flake-tools, in particular thick, steep-edged scrapers that show considerable evidence of repeated sharpening by several separate episodes of chipping. Artefacts of this period are directly preceded in time by Late Acheulean handaxe industries. In a few sites with occupations that correspond to the later part of this first period, several industries have been encountered that show a heavy emphasis on the manufacture of blades (long, slender, parallel-sided prismatic flakes), a practice more characteristic of the much later Upper Palaeolithic cultures. This initial period of the Middle Palaeolithic appears to date to at least the initial phases of the last glacial cycle (oxygen isotope stages 5d to 5a) approximately 110,000 to 80,000 years ago, and perhaps begins somewhat earlier.

The later Middle Palaeolithic period is characterized by an intensive use of the Levallois technique of flake manufacture (only rarely encountered in the earlier period) and an almost complete absence of handaxes and heavy scrapers. Two or perhaps three time phases seem to be represented by these industries. The earliest (on the basis of geological stratigraphy) shows an emphasis on the manufacture of flakes in the form of elongated points made using the Levallois technique, and also includes significant numbers of slender, parallel-edged prismatic blades made using the same technique. Industries of the second phase show a strong emphasis on the production of broad, thin, ovate Levallois flakes and few points or blades. A third phase has been proposed that includes more of a balance between the manufacture of broad flakes and relatively short points. While its relative stratigraphic position and radiocarbon dating suggest that this second Middle Palaeolithic period correlates with oxygen isotope stages 3 and 4 (approximately 80,000 to 40,000 years ago), the occurrence and time duration of the different phases seem to vary in different regions of the Levant.

It is important to bear in mind that much of our evidence of the time sequences and cultural activities of the Neanderthalers in western Asia has been derived from excavations in the deeply layered deposits preserved at the mouths of caves and under overhanging rock shelters. These localities are favoured by archaeologists, who know that these natural shelters are likely to protect the material they contain from erosion. This concentration of archaeological effort led in the past to the application of the term 'Cave Men' to the Neanderthalers and other Palaeolithic peoples. In fact, it is probable that such places were visited only intermittently in the Palaeolithic, and that the Palaeolithic artefacts in each geological layer of such sites represent the mixed residue of many brief visits rather than single long-term habitations. Such sites are valuable because of the increments of material that they preserve, in the form of accumulations of superimposed (stratified) layers of geological sediment and cultural artefacts over thousands of years. The interpretation of this stratigraphic succession allows archaeologists and geologists to reconstruct the time sequence of changes in the industries contained in the layers. Thus, such sites are primarily useful in archaeology for the information that they provide about long sequences of time and not because they were particularly favoured habitats of prehistoric peoples. (In this sense it is the archaeologist who has preferred such places and is more deserving of the epithet 'Cave Man'!) It is only relatively recently that occupation surfaces of Middle Palaeolithic age have been discovered in open-air sites, where isolated single periods of habitation can provide a better understanding of the distinct kinds of activities in which people were engaged. On the basis of the behaviour of recent peoples who live by hunting and gathering, it is probable that these open-air sites were the preferred places of habitation of Palaeolithic peoples. In reading the following survey it is important to remember that we do not yet have any studies of well-preserved living surfaces from any sites for the early Middle Palaeolithic in western Asia, and only a single study of a limited exposure of such surfaces in one open site at the end of the late Middle Palaeolithic.

THE EARLY MIDDLE PALAEOLITHIC IN THE LEVANT

The major part of our evidence of the early Middle Palaeolithic cultures has been derived from excavations in a few cave and rock shelter sites in Lebanon, Syria and Israel, although recently a few open-air sites of this period have also been discovered in north-eastern Syria. The two most important sites are the cave of Tabun on the Wadi Mughara at the western edge of Mount Carmel near Haifa, Israel, and the rock shelter of Jabrud I, on the eastern margin of the Anti-Lebanon mountains (*Jebel esh Sharqi*) about 60 km north of Damascus, Syria. These two sites have yielded similar long sequences of cultural industries, with early Middle Palaeolithic in their lower levels and late Middle Palaeolithic in their upper levels.

At Jabrud I, Alfred Rust, during a remarkable series of excavations in the 1930s (Rust, 1950), found numbers of superimposed layers in the earlier portion of the sequence that contained either many thick scrapers, or many handaxes, or a mixture of the two. He named the stone tool industry represented by the thick scrapers 'Jabrudian' and used the traditional name 'Acheulean' for the layers with handaxes. He called the industry with both kinds of tools 'Acheuleo-Jabrudian'. At about the same time that Rust was working at Jabrud I, Dorothy Garrod was conducting excavations at the Tabun cave (Garrod and Bate, 1937), where she found a deep deposit of 'Acheuleo-Jabrudian', with both handaxes and thick scrapers, overlying a layer with a typical late Acheulean handaxe industry.

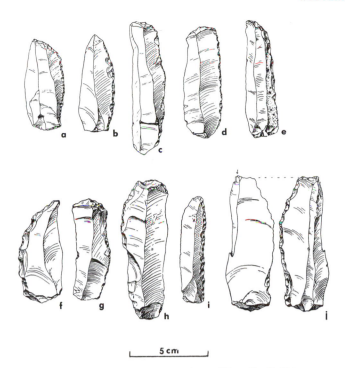

├——— 5 cm ———┤

Figure 28 Blade tools, Mugharan tradition ('Amudian'), Tabun cave (Israel). a, b, d–i, typical and atypical backed knives; c, end-scraper; j, burin on a backed prismatic blade (the arrow indicates the direction of the blow that produced the burin spall. (Garrod's layer Eb.) (After Garrod and Bate, 1937.)

At both sites, near the top of the early Middle Palaeolithic deposits, Rust and Garrod discovered concentrations of slender, parallel-edged prismatic flakes ('blades'), some of which had been made into a variety of tools (Fig. 28). At Tabun these tools were mostly backed knives, while chisel-edged 'burins' predominated at Jabrud I. These kinds of flakes and tools are typical of much later industries in Europe and western Asia, industries always associated with evolved *Homo sapiens*, anatomically identical to people in living human populations. The similarity of this material to the earliest of these industries in Europe, the Aurignacian, led Rust to call the industry at Jabrud I the 'pre-Aurignacian', a term that continues to be used in archaeology despite the now demonstrated lack of continuity between the Jabrud I and European or similar later western Asian industries. Garrod initially used this same term for the blade industries at Tabun, but later used the name 'Amudian' for these materials, a name derived from the Wadi Amud (Lebanon), where tools similar to those from Tabun had been discovered in a similar context, with handaxes and thick scrapers, in a rather primitive excavation by F. Turville-Petre at the Zut-tiyeh cave (Jordan valley) in 1925–6 (Turville-Petre, 1927). Garrod's decision to use this term to distinguish industries with backed knives was made after she discovered yet a third site with this kind of industry, the Zumoffen shelter near Adlun in southern Lebanon (Garrod and Kirkbride, 1961). Here the Amudian tools were found in ancient beach deposits in front of the shelter, and were overlain by a typical Jabrudian industry (Copeland, 1983).

One question that has occupied the attention of Palaeolithic archaeologists is that of the relationship between Garrod's Amudian and Rust's pre-Aurignacian industries. The environmental setting of Rust's site of Jabrud I, on the more arid eastern margin of the mountains bordering the Mediterranean, is quite different from that of Tabun and the Adlun sites on the coastal plain, or Zuttiyeh in the moist Jordan valley. Perhaps it was a different pattern of resource exploitation in this region that led to the different emphasis on the kinds of tools that were made on the blade of the pre-Aurignacian industry at Jabrud I (primarily burins). Here, as at Zumoffen, there are almost no heavy scrapers associated with the blade industry, although there is abundant evidence of the presence of handaxes in the form of broken tips and a curious group of flakes struck from the edges of handaxes. Despite the differences in emphasis in tool manufacture between the Amudian and the pre-Aurignacian, the techniques of blade manufacture in the two industries are quite similar. This, along with their similar position in the chronological and cultural sequence, suggests that they may well be two different aspects of a single phenomenon based in a relatively brief period of widespread manufacture of slender prismatic flakes.

More recent excavations at Tabun (Jelinek et al., 1973; Jelinek, 1982) have provided some additional insights into the relationships between the handaxe, thick scraper and blade industries encountered by Rust and Garrod. It can now be demonstrated that there is considerable variation in the ratio of bifaces to scrapers in the industries contained in the individual geological layers at Tabun, and that this variation is not random but follows a cyclical pattern. The estimated time span for this sequence and the length of the cycles suggest an approximate correspondence to the climatic changes reflected in the deep-sea oxygen isotope record (stages 5a–d). This correlation is supported to some degree by the geological record in the cave. It suggests that manufacture of the heavily retouched scrapers was most prevalent during warmer intervals and that biface manufacture corresponded to cooler intervals. If this correlation is correct, the blade industries of the Amudian were made during the culmination of the coldest interval in this portion of the sequence (stage 5b), following a long period of gradual increase in the relative frequency of bifaces. The recent excavations confirmed that these characteristic 'Upper Palaeolithic' artefacts were in geological association with thick Jabrudian scrapers and Acheulean-like handaxes. It also confirmed the presence of some quantity of both handaxes (Acheulean tools) and thick scrapers (Jabrudian tools) in virtually all of the early Middle Palaeolithic layers. It is now also clear that the Amudian industry is part of a long trend toward the manufacture of narrower flakes that culminated, technologically, in the manufacture of the slender blades upon which the Amudian tools were made.

This evidence of gradual changes in the manufacture of particular kinds of tools supports an interpretation of a single continuing cultural tradition, perhaps the work of a single human population through time. The interpretation is supported by basic continuities and gradual, unidirectional changes in the technology employed in manufacturing the chipped stone artefacts. The term 'Mugharan tradition' (from the Wadi Mughara) has been suggested for this single continuous tradition of stone tool manufacture (Jelinek, 1982). This explanation of the industrial variability at Tabun seems more likely (more economical) than an interpretation of separate populations of 'Acheulean people' and 'Jabrudian people' who maintained their social identity in the same small region over tens of thousands of years, and gradually changed the intensity with which they participated in the mutual use of particular sites. While the brief appearance and disappearance of the blade-based industries of the Amudian might be taken as a stronger case for the appearance and disappearance of a distinct human population (as Garrod and Rust believed), the basic aspects of flake production mentioned above, and the presence of characteristic Acheulean bifaces and Jabrudian scrapers in the Amudian layers, suggest that this industry at Tabun, like the Acheulean and Jabrudian, may simply be a facies of the continuing lithic tradition of a single human population.

The interpretation of these relationships in human terms is limited by the paucity of direct evidence for the use of the different kinds of implements. Neither animal bone nor macroscopic plant remains are well preserved in any of the deposits that have yielded Mugharan industries. The depositional evidence suggests that the flint artefacts were left in the sites during many brief periods of occupation. At Tabun it is likely that a spring or another source of moisture was available near the mouth of the cave. Spring-polished flints occur in the Mugharan layers and even at present the face of the centre of the profile under the arch of the cave is always moist. Thus a dependable source of water may have periodically drawn both people and animals to the site. This would have been especially important during the summers of the warmer climatic intervals, which may not have been very different from present rainless summers in this region. In general, it seems most reasonable to see the heavy scrapers as tools for processing plant materials, and the bifaces (which frequently have sharp transverse edges) and the blade tools as butchering implements. The slowly shifting relative frequencies of the different kinds of tools may reflect human responses to the gradually changing opportunities to utilize particular kinds of resources in the vicinity of the cave as the local environment also slowly shifted in response to global patterns of climatic change.

Thus, the Tabun cave, the Jabrud I shelter and the Adlun sites show that the early period of the Middle Palaeolithic, as represented by the Mugharan tradition with its specialized patterns of tool manufacture, contrasts with the more uniform and generalized Lower Palaeolithic Acheulean culture that preceded it. In a long-term view, these early patterns of specialization may reflect an increasing awareness of differences in the potential value and economy of utilization of particular environmental resources by groups of Middle Palaeolithic hunter-gatherers.

As well as the occurrences in the southern and central Levant, there have been several discoveries of early Middle Palaeolithic industries in the northern Levant, including finds of Jabrudian scrapers with and without associated handaxes in the Al-Kowm Basin of central Syria (Besançon et al., 1981). Here tentative age estimates using electron spin resonance (ESR) techniques suggest that the Jabrudian industries may date from as early as about 150,000 to somewhat later than 100,000 years ago. The earliest range of these dates is older than would be expected on the basis of geological correlations for similar industries in the coastal areas, and it is important to note that their tentative nature has been emphasized by the physicist who made the observations (Henning, in Henning and Hours, 1982). The Al-Kowm discoveries are of particular interest since they are associated with spring deposits that reflect locally favourable oasis environments, where both plant foods and animals were predictably available.

These Jabrudian finds and other reported occurrences of this industry in the northern Levant are based primarily on surface finds and shallow tests. Geological data collected on the surveys that produced these finds indicate that they are contemporary with Acheulean biface industries that show a significant emphasis on Levallois flaking and have a much wider distribution than does the Jabrudian (Copeland and Hours, 1981). Evidence is not yet at hand from this region

to demonstrate the nature of the relationship between these two industries; it is quite possible that they represent two facies of the same stone tool tradition, where the Jabrudian is associated with localities with more abundant plant resources and the Acheulean with a more diversified range of resources. The major difference between these industries and those of the cave and shelter sites of Jabrud I, Tabun, and Adlun is in the absence of Levallois flaking in the Acheulean components of the latter sites.

Thus evidence exists throughout the Levant for human habitation during the earliest phases of the last glacial cycle, contemporary with the Mousterian cultures of the Neanderthalers in western Europe. The lithic industries and their distribution suggest that a fundamental level of specialization in resource exploitation was already present at that time. An alternative explanation for the differences in the relative abundance of different kinds of tools is that distinct contemporary and coterminous social groups produced only particular kinds of tools for tens of thousands of years. On the basis of the overall evidence such an explanation appears to be significantly weaker than one based on the specialized exploitation of resources.

The biological and mental nature of the hominids that produced these industries remains virtually unknown. The only human fossil that can be assigned to this period, the 'Galilee skull', recovered at the base of Mugharan tradition layers at Zuttiyeh in the early excavation by Turville-Petre, has some physical resemblance to the later western Asian Neanderthalers, but is held to be distinct from them by some human palaeontologists. There is not yet any evidence of deliberate human burial in this period, but it should be pointed out that in most of the deposits that have produced these industries bone is either absent or poorly preserved. In contrast to the relatively sparse archaeological record for the early Middle Palaeolithic, the late Middle Palaeolithic in the Levant is represented at numerous sites throughout the region.

THE LATE MIDDLE PALAEOLITHIC IN THE LEVANT

The single dominant feature of the late Middle Palaeolithic industries in the Levant is the presence of the Levallois technique of flake manufacture at all known sites. This feature led to their designation as 'Levalloiso-Mousterian' by Garrod (1936). Because of the distinct nature of these industries in the Levant, and in view of the known presence of different Mousterian industries with heavy emphasis on Levallois flake production in Europe and North Africa, it is now preferable to replace the more generalized term of Levalloiso-Mousterian with 'Levantine Mousterian' to distinguish the Levant industries. With the appearance of these later Middle Palaeolithic industries, the manufacture of bifaces and of the characteristic thick steep scrapers of the Jabrudian industries virtually ceased. In addition to the disappearance of the bifaces, core tools in general become less frequent. The significance of this profound change in stone tool manufacture in human terms remains obscure.

The two deepest stratified sites that have produced sequences of Levantine Mousterian industries are Tabun and Jabrud I. At both sites there is evidence for an early appearance of a stone tool industry that emphasized the manufacture of long, triangular Levallois flakes, designated as Levallois points (Fig. 29), and prismatic blades with faceted striking platforms that appear to be by-products of the manu-

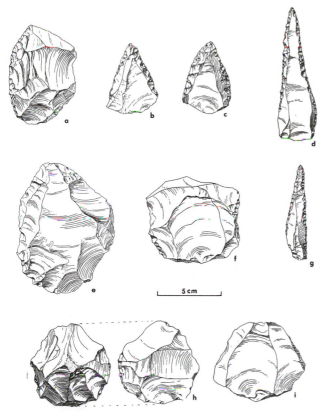

Figure 29 Levantine Mousterian tools, Levallois flakes and cores, Tabun cave (Israel). a, simple convex side-scraper on a Levallois flake; b, short retouched Levallois point; c, Mousterian point on short Levallois point; d and g, elongated Mousterian points on long Levallois points; e, large broad Levallois flake; f, h and i, Levallois cores. (d and g from Garrod's layer D (phase 1); a and e from Garrod's layer C (phase 2); b, c, h and i from Garrod's layer B and chimney (phase 3).) (After Garrod and Bate, 1937.)

facture of the points. This industry has been referred to as 'phase 1' Mousterian (Copeland, 1975) or 'layer D' or 'D-type' Mousterian, the latter terms taken from its position in Garrod's sequence at Tabun (Garrod and Bate, 1937, pp. 76–8). The more recent excavations at Tabun (Jelinek, 1982) have shown that this industry is preceded by a transition that shows a gradual increase in emphasis on Levallois flaking and a corresponding decrease in the frequency of characteristic earlier-period bifaces and heavy scrapers. The earliest horizons of this transition include both broad, radially prepared Levallois flakes and Levallois points. Later there are increasing frequencies of points and fewer and fewer broad flakes. This transition at Tabun seems to show that there was some continuity between the early and late Middle Palaeolithic industries. There is also some evidence from the Hummal locality at Al-Kowm for a transition to a phase 1 Levantine Mousterian following an earlier Jabrudian industry (Copeland, 1983).

At Tabun the phase 1 Mousterian is overlain by phase 2 ('layer C' or 'C-type') Mousterian, which includes many broad, thin, radially prepared Levallois flakes (Fig. 29) and relatively few Levallois points. There is a dramatic hiatus in the deposits at Tabun between layer D and layer C, caused by a period of karstic collapse of layer D sediments into a sink-hole in the inner chamber of the cave and a gradual filling of the immense pit in that chamber prior to the deposition of the layer C industry. There is some evidence for a gradual transition between these two kinds of industries at Jabrud I, and perhaps at Abou Zif in the Judean desert

south-east of Jerusalem (Neuville, 1951), but in general such evidence remains sparse.

A third phase of Levantine Mousterian, characterized by broad Levallois flakes and relatively short, broad-based, convex Levallois points (Fig. 29), has also been proposed (Copeland, 1975). The uppermost industries at Tabun (layer B and the Chimney levels) have been referred to this phase 3 (or 'Tabun B' or 'B-type' Mousterian), as have industries from other sites in the coastal and hill region of the southern and central Levant. It is important to note that between the deposition of layer C and layer B at Tabun a relatively rapid transition took place in the human utilization of the cave, which was caused by the collapse of the roof in the interior chamber. The layer C industry appears to be the product of a relatively intensive utilization of the terrace at the mouth of the cave for a range of domestic activities that included food processing and of the production at this spot of broad Levallois flakes (the whole range of manufacturing debris is present). The layer B and Chimney industries, on the other hand, were the result of a different set of activities: the butchering of animals (primarily *Dama*), apparently driven into the natural trap formed by the hole left by the collapsed roof. It is therefore possible that the different occupational circumstances at Tabun may be the primary factor responsible for the differences between the kinds of stone tools left in the layer C and layer B deposits. The geological evidence at the site suggests that very little time elapsed between the two kinds of occupations.

The geographical distribution of these three kinds of Levantine Mousterian industries is not random. In the southern and central Levant the phase 2 and 3 industries, with broad Levallois flakes, are largely confined to the coastal region and to the hill country to the north and west of the broad interior expanses of steppe and desert. Mousterian industries from the steppe–desert region are predominantly of the phase 1 type. In the northern Levant the broad flake industries are more widespread, particularly in the terraces of the Euphrates and other major drainages (Copeland, 1981).

The chronological relationships of the three proposed phases of Levantine Mousterian are not yet resolved. The absolute age of most of the Middle Palaeolithic lies beyond the range of present radiocarbon-dating techniques, and most of the 'finite' radiocarbon age determinations on the later Middle Palaeolithic should probably be treated as *minimal* ages, unless it can be demonstrated that the samples were collected under rigorous conditions and processed in facilities especially equipped to deal with materials older than 40,000 years. The few determinations that satisfy these criteria indicate that the phase 2 industries of layer C at Tabun are about 50,000 years old (Jelinek, 1982) and that the transition from phase 1 to Upper Palaeolithic industries in the Negev desert took place about 40,000 years ago (Marks, 1983). These are at present the limits of our knowledge of the chronology of the industries as revealed by consistent absolute dating techniques.

Stratigraphic evidence shows that phase 1 industries always underlie phase 2 or 3 or both when they are found in the same site. The general absence of phase 2 and 3 in the desert–steppe regions, and the apparent continuity of phase 1 in those regions up to the transition to Upper Palaeolithic industries at such sites as Boker Tachtit (Marks, 1983) in the central Negev, suggests that these two patterns of tool manufacture may have been related to distinct environmental adaptations. If this was the case then the basic pattern of development could have been one of an initial overall distribution of phase 1 industries, as the major technological advance in a generalized adaptation to a broad resource base, followed by the development of the phase 2 and 3 industries in regions of more abundant moisture and vegetation. Considering the size of the territories involved, this might reflect an eventual separation of two distinct Levantine Mousterian cultures into ethnically separate entities.

The basic chronology presented here for the Middle Palaeolithic industries rests, for the early part of the sequence, on the geological evidence of assumed stratigraphic correlations with the marine oxygen isotope stages and on an association of some of the industries at Adlun with beach deposits that reflect a relatively high level of the Mediterranean Sea. The general time frame for these cultures is supported by absolute dates from Al-Kowm and the basal travertine at Zuttiyeh. The early Levantine Mousterian industries at Tabun (phase 1) have been found in asssociation with cold climate rodents and pollen (Jelinek et al., 1973) that tend to support the geological correlation of these industries with oxygen isotope stage 4 at about 70,000 years ago. The radiocarbon dates of about 50,000 years ago for the phase 2 industries at Tabun are also consistent with climatic and geologogical evidence that suggests an oxygen isotope stage 3 placement. The earliest appearance of the Upper Palaeolithic and the disappearance of Middle Palaeolithic industries is currently documented at about 40,000 years ago by absolute dating in the Negev.

An alternative chronology to that given above has been based upon the relatively great age (up to 90,000 years) assigned to phase 2 industries at the coastal sites of Ras Al-Kelb and Naameh near Beirut, Lebanon, on the basis of apparent correlations of stone tools with raised Mediterranean beaches and (somewhat inconsistent) uranium–thorium dates for marine organisms in the beach deposits (Copeland, 1981). Another alternative scheme places the phase 3 industries of the Qafzeh cave, near Nazareth, Israel, at about 70,000 to 80,000 years ago (Bar Yosef and Vandermeersch, 1981). This chronological assignment is based upon an acceptance of the dates of the industrial association at Naameh, and upon the presence of two extinct species of rodents at Qafzeh that are not present in layer C at Tabun and one modern form of rodent in Tabun C that is absent at Qafzeh. If either of these chronological estimates proves to be correct it will indicate that the time assignments of the early Middle Palaeolithic industries at Tabun may be too conservative, and that the late Middle Palaeolithic industries were less consistent in their chronological appearance than has been assumed from the similar sequences at Tabun, Jabrud I and Adlun.

Perhaps the most striking new development in the late Middle Palaeolithic of the Levant is the presence of repeated instances of deliberate burial of the dead. No clear association of this practice with phase 1 industries is yet known. It is possible that the Tabun I burial belonged to this phase, but this cannot be conclusively demonstrated with present evidence. The burials associated with the Levantine Mousterian are of exceptional interest for the study of human biological evolution because they include both Neanderthalers and modern forms of *Homo sapiens sapiens*, as well as some individuals who exhibit features of both types. Burials of individuals with many features reminiscent of European Neanderthalers include the Tabun I female (McCown and Keith, 1939), the Amud male (Plate 17) (Suzuki and Takai, 1970) and the recently recovered Kebara male (Arensburg et al., 1985). The Amud and Kebara finds

are probably associated with phase 3 industries and Tabun I with phase 2 (see p. 157).

Burials of *Homo sapiens sapiens* similar to individuals in present-day populations, but also showing some archaic morphological features, were found on the terrace in front of the shelter of Skhul, a few hundred metres from Tabun (McCown and Keith, 1939), and in the lowest levels at Qafzeh (Qafzeh Hominid 11: Tillier, 1984). The industry at both of these sites appears to be phase 3. Finally, a number of burials of fully modern *Homo sapiens sapiens* have been found associated with a phase 3 industry at Qafzeh (Plate 25) (Vandermeersch, 1981).

As is obvious from the preceding discussion of chronology, the relative ages of these different kinds of humans are still in question. A technological trend, based on a gradual decrease in the relative thickness of flakes in the long sequence at Tabun, when applied to the industries at Qafzeh and Skhul (Jelinek, 1982), suggests that the Neanderthalers are earlier than the 'mixed' hominids, and that the fully modern forms are the most recent. The postulated early date for Qafzeh of 70,000 to 80,000 years ago (Bar Yosef and Vandermeersch, 1981) would, of course, imply that anatomically modern *Homo sapiens sapiens* was present there with a phase 3 industry at least 20,000 years prior to the Neanderthalers with a phase 2 industry at Tabun, 30 km to the west of Qafzeh. Here too, only reliable absolute dating will resolve the question.

One interesting point relevant to culture history that can be addressed with the current evidence is the fact that all of the industries associated with these burials are basically Levantine Mousterian, regardless of the state of the evolutionary development of the people. This seems to demonstrate that the biological potential of anatomically modern *Homo sapiens sapiens* for the dramatic cultural advances that characterize the Upper Palaeolithic was present in the Levant before (and perhaps long before) there is archaeological evidence of this cultural transition.

The evidence for a transition from Middle to Upper Palaeolithic in this region has been well reviewed by Marks (1983). Transitional industries have been proposed at several sites (chiefly Ksar Akil and Abu-Halka in Lebanon, and Boker Tachtit in the central Negev). Marks points out that this transition about 40,000 years ago was mainly a technological change to the manufacture of prismatic blades on unidirectional cores without evidence of Levallois preparation, and that the typological products of these transitional industries appear to differ in different localities. Within the small confines of the excavation area at Boker Tachtit, Marks found interesting contrasts between the Middle and Upper Palaeolithic occupations in the dispersal of the products of flaking of particular flint cores. These differences suggest, albeit very tentatively, that there may have been more effective social interaction between the Upper Palaeolithic people than between the Middle Palaeolithic people at the site. One important feature of the evidence put forward by Marks is that it demonstrates that there is continuity between some of the Mousterian industries and the following Upper Palaeolithic in the Levant. This obviates the need to postulate an intrusion of a 'foreign' Upper Palaeolithic population to account for this important cultural change. The interesting information derived from the Boker Tachtit open-air site excavation highlights the great future potential of such sites for the interpretation of the behaviour of the Neanderthalers and their contemporaries in this part of the world.

Thus, present evidence from the Middle Palaeolithic in the Levant seems to show a long slow evolution, typical of the *palaeocultural* behaviour that characterizes fossil human beings (Jelinek, 1977), which culminated in the presence of qualitatively different industries and hominids that exhibit all of the essential features of modern biological populations and fully cultural behaviour. While it is possible to interpret this sequence as a reflection of parallel biological and cultural evolution, this has not yet been firmly demonstrated. In any event, it is clear that the prehistoric sequence in the Levant has provided us with some of the most important available evidence relevant to the development of humanity during the period in which humans that looked and behaved like the peoples of today appeared.

THE ZAGROS MIDDLE PALAEOLITHIC

In contrast to the relatively abundant evidence and long stratigraphic records of Middle Palaeolithic cultures in the Levant, the valleys and foothills of the Zagros mountains to the north and east of the Mesopotamian plain have thus far yielded relatively little evidence of this phase of human development. In part this sparse record is probably due to the fact that there has been appreciably less archaeological exploration in that region. It is of interest to note that virtually every expedition that has searched for Middle Palaeolithic evidence in the Zagros area has discovered relevant sites.

The collections that have been recovered reveal a quite uniform group of lithic industries that differ significantly from any of the Middle Palaeolithic industries of the Levant. Because of their uniformity and distinctive character these industries are usually grouped under the name of 'Zagros Mousterian'. They were manufactured from relatively small nodules of chalcedony, radiolarite and similar materials. As a result, the tools, flakes and cores are generally smaller than those of the Levantine industries. Furthermore, in most of these industries tools were extensively reflaked until they were reduced to a size no longer practical for further use. Because of this intensive pattern of tool reduction it has been difficult to reconstruct technological patterns of flake manufacture at most sites, and our knowledge of this aspect of lithic production remains limited. It now appears that, contrary to earlier interpretations, there may have been a significant use of the Levallois technique in these industries, but that most of the Levallois flakes and cores were subject to such extensive resharpening that much of the evidence of the technique has been obliterated.

Very few Zagros Mousterian sites have been described in detail and no information is available on possible temporal or spatial differences in the industries. Only a few collections have been described in terms that allow quantitative comparisons. Pertinent here is the pioneering work of Skinner (1965) on materials from the Iraqi sites of Shanidar cave, layer D, and Hazar Merd, and the Iranian sites of Kunji and Bisitun. Other relevant studies are those of Akazawa (1975) for Shanidar D, Dibble (1984) for Bisitun and Bewley (1984) for Houmian (Iran). All of these studies describe industries with a strong emphasis on well-retouched Mousterian points, simple scrapers, convergent scrapers, and other heavily flaked small pieces (Fig. 30). Neither Skinner nor Akazawa found much evidence of Levallois technique in the industries that they examined, and this absence was taken by Skinner to be a feature of all of the Zagros Mousterian. Dibble, on the other hand, reported very high frequencies of this technique at Bisitun (45–60 per cent) and Bewley found 11 per cent at Houmian. The discrepancy between

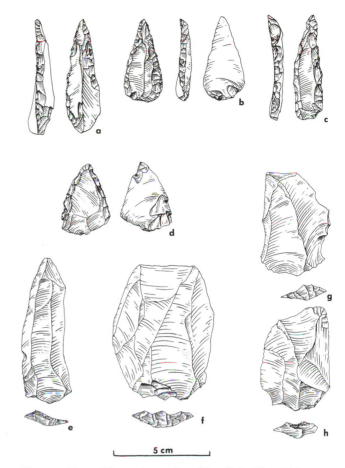

Figure 30 Zagros Mousterian tools and Levallois flakes, Bisitum cave (Iran). a–d, small convergent scrapers and Mousterian points; e–h, Levallois flakes. (After Dibble, 1984.)

the findings of Dibble and Skinner for the Bisitun industry may be due in part to the incomplete collection examined by Skinner and in part to his use of a more restricted definition of Levallois technique. The studies of Dibble and Bewley suggest that more variability may exist in the technology employed in the Zagros Mousterian industries than would be expected on the basis of earlier reports. However, the uniformity of the tools present in these industries remains unchallenged by recent work.

The age of the Zagros Mousterian industries remains an open question. The only site for which absolute dates are available is Shanidar cave. Here radiocarbon determination from samples near the top of Layer D approach the limits of the technique and suggest a minimal age of about 50,000 years. The full time range of the more than 8 metres of deposits in this layer has been estimated at about 50,000 years on the basis of sedimentation rates, palynology, and chemical analyses (Solecki, 1963), but this estimate is clearly in need of further verification. On the basis of palynological evidence, it has been suggested that the Houmian Middle Palaeolithic is probably earlier than Shanidar and may date to between 60,000 and 70,000 years ago (Bewley, 1984, p. 32). These limited data indicate that the Zagros Mousterian may equate in a general temporal sense with the Levantine Mousterian.

Only one site in the Zagros region has yielded evidence of human burials associated with Middle Palaeolithic materials. In the upper half of layer D of Shanidar cave two groups of human remains, representing a total of nine individuals, were discovered by Solecki in his excavations between 1951 and 1960 (Solecki, 1971). These remains have been thoroughly studied and reported by Trinkaus (1983). They are classified as Neanderthalers and comprise the largest sample of this type of hominid that has been recovered from any single site. This has allowed a more extensive interpretation than has been possible for other finds. Trinkaus sees an evolutionary change in the facial structure from the earlier to the later group that parallels similar development in Neanderthalers in western Europe. This trend suggests that broadly similar patterns of selection may have prevailed among the human populations of the western Old World in the earlier periods of the late Pleistocene. He interprets the robust structure of the Neanderthalers (relative to that of modern *Homo sapiens sapiens*) as evidence of a need for physical strength in activities that were later aided by the technological innovations of the Upper Palaeolithic. This interpretation, drawn from western Asian evidence, has far-reaching implications for human development everywhere.

Two burials at Shanidar are of particular interest for an understanding of human cultural development in this period. The Shanidar 1 hominid, an adult male who died at between 30 and 40 years of age, shows evidence of extensive injuries that resulted in loss of sight in one eye, probable paralysis of the right arm and a crippling of the right leg at least several years before his death. It seems unlikely that such an individual could have continued to fill a full adult economic role in the society after these injuries. Thus his survival appears to reflect a significant level of altruistic care and support by his social group. A second burial of interest is that of Shanidar hominid 4. A palynological analysis of sediments surrounding the burial discovered numerous clumped grains of pollen from plants characterized by bright, easily visible flowers. The clustered nature of the grains strongly suggests that the whole flowers were present and from this evidence considerable speculation has developed regarding the aesthetic propensities of the Neanderthalers. At present this is the only evidence available for the association of flowers with Neanderthal burials, and even here alternative explanations for the presence of the pollen are possible (Leroi-Gourhan, 1975).

As is the case with many other aspects of Palaeolithic research in the Zagros region, the transition from Middle to Upper Palaeolithic industries and the time of appearance of anatomically modern *Homo sapiens* are problems in culture history that remain to be explored. The Upper Palaeolithic 'Baradostian' industry, first defined at Shanidar (Solecki, 1956), has many features in common with the earlier Mousterian; in some respects it looks like a miniaturized version of that industry. It seems to occupy the same geographical range as the Zagros Mousterian and this combined limited evidence suggests a transition *in situ*. The radiocarbon dates of about 35,000 years ago for samples of bone from the Baradostian at Shanidar should probably be treated with caution, because these determinations were made before refined techniques of preparation of bone samples were available.

THE SIGNIFICANCE OF THE WESTERN ASIAN MIDDLE PALAEOLITHIC EVIDENCE

Most of our knowledge of the cultural activities and the biological nature of these Middle Palaeolithic peoples is derived from the human and animal bones and the remnants of industries of flaked stone tool manufacture that have been found in the protected deposits of cave mouths and rock shelters. Because of the restricted nature of the sites that have produced this archaeological record, the misconception has arisen that these kinds of sites were the preferred habitat of Middle Palaeolithic societies. A simple consideration of the amount of evidence of cultural activity that can be accounted for in these kinds of sites in any region over the 70,000-year time span of the Middle Palaeolithic is a sufficient illustration of the relatively minor importance of such sites in the life of these earlier hominids. This illustration shows the limits of our present evidence and how much remains to be learned about the behaviour and activities of the people who produced the Middle Palaeolithic industries.

On a more positive note, the western Asian region has provided us with some of the best-documented distributions and sequences of Middle Palaeolithic stone tool industries found to date. Industries generally similar to those of the western Asian Middle Palaeolithic have been well described for western Europe (Chapter 12). While similar kinds of tools and techniques are present in the two regions, there are clear and important differences as well. For example, an industry with the same kinds of tools as the Jabrudian, and in similar relative quantities, is known as the 'Quina Mousterian' in Europe. There, however, it is encountered chiefly in the later Middle Palaeolithic levels (contemporary with phase 1 of the Levantine Mousterian), where it is associated with evidence of very cold and rigorous environments. These kinds of contrasts highlight the problems of interpreting cultural systems with only the restricted evidence of their stone tool industries. The archaeological record from western Asia does reinforce the impression derived from evidence in Europe and other parts of the world of the Middle Palaeolithic as a prolonged period in which innovations seldom appear and the same restricted techniques and forms of flake and tool manufacture persist through many hundreds of human generations. The long sequence at Tabun and Jabrud I are some of the best illustrations of this phenomenon in the Levant, and perhaps the deep record at Shanidar will eventually provide comparable evidence from the Zagros region. The contrast between this record and that of the Upper Palaeolithic illustrates the profound differences in behaviour between these Middle Palaeolithic populations and peoples like ourselves.

Beyond this essentially palaeocultural industrial pattern, the western Asian evidence does reveal aspects of more complex behaviour. In particular, the deliberate human burials at Shanidar, Tabun, Skhul and Qafzeh suggest a concern for the future of the deceased. The extent and complexity of this concern are difficult to discern at present. The inclusion of objects with some burials (such as a boar's jaw at Skhul and a large deer antler at Qafzeh) has been interpreted as evidence for a concept of an after-life. However, most such objects, including the well-known goat horn cores at Teshik-Tash in Uzbekistan, can as easily be explained as discarded digging implements left in or on the grave. The flower pollen at Shanidar is more difficult to interpret, as is the curious deer burial from the phase 2 Levantine Mousterian levels at Nahr Ibrahim in Lebanon. These are tantalizing clues to aspects of behaviour not reflected in the stone tool industries, and only additional evidence will allow us to interpret them more fully.

Finally, the human burials from western Asia comprise a unique collection of physical remains of Middle Palaeolithic peoples. This record shows a wide range of variability in the biological morphology of individuals associated with later

Middle Palaeolithic industries, from the Neanderthalers of Shanidar and Tabun to fully modern *Homo sapiens sapiens* at Qafzeh. Whether these different kinds of hominids represent evidence of an evolution from Neanderthaler to humans of the Modern type or different contemporary populations will only be understood when a reliable absolute chronology is available.

BIBLIOGRAPHY

AKAZAWA, T. 1975. Preliminary Notes on the Middle Paleolithic Assemblage from the Shanidar Cave. *Sumer* (Baghdad), Vol. 31, Nos. 1–2, pp. 3–10.

ARENSBURG, B. et al. 1985. Une sépulture néanderthalienne dans la grotte de Kebara (Israël). *C. R. Acad. Sci.* (Paris), Vol. 300, No. 6, pp. 227–30.

BAR-YOSEF, O.; VANDERMEERSCH, B. 1981. Notes Concerning the Possible Age of the Mousterian Layers in Qafzeh Cave. In: CAUVIN, J.; SANLAVILLE, P. (eds), *Préhistoire du Levant*. Paris, CNRS. pp. 281–5.

BESANÇON, J. et al. 1981. La Paléolithique d'El Kowm, rapport préliminaire. *Paléorient*, Vol. 7, no. 1, pp. 33–5.

BEWLEY, R. H. 1984. The Cambridge University Archaeological Expedition to Iran 1969, Excavations in the Zagros Mountains: Houmian, Mir Malas and Barde Spid. *Iran* (London), Vol. 22, pp. 1–38.

COPELAND, L. 1975. The Middle and Upper Paleolithic of Lebanon and Syria in the Light of Recent Research. In: WENDORF, F.; MARKS, A. E. (eds), *Problems in Prehistory: North Africa and the Levant*. Dallas. pp. 317–50.

—— 1981. Chronology and Distribution of the Middle Paleolithic as Known in 1980, in Lebanon and Syria. In: CAUVIN, J.; SANLAVILLE, P. (eds), *Préhistoire du Levant*. Paris, CNRS. pp. 239–63.

—— 1983. The Stone Industries. In: ROE, D. A. (ed.), *Adlun in the Stone Age: The Excavations of D. A. E. Garrod in the Lebanon, 1958–1963*. Oxford. pp. 89–365. (BAR Int. Ser., 159).

COPELAND, L.; HOURS, F. 1981. La Fin de l'Acheuléen et l'avènement du Paléolithique Moyen en Syrie. In: CAUVIN, J.; SANLAVILLE, P. (eds), *Préhistoire du Levant*. Paris, CNRS. pp. 225–38.

DIBBLE, H. L. 1984. The Mousterian Industry from Bisitun Cave (Iran). *Paléorient*, Vol. 10, No. 2, pp. 23–34.

GARROD, D. A. E. 1936. A Summary of Seven Seasons' Work at the Wady el-Mughara. *Bull. Am. Sch. Prehist. Res.*, Vol. 12, pp. 125–30.

—— 1956. 'Acheuléo-Jabrudien' et 'Pré-Aurignacien' de la Grotte du Taboun (Mont Carmel): étude stratigraphique et chronologique. *Quaternaria* (Rome), Vol. 3, pp. 39–59.

GARROD, D. A. E.; BATE, B. M. A. 1937. *The Stone Age of Mount Carmel I*. Oxford.

GARROD, D. A. E.; KIRKBRIDE, D. 1961. Excavation of the Abri Zumoffen, a Paleolithic Rock-Shelter near Adlun, South Lebanon, 1958. *Bull. Mus. Beyrouth*, Vol. 16, pp. 7–46.

HENNING, G. J.; HOURS, F. 1982. Dates pour le passage entre l'Acheuléen et le Paléolithique moyen à El Kowm (Syrie). *Paléorient*, Vol. 8, No. 1, pp. 81–6.

JELINEK, A. J. 1977. The Lower Paleolithic: Current Evidence and Interpretations. *Annu. Rev. Anthropol.*, Vol. 6, pp. 11–32.

—— 1982. The Tabun Cave and Palaeolithic Man in the Levant. *Science* (Washington), Vol. 216, No. 4553, pp. 1369–75.

JELINEK, A. J. et al. 1973. Excavations at the Tabun Cave, Mount Carmel, Israel. *Paléorient*, Vol. 1, No. 2, pp. 151–83.

LEROI-GOURHAN, ARLETTE. 1975. Flowers Found with Shanidar IV, a Neanderthal Burial in Iraq. *Science* (Washington), Vol. 190, pp. 562–4.

MCCOWN, T. D.; KITH, A. 1939. *The Stone Age of Mount Carmel*. Oxford. Vol. 2.

MARKS, A. E. 1983. The Middle to Upper Palaeolithic Transition in the Levant. *Adv. World Archaeol.*, Vol. 2, pp. 51–98.

NEUVILLE, R. 1931. L'Acheuléen supérieur de la Grotte d'Oumm-Qatafa (Palestine). *Anthropologie* (Paris), Vol. 41, No. 1, pp. 13–51, No. 2, pp. 249–63.

—— 1951. Paléolithique et Mésolithique du désert de Judée. *Arch. Inst. Paléontol. Hum.* (Paris), Vol. 24, pp. 1–271.

RUST, A. 1950. *Die Höhlenfunde von Jabrud (Syrien)*. Neumünster.

SKINNER, J. 1965. *The Flake Industries of Southwest Asia: A Typological Study*. New York. (Doct. thesis, Columbia University.)

SOLECKI, R. S. 1956. The Baradostian Industry and the Upper Palaeolithic in the Near East. New York. (Doct. thesis, Columbia University.)

—— 1963. Prehistory in the Shanidar Valley, Northern Iraq. *Science* (Washington), Vol. 139, No. 3551, pp. 179–93.

—— 1971. *Shanidar. The First Flower People*. New York.

SUZUKI, H.; TAKAI, F. (eds) 1970. *The Amud Man and his Cave Site*. Tokyo.

TILLIER, A. M. 1984. L'Enfant Homo 11 de Qafzeh (Israël) et son apport à la compréhension des modalités de la croissance des squelettes moustériens. *Paléorient*, Vol. 10, No. 1, pp. 7–48.

TRINKAUS, E. 1983. *The Shanidar Neanderthals*. New York.

TURVILLE-PETRE, F. 1927. Researches in Prehistoric Galilee (1925–1926) and a Report on the Galilee Skull. *Bull. Br. Sch. Archaeol. Jerus.* (London), Vol. 14, pp. 1–119.

VANDERMEERSCH, B. 1981. *Les Hommes fossiles de Qafzeh (Israël)*. Paris, CNRS.

15

SOUTH ASIA

in the period of *Homo sapiens neanderthalensis* and contemporaries (Middle Palaeolithic)

Ramchandra V. Joshi

The cultures belonging to the period of *Homo sapiens neanderthalensis* are fairly well represented in south Asia except in Bangladesh, Bhutan, Myanmar (formerly Burma) and Sri Lanka. There is some confusion about the occurrence of these cultures in Nepal (Terai region) and Sri Lanka. In Pakistan the Soan and Peshawar regions are being freshly examined to determine the characteristics of the Late Soan industry, which show some influence of Clactonian and Levalloiso-Mousterian technology in the flake assemblages from Soan and Sanghao cave sites. Afghanistan has also yielded artefacts of such a culture, which is more closely allied to the cultures of the adjoining central Asian region.

Occurrences of Middle Palaeolithic artefacts are better known in India. Basically these belong to a flake industry with a few tools worked on nodules or cores and occasionally on blades. Although some glimpses of the Typical Mousterian of Europe are discernible in a few assemblages, by and large, the industry corresponds to the African Middle Palaeolithic (Middle Stone Age). There appear to be evolutionary trends towards this culture in the earlier Lower Palaeolithic and some continuity with the technology and typology of the following Upper Palaeolithic. A favourable environment and perhaps an increase in population at this cultural stage may have caused the extensive spread of this culture over almost all India.

Middle Palaeolithic hominid remains have been reported only from Afghanistan.

AFGHANISTAN

According to Davis (1978), out of several possible Middle Palaeolithic sites in Afghanistan that have been discovered, only the one at Dara-i-Kur can definitely be considered to be of this period. It has been radiometrically dated to around 30,000 years ago. This is a rock shelter site located in Badakhshan Province. It possesses a flake industry showing the Levallois technique in the manufacture of the artefacts (Fig. 31). This assemblage is made on basalt and a fairly high proportion of it consists of blades, recalling Upper Palaeolithic blade forms. Scrapers are rare and handaxes absent. This site has also yielded an incomplete hominid temporal bone. This is the only example of hominid material so far obtained from Afghanistan and it shows characteristics partly

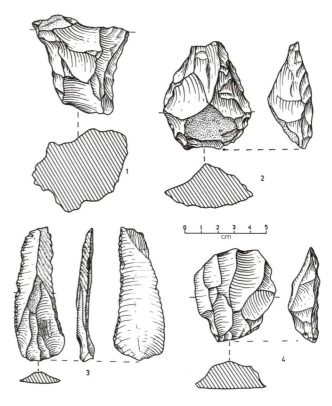

Figure 31 Middle Palaeolithic artefacts, Dara-i-Kur (Afghanistan). 1, flake core; 2, discoidal core; 3, retouched blade; 4, Levallois core. (After R. S. Davis, 1978; Courtesy Academic Press, Orlando.)

of Neanderthal and partly of Modern humans. There are a few traces of Palaeolithic sites at Kara Kamar and Ghar-i-Mordeh Gusfand, but in the opinion of Davis their Middle Palaeolithic aspects have not been firmly established. The Zagros mountains in Iraq and Iran have yielded Middle Palaeolithic material, as has the former Soviet region. Thus the region surrounding Afghanistan was occupied by a Middle Palaeolithic population. The Middle Palaeolithic economy was based on hunting, and, due to general aridity of the area, the population could not have been a large one.

The Hazar Sum industry from northern Afghanistan belongs to the flake industry complex of central and southern Asia. The tools comprise retouched Clactonian and proto-

Levalloisian flakes made into a variety of scrapers. Bifaces are absent so also are true Levallois flakes. The tools are made of dark brown flint.

PAKISTAN

The Late Soan industry shows some influence of Clactonian and Levalloiso-Mousterian technology in the flake assemblage, associated with the tools of Soan types. The excavations of the Sanghao cave in the Peshawar region have, however, yielded evidence of the Levalloiso-Mousterian (Middle Palaeolithic) culture in Pakistan, which Dani (1964) has placed in the Late Palaeolithic.

In a recent study, B. Allchin (1981a) has offered fresh evidence on Palaeolithic occurrences in the Potwar plateau and adjacent regions, with a view to attempting a re-examination of the stratigraphy and typology of the Palaeolithic sequence proposed earlier by de Terra and Paterson (1939). The sites have been located on the old eroded post-Siwalik land surface which developed upon the Lei conglomerate and on the Upper Siwalik conglomerates. These conglomerates are composed of pebbles and boulders of quartzite and limestone. The loess which overlies the Lei conglomerate has in places been eroded, exposing Palaeolithic factory sites. The artefacts and the associated debris are fresh. The tools are mostly composed of choppers and chopping tools and several flakes obtained from prepared cores as well as cleaver-cum-chopper types, scrapers, hammers and so on which indicate a hunting economy. Typological studies of this toolkit show mostly Middle Palaeolithic cultural traits and this culture has been tentatively dated to 40,000 years ago.

The Sanghao valley is a rugged area of undulating plains broken by *Khwara* (torrents). Here the limestone hill spurs are highly dissected resulting in canyon-like valleys locally called *darra*; several natural caves are formed in them.

The Parkho-derra cave contains nearly 5 m of cultural deposits and as many as five periods have been recognized. Of these, periods I to III yielded lithic material worked on quartz, consisting of cores, flakes and points. According to Dani, Sanghao flake industry is of a Levalloiso-Mousterian type (Middle Palaeolithic). Further, it is different from the Upper Soan but related to material from Afghanistan and western Asia. The industry implies a food-collecting economy.

It is interesting to note that the distribution of such sites in the Potwar region and the cave locations in the Sind area perhaps indicate a great diversity of life styles, for in the cave sites a succession of occupation has been traced from the Middle Palaeolithic to the Upper Palaeolithic, which is not the case at the open-air sites (B. Allchin, 1981a).

INDIA

The existence of the Middle Palaeolithic culture in India is now firmly established on the basis of its tool typology, the absolute radiometric dates of the associated deposits, and to a very limited extent by stratigraphic evidence. It is also possible to have some idea of the relationship of this culture to the earlier Lower Palaeolithic and the succeeding Upper Palaeolithic. The picture of the ecological setting of that time, as regards climate, vegetation and animal life is, however, not yet clear. Similarly, in view of the absence of human remains of the Middle Palaeolithic period nothing can be said about the human types to whom this culture

could be attributed. Since no large-scale excavations of primary sites have been possible, no data are available about Palaeolithic life-ways and settlement patterns.

This culture is dominated by small tools such as a variety of scrapers (straight, concave, convex, all round and so on), points (simple, shouldered or tanged and, rarely, bifacially worked) and borers, made on flakes, cores and nodules. There are a few combined-purpose tools like scrapers-cum-borers and borers-cum-points. The flakes are mostly obtained from unprepared cores and only a few show the use of the Levallois and Mousterian techniques. There is very limited retouch on the edges of the flakes to convert them into particular types of artefacts.

There is a marked change in the use of raw material after the Lower Palaeolithic stage. Now the most common lithic materials are a variety of siliceous minerals like chert, jasper, agate, chalcedony, quartz and the like, which have different colours, and occasionally even fine-grained rocks, i.e. quartzite and basalt.

Since the identification of this culture in 1954 at Nevasa on the Pravara river in Maharashtra, scores of Middle Palaeolithic sites have been found all over India (Sankalia, 1974), except in Kerala in the south-west. Typical Middle Palaeolithic artefacts often occur in Acheulean as well as Upper Palaeolithic and Mesolithic sites. They are generally found in fluvial sediments in the basins of the Luni (Rajasthan), Narmada, Godavari and Krishna rivers (Maharashtra, Andhra and Karnataka), and in exposed river sections the artefacts are usually found in finer gravel overlying the coarser pebbly gravel that contains Lower Palaeolithic material. However, the most common occurrences are factory sites located near the source of raw material. For example, in central India the Vindhyan conglomerates contain pebbles of jasper, agate and allied minerals, while in Maharashtra the volcanic basalt rock possesses veins of these minerals which held a very great attraction for early settlers in these areas. In Karnataka the sites are located on the high-level river gravel, while in Rajasthan they are found in association with sand dunes. Rock shelters (Bhimbetka, Adamgarh in Madhya Pradesh and Gudiyam in Tamil Nadu) have also yielded Middle Palaeolithic artefacts in excavations.

Owing to varied landscapes and equally varied climatic zones as well as the available raw material in India there are regional differences in the Middle Palaeolithic cultural material. The sizes of different tools vary from small (3 cm in length) to large (15 cm).

On the basis of the vertebrate fauna, which includes *Bos*, *Bubalus*, *Elephas maximus*, *Elephas namadicus*, *Equus namadicus*, and *Unio* and other fresh-water molluscs, obtained from the Narmada and Godavari rivers, this culture can be placed in the Upper Pleistocene, which is also corroborated by the carbon-14 dates.

In the absence of pollen material in the Middle Palaeolithic deposits no inferences can be drawn about the vegetation patterns which existed then. But since these sites are generally located in open woodland and grassland areas and are also accompanied by vertebrate faunal material, the character of the climate does not seem to have been very much different from that of India's present monsoonal climate. The associated fine sediments in river sections indicate a slightly wetter climate and this is also supported by the presence of a deeply weathered palaeosol in the Rajasthan dunes (Allchin et al., 1978).

Carbon-14 dates for organic material associated with the sediments yielding Middle Palaeolithic artefacts in Maharashtra range from about 38,000 to 20,000 years ago.

There are different views on the origin of this culture. Typologically the artefacts are closely comparable to the African Middle Stone Age industries (such as Zambezi, Zimbabwe; Joshi, 1966), while the occurrences of Mousterian forms at some sites in India and also from the excavation at Sanghon caves in Pakistan, within the south Asian subcontinent, suggest that the Middle Palaeolithic can be related to the classical Mousterian industries of Europe. However, from recent work in India, particularly the excavations at the Bhimbetka rock shelters as well as from riverine sites (Joshi, 1961), an indigenous origin has been traced for the Middle Palaeolithic culture of India. Continuity and typological evolution from the Lower Palaeolithic to the Middle Palaeolithic can be deduced from these new pieces of evidence.

In the wider geographical context, the Indian Middle Palaeolithic, which is basically characterized by a flake-blade industry, forms one of the components of the south Asian flake-blade tradition. The Upper Pleistocene age of the Middle Palaeolithic cultures of India, as well as its toolkit, comparable to that of the Middle Palaeolithic of Europe, suggest the existence of human beings of Neanderthal type in India.

BIBLIOGRAPHY

See Chapter 6.

16

CHINA

in the period of *Homo sapiens neanderthalensis* and contemporaries

Wu Rukang and Jia Lanpo

The period of the Neanderthal people is generally believed to have begun about 250,000 years ago and to have continued to about 25,000 years ago. It has a time span of more than 200,000 years. Its geographical distribution extended over a vast area from western Europe to central Asia and both north and south of the Mediterranean basin. As the fossil hominid specimens of this period found in east Asia and sub-Saharan Africa have different morphological features from the Neanderthalers, it is now usual to call hominids of this period early *Homo sapiens* or archaic *Homo sapiens*; their culture roughly corresponds to the Middle Palaeolithic Age.

In all, twenty-seven sites of this period have been found in China, nine of which have hominid fossils. A brief description is given here of the most important sites.

The earliest site of this period is Dali. The well-preserved Dali cranium was found in 1978 in a gravel layer at the base of the third terrace of the Luo river near Jiefang village in Duanjia People's Commune, Dali County, Shaanxi Province (Plate 22).

Associated with the cranium were a number of stone artefacts and more than ten species of fossil vertebrates including the thick-jawbone deer (*Megaceros pachyosteus*), the ancient horse (*Equus*) and a kind of ancient elephant (*Palaeoloxodon*), which suggest a late Middle Pleistocene age (Wu, 1981).

The cranium is large with robust supraorbital ridges and prominent temporal lines and other muscular markings. Judging from the morphological features, it belongs to a male individual aged less than 30 years. The transverse curvature and the relative cranial height indicate that the Dali hominid occupies an intermediate position between Peking Man (*H. erectus pekinensis*) and the early *H. sapiens* of western Europe. However, many features of the Dali cranium are diferent from the European Neanderthalers. The suture joining the frontal bone, the nasal bones and the frontal processes of the maxilla is arc-shaped. The nasal bones are narrow and flat and are orientated nearly vertically. The facial portion is not so prognathous as that of the Neanderthalers. The antero-lateral surface of the fronto-sphenoidal processes of the zygomatic bone face more anteriorly than those of the Neanderthalers. The orbital contour is not circular. All these features distinguish the Dali cranium from the Neanderthalers (Wu and Wu, 1985).

The stone artefacts are chiefly made of quartzite, vein quartz and flint. Most flakes are produced by simple direct percussion. Finished tools were fabricated mostly on small flakes and include scrapers, points, gravers and awls (Qiu, 1985).

The Xujiayao site is on the west bank of Liyikou, a small tributary of the Sangan river, about 1 km south-east of Xujiayao village in Yanggao County, Shaanxi Province. The site is dated by the uranium isotopes series method to be about 100,000 years old. Excavations in this site yielded over 30,000 stone and bone or antler artefacts, fragmentary vertebrate fossils, and the remains of more than ten human individuals in the sand concretion layer of a yellowish-green clay deposit about 8 m below the present ground surface (Jia et al., 1979).

The human fossils include eleven parietal fragments, two occipitals, one fragmentary left maxilla, one fragmentary right mandibular ramus and two isolated teeth. The Xujiayao hominid possesses a rather thick cranial vault, reaching the upper limit of the range of variation of this character of *H. erectus pekinensis*. The occipital torus is much less developed and in a higher position than that of the Zhoukoudian *erectus* specimens. The anterior nasal spine is clearly shown. In general the Xujiayao hominid seems to be transitional in morphology from *Homo erectus* to *Homo sapiens*.

The stone tools of Xujiayao include scrapers, points, gravers, anvils, choppers and spheroids: the thumbnail scrapers among them were not seen in lithic assemblage of earlier sites (Fig. 32). The Xujiayao stone spheroids are of particular interest. They may be divided into three categories according to size. It is thought that they may have been used as bolas or missile stones.

The hominid fossils recovered from Changyang County, Hubei Province, include a left maxilla fragment with the first premolar and first molar *in situ* and an isolated left lower second premolar. The alveolar portion of the maxilla is almost orthognathous. The anterior nasal spine is present though weak. The anterior wall of the maxillary sinus extends forward to a point anterior to the first premolar. These features are similar to Modern *Homo sapiens*.

The Changyang specimen also shows some primitive features. The inferior margin of the nasal aperture is relatively wide and its lateral wall is less curved than in modern humans. The canine eminence is very pronounced and extends upward beyond the nasal floor indicating that the

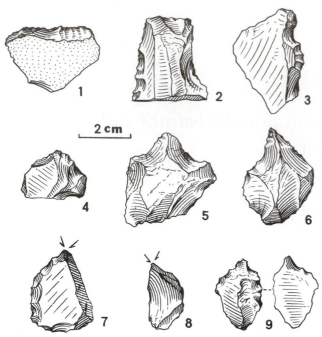

Figure 32 Artefacts, Xujiayao, Shaanxi (China). 1, straight side-scraper; 2, double-sided scraper; 3, concave scraper; 4, thumbnail scraper; 5–6, points; 7–8, burins; 9, borer.

root of the canine was well developed. Both the upper first premolar and first molar are large and the crenellations of their occlusal surfaces are complex.

Almost twenty species of fossil vertebrates of the *Ailuropoda–Stegodon* fauna were uncovered from this site. Its age was first thought to be Middle Pleistocene. After the discovery of the fossil hominid specimen, it appears that its age may extend to the early Late Pleistocene (Jia, 1957).

In 1958 a fossil hominid specimen and many mammalian fossils were found in a limestone cave on Shizi Hill south-east of Maba village in Shaoguan County, Guangdong Province.

The preserved specimen is a calotte comprising the two parietal bones and the frontal bone with fairly complete nasal bones and the right orbit. The cranial wall is fairly thick. The supra-orbital ridges are prominent. The medial parts project anteriorly more than their lateral margins and the ridges are thickest at the medial ends as well. The lateral margins clearly project postero-laterally to make the post-orbital constriction very marked. The orbit is rounded (Plate 23).

Although the Maba cranium shares some morphological features with *H. erectus*, it is on the whole a type of early *H. sapiens* (Wu and Peng, 1959).

Another two sites of this period have yielded many stone artefacts. One is the Shilongtou site in south China, the other is the Dingcun site in north China.

The Shilongtou site of Hubei Province is composed of clay deposits in a cave. The stone artefacts were fashioned mainly from quartzite, although a small proportion were of quartz and sandstone, and consist of cores, flakes, choppers and scrapers. Most of the implements had been produced by simple direct percussion. They seem to be much less advanced than the tools of the Dingcun culture mentioned below. The associated vertebrate fossils belong to the *Ailuropoda–Stegodon* fauna. Its geological age is of Middle to Upper Pleistocene, the same as the Changyang site of Hubei (Li et al., 1974).

The Dingcun material was uncovered from a sand layer with cross bedding under a loess-like deposit at Dingcun, Xiangfen County, Shaanxi Province. The human fossils consist of three teeth of an individual of 12 to 13 years of age and a parietal bone of a small child. In general, the morphological features are more advanced than those of Xujiayao and Changyang specimens.

A total of 2,000 stone artefacts were also collected at this site. The majority of the tools are fashioned from dark hornfels while the remaining minority were made of chert, limestone, basalt and quartzite. Most of the Dingcun artefacts are large flakes. The most common tool types are choppers. There are a few small scrapers and points. Of special interest are the bifaces and heavy trihedral points. The former occur only in this site of the period, but the latter were also found in the Kehe site of early Middle Pleistocene, which indicates some relation between the two cultures.

In conclusion, early *Homo sapiens* in China shares a number of morphological features with *H. erectus*, such as shovel-shaped incisors, the frequent presence of Inca bones, the presence of weak sagittal keeling on the skull, flattened nasal bones, forward-jutting cheek bones and others. These morphological traits distinguish China's early *H. sapiens* from the Neanderthalers in Europe. And some Neanderthal characteristics, such as the large, prognathous face, the lack of canine fossae, the nearly circular orbital contours and the bun-shaped supra-occipital region, are not found in Chinese early *H. sapiens*. The geographical variation in the early *H. sapiens* period seems well established.

The Chinese Middle Palaeolithic culture was extensively distributed in both north and south China. It seems to have developed directly out of the indigenous early Palaeolithic culture. Scrapers, points, choppers and chopping tools are the main artefact types. Most of them have only unifacial retouch. There are clearly regional and temporal variations, so that the Chinese Middle Palaeolithic should not be considered as a homogeneous entity as earlier publications suggested.

BIBLIOGRAPHY

JIA LANPO (CHIA, LAN-PO). 1957. Notes on the Human and Some Other Mammalian Remains from Changyang, Hupei. *Vertebr. PalAsiat.* (Beijing), Vol. 1, No. 3, pp. 247–58.

JIA LANPO (CHIA, LAN-PO); WEI QI; LI CHAORONG. 1979. Report on the Excavation of Hsuchiayao Man Site in 1976. *Vertebr. PalAsiat.* (Beijing), Vol. 17, No. 4, pp. 277–93.

LI YANXIAN et al. 1974. Report on the Excavation of a Palaeolithic Station Known as Shilongtou at Daye, Hubei. *Vertebr. PalAsiat.* (Beijing), Vol. 2, No. 2, pp. 139–57.

QIU ZHONGLANG. 1985. The Middle Palaeolithic of China. In: WU, RUKANG; OLSEN, J. W. (eds), *Palaeoanthropology and Palaeolithic Archaeology in the People's Republic of China.* Orlando. Vol. 10, pp. 187–210.

WU RUKANG (WOO, JU-KANG); PENG RUCE. 1959. Fossil Human Skull of Early Palaeoanthropologic Stage Found at Mapa, Shaokuan, Kwangtung Province. *Palaeovertebr. Palaeoanthropol* (Montpellier), Vol. 1, No. 4, pp. 159–64.

WU XINZHI. 1981. The Well-Preserved Cranium of an Early *Homo sapiens* from Dali, Shaanxi. *Sci. Sin.* (Beijing), Vol. 2, pp. 200–6.

WU XINZHI; WU MAOLIN. 1985. Early *Homo sapiens* in China. In: WU RUKANG; OLSEN, J. W. (eds), *Palaeoanthropology and Palaeolithic Archaeology in the People's Republic of China.* Orlando. Vol. 6, pp. 91–106.

17

INDONESIA

in the period of *Homo sapiens neanderthalensis* and contemporaries

Gert-Jan Bartstra

In 1931 it was announced that hominid cranial remains had been found at Ngandong, a small village in central Java, situated on the Solo river. This announcement caused a lot of excitement, for Java already possessed a reputation in the field of research on early humans. Almost half a century earlier, a fossil skull-cap and a femur had been found, also along the Solo river. This was the famous *Pithecanthropus erectus* or 'Java Man' (now *Homo erectus erectus*). Did the cranial remains from Ngandong originate from the same hominid?

The site of Ngandong was discovered by ter Haar, a mining engineer who was involved in the so-called 'Java-kaarteering', the detailed geographical and geological mapping of Java (ter Haar, 1934). For fieldwork the surroundings of Ngandong are difficult terrain: hilly, forested and with a clammy, oppressive climate. It was quite by chance that ter Haar found the fossiliferous deposits: the story goes that it was in the late afternoon when he suddenly saw the point of a vertebrate fossil sticking out of the ground.

Subsequently the name of Oppenoorth, the then director of the *Java-kaarteering*, become known. It was Oppenoorth who was in charge of the excavations that had been started at Ngandong, and who first described the hominid remains that came to light and gave them the name *Homo (Javanthropus) soloensis* (Oppenoorth, 1932) (Plate 24). Oppenoorth saw a strong resemblance to the Neanderthalers of Europe; afterwards he discarded the designation *Javanthropus* (Oppenoorth, 1937).

Since then many research workers have devoted their attention to this new fossil hominid from Java, 'Solo Man' or 'Ngandong Man', as it came to be known popularly; Weidenreich (1951) and von Koenigswald (1958) can be mentioned here. The fossil's age was supposedly Upper Pleistocene (a period between about 125,000 and 10,000 years ago). A recent and detailed study on the fossil remains from Ngandong is that of Santa Luca (1980), who proposes that the Solo remains, although clearly those of a hominid more advanced than *Pithecanthropus erectus*, nevertheless belong to an early human within the species *Homo erectus*, who can by no means be called Neanderthal or Neanderthal-like.

THE HILL OF NGEBUNG

While Oppenoorth was closely following the developments in Ngandong, von Koenigswald had become interested in Sangiran. A certain rivalry existed between the two men: both wanted to play a prominent role in the research into early humans on Java. As director of the *Java-kaarteering*, Oppenoorth had an advantage in this respect: he was able to take control of the situation in Ngandong, for example, and at first he tried to keep von Koenigswald away from the spot. The latter, however, was aware of the fact that the Ngandong fossils were definitely younger than *Homo erectus* of Trinil, and it was for more remains of the old *Homo erectus* that von Koenigswald was searching. In this quest he discovered Sangiran.

Sangiran lies further to the west than Ngandong and Trinil, but it is situated nevertheless in central Java. Sangiran is the name of a small village but the surrounding landscape is known by the same name. It is a desolate landscape, with bare hills that are subject to severe tropical erosion. One can find fossils in Sangiran, but they are not too abundant (there is no true bone-bed as at Trinil), and they have to be looked for systematically. Von Koenigswald knew that Dubois, who had found the *Homo erectus* remains at Trinil, had also once been in Sangiran; but Sangiran had made little impression on Dubois as a fossil locality or as a potential site for fossil hominid remains. Yet von Koenigswald had great expectations of Sangiran, and his search was rewarded in 1937 when a *Homo erectus* skull came to light (von Koenigswald, 1938).

Von Koenigswald had in fact begun his fieldwork in Sangiran in 1934, and in that year he found stone implements: small, inconspicuous, artificially worked flakes with a few irregular cores, made out of silicified limestone, above all coral limestone. Von Koenigswald found them on the top of the high hill of Ngebung, in the northern part of Sangiran. The artefacts lay there scattered in river gravel which caps tuffaceous sand deposits. Naturally von Koenigswald was very curious about the age of this gravel sheet and he found an indication of this in the form of a few heavily fossilized vertebrate bones.

Having found these bones, von Koenigswald was on familiar ground. For at that time he was trying to establish a vertebrate chronology for the Pliocene and Pleistocene of Java. He developed a scheme of successive faunas on the basis of the known sites of fossil vertebrates, using these fossil faunas to enable him to date deposits of unknown age. Thus the rich collection of vertebrates from Trinil became the Trinil fauna, dating from the Middle Pleistocene. The excavations at Ngandong provided the younger Ngandong fauna, of the Upper Pleistocene. And the collection of fossil vertebrates that came from Jetis, in East Java, was the Jetis (formerly Djetis) fauna of the Lower Pleistocene (von Koenigswald, 1935).

In the presentation of this chronology von Koenigswald stated emphatically that sediments could never be (relatively) dated on the basis of the vertebrate fossils alone, but that in addition other techniques should be employed, such as the mollusc percentage method (which was a well-established dating method on Java in the 1930s) or lithological and geomorphological research. With regard to Ngebung, however, von Koenigswald did not abide by his own rules, and he dated the river gravel using only the vertebrate fossils. The bones from the gravel were in his opinion Trinil fauna. The gravel thus had to be Middle Pleistocene and the artefacts too.

Despite this apparently surprising great age of the Ngebung artefacts, von Koenigswald did not devote any extensive publication to his finds (at least not in the years immediately following this discovery). This was perhaps due less to the inconspicuous and uninteresting appearance of the artefacts, than to a feeling of uneasiness and doubt on the part of von Koenigswald. Were these really the tools of 'Trinil Man', of *Homo erectus*?

It must therefore have come as a relief to him when handaxes were found at Pacitan (formerly Patjitan) on the south coast of central Java. There, in a landscape of limestone hills, flows the Baksoka river, and it was along the upper course of this stream that the prehistoric tools were found in 1935. Handaxes were the symbol of the Old Stone Age, and therefore von Koenigswald could confidently ascribe the artefacts from Pacitan to *Homo erectus*. This he did, a year after the discovery (von Koenigswald, 1936).

However, already before the outbreak of the Second World War in South-East Asia (after which fieldwork became impossible for many years) it was apparent that the handaxes of Pacitan are not very characteristic of this lithic industry as a whole (the so-called 'Pacitanian'). The handaxes are not only few in number, but the technique of their manufacture is completely different from any used in Europe and Africa. It also seemed that the 'Pacitanian' could well be of lesser antiquity than had been thought. Finally, with regard to the site of Ngebung in Sangiran it was concluded that the implementiferous gravel layer could by no means be of Middle Pleistocene age and that the fossils that von Koenigswald had used for dating must have been reworked (Lehmann, 1936; Teilhard de Chardin, 1938; de Terra, 1943).

With this last point von Koenigswald never agreed, however. The fossils from Ngebung remained for him evidence that the top gravel layer was Middle Pleistocene. A detailed publication concerning the artefacts did ultimately appear in the 1970s, in which von Koenigswald presented the tools from Ngebung as those of *Homo erectus* in Java. By then he too had become convinced that the 'Pacitanian' was younger than the tools from Ngebung; moreover, elsewhere in Indonesia (Flores, Timor) tools had been found (according to von Koenigswald in unmistakably Middle Pleistocene de-

posits) bearing a great resemblance to the Ngebung artefacts (von Koenigswald and Ghosh, 1973; von Koenigswald, 1978).

From a geological point of view the site of Ngebung is much more complicated than the literature would suggest. A system of hills can be discerned with complex slope profiles, where various alluvial deposits outcrop (Bartstra, 1985). The oldest of these are river-laid tuffaceous sands and gravels referred to as Kabuh beds, which according to radiometric age determinations date for the most part from the Middle Pleistocene (between 0.69 and 1.3 million years ago). On top of these Kabuh beds there lies elsewhere in Sangiran (though not in Ngebung) a lahar or volcanic mud stream deposit that can be correlated with the first period of activity of the Lawu volcano (approximately at the end of the Middle Pleistocene, 0.13 million years ago). But because this lahar is absent at Ngebung, at this particular locality it is not easy to trace boundaries in the sequence of cross-stratified sands and lenses of rounded pebbles, a sequence measuring tens of metres in thickness. Yet the top part of this Ngebung section must postdate the first Lawu activity (on the basis of geomorphological and lithological arguments) and thus it must postdate the Middle Pleistocene, despite the presence of fossil remains of vertebrates in the top part. The fossils are few in number, and they show a strong fluviatile wear. It is therefore indeed reasonable to assume that they originate from older strata.

In the post-Middle Pleistocene or Upper Pleistocene top section of Ngebung artefacts do occur *in situ*. One wonders whether these were perhaps the tools of *Homo soloensis*, who is also considered to date from the Upper Pleistocene. This question gains more significance when one realizes that the Ngebung top gravel is possibly a remnant of an old Solo river terrace, and that it was in such a terrace remnant that the cranial remains and tibiae of *Homo soloensis* were found.

THE SITE OF NGANDONG

A river terrace can be considered as a part of a former valley floor (floodplain) that is now to be found at some height above the present one as a result of down-cutting action by the river. If one assumes that this process of entrenchment did not always proceed at the same rate (because it was either the result of crust movements or of fluctuations in sea-level) then different terraces should now be visible at different heights on the valley slope. However, it appears that terraces do not develop everywhere, while later denudation may have eroded away terrace deposits that were once present. This means that tracing terrace levels is often a frustrating business, and is surely so along the Solo river in the Kendeng hills in central Java, where the presence of a dense forest is an additional complicating factor. Yet in the search for *Homo soloensis*, it is on these terraces that attention should be focused. Rivers were vital for prehistoric humans, and along the rivers they made their encampments. The remnants of these encampments became buried in the former floodplains, parts of which are now to be found as terraces on the valley slope.

Terraces are present in the Solo meander at Ngandong in the Kendung hills. Two clear levels can be distinguished, a high terrace and a low one (Lehmann, 1936), but on closer inspections it is possible to discern sublevels (de Terra, 1943). The high terrace at Ngandong lies at about 20 m above the Solo river; the fill itself (the sequence of terrace sediments) is about 3 m thick, and consists in the lower part of sandy deposits with small andesitic pebbles and at the top of more marly material. The volcanic pebbles show that one is concerned with a true terrace fill: previous bedload that must originate from the central Javanese volcanic zone, much further south of Ngandong. The top section of the terrace consists of local alluvium: the Kendeng hills at this place consist entirely of limestone and marl.

Fossil vertebrate remains, including the cranial remains of *Homo soloensis*, came from the lowermost terrace strata, according to reports made by eyewitnesses of the excavations at Ngandong, which were carried out from 1931 until 1933 (Oppenoorth, 1932; ter Haar, 1934). Unfortunately, this stratigraphic position can no longer be checked, because all fossiliferous deposits at Ngandong have disappeared. As for the part of the high terrace that was supposed to have been preserved after the excavations to permit inspection at a future date, this has now also disappeared, as a result of erosion accelerated by human agricultural and constructional activities.

Eyewitnesses also reported that the animal remains from the terrace strata at Ngandong could often be recovered in complete association (for instance well-preserved skulls with mandibles still attached, and complete vertebral columns). It is thus evident that little fluviatile transport has taken place since that would inevitably have resulted in the separation of heavy and light skeletal parts. On the other hand, Santa Luca points out that the hominid remains from Ngandong appear to present a completely different picture (Santa Luca, 1980). These hominid remains typically form a lag deposit, which can only suggest a great deal of fluviatile transport. Only the more durable skeletal elements of hominids have been found at Ngandong, such as tibiae, calvariae (skulls without the facial bones) and calottes (skulls without the facial bones and without a base). So what happened to the rest of the hominid skeletons?

Ter Haar had already found an explanation for this (ter Haar, 1934). For apart from the absence of light hominid skeletal parts, there is also the hydrodynamically unexplainable fact that the skulls in the terrace sediments had been found in a position in which they offered precisely the greatest resistance to the former stream current: namely with the concave basal side facing upwards instead of with the convex upper side, which is what one would expect as a result of a natural sorting process in the river. Ter Haar saw in this intentional human interference, and he assumed that the skulls of Ngandong bore witness to a cannibalistic feast. Von Koenigswald was also an adherent of this theory, and as further supporting evidence he pointed out the damaged condition of some of the skulls, suggesting that they had been purposely smashed (von Koenigswald, 1951).

Santa Luca, however, has little faith in this cannibalism theory. He mentions the fact that the skulls were not found in any particular area (as one would expect after a cannibalistic feast on the bank of the prehistoric Solo), but rather irregularly distributed throughout the excavations (Santa Luca, 1980). On the other hand, both ter Haar and Oppenoorth speak of a distinct fossiliferous level, namely at the bottom of the excavation pits, just above the bedrock. Santa Luca's 'irregularly distributed' can therefore not be meant in a vertical sense, but at most horizontally. But it should be pointed out that the terrace remnant at Ngandong yielded as many as eleven hominid skulls, a considerable number in view of the experiences in Trinil and Sangiran. There must be something special about Ngandong; and the possibility that one is here concerned with the remains of a cannibalistic or head-hunters' ritual is an exciting thought. If this is indeed the case then one is afforded a glimpse of

cultural and social life in the Old Stone Age, a realm that is for the most part a closed book.

According to Santa Luca the hominid cranial remains and the two tibiae from Ngandong could well have originated from older deposits, and then have ended up secondarily in the terrace fill (Santa Luca, 1980). In that case one would have to assume that a proportion also of the animal remains is older; in other words that the Ngandong fauna also is mixed and consists partly of reworked elements. Yet so far not one research worker concerned with the Ngandong animal remains has ever put forward ideas in this direction. Furthermore, the question must be asked where those older deposits actually are. In the transverse Solo valley in the Kendeng hills (in the surroundings of Ngandong) terrace deposits occur on top of the (Neogene) limestone and marl. Only much further south (beyond Ngawi) are old fluviatile sediments eroded by the Solo that are of the same age (Middle Pleistocene) as the Kabuh beds in Sangiran. Is it possible that it was from these sediments that the hominid skulls and tibiae were derived, subsequently to become transported far to the north, and ultimately to become deposited at Ngandong?

Santa Luca's remarks are related in a remarkable way to the problems (that have existed and that still exist) concerned with the find of the *Homo erectus* remains from Trinil. Dubois mentioned also that many skeletal remains from his excavations in Trinil had been recovered almost complete (skulls with mandibles still attached and so on), but that on the other hand different parts of the same skeleton had been found metres apart. Dubois ascribed all this to the activities of crocodiles, which tore cadavers apart in the river. In fact he was able to demonstrate damage on bones inflicted by the gnawing action of crocodiles (Dubois, 1908). Also interesting in this connection are the remarks of Oppenoorth and Carthaus, who took part in the Selenka expedition to Trinil in 1907. They stated that complete skeletons or complete parts of skeletons had never been found in the main bone-bearing horizon at the bottom of their excavation pits, from where the remains of *Homo erectus* also originated. However, complete and articulated parts of skeletons did come to light from higher up in the profile. Moreover, the fossils from the main bone-bearing horizon were heavily mineralized, while those from the top layers were brittle and badly preserved. Thus Oppenoorth and Carthaus pointed out the existence, at least in Trinil, of two fossil-bearing units (Oppenoorth, 1911; Carthaus, 1911). Later on this same situation could be ascertained elsewhere along the Solo (outside the Kendeng hills). But at Ngandong (in the Kendeng hills) the situation is different, for the terrace deposits (the only vertebrate-bearing unit) lie immediately on top of the Neogene limestone bedrock, and not, as in Trinil, on top of older fossiliferous fluviatile deposits.

With respect to the Ngandong death assemblage (thanatocoenosis) it is therefore advisable to maintain the *entia non sunt multiplicanda* and to assume that the entire fauna including the hominid remains is indeed only one single assemblage. The remarkable accumulation of cranial remains may have been caused artificially; the circumstances of the find and the damage on the bones together suggest that the idea of a cannibalistic ceremony is plausible. Finally, von Koenigswald, also an eyewitness of the excavation at Ngandong, who together with ter Haar in 1932 dug up the sixth skull, once stated emphatically that the preservation of the hominid remains was exactly the same as that of the numerous animal bones (von Koenigswald, 1951).

HOMO SOLOENSIS IN INDONESIA

The terraces of the Solo river near Ngandong have thus yielded the actual remains of *Homo soloensis*, and the hill of Ngebung in Sangiran the tools presumed to have been used by this hominid. The question now arrives whether it is possible to establish a clear association between the two localities. Have the Solo terraces near Ngandong ever yielded artefacts?

In some of his publications Oppenoorth does indeed mention implements found in Ngandong, made of bone and antler (Oppenoorth, 1936). It is now clear, however, that his 'osteodontokeratic culture' was wishful thinking. The only bone instrument that is repeatedly mentioned in the literature (although it was not found at Ngandong itself but much further south) is the harpoon of Sidorejo (formerly Sidoredjo). Yet it is highly questionable whether this artefact can indeed be associated with high-terrace sediments. Sidorejo, to the west of Ngawi, lies in the region (immediately adjacent to the southern border of the Kendeng) where complicated terrace intersections occur (with high terraces plunging under low ones), while the find circumstances of the Sidorejo harpoon have always remained rather vague.

Humanly worked chalcedony flakes have also been found in outcropping terrace gravels along the Solo (although again not at Ngandong itself, but further south). They have never been described in detail, but the name 'Ngandongian' or 'Ngandong-industry' has become attached to them (Movius, 1949; van Heekeren, 1972). Yet once again the question has to be asked whether these flakes do indeed occur *in situ* in genuine high-terrace fills, or whether they lie scattered on the surface. Excavations carried out with the sole aim of solving this question have so far not provided any clear results. The difficulty is that the artificial character of these small flakes is often barely recognizable. Not only does fluviatile wear play a role, but so does the fact that the artefacts belong to the notorious 'smash-and-grab' lithic industries, with hardly definable types.

In the literature reference is also made to round stone balls (resembling small stone cannon-balls) that are allegedly found in terrace sediments along the Solo. They are made of andesite, are not polished and measure on average 10 cm in diameter. They are associated with *Homo soloensis* (on account of their assumed stratigraphical position), and they are regarded as a primitive hunting weapon, which is why these stone balls are often referred to as bolas or sling-stones. Von Koenigswald even saw in them evidence for the Neanderthal character of the Solo hominids: similar stone balls do occur at such famous Neanderthal sites as La Quina (France) and Teshik-Tash (Uzbekistan) (von Koenigswald, 1951). In Sangiran too these stone balls are found (and they are displayed in the local museum); but around the hill of Ngebung it can be demonstrated that they certainly do not lie buried in high-terrace sediments. In Ngebung the stone balls can be associated with young, post-Pleistocene alluvial deposits (Bartstra, 1985). The question therefore arises whether the stone balls found along the Solo do not in fact originate also from recent sediments, and reflect the activities of Holocene hunters rather than those of ancient *Homo soloensis*.

The problem of hominid remains and artefacts along the Solo river could be better solved if we knew how old the terrace sediments are. In the literature they are mostly assigned an Upper Pleistocene age; in absolute terms that would mean an age between about 125,000 and 10,000 years ago (from the beginning of the Blake reversed event until

the generally accepted beginning of the Holocene). There is geomorphological evidence to suggest that the age of the terrace sediments does indeed fall within this range. As mentioned, the first period of activity of the Lawu volcano dates from towards the end of the Middle Pleistocene (the lahars and tuffs from this first Lawu phase still have a normal (Brunhes) palaeomagnetic polarity; Sémah, 1984). At that time the general drainage of the central Javanese lowland was directed southward. However, when that first period of active Lawu volcanism came to an end, at the beginning of the Upper Pleistocene and as a result of crust movements, certain basins sank deeper and mountain ridges rose higher, this southward-directed drainage gradually halted (the now dry river valley of Giritontro on the south coast of central Java can be studied as a geomorphological relic dating from that period). The water then began to flow towards the north, and in this way there originated the drainage pattern of the present-day Solo river. The oldest terrace fills along this river developed in this period.

It is important to seek confirmation for this geo-morphological scenario, for example with radiometric techniques. Unfortunately, however, research on Java has not yet progressed this far. Up until now attempts at radiometric age determination have been mostly concerned with older deposits (for example, in order to establish the precise Pliocene–Pleistocene boundary); besides, it is not easy to collect reliable samples from the younger fluviatile deposits of Java. Attempts have been made to date directly a few fossil remains of vertebrates from the Solo terraces (from high as well as low terraces), with the aid of the U-series method. The results are encouraging, and they do indeed indicate Upper Pleistocene and Holocene ages between 100,000 and 3,000 years ago, but many more samples will have to be analysed before it is possible to assign a particular age to a particular terrace level with any degree of certainty. Moreover it should be stressed that a study of the reworking of fossil components in the Solo sediments is prerequisite for such an analysis.

If one assumes that the older Solo terraces (with the remains of *Homo soloensis*) are indeed lower Upper Pleistocene, is this then not precisely the Neanderthal stage in Europe, and may one not picture the Solo hominids (also on the basis of certain morphological features) as a tropical Neanderthaler? Von Koenigswald always liked to do so (von Koenigswald, 1958); but his former colleagues of the Geological Service in Bandung had also already drawn comparisons with Neanderthalers (Oppenoorth, 1932; ter Haar, 1934). Only Oppenoorth later changed his opinion and then saw in *Homo soloensis* one of the oldest representatives of *Homo sapiens* (Oppenoorth, 1937).

In the 1930s the Neanderthalers were still seen as a distinct stage in human evolution. It is this idea that Santa Luca now dismisses as out of date in his study on the Ngandong skulls (Santa Luca, 1980). Consequently the term 'Neanderthaler' cannot simply be extrapolated as far as South-East Asia. According to Santa Luca the cranial remains and the tibiae from Ngandong are the remains of a late *Homo erectus* group, and one might therefore speak of *Homo erectus soloensis*. Besides Ngandong, in central Java there is only Sambung-macan, another village on the Solo river, where a skull of *Homo erectus soloensis* has been found (Jacob, 1978; Sartono, 1979). From the rest of Indonesia or insular South-East Asia no remains are known.

The question remains unanswered whether *Homo erectus soloensis* had already become adapted to living in the rain forests, or just ventured into them only now and then

(Hutterer, 1985; Pope, 1985). Important in this connection is Santa Luca's remark (in contradiction to Weidenreich, 1951) that there is no morphological relation between the skulls of Ngandong and those of Wajak (formerly Wadjak; Santa Luca, 1980). Wajak is a small village near the south coast of central Java, where proto-Australoid skulls have been found. These Wajak people are the first representative of *Homo sapiens* on Java (*Homo sapiens wadjakensis*; see also Shutler, 1984).

Culturally the discontinuity between Ngandong and Wajak could be visible in the small flakes of Ngebung and the large handaxes of Pacitan: two lithic industries that appear not to be related in any way.

BIBLIOGRAPHY

BARTSTRA, G.-J. 1985. Sangiran, the Stone Implements of Ngebung, and the Paleolithic of Java. *Mod. Quat. Res. SEAsia*, Vol. 9, pp. 99–113.

CARTHAUS, E. 1911. Zur Geologie von Java, insbesondere des Ausgrabungsgebietes. In: SELENKA, M. L.; BLANCKENHORN, M. (eds), *Die Pithecanthropus-Schichten auf Java*. Leipzig. pp. 1–33.

DUBOIS, E. 1908. Das geologische Alter der Kendeng- oder Trinilfauna. *Tijdschr. K. Ned. Aardrijkskd. Genoot.* (Amsterdam), Vol. 25, pp. 1235–70.

HAAR, C. TER. 1934. Homo-Soloënsis. *De Ing. in Ned.-Indië, Mijnb. Geol., de Mijningenieur*, Vol. 1, No. 4, pp. 51–7.

HEEKEREN, H. R. VAN. 1972. *The Stone Age of Indonesia*. 2nd rev. edn. (Verh. K. Inst. Taal-, Land-Volkenkd., 61.)

HUTTERER, K. L. 1985. The Pleistocene Archaeology of Southeast Asia in Regional Context. *Mod. Quat. Res. SEAsia*, Vol. 9, pp. 1–25.

JACOB, T. 1978. The Puzzle of Solo Man. *Mod. Quat. Res. SEAsia*, Vol. 4, pp. 31–40.

KOENIGSWALD, G. H. R. VON. 1935. Die fossilen Säugetierfaunen Javas. *Proc. K. Ned. Akad. Wet.* (Amsterdam), Vol. 38, pp. 188–98.

—— 1936. Early Palaeolithic Stone Implements from Java. *Bull. Raffles Mus.* (Singapore), Vol. 1, pp. 52–60.

—— 1938. Ein neuer Pithecanthropus-Schädel. *Proc. K. Ned. Akad. Wet.* (Amsterdam), Vol. 41, pp. 185–92.

—— 1951. Introduction. In: WEIDENREICH, F. Morphology of Solo Man. *Anthrop. Pap. Am. Mus. Nat. Hist.* (New York), Vol. 43, pp. 211–21.

—— 1958. Der Solo-Mensch von Java. Ein tropisches Neanderthaler. In: KOENIGSWALD, G. H. R. VON (ed.), *Hundert Jahre Neanderthaler 1856–1956*. Utrecht. pp. 21–6.

—— 1978. Lithic Industries of *Pithecanthropus erectus* of Java. In: IKAWA-SMITH, F. (ed.), *Early Paleolithic in South-East Asia*. The Hague. pp. 23–7.

KOENIGSWALD, G. H. R. VON.; GHOSH, A. K. 1973. Some Implements from the Trinil Beds of Sangiran, Central Java. *Proc. K. Ned. Akad. Wet.* (Amsterdam), Vol. 76, pp. 1–34.

LEHMANN, H. 1936. Morphologische Studien auf Java. *Geogr. Abh.* (Leipzig), Vol. 3, No. 9, pp. 1–114.

MOVIUS, H. L. 1949. The Lower Palaeolithic Cultures of Southern and Eastern Asia. *Trans. Am. Philos. Soc.* (Philadelphia, Pa.), Vol. 38, pp. 329–420.

OPPENOORTH, W. F. F. 1911. Arbeitsbericht über die Ausgrabungen; 1. Teil: Die Arbeiten des Jahres 1907 bis August. In: SELENKA, M. L.; BLANCKENHORN, M. (eds), *Die Pithecanthropus-Schichten auf Java*. Leipzig. pp.xxvi–xxxviii.

—— 1932. Homo (Javanthropus) soloensis, een plistoceene mensch van Java Homo soloensis – Javanthropus – a Pleistocene Hominid from Java. *Wet. med. Dienst v. d. Mijnb. Ned. Indië*, Vol. 20, pp. 49–63.

—— 1936. Een prehistorisch cultuurcentrum langs de Solo-rivier [A Cultural Prehistoric Center along the Solo River]. *Tijdschr. K. Ned. Aardrijkskd. Genoot.* (Amsterdam), Vol. 53, pp. 399–411.

—— 1937. The Place of *Homo soloensis* among Fossil Men. In: MACCURDY, G. G. (ed.), *Early Man*. Philadelphia. pp. 349–60.

POPE, G. G. 1985. Taxonomy, Dating, and Paleoenvironment: The Paleoecology of the Early Far Eastern Hominids. *Mod. Quat. Res. SEAsia*, Vol. 9, pp. 65–80.

SANTA LUCA, A. P. 1980. The Ngandong Fossil Hominids. *Yale Univ. Publ. Anthropol.* (New Haven), Vol. 78, pp. 1–175.

SARTONO, S. 1979. The Stratigraphy of the Sambungmacan Site in Central Java. *Mod. Quat. Res. SEAsia*, Vol. 5, pp. 83–8.

SÉMAH, F. 1984. The Sangiran Dome in the Javanese Plio-Pleistocene Chronology. *CFS, Cour. Forsch.inst. Senckenbg.* (Frankfurt/Main), Vol. 69, pp. 245–52.

SHUTLER, R., JR., 1984. The Emergence of *Homo sapiens* in Southeast Asia, and Other Aspects of Hominid Evolution in East Asia. In: ORR WHYTE, R. (ed.), *The Evolution of the East Asian Environment*. Hong Kong. Vol. 2, pp. 818–21.

TEILHARD DE CHARDIN, P. 1938. Deuxièmes notes sur la paléontologie humaine en Asie méridionale. *Anthropologie* (Paris), Vol. 48, pp. 452–6.

TERRA, H. DE. 1943. Pleistocene Geology and Early Man in Java. *Trans. Am. Philos. Soc.*, (Philadelphia, Pa.), NS, Vol. 32, No. 3, pp. 437–64.

WEIDENREICH, F. 1951. Morphology of Solo Man. *Anthropol. Pap. Am. Mus. Nat. Hist.* (New York), Vol. 43, pp. 205–90.

C: The period of *Homo sapiens sapiens* (Modern humans) to the beginnings of food production

CONTENTS

18

THE PERIOD OF *HOMO SAPIENS SAPIENS* TO THE BEGINNINGS OF FOOD PRODUCTION

An overview (excluding art)

Bohuslav Klima

The course of evolution of human society was gradual and continuous, sometimes with periods of stagnation, but also with important periods of rapid advance, especially under favourable conditions. Such evolution occurs as dialectical, repeated changes which give rise to sudden qualitative social advances. Owing to their revolutionary character, these changes are often called 'revolutions'. The new inventions were disseminated relatively quickly over wide areas and soon became commonly known. Such qualitative leaps can most clearly be observed in the primary economic sphere, that is in the preserved tools. This kind of evidence shows how and by what means prehistoric humankind worked, and which tools they used in their work, but is less informative about the final products. The changes already mentioned would naturally also be reflected in the superstructure, that is in social organizations and in spiritual life; however, in this latter sphere, rapid evolutionary advances cannot so easily be demonstrated.

One of the most important evolutionary changes, perhaps the most striking one, relates to the development of a fully evolved spiritual life, stimulated by advances in productive techniques. The consequences of this phenomenon were far-reaching. First of all, it opened a new and distinct historical period, the Upper Palaeolithic, the most recent part of the Old Stone Age. Some authors also use the term 'Miolithic', 'Leptolithic' or 'Höheres Jägertum', according to their preferred classificatory criteria. It is a period of accelerated evolution for humanity, a period when the prehistoric hunting societies, thanks to their technological progress, reached their peak of development, reflected among other things by important changes in the spiritual sphere.

During this period, humankind consciously inquired into nature; they discovered numerous natural laws and relationships and mastered a number of working approaches. Many human activities may justifiably be said to have been initiated at this time, from the evidence preserved. Several important discoveries took place: humans manufactured and used efficient working implements and other kinds of tools, which satisfied the requirements of everyday life so perfectly that their forms have needed no improvements to the present day. Furthermore, with these tools prehistoric hunters could overcome environmental constraints and, at the same time, were able to develop different technological and cultural traditions (the technological adaptation).

The rapid evolution of hunting cultures, in a period when obtaining food resources no longer presented a substantial problem, permitted further development of non-productive activities. As a result, cultural artefacts could be accumulated and, at the same time, cultural and functional specialization began. The people of that time reached the level not only of abstract thinking but also of aesthetic feeling. Such manifestations reflect the first theoretical ideas and emotions stimulated by efforts to ensure the survival of their group. The preserved objects are intelligible, convincing, technically perfect. This surprising perfection is well demonstrated by the fact that at the end of the last century, in the period when they were first excavated, it seemed incredible that Stone Age people could ever have created such evolved art. Recognizing that this was indeed prehistoric art can therefore be considered one of the most important discoveries of our time.

Scientific study of the Upper Palaeolithic period was widely influenced by the discoveries in western Europe, especially in the French caves. These caves were attractive as shelters to prehistoric people; furthermore, their fill has preserved well the remains of human settlement to our day. These remains were formerly the object of enthusiastic activities by collectors. Later, they were subjected to serious study, including the first attempts at systematic classification. It is only natural that these rich finds determined the course of research into the earliest patterns of settlement, not only in France but also in other countries, and that the ideas and views proclaimed in France were accepted abroad as generally valid.

Further excavations proved that important settlements occurred in the regions with caves outside France as well, and even in the open landscape. Furthermore, it was noted that loess deposits, peatbogs and aquatic sediments are equally suitable for the preservation of archaeological materials. The loess, by its sensitivity to the climatic changes, supplied further evidence about the circumstances of deposition, the environment and its evolution. When complemented by the data of other sciences (geology, geomorphology, pedology, palaeontology, anthropology and so on) this evidence has made it possible during the last years to refine our knowledge of Final Pleistocene stratigraphy as the basis for the chronology of the period under study.

The Upper Palaeolithic lasted for a relatively long period (from 40,000 to about 12,000 years ago). It is only natural that the advanced evolutionary level stimulated further cultural differentiation. The resulting units did not range over large territories of the Old World, as in the preceding periods, but were restricted to smaller regions. The Upper Palaeolithic complex can thus be divided into distinct evolutionary units. Their character, territorial spread and duration were widely influenced by the climatic changes that took place and by the geographical environment. The evolution of these units (which are to be understood as divisions made for the purpose of historical classification alone) with respect to their gradually improving command over productivity, was proceeding ever more rapidly.

This period represents the final part of the Last Glaciation (Würm or Weichsel). During this time, there were frequent fluctuations between colder and more temperate phases of different intensities, which, however, are sometimes difficult to separate one from another. The sequence of alternating stadials and interstadials is therefore being abandoned and replaced by the idea of climatic fluctuations and oscillations during the Würm glaciation.

These circumstances, representing the basic environmental conditions, greatly influenced the development of the Upper Palaeolithic and its division into the different units, most frequently known as 'cultures' (Châtelperronian, Aurignacian, Périgordian, Gravettian, Solutrean, Szeletian, Magdalenian). However, the basic features of economic and social life did not change during the Upper Palaeolithic. These cultures are differentiated on the basis of features of lesser importance and of smaller, relatively insignificant divergences whose character, territorial extent and duration depend always upon the immediate geographical conditions. Less important and territorially more limited units are considered as cultural groups, industries and so on (Grimaldian, Pavlovian, Hamburgian, Ahrensburgian). In order to avoid the term 'culture', especially in cases when only limited sources of information (the stone industry) are available, some authors prefer the terms 'industrial complex', 'techno-complex' and the like. Recent research has brought about a further, more detailed division of the Upper Palaeolithic to the Early, Middle and Late phases.

Climatic changes at the end of the Last Glaciation and related changes in landscape and faunal composition stimulated economic changes resulting in complete adaptation by human groups to the changed environment, especially by hunting the forest and forest–steppe animals and, later, by specialized fishing. These changes are reflected in the material culture, now known as the Late Palaeolithic. The Late Palaeolithic cultures, dated 12,000 to 10,000 years ago, witness continual evolution based on Upper Palaeolithic traditions (Azilian, Epimagdalenian, Epigravettian, and so on).

Similarly the Mesolithic, formerly defined as a separate historical period, is today understood as a natural final phase of the preceding social evolution. This is reflected in the suggested term Final Palaeolithic (10,000 to 5,000 years ago). Herbivores always represented the most important prey, but in restricted areas, where environmental conditions were optimal, fishing gained some importance. Throughout most of the large territories occupied by the Final Palaeolithic people, no important changes which would indicate a local transition to food production have been noted. In certain regions (western Asia, Egypt), however, the earliest evidence of settled life, early stock-breeding and agricultural production may be observed as early as 12,000 years ago. The organization of different hunting groups was already stabilized in the Final Palaeolithic; they were able to adapt their economies to any conditions and to survive. The level of communication and of information exchange was high. In the imaginative sphere, people were able to address themselves to supernatural forces for favour and help. The Palaeolithic hunters stood on the brink of a new historical epoch which is marked by an important evolutionary change, the invention of food production, often called 'the Neolithic revolution' (Chapters 36, 37 and 38).

ORIGINS AND PHYSICAL CHARACTERISTICS OF *HOMO SAPIENS SAPIENS*

The Upper Palaeolithic cultures are connected with humans of the *Homo sapiens sapiens* type, representing the result of a long and complicated process of hominid evolution and of the biological formation of the human genus. This subject is the field of study of physical anthropologists, who at the same time look for reliable explanations for these processes. Such studies depend not only upon new archaeological discoveries, but also upon contemporary scientific developments. From the morphological point of view hominid evolution embraces three functional complexes. The first group of features includes changes in the shape of the thorax and the related release of the upper extremities, allowing rotating movement in the shoulder joint. The second complex, influenced by the hunting way of life, is seen in erect stature and perfect bipedal locomotion, associated with morphological modifications of the pelvis and of the lower extremities. The third complex includes changes in the cranial morphology, especially increase in the cranial capacity and a shifting of the foramen magnum forwards and thus changes in the complex disposition of the head; furthermore it comprehends changes in dentition and, very important, final shaping of the hand. The hand itself, together with the whole arm, changed so much that it became able to throw objects with great force and accuracy, using the mobility of the trunk carried by the pelvis and strong legs, under direct control of the eyes. At the same time, the hand became sensitive enough to produce the most delicate objects, and to imitate the beauty people observed around them and enjoyed.

In the technological field the hand perfected its abilities as well. Human hands were able to carry out the most different and even complicated operations, to use different tools and to modify them as required by the tasks being performed. Hands became tools in the widest sense for work and cultural activities.

Animal hunting stimulated the progressive evolution of the brain and of broad intellectual activities as well. Human beings, in the search for their basic food resources, could not compete with all the other animals by physical strength only, so they were forced to employ other means, such as artifices and tricks, and to use different hunting aids and powerful weapons.

Primeval reflex behaviour, related to the simplest system

of signalling, was replaced by conscious behaviour, a more complex signalling system, which permitted generalizations and improvements in thought to the point of abstract thinking. Evolution of the larynx and lips, with the help of the tongue, gradually made possible complicated sonic expressions and, finally, speech – one of the important indications of an evolved nervous system. Fluent and articulated speech is evidenced by further anatomical features of the skull, such as the fully evolved chin. All these features, evolved over very long periods, and not always at the same time or the same rate, but were related to the cultural and social evolution.

The earliest forms of *Homo sapiens sapiens* appear about 40,000 years ago,[1] and they are still sometimes called *Homo sapiens fossilis*. Broadly speaking, however, these representatives of the Upper Palaeolithic hunting societies correspond in the morphology of their skeletons, their body length and their body structure to Modern humans. The earlier remains may perhaps show some traces of robustness, while in the more recent materials we can observe a more marked dimensional reduction in males than in females, and thus a decrease in sexual dimorphism in height. There are no significant differences in morphology however; those differences that occur are rather of individual or group significance and do not go beyond the range of normal variation. The hand acquires an even greater ability to move quickly and deftly, and the thumb is completely opposable to the other fingers. These changes had favourable consequences for the further development of working activities and production.

Even Modern humans, however, are not morphologically homogeneous. In the different regions and continents of the world we find various somatic differences, which led formerly to the definition of a Cro-Magnon, a Combe-Capelle or Brno human type (Plate 30). Considerable individual and geographical variability seems natural, but the different types do not exceed the limits of subspecies variation. Furthermore, the features formerly explained as differences among the artificially defined Upper Palaeolithic 'races' are now understood to be the result of general evolutionary process.

Local evolutionary trends in the major regions led, nevertheless, to the formation of geographical races, which without doubt took place after the appearance of Modern humans (*Homo sapiens sapiens*). The evidence for Mongoloids may be followed back to about 20,000 years ago. In Africa, the Boskop human type was defined, while the Proto-Australoid type is observed in South Asia and a Mongoloid variant of East Asian origin is documented in America. The most recent human type seems to be the Negroid one, which started its spread at the beginning of Holocene, about 10,000 years ago. Among the main human types may be seen some relatively striking differences in the colour of skin, eyes and hair, in the body proportions and further important features, both morphological and physiological. However, these differences are not genetically significant. All human groups may interbreed and belong to the same subspecies, *Homo sapiens sapiens*.

From the point of view of population genetics, the later populations may be considered as the result of adaptive selection, mutation, accidental drift, isolation or interbreeding, and of other genetic processes. There was a gradual decrease in the breadth of the skull, the height of the face and the general robustness of the body. These changes were stimulated by economic factors which appeared during the final Upper Palaeolithic, especially the emphasis on the hunting of smaller game and catching fish, the increased importance of plant gathering and, later, stock-breeding.

GEOGRAPHICAL DISTRIBUTION

Homo sapiens sapiens penetrated every continent of the world, venturing into their different and sometimes very distinct regions, and persisted there. Modern humans succeeded in an undertaking which had never before been achieved by any animal species. This was made possible only by the human ability to adapt very quickly and perfectly to changing conditions. Retreat occurred only when there was no hope of survival, and there was a return to the deserted areas as soon as the environmental conditions improved. In certain regions it is thus possible to observe population migrations that are synchronous with the climatic fluctuations of the Late Glacial.

In regions where humans survived under very hard conditions, groups lived in extreme isolation and their evolution was slow or even retarded. Sometimes they have continued as hunter-gatherers till the present time. This fact was documented by the numerous travellers in recent centuries who ventured into the tundras of the Far East and Alaska, or by sailors who reached the shores of Tierra del Fuego and other remote areas.

In penetrating everywhere it was possible to penetrate, human beings were able to overcome immense natural barriers, the most difficult of these being, of course, the large stretches of ocean. However, the glaciers during the cold phases of the Last Glacial locked up so great an amount of the world water reserves that the sea-level was considerably lowered, exposing major land bridges between islands and continents. In cases where the newly exposed land surfaces did not permit a direct land passage, they at least made it easier to reach the unknown shores on simple vessels and later on safer boats, which provided better control and were equally suitable for fishing. The boat is one of the most important discoveries of the final phases of this epoch.

The most substantial colonization was from east Siberia over the Bering Strait to the American continents, by hunting groups adapted to the cold steppes and tundras. The colonists penetrated Alaska about 45,000 years ago, before the most exteme cold oscillation of the Last Glacial, when the way to the south, free of glaciers, was still open. The ancestors of the Amerindians used archaic flake technology and made bifacially retouched leaf-points similar to those of their contemporaries in east Asia. Later, production of these tools was perfected in the American continents.

It was not before the final retreat of the glaciers that the first human groups entered the north, as far as the shores of Greenland, and as a result of specific evolution, influenced by adaptation to the cold polar environment, gave rise to the Inuit.

Humans established their position in the deserted steppes and in the woodlands of Africa, in the immense areas of Asia and colonized New Guinea, Australia and Tasmania. Adaptation to new environments was not always so difficult. This may be judged from the preserved remains, which continue the archaic techniques on the one hand, but introduced new approaches on the other, including the polishing of stone tools.

TECHNOLOGICAL PROGRESS

Stone tools and weapons, produced by chipping suitable rocks, retained their importance during the Upper Palaeolithic period. The technology of blade production was perfected, however, and gained wide importance. It allowed the production of long and narrow flakes – blades – from specially prepared cores, by using a soft hammerstone. The shape of the blades was regular, with parallel edges, so that they could serve as perfect knives even without further modifications. They were nevertheless considered as half-finished products and often processed subsequently by pressure-flaking with stone, bone and wood retouchers into many differently shaped tools, perfectly adapted to serve their functions.

The techniques used in the final shaping of blades were already differentiated according to the desired tool types, and some of them are even typical for certain cultures or geographical regions. Special importance was attached to the techniques of edge removal, which resulted in a short and strong point, suitable for engraving hard materials (the dihedral burins). A similar tool type was also produced simply by retouching the edge (the edged burins). Another technique, the production of backed implements, is characteristic especially of the Gravettian cultural complex. By-products of this working process were the numerous small chips of debitage from the removal of the smaller, marginal parts of blades by pressure-flaking using various tools, or from core preparation. Some of them could be used directly for different purposes as well.

The morphology of the different tool types, but also the examination of their functional parts and of the preserved use-wear traces, allows conclusions to be drawn about the most general ways in which they were used and sometimes even about very specialized activities. New weapons, meant not for hunting at close range or for fighting but for killing prey at a distance, had been invented, which means that humans had empirically detected some laws of mechanics: these weapons comprise the light spear, the spear-thrower and the bow and arrow. It is possible to distinguish hunting weapons, especially spearheads and arrowheads, tools for processing prey such as knives and scrapers, and implements for woodworking (notches, chisels) and bone-working (burins, becs), as well as small borers and saws, which could be used for perforating decorative objects and so on. Specialization progressed so far that within the tool categories mentioned and their range of variants it is possible to differentiate further special forms. Together with the very specialized tools appear general-purpose tools, fulfilling different functions without further modifications (leaf-points, some perfect knives and the like), but also, on the other hand, ingeniously composite tool types. Such composite tools included both those that combined several tools of the same type (such as double end-scrapers, double or triple burins and so on) and those that combined several different tool types.

An important advantage of the blade technology, in comparison with the previous simple method of flaking and toolworking, was in the more economical use of the raw material. It was now possible to obtain several tools from a single pebble or lump of stone, far more than in the previous periods.

Morphological differentiation of the stone tools not only is the result of increasing standardization, but was equally influenced by immediate needs and by environmental factors and conditions. Tool morphology and functional efficiency

were closely related to the raw material used, to its qualities (structure, hardness, suitability for flaking), but also to its accessibility, the necessity of transporting it and the means of distribution. These circumstances are reflected not only in the quantity of the lithic industries and of their by-products, but also in the techniques used to manufacture the different tool types.

The most suitable rocks were flint, different hornstones, radiolarite, lydite, quartzite and quartz. Among the materials of lower quality, the quartzitic sandstone, crystalline schists, claystones and limestone were of importance. Precious stones such as rock crystal, chalcedony, obsidian, opal, agate, jasper and so on were equally used.

These raw materials were sometimes brought to the living-sites from quite far away; however, they were more commonly collected in the places of their secondary deposition, mainly from river gravels, ancient gravel terraces or moraine deposits in the form of pebbles and boulders. They were also quarried from primary deposits, usually by simple freeing from the parent rock.

Some rare rocks were probably highly appreciated. This is reflected by the fact that they were selected for making special tool types only and served for special occasions. Such materials probably soon became the object of barter trade. Where the foreign materials are more numerous, they may indicate population movements and prospecting activities. On the other hand, local rocks were preferred for making the coarser tools used for rough work such as grinding or smashing, as bolas stones, discs, and so on. In areas around the sources of raw material appear sites specialized in the supply of this material, where it was concentrated, transformed into the pre-core form and flaked into the raw flakes and blades. Nevertheless, core preparation by which tools of a predetermined shape could be struck was more frequently concentrated in the permanent living-sites.

The influence of tradition is particularly to be seen in the technological sphere. While technology becomes more sophisticated, stylistical and aesthetic features appear alongside the purely functional ones. Their most obvious manifestation is in the regular and symmetrical form of the tools, which achieves admirable perfection and accuracy. Sometimes the tools become increasingly small, some of them reaching microlithic dimensions. The phenomenon is the result not only of the adaptation of tools to the changing environment and to hunting specialization, but equally of gradual refinement of manufacturing techniques. Thus we can observe 'microlithization' not only during the Late and Final Palaeolithic, when it is traditionally considered to have been an adaptation to hunting smaller animals, birds and fishes, but already during the Upper Palaeolithic.

The typology of Upper Palaeolithic stone tools is based on their presumed suitability for particular functions, supported by evidence of such use observable in use-wear traces. Recently studies of artefacts have included microwear analysis. Formerly the stone industries were evaluated only by means of the descriptive morphological method. However, consideration and comparison of industries by this method alone led sometimes to quite subjective judgements, including the selection of the artefacts to be analysed. After the Second World War, in an attempt to achieve a common and objective approach, the statistical method was gradually introduced, which required detailed metrical data. Use of such methods, however, presupposes a unified classification of the tool types, the matter about which the different authorities disagree up to the present time. Even attempts to produce a universal nomenclature for the Palaeolithic tool types and for obligatory principles for their classification have not helped to facilitate international understanding in this field.

At the present time the technological method is increasingly becoming standard practice, studying the different techniques of manufacture and modification of the stone tools. As documented by numerous experiments, these procedures were sometimes more complicated and more elaborate than might generally be expected. The final product was dependent not only on the quality of the raw material, but also on the core preparation, on the type and direction of pressure, blow or other application of force. In particular, the production of narrow blades and other sophisticated forms required an intermediary punch made of antler or bone instead of the direct use of the hammerstone, and the core itself was placed on an anvil made of different materials.

The Upper Palaeolithic stone tools were usually hafted into handles, holders or butts made from other materials, thus forming a more perfect functional unit. Such composite tools are more sophisticated than the artefacts of preceding periods. Composite tools reached their apogee during the Final Palaeolithic, when microliths were hafted side by side to form a single sharp edge, or harpoon barbs or as the heads of projectiles.

Tools made generally of stone served not only directly in hunting and in tasks related to the hunting, but to a certain extent even in producing and adapting the other important tools from organic materials. For this reason stone tools may be considered as the basic requirement for work. It was only with stone tools that the different parts of the animals killed, such as bones, horns, antlers, teeth and tusks could be worked. Such materials, typical components of the Upper Palaeolithic toolkit, are preserved only under favourable depositional conditions. Although organic materials were worked in the previous periods too, it was not until the Upper Palaeolithic that tools of these materials become, alongside the stone tools, a standard component of the full toolkit. These tools comprised standardized forms such as spearpoints, daggers, various points, picks, polishing tools, retouchers, pins, needles, awls, hammers, cylindrical grinding implements, shovel-like and spoon-like implements, clubs, perforated antlers and others which were designed for various important tasks. Some of them were composite tools or were lengthened by a handle.

While the lithic industries are studied in more and more detail, in the case of the bone industries the basic typology, content, nomenclature and terminology have not yet been elaborated. Similarly the technology, the methods employed in the preparation of the basic shape and in its further modifications by smashing, knocking and breaking as in stoneworking or splitting with wedges, scraping, perforating and polishing, and even the function of these tools are not always well understood. There are many forms, rarely represented but standardized, where it is not possible to demonstrate either their purpose or their significance. The use of ethnographic parallels and other comparisons, which usually cannot go beyond the speculative level, is limited as well. However, the use-wear traces on bone tools are more marked than on stone tools, thus encouraging the use of microwear analysis to explain their different functions. The evolved techniques of boneworking indicate that different working processes were involved and that for the first time useful, functionally and morphologically differentiated implements were being made. Sometimes the manufacture of a tool required a combination of several techniques; in

other cases it was sufficient to adapt the natural shape by simple polishing of the bone.

It is only natural that the tools, originally simple in shape, were gradually improved, as a result of experience built up by the end of the Upper Palaeolithic; the forms became very sophisticated (harpoons, points with blood grooves, and so on). Some of them were so perfect in shape (for example, needles) that they did not need further improvements in later periods. The techniques of polishing and perforating were soon adapted to lithic material as well, even if the mass employment of polished stone is not observed before the Neolithic.

By-products of boneworking are numerous chips and fragments; however, they usually cannot be differentiated from accidental remains of smashed bone. Their suitable forms meant that such fragments could also be used for different functions. The same is true of some natural pieces of bone, which could be successfully used even without modifications.

Mastery of lithic production, together with sophisticated and varied methods of boneworking, suggests that other materials, not preserved in the archaeological record, were processed similarly. One of the most important is wood. A very substantial part of the lithic industry was intended for woodworking. However, wood was probably used only in a limited way for complete tools. It was more frequently employed in composite tools as handles, or served directly in natural, accidental or only slightly modified forms.

Similarly the other inorganic and organic materials found in the environment could be modified and used. It was possible to introduce different technological approaches to make them easier to process or more suitable for their intended functions. By dipping them in water, mammoth tusks and reindeer antlers became pliable and could be straightened, while the points of wooden spears changed their structure in fire and became harder. Water and especially fire could serve in other working processes as well (exploitation of rocks). It was recognized as early as the Upper Palaeolithic that clay is able to keep its form after being dried and particularly if it is baked. In exceptional cases this discovery was used to model animal and human figures, which after being baked, became the most ancient ceramic products.

The Upper Palaeolithic people observed different materials in nature, recognized their utility, transported them to their living-sites and used them for a great variety of different purposes. Usually, the utilization of these materials became possible after modifications had been effected. In this process, people discovered physical and chemical laws. They were not able to explain these, but they could use them empirically.

During their collecting activities, people noticed striking and curious minerals or rocks, the origin of which may be in some cases unclear even today. In a certain sense it is possible to say that the first petrographical and mineralogical collections arose during this period. Apart from siliceous rocks used for flaking, other types of rocks were equally appreciated, such as rare fragments of pyrite, usable for making fire, agate and other soft rocks suitable for engraving and shaping, or, exceptionally, coal as fuel for maintaining fire. Concave parts of stone concretions and other dish-like shapes were used as containers for grease, which, together with a wick, could bring light and warmth into the caves and dwellings.

In the archaeological complexes at the living-sites stone beds are often observed which form 'working tables' associated with raw material, tools and by-products. These are explained as workshops. In such places specialized individuals most probably worked, who by their experience and skill reached a high level of mastery of their specialized field.

The functional and especially the technical perfection of the bone tools, and even of the stone tools, is sometimes called 'art'. However, such objects, even the most perfect ones, have nothing in common with real artistic expression and manifestations of aesthetic feelings (Chapters 19 and 23).

MEANS OF SUBSISTENCE

The picture of the material culture, as reflected in the archaeological evidence, is very limited and fragmentary. Most of the preserved objects are of inorganic substances and only very exceptionally organic materials, which usually decay. Nevertheless, the remains discovered and the circumstances of their deposition reflect a significant part of the work undertaken, the workforce involved and relations within production, that is social relations. Such evidence may therefore throw light on the way of life of the producers.

It is possible to conclude that Upper Palaeolithic people subsisted mainly on hunting, practised in a more advanced way than in previous periods. It was not before the end of this period that the hunting way of life reached its fullest development, and hunting techniques their peak of sophistication. Hunting was frequently specialized in taking particularly large prey, especially the herbivorous animals, herds of which moved with reliable regularity within given regions. This specialized hunting was connected with more sophisticated and more productive techniques, and with the primary division of labour, most probably on the basis of sex alone.

The archaeological evidence can supply only global information on the way of hunting. It is evident that people of this period were equipped with innate instincts and with experience collected over generations. They perhaps mastered all the methods used by recent hunting populations. The most common and most frequent one was the direct attack, using different weapons and hunting aids. It was a very natural way of hunting, most suitable for meeting the elementary requirements of food for survival. The hunters' skill in using different tricks to deceive animals evolved during generations by observing the characters and habits of the different animal species, while a good knowledge of their anatomy was gained from butchering the carcasses. Hunters built different traps, dug and masked pitfalls and laid snares. They were able to profit from favourable environmental conditions by using fire to drive the prey into ravines, over cliffs, into canyons or into swamps, where it was easier to approach and capture the animal.

Geographical conditions influenced the choice of living sites as well. Places where the presence of prey promised good hunting, such as river confluences and fords, animal paths and watering places, were preferentially selected. Patterns of animal migrations, especially seasonal movements, were equally taken into account.

Some of the small animal and bird bones were made into flutes and probably used to deceive the animals. On the other hand, there is no evidence of the hunting of large herbivores such as the mammoth using pitfalls, which have never been archaeologically demonstrated. Engravings and paintings in the caves of western Europe, known as 'tectiform signs', can hardly be explained as pitfalls either, because they depict dwellings rather than traps. Furthermore, it is difficult to imagine that the hunters with their tools could dig a pit of such dimensions that a mammoth would be trapped without any possibility of escape. The success of such methods would have been very uncertain as well.

In making a direct attack the hunter could rely upon powerful weapons, perfected during this period. This is evidenced by long points made of mammoth tusks and pointed mammoth ribs, imitating the shape of wooden spears with their sharpened extremities, hardened in fire. Naturally spears with bone points were important as well. Some of them have harpoon barbs, others have blood grooves, intensifying the debilitation of the wounded animal and enabling the hunter to follow its trail more easily. Similarly the spear-thrower was useful in extending the throwing range of the hunter's arm and facilitating and strengthening his throw. Other hunting techniques employed harpoons composed of three parts: a point with barbs, a central fastening part and a wooden handle. Swiftly moving animals were attacked with bolas, boomerangs, sling-stones and other weapons. This complex of weapons and techniques represents the climax of the prehistoric hunter's inventory.

The success of the hunt in these circumstances was dependent upon group co-operation. Similarly, since food remains accumulated in places used by the whole group, it seems that the food itself was obtained and shared communally. Only a small part of the food was left unused. All parts of the animals' bodies were exploited, and only the unusable bones, which could serve neither in toolmaking nor in building dwellings nor as fuel, were thrown away, especially in periods of competence. The meat was eaten after being cooked over the fire, probably only partly baked, and some parts of the entrails were consumed even in the raw state. It is possible that the food was prepared in leather bags and cooked using pit-boilers (stones heated and dropped in); it might also be dried and smoked, preserved in ash or frozen and stored against future need. The marrow was taken from the big bones and the brain extracted from the skulls. Some of these activities are indicated by deliberately smashed bones. Leather and skins were used in making dresses, head-dresses, and simple shoes, providing clothing, but were also employed to cover dwellings and to make various straps, belts and so on.

The bow is commonly supposed to have appeared only in the most recent periods of the Palaeolithic, and it is archaeologically evidenced as late as the end of this period. It could be used not only in hunting small animals and birds, but also in fishing: fish-bones are found in some numbers in the living-sites as well. Fishing must have taken place, even if no hooks, nets and other tackle are preserved. It is only natural that there were different techniques, means and weapons used for different types of animals, and that the methods used to obtain meat changed in relation to the climatic conditions and the structure of the biotope.

If specialization in hunting reached so high a level that the main prey animal predominated significantly, it is evident that the relationship between humans and their preferred animal was closer than the usual one of the hunter to the prey. It is possible to suppose a more permanent human–animal relationship and to look for the first indications leading subsequently to domestication and stock breeding. This relationship could take the form of interaction with a single herd or individual, to which the people offered food or shelter in a fold. This type of interconnection evolved especially in relation to the reindeer, in more temperate areas to the horse and in the mountains to the ibex. Sometimes an attractive animal might have been used to decoy the prey and to ensure the success of the hunting.

On the other hand, one should not overestimate the hunter's abilities and potential. Data from ethnographic studies among contemporary hunter-gatherers reveal that meat is not of overriding importance in meeting the requirements of the social unit, an important part of food resources being represented by plants. It is thus probable that as early as the Upper Palaeolithic, depending on the environmental conditions, we may postulate an intensification of the gathering of plant foods and of assuring that continuing productivity took place. This gained importance especially in the more temperate climatic zones, in a warmer climate and most notably during the Late and Final Palaeolithic, and took place with conscious regulation of conditions favourable to the spread of certain useful plants. Such activities increased in extent, especially when burning of the forest was introduced to provide more light for plant growth. Such human interference with natural conditions had revolutionary consequences during later evolution and led subsequently to permanent manipulation of natural events for human benefit and thus a change in the economic base.

It may be observed that important changes in the temperate (Postglacial) climate influenced not only flora and fauna, but human society as well, including the material culture and the way of life. While numerous animal species migrated or even became extinct, humans were able to adapt themselves to all the consequences of these changes. If, on the one hand, nature offered a broader choice of plants and of their fruits, society, on the other hand, changed methods of exploiting these food resources.

Humankind lived to the best of their ability as an integral part of nature till the very end of the Upper Palaeolithic. Our ancestors took everything they needed from nature, without having the interest, influence, potential or ability to enlarge their needs. Their economy was of a passive, non-productive character, and their needs were not as yet satisfied by direct food production, which would imply active interference with nature. Under the changed environmental conditions, however, the opportunity arose to use all the accumulated human experience and observations, and to create a more elaborate economic base, which meant the transition to a productive economy. An important indication was the use of plant resources, a more intensive relationship with certain animals and attempts at domestication of the first animal – the dog, which provides a proof that the hunting way of life still represented the main source of nourishment. However, this transition was still quite irregular and depended upon the environment. Under optimal conditions agricultural food production was introduced rather early, while in northern and mountainous regions we can observe a direct transition from hunting to a pastoral way of life.

SETTLEMENTS AND SOCIAL ORGANIZATION

One of the important innovations of the Upper Palaeolithic is the large-scale enforced building of artifical dwellings. During the past decades, archaeologists have succeeded in finding them in numerous places. After the first discoveries of such dwellings at Langmannersdorf (Austria) and of the dwelling arrangements at the cave of Fourneau-du-Diable (Dordogne, France), numerous proofs of the existence of early architecture were revealed by Soviet archaeologists in the large steppe-areas of eastern Europe (Gagarino, Buret, Kostenki). Recent excavations have brought to light new evidence, including dwellings of the Middle Palaeolithic period. Even earlier are the artificial shelters and dwelling arrangements discovered especially in the caves of western Europe and in the open-air sites of Africa. The remains of some Upper Palaeolithic dwellings bear witness to the surprisingly perfect and sophisticated construction of huts and their equipment, enabling reliable reconstructions to be made. Similarly surprising is the ingenious choice of locality, the basic disposition in the plan of the living site, and feeling for having a certain degree of order. Today, the number of excavated huts is so high that it is possible to compare and classify them. The new, detailed methods of research enable convincing interpretations of their importance to be made.

The majority of the dwellings are represented by the remains of tent-like shelters with a wooden framework covered by animal skins. Other building materials were bones, especially mammoth bones and reindeer antler, wood and earth; stones were also used for securing the skin covering the huts to the ground. The construction of these huts and shelters could draw on the wealth of technical expertise that had been developed for tool production. The stone blocks placed one next to the other and the piled-up schist plaques show traces of working. Another common approach was binding together or wedging shaped bones and wood. Building shelters involved digging as well. Sometimes only the posts or piles were entrenched in the earth, but sometimes the whole floor was dug out to a considerable depth. The so-called 'zemlyanka' or 'semi-zemlyanka' arose in this way. The preserved peripheral mounds, composed of remains of building materials from the walls, even include stone masonry or mammoth skulls, sometimes still with the tusks.

The Upper Palaeolithic dwellings are of different shapes, most frequently oval, kidney-shaped, circular or quite irregular. Their dimensions are variable as well: from quite small ones, probably winter shelters, to big structures which were difficult to roof with the available techniques, and which served probably as summer dwellings. Various modifications and the associated equipment indicate the difference in function of certain huts. Some of them clearly represent permanent dwellings in continuously settled living sites, while others are more probably light, tent-like structures, which could be easily transported and used by hunters following the animal herds. Prehistoric humans, who sheltered their closest living spaces by building dwellings, at the same time protected their own bodies against unfavourable external influences by making simple clothing, headgear and probably also shoes. As far as the dwellings and settlements occupied for a long time are concerned, it should not be concluded that the society was permanently settled. This would contradict the model generally accepted till recently, which assumes that the Palaeolithic people were highly mobile nomads given their hunting way of life. Some knowledge acquired through experience, especially technical expertise, could be transmitted only through contact with other groups. Some raw materials could also be obtained only by exchange or by movements over long distances. Some economies were transhumant, the hunting territories being abandoned to follow seasonal migrations of the game. Direct superpositions in the stratigraphy of cultural layers in the settlements show that certain groups preferred a longer stay at the site. It is even impossible to prove that these sites were really abandoned for a certain time. It is probable that at the end of the Upper Palaeolithic some feelings of close relation to a given region appear, feelings for a sort of 'home'. Such a tendency towards settled life is one of the important preconditions for further evolution to the Neolithic food-producing economy.

Walls and shelters were built not only in the open, but also in naturally roofed spaces such as cave entrances or rock shelters, protecting its inhabitants from the cold and wet. Here it was not necessary to dig in the earth, because stone was abundant and could be used to make different living accommodation, hearths, recesses, paved floors and so on.

Hearths inside or outside the living sites are an important component of building activities. They are frequently dug out, circular in shape, with a diameter of about 1 metre, sometimes walled with earth and stones, and even roofed. Exceptionally a sort of channel bringing the air supply to the fire is preserved. Not only wood, but also the bones of hunted animals were burned. Such hearths recall permanent fireplaces or ovens; their pits were repeatedly cleaned out when filled with ash, and the fire set again. In the vicinity of such features large ash deposits gradually accumulated.

Sometimes it is possible to observe small, cauldron-shaped pits, which could have been used as containers. From their contents and shape it is possible to conclude that in certain cases the meat was cooked here ('cooking pits'). This could have been done by putting heated stones, especially quartz pebbles, inside the holes lined with skins or in leather bags filled with ash or water. In other cases modified bone constructions suggest that the food could have been cooked here in the open fire by grilling.

On the periphery of permanently settled sites large refuse mounds developed, especially remarkable in cases when the mammoth bones were abandoned. They are proofs of the high productivity of hunting, but also an expression of the communal nature of the economy. They preceded the well-known *Kjøkkenmøddinger* (kitchen middens) of Denmark, and they are also frequently called thus.

With the increased numbers of dwellings discovered, our archaeological knowledge has evolved so far that it is now possible to study the associations of the huts and even groundplans of whole Palaeolithic settlements, which display general consistencies. Although speculative, they enable us nevertheless to consider the global structure of such permanent settlements, their internal organization and the serious economic, social and especially the organizational pattern at this evolutionary level.

It is becoming clear that typical mammoth-hunters' settlements (Gravettian) were composed of five or six independent shelters, not very durable and therefore frequently renovated. They represent the dwellings of basic social units, connected by close relationships. Prehistoric communities were composed of members of such matrilinear clans. If a household unit numbered about twenty people, the prehistoric community would have totalled 100 to 120. It seems that such a social unit could prosper under the prevailing conditions and at the level of economic evolution which had been attained. It made it possible to organize sufficiently large groups of hunters, adult males who could supply all inhabitants of the settlement with enough food.

During the final phases of the Upper Palaeolithic when hunting patterns changed, the number of members in a social unit decreased. There was rapid population decrease and community fragmentation, bringing about profound social changes. The circumstances would suggest a global population decrease, as reflected by a striking reduction in the accessible remains of the material culture. However,

life continued to develop, and it is only because of the unfavourable conditions of deposition that we do not have a sharper picture of its continuity. The groups of the Final Palaeolithic (Mesolithic) founded their sites on sandy deposits on the shores of rivers and lakes, where it was possible to take small animals, birds and fishes without much effort and more easily than in the preceding periods. This kind of hunting could be successfully undertaken by single individuals. Large groups were unnecessary now, but arrow and bow were useful aids in hunting.

METAPHYSICAL CONCERNS

The intense evolution of continuously improved tools is naturally reflected in the sphere of ideas, at a higher level in intellectual life, in evolved abilities for abstract thought. The most important result is articulated speech, together with other means of communication. This made possible the reciprocal exchange of experiences and information, the organization of social activities, and so on.

Apart from the single lines or cuts in bone and also on hard stone objects, more sophisticated signs appear, engraved or painted, and even very complicated and geometrically exact designs. In some cases, the decorative meaning of such designs is apparent. They are found on numerous useful objects, but also on discarded tools and weapons. Some of them are interpreted as devices recording a lunar calendar, while others are considered to be arithmetical marks developed from the use of the simplest mathematical aid – the human hand with its five fingers. This is the case for regularly arranged elements which could represent any concrete feature, immediate state, value or image, or even symbolize it in a schematic and stylized form.

Apart from these first forms of annotation, graphical expression and communication, which in their conceptual content are undoubtedly the precursors of the later invention of script, we meet in the Upper Palaeolithic an intense flowering of decorative objects, ornaments and various personal equipment.

Depending on their shape and function they are classified as pendants, necklaces, brooches, headbands, bracelets, rings and so on. However, their significance was not merely decorative, but had a deeper meaning, which cannot be determined with certainty but can be suggested with some confidence, especially on the basis of ethnographic parallels. Significance for these types of objects may be found even in modern times, when many are promoted or even personified, and connected with a sort of higher, supernatural force and power.

Such objects could probably mediate between humans and their environment, a sphere imagined as being inhabited and directed by invisible powers. Such imaginings originated in the powerless position of humanity faced with the external world and its unexplainable laws. Human beings thus tried to find an intermediary, a person able to gain the favour of these higher powers by means of magic rituals and sorcery such as shamanism, and to influence favourably current and future events. With similar intentions they made use of red pigment, coating corpses with it or showering it over them. This fact bears witness to the beliefs in a life after death, the pigment symbolically restoring blood to the corpse. The suspiciously small number of Upper Palaeolithic burials suggests that only prominent persons were given ritual burial. Most of the corpses were treated, so that their remains were not preserved. During the Final Palaeolithic it is also observed that sometimes only certain parts of the bodies, such as mandibles or skulls, were kept. Parts of animal bodies, especially the heads, were treated in a similar way and are taken to have been sacrifices.

Communication with the supernatural beings was arranged, among others, by the shaman or a precursor. This person tried to influence the greatest variety of social events, and lived most probably at the expense of society. Most frequently they assisted in ritual activities.

Prehistoric humans made and decorated various objects and ascribed to them the power of amulets and fetishes. Their purpose was to secure safety and help in the fight against harsh nature. People could even use quite simple objects and natural pieces, the significance of which need not be expressed. If such objects were trusted and if belief in their successful intervention were supported by circumstances, they would certainly be highly esteemed. However, if they failed or became inefficacious for some reason, they would be rejected or destroyed. In this way the earliest forms of religious beliefs influenced social evolution in the negative sense, since they impeded and retarded the development of proper human creative forces and capacities.

Some of the sophisticated engravings clearly go beyond mere accounting or recording information numerically or in inscriptions, while, on the other hand, many decorative objects are more than simple decoration. In addition they mostly demonstrate a profound aesthetic feeling on the part of the creator, and evoke a similar reaction from the observer. Thus they fall into the category of earliest art, even if artistic manifestations cannot always be differentiated from other objects by their form and content alone. In any case it is not possible to divide the two spheres by a precise boundary, since they overlap or form a continuum.

CONCLUSIONS

The Upper Palaeolithic may be defined as the period when *Homo sapiens sapiens*, the human genus evolved to its present state, established its position in nature, and at the same time completed the longest period of social history. During this period, humankind developed an advanced economy and started to create the first productive relationships with their resources.

The economy of the first human societies was based on hunting and gathering, and it is not possible to demonstrate that either food-procurement strategy was superior to the other. Both of them were needed. It is difficult to consider the past way of life on the basis of our modern experiences only, as it was influenced by numerous environmental stresses in different directions; natural evolution was still in progress, and the social formations were not yet stabilized. Qualitative differences between individual cultural periods and groups

were quite slight, but they were nevertheless of great significance for further evolution.

The spread of humankind over the whole world and the new climatic conditions and zones of the Postglacial forced numerous population groups to increase their adaptability and to create conditions for more effective physical, economic and cultural differentiation. This is the starting point for further diverse evolution.

NOTE

1 The views advanced here seem to be obsolete, except for Europe. In other regions the evolution from *Homo erectus* to Modern humans advanced much more quickly. In eastern and in southern Africa fully developed *Homo sapiens sapiens* appeared between 130,000 and 100,000 years ago (Kibish 2 in Ethiopia around 130,000 years ago, Border Cave in Natal around 115,000 years ago and Klasies River Mouth near Cape Town around 100,000 years ago); in western Asia *H. sapiens sapiens* appeared around 50,000 years ago (skulls of Qafzeh and Skhul in Israel). (See Chapters 2, 9, 11 and 14.) – Ed.

BIBLIOGRAPHY

BAYER, J. 1921. Der Mammutjägerhalt der Aurignacienzeit bei Langmannersdorf an der Perschling. *Mannus* (Würzburg), Vol. 13, pp. 76–81.

BOHMERS, A.; WOUTERS, A.G. 1956. Statistics and Graphs in the Study of Flint Assemblages. *Palaeohistoria* (Groningen), Vol. 5, pp. 1–39.

BORDES, F. (ed.) 1972. *The Origin of* Homo sapiens. Paris, UNESCO.

CHILDE, V.G. 1948. *Man Makes Himself*. London.

DUMOND, D.E. 1980. The Archaeology of Alaska and the Peopling of America. *Science* (Washington), Vol. 209, 29 Aug., pp. 248–80.

LAPLACE, G. 1964. Essai de typologie systématique. *Ann. Univ. Ferrara*, Section 15, Suppl. 2, p. 1.

LEVÊQUE, F.; VANDERMEERSCH, B. 1981. Le Néandertalien de Saint-Césaire. *Recherche* (Paris), Vol. 12, No. 119, pp. 242–4.

MARSHACK, A. 1970. *Notation dans les gravures du Paléolithique supérieur: nouvelles méthodes d'analyse*. Bordeaux. (Publ. Inst. préhist. Univ. Bordx., 8.)

MÜLLER-BECK, H. 1982. Der Mensch als Techniker. In: *Kindlers Enzyklopädie: Der Mensch*. Bonn. Vol. 2, pp. 147–200.

NARR, K. J. (ed.) 1966–85. *Handbuch der Urgeschichte*. Bern/Munich. 2 vols.

PEYRONY, D. 1928. Un Fond de hutte de l'époque solutréenne. In: *Institut International d'Anthropologie*. 3e session. Amsterdam. pp. 315–18.

PEYRONY, D.; PEYRONY, E. 1932. *Les Gisements préhistoriques de Bourdeilles*. Paris. (Arch. Inst. Paléontol. Hum., Mém. 10.)

SONNEVILLE-BORDES, D.; PERROT, J. 1953. Essai d'adaptation des méthodes statistiques au Paléolithique Supérieur. *Bull. Soc. préhist. fr.*, Vol. 50, pp. 323–33.

19

THE ORIGINS OF ART

An overview

Hans-Georg Bandi

The would-be student of the origins of art in our prehistoric past must be clear about two things. The first is that the only fields of creative activity that can be considered in the Upper Palaeolithic and Mesolithic periods are those of representational art. It is perfectly possible that, at the same time or possibly earlier, there were poetic productions (such as myths handed down by word of mouth) and early forms of music (for instance chants associated with ritual dances), but no archaeological proof of the existence of either is possible. The second point is that the artistic activity of prehistoric hunting societies has only external affinities with our present-day conceptions of representational art. When human beings, still wholly a part of the natural environment, engraved, sculpted and painted, they did not do so in any spirit of *ars gratia artis*, but for the most part as a function of their mental image of the supernatural powers on which their existence depended.

Up to now we have no secure evidence that *Homo sapiens neanderthalensis*, the carrier of the Middle Palaeolithic cultures, was capable of representational art.[1] The first to leave indubitable evidence of art was *Homo sapiens sapiens* of the Upper Palaeolithic, but what was produced was astonishing in quantity and impressive in quality. The mural and mobiliary art of the Upper Palaeolithic and its development from humble beginnings to fascinating masterpieces is an important feature of the advanced hunting cultures of the late Ice Age. Exactly where these highly specialized hunting and gathering societies developed from their Middle Palaeolithic antecedents is still not clear, but it is certain that nowhere did they flourish so vigorously during the Late Glacial as they did in Europe. This applies most particularly to the art that is the subject of our discussion here. There is evidence of Upper Palaeolithic art outside Europe, too, but what has been found proves little more than the fact that there were trends elsewhere among representatives of the advanced hunting cultures. What we know from finds in Europe points to an early and extremely impressive flowering of this art. On the other hand, evidence also exists of similar forms of artistic expression from later periods and other areas to which advanced hunting cultures spread; these certainly, in most cases, have an independent origin: the early beginnings of representational art in Europe were paralleled in later times by peoples with similar life-styles and a similar mentality. Since in this chapter we are concerned with the earliest beginnings of representational art, we can con-

centrate on the Upper Palaeolithic in Europe, which, as we shall see, was responsible for some extraordinary achievements, particularly in the west.

The reader of Chapter 18 will be already familiar with the various aspects of the advanced hunting cultures of the late Pleistocene belonging to *Homo sapiens sapiens*. In an environment similar to present conditions in the Arctic and subarctic for human beings, obtaining food and defeating the cold was a constant battle. They were challenged in many respects and the way they managed to ensure their existence and their survival makes an impressive story. Here there are three especially important aspects: first, the specialized hunting on animal species that are particularly numerous and high-yielding; second, the accumulation of material goods shown by the richness of the finds at Upper Palaeolithic settlement sites; and third, the differentiation in tools and weapons and related hunting methods. The basis of late Ice Age human existence was a completely adapted economy, one that remained adaptive and in use in the post-glacial age in some remote areas of Europe, especially in the north, near the Arctic Circle, but also around the mountains, up to seven or six millennia ago, when Mesolithic hunting and fishing societies, replacing the Upper Palaeolithic advanced hunting societies, enlarged the occupied area as the ice sheets gradually retreated.

At first sight it seems astonishing and scarcely credible that these peoples, having to fight a continuous and hazardous battle for existence, found time for artistic activities. Here, as already pointed out, we must first remember that the works of art they left behind were primarily intended to serve purposes that we admittedly do not understand clearly but in which artistic feelings certainly did not come first. A second point is that present-day hunting peoples living in arduous environments, such as the Inuit, also created many works we would describe as art long before they had any contact with modern civilization.

Before we embark on an interpretation of the representational art of the Upper Palaeolithic and Mesolithic ages, we shall look first at such aspects as forms of expression, production techniques, content, distribution and chronology.

A first point to consider is the division of the material into two main categories: mobiliary art and rock art. Mobiliary art consists of movable objects that may be works of art in their own right or else decorated tools and weapons.

They are made of stone (Plate 31), carbonaceous material, antler (Plate 32), bone (Plate 33), ivory and, more rarely, teeth. The astonishing thing about these artefacts, some of which possess a striking naturalism and considerable quality, is that they were made using simple tools, mainly of flint, to engrave and sculpt the generally hard materials (an exception being soapstone, which was also used occasionally). A distinct subcategory is constituted by the 'cut-out silhouette' figures fashioned from a flat piece of antler or bone and completed with engravings (Plates 32 and 33). In some isolated examples of mobiliary art, colour is used: ochre or some other dye has been rubbed on the whole article, engraved lines filled with coloured paste, or animal figures painted on flat stone. (We shall come back to the question of dyes and painting technique in connection with rock art; see below). Another point to be made about mobiliary art is that originally the use of colour probably played a greater part, but that this is no longer demonstrable in most cases because the objects have been buried so long in the earth. Finally there are a few small figures shaped from clay (mixed with carbonized, powdered bone or ivory) and hardened by fire. This was probably accidental because the late Ice Age peoples did not make pottery, which would have had no function in their nomadic existence, dictated as it was by hunting considerations. We may of course safely assume that wood and other perishable materials were also used to make or complete mobiliary art. What has finally come down to us represents the imperishable 'skeleton' of what was once a far more manifold and colourful inventory; the rest disappeared long ago. Most works of mobiliary art have been found in the dwelling places of the time.

That brings us to rock art, or 'cave art'. The latter term is not quite correct because, although there are many natural formations, particularly those used during the Upper Palaeolithic and which deserve to be called picture caves, many rock shelters were already being used at that time for representational art. Neither does the term 'mural art' altogether suffice, because not only the walls but also the ceilings and occasionally the floors of caves were used. A further distinction has to be drawn between engraved and painted figures and, more rarely, those executed in bas-relief. Relatively frequently, too, the natural shapes in the rock were incorporated in the representations or converted, by means of minor changes, into readily recognizable figures. This applies not only to the original rock parts but also to stalactites and stalagmites and other formations created by dripping water. In addition one is tempted to suppose that Ice Age people interpreted natural formations, modified by them in ways we cannot perceive, as though they were really figures. It is also possible that they gave them additional features in organic material so as to create the impression, in dark cave interiors lit by rudimentary light sources, that they were in the presence of beings from the world of the imagination of those ages. When we wander through the picture caves today, some of them kilometres long, we are often taken aback when our lights pick out rock formations giving the impression, without any visible intervention upon them by Ice Age hands, of animals or beings from the underworld. How much more strongly aroused, as they penetrated the darkness of the caves, must have been the imagination of those hunting people whose life and effort was so closely bound up with the Ice Age animal kingdom and the supernatural forces that reigned over it. The fact that they were at their ease in the subterranean labyrinths was certainly due only partly to the light sources they had at their command (tallow lamps or pitch torches – here too we

can only guess); an important role must have been played by the highly developed sense of orientation that these people close to nature possessed.

As for the technique used in these rock pictures, some are so-called finger drawings made by tracing the figure with a bare finger in the soft clay that covered parts of the rock. The majority, however, are engravings cut into the rock with flint burins, a task often assisted by the fact that the formations were limestone and not particularly hard. Other evidence to support this assumption is provided by the fact that various tools matching the engravings have been found on the ground in front of the pictures or wedged into nearby cracks in the rock. Here the surprising thing is that, from place to place alongside relatively coarse and deeply incised engravings, there are extremely finely traced drawings that are barely noticeable to the naked eye and very difficult to make out. How and for what purpose Ice Age people made these pictures and how they were able to recognize them in the darkness of the caves is not easy to explain. Lastly, another, though less frequently used, technique must be mentioned: it consisted not of engraving the lines of the design but in punching them into the rock using a stone implement.

There has already been much speculation about the colours used for painting and how they were prepared, applied and preserved. One known fact is that they were of mineral origin, in particular different variants of iron ochre, haematite, manganese ore and red ochre, plus perhaps wood charcoal and other materials. The colour spectrum therefore ranges from bright yellow via red and brown to black, with a complete absence of blue and green. Experiments have shown that the pigments were probably ground into powder and then mixed with a binding agent, possibilities here being grease, blood, egg-white, vegetable juices or wild honey. The paints may have been applied with the hand, with brush-like aids made from feathers, hair or blades of grass, or even perhaps with dabbers made from animal skins. Another possibility not to be excluded, as certain finds have shown, is the pastel technique using lumps of pigment sometimes sharpened like pencils. A further problem not yet completely solved is that of the preservation of the paintings. Local factors certainly played a major role. In many cases, deep inside the caves, the constant level of humidity of the decorated parts of the rock may have contributed to conservation, whereas in others precisely the reverse may have been true, a dry climate in the open rock shelters being responsible for the beneficial effects. In either case the important fact was that for thousands of years the conditions did not change, or at least changed very little and very gradually. Where abrupt changes were or are brought about through human intervention, there was and is a likelihood of damage to the paintings. Often the sinter that formed after the paintings or engravings were created, and which to a certain extent settled over the pictures like a protective film (but may also have concealed them completely), also helped. Clearly, given the circumstances, much has been lost forever but some, too, is still waiting to be discovered. This applies equally to mobiliary art, examples of which continue to be brought to light in excavations, and to rock pictures, since decorated caves and rock shelters bearing works of representational art continue to be discovered.

As already said, the centre of gravity of early representational (mobiliary and rock) art lay in western Europe. Only isolated instances of Upper Palaeolithic rock art have been found outside the Iberian peninsula and France, for instance in the south of Italy, Sicily and the Urals. Con-

Figure 33 Magdalenian cave bear (length 48 cm), Les Combarelles cave, Dordogne (France). (Centre National de Préhistoire, Périgueux.)

of smaller mammals, for example, that were hunted for their meat or skins, as well as birds, fish, reptiles, amphibians, and even insects (Plate 33), though pictures of these are very rare indeed. In most cases they seem to have been the subject of isolated representations in both mobiliary and rock art, but there is a danger that we may not always be able to discern relationships that were obvious in the Ice Age. In any case there are also group scenes (Fig. 34). Representations of human beings are more rare, although in mobiliary art there is a significantly large group of figurines (mostly female) (Fig. 35). Supplementing these are the engravings (and occasionally paintings) of human beings identified in rock art. Many figures are best described as anthropomorphic, being half-human, half-beast, hybrid creatures suggesting some of the ideas held by late Ice Age hunting societies. In this connection reference should be made to the so-called hand silhouettes which are executed in both positive and negative forms and in some cases possibly hint at ritual finger mutilation. Plant life is hardly represented at all, and interpretations are extremely uncertain in every case. Conversely, there are a relatively large number of signs, ranging from dots on their own or in rows to complicated chequer-board and maze-type designs, whose interpretation is particularly difficult.

temporary mobiliary art is present in western Europe, but a considerable number of pieces are known from central and eastern Europe, occurrences stretching as far eastwards as Lake Baikal. This is one of the factors that suggest that the advanced hunting cultures that spread over large parts of the Old World at the end of the Ice Age had parallel features which may not have been due only to environmental similarity but which point to a similar mental attitude.

As to the content of late Ice Age mobiliary and rock art, it is clear that the representation of animals prevails over everything else. Primarily these are large mammals like bison, aurochs, wild horses (Plate 34), mammoths, woolly rhinoceros, reindeer, red deer, ibex, cave bear (Fig. 33) and brown bear – all important as sources of food or for making clothes, tent coverings, tools, weapons, ornaments and other essentials for daily life such as hides and skins, antler, bone, ivory and sinew.

However, the list of animals drawn up on the basis of the bones that have been found and from the representations in home and rock art is much longer than this, and contains many animals that were killed much less frequently, including species that could not have had the slightest practical significance for the maintenance of life. There is a whole series

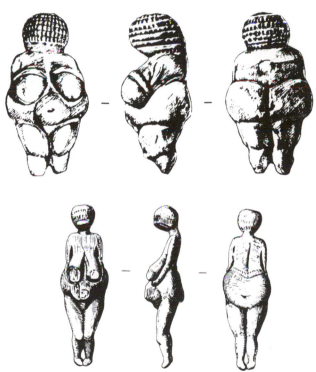

Figure 35 Willendorf 'Venus' (height 10.5 cm) (Austria) and Kostenki 'Venus' (Russian Federation). (After M. Otte.)

Lastly there are the clay figures, in relief or in the round, found in isolated cases in a limited number of caves. Here too the possibility that not all of them have been preserved has to be borne in mind. Some may have crumbled away during the thousands of intervening years and others may have been unwittingly or intentionally destroyed by visitors to the caves in more recent times.

A point to note in connection with rock art is that, generally, decorated caves were not places of settlement; it can be shown that where representations were located, dwelling places did not exist. The majority of rock pictures are found in the depths of caves, but it is possible that the

Figure 34 Rock-engravings, Grotte des Trois Frères, Ariège (France). Left to right: a reindeer, a hybrid animal with the body of a reindeer and the head of a bison, and a man (height 30 cm) disguised as an animal and playing a musical bow (possibly a group scene); Magdalenian.

Table 6 Stylistic evolution of Upper Palaeolithic art in Europe. (After André Leroi-Gourhan, 1965, fig. 6, and H. de Lumley, 1984, fig. 1.)

often considerably widened cave entrances were used for settlement, with representational art being practised in the remoter parts far from the presence of daylight. It is also possible that the use of specific parts of caves for dwelling and others for representational art alternated; here we have to bear in mind the considerable period of time during which Upper Palaeolithic humanity lived and worked. In the case of works of mobiliary art this broad-ranging distinction between daily life and specialized activities at a certain distance from the living quarters does not exist. The artefacts are to be found, mixed in with tools and refuse, where the hunters made their camps, for varying lengths of time. Often they are directly related to typical tools and weapons made of organic materials of which they are the decoration. Since stylistically they correspond with the rock pictures, they are of considerable relevance to the question of the chronology of Ice Age art, our next subject of study.

Very marked stylistic and technical differences can also be clearly distinguished in rock art, and though they are not of decisive significance in terms of absolute chronology, relative observations are sometimes possible on the succession of events based on overlying and overlapping positions. As is clear from Chapter 18, the Upper Palaeolithic cultures of the late Ice Age date from the period between 40,000 and 12,000 to 10,000 years ago. Although the possibility that forms of artistic expression that originated at the beginning of this period is not to be ruled out and the existence of

precursors of some kind must certainly be admitted, the documents accessible to us today suggest that the real 'birth of art' did not take place until around 30,000 years ago. This, therefore, gives us a period of over 20,000 years during which Ice Age rock and mobiliary art was practised. Although the pace of cultural development at the time was very slow (out of all comparison with its hectic tempo since the transition from the predatory to the productive form of economy between 10,000 and 6,000 years ago), the period is of a considerable length – long enough for representational art to develop from its hesitant beginnings to its full flowering and then to fall steadily into obscurity. Already during the post-glacial Mesolithic Age (10,000 to 6,000 years ago) the rock and mobiliary art of the hunting societies was confined to some cultures and areas, visibly losing vigour and originality.

According to A. Leroi-Gourhan (1965) (Table 6), apart from a largely prefigurative phase 0 corresponding to the Châtelperronian culture, which may be dated between 36,000 and 32,000 years ago, there are four main styles to be distinguished in Ice Age art. H. De Lumley (1984) describes the first and second as 'primitive', the third as 'archaic' and the fourth as 'classical'. Style I (about 32,000 to 23,000 years ago) belongs for the most part to the culture of the so-called typical Aurignacian but also extends into the following cultures of the Gravettian. Style II (about 23,000 to 17,000 years ago) lies between Gravettian and Solutrean and style

III between Solutrean and early Magdalenian, while style IV (about 13,000 years ago to the transition from the Upper Palaeolithic to the Mesolithic in the period between 12,000 and 10,000 years ago) corresponds to the middle and later Magdalenian. A closer look at the development of Ice Age art during this time is taken in Chapter 23.

Here we are going to concentrate on the difficult question of the aim and purpose of this early form of representational art in the context of the advanced hunting cultures of the late Ice Age. For a long time the problem was thought to have been largely solved by the work of H. Breuil and his school. Breuil (1952) contributed a great deal to research on Ice Art and the fact that there is such comprehensive documentary material available today is largely due to him. It is therefore easy to understand that his views on the meaning of Upper Palaeolithic art influenced research in a decisive way for a considerable time. This applies in particular to the rock pictures and to the question of the role played by the decorated caves in the life of western European hunting societies of the late Ice Age. Admittedly the interpretations concerned did not all stem from Breuil himself. A number of conjectures were made before his time by Reinach (1922), and other specialists also contributed to his theories. But it was because of Breuil's authority that his hypotheses gradually acquired the status of dogma. Much of their justification was taken from ethnographic information about more recent hunting societies – used on occasion somewhat arbitrarily. Breuil's theory was that Ice Age works of art, particularly the rock pictures, were there in the service of magical concepts and customs to which humankind at the advanced hunting stage of development attached great importance in the business of ensuring their survival. Hunting magic, embracing killing magic and procreation magic, was presented as the dominant motif: killing magic, represented by scenes in which Ice Age hunters are shown as having symbolically killed the animals they are hunting, the weapons or wounds sometimes being shown, in order to ensure their success in the hunt, and procreation magic being intended to preserve the stock of fauna so important to life by depicting mating or pregnant animals. On the thesis of the trends in interpretation dominated by Breuil it was later believed that fertility magic could also be perceived in connection with the far rarer representation of humans and sexual symbols. In addition, many anthropomorphic figures were guessed to represent personages of the priestly healer or shaman type, or ancestors or wood spirits or beings from the 'ruler of the animals' conceptual realm who kept watch over the animals hunted.

On sober reflection one cannot fail to recognize that all these ideas are of a hypothetical nature, even though many representations in both rock and mobiliary art seem to lend themselves to such interpretations. In any event, they can be accorded no evidential value. Even in Breuil's lifetime, but mainly after his death in 1961, attempts were made to review the problem area in order to see whether other explanations might not be possible. Particularly efficient work was done by A. Leroi-Gourhan (1965), who, on the basis of preparatory work by his pupil A. Laming-Emperaire (1962), came to wholly new conclusions. He began with rock art and, for the purpose, made an inventory of the representations in a considerable number of caves. The keystone of his theory is that in the placing of animal figures, human representations and signs in the form of engravings, paintings, bas-reliefs or clay sculptures, a clearly defined system was methodically followed (Fig. 36). A first feature is the spatial distribution of the figures in the individual caves in

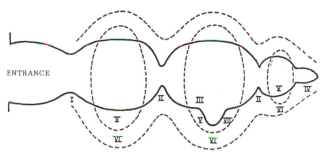

Figure 36 Topological position of engravings in a cave. I, situation at the first point where figures appear (often where darkness begins, or at the last point where the entrance is still visible, and always where there is a narrowing or a turn); II, positioning at turns, passages or narrowings leading from one hall to another; III, positioning at the entrance to fissures, blind recesses or alcoves; IV, situation at the last point reached by the decoration; V, positioning in the central part of the decorated walls of the halls or widened parts; VI, positioning on the margins of the central part; VII, positioning within fissures, blind recesses or alcoves leading on to halls. (After A. Leroi-Gourhan, 1965, fig. 8.)

which the following seven zones are distinguished: (I) the places where, on penetrating a cave, the first figures are placed; (II) communicating passages between larger parts of the caves; (III) places in the forward part of crevices, recesses or niches; (IV) the most remote, deepest-lying places with figures; (V) the central parts of those large cave halls or rooms that have figures; (VI) the marginal parts of the zones referred to under V; (VII) places in the interior of crevices, recesses or niches in the area of the central parts of caves referred to under zone V.

Considerable importance is attached to this distribution into seven zones. This applies first and foremost to the signs group, in which Leroi-Gourhan believes two categories can be identified, described by him as male and female sexual symbols. The balance of occurrence of the two categories in the seven cave zones falls into a complementary pattern: the male signs predominate in zones I to IV and VI while the female signs have a 90 per cent majority in zones V and VII. Practically all the female but only a third of the male symbols are therefore in the central areas of the caves, while only very few female and an abundance of male signs are in the peripheral areas. Leroi-Gourhan also puts forward similar observations with regard to the representations of human beings and animals. The representations of women, whose number is far fewer than those of animals, are preferentially in zone V, that is the central parts, as in the case of the sexual symbols, while the somewhat more numerous male figures occur almost exclusively in the remote parts of the caves, or otherwise in the marginal zones of central compositions.

Leroi-Gourhan's statistical investigations point also to a kind of dualism with regard to the animal figures. Two types of animal – bison and aurochs – occur, as do the female figures, almost exclusively (over 80 per cent) in the central parts of the caves. For this reason they are put together in a 'female' group B, regardless of whether males or females of the two species are portrayed. All other animals, in Leroi-Gourhan's view, represent the male element and constitute group A.

Even though Leroi-Gourhan's very cautiously formulated theory leaves many open questions and has been received with scepticism by many researchers, it has to be recognized that the assumption that Ice Age art could be based on the concept of a dualism of crucial importance for human existence cannot be dismissed without further investigation.

But whether it is solely a matter of the contrast between the male and female principle or whether other possibilities such as social factors, may not be involved, is another question. Neither has sufficient attention yet been accorded to the scientific interpretaion of symbols. Lastly, mobiliary art should be given a bigger place in the debate. It too contains much that could afford us access to the probably highly differentiated conceptual world of the advanced hunting cultures of the late Ice Age, intensely oriented as they were towards their environment and the supernatural powers. Particularly important for the study of mobiliary art (but also in some cases for that of rock art) are the investigative methods developed by A. Marshack (1972) in which special photography enables details to be perceived and relationships to be established that have previously been disregarded.

Another possible way of coming closer, step by step, to the correct interpretation of Ice Age art is to intensify the co-operation between prehistorians on the one hand and on the other zoologists and ethologists (behavioural scientists) in the evaluation of animal representations. In this way, not only would the determination of species, sex and age be made more accurate but also characteristics governed by the season, particularities dependent on the relevant style, and so on, could be elicited. A further point is that in the case of species that still exist – and this is true of many representatives of late Ice Age fauna – behavioural observation could throw some light on the ideas in the heads of Ice Age hunter–artists when they reproduced in specific poses these animals that were so familiar to them in every respect.

The number of late Ice Age works of mobiliary art is so great today, particularly in the field of the European Upper Palaeolithic, that the aid of electronic data processing is indispensable in such investigations. In this way it should become possible to have a better general perception of Ice Age art in all its fascination and to come gradually closer to the real meaning of its many-faceted content.

NOTE

1 It should, however, be mentioned that several Middle Palaeolithic sites have yielded pieces of bone and small slabs of stone bearing a series of engraved and more or less parallel lines, which were almost certainly drawn intentionally. They represent perhaps a first attempt at abstract art, although agreement with this interpretation is not unanimous. It is also possible that figurative art has its roots in the Middle Palaeolithic: a mammoth scapula, from Molodova I (Dniester Basin), is covered with entangled lines, which could perhaps represent a bull and a female symbol. More convincing is a piece of bone with the image of an animal carved on one side; it was found in a Mousterian layer of the Pronyatin site near Ternopol in Ukraine (Fig. 26) (see Chapters 10, 12 and 13). The problem is discussed briefly in Chapter 23 – Ed.

BIBLIOGRAPHY

ADAM, K. D.; KURZ, R. 1980. *Eiszeitkunst im süddeutschen Raum*. Stuttgart.

L'Art des cavernes. Atlas des grottes ornées paléolithiques françaises. 1984. Paris.

BANDI, H.-G.; MARINGER, J. 1952. *L'Art préhistorique: les cavernes, le Levant espagnol, les régions arctiques*. Basle.

BANDI, H.-G. et al. (eds) *La Contribution de la zoologie et de l'éthologie à l'interprétation de l'art des peuples chasseurs préhistoriques*. Fribourg.

BELTRAN MARTINEZ, A. 1968. *Arte rupestre levantino*. Zaragoza.

BREUIL, H. 1952. *Quatre cents siècles d'art pariétal*. Montignac.

BREZILLON, M. 1980. *Dictionnaire de la préhistoire*. Paris.

DAMS, L. 1984. *Les Peintures rupestres du Levant espagnol*. Paris.

Dänische Vorzeit. Führer durch das Nationalmuseum. 1972. Copenhagen.

DELPORTE, H. 1979. *L'Image de la femme dans l'art préhistorique*. Paris.

GJESSING, P. 1932. *Artiske Helleristninger i Nord-Norge* [Arctic Rock Carvings in North Norway]. Oslo.

GRAZIOSI, P. 1956. *L'arte'dell antica età della pietra*. Florence.

HALLSTRÖM, G. 1938. *Monumental Art of Northern Europe from the Stone Age*. Stockholm.

—— 1960. *Monumental Art of Northern Sweden from the Stone Age*. Stockholm.

KOENIGSWALD, W. VON; HANN, J. 1981. *Jagdtiere und Jäger der Eiszeit*. Stuttgart.

Kunst der Eiszeit in Deutschland und der Schweiz. 1985. Cologne.

LAMING-EMPERAIRE, A. 1962. *La Signification de l'art rupestre paléolithique*. Paris.

LEROI-GOURHAN, A. 1964. *Les Religions de la préhistoire*. 4th edn. Paris.

—— 1965. *Préhistoire de l'art occidental*. Paris.

LUMLEY, H. DE. (ed.) 1984. *Art et civilisation des chasseurs de la préhistoire: 34.000–7000 av. J.-C*. Paris.

MARSHACK, A. 1972. *The Roots of Civilisation*. New York.

MÜLLER-BECK, H. (ed.) 1983. *Urgeschichte in Baden-Württemberg*. Stuttgart.

MUSÉE DE L'HOMME. 1984. *Art et civilisations de chasseurs de la préhistoire*. Paris.

REINACH, S. 1922. *Cultes, mythes et religions*. 3rd edn. Paris. Vol. I.

SIEVEKING, A. 1972. *The Cave Artists*. London.

UCKO, P. J.; ROSENFELD A. 1967. *Palaeolithic Cave Art*. London.

WHYNER, J. 1982. *The Palaeolithic Age*. London.

ZERVOS, C. 1959. *L'Art de l'époque du Renne en France*. Paris.

20

AFRICA

from the appearance of *Homo sapiens sapiens* to the beginnings of food production

J. Desmond Clark

THE MIDDLE PALAEOLITHIC/MIDDLE STONE AGE AND THE POSSIBLE AFRICAN ORIGINS OF MODERN HUMANITY

On the basis of the few radiocarbon dates available before 1972 (Beaumont and Vogel, 1972) it appeared that the Middle Palaeolithic/Middle Stone Age technological mode in Africa was out of phase with that in Eurasia and was thought to have continued to as late as some 15,000 years ago and so to have been contemporary with the Upper Palaeolithic in Europe. Since 1972, however, the very early dates being obtained for well-stratified cultural and faunal sequences in widely separated regions of the African continent have shown this hypothesized time lag to be no longer tenable and it is now clear that the technological mode associated with the Middle Palaeolithic/Middle Stone Age in Africa began nearly 200,000 years ago and, in its unmodified form, had been replaced, by 35,000 years ago, by Upper Palaeolithic/Late Stone Age technologies. Middle Palaeolithic technologies in Africa, therefore, can now be seen to be contemporaneous with those in Eurasia and have lasted some 150,000 years or more.

Any attempt at phylogenetic reconstruction based on the finds of hominid fossils depends almost entirely on the dating of these fossils, which usually lies beyond the limit of the radiocarbon method. Consequently other, less reliable, radiometric and isotopic methods have to be used, but when the stratigraphic, faunal and cultural evidence is also taken into account most of the fossils can be dated with at least a modicum of confidence. In Eurasia, therefore, we find that the makers of the Mousterian and Levalloiso-Mousterian industries belonged to the Neanderthal physical stock until the late Middle Palaeolithic. At this time, evidence from western Asia shows that some populations associated with Mousterian industries were, physiologically, robust but Modern humans (Day, 1977, pp. 89–100). On the other hand, in Africa we can now see that Modern traits were already present in the Middle Pleistocene (about 0.7–0.2 million years ago) during the time of the later Acheulean (Brauer, 1984). These African fossils showing Modern traits have recently been chronologically classified into two groups (Brauer, 1984): an earlier, Middle Pleistocene, group (known as archaic *Homo sapiens*) and a later group belonging to the transition between the Middle and Upper Pleistocene and

to the early Last Glacial. Where associated artefacts are present, these are all of Middle Palaeolithic/Middle Stone Age type. This evidence is important in view of the awakened interest in the origins and spread of humans of the Modern type and the abandonment (Stringer, 1974; Brauer, 1984) of the pre-*sapiens* hypothesis that saw the origins of Modern humans in Europe, based on the no longer accepted assumption of the existence of two parallel lineages, the one leading to the Neanderthalers and the other to Cro-Magnons (Vallois, 1954).

Most recent work, however, on the biochemical evolutionary record contained within human genes has been regarded as strengthening the case for an African origin for Modern humans. One study (Wainscott et al., 1986) examines patterns of relatedness in a small segment of nuclear DNA in the β-globin gene cluster from four major world populations and shows that these patterns are consistent with the rapid spread of Modern humans from a single centre of origin, which is postulated to have been in Africa. An independent study by Cann et al. (1987), by calculating the slow changes (2 to 4 per cent every million years) that have taken place in human mitochondrial DNA over the millennia and which are inherited only through the mother, has suggested that all Modern humans are descended from a single female ancestor, or small group, that lived between 280,000 and 140,000 years ago, again probably in Africa. This molecular, biochemical evidence is clearly still controversial and needs to be refined, but it does show the greater likelihood that the Modern gene pool originated in one nuclear region, from which it spread very rapidly rather than that Modern humans evolved independently from archaic forms in each of the main regions of the Old World.

If the modern genotype evolved first in Africa, then the physical, intellectual, linguistic and technological advances with which it is associated should be manifest in the fossil and archaeological record there, though the recovery techniques at present available may not be specific enough to permit identification and interpretation except at the broadest level. However, so far as we can tell at present, the technological and typological changes observed in Africa from the beginning of the later Pleistocene were also manifest in Eurasia. Indeed, the observed changes seem to have been the general pattern of the times and not to have been confined to the African continent, though much of what distinguishes Modern humans from their archaic predecessors is concerned with traits that are not preserved in the archaeological record and that have to be inferred.

As a working hypothesis, therefore, it might be postulated that a nuclear Modern population evolved somewhere in southern or eastern Africa shortly after the close of the Middle Pleistocene, and from there spread into the Levant and into sub-Saharan Africa. Its success was due to a full language system that permitted transmission of precise information, abstract, ideological and symbolic thought and expression and new technology more advanced, not so much in the development of blade technology and composite-tool manufacture as in the ways in which the artefacts were used, which made possible the exploitation of new resources and increased skill in obtaining them as well as the preservation of the individuality of the societies themselves. It is quite certain that the intellectual and behavioural skills of early Modern humans must have been infinitely more efficient and successful than those possessed by any more archaic populations, so leading everywhere to the rapid extinction of the latter and their replacement by Modern humans. Although the evidence is increasing that the nuclear region may have been in Africa, this still remains a hypothesis which can be tested only when many more precise data have been recovered to which it can be rigorously applied.

THE UPPER PALAEOLITHIC/ LATER STONE AGE

Middle Stone Age technology based on various kinds of prepared and unprepared cores disappeared in Africa some 40,000 to 35,000 years ago, if not earlier. In parts of northeast Africa, the Mediterranean littoral and the Nile north of Asyut, the Middle Palaeolithic is succeeded by a true blade industry of Upper Palaeolithic type in which the most common forms of tools are backed blades, with burins (grooving/engraving tools) and end-scrapers. It appears to be relatively restricted in its distribution, being known, up to now, only from two cave sites in Cyrenaica (McBurney, 1967, pp. 135–84) and two sites along the Nile valley, at one of which the chert was mined from open, well-shaped pits (Vermeersch et al., 1982). Human remains from north Africa dating to between 40,000 and 20,000 years ago are generally lacking, but with one of the upper Nile sites at Nazlet Khater, dating to betweeen 35,000 and 30,000 years ago, were discovered two burials of individuals whose physical characteristics are robust but fully Modern (Vermeersch et al., 1984).

It might be thought that if Upper Palaeolithic tool technology was so greatly in advance of that of other traditions, it would have spread rapidly throughout the Old World. However, this is not so: it never spread to China or South-East Asia or Australia, for example, neither did it spread to the rest of the African continent. There, succeeding traditions in the late Pleistocene made use sometimes of blades, sometimes of flakes, sometimes of core tools, even though the makers were fully Modern humans (Clark, 1981). The explanation probably lies in stylistic preferences in tool morphology and technology that stem from traditional behaviour relating ultimately to resource procurement.

North Africa (Map 13)

Apart from the Cyrenaican and Nile valley sites mentioned above, there appears to be a relative dearth of assemblages that can be assigned to the period between 40,000 and 20,000 years ago in North Africa though, in the Maghreb, this may in part be due to inadequate dating evidence. Only two Maghrebian sites – those of Tamar Hat and Taforalt (lower level) – fall in the time range between 25,000 and 20,000 years ago and were occupied during the time of maximum low sea-level during the last glaciation (Saxon, 1974). Another, as yet undescribed bladelet industry from Atlantic Morocco is associated with a date of around 27,700 years ago (Close, 1986). Since the shore-line was some 90 m or more lower than it is today and would have been displaced several kilometres northward, it is likely that many of the localities occupied during this time would have been in the warmer zone close to the shore. The plateau, the eastern extension of the Atlas, was cold, windy and arid, which is probably why there are no sites known from this time range there, with the possible exception of the industry from the Horizon Collignon at Sidi Mansour (McBurney, 1960, pp. 215–17). The stone industry here is known as Ibero-maurusian or Oranian (Fig. 37) and it makes use of relatively small blades, backed and otherwise retouched for mounting in hafts in various different ways. Most of the Iberomaurusian sites and assemblages fall within the terminal Pleistocene between 14,000 and 10,000 years ago, and they are nearly all in the northern Maghreb along the coastal plain (Camps, 1974, pp. 52–99; Smith, 1982, pp. 377–82). The stone industry is characterized by small backed bladelets together with smaller numbers of end-scrapers, burins and borers. There are variable proportions of microliths, usually segments, and the micro-burin technique for breaking down blades is sometimes but not always found. A characteristic form of retouching (Ouchtata) is fine, abrupt, marginal nibbling, which may have been in part to make it easier to mount the bladelets by means of mastic or binding. With these stone artefacts are sometimes found bone awls and points, 'chisels' (tranchets) and, from one site (Taforalt), a fragment of what may be a barbed harpoon head (Fig. 37). Evidence of ornamentation is rare and simple and in the form of perforated sea-shells and stones and red and yellow pigment, presumably for body and artefact decorating since there is no evidence for art in the form of painting, though some stones with engraved lines from one site (Taforalt) may show the beginnings of this art-form. Ostrich eggs were used as containers for liquids and caches of these, such as were made until recently by San hunter-gatherer populations in the Kalahari, have been found in some of the northern Sahara oases.

The Iberomaurusian lasted for some 10,000 years but, while there is little evidence for any significant changes throughout this time, regionally there is considerable variation. The bladelets show a great deal of ingenuity in form and they were probably hafted in a variety of ways as the cutting and piercing points and barbs of composite tools and weapons of which the wooden handles have not survived. This early Epipalaeolithic population in the Maghreb hunted wild cattle and other large bovids, zebra, Barbary sheep, gazelle, pigs, giant deer, giant buffalo and rhinoceros. In addition, they probably exploited a wide range of other resources. Acorns, pine and pistachio nuts, wild grass and other plant seeds and tubers may have been processed using flat grinding-stones and digging sticks may have been weighted with perforated stones. The sites also sometimes yield evidence of land snails, shellfish, both freshwater and

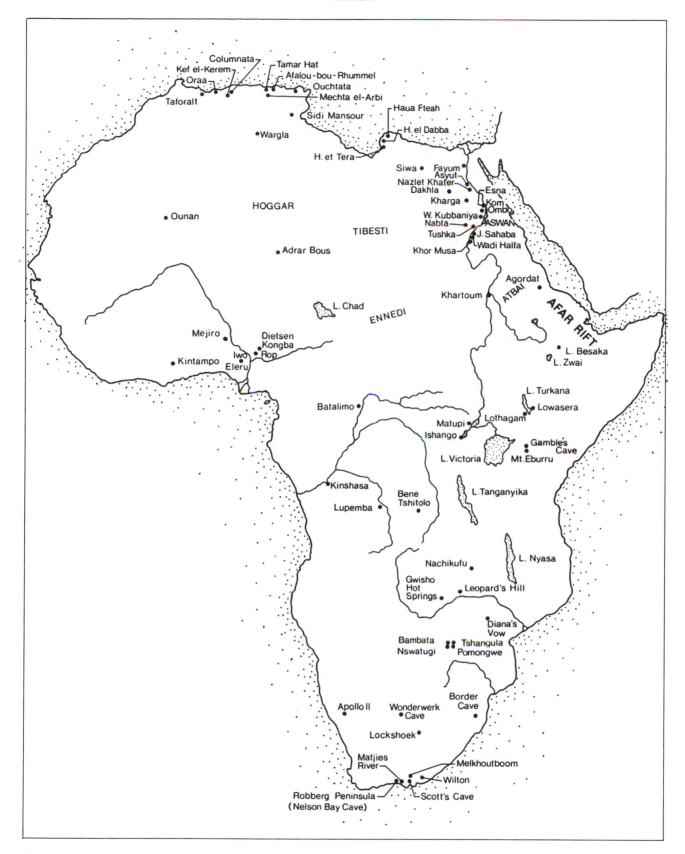

Map 13 Main African regions and sites referred to in the text.

marine, birds, rodents and fish. Much of the variety seen in the different regional assemblages may have been due to seasonal availability of the various food resources which would have given rise to movements of the population between the caves and rock shelters or favoured open localities in their home range. Seasonal movement would have been to the coast in the winter and inland, perhaps, to the border of the desert steppe in the spring and summer, as some evolved and later Iberomaurusian sites there suggest. As yet, however, little is known of the socio-economic patterning of these hunting and gathering peoples. The societies must, however, have been traditionally organized

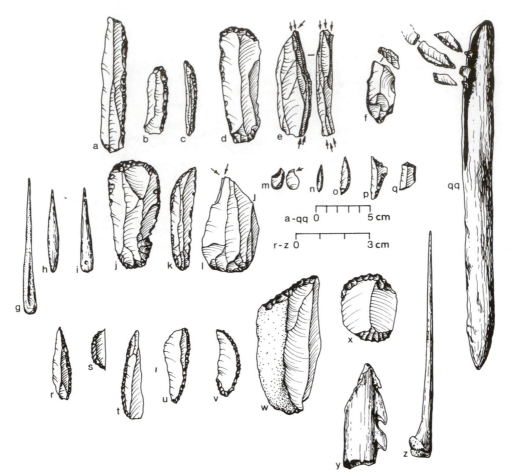

Figure 37 Later Stone Age industries, north Africa. Dabban industry artefacts from Haua Fteah cave (Cyrenaica): a–c, backed blades; d, end-scraper; e, burin; f, chamfered blade with resharpening spall. (After McBurney, 1960.) Capsian industrial complex artefacts from various sites in Tunisia and eastern Algeria: bone tools – g, awl; h, point; i, needle; stone artefacts – j, end-scraper; k, backed blade; l, burin end-scraper; m, micro-burin; n–q, geometric microliths, qq, slotted bone sickle handle and microlithic insets. (After Clark, 1978, p. 56.) Iberomaurusian (Oranian) industrial complex artefacts from Taforalt cave (Morocco): r–v, backed bladelets; w, truncated flake; x, double end-scraper, y, fragment of barbed bone harpoon; z, awl. (After Camps, 1974, p. 74.)

and well structured to deal with a regular pattern of seasonal movement within established territories, since several large cemeteries in caves, one with more than 200 burials, imply the presence of seasonally reoccupied base camps nearby at the optimum time for exploiting local resources. The hunting pattern at Tamar Hat is further evidence for this, since more than 90 per cent of the food remains come from Barbary sheep, the majority from young male and old female animals, a pattern that is believed to indicate some form of regular herd management over a long period of time (Saxon, 1974, pp. 79–82).

Much is known about the physical appearance of the Iberomaurusian peoples from the many skeletal remains. They belonged to a robust and fully Modern population known as the 'Mechta-Afalou race' after two of the main cemetery sites, and they have been compared with the Upper Palaeolithic Cro-Magnon race of western Europe. The skeletal remains show little evidence of trauma, but there is high incidence of infant mortality and health was sometimes poor, with evidence of dental caries and arthritis. Certain gene-related traits also suggest considerable inbreeding, from which it might be concluded that many of these groups were living in relative isolation, a situation not unlikely where demographic pressures were minimal (Camps, 1974, pp. 81–6; Smith, 1982, pp. 381–2, 401–4).

With the retreat of the continental ice-sheets at the end of the last glaciation 10,000 years ago, northern Africa experienced a significant amelioration of climate, the sea-level returned to close to where it is today and conditions warmer and moister than those pertaining at present were experienced as far south as the southern Sahara. The Maghreb plateau and the desert became very favourable regions for occupation by human populations and there was a significant shifting of the focus of settlement during the early postglacial (Lubell et al., 1984). In the Maghreb, this focus was on the more easterly parts of the plateau (Tunisia and eastern Algeria); in the Sahara it was along the stream courses and round the lakes, now high on account of the rain received from both northerly and tropical wind systems.

The new Epipalaeolithic industrial complex that superseded the Iberomaurusian is known as the Capsian (Fig. 37) and is centred on the eastern parts of the Atlas plateau (Camps, 1974, pp. 100–220; Lubell et al., 1975). A large number of sites are known and density is often considerable, suggesting, perhaps, a larger overall population and a more sedentary form of land-use. Many of these sites are large, open-air middens consisting of stone artefacts and manuports, charcoal and ash, soil and food refuse – mostly bones and the shells of *Helix* (the land snail) from which the middens have come to be known as *escargotières*. A good deal is now known about the subsistence of the makers of the Capsian industries, who were hunters and gatherers of the high plains. Although they hunted and ate antelope, wild cattle, Barbary sheep, gazelle, zebra, hare and tortoise (probably roasted with hot stones in earth ovens) there are never large quantities of bones at the sites, so that it has been suggested that the antelopes – in particular the hartebeeste – may have been manipulated or kept under some kind of control and selectively slaughtered. One possibly important source of protein was the land snail which was collected in large numbers, probably seasonally, and may have been boiled in clayed baskets or hide bags by dropping hot stones into the water, as many reddened and fractured 'pot-boiler' stones occur at the middens. Little has been preserved in the way of plant remains, but these can be expected to have been similar to those used by the earlier Iberomaurusian peoples. The importance of wild cereal grasses becomes more apparent from the artefacts that imply plant collecting and processing. Several slotted bone 'sickles' or reaping knives are known, some with microlith stone insets still in position; other small bladelet forms show evidence of lustre and gloss resulting from silica deposition on their cutting edges. Flat, lower grindstones and dimple-scarred upper hand stones attest to the grinding of plant foods. Capsian groups may also have possessed domestic dogs for, while the evidence in the eastern Maghreb is uncertain, domestic dog has now been identified from the contemporary and related Libyco-Capsian industry (10,000 to 7,000 years ago) in the Haua Fteah cave in Cyrenaica (Fig. 37) (Klein and Scott, 1986).

Two phases of the Capsian have been recognized (Typical and Upper) which, although at first thought of as being chronologically separate, are now seen to overlap to a considerable extent and may be a reflection of different activities. The raw material available was Eocene flint, which came in large nodules so that many Capsian tools are larger than those of the Iberomaurusian, which was often based on small cobbles. The tools consist of backed blades, end-scrapers, burins and other large tools struck from fine, prismatic cores, the blades being sometimes, it is thought, removed by pressure. While microliths are present throughout the Capsian, they are much commoner in the Upper Capsian. The micro–burin technique was extensively used to produce geometric microlithic forms – scalene triangles, lunates, rectangles and trapezes. Many more bone artefacts are present and the high degree of polish on some of the awls is thought to imply leatherworking. Ostrich-egg containers continue to be used and are now engraved with geometric and sometimes naturalistic designs. Small, portable art objects are also present, both engraved slabs of stone and carved reproductions of human and animal heads and phalli in soft limestone (Fig. 38). It is also possible that some of the early large animal rock engravings in the northern Sahara may date back to Capsian times and contemporary peoples in Cyrenaica and on the Nile (Kom Ombo) may have been responsible for the large engravings of wild cattle that are to be found there (Smith, 1982, pp. 397–400).

The Capsian population, as known from skeletal remains from the burials in the middens, are less robust and more gracile than the Mechta–Afalou peoples, though they are undoubtedly descended from them. They have been described as 'proto-Mediterranean'. Not a little body mutilation is to be seen. This takes the form of incisor tooth extraction (also a feature of the Iberomaurusian), skulls that were modified after death by sawing, cutting and drilling, in one instance to form a kind of mask or 'trophy skull'; there was a false tooth in one mandible and a human fibula had been made into a dagger.

The Iberomaurusian and the Capsian were not the only Epipalaeolithic variants in north-east Africa, but they are

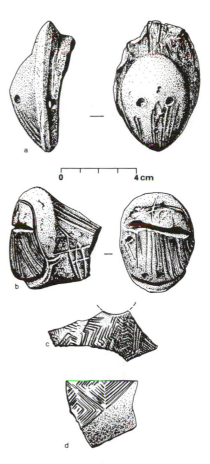

Figure 38 Upper Capsian art (Tunisia). El-Mekta: a, anthropomorphic and b, zoomorphic, carvings in soft limestone; c–d, engraved ostrich eggshell from other sites.

certainly the most important and best understood. In Morocco, which the Capsian never reached, a form of Iberomaurusian persisted. Elsewhere, more locally restricted variants or facies (such as the Keremian, Mellalian and el Oued facies) are found and sometimes the dimensions of the microlithic component are very small (Columnatan), but their relationship to the Capsian is unclear. Most of them are undated and they probably represent regional adaptations or special-purpose assemblages within the Capsian time span.

In Cyrenaica, the sequence seen in the Maghreb is repeated, though the industries exhibit regional characteristics. Succeeding the Upper Palaeolithic Dabban at Haua Fteah around 14,000 years ago is a new industry called the Eastern Oranian (Iberomaurusian) in which the dominant tool type is a small backed bladelet, often fully microlithic. The Barbary sheep was the main animal hunted on the coastal plain, while at another site (Hagfet et-Tera), on the edge of the desert, the chief food animal was the gazelle. These two sites are probably too far apart (200 km) for them to have been seasonally exploited by the same group, so that they possibly represent evidence for two distinct and locally adapted groups. Two human jaws associated with the Eastern Oranian at Haua Fteah show the human population to have been fully Modern (McBurney, 1967, pp. 185–228). About 10,000 years ago the Eastern Oranian was replaced by the Libyco-Capsian industry, so named for its affinity to the Capsian. Its makers appear to have been desert-oriented groups adjusted to the drier and warmer conditions pertaining at that time. They hunted mostly Barbary sheep and large bovids, collected snails and may have eaten ostrich

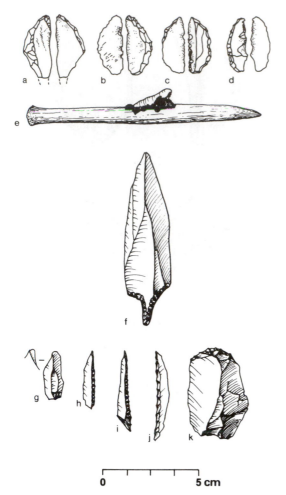

Figure 39 Backed microliths with silica lustre on the chord, indicated by stippling (a–d); hatching on b shows area covered by traces of mastic, Tushka (Nubia); e, probable method of hafting. (After Wendorf and Schild, 1976, p. 277.) f, Ounanian point, central Sahara (After Smith, 1982, p. 395.) g–k, Epipalaeolithic industry artefacts (Mellalian), Wargla Oasis (Algeria): g, micro-burin; h–j, straight-backed bladelets; k, end-scraper. (After Camps, 1974, p. 201.)

with sandy sediments near the edge of small, closed lake basins, or with stream courses or, as at Kharga, with artesian springs; clearly, a major consideration was the proximity to water. The sites were all small and may represent hunting camps though, since the arid nature of the Western Desert at this time was unfavourable to large mammals, the main animals hunted were gazelles and hares. Numerous grinding stones attest the importance of cereal grasses as a nutritional source in the desert, giving an indication of the time of year when these sites were probably occupied. That the population must have been highly mobile is suggested by the preferred use of the best stone (Eocene chert) which had to be transported considerable distances (Wendorf and Schild, 1980, pp. 257–64). These populations were occupying marginally favourable localities, but by 8,000 years ago others were settled round the edges of the central and southern Saharan lakes (see p. 198).

The Nile (Map 13)

The Nile was, and is, the single most important ecological entity in north-east Africa, surrounded as it is for hundreds of miles in the Sudan and Egypt by desert. It provided a very rich habitat for hunter-gatherers who were also using fish and freshwater molluscs from early in the later Pleistocene. An early blade industry was present in the northern part of Egypt over 30,000 years ago; to the south in Nubia, however, the old prepared core technology still persisted at first, but through time became associated with an increasing emphasis on blade technology and smaller artefacts that were fully microlithic 15,000 years ago. Settlement along the Nile was controlled by the climatic regime in Equatorial Africa, from where the water in the river is derived. Climatic oscillations produced alternating periods of high Nile with much silt deposited on the flood plain, and low Nile when the bed was being actively eroded. Only when Egypt experienced local rains did the tributary wadis flow. At times (usually high Nile) there was much grazing available while at others (low Nile) the grazing would have been considerably restricted with resulting competition for it.

A number of technologically and typologically distinct stone tool entities (industries) have been recognized (Wendorf, 1968; Wendorf and Schild, 1975; Smith, 1976), but the meaning of this variability is not clearly understood. Some may be special-purpose assemblages, others were specifically related to functional differences resulting from variation in seasonal resource exploitation. Others again could represent different ethnic populations, with distinctive stylistic tool traditions. The work that is the main basis for our knowledge was the rescue operation relating to the construction of the Aswan High Dam. Between 20,000 and 10,000 years ago the valley saw considerable cultural development, since the inhabitants were able to exploit a relatively stable ecosystem with several micro-environments. From the river were obtained, besides fish, molluscs and aquatic animals (hippopotamus, rodents, crocodiles and tortoise). From the gallery forest came wild cattle and antelopes, including hartebeeste, and from further back on the desert steppe, Barbary sheep and gazelle. This was a very rich environment, with especially favourable situations where the floodplain was broad. While conditions remained optimum, the human populations could experiment and remained relatively stable, but in times of climatic deterioration, as in the terminal Pleistocene, for example, the pressures and stress experienced by those groups in the more marginal areas

eggs, the shells being used as containers and decorated. Grinding equipment shows that plant foods, in particular cereal grasses, were collected and eaten (McBurney, 1967, pp. 229–70).

The Sahara began to be reoccupied by the large tropical (Ethiopian) game animals and by humans around 10,000 years ago. Sites dating to that time are rare and widely dispersed, perhaps an indication of the sparseness of population during this initial reoccupation phase. Siwa oasis was reoccupied 8,800 to 8,400 years ago (Hassan, 1978), as were the north-west Saharan oases, for example the Mellalian in Wargla Oasis (Fig. 39) (around 8,600 to 7,700 years ago) (Camps, 1974, pp. 200–3). Epipalaeolithic industries occur in northern Mali (Ounanian) (Fig. 39) and, again at Adrar Bous and in the Aïr, but they are undated (Clark, 1976a). In the oases and playas of the Western Desert and in Egypt (9,000 to 8,300 years ago), notably at Nabta Playa and in the Dyke area south of Dakhla and in Kharga oasis, the industries are characterized by similar microlithic forms, though in very differing proportions, together with small numbers of the characteristic Ounanian and Bou Saada points, which may represent early prototypes of arrowheads (Wendorf and Schild, 1980, pp. 103–28, 188–9). The sites are associated necessitated readjustment and sometimes resulted in open conflict to retain territory and a place in the valley.

More than 40,000 years ago, Upper Egypt and Nubia were occupied by an evolved form of Mousterian known as the Khormusan. The climate was dry and the people lived close to the river, hunting large terrestrial and aquatic animals and doing some fishing. An industry still using the Levallois flaking tradition followed between 19,000 and 15,000 years ago, named the Halfan. The flakes and blades are now quite small and the Ouchtata marginal and abrupt blunting retouch makes its appearance in the valley. Grindstones are present, showing that plant foods were important, but they are not nearly so common as at the locality of Wadi Kubbaniya, close to Aswan in Upper Egypt (Wendorf et al., 1980). The Kubbaniyan industry is associated with camps on dunes overlooking an embayment of a rising Nile during an arid period between 21,000 and 19,000 years ago. The stone industry shows a true micro-blade technology, though some Halfan elements are present and, again, Ouchtata retouch is much in evidence. A range of resources were exploited and it is likely that the locality was reoccupied more than once in the year. Besides the large mammal fauna, winter migrant birds were important at some of the sites, as were fish. There are many shallow grinding stones and also deepish mortars and stone pestles, attesting the importance of wild grain, seeds and other plant foods, but the barley and wheat, which were at first thought to be contemporary, have now been shown to be intrusive and probably no more than 6,000 years old (Wendorf et al., 1980; Wendorf and Schild, 1984, p. 61).

From 18,000 years ago a number of apparently distinctive industrial entities have been identified in Nubia and Upper Egypt (Wendorf and Schild, 1976, pp. 229–319). Between the Kom Ombo plain, north of Aswan, and Esna some 150 km further to the north, for example, there are no less than twelve industrial entities that have been recognized from the period between 16,000 and 10,000 years ago. Some of these are associated with large settlements, some with small, reoccupied camp sites; some have grindstones, some do not. Some (Sebilian) are characterized by large, wedge-shaped trapezes (tranchets), possibly, since they are found with wild cattle bones, part of some kind of hunting equipment. In some industries the tools are macrolithic (Sebekian, Menchian), in others (Silsilian) microliths predominate (Smith, 1976). At one large settlement dating to 15,000 years ago, the faunal assemblage suggests year-round occupation since some of the animals would only have been available during summer and some only during the winter months (Churcher and Smith, 1972). It would therefore seem that during the late Pleistocene in the Nile valley we can begin to see the onset of more sedentary behaviour and a greater, in-depth exploitation of the natural resources – large terrestrial and aquatic animals, fish and wildfowl – and intensified plant utilization with emphasis on cereal grasses. At Tushka in Nubia (Fig. 39) grinding stones and lustrous-edge microlithic flakes with traces of mastic still adhering are evidence of wild grain processing and demonstrate the method of mounting in a handle (Wendorf, 1968, p. 943). Another site dating to around 12,000 years ago, adjacent to an inter-dune pond on the floodplain near Esna in Upper Egypt, yielded a large number of grinding stones and some 15 per cent of backed bladelets showing lustre from cutting plant stems rich in silica. The way in which this lustre covered only a part of the tools shows again the method of hafting – obliquely with mastic in a wooden-handled reaping knife. Barley pollen has also been identified from this site.

This late Pleistocene evidence from the Nile is some of the earliest to show the systematic exploitation of freshwater fish and cereal grasses by broadly-based foragers.

It is apparent that by 12,000 to 10,000 years ago the Nile valley societies must have been territorially structured, for in Nubia two large cemeteries (Wendorf, 1968, pp. 954–95; Greene and Armelagos, 1972) have been found that, like those in the Maghreb, must relate to regularly occupied settlements. The burials are sometimes double ones, but a significant proportion of the skeletons have microliths and small bladelets associated with the bones, and sometimes actually sticking in a bone, such that it must be concluded that these individuals met with a violent death. In particular, the Jebel Sahaba cemetery burials are strongly suggestive of group aggression, so providing some of the earliest evidence for intergroup warfare. This is likely to have been brought about by increased population density, more intensive use of and greater reliance on an expanded range of resources and the acceleration of aridification and the resultant competition in the later part of the late Pleistocene. Of special interest in this connection is the discovery at Wadi Kubbaniya (Wendorf et al., 1986) of the burial of a young adult male, who appears to have met a violent death from a spear wound at some time between 25,000 and 20,000 years ago. Physically, the individual is comparable to the other late Palaeolithic population on the Nile (see Jebel Sahaba), which shows the considerable antiquity of this relatively unspecialized and robust race (Wendorf et al., 1986).

In summary, therefore, in the northern part of north Africa stone industries based on a true blade technology appeared between 40,000 and 30,000 years ago on the Mediterranean littoral and in the northern part of the Nile valley. Thereafter, there developed a number of regionally and chronologically specialized traditions all showing a steady trend towards microlithic proportions. In the more southerly parts of the Nile valley in Sudanese Nubia, the Middle Palaeolithic tradition persisted but became increasingly more bladelike and microlithic through time, perhaps as a result of the southerly spread of Upper Palaeolithic technology by northern ethnic groups moving up the valley. From at least 20,000 to 12,000 years ago the Sahara desert was hyperarid and there are no occupation sites known from this time period. Reoccupation after this period must have been rapid, however, and the very favourable environment in many parts of the desert, as also along the Nile, saw the development of a rich hunting, fishing and gathering economy, pre-adapted to food production when this became advantageous from the seventh millennium BP onwards.

THE PRE-NEOLITHIC HUNTING, FISHING AND COLLECTING TRADITION IN THE NILE VALLEY AND SAHARA FROM NINE TO SEVEN MILLENNIA AGO

First known from the Nile valley at Khartoum (Arkell, 1949), these so-called Khartoum Mesolithic sites (Fig. 40) are large settlements, no doubt seasonally occupied by hunters who significantly supplemented their food supply with aquatic resources, in particular, hippopotamus, fish and molluscs. The sites are distributed along the Nile for some 200 km north and south of Khartoum. The occupants collected and ground wild plant foods, as is well attested by the large number of lower and upper grindstones on their sites. They also hunted large terrestrial game animals, and it can be expected that they would have organized their seasonal

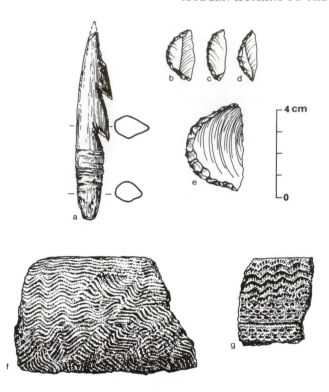

Figure 40 Mesolithic artefacts, 'early Khartoum' site (Sudan): a, bone harpoon; b–d, microliths; e, large lunate; f, sherd of 'Wavy Line' pottery; g, sherd of 'Dotted Wavy Line' pottery. (After Arkell, 1949.)

movements to coincide with those of the animals, as well as for the harvesting of plant foods as these became available. The characteristic material culture (Fig. 40) of these early Holocene foraging groups included, besides the microliths, the uniserial barbed bone point and other bone tools, together with grinding equipment and pottery. There is no reason to suppose that the manufacture of pottery was not a spontaneous development at this time on the upper Nile, and some of the earliest dates to nearly ten millennia ago. The 'Wavy Line' and 'Dotted Wavy Line' decoration that gives the pottery its name is not the only ceramic type found at this time, but it is the most characteristic. The vessels are large, deep, open bowls and it seems probable that they were produced for the processing of fish and the large freshwater gastropod *Pila*, the remains of which are very common at the settlements. Possibly the method of preparing fish oil and the production of 'cakes' of pounded fish were not unlike those of the Ichthyophagi described by the classical authors (Oldfather, 1979) and still practised today by the Bozo (Sorko) in the inland Niger delta (Ligers, 1966, pp. 202–3, plates 9 and 10).

The 'Mesolithic' population along the Nile were of a robust Sudanese Negro physical type, as is well attested from burials (Anderson, 1968; Greene and Armelagos, 1972). They share a number of characteristics in common with the Mechta-Afalou populations of the Maghreb, which can, perhaps, in view of the association of an early Mechta-Afalou individual with the Aterian in Morocco, be considered as representing the relatively unspecialized Upper Palaeolithic type in northern Africa generally, from which evolved in the late Pleistocene, through regional specialization and adaptation in isolation, the various indigenous northern African ethnic populations.

The 'Khartoum tradition' spread rapidly across the central

and southern Sahara and numerous sites yielding 'Wavy Line' and 'Dotted Wavy Line' pottery and bone harpoons and other characteristic items of the material culture are dispersed from the Western Desert of Egypt, Ennedi and the Aïr to Tibesti, Chad and the Hoggar massif (Clark, 1980a, pp. 562–7). The large settlements round the lakes and the then perennial stream courses can be seen as the base camps, where hippopotamus, crocodile and fish, in particular Nile perch, were taken during the dry season; the smaller, more temporary sites in the stabilized dune fields were the hunting camps occupied during the rains when the game was dispersed. Equally important also must have been the extensive stands of wild cereal grasses that the ubiquitous grinding equipment shows must have been regularly collected; as yet, however, there is no evidence that any of these collected plants were cultivated.

The Saharan population appears to have been a mixed one – of Mediterranean type in the north and Negroid in the centre and south (Chamla, 1968). This is not surprising, since the human populations can be expected to have moved into the desert from both directions as favourable habitats became available.

These Saharan hunting, fishing and collecting communities are sometimes grouped as an 'Old Neolithic' complex because of the presence of pottery and grinding equipment, but the term is unfortunate because, for many archaeologists 'Neolithic' is synonymous with food production and there is no evidence at these sites for any domestic animals or plants. In the central Sahara, the earliest site with domestic cattle does not occur before the end of the seventh millennium BP. In northern Egypt, the Fayum Neolithic with domestic cattle and sheep and cereals is dated from 7,000 to 6,500 years ago. In Cyrenaica and the Maghreb domestic sheep and goat are present eight millennia ago, while in the Western Desert an earlier date from 9,000 years ago is projected on the presence of pottery and sheep with an early Neolithic at Nabta Playa dating to around 8,000 years ago. The climax Neolithic in the Sahara is a pastoral economy, starting seven millennia ago, and based on domestic cattle and small stock. There is no certain proof that any of the plant foods used were domesticated and this nomadic pastoralism may have come about as a result of the pressures on the Negroid hunting, fishing and collecting populations that were attendant upon the increased desiccation that set in less than 7,000 years ago.

WEST AFRICA AND EQUATORIA (Map 13)

Little is known of the sequence of events in the west African savannahs and rain forest during the late Pleistocene, but during the glacial maximum, savannah woodland and grassland occupied the Niger delta and the shore-line (in the Niger delta area) was much further south than it is today (Sowunwi, 1981). The evergreen rain forest had retreated drastically to two main refuge areas in Nigeria and Sierra Leone. Much of southern Ghana, which was occupied by wooded grassland of montane character maintained by heavy cloud cover lasting for most of the year, was some 2 to 3 °C cooler and the rain forest did not become re-established there until 9,000 years ago (Talbot, 1983).

The few sites known from Ghana, Nigeria and Burkina Faso all produced microlithic industries, usually in quartz; they are mostly undated, of small extent and characterized by the informality of the retouched pieces. Nothing is known of the economy since bone is rarely preserved. At Mejiro cave in Nigeria occurs a microlithic industry without pottery, as it does at several other cave and rock shelter sites also, such as Iwo Eleru and Dietsen Kongba, Rop in Nigeria, Kamabai and Yengema in Sierra Leone and Rim in Burkina Faso. Sometime less than 5,000 years ago, perhaps no later than the fifth millennium BP, pottery and ground stone axes occur in the material culture in the upper levels in some of these rock shelters and might indicate that some incipient form of domestication of plants and animals was being practised.

These societies are all likely to have been small, isolated communities living in woodland savannah and grassland and hunting savannah animals. Much use would have been made of local wild plant staples – *Canarium*, oil palm, shea-butter, cola, *Parkia* and other fruits. Legumes and tubers would have been especially important, particularly the wild yams. Various cereal grasses, *Pennisetum*, *Sorghum*, *Brachiaria* and *Digitaria*, all present-day domesticates, are also likely to have been staples in pre-agricultural times in the several different regions of west Africa where they were growing wild and where they appear to have been first domesticated (Harlan, 1971), since there is no one paramount local domesticate that is universally grown. Some support for use of these cereals may come from the large 'chisels' (*tranchets*) or wedge-shaped trapezes with silica gloss from the lower levels at Iwo Eleru (Shaw, 1978, p. 49). The absence of any heavy-duty tools at this time also points to a savannah-adapted economy making little or no use of forest resources. Skeletal remains from a burial at Iwo Eleru dating to around 11,000 years ago and another from Rop show the physical type to have been Negro (Brothwell and Shaw, 1971).

Increasing desiccation in the desert (Talbot, 1980), no doubt hastened by over-stocking and bad land use, especially after 4,000 years ago, resulted, it is believed, in the southward movement of pastoralists with cattle, sheep and goats into the Sahel and the savannah (Clark, 1980b, pp. 53–66). Since, however, the tsetse fly effectively prevented cattle-owning people from permanently occupying the savannah zone, there was established the kind of symbiotic relationship between pastoralists and cultivators seen today in west Africa, which resulted in mutually beneficial interaction and exchange of animal and plant products. One early expression of what was probably incipient plant domestication in conjunction with goat and, perhaps, cattle herding, is to be seen in the Kintampo culture of Ghana dating from around 3,400 years ago. Village settlements with permanent dwellings are a feature of these sites and it would seem that by that date mutually beneficial interaction with pastoral nomads had already been established (Stahl, 1985).

Coastal resources began to be exploited earlier than 4,000 years ago in west and Equatorial Africa (Sutton, 1982, pp. 299–302). On the Atlantic coast of Mauretania and Senegal, large shell-mounds with a rich Neolithic culture show that, besides the large Ethiopian fauna, seed-food had now become more important, especially with the intensification of aridity 4,000 years ago. Individuals, physically comparable to the prehistoric Guanches of the Canary Islands, were buried in cemeteries, which suggests that some of their settlements may have been permanently occupied or, at least, seasonally reoccupied since other, inland, sites have many grindstones and may have been localities to which the population moved when wild grasses were available for harvesting (Petit-Maire, 1979). On the Gulf of Guinea there are middens with pottery and quartz artefacts that date from five and six millennia ago on the Ghana coast and from 2,500 years ago in Côte d'Ivoire; while middens dated as early as

the eighth and fifth millennia BP have been investigated in Gabon. Shell middens on the central Angola coast date from the fourth millennium BP and confirm that sea-food was by now a regular dietary supplement for groups who were geographically able to exploit it (de Maret, 1982; 1985).

To the east and south, in the great depression of the Zaire or Congo system, is to be found a totally different stone tool tradition based largely on the production of bifacially flaked core tools. This had its origins during the time of the Middle to Later Pleistocene transition when the forest began to retreat and woodland savannah and grassland replaced it over most of the Congo basin. The most characteristic artefacts made by the human populations moving into these empty niches left by the retreating forest between 40,000 and 12,000 years ago were core axes and long, bifacial, lanceolate points which belong to what is called the Lupemban industrial complex (Clark, 1982, pp. 286–93). Use-wear on the edge of the core axes indicates use for woodworking and digging in the ground. The lanceolates, which are among some of the finest Palaeolithic stone tools to be found anywhere, may have been, on analogy with the broad-based, elongated spear-heads used by the Pygmies and forest Negroes for hunting elephant, alternately spearhead and machete. Unfortunately, fauna is very rarely preserved at sites in Equatoria, so that almost nothing is known of the resources that were exploited. It seems likely that, besides fruits and tubers, these people may have extensively hunted and scavenged large animals: elephant and hippopotamus. The Lupemban complex is present in the Central African Republic, Cameroon, Gabon, Zaire and much of Angola, Ruanda and Burundi, and also extended into the Lake Victoria basin. Elsewhere, as at Matupi in the Ituri forest in north-eastern Zaire, a microlithic tradition in quartz had been present around 40,000 years ago and well-made microliths appear 20,000 years ago (van Noten, 1977). Although the site of Matupi today lies in rain forest, the associated fauna is essentially one of savannah animals.

About 14,000 to 12,000 years ago the Lupemban was replaced by the Tshitolian complex, which consists of smaller, finely made bifacial points, tanged points and many chisels (*tranchets*), together with more refined forms of core axe that were most probably hafted (Clark, 1963, pp. 133–70). The origins of the Tshitolian clearly lie in the Lupemban and this ancient core tool tradition continued for some 50,000 years until the appearance in Zaire of peoples making pottery and ground stone axes or hoes around 2,500 years ago.

It is of interest that the leaf-shaped and tanged projectile points are found usually at the plateau sites while, in the valleys, the tranchets are much commoner (Bequaert and Mortelmans, 1955). These wedge-shaped implements with a sharp cutting edge resemble the chisels and cutting 'points' used by present-day peoples like the Chokwe. The chisels are used in woodworking, in particular in hollowing out utensils, mortars for example. The chisel-edge 'point' is also the cutting part of a fall-trap. Secured to a foreshaft, it is set into a heavy log suspended from the bough of a tree over a game path. The 'point' is designed to pierce the cervical vertebrae of game, anything from an elephant downwards, when the trap is sprung and the device falls correctly. It is very probable that some of these Tshitolian *tranchets* were used in similar ways.

In the Cameroon grasslands a Later Stone Age microlithic industry dates from 9,000 years ago and the associated fauna shows that the makers were hunting forest animals (monkeys and gorillas). Of later age are village settlements with pottery, ground stone and palm nuts. These settlements were possibly agricultural and date from at least three millennia BP (de Maret, 1985). In the Ubangi–Uele basin and in lower Zaire there may have been some incipient cultivation, but no plant or animal remains and few dated settlement sites are known. A riverside settlement at Batalimo in Ubangi has yielded pottery and a ground stone axe with lithic industry and is dated to the fourth century AD (de Bayle des Hermens, 1975). In Fernando Po, an agricultural 'Neolithic' with ground axes survived up to the eleventh century AD or later, but in lower Zaire at Kinshasa and elsewhere it would seem that a 'Neolithic' with pottery and ground tools was present 3,000 years ago, though whether the makers were cultivators is not known (van Noten, 1982, pp. 57–65).

It therefore appears that at least two Later Stone Age stone tool traditions, the Tshitolian and a microlithic one, regionally distinct, continued until three millennia ago or earlier in northern and western Equatoria when new cultural elements (pottery and ground stone associated with possible village settlements) are suggestive of some form of agriculture supplementing or replacing the old hunting and gathering economy. Elsewhere in Equatoria the hunting and gathering way of life continued, certainly up to the coming of Iron Age cultivators, probably Bantu-speakers, from around 2,400 years ago and later. The materially beneficial symbiotic relationship established in the ecotone between forest and savannah, between the hunting and gathering Pygmies and the forest Negro cultivators, most probably goes back to the time of the first Iron Age immigrants.

ETHIOPIA AND EASTERN AFRICA (Map 13)

The earliest blade industry known as yet from the Horn comes from the Ethiopian Rift in the Lake Ziway basin, where an early backed blade industry in obsidian with fauna and human remains has been found at Bulbula dating from about 27,000 years ago (Gasse and Street, 1978, p. 290) and it would seem that prismatic blade production was clearly being practised in Ethiopia 30,000 years ago, if not before. The Lake Besaka area at the south-west corner of the Afar Rift has produced a long and evolving blade tradition based mostly on obsidian but sometimes elsewhere on chert (Fig. 41). This record can be tied into a climatic framework shown by fluctuations in lake-level and begins about 22,000 years ago. Retouched blades and small backed bladelets show that microlithic technology was already developed. Later stages were entirely microlithic and the associated fauna shows an economy based on hunting, fishing and gathering, though grindstones are not common. Marine shells from necklaces with burials from around 7,000 years ago indicate that there was already some kind of contact or exchange between these inland groups and the coast 500 km to the east. The stone technology of the last phase, 4,500 years ago, undergoes significant changes which, together with faunal associations, suggest that a pastoral economy had replaced that based on hunting and fishing. About 8,000 or 7,000 years ago the population may, but need not, have had Negroid affinities, judging by two burials where the crania show sub-alveolar prognathism (Clark and Williams, 1979; Brandt, 1982).

We do not yet know the precise time when food production became the dominant economy on the Ethiopian plateaux, but the village settlements near Agordat (Arkell, 1954) in the north show ceramics and other features that connect them with the mixed farming phases of the Atbai ceramic tradition in eastern Sudan (close to 4,000 to about 3,000 years ago) and suggest possible connections with Egypt via Punt (Fattovich et al., 1984). Pastoral peoples herding cattle were present in the Afar Rift 4,000 years ago or before and sometime, probably shortly after, fat-tailed sheep, depicted in the rock paintings of the south-eastern plateau escarpment, were acquired, presumably from Arabia (Clark, 1976b). But in many parts of plateau and rift, the hunting and gathering way of life appears to have persisted, the last vestiges of it to being seen in the so-called low-caste and minority groups such as the Waytu of Lake Tana, the Fuga of Sidama and the Midgan of Somalia.

The record in East Africa – Kenya, northern Tanzania and Uganda – is better known than in Ethiopia. In the lake basin of Turkana/Rudolf (Lothagam, Lowasera) (Barthelme, 1985; Robbins, 1974; Phillipson, 1977) and Edward (de Heinzelin, 1957) are found hunting, fishing and collecting communities associated with the early Holocene high lake stands. As in the Sahara and on the Nile, the most characteristic artefacts are barbed bone harpoons and, since all these lakes and rivers formed, or still form, part of the Nile drainage system, it is probable that Nile perch, which can reach 45 kg or more in weight, was the main species taken, though this was not the only use made of the harpoon. The lithic assemblages are variable. Microliths dominate in the Turkana basin, but the Ishango industry is one of informal flakes with little or no retouch. The Turkana sites date from ten millennia ago or earlier and that of Ishango from 8,500 to 8,000 years ago. They overlap in time, therefore, with the upper Nile valley and Sahara sites and, while Ishango is aceramic, some of the pottery from the Turkana sites has 'Wavy Line' decoration that calls to mind, but is not closely comparable to, the 'Khartoum Mesolithic' pottery. The first cattle pastoralists appear to have entered the north Turkana basin about 4,000 years ago, probably from Ethiopia.

The best-known area is the Kenya highlands and northern Tanzania, mostly grassland, well watered and with forest on the rift escarpments and high volcanic mountains. The late Pleistocene industrial complex was first investigated here and described by Louis Leakey in the late 1920s (Leakey, 1931) as 'Kenya Aurignacian'. Later the name was changed to 'Kenya Capsian' on account of the similarities between the two traditions and, still more recently, the industry was renamed Eburran after the volcanic highland where so many of the sites are located, overlooking the Naivasha and Nakuru lake basins (Fig. 41). The major features of the lithic industry are relatively large backed blades and bladelets making up some 50 per cent of tool classes, together with end-scrapers, burins and side scrapers, all based on blades struck from prismatic cores of obsidian. The Eburran probably began some time over 12,500 years ago. Five phases have been recognized (Ambrose, 1984). In the fifth phase (5,000–1,300 years ago) domestic as well as wild animals are present, this phase being contemporary with Savannah Pastoral peoples who had entered the highlands by around 3,000 years ago.

By the end of Eburran times, obsidian was obtained from sources often some considerable distance away from the settlements. Bone awls, a probable harpoon fragment and rare pottery are also part of the material culture. The camp sites appear to have been situated in or close to the ecotone

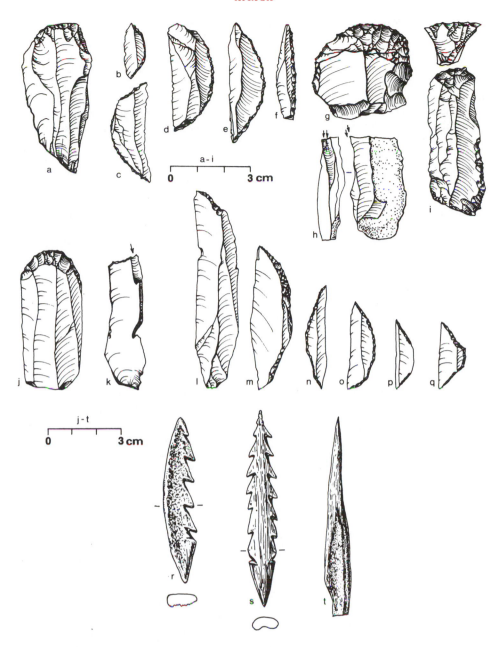

Figure 41 Later Stone Age industries (Ethiopia and eastern Africa). Artefacts from Ethiopian blade industry tradition, Lake Besaka (Ethiopia): a, opposed platform blade core; b, microlithic lunate; c–f, backed blades and bladelet; g and i, end-scrapers; h, burin. Ebburan Industrial Complex artefacts from Gamble's Cave (Kenya highlands): j, end-scraper; k, burin; l, truncated blade; m, backed blade; n–q, microliths; t, bone awl. (After Leakey, 1931.) From Lothagam, Lake Turkana Rift: r, uniserial barbed bone harpoon. (After Robbins, 1974.) From Ishango, Western Rift (Zaire): s, biserial barbed bone harpoon. (After de Heinzelin, 1957.)

between the grassland savannah and the forest and to have moved up and down in relation to climatic changes that brought about the advance and retreat of the montane forests. Eburran development is best seen at Gamble's Cave dating from between 8,600 and 4,000 years ago (Fig. 41). During this time the forest–savannah ecotone moved upwards 460 m with corresponding Eburran settlement movement to higher ground. Sites around the lakes themselves are generally small and suggest special-purpose foraging camps rather than base settlements. A present-day analogy for the Eburran life-style might be in the semi-sedentary Okiek of the ecotone areas, for whom honey is the main reason for foraging journeys. Skeletal remains in the Eburran are seen to be not dissimilar from those of the present-day Negroid inhabitants of East Africa. Again, it needs to be emphasized that in a few areas the hunting and gathering way of life still

continues in eastern Africa side by side with that of pastoralists and mixed farmers. The Sandawe only recently changed to mixed farming, perhaps in the last 200 years, and the Hadza are still hunters and collectors of fruits and tubers in the Eyassi Rift.

SOUTHERN AFRICA (Map 13)

Later Stone Age technology, based on the production of small flakes and bladelets struck from single-platform and bipolar blade cores, is first found in southern Africa about 40,000 years ago (Deacon, 1984). At Border Cave the early Later Stone Age dates from about 38,000 years ago. Somewhat later are several sites in the central and eastern Transvaal, Swaziland, the southern and eastern Cape and Lesotho.

The Nachikufu I from northern Zambia, dated from about 19,000 years ago, is technically the equivalent of these early bladelet industries. In Zimbabwe, a complex (Tshangulan) dating from between 25,000 and 13,000 years ago represents a blending of bladelet-based artefacts with Middle Stone Age technology and is probably a reflection of the continuing efficiency of Middle Stone Age point forms for large mammal hunting in the tropical woodland savannahs (Cooke, 1963). These need to be distinguished from the true microlithic assemblages of the late Pleistocene, which are characterized by many small bladelets, only rarely retouched. With them are small and some large scrapers, bone points, shell beads and bored stones. The bladelets were possibly mounted as the cutting parts of spears and knives. Those assemblages from the south coast caves (known as the Robberg industry) are dated from between 20,000 and 12,000 years ago, contemporary with the maximum regression of sea-level during the last glacial in oxygen isotope stages 3 and 2. At this time, an extensive area of the continental shelf was exposed, the shore-line being between 100 and 200 km south of its present position. Temperatures were 3 to 5 °C cooler than they are today and rainfall was reduced in the south, though further north in Botswana precipitation was higher. The habitat was one of grassland and the main food source was the large gregarious land mammals. Besides springbok, wildebeeste, quagga, bontebok, wart-hog and ostrich, there were a number of large animals that had become extinct by the end of the Pleistocene and early Holocene – these include the giant buffalo (*Pelorovis antiquus*), the giant Cape horse, a giant Alcelaphine, a pig and two springbok. It is possible that improved hunting techniques hastened the extinction of these species. Human groups are likely to have been large if game was regularly driven, and territories would have been correspondingly larger. It is unknown to what extent sea-food was used at this time, because the caves on the present coastline were then well inland and the then coastal sites are now all below sea-level.

In the terminal Pleistocene to early Holocene (12,000–8,000 years ago) the microlithic stone technology south of the Zambezi was replaced by one in which flakes from informal cores replace bladelet cores and the main tools are large scrapers, made either on cores or chunks or on large side-flakes. Bone tools are now numerous and some of these have been interpreted as fish gorges. Between 14,000 and 12,000 years ago the sea-level was rising and by 12,000 years ago the coastline would have been close by the caves. With the fish gorges are bone points, spatulae, bone and stone beads, an eyed matting needle (from Pomongwe), bored stones for digging-stick weights and engraved stones from Zimbabwe (Bambata) and the northern Cape (Wonderwerk cave) where the associated date is 10,000 years ago. Intentional burial of the dead is to be seen on the south coast (Matjes River) and in Zimbabwe (Nswatugi). Some of the large scrapers are those made on concavo-convex side-scrapers characteristic of what would be called Smithfield A from the Orange Free State, now renamed the Lockshoek industry. Local regional names are in use in different parts of the subcontinent, such as the Pomongwan in Zimbabwe and the Albany industry in the southern Cape.

A quantity of marine food sources now appear in the south coast caves – shellfish, birds and marine mammals, especially seals – and, on oxygen-isotope data, it is suggested that the sites were occupied in the winter and early spring. The land mammal fauna shows a trend away from large, gregarious antelopes towards smaller, more solitary ones, a trend that is consistent with the global warming in the early Holocene that changed the habitats from grassland to more closed bush. Hard-shelled plant foods now began to survive in archaeological horizons and, especially from the tropical parts, a range of indigenous fruits are known, most of which are still eaten today. These include the *marula* (*Sclerocarya* sp.), a cycad (*Encephalartos* sp.) and the monkey orange (*Strychnos* sp.), while the *nara* melon was used from 11,000 to 10,000 years ago in Namibia.

The reason for this technological change is unknown – it might be a reflection of adaptation to the changed early Holocene environment by new technological inventions. The bow and arrow are likely to have been in use in many parts of the continent by this time and the bone points are probably arrow points. Alternatively, this change might be the outcome of widespread stylistic preferences or, again, of other as yet unidentified causes.

The succeeding and main Holocene artefact assemblages are characterized by a return to 'microlithicness'. Whereas in the more southerly parts diminutive thumbnail scrapers dominate and backed microliths are generally not numerous, in Zimbabwe, Zambia and Malawi, for example, the proportions are reversed. The earliest dated assemblages are found in the north in Zambia (Nachikufu II), Zimbabwe (Diana's Vow) and Namibia (Apollo 11), where they date from between 10,000 and 9,000 years ago. By 6,000 years ago microlithic technology was widely spread in southern Africa and it has been suggested that the stimulus for this may have come from tropical parts. There appears, however, to have been a dearth of sites in the interior plateau of South Africa, and few are known between 9,500 and 4,500 years ago compared with those in other regions. This may be an indication that the drier interior was less hospitable during the mid-Holocene warming than were the sea-coasts and southern mountain region, or Natal, for example, so that population density was reduced on the interior plateau during that time.

The first excavated site to yield characteristic microlithic assemblages of this kind was the Wilton Rock shelter in the eastern Cape (Hewitt, 1921), and subsequent researchers extended the use of the term 'Wilton industry' as far north as Kenya and the Horn. Now many local terms are in use to describe the various regional expressions of the middle to late Holocene microlithic traditions.

The toolkits are now more varied and more complex than ever before. Besides a range of microlithic forms they include awls or borers, adzes (thick, backed flakes) for woodworking, bored stones and reamers, grooved stones, stone arm-rings and 'palettes', a rich bone component including, besides points and linkshafts, spatulate bone 'axes' and eyed needles. Objects of personal adornment include pierced sea-shells, pendants and beads made of ostrich eggshell and mollusc shell, bone and stone. There is also a much greater amount of perishable material preserved at these younger sites including wooden fragments from bows and arrows, fire-sticks, pegs, digging-sticks and arrow points and linkshafts. The site of Gwisho Hot Springs, in southern Zambia, dating from 4,500 years ago, has produced a large number of wooden artefacts and shows the importance of hardwoods, which largely replaced bone in the tropics for parts of composite arrows (Fagan and van Noten, 1971). Vegetable fibre was made into rope and string; leather was tanned and sewn into garments with sinew; and containers made from tortoise shells and ostrich eggs, the latter decorated, are commonly found. In addition, several examples are known of stone scrapers hafted

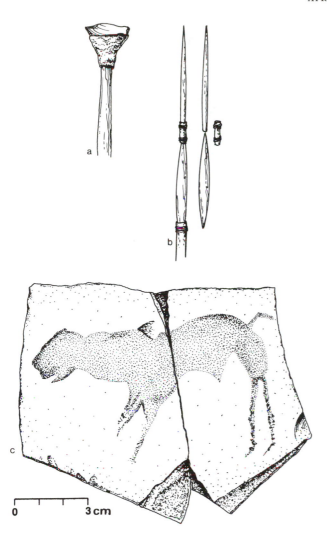

Figure 42 Later Stone Age, southern Africa. Methods of hafting: a, one method of hafting microliths as transverse arrowheads; b, bone arrow point, reed collar and link shaft of San arrow, showing method of hafting by Later Stone Age prehistoric populations in South Africa. (After Clark, 1959, pp. 195, 233.) Rock slab in two pieces with painting of feline with human-like hind legs, from archaeological horizon, dated to around 26,000 years ago, in Apollo 11 rock shelter (Namibia). (After Wendt, 1974, p. 27.)

Cape and probably also inland. Residues are preserved in some caves (Melkhoutboom, Scott's Cave) and show that these corms were stored in shallow, leaf-lined pits. These geophytes were available in the summer months, while fruits, berries and leaves became available in the winter months and were especially important in the tropics. Other important foods were honey, insects (especially termites and caterpillars), tortoises, snails, large lizards and snakes. Along the coast, marine foods became even more intensively exploited and many open-air midden sites are known round the coastline. Fish became more important and were perhaps mostly caught in tidal fish-weirs, though also by lines and spearing. Seals were taken and occasionally whales, though there is no convincing evidence that these were hunted and they were most likely scavenged. Regular seasonal movements to and from the coast are attested for the eastern and western Cape (Deacon, 1976; Parkington, 1984) and, while the coastal sites on the south coast were occupied in the summer, those on the west coast were occupied in the winter. This seeming paradox is explainable in terms of rainfall, which occurs in the winter in the western Cape and in the summer in the east.

Much can be learned about behaviour from the superb, naturalistic rock art that is preserved from central Tanzania down to the Cape. Although the motives behind this art must lie in the mythical or religious beliefs and ceremonies of the groups to which the artists belonged, their expression of these is, of necessity, in terms of their everyday behaviour, so that scenes depicting hunting, plant and honey collecting, camp life, fights, dances, rain magic, ceremonial activities and much besides help to fill out our knowledge of the Later Stone Age way of life as never before. The oldest art in the subcontinent is found in Namibia in the Apollo 11 rock shelter (Fig. 42). In a level transitional between the latest Middle Stone Age and a Later Stone Age large scraper assemblage were found several stone plaques that had been painted with representations of animals in black and red pigment. The horizon in which these occur has been dated to around 26,000 years ago (Wendt, 1974). Not only does this show the great antiquity of rock art in the continent, but these paintings rank as among the oldest dated examples in the world.

There can be no doubt that the present-day San peoples are the descendants of the Later Stone Age populations of southern Africa, though the use of modern analogues of behaviour requires greater caution in application the further back in time one goes. The hunting and gathering way of life continued with little change up to the second half of the nineteenth century in some parts of southern Africa. In tropical Zambia and Zimbabwe it was largely replaced in the first centuries of our era by early Iron Age Negroid peoples generally assumed to be Bantu-speaking agriculturalists. In the Cape, pottery and the remains of sheep are present in some of the Later Stone Age assemblages dating from the first few centuries AD; cattle remains occur later. The pottery is well made with pointed bases and sometimes spouts and lugs. Elsewhere (for instance Zimbabwe) are other pre-Iron Age pottery traditions with sheep remains but their associations are not generally understood. The southern African populations are identified with the historic Khoi or Hottentots who appear to have acquired pottery, sheep and, later, cattle and other traits, from some as yet unidentified source. They were nomadic pastoralists who continued, however, to use the traditional wild plant resources, as did, most probably, the 'Neolithic' pastoralists of the Sahara. It was

by means of mastic, as were the microliths used to form arrowheads.

Ethnographic and historical evidence has helped very greatly to fill out understanding of the way of life of the later Holocene hunting and gathering populations of southern Africa. These people belonged to the Khoi–San physical stock to be seen in the present-day 'Bush–Hottentot' peoples, the earliest evidence for which (Matjes River Cave) is at least 9,000 years old. Group size would have been generally small except when several groups came together for special purposes at certain times of the year – for ceremonies, exchange and so on. Territories would have been defined and would have varied in size depending on the geographical availability of resources. Hunting would have been with bow and arrow (Fig. 42), and poison was a significant part of one kind of hunting arrow. The game taken was clearly a mixture of large and medium to small antelopes and the latter are likely to have been captured by means of various kinds of traps. Plants were a very important food source and would have been collected by the women. The corms and bulbs of geophytes formed a staple in the winter-rainfall area of the therefore from some 2,000 years ago that the hunting and gathering peoples of the whole of the subcontinent began to share the savannah with pastoral and agricultural peoples, who, sometimes rapidly, sometimes more slowly, replaced them and, in a few instances, effected a mutually beneficial symbiotic relationship.

CONCLUSIONS

The human fossil record in Africa shows a steadily increasing number of Modern traits from around 500,000 years ago and the first fully Modern human remains are found in Middle Stone Age contexts dating from between 100,000 and 50,000 years ago. If the molecular biological evidence suggesting that Modern humans (*Homo sapiens sapiens*) originated in the African continent is confirmed, then it is reasonable to suppose a fairly rapid dispersal of small groups of Moderns into Eurasia, on a conservative estimate between 200,000 and 50,000 years ago. What was it that made Modern human beings dominate the world? Was it the possession of a full language system and all the intellectual and technical skills that this implies? What was the role of climatic and environmental change? What was the relationship with the Neanderthal and pre-Neanderthal populations of Eurasia? If a blade technology is the hallmark of *Homo sapiens sapiens*, why is it that Modern human fossils are also found with a Middle Palaeolithic/Middle Stone Age technology? Once the Modern genotype made its appearance, what was the mechanism for the replacement of the archaic hominids? To what extent was social selection a significant factor in bringing this about? Precise chronological correlation is crucial, as is also more archaeological evidence of the behavioural patterns belonging with the early cultural manifestations of the later Pleistocene, before we can hope to answer these kinds of questions. What is apparent, however, is that Modern humans were widely dispersed in Africa around 40,000 years ago and with them are present in the archaeological record a number of cultural indications that show the great intellectual and technical advances that had now taken place. While it is possible to see the emergence of these new skills in Middle Palaeolithic/Middle Stone Age contexts, their full expression, in Africa as in Eurasia, is found only with the specialized hunting and gathering societies of the Late Palaeolithic.

In the African continent, human societies evolved many ingenious and successful adaptations to enable them to exploit the very varied habitats and resources offered by the tropical and subtropical savannahs. During the 50,000 years or so of the late Pleistocene, the human populations of the continent were steadily evolving physiologically from a generalized physical stock – Mechta-Afalou (Cro-Magnon related) in the north and undifferentiated Khoisanoid–Negroid south of the Sahara – until, by some 10,000 years ago, populations representative of the main indigenous race of the continent can be recognized in north, west, east and south Africa.

During this time also, behaviour and material culture displayed, as we have seen, a great deal of variability in response to the need to make the most efficient uses of the resources being exploited, within the limits imposed by the technological skills of the prehistoric groups. As new inventions and innovative behaviour grafted on to inherited traditional skills developed, so these regionally specialized and largely isolated societies evolved ever more efficient ways of using their resources and enlarging the range that they exploited. The African savannah offered one of the richest biomasses in the world to hunters and gatherers and, when aquatic resources and storage of food became important in some ecosystems, a more sedentary life-style was possible that provided more security during the famine months so that population density increased as birth spacing was able to become shorter. Some relatively large settlements were now present, occupied seasonally if not permanently, so that such favoured societies were thus pre-adapted for the change to food production when this became expedient.

To a great extent, the Sahara is a key region during the late Pleistocene because of the major changes brought about by climatic fluctuations. During the glacial maximum, the desert was hyper-arid and apparently unoccupied. In the terminal Pleistocene/early Holocene much of it became a highly favoured habitat and was reoccupied from both north and south. With the return of desiccation about 5,000 years ago the movement of population out again to the south must have been a major cause of the interaction that took place in the Sahel and eventually brought about the complex of domesticated, indigenous plants in west Africa and the Horn after 5,000 years ago. Where such interaction was absent as in much of the rest of sub-Saharan Africa, the hunting and gathering way of life continued largely un-changed as long as the resources remained the same and were not over-exploited, up to the coming of food producers in the last centuries before the Christian era.

BIBLIOGRAPHY

AMBROSE, S. H. 1984. *Holocene Environments and Human Adaptations in the Central Rift Valley, Kenya.* Berkeley. (Ph.D. dissertation, Department of Anthropology, University of California.)

ANDERSON, J. E. 1968. Late Palaeolithic Skeletal Remains from Nubia. In: WENDORF, F. (ed.), *The Prehistory of Nubia.* Dallas. pp. 996–1040.

ARKELL, A. J. 1949. *Early Khartoum.* Oxford.

—— 1954. Four Occupation Sites at Agordat. *Kush* (Khartoum), Vol. 2, pp. 33–62.

BARTHELME, J. W. 1985. *Fisher-hunters and Neolithic Pastoralists in East Turkana, Kenya.* Oxford. (BAR Int. Ser., 254).

BAYLE DES HERMENS, R. DE. 1975. *Recherches préhistoriques en République Centrafricaine.* Nanterre.

BEAUMONT, P. B.; VOGEL, J. C. 1972. On a New Radiocarbon Chronology for Africa South of the Equator. *Afr. Stud.* (Johannesburg), Vol. 31, pp. 65–89, 155–82.

BEQUAERT, M.; MORTELMANS, G. 1955. *Le Tshitolien dans le Bassin du Congo.* Brussels. (Acad. R. Sci. Colon., Mém. 8, NS, II-5.)

BRANDT, S. A. 1982. *A Late Quaternary Cultural/Environmental Sequence from Lake Besaka, Southern Afar, Ethiopia.* Berkeley. (Ph.D. dissertation, Department of Anthropology, University of California.)

BRAUER, G. 1984. The 'Afro-European *Sapiens* Hypothesis' and Hominid Evolution in East Asia during the Late Middle and Upper Pleistocene. *CFS, Cour. Forsch.inst. Senckenb.* (Frankfurt/Main), Vol. 69, pp. 145–65.

BROTHWELL, D. R.; SHAW, T. 1971. A Late Upper Pleistocene Proto-West African Negro from Nigeria. *Man* (London), Vol. 6, pp. 221–7.

CAMPS, G. 1974. *Les Civilisations préhistoriques de l'Afrique du nord et du Sahara.* Paris.

CANN, R. L.; STONEKING, M.; WILSON, A. C. 1987. Mitochondrial DNA and Human Evolution. *Nature* (London), Vol. 325, pp. 31–6.

CHAMLA, M. C. 1968. *Les Populations anciennes du Sahara et des régions limitrophes.* Paris. CRAPE, Mém. 9.

CHURCHER, C. S.; SMITH, P. E. L. 1972. Kom Ombo: Preliminary

Report on the Fauna of Late Paleolithic Sites in Upper Egypt. *Science* (Washington), Vol. 177, pp. 259–61.

CLARK, J. D. 1963. *Prehistoric Cultures of Northeast Angola and their Significance in Tropical Africa*. Lisbon. (Pub. Cult., 62, Mus. Dundo.)

—— 1976a. Epi-palaeolithic Aggregates from Greboun Wadi, Air and Adrar Bous, Northwestern Tenere, Republic of Niger. In: ABEBE, B. (ed.), *Proc. 8th Afr. Cong. of Prehist. and Quat. Stud., Addis Ababa*. Addis Ababa. pp. 67–8.

—— 1976b. The Domestication Process in Sub-Saharan Africa with Special Reference to Ethiopia. In: HIGGS, E. (ed.), *Origine de l'élevage et de la domestication*. Paris. pp. 56–115. (Colloque XX, IXe Cong. UISPP, Nice.)

—— 1980a. Human Populations and Cultural Adaptations in the Sahara and Nile during Prehistoric Times. In: WILLIAMS, M. A. J.; FAURE, H. (eds), *Quaternary Environments and Prehistoric Occupation in Northern Africa*. Rotterdam. pp. 527–82.

—— 1980b. Early Human Occupation of African Savanna Environments. In: HARRIS, D. R. (ed.), *Human Ecology in Savanna Environments*. London. pp. 41–71.

—— 1981. New Men, Strange Faces, Other Minds: An Archaeologist's Perspective on Recent Discoveries Relating to the Origin and Spread of Modern Man. *Proc. Br. Acad.* (Oxford), Vol. 67, pp. 163–92.

—— 1982. The Cultures of the Middle Palaeolithic/Middle Stone Age. In: CLARK, J. D. (ed.), *The Cambridge History of Africa*. Vol. I: *From the Earliest Times to c.500 BC*. Cambridge. pp. 248–341.

CLARK, J. D.; WILLIAMS, M. A. J. 1979. Recent Archaeological Research in Southeastern Ethiopia (1974–1975): Some Preliminary Results. *Ann. Ethiop.* (Addis Ababa), Vol. 11, pp. 19–44.

CLOSE, A. 1986. The Place of the Haua Fteah in the Late Palaeolithic of North Africa. In: BAILEY, G. N.; CALLOW, P. (eds), *Stone Age Prehistory*. Cambridge. pp. 169–80.

COOKE, C. K. 1963. Report on Excavations at Pomongwe and Tshangula Caves, Matopos Hills, Southern Rhodesia. *S. Afr. Archaeol. Bull.* (Claremont), Vol. 18, pp. 73–151.

DAY, M. H. 1977. *Guide to Fossil Man: A Handbook of Human Paleontology*. Chicago.

DEACON, H. J. 1976. *Where Hunters Gathered: A Study of Holocene Stone Age People in the Eastern Cape*. Cape Town.

—— 1984. Later Stone Age People and their Descendants in Southern Africa. In: KLEIN, R. G. (ed.), *Southern African Prehistory and Palaeoenvironments*. Rotterdam. pp. 221–328.

FAGAN, B. M.; NOTEN, F. VAN. 1971. *The Hunter-Gatherers of Gwisho*. Tervuren.

FATTOVICH, R.; MARKS, A. E.; MOHAMMED-ALI, A. 1984. The Archaeology of the Eastern Sahel, Sudan: Preliminary Results. *Afr. Archaeol. Rev.*, Vol. 2, pp. 172–88.

GASSE, F.; STREET, F. A. 1978. Late Quaternary Lake Level Fluctuations and Environments of the Northern Rift Valley and Afar Region (Ethiopia and Djibouti). *Palaeogeogr. Palaeoclimatol. Palaeoecol.*, Vol. 24, pp. 279–325.

GREENE, D. L.; ARMELAGOS, G. J. 1972. *The Wadi Halfa Mesolithic Population*. University of Massachusetts.

HARLAN, J. R. 1971. Agricultural Origins: Centers and Non-Centers. *Science* (Washington), Vol. 174, pp. 468–74.

HASSAN, F. A. 1978. Archaeological Explorations of the Siwa Oasis Region, Egypt. *Curr. Anthropol.*, Vol. 19, pp. 146–8.

HEINZELIN DE BRAUCOURT, J. DE. 1957. *Les Fouilles d'Ishango*. Brussels.

HEWITT, J. 1921. On Several Implements and Ornaments from Strandlooper Sites in the Eastern Province. *S. Afr. J. Sci.* (Johannesburg), Vol. 18, pp. 454–67.

KLEIN, R. G.; SCOTT, K. 1986. Re-evaluation of Faunal Assemblages from the Haua Fteah and Other Late Quaternary Sites in Cyrenaican Libya. *J. Archaeol. Sci.*, Vol. 13, pp. 515–42.

LEAKEY, L. S. B. 1931. *The Stone Age Cultures of Kenya Colony*. Cambridge.

LIGERS, Z. 1966. *Les Sorko (Bozo), Maîtres du Niger*. Paris, CNRS.

LUBELL, D.; SHEPPARD, P.; JACKES, M. 1984. Continuity in the Epipalaeolithic of Northern Africa with Emphasis on the Maghreb. In: WENDORF, F.; CLOSE, A. (eds), *Advances in World Archaeology*. New York. Vol. 3, pp. 143–91.

LUBELL, D. et al. 1975. The Prehistoric Cultural Ecology of Capsian Escargotières. *Libyca* (Paris), Vol. 23, pp. 43–121.

MCBURNEY, C. B. M. 1960. *The Stone Age of Northern Africa*. Harmondsworth.

—— 1967. *The Haua Fteah (Cyrenaica) and the Stone Age of the Southeast Mediterranean*. Cambridge.

MARET, P. DE. 1982. New Survey of Archaeological Research and Dates for West-Central and North-Central Africa. *J. Afr. Hist.*, Vol. 23, pp. 1–15.

—— 1985. Recent Archaeological Research and Dates from Central Africa. *J. Afr. Hist.*, Vol. 26, pp. 129–48.

NOTEN, F. VAN. 1977. Excavation at Matupi Cave. *Antiquity*, Vol. 51, pp. 35–40.

—— 1982. *The Archaeology of Central Africa*. Graz.

OLDFATHER, C. H. (trans.) 1979. *Diodorus of Sicily*. 12 vols. Cambridge, Mass. Vol. 2, p. 127.

PARKINGTON, J. 1984. Changing Views of the Later Stone Age in South Africa. In: WENDORF, F.; CLOSE, A. (eds), *Advances in World Archaeology*. New York. Vol. 3, pp. 90–142.

PETIT-MAIRE, N. 1979. *Le Sahara atlantique à l'Holocène: peuplement et écologie*. Algiers.

PHILLIPSON, D. W. 1977. Lowasera. *Azania* (Nairobi), Vol. 12, pp. 1–32.

ROBBINS, L. H. 1974. *The Lothagam Site: A Late Stone Age Fishing Settlement in the Lake Rudolf Basin, Kenya*. East Lansing, Michigan State University.

SAXON, E. C. 1974. Results of Recent Investigations at Tamar Hat. *Libyca*, Vol. 22, pp. 49–82.

SHAW, T. 1978. *Nigeria: Its Archaeology and Early History*. London.

SMITH, P. E. L. 1976. Stone Age Man on the Nile. *Sci. Am.*, Vol. 235, pp. 30–8.

—— 1982. The Late Palaeolithic and Epi-palaeolithic of Northern Africa. In: CLARK, J. D. (ed.), *The Cambridge History of Africa*. Vol. I: *From the Earliest Times to c.500 BC*. Cambridge. pp. 342–409.

SOWUNMI, M. A. 1981. Nigerian Vegetational History from the Late Quaternary to the Present Day. *Palaeoecology of Africa and the Surrounding Islands*, Vol. 13, pp. 217–34.

STAHL, A. B. 1985. Reinvestigation of Kintampo 6 Rock Shelter, Ghana: Implications for the Nature of Culture Change. *Afr. Archaeol. Rev.*, Vol. 3, pp. 117–50.

STRINGER, C. B. 1974. Populationships of Later Pleistocene Hominids: A Multi-variate Study of Available Crania. *J. Archaeol. Sci.*, Vol. 1, pp. 317–42.

SUTTON, J. E. G. 1982. Archaeology in West Africa: A Review of Recent Work and a Further List of Radiocarbon Dates. *J. Afr. Hist.*, Vol. 23, pp. 291–314.

TALBOT, M. 1980. Environmental Responses to Climatic Change in the West African Sahel over the Past 20,000 Years. In: WILLIAMS, M. A. J.; FAURE, H. (eds), *The Sahara and the Nile*. Rotterdam. pp. 37–62.

—— 1983. Lake Bosuntwi, Ghana. *Nyame Akuma* (Calgary), Vol. 23, pp. 11 ff.

VALLOIS, H. V. 1954. Neanderthals and Praesapiens. *J.R. Anthropol. Inst. G.B. Irel.* (London), Vol. 84, pp. 111–30.

VERMEERSCH, P. M.; GIJSELINGS, G.; PAULISSEN, E. 1984. Discovery of the Nazlet Khater Man, Upper Egypt. *J. Hum. Evol.* (New York), Vol. 13, pp. 281–6.

VERMEERSCH, P. M. et al. 1982. Blade Technology in the Egyptian Nile Valley: Some New Evidence. *Science* (Washington), Vol. 216, pp. 626–8.

WAINSCOTT, J. S. et al. 1986. Evolutionary Relationships of Human Populations from an Analysis of Nuclear DNA Polymorphisms. *Nature* (London), Vol. 319, pp. 491–3.

WENDORF, F. (ed.) 1968. *The Prehistory of Nubia*. Dallas. 2 vols.

WENDORF, F.; SCHILD, R. 1975. The Palaeolithic of the Lower Nile Valley. In: WENDORF, F.; SCHILD, R. (eds), *Problems in Prehistory: North Africa and the Levant*. Dallas. pp. 127–69.

WENDORF, F.; SCHILD, R. (eds) 1976. *Prehistory of the Nile Valley*. New York.

—— 1980. *Prehistory of the Eastern Sahara*. New York.

—— 1984. The Emergence of Food-Production in the Egyptian Sahara. In: CLARK, J. D.; BRANDT, S. A. (eds), *From Hunters to Farmers*. Berkeley. pp. 93–101.

WENDORF, F.; SCHILD, R.; CLOSE, A. 1980. *Loaves and Fishes: The Prehistory of Wadi Kubbaniya*. Dallas.

—— 1986. *The Wadi Kubbaniya Skeleton: A Late Palaeolithic Burial from Southern Egypt*. Dallas. (The Prehistory of Wadi Kubbaniya, Vol. 1.)

WENDT, W. E. 1974. 'Art mobilier' aus der Apollo 11-Grotte in Südwest Afrika: Die ältesten datierten Kunstwerke Afrikas. *Acta Praehist. Archaeol.* (Berlin), Vol. 5, pp. 1–42.

21

EUROPE

during the Upper Palaeolithic and Mesolithic

Marcel Otte

THE PALAEOGEOGRAPHY OF EUROPE DURING THE UPPER PLEISTOCENE

During the different cold periods of the Quaternary and, more particularly, during the most recent, referred to as the Würm or Weichsel glaciation, a considerable mass of water from the atmosphere and the sea remained on the continents in the form of gigantic ice-caps. This deficit in ocean water led to a considerable lowering of world sea-level and a consequent recession of sea-shores in Europe. These changes in the coastline were particularly marked in northern Europe: the North Sea was virtually dry and the Atlantic coastline followed the edge of the continental shelf, hundreds of kilometres west of its present location. A vast plain was thus formed, taking in the channel joining Brittany to the British Isles, northern France, the Netherlands and the North Sea and stretching to the plains of central Germany, Poland and Belarus. During the greater part of the Ice Age this plain was hemmed in by the two main glaciers, that of the Alps in the south and that which, in the north, joined Scotland and Ireland to Scandinavia and northern Germany.

These geographic conditions quite naturally brought about significant climatic changes (see below) and determined the preferred communication routes between the different parts of Europe. These communication routes varied in accordance with the climatic rhythms which affected the distribution of the ecological areas attractive to Palaeolithic hunters. Communications between the different parts of the northern plain were no problem, whereas the Mediterranean and Balkan zones were more isolated than is the case today. These factors in large part determined the cultural distribution of the human groups, which adapted to the individual biotopes.

THE ENVIRONMENT

The general lowering of temperature and, more importantly, the changes in wind regimes due to the extension of the continental mass created climatic conditions which were very different from those of today and very variable from one part of Europe to another: from west to east, considerable drying of air masses from the Atlantic resulted in a longitudinal spread of ecological zones; there was a humid tundra to the west of the great plain, while a cold steppe extended eastwards. In these open, grassy plains large herds of herbivores proliferated, offering an abundance of game for Palaeolithic predators. The grassy steppes of the Ukraine and central Europe provided a constant supply of wild animals (Bovidae, Cervidae, Equidae) thanks to maximum sunshine, and were consequently zones with large concentrations of population. In the north-west, the tundra provided better subsistence for reindeer and animals able to withstand the cold, such as the mammoth, the woolly rhinoceros and the Arctic fox. Thanks to more varied and luxuriant biotopes, the southern regions of Europe (south-west France, the Mediterranean) were once again supporting more abundant animal life, some types of which, such as the ibex and the chamois, were adapted to mountainous conditions.

These palaeoclimatic reconstructions can be attempted not only on the basis of study of the bones of the animals themselves (particularly of microfauna, which is very sensitive to climatic variations) and that of geological deposits (sedimentology, pedology) but, above all, from the analysis of fossil pollen preserved in the sediments (palynology). The evolution of the European landscape (Table 7) can thus be reconstructed with a fair degree of precision. During the more severe periods, virtually treeless tundra occupied a large part of Europe, but when the climate improved, gallery forests appeared in the shelter provided by the large valleys, and wooded steppes developed on the plateaux.

These steppes sometimes had clumps of trees such as willow, pine and birch. When conditions improved these species could give way to hazel and alder and, in still more temperate periods, to elm, lime, hornbeam and oak.

The determination of climatic conditions and reconstructions of the landscape must take into account both the position of the sites (altitude, longitude, latitude) and their dating, since there were major changes from one period to another within the Würm or Weichsel glaciation. This reconstruction is none the less essential if we are to ascertain the way in which a given society maintained its equilibrium in a particular environment by means of its economy.

CHRONOLOGY

These variations in climate, which have been identified by palynologists or on the basis of deep-sea cores, provided

Table 7 Chronological position of the main cultural traditions of the Upper Palaeolithic in western Europe in relation to the climatic curve during the last Würm glacial period. (After Arlette Leroi-Gourhan.)

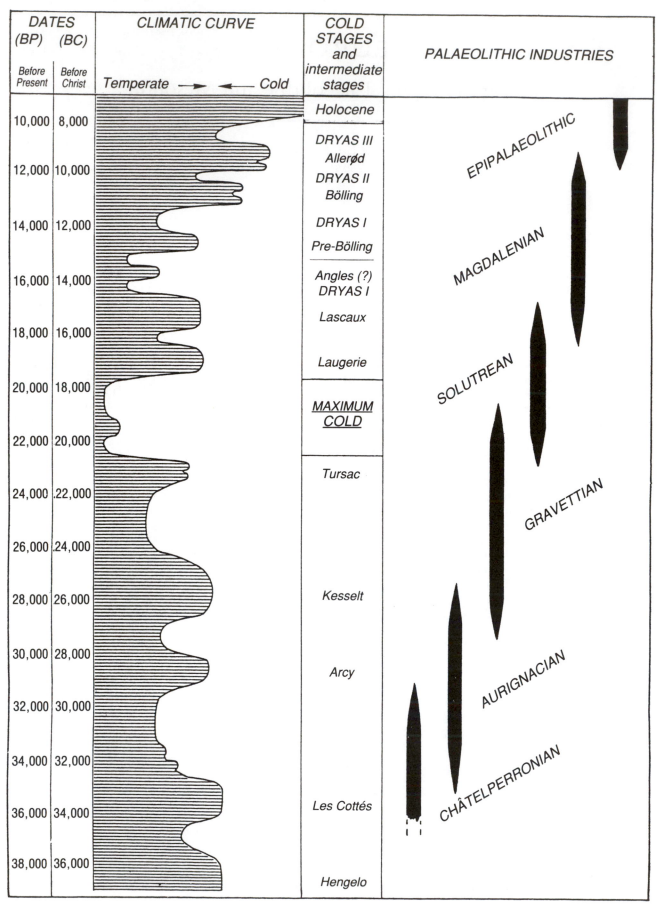

the context in which industrial groupings developed. And radiometric dates, available in increasingly large numbers for the Upper Palaeolithic, now locate each of these climatic variations and their accompanying human occupations on a detailed chronological scale. The pollen assemblages and associations of microfauna characteristic of each of the phases can be used for an approximate calculation of the relative position of the Palaeolithic cultural groups.

In Europe the Upper Palaeolithic appeared during a temperate climatic oscillation, approximately 35,000 years ago, that is, in about the middle of the last Ice Age. A series of climatic phases then followed which lasted until about 22,000 years ago, when a particularly cold spell started. The subsequent rise in temperature began very slowly, with more or less severe fluctuations, during what is called the Late Glacial stage, between about 18,000 and 8,000 years ago.

Next began a new geological era, the Holocene, which is still going on. Environmental conditions began to resemble those of the present time: temperate and humid. The Palaeolithic populations, adapting to tree vegetation and to the disappearance of steppe fauna, changed their technology although they continued to be predators – this was the Mesolithic (about 8,000 to 5,000 years ago). After this phase a new mode of life was invented or introduced from western Asia. Populations then became sedentary, cultivated certain plant species and reared animals – that was in the Neolithic, which is dealt with in Chapter 47.

THE ORIGINS OF THE UPPER PALAEOLITHIC IN EUROPE

The transition from the technology of the Middle Palaeolithic to that of the Upper Palaeolithic took different forms in different European regions. At the same time, there was an equally important evolution in human anatomy, as Neanderthalers were replaced by Modern humans.

These anatomical and technical changes are simply the reflection of more profound and less easily apprehended transformations in the system of social relationships, which are indicated by the development and complexity of settlements, the systematization of burial procedures, the development of abstract notations (ridges, notches: bones or stones with regular notching), and, lastly, the production of images reproducing a part of reality symbolically transposed by art.

Some of these innovations were introduced locally, as an extension of the Mousterian cultural substratum. Others seem to be derived from Eastern models which were imitated or transported by migrant populations.

It seems, in any case, that this new mode of social relationships, which no doubt encompassed a greater number of individuals organized in a more complex way, led to more efficient means of subsistence and therefore to an increase in population. This new technology, which was better adapted to more diverse environments, enabled the people of Upper Palaeolithic Europe to settle almost the entire continent and to withstand profound changes in climate.

THE CHÂTELPERRONIAN CULTURE (Map 14)

The cave at Châtelperron in the French department of Allier has given its name to an early culture which constituted a transition to the Upper Palaeolithic. The innovations are most noticeable in stone technology. In addition to the

production of flakes used to make archaic tools (side-scrapers, denticulated implements, points), there appeared elongated flakes known as blades which were used to make new, lighter and more precise tools: burins, knives and chisels. A characteristic implement is the 'Châtelperronian knife', which is made from a blade with one cutting edge, while the opposite edge is curved and blunted (Fig. 43).

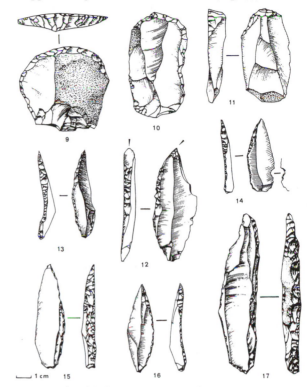

Figure 43 Early Châtelperronian stone industry (France): 9–11, scrapers; 12–17, knives or points with curved backs. (After F. Leveque.)

Several of these implements seem to have been associated with the working of bone, which also began at this time (awls, rods, tubes), thus diversifying the repertoire of existing weapons and tools.

The first evidence of symbolic thought also appears: bones with regular notches as if to record a calculation, perforated teeth used as pendants and colouring of the ground or of instruments with red ochre.

Clear, well-organized dwelling structures associated with this culture have been described in Arcy-sur-Cure (Yonne, France). These were circular dwellings created by the superposition of calcareous blocks around hearths, with postholes or mammoth tusks sunk into the ground. These humble remains clearly demonstrate a desire to modify the living environment in order to adapt it to the domestic needs of the group and to divide dwellings into different areas which were functionally distinct from one another.

Several authors have clearly emphasized the technical continuity linking this culture to the local Mousterian phases, and it is very probable that these beginnings of the Upper Palaeolithic in western Europe were independent of contemporary discoveries in western Asia. This seems all the more plausible today as a Châtelperronian tomb recently yielded the bones of a Neanderthaler (Saint-Césare, Charente, France). This discovery demonstrates the ability of this rather short-lived fossil race to create new techniques and a new mode of existence.

The Châtelperronian is an exclusively western European culture, since it extended over an area contained within the borders of present-day France and some parts of Spain and Italy (Map 14). It is chronologically situated between 35,000 (the Les Cottés interstadial) and 30,000 years ago (end of the next cold phase).

Given the limited number of recently excavated deposits, knowledge of its economy is still scant but, to judge by the lightness of the flake tools and the existence of bone implements, it is likely that a light spear came into use during this period and that it was used to hunt steppe animals.

LEAF-SHAPED POINT CULTURES

An entirely different tradition made its appearance in the northern regions of Europe during the Upper Palaeolithic (Map 14). During roughly the same period, that is during the Les Cottés interstadial, the cultures of the local Middle Palaeolithic also began to produce blades by flaking, but they used them to make projectile points or leaf-shaped knives by flat bifacial retouch (Fig. 44). Strangely, the shapes differed very little from those of the implements of the preceding cultures, but the new techniques enabled greater advantage to be taken of the material used, thus allowing for a lesser dependence on sources of supply.

These groups of hunters seem to have been well adjusted to the ecology of the great northern plain (from Britain to Russia) which, during this temperate oscillation, had a shrub steppe vegetation ideally suited to the needs of the great herds of herbivores.

It was in the caves of the plateaux on the southern edge of this vast plain that most of the discoveries were made: in England, Belgium, Germany (Thüringen) and Poland. A central (Szeletian) group discovered in Hungary and Moravia seems to be genetically related to this northern plain culture.

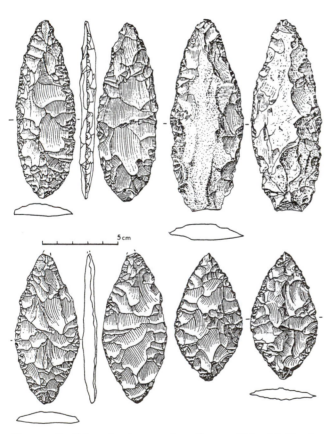

Figure 44 Leaf-shaped points, northern Europe. (After M. Otte.)

5cm

The founders of this culture have not yet been identified, although its local origin leads one to believe they were Neanderthalers, as with the Châtelperronian. No traces of dwelling structures have been found in these caves, which were excavated at a very early date and had been seriously eroded during later oscillations.

From about 38,000 years ago, this culture seems to have spread to the regions of the north during the Les Cottés interstadial, before falling back towards the south during the colder period that followed (34,000 to 32,000 years ago) and playing a part in the formation of the Gravettian complexes of central Europe (see p. 212).

THE AURIGNACIAN CULTURE
(Maps 14 and 15)

This culture is named after the site at Aurignac in the Haute-Garonne (France) where it was first discovered. It extended well beyond French territory, indeed it seems to have originated outside Europe (Maps 14 and 15).

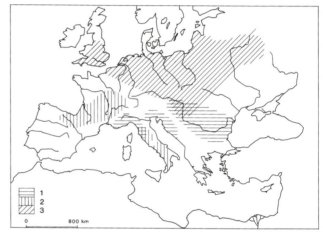

Map 14 Distribution of the principal cultures of the beginning of the European Upper Palaeolithic, between around 38,000 and 32,000 years ago. 1, Aurignacian; 2, Châtelperronian; 3, Northern leaf-shaped points.

The oldest dates show it as existing in the Balkans about 40,000 years ago, that is, in the cold phase which preceded Les Cottés (Bacho Kiro site in Bulgaria). Ancient traces are also to be found in Hungary (Istallöskö) and in Moravia (Vedrovice). Consequently, the most likely hypothesis now is that this cultural tradition originated in western Asia, where these techniques were also used.

A trail of archaic sites ('proto-Aurignacian') along the European side of the Mediterranean (Italy, south-east France) indicates the same influence being carried along a different route.

During the Les Cottés interstadial, the following cold phase and, lastly, the Arcy oscillation, this culture spread throughout Europe in an astonishing way, adapting to different types of environment, but mostly concentrating in the plateau regions of central Europe. In the course of the different stages which have been identified in its development it covered almost the whole of Europe except for Scandinavia, which was then covered with glaciers, and the Ukrainian–Russian plain, where its traces are very indistinct, probably as a result of the occupation density of other cultures (leaf-shaped points, followed by Gravettian).

In addition to the techniques used, its external origin is

also suggested by the association of this culture with a new anatomy, that of Modern or Cro-Magnon human type, more slender in frame than the Neanderthal, with a slightly larger cranial capacity and, above all, the high forehead and jutting chin of present-day humans.

By means of acculturation, interbreeding and population movements, the Aurignacians spread stone toolkits throughout Europe that were made from thick blades with scalar retouch or from blocks with lamellar retouch: beaked burins, keeled scrapers or nosed end-scrapers. This 'fashion', which was always grafted on to what was probably a variety of different ethnic substrata, was accompanied by the emergence of an ability to manufacture a great variety of bone tools: domestic utensils (polishers, awls, chisels) and hunting tools (points, light spears made from ivory or antler, lozenge-shaped with a split or solid base).

Aurignacian ornaments include a large number of pendants: ivory beads, drop-shaped pendants, rings, perforated teeth (Fig. 45). Notched bones are frequently seen: hollow bones covered with X- or V-shaped score-marks, a staff covered with cup marks which, it has been suggested, might be a 'lunar calendar'.

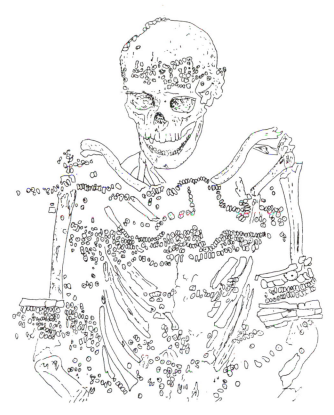

Figure 45 Burial from Sungir, near Moscow (Russian Federation). A great many beads and pendants seem to have come off garments on which they were sewn as decoration. (After Bader.)

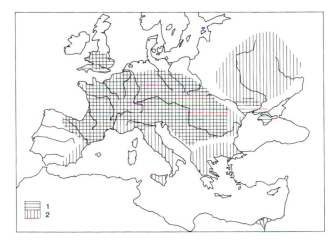

Map 15 The two principal cultures of Europe between about 32,000 and 22,000 years ago spread over the whole of the continent. The wide areas covered in central Europe contrast with the sporadic areas in Mediterranean and Eastern Europe. 1, Aurignacian; 2, Gravettian.

But the most evocative artefacts belong to the domain of figurative art. A group of admirable ivory figures was discovered in the caves of the Swabian Jura (Germany), depicting animal or human forms in the round.

The rock shelters of south-west France have yielded engraved slabs bearing schematic representations of animals and of signs interpreted as male and female sexual symbols.

Lastly, a number of caves in the same region contain the first cave engravings, attributed to the Aurignacian culture (Belcaire).

A set of elaborate symbolic concepts now clearly makes its entrance on the European scene. It would seem that a metaphysical world was being organized during the Aurignacian period which was to be developed in the subsequent Upper Palaeolithic.

A number of tombs have been discovered in Aurignacian contexts: a group burial in a Cro-Magnon shelter at Les Eyzies (Dordogne, France), unfortunately excavated too early, before the development of sound excavation techniques, a double burial in a flexed position in Grimaldi (Italy) and an individual burial in the Cueva Morin (Asturias, Spain).

Traces of living arrangements are also scarce because the caves which were the favourite habitat were excavated in the nineteenth century when methods were not geared to detecting them. Rounded and elongated pits have been discovered at Barca in Slovakia and a quadrangular pit in the Cueva Morin (Spain).

Above all, the Aurignacians were hunters of big game and species that are now extinct: the cave bear, mammoth and woolly rhinoceros, which they brought down with spears tipped with lozenge-shaped heads. No sufficiently detailed study is yet available to show how the spoils were shared out, but a large part of the prey was taken back to camp, and studies of the fauna in the latter have demonstrated the importance of the family group (about thirty persons), and the absence of any sharing out on the spot where the animal was killed.

Having progressed through a number of stages and expanded to cover a vast geographical area, the Aurignacian seems to have given way to a culture with which it was partially contemporary, the Gravettian culture.

THE GRAVETTIAN CULTURE (Map 15)

Present-day opinion is that this important technical tradition sprang up in a variety of centre. In the west, the Châtelperronian culture must have contributed, beyond the Aurignacian, to the formation of the local Gravettian facies, the Upper Perigordian. In the plains of northern Europe, the leaf-shaped point industries were a formative influence and in the eastern regions of Europe little-known technical groups at the beginning of the Upper Palaeolithic merit very serious consideration as contributors to the formation of the local Gravettian culture.

Be that as it may, in about the middle of the European Upper Palaeolithic, the continent witnessed the emergence and very rapid spread of new technical processes which were very different from those used by the Aurignacians, with which they were none the less largely contemporaneous. These new processes were apparently linked to a change in hunting techniques, which now concentrated more on the fauna of open country such as the great plains, rather than on that of the plateaux. Stone projectile points now consisted of thin blades sharpened by steep retouch over the whole of the rectilinear edge (these were known as 'Gravette points' after the French site in which they were first identified). These pieces were used to equip projectiles either pointing in the same direction as the shaft or laterally as barbs. Several other forms of light weapons also appeared in Gravettian times: flat, leaf-shaped 'darts', shouldered points in eastern areas, tanged points in the west, and straight-backed bladelets in most areas.

In order to produce these light tools, new techniques were adopted for preparing the block of raw material, and stone suitable for elaborate working had to be found. More than in Aurignacian times, good-quality stone was exported over considerable distances (no doubt encouraging contacts between groups) and activities were separated to a greater degree: sites included the sources of supply, the places where the block was prepared, storage areas and living areas.

In the large sites of central Europe, it seems that social organization was such that a part of the community could remain sedentary while other members of the group were securing supplies of raw material and game (for instance, Dolni-Vestonice and Pavlov in former Czechoslovakia).

These deposits have revealed veritable Gravettian 'villages' of rounded dwellings hollowed out of the loess. The presence of tombs and areas set aside for the making of figures also bears witness to the permanent nature of the settlements. In the northern regions (Poland), settlements made of accumulated mammoth bones have been found. It is supposed that they were temporary camps used during hunting expeditions or expeditions to acquire supplies of the stone which is plentiful in this region (Krakow-Spadzista). In western Europe groups settled both in natural shelters and in the open. Shelters made of flagstones piled up in a circle have recently been discovered in Vigne-Brun near Roanne in France. They, too, attest the existence of large settlements which were occupied from time to time.

Weapons made of bone are less common than in Aurignacian times, this material being used only for the long slender or biconical points used to tip projectiles. Conversely, domestic implements made of bone were developed to an extraordinary degree, for tools apparently used to make houses: scoops, picks, pickaxes made of bone or antler. These objects often have very finely engraved geometric decorations: meanders, herring-bone patterns or Greek frets.

The most spectacular feature of the Gravettian culture is without question its artistic creations, whose homogeneity over most of Europe confirms the impression of cultural unity, or at least of frequent contacts, gathered from the study of its stone tools. From southern Russia to the Pyrenees, a trail of Gravettian sites has yielded statuettes which are sometimes called 'Venuses', of females with adipose and stereotyped figures (Fig. 35): broad hips, pendulant breasts and prominent posteriors. The limbs are either broken off or very summarily executed. There is a noticeable absence of facial features, except in rare cases such as the famous *Dame à la capuche* (Hooded Lady), discovered at Brassempouy in the Pyrenees (Plate 35), and the Dolní-Věstonice face.

These statuettes are fashioned from various materials, depending on the region: soft stone, ivory or even terracotta in Moravia. In Moravia and Ukraine they are sometimes discovered alongside animal figurines, rhinoceros, mammoth and feline. The unity of theme and aesthetic canon demonstrates the transmission throughout Europe within the Gravettian culture of cults and religious practices associated with these images.

In south-west France and in Cantabria, the continuing growth of cave art was another characteristic of Gravettian times. What is defined as style II by A. Leroi-Gourhan belonged to this period and involved the accentuation of the cervical and dorsal outline characteristic of the different species: Pair-non-Pair in Gironde and Gargas in Ariège are important examples (Chapters 19 and 23).

The Gravettian cultural tradition, which covered an exceptionally large area and is associated with an apparently stable and very elaborate economic and social structure, underwent some complex changes from about 27,000 to 22,000 years ago, which this is not the place to examine in detail. These variations in time were accompanied by increasingly marked regional differences, indicating a degree of compartmentalization within this vast cultural complex. Towards the end of the period the worsening climate increased these regional differences by isolating particular geographical areas. Thus, while northern Europe seems to have been abandoned, the Gravettian tradition was continued in the Mediterranean regions until the post-glacial period. In the same way, in the Balkan peninsula and eastern Europe, now separated from the western regions, this culture continued over a very long period. In the west, profound climatic changes seem to have led to a cultural and technical intermixing from which the new Palaeolithic traditions were to emerge.

THE SOLUTREAN CULTURE (Map 16)

The Le Solutré deposit in Burgundy (France) has given its name to a distinctive culture, peculiar to the western regions, which developed during the coldest period of the last Ice Age, that is, from about 20,000 to 15,000 years ago. While Gravettian cultures were still in existence in the Mediterranean, new techniques for the fashioning of stone weapons and implements were developed in the Rhône

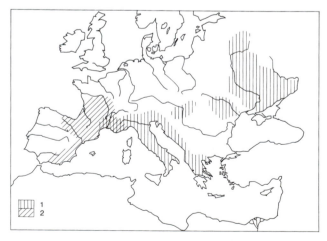

Map 16 Europe at the height of the Last Glaciation, from about 22,000 to 17,000 years ago. The area of occupation is reduced to the southern zones. 1, Late Gravettian; 2, Solutrean.

valley and in the Yonne. Flat retouch, apparently derived from the techniques of the ancient cultures of the northern regions and transmitted by certain Gravettian facies (Belgium and central Europe), was brought back into fashion in the 'proto-Solutrean' culture which abandoned most of the Gravettian blunt-backed techniques used in making weapons. This flat retouch, applied to larger and thicker blanks, led initially to the manufacture of domestic implements: pointed blades or uniface points of particularly regular outline. The Lower, Middle and Upper Solutrean cultures which followed (from 18,000 to 15,000 years ago) saw an improvement and diversification of the implements and weapons produced. The flat retouch, now bifacial, was ever more finely executed and regular, pressure-flaking being sometimes used in the later period. Laurel-leaf, willow-leaf and shouldered points were made in this way. This was without question the period of greatest technical achievement in stoneworking, one in which one senses that the stone-worker is seeking new challenges, new opportunities to excel, and also, probably, aesthetic refinement (Figs 46 and 47).

Once again, the uniformity of the technical processes employed over a vast area of land and the indications of continuity between the different stages illustrate the cultural

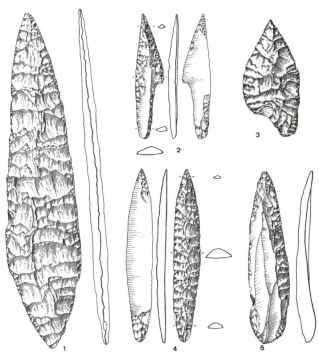

Figure 47 Solutrean stone points: 1, laurel-leaf point; 2, shouldered point; 3, asymmetrical point; 4, willow-leaf point; 5, uniface point. (After P. Smith.)

ties which existed between the occupants of the different Solutrean sites during the different periods.

This culture covered the greater part of present-day France and Spain. In the latter country, it produced remarkable stone weapons with tangs and barbs which foreshadowed Neolithic arrowheads some thousands of years later.

Bone toolkits were not highly developed and included slender spearheads. It was none the less the Solutreans who invented eyed needles, which they made from bone.

A detailed study has been conducted in the Asturias (Spain) (Strauss and Clark, 1983) of the life-style and means of subsistence of the Solutreans. It shows the opportunism of the hunters of this culture, the location of whose camps varied according to the time of year and the game sought. There were seasonal migrations to hunt the mountain ibex and the deer of the coastal plain.

A number of subcircular dwelling structures associated with this culture have been found, particularly in Chufin (Spain) where a circular low wall measured 2 metres in diameter.

Solutrean art is characterized by engraved plaquettes bearing more realistic representations than those of the Gravettian culture, for example the female deer and the horses found at Parpallo in Spain. Solutrean artists are also credited with a number of cave paintings and engravings, examples being Chabot in the Ariège and the Tête du Lion (Lion's Head), in the Ardèche (France). But the most outstanding feature of this culture is the bas-reliefs carved on blocks, representing pot-bellied, short-limbed animals (Leroi-Gourhan's style III), as can be found in the Fourneau-du-Diable in Bourdeilles (Dordogne) and in Roc-de-Sers (Charentes).

After this brilliant efflorescence, Solutrean culture mysteriously disappeared from western prehistory or gradually declined, leaving its mark on the later Gravettian groups of southern Spain, of Languedoc and Provence. Traces of its techniques also appear in one facies of the ancient Mag-

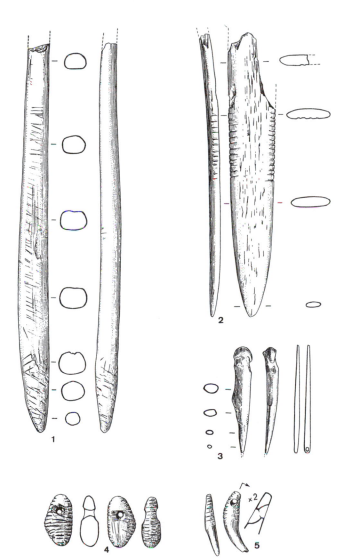

Figure 46 Bone and ivory Solutrean artefacts: 1, slender lower part of an incised bone lance-head; 2, notched smoothing bone plane; 3, bodkin and eyed bone needle; 4, incised ivory pendant; 5, notched and perforated fox tooth. (After P. Smith.)

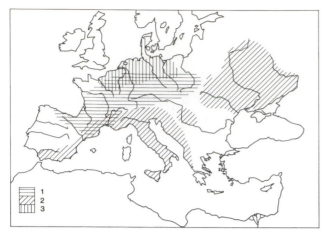

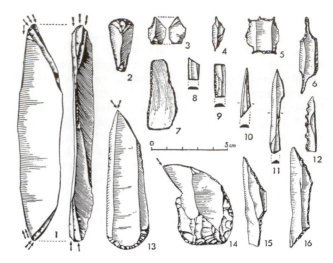

Map 17 Europe during the Late Palaeolithic, from about 17,000 to 12,000 years ago. Each region possesses its own group of hunters adapted to the different forms of environment. Areas at the southern and northern limits are covered episodically. 1, Magdalenian; 2, Late Gravettian; 3, northern groups with shouldered points.

dalenian culture (the Badegoulian). But its most important achievement was that it maintained a population substratum in the west during the period of most severe cold, and bequeathed its artistic techniques and all of the myths they illustrated to the later cultures of the Upper Palaeolithic.

THE MAGDALENIAN CULTURE (Map 17)

The Late Glacial period of approximately 18,000 to 8,000 years ago witnessed the growth of a culture that was particularly well adapted to the ecological conditions then prevailing over the greater part of the European continent. The Magdalenian culture apparently developed out of the Gravettian on to which what was left of the Solutrean had been grafted; it reached unparalleled heights of technical sophistication, introduced specialization into the organization of hunting and built complex settlements, and its many artistic achievements showed great refinement.

In the technical domain (Fig. 48) this period ushered in the production of microlithic projectile points which are perhaps related to the invention of the bow. There was also an increase in the number of composite tools made of different materials: bladelets whose backs were set into bone points which were in turn fitted into wooden shafts, and detachable harpoon-heads. For the first time, a machine, made up of two elements, was invented – the spear-thrower. This was a short shaft of antler with a lug at one end, which was swung to increase the force of the throw, on the same principle as a lever. A variety of spearheads were produced – slender points and points with a single or double bevelled base. Harpoon-heads with a single or double row of barbs were another technical landmark, apparently linked to particular hunting methods. The Magdalenian culture was the 'golden age' of bone tools, which were often decorated. A. Leroi-Gourhan distinguishes between objects used for long periods and those with a short life-span. The former (spear-throwers, perforated staffs, spatulas) bear representations of animals in the round or in high relief which may be related to the function of the object or may illustrate a myth (Plate 36). These representations include horses, ibexes in combat and compositions. The latter (spears, harpoons) bear a more

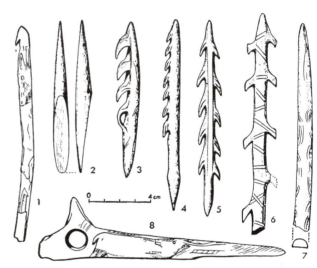

Figure 48 Stone and bone Magdalenian artefacts. Above – stone artefacts: 1, 14, burins; 2, 13, scrapers; 4–6, borers; 8–12, microlithic points; 15,16, straight-backed points. Below – bone artefacts: 1, thrower; 2, lance-head; 3–6, harpoons; 7, half-cylindrical wand; 8, decorated 'bâton de commandement'. (After D. de Sonneville-Bordes.)

schematic decoration linked to the function of the object or to the identity of the hunter.

Magdalenian culture, which very probably originated in the southern regions of France, expanded to cover a large area of central Europe during its early (17,000 to 16,000 years ago) and middle (16,000 to 14,000 years ago) stages. The site of Maszyska in Poland, dated to 14,500 years ago, illustrated the extremely extensive coverage of this new mode of cultural expression, even to the minute decorative motifs on bone objects. The identical culture also appears in Moravia (Pekarna), Thüringen (Nebra), in Bohemia (Hostim), in Austria, Germany, Belgium and Switzerland. But its period of greatest expansion in these regions was the later phase of its development (about 11,000 to 9,000 years ago).

In the southern part of Europe, Italy, which remained under the influence of Gravettian cultures, would only show indirect traces of Magdalenian culture. In Spain, on the other hand, it reached the height of its development.

The Magdalenians' nomadic way of life, following an annual cycle, was essentially governed by the movements of herd animals (reindeer, horses), and the settlements which they occupied for short periods are often well preserved. The tents and huts constructed each year provide a clear picture of the activities of the group during a particular period, whereas in long-term settlements the arrangements were modified in the course of occupation. When the natural deposits which have accumulated on top of these remains are light (brought by wind or gradual river action), the interpretation of their distribution after careful removal of the covering layer makes possible a substantial reconstruction of the pattern of life: light tent dwellings in Pincevent (near Paris) where domestic activities (slaughtering, tool-blank production, toolmaking) were clearly divided; felted cloth tents with vertical sides in Gönnersdorf in the Rhineland where the large number of decorated plaquettes seems to indicate a concentration of ritual activities.

In addition to decorating the mobile utilitarian objects mentioned above, Magdalenian artists produced animal and, more especially, female figurines made of stone and bone. The latter are very stylized and easily distinguishable from the adipose Gravettian shapes, merely representing silhouettes in profile with emphasis on the prominent buttocks.

The intensive development of cave art, which bears witness to the homogeneity of Magdalenian mythology and is often described in works on this period, is dealt with in Chapter 23.

NORTHERN GROUPS WITH SHOULDERED POINTS (Map 17)

During the temperate Bølling oscillation (about 13,500 to 12,000 years ago), Palaeolithic hunters reoccupied the great northern plain from which the glaciers had retreated. These populations were perfectly adapted to this tundra or cold steppe environment. Their highly specialized economy was based primarily on reindeer hunting. They either followed the animals' seasonal migratory movements or settled in places, such as fords, where they were bound to pass. These populations are estimated to have numbered several hundred families comprising some thousands of individuals who were divided into groups, each of which was about forty strong. Their settlements show signs of intermittent occupation in light structures, within which separate areas were used for the various activities.

The area occupied was very extensive, having been estimated at about 440,000 km², and including the plains of Poland, of north Germany, the Netherlands, Belgium, Britain and northern France. It thus overlapped with the area occupied by the Magdalenians in the later phase of their development, although the two cultures remain clearly separated from each other. Genetically these populations seem to have derived from the Magdalenians of central Europe (Poland, Thüringen) in their middle period, dated to the Dryas I cold oscillation. They may perhaps have reacted to pressure of population growth by adapting their technology and means of subsistence to the northern ecological zone, becoming specialized predators, developing an elaborate stone technology and leading a migratory existence. The main points of difference from the contemporary Magdalenian culture were the scarcity of their bone implements and the development of shouldered stone projectile points. This technique, which was very probably dictated by the method used to fix the tip to the haft, is applied not only to the actual weaponheads but also to different types of domestic utensil: knives, gravers and borers. For these last tools bits of a special type were developed

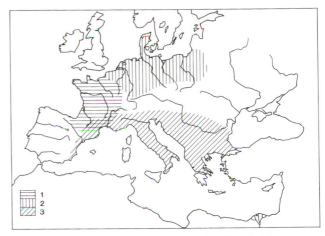

Map 18 Europe in the Late Glacial period (Allerød). Three principal cultural groups are distributed over the principal regions: 1, Azilian (in the west); 2, Federmesser cultures (in the north); 3, Epigravettian (in the south).

which were apparently suited to working reindeer antler. They each have bevelled cutting edges and are known by the German term *Zinken*.

In addition to the different stages of development of this culture, there were two main geographical groupings. These were the Creswellians in Belgium and Britain and the Hamburgians in Germany, Poland and the Netherlands (Fig. 49). Their expansion from the east to the western parts of the great plain is fairly clear during the Bølling interstadial. Towards the end of the latter, and even more markedly during the succeeding Dryas II cold period, these populations migrated southwards when the climate became more severe again. The resulting contacts with Magdalenian populations are reflected in the traces of acculturation observed in the stone implements. At the close of Dryas II, a new adaptation to the forest of the Allerød oscillation resulted in the formation of the 'Federmesser' group in the northern regions.

LATE GRAVETTIAN (Maps 16 and 17) AND EPIGRAVETTIAN (Maps 18 and 19)

Throughout the Late Glacial period and in continuity with earlier local cultures, a large part of Mediterranean and

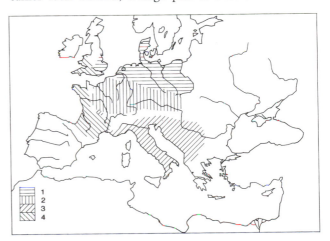

Map 19 The European Mesolithic. 1, Maglemosian (in northern Europe); 2, Beuronian (in central Europe); 3, Epigravettian (in the Mediterranean zone); 4, Sauveterrian (in western Europe).

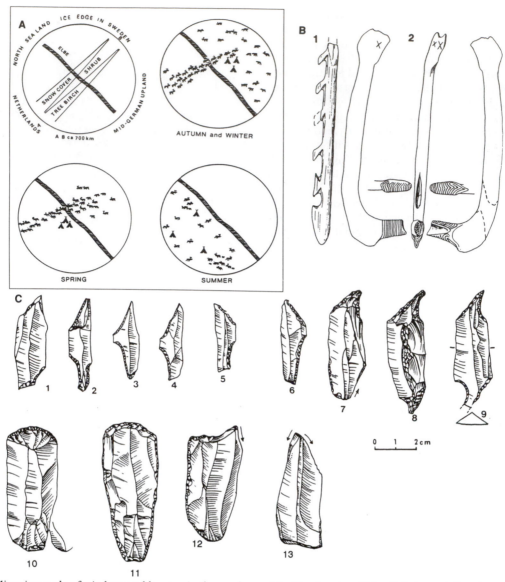

Figure 49 A, Migration cycle of reindeers and hunters in the northern plain, Hamburgian. (After Bokelmann.) B, 1, harpoon; 2, axe handle. C, 1–6, shouldered stone points; 7–9, *Zinken* and borers; 10, 11, scrapers; 12–13, burins. (After G. Clark.)

Balkan Europe kept alive Gravettian traditions. Toolmakers, who manufactured increasingly lightweight implements and replaced Palaeolithic blades with lamellar media, brought increased sophistication to light weaponheads by using the straight-backed technique. Different regional groups can be distinguished in Provence (Arenian, Bouverian), in Italy (Epigravettian), in Hungary (Sagvarian) and in the Balkan peninsula (in former Yugoslavia, Greece and Romania, Epigravettian or late Gravettian). Their economy was always varied and opportunistic, making the most of regional resources. Each of these groups led to a local early Mesolithic, and the evolutionary sequence followed and studied in the greatest detail to date is that of Italy. Here the early Epigravettian began with a leaf-shaped point phase (19,000 to 18,000 years ago), which was succeeded by a shouldered point phase (18,000 to 15,000 years ago). This, in turn, led to a final Epigravettian phase with many angular-backed pieces (from Dryas I to the Preboreal), tending to microliths: triangles, backed bladelets and points with curving backs or both sides blunted.

Traces of Magdalenian influence appear in the form of engraved plaquettes, with geometrical or figurative motifs, and a few engravings on cave walls, such as have been discovered in Addaura (Plate 37) and Levanzo. Animal themes occur again, but are here much more concerned with narrative scenes (dances and rituals), showing an interest in anecdote or a desire to portray the natural poses of the animals. Here, as elsewhere, the end of the Palaeolithic also signals the end of the artistic tradition of the Magdalenian hunters and art, losing its vigour, seems to perform a narrative rather than a religious function.

THE AZILIAN CULTURE (Map 18)

During the Allerød temperate oscillation (11,800 to 10,800 years ago) and then the Dryas III cold phase (10,800 to 10,200 years ago), changes took place in the western Magdalenian culture which gave birth to a new culture called the Azilian (after the Mas d'Azil in Ariège, in France) (Fig. 50). The dimensions of the stone industry were reduced and there were more microlithic projectile points. The most characteristic piece is a curved-backed point which was apparently used to tip arrows. Domestic implements, made from short blades, include a large

216

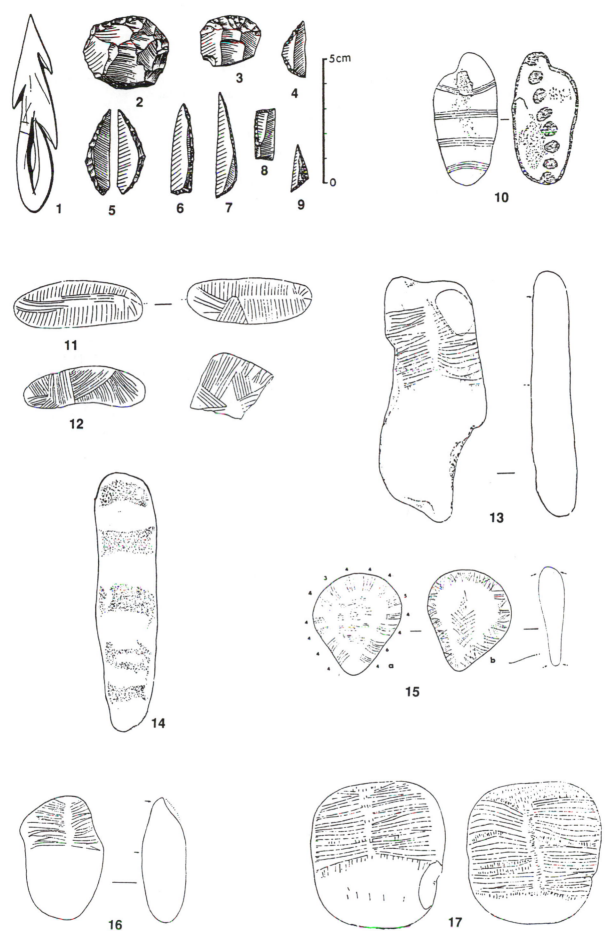

Figure 50 Azilian artefacts (France): 1, harpoon; 2, 3, scrapers; 4–9, points. (After D. de Sonneville-Bordes.) 10–17, pebbles, carved and painted with geometrical designs. (After A. Thevenin.)

number of small scrapers that are round or nail-shaped. This seems to have been linked to the new methods of hafting in wood, which enabled small pieces to be used and this business end of the tool to be easily replaced. A parallel link with the environment could explain the drastic diminution in the number of burins. The boneworking for which the latter tool was used lost ground to wood-working. All of this resulted from the changed climatic conditions of the Allerød period during which the hard-wood forest gradually replaced the cold steppe. Temperate species increased in number and included the red deer whose antlers were now used to make tools: broad, flat harpoons with perforated bases and not very protruding barbs.

In this widely scattered society, divided into different regional groups (the Pyrenees, Périgord, Rhône valley), long-distance links seem to have weakened. The almost complete disappearance of cave art was possibly a result of this. The impact of Palaeolithic religion seems to have changed and the cave 'sanctuaries' to have been superseded by open-air cult places. It was succeeded by a very degenerate mobiliary art: pebbles which were initially painted and later engraved can be found throughout the territory of the Azilians. Spots, transversals and zigzags were painted on the pebbles, while the engravings are mostly parallel lines arranged in one or two different patterns. Some kind of symbolism is clearly involved and careful statistical analysis reveals regularities in number and arrangement whose significance is still obscure. Were they used as cult objects or mnemonic devices?

This culture, which spread throughout France and a part of Spain, and was a logical sequel to the local Magdalenian, was still Palaeolithic in many ways (stone technology, means of subsistence). In its adaptation to the forest environment, development of light weaponheads and division of society into smaller groups, it also fore-shadowed, after the cold interval of Dryas III, the local forms of the Mesolithic.

THE NORTHERN GROUPS WITH CURVED-BACKED POINTS, THE *FEDERMESSER* (Map 18)

A comparable trend had begun in the cultural groups with shouldered points (Hamburgian, Creswellian) which inhabited the northern plains. The Allerød oscillation and the resulting economic changes led to the splitting of groups into small regional units. The more scattered settlements, which were less intensively occupied but more evenly distributed, have been the object of detailed research using reconstitution techniques (putting together pieces struck from a single core) and microscopic traces of utilization: Meer in Belgium and Calowine in Poland. They contain localities showing the distribution of the different activities which were successively carried out in the settlements: the production of flakes and antler tools, and the disposal area for worn out tools. Reconstruction of the blocks of raw material also indicates which pieces were in use at the same time and consequently, the existence of successive settlements on the same site.

These groups also appeared during the Allerød oscillation, stretching throughout the northern plains, from Britain to Poland. Everywhere, stone tools in general became smaller, and included short-end scrapers and transverse gravers. The characteristic weaponhead, a curved-backed point, gave its name to the entire group, Federmesser (penknives), which is geographically subdivided into a number of facies: Tjongerian in Belgium and the Netherlands (Fig. 51), Rissen and Wehlen in northern Germany. As with the Azilian culture, art objects are confined to a number of pebbles incised with transverse and parallel lines.

THE TANGED-POINT GROUPS OF THE NORTH

In the course of the last cold phase of the glaciation, Dryas III, a new group, which was apparently adapted to tundra conditions, made its appearance in northern Europe. The Ahrensburgians (named after Ahrensburg in northern Germany) (Fig. 52) concentrated on hunting the reindeer, which had extended its territory once again, and developed very light stone tools often made from bladelets. These narrow blanks (less than 12 mm) were used to make microlithic weaponheads, thus leading to their identification as Mesolithic by certain authors. This view was reinforced by some wooden arrowshafts discovered in Stellmoor (Germany) which still had their arrowheads attached. The main weaponhead consisted of a point opposite a short tang: the 'Ahrensburg point'. This culture, which was restricted to Dryas III and spread from northern Germany to Belgium, seems to have given rise to a form of local Mesolithic during the Preboreal. The repertoire of bone implements, on the other hand, is more reminiscent of the Palaeolithic, the harpoons having one or two rows of barbs made of antler and bulging bases around which the thong could be attached.

These different groups apparently migrated southwards and, as they were better adapted to the economy of the tundra, supplanted the Federmesser groups in some southern areas. Different territorial entities have been distinguished within the 'tanged-point cultures': Ahrensburgian in northern Germany and the Benelux countries, Brommian in Denmark and Swiderian in Poland.

In the latter country, a detailed study of the area of distribution of a given stone material has demonstrated the growth of social relations between the different tanged-point population groups during Dryas III. This distribution, which varied according to the product concerned (unworked blocks or finished tools), differed sharply from the method of distribution used during the Allerød among the Federmesser groups (distribution over shorter distances) and distribution arrangements during the Preboreal ('relaying' through intermediary sites).

THE EARLY AND MIDDLE MESOLITHIC (Map 19)

In most of the European regions, the different regional groups of the Late Palaeolithic underwent profound changes either during Dryas III or during the Preboreal (ten millennia ago). The marked reduction in the range of stone tools and the transition from blade technology to one based on the manufacture of small blades that were used as blanks reflect more fundamental socio-economic changes (Fig. 53). The now definitively established forest environment in central Europe led to the adjustment of hunting weaponry. The bow and arrow came into general use, being more effective than the spear in this type of environment, where animals were more mobile and widely dispersed than those of the steppe: the stag, roe-deer and wild boar. Although popu-

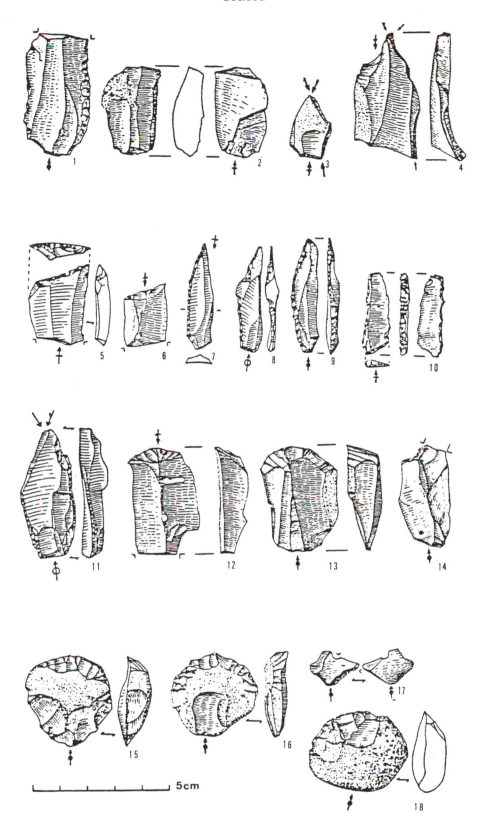

Figure 51 Tjongerian stone industry (*Federmesser* culture) (Belgium), Meer IV, according to M. Otte: 1, 2, retouched blades; 3, 4, 11, burins; 5, 6, truncated blades; 7–10, backed points; 12, 13, 15, 16, 18, scrapers.

lation density was stable, if not higher, it seems that settlements were more widely spread than in the Palaeolithic, that food resources were more diverse (gathering, fishing) and that the social groups were smaller.

In the Mediterranean the Late Gravettian evolved into the Epigravettian with straight-backed bladelets and geometric projectile points (triangle and segments). In western Europe the Azilian gave rise to the Sauveterrian with points whose two edges were curved and blunted and also to the development of geometric forms. Central Europe then witnessed the rise of the Beuronian (Early Tardenoisian) in which, alongside geometric forms (scalene triangles, segments), appeared triangular asymmetrical points with trimmed bases ('Tardenois points').

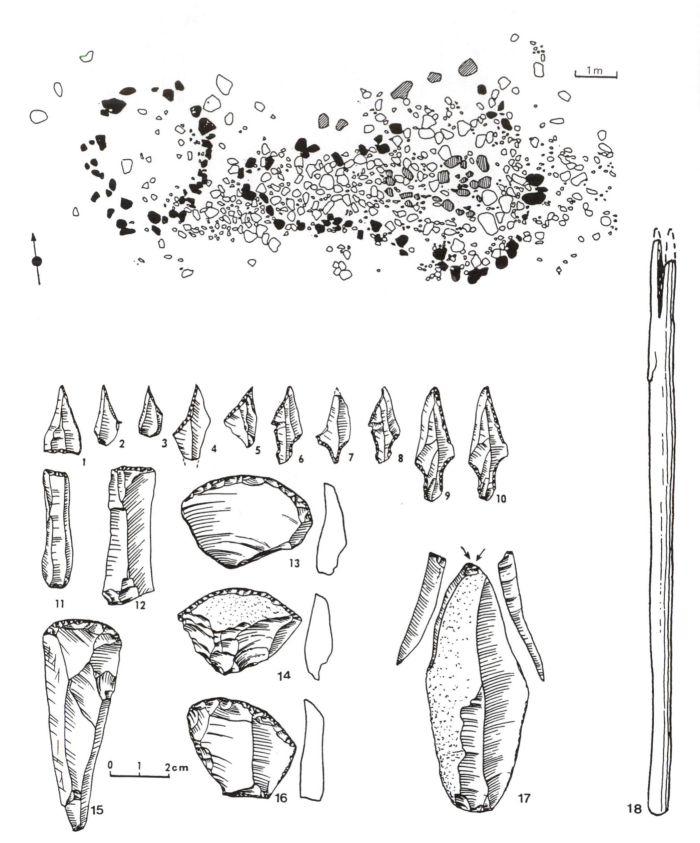

Figure 52 Ahrensburgian culture (Germany). Above – plan of tent habitation: the black stones indicate the limits of the partitions; the slanted hatching represents weights for runners; the vertical hatching represents firestones. Below – 1–10, points; 11–16, scrapers; 17, burin; 18, wooden shaft with slit for stone point. (After A. Rust.)

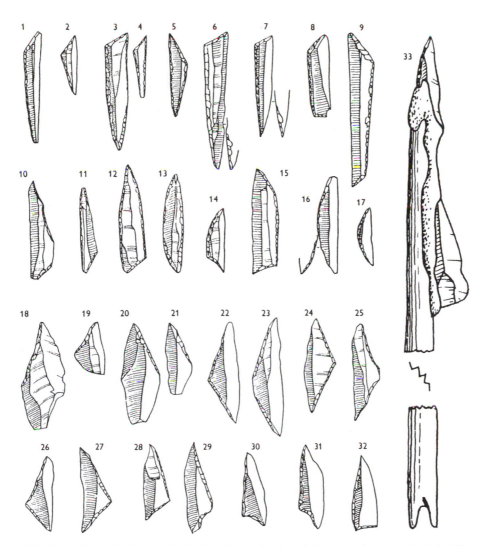

Figure 53 Early Mesolithic (Boreal period). Geometrically shaped arrowheads and sideprongs for arrow shafts held by resin on a pine stem. (After G. Clark.)

In northern Europe (southern Scandinavia and Britain) the Maglemosian, which was derived from the Ahrensburgian, made its appearance, as did the Duvensee and Komornica groups in north-central Europe.

The northern groups (Figs 54 and 55), which are well known thanks to the discoveries made in peatbogs, left behind, in addition to distinctive stone tools (hatchets and sculpted picks), large numbers of objects made of organic material: barbed points, axes, bone or antler chisels, canoes, nets and snares made of plant fibres. These regions also yield the rare works of art of the period (Fig. 56): in the Baltic, amber animal figures are found covered with fine geometric incisions, also schematic human representations and even some wall engravings (Chapter 23).

The characteristic common to all these groups is the use of the 'micro-burin' weaponhead manufacturing process whereby bladelets were snapped off from larger blades at the point where a notch had been made and finished by steep retouch.

In the domain of religion, there was a continuation of the Palaeolithic tradition of individual burial with funerary items: dusting with red ochre, pendants, bone or stone tools.

THE LATE MESOLITHIC

Between eight and seven millennia ago the form of the weaponheads used by the Mesolithic groups and the ways in which they were manufactured underwent fresh changes. The bladelets, obtained by pressure flaking, were more regular, with parallel edges and straight outlines. They were thus particularly well suited to the manufacture of the trapezoidal projectile points whose many and varied types are used to characterize the individual regional groups: Castelnovian in the south, Montbanian in the central regions, and Ertebølle-Ellerbek in Scandinavia and in northern Germany.

During this period, the first signs of a new era were beginning to appear, in different forms in south and central Europe. In the Mediterranean region the first domesticated species (sheep and goats) appeared and settlements were now becoming sedentary, possibly in response to population pressure.

On the Atlantic coasts (Hoëdic, Téviec) there were true villages and the tombs were grouped together in necropolises. The worship of skulls, which were all buried

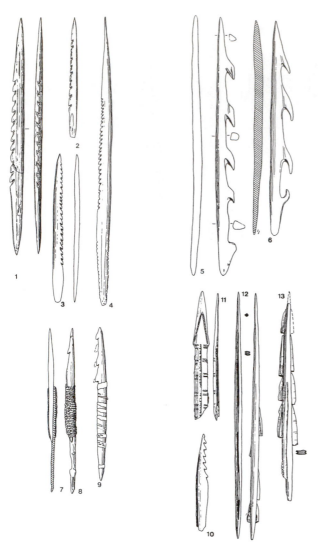

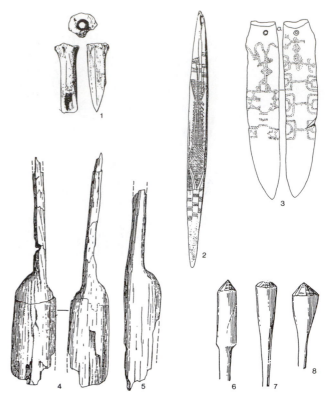

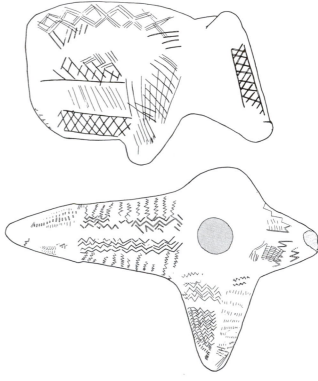

Figure 55 Bone and wood Mesolithic artefacts, Scandinavia: 1, bone chisel; 2, 3, spatula and knives decorated with geometrical designs; 4, 5, paddles; 6–8, wooden arrowheads for hunting birds. (After G. Clark.)

Figure 54 Bone and stag-horn points, northern Mesolithic: 1–4, barbed points; 5, 6, harpoon heads; 7, 8, 9, barbed points held in a hazel tree shaft; 10, with traces of resin; 11–13, bone points with flint bladelets inserted in grooves. (After G. Clark.)

together, as in Ofnet in Bavaria and among the Natufians of western Asia, seems to indicate a desire to mark the fixed nature of the settlement by emphasizing the hereditary occupation of the land.

This fixed nature of settlement and population pressure are even more marked in Scandinavia, where the coastal villages show a perfect adaptation to a mixed economy based on exploitation of the marine and forest environments; pottery-making techniques were soon acquired, probably through acculturation.

In Serbia large groups established a village on the banks of the Danube that was clearly sedentary. A house, discovered on this site, trapezoidal in design and with stone foundations, contained or was surrounded by tombs. This site of Lepenski Vir has also yielded impressive Mesolithic sculptures which are simply egg-shaped blocks on which are engraved facial features accompanied by geometric motifs (meanders, herring-bone patterns).

Figure 56 Mesolithic art, northern Europe: engraved amber animal figurine, finely carved soft stone axe. (After A. Marshack.)

The pace of change was more rapid in central Europe, however: the Bandkeramik culture, which began in the Balkans where the eastern Neolithic had been introduced, spread throughout the region as far as the Paris basin and Belgium, bringing with it, via migrating populations, a new means of subsistence based on food production (agriculture and animal husbandry). In these regions the advanced Mesolithic groups settled areas unfit for agriculture (dense forests on infertile land), with the result that peaceful contacts were established between the two populations and exchanges of technical skills could take place. Within the space of some millennia, the greater part of Europe had been 'accultured'; in other words it had adopted the new Neolithic economy, although in the very north of Europe, now liberated from the Scandinavian glaciers, the traditions of the hunting, fishing and food-gathering peoples survived for many centuries more (Fosna culture).

BIBLIOGRAPHY

BAILEY, G. (ed.) 1983. *Hunter-Gatherer Economy in Prehistory: A European perspective.* Cambridge.

BARTA, J. 1974. Kniektorym Historicko-Spolovenskym otazkam peleolituna Slovensku [On Historical-Sociological Problems of the Slovakian Palaeolithic]. *Slov. Archaeol.* (Bratislava), Vol. 22, pp. 9–32.

BORDES, F. 1968. *Le Paléolithique dans le Monde.* Paris.

—— (ed.) 1968. *La Préhistoire: problèmes et tendances.* Paris, CNRS.

BOSINSKI, G. (ed.) 1968–80. *Der Magdalenien-Fundplatz Gönnersdorf.* Wiesbaden. 5 vols.

BREZILLON, M. 1969. *Dictionnaire de la préhistoire.* Paris.

CAMPBELL, J. B. 1977. *The Upper Palaeolithic of Britain: A Study of Man and Nature in the Late Ice Age.* Oxford. 2 vols.

CESNOLA, A. PALMA DI (ed.) 1983. *La Position taxonomique et chronologique des industries à pointes à dos autour de la Méditerranée européenne.* Siena. (Colloque International de l'UISPP, Siena.)

CLARK, G. 1975. *The Earlier Stone Age Settlement of Scandinavia.* Cambridge.

—— 1977. *World Prehistory in New Perspective.* 3rd edn. Cambridge.

COLLOQUE INTERNATIONAL EN HOMMAGE AU PROFESSEUR ANDRÉ LEROI-GOURHAN. 1982. *Actes.* Roanne-Villerest. (Offprints.)

COMBIER, J. 1967. *Le Paléolithique de l'Ardèche dans son cadre paléoclimatique.* Bordeaux.

DE LAET, S. J. 1982. *La Belgique d'avant les Romains.* Wetteren.

DELPECH, F. 1983. *Les Faunes du Paléolithique supérieur dans le sudouest de la France.* Paris, CNRS. (Cah. Quat., 6.)

DELPORTE, H. 1979. *L'Image de la femme dans l'art préhistorique.* Paris.

ESCALON DE FONTON, M. 1966. Du Paléolithique supérieur au Mésolithique dans le Midi méditerranéen. *Bull. Soc. préhist. fr.,* Vol. 63, pp. 66–180.

FAGAN, B. M. 1970. *Introductory Readings in Archaeology.* Boston.

FORTEA PEREZ, J. 1973. *Los complejos microlaminares y geométricos del Epi-paleolítico mediterráneo español.* Salamanca.

FULLOLA I PERICOT, J. 1979. *Las industrias líticas del paleolítico superior ibérico.* Valencia.

GABORI, M.; GABORI, V. 1957. Études archéologiques et stratigraphiques dans les stations de loess paléolithiques de Hongrie. *Acta Archaeol. Acad. Sci. Hung.* (Budapest), Vol. 8, pp. 3–117.

GINTER, B. 1974. Wydobywanie, Przerworstwo i dystrykucja surowcow i wyrobow krzemiennych w schylkowym peleolicie polnocne czesci Europy srodkomej [The Extraction, Production and Distribution of Raw Material and Flint Products during the Late Palaeolithic in the Northern Part of Central Europe]. *Pr. Archeol.* (Poznań), Vol. 22, pp. 5–122.

GOB, A. 1981. *Le Mésolithique dans le bassin de l'Ourthe.* Liège.

HAESAERTS, P.; HEINZELIN, J. 1979. *Le Site paléolithique de Maisières-Canal.* Bruges.

HAHN, J. 1977. *Aurignacien: das ältere Jungpaläolithikum in Mittel- und Ost-Europa.* Cologne.

HASSAN, F. 1981. *Demographic Archaeology.* New York.

HOURS, F. 1982. *Les Civilisations du paléolithique.* Paris.

JULIEN, M. 1982. *Les Harpons magdaléniens.* Paris.

KLIMA, B. 1963. *Dolní Věstonice, Vyzkum taboriste lovcu mamutu v leteca 1947–1952* [Dolní Vestonice, Field Research into a Mammoth Hunting Place during 1947–1952]. Prague.

—— 1966. Le Peuplement paléolithique de la Tchécoslovaquie et sa chronologie. *Investigations archéologiques en Tchécoslovaquie,* Prague, pp. 11–20.

KOZLOWSKI, J. K. 1965. Studia nad zroznicowaniem Kulturowym w paleolicie gornym Europy srodkowej [Studies on the Cultural Differentiation in the Upper Palaeolithic of Central Europe]. *Pr. Archeol.,* Vol. 17.

—— 1969. Les Problèmes de la géochronologie du Paléolithique supérieur en Pologne. *Quaternaria,* Vol. 11, pp. 197–213.

—— 1976. Les Industries à pointes à cran en Europe Centre-Est. In: CONGRÈS UISPP, 9, Nice. *Colloque XV, Périgordien et Gravettien en Europe.* pp. 121–7.

KOZLOWSKI, J. K.; KOZLOWSKI, S. K. 1977. *Epoke Kamiena na ziemiach Polskich* [The Stone Age in Poland]. Warsaw.

—— 1979. *Upper Palaeolithic and Mesolithic in Europe: Taxonomy and Palaeohistory.* Warsaw.

—— 1981. *Préhistoire de la grande plaine de l'Europe.* Cracow.

KOZLOWSKI, S. K. (ed.) 1973. *The Mesolithic in Europe.* Warsaw.

—— 1975. *Cultural Differentiation of Europe from 10th to 5th Millennium BC.* Warsaw.

—— 1980. *Atlas of the Mesolithic in Europe.* Warsaw.

LAVILLE, H. 1973. *Climatologie et chronologie du paléolithique en Périgord: étude sédimentologique des dépôts en grottes et sous abris.* Bordeaux. 3 vols.

LEROI-GOURHAN, A. 1964. *Les Religions de la préhistoire.* Paris.

—— 1965. *Préhistoire de l'art occidental.* Paris.

LEROI-GOURHAN, A.; BREZILLON, M. 1972. *Fouilles de Pincevent. Essai d'analyse ethnographique d'un habitat magdalénien.* Paris, CNRS.

LEROI-GOURHAN, A. et al. 1968. *La Préhistoire.* Paris.

LUMLEY, H. DE. 1969. *La France anonyme au temps des mammouths.* Paris.

—— (ed.) 1976. *La Préhistoire française.* Vol. I: *Les Civilisations paléolithiques et mésolithiques de la France.* Paris, CNRS. 2 vols.

MARSHACK, A. 1972. *Les Racines de la civilisation.* Paris.

MOVIUS, H. L. 1975. *Excavations of the Abri Pataud, Les Eyzies (Dordogne).* Cambridge, Mass.

NOTEN, F. VAN. 1978. *Les Chasseurs de Meer.* Bruges. 2 vols.

ONORATINI, G. 1982. *Préhistoire, sédiments, climats du Würm III à l'Holocène dans le Sud-Est de la France.* Aix/Marseille. 2 vols.

OTTE, M. 1979. *Le Paléolithique supérieur ancien en Belgique.* Brussels.

—— 1981. *Le Gravettien en Europe centrale.* Bruges. 2 vols.

PALMER, S. 1977. *Mesolithic cultures of Britain.* London.

RÉUNION DE LA 10e COMMISSION DE L'UISPP, Nice, 1976. *Actes.* Liège, 1984.

—— Cracovie-Nitra 1980. *Actes.* Liège, 1982.

—— Mexico 1981. *Actes.* Liège, 1982.

ROZOY, J. G. 1978. *Les Derniers chasseurs, l'Epipaléolithique en France et en Belgique: essai de synthèse.* Charleville. 2 vols.

SCHILD, R. 1976. The Final Palaeolithic Settlements of the European Plain. *Sci. Am.,* Vol. 234, No. 2.

SCHMIDER, B. 1971. *Les Industries lithiques du Paléolithique supérieur en Île-de-France.* Paris.

SCHWABEDISSEN, H. 1954. *Die Federmesser-Gruppen der nordwest-europäischen Flachlandes.* Neumünster.

SKLENAR, K. 1976. Palaeolithic and Mesolithic Dwellings: An Essay in Classification. *Pamat. Archeol.* (Prague), Vol. 67.

SMITH, P. 1966. *Le Solutréen en France.* Bordeaux.

SONNEVILLE-BORDES, D. DE. 1960. *Le Paléolithique supérieur en Périgord.* Bordeaux. 2 vols.

—— 1966. L'Évolution du Paléolithique supérieur en Europe et sa signification. *Bull. Soc. préhist. fr. Etud. Trav.* (Paris), Vol. 63, pp. 3–34.

—— 1972. *La Préhistoire moderne: l'âge de la pierre taillée.* 2nd edn. Périgueux.

—— 1973. The Upper Palaeolithic (*c.*33,000–10,000 BC). In: PIGGOTT, S.; DANIEL, G.; MCBURNEY, C. (eds), *France before the Romans.* London. pp. 30–60.

—— (ed.) 1979. *La Fin des temps glaciaires en Europe: chrono-stratigraphie et écologie des cultures du Paléolithique final.* Paris. 2 vols. (Colloques du CNRS, 271.)

—— 1984. *Art et civilisations des chasseurs de la préhistoire (34.000–8.000 ans av. J.-C.).* Paris.

STRAUSS, L.; CLARK, G. 1983. *Late Pleistocene Hunter-Gatherer Adaptation in Cantabrian Spain.* Cambridge.

TAUTE, W. 1968. *Die Stielspitzen-Gruppen in nördlichen Mitteleuropa.* Cologne.

TESTART, A. 1982. *Les Chasseurs cueilleurs ou l'origine des inégalités.* Paris.

TRINKAUS, E. (ed.) 1983. *The Mousterian Legacy: Human Biocultural Change in the Upper Pleistocene.* Oxford. (BAR Int. Ser., 164.)

VALOCH, K. 1967. La Subdivision du Pléistocène récent et l'apparition du Paléolithique supérieur en Europe centrale. *Bull. Assoc. Fr. Etud. Quat.* (Paris), Vol. 4, pp. 263–9.

22

THE TERRITORY OF THE FORMER USSR

during the Upper Palaeolithic

Valeriy P. Alexeev

In the latest survey of Upper Palaeolithic remains in the European part of the former USSR (Rogachev and Anikovich, 1984) the beginning of the Upper Palaeolithic in that region is set at 40,000 to 42,000 years ago. Clearly this is an exaggeration: the actual dates of the layers containing Upper Palaeolithic industries go back no further than 36,000 to 37,000 years. A number of sites in the Caucasus with late Mousterian industries are of similar age. This means that on the territory of the former USSR, as in many parts of western Europe, some late forms of Mousterian industry were contemporaneous with early forms of Upper Palaeolithic techniques. The number of Upper Palaeolithic sites discovered is fairly high – over a thousand – but, like the Mousterian sites, they are distributed very unevenly. Most of them are concentrated in the southern areas of the European part of the former USSR and in the Caucasus (especially the western Caucasus). In central Asia there are very few sites, while in Siberia and the Far East they are to be found chiefly in the south, particularly in the Yenisei and Angara basins. Few Upper Palaeolithic sites have been discovered in the Amur basin. Special locations are the basin of the Aldan, a right-bank tributary of the Lena, where several sites have been found, and a single site in the centre of the Kamchatka.

Discoveries of human remains dating to the Upper Palaeolithic on the territory of the former USSR are even more sparse than are Upper Palaeolithic sites. They have been listed several times (Debetz, 1948; Vallois and Morins, 1952; Oakley, et al., 1975). Many of them are in such poor condition that either they are completely unsuitable for taxonomic diagnosis, or they allow us to say with certainty only that they belong to modern humans. We shall mention only those finds whose morphological completeness allows us to discuss early racial differentiation in the territory of the former USSR.

The westernmost group of finds are graves that were discovered near the villages of Kostenki and Borshevo on the Don. These contained the remains of two adults and two children. The chronological relationship between the two burial sites is unclear because, although the sites are close together, they have very complex stratigraphy, which is the object of constant debate (*Paleolit...*, 1982). The adult skeletons were found at the sites of Kostenki II and Kostenki XIV (Markina Gora). The skull from Kostenki II, which was masterfully reconstructed by M. M. Gerasimov, belongs to an elderly man (Debetz, 1955). The low, broad face with its very prominent nose and the elongated form of the cranium show the skull's similarity to the most typical morphological variant of the Upper Palaeolithic population of Europe, the classic example of which is the Cro-Magnon III skull. The similarity is evident also from Gerasimov's reconstruction of the face from the skull (1964).

More questions – which have still not been finally answered – were raised by the find of a skeleton, almost perfectly preserved, in the cultural layer of Kostenki XIV site (Debetz, 1955). The skull is so small and the skeleton so slender that only the indisputably male form of the pelvis establishes the sex as male. The exceptional prognathism and enormous breadth of the piriform opening set the skull apart from all the other Upper Palaeolithic skulls of Europe and call to mind the craniological traits of the Negroid race.

The reconstruction of the face from the skull, published in the atlas of Gerasimov (1964), is highly reminiscent of the modern Papuan, and G. F. Debetz, assessing the morphological type of human from the Kostenki XIV site, considered it to be evidence of the appearance of some group of people of East African origin on the eastern European plain. This conclusion became part of the archaeological literature and is quoted without any critical commentary (Rogachev and Anikovich, 1984).

In morphological terms, however, such is by no means self-evident: the skull from Kostenki XIV has very prominent nasal bones, while in Negroid peoples the nose is not at all prominent. It was for that reason that Debetz's diagnosis was immediately refuted in the anthropological literature (Roginski and Levin, 1963): it was demonstrated that the combination of such opposing traits as prognathism and a markedly broad and prominent nose were evidence rather that the races were not differentiated at that early stage. There is no need, in this case, to speak of a migration of people from East Africa to the eastern European plain.

The children's skulls are from the burial site of Kostenki XV (the Gorodtsovskaya site) and Kostenki XVIII (Pokrovski gully). Both skulls were discovered in fragments and have been heavily restored. One was described by V. P. Yakimov (1957) and the other by Debetz (1961). Given the poor state of preservation of the facial skeleton, Yakimov was compelled to base his taxonomy on the shape of the cranium. Going by the very elongated form of the cranium, he suggested that the skull had belonged to a child (of about 6 years of age) who was similar to the people of Předmosti (former Czechoslovakia), whom many specialists held to be an eastern Cro-Magnon group within the Upper Palaeolithic population. Considering that the find consists of a single item, and that the cranial index increases with age (and the basis for Yakimov's conclusion was precisely the very low cranial index), this thesis seems rather hypothetical. The state of preservation of the find is such that precise taxonomic diagnosis is impossible.

The skull from Kostenki XVIII belonged to a child of 9 to 11 years. It is better preserved, and its basic dimensions have been ascertained. Both the dimensions and the proportions suggest very strongly that the child belonged to the morphological type that predominated in the Upper Palaeolithic population of Europe. Extrapolation of 'adult' measurements using a scale showing changes in the dimensions of Modern humans (*Homo sapiens sapiens*) confirms this conclusion (Alexeev, 1978, 1981).

The second local group of Upper Palaeolithic graves that provided palaeoanthropological material was discovered at the site of Sungir on the Klyazma, a tributary of the upper Volga. This was evidently a burial ground, since a number of graves had been destroyed by quarrying before the excavation began (Fig. 45). The stratigraphy and topographical interrelations of separate burial pits are rather complex, but it is likely that what was excavated was only two graves, which contained five bodies between them (Bader, 1978). Three of them are well preserved and suitable for in-depth anthropological analysis. The skeleton of the adult male was first described by Debetz (1967). Its great height, the very broad shoulders and massive bones show that the Sungir man is similar to the people of the Grimaldi cave (Italy). The skull, too, is massive, distinguished by a very large face that is exceptional in height as well as breadth, which is not characteristic of European Upper Palaeolithic human remains. Going by this feature, and by a certain flatness in the facial skeleton, Debetz endorsed the idea that Mongoloids moved westward at an early stage, and did not discount the possibility that ancient Mongoloids had contributed to the anthropological composition of the people buried at the Sungir site. However, Gerasimov's reconstruction of the face from the skull shows a completely European cast of features without a trace of the Mongoloid. We need consider only the morphology of the skull to see that it would be difficult to detect the presence of such a trace. The great height of the facial skeleton may be an individual variation, and the skulls of Combe-Capelle (France) and Předmosti III (former Czechoslovakia) have a similar facial height. The variation in the horizontal profile of the face, too, is not unusual in the Upper Palaeolithic series, and the skull from Oberkassel (Germany) has a flatter facial skeleton. It seems, therefore, that V. V. Bunak (1973) was closer to the truth in considering that the Sungir man showed an aggregate of features that typified one of the local populations of the Upper Palaeolithic denizens of Europe, finding no evidence of a specific tendency towards the morphological combinations of one of several modern races. A special study of the Sungir skeleton by E. N. Khrisanfova (1980) tells us much about the details of the physical structure of Upper Palaeolithic humans, although in general terms it simply confirms the earlier deduction as to the massive and athletic build of its owner.

The two well-preserved skulls of children were described later. They were reconstructed by G. V. Lebedinskaya (1984). The boy had died at the age of 12 to 13, and the girl at 7 to 8. In these cases the sex was determined not from the skull (a method which is not precise at that stage of development) but from the inventory in the graves. The boy's skull showed some alveolar prognathism, while the girl's did not, which points to an individual peculiarity. The aggregate of features repeats by and large, without serious modification, the combination that characterizes an adult skull. One should, of course, extrapolate the 'adult' dimensions from the children's skulls with the aid of a scale showing the increase in dimensions for Modern humans: it should then be possible to confirm the general impression of typological uniformity in the population by comparison of statistics.

What general conclusion may be drawn from consideration of the morphological characteristics of the Upper Palaeolithic population of eastern Europe? Although as yet very few bone remains of Upper Palaeolithic people have been discovered, it is clear that they did not tend to resemble any specific Modern race. Closest of all to the Caucasians, the populations of the Upper Palaeolithic in the eastern European plain differed from them in the same way as did the Upper Palaeolithic populations of western Europe. At the same time each population or local group differed from the next, but these differences had not yet become established as definite racial complexes. V. V. Bunak (1959) calls this phenomenon 'craniological polymorphism' and considers it typical of the inchoation of races that occurred in the Upper Palaeolithic era.

Such is the sum of more or less fully preserved palaeoanthropological finds. In the interests of completeness we should mention two other sites that provided definable fragments. One is the Samarkand site in central Asia, within the city of Samarkand. It contained two adult lower jaws – one of a man, the other of a woman, which have been described by V. V. Ginzburg and I. I. Gokhman (1974). On the basis of certain morphological details the scholars likened the Samarkand fragments to finds in former Czechoslovakia – those on whose basis many specialists defined the eastern Cro-Magnon variant in the Upper Palaeolithic population of western Europe. In theory such a juxtaposition does not seem to be totally unjustified, although the morphological evidence in its favour does not weigh heavily, since racial features are not clearly expressed in the lower jaw.

The other site is Afontova Gora near the city of Krasnoyarsk on the Yenisei. During excavation of a section of this site in 1937 participants in the Seventeenth International Geological Congress discovered a fragment of a child's skull in the Upper Palaeolithic cultural layer; fortunately it was a piece of the frontal bone around the glabella, with fragments of the nasal bones attached. The flatness of the glabella is an important feature that differentiates modern Caucasians from Mongoloids. Remarking on the flatness of this part of the fragment, Debetz (1946) demonstrated that the fragment had belonged to a Mongoloid. The Afontova fragment is significant in that it shows that, while the Caucasian complex of features in the Upper Palaeolithic population of eastern Europe took shape, as we have seen, in morphological forms dissimilar to those of contemporary Caucasians, such a fundamental distinctive feature of the modern representatives of the Mongoloid races as the flat glabella had already formed during the Upper Palaeolithic in northern Asia.

Given the quantity and typological diversity of these sites it is impossible to characterize each of them and dwell on individual sites. The only feasible way of describing them is

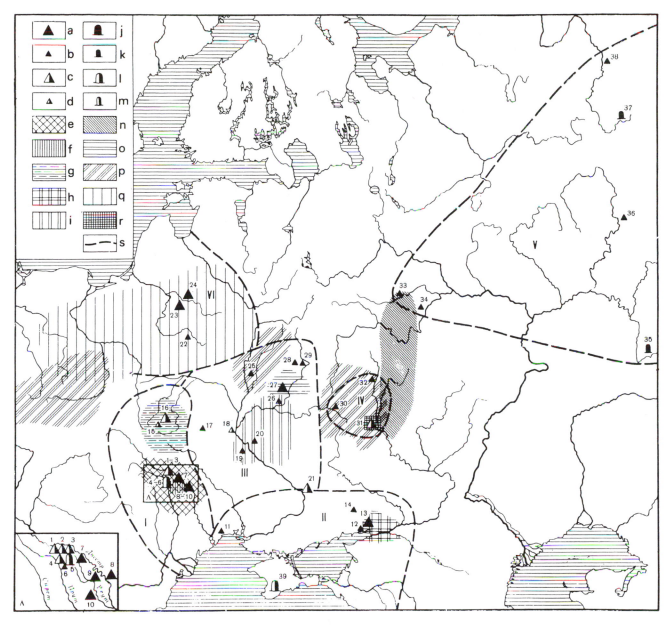

Map 20 Distribution of the principal groups of Upper Palaeolithic sites over the territory of the eastern European plain and in Crimea. I, South-western region: A, Region of the Dniester and the Prut. II, South-eastern region. III, Dnieper basin. IV, Middle Don region. V, North-eastern region. VI, North-western region. a, Group of open-air sites; b, isolated open-air sites; c, group of open-air sites with numerous horizons; d, isolated open-air sites with numerous horizons; e, Molodova culture; f, Brynzeni culture; g, Lipa culture; h, Kamennaya-Balka culture; i, Mezin and Mezhirich–Dobranichevka culture; j, group of cave sites; k, isolated cave sites; l, group of cave sites with numerous horizons; m, isolated cave sites with numerous horizons; n, Streletsko–Sungir culture; o, Pushkari culture; p, Willendorf–Kostenki culture; q, Swiderian culture; r, cultures found only in the Kostenki–Borshevo region; s, approximate regions of zones I–VI. (The numbers refer to a list of sites which is not available.) (After Rogachev and Anikovich, 1984.)

to outline the basic local tool inventories, going beyond particulars in an attempt to form some cultural and historical generalizations about them. The most recent classification and the richest in terms of material classified is by A. N. Rogachev and M. V. Anikovich (1984). It has been expressed in graphic form on Map 20. The classification is in several stages and on two levels: the authors begin by isolating areas of individual development of Upper Palaeolithic culture in eastern Europe, and go on to identify within each area the archaeological cultures in the narrow sense of the word. Sometimes it happens that one culture or another is represented not in one but in two neighbouring regions. Six areas have been identified: south-west, south-east (the steppe), the Dnieper area, the upper Don basin, north-east and north-west. Both this list and the map show that, in

spite of the vast scope of research operations, there are enormous expanses within which not one site has been discovered. This is true not only of east and north, but also of many central regions. Thus the following enumeration of what are called cultures, groups of sites with very similar or even nearly identical inventories – an indication of common origin and technology – must be understood as only a preliminary approach to the real situation.

Rogachev and Anikovich, who have synthesized the previous studies of separate local groups of sites, identify ten cultures with very different areas of diffusion: from huge areas covering, to take one example, the south of the eastern Baltic coast, the regions on the south of the Baltic Sea and also the middle Dnieper basin, to tiny micro-regions comprising single sites. It is quite obvious that similarity of inventory, when applied to sites in areas of such greatly differing size, is not always of the same order, and that all the cultures identified are groups at different hierarchical levels, which demonstrates once again the preliminary and highly relative nature of the entire classification. The ten cultures are as follows: Molodova, Brynzeny, Lipa, Kamennaya-Balka, Mezin and Mezhirich-Dobranichevka (a culture which includes well-known sites with a number of distinctive features), Streletsko–Sungir, Pushkari, Willendorf–Kostenki and Sviderian, a group of what we might call microcultures, characterized by one or two sites within the Kostenki locus of the Willendorf–Kostenki culture. It should be borne in mind that the cultures are named not in any consistent order, but after the area or the nearest settlement.

The south-western region incorporates three cultures: Brynzeny, Molodova and Lipa, all of which are named after typical sites. The Brynzeny culture covers a tiny area in the middle reaches of the Dniester, and yet it is represented by several sites. The distinctive feature of the inventory of these sites is the survival of Mousterian forms among typically Upper Palaeolithic forms; there is a wealth of blades and burins, of various sizes. Many authors have sought analogies to this collection of forms in the central regions of eastern Europe, and in the west, in the territory of central Europe and even western Europe, but it would seem that U. A. Borziyak (1978), a student of the sites of this culture, was nearer the truth in suggesting analogies with the Mousterian culture of that area and surrounding areas.

The principal site of the Molodova culture is that same many-layered site of Molodova V whose deeper layers served in the description of the Mousterian culture of the Dniester area. Its upper layers provided large amounts of Upper Palaeolithic material (Chernysh, 1959, 1973). Blades larger than those usually found in Upper Palaeolithic sites in the eastern European plain are a typical feature of the Upper Palaeolithic culture of Molodova. A large number of burins of various kinds were also discovered. Microlithic blades were discovered too, but in small quantities. There was an interesting profusion of bone implements. The tools were made of mammoth tusk and reindeer antler. There were also what are referred to as *bâtons de commandement*, antler axes of the Lyngby type, points and punches. One composite tool was found: a mammoth rib with a slot to receive flint inserts – a composite knife. The presence of a bone industry relates the Molodova culture sites to many central European and western European sites. The more general question of the origin of this culture, which is much more widespread than the Brynzeny culture, has not yet been satisfactorily answered in the literature. It is, in any event, sufficiently distinct from the Mousterian remains of that same area not to be derived totally from the Mousterian.

The Lipa archaeological culture was named after the village of Lipa, near which one of the sites of this culture was discovered (Ostrovski and Grigoriev, 1966; Grigoriev, 1970). The area covered by this culture in western Ukraine corresponds roughly to the area occupied by the Molodova culture in the Dniester basin. The inventory of the Lipa culture resembles that of the Molodova culture, and its sites, too, contain many bone implements, including composite knives of mammoth bone (Savich, 1969, 1975); there are many blade-tools. The main distinguishing feature is the variety of burins, which are the most numerous tools in the inventory. It should be noted that, in spite of the differences between the three above-mentioned cultures in terms of most frequently encountered tools, Rogachev and Ani-

kovich (1984) are obviously right in uniting them in a single, south-western area, with a definite and distinct historical and cultural unity. Being hunters, like all the Upper Palaeolithic populations, their principal quarry within that area was the horse, which was subsequently ousted by the reindeer. As well as horse they sometimes hunted red deer, aurochs, mammoth and woolly rhinoceros. Although caves were scarce, they were still used as dwellings, while on open-air sites dwellings were erected; it is difficult to reconstruct them, however, since it seems that they did not make use of the bones of large animals. In any case, no dwellings constructed with the bones of mammoth or large-hoofed animals have yet been discovered.

The next area in which we find a single, cultural and historical tradition is the Dnieper area, where the Pushkari and Mezin or Mezhirich-Dobranichevka cultures are located. The former is the earlier. Pushkari, after which the culture is named, is one of the richest sites on the eastern European plain (Boriskovski, 1953). Of the enormous variety of implements found on this site, perhaps the most numerous and typical are tools with a blunted edge – bladelets and points; both occur in a variety of forms: among the latter is a high percentage of asymmetrical points. Long, constructed dwellings with hearths placed along the entire length were typical of this culture.

The Mezin site is renowned among specialists in the European Upper Palaeolithic for its very rich inventory and its various artistic bone carvings, illustrations of which often feature in general surveys of European archaeology. Excavation of the site began in 1908, and a large area was examined and some 100,000 stone items collected, although only about 5 per cent of them were tools. All the implements are lamellar (Shovkoplyas, 1965), and there is a good variety of burins, flakes with blunted edges and punches. Chisel-shaped tools and bone implements were also found. The people of that culture lived in round dwellings built from the lower jaws of mammoths, which they must have covered with skins (Fig. 57). The hearth was in the middle. Female statuettes and other objects of art were discovered within the dwelling. Unlike other relics of western and eastern Europe, these statuettes are not realistic but very stylized (Fig. 58). Many bone artefacts bear ornamentation that suggests the existence of numerical rules, testifying to the use of a fairly complex calculation system in the Upper Palaeolithic (Frolov, 1974). A number of large mammoth bones found on the floor of one dwelling near an ornament painted with ochre were thought to be ancient musical percussion instruments (Bibikov, 1981).

The south-eastern area contains the Kamennaya-Balka culture (named after the site at Kamennaya-Balka), which consists of a number of sites with a poorly preserved cultural

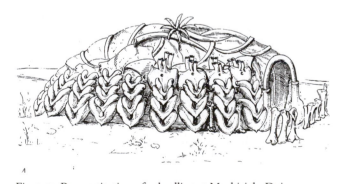

Figure 57 Reconstitution of a dwelling at Mezhirich, Dnieper area (Ukraine). (After I. G. Pidoplitchko.)

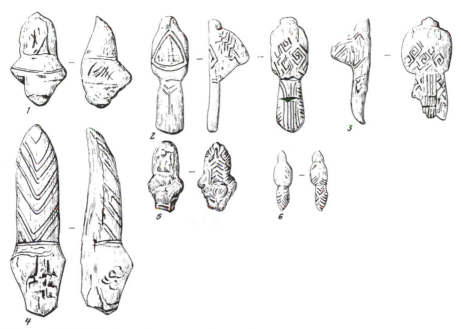

Figure 58 Stylized figurines of women, Mezin, Dnieper area.

layer (Boriskovski and Praslov, 1964). A huge pile of aurochs bones (of about a thousand animals) was found next to the site at the village of Ambrosievka; some of them bore the traces of incisions made by stone implements (Boriskovski, 1953). The vast majority of experts regard this heap of bones as a result of organized hunting by Upper Palaeolithic people. However, one other possible explanation has been put forward: the heap of bones could be the remains of a ritual site where some kind of magic rites were regularly enacted. On these sites the selection of implements is poor and there is no special form of artefact. It is curious to note that there is nothing to distinguish the tools found at the sites from those discovered on the pile of bones.

The cave of Syuren I in Crimea also comes within the south-eastern area, although of course it differs considerably from the Kamennaya-Balka sites. The cave dwellers hunted mainly saiga and giant deer. The stone inventory combines a large number of microblades with a proportion of archaic Mousterian forms (Vekilova, 1957). There are also bone implements and ornaments. A similar, though later, cultural complex was found in the neighbouring cave of Syuren II (Vekilova, 1961).

Although Rogachev and Anikovich (1984) look upon isolated historical and cultural traditions in the upper reaches of the Don as constituting a fourth area, they themselves have shown on a map (see Map 20) the proximity of its component cultures to the Streletsko–Sungir culture and the intersection of their areas of diffusion. In view of the considerable cultural similarity between the remains in the upper Don basin, especially the famous site near the villages of Kostenki and Borshevo and the site of Sungir on the Klyazma near the town of Vladimir, the geographical boundaries of that area should be extended and it should be renamed the central European area. It comprises two cultures, the Willendorf–Borshevo and the Streletsko–Sungir, as well as a number of unusual cultural variants identified and classified on the basis of study of separate sites within the Kostenki–Borshevo region; these variants differ sharply one from the other and do not fit into any wider typological framework. The name suggested for the culture of the sites concentrated in the vicinity of Kostenki

and Borshevo draws attention to its analogy with western Europe.

This is not the place for a description of each of the twenty or more huge sites with rich inventories in Kostenki and Borshevo; a series of monographs summarizes the available information (Boriskovski, 1953; *Paleolit...* , 1982; Rogachev and Anikovich, 1984). The region was inhabited throughout the Upper Palaeolithic, but each period within it is represented by different sites, and there is not one that was in use for the duration of the Upper Palaeolithic era. The inventory of these sites is very diverse, and there are sites with a preponderance of Aurignacian or Solutrean forms, but their chronological sequence is not the same as in France. The inventory of the early sites clearly evinces an archaic tradition that dates from the Mousterian era. The people hunted mainly the large animals of the steppe. The inhabitants of the area lived in long structures with hearths along the entire length, and the dwellings were surrounded by separate pits and holes that were evidently used for storage. The form of the structures varied from one site to another, and the inventories varied to such an extent that it was possible to identify a number of local variants of one culture, or even separate, purely local, cultures – such as the Gorodtsov and the Spitsin (which were named after great Russian archaeologists). It is clear that the inhabitants of separate sites were not connected through an unbroken succession of generations, for if they had been then the typological gap between the inventories would not have been so great. This goes to show that the Kostenki and Borshevo area was resettled several times. The burials, too, testify to definite cultural differences. Some were accompanied by a range of tools and others were not. Bone and soft stone were used for the fashioning of ornaments, female statuettes reminiscent of western European models and zoomorphic designs.

The principal site of the Streletsko–Sungir culture is the site of Sungir (p. 226) (Bader, 1978). The carbon-14 datings for bone and charcoal from the cultural layer of this site are from between 27,000 and 24,000 years ago. This means that the site dates approximately to the boundary between the

Early and Middle Upper Palaeolithic. The cultural layer is very rich and has provided a large collection of tools of a typical Upper Palaeolithic form, which nevertheless have their own distinctive features. There is an exceptional profusion of bone implements and ornaments (which were made also from various types of stone). A particularly large selection of bone implements and ornaments was found in graves. The positioning of the ornaments on the skeletons enabled archaeologists to reconstruct the clothing, which was of animal skins (Fig. 45).

Designation of the north-eastern area as a single cultural tradition is very much a relative matter, since in that enormous area only four sites have been discovered, which differ in terms of topography and cultural characteristics. Three sites contained material which, while not very rich, is analogous in certain respects to central European material. Bone implements were found as well as stone tools, which indicates the existence of insert techniques (Talitski, 1940; Gvozdover, 1952; Kanivets, 1976). The fourth site, Kapova (or Shulgantash) cave is much more important; here in 1959 A. V. Ryumin discovered multi-coloured drawings, which were later described by O. N. Bader (1965a). The cave is on the Belaya river in the southern Urals. The drawings depict mammoth, rhinoceros and horse (Plate 38). The type of animals depicted – there are about forty drawings – and the way they are drawn, with red ochre, point to the Palaeolithic, but it is impossible to date them more accurately. It would be difficult to exaggerate the significance of the drawings in the Kapova cave: they are the first indication of the existence of an artistic tradition in the eastern European Palaeolithic, and they show that archaeologists must seek and may find similar monuments far beyond the Franco-Cantabrian area.

Turning to the north-western area, we should note that it coincides entirely with the area of diffusion of a single archaeological culture – the Swiderian. Sites of the Ahrensburg type are to be encountered at the western extremities of this area, but they are in effect the easternmost examples of the Ahrensburg culture, whose centre is the western European part of the Baltic coastal region. The Swiderian sites do not have rich cultural deposits, and no trace of habitations remains (Gurina, 1985; Rimantene, 1971; Koltsov, 1977). Palaeogeographical study of the topology shows that the Swiderian sites are from the end of the Palaeolithic, and some may even be Mesolithic. The predominance of microlithic forms in the inventory tends to confirm that the site belongs to the late Upper Palaeolithic. The commonest form is the so-called Swiderian point (Fig. 59). Division of the Swiderian sites into three chronological phases has been attempted, but these are only preliminary attempts.

The recent survey by Bader (1984) makes it easier to characterize the Upper Palaeolithic in the Caucasus. The Upper Palaeolithic sites that have been studied are mainly in the western regions of the northern Caucasus, on the Black Sea coast and western Transcaucasia – in Imeritya, a historical and geographical division of western Georgia. The remains in eastern Transcaucasia have not been studied in depth; they consist of isolated sites to the north and the west of Lake Sevan. All of these are cave sites, sometimes with many layers, and the vast majority contained a rich flint inventory, although neither graves nor art have been found in the Caucasus. The only exception is the cave paintings in the Mgvimeni V cave in Imeritya (Zamyatnin, 1937). The fact that the stalagmite crust over the drawings contains Upper Palaeolithic implements proves that the drawings are from the Upper Palaeolithic. The images are painted on the cal-

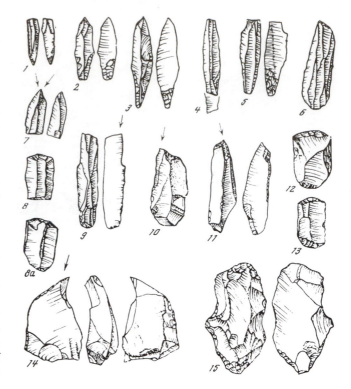

Figure 59 Swiderian stone artefacts, Mesolithic.

careous wall of the cave and consist of a more or less chaotic network of lines. Similar lines were drawn on the calcareous slab that was found together with the implements in the calc-sinter. Of course, the discovery of cave sites in the Caucasus, especially the northern Caucasus and the open spaces at the mouths of large rivers, does not mean that Upper Palaeolithic people in those regions did not settle in the open, but open-air sites have yet to be found. Those people lived mainly by hunting lone animals, which leads us to infer that hunting was a matter of individual pursuit. However, the bones of aurochs and cave bears have been discovered, which indicates that herd animals were hunted too. *Helix* shells, also, have been found, which points to the practice of gathering.

Zamyatnin (1935, 1957) has divided the Upper Palaeolithic sites in the Caucasus into three chronological phases, where the first phase sites contain Mousterian forms while the sites of phase 3 have some microlithic forms in their inventory. Since then a large number of remains have been discovered that add considerably to the results of previous excavations, and Bader (1984) has correctly stressed the need to elaborate Zamyatnin's division into periods, which is still valid as a chronological frame of reference. It should be noted also that a number of multi-layered sites were in use for lengthy periods and retained cultural layers relating to different periods in the Upper Palaeolithic era.

On the basis of known sites, two archaeological cultures – the Gubs and the Imeretiya – are recognized in the Caucasus. The former was identified and named after the Gubs rock shelter site by Bader (1965b). It contains a number of unusual forms, and also microliths and inserts. The sites of this culture relate primarily to the final stage of the Upper Palaeolithic culture. The Imeretiya sites have been studied by a number of archaeologists, who have shown them to be most unusual and quite unlike any of the other cultures within the former USSR discussed so far. It seems that they existed and evolved throughout the entire Upper Palaeolithic. Bader (1975, 1984) has argued that this culture was related to the Baradostian (Solecki, 1957) and Zarzian (Garrod, 1930) cultures of western Asia. They have in common many methods of primary fashioning and many forms of implements. Bader correctly remarks that the sites of the Imeretiya and western Asian cultures are separated by mountain ranges which cannot have been impassable barriers to Upper Palaeolithic people.

In her survey of the Palaeolithic in central Asia and Siberia, S. A. Abramova (1984) endorses D. A. Ranov's identification (1972) of three archaeological cultures, each of which is represented by a single site, and she adds a fourth culture, which is also represented by a single site. While it is true that each of these sites has analogies beyond the bounds of central Asia, and that each has a fairly unusual inventory, this is not sufficient justification for designating them independent archaeological cultures. The first of these sites is Yangadzha on the Krasnovodsk peninsula; strictly speaking, it is not a site but a workshop, and few completed tools were found there (Okladnikov, 1966). Of the other three sites, two are in the plains of Uzbekistan – the Samarkand site (Kholyushkin, 1981) and Kulbulak (Kasimov, 1972) – and the third is situated at a height of 2,000 m above sea-level in Tadjikistan (Ranov, 1973). The inhabitants of the last site hunted horse, cattle or bison, and sheep or goat. The denizens of the plain had a greater choice: Pleistocene ass, onager, primeval aurochs, Knoblock camel, Bukhara deer and red deer, steppe ram, cave hyena, and occasionally elephant or rhinoceros, wolf and wild boar. Each site contained forms that were absent from the others: in Shugnu there were corescrapers, in the Samarkand site chisel-shaped implements and in Kulbulak a number of Mousterian forms. The cultural traditions of the Upper Palaeolithic peoples of central Asia may originate in the culture of the Mousterian population, but there is as yet no very clear evidence for this assumption.

We can identify eight regions where Upper Palaeolithic remains were discovered in the territory of Siberia and the Far East (Abramova, 1984, map): the Altai, the upper reaches of the Yenisei, the area around Lake Baikal, the area east of Lake Baikal, the middle reaches of the Amur, the southern Primorskii area, the middle reaches of the Aldan (a left-bank tributary of the Lena) and the central regions of the Kamchatka. The sites discovered represent the entire Upper Palaeolithic era, but because they are scattered over thousands of kilometres it is impossible to deduce from them any specific mode of development for Upper Palaeolithic culture in the vast territory of northern Asia. We should observe only that the specific local character of individual sites and groups of sites is fairly clear, so that we must speak of local lines of development in separate areas; the genetic connections between these areas, and the genesis of separate local groups of the Upper Palaeolithic population, are not yet sufficiently clear (Derevyanko, 1975).

In addition to the Ust-Kan cave complex in the Altai there are several multi-layered cave sites with Upper Palaeolithic layers that have yielded a wide array of implements and even fragmentary human remains. This material is still being examined and has not yet entered the literature. The Afontova and Kokorevo cultures have been identified in the upper Yenisei basin on the basis of sites around Krasnoyarsk (Abramova, 1979a, 1979b), but statistical comparison of the inventory from the sites of these cultures did not confirm their independence (Kholyushkin, 1981). A series of sites has been discovered in Khakasia and Tuva, to the south of the sites of these two cultures, but the bulk of that material, also, is yet to be published.

The most famous sites near Lake Baikal are on the Angara – Malta (Gerasimov, 1931, 1935, 1958, 1961; Formozov, 1976a, 1976b) and Buret (Okladnikov, 1940, 1941). They are often amalgamated into a single Malta or Buret–Malta culture. Malta is larger and richer than Buret; it contained a great deal of carved bone: sculptural representations of birds, female statuettes, a bone bladelet with the outline of a mammoth etched upon it and another bone blade testifying to the existence of a counting and calendar system among the inhabitants of Malta (Larichev, 1984). It is interesting that the very well-sculptured face of one of the female statuettes from Malta has Mongoloid features (Plate 39). For a long time sculptural representations of women were the only known artistic objects from the Upper Palaeolithic in Siberia, and it is only recently that a stylized clay sculpture of a man was found in the cultural layer of the Majna site on the Yenisei. No similar finds have yet been made east of Lake Baikal or in the Amur basin or in the Primorskii area (Derevyanko, 1983).

A number of sites on the Aldan are dated to 37,000 to 35,000 years ago, and they are grouped together as the Dyuktaii culture, which is named after the key site and which, according to its discoverer, existed approximately 25,000 years ago (Motshanov, 1977). The inventory found at these sites is modest and does not allow archaeologists to trace the chronological development of the Dyuktaii culture. There is strong evidence that the early dates for this culture are an exaggeration and that all the sites in the Dyuktaii culture date from the final phase of the Upper Palaeolithic. They would seem to have been more or less contemporary with the group of sites at Ushki on the middle reaches of the Kamchatka river which were discovered and excavated by N. N. Dikov.

BIBLIOGRAPHY

ABRAMOVA, S. A. 1979a. Paleolit Eniseja, Kokorevskaja kul'tura [The Palaeolithic of the Yenisei Valley, the Kokorevo Culture]. Novosibirsk.

—— 1979b. Paleolit Eniseja, Afontovskaja kul'tura [The Palaeolithic of the Yenisei Valley, the Afontova Culture]. Novosibirsk.

—— 1979c. K voprosu o vozraste Aldanskoj kul'tury [On the Age of the Aldan Palaeolithic]. Sov. arheol., Vol. 4, pp. 5 ff.

—— 1984. Pozdnij paleolit aziatskoj časti SSSR [The Late Palaeolithic of the Asiatic Part of the USSR]. In: BORISKOVSKI, P. I. (ed.), Paleolit SSSR. Moscow. pp. 302–46.

ALEXEEV, V. P. 1978. Paleoantropologija zemnogo šara i formirovanija čelovečeskih ras. Paleolit [Palaeoanthropology of the World and the Formation of Human Races. Palaeolithic]. Moscow.

—— 1981. Fossil Man on the Territory of the USSR and Related Problems. In: FEREMBACH, D. (ed.), Les Processus de l'hominisation; l'évolution humaine. Les faits. Les modalités. Paris, CNRS. pp. 183. (Colloq. Internes CNRS, 599.)

BADER, O. N. 1965a. Kapovaja peščera [The Kapova Cave]. Moscow.

—— 1965b. Varianty kul'tury Kavkaza v konce verhnego paleolita – načale mezolita [The Variants of the Culture of the Caucasus at the End of the Palaeolithic and the Beginning of the Mesolithic]. Sov. arheol., Vol. 4, pp. 3–16.

—— 1975. Pozdnij paleolit Zagra i Imeretii [The Palaeolithic of the Zagros and Imeretiya]. In: Pamjatniki drevnejšej istorii Evrazii. Moscow. pp. 42–9.

—— 1978. Sungir-verhnepaleolitičeskaja stojanka [The Upper Palaeolithic Site of Sungir]. Moscow.

—— 1984. Pozdnij paleolit Kavkaza [The Late Palaeolithic of the Caucasus]. In: BORISKOVSKI, P. I. (ed.), Paleolit SSSR. Moscow. pp. 272–301.

BIBIKOV, S. N. 1981. Drevnejšij muzykal'nyj kompleks iz kostej mamonta

[The Most Ancient Musical Complex Made of Mammoth Bones]. Kiev.

BORISKOVSKI, P. I. 1953. *Paleolit Ukrainy* [The Palaeolithic of the Ukraine]. Moscow/Leningrad. (Mater. issled. arheol. SSSR, 40.)

BORISKOVSKI, P. I.; PRASLOV, H. D. 1964. *Paleolit bassejna Dnepra i Priazov'ja* [The Palaeolithic of the Dnieper Valley and Azov Sea Area]. Moscow.

BORZIYAK, U. A. 1978. *Pozdnij paleolit severo-zapada Moldavii* [The Late Palaeolithic of North-Western Moldavia]. Leningrad.

BUNAK, V. V. 1959. *Čerep čeloveka i stadii ego formirovanija u iskopaemyh ljudej i sovremennyh ras* [The Human Skull and the Stages of its Formation by Fossil Man and Modern Races]. Moscow. (Tr. Inst. etnogr., NS, 49.)

—— 1973. *Iskopaemyj čelovek iz stojanki Sungir i ego mesto sredi drugih iskopaemyh pozdnego paleolita* [Fossil Man from the Sungir Site and its Place among other Fossils of the Late Palaeolithic]. Moscow.

CHERNYSH, A. P. 1959. Pozdnij paleolit srednego Pridnestrov'ja [Late Palaeolithic of the Middle Dniester Valley]. In: *Paleolit srednego Pridnestrov'ja.* Moscow. pp. 5–214.

—— 1973. *Paleolit i mezolit Pridnestrov'ja* [The Palaeolithic and Mesolithic of the Dniester Valley]. Moscow.

DEBETZ, G. F. 1946. Fragment lobnoj kosti čeloveka iz kul'turnogo sloja stojanki 'Afontova gora II' pod Krasnojarskom [A Fragment of Human Forehead Bone from the Cultural Layer of the 'Afontova gora II' Site near Krasnoyarsk]. *Bjull. kom. izučeniju četvert. perioda* (Moscow), No. 8, pp. 73–7.

—— 1948. *Paleoantropologija SSSR* [Palaeoanthropology of the USSR]. Moscow/Leningrad. (Tr. Inst. etnogr., NS, 4.)

—— 1955. Paleoantropologěskie nahodki v Kostenkah [Palaeoanthropological Finds in Kostenki]. *Sov. etnogr.,* No. 2, pp. 43–53.

—— 1961. Čerep iz pozdnepaleolitičeskogo pogrebenija v Pokrovskom loge (Kostenki XVIII) [A Skull from a Late Palaeolithic Burial in the Pokrovskij Gully (Kostenki XVIII)]. *Kratk. soobsc. Inst. arheol.* (Moscow), No. 82, pp. 160–4.

—— 1967. Skelet pozdnepaleolitičeskogo čeloveka iz pogrebenija na Sungirskoj stojanke [Human Skeleton from a Late Palaeolithic Burial on the Sungir Site]. *Sov. arheol.,* No. 3, pp. 160–4.

DEREVYANKO, A. P. 1975. *Kamennyj vek Severnoj, Vostočnoj i Central'noj Azii* [The Stone Age of Northern, Eastern and Central Asia]. Novosibirsk.

—— 1983. *Paleolit Dal'nego Vostoka i Korei* [The Palaeolithic of the Far East and Korea]. Novosibirsk.

FORMOZOV, A. A. 1976a. Kharakteristike paleolitičeskogo poselenija Mal'ta [A Contribution to the Characteristics of the Palaeolithic Settlement of Malta]. *Sov. arheol.,* No. 2, pp. 205–10.

—— 1976b. Neopublikovannye proizvedenija iskusstva paleolitičeskoj stojanki Mal'ta [Unpublished Works of Art from the Palaeolithic Site of Malta]. *Sov. arheol.,* No. 4, pp. 180–4.

FROLOV, B. A. 1974. *Čisla v grafike paleolita* [Numbers in Palaeolithic Drawings]. Novosibirsk.

GARROD, D. A. 1930. Palaeolithic of Southern Kurdistan: Excavations in the Caves of Zarzi and Hazar Merd. *Bull. Am. Sch. Prehist. Res.* (Harvard), Vol. 6, pp. 32–76.

GERASIMOV, M. M. 1931. *Malta: paleolitičeskaja stojanka* [Malta, a Palaeolithic Site]. Irkutsk.

—— 1935. Raskopki paleolitičeskoj stojanki v sele Malta [Excavation of a Palaeolithic Site near the Village of Malta]. In: *Paleolit SSSR.* Moscow/Leningrad. pp. 78–124.

—— 1958. Paleolitičeskaja stojanka Malta [The Palaeolithic Site of Malta]. *Sov. etnogr.,* No. 3, pp. 28–52.

—— 1961. Krugloe žilišče stojanki Malta [A Round Dwelling on the Malta Site]. *Kratk. soobšč. Inst. arheol.* (Moscow), No. 82, pp. 128–34.

—— 1964. *Ljudi kamennogo veka* [The People of the Stone Age]. Moscow.

GINZBURG, V. V.; GOKHMAN, I. I. 1974. Kostnye ostatki čeloveka iz Samarkandskoj paleolitičeskoj stojanki [Human Skeleton Remains from the Samarkand Palaeolithic Site]. In: GOKHMAN, I. I. (ed.), *Problemy etniceskoj antropologii i morfologii čeloveka.* Leningrad. pp. 5–11.

GRIGORIEV, G. P. 1970. Verhnij paleolit [The Upper Palaeolithic]. In: FORMOZOV, A. A. (ed.), *Kamennyj vek na territorii SSSR.* Moscow. pp. 43–63. (Mater. issled. arheol. SSSR, 166.)

GURINA, N. N. 1985. Novye dannye o kamennom veke severo-zapadnoj Belorussii [New Data on the Stone Age of North-western Byelorussia]. In: *Paleolit i neolit SSSR.* Leningrad. Vol. 5, pp. 141–203. (Mater. issled. arheol. SSSR, 131.)

GVOZDOVER, M. D. 1952. Vkladyševyj nakonečnik s paleolitičeskoj stojanki Talickogo [An Inset Point from the Palaeolithic Site of Talitskij]. *Uč. zap. Mosk. Univ.* (Moscow), No. 158, pp. 107–10.

KANIVETS, V. I. 1976. *Paleolit krajnego severo-vostoka Evropy* [The Palaeolithic of Extreme North-Eastern Europe]. Moscow.

KASIMOV, M. P. 1972. Mnogoslojnaja paleolitičeskaja stojanka Kulbulak v Uzbekistane [Polystratigraphic Palaeolithic Site of Kulbulak in Uzbekistan]. In: *Paleolit i neolit SSSR.* Leningrad. Vol. 7, pp. 111–19. (Mater. issled. arheol. SSSR, 185.)

KHOLYUSHKIN, Y. P. 1981. *Problemy korreljacii pozdnepaleolitičeskih industrij Sibiri i Srednej Azii* [Correlation Problems Between Late Palaeolithic Industries in Siberia and Central Asia]. Novosibirsk.

KHRISANFOVA, E. N. 1980. Skelet verhnepaleolitičeskogo čeloveka iz Sungira [A Skeleton of the Upper Palaeolithic from Sungir]. *Vopr. antropol.,* Vol. 64, pp. 40–68.

KOLTSOV, A. V. 1977. *Finalnyj paleolit i mezolit Južnoj i Voctočnoj Pribaltiki* [Late Upper Palaeolithic and Mesolithic of the Southern and Eastern Baltic]. Moscow.

LARICHEV, V. E. 1984. *Lunno-solnečnaja sistema verhnepaleolitičeskogo čeloveka Sibiri* [The Lunar and Solar Calendar of Upper Palaeolithic Man in Siberia]. Novosibirsk.

LEBEDINSKAYA, G. V.; SURNINA, T. S. 1984. Portrety detej, pogrebënnyh na stojanke Sungir (plastičeskaja rekonstrukcija) [Plastic Reconstruction of the Portraits of Children Buried on the Sungir Site]. In: *Sungir: Anthropological Investigation.* Moscow. pp. 156–61.

MARSHAK, A. 1972. *The Roots of Civilization.* New York.

MOTSHANOV, Y. A. 1977. *Drevnejšye etapy zaselenija čelovekom Severo-Vostočnoj Azii* [The Earliest Peopling of North-Eastern Asia]. Novosibirsk.

OAKLEY, K.; CAMPBELL, B.; MOLLESON, T. (eds) 1975. *Catalogue of Fossil Hominids. America, Asia, Australia.* London. Vol. 3.

OKLADNIKOV, A. P. 1940. Buret, novaja paleolitičeskaja stojanka na Angare [Buret, a New Palaeolithic Site on the Angara River]. *Sov. arheol.,* Vol. 5, pp. 290–3.

—— 1941. Paleolitičeskoe žilišče v Burete [A Palaeolithic Dwelling at Buret]. *Kratk. soobšč. Inst. ist. mater. kul't.* (Moscow/Leningrad), No. 10, pp. 16–31.

—— 1966. Paleolit i mezolit Srednej Azii [The Palaeolithic and Mesolithic of Central Asia]. In: *Srednjaja Azija v epohu kamnja i bronzy.* Moscow/Leningrad. pp. 11–75.

OSTROVSKI, M. I.; GRIGORIEV, G. P. 1966. Lipskaja paleolitičeskaja kul'tura [The Lipa Palaeolithic Culture]. *Sov. arheol.,* No. 4, pp. 2–13.

Paleolit Kostenko-Borševskogo rajona na Donu [The Palaeolithic of the Kostenko-Borshevskij Area on the River Don]. Leningrad, 1982.

RANOV, D. A. 1972. K probleme vydelenija lokal'nyh paleolitičeskih kul'tur v Srednej Azii [The Problem of Local Palaeolithic Cultures in Central Asia]. In: *Kamennyj vek Srednej Azii i Kazahstana.* Tashkent. pp. 31–4.

—— 1973. Sugnu: mnogoslojnaja paleolitičeskaja stojanka v verhov'jah reki Yahsu (raskopki 1969–1970 gg) [Shugnu, a Polystratigraphic Palaeolithic Site in the Upper Yahsu River Valley: Excavations in 1969–1970]. *Arheol. rab. Tdzikystane* (Dushanbe), Vol. 10, pp. 42–61.

RIMANTENE, P. K. 1971. *Paleolit i mezolit Litvy* [The Palaeolithic and Mesolithic in Lithuania]. Vilnius.

ROGACHEV, A. N.; ANIKOVICH, M. V. 1984. Pozdnij paleolit Russkoj ravniny i Kryma [The Late Palaeolithic of the Russian Plain and the Crimea]. In: BORISKOVSKI, P. I. (ed.), *Paleolit SSSR.* Moscow. pp. 162–271.

ROGINSKIĬ, Y.; LEVIN, M. G. 1963. *Osnovy antropologii* [Fundamentals of Anthropology]. Moscow.

SAVICH, V. P. 1969. Kostjanye izdelija stojanki Lipa VI [Bone Artefacts from the Lipa VI Site]. *Bjull. kom. izučeniju četvert. perioda* (Moscow), No. 36, pp. 136–41.

—— 1975. *Piznopaleolitične naselennta pivdenno-zahidnoi Volyni* [The Late Palaeolithic Population of South-Western Volyn]. Kiev.

SHOVKOPLYAS, I. G. 1965. *Mezinskaja stojanka* [The Mezin Site]. Kiev.

SOLECKI, R. S. 1957. The 1956–1957 Season in Shanidar, Iran. *Quaternaria*, Vol. 4.

TALITSKI, M. V. 1940. Ostrovskaja paleolitičeskaja stojanka [The Ostrov Palaeolithic Site]. *Kratk. soobšč. Inst. ist. mater. kul't.* (Moscow/Leningrad), No. 4, pp. 41–2.

VALLOIS, H.; MORINS H. 1952. Catalogue des hommes fossiles. In: CONGRÈS GÉOLOGIQUE INTERNATIONAL, 19ᵉ, Paris, 1952. *Comptes-rendus*. Paris. Vol. 5, pp. 63–375.

VEKILOVA, E. A. 1957. Stojanka Syuren I i eë mesto sredi paleolitičeskih mestonahoždenij Kryma i bližajših territorij [The Syuren I Site and its Place Among the Palaeolithic Localities of the Crimea and Surrounding Territories]. In: *Paleolit i neolit SSSR*. Leningrad. Vol. 3, pp. 235–323. (Mater. issled. arheol. SSSR, 59.)

—— 1961. K voprosu o sviderskoj kul'ture v Krymu (stojanka Syuren II) [A Contribution to the Question of the Existence of the Swiderian Culture in the Crimea (Syuren II Site)]. *Kratk. soobšč. Inst. arheol.*, No. 82, pp. 143–9.

YAKIMOV, V. P. 1957. Pozdnepaleolitičeskij rebënok iz pogrebenija na Gorodcovskoj stojanke v Kostenkah [Late Palaeolithic Child from a Burial on the Gorodtsov Site in the Kostenki Area]. *Sb. Muz. antropol. etnogr.* (Moscow/Leningrad), Vol. 17, pp. 500–29.

ZAMYATNIN, S. N. 1935. Novye dannye po paleolitu Zakavkaz'ja [New Data on the Palaeolithic of the Transcaucasus]. *Sov. etnogr.*, Vol. 2, pp. 46–123.

—— 1937. Peščernye navesy Mgrimevi bliz Čiaturi [The Mgrimev Caves near Chiatura]. *Sov. arheol.*, Vol. 3, pp. 57–76.

—— 1957. Paleolit zapadnogo Zakavkaz'ja [The Palaeolithic of the Western Transcaucasus]. *Sb. Muz. antropol. etnogr.* (Moscow/Leningrad), Vol. 17, pp. 432–99.

ZHUKAKULOV, M. D. et al. 1980. Samarkandskaja stojanka i eë mesto v pozdnem paleolite Srednej Azii [The Samarkand Site and its Place in the Late Palaeolithic of Central Asia]. In: LARICHEV, V. E. (ed.), *Paleolit Srednej i Voctocnoj Azii*. Novosibirsk. pp. 51–95.

23

PALAEOLITHIC AND MESOLITHIC
ART IN EUROPE

Hans-Georg Bandi

Here, as in Chapter 19 on the origins of art, we can confine ourselves to questions of representational art, because in the case of poetry and music we have nothing to go on for these early periods; it is possible, however, that some mammoth skulls and other big bones discovered at Mezin in Ukraine had been used as percussion instruments. It must also be remembered that the factors inspiring people to artistic expression at this stage of the advanced hunting cultures were fundamentally different from those at work today.

When the Middle Palaeolithic cultures were supplanted by the Upper Palaeolithic in conjunction with the arrival of *Homo sapiens sapiens* between approximately 42,000 and 37,000 years ago the day of the birth of art was already dawning, but unfortunately the Châtelperronian (dated at between 37,000 to 36,000 and 32,000 to 31,000 years ago and formerly known as the Lower Perigordian) has left us practically no evidence of early representational art whether in the form of mobiliary art (works in their own right or the decoration of tools and weapons) or of rock art in caves and rock shelters. The only exception is formed by isolated pieces of bone and small slabs of stone bearing series of engraved and more or less parallel lines. We do not know their meaning, but it is certain that they were drawn there intentionally. Possibly other tentative attempts in the direction of representational art were also made for which no evidence has come down to us because of the perishable nature of the material used. Authors refer in this connection to a 'prefigurative phase' classed as style 0 or included in style I, depending on the writer. If the discovery of a carved bone at the Mousterian site of Pronyatin in Ukraine (Fig. 26) (Chapter 13) is confirmed there might even be the possibility of roots going back to the Middle Palaeolithic cultures.

AURIGNACIAN

The origins of representational art become more easily discernible with the Aurignacian (or typical Aurignacian) culture whose beginnings, largely overlapping with the Châtelperronian, are put at around 35,000 years ago, though there is a school of thought claiming that the origin of this second major culture of the Upper Palaeolithic age in Europe

has to be sought in western Asia and that it probably arrived in the Balkans around 42,000 years ago. The area it spread over is much larger than that of the Châtelperronian, which was definitely confined to western Europe, and stretched, to the best of our present knowledge, from Bulgaria and Hungary, via Germany, Belgium and France, to the Iberian peninsula. Here, the prominent style I of Upper Palaeolithic art which runs on into the early Gravettian is primarily characterized by the advent of plastic figures. H. de Lumley describes a phallus-shaped figure in aurochs or bison horn found in the Blanchard des Roches rock shelter (near Sergeac, Dordogne) as 'the most ancient piece of figurative art in France'. A piece of bone decorated with a dot-pattern from the same source is interpreted by A. Marshack as a lunar calendar, a theory that is still in dispute (Plate 40). Other significant finds have been made in southern Germany, some of them a long time ago but others more recently. In the Vogelherd cave near Heidenheim (Baden-Württemberg, Germany) a whole series of figures in mammoth ivory were found sculptured in the round and in one case in relief, including a particularly lifelike wild horse, several mammoths, a cave lion and the simplified shape of a man (Fig. 60). Similar works of mobiliary art have been found in the neighbouring sites of Geissenklösterle near Blaubeuren and Hohlenstein-Stadel in the Lohnetal.

There is also rock art that can be classified as Aurignacian and therefore belongs to style I, although such works have never, as yet, been discovered *in situ* in caves or rock shelters. Those that have been found are on blocks and slabs that may have broken off by accident a long time after the engravings or dots of colour were applied. Hence the term 'block art'. Their classification as Aurignacian is supported by stratigraphic observations at some sites, in particular La Ferrassie near Bugue in the Dordogne, France. Some of the figures are engraved in the rock, some executed by the punching technique. Occasionally sexual symbols can be recognized, mostly vulvae, exceptionally also phalli. They are generally associated with human beings but not inevitably so since hunters must also have been interested in the propagation of the game they hunted. The representations of animals have a schematic, stiff and clumsy appearance and reliable zoological identification is generally difficult, particularly since they are often limited to the head with, in some cases, a line

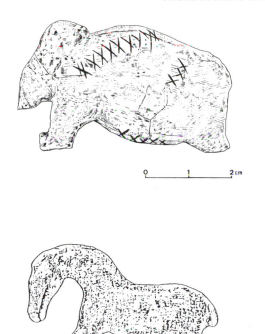

Figure 60 Two mammoth ivory figurines (mammoth, horse) (length of the horse 5 cm) from the Vogelherd cave, Baden-Württemberg (Germany), Aurignacian.

representing the back, complete animal figures being the exception (Plate 41). Although the works of mobiliary and 'block' art so far known to us suggest there must have been some kind of preliminary stage, there is no doubt that style I ascribed to the Aurignacian and early Gravettian approximates very closely to the origins of representational art.

GRAVETTIAN

A major advance is discernible in the works of art that have been found from the Gravettian (or 'Upper Perigordian') culture that then followed. Its beginnings around 29,000 years ago overlap the end of the typical Aurignacian, which is put at 28,000 years ago. The Gravettian lasted until between 21,000 and 20,000 years ago. As André Leroi-Gourhan points out, the area covered by the Gravettian represents the maximum spread of Upper Palaeolithic rock and mobiliary art in Europe, including the east of Spain and large parts of France. Other areas where related finds have been made range from the Apennine peninsula through Belgium and central Europe eastward as far as Ukraine. As already stated, style I, which we have seen to be associated with the typical Aurignacian, continues into the early Gravettian. In Leroi-Gourhan's view, style II evidently began only at an advanced stage in the Gravettian and at a time when there can be no doubt about the existence of very close cultural ties between western and eastern Europe.

To begin with, style I carried forward from the typical Aurignacian continues to dominate the Gravettian and no important changes in rock and mobiliary art are to be noted. Thereafter, however, innovations arise heralding a faster pace of development. While the number of caves and rock shelters

with rock art is still small, from the beginning of style II about 23,000 years ago there are already representations deep inside caves to which, as at Gargas in Hautes-Pyrénées, Leroi-Gourhan applies the term 'sanctuaries'. But for the most part, rock art continues to be found at cave entrances lit by daylight or just at the start of the dark part of the interior and also in rock shelters. Especially characteristic is the back line in the form of a horizontal 'S', to which the remaining parts of the body silhouette are added, whether the animal concerned is a bison, aurochs, ibex, horse, mammoth, stag or felid (Plate 42). This S-shaped back line even figures in the representations of women. The Gargas cave already referred to, not far from Montréjeau and St Bertrand-de-Comminges in Haute-Garonne, may be regarded as a typical example of an underground sanctuary, although this cave, 135 m long, and 20 to 40 m wide and consisting of many chambers, is known primarily for its very large number of hand silhouettes. Most of these are 'negative imprints' of hands of adults and young people that were held against the rock and then fixed for eternity with black or red paint (perhaps sprayed on by mouth). There are 'positive' imprints too, probably made by applying the paint-covered flat of the hand. In many cases, these hand silhouettes, which occur in greater number at Gargas than anywhere else, reveal mutilations with parts of or whole fingers missing. Various attempts have been made to interpret this phenomenon of hand imprints in Ice Age art. On the basis of ethnographic parallels they were at first believed to relate to ritual amputations. Leroi-Gourhan, whose views on Ice Age art are presented in Chapter 19, classifies these hand silhouettes with the symbols of a female nature on the evidence of their distribution in the various cave zones and their combination with other – in his view male – symbols. In Gargas, the hand imprints, whose dating within the period of Ice Age art is not entirely unproblematic, are not found at the same places as the approximately 150 animal pictures also discovered there. These, with very few exceptions, are in the furthermost parts of the cave. The techniques used vary. There are finger drawings on mud surfaces, engravings made with stone implements and a few isolated paintings. Bison and horses predominate, mammoths, aurochs, stags and ibex are fewer in number and carnivores and birds are rare. Generally these pictures are associated with the Gravettian. In Leroi-Gourhan's view, they mainly belong to his style II period, which covers the years between 23,000 and 17,000 years ago and therefore corresponds not only to the Gravettian we are now considering but also to the Solutrean – which came after and to which we shall return on p. 236. It is supposed that the Gargas rock pictures classified as style II were made over the course of a long period of time. This fits the findings of de Lumley, who distinguished twelve phases, which can be put into three major cycles, on the basis of an investigation of the superimposed layers. De Lumley also considers he has evidence showing that the faunas depicted in Gargas reveal a succession of species adapted first to moderate cold, then to extreme cold and finally to moderate cold again: while adaptable wild cattle species occur throughout the period, the wild horse is absent at the start and mammoth and elk are late to appear and do so for only a relatively short time. Chronologically, the matter is further complicated by the fact that, stylistically speaking, 'archaic' tendencies are again recognizable at the start, when species not pictured before make their debut, and these archaic representations are not superseded until after some time by the more highly developed forms of representation already in established use for other animals.

This reference to the observations in Gargas must suffice as an indication of the problems in the field of Gravettian rock art. In that connection not the least important factor contributing to the importance of Gargas is the fact that the relatively clear stratigraphic conditions in the cave reveal a sequence of cultures beginning in the Middle Palaeolithic and continuing, via the Châtelperronian and Aurignacian, to the Gravettian. A significant point is that the Gravettian layers were found to contain works of mobiliary art in the form of small stone slabs with animal engravings that correspond stylistically to some of the mural pictures. As de Lumley points out, Gargas therefore performs an important role in establishing the chronological position of the 'first' works of rock art.

Leroi-Gourhan stresses that style II art is directly based on the traditions of style I and that a striking degree of similarity is to be observed right across Europe, which is particularly manifest in the works of mobiliary art, from the lands in the east of our continent to the Pyrenees and the Iberian peninsula. This is particularly true of the 'Venus' figures (Fig. 35 and Plate 35). Practically all the figurines, mostly female, in ivory, bone or stone (and some isolated rather larger bas-reliefs found in rock shelters) that can be reliably dated belong to style II and display surprising affinities in spite of the considerable geographical distances separating them: heavy emphasis on the shape of the torso with breasts, hips and abdomen, whereas the face, arms and legs are given little attention and feet are almost always absent. To some extent they seem to depict a form of steatopygia found today with certain women of the 'Bushman' tribes of southern Africa. Leroi-Gourhan points out that this suggests the existence of a widespread conventionalism, the breasts, hips and belly forming a kind of circle bounded by a rhombus ending at the head and the legs. The figures are generally small, averaging 10 cm in height and rarely reaching 23 cm. Although their significance is not clear (theories include that they relate to fertility symbolism, that they are representations of a 'ruler of the animal world' or had a role of protector of home and hearth) they argue eloquently for the identity in conceptual approach at the time of Gravettian.

The mobiliary art of the Gravettian also includes representations of animals which now, to some extent, decorate objects in everyday use, like the two mammoths face to face on the *bâton de commandement* made of reindeer antler found at Laugerie-Haute in the Dordogne (Plate 43). The numerous plastic animal figures found in eastern Europe also deserve mention, some of them carved from organic materials and others shaped from a mixture of clay and bone debris and hardened – probably unintentionally – in the fire. The best known finds in this connection are those of Dolní Věstonice in Moravia.

SOLUTREAN

About 22,000 years ago the Gravettian begins to be supplanted by the Solutrean, another Upper Palaeolithic culture. However, this somewhat singular period overlaps not only with the outgoing Gravettian between 21,000 and 20,000 years ago but also with the dawning Magdalenian from around 18,000 years ago (about a thousand years before the final fading of the Solutrean about 17,000 years ago). So the period for which the Solutrean seems to have been the sole prevailing carrier of cultural development in western Europe was relatively short. It has to be borne in mind that, compared with both its predecessor the Gravettian and its suc-cessor the Magdalenian, the area over which the Solutrean spread was distinctly small, confined as it was to central France, the lower Rhône valley, eastern Spain and lastly an area stretching from the French Pyrenees to Asturia. In certain respects this once again purely hunting-oriented culture has a special place in our present context: its industry and in particular the stoneworking technique developed in what was, to some extent, a highly independent manner; the differences, however, are not so momentous as was at one time thought due, not least, to the fact that style II of Ice Age art, as already mentioned, was still characteristic at the beginning of the Solutrean period.

However that may be, the number of relevant finds in the field of art is so far very small. The situation does not change until part-way through the Solutrean with the beginning of style III, an event according to Leroi-Gourhan to be dated around 21,000 years ago. To this period we owe a considerable number of strikingly beautiful bas-reliefs executed on the walls or on large stone blocks upended in rock shelters. An example that may be quoted as particularly characteristic is the Roc-de-Sers shelter in Charente (southern France) made out of huge blocks of stone. Here eleven overturned blocks were found on which figures are represented in bas-relief and in some cases engraved. They include horses, bison, reindeer and human beings. This astonishing work of Solutrean art, which can now be admired at the Musée des Antiquités Nationales in Saint-Germain-en-Laye near Paris, is additionally interesting for the fact that some of the animals have been altered, no doubt by a later hand, bison having been changed into horses and a wild boar. In de Lumley's view, it is quite possible that a whole series of decorated caves should be classified as Solutrean, but this can very seldom be proved with any certainty. Examples are the paintings in the Grotte de la Tête du Lion in Ardèche and the engravings in the Grotte du Chabot near Aiguèze in Gard, both in southern France.

Solutrean mobiliary art is, generally speaking, of little significance, one exception being the finds made in the Parpalló cave near Gandia in the Spanish province of Valencia. Between older and younger deposits, various old layers of the Solutrean were discovered in a truly comprehensive sequence of Upper Palaeolithic industries. The investigation brought a considerable number of small stone slabs to light on which animals were represented, most of them engraved but some painted in red and black. Species include wild horses, stags, wild cattle and wild boar. Unfortunately these works of mobiliary art, like those in the Gravettian and Magdalenian layers above and below, yield no vital clues with regard to stylistic development.

MAGDALENIAN

Style III, which becomes increasingly pronounced towards the end of the Solutrean, continues up to the beginning of the Magdalenian culture around 18,000 years ago but is then supplanted by style IV. The area covered by the Magdalenian varies depending on whether we are concerned with an early, middle or late phase, but by and large it embraces the area from northern Spain across France and central Europe to Poland. While Leroi-Gourhan refers to style III as still an 'archaic' period, his adjective for style IV is 'classical'. Indeed much of what has come down to us from the middle and late Magdalenian, in both rock and mobiliary art, far surpasses anything of an earlier date in beauty, impact and rich variety. Shortly before its close – between 12,000 and 11,000 years

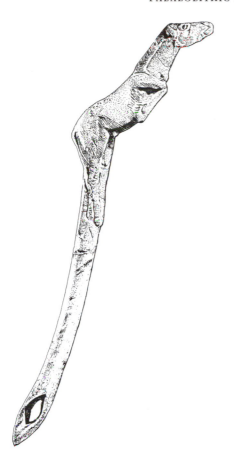

Figure 62 Reindeer antler carving of a male reindeer in rutting season (length 6.2 cm) on a *bâton de commandement*, Kesslerloch cave, near Thayngen, Schaffhausen Canton (Switzerland), Magdalenian.

Figure 61 Reindeer-antler spear-thrower ending in the figure of a leaping horse (length 28 cm). Abri Montastruc, Bruniquel, Tarn-et-Garonne (France), Magdalenian. (Drawing M. Otte.)

ago in Europe but rather later further east – Ice Age art here reaches its absolute peak.

Let us first turn to mobiliary art. In line with the large quantity of objects carved out of organic material and reindeer antler in particular, such as spearpoints, so-called harpoons, shaft-straighteners, spear-throwers and so on, there is also an abundance of works of art, some in the form of decorative adjuncts to objects used as weapons and tools (Figs 61 and 62; Plates 36 and 43) and others that are works of art in their own right (Plate 32). Their interest today lies mainly in their aesthetic qualities, although for their creators they probably – or at least also – had other associations. The same applies to the similarly plentiful works of mobiliary art in stone, including the many engraved small slabs. Whereas for the early Magdalenian no changes of any importance are to be noted as compared with the style-III-imbued artistic output of the Solutrean, the situation changes radically with the beginning of the middle phase of the Magdalenian, which was to some extent specialized in reindeer-hunting. For one thing, as already stated, we are dealing, from now until the close of the Magdalenian, with style IV, and for another the number of works of mobiliary art increases steeply. Leroi-Gourhan makes the point that, on the other hand, there is an appreciable decline in manifestations of rock art towards the end of style IV and feels justified in arguing on those grounds that the undergound sanctuaries had gradually lost their importance, whereas increasing significance was being attached by the late Ice Age hunting societies to mobiliary art.

For us, however, many of the engraved or three-dimensional decorations are simply ornaments, whereas

Magdalenian people may, at least partly, have credited them with magical powers or virtues as amulets. They include very many varyingly naturalistic representations of animals and – much more rarely – human beings, often singly but sometimes together in the same scene and often (at least as far as the animals are concerned) easily identified but sometimes extremely puzzling. To be associated with the engravings and sculptures in the case of the representations of animals are the so-called 'cut-out silhouettes': reproductions cut out from flat bones, mainly shoulder-blades or antlers (Plate 32). But whether engraved, carved or cut out, the works of mobiliary art of the Middle and Upper Magdalenian are of unbelievable originality, aesthetic quality and expressiveness. Admittedly the standard varies, but the number of masterpieces is high. Often naturalistic animal representations have been created, turning the conditions imposed by the material or the purpose of the object to be decorated to skilful account; these representations occur in most cases singly, but some times several are found on a single object. All the animals of the chase are there to meet us, from the mammoth to small animals (Plate 44), more rarely birds and fish, and occasionally even amphibia and insects (Plate 33). Often details of the eyes and nose, horns or antlers, hair and hooves or claws are meticulously and faithfully reproduced. Representations of human beings are also present, sometimes only heads or faces, but sometimes complete figures. Animals and people are occasionally shown together in the same picture. Towards the end of the Magdalenian an increasing tendency towards schematization is apparent. We may mention, for instance, the great number of engraved slabs from the famous site of Gönnersdorf near Koblenz in the Rhineland dating from the end of the eleventh millennium BP: there especially the representations of women are extremely schematic (Fig. 63).

This brings us to the engraved, painted and bas-relief representations in the subterranean sanctuaries of the Magdalenian. The best-known names here are those like Altamira near Santander in northern Spain, the 'Sistine Chapel of Ice Age art', known about since 1879 but long branded as a fake, and Lascaux near Montignac in the Dordogne (Plates 34 and 45), which has been described as 'the Prado of the Ice Age hunters' and was so endangered by the massive throngs of tourists that it had to be closed to the public (fortunately there exists in the vicinity an excellent replica of the whole cave which can be visited). But there are many other caves of the Magdalenian period, particularly in the

Figure 63 Highly stylized figure of a woman on a sheet of shale, Gönnersdorf near Neuwied (Germany), Magdalenian. (Drawing M. Otte.)

south of France and northern Spain as well as in other parts of western Europe. Altogether, today, the number of sites where a varying number of works of rock art have been found totals over 150. It is rare to find Magdalenian art in rock shelters, though one example is the very beautiful bas-relief frieze of horses, recalling the preceding Solutrean, at Cap Blanc not far from Les Eyzies in the Dordogne. But, unlike the much more widespread mobiliary art, no decorated caves have so far been discovered in other parts of the area covered by the Magdalenian.

The fact that the paintings in the Kapova (or Shulgantash) cave in the southern part of the Urals (mammoths and wild horses) (Plate 38) show affinities with Magdalenian art is difficult to explain, because we have no other evidence for an extension of this culture further east than Poland.

What we have learned from the finds in France and Spain is extremely impressive. Often there are life-size representations – sometimes larger than life – of the animals of the chase, mostly big game, together, as in mobiliary art, with smaller animals (Plate 44), birds and fish. It is clear from the shape of the lines in the engraved or painted figures that they were made with great assurance by the hunter-artists who produced these pictures thousands of years ago in the light shed by extremely inadequate sources of illumination. One can see that they had a thorough knowledge of the animals and their behaviour and were therefore able to reproduce them in the most naturalistic manner. Not infrequently, natural features in the rock were incorporated in the design, which suggests that people's imaginations were aroused by their sojourn in the loneliness of the caves and made receptive to the psychic world. The culminating point is constituted by the polychrome pictures of animals, so beautiful and perfect that, as has been said, people in the nineteenth century refused to believe they were genuinely ancient work. But then, at the very end of the Magdalenian, in other words around 12,000 years ago, rock art also loses momentum and declines in both quantity and quality as a result of various factors bound up with the changing environmental conditions at the end of the Ice Age.

EPIGRAVETTIAN

In parallel with the Magdalenian in western Europe, a cultural development of a somewhat different kind was taking place in the central and eastern parts of the European side of the Mediterranean. As mentioned by M. Otte in Chapter 21, this is known in the Apennine peninsula as the Epigravettian. A number of finds have been made of both mobiliary and rock art, the latter in Sicily (Plate 37) and Levanzo (a small island to the west of Sicily), bearing witness to this late Ice Age culture. The representations in some ways differ stylistically from Magdalenian art.

MESOLITHIC

It is also mentioned in Chapter 21 that in western Europe between 11,800 and 10,200 years ago (the Allerød and late Dryas age) a culture called the Azilian arose out of the Magdalenian, which was then in decline owing to environmental change. The later culture carried on the hunting traditions in an altered form; of interest to us is the fact that rock art is almost totally absent and 'painted pebbles', round stones striped and dotted with paint, are all that is left of the many-faceted mobiliary art of the Magdalenian.

This widespread absence of mobiliary and rock art is a general feature of Europe's Mesolithic societies, both among the 'epigonic' cultures, the western groups carrying on the Upper Palaeolithic traditions, and among the 'progressive' ones of the north where adaptation to the changed environmental conditions at the end of the Ice Age around 10,000 years ago led more quickly to the introduction of new techniques and implements. Even so, there are indications of mobiliary art from the Maglemosian culture which was strongly developed during the Boreal climatic period (8,800 to 7,500 years ago) in the area of Denmark and southern Sweden and also in England: on the one hand, geometrical ornaments (sometimes of an anthropomorphic or zoomorphic nature) (Fig. 64) and decorated articles of use and, on the other, occasional varyingly naturalistic figures of animals engraved or formed in the round.

In addition there are, during the still hunting-oriented Mesolithic Age in Europe, two important centres of highly interesting rock art whose roots may be attributed to the Upper Palaeolithic. To take northern Europe first, along the fjord-strewn coast of Norway from Finnmark north of the Arctic circle southwards to the neighbourhood of Oslo there is a group of rock pictures described as 'arctic' or 'huntsman's art'. The representations, most of them on exposed rock surfaces in all positions from the vertical to the horizontal, are markedly naturalistic, particularly in Finnmark, whereas towards the south they have an increasing tendency to be stylized and to resemble the later, in most cases Bronze Age, pictures also found there. The culture they belong to and therefore their date are not yet firmly established, but it may be safely assumed that this group of rock pictures comes from an at least predominantly hunting-oriented society. The naturalistic representations in Finnmark may possibly have affinities with the Komsa culture; the source of this group, characterized by peaks of style in the inventory of stone implements is still in dispute, its derivation from the Upper Palaeolithic culture of the western part of the former USSR (where there is the Kapova/Shulgantash cave in the southern Urals with painted representations of Ice Age animals (Plate 38), as mentioned above in relation with Magdalenian art) being for the moment, pure speculation. The representations in Finnmark are cut into the rock, are sometimes larger than life-size and most portray elk, reindeer, bears, whales, seals and water-birds, in other words the game that Mesolithic people hunted on land and water.

Figure 64 Stylized figures (height 2 cm) carved on a bone, Maglemose, Sjaelland (Denmark), Maglemosian.

Moving south, there is an extremely interesting group of rock pictures in eastern Spain, running from the province of Lerida in the north to that of Murcia in the south, to which the term 'Levant art' is applied. This is to be found partly in the hilly and mountainous hinterland of the coastal area of the east of Spain and partly more deeply inside the Pyrenean peninsula as far as the province of Teruel. Here too the culture and period to which the pictures are to be ascribed have long been unclear and in dispute. Today, their derivation from Ice Age art and classification with Epipalaeolithic or Mesolithic cultures is proving increasingly probable. The culture is definitely hunting-oriented but post-Ice Age. Furthermore, it is wholly possible that the people concerned clung to their hunting-oriented way of life based on a predatory economy at a time when animal husbandry and crop growing were already known in other parts of the Iberian peninsula.

Levant art comprises paintings applied to the walls of exposed rock shelters. Most of them are small, often only the size of a human hand. A few are larger and certain

Figure 65 Deer hunt (distance from upper right to lower left 18 cm) painted in black, Abrigo Mas d'en Josep, Valltorta, Castellon province (Spain). Art of the Levant, Mesolithic.

239

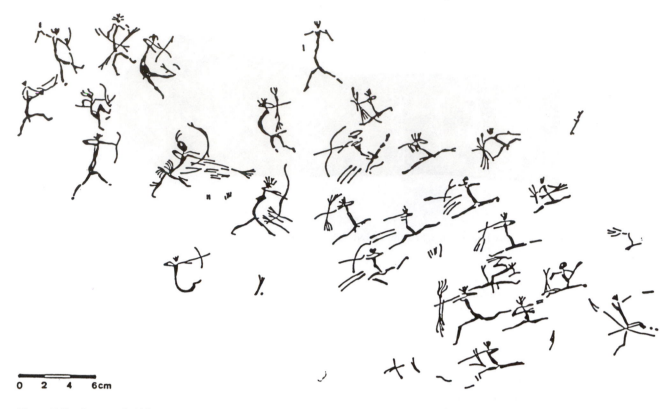

0 2 4 6cm

Figure 66 Battle scene (width 50 cm), painted in black, Abrigo Les Dogues, Gasulla, Castellon Province (Spain). Art of the Levant, Mesolithic.

exceptions are almost life-size. Although engraved lines occur in many places, painting predominates. Red, brown and black occur but white only occasionally. In contrast with Ice Age art, single one-figure representations are the exception and clearly belong primarily to an early stage of Levant art. Typical scenes are groups depicting events from the hunt (Fig. 65) and combat (Fig. 66), dancing and other activities in the life of a hunting and gathering society. Some pictures are extraordinarily alive and afford an interesting insight into the weapons, clothing, ornaments and hairstyles of the people who painted them. The pictures of animals, which portray what are clearly post-Ice Age fauna with stags, aurochs, wild boar and ibex predominating, are mostly naturalistic in character but in the human figures there is a varyingly strong trend towards stylization. We have no clues to the significance of Levant art. One is tempted to think of picture-stories but the fact that the paintings are often crowded into a particular niche in the rock, although there are equally suitable places nearby argues for the 'sanctuary' hypothesis, a theory supported by the fact that such niches, as in Cogul (Lerida province), bear more recent dedicative inscriptions, proving that they must still have been visited as places of worship in Iberian and Roman times.

BIBLIOGRAPHY

ADAM, K. D.; KURZ, R. 1980. *Eiszeitkunst im süddeutschen Raum.* Stuttgart.

L'Art des cavernes. Atlas des grottes ornées paléolithiques françaises. 1984. Paris.

BANDI, H.-G.; MARINGER, J. 1952. *L'Art préhistorique: les Cavernes, le Levant espagnol, les régions arctiques.* Basle.

BANDI, H.-G. et al. (eds) *La Contribution de la zoologie et de l'éthologie à l'interprétation de l'art des peuples chasseurs préhistoriques.* Fribourg.

BELTRAN MARTINEZ, A. 1968. *Arte rupestre levantino.* Zaragoza.

BREUIL, H. 1952. *Quatre cents siècles d'art pariétal.* Montignac.

BREZILLON, M. 1980. *Dictionnaire de la préhistoire.* Paris.

DAMS, L. 1984. *Les Peintures rupestres du Levant espagnol.* Paris.

Dänische Vorzeit. Führer durch das Nationalmuseum. 1972. Copenhagen.

DELPORTE, H. 1979. *L'Image de la femme dans l'art préhistorique.* Paris.

GJESSING, P. 1932. *Artiske Helleristninger i Nord-Norge* [Arctic Rock Carvings in North Norway]. Oslo.

GRAZIOSI, P. 1956. *L'arte'dell antica età della pietra.* Florence.

HALLSTRÖM, G. 1938. *Monumental Art of Northern Europe from the Stone Age.* Stockholm.

—— 1960. *Monumental Art of Northern Sweden from the Stone Age.* Stockholm.

KOENIGSWALD, W. VON; HANN, J. 1981. *Jagdtiere und Jäger der Eiszeit.* Stuttgart.

Kunst der Eiszeit in Deutschland und der Schweiz. 1985. Cologne.

LAMING-EMPERAIRE, A. 1962. *La Signification de l'art rupestre paleolithique.* Paris.

LEROI-GOURHAN, A. 1964. *Les Religions de la préhistoire.* 4th edn. Paris.

—— 1965. *Préhistoire de l'art occidental.* Paris.

LUMLEY, H. DE. (ed.) 1984. *Art et civilisation des chasseurs de la préhistoire: 34.000–7000 av. J.-C.* Paris.

MARSHACK, A. 1972. *The Roots of Civilisation.* New York.

MÜLLER-BECK, H. (ed.) 1983. *Urgeschichte in Baden-Württemberg.* Stuttgart.

MUSÉE DE L'HOMME. 1984. *Art et civilisations de chasseurs de la préhistoire.* Paris.

REINACH, S. 1922. *Cultes, mythes et religions.* 3rd edn. Paris. Vol. I.

SIEVEKING, A. 1972. *The Cave Artists.* London.

UCKO, P. J.; ROSENFELD A. 1967. *Palaeolithic Cave Art.* London.

WHYNER, J. 1982. *The Palaeolithic Age.* London.

ZERVOS, C. 1959. *L'Art de l'époque du Renne en France.* Paris.

24

WESTERN ASIA

from the end of the Middle Palaeolithic to the beginnings of food production

Ofer Bar-Yosef

THE DATE OF THE WESTERN ASIAN NEANDERTHALERS

The presence of anatomically Modern humans in the Mousterian contexts of western Asian sites was already recognized during the excavations of the Mt Carmel caves in the 1930s. Since then additional skeletons have been uncovered in Qafzeh cave (Israel), Shanidar (Iraq), Amud cave (Lebanon) and recently in Kebara cave (Trinkaus, 1983, 1984; Vandermeersch, 1981; Bar-Yosef et al., 1986). Anthropological observations indicate that two types existed during the first part of the Upper Pleistocene. One is often called Archaic *Homo sapiens* or 'proto-Cro-Magnon' while the other is known as 'Neanderthal' or 'advanced Neanderthal' (*Homo sapiens neanderthalensis*).

The definition and the dating of the Mousterian human remains of western Asia are inseparable from the problem of the European Neanderthalers and the emergence of *Homo sapiens sapiens*. While several scholars see a local phylogenetic evolution from European Neanderthalers to early Modern humans (Wolpoff, 1981), others prefer to interpret the archaeological–palaeontological situation as pointing to the replacement of the classic Neanderthalers by *Homo sapiens sapiens* (Stringer et al., 1984). Although Neanderthalers evolved from the time of Isotope Stage 6 (Riss III in French terminology), their presence or genetic imprint is seen at a much later date in Western Asia.

The bio-anthropological issue is complicated by the uncertainties in the dating of the Mousterian sequence in western Asia. This situation has been somewhat improved in recent years by the results of new excavations, detailed biostratigraphies and the first thermoluminescence dates (Jelinek, 1981; Bar-Yosef and Vandermeersch, 1981; Tchernov, 1981; Roe, 1983; Bar-Yosef et al., 1986).

The presence of Mousterian assemblages on the Lebanese transgressive shore-line (named Enfean II) with *Strombus bubonius* is well known (Sanlaville, 1981). This Enfean II shore-line is now tentatively dated to the 'last interglacial' or 130,000 to 120,000 years ago. One outcrop is radiometrically dated to between 90,000 and 93,000 years ago, but could be of a somewhat earlier age. This corresponds to other uranium-series dates of Mousterian age – travertines in Zuttiyeh cave (Galilee) and Ain Aqev (Negev), indicating an overall date of *c.*97,000 to 90,000

years ago (Schwarz et al., 1980). The preceding Acheulo-Jabrudian sequence (or the 'Mugharan tradition'), which contained the fragmentary skull of an archaic *Homo sapiens*, is dated to an earlier period (Gisis and Bar-Yosef, 1974) perhaps as far back as 150,000 to 140,000 years ago (Copeland and Hours, 1983). Thus the Mousterian sequence commenced around 115,000 to 110,000 years ago.

Dating the phases within the Mousterian sequence, which lasted until 40,000 years ago, is essential. The microfaunal stratigrapical sequences demonstrate that the Mousterian layers in Qafzeh cave which contained the burials of anatomically Modern humans preceded the Neanderthal woman from Tabun C or the Amud man. It means that the Neanderthalers, who developed in Europe and never reached North Africa, arrived in western Asia during Mousterian times.

This human movement or genetic flow probably resulted from the onset of oxygen isotope stage 4 (*c.*75,000 to 70,000 years ago), which was characterized on the continents by the rapid expansion of glaciers. The ecological changes, as reflected by the major shifts in the faunal spectra, forced the European Neanderthalers to readapt their survival techniques, the innovations including migration into new territories. South-west Asia, on the whole, was an ideal refuge area with large lakes and temperate climatic conditions. If this scenario is further substantiated, then the arrival of Neanderthal features in south-west Asia occurred during late Mousterian times. With the local selective forces acting against their physical features they disappeared after several thousands of years. Thus the presence of Modern humans around 40,000 years ago in western Asia was merely the continuation of local evolution.

THE TRANSITION FROM THE MIDDLE PALAEOLITHIC TO THE UPPER PALAEOLITHIC

Understanding the nature of the Middle to Upper Palaeolithic transition is commonly achieved by an overall comparison of various cultural aspects. Thus, before proceeding into the description of the actual transition, a general comparison is worthwhile.

Visually, the differences between the south-west Asian cultural achievements of the Middle Palaeolithic people and their Upper Palaeolithic descendants are less impressive when compared with their European contemporaries. The Upper Palaeolithic cultural remains in south-west Asia do not include numerous art works like those of the Franco-Cantabrian region or mobile art objects like those in central and eastern Europe. Part of this poverty can be explained by conditions of preservation in south-west Asian cave sites and rock shelters, and the relatively small number of excavated Upper Palaeolithic occurrences. Rare art objects uncovered recently, such as an animal engraving (possibly of a horse) from Hayonim cave (western Galilee, Israel) (Belfer-Cohen and Bar-Yosef, 1981), and the mobile art objects of the Natufian, which is a late Pleistocene culture, indicate that, with additional fieldwork, the picture might change.

The number of excavated Upper Palaeolithic sites is rather small. Many of those which have been studied in recent years are located in the semi-arid region of the Negev and Sinai and on the margins of the Syro-Arabian desert (Marks, 1977, 1983a; Bar-Yosef and Phillips, 1977; Gilead, 1983; Goring-Morris, 1985; Garrard et al., 1986). Only in rare cases are bones well preserved. More often, little can be learned from these sites, apart from details of the technology and typology of the lithic assemblages.

When Mousterian cave sites are compared with Upper Palaeolithic ones it seems that the former commonly used a larger space than the latter. In the semi-arid zone, Mousterian occupations convey an impression of having been more intensive than the Upper Palaeolithic ones, although this might have been the result of different aggradation and degradation processes. The Upper Palaeolithic occupations are interpreted as reflecting a highly mobile exploitation strategy (Marks, 1981).

Intentional, well-organized Mousterian burials are known from several south-west Asian sites. Upper Palaeolithic graves are scarce and only one (in Nahal Ein Gev I, Israel) was reported in detail (Arensburg, 1977). Incomplete human remains were retrieved in cave sites such as El Wad, Hayonim and Ksar Akil, but none indicate intentional burials.

The use of red ochre has been recorded in both Mousterian and Upper Palaeolithic contexts (Wreschner, 1983). Bone tools have been found only in Upper Palaeolithic sites, including open-air occurrences in *terra rosa* soils (Newcomer, 1974; Goring-Morris, 1980; Belfer-Cohen and Bar-Yosef, 1981). Although the use of marine shells is thought to have commenced in Upper Palaeolithic times, a few *Glycymeris* sp. shells were found in Skhul and Qafzeh caves, in the Mousterian levels. Intensive collection of marine shells increased considerably from 25,000 to 20,000 years ago onwards. Most, if not all, of these shells were used for decorations and not as food resources.

To sum up, the cultural differences between the south-west Asian Middle and Upper Palaeolithic are much less overwhelming than in Europe, and this impression is enhanced when the early phase of the Upper Palaeolithic sequence is examined. The archaeological record points to a continuous development in which changing trends in technology and typology can be observed.

The actual transition was studied in two areas, namely in Ksar Akil (wadi Antelias, Lebanon) and Boker Tachtit (Negev highlands, Israel) (Copeland, 1975; Copeland and Bergman, in Azoury, 1986; Marks, 1983a, 1983b).

The sequence in Ksar Akil may represent the central Mediterranean Levant. There, the Mousterian knapping strategy was basically oriented towards a unipolar Levallois technique. Flakes, blades and points, often with faceted platforms, were obtained from unipolar cores. The onset of the Upper Palaeolithic is determined when mainly blades, commonly with faceted platforms, were removed from unipolar blade-cores. These blanks were shaped into end-scrapers and burins, which form the characteristic tool types of Upper Palaeolithic assemblages.

In Ksar Akil, Abri Antelias and Abu-Halka cave (all within a distance of 60 km) a common tool type was the chamfered piece (*chanfrein*). This tool is a blade or a flake from which the distal end was removed by a transversal blow beginning from lateral retouch or a retouched notch. The transverse scar is visible on the dorsal face and the edge damage indicates their utilization as scrapers (Newcomer, 1970). This tool type is unknown in Israeli or Jordanian sites, but was found in a stratigraphic position of similar date in Cyrenaica (McBurney, 1967).

In the southern Levant the site of Boker Tachtit exhibits a similar transition, but the characteristic core type is bipolar. Levallois points and blades were detached from bipolar cores. The striking platform is mainly faceted in the lower level of the site (level 1), a feature which disappeared entirely in the upper level (Volkman, 1983).

A similar trend is exhibited by the retouched pieces. Levallois points made in level 1 by the bipolar technique became unipolar in level 4. End-scrapers and burins are the dominant tool types, while side-scrapers are very rare. Emireh points, considered by Garrod and Neuville to indicate the onset of the Upper Palaeolithic, are common in the earlier levels and disappear entirely in level 4 (Marks and Kaufman, 1983; Marks, 1983b; Volkman, 1983).

Since the 1930s excavations it has been apparent that Emireh points were found in both late Mousterian and Upper Palaeolithic archaeological contexts, although their occurrence was interpreted as resulting from a mixture. While the presence of Emireh points in Mousterian assemblages such as Shovakh cave (Wadi Amud) are as yet not satisfactorily clarified, the Boker Tachtit finds confirm the chronological position of this type (Volkman and Kaufman, 1983).

The site of Boker Tachtit is radiometrically dated to 40,000 to 43,000 years ago. If the radiocarbon dates of Mousterian assemblages such as Douarah, Ksar Akil, Geula and others can be reconciled with those of Boker Tachtit, it seems that the transition from the Middle Palaeolithic to the Upper Palaeolithic occurred around 40,000 years ago. It is hoped that with the advancement of the AMS (C^{14} accelerator mass spectrometry) dating a better chronological picture will emerge in a few years.

Most of the other transitional assemblages and sites, including the later ones (up to about 30,000 years ago), are not radiometrically dated. Their chronological assignment is derived from their stratigraphic position. Thus in Ksar Akil the transitional assemblages are those of layers 25 to 21, in Abu Halka IVF and IVE, in Abri Antelias layers VII to V, the deposit in Emireh cave, in Et-Tabun layer C and in El Wad layer F (Garrod and Bate, 1937; Neuville, 1951; Copeland, 1975).

The general picture of site size and the possible subdivision of sites according to seasonality or other factors is unclear. The excavations of the 1930s tended to expose the entire surface of the site, while the later ones left considerable unexcavated portions. Generally when the rate of sediments versus number of retrieved pieces is calculated, the semi-arid sites are poorer than those within the Mediterranean

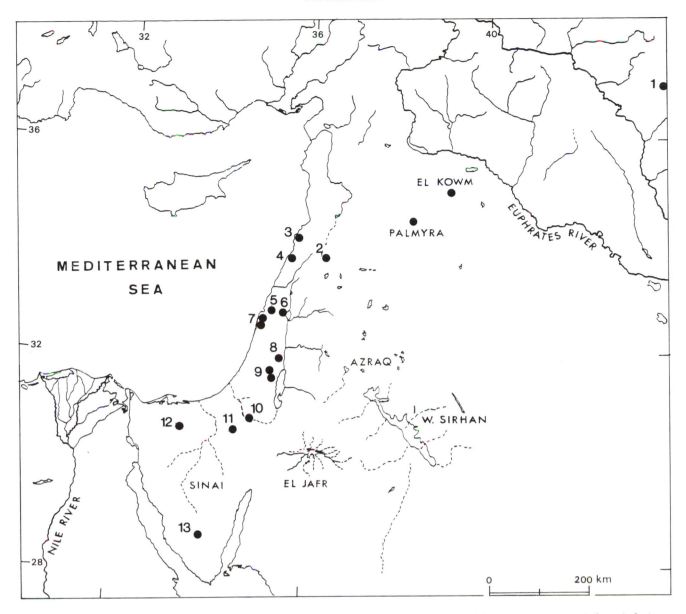

Map 21 Upper Palaeolithic sites in western Asia. 1, Shanidar; 2, Jabrud; 3, Abu Halka; 4, Ksar Akil; 5, Hayonim; 6, Emireh; 7, Sefunim, El-Wad, Kabara; 8, Fazeal IX and X; 9, Zeqel-Ahmar, El-Khiam; 10, Boker-Tachtit, Boker; 11, Kadesh Barnea; 12, Gebel Lagam; 13, Tarfat Kidrein.

vegetational belt. Repeated occupations in the same cave sites or rock shelters can be explained partially as resulting from a preference for prime locations or due to compelling topographic conditions. In the semi-arid area camping could have taken place on banks or terraces along wadi courses, many of which have since been eroded.

THE EARLY BLADE INDUSTRIES (Map 21)

The evolution of blade/bladelet industries stemmed directly from the transitional phase. The archaeological record presents a continuous sequence that unfortunately, until about 30,000 years ago, is not well dated.

This period, which according to carbon-14 dating lasted about 10,000 years, precedes the appearance of Levantine Aurignacian assemblages. The description of technological and other cultural achievements is based on Ksar Akil layers 20 to 15/14 (Copeland, 1975; Bergman, 1981) as well as layers 13 to 9, Qafzeh 9 to 7 (Ronen and Vandermeersch,

1972), Jabrud II layers 7 to 2 (Rust, 1950; Bakdach, 1982), Erq el Ahmar F, D (Neuville, 1951), Masraq en Naj D (Gilead, 1981), Boker A (Jones et al., 1983), and the Lagaman sites in northern Sinai (Bar-Yosef and Belfer, 1977; Gilead, 1983). The geographical extent of the distribution of blade industries includes the Nile Valley as well (Vermeersch et al., 1982).

More sites from this period were excavated in the Levantine desert zone than cave sites in the Mediterranean belt. The former provide data on aspects of site size and the presence of hearths. The average site size ranges from 10 to 100 m². In several occurrences hearths were exposed, in a few cases indicating the repeated occupation of the same locale.

The distribution of the Lagaman sites within the same ecological niche perhaps reflects a mixture of the contemporary camp sites of several families with specific task groups (Gilead, 1983). One may expect that when such a camp site is abandoned on a large terrace, natural agencies such as deflation and sheet wash would create a large 'site' of several thousands of square metres.

The use of red ochre is evidenced in the form of small lumps, large ochre-stained areas within the occupational horizon and ochre-stained artefacts. In most of the arid zone sites, bones were not preserved. The only evidence for gathering is broken ostrich eggshells (which could have served as water containers).

Cave sites and rock shelters, such as Ksar Akil, El-Wad, Jabrud II, Qafzeh and others, provide faunal assemblages. They clearly demonstrate the consumption of meat from the common animals in the vicinity of each site. Thus the mountainous forested area of Ksar Akil with its craggy environs supplied fallow deer, roe deer and ibex, while the hilly valley ecotone of Qafzeh had mainly fallow deer, wild oxen and gazelles (Hooijer, 1961; Bouchud, 1974). A similar picture emerges in El-Wad (Mt Carmel), where fallow deer predominated over gazelle or in Jabrud II (Anti-Lebanon mountains) in which wild ass and ibex were the only identifiable species (Garrard, 1982; Lehman, 1970).

Bones were occasionally used as the raw material for making tools (Newcomer, 1974; Newcomer and Watson, 1984), mostly awls. Marine shells are known only from Ksar Akil (Inizian and Gaillard, 1978) and a site in northern Sinai which is not well dated.

The stratified lithic assemblages of Ksar Akil exhibit quantitative changes through this period. End-scrapers outnumber burins throughout, except in layers 13 and 12. Carinated tools, including carinated scrapers and carinated burins, make their first dominant appearance in layer 12. Points were produced from blades, and the forerunners of El-Wad points (formerly Font Yves or Krems points) make their earliest appearance in layer 17 and are known as Ksar Akil points. Their profile demonstrates a shift from flat profile in layers 20 to 15 to the twisted one in layers 13 to 9 of Ksar Akil (Bergman, 1981).

The appearance of blade assemblages, sometimes with high frequencies of retouched bladelets (up to 40 per cent), at such an early date, was one of the surprises of the 1970s. Blade/bladelet industries were supposed to have preceded the Kebaran complex (late Upper Palaeolithic or Epipalaeolithic), but it became apparent that blade-knapping techniques commenced with the transitional industries. On the other hand, the presence of flake-dominated assemblages in cave sites, known as the 'Levantine Aurignacian', and of technologically (though not typologically) similar assemblages in the arid zone, has led to the conclusion that two technological traditions existed contemporaneously in the Levant (Bar-Yosef, 1980; Marks, 1981; Gilead, 1981). Each was given a different name. The blade/bladelet tradition was called Ahmarian (after the rock shelter of Erq el Ahmar in the Judean desert), while the term Aurignacian was often kept for the flake-dominated assemblages. However, it should be noted that the original definition of the Aurignacian had changed since the early days of D. Garrod (Garrod and Bate, 1937). In the 1970s L. Copeland updated the definition of the Levantine Aurignacian, subdividing it into three phases. Thus, Levantine Aurignacian A and B were, as presented in the type-sequence of Ksar Akil in layers 13 to 9, dominated by the production of blades and bladelets along with typical Aurignacian tool types such as carinated scrapers (Copeland, 1975; Copeland and Bergman, 1987). Only in layers 8 to 6 are flakes the dominant blanks, many of which were shaped into carinated tools. The latter assemblages are accompanied by many more bone and antler objects when compared to preceding and succeeding industries.

The contemporaneity of two cultural phyla is a much-debated subject in archaeological literature. Thus a further chronological clarification is needed. If western Asia is taken as a whole it is quite clear that the classical Aurignacian industry is absent from the southern desert areas. Continuous field research along the edge of the Syro-Arabian desert will enable us to outline the boundaries between this entity and its contemporaries. The presence of the Levantine Aurignacian in the Mediterranean vegetation belt and especially in the coastal hilly ranges requires an explanation. The 'immigration model' advocated by Garrod (1957) saw the special typological features such as nosed and carinated scrapers, Aurignacian blades and the relative proliferation of bone and antler tools as resulting from a penetration of European hunter-gatherers through Anatolia into the Levant. Without denying the possibility of long-range exchange networks, the Levantine Aurignacian and its derivatives can be seen as a 'short-term' adaptation (c.5,000 radiocarbon years) to the Levantine coastal hilly ranges. The contemporaneity of the Ahmarian and Aurignacian traditions, when carefully examined, despite the paucity of carbon-14 dates, seems overall to be of brief duration when viewed against the entire Upper Palaeolithic sequence, which lasted about 30,000 years. The Ahmarian or the complex of blade/bladelet-knapping techniques was probably the one practised by most of the south-west Asian hunter-gatherers of this period.

THE LEVANTINE AURIGNACIAN (Map 21)

In order to isolate the archaeological phenomenon of the Levantine Aurignacian, in its limited definition (Gilead, 1981), only the assemblages characterized by the following features will be considered (Fig. 67): that over 50 per cent of tools and debitage are flakes, that nosed and carinated scrapers are abundant, that Aurignacian blades are present, and, where there is good bone preservation, that a fair number of antler and bone tools occur. Other assemblages dominated by scrapers and burins commonly made on flakes could be interpreted as reflecting the continuation of the Aurignacian tradition. However, such a conclusion is open to debate, and these flake assemblages will not be referred to here as Aurignacian.

The distribution through time of sites along a north–south transect indicates that the Levantine Aurignacian as defined above is known at present from a limited area, namely that of the forested coastal central Levant. A few possible occurrences in southern Turkey point perhaps to a geographical spread which stretched into the Balkans.

Most of the known Levantine Aurignacian sites are either caves or rock shelters. In two of these (Ksar Akil and Hayonim cave) rich bone and antler assemblages were preserved (Newcomer, 1974; Newcomer and Watson, 1984; Belfer-Cohen and Bar-Yosef, 1981). Despite careful surveys in the Israeli coastal plain, no Aurignacian open-air sites were found; the suggestion that they were all flooded by the postglacial rise in sea-level is a mechanistic solution for the problem. Very few occurrences were noted in the Beqa'a and the Jordan Rift Valley or on the Syrian–Jordanian plateaux. Only Jabrud rock shelter II provided evidence for the presence of Aurignacian assemblages on the eastern flanks of the Anti-Lebanon mountains. No Aurignacian assemblages were recorded in Sinai and the Syro-Arabian desert.

The lithic assemblages of the central Levant demonstrate

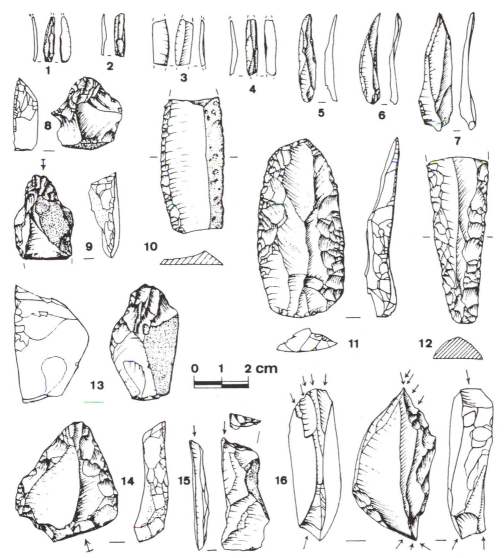

Figure 67 Levantine Aurignacian artefacts, Hayonim cave (Israel): 1–7, finely retouched bladelets; 8, 9, 14, nosed scrapers; 10, retouched blade; 11, double side scraper; 12, broken Aurignacian blade; 13, carinated scraper; 15, burin on concave truncation; 16, double dihedral burin.

the combined use of two knapping techniques. The dominant one produced thick flakes and thick blades. Most of these blanks were shaped into end-scrapers, carinated and nosed scrapers, burins and Aurignacian blades. The second, although not always frequent, resulted in the removal of delicate blade/bladelets. Many of these were retouched to form the El-Wad points. Stratigraphic observations indicate that El-Wad points tend to disappear in the later phase of the Levantine Aurignacian (Garrod, 1957). This point, which probably served as a spear or projectile point (Bergman, 1981; Bergman and Newcomer, 1983), was possibly replaced by antler bipoints. Nosed scrapers exhibit a similar trend. The frequencies of this type decreased through time. Its presence or absence in various assemblages, although traditionally interpreted as of cultural significance, can be explained in terms of hafting considerations. Thus, it is suggested that in sites or situations characterized by a scarcity of raw materials or by diminishing numbers of complete blanks, carinated scrapers were retouched several times while still hafted, resulting in nosed forms. In cases or places where raw material was abundant, hafted carinated scrapers were continuously replaced by new ones. The scarcity of blanks is often indicated by an increase in use of old, patinated

pieces, such as in Hayonim cave (Belfer-Cohen and Bar-Yosef, 1981). In the Negev, where hunting, collecting and habitation localities are close to flint sources, only thick end-scrapers were found and not the nosed version.

The flake assemblages which stratigraphically overlie the typical Levantine Aurignacian are often characterized by the proliferation of burins made on truncated flakes. This is demonstrated by the quantitative picture in Ksar Akil 6, Nahal Ein Gev I, Fazael IX, El-Khiam 10–11 and other sites (Newcomer, 1971; Goring-Morris, 1980; Echegaray, 1964/6). However, the dating of this phase, or even confirmation of the chronological and cultural relationship between the many open-air sites and the preceding Levantine Aurignacian, is far from being clear. Additional assemblages were collected from deflated sites in the Negev highlands (Marks and Ferring, 1977) and are sometimes termed the 'Arqov-Divshon' group (Gilead, 1981). Others were found in Kadesh-Barnea and western Sinai (Gilead, 1983).

The typical Levantine Aurignacian is thus far better known from the central Levant. As most assemblages were excavated in cave and rock shelter sites, the bone and antler industry was preserved. The European 'groove and splinter' technique was never found. The shaping of tools was done by flint knives which often left 'chattering marks' (Newcomer, 1974). Tool types are classified as awls, points, bipoints (often made of antler), spatulas and so on.

Almost every assemblage contained stone slabs which were used for mixing red and black pigments. In Hayonim cave two finely engraved limestone slabs exhibit the results of rare artistic activities. One slab (the better preserved) shows a form of an animal, possibly a horse (Belfer-Cohen and Bar-Yosef, 1981).

Scarce human remains, which might be the residues of unorganized burials, were noticed at El Wad, Hayonim and Kebara. The only grave was uncovered at Nahal Ein Gev I in the context of a burin-dominated industry. It was a flexed burial of a woman, 30 to 35 years of age, laid on her right side with a few gazelle horn-cores in the grave fill. Her physical attributes indicate close affinities with European Upper Palaeolithic humans and the later proto-Mediterranean south-west Asian population (Arensburg, 1977).

Animal bones are well preserved in cave sites and open-air sites within the Mediterranean vegetation belt (e.g. Hooijer, 1961; Davis, 1982). The faunal spectrum seems to represent the available game in each region. Thus the Ksar Akil forested mountainous environment provided mainly fallow deer, roe deer and ibex, while in Hayonim cave gazelles were dominant among the animals exploited. In the Ein Gev area (east of the Sea of Galilee) gazelle, red deer and fallow deer were hunted and in Fazael IX (Lower Jordan Valley) gazelles were prolific along with some fallow deer.

Given the environmental fluctuations during this period and the scarcity of detailed publications, little can be said about what cultural determinants dictated the fauna selected from the available spectrum. Current field projects in Israel, Jordan and Syria will in the future provide better data.

BLADE/BLADELET INDUSTRIES AND THE TRANSITION TO THE EPIPALAEOLITHIC

Stratigraphic evidence from Ksar Akil, Jabrud III and other sites indicates that the post-Levantine-Aurignacian flake industries are followed by assemblages dominated by blade/bladelets. These form the later phase of the Ahmarian tradition (Gilead, 1981; Marks, 1981). Although the production of flakes, which in every industry is part of the basic knapping technique, continued, it seems that in most assemblages blades were the chosen blanks for secondary trimming. Here and there a flake-dominated toolkit is to be found. Such is the case of Ain Aqev (radiometrically dated to 17,000 years ago), but the general trend involves a proliferation of blade/bladelet tools.

In the early sites assigned to this phase, El-Wad points are still found. However, the dominant tool forms are various retouched and backed blades and bladelets shaped by abrupt, semi-abrupt and fine retouch. In several assemblages carinated cores or carinated burins, from which twisted bladelets were removed, would be considered as the remnants of the Aurignacian technological tradition.

Bone tools are few and are mainly classified as points. A special point, on which five series of short transversal incisions were made, was found at Ksar Akil (Tixier, 1974). A somewhat similar object with a zigzag engraved pattern was found in Jaita II, layer II, considered to be contemporary with the Ksar Akil context (Copeland and Hours, 1977). Several grinding stones, often with red ochre stains, were retrieved in various sites.

The distribution of the sites and their size do not differ from the preceding period. They give the impression that the dichotomy between small sites (less than 100 m²) and large ones (several hundred square metres) persisted. The same can be said about hunting, as evidenced in the bone collections.

The transition to what is known in south-west Asia as the Epipalaeolithic was defined on the basis of a theory. Historically, microlithic industries in North Africa were labelled Epipalaeolithic before their radiometric age was known. This determination was followed by Perrot (1968), who suggested adopting this term for the microlithic industries of the Levant. Such a step seemed logical when the European formula of 'Mesolithic = microliths = Postglacial' was found to be inadequate for western Asia. Furthermore, during the 1960s it was not known that some Levantine Upper Palaeolithic industries contain high frequencies of retouched bladelets. Therefore, the microlithic Kebaran industry, as defined by D. Garrod and R. Neuville in the 1930s, was considered as the early Epipalaeolithic. In the 1970s it was demonstrated that the Kebaran (Fig. 68) actually incorporates two microlithic complexes. The earlier one, for which the term Kebaran was reserved, includes very few geometric microliths. The later complex was named Geometric Kebaran as its microlithic component is dominated by geometrics, mostly trapezes and rectangles and rarely triangles and lunates (Bar-Yosef, 1975).

With the few available radiocarbon dates for the Kebaran this subdivision meant that the Epipalaeolithic commenced approximately 19,000 years ago. The Kebaran was followed by the Geometric Kebaran and its contemporary industries (from about 14,500 to around 14,000 years ago), ending with the establishment of the Natufian culture about 12,500 years ago (Bar-Yosef, 1975, 1981; Henry, 1983). Recently it was proposed to rename the major phases Epipalaeolithic 1 (about 19,000 to 12,500 years ago) and Epipalaeolithic 2 (about 12,500 to 10,500 years ago) or the Natufian and its contemporaries (Moore, 1985). A different approach advocates defining the onset of the Epipalaeolithic as taking place when the more distinct typological change of the Geometric Kebaran occurs (Gilead, 1983). However, when settlement pattern, site size, economic activities, subsistence strategies and so on are taken as a combined yardstick for measuring socio-cultural changes, it is clear that the real shift from what was a typical Palaeolithic way of life to sedentary and perhaps even incipient cultivating communities comes only with the establishment of Natufian sites.

The term 'Epipalaeolithic' is still used in western Asia in its original meaning as coined in the 1960s. Within the framework of a survey of the complete Upper Palaeolithic sequence, the pre-Natufian Epipalaeolithic should be taken into account.

THE KEBARAN COMPLEX (Fig. 68)

The Kebaran complex was originally defined on the basis of its lithic characteristics, its chronological and stratigraphic position and its geographical distribution in the Mediterranean Levant.

Over thirty sites are known already in the Levant, including both stratified sites which contain several assemblages and isolated single culture sites. Of these, details of about fifty assemblages are available in the form of final or preliminary

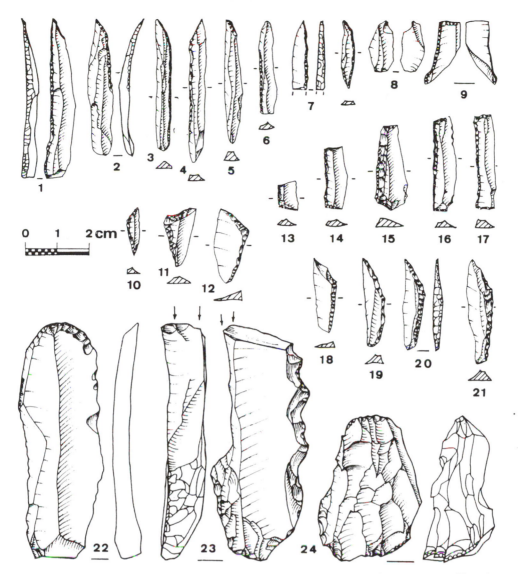

Figure 68 Kebaran, Geometric Kebaran and Mushabian artefacts, western Asia. Kebaran: 1, Falita point; 2–5, obliquely truncated and backed bladelets (Kebara points); 6, broken, partially backed bladelet; 7, broken microgravette point and small, curved micropoint; 8, microburin. Geometric Kebaran: 9, Krukowski burin; 10–12, triangles; 13, broken rectangle; 14, 16, 17, trapeze-rectangle; 15, asymmetric trapeze. Mushabian: 18, La Mouilla point; 19–21, curved arched backed bladelets. General: 22, end-scraper on blade; 23, burin on retouched and denticulate piece; 24, bladelet core.

reports (e.g. Rust, 1950; Hours, 1973, 1976; Saxon et al., 1978).

The basic technology of the Kebaran aimed at the removal of bladelets from cores, usually with one striking platform. From these bladelets various types of narrow microliths were shaped. The width of most of these microliths varies from 4 to 7 mm. Local regional variations in technology have not yet been studied in depth. Blade production was quite limited in the coastal Levantine province. Falita points, often made on blades, were manufactured mainly in Syria and Jordan and occur with other types of backed blades.

Among the shaping techniques, the retouch seems to indicate a linear change from fine and semi-abrupt retouch (obverse, inverse and alternate) to the dominance of abrupt retouch.

The presence of micro-burins in most of the Kebaran assemblages is considered accidental. However, in a few cases, such as Nahal Hadera V, layers 6 to 5, it seems to be intentional (Saxon et al., 1978) and is directly related to the production of triangles.

The typological variability within the Kebaran has not been fully investigated yet. The Israeli sites have been divided into four clusters, according to the dominant types among the entire groups of microliths, as follows (Bar-Yosef, 1981):

A   narrow curved micropoints, including a large number of pieces with basal truncation, accompanied by finely retouched bladelets;

B   curved and pointed backed and retouched bladelets, sometimes with basal truncations;

C   narrow curved micropoints and obliquely truncated backed bladelets;

D   obliquely truncated backed bladelets, sometimes along with narrow curved bladelets shaped by semi-abrupt or abrupt retouch.

Following the stratigraphic evidence from Jabrud III, Jiita, Hayonim cave, Nahal Hadera V and Fazael III, it seems that cluster D followed cluster C. Clusters A and B might be earlier but, owing to the close proximity of most cluster A sites (within a diameter of 50 km), a regional archaeological expression of an individual band of hunter-gatherers is the preferred interpretation to date. Additional evidence for a territorial variant comes from Ein Gev I and II, whose basic technology and, in particular, the appearance of the Falita point link them to the area east of the Jordan Valley. Two facies within the Late Kebaran sequence were defined in Jordan as Qalkhan and Early Hamran (Henry, 1983).

Only a few bone tools were found in Kebaran sites. These are generally points and burnishers. Among the bone points, a specimen from Jiita rock shelter decorated with a zigzag incised pattern is worth noting (Copeland and Hours, 1977).

With every new excavation of a Kebaran site ground-stone tools accumulate. The common types are mortars, bowls, cup-marked stones and different kinds of pestles. Pounding tools testify to the preparation of as yet undetermined plant foods as well as the processing of ochre. One may assume that mortars and bowls were used for pounding roasted pulses, wild cereal grains or acorns, but in the sites where those tools were found, even charcoal for dating was not preserved.

Scarce marine molluscs collected in Kebaran sites indicate a preference for Mediterranean shells. The frequencies of the bones of different animals in various sites reflect the local environments. For example, Ein Gev I hunters procured their game on the partially forested Golan plateau (fallow deer), the cliffs (ibex) and the narrow plain near the Sea of Galilee (gazelle). Avian remains are scanty.

Only one semi-flexed burial of a woman (30 to 35 years old) was uncovered at Ein Gev I (Arensburg and Bar-Yosef, 1973). Two more burials were recently uncovered in a site near Qasr Kharaneh, possibly of Kebaran age (Muheisen, 1983; Rolston, 1982). The first one was a young adult, perhaps a male. The second was a male, 35 to 45 years old, lying extended on his back with his hands by his sides. Two gazelle horn cores were found near the skull. A palaeo-pathological examination indicated that he had suffered from various bone infections before death.

The size of Kebaran sites is not easily determined due to the usually small extent of the excavated areas. However, from those sites that either have been totally excavated or where the edges of the site can be outlined, approximate dimensions can be obtained. Temporary camping sites indicate repeated ephemeral occupations (such as Hayonim and Sefunim caves), which cover an area of 14 to 25 m². In Ein Gev I, a shallow dug-out basin (5 to 7 m in diameter) was used repeatedly as a basis for a hut or shed built of organic substances. Taking into account the littered areas around it, a site size of 100 to 150 m² is reached. Surfaces of 200 to 350 m² were estimated for the occupations at Kebara cave, Jiita and Ksar Akil rock shelters, although in reality they might have been smaller. Estimating the size of open-air sites in the Israeli coastal plain represents a major problem. Many surface lithic distributions were distorted by the erosion which occurred during the Kebara period (between recurrent occupations) and in post-Kebaran times. The lack of structures and built-up features like fireplaces hampers a clear definition of the main activity areas and thus an estimate of the actual size of the site.

The location of Kebaran sites can be subdivided into lowland and highland situations. Most of the coastal plain sites are concentrated along wadi courses, often on the first *kurkar* (sandstone) ridge which lies within a few hundred metres of the shore-line. During Kebaran times (at the maximum of the Late Glacial), the shore-line was about 10 to 25 km further west and these sites were in the middle of the coastal plain, about 150 to 200 m above sea-level. Similar large or densely occupied sites are located near wadi outlets in the Jordan Valley and are also typical of lowlands location. Such clusters of sites along lowland wadi courses are considered to form the 'core area' of definable Kebaran territories (Bar-Yosef, 1975).

Sites in the hilly area are known much less frequently. They are located at altitudes of 400 to 1200 m above sea-level. Their small size (25 to 50 m²) might indicate that they were seasonal summer camps.

The geographical distribution of Kebaran sites as a whole exhibits a preference for the Mediterranean vegetation zone, indicating that cold and relatively dry conditions prevailed in the Levant during that period. Contemporary desert occupations were very rare, as is shown by recent large-scale surveys in Israel and Jordan.

THE GEOMETRIC KEBARAN (Fig. 68)

The dating of the Geometric Kebaran complex is based on its stratigraphic position, supported by numerous radiometric dates (14,500 to 12,500 years ago). The geometric components of the lithic assemblages are trapezes or rectangles. A few sites apparently of the same period are rich in triangles and lunates (such as the Middle and Late Hamran sites in Jordan), hinting at the possible existence of a different facies within the Geometric Kebaran Complex (Bar-Yosef, 1981) or contemporaneity of two cultural groups (Henry, 1983).

In its technological aspects, the Geometric Kebaran complex lacks uniformity. Its variability in aspects of both quantity and quality requires more detailed study. Following a preliminary examination, it was divided into two groups. The first is characterized by the production of narrow bladelets, a continuation of the Kebaran tradition, while the second exhibits wider bladelets and blades. This resulted, respectively, in narrower and wider trapezes/rectangles. The production of blades is also illustrated by the increased number of end-scrapers on blades.

Typologically one can discern a similar dichotomy between assemblages containing various types of microliths, dominated by trapezes/rectangles, and others with almost solely trapezes/rectangles. Sites of the latter group are common in the semi-arid regions of the Negev and northern Sinai (Bar-Yosef and Phillips, 1977; Goring-Morris, 1985).

Ground-stone tools have been uncovered in Geometric Kebaran sites within the Mediterranean vegetation belt. These include limestone and basalt pestles, bowls and mortars.

Shells were commonly obtained from the Mediterranean shores, again marking the continuation of the Kebaran tradition. Such shells were found in inland sites as far south as southern Sinai.

Recently a flexed human burial of a male 25 to 30 years old and lying on his right side, was uncovered in Neve David, near Haifa (Kaufman, 1985). The grave was marked by two rows of large stones including a broken mortar and a broken stone bowl. An additional flat grinding-stone was placed between the legs of the individual.

The limited size of excavations, the surface deflation of some sites and the bad preservation of bones in sandy deposits explain the scantiness of the information about the economic activities of the Geometric Kebaran hunter-gatherers. Ungulate remains include mainly gazelles with some fallow deer, wild boar and ibex.

The size of these sites seems to be similar to the size of those of the Kebaran. The smaller ones are 15 to 25 m², others reach 100 to 150 m². Sites within the Mediterranean forested areas are often larger and attain as much as 400 to 800 m².

The geographical dispersion of Geometric Kebaran sites encompasses north-east Syria, Lebanon, the Anti-Lebanon mountains, Galilee, Mt Carmel, the Jordan valley, the Trans-Jordan plateaux, the coastal plain, the Negev and Sinai. They are found in the mountains as well as the deserts. Dense occurrences are located in the lowlands of the coastal plain and the Jordan Valley and oasis situations in Jordan. The pattern as a whole indicates an exploitation of resources similar to that of the Kebaran. However, the distribution of Geometric Kebaran sites over semi-arid and arid zones seems to demonstrate the results of a climatic amelioration that enabled hunter-gatherers to expand into deserts.

To sum up, the size of the Geometric Kebaran band remained basically the same as during the Kebaran complex. There are clear indications of a continuous tradition accompanied by technological innovation during Geometric Kebaran times. The geographical distribution shows an expansion which is interpreted as reflecting an improvement in physical conditions which allowed traditional adaptive strategies to be carried into arid zones.

THE MUSHABIAN COMPLEX (Fig. 68)

The desert margins of the Mediterranean Levant have been the subject of intensive field study and laboratory research during recent years (Marks, 1977; Bar-Yosef and Phillips, 1977; Henry, 1983; Goring-Morris, 1985; Garrard et al., 1986). Several archaeological entities were identified on the basis of aspects of their technology and typology and were dated to the same, pre-Natufian, period (about 14,000 to 12,500 years ago). Of these, a well-defined entity is the Mushabian, of which a large number of surface and *in situ* sites were collected and excavated in the Negev and Sinai. Radiocarbon dates place it between 14,000 and 12,750 years ago. The lithic assemblages are characterized by the production of short and broad bladelets, modified to produce curved-backed bladelets, truncated-backed bladelets and La Mouillah points. Indices of the micro-burin technique are relatively high. In one of the sites in Gebel Maghara two bone tools were uncovered along with a broken pounding bowl, and a limestone pestle was found in a neighbouring site. The latter site was the only one showing evidence of repeated occupations and, due to its topographical situation, is interpreted as a winter camp. Most ephemeral sites varied in size between 50 m² and 150 m² and, among those which were well preserved, only one hearth was discovered.

The general resemblance between the Mushabian and certain North African industries is striking. The tradition of intensive use of the micro-burin technique and the production of La Mouillah points are considered to be of African origin.

The Late Mushabian (formerly known as the 'Negev Kebaran') in the Negev has been further subdivided into two phases: the Harif phase and the Helwan phase. Both phases contain backed bladelets, backed and obliquely truncated bladelets, among which concave backs are a common feature, and intensive use of the micro-burin technique. Helwan lunates (made by bifacial retouch) characterize the Helwan phase and are considered to indicate contemporaneity with Early Natufian.

Marine molluscs from these sites show both Mediterranean and Red Sea connections. Quartz pieces in Gebel Maghara indicate exchange with the region of southern Sinai.

In southern Jordan local entities were defined (Henry, 1983). The Qalkhan, a microlithic industry dominated by straight backed and truncated bladelets, has a special triangular point shaped by the micro-burin technique. The Hamran, subdivided into Early, Middle, Late and Final, seems to represent a sequence from very late Kebaran to the verge of Early Natufian. The Middle Hamran, somewhat similar to the Geometric Kebaran, exhibits high frequencies of abruptly retouched lunates which become the dominant form among the microliths of the Final Hamran.

The geographic distribution of the Mushabian and related industries is limited to the semi-arid and arid zones. Within their confines most of the sites are located in the lowlands and fewer in the highlands. The small size of the sites in the Negev, Sinai and southern Jordan should be stressed. They hardly exceed 150 m² before deflation and seem to indicate a small band size.

UPPER PALAEOLITHIC AND EPIPALAEOLITHIC IN IRAN

Unfortunately very little is known today about the Upper and Epipalaeolithic period in most regions of western Asia except for the Levant.

A few glimpses are given in the available literature of finds from Turkey and Iraq. Most of the information, however, comes from the Zagros area in Iran, which includes, in this survey, its studied portion in Iraq (Smith, 1986).

Extrapolations from palynological evidence point to the dominance of cold and dry conditions over most of this region. These prevailed until about 14,000 years ago when the Terminal Upper Pleistocene climatic changes began. Only the southern reaches, along the coast of the Persian Gulf, enjoyed a milder climate. The studied areas in the Zagros provide the archaeological evidence for a more or less continuous sequence of Upper and Epipalaeolithic industries. A thorough search along the Caspian coast and on the Iranian plateau failed to fulfil earlier expectations of the presence of very early Upper Palaeolithic manifestations. Carbon-14 dates indicate a commencement of the Upper Palaeolithic around 40,000 years ago, as in the Levantine region.

Upper Palaeolithic sites are known mainly from caves and rock shelters and a few surface sites. While the latter contained an as yet undefined blade/bladelet assemblage, the excavated caves have been reported in more detail. Thus the main sequence of lithic assemblages was named Baradostian (Solecki, 1963). This was for the present subdivided into an Early phase (40,000 to 32,000 years ago) and Late phase (32,000 to 22,000 years ago) (Hole and Flannery, 1967). The lithic assemblages are dominated by the production of blades and clearly exhibit the proliferation of bladelets through time. Burins seem to be the most frequent tool type. End-scrapers, a few carinated forms, retouched bladelets and Arjeneh points (similar to El-Wad points) make up the rest of the assemblages. Picks and choppers occur as well as grinding stones. The latter bear mainly red ochre stains but could have served for vegetal food processing as well. The rare bone tools are mainly points. Hunted game was mainly goat, sheep, red deer, cattle and onager.

The overall dispersal pattern of Upper Palaeolithic sites is not well known. Their small number (as in the Levant) is intriguing. Their topographic distribution may indicate occupation at higher altitudes during the summer. Thus the possibility that there are buried sites in colluvial and alluvial deposits cannot be ruled out as an explanation for their paucity, but the extremely cold condition which prevailed during the maximum of the Last Glacial (Emiliani Stage 2) probably limited potential occupation of the higher areas in the Zagros.

Epipalaeolithic sites, defined on the basis of their microlithic assemblages, supported by as yet very few radiometric dates, are more numerous. Among the various possible 'cultural facies' only the Zarzian is well known (Solecki and Solecki, 1983). Its age (15,000 to 12,000 years ago) corresponds to the beginning of a climatic amelioration, which brings an increase in annual temperatures and in precipitation in this region.

The early Zarzian industry is characterized by retouched and backed bladelets and the later phase by the introduction of geometrics, especially triangles, the use of the micro-burin technique, retouched and backed bladelets, borers, perforators, end-scrapers, notches and denticulates (Garrod, 1930; Braidwood and Howe, 1960; Young and Smith, 1966; Wahida, 1981). A rare form is the shouldered point. Grinding stones are present as well as pendants and beads. Marine shells were brought over long distances and obsidian from eastern Anatolia.

A degree of specialization is exhibited in the range of hunted animals. Thus goat, sheep and gazelle were common in Zarzi, goat and sheep in Shanidar, onager in Palegawra and Warwasi. Land snails were consumed and occasionally fish. In Palegawra domesticated dog was found (Turnbull and Reed, 1974).

Sites at lower and higher altitudes, in rock shelters and alluvial deposits indicate foraging over the entire Zagros area. The scanty evidence gives the same impression as in the Levant of a general dichotomy between winter and summer campsites (Smith, 1986).

THE NATUFIAN CULTURE AND ITS CONTEMPORARIES

The Natufian culture was originally defined by Garrod and Neuville on the basis of their finds in Mt Carmel and the Judean desert cave sites and rock shelters. During the 1950s and later, open-air sites were discovered, as well as Natufian layers in the lowermost levels of Neolithic mounds such as Jericho, Beidha, Mureybet and Abu Hureyra (Valla, 1975; Bar-Yosef, 1983). Thus the geographical distribution of the Natufian extends over the Mediterranean vegetation belt with some penetrations into the more arid Irano-Turanian belt. Small, ephemeral sites in the fringes of the Sinai and Syro-Arabian deserts indicate that this culture was basically dependent for its subsistence on the parkland region of the Mediterranean Levant. Earlier claims for Natufian remains in the Nile valley or in Anatolia were not confirmed.

The chronological framework of the Natufian culture is based on radiocarbon dates and typological considerations. Radiometric dates indicate early manifestations around 12,800 to 12,500 years ago and the later ones c.10,500 to 10,300 years ago (Bar-Yosef, 1983). The basic subdivision consists of the Early and Late Natufian (Garrod and Bate, 1937; Henry, 1983, Valla, 1984).

The Early Natufian is characterized by the presence of dwellings, single and communal burials, numerous stone pounders, art objects, and a rich bone industry (Fig. 69), and, among the lithic assemblages, by the predominance of microliths (often between 40 and 80 per cent) including Helwan lunates (Valla, 1984; Bar-Yosef, 1983). Among the technological traits, the dominance of short and broad bladelets, with high frequencies of flakes, gives the impression that the Natufians used fewer than their predecessors. The use of the micro-burin technique, once considered to be a chronological marker, is now seen as a 'group attribute' (Bar-Yosef and Valla, 1979), present or absent in both Early and Late Natufian contexts.

The Late Natufian exhibits similar features, with dwellings, single burials, art objects and perhaps an impoverished bone industry. Lithic assemblages are often more standardized, with lunates (with abrupt or bipolar retouch) dominant among the microliths.

A further subdivision based on a detailed analysis of the lunates and their dimensional traits was offered recently by Valla (1984). He distinguished Early, Late and Final Natufian phases and notes a decrease in the size of the lunates.

As the study of the Natufian began in what might have been its 'core area' (Stordeur, 1981) and proceeded into other regions, including the Negev and Syro-Arabian deserts and the Euphrates valley, additional sites were attributed to this entity on the basis of the presence of lunates. Thus, it seems essential to limit geographically the area of the Natufian culture. If 'base camps' or incipient villages are recognized, such as Eynan or Hayonim cave and terrace, then the settlement pattern may include seasonal or transitory camp sites situated within reasonable distances. Sites with microlithic toolkits, dominated by lunates and the use of the micro-burin technique, if found beyond 20 to 30 km from the Natufian nuclear area can be defined as possibly contemporary, but not necessarily Natufian.

Natufian base camps are often located on the ecotone, the boundary belt between the Mediterranean and Irano-Turanian vegetation zones (Henry, 1983; Bar-Yosef, 1983). The best example, excavated over an area of 400 m², is Eynan (Mallaha), where well-built dwellings were exposed (Perrot, 1966; Valla, 1981). The houses, built on a slope and constructed in undressed stone, are partially subterranean, 4 to 9 m in diameter; they exhibit the use of primitive plaster. In one house (Plate 46), several post-holes placed in a semicircle, about a metre away from the wall, hint at a possible way in which the roof was constructed (Valla, 1981). In Hayonim cave, a few round rooms, 2 to 3 m in diameter, were built inside the cave (Bar-Yosef and Goren, 1973). One structure served, during its later use, as a kiln for burning limestone. Sufficient remains on pestles in Hayonim cave, as well as in Eynan, to indicate that lime plaster was used by the Natufians.

Fragmentary structural remains, possibly of round and oval dwellings, were reported from Rosh Zin and Rosh Horesha in the Negev highlands (Henry, 1976; Marks and Larson, 1977). It is expected that excavations in Natufian sites in Jordan and Syria will provide additional evidence of Natufian building activities.

Natufian burials are a common feature of base camps, demonstrating ownership over a certain locale and the surrounding territory. Early Natufian graves are often collective, possibly belonging to particular families, and include a relatively large number of skeletons with their personal ornaments. The position of the corpse could be supine, semi-flexed or flexed (Perrot, 1966; Bar-Yosef and Goren, 1973). The Late Natufian burials are often single and flexed (Plate 47). In Hayonim cave, isolated cup marks on undressed

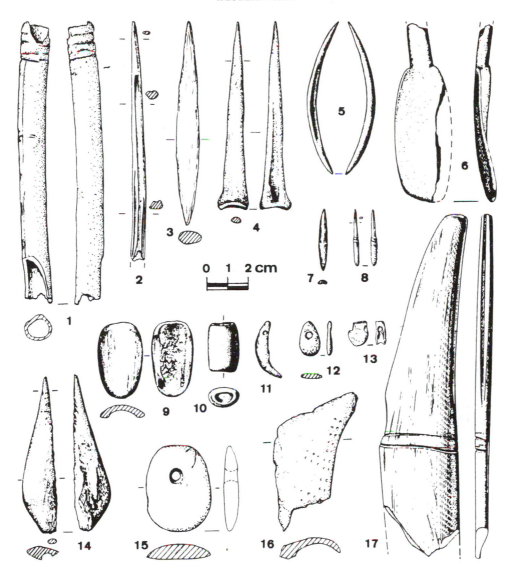

Figure 69 Natufian bone artefacts, western Asia: 1, incised bone; 2, 14, bone points; 3, 5, bipoints; 4, point with the articulation; 6, bone spoon; 7, 8, gorgets or mall bipoints; 9, non perforated oval object; 10, bone bead; 12, 15, pendants; 13, gazelle phalange pendant; 16, decorated bone by series of small partial drillings; 17, broken sickle haft.

rocks indicate the placement of the burials. Similar indications are given by the 'stone pipes' (measuring 60 to 80 cm in depth, and narrow, often with broken mortars) in Nahal Oren and Hayonim terrace. Signs of social hierarchy were recognized among the buried populations (Wright, 1978), indicating an increase in social complexity (Henry, 1985).

The assemblages of marine shells in most Natufian sites are directly related to decoration of the body and of utensils. They are dominated by Dentalium shells commonly collected from the Mediterranean shore-line, rarely from the Red Sea or as fossils from Plio-Miocene formations (Bar-Yosef, 1983). The Negev Natufian sites contain additional Red Sea species but the ratio remains in favour of the Mediterranean shells. The abundance of these shells indicates an increase in interactions within and between groups, which were an essential survival mechanism for the first sedentary communities.

Long-distance exchange included also the greenstone beads generally assigned a Syrian origin, the Anatolian obsidian in Eynan (uppermost layer) and the *Aspatharia* shells from the Nile (in Eynan; Reese et al., 1986). Most of these

commodities are found in negligible amounts (Valla, 1984; Bar-Yosef, 1983).

Art objects (Fig. 70) are few and include the carved young gazelles on sickle hafts, small human figures, rather schematic in character, as well as other portable animal figurines or representations such as the dog/owl from Nahal Oren, the tortoise from Eynan, the gazelle from Um-ez-Zuwetina and so on (Perrot, 1968; Stekelis and Yizraeli, 1963; Bar Yosef, 1983; Valla, 1975).

The Natufian bone industry reflects both technological and artistic skills. Often bovid bones were used, comprising splinters of long bones, phalanges and horn cores. Fox canines were perforated to serve as pendants. The bone tools for daily use comprised awls and points, many of which were used to perforate hides or skins, and others of which were used to make basketry. Bones were shaped into sickle hafts, as harpoons, gorges and fish-hooks (Bar-Yosef and Tchernov, 1970; Stordeur, 1981). The intensive use of bones as a raw material is undoubtedly a Natufian trait. Provisioning of suitable pieces led probably to their storage, as exemplified in a small, well-hidden cache revealed in Hayonim cave. It contained a few sawn bovid

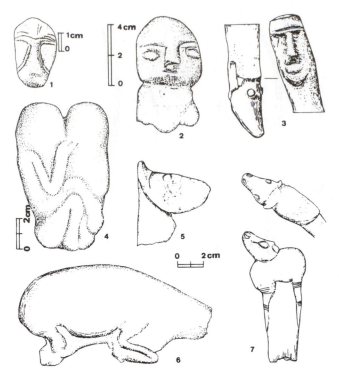

Figure 70 Natufian art objects, western Asia: 1, human face incised on a pebble (Mallaha); 2, human figurine made of limestone (El Wad); 3, double figure bone object depicting an ungulate face and a human face (Nahal Oren); 4, limestone figurine depicting a scene of intercourse (Ain Sakhri); 5, gazelle head made on bone (Nahal Oren); 6, limestone figurine of a kneeling gazelle (?) (Um ez-Zuweitina); 7, bone handle of a sickle with a carved young ungulate from El Wad.

ribs as well as a sickle haft which was in a primary stage of manufacture.

The use of bows and arrows and spears is indirectly attested in the archaeological evidence. Besides the well-shaped bone points and the microliths, grooved basalt pebbles which served as 'shaft straighteners' are found.

The Natufian subsistence strategy was based, as inferred from animal bone collections and rare plant remains, on hunting, fishing and gathering. Gazelles were the most frequent game, although fallow deer and wild boar played an important role in Eynan, in the Hula valley (Legge, 1977; Davis, 1982). Ibex and gazelle were hunted in the Negev highlands, and in most sites there is evidence for consumption of small mammals as well as reptiles. Fishing was intensive in the Hula Lake but was of some importance in the coastal sites such as El-Wad (new excavations) and Hayonim cave.

The almost total absence of plant remains is due to unfavourable conditions of preservation and the lack of systematic flotation in older excavations. The strontium : calcium ratios (Sillen, 1984), which reflect in human bone the relative proportions of vegetable food and meat in the diet, indicate that the Natufians were rather more seed consumers than meat eaters and, given the state of barley and wheat domestication ten millennia ago, it is not impossible that a few of them were incipient farmers. Intensive gathering of cereals is evidenced in the sheen on flint sickle blades, despite earlier debates (Anderson-Gerfaud, 1983).

The ground-stone industry was directly related to food-processing techniques. Although present in earlier Epipalaeolithic cultures, it seems that mortars, bowls, cup-marked stones, pestles, handstones and grinding slabs,

mullers and other such tools are more frequent in Natufian sites than before. Many objects made of basalt were transported over a distance greater than 30 km but an analysis to locate their source precisely has not been undertaken.

Storage facilities are hardly known in Natufian sites. A few plaster-lined pits were traced in Eynan (Perrot, 1966). If pulses, cereals and pistachio nuts were intensively collected, baskets were possibly used. Storage could have taken place either inside the dwellings or in underground pits outside the habitation area. The latter are often not within the targets of an ordinary excavation. More fieldwork is undoubtedly needed in order to resolve the question of Natufian storage habits.

To sum up, the Natufian, as an archaeological culture which occupied the woodland, parkland and occasionally the steppe belts of the Mediterranean Levant, marks an important change in human evolution. Sedentary communities were established which led, unlike those of other sedentary hunter-gatherers, towards the emergence of genuine farming villages. The sense of territoriality is expressed both in the dispersal pattern of Natufian sites and in the cemeteries within sites. Social hierarchy and social complexity can be traced in various archaeological aspects, including individuals who were found with their personal ornaments or special grave goods, the size of habitations, the differential use of pyrotechnology (a kiln for lime plaster) and other features.

While the Late Natufian phase in the Mediterranean belt was successful, the groups in the Negev and the northern Sinai region eleven millennia ago faced increasing environmental stress which then led to a new type of adaptation. The archaeological entity known as the Harifian (Bar-Yosef, 1975; Scott, 1977; Goring-Morris, 1985) shows in its technological and typological traits a continuation of the Negev Natufian tradition. The bulk of the artefacts were microlithic, mainly lunates and backed bladelets. The micro-burin technique was used to shape these as well as the Harif points, simple rhomboid-shaped projectile points. The geographical distribution of these points, in sites and as isolated finds, delineate an area that covers the Negev and northern Sinai (c.25,000 km²).

The subsistence strategy of the Harifian resembles an earlier Epipalaeolithic one, with dispersed winter camp sites in the lowlands and summer sites in the highlands. The major difference is that the winter camps are often small sites. Summer camps are large aggregations on the Har Harif plateau and its vicinity (900 to 1,000 m above sea-level). These sites contain subterranean round houses with a wealth of mortars, pestles, grinding stones and especially shallow cup-marked stones. It seems that the summers were relatively cooler than now, and the highlands were the source of pistachio nuts, wild barley and pulses, as well as ibex, gazelle and hare (Goring-Morris, 1985).

Marine shells were predominantly of Red Sea origin, but Mediterranean species make up to one-third of the assemblages. Greenstone beads occur together with phallic-shaped pestles, forms common also in southern Sinai at the end of the eleventh millennium BP.

Little is known in western Asia about industries or cultures that were contemporary with the Natufian. One expects to find sites with microlithic industries that are not Natufian in their other traits. Perhaps Belbasi and Beldibi caves in Anatolia, Turkey, can be related to this time span (Bostanci, 1965). Other candidates are mentioned briefly in various archaeological reports but with no radiocarbon dates (Aurenche et al., 1981; Moore, 1985). In the Caspian region a microlithic sequence was exposed and dated by McBurney (1968) in Ali Teppeh. It is only with the earliest Neolithic communities that archaeological data are available from almost the entire area of western Asia.

BIBLIOGRAPHY

ANDERSON-GERFAUD, P. 1983. A Consideration of the Uses of Certain Backed and 'Lustered' Stone Tools from Late Mesolithic and Natufian Levels of Aub Hureyra and Mureybit (Syria). In: CAUVIN, M. C. (ed.), *Traces d'utilisation sur les outils néolithiques du Proche Orient.* Lyons. pp. 77–106.

ARENSBURG, B. 1977. New Upper Paleolithic Remains from Israel. *Eretz-Isr.*, Vol. 13, pp. 208–15.

ARENSBURG, B.; BAR-YOSEF, O. 1973. Human Remains from Ein Gev I, Jordan Valley Israel. *Paléorient*, Vol. 1, pp. 201–6.

AURENCHE, O. et al. 1981. Chronologie et organisation de l'espace dans le Proche Orient de 12,000 à 5600 av. J.-C. (14,000 and 7,600 BP). In: CAUVIN, J.; SANLAVILLE, P. (eds), *Préhistoire du Levant.* Paris. pp. 571–601.

AZOURY, I. 1986. *Ksar Akil, Lebanon: A Technological and Typological Analysis of the Transitional and Early Upper Palaeolithic Levels of Ksar Akil and Abu Halka.* Vol. 1: *Levels XXV–XII.* Oxford. (BAR Int. Ser., 289.)

BAKDACH, J. 1982. *Das Jungpaläolithikum von Jabrud in Syrien.* Cologne. Ph.D. thesis, Universität Köln.

BAR-YOSEF, O. 1975. The Epi-palaeolithic in Palestine and Sinai. In: WENDORF, F.; MARKS, A. E. (eds), *Problems in Prehistory: North East Africa and the Levant.* Dallas. pp. 363–78.

—— 1980. The Prehistory of the Levant. *Annu. Rev. of Anthropol.*, Vol. 9, pp. 101–33.

—— 1981. The Epi-palaeolithic Complexes in the Southern Levant. In: CAUVIN, J.; SANLAVILLE, P. (eds), *Préhistoire du Levant.* Paris. pp. 389–408.

—— 1983. The Natufian in the Southern Levant. In: YOUNG, C. T.; SMITH, P. E. L.; MORTENSEN, P. (eds), *The Hilly Flanks and Beyond. Essays on the Prehistory of Southwestern Asia, Presented to R. J. Braidwood.* Chicago. pp. 11–42. (Stud. Anc. Orient. Civiliz., 36.)

BAR-YOSEF, O.; BELFER, A. 1977. The Lagaman Industry. In: BAR-YOSEF, O.; PHILLIPS, J. L. (eds), *Prehistoric Investigations in Gebel Maghara, Northern Sinai.* Jerusalem. pp. 42–84. (Qedem, Monogr. Inst. Archaeol. Jerus., Vol. 7.)

BAR-YOSEF, O.; GOREN, N. 1973. Natufian Remains in Hayonim Cave. *Paléorient*, Vol. 1, pp. 49–68.

BAR-YOSEF, O.; PHILLIPS, H. L. (eds) 1977. *Prehistoric Investigations in Gebel Maghara, Northern Sinai.* Jerusalem. (Qedem, Monogr. Inst. Archaeol. Jerus., 7.)

BAR-YOSEF, O.; TCHERNOV, E. 1970. The Natufian Bone Industry from Hayonim Cave. *Israel Explor. J.*, Vol. 20, pp. 141–50.

BAR-YOSEF, O.; VALLA, F. R. 1979. Évolution du Natoufien: nouvelles suggestions. *Paléorient*, Vol. 5, pp. 145–52.

BAR-YOSEF, O.; VANDERMEERSCH, B. 1981. Notes Concerning the Possible Age of the Mousterian Layers in Qafzeh Cave. In: CAUVIN, J.; SANLAVILLE, P. (eds), *Préhistoire du Levant.* Paris. pp. 281–6.

BAR-YOSEF, O. et al. 1986. New Data Concerning the Origins of Modern Man in the Levant. *Curr. Anthropol.*, Vol. 27, pp. 63–4.

BELFER-COHEN, A.; BAR-YOSEF, O. 1981. The Aurignacian at Hayonim Cave. *Paléorient*, Vol. 7, No. 2, pp. 19–42.

BERGMAN, C. A. 1981. Point Types in the Upper Palaeolithic Sequence at Ksar Akil, Lebanon. In: CAUVIN, J.; SANLAVILLE, P. (eds), *Préhistoire du Levant.* Paris. pp. 319–30.

BERGMAN, C. A.; NEWCOMER, M. 1983. Flint Arrowhead Breakage: Examples from Ksar Ajil, Lebanon. *J. Field Archaeol.*, Vol. 10, pp. 238–43.

BOSTANCI, E. 1965. The Mesolithic of Beldibi and Belbasi and the Relation with the Other Findings in Anatolia. *Antropoloji* (Ankara), Vol. 3, pp. 91–141.

BOUCHUD, J. 1974. Étude préliminaire de la Faune provenant de la grotte de Djebel Qafzeh, Israël. *Paléorient*, Vol. 2, pp. 87–102.

BRAIDWOOD, R. J.; HOWE, B. 1960. *Prehistoric Investigations in Iraqi-Kurdistan.* Chicago. (Stud. Orient. Civiliz., 31.)

COON, C. S. 1962. *The Origin of Races.* New York.

COPELAND, L. 1975. The Middle and Upper Palaeolithic of Lebanon and Syria in the Light of Recent Research. In: WENDORF, F.; MARKS, A. E. (eds), *Problems in Prehistory: North East Africa and the Levant.* Dallas. pp. 317–50.

COPELAND, L.; BERGMAN, C. A. 1987. *Ksar Akil, Lebanon.* Oxford. Vol. 2. (BAR Int. Ser., 329.)

COPELAND, L.; HOURS, F. 1977. Engraved and Plain Bone Tools from Jiita, Lebanon, and their Early Kebaran Context. *Proc. Prehist. Soc.*, Vol. 43, pp. 295–301.

—— 1983. Le Yabroudien d'El-Kown (Syrie) et sa place dans le paléolithique du Levant. *Paléorient*, Vol. 9, pp. 21–37.

DAVIS, S. J. M. 1982. Climate Change and the Advent of Domestication: The Succession of Ruminant Antidactyls in the Late Pleistocene-Holocene Period in the Israel Region. *Paléorient*, Vol. 8, pp. 5–16.

ECHEGARAY, J. G. 1964/6. *Excavaciones en la Terraza de 'El-Khiam' (Jordania).* Madrid. 2 vols.

GARRARD, A. N. 1982. The Environmental Implications of a Re-analysis of the Large Mammal Fauna from the Wadi el-Mughara Caves, Palestine. In: BINTLIFF, J. L.; ZEIST, W. VAN (eds), *Palaeo-climates, Palaeoenvironments and Human Communities in the Eastern Mediterranean Region in Later Prehistory.* Oxford. pp. 165–87. (BAR Int. Ser., 133.)

GARRARD, A. N.; BYRD, B.; BETTS, A. 1986. Prehistoric Environment and Settlement in the Azraq Basin: An Interim Report on the 1984 Excavation Season. *Levant* (London), Vol. 18, pp. 1–20.

GARROD, D. 1930. The Palaeolithic of Southern Kurdistan: Excavations in the Caves of Zarzi and Hazar Merd. *Bull. Am. Sch. Prehist. Res.*, Vol. 6, pp. 9–43.

—— 1957. Notes sur le Paléolithique supérieur du Moyen Orient. *Bull. Soc. Préhist. fr.*, Vol. 54, pp. 439–46.

GARROD, D.; BATE, D. 1937. *The Stone Age of Mount Carmel.* Oxford. Vol. 1.

GILEAD, I. 1981. Upper Palaeolithic Tool Assemblages from the Negev and Sinai. In: CAUVIN, J.; SANLAVILLE, P. (eds), *Préhistoire du Levant.* Paris. pp. 331–42.

—— 1983. Upper Palaeolithic occurrences in Sinai and the Transition to the Epi-palaeolithic in the Southern Levant. *Paléorient*, Vol. 9, pp. 39–54.

GISIS, I.; BAR-YOSEF, O. 1974. New Excavation in Zuttiyeh Cave, Wadi Amud, Israel. *Paléorient*, Vol. 2, pp. 175–80.

GORING-MORRIS, A. N. 1980. Palaeolithic Sites from Wadi Fazael. *Paléorient*, Vol. 6, pp. 173–92.

—— 1985. *Terminal Pleistocene Hunter-Gatherers in the Negev and Sinai.* Jerusalem. Unpublished Ph.D. thesis, The Hebrew University of Jerusalem.

HENRY, D. O. 1976. The Excavation of Hayonim Terrace: An Interim Report. *J. Field Archaeol.*, Vol. 3, No. 4, pp. 391–406.

—— 1983. Adaptive Evolution within the Epi-palaeolithic of the Near East. In: WENDORF, F.; CLOSE, A. (eds), *Advances in World Archaeology.* New York. Vol. 2, pp. 99–160.

—— 1985. Preagricultural Sedentism: The Natufian Example. In: PRICE, T. D.; BROWN, J. A. (eds), *Prehistoric Hunter-Gatherers: The Emergence of Cultural Complexity.* New York. pp. 365–84.

HOLE, F.; FLANNERY, K. V. 1967. The Prehistory of Southwestern Iran: A Preliminary Report. *Proc. Prehist. Soc.*, Vol. 33, pp. 147–206.

HOOIJER, D. 1961. The Fossil Vertebrates of Ksar Akil, a Palaeolithic Rock Shelter in Lebanon. *Zool. Verh.*, Vol. 49, pp. 4–65.

HOURS, F. 1973. Le Kabarien au Liban: réflexions à partir des fouilles de Jiita en 1972. *Paléorient*, Vol. 1, pp. 185–200.

—— 1976. L'Épi-paléolithique au Liban: résultats acquis en 1975. In: WENDORF, F. (ed.), *Second Symposium on Terminology of the Near East.* Nice. (Acts of the 9th International Congress for Pre- and Protohistoric Sciences, Nice.)

HOWELL, F. C. 1957. The Evolutionary Significance for Variation and Varieties of 'Neanderthal' Man. *Quarterly Rev. Biol.* (Baltimore), Vol. 32, pp. 330–47.

HOWELLS, W. W. 1976. Explaining Modern Men: Evolutionists versus Migrationists. *J. Hum. Evol.*, Vol. 5, pp. 477–96.

INIZIAN, M. L.; GAILLARD, J. M. 1978. Coquillages de Ksar Akil: éléments de parure? *Paléorient*, Vol. 4, pp. 295–306.

JELINEK, A. J. 1981. The Middle Palaeolithic in the Southern Levant from the Perspective of the Tabun Cave. In: CAUVIN, J.; SANLAVILLE, P. (eds), *Préhistoire du Levant*. Paris. pp. 265–80.

JONES, M.; MARKS, A. E.; KAUFMAN, D. 1983. Boker: The Artifacts. In: MARKS, A. E. (ed.), *Prehistory and Paleoenvironments in the Central Negev, Israel, III*. Dallas, pp. 283–332.

KAUFMAN, D. 1985. *Adaptive Changes in the Late Pleistocene of the Levant: The Evidence from Neveh David, Israel*. Denver. (Paper presented at the 50th Annual Meeting of the Soc. Am. Archaeol., Denver.)

LEGGE, A. J. 1977. The Origins of Agriculture in the Near East. In: MEGAW, J. V. S. (ed.), *Hunters, Gatherers and First Farmers beyond Europe*. Leicester. pp. 51–68.

LEHMANN, U. 1970. Die Tierreste aus den Höhlen von Jabrud (Syrien). *Frühe Menschheit und Umwelt*. Cologne. Part 1, pp. 181–6.

LEROI-GOURHAN, ARLETTE. 1980. Les Analyses polliniques au Moyen Orient. *Paléorient*, Vol. 6, pp. 79–92.

MCBURNEY, C. B. M. 1967. *The Haua Fteah (Cyrenaica) and the Stone Age of the Southwest Mediterranean*. Cambridge.

—— 1968. The Cave of Ali Tappeh and the Epi-Palaeolithic in North-West Iran. *Proc. Prehist. Soc.*, Vol. 34, pp. 385–413.

MARKS, A. E. (ed.) 1977. *Prehistory and Palaeoenvironments in the Central Negev, Israel: The Avdat/Agev Area*. Dallas. Vol. 2.

—— 1981. The Upper Palaeolithic of the Negev. In: CAUVIN, J.; SANLAVILLE, P. (eds), *Préhistoire du Levant*. Paris. pp. 343–52.

—— (ed.) 1983a. *Prehistory and Palaeoenvironments in the Central Negev, Israel: The Avdat/Agev Area*. Dallas. Vol. 3.

—— 1983b. The Middle to Upper Palaeolithic Transition in the Levant. In: WENDORF, F.; CLOSE, A. (eds), *Advances in World Archaeology*. New York. Vol. 2, pp. 51–98.

MARKS, A. E.; FERRING, R. C. 1977. Upper Palaeolithic Occupation Near Avdat, Central Negev, Israel. *Eretz-Isr.*, Vol. 13, pp. 191–207.

MARKS, A. E.; KAUFMAN, D. 1983. Boker Tachtit: The Artifacts. In: MARKS, A. E. (ed.), *Prehistory and Palaeoenvironments in the Central Negev, Israel*. Dallas. Vol. 3, pp. 96–126.

MARKS, A. E.; LARSON, P. A., JR. 1977. Test Excavations at the Natufian Site of Roshe Horesha. In: MARKS, A. E. (ed.), *Prehistory and Palaeoenvironments in the Central Negev, Israel*. Dallas. Vol. 3, pp. 191–232.

MOORE, A. M. T. 1985. The Development of Neolithic Societies in the Near East. In: WENDORF, F.; CLOSE, A. (eds), *Advances in World Archaeology*. New York. Vol. 4, pp. 1–69.

MUHEISEN, M. 1983. *La Préhistoire en Jordanie: recherches sur l'Ep-ipaléolithique – l'exemple du gizement de Kharaneh IV*. Bordeaux. Unpublished Ph.D. thesis, Université de Bordeaux.

NEUVILLE, R. 1951. *Le Paléolithique et le mésolithique du désert de Judée*. Paris. (Archives de l'Institut de Paléontologie humaine, Mémoire, 24.)

NEWCOMER, M. H. 1970. The Chamfered Pieces from Ksar Akil. *Bull. Inst. Archaeol.* (London), Vol. 8/9, pp. 177–91.

—— 1971. Un Nouveau Type de burin à Ksar Akil. *Bull. Soc. préhist. fr.*, Vol. 68, pp. 267–72.

—— 1974. Study and Replication of Bone Tools from Ksar Akil. *World Archaeol.*, Vol. 6, pp. 138–53.

NEWCOMER, M. H.; WATSON, J. 1984. Bone Artefacts from Ksar Akil (Lebanon). *Paléorient*, Vol. 10, pp. 143–8.

PERROT, J. 1966. Le Gisement Natoufien de Mallaha (Eynan), Israel. *Anthropologie* (Paris), Vol. 70, pp. 437–84.

—— 1968. La Préhistoire palestinienne. In: *Supplément au dictionnaire de la Bible*. Paris. Vol. 8, cols 286–446.

REESE, D. S.; MIENIS, H. K.; WOODWARD, F. R. 1986. On the Trade of Shells and Fish from the Nile River. *Bull. Am. Sch. Orient. Res.*, Vol. 264, pp. 79–84.

ROE, D. A. (ed.) 1983. *Adlun in the Stone Age: The Excavations of D. A. E. Garrod in Lebanon, 1958–1963*. Oxford. 2 vols. (BAR Int. Ser., 159.)

ROLSTON, S. L. 1982. Two Prehistoric Burials from Qasr Kharaneh. *Annu. Dep. Antiq. Jordan* (Amman), Vol. 26, pp. 221–9.

RONEN, A.; VANDERMEERSCH, B. 1972. The Upper Palaeolithic Sequence in the Cave of Qafza (Israel). *Quaternaria*, Vol. 16, pp. 189–202.

RUST, A. 1950. *Die Höhlenfunde von Jabrud (Syrien)*. Neumünster.

SANLAVILLE, P. 1981. Stratigraphie et chronologie du quaternaire marin du Levant. In: CAUVAN, J.; SANLAVILLE, P. (eds), *Préhistoire du Levant*. Paris. pp. 21–32.

SAXON, E. C.; MARTIN, G.; BAR-YOSEF, O. 1978. Nahal Adera V: An Open-air Site on the Israeli Littoral. *Paléorient*, Vol. 4, pp. 253–66.

SCHWARZ, H.; GOLDBERG, P.; BLACKWELL, B. 1980. Uranium Series Dating of Archaeological Sites in Israel. *J. Earth Sc.*, Vol. 29, pp. 157–65.

SCOTT, T. R. 1977. The Harifian of the Central Negev. In: MARKS, A. E. (ed.), *Prehistory and Palaeoenvironments in the Central Negev, Israel*. Dallas. Vol. 2, pp. 271–322.

SILLEN, A. 1984. Dietary Variability in the Epipalaeolithic of the Levant: The Sr/Ca Evidence. *Paléorient*, Vol. 10, pp. 149–55.

SMITH, P. E. L. 1986. *Palaeolithic Archaeology in Iran*. Philadelphia.

SOLECKI, R. L.; SOLECKI, R. S. 1983. Late Pleistocene–Early Holocene Cultural Traditions in the Zagros and the Levant. In: YOUNG, T. C.; SMITH, P. E. L.; MORTENSEN, P. (eds), *The Hilly Flanks and Beyond: Essays on the Prehistory of Southwestern Asia, Presented to R. J. Braidwood*. Chicago. pp. 123–37.

SOLECKI, R. S. 1963. Prehistory of the Shanidar Valley, Northern Iraq. *Science* (Washington), Vol. 139, pp. 177–93.

STEKELIS, M.; YIZRAELI, T. 1963. Excavations at Nahal Oren: Preliminary Report. *Isr. Explor. J.*, Vol. 13, pp. 1–12.

STORDEUR, D. 1981. La Contribution de l'industrie de l'os à la délimitation des aires culturelles: l'example du Natoufien. In: CAUVIN, J.; SANLAVILLE, P. (eds), *Préhistoire du Levant*. Paris. pp. 433–8.

STRINGER, C. B.; HUBLIN, J. J.; VANDERMEERSCH, B. 1984. The Origin of Anatomically Modern Humans in Western Europe. In: SMITH, F. H.; SPENCER, F. (eds), *The Origins of Modern Humans: A World Survey of the Fossil Evidence*. New York. pp. 51–135.

TCHERNOV, E. 1981. The Biostratigraphy of the Middle East. In: CAUVIN, J.; SANLAVILLE, P. (eds), *Préhistoire du Levant*. Paris. pp. 67–98.

TIXIER, J. 1974. Os incisé de Ksar Akil, Liban. *Paléorient*, Vol. 2, pp. 123–32.

TRINKAUS, E. 1983. *The Shanidar Neanderthals*. New York.

—— 1984. Western Asia. In: SMITH, F. H.; SPENCER, F. (eds), *The Origins of Modern Humans: A World Survey of the Fossil Evidence*. New York. pp. 251–93.

TURNBULL, P. F.; REED, C. A. 1974. *The Fauna from the Terminal Pleistocene of Palegawra Cave, a Zarzian Occupation Site in the Northeastern Iraq*. Chicago. (Fieldiana: Anthropol., 63.)

VALLA, F. R. 1975. *Le Natoufien: une culture préhistorique en Palestine*. Paris. (Cah. Rev. Biblique, 15.)

—— 1981. Les Établissements natoufiens dans le nord d'Israel. In: CAUVIN, J.; SANLAVILLE, P. (eds), *Préhistoire du Levant*. Paris.

—— 1984. *Les Industries du silex de Mallaha (Eynan) et du Natoufien dans le Levant*. Paris. (Mém. trav. Cent. rech. fr. Jérus., 3.)

VANDERMEERSCH, B. 1981. *Les Hommes fossiles de Qafzeh (Israel)*. Paris.

VERMEERSCH, P. M. et al. 1982. Blade Technology in the Egyptian Nile Valley: Some New Evidence. *Science* (Washington), Vol. 216, pp. 626–8.

VOLKMAN, P. 1983. Boker Tachtit: Core Reconstructions. In: MARKS, A. E. (ed.), *Prehistory and Palaeoenvironments in the Central Negev, Israel*. Dallas. Vol. 3, pp. 127–90.

VOLKMAN, P.; KAUFMAN, D. 1983. A Reassessment of the Emireh Point as a Possible Type-fossil for the Technological Shift from the Middle to the Upper Palaeolithic in the Levant. In: TRINKAUS, E. (ed.), *The Mousterian Legacy: Human Biocultural Change in the Upper Pleistocene*. Oxford. (BAR Int. Ser., 164.)

WAHIDA, G. 1981. The Re-excavation of Zarzi, 1971. *Proc. Prehist. Soc.*, Vol. 47, pp. 19–40.

WOLPOFF, M. H. 1981. *Palaeoanthropology.* New York.

WRESCHNER, E. 1983. *Studies in Prehistoric Ochre Technology.* Jerusalem. Unpublished Ph.D. thesis, The Hebrew University of Jerusalem.

WRIGHT, G. A. 1978. Social Differentiation in the Early Natufian. In: REDMAN, C. L. et al. (eds), *Social Archaeology, Beyond Subsistence and Dating.* London. pp. 201–33.

YOUNG, T. S.; SMITH, P. E. L. 1966. Research in the Prehistory of Central Western Iran. *Science* (Washington), Vol. 153, pp. 398–91.

25

SOUTH ASIA

in the period of *Homo sapiens sapiens* up to the beginnings of food production (Upper Palaeolithic and Mesolithic)

Ramchandra V. Joshi

Occurrences of Upper Palaeolithic material have been noticed in Afghanistan, India and Pakistan. For other regions of south Asia no information about these cultures is so far available. The most common and widespread feature of these cultures is the use of flake-blades and blades for manufacturing lithic artefacts. There have been no finds of human remains associated with these cultures, but almost all other aspects like their palaeoecology, their chronology, the typology of their artefacts and the distribution of their sites are well documented in the Indian region. Such details are, however, lacking for Afghanistan and Pakistan.

Upper Palaeolithic cultures show a directional change towards the manufacture of microliths (Mesolithic), particularly in India, and in the succeeding Mesolithic cultural level physical remains of *Homo sapiens sapiens* begin to appear. In addition, excavations of Mesolithic sites have yielded information on chronology, social aspects and settlement patterns.

The recently explored Terai region of Nepal has provided lithic material but its identity has not been established. Some of the artefacts show microlithic characteristics.

The evidence of Mesolithic cultures from Sri Lanka is very interesting. They have been dated to about 28,000 to 10,000 years ago, which chronologically should correspond to the Upper Palaeolithic period, but the tool typology is distinctly microlithic: this seems rather enigmatic.

AFGHANISTAN

The Upper Palaeolithic (Late Palaeolithic) sites lie in the semi-arid region north of the Hindu Kush. The palaeo-environment during the late Upper Pleistocene and the early Holocene is not yet properly known, but during this period the climate in general was apparently colder and more arid than that of today.

Among the several sites of this period that at Kara Kamar is well studied. The third level (Kara Kamar III) has yielded a very early Upper Palaeolithic industry in association with the loess deposits derived from the fine alluvium of the Amu-darya. This industry can be placed between 32,000 and 25,000 years ago or even earlier. The raw material used

for this lithic industry is the locally available flint. The material is composed of blades and bladelets and some of the retouched specimens recall the carinated end-scraper types of the Aurignacian industry. No burins have been found and among the retouched blades some are notched pieces. In the Zagros mountains of Iraq and Iran a roughly parallel Palaeolithic industry (Baradostian) has been found, but it does not show typological similarities to the Kara Kamar industry.

The Epipalaeolithic culture of Afghanistan is very rich and follows the Kara Kamar (III) culture after about 15,000 years. It is basically microlithic in character and appears to represent the final stages of the Upper Palaeolithic. Several localities were discovered and later excavated near the town of Aq Kupruk in Balkh Province by Louis Dupree. The stratigraphy, which is rather complex, consists of limestone rock shelter rubble, loess and alluvium. Since no pollen analysis has been done, no palaeoclimatic deductions can be made.

The artefacts include a high proportion of microblades obtained from flint cores but no geometric microliths. Since the microblade collections occur in rock shelters as well as in open sites, they seem to be used not only at the base camps but also for some other activities such as barbs on a shaft for hunting.

A variety of burins and edge-retouched blades are common tools in this assemblage. The faunal remains associated with the deposit are dominantly of sheep and goat.

Several sites of this culture have been discovered and some regional variations are noticed in their tool types. An interesting recent discovery was made by Louis Dupree and Davis in 1976 in the Dasht-Nawar area, where two surface concentrations of obsidian tools were obtained, which on typological grounds can be assigned to the Epipalaeolithic.

PAKISTAN

In the Soan region no clear Upper Palaeolithic site has yet been found. The tools of Evolved Soan may be related to Late Soan B. The Sanghao cave excavations have,

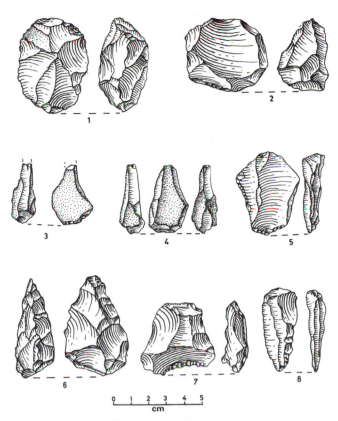

Figure 71 Middle and Upper Palaeolithic artefacts, Sanghao cave (Pakistan): 1, 2, cores; 3, 4, burins; 5, flake; 6, handaxe; 7, hollow scraper; 8, pointed flake. (After Allchin and Allchin, 1983, p. 53.)

however, yielded blade and burin industries on quartz in varying proportions from all the layers (Allchin, 1973) (Fig. 71).

INDIA

The existence of Upper Palaeolithic cultures in India was firmly established only as long ago as 1968 by Murty (1985) in coastal Andhra Pradesh in south India. The area had also yielded Lower Palaeolithic and Middle Palaeolithic artefacts. Earlier discoveries of blade-tool assemblages indicating Upper Palaeolithic traits were made by Cammiade and Burkitt and by Foote, who found bone artefacts in the limestone caves in Kurnool. The last phase of the Palaeolithic cultures in India was for a long time known as the Late Stone Age and comprised mostly Mesolithic implements (Mesolithic period). As in Europe the authors of the Upper Palaeolithic cultures of India were *Homo sapiens sapiens*, though no fossil of this human group has yet been found anywhere in India. However, the discoveries of animal fossils and bone tools and the radiocarbon dates of the deposits associated with the lithic artefacts of these cultures provide ample proof of their definite identity as Stone Age cultures belonging to a period from late Upper Pleistocene to Early Holocene. The Upper Palaeolithic sites in India have been located in habitats as varied as desert areas, hilly regions, river basins, rock outcrops, coastal tracts and caves and rock shelters.

Blade technology is the hallmark of this culture, although flakes and core-remnants have also been used for producing the finished tools, which comprise simple as well as partially or wholly marginally retouched blades, scrapers (side, end, concave, convex and multiple varieties), points, borers and burins. Some assemblages also contain Mesolithic artefacts like lunates, trapezes and triangles. Typologically two traditions can be distinguished in the regional occurrences: early Upper Palaeolithic and late Upper Palaeolithic, the latter showing Mesolithic characteristics. Its attribution to this period is to some extent supported by the available radiocarbon data.

The prismatic technique used for the production of blades by the Upper Palaeolithic culture shows it to have been technically advanced. The blades made by Middle Palaeolithic (for instance, from the Bhimbetka rock shelters in central India) or even by Lower Palaeolithic cultures (such as those from the Gudiyam caves in Tamilnadu, south India) are of a larger size and rarely carry delicate retouch and blunting as do Upper Palaeolithic blades.

The most common raw materials used to make these artefacts are siliceous minerals like chert, jasper and chalcedony, but in some sites fine-grained quartzite and lidianite have also been used. The size of the resultant finished tool was dependent on the size of the available raw material, and since the fine-grained siliceous minerals occur in small nodules Upper Palaeolithic tools in general are smaller in size than the blade-tools of Middle Palaeolithic and Lower Palaeolithic cultures, which were made on rocks like quartzite and basalt.

In recent excavations the limestone caves in the Kurnool area in south India have yielded bone artefactual remains consisting of over 1,700 pieces of worked and cut bone (mostly of bovids), of which nearly 200 are tools comprising scrapers, perforators, chisels and shouldered points: several bone blanks, cut bones and splinters. As a whole this bone industry is crude compared with the fine artistic specimens obtained from European Upper Palaeolithic cave sites.

Murty (1985) has attempted to differentiate the various sites of this culture on the basis of typological and technological criteria into three groups: (1) a flake-blade group, (2) a blade group and (3) a blade and burin group (Plate 48). This classification indicates regional variations in this cultural toolkit but does not necessarily show sequential development or evolutionary trends.

The Upper Palaeolithic sites usually occur in association with riverine or colluvial sediments. Wherever the stratigraphical horizon could be determined, as in Belan valley (Uttar Pradesh), Patne (Maharashtra) and river sections in the Andhra area, these tools occur in sediments overlying those bearing Middle Palaeolithic artefacts. The Mesolithic cultural deposits overlie Upper Palaeolithic horizons. Occurrences of this culture in natural caves or rock shelters are rather rare, the most important cave sites being Bhimbetka and Adamgarh (Madhya Pradesh) and Muchchatla Chintamanu Gavi (Andhra Pradesh). Recently this culture has also been found in association with sand dunes in Rajasthan. The radiocarbon dates of this culture which are now available range broadly from 30,000 to 10,000 years ago.

Some glimpses of the palaeoecology of this culture can be had from the fossil fauna from Kurnool cave, which includes several species belonging to the orders Primates, Carnivora, Insectivora, Perissodactyla, Artiodactyla, Crocodilia and so on. The fossils from the river sediments at Ghod (Maharashtra) include *Hexaprotodon palaeindicus*, *Equus namadicus*, *Elephas* sp., *Bos* sp., *Bubalus* sp. and *Cervus* sp. This faunal material indicates a grassland vegetation of savannah type with pockets of forest and swamp and shows a time range from the later part of the Upper Pleistocene to the early Holocene. There also occur ostrich shells in large numbers at Patne in Maharashtra and several localities in west central India.

Recent geomorphological and sedimentological studies indicate that the blade and burin complex in Rajasthan and Gujarat existed during a period of greater aridity than today (Allchin et al., 1978). The Indian climate during Upper Pleistocene showed a general tendency towards drier conditions (Rajaguru, 1973). But such changes were by and large of degree only and not of kind, at least in other geographical regions of India. The occurrence of fossils of crocodile, elephant, rhinoceros or hippopotamus at some localities indicates the existence of a few favourable habitats for such animals during the Upper Palaeolithic period.

A few objects like the bone figurine from the Belan valley (Uttar Pradesh) and engraved fragments of ostrich shell from Patne (Maharashtra) and Rajota (Madhya Pradesh) are the only evidence of Upper Palaeolithic art from the Indian region. Some of the paintings in rock shelters from central India are likely to be of Upper Palaeolithic date, but this requires further studies. There is evidence of fires and of the use of fire to harden the tips of some bone objects.

From the distribution of these sites in all kinds of environments in the monsoonal climate areas of India it is evident that the makers of this culture adapted to a variety of environments. These sites occur as surface scatters, as well as cave or rock shelter occupations. In the latter type the cave sediments are not thick and the artefactual material is not abundant. These cave occupations appear to be of a transitory nature. The open camps with thick clusters of artefacts and the evidence of large blocks of rocks and some heavy-duty tools seem to represent sedentary or seasonal occupations. At some sites in Andhra Pradesh and in Maharashtra where excavations have been carried out, the Upper Palaeolithic cultures gradually evolve into the succeeding Mesolithic phase. In rock shelter sites like Bhimbetka in central India we have evidence of the Middle Palaeolithic culture giving rise to the Upper Palaeolithic. Thus it is possible to trace the evolution of these lithic cultures. The economy at this Palaeolithic stage was based on hunting and food gathering, the evidence for the former activity in the form of faunal remains being recorded in cave sites of this culture.

NEPAL

In 1985 Gudrun Corvinus started explorations in the foothills of the Himalayan region in the Siwaliks (Churias) of western Nepal. At present (1993) studies are in progress on the geology and stratigraphy of the Siwaliks south of the Deokhuri valley between Nepal and Shivpur. Another interesting area is the Chitwan valley, where terraces have been located at heights of 25 m and 45 m. None of them, however, have as yet yielded any Palaeolithic artefacts.

In the Deokhuri and Dang valleys both on and within the fan deposits archaeological material was obtained most of which is microlithic and worked on chert, quartz and quartzite. Tools of a larger size have also been found, made on flakes and pebbles; among the latter are unifacial chopper types. The exact cultural level and chronology of these various assemblages has yet to be understood.

SRI LANKA

The Quaternary sediments at Bandala in southern Sri Lanka which occur in the coastal tracts of the semi-arid zone consist of sheet gravels capped by sands (Iranamadu formation). These excavations yielded Stone Age occupation horizons within both the gravels and the overlying sands. The artefacts from gravels were typologically indeterminate, but those from the sands are clearly microlithic, with geometric forms a major element.

No organic remains were found, but thermoluminescence dating of the sands places these sediments and hence the microlithic (Mesolithic) culture of Sri Lanka at 28,000 years BP. The geometric microliths from Kitulgala Belilena cave have carbon-14 dates of between 21,500 and 10,500 years. Microliths from Zaire and Zambia in Africa have been dated to 28,000 years ago, which is comparable to the date of those from Sri Lanka.

In peninsular India, Upper and Middle Palaeolithic artefacts have been found in late Pleistocene deposits that could be dated to about 25,000 years ago (Rajaguru et al., 1980). The microliths from the same area have been dated to 12,000 years ago. There is therefore a possibility that some of the artefacts from Sri Lanka, although typologically microlithic, are of great antiquity and thus may be elements of an Upper Palaeolithic culture.

BIBLIOGRAPHY

See Chapter 6.

26

CHINA
in the period of *Homo sapiens sapiens* up to the beginnings of food production

Jia Lanpo and Wu Rukang

The period of *Homo sapiens sapiens*, or late *Homo sapiens*, before the beginnings of food production, extended from about 40,000 to 10,000 years ago. Morphologically, these hominids are anatomically Modern. Their culture belongs to the Late Palaeolithic, roughly corresponding to the Châtelperronian to Magdalenian in Europe. Altogether 110 sites of this period have been found in China, of which thirty-five contain human fossils.

The earliest human fossils of this period were found in the Tongtianyan cave, Liujiang County, Guangxi Zhuang Autonomous Region. The fossil materials consist of a well-preserved cranium, the lower four thoracic vertebrae, all five lumbar vertebrae, the sacrum, the right innominate bone and two femur fragments.

The morphological features of the Liujiang cranium show both Mongoloid and Australoid affinities. The superciliary arches are well developed. The supraoccipital region is slightly bulging in a bun-shaped structure somewhat similar to that of the Neanderthalers of western Europe. The cranial height is moderate. The mandibular fossae are shallow, and the foramen magnum is small, but the occipital condyles are relatively massive. The face in general is broad and short. The orbits are wide and low. The nasals are also wide, and the lower margin of the nasal aperture is especially broad. The anterolateral surface of the frontal process of the malar is rotated forward as in Mongoloids. The upper right lateral incisor is shovel-shaped, one central incisor was missing and the other is too worn to allow accurate assessment of this feature. The maxillary third molars have not erupted, which is of special interest since this individual is estimated to have been 40 years old (Wu, 1959). The postcranial remains show some features of the Australoids.

No cultural remains were uncovered from this site. Animal fossils associated with the cranium belong to the *Ailuropoda-Stegodon* fauna.

Other important human fossils of this period are the Ziyang and Upper Cave skulls. The Ziyang skull was found during construction of the Chengdu-Chongqing Railway in Ziyang county, Sichuan Province. The specimen consists of the palate and partial maxilla along with small fragments of the nasals attached to a complete calvarium. The cranium is small and smooth and all its principal morphometric indices fall within the range of modern *H. sapiens*. The superciliary arches are well developed and their medial ends

unite over the nasal root to form a transverse ridge.

That the Ziyang hominid is somewhat more primitive than those discovered in the Upper Cave at Zhoukoudian (Choukoutien) is demonstrated by such morphological features as the height of the calvarium, the position of bregma, and the bregma and frontal angles. No stone artefacts were found in unquestionable association with either the Ziyang hominid specimen or the faunal components.

The Upper Cave (or Shandingdong) at Zhoukoudian yielded human remains of at least eight individuals, finely crafted ornaments, a bone needle and many fossil animals of Upper Pleistocene age.

The human fossils include three fairly complete crania, a maxilla fragment, four mandibles and fragments of radius, femur and patella.

The first skull (no. 101) was suggested by Weidenreich (1939) to have features of both Western Europeans and Mongoloids; the second skull (no. 102) was believed to be of Melanesoid type and the third one to be Eskimoid. However, Wu (1960) reanalysed casts of the Upper Cave skulls and concluded that all of them are consistent with an essentially homogeneous Mongoloid population.

Few stone implements were found in this cave, but there were many perforated animal teeth, shells, fish bones, stone beads apparently used as ornaments and a bone needle apparently for sewing. These cultural remains are quite similar to those of the Magdalenian in Europe. There is definite evidence of intentional human burials here.

Two radiocarbon dates have been given for this cave. The sample from the lower chamber dates from about 10,500 years ago and that from the lower recess from about 18,900 years ago. It is suggested that the former date probably more closely approximates the time of interment.

Sites with Late Palaeolithic cultural remains are relatively widespread all over China. The main sites are Salawusu (Sjara-osso-gol), Shiyu, Shuidonggou, Xiachuan and Xiaonanhai, and Hutouliang which is a site transitional from the Late Palaeolithic to the Neolithic. The majority of the sites in south China yield stone implements of large size and roughly fabricated. The technique is even more primitive than that of Peking Man.

The Salawusu site is situated near Dagouwan village, Ordos plateau in Inner Mongolia. It has been excavated many times. More than twenty pieces of human skeletal remains of Modern type bearing some primitive features, several hundred stone implements and many fossil vertebrates of forty-six species were uncovered. The salient feature of the artefacts is their particularly minute size. Typical implements include points, borers, side-scrapers, nosed end-scrapers, thumbnail scrapers and burins. A carbon-14 date places this site at about 35,000 years ago (Huang and Wei, 1981).

An interesting site is Shiyu, which was found near Shiyu Village, Suxian County, in northern Shaanxi Province. Besides a piece of modern human occipital bone, it yielded more than 15,000 stone artefacts, one polished and per-forated ornament of graphite and sixteen species of vertebrate fossils of the Late Palaeolithic period. The radio-carbon dates are about 31,000 and 28,100 years ago.

The Shiyu artefacts are predominantly made on pebbles of vein quartz, quartzite of different colours, agates and siliceous limestones. The majority of the artefacts are of small types, principally bipolar cores, polyhedral nuclei and slender blades made by indirect percussion. Points and scrapers become more complicated. Some of the scrapers such as double-sided scrapers, end-scrapers with rounded edges and thumbnail-shaped scrapers already known from the Xujiayao site were found. Typical burins also occurred (Fig. 72).

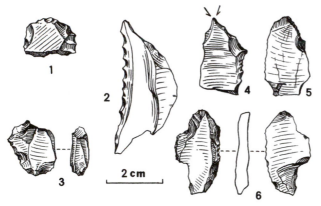

Figure 72 Artefacts, Shiyu, Shaanxi (China): 1, thumbnail scraper; 2, concave scraper 3, wedge-shaped microblade core; 4, burin; 5, arrowhead; 6, axe-like knife.

Gobi cores, frequently found in the microlithic sites of north-east China, east Siberia and North America, were also uncovered in this site. These seem to be linked with the microlithic cultural tradition of this area. Of special interest are arrowheads made of thin flint.

Another variant of Late Palaeolithic culture in north China is represented by the Shuidonggou site in Lingwu County, the Ningxia Hui Autonomous Region. A rich assemblage of stone artefacts was discovered, fashioned mainly on quartzite, siliceous limestones and marlites, and felsoporphyre.

Large implements dominate the Shuidonggou culture, which bears some resemblance to Mousterian and Aurig-nacian cultures in western Europe. In particular, the trihedral points of Shuidonggou are essentially identical to Mousterian points and the semi-lunar scrapers closely resemble such implements in the Aurignacian. Boule et al. (1928) remarked that the Shuidonggou culture resembled a highly evolved Mousterian and an incipient Aurignacian culture, or perhaps a combination of the two. Jia et al. (1964) came to the same conclusion and pointed out that it is very rare in other sites in China. Radiocarbon dating gives it an age of about 26,200 years.

The earliest and richest of the microlithic sites is the Xiachuan site. It is located in Qinshui County, Shaanxi Province. The Palaeolithic remains are distributed widely in river sediments in this area. Cores include different types, such as the conical microblade core, the cylindrical micro-blade core, the funnel-shaped core and the Gobi core. The breadth-to-length ratio of the stone blades is mostly about 1 : 4. Many stone blades were truncated at both ends, apparently to allow them to be set together as a knife blade inserted in a bone handle. Some kinds of burins are commonly seen in this microlithic culture. The small trihedral points with a rounded or pointed base may have been used as arrowheads (Wang et al., 1978). In general, the Xiachuan stone implements approach more nearly to those of the Neolithic period than the microlithic tools of other Palaeolithic sites. Radiocarbon dates for the site are around 21,000, 20,100 and 16,000 years ago.

The succeeding culture is the Hutouliang culture. The site is in the Nihewan basin of Yangyuan County, Hebei Province (Gai and Wei, 1977). The stone implements are similar to Xiachuan. A single radiocarbon date is about 11,000 years ago.

The Xiaonanhai cave site of Henan Province also belongs to the microlithic culture (An, 1965). More than 7,000 stone artefacts were collected, but only a small proportion of them were retouched. A radiocarbon date from this site is about 11,000 years ago.

At present, the Palaeolithic culture in north China may be divided into two major systems. One is characterized by large stone tools and trihedral points of the 'Kehe-Dingcun lineage'. Its sequence is Xihoudu → Kehe → Dingcun → E'maokou of the Early Neolithic (Jia and You, 1973). The other system is characterized by the microlithic culture of the 'Zhoukoudian Locality 1-Shiyu lineage'. Its sequence is Donggutuo → Zhoukoudian Locality 1 → Xujiayao → Salawusu → Shiyu → Xiaonanhai. The Shuidonggou, Xia-chuan and Hutouliang cultures seem to have derived from these two systems in the Middle Palaeolithic period. And in the beginning of the Neolithic period, in combination with the Xiaonanhai culture, they form the Neolithic culture widespread in north China. The Palaeolithic culture in south China may belong to another system and at present it is still difficult to assess.

About 10,000 years ago the technique of pottery-making began to develop. In the Hemudu (Ho-mu-tu) site of Yuyao County, Zhejiang Province, much evidence of rice and a bone spade made from a vertebrate scapula were found; it dates from 7,000 to 6,000 years ago. In the possibly earlier site of E'maokou, stone spades and stone sickles were found. This indicates that the origin of agriculture is much earlier than is generally suggested. If one takes pottery, agriculture and the domestication of wild animals to be the hallmarks of the Neolithic period, it should begin about 10,000 years ago.

BIBLIOGRAPHY

AN ZHIMIN. 1965. [Trial excavations of the Palaeolithic cave of Xiaonanhai in Anyang, Honan.] *Acta Archaeologica Sinica*, Vol. 1, pp. 1–28.

BOULE, M. et al. 1928. *Le Paléolithique de la Chine*. Paris, Archives de l'Institut de Paléontologie Humaine. Vol. 4, pp. 1–138.

GAI PEI; WEI QI. 1977. Discovery of the Late Palaeolithic Site of Hutouliang, Hebei. *Vertebrata PalAsiatica*, Vol. 15, No. 4, pp. 287–300.

HUANG WEIWEN; WEI QI. 1981. [New Discovery of Human Bones

and Stone Artifacts from Ordos.] In: 'Inner Mongolian Agriculture and Animal Husbandry.' Yikezhao League Cultural Relics Work Station Hohhot, Head Office. *E'erduosi Wenwu Kaogu Wenj.* pp. 24–32.

JIA LANPO; YOU YUCHU. 1973. [The Remains of a Stone Workshop at Ngo-mao-kou in Huaijen County, Shensi Province.] *Acta Archaeologica Sinica*, Vol. 2, pp. 13–26.

JIA LANPO; GAI PEI; LI YANXIAN. 1964. New Material from Shuidonggou Palaeolithic site. *Vertebrata PalAsiatica*, Vol. 8, No. 1, pp. 75–83.

WANG JAIN; WANG XIANGQIAN; CHEN ZHEYING. 1978. [Archae-

ological Reconnaissance in Hsia Chuan in Chin Shui County, Shansi Province.] *Acta Archaeologica Sinica*, Vol. 3, pp. 259–88.

WEIDENREICH, F. 1939. On the Earliest Representative of Modern Mankind Recovered on the Soil of East Asia. *Bulletin of the Natural History Society of Peking*, Vol. 13, No. 3, pp. 161–74.

WU RUKANG. 1959. Human Fossils Found in Liukiang, Kwangsi, China. *Palaeovertebrata et Palaeoanthropologia*, Vol. 1, No. 3, pp. 97–103.

WU XINZHI. 1960. On the Racial Type of Upper Cave Man of Choukoutien. *Palaeovertebrata et Palaeoanthropologia*, Vol. 2, No. 2, pp. 141–9.

27

SOUTH-EAST ASIA AND JAPAN

in the period of *Homo sapiens sapiens* up to the beginnings of food production

Karl L. Hutterer

Although research on the Pleistocene archaeology of South-East Asia began in the late nineteenth century and has been pursued almost continuously since then, our knowledge of the origins and development of the culture of *Homo sapiens sapiens* in this region remains remarkably inadequate. Geographical coverage of the region is uneven, and new research continues to produce unexpected findings that force frequent reassessment of previous reconstruction.

By contrast, credible research on Pleistocene cultures in Japan started only in the 1950s. Until that time it was widely assumed that the Japanese islands had been settled in mid-Holocene times by Jomon populations, who were often considered Neolithic on the basis of their use of pottery and edge-ground stone tools. Although the existence of a pre-ceramic period was not universally accepted by Japanese archaeologists until quite recently, research in this area has progressed rapidly. Today, more than a thousand pre-ceramic sites are known and have to some degree been investigated, and a reasonably reliable and detailed picture of at least some aspects of late Upper Pleistocene human life and settlement in Japan has emerged.

Basing their hypothesis on formal similarities in some stone tools, and perhaps even in some of the earliest pottery, some investigators have raised the question of possible prehistoric connections between South-East Asia and Japan (for instance, Bellwood, 1979; Maringer, 1957*a*, 1957*b*). While the possibility of such connections cannot be rejected out of hand, present evidence is insufficient to pursue such an argument. In general, the overall picture of cultural development in the two regions in the late Pleistocene and early Holocene differs substantially. Given the disparity in the data available for South-East Asia and Japan and the dissimilarities of cultural and social development, at least on a gross scale, this chapter will treat the two regions in separate sections.

SOUTH-EAST ASIA

Late Pleistocene archaeology

To set the topic of this chapter into an appropriate context, it is necessary to reiterate a few points already made in Chapters 8 and 17. Geographically, South-East Asia is com-monly divided into a 'mainland' and an 'island' component. However, the present configuration of land and sea masks the fact that, geographically, the Asian landmass extends out in a broad shelf (the Sunda shelf) which is now largely submerged. Several times during the Pleistocene sea-levels dropped sufficiently to expose large reaches of that shelf and, thus, to incorporate the islands of Sumatra, Java and Borneo (and occasionally Palawan) into the Asian landmass. It was at such times of lowered sea-levels that *Homo erectus* populations dispersed from continental South-East Asia into the Sunda islands as far as Java.

Eastern Indonesia, Sulawesi (Celebes) and the main Philippine island groups most probably were not part of the Asian landmass at any time during the Pleistocene (see Heaney, 1985). Although a variety of stone tools from these islands have been claimed to be of Middle or early Upper Pleistocene age (see, for instance, Fox, 1978; Heekeren, 1958; Maringer, 1970), this dating is suspect on stratigraphic grounds (Hutterer, 1977). It is noteworthy that no hominid remains have ever been found on the oceanic islands other than those of *Homo sapiens sapiens*. Thus, although we have only negative evidence to base an argument on, it seems unlikely that pre-*sapiens* hominids reached the oceanic islands. There is, however, definitive evidence of the presence of humans on the oceanic islands by at least 30,000 years ago (I. C. Glover, 1981). Together with evidence for the first settlement of Australia and New Guinea about 30,000 to 35,000 years ago (or perhaps slightly earlier) (White and O'Connell, 1982), this may be seen as reflecting a landmark technological development on the *Homo sapiens sapiens* level, the development of means to cross large spaces of open water.

Biological evidence of early *Homo sapiens sapiens* populations in South-East Asia is still rather slim. Three sets of fossil finds have been reported, all of them from the continental islands: two skulls found at the site of Wajak (Wadjak) in Java in 1889 at a limestone quarry are undated (Dubois, 1920–1); a skull found at Niah cave in Sarawak (Borneo) has been tentatively associated with radiocarbon dates around 41,500 and 39,600 years ago (Harrisson, 1970), while a carbon-14 date of 21,000 years ago has been tentatively attributed to a skull found in Tabon cave on Palawan Island, Philippines (Fox, 1970). Although the validity of these dates is uncertain because of doubts regarding stratigraphic association, all three fossil sets are most likely of late Upper Pleistocene age.

The finds are of intense interest, as they have a bearing on our understanding of the development of contemporary racial variability in eastern Asia and Oceania. Unfortunately, the small number of finds and their uncertain dating has led to a series of diverging and often contradictory interpretations. Different investigators have variously seen similarities between the South-East Asian specimens and earlier *Homo erectus* fossil finds in the region, *Homo sapiens sapiens* fossils from Australia and from the Upper Cave at Zhoukoudian (Choukoutien) in China, and modern Negrito populations in South-East Asia (Brothwell, 1960; Howells, 1973, 1976). These differing views influence interpretations of the fossil record as reflecting either a continuous evolutionary process *in situ* or a replacement of earlier primitive populations with Modern humans diffusing from a source further north in Asia. Thorne and Wolpoff (1981; Wolpoff et al., 1984) have recently argued that both processes occurred and interacted with each other (see also Brace, 1978; Brace and Hinton, 1981, Brace and Vitztnum, 1984; Bulbeck, 1981).

What was the environment like that the early *Homo sapiens sapiens* populations had to contend with in South-East Asia? Again, our knowledge is fragmentary at best. We do know that we are dealing with what was, in temperate latitudes and higher altitudes, the last major period of Pleistocene glaciation. Thus, it would also have been a period of reduced sea-levels, although the precise magnitude and fluctuations of the lowering have not been definitively clarified. It seems that during the late Pleistocene mean sea-level was at least 120 m below its present position (Donn et al., 1962; Hopkins, 1982), although drops of 160 m and even 200 m have been suggested (Chappell, 1976). Using the more conservative estimate, a reconstruction of continental and island geography for that period is shown in Map 22.

We are less certain about climate and vegetation. A variety of avenues of research suggest that, with the global lowering of temperatures during the cool periods of the Pleistocene, average annual temperatures in the Equatorial portion of South-East Asia may have been about 2 °C lower than they are at present (CLIMAP, 1976; Flenley, 1985). This may not have had a very significant direct effect on life in the region, but in connection with major changes in the distribution of land and water, it may well have had a notable effect on the patterns of prevailing winds and precipitation, and thus on vegetation and animals. Most likely, regional and local climates in the late Pleistocene were drier than they are now (van Zeist, 1983–4; Verstappen, 1975). As a result, humid evergreen rain forests were probably less widely distributed, and larger portions of the region were covered with deciduous tropical forests and savannah-type vegetation.

Only a small number of sites have been studied (and published) so far that can be securely dated to the late Pleistocene. They include both caves and open sites. Niah cave in Sarawak, East Malaysia (Borneo), and Tabon cave are perhaps the best known. Niah is a very large cavern with deep deposits. Based on several radiocarbon dates, the cultural sequence at Niah is said to start around 40,000 years ago (Harrisson, 1970); a restudy of the site raises the possibility that this date may have to be revised upward (Zuraina, 1982). The Niah sequence extends up to the present. The Pleistocene portion of the sequence is characterized by a lithic assemblage that consists predominantly of flake-tools with little morphological patterning and a low incidence of retouch, and a small percentage of pebble-tools (less than 2 per cent). The archaeological deposits

Map 22 South-East Asia: the extent of the late Pleistocene land bridges, and the archaeological sites referred to in the text: 1, present coastline; 2, Pleistocene coastline. (After Hutterer.)

also contain ample animal bone as well as the remains of freshwater and marine shellfish (Niah cave is today 16 km from the sea-shore!) and seeds of several species of forest trees that yield edible fruits or raw materials. Even if not all these biological materials were brought into the cave by humans, the assemblage as a whole suggests exploitation of a very broad range of resources through hunting and gathering.

Tabon cave today overlooks the South China Sea but during periods of lower Pleistocene, sea-level may have been 30 km or more removed from the coast. Its occupational sequence is estimated to start around 45,000 years ago (although the earliest radiocarbon date is around 30,500 years ago: Fox, 1970, p. 24) and ends around 9,000 years ago. The excavators divided the cultural deposits into a series of five distinct flake assemblages which are, however, very similar to each other. Overall, the stone tool technology resembles strongly that of Niah, consisting primarily of flakes, with a small pebble-tool component. Steep-edged domed scrapers, a tool form found widely distributed throughout South-East Asia and the Pacific, are prominent in the assemblage (Peralta, 1981). While there are significant differences in the list of animal species found as food remains in Niah and Tabon, there is a generic resemblance in that the Tabon finds also indicate exploitation of a broad spectrum of the available resources.

A third site, Leang Burung 2, is a rock shelter in southern Sulawesi (Heekeren, 1972; I. C. Glover, 1981). The shelter contained deposits radiocarbon dated from around 31,000 to 20,000 years ago, with the actual dates for earliest and latest occupation probably exceeding these dates in either direction. The shelter contains a flake-tool assemblage that differs in several respects from the assemblages of Niah and Tabon: it contains points made by the Levallois technique (Fig. 73 (A)); it does not contain any pebble-tools; and it contains flakes with phytolith (or silica) gloss, a gloss produced by working siliceous plant materials. Animal bones and remains of freshwater shellfish and snails were found as well. The latter seem to indicate environmental stability during the period of occupation (E. Glover, 1981).

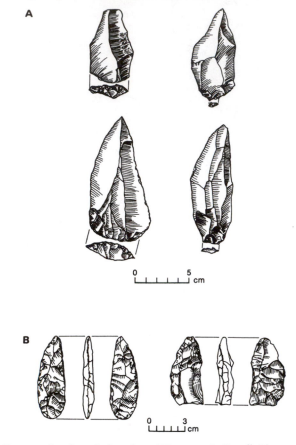

Figure 73 Artefacts, Indonesia and Borneo: A, 'Levallois' type flakes, Leang Burung 2, Sulawesi (Indonesia). (After I. C. Glover, 1981, p. 24); B, bifacially flaked lanceolate points, Tingkayu, Sabah, East Malaysia, Borneo (Indonesia). (After Bellwood, 1984, p. 41.)

Yet another element is added by a series of open sites and rock shelters situated near Tingkayu, in Sabah, West Malaysia (Borneo), along the shores of a dried-up former lake (Bellwood, 1984). Occupation of the open sites seems chronologically defined by a lava flow that dammed the Tingkayu river around 28,000 years ago and the draining of the lake sometime over 17,000 years ago. In the Tingkayu sites, a stone industry is found that contains, besides pebble-tools, cores and utilized irregular flakes, highly sophisticated, bifacially flaked, lanceolate points (Fig. 73 (B)). The latter are so far unique in South-East Asian prehistory. Interestingly, the nearby Bagop Bilo rock shelter, occupied 17,000 to 12,000 years ago, yields no bifacial tools but a more typical South-East Asian array of flake-tools, steep-edge scrapers, cores and pebble-tools. A special element in the latter case is represented by 'blade-like knives' (Bellwood, 1984, p. 45) with phytolith gloss. No organic remains survived in the open Tingkayu sites, while again a broad range of mammal, bird, reptile, and fish remains were found in the Bagop Bilo rock shelter.

On the South-East Asian mainland, sites dating to the period under discussion are so far known only from Vietnam. Over 130 open sites and caves have been found yielding lithic assemblages termed Son Vi (Ha, 1980, 1985). Assemblages of this sort are characterized by the presence of unifacially flaked pebble-tools, but by the absence of what are considered to be typical Hoabinhian tools (see p. 265) such as sumatraliths. It is not clear from available reports what the complete composition of these lithic assemblages is. Excavations at Con Moong cave demonstrated that Son Vi stratigraphically underlies Hoabinhian deposits (Pham, 1980). A series of radiocarbon dates from other cave sites locates this industry between 18,000 and 13,000 years ago (Ha, 1980, p. 118). Summary reports seem to indicate that a similar broad range of animals is found in Son Vian sites as in later Hoabinhian sites.

Quite recently, a flake and blade industry was found underlying a Son Vian deposit in the Nguom rock shelter, dating from around 18,600 years ago and before, with a basal age estimated to be around 30,000 years (Ha, 1985). It appears that many of the tools are made on flakes that retain some of the original surface of the pebble from which they were struck, while actual pebble-tools are apparently absent.

It is difficult to distill from such fragmentary information a coherent picture of late Pleistocene societies and cultures. It is impossible to say, for instance, whether differences between lithic assemblages indicate actual differences in cultural tradition, technological adaptations to different environmental conditions, or perhaps a particular range of activities carried out in a given site. What we can say with some assurance is that *Homo sapiens sapiens* was present throughout South-East Asia, on the mainland as well as the major islands, and that their subsistence seems to have been based on hunting and collecting a broad diversity of resources from a range of tropical habitats. For the most part, the stone tool technology utilized was remarkably simple. The fact that a few more complex stone-tool technologies do exist, however, indicates that such simplicity was not based on lack of technological ability. Rather, as a number of scholars have suggested (for instance, Hayden, 1977; Hutterer, 1977; Solheim, 1969), the simple lithic technology was probably complemented by a far more elaborate and specialized one employing organic raw materials, particularly wood.

Post-Pleistocene hunting cultures (to around 5,000 years ago)

With the end of the last Pleistocene glaciation around 10,000 years ago, world-wide annual temperatures increased, the glaciers of the higher latitudes receded, and sea-levels rose. The most visible effect of these changes was a reduction of the land area of mainland South-East Asia by about 50 per cent. In very broad terms, the monsoonal climatic pattern of the region, and the corresponding vegetational and faunal environments (such as lowland and upland rain forests, deciduous monsoonal forests, coastal mangrove forests and so on) as we now know them, became established at that time, although minor climatic fluctuations continued throughout the Holocene period. The effects of these fluctuations varied locally but, in general, involved episodes of warmer and cooler temperatures, wetter and drier periods, and fluctuations of the sea-level of up to several metres above or below its present situation (Huang et al., 1984; Yang and Xie, 1984).

South-East Asian archaeologists have debated extensively the magnitude of the environmental changes that took place at the end of the Pleistocene and the adaptive adjustments they may have necessitated among human communities. A reasonably large number of sites with occupations straddling the transitional period are known throughout the region. The evidence that has survived in them does not seem to indicate any dramatic cultural discontinuities, at least in terms of stone tool technology. However, there are many other aspects of cultural organization about which we know very little so far and which may well have been much more sensitive to environmental shifts.

A cultural complex dating to the Pleistocene–Holocene boundary was first identified by French archaeologists in the 1920s, working in what was then known as Indochina (Colani, 1927, 1939; Patte, 1925, 1936; Matthews, 1966). Cave sites and coastal shell-mounds have yielded unifacially flaked pebble-tools of characteristic and predictable shapes, flake-tools of irregular shapes and with little retouch, grinding stones, often lumps of haematite and remains of mammals, reptiles, birds and shellfish.

In early definitions of the Hoabinhian complex or 'culture', great emphasis was put on the presence of specific types of pebble-tools, among them so-called 'sumatraliths' (flat water-worn pebbles of oval, almond or disc shape, flaked completely over one surface), 'short-axes' (short, stubby pebbles with a unifacially flaked working edge) and others (Fig. 74). In upper layers of Hoabinhian deposits, pebble-tools were often found to have ground working edges. Hoabinhian sites have been found in Vietnam (Ha, 1978, 1980; Pham, 1978), Laos (Matthews, 1966), Cambodia (for instance Laang Spean: Mourer, 1977), Thailand (such as Spirit Cave (Gorman, 1970) and Sai Yok (Heekeren and Knuth, 1967), Myanmar (formerly Burma) (Padah-lin (Aung, 1971)), the Malay Peninsula (Matthews, 1961), Gua Cha (Sieveking, 1955), Sumatra (Heekeren, 1972) and south China (Aigner, 1979; Jiangxi Provincial Museum, 1976; CPAM, Guangxi Province, 1976; Zhu, 1984).

In spite of much work that has been done on the Hoab-

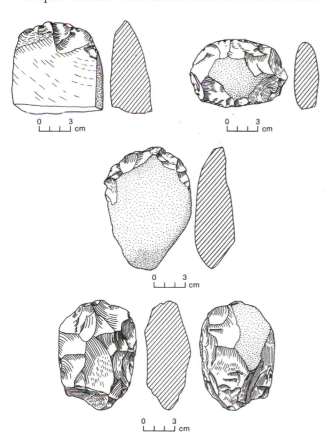

Figure 74 Hoabinhian pebble-tools (Vietnam). (After Pham Huy Thong, 1978.)

inhian, there remain unsolved problems. Based on selected radiocarbon determinations, Vietnamese prehistorians define the Hoabinhian period as dating from 12,000 to 8,000 or 6,000 years ago (Davidson, 1975, 1979; Ha, 1980). Others consider a starting date as early as 40,000 years ago, viewing assemblages of the Son Vi type as an early Hoabinhian stage (Solheim, 1972, 1980), while dates as late as 1,200 years ago have been reported for some sites (Yen, 1977). Another open question concerns subsistence. Animal remains, freshwater fauna and marine shellfish found in many sites indicate that their inhabitants hunted, trapped, and collected a broad range of animals, including such different forms as rhinoceros, deer, pig, squirrel, birds, reptiles, fish and shellfish. Excavations at Spirit Cave in northern Thailand yielded plant remains which raised the possibility that initial steps toward domestication and cultivation had been taken by 10,000 years ago (Gorman, 1969, 1970, 1971; Solheim, 1969, 1970, 1972). Unfortunately, botanical studies have not been able to substantiate this claim (Yen, 1977). Nevertheless, some Vietnamese archaeologists have incorporated the assumption of horticultural activity into the concept of the Hoabinhian (Hoang, 1984).

Finally, there is the question of the geographic distribution of the Hoabinhian. It had long been believed that the occurrence of Hoabinhian sites is limited to the South-East Asian mainland and the east coast of Sumatra (Solheim, 1974). Recently, however, Hoabinhian sites have also been found in the Philippines (Peterson, 1974) and it appears that many unifacially flaked pebble-tools collected from the surface throughout Indonesia, and previously considered to be of Palaeolithic age, may in fact be of post-Pleistocene date (Bartstra, 1983; Heekeren, 1972). Thus, if the main emphasis in defining the Hoabinhian is on pebble-tools, assemblages with Hoabinhian elements can be seen as occurring throughout the South-East Asian region.

Turning to the South-East Asian islands, a large number of early or middle Holocene sites are known with stone tool assemblages that are variously described as 'amorphous' flake-tool industries and as flake-and-blade tool industries. Such sites are found in Timor (I. C. Glover, 1971, 1972); Flores (Verhoeven, 1953); Sumatra (Bronson and Asmar, 1975); Borneo (Bellwood, 1985); Sulawesi (Bellwood, 1976); Mindanao (Solheim et al., 1979; Spoehr, 1973); Palawan (Fox, 1970); central Philippines (Coutts, 1983; Tuggle and Hutterer, 1972); and northern Luzon (Peterson, 1974; Ronquillo, 1981; Thiel, 1980). Many of these sites have long occupational sequences lasting up to 10,000 years, with the oldest occupations recorded at around 13,500 years ago (Uai Bobo 2, Timor (I. C. Glover, 1972)), and the youngest around 400 years ago (Sohoton, Samar, Philippines (Tuggle and Hutterer, 1972)). The great majority of the sites are caves and rock shelters, although open sites are known as well.

The stone tools found in these sites range from industries that seem to involve an almost random flaking or smashing of cores to produce chips from which suitable specimens were then selected as tools sometimes (although somewhat inaccurately) described as 'smash-and-grab' industries, to industries that entail some degree of core preparation and more highly controlled flaking, producing flakes of more standardized shapes, including often a small proportion of elongated or blade-like flakes. It is difficult at present to say whether the industries in question can be divided into two or more distinct types, or whether we are dealing with a situation of more or less continuous variability. Deliberate retouch is rare in any of the assemblages.

In a number of cases, some of the flakes have phytolith gloss along one or more working edges, indicating that they were used to cut or trim some kind of plant materials containing silica. Not infrequently, the stone tools are associated with bone tools, mostly awls or needles. After about 4,000 to 5,000 years ago, ceramics are commonly added to the archaeological assemblages.

Plant and animal remains suggest generally that the inhabitants of these sites engaged in an intensive and broad-spectrum exploitation of localized resources. In a number of instances, site occupation continues beyond the point when agriculture appeared in the area. At this juncture, the nature of site occupation often changes in terms of the intensity of site use, the composition of the lithic tool assemblage, the addition of new technological elements such as ceramics and the appearance of domesticated or introduced species among the faunal remains. Nevertheless, these sites generally continue to reflect a hunting and collecting existence. The question of technological change in mid-Holocene times, possibly in connection with the appearance of agriculture, is brought into closer focus by a few rather highly specialized lithic industries found primarily in central Indonesia and the Philippines. Among them are some with a large component of true blades, flaked from conical or cylindrical cores, and sometimes quite small in size (for instance, at Leang Tuwo Mane'e, Talaud Island, Indonesia: Bellwood, 1976; Buad Island, Philippines: Scheans et al., 1970). As a rule, many of the blades, and sometimes also flakes, have phytolith gloss. The blade industries seem to appear before pottery but overlap with the introduction of ceramics. At Leang Tuwo Mane'e, blade tools appear around 5,500 years ago but decline in frequency after pottery is added to the assemblage around 4,500 years ago (Bellwood, 1976, 1985).

Other specialized industries, so far limited in their occurrence to Sulawesi and Java, involve microliths and bifacially

flaked projectile points. Industries of this sort reported from southern Sulawesi include small blades as well as triangular or trapezoidal sections of blades or flakes with a steep, blunting retouch along one edge ('backed blades' and 'geometric microliths'; see Fig. 75 (A)) and so-called 'Maros points': small triangular flakes or blades, retouched to form a concave notch at the bulbar end and with unifacial or bifacial retouch along the sides to form either smooth or serrated edges (Fig. 75 (B)) (for instance, at Ulu Leang 1, Sulawesi, Indonesia (I. C. Glover, 1976; Glover and Presland, 1985)). Backed blades and geometrics appear sometime around 7,000 to 6,000 years ago, and Maros points are added to the repertoire of stone tools around 4,000 years ago. Both tool types seem to disappear again around 2,000 years ago. Microliths and bifacially flaked points are also known from undated sites in central and western Java (Fig. 76) (Bandi, 1951; Heekeren, 1972).

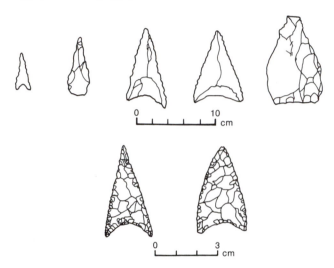

Figure 76 Bifacially flaked projectile points, Java (Indonesia). (After Heekeren, 1972; Glover, 1973*a*.)

Although a number of attempts have been made to link the post-Pleistocene lithic industries of South-East Asia with origins elsewhere (Bellwood, 1979, 1985; I. C. Glover, 1973*b*; Glover and Presland, 1985), they have not been very successful to date and it is doubtful if they ever will. Attempting a more general interpretation of the archaeological findings, it appears that the last few thousand years of South-East Asian prehistory saw in many areas of the region the development of a complex mosaic of subsistence modes, with hunting and collecting economies persisting after agricultural economies became established. There is evidence in several of the later sites of some form of interaction with farming populations (Dunn, 1975; Hutterer, 1976) and it may well be that some of the more specialized stone industries reflect specialized forms of forest exploitation, somehow tied to, or interacting with, agricultural economies.

JAPAN

Pre-ceramic cultures

As alluded to at the beginning of this chapter, Palaeolithic archaeology in the proper sense had a relatively late beginning in Japan. Definitive evidence of the existence of a pre-ceramic culture, with a Pleistocene antiquity, was not established until the amateur archaeologist Aizawa Tadahiro

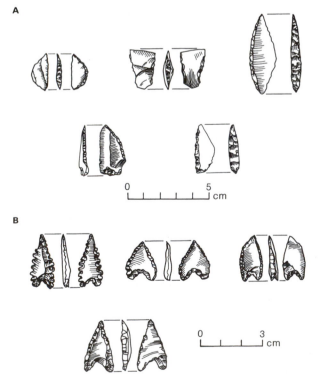

Figure 75 Artefacts, Ulu Leang, Sulawesi (Indonesia): A, backed blades and microliths; B, 'Maros points'. (After Glover and Presland, 1985.)

discovered stone tools in Pleistocene loam deposits at Iwajuku, about 90 km north of Tokyo (Ikawa, 1964). Subsequent excavations by Sugihara (1956) confirmed the stratigraphic position of the artefacts in a Pleistocene horizon underlying a Jomon deposit. Since that time, over a thousand preceramic sites have been found and investigated (Ikawa-Smith, 1978a). Archaeological findings together with a wealth of studies in related disciplines have contributed toward establishing a relatively detailed picture of at least some aspects of the Japanese Palaeolithic.

With the lowering of sea-levels during cold periods of the Pleistocene discussed earlier, the Japanese islands were not only linked to the Asian mainland several times, but the islands themselves changed in shape and size, coalescing and dividing with the receding and rising waters. Since they formed a long-stretched arc, the islands could be linked to two environmentally very different parts of the continent, namely Siberia (via Hokkaido and Sakhalin) and the north China plain (via Kyushu and Korea) (Kotani, 1969; Minato et al., 1965). From these diverse source areas, very different animals and plants came into Japan. Tracking the presence of different animal and plant species during different parts of the Pleistocene provides important evidence for land connections. On this basis, it appears that during the last glacial period Hokkaido was firmly joined with Siberia, while the other islands formed one long solid stretch of land that was briefly joined by narrow connections to Hokkaido in the north and Korea in the south (Map 23). The islands became completely severed from the continent sometime between 18,000 and 12,000 years ago (Kotani, 1969).

Unlike continental areas of the same latitude, only high mountain peaks in the Japanese islands were covered with glaciers even at the height of cold periods, owing to the

ameliorating influence of warm ocean currents. During the last glaciation, Japan was dominated by a boreal coniferous forest, indicating a considerably cooler, and probably somewhat drier, climate than at present (Tsukada, 1986). The boreal forest was poor in edible plant resources as well as in game, although some large animals (such as woolly mammoth, Nauman's elephant, giant deer) were present. Mixed forests and deciduous broadleaf forests, with their important resources of acorns, beechmast, walnuts and chestnuts, were limited to the south and to a narrow strip along the Pacific coast (see also Yasuda, 1978). A warming trend began to set in around 15,000 years ago, and about 12,000 years ago the deciduous broadleaf forest started to move northward, replacing the coniferous forests. During the Holocene, mixed coniferous and broadleaf forests are typical of Hokkaido, while cool-temperate deciduous broadleaf forests took over in eastern Honshu, and warm-temperate evergreen broadleaf forests established themselves in Kyushu, Shikoku, and western Honshu.

Palaeolithic studies in Japan are closely linked with geological research on Pleistocene stratigraphy and sedimentation. Two avenues of research have been particularly important in this respect: studies of loam deposits in plains abutting major volcanic formations and investigation of marine terraces along the coast. The loam formations are the result of weathering of volcanic ash deposits. They are subdivided by pumice layers, buried soils, gravels and erosion surfaces and can be dated by radiometric means. The early studies of loam sequences were carried out in the Kanto plain, and attempts have been made to establish correlations between different regions. Unfortunately, long-distance correlations between either loam sequences or marine terraces are difficult in Japan because of the tectonic instability of the islands resulting in complex patterns of local uplift. Nevertheless, the basic outlines of Pleistocene stratigraphy from about 100,000 years ago onward seem to be pretty well established (Table 8; Ikawa-Smith, 1978b).

Possibly because of the acidity of the volcanic loam soils, the great majority of Palaeolithic sites in the islands are essentially devoid of organic materials. This limits archaeological research to the study of stone tools. Straightforward as this may seem, there has been a lively debate over the nature and age of the earliest stone tools, reminiscent in some ways of European debate in the early part of this century over 'eoliths'. Serizawa Chosuke, one of the pioneers of Palaeolithic research in Japan, has been advocating recognition of an 'Early Palaeolithic' period dating to the early Upper Pleistocene (130,000 to 60,000 years ago) or earlier (Ikawa-Smith, 1978a; Serizawa, 1978). Three sites, excavated or re-excavated by Serizawa, figure particularly prominently in the debate: Sozudai, Hoshino and Iwajuku. Sozudai, located on a marine terrace in north-eastern Kyushu, yielded materials from a gravel layer that were described in terms of choppers, chopping-tools, proto-handaxes and so on and compared with Lower Palaeolithic tools from China (Zhoukoudian) and Java (Serizawa, 1965). At Hoshino, a site in the northern Kanto plain, Serizawa distinguished eleven cultural horizons. All but the two topmost horizons were thought to predate 30,000 years ago, with horizons 7 to 11 predating 60,000 years ago, and comparisons were again made with Zhoukoudian (Serizawa, 1969, 1976). Finally, in 1970 Serizawa re-excavated Iwajuku, the first site that had been definitively identified as Palaeolithic. Below two horizons established earlier by Sugihara, Serizawa defined a horizon 0, containing what he described

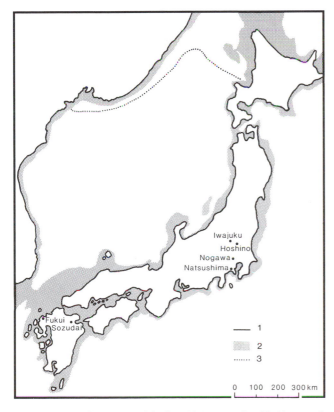

Map 23 Japan: the extent of the late Pleistocene land bridges, and the archaeological sites referred to in the text: 1, present coastline; 2, Pleistocene coastline; 3, southern limit of ice-sheet. (After Hutterer.)

Table 8 Sequence of Upper Pleistocene geological horizons and Palaeolithic cultures in Japan.

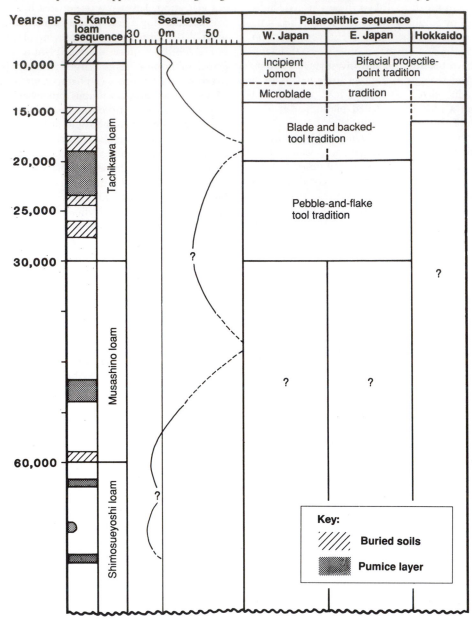

as choppers, pointed flakes, burins and cores, and again earlier than 50,000 years ago.

There are serious doubts about the artefactual nature of virtually all of the stone specimens from the three sites attributed by Serizawa to the Early Palaeolithic (Bleed, 1977; Ohyi, 1978), and few Japanese archaeologists today accept them as valid evidence. The presence of Lower Palaeolithic materials has also been claimed for a number of other sites, but in all cases the specimens in question are either of uncertain stratigraphic provenance and date, or it is doubtful that they were produced by humans (Ikawa-Smith, 1978a; Aikens and Higuchi, 1982). There is no intrinsic reason why *Homo erectus* or primitive *Homo sapiens* could not have reached Japan. The evidence available at present, however, does not demonstrate that this did in fact happen. The earliest solid evidence for human occupation of the Japanese islands dates from around 30,000 years ago.

Oda and Keally (1979) have recently worked out a comprehensive sequence for the Japanese Palaeolithic, based on a detailed analysis of some 200 Palaeolithic sites. This scheme is supported by extensive stratigraphic studies as well as a

detailed typological analysis of the assemblages of twelve important type-sites by Akazawa et al. (1980). The first phase, dating to approximately 30,000 to 20,000 years ago, is characterized by pebble- and flake-tool assemblages. Although there is little standardization among the tools of this phase, it is possible to see some change over the 10,000 years involved. The earliest assemblages, found in the Kanto and Chubu regions, are characterized by small flake industries associated with crude pebble-tools and large flakes. Similar late Palaeolithic assemblages found in the Ordos region of north-west China (Ikawa-Smith, 1982b; Jia and Huang, 1985) are considered as possible continental ancestors. Around 27,000 years ago, blade-like flakes and bifacially chipped ovoid tools are added to the existing technology. Pebble-tools become rare around 23,000 years ago, while blade-like flakes with a steep backing retouch along one margin appear in some sites (Fig. 77). Sites of phase I are found primarily in central and western Honshu, Shikoku and Kyushu. Only toward the end of the phase are sites found also in northern Honshu and southern Hokkaido, suggesting that the latter areas were settled by population

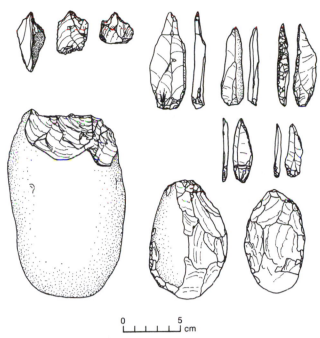

Figure 77 Stone tools of the Japanese Palaeolithic, phase I. (After Oda and Keally, 1979.)

expansion within Japan, after climatic amelioration made them suitable for settlement.

Phase II, starting approximately 20,000 years ago, is characterized by a variety of temporally and regionally distinctive technologies producing blades and blade-like flakes, some of them evocative of Upper Palaeolithic industries in Eurasia, particularly of the Aurignacian (Chard, 1974). Two basically different approaches to flake production were used (Morlan, 1971). One involved the Setouchi technique of preparing a flat core which was then struck on the wide side, producing a flake that is wider than it is long (measured from the butt to the cutting edge). Such side-struck blade-like flakes are often slightly triangular in outline (Fig. 78 (a)). They are frequently retouched in a distinctive fashion to form a series of highly standardized types of knives (for example, the Ko knife and the Kiridashi knife: Fig. 78 (b)). The second approach involved a variety of techniques for preparing blade cores which were then struck on the small end, producing long, narrow, end-struck blades and elongated flakes (Fig. 78 (d)). Again, many of these are retouched into distinctive knife forms (for instance, the Moro knife (Fig. 78 (c)) and the Higashiyama knife). Besides knives, there are also a variety of other specialized tool forms, particularly burins. During phase II, there is for the first time good evidence for regional differentiation within Japan. A major dividing line runs through the mountains of central Honshu, an area which has remained a boundary of sorts in regional cultural variation ever since (Aikens and Higuchi, 1982).

Starting perhaps 15,000 years ago, a marked microlithic tendency becomes evident, leading into phase III by 13,000 years ago. This phase is very brief, lasting only for about one or two thousand years. Strong regional differences in technology are apparent: in western Japan (Honshu south from the Kanto; Kyushu), small blades and bladelets are struck from conical and subconical microcores, while in eastern Japan (Honshu north of Kanto; Hokkaido) wedge-shaped or boat-shaped microcores are prepared by the Yubetsu technique. There are again variations in the way in

which the basic Yubetsu technique is approached. Micro-blades are largely unmodified, except that both ends are often snapped off; micro-burins are a common occurrence. In general, assemblages of phase III tend to be highly internally homogeneous, while there is considerable variation between assemblages.

By about 12,000 years ago, important technological innovations occur that mark the transition into the Jomon period. Thus, the period between 12,000 and 10,000 years ago has variously been considered as the final phase of the Palaeolithic, the Epipalaeolithic, the Mesolithic, or the incipient phase of the Jomon period. It is marked by the occurrence of large pebble- and flake-tools, bifacially flaked projectile points, chipped and partially ground stone axes, and the first appearance of pottery. Bifacial projectile points occur first at the Nogawa site in Tokyo (Kidder et al., 1970) and continue throughout most of the Jomon period. Edge-ground stone tools occur as early as 30,000 years ago, but they change in size and form and are far more common during this final phase (Oda and Keally, 1973, Ikawa-Smith, 1986). Partially and completely ground stone tools occur also, of course, during the Jomon period.

Studies of the Japanese Palaeolithic have been hampered to some extent by the fact that few organic remains have been found. Human skeletal remains are exceedingly scarce (Suzuku and Hanihara, 1982), impeding studies of the racial relationships of the Palaeolithic inhabitants of the islands. Similarly, the lack of food debris in pre-ceramic sites makes it difficult to address the question of economic subsistence beyond general inferences based on the assumption of hunting and collecting in the broadly known environmental zones of post-Pleistocene Japan (Tsukada, 1986; Yasuda, 1978). In the absence of organic evidence, Japanese archaeologists have concentrated mainly on producing a series of excellent typological and technological studies (for instance Akazawa et al., 1980). Recently, attempts have also been made to derive information from the geographic distribution of sites and from the spatial distribution of artefacts within

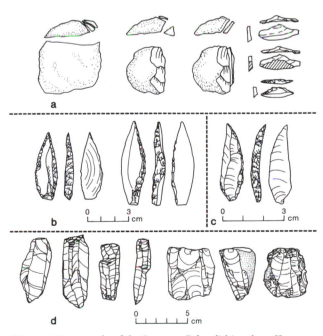

Figure 78 Stone tools of the Japanese Palaeolithic, phase II: a, Setouchi technique; b, Kiridashi knives; c, Moro knives (after Akazawa et al., 1980); d, end-struck blades. (After Oda and Keally, 1979.)

sites (Ikawa-Smith, 1975; Pearson, 1986b; Reynolds and Barnes, 1984).

Considerable efforts have been expended in considering the relationships of Palaeolithic technologies and cultures in Japan with others in north-east Asia (Chard, 1974) as well as with regions further afield such as South-East Asia (for instance, Maringer, 1957a, 1957b), Australia (for example, Blundell and Bleed, 1974; Oda and Keally, 1973), and north-western North America (for instance, Aikens and Dumond, 1986; Hayashi, 1968; Ikawa-Smith, 1982b; Morlan, 1976). There is little doubt about historical relationships to Upper Palaeolithic industries on the Asian mainland (see, for example, Shackley, 1984; Olson and Wu, 1985; Yi and Clark, 1985), particularly for phases I and III of the Japanese sequence (Oda and Kealley, 1979, p. 17). Similarities with Palaeoindian technologies in North America are evidently caused by the fact that some industries in Japan and North America share common ancestors on the Asian mainland. Similarities with South-East Asia and Australia, on the other hand, focus mostly on individual tool types rather than on whole industries and reflect probably no more than either functional or accidental parallels.

Hunting and gathering cultures of the Jomon period

In the early years of Palaeolithic research in Japan, a major cultural discontinuity was perceived between the Palaeolithic and the succeeding Jomon period. A number of sites with long sequences of occupation have more recently made it possible to see not only long-term continuous evolution within the Palaeolithic itself but also a gradual transition into the post-Pleistocene phase of cultural development (Ikawa, 1964). As noted above, this transitional phase is marked by bifacially flaked projectile points in the stone toolkit, indicating an apparent change in hunting technology, and by the appearance of pottery.

The earliest pottery comes from Fukui cave in Kyushu and is radiocarbon dated at around 12,700 years ago (Aikens and Higuchi, 1982; Kamaki and Serizawa, 1967). Unlike later Jomon pottery, it consists of round-bottomed, plain vessels with thin raised lines (linear relief pottery) and (slightly later) fingernail impressions below the rim. A number of other sites have been found with similar pottery and dates, all of them in southern Japan. It is evident that the transitional technologies and the subsequent Jomon tradition itself have their starting point in the south. This has naturally led to a search for continental roots for the new developments, with the assumption that they would have entered Kyushu from Korea. Early pottery has recently been reported from the Xianren cave in Jiangxi Province (with a radiocarbon date of around 10,800 years ago), Zengpiyan cave in Guangxi Province and several other cave sites in southern China (CPAM, 1976; Esaka, 1986; Jiangxi Provincial Museum, 1976; Zhu, 1984). However, the dating of the Chinese sites remains somewhat controversial, and, as mentioned earlier, their assemblages resemble less those of the Incipient Jomon than those of the Hoabinhian in South-East Asia. It is entirely conceivable that pottery arose in Japan independently of any influence from the Asian mainland in the context of adjustments to post-Pleistocene environmental conditions (Ikawa-Smith, 1980).

The most important environmental changes associated with the climatic warming trends of the Holocene were the expansion of cool-temperate and warm-temperate broadleaf forests (Pearson, 1977; Tsukada, 1986; Yasuda, 1978). These forests harboured rich animal communities of wild pig, deer, various small game and birds. On the coast, warm currents favoured the propagation of shellfish beds in drowned inlets and on shallow shelves, while further offshore pelagic fish and sea-mammals represented a potential resource of almost inexhaustible magnitude. Like other parts of the world, Japanese climates continued to fluctuate throughout the Holocene, with a climatic optimum between 7,000 and 4,000 years ago associated with a rise in sea-level of perhaps several metres (Huang et al., 1984; Pearson, 1977, 1986a; Tsukada, 1986; Yang and Xie, 1984; Yasuda, 1978). Human adjustments to the environmental changes these fluctuations entailed are reflected throughout most of the Jomon in patterns of technology, location of settlements, house construction and other aspects of life (Ikawa-Smith, 1986; Yasuda, 1980).

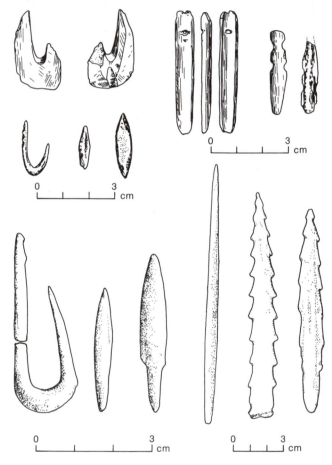

Figure 79 Selected Jomon bone artefacts (Japan). (After Aikens and Higuchi, 1982.)

The term 'Jomon' refers to cord-marked pottery, typical of much (though by no means all) of the ceramics of the period. Typological studies of the pottery, beginning before the turn of this century, have resulted in the establishment of detailed local and regional sequences. It is possible to abstract from them a general chronological framework of the Jomon period:

Incipient Jomon	13,000–9,500 years ago
Earliest Jomon	9,500–7,300 years ago
Early Jomon	7,300–5,600 years ago
Middle Jomon	5,600–4,500 years ago
Late Jomon	4,500–3,000 years ago
Latest Jomon	3,000–2,250 years ago

It must be kept in mind, however, that this broad framework ignores a great deal of regional cultural variation, including variation in the chronological structure of regional and local sequences. This, together with the vast amount of archaeological data available, makes it difficult to summarize the cultural developments of the Jomon period. This chapter will therefore concentrate only on a few very general points regarding hunting and collecting economy and associated aspects of technology and social organization.

Jomon culture first became known from the two to three thousand shell-mounds scattered along the coast of the Inland Sea and Pacific Ocean. These sites indicate a very intensive exploitation of the rich resources found in the littoral and inshore environmental zones. Already in the Earliest and Early Jomon, however, there are indications of

the ability to leave the coastal environments and take advantage of pelagic resources. At the famous Natsushima shell-mound, for instance, remains of deep-sea fish and marine mammals (dolphin) were found (Sugihara and Serizawa, 1957). Broadly speaking, exploitation of marine resources was more important in eastern Japan than in the west (Akazawa, 1980, 1981, 1982, 1986). Over time, there is an evident tendency towards increasing emphasis on a smaller number of shellfish species and the increasing importance of deep-sea fishing and the hunting of marine mammals (Pearson, 1977).

Besides remains of marine resources, the shell-mounds contain also bones of wild land mammals, especially deer,

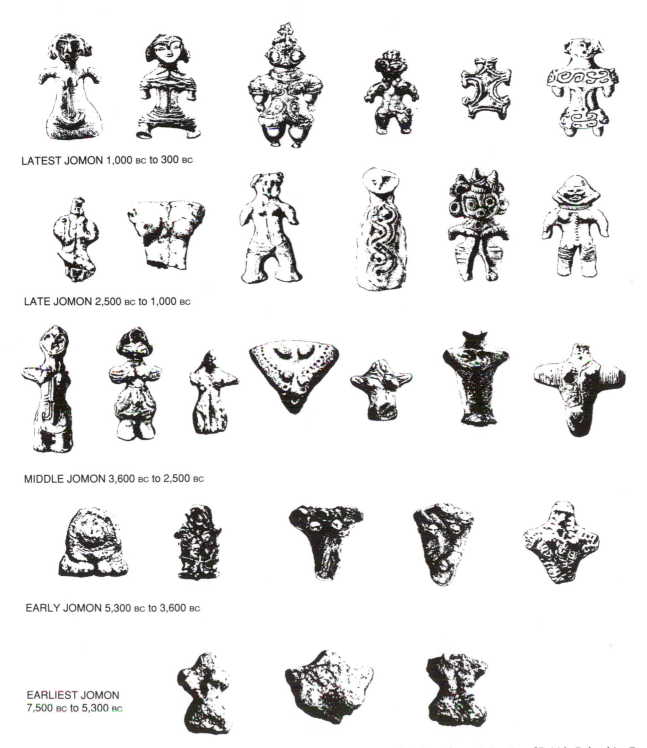

LATEST JOMON 1,000 BC to 300 BC

LATE JOMON 2,500 BC to 1,000 BC

MIDDLE JOMON 3,600 BC to 2,500 BC

EARLY JOMON 5,300 BC to 3,600 BC

EARLIEST JOMON
7,500 BC to 5,300 BC

Figure 80 Ceramic figurines of the Jomon period (Japan). (Courtesy Museum of Anthropology, University of British Columbia, Canada.)

wild boar, hare and some birds as well as a wide range of plant remains, particularly a variety of nuts and seeds (Pearson and Pearson, 1978), indicating that the subsistence economy even of the coastal sites included a combination of marine and terrestrial foods. There are, however, also a large number of interior sites with remains of wild game and a broad range of plant foods, the most important among them being acorns, walnuts and chestnuts as well as other nuts and seeds (Pearson and Pearson, 1978). A number of archaeological and ethnoarchaeological studies (for example, Koyama, 1981; Matsuyama, 1981) indicate that the collecting and processing of these plants involved a very intensive interaction with the natural environment and may, at least in western Japan, well have constituted a pre-adaptation to the introduction of agriculture (Akazawa, 1981, 1982; Nishida, 1983).

The hunting, fishing and collecting economy of Jomon populations was made possible by an elaborate and rather highly specialized technology, which included a variety of chipped and ground stone tools for the processing of meat, shellfish and plant foods, several regionally and chronologically distinct styles of chipped stone arrowheads, fishhooks, fish gorges and harpoon heads made of bone, and of course an elaborate ceramic assemblage (Aikens and Higuchi, 1982) (Fig. 79). The pottery clearly fulfils a series of important functional roles in the subsistence and economy of Jomon populations (Ikawa-Smith, 1986). Beyond this, however, the great formal and decorative elaboration of ceramics, particularly during the Middle Jomon period, indicates that they were evidently also invested with social and symbolic functions. After decades of typological studies, Japanese archaeologists are just beginning to explore these aspects (for example, Ueno, 1980). Ritual significance is ascribed in particular to ceramic figurines manufactured throughout most of Jomon period (Nagamine, 1986) (Fig. 80).

There is evidence of population growth during the Jomon period and the formation of rather large settlement sites with remains of more than a hundred house structures. Although only a small number of the houses would have been used simultaneously at any one period of site occupation, detailed analyses indicate considerable residential stability, with many coastal as well as interior sites occupied on a year-round basis (Koike, 1980a, 1980b; Watanabe, 1986). While there is again a great deal of regional and chronological variation (Chard, 1974), the majority of dwellings are semisubterranean structures (pit houses) with either square or round floor plans.

Because of the size of some of the sites, the high degree of residential stability and the elaboration in some aspects of the material culture (particularly pottery), it has been suggested that some Jomon communities may have developed some degree of status differentiation. Archaeologists have also discussed questions of territoriality and interaction among communities. Although these questions are far from resolved, they are of interest beyond the boundaries of Japan in a comparative context, because of the extensive similarities that are seen in resource patterns, settlements and regional exchange systems between Jomon Japan on the one hand and prehistoric societies in the coastal regions of North America on the other (Aikens, 1981; Aikens and Dumond, 1986).

It had at one time been considered as given that agriculture, in the form of rice cultivation, came into Japan very late, at the end of the Latest Jomon phase or at the beginning of the succeeding Yayoi period. Increasing sophistication in archaeological research techniques has produced new information that makes it necessary to revise this view. While it remains clear that rice cultivation came to the islands from the Asian continent and entered through southern Japan, it now appears that its first appearance may have been earlier than previously thought. Even more important, there is now reason to believe that the transformation to fully agricultural economies was preceded by a long period of local experimentation with indigenous resources (Akazawa, 1982, 1986; Crawford, 1983; Crawford et al., 1976; Nishida, 1983; Rowley-Conwy, 1984).

The overall assessment is, then, that the Jomon period represents a settling-in phase in the prehistory of Japan: adjustment to relatively aggregated, and often rather stable, resources and evolution of regionally and locally distinctive, but broadly similar and interactive, cultural traditions. Although hunting, fishing and collecting economies constitute the basis for the maintenance of Jomon populations, there is increasing experimentation with horticultural strategies. On the other hand, the stable resource base in several areas of Japan may have allowed the emergence of some degree of social complexity. Both of the latter elements constitute important foundations for the conversion to fully agricultural economies and the rapid evolution of complex societies after the Jomon period.

BIBLIOGRAPHY

AIGNER, J. S. 1979. Pleistocene Ecology and Palaeolithic Assemblages in South China. *J. Hong-Kong Archaeol. Soc.*, Vol. 8, pp. 52–73.

AIKENS, C. M. 1981. The Last 10,000 Years in Japan and Eastern North America: Parallels in Environment, Economic Adaptation, Growth of Social Complexity and the Adoption of Agriculture. In: KOYAMA, S.; THOMAS, D. H. (eds), *Affluent Foragers*, pp. 261–73. (Senri Ethnol. Stud., 9.)

AIKENS, C. M.; DUMOND, D. E. 1986. Convergence and Common Heritage: Some Parallels in the Archaeology of Japan and Western North America. In: PEARSON, R. (ed.), *Studies in Japanese Archaeology*. Ann Arbor.

AIKENS, C. M.; HIGUCHI, T. 1982. *Prehistory of Japan*. New York.

AKAZAWA, T. 1980. Fishing Adaptation of Prehistoric Hunter-Gatherers at the Nittano Site, Japan. *J. Archaeol. Sci.*, Vol. 7, pp. 325–44.

—— 1981. Maritime Adaptation of Prehistoric Hunter-Gatherers and their Transition to Agriculture in Japan. In: KOYAMA, S.; THOMAS, D. H. (eds), *Affluent Foragers*. pp. 213–58. (Senri Ethnol. Stud., 9.)

—— 1982. Cultural Change in Prehistoric Japan: Receptivity to Rice Agriculture in the Japanese Archipelago. *Rec. Adv. World Archaeol.* (Orlando, Fla.), Vol. 1, pp. 151–211.

—— 1986. Discriminant Function Analysis of Later Jomon Settlements. In: PEARSON, R. (ed.), *Studies in Japanese Archaeology*. Ann Arbor.

AKAZAWA, T.; ODA, S.; YAMANAKA, I. 1980. *The Japanese Palaeolithic: A Techno-typological Study*. Tokyo.

AUNG, T. 1971. The 'Neolithic' Culture of the Padahlin Caves. *Asian Perspect.*, Vol. 14, pp. 123–33.

BANDI, H. G. 1951. Die Obsidianindustrie der Umgebung von Bandung in West Java. *Südsee Studien*, pp. 127–61.

BARTSTRA, G. J. 1983. Some Remarks upon Fossil Man from Java, his Age, and his Tools. *Bijdragen tot de Taal-, Land- en Volkenkunde* (Dordrecht), Vol. 139, pp. 421–34.

BELLWOOD, P. 1976. Archaeological Research in Minahasa and the Talaud Islands, North-Eastern Indonesia. *Asian Perspect.*, Vol. 19, pp. 240–88.

—— 1979. *Man's Conquest of the Pacific*. Oxford.

—— 1984. Archaeological Research in the Madai-Baturong Region, Sabah. *Indo Pac. Prehist. Assoc. Bull.*, Vol. 5, pp. 38–54.

—— 1985. Holocene Flake and Blade Industries of Wallacea and their Predecessors. In: MISRA, V. N.; BELLWOOD, P. (eds), *Recent Advances in Indo-Pacific Prehistory*. Leiden. pp. 197–205.

BLEED, P. 1977. Early Flakes from Sozudai, Japan: Are they Man-made? *Science* (Washington), Vol. 197, pp. 1357–9.

BLUNDELL, V. M.; BLEED, P. 1974. 'Ground' Stone Artefacts from Late Pleistocene and Early Holocene Japan. *Archaeol. Phys. Anthropol. Oceania*, Vol. 9, pp. 203–19.

BRACE, C. L. 1978. Tooth Reduction in the Orient. *Asian Perspect.*, Vol. 19, pp. 203–19.

BRACE, C. L.; HINTON, R. J. 1981. Oceanic Tooth-Size Variation as a Reflection of Biological and Cultural Mixing. *Curr. Anthropol.*, Vol. 22, pp. 549–69.

BRACE, C. L.; VITZTNUM, V. 1984. Human Tooth Size at Mesolithic, Neolithic and Modern Levels at Niah Cave, Sarawak: Comparisons with Other Asia Populations. *Sarawak Mus. J.*, Vol. 33, pp. 75–82.

BRONSON, B.; ASMAR, T. 1975. Prehistoric Investigations at Tiangko Panjang Cave, Sumatra. *Asian Perspect.*, Vol. 18, pp. 128–44.

BROTHWELL, D. R. 1960. Upper Pleistocene Human Skull from Niah Caves, Sarawak. *Sarawak Mus. J.*, Vol. 9, pp. 323–49.

BULBECK, F. D. 1981. *Continuities in Southeast Asian Evolution since the Late Pleistocene*. Canberra. (MA thesis, Australian National University.)

CHAPPELL, J. 1976. Aspects of Late Quaternary Palaeogeography of the Australian-East Indonesian Region. In: KIRK, R. L.; THORNE, A. B. (eds), *The Origin of the Australians*. Canberra. pp. 11–28.

CHARD, C. S. 1974. *Northeast Asia in Prehistory*. Madison.

CLIMAP PROJECT MEMBERS. 1976. The Surface of the Ice-Age Earth. *Science* (Washington), Vol. 191, pp. 1131–7.

COLANI, M. 1927. L'Âge de la pierre dans la province de Hoa-Binh, Tonkin. *Mém. Serv. géol. Indochine* (Hanoi), Vol. 14, pp. 1–47.

—— 1939. La Civilisation hoabinhienne extrême-orientale. *Bull. Soc. préhist. fr.*, Vol. 36, pp. 170–4.

COUTTS, P. J. F. 1983. *An Archaeological Perspective of Panay Island, Philippines*. Cebu City.

CPAM, GUANGXI PROVINCE. 1976. Test Excavation of a Cave Site at Zengpiyan in Guilin, Guangxi. *Kao Gu* (Beijing), Vol. 20, pp. 175–9.

CRAWFORD, G. W. 1983. *Palaeoethnobotany of the Kameda Peninsula Jomon*. Ann Arbor.

CRAWFORD, G. M.; MURLEY, W. H.; MASAKAZU, Y. 1976. Implications of Plant Remains from the Early Jomon Hamanasuno Site. *Asian Perspect.*, Vol. 19, pp. 145–55.

DAVIDSON, J. H. C. S. 1975. Recent Archaeological Activity in Viet-Nam. *J. Hong Kong Archaeol. Soc.*, Vol. 6, pp. 80–99.

—— 1979. Archaeology in Northern Viet Nam. *J. Hong Kong Archaeol. Soc.*, Vol. 10, pp. 80–99.

DONN, W. L.; FARRAND, W. L.; EWING, M. 1962. Pleistocene Ice Volumes and Sea Level Lowering. *J. Geol.* (Chicago), Vol. 70, pp. 206–14.

DUBOIS, E. 1920–1. De proto-Australische fossiele mensch van Wadjak. *Kon. Akad. Wetenschappen, Wis- en Natuurkundige Afdeeling*, Vol. 29, pp. 88–105, 866–87.

DUNN, F. L. 1975. *Rain-Forest Collectors and Traders: A Study of Resource Utilization in Modern and Ancient Malaya*. Kuala Lumpur. (Monogr. Malays. Branch, R. Asiatic Soc., 5.)

ESAKA, T. 1986. The Origins and Characteristics of Jomon Culture. In: PEARSON, R. (ed.), *Studies in Japanese Archaeology*. Ann Arbor.

FLENLEY, J. R. 1985. Quaternary Vegetational and Climatic History of Island Southeast Asia. *Mod. Quat. Res. SEAsia*, Vol. 9, pp. 55–63.

FOX, R. B. 1970. *The Tabon Caves*. Manila.

—— 1978. The Philippine Palaeolithic. In: IKAWA-SMITH, F. (ed.), *Early Palaeolithic in South and East Asia*. The Hague. pp. 59–85.

GLOVER, E. 1981. Leang Burung 2: Shell Analysis. *Mod. Quat. Res. SEAsia*, Vol. 6, pp. 45–50.

GLOVER, I. C. 1971. Prehistoric Research in Timor. In: MULVANEY, D. J.; GOLSON, J. (eds), *Aboriginal Man and Environment in Australia*. Canberra. pp. 158–81.

—— 1972. *Excavations in Timor*. (Ph.D. dissertation, Australian National University.)

—— 1973a. Island Southeast Asia and the Settlement of Australia. In: STRING, D. (ed.), *Archaeological Theory and Practice*. London. pp. 105–29.

—— 1973b. Late Stone Age Traditions in South-East Asia. In: HAMMOND, N. (ed.), *South Asian Archaeology*. London. pp. 51–66.

—— 1976. Ulu Leang Cave, Maros: A Preliminary Sequence of Post-Pleistocene Cultural Development in South Sulawesi. *Archipel* (Paris), Vol. 11, pp. 113–54.

—— 1981. Leang Burung 2: An Upper Palaeolithic Rock Shelter in South Sulawasi, Indonesia. *Mod. Quat. Res. SEAsia*, Vol. 6, pp. 1–38.

GLOVER, I. C.; PRESLAND, G. 1985. Microliths in Indonesian Flaked Stone Industries. In: MISRA, V. N.; BELLWOOD, P. (eds), *Recent Advances in Indo-Pacific Prehistory*. Leiden. pp. 185–95.

GORMAN, C. F. 1969. Hoabinhian: A Pebble-Tool Complex with Early Plant Associations in Southeast Asia. *Science* (Washington), Vol. 163, pp. 671–3.

—— 1970. Excavations at Spirit Cave, North Thailand. *Asian Perspect.*, Vol. 13, pp. 79–107.

—— 1971. The Hoabinhian and After: Subsistence Patterns in Southeast Asia during the Late Pleistocene and Early Recent Periods. *World Archaeol.*, Vol. 2, pp. 300–20.

HA VAN TAN. 1978. The Hoabinhian in the Context of Viet Nam. *Vietnamese Stud.*, Vol. 12, No. 46, pp. 127–97.

—— 1980. Nouvelles Recherches préhistoriques et protohistoriques au Vietnam. *Bull. Ec. fr. Extrême Orient* (Hanoi), Vol. 68, pp. 115–54.

—— 1985. Late Pleistocene Climate in Southeast Asia: New Data from Vietnam. *Mod. Quat. Res. SEAsia*, Vol. 9, pp. 81–6.

HARRISSON, T. 1970. The Prehistory of Borneo. *Asian Perspect.*, Vol. 13, pp. 17–46.

HAYASHI, K. 1968. The Fukui Microblade Technology and its Relationship to Northeast Asia and North America. *Arctic Anthropol.*, Vol. 5, pp. 128–90.

HAYDEN, B. 1977. Sticks and Stones and Ground Edge Axes: The Upper Palaeolithic in Southeast Asia. In: ALLEN, J.; GOLSON, J.; JONES, R. (eds), *Sunda and Sahul: Prehistoric Studies in Southeast Asia, Melanesia and Australia*. London/New York. pp. 73–109.

HEANEY, L. R. 1985. Zoogeographic Evidence for Middle and Late Pleistocene Land Bridges to the Philippine Islands. *Mod. Quat. Res. SEAsia*, Vol. 9, pp. 127–43.

HEEKEREN, H. R. VAN. 1958. The Tjabenge Flake Industry from South Celebes. *Asian Perspect.*, Vol. 2, pp. 77–81.

—— 1972. *The Stone Age of Indonesia*. 2nd edn. The Hague.

HEEKEREN, H. R. VAN; KNUTH, C. E. 1967. *Archaeological Excavations in Thailand*. Copenhagen. Vol. 1.

HOANG XUAN CHINH. 1984. Hoabinhian Culture and the Birth of Botanical Domestication in Viet Nam. In: BAYARD, D. (ed.), *Southeast Asian Archaeology at the XV Pacific Science Congress*. Dunedin. pp. 169–77.

HOPKINS, D. M. 1982. Aspects of the Palaeoecology of Beringia during the Late Pleistocene. In: HOPKINS, D. M. et al. (eds), *Palaeoecology of Beringia*. New York. pp. 3–28.

HOWELLS, W. W. 1973. *Cranial Variation in Man*. Cambridge. (Pap. Peabody Mus., Harvard Univ., 67.)

—— 1976. Physical Variation and Prehistory in Melanesia and Australia. *Am. J. Phys. Anthropol.*, Vol. 45, pp. 641–50.

HUANG, Y. et al. 1984. Holocene Sea Level Changes and Recent Crustal Movements along the Northern Coasts of the South China Sea. In: WHYTE, R. O. (ed.), *The Evolution of the East Asian Environment*. Hong Kong. pp. 269–87.

HUTTERER, K. L. 1976. An Evolutionary Approach to the Southeast Asian Cultural Sequence. *Curr. Anthropol.*, Vol. 17, pp. 221–42.

—— 1977. Reinterpreting the Southeast Asian Palaeolithic. In: ALLEN, J.; GOLSON, J.; JONES, R. (eds), *Sunda and Sahul: Prehistoric Studies in Southeast Asia, Melanesia and Australia*. London. pp. 31–71.

—— 1985. The Pleistocene Archaeology of Southeast Asia in Regional Perspective. *Mod. Quat. Res. SEAsia*, Vol. 9, pp. 1–23.

IKAWA, F. 1964. The Continuity of Non-Ceramic to Ceramic Cultures in Japan. *Arctic Anthropol.*, Vol. 2, pp. 95–119.

IKAWA-SMITH, F. 1975. Japanese Ancestors and Palaeolithic Archaeology. *Asian Perspect.*, Vol. 18, pp. 15–25.

—— 1978a. The History of Early Palaeolithic Research in Japan. In: IKAWA-SMITH, F. (ed.), *Early Palaeolithic in South and East Asia.* The Hague. pp. 247–86.

—— 1978b. Lithic Assemblages from the Early and Middle Upper Pleistocene Formations in Japan. In: BRYAN, A. L. (ed.), *Early Man in America from a Circum-Pacific Perspective.* Edmonton, University of Alberta. pp. 22–35.

—— 1980. Current Issues in Japanese Archaeology. *Am. Sci.* (New Haven), Vol. 68, pp. 134–45.

—— 1982a. Co-traditions in Japanese Archaeology. *World Archaeol.*, Vol. 13, pp. 296–309.

—— 1982b. The Early Prehistory of the Americas as Seen from Northeast Asia. In: ERICSON, J. E.; TAYLOR, R. E.; BERGER, R. (eds), *Peopling of the New World.* Los Altos, Calif. pp. 15–33.

—— 1986. Late Pleistocene and Early Holocene Technologies. In: PEARSON, R. (ed.), *Windows in the Japanese Past.* Ann Arbor. pp. 199–214.

JIA, L.; HUANG, W. 1985. The Late Palaeolithic in China. In: WU, R.; OLSON, J. W. (eds), *Palaeoanthropology and Palaeolithic Archaeology in the People's Republic of China.* Orlando. pp. 211–23.

JIANGXI PROVINCIAL MUSEUM. 1976. Excavation (Second Season) of the Neolithic Site of Xianren at Dayuan in Wannian, Jiangxi. *Wen wu* (Beijing), Vol. 20, pp. 23–35.

KAMAKI, Y.; SERIZAWA, C. 1967. Nagasaki-ken Fukui doketsu [Fukui Cave, Nagasaki Prefecture]. In: NIPPON KOKOGAKU KYOKAI DOLETSU ISEKI CHOSA TOKUBETSU INKAI. *Nippon no doketsu iseki* [Cave Sites in Japan]. Tokyo. pp. 256–65.

KIDDER, J. E. et al. 1970. Preceramic Chronology of the Kanto: ICU Loc. 28 C. *Zinruigaku Zassi* [J. Anthropol. Soc. Nippon] (Tokyo), Vol. 78, pp. 140–56.

KOIKE, H. 1980a. *Seasonal Dating by Growth-Line Analysis of the Clam Heretrix Lusoria: Towards a Reconstruction of Prehistoric Shell-Collecting Activities in Japan.* Tokyo. (Tokyo Univ. Mus. Bull., 18.)

—— 1980b. Jomon Shell Mounds and Growth-Line Analysis of Molluscan Shells. In: PEARSON, R. (ed.), *Windows in the Japanese Past.* Ann Arbor. pp. 267–78.

KOTANI, Y. 1969. Upper Pleistocene and Holocene Environmental Conditions in Japan. *Arctic Anthropol.*, Vol. 5, pp. 133–58.

KOYAMA, S. 1981. A Quantitative Study of Wild Food Resources: An Example from Hida. In: KOYAMA, S.; THOMAS, D. H. (eds), *Affluent Foragers.* pp. 91–115. (Senri Ethonol. Stud., 9.)

MARINGER, J. 1957a. A Stone Industry of Patjitanian Tradition from Central Japan. *Kokogalu Zassi* [J. Archaeol. Soc. Nippon] (Tokyo), Vol. 42, No. 2, pp. 1–8.

—— 1957b. Some Stone Tools of Early Hoabinhian Type from Central Japan. *Man* (London), Vol. 57, pp. 1–4.

—— 1970. Die Steinartefakte aus der Stegodon-Fossilschicht von Mengerude auf Flores, Indonesien. *Anthropos* (Vienna), Vol. 65, pp. 229–47.

MATSUYAMA, T. 1981. Nut Gathering and Processing Methods in Traditional Japanese Villages. In: KOYAMA, S.; THOMAS, D. H. (eds), *Affluent Foragers,* pp. 117–39. (Senri Ethnol. Stud., 9.)

MATTHEWS, J. M. 1961. *A Check-List of 'Hoabinhian' Sites Excavated in Malaya 1860–1939.* Singapore.

—— 1966. A Review of the 'Hoabinhian' in Indo-China. *Asian Perspect.*, Vol. 9, pp. 86–95.

MINATO, M. et al. 1965. *The Geological Development of the Japanese Islands.* Tokyo.

MORLAN, R. E. 1976. Technological Characteristics of Some Wedge Shaped Cores in North-Western North America and Northeast Asia. *Asian Perspect.*, Vol. 19, pp. 96–106.

MORLAN, V. J. 1971. The Preceramic Period in Japan: Honshu, Shikoku and Kyushu. *Arctic Anthropol.*, Vol. 8, pp. 136–70.

MOURER, R. 1977. Laang Spean and the Prehistory of Cambodia. *Mod. Quat. Res. SEAsia*, Vol. 3, pp. 28–56.

NAGAMINE, M. 1986. Clay Figurines and Jomon Society. In: PEARSON, R. (ed.), *Windows in the Japanese Past.* Ann Arbor. pp. 255–66.

NISHIDA, M. 1983. The Emergence of Food Production in Neolithic Japan. *J. Anthropol. Archaeol.*, Vol. 2, pp. 305–22.

ODA, S.; KEALLY, C. T. 1973. Edge-Ground Tools from the Japanese Preceramic Culture. *Busshitsu Bunka* [Material Culture], Vol. 22, pp. 1–26.

—— 1979. *Japanese Paleolithic Cultural Chronology.* (Paper presented at the 14th Pacific Science Congress, Khabarovsk.)

OHYI, H. 1978. Some Comments on the Early Palaeolithic of Japan. In: IKAWA-SMITH, F. (ed.), *Early Palaeolithic in South and East Asia.* The Hague. pp. 299–301.

OLSON, J. W.; WU, R. (eds) 1985. *Palaeoanthropology and Palaeolithic Archaeology in the People's Republic of China.* Orlando.

PATTE, E. 1925. Le Kjokkenmodding néolithique du Bau Tro a Tam Tao près de Dong-Hoi (Annam). *Bull. Ec. fr. Extrême Orient* (Hanoi), Vol. 24, Nos. 3–4.

—— 1936. L'Indochine préhistorique. *Rev. Anthropol.* (Paris), Vol. 46, pp. 277–314.

PEARSON, R. 1977. Palaeoenvironment and Human Settlement in Japan and Korea. *Science* (Washington), Vol. 197, pp. 1239–46.

—— 1986a. Introduction. In: PEARSON, R. (ed.), *Windows in the Japanese Past.* Ann Arbor. pp. 1–5.

—— 1986b. The Palaeolithic: Introduction. In: PEARSON, R. (ed.), *Windows in the Japanese Past.* Ann Arbor. pp. 187–9.

PEARSON, R.; PEARSON, K. 1978. Some Problems in the Study of Jomon Subsistence. *Antiquity*, Vol. 52, pp. 21–7.

PERALTA, J. T. 1981. *The Philippine Lithic Tradition.* Manila.

PETERSON, W. E. 1974. Summary Report of Two Archaeological Sites from North-Eastern Luzon. *Archaeol. Phys. Anthropol. Oceania*, Vol. 9, pp. 26–35.

PHAM HUY THONG. 1978. Our Stone Age: From the Mount Do Industry to the Hoa Binh Industry. *Vietnamese Stud.*, Vol. 12, No. 46, pp. 9–49.

—— 1980. Con Moong Cave. *Asian Perspect.*, Vol. 23, pp. 17–21.

REYNOLDS, T. E. G.; BARNES, G. L. 1984. The Japanese Palaeolithic: A review. *Proc. Prehist. Soc.*, Vol. 50, pp. 49–62.

RONQUILLO, W. P. 1981. *The Technological and Functional Analyses of the Lithic Flake Tools from Rabel Cave, Northern Luzon, Philippines.* Manila.

ROWLEY-CONWY, P. 1984. Postglacial Foraging and Early Farming Economies in Japan and Korea: A West European Perspective. *World Archaeol.*, Vol. 16, pp. 28–42.

SCHEANS, D. J.; HUTTERER, K. L.; CHERRY, R. L. 1970. A Newly Discovered Blade Tool Industry from the Central Philippines. *Asian Perspect.*, Vol. 13, pp. 179–81.

SERIZAWA, C. 1965. Oita-ken Sozudai ni okeru zenki kyusekki no kenkyu [A Lower Palaeolithic Industry from the Sozudai Site, Oita Prefecture]. *Tohoku Daigaku Nippon Bunka Kenkyusho Kenkyu Hokoku* [Rep. Res. Inst. Japan. Culture, Tohoku Univ.], Vol. 1, pp. 1–119.

—— 1969. *Tochigi-shi Hoshino izeki – Daisan-ji hakkutsu chosa hokoku* [The Hoshino Site, Tochigi City – Report of the Third Excavation]. Toshigi.

—— 1976. The Stone Age of Japan. *Asian Perspect.*, Vol. 19, pp. 1–14.

—— 1978. The Early Palaeolithic of Japan. In: IKAWA-SMITH, F. (ed.), *Early Palaeolithic in South and East Asia.* The Hague. pp. 287–97.

SHACKLEY, M. 1984. Palaeolithic Archaeology in the Mongolian People's Republic: A Report of the State of the Art. *Proc. Prehist. Soc.*, Vol. 50, pp. 23–34.

SIEVEKING, G. DE G. 1955. Excavations at Gua Cha, Kelantan, 1954. *Fed. Mus. J.* (Kuala Lumpar), Vols 1–2, pp. 75–138.

SMITH, R. B.; WATSON, W. (eds) 1939. *Early South East Asia.* Oxford.

SOEJONO, R. P. 1982. Trends in Prehistoric Research in Indonesia. *Mod. Quat. Res. SEAsia*, Vol. 7, pp. 25–31.

SOLHEIM, W. G. II. 1969. Reworking Southeast Asian Prehistory. *Paideuma* (Wiesbaden), Vol. 15, pp. 125–39.

—— 1970. Northern Thailand, Southeast Asia, and World Prehistory. *Asian Perspect.*, Vol. 13, pp. 45–57.

—— 1972. An Earlier Agricultural Revolution. *Sci. Am.*, Vol. 226, No. 4, pp. 34–41.

—— 1974. The Hoabinhian and Island Southeast Asia. In: REGIONAL SEMINAR ON SOUTHEAST ASIAN PREHISTORY AND ARCHAEOLOGY, 1, Manila. *Proceedings*, pp. 19–26.

—— 1980. Review Article of 'Recent Discoveries and New Views on Some Archaeological Problems in Vietnam'. *Asian Perspect.*, Vol. 23, pp. 9–16.

SOLHEIM, W. G., II; LEGASPI, A. M.; NERI, J. S. 1979. *Archaeological Survey in Southeastern Mindanao.* Manila.

SPOEHR, A. 1973. *Zamboango and Sulu.* Pittsburgh.

SUGIHARA, S. 1956. *Gumma-ken Iwajuku hakken no sekki jidai bunka* [The Stone Age Remains Found at Iwajuku, Summa Prefecture, Japan]. Tokyo.

SUGIHARA, S.; SERIZAWA, C. 1957. *Kanagawa-ken Natsushima ni okeru Jomon bunka shoto no kaizuka* [Shell Mounds of the Earliest Jomon Culture at Natsushima, Kanagawa Prefecture]. Tokyo.

SUZUKU, H.; HANIHARA, K. (eds) 1982. *The Minatogawa Man: The Upper Pleistocene Man from the Island of Okinawa.* Tokyo.

THIEL, B. 1980. Excavations in the Pinacanauan Valley, Northern Luzon. *Indo Pac. Prehist. Assoc. Bull.*, Vol. 20, pp. 40–8.

THORNE, A. G.; WOLPOFF, M. H. 1981. Regional Continuity in Australasian Pleistocene Hominid Evolution. *Am. J. Phys. Anthropol.*, Vol. 55, pp. 337–49.

TSUKADA, M. 1986. Vegetation in Prehistory: The Last 20,000 years. In: PEARSON, R. (ed.), *Windows in the Japanese Past.* Ann Arbor. pp. 11–56.

TUGGLE, H. D.; HUTTERER, K. L. 1972. *Archaeology of the Sohoton Area, Southwestern Sahar, Philippines.* Tacloban City. (Leyte-Samar Stud., 6 (2).)

UENO, Y. 1980. Joho no nagare toshite no Jomon-doki keishiki no dempa [Diffusion of Jomon Pottery Types as Information Flow]. *Minjoku-gaku Kenkyu* [Ethnol. Stud.], Vol. 44, pp. 335–65.

VERHOEVEN, T. 1953. Eine Mikrolithenkultur in Mittel- und West-Flores. *Anthropos* (Vienna), Vol. 48, pp. 597–612.

VERSTAPPEN, H. T. 1975. On Paleo-Climates and Landform Development in Malesia. *Mod. Quat. Res. SEAsia*, Vol. 1, pp. 33–5.

WATANABE, H. 1986. Community Habitation and Food Gathering in Prehistoric Japan: An Ethnographic Interpretation of the Archaeological Evidence. In: PEARSON, F. (ed.), *Windows in the Japanese Past.* Ann Arbor. pp. 229–54.

WHITE, J. P.; O'CONNELL, J. F. 1982. *A Prehistory of Australia, New Guinea and Sahul.* Sydney.

WOLPOFF, M. H.; WU XIN ZHI; THORNE, A. B. 1984. Modern *Homo sapiens* Origins: A General Theory of Hominid Evolution Involving the Fossil Evidence from East Asia. In: SMITH, F. H.; SPENCER, F. (eds), *The Origins of Modern Humans.* New York. pp. 111–201.

YANG HUAI-JEN; XIE ZH. 1984. Sea-Level Changes in East China Over the Past 20,000 Years. In: WHYTE, R. O. (ed.), *The Evolution of the East Asian Environment.* Hong Kong. pp. 288–308.

YASUDA, Y. 1978. *Prehistoric Environment in Japan: Palynological Approach.* Tohoku.

—— 1980. *Kankyo ko kogaku kotohajime: Nihon retto ni man nen* [Introduction to Environmental Archaeology: The Japanese Archipelago in the Past 20,000 Years]. Tokyo.

YEN, D. H. 1977. Hoabinhian Horticulture: The Evidence and the Questions from North-West Thailand. In: ALLEN, J.; GOLSON, J.; JONES, R. (eds), *Sunda and Sahul: Prehistoric Studies in Southeast Asia, Melanesia and Australia.* London/New York. pp. 567–99.

YI, S.; CLARK, G. 1985. The 'Dyuktai Culture' and New World Origins. *Curr. Anthropol.*, Vol. 26, pp. 1–20.

ZEIST, W. VAN. 1983–4. The Prospects of Palynology for the Study of Prehistoric Man in Southeast Asia. *Mod. Quat. Res. SEAsia*, Vol. 8, pp. 1–15.

ZHU, F. 1984. Several Problems Related to the Archaeology of Neolithic Guangdong. In: *Archaeological Finds from Pre-Qin Sites in Guangdong.* Hong Kong. pp. 30–42.

ZURAINA, M. 1982. *The West Mouth, Niah, in the Prehistory of Southeast Asia.* Sarawak.

28

AUSTRALIA AND NEW GUINEA

in the period of *Homo sapiens sapiens* up to about 5,000 years ago

Josephine M. Flood

ORIGINS

The earliest evidence of human presence in Australia comes from camp sites dated to about 38,000 years ago. These camp sites are in the south of the continent, so archaeologists have suggested that the first humans reached the Australian continent some time before 40,000 years ago. Most Australian Aborigines, however, do not accept this theory, and believe that their ancestors have always been here since the Dreamtime, the time of creation. There are many Aboriginal oral traditions supporting this view, but there are others that suggest an overseas origin for these ancestral beings. Some have been recounted by the Aboriginal elder Wandjuk Marika, who says:

> The truth is, of course, that my own people, the Rir-atjingu, are descended from the great Djankawu who came from the island of Baralku far across the sea. Our spirits return to Baralku when we die. Djankawu came in his canoe with his two sisters, following the morning star which guided them to the shores of Yelangbara on the eastern coast of Arnhem Land. They walked far across the country following the rain clouds. When they wanted water they plunged their digging stick into the ground and fresh water flowed. From them we learnt the names of all creatures on the land and they taught us all our Law.

That is just a little bit of the truth, Aboriginal people in other parts of Australia have different origins and will tell you their own stories of how the mountains came to be, and the rivers, and how the tribes grew and followed the way of life of their Spirit Ancestors.

The huge Wandjina, makers of thunder, rain and lightning, soared over the sea to Western Australia. Their faces stare at us from the cave walls of the Kimberley Ranges and the spears that fought their giant battles are still in the sands on the coast north of Derby. The giant Rainbow Serpent emerged from beneath the earth and as she moved, winding from side to side, she forced her way through the soil and rocks, making the great rivers flow in her path, and carving through mountains she made the gorges of northern Australia. From the Rainbow Serpent sprang many tribes, and tales about her are told all over Arnhem Land – over to Western Australia, in central Australia and even to New South Wales. Our paintings on rocks illustrate this true story about one of our Ancestors . . . .

In Queensland Giroo Gurrll, part man and part eel, rose out of the water near Hinchinbrook Island and named the animals, birds and all the places there, while the great Ancestor Chivaree the Seagull paddled his canoe from the Torres Islands down the western coast of Cape York to Sandy Beach where his canoe turned into stone.

(Isaacs, 1980, p. 5)

Whatever the origin of their creation heroes, Aboriginal people see themselves as indigenous rather than Australia's first migrants, in the sense that they have no other race history except from the place where they live (Willmot, 1985, p. 45).

There are two main reasons why scientists believe that the earliest *Homo sapiens sapiens* found in the Australian continent came from overseas. These are the lack of anthropoid or pongid ancestors in Australia from whom they could be descended and the fact that all remains of human occupation found so far in Australia belong to the late Pleistocene.

Where did these earliest Australians originate? Neighbouring South-East Asia has been occupied by humans for more than a million years, so it would theoretically have been possible for the Australian continent to have been colonized any time during this period. However, at no time during the last 3 million years has there been a complete land bridge between the Asian and Australian continents, and the complete lack of Asian animals in Australia signifies that there has always been a substantial sea barrier between the two. The only mammals that made this crossing in prehistoric times were, apart birds and bats, humans, rats, mice and the dingo (*Canis familiaris dingo*). (The last is thought to have been brought to Australia by human seafarers about 4,000 years ago.) (Gollan, 1983).

Throughout the Pleistocene epoch the sea gap isolating the Australian continent from Asia is thought never to have been less than 50 km wide. During this period the sea-level fluctuated dramatically, and dropped to as low as 140 m below present sea-level (Table 9). At times of low sea-level an isthmus of land was exposed joining New Guinea to the Australian land mass in the north, and Tasmania similarly became part of the Australian continent in the south. This

Table 9 Sea-levels of the last 140,000 years in the northern Australasian region, based on Huon peninsula, Papua-New Guinea: stippled area, times when Torres Strait was open; hachured area, times when Gulf of Carpentaria was cut off from the sea; small boxes, error estimates.

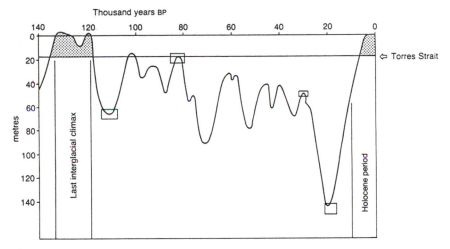

Source: Chappell, 1982, fig. 1.

enlarged continent, which existed during most of the Pleistocene period, has been termed 'Greater Australia'.

When the drop in sea-level was only 65 m, it was possible to walk from Myanmar (formerly Burma) to Bali, but the gap between Indonesia and Greater Australia remained a substantial water barrier.

The continental shelf fringing Asia is known as Sunda Land and the Australian shelf as Sahul Land. The south-eastern boundary of the oriental faunal region is marked by the edge of the Sunda shelf, and the Sahul shelf marks the boundary of the Australian faunal region. A zone of islands, usually termed Wallacea after the nineteenth-century geographer A. W. Wallace, lies in between. Wallacea is a geologically unstable area, and the distribution of fossil land mammals such as the extinct pygmy 'elephant', *Stegodon*, on islands such as Timor, Flores, Sulawesi and the Philippines suggests that water barriers between these islands and Sunda Land were much less at some time in the Pleistocene than they are at present. The antiquity of occupation on the islands of Wallacea is still unclear (White and O'Connell, 1982, pp. 45–6).

PLEISTOCENE VOYAGERS

There is no doubt that the first humans to arrive in Australia must have come by sea. Whether the voyages were accidental or deliberate we do not know, nor what sort of watercraft were used. No archaeological evidence of Pleistocene watercraft has yet been found in Australia, nor do any of the canoes or rafts in existence at the time of European settlement in Australia seem likely candidates, since all lack the necessary buoyancy and seaworthiness for long sea voyages. Yet we know that in the Pleistocene people managed to make voyages across more than 50 km of open sea.

The most likely explanation seems to be that bamboo rafts were used. Bamboo shafts are coated in silica and thus impervious to water and very buoyant. Bamboo was certainly present in the islands of Indonesia and Sulawesi and Kalimantan, but was not available in Australia. This lack of good boatbuilding material in Australia would account for the apparent arrival of people by watercraft in Pleistocene Australia, but absence of any adequate sea-going craft in more recent times.

Fire may also have been taken on deliberate voyages, the fire being kept alight on a clay hearth in the bottom of the craft and used to cook fish and to keep warm, as was the custom among Tasmanian and mainland Aborigines.

The concept of deliberate voyages in seaworthy watercraft at a period in excess of 40,000 years ago is a reasonable hypothesis, in view of the extremely high level of early technology recently revealed by archaeological work in Papua-New Guinea and Australia, and described on pp. 278–9, 280 ff. The stimulus for expansion of population out of South-East Asia may have been demographic pressures caused by the expansion and subsequent contraction of areas of habitable land as the sea fell and rose again. Or it may have been the volcanic activity for which this part of the Pacific 'ring of fire' is notorious.

Smoke from natural bush fires in Australia could occasionally have been visible from some of the islands of Indonesia at any time in the Pleistocene, and at times of low sea-level this is a distinct possibility. This would have provided an incentive for deliberate voyages to Australia.

The routes such voyages may have followed have been analysed in detail by Birdsell (1977, pp. 113–67), who concluded that at the time of lowest sea-level the shortest route across Wallacea involved eight voyages. The most likely routes were either a northern one through Kalimantan and Sulawesi to land on the Sahul shelf near the north-western tip of New Guinea, involving eight stages with none greater than 70 km, or a southern route via Java, Flores and Timor, with eight stages of less than 30 km except for the last crossing of some 87 km from Timor to the Sahul shelf. Both these routes would have been much more difficult, but not impossible, at other times during the glacial period when sea-level was perhaps only some 50 m below its modern level.

On present evidence the most likely time for the earliest human landfall in Australia is generally thought to be the period of low sea-level (a drop of about 120 m below present level) which occurred about 52,000 years ago or the previous one about 70,000 years ago (Chappell, 1983). The lowest sea-level since the last interglacial 120,000 years ago occurred about 18,000 years ago, with a drop to minus 140 m. This was thought to be the most likely time for human colonization of Australia, until archaeological evidence revealed the presence of humankind in the continent by 40,000 years ago.

This is not to exclude the possibility that humans were in

Australia earlier, but there is as yet no firm evidence for human presence before 40,000 years ago. Nevertheless, it is possible that castaways clinging to logs or clumps of vegetation occasionally made landfall on the Australian continent long before this.

Some intriguing evidence suggestive of earlier human arrival is contained in two pollen sequences. In north Queensland in Lynch's Crater on the Atherton Tableland a huge increase in the amount of charcoal occurred 45,000 years ago, at the same time as the local vegetation changed from rain forest to fire-adapted *Eucalyptus*. This change is only explicable, according to the palynologist Kershaw, by the arrival of humans with their firesticks (Singh, Kershaw and Clarke, 1981, pp. 23–54). This suggests that people were in north Queensland by 45,000 years ago, but even more startling is the evidence from Lake George near Canberra in the south-east of the continent. There a 350,000-year-long pollen sequence revealed a huge increase in the amount of charcoal present during the last interglacial period, about 120,000 years ago (Singh, Opdyke and Bowler 1981; Flood, 1983, pp. 98–102). This indicates a much higher incidence of fires than before and a sudden change to a fire-tolerant vegetation dominated by *Eucalyptus*. Singh et al. maintain that nothing can explain this sudden change except the arrival of a new factor in the equation: hunter-gatherers. Unfortunately, archaeological evidence to support this theory of human presence during the last interglacial or indeed before 40,000 years ago has so far proved elusive, so the question of the date of the first human occupation of Australia must remain open.

NEW GUINEA (Map 24)

The island of New Guinea formed part of the same land mass as Australia throughout most of human history, and also lay on the route from Asia to Australia. The coast of New Guinea would have presented a familiar environment to coastal, maritime-adapted people from the rain forest clad islands of Wallacea.

Exciting new evidence shows that the human settlement of New Guinea has an antiquity equal to that of Australia, together with even more startling implications regarding the beginning of horticulture. The evidence comes from uplifted limestone sea-shore terraces on the Huon peninsula, north-east of Lae.

The Huon terraces are one of the best sets of fossil Pleistocene coastlines anywhere in the world. The terraces rise like a giant flight of steps out of the sea; each 'tread' is an ancient coral reef now raised up high above modern sea-level.

The Huon peninsula is bounded by offshore volcanoes and lies at the collision point between three of the earth's plates. Massive earth movements, earthquakes and volcanic eruptions to which New Guinea is subject have raised the coral reef formed at the shoreline 120,000 years ago to 400 m above sea-level. The rate of uplift is 4 mm per year, or about 4 m every thousand years. On one of the lower terraces, 80 m above sea-level, more than twenty-four weathered axes have been found. These 'waisted axes' are large, heavy, stone tools with a flaked cutting edge. A notch flaked out of each side edge gives them a 'waist', or an hour-glass shape. The notches are not simply to provide a grip on hand-held stone tools, since some of them are too wide apart for even the largest hand to stretch across. The notches were probably made to aid the attachment of a handle by hafting.

These waisted axes were found in a terrace formed 45,000 to 55,000 years ago. With each volcanic episode layers of ash fell on the landscape, encasing the evidence of human occupation. On this terrace under 2 m of tephra were found two waisted axes (Plate 49), a core and some flakes (Groube et al., 1986). These stone artefacts are covered by a layer of tephra dated to an absolute minimum age of 35,000 years, and lie on another tephra layer dated to in excess of 37,000 years. (The dates are thermoluminescence dates obtained by the Australian National University and are regarded by Chappell as reliable (personal communication).)

The absolute minimum age for these artefacts is regarded by Chappell and Groube as 37,000 years, and they are probably a few millennia older. This is the first evidence that human occupation of New Guinea is as old as that of Australia. The environment of the camp site on the Huon terrace was probably similar to that of today, with an average annual rainfall of over 2,500 mm (100 inches). The natural vegetation is coastal rain forest, although much of this has been cleared and the region now contains anthropogenic grasslands. About 40,000 years ago the area was probably clad in rain forest, possibly with some sago and mangroves present (Chappell, personal communication).

Fire is the main tool used to clear such rain forest nowadays by the slash-and-burn method. It may be that the massive stone axes found by Joe Mangi, a Papua-New Guinean teaching fellow at the University of Port Moresby, and Groube were used for primitive horticulture. In an interview with Groube, the journalist Reinhardt reported:

Groube is convinced the Huon axes were used for primitive agriculture. His argument is advanced cautiously into the uncertain along the following lines:

'The opening up of the dense coastal rain forests must have been an immense problem for the earliest settlers in New Guinea which the massiveness of the Huon tools may reflect.'

'Why these early colonists were attempting to trim back the forest edges, however, is unclear, whether to facilitate hunting or as an early trend towards utilizing the forest plant resources is unknown.'

But in contemporary Papua-New Guinea, Groube points to isolated clans in the remote west of the country who cultivate bananas in the middle of rain forests, simply by axing back enough vegetation cover for sunlight to reach a banana clump.

'The possiblity undreamt of a few years ago, that the manipulation of rain forest resources, a form of casual "gardening", might have a Pleistocene antiquity must be seriously considered, altering our views of the emergence of systematic gardening' he says.

'The evidence of botanists that many important garden plants are of New Guinea origin, e.g. sugar cane, pandanus, breadfruit, probably one of the bananas, perhaps coconuts, possibly the swamp taro and many tree crops, strengthen these hints.'

(Reinhardt, 1985, p. 91)

Agriculture was being practised in the highlands of New Guinea 9,000 years ago. The evidence comes from the Wahgi Valley in the central highlands near Mount Hagen (Golson, 1977). When some tea planters drained a swamp in the late 1960s they discovered ancient digging-sticks, wooden paddle-shaped spades and stone axes. These artefacts were associated with many water-control ditches, probably dug to aid the growing of taro (*Colocasia esculenta*), cultivated for its edible, starchy tuberous root. The earliest ditch, 1 m deep

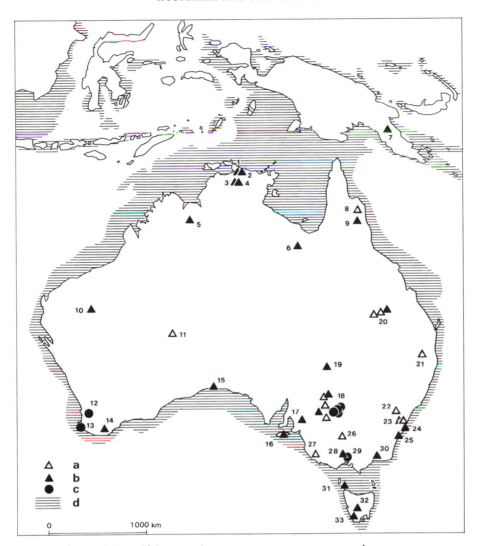

Map 24 Australia, Tasmania and New Guinea: Pleistocene sites. a, 10,000 to 15,000 years ago; b, 15,000 to 30,000 years ago; c, more than 30,000 years ago; d, −200 m sea-level. 1, Nawamoyn; 2, Malangangerr; 3, Malakunanja; 4, Nawalabilla; 5, Miriwun; 6, Colless Ck; 7, Kosipe; 8, Early Man; 9, Walkunder Arch; 10, Mt Newman; 11, Puntutjarpa; 12, Upper Swan Bridge; 13, Devil's Lair; 14, Kalgan Hall; 15, Koonalda; 16, Seton; 17, Roonka; 18, Willandra Lakes; 19, L. Yantara; 20, Kenniff; 21, Talgai; 22, Noola; 23, Kings Table; 24, Bass Point; 25, Burrill Lake; 26, Kow Swamp; 27, Wyrie Swamp; 28, Lancefield; 29, Keilor; 30, Cloggs Cave; 31, Cave Bay Cave; 32, Beginners Luck; 33, Kutikina Cave.

by 2 m wide and some 450 m long, was radiocarbon dated to about 9,000 years ago. Taro, like the pig, is not native to New Guinea, so it must have been introduced. Other archaeological evidence in New Guinea shows that by 5,000 to 6,000 years ago plant cultivation, based on both native and non-native species, forest clearance, relatively permanent village settlements and complex water-management systems had already been developed.

Elsewhere in New Guinea evidence of early human activity has come to light. The Huon artefacts are similar in some respects to 26,000-year-old tools from Kosipe – the earliest site previously known in New Guinea (White et al., 1970). The discovery of Pleistocene occupation at Kosipe was a surprise, for it lies in the south-east corner of New Guinea some 1,400 km from the western Ice Age coastline and in the highlands at 2,000 m above the present sea-level. Kosipe is an open camp site on a flat-topped, steep-sided ridge on the southern slopes of Mt Albert Edward, a 3,990 m peak on which there was a glacier and substantial ice area during the late Pleistocene.

It thus seems clear that humans were paying at least seasonal visits to the highlands of south-east New Guinea 26,000 years ago, when the snow-line was only some 1,000 m

above the camp site and the temperature would have been about 6 °C lower than at present.

PLEISTOCENE TECHNOLOGY

The Huon axes are distinguished by their general massiveness, extremely weathered appearance, flaked edges and the presence of waisting on some specimens. Wear marks are obvious to the naked eye on the 37,000-year-old specimen, indicating that the continuous groove around the body of the axe must have been for a cane or vine binding to a handle. This type of hafting of massive stone axeheads to wooden handles by means of canes or vines is known from the ethnographic present in tropical Australia, the island of Bougainville and elsewhere in the New Guinea region.

The Kosipe artefacts follow in the same tradition as those from the Huon terrace. They are smaller than the Huon axes, but some bear the same hafting notches or grooves. An innovation found in the Kosipe assemblage is the use of edge-grinding, in which the working edge of a tool is ground to a chisel-like bevel for better cutting properties.

There are parallels in Pleistocene Australia for both the Kosipe and Huon artefacts. Some waisted stone tools with flaked edges have been found in South Australia on surface sites in the Flinders Ranges and on what is now Kangaroo Island (Lampert, 1975, 1981). The average length of twenty-four from Kangaroo Island is 19 cm and one is an exceptional 27 cm long. Similar massive waisted artefacts occur in undated contexts in the Mackay district of Queensland.

The use of these waisted tools in Australia is unknown. Lampert has remarked on their resemblance to the sago-pounders of New Guinea and thinks they may have been used to pound some hard foodstuff. Tindale (1981b, pp. 1772–3) has suggested that they were used to kill large animals caught in fall-traps, citing the Aboriginal practice in the Queensland rain forest in recent times of using large, heavy-bladed, sometimes grooved stone axes, with very long handles of the so-called 'lawyer cane' wrapped around the axe head and bound with cane lashings, to kill animals caught in pitfall traps. It may also be that they were used for forest clearance, as seems the most likely explanation in New Guinea.

The Huon waisted artefacts are the earliest hafted stone axes known in the world. They bear witness that the early occupants were technically far more accomplished than was hitherto suspected. The close similarity between these New Guinea artefacts and those from Kangaroo Island and elsewhere in Australia is the clearest evidence yet of the cultural unity of Sahul Land or Greater Australia in the Pleistocene.

Figure 81 Pleistocene ground-edge axes from Arnhem Land, Northern Territory (Australia). All are bifacially flaked and the cutting edge is ground to a bevel; the grooves presumably assisted the attachment of handles. Left: axe from Malangangerr, made of hornfels, grooved on one surface (23,000 to 19,000 years ago). Centre: axe from Nawamoyn, made of porphyritic dolorite, grooved on one surface and one broken margin (21,500 years ago). Right: waisted axe from Nawamoyn, made of hornfels, indented on both margins (21,500 years ago). (After White, 1967.)

The technological parallels continue, with edge-ground tools occurring in New Guinea and in Arnhem Land in northern Australia around 26,000 to 20,000 years ago. Fifteen axes with ground cutting edges have been found in Pleistocene rock shelter deposits in Arnhem Land (White, 1967) (Fig. 81). Grinding of the working edge produces a much more effective cutting edge than flaking, and several of the axes also bear grooves or notches to facilitate hafting. They were manufactured by the 'pecking' technique, which involves fashioning them with a stone hammer or 'hammer-dressing'.

Two features of the Arnhem Land edge-ground artefacts support the idea that they originate locally rather than being imported. First, unlike the edge-ground tools from Asia, the Australian artefacts are hatchets rather than axes (Dickson, 1981). Hatchets differ from true axes in being employed with one hand instead of two and in having a lower mass and shorter handle. The small size and light weight of the Arnhem Land examples make it clear that they should be termed hatchets rather than axes. (However, for convenience the traditional term 'axes' has been retained here.) Second, the early use of hammer dressing on edge-ground tools is confined to northern Australia.

These Arnhem Land axes have provided among the world's oldest evidence for shaping stone by hammer dressing or pecking. And so far only in Japan does the technology of grinding stone to make a sharp, chisel-like cutting edge have a similar antiquity, although edge-ground tools do occur in what may be equally early South-East Asian contexts. These significant technological innovations of hafting, grinding and hammer dressing thus appear to be older in the Australasian region than in Africa, Europe or western Asia.

The first Australians seem to have been the world's earliest ocean voyagers, or at least the first successful castaways. People had reached the necessary technological level to cross substantial bodies of open sea and adapt to a new continent more than 40,000 years ago. The adaptation to a strange, new continent at such an early date must be counted as one of the major achievements in the world's human story. Furthermore, the colonization of Australia marked the first human expansion beyond the single landmass comprising Africa, Europe and Asia.

AUSTRALIA (Map 24)

Physical and biological development

Physically, Australian Aboriginal people are sufficiently distinctive from other peoples of the world to have been given a separate name: Australoid. While New Guineans are distinct from Australians, there appears to be a common Sahul substratum on the evidence of measurements of modern crania (Howells, 1976; Giles, 1976) and from biochemical evidence (Kirk, 1976, p. 341). On a global basis, therefore, the Sahul populations of Australia, New Guinea and Tasmania form a distinctive entity.

All Australian skeletal remains so far found belong to the youngest form of the human race, *Homo sapiens sapiens*. There are some hundred fossil human remains in Australia older than 6,000 years, but detailed analysis has been carried out on less than half this number. This analysis has revealed considerable heterogeneity, particularly in facial characteristics.

The extreme diversity in contemporaneous prehistoric populations in Australia has been described by Thorne (1976, 1977, 1980; Thorne and Wilson, 1977; Thorne and Wolpoff, 1981). He has suggested that two principal groups can be identified: the robust group, exemplified by the Kow Swamp population (Thorne and Macumber, 1972), and the gracile, represented by Mungo I and III (Bowler et al., 1970) and the Keilor skull (Gill, 1966). The robust group are more archaic in appearance, being large, heavy and thick-boned, with massive teeth and mandibles and pronounced supra-orbital brow ridges. In contrast, the gracile group are lightly built and thin-boned, with less sloping foreheads and smaller dentition (Plate 50).

Comparison of fossil and Modern Aboriginal crania reveals the remarkable facts that the Kow Swamp people were more robust and larger than Modern Aborigines and that the Mungo–Keilor group were more gracile and del-

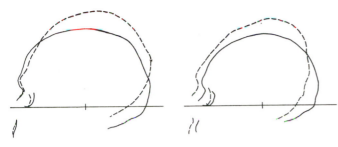

Figure 82 Kow Swamp 5 skull (Australia) compared with Modern artificially deformed and undeformed skulls. Left: midline cranial contours of Kow Swamp 5 (dashed line) and a Modern Murray valley male Aborigine. Right: midline cranial contours of an artificially deformed Arawa male (dashed line) and an undeformed male from northern New Britain. (After Brown, 1981.)

icate, so that they too lie outside the Modern range. This applies to both males and females (Fig. 82).

There are thus significant physical differences both between prehistoric groups and between Modern Aborigines and prehistoric ones. Skull size in Pleistocene Australians was significantly greater than in more recent Aborigines, and other morphological changes have occurred in the Aboriginal cranium over the last 10,000 years, particularly in the form of the forehead and face.

The main differences between the rugged, robust Kow Swamp and the lightly built Mungo groups, which lie only 300 km apart, are in size, facial characteristics and bone thickness. All the Australian Pleistocene hominid remains lie outside the range of present-day Aboriginal skeletal forms of the appropriate sex, but they fall into two contrasting groups, one more lightly built than any Modern Australian Aborigines, the other more rugged and archaic-looking.

Lake Mungo

It is now clear from archaeological evidence that these two groups, the robust and gracile, coexisted for a very long time in prehistoric Australia. Evidence from the Lake Mungo region suggests that around 30,000 years ago both groups had occupied that part of inland Australia. The area is known as the Willandra Lakes region and is now on the World Heritage list on account of its high archaeological and geomorphological significance (Australian Heritage Commission, 1981). Now a semi-arid belt of fossil lakes fringing the desert core of Australia, the Willandra Lakes during the late Pleistocene were full of fresh water and teeming with large fish and shellfish. On the lee side of the lakes crescent-shaped aeolian sand dunes or lunettes provided sheltered camp sites by the lake shores.

The study of the deposits downwind of these fossil lakes by Bowler and others has elucidated the past climate and environment not only of the semi-arid Willandra area but also of the whole of inland Australia (Bowler et al., 1976). Australia is the world's driest inhabited continent; on over 75 per cent of its surface annual rainfall is exceeded by potential annual evaporation. This was not always the case, for great changes in the Australian climate occurred during the Pleistocene. The Willandra Lakes region, and Lake Mungo in particular, is one of the key areas where both climatic changes and early human occupation have been documented. Some of the earliest evidence at present of human occupation in Australia comes from this zone in the south-east of the continent, in the far west of southern New South Wales.

Research in the fossil lake system has concentrated on Lake Mungo, which has suffered extensive erosion of its lunette, exposing 600 hectares of its core and partially exposing much of the rest. The Mungo lunette is 25 km long and before deflation was up to 40 m high. It is visible from several kilometres distant as a long, low white hill among the brown plains. The earliest sediments at Lake Mungo, called the Golgol sediments, were laid down about 150,000 to 120,000 years ago, when the lake was full. No evidence of human presence has ever been found in the Golgol sediments, and it seems that people did not begin to camp at Lake Mungo until the latest full-water phase, which began about 45,000 years ago. During the lake-full stage, from about 45,000 to 26,000 years ago, sand was blown up from lake-side beaches to form a lunette on the eastern shore. This dune is known as the Mungo unit. Over the next 10,000 years the lakes gradually dried up, and the increasingly arid environment is reflected in the Upper Mungo and Zanci sediments.

Most of the earliest traces of human occupation in Australia come from the Lake Mungo area. Several sites containing stone artefacts and middens of freshwater mussel shells (*Velesunio ambiguus*) have been radiocarbon dated to more than 30,000 years. A midden containing mussel shell, ash and charcoal at Lake Outer Arumpo was dated to about 35,600 years ago, and at Lake Mungo shells associated with stone tools eroding out of the Mungo unit have yielded dates ranging back to about 32,750 years ago.

Within the Mungo unit in the period between 33,000 and 24,000 years ago a series of stone tool assemblages have been found, and Mungo is the type site of the Australian core tool and scraper tradition, a tradition of hand-held, steep-edged core- and flake-tools, probably used for heavy-duty planing, pounding or scraping activities and the manufacture of wooden artefacts such as spears and carrying dishes. Also occurring are pieces of ochre with facets ground down by use, and both fireplaces and evidence of earth ovens, together with cooking 'stones' made out of moulded lumps of clay, there being in the Mungo region a shortage of the stone cobbles or pebbles that are used for cooking stones in ground ovens in the ethographic present in Australia.

Remains of more than fifty hominids have been found in the Willandra Lakes region. They include remains of the robust group, exemplified by Willandra Lakes Hominid 50 (Thorne, personal communication; for a brief description see Flood, 1983, pp. 67–8), and the gracile group, characterized by Mungo I and III. Mungo I is the cremated remains of a woman between 20 and 25 years old, dated to about 26,250 years ago, and Mungo III is the complete, extended skeleton of an adult male who was interred within the Mungo sediments about 30,000 years ago, being dated by the burial's position within the Mungo sediments. Morphologically Mungo I and III (and the very fragmentary remains of Mungo II found with Mungo I) are extreme examples of gracility, being lightly built, with very thin cranial bone, no marked eyebrow ridges, and small, light mandibles and teeth.

Kow Swamp

Conversely, the robust people of Kow Swamp and other sites such as Cohuna, Talgai, Mossgiel and Cossack (described in Flood, 1983, pp. 55–66) were large, rugged and thick-boned, with flat receding foreheads. More than forty individuals were excavated by Thorne from the Kow Swamp burial ground in the Murray river valley in Victoria. They included men, women, juveniles and infants, and the burials were dated between about 13,000 and 9,000 years ago. This burial complex is at present the largest single population from the late Pleistocene excavated in one locality anywhere in the world, and is thus of immense importance in the global study of human physical development.

Long, sloping foreheads or extreme frontal recession are a feature of some of the Kow Swamp and other robust skulls. A study by Brown (1981) has established that some of these skulls have been artificially flattened or deformed. Among Australian Aborigines only three groups are recorded in historical times as practising intentional head deformation. These are groups in northern Victoria, Cape York and Mabuiag in Torres Strait. The type of head deformation used in Victoria is unknown, but the other two societies practised pressing rather than binding of the infant's head. In Cape York an observer in 1852 recorded that 'Pressure is made by the mother with her hands ... one being applied to the forehead and the other to the occiput, both of which are thereby flattened, while the skull is rendered proportionally broader and longer than it would naturally have been' (Macgillivray, quoted in Brown, 1981, p. 165).

Head pressing produces more variable deformation than head binding, and at Kow Swamp there is a gradation from clearly deformed skulls to those showing no evidence at all of deformation. Deformation was applied to some skulls of both sexes. The most significant implication of this evidence is that concern about physical beauty in both sexes goes back into the Pleistocene. The concern must be on aesthetic grounds, since there is no practical reason for making a child long-headed. The oldest example of this practice of artificial head deformation in Australia is the Kow Swamp V skull (Fig. 82), dated to about 13,000 years ago, radiocarbon dated on shells within the grave.

The peopling of Australia

What is the explanation for the apparent coexistence of the gracile and robust groups in the same area of prehistoric Australia? There would seem to be three different possibilities. The first is that two distinct groups entered Australia at markedly different times and later merged or hybridized to form the modern Aboriginal population. The archaeologist Rhys Jones explains the problem in terms of gradual interbreeding:

> I think we are seeing the obvious, that the Kow Swamp people reflect a relict group of the original inhabitants of Australia, an archaic race of Homo sapiens who first colonized the continent at least 50,000 years ago. They occupied the well-watered regions and survived intact for tens of thousands of years. Australia was then occupied by a second group of modern Homo sapiens, the Mungo people. They came from south-east Asia and because of their superior technological powers they were able to inhabit large areas of the continent. Eventually the two groups met, and intermarriage between them led to a new group, from which evolved the modern Aborigine.
>
> (quoted in Stokes, 1981)

The second possiblility is that the two groups reached Australia at a similar time but from different places and, again, later merged to form the present population. Both these explanations involve the selective extinction of the extremes of Pleistocene physical characteristics (exemplified by the

marked contrast between the Mungo and Kow Swamp people) when the two groups hybridized to form the contemporary Aboriginal population. The Aborigines of Australia are physically among the world's most variable people, and it may be that this great diversity was even greater in the Pleistocene.

The third possiblility is that a single founding population already containing much physical variation entered Australia a very long time ago, perhaps as much as 100,000 years, and underwent considerable change and diversification within Australia, leading to both the Mungo and Kow Swamp physiques, and some morphologically intermediate varieties.

Considerable attention has been given to the examination of possible biological, linguistic and cultural links between Australian Aborigines and other populations in the Asian region. However, the great time lapse since the first human settlement of the Australian continent means that such links cannot now be identified with any certainty. What seems clear is that the first Australians were among the earliest, most generalized representatives of modern humankind. The basic modern Aboriginal skeletal form is robust rather than gracile and so are the majority of Australian prehistoric remains. Thorne (1980; Thorne and Wolpoff, 1981) has argued for derivation of the robust group from Homo soloensis in Indonesia and a later migration of gracile people from the region of south China, but such ancestral links remain to be substantiated. The emphasis in physical anthropological studies has tended to be on morphological variation in Pleistocene Australians, but similar emphasis must be given to the basic unity and long continuity of the Australian Aboriginal population and culture.

The pattern of settlement

There is considerable uncertainty at present whether the coasts of Australia were colonized earlier than the centre of the continent by people with marine-adapted economy and technology, as argued by Bowdler (1977), or whether the contrary is correct, as hypothesized by Birdsell (1957). So little archaeological work has been done in central Australia that it is perhaps premature to try to establish the pattern of colonization. Likewise, Aboriginal population numbers both in prehistoric and early historic times are extremely uncertain, although it seems clear from Butlin's work (1983) that the traditional figure of about 300,000 Aborigines in Australia at the time of first European settlement in 1788 must be revised upwards to at least a million.

What has become clear from archaeological work over the last decade is that by 20,000 years ago Aboriginal people were occupying a wide range of different environments all over Australia, including the desert core of the continent. In the tropical north they utilized the rock shelters of Arnhem Land, the Kimberley and Pilbara, coexisting with crocodiles, the pied goose (Anseranas semipalmata) and the Tasmanian 'tiger' (Thylacinus cynocephalus), now extinct in mainland Australia.

In temperate Australia Pleistocene sites have been found in the highlands of central Queensland (Kenniff's Cave: Mulvaney and Joyce, 1965), on the coast near modern Sydney (Burrill Lake rock shelter: Lampert, 1971) in the foothills of the south-eastern highlands (Cloggs Cave: Flood, 1974) and elsewhere (Mulvaney, 1975; Flood, 1983, pp. 24–159, 251–3).

Australia's oldest firmly dated human occupation site at present lies in Western Australia near Perth. It is the Upper

Swan Bridge camp site, where charcoal associated with a stone tool assemblage has given reliable radiocarbon dates of about 39,500 and 37,100 years ago (Pearce and Barbetti, 1981, p. 178).

In the extreme south-west corner of the continent the limestone cave of Devil's Lair has produced valuable evidence about human lifeways some 30,000 years ago (Dortch, 1979a). As well as stone tools, the occupants were using bone points, evidently to make skin cloaks, and were also concerned with self-adornment, as described later in this paper. They apparently lived well, exploiting shellfish, emu eggs, birds, bats, lizards, snakes, small and medium-sized animals such as possums and wallabies, and probably the giant kangaroos, *Protemnodon* and *Sthenurus*, now extinct.

The role played by human hunters in the extinction of the Australian megafauna has been the subject of much debate (Hope, 1978). What has become clear is that human hunter-gatherers and megafauna coexisted in Australia for many millennia. Although no 'kill sites' have yet been found, evidence is mounting that hunters did exploit the giant kangaroos, rhinoceros-sized wombat-like *Diprotodon* and other elements of the megafauna. Human agency, however, is most unlikely to have been the sole factor which caused their demise; it seems certain that climatic changes, such as the drying up of Pleistocene lakes and habitat alteration, must also have played a part.

TASMANIA (Map 24)

Tasmanian Aborigines of the nineteenth century were dubbed by anthropologists 'the world's most primitive people', but their most remarkable achievement was that they survived a hundred centuries of glacial conditions, followed by a hundred centuries of complete isolation from any other people. Moreover, not only did they survive but also they preserved and developed the rich cultural tradition which the first migrants had carried across the land bridge into Tasmania. Engravings in Pleistocene style were still being made 20,000 years later, ritual cremations were carried out, ceremonies, songs and dances performed.

In the Pleistocene the most southerly part of the Australian continent was the South East Cape region of Tasmania. A drop in sea-level of only some 60 m exposed the floor of what is now Bass Strait, producing a land bridge of 15 million hectares.

Archaeological evidence has now demonstrated that humans were present at Cave Bay cave on what is now Hunter Island off north-west Tasmania about 22,750 years ago. This is only about one millennium after the land bridge became open, since from about 50,000 until 24,000 years ago Tasmania was an island. While the possibility of occupation of Tasmania as early as 50,000 years ago cannot be entirely discounted, on present evidence it seems more likely that it was the later drop in sea level about 24,000 years ago that saw the move southwards.

Tasmania is further south than any other region in the Southern Hemisphere inhabited during the Pleistocene. There were glaciers on its mountains, and icebergs would have come floating up the coast from the great Antarctic ice-sheet only 1,000 km to the south. Into this freezing toe on the foot of the world moved the Aborigines, perhaps impelled into empty space by an urge to explore, or in search of better summer hunting grounds.

Hunters were present in the interior river valleys of south-west Tasmania at the climax of the last glaciation about 18,000 years ago. They were, it seems, highly specialized hunters, on the evidence of Kutikina, Deena Reena and the other newly discovered limestone caves in the Franklin river region (Kiernan et al., 1983). The bone deposits in these caves give us a unique picture of the hunting strategies of Pleistocene Tasmanians. Most striking is the evidence for a tight, targeting strategy concentrating on one or two species. The people were eating mainly wallabies, especially Bennett's or the red-necked wallaby (*Macropus rufogriseus*), some wombats and a few echidna. In Kutikina cave the bones must be the result of human meals for the long bones are smashed to extract the marrow, almost all the bones have been charred, and only certain body parts are present.

Kutikina cave is huge, with a floor area of about 100 m², covered with a 1–2 m-deep carpet of bone debris, stone and bone tools, and fireplaces. It probably served as a base camp occupied by twenty to thirty people for a few weeks each year. Twenty thousand years ago there were alpine grasslands in the Franklin valley instead of the present rain forest. Glaciers flowed down the high mountain valleys and the only trees were bands of forest along the rivers in sheltered valleys, which would have provided Bennett's wallabies with a habitat of forest and grassland similar to their modern habitat; they still roam the more open parts of the south-west today.

The open grasslands would have been comparable to the present cold, dry arctic tundra of Alaska, the Yukon or Russia and, like their contemporaries in the northern hemisphere, the Ice Age hunters of Tasmania made use of deep caves to survive the glacial temperatures.

Kutikina cave is an incredibly rich site. It has been estimated that there are 10 million artefacts in its earth floor. Only 1 m³ has yet been excavated, and even this has yielded scientific evidence of world significance concerning past climate, environment and human adaptation. As the southernmost Pleistocene sites in the world, these caves in south-west Tasmania are of incalculable importance in tracing the history of mankind. The whole region is on the World Heritage list, and the scientific and symbolic significance of Kutikina and the other Pleistocene occupation sites was a large contributing factor in the successful campaign to save the Franklin valley from the threat of destruction by a hydro-electric scheme. The skill and courage of the Tasmanian Aborigines, who braved snow, ice and freezing cold to hunt within sight of glaciers, bears witness to the indomitable spirit of humankind, and is an inspiration to the several thousand people of Aboriginal descent who still inhabit Tasmania.

As the ice receded, the climate grew warmer and rain forest took over the grasslands, the cave-dwellers moved out of south-west Tasmania. Around 12,000 years ago the land bridge to the mainland was severed, and since that time Tasmanian Aborigines have lived in complete isolation from the rest of the world.

No other surviving human society has ever been isolated so completely or so long as were the Tasmanian Aborigines over the last 12,000 years. The stormy ocean of Bass Strait ensured that there was no contact with the mainland 250 km away, and none of the new developments there such as the boomerang and spear-thrower penetrated Tasmania. Nor did the dingo reach Tasmania. Dingoes were found all over Australia in historic times but were completely absent from Tasmania, so their arrival in south-east Australia must postdate the disappearance of the land bridge.

What effect did 12,000 years of isolation have on the culture of these 3,000 to 4,000 Aborigines, stranded on an island of 67,870 km² (about the same size as Sri Lanka)? This is a controversial question. Some archaeologists such as Jones (1977a, 1978) have argued for a gradual cultural and economic decline; others, like Vanderwal (1978) and Lourandos (1977) have suggested the reverse.

Tasmanian traditional material culture at the time of European settlement included only about two dozen items: wooden spears with fire-hardened tips, throwing clubs, the women's club–chisel–digging-stick, wooden wedges or spatulae, baskets woven from grass or rushes, possum-skin pouch bags, water buckets made from kelp, fire-sticks, kangaroo-skin cloaks, shell necklaces, canoe rafts, huts and a few stone tools.

That the simplest material culture should be found among the people who experienced the longest isolation in the world is significant according to Jones, who sees analogies with the reduction in the number of faunal species on islands that become separated from their parent continents. He believes that the 4,000 people isolated on Tasmania and divided into several different language groups were too few to maintain indefinitely their Pleistocene culture, and that they were therefore 'doomed to a slow strangulation of the mind' (Jones, 1977a, p. 203).

In contrast to the degeneration-and-doomed-people theory, the opposite case has been made by Bowdler (1980), Vanderwal (1978) and others that the Tasmanian population was on the increase and that the society, rather than deteriorating, was branching out in new directions over the last 2,000 years. It may be that Tasmanian watercraft were invented only about 200 years ago, on the west coast where they were most needed, and this is the reason, rather than loss of useful arts, that they are not found in eastern Tasmania. This theory is supported by some cultural developments in the same period. During the last thousand years, some new initiatives related to religious life were taken, such as the construction of stone arrangements for ceremonial purposes.

Prehistoric Tasmanian Aborigines may have had a simple material culture, but they survived more than twenty millennia on their rugged island, they successfully weathered the glacial cold further south than any other people in the world, they produced some of Australia's finest rock engravings, and they achieved a successful balance between hunters and land and a population density similar to that on the Australian mainland.

CULTURE OF ICE AGE AUSTRALIANS

Cultural life

Cultural life in the distant past is so much less knowable than economic life as to be almost invisible to the archaeologist: almost, but not quite, invisible, that is, for there are a few fragments of evidence that give us at least a glimpse of the ritual and artistic tradition of the earliest Australians. These hints at the great antiquity of Aboriginal culture hold high significance for present-day Aborigines, who can now demonstrate that their complex rituals, symbolism and art have their roots in the Ice Age.

It has long been suspected that the life of prehistoric Aborigines, as of those at the time of European settlement, was more than just a constant struggle for survival. Views of Aboriginal society have always tended to be coloured by the bias of the observer. They have varied from that which saw hunters' lives as 'nasty, brutish and short' to the portrayal of 'the noble savage' and 'the original affluent society'. Modern

archaeological evidence shows that the latter two descriptions are the more accurate. Whether Ice Age hunter-gatherers were 'affluent' or not, it is at least now certain that their life included much more than just the endless food quest and the manufacture of essential tools. The French anthropologist Lévi-Strauss has called Australian Aborigines the intellectual aristocrats of the prehistoric world and the archaeological evidence bears him out.

Ritual

The earliest evidence of ritual comes from Lake Mungo in western New South Wales. It is connected with the burial of a man some 30,000 years ago. This tall man, Mungo III, was unquestionably of fully Modern *Homo sapiens sapiens* stock, and this is one of the earliest burials of Modern humans known in the world (Bowler et al., 1970; Bowler and Thorne, 1976). He was placed in a grave on his side with his hands clasped. The corpse had been covered with a thick coating of red ochre, now indicated by deep red staining on the bones and surrounding soil.

The significance of this ochred burial 300 centuries ago is that it shows that such rituals go back at least as far in Australia as in other parts of the world such as Mediterranean Europe, where ochred burials have been found, for instance in Grimaldi cave (Liguria, Italy) at a similar period. In fact at Mungo red colouring pigment was in use even earlier, for lumps of ochre and stone artefacts were found deep below the ashes of a fire lit 32,000 years ago (Australian Heritage Commission, 1981). This ochre did not occur naturally at Mungo, but must have been deliberately carried there from some distance away.

Similar lumps of pigment, some of them bearing ground facets indicating use, have been found in Ice Age levels in several other widely separated sites such as Kenniff Cave in Queensland, Cloggs Cave in Victoria, Miriwun in Western Australia, and several Arnhem Land rock shelters. At one of the latter, Malakunanja II, a large grinding stone was impregnated with red and white pigment, showing that lumps of pigments were ground up into a powder paint 19,000 years ago. Ochre has no utilitarian functions such as medicinal use; it is simply a pigment used (at least in the recent past) to decorate rock walls, artefacts, dancers' bodies in ceremonies and corpses during some burial rites. Its use in burial ritual is the only use documented so far in Ice Age sites, but no doubt then as now ochre was also used for other purposes.

Stronger evidence of ritual behaviour comes from the 26,000-year-old Mungo cremation. There is no doubt that it was a cremation: the young woman's body was burned on the lake-shore, then the bones were smashed and interred in a small round pit. In Aboriginal Australia the tradition of cremation extends from the Ice Age to the present day. That cremation was widespread in Tasmania may signify that this elaborate ritual was part of the culture of the earliest migrants, since Tasmania was cut off from the rest of the world by rising post-glacial seas about 12,000 years ago.

It is interesting that it is a woman who was cremated. While no conclusions can be drawn from a sample of one, it at least shows that 260 centuries ago women were considered worthy of complex burial rites. What emotions inspired these rites – love, fear or religious awe – we will never know, but all show a concern for the deceased which is the essence of humanity.

A remarkable variety of burial practices were in use by Aborigines at the time of first European contact. In addition to inhumation in a grave or mound and cremation, corpses were exposed on platforms in trees, laid out in caves, and put in hollow trees. Burial might be immediate or delayed, delayed burial involving desiccation and later dismemberment of the body, the remains being carried around, ritually eaten, or packed into rock crevices, skin bundles or bark cylinders.

Grave goods were found by Thorne and Macumber (1972) with several of the 10,000- to 13,000-year-old Kow Swamp burials. These were ochre, shells, marsupial teeth and stone artefacts, and one body was laid to rest on a bed of mussel shells. As at Mungo 20,000 years earlier, ochre was powdered over a corpse, which shows the long continuity of such customs.

The presence of grave goods may mean simply that the corpses were being buried with their normal equipment in everyday life, but there are indications that special non-utilitarian regalia were also sometimes included. One body buried at Kow Swamp some 12,000 years ago wore a band of kangaroo incisor teeth round the head. Traces of resin on the teeth showed that they had been stuck together in a band. Similar headbands of kangaroo teeth, plant fibre and resin were worn by Central Desert Aborigines – both men and women – in the nineteenth century.

One of the most spectacular finds of this kind was the huge pierced tooth necklace slung from the neck of a man buried in a sandy dune beside the relict Lake Nitchie in western New South Wales (Macintosh, 1971). No fewer than 178 pierced teeth of the Tasmanian devil (*Sarcophilus*) made up the necklace (Plate 51). The teeth must derive from a minimum of forty-seven individual animals, which are now extinct on the Australian mainland. Indeed, if such necklaces were common, it is not surprising that Tasmanian devils became extinct.

Each tooth is pierced by a hole that was ground and gouged, involving a tremendous amount of labour. This pierced tooth necklace is unique both in present Aboriginal culture and in prehistoric Australia.

The Nitchie burial has other important features. The skeleton was compressed downwards into a shaft-like pit, there were ochre pellets in the grave, and the tall man lacked his two central upper front teeth. This indicates prehistoric tooth avulsion – the widespread practice in male initiation rites of knocking out one or two of the novice's upper incisors. If so, this ritual practice goes back at least some 6,500 to 7,000 years, the age of the Lake Nitchie burial.

Ornaments

The wearing of ornaments has recently been shown to be an age-old custom, for at Devil's Lair in Western Australia three pierced bone beads occurred in layers dated to between 12,000 and 15,000 years ago (Dortch, 1979a, 1979b) (Plate 52). These beads are segments of kangaroo fibulae cut with stone tools, and show wear on their ends indicating friction from a threaded sinew. Such beads do not exist in Aboriginal material culture in the ethnographic present.

Another remarkable find at Devil's Lair, in a 14,000-year-old layer, was a perforated fragment of soft marl which is foreign to the locality (Dortch, 1980). This is thought to be an ornamental pendant, but the perforation could also have served to polish the tips of shafts of wooden spears or bone awls. Its shape resembles a bird's head; the base of the 'neck' appears to have been fractured so was probably originally longer.

Personal adornment was widespread in prehistoric Abo-

riginal Australia, and has its roots in the Ice Age. Ochre has been in use as a paint for more than 30,000 years, bone beads and headbands of kangaroo teeth for over 12,000, long necklaces of Tasmanian devil teeth for over 6,000 years and pendants of bone, shell and opal for at least 5,000. And Tasmania shell necklaces, made from hundreds of tiny shells, are one of the most distinctive features of Aboriginal culture, which may well have a long ancestry.

The wearing of ornaments reflects the self-awareness, individuality and cult of personality of these early Australians, and hints at long-enduring decorative arts, aesthetic traditions and belief systems.

Aboriginal traditions that appear extremely ancient are the practice of delayed burial, cremation, infanticide, tooth avulsion in initiation ceremonies, the wearing of headbands by initiated men and wearing of ornaments such as pendants and beads.

Development of art

Aboriginal art likewise has its roots in the Pleistocene epoch. One of the most remarkable discoveries yet made in Australia is the presence of Ice Age art in total darkness inside Koonalda cave far below the arid Nullarbor plain in South Australia (Wright, 1971). Koonalda cave is a crater-like doline (limestone sink-hole), which was used as a flint mine between 15,000 and 23,000 years ago. Hearths, charcoal, stone artefacts and flint-quarrying debris were excavated from a dimly lit chamber about 100 m inside the entrance. In total darkness some 300 m inside the cave, wall markings were found. These were scratched with fingers, sticks, bones or stone artefacts into the limestone walls, which vary in texture from very soft to hard (Plate 53).

Some large, flat wall panels are totally covered with diagonal criss-crossing sets of parallel finger-markings. Large groups of vertical and sometimes horizontal lines occur, together with a few definite designs, such as regularly spaced grids or lattices. There are also two sets of four concentric circles, both about 20 cm in diameter. The most remarkable design of all is a 120 cm-long herringbone design, consisting of a row of seventy-four diagonal incised lines below thirty-seven short finger-markings. The fact that the number of the former is exactly twice the number of finger markings can scarcely be chance; this is probably a deliberate design with symbolic significance.

This 'art' is believed to date to around 20,000 or more years ago, on several grounds: all radiocarbon dates for human use of the site are from this period; there is no evidence of later re-use of the cave; a small fragment of incised limestone wall occurred in the excavated occupation deposit; and charcoal from just below a panel of wall markings gave a date of 20,000 years ago. (The charcoal is thought to have come from hand-held torches used to light the way into these deepest recesses of the cave.)

The wall markings at Koonalda and other caves such as Snowy River Cave in eastern Victoria (Flood, 1983, pp. 121–40) resemble the so-called 'macaroni style' found in the earliest cave art in Europe. While no link between the two is being suggested, such markings mirror the instinctive human impulse to make marks on blank surfaces. This is a well-documented reaction, common to *Homo sapiens* all over the globe, which may be the first step in the development of art in all societies. The markings may also be symbols produced in the course of ceremonial activity. In hunter-gatherer societies most art forms are part of religious ritual, and this is certainly true of traditional Aboriginal society in more recent times. Likewise, remote, inaccessible places like the depths of caves or mountain tops tend to be used for ceremonies, such as the initiation of boys into manhood.

Early Australian art tends to be abstract, with the circle and tracks of animals and birds being the predominant motifs. A number of engravings (or petroglyphs) have been dated to the Pleistocene; the best evidence has come from Early Man Shelter in north Queensland (Rosenfeld et al., 1981). These engravings were sealed in by archaeological deposits dating from about 13,200 years ago. They are pecked out on the shelter wall to form a long frieze, which rises obliquely, parallel to the natural bedding planes of the rock. The designs have been influenced by the natural contours of the rock surface; hollows have been engraved or emphasized by outlining. Most common are gridded designs, simple three-pronged 'bird tracks', circles and extensive maze-like patterns of lines (Plate 54).

Over much of central and eastern Australia a similar style of engravings, dating at least from the terminal Pleistocene, has been found (Maynard, 1979). This has become known as the Panaramitee style after the type site in South Australia (Mountford and Edwards, 1963; Edwards, 1971). Recurrent features of these engravings sites are proximity to water, association with human occupation, advanced weathering and surface patination including desert varnish, the use of the pecking (hammer dressing by percussion) technique, a predominance of tracks of macropods (kangaroos and wallabies) and birds, and the presence of circles. The circles take many forms, and include vulva-like designs which certainly seem to be sexual symbols.

There is every reason to believe that the art of painting has an antiquity similar to that of engraving in Australia, but firm evidence has so far been lacking. Some indications, however, have been found in Arnhem Land in the Northern Territory, which contains some of the world's most complex and prolific rock paintings. The paintings are generally naturalistic, and thus document local material culture, life-style and environment.

There are strong indications that this art has a Pleistocene antiquity (Chaloupka, 1984). Major factors are that pieces of ochre with ground facets have been found in a 19,000-year-old layer in a local rock shelter (Naulabila); an ochre-impregnated grindstone was excavated in an 18,000-year-old layer in Malakunanja II rock shelter; paintings of locally extinct animals, such as the Tasmanian 'tiger', *Thylacinus*, and the long-beaked echidna, *Zaglossus*, occur, and some paintings are covered by transparent siliceous concretions which geologists think may have formed at the height of the last glaciation about 18,000 years ago.

On the basis of superimposition and changes in style and motifs, Chaloupka has proposed a sequence of four styles. The earliest art (the 'dynamic style') is considered to predate the post-glacial rise in sea-level some 9,000 to 7,000 years ago. Its subject matter is dominated by animals and human beings. A fascinating aspect of the paintings of humans in the dynamic style is the evidence of personal adornment in the form of armlets, neck ornaments and head-dresses decorated with tassels and feathers (Figs 83 and 84). There even seems to be a stencil of a tooth necklace, reminiscent of that found on the Nitchie burial. Another remarkable feature is the portrayal of zoomorphs: human figures with animal heads, some of which may represent flying foxes.

There are many small, superbly drawn scenes of people and animals in narrative composition from everyday life, such as dances and kangaroo hunts. As many as sixty figures appear in one painting, and the scenes are full of expressive

Figure 83 Hunter spearing emu. Painting in the dynamic style, from Kakadu National Park, Arnhem Land (Australia). The hunter, hidden behind a bunch of grass, stalks an emu and successfully spears it. The hunter has a large head-dress and a waist hair belt. The body, legs and feather coat of the emu are faithfully depicted. There is also a suggestion of the non-visual aspects of the event. The power with which the spear was thrown is implied by the dashed line drawn underneath the spear from the man's hand to where the body of the emu is pierced. Dashes in front of the hunter and the head of the emu perhaps indicate the hunter calling in triumph and the emu in pain. (Drawing and interpretation by G. Chaloupka.)

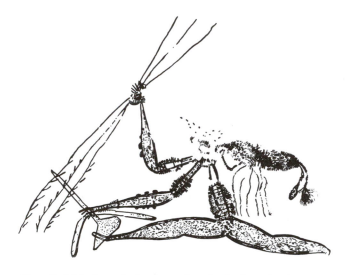

Figure 84 Male figure in the dynamic style. Arnhem Land, Northern Territory (Australia). This hunter from Kolondjoruk site 2, Deaf Adder creek, wears a long, tasselled ceremonial head-dress and holds barbed spears, a boomerang and a hafted stone axe. (After Brandl, 1973, courtesy of the Australian Institute of Aboriginal Studies.)

movement, which is why Chaloupka has named this the dynamic style. Previously it was known as *Mimi* art, because Aborigines had no direct knowledge of the paintings but described them as being the work of *Mimi* spirit people who live in the rocks.

Considerable change took place in the development of this rock art, culminating in the well-known polychrome 'X-ray' paintings, which depict the internal anatomical details of figures as well as their exterior. The post-glacial rise in sea-level, which had a dramatic effect on the coastal plains of northern Australia, may have led to the myth of the Rainbow Serpent.

The Rainbow Serpent is usually depicted as a snake with ears or antler-like projections on its head and is generally associated in northern Australia with myths concerning rain and floods. These could reflect the encroaching sea, which has been estimated to have swallowed up several hundred metres of land each decade. The change from pre-estuarine to estuarine conditions and the appearance of the Rainbow

Serpent in rock art belong to between 9,000 and 7,000 years ago, which would make the Rainbow Serpent myth the longest continuing religious belief documented in the world.

Many uncertainties are inevitable in attempting to identify tangible evidence of the awakening of the human intellect. The oldest 'art' in Australia is barely distinguishable from random finger markings, yet these tentative beginnings were to flower into the naturalistic narrative art of northern Australia in the late Pleistocene. The scenes of hunting, dancing and battles in this dynamic style may be the world's earliest known narrative paintings.

While comparatively few traces remain of the Pleistocene art of Aboriginal Australia, the great diversity, quality, vigour, complexity and symbolism of recent Aboriginal art are evidence of strong artistic and religious traditions of great antiquity.

TECHNOLOGY

The emerging picture of Pleistocene technology is of an efficient toolkit, including stone, bone and wooden tools and no doubt many other items made of organic materials that have not survived in the archaeological record. The stone tools are similar all over the continent, even when made from very different raw materials, and they appear to belong to a single technological tradition. This Australian core tool and scraper tradition is characterized by pebble choppers, horse-hoof cores, and steep-edged, notched and other scrapers. They were primarily tools to make tools, and were used for manufacturing, maintenance and processing tasks, and some preparation of animal and vegetable food.

Aboriginal prehistoric technology was not static, but there was a gradual development towards less massive, more efficient and more varied tools. Later Pleistocene industries have fewer core-tools, smaller scrapers and a greater range of types. This decrease in size reflects progress towards greater efficiency in the use of raw material. Holocene assemblages are even more varied, reflecting a trend towards ever greater diversity in Aboriginal material culture.

Stone tools played a relatively small part in traditional Aboriginal equipment, but of Ice Age wooden technology we have but a single glimpse: the twenty-five wooden artefacts preserved in a 10,000-year-old layer in Wyrie Swamp, a peat bog in South Australia (Luebbers, 1975). These represent the characteristic equipment of traditional Aboriginal Australia. Women were equipped with digging-sticks, men with spears and boomerangs. A strong wooden spear with a fire-hardened tip was a highly effective weapon which has been used throughout Aboriginal occupation of the continent. The barbed, javelin-type spear was a refinement that was unexpected 10,000 years ago, but it would have been an effective weapon for spearing large kangaroos. When such barbed spears enter an animal they are difficult to dislodge, and tend to cause death through loss of blood.

The boomerangs from Wyrie Swamp are even more sophisticated weapons than the barbed spears (Plate 55). They are clearly the returning type of boomerang; the two ends are oriented in different aerodynamic planes, and their lateral twist and curvature are the classic properties of a well-designed aerodynamic missile. It is fitting that the world's oldest known boomerangs have been found in Australia. So-called boomerangs have been found elsewhere, such as in Egypt and Florida; these were not true returning boom-

erangs, but throwing sticks. Another independent invention in Australia was the spear-thrower, which seems to have been developed after the post-glacial sea-level rise, since it was not used in Tasmania.

In summary, prehistoric technology in Australia was neither primitive nor simple. Material equipment was limited in diversity and highly portable, but it was adapted to cope successfully with a wide variety of environments and harsh conditions which, 20,000 years later, were to prove too much for many European 'explorers' and farmers.

THE PLEISTOCENE–HOLOCENE TRANSITION

Australia was the only continent where the end of the Pleistocene did not herald major cultural changes, such as the development of agriculture and urbanization. Australia remained a land of nomadic hunter-gatherers while most people in the rest of the world, including nearby Papua-New Guinea, became farmers, horticulturalists or herdsmen. Other traits that never developed in the fifth continent were the bow and arrow, pottery or the use of metals.

The reasons why Australian Aborigines did not become farmers or horticulturalists or domesticate animals are complex. One factor is that basic human adaptation to the Australian environment took place when the continent was first occupied, another that the environment was to a remarkable degree modified by its prehistoric occupants, particularly by 'fire-stick farming'. The hunter-gatherer way of life was ideally suited to Australia, the world's driest inhabited continent, and Aboriginal people lived well in a range of harsh environments where European agriculture later proved an abysmal failure.

Once the nomadic way of life had become well established, with its consequent need to travel light, it was unlikely that agriculture or horticulture, pottery or sedentary life would be adopted, except in response to major environmental or other changes, but environmental changes at the Pleistocene–Holocene boundary were relatively minor compared with those in the northern hemisphere. The main change was the inundation of about one-seventh of the landmass of Greater Australia (some 2.5 million km²) by the rising glacial melt-water.

One effect of this drastic loss of land seems to have been to push occupation into less favourable zones, which had previously been uninhabited or visited only occasionally. Other areas became less favourable for human occupation because of habitat alteration due to climatic change at the end of the Pleistocene. In central Australia higher temperatures caused the Pleistocene lakes to dry up, inducing a change in local Aboriginal food staples from freshwater aquatic foods such as fish and mussels to flour made from wild seeds. In south-west Tasmania climatic change converted alpine grasslands into rain forest, and the Pleistocene Aboriginal occupants of caves such as Kutikina on the Franklin river vacated the area. In other words, in regions such as these the climatic change at the end of the Pleistocene caused environmental deterioration rather than amelioration from the hunter-gatherer point of view.

While some major environmental changes did occur at the beginning of the Holocene, in a continent the size of Australia it was possible for prehistoric people to respond to regional environmental changes by moving elsewhere rather than by major cultural adaptation. The archaeological record shows considerable continuity in technology and economy across the Pleistocene–Holocene boundary, with which no major cultural changes are associated. The greatest changes in prehistoric Aboriginal society seem to occur later, when in the mid-Holocene between about 4,000 and 3,000 years ago new, specialized, small tools appear together with the dingo, an apparent increase in population and intensification of food-harvesting techniques.

The broadly based economic systems of Australian Aborigines which were developed during the Pleistocene era allowed them the flexibility not only to survive but to flourish in reasonable affluence, and to adapt to the post-Pleistocene diminution and desiccation of the Australian continent without major changes in their economy or lifestyle.

Prehistoric Aboriginal society was dynamic; neither the land nor the people were unchanging, and constant adaptation was made to environmental fluctuations. In contrast with other continents, however, there has also been basic stability and continuity of the hunter-gatherer way of life, from more than 40,000 years ago till the present.

BIBLIOGRAPHY

AUSTRALIAN HERITAGE COMMISSION. 1981. *Nomination of the Willandra Lakes Region for Inclusion in the World Heritage List.* Canberra.

BIRDSELL, J. B. 1957. Some Population Problems Involving Pleistocene Man. *Cold Spring Harbor Lab. Symp. Quant. Biol.* (New York), Vol. 22, pp. 47–70.

—— 1977. The Recalibration of a Paradigm for the First Peopling of Greater Australia. In: ALLEN, J.; GOLSON, J.; JONES, R. (eds), *Sunda and Sahul: Prehistoric Studies in Southeast Asia, Melanesia and Australia.* London/New York. pp. 113–67.

BOWDLER, S. 1977. The Coastal Colonisation of Australia. In: ALLEN, J.; GOLSON, J.; JONES, R. (eds), *Sunda and Sahul: Prehistoric Studies in Southeast Asia, Melanesia and Australia.* London/New York. pp. 205–46.

—— 1980. Fish and Culture: A Tasmanian Polemic. *Mankind* (Sydney), Vol. 12, pp. 334–40.

BOWLER, J. M.; THORNE, A. G. 1976. Human Remains from Lake Mungo: Discovery and Excavation of Lake Mungo III. In: KIRK, R. L.; THORNE, A. G. (eds), *The Origin of the Australians.* Canberra. pp. 127–38.

BOWLER, J. M. et al. 1970. Pleistocene Human Remains from Australia: A Living Site and Human Cremation from Lake Mungo, Western New South Wales. *World Archaeol.,* Vol. 2, pp. 39–60.

—— 1976. Late Quaternary Climates of Australia and New Guinea. *Quat. Res.,* Vol. 6, pp. 359–94.

BROWN, P. 1981. Artificial Cranial Deformation: A Component in the Variation in Pleistocene Australian Aboriginal Crania. *Archaeol. Ocean.* (Sydney), Vol. 16, pp. 156–67.

BUTLIN, N. 1983. *Our Original Aggression.* Sydney.

CHALOUPKA, G. 1984. *From Palaeoart to Casual Paintings.* Darwin.

CHAPPELL, J. 1982. Sea Levels and Sediments: Some Features of the Context of Coastal Archaeological Sites in the Tropics. *Archaeol. Ocean.* (Sydney), Vol. 17, No. 2, pp. 69–78.

—— 1983. A Revised Sea-level Record for the Last 300,000 Years from Papua New Guinea. *Search* (East Lansing, Mich.), Vol. 14, Nos. 3–4, pp. 99–101.

DICKSON, F. P. 1981. *Australian Stone Hatchets: A Study of Design and Dynamics.* Sydney.

DORTCH, C. 1979a. Devil's Lair: An Example of Prolonged Cave Use in South-Western Australia. *World Archaeol.,* Vol. 10, pp. 258–79.

—— 1979b. Australia's Oldest Known Ornaments. *Antiquity,* Vol. 53, pp. 39–43.

—— 1980. A Possible Pendant of Marl from Devil's Lair, Western Australia. *Rec. West. Aust. Mus.* (Perth), Vol. 8, pp. 401–3.

EDWARDS, R. 1971. Art and Aboriginal Prehistory. In: MULVANEY, D. J.; GOLSON, J. (eds), *Aboriginal Man and Environment in Australia.* Canberra. pp. 356–67.

FLOOD, J. 1974. Pleistocene Man at Cloggs Cave: His Toolkit and Environment. *Mankind,* Vol. 9, pp. 175–88.

—— 1983. *Archaeology of the Dreamtime.* Sydney.

GILES, E. 1976. Cranial Variation in Australia and Neighbouring Areas. In: KIRK, R. L.; THORNE, A. G. (eds), *The Origin of the Australians.* Canberra. pp. 161–72.

GILL, E. D. 1966. Provenance and Age of the Keilor Cranium: Oldest Known Human Skeletal Remains in Australia. *Curr. Anthropol.,* Vol. 7, pp. 581–4.

GOLLAN, K. 1983. *Prehistoric Dingo in Australia.* Canberra. (Ph.D. thesis, Australian National University.)

GOLSON, J. 1977. No Room at the Top: Agricultural Intensification in the New Guinea Highlands. In: ALLEN, J.; GOLSON, J.; JONES, R. (eds), *Sunda and Sahul: Prehistoric Studies in Southeast Asia, Melanesia and Australia.* London/New York. pp. 601–38.

GROUBE, L. et al. 1986. A 40,000 Year Old Human Occupation Site at Huon Peninsula, Papua New Guinea. *Nature* (London), Vol. 304.

HOPE, J. H. 1978. Pleistocene Mammal Extinctions: The Problem of Mungo and Menindee, New South Wales. *Alcheringa* (Sydney), Vol. 2, pp. 65–82.

HOWELLS, W. W. 1976. Metrical Analysis in the Problem of Australian Origins. In: KIRK, R. L.; THORNE, A. G. (eds), *The Origin of the Australians.* Canberra. pp. 141–60.

ISAACS, J. (ed.) 1980. *Australian Dreaming: 40,000 Years of Aboriginal History.* Sydney.

JONES, R. 1968. The Geographical Background to the Arrival of Man in Australia and Tasmania. *Archaeol. Phys. Anthropol. Ocean.,* Vol. 3, pp. 186–215.

—— 1977a. The Tasmanian Paradox. In: WRIGHT, R. V. S. (ed.), *Stone Tools as Culture Markers: Change, Evolution, Complexity.* Canberra. pp. 189–204.

—— 1977b. Man as an Element of a Continental Fauna: The Case of the Sundering of the Bassian Bridge. In: ALLEN, J.; GOLSON, J.; JONES, R. (eds), *Sunda and Sahul: Prehistoric Studies in Southeast Asia, Melanesia and Australia.* London/New York. pp. 317–86.

—— 1978. Why Did the Tasmanians Stop Eating Fish? In: GOULD, R. (ed.), *Explorations in Ethnoarchaeology.* Albuquerque. pp. 11–48.

KIERNAN, M.; JONES, R.; RANSON, D. 1983. New Evidence for Glacial Age Man in South-West Tasmania. *Nature* (London), Vol. 301, pp. 28–32.

KIRK, R. L. 1976. Serum Protein and Enzyme Markers as Indicators of Population Affinities in Australia. In: KIRK, R. L.; THORNE, A. G. (eds), *The Origin of the Australians.* Canberra. pp. 329–46.

LAMPERT, R. J. 1971. *Burrill Lake and Currarong.* Canberra. (Terra Aust., 1.)

—— 1975. A Preliminary Report on Some Waisted Blades Found on Kangaroo Island, South Australia. *Aust. Archaeol.* (Canberra), Vol. 2, pp. 45–7.

—— 1981. *The Great Kartan Mystery.* Canberra. (Terra Austr., 5.)

LOURANDOS, H. 1977. Aboriginal Spatial Organization and Population: South-Western Victoria Reconsidered. *Archaeol. Phys. Anthropol. Ocean.,* Vol. 12, pp. 202–25.

LUEBBERS, R. A. 1975. Ancient Boomerangs Discovered in South Australia. *Nature* (London), Vol. 253, p. 39.

MACINTOSH, N. W. G. 1971. Analysis of an Aboriginal Skeleton and a Pierced Tooth Necklace from Lake Nitchie, Australia. *Anthropologie* (Brno), Vol. 9, pp. 49–62.

MAYNARD, L. 1979. The Archaeology of Australian Aborignal Art. In: MEAD, S. M. (ed.), *Exploring the Visual Art of Oceania.* Honolulu. pp. 83–110.

MOUNTFORD, C. P.; EDWARDS, R. 1963. Rock Engravings of Panaramitee Station. *Trans. R. Soc. South Aust.* (Adelaide), Vol. 86, pp. 131–46.

MULVANEY, D. J. 1975. *The Prehistory of Australia.* 2nd edn. Melbourne.

MULVANEY, D. J.; JOYCE, E. B. 1965. Archaeological and Geomorphological Investigations on Mt Moffatt Station, Queensland, Australia. *Proc. Prehist. Soc.,* Vol. 31, pp. 147–212.

PEARCE, R. H.; BARBETTI, M. 1981. A 38,000 Year Old Archaeological

Site at Upper Swan, Western Australia. *Archaeol. Ocean.* (Sydney), Vol. 16, pp. 173–8.

REINHARDT, D. 1985. The Cradle of Civilisation is Heading Our Way. *The Bulletin*, 18 June, pp. 88–91.

ROSENFELD, A.; HORTON, D. R.; WINTER, J. W. 1981. *Art and Archaeology in the Laura Area, North Australia*. Canberra. (Terr. Aust., 6.)

SINGH, G.; KERSHAW, A. P.; CLARK, R. 1981. Quaternary Vegetation and Fire History in Australia. In: GILL, A. M.; GROVES, R. H.; NOBLE, J. R. (eds), *Fire and the Australian Biota*. Canberra. pp. 23–54.

SINGH, G.; OPDYKE, N. D.; BOWLER, J. M. 1981. Late Cainozoic Stratigraphy, Palaeomagnetic Chronology and Vegetational History from Lake George, NSW. *J. Geol. Soc. Aust.* (Sydney), Vol. 28, No. 4, pp. 435–52.

STOKES, E. 1981. Skeletons in the Sand. *Geo*, Vol. 3, No. 3, pp. 27–49.

THORNE, A. G. 1976. Morphological Contrasts in Pleistocene Australians. In: KIRK, R. L.; THORNE, A. G. (eds), *The Origin of the Australians*. Canberra. pp. 95–112.

—— 1977. Separation or Reconciliation? Biological Clues to the Development of Australian Society. In: ALLEN, J.; GOLSON, J.; JONES, R. (eds), *Sunda and Sahul: Prehistoric Studies in Southeast Asia, Melanesia and Australia*. London/New York. pp. 187–204.

—— 1980. The Longest Link: Human Evolution in Southeast Asia. In: FOX, J. J. et al. (eds), *Indonesia: Australian Perspectives*. Canberra. pp. 35–43.

THORNE, A. G.; MACUMBER, P. G. 1972. Discoveries of Late Pleistocene Man at Kow Swamp, Australia. *Nature* (London), Vol. 238, pp. 316–19.

THORNE, A. G.; WILSON, S. R. 1977. Pleistocene and Recent Australians: A Multivariate Comparison. *J. Hum. Evol.*, Vol. 6, pp. 393–402.

THORNE, A. G.; WOLPOFF, M. H. 1981. Regional Continuity in Australasian Pleistocene Hominid Evolution. *Am. J. Phys. Anthropol.*, Vol. 55, pp. 337–41.

TINDALE, N. B. 1981a. The Aborigines: An Introduction. In: KEAST, A. L. (ed.), *Ecological Biogeography of Australia*. The Hague. pp. 1743–8.

—— 1981b. Prehistory of the Aborigines: Some Interesting Considerations. In: KEAST, A. L. (ed.), *Ecological Biogeography in Australia*. The Hague. pp. 1761–98.

VANDERWALL, R. L. 1978. Adaptive Technology in Southwest Tasmania. *Aust. Archaeol.* (Canberra), Vol. 8, pp. 107–26.

WHITE, C. 1967. Early Stone Axes in Arnhem Land. *Antiquity*, Vol. 41, pp. 149–52.

WHITE, J. P.; O'CONNELL, J. F. 1982. *A Prehistory of Australia, New Guinea and Sahul*. London.

WHITE, J. P.; CROOK, K. A. W.; RUXTON, B. P. 1970. Kosipe: A Late Pleistocene Site in the Papuan Highlands. *Proc. Prehist. Soc.*, Vol. 36, pp. 152–70.

WILLMOT, E. 1985. The Dragon Principle. In: MCBRYDE, I. (ed.), *Who Owns the Past?* Oxford. pp. 41–8.

WRIGHT, R. V. S. 1971. *The Archaeology of the Gallus Site, Koonalda Cave*. Canberra.

29

THE ORIGINS OF HUMANITY
IN AMERICA[1]

José L. Lorenzo

THE PROBLEM OF TRANSOCEANIC CONTACTS BETWEEN THE FIRST INHABITANTS OF AMERICA AND PEOPLE FROM OTHER CONTINENTS

The origins of humanity in America are a subject that has filled thousands of pages and dozens, if not hundreds, of books. Theories range from Ameghino's improbable one of the autochthonous origin of indigenous Americans, which is impossible from a phylogenetic point of view, to those about the Phoenicians, Carthaginians, Greeks, Hebrews, Romans and other peoples, and going so far as to include the arrival of extra-terrestrial beings.

Given such a proliferation of theories, it seems that the problem to be solved is twofold: first, to determine who the original inhabitants were and how and when they came and, second, to establish whether at a later date there were trans-oceanic contacts and, if so, when they took place, who made them and what their contribution was to the cultures that were already developing along their own original lines on the American continent.

In the following pages the first aspect of the problem will be dealt with, but we should also like to set forth some ideas on the second. Without denying the possibility in later times of people from other continents being shipwrecked there, it should be pointed out that long-distance sea voyages were well beyond human capacities in early times, and even in much later times they should be regarded as by no means the rule. In other words they were impossible for early humans, and virtually so even at later periods. While it is a fact that certain ocean currents assist sea travel towards the West Indies from north-western Africa and south-western Europe, it is equally true that this journey takes several days and that the ships used by those who are thought to have arrived there were not equipped for such journeys. This does not rule out the possibility of the forced landing of some group of exhausted sailors driven by storms or other circumstances on to the coasts of America. This is, in fact, far more likely from the west than from the east; the voyage of the *Kon Tiki* proved that one could reach the Pacific islands from Ecuador, whereas it has been found to be impossible to sail in the opposite direction at the same latitude. Suffice it to recall the long voyage which Spanish ships had to make from Manila in the Philippines to reach the port of Acapulco in Mexico. Taking advantage first of all of the Kuroshio Current and than of its Extension, subsequently following the Aleutian Current or the North Pacific Current and finally the California Current, they were forced to go as far north as the forty-fifth parallel. All this was done in large ships that were equipped for such long voyages and yet, even so, there was considerable loss of life among crews and passengers, not to mention the ships that were also lost.

It emerges from the above that if there were transatlantic or transpacific contacts, they were the result more of chance than of any definite plan, and the idea that there were constant lines of communication involving safe journeys to and fro is wholly inconceivable.

Thus we must exclude the 'diffusionist' theory, with its ideas of regular long-distance contacts in both directions, and accept the possibility, improbable though it may be, of forced landings. But then another question arises: what kind of contribution could such shipwrecks make to the local cultures? If we look at the composition of a ship's crew we find that it includes sailors and traders. Given the character of Neolithic culture, with its self-sufficiency in many fields, it is possible that there were potters, and also other craftsmen whose work has left no archaeological trace. It is highly unlikely that castaways included people sufficiently evolved to be called priests, still less architects or mathematicians.

Even making such an assumption, one must take into account a society's capacity to admit newcomers, hence the possibility of assimilating them. The same or at least a broadly similar level of development would be necessary, because otherwise the host society would be completely unable to assimilate something new and completely different. Let us take the case of metalworking. In the first place, metalworking involves a range of techniques: the ability, acquired from experience and knowledge of one's territory, to find mineral deposits, and the techniques of extracting, smelting and casting. Some of these functions may be carried out by one and the same person, but not all of them. And even if one single person possessed all these abilities and if – an extremely unlikely occurrence – they were a member of the crew, it is certain that in a completely new environment it would be a long time before they were able to make metal objects, assuming that they ever tried to do so.

To resume: if there were forced landings on the coasts of America by people from other cultures, their impact was limited to coastal areas and lasted for only short periods; and we should avoid making the simplistic deduction that contacts were thereby established.

In other words, although there is evidence that contacts may have taken place, there is no proof of any cultural inputs by newcomers, nor of any massive influx of groups that modified or changed the existing racial patterns.

THE CROSSING OF THE LAND BRIDGE (BERINGIA) BETWEEN ASIA AND AMERICA

Physiography and hydrology of Beringia

However, let us leave this particular subject in the hands of scholars engaged in the study of mixed populations and their cultural linkages, and turn to the first aspect: that of the early original inhabitants, the times in which they lived and the problems they had to face.

Let us take as our starting-point the hypothesis, which is increasingly becoming an accepted fact, that the earliest and most ancient populations of America arrived in that continent via the Bering Strait at the end of the Pleistocene epoch.

If we examine the fluctuations in sea-level in the Bering Sea during the last Ice Age we find that there were two major glacial phases when advances of ice occurred. The first took place between 70,000 and 32,000 years ago, and was accompanied by a fall in sea-level which led to the two continents of Asia and America being joined together between 63,000 and 45,000 years ago (Map 25 (A)). This was followed by a slight rise in sea-level, which perhaps severed the land bridge between the two continental masses during the period from 45,000 to 35,000 years ago. The land then once again emerged above sea-level, completely uniting the two continents between 35,000 and 10,000 years ago (Map 25 (B)).

During the first phase (the York-Knik in Alaska and the Altonian in the central lobe of the North American ice-sheet), which was of relatively lesser intensity, the ice-sheet did not extend as far as the glaciers that descended towards the east from the Rocky Mountains, and thus an open corridor was left between the two masses of ice. This produced a series of pro-glacial lakes in this corridor, formed from the rivers which, originating in the glaciers on the eastern slopes of the Rockies bordering on the western edge of the Laurentide ice-sheet, were unable to drain away naturally. In spite of the lower temperatures then prevailing, these lakes must have had a considerable fauna of birds and fish, not to mention the mammals that took refuge on the land not covered by ice or water. At a later date, between 63,000 and 45,000 years ago, conditions existed that would have allowed people to penetrate towards the south.

These people originated in the sub-arctic climatic fringe, in the far north-east of Asia, and had passed across the land bridge that was formed between Asia and America – Beringia - when the sea-level fell below 45 m. They penetrated into America by the Yukon valley, which was not glaciated, and, by the same route, gained the head-waters of the same river system before going on to reach the corridor.

The same thing happened between 45,000 and some

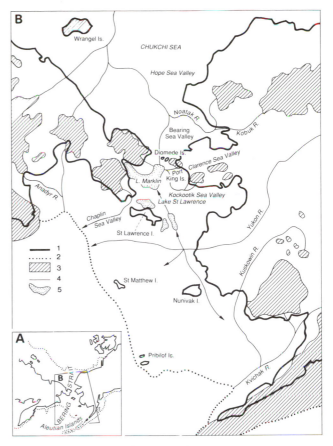

Map 25 A – Beringia in the Upper Pleistocene. B – Beringia during the Woodfordian substage (c.20,000–14,000 years ago): 1, present-day coast; 2, limit of ice-sheet during the Woodfordian; 3, emerged land during the Woodfordian; 4, rivers during the Woodfordian; 5, lakes during the Woodfordian. (After J. L. Lorenzo.)

35,000 years ago, during the Woronzof interstadial in Alaska and the Farmdalian interglacial stage in the centre of North America, since even when the sea-level subsequently rose again these people remained on the American side. They were able to continue their migration towards the south, where the corridor had widened and thus afforded greater possibilities for population movements.

During the Mint River–Naptowne glacial phase in Alaska and the Woodfordian substage in the centre of North America conditions changed, as the glaciation was much greater. All the information available indicates that between 35,000 and 10,000 years ago the corridor was closed as a result of the ice-sheet expanding to join up with the ice on the mountain ranges, though it is possible that for several thousand years at both the beginning and the end of this period it was possible to pass between them (Map 26).

The coalescence of the two ice masses was not total, and left areas uncovered at both the south and the north, but the ice covered an area at least 2,000 km long, and thus migration was made very much more difficult.

Another hypothesis put forward by some writers is that migration towards the south took place along the north-western coast of North America – the Pacific coast of present-day Canada and the north-west of the United States of America. Owing to the fall in sea-level and in spite of there being virtually no continental shelf in that region, it would seem likely that some areas above sea-level remained ice free and extended as far as zones which were not subject

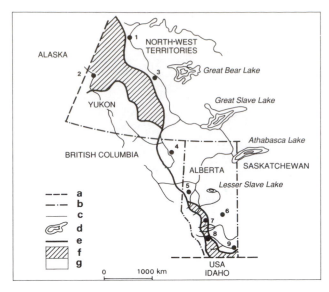

Map 26 Limits of the ice-sheets in the north-west of North America during the period of maximum extension of the Woodfordian substage: a, national border; b, provincial border; c, present-day rivers and streams; d, present-day lakes; e, limit of the ice-sheets; f, zone free of ice-sheets; g, glacial mass. 1, Inuvik; 2, Dawson; 3, Norman Wells; 4, Fort Nelson; 5, Fort St John; 6, Edmonton; 7, Grande Prairie; 8, Calgary; 9, Medicine Hat. (After Rutter, 1980.)

to glaciation, thereby facilitating migration combined with the economic exploitation of the coastal resources.

However, this hypothesis does not take two factors sufficiently into account. The first is that it is precisely along this coast that we find glaciers (of which the Malaspina glacier is a typical example), which, having emerged from the valleys on the western slope of the Rocky Mountains, spread out over the plain, forming large ice-fields. It seems highly likely that during the Ice Ages these ice-fields were much more numerous and more extensive, and that through a process of anastomosis the tongues of the glaciers joined to form a continuous or almost continuous belt, which would leave hardly any areas free of ice.

The second factor raises an even greater objection. In support of this hypothesis scholars have produced maps showing the coastal zones to be free of ice, but although this can be accepted as a theory, they have not been able to show how people reached these areas from the centre of Alaska or from the then existing Beringia.

Between the coast of the Gulf of Alaska, the beginning of the chain of emergent territory, and Beringia or central Alaska, there lay a vast zone of glaciers where the Aleutian range is situated. The hypothesis does not take into account either the geographical position of these glaciers or their size and thus, even if we allow the possibility of there having been a coastal corridor running along the Pacific coast of North America, there would appear to be no way of gaining access to it, and it is on this account that the whole theory loses its credibility.

However, there remains Beringia, the enormous area of land that united Asia and America as a result of the fall in sea-level during the Ice Ages. We should remember that this fall in sea-level was a slow process over thousands of years, and that the sea then remained at its lowest level for several thousand years more. During this long period plants and then animals gradually spread over the recently emerged areas. This increased the habitable lands, so that Asian people

were able to advance gradually towards the east and eventually become, without knowing it, the first inhabitants of the American continent.

There were no difficulties in the way of this migration, since it consisted of movement within a single ecosystem which humans were already able to exploit on the basis of cultural patterns established in the area from which they came.

Countless soundings and deep-sea drillings in the Bering Sea, the North Pacific and the Chukotka Sea have provided information that, while somewhat sketchy, is sufficient to give us a good idea of what this intercontinental land bridge must have been like during the Ice Ages. Naturally, the most reliable information concerns the situation during the final glacial phase between 35,000 and 10,000 years ago, but it seems reasonable to suppose that conditions were broadly similar during the penultimate glacial phase which occurred between 63,000 and 45,000 years ago.

The two continents of Asia and America come very close together at the Bering Strait, since Cape Dezhnev, the easternmost point of Siberia in the Chukotka peninsula, and Cape Prince of Wales, the westernmost point of Alaska, are only about 90 km apart. Lying about halfway between them are the Little and Great Diomede Islands.

When Beringia emerged, it brought into being a new landscape in which the present Diomede, King, St Lawrence, St Matthew, Nunivak and Pribilov Islands stood out as mountains, since it was not a vast plain, but a mountainous area with rivers and lakes. On the Siberian side watercourses, originating in the glaciers which covered the Kolymsky and Chukotka ranges, came together at the latitude of Wrangel Island, which was then a mountainous massif covered with glaciers, to form a river which flowed into the Arctic Sea. This river also captured the waters of another river formed by the Kobuk and Noatak rivers, which originated in the glaciers of the Brooks range in Alaska, and joined with it to flow northwards along what is now the Bering sea valley which, further north, becomes the Hope sea valley.

To the south of the Chukotka peninsula a large lake formed – Lake Marklin – which received water from various sources: from the east along the present-day sea valleys of Port Clarence and King Island; from the west from the glaciers of the Chukotka range and from the south from a tributary of the Yukon river in Alaska whose course followed several different channels, although it has not been possible to identify the course of these tributaries at specific times.

To the south of Lake Marklin and to the north of St Lawrence island there was another lake, which has been given the same name as the island, and which was joined to Marklin Lake in the north by the Kookootik sea valley. On the Siberian side smaller watercourses originating in the glaciers of the Chukotsky, Kolymsky and Koryanksky mountains descended to flow into the Anadyr river, whose course followed what is now the gulf of the same name. Further eastwards, there flowed another river which originated in the glaciers of the Chukotsky range and followed the course of the present-day Chaplin sea valley. From Alaska, in addition to the tributaries of the lower Yukon, one of which flowed northwards and formed a small lake, there were two others which flowed westwards. Yet a third flowed towards the south-east, passing to the east of Nunivak Island, and possibly joined the extension of the Kuskokwin river, which further downstream joined the Kvichak river to flow into the open sea to the north-east of the present-day Aleutian Islands.

Beringia's food resources

The climate was harsh, extreme and dry, with short, almost warm summers and long, severely cold winters with strong winds. Throughout the year conditions were more extreme in the northern part, washed by the waters of the Arctic Sea, which was, as today, an enormous mass of ice. On the southern side, towards the north Pacific, it is possible that the climate was somewhat better, somewhat warmer and wetter, since the emergence of Beringia had cut off the Arctic current which now flows southward through the Bering Strait to meet the warm Kuroshio Current, diverting it towards the east and preventing it from flowing northwards. If, however, as we suppose, the Arctic current was cut off, the warm waters of the Kuroshio would then have reached the southern coast of Beringia. There is however another, contrary hypothesis according to which, for meteorological reasons, there was a floating mass of ice between the southern coast of Beringia and the chain of the Aleutian Islands.

Under these climatic conditions there developed a type of vegetation typical of steppe and tundra lands, both of which are arctic or sub-arctic in character, with copses of small trees extending along the banks of watercourses. In this kind of vegetation at the right season of the year there were abundant edible berries and also tender buds and bulbs that could be eaten: for some part of the year there was thus no lack of food that could be gathered.

As far as animal life was concerned, the herbivores alone must have included large herds of reindeer, horse, bison and elk and also the huge mammoths, together with a wide variety of smaller animals, such as the arctic hare. The sea, particularly on the southern coast, teamed with various kinds of sea-mammals, shellfish and fish, including salmon, particularly abundant at certain times of the year. Preserving food by the use of such processes as smoking, salting, drying in the sun and freezing must have been known to the inhabitants of this region, since it was necessary to preserve a large part of the food that was so abundant in summer for the long hard winters.

There was also no lack of wood from the trees, albeit small ones, growing in some parts of Beringia for the manufacture of particular kinds of objects; there were likewise plentiful supplies of fibrous plants and bark that could be used for making rope or, in the case of the bark of the birch tree, used directly. To these resources should be added the furs, skins, sinews and entrails of animals, used for a great variety of purposes.

The rocky terrain of the region probably provided material which could be shaped by percussion, such as flint and other micro-crystalline rocks. Thus while far from being an earthly paradise, the region did at least yield the basic means of subsistence, as is shown by the survival of present-day groups of human beings living in the Arctic Circle, where they have established a kind of symbiotic or integrated relationship with the ecosystem. This should be taken into account when attempting to explain the passage or movement of human beings through this region.

Human migration from Alaska to Patagonia (Map 27)

These, then, were the main features of the region through which humans penetrated into America. The arrival of humans took place, as we have seen, in two phases, a first, more ancient but easier passage – because of the existence

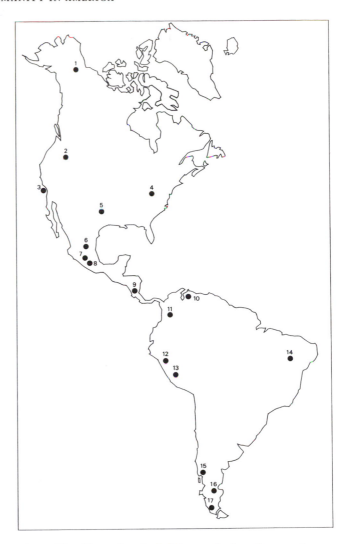

Map 27 The oldest archaeological sites on the American continent: 1, Old Crow, 40,000 years BP; 2, American Falls, <43,000; 3, Sta Rosa, <40,000; 4, Meadowcroft, 20,000; 5, Coopertown, 20,000; 6, El Cedral, 31,000; 7, Tlapacoya, 21,000; 8, Caulapan, 21,000; 9, El Bosque, 20,000; 10, Taima-Taima, 16,000; 11, El Abra, 12,400; 12, Guitarrero, 12,500; 13, Pikimachay, 18,000; 14, Toca do Boqueirão, 31,000; 15, Monte Verde, 13,000; 16, Los Toldos, 12,600; 17, Cueva Fell, 11,000.

of an ice-free corridor – lasting from 65,000 to 45,000 years ago, and a second phase from 35,000 to 10,000 years ago. In the second phase occupation was limited, in addition to Beringia itself, to the Yukon valley in the interior of Alaska, although probably from 15,000 years ago onwards movement southwards into the continent became possible.

Some scholars exclude the first phase from consideration as being too early and, furthermore, in their opinion, the corroborative archaeological evidence is too weak. While it is true that the evidence is extremely scanty, some sites provide abundant material that clearly indicates a general movement from north to south.

The most northerly finds are the collection of carved bones found at various sites at Old Crow Flats in Canada and dating from 40,000 years ago, while artefacts attributable to human beings have been found at American Falls (United States) over 40,000 years old. Then there are traces of hearths dated as being over 40,000 years old on Santa Rosa island, California (United States); remains of human settlement in Meadowcroft (United States) from 20,000 years ago; marks and cuts on the bones of a proboscidean in Coopertown, from 20,000 years ago; traces of fire and bone fragments in El Cedral, Mexico, 31,000 years old; traces of fire and heaps of charred animal bones in Tlapacoya, Mexico, 21,000 years old; a scraper in Caulapán, Mexico, 21,000 years old; stone objects associated with Pleistocene fauna at El Bosque, Nicaragua, from 20,000 years ago; artefacts associated with extinct fauna in Taima-Taima, Venezuela, 13,000 years old; evidence of settlement with artefacts and traces of hearths in El Abra, Colombia, 12,400 years old; similar finds in the caves of Guitarrero, Peru, from 12,500 years ago; occupation layers, traces of fire and a lithic industry in Toca de Boqueirão, Brazil, 31,000 years old; remains of settlement and artefacts in Pikimachay, Peru, from 18,000 years ago; abundant remains of settlement in Monte Verde, Chile, from 13,000 years ago; an occupation layer with a lithic industry in Los Toldos, Argentina, 12,600 years old; and also remains of human settlement in the Fell cave, Chile, from 11,000 years ago.

The general movement from north to south indicated on p. 293 shows variations in the speed at which it advanced, but it is clear that if the finds dated from 13,000, 12,600 and 11,000 years ago in the extreme south of the continent are correct, then the thesis that humans could not have arrived in America earlier than 15,000 years ago must be discarded.

The migration of groups of hunters and food-gatherers from Alaska to Patagonia could only have been an extremely slow process, since the distance is enormous. In addition there were the problems of forced acclimatization and the technological changes necessary to survive in passing through so many different ecosystems. There seems to be no explanation or reason whatsoever for the speed at which people migrated southwards – a comparison of dates shows that it took 2,000 years between 15,000 and 13,000 years ago to cover a distance about 15,000 km – particularly when we bear in mind the fact that many regions possessed a wealth of food resources that would normally have given rise to longer stays, not to constant movement.

Nor is there any reason to believe in the existence of violent demographic pressures that forced peoples to keep on the move, since judging from the few traces remaining from these periods it seems clear that populations were sufficiently scattered to be able to exploit extensive territories without any danger of conflict.

Although few examples of the tools used by these early people at that time have been found, it seems clear that they did not have stone-tipped projectiles and would probably have used sticks instead, which were sharpened or tipped with perishable materials. There are frequent examples of objects made of bone, roughly worked so as to sharpen them to a point, or to produce cutting or scraping edges. The lithic industry used a percussion technique with a minimum of finishing and no specific form. It seems that no great preference was shown in the choice of the basic material; tools were made with a scraping or a cutting edge and then discarded.

WHO WERE AMERICA'S FIRST INHABITANTS?

We now come to the inevitable question: who were these people? In the first place, though no human remains from such early periods have yet been found, the general opinion is that the original inhabitants of America were Mongoloids, but that they also included other types with Australoid and Melanesian characteristics; some scientists have also identified Caucasoid characteristics.

It is not easy to advance in such difficult territory, since the basic criteria for making valid judgements are lacking, and it seems possible that the theory put forward by Birdsell (1951) some years ago, which was widely challenged, now needs to be reconsidered in the light of a different chronology from the one formerly accepted.

In Birdsell's opinion the methods previously used to solve the problem had proved to be inadequate, and it was necessary to seek new ones. The origin of the non-Mongoloid types had been studied through a detailed analysis of American material, but Birdsell argued that it was necessary to identify, within wide margins of possibility, the racial types that existed in Asia at the time of the early migrations across the Bering Strait. His reasoning was as follows: first, the evidence available indicated that the Mongoloid race reached its present geographical distribution as a result of an extremely rapid or perhaps even explosive expansion; second, it is a generally accepted fact that the presence of Neolithic cultivators strongly modifies the distributional pattern of food-gatherers and hunters, with important consequences for the genetic make-up of populations. In view of the cultivators' potential for achieving a higher population density, it is possible that the appearance of agriculture and the expansion of the Mongoloids through Asia were not separate phenomena, but took place simultaneously. Consequently, the peoples now living in Asia cannot provide the necessary evidence to solve the problem of the racial origin of the Americans.

Starting from the theory that marginal areas provide refuges in which early populations may be preserved, we find that, for an understanding of eastern Asia, there exist two major areas possessing these characteristics: America and Australia. Strange though it may seem, the study – with all due caution – of how Australia and Melanesia were populated may well provide us with information on the nature of the racial groups that existed in Asia and which also migrated to the New World at the end of the Pleistocene and even in more recent times.

On the basis of his own studies in Melanesia and, above all, in Australia, Birdsell concluded that there were three distinct populations: the Oceanic Negritos, who would have formed the first wave; the Murrayians, the second wave, and the Carpentarians, the third wave. The Negritos, the first wave of *Homo sapiens*, have a clear affinity for wet and forested tropical regions and it would seem from their distribution that at no time did they move northwards out of this zone. The Murrayians found in Australia are closely related to the Ainu and, from the evidence of excavations in Australia, must have arrived there during the last glacial period. Birdsell believes that the area around the Amur river must have contained a racial type similar to the Ainu, which he calls the Amurians. These are a not very clearly established type of proto-Caucasoids or palaeo-Caucasoids, from which he considers the Mongoloids to have been derived. The third people to occupy Australia were the Carpentarians, though at a much later date, since they arrived at the end of the last glacial period.

Birdsell considers that the human remains in the upper cave at Zhoukoudian (Choukoutien) are the only vestiges that can give us any information on the human types that settled in America, since they represent the types existing in north-eastern Asia at the end of the Pleistocene and the beginning of the Holocene. As against the interpretations put forward by Hooten and Weindenreich, he maintains his own theory that 'skull 101' (the old man) is Murrayian. He also rejects a number of features that led other authors to regard it as a Mongoloid hybridization, and shows that these features also existed among the Murrayians. In Birdsell's view 'Woman 102', 'thought to be Melanesian', is a hybrid of a long, high Mongoloid skull with the long, low Amurian skull; and 'Woman 103' (thought to be 'Eskimoid') is a Mongoloid with a very long and relatively high skull with Ainoid features. To sum up, the upper Zhoukoudian population displays two distict racial elements: (1) an archaic, possibly ancestral Caucasoid type related to both the Murrayians and the Ainu, and (2) a Mongoloid type with a long, narrow skull.[2]

At the beginnning of the fourth and last glaciation a hypothetical reconstruction of the human population in eastern Asia suggests the presence of three major racial groups: the Negritos and the Carpentarians, both in the tropical zones, and the Amurians (Murrayians) in the temperate zones. This assertion rests on the fact that no traces have been found in eastern continental Asia of either Negroids, Papuans and Melanesians or elements of the Mediterranean branch of the Caucasoids, all of which, according to some authors, are present in the American population.

At the end of the Pleistocene the Mongoloids evolved somewhere in north-east Asia in a dry and very extreme arctic environment. It is Birdsell's theory that the Mongoloids developed from the earliest Caucasoids.

The distribution of the peoples of eastern Asia, and also the scanty archaeological evidence available, suggest a hybrid origin for the indigenous American Indians. The two racial elements present at the appropriate time and place to populate America were the Amurians and the Mongoloids. If human beings arrived in the American continent during the third interglacial period they must have been Caucasoid, that is to say pure Amurian. Conversely, any group that migrated in postglacial times must have been hybrid in origin; at the beginning of this period the Mongoloid element would have been weak and the Amurian more pronounced, while at the end of the period the Amurian would have been weak and the Mongoloid more pronounced.

On this basis of the information so far available, study of the skulls found in America has provided little evidence of hybridism, although Amurian features have been identified among groups of present-day Indians such as the Cahuilla in the south and the Pomo and Yuki in the north of California. Such then is Birdsell's theory.

In a study on the origins of human races and the differences between them, which contains a phylogenetic analysis based on genetic polymorphism, Cavalli-Sforza (1973) arrives at conclusions that reinforce Birdsell's theory with regard to the settlement of the American continent. From a study of five blood groups and a total of twenty alleles from among fifteen human groups representative of all parts of the world he drew up a tree of descent. In one of the main branches of this phylogenetic tree three African groups were clearly separated from three European groups, while the other branch, although more heterogenous in aspect, contained features from which it was possible to identify relationships between, on the one hand, the groups in Australia and in New Guinea and, on the other, the Indians of Venezuela, the Inuit and the Indians of Arizona.

Several years after this study, and drawing upon others in this field, Cavalli-Sforza carried out yet another study in which he selected population groups which were different from those used before, but also representative of all five continents and characterized by high polymorphism. In addition to the five blood groups which had been used, namely ABO, MN, Rh, Fy and Diego, four markers were introduced, Hp, Tb, PGM and AK. The results obtained were essentially the same, although the heterogeneity that had emerged in part of the previous work became even clearer, with greater definition and separation, so that all the human groups occupying the far east of Asia, Australia, Melanesia and the American continent clearly appear to form one single branch.

From the studies of Birdsell and Cavalli-Sforza it appears highly probable that the original population of America was of Amurian origin; that the subsequent human groups were increasingly Mongoloid in character, and that they all came from the same original stock from which Australians and Melanesians also developed, a fact that would explain many of the problems arising from the presence in America of racial elements thought to have these origins.

Apart from some characteristics that are repeated, we must attribute the diversity of the inhabitants of the New World to the possibility of large-scale genetic drift, resulting from the isolation of small groups over thousands of years. This is in no way to ignore the potentialities of dominant and recessive characteristics, but merely to emphasize the effects of prolonged isolation on a population group.

In conclusion, we may state that in many respects Birdsell's theory, and its corroboration by Cavalli-Sforza, accords well with the situation observed in America. The fact that in America and in Australia there are frequent dolicoid groups of hunters and food-gatherers living in marginal areas that are little or not at all suited to agriculture means that it may well have been populated in earlier times by a population that was later 'centrifuged', so to speak, or driven out to more inhospitable regions on the periphery by an agricultural population.

This may appear to be a somewhat wild hypothesis, but the fact that America and Australia were populated simultaneously, together with the appearance of *Homo sapiens sapiens* in Europe, combined with the ancestral links of the Caucasoid type, helps to explain or corroborate demographic movements; while the geographical isolation of these groups explains present-day differences, since, as we have seen, there were three basic movements which took place in completely separate areas: one through the Arctic zone, another through the temperate steppes and a third through the tropical zone.

This is, very briefly, a possible theory of the origins of humanity in America.

NOTES

1 Chapters 29–35 inclusive cover the immense extent of the territory of the American continent, from Alaska to the Archipelago and Patagonia, and the many millennia separating the arrival of the first humans in America from the beginnings of food production. Co-Editor José L. Lorenzo acted as co-ordinator for these regional chapters – Ed.

2 For divergent opinions on the subject, see Chapters 2, 6, 9, 26, 28 and 30 – Ed.

BIBLIOGRAPHY

BIRDSELL, J. B. 1951. The Problem of the Early Peopling of the Americas as Viewed from Asia. In: LAUGHLIN, W. S. (ed.), *Papers in Physical Anthropology of American 'Indians'*. New York. pp. 1–68.

BLACK, R. F.; GOLDTWAIT, R. P.; WILLMAN, H. B. 1973. *The Wisconsin Stage*. Boulder.

CAVALLI-SFORZA, L. L. 1973. Origin and Differentiation of Human Races. *Proc. R. Anthropol. Inst. G.B. for 1972*. London. pp. 15–25.

FLADMARK, K. R. 1979. Routes: Alernate Migration Corridors for Early Man in North America. *Am. Antiq.*, Vol. 44, No. 1, pp. 55–69.

HOPKINS, D. M. (ed.) 1967. *The Bering Land Bridge*. Stanford.

HOPKINS, D. M. et al. (eds) 1962. *Palaeoecology of Beringia*. New York.

HUMPHREY, R. L.; STANFORD, D. 1979. *Pre-Llano Cultures of the Americas: Paradoxes and Possibilities*. Washington.

JENNINGS, J. D. (ed.), 1978. *Ancient Native Americans*. San Francisco.

LAMING-EMPERAIRE, A. 1980. *Le Problème des origines américaines*. Paris.

LORENZO, J. L. 1970. Los origines mexicanos. In: *Historia General de México* (Mexico, DF), Vol. 1, pp. 83–123.

—— 1974. Poblamiento del continente americano. In: *Historia de México* (Mexico, DF), Vol. 1, pp. 27–54.

—— 1986. Los primeros americanos: la etapa lítica en México y Centroamerica. In: *Historia General de America* (Caracas), Vol. 1.

—— *Los origines americanos y los primeros pobladores* (Caracas). (In press.)

RUTTER, N. W. 1980. Late Pleistocene History of the Western Canadian Ice-Free Corridor. *Can. J. Anthropol.* (Edmonton), Vol. 1, No. 1, pp. 1–8.

30

PREHISTORY OF NORTH AMERICA

Alan L. Bryan

The primary culture historical problem about the time and circumstance of the original peopling of the Americas remains unresolved, so some discussion is necessary to explain the temporal scope of this survey of North America prehistory to about 5,000 years ago.

Considerable antiquity is suggested by the tremendous linguistic diversity within the Americas (a dozen language stocks as well as many more unrelated and isolated languages) and the fact that no American languages except Inuit-Aleut can be related to Old World languages. Although some genetic traits set them apart (such as the highest incidence of blood O–Rh$^+$ in the world), Amerindians are also characterized by considerable biological diversity. How long it might take for such diversity to develop remains a matter of opinion, however. Two contending models exist which defy resolution because of basically different premises. The prevailing model assumes that the earliest humans entered the New World with sophisticated technology on an Upper or perhaps a developed Middle Palaeolithic ('Mousteroid') level that enabled them to traverse the subarctic regions of Siberia and north-western North America. The alternative model postulates that the earliest people were ingenious enough to be able to adapt to subarctic climates, especially along the Pacific coast, as long as they had fire, furred animal skins for body coverings, sufficient protein and simple flaked stone technology that need not have been above a Lower Palaeolithic level. The prevailing model allows for initial entry sometime between 13,000 and a maximum of 30,000 years ago, assuming time for migration from a north-eastern Eurasian source. No fixed time limit is suggested by proponents of the alternative model, who argue that the actual archaeological data take precedence over untestable assumptions and preconceptions about when the first people arrived and what technological equipment they brought with them to America. Rather, it is necessary to develop testable hypotheses within a model designed to explain the available evidence.

After more than a century of controversy over this complex question an impasse has been reached. Sceptics reject all archaeological evidence that does not fit the prevailing model according to which the only acceptable evidence should refer to big-game hunters who made sophisticated artefacts by methods which should include advanced flaking techniques. The sceptics apply more rigorous standards for recognition of suggested early sites than they would to those within the generally accepted time-range, a process they claim is being properly scientific, and by this means manage to discount these sites (for instance: Dincauze, 1984; Owen, 1984; Waters, 1985). The earliest generally accepted evidence for big-game hunters in North America has long been recognized at several mammoth and giant bison kill-sites on the Great Plains about 11,500–11,000 years ago. The hunters who occupied these sites have become known as the classic Palaeoindians, who manufactured a technological complex composed of diagnostic (meaning carefully shaped artefacts belonging to readily definable standard categories) stone and bone tools identified as the Clovis culture.

Most American archaeologists agree that prehistoric Amerindians developed their culture and civilizations independently of Old World civilizations. Occasional pre-Norse transoceanic contacts undoubtedly occurred, but they left little concrete archaeological evidence that these foreign contacts had had any significant impact on American cultural developments. Likewise, it is clear that indigenous plants and animals were domesticated in America, so food production was clearly also an independent development. Pottery is another example of independent technological invention in America. Ceramic vessels were never used in a vast area west of the northern Rocky Mountains, nor anywhere along the Pacific coast between Alaska and southern California. Alaskan pottery was derived from Asia only about 2,500 years ago. The earliest known pottery appeared more than 5,000 years ago in several places in northern South America and soon thereafter in south-eastern North America. Hypotheses of direct transoceanic contact as an agent for the diffusion of pottery have been disproved because apparent stylistic similarities occurred at quite different times on opposite sides of the oceans. All the archaeological evidence indicates that prehistoric Amerindians were highly innovative. They developed distinctive cultural adaptations to the many highly diversified environmental conditions within the Americas, without external stimuli. A model of multilinear cultural evolution by adaptive radiation can explain later American cultural history.

The available archaeological evidence suggests that this evolutionary model can be extended back to the late Pleistocene. The evidence indicates that the Upper Palaeolithic level of technology attained by the people who made Clovis points developed in south central North America as part of an adaptation to the predictable availability of herds of migratory mammals. Attempts to find specific technological antecedents for Clovis in north-east Asia have been unsuccessful.

North American archaeologists have traditionally looked back to northern Asia for cultural origins because of the clear evidence that Amerindians are biologically most closely related to north-east Asians. The lack of any archaeological evidence for the occupation of any isolated ('far') Oceanic islands during the Pleistocene indicates that the generally accepted route of entry from north-east Asia to north-western America is correct. The earliest entrants may have been adapted to the North Pacific coast with relatively mild climatic conditions rather than to the continental interior, but there is little chance that the initial peopling was by open ocean watercraft across either the Atlantic or the Pacific oceans. The latter improbable hypothesis has recently resurfaced in order to explain the presence of several sites in various parts of South America predating the Clovis manifestation in North America, which became archaeologically visible about 11,500 years ago. Archaeological remains from several South American sites are not only older, but they lack any technological relationship with Clovis. They also differ significantly from each other, a fact that suggests that sufficient time had elapsed for several independent developments to have occurred as adaptations to local environments. As in North America, technological traditions (referring to distinctive procedures for making something, as distinct from a cultural tradition, which would include many specific technological traditions) for manufacturing bifacial projectile points were developed by different innovative groups of descendants of the original colonists as effective adaptations to several South American ecosystems between about 13,000 and 11,000 years ago. Only at this stage of technological development are all archaeologists confident that they are dealing with human handiwork and not some possibly natural agencies of fabrication. However, the presence of unequivocal sites in South America 12,000 or more years old means that the ancestors of these early South Americans must have occupied earlier sites in North America.

In Chapter 29 an attempt has been made to provide the hemisphere-wide perspective that is essential to the proper understanding of early North American prehistory. Available evidence supports a model of effective socio-economic adaptation to diverse environmental conditions by general foragers using an uncomplicated but readily modifiable material culture that included many multi-purpose cores and flakes with useful edges but few specialized tools. The largely non-lithic material culture of lowland South American Indians supports the assumption that most of their ancestors' tools were probably made of perishable materials such as wood, bark, fibre, hide, sinew and feathers. Therefore the tools, except under unusual conditions of preservation, are very simple and easily overlooked by archaeologists attuned to finding standardized types of shaped tools. Some perishable elements of the material culture may have been highly developed, but normally only the non-perishable worked stone and occasionally bone have been preserved to be studied. As in large parts of east Asia and Australia, this unifacial stone technology remained on a general level of development which in the Old World is generally referred to as the Lower rather than the Upper Palaeolithic. For historical reasons, such terms are not used in the Americas in order to avoid any implication of great antiquity. Two other facts should be kept in mind: (1) as described in the

literature, the Lower Palaeolithic flaked stone technology from the western Old World is characterized by abundant bifacial tools. This western handaxe tradition differed significantly from contemporary east Asian industries, where bifaces form a minor proportion of the total artefact assemblages. Also, (2) the aborigines of Australia and America did not come from western Eurasia, but from east Asia, a vast region characterized by unifacial flaked stone industries, although bifacial industries developed locally during the Palaeolithic.

Figure 85 Left: Clovis point, Arizona (USA); right: Folsom point, Colorado (USA). (After Alicia Castro.)

In North America, the earliest generally recognized complex of technological traditions is often identified as the Clovis culture (Haynes, 1980) (Fig. 85). Because no similar bifacial thinning technology has been found stratigraphically beneath known Clovis kill-sites on the Great Plains, the search for technological antecedents has led to adoption of the assumption that a diagnostic artefact type identifies a specific cultural group as if it were its trademark. Despite the fact that Clovis kill-sites have been found only on the Great Plains and adjacent areas with similar past environments, it is generally assumed that projectile points of a range of shape and size identifiable as Clovis were made by the same cultural group of hunters who pursued herds of large mammals from coast to coast. These implicit assumptions form the basis of the generally accepted model that specialized Palaeoindian hunters preceded adaptations by general foragers. (In other words, the Palaeoindians' specialized hunting stage preceded the foraging stage of economic organization known as the Archaic throughout North America.) However, one basic assumption, that the same group of people made all the Clovis points, has recently been disproven (Young and Bonnichsen, 1985). Replication experiments have shown that very different flaking procedures were used by people in Montana and Maine to knap what archaeologists categorize as Clovis fluted points on the basis of form and the presence of fluting.

As different cultures applied their distinctive traditional knapping techniques to making fluted points of similar shape and size, it is clear that diverse flaking traditions had already been developed by local populations before Clovis points appeared in various parts of North America. Evidently the spread of large fluted points, the earliest recognized bifacial projectile points in North America, came about more by a process of diffusion of ideas about style and hafting techniques than by population movement. In order to clarify what cultural processes actually occurred in certain areas, it is necessary first to identify technological traditions, however defined, and not simply to assume the existence of cultures or cultural traditions without demonstrating their reality.

The term Archaeolithic has been adopted in this book to refer to the hypothetical period, for which there is widespread evidence, of people in North America before the invention of flaked stone projectile points in the Cenolithic stage. The reality of the Archaeolithic stage has not been demonstrated to the satisfaction of most North American archaeologists. A major reason why most are sceptical of all claims for earlier evidence is because they cling to an outdated model which assumes that the first Americans brought with them an economy that emphasized big-game hunting, which they imposed upon all regions of the continent. Only later, this model holds, after many of the readily available herds of mammals had been depleted, did they adapt themselves efficiently to local ecosystems. However, the available evidence for an Archaeolithic stage can be explained better by adoption of a multi-linear evolutionary model that recognizes that innovative colonists entering any ecosystem devoid of human competitors had the intellectual capacity to alter and adapt their elementary technological skills by experimenting with locally available food resources and materials for obtaining and processing those resources.

NORTH-WESTERN NORTH AMERICA

Although the earliest American sites should be in Alaska and the Yukon, available evidence from this unglaciated portion of eastern Beringia is disappointing. Although permanently frozen ground can result in perfect preservation of normally perishable organic remains, permafrost and other geological phenomena present in the region make it exceedingly difficult to find undisturbed archaeological contexts in Pleistocene deposits. Permafrost combined with solifluction, when the saturated surface layer melts in the sun, can cause denudation of hills and rapid colluviation and alluviation of valleys. Also, frequent earthquakes often cause the collapse of habitable caves. Most importantly, the vast Bering land bridge, as well as the narrower Pacific continental shelves, are now inaccessible because they have been submerged by the postglacial rise in sea-level. Thus archaeological support for the logically reasonable early maritime coastal way of life is unavailable for investigation. Most probably, the earliest people first adapted to the Siberian subarctic during a warm interval, and unknowingly entered what is now America along the southern shore of the Bering land bridge. Some evidence, summarized by Gruhn (1989), suggests that there was a period between 60,000 and 50,000 years ago when the climate of Alaska was as warm as now, but the sea-level was low enough for pedestrians to cross between the continents. It seems more likely that the first people would have expanded their territory eastward into Alaska during such a warm period than that they would have done so after the climate had become significantly colder during the last phases of the last glacial period.

Quite possibly the earliest human groups had adapted a general foraging economy to the relatively mild and economically productive North Pacific shores, and they seasonally hunted several species of large herd mammals (including bison, horse, mammoth and saiga antelope) which lived farther inland. Eventually, some of these groups probably became permanent occupants of the continental interior, which in the winter provided abundant frozen meat and even preprocessed vegetable food in the stomachs of the herbivores. One or two mammoths would provide sustenance for a small human group throughout a long frozen winter season. Available snow and ice meant that water was no problem as long as people were able to build and maintain a fire, using herbivore dung for fuel. A shelter could easily be erected from the bones and hides of the large beasts. Clothing could also be cut from hides with a sharp flake or naturally sharp-edged rock, and sewn with sinew and bone splinter awls. Sophisticated, bifacially retouched projectile points or knives were not necessary; wooden spears tipped with sharpened bone splinters or simple unretouched flakes would suffice. These ingenious people were able to drive animals over cliffs or into crevasses or large frost cracks. In fact, occasional naturally trapped animals could easily have been exploited without having to chase them. The above scenario, which presupposes only that the early people soon acquired a detailed body of knowledge of their ecosystem and how to live in it, should be considered as an alternative hypothesis to the generally accepted assumption that the earliest people must have had highly specialized flaked-stone technology in order to survive in Beringia. This alternative hypothesis would explain the presence of the many diverse assemblages of unsophisticated non-perishable artefacts found throughout the Americas, including eastern Beringia. Even in late prehistoric times, the occupants of interior Alaska and Yukon had simple basic flaked stone tools, complemented by hide, wood, bone and antler artefacts which were often quite elaborate (LeBlanc, 1984).

The oldest radiocarbon-dated artifically modified objects so far found in the Americas have been collected from the Old Crow river valley in northern Yukon Territory, in extreme north-west Canada. A serrated caribou tibia end-scraper, collected in 1966 with mammoth and other fossilized bone of extinct Pleistocene animals, precipitated an intensive search for artefacts in undisturbed contexts when the apatite content of the scraper was dated to 27,000 years ago. Later, fossilized bones of mammoths and other animals, flaked while fresh, were recovered from an ancient eroded surface now dated to about 35,000 years ago (Charles Schweger, personal communication, 1987). The flaked bones had been redeposited from their original contexts, and no flaked stone artefacts have ever been found directly associated with the modified bones.

Sceptics have hypothesized that the Old Crow Flats bones could have been flaked, cut, polished, grooved and faceted by natural processes, although so far no convincing replicas have been made by attempts at reproducing natural causes. Rigorous reanalysis with hypothetical natural causes in mind has led to the conclusion that it is not possible either to prove or to disprove that people lived on the ancient surface. However, the collagen content of several bones collected from other localities that appear to have been cut or flaked repeatedly in a patterned way, in an accelerator counter yielded ages of between 45,000 and 25,000 years, which bracket a relatively warm interstadial period prior to the final cold period (Morlan, 1986).

Ironically, the original tibia end-scraper that precipitated the prolonged search has been redated by the new accelerator method to 1,350 years ago (Richard Morlan, personal communication, 1986), so none of the early dated bone artefacts are deliberately shaped tools. Many archaeologists will continue to doubt the evidence from Old Crow Flats because of the lack of standardized types and undisturbed cultural contexts; however, directly dated humanly altered bones constitute concrete evidence that cannot be ignored.

Microblades removed from specialized cores constitute the only diagnostic technological tradition found in north-western America that can definitely be traced back to north-east Asia. This specialized technology is known from late Palaeolithic contexts throughout north-east Asia, and is dated in eastern Siberia between about 35,000 and 11,000 years ago (Mochanov, 1978). The technological tradition evidently arrived in eastern Beringia in final Pleistocene times earlier than 14,000 years ago when the Bering land bridge became submerged for the last time. A microblade core has been recovered from Bluefish cave, south of Old Crow Flats, in the oldest primary archaeological context in eastern Beringia. Also recovered from this zone are a burin made on a blade, a burin spall, a hammerstone and chert flakes, in addition to many modified (whittled, scraped and cut) bones and antlers of mountain sheep and caribou. Worked mammoth and horse bones from this zone have yielded dates between 23,000 and 15,000 years ago, which indicates that the cave was occupied occasionally during the last glacial maximum (J. Cinq-Mars and R. Morlan, personal communications, 1987). Although blades and burins are known from early contexts south of the continentally glaciated region, micro-blades removed from specialized cores are unknown south of the continental glaciers until long after the ice had melted. Significantly, Clovis hunters never used micro-blades, which suggests that Clovis technology did not immediately come from Beringia, as is often assumed. Soon after this terminal occupation of the Beringian steppe tundra, the environment of central Alaska and the Yukon gave way to a moister shrub tundra which evidently was associated with a rapid decline of the late Pleistocene megafauna.

Not all of the earliest dated (about 11,000 years ago) occupations of central Alaska contain microblades, however. Blades, burins, and lanceolate and thin, triangular projectile points are present at some sites about 11,000 years ago, and microblades become common after 10,500 years ago. The projectile points are quite different from the earlier Siberian willow-leaf-shaped points; and although some examples have been basally thinned, they only vaguely resemble true fluted points. Although present in Alaska and Yukon, fluted points have not been obtained from well-dated contexts (Clark, 1981). However, a stubby fluted point, looking very similar to many Alaskan speci-mens, has been excavated from a 10,500-year-old level of Charlie Lake cave in north-eastern British Columbia (Fladmark et al., 1988). This stubby variety is the most common form of fluted point found east of the Rocky Mountains in north-eastern British Columbia and Alberta. Most probably, fluted points were adopted by people who were expanding their hunting territory north-westward up the eastern flanks of the Rocky Mountains into central Alaska soon after the deglaciation of north-eastern British Columbia and southern Yukon. The long lanceolate and thin triangular points probably evolved in unglaciated central Alaska before the arrival of fluted points from the south.

Although the spread of the fluted point tradition might have been associated with the initial northward expansion into formerly glaciated territory by Plains bison hunters, better dated evidence for an initial occupation of recently deglaciated territory is found somewhat later farther east. Willow-leaf-shaped Agate Basin points appear in the Mackenzie and Keewatin Districts west of Hudson Bay about 8,000 years ago (Wright, 1981). Probably the pioneers who used these points had been hunting caribou herds who were following the edge of the melting glaciers north-eastward.

Fluted points had been replaced by Agate Basin and similar stemmed points (known collectively as Plano points and referred to as the stemmed point tradition) belonging to bison hunters on the High Plains of Wyoming about 10,000 years ago, and soon thereafter in southern Alberta (Bryan, 1980). As will be discussed later, stemmed points have been dated to 11,000 years ago and earlier in the Great Basin west of the Rocky Mountains. Probably this north-eastward expansion does not represent a movement of a group of hunters from the Great Basin on to the High Plains and then northward to the Barrenlands, but rather widespread acceptance by local hunting groups of a popular style of effective projectile points for insertion into socketed hafts.

Side-notched points, reflecting a more efficient method of hafting projectile points with a wrap-around tie, were already replacing Plano points in southern Alberta 8,000 years ago. Evidently the notched point technological tra-dition diffused rapidly north-westward, as it appeared in western Alaska 7,000 years ago.

Meanwhile, west of the Rocky Mountains, the north-east Asian microblade tradition can be traced southward into deglaciated central British Columbia by 6,600 years ago, where microblades persisted until about 4,000 years ago. On the British Columbian coast (at Namu near Bella Bella), microblades were already present 9,700 years ago, apparently reflecting earlier acceptance of the technological tradition on the Northwest Coast than on the British Columbian plateau (Fladmark, 1982).

The present unbroken distribution of Athapaskan lan-guages throughout the interior of Alaska and north-western Canada suggests the likelihood that the first colonists to re-enter formerly glaciated northern British Columbia spoke Athapaskan languages. Very probably these colonists brought microblades with them; however, a one-to-one association between language and microblade technology is not demonstrable, because most Northwest Coast people speak a variety of non-Athapaskan languages. Evidently microblade technology was adopted by people speaking many different languages. A rich microblade industry appeared on the isolated Queen Charlotte islands between 7,400 and 5,500 years ago (Fladmark, 1982). These islands were only partly glaciated, and most ice probably had melted by 12,000 years ago, suggesting the hypothesis that the Haida, who occupy the Charlottes, cannot be related linguistically to any other group because they may have occupied the islands while most of British Columbia was still buried by ice. Evidence for an early occupation of the islands is suggested by simple pebble and flake artefacts recovered from an undatable context discovered in a raised beach deposit (Fladmark, 1982).

Although microblades are useful for tracing a diagnostic technological tradition from north-east Asia to north-west America on the Pleistocene–Holocene boundary, most likely they were simply a useful piece of material equipment adopted by various people, rather than the trademark of a particular expanding population. The use of microblades made on specialized cores persisted for many millennia in the interior subarctic zone from central Alaska to the Hudson Bay (Clark, 1981; Wright, 1981). Microblades, miniature burins and small stemmed projectile points also became characteristic components of the Arctic small tool tradition (ASTT), which was carried rapidly eastward by specialized sea-mammal and caribou hunters who became the initial occupants of the Canadian High Arctic islands and Greenland about 4,000 years ago (Hickey, 1986). This spectacular migration by specialized hunters is what many scholars think of when they model the initial peopling of temperate North America. However, the ASTT expansion is the first time in North America that a complex of technological traditions can be linked with an identifiable cultural traditon (ASTT) that can be clearly traced in space and time as it spread into virgin territory by rapid population expansion.

Leaf-shaped and stemmed projectile points that can be related to the stemmed point tradition of the Great Basin indicate that the recolonization of deglaciated southern British Columbia was from the south. Stemmed points were used at the deeply stratified Milliken site near Hell's Gate at the fall line of the Fraser river as early as 9,000 years ago. Bifacial knives, scrapers, blades, gravers, pebble-tools and grinding stones (mullers) were all suitable for hunting, gathering and fishing at this excellent fishing locale (Fladmark, 1982). Already in early postglacial times, salmon fishing probably had become part of a seasonal round that took people from hunting to fishing localities and to places where they gathered roots and berries. Although these people occupied mountainous British Columbia while Palaeoindian bison hunters were still ranging the Great Plains, migratory herds were scarce in their environment; neverthelesss, a great variety of food sources was available, so these people developed and maintained a less specialized economy.

The earliest dated site on the Northwest Coast is on the Olympic peninsula in north-western Washington State overlooking the Strait of Juan de Fuca and Vancouver Island (Gustafson et al., 1979). Almost 12,000 years ago a mastodon died near stagnant glacial ice. At first the presence of a pointed bone deeply imbedded in a vertebra was believed to be evidence that hunters had killed the animal, but X-rays proved that the wound had healed before death. Several bones had cut marks, and the skull had been smashed and turned upside down. A pebble flake was also recovered during the fastidious excavations at the Manis mastodon site, but one of the best clues that people had been present was the fact that one of the two broken fragments of the outer enamel of a tusk exhibits scrape marks and bevelling, while the piece that fitted on to the modified fragment lacks any sign of use (C. Gustafson, personal communication). Although they may earlier have tried to kill the animal, there is no evidence that hunters actually did so, only that they utilized parts of the dead beast.

The story of the development of the famous Northwest Coast culture with its spectacular art style and complex social ranking system remains unclear because few occupation sites have been found between about 7,000 and 5,000 years ago, when the first shell-middens appear. It seems unlikely that people would not have utilized shellfish earlier as a staple resource. Probably, the complex relationship between eustatic rise in sea-level and isostatic recovery of deglaciated land finally stabilized about 5,000 years ago, allowing shellfish to become established. However, coastal people always had been able to rely on salmon, other fish, both sea and land mammals, and abundant berries; so it can be anticipated that archaeological evidence before 5,000 years ago for increasing technological and social complexity will be found. The first good evidence for the development of social classes occurs about 4,500 years ago

at Namu, where few offerings are associated with flexed burials, while extended burials had many associated artefacts. After this time, throughout the Northwest Coast, there are not only more but larger settlements, reflecting rapid population increase. Many new artefact types, including antler wedges, ground-stone celts and other wood-working tools, as well as increased elaboration of decorative art in bone and stone occur between 4,500 and 3,000 years ago. During this period evidence of the introduction of ideas from various directions indicates that these people became part of the widespread North American exchange network but nevertheless continued to maintain their distinctive cultural traditions, which are reflected in developing regional art styles (Fladmark, 1982).

COLUMBIA PLATEAU

Although glacial ice never extended into the more open semi-arid Columbia basin of eastern Washington State, the melting of the glaciers had created huge lakes on tributaries of the Columbia in western Montana, which periodically scoured all low-lying areas of eastern Washington with a sudden wall of water. The last flood, c.13,000 years ago, either swept away or deeply buried earlier evidence of occupation. A few probable artefacts have been found beneath the flood deposits. The earliest dated evidence for reoccupation is a cache of Clovis points near Wenatchee lying directly on volcanic ash from the Glacier Peak eruption which occurred 11,250 years ago (Mehringer and Foit, 1990). At Marmes rock shelter near the confluence of the Snake with the Columbia human skeletal remains were found with artefacts in 10,000-year-old sediments (Bryan, 1980). Occupants of Marmes rock shelter used tiny, eyed, bone needles as well as stemmed projectile points resembling those from the Milliken site in the Fraser canyon of British Columbia. In the heart of the Columbia basin at Lind Coulee, bison were hunted in the spring about 9,000 years ago by people who used similar stemmed spearpoints, peculiar flaked stone crescents, side-scrapers and end-scrapers, grinding stones, and barbed bone points. Perhaps the same group gathered in the autumn at the fall line of the Columbia river at The Dalles, Oregon, to spear salmon with barbed bone and antler points. They also used bolas and flaked stemmed points, blades and burins. The presence of abundant haematite and bones of cormorants, eagles, vultures and condors suggests that red paint and feathers were used during rituals. Seasonally, these same people probably also dug for roots and picked berries in the mountains. These early people had already established an economically efficient annual round of the kind maintained by the Plateau Indians into the twentieth century.

In southern Idaho, north of the Snake river, the major southern tributary of the Columbia, people occupied Wilson Butte cave near the end of the Pleistocene. A blade, a burin made on a flake, a small thick biface and cut bones of camel and horse were found in 15,000- to 14,500-year-old deposits (Gruhn, 1961, 1965). Stemmed and willow leaf-shaped points occur in later deposits before camels became extinct. Wilson Butte cave not only is one of the earliest radiocarbon-dated sites in North America, but it contains the earliest such evidence for bifacial tools. The site also indicates that large blades and burins were already present south of the continental glaciers, and were not introduced from Siberia with microblades in the final Pleistocene times.

THE GREAT BASIN

The stemmed point tradition (Fig. 86) originated further south in the now-arid Great Basin, which differs ecologically from the Columbia plateau mainly in that it lacks the predictable and highly productive seasonal salmon runs, winter village sites never developed in this vast area of internal drainage. The ecology of the two regions differed more significantly during the Pleistocene, when increased precipitation in the basin created many freshwater lakes, some vast and deep but most shallow and marshy. Certainly the Great Basin at this time would have been one of the most productive habitats in North America, with abundant fish, waterfowl and large mammals, as well as edible seeds and marsh plants. The Basin environment became drier and less productive at the end of the Pleistocene; however, a seasonal round from the riparian shores up through the productive pinyon pine zone to higher altitude sheep-hunting camps was established early and maintained into this century.

The lowest occupation at Fort Rock cave in a small lake basin in south-central Oregon was dated to 13,200 years ago on material from a hearth associated with a short stemmed point and a stubby point with a concave base. These, the earliest dated projectile points in North America, were associated with eleven nondescript flaked tools and a *mano* (upper grinding stone), indicating that plant foods formed part of the diet (Bedwell, 1973). More carefully shaped stemmed points came from higher levels in the cave. Several sites in the basin have yielded simple stone and bone artefacts associated with the remains of extinct animals, but so far no kill-sites of extinct mammals have been found associated with diagnostic projectile points, such as have often been discovered farther east on the Great Plains. Certainly there must have been kill-sites; but the implication from this as well as from other evidence is that early occupants of the Great Basin did not specialize in hunting big-game animals as did their contemporaries on the High Plains, but instead had developed an effective general foraging economy revolving around the pluvial lakes and the seasonally productive ecotones in the surrounding mountains.

Clovis fluted points do occur, especially in southern Idaho and the western Great Basin, but they also are associated with pluvial lake environments and so far not with mammoth kill-sites. The cultural and chronological relationships between fluted and stemmed points in the Great Basin have not been determined because fluted points have rarely been found in radiocarbon-dated contexts in the Basin, and then only in contexts dated later than 9,000 years ago (Bryan,

1988). Stemmed and Clovis fluted points collected from the undated Dietz site in south-eastern Oregon have discrete distributions, suggesting that they were used at different times or by different people or both (Judy Willig, personal communications, 1986, 1987).

As fluted points are known to be earlier than stemmed points on the High Plains, it is generally assumed that fluted points somehow evolved into stemmed points, probably on the Plains. The hypothesis that stemmed points were developed in the Basin and later spread on to the Plains (Bryan, 1980) has not been properly evaluated. In order to maintain the accepted model that fluted points are earliest everywhere, the presence of the 13,000-year-old stemmed point in Fort Rock cave is usually ignored, as are stemmed points reported from other contexts dated earlier than or contemporary with Clovis. However, the presence of stemmed points on occupation floors dated to between 13,000 and 10,000 years ago in several caves suggests the possibility that stemmed points were developed quite independently in the Great Basin as part of an indigenous adaptation to the productive late Pleistocene environments here (Bryan, 1988).

In addition to Fort Rock cave, an intensively used occupation zone in Smith Creek cave, eastern Nevada, has yielded a dozen dates on charcoal and wood ranging between 12,000 and 10,000 years ago, from deposits that also yielded stemmed point bases, flake scrapers and many perishables, including artiodactyl, bison, and camelid hair (Bryan, 1979). Neither bison nor camels would have entered the inaccessible cave voluntarily, so their hair evidently was removed during hide preparation. Sceptics (for example, Thompson, 1985) have argued that all wood and charcoal dates older than 11,000 years must be too old for various reasons, the most cogent of which is that people might have collected old wood preserved for thousands of years in this desert environment. In response to this possibility, hair samples were submitted for dating by the accelerator method. The results confirm the dates on charcoal and wood (Bryan, 1988). In north-western Nevada, bovid and human hair was found in Handprint cave associated with a square-based stemmed point (Fig. 86). Directly associated charcoal yielded a date of around 10,700 years ago. All of these dated occupation contexts indicate that stemmed points were used in the Great Basin during as well as before the time (*c.*11,500 to 10,000 years ago) that fluted points were used to hunt extinct herd mammals on the High Plains and in environmentally similar areas just west of the continental divide. It is possible that some Plains hunters who made fluted points moved into the Great Basin to exploit the pluvial lake environments after the mammoths had become extinct, although it is also possible that some local groups simply adopted the fluted-point hafting technology. Detailed analysis of flaking techniques, such as was used to demonstrate that Clovis points from Maine and Montana were flaked by different cultural groups, may help resolve this problem.

The cultural adaptation to the wetland environments spanning the Pleistocene–Holocene boundary is referred to as the Western Pluvial Lakes tradition, which persisted until most lakes had dried up, about 7,000 years ago (Bedwell, 1973). Some descendants of these people adapted to an environment whose carrying capacity was reduced under the harsher Holocene desert conditions, while others moved out of the Basin into more favourable environments.

The productive Pleistocene ecosystems of the Great Basin certainly could be expected to have been amongst the very best places for people to have lived before projectile points

Figure 86 Square-based stemmed point, Handprint Cave, Nevada (USA). (After Margaret Brown.)

were innovated. Although earlier occupations have not been demonstrated to the satisfaction of sceptics, many open sites exist, often associated with pluvial lake shore-lines, which contain superficial clusters of artefacts. Some clusters contain small bifaces, while other assemblages yield only unifacially flaked artefacts, which suggest the possibility that technological development occurred in the Great Basin from primarily unifacial industries into industries containing bifacially flaked artefacts. Most of these surface scatters are in wind-deflated desert pavements, which lack datable charcoal. Consequently, very few have been test-excavated, because it is generally assumed that everything has been deflated to the same level. Nevertheless, features and other cultural associations have been demonstrated at some sites, which appear never to have been disturbed since the occupants left.

East Rim is an example of an excavated surface site which yielded eighteen types of both bifacially and unifacially flaked woodworking and hide-processing artefacts, but no projectile points or other types characteristic of Holocene assemblages in the area. This and related sites are located only above the 520 m beach of Pleistocene Lake Manix near Barstow in the Mojave desert of southern California. Tufa that formed on the shore has been dated to around 19,750 years ago, a date suggesting that the people who made the Lake Manix industry lived near the lake about 20,000 years ago, during full glacial times. Verification of this estimate was obtained at the East Rim site from analysis of pollen collected from subsurface sediments in association with artefacts (Alsoszathei-Petheo, 1975). The pollen assemblage includes pine and fir, which were probably growing on the nearby hills, local grasses and marshland plants, as well as desert plants, which are the only modern survivals. The Pleistocene plant community has been dated in lake cores elsewhere in the Mojave desert to between 37,000 and 18,000 years ago.

Calico, overlooking Pleistocene Lake Manix, has become the most controversial site in North America because of its apparently great antiquity. Calico is a stratified deposit containing silicates suitable for making flake-tools (chert and chalcedony) in an ancient alluvial fan which became separated from its mountain source by faulting in this tectonically active area. Most of the flaked objects interpreted as tools have been found up to 10 m below the surface in sediments deposited by mud flows and fluvial processes (Simpson et al., 1986). Unfortunately many of the objects that have been exhibited at archaeological conferences as tools have in fact assumed the shape of characteristic artefacts by natural processes. Such objects are encountered at many archaeological sites; but usually they are discarded in the field, or simply ignored during the process of artefact analysis because an abundance of unquestionably genuine artefacts means that there is no reason to deal with problematical objects, which may or may not have been picked up and used by prehistoric people.

Although other activities undoubtedly took place, Calico was primarily a quarry and workshop site. Recent analysis of the flaked objects from Calico has demonstrated that original cortical surfaces have been completely removed from many percussion flakes that have prominent bulbs (Patterson et al., 1987). Many flakes and blades also exhibit sequential flake removal, and cores also show multiple scars where flakes were removed from the same platforms. Some cores were flaked on both faces; but otherwise there are no shaped bifaces from deeply buried deposits, which yielded most of the artefacts. Many of the flakes and cores were found in clusters up to 3 m in diameter, and nearly all have sharp edges, showing that they were not carried far by water action. The clusters are similar to flaking debris that accumulates around a knapper. Although some archaeologists admit that real artefacts, including blades and gravers, are present, they are unable to accept the possibility of extreme antiquity. Soil-stratigraphic age estimates for the sediments enclosing the flaked stones range between 125,000 and 200,000 years, and this estimate has been substantiated by uranium–thorium disequilibrium dates of 200,000 years on calcrete coating flaked objects at the base of the deposits (Simpson, Patterson and Singer, 1986; Patterson et al., 1987). Such an estimated maximum age is too old for most North American archaeologists, who therefore conclude either that the artefacts must be intrusive or that nature was somehow able to fabricate what appear to be genuine artefacts. Although Calico, like many other sites, contains a great many objects that could be the work either of nature or humans, it is not logical to conclude that repetitive patterned flaking must be natural simply because the geological context is too old to fit the prevailing model of the final-Pleistocene entry of human beings.

The large temporal gap between the Lake Manix industry and Calico must be filled before the evidence from Calico will be considered feasible. Several other sites in southern California, especially around San Diego, have been reported to contain evidence for the presence of people as early as the last interglacial (Reeves et al., 1986). However, no descriptive site reports are available, so archaeologists cannot properly evaluate these claims. Considerable evidence does exist in south-eastern California for occupations that lack bifacial projectile points, and eventually a more complete picture of the Pleistocene prehistory of this rich environmental region should emerge.

CALIFORNIA

California west of the Sierra Nevada mountains has always been one of the most productive environmental regions of North America. Several Pleistocene pluvial lakes were utilized in the central valley as well as east of the Sierras, but dating these occupations remains a problem. The central valley also contains rich riverine environments, and is flanked by oak-covered hills which provide a habitat for many mammal and bird species. But most importantly, indigenous people learned how to process the abundant acorns into a staple food resource which at the time of contact supported the densest aboriginal population north of central Mexico, without the assistance of domesticated food plants.

Because of the lack of excavated dated evidence, it has been assumed that prehistoric Californians did not learn how to process acorns and other edible seeds until after the Pleistocene. Processing this important staple food may have occurred earlier in the Holocene than previously believed, however. An obvious geomorphological reason for the lack of evidence is now being verified. Rising sea-levels not only drowned all early Holocene coastal sites, but caused tremendous postglacial alluviation of the central valley of California. Easily recoverable archaeological remains in the alluviated central valley are thereby restricted to those originating within the last 4,500 years (Moratto, 1984).

Recent excavations in the coast range west of the central valley have encountered important deeply stratified sites which help fill the gap until the late Pleistocene. The Mostin site near Clear Lake north of San Francisco Bay has yielded several human burials. Dates on the collagen content of human bone from four burials range from 10,500 to 7,750 years ago, but associated charcoal dated 7,700 and 7,500 years ago suggests that the occupation was probably not earlier than eight millennia ago (David Frederickson, Stephen Robinson and Gregory White, personal communications, 1986). Artefacts from the site include thick pentagonal points, large percussion-flaked bifaces of obsidian and chert, bone points, two rectangular ground-stone tablets, one of which is perforated, and a well-made pestle (Moratto, 1984). The evidence from the Mostin site suggests that these early people hunted animals and birds, fished, and collected shellfish and plant foods at an earlier time than previously recognized in central California. Another stratified site near Santa Clara has yielded dates between 10,000 and 8,000 years ago. Ground-stone artefacts, including a *mano* for preparing plant food, have been recovered. An *Olivella* shell bead and obsidian, the nearest source of which is 200 km north near Clear Lake, suggest that valuable foods were obtained from considerable distances at least by 8,000 years ago (Moratto, 1984).

The earliest well-dated evidence for projectile points west of the Sierras is in the far south, where it is known as the San Dieguito complex. Many kinds of scrapers, knives and projectile points related to the stemmed point tradition have been dated to between 9,000 and 8,500 years ago on the San Dieguito river, while similar less carefully flaked points have come from 8,000-year-old contexts at nearby coastal sites (Moratto, 1984). Probably these hunters decided to move from the southern Great Basin after the pluvial lakes dried up. Above the San Dieguito levels are milling stones and other tools indicating that these later La Jollan people were grinding seeds, hunting small game and collecting shellfish about 6,000 years ago. It is usually assumed that the former hunters had gradually adapted themselves to a generalized foraging economy after they had moved to the coast; however, the evidence from central California suggests that a foraging economy was already well established in that area long before the San Dieguito hunters arrived. The possibility that the general foraging economy was also earlier in the San Diego area is supported by the recovery of many milling stones on the continental shelf by scuba divers, although many of these milling stones may be more recent. Evidence for any early coastal foraging adaptation is not readily available because coastal sites older than 8,000 years have been drowned by the rising sea-level.

Rich ecosystems have always been available in California west of the Sierras, unlike the situation further east in the Basin where the climate deteriorated rapidly as the pluvial lakes dried up. However, there was never any environmental reason why people on either side of the Sierras had to specialize in hunting large mammals; and indeed there is no compelling archaeological evidence that these westerners were ever anything other than highly successful foragers. Because of environmental advantages, the early central Californians may be expected to have developed their successful adaptation just as early as the people around the Basin pluvial lakes. The major difference is that while the carrying capacity was drastically reduced in the Basin as the pluvial lakes dried up, people west of the Sierras probably were able to develop their sucessful adaptation to their rich environment, with the highest carrying capacity north of central Mexico, earlier than most other areas in North America. By 4,500 years ago, after the postglacial sea-level had stabilized, a rich picture of diverse local cultural traditions emerges, with established barter relations to take advantage of local environmental variations. Fancy shell, flaked and ground stone, and ground bone objects are ornamental and ceremonial items associated with burials, although utility goods, including stemmed projectile points, were exchanged as well. But earlier evidence for exchange of valuable goods as an indicator of wealth implies that the rich California tradition was developing long before it became archaeologically fully visible about 4,500 years ago.

THE SOUTHWEST

The Southwest is an environmentally diverse region east of California and south of the Great Basin. It includes the high Colorado plateau through which the Colorado river has sliced its deep canyon, the northern Sonoran desert to the south and the mountainous region to the east where the Rocky Mountains disappear into the high desert plateau of north-central Mexico.

The early economic adaptation was like that in the Great Basin, with evidence for general hunting and gathering cultures. The earliest (*c.*11,500 to 11,000 years ago) generally accepted sites, however, are Clovis kill-sites in south-eastern Arizona. Nevertheless, the available evidence suggests that the indigenous economy was general foraging, including the use of milling stones for processing plant foods and, often at separate sites, stemmed and notched points for hunting large and small game. As in the Basin, an annual round of economic activities evidently had been established early. The fluted point tradition might represent a temporary incursion into the area about 11,000 years ago by a group of specialized big-game hunters; but it is also possible that fluted points were adopted by local Cochise foragers to dispatch the last remnants of the mammoth herds.

The best evidence that general foragers were already resident in the region at the time that Clovis points were used to hunt mammoths comes from south-western Arizona in Ventana cave, which was excavated before the introduction of radiocarbon dating (Haury, 1950). A small chunk of charcoal, collected after the final report was published, yielded a date of about 11,300 years ago, which indicates contemporaneity of at least part of the volcanic debris layer with the Clovis kill-sites further east (Haury, 1975). Horse, tapir, bison and an extinct antelope are present in the volcanic debris layer. Associated artefacts include thick unifacial scrapers, pebble choppers and planes which are evidently related to the tools in many undated surface assemblages found further west and north in the Great Basin. In addition, there are a carefully shaped discoidal stone, a hammerstone, bifacial knives and two small projectile points, one with shallow corner notches and the other with a concave base. Marine shells indicate that trade relations had already been established with people living further west. The underlying conglomerate layer yielded a few artefacts and flakes as well as bone carbonate dated to around 12,600 years ago, and constitutes an often overlooked 'pre-Clovis' occupation.

Evidently Ventana cave was used occasionally by foragers considerably before the local extinction of the Pleistocene fauna, but there is no evidence that these people were a primary cause of their demise. About 10,000 years ago, southern Arizona became hotter and more arid, and the Cochise foragers increasingly emphasized plant collecting and seed grinding with milling stones. Considerable accumulation of midden debris in open sites as early as 6,000 years ago suggests that they may have been deliberately cultivating native plants, including chenopods and amaranth, long before the introduction of domesticates from central Mexico.

already learned special techniques for preserving surplus food.

THE GREAT PLAINS

The Great Plains extend from the southern prairie provinces of Canada to north-west Texas and eastern New Mexico. This vast grassland is divisible into the short-grass High Plains just east of the Rocky Mountains and the tall-grass prairies east of the ninety-eighth meridian to the edge of the Eastern Woodlands. The prairies now extend east of the Mississippi river in Minnesota, and extended much farther east in early Holocene times. The High Plains can be gently rolling or locally quite mountainous, possibly with forest cover, whereas the tall grass prairies are generally quite flat except where they are dissected near the forested river valleys.

Until the advent of the steel plough, the only way to make a living on the High Plains was to hunt large game animals, most importantly bison. Even now, the region supports more cattle ranchers than grain farmers. This fact explains why nearly all bison and mammoth kill-sites throughout prehistory are located on the High Plains. It is surprising, therefore, that the presence of Clovis mammoth kills and later bison kills with Folsom and Plano points, all on or near the High Plains, have been used to define an early (Palaeoindian) period of specialized big-game hunting which has been assumed to characterize all of North America before about 10,000 years ago. Around 8,000 years ago Plains hunters increasingly used side-notched instead of stemmed points to kill bison. Although the specialized economy did not change, the change in projectile point technology has led to the use of the term Plains Archaic because notched points are associated with the Eastern Archaic, which clearly was based on a general foraging economy.

Between about 7,000 and 5,000 years ago a widespread drought reduced the Plains bison herds. As a result, most people were forced to retreat to the mountains and the prairies to the east and north where they could hunt small game, gather plants and catch fish. About 5,000 years ago, many people returned to the High Plains to hunt bison, increasingly using special techniques for driving bison herds into stockaded pounds and over cliffs.

An unexpected development occurred in the prairie-parkland zone of transition to the boreal forest in southern Alberta and Saskatchewan as the Altithermal drought was drawing to a close and plants and animals became more abundant. About 6,000 years ago a distinctive side-notched point with a concave base creating 'ears' became characteristic of the Oxbow culture. It is possible to identify an Oxbow culture (not just a technological tradition) because the same group of people repeatedly buried their dead in a particular cemetery near Swift Current for more than 2,000 years, starting about 5,200 years ago (Millar, 1978). Most of the burials are secondary; evidently the bodies had been covered with red ochre, packed in hide bundles and transported to the cemetery. Further indication that religious ideas were a significant part of life is suggested by the presence in graves of bird and animal bones, which were probably items included in medicine bundles. Associated artefacts include Oxbow points, knives, scrapers and grooved stone mauls of the type used for preparing pemmican (a mixture of berries and dried meat, which preserves for prolonged periods when pounded). Although the Oxbow people were nomadic hunters, they had

THE EASTERN WOODLANDS

The Eastern Woodlands (mixed pine and deciduous trees giving way northward to the less productive Boreal Forest) is a vast area encompassing all of eastern North America south of the Barrenlands. Environmentally, this zone is relatively much more uniform and culturally less diverse than western North America, so it is appropriate to consider it as a single region. The primary physiographic features are the Mississippi river system, which empties into the Gulf of Mexico, and the Great Lakes, which drain eastward into the St Lawrence river. The St Lawrence bisects the much-eroded Laurentian–Appalachian mountain system, which parallels the Atlantic coastal plain. South of the mountains, the Florida peninsula is ecologically distinctive because it extends into the subtropical zone, and has an exceptionally high water-table caused by the postglacial rise in sea-level. Many early artefacts, including Clovis points and ground bone points, as well as human bones, have been found by Florida scuba divers in apparent association with extinct fauna, and there is a good chance that an early waterlogged occupation site will one day be located in Florida. The potential for such an important discovery is indicated at Little Salt Springs, where an extinct giant tortoise had evidently been impaled with a sharpened wooden stake which dated to around 12,000 years ago (MacDonald, 1983, p. 106).

The Pleistocene prehistory of the Eastern Woodlands is not well understood, because there are few deposits that are not deeply buried in river valleys and few in rock shelters and caves that have not collapsed. The postglacial palaeo-environmental sequence is also not well understood; but there is less evidence than expected that the Pleistocene climate was substantially different from now, especially in areas very far from the ice that blanketed Canada and the northern portion of the United States until it started melting rapidly about 15,000 years ago.

Meadowcroft rock shelter in south-western Pennsylvania is the prime site in the Eastern Woodlands containing evidence for occupations earlier than Clovis (Carlisle and Adovasio, 1982). The large overhang above a small stream was located about 80 km from the maximum advance of the late Pleistocene glacier about 18,000 years ago. The cultural sequence, which is dated by fifty stratigraphically consistent radiocarbon dates, ranges from an historic firepit to 20,000-year-old charred basketry fragments. Although the dates of the Holocene sequence are all reasonable and never have been challenged, sceptics have argued that the radiocarbon samples from the Pleistocene occupation floors (> 12,000 years ago) must have been contaminated. The artefacts from the Pleistocene deposits consist mainly of unifacially retouched flakes, although a few bifacial thinning flakes have been identified. The lowermost cultural material is reported to be a charred basket, which itself yielded a date of about 19,600 years ago.

Large fluted points are more numerous in the Ohio–Tennessee drainage basin than elsewhere in North America. In contrast to the Plains, however, kill-sites have never been identified here, although a Clovis point has been found with mastodon remains at the Kimmswick site near St Louis (MacDonald, 1983). Mastodons evidently survived in the Eastern Woodlands until about 8,000 years ago, long after mammoths had become extinct. Bones of some mastodons have cut and gouge marks evidently caused by dismembering the dead animals (Fischer, 1984), while cut wood is reported to have been associated with others. Perhaps the lack of associated projectile points is because these mastodons were not migratory herd animals, and therefore were not slain by organized hunting parties at predictable places. Rather, when the opportunity presented itself, people attacked a solitary beast. It is also possible that, as probably happened with the Manis mastodon, people simply scavenged the remains of a dead animal, whether or not they had hastened its demise.

It is usually assumed that fluted points are always older than stemmed or notched points. However, increasing numbers of stratified sites throughout the south-east, especially in Texas, contain notched and stemmed points stratigraphically associated with or actually beneath fluted points (see, for instance, Patterson and Hudgins, 1985). These cases are usually ignored or explained away by hypothesizing that later people collected earlier points. Alternative hypotheses can be suggested. Perhaps fluted points persisted in some areas after the innovation of stemmed and notched points. It is also possible that fluted points were used by the same people who used stemmed and notched points for different purposes. Until these alternative possibilities are adequately tested, the best policy is to consider each form as simply representing a hafting method (specific technological tradition) that was developed originally as part of an efficient adaptation to locally available resources, rather than assuming that a point sequence (fluted → stemmed → notched), that has been established in one area (the High Plains), can be extrapolated to all areas.

Nevertheless, it is evident that some early native Americans emphasized hunting, although they never completely abandoned fishing and gathering. Most probably, they learned by observation the behaviour of migratory herd animals. After repeated successful communal hunts at game crossings they developed a specialized technological complex which included fluted points. Most probably this development occurred first in the prairie grasslands on the eastern margins of the plains. Some bands then seasonally ranged westward on to the High Plains to apply their specialized hunting techniques to the pursuit of mammoth and bison herds.

The technological complex often found associated with fluted points in the east includes steep end-scrapers, often with lateral graver spurs, side-scrapers, blade-like flakes, bifacial knives, drills and perforators, bipolarly flaked wedges (pièces esquillées) and characteristic channel flakes removed from the fluted point bases (MacDonald, 1983). As this specialized hunting, bone-breaking and meat-processing technology was dependent on good stone suitable for flaking, sites where such stone could be quarried were located, and material was reduced to bifacial rough-outs and traced widely among various cultural groups who made fluted points. As bone does not preserve in acidic forest soils, there is little direct information about which animals these hunting groups slew, although caribou herds were probably the most common game. Fluted points are rarely found in caves anywhere in North America, but one fluted point from the tiny Dutchess Quarry cave in southern New York State was found with caribou. An associated date of 12,500 years ago is unexpectedly early; however, if correct, it would support the hypothesis that the fluted point tradition began somewhere south of the ice-dammed Great Lakes in the region containing the greatest concentration of fluted points. Extensive occupation sites containing the characteristic tech-

nological complex associated with fluted points have been excavated in Virginia, Pennsylvania, New Jersey, Connecticut, Maine and Nova Scotia. Most radiocarbon dates from these sites range between 11,000 and 10,000 years ago (MacDonald, 1983). These large occupation sites suggest that several nomadic hunting bands seasonally congregated for ceremonial and social purposes.

Most sites with fluted points are small temporary camp sites. Several camp sites have been located in southern Ontario on and above Pleistocene Lake Algonquin beaches before Lakes Huron and Erie attained their present form (MacDonald, 1983). These sites could have been occupied by a few bands of caribou hunters. Lower terraces have yielded stemmed points related to Plano forms of the west. This late Plano manifestation most likely represents a new projectile point technology that diffused from the west, rather than a new migration. These stemmed points are mainly distributed near the Great Lakes waterways as far east as the mouth of the St Lawrence. Caribou hunters presumably continued to occupy the old lake shores and river crossings during the period of rapid postglacial isostatic recovery from the weight of the former glaciers.

Encroaching forests eventually forced most of these people to readapt their economy to a general foraging way of life, which included hunting deer, moose, and woodland caribou. However, far to the north-east, beyond the boreal forest, one group of specialized hunters made a remarkable adaptation to hunting sea-mammals, especially seals, on floe ice off southern Labrador. Evidently these sea-mammal hunters were remarkably successful because about 7,500 years ago they constructed the oldest known burial mound in North America at L'Anse Amour on the Straits of Belle Isle (McGhee and Tuck, 1975). A young teenager was buried with a walrus tusk, several notched projectile points, stemmed knives shaped like Plano points, ground slate points, a bone pendant, a bird-bone flute, a beautifully carved antler toggle and the earliest known toggling harpoon. The pit was backfilled and then marked with two parallel lines of upright stone slabs, between which were found charcoal and a few fish bones, presumably remnants of a ceremony. Everything was covered by a low mound of boulders, 8 m in diameter. The toggling harpoon, which is designed to turn parallel to the animal's hide after penetration, is particularly significant because its invention allowed specialized hunters to invade a new arctic maritime ecosystem teeming with sea-mammals as well as fish.

Because these early sea-mammal hunters of southern Labrador had already adopted notched projectile points, they are arbitrarily classified as Maritime Archaic rather than late Palaeoindian. By 6,500 years ago these arctic maritime hunters had penetrated to northern Labrador, where they discovered a source of fine translucent quartzite which they quarried and exchanged throughout the Maritime provinces and up the St Lawrence. These Maritime Archaic people also started grinding slate into long spearheads, daggers and knives, which were also much valued by Laurentian Archaic people in the Lower Great Lakes region for use as fancy grave goods after about 6,000 years ago. The increasingly successful foraging economy that various Archaic peoples developed between about 10,000 and 4,000 years ago has been termed 'primary forest efficiency'. It reflects intensive adaptation to the available local resources by larger groups of people who increasingly emphasized plant foods rather than hunting. Concern for the dead accelerated throughout the Late Archaic, especially in the Great Lakes region and the Ohio and Mississippi valleys. A complex system of exchange became established throughout this region, and extended far to the south and west. Cold-hammered native copper from western Lake Superior, conch shells from the Gulf of Mexico, shell beads from the Atlantic, and exotic ground and flaked-stone artefacts from many dispersed locales were obtained for burial with special personages. A great variety of utilitarian objects, including ground-stone woodworking and hunting tools, were also manufactured and traded widely by Archaic foragers.

SUMMARY

Asians with a Palaeolithic (Archaeolithic) stone technology expanded across Beringia sometime during the late Pleistocene. Some people stayed because they were adapted to Beringian environments. However, population pressures ultimately caused some bands to bud off and move into neighbouring ecosystems. Eventually, the slow process of population expansion into virgin territories resulted in the peopling of all regions of the Americas.

When the stage was reached where population pressures could no longer be relieved simply by budding off to occupy virgin environments, people had to adapt more closely to their ecosystem. During this Cenolithic stage, experimentation with new methods for utilizing available food sources resulted in the introduction of more specialized technological equipment, including in some areas the development of bifacially flaked stone projectile points for hunting migratory herd animals. Equally ingenious people in other areas hunted with nets and traps, while others developed milling stones for processing seeds and roots. More than one specialized economic adaptation was developed as a response to local food resources by people gaining an ever-expanding knowledge of their ecosystem. The specialized big-game hunting adaptation that developed on the High Plains is just one example of the ingenuity of early Americans. Some effective adaptations that developed in one region were adopted by people in neighbouring regions. Before about 5,000 years ago there is little evidence that cultural groups with an effective economic adaptation actually migrated to neighbouring areas which were already occupied, except when climatic deterioration forced them out of one area into more productive environments.

Preparation and storage of staple foods allowed the development of networks of exchange of valuable goods and more permanent settlements between about 11,000 and 9,000 years ago in California, the Plateau, the Southwest, and the Eastern Woodlands, leading to domestication of a few local staple plants in the latter two areas about 5,000 years ago. During all this time indigenous North Americans were establishing their own distinctive regional cultural traditions without significant cultural stimuli from elsewhere.

BIBLIOGRAPHY

ALSOSZATHEI-PETHEO, J. A. 1975. *The East Rim Site*. (Unpublished Master's thesis, Eastern New Mexico University, Portales.)

BEDWELL, S. F. 1973. *Fort Rock Basin: Prehistory and Environment*. Eugene, University of Oregon.

BRYAN, A. L. 1979. Smith Creek Cave. *Anthrop. Pap. Nevada State Mus.* (Carson City), Vol. 17, pp. 164–251.

—— 1980. The Stemmed Point Tradition: An Early Technological Tradition in Western North America. In: HARTEN, L. B. et al. (eds), *Anthropological Papers in Memory of Earl H. Swanson Jr.* Pocatello. pp. 77–107.

—— 1988. The Relationship of the Stemmed and Fluted Point Traditions in the Great Basin. *Anthrop. Pap. Nevada Mus.* (Carson City), Vol. 21, pp. 53–74.

CARLISLE, R. C.; ADOVASIO, J. M. 1982. *Meadowcroft*. Pittsburgh.

CLARK, D. W. 1981. Prehistory of the Western Subarctic. In: HELM, J. (ed.), *Handbook of North American Indians*. Washington, DC. Vol. 6, pp. 107–29.

DINCAUZE, D. F. 1984. An Archaeo-Logical Evaluation of the Case for Pre-Clovis Occupations. *Adv. World Archaeol.*, Vol. 3, pp. 275–323.

FISCHER, D. C. 1984. Taphonomic Analysis of Late Pleistocene Mastodon Occurrences: Evidence of Butchery by North-American Paleo-Indians. *Palaeobiology* (Jacksonville), Vol. 10, No. 3, pp. 338–57.

FLADMARK, K. 1982. An Introduction to the Prehistory of British Columbia. *Can. J. Archaeol.* (Edmonton), Vol. 6, pp. 95–156.

FLADMARK, K.; DRIVER, J. C.; ALEXANDER, D. 1988. The Paleoindian Component at Charlie Lake Cave (HbRf39). *Am. Antiq.*, Vol. 53, No. 2, pp. 371–84.

GRUHN, R. 1961. *The Archaeology of Wilson Butte Cave, South-Central Idaho*. Pocatello.

—— 1965. Two Early Radiocarbon Dates from the Lower Levels of Wilson Butte Cave, South-Central Idaho. *Tebiwa* (Pocatello), Vol. 8, No. 2, p. 57.

—— 1989. *The Pacific Coast Route of Initial Entry: An Overview.* (Paper presented in the First World Summit Conference on the Peopling of the America, Orono.)

GUSTAFSON, C.; DAUGHERTY, R.; GILBOW, D. 1979. The Manis Mastodon Site: Early Man on the Olympic Peninsula. *Can. J. Archaeol.*, Vol. 3, pp. 157–64.

HAURY, E. 1950. *Ventana Cave*. Tucson/Albuquerque. (2nd edn 1975.)

HAYNES, C. V., JR. 1980. The Clovis Culture. *Can. J. Anthropol.*, Vol. 1, pp. 115–21.

HICKEY, C. 1986. The Archaeology of Arctic Canada. In: MORRISON, R. B.; WILSON, C. R. (eds), *Native Peoples: The Canadian Experience*. Toronto. pp. 73–97.

LEBLANC, R. J. 1984. *The Rat Indian Creek Site and the Late Prehistoric Period in the Interior Northern Yukon*. Ottawa.

MACDONALD, G. F. 1983. Eastern North America. In: SHUTLER, R., JR (ed.), *Early Man in the New World*. Beverly Hills. pp. 97–108.

MCGHEE, R.; TUCK, J. A. 1975. *An Archaic Sequence from the Strait of Belle Isle, Labrador*. Ottawa.

MEHRINGER, P. J., JR; FOIT F. F., JR. 1990. Volcanic Ash Dating of the Clovis Cache at East Wenatchee, Washington. *Natl Geogr. Res.* (Washington), Vol. 6, pp. 495–503.

MILLAR, J. F. V. 1978. *The Gray Site: An Early Plains Burial Ground, Parks Canada*. Ottawa. (Manuscript Report, 304.)

MOCHANOV, I. A. 1978. Stratigraphy and Absolute Chronology of the Paleolithic of Northeast Asia, According to the Work of 1963–1973. In: BRYAN, A. L. (ed.), *Early Man in America from a Circum-Pacific Perspective*. Edmonton. pp. 54–66.

MORATTO, M. J. 1984. *California Archaeology*. Orlando.

MORLAN, R. E. 1986. Pleistocene Archaeology in the Old Crow Basin: A Critical Reappraisal. In: BRYAN, A. L. (ed.), *New Evidence for the Pleistocene Peopling of the Americas*. Orono. pp. 27–48.

OWEN, R. C. 1984. The Americas: The Case Against an Ice-Age Human Population. In: SMITH, F. H.; SPENCER, F. (eds), *The Origins of Modern Humans: A World Survey of the Fossil Evidence*. New York. pp. 517–63.

PATTERSON, L. W.; HUDGINS, J. D. 1985. Paleo-Indian Occupations in Wharton County, Texas. *Bull. Tex. Archaeol. Soc.* (Austin), Vol. 56, pp. 155–70.

PATTERSON, L. W. et al. 1987. Analysis of Lithic Flakes at the Calico Site, California. *J. Field Archaeol.*, Vol. 14, pp. 91–106.

REEVES, B.; POHL, J. M. D.; SMITH, J. W. 1986. The Mission Ridge Site and the Texas Street Question. In: BRYAN, A. L. (ed.), *New Evidence for the Pleistocene Peopling of the Americas*. Orono. pp. 65–80.

SIMPSON, R. D.; PATTERSON, L. W.; SINGER, C. A. 1986. Lithic Technology of the Calico Mountains Site, Southern California. In: BRYAN, A. L. (ed.), *New Evidence for the Pleistocene Peopling of the Americas*. Orono. pp. 89–105.

THOMPSON, R. S. 1985. The Age and Environment of the Mount Moriah (Lake Mohave) Occupation at Smith Creek Cave, Nevada. In: MEAD, J. I.; MELTZER, D. J. (eds), *Environments and Extinctions: Man in Late Glacial North America.* Orono. pp. 111–19.

WATERS, M. S. 1985. Early Man in the New World: An Evaluation of the Radiocarbon-dated Pre-Clovis Sites in the Americas. In: MEAD, J. I.; MELTZER, D. J. (eds), *Environments and Extinc-* *tion: Man in Late Glacial North America.* Orono. pp. 125–43.

WRIGHT, J. V. 1981. Prehistory of the Canadian Shield. In: HELM, J. (ed.), *Handbook of North American Indians.* Washington, DC. Vol. 6, pp. 86–96.

YOUNG, D. F.; BONNICHSEN, R. 1985. Cognition, Behavior and Material Culture. In: *Stone Tool Analysis: Essays in Honor of Don E. Crabtree.* Albuquerque. pp. 91–131.

31

MEXICO AND CENTRAL AMERICA

from the arrival of humans to the beginnings of food production

José L. Lorenzo

Our point of departure is the unobjectionable supposition that the first inhabitants of what is now Mexico and Central America came from the north. They moved slowly and were few in number, judging by the sparse traces of their presence that have been found.

To gain a better understanding of the arrival of human groups in this part of America, it is essential to be acquainted with the physical geography of the area and the natural routes of access.

A glance at a map showing the physical geography of Mexico will reveal that the territory may have been penetrated from the north via the peninsula of Baja California, a route which reached an impasse. Another way may have led along the Sonora coast and across the northern plateau between the two chains of the Sierra Madre, joining the littoral plain of the Gulf of Mexico. Human groups engaged in exploiting marine resources must certainly have left traces of their passage in places now lying thirty metres or more under water.

The land reached by these various possible routes forms a kind of triangle, or funnel, with the apex pointing south. Athwart it, beyond the Tropic of Cancer, lies the Trans-Mexican volcanic axis, a great mountainous zone running from east to west. Some of the peaks of this unbroken mass of volcanoes rise more than 5,000 m above sea-level and are still covered in glaciers. These are Iztaccihuatl, Popocatepetl and Citlaltepetl. Other peaks more than 4,000 m high and many over 3,500 m bear evidence that their slopes were also ice-covered at some stage. The region south of the present border between the United States and Mexico is marked by the vestiges of an extensive group of Pleistocene lakes, which have not yet received thorough study. In the central volcanic region are bolsons which still contain, or once contained, lakes, a highly favourable habitat for early humans. Beyond the volcanic fringe a complex chain of mountains continues southwards, cleft by deep valleys and a few tectonic depressions as far as the isthmus of Tehuantepec, which some geographers and geologists claim to be the dividing line between North and Central America. Both coasts extending from the North American frontier are lined with plains. These are broader along the Gulf of Mexico than on the Pacific, where there are steep cliffs affected by powerful tectonic movements.

The isthmus of Tehuantepec, which interrupts the oro-graphic system from the north, links up with another system in the south, extending the mountain chain and central depression of Chiapas practically without a break through the various ramifications of Central America to meet the northern extremity of the Andean system in the north-east of Colombia, or Panama, as some authors claim. The Central American landscape consists of plateaux, coastal plains, mountains and various topographical accidents. Finally there is the peninsula of Yucatán, a flat expanse of recently emerged marine limestone deposits, on a karst hydrological pattern very different from the rest.

A fact to be borne carefully in mind is that the Central American isthmus narrows towards the south. This means that the territory is influenced more and more by both maritime masses, the Caribbean and the Pacific, as latitude decreases.

It is reasonable to suppose that the geographical differences in the territory we are studying are significant, and therefore that different cultural patterns were induced by the need to adapt to different ecosystems. In other words, as they advanced from north to south, doubtless at a very slow rate because there were not very many people in those days according to the number of finds, the human groups met with a variety of conditions in addition to the ecosystems produced by major climatic alterations that accompanied their itineraries.

As will be explained in more detail below, the earliest traces left by human beings in this region date back to more than 30,000 years ago. This means that major climatic changes must be taken into account, as those changes affected the ecosystems in areas where human beings settled temporarily or which they crossed in their nomadic migrations. The great variations in climate in Mexico and Central America today are the outcome of the substantial modifications that took place during those 30,000 years, transforming landscapes and their botanical and zoological features.

Where palaeoclimatology is concerned, very few reliable studies are available. The most complete so far, relating to water levels and glacier movements in central Mexico, reveals odd discrepancies between these two elements together with natural coincidences; most important of all, it shows a definite dephasing between tropical glaciation and glaciation at high latitudes.

In the regions outside the tropics the general sequence of climatic changes has been fairly well established, thanks to the very plentiful studies conducted on this topic for many years. Information on the tropical and Equatorial regions is still scarce, but major hypotheses can nevertheless be put forward, such as that high latitude glaciation is matched by a period of aridity and cold temperatures at lower latitudes, and in the specific case of Mexico and Central America by a disappearance or marked diminution of the so-called hurricanes which are precisely the bringers of heavy summer and autumn rains.

In order to grasp the order and content of the earliest phases of human presence, it is essential to work out a system of stages so that chronological and cultural factors may be interrelated, on a very broad scale, of course. Since we are dealing with a New World (though its human origins lie in the Old - in Asia, in point of fact) the vocabulary used to classify homotaxial cultural stages in the western and even the Asian world is inapplicable, because it could create unnecessary confusion.

Several stages of development have been identified, largely on the strength of the evidence provided by the prehistoric material found in North America and also in Mexico, Central America and South America. The most appropriate division is that adopted by Willey and Phillips (1958), who grouped everything that outside America has been called Palaeolithic under the label Lithic Period; where we are concerned, this also encompasses what they call the Archaic and Formative Periods.

To speak of a Lithic Period is helpful in so far as the term contains the concept of a type of material, namely stone, the most conspicuous among the finds. Nevertheless, it is certain that in the remotest times and in some regions, wood, bone and ivory also played a very prominent role as raw materials in the manufacture of artefacts.

The Lithic Period falls into what we call horizons, which can be identified on the basis of changes in household items and effects and in methods of exploitation. To some extent they follow a temporal sequence which suggests cultural evolution. The horizons are denoted by neologisms already used in Europe but later abandoned, some because they went out of fashion and others because they were rejected by the scientific community. These etymological terms, which is what they really are, answer the descriptive needs of our area of study.

Something which should be pointed out is that there are disparities in the extent and rate of cultural development within the New World: in the sixteenth century, for example, groups of hunters and gatherers were found living in the immediate vicinity of high Mesoamerican culture. Such extreme cultural variants occurring side by side and contemporaneously seem to suggest climatic causes related to the possibility of agriculture, but, whatever the reason, they show how unrealistic it is to establish rigidly sequential stages of evolution that admit of no exceptions.

The system followed here accordingly covers broad periods of time. The fact that certain ways of life established at a given period persisted beyond it, even though among minorities and in peripheral situations, justifies this approach.

Over such a vast territory with very varied ecosystems in close proximity, it is possible that specialized tools came to be made in different regions which nevertheless shared certain general features. However, the scarcity of materials in most cases, including many surface finds, compared with a few sites which have yielded a great wealth of artefacts, makes regional classification within the same horizon hazardous except in respect of coastal activities, which, moreover, may have been no more than seasonal occurrences.

The term 'Archaeolithic', used for the first time by Morgan (1947), refers to 'old stone' - the oldest. From the evidence obtained in our region so far this horizon ranges from slightly earlier than 30,000 to 14,000 years ago. The people's way of life seems to have been based on the gathering of certain items which catered for their principal needs, whereas hunting, mainly of small and medium-sized animals, remained a secondary activity.

'Cenolithic', a neologism used by Hodder Westropp in 1872 (Daniel, 1981), means 'recent stone'. The lower phase of this horizon, ranging from 14,000 to 9,000 years ago, was dominated by hunting, including that of large game, although gathering continued. There appears to have been a systematic use of coastal resources, but this may have been merely a seasonal activity. The Upper Cenolithic horizon, from 9,000 to 7,000 years ago, differs from the previous stage, owing quite definitely to the change in all climatic and biotic aspects that occurred at the end of the Pleistocene and the beginning of the Holocene. Large animals disappeared almost entirely and the hunting of medium-sized and small animals increased. There are some indications that the domestication of plants may have begun, while coastal activities were prevalent, particularly in the lagoons. On the Proto-Neolithic horizon, see Chapter 57.

ARCHAEOLITHIC PERIOD (Map 28)

The Archaeolithic Period is known for its large artefacts struck by the impact of stone against stone. There are some signs of bifacial chipping on the cutting edges of these implements and on the rarer small artefacts. The small pieces consist of thick, broad flakes which were used as side- and end-scrapers, and for cutting and piercing holes. Some denticulates have also been found, frequently displaying a very wide-angled fracture like that typical of the Clactonian technique. There are no milling tools and a characteristic lack of stone projectile points, although points in materials like bone, wood or ivory may well have existed (Plate 56). Bone artefacts, likewise struck by direct percussion, are very plentiful and in some cases show signs of shaping by polishing. However, they may also have become polished with use.

On the whole, typology is flimsy, so much so that it is hard to establish at all, save in very general terms. The objective of the makers of the tools would appear to have been functionality rather than the creation of regular forms. A cutting or scraping edge obtained by chipping was enough. These tools may be regarded as non-specialized artefacts used for various primary purposes, and they indicate that this was probably a gathering stage with little hunting.

A few authors have raised the possiblity of a derivation of the tools from 'core and flake' industries brought from South-East Asia. In our opinion this equation is unrealistic, as technologically there would have been no flakes without cores and no cores without the flakes that had been chipped off them. This is a binomial expression found throughout lithic cultures. To speak of a core and flake industry as something distinct and separate would therefore be inappropriate, although admittedly some cultures made greater use of flakes and others of cores.

Representative sites of this horizon are few and in most cases have yielded few artefacts, yet the majority are

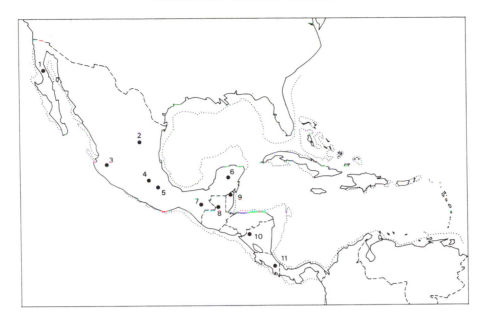

Map 28 Mexico and Central America in the Archaeolithic. ......, isobath of −100 m; ★, radiocarbon-dated sites. 1, Laguna Chapala★ (Baja California (Norte)); 2, El Cedral★ (San Luis Potosí); 3, Chapala-Zacoalco (Jalisco); 4, Tlapacoya★ (Estdao de Mexico); 5, Caulapan★ (Puebla); 6, Loltun★ (Yucatán); 7, Teopisca-Ahuacatenango★ (Chiapas); 8, Richmond Hill (Belize); 9, Río La Pasión (Guatemala); 10, El Bosque★ (Nicaragua); 11, Turrialba (Costa Rica).

radiocarbon dated and the remainder are included on account of the typological character of the pieces, despite the later dating. They are apparently not the only examples of a cultural backwater or a failure to evolve due to total adjustment to a way of life.

The geographical order that we have adopted in describing the sites progresses from north to south and from west to east – like writing on a page, as it were.

On the Baja California peninsula there are traces of what was once a medium-sized lagoon, Lake Chapala, which still collects water in some seasons. Its terraces, indicating former fluctuations in the water-level, have turned up a large number of stone artefacts. One of the terraces, lying 8.5 m above the bed of the lagoon, has yielded a date of about 14,600 years ago (Ritter, 1976) in a limestone crust, which suggests that when the crust formed the water was below that level and created the third terrace at 4.5 m. This explains why the cultural material associated with the second terrace is of an earlier date and consists of large bifacial tools, flakes that are also large, and the choppers and cutters that in fact predominated (Arnold, 1957).

On the Amapola Ranch in El Cedral, San Luis Potosí, hearths dated to about 31,000 to 21,000 years ago have been found, and a discoid scraper from a stratum dated to about 33,000 years ago. Other items include bone and stone artefacts with dates varying between 25,000 and 17,000 years ago, these being the dates of the strata in which they were found (Lorenzo and Alvarez, 1979; Lorenzo and Mirambell, 1978, 1979, 1980, 1982, 1983).

The central region of the state of Jalisco has yielded a total of thirty bone artefacts described by Solórzano (1976). Fifteen came from the shores of Lake Chapala, and as many from Lake Zacoalco. All show signs of having been fashioned by striking, polishing and perforation, and are highly mineralized. The same author (Solórzano, 1962) reported other artefacts and some human bone fragments with a similar degree of mineralization. The human remains were a lower right second large molar, belonging to an individual at least 50 years old, and a fragment of a right jawbone with what

may be the second premolar. Both specimens were found in the region of Lake Chapala and are highly mineralized.

On a Pleistocene shore of what was formerly Lake Chalco in Tlapacoya near Mexico City, radiocarbon dates have placed two hearths at about 24,000 and 22,000 years ago, respectively. In direct association with the two hearths and one other, undated, were accumulations of bones, including those of animals now extinct, three obsidian blades, whose dating according to their degree of hydration was found to tally with the radiocarbon assessment, and two carved bones (Lorenzo, 1972; Mirambell, 1978; Lorenzo and Mirambell, 1984).

To the north of the Valsequillo dam near Puebla, in an alluvial layer in the gorge of Caulapan, a side-scraper was found, associated with molluscs in the same layer dated to about 22,000 years ago (Szabo et al., 1969). Discovery of a group of very ancient stone artefacts in the region of Teopisca-Aguacatenango in the highlands of the State of Chiapas (Lorenzo, 1977a) promoted subsequent excavation. Guevara Sánchez (1981), after examining the surface materials on the shores of Lake Aguacatenango, outlined a typical industry, which García-Bárcena pursued further with more excavations. This revealed two horizons of occupation for the same industry, with very few variants and the peculiarity that the older of the two is associated with Pleistocene fauna, mammoth and extinct horse (García-Bárcena, 1982).

Excavations in Yucatán at Huechil in the Loltun caves complex brought to light Pleistocene fauna, *Equus conversidens* and *Bison bison* among other species, together with traces of a great many human occupations and a flint industry. The tephrite layer underlying these finds has been identified as Roseau's volcanic ash, which originated in Dominica, dating from 30,000 years ago. So far no datable material has been found in the layers indicating occupations (personal communication from the excavator, N. González Crespo).

The industry of Teopisca-Aguacatenango appears to have extended as far as Belize, since a site called Richmond Hill (Puleston, 1975) has yielded retouched flakers, scrapers and

311

denticulates but no stone projectile points. All the items tend to be small, of a size comparable with those of Teopisca-Aguacatenango. The same industry has also been found in the north of Belize, along with others of more recent date (MacNeish et al., 1980).

Even, without the knowledge derived from direct dating, when this can be done, the typological characteristics of this industry would warrant its inclusion, albeit tentative, in the Archaeolithic horizon. This may seem an over-simplification, but the evidence is systematic and coherent and it would be hard to apply another criterion without more and better information. Our theory is that some lithic traditions may have lasted over long periods of time.

When we leave Mexico and enter Central America, few finds can be attributed to the Archaeolithic horizon, and some of those that can are doubtful, such as the fossils of camel, mastodon, megatherium and glyptodon and the stone flakes yielded by the river La Pasión in Peten in Guatemala (Shook, 1961). One of the bones had three notches forming a V-shaped section, caused by a hard cutting object such as the edge of a blade.

In Nicaragua, in El Bosque, a collection of remains of Pleistocene fauna, eminently South American in character, was found together with a few stones (eoliths). Apatite analysis of these bones has given dates ranging from more than 32,000 to about 23,000 years ago (Espinosa, 1976).

Part of the stone collections found by Snarkis (1979) in Turrialba, Costa Rica, may well belong to the Archaeolithic period, but so far the evidence is not sufficient for us to form an opinion.

Owing to their rarity and the importance of their dates which corroborate the very early presence of human beings in the region, the sites of the Archaeolithic period have been discussed in detail. This will not be feasible for the other horizons, where the sites become increasingly numerous as time advances and more complex in their cultural content.

LOWER CENOLITHIC (Map 29)

It is still hard to establish the phases of transition in the Lithic Period, and much simpler to identify the horizons by their periods of highest development. Where the transition from the Archaeolithic to the Lower Cenolithic is concerned, however, the problem does not arise, because the change is total, indeed there are no lines of development leading from one horizon to another, but just an abrupt break, a complete transformation.

In theory, this may lead us to suppose that we are dealing with another people, a human group or groups of different cultural origin. The idea is legitimate in so far as the peoples who could have crossed the Bering Strait between 64,000 and 45,000 years ago may have been followed by others between 35,000 and 10,000 years ago. The bringers of what we call the Archaeolithic culture could therefore have arrived in the earliest times and proceeded unhindered to the south; those of the Lower Cenolithic Period would have reached the areas and a possible route southwards later.

Whatever the cause of the change, and regardless of the importance to be attached to the foregoing hypothesis, the fact remains that there is concrete evidence of a new way of life, represented by artefacts far more elaborate than those of the earlier horizon. The period begins 14,000 years ago and ends 9,000 years ago and, in the light of existing knowledge, has also been called the stage of the 'megafauna hunters'. Archaeologically this is the most salient feature for which

there is proof, but if we bear in mind the efficacy of the projectiles and the means of propulsion available at that time, the slaying of a mammoth or a mastodon cannot have been frequent. In all likelihood it was the result of teamwork, luring the animal into a swampy zone or gorge where it would be powerless and soon overcome. If this were so, as is possible, such an activity cannot be elevated to the category of basic cultural pattern.

The gradual improvement in climate characteristic of the Lower Cenolithic horizon brought about the steady retreat of the glaciers and culminated in the end of the Pleistocene and the beginning of the Holocene. This signified wide-spread changes in flora and fauna and, in consequence, human adaptation to new methods of working and new ways of life.

Among the objects distinguishing the Lower Cenolithic are fluted points, the earliest being Clovis points. These were followed chronologically by Folsom and fish-tail points (Plate 57).

Though less distinctive, other projectile points belonging to the same horizon show angular notches at the base, sometimes forming a stem, or notching on one side only, in a manner recalling that of the Solutrean points. Finally, some bifacial and leaf-shaped points, the simplest way of making a point and affording scope for many variants by retouching, date from the same period.

It is important to remember that very many finds corresponding to the Lower Cenolithic come from North America and from sites fairly rich in materials. The flint industry produced side- and end-scrapers, blades, retouched flakes, gravers, burins and miscellaneous artefacts as well as the classic fluted and other points. There are also bone perforators and scrapers and bone and ivory projectile points with hafts in the same materials, very similar to those of the Aurignacian in the European Upper Palaeolithic, although this does not mean that there was any form of contact or relation between them. Secondary human burials with bones dyed with red ochre have also been found.

In Mexico and Central America, most of the discoveries belonging to this horizon are surface finds. They have been attributed to the Lower Cenolithic on account of their fluted points, since their other attributes are not clearly defined.

Guided by that definition, García Bárcena, who carried out a detailed analysis (1979; 1982) of the North American Clovis point ranging from 11,500 to 10,800 years ago, found two fundamental types: the typical Clovis point and the Clovis point with concave sides, as well as a pentagonal-shaped variant of the former. Typical Clovis points have been found in central and western North America and as far as Turrialba in Costa Rica, across the western highlands of Mexico and Central America; they are most densely concentrated in north-west Mexico, northern Baja California and Sonora.

The pentagonal Clovis point from the south-western part of North America seems to have taken the same route but penetrated no further than western-central Mexico.

Clovis points with concave sides have been found throughout the region from western-central Mexico to Guatemala.

The so-called fish-tail points with a stem shaped by concave lateral retouch in the lower third but not at the base, itself slightly concave, show some fluting on one side or both. These were once thought to be variants of the Clovis points, but are now believed to have originated in South America, possibly in the Paraná basin, in view of the plentiful finds in that zone (Schobinger, 1973). From there they seem

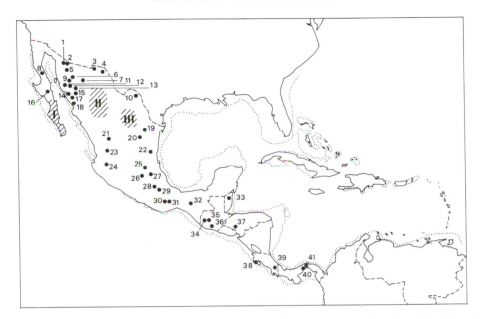

Map 29 Mexico and Central America in the Lower Cenolithic: ......, isobath of −100 m; ★, radiocarbon-dated sites. I, Las Palmas Culture (Baja California (Sur)); II, Cazador Complex (Chihuahua); III, Ciénegas Complex (Coahuila). 1, El Plombo (Sonora); 2, Sásabe (Sonora); 3, Rancho Colorado (Chihuahua); 4, Samalayucan (Chihuahua); 5, La Playa (Sonora); 6, El Bajio (Sonora); 7, Huasabas (Sonora); 8, Laguna Chapala (Baja California (Norte)); 9, Pozo Valdés (Sonora); 10, La Chuparrosa (Coahuila); 11, Los Janos (Sonora); 12, Cerro Izabal (Sonora); 13, Rancho Pimas y Aigame (Sonora); 14, Tastiota (Sonora); 15, Las Peñitas (Sonora); 16, S. Joaquin (Baja California (Sur)); 17, Cerro Prieto (Sonora); 18, Cerro Guaymas (Sonora); 19, Puntita Negra (Sonora); 20, La Calzada★ (Nuevo León); 21, Sitio Wicker (Durango); 22, Cueva del Diablo★ (Tamaulipas); 23, San Sebastian Teponahuastlan (Jalisco); 24, Zacoalco y San Marcos (Jalisco); 25, Tecolote (Hildago); 26, San Bartolo Atepehuacan★ (Federal District); 27, San Juan Chaucingo★ (Tlaxcala); 28, El Riego★ (Puebla); 29, Coxcatlan★ (Puebla); 30, Cueva Blanca★ (Oaxaca); 31, Guila Naquitz★ (Oaxaca); 32, Los Grifos★ (Chiapas); 33, Sand Hill and Ladyville (Belize); 34, Los Tapiales, Piedra del Coyote★ (Guatemala); 35, Quiche (Guatemala); 36, Sn Rafael (Guatemala); 37, La Esperanza (Honduras); 38, Las Huacas (Costa Rica); 39, Turrialba (Costa Rica); 40, Balboa (Panama); 41, Lago Madden (Panama).

to have spread as far as Patagonia, where the finds show dates similar to those of the North American Clovis point, about 11,000 years ago, and subsequently to have reached the south of Mexico, in particular Los Grifos shelter, Chiapas, about 9,000 years ago. We have some information on these points found in association with Folsom points in New Mexico (personal communication by Dr Dennis Stanford).

The other typical fluted point is the Folsom point, generally smaller than the Clovis, flatter and sometimes with a small projection at the centre of the notch in the base. Folsom points have been dated to between 11,000 and 9,800 years ago and did not penetrate into Mexico to any great extent, even in the north.

The typical Clovis points found in Mexico come from San Joaquín (Baja California (Sur)), Cerro Guaymas, Pozo Valdés, Las Peñitas, San José de Pimas, Cerro de Izabel, El Aigame and Cerro Prieto (all in Sonora); San Juan Chaucingo, Tlaxcala, Ladyville (the most easterly part of Belize); Los Tapiales and Sacapulas (Guatemala); and Turrialba (Costa Rica).

The variant of this, the pentagonal point, is represented in Tastiota Los Janos, El Bajio and Huasabe (Sonora) and San Sebastián Teponahustlan and San Marcos (Jalisco).

Clovis points with concave sides are found from Sitio Weicker (Durango, Mexico), Los Grifos (Chiapas, Mexico) to San Rafael and Santa Rosa Chujub (Guatemala), Las Huacas and Turrialba (Costa Rica), and Lake Madden (Panama).

The order of siting should be reversed in the case of the fish-tail points, starting in the south, since they came from South America and therefore travelled from south to north. They have been found at Lake Madden and Balboa (Panama), in Turrialba (Costa Rica), La Esperanza (Honduras), Sand

Hill and Ladyville (Belize) and Los Grifos (Chiapas, Mexico) as well as the points already mentioned found in New Mexico (United States).

Folsom points follow chronologically, although they also overlap to a great extent and, as already stated, the finds outside North America are very scarce and even somewhat dubious. The sites, lying in the far north of Mexico only, are La Mota Samalayucan (Chihuahua), La Chuparrosa (Coahuila) and Puntita Negra (Nuevo León), the most southerly area.

As far as we know, the distribution of fluted points obeys a definite pattern: they are found in the highlands. This may be a sign of adaptation to a given ecosystem, in the course of which there was movement from north to south. Fish-tail points, as we have seen, fall into a separate category and follow a south-to-north movement.

More sites unassociated with fluted points have been attributed to the same horizon by their dating, the stratigraphic position of certain materials and their link with Pleistocene fauna. They are as follows: Mexico: Lake Chapala (northern Baja California), Las Palmas culture (Baja California (Sur)), Cazador complex (Chihuahua), Ciénagas and Coahuila complexes (Coahuila), La Calzada (Nuevo León), Diablo cave and the first phase of the coastal complex (Tamaulipas), El Tecolote cave (Hidalgo), San Bartolo Atepehuacan (Federal District), El Riego and Coxcatlan (Puebla), Blanca and Guila Naquitz caves (Oaxaca); Guatemala: Piedra del Coyote.

In the arid zones some of these sites have yielded fairly plentiful remains of artefacts made of organic material such as wood and plant fibres; leather, nets, sandals, bags, various rope artefacts and baskets, and many more, including simple, small wooden objects made from twigs or bushes. Stone artefacts have also been discovered: scrapers, blades, burins, denticulates, retouched flakes, bifacial knives and others, but scarcity of sites has prevented any systematic study of the areas occupied by these cultures and complexes.

Without a doubt, the passage from the Lower Cenolithic to the Upper Cenolithic was a transition period, not a break. With the discovery of more productive sites it will appear as a horizon displaying typical features of the Lower Cenolithic in increasing association with those of the Upper Cenolithic.

The Upper Cenolithic horizon brings us into the Holocene, although the intermediate phase was of long duration in the lower latitudes and the change properly so called took place about 7,000 years ago.

shape, and there is a remarkable proliferation of stemmed projectile points with ear-like projections, which leaves open the distinct possibility that bows and arrows may have been in use (Plate 58). Milling implements appear, both mortars and querns, and a variety of tools attesting to the techniques of stone polishing. The technological complexity of the time is undeniable, judging by the many different types of tools that existed, and it is possible that at this stage the foundations of ethnic differences began to be laid.

With the disappearance of the Pleistocene fauna, gathering seems to have prospered proportionately, including the collecting of snails, reptiles, amphibia and other species by means of a cane or a sharp stick. The first steps were taken

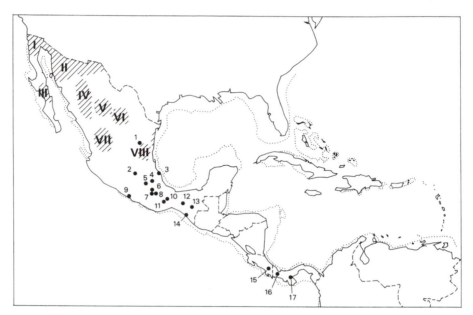

Map 30 Mexico and Central America in the Upper Cenolithic: ......, isobath of −100 m; ★, radiocarbon-dated sites. I, San Dieguito complex★ (Baja California (Norte)); II, Cochise complex★ (Baja California (Norte), Sonora and north of Chihuahua); III, Comodu culture★ (Baja California (Sud)); IV, Per. Forrajero★ (Chihuahua); V, Las Nievas culture (Chihuahua and y Coahuila); VI, Joa and Mairan complexes★ (Coahuila); VII, Caracoles and Las Chivas cultures★ (Durango and Zacatecas); VIII, Nogales, Ocampo and La Perra complexes★ (Tamaulipas). 1, Sn Isidro★ (Nuevo León); 2, San Nicolas (Querétaro); 3, Centro de Veracruz★; 4, Tecolote (Hidalgo); 5, Santa Isabel Iztapan I and II★ (Estado de Mexico); 6, El Riego★ (Puebla); 7, Abejas★ (Puebla); 8, Coxcatlan★ (Puebla); 9, Tecpan★ (Guerrero); 10, Guila Naquitz★ (Oaxaca); 11, Cueva Blanca★ (Oaxaca); 12, Los Grifos and Santa Marta★ (Chiapas); 13, Aguacatenango★ (Chiapas); 14, Chantuto★ (Chiapas); 15, Turrialba (Costa Rica); 16, Chiriqui★ (Chiapas); 17, Cerro Mogote★ (Panama).

UPPER CENOLITHIC (Map 30)

This marks a clear development from the previous horizon. Without any doubt, the diversity in representations and items of everyday use was the result of the improvement in climate distinguishing the Holocene from the Pleistocene. The far-reaching changes in flora and fauna brought a modification of the systems and techniques of acquisition and above all a transformation of subsistence raw materials, and hence new methods of treating them. The swing away from a gathering towards a hunting economy apparent in the Lower Cenolithic seems to have been reversed to some extent, with greater use being made of plant resources. However, this may also be explained by the fact that our evidence of these possible modifications consists almost exclusively of the remains of material culture, the comparatively recent date of which has allowed more organic material to be preserved than in earlier horizons.

The Upper Cenolithic horizon has yielded a quantity of stone items struck by heavy percussion and by pressure techniques, which may have been in existence since the late Lower Cenolithic. Care has been taken over both finish and

in the domestication of plants such as squash, chili, amaranth, maize and perhaps beans (Chapter 57). It is also likely that milling implements had several uses and were not solely employed for the preparation of cultivated plant products.

It is difficult, even so, to set a specific date for the transition from one horizon to another. In view of the survival of many elements, this period may be regarded as stretching, broadly speaking, from 9,000 to 7,000 years ago.

The large number of sites yielding distinctive features for this horizon suggests that there was a definite increase in the population, or else that these sites have been more easily located, which would not be incompatible with the former conclusion.

Only a few of the plentiful sites are mentioned here, but all those known are shown on the map. No clear boundaries have been determined for the complexes and cultures named. This is to some extent natural, since poor communications and sparse population in the areas where they are found have restricted the scope of research and also rendered it very costly.

During the Upper Cenolithic, northern Mexico belonged to the cultures found in what is now the south and southeast of North America, since they were affected by the same ecosystems. As this had been an arid or semi-arid zone for several thousands of years, finds of archaeological remains of organic materials are frequent, especially in caves, and enrich our knowledge of the material culture of human groups which, for the most part, remained at the same stage of development until the sixteenth, seventeenth or eighteenth centuries of the Christian era, depending on the region, when they came into contact with the Spaniards.

Proceeding from north to south and from west to east, we encounter the first site in the form of the San Dieguito complex, phase II in north Baja California. Further south, it borders on the Comondu culture in south Baja California. The Cochise complex, known locally as the Peralta complex, stretches eastwards towards Sonora, and the Forrajero culture of plant gatherers lies even further to the east in Chihuahua. The Las Nieves culture, with evidence of a fishing industry, covers the area to the south as far as Durango and to the east as far as Coahuila. The Las Chivas culture, derived from its equivalent in North America, is found in the northern part of Chihuahua.

Derivative or local forms of what are called the Cochise and Desert cultures in the south-west of North America are found throughout the region. The term is odd, because at the time when the culture formed and spread, the land was not as desert-like as it is now.

Near Coahuila, to the east of the previous zone, are the late Jora and Mayrán cultural complexes, and in Tamaulipas the Los Nogales, Ocampo and La Perra complexes, as well as the coastal variant.

The site of San Isidro in Nuevo Léon can also be ascribed to this horizon, but beyond it there is a great gap in our knowledge as far south as the San Nicolás cave in Querétaro. Two sites, Santa Isabel Ixtapan I and II, in the Federal District, have been included on account of their associated materials although there is also evidence of mammoths.

Then there is El Tecolote cave in Hidalgo and a coastal variant in central Veracruz, similar but not identical to the finds from a shell-mound on the coast of Guerrero, in Tecpan.

The sites of Texcal, Coxcatlan, Abejas and El Riego in the State of Puebla have yielded much material of similar type to that found in the Guila Naquitz and Blanca caves in Oaxaca.

Two different types of environment characterize Chiapas, the highlands with the upper phase of Los Grifos, Santa Marta and Aguacatenango and the coasts centred round the Chantuto shell-mound. It is very likely that the use of coastal resources and the salt lagoons was merely a seasonal occupation for inland peoples.

All the above-mentioned sites are in Mexico. Entering Central America, to the south and south-east, we find Pedra del Coyote in Guatemala, La Esperanza in Honduras, some material from the great site of Turrialba in Costa Rica, and again two different aspects, one inland, in the upper basin of the river Chiriquí, and the other in the coastal zone of Cerro Mangote and Monagrillo in Panama.

No less than 30,000 years or so of human presence in what is now Mexico, Belize, Guatemala, Honduras, El Salvador, Nicaragua, Costa Rica and Panama have been summed up in this chapter.

BIBLIOGRAPHY

ALVÁREZ, T.; CASAMIQUELA, R.; POLACO, O. 1977. *Informe de la 1er temporada de excavaciones realizadas en El Cedral, SLP.* México, DF, INAH.

ARNOLD, B. A. 1957. Late Pleistocene and Recent Changes in Land Form, Climate and Archaeology in Central Baja California. *Univ. Calif. Pub. Geogr.* (Berkeley), Vol. 10, No. 4, pp. 201–318.

BANERJEE, U. C.; BARGHOORN, E. S. 1972. Fine Structure of Pollen Grain Ektextine of Maize, Teosinte and Tripsacum. In: *Thirtieth Annual Proceedings of the Electro-Microscopy Society of America.* Los Angeles. pp. 226–7.

BARGHOORN, E. S.; WOLFE, M. K.; CLISBY, K. H. 1954. Fossil Maize from the Valley of Mexico. *Bot. Mus. Leafl., Harv. Univ.* (Cambridge, Mass.), Vol. 16, pp. 229–40.

BEADLE, G. W. 1977. The Origin of *Zea mays.* In: REED, C. A. (ed.), *Origins of Agriculture.* The Hague. pp. 615–35.

—— 1980. The Ancestry of Corn. *Sci. Am.*, Vol. 242, pp. 96–103.

DANIEL, G. E. 1981. *A Short History of Archaeology.* London.

ESPINOSA ESTRADA, J. 1976. *Excavaciones arqueológicas en 'El Bosque'.* Managua.

GALINAT, W. C. 1975. The Evolutionary Emergence of Maize. *Bull. Torrey Bot. Club*, Vol. 102, No. 5, pp. 313–24.

—— 1977. The Origin of Corn. In: SPRAGUE, F. (ed.), *Corn and Corn Improvement.* Madison. pp. 1–47.

GARCÍA-BÁRCENA, J. 1979. *Una Punta Acanalada de la Cueva Los Grifos, Ocozocoautla, Chiapas.* Mexico, DF, INAH.

—— 1982. *El Precerámico de Aguacatenango, Chiapas, México.* Mexico.

GUEVARA SÁNCHEZ, A. 1981. *Los Talleres líticos de Aguatenango, Chiapas.* Mexico.

LORENZO, J. L. 1972. Problèmes du peuplement de l'Amérique à la lumière des découvertes de Tlapacoya. In: UNESCO. *Proceedings of the Colloquium on the Homo sapiens Origins.* Paris. pp. 261–4.

—— 1977a. *Un conjunto lítico de Teopisca, Chiapas.* Mexico, DF, INAH.

—— 1977b. Agroecosistemas prehistóricos. In: HERNANDEZ XOCOLOTZI, E. (ed.), *Agrocistemas de México: contribuciones a la enseñanza, investigación y divulgación agrícola.* Chapingo, Collegio de Postgraduados.

—— 1986. Conclusiones. In: LORENZO, J. L.; MIRAMBELL, L. (eds), *Treintaicinco mil años del Lago de Chalco.* Mexico, DF, INAH. pp. 225–87.

LORENZO, J. L.; ALVAREZ, T. 1979. Presencia del Hombre en México hace mas de 30,000 años. *Cienc. Desarrolo.* Mexico, Vol. 26, pp. 114–15.

LORENZO, J. L.; MIRAMBELL, L. 1978. *Informe de 2a. temporada de excavaciones realizadas en El Cedral, San Luis Potosí.* Mexico.

—— 1979. *Informe de la 3a. temporada de excavaciones realizadas en El Cedral, San Luis Potosí.* Mexico.

—— 1980. *Informe de la 4a. temporada de excavaciones realizadas en El Cedral, San Luis Potosí.* Mexico.

—— 1982. *Informe de la 5a. temporada de excavaciones realizadas en El Cedral, San Luis Potosí.* Mexico.

—— 1983. *Informe de la 6a. temporada de excavaciones realizadas en El Cedral, San Luis Potosí.* Mexico.

—— 1984. *Informe de la 7a. temporada de excavaciones realizadas en El Cedral, San Luis Potosí.* Mexico.

MACNEISH, R. S. (ed.) 1972. *The Prehistory of the Tehuacan Valley. 4. Chronology and Irrigation.* Austin.

MACNEISH, R. S.; WILKERSON, S. J.; NELKEN, A. 1980. *First Annual Report on the Belize Archaeological Reconnaisance.* Andover.

MIRAMBELL, L. 1978. Tlapacoya: A Late Pleistocene Site in Central Mexico. In: BRYAN, A. L. (ed.), *Early Man in America from a Circum-Pacific Perspective.* Edmonton. pp. 221–30.

MORGAN, J. DE. 1947. *La humanidad prehistórica.* Barcelona. (Trad. 2nd French edn.)

OBERMAIER, H. 1925. *El hombre fosil.* 2nd edn. Madrid.

PICKERSGILL, B. 1977. Taxonomy and the Origin and Evolution of Cultivated Plants in the New World. *Nature* (London), Vol. 268, No. 5621, pp. 591–5.

PULESTON, D. E. 1975. Richmond Hill, a Probable Early Man Site in the Maya Lowlands. In: *Acts XLI Congr. Intern. Americas.* Mexico, DF. Vol. 1, pp. 522–33.

RITTER, E. W. 1976. The Antiquity of Man in the Laguna Seca Chapala Basin of Baja California. *Pacific Coast Archaeol. Soc. Quart.*, Vol. 12, No. 1, pp. 39–46.

SCHOBINGER, J. 1973. Nuevos hallazgos de puntas 'Cola de Pescado' y consideraciones en torno al origen y dispersión de la cultura de los cazadores superiores toldense (Fell II) en Sudamérica. In: *Atti XL Congr. Intern. Americ.* Rome. Vol. 1, pp. 33–50.

SHOOK, E. M. 1961. The Present Status of Research in the Preclassic Horizons of Guatemala. In: TAX, S. (ed.), *The Civilizations of Ancient America.* Chicago. pp. 93–100. (Selected papers XXIX Int. Congr. Americanists.)

SNARKIS, M. J. 1979. Turrialba: A Paleoindian Quarry and Workshop Site in Eastern Costa Rica. *Amer. Antiq.,* Vol. 44, No. 1, pp. 125–38.

SOLÓRZANO, F. A. 1962. *Reporte preliminar sobre el estudio de artefactos y huesos humanos fosilizados procedentes dela zona de Chapala.* Guadalajara.

—— 1976. *Artefactos prehistóricos de huseco del Occidente de México.* Guadalajara.

SZABO, B. J.; MALDE, H.; IRWIN-WILLIAMS, C. 1969. Dilemma Posed by Uranium Series Dates of Archaeological Significant Bones from Valsequillo, Puebla, Mexico. *Earth and Planetary Science Letters,* Amsterdam, Vol. 6, pp. 237–44.

WEST, R. C. 1964. The Natural Regions of Middle America. In: WAUCHOPE, R. (ed.), *Handbook of Middle American Indians.* Vol. 1, pp. 363–83.

WILKES, M. G. 1967. *Teosinte: The Closest Relative to Maize.* Cambridge.

WILLEY, G. R.; PHILLIPS, P. 1958. *Methods and Theory in American Archaeology.* Chicago.

CENTRAL AMERICA, THE CARIBBEAN, NORTHERN SOUTH AMERICA AND THE AMAZON

The way of life of the ancient hunters

Mario Sanoja Obediente

Human groups first entered the South American subcontinent by land across the Central American isthmus. Populations of ancient hunters seem to have migrated from North America, entering South America through the territory that now corresponds to the Republic of Colombia. From there, they seem to have travelled both towards the south, along the mountain chain and the coast of northwest South America until they arrived at the tip of the continent, and towards the north-east region of South America (Lynch, 1978, pp. 466–7).

In general, the remains left by these ancient groups show a considerable variety of artefacts, tool manufacturing techniques and ways of life. This suggests that the groups were not integrated as a culturally homogeneous population, but represented both technological traditions already known in Asia and North America and local cultural advances, technological traditions and economies that developed during the process of adaptation to the different environments characterizing the geography of Central America and northern South America. The economies that evolved in the region developed increasingly complex subsistence practices which culminated in the appearance of sedentary agricultural societies. These formed the economic basis that was to characterize the early agricultural and pottery-making societies of northern South America and of Central America.

PHYSICAL CHARACTERISTICS OF THE FIRST INHABITANTS

The work undertaken by Peter W. Lund in the State of Minas Gerais, Brazil, towards the middle of the last century drew attention to the existence of human remains in the Soumidouro caves in the Lagoa Santa region, which were estimated to be at least 10,000 years old (Hurt and Blasi, 1969). At the time, Lund stated that these remains were associated with fossil fauna; at present, it is not possible to confirm this association in the absence of stratigraphic checking of his work. Current research, however, has made it possible to determine the presence of a level with an extinct Quaternary fauna in various caves in the region where a very rudimentary quartz flake industry has been found. The anthropometric analysis of the Lagoa Santa skulls in Brazil is 74.56 for the horizontal cranial index, placing them in the dolichocranial category (Steward and Newman, 1950). These authors also confirm the significant dolichocephaly of a series of skulls studied in Tierra del Fuego, Argentina, and in Ecuador, Guyana and Paraguay.

Additional data have come from the excavation of dwelling sites of the hunter-gatherer groups of Colombia by Correal and Van der Hammen (1977) and by Correal (1979). These authors found a series of graves in clearly defined cultural contexts in the rock shelters of Tequendama. In virtually all cases the skulls had a horizontal cranial index of less than 74.9, which places them in the dolichocranial category. The Tequendama skeletons go back 8,000 years, a date which correlates with the skull discovered by Correal in the Sueva cave, which is also dolichocephalic and dates back to ten millennia ago (Correal, 1979, p. 240). The lithic industry found in the context of these caves is also very rudimentary, particularly the artefacts obtained by flaking a stone core, as are the bone implements.

These associations are important since they could indicate the possible presence of ancient groups of hunters who shared specific physical characteristics and also, in several cases, a technical tradition for the very rudimentary manufacture of stone tools.

CULTURAL EVIDENCE

The cultural evidence indicating the early presence of humans in the area under study reflects many of the questions emerging from the examination of the remains left by the ancient hunting societies of North America. These include the existence of an undifferentiated lithic industry horizon, to which Krieger gave the name of the 'pre-projectile point horizon' (1962, pp. 130–43). This apparently precedes the bifacial laminar industries usually associated with the hunting of large fauna.

Without entering into discussion on the chronological issue, it would seem clear that non-specialized economic or technical traditions existed, as well as industries specialized in the manufacture of tools for specific purposes within the subsistence activities of the ancient hunting and gathering societies. However, the absence of projectile points manufactured in stone does not prove that there were no pointed artefacts with a similar function. As indicated further on, sites linked with this tradition of undifferentiated tools also exist in Colombia, associated with the hunting of large Pleistocene fauna in periods of similar date (Correal, 1981).

It can be concluded from the above that two major technical traditions in the manufacture of artefacts existed side by side, at least in the area under study: one defined by crudely manufactured, multi-purpose tools, without stone projectile points, which may have developed specialized artefacts of fibrous raw materials (bone, wood and so on), and the other identified by laminar bifacially flaked artefacts, with stone projectile points, for all of which the basic raw material was stone. These in fact represent different economic practices which imply different subsistence strategies within the way of life characteristic of the ancient hunters.

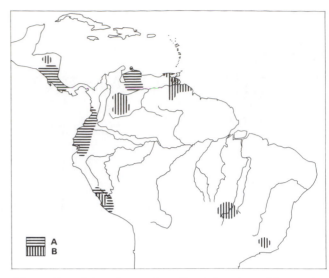

Map 31 Central America, northern South America and Amazonia: A, bifacial blade industries; B, undifferentiated industries.

Table 10 Chronologic position of the most important sites relating to early hunter-gatherer communities: italic type, undifferentiated industries; roman type, laminar bifacial industries.

Years BP	Mesoamerica	Venezuela	Colombia	Brazil
3000				
4000				
5000				
6000		*Guayana-Ño Carlos*		
			Chía	
7000		*Tpukén*		
	Cofradía			
8000	*Alajuela (Madden)*			
	Acahualinca	La Hundicion		
9000		Las Mesas	*Nemocón*	
			Sueva	*Tapajóz*
10,000				*Lagoa Santa*
				Abrigo do Sol
11,000				
12,000				
		Montecano	Tequendama	
13,000		Manzanillo	El Abra	
		Taima-Taima		
14,000		El Jobo		
18,000				
20,000				
28,000	*El Bosque*			

LITHIC TRADITIONS

The tradition of non-specialized lithic artefacts in Central America (Table 10 and Map 31)

The most northerly evidence of the presence of ancient hunting groups in Central America was found at the El Bosque site, near Pueblo Nuevo in the Estelí district of north-west Nicaragua (Espinoza, 1976). The stratigraphic features of the site indicate the presence of a lower layer containing numerous bones of large mammals identified by

Miller and Lundelius (1976) as belonging to the species of *Eremotherium* (a huge ground-sloth), *Megalonychil* (a species of horse) and *Odocoileus* (deer), and also bones of Chelonians and small mammals. The artefacts associated with these fauna were manufactured in chert, flaked in a very rudimentary fashion, in particular unifacial tabular flakes. According to various scientists who took part in excavating the site, many of the supposed stone artefacts at El Bosque could have been produced by the mechanical action of the rocks and large boulders on the site, although others consider that the source of raw material for these artefacts is not local, implying that it could have been brought to the site by human activity (Gruhn, 1976).

The radiocarbon dates obtained from the El Bosque material were obtained from apatite from the bones, and form a series dating from 22,600 back to at least 32,000 years ago. These dates have been queried by various authors, although other assays, this time on the basis of carbon samples, have produced dates between 10,100 and 35,000 years ago (Page, 1978, pp. 252–6).

The tradition of bifacial lithic artefacts in Central America (Map 31)

Other important evidence related to the life of the hunting and gathering societies of Nicaragua is found in the frequent presence of human footprints in fresh volcanic mud deposits which formed near Lakes Managua and Nicaragua. One of these deposits is at the Acahualinca site (Flint, 1885; Matillo, 1977), on the outskirts of the city of Managua.

Excavations carried out at this site in 1874 brought to light the existence of footprints of possibly a small group of individuals composed apparently of children and adults. Some of them seem to have been carrying heavy loads which they were transporting with them during their journey towards the shores of Lake Managua. This is demonstrated by the different depth of the footprints and their size.

In other similar deposits in the region, the footprints of members of such groups of people are found along with those of bison and other mammals, which may have been among the fauna hunted by them.

Authors such as Crawford (1891, pp. 160–6) claim that in Acahualinca they found remains of projectile points and stone axes associated with the volcanic mud layer containing the human footprints. Unfortunately these finds, if they existed, were not preserved.

Alan Bryan (1973) obtained an absolute dating for the layer in which the Acahualinca human footsteps were found, by using earth lying below the level of the deposit. This indicated that the assumed hunters and gatherers travelled towards the shores of the lake around 8,000 years ago (Matillo Vila, 1977, pp. 57–8), a time at which, for other contemporary hunting and gathering societies such as those in the north of Colombia (see below), it is suggested that there were the best possible climatic conditions and a relative increase in the animal resources on which they subsisted.

Although the remains have not yet provided more information, it can be reliably argued that there were groups of early hunter-gatherers on the Pacific coast of Nicaragua, associated with extinct fauna such as bison.

Collections of lithic artefacts at the Instituto de Patrimonio Cultural de Nicaragua that have not yet been examined indicate the presence at the Cofradía site in the Pacific region of a complex of bifacial artefacts chipped from flint which includes oval blanks, flaked cores, large flakes, some with retouched sides, biface lanceolate points, uniface end-scrapers and triangular bifaces, generally worked with the flat flaking technique. The general aspect of the artefact complex is reminiscent of the bifacial tradition of El Jobo in north-west Venezuela in the morphology of the objects and in the flaking technique, providing potentially significant cultural evidence concerning the likely association between bands of hunters and extinct fauna such as bison.

In Costa Rica there appears to be no evidence of human presence earlier than 13,000 years ago. Remains from that date were found at the Turrialba site, on the eastern slope of the Costa Rican central cordillera, at an altitude of 700 m above sea-level, above the ravines formed on the banks of the Reventazón river.

The remains include eighteen complete or broken elongated projectile points, as well as blanks, keeled, side and unguiform scrapers, blades and burins. In addition, stone artefacts that could belong typologically to later periods were found in Costa Rica and Nicaragua, and a pottery site, El Bosque, where atypical assemblages of flint artefacts have also been found. Among these should be noted the stemmed or triangular projectile points characteristic of the gatherer groups of Panama or of the Costa Rican potters (Snarkis, 1984).

In Panama the most important collection of remains associated with the early presence of man has been located in the sediment of Lake Alajuela (or Madden) (Bird and Cooke, 1977, 1978). One of the projectile points, apparently located in its context, seems to indicate that the hunter tried to capture a prey in the waters or on the banks of the Chagras river. Since no evidence exists of large fauna associated with these finds, it could be considered that the ancient hunters of Lake Alajuela also tried to capture the fauna that frequented the shores of the lake or lived in the water of its tributaries.

According to Bird and Cooke, the fish-tail projectile points from Lake Madden seem to have most morphological and technological similarity to those discovered at El Inga, Ecuador, Cueva Fell and Pallí Aike, near the Magellan Straits, and others found in Brazil, Uruguay and Peru. This would show that these groups of hunters were associated with the fish-tail projectile point tradition that – according to several authors – developed in the southern tip of South America as a kind of parallel or independent invention to those found as far away as North America (Meyer-Oakes, 1974, 1981). Although no absolute dates exist for the Lake Madden discoveries, the fact that similar implements are not found in the more recent archaeological sites associated with the gatherer groups of the interior of Panama seems to indicate that they are of considerable antiquity.

The tradition of bifacial lithic artefacts in northern South America

The fish-tail projectile-point hunters in Colombia and Venezuela

In Colombia the presence of populations associated with the bifacial lithic artefact tradition has been indicated up to now only by isolated finds, which include fish-tail projectile points similar to those of Lake Madden and El Inga, and a great variety of stemmed points. These finds are distributed over an area from El Darién, the Colombian Atlantic coast and the Cauca valley to the Pacific Ocean. Méndez Gutiérrez (1984) describes various sites in the Cajibío district in the Cauca valley which contain crudely manufactured stemmed and fish-tail bifacial projectile points. He also describes a cultural sequence that could be interpreted as a progression towards more diversified forms of subsistence based on hunting and the gathering and processing of food of vegetable origin, which as already noted on p. 318 also occurred in other regions of South America.

Other research relating to the study of these groups of hunters associated with the fish-tail projectile-point tradition in South America is being undertaken currently by the Archaeological Museum of Quíbor near Lake Yai in the State of Lara, Venezuela (Pantel, 1983).

The deposit, called La Hundición, is situated in the mountains surrounding the Quíbor valley, at an altitude of 900 m above sea-level. These mountains form the northern foothills of the Venezuelan Andes, separated from the coastal cordillera by a series of interior valleys surrounded by low ranges.

The La Hundición site lies to the west of Sanare, capital of the Andrés Eloy Blanco district. Its co-ordinates are latitude 9°46'10" S and longitude 69°41'30" E. The site looks like a small depression in a limited concave section of land near Lake Yai. The floor of the depression is some 6 m below the surrounding surface.

In general the deposit looks like a very much eroded depression in which the ancient strata have been exposed by the action of run-off water. The floor of the depression was completely covered with pebbles from which it was possible to recover at the first excavation a fish-tail projectile point blank, uniface scrapers, oval biface scrapers and a large number of small flakes.

Most of the objects at La Hundición were manufactured from fine sandstone. Associated remains of fauna, later identified as the vertebrae and major bones of the species of *Eremotherium*, were found in the area surveyed.

During a second excavation of the site, soundings were taken around the collections of *Eremotherium* bones and shallow lithic material.

One of the most significant discoveries was a basal fragment of an elongated fish-tail projectile point made from fine-grained siliceous chert. It seems to be a classic example, resembling those already recorded in El Inga (Ecuador) and Cueva Fell (Chile). A borer and what appear to be two bifacially worked blanks were also found.

A large number of ribs were found in the main collection of faunal remains, possible evidence of the existence of a dwelling area, together with hearths, indicated by the matrix, like an ancient, burnt, grey-coloured soil, surrounding the bones.

The presence of abundant stone rejects of the same raw material as that from which the points were manufactured seems to indicate that the points could have been worked at the site. The way that the bone and stone remains are scattered suggests that this could have been a place for slaughtering animals. No absolute dates have been determined as yet, although the Smithsonian Institution in Washington (United States) is proceeding with datings based on the collagen in the bones. Other sites containing Pleistocene fauna, particularly mastodons and megatheria, located in the Quibor valley, have been dated on the basis of vegetable carbon samples at around 11,000 to 9,000 years ago. There are no associations however with the bone remains and stone material found in La Hundición.

THE HUNTERS OF THE JOBO CULTURE, VENEZUELA

One of the regions in the north of South America in which the largest accumulation of stone artefacts linked to the ancient hunting society has been found – and on which the most opposing views are held – is in the State of Falcón in north-west Venezuela, where the so-called El Jobo industry or tradition has been identified.

Research on the presence of ancient hunters started in 1956 (Royo y Gómez, 1956), when the existence of extensive fossiliferous beds was brought to light in the Muaco deposit. Their contents indicated the presence of mastodons, stegomastodons, megatheria, horses, glyptodons, toxodons, athocterium, cameloids, wolves, jaguars, lynxes, rabbits, mustelidae and mylodons. Some bones seem to bear traces of exposure to fire, or of deliberate cuts made with stone implements. A radiocarbon date of around 16,900 years ago was obtained, which was queried on account of the uncertainty of the stratigraphic context, clearly altered by the process of entrainment (Royo y Gómes, 1960a, 1960b; Cruxent, 1961; Lynch, 1978, p. 476).

The aim of this initial research was to prove that the people who had manufactured the El Jobo stone material were contemporary with the extinct fauna. Later research on these lines in the area uncovered a new deposit situated near the Cucuruchú river, which produced fragments of lanceolate projectile points of the El Jobo type in a layer of fossilized bones of *Haplomastodon guayanensis*, *Eremotherium rusconii* and *Glyptodon clavipedes* Owens, also disturbed by entrainment and deposited in a layer of Miocene–Pliocene clay much older than humans themselves. Setting aside the traces of the disturbance, it was considered that since this layer was sealed by a bed of lacustrine clay, it proved without doubt the association of the El Jobo lithic industry with large Pleistocene fauna (Cruxent, 1970). This hypothesis is criticized on the grounds that the context indicated only that the bones and the projectile points dated from earlier than the time at which the lacustrine clay was deposited, and that there was no evidence to indicate an association between the two elements (Bate, 1983, p. 11).

Further research was subsequently carried out at the Taima-Taima site, also in the State of Falcón, led by the specialized archaeologists Alan Bryan and Ruth Gruhn, together with J. M. Cruxent. They finally located the skeleton of a young *Haplomastodon*, partly dismembered and bearing traces of deliberate cuts, likely evidence of butchering. A quartzite projectile point of El Jobo type, a jasper

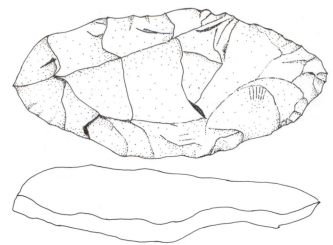

Figure 87 Biface, El Jobo industry, El Altico (Venezuela).

flake and a pointed stone were found inside the pelvic cavity of the mastodon. The remains of shoots ingested by the animal, which were still in its stomach at the moment of its death and were preserved by favourable soil conditions, were used to date the discovery. Carbon-14 assays gave dates of about 13,000, 13,200 and 13,900 years ago, that is 1,500 years earlier than existing dates for the mammoth hunters in North America who used Clovis projectile points (Bryan et al, 1978).

Another purpose of the study of the stone material associated with the way of life of the ancient hunters in the State of Falcón was to build a technological evolution model based on the investigation of the Pedregal river terraces carried out by Petzall (Cruxent and Rouse, 1963, p. 29; Bryan, 1973, p. 249). This was based on the collections of artefacts gathered near the surface in different parts of the terraces, and also on the nature of the discrete contexts in which they were found. The collections of artefacts appeared to demonstrate an evolutionary sequence which started with very crudely manufactured artefacts, of which the bifaces from the El Camare site represented the oldest stage of the process (Fig. 87), and included choppers (Fig. 88) and large chipped flakes, some of them looking like scrapers (Fig. 90). The so-called Las Lagunas complex, where smaller bifaces apparently existed, seemed to follow on from the El Camare site. The next complex, called El Jobo, was situated in the lowest terraces of the Pedregal river, and was identified by the presence of biface lanceolate points, some with a flat or concave base and, in some cases, with denticulate edges (Figs 89 and 90). Triangular stemmed points were found in the lowest terrace, in the so-called Las Casitas complex, in addition to the complex of artefacts already mentioned.

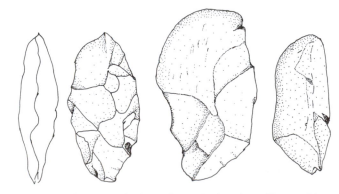

Figure 88 Choppers, El Jobo industry, E. do Falcon (Venezuela).

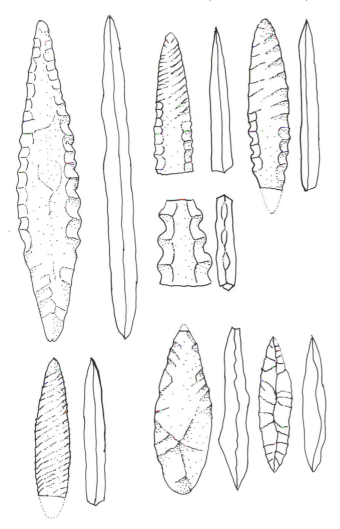

Figure 89 Denticulates and lanceolate biface points, El Jobo industry (Venezuela).

Dating the material composing the various complexes mentioned above was hampered by the fact that they were found on the surface with indications of entrainment by the water cycles and that there were no organic remains that would have made it possible to date the various groups of artefacts.

Some current research, such as that of Charles Alexander, seeks to establish geomorphologic evidence about the origin, number and chronology of the Pedregal river terraces. However, this evidence provides only a basis from which archaeological research might proceed to clarify the cultural characteristics of the ancient hunting societies of north-west Venezuela, since establishing the position of the artefacts in the terraces does not necessarily provide indications that El Camare and Las Lagunas are older than El Jobo and Las Casitas, especially as it has not been proved that the formation of river terraces is not due to tectonic movements.

Based on the author's experience with material from the different complexes exhibited in various museums in the United States, the collections of artefacts, arranged to form a logical technological series, indicate an evolution in complexity and in quality of manufacture that culminates with the El Jobo and Las Casitas material. Technological logic has to coincide with historical logic, however. As long as this coincidence is not proved, the technical evolution cannot be automatically assumed to be the same as the Lower

Palaeolithic–Middle Palaeolithic–Upper Palaeolithic historical process of the Old World. It is more likely that it is a succession of stages in tool manufacture, ranging from the chipping of cores for the preparation of blanks up to the final elaboration of the most advanced implements such as points, knives, scrapers and so on.

One of the criticisms made in this respect relates to the way in which the samples of the materials were apparently collected, many of them having been bought from local peasants without any real control of their origin or contextual characteristics (Bate, 1983, pp. 1–125). In addition, an alternative explanation for the process mentioned above has been suggested by Bate (1983, pp. 1–125), Morganti and Rodríguez (1983) and Rodríguez (1985). This is that there may have been not only tool-working sites on the terraces, but also camps where the hunters finished chipping the blanks to obtain points and other tools and at the same time repaired projectiles damaged during hunting. In this case it is very likely that the hunters installed their camps near the river, that is, at the bottom of the Pedregal valley, where animals would gather to drink water and seek food. This would explain the presence of a large number of projectile points in the lower terraces. These assumptions are apparently substantiated by the work of Morganti and Rodríguez (1983) in the Monte Cano site, a deposit situated in the Paraguaná peninsula in the State of Falcón, identified by the presence of a lithic industry of El Jobo type using quartz. In the tool complex at Monte Cano finds of the same technological elements define the different stages of the El-Camare–Las Lagunas–El-Jobo–Las-Casitas sequence, including the morphological and functional elements, except

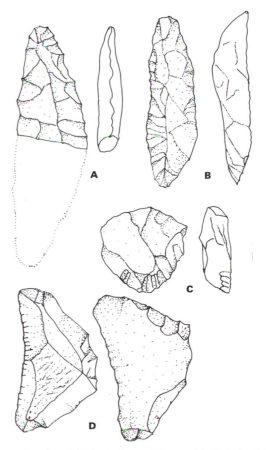

Figure 90 Artefacts, El Jobo industry (Venezuela): A, biface blade; B, scraper on uniface blade; C, uniface disc-shaped scraper; D, biface lateral scraper.

that the work of chipping the cores is conditioned by the kind of raw material used.

At the Monte Cano site an association can be observed between the large bifaces of Camare and Manzanillo types (Manzanillo is a deposit situated on the north-west edge of Lake Maracaibo) and the leaf-shaped points at El Jobo. An important characteristic of this site is the distribution of archaeological material over the area of the deposit, which seems to represent different stages in the process of manufacturing tools. At Monte Cano large bifaces are found in sector D, smaller blanks in sector C, and virtually nothing but waste flakes in sectors A and B; the knives or blades and projectile points are located in sector E of the deposit.

The above associations seem to indicate that there are grounds for challenging the chronology suggested to demonstrate local evolutionary development based on the chronological superimposition of various kinds of artefacts in the Pedregal river terraces. As already mentioned (p. 320), they may well represent stages in the processing of the raw materials, rather than sets of tools to exploit environmental resources, whose forms changed progressively with changing socio-historic conditions (Rodríguez, 1985, pp. 47–8).

Interpretation of the material remains left by the ancient hunters of the bifacial tradition, particularly in the Falcón area, is hampered by the lack of detailed studies that could contest the typological–technological framework that has characterized virtually all publications related to this area. It could be considered, nevertheless, that the appearance of the first ancient hunters may have coincided with the existence of a humid climate and sufficient vegetation to feed the large herbivores still surviving towards the end of the Pleistocene era. The projectile points, although they were still large and heavy, could have been set in wooden hafts to be used as missiles over short distances, while the stemmed points could have been those of arrows or darts projected by a throwing stick. In some cases the El Jobo lithic instruments also include flakes bearing notches of various diameters that could have been used for the manufacture of wooden handles or hafts for the different artefacts – triangular blades, projectile points and so on – used in the various stages of hunting and butchering prey. In the same way, the flake scrapers also included among the stone tools could well be associated with woodworking itself, or the preparation of the skins of hunted animals. Another important element is the presence of possible grinding stones and the use of large bifaces, not only as blanks for the manufacture of smaller tools, but also as hoes for unearthing tubers and other edible roots that must certainly have been part of the ancient hunters' diet, as seems to have been the case in the Sangoan and Lupemban industries in the central Congo and west Africa. Here studies of the work methods of the African hunter-gatherers adapted to the exploitation of woodland and savannah environments should be taken as a reference for understanding the bifacial industrial complexes of the north of South America such as El Jobo, which represent an evolution *in situ* of the various complexes or artefacts apparently related to the changes in climate, temperature and rainfall in the area up to 11,000 years ago (Coursey, 1976, p. 399; Sanoja, 1982*b*, p. 27).

Generally speaking, the diversity of tools characterizing the El Jobo culture seems to indicate the existence of a number of activities ranging possibly from the working and processing of wood to the gathering of plant food and the development of hunting activity, the use of javelins with heavy points to penetrate the hides of animals at close quarters, darts or arrows for projecting at a distance and sharp-edged instruments with wooden handles for slaughtering

prey. This would have made it possible to hunt in a more varied range of environments and to include medium- and small-sized animals that were easier to hunt and capture than large herbivores. Thus there would have been comparative freedom from the environmental constraints that determine the way of life of hunters, transforming the natural surroundings into a more productive, safer and better-controlled medium in which to work.

The survival of the form of social organization and the system of acquiring food resources characteristic of these ancient hunting groups must have been conditioned by the existence of an abundance of large animals that seem to have become extinct between 10,000 and 8,000 years ago. The arid coastal regions of Falcón State and the semi-desert valleys and northern foothills of the Andes in Lara State, where nearly all the archaeological deposits related to these groups have been found, as well as the most varied and dense accumulation of palaeontological remains, could have been covered in previous eras with a vegetation more suited to the survival of large herbivores. These seem to have disappeared later, either killed off by hunters or possibly as a result of the climatic changes that affected Equatorial America during the Holocene period. By applying the palaeoclimatic models suggested by Lynch (1978, pp. 466–7) for the Pacific coast of Central America and the north of South America to the north-west region of Venezuela, it could be considered that the drop in the sea-level that took place between 15,000 and 12,000 years ago may also have determined the formation of coastal savannahs covered with gramineae and broken up by high forests that formed along the river banks. This favoured a greater concentration of fauna in these regions, giving the ancient hunting populations a better chance of securing food. Here it is interesting to note the conclusions of the palynological work of Salgado-Laboriu (1982, pp. 74–7) carried out in the region adjoining the centre of the coast of Venezuela. The study of fossil pollen discovered in the deep sediment of Lake Valencia shows that towards the end of the Pleistocene era, about 13,000 years ago according to radiocarbon dating, the lake finally dried up, the climate became very arid and the whole region was covered with semi-arid vegetation, mostly gramineae and grasses (Salgado-Laboriu, 1982, fig. 7.2), while the mountainous areas surrounding the lake could have been covered with drought-resistant forests. This drying-up process was subsequently reversed, with a return to a more humid climate about 10,000 years ago. Lake Valencia reappeared, together with a more profuse growth of brackish-water vegetation such as scrub or thorn-bushes.

Climatic circumstances such as those indicated for northwest Venezuela would be consistent with the model proposed by Morganti and Rodríguez (1983) to explain the concentration of stone-working sites and tools on the banks of the Pedregal river in the State of Falcón. This might also explain the apparent spread of the ancient hunting populations in various valleys further south, in the State of Lara, as demonstrated by the findings of Molina (1985). At the Las Mesas site in the Carora valley, Molina located various deposits that yielded complexes of tools related to the El Jobo bifacial tradition, particularly leaf-shaped points with notches or retouched edges, knives, flake scrapers and a large number of waste flakes. In the nearby Quibor valley, Molina also reported the presence of large bifaces, hammers, scrapers and prismatic flakes, as well as fragments of projectile points similar to those already mentioned at the La Hundición site. In some sites still under study, the material related to the El Jobo culture could be linked to remains of extinct fauna and to sources of raw materials, particularly quartzite, from which the artefacts were manufactured.

Other evidence related to the way of life of the ancient hunters has also been discovered on the north-west coast of Lake Maracaibo (Cruxent, 1962) at the Manzanillo site. This is characterized by the presence of artefacts, possibly in their initial chipping stage, which are manufactured from fossil wood; these include biface and uniface implements, large flakes and crude-looking scrapers which may have been blanks for subsequent finishing as tools in the area where they were to be used. Taking the model suggested by Morganti and Rodríguez (1983), this last stage would have been performed in camps or working sites which may now be submerged below the waters of Lake Maracaibo or lie under the sediment of the rivers flowing into it.

THE ANCIENT HUNTING COMMUNITY OF NORTH-WEST VENEZUELA

The present distribution of the tool complexes associated with the ancient hunting community of north-west Venezuela seems to suggest the existence of nomadic groups, apparently moving around within more or less well-defined territories, which can be identified with the so-called 'restricted nomadic community' model (Beardsley et al., 1955). According to this hypothesis, the members of these communities lived itinerant lives within a specific territory delimited as their own, holding exclusive rights over certain kinds of food resources. Movements within the territory could be erratic or could follow a seasonal cycle according to the type of food hunted and gathered, as a way of making the best use of the work force by moving it to areas with greater food resources.

The 'restricted nomadic' type communities usually had a small population, typically less than a hundred persons. These groups were composed of nuclear or extended families which moved together from one place to another either all the year round or for part of it.

According to current data, there is no direct evidence that would make it possible to deduce the length of time that the ancient hunters spent in any particular encampment. It seems clear, however, that the accumulation of more than a ton of artefacts and waste flakes in some important sites must have required continuous occupation or reoccupation over a long period, particularly at places that were camps or working sites, or necessary points of transit for various species of animals (Sanoja and Vargas, 1979, p. 94).

Owing to the nature and requirements of the hunting way of life, the training and preparation of the youngest members of the social group as individual or collective hunters must have needed the advice of individual adults. This implies the existence of blood or kinship relationships, at least until a youth was considered an adult. A hunter's training required a long apprenticeship to learn how to handle the various weapons and tools related to hunting activities, the habits and customs of the animals that the social group considered useful for their subsistence, and the tactics needed to hunt and kill them. In addition, a hunter needed to know certain basic facts about animal anatomy to enable him to choose the parts of the body where wounds caused by his weapon would be the most lethal; also how to butcher and skin the animals to make the best use of their meat, bones and hides.

THE BIFACIAL TRADITION AND THE EARLY POPULATION OF AMERICA

Material evidence obtained so far in north-west Venezuela, particularly that originating from the various sites in the State of Falcón, has been interpreted by various authors within the general hypothetical framework which attempts to explain the early population of the New World.

Bryan (1978) argues that the origin of the bifacial industries in South America, particularly the El Jobo culture, was the result of independent developments whose remotest antecedents go back not to the Mousterian traditions that supposedly appeared in the north of Siberia between 30,000 and 10,000 years ago, but to the crude techniques of human groups which arrived very much earlier. It was apparently from these techniques that a crude bifacial industry subsequently developed, producing better and more specialized forms, including projectile points. Proof of this process would be the bone artefacts located in sites such as Old Crow Flats and the stone artefacts and the hearths of Meadowcroft shelter in the United States, with dates of about 27,000 years ago for the former and 19,700 and as far back as perhaps 37,000 or 21,500 years ago for the latter. This well-documented evidence seems to indicate that human settlements already existed to the south of the glacial zone which covered the far north-west of North America more than 12,000 years ago; it also coincides with Krieger's hypothesis of the existence of a pre-projectile point horizon in the New World (Krieger, 1962, 1964). On the other hand, Bryan (1978) stresses that the North American Clovis points designed to be inserted into a cut in the shaft of a javelin or other projectile could not technically precede the El Jobo type bifacial lanceolate points apparently designed to be inserted in a hollow-ended shaft. For this reason the development of both kinds of head should be understood as the result of separate inventions within a multi-evolutionary context.

Authors such as Lynch (1978) maintain that there can be no doubt as to the technological continuity between the artefact industries of the North American hunting culture and those of its South American descendants. Lynch argues that it is unlikely that the bifacial projectile point could have been invented independently, by accident, in both subcontinents with a chronological difference of several hundred years. It is also unlikely that the North American fluted points and the fluted fish-tail points of South America developed in parallel at either end of the continent, since the rest of the artefacts composing these early industries are almost identical: end-scrapers, unguiform scrapers, burins, notched artefacts, biface scrapers, flaked scrapers with side retouches and so on. Although this might possibly be due to different subsistence strategies, the fact that all these peoples used a set of technologically related tools suggests rather that the two traditions may represent complementary and coexistent methods of work, a process typified by the findings of Molina in the Quibor valley and of Pantel and Molina in the foothills of the mountains surrounding the valley (Pantel, 1983).

In the same way Bell (1965, p. 30) considers that the fluted fish-tail projectile point tradition of South America could have originated in the Clovis complex, as a parallel development that broke away from the fluted point tradition. Bell (1965, p. 318) also expounds the stratigraphic origin of the fish-tail points of Cueva Fell type, which are apparently the characteristic component of El Inga I, whereas oval and lanceolate points, together with stemmed points, are present in El Inga II; El Inga I apparently represents a complex of tools more similar to the so-called Magallanes I at Cueva Fell and Pallí Aike, in the south of Patagonia (Bird, 1938, 1946), whereas El Inga II contains lanceolate point shapes that exist in a large number of sites in the north and north-west of South America. This suggests that this shape developed from very crude unifaces to reach a high degree of bifacial flaking and a very small size (Bell, 1965, pp. 318–21).

With respect to the elongated fish-tail points, examples of which have been discovered in the La Hundición site, State of Lara, Venezuela, Meyer-Oakes also suggests the hypothesis of the existence of a tradition of this kind of implement originating in the extreme south of South America and subsequently spreading towards the north of the subcontinent.

On the other hand Bate (1983, pp. 1–11, p. 208) considers that the fish-tail points represent a Toldo culture or tradition dating from 12,600 years ago, mainly located in the eastern plains and plateaux of the Southern Cone, especially in the extreme south. This sets aside the more northern discoveries, such as El Inga and Papallacta, as being related possibly to the El Llano tradition, through sites such as Los Grifos in south-west Mexico, Lake Madden in Panama, isolated finds in Colombia and now, perhaps, those of La Hundición in north-west Venezuela.

Bate (1983, pp. 2–11, p. 210) considers that towards 6,500 years ago the fish-tail projectile point cultures from the extreme south could have mixed with groups from the Andean region and south-east Brazil as a result of agricultural tribal developments in these areas.

With respect to the possible spread of the El Jobo culture in the north-west region of South America, Patterson and Lanning (1974) consider that the lithic industries of El Camare and Manzanillo, the latter with a possible carbon-14 date of about 12,000 years ago, could have been the predecessors of a bifacial Andean horizon that could have extended towards the south across the Venezuelan and Colombian Andes, replacing an ancient burin industry which may have predominated in these regions from at least 12,000 years ago. This industry is typified especially by the Oquendo complex situated on the northern coast of Peru, composed mainly of choppers, burins, denticulate artefacts and bifacial artefacts; so far no projectile points have been found. According to Patterson, this complex is more likely to be associated with hunters and plant gatherers who used wooden javelins in a non-specialized way of life. He also argues that similar complexes could perhaps be located in North America in pre-Clovis periods.

UNDIFFERENTIATED LITHIC INDUSTRIES IN NORTHERN SOUTH AMERICA

Systematic research carried out in recent years in the territory that is now the Republic of Colombia has opened up a next stage in knowledge about the ancient hunting societies in northern South America. It stresses the existence of human groups with a complex of tools distinct from the flaked-stone traditions whose characteristics, as seen above, relate them more to the North American traditions.

This undifferentiated industry comprises implements that were obtained by flaking a core. The resulting fragments or flakes, which were most suitable for the operations of cutting, scraping or boring, were then either adapted by flaking or used in their original state.

The first stratigraphic investigations of dwelling sites belonging to this lithic tradition were undertaken at El Abra in the Bogota plateau (Hurt et al., 1972). They located flake artefacts in a layer that yielded a radiocabon date of about 12,400 years ago, placing this tradition at a period similar to that of Taima-Taima in Venezuela (Bryan et al., 1978, p. 306). Research made it possible to identify dwelling areas with hearths and a chronological sequence that lasted until the appearance of pottery, evidence not only of astonishing occupational stability but also of striking continuity in production techniques.

All the artefacts of the El Abra technique are identified by work on only one of the side edges, producing end-, side-, ovoid and diamond-shaped scrapers, perforators, and the like, which could have been used for the preparation of skins and wood. There are no stone projectile points; given the suggested functions of the tools mentioned above, these could have been manufactured in bone or wood.

Palynological studies indicate that the occupation of the Bogota plateau by individuals of the El Abra tradition occurred at a time when the climate was very much colder than now, corresponding to the later period of the last glaciation and to the Guantiva interstadial period, approximately from 21,500 to 11,000 years ago. Between 11,000 and 10,000 to 9,500 years ago the climate again became much colder, defining the El Abra stage (Correal and Van der Hammen, 1977). New dwelling sites appeared approximately during this period in the Tequendama caves in the Bogota plateau, where the first stages – known as Tequendama I – indicate the presence of bifacial blades, flakes, laminar knives, scrapers, hammers and pebbles, for which the raw material was chert; there are also a large number of haematite nodules.

At the same time a bone industry also existed, for which the epiphyses of deer long bones were used. The artefacts are knives, scrapers, perforators and sharpened splinters (perhaps used as awls). Some artefacts classified by Correal and Van der Hammen (1977, Photo 46) as lanceolate bone scrapers could, in fact, have been projectile points which the natural grooving of the epiphysis would have made it easier to set in the handle. Among the collection of stone artefacts, some pieces were manufactured with a more refined technique and a better finish, particularly the apparently leaf-shaped projectile points and keeled scrapers present only in the initial stage of Tequendama.

The domestic spaces in the caves that served as shelter and homes for the Tequendama hunters seem also to have been used as workshops for the manufacture of stone or bone artefacts, and possibly for processing the skins of the animals hunted. Most of these work areas were close to the hearths.

The hunters of the Bogota plateau used to bury their dead within the domestic space. In some graves the bodies were accompanied by grave goods, apparently testifying to the activity carried out by the dead person within the community: stone and bone artefacts, land snails, fragments of haematite and deer horns. In general the tombs were elongated and oval-shaped; skeletons of children were found buried inside circular pits in a crouched position as if they were in the maternal womb.

Another feature also associated with the Bogota plateau burials is the presence of ochre. In many cases this was applied as pigment on the bones, a custom that was widespread both in the Old and the New World, associated, perhaps, with beliefs about preserving the vital force of the dead. There are also indications of secondary burials and the cremation of human remains in Sueva (Correal, 1979, p. 116). In addition, remains show that in the various caves examined in the Bogota plateau, the human skeletons contain arthritic lesions in their joints and degenerative processes in the jawbones due perhaps to the diet of hard food typical of the hunters (Correal and Van der Hammen, 1977; Correal, 1979).

The Bogota plateau hunters exploited in particular faunal resources such as *Odocoyleus virginianus* and the American mazama, as well as smaller fauna such as rabbits, wild rats, dasyproctas, agoutis, armadillos and guinea pigs, the latter perhaps evidence of an early process of animal domestication. At the same time there is also evidence at other sites in the Bogota plateau such as Tinito – dated to about 11,750 years ago – of the hunting and butchering of large Pleistocene fauna such as mastodons (*Cuvieronis Hyodon* and *Haplomastodon*), horses (*Equus americanus*) and – on a smaller scale – deer (*Odocoyleus virginianus*) by individuals associated with the hunting community which lived in the Bogota plain. These individuals also possessed tools made from flakes and bones, but without stone projectile points. They were, however, able to capture and butcher large animals such as those mentioned above, although the contexts studied suggest that these were very exceptional activities (Correal, 1981).

This tradition of hunters with an undifferentiated bone and stone industry also extended apparently as far as the Magdalena valley and the Atlantic coast of Colombia. It is possible that the populations related to this tradition also extended to other regions of north-east South America. Their existence is proved by the presence of large conchiferous deposits with a lithic industry situated in the Paria Peninsula and rocky caves in the south of Venezuelan Guyana, complexes of lithic material such as those at Tupuken and Canaima, also in the south of Venezuelan Guyana, which have not yet undergone much study, the early stages of the Banwari conchiferous deposit, the Alaka stage, and the complexes of crudely manufactured material at Rupununi in Guyana. In some cases, such as along the Atlantic coast of Colombia and the Paria Peninsula, self-generating processes seem subsequently to have occurred among these populations, which culminated in agriculture and the production of food (Sanoja, 1980, 1982a, 1982b, 1984, 1985; Sanoja et al., 1982; Sanoja and Vargas, 1979, 1983; Evans and Meggers, 1960; Cruxent, 1971, p. 32; Cruxent and Rouse, 1963, pp. 42–3).

THE WAY OF LIFE OF HUNTERS IN THE BRAZILIAN AMAZON

The data so far available suggest that the Amazon basin was not affected by the processes which set on their travels the ancient hunting societies of the north of South America, Central America and the Caribbean. It is possible nevertheless that some human groups related to those in the eastern foothills of the Andes reached the head-waters of tributaries of the Amazon river such as the Marañon and the Napo, as seems to be attested by the archaeological sites at La Cumbre in Peru, and Papallacta and El Inga in Ecuador (Schobinger, 1973; Lynch, 1978; Bate, 1983, p. 149). This movement could have occurred before the growth of the postglacial Amazonian forest. This hypothesis may be supported by the work of Van der Hammen (1972, 1974, 1982) and Simpson-Vuillemier (1971), who suggest that the glacial advances in the Amazon basin would have had the effect of replacing the forest vegetation with dry savannah formations at different times during the Pleistocene epoch, in particular between 21,000 and 12,500 years ago. On the other hand, these cyclical changes could also have happened on a smaller scale during more recent periods such as 4,000 and 2,000 years ago (Bigarella and Andrade, 1982; Absy, 1982). In these conditions, the groups of ancient hunters could have found a more suitable environment in the region for developing their way of life.

Although there are so far virtually no archaeological records of this hunting society, it is possible either that many remains were buried below thick alluvial layers deposited by the major rivers of the Amazon basin or destroyed by excessive humidity, or else simply that archaeological research has not managed to produce sufficient knowledge about such a huge area (Meggers, 1982, pp. 485–6). In this respect, the results of the last research project at the Pronapapa camp, under the co-ordination of Betty Meggers from the Smithsonian Institution, have established the existence of a conchiferous deposit formed by an accumulation of land gastropods in the head-waters of the Tapajoz river, with a cultural layer 10 m thick. The upper part of the archaeological deposit is typified by the presence of pottery, which includes among its decorative techniques incision and areas of crossed incisions. The eight lower layers of the deposit indicate an industry without pottery, identified only by artefacts manufactured from large mammal bones, particularly pointed implements. There is also another industry composed of stone artefacts manufactured from crude flakes similar to the flaked stone technique characterizing the non-specialized lithic industries found, as seen above, in various regions in the north of South America.

Although there are not yet any absolute dates, the Abrigo do Sol has been excavated near the deposit. It is also defined by a crude lithic industry with a date of 10,400 years ago, which could provide a reference for dating the material from the lower levels of the Tapajoz river conchiferous deposit.

Other sites prospected under the Pronapapa project in various areas in the Amazon basin seem to contain camp fires, but it has not been possible to find any trace of artefacts. A series of carbon-14 dates exists, which goes from about 7,400 to 5,200 years ago in Rondônia, to 4,600 years ago in the middle Amazon, and to 4,100 years ago in Rio Negro (Betty Meggers, personal communication, 1985), although their significance is not yet clear.

If the existing dates in the Pronapapa project mentioned above are confirmed, the presence of ancient hunter-gatherers in the Amazon basin would be consistent with the dates already obtained for the Mato Grosso, Minas Gerais and other areas of Brazil, where findings include the Paranaiba and Serranopolis stages with datings of 9,000 years ago, and Lapa Vermelha, 9,600 years ago.

BIBLIOGRAPHY

ABSY, M. L. 1982. Quaternary Palynological Studies in the Amazon Basin. In: PRANCE, G. T. (ed.), *Biological Diversification in the Tropics*. New York. pp. 67–73.

ANDERSON, D. 1974. A Stone Campsite at the Gateway to America. In: ZUBROW, E. et al. (eds), *New World Archaeology: Readings from Scientific American*. San Francisco.

AVELEYRA DE ANDA, L. 1964. The Primitive Hunters. In: WAUCHOPE, R. (ed.), *Handbook of Middle American Indians*. Dallas. Vol. I, pp. 384–412.

BATE, L. P. 1983. Comunidades primitivas de cazadores recolectores en Sudamérica. In: *História General de América*. Caracas. Vol. 2–1–2–II.

BEARDSLEY, R. et al. 1955. In: WAUCHOPE, R. (ed.), *Seminars in Archaeology: 1955*. Salt Lake City. (Mem. Soc. Am. Archaeol., No. 11, Vol. 22, No. 2, Part 2.)

BELL, R. E. 1965. *Investigaciones arqueológicas en el sitio El Inga, Ecuador*. Quito.

BIGARELLA, J. J.; ANDRADE LIMA, D. DE. 1982. The Paleoclimate and Palaeoecology of Brazilian Amazonia. In: PRANCE, G. T. (ed.), *Biological Diversification in the Tropics*. New York. pp. 27–40.

BIRD, J. 1938. Antiquity and Migration of the Early Inhabitants of Patagonia. *Geogr. J.* (New York), Vol. 28, pp. 250–75.

—— 1946. The Cultural Sequence in the North Chilean Coast. In: *Handbook of South American Indians*. Vol. 1, pp. 17–24.

BIRD, J.; COOKE, R. 1977. Los artefactos mas antiguos de Panamá. *Rev. Nac. Cult.* (Panama), No. 6.

—— 1978. The Occurrence in Panama of Two Types of Palaeo-indian Projectile Points. In: BRYAN, A. L. (ed.), *Early Man in America from a Circum-Pacific Perspective*. Edmonton.

BRYAN, A. L. 1973. New Light on Ancient Nicaraguan Footprints. *Archeology* (New York), Vol. 26.

—— 1978. An Overview of Palaeoamerican Prehistory from a Circum-Pacific Perspective. In: BRYAN, A. L. (ed.), *Early Man in America from a Circum-Pacific Perspective*. Edmonton. pp. 306–27.

BRYAN, A. L. et al. 1978. *An 'El Jobo' Mastodon Kill Site at Taima-Taima, Northern Venezuela*.

COLLINS, M. B. 1981. The Implications of the Lithic Assemblage from Monte Verde, Chile, for Early Man Studies. In: CONGRESO DE LA UISPP, 10, Mexico. *Actas*. Mexico.

CORREAL, G. 1979. *Investigaciones en Abrigos Rocosos de Nemocon y Sueva*. Bogota.

—— 1981. *Evidencias culturales y megafauna Pleistocenica en Colombia*. Bogota.

CORREAL, G.; HAMMEN, T. VAN DER. 1977. *Artefactos líticos de las Abrigos Rocosos del Tequendama*. Bogota.

COURSEY, D. G. 1976. The Origins and Domestication of Yams in Africa. In: HARLAN, J.; QET, A. M. J. DE; STEMMLER, A. B. L. (eds), *Origins of African Plant Domestication*. The Hague. pp. 383–408.

CRAWFORD, 1891. Neolithic Man in Nicaragua. *Am. Geol.* (Minneapolis), Vol. 8, pp. 160–6.

CRUXENT, J. M. 1961. Huesos quemados en el yacimiento pre-histórico de Muaco, Estade Falcon. *Inst. Venez. Invest. Cient., Dep. Antropol. Bol. Inf.* (Caracas), No. 2, pp. 20–1.

—— 1962. Artifacts of Paleoindian Type, Maracaibo, Zulia, Venezuela. *Ame. Antiq.*, Vol. 27, pp. 576–9.

—— 1970. Projectile Points with Pleistocene Mammals in Venezuela. *Antiquity*, Vol. 175, pp. 223–6.

—— 1971. Apuntes sovre arqueología Venezolana. In: *Arte Prehispanico de Venezuela*. Caracas.

CRUXENT, J. M.; ROUSE, I. 1961. *Arqueolgía chronológica de Venezuela*. Washington, Unión Panamericana.

—— 1963. *Venezuelan Archaeology*. New Haven/London.

DEREVIANKO, A. P. 1979. On the Immigration of Ancient Man from the Asian Pleistocene. In: BRYAN, A. L. (ed.), *Early Man in America from a Circum-Pacific Perspective*. Edmonton.

DIKOV, N. N. 1978. Ancestors of Paleoindians and Proto-Eskimos Aleuts in the Palaeolithic of Kamchatka. In: BRYAN, A. L. (ed.), *Early Man in America from a Circum-Pacific Perspective*. Edmonton.

DILLEHAY, T. 1981. Early Man in South Central Andes, Monte Verde. In: CONGRESO DE LA UISPP, 10, Mexico. *Actas*. Mexico.

ESPINOZA, E. J. 1976. *Excavaciones en El Bosque: informe no. 1*. Managua.

EVANS, C.; MEGGERS, B. 1960. *Archaeological Investigations in British Guiana*. Washington. (Smithson. Inst., Bull., 177.)

FLINT, E. 1885. Human Footprints in Nicaragua. *Am. Antiq.* (Chicago), Vol. 7, pp. 112–4.

GONZÁLES, A. R. 1952. Antiguo horizonte preceráamica en las Sierras Centrales de la Argentina. *Runa* (Buenos Aires), Vol. 5, pp. 110–33.

—— 1960. La Estratigrafía de la Gruta de Itihuasi (Provincia de San Luis, RA) y sus relaciones con otros sitios precerámicos de Sudamérica. *Rev. Inst. Anthropol., Univ. Nac. Cordoba*, Vol. 1.

GRUHN, R. 1976. A Note on Excavations at El Bosque, Nicaragua, in 1975. In: BRYAN, A. L. (ed.), *Early Man in America from a Circum-Pacific Perspective*. Edmonton.

GRUHN, R.; BRYAN, A. 1981. A Summary and Implications of the Taima-Taima Mastodon Kill Site, Northern Venezuela. In: CONGRESO DE LA UISPP, 10, Mexico. *Actas*. Mexico.

HAMMEN, T. VAN DER. 1972. Changes in Vegetation and Climate in the Amazon Basin and Surrounding Areas during the Pleistocene. *Geol. Mijnb.* (Dordrecht), Vol. 51, pp. 641–3.

—— 1974. The Pleistocene Changes of Vegetation and Climate in Tropical South America. *J. Biogeog.* (Oxford), Vol. 1, pp. 3–26.

—— 1982. Palaeoecology of Tropical South America. In: PRANCE, G. T. (ed.), *Biological Differentiation in the Tropics*. New York. pp. 60–6.

HURT, W. R.; BLASI, O. 1969. *O projeto arqueológico Lagoa Santa, Minas Gerais, Brasil*. Curitiba. (Arq. Mus. Paranaense, 4.)

HURT, W. R.; HAMMEN, T. VAN DER; CORREAL, G. 1972. Preceramic Sequences in the El Abra Rock, Colombia. *Science* (Washington), Vol. 175, pp. 1106–8.

KRIEGER, A. 1962. The Earliest Cultures in the Western United States. *Am. Antiq.*, Vol. 28, No. 2, pp. 138–43.

—— 1964. Early Man in the New World. In: JENNINGS, J.; NORBECK, E. (eds), *Prehistoric Man in the New World*. Chicago.

LEROI-GOURHAN, A. 1946. *Archéologie du Pacifique Nord*. Paris, Musée de l'Homme.

LYNCH, T. F. 1978. The South American Palaeoindians. In: JENNINGS, J.; FREEMAN, W. H. (eds), *Ancient Native Americans*. San Francisco.

MATILLO, V. J. 1977. *Acahualinca en el panorama arqueológico de Nicaragua*. Managua.

MEGGERS, B. J. 1982. Archaeological and Ethnographic Evidences Compatible with the Model of Forest Fragmentation. In: PRANCE, G. T. (ed.), *Biological Differentiation in the Tropics*. New York. pp. 483–96.

MÉNDEZ GUTIÉRREZ, M. 1984. *Puntas de proyectil de Cajibio, Cauca, Colombia*. Popayan.

MEYER-OAKES, W. 1974. Early Man in the Andes. In: SUBROW, E. et al. (ed.), *New World Archaeology: Theoretical and Cultural Transformation*. San Francisco.

—— 1981. Early Man Projectile Points and Lithic Technology in the Ecuadorian Sierra. In: CONGRESO DE LA UISPP, 10, Mexico. *Actas*. Mexico.

MILLER, W.; LUNDELIUS, E. 1976. The Fossils from El Bosque: A Preliminary Report to Jorge Espinoza. In: ESPINOZA, E. J. *Excavaciones en El Bosque: informe no. 1*. Managua. pp. 22–9.

MOCHANOV, Y. A. 1978. Stratigraphy and Absolute Chronology of the Palaeolithic of Northeastern Asia According to the Work of 1963–1973. In: BRYAN, A. (ed.), *Early Man in America from a Circum-Pacific Perspective*. Edmonton. pp. 54–66.

MOLINA, L. 1985. *Wachakaresai: la história que duerme bajo tierra*. Caracas.

MORGANTI, A.; RODRÍGUEZ, M. H. 1983. *Cazadores recolectores de Monte Cano, Paraguana, Venezuela*.

MÜLLER-BECK, H. 1966. Palaeohunters in America: Origins and Diffusion. *Science* (Washington), Vol. 52, pp. 1191–210.

—— 1967. On Migrations of Hunters across the Behring Land Bridge in the Upper Pleistocene. In: HOPKINS, D. M. (ed.), *The Behring Landbridge*. Stanford. pp. 373–408.

PAGE, W. 1978. Geology of El Bosque Archaeological Site. In: BRYAN, A. L. (ed.), *Early Man in America from a Circum-Pacific Perspective*. Edmonton.

PANTEL, A. 1983. *La Hundición, Estado Lara, Venezuela: Draft Field and Labor, Report*. San Juan, MS. Fundación Arqueo. Puerto Rico.

PATTERSON, T.; LANNING, E. P. 1974. Early Man in South America. In: ZUBROW, E. et al. (eds), *New World Archaeology: Readings from Scientific American*. San Francisco. pp. 44–50.

RODRÍGUEZ, M. E. 1985. Grupos precerámicos del Noroccidente de Venezuela y su relación con la Cuenca del Lago de Maracaibo. *Rev. GENS*, Vol. 1, No. 2, pp. 38–53.

ROYO Y GÓMEZ, J. 1956. El Cuaternario en Venezuela. *Bol. Geol. Publ. Espec. No. 1, Lexico Estratigráfico de Venezuela* (Caracas), pp. 199–204.

—— 1960a. Características Paleontológicas y Geológicas del yacimiento de vertebrados de Muaco, Estado Falcon, con industria lítica humana. *Boletín de Geología Publ. Espec. No. 3: Memórias III. Congreso Geológico Venezolano II* (Caracas) pp. 501–5.

—— 1960b. El Yacimiento de vertebrados Pleistocenos de Muaco, Estado Falcon, Venezuela, con industria humana lítica. In: INTERNATIONAL CONGRESS OF GEOLOGY, 21, Copenhagen. *Report.* Copenhagen. Vol. 14, pp. 154–7.

SALGADO-LABORIU, M. L. 1982. Climatic Change at the Pleistocene Holocene Boundary. In: PRANCE, G. T. (ed.), *Biological Differentiation in the Tropics.* New York.

SANOJA, M. 1980. Los recolectores tempranos del Golfo de Paria, Estado Sucre, Venezuela. In: CIPECPAN, 8, St Kitts. *Actas.* pp. 139–51.

—— 1982a. *Los hombres de la yaca y del maïz.* Caracas.

—— 1982b. De la recolección a la agricultura. In: *Historia General de América.* Caracas. Vol. 3.

—— 1984. Problemas de la Arqueología del Noreste de Venezuela. In: *Los Problemas de la Arqueología de América Latina.* (Inst. Arqueol., Acad. Cienc. URSS.)

—— 1985. Preceramic Sites in Eastern Venezuela. *Nat. Geogr. Res. Rep.* (Washington, DC), Vol. 18, pp. 663–8.

SANOJA, M.; ROMERO, L.; RONDON, J. 1982. Investigaciones arqueológicas en los Concheros, Guayana, El Bajo y Las Varas, Estado Sucre, Venezuela. *Acta Cient. Venez.* (Caracas), Vol. 33, suppl.

SANOJA, M.; VARGAS, I. 1979. *Antiguas formaciones y modos de producción venezolanos.* 2nd edn. Caracas.

—— 1983. New Light on the Prehistory of Eastern Venezuela. In:

WENDORF, F.; CLOSE, A. (eds), *Advances in World Archaeology.* New York. Vol. 2, pp. 205–44.

SCHOBINGER, J. 1973. Nuevos hallazgos de puntas 'Cola de Pescado' y consideraciones en torno al origen y dispersión de la cultura de los cazadores superiores Toldenses (Fell I) en Sudamérica. In: CONGRESSO INTERNATIONAL DEGLI AMERICANISTI, 40, Rome, Genova. *Atti.* Vol. 1, pp. 33–50.

SIMPSON-VUILLEMIER, B. 1971. Pleistocene Changes in the Fauna and Flora of South-America. *Science* (Washington), Vol. 173, pp. 771–80.

SNARKIS, M. 1984. Central America: The Lower Caribbean. In: LANGE, F. W.; STONE, D. Z. (eds), *The Archaeology of Lower Central America.* Albuquerque.

STEWARD, T.; NEWMAN, M. 1950. Anthropometry of Southamerican Indians: Skeletal Remains. In: STEWARD, T. (ed.), *Handbook of South American Indians.* Washington. (Smithson. Inst., Bull., 6.)

VELOZ MAGGIOLO, M. et al. 1982. Las Técnicas Unifaciales de los yacimientos de El Jobo y sus similitudes con el Paleoarcaico Antillano. *Bol. Mus. Hombre Dominicano* (Santo Domingo), Vol. 18.

WILLEY, G. 1966. *An Introduction to American Archaeology.* Vol. I: *North and Middle America.* New Jersey.

—— 1971. *An Introduction to American Archaeology.* Vol. II: *South America.* New Jersey.

WILSEM, E. 1964. Flake Tools in the American Arctic: Some Speculations. *Am. Antiq.*, Vol. 29, pp. 338–44.

WORMINGTON, H. M. 1961. Prehistoric Cultural Stages of Alberta, Canada. In: *Homenajes a Pablo Martinez del Rio; 25. Aniversario de la Edición de los Origines.* Mexico, DF. pp. 163–71.

33

PREHISTORY OF THE NON-ANDEAN REGION OF SOUTH AMERICA

(Brazil, Paraguay, Uruguay and Argentina, 31,000–5,000 years ago)

Osvaldo R. Heredia

The Brazilian territory encloses within its boundaries a great variety of environments and vegetal formations which can explain, to a certain extent, the characteristics of the human groups that in prehistoric times lived in it. The thick Amazonian jungles in the west and north, with their *varzeas* liable to floods, the xerophytic mountains (*caatingas* and *cerrados*) of the north-west and centre, the eastern *florestas* connected to the Serra do Mar, the araucaria woods of the central south and forests alternating with prairies (*campos*) in the south, all form a mosaic of regions to which different people with their specific cultural patterns were attached. The coastal regions alone, which were recently occupied, are characterized by open beaches dominated by *restinga* vegetation, thick *florestas* near the slopes of the coastal ranges or calm coves and bays generally covered at their ends by mangrove formations.

Systematic archaeological research in Brazil is relatively recent, undertaken really only in the last twenty years, and the information has as yet not been analysed in detail. During this time many cultural divisions have been proposed, spatial, chronological or both, and very many have been suggested for the pottery-making agricultural groups. The majority were defined only on the basis of artefact collections, basically sherds, so the cultural entities thus distinguished have merely an operational value for the archaeologist, as the criteria applied are so universal that very seldom do possible specific distinguishing features appear. By these means an integrated picture of Brazilian archaeology has been produced, but one that unites large groups of cultural traits – so-called 'traditions' – which relate peoples distributed over very wide areas all too often separated by thousands of years. At the same time some cultural objects were radiocarbon dated, producing an extensive list of chronological markers that relate to few clearly significant events that mark changes in cultural patterns, suitable for distinguishing cultural distribution, periods or phases. In this way it appeared that through almost 30,000 years the Brazilian territory was occupied exclusively by hunter-gatherers, a long time, in which it is difficult to establish socially important chronological differences. During this long time span adoptions of or innovations in technology or in full economic systems do not appear, or are not visible in the data available.

We consider as not valid such a scheme of cultural development dividing this hunter-gatherer period into three stages, as has been suggested. The first of them, from about 30,000 to 12,000 years ago, would include the hunters of the extinct Pleistocene megafauna. Many reasons make it difficult to accept this proposed stage. First and most important is that until now no unquestionable evidence has been obtained in Brazilian territory showing a clear association between human beings and this extinct fauna. In some cases, as in Lagoa do Carro or Ibicui, there are some artefacts found in the same geological beds, but no direct associations. Strong erosional processes and the transport of sediments from one place to another are factors which up to now have prevented any clear confirmation. We should accept, however, that during this long period humans coexisted with some of the large animals in some areas and some of them will have become extinct recently, in Holocene times. Nevertheless, if the animals were hunted, this hunting was opportunistic, not systematic. The hunters would have taken advantage of special situations, such as sickness, old age, immobility in swamps or mud, as happens on the sea-shore with whales that land to die on beaches and are exploited by coastal populations. At the same time the archaeological data do not include weapons capable of killing animals of these kinds. Consequently, we cannot accept a Pleistocene megafauna hunter stage in which large animals formed the main source of subsistence for those groups; insistence upon this economic hypothesis prevents proper understanding of this early period.

Between 12,000 and 7,000 years ago it seems that there was a degree of continuity in ways of life and subsistence patterns, even though during this time the environment underwent marked alterations. But the change cannot have been from a hunting economy based on killing large animals to one based on killing medium and small animals. It simply reflects change in the species available. It should be borne in mind that none of the sites older than 12,000 years contain remains of extinct fauna, probably because the *caatinga* and *cerrado* areas no longer offered conditions suitable for this kind of fauna, and had probably not done so for thousands of years prior to man's presence in those areas. In some regions such fauna persisted, as in Ibicui, where the necessary environmental conditions existed. On the other hand, in fossil-bearing beds there were also numerous bones of recent fauna that should have been the preferred prey of the early inhabitants of Brazil.

Unlike in the regions under the direct influence of Ice Age conditions, where the movements of the ice-sheets in Pleistocene times opened or closed areas to human habitation, in tropical or subtropical regions there were advances and retreats of the woodland and other major vegetation types. The *florestas* retreated and in consequence generally the *campos* advanced; in the same way the *caatinga* advanced and the *cerrados* shrank or became altered. It seems that deserts incapable of supporting life, and in particular that of human groups, never formed. Probably it is for these reasons that drastic technological changes, which are found with extreme environmental changes, were not necessary.

If we consider that the stone tools obtained from excavations were used to process different raw materials rather than as weapons, we may suppose that for hunting they were using wooden darts and spearheads. As no vestiges of these appear in the archaeological record, there is no way of studying alterations in their design or typology as a result of environmental change. It is clear that the presence or absence of projectile points cannot be considered diagnostic.

A third major epoch or stage of development is said to be one in which gathering plant foods took first place and was more important than hunting. This phase, called Archaic, is supposed to be significantly different from the previous phase in which gathered foods were not so important in the diet as were the products of hunting. However, there is no concrete evidence to prove that hunting diminished in intensity (the remains showing its presence are always poor), or that if hunting remained important then gathering wild plant foods became increasingly so. Probably, the new Holocene environment saw the appearance of new plant species which humans started to use as food, adding them to the range of plant foods they already knew; but nevertheless they went on hunting wherever it was necessary or possible. In other words, there was no abandonment of former ways of subsistence, but only a change in emphasis, owing to the scarcity of some animals, combined with an increase in potential plant foods. Nevertheless, this situation is not clearly marked by any significant technological change that could be used to distinguish this stage. It is our hypothesis that these early inhabitants of Brazil always depended more on gathering (of fruits, tubers and rhyzomes) than on hunting or, at least, they practised both activities with the same intensity.

In other areas of South America in some cases there were truly specialized hunters of some gregarious animals (pampas de Junin: vicuña and guanaco; Los Toldos: guanaco; Pampas: ñandu, to the point of inventing a special weapon for hunting swift animals, the boleadora), maintaining for millennia their reliance for basic subsistence practically on a single resource, or using it as the main economic base. As the animals of tropical or subtropical regions are not gregarious, or at least do not form substantial flocks, this kind of specialization was not possible, so neither was there a specific toolkit created for this purpose. Thus, the concept that 'specialized' hunters necessarily contrasted with 'unspecialized' hunters is not useful as a stage marker for the region under analysis. Either all of them were 'unspecialized' or they 'specialized' in the exploitation of a kind of environment offering a wide range of resources (which were not necessarily abundant) either at

the same time or alternating (depending on the ecological niches present or the major changes in environment). Genuine specialization came later, when man decided to settle in maritime, lagunal or estuarine environments.

Following this idea, when considering the prehistoric peopling of the tropical and subtropical areas, we prefer to go by regions, e.g. the 'north-east and central *caatinga* and *cerrado* region' and 'south Brazil and north-east Argentina *florestas* and *campos* region', rather than by developmental stages which as yet are badly defined and have arbitrary chronological boundaries. Although there is a risk that some important change in this development could be missed or remain obscure, we believe that the existing information does not allow one to attempt any culturally significant division. It seems obvious that in 30,000 years of history there must have been important modifications, even of the environment, that were able to produce important influences on and changes in technologies, but such differences are visible neither in the tools nor in the environments.

Such a situation appears in other regions considered here, where clear indicators of cultural change are not found either. Undoubtedly a clear significant feature is the appearance, around 7,000 years ago, in the pampas of Argentina and Uruguay, of stone balls for boleadoras. Various deer and ñandu were probably hunted with this weapon, suggesting the invention of a tool for a specific and well-defined environment: the pampas plains where the boleadora can be thrown long distances. However, there are no major indications that this tool meant a revolution in technology or that it efficiently modified the previous way of life. The problem of the 'megafauna hunters' is again present in the Argentinian pampa, where around 10,000 years ago this early fauna was contemporary with man and where too its exploitation eventually took place.

The Patagonian date informs us about groups of hunters around 12,000 years ago, fairly specialized in guanaco hunting (Los Toldos), but this basic diet prevailed for thousands of years, so this kind of information is not enough to establish cultural horizons, even though some changes took place in the tool-kit. In other words, we do not consider that it was of particular importance that the guanaco hunting was undertaken first with weapons that included projectile points and later with boleadoras, because both ways proved to be equally efficient.

CAATINGA AND SERTÃO REGIONS OF NORTH-EASTERN AND CENTRAL BRAZIL (Map 32)

The first inhabitants of Brazil

The earliest known inhabitants of Brazil settled in the south-east of the State of Piauí (north-eastern Brazil) between 25,000 and 30,000 years ago, occupying in succession different levels of limestone caves and shelters in the Serra Bom Jesus de Gurgueia. This mountain range varies in altitude between 500 and 800 m above sea-level, but the salient neighbouring areas rise to only between 200 and 500 m. Today the climate is semi-arid, hot, with rain in summer, and an average annual temperature of 25 °C, the rainfall amounting to 750 mm. These and other factors make for a dry region in which the dominant vegetation is *caatinga* (scrub forest), deciduous, spiny formations ranging from dense forest to sometimes very sparse woodland (Emperaire, 1983). However, these general characteristics vary in some

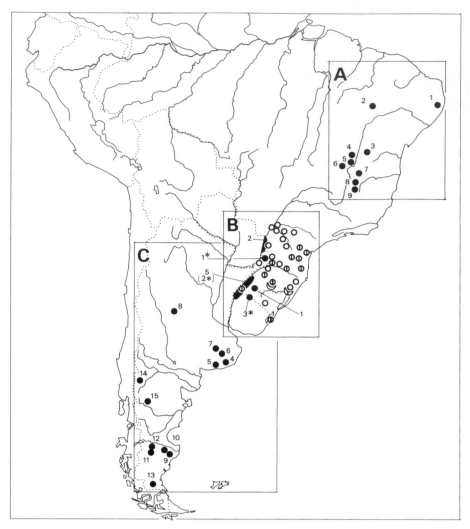

Map 32 Archaeological cultures and sites mentioned in the text. A, north-east and central Brazil: 1, Itaparica–Pedra do Caboclo; 2, south-west of Piauí; 3, Iuiu; 4, Montaluania; 5, Januária; 6, Lapas do Gentio y da Foice; 7, Lapa Pequena; 8, Serra do Cipó; 9, Lagoa Santa. B, south Brazil: 1, Touro Passo (Ibicuí); 2, Vinitu culture; 3, Umbú culture; 4, Humaitá culture; 5, Uruguay Culture. C, south Brazil, Argentina, Uruguay, Paraguay: 1★, Humaitá or Altoparanaense; 2★, Uruguay or Catalanense; 3★, Cuareimense; 4, Cerro La China; 5, Arroyo Seco; 6, Tandiliense; 7, Estancia la Moderna; 8, Intihuasi; 9, El Ceibo; 10, Los Toldos; 11, Rio Pinturas; 12, Arroyo Feo; 13, Las Buitreras; 14, Traful; 15, Piedra Parada. ★, Sites of Map C (2★ is also no. 5 of Map B).

specific parts of the region, producing valleys or tablelands with succulents (Cactaceae) and herbs (Bromeliaceae), but never epiphytes or lianas. Although no systematic studies have been carried out on the palaeoclimate, it is likely that the prevailing conditions began to form and predominate 10,000 years ago and also that, even earlier, the climate was more humid, with consequences for the vegetation (Ab'Sáber, 1983, quoted by Schmitz, 1984).

The first human settlement discovered was a temporary hunting encampment in the Boqueirâo da Pedra Furada cave, found by Guidon (1984), who unearthed various occupation levels from 1978 onwards. The oldest, corresponding to bed XIX, revealed hearths whose charcoal, tested at Gif-sur-Yvette (France), dated back to about 31,500 and 24,600 years ago. The cultural objects do not include finished artefacts, but the writer considers the prepared cores and quartz and quartzite flakes found at the lowest levels to have been made by human hand. However, in later occupation layers, but still within the same period, genuine artefacts were found, particularly a side-scraper on a quartz flake and a quartzite knife, both retouched.

Stoneworking techniques were of high quality around 25,000 years ago, although the models of tools remain unchanged, without much variation in type, and the functions for which they were used do not indicate the emergence of new needs. Among the finds was a side-scraper with edge-trimming to form a file and a number of flakes and cores. A dating of 17,000 years ago in the same stratigraphic sequence marks another period of occupation of the cave, which also contains waste flakes in the form of flakes and cores.

Although human presence is very well documented for this period of 13,000 years from 30,000 to 17,000 years ago, not much evidence has come to light from which to reconstruct the life-styles of these ancient groups. So far there have been few finds to indicate the natural resources they used for food, but we may suppose that they hunted and gathered wild fruit. In view of the datings made, these camps obviously correspond to the Pleistocene period, when species of large animals were still in existence. However, the shape of the stone tools discovered suggest that they were not sufficiently developed to cope with hunting on such a scale. All the same, it is true that there have not been any palaeontological studies in the area showing that human beings were contemporary with the Pleistocene megafauna, and even fewer indications that they used them for food, but the characteristics of the tools of this period suggest that they were unsuitable for this purpose. The artefacts found seem to have been designed for processing various raw materials, such as wood or leather, or possibly for making other tools to be used for obtaining food, but no remains have been found on the camp sites. At the same time, unlike later periods when flint was very much in use as a raw material, during the period in question only quartz and quartzite were used, from which we may infer that those materials were probably collected around the caves and not in specially selected quarries.

Most of the caves and rock shelters in the region contain rock art on their walls. These paintings have been classified according to styles that belong to traditions variously distributed in space and time. But in the Gruta Boqueirão da Pedra Furada were found deposits containing small blocks with traces of red paint, the older one being found in a layer dated 25,400 years ago and the other a stone that formed part of a hearth dated 17,000 years ago. This clearly indicates that these very ancient hunters were already familiar with the use of pigments, probably for wall painting.

The same caatinga region south-east of Piauí continued to be occupied by small groups of hunters whose remains are still to be found in various localities. In the cave of Caldeirão do Rodrigues I the first occupants (bed VIII) arrived 18,600 years ago, or even earlier, since fertile sediments are still found at the lowest level. The cave was unsuitable for habitation because of its limited open spaces, but in any event hearths have been found, in some cases marked out with stones. Although no stone artefacts have been found at the lowest levels, there is no doubt that this place was occupied by human beings. Given its degree of inhabitability, this cave was probably occupied only temporarily and sporadically, since the next settlement level (bed VII) appeared 9,000 years later.

These hunting societies continued to live in Piauí between 15,000 and 12,000 years ago. Remains from this period have been found in the cave of the Meio site, where the first occupants arrived around 14,300 years ago and remained until around 12,000 years ago; they had a homogeneous technology very similar to the older ones in the region. Several stone objects show signs of use; these include flakes, cores or anvils bearing marks where they were struck. But there are also tools with edge-trimming, such as sidescrapers, one of which is bifacial. Although chert and flint were found in use on this site, together with quartz and quartzite, there was still no effort to obtain particular raw materials, since chert is a part of the natural formation of the walls of the shelter and there are very few flint objects.

Although the findings on the food remains have not yet been published, the information considered so far points to the fact that for approximately 20,000 years the peoples that lived in south-eastern Piauí maintained a relatively stable balance with the environment from which they probably extracted necessary and sufficient resources for their survival. Throughout this period there were no technological innovations to indicate better or greater use of resources. It is obvious, too, that these resources never allowed the human groups to expand beyond certain limits, since no concentrations of artefacts or other remains to suggest greater population density have been found in any of the camp sites investigated. Despite indications that in very ancient times the climate was more humid and favoured denser vegetation, the resources provided by the environment must have been limited and became even scarcer with the passage of time when the caatinga encroached on the pastures and woods.

Cultures subsequent to 12,000 years ago

From 12,000 years ago onwards the population of Brazil became diversified, with various groups occupying territories remote from south-eastern Piauí.

The first hunters and gatherers to settle in the central region of Brazil (Minas Gerais) occupied the great rock shelter of Santana do Riacho. The region is dominated by the Serra do Cipó, rising to altitudes of 1,100 m, at the foot of which spread undulating plateaux or valleys in which limestone formations predominate. The tropical climate, with temperate winters, is arid, with rainfall of approximately 1,100 mm concentrated between October and March. These environmental characteristics make for an open forest vegetation of isolated trees and bushes with short, twisted trunks and branches and a thick xerophilous bark, a formation known regionally as cerrado, and in its most developed form, cerradão, usually found together with open grassy spaces.

In Santana do Riacho, Prous (1980–1) dated traces to about 12,000 years ago of the first occupants of the cave, which were found in a hearth approximately 2 m in diameter. At this level only one small quartz flake and traces of pigments were found, but nothing to indicate what they used for food. Although this dating of the very earliest settlements on the central Brazilian plateau is still somewhat uncertain, there is no doubt that human beings lived there at least 12,000 years ago.

There is evidence of occupation during more or less the same period, or very shortly thereafter, in the northern region of Minas Gerais, to the west of the river São Francisco, including the valley of the river Peruaçú and the Januária region. This area has an average annual temperature of 24 °C, fluctuating between 16 and 34 °C, and an annual rainfall ranging from 850 to 950 mm. There are two typical forms of vegetation: the cerrado and the caatinga, so set out that neither is uniform. In the Peruaçu Valley the oldest settlement was established on the terraces formed by erosion in the vicinity of the river, which provided shelter from the rocky cliffs, but open camp sites at least 2 km away from the river have also been found. In 1984 Prous, Junqueira and Malta excavated ancient levels in the Gruta do Boquete, where flint was the main material used for manufacturing end-scrapers and plano-convex scrapers from large thick flakes as well as other types from short flakes. Other unworked flakes showing signs of use were also discovered along with natural limestone slabs, the edges of which had been dressed with marginal flaking. Here there are indications of the use of bone as a raw material for making a sort of dagger from the diaphysis of a deer, using the epiphysis as a haft. The only food remains found were river and land molluscs, but the diet was probably supplemented by other foodstuffs that have gone unrecorded as yet.

The same type of industry was also found at the lower levels of the Gruta do Dragão in the Montalvânia region, where ceremonial sites can clearly be distinguished from the living sites. The former, adorned with paintings, are situated in shelters, while the living sites are located in various other caves and on the hilly slopes or their plateaux.

In Iuiú, a region adjacent to the one previously described, but in the State of Bahia, we find remains of a typologically similar occupation, which must date from the same period. The environment of this region is very like that in Januária and Montalvânia, but the vegetation is predominantly caatinga. However, the living sites investigated are situated on a mountain range with an average altitude of some 600 m and here, in the more remote and humid areas, the *caatinga* is relieved by a greater abundance of trees and more luxuriant grass. The deeper levels of the caves and shelters investigated – Toca da Onça and Toca do Mal Assombrado – yielded remains of an industry with the same technological characteristics as the Minas Gerais sites, although only a very few complete artefacts were recovered. However, this comparison is made inevitable by the presence of flakes, cores and the few artefacts with side-trimming, in addition to the abundant use of flint as a raw material. All this material from northern Minas Gerais and southern Bahia shows typological similarities with the Paranaíba hunting culture studied by Schmitz (1980), particularly the above-mentioned materials from Boquete (p. 331). However, a word should be said here about another area to which we shall return later. This consists of various archaeological sites in the state of Pernambuco (north-eastern Brazil), where sets of stone tools called Itaparica date from the same period as those of the Paranaíba culture, to which they also have typological similarities.

Differences were noted in the Paranaíba Culture in the deepest cave levels, especially in shelter GO-JA-01 in the south-west of the State of Goiás on one of the tributaries of the Paranaíba that forms part of the basin of the river Parana. As far as we know at present, the earliest inhabitants of the region settled in the caves around 10,750 years ago. The environment of the neighbouring region nowadays has four main features:

1 *campos* with grassy vegetation, few bushes and little in the way of vegetable food resources;
2 the *cerrados* situated between the *campos* and the woods and providing a large variety of fruit;
3 *matas cerradas* with tall trees with little fruit;
4 the marshes and river banks with reeds and little fruit, but with abundant land mammals and fish, jacares, river turtles and molluscs. This environment is not thought to have been essentially different 11,000 years ago, except that the *campos* and *cerrados* would have extended over larger areas because of the drier climate that brought about a reduction in wooded areas (Schmitz, 1980).

These ancient inhabitants of south-western Goiás also opted for the protection of shelters for their temporary camps. However, judging from the larger quantity of remains of food and industries found in them, the caves they chose were occupied for longer periods during the year and probably by larger groups. Although various types of quartzite artefacts were identified, most of them have characteristics in common: they are elongated, unifacial, usually symmetrical scrapers made from narrow, thick blades either worked along the entire margin or maintaining the original striking platform; on the inside surface only the bulb of percussion was removed. Furthermore, small, thick flints with one protruding end that may have been borers, and small discoid hammerstones polished and pecked, all form part of this people's equipment. The people who inhabited the shelters during the Paranaíba period also used bone as a raw projectile material for making points, which they probably used for hunting, although not many specimens have been found. Statistical research on the fauna in a single section of this site (Jacobus, 1983) reveals that during this period 90 per cent of the animals hunted were land mammals, more than 8 per cent reptiles and birds in equal proportions, while fish account for less than 2 per cent; land molluscs were occasionally eaten. The main mammals were deer (Cervidae), but there were also specimens of armadillos (Dasypodidae sp.), carnivores,

opossum (Didelphidae) and capybara (Hydrochaeridae). Among the reptiles were river turtles (Chelonia), jacares (Crocodilia) and lizards. The small fish vertebrae found suggest that they weighed no more than half a kilo. Oddly enough, there are no signs of the paca (*Agouti paca*), tapir (*Tapirus terrestris*) or monkey with which the region abounds today.

As regards plants, only a few small palm nuts and other as yet unidentified fruits have been found on this site.

None of the stone artefacts seems to have been efficient enough to hunt the animals whose remains are to be found on the site. The bone arrowheads may have been useful for hunting some species of animals, but not all. When we consider that the main food represented is deer, a nervous, swift animal that is very apt to make sudden changes of direction when running, we may assume that catching it was no easy task. It is probable that the stone tools discovered were used, as well as for preparing hides for various purposes, to make the real weapons, which were very likely of wood. It was observed that the stone artefacts called scrapers were worn at the edges, suggesting a dual function: scraping and cutting; but they were never used for cleaving or boring, unless the small specialized borers were used for that purpose. At the same time it is clear that no stone projectile points are to be found here.

Although this industry is unifacial, it displays a degree of sophistication that suggests a sufficiently thorough knowledge of the raw material to be able to obtain the long, thick flakes needed to produce the final object. The secondary flaking on the back of the object formed symmetrical shapes when desired; the removal of the bulb of percussion from the inside surface of the flake also points to the same conclusion. The fauna on the sites all belong to the recent Holocene period, and it seems clear that the original inhabitants of this region had no need to depend on the last survivors of the megafauna, if indeed they existed until that period.

The first settlers arrived in the north-eastern State of Pernambuco around 11,000 years ago and established themselves in Pedra do Caboclo in the flat Agreste region, albeit in a site situated between huge rocks which formed shelters and small caves. The vegetation here is of an intermediate kind between the *caatinga* and the non-spiny *Floresta caducifolia* associated with a gently rolling landscape. The humidity is higher than in the *caatinga* and the climate may be described as semi-humid or semi-arid, with dry seasons lasting from four to six months and an average annual rainfall of 1,010 mm (Laroche, 1970).

Although 11,000 years ago is the date which has been obtained for the first human occupation in Pernambuco, it is known that traces of an earlier quartz industry have been found beneath the levels that correspond to that period. They include untrimmed artefacts hewn by direct percussion from blocks or polyhedral flakes, some of which would appear to be choppers. However, there is no further information nor any radiocarbon dating of this possible earlier level to confirm its antiquity.

As we have said, 11,000 years ago the Itaparica culture took root in the region with the manufacture of artefacts similar to those already described as belonging to the Paranaíba culture of south-western Goiás. These are unifacial plano-convex stone tools, mostly leaf-shaped, some with parallel pressure-flaking along the edges and back of long, thick flakes. These artefacts vary between 5 and 11 cm in length and 3 and 4.5 cm in width; they may also be spear-shaped or triangular. Flint is the main raw material used but quartz artefacts also exist.

The same industry had already been discovered by Calderón (1969) in the Gruta do Padre in the State of Bahia, near Petrolândia, where the objects dating from 7,600 years ago show a continuity of at least 3,500 years, and in Lapa da Foice (western Minas Gerais), where artefacts of this type were still in use until 4,000 to 5,000 years ago (Dias, 1980).

The people who inhabited Santana do Riacho around 9,500 years ago manufactured a more recognizable industry than that found at a lower level on the same site. This is also the date of the earliest known tombs in Brazil, recognized as belonging to the so-called Lagoa Santa race. These people were of relatively light complexion and slender build, rather short, with delicate limbs; however, the lower limbs had insertions that suggest great muscular development. The cranial capacity was average in a dolichocephalic or hyper-dolichocephalic skull, the forehead wide and the nose broad and short in a prognathous or mesognathous face. The pelvis was narrow and high, the hands and feet small, and there was moderately marked sexual dimorphism (Alvim, et al., 1977). The burials in Santa do Riacho are mostly primary in circular or oval graves hollowed out of the ground to a depth of 20 to 30 cm. The bodies were sometimes placed in a kind of stone coffer, while others were placed in the middle of large blocks of stone already existing in the area. The head usually rests on a stone and the skull has in many cases been crushed by another block. The skeleton is in a flexed position with one arm over the head and the other on the stomach, probably because it was wrapped in a net or hammock (traces of these are present in more recent levels). Quartz scrapers or flakes and bone projectile points have been found next to the skeletons and, in one case, a bone fish-hook and necklaces made of seeds or vegetable fibres. They were single grave or multiple burials, containing several children or a child and an adult. The corpses represent equal proportions of men and women and children and adults, but very few adolescents. The average age of the women's skeletons is 30 years and the bodies are often associated with deposits of red pigments.

All this information is important in determining the characteristics of a population that lived in a *cerrado* environment and ate the flesh and kernel of the *pequi* (*Caryocar brasiliense*) along with the *sicupira* (*Pterodon abruptus*). Animal remains discovered on the site suggest that the population hunted armadillos, small deer and various rodents, including the paca (*Agouti paca*); to a lesser extent, they hunted birds, tortoises and small fish. A large land snail, the *Strophocheilus*, also appears to have been used for food, since remains of it are found burnt among the ashes and cinders in the hearths.

The industry on this site is composed of quartz, particularly glassy quartz, artefacts in the form of flakes or blades obtained from polyhedral cores. There are tall carinated scrapers, burins with signs of use on the dihedral angle and borers, particularly in an unusual form resembling gouges or 'zinken' (Prous, 1980–1). One significant find was a bifacial projectile-head that had been left uncompleted. The completed tools seem, on the whole, to have been used for scraping rather than cutting, considering the thickness of their edges; the glassy quartz flakes with their natural strong edge would have been used for cutting.

In another part of the cave, dating from around 9,000 years ago, next to the quartz industry another industry was discovered which used flakes of quartzite transported from 3 km away, out of which they made scrapers with marginal retouch that recall the Paranaíba industry of Goiás. In addition to stone artefacts, they also manufactured a few bone implements which were found in the tombs. These consist of three small points of a circular or semicircular section of mammal bone, two objects that are probably needles and a fragment of a hook, suggesting that fishing had begun even at this early date.

The cave continued to be occupied for a long time and shows great homogeneity in the types of tools used at least until 4,000 years ago. However, glassy quartz ceased to be the main raw material and was supplanted by the milky variety.

In a site not far from Santana do Riacho there is the Lapa Vermelha, in the Lagoa Santa region, where A. Emperaire (1983) dated human occupation layers to about 11,700 to 9,600 years ago. However, the presence of human beings is poorly represented by a quartz stone industry with imprecisely defined artefacts, a number of hearths and a few food remains. Some older radiocarbon dates that may be as much as 25,000 years old are still awaiting confirmation, since the stratigraphy is being reinterpreted. But it is certain that in various caves in this region of Lagoa Santa there was a stone industry of which crystalline or glassy quartz was the predominant raw material.

A unifacial industry with relatively similar characteristics, using small prismatic flakes, obtained from quartz crystal and flint flakes can be found in the deposits, particularly the deeper ones, of the Lapa Pequena near Montes Claros in the north of Minas Gerais, dating from about 8,200 to 7,600 years ago. This region, like others already mentioned, belongs to the *cerrado* type of vegetation. This site, investigated by Bryan and Gruhn (1978) has yielded some significant information. First, it has revealed the existence of a considerable number of stone objects with a small depression on one or two of their surfaces, known in the Brazilian archaeological lexicon as 'quebra-cocos' (they could be used to anchor the nuts of the coquito palm and break them with one blow), but which are really associated with bipolar flaking, especially of quartz; flakes of this kind abound on the site. Second, the scarcity of finished retouched artefacts suggests that most of the flakes were used by taking advantage of the natural edge obtained from the flaking process. Also significant is the presence of haematite cores associated with an artefact in the shape of a gouge or 'zinken' which according to Prous (1978–80) were probably used for scraping pigments. Some objects with signs of blows were also found in addition to a few bone projectile-heads and shell scrapers. We know very little about the use to which these implements were put, since the food remains in the Lapa Pequena are very sparse. The authors suggest that although the technology was rudimentary, it enabled the cave's inhabitants to survive for millennia on a diet based on land molluscs and the coquito palm. In our view, this seems somewhat far-fetched; other foodstuff that has not been preserved on the site must have been available. It is possible that the cave was inhabited only at certain times of the year in order to make use of the resources available in the vicinity.

In Cerca Grande, in the Lagoa Santa region, a crystal and quartz flake industry, comprising artefacts for cutting and scraping, already existed around 9,700 years ago. Also found in this Stone Age complex were bifacial stone projectile-heads with peduncle and barbs, probably the oldest known in Brazil, accompanied by points made of bone (Hurt and Blasi, 1969). However, the most widely accepted age of these stone points is between 4,000 and 5,000 years.

The caves and shelters of south-western Piauí were occupied continuously, so that by approximately 10,000 years ago their inhabitants were already manufacturing and using the scrapers and other artefacts typologically linked to the Itaparica culture, with flint tools predominating. In Pernambuco, the Chá do Caboclo also continued with a population of the same culture until approximately 5,000 years ago. During this period the territories to the north of Pernambuco (State of Rio Grande do Norte) were probably also populated by peoples using an Itaparica-type industry. In the west of Minas Gerais, in the Lapa da Foice and the Lapa do Gentio, carinated flint scrapers of the Itaparica type, associated with burials (Dias, 1979–80), have also been found, dating from about 8,600 years ago.

An important fact now emerging is that the industries, especially the flint industry, of the cultures whose technological equipment included an artefact like the carinated scraper, are found spread over a wide area of the Brazilian territory that coincides with the high tableland regions and those of *cerrado* and *caatinga* vegetation. With a few doubtful exceptions, there were no stone projectile-heads during this period. One of the uses of the carinated scrapers and other artefacts that usually accompany them must have been to manufacture wood weapons, and they must have been used as implements to cope with an environment that underwent no major changes for several millennia. Any of these artefacts dating from later than 6,000–5,000 years ago were probably survivals into periods when the environmental conditions began to change and new tools were required. These scrapers would thus have been most used during a period sometime between 11,000 and 6000 years ago. The beginning of this period is marked by the survival of some examples of Pleistocene megafauna found embedded in shallow wells or watering places on various sites. However, such fauna does not seem to have played an important part in the daily life of the inhabitants of this period.

Nevertheless, at periods that are partly contemporary with the manufacturers of the Itaparica industry, some sites contain other evidence of occupation by peoples with different equipment, typified by small quartz or flint flakes or blades. Until evidence is found to the contrary, we may consider that these tools satisfied only the local or regional requirements of the Itaparica themselves, who in some places did not need the typical carinated scrapers. However, it is always possible that they were really independent groups adapted to a similar environment but beginning to develop a tradition that first emerged in the Lagoa Santa region, with the small quartz and flint artefacts marking a new technological era in response to other needs.

According to this thesis, the Itaparica and their industry apparently appeared at different sites and at different times, but not everywhere.

In south-western Goiás, where the local sequence was well established, the Itaparica or Paranaiba culture of re-touched carinated scrapers was replaced around 7,400 years ago by another cultural level called Serranópolis with no clearly defined types of stone tool; there are gouges, picks, borers and small scrapers made from irregular flakes. The waste flakes are considerably larger and coarser than those of the preceding period. A tendency has also been observed to use less quartzite and more chalcedony as a raw material. Bone heads with hooks also made of bone continued to be made, indicating specialization in one type of activity, namely, river fishing. However, the most remarkable aspect is the use of land molluscs (Strophocheilidae) for food. Specimens of these have been found in large numbers in the floors occupied during this period; their shells were used as scrapers (Schmitz, 1980). This trend ran parallel with a considerable reduction in the consumption of land mammals, suggesting that this was an era when hunting was giving way to new feeding habits based much more on fruit, fish and mollusc-gathering. A similar situation has been observed in Lapa Vermelha and in the Gruta da Foice and the Gruta do Gentio where, alongside the nuts of the coquito palm, there is evidence of small-scale hunting of armadillo, lizard, land turtle and deer. However, mollusc-gathering played an important part in the diet of this period: on some sites vast heaps of their shells have been found inside the caves. Most of the sites investigated have provided evidence of greater consumption of wild fruit, indicating greater dependence on plant resources and a more diversified use of these.

This period of more active gathering of molluscs and plants, supplemented by the hunting of small and sometimes medium-sized animals, must have started during a period when the atmosphere was drier. However, the molluscs did not disappear, and they must have sought refuge in the darker, damper parts of the caves, going to meet, so to speak, hunters who found their sources of food reduced by the impoverishment of their hunting grounds. These conditions also called for a more systematic diversification of the use of fruit, which previously had been consumed only occasionally. Possibly medium-sized animals such as deer also tended to disappear from areas that provided few plants on which they could feed. They were therefore more sought after and different weapons were needed for capturing them, such as the long-distance bow and arrow. Stone projectile heads seem to have originated at some point during this period about 6,000 years ago. Although in later periods new humid conditions may have prevailed, the ancient forms of economy did not reappear and this type of diversified gathering economy, along with fishing and hunting, finally took root and developed.

It was probably just such an environmental situation (which took the Itaparica hunters, with their very specialized but inflexible strategies for coping with the *caatinga* and *cerrado* environments by surprise, around 7,000 to 6,000 years ago) that prompted some groups to move towards richer environments, such as the sea-shore. Here they probably continued to live by mollusc gathering and fishing, developing a totally different style of adaptation by about 5,000 years ago.

In the north-eastern part of the State of São Paulo and its natural prolongation, the south of the State of Minas Gerais, industries of large artefacts similar to handaxes and planes have been discussed, but their date has not yet been determined. The inhabitants of this region later adopted a more sophisticated industry comprising carinated and side scrapers, the latter with flaked marginal retouch along their entire outer edges; there are also finely executed blades with retouching over their whole surface (Carderelli, 1978–80). Further south, in the Rio Claro region, carinated scrapers and pedunculated projectile-heads have been dated at approximately 6,000 years ago. On the Água Ronca site a set of stone flake-tools has been dated to about 6,200 years ago, while in Pau d'Alho hearths with stone material based on cores and flakes obtained by direct percussion date from about 5,500 years ago. To the south of São Paulo, the Paranapanema region was probably first inhabited around the same period, since on the Camargo site a rather elaborate industry of bifacially worked artefacts and pedunculated points has been found, dated to about 4,650 years ago (Pallestrini and Chiara, 1978).

THE FORESTS AND PLAINS OF SOUTHERN BRAZIL AND NORTH-EASTERN ARGENTINA (Map 32)

The southern region of Brazil

The southern region of Brazil (approximate latitude 26° S) shows traces of prehistoric occupation differing somewhat from that of the *cerrado* and *caatinga* region of the centre and north-east. This area was first occupied by human beings approximately 13,000 years ago.

Generally speaking, the region features low, rolling countryside with an altitude of less than 400 m; this dominant topography stretches southwards to Uruguay and westwards to Argentina. The eastern area is covered by a narrow coastal plain, with lowlands bounded by the ocean and the Serra do Mar. In the north, higher ground predominates (up to 2,000 m) and covers the southern part of the Brazilian *planalto*, extending to north-eastern Argentina.

The climate in this region is mesothermal and humid, with heavy rainfall in the autumn–winter season, although it rains all year round, with a precipitation of 2,000 mm in the Serra do Mar and 1,250 mm in the plains. The average temperature nowadays is 22 °C, but minimum temperatures are fairly low. The vegetation can be divided into three main types: a relatively dense forest of broad-leafed trees in the river valleys, on the slopes of the Serra do Mar and along the edge of the *planalto*; a sparser subtropical forest with araucaria (*Araucaria angustifolia*) less close, typical of the higher areas; and clear grassy fields, sometimes with park formations, occupying the southern areas and part of the heights of the *planalto*.

Regional geological studies conducted in Touro Passo (Rio Grande do Sul) by Bombin (1976) reveal that between 20,000 and 14,000 years ago, during a period corresponding to the last stage of the alpine Würm glaciation, the climate was cold and dry as a consequence of the predominant Pacific anticyclone. A period of seasonally concentrated rains occurred between 14,000 and 12,000 years ago, and the climate was humid with the prevailing Atlantic anticyclone between 12,000 and 5,000 years ago, which included the 'climatic optimum'.

The oldest remains suggesting human occupation of the region belong to the second of these periods, from which several examples of different species of extinct fauna were found: they include *Glossotherium robustum* (giant sloth), Glyptodons (giant armadillo), *Toxodon platensis* (ancient hippopotamus), *Stegomastodon humboldtii* (large elephant), *Equus curvidens* (horse), *Paleolama paradoxa* (camelid) and specimens of fauna still extant.

The skull of a *Glossotherium robustum* was found at the same level as the remains of a stone industry consisting of two thick discoid bifaces, two tabular objects with marks of use on their edges and four flakes with similar marks. They are rough tools worked by percussion and pressure-flaking on basalt cores and natural sandstone blades, and represent non-specialized artefacts. This association of human industry and extinct fauna dates back to about 12,800 years ago in the gorges of the Ibicuí river.

Various camp sites are concentrated on the Brazilian banks of the Uruguay river on the border with Argentina and even as far as the Uruguayan border. Here a stone industry – the Uruguay culture – was found, consisting of knives with pressure retouch, small circular scrapers, side-scrapers and end-scrapers, rough-hewn spear-shaped handaxes and a large number of flakes of various sizes, some of them débitage of pressure retouch. These tools also include several types of small and medium-sized pedunculated biface stone projectile points; they are usually narrow with pressure retouch. These remains belong to a population that settled at the confluence of small streams with the river Uruguay at some time between 10,400 and 8,600 years ago. The datings indicate that they are the oldest projectile-heads discovered on Brazilian soil. The sites have not yielded many food remains except for a few bones and charred fruit.

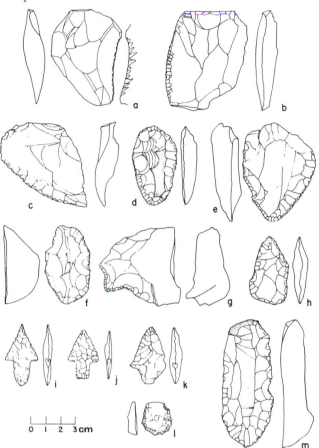

Figure 91 Stone artefacts, the Vinitu stage (Brazil): a, flake used; b–k, 'retouched' flakes; l, retouched microlith; m, retouched blade. a, plane; b, side-scraper; c, end-scraper; d, oval scraper; e and m, pointed scrapers; f, plano-convex scraper; g, beak-shaped scraper; h, leaf-shaped projectile head; i–k, projectile heads with neck (k, an artefact in the making); l, hook-shaped scraper.

In the north-western part of the region, on Brazil's border with Paraguay, numerous camp sites have been found on rivers that flow into the Paraná. Although they have not been radiocarbon dated, they are attributed to the period between 9,000 and 8,000 years ago. The tools of this culture, the Vinitu (Fig. 91), consist of stone implements fashioned on flakes and blades and comprise mainly leaf-shaped pedunculated projectile points and a variety of scrapers, knives, handaxes, choppers and so forth. Among the material collected on surface sites were a few examples of the fish-tail projectile points that abound throughout the South American continent, although only one of them was actually found in context (Chmyz, 1982).

About 7,000 years ago the Umbú culture (Fig. 92), which used artefacts probably derived from the two earlier cultures already mentioned, extended over a vast area of southern Brazil. These people's camps were situated in open sites on the borders between *florestas* and *campos*, but they also occupied shelters in the *planalto* area. Thus, camp sites have existed alongside the Umbú culture in the same region of southern Brazil, but their camp sites are found on terraces and hills flanking rivers and streams in areas with an average altitude of 200 m in a tropical and subtropical environment. Occasionally this culture has been found in caves or shelters. They are usually surface sites that occasionally reach a depth of between 20 and 30 cm, suggesting that they were occupied only on a temporary basis. The stone tools include artefacts made of sandstone or basalt, depending on the material available locally, and comprise different types of scraper, knives, choppers, borers, handaxes and pick-shaped instruments, manufactured and retouched by direct percussion (Schmitz, 1984). The instruments are all large, heavy and rudimentary. The most characteristic of these artefacts is the curved biface, commonly known as a 'boomerang' because of its relative similarity to that implement. Also significant is the virtual lack of stone projectile points of which there are only rare examples on a very few sites. Some polished stone objects, such as the bolas, were already known at this period.

It seems clear that the association of the living-sites with an environment of dense vegetation and the diversity of the artefacts' shapes and functions are two terms of a single equation.

These cultures, the Umbú and Humaitá, lasted with their more general features until at least 3,000 years ago and in some places even later. Their cultural patterns also extended to the adjacent regions of eastern Paraguay and north-eastern Argentina. In this latter area there have been discoveries of sites probably linked to those of the Uruguay and Umbú

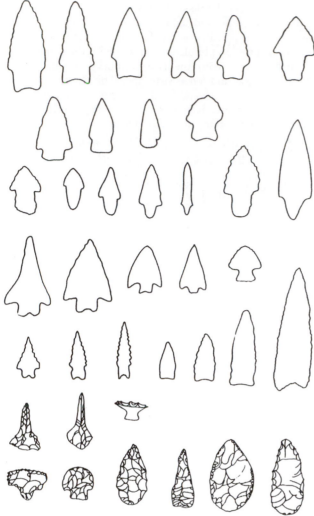

Figure 92 Stone artefacts, Umbú culture (Brazil): projectile points, borers, small stemmed scrapers, small biface leaf-shaped points.

been found at altitudes of over 600 m and under 200 m (Kern, 1981–2). This culture also used pedunculated stone projectile-heads with triangular or leaf-shaped barbs, as well as knives, various forms of scraper, borers, handaxes and other implements. Less common is the appearance of laminate end-scrapers, burins, choppers and large bifaces. In some sites bolas from *boleadoras*, with or without perimetrical grooves, as well as axes, were found. There are also bone artefacts such as scrapers, double-tapered points, spatulas, hooks, needles, scrapers and pierced animal teeth.

These hunters appear to have been more successful with their hunting gear, since remains of animals hunted by them are found on some camp sites: anta (Tapiridae), various species of deer (Cervidae), peccary (Tayassuidae), paca (Agoutidae), monkeys of different species (Cebidae), small and medium-sized rodents, armadillos (Dasypodidae), some felines (Felidae), land turtles (Chelonia) and lizards (Sauria). In some camps, fish bones and land molluscs also appear. The fruit consumed was the small nut of various palm trees and the araucaria pine. Some sites were situated on the banks of lagoons, apparently for seasonal fishing and crustacean collection, not ignoring the land fauna. The existence of marine remains on sites in the interior suggest that the people who lived there at this period exploited marine resources on a seasonal basis and pitched their camps near the sea.

The Humaitá culture (Fig. 93), around 6,900 years ago,

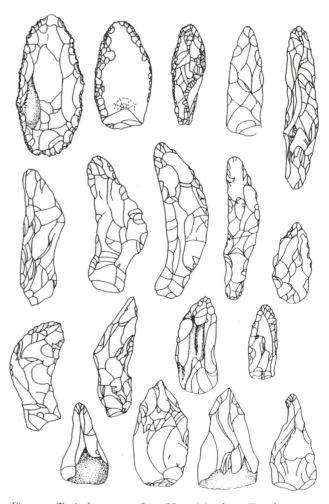

Figure 93 Typical stone artefacts, Humaitá culture (Brazil).

cultures, since they include convex-based triangular projectile-heads with peduncles and barbs.

Defined by Menghin in 1955, the Altoparanaense culture is Argentina's equivalent to the Humaitá culture of Brazil. It spanned the period from approximately 10,000 to 4,000 years ago, passing through various stages. The earliest stage possessed only a stone industry of thick plano-convex flakes. The following stage, Classical Altoparanaense or Alto-paranaense II, was already producing bifacially worked arte-facts of which the most outstanding are curved bifaces or clubs, oval scrapers and picks. Remains have been found in the Tres de Mayo cave in the province of Misiones, where, in addition to the typical stone industry including the 'boomerangs' or clubs, remains of existing fauna have also been found, mostly tapir or anta (*Tapirus terrestris*) and deer (*Mazama* sp.). There are also large quantities of fish remains found together with bone hooks; bone was also used to manufacture projectile-heads, needles and borers. The land snail (*Strophecheilus*) was eaten and its shell used for planing wood through holes made in its back.

This stone tradition continued until the periods when ceramics and cultivation were adopted as a form of sub-sistence, around 2,000 years ago.

The Uruguayan and Argentine pampas (Map 32)

The plains of southern Brazil extend naturally into Uru-guayan territory, where hunters and gatherers settled on the banks of the rivers and streams that flow into the river Uruguay. Their culture is known here as the Catalanense culture, but in reality it is a southern extension of the Uruguay culture found on Brazilian territory which dates from 10,000 years ago.

The tools made of silicified sandstone include end-scrapers, side-scrapers and various kinds of knives worked bifacially with percussion retouch. The projectile-heads are unevenly distributed among the various sites and are totally absent from some (Taddei, 1980).

In some camps on the river Cuareim (the Uruguay–Brazil boundary) a poorly defined industry has been found, comprising scrapers, planes and flakes with signs of use, in which there is very little percussion retouch. The artefacts are coarser and larger than in the Catalanense and there is a remarkable lack of stone heads and bolas. It is likely that this culture, called Cuareimense, is merely a less elaborate offshoot of the Catalanense and dates from between 8,000 and 7,000 years ago.

In central Uruguay, other, more recent manifestations of hunters have been found with stone implements comprising mainly pedunculated, barbed projectile points worked bifacially with various forms of pressure retouch. Points without peduncles, bifaces, bola stones and sling stones, querns, with their handles, side-scrapers, end-scrapers and so forth have also been found. It is estimated that these hunters lived at around 5,000 years ago and their surface camps are scattered throughout Uruguay; one has even been discovered on the sea-shore. Although they were not involved in agriculture to begin with, some later tools have been found in association with agricultural levels. The bolas and sling stones indicate a type of equipment adapted to the prairies or plains where ñandu (*Rhea americana*) were abundant. The querns, on the other hand, suggest a different type of processing of the vegetable resources available.

The humid pampa area situated in east-central Argentina was first populated, according to available data, around 10,700 years ago in Cerro La China. This has yielded cultural remains that are probably connected with the typical fish-tail projectile points discovered in the area, although out of context (Cardich, 1984).

Further south, a group settled on the Arroyo Seco 2 site (Tres Arroyos, Province of Buenos Aires) c.8,500 years ago, living in the same environment as the now extinct fauna and using it for food. At the lower levels of the camp site there was a unifacial industry, worked predominantly on quartzite and basalt flakes, although blades were also used. A few end-scrapers were made from quartzite cores. According to the information available, this industry did not include any stone points. Remains of existing fauna have been found in associ-ation with this industry: guanaco, deer, ñandu, hare and armadillo, and also of extinct species such as *Megatherium*, *Mylodon*, *Macrauchenia*, *Eutatus*, *Equus* and a species of the *Hippidion–Onohippidium* (horse) complex.

From this period onwards there is a gap in our knowledge, since the typical hunting cultures of the Pampas, which are identified by their different names, emerged only much later.

The best known of these cultures, the Tandiliense, used quartzite as a raw material for manufacturing implements such as thick end-scrapers, flakes with marginal retouch, side-scrapers and 'parrot-beak' flakes. They lived on the typical animals of the pampa, such as ñandu, armadillo, deer, and so on, but no projectile-points have been found in association with this context.

There is some dissent about this culture's real age. Menghin and Bormida, who discovered this culture, pro-posed a date of about 7,000 years ago, based on geological considerations. Madrazo, on the other hand, has pointed out that the Tandiliense material in other places appears associated with materials that postdate the Hispanic con-quest. However, other authors (for instance, Orquera, 1980) contest this position and, at least for one site, confirm the original chronology.

The most typical hunters of this area, who used projectile-heads and bolas, possibly revealing influences of different origins, were to develop after 5,000 years ago.

The Sierras Centrales of Argentina, extending across the provinces of Córdoba and San Luis, are situated to the west of the humid pampa region. Rex González (1960) identified a level of guanaco and deer hunters and gatherers extending back to 8,000 years ago at various sites in those central mountains, but particularly in the Intihuasi cave. Its most characteristic implement is a spear-shaped projectile-head for a throwing spear accompanied by large end-scrapers, side-scrapers, flat querns, and so on. This industry coincides with an area extending from the Andean regions (Chapter 34).

EASTERN PATAGONIA

The region of the South American continent that lies south of the thirty-eighth parallel is called Patagonia and comprises three subregions: western or Chilean Patagonia, the Pat-agonian Andes or the Cordillera of the southern Andes and eastern Patagonia. The last is the largest of the three terri-tories and mainly features terraces and plateaux stretching to the Atlantic Ocean, gradually losing altitude. This great plain is seamed with valleys and ravines with deep gullies – some containing rivers – interspersed with low-lying areas con-taining lagoons. Here and there rise chains of low mountains, hills of volcanic origin or occasional rocky cliffs. The typical climate is dry, semi-arid, cold and buffeted by strong westerly winds. The landscape is mainly semi-desert steppe, with vegetation of sparse bush, some grassy patches and small cacti. This vegetation becomes denser in lower-lying areas and in the gullies, which afford some degree of protection. The most typical animals of the area are the guanaco (*Lama guanicoe*), a type of small deer called the huemul (*Hippocamelus bisulcus*), the ñandu (*Pterocnemia pennata*) and the puma (*Felis concolor*). The Patagonian coast is composed of huge escarpments in some parts and sweeping beaches in others with a gentle prolongation into the submarine shelf, which is shallow and level.

The ice-sheets of the last Pleistocene glaciation covered a limited part of eastern Patagonia, except in the extreme south. According to the latest available data, a considerable advance of the ice-sheets occurred about 19,500 years ago, coinciding with a similar occurrence in other parts of the world. Approximately 16,200 years ago there was a retreat, followed by a readvance that seems to have lasted from 15,000 to 11,000 years ago. The ice mass then began a further retreat, and stabilized at its present position *c.*11,000 years ago.

These chronological pointers are important, because they indicate the conditions found by human beings when they settled in the region around 12,000 years ago or even a little earlier. These groups of hunters found a gentler climate with higher temperature, at least until the Neoglacial period (*c.*4,500 years ago), when the ice-sheets again advanced and retreated, though more moderately. Nevertheless, Auer's pollinic studies show that between 11,000 and 10,000 years ago the atmosphere cooled as a consequence of an advance of the ice-sheets, but as yet no glaciological data have come to light to validate this theory.

What is certain, however, is that around 12,600 years ago groups of hunters arrived at the Cañadón de las Cuevas in the Province of Santa Cruz in the southern part of Eastern Patagonia. We still do not know where they came from or what route they took, since this is the earliest known occupation in the continent's entire southern cone. It is likely that their origins, still to be discovered, were Andean or sub-Andean from further north. These original occupants of the region settled at the lower levels (level 11) of cave 3 of the site known as Los Toldos, situated in the above-mentioned Cañadón, when the floor of the cave was approximately 2 m lower than it is at present. They left behind them an industry of stone artefacts (called 'Industry of Level 11') typified by its unifacial marginal retouch by direct percussion and, to a lesser extent, by pressure-flaking on large thick flakes besides two lithic projectile-points. By these methods they manufactured knives, scrapers and graters, irregular in shape. They used scaler retouch, but also parallel and sub-parallel flaking, and there are a few examples of invasive retouch. The same industry was discovered in layer 12 of cave 7 at El Ceibo, 150 km south of Los Toldos, where deeper deposits were found, sealed in by stones from a massive erosion, which separates them from subsequent deposits above and from later cultures.

Analysis of the El Ceibo artefacts (Fig. 94) gave rise to some significant conclusions on their functions and the activities for which they were used. The loss of small flakes from the edges of the tools, which would substantiate the theory that they were 'used', was disregarded, because such losses could also be attributed to natural causes, and a study was made of the micro-polishings and the various tiny grooves left by the friction of the implements against different raw materials: wood, non-woody plants, dry leather, fresh skin, flesh, antler or bone, shell, and so on. All this would suggest that the artefacts made by these groups had no shafts

and were held directly in the hand; most of them were used to work fresh or dry skins and for cutting flesh; only a few were used to work on wood. Those used for flesh were not sharp enough to sever tendons, nor did they cut to the bone. There are other indications that each of the various types of tool served a unique purpose, that is, it was used to process a single type of material (Mansur-Franchomme, in Cardich, 1984).

Some animal remains show that the caves' inhabitants were hunters. In Los Toldos 3, for instance, guanaco bones (*Lama guanicoe*) have been found in abundance and, subsequently, extinct horse (*Onohippidium* sp.), remains of other camelids, different from the guanaco, probably *Lama gracilis*, already extinct in the Upper Pleistocene, and puma (*Felis concolor*); there are also smaller bones of rodents that have yet to be identified (Cardich et al., 1973; Cardich, 1984).

The discovery of two projectile points in this same context suggests that this instrument was used for hunting the animals found. The fact that very few have been found in Los Toldos and in El Ceibo corroborates the hypothesis that the caves were not primarily workshops where instruments were manufactured, but camps where people lived, processed skins and engaged in other domestic activities. These sites yield up few cores or flaking rejects; the points would have gone directly from the workshops to the hunting camps.

The same region was occupied by the Toldense culture around 9,300 years ago. Identified by Menghin in 1952 in Los Toldos, it was later more clearly defined in this cave's second occupation layer (Cardich et al., 1973) and in various other sites in the Rio Pinturas area, such as Cueva de las Manos (around 9,300 years ago) and Cueva Grande del Arroyo Feo (around 9,300 years ago) (Gradin et al., 1976, 1979; Aguerre, 1981–2). The Toldenses also hunted guanaco, which they supplemented with the hunting of birds such as the martineta (*Eudromia* sp.), small ñandu (*Pterocnemia pennata*) and larger ñandu (*Rhea america*) that normally live further north; horse (*Parahipparion*) was hunted from time to time. This era's stone industry (Fig. 95) is one of artefacts manufactured on obsidian and flint of medium-sized and large flakes with marginal retouch: end-scrapers, side-scrapers, borers and knives. However, the most characteristic instrument is the triangular projectile-head without peduncle, with a straight or slightly convex base, with bifacial scalar and subparallel steep retouch applied by percussion and pressure, the very distinctive characteristic of Los Toldos culture. Some stone bolas have been found in the same

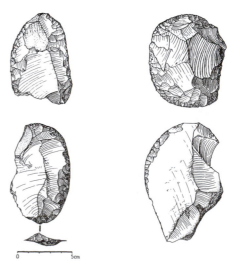

Figure 94 Earliest stone artefacts, El Ceibo, Patagonia (Argentina): different types of scrapers.

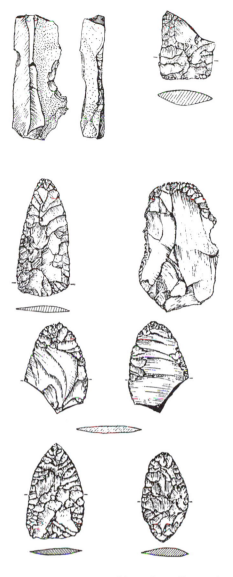

crystalline gypsum, were part of the paintings; by their stratigraphical position these materials are contemporaneous with the tools of the same origin. We follow Gradin's chronological sequence (1984): he divides the wall paintings into three main groups: (1) archaic paintings, with guanaco hunting scenes, hunters and weapons, hands in negative and simple geometric and abstract patterns (points, circles and straight lines); (2) engraved curvilinear patterns, ñandu, puma and guanaco footprints, human hands and feet, guanaco silhouettes, lizards and some anthropomorphic figures; (3) abstract or geometric paintings, rectilinear (in echelon), sometimes in association with positive hands and tridigits, schematic anthropomorphic figures, miniature geometric designs, parallel lines and people on horseback (Hispanic).

Gradin (1984) says that since twelve millennia ago hunting groups reached the area between the Deseado and Santa Cruz rivers; they made parietal art that is basically representational and which included hands in negative and hunting scenes. Its development seems to indicate a stylistic progression from naturalistic to schematic representation. Black, yellow, ochre, red, purple and white are all used for painting. He notes that at least since seven millennia ago many sites of this extensive Patagonian territory have some of these abstract paintings which are essentially geometric, all of simple form, usually executed in red. They have been recorded in several places, especially at the tip of mainland Chile, in Chubut province, and in the transitional pampa–patagonian area.

The Toldense culture disappeared from the Cueva de Los Toldos around 8,750 years ago, but continued in the area around the Rio Pinturas until around 7,300 years ago, which suggests the Toldenses abandoned the intermediate zone between *cordillera* and the ocean, and in the former, the Patagonian hunters continued to exist with an economy much the same as that of the preceding period and used tools which show evidence of a continuation of Toldense techniques.

In the Patagonian north-west sector, against the Andean *Cordillera*, that is away from the plains, guanaco hunters were inhabiting Traful cave around 9,300 years ago and this occupation persisted until more or less five millennia ago. Their tools included very elaborated triangular projectile points.

After 1,500 years of neglect, the Los Toldos cave was once more occupied around 7,250 years ago by other guanaco hunters, who were much more expert in this type of hunting. While the stone industry of these new inhabitants (Fig. 96) – called the Casapedrenses – does not include the stone projectile point, it does contain the stone bola, which must have been its most effective weapon. This was accompanied by blades with edge retouch for manufacturing scrapers and knives, and worked on one surface only; there are also blades with marginal notches. On this site at least guanaco flesh was the only meat consumed. This site was probably occupied by the Casapedrenses as a base camp for guanaco hunting in the particularly favourable adjacent areas, but the discovery of the bones of guanacos of all ages suggests that the cave was occupied throughout the year and the presence of all parts of the animal indicates that it was consumed in its entirety on the spot (Cardich, 1984).

The Casapedrense culture also abandoned Los Toldos suddenly, probably driven out by volcanic eruptions in nearby areas, which covered the floor of the cave with ash. This phenomenon seems to correspond to the second eruptive period defined by Auer, which occurred 4,800 years

Figure 95 Stone artefacts, Los Toldos culture, Patagonia (Argentina): points, knife and scrapers.

context, confirming their relative antiquity. There was a parallel industry of bone artefacts comprising borers and spatulas. At the levels corresponding to this culture remains have been found of the typical pictographs of the area: fragments of ochre and stones loosened from the ceilings of the caves with traces of red-pigment painting, as well as other indications (Gradin, 1984). Attention must be drawn here to the chronological and typological similarity, indicated by the triangular points without peduncle, between the culture of the Toldense hunters and that of the occupants of level III of Fell's cave and the Palli Aike cave in the extreme south of Chile (Chapter 35).

The Patagonian cave walls on which floors and strata of the different cultures described in this chapter have been found are crowded with innumerable paintings. Probably they were related to individual or group rituals, part of the inhabitants' life cycle. Abstract geometrical drawings, and even the figurative drawings, have no clear significance for us, but they surely were of vital importance to their makers and their communities.

It is just at this moment, in the period of Toldense culture, when there appears in Patagonia the first evidence of cave paintings. Such traces are present as pigment fragments in the stratigraphical layers, and other raw materials, such as

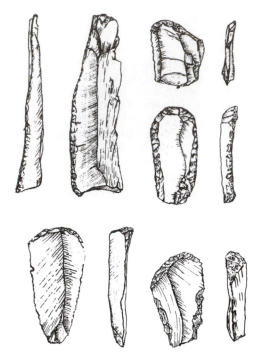

Figure 96 Stone artefacts, Casapredense culture, Patagonia (Argentina): knife and scrapers.

ago. However, the Casapendrenses' bladecraft was to emerge in later cultures in the region after 5,000 to 4,500 years ago.

The Casapedrense technology extended to certain areas north of the Los Toldos region. In the Piedra Parada region, on Chubet river, artefacts corresponding to the Casapedrense culture in their characteristics were found, and it is considered they are of the same age.

In the far south of the continent, in the Cueva de las Buitreras, 80 km from the sea, there was also a stone flake industry with signs of use on the edges, as well as bones showing the same signs, associated with extinct fauna such as *Mylodon* and *Hippidium* and existing fauna: guanaco, foxes, birds and small rodents. A carbon-14 date indicates that the lower levels, where this extinct fauna appears, date as far back as 10,000 years ago. The presence of a Delphinidae bone (dolphin) indicates that its inhabitants went in for sea-fishing, although probably sporadically.

Occupation of the sea-coast poses a number of chronological problems, mainly because the antiquity attributed to the occupational evidence has been based on that of the various levels of the marine terraces on which the camps were built. Auer's estimated dates for these terraces are now disputed, although no new dates have been suggested (Orquera, 1980). Two of the supposedly oldest cultural manifestations, the Oliviense (12,000 years ago) and the Solanense (11,000 years ago) are challenged by Borrero and Caviglia (1978) and Borrero (1980). They have carried out soundings in Bahia Solano and concluded that the populations that settled nearest to the sea in order to make use of its resources did so around 5,000 years ago. Similar problems in calculating antiquity on the basis of marine terraces are encountered all along the Patagonian coast; we have therefore chosen to consider these occupations as belonging to later periods, to be discussed in Volume II.

BIBLIOGRAPHY

AB'SÁBER, A. N. 1983. Mecanismos das migrações préhistóricas na América do Sul: busca de correlações paleoclimáticas. In: ENCONTRO DA SOCIEDADE BRASILEIRA PARA O PROGRESSO DA CIÊNCIA, 35, Belém. *Atas.*

AGUERRE, A. M. 1981–2. *The Lower Levels of Cueva Grande (Arroyo Feo) Rio Pinturas Area, Province of Santa Cruz.* Buenos Aires. (Rep. Argentine Anthropol. Soc., 14, NS, No. 2.)

ALVIM, M. et al. 1977. *The Ancient Inhabitants of the Lagoa Santa Area, Minas Gerais, Brazil: Morphological Study.* Belo Horizonte, UFMG. (Arch. Nat. Hist. Mus., 2.)

BOMBIN, M. 1976. *Evolutionary Paleo-Ecological Model for the Neo-quarternary of the Campanha Region, West of Rio Grande do Sul (Brazil): The Touro Passo Formation, its Fossil Content, and Post-depositional Pedogenesis.* Porto Alegre, Pontificia Universidade Católica do Rio Grande do Sul.

BORRERO, L. A. 1980. *Geomorphological and Chronological Problems Relating to Archaeological Materials Attributed to the Solanense and Oliviense Industries.* Buenos Aires, Archaeol. Museum Dr. O. F. A. Menghin.

BORRERO, L. A.; CAVIGLIA, S. E. 1978. Stratigraphy of the Concheros de Bahia Solano: Campaign 1976–1977. In: CONGRESO NACIONAL DE ARQUEOLOGIA ARGENTINA, 5, San Juan.

BRYAN, A. L.; GRUHN, R. 1978. Results of a Test Excavation at Lapa Pequena. *Arq. Mus. Hist. Nat.* (Belo Horizonte), Vol. 3.

CARDERELLI, S. 1978–80. Temas de arqueologia brasileira: 2 – arcaico do interior. *Anu. Divulg. Cient. Univ. Catol. Goiás* (Goiânia).

CALDERÓN, V. 1969. Preliminary Note on the Archaeology of the Central and Southwestern Regions of the State of Bahia. *Pronapa*, No. 2.

CARDICH, A. 1984. Palaeo-Environments and the Earliest Human Presence. In: SEMINARIO SOBRE LA SITUACION DE LA INVESTIGACION DE LAS CULTURAS INDIGENAS DE LA PATAGONIA. *Las culturas de América en la epoca del descubrimiento.* Madrid. (Bibl. V Cent.)

CARDICH, A.; CARDICH, L. A.; HAJDUK, A. 1973. *Archaeological Sequence and Radiocarbon Chronology of Cave 3 of Los Toldos.* Buenos Aires. (Rep. Argent. Anthropol. Soc., 7.)

CHMYZ, I. 1982. Estado atual das pesquisas arqueológicas na margem esquerda do Rio Paraná. *Estud. Brasil.* (Curitiba), Vol. 8.

DIAS, O. 1978–80. Temas de arqueologia brasileira: 1 – Paleo-índio [The Palaeo-Indian in Minas Gerais]. *Anu. Divulg. Cient. Univ. Catol. Goiás* (Goiânia).

EMPERAIRE, A. 1983. *La Caatinga du Sud-Est du Piaui (Brésil): étude Ethnobotanique.* Paris.

GONZALES, A. 1960. La estratigrafia de la Gruta de Intihuasi y sus relaciones con otros sitios precerámicos de Sud-América. *Rev. Inst. Anthropol. Univ. nac. Cordoba,* Vol. 1.

GRADIN, C. 1984. Arqueología y arte rupestre de los cazadores de la Patagonia. In: SEMINARIO SOBRE LA SITUACION DE LA INVESTIGACION DE LAS CULTURAS INDIGENAS DE LA PATAGONIA. *Las culturals de América en la epoca del descubrimiento.* Madrid. (Bibl. V Cent.)

GRADIN, C. J.; ASCHERO, C. A.; AGUERRE, A. M. 1976. *Investigaciones arqueológicas en la Cueva de las Manos, espacia Alto Rio Pinturas, Prov. de Santa Cruz.* Buenos Aires. (Rep. Argent. Anthropol. Soc., 10.)

—— 1979. *Arqueología del area Rio Pinturas, Prov. de Santa Cruz.* Buenos Aires. (Rep. Argent. Anthropol. Soc., 13.)

GUIDON, N. 1981. Datações pelo C.14 de sítios arqueológicos em São Raimundo Nonato, sudeste do Piauí. *Clio IV, Univ. Fed. Pernambuco* (Recife).

—— 1984. As primeiras ocupações humanas da área arqueológica de São Raimundo Nonato, Piauí. *Rev. Arqueol.* (Belém), Vol. 2, No. 1.

HURT, W. R.; BLASI, O. 1969. O projeto arqueológico de Lagoa Santa, Minas Gerais, Brasil (nota final). *Arq. Mus. Paran. Arqueol.* (Curitiba), No. 4.

JACOBUS, A. L. 1983. *Restos alimentares do sítio GO-JA-01, Serranópolis, Goiás.* São Leopoldo, Instituto Anchietano de Pesquisas, Unisinos.

KERN, A. 1981–2. Variáveis para a definição e a caracterização das tradições pre-cerámicas Humaitá e Umbú. *Arq. Mus. Hist. Nat.* (Belo Horizonte), Vol. 6–7.

LAROCHE, A. 1970. *O sítio arqueológico da Pedra do Caboclo.* Recife.

ORQUERA, L. A. 1980. Geocronología del cuaternario en Patagonia. *Sapiens, Mus. Arqueol. Dr. O. F. A. Menghin* (Buenos Aires), No. 4.

PALLESTRINI, L.; CHIARA, P. 1978. *Indústria lítica de 'Camargo 76', Pirajú, Est. São Paulo.* São Paulo. (Coleção de Estudos em Homenagem a Annette Lamming-Emperaire.)

PROUS, A. 1978–80. Temas de arqueologia brasileira: 1 – Paleoíndio, o paleo-índio em Minas Gerais. *Anu. Divulg. Cient. Univ. Catol. Goiás* (Goiânia).

—— 1980–1. Fouilles du Grand Abri de Santana do Riacho (MG), Brésil. *Journal de la Soc. des Américanistes*, Paris.

PROUS, A.; JUNQUEIRA, F.; MALTA, I. 1984. Arqueologia do Alto Médio São Francisco, região de Januária e Moltalvânia. *Rev. Arqueol.* (Belém), No. 2.

SCHMITZ, P. I. 1980. A evolução da cultura do sudoeste de Goiás. *Pesqui., Antropol.* (São Leopoldo), No. 31.

—— 1984. *Caçadores e coletores da pré-história do Brasil.* São Leopoldo.

TADDEI, A. 1980. Carácter y contenido de algunas industrias precerámicas del territorio Uruguayo. *Sapiens, Mus. Arqueol. Dr O. F. A. Menghin* (Buenos Aires), No. 4.

34

THE EQUATORIAL AND TROPICAL ANDES

from the arrival of humans to the beginnings of food production

Luis G. Lumbreras Salcedo

The area known as the central Andes falls within what is now Peru. It is a region that extends between latitudes 6° S and 15° S approximately, which places it within the earth's tropical belt. To the north, between latitudes 6° S and 4° N, lie the northern Andes, which are right in the middle of the Equatorial belt.

This would indicate tropical climatic and ecological features, with wet evergreen forests and heavy rainfall, as found in most of tropical America, particularly in the Amazon basin, which stretches to the east of the Andes across the broadest part of South America. But the effects of latitudinal geographical position are considerably altered by the high altitude of the Andes, a range in which some of the highest mountains are more than 6,500 m above sea-level and which lies mainly between 2,500 and 4,000 m above sea-level.

The Andean mountain range runs the full length of the western flank of Southern America, but its effects are obviously most marked in the tropical zone, which boasts the greatest possible variety of scenery and climate. Every type of climate, vegetation, soil type and land-form found at any latitude, from the ice-cold polar regions to steaming hot rain forest, is represented in this area. This characteristic variety of land-form obviously brings with it a network of ecological, climatic and territorial interrelations and influences very different from any that have been formed in other latitudes.

One feature is that the most varied landscapes are found side by side, so that the steppes or the cold high plateaux (*paramos*), with their own characteristic plants and animals, are in close communication with the temperate inter-Andean valleys or the surrounding savannah. A good account of the close proximity of these different landscapes was given by Spanish chroniclers who arrived in Peru during the sixteenth century, and wrote that in a single day's journey on horseback travellers could move from winter to summer between one region and another, the one cold and rainy and the other hot and dry. Likewise, in one day, one could leave near-absolute deserts for well-watered valleys and tundra for woodland.

This scenic variety is matched by an equally unusual climatic system. Seasonal temperature changes in the tropical region are known to be always very small, the difference

between winter and summer and the intermediate seasons being hardly noticeable in terms of temperature. Seasons are usually defined in terms of higher or lower rainfall – 'dry' and 'rainy' seasons – and changes in wind magnitude and force. In the Andes the *cordillera* modifies these typical tropical conditions: in the highest areas daily fluctuations in temperature are considerable, temperatures falling below 0 °C at night and sometimes rising to more than 20 °C during the day, whereas in these same regions the difference in temperature from one season to the other is no more than 1 °C.

From the ecological point of view, it should be pointed out that this scenic 'mosaic' taken as a whole constitutes a biotic macrosystem of an endemic nature, which is isolated from the rest of the continent because the mountain range forms a barrier which places the Andean landmass in a somewhat marginal position in relation to other eastern South American regions and the '*chaco*' or the pampas to the south.

Many factors in addition to altitude combine to produce these and other anomalies; most outstanding are the Humboldt and El Niño ocean currents, the former cold and the latter hot, which pass close to the coasts of Ecuador and Peru. The passage of the cold current cools the western flank of the mountain range and consequently the coast washed by the Pacific Ocean, having a dramatic effect on the tropical climate that would otherwise be found in the lowlands, and producing year-round desert conditions which are relieved only by streams running down from the mountain range towards the sea, giving rise on alluvial material to fertile, oasis-like valleys crossing the broad coastal strip of sandy desert which are watered by irrigation only.

This is the environment that hunters and gatherers arriving some 20,000 years ago would have been confronted with, although much of the landscape was obviously different then, in terms of both geographical extension and ecosystems. This much can be inferred from the as yet insufficient studies on the Andean Pleistocene.

It is supposed that during the late Pleistocene, known here as the Andean glaciation or Lauricocha glaciation, with its Antacallanca, Agrapa, Magapata and Antarragá stadials

(Cardich, 1964, p. 8), the Peruvian seaboard was much wider, owing to a fall of more than 100 m in the sea-level and in addition, the climate must have been as dry as it is today or even more so. Dollfus (1981, p. 60) says that in the Peruvian desert there was less coastal mist, a less severe cold current and probably heavy downpours from time to time connected with the increase in convection between the high, cold mountains and the hot plains. As for the mountain range itself, temperature indicators point to a situation 5 or 7 °C colder, which means that the perpetual snow cover, found today at about 4,700 m above sea-level, would start several hundred metres lower, as low as 4,000 to 4,500 m, and in periods before the Antarraga stadial as low as 3,400 to 3,700 m. This would obviously have a marked effect on adjacent areas, so that the dry environment of the puna, which is confined today to the centre and south of Peru, would extend much further to the north.

Data existing for the coast (Craig and Psuty, 1968; Lemon and Churcher, 1961) indicate, on the other hand, that the waters of the Humboldt current had the same effect on the coastal plains then as now, creating desert conditions. This also implies of course that frequent changes or climatic modifications would be caused, as now, by fluctuations in the movement of this ocean current.

On the other hand, the larger number of glaciers, with their characteristic lacustrine environment of woodlands and cold high plateaux, also gave rise to a larger number of watercourses, so that areas that are now deserts would then have been well watered. This explains why remains of flourishing flora and fauna are often found in areas that are now complete deserts; Cardich (1964, p. 36) states that the irrigated basin of the river Chillón was considerably more extensive, including the now completely dried up Ancón valley according to studies by the engineer Harold Conkling.

Conditions then were undoubtedly different from today, especially considering the evidence of a fauna comprising species now extinct, such as giant sloths (*Megatherium americanum* and *Mylodon*), mastodons or South American elephants (*Mastodon andium*), horses (*Parahipparion saldose, Onohippidium peruanum* and *Equus curvidens*), cervids that are now extinct (*Cervus brachyceros* and *Cervus dubius*), camelids that have also disappeared such as 'palaeo-lama' (*Macro auchenia?*), sabre-toothed felines (*Smylodon* sp.) and various types of canids among others. The primarily herbivorous animals required plant cover which in its present-day state could only meet part of their requirements; moreover their remains are found in semi-desert regions like Ayacucho, where there must have been many more watercourses flowing steadily from nearby glaciers, today virtually non-existent, which nurtured plant resources that are now no longer to be found.

All this does not however imply dramatic climatic changes; specialists consider that differences of degree can be assumed, but with ecosystemic characteristics similar to those of today which, among other things, implies a mosaic of landscapes similar to today's, with deserts, woodlands and barren plateaux that would differ in terms of area and specific location, but were similar in structure and effect. With regard to animals of the so-called megafauna types, such as mastodons, megatheria or horses that are now extinct, it can be presumed that their chances of finding food diminished as the overall temperature rose.

When human groups arrived in the Andes, the retreat of the glaciers and the easing of the cold were under way. According to Wright and Bradbury (1975), it seems that in Junín, in the central range of Peru, the major glaciers in the

centre of Peru probably began to melt around 16,500 years ago. This process must have been completed around 13,000 years ago, causing temperatures to rise substantially, reaching their highest levels between 8,000 and 5,000 years ago.

Although the presence of human beings has been established during the process of glacier retreat between 16,000 and 14,000 years ago, nothing would have prevented hunter-gatherers from reaching the area before that time, at the height of the glacial period, for even during the coldest periods there were valleys and woodlands that could support human life. In any event, it can be assumed that the deglaciation process with attendant changes in the linkages of the different ecosystems was the factor that accelerated the movement of humans and animals in one direction or the other in search of habitable areas.

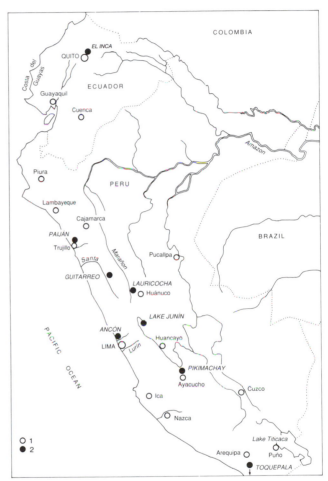

Map 33 The principal archaeological sites of hunter-gatherers of the Andean region, between 16,000 and 10,000 years ago. 1, modern towns; 2, archaeological sites. (After L. G. Lumbreras.)

UNDIFFERENTIATED GATHERERS OF THE ARCHAEOLITHIC (Map 33)

As for the entire continent, information on the first peoples to arrive in the Andes is meagre and fragmentary. There is no doubt that they came during the late Pleistocene period, or that human beings coexisted with the extinct Pleistocene 'megafauna'. Proof of the age of the oldest finds is insufficient and does not convince all prehistorians; these are remains excavated by Richard S. MacNeish in the Pikimachay cave in Ayacucho. In the Pikimachay cave, MacNeish identified the major components or phases of human occupation associated with extinct animals, which he has named the Pacaicasa and Ayacucho components.

The first and oldest component – Pacaicasa – was found in constant association with the remains of extinct megatheria, horses and cervidae, and is identified by crude core tools, 'choppers' and big, thin flakes apparently worked in a very simple manner; as MacNeish himself pointed out when he defined it for the first time, they are a heterogeneous collection made primarily of volcanic tuff probably from the walls of the cave itself (MacNeish, Nelken-Turner and Garcia Cook, 1970, p. 31). According to its discoverer, the Pacaicasa phase started around 23,000 years ago and lasted until nearly 16,000 years ago; associated radiocarbon dates indicate that this is probable, and in fact it is conservatively regarded as likely that human beings made their first inroads into the Andes during this period. This is the view of MacNeish, who places the Pacaicasa 'industry' within the core-tool tradition, which would correspond with the first wave of American inhabitants.

The crude Pacaicasa toolkit, apparently used to prepare food and work animal skins, tree-bark, and so on, does not include projectile points or other stone artefacts for hunting, so there must also have been specifically hunting and gathering gear made of perishable materials.

However, though we all know today that the absence of stone tools does not indicate a 'primitive' gathering economy without any type of hunting whatsoever, many prehistorians do not agree with the technological conclusions of MacNeish and his team, and believe that the few stone objects exhibited by this archaeologist are not really tools but mere fragments of local volcanic rock fractured by natural accident, and that consequently there is no proof of human presence in the layers attributed to the Pacaicasa phase. If these observations are correct and the radiocarbon dates are valid, the Pikimachay cave, with its remains of horses and giant sloths, would have remained uninhabited until at the earliest some 16,000 years ago.

The second component, dubbed Ayacucho, has a single radiocarbon date of about 14,200 years ago. The Ayacucho phase, made up of thin handaxes and bone instruments would, according to MacNeish (1971, p. 44) represent the emergence of a new flake and bone tool tradition, which nevertheless bears some resemblance to the preceding Pacaicasa phase.

The most important difference between the two lies in the fact that in the Ayacucho period some unifacial stone points and triangular points made of the bones of extinct animals appeared; both, however, occurred late in the period. The 'unifacial points' need not have been hunting instruments. The Ayacucho industry included nearly all the types found in the preceding phase in addition to new ones. In particular, it used a greater variety of materials, some of which must have been found at some distance from the cave. The similarity with the Pacaicasa period led MacNeish to comment (MacNeish, Nelken-Terner and Garcia Cook, 1970, p. 33) that the possibility should be ruled out that Pacaicasa was no more than an early and incomplete example of an Ayacucho toolkit, although, as stated earlier, it seems from his most recent studies that he is prepared to establish the difference between them more firmly, and even to consider them as traditions with separate extra-continental origins. Most prehistorians are prepared to consider the Ayacucho finds, but there is not the same consensus for the Pacaicasa.

The remains of giant sloths of the *Scelidotherium* and *Megatherium tarijense* species, horses (*Equus andium*) and other animals of extinct species or species still extant, such as the puma (*Felis concolor*), and of various carnivorous animals have been found in association with Ayacucho tools (MacNeish, Patterson and Browman, 1975, p. 15).

MacNeish divides the Ayacucho stone industry into five major categories: unifacial tools consisting of knives or scrapers and points; denticulate tools; pebble-tools consisting mainly of choppers; burinoid flakes and handaxes. The first category of tools is the best represented. Bone instruments are nearly as common and include long, triangular-shaped projectile points, and antler punch or flaker and scrapers.

Very little additional contextual information can be provided for this era; in fact the only other known sequence is based on finds on the Peruvian coast near Lima, in the vicinity of Ancón and the Chillón Valley. This sequence contains three components considered to belong to the Pleistocene epoch: Zona Roja, Chivateros and Oquendo. It was derived from two sites located on mountain tops with outcrops of metavolcanic rock. Zona Roja, and Chivateros I and II are stratigraphically superimposed, while Oquendo was found isolated in another site; however, Edward Lanning and his students have formulated a continuous sequence with the Zona Roja component as the oldest, followed by Oquendo and then Chivateros I and II. The insertion of Oquendo is based on typological considerations and is not widely supported. The only two radiocarbon dates that have been obtained are for the Chivateros I phase and give an age of about 10,400 years ago, which implies that all phases regarded as earlier than this must have occurred prior to the eleventh millennium BP.

Apart from observations about chronological aspects, the artefacts used to identify the phases also call for comment. First of all, it should be noted that the sites of origin are quarries and that the materials are blanks and not finished tools. Second, many of the flakes are rejects and taken as a whole do not constitute an 'industry', and therefore cannot in any way be attributed to a 'pre-projectile-point' stage.

Claude Chauchat (1975) has identified identical quarries to Chivateros on the northern coast in association with a clearly defined industry of pedunculate projectile points known as Paiján. On the other hand, the chronological presumption that this entire complex – with its three components – dates back to about 10,000 to 12,000 years ago seems acceptable, although the association of dated plant remains with the artefacts is also called into question; at any rate, this places it in the transitional period between the Pleistocene and the Holocene.

This period of great change in terms of fauna and the geographical balance of landscapes also seems to have been a time of intense population mobility. For the time being, there is little evidence of obviously migratory groups of hunters, though the few finds are significant.

The artefacts and blanks from the Ancón–Chillón coastal area, both from the Oquendo and Chivateros epochs, were struck directly from unprepared cores; in actual fact, they are all rejects, abandoned cores with some half-finished and broken tools. According to Patterson (1966, p. 146), Oquendo was an industry with a predominance of burins produced from flakes removed from pyramidal cores, which retained a small part of the original striking platform at the near end, near the bulb of percussion. In fact, it is not the type of artefact that other prehistorians call a burin although it resembles it; however, Oquendo appears to be a more homogeneous industry than that formed by the Chivateros blanks. Most of the instruments identified there are unifacial, including the so-called burins (various types), some asymmetrical denticulate artefacts, side-scrapers and also end-scrapers. Given the nature of the sites, excavated nearly at surface level, it has not been possible to obtain information about the associated fauna and other important details; in fact all we know is that they are workshops situated on open sites, on crags separated from the sea by a few kilometres of arid land. At present, various sites of similar nature and character have been found on the coast between Trujillo (Paiján) and Lima (in Lurín). Lanning himself has also found similar workshops on the Guayas coast in Ecuador with complexes known as Exacto and Manantial, which correspond in every respect to the Zona Roja and Chivateros finds. Lanning has also located others in the north of Chile.

There is evidence, coetaneous with these finds, which suggests a 'pre-projectile-point' stage of hunters who produced beautiful well-finished pedunculate points and who used stone from these quarries to make them, as has been proved for the Paiján industry, according to C. Chauchat (1975).

MORE ADVANCED HUNTERS OF THE UPPER CENOLITHIC (Map 33)

At least three complexes with clearly defined toolkits and satisfactory associations belong to this transitional epoch: Paiján in the northern coast, Guitarrero I in the northern mountain range and Puente in the Ayacucho region. However, a fourth should be added which, although it is not fully documented as regards associations, certainly belongs to this period and can even be considered to precede these complexes, certainly being contemporaneous with the last millennia of the Ayacucho phase: this is the fish-tail point complex.

The name site of this complex is at El Inga in Ecuador, in the Equatorial Andes, estimated to date from 12,000 to 13,000 years ago. Unfortunately, the age of this culture has not been sufficiently substantiated, as finds were made on the surface; the maximum radiocarbon age is about 9,000 years ago (Schobinger, 1969, p. 115) and obsidian-based datings range from 12,000 to 7,000 years ago, a very wide time span indeed.

However, the fish-tail points are very unusual and, over and above a hunting industry, identify a style, indicating that all those who made them were closely related. There is evidence of this type of point being manufactured in America from the extreme south, in Patagonia, up to south Mexico at least, in the isthmus that connects South with North America. Existing ages, from Patagonia, for these unique South American tools are 13,000 and 12,000 years, which indicates the late Pleistocene.

This style has also been found in the tropical Andes, in the Pikimachay cave, in the upper part of a stratum corresponding to the Ayacucho phase, which it was possibly associated with or may have replaced, or both. MacNeish, Nelken-Terner and Garcia Cook (1970, p. 34) were trying to propound a phase called the 'Huanta' on the basis of this evidence, but it seems that they preferred to suspend this hypothesis pending further studies. Paul Ossa (1975, p. 97) has identified a fish-tail point near the Moche valley, and C. Chauchat and J. Zevallos (1979) found another one in Piura. There are certainly many others in other areas, and one hopes that some day they will be found at deeper levels.

In any event, if at any time these different finds are proved to be relatively or absolutely coetaneous, it could be presumed that their makers travelled widely up and down

South and Central America. It is assumed that they were associated with the hunting of Pleistocene animals. In fact, it is not merely a matter of projectile points: and besides, it seems that they were also associated with other types and forms of artefacts including triangular and pedunculate points. The typical points are very finely finished in the form of a fish, with a rather broad edge and a stem in the form of a fish-tail, in some cases – as at El Inga in Ecuador – with a small groove along the stem just like the North American Clovis points. Some archaeologists therefore believe that this fish-tail complex could be considered to be a South American version of the Clovis tradition of North America.

The Paiján complex is much better known and according to C. Chauchat (1975, p. 85) includes a variety of pedunculate projectile points, handaxes, side-scrapers, denticulated and pebble-tools. Various sites have been identified for this culture, sometimes closely associated with human remains; some are living sites and there are also quarries and stone workshops where a carbon-14 date gives an age of 10,200 years ago, which is quite acceptable (Chauchat and Lacombe, 1984, p. 5).

Paiján further poses the problem of the racial characteristics of the first American peoples. It is in fact associated with one of the oldest finds of human remains: Chauchat and Lacombe (1984) found two skeletons, a child and an adult. These two skeletons, according to these researchers, have physical features that differ from those of other South American skeletons of that period (Lauricocha, Punin and Lagoa Santa), which would raise the possibility of differences other than cultural differences among the early American inhabitants, with a racial diversity that may imply both several 'waves' of hunters and an accelerated process of racial diversification. Paiján people were tall (1.70 m) and brachycephalic in tendency, unlike what seems to be the usual form of the early Americans, who were obviously dolichocephalic.

Paiján people had another important characteristic: they were indeed hunters, but hunters with close links to the sea, for it seems that their weapons were used mainly for harpoon fishing. Chauchat and Lacombe (1984, p. 6) say that Paiján people gathered plants and small land fauna and fished. This was not wholly unexpected on the Peruvian coast, but would necessitate a revision of the schedule for the emergence of the exploitation of marine resources, indicating that this occurred, not in the complex, sedentary societies of the Late Pre-ceramic but much earlier, among small nomadic groups that used tools that were still Palaeolithic. A culture similar to that of Paiján was found to extend nearly to the coast of the department of Lima, where a similar complex called Luz has been identified; for the time being, this would seem to be associated with a maritime form of hunter-gatherer, apparently with stable links with the sea.

In the mountains, the Guitarrero I and Puente complexes in the Callejón de Huaylas and in Ayacucho respectively, both at some 3,000 m above sea-level, are well known.

The Guitarrero I industry is almost exclusively composed of flake tools; the big handaxes and 'burins' of its coastal contemporaries are not found in this complex, though there are scrapers and a few choppers, hammerstones and lamellar flakes. Thomas Lynch (1980, p. 295) thinks that it could be compared to the Ayacucho phase, although this has pedunculate points. The carbon-14 dates (Lynch, 1980, p. 32) for Guitarrero I range between 12,500 and 9,000 years ago.

Information on the fauna indicates that the Guitarrero cave dwellers were already associated with modern animals, which implies that at the time, in the Huaylas mountain range at least, typically Pleistocene animals had already disappeared; in addition, they gathered plants and small animals. Apparently however, the consumption of Andean camelids was not significant.

The Puente phase of the Ayacucho, roughly contemporaneous with Paiján and Guitarrero, though it came slightly later, has been identified in various places in the central mountain range, and seems to be associated primarily with the hunting of camelids (guanaco and vicuña), which from then on were the main animals hunted, together with Andean deer, viscacha (*Lagidium* sp.), a rodent the size of a rabbit, and other small animals.

Lastly, a series of groups of hunters that occupied practically every type of environment on the coast and in the Andes ranges between 10,000 and 8000 years ago has been identified; some common features, such as the tendency to standardize projectile points into leaf shapes, could reflect constant interregional exchanges. On the other hand, as apparently was the case in Junín (Rick, 1980), a noteworthy process of adaptation to particular Andean environments started with forms of relative sedentarization in association with the camelid-rich high plateaux and steppes and also seasonal transhumance to temperate coastal woodlands called 'lomas' that were lush for four or five months each year in the winter.

It was at this time that the Lauricocha caves in the sierra de Huánuco, the first to be explored and defined in terms of the ancient 'preceramic' Andean inhabitants, were occupied.

It is also possible that this epoch, the early Holocene, marked the beginning of rock painting, the best-known examples of which are in Lauricocha (Huánuco) and in the south at Toquepala, with representations of camelid-hunting scenes.

It was also a period of great discoveries that led subsequently to the domestication of plants and animals (see Chapter 59).

BIBLIOGRAPHY

ADOVASIO, J. M.; MASLOWSKI, R. 1980. Cordage, Basketry and Textiles. In: LYNCH, T. (ed.), *Guitarrero Cave*. Ann Arbor.

BELL, R. E. 1965. *Investigaciones arqueológicas en el Sitio de El Inga, Ecuador*. Quito.

CARDICH, A. 1958. Los yacimientos de Lauricocha y la nueva interpretación de la prehistoria Peruana. *Stud. Praehist.* (Buenos Aires), No. 1.

—— 1964. Lauricocha: fundamentos para una prehistoria de los Andes Centrales. *Stud. Praehist.* (Buenos Aires), No. 3.

CHAUCHAT, C. 1975. The Paiján Complex, Pampa de Cupisnique, Peru. *Ñawpa Pacha* (Berkeley), No. 13, pp. 85–96.

CHAUCHAT, C.; LACOMBE, J. P. 1984. El hombre de Paiján? El más antiguo Peruano? *Gac. Arqueol. Andina* (Lima), Vol. 11, pp. 4–6, 12.

CHAUCHAT, C.; ZEVALLOS, J. 1979. Una punta en cola de pescado procedente de la Costa Norte del Perú. *Ñawpa Pacha* (Berkeley), No. 17, pp. 143–6.

COHEN, M. N. 1981. *La Crisis alimentaria de la prehistoria*. Madrid.

CRAIG, A. K.; PSUTY, N. P. 1968. *The Paracas Papers: Studies in Marine Desert-Ecology I, Reconnaissance Report*. Boca Raton. (Dep. Geogr., Fla. Atl. Univ., Occasi. Publ., 1.)

DOLLFUS, O. 1981. *El reto del Espacio Andino*. Lima.

DONNAN, C. B. 1964. An Early House from Chilca, Peru. *Am. Antiq.*, Vol. 30, pp. 137–44.

ENGEL, F. 1966. *Paracas: cien siglos de historia Peruana*. Lima.

—— 1972. New Facts about Pre-Columbian Life in the Andean Lomas. *Curr. Anthropol.*, Vol. 14, pp. 271–80.

FUNG, P.; CENZANO, C. F.; ZAVALETA, A. 1972. El taller lítico de Chivateros, Valle de Chillon. *Rev. Mus. Nac.* (Lima), Vol. 38, pp. 61–72.

HAWKES, J. G. 1967. The History of the Potato. *J. R. Hortic. Soc.* (London), Vol. 92, pp. 207–24, 249–62, 288–302, 364–5.

HESTER, J. J. 1973. Late Pleistocene Environments and Early Man in South America. In: GROSS, D. (ed.), *Peoples and Cultures of Native South America*. New York. pp. 4–18.

KAPLAN, L. 1965. Archaeology and Domestication of American Phaseolus (Beans). *Econ. Bot.*, Vol. 19, pp. 358–68.

—— 1980. Variation in the Cultivated Beans. In: LYNCH, T. (ed.), *Guitarrero Cave*. Ann Arbor.

LANNING, E. P. 1963. A Pre-agricultural Occupation of the Central Coast of Peru. *Am. Antiq.*, Vol. 28, pp. 360–71.

—— 1965. Early Man in Peru. *Sci. Am.*, Vol. 213, pp. 68–76.

—— 1967. *Peru before the Incas*. New Jersey.

—— 1970. Pleistocene Man in South America. *World Archaeol.*, Vol. 2, pp. 90–111.

LANNING, E. P.; HAMMEL, E. 1961. Early Lithic Industries in Western South America. *Am. Antiq.*, Vol. 27, pp. 139–54.

LANNING, E. P.; PATTERSON, T. C. 1967. Early Man in South America. *Sci. Am.*, Vol. 217, pp. 44–50.

LAVALLÉE, D.; JULIAN, M. 1975. El habitat prehistórico en la zona de San Pedro de Cajas, Junín. *Rev. Mus. Nac.* (Lima), Vol. 41, pp. 81–127.

LEMON, R. H.; CHURCHER, C. S. 1961. Pleistocene Geology and Palaeontology of the Talara Region, North West Peru. *Am. J. Sci.* (New Haven), Vol. 259, pp. 410–29.

LUMBRERAS, L. G. 1974. La evidencia etnobotánica en el tránsito de la economía recolectora a la producción de alimentos. In: *La Arqueología como Ciencia Social*. Lima. pp. 177–209.

—— 1976. *The Peoples and Cultures of Ancient Peru*. Washington, DC.

LYNCH, T. F. 1967. *The Nature of the Andean Preceramic*. Pocatello. (Idaho State Univ. Mus., Occas. Pap., 21.)

—— 1970. *Excavation at Quishqui Puncu in the Callejon de Huaylas, Peru*. Pocatello. (Idaho State Univ. Mus., Occas. Pap., 26.)

—— 1971. Preceramic Transhumance in the Callejon de Huaylas, Peru. *Am. Antiq.*, Vol. 36, pp. 139–48.

—— 1974. The Antiquity of Man in South America. *Quat. Res.*, Vol. 4, pp. 356–77.

—— (ed.) 1980. *Guitarrero Cave: Early Man in the Andes*. New York.

MACNEISH, R. S. 1969. *First Report of the Ayacucho Archaeological-Botanical Project*. Andover.

—— 1971. Early Man in the Andes. *Sci. Am.*, Vol. 224, pp. 36–46.

—— 1979. The Early Man Remains from Pikimachay Cave. In: HUMPHREY, R. L.; STANFORD, D. (eds), *Pre-llano Cultures of the Americas*. Washington, DC.

MACNEISH, R. S.; NELKEN-TERNER, A.; GARCIA COOK, A. 1970. *Second Annual Report of the Ayacucho Archaeological Project*. Andover.

MACNEISH, R. S.; PATTERSON, T. C.; BROWMAN, D. L. 1975. *The Central Peruvian Interaction Sphere*. Andover.

MACNEISH, R. S. et al. 1980. *Prehistory of the Ayacucho Basin, Peru*. Ann Arbor. Vol. 3.

—— 1981. *Prehistory of the Ayacucho Basin, Peru*. Ann Arbor. Vol. 2.

MATOS, M. R.; RICK, J. W. 1980. Los recursos naturales y el poblamiento precerámico de la Puna de Junín. *Rev. Mus. Nac.* (Lima), Vol. 44, pp. 23–64.

MAYER-OAKES, W. J. 1966. El Inga Projectile Points: Surface Collections. *Am. Antiq.*, Vol. 31, pp. 644–61.

OSSA, P. 1975. Fluted 'Fishtail' Projectile Point from La Cumbre, Peru. *Ñawpa Pacha* (Berkeley), Vol. 13, pp. 97–8.

OSSA, P.; MOSELEY, M. E. 1971. La Cumbre: A Preliminary Report on Research into the Early Lithic Occupation of the Moche Valley, Peru. *Ñawpa Pacha* (Berkeley), Vol. 9, pp. 1–16.

PATTERSON, T. C. 1966. Early Cultural Remains on the Central Coast of Peru. *Ñawpa Pacha* (Berkeley), Vol. 4, pp. 145–53.

—— 1971. Central Peru: Its Population and Economy. *Archaeology* (New York), Vol. 24, pp. 316–21.

PICKERSGILL, B. 1969. The Archaeological Record of Chili Peppers (*Capsicum* sp.) and the Sequence of Plant Domestication in Peru. *Am. Antiq.*, Vol. 34, pp. 54–66.

RICHARDSON, J. B., III. 1972. The Preceramic Sequence and the Pleistocene and Post-Pleistocene Climate of Northwest Peru. In: LATHRAP, D.; DOUGLAS, J. (eds), *Variation in Anthropology.* Urbana.

RICK, J. W. 1980. *Prehistoric Hunters of the High Andes.* New York.

—— 1983. *Cronología, clima y subsistencia en el precerámico Peruano.* Lima.

SCHOBINGER, J. 1969. *Prehistoria de Sudamérica.* Madrid.

SMITH, C. E. 1980. Plant Remains from Guitarrero Cave. In: LYNCH, T. H. (ed.), *Guitarrero Cave.* Ann Arbor. pp. 87–120.

STEINMANN, H. 1930. *Geología del Perú.* Lima.

TOSI, J. A. 1960. *Zonas de vida natural en el Perú.* Lima. (Inst. Interam. Cienc. Agríc., Zona Andina, Bol. Téc., 15.)

TOWLE, M. A. 1961. *The Ethnobotany of Pre-Columbian Peru.* Chicago.

WILLEY, G. R. 1971. *An Introduction to American Archaeology: South America.* New Jersey. Vol. 2.

WING, E. 1977. Animal Domestication in the Andes. In: REED, C. A. (ed.), *The Origins of Agriculture.* The Hague. pp. 837–60.

—— 1980. Faunal Remains. In: LYNCH, T. H. (ed.), *Guitarrero Cave.* Ann Arbor. pp. 149–71.

WRIGHT, H. A.; BRADBURY, J. P. 1975. Historia ambiental del Cuaternario tardio en el area de la Planicie de Junín, Perú. *Rev. Mus. Nac.* (Lima), Vol. 41, pp. 75–6.

35

THE WESTERN PART OF SOUTH AMERICA

(southern Peru, Bolivia, north-west Argentina and Chile) during the Stone Age

Lautaro Núñez Atencio

GEOGRAPHICAL DIVERSITY (Map 34)

This area, in which the Andes and the southern Pacific constitute the predominant features, comprises a large variety of environments, owing to the diversity of altitudes and latitudes, ranging from the desert to sub-antarctic woods and steppes (latitude 17° to 55° S). Various processes of adaptation took place during the Stone Age in the exploitation of natural resources, giving rise to different cultural entities and involving interaction between the eastern forest, the highlands, the valleys and the Pacific.

The southern central area includes a large part of the highlands (over 3,000 m), with a biomass potential that diminishes from north to south: steppes, valleys and lakes. Adaptation to altitude made it possible to domesticate Andean resources (such as camelids and tubers) and led to the emergence of the agricultural and herding societies which spread through the Andes, forming a link between the tropical forest and the Pacific Ocean, along the valleys or transit points that made interaction possible and whose ecological layers ranged from the cold and rainy mountain range to the hot coastal deserts (latitude 17° to 26° S).

The southern Andean area includes marginal zones: the middle-level and low valleys, tropical forests and the almost desert steppes in Argentina. We shall consider here the western valleys that drain into the Pacific, and the longitudinal valley that stretches parallel to the Andes and the coast (latitude 26° to 38° S) with considerable natural resources.

The longitudinal valley continues in the southern extremity of the Andes (latitude 36° to 42° S) with a high rainfall pattern and extensive networks of rivers and lakes, intermingled with sub-Andean woods.

The panorama ends in the Archipelago–Patagonia region, with extreme environmental conditions – high rainfall, low temperatures and glacial erosion. Natural resources are sub-antarctic, with woods and steppes whose vegetation sustained abundant wildlife but provided minimal possibilities for food gathering.

In all, four environments with potential resources stand out in the region: the highlands, the sub-Andean valleys, the Patagonian region and the Pacific coast. The highlands,

a narrow band stretching from the southern central area towards the south, has native animal and plant species suitable for hunting, gathering and domestication. As the influence of altitude diminished in the south (southern area), the resources of the sub-Andean valleys became more attractive, from desert interfluves to fertile basins in which the interlacing network of rivers created a rich biomass typical of the lowlands of central Chile. In the Patagonian region the predominant features – woods, steppes and ocean – with abundant wildlife, gave rise in particular to hunting and fishing. The whole of the Pacific shore had a high food potential owing to the cold currents found along the coast from the desert to the southern archipelago. It was extensively exploited, with greater continuity and less fluctuation than the seasonal resources of the continental habitats.

THE EARLY PLEISTOCENE SETTLEMENTS (15,000 TO 13,000 YEARS AGO) (Table 11)

To date little is known about the earliest probable settlements. The encroachments of the sea have covered their sites, and the desert was very stable, forming an effective barrier to expansion. Nevertheless, the highlands in the southern central area include Pleistocene steppes and lakes where megafauna concentrated that could possibly have been exploited (Phillipi, 1983). A transit point or corridor existed in the semi-desert steppe close to the Atlantic slope (latitude 21° to 24° S), linking the Amazon Basin with the Patagonia–Pampa region, and approaching the low-lying western lakes (southern central Chile) by different mountain passes until it reaches the southern 'cul de sac' from both sides of the watershed.

Settlements in this hemisphere existed earlier than 12,000 years ago (Bryan, 1978), and there are indications that they were already present in South America between the thirtieth and the twelfth millennia (Schmitz, 1984), probably during the middle Würm glacial period (according to European terminology). Their remains have not been well identified in the central Andes and the southern-central area. Non-specialized traditions in flakes, choppers, burins and biface

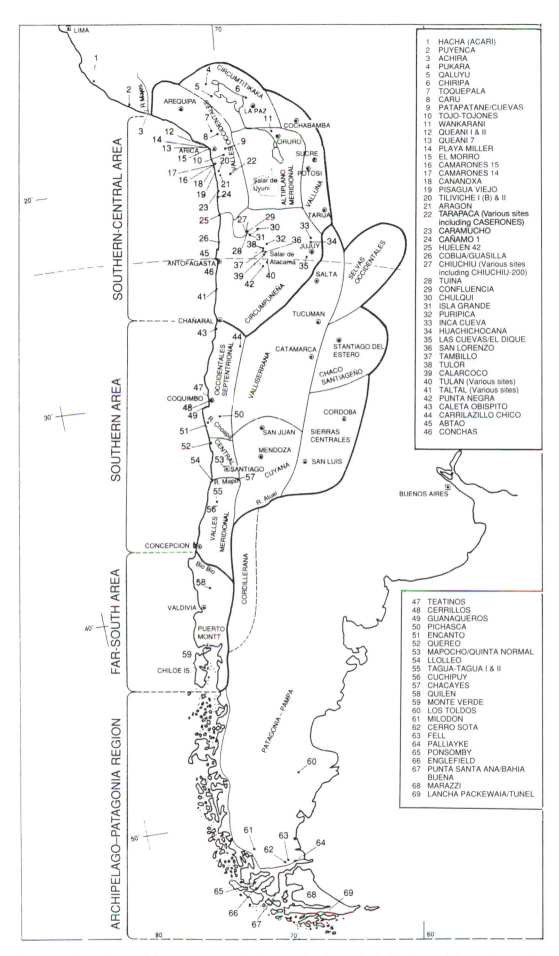

1   HACHA (ACARI)
2   PUYENCA
3   ACHIRA
4   PUKARA
5   QALUYU
6   CHIRIPA
7   TOQUEPALA
8   CARU
9   PATAPATANE/CUEVAS
10 TOJO-TOJONES
11 WANKARANI
12 QUEANI I & II
13 QUEANI 7
14 PLAYA MILLER
15 EL MORRO
16 CAMARONES 15
17 CAMARONES 14
18 CANANOXA
19 PISAGUA VIEJO
20 TILIVICHE I (B) & II
21 ARAGON
22 TARAPACA (Various sites
    including CASERONES)
23 CARAMUCHO
24 CAÑAMO 1
25 HUELEN 42
26 COBIJA/GUASILLA
27 CHIUCHIU (Various sites
    including CHIUCHIU-200)
28 TUINA
29 CONFLUENCIA
30 CHULQUI
31 ISLA GRANDE
32 PURIPICA
33 INCA CUEVA
34 HUACHICHOCANA
35 LAS CUEVAS/EL DIQUE
36 SAN LORENZO
37 TAMBILLO
38 TULOR
39 CALARCOCO
40 TULAN (Various sites)
41 TALTAL (Various sites)
42 PUNTA NEGRA
43 CALETA OBISPITO
44 CARRILAZILLO CHICO
45 ABTAO
46 CONCHAS

47 TEATINOS
48 CERRILLOS
49 GUANAQUEROS
50 PICHASCA
51 ENCANTO
52 QUEREO
53 MAPOCHO/QUINTA NORMAL
54 LLOLLEO
55 TAGUA-TAGUA I & II
56 CUCHIPUY
57 CHACAYES
58 QUILEN
59 MONTE VERDE
60 LOS TOLDOS
61 MILODON
62 CERRO SOTA
63 FELL
64 PALLIAYKE
65 PONSOMBY
66 ENGLEFIELD
67 PUNTA SANTA ANA/BAHIA
    BUENA
68 MARAZZI
69 LANCHA PACKEWAIA/TUNEL

Map 34 Southern–central, southern and far-south zones of the Andes and region of the Archipelago and Patagonia: location of the principal archaeological sites. (After L. Núñez, 1985.)

Table 11 Chronological position of the most important archaeological sites of the western part of South America: southern Peru–Bolivia–north-west Argentina–Chile.

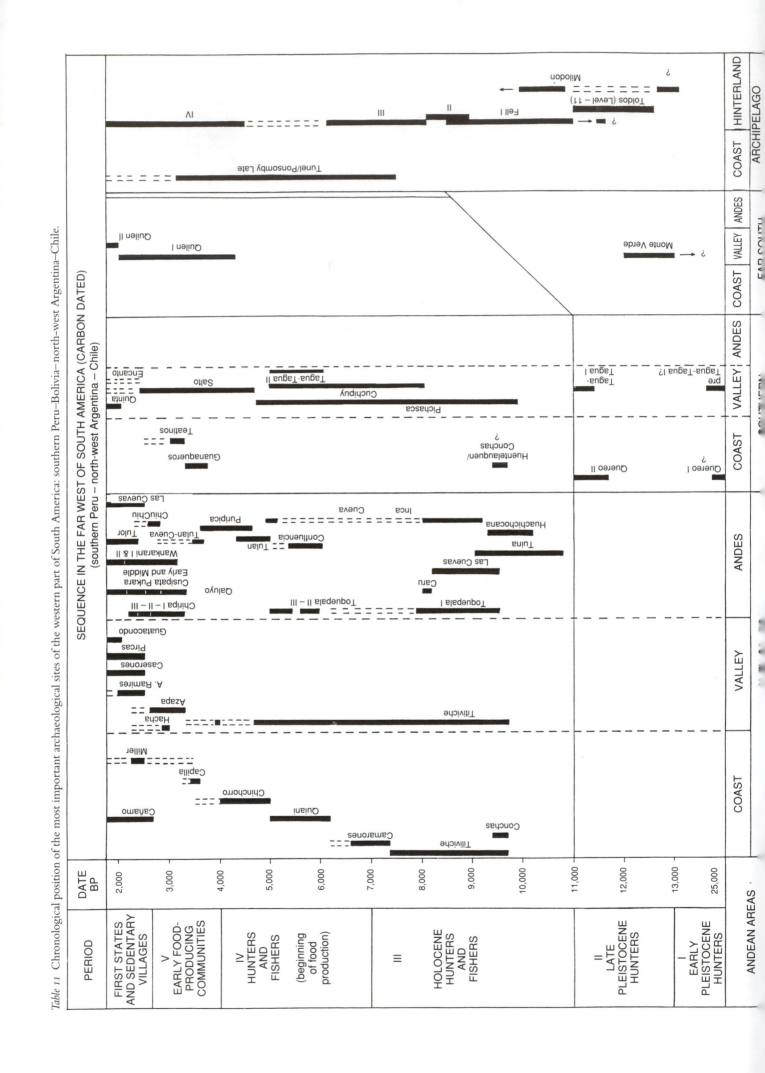

SEQUENCE IN THE FAR WEST OF SOUTH AMERICA (CARBON DATED)
(southern Peru – north-west Argentina – Chile)

tools of the 'pre-projectile-point' kind have been described, dating from before the eleventh millennium BP (Lanning, 1967; Krieger, 1964). But for the most part these industries come from surface sites and quarries without chrono-stratigraphic associations. Their estimated considerable age is based on palaeogeographic and typological-chronological criteria with reference to the Palaeolithic age in the Old World (Meltzer, 1969). It has been proved, however, that these examples (such as bifaces) are rough blanks or waste flakes from the flaking process, while others are connected with postglacial periods, and are not known from Pleistocene contexts (Fung et al., 1972; Núñez, 1983b).

According to Lynch (1985), it is likely that early hunters arrived here before the eleventh millennium BP, around the freshwater Pleistocene lakes (highland saline basins). Certain chronostratigraphic evidence from the Pleistocene lakes in the southern Andean area could support this assumption. In fact, a possible butchering site has been recorded at Quereo I, among lacustrine deposits, associated with hammered bones and a horse skull marked by a naso-frontal blow, together with altered natural stones. Remains were found of horse (Equus sp.), deer (Antifer niemeyeri), Palaeolama sp. and Mylodon sp., which existed in a semi-desert climate somewhat similar to that of today. These remains have been associated with those of a wood (Dayphillum excelsum) which formed a limited habitat attracting the large herbivores towards an ideal spot for hunters. Present groundwater resources have given earlier datings to the Quereo I site; that it was, in fact, an earlier period is confirmed by differentiated sedimentation, stratigraphic position and proximity to a sea-board that lay 5 to 10 m above the present one in the Laufen interstadial period, about the twenty-fifth to twenty-second millennium BP (Núñez et al., 1983).

A similar event occurred in the Tagua-Tagua lagoon, another butchering site, where mastodons and deer remains have been recorded (below the eleventh millennium BP level), as well as hearths left perhaps by hunters, dated between the thirtieth and twenty-first millennia BP (Montané, 1968; Heusser, 1983). This also occurred in a warm and dry climate with resources restricted to an 'oasis'. After these possible traces of 'precursors', a moist climate returned at Quereo I and Tagua-Tagua (pre-level I), with a greater predominance of lakes. Natural resources thus expanded, and with them the dispersion of the megafauna and their hunters.

In Patagonia the earliest occupation has been identified as occurring in about the thirteenth millennium BP (Cardich, 1977). It is possible, however, that other groups arrived before then, judging from the presence of Mylodon sp. in the early deposits in the Fell and Milodón caves (Bird, 1938; Borrero, 1981). These were hunted in the eleventh millennium BP, but some Mylodon bones which had been altered by human hand occurred in the Milodón cave, dating possibly from the thirteenth millennium BP.

THE LATE PLEISTOCENE HUNTERS (13,000 TO 8,600 YEARS AGO) (Table 11)

Settlements in the southern-central Andean area during this period are unknown, although there are indications of surface industries of unspecified age (such as Viscachani). Hunting sites exist, however, near the sub-Andean lakes in the southern area and in the Patagonian caves, associated unmistakably with extinct fauna.

These hunters existed from the end of the Pleistocene to the beginning of the postglacial period, adapting to different environments through specialized and generalized activities according to regional conditions. Their technological and economic traits tend to be homogeneous and synchronous throughout the hemisphere.

Findings in the southern Andean area and the far south

Quereo II

A group of megafauna hunters lived on the edge of a lake to the south of Los Vilos, near a water-hole where large herbivores came to drink: mastodon (Cuvieronius sp.), horse (Equus sp.), deer (Antifer sp.), camelids (Lama sp.) and giant sloth, Mylodon sp. or Glossotherium sp. or both. Remains found in a plastic sandy matrix indicate that hunters had killed their prey with lumps of stone between 11,400 and 11,100 years ago, at a time when the lagoon had become a marsh with sandy shores; here two horses were killed at the same time (Núñez et al., 1983).

The climate was less cold and rainy (the so-called Allerød interstadial period) compared with that of the lower level, so that droughts again occurred, reducing resources to one site, and concentrating the range of fauna and plant life. The thornbush-covered steppe contracted, limiting the expansion of proboscideans. A sclerophyll wood composed of Lithraea, Escallonia, Maytenus and Azara microphylla was situated nearby, close to wetlands and swamps with plants such as sedge (Cyperacea) and bulrushes (Typha), according to the pollen evidence.

The hunters used to surprise their prey in the gorge on soft ground where the use of tipped projectiles was not necessary. The butchering was carried out with cutting stones and bone artefacts, by-products of hunting. It is likely that given the sparse hunting groups, the killing of no more than a few animals sufficed. Although the sea was just 200 m away only two molluscs have been recorded (Concholepas sp.).

Traces of human activity can be seen in fragments of bone bearing knife marks (butchering), broken bones, hammered and polished bone artefacts (Fig. 97 (o)), lumps of stone close to sites of skeletons and laminar flakes bearing traces of use (Núñez, 1983a, 1983b).

Tagua-Tagua I

Another butchering site is situated in a basin near the coast (Cachapoal valley) at the edge of a lake (Montané, 1968). Extinct fauna and a few stone artefacts have been identified, dated from the twelfth millennium BP, together with remains of deer (Antifer sp.), mastodon (Cuvieronius humboldtii) and horse (Equus sp.) (Montané, 1968; Casamiquela et al., 1976).

When the lake retreated towards the centre of the basin, butchering took place in warm conditions, with scarce rainfall (the so-called Allerød interstadial period). On the shores of this lake-swamp, hunters struck the skull of a mastodon with lumps of stone (there is an absence of projectile points). The butchering took place in situ since, as in Quereo, bones with knife marks have been found. In Tagua-Tagua I, however, the stone implements are more varied: an obsidian alternately flaked knife-scraper (Fig. 97 (u)), alternately edge flakes, and unifacially retouched end-scrapers similar to those found in Patagonia. Artefacts occasionally found include uniface flakes, granite hammerstones and pounders, and

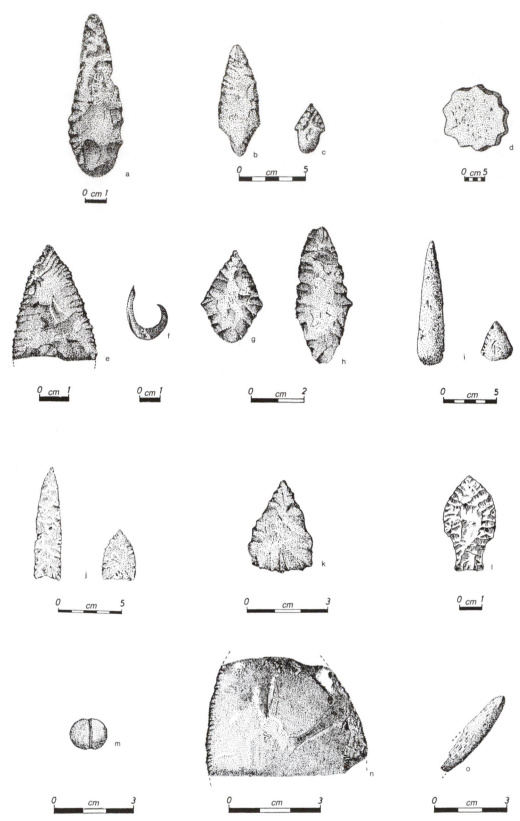

Figure 97 Typical artefacts of the Pleistocene and the Holocene hunters' periods, western part of South America: a, biface leaf-shaped point, Tiliviche I-B, intermediate stratigraphical horizon camp site (7,850 to 6,900 years ago) (after Núñez, 1983); b–c, stemmed points, Cuchipuy site zone of the early graves (8,070 to 5,000 years ago) (after Kaltwasser et al., 1983); d, polygonal stone (cog stone), Las Conchas/Huentelauquen camp site (about 9,680 to 9,400 years ago) (after Carevic, 1978); e, asymmetrical leaf-shaped biface knife, Tiliviche I-B, early stratigraphical horizon (9,760 to 7,850 years ago) (after Núñez, 1983); f, shell fish-hook (*Choro mytilus*), Tiliviche I-B, intermediate stratigraphical horizon (after Núñez, 1983); g, pentagonal biface point, Patapatane site, early stratigraphical horizon (around 8,200 years ago) (after Santoro MS.); h, leaf-shaped point, Patapatane, early stratigraphical horizon (after Santoro MS.); i, leaf-shaped and triangular points, Fell site, level III (8,200 to 6,400 years ago) (after Bird, 1938); j, triangular points, Pichasca site, early stratigraphical horizon (9,890 to 7,050 years ago) (after Ampuero and Rivera, 1971); k, triangular biface point, Tuina site, early stratigraphical horizon (10,820 to 9,080 years ago) (after Núñez, 1983); l, Fell fish-tail biface point, Fell site, early stratigraphical horizon (about 11,000 years ago) (after Bird, 1938); m, bola stone, Monte Verde site, occupation level (13,000 to 12,000 years ago) (after Dillehay, 1984); n, fragment of obsidian biface knife, Tagua-Tagua site, level I (11,380 to 11,000 years ago) (after Montané, 1968); o, fragment of polished bone artefact, Quereo site, level II, intermediate stratigraphical horizon (about 11,400 years ago) (after Núñez).

polished and grooved bone gravers (flakers and hammer-stones). Flakers were used to sharpen the butchering implements, since percussion and pressure-flaking rejects were found *in situ*. In addition, the presence of charcoal and charred bones suggests the proximity of hearths.

A plant cover of Chenopodiaceae–Amaranthaceae existed during this period, confirming the existence of a hot and dry climate, similar to an oasis, with dry periods and low lake-level (Heusser, 1983). At the same time, the scarcity of false beech (*Nothofagus*) (implying increasing humidity) and of Compositae and Gramineae confirms that evaporation increased at the same time as the temperature, in comparison with present conditions. Mastodons therefore had little forage to eat and concentrated in narrow tracts suitable for intensive hunting.

Monte Verde

Towards the far south, at the extreme limit of the longitudinal valley, a gradual improvement in climatic conditions took place after the last glacial advances, from the thirteenth millennium BP (Heusser, 1960). During the twelfth millennium BP (latitude 40° S), the glaciers were limited by the cordillera and, as in the case of the lakes, in the eleventh millennium BP were already at their present level (Mercer, 1970).

A chain of piedmont lakes, wet forests and grassy prairies were available for the large herbivores that advanced further south during the so-called Allerød interstadial period.

In fact, a camp of mastodon hunters from outside the region has been found near Puerto Montt, the southernmost location in America. Dillehay has described (1984) an occupation level situated in a pebble layer. The Monte Verde episode has been dated as between the fourteenth and twelfth millennia BP and is associated with rectangular dwellings with felled trunks and hearths. The remains of mastodons and palaeocamelidae were brought there, but the non-seasonal gathering of seeds, tubers, shoots, leaves, club rushes (*Scirpus* sp.), boldo and the like predominated.

The production of stone tools would probably have been undertaken by means of percussion, chipping and polishing techniques, with emphasis on the use of pebbles.

A few bifacial flakes were also used, in particular a biface doubtfully linked to the occupational level and two natural stone spheres with grooves similar to bola stones (Fig. 97 (m))

This camp could be an indication of the adaptation of mastodon hunters to gathering activities in the cold, wet subantarctic woods at the end of the Ice Age, through a more generalized strategy of hunting and gathering.

The hunters of the Patagonian region

During the twelfth and eleventh millennia BP, when the first inhabitants arrived at the southernmost extremity of the continent, the glaciers were contracting, their meltwaters producing networks of rivers and lakes. There were no obstacles to the migratory flow which descended to the south under pressure from the new, dry Postglacial conditions.

In the eleventh millennium BP, steppes were predominant due to the warm and dry Allerød environment and this caused humans and herbivores to draw closer together in a substantial grassland plateau, where hunting skills reached their peak. The two stages that represent the beginning of the process of adaptation to subantarctic conditions are described below.

Early Toldos stage (13,000 to 11,000 years ago) Los Toldos cave-3 (level 11) is situated in Argentine Patagonia near the Deseado river. It sheltered hunters who adapted to the Patagonian steppe around 13,000 years ago and who were spread over a large geographical area (Menghin, 1952; Cardich, 1977; Cardich et al., 1973; Cardich and Flegenheimer 1978). Stone tools include thick flakes with a unifacial retouch, side-scrapers and end-scrapers, retouched knives and subtriangular unifacial points. They hunted horse (*Parahipparion*) and camelids (*Lama gracilis*) among the now extinct species, and guanacos (*Lama guanicoe*) and rodents among the modern species. This period lasted almost up to the eleventh millennium BP, and provided the technological framework for subsequent developments.

Other settlements have been recorded in Argentina: the Arroyo Feo cave, in an affluent of the Pinturas river (Gradín et al., 1976; Silveira, 1979); El Buho cave in the Pinturas river (Gradín et al., 1976); and El Ceibo-7 cave near the Deseado river (Cardich et al., 1981–2).

The Fell stage (11,000–8,600 years ago) This includes sites on both slopes, among them Fell's cave, characteristic of Chilean Patagonia.

Los Toldos Classic Los Toldos cave-3 was occupied again (levels 9–10) in the eleventh millennium BP, and end-scrapers, tanged subtriangular points, bifacial cores, bone spatulae and bifacial knives have been found. This period has been related to the beginning of activities in Fell's cave (Cardich, 1977) on account of the presence of polished disc-shaped stones and fragments somewhat similar to the fish-tail points. A roof-fall bearing remains of painting made it possible to attribute complex wall art to this period ('painted hands' style). Horses were still hunted (*Parahipparion*), as well as now extinct camelids (*Lama gracilis*), guanaco (*Lama guanicoe*), tinamou (*Eudromia* sp.), small ñandu (Rheidae/*Prerocnemeiapennata*), pampa ñandú (*Rhea americana*), canids and rodents (*Cavidae* sp.).

The site was abandoned about 8,750 years ago on account of a period of comparative dryness, but a third occupation occurred subsequently with the arrival of Casapedrense groups, as from 7,200 years ago. They used laminar flakes and blades with unifacial retouches, bola stones, denticulates and a few bifacial tools, and increased the number of guanacos killed possibly with the help of dogs (*Canis familiaris*).

Although the Toldos Classic and early Fell groups are not completely identical, the polished disc-shaped stones, the size of the end-scrapers and side-scrapers, and the similarity between the fauna – extinct and Modern – hunted by both groups, suggest the existence of a socio-cultural matrix shared by both. It is likely that, given the different conditions under which activities took place, fairly independent dwelling and technological processes were developed on either side of the watershed, as may be inferred from the different types of points found in both sites.

The groups were more populous compared with previous periods, adapting better to the open areas where adult guanacos, a preferred catch, would roam. Paintings of hand 'negatives' bear witness to their rites involving productive magic (Menghin, 1957; Cardich and Flegenheimer, 1978).

Other shelters have been recorded in Los Toldos-2, containing Fell points, a polished disc and a fossil horse tooth (Menghin, 1952). They include the Las Manos cave, containing tanged points of the classic Toldos type, but no remains of extinct fauna. These groups enhanced their rupestrian art with 'painted hands' and polychrome hunting scenes, from which it can be seen that they drove animals into large gulleys with the help of bola stones and darts (Gradín et al., 1976). Since the number of caves was limited, these groups were not very populous; nevertheless the scenes from the Pinturas river suggest collective hunts, with fifty-four hunters surrounding seventeen guanacos, so that there must have been a sharing of work between groups.

Another site is the Buitreras cave, also in Argentina, containing remains of horse (*Hippidium–Onohippidium*), guanaco (*Lama guanicoe*), fox (*Dusicyon avus*) and mylodon (*Mylodon* sp.), associated with short-lived human activity (Sanguinetti and Borrero, 1977).

Five periods have been identified in Fell's cave, situated on the Chilean side of the watershed, near the Chico de Magallanes river (Bird, 1938, 1946; Emperaire et al., 1963). Level 1 belongs to the eleventh millennium BP; it was sealed by ash from the first cycle of volcanic activity (Auer, 1970). The cultural traits include polished, disc-shaped stones, high-backed front-scrapers, thick flakes, a bifacial leaf-shaped knife, double-ended side-scraper, pebble choppers, gravers and bone flakers. Various animals were hunted: the giant sloth (*Mylodon listai*), horse (*Parahipparion saldasi*), guanaco (*Lama guanicoe*), fox, puma, birds and rodents; and ostrich eggs were collected (Bird, 1938). In other words, remains of modern species were associated with those of extinct fauna and a few traces of gathering; there was an absence of food derived from the seaboard. The Fell (fish-tail) points were located here, together with hearths where horse-flesh was roasted. They dated from between the eleventh and tenth millennia BP and stretched over a large geographical area (Fig. 97 (l)). It has been suggested, however, that these points originated in more northerly regions, where similar forms have been identified, such as examples from Lake Madden (Alajuela) in Panama and El Inga in Ecuador (Bird, 1969). Nevertheless, comparisons proposed at the South American level are not based on Pleistocene contexts or specific chronologies. It would therefore be interesting to investigate further the possibility of a migratory corridor with Fell points on the Atlantic slope of the watershed (Pampa–Patagonia) where several successive camping places have been recorded (Bate, 1982).

The later Fell occupation period (period II) occurred in the ninth millennium BP, and from this moment the hunters of land animals evolved their economic strategies towards exploiting a combination of resources, including the Pacific area in their sphere of interaction.

Pallí Aike, 26 km from Fell (Chilean–Argentine border), is another shelter containing traces of extinct fauna and similar cultural remains to Fell (Bird, 1938). It has been accepted that the charred human skeletons, lying on ash dated from the ninth millennium BP, come from this deposit.

The chronological span between Fell and Pallí Aike is a little more than two millennia, corresponding to a prolonged occupation period extending up to the ninth millennium BP, when the hunters in the northern regions were fully adapted to the Holocene pattern without extinct fauna. This suggests a time lag in the south with respect to the survival of Pleistocene fauna.

A deposit of calcined human skeletons also exists in Cerro Sota, a hollowed-out rock shelter situated near Fell, which is likely to be contemporaneous with the period of horse hunting. Despite the lack of dates, these bodies are likely to be the oldest in Patagonia, although their links with Pleistocene fauna are not necessarily an indication of their age, since horse and mylodon persisted throughout the sequence in Pallí Aike. The skeletons are of a family group

in a good state of health, with skulls combining both ancient and modern traits, who withdrew into this 'cul-de-sac' as a result of the arrival of different migrating peoples (Munizaga, 1976).

A hollowed-out shelter exists in Marazzi (Isla Grande de Tierra del Fuego) with remains of hunters – probably hunters of terrestrial species, despite the fact that they were located close to the coast where they started to procure additional supplies (Laming-Emperaire et al., 1972). Finally, in the Milodón cave (Seno de Ultima Esperanza), mylodon remains have been recorded bearing traces of butchering (Borrero, 1981). It has been observed that these sloths could have been hunted during the Pleistocene and the Holocene since they were located in high and low strata. However, this large shelter is cold even in summer, so it was not intensely occupied. The Patagonian megafauna were part of the preferred diet of the hunters, but they gradually became extinct for various reasons.

The reduction of woods containing conifers (*Podocarpus andinus*), false beech (*Nothofagus dombeyi*) and *N. oblicua* (Heusser, 1983) at Tagua-Tagua indicate that a radical change took place in the diet of herbivores (such as mastodon) at the beginning of the eleventh millennium BP. The assumption that the megafauna moved towards the south between the eleventh and ninth millennia BP could be correct, since 'Pleistocene' conditions would have been better maintained in the far south and Patagonia, compared with the dry northern climate (Tagua-Tagua and Quereo). It has been suggested that the fluctuations in resources and over-extensive hunting practices wiped out the megafauna in the Americas in a short period of time (Martín, 1973). Nevertheless, it has been shown that the people of this period lived by hunting between 13,000 and 8,600 years ago, judging from their association with extinct fauna, so that this hypothesis of sudden overkilling does not seem convincing.

Markgraf (1985) analysed mylodon coprolites and concluded that a large-scale reduction of the grassy steppe occurred in Fuego–Patagonia around the tenth millennium BP, coinciding with the extinction of the large herbivores under pressure from hunting. In fact, the graminaceous and herbaceous cover of the cold steppe evolved between the eleventh and eighth millennia BP and came to form an arid steppe and desert scrubland. This change towards 'modern vegetation' corresponds to a rise in temperature and a drop in rainfall which affected the diet of the mylodon, which was basically grasses. The large herbivores were unable to cope with the adjustment to Holocene conditions in this new ecological framework, so the guanacos, with a less specialized diet, became predominant and were the means of support for the later continental hunters.

It is reasonable to accept that the causes of extinction were many and interrelated: biological, ecological and cultural (Borrero, 1977; Saxon, 1978; Massone, 1981; Bate, 1982). Apart from the role played by the hunters, the first cycle of volcanic activity hastened the process of disruption, since it contaminated both drinking water and the forage itself. In addition, the competition for pasture between mylodons, horses and guanacos (Pleistocene versus Modern) in a context of drastic change in plant life was also crucial.

During the last period for hunting southern Pleistocene fauna (about the ninth millennium BP), the hunters in the southern-central and southern areas had already started to adapt to Postglacial conditions and evolved towards the exploitation of Holocene camelids, together with Andean and valley plant resources, while the Pacific shore was already occupied by the first fisherfolk.

HOLOCENE HUNTERS AND FISHERFOLK: TOWARDS THE BEGINNING OF FOOD PRODUCTION (10,000 TO 4,000 YEARS AGO) (Table 11)

During the Postglacial period the hunter-gatherers adapted to the new, increasingly dry, Holocene conditions, which confined resources to isolated and more highly contrasted ecozones on the Andean–coastal slope (from about the eleventh to the tenth millennium BP). Resources lacked continuity and became more differentiated because of greater ecological variety deriving from changes in altitude, which stimulated the emergence of various patterns of mobility between levels. The pasture lands reflected this transformation of the environment to a greater extent, and there was an early migrational descent towards the coast or transhumance or both.

Hunters existed in the areas adjoining the puna (*Circumpuna*) around the eleventh millennium BP, while the Pacific coast was occupied in the tenth millennium and as late as the seventh on the Magellan seaboard. This period was characterized by adaptation to the abundant marine biomass offering a protein diet that did not require mobility, since the resources were continuously available with only minor seasonal variations. Nevertheless, at the highest levels, a transhumance pattern predominated (seasonal nomadism) with greater mobility in the search for food and raw materials descending from 4,500 m towards the western and eastern slopes.

In the fertile puna in the heart of the Andes, the hunters maintained semi-sedentary camps; in the *altiplano* and the heads of the western valleys in the southern-central region, the high concentration and year-round stability of forage made semi-sedentary activities possible, but with transhumance which meant adjustment to a greater variety of geographical conditions.

This mobility increased in the *Circumpuna* lands, because at over 3,500 m seasonal changes were rigidly marked and winters unbearable for animals and humans. In addition, Andean resources here were dispersed and their importance diminished from north to south. Once the longitudinal valley of Chile was reached, the continuity and stability of continental resources with additional Andean and coastal inputs supported more sedentary populations and there was less dependence on transhumance. This situation changed drastically, however, in the uniform Patagonian region, where the absence of plant gathering and the abundance of fauna in open land and ravines stimulated hunting that was independent of seasonal fluctuations.

As a result, the stone industries on the Pacific coast tended to specialize early on account of the large variety of predictable activities around base camps. Inland areas, however, were affected by greater ecological and seasonal disruption (volcanic activity, drought and so on), so less specialized industries developed for specific subsistence activities. Responses were wide-ranging, according to the kind of level exploited, with more technological flexibility and access as necessary to various ecozones. The population increased and circuits were established over an area that was large enough to support the existence of groups in base camps, now associated with many secondary stopping places.

In all, a patchwork of additional resources was established, for whereas in the highlands hunting prevailed over plant gathering, in the valleys that descended to the Pacific the situation was either reversed or in equilibrium, with emphasis on the use of grinding tools. On the coast, the balance was clearer, but there was also dependence on the fertile ecozones when there were no neighbouring rivers.

This mobility gradually brought about an improved knowledge of the environment: animal behaviour, the productive processes of wild crops, assessment of new raw materials and so on. The sites with the widest choice of foods were situated in the Andes, the Pacific coast and the low continental regions where large rivers provided a continuity of resources (southern area and far south).

This mobility is important in order to understand the emergence of an Andean approach to life that tended to rationalize human energy through more sedentary work, which meant dietary improvements. The beginning of domestication or adoption of native species was particularly important; examples occurred in the southern-central area and the south between the sixth and fourth millennia BP of the domestication of llamas (*Lama* sp.) and guinea pigs (*Cavia* sp.), and the adoption of maize (*Zea mays*), beans (*Phaseolus vulgaris*), quinoa (*Chenopodium quinoa*), cucurbita and other species, in hunter-gatherer contexts (Hesse, 1982; Núñez, 1983a, 1983b; Ampuero and Rivera, 1971).

The various stages that prevailed from the Andes to the seaboard are described in chronological order in Table 11.

Andean hunters

Andean hunters in the southern-central Andean region

The first postglacial periods have been identified in the *Circumpuna* zone in the ravines which descend to the east and west of the Atacama plateau around the eleventh millennium BP, even though it is possible that before then the shores of the adjoining freshwater lakes were inhabited (Núñez, 1983b; Lynch, 1985).

The hunters of the *Circumpuna* tradition lived in caves at moderate altitudes below 3500 m; through their movements they linked up the high puna floor with the intermediate valleys, oases and wetlands of the Atacama basin. A good example is found in an area near Calama in the mountainous region of Tuina (2,800 m) which was occupied between 10,800 and 9,100 years ago. The population lived from hunting camelids and rodents (*Lagidium viscasia*), using tools made in open workshops: obsidian triangular points (Fig. 97 (k)), disc-shaped side-scrapers, flat anvil-stones and numerous high-backed end-scrapers. Another group was installed in the San Lorenzo cave (2,500 m) in a valley close to Toconao, between 10,400 and 10,000 years ago (Núñez, 1983b); while at a higher altitude, in the Chulqui shelter (3,280 m) the same fauna were exploited as at Tuina about 9,500 years ago (Sinclaire, MS).

On the eastern slope of the Atacama puna other groups, also with low population density, exploited from the sheltered valleys different ecozones at a higher altitude, including the eastern forest, thus giving a broader scope to the transhumance patterns. The inhabitants of the Huachichocana cave III (3,400 m) hunted the same species as in Tuina, but intensified plant gathering: bulbs, roots, tubers, Leguminosae, Gramineae, and the like, using tools such as end-scrapers, unifaces and triangular points associated with a few leaf-shaped points; their occupation is dated to between 10,200 and 8,400 years ago. Traces of cultivable plants as important as maize have been found together with complex artefacts of leather and plant fibres (Fernández Distel, 1974), but it is not yet clear whether these were gathered in their natural state, since the lowlands of north-east Argentina are rich in wild food plants (Yacobaccio, 1983).

Another dwelling site of this kind was discovered in Inca cave-4 (3,600 m), dating from the eleventh millennium BP. It is situated in a ravine at Jujuy, with a dug-out interior chamber that repeats an unusual trait of the first dwellings in the area. Sophisticated fibre artefacts for ropemaking and plaited baskets have been found along with triangular points, end-scrapers and side-scrapers. Creativity was highly developed, as was the abstract rock art, and there are even some remains of llama (*Lama* sp.), possibly in the process of domestication (Aschero, 1984).

This *Circumpuna* tradition led later to considerable achievements: a greater mastery of cultivable plants from the lowlands and mesothermal valleys, and the domestication of camelids and Andean plants. Funeral practices also developed, for in a nearby rock shelter (Inca cave-7), dated from the fourth millennium BP, a complicated cult of the dead appeared, with offerings reflecting new cultural traits: cucurbitae, semi-woven cloth, coiled baskets, carved wooden artefacts, pipes, flutes and cebil (*Anadenanthera macrocarpa*), a hallucinogen that was to be widely used later on (Aschero, 1984).

A second highland–*altiplano* Andean hunting tradition occurred in the highlands of the western valleys between the ninth and eighth millennia BP. It is difficult to recognize links with previous periods, but in the Arica sierra, triangular points have also been dated from the tenth and ninth millennia BP, and further south, in Pichasca (southern area), other similar objects have been dated within the same time span (Fig. 97 (j)). It is assumed that these assemblages originated in the central Andean highlands, since triangular points have been recorded between the eleventh and eighth millennia BP both in the Guitarreros cave and in Pachamachay (Lynch, 1983; Rick, 1980), but this is still open to doubt.

In the Arica sierra a small group that sheltered in Las Cuevas used triangular, leaf-shaped and tanged points for hunting camelids, rodents and birds, their pattern of transhument exploitation including the pre-puna level (summer camps) and the *altiplano* (winter camps). In other words, they alternated between sheltered highland regions and open or Andean paramo regions, between 9,600 and 8,250 years ago (Santoro, MS). The highland–*altiplano* area offered greater stability on account of its permanent forage, with only minor seasonal variations, which supported a larger camelid population and allowed a semi-sedentary life-style. Transhumance activities were concentrated on the exploitation of the rich biomass of the highlands. Nevertheless, the presence of a Pacific shark's tooth introduces the possibility that some movement existed along the valleys.

It is likely that while occupation of Las Cuevas was going on, another wave of hunters arrived from the central Andes, moving along the mountainous country of southern Peru. This is the Toquepala I period, characterized by camelid hunting, and involving hunting magic in the form of an unusually naturalistic rupestrian art style. Leaf-shaped points, asymmetrical knives and Pacific shells have been recorded which indicate possible transhumance to the coast between 9,500 and 7,850 years ago (Ravines, 1972). This wave reached the Arica sierra, judging from the remains in the Tojo-Tojones cave: camelids, deer (*Hyppocamelus antisiensis*), rodents, leaf-shaped points and the so-called 'ichuña' barbed points with serrated edges dated to 9,600 years ago (Dauelsberg, 1983). It has been suggested that these hunters also descended to the coast, as leaf-shaped points and Andean scrapers on the Achira (Camaná) coast have been dated to about 8,765 years ago (Ravines, 1972). In addition, similar points have been recorded on the Camarones-Norte shore

(Dauelsberg, 1983) and Tiliviche near the Pisagua coast during the same time span (Núñez, 1983a).

A later wave of camelid hunters covered the mountainous regions of Peru, living for example in shelters in Caru, where rhomboid, tanged and barbed points have been dated to about 8,200 years ago (Ravines, 1967), and moving down to the coast at Puyenca (north of Camaná). Their obsidian industry was situated there, dated between 8,100 and 7,850 years ago. They progressed as far as the Arica sierra, where, in the Patapatane cave, remains of camelids, rodents and pentagonal points with broad tangs and barbs have been recorded, associated with leaf-shaped pieces, dated 8,200 years ago (Fig. 97 (g, h)).

It is still difficult to confirm where they originally came from, but it is assumed that there is a correlation with the tanged points from the Puente de Ayacucho stage, dated around the ninth millennium BP, and those of Pachamachay, in the Junín puna (MacNeish, 1969).

The Patapatane stage is linked with the intensive use of stable resources at high altitude (puna level) – steppes, lakes and swamps vegetation (3,600 m) – through longitudinal transhumance at high level, and even transversal movements towards the coast, since Pacific shell (*Choro mytilus*) artefacts have been recorded (Santoro, MS). In this way, there was greater occupation of the puna and less dependence on the lowlands, but given the short-lived nature of their settlements, these hunters did not manage to develop a sedentary life-style, as occurred in the rich Junín puna (Rick, 1980). Nevertheless, unlike the situation of the *Circumpuna* hunters, their settlements in the highlands at the head of the Western Valleys could be used all year round, without climatic limitations, for they were supported by a more stable fauna and flora.

We do not know how this highland–*altiplano* tradition developed in terms of growing complexity. The development of greater control over camelids and Andean plants should have had an effect on the processes of domestication, echoing similar changes, as yet undated, in the circum-Titikaka and the southern *altiplano* zones. For the moment a hiatus has been observed between these early periods and the beginning of Andean food production. Some evidence indicates that both in Patapatane and Tojo-Tojones the shelters were in use again around 4,900 and 3,750 years ago respectively, owing to better exploitation of the valley flora (*chacu* or *rodeo* hunting), cultivation of tubers and llama herding (Santoro, MS).

After these early Andean periods of occupation, dispersed in the eighth millennium BP, settlements reappeared following a hiatus, in Toquepala II (6,000 to 5,650 years ago), where rhomboid points, oval knives and serrated tanged points were used, and transhumance to the coast increased (indicated, for instance, by Pacific shells). In fact the coastal slopes supported intermittent forage reserves upon which the Andean herbivores and their highland hunters converged, between the Majes river and the Arica coast.

This 'archaeological silence' also existed in the *Circumpuna* lands between the eighth and sixth millennia BP. It is likely that long dry periods or Holocene volcanic events or both disrupted the Andean habitat, as occurred in the Bolivian *altiplano* (Avila, 1978). In the *Circumpuna* zone, a third tradition of river–puna hunters appeared after the hiatus (lack of survey?). They linked up different stages in the Loa river environment and that of the streams which flowed down to the salt basin; there was seasonal access to the high Atacama puna.

The first indications come from the camp sites with dwellings dug out below ground level in Confluencia (5,400 years ago) and Isla Grande (6,000 years ago), established in the Loa. Despite the fact that tools are compatible with the exploitation of higher lands (such as leaf-shaped points and grinding tools), they have only been located near the fertile wetlands in the middle Loa, where resources contracted during the dry periods, when the seasonal migrations to higher lands became more important.

This transhumance pattern is clearer in the nearby Atacama basin, along the high puna-Atacama salt basin strip, between the fifth and fourth millennia BP. The seasonal resources of the high puna (4,000 m) were exploited at the head of the Tulán valley - camelids, obsidian and aquatic and flightless birds which supported settlements in the hot season around the Meniques and Miscanti lagoons (Niemeyer and Schiappacasse, 1976). Nevertheless, more sedentary camps with groups of circular dwellings, substantial refuse deposits and workshops were located lower down in the sheltered Tulán valley (2,925 m). The existence of drainage basins, forage and quarries enabled the population to establish a number of camps for the hunting of adult camelids, supplemented by local rodents and birds. The presence of numerous grinding pestles and mortars suggests a greater use of plant resources (undetermined). One of these blade workshops (Tulán-51) has been dated to 5,000 years ago, while a base camp (Tulán-52) has been assigned a date of around 4,350 years ago. The first underground deposits have been identified in these stone-walled dwellings dug out below ground level, together with evidence of the flaking of stone using blanks brought from nearby quarries, where numerous bifaces and discarded blades have been found (Tulán Cerros). The stone industry is highly varied, with leaf-shaped points, side-scrapers, end-scrapers, microliths and blade knives. The exploitation of the high puna was continuous, as indicated by the intensive use of Andean obsidian, while adult camelid remains suggest that the pattern of semi-sedentary life was based on specialized hunting (*chacu*) of these animals on the ravine floor, supplemented by local rodents: mountain viscacha (*Lagidium* sp.), tuco-tuco (*Ctenomys* sp.) and chinchilla (*Chinchilla* sp.). Groups of similar dwellings were situated lower down, on the shores of the present Atacama salt basin (2,500 m). In fact, the Tulán hunters established themselves temporarily alongside the piedmont oases, fertile wetlands and small lakes. The concentration of Andean birds and local rodents in the wetlands and lagoons of the salt basin encouraged seasonal access, and camps such as Tambillo appeared, where a burial ground has been recorded with dolichoid skulls associated with mortars. A similar occupation has been dated in Calarcoco to 5,100 years ago; and in the interior of Toconao another ravine indicates a similar pattern of transhumance (Núñez, 1980; Serracino and Pereyea, 1977).

A similar seasonal round has been identified along the Puripica river gorge (3,200 m) in the far north of the Atacama basin, confirming the broad geographical scope of these transversal movements. A base camp dated 4,800 to 4,050 years ago is situated here. Although the Puripica stone and grinding industries remain similar to those of Tulán, there is a marked absence of blades, which are replaced by local basalt flakes. The large number of knives, boring tools and microliths suggest an activity linked with butchering and the preparation of camelid skins, whereas the reduction of leaf-shaped points indicates that there was less hunting. Up to this point there was a high concentration of vicuña (*Vicugna vicugna*) in this region, as corroborated by archaeological evidence. The large amount of bone remains of young

and new-born camelids (osteometric evidence) suggests the beginning of a meat-producing economy, through domestication. Breeding in captivity caused disease, reflected in a high rate of early death. In addition to this evidence, there are the new functions of the stone industry mentioned above, together with the only record of stone pieces with engravings of camelids, linked to the cult of domestic llamas. It is likely that this camp was used more during the summer (camelid breeding), and that the inhabitants then moved along the Puripica river and even towards the Loa. In fact camps have been recorded in this last area at the Chiuchiu complex, with dates of between 4,500 and 3,600 years ago. The semi-underground circular dwellings, leaf-shaped points, grinding tools and microliths repeat the Puripica model, situated at 2,300 m. It can be accepted therefore that the hunter-gatherer communities of the Puripica/Chiuchiu stage established transhumance circuits related to camelids that included the highlands, hunting in the high *puna*, domesticating llamas in the ravines and keeping flocks, hunting and gathering plants in the low wetlands of the Loa river (when these resources were not affected by periodic drought).

These early pastoral activities were constituting the beginning of an increasingly complex life-style with regional repercussions, if it is accepted that the presence of shells in Puripica/Chiuchiu indicates contact with the alternative resources of the *Circumpuna* coast (Núñez, 1980; Hesse, 1982; Druss, 1977).

It can therefore be suggested convincingly that during the fifth and fourth millennia BP the highlands of the southern-central Andean region sustained large groups with greater communal cohesion around sites with resources. There are some indications of ethnic identity in more clearly delimited regions such as at the heads of the western valleys and in the *Circumpuna* area, where horticulture and early livestock-raising activities (llamas) complemented traditional hunting and gathering. The late periods in this time span, at Toquepala III, Las Cuevas, Huachichocana, Inca cave-7 and the western *Circumpuna* sites already mentioned indicate a more effective process of adaptation in terms of incipient food production, based on better-ordered transhumance movements. These covered the different Andean regions – the moderate altitude habitat, together with other areas stretching towards both the Pacific and the tropical forest – within a broad sphere of complementary interaction which facilitated the approach to the threshold of civilization, the result of the quickening of productive forces leading to the establishment of new sedentary life-styles and supported by such advanced activities as agriculture and livestock-raising.

Andean hunters of the southern area and the far south

So far no settlement has been dated over 2,500 m in the zone of the western valleys, which covers the present semi-arid and fertile Chilean territory, with its characteristic transversal valleys and broad basins situated below the narrow Andean heights. The continental distribution of the Cárcamo industry, with its unusual tanged points, suggests that the Huentelauquén communities practised transhumance from the coast towards the high pastures where the Andean birds concentrated during the summer season. The Andean cordillera served as a bridge for the flow of hunters who moved in search of high altitude hunting sites. The Fortuna industry has been identified precisely in the Cuyana zone, with identical tanged points dated at around 8,100 years ago (Gambier, 1974; Silva and Wiesner, 1972–3; Iribarren, 1961). This access to additional resources continued, judging from the mobility of the Morillos transandean culture. These hunters, who practised transhumance, exploited Andean resources (such as camelids) and those of lower altitudes (like carob). They also moved towards the Pacific where they assimilated local handicrafts (Gambier, 1974). This period occurred between the eighth and fourth millennia BP, at the same time as the occupation of Cuchipuy and Tagua-Tagua II, where similar pierced stones and triangular points have been recorded in comparable contexts.

In the zone of the western valleys and in the far south, the subandean populations, situated in the networks of rivers and lakes, maintained abundant resources which slightly reduced the transhumance movements towards the Andes. The number of hunting sites recorded in the Santiago piedmont suggests that even if an ample stock of camelids existed it did not contribute decisively to the cultural process (Stehberg, 1984).

Andean hunters of the Patagonian region

The reappearance of Andean fauna (such as *Lama guanicoe*) in this broad continental plateau suggests that more than one element of the areas mentioned above, on both sides of the Andes, could have spread towards the Patagonian region.

Continental hunters of the inter-montane basins and valleys

Hunters of the southern-central valleys

Camps were established in the lower western valleys, with circular, dug-out chambers and posts for supporting roofs; semi-sedentary activities here were complementary to exploitation of the coastal habitat. This was an unusual fluvial–coastal economy aimed at providing food and raw materials for the communities settled on the Pacific coast, covering an extended sequence below 1500 m.

A first period has been identified in the Tiliviche oasis linked to the Pisagua and Camarones coast, from where coastal produce was brought to supplement local hunting and gathering. The predominant activity was stone flaking, stone being brought to the coast where there was a lack of this resource. The presence of leaf-shaped points, asymmetrical knives, grinding tools, end-scrapers, scraping-planes and shell fish-hooks (Fig. 97 (a, e, f,) and so on, confirm that the nearby coast was occupied simultaneously from 9,750 to 7,850 years ago. The cultivation of maize and the raising of guinea pigs (*Cavia* sp.) began at a later stage (6,050 to 4,650 years ago). This densely populated camp was built up in an intermittent fashion between the tenth and the fourth millennia BP. Mixed refuse from both coast and valley (such as fish, sea-food, edible roots, club rushes (*Scirpus* sp.)) was found, indicating that this oasis came within the sphere of interaction with the coast. A period of post-Chinchorro coastal tombs indicates that the latest occupation took place around 3,870 years ago (Núñez, 1983*b*). Another late camp of this type has been located in the mouth of the Camarones river (Cononoxa), with similar activities (Niemeyer and Schiappacasse, 1963).

The Aragón camp (8,650 to 4,500 years ago) covers two stages in this long sequence, with coastal complementarity playing a similar role. In the Tarapacá ravine, the camps furthest away from the coast (80 km) confirm that this circuit was in use between 6,850 and 3,900 years ago, with similar stone industries. It was possible to transport marine produce up to this point to supplement the exploitation of coastal resources. The cultivation of maize in particular provided an important innovation in the hunters' diet (Núñez and Zlatar, 1976; True et al., 1970).

Hunters of the southern-area valleys

The Pichasca cave is situated in the centre of the western valleys, in an affluent of the Hurtado river. Remains of hunting have been found (camelids, deer, rodents) with evidence of darts and throwing sticks, as well as of active plant gathering, including fibre for coiled baskets. Numerous triangular points were flaked (Fig. 97 (j)), dated to about 9,900 years ago (Ampuero and Rivera, 1971). The inhabitants moved towards the Pacific because there they obtained resources and shells (*Choro mytilus*) which they used as tools. These semi-arid valleys were ideal for the introduction of horticulture, in a context of hunting and gathering. Thus maize (*Zea mays*) and beans (*Phaseolus vulgaris*) existed at Pichasca from its middle to late periods, between 7,050 and 4,700 years ago.

These activities aimed at food production increased at the El Salto shelter and extended through the middle and late Pichasca sequence, with indications of horticulture in the coastal hinterland. It is not yet possible to confirm if the interconnection between these valleys served as a support for the coastal communities, like the fluvial–coastal economy of the southern-central area. The origins of Pichasca have not yet been ascertained, but they could be related to the triangular points from the *Circumpuna* zone or the triangular pieces from the Pampa–Patagonia region, from where the rupestrian art motif of painted hands present in the cave may have come.

Further south, in the longitudinal valley, the Cuchipuy burial ground close to the Tagua-Tagua lagoon belongs to the people of the fluvial–lacustrine economy. Here the coastal–transcordillera transhumance movement located an important site of stable lacustrine resources, inducing a greater degree of sedentism in their semi-nomadic life. The burial ground is crowded, suggesting the establishment of base camps (Kaltwasser et al., 1983). Burials (in a flexed position), dated from around 8,100 years ago, began in zone 4. Remains have ultra-dolichocephalic craniometric traits, and are associated with tanged points (Fig. 97 (b)) similar to those of the Huentelauquén coast, and those of the Andes at Fortuna and Patapatane. Zone 3 contained tanged points and throwing sticks, dated to 7,600 and 6,150 years ago, while in zone 2, 5,750 years ago, the bodies were associated with stone debris, leaf-shaped and triangular points, flat grinding anvil-stones, mortars, pestles, bone gravers and pierced stones. The growing number of obsidian artefacts (common in zone 2) suggest that the tenuous transhumance movements in the Andean–coastal section were controlled from Cuchipuy, within a broad sphere of interaction whose peak seems to have been in the sixth millennium BP.

A much later camp has been recorded in the same lagoon, dated to between 6,150 and 5,050 years ago (Tagua-Tagua II), containing tanged and triangular points, stone polishers, grinding tools, hammerstones, end-scrapers and pierced stone (Durán, 1980). It is accepted that these groups, as well as exploiting resources from rivers and lakes, were in contact with the neighbouring coast (indicated by the presence of Pacific shells) and would correspond to the Cuchipuy zone 2 burials.

Hunters in the valleys of the far south

An occupational level has been found below the Quilem cliff overhang in the sub-Andean region of Araucanía, dated to 4,700 years ago, with stone-flaking activities that could be linked with hunting and the last traces of predominant plant gathering (Sánchez and Valdes, 1982).

Pacific fisherfolk

Fisherfolk of the southern-central Andean area

Two different economic traditions of coastal populations have been identified in the zones of the western valleys and the *Circumpuna*, both dating from around the tenth millennium BP. In the first case, the Tiliviche camp, according to its artefacts and the foodstuffs brought from the Pacific, unmistakably indicates that there were fisherfolk on the neighbouring coast (for instance, at Pisagua and Camarones) from about 9,800 years ago.

In the second case, Las Conchas camp was established on the desert coast of Antofagasta and contained tanged points, anvil-stones, pestles, tropical fish and polygonal or cog stones (Fig. 97 (d)), dated around 9,700 years ago (Llagostera, 1979). This period included the most northerly extent of the Huentelauquén population, centred in the coast of the southern area. There is a hiatus before later occupations of the *Circumpuna* coast, which began by the sixth to fifth millennium BP.

After the Tiliviche stage on the coast (about the tenth millennium BP), exploitation of ecozones in the mouths of rivers increased during the Camarones stage (seventh millennium BP), with similar artefacts and dwelling remains. Continuity of population has been observed; presumably people who had arrived at the coast through an extension of the Andean hunters' migrations or transhumance or both and adapted their economic practices to exploit the coastal resources of the Postglacial era.

During the Camerones stage (between 7,000 and 6,600 years ago) base camps and secondary camps were dispersed in coastal sites where a semi-sedentary life-style was centred, since the relative stability of resources required less energy expenditure (Schiappacasse and Niemeyer, 1984). This was a biologically homogeneous population, with high fertility and infant mortality rates, since they were living in a social and ecological readaptation. Efficient implements for the coastal surroundings emerged, along with leaf-shaped points, grinding tools and shell fish-hooks, which enabled this population to apply first hunting and fishing techniques (a low-calorie diet) and then include the gathering of molluscs as an additional input. The organization of work was divided by age and sex with an egalitarian distribution of tasks, including journeys to inland oases such as Tiliviche, which provided stone blanks, carob (*Prosopis juliflora*) wood, camelids and rodents. The first artificially mummified human bodies came from the Camarones-14 camp, indicating the beginning of an unusual cult of the dead which gave a greater ideological coherence to the later population.

The Quiani (Arica) stage, revealed by a shell-midden assigned a date of around 6,150 years ago (Bird, 1943), developed from the previous stage through greater specialization. Its features included shell fish-hooks and other characteristics which continued with few changes (including artificial human mummification, with a filling of the thorax and the covering of the body with clay). These burials reached their peak in the fifth millennium BP and continued up to the fourth millennium BP (Chinchorro stage), spread-ing from Antofagasta to Mollendo with a clear focal point between Camarones and Arica.

In chronological terms, the population with shell fish-hooks established itself on the coast of the western valleys between the seventh and sixth millennia BP, moving gradually through the coast of the *Circumpuna* zone with a certain time lag. Intermediate stages in this movement reached Caramucho, Cobija, Abtao and Taltal by the sixth millennium BP, the southern coast at Guanaqueros being arrived at around the fourth millennium BP accompanied by the development of different regional expressions. This southern limit seems to be compatible with contact with the populous hunting-gathering communities which had spread through the longitudinal valley and the coast (for instance at Cuchipuy) with strong continental development.

The Chinchorro stage was concentrated on the coast of the western valleys in the fifth and fourth millennia BP, a peak being reached in the preparation of mummies and cactus-spine fish-hooks. This population still showed signs of poor adaptation to the environment (such as injury while carrying out productive tasks, high fertility rate and high female death rate due to calcium deficiency), although its activities were semi-sedentary and socially well balanced (for instance, note the absence of injury resulting from violence). The crowded burial grounds imply a dispersion of settlements closely linked by a shared funeral ritual, suggesting an incipient ethnic identity. Work was hierarchically structured, with certain specialization of functions which even included divers (a high level of auditive osteoma), hunters expert with harpoons and throwing-sticks, and 'priests' responsible for mummification and so on (Standen et al., 1984; Allison, 1985).

The practice of artificial mummification, a sign of the spirit of continuity, lasted from the seventh to the fourth millennium BP, perhaps one of the earliest examples in the world. It has been suggested that genetically these groups were migrants originating in the tropical forests, via the *altiplano* (traces of vicuña and quinoa) (Rivera and Rothhamer, 1985; Núñez, 1983*b*). The mummification technique was not selective (both young children and adults). It consisted of skinning the corpse, removing the flesh, and disembowelling. The cavities were dried by fire and rubbed with ashes. They were later filled with vegetable fibre, ashes and clay, a basis for replacing the skin as if the body were intact. For this purpose pieces of wood were inserted between the skin and bones from the ankles to the skull through the foramen magnum. The outside of the body was then modelled with clay, with facial expression, genitals and breasts, and included false hair and layers of paint on the death mask. A wrapping of straw matting gave it the appearance of a stiff, small package which could be presented as a small statue for the purposes of the ceremony. Mummified birds, fish, human foetuses and dogs indicate that this practice was broad in scope, and it was associated with non-mummified bodies (Uhle, 1919; Allison et al., 1984).

After the Chinchorro stage, the coast was inhabited by communities deriving from it (indicated, for instance, by the persistence of facial death masks) which clustered around burial grounds. They were more sedentary to the south of the Loa river. On the *Circumpuna* coast, however, an overlapping of coastal and Andean traits occurred between Huelén-42 (Loa river mouth) and Taltal, for camps were built in circular enclosures following the highland tradition (such as Tulán-52). The presence in Huelén of cordillera parakeet feathers (*Psilopsiagon aurifrons*) and obsidian, as well as the similarity of artefacts, suggest that the Andean hunters of the fluvial–puna tradition may have occupied the coast at the same time, according to the various coastal datings between the fifth and second millennia BP (Núñez, 1983*b*; Bittman, 1982).

Hunter-fisher-gatherers in the southern area

The Huentelauquén stage could include the first Postglacial periods of the western valleys. In fact, the shell-middens of this population were distributed from the Choapa river mouth towards the south by Los Vilos and towards the north up to the *Circumpuna* coast (Caleta del Obispito and Las Conchas). The Huentelauquén sites of the southern coast include tanged and leaf-shaped points, grinding tools, flakers, throwing sticks, pebble industries and polygonal or cog stones. Although there is no dating for this population on the southern coast, it is assumed that this was an early period (around the tenth millennium BP) and could overlap with the arrival on the coast of the ancient Pichasca hunters (Ampuero and Hildalgo, 1976). It has also been suggested that these fisherfolk moved inland under the impetus of transhumance movements, although no cog stones have been recorded away from the coast, apart from one exceptional case, but their tanged points have been identified.

Following this period there was a chronological hiatus on the southern coast and activity reoccurred only in the fourth millennium with specialized fishermen, constituting the Guanaqueros and Teatinos stages respectively.

No specific coastal periods have been dated to the south of the Choapa river, but the high degree of dispersion of shell-middens could indicate that they included a sequence related to Cuchipuy, Huentelauquén, Tagua-Tagua II or to later events such as Papudo, Bellavista and Gamboa. The extension of these occupations towards the Archipelago–Patagonia region is not confirmed, but the 'Casa-Pozo' (pit-house) and 'Cuchillo de Concha' (shell-knife) canoeists could have reproduced certain elements from this area.

Hunters and fisherfolk of the archipelago–Patagonia region

After the Pleistocene occupations, a wave of hunters of Andean descent constituted the Fell III period, from 8,200 to about 6,400 years ago. Their remains include small end-scrapers, bola stones, and leaf-shaped and triangular points. Their dispersion in the Magellan region is indicated by camps, collective tombs, hollowed-out shelters, and their unusual rock art of ostrich 'footprints'. Between the seventh and sixth millennia BP these populations began a specific process of readaptation to Pacific resources.

In fact, the late Túnel–Ponsomby stage included various sites adjoining the coast, with activities leading to specialization: Túnel, Lancha, Late Ponsomby, Englefield, Bahía Buena and Punta Santa Ana. Leaf-shaped and triangular points associated with characteristic bone harpoons dated between 6,400 and 5,200 years ago (Orquera et al., 1979; Ortíz-Troncoso, 1979) have been recorded here. Thus, from the seventh millennium BP the life-style of the hunters from the interior and that of the coastal canoeists began to coexist, like land and sea nomads respectively.

During the fifth and fourth millennia BP, these lake hunters occupied various sites between Laguna Timone and Monte Aymond. Their remains include broad-tanged notched points with barbs. Guanaco and ñandú were hunted with large bola stones, while leather working improved with better scrapers. They lived in shelters and left remains of butchering along the path of their movements between the

pampa and the Magellan regions, where they left numerous shell-middens. Finally these hunting traditions gave rise to the first ethnic expression of the Proto-Tehuelche or *Aonikenk* kind (Massone, 1981).

BIBLIOGRAPHY

ALLISON, M. 1985. La salud de las poblaciones arcaicas. In: CONGRESO NACIONAL DE ARQUEOLOGIA CHILENA, Arica. *Resumenes de Ponencias.*

ALLISON, M. J. et al. 1984. Chinchorro, momias de preparación complicada: métodos de momificación. *Chungara* (Arica), Vol. 13, pp. 155–73.

AMPUERO, G.; HILDALGO, J. 1976. Estructura y proceso en la prehistoria y protohistoria del Norte Chico. *Chungara* (Arica), Vol. 5, pp. 87–124.

AMPUERO, G.; RIVERA, M. 1971. Secuencia arqueologica del alero de San Pedro Viejo – Puchasca. *Bol. Mus. Arqueol. Serena*, Vol. 14, pp. 45–69.

ASCHERO, C. M. 1984. El sitio ICC-4: un asentamiento precerámico en la quebrada de Inca Cueva. In: SIMPOSIO DE ARQUEOLOGÍA ATACAMEÑA, San Pedro de Atacama. pp. 62–72.

AUER, V. 1970. The Pleistocene of Fuego-Patagonia; Part V: Quaternary Problems of Southern South America. *Ann. Acad. Sci. Fenn.* (Helsinki), Ser. A, Vol. 3, No. 100.

AVILA, S. W. 1978. Consideraciones sobre el vulcanismo Cenozoico en la Cordillera Occidental de Bolivia. *Bol. Serv. Geol. Boliv.* (La Paz), Vol. 2, pp. 31–56.

BATE, F. 1982. *Orígenes de la comunidad primitiva en Patagonia.* Mexico.

BIRD, J. 1938. Antiquity and Migration of the Early Inhabitants of Patagonia. *Geogr. Rev.* (New York), Vol. 281, pp. 250–75.

—— 1943. Excavations in Northern Chile. *Anthropol. Pap. Am. Mus. Nat. Hist.*, Vol. 38, No. 4, pp. 171–318.

—— 1946. The Archaeology of Patagonia. In: STEWARD, J. (ed.), *Handbook of South American Indians.* Washington, DC. pp. 17–24.

—— 1951. South American Radiocarbon Dates. *Mem. Soc. Am. Archaeol.* (Washington), Vol. 8.

——. 1969. A Comparison of South Chilean and Ecuatorian Fishtail Projectile Points. *Kroeber Anthropol. Soc. Pap.* (Berkeley), Vol. 40, pp. 52–71.

BIRD, J.; COOKE, R. 1978. The Occurrence in Panama of Two Types of Palaeo-Indian Projectile Points. In: BRYAN, A. L. (ed.), *Early Man in America from a Circum-Pacific Perspective.* Edmonton. pp. 263–72.

BITTMANN, B. 1982. El proyecto Cobija: investigaciones antropológicas en la costa del Desierto de Atacama. In: SIMPOSIO DE CULTURAS ATACAMEÑAS, San Pedro de Atacama, Manchester. *Anales.* San Pedro de Atacama. pp. 99–146.

BORRERO, L. A. 1977. La extinción de la megafauna: su explicación por factores recurrentes: la situación en Patagonia Austral. *An. Inst. Patagonia* (Punta Arenas), Vol. 8, pp. 81–93.

—— 1981. El poblamiento de la Patagonia Austral: revalorización de los cazadores de Mylodon. In: CONGRESO DE LA UISPP, 10, Mexico. *Comisión 12.* pp. 90–3.

BRYAN, A. L. 1978. An Overview of Palaeo-American Prehistory from a Circum-Pacific Perspective. In: BRYAN, A. L. (ed.), *Early Man in America from a Circum-Pacific Perspective.* Edmonton. pp. 306–27.

CARDICH, A. 1977. Las cultura Pleistocenicas y Postpleistocenicas de Los Toldos y un bosquejo de la prehistoria de Sudamérica. In: *Obra del Centenario del Museo de la Plata.* La Plata. Vol. 2, pp. 149–72.

CARDICH, A.; FLEGENHEIMER, N. 1978. Recent Excavation at Lauricocha (Central Andes) and Los Toldos (Patagonia). In: BRYAN, A. (ed.), *Early Man in America from a Circum-Pacific Perspective.* Edmonton. pp. 296–302.

CARDICH, A.; CARDICH, L.; HAJDUK, A. 1973. Secuencia arqueológica y cronología radiocarbónica de la cueva 3 de Los Toldos. *Relac. Soc. argent. Antropol.* (Buenos Aires), Vol. 7, pp. 85–123.

CARDICH, A. et al. 1981–2. Arqueología de la cuevas de El Ceibo.

Relac. Soc. argent. Antropol. (Buenos Aires), Vol. 14, No. 2, pp. 173–209.

CASAMIQUELA, R.; MONTANE, J.; SANTANA, R. 1976. Convivencia del hombre con el mastodonte en Chile central: noticias sobre las investigaciones en la laguna de Tagua Tagua. *Notic. Mens.* (Santiago del Chile), Vol. 132, pp. 1–5.

DAUELSBERG, P. 1983. Tojo-Tojone: un paradero de cazadores arcaicos. *Chungara* (Arica), Vol. 11, pp. 11–30.

DILLEHAY, T. D. 1984. A Late Ice-Age Settlement in Southern Chile. *Sci. Am.*, Vol. 251, pp. 106–17.

DRUSS, M. 1977. Computer Analysis of ChiuChiu Complex Settlement Pattern. *El Dorado* (Greeley), Vol. 2, No. 3, pp. 51–73.

DURAN, E. 1980. Tagua Tagua II, Nivel de 6.130 años: descripción y relaciones. *Bol. Mus. Nac. Hist. Nat.* (Santiago de Chile), Vol. 37, pp. 75–86.

EMPERAIRE, J.; LAMING-EMPERAIRE, A.; REINCHELEN, A. 1963. La grotte Fell et autres sites de la région volcanique de la Pagatonie Chilienne. *J. Soc. Américanist.* (Paris), Vol. 52, pp. 189–254.

FERNÁNDEZ DISTEL, A. A. 1974. Excavaciones arqueológicas en las cuevas de Huachichocana, Dep. de Tumbaya, Prov. de Jujuy, Argentina. *Relac. Soc. argent. Antropol.* (Buenos Aires), Vol. 8, pp. 101–27.

FUNG, R.; CENZANO, C.; ZAVALETA, A. 1972. El taller lítico de Chivateros, valle de Chillon. *Rev. Mus. Nac.* (Lima), Vol. 38, pp. 62–72.

GAMBIER, M. 1974. Horizonte de cazadores tempranos en las Andes Centrales Argentinos-Chilenos. *Rev. Huruc Huar* (San Juan), Vol. 11, pp. 44–103.

GRADÍN, C. J.; ASCHERO, C.; AGUERRE, A. M. 1976. Investigaciones arqueológicas en la cueva de las Manos Puntadas, Estancia Alto Rio Pinturas. *Relac. Soc. argent. Antropol.* (Buenos Aires), Vol. 13.

HESSE, B. 1982. Archaeological Evidence for Camelid Exploitation in the Chilean Andes. *Säugetierkundl. Mitt.* (Munich), Vol. 3, pp. 201–11.

HEUSSER, C. J. 1960. Late Pleistocene Environment of the Laguna de San Rafael, Chile. *Geogr. Rev.* (New York), Vol. 1, No. 4.

—— 1983. Quaternary Pollen Record from Laguna Tagua Tagua, Chile. *Science* (Washington), Vol. 219, pp. 1469–82.

IRIBARREN, J. 1961. La cultura Huentelauquen y sus relaciones. *Contrib. Arqueol., Mus. Arqueol. Chile* (La Serena), No. 1.

KALTWASSER, J.; MEDINA, A.; MUNIZAGA, J. 1983. Estudio de once fechas de RC-14 relacionadas con el Hombre de Cuchipuy. *Bol. Prehist. Chile* (Santiago de Chile), Vol. 9, pp. 9–13.

KRIEGER, A. 1964. Early Man in the New World. In: JENNINGS, J. D.; NORBECK, E. (eds), *Prehistoric Man in the New World*. Chicago. pp. 28–81.

LAMING-EMPERAIRE, A.; LAVALLEE, D.; HUMBERT, R. 1972. Le Site de Marassi en terre du feu. *Objets Mondes* (Paris), Vol. 12, No. 2, pp. 225–44.

LANNING, E. P. 1967. Early Man in South America. *Sci. Am.*, Vol. 217, pp. 44–50.

LLAGOSTERA, A. 1979. 9700 Years of Maritime Subsistence on the Pacific: An Analysis by Means of Bioindicator in the North of Chile. *American Antiquity*, Vol. 44, No. 2, pp. 309–24.

LYNCH, T. F. 1983. The Paleo-Indians. In: JENNINGS, J. D.; FREEMAN, W. F. (eds), *Ancient South Americans*. San Francisco. pp. 87–137.

—— 1985. Un reconocimiento del salar de Punta Negra, segunda región. In: CONGRESO DE ARQUEOLOGIA CHILENA, 10, Arica. *Resumen de Ponencia*. Arica.

MACNEISH, R. S. 1969. *First Annual Report of the Ayacucho Archaeological-Botanical Project*. Andover.

MARKGRAF, V. 1985. Late Pleistocene Faunal Extinctions in Southern Patagonia. *Science* (Washington), Vol. 228, pp. 1110–12.

MARTÍN, P. S. 1973. The Discovery of America. *Science* (Washington), Vol. 179, pp. 969–74.

MASSONE, M. M. 1981. Arqueología de la región volcánica de Palli-Aike (Patagonia Meridionale Chilena). *An. Inst. Patagonia* (Punta Arenas), Vol. 12, pp. 95–124.

MENGHIN, O. 1952. Fundamentos cronológicos de la prehistoria de Patagonia. *Runa* (Buenos Aires), Vol. 5, pp. 1–23.

—— 1957. Los estilos de arte rupestre de Patagonia. *Acta Prehist.* (Buenos Aires), Vol. 1.

MELTZER, S. 1969. The Salar de Talabre, Northern Chile: A Tentative Ecological Reconstruction and Serration of Archaeological Remains, San Pedro de Atacama, Chile. In: CONFERENCE OF PLEISTOCENE MAN IN LATIN AMERICA. *Acta*.

MERCER, J. 1970. Variation of some Patagonian Glaciers since the Late Glacial. *Am. J. Sci.* (New Haven), Vol. 269, pp. 1–25.

MONTANÉ, J. 1968. Palaeo-Indian Remains from Laguna de Tagua Tagua, Central Chile. *Science* (Washington), Vol. 161, pp. 1137–8.

MUNIZAGA, J. 1976. Paleoindio en Sudamérica: restos humanos de las cuevas de Palli Aike y Cerro Sota, Prov. de Magallanes, Chile. In: *Volumen de Homenaje al Dr Gustavo Le Paige, S.J.* Antofagasta, Universidad del Norte. pp. 19–30.

NIEMEYER, H.; SCHIAPPACASSE, V. 1963. Investigaciones arqueológicas en las terrazas de Conanoxa, Valle de Camarones (Prov. Tarapaca). *Rev. Univ., Univ. Catól. Chile* (Santiago de Chile), Vol. 26, pp. 102–66.

—— 1976. Los yacimientos arqueológicos en la Laguna de Meniques, Antofagasta. In: *Volumen de Homenaje al Dr Gustavo Le Paige, S.J.* Antofagasta, Universidad del Norte. pp. 31–57.

NÚÑEZ, L. 1980. Asentamiento de cazadores-recolectores tardios en la Puna de Atacama: hacia el sedentarismo. *Chungara* (Arica), Vol. 8, pp. 137–68.

—— 1983a. Palaeoindian and Archaic Cultural Periods in the Arid and Semiarid Regions of Northern Chile. *Adv. World Archaeol.*, Vol. 2, pp. 161–203.

—— 1983b. *Paleoindio y arcaico en Chile: diversidad, secuencia y proceso.* Mexico.

NÚÑEZ, L.; CASAMIQUELA, R.; VARELA, J. 1983. *Ocupación paleoindio in Quereo: reconstrucción multidisciplinaria en el territorio semiarido de Chile.* Antofagasta, Universidad del Norte.

NÚÑEZ, P.; ZLATAR, V. 1976. Radiometria de Aragon – y su implicancia en el precerámico costero del Norte de Chile. In: CONGRESO DE ARQUEOLOGICA ARGENTINA, 4, San Rafael. *Actas*.

ORQUERA, L. et al. 1979. 8.000 años de historia en el canal de Beagle. *Rev. Proy. Bouchard* (Buenos Aires), Vol. 1, pp. 10–23.

ORTÍZ-TRONCOSO, O. 1979. Punta Santa Ana et Bahia Buena: deux gisements sur une ancienne ligne de rivage dans le détroit de Magallan. *Soc. Mus. Homme* (Paris), Vol. 67, pp. 133–204.

PHILLIPI, R. 1983. Noticias preliminares sobre los huesos fosiles de Ulloma. *An. Univ. Chile* (Santiago de Chile), Vol. 82.

RAVINES, R. 1967. El abrigo de Caru y sus relaciones con otros sitios tempranos del Sur del Perú. *Nawpa Pacha* (Berkeley), Vol. 8, pp. 39–57.

—— 1972. Secuencia y cambio en los artefactos líticos del Sur del Perú. *Rev. Mus. Nac.* (Lima), Vol. 37, pp. 133–84.

RICK, J. W. 1980. *Prehistoric Hunters of the High Andes.* New York.

RIVERA, M.; ROTHHAMER, F. 1985. Evaluación biológica cultural de poblaciones Chinchorro: nuevos elementos para la hipótesis de contactos transaltiplanicos, Cuenca del Amazona, Costa del Pacífico. In: CONGRESO DE ARQUEOLOGIA CHILENA, 10, Arica. *Resumen*. Arica.

SÁNCHEZ, M.; VALDES, C. 1982. Excavaciones arqueológicas en Cautin: Alero Quillem I. In: CONGRESO NACIONAL DE ARQUEOLOGIA CHILENA, 9, La Serena. *Resumen*. La Serena.

SANGUINETTI, A. C.; BORRERO, L. A. 1977. Los niveles con fauna extinta de la cueva de las Buitreras. *Relac. Soc. Argent. Antropol.* (Buenos Aires), Vol. 9.

SANTORO, C.; CHACAMA, J. 1982. Secuencia cultural de las terras altas del area Centro Sur Andina. *Chungara* (Arica), Vol. 9, pp. 22–45.

—— 1984. Secuencia de asentamientos precerámicos del extremo Norte de Chile. In: SIMPOSIO DE ARQUEOLOGIA ATACAMEÑA, San Pedro de Atacama. pp. 85–103.

SAXON, E. C. 1978. La prehistoria de Fuego-Patagonia: colonización de un habitat marginal. *An. Inst. Patagonia* (Punta Arenas), Vol. 12, pp. 63–74.

SCHIAPPACASSE, V.; NIEMEYER, H. 1984. *Descripción y análisis interpretativo de un sitio arcaico temprano en la Quebrada de Camarones,*

Santiago de Chile. (Mus. Nac. Hist. Nat., Publ. Ocass., 41.)

SCHMITZ, P. I. 1984. *Caçadores e coletores de pré-história do Brasil.* São Leopoldo.

SERRACINO, G.; PEREYEA, F. 1977. Tumbre: sitios estacionales de la industria Tambilliense, San Pedro de Atacama. *Estud. Atacam.* (Antofagasta), No. 5, pp. 5–17.

SILVA, J.; WIESNER, R. 1972–3. La forma de subsistencia de un grupo cazador recolector del post glacial en los valles transversales del area Meridional Andina. In: CONGRESO NACIONAL DE ARQUE-OLOGIA CHILENA, 6, Santiago de Chile. *Actas.* Santiago de Chile. pp. 353–70.

SILVEIRA, M. 1979. Análisis e interpretación de los restos faunísticos de la Cueva Grande del Arroyo Feo. *Relac. Soc. Argent. Antropol.* (Buenos Aires), Vol. 13.

STANDEN, B.; ALLISON, M.; ARRIAZA, B. 1984. Pantologías oseas de la población Morro-1, associada al coplejo Chinchorro, norte de Chile. *Chungara* (Arica), Vol. 13, pp. 175–85.

STEHBERG, R. 1984. Arqueología de Chile Central. *Gac. Arqueol. Andina* (Lima), Vol. 12, pp. 4–5, 15.

TRUE, D.; NÚÑEZ, L.; NÚÑEZ, P. 1970. Archaeological Investigations in Northern Chile: Tarapaca Project, Preceramic Resource. *Am. Antiq.*, Vol. 35, pp. 170–84.

UHLE, M. 1919. La arqueología de Arica y Tacna. *Bol.Soc. Ecuator. Estud. Hist. Am.* (Quito).

YACOBACCIO, H. 1982. Consideraciones sobre los asentamientos de cazadores-recolectores post-pleistocénicos en zonas aridas (Provincia de Jujuy, Argentina). In: REUNION NACIONAL DE CIEN-CIAS DEL HOMBRE EN ZONAS ARIDAS, 1, Mendoza.

—— 1983. Explotación complementaria de recursos en sociedades cazadoras-recolectoras surandinas. (Manuscript.)

—— 1984. Aproximaxión a la función de los asentamientos pre-cerámicos en la Puna y su borde oriental (Jujuy, Argentina). In: SIMPOSIO DE LA ARQUEOLOGIA ATACAMEÑA, San Pedro de Atacama. *Ponencia.* pp. 73–84.

Part II

FROM THE BEGINNINGS OF FOOD PRODUCTION TO THE FIRST STATES

CONTENTS

36

FROM THE BEGINNINGS OF
FOOD PRODUCTION TO THE FIRST STATES

An overview

Sigfried J. De Laet

There was a temptation, in preparing the outline for this volume, to give this second part the title: 'From the Neolithic Revolution to the Urban Revolution'.

These two concise terms were coined about fifty years ago by V. Gordon Childe and are still in frequent use today. However, an increasing number of historians have raised serious objections to the word 'revolution', for it is rather ambiguous and may give rise to confusion. Both in English and in French it suggests a sudden, significant change, and whereas in Childe's time it could still be believed that the transition to the Neolithic way of life based on food production had been fairly rapid, it is now known that it was the result of a long process of evolution extending over many centuries. Similarly, the first city-states were the end product of a long process of development. On the other hand, prehistorians who continue to use the term 'revolution' want first and foremost to lay emphasis on its connotation of 'extensive or indeed total transformation' without stressing the length of time required for this transformation. They consider that the term is still fully justified today, for the consequences, first, of the transition to agriculture and stock-raising and, second, of the birth of the first city-states were so important for the social and economic organization of human communities that both the 'Neolithic revolution' and the 'urban revolution' are rightly regarded as fundamental turning-points in the development of civilization.

We may usefully dwell a moment on the concept of 'Neolithic'. Only a few decades after the Danish archaeologist C. J. Thomsen had suggested, in 1819, subdividing the prehistoric period into 'three ages' (see Introduction), it was noted that his 'Stone Age' included cultures that had attained very different levels of cultural development. A distinction was therefore drawn between the early period, the 'age of chipped stone' (a period dating from the Pleistocene, in which humans, dwelling alongside a now extinct megafauna, lived exclusively by hunting, fishing and gathering) and the later period, the 'age of polished stone', (a period dating from the Holocene in which present-day fauna and flora already existed and humans practised agriculture and stock-raising, made pottery, engaged in weaving and polished some of their stone artefacts). In 1865 John Lubbock proposed that these terms be replaced by 'Palaeo-lithic' and 'Neolithic', which very soon were generally adopted. It was felt that the two earlier terms were inadequate, as stone chipping occurred throughout the prehistoric period and there are known to have been Neolithic cultures without polished axes. For some years it was believed that there had been a gap between the two periods; increasingly, however, traces were found of cultures dating back to the beginnings of the Holocene, but without knowledge of stock-raising or agriculture. This intermediate period was then referred to as the 'Mesolithic' period, a term that is falling increasingly into disuse today, for the earliest Mesolithic cultures are but the continuation of cultures of the Upper Palaeolithic. They are now generally designated by the term 'Late Palaeolithic', while other, more recent ones may be described as 'Pre-' or 'Proto-Neolithic', for in those cultures are to be found traces of the long process, mentioned above, that led to the Neolithic way of life.

Today 'Neolithic' designates a stage of cultural development at which the subsistence economy was based essentially on farming and stock-raising, and metals were not yet used to make tools and weapons. Consequently, this second part of the volume will focus mainly on the Neolithic. It is necessary, however, to start off by reminding the reader of what was said in the Introduction about the asynchronous development of the different cultural stages. The Neolithic did not begin everywhere at around the same time. In south-west Asia it began some 12,000 years before the present, but it was not until 3,000 years later that the first farming communities were formed in Europe. To this is to be added the fact that around 5,000 years ago, the cut-off date for this volume, many regions were still at the hunting and gathering stage,[1] whereas at the same date other regions were already producing copper weapons and tools and had already attained the Chalcolithic stage. We shall consider these matters in greater detail below.

FROM THE PLEISTOCENE TO THE HOLOCENE: THE DAWN OF A NEW AGE

To grasp the full importance of the transition to food production, we may usefully summarize what we know about the way of life of human beings at the end of the last Ice

Age, even if such an outline is bound to be all too generalized and highly approximate.

Towards the end of the Pleistocene humans already inhabited the greater part of the earth, where they lived in ecological niches that varied a great deal according to region and climate. A considerable proportion of the temperate zones of Europe was subject to a very harsh periglacial climate, characterized by tundra and steppe. As for the warmer zones – subtropical, tropical and Equatorial – the temperature there was 5° to 8°C lower than it is today, but rainfall was less abundant, so that there was more savannah and less forest than at the present time.

In so far as the possibilities of their environment permitted, people lived exclusively by hunting and fishing; food gathering was probably practised as well, but we possess very little concrete evidence of it. Humans everywhere, like the fauna and the flora, were still subject to the laws of biological balance. As early as the Lower Palaeolithic they had become predators, but through their mastery of fire and the invention of projectile weapons they no longer had much to fear from other predators, with the result that they no longer had many natural enemies. Human groups were, however, still too few to disturb the biological balance of their biotopes.

With regard to social organization, the fact that humans seemed to prefer to hunt megafauna and animals living in herds suggests the collaboration of a number of hunters extending beyond the limits of the nuclear family, which might indicate that the basic social unit was composed of several families, the number of which can hardly be assessed. As with all the higher animals, especially those living in groups, human beings must have been subject to territorial and hierarchical instincts. It is therefore likely that each group had its own hunting territory and that it was led by a 'chief' (or, in ethological terms, by a 'dominant male'). The latter probably owed his rank to the fact that he was the most vigorous or the most cunning hunter. It might also be thought that the role of the chief would fall to the most experienced elder, but this would be to overlook the fact that among the higher animals closest to the genus *Homo* the 'dominant male' ceases to enjoy this status when his strength starts declining. Furthermore, there could hardly have been any old men because human life in the Palaeolithic seldom extended beyond 30 years and only exceptionally reached 40. Alongside the 'chief', another person dominated the group: the 'sorcerer' or 'shaman', who was thought to have the gift of being able to enter into communication with spirits and supernatural beings. Through the practice of magic, this person (male *or* female) was supposed to ensure the group's survival, for instance by guaranteeing successful hunting and an abundance of game.

According to one very plausible hypothesis, the caves in which cave art flourished were community meeting-places where different groups came together to take part in religious or magical ceremonies; it is thought, then, that the role of the 'sorcerer' was more important than that of the 'chief'. The different groups united by these common beliefs were probably linked to one another by blood ties (or by totemic bonds) and practised exogamy among themselves. However that may be, the social and economic organization of the Upper Palaeolithic hunter-gatherers was fairly simple and has been described as 'primitive communism'.

The profound and relatively rapid climatic changes at the end of the Pleistocene and the beginnings of the Holocene led nearly everywhere to significant modifications both in geomorphology and in the fauna and flora, and had tremendous consequences for the way people lived. The fairly rapid melting of the northern ice-cap and the enormous glaciers covering high mountains was responsible not only for a considerable rise in the sea-level and the submersion of vast stretches of lowland but also for isostatic movements in the earth's crust that, in some regions, considerably raised the old shore-lines. The whole face of the earth was thus radically changed.

In Eurasia and North America the periglacial zones of the last glaciation now benefited from a temperate climate, and forests had gradually replaced the steppes and tundras; the latter now covered the more northern regions previously covered by the Arctic ice-cap. As for the more southern zones, it will be recalled that the mean temperature there had increased by between 5 and 8°C and that, as a result of more abundant rainfall, the forest had spread, encroaching upon the savannah.

The fauna too had considerably changed. Some species that in earlier periods had played no small role in ensuring human subsistence, such as the mammoth, the woolly rhinoceros, the cave bear and so on, but that were already dying out towards the end of the Pleistocene had now become extinct. Others, having adapted to a periglacial environment, like the reindeer, had migrated to more northern regions in pursuit of the tundra. The spread of the forest in large parts of the temperate, subtropical, tropical and Equatorial zones had brought about considerable changes in the animal life there. Only those regions where varied natural conditions – nature of the soil, altitude, less abundant rainfall - had helped to create steppes, grasslands or savannah contained animals that scarcely differed from those of the late Pleistocene. It may further be noted that the desertification of vast areas of Africa and Asia did not begin until many centuries later.

All these far-reaching changes in their environment considerably affected human communities, most of which had to cope with a critical situation. Some of them, not wanting to adapt to the new circumstances, had followed their favourite game animals – the herds of reindeer – in their migration northwards and settled in the regions of northern Europe, Asia and America that were no longer under the ice-cap, and there for a very long time yet they continued their traditional way of life as predators, based on fishing and the hunting of reindeer, walruses and other arctic species. These first inhabitants of the Far North were the predecessors (but probably not the ancestors) of the Sams (Lapps), the Samoyeds, the Inuit and the other peoples that currently live in those regions.

The other human groups, especially those in the regions now covered with forests of the temperate zone, passed through a period of disarray (which is reflected in the cultures of the Late Palaeolithic referred to on p. 366), but were able subsequently to adjust fairly rapidly to their new environment. Most noteworthy is the very great change in the sources of subsistence of those communities. Hunting still played an important, though no longer essential, role in the securing of food. The hunting of big game living in large herds in the steppes and tundras had given way to the hunting of forest animals living in smaller herds or even as isolated individuals (such as red deer, roe deer, aurochs and wild boar). Only in the savannah and grassland regions mentioned earlier was it possible to go on hunting animals living in herds, such as the bison or the gazelle. In the forests, game animals were also far more difficult to track down. No wonder then that hunters made increasing or indeed exclusive use of the bow and arrow – a weapon that had been invented in the Upper Palaeolithic. This is attested by the abundance of microliths, which served as arrowheads, in the lithic industry of those communities. For the same reasons, in several regions lying at some distance from one another humans tamed and gradually domesticated the wolf (the ancestor of the dog), which provided valuable assistance in hunting by tracking down game in forests and thickets. In some communities people also reared dogs to eat their flesh (Chapter 38). It was certainly more difficult and less profitable to hunt in the forest than it had been to hunt reindeer in the previous period. This is probably why there was a growing tendency to hunt small game, such as aquatic birds. This poor yield from hunting may have had social consequences. Human communities probably consisted of fewer families than formerly, since forest hunting called for a smaller number of hunters and no longer brought in enough food to feed a large group. Furthermore, fishing had assumed far more importance, as is evidenced by a large number of finds: barbed points made from bone or deer antlers that were parts of fish spears or prongs, hooks, wickerwork nets and pirogues made from tree trunks hollowed out by burning. Some communities even settled on the banks of rivers and lakes, and others beside the sea, where they lived mainly by fishing, collecting shellfish and hunting seals. Lastly, the change in the environment provided fresh sources of subsistence – and people took advantage of them. They stole eggs from birds' nests, they gathered snails and other molluscs and they gave greater variety to their diet by gathering fruits, harvesting a large number of edible plants and digging up roots.

In this way human groups were able gradually to make the most of their environment. In several regions the territory of such a Mesolithic community has been found to have contained three kinds of habitation sites: a base camp, where all the activities essential to the community's subsistence took place and which was occupied for relatively long periods; less extensive 'satellite camps' where more specialized, seasonal activities were carried out; and simple camps where a few hunters spent one or two nights. It may be assumed on the basis of ethnological parallels that within its territory each community possessed a more or less permanent base camp and a number of satellite camps, so as to exploit to the maximum, and in a rational manner, all the plant and animal resources of that territory. The non-permanent character of the satellite camps suggests some degree of mobility and no doubt a regular and perhaps annual migratory cycle.

Extremely important is the fact that some communities practised a form of hunting that was not only specialized, in that it was restricted to one or two kinds of game (a practice already frequent in the Upper Palaeolithic), but also selective: the hunters tended to go for old animals and young males, sparing the females so as not to endanger the reproduction of the species. Such selective hunting presupposes a sound knowledge on the part of the hunters of the behaviour, biology and physiology of the game.

In other communities the women, who were responsible for maintaining a supply of vegetable food, selectively gathered or dug up certain plants, fruits or roots in preference to others, either because they felt them to be more nourishing or because they had a more agreeable taste. And so these women must have taken similar steps, in order to ensure the survival and propagation of the desired plants, for instance by taking care not to harvest all the seeds. Such a practice, for which a fair number of ethnographic parallels are known to exist among modern hunter-gatherers (Chapter 37), obviously requires solid empirical knowledge of the biological cycle of those plants: seed dispersal, germination, maturation and so on.

While the remote origins of the Neolithic way of life, based on agriculture and stock-raising, date back to the transitional period between the Pleistocene and Holocene and to the resulting upheavals in the economy of human communities, the direct origins are to be sought in the Pre-Neolithic groups that practised selective hunting or the selective harvesting of edible plants or both. It is for this reason that there is a growing tendency today to describe these Mesolithic communities as 'Pre-Neolithic' or 'Proto-Neolithic'. It should, be emphasized however, that this Neolithic stage may have lasted several centuries in some cases and that not all the Pre-Neolithic communities necessarily moved on independently to the stage of food production.

WHY AND HOW THE TRANSITION TO FOOD PRODUCTION OCCURRED

The ways in which the transition to food production occurred are described in detail in the following two chapters, prepared by J. R. Harlan (Chapter 37, on the domestication of plants) and S. Bökönyi (Chapter 38, on the domestication of animals).

At the time when V. Gordon Childe launched his theory of the 'Neolithic revolution' it was thought that, at least where the ancient world was concerned, agriculture and stock-raising had been invented in a single 'nuclear region', south-west Asia, from where the Neolithic way of life had spread to Europe, Africa and the other regions of Asia all the way to China. We now know that food production began in several regions absolutely independently. As archaeological excavations have not been conducted everywhere in the same intensive, systematic way, the list given below is by no means exhaustive and may need to be added to following further research. For the same reasons, the information available to us for each of these nuclear regions is not always equally reliable and may be subject to debate and differences of opinion.

The oldest nuclear region extends in western Asia from the Levant in the west to the Taurus mountains in the north and the slopes of the Zagros mountains in the east. It is the region where the Neolithic has occasioned by far the greatest amount of research and that has provided us with the most reliable data. Food production there began soon after 12,000 years BP. Bones of domestic sheep have been discovered there that date back to the beginnings of the eleventh millennium BP and the remains of domestic goats from the following millennium. Pigs are more recent, and cattle do not seem to have been domesticated in that region until around the middle of the ninth millennium BP. As for plants, a large number of cereals and leguminous plants together with flax were already being grown. It was from this nuclear region that the Neolithic way of life spread to Anatolia, Europe, the Mediterranean part of Africa and the whole of western and southern Asia all the way to the Indian subcontinent.

A second nuclear region can probably be located in Upper Egypt or in the south-eastern Sahara, which at that time had not yet been affected by desertification. Remains of domesticated animals of the Bovidae family dating back to the tenth millennium BP (and therefore about 1,000 years older than those discovered in western Asia) have been found in what is now the western part of the Egyptian desert. Local domestication of the aurochs is highly plausible, as it was already specifically hunted in that region during the Upper Palaeolithic. In the same region barley may have been domesticated some time in the ninth millennium BP, for it was already picked wild between the fifteenth and thirteenth millennia BP. Later, about 6,000 years ago, the donkey was domesticated in the same region. However, other animals (sheep, goats and pigs) and wheat and flax were imported, already domesticated, from western Asia. It is not impossible that the Neolithic way of life spread from this second nuclear region to Sudan, Ethiopia and East Africa and also to West Africa and was associated with the domestication of new indigenous plants (sorghum, millet, African rice, gourds, calabashes, yams and others) in each region. In all these regions the Neolithic got off to a fairly late start, and the manner in which it spread from the Sahara and Upper Egypt has still not been elucidated (Chapter 40).

Two nuclear regions can be located in China. The first is formed by the Huanghe (Yellow river) basin. The beginnings of food production there date from the first half of the eighth millennium BP. Agriculture there was based on two kinds of millet, foxtail and panic, while domestic animals were limited to the dog, the pig, the duck and the chicken. The first Neolithic cultures (Peiligang, Cishan and Dadiwan) were followed there by the Yangshao culture, which may, although this is not certain, have been marked by rice-growing and the presence of domestic sheep and other animals of the Bovidae family. From the Huanghe valley the Neolithic way of life spread to inner Mongolia and to the steppelands of northern China.

The second Chinese nuclear region includes the middle and lower Changjiang (Yangtze or Blue river) basin. Food production began there at about the same time as in the Huanghe basin. Especially noteworthy is the fact that it was there that rice (which was to become the main food staple in vast areas) started to be grown and that the technique of paddy field cultivation was invented. Rice growing spread from the Changjiang basin to the regions south of that river and also westwards, to Yunnan and Assam in India, and from there to Myanmar (formerly Burma), Thailand, Laos, Cambodia, Vietnam and Malaysia.

Another nuclear region was South-East Asia (a region that, where the Neolithic way of life was concerned, also included the hilly area of southern China, the Philippines, Indonesia and Papua). Vegetable food production there was marked by distinctive features, which were probably due to the subtropical and tropical climate of the area. The first food growers there did not begin by laying out fields and scattering vast quantities of seeds in them, but went in first for horticulture, planting the seeds in small quantities in small, specially dug hollows where the fruit trees received individual attention. The first cultivated plants were tubers, mainly taro and yam, and fruit trees. This food production began between the eighth and seventh millennia BP. Later, South-East Asia saw the introduction of millet growing (from the Huanghe basin) and of rice cultivation (from the Changjiang basin, probably via Yunnan and Assam).

Two last nuclear regions were situated in America: one in Mexico and Central America; the other in the region of the Andes.

In Mesoamerica specialized food-gathering had long been practised. From about 7,000 years ago there was a gradual transition towards a rather limited form of agriculture. This period of adaptation to the new way of life lasted quite a long time, and it was not until about 4,500 years ago that the Neolithic truly began in the region, with permanent crops and established villages (Chapter 57).

However, according to some archaeologists the starting date for the beginnings of agriculture should be set a thousand years earlier (Chapter 37), and thus there is no agreement here. The first domesticated plants were not cultivated very intensively and helped only very partially to meet food needs, which accounts for the length of the period of adaptation just referred to. Cultivated plants included gourds, beans and maize (concerning this gramineous plant and its relationship to teosinte, see Chapter 57). During the same period amaranth, avocado, peppers and cotton were also domesticated. Little interest was taken in the domestication of animals in Mesoamerica. The dog had already been domesticated at the end of the Lithic Period and was joined only by the turkey, domesticated at the beginning of the fifth millennium BP and the duck. Knowledge of agriculture spread from Mexico to the south-western part of North America.

As regards the region of the Andes, little in the way of reliable data is available as yet. This is due to the fact that excavations of prehistoric sites have centred on the coastal areas, which were not very suitable for the development of agriculture. However, thanks to excavations carried out in the Guitarrero cave, in an Andean valley in Peru (Chapters 34 and 59), it has been established that in this region of the Andes, around the beginning of the eighth millennium BP, various kinds of beans were already being grown. The first attempts to domesticate the llama, the guanaco and the vicuña can be dated to about the middle of the eighth millennium BP; in the seventh millennium BP this domestication was fully completed.

In the foregoing paragraphs the approximate date generally acknowledged for the beginnings of food production has been given for each nuclear region. It must however be stressed that these dates are the earliest ones for which bones of animals or vestiges of plants belonging to domesticated species have been found, since, among animals and plants alike, domestication led to certain mutations; this phenomenon will be dealt with at greater length in the following two chapters (Chapters 37 and 38). What is important here is that these mutations did not occur until after some time, of variable length, had elapsed and that the starting-dates mentioned above are but dates *post quem*, the real dates for the beginnings of domestication being certainly earlier.

At this point in the present account there arise several questions to which no wholly satisfactory answers have yet been given. These are as follows.

First, why, at a particular moment in time, did certain communities cease to engage in selective hunting and food-gathering and go on to stock-raising and agriculture? Some twenty years ago there seemed to be a simple answer to this question. It was believed that the lives of hunter-gatherers were dominated practically all the time by the need to find their daily subsistence and that the Neolithic way of life delivered them from this constant obsession: grain in the barn and livestock in the stable were thought to have reassured them about their immediate future. Ethnographic parallels have shown, however, that in reality the life of hunter-gatherers was far less harsh than that of farmers or stock-breeders and that constant concern about food was far more acute among the latter. It is now thought that it was under the pressure of certain circumstances that Pre-Neolithic Mesolithic groups were forced to change their way of life radically. Many authors consider that it was population pressure that played the essential role in this process. This idea may seem tempting at first sight, but it hardly rests on concrete facts. There is no evidence of a population explosion among these Pre-Neolithic communities; ethnology reveals, on the contrary, that hunter-gatherer tribes of modern times tend rather to practise some form or other of birth control and that a large population increase is to be expected more among farmers, where all additions to the labour force are welcome. According to another hypothesis, the practice of selective hunting and gathering maintains a fragile biological balance, which may be disturbed by unforeseen circumstances. If that happens, human communities may be plunged into a state of crisis and be forced to change over to the production of food. It now seems to be generally agreed that the Pre-Neolithic communities did not spontaneously adopt the Neolithic way of life but did so merely in response to a crisis situation.

Second, many groups of Pre-Neolithic hunter-gatherers had a sufficient knowledge of botany and animal biology to be able easily to move on to the stage of food production, but only some of them did so. Why this should have been is a question to which an answer very close to that suggested for the previous question can probably be given. It seems that as long as a community lived in harmony with its natural environment, without suffering, for various reasons, any pressure on the availability of its food, it preferred to preserve its traditional way of life, even if neighbouring communities had begun to engage in farming and stock-raising. This was true, for instance, of the groups referred to earlier that had settled beside seas, lakes or rivers and lived by fishing, hunting aquatic mammals and gathering shellfish, who adopted the Neolithic way of life (and then only partially) long after neighbouring groups had taken up farming. Other groups of hunter-gatherers lived in close association with Neolithic farmers with whom they regularly bartered the product of their hunting for agriculture produce without ever themselves trying to engage in agriculture. A typical example is provided by the thousands of years of contacts that existed (and still exist) between Aborigine groups in northern Australia and Neolithic tribes in the south of New Guinea, although they had to cross the Torres Strait, which, at its narrowest, is 160 km wide! In Zaire, in the Equatorial forest region, such bartering is still common between the Pygmies living by hunting and gathering and Bantu farmers. Lastly, among some groups of hunter-gatherers it frequently happens that a small quantity of edible plants are sown or planted and then left without special care until harvesting time. These plants stay wild and never form the staple food of such groups but are merely an extra. Such practices can scarcely be described as agriculture but are more of the nature of a hobby. J. R. Harlan cites several examples among modern hunter-gatherers (Chapter 37). It is not unlikely that such practices already existed in prehistoric times. It will be recalled that in the nuclear region of Mesoamerica (see p. 369) the first cultivated plants were not grown intensively and covered food needs only to a very small extent, which also explains why between 2,000 and 3,000 years elapsed there between the appearance of the first cultivated plants and the beginnings of a truly Neolithic culture, with permanent crops.

A third question concerns the manner in which the Neolithic way of life was transmitted from the different nuclear regions to other areas. As this problem has been considered mainly with respect to Europe it will be dealt with in greater detail in Chapter 47. However, the findings with regard to Europe can more than probably be extrapolated to other regions for which fewer data are available. Suffice it to say here that three models (or three types of model) have been proposed. The first has been advocated by V. Gordon Childe, who thought that the Neolithic way of life had been transmitted from western Asia to Europe by successive waves of immigrants, colonizers in search of new arable land. The indigenous Mesolithic peoples were considered to have played only a negligible role in the adoption of the Neolithic way of life in Europe. It may be noted that this theory has now been abandoned by most prehistorians but that in a more qualified, less categorical form it still has a few supporters. The second model, in its extreme form, is almost diametrically opposed to the first. The colonizers (whose existence has to be admitted to explain how animals and plants that did not exist in the wild in Europe were introduced to that part of the world already domesticated) are claimed to have been very few and their role to have been far less important than that of the indigenous Mesolithic population. Finally, the third model is halfway between the two previous ones. The adoption of the Neolithic way of life is thought to have been the result of the acculturation of the indigenous population by Neolithic people from Anatolia who started the process by colonizing the Aegean and part of the Balkans. Subsequently, however, indigenous groups who had already become Neolithic are believed to have gradually spread the new way of life to other regions. It will be noted that the adoption of the Neolithic way of life in Europe did not occur as an uninterrupted process but that periods of change in this direction alternated with periods of stability. It seems likely that the Neolithic way of life spread to new regions only when the Mesolithic economy of the inhabitants of those regions was disrupted by various factors (such as climatic change) that generated tension and a state of crisis.

CONSEQUENCES OF THE TRANSITION TO FOOD PRODUCTION

Before going on to consider the consequences of the adoption of the Neolithic way of life, we should recall that this way of life is often defined still in such a way as to include, alongside the production of food, the making of pottery, knowledge of weaving and the polishing of certain stone artefacts. Originally (p. 366) this last characteristic was accorded a significance out of all proportion to its real importance, for the polishing of stone was no more than a minor innovation, involving the application to stone of a technique for working bone that had been known since the Upper Palaeolithic, or perhaps even earlier. In addition, it is not even very characteristic of the Neolithic, since in Japan the cutting edges of certain stone artefacts were already polished about 20,000 years ago, long before the Neolithic, and furthermore, during the Neolithic only certain artefacts used for cutting, like axes or adzes, were polished, whereas daggers or knives were not.

As regards pottery, some groups of hunter-gatherers of the Upper Palaeolithic had already observed that clay hardens on contact with fire, as evidenced by the terracotta figurines made by the mammoth hunters of Moravia; it was not until the Neolithic, however, that terracotta receptacles started to be made. Nevertheless, it is far more difficult to make a ceramic vessel than a small figurine only a few centimetres high. It is necessary to learn how to purify the clay, mix it with straw or small fragments of stone or shell in order to temper it and prevent it from cracking during firing, mould the vessel and fire it at a high temperature in a pit or primitive kiln. The earliest known pottery dates back to 12,500 years BP, in Japan, still well before the end of the Palaeolithic period.

Elsewhere pottery made its appearance during the Neolithic, but not always at the beginning of that period, since in Anatolia, in Greece and in South America evidence has been found of aceramic cultures. Before the invention of pottery, in order to preserve and transport liquids, people used either hollowed-out calabashes or bottles made of skin, and for solids wickerwork baskets. The first ceramic vessels very often imitated the form of these receptacles that preceded them, or they were decorated in the same way.

Pottery is extremely important for the archaeologist, especially for the identification of different cultures, because of the very different ways in which ceramic vessels can be shaped and decorated. Like all traditional peoples, the Neolithic communities were strongly bound by ancestral customs. It is not impossible that among some of those communities (as revealed by certain ethnographic parallels), the decoration of the pottery had a religious, magical, symbolic or ethnic significance. Once the form and decoration of the pottery had been fixed by tradition in a given human group they remained almost unalterable and changed only very slowly, with the result that pottery is one of the best index fossils for the identification of particular cultures or to determine a period or stage of evolution within those cultures. There has been much debate about the reasons that might have prompted certain Neolithic groups suddenly to cease decorating their pottery or to start decorating it in radically different ways, but such speculation has remained at the theoretical level.

The domestication of the goat and sheep in the ancient world, and of the llama, guanaco and vicuña in the region of the Andes, led to the invention of weaving, but only after some time, for the fleece of these animals was not suitable for spinning and weaving until certain mutations had occurred as a result of domestication. Gradually the leather and fur garments formerly worn were largely replaced by woollen clothes. Very soon ways were also learned of using certain textile plants, like flax, which had first been grown as an oleaginous plant in western Asia, Egypt and Europe, and cotton, which was grown very early on in India and Mesoamerica.

One of the first consequences of the Neolithic way of life was a radical change in human diet. Whereas in the Palaeolithic it had been mainly meat-based, it became more diversified in the Mesolithic. Now, in the Neolithic, it was based primarily on cereals – corn in western Asia and Europe, rice in southern and eastern Asia, sorghum and millet in Africa, maize in America. These cereals were eaten in the form of gruel, biscuits or bread. There was a considerable decrease in meat consumption. On the other hand, the domestication of animals added an entirely new and important item to the daily diet: milk and its derivatives (butter and cheese). Finally, the invention of pottery made it possible to cook or boil food. It must however be noted that already before that time meat was often roasted, and that in some communities it was boiled in 'cooking pits': a skin bag or a tight wickerwork basket was placed in a pit and filled with water, in which heated pebbles were dropped to bring it to boiling temperature; the meat was then boiled in the bag or the basket.

It may also be noted that the replacement of a meat diet by a largely vegetable one necessitated the use of salt (which very quickly became an item of trade, and sometimes of long-distance trade). This is considered at greater length in Chapter 47, as we know more about the role of salt in Neolithic Europe than in the other regions. These radical changes in diet certainly had consequences for human metabolism; this, however, is an area that has so far been little explored. This is also true of the diseases that may have resulted from the new diet. There is still a vast area to be explored here by palaeopathology.

The Neolithic way of life clearly appears to have had not inconsiderable demographic consequences. Nearly everywhere it is found that the number and size of the settlements and the number of cemeteries considerably increased in the Neolithic compared with earlier periods. This of course is no more than an impression, for which no reliable figures or statistics are available.

The consequences of food production are most apparent in the social and economic sphere.

One of the main consequences was the adoption of a sedentary way of life. Villages sprang up everywhere. In the Upper Palaeolithic and the Mesolithic hunter-gatherers often practised a seasonal form of nomadism within the group's territory and, to follow game in its seasonal migrations or to make the most of the territory's plant resources, they adopted a regular, probably annual, migratory cycle. It is true that some Mesolithic groups already possessed permanent dwellings, for instance, the groups that had settled beside a sea or lake, living there by fishing, collecting shellfish and so on, but these were the exception. Farmers, however, are tied to their fields and are virtually obliged to set up permanent homes near to them. One consequence of their settled way of life was that they began to build houses, barns and stables of wattle and daub, and sometimes even of drystone, that were far more durable than the simple huts of earlier periods. In many Neolithic habitation sites excavations reveal a complex stratigraphy pointing to the almost uninterrupted occupation of the site, sometimes for a period of centuries.

In these villages there were increasing divisions between the different social categories. On the one hand, there was more marked occupational specialization and, on the other, there was increasingly complex social stratification, which we now consider. First, social specialization increased to an extent unmatched in earlier times. In the Upper Palaeolithic there was but one specialist, the sorcerer-shaman, while all the other members of the community shared the same activities: the manufacture of artefacts, hunting, fishing and so on. In the Neolithic village, on the other hand, there were farmers, stock-breeders or herdsmen, potters, weavers, stoneworkers, carpenters and, in the following centuries, wheelwrights, traders and the first metallurgists (see pp. 373–4). It has rightly been pointed out that craft specialization was the direct result of sedentism. There probably existed a division of labour between the sexes, and certain activities may have been reserved for women, such as potting, basket making and, at least at the beginning of the period (before the invention of the ard, when the fields were worked exclusively with a hoe, and before the domestication of cattle), farming and stock-raising. However, the invention of the ard and the domestication of cattle caused farming and stock-raising to become exclusively men's work.

Second, social stratification, not yet very pronounced at the beginning of the period, gradually became quite complex. It was suggested above (p. 367) that the communities of hunter-gatherers were led by a 'chief' – the most vigorous and cunning hunter – whose authority was in no way tyrannical, however, and who should probably be regarded as a first among equals. What we know about the hierarchical instinct among primates leads us to believe that in the Palaeolithic and Mesolithic communities this position of chief was by no means hereditary. From the Neolithic onwards the role of the chief and that of the sorcerer changed radically. The 'chief' became the 'monarch', whose powers became increasingly military while also taking on a religious character and whose functions became hereditary. As for the 'sorcerer', this person became the 'priest', whose religious power was combined with secular, economic and political power.

On the basis of ethnographic parallels taken mainly from Africa, it may be assumed that the communities of hunter-gatherers shared equally among themselves the products of hunting and gathering. The transition to food production put an end to this solidarity and to this pattern of reciprocity, which were replaced by competition to possess as much in the way of resources as possible. 'Property' came into existence. No doubt the concept existed in embryonic form among the hunter-gatherers, where each community possessed 'its own' hunting territory. Among farmers, however, the idea of property assumed considerable importance: every farmer had their 'own' fields, their 'own' cattle, their 'own' house and their 'own' tools. At the same time, the other face of property was revealed, for it led to theft, pillage and also war. A community whose harvest had been destroyed by bad weather would be only too easily tempted to go and plunder the barns of a more fortunate neighbouring village community, but the latter would of course defend its possessions by force. Such wars must have been fairly numerous, as is shown by the fact that most Neolithic villages were fortified (see p. 375). A class of professional warriors gradually came into being, responsible for defending the village while the farmers and shepherds were in the fields. It may well be imagined that initially all able-bodied men took up arms in cases of danger but that soon a few men were made permanently responsible for maintaining security. Such military activities called for a commander, and this role naturally fell to the village chief, whose powers, as noted earlier, thus took on a military character.

A Neolithic village, with its highly varied activities, faced with the problem of the relations between farmers and the first specialized craftsmen, who had to be paid for their work, and with the need to undertake certain large-scale collective operations (such as the building of village fortifications), required fixed, commonly accepted customs to ensure smooth relations among its inhabitants. In this *mos majorum*, this unwritten legislation, lie the deepest roots of the laws of the historical period. Responsibility for ensuring that those rules were respected fell either to the village chief or to the priest.

It may be wondered that links bound together villages belonging to the same culture. It is likely that they shared common technological traditions, a common religion and probably also a common language. The inhabitants of those different villages may have come together for seasonal religious ceremonies. There is some indication that this was the case in Europe (Chapter 47).

Religious beliefs were also influenced by the new way of life. Because these beliefs varied greatly from one region to another, the reader is referred to the different regional chapters for more detail. Suffice it here to note that these religions do seem nevertheless to have certain broad features in common. The religions of the Neolithic were clearly fertility cults, with dual male (sky, sun, rain) and female (earth, moon) principles. At the beginning of the Neolithic, so long as farming continued to be essentially women's work, the female principle dominated. Nearly everywhere a very large number of representations of a goddess of fertility have been found, the indisputable ancestor of the great mother goddesses of the early historical period. However, when the

development of agricultural techniques (tilling with the ard, drainage and irrigation) made it too hard for women to work in the fields and when domestication of the aurochs made stock-raising too dangerous for them, the male principle (in the form of solar or astral divinities, bull-gods, phallic representation and the like) gradually took on greater importance. Emphasis should also be laid on the growing importance of religion and religious practices in everyday life, which accentuated social distinctions to the advantage of the priests, considered to be the earthly representatives of the gods.

All the inventions that marked the beginnings of the Neolithic show that the power of observation – which was already highly developed in the pre-Neolithic communities, as is demonstrated by the knowledge of botany and animal biology underlying the domestication of plants and animals – had gone on to become considerably more refined and far-reaching. People began to ask themselves questions, many of which were not strictly practical, about the phenomena they observed. They speculated about the causes of the mysterious changes they noted around them. Why sow in one season rather than in another? Why does seed germinate? Why does clay harden on contact with fire? Why do the moon and stars change position in the sky? What is the relationship between the position of the stars and the propitious moment for any particular agricultural activity? If the position of the stars in the sky has an influence on the lives of plants, does it also have an influence on the lives of human beings? In these questions and in the answers given (even if in most cases they are still irrational) are to be found the first germs of the scientific mind.

So it is then that political and social institutions, law, the spirit of observation and embryonic scientific thought were all linked more or less directly to the introduction of the Neolithic way of life, as indeed were war and social stratification, characterized by the domination (often lasting for millennia) exercised by the military and priestly castes. It is in this sense that it is still possible to speak of a 'revolution'. It was in fact the most significant turning-point in the development of human civilization.

FROM THE NEOLITHIC VILLAGE TO THE FIRST CITY-STATES

Before broadly outlining the process of socio-economic change that led from the Neolithic village to the first city-states, it may be useful first to define briefly what is understood here by the terms 'village' and 'city'.

A village in the Neolithic period was generally a rather small settlement, inhabited mainly by persons in the 'primary sector', namely food producers, farmers and stock-raisers; such a village might possibly contain, in addition, a small minority of individuals belonging to the 'secondary sector', i.e. the few specialized craftspeople referred to earlier.

A city was generally bigger than a village and contained a larger number of inhabitants. More important is the fact that the first cities dominated a fairly extensive territory where a number of villages were to be found. A city formed the political centre of a state. Just as important were the social and economic characteristics of a city, which were totally different from those of a village. One of the pre-conditions for the birth of a city was the existence of a marked degree of social stratification, with dominant civil, military and religious classes. In the earliest cities civil power and military power were usually in the hands of the same dominant class.

Such classes exercised their power with the help or through the agency of persons belonging to the 'tertiary sector': soldiers, civil servants or religious officials. The governing classes – military chiefs and religious chiefs, successors to the village chiefs and priest-sorcerers of the farming communities discussed earlier – subjected persons in the primary sector to their domination, robbed them of their fields and pastures, reduced them to the rank of semi-free tenant farmers or even slaves, and forced them to pay as rent for the use of those fields and pastures a not inconsiderable portion of their crops and a number of animals from their herds. With the proceeds from this taxation the governing classes paid in kind not only their soldiers and officials but also most of the people in the secondary sector, who found it more profitable to work for the governing classes than for the people in the primary sector. To the craftspeople already mentioned who were to be found in the Neolithic villages, such as potters, weavers, stoneworkers and carpenters, were added cartwrights and metalworkers (see below and p. 374). Lastly, the tertiary sector included not only soldiers and functionaries but also carriers and traders. The role of the latter was steadily to increase with time. From the beginnings of the Neolithic there was long-distance trade in certain raw materials much sought after for the manufacture of artefacts, such as flint or obsidian; soon these included ores as well. Later on the governing classes, the better to mark themselves off from the lower classes and to enhance their prestige, had impressive palaces and magnificent temples built (of material which often had to be imported from afar); the members of those classes themselves wore, as a symbol of their high rank, fine raiments, jewels and precious stones and other 'prestige items', sometimes imported from very far away. As a result of this trade in raw materials and luxury goods, carriers and traders very soon occupied a privileged rank in society. Officials too held a privileged position. The renting of land to the farmers and the recovery of taxes in kind mentioned earlier required a fairly sophisticated system of accounting and also a system for the registration of rental and tax payment contracts. Thus, for the needs of bureaucracy, mathematics and writing came into being and developed. Nearly everywhere the invention of writing – which much later came to be regarded as marking the beginning of the historical period (see in this connection the Introduction to this volume) – coincided with the rise of the first city-states. Incidentally, however, it is to be noted that some cities did come into being, chiefly in the Andean region of South America, in which writing was unknown but where another, rather complicated, mnemonic system of recording was invented, based on the use of knotted string. As for mathematics, it was not used solely for administrative and financial purposes but, around the same period, was considerably developed by astrologists or astronomers to compute precisely the course of the sun, moon and stars. These calculating and writing systems were very complicated – the first writing systems including several hundreds of different signs – and to learn them took several years. As a result there were only very few cultured people, 'scholars' (the 'mandarins' of China), and they held a privileged rank.

The city-states constituted not only the beginning of a new stage in the scientific and cultural development of humanity, but also the culmination of the long period of development leading from the 'Neolithic revolution' to the 'urban revolution'. The following outline is based mainly on what is known about this process of development in western Asia and Egypt, regions that up to now have been the sources of the greatest amount of information on the subject. With some minor differences, a parallel process occurred in China. As for the Americas, the transition to urban life came later.

The development of villages into city-states was determined essentially by three factors, which are analysed below:

1 a series of inventions and technical advances achieved during the centuries following the transition to food production;
2 the end of the economic self-sufficiency of the Neolithic village;
3 the concentration of economic and political power in the hands of the military class and the priesthood.

Let us consider these three factors in greater detail. First, in the centuries that followed the beginnings of the Neolithic way of life new food plants and textile plants were domesticated, as were new animal species. These plants and animals obviously differed from one nuclear region to another and cannot be listed in detail here. Mention may be made, however, of flax, cotton, olive trees, vines, fig trees and date palms. Where animals are concerned, the domestication of the dog, the sheep and the goat were followed by that of the ox (end of the ninth millennium BP), the donkey and the horse (sixth millennium BP), and later of the camel and the dromedary. Very soon human intervention resulted in genetic mutations in plants and animals. Already in the period of concern to us here it was the custom to geld bulls to make them more docile and enable them to be used as draught animals. Agricultural techniques advanced rapidly. The hoe and the digging-stick were soon replaced by the ard, a primitive plough without wheels or mouldboard and with a share made from deer antler or stone, which cut furrows but did not turn the sod. Of great importance was the invention of irrigation and drainage. Formerly agriculture had been limited to regions where there was sufficient annual rainfall for crops to be grown without extra watering. The earliest traces of irrigation go back to the end of the ninth millennium BP (Çatal Hüyük in Anatolia). The irrigation of excessively dry land and the drainage of excessively wet or marshy land necessitated large-scale collective works requiring the collaboration of the entire community: the digging of ditches and channels, the building of dykes and so on. It was through such works that in Asia rice could be grown in paddy fields, but also, and above all, that the valleys of some major rivers (the Nile in Egypt, the Tigris and the Euphrates in western Asia, the Indus in southern Asia, the Huanghe and the Changjiang in China), previously unusable, despite their fertility, because of flooding and their often marshy land, could be brought under cultivation. These rapidly became the culturally most advanced areas in the period which followed (see Volume II). One of the most important consequences of these advances in agriculture and stock-raising was that the farming communities now had the possibility and very soon the duty to produce more food than was necessary for their own needs. We shall see further on the essential role played by this surplus in social and economic development.

In other areas, too, remarkable progress was made, and especially in overland and maritime transport. During the sixth millennium BP, or perhaps even earlier, the wheel was invented. It was used by potters to make more regularly shaped ceramic vessels, but, most important, it became the essential part of the wagon to which donkeys, oxen and horses were harnessed, making it possible to transport loads, sometimes of considerable size, over long distances. The use of the wheel spread very fast in the Ancient World, but it remained unknown in America, where the llama was sometimes used as a pack animal, but only for light loads, and where, until the European colonization, overland transport was otherwise effected exclusively by human porters. It was around the same period that the sail was invented in Egypt. Boats had long been known, but now for the first time the driving force of the wind was used. The sail and the wheel greatly facilitated long-distance transport and trading relations. It is true that over the centuries improvements were introduced in the technology of wagons and sailing boats, but these vessels and vehicles did not undergo any essential change until the eighteenth century of the Christian era.

A few words still need to be said about one of the major inventions made right at the very beginning of the Neolithic period, namely, metalworking. In western Asia, in sites dating from the Pre-pottery Neolithic period B (around the middle of the ninth millennium BP), copper objects have been found. In eastern Anatolia deposits of almost pure native copper are to be found. It was very soon realized that this 'kind of stone' could be shaped by hammering while cold and even more easily by hammering while hot. The first copper objects obtained in this way were still very simple: awls, wire that could be coiled to make rings or bracelets, and so on. The next stage was not reached until during the seventh millennium BP, when it was discovered that copper could not only be hammered but also, when it had been brought to a very high temperature, melted and poured into moulds, thereby producing larger objects with more complicated shapes. Still later people learned how to extract copper from less pure ores by means of successive smeltings to remove the dross and impurities. Around the same period other metals, such as gold, silver, lead and tin, started to be used.

Towards the end of the sixth millennium BP the techniques of metal-working were discovered quite independently in the Balkans and, about a thousand years later, also independently, in Italy and the Iberian peninsula (Chapter 47). In eastern Asia (China and Thailand) metalworking also started independently, but not within the period of time covered by the present volume. It is not impossible that yet other areas will be discovered where metalworking developed independently, without outside influences.

Copper has several major defects: it is rather a soft metal, and the cutting edge of copper tools and weapons soon becomes blunted and needs frequently to be rehammered to regain its keenness; copper objects break easily; and, lastly, copper melts only at a very high temperature. For these reasons efforts were made in western Asia, in the sixth millennium BP, to remedy these defects by mixing copper with other metals. It is possible that the first alloys were discovered by pure luck, from the use of impure ore, but very quickly metallurgists started experimenting by intentionally mixing copper with arsenic, antimony and other metals. Finally, after numerous attempts, it was discovered that by mixing copper (85 to 90 per cent), with tin (10 to 15 per cent), an alloy, bronze, is obtained that is much harder, more solid and less brittle, and the melting-point of which is considerably lower than that of pure copper. The use of bronze coincided roughly with the beginnings of the period of city-states, hence the story of bronze technology is dealt with in Volume II. Metallurgy gave rise to a new social complex: some people now specialized in prospecting, investigating new deposits of copper, tin, gold, silver, lead and so on. Mining techniques, already developed for extracting flint (Chapter 56), were now adapted to the extraction of mineral ores. Luxury items in bronze, gold and silver were the objects of a lucrative trade. However, it was the metallurgists themselves who played the first part in this new social complex.

The techniques of metalworking must have seemed extremely mysterious to the vast majority of people of the time, and those capable of such alchemy must certainly have appeared in their eyes to have possessed supernatural powers and must therefore have enjoyed great prestige. Ethnographic parallels suggest that the metallurgists formed a kind of closed caste and that the secrets of the craft were transmitted only to initiates. It is obvious that, among craftsmen, metalworkers occupied a special place and that the governing classes availed themselves of their services.

Second, at the beginning of the Neolithic each village was virtually self-sufficient, and trading was probably limited to a few rather insignificant exchanges with nearby villages. Several factors contributed to the decline of this self-sufficient economy:

1 improved farming methods enabled a surplus to be produced that served as a currency to obtain consumer goods, raw materials and soon the luxury items that were desired as well;
2 improved means of transport, making long-distance trade possible;
3 social stratification become increasingly complex, with the cornering of the agricultural surplus by the military and religious chiefs, which enabled them to finance trading expeditions, often to distant regions, to obtain the luxury articles they wished to possess in order to increase their social prestige.

Very soon certain settlements owed their economic prosperity largely to their trading activities, for instance the agglomeration of Çatal Hüyük in Anatolia (Chapter 41).

Third, the concentration of economic and political power in the hands of the priests and warriors, referred to on p. 372, should be considered at greater length; but it should be borne in mind that the model presented here is still in many respects hypothetical.

Mention was made earlier of the growing importance of priests and warriors in the Neolithic communities. In the first city-states the priests formed a distinct and exclusive social class: a caste that took advantage of the religious emotions of the other members of the community to increase its own power. They now dominated the lower classes not only in the religious sphere but also in the economic and even in the political sphere. The land was declared to be the property of the gods, which in practice meant that it was the property of the temples and that it was administered by the priests on behalf of the gods. As for the warriors, they had managed by force of arms to dominate their fellow-citizens, and their chiefs had become monarchs. There was a close alliance between the priests and the monarchs, and the latter were not only military leaders: they were nothing less than representatives of the gods on earth (in Egypt they even became incarnations of the gods), and as such they, along with the priests, were joint owners of all the fields. As noted earlier, the farmers no longer owned the fields they tilled, nor the cattle they bred; they were reduced to the rank of tenant farmers who were required to pay annual rent to the monarch and the temple (this rent often amounted to one-eighth or one-seventh of the crop).

The submission of the great mass of the population to a small minority and the emergence of a strong central authority had immediate consequences:

1 only a strong authority could have large-scale irrigation and drainage work carried out to increase the surface area and profitability of the fields;

2 such large-scale work, which was needed in order to make use of the marshy valleys of the great rivers (see p. 373), was out of the question in a Neolithic community that lacked a powerful central authority;

3 the central authority forced the rural masses to over-produce, or in other words to produce more than was necessary for their own needs. This surplus found its way into the hands of the governing classes through the rent that the farmers had to pay the monarch and the temple. Wealth thus became concentrated in the hands of the monarchs and priests. The temples were no longer merely places of worship but now comprised, alongside the sanctuary proper, granaries, barns, store-houses, stables and workshops; the royal palace was also flanked by the same out-buildings.

Some specialized craftsmen still worked partly for people in the primary sector (who would 'buy' a ceramic pot in exchange for a certain amount of corn), but the craftsmen worked mainly for the temple or for the palace, for the monarchs and the priests were the only ones who could afford 'expensive' products (like, for instance, metal objects, especially weapons, with which the soldiers were now equipped). They were of course paid for their work in kind: in corn or a variety of products taken from the surplus accumulated in the temple or palace.

Thus an entire social pyramid came into being. At the base of this pyramid were of course the peasants, half-free tenant farmers, sometimes indeed reduced to slavery (see p. 373). Slightly more privileged were the craftsmen, some of whom still worked for the peasants but most of whom were in the service of the temple or the palace. Among them the metalworkers, thanks to the secrets of their trade, formed a privileged group in the exclusive employ of the governing class, the only one able to afford their precious services. At a higher echelon were those in the tertiary sector, primarily the warriors paid by the monarch and in the exclusively royal service and the officials needed by the administration. Only one category of people had managed to remain relatively independent of the monarchs and priests: the traders. The rulers and high priests, in order to increase their prestige and display their wealth and power, had to build temples and monumental palaces, with every luxury and amenity, and to decorate them with rare and precious materials; they themselves, their consorts and courtiers wore jewels made of gold and silver, ivory, mother-of-pearl, jade, amber, lapis lazuli, turquoise, chalcedony and other valued substances. All this had to be imported, often from very far away, as indeed did many raw materials: copper, tin, lead, gold and silver ores and also, in some cases, the stone needed for the building of monuments and on occasion even the wood for structural work. This accounts for the growing importance of the class of traders. Caravans went off in search of these rare or precious materials, and such undertakings were organized as real expeditions. It was necessary to carry out not only food for the members of the caravan and fodder for the pack and draught animals but also presents to be given in order to obtain free passage across the territory of communities living on the route to be followed and trading items (very often slaves) to be bartered for materials that were in demand. Such caravans were accompanied by a detachment of armed guards responsible for protecting the expedition against the raids of looters or, weapons in hand,

for clearing a way for the caravan across enemy country. Only royalty and high-ranking priests could finance such undertakings, but the traders who headed them charged a very high price for their services.

It was emphasized earlier that warfare was one of the adverse consequences of the Neolithic way of life and that it was responsible for the emergence of a class of warriors and for their power. As the power and wealth of the ruling classes increased, so their desire to acquire yet greater power became more imperious. There must have been frequent cases of rulers undertaking the conquest of territories belonging to neighbouring communities in order to gain possession of the surpluses produced in those territories or of the natural resources to be found there. The increasingly strong and increasingly sophisticated fortifications that protected settlements, or at least the most important ones, in western Asia, China and Europe alike, attest the general insecurity created by such conflicts. By the end of the period dealt with here certain major settlements already held sway over very extensive areas. The most striking example is that of Egypt, which was entirely unified, after many a war, by the end of the Pre-dynastic period. Imperialism, understood as the policy of a state seeking to bring other states under its political and economic domination, thus came into being during this period of transition between the Neolithic village and the city-state.

NOTE

1 It is to be noted that the regions that had not yet attained the Neolithic stage by around 5,000 years ago are not dealt with in this second part of the volume: in the chapters about them in the first part the account goes up to that date. It should be borne in mind that even at the present time certain populations have not yet gone past the hunting and gathering stage, while others are still at the Neolithic stage. They will be covered in the following volumes of the work.

BIBLIOGRAPHY

BANKS, K. N. 1984. *Climates, Cultures and Cattle: The Holocene Archaeology of the Eastern Sahara*. Dallas.

BENDER, B. 1975. *Farming in Prehistory: From Hunter-Gatherer to Food Producer*. London.

—— 1978. Gatherer-Hunter to Farmer: A Social Perspective. *World Archaeology*, Vol. 10, pp. 204–22.

BLOCH, M. R. 1963. The Social Influence of Salt. *Sci. Am.*, Vol. 209, No. 1, pp. 88–96.

BÖKÖNYI, S. 1974. *History of Domestic Mammals in Central and Eastern Europe*. Budapest.

BRAIDWOOD, R. J. 1960. The Agricultural Revolution. *Sci. Am.*, Vol. 203, pp. 130–48.

BRAIDWOOD, R. J.; WILLEY, G. (eds) 1962. *Courses Towards Urban Life*. Chicago.

CHILDE, V. G. 1950. The Urban Revolution. *Town Plann. Rev.* (Liverpool), Vol. 21, No. 1, pp. 1–17.

—— 1951. *Social Evolution*. London.

—— 1952. *New Light on the Most Ancient East*. London.

—— 1954. *What Happened in History*. Harmondsworth.

CLARK, J. D.; BRANDT, S. A. (eds) 1984. *From Hunters to Farmers: The Causes and Consequences of Food-Production in Africa*. Berkeley.

CLARK, J. G. D. 1952. *Prehistoric Europe: The Economic Basis*. London.

—— 1966. *Symbols of Excellence*. Cambridge.

CLASON, A. T. (ed.) 1975. *Archaeozoological Studies*. Amsterdam.

CLUTTON-BROCK, J. 1981. *Domesticated Animals from Early Times*. London.

COHEN, M. N. 1977. *The Food Crisis in Prehistory: Overpopulation and the Origins of Agriculture*. Yale.

COLES, S. 1959. *The Neolithic Revolution*. London. (7th edn 1970.)

COULBORN, R. 1959. *The Origin of Civilized Societies*. Princeton.

CURWEN, E. C.; HATT, G. 1953. *Plough and Pasture: The Early History of Farming*. New York.

DENNELL, R. W. 1983. *European Economic Prehistory*. London/New York.

DIRINGER, R. 1962. *Writing*. London.

DOLUKHANOV, P. M. 1979. *Ecology and Economy in Neolithic Eastern Europe*. London.

EPSTEIN, H. 1971. *The Origin of Domestic Animals in Africa*. New York.

GLOB, P. V. 1951. *Ard og Plov in Nordens Oldtid* [Hoe and Plough in Nordic Prehistory]. Aarhus.

GUILAINE, J. 1976. *Premiers bergers et paysans de l'Occident méditerranéen*. Paris.

HARLAN, J. R.; DE WET, J. M. R.; STEMLER, A. B. L. (eds) 1976. *Origins of African Plant Domestication*. The Hague.

HIGGS, E. (ed.) 1972. *Papers in Economic Prehistory*. Cambridge.

—— (ed.) 1975. *Palaeoeconomy*. Cambridge.

HODDER, I.; ISAAC, G. L.; HAMMOND, N. (eds) 1981. *Patterns of the Past: Studies in Memory of David Clarke*. Cambridge.

INGOLD, T. 1980. *Hunters, Pastoralists and Ranchers*. Cambridge.

INTERNATIONALES SYMPOSIUM IN KIEL, 1961, 1962. *Zur Domestikation und Frühgeschichte der Haustiere*. Hamburg.

JARMAN, M. R.; BAILEY, G. N.; JARMAN, H. N. (ed.) 1982. *Early European Agriculture: Its Foundations and Developments*. Cambridge.

KUBASIEWICZ, M. (ed.) 1978. *Archaeozoology*. Szczecin.

MELLAART, J. 1975. *The Neolithic of the Near East*. London. (2nd edn 1981.)

MERCER, S. A. B. 1959. *The Origin of Writing and Our Alphabet*. London.

MÜLLER, H. H. 1984. *Bibliographie zur Archäologie und Geschichte der Haustiere (1971–1982)*. Berlin.

MULTHAUF, R. P. 1978. *Neptune's Gift: A History of Common Salt*. Baltimore.

MURRAY, J. 1970. *The First European Agriculture: A Study of the Osteological and Botanical Evidence until 2000 BC*. Edinburgh.

PHILLIPS, P. 1985. *Early Farmers of West Mediterranean Europe*. London.

PIGGOTT, S. (ed.) 1961. *The Dawn of Civilization*. London.

—— 1983. *The Earliest Wheeled Transport*. London.

PING, TI HO. 1977. The Indigenous Origins of Chinese Agriculture. In: REED, C. A. (ed.), *The Origins of Agriculture*. The Hague. pp. 413–84.

REED, C. A. (ed.) 1977. *The Origins of Agriculture*. The Hague.

RENFREW, C. 1972. *The Emergence of Civilization*. London.

—— 1974. *Before Civilization*. London.

—— 1979. *Problems in European Prehistory*. Edinburgh.

RENFREW, J. M. 1969. The Archaeological Evidence for the Domestication of Plants: Methods and Problems. In: UCKO, P.; DIMBLEBY, G. W. (eds), *The Domestication and Exploitation of Plants and Animals*. London. pp. 149–72.

—— 1983. *Palaeoethnobotany: The Prehistoric Food-Plants of the Near East and Europe*. London.

RYDER, M. J. 1969. Changes in the Fleece Following Domestication. In: UCKO, P.; DIMBLEBY, G. W. (eds), *The Domestication and Exploitation of Plants and Animals*. London.

SAUER, C. O. 1952. *Agricultural Origins and Dispersals*. Cambridge, Mass.

SCHWABEDISSEN, H. (ed.) 1972–6. *Die Anfänge des Neolithikums vom Orient bis Nordeuropa*. Cologne/Vienna. 4 vols.

SHERRATT, A. G. 1981. Plough and Pastoralism: Aspects of the Secondary Products Revolution. In: HODDER, I.; ISAAC, G. L.; HAMMOND, N. (eds), *Patterns of the Past: Studies in Honour of David Clarke*. Cambridge. pp. 261–305.

SINGH, P. 1971. *Neolithic Cultures of Western Asia*. London/New York.

TRINGHAM, R. 1971. *Hunters, Fishers and Farmers of Eastern Europe, 6000–3000 BC*. London.

UCKO, P.; DIMBLEBY, G. W. (eds) 1969. *The Domestication and Exploitation of Plants and Animals*. London.

UCKO, P.; TRINGHAM, E.; DIMBLEBY, G. W. (eds) 1972. *Man, Settlement and Urbanism*. London.

VAVILOV, N. I. 1951. *The Origins, Variation, Immunity and Breeding of Cultivated Plants*. Chester. (Trans. K. Starr.)

WERTH, E. 1954. *Grabstock, Hacke und Pflug*. Ludwigsburg.

WHITTLE, A. 1988. *Problems in Neolithic Archaeology*. Cambridge.

ZEUNER, F. E. 1963. *A History of Domesticated Animals*. London.

ZVELEBIL, M. (ed.) 1986. *Hunters in Transition: Mesolithic Societies of Temperate Eurasia and their Transition to Farming*. London.

37

PLANT DOMESTICATION

An overview

Jack R. Harlan

In order to understand how plant domestication came about, it is first necessary to divest oneself of some ancient myths or their implications. It should not be necessary, late in the twentieth century, to discount ancient mythologies, but unfortunately their legacies still condition the thinking of some scientists and the public at large. We need to make a fresh start from a less biased viewpoint.

The subject was of interest to the ancients and all the earliest literatures and many oral traditions contain myths about the origins of agriculture and the source of domestic plants. In the Mediterranean world, the prime source centred on a goddess – Isis in Egypt, Demeter in Greece, Ceres in Rome – who taught humans how to cultivate and showed them the uses of barley and wheat. In Mesopotamia it was a god named On, half man and half fish. In China, it was an ox-headed god named Shen-Nung who was later called an emperor and given a fictitious date, usually about 4,800 years ago (Christle, 1968). To the Aztecs it was Quetzalcóatl, the plumed serpent, and to the Incas it was the first Inca and his queen Coya who were sent by Father Sun to instruct mankind in the arts of agriculture and civilization (Vega, 1961). A constituent part of each of these mythologies is that the god or goddess not only brought the domestic plants and instructed humans in their use, but was in addition a civilizing force teaching law, justice and various arts of civilized society.

There are, of course, other myths and legends in the folklore of other peoples around the world. Many have the same content. The persistent theme is that the arts of agriculture and the domestic plants required for their practice are gifts of the divine. Humans are, somehow, incapable of developing them without supernatural intervention. Further, agricultural people were civilized and non-agricultural people were savages and lived like animals from natural products.

The traditional view, stretching back to prehistoric times, has three basic elements. First: agriculture is an 'invention' or 'discovery', a gift of the gods; it was due to an 'idea' or 'conception'; one must learn to put the seeds in the ground or plant a tuber. The reverse side of the coin is that not farming is due to 'ignorance', 'lack of intelligence', 'an inability to observe or reason' and the like. This element automatically leads to the second: farming is superior to not farming and therefore farmers are superior to hunter-gatherers. The latter are ignorant savages who do not know how to put seeds in the ground or plant a tuber. This element automatically leads to the third: farming, once conceived, is so superior to hunting-gathering that it would diffuse readily around the world. People would adopt it with relief and pleasure because it is so obviously a better way to live.

All elements of the traditional view are completely false and it is long past time to discard them. Echoes, however, still persist in the current literature and thinking. We must disabuse ourselves of these archaic ideas and develop a more reasonable view of the real world. Much of our prejudice has derived from our own ignorance of hunter-gatherers. After all, they were the people who began the process of plant domestication and we cannot understand the process without some understanding of the people involved. We who live by the fruits of farming are all descendants of hunter-gatherers. We have the same genes, possibly in different frequencies, but there is no reason to suppose that we are any more or less intelligent than our ancestors of a few millennia ago. They had the same powers of observation and the same ability to reason.

A critical issue is the botanical knowledge of hunter-gatherers. Did they really need to be taught how to put seeds in the ground or to plant a tuber? A survey of those hunter-gatherers who have survived into the ethnographic present shows that many of them did both.

Of nineteen tribes studied by Steward (1934, 1941) in the Great Basin of North America, seven planted seeds. The species sown were wild and never domesticated. The procedure was to burn a convenient patch of vegetation in the autumn and to broadcast the desired seeds in the burned-over area the following spring. On the western margin of the region, the Paiute of Owens Valley, California, irrigated substantial tracts of land to increase their yield (Steward, 1934; Lawton et al., 1976). One block was over 5 km² in size and another about 13 km². Sometimes seeds from wild harvests were planted to thicken up stands, but none of the species were domesticated. It might be argued that these Indians had contact with agricultural people and obtained the concept of planting and irrigation from them. However, half-way around the world, we find Australian Aborigines doing much the same thing (Campbell, 1965), and also tribes without contact with farmers.

Eleven Californian Indian tribes grew tobacco but no other crop (Klimek, 1935). Other tribes in Oregon,

Washington and British Columbia did the same (Drucker, 1963). The tobaccos were local native species, usually *Nicotiana attenuata* or *N. bigelovii*, and not the tobacco of commerce today. The Karuk vocabulary is of interest here. A tobacco garden was called 'to put seed' and was established by burning logs in the forest and broadcasting seeds in the ashes. The Karuk had terms for wild tobacco, cultivated tobacco, roots, stems, bark, leaf, branch, leaf branch, pith, gum, buds, flowers, seed pods, seeds, flower stems, clusters of flowers, sepals and calyx. There was no word for petal, but descriptive terms were used, as for example, the white-flowered *N. bigelovii* was said to have 'five white ones sticking out'. The stamens and pistil were described as 'sticking out in the middle of every flower where the seeds are going to be'. Stamens were called 'flower whiskers', 'flower threads' or 'flower hairs'. Pollen was 'flower dust'. Nine stages from flowering to seed setting were recognised with descriptive terms (Harrington, 1932). How did we ever get the idea that hunter-gatherers did not know about seeds and plant reproduction?

Tobacco seeds and seedlings are very small, but the Karuk were aware that germination was epigeal and the first leaves (cotyledons) were paired and different from other leaves. The Karuk fertilized (with ashes), sowed, weeded, harvested, selected (for strength), cured, stored and sold tobacco, but no other crop. Clearly, the concept or idea of planting was in no way revolutionary and did not lead to food production (Harrington, 1932).

Observers of the Australian Aborigines have repeatedly been impressed by their knowledge of botanical lore. They were well aware that seeds germinated and gave rise to plants after their kind. Sir George Grey (1841) noted that some had taboos against harvesting certain plants until after the seed is mature so that the species would reseed itself. Several observers noted that the women, when digging yams, replaced the top in the hole just dug to ensure production in the next season (Berndt and Berndt, 1951; McCarthy, 1957). Even large yams may be scolded for not growing big enough, and the head planted with the admonition to do better next time (Tindale, 1974). Replacing the tops of yams at digging time has been recorded for hunter-gatherers in the Andaman Islands (Bengal Gulf) (Coon, 1971), and Africa (Chevalier, 1936).

The number of useful plants known to hunter-gatherers is impressive and some measure of their botanical knowledge. Yanovsky (1936) in his *Food Plants of the North American Indians* lists 1,112 species of 444 genera belonging to 120 families. Only about 10 per cent of these are domesticates or imported weeds; the rest were harvested for food by hunting-gathering tribes. Jardin (1967) compiled a very useful *List of Foods Used in Africa*. Many of these are native plants harvested in the wild by farming people and it is difficult to sort out the cultures using different species. But after removing cultigens, introductions and synonyms as best one can, there still remain some 1,400 species of native African plants collected from the wild and consumed for food. Perhaps nothing could show more clearly the non-revolutionary nature of agriculture than this fact. After farming has been fully established for thousands of years, it is still worth while to gather food from the bush. Golson (1971) listed some 277 genera known and used for food by the Australian Aborigines. Lévi-Strauss (1950) provided a partial list of wild plants used for food in South America.

Perhaps even more striking is the widespread practice of detoxification of poisonous plants so they can be used for food. Hunter-gatherers on every continent knew about methods of soaking, leaching, heating or other techniques for rendering poisonous foods safe. Some procedures required an alkaline leach using wood ashes; some involved boiling for extended periods in several changes of water; others involved the use of clays, fermentation, enzymatic incubation and so on. As, perhaps, a corollary, botanical knowledge extended to drugs for healing and poisons for killing (Coon, 1971; McCarthy, 1957; Tindale, 1974; Berndt and Berndt, 1951).

The more one learns of the botanical lore of hunter-gatherers the more one is impressed by its depth and coverage. These people are and were practising economic botanists. They knew all about life-cycles of plants and knew they could rear them from seeds, tubers or cuttings. No revelation was necessary; they needed no special instruction to practise agriculture. The information required was common knowledge and was probably widely available well back into the Pleistocene Palaeolithic. Plant domestication began on a base of knowledge, not on one of ignorance.

Since agriculture and plant domestication are not the result of an 'idea' or 'invention', the old notion that it would be readily diffusible is also in error. It can be documented, in fact, that agriculture is not a very diffusible system. It is true that occasionally hunting-gathering people take up agriculture, especially under duress, but it is also true that some tribes abandon agriculture and take up the alternative mode of subsistence. Some anthropologists (for instance Levi-Strauss, 1950; Lathrap, 1968) have suggested that many if not all non-farming tribes of tropical America that do not practise agriculture now have done so at some time in the past. Most of the diffusion of agriculture is accomplished by the diffusion of farmers, not by the spread of an idea.

The Aborigines of northern Australia represent a classic case of non-diffusion. Those on the Cape York peninsula and on islands in the Torres Strait have been in contact with agricultural Papuans for millennia. Farmers married non-farmers. Melanesian physical traits are found in the Aboriginal population. Cultural elements such as initiation rites, hero cults, carving in the round, certain types of drums and the bow and arrow were introduced from Papua to Cape York, but not agriculture (White, 1971; Walker, 1972; Tindale, 1974).

The Aborigines of north-west Australia had had contact with agricultural Indonesian traders for at least a few centuries before European contact. It was common for the proas to recruit Aborigine sailors and take them to Indonesia, to be returned on later visits. Cultural traits such as dug-out canoes with outriggers and sails, opium-type smoking pipes, use of metal tools, types of ceremonial grounds and floral art representation were transferred from Indonesia to Australia. The Berndts even found evidence that the Australians were making pottery to trade to Indonesians even though they did not use it themselves (McCarthy, 1957; Berndt and Berndt, 1951). Yet food production was not introduced.

There are, of course, many examples both modern and prehistoric of hunter-gatherers living in close contact with farming people without transmission of agriculture, such as the pygmies, !Kung, Hadza, Toda, Negrito, Plains Indians of North America and Mesolithic tribes of Europe. Indeed, all surviving hunter-gatherers are now constrained by agriculturalists. Only a few have taken up agriculture.

Not only is botanical lore well developed among hunter-gatherers but the tools and technology require little or no change. Non-farmers do virtually everything that farmers do. One tribe or another may prepare seed beds, sow seeds, plant tubers, modify vegetation with fire, irrigate wild plants, live in settled villages, own property such as land, trees, groves, springs, mines or slaves, make pottery, conduct first-fruit ceremonies, pray for rain, sacrifice for abundant production, participate in long-distance trade, detoxify poisonous plants, prepare and use drugs to heal or kill or for hallucinogenic purposes. There is, in fact, nothing that farmers do that non-farmers have not also done somewhere, sometime.

It is only when we make it clear that hunting-gathering is a perfectly valid alternative to agriculture that we can begin our discussion of how, when, where and why plant domestication began. Since hunter-gatherers are professional economic botanists with an enormous command of botanical lore, plant domestication could begin almost anywhere within reasonable ecological limits and at almost any time after Pleistocene. This is, in fact, the picture that is beginning to emerge. Further, the discussion in which vegetatively propagated 'horticulture' is contrasted with seed propagated 'agriculture' is basically irrelevant. Hunter-gatherers know all about both kinds of reproduction and people who plant tubers also plant seeds and people practising seed agriculture also reproduce plants vegetatively. The subject was originally introduced out of the traditional prejudice that 'horticulture' was easier to learn and, therefore, *should* come first; the 'savages' would not at first be capable of planting seeds!

Plant domestication evolved from an intimate association between plants and humans. Such associations probably developed far back in Palaeolithic times – we have no source of evidence. Indeed, since hominid teeth lack a carnivorous character, the close association with plants may have been a legacy of pre-*Homo* ancestors. At any rate, the association seems to have intensified with human adaptation to Post-Pleistocene conditions (the 'Mesolithic' age). During this period, there seems to have been a widespread tendency to emphasize plant foods more than previously, and people surely learned all they needed to know about plant reproduction in order to practise both seed agriculture and vegetative reproduction. As a consequence of such general knowledge, plant domestication could take place almost anywhere or at any time that people chose to cultivate plants for food, fibre, ritual, magic or other purposes. Archaeological evidence suggests that plant domestication did begin in several diverse parts of the world at roughly contemporaneous times. The evidence does not support the suggestion of one or a few 'inventions' followed by diffusion around the world. However, see Carter (1977) for an opposite view.

If we are willing to admit that hunter-gatherers were well-informed applied botanists with the knowledge to grow food plants at any time and anywhere they chose to do so, within reasonable ecological constraints, it follows that we will not and cannot find a time or a place where agriculture originated. We cannot find a place because people were manipulating plants in one way or another over vast reaches across whole continents. We will not find a time because we are dealing with ranges over millennia and we cannot even define agriculture until after it has evolved.

Cultivating a non-food plant like tobacco obviously does not alter the food procurement system. Cultivating a few squash plants in summer camp to provide less than 5 per cent of the diet is hardly a revolutionary change in the food

supply either. Yet, Indians in ancient Mexico followed this practice for several millennia, gradually adding more cultigens and slowly becoming more dependent on them. At what stage can agriculture be said to have originated? When 15 per cent of the diet was provided by domesticated plants? Or 20 per cent? Or 50 per cent? Archaeologists in recent years have become much more cautious than formerly about identification of boundaries between hunter-gatherers and farmers and many complain of the difficulties and uncertainties of such interpretations (Bender, 1975; Bray, 1977; Hutterer, 1983; Moore, 1982). It is in the nature of the problem that there is no genuine 'time', since we are dealing with processes that lasted for millennia and are still continuing.

If we cannot identify times and places where agriculture originated, what can we do? We can describe the evolution of agriculture as revealed by the archaeological record for various geographical regions that have been studied. We can also examine the nature of the domestication processes and relate them to the other evidence. In the pages that follow a selected set of descriptions will be presented.[1] It will become apparent that many of the questions we have been asking are really irrelevant and grounded in false perceptions of prehistory and the nature of agricultural origins. In a later section some observations on plant domestication will be presented.

WESTERN ASIA

The earliest firm evidence that we have to date comes from western Asian sites such as Çayönü, Ramad, Beidha, Ali Kosh, PPN Jericho, PPN Nahal Oren, Haçilar, Mehrgarh, Can Hasan III, Ain Ghazal, and so on (Map 35). We consider the evidence to be 'firm' because at least some of the plant remains have the morphologies of domesticated plants rather than those of their wild relatives. An increase in the abundance of artefacts associated with agriculture, such as sickle blades with silica gloss, grinding-stones and so on is suggestive but not completely diagnostic, since they could be used for harvesting wild plants as well. Osteopathology may also be suggestive, since agriculture is often associated with an increase in dental caries, more rapid tooth wear and a greater incidence of chronic diseases some of which leave traces in bones or teeth. Abrupt changes in vegetation as revealed by

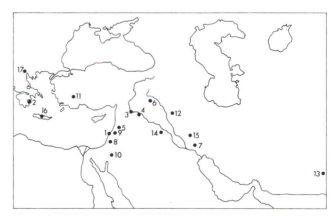

Map 35 Sites of south-west Asia and south-east Europe with domesticated plant remains dating to 8,000 years ago or earlier. 1, Nahal Oren; 2, Franchthi cave; 3, Mureybet; 4, Tell Abu Hureyra; 5, Tell Aswad; 6, Çayönü; 7, Ali Kosh; 8, Jericho; 9, Ramad; 10, Beida; 11, Haçilar; 12, Jarmo; 13, Mehrgarh; 14, Bouqras; 15, Tepe Guran; 16, Knossos; 17, Nea Nikomedeia.

changes in pollen frequencies have been used to indicate the arrival of agriculture (Godwin, 1965), but they are not likely to tell us much about ultimate origins. The most reliable direct evidence comes from plant morphology.

The morphologies of domesticates most readily detected in archaeological plant material are as follows. For details and more examples, see Harlan et al. (1973).

1 Inflorescences of cereals that do not shatter at maturity.
   (a) Wheat, barley, rye have spikes; rachis joints fragment in wild races and remain intact in cultivated races. Rachis joints that fragment naturally tend to be smooth; non-shattering races show ragged breaks between joints.
   (b) Oats, panic, foxtail millet and so on have panicles: spikelets are shed in wild races and are more tenacious in cultivated ones. Those that shed naturally usually have a characteristic scar where the abscission layer was formed. The tip of the pedicel may have a 'sucker mouth' which is easily recognized, but it may not be possible to separate weed races from wild ones.
2 Size and shape of grains.
   (a) Cultivated races of seed crops usually have larger grains than wild races, but this is not *always* true and great caution is advised. In some cases, such as that of the large-seeded fava bean (broad bean), there is no question and domesticated seeds are identifiable at a glance.
   (b) Cultivated grains may be plumper, better filled, or otherwise of a different shape from wild ones. If the material is carbonized – and often that is the only material that survives - distortion during carbonization can cause misidentification. Many laboratories char grains artificially for reference specimens.
3 Pods and capsules that do not dehisce.
   (a) Most wild legumes open explosively at maturity, flinging the seeds some distance from the parent plant. The pod twists at the same time because the inner tissues are laid down at an angle to the central and outer tissues and do not dry at the same rate. This feature is suppressed in cultivated legumes either by reduction of the inner tissues or by their elimination.
   (b) Plants with capsules (flax, rape, mustard, opium and the like) may developed sutures or pores that do not open at maturity. This may be quantitative, however, and in some material is a dubious characteristic.
4 Other, more subtle characteristics may be used on occasion, and some crops such as maize have their own special morphologies that can be used.

In addition, geographical and ecological limitations may be used. Grapes are vines of rather mesic habitats. If we find grape pips near the Dead Sea or in Egypt they are most probably from cultivated plants. The sycamore (*Ficus sycomorus*) does not produce seed in Egypt, the Levant or North America for want of the proper species of wasp. The plants in this region are propagated by humans only.

Some early sites with domesticated plants and their time ranges are shown in Table 12, and their locations are given in Map 35.

Earlier sites, such as Mureybet and Tell Abu Hureyra, indicate extensive harvesting of wild material, or possibly some form of incipient cultivation of plants with wild morphologies (Cauvin, 1977). It may never be possible correctly to interpret such material. The Natufian culture, so far as we can tell from the evidence, did not practise agriculture but flourished long after other nearby cultures were producing food by this method. Natufians lived in areas where wild cereal harvests could have supplied ample food and cultivation may have been unnecessary (Perrot, 1966; Harlan, 1967).

Later sites indicate a substantial increase in human population and a diffusion of a western Asian agricultural complex out of the nuclear zone. A farming village way of life spread into the Mesopotamian alluvium with the development of irrigation. It spread along the shores of the Mediterranean,

Table 12 Western Asian sites with plant remains dated to 8,000 years ago or earlier.

Time ranges in millennia BP (uncalibrated C^{14} dates)	Site	Plant remains	Reference (senior author only given here)
16.8–15.8	Nahal Oren (Kebaran), Israel	Em, v, v, fig, grape	Noy, 1973
c.12.0	Franchthi cave, Greece	b, o, l, v, pistachio, almond	Hansen, 1978
c.8.0	Franchthi cave, Greece	Em, B, L, V, pistachio, almond	Hansen, 1978
11.0–9.0	Mureybet, Syria	ek, b	Van Zeist, 1968
11.0–10.0	Tell Abu Hureyra, Syria	ek, b, l, v, v, +	Hillman, 1975
9.8–9.0	Tell Aswad, Syria	Em, B, P, L	Van Zeist, 1979
9.5–8.5	Çayönü, Turkey	ek, Ek, em, Em, P, L, V, F	Van Zeist, 1972
9.5–8.75	Ali Kosh (B.M.), Iran	ek, Ek, Em, b, B?, F	Helbaek, 1969
8.75–8.0	Ali Kosh (M.J.), Iran	Em, B, o	Helbaek, 1969
8.0–7.6	Ali Kosh (M.J.) Iran	Em, B, o	Helbaek, 1969
9.0–8.0	Jericho, Palestine	Ek, Em, B, P, L, V	Hopf, 1969
9.0–8.5	Ramad, Syria	Ek, Em, NW, B, L, V, pistachio, almond	Van Zeist, 1966
9.0–8.5	Beidha, Jordan	Em, b, B?, o, V	Helbaek, 1966
c.9.0	Aceramic Haçilar, Turkey	ek, Em	Helbaek, 1969
8.8–8.5	Jarmo, Iraq	ek, Ek, em, Em, B, P, L, V	Helbaek, 1969
8.5–8.0	Mehrgarh, Pakistan	Ek, Em, NW, jujube, date	Jarrige, 1980
8.5–8.0	Bouqras, Syria	Em, NW, B, +	Akkermans, 1983
8.2–7.5	Tepe Guran, Iran	b, B	Renfrew, 1969
c.8.0	Knossos (stratum X), Greece	Ek, Em, NW, B, L	Evans, 1968
c.8.0	Nea Nikomedeia, Greece	Ek, Em, B, o, V, L, oak, almond	Renfrew, 1979

Capital letters = cultivated races; lower case = wild race. ek = einkorn; em = emmer; b = barley; o = oats; p = pea; l = lentil; f = flax; nw = naked wheat; v = vetch; vv = two species of *Vicia*; + = many weed species present.

across the Balkans, up the Danube and down the Rhine (Clark, 1965). It flourished across what is now the Sahara desert and became firmly established in Egypt 7,000 years ago. Diffusion across Iran into central Asia and into the Indus valley can also be traced (Jarrige and Meadow, 1980).

The question of a 'centre of origin', however, is not altogether settled. The evidence, as far as it goes, indicates a nuclear area along the rain-fed oak woodland formation extending from the Levant to the Taurus and southward along the Zagros at mid-elevations. There, the agricultural complex that we recognize as characteristically Western Asian evolved and from there it spread out. But, we are not yet sure what it spread against. Were other people practising a less successful form of agriculture at this time? Is our centre of origin an artefact due to a concentration of archaeologists in the nuclear area? Are we still biased by the concept that agriculture was an 'invention' or gift of the gods (Isis, Demeter, Ceres) and, therefore, *ought* to have a centre? Some recent evidence suggests that the indigenous Europeans of the time were doing more than simple hunting and gathering of forest products (Renfrew, 1970; Bender, 1975; Hansen and Renfrew, 1978).

CHINA

A nuclear area in north China also has the appearance of a centre of origin. The earliest Neolithic cultures in China were found quite recently in the Huanghe valley: the Cishan culture (dated from about 8,000 to about 7,700 years ago), the Peiligang culture (dated from about 8,000 to about 7,500 years ago) and the Dadiwan culture (dated from about 7,800 to about 7,600 years ago). Amongst the signs of their agricultural economy there are querns, cylindrical rollers, spades and sickles. The cultivation of foxtail millet (*Setaria italica*) in the Cishan culture, and of broomcorn millet (*Panicum miliaceum*) and of rapeseeds (*Brassica*) in the Dadiwan culture are attested (Chapter 46).

These cultures are all forerunners of the Yangshao culture, which is represented by a large number of village sites found on terraces of the loess highlands in the area where the Fenko and Weishui rivers join the Huanghe, that is in Shensi, Shansi and Honan provinces. The villages were definitely based on the cultivation of millets and some of the later ones had rice as well. Some of them were rather large and the pottery was made with considerable flair. Domestic animals included a range of animals: pigs, cattle, sheep, dogs and chickens. The culture, as we know it, appears to be highly sophisticated for the very first stages of agricultural development. It is dated into the late eighth millennium BP and is, therefore, later than the early farming cultures of western Asia (Chang, 1977).

Diffusion from the nuclear area can be documented by sites of a later Longshanoid character. These are relatively abundant and spread into the coastal plains and southward along the coast opposite Taiwan island, where it jumped the water gap and became established on the island. An intermediate Miaodigou (Miao-ti-kou) II culture is also found in the nuclear area later than Yangshao and earlier than Longshan (Chang, 1977).

While the North Chinese Neolithic cultures appear to have evolved in the nuclear area and spread out from there, it is not yet clear what other Chinese cultures were doing in terms of subsistence. Something had been going on in South-East Asia in terms of plant domestication,

but our evidence is still tenous. The Dapenkeng (Ta-p'en-k'eng) culture of south-east coastal China is characterized by a distinctive cord-marked pottery that may have some connection with the Hoabinhian culture of Vietnam and Thailand. Dapenkeng is dated to about the same age as the Yangshao but there is no evidence to suppose that either one was derived from the other (Chang, 1977). The Chinese pattern will no doubt turn out to be much more complex than the current picture. There is a recent report of a Hemudu (Ho-mu-tu) culture with abundant rice remains and dated to approximately 7,000 years ago (Sun et al. 1981). The site is near the coast of Zhejiang Shen, south of Shanghai. Once again, the archaeological evidence suggests origins that are diffuse in both time and space.

SOUTH-EAST ASIA AND THE SOUTH PACIFIC

Key sites of the region are shown on Map 36. The Spirit cave site proved to be rich in plant remains (Gorman, 1969). In the time range from 11,500 to 7,500 years ago, remains were found of *Aleurites, Canarium, Madhuca, Prunus, Terminalia, Castanopsis, Cucumis, Lagenaria, Trapa, Areca* and *Piper*, all of tropical affinities. The presence of the Mediterranean genera *Pisum* and *Vicia* was also reported but challenged on the basis of geography and adaptation. Later excavations added *Celtis, Ricinus, Mamordica, Nelumbium, Trichosanthes* and *Luffa* to the list, all of tropical adaptation. Nearby caves contributed *Mangifera* and *Oryza*. These finds are particularly significant because it had previously been thought that plant materials could not persist in tropical climates. There is no firm evidence indicating that these materials came from domesticated plants, however (Hutterer, 1983).

The Lie Siri and Vai Bobo caves on Timor yielded a shorter list of somewhat similar plants. Remains dated earlier than 5000 years ago included *Aleurites, Celtis, Areca, Piper* and *Coix*. Afterwards *Inocarpus, Bambusa, Lagenaria* and possibly *Setaria* were added (Glover, 1977; Hutterer, 1983). The Ulu Leang site in southern Sulawesi had remains of *Panicum, Ficus, Canarium* and *Bidens* and much rice by 6,000 years ago. It has not yet been determined if the rice was wild or domesticated (Glover, 1977).

The Hoa Binh site is typical for a number of sites found widely in the region and represented by a technology like that in Spirit cave. The culture was probably based on broad-spectrum intensive food gathering and hunting and very likely gave rise to the local Neolithic cultures that followed. Ban Chiang and Non Nok Tha are examples. The dating of these two sites has been a problem, but this may now be resolved by correlation with the site of Ban Nadi (Higham et al., 1982). At any rate, such evidence as we have does no damage to the idea of an indigenous agriculture developing in South-East Asia and adjacent islands.

Very early agriculture has been claimed for the Kuk valley in New Guinea where altered land forms have been found beneath a peat deposit (Golson, 1984). The earliest land forms, about 9,000 years ago are somewhat tenuous and difficult to interpret, but later ones seem clearly to represent some form of raised tables surrounded by drainage/irrigation ditches. These are quite extensive and one canal is some 10 km long, 1 m deep and 10 m wide, a rather monumental construction. What appear to be pig wallows were also found. If it is true that the pig is not indigenous to New

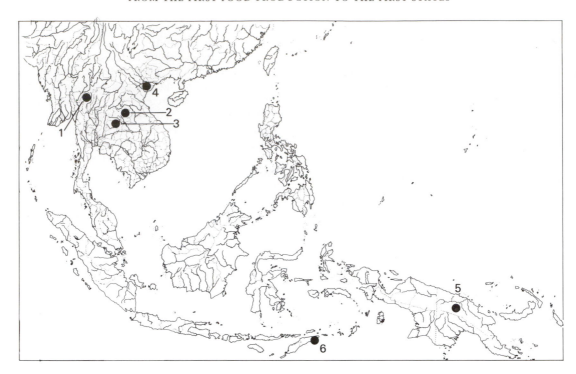

Map 36 Map of the most ancient Neolithic sites in South-East Asia and the South Pacific: 1, Spirit Cave; 2, Ban Chiang; 3, Non Nok Tha; 4, Hoa Binh; 5, Kuk; 6, Lie Siri and Vai Bobo caves, Timor.

Guinea, then they were imported by humans and were at least feral if not fully domesticated. The crops raised are unknown, but taro (*Colocasia*) would fit the environment well. It should be noted, however, that Australian Aborigine hunter-gatherers also modified land forms on a comparable scale, probably for eeling (Lourandos, 1980).

The general impression from the work done so far is one of intensified plant manipulation widely practised over the region, probably going back to the terminal Pleistocene. To attempt to assess where and when plants were first domesticated in the region is probably a meaningless exercise.

INDIA–PAKISTAN–BANGLADESH

Recent evidence suggests that plant domestication in South Asia was simultaneous in time with western Asia. In greater parts of India the Neolithic was contemporaneous with the Harappan civilization (Vishnu-Mittre, 1977) and in some regions, such as south India, even later (Agrawal and Ghosh, 1973). In Baluchistan, however, wheat-based agriculture goes back to at least 9,000 years ago (Jarrige and Meadow, 1980), while rice-centred agriculture has been traced to between 10,000 and 9,000 years ago in the Belan valley (Sharma, 1983). There are again other cultigens that are undeniably Indian in origin, such as egg-plant, sesame, pigeon pea, possibly cucumber, and several minor millets, tubers, pulses and others. The north Indian sugarcanes may represent an independent domestication of that crop. (The noble canes probably originated in New Guinea.) The timing and sequences of these developments are not well worked out.

Again, it may be possible that indigenous Indians were already growing crops when wheat and rice agriculture arrived, but also that the latter in south Asia is much older than had been previously believed.

AFRICA

A complete suite of cultivated plants was domesticated in sub-Saharan Africa including cereals, pulses, tubers, oil crops, vegetables, fruits, nuts, fibre plants, and plants for medical and religious purposes. Some of the most important include sorghum, pearl millet, finger millet, teff, fonio, cowpea, Bamara groundnut, African rice, African yams, water-melon, okra, cola nuts, coffee and oil palm (Harlan et al., 1976). Several reviews of the botanical and archaeological evidence have been published (Clark, 1976; Shaw, 1976, 1977; Phillipson, 1982; Harlan, 1982). Unfortunately, the archaeological evidence so far obtained tells us very little about the earliest phases of plant domestication in Africa. The agricultural sites excavated up to now have been rather late (Close, 1984) and earlier developments have not been documented.

The earliest plant remains that are clearly domesticated are seeds of finger millet found in a rock shelter in Ethiopia (Phillipson, 1977). The dating is not very precise but could belong to the sixth millennium BP. On the whole, firm evidence for food production comes late, and in southern Africa seems to be associated with Iron Age settlements (Phillipson, 1982). No doubt, earlier finds will appear as more research is conducted, but for the present the story of plant domestication in Africa must rely largely on botanical evidence.

The botanical evidence is consistent in indicating that plants were domesticated right across the entire continent from the Atlantic to the Indian Ocean, south of the Sahara and north of the Equator. At least three centres have been proposed: Ethiopia (Vavilov, 1926), the bend of the Niger (Murdock, 1959) and the Sahara (Chevalier, 1938; Portères, 1951). These theories do not fit the facts, although a few plants were probably domesticated in each. Plants that are probably Ethiopian include ensete, noog, finger millet, coffee and perhaps teff. West African crops include African

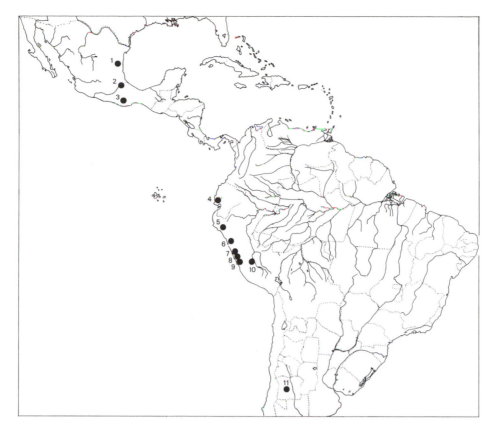

Map 37 The most ancient Neolithic sites in America: 1, Ocampo caves, Tamaulipas, Mexico; 2, Tehuacán valley, Mexico; 3, Guila Naquitz cave, Oaxaca, Mexico; 4, Valdivia sites, Ecuador; 5, Huaca Prieta, Peru; 6, Guitarrero cave, Peru; 7, Pampa site, Peru; 8, Ancón, Peru; 9, Chilca, Peru; 10, Ayacucho, Peru; 11, Gruta del Indio, Patagonia, Argentina.

rice, African yams, fonio, sorghum, okra, cowpea, Bambara groundnut and oil palm, but not necessarily from a centre at the bend of the Niger. The most likely candidate for domestication in the Sahara is pearl millet (Brunken et al., 1977). In fact, the most conspicuous feature of African plant domestication is its non-centric character (Harlan, 1971; Harlan et al., 1976). The time range is probably as diffuse as the geography.

MESOAMERICA (Map 37 and Table 13)

Early agriculture in Mesoamerica is documented by sites in Tamaulípas (MacNeish, 1958), Puebla (MacNeish, 1967) and Oaxaca in Mexico (Flannery, 1968). The results of these studies have been summarized by Bray (1977). The earliest traces are not very well dated, but may extend to about 8,000 years ago in Tehuacán and earlier in Tamaulípas. A characteristic feature of these archaeological sequences is that domesticated plants contributed very little to the human diet for some millennia. Species of *Cucurbita* were among the first cultigens, but these were grown on a small scale in summer camp when wild harvests were abundant. The cultivation would seem to be more of a hobby than a necessity.

In the Tehuacán valley a complex of squash, bean and maize was established a little before 7,000 years ago but it still represented a minor portion of the diet. Unless the climate there was different then from what it is now, it is very unlikely that the Tehuacán valley was in the mainstream of agricultural evolution, and this is probably true of Oaxaca

as well. Both valleys are dry enough to be marginal without supplementary irrigation. The cultivated plants appearing in the archaeological record probably represent the products of evolution taking place in more favoured locations in other valleys.

The variety of plant remains recovered and identified in the Tehuacán studies is unusual. In the Coaxcatlán phase about 7,000 to 5,400 years ago, when agriculture began to become effective, some eighteen species were identified, half of them domesticated. By 3,500 years ago with the Ajalpan phase another half-dozen cultigens had been added. The picture obtained from all three sequences is one of an early, casual cultivation of a few plants that did not contribute much toward feeding the people, followed by a slow, seemingly reluctant, acceptance of other cultigens until viable agriculture eventually evolved. The earliest experiments may have been about 9,000 years ago and fully effective agriculture did not develop until the mid to late fourth millennium BP (Bray, 1977).

Mesoamerica has the appearance of a centre of origin, being a relatively small region in which an agricultural complex evolved and out of which it diffused. The diffusion, however, was not always into cultures entirely devoid of cultivated plants. Indians in eastern North America were raising squash, gourds, tobacco, sunflowers and probably *Iva*, *Phalaris* and *Chenopodium* before maize and beans arrived from Mexico. Further, the Mesoamerican complex seems to have arrived piecemeal. Beans (*Phaseolus vulgaris*) arrived later than maize in the Mississippi Valley, while squash and gourds were being grown by the sixth millennium BP or earlier (Stothers and Yarnell, 1977).

Table 13 The main tropical American sites with plant remains dated to 4,000 years ago or earlier.

Time ranges in millennia BP (uncalibrated C¹⁴ dates)	Site	Plant remains
10.7–9.8	Guila Naquitz cave, Oaxaca, Mexico	*Cucurbita pepo* (1 seed fragment)
9.4–9.2	Guila Naquitz cave, Oaxaca, Mexico	*Curcurbita pepo* (seeds + peduncles)
c.9.0	Ocampo caves, Tamaulípas, Mexico	*Lagenaria siceraria*
9.0–7.5	Ocampo caves, Tamaulípas, Mexico	*Phaseolus coccineus*
8.5–7.5	Tehuacán, Puebla, Mexico	*Capsicum*
8.0–6.0	Coastal Peru	*Lagenaria*
c.7.7	Guitarrero cave, Peru	*Phaseolus vulgaris; Phaseolus lunatus*
c.7.5	Tehuacán, Mexico	*Lagenaria, Zea*
	Pero Ayacucho, Peru	*Lagenaria*
c.6.0	Tamaulípas, Mexico	*Phaseolus vulgaris*
c.5.5	Tehuacán, Mexico	*Gossypium, Amaranthus cruentus*
c.5.3	Real Alto (Valdivia), Ecuador	*Canna, Canavalia, Gossypium, Zea*
c.5.3	Chilca (coastal), Peru	*Phaseolus lunatus*
c.5.3	Pampa site (coastal), Peru	*Cucurbita ecuadoriense; C. andreana; C. ficifolia*
c.4.5	Ancón (coastal), Peru	*C. moschata*
	Huaca Prieta, Peru	*Phaseolus lunatus; Capsicum; Gossypium*
c.4.3	Huaca Prieta, Peru	*Canna edulis; Ipomoea batatas*
c.4.0	Huaca Prieta, Peru	*Canavalia plagiospermum*

Source: Pickersgill and Heisen, 1977, with additions.

SOUTH AMERICA (Map 37 and Table 13)

Early plant domestication is documented by cultivated beans (*Phaseolus vulgaris*) and lima beans (*P. lunatus*) dated to about 8000 years ago in Guitarrero cave, Peru (Kaplan et al., 1973). These were found in an intermontane valley of the western slopes, and the nearest known wild races grow at intermediate elevation on the eastern slopes of the Andes. Since the beans are morphologically fully domesticated and well removed geographically from their wild relatives, one may presume that plants were being domesticated well before 8,000 years ago.

Unfortunately most of the archaeological work done so far in South America has concentrated on the Pacific coast. In coastal Peru, the climate is virtually rainless and preservation of plant residues, textiles, featherwork and human bodies is superb. This provides excellent material for study, and is perhaps the main reason for the focus of archaeological research. But, the climate is too dry for agriculture without irrigation or some other device to supplement soil moisture. This is not the place for plant domestication and what one finds on the coast represents products that evolved elsewhere. Too few sites have been excavated in rain-fed agricultural areas to give an adequate picture of plant domestication in South America.

At present, the earliest domesticates found on the coast are in Valdivian villages of Ecuador. The earliest, period A, dates from about 5,300 to 4,300 years ago (Damp et al., 1981; Damp, 1984). Plant remains include achira (*Canna*), *Canavalia*, bottle gourd, cotton and maize. If maize is indeed of Mexican origin, as seems to be the current consensus, then the Valdivians were far removed from the beginnings of agriculture in Latin America. Somewhat later sites in coastal Peru add squash (*C. moschata, C. ficifolia*) and lima beans. By 4,000 years ago chili peppers (*Capsicum*), guava (*Psidium*), peanut (*Arachis*), cassava (manioc), *Inga, Lucuma* and *Pachyrrhizus* were added to the list (Rowe and Menzel, 1967). Heiser (1979) has reviewed the origins of a select list of American plant domesticates, and more details may be found there.

Plants were domesticated over very wide regions of South America. There is a highland complex including several tubers that undoubtedly evolved in the Andes from Bolivia to Colombia but does not appear to be very early. The peanut (*Arachis*) probably was domesticated in or near Jujuy province of Argentina. Cassava (manioc) was probably first grown along the savannah–forest ecotone. A number of similar plants were domesticated in both Mesoamerica and South America. There were multiple domestications of the cottons (2 species), chili peppers (5), *Cucurbita* (5), *Phaseolus* (4), *Solanum* (4), *Annona* (7), *Chenopodium* (3), *Amaranthus* (3) and so on (Harlan, 1975).

GENETIC LIMITATIONS

The several archaeological sequences available all indicate that agriculture evolved slowly and that it took several millennia from first evidences to an effective food procurement system. This has led a number of students of the problem to state that the slowness is due to genetic limitations of the target species and that agriculture is slow to evolve because crop plants are slow to evolve (Bray, 1977). Recent and current experience with plant and animal domestication indicate that this is simply not true. Both plants and animals have been successfully domesticated in this century and several species have yielded domesticated races in a very short time.

Vegetative propagation is a device that can lead to 'instant domestication'. The 'Concord' grape (*Vitis labrusca*) has been very popular in North America for well over a century. It appeared as a seedling in the pasture of Mr E. W. Bull of Concord, Massachussetts, in 1843. It was selected in 1849 and has been propagated on a substantial scale ever since (Hedrick, 1922). By 1869, Downing listed more than 100 cultivars of American grapes selected from spontaneous sources. Most of the 'paper shelled' pecans (*Carya pecan*) grown in USA are simple selections from native populations growing wild in the bottomlands of the southern Mississippi watershed. The bulk of the yearly harvest is still from wild trees.

'Coastal' bermudagrass (*Cynodon dactylon*) is a single plant selected from an F1 population of hybrids between a naturalized clone from Georgia (USA) and an introduced clone from South Africa. Both parents were undeveloped wild-type plants. The cultivar is now established on some 4.5

million ha. A number of cultivars of ornamentals have been introduced into cultivation directly from the wild by vegetative propagation. These include, tulips, iris, rose, clematis, crocus and so on. Vegetative propagation permits domestication in a single generation.

Although the *Hevea* rubber tree had been used by native Americans, perhaps for millennia, it did not become a domesticated plantation crop until about the turn of the twentieth century. In many modern plantations each tree consists of three genotypes. A high-yielding clone is grafted on selected wild-type seedlings to provide a tapping panel. This is, in turn, top grafted with disease-resistant clones selected from wild trees. The high-yielding panel may yield several times as much latex as unselected wild trees, but it is the only part of the tri-partite tree requiring plant breeding procedures.

The cacao of commerce is no longer based on the cultivars of the ancient Mesoamerican Indians but on material taken from wild populations in northern South America and Amazonia. The modern, high-yielding octoploid strawberry is a recent product that combines wild strains from Canada, Virginia, California and Chile (Wilhelm, 1974).

Professor Gladstones (1970, 1980) has domesticated two species of lupin, *Lupinus angustifolius* and *L. consentinii* in his career at Perth, Western Australia. He started with material of wild type that shattered its seed at maturity. The seeds were hard, dark coloured, highly dormant and high in alkaloids. He developed cultivars that are relatively non-shattering with soft, non-dormant, white seed and with low alkaloid content. White flowers were obtained as well, as a marker. It may be argued that he had a goal in mind, knew the principles of genetics, had access to a sizeable collection of plants and had the co-operation of colleagues. This may speed up the development somewhat, but the facts are that the desired variations occur spontaneously and one needs only to combine them. This is not beyond the 'primitive' farmer with his deep appreciation for the plants he grows.

The present writer has had some personal experience with the semi-domestication of perennial grasses native to the southern Great Plains of the USA. Since these were to be used for forage, full domestication was not a goal, but seed supplies were often limiting and this led to the establishment of a grass seed laboratory and considerable research on seed production and seed characteristics.

With several species we were able to harvest one ton or more of grain per hectare with a combine harvester. This is comparable to yields of most annual domesticated cereals under subsistence farming conditions. Wild races are too often underrated with respect to productivity. We found that seed retention could be greatly improved simply by harvesting late in the season after most of the seed had shattered. Those plants that did not shatter provided seed for the next generation. Among the cereals that have been studied, including barley, sorghum, maize, rice and so on, non-shattering is usually controlled by a single gene or by two or three genes any one of which suppresses shattering.

Seedlings from large seeds can emerge from greater depths than seedlings from small seeds. One can readily select for seed size by deep planting. Dormancy can be reduced rapidly by repeated sowings. The dormant genotypes do not contribute to the next generation, but the non-dormant genotypes do. These features are among the most important in the domestication of cereals, and appear to be under simple genetic controls or are highly heritable. The natural cycles of sowing and reaping automatically select toward domesticated

types and rapid progress can be demonstrated in only a few cycles (Hilu and de Wet, 1980). (For more detail, see Harlan, 1975; Harlan et al., 1973.)

If the evolutionary capacity of crop plants is not limiting to the development of agriculture, why did it take so long for agriculture to evolve? This is a question that clearly needs further study, but the answer would seem to lie on the human side of the equation (Bender, 1978) rather than in the genetic response of cultigens to the pressure of selection.

ECOLOGICAL LIMITATIONS

In principle, the process of plant domestication could have started almost anywhere within the latitudes of 45° N and 45° S; in practice there were ecological constraints that made the process more selective. Agriculture came late, for example, to the temperate prairie grasslands of the world. The soils are among the richest of agricultural resources, but the prairie sod was too difficult to manage with primitive tools. The prairies of the world were broken open for farming only in the last century or so. Soils high in clay and temperate wetlands were generally avoided for the same reason. The agriculturally marginal semi-arid steppes were also not well suited to early farming, but were well suited to exploitation by nomadic herdsmen. Few important domesticates can be traced to these ecological environments (Harlan, 1981).

Tropical rain forests are difficult environments for humans, and many of them remain sparsely settled to this day. Forests with pronounced wet and dry seasons, gallery forests and forest–savannah ecotones, however, are much more easily exploited and provide a setting for agricultural innovation. Many tropical domesticates, especially fruits and roots, can be traced to these environments.

The easiest environments to exploit in primitive agriculture seem to be open woodlands or savannahs characterized by widely spaced trees and herbaceous, mostly grassy, vegetation between. Most of the Western Asian nuclear area was an oak-park woodland, although parts of it may have been covered with a more shrubby maquis or chaparral growth. Indigenous African agriculture has a savannah character. Even the native rice and yams, now grown in the wet forest zone, had savannah origins (Harlan et al., 1976). The vegetation in the north China nuclear area at the time of Yangshao development is still in dispute. Ho (1977) describes it as a semi-arid steppe, rich in *Artemisia*, while Chang (1977) and others claim it was forested. Unless the climate has changed dramatically, it seems unlikely that the loess highlands were really forested, although the steep slopes of ravines and stream banks no doubt supported trees, as they do now. The upland plains could well have been open woodland, but the question awaits further evidence. So far as we now know Mesoamerican agriculture first began to develop in savannah type woodland formations, but our archaeological sampling has been biased in that direction.

An ecological setting much favoured by geographers is a tropical riverine environment. This can be traced, primarily, to the influence of Carl O. Sauer (1952), who proposed that the first tentative steps towards plant domestication would have been taken by sedentary fishing folk who lived in villages near streams supplying fish year round. These people, secure in their food supply and freed from nomadism, would have the leisure to experiment with plant domestication. There is logic to the argument, but it was rooted, in part, in the concept that farming is something that must be learned or invented. Sauer thought that vegetative reproduction preceded seed planting because it was simpler to learn. We have yet to find archaeological evidence for agricultural origins of this type, although the activities in Kuk swamp in New Guinea may have had such a character.

We do have evidence to suggest that some ecological settings were so rich in resources that agriculture was taken up at a late date, and this by introduction from the outside. Temperate forest zones are typical of this class. Jomon of Japan, Indians of the west coasts of North America and of eastern North America and some Mesolithic European groups are examples. The Jomon of Japan and the west coast Indians, in particular, developed high population densities living on fish, roots, acorns, nuts and other natural products. They lived in villages and developed native arts to a high degree but did not grow food plants until invaded by outside agricultural people. The coast Indians did, indeed, experiment with plant domestication and grew native tobacco, but these sedentary fishing folk at least, did not opt for farming.

A global survey suggests that some ecological settings are more suited to plant domestication and the development of agriculture than others (Harlan, 1981). Some environments were too rich and farming was unnecessary (temperate forests, some savannahs); some were marginal and required too much mobility (deserts, steppes, taiga); some were too difficult to manage (prairie grasslands, rain forest). The most suitable environments (woodlands, savannahs, savannah–forest ecotones) began to be exploited at about the same time in various parts of the world. It is the ecological constraints, more than anything else, that give the appearance of 'centres of origin', not the constraints of knowledge, discovery and diffusion.

NOTE

1 With the agreement of the author, the texts concerning China and India, and Pakistan and Bangladesh have been slightly modified to take into account new data provided by An Zhimin (see Chapter 46) and by Co-Editor A. H. Dani – Ed.

BIBLIOGRAPHY

AGRAWAL, D. P; GHOSH, A. (eds) 1973. *Radiocarbon and Indian Archaeology.* Bombay.

AKKERMANS, P. A. et al. 1983. Bouqras Revisited: Preliminary Report on a Project in Eastern Syria. *Proc. Prehist. Soc.*, Vol. 49, pp. 335–72.

BENDER, B. 1975. *Farming in Prehistory: From Hunter-Gatherer to Food Producer.* London.

—— 1978. Gatherer-Hunter to Farmer: A Social Perspective. *World Archaeol.*, Vol. 10, pp. 204–22.

BERNDT, R. M.; BERNDT, C. H. 1951. *Man, Land and Myth in Northern Australia.* East Lansing.

BRAY, W. 1977. From Foraging to Farming in Early Mexico. In: MEGAW, J. V. S. (ed.), *Hunters, Gatherers and First Farmers beyond Europe.* Leicester. pp. 225–50.

BRUNKEN, J. N.; DE WET, J. M. J.; HARLAN, J. R. 1977. The Morphology and Domestication of Pearl Millet. *Econ. Bot.* (Lancaster, Pa.), Vol. 31, pp. 163–74.

CAMPBELL, A. H. 1965. Elementary Food Production by the Australian Aborigines. *Mankind* (Sydney), Vol. 6, pp. 206–11.

CARTER, G. F. 1977. A Hypothesis Suggesting a Single Origin of Agriculture. In: REED, C. A. (ed.), *Origins of Agriculture.* The Hague. pp. 89–133.

CAUVIN, J. 1977. Les Fouilles de Mureybet (1971–1974) et leur signification pour les origines de la sedentarisation au Proche-Orient. *Ann. Am. Sch. Orient. Res.* (Baltimore), Vol. 44, pp. 19–48.

CHANG, K.-C. 1977. *The Archaeology of Ancient China.* 3rd edn, rev. New Haven.

CHEVALIER, A. 1936. Contribution à l'étude de quelques espèces africaines du genre *Discorea. Bull. Mus. Hist. Nat.* (Paris), 2nd series, Vol. 8, pp. 520–51.

—— 1938. Le Sahara, centre d'origine de plantes cultivées. *Soc. Biogéogr. Mém.* (Paris), No. 6, pp. 307–22.

CHRISTLE, A. 1968. *Chinese Mythology.* Fetham.

CLARK, J. D. 1976. The Domestication Process in Sub-Saharan Africa with Special Reference to Ethiopia. In: HIGGS, E. (ed.), *Colloque XX: origine de l'élevage et de la domestication.* Nice. (IX Congrès de l'UISPP, Nice.)

CLARK, J. G. D. 1965. Radiocarbon Dating and the Spread of Farming Economy. *Antiquity*, Vol. 39, pp. 45–8.

CLOSE, A. E. 1984. Current Research and Recent Radiocarbon Dates from Northern Africa II. *J. Afr. Hist.*, Vol. 25, pp. 1–24.

COON, C. S. 1971. *The Hunting Peoples.* Boston.

DAMP, J. E. 1984. Environmental Variation, Agriculture, and Settlement Process in Coastal Ecuador (3300–1500 BC). *Curr. Anthropol.*, Vol. 25, pp. 106–11.

DAMP, J. E.; PEARSALL, D. M.; KAPLAN, L. T. 1981. Beans for Valdivia. *Science* (Washington), Vol. 212, pp. 811–12.

DOWNING, A. J. 1869. *The Fruits and Fruit Trees of America.* New York.

DRUCKER, P. 1963. *Indians of the Northwest Coast.* Garden City, NY.

EVANS, J. D. 1968. Knossos Neolithic, Part II. *Ann. Br. Sch. Archaeol. Athens* (London), Vol. 63, pp. 239–76.

FLANNERY, K. V. 1968. Archaeological Systems Theory and Early Mesoamerica. In: MEGGERS, B. J. (ed.), *Anthropological Archaeology in the Americas.* Washington, DC. pp. 67–87.

GLADSTONES, J. S. 1970. Lupins as Crop Plants. *Field Crop Abstr.* (Farnham Royal), Vol. 23, pp. 123–48.

—— 1980. Recent Developments in the Understanding, Improvement and Use of *Lupinus.* In: SUMMERFIELD, R. J.; BUNTING, A. H. (eds), *Advances in Legume Science.* Kew. pp. 603–11.

GLOVER, I. C. 1977. The Late Stone Age in Eastern Indonesia. *World Archaeol.*, Vol. 9, pp. 42–61.

GODWIN, H. 1965. The Beginnings of Agriculture in Northwest Europe. In: HUTCHINSON, J. (ed.), *Essays on Crop Plant Evolution*, Cambridge. pp. 1–22.

GOLSON, J. 1971. Australian Aboriginal Food Plants: Some Ecological and Culture – Historical Implications. In: MULVANEY, D. J.; GOLSON, J. (eds), *Aboriginal Man and Environment in Australia.* Canberra. pp. 196–238.

—— 1984. New Guinea Agricultural History: A Case Study. In: DENOON, D.; SNOWDEN, G. (eds), *A Time to Plant and a Time to Uproot: A History of Agriculture in Papua New Guinea.* Institute of Papua New Guinea Studies. pp. 55–64.

GORMAN, C. 1969. Hoabinhian: A Pebble-Tool Complex with Early Plant Associations in Southeast Asia. *Science* (Washington), Vol. 163, pp. 671–3.

GREY, G. 1841. *Journals of Two Expeditions of Discovery in Northwest and Western Australia during the Years 1837, 38 and 39.* London. 2 vols.

HANSEN, J.; RENFREW, J. M. 1978. Palaeolithic–Neolithic Seed Remains at Franchthi Cave, Greece. *Nature* (London), Vol. 271, pp. 349–52.

HARLAN, J. R. 1967. A Wild Wheat Harvest in Turkey. *Archaeology* (New York), Vol. 20, pp. 197–201.

—— 1971. Agricultural Origins: Centers and Noncenters. *Science* (Washington), Vol. 174, pp. 468–74.

—— 1975. *Crops and Man.* Madison.

—— 1981. Ecological Settings for the Emergence of Agriculture. In: THRESH, J. M. (eds), *Pests, Pathogens and Vegetation.* London. pp. 3–22.

—— 1982. The Origins of Indigenous African Agriculture. In: CLARK, J. D. (ed.), *Cambridge History of Africa,* Vol. I: *From Earliest Times to c.500 BC.* Cambridge. pp. 624–57.

HARLAN, J. R.; DE WET, J. M. J.; PRICE, E. G. 1973. Comparative Evolution of Cereals. *Evolution,* Vol. 27, pp. 311–25.

HARLAN, J. R.; DE WET, J. M. J.; STEMLER, A. (eds) 1976. *The Origins of African Plant Domestication.* The Hague.

HARRINGTON, J. P. 1932. Tobacco among the Karuk Indians of California. *Bul. Smithson. Inst. Bur. Am. Ethnol.* (Washington), Vol. 94, p. 284.

HEDRICK, V. P. 1922. *Cyclopedia of Hardy Fruits.* New York.

HEISER, C. B. 1979. Origins of Some Cultivated New World Plants. *Annu. Rev. Ecol. Syst.* (Palo Alto), Vol. 10, pp. 309–26.

HELBAEK, H. 1966. Commentary on the Phylogenesis of *Triticum* and *Hordeum. Econ. Bot.* (Lancaster, Pa.), Vol. 20, pp. 350–60.

—— 1969. Plant Collecting, Dry-Farming, and Irrigation Agriculture in Prehistoric Deh Luran. In: HOLE, F.; FLANNERY, K. V.; NEELY, J. A. *Prehistory and Human Ecology of the Deh Luran Plain: An Early Village Sequence from Khuzistan, Iran.* Ann Arbor. pp. 383–426. (Mem. Mus. Anthropol., Univ. Mich., I.)

HIGHAM, C. F. W.; KIJNGAM, A.; MANLY, B. F. J. 1982. Site Location and Site Hierarchy in Prehistoric Thailand. *Proc. Prehist. Soc.,* Vol. 48, pp. 1–27.

HILLMAN, G. 1975. Plant Remains from Tell Abu Hureyra. *Proc. Prehist. Soc.,* Vol. 41, pp. 80–3.

HILU, K. W.; DE WET, J. M. J. 1980. Effect of Artificial Selection on Grain Dormancy in *Eleusine* (Gramineae). *Syst. Bot. Monogr.* (Ann Arbor), Vol. 5, pp. 54–60.

HO, PING-TI. 1977. The Indigenous Origins of Chinese Agriculture. In: REED, C. A. (ed.), *The Origins of Agriculture.* The Hague. pp. 413–84.

HOPF, M. 1969. Plant Remains and Early Farming at Jericho. In: UCKO, P. J.; DIMBLEBY, G. W. (eds), *The Domestication and Exploitation of Plants and Animals.* Chicago. pp. 355–60.

HUTTERER, K. L. 1983. The Natural and Cultural History of Southeast Asian Agriculture: Ecological and Evolutionary Considerations. *Anthropos,* Vol. 78, pp. 169–212.

JARDIN, C. 1967. *List of Foods Used in Africa.* Rome, FAO.

JARRIGE, J. F.; MEADOW, R. H. 1980. The Antecedents of Civilization in the Indus Valley. *Sci. Am.,* Vol. 243, No. 2, pp. 122–32.

KAPLAN, L.; LYNCH, T. F.; SMITH, C. E., JR. 1973. Early Cultivated Beans (*Phaseolus vulgaris*) from an Intermontane Peruvian Valley. *Science* (Washington), Vol. 179, pp. 76–7.

KLIMEK, S. 1935. Culture Element Distributions: I. The Structure of California Indian Culture. *Am. Archaeol. Ethnol.* (Berkeley), Vol. 37, pp. 1–70.

LATHRAP, D. W. 1968. The 'Hunting' Economies of the Tropical Forest Zone of South America: An Attempt at Historical Perspective. In: LEE, R. B.; DE VORE, I. (eds), *Man the Hunter.* Chicago. pp. 23–9.

LAWTON, H. W. et al. 1976. Agriculture among the Paiute of Owens Valley. *J. Calif. Anthropol.* (Banning, Calif.), Vol. 3, pp. 13–50.

LEVI-STRAUSS, C. 1950. The Use of Wild Plants in Tropical South America. In: STEWARD, J. (ed.), *Handbook of South American Indians.* Washington, DC. Vol. 6, pp. 465–86. (Bull. Smithson. Inst. Bur. Am. Ethnol., Vol. 143.)

LOURANDOS, H. 1980. Change or Stability? Hydraulics, Hunter-Gatherers, and Population in Temperate Australia. *World Archaeol.,* Vol. 11, pp. 245–64.

MACNEISH, R. S. 1958. Preliminary Archaeological Investigations in the Sierra de Tamaulipas, Mexico. *Trans. Am. Phil. Soc.* (Philadelphia, Pa.), NS, Vol. 48, No. 6.

—— 1967. Summary of the Subsistence. In: BYERS, D. S. (ed.), *The Prehistory of the Tehuacan Valley,* Vol. I: *Environment and Subsistence.* Austin. pp. 290–309.

MCCARTHY, F. D. 1957. *Australia's Aborigines, Their Life and Culture.* Melbourne.

MOORE, A. M. T. 1982. Agricultural Origins in the Near East: A Model for the 1980s. *World Archaeol.,* Vol. 14, pp. 224–36.

MURDOCK, G. P. 1959. *Africa, Its Peoples and their Culture History.* New York.

NOY, T.; LEGGE, A. J.; HIGGS, E. S. 1973. Recent Excavations at Nahal Oren, Israel. *Proc. Prehist. Soc.,* Vol. 39, pp. 75–99.

PERROT, J. 1966. Le Gisement Natoufien de Mallaha (Eynan), Israel. *Anthropologie* (Paris), Vol. 70, pp. 437–84.

PHILLIPSON, D. W. 1977. The Excavation of Gobedra Rock-Shelter, Axum: An Early Occurrence of Cultivated Finger Millet in Northern Ethiopia. *Azania* (Nairobi), Vol. 12, pp. 53–82.

—— 1982. Early Food Production in Sub-Saharan Africa. In: CLARK, J. D. (ed.), *Cambridge History of Africa,* Vol. I: *From Earliest Times to c.500 BC.* Cambridge. pp. 770–829.

PICKERSGILL, B.; HEISER, C. B. JR, 1977. Origins and Distribution of Plants Domesticated in the New World Tropics. In: REED, C. A. (ed.), *Origins of Agriculture.* The Hague. pp. 803–35.

PORTÈRES, R. 1951. Géographie alimentaire, berceaux agricoles et migration des plantes cultivées en Afrique intertropicale. *C. R. Soc. Biogéogr.* (Paris), No. 239, pp. 16–21.

RENFREW, C. 1970. Tree-ring Calibration of Radiocarbon: An Archaeological Evaluation. *Proc. Prehist. Soc.,* Vol. 36, pp. 280–311.

RENFREW, J. M. 1969. The Archaeological Evidence for the Domestication of Plants: Methods and Problems. In: UCKO, P. J.; DIMBLEBY, G. W. (eds), *The Domestication and Exploitation of Plants and Animals.* Chicago. pp. 149–72.

—— 1979. The First Farmers in South East Europe. In: KÖRBER-GROHNE, U. (ed.), *Festschrift Maria Hopf.* Cologne. pp. 243–65.

ROWE, J. H.; MENZEL, D. 1967. *Peruvian Archaeology.* Palo Alto, Calif.

SAUER, C. O. 1952. *Agricultural Origins and Dispersals.* Cambridge, Mass.

SHARMA, G. R. 1983. Beginnings of Agriculture: New Light on the Transformations from Hunting and Food Gathering to the Domestication of Plants and Animals. *J. Cent. Asia* (Islamabad), Vol. 6, No. I, pp. 51–64.

SHAW, T. 1976. Early Crops in Africa: A Review of the Evidence. In: HARLAN, J. R.; DE WET, J. M. J.; STEMLER, A. B. L. (eds), *Origins of African Plant Domestication.* The Hague. pp. 107–53.

—— 1977. Hunters, Gatherers and First Farmers in West Africa. In: MEGAW, J. V. S. (ed.), *Hunters, Gatherers and First Farmers beyond Europe.* Leicester. pp. 69–125.

STEWARD, J. H. 1934. Ethnography of the Owens Valley Paiute. *Am. Archaeol. and Ethnol.* (Berkeley), Vol. 33, pp. 233–340.

—— 1941. Culture Element Distributions: XIII Nevada Shoshoni. *Univ. Calif. Anthropol. Rec.,* Vol. 4, pp. 209–359.

STOTHERS, D. M.; YARNELL, R. A. 1977. An Agricultural Revolution in the Lower Great Lakes. In: ROMANS, R. C. (ed.), *Geobotany.* New York. pp. 209–32.

SUN, XIANG-JUN; DU, NAI-QIU; CHEN, MING-HONG. 1981. The Paleovegetation and Paleoclimate during Time of Homudu People. *Acta Bot. Sin.* (Beijing), Vol. 23, No. 2, pp. 146–51.

TINDALE, N. B. 1974. *Aboriginal Tribes of Australia.* Berkeley.

VAVILOV, N. I. 1926. *Studies on the Origin of Cultivated Plants.* Leningrad, Inst. Appl. Bot. Genet. Pl. Breed.

VEGA, G. DE LA. 1961. *The Royal Commentaries of the Inca Garcilaso de la vega.* New York.

VISHNU-MITTRE. 1977. Changing Economy in Ancient India. In: REED, C. A. (ed.), *Origins of Agriculture.* The Hague. pp. 569–88.

WALKER, D. 1972. *Bridge and Barrier: The Natural and Cultural History of Torres Strait.* Canberra.

WHITE, J. P. 1971. New Guinea and Australian Prehistory: The Neolithic Problem. In: MULVANEY, D. J.; GOLSON, J. (eds), *Aboriginal Man and Environment in Australia*. Canberra. pp. 182–85.

WILHELM, S. 1974. The Garden Strawberry: A Study of its Origin. *Am. Sci.* (New Haven), Vol. 62, pp. 264–71.

YANOVSKY, E. 1936. *Food Plants of the North American Indians.* (USDA Misc. Publ., 237.)

ZEIST, W. VAN. 1972. Palaeobotanical Results of the 1970 Season at Cayönü, Turkey. *Helinium* (Wetteren), Vol. 12, pp. 1–19.

—— 1976. On Macroscopic Traces of Food Plants in Southwestern Asia (With Some Reference to Pollen Data). *Phil. Trans. R. Soc.* (London), B, Vol. 275, pp. 27–41.

ZEIST, W. VAN; BAKKER-HEERES, J. A. H. 1979. Some Economic and Ecological Aspects of the Plant Husbandry of Tell Aswad. *Paléorient*, Vol. 5, pp. 161–7.

ZEIST, W. VAN; BOTTEMA, S. 1966. Palaeobotanical Investigations at Ramad. *Ann. archéol. arab. syr.*, Vol. 16, pp. 179–80.

ZEIST, W. VAN; CASPARIE, W. A. 1968. Wild Einkorn and Barley from Tel Mureybet in Northern Syria. *Acta Bot. Neerl.* (Amsterdam), Vol. 17, pp. 45–55.

38

DOMESTICATION OF ANIMALS

from the beginnings of food production up to about 5,000 years ago
An overview

Sandor Bökönyi

THE DEFINITION OF DOMESTICATION

The essence of the Neolithic is not the changeover from chipped to polished stone or the absence or presence of pottery but the changeover from hunting, fishing and collecting to food production. This economic transformation was the most important element of the 'Neolithic revolution', a term introduced by V. G. Childe (1957) by which he signified a qualitative change not only in the tools but also in the productive forces of society as a whole and thus in the means of social production although without the appearance of a new form of society.

One of the crucial elements of the Neolithic revolution was the domestication of animals and plants that made possible this transformation, the essence of which was the shift from hunting, fishing and gathering to food production: from the simple exploitation of nature to active involvement in reproduction through plant cultivation and animal breeding.

With domestication (from now on in this chapter this expression means animal domestication) individuals of species with certain psychological characteristics are captured and tamed, taken out of their natural habitat and breeding community, kept and bred under human control and for human benefit, though they are given food and protection at the same time (Bökönyi, 1969, p. 219).

It is a long and complicated process. Animal domestication was the culmination of experience and knowledge gained through tens of thousands of generations of hunting, about the anatomy, biology, physiology, behaviour and so on of a number of wild animal species. The domestication itself was not a process that occurred from one animal generation to the other but took several and sometimes up to thirty generations.

Looking more closely at the above definition, we see that its first point is that for domestication, animals had to be captured. According to both antique sources and modern experiments only young animals could be domesticated, so it was these that had to be captured. However, in European and western Asian sites where large-scale domestication of one or more species was being carried out, one finds almost exclusively bones of adult individuals from the wild species under domestication. The explanation is quite simple: the young individuals were not killed but captured, but the adult

ones had to be killed, both for their meat and because they tried to protect their young.

After capture, the animals had to be tamed because only in this way could they be kept. Keeping aggressive animals would be dangerous. In most cases it was not a particularly difficult job for, with enough patience and by giving each animal individual treatment, every young wild animal – including carnivores – can be tamed, though this taming does not necessarily develop into true domestication.

An absolutely essential part of the above definition is that only individuals of species with special psychological characteristics can be domesticated. One may well ask what makes one species domesticable and prevents another from being domesticated. The answer is not simple. First of all, domesticable species are herd animals, although not all of them can be domesticated. Every one of our domestic species is a herd animal, the only exception being the cat, which is a solitary animal and as such has not become as fully domesticated as the others, retaining a lot of its independence. It is a fact that herd animals join more easily to a new breeding community (such as a domestic herd) or even to humans. Nevertheless, not every herd animal is a good subject for domestication. Old Egyptian representations prove that unsuccessful attempts at domesticating several antelope species (all of them herd animals) were carried out there.

In fact, the domesticability of different herd animal species is not all connected with their systematic position. For instance, the aurochs (the wild ancestor of our domestic cattle) and the bison are both systematically and osteologically very close to each other: in spite of this, of the two only the aurochs could be domesticated. The case is similar with the four subgenera (horses, asses, half-asses and zebras) of equids: the first two alone could be domesticated. As far as it can be seen now, in the domesticable species some key psychological feature or features are present, or conversely are missing, but nobody knows what these are.

With domestication, humans take certain individuals out of the typical habitat and breeding community of the species in question. The habitat is the ideal living place for the species determined by soil, climate, vegetation, competing species, predators and so on. The domesticating human takes the animals out of these and puts them into basically different new environmental types. Something similar happens to domesticated animals, when humans remove them from their original breeding community, the small herd, and keep them in large herds, under new genetic conditions (using a primitive type of breeding selection through the early introduction of castration, eliminating natural selection and so on). By keeping and breeding the domesticated animals under their own control, humans basically change the social and sexual structure of the wild forms.

The crucial point of the above definition is, however, that humans breed, and thus propagate, the captured animals. And this is the main difference between taming and domestication: while the former refers only to one individual (which nevertheless can come from any species), the latter supposes breeding in captivity. And without this, domestication cannot exist.

And finally it is quite obvious that humans kept their own benefit in mind first and foremost when they domesticated animals, though at the same time they provided them with food and protection. Domestication was not a pastime for humans, but the consequence of hard economic necessity; it is therefore not at all surprising that they wanted to enjoy its benefits; but it is also true that the animals in question enjoyed its benefits too. In fact some of the species would not have survived without domestication. One can thus consider domestication to be a special kind of long symbiosis between human beings and certain animal species. From domestication animal husbandry arose. In its development it has two main phases: (1) animal keeping and (2) animal breeding.

Animal keeping is a primitive, initial form of animal husbandry in which conscious breeding is missing and feeding is both qualitatively and quantitatively unsatisfactory. Its main characteristics are as follows: (1) in a population there exists only one breed, although it is very variable; (2) the domestic animals are of primitive type and their size falls far below that of their wild form. Nevertheless a certain kind of primitive breeding selection existed in this phase too, for instance through the introduction of the castration of bulls and the killing of rams, bucks and boars, mainly at a young age, certain individuals were *ab ovo* excluded from breeding already by Neolithic times. But this does not seem to have been conscious selection aimed at higher productivity (more meat, milk, draught power, speed, more or finer wool and so on), since such effects cannot be observed in early periods.

How this unconscious selection functioned can be seen in Table 14.

Table 14 Age and sex group frequencies of faunal remains from an Early and Middle Neolithic site at Anzabegovo (former Yugoslavia). (After Bökönyi, 1976b, p. 15.)

Age	Sex No. (% killed)			
	Female	Male	Undetermined	Total
Juvenile	0 (0)	33 (64.7)	4 (66.7)	37 (44.1)
Subadult	22 (81.5)	14 (27.5)	1 (16.5)	37 (44.1)
Adult	5 (18.5)	4 (7.8)	1 (16.7)	10 (11.9)
Undetermined	43 (–)	19 (–)	4 (–)	66 (–)
Total	70	70	10	150

This clearly demonstrates that the breeders did not kill any juvenile female, while at the same time they killed about two-thirds of the males at that age. Most of the females were killed in their subadulthood (between one and two years) when they could be used once for lambing. At this age a quarter of the males were killed, and less than 10 per cent of the males in comparison with almost 20 per cent of the females reached their adult age to form the precious breeding stock. Similar phenomena can be observed in other Neolithic sites.

The second phase, animal breeding, was based on conscious breeding selection and satisfactory feeding in both the quantitative and qualitative meaning of the word. Animal breeding started at that time when people first began to handle domestic animals as individuals and not as a herd. Its main characteristics are: (1) in a population there are several breeds living together; (2) the size of the animals increases in certain breeds (horse, hen and so on), exceeding even that of their wild forms, while at the same time dwarf breeds can also appear; and (3) the productivity of domestic animals also increases.

The main cause of animal domestication undoubtedly was the drastic decrease in wild stock after the end of the Pleistocene, although whether it was connected with a period of desiccation or not is still an open question. Animal domestication was closely connected with settled life as were other components of the Neolithic revolution. Nevertheless, settled life was not an indispensable precondition for animal domestication. It can also happen – and in fact did – without settled life, but only under extreme environmental conditions, for instance in the case of reindeer domestication by northern nomads; in such circumstances, however, real animal husbandry with a wide range of domesticated species could not develop at all or rarely did so.

It seems to be impossible to answer the question whether settled life made animal domestication possible, or vice versa. It is not impossible that both are true: one can hardly imagine that keeping, taming and breeding a large number of wild animals could have taken place without corrals or some primitive kind of stalls, and such structures would presuppose a temporarily settled life at least. And what is more, supplying a larger, settled community with food is hardly imaginable without animal domestication and stock-keeping or at least their forerunner, the control of herds of domesticable wild species.

At the same time it is quite obvious that demographic pressure also played an essential part in animal domestication as one of the main factors in the development of food production.

For the increase of human population necessarily brought about changes in technology and one such basic change was the domestication of animals. Other causes, like political pressure from developed communities, the attraction of the products of groups who were already producing food or simply the copying of new customs, were only of secondary or tertiary importance in this respect.

Nevertheless, it cannot be explained why one hunting group should have domesticated animals and another group practising the same type of hunting should not. The difference may be in the social-cultural state of the two peoples (Down, 1960, p. 42) or in the frequency of the hunted species.

The main aim of domestication was that people wanted to make themselves independent from the chanciness of hunting, which had become more and more unreliable along with the decrease in the numbers of wild animals around human settlements. In this respect the first domestic animals were nothing but living food reserves which could be used any time when it was necessary. (At the same time people were able to invest and accumulate capital in the form of domestic animals.) The fact that the wild ancestors of four out of the five Neolithic domestic animals (wild sheep, bezoar goat, wild boar and aurochs) had already been hunted for their meat before domestication, and that the meat of all five Neolithic domestic species was eaten, clearly proves this.

Nevertheless there could be other reasons for the domestication of animals, one of the strongest being their potential use as sacrificial animals. The use of domestic cattle as a sacrificial animal replacing the wild aurochs can excellently be demonstrated in the ninth to eighth millennium BP in Çatal Hüyük, Anatolia (Mellaart, 1967) and early domestic dogs were also used as sacrificial animals some thousand years later in Lepenski Vir in the Iron Gates gorge of the Danube (Srejovic, 1966, 1972; Bökönyi, 1970, p. 1703), while dogs had already been placed in human graves in the Magdalenian of central Europe (Nobis, 1981, p. 49, 1984, p. 73) or the Natufian of Palestine (Davis and Valla, 1978, p. 608).

There were several ways that all led to (not necessarily successful) domestication. These include the keeping of pets, a very ancient practice that persists today, and the keeping of pronghorn antelopes by American Indians which never resulted in a true domestication (Down, 1960, p. 43). The seemingly most efficient form of hunting, which led in many cases to domestication, was the specialized kind where humans followed one or more herds of an animal species (Pohlhausen, 1953, pp. 67 ff.) on their seasonal wanderings, protecting them from their natural enemies (including other human hunter groups). In fact the hunters considered such herds their own property and began to husband with them by regulating their hunting first of all through the killing of the superfluous males. Later, humans tried to limit the seasonal wanderings of the herd or herds, but never attempted to force them to leave their natural habitat. This was probably the time when they began to capture, tame and domesticate young individuals. To prove this model one can find enough examples for cattle in the Hungarian Middle and Late Neolithic (Bökönyi, 1959, pp. 80 ff., 1969, p. 222, 1974, p. 29) and for goat in the Early Neolithic of Iran (Bökönyi, 1973a, pp. 71 ff., 1977, p. 20).

CHANGES CAUSED BY DOMESTICATION

In defining domestication (p. 389) we have already pointed out that it was a special kind of symbiosis in which both partners significantly influenced each other. In this respect, human influence was stronger, so the domestic animals underwent considerable changes. These changes, which were first studied in detail by Darwin (1868), show that with domestication a series of new stresses affected the species in question and caused changes never known before. In fact there is not a part or organ of the animals that would not have responded to these stresses.

With domestication the variability of animals in comparison to that of their wild forms enormously increases. This can be seen in every species, and is the basis of that richness of breeds that can be observed in many domestic species. Darwin already knew of more than 150 breeds of domestic pigeon, while today dog breeds number over 300 and breeds of domestic rabbit over 500. One must add that the speed of evolution has considerably increased through

domestication, resulting in a much quicker development of new varieties. Likewise, the occurrence of mutations has become more frequent, causing radical changes or creating basically new exploitation types in domestic animals.

Probably the most interesting group of changes caused by domestication comprises the so-called parallel changes that occurred in all or at least several domestic animal species. These include a decrease in size (on this basis one can reliably distinguish the bones of early domestic animals from those of wild ones in prehistoric sites) and a change in body proportions, with a shortening of the skull (sometimes connected with a concave profile line), particularly of its facial part, along with the crowding of the premolar teeth (and the disappearance of the first lower premolar on the last column, with a size decrease in the third lower molar). Other changes are a twisting of the horns, the complete disappearance of horns, changes in the form and fine structure of bones, a refining of the skin connected with general or local fat accumulation and a refinement of the hair along with the disappearance of pigmentation or, conversely, appearance of different coloration types. The most important change in this latter respect is the appearance of long wool, caused by a sudden mutation that stopped the yearly change of wool fibres. Many changes were caused by domestication to the internal organs, in their biology, physiology, psychology, behaviour and even their pathology (there are certain diseases that are connected with domestication).

EARLIEST ANIMAL DOMESTICATION IN EUROPE AND SOUTH-WEST ASIA

Today it is more and more obvious that domestication did not begin in one single centre. On the contrary, as soon as humankind reached a certain level of cultural and economic development in an area, it began the domestication of the locally available wild animal species. This means that centres of domestication could exist in different places at the same time. Each domestic species could be domesticated anywhere and in several places within the area of distribution of its wild form, and what is considered to be the place of the earliest domestication of a given domestic animal species can easily be so simply as the result of more thorough archaeological exploration there or just of lucky finds. Another problem is that domestication did not end with the acquisition of the first domestic animals. It played an essential part in the increase of the domestic stock during the whole of the Neolithic and existed even in later prehistoric periods, as well as medieval times, particularly when epidemics decimated or completely destroyed the domestic stock of a species in a given region. In fact, domestication is still being carried out in certain parts of the world.

For a long time it was an axiom that animal domestication had started at the dawn of the Neolithic, but recently more and more data have emerged which show that the earliest traces of domestication went back as far as the Mesolithic or even the Late Palaeolithic. Nevertheless, it is also true that in both these early periods these were isolated attempts to tame and keep individuals of a particular animal species, but these never led to true animal husbandry and the keeping of several domestic species. The common characteristic of these attempts was that their subject was the dog or (rarely) the pig, two species whose food requirements were very similar to those of humans and which consequently could survive on kitchen remnants (Turnbull and Reed, 1974, pp. 84 ff.;

Table 15 Species frequencies in Early Neolithic faunas of southern Europe. Greece: 1, Argissa Magula; 2, Nea Nikomedia; 3, Knossos; 4, Achilleion. Former Yugoslavia: 5, Anzabegovo I–III; 6, Divostin; 7, Lepenski Vir III; 8, Mihajlovac–Knjepište; 9, Nosa–Gyöngypart; 10, Ludaz–Budžak. Hungary: 11, Endröd-35; 12, Endröd-39; 13, Szarvas-8; 14, Szarvas-23; 15, Röszke-Ludvár; 16, Szolnok-Szanda; 17, Szentpéterszeg. Southern Italy: 18, Scaloria cave; 19, Rendina; Southern France: 20, Grotte de St Pierre de la Fage.

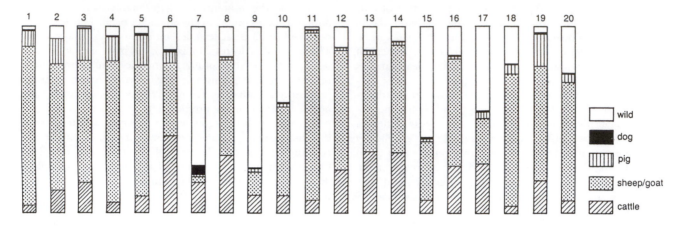

Bökönyi, 1976a, p. 20; Nobis, 1984, p. 74). In fact they were dead-ends in the history of domestication, because the fact that they needed the same food as humans became an obstacle to their domestication on a large scale.

In the Old World, south-west Asia was an ideal nuclear area for the beginning of domestication for a number of reasons:

1 the wild forms of all five Neolithic domestic species lived there;
2 particularly important was that wild sheep and goats were present there, because these two species were the best subjects for experiments in domestication, since (a) they were ruminants and could thus survive on fodder rich in cellulose (straw and hay as by-products of early agriculture), thus producing meat from a food that could not be used either by humans or by dog and pig; (b) they were small-sized animals and their capture and keeping did not involve serious dangers for humans; and (c) their undemanding feeding habits are unprecedented even among ruminants, which could be a very valuable feature in the circumstances of primitive animal husbandry;
3 in south-west Asia the wild forms of cereals were also present and their cultivation started at about the same time as animal domestication, and the two processes went hand in hand there. As a matter of fact, the domestication of three out of the five Neolithic domesticates – dog, cattle and pig – could have happened in other areas where their wild forms also lived, for example in Europe (Table 15), but owing to the lack of cultural–economic development it did not, except for some early attempts at domesticating the dog.

According to our most recent knowledge, the domestication of the five Neolithic domestic animal species happened in the following order. First the dog was domesticated, its wild ancestor being the wolf (Map 38); the site that has yielded the earliest dog bones is the Palegawra cave in north-east Iraq and the period of domestication was the terminal Pleistocene Zarzian about 14,000 years ago (Turnbull and Reed, 1974, pp. 84 ff.). The earliest possibly domesticated sheep (Map 39) have been found in Zawi Chemi Shanidar, again in north-east Iraq, from the early eleventh millennium BP (Perkins, 1964, pp. 1565 ff.), but the earliest undoubtedly domesticated sheep remains came from Ali Kosh, western Iran, about 9,500 to 8,750 years ago (Hole and Flannery, 1967, pp. 171 ff.).

Two sites in western Iran, Asiab and Ganj Dareh of the Kermanshah valley, have produced the remains of the earliest domestic goats (Map 39) from the tenth millennium BP (Bökönyi, 1973a, pp. 71 ff., 1977, pp. 19 ff.; Perkins, 1973, pp. 279 ff.), but domestic goats were found certainly in Jericho (Clutton-Brock, 1971, pp. 48 ff.) and probably in Ali Kosh (Hole and Flannery, 1967, pp. 171 ff.), also in the same period. In contrast to these three species, the earliest domestic pigs (Map 40) were found in Qala'at Jarmo, north-east Iraq, about 8,750 years ago (Stampfli, 1983, p. 454) and the first domesticated cattle (Map 40) appeared in Çatal Hüyük, Anatolia, about 8,400 years ago (Perkins, 1969, pp. 177 ff.).

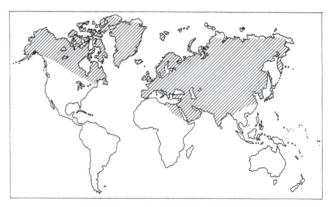

Map 38 Area of distribution of the wolf.

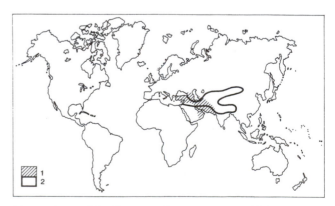

Map 39 Areas of distribution: 1, bezoar goat; 2, wild sheep.

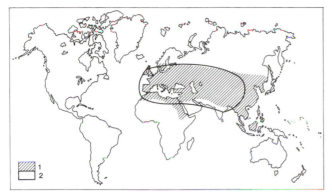

Map 40 Areas of distribution: 1, wild boar; 2, aurochs.

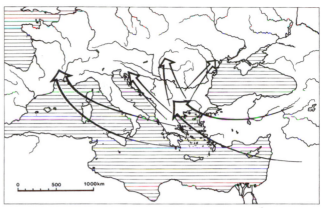

Map 42 Expansion of caprovine-based animal husbandry in southern Europe in the Early Neolithic.

These data together mean that by the middle of the ninth millennium BP all five domestic animal species had already been acquired. They were found in different combinations, but the five did not appear together as far as is now known, before 8,000 years ago (Map 41) (Bökönyi, 1976a, p. 22; 1978, p. 57; 1983, p. 27).

Interestingly enough, this complete Neolithic domestic fauna containing all five domestic species appeared in south-east Europe some 500 years earlier, around 8,500 years ago (Map 42). This seems something of a contradiction, because this earliest European animal husbandry is clearly of south-west Asian origin since its leading species, the caprovines (sheep and goat), could only be domesticated there. The solution to the problem may lie in two points: (1) we know nothing about the Pre-pottery Neolithic domestic fauna of western Anatolia, which was the part of south-west Asia with the strongest connections with the Early Neolithic of south-east Europe; (2) there must be some confusion in the radiocarbon dates, because the earliest pottery Neolithic cultures of south-west Asia certainly preceded those of south-east Europe, although their radiocarbon dates are lower than those of the European ones.

Anyway, the earliest complete animal husbandry in south-west Asia was primarily based on caprovines, which form the overwhelming majority of the domestic stock in every site. This is not surprising, because here they had optimun environmental conditions, whereas cattle needed richer pastures and pigs water in abundance. At the beginning, the frequencies of sheep versus goat were varied according to the geographical situation: in plains and hilly regions sheep were more abundant, while in mountains goats were more common. Later, however, sheep generally outnumbered goats because of two advantages they had: they provided wool and they were able to withstand heat much better than goats.

There was wide variation in the success this kind of animal husbandry enjoyed in the different regions of south-west Asia. It flourished in fertile valleys, along major rivers and in piedmonts of large mountains. In such areas hunting was hardly needed in order to make the animal protein diet of humans complete. In the mountains themselves, where the environmental circumstances were harder, animal husbandry was less successful and people had to hunt more. Under the extremely harsh conditions of salty steppes hunting on a large scale was obligatory, in spite of having the complete range of domestic fauna (Bökönyi, 1977).

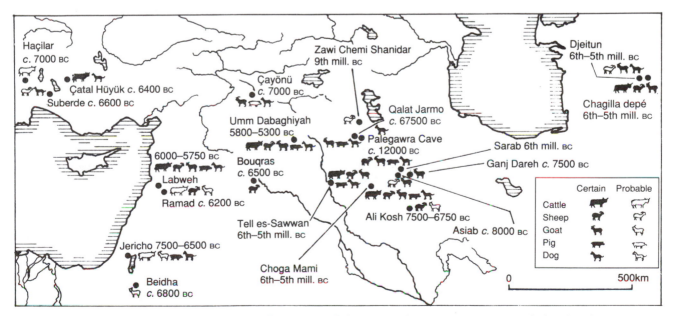

Map 41 Early occurrences of domestic animals in south-west Asia (all the dates on this map are given in years before the Christian era). (Mill. – millennia/millennium.)

THE EARLIEST DOMESTIC FAUNA OF EUROPE (Table 15)

The earliest domestic fauna of Europe, which appeared in the south of the Balkans in the middle of the ninth millennium BP, was very similar to that of early south-west Asia: caprovines made up as much as 75 to 80 per cent of the domestic stock, followed by much smaller numbers of pig and cattle, and dog was always the least common. From the start the western Asian origins of this animal husbandry meant that it included a high frequency of caprovines, and the similarity of the environment of Greece (where this domestic fauna first appeared) merely reinforced this. In that hot and dry environment this animal husbandry could not only survive but could develop further, too. As a result it was able to provide enough food of animal origin for the human population and it was hardly necessary for these people to hunt or fish in order to get enough animal protein. This is clearly shown by the fact that in early Greek Neolithic sites the number of wild animal and fish bones is always very low (Boessneck, 1962; Higgs, 1962; Jarman and Jarman, 1968, Bökönyi, 1973b, 1974, 1983).

This caprovine-based animal husbandry started its advance to the north-east and west as early as the second half of the ninth millennium BP, probably helped by the 'climatic optimum' of that period, which meant that, since the average temperature was 3 to 4 °C higher, southern forms easily extended into the southern territories of central and eastern Europe. Still, before the end of the ninth millennium BP this animal husbandry reached Macedonia (Bökönyi, 1976b) and in the middle of the eighth millennium BP the central part of former Yugoslavia (Bökönyi, 1976c) and Bulgaria (Dennel, 1972). There is a minor problem with the samples from former Yugoslavia, because in those sites the ratio of cattle bones was a little higher than those of caprovines. It was not possible to determine whether ethnic–cultural elements or a more forested environment were responsible for this situation, but the most recent excavations with very careful bone collecting proved that there was no difference between central former Yugoslavia and the neighbouring regions. Right before the end of the eighth millennium BP this type of animal husbandry arrived in the Carpathian Basin (Bökönyi, 1969, 1974, 1983) and reached Moldavia and the south-east Ukraine in the seventh millennium BP (Tringham, 1969). It is quite interesting that, while throughout the Balkans fully Neolithic animal husbandry was flourishing, in inaccessible places like the Iron Gates gorge of the Danube the surviving Mesolithic population was still living by hunting and gathering, and only made isolated attempts at dog or pig domestication (Bökönyi, 1970, 1975, 1978; Bolomey, 1973).

Westwards, animal husbandry occurred in southern Italy in the seventh millennium BP (Bökönyi, 1977, p. 82, 1983) and in southern France around 6,000 years ago (Poulain-Josien, 1975, 1978; Bökönyi, 1983), reaching eastern Spain a little later.

These regions were the northernmost points attained by this animal husbandry of basically western Asian character. Parts of Europe located north or north-west of these regions could only acquire domestic animals by importing them from these regions, but certainly they very quickly did so because all five Neolithic domestic species were to be found throughout the temperate belt of Europe in the course of the sixth millennium BP.

In the meantime, interesting changes in animal husbandry were taking place in the southern part of Europe. It is well known that animal husbandry depends strongly on environmental conditions even now, so one can imagine just how strong this dependence was in the early phases of its development. In Greece the pattern of husbandry did not change much because the environment was favourable. But in the temperate zone of Europe caprovine-based animal husbandry was alien and incapable of further development. It was alien because its main species, the sheep and goat, did not find favourable conditions and consequently did not breed well there. It was incapable of further development because the wild forms of its leading species did not live on the European mainland and the stock of caprovines could therefore not be increased by local domestication. This was a crucial disadvantage, because under the primitive conditions of Neolithic animal husbandry the natural offspring of the domestic animals alone could not provide enough food for the growing human population and increase the numbers of domestic stock at the same time.

Thus humans had to base their economy in this region primarily on domestic animals that both were well suited to the environmental conditions of temperate Europe and also had locally domesticable wild forms. They found them in cattle and pigs, and at the end of the Early Neolithic they started the change-over to these latter species. From this time on, cattle and pig domestication grew enormously in importance in most parts of Europe. In certain regions, such as the Carpathian basin, real cattle-domestication centres developed. As a result the cattle population multiplied greatly and cattle became the leading species all over the temperate belt of Europe. Pig domestication never equalled that of cattle in importance, but despite this it was of considerable significance and made pigs as common as caprovines or even more important. This picture can be observed very well in the sites of the Bandkeramik culture and its related groups, where cattle generally took the leading part and pigs and caprovines alternately stood in second place.

Up to the end of the Early Neolithic, domestic animals had only one use (apart from their sporadic use as sacrificial animals, hunting companions, herd or watch dogs and so on): to supply meat. Then their secondary uses to provide milk, wool, draught power and so on were discovered. This was almost another 'revolutionary' step and started a 'domestication fever' in the second half of the Neolithic, when humans tried to increase the number of their domesticates by all means in their power (Bökönyi, 1971, p. 643; 1974, p. 27 ff., 1983, p. 32; Sherratt, 1983, pp. 90 ff.). The best examples of the large-scale domestication of the Late Neolithic can be found in the Tisza, Herpály and Lengyel cultures of the Carpathian basin in the sixth millennium BP.

The meat of all domestic animals, including that of the dog, was consumed, as is proved by the occurrence of skulls with opened brain-cases (brain was a delicacy even in those times) and of extremity bones broken for the marrow. In fact, people stopped eating dog flesh only at the end of the Bronze Age, and this was probably the first food avoidance in Europe.

Throughout the Neolithic cattle were the main meat suppliers even in areas where sheep and goat outnumbered them by far. One must not forget that the meat yield of a cow was equivalent to that of seven caprovines or four to five pigs. In this way, about 40 per cent of all domestic animal meat came from cattle, even in caprovine-dominated animal economies. In economies where cattle were most frequent this ratio could go up to 75 to 90 per cent. In the Early Neolithic caprovine meat was also important but from the

Middle Neolithic onward pork became the second most important meat after beef (Bökönyi, 1983, p. 14).

With that period the Neolithic development of animal husbandry came to an end. Animal husbandry was by now so well developed that hunting and domestication lost most of their importance. In addition, the increase in the human population brought about an increase in the land under cultivation, thus destroying the habitats of wild animals.

Among the domestic animals new species – horse and ass – appeared; these were intentionally domesticated for work. In addition, the first elements of conscious animal breeding occurred in Mesopotamia, which certainly influenced the animal husbandry of Europe too; though new methods were not adopted, there was an improvement of certain domestic species through new waves of improved breeds (sheep).

CHINA AND SOUTH-EAST ASIA

Our knowledge about the beginnings of animal domestication and early animal husbandry in this part of the world is rather scanty. Out of the five species of early domestication wolves, pigs and probably sheep had wild forms in China, and pigs in South-East Asia. At the same time, China had strong contacts with western Asia, while those of South-East Asia with the Indian subcontinent were much weaker and became stronger only from about the beginning of the first century of the Christian era (Higham, 1977, p. 387).

In China, in the earliest Neolithic cultures (Cishan, Peiligang and Dadiwan cultures, dated before the eighth millennium BP), pigs, dogs and chickens had already been domesticated (Chapter 46). In the following Early Neolithic Yangshao (Yang Shao) and Longshan (Lung Shan) cultures, as well as pigs, dogs and chickens, other domestic species appeared: cattle, sheep and goats (Watson, 1969, pp. 392 ff.; Ping-Ti Ho, 1977, pp. 413 ff.). In general, pigs were the most important domestic animals, although in some of the sites caprovines are not uncommon either. The high frequency of pigs may be a result of local domestication, though direct evidence of this has not yet been found there. In one of the Yangshao sites a horse tooth also was found, but this cannot give any evidence for the domesticated or non-domesticated status of the animal. In fact, it probably was the tooth of a wild Przevalsky horse of the area.

In South-East Asia the osteological evidence is particularly scanty. There, cattle seem to occur about 7,000 years ago, certainly around 5,000 years ago, and possible pig and dog keeping appears around 5,500 years ago (Higham, 1977, pp. 388, 405). Other domestic species were introduced later (from India or China or both), or were locally domesticated.

In South-East Asia and China the first domesticates were also meat animals. The abundant resources of the rain forests made it unnecessary for man to keep domestic stock; this is probably why domestication started there later and was of less significance than in south-west Asia. Exploration for secondary products probably began no earlier than the end of this initial phase.

THE UPPER NILE VALLEY AND THE EASTERN SAHARA

Nowadays when archaeological interest in north-east Africa is growing, data on animal domestication in that area have been increasing. In the light of these new evidences we have to abandon the old model that all domestic species of north-east Africa originated in south-west Asia. Although it is true for sheep, goat, dog and possibly pig, cattle were seemingly kept in the eastern Sahara from the period between 9,800 and 8,000 years ago (Krzyzaniak, 1981, p. 694; Gautier, 1984a, pp. 59 ff., 69 ff.; Wendorf and Schild, 1984, pp. 420 ff.). These cattle showed well-expressed changes in size caused by domestication.

The key to the problem lies in a climatic amelioration between 12,000 and 5,000 years ago, when the Sahel and Sudanic vegetation belts may have extended as much as 4 degrees north of their present limits. Nevertheless, wild cattle could not exist even under such circumstances in the desert, thus they must have been domesticated somewhere in the Nile valley in spite of the fact that the first appearance of domesticated cattle along the Nile is in the Predynastic period (Gautier, 1984a, p. 71; Wendorf and Schild, 1984, p. 422). According to Gautier's explanation, cattle might have been reintroduced along the Nile as a fully domesticated species when climatic deterioration forced desert cattle pastoralists into peripheral regions (Hassan et al., 1981, pp. 28 ff.). This may be true, but local cattle domestication from aurochs that survived up to Dynastic times cannot be excluded either. At any rate, this part of Africa became one of the most important centres of origin of humped cattle.

Shortly after cattle were domesticated the domestic dog also appeared (Gautier, 1984a, pp. 55 ff.), and in Middle Neolithic sites caprovines were also found (Krzyzaniak, 1981, p. 694). In the Predynastic period all five domestic species of the Neolithic were present at least in the Nile valley, where even pigs could find a reasonably good area for living (Gautier, 1984b, p. 47), but from that time on caprovines became the most common species in the animal husbandry because they best suited the increasingly arid climate.

At the end of the sixth millennium BP a new species, the donkey, completed the list of domesticates. It had a local wild form, the Nubian wild ass. While the earlier domestic animals were kept mainly for their meat or milk (cattle being kept probably for their milk and blood as they are today by the nomadic cattle keepers of Africa), the donkey probably belonged to the group of working animals, being used as a beast of burden.

SOUTH AMERICA

Apart from the dog, which is probably the earliest domestic animal of South America, wild llamas (camelids), the guanaco (*Lama guanicoe* Muller) and the vicuña (*Vicugna vicugna* Mol.), and the guinea-pig (*Cavia porcellus* L.) were domesticated, all three in the Peruvian Andes. Out of them the camelids are those whose domestication and history is best known.

According to Wing (1975, p. 302) the guanaco lives at over 3,000 m elevation, and the vicuña's habitat is the highest part of the mountains; therefore their domestication happened there. The domestication is signalled by the shift from cervids to camelids as prey (Wing, 1975, p. 305). First 'an intense use and beginnings of control of camelid herds' could be observed in the high elevation sites of the central Andes from 7,500 to 4,500 years ago, followed by real domestication around 6,000 years ago (Novoa and Wheeler, 1984, p. 123) or between 4,500 and 3,750 years ago (Wing, 1979, p. 212). The domesticated llamas were mainly kept in the valleys, and at the end of this period they and the guinea pig even reached the central Peruvian coast, thus arriving in ecological zones where their wild forms had never lived. The proofs of early domestication are (1) the appearance of alpaca-type incisors, (2) morphological changes in some lower molars and (3) the increase in the remains of new-born individuals (Novoa and Wheeler, 1984, pp. 123 ff.).

Breeders put different kinds of emphasis on domestic llama herds in different settlements, and this is very well reflected in the age structure. In sites with 56 per cent juveniles they were undoubtedly used as meat animals; in others with only 22 per cent they probably served as beasts of burden (Wing, 1975, pp. 306 ff.). The llama as pack animal can carry loads of 25 to 30 kg in a slow way over 15 to 20 km a day and today is still in use even for long-distance transport. Its wool is also used, though alpacas provide the really fine-quality wool.

The time of domestication of the guinea-pig is not exactly known; its appearance on the Peruvian coast around 3,750 years ago certainly does not represent its earliest domestication. The wild form lives in a large area from eastern Brazil and Paraguay west through Argentina and in the Andes north to Colombia. There were at least two centres of domestication: in central Peru around 6,000 years ago and in Colombia around 5,000 years ago (Wing, 1983, p. 34). It was exlusively kept for its meat and as a sacrificial animal. It was only after the Spanish conquest that it appeared to spread out to other parts of the world.

BIBLIOGRAPHY

BOESSNECK, J. 1962. Die Tierreste aus der Argissa-Magula vom präkeramischen Neolithikum bis zur mittleren Bronzezeit. In: MILOJCIC, V.; BOESSNECK, J.; HOPF, M. (eds), *Die deutschen Ausgrabungen auf der Argissa-Magula in Thessalien*. Bonn. Vol. 1, pp. 27–99.

BÖYKÖYNYI, S. 1959. Die frühalluviale Wirbeltierfauna Ungarns. *Acta Archaeol. Acad. Sci. Hung.* (Budapest), Vol. 11, pp. 39–102.

—— 1969. Archaeological Problems and Methods of Recognizing Animal Domestication. In: UCKO, P. J.; DIMBLEBY, G. W. (eds), *The Domestication and Exploitation of Plants and Animals*. London. pp. 219–29.

—— 1970. Animal Remains of Lepenski Vir. *Science* (Washington), Vol. 167, No. 3926, pp. 1702–4.

—— 1971. The Development and History of Domestic Animals in Hungary. *Am. Anthropol.* (Washington), Vol. 73, No. 2, pp. 640–74.

—— 1973a. Some Problems of Animal Domestication in the Middle East. In: MATOLCSI, J. (ed.), *Domestikationsforschung und Geschichte der Haustiere*. Budapest. pp. 69–75. (Internationales Symposion in Budapest, 1971.)

—— 1973b. Stock Breeding. In: THEOCHARIS, D. R. (ed.), *Neolithic Greece*. Athens. pp. 165–78.

—— 1974. *History of Domestic Mammals in Central and Eastern Europe*. Budapest.

—— 1975. Vlassac: An Early Site of Dog Domestication. In: CLASON, A. T. (ed.), *Archaeozoological Studies*. Amsterdam/Oxford/New York. pp. 167–78.

—— 1976a. Development of Early Stock Rearing in the Near East. *Nature* (London), Vol. 264, No. 5581, pp. 19–23.

—— 1976b. The Vertebrate Fauna from Anza. In: GIMBUTAS, M. (ed.), *Neolithic Macedonia*. Los Angeles. Vol. 1, pp. 313–63.

—— 1976c. The Vertebrate Fauna of Obre. *Wiss. Mitt. Bosn.-Herzegow. Landesmus.* (Sarajevo), Vol. 4A, pp. 55–154.

—— 1977. *Animal Remains from the Kermanshah Valley, Iran*. Oxford. (BAR Int. Ser., 34.)

—— 1978. Environmental and Cultural Differences as Reflected in the Animal Bone Samples from Five Early Neolithic Sites in South-East Asia. In: MEADOW, R. H.; ZEDER, M. A. (eds), *Approaches to Faunal Analysis in the Middle East*. Cambridge, Mass. pp. 57–60.

—— 1977–82. The Early Neolithic Fauna of Rendina. *Origini*. (Rome), Vol. 11, pp. 345–54.

—— 1983. Domestication, Dispersal and Use of Animals in Europe. In: PEEL, L.; TRIBE, D. E. (eds), *World Animal Science*, Vol. A1: *Domestication, Conservation and Use of Animal Resources*. Amsterdam. pp. 1–20.

BOLOMEY, A. 1973. The Present Stage of Knowledge of Mammal Exploitation during the Epipalaeolithic in the Territory of Romania. In: MATOLCSI, J. (ed.), *Domestikationsforschung und Geschichte der Haustiere*. Budapest. pp. 197–203. (Internationales Symposion in Budapest, 1971.)

CHILDE, V. G. 1957. *The Dawn of European Civilization*. London/New York.

CLUTTON-BROCK, J. 1971. The Primary Food Animals of the Jericho Tell from the Proto-Neolithic to the Byzantine Period. *Levant* (London), Vol. 3, pp. 41–55.

DARWIN, C. 1868. *The Variation of Animals and Plants under Domestication*. London. 2 vols. (2nd edn 1885.)

DAVIS, S. J. M.; VALLA, F. R. 1978. Evidence for Domestication of the Dog 12,000 Years Ago in the Natufian of Israel. *Nature* (London), Vol. 276, No. 5688, pp. 608–10.

DENNEL, R. W. 1972. Stone Age Farming in Bulgaria. *Illus. Lond. News*, Sept., pp. 61–2.

DOWN, J. F. 1960. Domestication: An Examination of the Changing Social Relationships between Man and Animals. *Kroeber Archaeol. Soc.* (Berkeley), pp. 18–67.

GAUTIER, A. 1984a. Archaeozoology of the Bir Kiseiba Region, Eastern Sahara. In: WENDORF, F.; SCHILD, R.; CLOSE, A. (eds), *Cattle Keepers of the Eastern Sahara: The Neolithic of Bir Kiseiba*. Dallas. pp. 49–72.

—— 1984b. Quaternary Mammals and Archaeolozoology of Egypt and the Sudan: A Survey. In: KRZYZANIAK, L.; KOBUSIEWICZ, M. (eds), *Origin and Early Development of Food-Production Cultures in North-Eastern Africa*. Poznan. pp. 43–56.

HASSAN, F. A. et al. 1981. Agricultural Developments in the Nagada Region during the Predynastic Period. *Nyama Akuma* (Calgary), Vol. 17, pp. 28–33.

HIGGS, E. S. 1962. The Fauna of the Early Neolithic Site at Nea Kilomedeia (Greek Macedonia). *Proc. Prehist. Soc.*, Vol. 28, pp. 271–4.

HIGHAM, C. F. W. 1977. Economic Change in Prehistoric Thailand. In: REED, C. A. (ed.), *Origins of Agriculture*. The Hague. pp. 385–412.

HOLE, F.; FLANNERY, K. V. 1967. The Prehistory of South-Western Iran: A Preliminary Report. *Proc. Prehist. Soc.*, Vol. 33, pp. 147–206.

JARMAN, M. R.; JARMAN, J. N. 1968. The Fauna and Economy of Early Neolithic Knossos. *Ann. Br. Sch. Archaeol. Athens* (London), Vol. 63, pp. 241–64.

KRZYZANIAK, L. 1981. Origin and Early Development of Food-Producing Cultures in North-Eastern Africa. *Curr. Anthropol.*, Vol. 22, pp. 693–4.

MELLAART, J. 1967. *Çatal Hüyük, a Neolithic Town in Anatolia*. London.

MUZZOLINI, A. 1983. *L'Art rupestre du Sahara Central: classification et chronologie: le boeuf dans la préhistoire africaine*. Toulouse. (Ph.D. thesis, Université de Toulouse.)

—— 1986. *L'Art rupestre préhistorique des massifs centraux sahariens*. Oxford. (BAR Int. Ser., 318.)

NOBIS, G. 1981. Aus Bonn: das älteste Haustier des Menschen: Unterkiefer eines Hundes aus dem Magdaleniengrab von Bonn-Oberkassel. *Berichte aus der Arbeit des Museums*, Vol. 4, pp. 49–50.

—— 1984. Die Haustiere im Neolithikum Zentraleuropas. In: NOBIS, G. (ed.), *Die Anfänge des Neolithikums vom Orient bis Norden Europas*, Vol. 9: *Der Beginn der Haustiererhaltung in der 'Alten Welt'*. Cologne/Vienna. pp. 73–105.

NOVOA, C.; WHEELER, J. C. 1984. Llama and Alpaca. In: MASON, I. L. (ed.), *Evolution of Domesticated Animals*. London/New York. pp. 116–28.

PERKINS, D. 1964. Prehistoric Fauna from Shanidar, Iraq. *Science* (Washington), Vol. 144, pp. 1565–6.

—— 1969. Fauna of Çatal Hüyük: Evidence for Early Cattle Domestication in Anatolia. *Science* (Washington), Vol. 164, pp. 177–9.

—— 1973. The Beginnings of Animal Domestication in the Near East. *Am. J. Archaeol.* (New York), Vol. 77, pp. 179–82.

PING-TI HO. 1977. The Indigenous Origins of Chinese Agriculture. In: REED, C. A. (ed.), *Origins of Agriculture*. The Hague. pp. 413–84.

POHLKAUSEN, H. 1953. Nachweisbare Ansitze zum Wanderhirtentum in der niederdeutschen Mittelsteinzeit. *Z. Ethnol.* (Berlin), Vol. 78, pp. 64–82.

POULAIN-JOSIEN, T. 1975. Les Animaux domestiques en France à l'époque néolithique. In: COLLOQUE D'ETHNOZOOLOGIE, 1, Paris. *L'Homme et l'animal*. Paris. pp. 409–15.

—— 1978. L'Élevage ovin en France à l'époque préhistorique. *Ethnozootech.* (Paris), Vol. 28, pp. 95–102.

SHERRATT, A. 1983. The Secondary Exploitation of Animals in the Old World. *World Archaeol.*, Vol. 15, pp. 90–104.

SREJOVIC, D. 1966. Lepenski Vir, a New Prehistoric Culture in the Danubian Region. *Archaeol. Iugosl.* (Beograd), Vol. 7, pp. 13–7.

—— 1972. *Europe's First Monumental Sculpture: New Discoveries at Lepenski Vir*. London.

STAMPFLI, H. R. 1983. The Fauna of Jarmo with Notes on Animal Bones from Matarrah, the Amuq and Karim Shahir. In: BRAID-

WOOD, L. S. et al. (eds), *Prehistoric Archaeology along the Zagros Flanks*. Chicago. pp. 431–83.

TRINGHAM, R. 1969. Animal Domestication in the Neolithic Cultures of the South-West Part of European USSR. In: UCKO, P.; DIMBLEBY, G. W. (eds), *The Domestication and Exploitation of Plants and Animals*. London. pp. 381–92.

TURNBULL, F.; REED, C. A. 1974. The Fauna from the Terminal Pleistocene of Palegawra Cave, a Zarzian Occupation Site in North-Eastern Iraq. *Fieldiana Anthropol.* (Chicago), Vol. 63, pp. 81–146.

WATSON, W. 1969. Early Animal Domestication in China. In: UCKO, P. J.; DIMBLEBY, G. W. (eds), *The Domestication and Exploitation of Plants and Animals*. London. pp. 393–95.

WENDORF, D.; SCHILD, R. 1984. Conclusions. In: WENDORF, F.; SCHILD, R.; CLOSE, A. (eds), *Cattle Keepers of the Eastern Sahara: The Neolithic of Bir Kiseiba*. Dallas. pp. 404–28.

WING, E. 1975. Hunting and Herding in the Peruvian Andes. In: CLASON, A. T. (ed.), *Archaeozoological Studies*. Amsterdam. pp. 302–8.

—— 1979. Spread of the Use of South American Camels (Camelidae). In: KUBASIEWICZ, M. (ed.), *Archaeozoology*. Szczecin. Vol. 1, pp. 201–15.

—— 1983. Domestication and Use of Animals in the Americas. In: PEEL, L.; TRIBE, D. E. (eds), *World Animal Science*, Vol. A1: *Domestication, Conservation and Use of Animal Resources*. Amsterdam. Vol. 1, pp. 21–39.

ZEUNER, F. E. 1963. *A History of Domesticated Animals*. London.

39

LATE PREHISTORY OF EGYPT

Lech Krzyzaniak

Few parts of the world are comparable to Egypt in the importance of their local late prehistory. This is because in Egypt the period in question produced two phenomena of exceptional historical consequence: the oldest food-producing (Neolithic) economy in Africa (and, at the same time, one of the oldest in the Old World) and the beginnings of the process of the formation of one of the first stratified (complex) societies in the whole world.

Their early date and the specific character of these two revolutionary phenomena, which are of great consequence not only for Egypt but also for the neighbouring areas, make the late prehistory of the lower Nile a particularly interesting field of research not only for prehistorians. Egyptologists (that is, students of the history and culture of Pharaonic (i.e. Dynastic) Egypt) also often look at developments during the Predynastic period (the time immediately preceding the unification of Egypt into one state about 5,100 years ago) in order to explain the origins of many processes occurring in later periods.

The combination of all these factors makes late prehistory a separate and important period in the development of the societies living in Egypt in the past. Its beginnings are dated to the emergence of a food-producing (Neolithic) economy some ten millennia ago but the roots of this economy – the origins of the domestication of animals and plants – are clearly in the Late Palaeolithic, in the period of some twenty to ten millennia ago. The end of prehistory in Egypt is traditionally associated with the political unification of this country by the founder of the First Dynasty around 5,100 years ago. At that time, and perhaps even somewhat earlier, appeared the first elements of hieroglyphic writing and from then onwards they provide us with more and more information on the development of Egyptian history and culture, although the archaeological evidence, dominant until then, will have remained for a very long time an important source of relevant information. As in other parts of the world, the appearance of writing in Egypt therefore marks the boundary between prehistory and history.

ORIGINS OF THE DOMESTICATION OF ANIMALS AND PLANTS

The oldest food-producing economy in Egypt, practised in Neolithic and Predynastic times, was based on the husbandry of domestic animals and cereals. Present archaeological evidence indicates that Egypt was one of the few major centres of domestication in the Old World. When did domestic animals and plants first appear in Egypt and which species were they?

The most recent evidence suggests that the earliest domestic animals in Egypt were cattle and that they appeared ten millennia ago. The earliest domestic plant in Egypt – barley – started to be cultivated nine millennia ago. However, in order to explain the origins of the domestication of animals and plants one must turn back to the Late Palaeolithic that precedes the Neolithic in Egypt. It seems that in this period the relationship between the human inhabitants of Egypt and the local wild animals and plants was of such a character that it could have led to their intensive exploitation and control, and the eventual domestication of some of them.

The oldest domesticated and economically most important animals in the Old World are cattle, sheep, goats and pigs. Of these, cattle could have been domesticated in Egypt from the indigenous aurochs. It seems that the pig may also have been domesticated from the local wild boar, but there is no adequate evidence for the wild forms of sheep and goat among the prehistoric fauna on the lower Nile, and consequently these animals could not have been domesticated in Egypt.

As in other parts of the Old World, in Egypt the domestication of cattle must have been the result of a long and complex relationship between the social group of hunters and the herds of aurochs, involving their exploitation and control.

It is clear from the archaeological evidence that the tradition of hunting aurochs in Egypt goes back to the Middle Palaeolithic and lasted till the New Kingdom. Yet from the point of view of the origin of domestication, the process of the exploitation and control of the aurochs by groups of hunters must have had its most important consequences in the Late Palaeolithic, some twenty to ten millennia ago. It seems that during this period some groups were specializing in hunting herds of aurochs while others were hunting a wider spectrum of the wild fauna.

A good example of the Upper Palaeolithic sites in the lower Nubian Nile valley containing numerous remains of hunted aurochs is Wadi Kubbaniya, dated to the seventeenth or the eighteenth millennium BP (Wendorf et al., 1980). It is estimated by archaeozoologists that the flesh of these aurochs constituted some 67 per cent of all meat eaten by this specialized hunting group (Gautier et al., 1980, p. 292). In a context of particular interest were found the remains of aurochs in the Upper Palaeolithic site 8905 at Tushka, in the lower Nubian Nile valley (Wendorf, 1968, p. 875; Gautier, 1984, p. 71). A burial ground was found at this site dated to around 14,500 years ago; it contained, among other inhumations, three human interments in clear association with large horn-cores of aurochs which apparently were used as grave markers (Gautier, 1968, p. 88–9). It is thought (Gautier, 1984, p. 71) that this association indicated 'special status' of the aurochs among Late Palaeolithic social groups in northern Nubia, at least in the funerary rites of these groups. Future research may answer the question whether the important role played in the funerary rites could have led to the taming and domestication of the aurochs in Egypt. It seems, therefore, that the Upper Palaeolithic specialized hunters gradually became acquainted with the habitat, physiology and behaviour of the aurochs over the millennia and may have tamed captured calves, which eventually led to their domestication.

It is now thought (Gautier, 1984, p. 72; Wendorf and Schild, 1984b, p. 420; Banks, 1984, pp. 223–9) that cattle were first domesticated in Egypt by groups of immigrants from the Nile valley who were colonizing the Western Desert from around 9,350 years ago, at the advent of a moister climate in the eastern Sahara.

These domesticated cattle seem to have been the earliest in Africa, but they soon appeared in the central Sahara (Banks, 1984, pp. 223–9).

It is significant that the oldest remains of domestic cattle in the Nile valley seem to be dated later than in the Western Desert. In the Upper and Middle Egyptian Nile valley they are dated not earlier than the seventh millennium BP (Badarian), in the Fayum Oasis about 7,000 to 6,800 years ago (Fayum A) and in the Nile Delta in the earlier half of the seventh millennium BP (Merimde). It is suggested by the authors of this hypothesis that cattle were introduced into the Nile valley from the Western Desert by groups of pastoral herders who arrived there in the course of several short but severe Holocene arid subperiods.

Domestic cattle were known in western Asia and in the eastern Mediterranean from the eighth millennium BP, if not from the ninth. Domestic cattle may have existed in the Levant as long as 8,000 years ago (Singh, 1974, p. 54); in Anatolia they were domesticated around 7,700 to 7,600 if not about 8,100 years ago (Singh, 1974, p. 102). In the second half of the ninth millennium BP domestic cattle appear in mainland Greece (von den Driesch and Boessneck, 1985, p. 6). Shortly afterwards they appeared on the previously uninhabited island of Crete, transported by Neolithic colonists arriving there by watercraft around 8,000 years ago (Evans, 1971, p. 99 to 107). The Neolithic colonists travelling around the eastern Mediterranean may also have easily landed on the Egyptian coast in the earlier half of the eighth millennium BP, bringing with them domestic sheep, goat and wheat, which, as we know, could not have been domesticated in Egypt. Such may have been the origin of the domestic sheep and goat reported from the Neolithic site at Haua Fteah in Cyrenaica (present Libya) dated to around 6,800 years ago (McBurney, 1967, pp. 271 ff., 327–8). Of course, the domestic forms of cattle and pig of south-west Asian origin may also have been brought to Egypt by these colonists.

As with the animals, the beginnings of the exploitation – and perhaps the control – of plants in Egypt seems to be dated to Upper Palaeolithic times (Wendorf et al., 1980, p. 273, 278–9). It is known that while wild wheat has never been native to Egypt, barley was. The first indications of the exploitation of cereals may be the use of harvesting knives (proto-sickles) and grinding stones in the period between the fifteenth and twelfth millennia BP in the Upper Egyptian and lower Nubian Nile valley. Among the remains of camps from this period, particularly in the area of Esna and El-Khril in Upper Egypt, flint sickle blades hafted in such composite harvesting knives were found; a characteristic trait of these blades is the sickle gloss interpreted as an effect of cutting the stems or spikelets of cereals and perhaps also other grasses. Numerous grinding stones – upper (handstones) and lower (mortars) – occur in these sites and are interpreted as being used for grinding the grain before its further processing and consumption. However, no actual cereal grain has been found so far in these camps. That stands of barley were growing on the slopes of the Nile valley is indicated by the high frequency – 10 to 15 per cent – of barley pollen found in a pollen diagram from this period (Krzyzaniak, 1977, p. 41). Harvesting knives were also used in this period in the lower Nubian Nile valley (Wendorf, 1968, pp. 942–3) (Fig. 98). We have no evidence so far of any form of control that may have been exercised on the stands of wild barley by the earliest cereal harvesters in Egypt (such as the removal of weeds, protection against pests and even artificial watering, which are known to be practised by present-day grain collectors).

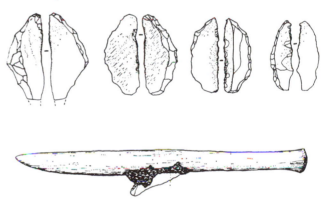

Figure 98 Stone bladelets showing sickle gloss. Reconstruction of the earliest harvesting knife in Egypt (about 12,500 years ago). (After F. Wendorf.)

Nor have we any information so far on the exploitation of plants in Egypt between eleven and nine millennia ago. It seems possible that the harvesting of wild barley was still being practised in this period at the apex of the Delta and in the wadis of the Red Sea hills, as was the case among the contemporaneous Natufians in neighbouring Palestine, who specialized in collecting wild wheat and barley; some artefacts similar to those used by the Natufians have been found in these parts of Egypt, but no direct or indirect remains of wild harvests have been detected.

The earliest known evidence for the cultivation of cereals in Egypt comes from the Western Desert and dates to between 8,200 and 7,900 years ago (Wendorf and Schild, 1984b, p. 422). In the Delta these cereals – wheat and barley – appeared for the first time in the Neolithic settlement at Merimde dated to the first half of the seventh millennium BP (Krzyzaniak, 1977, p. 89), in the Fayum oasis around 7,000–6,800 years ago (Fayum A) (Krzyzaniak, 1977, pp. 58–9) and in the middle and Upper Egyptian Nile valley in the second half of the seventh millennium BP (Badarian)

(Krzyzaniak, 1977, pp. 69–71). Domesticated barley of a sophisticated form – six-rowed, a form requiring much more moisture for growth than the two-rowed variety – started to be cultivated in the Western Desert already from about 8,200 to 7,900 years ago and wheat from about eight millennia ago (Wendorf and Schild, 1984a, pp. 7–8); that is, later than in south-west Asia, where wheat was cultivated from the tenth millennium BP (Singh, 1974, p. 208). However, we do not know for certain if the domestic barley from the Western Desert was domesticated in the Nile valley, the Delta or the Mediterranean littoral and brought to the present deserts by the earliest Holocene colonists, or was of foreign origin and was introduced to Egypt from south-west Asia.

It seems from this overview that cattle may have been locally domesticated in Egypt; the donkey may have been the result of domestication of the wild ass, which is indigenous to Egypt and Nubia. In contrast to these species, there is no evidence among the Egyptian prehistoric fauna for the presence of wild sheep and goats; their domestic forms must, therefore, have been introduced to Egypt from outside, certainly from south-west Asia where they were herded from the eleventh or the tenth millennium BP (Singh, 1974, pp. 209–11). The earliest sheep and goats in Egypt are known from the Western Desert and are dated to the eighth millennium BP (Wendorf and Schild, 1984a, pp. 7–8). The oldest domestic pig in Egypt was found in the Neolithic settlement of Merimde and is dated to the first half of the seventhth millennium BP (von den Driesch and Boessneck, 1985, pp. 23–5). The Delta seems to have been a particularly favourable environment for the herds of wild boar and could have been the place of their eventual domestication, but the data for the occurrence of wild boar in prehistoric Egypt are uncertain. Domestic pig may also have been introduced to Egypt from south-west Asia, where it was herded from the earlier half of the ninth millennium BP (Singh, 1974, p. 211).

When undertaking a review of the successful attempts at domestication in Egypt we should also take into account the apparently unsuccessful attempts in this field, which seem to have concerned both animals (such as hyena, hartebeeste, gazelles, antelopes, giraffe, ostrich, cranes) and probably also plants (grasses) (Clark, 1971; Smith, 1969).

EARLIEST FARMERS: THE NEOLITHIC (Map 43)

The most recent archaeological evidence indicates that the earliest food-producing economy in Egypt – the Neolithic – based on the exploitation of domestic animals and the cultivation of plants, started to be practised in the Western Desert in the tenth or the ninth millennium BP. It seems that it was of autochthonous origin and character. Similar developments may have taken place in the Eastern Desert, but no archaeological data – apart from the rock art – have been available from this area so far. The earliest production of food in Lower Egypt (the Delta and the Fayum oasis), which started in the earlier half of the seventh millennium BP, seems to have its roots, at least in part, in south-west Asia and the eastern Mediterranean. The chronology of the earliest food-producing economy in the Upper Egyptian Nile valley is rather obscure and seems to be somewhat later than in the surrounding deserts; recent radiocarbon measurements suggest a date in the later half of the seventh millennium BP.

The Holocene archaeological sequence from the southern part of the Western Desert pertaining to the earliest pro-

duction of food is divided into three periods: Early, Middle and Late Neolithic (Wendorf et al., 1984; Banks, 1984). The Early Neolithic is dated to between 9,800 and 7,900 years ago. It is assumed that the earliest Neolithic colonists arrived in an area of lakes that then existed in the steppe environment of the present desert. They inhabited small, seasonal camps on the shores of the lakes after the summer rains; it is thought that the base camps of these groups were still situated in the Nile valley and were occupied in the summer for fishing – particularly after the period of the annual inundation of the river – and for hunting at watering places in the winter and spring when these strategies were most productive. These social groups led a transhumant way of life while exploiting the expansive steppe of the Western Desert. Some of those camps (at Nabta) seem to have been larger villages built on a regular plan with rows of dwellings (round houses with associated pits and walk-in wells, and pits arranged in an arc) and were occupied for most of the year. The Early Neolithic archaeological assemblages have been classified into four 'types' (taxonomic units) (Al-Adam, El-Kortein, El-Ghorab and El-Nabta) and may reflect socio-economic and spatial differences prevailing in this area, rather than other phenomena (for instance, ethnic identity). The economy of these social groups comprised the exploitation of the new domestic stock (cattle) – probably not only its occasional butchering but also milking – as well as the cultivation of barley, the hunting of hares and gazelles and probably also the collecting of wild plants. The barley was of a naked, six-row form that requires a considerable amount of moisture for its growth; it was probably planted on the edges of lakes. These human groups were already making – albeit sporadically – the earliest ceramic vessels in Africa, chiefly bowls, decorated on the outer surface with incised and comb-impressed designs. The 'Dotted Wavy Line' motif was already in use in this decoration. The developed technology employed in making this pottery seems to suggest that it was a continuation of an earlier tradition, rather than a newly discovered skill. It was a well-fired pottery, technologically and stylistically within the so-called Saharo-Sudanese ceramic tradition which occurs on expansive areas of the southern and central Sahara and the northern savannahs. Tools were made from good-quality Egyptian flint, using the evolved bladelet technology. This raw material was certainly brought from a distant source, another piece of evidence for the mobile way of life led by the human groups in question. The toolkit of these groups was mostly composed of pointed-backed bladelets and geometric microliths, chiefly triangles. Grain was ground on grinding stones composed of large lower stones, often with deep grinding basins, and upper handstones. Ostrich eggshells were used as containers and for manufacturing beads. Decorated eggshells, which were perhaps used for storing water, were found, with red ochre filling the incised decoration. The Early Neolithic occupation of the Western Desert came to an end about 7,900 years ago with the advent of hyperarid conditions.

The Middle Neolithic of the Western Desert is dated to the eighth millennium BP. This area, deserted by the earliest Neolithic colonists a few centuries earlier, was again populated by groups of peoples arriving from the Upper Egyptian and lower Nubian Nile valley with the onset of a new period of rain and better living conditions. This period witnessed the most intensive and successful human settlement in Holocene times in the Western Desert. Settlements were situated on the edges of lakes and at least some of them may have been repeatedly seasonally reoccupied, as large numbers of superimposed hearths and pits seem to indicate. In general,

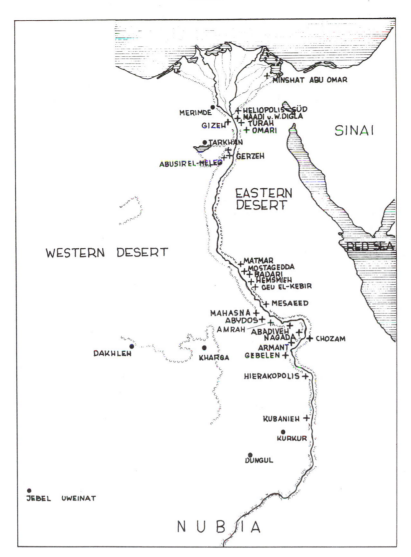

Map 43 Egypt: major Neolithic and Predynastic archaeological sites. (After Kaiser, with modifications by Krzyzaniak.)

the settlements tend to be much larger than in the preceding period. One of them, an exceptionally large site, E-75–8, situated on a dune which formed a peninsula in the lake, seems to have covered some 8 hectares (400 by 200 m)! Larger settlements were composed of houses, hearths and storage pits. It is suggested by the excavators that large settlements similar to E-75–8 were inhabited by the maximum number of members of the local social group who gathered here in the rainy season, possibly for social and ritual purposes. The high frequency of cattle bones found in this site suggests that cattle were slaughtered and eaten on the spot, and this also may have taken place as part of a social and ritual occasion. Other contemporary sites in this area are medium-sized or small and may be the remains of habitations of smaller groups, probably task forces involved in cattle herding after the rainy season. It is thought that crops (cereals) were planted only near larger settlements, on the edges of the lakes.

Direct evidence suggests that the economy of this period comprised the husbandry of the domestic cattle and most probably of sheep and goat, as well as the cultivation of domestic barley and wheat; some hunting (gazelle and hare) and collecting continued to be practised. There was a dramatic shift in this period as regards the technology and style of manufacturing lithic tools and in the raw material used. Local lithic material such as quartz and chert began to be

used instead of the Early Neolithic high-quality Egyptian flint suitable for blade technology. Flake technology became dominant and retouched flakes, perforators, denticulates and notches as well as lunates dominate the toolkit. The first bifacial tools, concave-based arrowheads, appeared, as did the first ground tools in Egypt, ground and polished axeheads (celts). Cereal grains were crushed and ground for food on grinding stones composed of large, oval lower stones with deep basins and round to oval handstones.

Pottery vessels of this period are still within the Early Neolithic Saharo-Sudanese technological and stylistic tradition, but their exterior surface is now decorated with the impressed Woven Mat motif. Finds of cowrie shells, which were used as beads, indicate contacts with the Red Sea area, undoubtedly via the Nile valley, from which also originate occasional freshwater shells.

The Late Neolithic of the Western Desert is dated to around 6,900 to 5,500 years ago and occurred after a short period of dry conditions. The human groups seem to have further developed their food-producing economy in this period. The settlement patterns are similar to those of the Middle Neolithic, and are characterized by habitations of different size and apparently with different socio-economic functions. In addition to the exploitation of domestic cattle, that of domestic sheep and goats was certainly also practised in this period, and there is evidence of the domestic dog.

Apart from the exploitation of domestic stock and the possible cultivation of cereals, hunting was also practised and was concentrated on hare and smaller gazelles. It is still not clear if the 'Ethiopian megafauna' (elephant, ostrich, wild ass, addax and other larger antelopes, giraffe) frequently depicted in the rock art in the higher parts of the Western Desert (and also in the Eastern Desert), was a sizeable component of the wild fauna on the steppe plains.

The toolkit of these Late Neolithic peoples was based on the exploitation of quartzes and chert as their raw material and on the manufacturing of tools on flakes; among these notches, denticulates and retouched pieces dominate; lunates, trapezes and triangles occur among the geometric pieces, as well as bifacial arrowheads and side-blow flakes. Grindstones as well as ground and polished stone axeheads (celts) are as common as in the Middle Neolithic; the first palettes for pulverizing pigment occur in this period.

In the ceramic technology the most notable innovation is the introduction of burnishing and smudging of the walls of vessels. The traditional incised and impressed designs are now limited to geometric motifs below or on the rim. It seems that the decoration of this pottery became different from the traditional Saharo-Sudanese ornamental style.

Late Neolithic sites are known also from other localities in the Western Desert such as the Kharga, Dakhla and Fayum oases, but they are, as yet, rather poorly known. Nevertheless, they seem to differ technologically and stylistically from the Late Neolithic sites in the southern part of the Western Desert.

The first burials of the Holocene inhabitants of the Western Desert, dated to this period, have recently been found (Banks, 1984, pp. 200–1). The corpses seem to have been laid in the grave pit in a loose position, and in one instance a clay amulet was found in a double burial.

The end of substantial human settlement in the Western Desert in the sixth and in the first half of the fifth millennium BP was caused by the advent of the hyperarid conditions; this confined human groups to larger oases.

The archaeological remains excavated or recorded on the surface of the ground in the Western Desert are considerably enriched by the information available from prehistoric rock art, which sheds additional light on the life of the earliest food producers in this area. Rock art is known from the Upper Egyptian and lower Nubian Nile valley and the Western and Eastern Deserts (Winkler, 1938–1939; Resch, 1967; van Noten, 1978). Although the evidence is not conclusive, it seems possible to associate major styles of this art with the three stages of the Neolithic development in the Western Desert.

The oldest rock art is represented by zoomorphic drawings, geometric symbols and drawings of fishing and hunting traps; this style could be dated to the period starting from around 9,350 years ago and it is known mainly from the lower Nubian Nile valley. Perhaps already from the beginnings of the Neolithic, along with the geometric motifs, drawings on the sunny side of large rocks were executed, most frequently depicting giraffes, but also lions, antelopes, gazelles, Barbary sheep, birds and crocodiles. In the Eastern Desert drawings of elephants also occur. This apparently Early Neolithic style in the development of the rock art in the Upper Egyptian and lower Nubian Nile valley and the Eastern and Western Deserts is known as the 'Earliest Hunters' style (Plate 59). However, it is puzzling that the bones of these, mostly large, wild animals ('Ethiopian megafauna') have apparently not been found so far among the remains in the Neolithic sites in the steppe plains of these deserts or in the Nile valley.

Some drawings show figures of humans depicted in clear association with wild animals. Although rare, these show the hunter with a bow and a dog on a lead or humans in dancing scenes, probably of a ritual nature. The drawings showing a wild animal being followed by humans may have been associated with hunting magic; the man and the beast are connected by lines, which may suggest keeping a captured animal on a rope or an attempt to catch a wounded animal; or else the lines may symbolize the bleeding caused by projectiles shot by the hunter. These hunters, when they are depicted dancing, sometimes wear animal masks on their heads and frequently have feathers in their hair and penis-sheaths.

The second stage in the development of the prehistoric rock art in Egypt seems to include both drawings (the Eastern and Western Deserts and the Nile valley) and paintings (the Western Desert – the mountains of Jebel Uweinat) with cattle as their main theme, although hunting scenes continue to occur. This is known as the 'Autochthonous Mountain Dwellers' style and dates probably to the peak of the development of the food-producing economy in general, and cattle husbandry in particular, in southern Egypt (Middle and Late Neolithic, eighth to sixth millennium BP). The cattle depicted in this art are often of the long-horned breed, sometimes with deformed horns, branded and decorated with amulets and a disc placed between the horns; well-shaped udders are deliberately drawn, which seems to suggest the practice of milking the cows. It is interesting to note that scenes of cattle hunting (using bows and arrows) and of capturing bulls and cows with a lasso were also executed. In the hunting scenes, in addition to the species already recorded in the 'Earliest Hunters' style, the new style in the Eastern Desert also includes the drawings of lions, possibly of wild boar and asses and perhaps of wild cattle. Apparently dogs and traps were used in hunting. Corpses of humans, mostly men with penis-sheaths, were drawn or painted in the shape of a wedge.

The beautiful art of the cattle herders from the Jebel Uweinat (Plate 60) may be compared to the art produced in the best centres of the Saharan rock art and is known as the 'Uweinat Cattle Breeders' style. Paintings of cows with well-developed udders, huts with vessels filled with a white substance, undoubtedly milk, scenes of copulating cattle, frequently decorated with necklaces, amulets and ornaments hanging on their horns, as well as figures of men attending the cattle, are the characteristic elements of this style. It is interesting that paintings of men wearing cattle skins and decorated with cattle tails (a trait known from the Dynastic art in Egypt) also occur in these scenes.

Probably contemporary with the 'Autochthonous Mountain Dwellers' and 'Uweinat Cattle Breeders' styles is one from the Dakhla oasis known as the 'Early Oasis Dwellers' style. The most characteristic element of this art is a drawing of a sitting woman wearing a long robe, or a woman in a sitting or standing position with a heavy steatopyga. It seems that this style is not very distant from the artistic tradition of the Mediterranean Neolithic.

Neolithic food producers may have also been present in the Eastern Desert from ten to five milllennia ago, as its rock art is in many ways similar to that of its western counterpart (although rock paintings do not occur here), but as yet we have virtually no archaeological information from this area.

The chronology of the beginnings of the farming life in the Egyptian Nile valley seems puzzling. This is due largely to the scantiness of archaeological evidence pertaining to the crucial period between the intensive exploitation of grains of wild grasses fifteen to twelve millennia ago and the apparently sudden appearance of fully developed food production in the late seventh millennium BP, represented by the Badarian (see p. 404).

It now seems that this section of the Nile valley may have been exploited seasonally by transhumant Neolithic groups that herded domestic stock and practised cultivation dependent upon summer rainfall, arriving seasonally at the river from the steppes of the Western and Eastern Deserts ten to seven millennia ago only to gather food. For some unknown reason they apparently did not start exploiting the effects of the river inundation for agriculture.

In contrast to the situation in southern Egypt, where indigenous food production originated in the tenth to the ninth millennium BP, it seems that food production was at least in part introduced to Lower Egypt from south-west Asia and the eastern Mediterranean. An already fully developed food-producing economy with some non-Egyptian traits appeared in the first half of the seventh millennium BP on the western edge of the Delta (Merimde) and in the Fayum oasis. It appears that the Mediterranean and the Upper Egyptian farming tradition may have met somewhere in Middle Egypt shortly after that date.

The Neolithic settlement at Merimde Beni Salame, located on the western edge of the Nile Delta, provides us with a great deal of information on the earliest food-production economy in Lower Egypt (Eiwanger, 1984; von den Driesch and Boessneck, 1985; see also Krzyzaniak, 1977, pp. 87–98). The earliest Neolithic settlement (layer I) may have been established in the earlier half of the seventh millennium BP, as suggested by the available, preliminary radio-carbon measurements (von den Driesch and Boessneck, 1985, p. 2). These earliest Merimdians were already exploiting domestic cattle, sheep, goats and pigs as well as cultivating wheat, barley and other plants. Sheep, goat and wheat, being alien to the wild fauna and flora of Egypt and, therefore not available for indigenous domestication, must have been introduced to the Delta from outside, either through inter-group contacts (such as barter trade along the coast by watercraft or overland) or by groups of foreign farmers colonizing the Delta. As the settlement with its cultivated fields and pastures was situated on the edge of the Delta, the earliest Merimdians must have had the skill necessary to exploit the effects of the annual inundation of the soil by the Nile waters. A certain amount of food was also acquired through fishing and hunting. Merimdian tools were manufactured from local flint nodules using blade technology. Ground and polished axeheads (celts) and grinding stones were also used. Some pottery vessels had flat bottoms, a trait characteristic of the Neolithic tradition in south-west Asia and alien to Egypt.

The earliest settlement seems to have been as large as a few hectares in surface area; hearths are its only preserved feature. A part of the area within the settlement was used as a burial ground for the earliest Merimdians. Several tens of poorly furnished graves containing skeletons laid in a contracted position were found in this cemetery. Anthropomorphic and zoomorphic figurines were found in the settlement, probably used for ritual practices (Plate 61).

Layer II at Merimde represents a settlement that was found after a hiatus of an unknown duration in occupation of the site. Layers III to V, dated to the middle of the seventh millennium BP, contain such features as dwellings, grain storage in baskets and pots, lithic tools manufactured using flake technology, bifacially retouched tools and other artefacts similar to those manufactured by the earliest farmers in the Fayum oasis (Fayum Neolithic A). In summary, the Merimde cultural development seems to show a mixture of traits traditionally regarded as African and Mediterranean or south-west Asian in origin.

The first farmers in the Fayum oasis appeared at the beginning of the seventh millennium BP. Their settlements have been excavated mainly on the shores of the huge Lake Moeris which then existed, of which present-day Birket Qarun is only a small remnant. The economy and other traits of the material culture of these farmers are so similar to the younger strata of the Merimde sequence that it seems reasonable to suggest that the culture of the earliest farmers in the Fayum oasis as a whole may also have been similar to that of the inhabitants of the Delta.

The archaeological remains of these earliest farmers are known as the Fayum A assemblages (Caton-Thompson and Gardner, 1934; Said et al., 1972; see also Krzyzaniak, 1977, pp. 57–68). They are dated to around 7,000 to 6,600 years ago. The Neolithic Fayumians cultivated wheat, three forms of barley and flax, undoubtedly on the seasonally inundated shores of the lake fed by the Nile waters through the Bahr Yousef branch of the river. They also kept cattle, sheep, goats, pigs and dogs. In addition, fishing played an important role (fish was also probably dried), as did hunting hippopotamus, elephant, turtle, waterfowl and crocodile and collecting land snails. The lithic toolkit of the Fayumians was manufactured using flake technology, and consisted of bifacially retouched and ground tools. Bone harpoons and fish-hooks were also used, as well as wooden artefacts. The best known agricultural artefacts of the Neolithic Fayumians are the harvesting sickles, wooden sticks for threshing grain, baskets for storing grain and stone querns. The sickles consist of a wooden haft into which several denticulated, bifacially flaked flint bladelets were mounted (Fig. 99). The Fayum evidence provides us with exceptionally rich information on grain storage. This was done in groups of subterranean containers (silos) made of plaited straw. It is estimated that each container may have contained up to 400 kg of grain, which could have represented a yield of a plot of land of about half a hectare. Groups of up to more than one hundred such containers – called granaries – were found in apparent association with the settlement, and may have originally been the 'property' of a given social group. Remains of equipment for transporting, threshing, parching and grinding the grain were also found in or near the containers; these are groups of wide-mouthed vessels for parching which stand in ashes, harvesting sickles, lower and upper grindstones, baskets made of woven straw (Fig. 99), linen sacks and wooden sticks for threshing. The Neolithic Fayumians also participated – as did other Neolithic groups in Egypt – in the large exchange network through which Red Sea

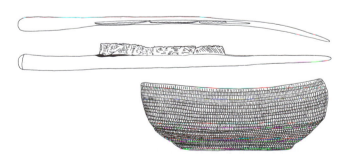

Figure 99 Neolithic agricultural items (harvesting knife and basket), Fayum oasis (Egypt) (about 6,500 years ago). (After Caton-Thompson and Gardner.)

shells as well as turquoise and amazonite from the Red Sea hills and the Sinai (used for manufacturing beads) were acquired.

THE BEGINNINGS OF STRATIFIED SOCIETY: THE PREDYNASTIC PERIOD

The terminal prehistory of Egypt (that is, the last several hundred years or so before the emergence of a unified state about 5,100 years ago) is most often known to prehistorians and Egyptologists as the Predynastic period. It is characterized by a succession of three so-called archaeological cultures occurring in the Nile valley: Badarian, Amratian (Naqada I) and Gerzean (Naqada II). A remarkable continuity of archaeological traits can be seen in this development, which is characterized by an accelerating rate of change in the technology, style and frequency of different artefacts. This is in obvious contrast to the situation observed in Egypt prior to the sixth millennium BP, when technological and stylistic changes were relatively slower.

The Badarian archaeological assemblages occur in the Upper and Middle Egyptian Nile valley (Brunton and Caton-Thompson, 1928; Brunton, 1938; see also Krzyzaniak, 1977, pp. 68–84) and are now seen to be dated to about 6,100 to 5,600 years ago (Hays, 1984). The Bandarian assemblages (Fig. 100) are the remains left by the first fully developed farming cultures in the Egyptian Nile valley, possibly the descendants of the desert peoples who moved to the river at the beginning of a major arid period. Although very few settlements have been excavated so far, it is known that these people cultivated two forms of wheat and two forms of barley and most probably also herded cattle, sheep and goats. The Badarians in their cultivation were undoubtedly exploiting the effect of the natural irrigation of the floor of the Nile valley by the annual river flood. Fishing, hunting and collecting played a secondary role in their subsistence. Tools were made mostly of flakes or chert and flint, using bifacial flaking or grinding and polishing. The toolkit of the Badarians consisted of sickles made of flint bladelets inserted into a straight haft, grinding stones, fish-hooks made mostly of bone, flint scrapers, axeheads (celts) of different sizes, bows and arrows pointed with flint heads, spears with flint heads, throwing sticks of wood and borers. The rich evidence from the cemeteries indicates woven and skin clothing as well as mats. The Badarian pottery vessels, mostly bowls, were the start of the excellent Predynastic ceramic tradition. They were hand-made of Nile silt and burnished. A characteristic trait of this pottery was the decoration known as 'rippling' and 'black-topping'. The first stone vessels occur at the same time. Personal adornments included strings of beads (necklaces, anklets) made of stone (carnelian, jasper, turquoise and the like), glazed steatite or Red Sea shells, lip-studs of pottery, feathers, combs for decoration of the head and bracelets made of ivory. The first copper artefacts in Egypt – beads – appear in this period.

Another typical Predynastic trait started by the Badarians was the use of the cosmetic set composed of a flat stone (usually slate) palette for pulverizing lumps of pigment (malachite, ochre, galena), small ivory vessels for mixing and storing it, and ivory or bone spoons for the extraction of the pigment from the vessel. Pieces of the mobile Badarian art such as zoomorphic vessels and female figurines of ivory or clay were probably used in ritual activities.

It seems that the Badarian settlements were relatively small, as were their burial grounds, where perhaps up to a hundred individuals had been originally interred. The corpses were laid in the grave pit in the contracted position on their side. It is interesting that the deliberate burials of animals (cattle, sheep, pig and dog or jackal) occur among the human interments.

The Amratian (Naqada I) archaeological assemblages follow the Badarian ones in the Predynastic sequence (Petrie, 1920; Kaiser, 1956; Baumgartel, 1955, 1960; Krzyzaniak, 1977, pp. 101–23). They seem now to occur in the Nile valley as far north as the environs of Cairo (Rizkana and Seeher, 1984, p. 251). The Amratian evidence comes mostly from cemeteries (Fig. 101). It seems that these assemblages date to the times immediately following the Badarian and may be dated to around 5,800 to 5,500 years ago (Hoffman, 1984, p. 237). The subsistence economy of the Amratians seems to be similar to that of the Badarians, and was composed of the cultivation of winter cereals and, perhaps, also of vegetables and stock-raising, supplemented by fishing, collecting and hunting (with dogs). The toolkit of the Amratians was not very different from that of the Badarians. However, an innovation in the lithic technology was the introduction of bifacial pressure-flaking (retouching), which enabled fine cutting tools and weapons to be manufactured. A new component of the lithic toolkit was a fine flint fish-tailed point (possibly of a dagger) and a discoidal macehead made of stone. Copper and gold working (hammering) was also introduced, mostly for making personal ornaments (beads) and for manufacturing some light-duty tools (harpoons, borers, chisels, pins).

Amratian funerary pottery was in many ways similar to that of the Badarians, although more types of vessels were manufactured and, judging from the number found in the cemeteries, production was bigger than in the preceding period. The 'rippled' kind of decoration of the surface of pots went out of fashion but some funerary vessels now started to be painted white on the red (coated with haematite) outer surface ('white-lined' pottery) (Fig. 102). Geometric designs and figurative scenes (hunting and ritual dancing) were painted on the vessels. More cylindrical stone vessels and of more diversified types were manufactured by the Amratians than in Badarian times. Such lithic raw materials as alabaster (calcite), basalt, marble and limestone were used for their manufacture. Basketry formed a traditionally important branch of the manufacture of receptacles.

Amratian corpses were interred with a much larger number of personal adornments, many of them of a new type and form, than were Badarian ones. Some of these adornments look like art objects. Strings of beads composing necklaces and bracelets were made of ostrich eggshell, semi-precious stones (carnelian, garnet, only sporadically lapis lazuli), glazed steatite, faience, copper, gold and colourful marine shells; bracelets made of a single piece of material (for instance ivory), armlets, finger rings, lip and nose studs, pins, decorated (carved) hair combs and hair pins were also found in Amratian graves. Traditional cosmetic sets are now composed of slate palettes of rhomboidal, zoomorphic or boat-like forms as well as of new containers for pulverizing pigment – so-called tusks, often carved in the form of a human head. Judging from the clay figurines found in graves, Amratian females seem to have worn only a linen woven skirt, while the males wore only a penis-sheath.

Paintings on the funerary vessels indicate that the Amratians were familiar with the domestic donkey and with rowboats. This might have helped further to develop trade and other intergroup contacts with areas more distant than

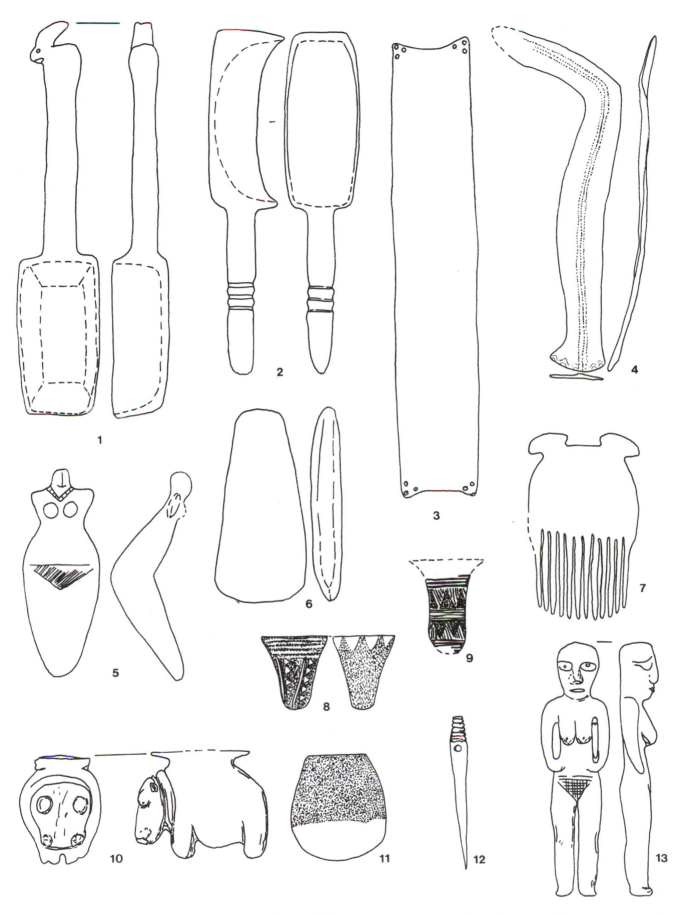

Figure 100 Artefacts found among Badarian grave goods (Egypt) (about 6,500 to 6,000 years ago): 1, 2, ivory cosmetic spoons; 3, cosmetic palette; 4, wooden throwing-stick; 5, 13, clay and ivory anthropomorphic figurines; 6, stone head of axe; 7, ivory comb; 8, 9, decorated ceramic beakers; 10, ivory hippopotamus figurine; 11, black-topped ceramic vessel; 12, bone needle. (Not to scale.) (After Krzyzaniak, 1977.)

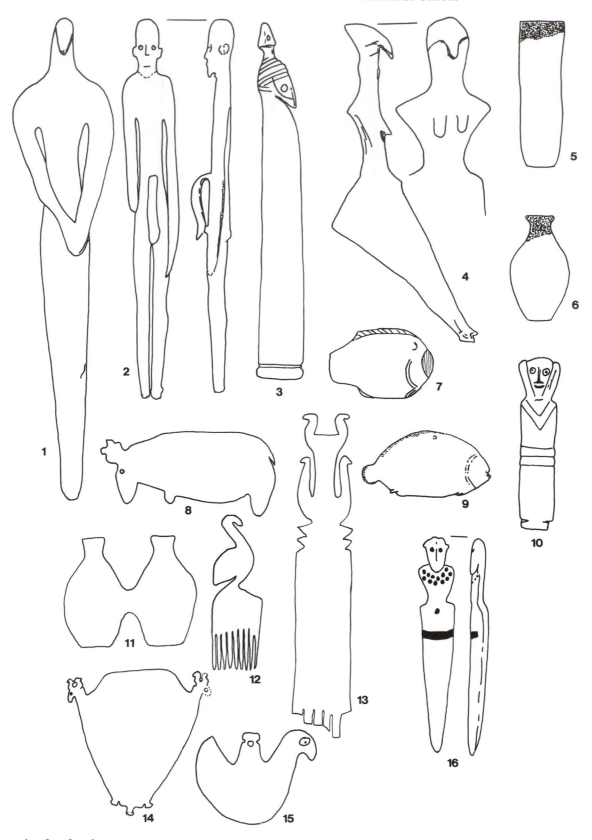

Figure 101 Artefacts found among Amratian grave goods (Egypt) (about 6,000 to 5,500 years ago): 1, 2, 4, clay and ivory anthropomorphic figurines; 3, 10, 16, anthropomorphic artefacts of unclear function; 5, 6, black-topped ceramic vessels; 7, 8, 9, 14, 15, cosmetic palettes; 11, fancy ceramic vessel; 12, 13, ivory combs. (Not to scale.) (After Krzyzaniak, 1977.)

before. The places of origin of foreign goods (malachite, marine shells, lapis lazuli, copper, gold, ivory, galena) indicate the growth of a far-flung exchange of material goods in this period.

Amratian settlement patterns seem to indicate an econ-

omic exploitation of the floor and slopes of the Nile valley mostly by farming and animal herding; excavations revealed small settlements composed of simple dwellings with hearths and storage containers, built of wooden branches and poles, silt, straw, reed and pieces of rock as well as windbreaks,

Figure 102 Motifs painted white on Amratian pottery vessels (Egypt). (After Krzyzaniak, 1977.)

groups of vessels for parching grain and threshing floors. The archaeological material also suggests that the Amratians engaged in some ritual practices. It is widely accepted that such objects as anthropomorphic figurines (male and female) may have been used in cult practices; dancing scenes painted on vessels also seem to be associated with them.

It seems that remarkable continuity in the existence of social groups in Upper and Middle Egypt can be traced from the Amratian times onwards. Many of the large cemeteries started to be used from this period and continued to be used, apparently without interruption, throughout Early Dynastic and even Old Kingdom times. This may have been the result of an existence of a social group with a long tradition of settlement in the same area and bound together by social and ritual ties including the burial of its members in the same ground; it looks then as if the Amratians were the ancestors of the terminal Predynastic and Dynastic Egyptians, and may already have spoken a language not very different from that of the latter. Similarly to the Badarian custom, animals – both domestic and wild – were interred in the Amratian cemeteries.

The Gerzean (Naqada II) archaeological assemblages superseded the Amratian ones (Petrie, 1920; Kaiser, 1956; Baumgartel, 1955, 1960; Krzyzaniak, 1977, pp. 138–64). They occur in the whole of the Nile valley and also in the Delta (Wildung, 1984). The Gerzean (Fig. 103) is the latest so-called archaeological culture of Predynastic Egypt and its chronology lies between about 5,500 years ago and the moment of unification of Egypt into one state by the founding king of the First Dynasty; most scholars believe now that this took place about 5,100 years ago (Barta, 1979, p. 14; Hassan, 1980, p. 204). Some scholars also distinguish the Naqada III period, which spans a comparatively short period of time dating from immediately prior to the political unification of Egypt and covering the beginning of Dynastic times. The Gerzean evidence comes almost exclusively from the cemeteries, which contain sometimes hundreds or even thousands of burials.

In general, the economy of the Gerzean was a development of that practised by the Amratians. However, in this period considerable socio-economic transformations took place (see pp. 409–10). A number of important technological innovations were also introduced. It is thought by the present writer (Krzyzaniak, 1977, pp. 131–2) that the beginning of the control of the annual inundation of the river may have occurred in this period, although we need more evidence

to substantiate this hypothesis. If this was so, however, then such a control would considerably enhance the agricultural output, its regularity and surplus. A considerable demographic growth of accelerating magnitude seems to have taken place at this time. It is thought that the population of Egypt may have increased from around 350,000 people about 6,000 years ago to some 870,000 by 5,000 years ago (Butzer, 1976, p. 83). Significant technological progress was made in pottery making and in copper and flint working, and there was also an increase in the quantity of the goods produced: mass-production of funerary vessels seems to have been started. Far-flung trade was also developing in the Gerzean times at a considerable rate.

Among the higher quality funerary pots of the Gerzean period, so-called Qena ware shows the development of new technology in its manufacture, which required that the pots be fired in kilns at about 1,200 °C. The kiln firing of the painted pots and the mass-production of most of the wares – some of it probably using a slowly rotating turntable – suggest that pottery making became a separate craft in this period. Also, the mass-manufacturing of typologically diversified stone vessels and personal adornments toward the end of this period point to the higher social status of this production. In the copper, silver and gold metallurgy there is evidence of indigenous smelting, casting and hammering of the products, which became more diverse and more common than in the Amratian times. However, the Gerzean toolkit was still dominated by lithic tools, which played an important role in Egypt deep into Dynastic times. The lithic tools started to be manufactured from tabular flint obtained from quarries in the deserts. In the lithic technology the most important innovation was the introduction of the blade technique, which permitted mass-production of refined, light-duty tools; the traditional flake technology – including bifacial flaking – was also used, as well as the grinding and polishing of stone.

A new component of the Gerzean toolkit was copper and silver adzeheads, copper heads of gouges and blades of knives, saws, stone apple- or pear-shaped maceheads, very fine, bifacially 'ripple-flaked' (pressure-flaked) flint knives with curved edges and backs, daggers with silver or copper blades as well as copper, gold or meteoric iron beads and copper bracelets. Copper vessels seem to have been more frequently used and locally made towards the end of this period. Traditional sets of cosmetic utensils were still used; it seems that at the very end of this period or at the start of the First

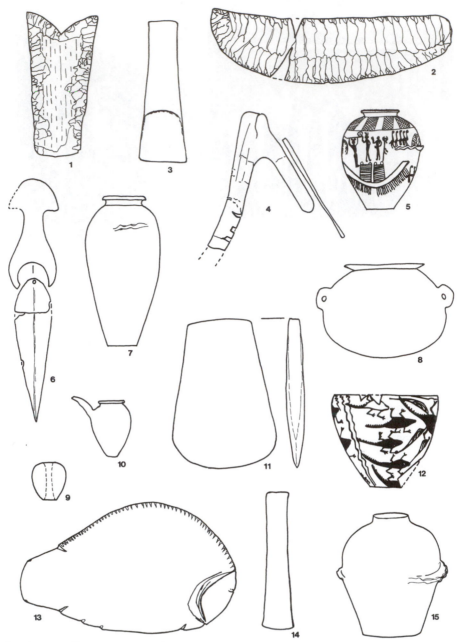

Figure 103 Artefacts found among Gerzean grave goods, Upper and Middle Egypt (about 5,500 to 5,100 years ago): 1, head of projectile or dagger of flaked and ground flint; 2, fine flint knife made with ripple flaking; 3, 11, 14, heads of copper adzes; 4, wooden hoe with stone blade; 5, 12. ceramic vessels with painted decoration; 6, dagger with silver blade; 7, 15, ceramic vessels with wavy-handles; 8, stone vessel; 9, macehead of stone; 10, fancy pottery vessel, probably imported from Palestine; 13, stone cosmetic palette. (Not to scale). (After Krzyzaniak, 1977.)

Dynasty (Naqada III) some of the slate palettes (said to be ceremonial) were decorated with flat carved motifs.

Items of foreign origin or their Egyptian imitations started to occur more frequently in this period. It seems that a particularly intensive Gerzean far-flung trade was going on with Palestine and Nubia. Studies of the Gerzean settlement patterns in the Nile valley indicate that, while burial grounds were traditionally founded on the higher terraces of the valley, permanent settlements – which so far have been practically not located – must have been situated on the floor of the alluvial valley. This suggests that either the level of the annual inundation and human settlement was considerably lower than is the case at present, or the Gerzeans had already mastered the art of protecting their habitations – probably located on mounds of silt like today – with dykes and the like against the rising water. The known Gerzean settlement

remains bear characteristics of a camp and seem to resemble those of the Amratians.

The archaeological evidence indicates the existence in Gerzean times of many cult practices that are reminiscent of those known from the Early Dynastic period. It seems that magic in particular, a characteristic component of the ancient Egyptian religion, may have been practised by the Gerzeans. A magical function may have been allotted to the anthropomorphic figurines used in Egypt since Badarian times. Ritual dances and scenes seem to have been the usual theme of figurative paintings on the Gerzean funerary pottery known as Decorated Ware. They show men and women usually represented larger than life-size (Fig. 104). Symbols of some gods ('tribal' deities) worshipped in Dynastic times (Horus, Min, Neith, Hathor) were carved on the palettes or painted on the funerary pots. A particularly frequent subject

Figure 104 Ritual dances painted on Gerzean funerary pottery vessels (Egypt). (After Krzyzaniak, 1977.)

in Gerzean art is a boat, probably funerary, represented in paintings or as small models (Plate 62).

A rich source of our knowledge of Gerzean funerary practices is provided by the numerous cemeteries known from the Nile valley and the Delta. The recently excavated cemetery of Minshat Abu Omar, in the eastern Delta (Plate 63), yielded particularly complex evidence of these practices and of the social composition of a Late Gerzean human group (Wildung, 1984). Like the Amratians, the Gerzeans interred animals in their burial grounds.

It seems that the rock art style known as the 'Eastern Invaders' style, which occurs in the Upper Egyptian Nile valley and the Eastern Desert (Winkler, 1938, 1939; Resch, 1967), may be contemporary with the Gerzeans. Frequent motifs of this art are drawings of the Nile boats and battle scenes (Plate 62).

It was during Gerzean times that Egyptian cultural influences were for the first time strongly felt in lower Nubia. Products of Egyptian origin started to be a frequent element among the funerary offerings in this southernmost part of Egypt (it is considered that ethnic Nubia starts at Gebel Silsila to the north of Aswan). Trade contacts with Egypt were probably responsible for the development of the A-Group archaeological culture (Trigger, 1976, pp. 32–46).

It is considered that in Predynastic times the cornerstone of the long process of cultural development in the Dynastic period was laid. It was traditionally believed by most researchers that this succession of archaeological cultures was the result of an invasion by foreign peoples who – through peaceful colonization or conquest – were introducing new cultural values and goods into Egypt (Petrie, 1920). In more recent years, however, scholars have been trying to find the explanation for Predynastic developments in cultural processes occurring in Egypt itself (Childe, 1935; Baumgartel, 1955, 1960; Hayes, 1965; Trigger, 1985; Hoffman, 1979; Vercoutter, 1981; Krzyzaniak, 1977). It seems obvious today that the most important aspect of this development was relatively rapid social change.

In contrast to the preceding Neolithic period, the Predynastic archaeological evidence is dominated by data originating from cemeteries. While evidence of this kind sheds relatively little light on such human activities as the subsistence economy, it is a valuable source of information about social phenomena. The most important phenomenon in the whole Predynastic period in Egypt was certainly the process of the concentration of power and goods and, as a result, the beginnings of social stratification. This was manifested by the emergence of the earliest social

élite and the political organization of a (proto-)state. Clear symptoms of these changes, it seems, can be traced to the end of this period.

The social development in Egypt in the Predynastic times has been described by Atzler (1981). On the basis of a careful and systematic analysis of the size and construction of the graves and of the offerings they contain, it is possible to date the moment of emergence of the social élite from the tribal society. One basis of this study was the classification of thousands of Predynastic graves into three different classes in terms of their size, construction and grave goods. The very beginnings of the appearance of a class of very large, complex and rich graves date already to Amratian times, but they become more established in the Gerzean period when – at its end – a small group of graves of outstanding construction and lavishly furnished appeared. It is believed that the two poorer classes of graves contain the remains of the members of Predynastic household communities – basic social units of production and distribution; the heads of these units may have had somewhat richer burials. The first real social élite in Egypt was interred in the richest class of graves. Its emergence coincided with a general rise in productivity and the introduction of new technologies on the Lower Nile, an increase in the level of social co-operation and organization which included specialization in the production of goods. It is thought that the burials of the leaders of the larger social groups and their relatives were interred in this class of graves. At the end of the Gerzean times (from subperiod Naqada IIc to Naqada III) a small group of exceptionally rich graves appeared within this class, even more outstandingly constructed and furnished, clear evidence of an extensive accumulation of power and goods by the individuals who were interred in these burials. A good example of such a burial is the famous Tomb 100 at Hierakonpolis and the large and originally rich tombs in cemeteries B and T at Naqada which are frequently called 'royal cemeteries'. It is believed that the leaders of larger territorial organizations – kings of the (proto-)states – were interred in these graves which contain their property and symbolic equipment. We have scanty information about the actual existence of these leaders in the earliest written records of the Dynastic chronology, which clearly refer to the kings ruling before the founder of the First Dynasty. Major centres of such territorial organization in Gerzean times seem to have existed at Hierakonpolis, Naqada and Thinis (Abydos) in Upper Egypt, and they undoubtedly were also in existence in the Delta (Plate 63). Written Dynastic evidence indicates such centres at Sais, Buto and Mendez (Vercoutter, 1981, pp. 717–18), but they were certainly more numerous, as recent fieldwork seems to suggest (Wildung, 1984; Krzyzaniak, 1989). The contents of these extremely complex and rich terminal Predynastic graves indicate not only an efficient and successful stratified social and political organization, and concentration of the material surplus, but indirectly also the effectiveness of this system for the growth of the economy through, for instance, the emergence of the first full-time specialists – craftsmen and artisans producing goods for the new élite. It can be envisaged that the centres of terminal Predynastic settlement – the first towns – were the places of residence of the new social élite, as well as of the first full-time specialists and individuals involved 'professionally' in cult practices.

CONCLUSION

When assessing social development in the late prehistoric Egypt, it can be seen that it was characterized by an astonishing acceleration in the rate of cultural change and growth in the last several hundred years before Dynastic times. After relatively slow development in the Neolithic period in the tenth to eighth millennium BP, the sixth millennium BP witnessed important economic and social changes, characterized by the concentration of power and goods and resulting in the emergence of the earliest stratified society, which became a leading force in this part of the Old World for the next few millennia.

BIBLIOGRAPHY

ATZLER, M. 1981. *Untersuchungen zur Herausbildung von Herrschaftsformen in Ägypten*. Hildesheim.

BANKS, K. N. 1984. *Climates, Cultures and Cattle: The Holocene Archaeology of the Eastern Sahara*. Dallas.

BARTA, W. 1979. Bemerkungen zu den Summenangaben des Turiner Königspapyrus für die Frühzeit und das Alte Reich. *Mitt. Dtsch Archäol. Inst. Abt. Kairo* (Mainz), Vol. 35, pp. 11–4.

BAUMGARTEL, E. J. 1955. *The Cultures of Prehistoric Egypt*. rev. edn. London/Oxford. Vol. 1.

—— 1960. *The Cultures of Prehistoric Egypt*. London/Oxford. Vol. 2.

BRUNTON, G. 1938. *Mostagedda and the Tasian Culture*. London, British School of Archaeology in Egypt.

BRUNTON, G.; CATON-THOMPSON, C. 1928. *The Badarian Civilization and the Predynastic Remains near Badari*. London, British School of Archaeology in Egypt.

BUTZER, K. W. 1976. *Early Hydraulic Civilization in Egypt: A Study of Cultural Archaeology*. Chicago/London.

CATON-THOMPSON, C.; GARDNER, E. W. 1934. *The Desert Fayum*. London.

CHILDE, V. G. 1935. *New Light on the Most Ancient Near East: The Oriental Prelude to European Prehistory*. London.

CLARK, J. D. 1971. A Re-examination of the Evidence for Agricultural Origins in the Nile Valley. *Proc. Prehist. Soc.*, Vol. 37, pp. 34–79.

DRIESCH, A. VON DEN; BOESSNECK, J. 1985. *Die Tierknochenfunde aus der neolithischen Siedlung von Merimde-Benisalame am westlichen Nildelta*. Munich.

EIWANGER, J. 1984. *Merimde-Benisalame I – Die Funde der Urschicht*. Mainz.

EVANS, J. D. 1971. Neolithic Knossos: The Growth of a Settlement. *Proc. Prehist. Soc.*, Vol. 37, pp. 95–117.

GAUTIER, A. 1968. Mammalian Remains of the Northern Sudan and Southern Egypt. In: WENDORF, F. (ed.), *The Prehistory of Nubia I*. Dallas. pp. 80–99.

—— 1984. Archaeozoology of the Bir Kiseiba Region, Eastern Sahara. In: WENDORF, F.; SCHILD, R.; CLOSE, A. E. (eds), *Cattle-Keepers of the Eastern Sahara: The Neolithic of Bir Kiseiba*. Dallas. pp. 49–72.

GAUTIER, A.; BALLMANN, P.; NEER, W. VAN. 1980. Molluscs, Fish, Birds and Mammals from the Late Palaeolithic Site in Wadi Kubbaniya. In: WENDORF, F.; SCHILD, R.; CLOSE, A. E. (eds), *Loaves and Fishes: The Prehistory of Wadi Kubbaniya*. Dallas. pp. 281–93.

HASSAN, F. 1980. Radiocarbon Chronology of Archaic Egypt. *J. Near East. Stud.* (Chicago), Vol. 39, pp. 203–7.

HAYES, W. C. 1965. *Most Ancient Egypt*. (Ed. K. C. Steele.) Chicago/London.

HAYS, T. R. 1984. Predynastic Development in Upper Egypt. In: KRZYZANIAK, L.; KOBUSIEWICZ, M. (eds), *Origin and Early Development of Food-Production Cultures in North-Eastern Africa*. Poznań. pp. 211–9.

HOFFMAN, M. A. 1979. *Egypt before the Pharaohs: The Prehistoric Foundations of Egyptian Civilization*. New York.

—— 1984. Predynastic Cultural Ecology and Patterns of Settlement in Upper Egypt as Viewed from Hierakonpolis. In: KRZYZANIAK, L.; KOBUSIEWICZ, M. (eds), *Origin and Early Development of Food-Production Cultures in North-Eastern Africa*. Poznań. pp. 235–45.

KAISER, W. 1956. Stand und Probleme der ägyptischen Vorgeschichtsforschung. *Z. ägypt. Sprache Altertkd.* (Berlin), Vol. 81, pp. 87–109.

KRZYZANIAK, L. 1977. *Early Farming Cultures on the Lower Nile: The Predynastic Period in Egypt*. Warsaw.

—— 1989. Recent Archaeological Evidence on the Earliest Settlement in the Eastern Nile Delta. In: KRZYZANIAK, L.; KOBUSIEWICZ, M. (eds), *Late Prehistory of the Nile Basin and the Sahara*. Poznań. pp. 267–85.

MCBURNEY, C. B. M. 1967. *The Haua Fteah (Cyrenaica) and the Stone Age of the South-East Mediterranean*. Cambridge.

NOTEN, F. VAN. 1978. *Rock Art of the Jebel Uweinat (Libyan Sahara)*. Graz.

PETRIE, W. M. F. 1920. *Prehistoric Egypt*. London, British School of Archaeology in Egypt.

RESCH, W. F. E. 1967. *Die Felsbilder Nubiens: eine Dokumentation der ostägyptischen und nubischen Petroglyphen*. Graz.

RIZKANA, L.; SEEHER, J. 1984. New Light in the Relation of Maadi to the Upper Egyptian Cultural Sequence. *Mitt. Dtsch. Archäol. Inst. Abt. Kairo* (Mainz), Vol. 40, pp. 237–52.

SAID, R. et al. 1972. Remarks on the Holocene Geology and Archaeozoology of the Northern Fayum Desert. *Archaeol. Polona* (Wroclaw), Vol. 13, pp. 7–22.

SINGH, P. 1974. *Neolithic Cultures of Western Asia*. London.

SMITH, H. 1969. Animal Domestication and Animal Cult in Dynastic Egypt. In: UCKO, P. J.; DIMBLEBY, G. W. (eds), *The Domestication and Exploitation of Plants and Animals*. Chicago. pp. 307–16.

TRIGGER, G. G. 1976. *Nubia under the Pharaohs*. London.

—— 1985. The Rise of Egyptian Civilization. In: *Ancient Egypt: A Social History*. Cambridge. pp. 1–70.

VERCOUTTER, J. 1981. Discovery and Diffusion of Metals and Development of Social Systems up to the Fifth Century before Our Era. In: KI-ZERBO, J. (ed.), *General History of Africa*, Vol. 1: *Methodology and African Prehistory*. Paris, UNESCO. pp. 706–28.

WENDORF, F. 1968. Late Palaeolithic Sites in Egyptian Nubia. In: WENDORF, F. (ed.), *The Prehistory of Nubia II*. Dallas. pp. 791–953.

WENDORF, F.; SCHILD, R. 1984a. Introduction. In: WENDORF, F.; SCHILD, R.; CLOSE, A. E. (eds), *Cattle-Keepers of the Eastern Sahara: The Neolithic of Bir Kiseiba*. Dallas. pp. 1–18.

—— 1984b. Conclusions. In: WENDORF, F.; SCHILD, R.; CLOSE, A. E. (eds), *Cattle-Keepers of the Eastern Sahara: The Neolithic of Bir Kiseiba*. Dallas. pp. 404–28.

WENDORF, F.; SCHILD, R.; CLOSE, A. E. (eds) 1980. *Loaves and Fishes: The Prehistory of Wadi Kubbaniya*. Dallas.

—— (eds) 1984. *Cattle-Keepers of the Eastern Sahara: The Neolithic of Bir Kiseiba*. Dallas.

WILDUNG, D. 1984. Terminal Prehistory of the Nile Delta: Theses. In: KRZYZANIAK, L.; KOBUSIEWICZ, M. (eds), *Origin and Early Development of Food-Production Cultures in North-Eastern Africa*. Poznań. pp. 265–69.

WINKLER, H. A. 1938–9. *Rock-Drawings of Southern Upper Egypt*. London. 2 vols. (Vol. 1, 1938; Vol. 2, 1939.)

40

AFRICA (EXCLUDING EGYPT)

from the beginnings of food production up to about 5,000 years ago

David W. Phillipson

AFRICAN FOOD PRODUCTION

In comparison with much of western Asia and parts of Europe, Africa was slow to adopt techniques of food production. This fact may at first seem puzzling in view of the very early development in parts of Africa of the intensive exploitation of wild food resources, examples of which are best known from the Egyptian Nile valley and, less certainly, from the coastal plains of Algeria. In the former region, for instance at Esna (Wendorf and Schild, 1976), wild cereals, notably barley, were evidently harvested in substantial quantities and processed for food as early as 12,000 years ago. Later, there was widespread experimentation with the control of wild animals, including numerous species that were not subsequently domesticated, such as giraffe, various antelope, lions, monkeys, etc. (H. S. Smith, 1969). It is tempting to speculate that such practices may have been far more frequent in northern Africa than is currently appreciated, in view of the suggestion (Saxon, 1974) that hunters in coastal Algeria, as at Tamar Hat earlier than 10,000 years ago, practised selective slaughter of Barbary sheep in order to maintain the size of the herds.

In considering these African percursors to food production we should draw attention to several factors that illuminate the nature of the transition from hunting and gathering to farming and help us to understand its specifically African significance. First, the dividing line between wild plants and animals on the one hand and their domestic counterparts on the other is extremely vague and ill defined. It can only be recognized by the botanist or zoologist using genetic or morphological criteria, yet its principal implications are for the study of human behaviour. Many attempts by men and women to secure the safety, welfare and productivity of their plant and animal food-sources could have yielded major economic benefit over many generations without resulting in discernible change to the species concerned. Examples from the fringes of the African Equatorial forest are cited on p. 414.

The preservation of actual remains of animals and, especially, plants is often rare in the physical and chemical conditions that prevail on archaeological sites in many parts of Africa. Even when they are preserved, specialists frequently encounter considerable difficulty in distinguishing domestic from wild varieties. Most bones of domestic cattle, for example, cannot readily be differentiated from those of wild buffalo (A. B. Smith, 1986). The pollen grains of cultivated cereals, too, are notoriously difficult to recognize (Higgs, 1972). It is only when domestication has resulted in a major expansion in a species's area of distribution that designations of domestication are safely removed from the realms of controversy. But, again, there are important varieties of African food plants, most notably the yam, the enset and the banana, whose traces will hardly ever survive in the archaeological record, and the prehistorian must rely upon botanical arguments to illustrate the early stages of the history of these crops (Harlan, 1982).

Although the history of plant and animal domestication is generally considered in terms of food production, it is important to realize that it was not exclusively as food that these wild species were brought under human control. Domestic animals also provide haulage and transport for goods and personnel, act as guards and assist in hunting and other pursuits. They provide materials for making clothing and for other crafts. Among many African peoples they serve as the repositories and embodiment of a society's wealth. Plants not only provide food, but also narcotics and stimulants, fibres and dyes, together with substances of medical and magical importance. None of these functions should be assumed, however, to be a prerogative of domestic varieties.

Before considering the advantages and stimuli that may have led to the adoption of food production in the various regions of Africa, it will be useful to enumerate the principal animals and plants that are involved.

The animals are comparatively few and simple to list (Zeuner, 1963; Epstein, 1971; Clark and Brandt, 1984). Goats, sheep and cattle are widespread through most regions of the continent. The first two (which cannot easily be differentiated one from the other on the basis of the bones recovered from archaeological sites) have no wild prototype known in Africa, and may be assumed to have been introduced into that continent in an already domesticated form, presumably from south-western Asia where their domestication is known to predate any African occurrence. Cattle are more problematic. There is an increasing body of evidence that the earliest African domestic cattle, those of the Sahara, are derived from a local wild prototype, *Bos primigenius*. Their subsequent dispersal to more southerly parts of Africa was often restricted by the presence of tsetse flies, carriers of trypanosomiasis to which most breeds of domestic cattle are highly susceptible. Other varieties of cattle, notably the humped short-horned zebu, may have been introduced from the east at a later date, but until further research has been undertaken on the prehistory of African cattle breeds one can do little more than speculate on these questions.

The pig (*Sus*) was included among the stock of the earliest Lower Egyptian farmers and evidently derived from south-western Asia. By Roman times it was widespread in northern Africa, but its distribution has since been curtailed by the spread of Islam and Ethiopian Christianity, both of which follow a more ancient Semitic prohibition on the eating of pork. The antiquity of domestic pigs in the coastal regions of West Africa is uncertain. The Zande and their neighbours of the Nile–Congo watershed area are reported to have tamed the local bush-pig (*Potamochoerus*). Further to the south, domestic pigs were not known prior to European colonization.

Of other African domestic animals, the donkey is attested in Egypt from at least the mid-sixth millennium BP, and is represented in rock art – probably of a somewhat later date – as far west as the Atlas mountains. Its use had reached southern Nubia by about 2,700 years ago and eventually reached the areas of East Africa under the influence of Nilotic-speakers. The camel is generally believed to have been introduced to north-eastern Africa from Arabia little more than 2,000 years ago: certainly it was exceedingly rare in Egypt until that time, although indications have recently been discerned that it may have been present in parts of the Horn of Africa at a significantly earlier date (Phillipson, 1984). The cat was probably originally domesticated in south-west Asia or in Egypt or in both as an aid to hunting: by New Kingdom times it had obtained sacred status in the latter area but remained unknown elsewhere in Africa.

Horses were imported to Egypt from about 3,600 years ago and were used for pulling wheeled vehicles and, occasionally, for riding. They were known in Nubia 2,700 years ago and through much of north Africa and the Sahara at the same time or somewhat earlier, the primary evidence being derived from undated rock art representaions. The horses of the Maghreb probably derive from this stock, established prior to the arrival of Arab horses. The southernmost presence of horses in pre-colonial Africa was in the sub-Saharan Sudanic savannah, whither they were presumably introduced from the Maghreb by the late first millennium of the Christian era.

Remarkably little attention has so far been paid to the domestic fowl (*Gallus*), which was widespread in Roman north Africa. Its presence south of the Sahara is often assumed to have been due to introduction via the Indian Ocean coastal settlements during the late first millennium of the Christian era, but there is little convincing evidence for this. The Guinea fowl (*Numida meleagris*) was also familiar to the Romans in north Africa, whence it was exported to Europe. It is of African origin, widely distributed, but where and when it was domesticated remains unknown. It was 'rediscovered' by the Portuguese on the west African coast in the sixteenth century.

The most commonly and widely known of all domestic animals, the dog, was widespread in Africa where, as in many parts of the world, it appears to be one of the oldest domestic animals. In both Egypt and the Sudan it is represented on the sites of the first farming peoples. In southern Africa it is depicted in rock art which may predate the local appearance of other domestic animals.

It emerges from the summaries given above that the domestic animals for which a local African ancestor may be postulated on zoological grounds include certain breeds of cattle, the donkey and the Guinea fowl (although there is no proof that the latter was ever domesticated in Africa in early times). The dog and cat are also candidates for local domestication. The remaining animals noted – sheep, goat, pig, horse, camel and fowl – all appear to have been introduced to Africa in a domesticated form, although at least the first four on the list ultimately gave rise to characteristically African varieties.

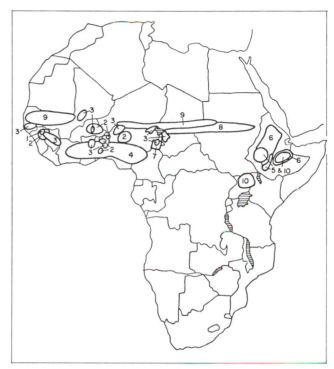

Map 44 General distribution of wild precursors of African cultivated plants. 1, *Brachiaria deflexa*; 2, *Digitaria exilis* and *Digitaria iburua*; 3, *Oryza glaberrima*; 4, *Dioscorea rotundata*; 5, *Musa ensete* and *Guizotia abyssinica*; 6, *Eragrostis tef*; 7, *Voandzeia* and *Kerstingiella*; 8, *Sorghum bicolor*; 9, *Pennisetum americanum*; 10, *Eleusine coracana*. (After Harlan, 1971, Fig. 5.)

It is now appropriate to turn to a consideration of plants, where we are faced with a far greater variety of types (Harlan et al., 1976) (Map 44). First, there are the winter-rainfall cereals, wheat and barley, which have been cultivated for many millennia in north Africa and Ethiopia, where the climatic conditions are suitable. These crops, together with flax, appear to have been introduced to Africa from south-western Asia, where their cultivation is attested at a date significantly earlier than any such evidence from Africa. However, the distribution of wild barley extends into Egypt, and it is possible that future research will reveal exploitation leading to local domestication in this area.

Winter rainfall in Africa does not extend at the present time south of the region around latitude 23° N (except for a restricted area in the Cape Province of South Africa). Fluctuations in this pattern during the Holocene have probably been minor. In the summer-rainfall regions wheat and barley can rarely be cultivated successfully without substantial irrigation, and the principal crops grown there are, with the exception of some comparatively recent introductions from Indonesia and the Americas, of indigenous origin. They may be summarily divided into three categories.

The sub-Saharan savannah crops are primarily cereals. They include sorghum, bulrush or pearl millet (*Pennisetum*), and fonio and its relatives (*Digitaria*). Also in this category should be included African rice (*Oryza glaberrima*). Minor crops which accompany these cereals are the Bambara groundnut (*Voandzeia subterranea*), some varieties of squash (*Citrullus*) and cotton (*Gossypium herbaceum*), gourd (*Lagenaria*) and cola nut (*Cola*).

The plants listed above are essentially those of the lowland Sahel and savannah north of the Equatorial forest. In highland Ethiopia, east of the Nile, a distinctive suite of crops is grown. The cereals include wheat and barley, together with finger millet (*Eleusine*), of which the last may have originated in the north-east African highlands. The preferred cereal is, however, teff (*Eragrostis tef*) which is an exclusively Ethiopian cultigen. Also widely grown in this area are the oil-yielding noog (*Guizotia abyssinica*) and the narcotic chat (*Catha edulis*). In the south of Ethiopia the staple food crop is the enset (*Ensete ventricosa*), a banana-like plant of which the stems and leaf-bases are made into a bread-like substance. These Ethiopian plants are of restricted distribution and were undoubtedly domesticated locally: their antiquity will be discussed below.

Lastly, we must consider the crops of the Equatorial forest and, more importantly, the forest margins. These are primarily vegetatively propagated, non-cereal crops. Pride of place must go to the African yam (*Dioscorea*) species and, second, to the cowpea (*Vigna unguiculata*). This is the place also to note a group of trees, notably the oil palm (*Elaeis guineensis*) and shea butter tree (*Butyrospermum paradoxum*). These are important sources of oil, which is regularly collected, but it is debatable whether the trees are formally cultivated rather than tended and protected. Likewise, *Canarium schweinfurthii* and *Celtis integrifolia* are wild forest trees, often protected, while the baobab (*Adansonia digitata*) enjoys similar status in the low-lying savannahs. Most of these plants are difficult to trace as cultigens in the archaeological record, either because – as with yams – they have no hard parts likely to be preserved, or because they are morphologically indistinguishable from their fully wild counterparts.

For the sake of completeness, it is useful here to note briefly some of the major cultivated plants that have been introduced to sub-Saharan Africa within comparatively recent times, since several of these have had a major impact upon indigenous farming practices and dietary preferences. The most widespread are two crops of New World origin, introduced since the early sixteenth century: maize and cassava (or manioc) which have been widely adopted as staples. Tobacco shares this origin, as do a variety of beans and pumpkins, the sweet potato, the chilli pepper, the guava and the papaw. More problematic and harder to date is a group of plants introduced to Africa from across the Indian Ocean. The most important of these crops is the banana, now a major staple in the Lake Victoria region. Others include the coconut, sugarcane, Asian rice, the betel nut and, probably, cannabis.

It will be seen from the foregoing that the variety of indigenous African crops is much greater than that of locally domesticated animals. In the former case, the foci of innovation appear, on botanical grounds, to have been centred between latitudes 18° and 5° N, between the southern Sahara and the northern margins of the Equatorial forest, and to have included the distinctive environments of the Ethiopian highlands on the eastern side of the continent. More southerly parts of Africa lack wild prototypes of domesticated species, and appear to have adopted domestic plants and animals that had originated further to the north. As is shown later in this chapter, the picture receives some confirmation from the very incomplete archaeological evidence that is currently available. Archaeological discoveries do illustrate the local development and adoption of food production techniques in Africa north of the Equator during the period from 8,000 to 3,500 years ago. They also support the view that it was not until substantially later that these techniques, with the plants and animals on which they depended, were transmitted to more southerly regions. It is necessary to seek an explanation for this apparent tardiness.

The advantages afforded by food production are often taken for granted as self-evident. In fact, the richness of the African biome, providing an enormous variety of wild plant and animal foods in a continent that supported, until very recently, a fairly sparse human population is such as to call the advantages of farming seriously into question. Even in the less productive regions, recent studies have shown that hunting and gathering provide a substantially higher level of nutrition for the expenditure of less time and physical effort than does herding or agriculture (Hitchcock and Ebert, 1984). It appears that, at least under African conditions, an unusual stimulus may be needed to initiate the adoption of food production. Once the transition has been made, however, there are pressures against reversion to an earlier life-style.

A widespread feature of African hunter-gatherer societies is the egalitarian sharing of resources. In such a context, there are built-in pressures against the partial or temporary adoption of food production, which would tend to remove its practitioners from the cycle of reciprocity. Once released from this cycle, and with competition for resources substituted for intra-group sharing, a population may be expected to increase rapidly towards the maximum carrying capacity of the available territory. The significance of sedentism in these processes is examined below.

SETTLED LIFE AND EARLY AFRICAN FOOD PRODUCTION

It is instructive also to examine some of the other changes in life-style which may be considered as dependent upon the adoption of food production. The breakdown of communal food sharing has just been noted. Related to this is a potential shift in gender roles, with a possible reduction in women's food-getting activities. This in itself may be related to the population increase, which, as we have seen, generally seems to have accompanied the adoption of food production. Sedentism is another important factor in this, and one which also permitted the accumulation of personal possessions with wealth and power as natural accompaniments. It is this wide-ranging set of 'side effects' that helps to explain the often irreversible nature of the transition from hunter-gatherer to farmer. It may also be noted that these effects are markedly greater in the case of agricultural societies than for those which rely exclusively upon pastoralism.

The adoption of food production should not therefore be considered alone, or seen as a desirable end in itself. Innate conservatism may often have combined with the bounty of the natural African environment to delay the adoption of agriculture, herding or mixed farming, but there are varied, less tangible reasons why the adoption of such practices should often have been delayed. We can understand much better the nature of the eventual transition, and its general irreversibility, if we consider the full package of cultural change which, it has been argued, may be expected to have accompanied the adoption of food production on any substantial scale. It follows from this that many influences may have been simultaneously in operation: change in this complex area should not be seen as monocausal. Once this change in emphasis is made, the archaeological evidence from African sites may be interpreted to yield a picture both more comprehensive and more comprehensible.

Cause and effect must not be confused, however. It has often been suggested that some of the major long-term contributions to human development provided by the adoption of food production were made because farming facilitated – or required – a sedentary life-style and thus the establishment of long-lasting buildings, the accumulation of possessions and so forth. The African archaeological data are of particular interest in this connection because they indicate that, over large areas of that continent, the opposite situation prevailed. Here it seems that settled communities were established many centuries before there is any evidence for the practice of any form of food production (Sutton, 1974). Their economic basis was not primarily the hunting of animals or the collecting of edible plants (although both activities were practised), but fishing. Lakes well stocked with fish provide an assured year-round supply of nutritious food in a single location, and such lakes were widespread over those parts of Africa that now comprise the southern Sahara and Sahel, with an extension into northern areas of East Africa, during the early Holocene.

It was, so the archaeological evidence now indicates, among the settled communities supported by these lakes that sub-Saharan African peoples first adopted domestic animals – both those of foreign northerly origin and those descended from local wild species gradually brought under human control – and began the care and cultivation of local food plants (see p. 419).

NORTH AFRICA

The northern coastlands of Africa face on to the Mediterranean Sea and have for millennia seen contacts between African peoples and those from other parts of the Mediterranean world. Egypt in particular has been a focus of interaction, having land links with south-west Asia as well as with north Africa and the Sahara and, via the Nile, with more southerly regions also. Although the later prehistory of Egypt falls outside the scope of this chapter, it is impossible to explain the impact of food production in Africa without reference to the developments that took place in the north-easternmost part of the continent.

During the early Holocene the north African littoral was inhabited by hunter-gatherer peoples whose predominantly microlithic industries are generally designated Capsian in the Maghreb and Libyco-Capsian further to the east. Hunting, notably of the Barbary sheep, and collecting edible snails appear to have provided the mainstay of the Capsian economy, in an environment from which the oak and pine forests of the final Pleistocene were rapidly retreating (Camps, 1974; McBurney, 1967). It is in this context that evidence for food production may first be discerned about 7,800 years ago, when domestic sheep or goat or both are represented at the Haua Fteah cave in Cyrenaica. There was no significant change in the associated stone industry at this time, and pottery did not make its appearance until later. The domestic small stock (i.e. sheep and goat) were clearly not derived from the Barbary sheep, the only local animal

that could be considered a possible progenitor, and it may safely be concluded that they were introduced to the area from elsewhere. This view is strengthened by the broad contemporaneity of the earliest evidence for herding in Cyrenaica with the advent of farming in the Nile Delta (Chapter 39). Cereal agriculture was practised in the Delta settlements, with both wheat and barley being cultivated, but is not indicated further to the west at this time. It may reasonably be concluded that, since a mixed farming economy exploiting domestic wheat, barley, flax, pigs and small stock had reached lower Egypt in the first half of the eighth millennium BP, small stock were also rapidly adopted by the inhabitants of the Libyan coastlands.

Further to the west, beyond the Gulf of Sirte, small stock were also present as early as the seventh millennium BP. This, it may be observed, is broadly contemporary with their appearance in several western Mediterranean coastal areas in France, Spain, Sardinia and Italy, at sites that are also marked by the presence of pottery decorated with characteristic shell impressions. Pottery of this type also occurs on the African coast in parts of northern Morocco, as at El Khril (Jodin, 1959), with related material also in Algeria.

It may be seen from the foregoing that the north African coastlands shared with other areas bordering the central and western Mediterranean the introduction of domestic small stock by both land and maritime routes from an ultimate source in south-west Asia. The subsequent development in the Maghreb of a complex pattern of transhumant pastoralism, in which cattle were also ultimately exploited, is discussed on p. 419. The date at which cereal agriculture, based presumably on both wheat and barley, began in Mediterranean Africa outside Egypt remains unknown and is an important focus for future research.

THE SAHARA AND THE CENTRAL SUDANESE NILE VALLEY (Map 45)

These regions must occupy a key position in any study of early African food production. During the period we are concerned with here there is evidence for substantial environmental change, of which at least the general trends are now reasonably well understood. In the central and southern Sahara, from Mali to the Western Desert of Egypt, lakes and watercourses developed during the early Holocene and were accompanied by fauna and flora quite distinct from those that prevail in these areas today. Hippopotamus and crocodile, for example, with antelope which feed on lush well-watered vegetation, flourished in regions that are now exceedingly arid. It is important, however, not to visualize the early Holocene Sahara as a continuous zone of well-watered terrain, but rather as a mosaic in which highland areas of increased precipitation, and the country watered by their run-off, interdigitated with zones whose desert conditions differed only in extent from those of today. Short periods of desiccation are attested over wide areas around 8,200 and 6,800 years ago and became progressively more general after about 5,700 years ago, although regional variation may readily be detected.

Two major factors should be taken into account in evaluating the scale of the environmental contrast between mid-Holocene conditions and those of today. Firstly, the extent of surface water was very greatly increased. Lake Chad, for example, reached a maximum extent about 12,000–7,000 years ago of over 400,000 km^2, more than fifteen times its recent area. Numerous other lakes existed that are now

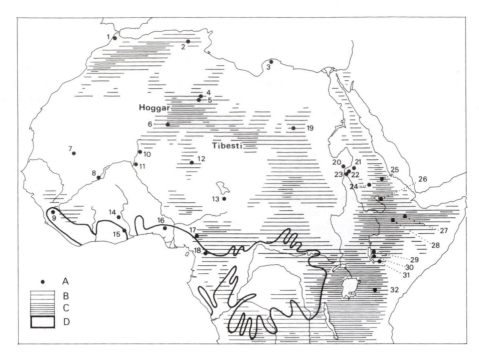

Map 45 Saharan, west African and eastern African sites illustrating early food production: A, archaeological sites mentioned in the text; B, land over 500 m; C, land over 1,000 m; D, modern extent of equatorial forest. 1, El Khril; 2, Capeletti; 3, Haua Fteah; 4, Van Muhüggiag; 5, Ti-n-Torha; 6, Amekni; 7, Dhar Tichitt; 8, Jenne-Jeno; 9, Kamabai; 10, Asselar; 11, Karkarichinkat; 12, Adrar Bous; 13, Daïma; 14, Kintampo; 15, Bosumpra; 16, Iwo Eleru; 17, Shum Laka; 18, Obobogo; 19, Jebel Uweinat; 20, Esh Shaheinab; 21, Shagadud; 22, Kadero; 23, Early Khartoum; 24, Kashm el Girba; 25, Gobedra; 26, Lalibela cave; 27, Laga Oda; 28, Lake Besaka; 29, Lleret; 30, Dongonien; 31, Ele Bor; 32, Lukenya Hill.

completely dry, as at Adrar Bous in Niger, and water flowed year-round or seasonally in channels which are today subject only to very rare floods. Such a greatly expanded occurrence of surface water and its accompanying vegetation increased rates of evaporation, water vapour in the atmosphere and local rainfall. Together with other climatic factors, such as shifts in the inter-tropical convergence zone, which remain imperfectly understood, these conditions resulted in the location of vegetational zones considerably closer to the central Sahara than their current position. During the Holocene climatic optimum, to cite but one example, it appears that the northern forest margin, now located near the Nile–Congo watershed in the southernmost Sudan, lay some 600 km further to the north, with savannah extending almost to southern Nubia (Mohammed-Ali, 1982). Such shifts in ecological zones must inevitably have resulted in movement of human populations. Indeed, the activities of these populations, through vegetation clearance both on their own account and, in due course, through the activities of their herds of domestic animals, must have accelerated the processes of change. These are magnifications of processes which occur constantly on a seasonal or short-term scale, as transhumant savannah pastoralists move northwards towards the Sahara at times of rainfall and retreat southwards during drought (Connah, 1981).

The late Palaeolithic peoples of the Nile valley in Upper Egypt had, as indicated in Chapter 39, engaged in the intensive use of wild cereal foods, notably barley. However, there is no clear evidence for the formal cultivation of cereals in the Egyptian Western Desert earlier than about 8,000 years ago or in the Nile valley before about 7,000 years ago. Corresponding innovation elsewhere in northern Africa was probably contemporary or later (Wendorf and Hassan, 1980; Hassan, 1985; A. B. Smith, 1984). Evidence for the herding of domestic animals in Egypt shows a similar pattern; else-

where this practice may have been adopted substantially earlier than the cultivation of food crops, although in evaluating the possibility it is important to remember the differential preservation of the primary evidence, animal bones being much more readily preserved and recovered from archaeological sites than are remains of plants.

Upstream, in the Sudanese Nile valley, the period from about 8,200 years ago until 7,400 years ago was marked by the complex known variously as the Early Khartoum industry or the Khartoum Mesolithic. Its distribution is now known to extend along 500 km of the valley centred on Khartoum, from Kosti in the south to around Shendi in the north. The only significant occurrences that are known away from the Nile are at Shaqadud in the Butana plain and near Kashm el Girba on the Atbara (Fattovich et al., 1984; Marks et al., 1985). Just as the local antecedents of this complex remain unknown, so do any contemporary occupations of the surrounding areas: it is uncertain how far this apparent isolation represents merely the uneven pattern of current research into Sudanese prehistory.

The Khartoum Mesolithic people established settlements on or near the banks of the Nile which appear to have covered up to 700 m² and to have seen prolonged occupation, as is indicated by fragments of clay daub and the accumulation of archaeological deposits up to 2.5 m deep. The faunal remains, which include no trace of domestic animals, show that fish and other aquatic creatures were the mainstay of the economy. Fishing equipment included barbed bone harpoonheads and grooved stones that have been interpreted as net-sinkers. Land animals that were hunted comprised species which frequent well-watered riverine environments. These combine with evidence from molluscs, wild nuts and geomorphological data to indicate a much moister, more wooded situation than that which prevails in the Khartoum area today, with the Nile then flowing at a significantly higher level. Flaked stone tools included backed microliths; there were no edge-ground implements. Pottery bowls were characterized by 'Wavy Line' decoration, apparently executed by dragging a catfish spine over the soft surface of the clay. Rubbing or grinding stones suggest that grains may have been exploited but, apart from the presence of oil palm nuts, there was no conclusive evidence for the use of vegetable foods (Arkell, 1949; Mohammed-Ali, 1982).

Despite the apparent isolation of the Khartoum Mesolithic province in the Sudanese Nile valley, broadly contemporary archaeological assemblages have been recovered in parts of East Africa (see pp. 421–2) and over a wide area of the central and southern Sahara. By the ninth millennium BP the hunting and grain-collecting life-style of earlier times had in numerous areas been modified by the establishment of settlements beside lake shores and other water sources, where the ready availability of aquatic foodstuffs, notably fish, permitted semi-permanent habitation. The fishing technology, based upon the use of harpoons with barbed bone heads, was analogous to that of the Khartoum Mesolithic (Sutton, 1974). These Saharan sites are also marked by the presence of pottery, which, again, is closely similar to that of the 'Wavy Line' or 'Dotted Wavy Line' styles characteristic of the contemporary sites in the Sudanese Nile valley. This was not, however, the only Saharan pottery tradition at this time: the vessels from such sites as Amekni in the Hoggar of south-eastern Algeria, dating back as far as 8,700 years ago, include vessels decorated with a walking stamp to produce a repeatedly impressed zigzag line (Camps, 1969, 1974).

It is against this background that the beginnings of food production in the Sahara and in the Sudanese Nile valley should be considered. It will be convenient to discuss separately the exploitation of cultivated plants and that of domestic animals, since it should be appreciated that the two practices were not necessarily linked.

The principal domestic animals of this area are cattle, sheep and goats. Since the last two are difficult to differentiate osteologically, they are here referred to collectively as small stock. There are no known local wild species in Africa from which domestic small stock could have been descended (the Barbary sheep *Ovis ammotragus* may for genetic reasons be excluded) and it may therefore be assumed, as noted on p. 415, that small stock were introduced from south-west Asia in an already domesticated form. A similar foreign origin was at one time postulated for the domestic cattle, but it now appears that there are no valid reasons why these may not have been derived from the local Saharan wild cattle *Bos primigenius* (A. B. Smith, 1980a). More detailed osteological studies will be required before the controversy may be resolved.

It will be noted below how sparse is the datable osteological evidence for early Saharan domestic animals from excavations. Fortunately, these data may be supplemented by reference to the many rock paintings and petroglyphs which are widely distributed, notably in the highlands. It is only in exceptional circumstances that an absolute chronology may be established for the rock art. Several attempts have, however, been made to distinguish stylistic sequences, notably in the Hoggar, Acacus and Tibesti highlands. These sequences may then tentatively be linked by their subject matter with the archaeological successions to produce a provisional chronology. That most widely accepted sees an initial phase of art with line engravings depicting exclusively wild animals, for which an age extending back at least nine millennia has been proposed. The later paintings show human figures with characteristic round heads (perhaps eight millennia BP) overlapping in time with the so-called 'bovidean' paintings in which pastoral scenes are predominant and which are thought to date between the eighth and fourth millennia BP. Later styles are defined by the successive appearance of horses and camels (P. E. L. Smith, 1968; Willcox, 1984). Despite their chronological uncertainty, the Saharan rock paintings do have the potential to provide substantial detailed amplification of our knowledge of prehistoric pastoralism in that part of Africa. Breeds of cattle may, for example, be recognized, as may the practice of artificial deformation of the horns which has continued in the Sahara, as in parts of East Africa, into recent times. Milking and use of cattle for riding are also depicted. The art shows many details of clothing and illustrations of the domestic, social and ritual life of the Saharan herders (Lhote, 1959; Mori, 1965; Stehli, 1978; Muzzolini, 1986).

In this connection, particular interest attaches to the undated rock peckings at Jebel Uweinat in south-eastern Libya. Here, several wild species, notably giraffe and ostrich, are depicted tethered and being led by halters (Fig. 105) (van Noten, 1978). Taken in conjuction with evidence from the Egyptian Nile valley (Chapter 39), this provides a clear indication that experiments were conducted in north-eastern Africa with the control of many animal species additional to those that eventually became fully domesticated (Clark, 1971).

Data relating to plant cultivation are very much more elusive. The winter rainfall area of the northern Sahara falls, with the northern coastal regions, in the territory where wheat and barley may have been grown, given suitable local conditions. Beyond Egypt and Nubia, however, there is virtually no convincing evidence for their cultivation in the period with which we are here concerned. To the south, in the summer rainfall areas, the south-west Asian cereal crops would not flourish and any prehistoric agriculture may be expected to have been based upon local plants. There are in this region a very large number of wild grasses, of such genera as *Sorghum*, *Pennisetum*, *Panicum* and *Eragrostis* to name but a few, whose exploitation for food has been recorded in recent times. Some, notably the first two, include species that have been brought under cultivation and, in that form, they are attested in later times in more southerly regions. Certain artefacts, notably grinding stones, were probably often used in the preparation of cereal foods, but it is impossible to ascertain whether these foods came from cultivated or wild plants unless remains of the plants themselves are preserved. Even then it may be difficult to be sure whether there are any morphological changes present that must be attributed to the processes of cultivation: as already noted (p. 412), the distinction between wild and cultivated plants cannot be precisely defined. Grinding stones are abundant on Saharan and Nile valley sites from at least the ninth millennium BP, but no absolutely convincing remains of cultivated plants are recorded from contexts which predate the fifth millennium BP.

Several localities in the central Sahara provide archaeological sequences that cover the period of the inception of food production, although the precise nature of the economic developments that took place at this time generally remain poorly understood. In the Tadrart Acacus massif of the Libyan Sahara, for example, research by Barich (1984) in the Wadi Ti-n-Torha has demonstrated two successive phases of early to mid-Holocene occupation. The earlier, dated to about 9,400 to 7,200 years ago, has a well-developed lithic industry dominated by pointed backed bladelets; pottery,

Figure 105 Two giraffes and an ostrich tied up. Rock carving, Jebel Uweinat (Libya). (After F. Van Noten.)

where present, is of the 'Dotted Wavy Line' tradition. Barich (1984, p. 684) attributes this material to 'semisedentary hunter-fishers engaged in an extensive exploitation of their habitat that included incipient domestication of plant and animal species'. Later, eight to seven millennia ago, lithic tools were less specialized (apart from a small number of arrowheads), but pottery was plentiful, being apparently developed from the stylistic tradition represented in the earlier phase. Faunal remains indicate that both cattle and goats were by now domesticated. This research sets in their context the earlier findings of Mori (1965), who at Uan Muhuggiag located the skull of a domestic short-horn ox dated to about 7,500 years ago, together with remains of small stock.

By contrast, the archaeological succession of this period in the Sudanese Nile valley is comparatively well known, thanks to recent intensive research. The former belief, based upon Arkell's (1953) excavations at Esh Shaheinab, on the west bank of the Nile some 70 km north of Khartoum, that the local herding of domestic animals began on a very small scale six millennia ago, has been shown to be erroneous. It now appears that from about 6,400 to 5,700 years ago (Hassan, 1986) the successors to the Khartoum Mesolithic had developed a complex pattern of seasonal resource exploitation over a territory that, unlike that of their predecessors, extended for some distance away from the river on either bank. As in earlier times, aquatic foods were an important resource for the Khartoum Neolithic people, especially in the dry season; but large herds of cattle and small stock were also maintained at settlements away from the river. The best known of these pastoral sites is at Kadero, 18 km north-east of Khartoum (Krzyzaniak, 1978). Here also, huge numbers of heavily used grinding stones strongly suggest the extensive use of plant foods. There are numerous grain impresssions on the pottery, but so far no convincing case has been made that any of these plants were cultivated. Links with the central Sahara at this time are indicated by the distribution of exotic raw materials for stone-tool manufacture. Later developments in the central Nile valley are poorly understood: indeed, after about 5,500 years ago the ancient inhabitants of the central Sudan remain totally unknown. Only at Shaqadud in the Butana plain is there any indication that the

Khartoum Neolithic tradition continued into later times (Marks et al., 1985).

To the north, in Sudanese Nubia, arid conditions probably prevailed throughout the Holocene, and human settlement was restricted to the very narrow strip of the Nile valley itself, where high river levels would have rendered extensive tracts suitable for grazing or cultivation or both. The earliest occupation of this region relevant to the present discussion is that marked by the stone industry known as Shamarkian, which shows typological affinities with contemporary Saharan occurrences. By around 7,800 years ago fishing (which had played an important part in the Nubian economy from far earlier times) was undertaken by means of harpoons with barbed bone heads akin to those of the Khartoum Mesolithic (Wendt, 1966). The succeeding Abkan industries, sometimes associated with pottery of a style similar to that of the Khartoum Neolithic, mark the start of demonstrable food production in Nubia; the indigenous economy is poorly known, but strong Egyptian contacts are demonstrated for the period around 6,500 to 4,900 years ago. The relevant archaeological material, designated 'A Group' (Adams, 1977), comes mainly from graves and provides evidence for the cultivation of wheat and barley and the herding of sheep and goats, with lesser numbers of cattle − in other words for a type of river-valley farming similar to contemporary practices in Predynastic Egypt further downstream. As in more southerly regions, the later prehistory of the area during much of the mid-fifth millennium BP remains poorly known.

In the central Sahara, one of the most thoroughly investigated regions is in Air, central Niger, where the sites at Adrar Bous lie only 600 km to the south-west of Acacus, noted above. Here there was a harpoon industry with 'Dotted Wavy Line' pottery predated 7,300 years ago (A. B. Smith, 1980b), and was associated with a lake-shore environment. By about 7,500 years ago the lake had largely dried up and the artefactual remains consist primarily of hunting equipment, while grinding stones suggest the utilization of (probably wild) grasses. The pottery of this phase often bore rocker-stamp decoration. The near-complete skeleton of a domestic short-horn ox indicates that stock were herded 6,500 years ago. Hunting continued and antelope, warthog, hippopotamus and rhinoceros fell prey to the finely flaked stone projectile points that are characteristic of the 'Tenerean' sites. Other features of Tenerean assemblages include grooved stone axe–adzes, ivory bangles and beads of ostrich eggshell. Stone was obtained from sources in the Hoggar, 500 km to the north-west, where cattle bones have also been recovered in contexts dated from about 6,000 years ago (Camps, 1974). Grinding stones continued in use from earlier times; a single impression of a sorghum grain has been identified on a potsherd from Adrar Bous, but there is no reason to believe that the cereal was cultivated. With increased desiccation, Adrar Bous was abandoned around 5,200 years ago.

In more northerly regions of the Sahara and in the inland areas of the Maghreb, archaeological research has provided a significantly different picture. The prehistoric industries generally known as the 'Neolithic of Capsian Tradition' are widely distributed in the Maghreb from Tunisia westwards to Morocco and southwards to about latitude 28° N. It has usually been distinguished from its predecessors not by evidence for the practice of food production but by the presence of pottery, which in this region may be dated back to the eighth millennium BP (Camps, 1982). Important research by Roubet (1979) at Capeletti cave in the Aures mountains of eastern Algeria has demonstrated the transhumant herding of small stock from the eighth millennium BP onwards. The inhabitants of this site appear not to have been cultivators of cereals, and domestic cattle do not seem to have played a significant part in the economy prior to the sixth millennium BP. It should be emphasized, however, that these conclusions are based upon the investigation of a single site, and it would be premature to assume that the practices demonstrated there were necessarily characteristic of the Maghreb region as a whole. Nevertheless, it does appear that the early pastoral communities of this north-western region belonged to a technological tradition that was in several ways distinct from that of the central and southern Sahara.

Corresponding events in more westerly Saharan regions are currently not well understood. Hunting and, where appropriate, fishing were practised throughout the early Holocene, and it is reasonable to assume, although precise evidence is (as so often) lacking, that vegetable foods were also exploited. Much attention has been given to the complex of archaeological occurrences at Dhar Tichitt in south-central Mauritania. This has conventionally been interpreted as representing a rapid and late adoption of food production during the fourth millennium BP (Munson, 1976): around 4,500 years ago hunter-fishers lived beside extensive lakes, but by 3,200 years ago the lakes had dried up and there was heavy reliance upon the cultivation of bulrush millet (*Pennisetum*), which had apparently initially been domesticated elsewhere, although this particular area does lie within the distribution of the wild form. A re-evaluation of the Dhar Tichitt evidence by Holl (1985), however, has drawn attention to an alternative interpretation, which emphasizes the contrasting environments that were exploited at different seasons: millet cultivation and livestock herding near main settlements in the wet season, with fishing and the gathering of wild plant foods (as well as herding) in the dry season when temporary camps were located near the water sources. If this view is confirmed, it will explain the apparent suddenness of the start of millet cultivation at Dhar Tichitt, while leaving the earliest development of that practice, there or elsewhere, to be elucidated by future research.

Throughout the present Sahelian zone from Mali to Sudan, it seems that the period 5,200 to 3,900 years ago saw the adoption of food production in progressively more southerly regions. It is presumably significant that this process was broadly contemporaneous with the main period of Saharan desiccation, when several areas previously inhabited, such as Adrar Bous, were effectively abandoned. Connah (1981) has likened the Sahara at this time to a bellows, drawing farming peoples into itself during periods when well-watered conditions prevailed, and forcing their movement southward when aridity increased. The process is clearly seen in the Tilemsi valley, which extends southward from Adrar des Iforas to a confluence near the northern Niger bend. At Asselar in the northerly part of the valley there is evidence that domestic cattle were herded about 5,300 years ago. At Karkarichinkat in the south, close to the confluence with the Niger, cattle herding is not indicated prior to the beginning of the fourth millennium BP (A. B. Smith, 1974). Several features of the associated artefacts, both the flaked stone and the pottery, suggest affinities with more northerly industries. In view of the west African evidence, discussed below, it seems reasonable to interpret these observations as indicating the gradual southwards movement of herders and their herds; and it is necessary now to consider the relevance of these processes to the early development of food production in west Africa.

WEST AFRICA (Map 45)

Consideration of the early development of food production in west Africa must take account of the variety of relevant techniques that have been practised in the region during more recent times. In contrast with the more northerly areas already discussed, we are concerned here not only with the herding of domestic animals and with the cultivation of dry savannah cereals but also with two more localized crops – African rice and the varied yams of the genus *Dioscorea*. Unfortunately, the archaeological evidence relating to these different modes of food production is sparse and of very variable reliability.

The indigenous cultivated food plants of west Africa originate in several distinct regions. Of the dry-land cereals, the most widespread are sorghum and bulrush millet which, as discussed above, are derived from wild species occurring between latitudes 18° and 10° N, from where their cultivated forms ultimately became dispersed through most of the sub-Saharan regions. A further dry-land cereal, fonio or *Digitaria*, is of much more restricted, specifically west African, distribution. On botanical grounds, its origin may be placed near the areas where it has been cultivated in recent times, in the savannah country west of Lake Chad. *Digitaria deflexa* is a particularly restricted form, being grown only in the Fouta Djallon region of Guinea (Harlan, 1982). African rice, *Oryza glaberrima*, was apparently first developed by cultivation around the annually flooded areas of the inland Niger delta from the wild savannah form *O. barthii*; secondary centres of cultivation apparently developed near the upper Niger and in the Senegal valley and the crop is now widely grown in west Africa to the west of longitude 5° W, with intermittent cultivation further to the east, as far as Lake Chad.

The yam (*Dioscorea* spp.) is, by contrast, a crop of the forest and the forest/savannah ecotone. The greatest diversity of varieties coincides with the most dense concentration of yam-dependent population, in what is now eastern Nigeria. The yam belt extends westward through the west African coastlands as far as the Bandama river in Côte d'Ivoire, which today forms a clear boundary between the yam cultivators on the east and the rice growers on the west (Miege, 1954). The forest margin is also the wild habitat of the oil palm *Elaeis guineensis* which, although arguably never cultivated in the strict sense of the term, is protected and encouraged when other forest trees are cleared: it is through such clearance that the oil palm has been enabled to penetrate into the forest zone itself.

The details outlined above give some indications of the geographical settings of certain developments in the history of west African food production. They provide virtually no evidence for the chronology, relative or absolute, of those processes. Before considering the extremely sparse primary data relevant to such chronologies, it will be useful to outline in general terms the local archaeological succession of the mid-Holocene.

In many of the regions of west Africa that have been archaeologically investigated, microlithic industries (cf. Chapter 11) were made throughout this period and lasted with little discernible typological change until the development of metalworking technology in the third millennium BP, or later in some areas. From about 6,200 years ago two important innovations occurred, however: pottery and ground-stone artefacts that resemble hoes or axes. The appearance of these new artefact types is best illustrated and dated at Bosumpra cave near Abetifi in southern Ghana, at Iwo Eleru rock shelter in south-western Nigeria, and at Shum Laka near Bamenda in Cameroon (Shaw, 1944, 1969; A. B. Smith, 1975; de Maret, 1980). Pottery was also present at this time at settlement sites on the coast of Ghana, where marine foodstuffs were collected. Further west, the corresponding technological developments may have taken place rather later, as at Yagala and Kamabai rock shelters in Sierra Leone and at both inland and coastal sites in Côte d'Ivoire where they are dated to the sixth or fifth millennia BP (Atherton, 1972; Calvocoressi and David, 1979).

It has not infrequently been assumed that the presence of pottery on these early sites indicates that some form of food production was being practised by their inhabitants. However, there is no convincing evidence that this was the case. As the Saharan data discussed above have demonstrated, pottery can and does occur in contexts which predated the local development of food production. It is true that pottery, providing a heavy and fragile type of container, will rarely be adopted by a community whose life-style requires a high degree of mobility. The earliest Saharan, Nile valley and East African pottery was made by people who, while not so far as we know food producers, had nevertheless become dependent on a local concentration of available wild food, such as fish and other aquatic food resources, which enabled them to adopt a sedentary domicile. A similar situation may have prevailed on the west African coasts where midden deposits, as in Ghana, Côte d'Ivoire and Senegal, represent some degree of sedentary reliance upon marine food resources. In the absence, so far, of detailed evidence, it would be unwise to assume that the earliest potters of the west African interior were necessarily farmers.

The one archaeological sequence from west Africa that appears to illustrate the local beginning of food production is that from the Kintampo region of Ghana, located on the northern forest margin. Here a series of excavated rock shelters and open sites have preserved materials of the fourth to the third millennium BP associated with evidence for domestic animals (small stock and possibly cattle). Cowpeas (*Vigna unguiculata*) were present and may have been cul-

tivated. Nuts of celtis and oil palm were also preserved. The suggestion of earlier excavators that the food-producing Kintampo industry represented the arrival of a new population of northern origin who replaced the earlier Punpun inhabitants around 4,000 years ago is queried by Stahl (1985, p. 117) who tentatively attributes the Kintampo industry to 'coalescence of autochthonous and northern elements'. Stone grater-like objects that are characteristic of Kintampo assemblages are of uncertain purpose: interpretations which have been proposed include use in the manufacture of pottery or in the culinary preparation of yams. There is no clear evidence in support of the latter suggestion, however, and their connection with any food production process must be regarded as completely unproved.

The Kintampo sequence, being at present isolated and unsupported by comparable discoveries in adjacent regions, should not necessarily be interpreted as indicating that west African agriculture does not predate the fourth millennium BP. In the case of several crops, the only archaeological occurrences so far known are of very late date: African rice, for example, is first attested at Jenné-jeno in Mali about the first century of the Christian era, while the oldest west African remains of sorghum are at Daima in north-eastern Nigeria, dated to about the mid-first millennium of the Christian era (McIntosh and McIntosh, 1981; Connah, 1981). But again, it is to be expected that much older attestations will in due course be brought to light. For the yam, an exceedingly important crop and one capable of supporting a very high population density, we have no primary archaeological data at all. The techniques of yam cultivation are so distinct from those employed for cereals, however, that there seems no reason to assume that yams were not the earliest of west African cultivated crops; certainly, the great range of varieties that has developed, together with the ritual significance of yams in some areas, would lend support to such a suggestion. It would also provide a plausible interpretation of the stone axes or hoes with heavy end-use that were present in the Cameroon grassfields as early as about 7,800 years ago (when the northern forest margin would have been located significantly to the north of its present position), later occurring in forest-edge regions further to the west. By the third millennium BP large village sites such as Obobogo near Yaoundé suggest that an agricultural life-style was gradually being introduced into the northern forest regions of central Africa (Phillipson, 1985a).

ETHIOPIA (Map 45)

Recent traditional agriculture in Ethiopia preserves several unique features, but archaeological data relevant to its prehistory remain extremely sparse. The Ethiopian highlands include the very few areas in sub-Saharan Africa where winter-rainfall cereal crops of south-west Asian origin – notably wheat and barley – may successfully be cultivated. They are grown alongside local crops, including the cereal teff, for several of which specifically Ethiopian origins may be demonstrated (Harlan, 1969).

The suggestion that teff was brought under cultivation before the introduction of wheat and barley to Ethiopia is based upon the view that such a small grain would not have attracted attention at a time when higher-yielding domesticated species were available. Such an argument ignores the drought-resisting properties of *Eragrostis*, and also its desirable flavour and nutritional qualities. There appears to be no convincing evidence as to whether or not cultivation of teff preceded the introduction of wheat and barley. The large number of local varieties of the two latter cereals, some of which have exclusively Ethiopian distributions, may be taken as indicative of the long period during which these crops have been cultivated there. However, there is as yet virtually no evidence for the actual period at which Ethiopian agriculture developed. Linguistic data indicate that speakers of Semitic languages, for whose presence in the country there is epigraphic evidence from the middle of the third millennium BP, borrowed from Cushitic-speaking indigenes vocabulary relating to the use of the plough and to the cultivation of cereals, suggesting that these practices were already well established in Ethiopia at that time. But for how many centuries, or indeed millennia, before that time cereal and plough agriculture had been carried on, we currently do not know (Ehret, 1979).

Archaeological evidence demonstrably relating to food production in Ethiopia prior to four millennia ago is effectively lacking. Gobedra rock shelter near Axum provides a sample through the only mid-Holocene sequence yet investigated and shows the first appearance of pottery in a microlithic industry of around the sixth or fifth millennium BP. Seeds of finger millet recovered from the same level (Phillipson, 1977a) have now been shown to be intrusive and less than a thousand years old. The only other excavated plant remains of which the present writer is aware come from Lalibela cave near the south-eastern side of Lake Tana: they do not predate the mid-third millennium BP and are associated with bones of domestic cattle and small stock (Dombrowski, 1970). At Laga Oda rock shelter near the Chercher mountains west of Harar, a microlithic industry includes several specimens displaying edge gloss that may best be replicated by use to cut grass. There is thus some indication that cereals, cultivated or wild, may have been harvested from the fourth millennium BP onwards. Domestic cattle are first represented in the Laga Oda sequence, and at Lake Besaka some 250 km to the west, at approximately this period (Clark and Williams, 1978; Clark and Prince, 1978). The oldest archaeological attestation of cultivated teff comes, in fact, not from Ethiopia but from Hajar bin Humeid in south Yemen, in a context dated to the third millennium BP (van Beek, 1969). It seems probable that the grain had been transported across the Red Sea or Gulf of Aden, either as produce or as a crop, from an earlier area of cultivation in Ethiopia.

Some further evidence for prehistoric food production in Ethiopia – and in Somalia – may be obtained from the rock paintings, notably in the northern and eastern areas. Here again, however, there are virtually no convincing chronological indicators. In both areas the most numerous paintings are those of long-horned humpless cattle attended by herders armed with spears. The prominence given to the cows' udders may suggest that herds were kept for milk production. Paintings that are judged to be later on the bases of patination or weathering and of superimposition include representations of humped cattle and of camels. On the assumption that the cattle of South Arabia were predominantly short-horned it has been suggested that the earlier Ethiopian paintings may predate the main incursions from that area which took place in the mid-third millennium BP; but such arguments are far from persuasive (cf. Willcox, 1984, and references).

In total, it must be admitted that the archaeological evidence for the early development of Ethiopian food production is very inadequate. It is clear from botanical, environmental, ethnographic and, to some extent, linguistic

studies that Ethiopian agriculture developed many independent features as well as absorbing crops and techniques that had been developed elsewhere. The absolute (or relative) chronology of these processes cannot be demonstrated from the evidence currently available. It would seem highly probable that the formative processes of Ethiopian agriculture extend back for several millennia before the period to which the earliest conclusive data are attributed (third millennium BP).

EAST AFRICA (Map 45)

To the south of the Ethiopian highlands, the arid northern Kenya plains to the east of Lake Turkana are a geomorphological extension of the Somali lowlands. Further south again, the central Rift Valley and adjacent highlands, together with the Lake Victoria region, provide varied rich and reasonably well-watered environments. Since the development of food production here probably took place after the time period with which this chapter is concerned, the following outline will be brief.

The Lake Turkana littoral is the region of north Kenya that has been most intensively investigated archaeologically. During the early and mid-Holocene the waters of the lake (which currently has no outlet) often reached a height of 80 metres above their present level, at which amplitude Lake Turkana maintained an overflow channel to the north-west, via the Sobat valley, to the Nile. The shores of this greatly enlarged lake were frequented by hunter-fishers whose technology, including at first 'Wavy Line' pottery, shares many features with that of the Khartoum Mesolithic (Phillipson, 1977b). By the late fifth millennium BP the water level was steadily falling, and parts of the Lake Turkana basin provide archaeological evidence for the presence at this time of East Africa's earliest known food-producing peoples.

Inland from Koobi Fora, near the eastern shore of the lake, the Dongodien site preserves evidence for settlement about 4,500 years ago by makers of a microlithic industry and of the finely decorated internally scored pottery known as Nderit ware. These people herded small stock and possibly cattle also. To the north a probably broadly contemporary site near Ileret has pottery of a different tradition, microlith tools and bones of domestic cattle and probable small stock. Of particular interest here are several stone bowls of a type commonly represented on pastoralist sites of the third millennium BP in the Rift Valley highlands further to the south. The herders at Ileret also exploited the rich fish resources provided by the shrinking waters of Lake Turkana (Barthelme, 1985).

Similar indications for the herding of domestic animals at a relatively early date come from Ele Bor, a series of rocky outcrops in an at present arid location close to the foothills of the Ethiopian escarpment, where a number of rock shelters provide a long archaeological sequence probably extending back nine millennia ago. Although hunting seems to have provided the basis for the local economy throughout this period, the faunal species represented indicate that climatic conditions somewhat wetter than those of today prevailed until about 2000 years ago. The first pottery occurs at a level that is provisionally dated to the fourth or fifth millennium BP, associated with bones of small stock and, interestingly, a camel tooth. At the same time, large grinding stones were extensively used in substantial numbers; it is tempting to suggest that they may have served a function connected with the preparation of cereal foods. Grains attributed to the genera *Eragrostis* and *Sporobolus* were recovered, but there was no evidence that they were cultivated, nor were any of the flaked-stone tools suitable for use in cultivation. With the onset of drier climatic conditions, grinding stones were no longer used at Ele Bor and pottery became significantly less common (Phillipson, 1984).

In the East African highland regions, pastoralism is not attested until very late in the fourth millennium BP. The archaeological data on which this statement is based is summarized below. First, however, it is necessary to note that claims have recently been made that domestic cattle were present in the East African highlands during significantly earlier times (Nelson and Kimengich, 1984). The sites on which these claims are based are at Salasun near Naivasha and at Likenya hill east of Nairobi, both in Kenya. In neither case are the stratigraphy, dating or osteological identification beyond dispute, and it is the present writer's opinion that these claims should be discounted pending the recovery of further evidence.

The early pastoralist inhabitants of the East African highlands must be viewed against the diversity of the environments which they exploited (Ambrose, 1984). These are the most intensively investigated Stone Age farming people in sub-Saharan Africa, but nevertheless many details of their archaeology remain poorly understood. At least two cultural variants may be recognized. The Elmenteitan industry is distinguished by its stone industry, pottery typology, burial customs and geographical distribution centred on the Mau escarpment. The remaining varied manifestations are usually grouped together under the name of 'savannah Pastoral Neolithic'. There is much variation in the pottery and flaked stone artefacts, the significance of which is not well understood. In contrast with the Elmenteitan cremation practices, the dead were buried under stone cairns. Some settlements were large, and it is likely that future research will demonstrate a complex system of seasonal resource exploitation. Cattle and small stock were herded in large numbers and some hunting was also conducted at most sites. Stone bowls, pestles and platters are frequently recovered both on settlement sites and in burials. Their function is not known, although it has been suggested that they may have been used for the preparation of pigment or of vegetable foods. Historical linguistic studies suggest that some of the Pastoral Neolithic people may have spoken a Southern Cushitic language. There is linguistic evidence that these people were cultivators as well as herders, but no archaeological evidence for food crops has yet been recovered. Pastoral Neolithic settlement is known as far south as the Serengeti plain in northern Tanzania. It is possible that food production also began at this time in the Lake Victoria basin, but conclusive evidence is so far lacking. In more southerly regions of Africa there is no indication that any form of food production was practised before the start of metal-working around two thousand years ago.

AFRICA SOUTH OF THE EQUATOR

The earliest evidence for food production in more southerly regions of Africa falls far outside the chronological scope of this chapter. For the sake of completeness, however, it is pertinent to note that throughout the period here considered the inhabitants of the southern half of Africa continued the hunter-gatherer life-style of their predecessors. Except in coastal regions where major fluctuations in sea-level were experienced and at high altitudes beyond regular human settlement, post-Pleistocene environmental changes were probably minor in comparison with those experienced in more northerly latitudes.

During the third millennium BP it is probable that the gradual penetration of the central African Equatorial forest by people who cultivated food crops, notably yams, and probably maintained some herds of domestic goats continued the earlier processes already noted. The archaeological data available from this region are both rare and imprecise, so the provisional reconstructions that have been proposed rest to a large extent upon linguistic studies. In the savannah regions of eastern and southern Africa a far greater amount of archaeological research has been undertaken: here it appears that the earliest food producers were metal-using, mixed-farming peoples who are shown to have spread with great rapidity through much of the territory previously occupied by stone-tool-using hunter-gatherers. There is broad agreement that this process involved a substantial element of population movement and that the people were probably speakers of Bantu languages (Phillipson, 1985a, 1985b). These major historical developments will be discussed in detail in a later volume of this work.

CONCLUSION

Three major processes have been recognized in the early history of African food production outlined above.

Some elements of north African food production appear to be derived from earlier developments in south-western Asia. Of these elements, only domestic small stock were to have a major impact in areas south of the Sahara.

There is little doubt that the earliest manifestation of food production in sub-Saharan Africa occurred in the southern Sahara and adjacent parts of the Nile valley by the start of the sixth millennium BP. Domestic animals are well attested, cultivated plants less convincingly. At least in the Sudanese Nile valley, and probably elsewhere, a complex system of seasonal resource exploitation, involving at least some degree of cyclical migration, is now demonstrated. Climatic deterioration may be regarded as a major factor contributing to the spread of domestic herds southwards into the savannah by the fourth millennium BP and into northern Kenya somewhat earlier. Such a model would imply some southward shift by the human populations also, perhaps by nothing more than a gradual extension of the cyclical migration pattern. To what extent there had been in west Africa an earlier indigenous development of agriculture involving non-cereal crops and perhaps rice, remains unknown, as does the relationship between early Ethiopian food production and that of more westerly regions. Whatever the regional picture, sub-Saharan agriculture as a whole must be seen as an indigenous development.

By about 3,200 years ago it seems likely that farming peoples were widely distributed through most of sub-Saharan Africa north of the Equator, the most southerly representatives being the pastoralists of the East African highlands. Along this general line, at least in the eastern part of the continent, the spread of food-production appears to have halted, perhaps for as long as a thousand years. South of the Equator the adoption of food production, when it came, took a very different guise – a major southward expansion of metal-using mixed farmers who rapidly brought as far as the Cape the crops and herds that had been brought under domestication in more northerly parts of Africa.

BIBLIOGRAPHY

ADAMS, W. Y. 1977. *Nubia: Corridor to Africa.* London.

AMBROSE, S. H. 1984. The Introduction of Pastoral Adaptations to the Highlands of East Africa. In: CLARK, J. D.; BRANDT, S. A. (eds), *From Hunters to Farmers.* Berkeley. pp. 212–39.

ARKELL, A. J. 1949. *Early Khartoum.* Oxford.

—— 1953. *Shaheinab.* Oxford.

ATHERTON, J. H. 1972. Excavations at Kamabai and Yagala Rock Shelters, Sierra Leone. *West Afr. J. Archaeol.* (Ibadan), Vol. 2, pp. 39–74.

BARICH, B. E. 1984. Fieldwork in the Tadrart Acacus and the 'Neolithic' of the Sahara. *Curr. Anthropol.,* Vol. 25, pp. 683–6.

BARTHELME, J. W. 1985. *Fisher-Hunters and Neolithic Pastoralists in East Turkana, Kenya.* Oxford. (BAR Int. Ser., 254.)

BEEK, G. VAN. 1969. *Hajar bin Humeid.* Baltimore.

CALVOCORESSI, D.; DAVID, N. 1979. A New Survey of Radiocarbon and Thermoluminescence Dates for West Africa. *J. Afr. Hist.,* Vol. 20, pp. 1–29.

CAMPS, G. 1969. *Amekni, néolithique ancien du Hoggar.* Paris. (Mém. Cent. Rech. Anthropol. Préhist. Ethnogr., 10.)

—— 1974. *Les Civilizations préhistoriques de l'Afrique du Nord et du Sahara.* Paris.

—— 1982. Beginnings of Pastoralism and Cultivation in North West Africa and the Sahara. In: CLARK, J. D. (ed.), *Cambridge History of Africa.* Cambridge. Vol. 1, pp. 548–623.

CLARK, J. D. 1971. A Re-examination of the Evidence for Agricultural Origins in the Nile Valley. *Proc. Prehist. Soc.,* Vol. 37, pp. 34–79.

CLARK, J. D.; BRANDT, S. A. (eds) 1984. *From Hunters to Farmers: The Causes and Consequences of Food Production in Africa.* Berkeley.

CLARK, D. J.; PRINCE, G. R. 1978. Use-Wear on Later Stone Age Microliths from Laga Oda, Haraghi, Ethiopia. *Azania* (Nairobi), Vol. 13, pp. 101–10.

CLARK, D. J.; WILLIAMS, M. A. J. 1978. Recent Archaeological Research in South-Eastern Ethiopia, 1974–5. *Ann. Ethiopie* (Addis Ababa), Vol. 11, pp. 19–42.

CONNAH, G. 1981. *Three Thousand Years in Africa.* Cambridge.

DOMBROWSKI, J. 1970. Preliminary Report on Excavations in Lalibela and Natchabiet Caves, Begemeder. *Ann. Ethiopie* (Addis Ababa), Vol. 8, pp. 21–9.

EHRET, C. 1979. On the Antiquity of Agricultures in Ethiopia. *J. Afr. Hist.,* Vol. 20, pp. 161–77.

EPSTEIN, H. 1971. *The Origin of the Domestic Animals of Africa.* New York.

FATTOVICH, R.; MARKS, A. E.; MOHAMMED-ALI, A. 1984. The Archaeology of the Eastern Sahel, Sudan: Preliminary Results. *Afr. Archaeol. Rev.,* Vol. 2, pp. 173–88.

HARLAN, J. R. 1969. Ethiopia, a Centre of Diversity. *Econ. Bot.* (Lancaster), Vol. 23, pp. 309–14.

—— 1971. Agricultural Origins: Centers and Noncenters. *Science* (Washington), Vol. 174, pp. 468–74.

—— 1982. The Origins of Indigenous African Agriculture. In: CLARK, J. D. (ed.), *Cambridge History of Africa.* Cambridge. Vol. 1, pp. 624–57.

HARLAN, J. R.; WET, J. M. J. DE; STEMLER, A. B. L. (eds) 1976. *Origins of African Plant Domestication.* The Hague.

HASSAN, F. A. 1985. Radiocarbon Chronology of Neolithic and Predynastic Sites in Upper Egypt and the Delta. *Afr. Archaeol. Rev.,* Vol. 3, pp. 95–116.

—— 1986. Chronology of the Khartoum 'Mesolithic' and 'Neolithic' and Related Sites in the Sudan. *Afr. Archaeol. Rev.,* Vol. 4, pp. 83–102.

HIGGS, E. S. (ed.) 1972. *Papers in Economic Prehistory.* Cambridge.

HITCHCOCK, R. K.; EBERT, J. I. 1984. Foraging and Food Production among Kalahari Hunter-Gatherers. In: CLARK, J. D.; BRANDT, S. A. (eds), *From Hunters to Farmers.* Berkeley. pp. 328–48.

HOLL, A. 1985. Subsistence Patterns of the Dhar Tichitt Neolithic, Mauretania. *Afr. Archaeol. Rev.,* Vol. 3, pp. 151–62.

JODIN, A. 1959. Les Grottes d'El Khrill à Achakar, province de Tanger. *Bull. archéol. maroc.* (Rabat), Vol. 3, pp. 249–313.

KRZYZANIAK, L. 1978. New Light on Early Food Production in the Central Sudan. *J. Afr. Hist.,* Vol. 19, pp. 159–72.

LHOTE, H. 1959. *The Search for the Tassili Frescoes.* London.

MCBURNEY, C. B. M. 1967. *The Haua Fteah (Cyrenaica) and the Stone Age of the Southwest Mediterranean.* Cambridge.

MCINTOSH, R. J.; MCINTOSH, S. K. 1981. The Inland Niger Delta before the Empire of Mali: Evidence from Jenné-jeno. *J. Afr. Hist.,* Vol. 22, pp. 1–22.

MARET, P. DE. 1980. Preliminary Report on 1980 Fieldwork in the Grassfields and Yaounde, Cameroon. *Nyame Akuma* (Calgari), Vol. 17, pp. 10–12.

MARKS, A. E. et al. 1985. The Prehistory of the Central Nile Valley as Seen from its Eastern Hinterlands. *J. Field Archaeol.,* Vol. 12, pp. 261–78.

MIEGE, J. 1954. Les Cultures vivrières en Afrique occidentale. *Cah. Outre-Mer* (Bordeaux), Vol. 7, pp. 25–50.

MOHAMMED-ALI, A. 1982. *The Neolithic Period in the Sudan, c.6000–2500 BC.* Oxford. (BAR Int. Ser., 139.)

MORI, F. 1965. *Tadrart Acacus: arte rupestre e culture del Sahara preistorico.* Torino.

MUNSON, P. J. 1976. Archaeological Data on the Origins of Cultivation in the South-Western Sahara and their Implications for West Africa. In: HARLAN, J. R. et al. (eds), *Origins of African Plant Domestication.* The Hague. pp. 187–210.

MUZZOLINI, A. 1986. *L'Art rupestre préhistorique des massifs centraux sahariens.* Oxford. (BAR Int. Ser., 318.)

NELSON, C. M.; KIMENGICH, J. 1984. Early Phases of Pastoral Adaptation in the Central Highlands of Kenya. In: KRZYZANIAK, L.; KOBUSIEWICZ, M. (eds), *Origin and Early Development of Food-Production Cultures in North-East Africa.* Poznań. pp. 481–7.

NOTEN, F. VAN. 1978. *Rock Art of the Jebel Uweinat, Libyan Sahara.* Graz.

PHILLIPSON, D. W. 1977a. The Excavation of Gobedra Rock Shelter, Axum. *Azania* (Nairobi), Vol. 12, pp. 53–82.

—— 1977b. Lowasera. *Azania* (Nairobi), Vol. 12, pp. 1–32.

—— 1984. Aspects of Early Food Production in Northern Kenya. In: KRZYZANIAK, L.; KOBUSIEWICZ, M. (eds), *Origin and Early Development of Food-Production Cultures in North-East Africa.* Poznań. pp. 489–95.

—— 1985a. An Archaeological Reconsideration of Bantu Expansion. *Muntu* (Paris), Vol. 2, pp. 69–84.

—— 1985b. *African Archaeology.* Cambridge.

ROUBET, C. 1979. *Économie pastorale préagricole en Algérie orientale: le néolithique de tradition capsienne.* Paris, CNRS.

SAXON, E. C. 1974. Results of Recent Investigations at Tamar Hat. *Libyca* (Paris), Vol. 22, pp. 49–91.

SHAW, T. 1944. Report on Excavations Carried Out in the Cave Known as Bosumpra at Abetifi, Kwahu, Gold Coast Colony. *Proc. Prehist. Soc.,* Vol. 10, pp. 1–67.

—— 1969. The Late Stone Age of the Nigerian Forest. In: LEBEUF, J. (ed.), *Actes 1er Colloque international d'archéologie africaine.* Fort-Lamy. pp. 364–73.

SMITH, A. B. 1974. Preliminary Report of Excavations at Karkarichinkat, Mali. *West Afr. J. Archaeol.* (Ibadan), Vol. 4, pp. 33–55.

—— 1975. Radiocarbon Dates from Bosumpra Cave, Abetifi, Ghana. *Proc. Prehist. Soc.,* Vol. 41, pp. 179–82.

—— 1980a. Domesticated Cattle in the Sahara and their Introduction into West Africa. In: WILLIAMS, M. A. J.; FAURE, H. (eds), *The Sahara and the Nile.* Rotterdam. pp. 489–501.

—— 1980b. The Neolithic Tradition in the Sahara. In: WILLIAMS, M. A. J.; FAURE, H. (eds), *The Sahara and the Nile.* Rotterdam. pp. 451–65.

—— 1984. Origins of the Neolithic in the Sahara. In: CLARK, J. D.; BRANDT, S. A. (eds), *From Hunters to Farmers.* Berkeley. pp. 84–92.

—— 1986. Cattle Domestication in North Africa. *Afr. Archaeol. Rev.,* Vol. 4, pp. 197–203.

SMITH, H. S. 1969. Animal Domestication and Animal Cult in Dynastic Egypt. In: UCKO, P. J.; DIMBLEBY, G. W. (eds), *The Domestication and Exploitation of Plants and Animals.* London. pp. 307–14.

SMITH, P. E. L. 1968. Problems and Possibilities of the Prehistoric Rock Art of Northern Africa. *Afr. Hist. Stud.* (Boston), Vol. 1, pp. 1–39.

STAHL, A. B. 1985. Reinvestigation of Kintampo 6 Rock Shelter, Ghana: Implications for the Nature of Culture Change. *African Archaeological Review,* Vol. 3, pp. 117–50.

STEHLI, P. (ed.) 1978. *Sahara.* Cologne.

SUTTON, J. E. G. 1974. The Aquatic Civilization of Middle Africa. *J. Afr. Hist.,* Vol. 15, pp. 527–46.

WENDORF, F.; HASSAN, F. A. 1980. Holocene Ecology and Prehistory in the Egyptian Sahara. In: WILLIAMS, M. A. J.; FAURE, H. (eds), *The Sahara and the Nile.* Rotterdam. pp. 407–19.

WENDORF, F.; SCHILD, R. (eds) 1976. *Prehistory of the Nile Valley.* New York.

WENDT, W. E. 1966. Two Prehistoric Archaeological Sites in Egyptian Nubia. *Postilla* (New Haven, Conn.), Vol. 102, pp. 1–46.

WILLCOX, A. R. 1984. *The Rock Art of Africa.* London.

ZEUNER, F. 1963. *History of Domesticated Animals.* London.

41

WESTERN ASIA

during the Neolithic and the Chalcolithic (about 12,000–5,000 years ago)

James Mellaart

Archaeological discoveries over the last forty years in western Asia and adjacent regions have greatly altered the conventional picture of primary and secondary centres, the role of cultural diffusion from the former and the vexed question of the rise of civilization, previously confined to Egypt, lower Mesopotamia and the vast plains of the Indus. By extending the archaeological range far beyond the threshold of civilization, conventionally placed about 5,000 and up to around 12,000 years ago, we now are able to see cultural development in all its diversity during the previous seven millennia and not just in Egypt, Iraq and Pakistan–India, but also in all the other territories that comprise ancient western Asia, which form a cultural continuum.

Co-operation with scientists, be they zoologists, botanists or physicists, has greatly benefited archaeology in the search for the origins of farming and animal domestication and the establishment of an absolute chronology, based on dendro-chronologically calibrated radiocarbon measurements. The new timescale is something no archaeologist can now afford to ignore.

The impact of some forty years of discovery, much of it not yet fully published or digested, on archaeological theory as established in the 1920s to 1940s has shattered most of its foundations. Many archaeologists have not yet come to terms with the new evidence and continue to fight rearguard actions to save their cherished theories. Others, more forward-looking, maintain that the new evidence demands a new interpretation, based on facts rather than on outmoded and discredited ideas formulated at a time when little was known and much was therefore assumed. The present author prefers to base himself on evidence.

The 7,000 years of cultural development that form the subject of this chapter fall, but for the last few centuries, entirely in the prehistoric period. Its relative chronology derives from stratified sequences, its absolute chronology from calibrated radiocarbon dates. Calibration has not yet proceeded beyond a true age of 9,200 years ago (which equals an uncalibrated *raw* date of 8,250 years BP); earlier 'true' dates, older than 9,200 years ago, are therefore provisional, which must be borne in mind. Pending refinements, a simplified chronological table now looks like that shown as Table 16.

The easiest way to deal with this period is in millennia and to avoid such local terms as create confusion, such as 'Mesolithic', 'Chalcolithic', 'Copper Age', devised for technological stages in the tools and weapons of various cultures and which new discoveries have rendered obsolete. Not a few western Asian cultures are known to have lasted a thousand years (or more), so that the use of, say, 'eight millennia ago' has a universal value. Individual dates for cultures do not of course fit so nicely, but that is something all archaeologists have learnt to live with.

The crucial importance of the seven millennia (from about 12,000 to 5,000 years ago) in western Asia lies in the fact that it was there that Upper Palaeolithic people became aware of the possibility of food production in addition to the time-honoured traditions of food collection: hunting, fishing, fowling and gathering. The realization that foodstuffs like cereals and pulses can be grown from seed and kept in storage, and that certain animals can be domesticated and stored on the hoof, opened up the way to mixed farming, the economic basis for the development of cultures and civilizations. As the famous palaeoethnobotanist Hans Helbaek put it: 'Grain is man's most precious artefact.' V. Gordon Childe called this development 'the Neolithic Revolution' and thought that it arose in the river basins of the Nile in Egypt, the Tigris and Euphrates in Mesopotamia, and the Indus in Pakistan, the areas of the three riverine (but much later) civilizations, and as a result of gradual desiccation at the end of the Ice Age; this is the so-called 'Oasis Theory'.

The idea of population increase causing a food crisis which could be solved only by developing new food resources is

Table 16 Chronological table of the Pre-Neolithic and Neolithic period in western Asia.

End Halaf/beginning Ubaid 3	*c.*7,250 to 7,000 years ago
Beginning of Halaf, Hassuna, Samarra	*c.*8,250 years ago
Late PPNB, Çatal Hüyük, Bougras, Umm Dabaghiyah	*c.*9,250 to 8,250 years ago
Early PPNB	*c.*10,500 to 9,250 years ago
PPNA	*c.*11,000 to 10,500/10,250 years ago
Late Natufian	*c.*11,700 to 11,000 years ago
Early Natufian	*c.*12,750? years ago
Geometric Kebaran	*c.*14,500? to 12,750? years ago
Kebaran	*c.*19,000 to 14,500 years ago

still popular, but not supported by the evidence. The end of the Ice Age in more northern latitudes is unlikely to have been the cause of something that started long before: it came after the end of the Natufian culture of the Levant about 11,000 years ago, by which time Mureybet, east of Aleppo on the Euphrates, was already practising agriculture! The oasis theory has been abandoned and the idea of a Neolithic revolution likewise now seems naive, as it was neither sudden nor 'Neolithic'. It cannot be stressed too much that we are dealing with a very long and evolutionary process starting, on the evidence of the site of Ein Gev (radiocarbon dated to about 15,700 years ago), in the Late Kebaran period, gathering momentum during the Natufian (about 12,750 to 11,000 years ago) and emerging with fully domesticated emmer wheat and two-row hulled barley in Jericho PPNA (Pre-pottery Neolithic A) around 11,000 years ago – a chronological span of some 5,000 years or more.

The people who experimented with early agriculture were not newcomers with special gifts, but descendants of those who previously practised hunting and gathering during the Upper Palaeolithic: in other words, the development was indigenous. Keen observers of gazelle and goat, which provided them with most of their meat, they appear to have taken the first step towards domestication, namely herding during the Late Kebaran period and observing the feeding habits of these animals. They may well have understood that cereals could be of nutritional value to humans also. Sooner or later bands of hunters must have realized that herding solved some of their dietary problems, the other half of which could be alleviated by planting the seeds of wheat and barley, native to their area, previously only consumed by animals, but a potential source of food once the proper tools for their preparation had been devised: pestles and mortars to remove the husks, grinding stones (querns) to turn the grains into flour, and clay-lined storage pits to store the grain and prevent damp, which causes germination and makes the grain unfit for consumption. Another early way for removing the grain from the tight-fitting husks was to roast it in pits, later in ovens; the application of fire has led to carbonization, and thus preservation of our earliest specimens at the sites of Mureybet and Abu Hureyra. Technically these may belong to the beginning of the post-Natufian phase, the PPNA tradition, itself developed out of the Natufian, from which actual finds of grain have not yet been reported. There is, however, little point in doubting that such will be forthcoming; the technical equipment is there (mortars, pestles, querns, grain pits), the teeth of many skeletons at Ain Mallaha (Eynan) are worn down as a result of a gritty cereal diet, the presence of commensal animals, such as mice and rats, has been noted at Natufian sites and the choice of location of those sites, in contrast to the previous period, is linked to the oak and pistachio woodland habitat below which wild emmer, wheat and two-row barley grew. These facts clearly show that the Natufians were interested in wild cereals, like some Kabarans even earlier (Ein Gev), made equipment to process them, stored them and ate them. What is not yet clear is whether they only gathered the wild crops, or whether they already planted the seeds around their settlements, thus practising agriculture and moving into the Neolithic period by definition.

The importance of sedentism in the Natufian culture is evident and from such early beginnings permanent settlements arose as early as the late Natufian at Mureybet, one of the earliest tells. None of the Natufian sites show much permanency; even with subphases, the three superimposed building-levels at Ain Mallaha are most unlikely to span 1,500 years. Nor were any of great dimensions; Ain Mallaha is now thought to contain only fifty round houses, suggesting a population of a few hundred people at best. Moreover, there are Natufian sites of a less permanent nature: summer or winter habitations occupied during hunting or gathering expeditions, lacking the installations for the preparation of plant foods and significantly, lacking burials. It appears that those who died away from home were either temporarily buried or exposed and given reburial in the permanent site alongside their relatives; hence the use of two different burial customs: primary burials and secondary ones, the latter frequently incomplete.

The use of red ochre – simulating blood – is widespread in burials, occurring in Upper Palaeolithic Europe, at Çatal Hüyük (Anatolia) nine millennia ago, possibly at Haçilar I and at Aceramic Neolithic Mehrgarh in Pakistan. In contrast to the hunters of the Kebaran, the semi-sedentary Natufians practised intramural burial; evidently the idea of *home* had developed. There is good evidence for funerary gifts, dentalium shells from the Mediterranean or the Red Sea being particularly prominent sewn onto caps, or fashioned into jewellery (bracelets, anklets, necklaces, etc.) probably also worn during life. There are phallic beads and beads made out of gazelle toe-bones (phalanges) and there are artistic carvings of gazelle in stone or on bone 'reaping knives' (their use as sickles is disputed). Human figurines occur, but are still very rare and no examples of an undoubted cult room has yet been found, though one building in Ain Mallaha had red plastered walls and a parapet and another round house was provided with a circle of wooden posts. Mud-brick is not yet in use and though there are baked-clay figurines, pottery is still unknown. Clothing presumably consisted of animal skins and furs, and possibly felt, but no animal was yet definitely domesticated, though claims have been made for dogs, and gazelle may have been tamed.

The Natufian culture, then, is a prime example of the last phase of the Upper Palaeolithic standing at the threshold of a new age (the agricultural Neolithic), or already in the process of crossing it. There is here a mixed economy of hunting, fishing, fowling and gathering, and a possible beginning of cereal manipulation in favourable locations, where emmer, wheat and barley grew wild around them. In areas where this was not so, the old traditions of hunting and gathering continued, by both Natufians and descendants of the ancestral Kebaran culture.

The distribution of the Natufian culture (or, if one prefers, its typical flint tools and weapons) is not confined to Palestine, but reaches from north Syria to the Negev with isolated occurrences at Helwan and in the Fayum in Lower Egypt. Similar material is also known from the Antalya area on the south coast of Anatolia, where a related sequence (Beldibi) follows upon an earlier phase (Belbaşi) just as Natufian followed Kebaran. As these links go back in other sites even to the Lower Palaeolithic, the possibility of a circum-east-Mediterranean complex having existed in early times should be borne in mind. It is possible that during the more severe cold phases of the Ice Age Syria and Palestine served as a refuge for the inhabitants of Anatolia. With the onset of warmer conditions they may have returned to their former dwelling sites, yet kept open relations with the Levant, as we will see.

THE PPNA (PRE-POTTERY NEOLITHIC A) PERIOD, ABOUT 11,000/10,500 TO 10,250 YEARS AGO, OF THE LEVANT (Map 46)

This culture is clearly derived from the Natufian and continues its stonework traditions, its round huts, its flexed burials, individual or collective, the use of red ochre and the special importance attached to skulls, and its taste for gazelle (with an occasional fox or goat). Hunting still provides the bulk of the food, and arrowheads now appear (Khiamian type). Other innovations are flint axes, greenstone small axes and chisels for woodwork, a flourishing bone industry, a few stone vessels and presumably a continuation of containers made of perishable materials: wood, skin and leather, and basketry coated for protection with gypsum or asphalt (bitumen). At Mureybet III about 10,000 years ago a number of sun-baked pots appear, hardened in a fire that destroyed the building in which they were found. Sun-baked bricks of plano-convex shape (*hog-backed*) now serve as building material, at Jericho and Tell Aswad on Lake Ateibe, for platforms between pit-dwellings with wattle and daub structures of the zafira type. In the earliest phases of this period (in Proto-Neolithic Jericho) similar structures were characteristic until supplanted by mud-brick round huts, possibly domed.

Such round or oval structures on stone foundations are typical for PPNA (Jericho (Fig. 106 (B)), Netiv Hagdud and Nahal Oren (Wadi Fallah)) and derive from Natufian prototypes. Permanent settlements forming tells are now much more common and more sophisticated features appear, such as red clay plaster and stone pavings in Mureybet II, a black-on-yellow wall painting of horizontal chevrons in a 'shrine' at Mureybet III, which contained a burial with an obsidian dagger, and a tendency to divide the circular space within the house by platforms and

partitions, again in Mureybet III (Fig. 107). Around the same time rectangular structures appear there and in Sheikh Hasan, built in stone and brick, and apparently entered from the roof. These may have been communal storage buildings for agricultural products.

At Nahal Oren, houses are set on terraces with stone retaining walls, but the wonder of the age was the fortified town of Jericho with its rock-cut ditch, stone curtain wall, twice rebuilt, until it rose to a height of 5 m, and its great stone tower, inside the wall and perhaps acting as a lookout post (Fig. 106 (A)). This was provided with an interior staircase and adjacent mud-brick storage rooms, one of which contained the earliest domesticated emmer wheat and barley. K. Kenyon estimated the population of PPNA Jericho at around 2,000, whereas Mureybet may have had 200 houses, and was already large for the period, Nahal Oren having but thirteen (surviving) houses. The expansion of population and the increase in sedentism are easily explained as the result of the introduction of agriculture, which characterizes this period. The three sites which have produced plant remains (Mureybet II and III with cultivated wild einkorn wheat, barley, lentil and pea, almond, pistachio and fig, and PPNA Jericho with domestic emmer, domestic barley, lentil and fig) all have abundant water supplies in the Euphrates river, the Ateibe lake and the great spring of Jericho (Ain es Sultan). Jericho's need for fortification is in itself an indication of the presence of envious neighbours, and attempts to see Jericho as a great trading centre for salt, sulphur and bitumen find little support in the finds from the site. What did get through from the north was obsidian from the Ciftlik source in central Anatolia, from the very beginning of the period about 11,000 years ago, and it evidently reached Palestine through north Syria, where obsidian had sporadically appeared as early as the Kebaran period (Nahr Homr). Jericho's main export may have been seeds and plant

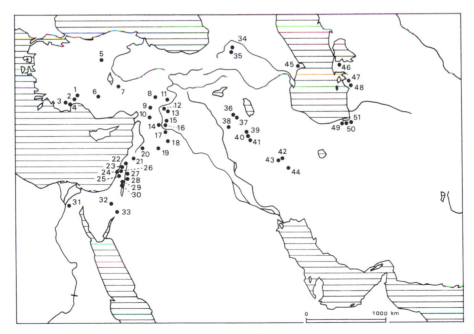

Map 46 Western Asia from about 11,000/10,500 to 10,250 years ago. 1, Öküzlü 'In; 2, Kara 'In; 3, Belbaşi; 4, Beldibi caves; 5, Macun Çay; 6, Çatal Hüyük; 7, Tepesi-Çiftlik; 8, Direkli cave; 9, Şarkli cave; 10, Qaramel; 11, Palanli caves; 12, Söğüttarlasi; 13, Biriş Hezalliği; 14, Nahr Hohr; 15, Sheikh Hasan; 16, Mureybet; 17, Tell Abu Hureyra; 18, Al-Kowm; 19, Palmyra sites; 20, Jabrud; 21, Tell Aswad; 22, Ain Mallaha; 23, Hayonim; 24, El Wad; 25, Kebara; 26, Nahal Oren; 27, Aingey; 28, Wadi Hammeh; 29, Jericho; 30, Gilgal, Netif Hagdud; 31, Helwan; 32, Koshzin; 33, Beidha; 34, Dzermuxh; 35, Edzani; 36, Zawi Chemi; 37, Shanidar cave; 38, M'Lefaat; 39, Zarzi cave; 40, Pelagawra cave; 41, Karimshahir; 42, Ganjdareh; 43, Tepe Asiab; 44, Pa Sangar cave; 45, Kobystan; 46, Kailu cave; 47, Jebel cave; 48, Damdam Cheshme cave; 49, Ali Tape; 50, Hotu cave; 51, Belt cave.

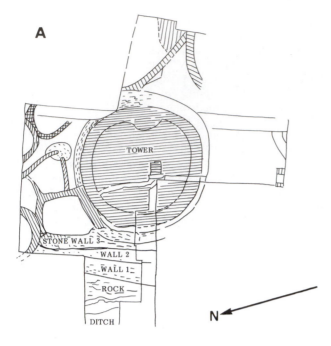

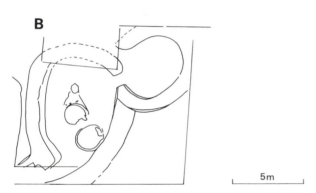

Figure 106 Jericho, PPNA: A, tower (ground plan); B, round houses (ground plan). (After Kenyon, 1980, Pls 209, 277*b* and 278*b*.)

food technology, more precious at this period to people than riches.

The limited exposure of remains of this period severely restricts one's knowledge of art, religion and social structures, and one only has a glimpse of the potentiality of this vital period, yet even this is quite remarkable. No archaeological theorist could have predicted the existence of PPNA Jericho; to dismiss it as a freak, as some have done, is quite unwarranted. It is such exceptional sites that provide the highlights of archaeology and remind us how much remains to be learnt.

THE ZAGROS ZONE FROM 12,000 TO 9,500 YEARS AGO

In view of the spectacular developments that were to take place in the later tenth and ninth millennium BP over a much broader area, we must briefly sketch the cultural developments that took place east of the Levant, in the Zagros zone, the counterpart of the Natufian–PPNA tradition. So far there has been little pioneering research in this vital area on the borders of Iraq and Iran, and the lack of intermediary sites makes it impossible to say whether the

Natufian tradition of the west had any connection with the Zawi Chemi–Shanidar tradition of the Zagros in the east. It would be surprising indeed if there was no such connection, but the evidence is not yet there. The sequence starts with the Zarzian, about 22,000 to 10,600 years ago, with a strong microlithic element, the equivalent of Kebaran plus the Natufian, mostly found in caves and rock shelters, but with an open-air complement (Zawi Chemi) for nearby Shanidar cave, with a radiocarbon date of about 11,000 years ago. Curvilinear structures and storage pits are flimsy and indistinct and there is no evidence for mud-brick. The general run of tools and implements is comparable to those in the west and contracted burials are found below floors. Remains of plant food have not been recovered, but the equipment for preparing cereals is there, and Zawi Chemi skeletons have the same worn-down teeth as are found at Ain Mallaha. They also suffered from *falciparum* malaria. Although hunting (of goat, deer, gazelle, onager, cattle and other animals) provided these people with the bulk of their food, Zawi Chemi shows incipient domestication of sheep. Domestic dog is present in the area from about 15,000 to 14,000 years ago (Palegawra cave). Wings of large birds found in a room at Zawi Chemi must have been used for some ritual function. Domestic goat is attested in the flint-knapping site of Tepe Asiab dating to about 10,000 years ago. Evidence for exchange comes from Shanidar in the form of obsidian from the Van area, as well as a posssibly native(?) copper bead that

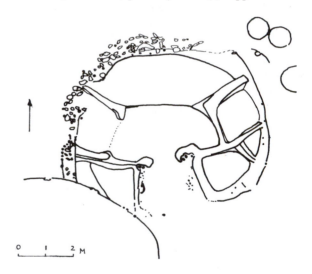

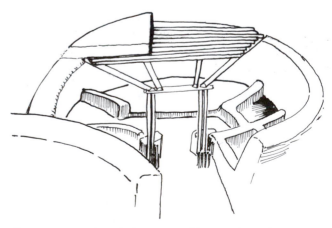

Figure 107 Mureybet III (Syria): round house, plan and reconstruction. (After Cauvin, 1977.)

428

points to Ergani Maden near Diyarbekir. Clay figurines start to appear and limestone is used for the manufacture of bracelets – both at Karim Shahir.

Although the list of remarkable items is still short, they point to significant developments to come after about 9,500 years ago. The distribution of this culture is not well known; at present it extends from north-east Iraq to Fars, a vast area. Links are also suspected with the Caspian 'Mesolithic' and the Transcaucasian area, which includes the fascinating site of Kobistan near Baku with its rock engravings. The later development of Neolithic agricultural communities in these areas strongly suggests not so much diffusion as local Epi-palaeolithic ('Mesolithic') origins about which much more remains to be learnt before we can fit them convincingly into our cultural mosaic.

THE PRE-POTTERY NEOLITHIC B OF THE LEVANT, ABOUT 10,500 TO ABOUT 8,250 YEARS AGO (Map 47)

Lasting for two millennia or more, this period is of funda-mental importance in western Asia, because, in addition to plant domestication, most of the five animal domesticates (dog, goat, sheep, cattle and pig) are domestic when the period ends, though not of course everywhere. Pastoralism is another feature of this period, and so is weaving in all its forms and in a variety of materials, both in plant fibres, (reeds, rushes and flax (linen)) and in wool. Stone vessels become widespread and sophisticated, and are imitated in white ware, a mixture of marl and ashes, baked like the earliest pottery, which now appears, some of it painted. Wall-paintings are produced at a number of sites, and fam-iliarity with clay leads to the production, hesitant before, of numerous figurines, statuettes and plaster reliefs, or even free-standing figures, half human size, or human skulls with the facial features restored in painted plaster. Red-painted floors, carefully burnished, are a feature of the period; ter-razzo stone mosaic is a more durable adaptation. Plastered-over animal skulls decorate buildings with presumably ritual functions. The first metal trinkets appear, in copper and lead, and beadmaking, in a variety of materials, flourishes; so does exchange and trade. Tools and weapons are produced in great varieties in various choice flints and in imported obsidian. Baked-clay counters of various shapes suggest numeracy and elementary accounting.

Architecture is now predominantly rectangular with large and small rooms, hearths, ovens, chimneys, stairs and cup-boards or niches; sometimes platforms become standard accessories, and posts or pillars may support flat roofs or an upper storey. Retaining terrace walls are not unusual, fortifications are. Settlements now come in any size, from camp and flint-knapping sites, trading posts and manu-facturing sites to large central places with thousands of inhabitants. Evidently some hierarchy of settlement is in the process of development, or has already been achieved.

The PPNB culture of the Levant – it stretches from southern Sinai to the Euphrates gorge in the Taurus moun-tains and deep into the oases of inland Jordan, Syria and into the North Mesopotamian steppe – covers a much larger area than its predecessor. The expansion into the Syrian interior and northern Mesopotamia appears to have come from the PPNA region around Mureybet and Aleppo, and it is generally agreed that many of the innovations that charac-terize PPNB are of 'Syrian' rather than 'Palestinian' origin. This gradual shift in the balance towards the north is linked by some to climatic deterioration, by others to the discovery of the great agricultural and pastoral potential of the Syrian and north Mesopotamian plains. A combination of both theories could explain the developments observed. The opening up of these vast territories established better links with the surrounding areas – southern Anatolia, Trans-caucasia and the Zagros zone of Iraq and Iran – with all the benefits: raw materials and, more important, human contacts that would have been entailed. Such cultural cross-fertilization would appear to have started in this period to gain momentum in its second half, say from 9,250 to 8,250 years ago and to continue with unabated vigour into our third phase: the classical age of painted-pottery cultures, the heirs of this development, the so-called Early Chalcolithic, about 8,250 to 7,000 years ago.

Compared with PPNA, PPNB is undoubtedly soph-isticated: archaic features such as microliths, plano-convex bricks and round buildings, with notable exception in the south of Palestine (Beidha and Sinai), tend to disappear. Roasting pits, communal-like grain storage, give way to ovens and bins in private houses which, when rebuilt, fre-quently are superimposed on their predecessors, an indi-cation of private property that presumably also included fields, vineyards and orchards. Differentiation of function by size – typical of later periods – is rarely observed; its place seems taken by unusual decoration like animal heads or reliefs, different contents, or richer burials than are found in ordinary dwellings. It may be surmised that the dividing line between sacred and profane was, if it existed at all, a very blurred one.

PPNB falls into two phases: an early one before about 9,250 years ago and a late one after that date, when pottery starts appearing in north Syria and the Mesopotamian steppe, but not in south Syria or Palestine. White lime ware, typical of the later phase, does however reach here (Ain Ghazal, Munhata) from the Beqa'a valley to the north (in Lebanon) and Tell Ramad II in the Damascus area.

The use of plaster is characteristic of this period; it covers walls and floors on a bed of pebbles; it can be left white, or painted red, buff, brown or black and burnished, or it will take wall paintings, left matt. It can be modelled into vessels or cover clay reliefs, statues or skulls, with or without the addition of paint. In short, it is a forerunner of clay, pottery and terracotta, but only by a little; a matter of half a mil-lennium or so. It has one disadvantage: being soft and brittle it lacks durability.

Before the invention of baked pottery, stone vessels were used, right back to the Natufian. When pottery becomes fully established the white lime ware is dropped and the plaster floors soon go out of fashion; so do wall paintings and plaster reliefs, their place being taken by painted or modelled pottery or textiles. Stone vessels, however, especially those in semi-precious or attractively veined rocks, never went out of fashion, but unlike wooden vessels or baskets they became luxury goods.

With even, flat floors it is not surprising that the first pottery, coil-built like baskets, is flat-bottomed; it is usually heavy, not well fired, and is of a buff or mottled colour, often burnished. It is used for cooking, storage of solids and, more important, liquids, and is on the whole utilitarian. Decoration is rare, a plain red wash, a few daubs or streaks of paint, a red self-slip or none at all, but there is burnish for the finer wares or, on some coarser vessels, there are a few incisions, impressions or applied ornaments of animal heads, figures, human and animal, knobs and warts and, rarest of all, painted motifs. Many shapes imitate vessels in other

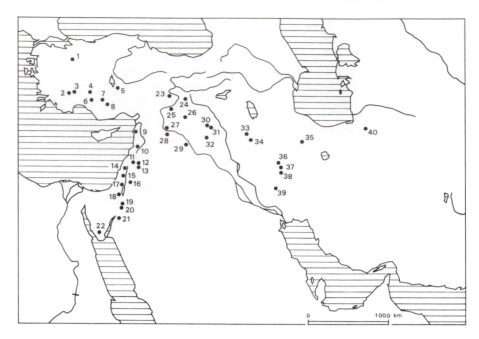

Map 47 Western Asia from about 10,500 to around 8,250 years ago. 1, Demirci Hüyük; 2, Haçilar; 3, Kuruçay; 4, Erbaba; 5, Aşikli Hüyük; 6, Suberde; 7, Çatal Hüyük; 8, Can Hasan; 9, Ras Shamra; 10, Labwe; 11, Tell Ramad; 12, Ghoraife; 13, Tell Aswad; 14, Beisamoun; 15, Munhata; 16, Ain Ghassul; 17, Jericho; 18, Nahal Hemar; 19, Basta; 20, Beidha; 21, Wadi Rum; 22, Tbeiq; 23, Cafer H; 24, Çayönü Tepesi; 25, Nevalaçori; 26, Tell Asouad; 27, Mureybet; 28, Tell Abu Hureyra; 29, Bouqras; 30, Tell Magzaliyah; 31, Tell Soto; 32, Tell Ettalathat Umm Dabaghiyah; 33, Tell Shimshara; 34, Jarmo; 35, Zaghe; 36, Ganjdareh; 37, Tepe Abdul Hosein; 38, Tepe Guran; 39, Ali Kosh (Bus Mordeh); 40, Tepe Sang-I-Chakùakh.

materials: stone or wooden bowls, baskets, vessels of bark or leather. The art of potting evidently goes back much before the PPNB, as already indicated; what was lacking before was its firing, so that unless accidentally burned it did not normally survive.

The production of figurines, mostly of females, but with a good number of horned animals and occasionally dogs, shows the same variations: unbaked or baked clay, gypsum or chalk, and mostly the finer examples in carved bone or stone. An increased use of firing techniques also led to the beginnings of metallurgy. Instead of studying these varied categories of artefacts separately, integrated studies promise better results and understanding.

Of particular interest are the PPNB finds from a possibly sacred cave in Nahal Hemar near the southern end of the Dead Sea, where the dry climate has preserved many perishable objects in association with human skulls, decorated with an asphalt (bitumen) net pattern or modelled clay features, painted limestone masks, a plaster statue (human) with painted eyes, small painted human heads of bone and stone animal figurines. There are numerous wooden and bone tools, thought to have been used in the manufacture of basketry, textiles, leather and so on. A fine belt hook of bone has Anatolian parallels at Aşikli and Çatal Hüyük; a straight, double-sided reaping knife has two sets of flint blades secured with resin. Flint blades with notches for hafting in bone handles bear traces of bitumen, suggesting that they were used for applying this material to coat containers.

Wooden arrowheads occur; other tools still have traces of malachite powder on them; some resemble spear-throwers, and so on. Particularly numerous are remains of baskets of reeds and rushes, showing coiling bands, plaiting and close and spaced twining. Bands and chequerboard motifs are composed in different natural colours. Thick mats also occur, as well as containers made of cordage, coated with asphalt.

There are ropes, knotless and knotted nets, knotted bags with shells or a green bead sown on to them, a weft-twined napkin, and a number of examples of harvested flax (such as linen) and other bast fibres, woven on a loom in tabby weave, some of the fragments having been dyed blue. The excavators regard these earliest textiles as having served a ritual rather than daily use. A few centuries later the people of Çatal Hüyük VI in Anatolia wore and were buried in linen (and woollen) garments.

Red and green painted wooden and clay beads (with thread) and an abundant use of sea-shells, including cowries, characterize Nahal Hemar's wide-ranging connections; some of the shells are Red Sea ones, the others Mediterranean, and the use of greenstone beads apparently points to Jordan, to Cyprus, or to the north of Syria or Anatolia. One might note the discovery of turquoise matrix (probably from Sinai) in PPNB Jericho. The presence of wooden beads is interesting: archaeologists too often report burials without any grave goods. Perhaps the word 'imperishable' should be added, as the idea of burying naked corpses is inherently unlikely, and reserved for enemies.

It should probably also be pointed out that the fine crafting of the perishable material found at Nahal Hemar may indicate much earlier origins of which we have as yet no inkling. It would not be in the least surprising to see similar material in association with Natufian or even Kebaran flints! Where estimating the age of a phenomenon is concerned, most scholars tend to err, through caution, on the low side, as radiocarbon dating has clearly demonstrated. The inventive potential of the Palaeolithic is consistently underrated, as was once the length and importance of the Precambrian by geologists. It would appear that, deprived of a scientific yardstick of time, prehistorians were unable to guess accurately how long any particular development took, and have unduly telescoped the timescale.

The various economies of the PPNB people are reflected

in their buildings from hunting camps and animal traps (*kites*) in the Transjordanian desert to summer and winter camps with round houses and bell-shaped pits of nomads in Sinai containing a stone equipment like that of the permanent agricultural settlement of Beidha near Petra, which with its neighbours specialized in the manufacture of and trade in beads, bracelets, bone tools and the like. Beidha has large houses and workshops and some special (perhaps ritual) places, and was protected by a retaining wall. It appears to date from Late PPNB and shows a unique sequence of round houses developing into spacious rectangular ones. At Jericho the entire PPNB sequence of over twenty building-levels exhibits rectangular mud-brick architecture and sophisticated buildings, but little of the planning of this large site, owing to insufficient exposure.

Ain Ghazal promises to be interesting, because the fine group of statues found in a pit suggests the presence of a sanctuary. Munhata has smaller houses than Jericho and a simpler layout and in the top level a round structure, otherwise unknown in the PPNB, with rooms around a central courtyard. In the Damascus area Tell Aswad and Ghoraife yield a fine series of figurines and economic details but no architecture, people living instead in reed shelters, whereas the late PPNB site of Tell Ramad that follows starts off with similar pits and then develops into plaster-covered rectangular rooms and covered passages. Beisamoun, a little further south, is said to be very large and like Ramad. Ghazal, Jericho and Nahal Hemar contain plastered skulls. No plans have yet been published. Rectangular houses with plaster floors also occur at Labweh in the Beqa'a and at T. Suqas and Ras Shamra on the Syrian coast. They occur in Mureybet IV and as far north as Gritille near Samsat, and a group of houses was dug at Tell Abu Hureyra (not yet published) and in the oasis of Al-Kowm.

The richest architectural harvest, however, comes from such remote sites as Bouqras, near the confluence of the Khabur with the Euphrates (Syria) (Fig. 108), Umm Dab-

aghiyah in the steppe south of the Jebel Sinjar (Iraq) and Çayönü, almost at the foot of the Taurus Mountains near Ergani Maden in Turkey.

Whereas Çayönü with its agriculture (emmer wheat, introduced einkorn, flax, lentil, pea, vetch and bitter vetch, vine and acorns, but no barley) but animal hunting, predominantly of cattle and pig, assisted by domestic dog, and domestic sheep and goat only in the top level and brought in from elsewhere, belongs to the early PPNB, Bouqras and Umm Dabaghiyah belong to the later phase.

At these sites agriculture was of little economic importance, but emmer and einkorn wheat, bread wheat, hulled and naked barley, peas and lentils were found, imported from further north at Umm Dabaghiyah, and perhaps grown around Bouqras. It is tempting to suggest that irrigation agriculture may have been invented thereabouts, but there is no formal proof. Yet Bouqras, occupying an area of 2.75 hectares, with an estimated population of about 850 people, flourished over a period of at least 600 years and had ovens, grain bins, querns and other equipment for cereal preparation, though very few sickle blades. Conceivably all the plant food found was imported. Both sites had the full range of domestic animals, with a preponderance of sheep, four times as common as goat, and some cattle and pigs as well as dogs. A pastoral economy of sheep-breeding – there are wild sheep as well in the area – accounts for the Bouqras economy; that of Umm Dabaghiyah depended on hunting onagers for meat and skins, exchanged with Jeber Sinjar sites for supplies of plant food. In the same way, Bouqras may have been an offshoot of Tell Abu Hureyra.

One sees here the beginnings of a settlement hierarchy with key sites, satellite towns and villages and, though hard to recognize, hunting camps, flint-knapping sites and so on. Exchange and trade were hardly secondary considerations. Bouqras is well sited for the obsidian trade from the Lake Van area coming down the river Habur; Umm Dabaghiyah and at least six neighbours lie on the southern edge of the Jebel Sinjar area, where we have Tell Sotto and a little further east Telul et Talathat, normal agricultural establishments. There is indirect evidence that the same pattern existed in the Habur triangle and the Balih valley. Throughout the Umm Dabaghiyah sequence (twelve building-levels) pottery is present, accompanied by white ware vessels of gypsum; at Bouqras, pottery, white ware and miniature stone vessels characterize at least the upper part of the sequence of ten building-levels; all three exist side by side and none can claim chronological precedence. Among the pottery, none looks as early as that of Tell Aswad on the Balih, dated about 9,000 years ago. Some of it is clearly Amuq A ware, burnished or red slipped and derived from western Syria (Amuq–Quweig–Jabbul), but the bulk is local, coarse and badly fired and consists of storage vessels. There are some finer wares, painted in red on buff, or incised in the latest levels. At Umm Dabaghiyah (less so at Bouqras) applied ornament in the form of animals, animal heads and human figures occurs and this new assemblage is clearly ancestral to the painted pottery cultures of the next period. Compared with Palestine and south Syria, Late PPNB in the north is no longer pre-ceramic, but fully ceramic, from about 9,000 years ago or soon thereafter. Evidence from southern Anatolia and Iran supports a similar development there. The invention of pottery was hardly revolutionary, but made both cooking and storage easier; it kept the soup in and the mice out, and could be refined to compete with traditional containers in wood, skin, basketry and stone.

Equally remarkable was the development in housing. At

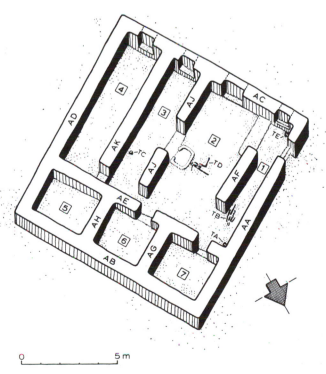

Figure 108 Bouqras (Syria): rectangular structure ('House 12'). (After Akkermans et al., 1983, p. 367.)

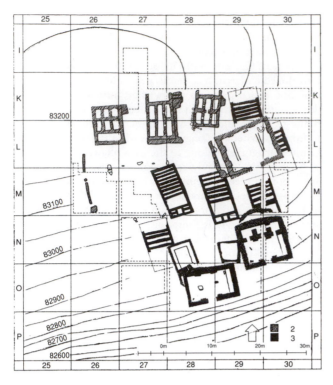

Figure 109 Çayönü Tepesi (Turkey): plan of the oriental part of the excavation: structures of levels 2 and 3. (After Çambel and Braidwood, 1983.)

Çayönü (Fig. 109), in an early PPNB context, the earliest settlers lived in sub-rectangular sunken huts, perhaps a relict of the PPNA tradition of Mureybet. These give way to half a dozen phases (period 3) with rectangular free-standing houses of 'grill plan' with a light superstructure of several rooms and plaster floors raised on parallel stone walls against damp. In turn, these houses are succeeded by another five to six phases of 'cell plan' (period 2) houses, and finally in the top building-level (period 1) mud-brick buildings make their appearance.

Side by side with grill and cell plan buildings there are others of more monumental appearance: the 'stone building', with a stone paved floor and two large stones to support the roof (period 3), a red-plastered 'skull building', thus named because of a deposit of forty skulls found in a room, and the 'terrazzo building' with a polished pebble floor in pink with white bands (period 2) and internal buttresses. Some special functions seem indicated for these structures. There is also a courtyard with rows of standing stones. Burials below floors, sophisticated stone tools and the earliest use of copper as well as some attempts at making pottery are other interesting features of this culture, which seems to extend from the Malatya area (Çafer Hüyük) via the Habur and Jebel Sinjar (Tell Magzaliyah with fortifications) to Tell Shimshara on the Little Zab river in the Zagros zone. Its distribution is predominantly lowland, but it has trading links with the Lake Van area for obsidian and other rocks and with the south Mediterranean for shells, stone vessels, white ware and so on.

Bouqras presents us with the most extensive settlement plan of the 'Late PPNB' period in the north and with a variety of buildings: spacious private houses with mud-brick walls and foundations, plastered in white gypsum, sometimes stained red and with occasional wall painting (cranes or ostriches) or relief in the form of a human head with obsidian-inlaid eyes. Many of the houses have a spacious

courtyard with an oven in a corner and a hearth in front of a wide doorway leading into a living room and another at the back; a row of store-rooms or workrooms is added. Doorways are narrow and low – one had to crawl into the house – and burials occur below the floors. Other structures consist of three or four rows of store-rooms, like the Çayönü cell plan. Others still consist of a series of corridors, reminiscent of grill plan structures. As at Çayönü all these buildings are large: 10 m or more in length and occasionally twice that size. Presumably they belonged to well-to-do citizens. No shrines or temples have yet been recognized, and one might note that the architectural layout of the settlement shows unmistakable signs of planning. When rebuilding takes place, the new house uses the walls of the old as foundations. There are no signs of fortification, but houses are very close to each other, presenting long stretches of unbroken wall; the low doorways (*c*.70 cm) also would discourage attack.

Umm Dabaghiyah, out in the desolate steppe, has its own peculiarities. The central building consists of small store-rooms entered from the roof. Houses are small but contain several rooms, and have arches and hooded chimneys and a number of steps and toe-holes leading to the roof from which they are entered. Mud-brick and gypsum plaster are the normal building materials; there are niches and cupboards, bins and hearths, benches, red plastered floors and again a number of wall paintings of onager hunting, humans, probably spiders, probably birds, and stick-like human figures in red ochre, as well as geometric patterns. The presence of such sophisticated features on a specialized hunting site bodes well for future excavations of the parent sites on which sites like Umm Dabaghiyah depended. It has now become abundantly clear that the 'hilly flanks theory' (no descent into the alluvium before the end of Jarmo) seriously underestimated human ingenuity.

The discovery of settlement from the eleventh millennium BP onward on the Syro-Mesopotamian alluvian (instead of a postulated descent in the eighth) removes a spurious backwardness and should act as a stimulant towards more thorough exploration in those parts, hitherto considered unfit for human habitation, because of a theory! The signal failure of the 'hilly flanks theory', as that of the 'oasis theory' before, has had its silver lining, an interest in the mountains and uplands, hitherto unexplored, of Iran and Anatolia.

IRAN

Excavations in the central Zagros zone, both on and off the Iranian plateau, present a similar picture, roughly contemporary with Early and Late PPNB. Here Ganj Dareh (D-A) and Bus Mordeh, the former in an intramontane valley near Bisitun, the latter on the alluvial plain near Deh Luran, were established about 9,500 years ago, and other Aceramic sites are known to exist in the Khuzistan plain. In the second half of the period, from around 9,000 years ago onwards, there are the sites of Jarmo, Tepe Guran, Tepe Sarab, Tepe Abdul Hosein, the Ali Kosh phase that follows Bus Mordeh, and on the north-central and east Iranian plateau, Zaghe and Sang-i Chakhmaq, the progenitors of the later Sialk and Djeitun cultures. Nothing quite as early has yet been excavated in southern Iran, whether in Fars, Kerman, Seistan or Baluchistan, but the site of Mehrgarh at the foot of the Bolan pass (and the bottom layers of Kili Ghul Mohammad near Quetta), dating from at least the ninth millennium suggest that future excavations may well close the gap. In view of the vast distribution of an Aceramic

Neolithic beyond the Zagros, the use of the term 'Greater Mesopotamia' is inappropriate, and the same applies to 'Syro-Cilicia'.

On the evidence of the stone industries it seems that Ganj Dareh and Bus Mordeh developed from the earlier Zawi Chemi Shanidar Karim Shahir complex. Domestic sheep and goat are attested in Bus Mordeh, goat only at Ganj Dareh (as before in neighbouring Asiab), sheep, however, like other animals being hunted. Wheats and barleys, peas and lentils and other crops now make their appearance in varying strains and proportions, as further west. Domestication of plants and animals is evidently well under way, but the presence of a settlement does not of course indicate that it was occupied all the year round and in the case of the Bus Mordeh phase at Ali Kosh it is thought to represent the winter quarters of a group exploiting the rich pasture lands of the Khuzistan lowlands who had summer quarters elsewhere and higher up in a valley of the Zagros, still undiscovered.

Characteristic of the period are rectangular mud-brick houses with plaster floors and several rooms, passages and courtyards (Bus Mordeh) or a more compact settlement with numerous small basement rooms used for storage and cult(?) purposes, with living quarters extending over them at a higher level (Ganj Dareh), in other words two-storey buildings. The two heads of wild sheep set in a niche one above the other discovered at this site are reminiscent of similar occurrences at Mureybet, Zaghe, Çatal Hüyük and Tell Aswad, and are unlikely merely to represent hunters' trophies. A cult seems more likely to lie at the root of such practices, and similar representations in relief on pots (Umm Dabaghiyah, Shulaveri culture, Haçilar, Can Hasan, Kösk cultures) strengthen this belief.

Ganj Dareh D, burnt and well preserved, yields some of the earliest pottery in western Asia, mainly in the form of containers for storage and apparently well before Tell Aswad, Bouqras and Umm Dabaghiyah. It is interesting to notice that the manufacture of pottery did not spread like wildfire as might have been expected; some communities managed it, others tried and gave up and borrowed at a later date. The division between aceramic and ceramic provides no useful chronological criterion; once again theory is in conflict with the evidence. There is no white ware in the Zagros zone at this period and stone vessels seem rare.

This changes in the better-known next phase, when for instance Tepe Guran shows a fine pottery development, perhaps derived from Ganj Dareh, with elegant shapes and painted patterns; whereas contemporary Jarmo makes fine stone vessels and handsome baked figurines, excelled only by those of Tepe Sarab. Ali Kosh, down in the torrid plain, has neither; at this period settlements go their own way, and no one site can be regarded as typical of the rest. The soundings at Guran, Sarab, Jarmo and Ali Kosh, all restricted in size, have yielded little in the way of architectural layouts; Jarmo, in particular, a small site with an estimated population of 150 people and an unknown number of houses (none complete), is disappointing. Far more rewarding are the as yet only partially published sites of Zaghe and Sang-i Chakhmaq (western mound), plateau sites with greater agricultural potential, in the plains of Qazvin or Shahrud. Zaghe 5–17 is aceramic, but 4–2 marks the beginning of coarse, sometimes painted archaic ware, copper smelting in an industrial complex, a temple in level 4 and interesting houses in level 2, built in mud-bricks and pisé (chineh). Typical are rectangular structures some 10 m long with walled courtyards and three roofed structures: main living room, store-room

and kitchen with bread-ovens. A water supply in a pot sunk in the courtyard, numerous working platforms, sometimes red plastered, and extended burials on a red-ochre-strewn floor are typical. Economic details are not yet available, but we are evidently dealing with farming communities. The temple structure is similar in plan, but the courtyard is here roofed over and contains a huge (probably ritual) fireplace; many female figurines were found, but the most striking feature is the decoration of the central room with a large meander pattern in black and white on a red ground and skulls and horns of mountain goats, eighteen in all, fixed onto the wall. Here again, as at Bouqras, high and low doorways were found intact. The temple dates probably to about 8,700 years ago.

At Sang-i Chakhmaq – western mound (second half of the ninth millennium BP) – five building-levels of neatly constructed houses were found with a standardized sequence of main connecting rooms; the central one with a raised floor, often with red-stained lime plaster, an earth floor in the kitchen with an oven for baking bread, and a lower area, perhaps for sleeping. Alcoves, bins and benches are an integral part of the architecture. These units are combined in blocks with open spaces in between. Pottery exists but is rare, and there are clay female figurines. The flint industry contains blades, cores and awls, but no microlithic element. Obsidian, as in the contemporary Zagros sites, is imported. Burials have not yet been reported. The presence of these early cultures on the north Iranian plateau is matched by material of similar date in southern Anatolia (Turkey).

ANATOLIA

At present there appears to be a hiatus between the Kebaran and Natufian-like occupation of the rock shelters of Belbaşi and Beldibi on the south coast and the establishment of permanent settlements on the Anatolian plateau roughly at the period of early PPNB, around 9,600 or 9,500 years ago. In other words, the equivalent of the PPNA is still missing, though the exportation of Ciftlik obsidian to the Levant during this period is well attested. It is presumably only a matter of time before settlements of this period will be discovered. The equivalents of Early PPNB on the Anatolian plateau are Asikli Hüyük and, somewhat later, Aceramic Haçilar, followed, after about 9,000 years ago, by Aceramic Can Hasan, Suberbe (still without pottery) and Aceramic Çatal Hüyük XIII-O.

As long as the key site for the earlier phase, Asikli Hüyük, remains unexcavated, little positive evidence can be derived from it except that it is large, has mud-brick buildings and red plaster floors (with burials below the floors), has a distinct obsidian industry of its own and no microliths; though it may show evidence for plant domestication, the animal bones collected show no domesticated species. It is roughly the contemporary of Çayönü and a possible ancestor of Çatal Hüyük.

Of the other aceramic sites, Aceramic Haçilar shows dry farming, domestic dog and potential domestication of sheep and goat; Suberbe probably the same, but Can Hasan III adds to this, irrigation crops (naked six-row barley and bread wheat) as well as collected fruits, grapes and walnuts. Like Aceramic Haçilar and Çatal Hüyük, Can Hassan III has rectangular architecture with entry from the roof, mud or plaster floors, often stained red, and traces of wall painting. Unlike at Asikli and Çatal Hüyük burials were not found below the floors on these sites, but human skulls were found in ritual positions at Aceramic Haçilar. Stone industries differ from Asikli and Çatal Hüyük; microlithic tools are said to occur at Can Hasan and Suberde. The evidence is at present insufficient to draw broad conclusions from mere soundings.

Last but not least comes the site of Çatal Hüyük, covering at least 15 ha with an estimated 25 m or more of Neolithic deposits. Only one-thirtieth of the site was dug and the lower levels remained untouched. Fourteen building-levels are radiocarbon dated to about 8,700 to 8,100 years ago; all yielded pottery, mud-brick architecture, white plaster floors (and some red ones) and wall paintings. On the basis of five to seven occupants per house, the population estimate is between five and seven thousand people, allowing for half the site to be covered by open spaces. The basis of the economy was simple irrigation agriculture and the domestication of cattle; sheep and goat still being morphologically wild. Domestic dogs were kept, but hunting appears to have lost its importance, and like fishing and fowling is mainly known from the wall paintings, which may record, not contemporary ways of life, but those of their ancestors centuries before. Likewise, the food remains found in an élite quarter tell us nothing of what the rest of the population fed on and we cannot just assume that at Çatal Hüyük everybody indulged in beef-eating. At this site a great number of arts and crafts are documented, but only in the form of finished products found in the élite quarter excavated; the workshops have not been found and should be sought elsewhere on the site. Most raw materials, clay, plaster, reeds and food excepted, came from elsewhere and the area of the Çatal Hüyük culture is correspondingly large, taking in the greater part of southern Anatolia. Links with Cilicia and north Syria are close and among the imports are Syrian tabular flint, white ware, small stone vessels of Bouqras type, Red Sea cowries (set in the eye-sockets of a skeleton) and probably linen (flax) garments, which together with woollen ones were found covering burials. Mediterranean shells, dentalium, cardium and whelks are by no means rare; obsidian and pumice came from Acigöl, east of Aksaray; stalactites, lead and copper probably from the Taurus, blue beads of apatite (looking like turquoise) and marble from metamorphic or igneous rocks in the Nigde area; cannabar from there or from Sizma, north of Konya; salt and sulphur from the Salt Lake region, and so on. There is little doubt that exchange and trade as well as manufactured goods contributed substantially to Çatal Hüyük's opulence and social development.

There is good evidence here for private property, for unequal distribution of wealth in the burials and their grave goods, for a consistent set of measures, for town-planning, rules and regulations, and, most important of all, for religious observance, art and symbolism on a scale unrevealed at any other site of this period. At Çatal Hüyük we are presented with the thought of a Neolithic people, long before writing, but more eloquently expressed in their reliefs and wall paintings. Crude figurines, familiar from all the other cultures discussed before, are here augmented by stone statuettes, often in groups, accompanied by stalactites – like a Christmas crib or translated into plaster reliefs of monumental size; there are also intricate wall paintings with deities, each with their symbols in a row like a Byzantine iconostasis. Most of these component elements are known before; here they are enhanced and enriched and combined into elaborate compositions in stone, clay, plaster, paint and probably textiles copied in paint. These people only buried their dead after vultures had stripped off the flesh, and wrapped up the bones in cloth, mats or baskets, and left wall paintings

showing the process. Red ochre burials still occur at Çatal Hüyük and blue and green paint is also used to emphasize features on skulls. From the study of several hundred skeletons the composition of the population emerges; over half are long-headed Eurafrican (like the Natufians, descendants of an Upper Palaeolithic race), less than a quarter are gracile long-headed Mediterraneans (as at Tell Ramad in Syria), the others are round-headed Alpine types. All are happily intermixed, a biological key to success.

THE FLORUIT OF PAINTED POTTERY CULTURES – FIRST PHASE (APPROXIMATELY EIGHT MILLENNIA AGO) (Map 48)

The most outstanding feature of this period is the proliferation of painted pottery, throughout the greater part of western Asia. Economically, the processes of domestication of plants and animals, achieved by the end of the previous period, were now consolidated, and simple irrigation agriculture allowed the cultivation of previously unfavourable environments, such as middle and lower Mesopotamia, the Solduz area in the Urmia basin, the foothill zone of the Kopet Dagh on the edge of the Karakum desert and finally Egypt. The first settled cultures start to appear in Transcaucasia, along the eastern flanks of the central Zagros mountains and in Fars. The cultural mechanics of such an expansion remain unknown; the success of farming may have tempted former hunters, gatherers and pastoralists to settle; in other cases settlements may have developed from earlier trading posts, desiccation of the more arid parts of western Asia about 8,000 years ago may have led to emigration in search of better land and so forth. What is not demonstrable is evidence for over-population, or widespread climatic change.

In contrast to ninth millennium BP sites, many sites of this period continued to be inhabited for millennia to come, severely restricting archaeological research, which has tended to concentrate on small and accessible sites without a later overburden, or satisfied itself with deep soundings. The architectural remains so far discovered are thus usually somewhat disappointing, and the prevailing idea that we are now dealing mainly with 'villages' rather than 'towns or cities' needs to be corrected; there are huge settlements in this period as before, both accessible and inaccessible, but they have not yet been excavated. Until they are, our interpretation is bound to suffer and will tend to underestimate the real achievements of this period, and the one which follows in the seventh millennium BP. Comparison is the main archaeological task: because already in the tenth and ninth millennia BP there were large and small settlements (the bulk) as well as sites of (later) city size side by side with mere hamlets or camping sites, one must expect to find a great variety of economic and, especially, cultural development. The old sequence 'from Cave to Empire' too often suggests a regular progress of evolution, which is not borne out by the facts, be they archaeological or historical. Cultural progress was erratic and whereas in the eighth millennium BP there were many fascinating painted pottery cultures, there were areas on the fringe where painting was not adopted, perhaps for technological reasons – an inability to make light-coloured wares on which alone painting was efficient – or out of disdain for new-fangled products born from innate conservatism. Transcaucasia's Shulaveri culture and the Keban area in eastern Turkey shunned painting, as

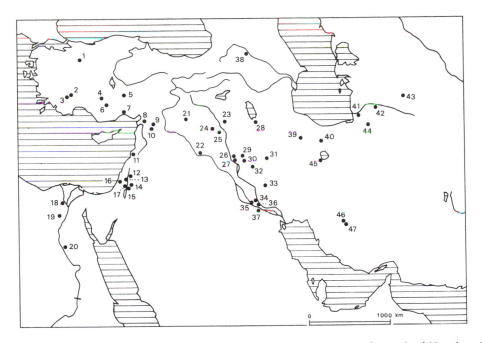

Map 48 Western Asia during the eighth millennium BP. 1, Demirci Hüyük; 2, Kuruçay; 3, Haçilar; 4, Çatal Hüyük; 5, Kösk; 6, Can Hasan; 7, Mersin; 8, Amuq; 9, Qouweiq; 10, Tell Berne; 11, Byblos; 12, Sha'ar Ha Golan; 13, Munhata; 14, Ain Ghassul; 15, Ghrubba; 16, Wadi Rabah; 17, Jericho; 18, Merimde; 19, Fayum 'A' 20, Badari; 21, Tell Halaf; 22, Baghouz; 23, Tell Arpachiyah; 24, Yarim Tepe; 25, Tell Hassuna; 26, Samarra; 27, Tell es-Sawwan; 28, Hajji Firuz; 29, T. Songor; 30, Abada; 31, Mahidasht (J.); 32, Chogha Mami; 33, Chogha Sefq; 34, Hajji Muhammad; 35, Uruk; 36, T. Oueli; 37, Eridu; 38, Shulaveri; 39, Zaghe; 40, Cheshmeh Ali; 41, Tureng Tepe; 42, Yarim Tepe; 43, Jeitun; 44, Sang-I Chakmakh; 45, Tepe Siyalk (I–II); 46, T. Mushki; 47, T. Jarri 'B'.

did the PPNB-derived cultures on the coast of Syria, Lebanon and Palestinian coast, as well as Fayum A and Merimde in Lower Egypt and the Badarian of Upper Egypt. Old and new nearly always go together; in one form or another they can be found throughout the eighth millennium BP. What is becoming abundantly clear is that underneath the changing fashions of this period we are dealing with local or regional developments from the previous period. Continuity and change is the keynote.

With the triumph of agriculture and stock-breeding there is a marked decline in hunting, reflected by the stone industries: microliths disappear, projectile points (spear, javelin and arrow-heads) decline, and the mace (club) and slinger-stone take their place. Sickles replace straight reaping knives, hoes gain popularity for weeding and blocking irrigation ditches; ovens for parching cereals and for more sophisticated cooking, now that pottery is common, are indispensable. Kilns appear to produce well-fired pots. The greater use of baked clay now produces spindle-whorls and loom-weights to facilitate weaving; copperworking changes from the production of trinkets to that of simple tools: pins, needles, chisels and an occasional axe. As metal is normally reused, its archaeological record is poor. Clay counters, used from about 10,000 years ago continue, as expected, and small stamp seals are now used to mark private property or seal store-rooms or houses. With the widespread use of pottery the white ware disappears, but stone vessels become a luxury product. Pottery and terracotta figurines supplant plaster reliefs and wall paintings, and become our sole source for religious beliefs. Burials, now deprived of excarnation or treatment with ochre, still occur below floors or, as an innovation in extramural cemeteries, accompanied by grave goods. The cult of the human skull disappears. To all these statements there are of course exceptions, but such is the general pattern. As wall paintings are a great source of information, the excavation of more architecture may

eventually redress the balance. No western Asian society was ever irreligious. Extramural burial, of course, reduces the possibility of having perishable materials preserved in graves. Similarly, the transference of wall painting and relief decoration current in the ninth millennium BP to the much-reduced scale of pot painting robs us of much vital information. On the other hand, the vast extension of painted pottery, often decorated with patterns deriving from felt or textiles, shows how widespread and how important the textile industry was in this period. From about 8,000 years ago, if not before, woven garments take the place of animal skins, and this was to become a basic development and industry of western Asia, where pottery and textiles were major and not minor arts.

If, on the other hand, the architectural development in this period seems undistinguished, it may be for the reasons outlined above: the digging of 'villages' rather than 'urban' sites. In general, rectangular structures now prevail except in the Shulaveri culture of Transcaucasia, which has round houses and monochrome pottery with applied decoration, like at Umm Dabaghiyah, and fine figurines. In the Halaf culture of north Syro-Mesopotamia round houses appear in the earliest strata and later are combined with rectangular rooms, courtyards and storage buildings, especially at Yarim Tepe. A survey in the Quweiq valley north of Aleppo shows that the Halaf pottery there is clearly a local development from Amuq A and B pottery of the ninth millennium BP. In north Iraq, the Umm Dabaghiyah painted pottery may have influenced the first Halaf painted wares, whereas its architecture influenced that of the Hassuna culture (Yarim Tepe I). The resurgence of round houses is as yet unexplained, as no suitable ancestor has been found. Surveys in eastern Anatolia lend no support to an origin in those regions; contrary to expectations, Halaf pottery is rare. The vast extent of the culture appears to date from its beginning and is not the result of later expansions as new work at Arpachiyah,

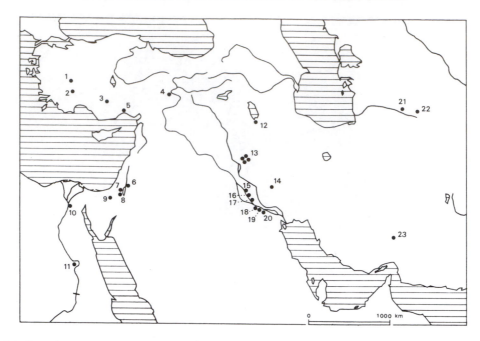

Map 49 Western Asia from about 7,250 or 7,000 to around 6,000 years ago: 1, Beycesultan; 2, Kuruçay; 3, Can Hasan I; 4, Değirmen Tepe; 5, Mersin; 6, T. Ghassul; 7, Engedi; 8, Nahal Mishmar; 9, Beersheba sites; 10, El Omari; 11, Negade I; 12, Dalma; 13, Hamrin sites: Abada, Madhur, Songor, Kheit Qasim; 14, Tepe Sabz Ghogha Sefq (Khazineh, Mehme, Bayat); 15, Hajji Muhammad; 16, Uruk; 17, T. Oueli; 18, Eridu; 19, Ubaid; 20, Ur; 21, Anauja; 22, Namazga; 23, Tepe Yahya.

combined with field exploration, has shown. Halaf imports occur in Haçilar VI and I, in south-western Anatolia, in the Keban area and Malatya, and even in the Kur and Araxes valleys. Offshoots reach Lebanon and Palestine (Wadi Rabah) and the Mahi Dasht near Kermanshah ('J ware'). In other words, Halaf appears as the successor of PPNB or Early Ceramic in the dry farming belt. Its southern neighbour, practising irrigation, is the Samarra culture, best known from Tell es Sawwan, but also known at Baghouz and Choga Mami. Elaborate, T-shaped houses are reminiscent of Bouqras; its early stone vessels betray a similar origin, though its statuettes do not. The painted pottery influenced the Hassuna culture, and was traded up the Euphrates into Syria. In the Hamrin area where Halaf and Samarra met, Eridu and Hajji Muhammad (Ubaid 1 and 2) have now also been found. These are typical of the first settlements on the lower Mesopotamian alluvium from about 7,500 years ago with its irrigation agriculture and cattle- and sheep-breeding, date palm cultivation and fisheries: the origins of Sumer and Akkad, and probably also of Susiana (Elam).

These two large cultures and their offshoots come to dominate the centre of the stage – Syria and Mesopotamia – whereas the surrounding mountain areas developed their own way and continued to supply raw materials such as obsidian, copper, and various semi-precious stones for seals, beads, amulets and small stone vessels. In Palestine various groups replace the Late PPNB; the Byblos Neolithic is derived from it and painted pottery cultures spread through southern Anatolia: Haçilar, Çatal West, Can Hasan, Mersin, and one other, Kösk, which specialized in low relief, but little painting. All are rooted in the Çatal Hüyük complex. In Iran the picture is similar: Cheshme Ali and Sialk I-II follow Zaghe, Djeitun develops out of Sang-i Chakhmaq. The Hajji Firuz culture resembles Hassuna somewhat and Tal-i Mushki and Tal-i Jarri B follow each other in Fars; their origin is still unknown.

FROM PAINTED POTTERY TO PLAIN WARES (ABOUT 7,250/7,000 TO 5,000 YEARS AGO) (Map 49)

From about 7,500 years ago onwards changes are taking place in southern Anatolia, where Late Chalcolithic burnished wares replace painted pottery (Kuruçay, Beycesultan, Can Hasan I) or, as at Mersin XVII–XVI, gain in volume without ousting it. Beyond the Euphrates, the old, dark burnished wares show little change. In north Syria, the later Halaf period ('Amuq' D) like Mersin shows much more burnished ware than painted pottery, and the former unity of Halaf culture breaks down. Late Halaf seems rare west of Jebel Sinjar. Then, about 7,000 years ago this splendid culture disappears in somewhat mysterious circumstances. What follows is either pure Ubaid 3 (or Early Ubaid in older books) or perhaps more often Ubaid 3 wares, matt-painted as in the south but with local peculiarities and patterns which derive from Halaf. The usual explanation is that the Ubaid people from the south of Mesopotamia overran the north and replaced Halaf with their own culture. Along the foothills of the Zagros similar changes take place at the same time as Khazineh (close to Hajji Muhammad) is transformed into Mehmeh and Bayat, roughly the equivalents of Ubaid 3 and 4, with repercussions also in the Mahi Dasht and beyond in the Sialk culture with so-called Ubaid-like wares in a new phase (Sialk III). Similarly Namazga I in Turkmenistan follows Anau IA with its Sailk II inspired wares. Evidently changes are in the air and simpler, matt-painted pottery in black or brown on buff replaced the gaudy and finer pottery, polychrome or bichrome of the Halaf age.

It is hard to believe that this is due to territorial expansion from southern Mesopotamia; it looks more like a change in taste and fashion brought in the wake of Sumerian and Elamite traders searching for raw materials and offering perhaps patterned garments in exchange. An intensification of trade, technological novelties like pottery thrown on the wheel, the spread of stamp seals and a steady increase in metal ornaments and tools mark this period. Much of the Northern Ubaid is probably made by the Halaf people, rather than by southerners, and these northern types in turn penetrate to the Syrian coast (Ras Shamra), Cilicia (Mersin) and the Antitaurus region (Elbistan and Malatya areas), hitherto within the Halaf orbit. Commercial enterprise now also spreads into the Gulf, and Ubaid pottery occurs on a score of sites along the Saudi Arabian coast to Bahrain, and one sherd comes from Tepe Yahya in Kerman. Dalma pottery of the north Zagros was found on Ubaid 3 sites in the Hamrin, eloquent evidence of contacts, already known to exist with Tepe Giyan and its Hajji Muhammad (Ubaid 2) patterns. In the Urmia region, Dalma follows upon Hajji Firuz.

What we are witnessing is the opening up of western Asia to trade, probably with the establishment of trading posts, and in its wake more widespread cultural resemblances and assimilations than had existed during the previous periods. The Anatolian plateau, Transcaucasia, Iran beyond the Zagros, Lebanon and Palestine and, of course, Egypt remain aloof from these developments. They were to develop along native lines and produced by the end of the Ubaid period if not before, centres of metallurgy that generated an even more intensive phase of commercial activity during the Uruk period in the sixth millennium BP.

The architectural hallmark of the Ubaid period is a building of tripartite form consisting of a central hall with rows of small rooms on either side: it is the basic form of both temples (Eridu, Warka, Tepe Gawra) and houses (for example T. Oueli Awaili, T. Abada (Fig. 110), Kheit Qasim, T. Madhhur, T. Songor and Degirmentepe), often with T-shaped ends. Houses are as large and elaborate as temples and both are provided with buttresses where appropriate. Other structures clearly served for storage (T. Oueli). Fragments of wall paintings are reported; typical for Ubaid 4 are lizard-headed female and male clay figurines, but only in south Mesopotamia. Burial customs vary, intramural burial

and extramural cemeteries both occurring. Metal remains exceedingly rare; so are rich burials and any other signs of a stratified society. Fortifications, or weapons other than a few mace heads, are likewise conspicuous by their absence. Successful trade depends on peaceful relations and it is not impossible that the Halaf and Ubaid peoples understood this already.

The Ghassulian culture of Palestine (and possibly Sinai) provides a welcome contrast. Descended from the Late Neolithic Wadi Rabah culture, an offshoot of Syrian Halaf, it probably practised irrigation agriculture, had domesticated donkeys, and had large settlements (T. Ghassul) where blocks of houses were arranged to form a blank wall against the enemy, impressive temples (Ein Gedi, Megiddo), a flourishing art of wall painting, though somewhat mediocre pottery, ritual stone vessels and a variety of burial habits, one of which employed pots or ossuaries in house form as containers for the bones of secondary burials. Yet its most striking features are accomplished ivory carvings of male and female deities (as in contemporary Egypt) and a most sophisticated metallurgy in arsenical copper as revealed by the Nahar Mishmar hoard, probably the treasures of the Ein Gedi temple, evacuated for safekeeping, and dated to the end of the Ghassulian period, 6,000 years ago or thereabouts. Sceptres, staffs, battle axes, crowns, copper vessels, and hundreds of maceheads of various types (with Egyptian parallels) show hitherto unsuspected wealth and advanced technology, such as lost-wax casting. Behind this must lie much previous expertise in prospecting and mining in Sinai, whose origins remain to be elucidated.

THE SIXTH MILLENNIUM BP: URUK (Map 50)

The sixth millennium BP technically marks the climax of prehistoric development in southern Mesopotamia and Egypt, ending with the appearance of script and bureaucratic records, euphemistically termed 'history'. Actual historical information, apart from kings' names, is frustratingly scarce in Egypt and absent in Mesopotamia. The Uruk period developed from Ubaid with the decrease in painted and a vast increase in coarse buff and pink ware, hand-made at first, and some fine red and grey ware. Spouted vessels are a notable innovation and reach even Egypt at the beginnning of Negade II, as well as Palestine. In Syria the early phase is known as 'Amuq F' best known for its reserve slip ware and fine gabled seals, about 5,500 years ago. A century or so of Sumerian colonization brings 'middle' or 'classical' Uruk culture to the Syrian Euphrates between the Taurus gorge and the eastward bend opposite Aleppo. Other colonies include T. Brak, T. Leyland, Grai Resh, Nineve and Qalinj Agha in the territory of the native Gawra cultures, another Ubaid offshoot, Qraya near Mari on the middle Euphrates, and extend into Susiana (Susa, Chogha Mish) and Faru-khabad (Den Luran), with trading posts well into Iran (Godin Tepe, Ghabristan and possibly even Tal-i Iblis in Kerman). Bevelled-rim bowls act as guide fossils for Sumerian expansion. Uruk trade encompasses the entire Fertile Crescent and acts as a catalyst in many neighbouring regions now, brought into closer contact with Sumerian and Elamite merchants. Numerical tablets and sealed clay balls with tokens (one reportedly from Dahran in Saudi Arabia) testify to the trade in grain, oil, wool, cloth and lapis lazuli in exchange for timber and metals. Writing at this stage is still

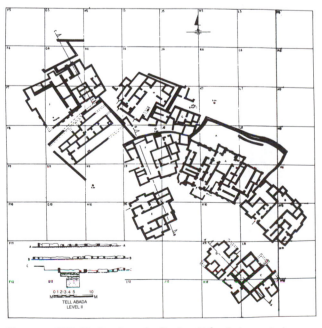

Figure 110 Tell Abada: plan of a district. (After Jasim, 1984.)

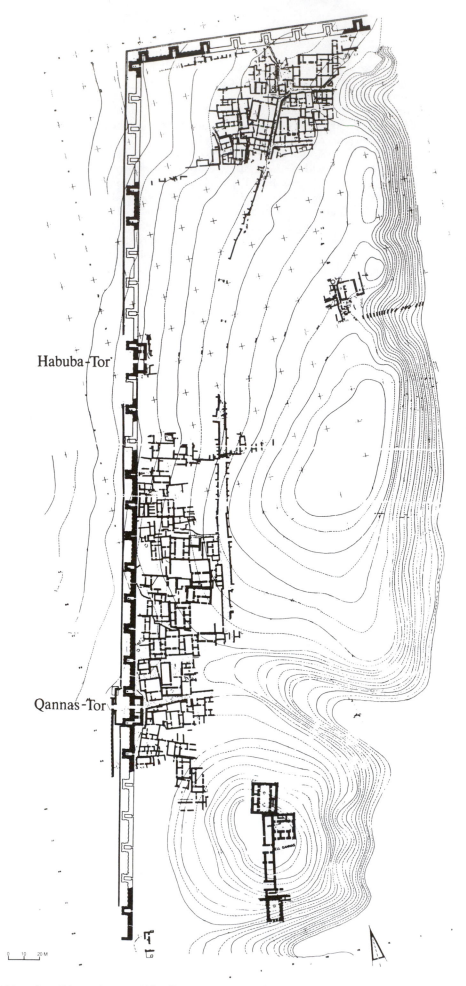

Habuba-Tor

Qannas-Tor

0 10 20 M

Figure 111 Habuba Kebira: plan of the settlement. (After Strommenger, 1980.)

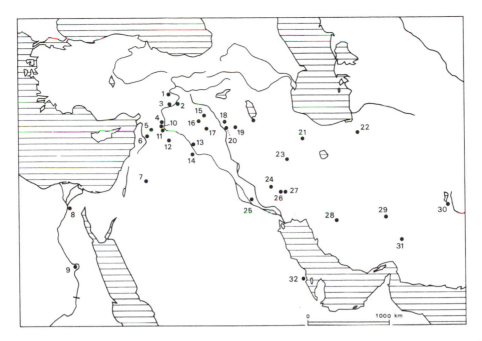

Map 50 Western Asia during the sixth millennium BP: 1, Arslan Tepe; 2, Hassek; 3, Samsat; 4, J. Aruda; 5, T. Berne; 6, Hama; 7, T. Jawa; 8, Ma'adi; 9, Negade II; 10, Habuba Kebira; 11, T. Qannas; 12, Al-Kowm; 13, T. Qraya; 14, Mari; 15, T. Leylan; 16, T. Brak; 17, Grai Resh; 18, Tepe Gawra; 19, Qalinj Agha; 20, Ninive; 21, Ghabrestan; 22, Tepe Hisar; 23, Godin VI; 24, Farukh Abad; 25, Uruk; 26, Susa; 27, Chogha Mish; 28, T. Maliyan; 29, T. I. Iblis; 30, Shahri Sokhta; 31, Tepe Yahya; 32, Dahran.

unknown, but cylinder seals are already in use. Local cultures preferred stamp seals, as in the Ubaid period.

The architectural remains of Habuba Kebira, J. Aruda, Samsat, T. Hassek and Brak are impressive. Habuba (Fig. 111) stretches over a kilometre along the banks of the Euphrates and is fortified on the landward side. Its administrative centre (T. Qannas) dominates a well-planned town laid out on a rectangular plan with blocks of tripartite houses, of various dimensions. J. Aruda is similar and contains small temples of south Mesopotamian plan. the eye temple at brak, with stone reliefs, strips of gold, stone rosettes and so on, shows great wealth, and at other sites (Qannas, Samsat, Hassek) cone mosaics, a typical Uruk feature were found. Canal-ization, brick vaulting, Riemchen bricks and other features, all testify to the presence of south Mesopotamian colonists. An exact chronological linkage with Uruk itself is still dis-puted; the White Temple on the Anu 'ziggurat' and the buildings below it would seem to be contemporary, as well as Eanna VI Stone Mosaic Temple and earlier levels. Early Uruk architecture is virtually unknown and it is in the later (post-colonial) phases (Eanna V-III), the Late Uruk (not Jemdet Nasr) period about 5,400 to 5,100 or 5,000 years ago, that monumental architecture develops (Figs 112 and 113), with the well-known sequence 'Limestone temple' (V), mosaic hall, great hall and so on (IV A), as well as an administrative building, misnamed the Red Temple (IV A) in which the first inscribed tablets were found. Most of the principal buildings of Uruk III remain to be excavated or stood on the denuded Anu Ziggurat. Tablets from this period are in (partly) readable Sumerian; evidently the IV A ones are in the same language.

The spread of Sumerian and Elamite motifs to Egypt, prior to the First Dynasty, dated from this Late Uruk period; its short-lived impact on Egypt has, in the present writer's opinion, been grossly exaggerated. The liberation of Elam (or rather Susiana) from Uruk domination ushered in the Proto-Elamite period whose commercial tentacles soon embraced the greater part of Iran, both north (Sialk

IV, Tepe Hissar) and south (Tal-i Malyan – Anshan, Tepe Yahya IV C and even Shahr-i Sokhta 1), where sites have yielded Proto-Elamite tablets, an eloquent testimony to far-reaching trade, which now also included the coasts of the Gulf and copper-rich Oman. The rise of Proto-Elamite Iran was at Sumer's expense; the Uruk civilization perished, and the following Early Dynastic I period is drab and undistinguished. Only on the Diyala and in the Hamrin, close to Elam and within its suzerainty did artistry survive, as a result of Iranian influence. Only in Early

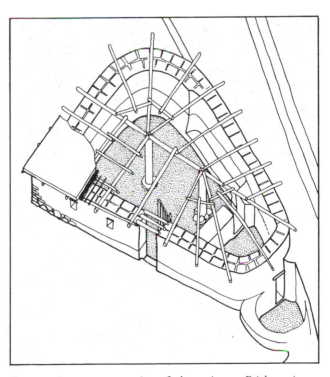

Figure 112 Jawa: reconstruction of a house in area F (phase 3). (After Helms, 1981.)

Dynastic II, and especially in Early Dynastic III did southern Mesopotamia redress the balance.

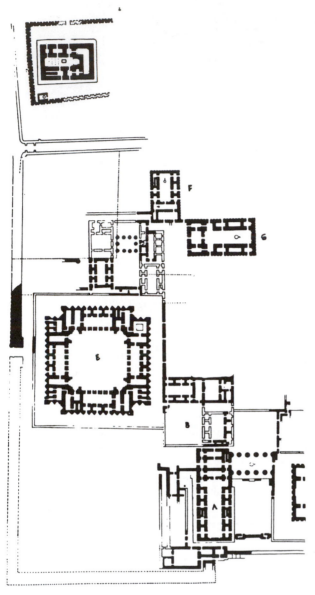

Figure 113 Uruk, Warka (Iraq): plan of level IVB in the Eanna complex. (After Mellaart, 1979.)

BIBLIOGRAPHY

AKKERMANS, P. et al. 1983. Bouqras Revisited. *Proc. Prehist. Soc.*, Vol. 49, pp. 335–72.

BAR-ADON, B. 1980. *The Cave of the Treasure: Finds from the Caves in the Nahal Mishmar.* Jerusalem.

BAR-YOSEF, O. 1985. *A Cave in the Desert: Nahal Hemar.* Jerusalem.

ÇAMBEL, H.; BRAIDWOOD, R. J. 1983. Çayönü Tepesi. In: BOEHMER, R. M.; HAUPTMANN, H. (ed.), *Festscrift für Kurt Bittel.* Mainz. pp. 155–77.

CAMERON, D. O. 1981. *The Ghassulian Wall Paintings.* London.

CAUVIN, J. 1977. Les Fouilles de Mureybet, 1971–1974 et leur signification pour les origines de la sédentarisation au Proche-Orient. *Annu. Amer. Sch. Orient. Res.* (Cambridge, Mass.), Vol. 44, pp. 19–48.

CONTENSON, H. DE. 1983. Early Agricultural in Western Syria. In: *The Hilly Flanks and Beyond.* Chicago.

DRIEL, G. VAN DEN. 1978. Jebel Aruda. *Akkadica* (Brussels), Vol. 12, pp. 2–28.

HEINRICH, E. 1982. *Die Tempel und Heiligtümer im alten Mesopotamien.* Berlin.

HELMS, S. W. 1981. *Jawa: Lost City of the Black Desert.* London.

HIJJARA, I. 1978. Three New Graves at Arpachiyah. *World Archaeol.*, Vol. 10, pp. 125–8.

JASIM, A. 1984. *Tell Abada.* Oxford. (BAR Int. Ser.)

—— 1985. *The Ubaid Period in Iraq.* Oxford. (BAR Int. Ser., 267.)

KENYON, K. M. 1980. *Jericho III.* London.

KOHL, P. L. 1984. *Central Asia: Palaeolithic Beginnings to the Iron Age.* Paris.

MELLAART, J. 1967. *Çatal Hüyük, a Neolithic Town in Anatolia.* London.

—— 1970. *Excavations at Haçilar.* Edinburgh.

—— 1975. *The Neolithic of the Near East.* London. (2nd edn 1981.)

—— 1979. Early Urban Communities in the Near East. In: *The Origins of Civilization.* Oxford.

—— 1981. In: MATTHERS, J. (ed.) *The River Quweiq.* Oxford. Part I, pp. 131 ff. (BAR Int. Ser., 98.)

MOORE, A. M. T. 1979. A Pre-Neolithic Farmers Village on the Euphrates. *Sci. Am.*, Vol. 241, pp. 50–8.

NEGABHAN, E. O. 1979. The Painted Building at Zaghe. *Paleorient*, Vol. 5, pp. 239–50.

ROLLEFSON, G. O. 1985. The 1983 Season at the Early Neolithic Site of Ain Ghazal. *Natl. Geogr. Res.* (Washington), Vol. 1, pp. 44–62.

SAFAR, F. et al. 1981. *Eridu.* Baghdad.

SCHIRMER, W. 1983. Drei Bauten des Çayönü Tepesi. In: BITTEL, K. (ed.), *Beiträge zur Altertumskunde Kleinasiens.* Mainz. pp. 463–76.

STROMMENGER, E. 1980. *Habuba Kebira.* Mainz.

VOIGT, M. 1983. *Hajji Firuz Tepe: The Neolithic Settlement.* Philadelphia.

—— 1985. *The Ubaid Period in Iraq.* Oxford. (BAR Int. Ser., 267.)

42

PREHISTORY OF THE ARABIAN PENINSULA

Abdullah Hassan Masry, with the collaboration of Ahmad Hasan Dani

Prehistoric research in the Arabian peninsula is in a preliminary stage. As survey work is now proceeding in all the states of the peninsula, more and more material is accumulating from exploration and also from excavations. Investigations are concentrated on two distinct lines: the first is geological, primarily related to the study of the advance of desert in the area and consequent adaptation of man to the changing environmental conditions; the second is cultural, deriving its source from the neighbouring high cultures in the valleys of the Tigris–Euphrates and the Nile and further afield in the Indus region. In this second phase, which actually belongs to the period of urban development and distant trade connections, it is the eastern and south–eastern coastal areas that play a dominant role and yet the other parts of the peninsula were not blank. In what way the human populations in these parts acted and reacted in relation to coastal settlements are questions that are being examined at present. However, two zones, that of Yemen in the south and another in the north-west, show evidence of local cultural development.

Map 51 presents an archaeological picture of the peninsula and shows the state of the present investigations. As the earliest finds are based on surface collections, it is difficult to be dogmatic about their definite chronology. Those results that have been obtained from laboratory work are given in Table 17, which attempts to view the phenomenon of early man in Arabia and his culture in geological time. It presents a preliminary analysis of the archaeological development in the peninsula. Typical and major sites are referred to by name, and these, with the other sites referred to directly in this chapter, will be found on Map 51. In order to provide a consistent account, an attempt is made to describe the scientific position as it stands at present. However, particularly with regard to the chronological classification of lithic artefacts, entering slightly into details of the recent history of research is unavoidable.

A multi-group classification of lithics was proposed by J. Kapel, who identified Acheulean (Lower Palaeolithic) handaxes, basing his arguments on finds from Qatar (Kapel, 1967) and from the vicinity of Thaj (Kapel, 1973). This material belonged to a so-called 'A-Group', which was supposed also to have Mousterian affinities. It stood in distinction to the 'C- and D-Groups', of similar suggested age, and to a later 'B-Group', which involved a basic blade industry incorporating modified projectile points and other examples of sophistication pointing to the Pre-pottery Neolithic. Examples from the Eastern Province (such as Ain Qannas) of Saudi Arabia facilitate dating to around 7,000 years ago (Masry, 1974, pp. 222–4). Parallels from the Pre-pottery Neolithic in Palestine and Syria were readily available. Technologically, Kapel's classification represents definable types, but the dating is probably complicated by the problematic existence in many periods of a mixed cultural horizon, reflected also in the co-existence of different technologies. Thus, more recent research has led to serious modifications. J. Tixier (1980) has suggested recategorization of the A-Group materials to the Ubaid Neolithic. This ties in with earlier work in Qatar (G. H. Smith, 1978, pp. 36 ff.) and stems in part from radiocarbon dating of handaxe material from Khor Ruri (Qatar) to the seventh millennium BP (Inizan, 1980, pp. 51 ff.).

Some of the problems of the older lithic material can be approached on the basis of the broad results of the Saudi Arabian survey. A total of 110 sites were identified as Acheulean, it being occasionally possible to distinguish between upper and lower phases. Distinguished from these in turn were a further 195 sites thought to be Mousterian, and to these must be related a few which were included simply under the rubric Middle Palaeolithic. One site was recognizably different, and tentatively identified as Oldowan; this point is returned to later. To be associated with the technology of Mousterian type were nine Levallois sites, and one diagnosed as Kebaran. What emerges from this is the existence of an extensive and varied spectrum of Palaeolithic sites and material. Looking forward on the chronological scale, one finds, in simple statistical terms, much less which relates clearly to the Upper Palaeolithic, Mesolithic, and immediately pre-Neolithic periods. It is not yet possible to propose a solution to this problem, but its complexity suggests a number of factors, including the problem of using specific fossil indices for artefact identification and the question of changes in population groups. This can be solved

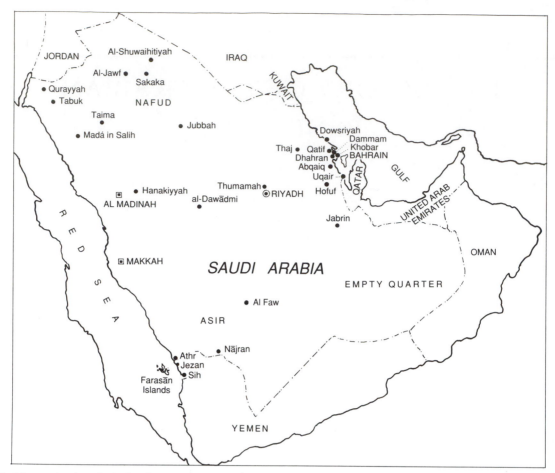

Map 51 Arabian peninsula: principal prehistoric sites.

only with more detailed analysis of the catalogued materials. The critical nature of the subject is illustrated by the reinterpretation of Kapel's A-Group data referred to above. A cautious approach is to separate, as far as possible, the cultural/technological definition based on recognized type sites from the chronological framework based on the classic evolutionary approach.

Recognizing this, the trend in Saudi Arabia has been to stress the need to use absolute physical dating methods wherever possible or feasible, as has been the case at the important Acheulean site of Saffaqah-Dawadmi where K–

Ar methods were employed, with successful results substantiating the date anticipated on the basis of technological type analysis.

To conclude the statistical overview of site identification, 117 sites were identified as Neolithic, and 66 as Chalcolithic. This account brings our review for Saudi Arabia down to the historical period, which is the limit of the present inquiry. However, before moving on to a more detailed discussion, something must be said of the southern areas of the Arabian peninsula which form part of this land mass and the progress of research in the present-day states in that region.

Table 17 Early humans in Arabia and their culture in geological time.

Geological age	Culture	Estimated dates	Examples	Notes
Miocene		17 to 15 million years ago	Dryopithecine primate at Sarrar, NE Arabia	
Pliocene				
Pleistocene	Lower Palaeolithic	500,000, to 70,000 years ago	Jabrin, Dawadmi, Wadi Tathlith, Shuwaihitiyah	Bifaces, etc.; potassium–argon dates obtained c.280,000 at Dawadmi
	Middle Palaeolithic	70,000 to 30,000 years ago	Bir Hima, Abu Arish, Uwa irid	Cf. Shanidar
	Upper Palaeolithic	30,000 to 12,000 years ago	Afif, Muwahy, Bir Hima	Disc cores, small bifaces, etc.
Holocene	Pre-pottery Neolithic	12,000 to 8,000 years ago	Rub' al-Khali sites, Sulayyil, 'Ain Qannas	Arrowheads etc.; earliest structures
	Neolithic	8,000 to 4,000 years ago	Abu Khamis, Dowsariyah, Ain Qannas, Sihi, Rjajil, Jubbah, Thumamah	Abundant carbon-14 corroboration of dates

In Yemen, emphasis has traditionally been focused on the classic urban civilization based on the wadis surrounding the central desert regions. Several major expeditions have taken place, and, supplemented by the multitude of miscellaneous discoveries, these show the potential of the area while leaving many important questions unanswered about both the chronology of the early urban phases and the nature of the earlier prehistoric developments. As shown by A. Masry (1983), these are key issues for understanding the fundamental basis of Arabian prehistory. The first systematic excavation in the Yemen was that at Hureidha in the Hadramawt (Caton-Thompson, 1944).

The achievements of the 'American Foundation for the Study of Man' expedition associated with Wendell Phillips, W. F. Albright, F. P. Albright, and R. Le Baron Bowen are conveniently summarized by G. van Beek (1968). Work was done in Wadi Baihan, Sohar and Marib. Excavations at Timna and Hajar Bin Humaid identified sixteen occupation levels, and provided some basis for chronology. Flint sites have been noted from the Yemen central desert (Sayhad) regions eastward to Oman (Pullar, 1974), taking in over 100 knapping sites in the Hadramawt (van Beek, 1968). Similar material has been recorded in Oman in association with the typical beehive tombs at Qubur Juhhal, Amlah and Miskin (de Cardi, 1976). In spite of the scattered and disparate nature of the evidence, it is clear that it has a crucial relevance for the rest of Arabia. It seems advisable to think in terms of a proto-urban phase, and to attempt to anticipate the potential relevance of this as a conceptual tool.

The early initiative in Bahrain and the rest of the Gulf was largely due to the Danish Archaeological Expedition, the work of which is described in some detail by T. G. Bibby (1969–70), and a more recent overview, also citing the latest research, is provided by M. Rice (1985). Earlier, during the latter part of the nineteenth and early twentieth centuries, the Island of Bahrain was the focus of Sumerologists who were preoccupied with the question of identifying ancient Dilmun – the 'Paradise Land' of the ancient Sumerians (Cornwall, 1946).

The work of the Danish expedition was initially concentrated on Ra's al-Qalcah and the tumuli fields. They were able to establish sequences associated with known sequences in Iraq and identifiable in Saudi Arabia where they also examined the coastal areas. Later, they extended their work into Oman, with highly important results at Umm an-Nar, Hafit, and Buraimi (*Kuml* vols 1962, 1965–70 and also the *Journal of Oman Studies*, generally). For the United Arab Emirates the work of H. Takriti should be mentioned, as well as the discoveries of S. Cleaziou at Hili near al-Ain. The Ubaid period has been definitively identified at Qatar (al-Daasa, Ra's Abaruk, Khor; Oates, 1978, p. 39; Inizan, 1980) and at al-Markh on Bahrain (Roaf, 1974, 1976). In general, the Mesopotamian Early Dynastic I to III is well represented in the Gulf. It is the period in which a distinctive East Arabian–Gulf culture emerges, although the later period (Barbar) in Bahrain also has its parallels on the east Arabia littoral (Tarut, Dhahran Tomb-fields, Khobar middens, Umm al-Nussi).

To return now to our detailed discussion of the sequence from the earliest periods, we can state that physical evidence for the actual presence of the earliest types of man in Arabia is mainly of a cultural rather than direct nature. However, fossil evidence for hominoid primates has been identified in the vicinity of Sarrar in eastern Arabia, in the context of rich fauna dating to the Dam Formation (Lower Miocene, 17–15 million years ago). These involve fragments of Dry-

opithecine primate fossils (Andrews et al., 1978; Hamilton et al., 1978). Little can be said about this, apart from the obvious comment that parallels could be adduced on either side of the peninsula. More promising is the major accumulation of the considerably later evidence from the Ubaid phases and the tumuli phenomena in eastern Arabia and the Arabian Gulf countries. The statistical scale and frequently good state of preservation of the tumuli open major possibilities for the archaeological study of population dynamics and human osteology in the Gulf area for comparison with similar data from lower Mesopotamia and western Iran (ancient Elam and Persia).

Another rich field for future research involves the themes of cultural ecology and Pleistocene archaeology. One interesting example is that of Kahman (site no. 216-208) along the southern shores of the Red Sea in Saudi Arabia. At this site, a corraline terrace some two metres above the present sea-level contains Mousterian tools. This is due to the existence of a complex fringing reef system extending several kilometres inland and the attested fluctuation in sea-level due to polar glaciation. The same phenomenon can be observed in the Farasan islands. For Bahrain, a pioneering study of geo-archaeology has been made by Larsen (1983), who cites also material relating to the east Arabian littoral. While some of the basis for his enquiry necessarily involves geological or geophysical issues that are not yet completely understood, such as fluctuation in water-levels, there can be no doubt as to the fruitfulness of this line of enquiry. In this connection we should also mention the important study of J. Dayton on the historical significance of even small changes, where the evidence of this complex issue is carefully reviewed (Dayton, 1975, 1979, the same author's study of the hydrology of the Marib Dam in Yemen).

Following this Palaeolithic cultural phase we may also refer to the prehistoric rock art that is widespread in Arabia. The art includes carvings and engravings in high and low relief and some also show painting. The oldest rock art is found at Kilwa and in the vicinity of the Romano-Nabataean site of Rawwafa. They depict ibexes, wild buffaloes and other indistinct animals (Plate 64). One carving (Plate 65) shows a running man with dishevelled hair, grasping weapons in his hands. It is possible that the art, as depicted here, forms part of a new economic way of life, involving multiple economic systems, such as hunting and gathering and nomadism.

It will be an interesting study to determine how these nomads fared when they came in contact with the trading entrepreneurs from the urban centres in the river valleys. These traders were in search of raw material and of intermediate places for rest and recuperation before their onward journey. It is in this context that the Babylonian texts referring to Dilmun, Magan and Meluhha are important. From the archaeological angle the cultural tie is provided by the discovery of Ubaid pottery (Fig. 114) all over the region. For the earliest period, the relevant sites are Qurayyah and Taima, which have produced painted pottery comparable to that from sites in Palestine. Evidence also comes from Thaj in eastern Arabia, Najran and Qaryat al-Faw in the southwest, Dumat al Jandal in the north and Taima, al-Hijr and Rurayyah in the west.

The Ubaid period has been definitely identified in Qatar and at al-Markh in Bahrain. It is the period in which a distinctive East Arabian Gulf culture emerges. The Ubaid sites now total nearly forty in Saudi Arabia (Masry, 1974), and relate to the sites in Bahrain and Qatar. In this culture two varieties of pottery are distinctively finished. One has black paint on a greenish slip and the other is a chaff-tempered, hand-made red ware. It is the first variety of pottery that is related to the Mesopotamian examples. Other elements in this cultural complex include grinding stones, plastered walls, domesticated cattle and caprids, domesticated cereals and a lithic repertoire of tanged, barbed arrowheads, and scrapers with fine pressure retouch. However, some sites do not have pottery at all.

Figure 114 Five ceramic vessels of the Ubaid type (Saudi Arabia.)

In general, the range and number of sites show that the culture was well established in eastern Arabia and that it was brought into close contact with Sumerian and Elamite merchants. Many tablets, including one from Dhahran in Saudi Arabia, have been found, testifying to the trade in household commodities, precious stones, timber and metals. However, the sites need not all belong to one uniform culture and to one chronological period. An important variation is seen in the Neolithic site of Thumamah in central Arabia, which exhibits a lithic technology of advanced type in association with circular dwellings and querns. From the sites of Sihi and Muwassan near the modern port and fishing centre of Jizan in the south-western province come pottery types characterized by semi-tempered wares with out-turned rims, ring bases and spouts (Zarins et al., 1981). They have been recovered from shell-middens.

In Yemen the first systematic excavation was carried out at Hureidha in the Hadramawt (Caton Thompson, 1944). It was followed by work (van Beek, 1968) in the Wadi Baihan, Sohar and Marib. The object of these excavations was to trace the antecedents of the urban phase in Yemen that is associated with the great dam at Marib. The result was the identification of sixteen occupation levels at Timna and Hajar bin Humaid and over a hundred knapping sites in the Hadramawt. Similar material has been recorded in Oman in association with the typical beehive tombs at Qubur Juhhal, Amlah and Midcin (de Cardi, 1976). It is these discoveries that have led to extensive excavations in Oman by M. Tosi, who has discovered an indisputable connection with the Indus valley. Indus-type seals have also been discovered at some sites in Bahrain, and one Bahrain seal has been found

at the Indian coastal city of Lothal, thus suggesting a widespread sea trade connection over the Arabian sea. Bahrain is rich in tumuli of different periods and so are its urban settlement sites. The present excavations have opened up new prospects of establishing close relations among the littoral countries of the Arabian Sea.

BIBLIOGRAPHY

Main periodicals

ATLAL. *Journal of Saudi Arabian Archaeology* (1977; Riyadh).
Journal of Oman Studies (Muscat).
Proceedings of the Seminar for Arabian Studies (1970; London).
RYDAN. *Journal of Ancient Yemeni Antiquities and Epigraphy* (1978).

References and further reading

ANDREWS, P.; HAMILTON, W. R.; WHYBROW, R. J. 1978. Dryopithecine from the Miocene of Saudi Arabia. *Nature* (London), Vol. 224, pp. 249–51.
ANSARI, A. 1982. *Qaryat al-Faw: A Portrait of Pre-Islamic Civilization in Saudi Arabia*. Riyadh.
BAHRAIN EDUCATION DEPARTMENT. ANTIQUITIES DIVISION. 1971. *Antiquities of Bahrain*. Manamah.
BEEK, G. W. VAN. 1968. *Hajar bin Humeid*. Baltimore.
BIBBY, T. G. 1969–70. *Looking for Dilmun*. New York/London.
BRAIDWOOD, R. J.; HOWE, B. 1960. *Prehistoric Investigations in Iraqi Kurdistan*. Chicago.
CARDI, B. DE. 1976. Ras al-Khaimah: Further Archaeological Discoveries. *Antiquity*, Vol. 50, pp. 216–22.
CATON THOMPSON, G. 1944. *Tombs and Moon Temple of Hureidha (Hadramawt)*. Oxford.
CLEZIOU, S. 1980. Three Seasons at Hili. *Proc. Semin. Arab. Stud.*, Vol. 10, pp. 19–32.
CORNWALL, P. B. 1946. Ancient Arabia: Explorations in Hasa 1940–41. *Geogr. J.*, Vol. 107, pp. 28–50.
DAYTON, J. E. 1975. The Problems of Climatic Change in the Arabian Peninsula. *Proc. Semin. Arab. Stud.*, Vol. 5, pp. 33–76.
—— 1979. A Discussion of the Hydrology of Marib. *Proc. Semin. Arab. Stud.*, Vol. 9, pp. 124–9.
FATCHRY, J. 1948. Les Antiquités du Yemen. *Muséon* (Leuven), Vol. 61, pp. 215–26.
FATCHRY, A.; RYCKMANS, G. 1952. *An Archaeological Journey to the Yemen*. Cairo, Service des Antiquités de l'Égypte. 3 vols.
FIELD, H. 1971. *Contributions to the Anthropology of Saudi Arabia*. Miami, Fl. (Field Res. Proj.)
FRÖHLICH, B.; MUGHANNAN, A. 1985. Excavations of the Dhahran Burial Mounds. *Atlal* (Riyadh), Vol. 9, pp. 9–40.
HAMILTON, W. R.; WHYBROW, R. J.; MCCLURE, H. A. 1978. Fauna of Fossil Mammals from the Miocene of Saudi Arabia. *Nature* (London), Vol. 274, pp. 248–9.
INIZAN, M. L. 1980. Premiers Résultats des fouilles préhistoriques de la région de Khor. In: TIXIER, J. (ed.), *Mission archéologique française à Qatar*. Qatar. Vol. 1.
KAPEL, J. 1967. *Atlas of the Stone Age Cultures of Qatar*. Aarhus. (Publ. Jutl. Archaeol. Soc., 6.)
—— 1973. Stone Age Survey. In: BIBBY, G. (ed.), *Preliminary Survey in East Arabia, 1968*. Aarhus.
KING SAUD UNIVERSITY. 1979. Sources for the History of Arabia. *Studies in the History of Arabia*. Riyadh. Vol. 1.
—— 1984. Pre-Islamic Arabia. *Studies in the History of Arabia*. Riyadh. Vol. 2.
LARSEN, C. E. 1983. *Life and Land of the Bahrain Islands*. Chicago.
MCCLURE, H. A. 1971. *The Arabian Peninsula and Prehistoric Populations*. Coconut Grove. (Field Res. Publ.)
MASRY, A. H. 1973. Factors of Growth of Southwestern Arabia: An Ethno-Ecological Approach. *Bull. Fac. Arts, Univ. Riyadh*, Vol. 3, pp. 41–65.

—— 1974. *Prehistory of Northeastern Arabia: The Problem of Inter-regional Interaction.* Miami.

—— 1976. Introduction. *Atlal* (Riyadh), Vol. 1.

—— 1983. Introduction. *Atlal* (Riyadh), Vol. 7.

OATES, J. 1978. Ubaid Mesopotamia and its Relations to Gulf Countries. In: CARDI, B. DE (ed.), *Qatar Archaeological Reports, Excavations 1973.* Oxford. pp. 39–52.

PARR, P. J. 1970. Preliminary Survey in Northeastern Arabia, 1968. *Bull. Inst. Archaeol.* (London), Vol. 8/9, pp. 193–242.

—— 1972. Preliminary Survey in Northeastern Arabia, 1968. *Bull. Inst. Archaeol.* (London), Vol. 10, pp. 23–61.

PARR, P. J.; GAZDER, M. 1980. A Report of the Soundings at Zubaydah (Al-Amarah) in the Al-Qasim Region. *Atlal* (Riyadh), Vol. 4, pp. 107–17.

POTTS, D. 1983. Thaj in the Light of Recent Research. *Atlal* (Riyadh), Vol. 7, pp. 86–101.

PULLAR, J. 1974. Harvard Archaeological Society in Oman, 1973. *Proc. Semin. Arab. Stud.* (London), Vol. 4, pp. 33–48.

RICE, M. 1985. *Dilmun Discovered.* London/New York.

ROAF, M. 1974. Excavations at Al Markh, Bahrain: A Fish Midden of the Fourth Millennium BC. *Paléorient*, Vol. 2, pp. 499–501.

—— 1976. Excavations at Al-Markh, Bahrain. *Proc. Semin. Arab. Stud.* (London), Vol. 6, pp. 144–60.

SMITH, G. H. 1978. The Stone Industries of Qatar. In: CARDI, B. DE (ed.), *Qatar Archaeological Reports.* Oxford. pp. 36–8, 53–75 (Da'ara), 80–106 (Ras Abaruk).

TIXIER, J. (ed.), 1980. *Mission archéologique française à Qatar.* Qatar. Vol. 1.

WHALEN, N. et al. 1983. Excavations of Acheulean Sites near Saffaqah in al-Dawadmi (1402/1982). *Atlal* (Riyadh), Vol. 7, pp. 9–21.

ZARINS, J. et al. 1981. Comprehensive Archaeological Survey Program on the Southwestern Province. *Atlal* (Riyadh), Vol. 5, pp. 9–42.

—— 1982. Preliminary Report on the Archaeological Survey of the Riyadh Area. *Atlal* (Riyadh), Vol. 6, pp. 25–38.

43

SOUTHERN ASIA

during the Neolithic and to the beginnings of the Bronze Age

Ahmad Hasan Dani

GEOGRAPHICAL PATTERNS (Map 52)

From the great deserts of Iran in the west to the thickly forested hills of Assam in the east, and from the great heights of the Himalayas, Karakorum and the Hindu Kush in the north to the Indian Ocean, this vast stretch of south Asian mainland is a varied geographical mass of contrasts, where hills and valleys, deserts and plains, and the Indian peninsular plateau vie with one another to share the sunny climate of the Indian monsoon and the Mediterranean winter rain of the west. Protected by the majestic heights of the Himalayas to the north, the entire zone has developed patterns of living that are different from those of central and northern Asia, and yet they participate in the development of human cultures that have evolved in Asia right from the earliest times. This sharing in a common human cultural heritage is amply evidenced by the material of Neolithic cultures and Early Bronze Age developments, recovered from recent explorations and excavations of archaeological sites and caves. Human interrelationships within Asia have been so strong that early interpreters thought that the Neolithic culture of

India had derived from southern China and South-East Asia (Worman, 1949, pp. 181–200; Wheeler, 1947, p. 295, Fig. 51). Similarly the Neolithic culture of Kashmir was thought to have its source and inspiration in north China (Dikshit, 1982, pp. 30–6). On the other hand, the first food-producing communities and Early Bronze Age settlers in the Indus valley were believed to owe their technological knowledge to borrowings from western Asia (Fairservis, 1975). However, the interconnection with central Asia, particularly with the Ghissar culture (Ranov, 1982, pp. 63–71) of Tajikistan and the cultural developments of Turkmenistan (Masson and Sarianidi, 1972) can no longer be overlooked. While accepting the existence of all these interrelationships, we can now better understand how Neolithic and Early Bronze Age developments in the entire zone relate to its geographical pattern, since archaeology has deepened our knowledge of human ability and efforts to profit by the natural conditions of each region and to evolve a life-style appropriate to them.

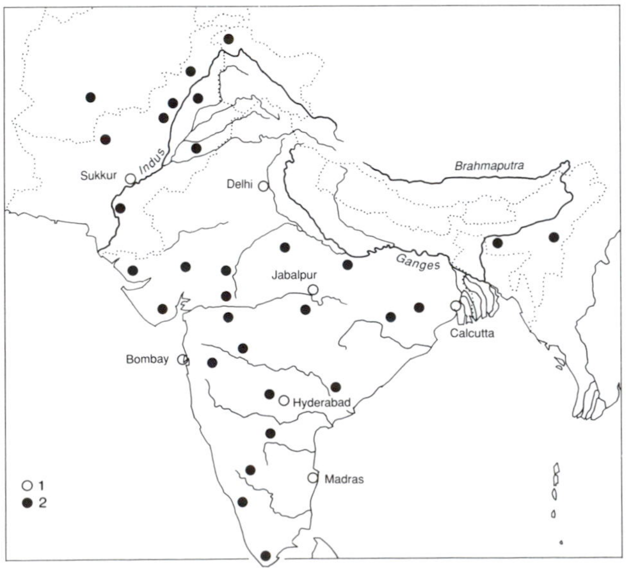

From this standpoint the entire zone can be subdivided into smaller geographical regions, so as to give a better perspective on the cultural developments. In this division chronology cannot be expected to be uniform. There is much cultural disparity even in the Neolithic patterns, and when we come to Bronze Age developments the variation is still greater. The primitive food producers continued their life-style in the hilly and backward regions much longer than the plains people, who transformed their ways of life within an early urban setting and in little kingdoms. We describe the developments as seen in eastern India, central India, south India and in the western regions.

Map 52 Distribution of Neolithic sites in southern Asia: 1, modern towns; 2, Neolithic sites. (After A. H. Dani.)

THE NEOLITHIC PATTERN OF NORTH-EASTERN INDIA

In this region great attention has been paid to the area that was formerly included under the geographical name of Assam: an area that includes the Brahmaputra valley and the neighbouring hill plateaux that border on Myanmar (formerly Burma) in the south and east and on the Yunnan province of south China. Earlier the material collected from the surface was studied on a geographical basis (Dani, 1960) and an attempt was made to understand the lithic tradition against the background of the evidence known from South-East Asia and India. The study did not accept E. C. Worman's thesis, where it is maintained: 'On the basis of their typology and distribution, Indian smoothed stone celts of "neolithic" type appear to have derived from eastward.' There are certainly some tool types that are derived from South-East Asia, but so far no evidence has been presented to show that all the 'Indian smoothed stone celts' are derived from the east.

Some excavations conducted in former Assam enable us to have a better picture of the Neolithic culture of that region today. In the Garo hills, one excavation has been conducted at Selbagiri (*Indian Archaeology: A Review*, 1976–8, p. 8). Here two levels were detected. In the earlier level only microliths were found and in the upper level only two types of tools have been recovered, along with plain, hand-made pottery. The tools from the Garo hills comprise hoe-blades and shouldered celts, all made of the igneous rock called dolerite (T. C. Sharma, 1977, p. 42). Unfortunately it is not clear how change from microlithic cultures to Neolithic took place in this sub-area and how other woodworking activities were performed by the local people. Further excavations may produce material that can give a better understanding of the transition from the microlithic to the Neolithic stage. On the present evidence the two advanced types of ground stone tools are linked with the South-East Asian tradition.

The second area where excavations have been conducted is located in the North Cachar hills and Kamrup zone; the actual sites are Daojali Hading and Sarutaru. At the former site only the middle layer had cultural material which included pottery and stone implements. Out of over 600 sherds, 595 were of cord-impressed ware, 19 of a stamped dull-red ware and 11 of a brick-red ware. The last type may have been derived from Szechwan in China. The cord-impressed pottery is hand-made and may have been derived from South-East Asia, either Thailand or Myanmar (Surin Pookajorn, 1984, pp. 16–19 for Myanmar, pp. 23–5 for Thailand), but the second ware appears to have been made on a wheel or turntable. The stone tools include edge-ground and fully ground tools, grinding stones, querns and mealing troughs, mullers and quartzite pebbles and fossil wood. The ground-stone tools comprise a shouldered variety and small celts including quadrangular adzes. An edge-ground chisel of fossil wood was also found at Daojali Hading. From the surface were recovered some elegant specimens of jadeite, most probably imported from China. The whole material speaks of borrowings from southern China and South-East Asia. Sarutaru (Rao, 1977, pp. 39–41) again produced nine celts: seven of the shouldered variety and two rounded-butt axes, along with numerous cord-impressed potsherds, all hand-made and brown or grey in colour.

The other sub-areas of Assam, like the Naga hills, the Khasi hills and the Sibsagar district, have so far yielded tools only on the surface. In the Naga hills the material used is green stone, shale and jadeite, the last obviously imported from China (T. C. Sharma, 1977, p. 48). For working hard materials like jadeite a pecking technique is said to have been used, but the jadeite tools might have been imports. Thus the best-known techniques are flaking and grinding, the last used in two ways, to make either edge-ground or fully ground tools. Among the types are the usual tanged or shouldered celts, quadrangular adzes and chisels. One important type is the pointed-butt axe – a type very well known in peninsular India, the main type in the South

Indian Neolithic tools assemblage. Two types are worth mentioning: one described as a 'cleaver' and traced to Hoab-inhian examples and the other a quadrangular type, very well known in China. Thus the tool complex in the Naga hills is a mixed material showing types and techniques borrowed from India as well as from China and South-East Asia. The position is no different in the other sub-areas of Assam, where tool types are almost identical. One new type is the grooved hammerstone, very common in China, and found here in the Darang district. On the whole the Neolithic culture of Assam shows firm contacts with the neighbouring areas of China and South-East Asia. Contacts with other parts of India are impeded by the great deltaic Bengal zone. However, Sharma is forced to conclude:

> The eastern Asiatic bias of the neolithic culture of Assam should not, however, prevent us from accepting the fact that Assam, being a part of the Indian subcontinent, has shared the cultural life of the subcontinent throughout the ages. The discovery of the hand-axe–cleaver industry as well as the flake and blade tool industry of the pre-neolithic periods in several parts of N.E. India showing very clear Indian and Western affinities, is a strong case to argue that Assam did not remain totally cut off from India during the neolithic period also.
>
> (Sharma, 1977, p. 48)

The implication appears to be that the Assam Neolithic culture gained some variety in its material culture by the addition of cultural traits from China and South-East Asia but otherwise must be understood in the wider context of Neolithic development in India as a whole.

BENGAL, BIHAR AND ORISSA

The region (Dani, 1960, Ch. V; Krishnaswami, 1960, pp. 55–9) consists primarily of the lower Ganges valley that slopes westward into the peneplain of West Bengal, verging on the Bengal delta. In the north it touches the submontane region of the Himalayas and hence the lower Himalayan system in which lies the Darjeeling district, which has cultural relations with Bengal and Bihar. The second subregion is the Mahanadi valley, which is historic Orissa. The two subregions merge imperceptibly into the traditional zone of the Chota-Nagpur plateau in South Bihar. To the east of the Bengal delta lies the Chittagong zone which is culturally related to Assam, as the discovery of a few faceted tools clearly suggests. On the hill terraces and slopes of the higher regions in Darjeeling the main tool varieties include faceted tools, rounded-butt axes, and wedge-shaped axes as well as chisels and hammerstones. In the plains of Bihar and Orissa the evidence is more definite and it shows that there was a diversity of tools and other cultural traits. The Neolithic cultures are represented by ground-stone tools, pottery and the cultivation of cereals. The older view of Gordon (Gordon, 1950, p. 83) that they represent 'a chalcolithic culture similar to that of Māski and Brahmagiri' no longer holds good. The excavations at Pandu Rajar Dhibi (Dasgupta, 1964) in West Bengal show a settlement pattern based on rice cultivation and exploiting fish, molluscs and animal food such as pork, mutton, beef and venison. It is in the first two early layers that protohistoric culture was found. Period I produced hand-made, drab or thick grey ware, showing impressions of paddy husks. Very few tools were found in period I, but they increase in period II and include crested-ridge blades, scrapers, flakes and fluted cores.

Ground-stone axes appear for the first time in period III. In Orissa the evidence corroborates the observations at Pandu Rajar Dhibi. One excavation at Kuchai (Sankalia, 1974, pp. 312–13) shows a typical pattern, producing grey–black, brownish red pottery as well as polished stone tools of phyllite, with both the shouldered variety and the rounded-butt variety, the latter being very common. In the Sanjai valley the pottery paste shows a mixture with husks of grain. The site from which celts were recovered has been noted to lie here on high ground above the alluvial floodplain. In fact the alluvial deposits bank against this high ground, suggesting that the Neolithic people lived on the older level surface. The artefacts consist of axes, wedges, chisels, perforated stones and hammerstones or pounders. Three different techniques – chipping, pecking or hammering, and grinding – have been used either singly or in combination to produce these tools. There are also miniature faceted tools in jadeite found at Lohardaga in Ranchi which are obviously imports from China.

Excavations at Chirand (Verma, 1970–1, pp. 19–23), district Saran, in Bihar, situated near the confluence of the Ghagra and the Ganges, have yielded a truly Neolithic assemblage, with varieties of bone tools. A radiocarbon date for the upper level of the Neolithic is given as 3,650 years ago, but the early level is said to have a date of *c.*3,750 years ago and hence the lowest deposit is calculated to be somewhere around 4,500 years old.

No complete plans of houses were recovered, but the house floors were paved and the walls made of clay or mud plastered over a bamboo screen both outside and inside. The late phase yielded a circular paved floor, 4 m in diameter. In this phase a semi-circular hut with several oblong ovens and also postholes were noted. Rice was known, as paddy-husk impressions were found. Charred rice along with charred wheat, *moong*, *masoor* and barley were also found. Bones of animals included elephant, rhino, buffalo, cattle, stag and deer. The finds also included the bones of birds and fish, clusters of fish-scales, shells and snails. Antiquities include bone and antler implements: different types of celts, scrapers, chisels, hammers, needles, points, borers, awls, diggers, a shaft-straightner, pins, styli, arrowheads (both tanged and socketed) and many unfinished implements, such as a shoulder bone of an ox. Bone ornaments consisted of pendants, earrings, bangles, discs and combs. The stone tools were made of quartzite, basalt and granite. Microlithic industry was an integral part of the Neolithic culture of Chirand. The microliths included parallel-sided microblades, scrapers, arrowheads, serrated points, notched blades, points, lunates, borers and so on. The materials were chalcedony, chert, agate and jasper. Not a single blade was of the crested ridge type. Beads were also locally manufactured. They were long tubular, long barrel, short barrel, cylindrical, triangular and disc-shaped beads of chalcedony, agate, jasper, marble, steatite and faience. Terracotta figurines of humped bulls, birds and *nagas* (snake deifies), terracotta bangles, beads, perforated decorated objects and balls and rectangular pendants, one terracotta wheel-shaped object without a hole and terracotta discs with central holes (probably spindle-whorls) were recovered. Of great importance is the find of terracotta figurines of *nagas* (snake deities), which indicate a serpent cult in Bihar. Of the bone tools H. D. Sankalia remarks:

This is the first time that in a Stone Age site in India, so many varied types of bone tools have been found. Hence we can easily picture the life of the Neolithic Bihari.

Unlike many of his senior and junior contemporaries in Assam-Meghalaya towards the east, Kashmir in the north, and Andhra-Karnataka in the south, south-west and Baluchistan in the west-north-west, he lived right in the vast alluvial plains of the Ganga, whereas others lived on plateaus and hills. The only comparable site would be T. Narasipur on the river Cauvery (Kaveri). For his manifold daily needs of hunting, skinning, weaving, stitching, digging, he utilized the long bones and antlers of animals he hunted or butchered on the site after trapping. He was obliged to do this because suitable raw material for larger stone tools was not available.

(Sankalia, 1974, p. 305)

Pottery also makes an interesting study. Hand-made pottery was very common but some may have been produced on a turntable. The majority were red ware, but grey, black and black-and-red wares were also in use. The inverted firing technique was known to these people. The forms of black-and-red ware found here are different from the black-and-red ware of the Chalcolithic period. Some of them were burnished on the surface. Types included vases with a broad mouth and narrow neck, spouted vases, bowls, lipped bowls, perforated bowls, footed bowls, oval bowls with a broad lip, bowls on a stand, lugged bowls, footed cups, channel spouts, miniature pots, spoons or ladles and knobbed pottery. One sherd showed mat impressions. Post-firing painting in red ochre on grey and rarely on red has been noted. Designs include criss-cross pattern in groups of five lines, concentric semicircles and wavy lines. These excavated materials at Chirand for the first time place the earlier surface collections from Bihar and the Chota Nagpur plateau in their proper cultural context and indicate the continuation of the Neolithic cultural complex in the fourth millennium BP when other parts of India had already adopted metal technology.

THE MID-WESTERN GANGETIC REGION COVERING BELAN VALLEY

The mid-western Gangetic region is the first in India that has provided a continuous sequence of transition from the stage of intensified food gathering and selective hunting through incipient food production to settled village farming. The excavations conducted by G. R. Sharma (1983, pp. 51–64) at Chopani Mando, Koldihawa and Mahagara in the Belan valley and the Vindhyan plateau have established the primacy of Neolithic culture in this region, particularly in the light of the proposed chronology (nine to seven millennia ago).

Chopani-Mando is located on the left bank of an old bed of the Belan, 77 km east-south-east of Allahabad. The excavators recognized three cultural phases: the first two are distinguished by the occurrence of particular tool types, such as blades, non-geometric and geometric microliths, and their gradual reduction in size and change in raw material from chert to chalcedony and carnelian. In the last phase of the advanced Mesolithic the cultural repertoire included tranchets, ground-stone tools like hammerstones, querns, mullers and ring-stones, and still more important, hand-made pottery, red ware and brownish-grey ware, sometimes decorated with impressed designs. Of greater importance is the discovery of hut foundations and hearths. Thirteen huts belonging to the advanced Neolithic were exposed. These were either round or oval in plan, with a diameter ranging between 5.7 and 3.5 m. The huts were closely placed in a beehive fashion. As the hut floors yielded large numbers of microliths, anvils, hammerstones, sling stones, mullers, querns, fragments of burnt clay, animal bones and potsherds, the economy of the people is inferred to have been gathering and hunting. There is no evidence for the domestication of animals or plants. However, the presence of querns and mullers are taken to point to incipient cultivation.

The excavation also produced remains of wild rice (carbonized or embedded in lumps of burnt clay) and bones of wild cattle and goat or sheep. This Neolithic period is ascribed to the eleventh to the tenth millennium BP.

The continuation of this cultural complex is seen at Koldihawa, situated on the left bank of the Belan river, only 3 km from Chopani Mando. Here three cultural phases have been recognized, which are attributed to the Neolithic, Chalcolithic and Iron Age. The Neolithic phase was characterized by ground-stone tools, including celts and microliths, and hand-made pottery of three varieties, cord-impressed, rusticated and burnished wares. Palaeobotanical discoveries have added remarkable information. The rice-husks used in the paste of the pottery are of the domesticated variety of rice and have been radiocarbon dated to the ninth to the seventh millennium BP. This is the earliest evidence so far known of rice in south Asia.

The third site of Mahagara is situated on the right bank of the Belan river, the opposite side to Koldihawa. It is a single-period site, with six structural subphases. Excavation has produced twenty huts represented by floors and postholes. Of these, eighteen huts, which are referred to the last constructional subphase, were retained by wattle and daub screens, as evidenced by the presence of burnt fragments of daub bearing impressions of reed or bamboo. All these huts belong to eight houses, linked together in a form of ring. Their floors have yielded Neolithic blades and microliths, pottery, querns, mullers, sling stones, celts, bone arrowheads, terracotta beads and bones of animals. An interesting discovery was a cattle-pen, irregularly rectangular in plan, measuring 12.5 by 7.5 m, with the longer axis running north to south. This pen was fenced by twenty uprights, indicated by the remains of postholes. Here no pottery was found, but a large number of hoof impressions of cattle of different ages were noted. Again outside the pen, near the cluster of huts, were observed hoofmarks of sheep or goats. The Neolithic pottery is of four varieties. The economy of the people depended on both hunting and farming, as is clear from the presence of both wild cattle (as well as wild horses) and domesticated cattle (in addition to sheep and goat) and rice (Thapar, 1984, pp. 195–7). On the cultivation of rice, G. R. Sharma points out that it has been found in the form of rice-husks as well as carbonized, and has been identified as the domesticated variety, *Oryza sativa*. 'The discovery of wild rice in the Mesolithic (Chopani Mando) and in cultivation in the Neolithic (Koldihawa) has fully confirmed Vavilov's theory that India was the original and primary centre of cultivation of *Oryza sativa*.' B. K. Thapar makes a pertinent general observation:

As regards similarities of the Neolithic culture of the Belan Valley with other Neolithic regional and extra regional cultures we find that cord-impressed ware alone provides some comparative basis. In India this ware has been reported from Daojali Hading, a Neolithic site of the north-eastern region. But in surface colour and the range of decoration pattern, the wares of the two regions differ

from each other. Furthermore the Neolithic culture of the north-eastern region, besides being younger than that of the Vindhyan, shows complete absence of the stone blade industry which is an integral part of the Vindhyan Neolithic. Outside the sub-continent, cord-impressed ware has been found in Neolithic contexts over a wide ranging territory in east and south-east Asia.

(Thapar, 1984)

THE SOUTH INDIAN PENINSULAR COMPLEX

This is not one homogenous region, except that the entire south lies outside the Indo-Gangetic plain, to the south of the Vindhyan mountain range, which divides northern India from southern. The whole of peninsular India can be subdivided into three sub-areas: the Deccan trap zone of Maharashtra and the coastal belt of Gujarat and Kathiawad, the undulating hilly sub-area of Andhra–Karnataka, and the extreme southern zone.

Gujarat, Kathiawad, the Narbada valley and the Banas valley

It is in the first sub-area that most work has been done (Sankalia, 1974, pp. 259–512). But here the material has been studied against the background of the Bronze Age influences that appear to have come from the Indus region early in the fifth millennium BP. Along with bronze material we find painted pottery, a parallel-sided ribbon flake industry and associated material, which seem to have been mixed with the earlier microlithic tool types of the region. However, the site of Langhnaj is of great importance, because it not only represented the typical microlithic culture widely spread in northern and central Gujarat but also presents evidence of successive cultures that show continuity from the earlier Mesolithic age into the new emerging agricultural stage when the hunting economy was being transformed into a pattern of incipient food production by the adoption of new techniques of agriculture, ground-stone tools and pottery making. Unfortunately the evidence is not conclusive and observations have not been successful in pinpointing the process of change. However, it is clear that the microlith-using people of this region were experiencing a technical and social transformation some time in the sixth millennium BP that was to affect the entire zone of Gujarat and Maharashtra. In what manner the microlith-using people adopted the new process of food production is at present difficult to say. The Langhnaj material can be compared with the remains in the caves and rock shelters of the sandstone formations above the Narbada valley. The most important rock shelter is at Adamgarh in Hoshangabad district. Here both microlithic tools and animal remains have been found. In the words of Sankalia (1974, p. 259), 'industrially and faunistically Adamgarh microlithic culture seems to be more advanced than the Langhnaj culture. It can be described well on the way to the food-producing stage or the Neolithic.' The third comparable site is Bagor in the Banas valley, just in the shadow of the Aravalli hills. Of the three phases observed by the excavators, the earliest is dated to 7,000 to 4,800 years ago. It is characterized by a microlithic industry and animal remains, suggesting a mixed economy of hunting and gathering and herding. The second phase is dated to 4,800 to 2,600 years ago. Here the microliths declined and were accompanied by copper tools and hand-made pottery. The pottery shows some affinity with the Ahar culture in Mewar.

Andhra–Karnataka zone

On the other hand, when we move to the sub-area of Andhra–Karnataka the evidence is still varied and shows a pattern that is characterized by an earlier flake-blade industry of microlithic age and a later succeeding culture with a pastoral and agricultural economy. It is in the second phase that, probably as a result of contact with the sub-area of Maharashtra and Gujarat, some copper material and painted pottery are occasionally found in some places. However, the Andhra–Karnataka region can be taken to be a primary and nuclear region for the peninsular Neolithic cultural complex.

The extreme southern zone

Further south in the Tamil- and Malayalam-speaking sub-area the earlier flake industry appears to have been mixed up with the pointed-butt axe industry of the Neolithic age, as evidenced by Paiyampalli and T. Narasipur on the Cauvery river, and this cultural complex continued until it became integrated into the iron-using Megalithic culture of the south. But the observation of Krishnaswami still holds good for this sub-area.

> The next largest collection of polished axes farther south comes from the Shevroy hills in Salem District, where, as in Bellary, there are large dykes of basalt that provided the requisite raw material. A few celts have also been collected from beyond Salem. The total absence of celts in the region south of the Cauvery should be attributed to the rarity of basaltic dykes in that region. A flat stone axe, similar to the one from Brahmagiri I A, reported by Foote in the Shevroy hills, may perhaps indicate the extension of the chalcolithic influence as far south as Salem.
>
> (Krishnaswami, 1960, p. 51)

Andhra–Karnataka

It is mainly the middle sub-area of Andhra–Karnataka that has provided the most varied stratified material and this even, therefore, gives the fullest picture of the Neolithic culture of southern India. This pastoral and agricultural pattern, which was previously thought to dominate numerous granitic hills around 4,000 years ago, is now safely pushed back by at least 500 years by radiocarbon dates and there is a possibility of tracing much earlier beginnings in this part. The excavations at Brahmagiri (Wheeler, 1947), Maski (Thapar, 1957, pp. 4–142) and Piklihal (Allchin, 1960) provided a glimpse of the Neolithic culture, but later excavations at Tekkalakota (Nagaraja Rao, 1965), Sanganakallu (Subba Rao, 1948) and Hallur (Nagaraja Rao, 1971) have now given a better picture of the plans of houses and of the settlement pattern. New explorations have established an inseparable association between ashmounds and habitation sites, uncovered skeletal material and multiplied the evidence related to houses, arts and crafts, food habits, burial customs and also chronology.

On granitic hills west-south-west of the Tekkalakota area a series of nineteen Neolithic sites were excavated. These have revealed three kinds of houses: (1) on the red *murrum* surface a circular free-standing house, the lower portion of the walls of which were built with wattle and daub and the upper portion, including a conical roof. was thatched; (2) a circular house supported by a natural circle of boulders; and (3) a square or rectangular house built against or with the help of boulders. Similarly at Sanganakallu the house, which was built on the *murrum* surface, had thirteen wooden posts, placed irregularly, to support a screen of split bamboo, plastered with clay. Four burials were found in one of the houses at Tekkalakota - one of an adult and three of children. One child was buried under the floor while two were outside. The adult was found under the rock at the northern end. At Tekkalakota and Kodekal the evidence suggests that the floor was covered with interwoven mat, made of bamboo strips or date-palm leaves. Here two main periods were observed: phase I, called Neolithic–Chalcolithic; and phase II, Megalithic (Iron Age). No difference in the house plans or building materials was visible. The same two cultural periods have been noted at other sites. In phase I all the pottery is handmade but in some cases the use of a turntable is postulated. There is a very small percentage of painted ware from the earliest layers at Brahmagiri, Piklihal and Maski. The second element of the culture is the ground-stone industry. It is now clear that right from the beginning the Neolithic folk possessed the knowledge of making pottery, ground-stone tools and also stone blades. The blades were made by every family irrespective of actual site or habitation, as seen at Tekkalakota. Terracotta head-rests have also been found. For ornaments, a variety of beads of shell, magnesite or steatite, agate and carnelian, terracotta, gold and copper have been recovered. As far as the burial practice was concerned, the adults were buried in specially dug pits in an extended position with a few pottery vessels and sometimes stone blades and polished axes. In phase II the adults were buried in pots in association with black-and-red ware. The children were buried within the house floor, usually in one or two urns. As far as art is concerned these Neolithic hill dwellers practised rock painting, pecking and etching. Their domestic art consisted of painting and pin-hole decoration on pottery. Tekkalakota has produced a magnificent bull on a rock and a human palm on a rock. Paintings, as evidenced at Piklihal, are in red over a white background, or simply in white as a lime wash, and finally only in red. The painted subjects include bulls, sambur (Indian elk), deer, gazelle, sheep and goat, horse, stylized humans and, rarely, trees and flowers. Bone and shell objects are found in several sites.

The evidence from Tekkalakota further suggests that the Neolithic people selected undulating hills, and not plain hills. They command the cultivable tract around their foot. The castellation provided a natural fortification and protection. The earliest settlers had first to clear the vegetation on the flat faces of the hills and prepare habitable ground. Here the houses were built with storage bins on legs for reasons of hygiene. The earliest radiocarbon date (Agrawal, 1947, p. 66) for Tekkalakota is 3,800 years ago.

Further remarkable archaeological data relates to the ashmounds seen in the northern parts of Andhra and Karnataka. These mounds have been dated between 4,000 years ago and 2,700 years ago. Some have taken them to be sites of gold and iron smelting but no archaeological proof for such an assumption is available. Others have taken them to be cattle-pens. The excavation at Kupgal near Bellary in Karnataka has now proved 'that these mounds originated from the burning of cow dung by the Neolithic pastorals.... The cause of burning was found to be definitely not due to any industrial activity but probably due to ritual practices' (Majumdar and Rajaguru, 1966, p. 47).

THE NORTHERN INDUS REGION INCLUDING KASHMIR, SWAT AND THE POTWAR PLATEAU

The northern Indus region of Gilgit, Baltistan, Swat, Kashmir and Panjab includes the trans-Himalayan zone of the upper Indus valley as well as the cis-Himalayan zone of the mid-Indus valley. The entire region was glacially affected. Moraines spread down into the Potwar plateau of Panjab, while mud flows and wind-blown deposition of soil in the Pleistocene period mark the varied features of the land surface. Uneven research in the region has not produced a complete sequence and hence transition from the Mesolithic to the fully developed Neolithic is not completely documented. However, the Taxila valley in Rawalpindi district has produced a microlithic cave site called Khanpur cave, which is characterized by a flake-blade industry. How this Khanpur cave culture was transformed into the Early Neolithic, as seen at Sarai Khola in the same valley, is not definitely known. However, still less explored is the Gilgit–Baltistan zone of the trans-Himalayan area, where evidence is limited to rock engravings (Dani, 1983, Ch. II). Their interrelationship with the trans-Pamir region of Kirgizia (Mu Shunying, 1984, pp. 55–72) and the trans-Kunlum region of Xin-Kiang is well established. This nomadic culture of the hunter-gatherer people could be dated from the sixth millennium BP onwards. Only in the later stages did the culture show other features: domestication of animals, like dog and cattle, using rafts for crossing rivers, life in small families or communities, fencing, covering the body with animal skins and the worship of rocks, emblems and even palm impressions and foot prints. Their equipment continued to be the bow and arrows tipped with microliths. But some of the human representations suggest a date in the Bronze Age of the fourth millennium BP.

In Dir and Swat excavated material is now accumulating that indicates continuity from the Late Stone Age culture, as evidenced from the early levels in the Ghaligai cave (Stacul, 1969, pp. 44–91). The cave dwellers were using pebble-tools and were initially without pottery, though later they made burnished hand-made grey pottery. Some of these pots showed mat impressions at their base and some forms are comparable to the Chalcolithic pottery of Turkmenistan. The stone tools are again made of pebbles. Animal bones, particularly antler and boar tusks, were also used for making tools. The ceramic ware closely parallels that known from Kashmir and at the site of Sarai Khola. The radiocarbon dates fall around 5,000 years ago. Similar pottery and ground-stone tools have been found in the deep pits excavated at Damkot near Chakdara in Dir. From Swat at the site of Loebanr III evidence for pit dwellings has also been gathered. G. Stacul comments:

> The largest hollow formed a hut foundation with a large fire-place and ample traces of floor-levels. The great number of artifacts and fragments of animal bones collected here is clear evidence of an intense settled activity. The large quantities of daub fragments were most probably in relation to wooden roofing materials (reed or stake impressions are clear on one side of the clay daub).
>
> (Stacul, 1977, p. 250)

The pottery found here was of the same kind as noted in the earlier excavations. Of particular interest was the discovery of some human terracotta figurines and some polished bone objects and the presence of green jade and lapis lazuli. The excavation at Birkot has established the contemporaneity of this Neolithic phase with the mature phase of the Bronze Age civilization in the Indus valley. The jade material and the pit dwellings are thought to establish a connection with China.

In the main Kashmir valley (Thapar, 1964; Khazanehi, 1977; Sharma, 1982, pp. 19–25) the Neolithic culture is represented by nearly three dozen sites, all located on the elevated flats of the Karewas, overlooking streams and lakes. Of these sites Burzahom, 16 km north-east of Srinagar, and Gufkral, 41 km south-east of Srinagar, have been systematically excavated. At both these sites three phases of Neolithic culture have been distinguished below later settlements. The first phase, I A, is aceramic and is characterized by a settlement pattern consisting of large and small dwelling pits dug into the loessic deposits above the Karewas. The pits are circular or oval in plan. They were surrounded by storage pits and hearths. A number of postholes are also seen around them. The floors of the pits were painted in red ochre. Rectangular or square pits or chambers were also dug in the loessic soil and had postholes at the corners for supporting a roof. In the next phase, I B, underground pits and chambers continued to be used by widening the sides and renewing the floors. At Burzahom as many as thirty-seven circular pits and forty-five pit-chambers have been exposed. The largest of the circular pits, which are 3.95 m in depth, were provided with steps. Some of the pit-chambers had depressions on all four sides and storage pits and hearths in the centre. The last phase of the Neolithic culture (I C) shows an abandonment of the underground dwelling pits and chambers. In their place dwelling units were now built above ground in either mud or mud-bricks. The presence of postholes, as many as forty-nine in one instance at Burzahom, indicates timber structures. Floors were made of rammed earth, coated with red ochre.

The subsistence economy of the people is characterized by specialized food-gathering and cereal farming, including stock-raising. Gufkral has produced evidence of both wild animals (such as ibex, bear, sheep, goat, cattle, wolf and Kashmir stag) and domesticated ones (sheep and goat) and grains of wheat, barley and lentil. In the first phase the bone tools consisted of points, needles and scrapers and the stone tools of axes, drills, picks, pounders, querns and maceheads. Tools were also made of antler. In the next phase, I B, among the animals, cattle and dog were additional domesticates and among the plants the common pea. In I B the most important addition was that of pottery. Three main fabrics, all hand-made, were in use. The pottery is made by the strip or coil technique and has burnishing on the surface produced by rubbing with twigs or bundles of grass. The main forms are jars and basins, with disc bases, often bearing mat impressions. The impressions suggest that people wove mats and twined baskets. The fine grey ware is comparatively thinner in section. It shows nail-tip decoration on the rim. The third ware, which is prepared out of coarse paste, is represented by jars, deep bowls and basins. The last phase makes a complete change as the structures are seen on the ground surface. The subsistence economy also progressively changed, perhaps through contacts with other neighbouring cultures. The tools have a better finish. New types include a long bone needle with or without an eye, small-sized bone points, the double-edged pick, spindle whorls and a harvester, a rectangular or semi-lunate knife with holes – a type very well known in the Yangshao culture of China. The ceramic repertoire of this phase has the addition of a burnished grey ware with types of high-necked, globular jars, dishes with hollow stand, stems with triangular perforations, bowls and basins. In this phase the fine grey ware and the burnished grey ware became the dominant pottery.

Burial practices are evidenced by six human interments at Burzahom, which comprise four primary and two secondary interments. The grave pits were oval in shape, dug either inside the house or in the compound, and plastered with lime on the sides. In the primary burials two bodies were found in a crouched position, an adult in an extended position and a child in a foetal position. Only three burials had grave goods: a small, barrel-shaped paste bead, animal bones, skull and pieces of antler, a soapstone circular disc and five carnelian barrel-shaped beads. Red ochre was applied on the interred human and animal bones. One skull had eleven trephined areas – six complete circular holes and five shallow depressions. On the basis of physical analysis it is suggested that the ethnic type resembles the skull of the mature Harappan people. One burial of dogs, which had been sacrificed, along with two antlers of *barasingha* (of the family Cervidae), is also evidenced.

From the point of view of cultural contacts the system of pit-dwelling seen in Kashmir, the use of crescent-shaped harvester and mat-impressed burnished ware have provided a basis for comparison with the Chinese Neolithic culture. However, in the lower levels of Burzahom a significant find is of a wheel-made vase of orange-slipped ware, painted in black with a horned figure. The pot and the design leave little room for doubt that it is an import from the Kot Dijian culture, as known from Sarai Khola in Taxila. The upper levels of Burzahom also produced a wheel-made red ware pot, containing 950 beads of agate and carnelian, again imports from the Indus plains. Similarly a few copper arrowheads, ring bangle fragments and a pin, discovered in phase I C at Burzahom, and a pin from Gufkral again appear to be imports. Of special importance is the find of two engraved stone slabs, fixed to a rectangular structure of a late tank. One stone shows a hunting scene – a stag pierced by a long spear from behind and struck by an arrow by two hunters in front. The upper part of the stone shows two sun symbols and a dog. The other stone has a tectiform pattern. Both these engraved stones are comparable to the rock engravings seen in the trans-Himalayan region of Gilgit and Baltistan.

Radiocarbon dates indicate that the earliest evidence for I B phase at Burzahom is around 4,759 to 4,600 years ago (after calibration), and the latest for I C around 4,100 years ago (after calibration).

In the third important sub-area of Potwar the typical settlement site is Sarai Khola (Halim, 1970–1, pp. 23–89; 1972, pp. 1–112), standing on the southern bank of Kala rivulet, about 3 km south-west of the Bhir mound of Taxila. Below the Kot Diji level of this mound the earliest occupation deposit has produced material of an indubitably Neolithic culture. The material consisted of ground-stone axes, a stone blade industry, bone tools and burnished pottery with mat impressions on the base of the pots. The pottery is coarse, red–brown and hand-made, or probably made on a simple turntable. The nearby ground perhaps preserves the fields of the Neolithic farmers. This was the first important site that produced evidence of pre-Bronze Age Neolithic culture in the upper Indus valley. The connection with Burzahom and the Swat cultural complex is provided by the mat-impressed pottery, the blade industry, the ground-stone tools and pit dwellings. All such contacts at present appear to have been at a time when the Bronze Age influences had penetrated this region, but earlier cultural contact is not ruled out. As far as the origin of the Neolithic culture of

this region is concerned, archaeologists have pointed out some comparative material from the Yangshao culture of China and have suggested a southward penetration of Chinese influences. Although Chinese borrowings through trade are not ruled out, yet the Neolithic cultural pattern of the region has a distinctive character of its own which appears to have been rooted in the natural geography of the Himalayan zone. As the rock engravings show, its natural cultural origins should be sought in the Trans-Pamir zone rather than further afield.

THE SOUTHERN INDUS REGION, INCLUDING BALUCHISTAN AND THE GOMAL PLAIN

The southern Indus region includes the southern alluvial plain of the Punjab, the Gomal and Bannu plains of the North-West Frontier Province, the Kachchni plain of Baluchistan outside the Bolan pass and the Baluchistan plateau, characterized by smaller valleys and punctuated by deserts, and the watery Zhob–Loralai sub-area of the north. It was in the Quetta valley of Baluchistan plateau that Walter A. Fairservis (1956) revealed a cultural complex at the site of Kili Ghul Mohammad – a complex which showed occupation in the earlier two levels below the earliest appearance of bronze material. Samples from a hearth of the uppermost levels gave C^{14} dates of c.6,400 and 6,100 years ago. The earlier nomadic people domesticated sheep, goats and cattle but had no pottery at all. At the end of the period they built houses of mud-brick or hard-packed clay. They used blades of chert, jasper or chalcedony and also rubbed or ground stone as well as awls or points of bone. This first phase is indubitably aceramic. It is only in period II, along with the initial construction of houses, that crude, handmade, basket-marked pottery was found. In period III painted pottery, wheel-made, with simple geometric motifs, was discovered.

This discovery of an aceramic nomadic culture is also matched by an aceramic flake-blade industry discovered in the ash-pits at Gumla (Dani, 1972) in the Gomal plain. But at Jalilpur (Mughal, 1972, pp. 117–24), 65 km south-west of Harappa, the occupation levels of period I, which are called Neolithic, revealed substantial structural remains of mud-brick and mud floor and also pottery, hand-made, of bright-red clay, showing mat impressions, a rectangular bead of gold sheet, terracotta net-sinkers, chert blades, bone points and a large number of bones of cattle, sheep, goat and gazelle.

The most important discovery in recent years is the site of Mehrgarh (Jarrige and Meadow, 1980, pp. 122–33; Jarrige and Lechevallier, 1979, pp. 463–535) at the head of the Kachchni plain, at the mouth of the Bolan pass, about 150 km from Quetta – a transition zone between the uplands of Baluchistan and Iran on the one hand and the plains of the southern Indus delta on the other. The excavations have produced the earliest evidence for settled agriculture in south Asia, dated to 10,000 to 9,000 years ago on the basis of radiocarbon dates. Seven stratigraphic periods have been distinguished at this site, of which four are located in the upper mound and three below the plain belonging to the Neolithic people. The northern end of the site has revealed the plan of the last farming village. In this period I, which is an aceramic period, the settlement consisted of multiform rectangular mud-brick units separated from one another by open spaces that held numerous human burials. Some structures appear to be smaller square compartments for storage. The artefacts include grinding stones and small flint blades with sickle gloss, which is suggestive of the earliest agriculture. Impressions of cereal grains in the mud debris have revealed different kinds of grain: two-row hulled barley (*Hordeum distichum*), six-row barley (*H. vulgare* and *H. vulgare* var. *nudum*), einkorn wheat (*Triticum monococcum*), emmer (*T. dicoccum*) and bread wheat (*T. durum* or *T. aestivum*). In the same deposits of period I, charred seeds of the plum-like jujube fruit (*Zizyphus jujuba*) and the stones of dates (*Phoenix dactylifera*) have been recovered, indicating that both trees were sources of food at this time.

Again the top 2 m of the Neolithic deposit show marked change in the faunal assemblages, the earlier having bones of wild animals, like gazelle (*Gazella dercas*), wild sheep (*Ovis orientalis*), wild goats (*Capra aegagrus*), swamp deer (*Cervus duvauceli*), large antelopes (*Boselaphus tragocamelus*) and wild cattle (*Bos*, perhaps the species *namadicus*), and the later having domesticated cattle (*Bos*, perhaps the species *indicus*) and goats (*Capra hircus*). By the end of the period a few remains of gazelle, wild boar and onager are present, but by far the majority of the bones are those of domesticated cattle, goats and sheep. It appears that the Neolithic people had undertaken a process of domestication of the wild animals locally available. Thus animal husbandry at Mehrgarh appears to be of the same age as in western Asia. Bones of water buffalo (*Bubalus bubalis*) have also been found outside eastern China. It must, however, be noted that in contrast to the domestication of sheep or goats in western Asia, here at Mehrgarh it is cattle that seem to have been domesticated first.

Associated with period I were two groups of graves, in which bodies were buried both flexed and extended, covered with red ochre. The grave goods included bead necklaces, anklets and belts. The most abundant objects of the period are flint tools, of which nearly 15,000 pieces were recoverd. The tools belong to a blade industry. The cores are small, pointed and either flat or conical. They comprise mainly retouched blades with various types of retouch, including notched blades and truncated blades, some end-scrapers, but include hardly any burins. The most characteristic tools are borers and geometric microliths, the latter of three types: lunates, triangles and trapezes. Sickle blades are present in small numbers. On the whole the evidence so far available suggests that the microlithic flint industry, although it shares some common traits with the Indian Late Stone Age, is connected with the early villages of the Zagros and the Epipalaeolithic industries of western central Asia.

Period II of Mehrgarh shows continuity with period I. Its lowest levels have produced a few potsherds of a coarse, hand-made ware, but in the upper levels pottery is plentiful and also painted. Here we find basket-marked sherds, and the painted decorations have parallels at Mundigak I and Kili Ghul Mohammad I. One set of ten sickle blades was found hafted in a bitumen matrix. Long-distance trade is evidenced by finds of conch shells and objects of turquoise. Beads of lapis lazuli have been found. A small unbaked clay figurine of a male torso was also found.

Period III at Mehrgarh has revealed great quantities of pottery. The painted motifs, particularly in the later stages, assignable to the first half of the sixth millennium BP, resemble those of Kili Ghul Mohammad II and III, Mundigak and Togau 'A' wares. Beads of lapis lazuli, turquoise and other semi-precious stones, as well as fragments of conch shell, have also been found. This continuity of life at Mehrgarh from the early beginnings of domestication of animals and cultivation of plants compares very well with

the chronological table of the Neolithic in western Asia (see Chapter 41, Table 16).

IRAN AND AFGHANISTAN

In Afghanistan (Dupree, 1972) two distinct patterns are seen: one in northern Afghanistan and another in southern Afghanistan. In the north the foothills of the Hindu Kush merge with the plains of Bactria. Here in the grottoes, caves and rock shelters, such as Kara Kamar and Aq Kupruk, a transition is seen from the Neolithic life of the groups who practised specialized hunting and later domestication of animals. In the eleventh millennium BP Kara Kamar has produced flint flakes and a wealth of animal remains of wild sheep, gazelle, fox and bird, suggesting an advance of the Mesolithic people from the Zagros mountains towards the Hindu Kush. In Ghar-e-Mar cave of Aq Kupruk, stratum A, which is dated to about 8,700 years ago, tools are represented by sickle blades, scrapers, piercers and chisels. There are also bone awls and burnishers. Here bones of domesticated sheep or goats have been found. The later stratum B of this cave has hoes, grinding stones and steatite and stone vessels. Similarly Ghar-i-Asp cave has yielded comparable material, dated to about 10,200 years ago. These objects indicate sedentary farming communities. Side by side with this new development, hunting continued, as is proved by the discovery of the bones of red deer, gazelle and wild sheep. A still later stage in these two caves is dated to about 4,500 years ago and has produced pottery and flint tools, like sickle blades, flakes, scrapers and chisels, and bone artefacts, awls, needles, piercers and burnishers. We also have here slate hoes, grinding stones, pestles, axes and fragments of steatite vessels. Of particular interest is the occurrence of pottery made of a brittle paste mixed with straw. Besides domesticated sheep and goats, there is a wide range of wild animals: onager, gazelle and bull. At Dara-i-kur cave in Badakhshan the Neolithic stratum revealed sickle blades, polished axes, a slate knife and scrapers, a basalt hammer, pebble-tools and fragments of copperware. Black-and-red pots, decorated with zigzags, chevrons, triangles and finger impressions, were found. Three pits contained goats buried with bones of children. The radiocarbon dates are about 5,900 years ago. Southern Afghanistan revealed a highly advanced agricultural economy in the lower strata of Mundigak (Casal, 1961) and Said Qala. At Mundigak I the earliest period showed brick constructions and wheel-made pottery and even copper ware.

In the north-eastern part of Iran (McBurney, 1969) several caves and rock shelters have been located. At Ghar-e-Kamarband the Neolithic stratum has produced geometric flint tools, some used as arrowpoints or javelin heads, and bones of gazelle and bull. One grave of a girl was sprinkled with red ochre. Ornaments included pendants of polished stone, animal teeth and pierced shells. Clay cones were also discovered. In the later strata of the cave sheep and goats were of domesticated types. Turang Tepe I produced a cultural complex comparable to the Djeitun culture of Turkmenistan. Similarly Yarim Tepe in the Gorgan valley has produced material typical of the Djeitun culture. The similarity leaves little doubt that here the economy of the Neolithic settlement was based on food production. The excavations at Sang-i Chakmaq have produced two types of structures with carefully made floors, one of them yielding clay figurines of mother goddesses and animal statuettes. Three ceramic sherds were also found along with flint flakes, microliths and obsidian blades. The neighbouring mound on the east also produced built constructions of clay and three graves of women and babies. Large quantities of ceramics were found, some of them painted. In the pottery of the upper stratum animal motifs are seen. Transition from an earlier economy to a food-producing system can be seen from the western mound to the eastern in the Gorgan valley. Underneath the later Bronze Age remains of Tepe Hissar earlier material still lies buried. The settlement of Shir-e-Shayn contains ceramics that are handmade and painted with line drawings, such as zigzags, similar to the early material from Djeitun. In fact the caves and shelters in the Gorgan valley indicate the presence of Mesolithic hunters, who moved into the plains and passed on to the stage of food production that later created the developed settlements at Tepe Hissar and Sialk.

ADVENT OF THE METAL AGE

Mehrgarh has now provided us with a complete sequence that enables us to understand the whole process of evolution from Neolithic to Early Bronze Age in the Indus region. Actually there are three important sites, Mehrgarh, Nowshero and Pirak (including Sibi), which together make up a continuous history from the tenth millennium BP down to the early historic period. While Pirak supplies the material for the post-Indus phase, Nowshero adds to the material of the Indus civilization and Mehrgarh lays bare the antecedents of this civilization. It is only in period II at Mehrgarh that hunting and gathering were almost replaced by the cultivation of cereal crops and animal husbandry. Here also one copper ring and one copper bead were found and hence the excavators named the cultural period Chalcolithic. It is dated to the seventh millennium BP. Several hundred charred seeds were found in a large burned area. They included different varieties of wheat and barley and some seeds of cotton. This is the earliest evidence for the cultivation of cotton in the region. The painted, wheel-turned pottery (Plate 66) has parallels at Kili Ghul Mohammad in the Quetta valley and at Mundigak in period I.2. Similarly we find here stone bowls. All this indicates that by the end of the seventh millennium and the beginning of the sixth millennium BP, the major communication axis connecting the Kachchni plain, the Quetta valley and the plain of Kandahar, wherein lies Mundigak, through the Bolan and Khojak passes did correspond to a vast zone of cultural interaction.

In the next period, III, the wheel-thrown pottery at Mehrgarh is mass-produced. Continuity from the earlier period is noted in the geometric motifs and also in the painted bangles. For the first time animal representation is now seen. The paintings show rows of processing caprids or birds among registers of geometric motifs. The excavators see in these motifs the source of some of the designs found in the Surab region of Baluchistan. A wider horizon is thus visualized by the excavators:

> the sudden occurrence of painted animal designs on potteries from sites which previously yielded only sherds decorated with simple geometrical motifs has been observed in Iran, in the levels of Sialk III and Hissar I B and I C, in Southern Turkmenia with the beginning of phase Namazga II and in Baluchistan in Period III at Mehrgarh, in phase Togan A in Surab region.
>
> (Jarrige and Lechevallier, 1979, p. 485)

Period IV has produced the earliest specimens of terracotta human figurines (Plate 67). They have a tubular head with a pinched nose, no arms but pendant breasts, heavy hips and jointed legs with a tapering end in a seated position. This period, the beginning of which is dated to 5,500 years ago, has produced pottery remarkable for fineness or sturdiness, but by now the goat and bird motifs of period II have disappeared. Very fine and fragile goblets in greenish ware and medium-sized carinated jars in wet ware are found along with big jars. Basins made in greenish buff ware are obtained all over the place. The painted motifs found here show a great variety and include designs that previously have been unnecessarily localized in one or the other subregion of Baluchistan, thus falsifying the earlier notion of different cultural subregions in Baluchistan. These designs again point to contacts and interactions between several ceramic production centres.

Period V at Mehrgarh begins about 5,200 years ago and thus brings into correct perspective the whole extensive phase of the Early Bronze Age cultures in Baluchistan, Punjab, Sind and also in the western regions of India now included in East Punjab, Rajasthan and Gujarat. Jarrige and Meadow rightly observe:

> Indeed, before even the earlier cultural phases at Mehrgarh were known the end of the fourth millennium BC was considered to mark the real beginning of developed farming economies in Southern Asia. The impetus for change in Baluchistan was then thought of as coming from sites in Central Asia belonging to Namazga III phase of cultural development, an impetus that had been mediated by such sites as Shahr-i-Sokhta in Iran and Mundigak in Afghanistan. It is now clear, however, that indigenous peoples, among them the residents of Mehrgarh, played an active role rather than a passive one in the transformation of this part of Asia in the first half of the fourth millennium BC.
>
> (Jarrige and Meadow, 1980)

It is in this period that wider interchange is reflected in the similar styles of artefacts. We now see similar compartmented stamp seals and a number of complex motifs for the decoration of pottery.

Period VI is dated between 5,000 and 4,700 years ago. This period has revealed plans of rooms and yards full of storage jars, complete pots, grinding stones, mortars and pestles around fire places. Circular kilns have also been found. Other objects include leaf-shaped arrowheads, compartmented seals in terracotta, one in stone and one double spiral-headed copper and bronze pin. For the first time beads of lapis lazuli, along with a few turquoise beads, are met. Human figurines in terracotta have been found in good numbers. These figurines are very elaborate and show a well-established local type distinct from the roughly-shaped figurines from Shahr-i-Sokhta or Mundigak.

Period VII is the last phase just before the development of the Indus civilization. This is divided into two subphases: an earlier with a huge monumental mud-brick platform with pilasters, and a later with intricate buildings, fitted with storage jars and complete pots. A grave found here associated grave goods of two plates and one necklace of white baked kaolin beads alternating with carnelian and lapis lazuli beads. This period revealed mass production of plain standardized pots, fine tulip shaped goblets, 'brandy glasses', piles of plates, storage jars with collared rims and a Harappan type of jars. Painted pottery shows leaf designs. A spectacular pottery is the grey ware painted in black. Animal, vegetal and geometric designs are remarkable for their quality and variety. This grey ware painted pottery has a wide distribution from Bampur to Baluchistan, through Tepe Yahya and Shahr-i Sokhta in Iran. Now terracotta human figurines become naturalistic with delicate hands, goggle eyes and neck bands. By the end of period VII the figurines became very rigid and were of the same type as the well-known Zhob mother goddesses. Compartmented stamp seals in terracotta, flat with two suspension holes, follow the tradition already seen in period VI; one has a swastika. A few circular seals or square seals bear cruciform motifs. One exceptional example bears a running animal, possibly a humped bull. The lithic industry shows the survival until the middle of the fifth millennium BP of the former flaking traditions. This material from period VII of Mehrgarh led on to the Harappan material culture seen at the site of Nowshero. At Mehrgarh no mature Harappan find has been noted, except for perforated pots on the surface. But painted bands in the Kot Diji style occur around the neck of vases found in the uppermost layers at Mehrgarh.

The type site of Kot Diji (Khan, 1965, pp. 11–85) is situated on the national highway 15 miles south of Kairpur town, under the shadow of the mediaevel Diji fort built on a rocky precipice on the south. The culture unearthed here has been taken to be one of the forerunners of the Indus civilization and hence some archaeologists have used the phrase 'Early Indus culture' for this type of cultural development that is now seen at two sites in Taxila, several sites in the Punjab, at the important sites of Gumla and Rahman Dheri, west of the Indus, at Kalibangan in Indian Rajasthan and many sites in Indian Punjab. This is no doubt the first major Bronze Age development seen in such an extensive area, but the culture again has local variations and there are important elements of the mature Indus civilization that hardly find a precursor here. The most important of these, unknown here, are the Indus system of writing, the grid planning of the city, the elaborate sanitary arrangement and the basic idea of a godhead as seen in the seals of the Indus. This is certainly a pre-Indus culture and in terms of anthropological cultural evolution it must be placed as an antecedent of the Indus civilization. Jarrige has shown in his excavations at Mehrgarh several other antecedent cultural periods which now provide a true chronological perspective for the various sequences built in the village cultures of Baluchistan, as proposed by W. A. Fairservis (1975). In the light of the new discoveries the entire material needs new interpretation; this will be fully discussed in the next volume.

SRI LANKA

The prehistory of Sri Lanka begins with the red coastal dunes, locally called *Teris*, with which stone artefacts have been associated. The hunters who used these tools continued in Sri Lanka well into the Holocene age. The Neolithic probably appeared only as a result of cultural spread from peninsular India: it is believed that early agriculturalists and pastoralists crossed over to Sri Lanka, perhaps in the fifth or fourth millennium BP, and introduced Neolithic elements to the otherwise Mesolithic communities in the island. The transition from Mesolithic to Neolithic is not yet clearly defined, although stray ground-stone axes have been reported here. A further development of the settled communities is associated with the introduction of megalithic

burials, but this cultural phase is related to the development of the Iron Age, which is also known from south India (Allchin and Allchin, 1962).

BIBLIOGRAPHY

AGRAWAL, D. P. 1947. *Prehistoric Chronology and Radio-Carbon Dating in India.* New Delhi.

ALLCHIN, B.; ALLCHIN, R. 1982. *The Rise of Civilization in India and Pakistan.* London.

ALLCHIN, F. R. 1960. *Piklihal Excavations.* Hyderabad.

CASAL, J. M. 1961. *Fouilles de Mundigak.* Paris.

DANI, A. H. 1960. *Prehistory and Protohistory of Eastern India.* Calcutta.

—— 1972. Excavations in the Gomal Valley. *Anc. Pakist.* (Peshawar), Vol. 5, pp. 1–177. (Special number.)

—— 1983. *Chilas, the City of Nanga Parvat.* Islamabad.

DASGUPTA, P. C. 1964. *The Excavations at Pandu Rajardhibi.* Calcutta.

DIKSHIT, K. N. 1982. The Neolithic Cultural Frontiers of Kashmir. *Man Environ.* (New Delhi), Vol. 6, pp. 30–6.

DUPREE, L. 1972. *Prehistoric Research in Afghanistan.* Philadelphia. (Trans. Am. Philos. Soc., Vol. 62, No. 2.)

FAIRSERVIS, W. A. 1956. *Excavations in the Quetta Valley.* New York.

—— 1975. *The Roots of Ancient India.* Chicago.

GORDON, D. H. 1950. The Stone Industries of the Holocene in India and Pakistan. *Anc. India,* Vol. 6, pp. 64–90.

HALIM, M. A. 1970–1. Excavations at Saraikhola. *Pakist. Archaeol.* (Karachi), Vol. 7, pp. 23–89.

—— 1972. Excavations at Saraikhola. *Pakist. Archaeol.* (Karachi), Vol. 8, pp. 1–112.

JARRIGE, J. F.; LECHEVALLIER, M. 1979. Excavations at Mehrgahr: Their Significance in the Prehistorical Context of the Indo Pakistan Borderlands. In: TADDEI, M. (ed.), *South Asian Archaeology.* Napoli. pp. 463–535.

JARRIGE, J. F.; MEADOW, R. 1980. The Antecedents of Civilization in the Indus Valley. *Sci. Am.,* Vol. 243, pp. 122–33.

KHAN, F. A. 1965. Excavations at Kot Diji. *Pakist. Archaeol.* (Karachi), Vol. 2, pp. 11–85.

KHAZANEHI, T. N. 1977. North-Western Neolithic Cultures of India. *Indian Inst. Adv. Stud. Newsl.* (Simla), Nos. 7–8.

KRISHNASWAMI, V. D. 1960. The Neolithic Pattern of India. *Anc. India,* Vol. 16, pp. 25–64.

MCBURNEY, C. B. M. 1969. The Cave of Ali Tappeh and the Epi-Palaeolithic in North-Eastern Iran. *Proc. Prehist. Soc.,* Vol. 34, pp. 385–413.

MAJUMDAR, G. G.; RAJAGURU, S. N. 1966. *Ashmound Excavations at Kupgal.* Poona.

MASSON, V. M.; SARIANIDI, V. I. 1972. *Central Asia.* New York.

MU SHUNYING. 1984. Development and Achievement of Archaeology in Sinjiang since the Founding of New China. *J. Cent. Asia* (Islamabad), Vol. 7, pp. 55–72.

MUGHAL, M. R. 1972. Excavations at Jalilpur. *Pakist. Archaeol.* (Karachi), Vol. 8, pp. 117–24.

NAGARAJA RAO, M. S. 1965. *The Stone Age Hill Dwellers of Tekkalakota.* Poona.

—— 1971. *Protohistoric Cultures of the Tungabhadra Valley: A Report of Halbur Excavations.* Bangalore.

RANOV, V. A. 1982. The Hissar Neolithic Culture of Soviet Central Asia. *Man Eviron.* (New Delhi), Vol. 6, pp. 63–71.

RAO, S. N. 1977. Excavations at Sarutaru: A Neolithic Site in Assam. *Man Environ.* (New Delhi), Vol. 1, pp. 39–41.

SANKALIA, H. D. 1974. *Prehistory and Protohistory of India and Pakistan.* 2nd edn. Poona.

SHARMA, A. K. 1982. Excavations at Crufkal, 1981. *Puratattva* (New Delhi), No. 11, pp. 19–25.

SHARMA, G. R. 1983. Beginnings of Agriculture: New Light on Transformation from Hunting and Food Gathering to the Domestication of Plants and Animals – India Primary and Nuclear Centre. *J. Cent. Asia* (Islamabad), Vol. 6, pp. 51–64.

SHARMA, T. C. 1977. The Neolithic Pattern of North-East India. In: MAHDU (ed.), *Recent Researches in Indian Archaeology and Art History.* Delhi.

STACUL, G. 1969. Excavations near Ghaligai (1968) and Chronological Sequence of Protohistoric Cultures in the Swat Valley. *East West* (Rome), Vol. 19, pp. 44–91.

—— 1977. Dwelling and Storage Pits at Loebanr III. *East West* (Rome), Vol. 26, pp. 227–54.

SUBBA RAO, B. 1948. *Stone Age Cultures of Bellary.* Poona.

SURIN POOKAJORN. 1984. *The Hoabinhian Mainland South East Asia: New Data from the Recent Thai Excavations in the Van Kao Area.* Bangkok.

THAPAR, B. K. 1957. Maski-1954: A Chalcolithic Site in the Southern Deccan. *Anc. India*, Vol. 13, pp. 4–142.

—— 1964. Neolithic Problems in India. In: MISRA, V. N.; MATE, M. S. (eds), *Indian Prehistory.* Poona.

—— 1984. Fresh Light on the Neolithic Cultures of India. *J. Cent. Asia* (Islamabad), Vol. 7, pp. 195–7.

VERMA, B. S. 1970–1. Excavations at Chirand: New Light on the Indian Neolithic Culture Complex. *Puratattva* (New Delhi), Vol. 4, pp. 19–23.

WHEELER, R. E. M. 1947. Brahmagiri and Chandravalli 1947: Megalithic and Other Cultures in Mysore. *Anc. India*, Vol. 4, pp. 295 ff.

WORMAN, E. C. 1949. The Neolithic Problem in the Prehistory of India. *J. Wash. Acad. Sc.*, Vol. 39, No. 6, pp. 181–200.

44

CENTRAL AND NORTHERN ASIA

during the Neolithic

Anatoly P. Derevyanko

The vast territory of central and northern Asia, which covers roughly 20 million km², comprises several large areas with individual Neolithic cultures (Map 53). They are Mongolia, south Siberia (Tuva and Khakasia), west Siberia, north-east Asia and Yakutia, south of the former Soviet Far East. Each can be regarded as the result of the interaction of consecutive cultures and individual localities with specific patterns of cultural development.

The Neolithic cultures of the region took shape in the context of mainly modern faunal and floral complexes. These vast expanses exhibited a great variety of landscapes and environments. It is therefore, no accident, that during the Neolithic the region aready contained a motley assortment of cultures. At the same time, the Neolithic tribes, who remained largely dependent on hunting and fishing, constantly roamed their immense territory, thus transmitting many elements of both the material and the non-material culture.

MONGOLIA (Fig. 115)

East and central Mongolia

The Mongolian Neolithic is genetically connected with the preceding Mesolithic. The Khereul Mesolithic culture, which marked the beginning of blade techniques, was the main contributor to the development of Early Neolithic sites (Derevyanko and Okladnikov, 1969; Dorzh and Derevyanko, 1970; Okladnikov and Derevyanko, 1970; Dorzh, 1971).

Settlements at Yamat-nuur lake in eastern Mongolia and other sites of this type, which are identified as the Yamat-nuur culture, can be classed among the Early Neolithic sites. All finds exhibit specific and well-defined features. Cores were mainly used for making micro- and macroblades. Prismatic, nearly prismatic and wedge-shaped nodules make up the greater part of the finds. The number of blade flakes and blades was also considerable. Among the finished articles mention should be made of end-scrapers, backed blades and burins. Particular adze-like implements make up a separate group. They are nearly triangular in section, with one side trimmed by removing broad flakes over the entire surface. This settlement group manifests quite a few archaic features such as core-scrapers, burins and composite implements which have analogies among the finds from the Khereul sites. Composite implements shaped like adzes–racloirs also

relate to the earlier period. The sites of this type are dated between the seventh and early sixth millennia BP and are found mainly in eastern and central Mongolia.

The sites that yield corded ware are dated to a later period. This ornamental type, popular in eastern and northern Asia, has a number of variants, but what is important here is the fact that it is found in Mongolia as well. The late sixth to early fifth millennium BP in eastern and central Mongolia is represented by settlements on the Ovoot mountain, Tamtsag-Bulak and others that are included in the Tamtsag-Bulak culture. A settlement 7 km to the east of Tamtsag-Bulak is especially interesting. It occupied a high fluvial terrace above the floodplain (10 to 12 m high), at the foot of which a spring of cold, clear water is to be found.

The settlement comprised several scores of dwellings. The Soviet–Mongolian expedition laid bare some large (40 m² and more) semi-subterranean dwellings. The space at the top through which the smoke escaped probably served as an exit, its use facilitated by a notched log. Archaeologists have already seen similar entrances in Neolithic and later settlements in the north and east of Asia.

The stone industry discovered in Tamtsag-Bulak is a vivid illustration of a definite stage in the development of early east Mongolian tribes. Wedge-like and nearly prismatic cores with blade-flaking on one or two sides are most typical in this settlement. Excavation in dwellings has yielded many implements made on blades: burins, knives, backed blades, awls and scrapers. Implements made on blades form an absolute majority. The settlement has also yielded many backed blades that were hafted as knives and daggers. Grinding stones for grain, portars, pestles and weights for digging sticks were found in the dwellings. Bone was widely used by the inhabitants. They made arrowheads, knife and dagger hafts and ornaments.

Pottery is not abundant. All sherds are thick and poorly shaped. Most of them are ornamented with parallel, deeply cut lines. The paste contained additions of fine sand and shells, was well mixed and was light yellow or dark grey in section.

The third stage (between the fifth and the early fourth millennia BP) in eastern and central Mongolia is marked by the sites on which bifacially worked artefacts replaced tools manufactured on blades. Some of the sites are dated to within the Early Bronze Age, and this is supported by finds at Khuityn-Bulak Lake, 130 km from the town of Choibolsan.

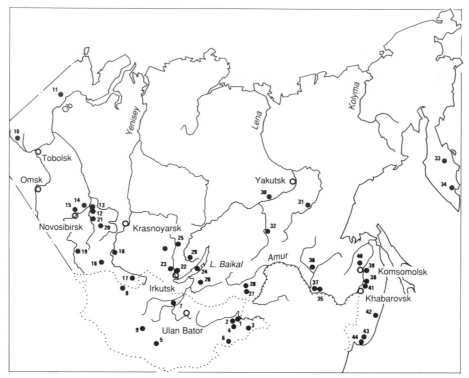

Map 53 Distribution of the most important Neolithic sites in central and northern Asia: 1, Yamat-Nuur; 2, Ovoot; 3, Tamtsag-Bulak; 4, Khuityn-Boulak; 5, Shabarik-Oussou; 6, Dariganga; 7, Archan-Khad; 8, Tchandman; 9, Ouldzit; 10, Andreevskoe lake; 11, Tches-tyi-yg; 12, the Samous burial; 13, the Tomske burial; 14, Alexandrovskoe; 15, Zavjalovo; 16, Khemtchik; 17, Toorakhem; 18, Khadyynykh; 19, Kouyoum; 20, the Vaskovskoe burial; 21, the Tomske petroglyphs; 22, Lenkovka; 23, the Tchastaya and Kinskaya valleys; 24, Olkhon; 25, Kamennaye isles; 26, Moukhinskoe; 27, Tchindant; 28, Boudoulan; 29, Chichkino; 30, Koullaty; 31, Belkatchi; 32, Krestyakh; 33, Ouchkovskoja; 34, Tarya; 35, Novopetrovka; 36, Gromatoukha; 37, Osinoub lake; 38, Malyshevo; 39, Vosnessenovka; 40, London; 41, Sakatchi-Alyan; 42, Roudnaya; 43, Zaisanovska; 44, Kirovskoe.

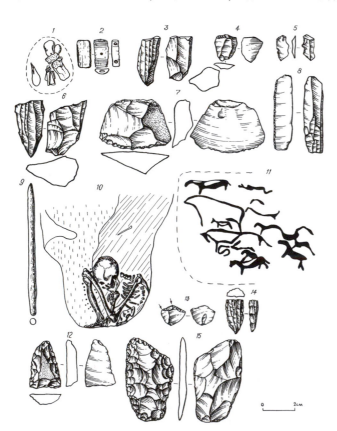

Figure 115 Typical Neolithic remains (Mongolia): 1, collection of animal bones and ornaments from a dwelling in Tamtsag-Bulak; 2, bone bead from Tamtsag-Bulak; 3–8 and 12–15, stone industry from Mongolian Neolithic settlements; 9, bone awl; 10, burial from Tamtsag-Bulak; 11, rock drawings on the Chandman mount.

South Mongolia and the Gobi Desert

Another vast area of central Asia with individual Neolithic cultures lies in the south of Mongolia and the Gobi Desert, where people had to adapt themselves to these peculiar landscapes and environments. In its Neolithic development this region had gone through three main stages as well.

The earliest complexes relate to the *Baindzak* culture, dated to the late Mesolithic and early Neolithic. Their basic characteristics are advanced blade techniques and numerous artefacts on blades. The camp sites at Baindzak or Shabarak-usu in the central Gobi, discovered in the 1920s by the American central Asian expedition led by R. C. Andrews, are well studied (Berkeley and Nelson, 1926; Maringer, 1950). The early complexes in the region are associated with the dune range covering the bottom of a huge ancient basin. The cultural layer is exposed in places where the sand has been blown away by the wind. The finds concentrated around fireplaces and formed small groups. Archaeologists have revealed two horizons testifying to definite periods in the development of the local Neolithic.

The lower horizon shows a wide use of wedge-shaped cores termed the Gobian, after the region in which they were found. They and other core shapes (prismatic, conical and others) served as a source of blades which were commonly used for manufacturing scrapers, burins, knives and multifunctional implements. The horizon also contained small disc beads made of ostrich eggshells.

The upper horizon contained cores and tools made on blades whose shapes and techniques resembled the earlier ones. Clay egg-shaped vessels bear witness to major cultural shifts. Their outer surfaces carried textile imprints, including twining patterns typical of the Baikal region.

The next Neolithic stage in southern Mongolia is also complicated. Its cultural layers are found directly in the dunes and are associated with the rather thick strata of buried soils divided by sands. Artefacts made on blades persisted, but they were to a considerable degree ousted by bifacially worked tools. Pottery changed its appearance as well: it had thin walls, fully developed profiles and flat bases. Painted ware made its appearance at the same time. For the most part vessels were painted red, though there are fragments carrying genuine ornamental designs in black on a red background. In some places such patterns were executed in black against a yellow background. Painted ceramics are a common feature of the south Gobi Neolithic sites.

It was a period of significant economic changes. Grinding stones for grain, mortars and pestles were quite frequent finds in the settlements. As has already been pointed out, the cultural layers of this period are mainly found in the buried soils. This is especially clear at the settlement of Dariganga in the south-eastern part of the Gobi Desert. It is hardly possible to distinguish between them both stratigraphically and chronologically. The settlements contained pottery of three types: corded vessels, vessels with smooth walls and slightly curved and thickened rims and vessels with thin walls ornamented with horizontal lines and applied rolls. The stone industry comprises both artefacts made on blades and bifacially worked tools.

Towards the end of the period, in the late fifth to the early fourth millennium BP, the climate became much drier. Tools on blades almost completely disappeared, to be replaced by bifacially worked implements. People continued their nomadic lifestyle, living in temporary dwellings. In fact, at that time a way of life characteristic of the nomads emerged.

Religion and art in Neolithic Mongolia

Investigation of the Mongolian Neolithic sites has shed some light on questions connected with the religious beliefs and art of the early population. All burials found in eastern Mongolia testify to a uniform burial rite over this vast territory, and hence to the definite ethnic unity of its population. The dead were placed in a sitting position, east- or west-oriented, in small, narrow graves. All the burials are exceedingly poor, with a sole exception in Tamtsag-Bulak which contained ornaments and bone daggers with backed blades.

An animal cult was typical of the Mongolian Neolithic tribes. Thus, archaeologists found in Tamtsag-Bulak a place where the skull of a small animal, ornamented bone beads and beads made of maral (hart) teeth were collected. Another such collection of bones of some large animal placed in a small pit, was, in all probability, a cult burial. Camp sites along the Kerulen river yielded some ritual burials of bones of wild animals.

Some of the petroglyphs from the enormous Stone Age gallery in Arshan-Khad in the Onon river valley, on the Chandman mountain, in the basin of the great lakes, at the Uldzit settlement in central Gobi and in other places are dated to the Neolithic (Novgorosova, 1984). Scores of animal and human images cover the sand-polished slate surfaces darkened with 'rock tan'. Many of them are tanned to the same degree as the rocks they are carved on. The earliest images depict the wild horse, its sexual features being especially prominent. They, undoubtedly, reflect the ancient idea of animal fertility as the main source of livelihood for the hunting tribes of hoary antiquity.

The Early Neolithic Mongolian tribes were engaged in food gathering, being mainly hunters and fishers. The Middle Neolithic (from the late sixth to the mid-fifth millennium BP) witnessed the emergence of semi-subterranean dwellings and implements for tilling the land. In the Gobi Desert these settlements are connected with thick layers of buried soil. Cultivation was not a widespread phenomenon in Mongolia, some tribes being still engaged in food gathering. Cattle-breeding and the beginning of nomadism coincided with the end of the Neolithic.

SIBERIA

Western Siberia (Fig. 116)

Neolithic tribes inhabiting western Siberia along its borders with the Ural and Kazakhstan shared common features with the population of these regions. The earliest Neolithic site at Lake Andreyevskoe, near Tyumen, produced backed blades, end-scrapers and arrowheads (Okladnikov, 1968; Chernetsov, 1953). All of them bear a great resemblance to artefacts of the same type found in Turkmenia and belonging to the Kelteminar culture.

The Early Neolithic period in the region is illustrated by finds from Lake Andreyevskoe, the sites at the Kozlov pereima and others. Vessels with round or conical bases, egg-shaped and parabolic in their vertical section, marked this stage. Comb and pit-comb ornaments, arranged in various patterns, decorated these vessels. The conical base often carried narrow patterns radiating from the centre. People continued to use blades, though a large number of flakes and blanks were also found.

In the northern reaches of the Ob River archaeologists studied an interesting settlement situated on an islet with the Zyrian name Ches-tyi-yag. It is located on a marshy floodplain terrace on the left bank of the Lyapin River, a tributary of the Ob. In the south-western part of the islet there was a cluster of seventeen dug-out structures. In most cases they were rectangular, nearly square dwellings, measuring from 9 by 9 m to 20 by 20 m. Some of them exceeded 600 m². The dwellings were 3 or 4 m deep. In general, they were very large semi-subterranean dwellings.

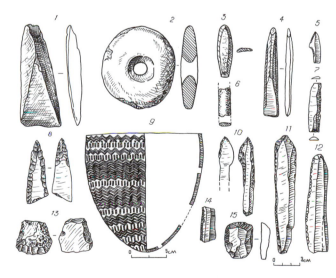

Figure 116 Typical Neolithic remains (western Siberia). Northern Sosva: 1, 4, adze; 2, disc-shaped implement; 3, arrowhead; 6, bead. Ches-tyi-yaga: 9, ceramic vessel. Andreyevskoe Lake: 5, 8, 10, arrowheads; 7, 14, backed blades; 11, 12, retouched blades; 13–15, scrapers.

Excavations at the settlement revealed adzes, chisels, and carefully polished nephrite knives. Arrowheads were also polished. In addition, the site produced bifacially worked tools.

Many earthenware vessels of different sizes were discovered at the settlement. They were parabolic or, more often, egg-shaped. The entire surface of the vessels was covered with decoration: in most cases it was comb-stamped. Analogous wares were found in other sites along the Severnaya Sosva river. The people who lived there also made extensive use of nephrite tools.

The Neolithic sites in the lower reaches of the Ob river do not fit the general pattern of the west Siberian Neolithic cultures. They make up a particular culture based, probably, on fishing, with hunting being of secondary importance. The surmise is supported by the existence of large settlements with dwellings of the dug-out type. Evidently, such a settled way of life there could be supported only by fishing.

The Upper Ob Neolithic culture occupied the region in the south of Western Siberia, in the upper reaches of the Ob. Its sites are to be found over the entire territory of the forest–steppe and the forest zone of the Ob basin, from the upper Ob and the Tomsk river up to the village of Alexandrovskoe on the Ob (Molodin, 1977). All in all, 100 sites of this type are known to date: they are burials, camp sites and places where isolated Neolithic artefacts were found. The Upper Ob culture is dated to between the sixth and the fifth millennia BP. Samus, Tomsk and other burial grounds and settlements represent the latest stage of this culture.

Almond-shaped racloirs, scrapers, knives, arrowheads and small stone notched rods which were parts of composite fish-hooks were typical of that culture.

These people buried their dead in collective graves, which at first were evidently covered with wooden planks. The culture's most striking feature is the contemporary use of inhumation and cremation. The people sometimes held funeral feasts and purified the burial place with fire. The grave goods include flat-bottomed vessels, implements and weapons.

The vessels had flat bases and rims delineated by horizontal rows of pits. Ornaments usually filled the entire side surface of the vessel and most often consisted of rows of stick impressions.

The number of polished implements has greatly increased in the burials of the Samus burial ground. Well-polished knives with concave blades were associated with the previously known large asymmetrical knives with convex blades and almond-shaped ones made on flakes. New narrow spear-heads with a rhombic section were added to the earlier laurel-leaf-shaped spearheads. The burials yielded chopping tools: adzes and axes. Round- and conical-based vessels carried complicated decorative patterns of comb impressions.

Tuva and Altai (Fig. 117)

The earliest stage of the Tuvinian Neolithic is associated with sites that have yielded microliths, commonly found in the steppe and the intermontane depressions of central Asia. The best studied among them is Ust-Khemchik 3, a site on the right bank of the Yenisey, just opposite the river Khemchik (Kyzlasov, 1982). It possessed a microlith industry and has a total lack of pottery and polished stone tools. Archaeologists found many microblades, some of

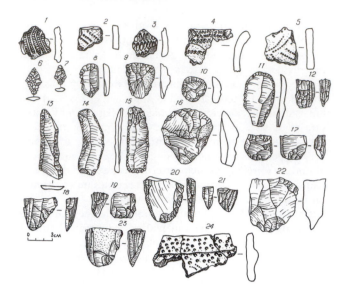

Figure 117 Typical Neolithic remains (Tuva). The Khadynnykh I camp: 1–5, 24, pottery sherds. Tooro-Khem (the second stage): 6, 7, arrowheads; 8–11, 16, scrapers; 12, 17–23, cores; 13–15, knife-like blades.

which had one edge blunted by the removal of tiny flakes. They were used to make hafted implements, knives, lances and spears. Bifacially worked arrowheads with asymmetrical hollows at their bases resemble the Isakovo ones from the Baikal region. In all probability, the Ust-Khemchik 3 site was a camp of a comparatively small group of hunters of the Siberian wild goat. Jawbones of these animals were discovered in the cultural deposit. Radiocarbon dating related the site to the mid-seventh millennium BP. However, microliths were in use in the region up to the end of the sixth millennium BP.

Hunting communities, which appeared in the region together with the microlith industry, most probably inhabited the central Tuvinian depression, the piedmont regions of Tanny-Ola and the Khemchik valley. From the ethnocultural point of view the tribes that lived in Tuva at that time shared many traits with the hunting and fishing peoples from the neighbouring regions of Mongolia and Altai.

Excavations in Todzha and Toorakhem (Fig. 117) shed light on the following stage of the Tuvinian Neolithic. People used pottery at that time. Archaeologists found fragments of round-based vessels, decorated with 'maggot' stamps of stick impressions, bracket-shaped and fine-toothed stamps.

The stone industry is genetically connected with that of the preceding stage. The cores are conical or pencil-shaped and were used for striking microblades. The arrowheads were hollow-based.

One group of sites has been discovered in the Sayan gorge at the Yenisey. The most interesting among them was a site on the Yenisey's right bank, 1.5 km below the mouth of the Khadynnykh brook. The camp was probably used by nomadic hunters and stock-breeders. Animal bones from the cultural layers belonged to wild goat, maral, roe deer, goat, sheep, horse and cattle. As we see, the list includes domestic animals as well. It seems that these people's activities were concentrated around the four hearths surrounded by stones in the centre of the camp.

Vessels with varied rims and decoration were made of carefully prepared clay. The most common was a pattern made using a tubular bone. As a rule, the decoration covered the entire external surface of the vessel and its rim. A decorative stamp, a triangular slate plate with nine small teeth of different sizes, was also found.

While the majority of Tuvinian camps and settlements yielded microliths, this camp had clumsy, chopper-like cores from which massive flakes–blanks were obtained for making implements and weapons such as arrowheads, knives, scrapers and blades.

Neolithic development in the Altai had much in common with that in Tuva. Excavation of the multilayer camp in the Kuyum gorge afforded an insight into stoneworking techniques and shapes of tools from the late Pleistocene to the early Holocene which were tending towards microlithic forms. Already the upper Kuyum layers produced bifacially worked stem- and closely similar leaf-shaped arrowheads, which attests that as early as the beginning of the Holocene the south Siberian tribes switched to the use of the bow and arrow.

Figure 118 The bear and the elk in west Siberian Neolithic art: 1, 4–9, 11, the Vaskovskoye burial ground; 2, 10, the Tom petroglyph; 3, the Old Muslim cemetery.

A highly individual art style represented by bone and stone sculptures and petroglyphs is a most typical feature of the western Siberian Neolithic tribes. A Neolithic burial ground at the village of Vaskovskoe (Kemerovo region) (Fig. 118) contained interesting figures of bears and an elk's head. One of the bears, with the stretched muzzle and strained body, seems to be walking.

The same burial contained more than 200 pendants made of animal incisor and canine teeth. An original necklace composed of thin polished bone pendants lay on the neck and chest of a skeleton of a 10- or 12-year-old girl.

A remarkable 'picture gallery' at the village of Pisanaya on the bank of the Tomsk offers thought-provoking material for the study of south Siberian Neolithic art (Okladnikov

and Martynov, 1972). The petroglyphs depicts mainly animal images. It can be said that all petroglyphs are, so to speak, a fragment of an early animal epos hardened into stone, a poem about animals. Elk images hold the central place among other drawings, because elks were the main animal hunted during the Neolithic. The animals are presented in movement; they have short, heavy bodies with large humps and lean croups. Laconic and vivid representations of the muzzles seem to be made in relief. Bears and birds are also present in the petroglyphs.

The Tomsk petroglyphs and other sculptures of birds and animals are graphic illustrations of the strivings and wishes of Neolithic people, their life-style being inseparably connected with hunting. There is no doubt that these pictures were created for prehistoric hunting magic.

The Taiga, the Angara and Lena basins, the Baikal region

Another world, distinct from that of western Siberia, the world of the Neolithic taiga hunters and fishers, was discovered and studied in the Angara and Lena basins, where one complex of hunting and fishing tribes took shape some 6,000 or 7,000 years ago. It differs greatly from the world of the Far Eastern settled fishers and cultivators or the nomads of the steppe–forest and steppe belt of western and southern Siberia.

The Baikal region reveals a most complete picture of historical development in the Neolithic. Several stages have been identified in the Neolithic of the upper Lena, in the Angara valley, between Irkutsk and Bratsk, and also around Lake Baikal (Okladnikov, 1950, 1965). The first stage, that of transition from the Palaeolithic to the Neolithic, is represented by multi-layered settlements at the mouth of the Belaya and in the Lenkovka valley, and by burials in the Chastaya and the Khinskaya valleys on the Angara. It can be surmised that the settlements on the island of Olkhon and the Baikal coast nearest to it, which have not yet been properly studied, are related to the transition period. The people living there were still ignorant of ceramics. But, judging by the finds from the mouth of the Belaya, they had already started to polish stone, which was one of the technological devices for making stone chopping tools, including those from nephrite. This was the period when the first arrowheads appeared. The archaic technique of making them from blades barely retouched along the edges was employed. Such basically Mesolithic arrowheads have been found in the Chastaya and Khinskaya valleys.

In the next, or Isakovo period, in the sixth millennium BP, the cultural complex of the Baikal Neolithic took its final shape (Fig. 119). Prominent local shapes of polished adzes appeared, which had triangular and trapezoidal sections. The vessels were parabolic in their vertical section and were covered with twining impressions. Bifacially worked arrowheads, with asymmetrical barbs and bases shaped like a sparrow's tail, large lunate racloirs, backed blades and points and a tendency to make hunting appliances out of mammoth tusks are strong evidences of persisting Palaeolithic traditions. Green Sayan nephrite came into wide use, together with grey siliceous schist. Small sculptures of bone or stone fish-lures became a common feature of grave goods.

The Serovo stage (Figs 119 and 120), dated to the first half of the fifth millennium BP, was a further evolution of basically the same culture. The vessels acquired more distinct shapes, with necks and rims being elaborately made, and more exquisite decoration. The simple horizontal belt of

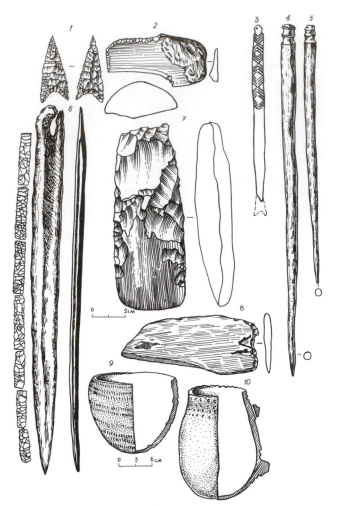

Figure 119 Artefacts from the Baikal area (Russian Federation). The Isakovo culture: 1, arrowhead; 2, schist knife; 3, bone artefact; 4–5, bone pins; 7, adze; 8, nephrite knife. The Serovo culture: 6, bone dagger with backed blades; 9–10, ceramic vessels.

angular nephrite knife-points, flat claystone knives the blades of which were made still flatter with the help of broad diagonal facets of pressed retouch, and also sandstone 'arrow-straighteners', burnishers, round stone plates and other objects (Fig. 120), among which white marble rings can be singled out.

Realistic art, basically animalistic, continued to progress further. The Kitoi burials contained fish images, including flat bone sculptures, which, in all probability, were shamanistic amulets. Representations of elk heads perhaps crowned shamans' staves resembling the Buryat shaman horse-staves. This period marked the appearance of anthropomorphic sculptures, direct predecessors of human sculptures typical of the age of metal.

The most graphic and complete picture of Neolithic art can be obtained on the Angara river, on the famous Kamennye islands. All three islands are full of splendid drawings. Some of them were cut in stone, others made with paint. Side by side with the completed representations of animals there are, so to speak, sketches, as if an ancient master needed only parts of the composition to visualize the whole.

There are many peculiarly stylized anthropomorphic figures, fish images and enigmatic signs on the islands. This amazing Stone Age picture gallery stretches for scores of metres. Sometimes the drawings were superimposed. Dozens of generations succeeded one another and each added new drawings to those already existing.

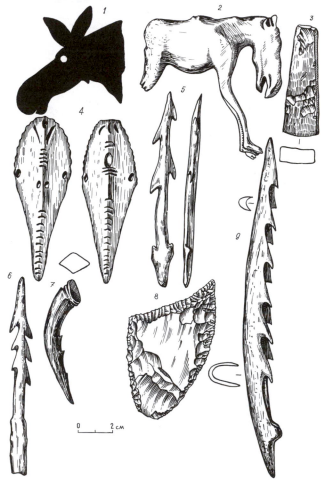

Figure 120 Elements from the Baikal area (Russian Federation). The Serovo culture: 1, representation of an elk (Shishkino); 2, a bone elk figurine (Bazaikha on the Yenisey river); 3, adze; 4, representation of a fish; 5, 9, harpoons; 8, knife. The Kitoi culture: 6, harpoon; 7, fish-hook.

pits under the rim gave place to either comb-stamped dotted or zigzag lines arranged in parallel rows.

The Serovo population used an improved type of bow. Many burials contained bone bow plates. Judging from the extant fragments, the Serovo bows were one and a half metres high. Bows in the burials are often accompanied by collections of arrowheads, there being sometimes as many as several score artefacts. Daggers and spearheads continued to be the most commonly used types of weapons. All of them are elaborately finished. The burials also yielded well-preserved composite knives and daggers, the backed blades of which were carefully chipped on both sides to fit the bone haft.

Besides hunting, the Serovo population was also engaged in fishing. They used varied tackle including bone and wooden hooks. At a later period they switched to composite hooks consisting of small slate or algamalite rods to which people tied bone or wooden barbs. Harpoons and bone or stone lures shaped to look like fish were also employed for fishing. Numerous weights testify to the use of fishing nets.

The Kitoi stage differed from others by the absence of masonry from the burials and by the lavish employment of ochre in them which symbolized the living principle, 'the blood of the dead'. The main typological feature of the Kitoi burials was a particular type of fishing rod that had semicircular protuberances at both ends. More common tools include nephrite adzes, lens-shaped in section, tri-

The trans-Baikal region

During the Neolithic the trans-Baikal region differed from the Baikal region in ethnocultural respects. Both western and eastern trans-Baikal areas comprised several well-correlated cultures.

In the Early Neolithic (between the late seventh and early sixth millennia BP) in western areas there existed the Mukhinskoe culture, while in eastern areas we find the Chindant culture; both were, in essence, a single ethnocultural complex (Okladnikov and Kirillov, 1980). The Early Neolithic is genetically connected with the local Mesolithic.

Among the cores, which are typical for the Early Neolithic, there are wedge-like cores, end cores and prismatic ones. They were used to make blades and microblades. Tools were mainly made on blades. The most characteristic feature was the common use of end-scrapers, awl-scrapers, varied awl-like instruments, arrowheads made on blades chipped along the two sides, with hollow bases and asymmetric barbs.

Adze- and racloir-like implements trimmed in a rough way along two sides and finely retouched along the edge became more numerous. Their closest analogies can be met with among the implements of the Gromatukha culture in the middle reaches of the Amur. They are the hallmark of the early trans-Baikal Neolithic in the same way as nephrite polished axes and adzes are for the Baikal Neolithic.

The simple shape of the vessels was close to that of an egg with a slightly pointed bottom. The rim is hardly identifiable. Besides traces of their manufacture restricted mainly to the upper part, the vessels had ornaments formed by round impressions of a narrow comb or some other stamp.

The developed Neolithic (between the sixth and the mid-fifth millennia BP) is represented by the sites of the Nizhne-Berezovo culture in the west of the trans-Baikal area and of the Budulan culture in the east. On the whole, it shows continuity with the preceding stage.

The developed Neolithic witnessed the blossoming of stoneworking techniques and of the blade industry. The most typical feature of the camps and settlements of the developed Neolithic in the trans-Baikal area is a large number of prismatic end cores used for striking blades. These blades and tools made on blades comprise a considerable part of the finds. The most typical tools were blades to be hafted to make a composite implement, burins of all types made on blades, end-scrapers, awls and saws. The tradition of adze- and racloir-like implements continued.

New cultural elements appeared at that time. What is most significant is the appearance of polished stone artefacts: axes and adzes, ornaments. Many sites yielded pestles, burnishers, mortars, rectangular and oval slabs used for grinding grain, oval discs with biconical holes in the centre which served as weights for digging-sticks, and stone and bone hoes.

Bone objects were made for diverse purposes: needles and awls, ornamental stamps, hafts for knives and daggers, harpoons and arrowheads. Bone and shell ornaments, pendants made from wild boar and maral teeth, rings and beads comprise a separate group.

The final stage of the trans-Baikal Neolithic (the Amagolon culture, late fifth millennium BP) saw the flowering of the tendencies apparent at the preceding stage. The number of objects made on blades sharply decreased, ceding their place to implements made on flakes: microscrapers, awls with beaked points, bifacially worked arrowheads with asymmetric and symmetric barbs, a straight base and a stem. Rectangular blunted blades and almond-shaped and nearly triangular knives retouched on the two sides were novel features. Though scarce, bone and shell artefacts are especially impressive. They are mostly associated with burials: blunted knives and daggers, harpoons, needle cases, pendants made from maral and wild boar teeth, hemispherical shell buttons and mother-of-pearl beads.

The economy of the Neolithic trans-Baikal tribes underwent considerable changes due to the introduction of cultivation and stock-breeding. In the earlier Neolithic, the tribes engaged in hunting and food gathering were, naturally, nomads. They hunted roe-deer, horse, onager, Mongolian gazelle, bison, deer and elk. The developed Neolithic brought with it finds of agricultural implements: hoes, weights for digging-sticks, pestles, mortars, grain grinders. Among the faunal remains there were canine bones and also bones of pigs, sheep, horses and cattle. Judging by pollen analysis, the climate in the Late Neolithic tended to aridity. Progress in agriculture and its enhanced economic significance are evidenced by a greater number of agricultural implements among the finds. Cattle-breeding advanced as well, though hunting and fishing retained some importance in the Late Neolithic economy.

Among the sites dated to the developed and Late Neolithic there are burial grounds where the dead were placed in stone boxes in a contracted or sitting position. The burials yielded vessels, ornaments, tools and weapons.

Yakutia

In Yakutia the Early Neolithic is represented by the Syalakh culture (Mochanov, 1978). Its sites are distributed over a vast territory along the Lena, Aldan and Vilyui, and beyond the Arctic circle. The culture spans the sixth millennium BP.

The Early Neolithic stone industry of Yakutia was mainly made on blades, with prismatic cores predominating. End-scrapers, scrapers on flakes, some of which were complete with small lug-shaped protuberances at the edge, unifacially worked racloirs and arrowheads on blades with triangular sections were also represented. The final stage is marked by leaf-shaped arrowheads with two trimmed sides, some of them with a tang at the base. Chopping-tools were present in great variety: chisel-shaped rectangular polished adzes and bifacially worked axes. Burins of different shapes were widely used: side, angle burins on retouched truncations, median and multifaceted ones.

People widely used bone unifacially worked harpoons with flat mounts and several barbs; some of them had holes for lines in their bases. Bone spearheads with lengthwise grooves for backed blades, as well as awls, points and needles were also found.

Vessels of the Syalakh culture were egg-shaped, with twining impressions on their external faces which came from the baskets in which the vessels were made. Rows of pierced round holes immediately above the rim served as decorations.

The Belkachi culture, genetically connected with the Syalakh culture, represents the Middle Neolithic in Yakutia (early fifth to early fourth millennium BP). The stone industry continued to be made on blades (65 per cent of all tools). At the same time a tendency towards a greater number of tools made on flakes also became prominent. The Belkachi culture is marked by backed blades, awls on blades, blades with bevelled sides, end-scrapers on narrow blades, angle- and side-scrapers on blades, burins with core-like handles, chisel-like implements on flakes, end-scrapers, pebble net weights, polished bone needles, awls and hafts.

The Belkachi vessels were egg-shaped with rounded bases and straight rims, under which a row of pierced holes was made. The form and ornamentation bring them close to the Syalakh vessels. Indented stamped decorations on the rims combined with impressions of twisted cord on the vessel's body were a novel feature in pottery decoration.

The Neolithic life-style in Yakutia was dictated by the prevailing economy. Archaeologists found no permanent dwellings of the dug-out type. People lived in *chums* (semi-permanent tents), sometimes staying for a long time at a single place or regularly returning to the same place, which accounts for the rich cultural layers. This relatively settled way of life depended upon hunting and fishing.

Rock drawings and burials provide thought-provoking information on the world outlook of the Neolithic population. The Early Neolithic Uolba burial ground contained two burials: one of a grown-up and the other of a child. The bodies were placed in communal graves on their backs and were oriented towards the north-east. All of them were covered with red ochre which, according to the ancient people, symbolized life.

At a later stage the dead were also buried in communal graves, up to five dead in one grave. The burials had no surface or internal structures. The dead were placed on their backs, their hands placed on the lower part of the abdomen. In a number of burials a child skeleton was found between the feet of two grown-ups. Grave furnitures consisted of tools, bows, arrows, pottery, in short objects indispensable for life in the other world.

In Yakutia, Neolithic rock drawings were found in the Olekma and Aldan basins. Rocks along the Olekma near the mouth of the Krestyakh river carry elk images and anthromoporphic figures. The elks are executed in light-red ochre. The ancient painter managed to achieve a realistic representation of the animals. The anthropomorphic figures are elongated and have horns, lowered hands, feet planted apart and a phallus. The Neolithic drawings on the Aldan mainly represent realistically depicted elks and deers with emphasis on the strength of the animals.

Kamchatka

The Neolithic of Kamchatka and the Chukotka peninsular shares many features with Yakutia. Materials found at Ushkovskaya Lake where two archaeological cultures have been identified form the foundation for the periodization of the Neolithic culture of the north-east of Asia (Dikov, 1974).

He relates the first Ushkovskaya culture, characterized by all kinds of prismatic and conical cores, to the Early Neolithic. A considerable number of tools were made on blades, including side- and median scrapers, backed blades, knives and other objects. Scrapers became more numerous and diversified while arrowheads were made in two types, tanged or leaf-shaped. It was an aceramic culture existing within the sixth to the fifth millennium BP.

The second Ushkovskaya culture is closely associated with the first in types of tools and techniques of manufacture.

The former Soviet Far East

The south of the former Soviet Far East exhibits a distinctive Neolithic development with three specific regions – the middle Amur, the lower Amur and the Maritime area – each of them marked by original Neolithic features.

The middle Amur

The middle Amur was the home of three Neolithic cultures – the Novopetrovka, the Gromatukha and the Osinovoe Ozero cultures.

The Novopetrovka culture's stone industry is a distinctive and integral cultural entity (Derevyanko, 1970). For the most part the stone implements were made on blades: arrowheads, lances, scrapers, burins and knives (Fig. 121). Stoneworking implements such as striking and flaking implements and small anvils were also discovered. Chopping tools are represented by adzes with rectangular sections and small hoes used, probably, for digging out dwellings. The settlement also yielded a large number of stone weights. Flat-bottomed vessels were ornamented with applied rollers.

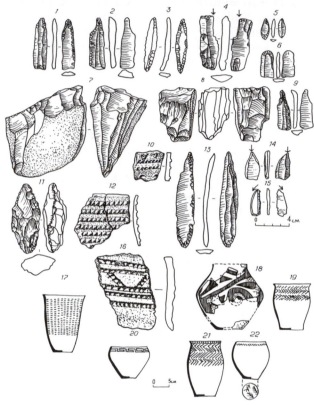

Figure 121 Novopetrovka Neolithic culture (Russian Federation): 1, 3, 5, arrowheads; 2, 9, beaked scrapers; 4, 14, 15, burins; 6, end-scraper; 7, 8, cores; 10, 12, 16, pottery sherds; 13, knife; 11, retouching implement. Maritime area: 17–22, Neolithic ceramic vessels.

Hunting and fishing dictated a settled way of life. The Novopetrovka tribes lived in rectangular dug-outs with rounded corners. The opening through which the smoke escaped served as the entrance. The culture, dated between the eighth and seventh millennia BP, is one of the earliest in the Far East.

The Gromatukha culture (seventh to sixth millennium BP) provided a considerably greater number of bifacially worked tools. The cores from which blades were struck are wedge-shaped, nearly prismatic and prismatic. Archaeologists have found large quantities of nodules that were used for flaking. Large pebble-tools predominated; they were adze- or chisel-like instruments with one side carefully chipped and re-touched along the edge while the other was left untouched.

The second group of stone artefacts comprised knives and spearheads with careful bifacial working and retouch along the edges. Spear- and lanceheads, between 4 and 15 cm long, had leaf shapes with somewhat elongated mounts. The blades also served to manufacture willow-leaf arrowheads, awls, backed blades for knives, end-scrapers and burins. A considerable portion of the stone tools is comprised of composite implements: knives-burins, scrapers-awls, scrapers-burins.

Though scarce, the pottery from the Gromatukha culture sites exhibits a variety of decorations, two patterns being the most popular ones: a design made by a beetle wrapped in grass or in a piece of rough textile, and a design consisting of lozenge, rectangular and rounded pits arranged in belts. A dotted comb ornament produced with the help of a cogwheel, applied rollers, and all kinds of line combinations can also be observed.

The Osinovoe Ozero culture relates to the developed Neolithic (late sixth to mid-fifth millennium BP). The stone industry is not varied or numerous; there are no cores of identifiable shapes, their place being taken by flint and chalcedony nodules bearing traces of random flaking unaccompanied by additional shaping. Flakes were used to manufacture arrowheads, backed blades, scrapers and awls.

Stoneworking further improved among the Osinoe Ozero population. All implements found on the sites had fine bifacial working. By that time, blades and implements made of them disappear from the middle Amur Neolithic. Arrowheads, knives and other objects were worked bifacially. Also found were agricultural implements such as pestles, mortars, grain grinders and weights for digging-sticks. It was a settled population with people living in dug-out huts.

The lower Amur

On the lower Amur, archaeologists have identified three cultures, the Malyshevo, the Kondon and the Voznesenska (Okladnikov and Derevyanko, 1973).

The Malyshevo culture is the earliest among them (the seventh to the mid-sixth millennium BP), and is marked by the earliest methods of stoneworking: nearly prismatic and prismatic cores are found, wedge-shaped cores being rare, as well as arrowheads and other implements made on blades. Bifacial working received a fresh impetus, backed blades, knives, scrapers and racloirs being manufactured from blanks. The settlements of this type yielded an appreciable amount of convex axe-adzes with oval sections. Most probably, they were used for erecting dwellings and constructing other things such as fish traps and other fishing devices and, perhaps, for making dug-out boats.

Two types of pottery relate to this period. The first embraces well-profiled vessels lavishly ornamented with stamped designs of inscribed triangles. Some of the vessels carry imprints made by a beetle covered with cord. Several vessels were painted red. The second type includes poorly profiled vessels, often of a truncated conical shape. The main ornamental design was of horizontal belts of comb stamp. The radiocarbon date for the lower level of the multilayer settlement at the village of Voznesenska is around 5,200 years ago.

The Kondon culture is genetically connected with the preceding one. Excavations revealed willow-leaf arrowheads and artefacts on blades and prismatic cores. However, the number of implements on blades is insignificant compared with that of bifacially worked tools. Arrowheads, backed blades, scrapers and other similar objects were manufactured from blades and finely retouched.

This stage is marked by diversified ceramics. Most interesting among them are situla-shaped, thick-walled vessels with wide rims embellished with combinations of spiral and twining designs. Most frequently the Amur twining pattern

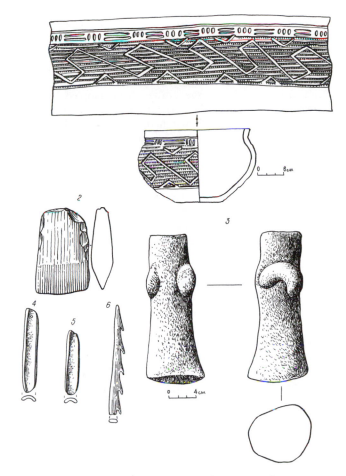

Figure 122 Kondon culture: 1, vessel with ornamental development; 2, adze; 4–5, spoon bait. Voznesenska culture: 3, pestle; 6, harpoon.

was superimposed on a net background. Vessels dated to this stage often carried meanders (Fig. 122). The date for the Neolithic Kondon settlement is around 4,500 years ago. On the whole, this culture in all probability relates to the period from the late sixth to the first half of the fifth millennium BP.

A highly individual culture, the Voznesenska, made its appearance in the final stage of the Neolithic in the lower Amur (mid-fifth to late fifth millennium BP). It is marked by the total absence of blade techniques, its place being taken by bifacial retouch. Arrowheads, backed blades, scrapers, racloirs, knives and other tools were manufactured from blanks and carefully retouched on both sides.

The technique of polishing stone became widespread at this stage of the lower Amur Neolithic. Settlements of the later Neolithic abundantly yield not only polished stone adzes but also arrowheads and knives, to which daggers were added in the concluding stage.

Vessels of the final stage of the Neolithic are of great interest to the archaeologist. For the most part they had a poor profile and were lavishly decorated with rocker patterns or net stamp. One can identify vessels designed, most likely, for rituals. Their walls were carefully burnished and painted red. Prior to firing the raw clay was covered with varied designs including facial masks (Plate 68). They closely resemble the faces found in the lower Amur petroglyphs. It was the period when a large ethnical centre took shape in the lower Amur, which exerted a great influence on the cultures in the neighbouring territories. At the end of the fifth millennium BP some of the lower Amur tribes advanced along the Amur, as far as its upper reaches.

In this way the lower Amur tribes at the final stage of the Neolithic penetrated the lower and middle reaches of the Ussuri river and the middle Amur. It is interesting to note that precisely at that time agricultural implements and, most likely, cultivation appeared on the lower Amur. The lower Amur tribes, the Stone Age ichthyophagi, adopted the new type of economy from the agricultural tribes of the middle Amur and the Ussuri and switched to cultivating the land.

With the exception of the Gromatukha tribes, the Neolithic population of the Amur basin lived in large settlements made up of semi-subterranean houses. Excavations on the lower and middle Amur have proved that the dwellings of all the Neolithic tribes in that territory were very much alike, being semi-subterranean homes entered through the smoke opening.

The settled way of life of the tribes who inhabited the lower and middle Amur in the Early and developed Neolithic was based on fishing. Large and small tributaries of the Amur are extremely rich in fish and it is not surprising that the spoon-bait was invented in these parts. Economically most important was salmon spawning.

The highly individual and vivid art of the Amur tribes is evident not only from pottery ornamentation, extremely varied and rich as it is, but also in petroglyphs. Today we are aware of several Stone Age 'picture galleries', the most interesting among them being the petroglyphs at the Nanai village of Sakachi-Alyan, on the banks of the Kie, Ussuri and in other places. The most numerous works are drawings found on individual stones along the Amur above the Sakachi-Alyan village, 80 km from Khabarovsk (Fig. 123).

Anthropomorphic facial masks hold the central place among hundreds of the earliest drawings. There are also images of birds, animals, snakes and hunting scenes. Snakes, which are represented in combinations with other drawings, form part of the combined anthropomorphic masks.

All the masks are treated in a more or less similar manner: they are oval and have a halo of short lines pointing in all directions. A head-dress is represented by several short lines. The faces are depicted in a particular way: on the forehead there are transversal lines, or often double or single arcs. Eyes received an identical treatment: they are drawn with small circles; mouths are sometimes also shown as an oval or a circle. The facial masks found on vessels differ somewhat from those on the petroglyphs but, combined, they are nevertheless an integral whole and form part of the ancient world outlook of their executors.

Boats held a special place among the drawings. In Sakachi-Alyan the boat formed part of a vast composition cut on a large boulder. Its centre is taken by a facial mask, while a spiral, most probably depicting a snake, is placed above it. Arched boats with people in them are seen on the flanks. An expressive series of boat drawings are found at the village of Sheremetyevo on the Ussuri river.

The earliest Amur art is highly ornamented, being subordinated to the play of curves and endless spirals. The petroglyphs are static: this is true not only of facial masks but also of the deer.

In contrast, in the petroglyphs of the Angara and Lena the elks are dynamic: they walk one after another, run or gallop on their long legs. Sometimes they bellow with stretched necks as if stricken by pain or passion. The elks from the Amur petroglyphs are absolutely static. An analysis of the Amur drawings provides a fuller picture of the social life in the region and their authors' psychology.

What distinguishes the Amur petroglyphs from other rock art of the same kind are the anthropomorphic facial masks,

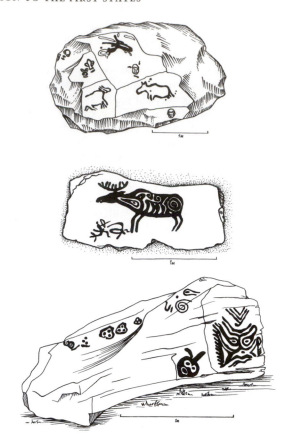

Figure 123 Petroglyphs, Sakachi-Alyan, Amur basin (Russian Federation).

which, in all probablility, are representations of masks widely used by many ancient peoples to imitate man's reincarnation as a spirit and were indispensable for the performance of rites and other religious acts. The masks were important in the social life of prehistoric communities as well. Suffice it to recall the place they held in the activities of secret male unions as a means of intimidation and maintenance of the power of their heads.

The Maritime area

The Maritime Neolithic tribes exhibit many common features with the lower Amur Neolithic. In that region, too, from the Early Neolithic, people led a settled life in large semi-subterranean dwellings. Excavations of the settlements of the Rudnaya culture provide ample information on the life-style of its inhabitants. Coil-built pottery with flat, narrow and sometimes conical bases and ornamental belts of twined rolls along the rims was a most typical feature of the culture.

The Rudnaya population made large stone implements on pebbles using, in some cases, fine pressure-flaking and polishing them first on rough and then on fine-grained sandstone plates. Smaller objects from volcanic tuff and siliceous schist were manufactured by amazingly precise pressure-flaking. Polished plano-convex adzes were accompanied by bifacially worked knives and heads whose shapes resembled the earliest ones from the Baikal area. The stone industry included scrapers and carefully retouched elongated rectangular backed blades which were hafted to wooden or bone knives and daggers.

The earliest Rudnaya settlement yielded art objects: a schematically presented flint bird made by pressure-flaking and a chalcedony human figure. The Rudnaya culture spans the period between the late seventh and mid-sixth millennia BP. It was replaced by the Zaisanovka culture, the sites of which are among the best studied in the south of the Maritime area. Its population also lived in semi-subterranean dwellings, each settlement comprising from ten to twenty such houses. The culture is marked by schist tools, smaller obsidian implements and pottery ornamented with parallel rocker patterns made either by comb stamps or by incision. Clay figurines of man, turtle and other animals are of particular interest. The stone industry comprises chopping tools, arrowheads, knives, scrapers, racloirs and backed blades.

The Kirovskoe culture emerged in the mid-fifth millennium BP. It had a lot of features in common with its predecessor, the Zaisanovka culture. Archaeologists have found chopping-tools, arrowheads, knives and scrapers, but also a high percentage of polished stone implements: arrowheads, knives and spears. Vessels were ornamented with vertical rocker designs, spirals and meanders and sometimes painted red. Clay spindle whorls were found in the settlements.

The Early Neolithic tribes of the Maritime area were hunters, fishers and food gatherers. Gathering sea-products (molluscs, seaweeds, trepangs and crabs) was important. The developed and later Neolithic exhibited traces of cultivation of the land.

Excavations offer a more or less complete picture of the tribes' social order. Archaeologists have managed to identify dwellings in the settlement at the mouth of the Rudnaya river where people were engaged in household activities; this is borne out by objects of everyday use found there and also by storage pits, cooking stoves and so on. A special construction much larger than the common dwellings was discovered in the settlement's centre. Its organization resembles the so-called men's houses, or houses for meetings, which were well studied among North Asian and North American peoples by ethnographers in the seventeenth to the nineteenth centuries.

CONCLUSION

Our brief survey of the Neolithic development in central and northern Asia can be concluded with an observation that this vast territory was, for many millennia, home to many original cultures. Thus, in the Early Neolithic, Mongolian tribes frequently changed their places of habitation: this was dictated by the way they lived and by their economy. They switched to a settled life-style in the later period, and at the turn of the Early Metal Age a specific nomadic way of life appeared among them, brought into existence by the progress of cattle-breeding. This nomadic life-style has survived without noticeable changes up to our own day.

Northern Asia has likewise produced many original features in the material and non-material culture. Throughout the Neolithic, people remained mainly hunters and fishers and roamed large territories. But in places where fishing provided them with a considerable amount of food (in the lower reaches of the Ob or along the Pacific coast) Neolithic tribes adopted a settled life. The developed Neolithic witnessed the transition to a food-producing economy in some regions of central and northern Asia.

Highly individual and vivid art is a feature shared by all the Neolithic tribes of the region, reflected in pottery and bone ornamentation and, particularly, in petroglyphs.

Neolithic studies of this vast region have just begun and many new and unexpected things will undoubtedly be discovered.

BIBLIOGRAPHY

BERKELEY, C. P.; NELSON, N. C. 1926. Geology and Prehistoric Archaeology of the Gobi Desert. *Am. Mus. Novit.* (New York), Vol. 222, pp. 3–18.

CHERNETSOV, V. N. 1953. *Drevnjaja istorija Niznego Priob'ja* [The Early History of the Low Ob Basin]. Moscow. pp. 25–8.

DEREVYANKO, A. P. 1970. *Novopetrovskaja kul'tura Srednego Amura* [The Novopetrovka Culture in the Middle Amur]. Novosibirsk.

DEREVYANKO, A. P.; OKLADNIKOV, A. P. 1969. Drevnie kul'tury voctočnyh rajonov Mongolii [The Ancient Cultures of Eastern Mongolia]. *Sov. arheol.*, Vol. 4, pp. 141–51.

DIKOV, N. N. 1974. *Drevnie kul'tury Severo-Vostoka Azii* [The Ancient Cultures of North-Eastern Asia]. Moscow.

DORZH, D. 1971. *Neolit Vostočnoj Mongolii* [The Neolithic of Eastern Mongolia]. Ulan Bator.

DORZH, D.; DEREVYANKO, A. P. 1970. Novoe v izučenii neolita vostočnoj Mongolii [New Facts on the Neolithic of Eastern Mongolia]. *Vest. (Bull.) Mongol. Acad. Sci.* (Ulan Bator), pp. 43–56.

KYZLASOV, L. P. 1982. *Drevnjaja Tuva* (Ancient Tuva). Moscow.

MARINGER, I. 1950. *Contribution to the Prehistory of Mongolia*. Stockholm.

MOCHANOV, Y. A. 1978. *Drevnejšie ětapy zaselenija čelovekom Severo-Vostočnoj Azii* [The Earliest Stages of the Settlement of North-East Asia]. Novosibirsk.

MOLODIN, V. I. 1977. *Ěpoha neolita i bronzy lesostepnogo Ob-Irtyš'ja* [The Neolithic and the Bronze Age of the Forest and Steppe Belt of the Ob and Irtysh Basins]. Novosibirsk.

NOVGOROSOVA, E. A. 1984. *Petroglify Mongolii* [Petroglyphs of Mongolia]. Moscow.

OKLADNIKOV, A. P. 1950. *Neolit i bronzovyj vek Pribajkalja* [The Neolithic and the Bronze Age of the Baikal Region]. Moscow/Leningrad. (Mater. issled. arheol. SSSR, 18.)

—— 1965. *Petroglify Angary* [The Petroglyphs of the Angara]. Moscow/Leningrad.

—— (ed.) 1968. *Istorija Sibiri. I. Drevnjaja Sibir'* [History of Siberia. I. Siberia in Ancient Times]. Leningrad.

OKLADNIKOV, A. P.; DEREVYANKO, A. P. 1970. Tamcag-Bulak - neolitičeskaja kul'tura Vostočnoj Mongolii [Tamtsag-Bulak, a Neolithic Culture of Eastern Mongolia]. *Mater. istor. filol. Cent. Azii* (Ulan-Ude), Vol. 5, pp. 3–20.

—— 1973. *Daljokoe prošloe Primor'ja i Priamur'ja* [The Distant Past of the Maritime and Amur Area]. Vladivostok.

OKLADNIKOV, A. P.; KIRILLOV, I. I. 1980. *Jugo-Vostočnoe Zabajkal'e v epohu kamnja i rannej bronzy* [The South-Eastern Trans-Baikal Region in the Stone and Bronze Age]. Novosibirsk.

OKLADNIKOV, A. P.; MARTYNOV, A. I. 1972. *Sokroviš̌a Tomskoj pisanicy* [Treasures of the Tomsk Petroglyphs]. Moscow.

45

SOUTH-EAST ASIA AND KOREA

from the beginnings of food production to the first states

Wilhelm G. Solheim, II

The area included in South-East Asia as a cultural region does not match what is now considered to be South-East Asia, and its boundaries have changed considerably through time. The South-East Asian cultural area would include Myanmar (formerly Burma), Laos, Thailand, Cambodia, Vietnam, west Malaysia, portions of Assam and Bangladesh, and south China, from the northern boundary of the Changjiang (Yangtze) river drainage to the south, as mainland South-East Asia, and the Andaman and Nicobar islands, Indonesia, Sarawak and Sabah of east Malaysia, Brunei, the Philippines and Taiwan as island South-East Asia (Map 54).

The amount and quality of archaeological research vary greatly from country to country and region to region.

Prehistoric archaeology was relatively little researched in South-East Asia until 1950. Myanmar, Laos, Cambodia, and the Andaman and Nicobar islands have had very little work done on the prehistoric period. Considerable research was carried out in portions of Vietnam, Indonesia and west Malaysia before the Second World War but by present-day standards the quality is low. For the last fifteen years both the quality and quantity of research have been improving rapidly in Thailand, Indonesia, Vietnam and the Philippines, but little of this has been published, except in Thailand and the Philippines, in English or French. There has been relatively little research done in Brunei and Sabah, while more has been done in Sarawak.

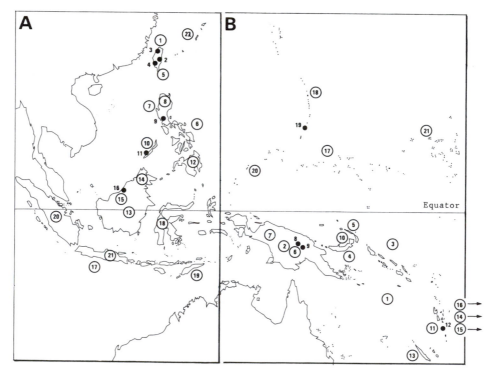

Map 54 Island South-East Asia, Melanesia and Micronesia, with location of geographic names mentioned in the text. Encircled numbers: countries, regions or islands. Non-encircled numbers: towns or archaeological sites. A – Island South-East Asia: 1, Taiwan; 2, Changpinian cave sites; 3, Tapenkeng; 4, Fengpitou; 5, O-Luan-Pi Park; 6, Philippines; 7, Luzon; 8, Cagayan valley; 9, Manila; 10, Palawan; 11, Tabon cave site; 12, Mindanao; 13, Borneo; 14, Sabah; 15, Sarawak; 16, Niah caves; 17, Indonesia; 18, Sulawesi; 19, Timor; 20, Sumatra; 21, Java; 22, Ryukyus. B – Melanesia and Micronesia: 1, Melanesia 2, New Guinea; 3, Island Melanesia; 4, New Britain; 5, New Ireland; 6, Papua New Guinea; 7, Irian Jaya; 8, Wanlek; 9, Kuk Swamp; 10, Bismark archipelago; 11, New Hebrides; 12, Mangassi; 13, New Caledonia; 14, Fiji; 15, Tonga; 16, Samoa; 17, Micronesia; 18, Marianas; 19, Guam; 20, Palau; 21, Bikini Atoll.

FOOD PRODUCTION

The beginning of food production

Controversy (where there is not a total lack of data) surrounds the beginnings of food production throughout this area. The term 'Neolithic' has been used to refer to the practice of grinding and polishing stone tools and the manufacture and use of pottery. Whether any form of food production was associated with these artefacts was not in question. In order to have some consistency with the coverage of other regions of the world, we cover here the period from the beginning of ground or polished stone tools and the manufacture of pottery.

Several archaeologists specializing in the study of South-East Asia have argued that the traditional sequences of stages named and used for Europe, Africa and western Asia do not fit this area (Solheim, 1969). What appears to be a different evolution of food production from that further west presents one of the difficulties in using those traditional stages.

The word 'agriculture' combines two Latin words, *ager* (field) and *cultura* (cultivation). Ordinarily agriculture refers to the growing of domesticated plants in fields, with the plants germinating directly from seeds which are distributed in the fields in large numbers (hundreds and thousands). This kind of farming has only become common in South-East Asia during the last twenty-five to thirty-five years. In South-East Asia horticulture was the common method of farming – from *hortus* (garden) and *cultura* (cultivation). Seeds, when planted directly in the ground, were planted two to four or five seeds at a time in a prepared hole. Fruit and nut trees were possible early domesticates, or at least were probably cared for. Tubers were not planted as seed. In general plants were handled singly and given individual attention, as in a garden. Wet rice was started from seeds in a very small field and then transplanted, two or three plants at a time, by hand into a larger field. The ecological conditions in the tropics were very different from those in the temperate zones, presenting different problems and requiring a different line of development for the organization of both plant and animal food production.

Plant food production

Domestication of plants

Domestication of plants used to be thought a necessity for the growing of plants for food. Archaeologists tended to think of domestication as something that happened rapidly. Communication between archaeologists and botanists led the archaeologists to the realization that domestication was a process, not an event, and that this process took many years. We have also come to realize from ethnographic sources that wild plants can be planted or tended to produce food and that wild or domesticated plants can be planted and then left without care while the planters move elsewhere, to return when the plants are ready for harvesting. If the plants have prospered they provide an extra supply of food for the taking and if they did not then their failure presents no great hardship.

Field agriculture

Two types of fields are used in South-East Asia today – wet and dry. The wet fields, under water for only part of a year, have raised boundaries to hold in the water and may receive their water from natural rainfall or irrigation. While they hold water they are used to grow rice and when dry may be used for some other crop. The dry fields are used for slash-and-burn – now commonly called swidden – agriculture on hill and mountainside. As commercialized agriculture becomes more widespread today, dry fields on the flat are becoming common. The use of slopes for wet and dry agriculture goes well back into prehistory. No such fields have been excavated, and it has been controversial whether wet or dry cultivation came first. Genetic research on rice indicates that dry rices are biologically the most advanced and thus evolved later than wet rice (T. Chang, 1984–5).

The dry fields on slopes were planted with many different crops mixed together and these crops were harvested at different times. The dry field ecosystem was much like the natural tropical forest that surrounded it, with a great variety of species. The major problem in identifying any such fields archaeologically is that they are carved from the forest, burned, planted and, unlike in temperate areas (as in Europe), used for only one or two years, then abandoned to return to forest. This is a gross over-simplification of swidden agriculture. This system of rotating field agriculture in tropical areas has been the subject of many articles (see, for instance, Conklin, 1957; Freeman, 1955; Harris, 1972a; Spencer, 1966).

The plants

Botanists and geographers have long felt that vegetative planting preceded the planting of seeds. For South-East Asia this would mean tubers were planted before rice or millet. The two major South-East Asian tubers are taro and yams. We modify Harris (1972b) and follow his reasoning on the sequence of development proposed here: first tubers, tree fruits and nuts, then the addition of rice as a wet crop and millet as a dry crop, followed by swiddening combining millet, tuber and tree crops, dry rice developing and being added to swiddening. These developments did not all happen in this order in any one area. The two major yams (the greater and the lesser) originated somewhere in mainland South-East Asia and northern mainland South-East Asia, while taro's origin was somewhere in South-East Asia as a whole. It has been said that yam domestication in South-East Asia was late (post-fourth millennium BP: Alexander and Coursey, 1969, pp. 415–16). More recent data have changed this belief.

The major millets important in South-East Asia supposedly originated in northern China (Harris, 1972b, p. 190). The wild ancestor of rice is hypothesized to have developed at the south-eastern foot of the Himalayas in Assam and western Yunnan and spread in its wild forms eastward through northern Myanmar, Thailand, Laos, Vietnam and south China, well south of the Changjiang (Yangtze), to the south China coast. Domestication then took place somewhere in this area. Chang T. (1984–5) states that the wet rice grown in Taiwan and northern Luzon terraces are *Javonica* varieties which developed in Java and Bali out of *Indica* varieties from the Assam area. Another early domesticate was sugarcane probably in New Guinea (Yen, 1984, p. 319).

From an ecological point of view swidden cultivation has a greater tendency to expand than vegeculture. The latter produces little protein for humans and so needs animal proteins and fats for a balanced diet, giving reason for a continuation of hunting and fishing and for living in ecotone situations where these sources of protein are optimal. Seed cultivation, not being so dependent on animal protein, can expand into areas where wild animals and fish are less abudant. Thus seed cultivation would expand more widely (Harris, 1972b, p. 188).

There is no direct archaeological evidence for this proposed sequence of plant food development.

> But pollen collections from Hoabinhian cultural deposits in Viet Nam as well as in Thailand show mainly evidence of tubers, and no *Oryza sativa* (rice). Moreover, the limestone mountains, hills, and mounds of the Hoabinhian environment were very favourable for growing tubers. In the highlands around Vietnamese Hoabinhian sites at present one can find several wild legumes and tubers as beans, *Dioscorea alata, D. persimilis* (yams), taro, etc.
>
> (Chinh, 1984, p. 171)

We have no idea when rice cultivation began in Vietnam, but its beginning could be associated with the rapid development of the shouldered adze as a hoe around 5,500 years ago. From linguistic studies Duong (1982) has proposed that most of the words in Vietnamese connected with rice cultivation came from the Thai languages. Different Thai-speaking peoples were probably scattered through northernmost Vietnam, Laos and adjacent south China at this time, well within the area proposed by the rice specialists as the original area for the domestication of rice.

Animal food production

We can say even less about food production from animals than about that from plants. Until the last twenty years there was no attempt to examine the animal bones recovered in excavation to see if they were from domesticated animals or to determine the sex, age and number of the animals represented. Only in Thailand has there been a start in this analysis.

Ethnographic data can again be useful. Until recently in many areas distant from urbanized localities boar pigs were not kept for breeding. Wild boars were depended upon to provide this service. The same practice was used with chickens, where wild cocks were not far from the domesticated hens. A major need for roosters in South-East Asia, however, is for cock-fighting. Potential fighting cocks were then and are now bred and well cared for.

The most common kind of domesticated animals kept in South-East Asia have been household animals, that is, dogs, pigs, chickens and ducks; it is hypothesized that these were domesticated here as well (Sauer, 1969, p. 28). Even South-East Asian cattle and water buffalo, which at times gather in small herds in the wild, are owned in such small numbers by individuals or families in South-East Asia that they are like household animals rather than herd animals. Without natural open prairies or grasslands in the tropical and subtropical regions of South-East Asia there was no ecological niche for herd animals. We know from ethnographic data that South-East Asian hunters commonly burn portions of the forest and grasslands shortly before the beginning of the rainy season, so that new grass and young plants of other kinds may furnish rich food sources for wild grazing animals and, by bringing them together, provide easy hunting. When this practice was started – probably well back in the Pleistocene – it provided scattered cleared areas around and in the tropical forest. In these areas wild cattle did best and it was from them that South-East Asian cattle were domesticated (Wharton, 1968), probably well before the earliest dating of domesticated cattle in north-eastern Thailand.

It is hypothesized that the smaller household animals were domesticated through being kept as pets when very young and growing up as part of the family of their human owners (Sauer, 1969, pp. 30–2). Most of the domesticated animals in the non-Buddhist, non-Islamic and non-Christian areas were important for sacrifices on occasions when ceremonies were held in which local spirits and ancestors needed to be contacted and consulted. Before the high religions were brought into the area such ceremonies were universal in South-East Asia, and it has been hypothesized that these animals were important as domesticates so as to have a ready supply for the necessary ceremonies. After the sacrifice and reading the livers or other vital organs for the purposes of divination had taken place, the meat was cooked and offered to the spirits and ancestors. Once they had had their fill of the spirit of the meat, it was divided into portions and presented to those taking part in or attending the ceremony, to eat then or later.

Summary

The boundaries of South-East Asia as a cultural region have varied considerably through time. The initial dates for food production vary by as much as 8,000 years. These beginnings in the northern portion of mainland South-East Asia may well have been in the late Upper Pleistocene. Some cultural groups in South-East Asia continued as hunters, gatherers or both until today but, with very few exceptions, living symbiotically with neighbouring agriculturists or traders. The quality and quantity of the data from which we can reconstruct prehistory vary tremendously.

SOUTH-EAST ASIA, 10,000 TO 5,000 YEARS AGO

Changes in climate and shore-lines

There is much overlap in time between this portion of this chapter and Chapter 27, but as the focus is different we feel it worth while to keep the overlapping portions.

The time span here covered extends from sometime after the end of the Pleistocene to about the end of a 2,000- or 3,000-year period of slightly warmer weather than we have today. Unlike in temperate areas of the world, the temperature and climate of most of South-East Asia during the Pleistocene was not drastically different from what it had been in the Holocene. There may have been as much as 6 °C lower average temperature during the coldest portion of the Pleistocene from that of the Holocene, but the difference of most importance to the ecology of that time was somewhat less rainfall. Since there was a much larger land area, including the Sunda shelf, resulting from the lower sea-level, the winds blew over much more land than at later times and carried less moisture for rain. This is shown by fossils of savannah fauna in some considerable areas of the Sunda shelf, indicating relatively open grasslands instead of tropical forest.

The shore-line of the Sunda shelf would have been much shorter during the late Pleistocene than it became during the Holocene with the break-up of about half of the large landmass into many islands (Map 54). It is likely that during the late Pleistocene varieties of *Homo sapiens* were living along the shore in many areas and gathering shellfish as a major portion of their diet. With the rapidly rising sea-levels of the late Pleistocene the sea-shores of the broad Sunda and Sahul shelves were retreating rapidly, several hundred metres per decade (Chappell and Thom, 1977, p. 283). These rapid changes, whether relatively constant or periodic, must have had major effects on the resident population. As those areas where we assume people were living are now up to 150 m below sea-level, there is no reliable way in which we can locate and excavate the sites and take these people and their culture into account.

Physical anthropological data and interpretation

The Melanesians, the Negritos and the Southern Mongoloids were the major and most distinct physical subdivisions of the human population in South-East Asia at the time of European arrival in the area. The Melanesians were in New Guinea and eastern Indonesia, the few small Negrito groups were in the Andaman islands, in the Malay peninsula and an unknown distance to the north in the limestone mountain extension of the peninsular mountains, and in scattered islands of the Philippines. The Southern Mongoloids, by far the majority, were spread over most of South-East Asia (Jacob, 1967, p. 903; Howells, 1973, pp. 171–9; Glinka, 1981, pp. 90, 106, 108–10; Bulbeck, 1982).

The Negritos

The Negrito is the smallest variety, in number and in size, and the most controversial in its origin. It was considered that the Negritos were the first to arrive in South-East Asia, and that they had a common origin. Now it seems likely that they are recently evolved and have Australo-Melanesian ancestry. No definite Negrito remains have ever been found in Indonesia, nor are they known from any South-East Asian prehistoric site (Jacob, 1967, p. 903; Howells, 1973, pp. 174–6; Glinka, 1981, pp. 99–103; Solheim, 1980a, p. 69). It is likely that small Negrito or Negrito-like groups were living a collecting and hunting life on the edges of the lowland, tropical rain forest, near the coasts and along the rivers in South-East Asia during the period covered here. It is also likely that they were trading rain-forest products with neighbouring agriculturists, where there were such, during the last 1,000 to 2,000 years of this period.

Australo-Melanesians and southern Mongoloids

The most recent hypothesis is that the differentiation into the present observable varieties came about through local evolution from a genetically variable ancestral population. The three earliest *Homo sapiens* remains in South-East Asia are from Tabon cave (Palawan, Philippines), the Great Cave at Niah (Sarawak, east Malaysia) and Wajak (east Java, Indonesia). These are dated to about 40,000 years ago for the earliest (Kennedy, 1977; Solheim, 1977, p. 39, 1983, pp. 43–4). Jacob (1979, pp. 8–9) grouped these remains as 'Wajak Man' (see also Bulbeck, 1982, p. 17), which through local micro-evolution developed into the Malay-Indonesian and Australo-Melanesian peoples.

Dating the start of this development somewhat earlier, Solheim (1980a, pp. 69–70) hypothesized that from a widespread but small population, distributed from Sri Lanka through eastern India to south China and Sunda Land, sharing a common but variable gene pool 50,000 years ago, evolved the Hoabinhian populations and related people of island South-East Asia. From this evolutionary centre the ancestors of the Papuans and Australians moved into their respective areas. Thus, before 50,000 years ago all of these people would have had a common ancestry.

Concerning the Li people on Hainan Island, just east of

northern Vietnam, Zhang and Zhang (1982, p. 71) have said: 'The results of comparison ... revealed that Li most closely affiliated with Han nationalities living in Guangxi, Guangdong, and Fujian, and also closely affiliates with Atayal, Ami and Peipu tribes living in Taiwan Province [the latter three are Austronesian speakers]'. From a genetic survey of blood groups on Hainan, Xu (1982, p. 79) concluded: 'It is supposed from the high M gene frequencies that there may be close racial relations between peoples of South China and South Asia.' On the basis of dental comparisons it has been suggested that northern Mongoloid tooth form (and probably northern Mongoloids) evolved out of southern Mongoloid tooth form (and southern Mongoloids).

Linguistic data

It has become customary in the last decade in South-East Asia and the Pacific to use new methods of linguistic analysis combined with archaeological data to hypothesize origins for and movements of the different language families and their speakers.

Languages from three major language families are spoken in South-East Asia today by ethnic groups native to the region. Burmese was thought to have arrived in northern Myanmar a little over 1,000 years ago. Burmese is a subdivision of Tibeto-Burman, which in turn is considered to be a subdivision of the Sino-Tibetan language family. It is now recognized that Pyu, a major language and culture in central Myanmar before Burmese, is related to Burmese. Pyu culture has been tentatively traced back in Myanmar to some time before 2,000 years ago, but whether it was a locally evolved culture is not known. This leaves Austro-Asiatic and Austronesian (AN) as two language families that probably originated in South-East Asia during the time period covered here.

It was long ago proposed that Austronesian and Austro-Asiatic were the two descendants of one superstock, Austric (Schmidt, 1906). This theory received little support from linguists and the idea was virtually dropped. Recently it has been revived, however, and now there is some supporting evidence (Reid, 1984–5). The Austro-Asiatic languages consisted of Mon and Khmer, Mon spoken in southern Myanmar and probably in much of Thailand, and Khmer in Cambodia, with related languages in west Malaysia spoken by some of the Orang Asli groups, Khasi in north-eastern India and Munda in eastern-central India. The Austronesian languages are spoken in island South-East Asia, Madagascar to the west, Micronesia, Polynesia and portions of island Melanesia and coastal New Guinea, and include a few languages in Vietnam, primarily Cham.

Much more research has been centred on the Austronesian languages than on the Austro-Asiatic. Two different types of studies are of the most interest for reconstructing prehistory, one concerned with the 'genetic' relationship between languages, and the other, through reconstruction of proto-languages, providing evidence on the culture of the people who spoke these protolanguages. Two of the latter type of study have recently been made of Proto-Austronesian (PAN). The people speaking this language lived in a tropical or subtropical area somewhere in South-East Asia around 7,000 years ago.

Pawley and Green had the following to say about this culture:

[They] had a mixed economy, based on agriculture and fishing, but supplemented by hunting and arboriculture.

Cultivated crops included taro, yams, banana, sugar-cane, breadfruit, coconut, the aroids Cytosperma and Alocasia, sago, and (probably) rice. They kept pigs, and probably dogs and chickens, and made pottery. They exploited a maritime environment, gathering shellfish and using a variety of fishing techniques and gear including nets, basket traps, hooks, and Derris poison. They sailed outrigger canoes. Their tools were of stone, wood, and shell; terms for metallurgy are not sufficently widespread to be attributed with any confidence to Proto-Austronesian.

(Pawley and Green, 1975, pp. 35–6)

In another reconstruction, Blust stated:

the broad outlines of AN culture history can be summarized as follows: PAN speakers occupied settled villages which contained both dwelling units ... and some kind of public building.... Dwelling units were evidently raised on posts ... and entered by a (probably notched log) ladder.... The roof (which was, therefore, gabled) contained a ridgepole ... possibly covered by an inverted log or bamboo rain shield ... and was thatched, probably with sago leaf.... A hearth ... was built on the floor (probably in one corner) and one or more storage shelves for pots, firewood etc., above it.... The inhabitants slept using a wooden pillow or headrest.... They possessed the pig ... fowl ... and dog ..., but also hunted ...; made pottery ..., plaited (presumably) mats and baskets ..., but also wove true fabrics on a (probably simple back) loom ..., chewed betel... and evidently had a form of intoxicating drink.... Iron was apparently known ..., though its uses remain unclear. In addition, some form of native script may have been invented, and used on perishable materials....

There is persuasive evidence that PAN speakers possessed a well-developed maritime technology...., cultivated a variety of root and tree crops ..., rice ... and possibly millet.... Cereal crops were hulled by pounding in a wooden mortar.

(Blust, 1976, p. 36)

In his most recent paper on this subject Blust (1984–5) has presented data suggesting that the Austronesian homeland is only marginally tropical. To fit this climate he suggests either Taiwan or the adjacent mainland of China as the Austronesian homeland.

The most popular reconstruction of Austronesian origins and movements proposes that the Austronesian homeland was in Taiwan or south China, and if the latter then the first movement was to Taiwan. Migration would then have been from Taiwan to the Philippines, south through the Philippines and then, around 5,000 years ago, both southeast and south-west from southern Mindanao into Indonesia and the western Pacific (Shutler and Marck, 1975; Blust, 1984–5).

A different reconstruction has been made by Solheim (1975, p. 152) to fit the archaeological data as he interprets it; this is further modified here. It is hypothesized that Austric languages were spoken throughout South-East Asia, including Sunda Land, during the late Pleistocene. With the rising of sea-levels and the conversion of Sunda Land into the islands of today, the eastern third of South-East Asia became separated from the western and northern two-thirds, isolating the speakers in the east from those to the west and north. This isolation led to Pre-Austro-Asian developing on the mainland and Sumatra and Pre-Austronesian developing in Java and the eastern islands. Those people to the west on the mainland and Sumatra would become more land-oriented relative to those on the east, who would become more marine-oriented as their land turned into many islands, often within sight of each other.

For archaeological reasons, it is hypothesized that Pre-Austronesian developed primarily in Mindanao and north-eastern Indonesia (Solheim, 1976a, pp. 36–7; 1976b, p. 138) and was carried north by a developing maritime population through the Philippine islands to Taiwan, and across to south China and then north and south along the coast. Proto-Austronesian developed in the northern Luzon, Taiwan and south China coast area. Austronesian then developed among this maritime people of the northern Philippines, Taiwan and coastal south China, serving at first as a trade language. These people intermarried with coastal people, making a distinct coastal population along the western shore of the South China Sea where safe anchorage and fresh water were available, with words in this trade language from both the southern islands and the northern mainland for plants such as rice. Soon after this development Taiwan became relatively isolated and its Austronesian languages evolved locally with relatively little input from outside. On the other hand, the subregionally developing Austronesian languages maintained contact with each other through the maritime traders and evolved away from each other more slowly. This hypothesis would agree with the first in having the Austronesian languages, and its speakers, moving east and west from Mindanao and north-eastern Indonesia starting around 5,000 years ago, after contact from the central coast of Vietnam was made by these people with Borneo and the southern Philippines. This second hypothesis would also have a trading movement north from the south China coast to southern Korea and Kyushu, Japan.

Archaeological and ethnoarchaeological data

There were two major technocomplexes in South-East Asia by 10,000 years BP, both of them with generalized beginnings well before this date in the same areas where they are found at 10,000 years BP. On the mainland is the Hoabinhian technocomplex, previously considered a long-lasting, primitive culture. Hoabinhian sites have been found in mountainous areas and a few coastal locations from Myanmar (and possibly as far west as Assam) through south China, Laos, Vietnam, Thailand, Cambodia and west Malaysia. The only mainland areas where they have not been found are the southern third of west Malaysia, eastern Cambodia and southern Vietnam. A few coastal Hoabinhian sites have been found in north-eastern Sumatra. The second technocomplex is found in island South-East Asia and the southern half of Sumatra. Both technocomplexes may have been involved in the domestication of plants and animals, but the people were primarily hunters and collectors of a broad spectrum of plants and animals.

The Hoabinhian technocomplex

The first Hoabinhian sites were discovered in northern Vietnam (Colani, 1927, 1929). Soon afterwards, similar sites were recognized and reported in Malaya (Matthews, 1961) and Laos (Fromaget, 1940; Saurin, 1966). Since 1950 Hoabinhian sites have been reported in western Cambodia (Mourer and Mourer, 1970, 1971), Thailand (Heekeren and Knuth, 1967; Gorman, 1969, 1970), Myanmar (Thaw, 1971),

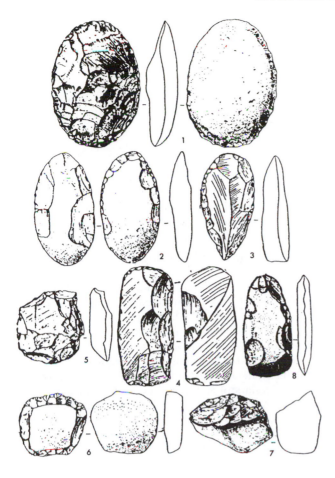

Figure 124 Chief types of Hoabinhian stone tools: 1, Sumatralith axe (Salt cave); 2, Sumatra-type axe, partly chipped on both surfaces (Lang Vanh); 3, pointed oval chopping tool (Salt cave); 4, elongated, pick-like axe (Hang-tung); 5, 'hache courte' (Muong Kham); 6, disc-like scraper with blade all around (Phy-vc); 7, scraper with blade on one side (Salt cave); 8, Bacsonian axe (Lang Cuom). (After Boriskovskii, 1970.)

south China (Aigner, 1981), and recognized in Sumatra (Heekeren, 1972, pp. 85–91; Brandt, 1976). Many more sites have been excavated in northern Vietnam (Boriskovskii, 1970; Chinh, 1979; Solheim, 1980b, pp. 10–11; Tan, 1980, pp. 117–19). There have been four summary reports on the Hoabinhian, three for the area as a whole (Gorman, 1971; Solheim, 1974; Bellwood, 1979, pp. 64–71), and one for Vietnam (Matthews, 1966).

Key traits (Gorman, 1970, p. 82) for the Hoabinhian include (Fig. 124):

1 a generally unifacial flaked tool tradition made primarily on water-rounded pebbles and large flakes detached from these pebbles;
2 core tools (Sumatraliths) made by complete flaking on one side of a pebble and grinding stones also made on rounded pebbles, usually in association with iron oxide;
3 a high incidence of utilized flakes;
4 fairly similar assemblages of food remains including remains of extant shellfish, fish, and small and medium-sized animals;
5 a cultural and ecological orientation to the use of rock shelters generally occurring near freshwater streams in an upland karstic topography (though Hoabinhian shell middens do indicate at least one other ecological orientation);

6 edge-grinding and cord-marked ceramics occurring individually or together, in the upper layers of Hoabinhian deposits.

It was argued that pottery found in the upper layers of a large number of Hoabinhian sites was intrusive and that the users of such crude stone tools could not have known how to make pottery. No contemporary non-Hoabinhian sites are known, so no potential source other than Hoabinhian is known. From the site of Gua Kechil in west Malaysia, Dunn (1964, pp. 100–13, 119–22) demonstrated an evolution of pottery, stratified in association with typical Hoabinhian stone tools. There is little doubt that pottery was independently invented in one or more locations of the Hoabinhian technocomplex.

Hoabinhian pottery is commonly cord-marked, and less commonly has impressions from nets resulting from a paddle wrapped with cord or netting used in the paddle-and-anvil technique of manufacture (Gorman, 1970, pp. 96–7). This suggests that cordage and nets were being used in other ways as well, possibly for fishing and hunting (Solheim, 1969, p. 132).

The primary reason that the Hoabinhian was considered a backward culture was its use of crude, unifacially flaked and seldom retouched stone tools. First hypothesized (Solheim, 1970, p. 153) and then tested for by micro-analysis of edge damage (Gorman, 1970), it appears likely that several of the variety of stone tools were used to manufacture wooden tools and that the development of tools went on in wood rather than stone.

The excavation of Spirit cave in north-western Thailand was the first Hoabinhian excavation conducted to save plant remains (Gorman, 1970, pp. 80, 92) and to test Sauer's hypothesis of early agriculture. A number of different seeds, shells and fruit remains were found derived from types of trees and plants tended or grown today in the area (Gorman, 1970, p. 100; Yen, 1977). No indication of tubers was found. 'The bottle gourd (Lagenaria), the Cucumis, a cucumber type, the Chinese water chestnut (Trapa), and the leguminous beans, however, form a group of food plants suggesting a botanical orientation beyond simple food gathering' (Gorman, 1970, p. 102). Excavation of two more Hoabinhian sites by Gorman led to further plant finds. Examination of this plant material does not advance the case for early horticulture beyond what it was when first published and speculated upon (Yen, 1977, p. 594). Pollen analysis of deposits from Son Vi and Hoabinhian sites in Vietnam indicate a change in vegetative patterns from the preceding Son Vi to the Hoabinhian. From this a period of plant domestication is hypothesized for the Hoabinhian of these sites (Chinh, 1984, pp. 170–1).

A considerable number of radiocarbon dates have come from Hoabinhian sites in South-East Asia. Spirit cave remains the best-dated site with thirteen dates from charcoal that are internally consistent. Pre-pottery dates range from around 11,350 to 8,500 years ago, while dates associated with pottery range from 8,550 to 7,400 years ago (Gorman, 1970, Table 2). Most of the Vietnamese dates are consistent, ranging from 11,350 to 7,600 years ago (Kohl and Quitta, 1978, pp. 389–91; Bayard, 1984, p. 308; Chinh, 1979; Solheim, 1980b, p. 10).

An archaeological culture differing from the Hoabinhian only in its higher percentage of edge-ground stone tools is called the Bacsonian. Some consider the Bacsonian a specialized and late Hoabinhian (Chinh, 1979) while others consider it a separate culture that developed out of the

Hoabinhian. The dating of Bacsonian sites is little different from Hoabinhian sites, with a range of about 10,300 to 7,900 years ago (Kohl and Quitta, 1978, p. 391).

Two charcoal dates from the Hoabinhian of Padah-lin cave in eastern Myanmar are around 7,750 and 6,600 years ago (Thaw, 1971, p. 133). The date for the approximate end of the Hoabinhian as it evolved into the early Malayan Neolithic at Gua Kechil is about 4,800 years ago (Dunn, 1966, p. 351). Laang Spean cave in western Cambodia has a date of around 6,250 years ago associated with pottery (Mourer, 1977, p. 32). There are no dates for the Sumatran sites, but many of them are shell-middens situated along an old shore-line now 10 to 15 kilometres inland (Brandt, 1976, p. 50). This probably means they were deposited during the climatic optimum of higher sea-level (Chappell and Thom, 1977, p. 282), about the time of the site of Da But, a coastal site when occupied around 6,000 years ago (Kohl and Quitta, 1978, p. 392; Jamieson, 1981, p. 190).

The Hoabinhian of Vietnam is considered by the Vietnamese to have developed directly out of the Son Vi culture of the Late Pleistocene and was ancestral to the later cultures of Vietnam (Tan, 1980, pp. 117–20). For the rest of South-East Asia, as for Vietnam before the discovery of Son Vi culture, it has been hypothesized that the Early Hoabinhian started around 42,000 years ago and developed directly out of the earlier Chopper–Chopping-Tool tradition (Solheim, 1969, p. 129; 1970, pp. 149–50). It would appear that all later cultures of mainland South-East Asia developed from a Hoabinhian technocomplex base. While Hoabinhian sites have not been dated later than about 7,500 years ago in Vietnam, there are many that are later in other mainland areas. Banyan valley cave in north-western Thailand has dates ranging from 5,500 to 1,250 years ago (Yen, 1977, p. 591). From trade materials in Late Hoabinhian sites it would appear that the Hoabinhian way of life continued in a symbiotic relationship with fully agricultural peoples well into the first millennium of the Christian era.

The island South-East Asian flake tradition

Two regional variants of the island South-East Asian flake tradition are apparent, so whether this should be considered as one or two technocomplexes is not clear. The variant to the east developed out of a single tradition for the whole area, possibly with outside input.

Four restricted areas in island South-East Asia have reliably dated sequences going back into the Upper Pleistocene. From all of these areas, utilized flakes are the predominant stone tool type. The longest sequence is from the Great Niah cave in Sarawak where it starts at about 40,000 years ago, with artefacts well below the level of this date (T. Harrisson, 1970, p. 40; Solheim, 1958, pp. 84–6). The second sequence is from the Tabon caves, on the west coast of Palawan (Philippines), where Fox (1970, pp. 22–37) described five different flake assemblages extending up to about 9,000 years ago. The third is from eastern Sabah with a sequence dated from 17,000 years ago (Bellwood, 1984, pp. 40–5). The fourth is a sequence for the north coast of eastern Timor (Indonesia), starting at about 14,000 years ago (Glover, 1977, p. 34). There are other sites with predominantly flake-tools either less well dated or without dates but that are thought to be Upper Pleistocene. It is obvious that a flake-tool tradition, with a few core tools similar to the chopper–chopping-tools of the mainland, was widely present during the Upper Pleistocene of island South-East Asia except possibly for Sumatra. Amongst these, blade-like

flakes were present in the central islands of Indonesia. Most of these cultures continued into the Holocene. The same four dated sequences referred to above are also the best dated for the 10,000 to 5,000 years ago period.

There is detailed information for the burials in the Great Cave of Niah (B. Harrisson, 1967, 1968; Brooks et al., 1977; Solheim, 1983, p. 44). The burials were summarized as follows by B. Harrisson:

> The 'mesolithic' period comprises three burial categories: flexed (18), seated (4) and mutilations (17). Material associations consist of stone (choppers, edge-ground pebbles, fire strikers), bone tools and ritual shell (Cyrena). Skeletal material and funerary objects are haematited, especially in flexed burials.
>
> (Harrisson, 1967, p. 188)

Dating for the 'mesolithic' burials goes back to about 11,400 years BP (Brooks et al., 1977, p. 28). It would be reasonable to say that the culture represented here, as indicated by the burials, had a religion that included a belief in an after-life, with ceremony at burial including preparation of the body before burial in a tightly flexed position, the placing of powdered haematite on the body and the possible association of a fire close to the body but not cremating it.

The diet of these people included a variety of large (orang-utan were common) and small land and tree mammals, pig and monkey being the most common, with bats, birds, turtles, amphibians, fish and shellfish from fresh and brackish water. With no local fine-grained stone, the small number of stone tools made in such material indicates either that the people travelled rather widely or that there was trade in this stone. There is no indication of whether the occupation of this cave was a sedentary one, seasonal or occasional. This is a low, swampy area today and during the time of only slightly higher sea-level could have been reached by boat, though it is several kilometres from the sea-shore today.

Life in the Tabon caves of Palawan appears to have been no different in the early Holocene from what it was in the Upper Pleistocene. The flake industry of the late Upper Pleistocene continues and is present in full in the main Tabon cave until after a radiocarbon date of about 9,250 years BP (Fox, 1970, pp. 24–6). The first change is the sudden appearance of a sea-shell midden after the 9,000-year dating and before a 7,000-year dating from Duyong cave (Fox, 1970, p. 54), indicating that the sea-level reached approximately its present level just below the caves some time between 9,000 and 8,000 years ago. The first occupation of another of the Tabon caves had a shell-midden and a flake-tools industry like that of the main Tabon cave except for a few blade tools in the upper levels and prepared cores to make the blades (Fox, 1970, p. 48). The small flake and blade industry in Duyong cave, starting about 7,000 years ago (Fox, 1970, pp. 54–60), is a different tradition from that of Tabon and other earlier caves, with the flakes from the latter caves being held in the hand when used while those from Duyong, and many other later caves, were said to have been hafted (Fox, 1970, pp. 48–50). In the small flake and blade sites there is much less animal bone than in the main Tabon cave flake industry (Fox, 1970, pp. 56–9), so the shellfish, and possibly more plant food, must have formed a major portion of the diet. The two industries continue side by side for some time, and Fox (1970, p. 50) felt that the new tradition was brought into the area by a new people. This small flake and blade tradition has been found in other Philippine areas.

Somewhat later in Duyong cave appeared what Fox (1970, pp. 60–4) called a 'Neolithic' culture. From charcoal recovered in a fire hearth a date of about 5,700 years ago was obtained. From this thin scattered 'Neolithic' level were recovered artefacts made of *Tridacna* shell, shell discs believed to be ear pendants and hearth-like areas. A burial from this level, with a date of around 4,600 years ago, had associated with it a large polished stone adze–axe, four *Tridacna* shell adze–axes, two centrally perforated shell discs (one next to the right ear so they were probably used as ear ornaments as they are today in north-eastern Luzon), a possible perforated shell pendant and six whole *Arca* shells placed near the feet, one having a round hole near its apex and being filled with lime, strongly suggesting the South-East Asian custom of betel chewing. The corpse was flexed and lying on its face (Evangelista, 1963, Pl. Ia). It was a muscular male with a reconstructed stature of 1.79 m, well above that of Negritos (Fox, 1970, pp. 60–3). People of the flake and small flake and blade cultures used these caves for habitation, while the people making the shell and stone adze-axes appeared to have used them for temporary shelter and burial but not for living (Fox, 1970, pp. 62–4).

In eastern Sabah an archaeological culture found in caves follows the earlier flake culture. It is dated from 11,000 to 7,000 years ago and is similar to the earlier flake culture, except that there were no blades and there was an emphasis on pebble-tools not present before. Many of the utilized flakes have an edge gloss from cutting a grass, rattan or bamboo with considerable silica in the stem. Hammerstones and pitted anvils or grinding stones, some coated with haematite, are present. Food remains are much the same, but with the addition of estuarine mangrove bivalves to the freshwater shellfish and to the smaller animals indicated before some larger mammals such as orang-utan, cattle and two species of rhinoceros. Bone tools were very rare in both cultures (Bellwood, 1984, pp. 45–8).

The Sabah sequence fits in with a sequence on the eastern tip of the Minahasa peninsula of Sulawesi and the Talaud Islands to the north-east (Bellwood, 1976). In a shell-mound were found obsidian flakes (no blades), bone tools, animal bones and haematite. The flakes are often high-angled, made by smashing obsidian nodules and selecting the resulting flakes for their natural edges. Bone tools probably served as awls or needles (Bellwood, 1976, pp. 243–54). A rock shelter on one of the Talaud Islands had a preceramic layer from which was recovered a flake and blade industry made on chert. A shell date for this is about 5,000 years BP (Bellwood, 1976, pp. 255–67).

The cave site sequence in eastern Timor shows little change. Interior and coastal sites are much the same. A concave-edge, steep-edge scraper is distinctive. Flakes and rare blades of flint or chert often have traces of edge gloss (Glover, 1971, 1977). The fauna is dominated by several species of extinct giant rats, with fruit bats, snakes, reptiles and, on the coast, fish and shellfish. Plant remains include seeds or fragments of *Celtis*, Job's Tears, betel vine, Polynesian chestnut (*Inocarpus*), Aleurites or candle nut, and bamboo (Glover, 1977, p. 43). These sites date from about 7,300 years ago and continue in use beyond our period (Glover, 1971, pp. 167–8).

There is little information from Taiwan. On the east coast the Changpinian culture was recovered from the Caves of the Eight Immortals. From the latest use of these caves four radiocarbon dates range between about 5,500 and 4,800 years ago. Dates for earlier sites are in the late Upper Pleistocene. The most common tools are utilized flakes with no blades. Core tools are more common in the earlier caves. A number of bone tools were also recovered of types

suggesting that both hunting and fishing were important (Chang, 1969, pp. 134–5).

For the Corded Ware culture there is one date of about 5,500 years ago. Chang suggests a dating of 8,000 to 5,000 years ago for this culture (Chang et al., 1974, p. 49). It has been found near the coast in north-west, south-west and south-east Taiwan. From these sites have been recovered cord-marked pottery, often with incised decoration on the rims and the upper part of shoulders, worked pebbles probably used as net-sinkers, rectangular polished stone adzes and small, triangular slate points. No flakes or blades were found. Chang (Chang et al., 1969, pp. 248–9) considers the people of this culture to have been hunters, fishers and horticulturists and that they came to Taiwan from south-western China, with a probable Hoabinhian origin.

Two published cave sites in the Cagayan valley of Luzon, Philippines, have dates between 12,000 and 5,000 years ago. From one of these sites, out of 273 utilized flakes four were blade-like. 'The edge damage on the tools shows use as scrapers on wood, bamboo and possibly hides; knives for whittling on wood, bamboo, and bone; animal butchering; drills or awls on wood, bone and possibly hides; spokeshaves; and saws on wood, bamboo, and bone' (Thiel, 1980a, p. 44). Probably present in this layer previous to 5,000 years ago were some human bone, pottery, bone points, fired clay earrings and cowrie shells. The site was probably used as shelter by hunters and gatherers while gathering shellfish. The cowrie shells may indicate trade (Thiel, 1980a, pp. 43–7).

The second cave came into use around 5,500 years ago. Stone tools recovered included 'utilized flakes, waste flakes, chips, primary cores, cobble tools and hammerstones' (Ronquillo, 1981, p. 6). No blades were recovered. From the functional analysis it was concluded that a majority of the flakes were used for butchering and a few for woodworking, and that they were probably not hafted. A considerable quantity of bones and teeth of birds, bats, monkeys and pigs was associated with the flakes. Pottery and river shell were also present (Ronquillo, 1981, pp. 10–11, 13).

The presence of purposeful blades in the Cagayan valley is highly questionable. No prepared cores were found.

There are no archaeological sites dated to our period from central Luzon. Many sites with flakes were recorded by Beyer from this area, but none of them included blades (Fox, 1970, p. 59). Numerous edge-ground stone tools were reported as surface finds (Beyer, 1948, pp. 17–19). From a site near Manila utilized flakes were recovered, but most of the common tools were small edge-ground artefacts plus an edge-ground stone axe. Postholes were found, suggesting a dwelling. Numerous seeds were recovered, either carbonized or partially mineralized; they were usually found in hearth areas. Some of these are from possible food or medicinal plants. This site is quite possibly early Holocene (Peterson et al., 1979, pp. 127–34).

Survey and excavation in the central Philippine islands has recovered flakes and blades *in situ* and from surface finds. In Samar the use of flakes has been dated to as far back as about 10,500 years ago (Tuggle and Hutterer, 1972, p. 11). Blade tools made on prepared cores were recovered from two sites, presumably of a later date (Hutterer, 1969, pp. 49–50; Scheans et al., 1970). From a site south of Cebu City blades from stone and oyster shell were reported (Tenazas, 1985, pp. 208–9).

Two sites in the far southern Philippines have produced utilized flakes. From Sanga Sang rock shelter (Spoehr, 1973, pp. 106–11), two radiocarbon dates of about 8,000 and 6,500 years ago came from shell that might have been fossilized and was therefore not useful for dating (Solheim et al., 1979, p. 117). The dates are probably not far wrong however. Utilized flakes were common but no blades were reported. Several, partly ground, shell adzes and other shell artefacts were found, the whole assemblage considered to be similar to that of Duyong cave on Palawan (Spoehr, 1973, pp. 255–66). A plain brown pottery and a rare red-slipped pottery with impressed circles were also recovered, and were possibly as early as the later date (Spoehr, 1973, pp. 184–91). Worked bone was also present.

Even less is known about Kamuanan cave site on Talikod Island in south-eastern Mindanao. Here were found a few small utilized stone flakes and utilized flakes and blades of shell (Solheim et al., 1979, p. 111, plates 28 and 29). Two shell dates from the same sample are dated to about 4,000 years ago, with much midden below the dated shell which was not tested.

Very little archaeological research has been done in Sumatra. The few known non-Hoabinhian lithic sites are from southern Sumatra (Bronson and Asmar, 1975, p. 131; Heekeren, 1972, pp. 137–9), dating to about 9,500 years ago. The primary artefacts are utilized obsidian flakes with a few potsherds from well above the latest date but associated with the same materials as the dated charcoal. Most of the sherds had impressions of a flexible material like straw from a bound paddle, and a few cord-marked sherds were found. Identified fauna included large deer or young bovids, bats, turtle, birds, reptiles, fish, rodents and possibly frogs, and there were large quantities of fresh-water snail shell. No tools for plant processing of food were found, so the people appear to have depended on hunting, fishing and gathering (Bronson and Asmar, 1975, pp. 136–42).

Numerous obsidian flakes and a few rare blades have been recovered from surface localities near Bandung in western Java (Heekeren, 1972, pp. 135–7; Subagus, 1979). From east Java,

> [t]he Sampung bone industry is characterized by a great proportion of bone, antler and shell tools of various types, and further by pestles and mortars, primary flakes and blades (used but not retouched), projectile points of stone with rounded base, shell ornaments, red pigment and flexed burials, and a few cord-marked potsherds.
>
> (Heekeren, 1972, p. 92)

Nineteen of these sites have been reported. Typical tools of horn are spatulas and daggers. Well-made projectile points are rounded or concave-based and similar to those from south-western Sulawesi. Bone tools include awls and fish-hooks (Fig. 125). Shell was used for scrapers and ornaments. Human remains from these sites are predominantly Melanesian with some Australoid features. A variety of large and small animals including ungulata, primates, carnivora and rodentia were represented (Heekeren, 1972, pp. 92–106).

A very important sequence has been developing for south-western Sulawesi. The sites, first referred to as Toalean, are all in limestone caves with a variety of flake artefacts (Heekeren, 1972, pp. 106–25). Three sites present a sequence from about 31,000 (Glover, 1981, p. 16) into the third millennium BP but with a gap from about 19,500 to 11,000 years ago. Utilized flakes are a part of the stone industry from the beginning and blade-like tools start close to the end of the Pleistocene (Glover, 1977) but there is no true blade tradition (Glover and Presland, 1985, p. 193). The middle of the three caves and other sites in south-western Sulawesi are the only

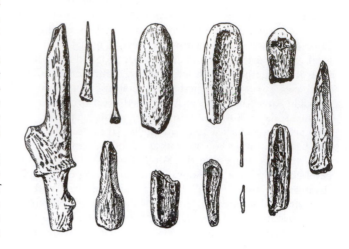

Figure 125 Bone tools, Sampung, Java (Indonesia). (Heekeren, 1972.)

known sites in South-East Asia with true microliths. These first appear around 6,500 years ago. There are several different forms (Fig. 126), some of them very similar to Australian microliths. The concave-based points (Maros points) are found in four varieties, including one with denticulate edges (Glover and Presland, 1985, pp. 190–3). These points are not common until about 4,500 years ago. Whether this very localized microlithic industry results from independent invention or through diffusion from Japan, where very similar forms (made by a different technique) are found at an earlier date, is controversial.

All the sites are freshwater shellfish middens. 'The most important food animals are pigs ... followed by a dwarf bovid (anoa), with monkey, snakes, bats, rodents, phalangers and lizards and squirrels appearing in small numbers. Birds and fish are surprisingly rare' (Glover, 1977, p. 51). Preliminary botanical identification indicates some plant gathering for food and possible medicinal uses.

There has been very little archaeological research in eastern Sulawesi, the Moluccas and other small islands of eastern Indonesia and Irian Jaya (Indonesian New Guinea). Utilized flakes and blades have been reported from surface collections (Glover and Ellen, 1975, 1977). Blades, while present, are in very small quantity. Flakes and blades were also found in a cave on an island in Berau Bay, Irian Jaya, from the deepest cultural layer. From the middle layer were recovered red sherds and some flakes and blades, some with faceted striking platforms (Heekeren, 1972, p. 133). We can surmise that at least a portion of the bottom layer dates from our period.

From the same caves in Irian Jaya many rock paintings have been reported, possibly dating from our period. Similar paintings have been found on Seram and the Kei islands. These include naturalistic fish and lizards, dancing humans and apparent masked figures, hand stencils and many varieties of geometric designs (Fig. 127) (Heekeren, 1972, pp. 127–33).

The Upper Pleistocene adaptation to similar ecological situations as the Early Hoabinhian suggests a mainland origin for the flake technocomplex. Solheim (1974, pp. 23–5) has hypothesized that this flake tradition developed out of the south China Early Hoabinhian with its emphasis on flake-tools relative to the emphasis on core tools of the more southerly and westerly Hoabinhian of the mainland. In eastern Indonesia there was a development of blade-like tools and in some areas true blades. This blade component of the flake industry spread north into the Philippines around 7,000 years ago but did not reach Taiwan or northern Luzon. This general flake technocomplex was used by hunters, gatherers, fishers and shellfish collectors, who may have developed horticulture like their mainland Hoabinhian cousins. We know that there was development of horticulture in Papua New Guinea at this time (Chapter 28) and the likely presence of domesticated pig. How far to the west and north does this early horticulture extend?

The post-Hoabinhian in mainland South-East Asia

Hoabinhian cultures continued in interior, mountainous areas of west Malaysia, Cambodia and Thailand long after 5000 BP but other cultures were appearing in some areas before that time. The site of Gua Kechil in Pahang, west Malaysia, contained evidence for the change from a Late Hoabinhian site to what has been called the Malayan Neolithic; there is a radiocarbon date of about 6500 BP for a portion of this change (Dunn, 1966). The middle stage of this progression suggests contact between the Hoabinhian inhabitants and people of the Malayan Neolithic, while the third stage suggests intermarriage and a junction of the two cultures forming a new, third (Orang Asli) culture (Solheim, 1980a). The reason for contact between the people of these two cultures may well have been trade. Dunn (1975, p. 132) has pointed out that marine molluscs appear at all levels in inland cave sites, indicating that shells must have been traded.

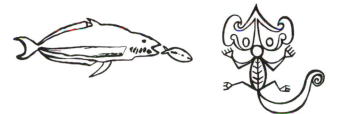

Figure 127 Graphic representations, Arguni Island (Indonesia): fish, lizard.

Traded for what we do not know, but we can guess that resins, bark cloth, haematite and *rotan* (*Calamus rotan*) were included.

Following excavations at Ban Chiang, north-eastern Thailand, it was thought that bronze artefacts were present in a burial from the bottom level of around 6,000 years ago (Gorman and Charoenwongsa, 1976, pp. 17–20). With analysis of the pottery it was apparent that this burial was from a later level and that the earliest bronze at Ban Chiang was around 4,000 years ago (White, 1982, p. 77). The earliest burials at Ban Chiang were usually supine, with a few flexed burials. One or two cord-marked or burnished pots with incised and impressed patterns and often low ring feet were placed at the head or feet, and occasionally ornaments or tools were present. The patterns included curvilinear scrolls and angular meanders. Rice was grown from the first occupation, a rice intermediate between a wild and a weed rice (Yen, 1982, pp. 62–3), probably a wet rice. No dry rice is grown in the area today and the area is not generally suitable for dry rice. Tubers and vegetables were probably important in the diet, including both domesticated and wild yams (White, 1984, pp. 28–33). Until twenty years ago both wild plants and animals were important in the diet, some gathered and hunted food even being found in town markets. From identified animal remains, we see that broad-spectrum trapping, hunting and collecting were important. Domesticated animals included pigs, dogs, chickens and probably cattle (Higham and Kijngam, 1985, pp. 419–23).

Although the Bac Son culture is of almost the same date as the Hoabinhian, most summary reports on Vietnamese prehistory separate it from the Hoabinhian, treating it as the first full Neolithic culture (Davidson, 1975, p. 84; Hao, 1979, pp. 21–2; Long, 1975, pp. 36–41; Tan, 1980, pp. 119–20). The Bacsonian sites had less pottery than the Late Hoabinhian sites. Sites similar to those of the Bacsonian have been found on the coast and on offshore limestone islands in north-eastern Vietnam (Hao, 1979, p. 22).

Another group of sites is considered by some as Late Bacsonian. The earliest of these is Da But, south of Hanoi. Although it is now some distance from the ocean, when inhabited it was close to the shore (Jamieson, 1981, pp. 188, 190). The Da But sites are open shell-middens. The later the site the closer it is to the present sea-coast (Davidson, 1975, p. 84; Hao, 1979, pp. 23–4; Tan, 1980, pp. 119–20).

A third culture following the Bacsonian was the Quynh Van, found in numerous sites south of Da But. Two features of the material culture make this look very different from any of the other cultures of Vietnam at that time: stone tools are made from basalt and are flaked instead of ground and polished, and the pottery is totally different. The early form is a large, cylindrical body with no rim and a pointed base, while all the other cultures and later Quynh Van sites have pottery with rounded bases and short rims. These appear to have been finished with a carved paddle producing parallel

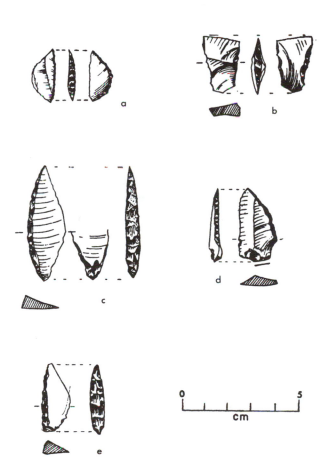

Figure 126 Microliths, Ulu Leang (Indonesia): a, geometric; b, tranchet; c, elongated point; d, oblique point; e, rectangular-backed flake. (After Glover and Presland, 1985.)

grooves and ridges (Hao, 1979, p. 24). The sites are large, open shell-middens. Burials in the middens are similar to the midden burials at Da But (Tan, 1980, p. 120). The two radiocarbon dates, around 6,500 years BP, are controversial. They are considered much too late.

The Bau Tro culture developed out of the Quynh Van culture, in the same area. There are no dates for this culture but we might estimate it at about 5,500 to 4,500 years ago. The major change is the development of the shouldered adze, which is interpreted as a hoe, an interpretation implying a much greater dependence on agriculture. The shouldered adze is also found in cultures in the north and to the west as far as Assam. Stages of development of this form are found throughout the area of south China and northern mainland South-East Asia. Portions of these adzes are often worn asymmetrically, a further indication that they were used as hoes (Roy, 1981, pp. 203–15). Another development in this culture and others at the same time in Vietnam and Thailand is increasing variation in the form and decoration of pottery (Hao, 1979, pp. 25–6; Tan, 1980, pp. 121–3), these forms and decoration continuing for over 3,000 years and spreading throughout South-East Asia and the western Pacific.

Development of South-East Asian maritime cultures

Little has been written about the maritime cultures of South-East Asia of the recent or historic past. We know a bit about the Sea Gypsies of west Malaysia and north-western Indonesia, and others of the Philippines, Borneo and eastern Indonesia (Sopher, 1977). We know about the history of the early trading empires such as Srivijaya and Majapahit, but very little about the maritime component of these 'empires'. From recent research we know that during the third millennium BP there was widespread maritime trade in South-East Asia (Loofs-Wissowa, 1980–1; Solheim, 1982–3). It has been proposed that the origins of the maritime cultures carrying on this trade go back around 7,000 years (Solheim, 1979, pp. 195–7).

There is much debate over interpretation of the archaeological findings of the 1960s, 1970s and 1980s and much more research in all fields pertaining to prehistory is needed before these controversies can be settled.

Korea

Archaeology in Korea is still in the early data-gathering stage with neither trustworthy dated sequences nor areal relationships worked out. Some traditionally accepted origins and relationships are now being questioned. One thing that has become clear is that a little before 3,000 years ago paddy rice culture from a South-East Asian cultural tradition starts to enter Korea and then Japan, starting a time of close relationships between southern Korea and Kyushu, Japan, that lasted for well over 1,000 years.

The Tongsamdong site is the only Korean site we are acquainted with for which dates have been published in English reports that fall in our period. The report refers to three other sites, one in the Democratic People's Republic of Korea. The Tongsamdong site is a shell-mound on a small island in Pusan Bay. The earliest pottery (Fig. 128) here, and in Japan, has an *appliqué* decoration forming hachured triangles or zigzag lines. At Tongsamdong this is found in the bottom layer (4) with some plain and comb-pattern (hereafter called geometric) pottery which increases in quantity to the top layer. Similar appliqué pottery decreases and is absent in the top layer. Similar appliqué pottery from a

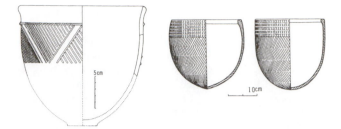

Figure 128 Three ceramic vessels, Tongsamdong (Republic of Korea). (After Kim Won-yong, 1983.)

site north of Pusan has a date of about 7,000 years ago. From layer 4 was recovered some Early Jomon pottery of Japan called Tokoroki, which is dated to the second half of the seventh millennium BP. Also from this layer was recovered obsidian from quarries in north-western Kyushu. 'These people engaged in extensive deep-sea and bay fishing... and they also caught sea-lions and occasionally stranded whales.... Land mammals such as river deer and wild boar were also hunted' (Kim W.-Y., 1983, p. 15).

Layer 3 at Tongsamdong dates from about 5,000 years ago. From this layer early Jomon pottery called Sobata was recovered, which in Japan is dated to the second half of the sixth millennium BP. The Sobata pottery is found in the north-eastern coastal area of Kyushu. Also recovered from layer 3 were bone fish-hooks, projectile points, harpoons, and so on and a scallop shell with three holes punched to form a face (Fig. 129) similar to shells found in Kyushu (Kim W.-Y., 1983, pp. 11–19). A west coast site in northern Korea has typical geometric pottery from around 6,000 years ago (Kim Jeong-hak, 1978, 26–30).

Figure 129 Scallop mask, Tongsamdong (Republic of Korea). (After Kim Won-Yong, 1983.)

ACKNOWLEDGEMENTS

I would like to thank Dr Erika Kaneko for suggestions concerning the data on Japan, Korea and Taiwan and Freda Hellinger for assistance in final typing. Any errors of omission or commission are the author's responsibility.

BIBLIOGRAPHY

AIGNER, J. 1981. The Hoabinhian in China. In: GOSH, A. K.; SOLHEIM, W. G., II (eds), *Festschrift in Honor of Hallam Movius Jr.* Calcutta.

ALEXANDER, S.; COURSEY, D. G. 1969. The Origins of Yam Cultivation. In: UCKO, P.; DIMBLEBY, G. W. (eds), *The Domestication and Exploitation of Plants and Animals*. Chicago. pp. 404–25.

BAYARD, D. 1984. A Checklist of Vietnamese Radiocarbon dates. In: BAYARD, D. (ed.), *Southeast Asian Archaeology at the XV Pacific Science Congress*. Dunedin. pp. 305–32.

BELLWOOD, P. 1976. Archaeological Research in Minahasa and the Talaud Islands, Northeastern Indonesia. *Asian Perspect.*, Vol. 19, pp. 240–88.

—— 1979. *Man's Conquest of the Pacific: The Prehistory of Southeast Asia and Oceania*. Oxford.

—— 1984. Archaeological Research in the Madai-Baturong Region, Sabah. *Indo Pac. Prehist. Assoc. Bull.*, Vol. 5, pp. 38–54.

BEYER, H. O. 1948. *Philippine and East Asian Archaeology and its Relation to the Pacific Islands Population*. Quezon.

BLUST, R. 1976. Austronesian Culture History: Some Linguistic Inferences and their Relation to the Archaeological Record. *World Archaeol.*, Vol. 8, pp. 19–43.

—— 1984–5. Austronesian Homeland: A Linguistic Perspective. *Asian Perspect.*, Vol. 26, pp. 45–67.

BORISKOVSKII, P. I. 1970. Vietnam in Primeval Times. Part IV: The Mesolithic. The Hoa-Binhian Culture. *Sov. Anthropol. Archaeol.* (New York), Vol. 8, No. 3, pp. 214–57.

BRANDT, R. W. 1976. The Hoabinhian of Sumatra: Some Remarks. *Mod. Quat. Res. SEAsia*, Vol. 2, pp. 49–52.

BRONSON, B.; ASMAR, T. 1975. Prehistoric Investigations at Tianko Panjang Cave, Sumatra. *Asian Perspect.*, Vol. 18, pp. 128–45.

BROOKS, S. T.; HEGLAR, R.; BROOKS, R. H. 1977. Radiocarbon Dating and Palaeoserology of a Selected Burial Series from the Great Cave of Niah, Sarawak, Malaysia. *Asian Perspect.*, Vol. 20, pp. 21–31.

BULBECK, D. 1982. A Re-evaluation of Possible Evolutionary Processes in Southeast Asia since the Late Pleistocene. *Indo Pac. Prehist. Assoc. Bull.*, Vol. 3, pp. 1–21.

CHANG KWANG-CHIH. 1969. Review Article of SUNG Wen-hsun, Changpinian: A Newly Discovered Preceramic Culture from the Agglomerate Caves on the East Coast of Taiwan (Preliminary Report). *Asian Perspect.*, Vol. 12, pp. 133–6.

CHANG KWANG-CHIH et al. 1969. *Fengpitou, Tapenkeng, and the Prehistory of Taiwan*. New Haven. (Yale Univ. Publ. Anthropol., 73.)

—— 1974. Man in the Chosui and Tatu River Valleys in Central Taiwan: Preliminary Report of an Interdisciplinary Project, 1972–1973 Season. *Asian Perspect.*, Vol. 17, pp. 36–55.

CHANG TE-TZU. 1984–5. The Ethnobotany of Rice in Island Southeast Asia. *Asian Perspect.*, Vol. 26, No. 1, pp. 69–76.

CHAPPELL, J.; THOM, B. G. 1977. Sea Levels and Coasts. In: ALLEN, J.; GOLSON, J.; JONES, R. (eds), *Sunda and Sahul: Prehistoric Studies in Southeast Asia, Melanesia and Australia*. London. pp. 275–91.

CHINH HOANG XUAN. 1979. A Few Remarks on Hoabinh Cultures Basing on New Documents. In: *Recent Discoveries and New Views on Some Archaeological Problems in Vietnam*. Hanoi. pp. 9–13.

—— 1984. Hoabinhian Culture and the Birth of Botanical Domestication in Viet Nam. In: BAYARD, D. (ed.), *Southeast Asian Archaeology at the XV Pacific Science Congress*. Dunedin. pp. 169–72.

COLANI, M. 1927. L'Âge de la pierre dans la province de Hoa Binh (Tonkin). *Mém. Serv. Géol. Indoch.* (Hanoi), Vol. 41, pp. 1–86.

—— 1929. Quelques stations Hoabinhiennes: Note préliminaire. *Bull. éc. fr. Extrême Orient*, Vol. 29, pp. 261–72.

CONKLIN, H. C. 1957. *Hanunoo Agriculture in the Philippines*. Rome, FAO.

DAVIDSON, J. H. C. S. 1975. Recent Archaeological Activity in Viet-Nam. *J. Hong Kong Archaeol. Soc.*, Vol. 6, pp. 80–99.

DUNN, F. L. 1964. Excavations at Gua Kechil, Pahang. *J. Malays. Branch R. Asiat. Soc.* (Kuala Lumpur), Vol. 37, pp. 87–124.

—— 1966. Radiocarbon Dating of the Malayan Neolithic. *Proc. Prehist. Soc.*, Vol. 32, pp. 352–3.

—— 1975. *Rain-forest Collectors and Traders: A Study of Resource Utilization in Modern and Ancient Malaya*. Kuala Lumpur. (Monogr. Malays. Branch R. Asiat. Soc., 5.)

DUONG PHAM DUC. 1982. The Origin of Wet Rice Socio-Cultural Model of the Viets through Linguistical Data. In: *Studies in History and Culture of Southeast Asia Environment and Human Life*. Hanoi. pp. 10–31.

EVANGELISTA, A. E. 1963. Philippines. *Asian Perspect.*, Vol. 7, pp. 52–6.

FOX, R. B. 1970. *The Tabon Caves*. Manila.

FREEMAN, D. 1955. *Iban Agriculture: A Report on the Shifting Cultivation of Hill Rice by the Iban of Sarawak*. London.

FROMAGET, J. 1940. La Stratigraphie des dépôts pré-historiques de Tam-Hang (Chaîne Annamitique septentrionale) et ses difficultés. In: CHASEN, F. N.; TWEEDIE, M. W. F. (eds), *Proceedings of the Third Congress of Prehistorians of the Far East*. Singapore. pp. 60–70.

GLINKA, J. 1981. Racial History of Indonesia. In: SCHWIDENTZKY, I. (ed.), *Rassengeschichte der Menschheit, 8. Lieferung Asien 1: Japan, Indonesien, Ozeanien*. Munich. pp. 79–113.

GLOVER, I. C. 1971. Prehistoric Research in Timor. In: MULVANEY, D. J.; GOLSON, J. (eds), *Aboriginal Man and Environment in Australia*. Canberra. pp. 158–81.

—— 1977. The Late Stone Age in Eastern Indonesia. *World Archaeol.*, Vol. 9, pp. 42–61.

—— 1981. Leang Burung 2: An Upper Palaeolithic Rock Shelter in Sulawesi, Indonesia. *Mod. Quat. Res. SEAsia*, Vol. 6, pp. 1–38.

GLOVER, I. C.; ELLEN, R. F. 1975. Ethnographic and Archaeological Aspects of a Flaked Stone Collection from Seram, Eastern Indonesia. *Asian Perspect.*, Vol. 18, pp. 51–60.

—— 1977. A Further Note on Flaked Stone Material from Seram, Eastern Indonesia. *Asian Perspect.*, Vol. 20, pp. 236–40.

GLOVER, I. C.; PRESLAND, G. 1985. Microliths in Indonesian Flaked Stone Industries. In: MISRA, V. M.; BELLWOOD, P. (eds), *Recent Advances in Indo-Pacific Prehistory*. New Delhi. pp. 185–205.

GORMAN, C. 1969. Hoabinhian: A Pebble-Tool Complex with Early Plant Associations in Southeast Asia. *Science* (Washington), Vol. 163, No. 3868, pp. 671–3.

—— 1970. Excavations at Spirit Cave, North Thailand: Some Interim Interpretations. *Asian Perspect.*, Vol. 13, pp. 79–107.

—— 1971. The Hoabinhian and After: Subsistence Patterns in South-East Asia during the Late Pleistocene and Early Recent Periods. *World Archaeol.*, Vol. 2, pp. 300–20.

GORMAN, C.; CHAROENWONGSA, P. 1976. Ban Chiang: A Mosaic of Impressions from the First Two Years. *Expedition, Univ. Pa. Mus.* (Philadelphia, Pa.), Vol. 18, pp. 14–26.

HAO NGUYEN VAN. 1979. Neolithic Age in Vietnam and its Evolution. In: *Recent Discoveries and New Views on Some Archaeological Problems in Vietnam*. Hanoi. pp. 21–5.

HARRIS, D. R. 1972a. Swidden Systems and Settlement. In: UCKO, P.; TRINGHAM, R.; DIMBLEBY, G. W. (eds), *Man, Settlements and Urbanism*. London. pp. 245–62.

—— 1972b. The Origins of Agriculture in the Tropics. *Am. Sci.* (New Haven), Vol. 60, pp. 180–93.

HARRISSON, B. 1967. A Classification of Stone Age Burials from Niah Great Cave, Sarawak. *Sarawak Mus. J.* (Kuching), NS, Vol. 15, Nos. 30–1, pp. 126–200.

—— 1968. A Niah Stone-Age Burial C¹⁴ Dated. *Sarawak Mus. J.* (Kuching), NS, Vol. 15, pp. 64–6.

HARRISSON, T. 1970. The Prehistory of Borneo. *Asian Perspect.*, Vol. 13, pp. 17–45.

HARRISSON, T.; MEDWAY, LORD. 1962. A First Classification of Prehistoric Bone and Tooth Artifacts Based on Material from Niah Great Cave. *Asian Perspect.*, Vol. 6, pp. 219–29.

HEEKEREN, H. R. VAN. 1972. *The Stone Age of Indonesia*. The Hague.

HEEKEREN, H. R. VAN; KNUTH, E. 1967. *Archaeological Excavations in Thailand. I. Sai Yok*. Copenhagen.

HIGHAM, C. F. W.; KIJNGAM, A. 1985. New Evidence for Agriculture and Stockraising in Monsoonal Southeast Asia. In: MISRA, V. N.; BELLWOOD, P. (eds), *Recent Advances in Indo-Pacific Prehistory*. New Delhi. pp. 419–23.

HOWELLS, W. 1973. *The Pacific Islanders*. London.

HUTTERER, K. 1969. Preliminary Report on Archaeological Fieldwork in Southwestern Samar. *Leyte-Samar Stud.* (Tacloban City), Vol. 3, pp. 37–56.

JACOB, T. 1967. Racial Identification of the Bronze Age Human Dentitions from Bali, Indonesia. *J. Dent. Res.* (Houston), Vol. 46, No. 5, pp. 903–10.

—— 1974. Studies on Human Variation in Indonesia. *J. Natl. Med. Assoc.* (East Norwalk), Vol. 66, No. 5, pp. 389–99.

—— 1979. Hominine Evolution in South East Asia. *Archaeol. Phys. Anthropol. Ocean.* (Sydney), Vol. 14, pp. 1–10.

JAMIESON, N. 1981. A Perspective of Vietnamese Prehistory Based upon the Relationship between Geological and Archaeological Data: Summary of an Earlier Article by Nguyen Duc Tam. *Asian Perspect.*, Vol. 24, pp. 187–92.

KENNEDY, K. A. R. 1977. The Deep Skull of Niah: An Assessment of Twenty Years of Speculation Concerning its Evolutionary Significance. *Asian Perspect.*, Vol. 20, pp. 32–50.

KIM JEONG-HAK. 1978. *The Prehistory of Korea.* Honolulu.

KIM WON-YONG. 1983. *Recent Archaeological discoveries in the Republic of Korea.* Paris/Tokyo.

KOHL, G.; QUITTA, H. 1978. Berlin Radiocarbon Dates V. *Radiocarbon* (New Haven), Vol. 20, No. 2, pp. 386–97.

LONG NGUYEN PHUC. 1975. Les Nouvelles Recherches archéologiques au Vietnam. *Arts Asiat.* (Paris), Vol. 31, p. 294.

LOOFS-WISSOWA, H. H. E. 1980–1. Prehistoric and Protohistoric Links between the Indochinese Peninsula and the Philippines, as Exemplified by Two Types of Ear-ornaments. *J. Hong Kong Archaeol. Soc.*, Vol. 9, pp. 57–76.

MAJID, Z. 1982. The West Mouth, Niah, in the Prehistory of Southeast Asia. *Sarawak Mus. J.* (Kuching), Vol. 31, No. 52, pp. 1–200.

MATTHEWS, J. M. 1961. *A Check-List of 'Hoabinhian' Sites Excavated in Malaya 1860–1939.* Kuala Lumpur.

—— 1966. A Review of the 'Hoabinhian' in Indo-China. *Asian Perspect.*, Vol. 9, pp. 86–95.

MOURER, C.; MOURER, R. 1970. The Prehistoric Industry of Laang Spean, Province of Battambang, Cambodia. *Archaeol. Phys. Anthropol. Ocean.* (Sydney), Vol. 5, No. 2, pp. 128–46.

—— 1971. Prehistoric Research in Cambodia during the Last Ten Years. *Asia Perspect.*, Vol. 14, pp. 35–42.

MOURER, R. 1977. Laang Spean and the Prehistory of Cambodia. *Mod. Quat. Res. SEAsia*, Vol. 3, pp. 29–56.

PAWLEY, A. K.; GREEN, R. C. 1975. Dating the Dispersal of the Oceanic Languages. *Ocean. Linguist.* (Honolulu), Vol. 21, pp. 1–67.

PETERSON, W. 1979. Archaeological Research in the Noviliches Watershed, Philippines. *Asian Perspect.*, Vol. 22, pp. 120–39.

REID, L. A. 1984–5. Bentedict's Austro-Thai Hypothesis – an Evaluation. *Asian Perspect.*, Vol. 26, pp. 19–34.

RONQUILLO, W. P. 1981. *The Technological and Functional Analysis of the Lithic Flake Tools from Rabel Cave, Northern Luzon, Philippines.* Manila.

ROY, S. K. 1981. Aspects of Neolithic Agriculture and Shifting Cultivation, Garo Hills, Meghalaya. *Asian Perspect.*, Vol. 24, pp. 193–321.

SAUER, C. O. 1969. *Agricultural Origins and Dispersals.* Cambridge, Mass./London.

SAURIN, E. 1966. Le Mobilier préhistorique de l'abri-sous-roche de Tam Pong (Haut Laos). *Bull. Soc. Etud. indoch.* (Saigon), Vol. 41, pp. 106–18.

SCHEANS, D. J.; HUTTERER, K. L.; CHERRY, R. L. 1970. A Newly Discovered Blade Tool Industry from the Central Philippines. *Asian Perspect.*, Vol. 13, pp. 179–81.

SCHMIDT, W. 1906. Die Mon-Khmer-Völker, ein Bindeglied zwischen Völkern Zentralasiens und Austronesiens. *Arch. Anthropol.* (Braunschweig), Vol. 33, pp. 59–109.

SHUTLER, R.; MARCK, J. C. 1975. On the Dispersal of the Austronesian Horticulturalists. *Archaeol. Phys. Anthropol. Ocean.*, Vol. 10, pp. 81–113.

SOLHEIM, W. F., II. 1958. The Present Status of the 'Palaeolithic' in Borneo. *Asian Perspect.*, Vol. 2, pp. 83–90.

—— 1969. Reworking Southeast Asian Prehistory. *Paideuma* (Wiesbaden), Vol. 15, pp. 125–39.

—— 1970. Northern Thailand, Southeast Asia and World Prehistory. *Asian Perspect.*, Vol. 13, pp. 145–62.

—— 1974. The Hoabinhian and Island Southeast Asia. In: TANTOCO, R. B. (ed.), *Proceedings of the First Regional Seminar on Southeast Asian Prehistory and Archaeology.* Manila. pp. 19–26.

—— 1975. Reflections on the New Data of Southeast Asian Prehistory: Austronesian Origins and Consequence. *Asian Perspect.*, Vol. 18, pp. 146–60.

—— 1976a. Coastal Irian Jaya and the Origin of the Nusantao (Austronesian Speaking People). In: SEROZAWA, C. (ed.), *Colloque 18: le premier peuplement de l'archipel nippon et des Îles du Pacifique: chronologie, paléogéographie, industries.* Nice. pp. 32–42. (9th International Congress of Prehistoric and Protohistoric Sciences.)

—— 1976b. Prehistory of Southeast Asia with Reference to Oceania. In: GARANGER, J. (ed.), *Colloque 9: la préhistoire oceanienne.* Nice. pp. 135–51. (9th International Congress of Prehistoric and Protohistoric Sciences.)

—— 1977. The Niah Research Program. *J. Malays. Branch R. Asiat. Soc.* (Kuala Lumpur), Vol. 50, pp. 28–40.

—— 1979. A Look at 'L'Art Prébouddhique de la Chine et de l'Asie du Sud-Est et son influence en Océanie' Forty Years After. *Asian Perspect.*, Vol. 22, pp. 165–205.

—— 1980a. Searching for the Origins of the Orang Asli. *Fed. Mus. J.* (Kuala Lumpur), Vol. 15, pp. 61–75.

—— 1980b. Review Article: Recent Discoveries and New Views on Some Archaeological Problems in Vietnam. *Asian Perspect.*, Vol. 23, pp. 9–16.

—— 1982–3. Remarks on the Lingling-o and Biècephalous Ornaments. *J. Hong Kong Archaeol. Soc.*, Vol. 10, pp. 107–11.

—— 1983. Archaeological Research in Sarawak, Past and Future. *Sarawak Mus. J.* (Kuching), NS, Vol. 23, No. 53, pp. 35–58.

—— 1985a. ' "Southeast Asia": What's in a Name?', Another Point of View. *J. SEAsian Stud.* (Singapore), Vol. 16, pp. 141–7.

—— 1985b. Nusantao Traders beyond Southeast Asia. (Paper presented at Research Conference on Early Southeast Asia, Thailand, April, 1985.)

SOLHEIM, W. G., II; LEGASPI, A. M.; NERI, J. S. 1979. *Archaeological Survey in Southeastern Mindanao.* Manila.

SOPHER, D. E. 1977. *The Sea Nomads: A Study of the Maritime Boat People of Southeast Asia.* Singapore.

SPENCER, J. E. 1966. Shifting Cultivation in Southeastern Asia. *Univ. Calif. Publ. Geogr.* (Berkeley/Los Angeles), Vol. 19, pp. 110–122.

SPOEHR, A. 1973. *Zamboanga and Sulu: An Archaeological Approach to Ethnic Diversity.* Pittsburgh.

SUBAGUS, N. A. 1979. Obisidian Industry in Leles, West Java. Preliminary Report. *Mod. Quat. Res. SEAsia*, Vol. 5, pp. 35–41.

SUZUKI, H. 1981. Racial History of the Japanese. In: SCHWIDENTZKY, I. (ed.), *Rassengeschichte der Menschheit 8. Lieferung Asien I: Japan, Indonesien, Ozeanien.* Munich. pp. 7–69.

—— 1983. Pleistocene Man in Japan. *Recent Prog. Nat. Sci. Jpn.*, Vol. 8, pp. 13–17.

TAN HA VAN. 1980. Nouvelles Recherches préhistoriques et protohistoriques au Vietnam. *Bull. éc. fr. Extrême Orient* (Paris), Vol. 68, pp. 115–43.

TENAZAS, R. 1985. A Note on Stone and Shell Instruments from Late Palaeolithic and Neolithic Sites in Carcar, Cebu, Philippines. In: MISRA, V. N.; BELLWOOD, P. (ed.), *Recent Advances in Indo-Pacific Prehistory.* New Delhi. pp. 207–9.

THAW AUNG. 1971. The 'Neolithic' Culture in the Padah-lin Caves. *Asian Perspect.*, Vol. 14, pp. 123–33.

THIEL, B. 1980a. Excavations in the Pinacanauan Valley, Northern Luzon. *Indo Pac. Prehist. Assoc. Bull.*, Vol. 2, pp. 40–8.

—— 1980b. *Subsistence Change and Continuity in Southeast Asian Prehistory.* Urbana-Champaign. (Ph.D. thesis, University of Illinois.)

TUGGLE, H. D.; HUTTERER, K. L. 1972. Introduction. In: Archaeology of the Sohotan Area, Southwestern Samar, Philippines. *Leyte-Samar Stud.* (Tacloban City), Vol. 6, No. 2, pp. 5–12.

WHARTON, C. H. 1968. Man, Fire and Wild Cattle in Southeast Asia. In: TALL TIMBERS FIRE ECOLOGY CONFERENCE, 8. Tallahassee. *Proceedings Annual.* pp. 107–67.

WHITE, J. C. 1982. *Ban Chiang: Discovery of a Lost Bronze Age.* Philadelphia, University of Pennsylvania Museum.

—— 1984. Origins of Plant Domestication in Southeast Asia: Ethnoecological Contribution from Ban Chiang. In: BAYARD, D. (ed.), *Southeast Asian Archaeology at the XV Pacific Science Congress*. Dunedin. pp. 26–35.

XU WENLONG. 1982. A Genetic Survey of ABO, MN Blood Groups of the Inhabitants in Hainan Island, Guangdong Province. *Acta Anthropol. Sin.* (Beijing), Vol. 1, No. 1, p. 79.

YAMAGUCHI, B. 1983. Microevolutionary Change of the Japanese. *Recent Progr. Nat. Sci. Jpn*, Vol. 8, pp. 19–23.

YEN, D. E. 1977. Hoabinhian Horticulture? The Evidence and the Questions from Northwest Thailand. In: ALLEN, J.;

GOLSON, J.; JONES, R. (eds), *Sunda and Sahul: Prehistoric Studies in Southeast Asia, Melanesia and Australia*. London/New York. pp. 567–99.

—— 1982. Ban Chiang Pottery and Rice. *Expedition, Univ. Pa. Mus.* (Philadelphia), Vol. 24, No. 4, pp. 51–64.

—— 1984. Wild Plants and Domestication in Pacific Islands. In: MISRA, V. N.; BELLWOOD, P. (eds), *Recent Advances in Indo-Pacific Prehistory*. New Delhi. pp. 315–26.

ZHANG XHENBIAO; ZHANG JIANJUN. 1982. Anthropological Studies on Li Nationality in Hainan Island, China. *Acta Anthropol. Sin.* (Beijing), Vol. 1, No. 1, pp. 70–1.

46

CHINA
during the Neolithic

An Zhimin

China lies in the east of Asia and has a total area of about 9,600,000 km². Within this vast land there are grand mountains, broad plateaux, large basins, expansive plains, numerous rivers and lakes, and a long coastline. The climate varies from region to region, ranging from tropical in the south to temperate in the north and with the temperature increasing from the coastal south-east to the interior north-west. As the rainfall decreases progressively from south to north, such landscapes as forests, steppes and deserts appear in different areas. All these topographical, climatic and botanical variations determined to a certain degree the economic and cultural development of prehistoric China.

Neolithic remains of human activities are distributed throughout the territory of China. According to the geographical and ecological environments and the economic and cultural development, they can roughly be divided into four regional groups which occupy the Huanghe (Yellow river) valley, the northern steppe, the Changjiang (Yangtze) river middle and lower reaches and the southern hilly land respectively. The Huanghe valley, where Neolithic settlements were distributed most densely, was the centre of origin of Chinese agriculture and civilization, and the other regions, of course, also had very old complexes and very long traditions. They displayed quite complex cultural aspects in their long development and mutual influence.

THE HUANGHE VALLEY

The Huanghe river is the most famous watercourse in north China; its reaches cover an area of about 750,000 km², including the loess plateau in the west, the alluvial plain in the east, and the hilly land on the Shangdong peninsula. Its warm climate and moderate rainfall (400 to 800 mm per annum) were instrumental in the development of primitive agriculture represented by foxtail and broomcorn millet cultivation. There was a wide distribution of Mesolithic complexes with a microlithic tradition in this area. With regard to the early Neolithic here, although there are still gaps in the sequence of development, the emergence of advanced agricultural settlements 8,000 to 7,000 years ago implies that the beginning of agricultural life can be traced back to an even earlier period. It is also in this area that the continuity of the Neolithic development in China and its close connection with the historical times are presented most distinctly.

For several decades people acquired knowledge of the Neolithic period in the Huanghe valley mainly by studying the Yangshao (Yang-shao) and Longshan (Lung-shan) cultures, until recently a number of earlier remains were brought to light, which was a remarkable breakthrough. These remains belong to the Cishan, Peiligang or Dadiwan cultures, which were first found in 1976, 1977 and 1979 respectively and later identified as parallel developments on the loess plateau and the north China plain. These cultures had something in common with each other, which indicated interactions.

The sites are distributed along small or medium rivers and situated generally 30 to 40 m above today's river-beds, though some are on the banks of old river courses. Each site has an area of more than 10,000 m², and house foundations, storage pits, a pottery-making kiln, tombs and other remains have been uncovered, which indicates the existence of settled villages at that time. The layout of settlements is not yet clear. Dwellings have been found in small numbers. Most of them are semi-subterranean houses, round or square in plan, each with a narrow doorway in the front and postholes along the lines of walls marking the remains of a wooden structure. The storage pits are mainly round, small and shallow; but at Cishan there are rectangular ones, 5 m deep, with piles of foxtail millet grains unearthed, showing clearly their function. At Peiligang a ruined horizontal pottery kiln has been dug out; it is the earliest known so far. Burial customs are reflected in the tombs discovered at the same site. Numbering more than one hundred, they formed a dense community cemetery near the settlement. Most of them are single burials, double ones being found rarely. The majority of the dead were provided with funerary objects of pottery and stone. Among them a quern with a roller and a spade with a sickle occur as two separate sets of stone tools and are not associated with each other, except in the double burial; thus it may be considered that they belonged respectively to females and males, but unfortunately the skeletons are too rotten to be identified. A few tombs have also been discovered from the Cishan and Dadiwan cultures. However, they are not so dense in distribution and not so rich and characteristic in tomb furniture as those of the Peiligang culture.

There are striking signs of an agricultural economy. Stone tools such as the well-polished legged quern, the cylindrical roller, the narrow and thin spade with a double-arced edge, and the serrated sickle were all typical agricultural implements of the Peiligang and Cishan cultures. Among them those of the Cishan culture were polished somewhat roughly, and its sickles are seldom found and are unserrated. The Dadiwan culture had another set of farming tools: the stone implements found so far are all rough spades and knives; besides, shell artefacts of the types of knife and serrated sickle have been unearthed in some cases. Species of crops have been identified quite clearly. The Cishan site has yielded rotten grains of foxtail millet (*Setaria italica*); the Dadiwan site, samples of broomcorn millet (*Panicum miliaceum*) and seeds of rape (*Brassica*). These discoveries prove that foxtail and broomcorn millet, drought-enduring and suitable to loess areas, were domesticated quite early and have been cultivated as traditional crops in north China for a long time. As for animal husbandry, we have evidence such as the pigs' bones and the life-like pottery sculpture in the shape of a pig's head from the Peiligang site, the numerous pigs' and dogs' skeletons and even the chickens' remains from the Cishan site, and the pigs' mandibles from tombs of the Dadiwan site, suggesting that the pig and the dog were the main domestic animals at that time. It can be concluded from the above that an agricultural economy had become the main means of living of the people of that time, although the discovery of walnut (*Juglans regia*), hazelnut (*Corylus heterophylla*) and hackberry (*Celtis bungeana*) seeds, and of abundant remains of fish and game from some sites, shows that gathering, fishing and hunting played a certain role in economic life.

With regard to the stone tool industry of this period, the implements in the Peiligang culture were mainly polished and well retouched (Fig. 130), while those in the Cishan and Dadiwan cultures were overwhelmingly chipped types, such as choppers, scrapers, axe-shaped tools and so on, with polished artefacts being relatively rough. It is notable that small stone blades and well-retouched scrapers have been found from the Peiligang and Dadiwan cultures, implying the survival of a microlithic tradition at that time.

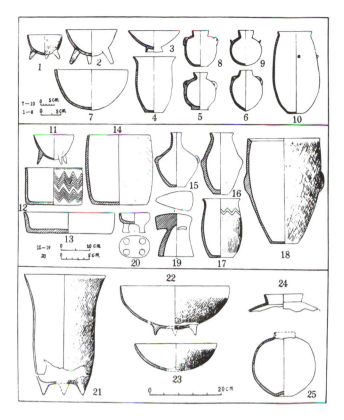

Figure 131 Pottery of Early Neolithic cultures (north China): 1–10, Peiligang culture; 11–20, Cishan culture; 21–25, Dadiwan culture.

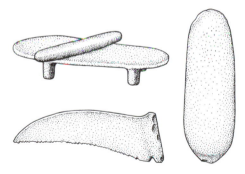

Figure 130 Stone implements, Peiligang culture (China).

The pottery (Fig. 131) was relatively primitive, hand-made and with walls of uneven thickness. The firing temperature was a little lower than that of the subsequent Yangshao culture, namely 900 to 960 °C in the Peiligang culture and 700 to 930 °C in the Cishan culture. The pottery kiln of the Peiligang culture was similar to that of the Yangshao culture, suggesting that the craft of pottery making laid a foundation for further development. The typology of vessels shows a certain similarity existed among the pottery industries of various regions. For example, round-bottomed, three-legged bowls (*bo*) and wide-mouthed, deep-bellied jars (*guan*) have been discovered from all three cultures and

are basically of the same shapes. Nevertheless, all the cultures had features of their own. In respect of the shape of vessels, the Peiligang culture was characterized by the two-lunate eared jar (*hu*) with a round bottom and the tripod (*ding*); the Cishan culture by the wide-mouthed, vertical-walled container (*yü*), the boot-shaped supporting feet for a vessel and the two-eared jar (*hu*), different from that of the Peiligang culture, with a narrow neck and a flat bottom; the Dadiwan culture, by the three-legged jar (*guan*) with a wide mouth and deep belly, the small-mouthed jar (*hu*) with a round bottom, often with an attached ring foot. Distinctions can also be detected in paste texture. In the Peiligang and Cishan cultures there prevailed a red, coarse sandy ware, with a certain amount of red clay ware. In the Dadiwan culture, a red, coarse ware with fine sand temper made up the major part of the pottery, while red clay ware occurs occasionally. Because of the improper control of temperature during firing, vessels often assume a greyish-brown colour in section and the surface is also impure in colour, sometimes with greyish-black spots. As for surface retouching and decoration, there was a striking disparity among the cultures. For instance, in the Peiligang culture, pottery was largely plain and undecorated; clay ware was usually burnished and its finest examples can match those of the Yangshao culture; a potsherd with simple patterns in black indicates the existence of painted pottery; and, in addition, comb-marks, incisions and nipples occur sometimes. The Cishan pottery was also plain for the most part and occasionally decorated with comb-marks, incisions and nipples. However, it was often impressed with cord marks, and parallel zigzags painted in red have been found on a sherd. In the Dadiwan culture, pottery was commonly decorated with crisscrossing, grid-shaped cord impressions. Plain retouching was used only on round-bottmed jars (*hu*) and a few other vessels. The cord marks along the mouth of three-legged bowls (*bo*) were often smoothed and painted with red bands. Judging from the above, the three potteries differ from rather than resemble each other, and thus should be held to be distinctive signs of different cultural systems.

Stratigraphical details and radiocarbon dates prove that all the complexes belong to a comparatively early period. At a number of sites, layers of the Peiligang and Cishan cultures are buried under those of the Yangshao culture. Radiocarbon dates provide even clearer evidence. The Peiligang culture dates from between *c*.8,000 and 7,500 years ago, the Cishan to between *c*.8,000 and 7,700 years ago and the Dadiwan to between *c*.7,800 and 7,600 years ago. They all preceded the Yangshao culture and existed roughly contemporaneously.

The Peiligang, Cishan and Dadiwan cultures were developed in the Huanghe valley relatively early and, moreover, had a close connection with the Yangshao culture, as is shown by the similarities in the distribution of settlements, the shape of houses and kilns and the arrangement of tombs, and, especially, by the clear succession of stone tools, pottery objects and other cultural elements. All this indicates that they were forerunners of the Yangshao culture.

The Yangshao culture is named after the first discovery of its remains at Yangshao Village in Mianchi County, Henan Province, in 1921. Formerly, there were many vague ideas about it. It was called the 'Painted Pottery culture' after just one of its features, which resulted in confusing a great number of culturally different remains that included painted pottery and obscuring the essential characters of the culture itself. Chronologically, it was estimated to be rather late and generally taken as a Late Neolithic culture. Archaeological work conducted broadly and intensively for the past thirty years has led to a more complete understanding of the Yangshao culture. It has become clear that, with the loess plateau as its centre, it stretched across the middle reaches of the Huanghe during Neolithic times. According to radiocarbon dates, it goes back to *c*.7,100 to 4,900 years ago, lasting more than 2,000 years. Moreover, its cultural characteristics and its origin and further development have been revealed.

Owing to cultural differences caused by the extensive geographical distribution and the wide chronological span, the Yangshao culture is generally classified into several types to reflect the distinction. For example, on the loess plateau four types have been distinguished: Beishouling, Banpo (Pan-p'o), Miaodigou (Miao-ti-kou), and Xiwangcun; on the north China plain, Miaodigou and Dahecun or Hougang and Dasikongcun. The chronological sequences and correlations of the types can be determined by combinative analysis of stratigraphical evidence, cultural features and radiocarbon dates.

Life had then become rather sedentary, and large settlements had been formed, measuring from tens of thousands to a hundred thousand or more square metres. Excavation at Jiangzhai in Lintong County, Shaanxi Province, has nearly completely revealed a whole site, which was laid out as a village over an area of more than 50,000 m², surrounded by a defensive moat, and with an open space sloping slightly down to the centre and encircled by densely packed houses, which can be divided into five complexes each with a big house as the main building and ten to twenty-odd small or medium-sized ones in its vicinity, as well as storage pits in groups. Three cemeteries have been found to the east of the moat, including 175 densely arranged adults' tombs with the heads of the dead pointing generally to the west and occasionally to the north-west and funerary objects con-

sisting of pottery, stone implements and other articles for daily use. Children were buried in urns, of which some are scattered in the cemeteries and most are gathered around the houses; they total as many as 190. The discovery of the settlement provides a vivid picture of the Yangshao people's daily life.

The houses were either semi-subterranean or surface buildings of wooden construction. Only their foundations remain in fairly good condition. Semi-subterranean houses were more popular; they are square, rectangular or round in plan and have an area of about 20 m². A large house has been found at the Banpo site near Xi'an City, Shaanxi Province; it remains in an area of more than 100 m² and must have been a public place where members of a community used to gather. Surface houses are either round or rectangular. The former must have had a cone-shaped roof as shown by the pottery house models unearthed; as for the latter, we can cite as an example the remains of a house discovered at Dahecun, Zhengzhou, Henan. It has three rooms linked together and a partition in the biggest room, with a total area of over 70 m². All this shows that the Yangshao culture reached a high level of competence in house building.

The agricultural economy was well developed. Remains of drought-resistant crops such as foxtail and broomcorn millet, along with vegetable seeds, have been found at many sites; and very rare examples have been identified as rice, but need further identification. There were simple farming tools such as stone spades for digging and stone and pottery sickles for harvesting. The stone quern which had prevailed before was gradually disappearing. The stone axe and adze, unearthed in large numbers, were suitable for cutting down woods and opening up plots and must have had a certain connection with farming. Animal husbandry was still on a lower level, with the pig and the dog the main domestic animals; the remains of sheep and cattle uncovered in some cases cannot yet be identified with certainty as domesticated species. Bone arrowheads, harpoons and fish-hooks, as well as remains of wild animals and plants, are often found, suggesting that hunting, fishing and gathering still played a certain part. Yet the extension of settlements, the prolongation of settled life and the frequent discovery of cereals and farming tools all indicate that the agricultural economy made greater progress than before.

The pottery-making industry of the Yangshao culture (Fig. 132) made a mighty advance. The kilns found so far were all built near settlements, separated from living-quarters, perhaps to guard against fire. Their construction is simple, horizontal or vertical in type, generally small in size, unhermetic at the top, and thus convenient for controlling the firing temperature and oxidizing atmosphere. Such kilns were capable of producing a red ware of hard texture, with a firing temperature of 900 to 1,050 °C, and reached quite a high technical level. Pottery remained hand-made and was touched up on a slow-wheel along the rim to obtain a neat form; the fast-wheel, however, had not yet appeared. The pottery has striking features in shape and decoration. The common pottery vessels include flat-bottomed or ring-footed bowls (*wan*), round-bottomed bowls, small mouthed jars (*hu*), wide-mouthed jars (*guan*), tripods (*ding*), and small-mouthed, pointed-bottomed bottles (*ping*). In respect of decoration, the most characteristic type was pottery painted with red-and-black patterns on a burnished surface. It varied in quantity and style from region to region and from period to period. Taking the loess plateau as an example, in the Beishouling type of the early period, painted pottery was rare except for some round-bottomed bowls with painted

Figure 132 Painted pottery, Yangshao culture (China).

rims. In the Banpo type, painted pottery increased in quantity and was often decorated with different triangular motifs as well as with lifelike human faces and animal motifs representing fish, birds and frogs. In the Miaodigou type, painted pottery was even more popular, with such motifs as round dots, triangular whorls and arcs, producing a strongly stylized effect. Some vessels were decorated with animal motifs of frogs and birds, and some were first coated with white slip and then painted in both red and black, thus adding to their artistic quality. In the Xiwangcun type of the late period, painted pottery was on the decline both in quantity and in pattern. The changes described above reflect the basic pattern of development of the Yangshao painted pottery.

The development of the Yangshao culture in the Huanghe valley, which began early and lasted for a long time, served as a link between the preceding and following cultures: on the one hand it succeeded the earlier stage represented by the Peiligang culture; on the other, it heralded the development of the Longshan culture. Furthermore, the Yangshao culture exerted a great influence on nearby regions. For example, the Majiayao culture in the upper reaches of the Huanghe and the Dawenkou culture in the lower reaches were both variations of the Yangshao culture; the Hongshan

culture in Inner Mongolia and both the Daxi and Qujialing cultures in the middle reaches of the Changjiang river, to judge by the appearance of painted pottery in them, were all related to the Yangshao culture. All this shows the important role of the Yangshao culture in the history of the cultural development of China.

THE NORTHERN STEPPE

The vast northern highland from the north-east via Inner Mongolia to Xinjiang Province and its vicinity, and including the Qinghai–Tibet plateau, is basically a steppe-desert zone, except for part of the north-east. The rainfall in most of the zone is below 100 mm per annum. Such harsh natural conditions directly influence human economic life and cultural development. The Neolithic there is represented on the whole by a microlithic tradition.

The microlithic tradition was a peculiar industry developed from the industries of the Upper Palaeolithic in north China and is represented by microblades, their cores and compound tools made of microblades. In the Huanghe valley, the microlithic tradition disappeared after the advent of agriculture, while in the steppe zone it continued to flourish during the Neolithic and even lasted into a later period.

As a result of the diversity of natural conditions and economic activities, the microlithic tradition in the northern steppe fell into two types. One of them was dominated by fishing, hunting and nomadism. Its people were constantly on the move and camped somewhere briefly or seasonally, leaving behind sites generally of small size and without clear cultural deposits. The people of the other type had taken up farming and led a sedentary life in settlements. Although both of them were characterized by microliths, they were quite different from each other in cultural aspect.

The first type of remains is represented by such sites as Qijiaojing in Hami County, Xinjiang Province, Shuanghu in Xainza County, Tibet, Layihai in Guinan County, Qinghai, and Songshan in Hailar City, Inner Mongolia. They are commonly characterized by an abundance of microliths, the occasional appearance of chipped stone tools and the absence of polished stone implements and pottery. Economically, these sites can be assigned to the Mesolithic. Chronologically, however, they were somewhat later than ordinary Mesolithic complexes. For instance, the Layihai site has been radiocarbon dated to as late as c.7,000 years ago. Thus it can be concluded that while the Huanghe valley was going through the development of agriculture, some other areas were still in the more primitive stage of fishing, hunting and nomadism. A number of polished stone tools and pottery vessels, of course, have been found at a few somewhat later sites, but microliths still make up the majority of the implements unearthed.

The second type included the settlements where farming was the main means of subsistence and the microlithic tradition was maintained to a certain extent. These sites are distributed mainly in the east of Inner Mongolia and in the west of Liaoning Province. The Xinglongwa culture, dated from the eighth millennium BP, had settlements, each surrounded by a moat, and subterranean dwellings, arranged densely in rows. Thus the culture was similar to the Yangshao culture in the Huanghe valley both in the layout of its settlements and in the structure of its houses. Its stone tools were mainly chipped, although polished ones were also represented in large numbers; microliths, however, were not so many. The pottery (Fig. 133), represented by a comb-marked ware, developed for a long time as a distinct feature in the area of the culture and its vicinity. The settlements and the tools show that agriculture held the main position

in the economy, though fishing, hunting and gathering still contributed a considerable proportion of the food. The subsequent Xinle and Hongshan cultures shared the same characteristics; even painted pottery appeared in the latter, suggesting closer relations with the Yangshao culture.

Under the gradual influence of agriculture after its appearance in the Huanghe valley, the northern steppe finally saw the advent of farming and settled life. At the same time, the microlithic tradition began to decline. Nevertheless, it still occupied the leading position in some non-agricultural regions.

MIDDLE AND LOWER REACHES OF THE CHANGJIANG RIVER

The Changjiang river is the longest in China. Rising from its source in the Qinghai–Tibet plateau, it flows through Sichuan Province, and, leaving the three narrow gorges and entering the alluvial plains along its middle and lower courses, it forms complex systems consisting of the main river channel, many tributaries, lakes, and marshes before emptying into the sea. The area of the middle and lower reaches of the river totals about 800,000 km². Here the rainfall measures 800 to 1,600 mm per annum, and the climate is warm and moist. All this contributes to rice cultivation originating in this region.

Remains from an earlier period of the Neolithic age in this region have been found in Linli County, Hunan Province, and in Zigui County, Hubei Province. Chronologically they correspond to the period of the Peiligang culture in the Huanghe valley. The paucity of available evidence, however, makes it impossible to understand the cultural aspects of the remains. In contrast, the Hemudu (Ho-mu-tu) culture in the lower reaches of the Changjiang river has clearly been indentified as a characteristic regional complex.

The Hemudu culture was first discovered in 1973. It was distributed mainly along Hangzhou Bay and in the adjoining area. The culture is represented by the lower layers of the Hemudu site in Yüyao County, Zhejiang Province, and goes back to about 7,000 to 6,000 years according to radiocarbon dates. The upper layers of the site belong to the Majiabang and Songze cultures, both of which were some time later than and distinctly different from the Hemudu culture.

The Hemudu site has yielded a large number of remains of wooden buildings, including piles, planks, beams, pillars and other structural members. Traces of cutting with stone axes and adzes are easily distinguished; a lot of members are of tenon-and-mortise construction, allowing them to be joined together tightly, which shows a high level of skill in the craft of building in wood. Judging from the depositional context of the finds, there must have been so-called 'pile dwellings', raised above the ground on piles. However, in general it is difficult to reconstruct their shape owing to the poor state of preservation. One of the buildings which has been found is rectangular in plan and must have been constructed on piles arranged closely in rows. Around 200 piles remain *in situ*, arranged in four rows in an area of 23 m by 7 m, representing a large-sized house of about 160 m². The 'pile dwelling' was one of the main architectural types along the Changjiang and to the south of the river in the Neolithic and early historical ages. The remains at the Hemudu site are the earliest known so far. Although it is hard to make out their structure, some information can be obtained from findings of a later period. For instance, the pottery model from Yingpanli in Qingjiang County, Jiangxi

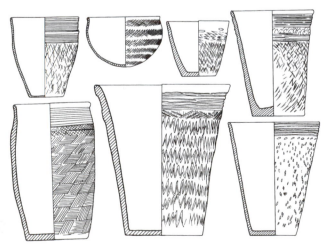

Figure 133 Pottery, Xinglongwa culture (China).

Province, and the bronze ones from Shizhaishan in Jinning County, Yünnan Province, present the house raised above the ground and covered by a roof with a ridge longer than its eaves, which might basically have retained the shape of the pile-dwelling in the Hemudu culture.

Twenty-seven tombs have been discovered at the site. The skeletons are preserved in a poor condition; they are all single burials, except for three double ones. Most of the grave goods consist of pottery and bone objects, with stone chisels and spindle whorls and semi-annular and penannular jade ornaments (*huang* and *jue*) occurring occasionally, but about half of the tombs contained no funerary objects. In some cases, human bones are separated, with even skulls and leg bones missing, which indicates a peculiar burial custom.

The stone tools from the site are simple in type. They are generally polished roughly, often with traces of pecking. The most characteristic types are a trapezoidal axe with an asymmetrical edge and a thick adze with an arched back; the latter may have been the prototype of the stepped stone adze. In addition, there are elbow-shaped antler or wooden handles with the thicker end made into a tenon to be bound with the tool body. All of them were doubtlessly among the main woodworking implements.

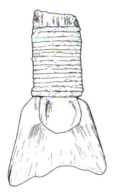

Figure 134 Spade-shaped bone digging-tool (*si*), Hemudu culture (China).

A great number of bone objects have been uncovered, among them the spade-shaped digging tool (*si*), one of the main farming implements; this is especially characteristic of the Hemudu culture (Fig. 134). It is made of a buffalo or deer scapula, with a horizontal tube chiselled out at the joint, a shallow vertical groove cut out along the axis of the body and two holes on the sides of the groove, and thus should have been fixed to a wooden handle. This has been proved by the example found together with its handle, which is bound in the groove with a rattan passing through the horizontal tube and the holes. The top of handles, to facilitate handling, was made T-shaped or triangular, as is shown in this and some other cases. The other bone artefacts (Fig. 135) include arrowheads, harpoons, awls, needles, hairpins, spoons and so on. Arrowheads predominate; they were used for hunting and maybe for fishing, thus indicating that hunting and fishing still played some part in the economy. In addition, there are some bone objects engraved with basketry or double-bird patterns, as well as a number of bird-shaped spoons and small cups made of ivory and decorated with openwork; these all reached a high artistic level.

There are many types of wooden objects, including spades, pestles, hammers, spears, oars and weaving implements such as a beater made of a wooden strip (*weidao*) and a roller for winding cloth. It is noteworthy that a wooden bowl has been found with a thin red coat, which, although badly worn, remains lustrous in part. It has been identified

as raw lacquer by chemical and spectral analysis. The bowl, therefore, is the earliest lacquered object known so far.

The pottery (Fig. 135) is strikingly distinctive, with a black charcoal ware predominating. Because the clay was commonly mixed with a large quantity of rice husks and fragmented rice stems and leaves as temper, the paste was carbonized in the reducing atmosphere during firing. As a result, the ware was made fragile in texture, light in weight and absorbent. The firing temperature was low, generally about 800 to 850 °C. The pottery could have been fired in a bonfire rather than in a kiln, which may not yet have appeared. The pottery types are simple, including cauldrons (*fu*), jars, bowls, plates, basins, vessel-supporting feet and so on, of which the cauldron in combination with its supporting feet was the characteristic cooking vessel in the culture. The surface of the pottery is mainly decorated with cord impressions, incisions and geometric patterns consisting of dots and stripes, as well as realistic figures of rice ears, algae and pigs in rare cases. It is interesting that three sherds are decorated with painted designs. They are fragments of vessels of the black charcoal ware with the cord impressions smoothed and coated by a white slip, on which geometric patterns are painted in reddish- and blackish-brown. Being uncommon in the Hemudu culture, the finds should reflect some relationship with the Yangshao culture in the Huanghe valley.

Another feature of the culture was the appearance of jade ornaments, such as penannular earrings (*jue*), semi-annular pendants (*huang*), tubes and beads, all finely polished. The penannular jade earring appeared first in this very culture. Often associated with the semiannular jade pendant used as a neck ornament, it had a wide distribution in the middle and lower reaches of the Changjiang river and their vicinity. This kind of ornament did not appear in the Huanghe valley until later. Therefore it must have originated from the area centred on the middle and lower reaches of the Changjiang river.

Leading a settled life near bodies of water on the plain and building wooden houses such as pile dwellings, the Hemudu people engaged mainly in rice cultivation, along with other productive activities. Besides a large number of bone, wooden and stone farming implements, mixed deposits of rice grains, husks, stems and leaves are often uncovered in the living area of the site, the greatest thickness being over 1 m. The species of long-grained non-glutinous rice (*indica* type) and round-grained non-glutinous rice (*japanica* type) have been identified. The great amount and good preservation of the rice remains here is rarely paralleled in other cultures. There is also evidence about the environment of the Hemudu culture, such as peat deposits of lakes and marshes uncovered near the settlement and water chestnuts, pollen of aquatic herbs, bones of water fowl and remains of animals dwelling in reed marshes all unearthed from the cultural layers of the site. These findings suggest that paddy fields were then cultivated near marshes.

The Hemudu culture and its successor, the Majiabang culture, displayed a strong regionalism as Neolithic cultures in the lower reaches of the Changjiang river. The rice farming, pile dwelling construction, pottery making and stone-tool industry here exerted a broad influence upon other parts of the Changjiang river reaches and regions south of the river. The emergence of painted pottery and the pottery tripod (*ding*) in the cultures in its turn indicates some contact and communication with the Huanghe valley. With regard to this, the Daxi culture in the middle reaches of the Changjiang river adopted more elements of the Yangshao

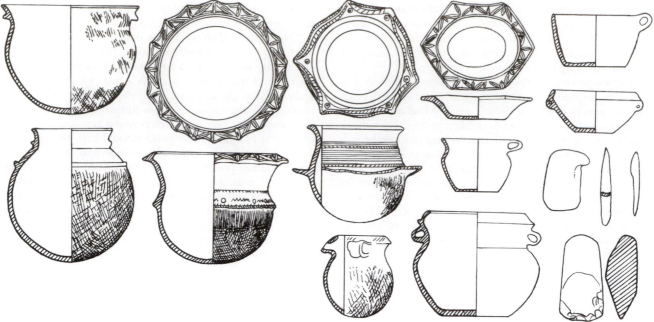

Figure 135 Pottery, bone and stone artefacts, Hemudu culture (China).

culture, which seems to indicate that the Daxi culture was related mainly to the Huanghe valley.

HILLY LAND IN SOUTH CHINA

The south-eastern coastal region of China includes the provinces of Fujian, Taiwan, Guangdong and Guangxi, covering an area of 400,000 km². It has a high temperature, much rainfall (1,600 mm per annum), and dense and rainy tropical forests. Such environments exerted a delaying influence on the advent of agriculture.

The Early Neolithic development is represented by cave dwellings, shell-mounds and terrace sites; the living areas are generally narrow and settlements are little known so far. Being widely distributed, the remains maybe belong to different cultural types. As their common features, it can be pointed out that great numbers of chipped stone tools existed in association with polished ones, a coarse pottery ware in simple shapes and with cord marks was quite popular, gathering, fishing and hunting played the main role in economic life, while farming and animal husbandry were so poorly represented that we can hardly make any comments on them. All this displays a considerable cultural primitivity, which should by no means be attributed to great antiquity, but reflects the environments and ecosystem in which people lived.

The tools are largely, even entirely at rare sites, of chipped stone. The common types include choppers, scrapers, points and discs. Polished stone tools are present in small numbers, among which piercers, awls, axes, adzes, knives and some other types being distinguished. There is no necessary connection between the proportion of chipped artefacts to polished ones and the chronological position of a site.

The pottery was all of red, coarse sandy ware of impure colour and low firing temperatures (only 680 °C for the potsherds from Zenpiyan in Guilin, Guangxi Province, and from Qingtang in Yingde, Guangdong). The kiln cannot have been known. The surface of objects was decorated with cord impressions, along with incisions, comb marks and basketry patterns and, perhaps later, was partly painted in red or coated with slip. Vessels are generally found in small numbers and as fragmentary sherds, which can scarcely be pieced together to indicate their complete shapes.

People then lived by rivers or on the sea-shore and engaged mainly in gathering, fishing and hunting, as shown by the piles of shells in cave sites and shell-mounds consisting of the remains of freshwater or marine shellfish, as well as by the excavated bones of wild animals and implements for fishing and hunting, such as bone arrowheads and harpoons, stone net-weights and so on. Farming and animal husbandry were not apparent yet. It cannot be excluded that tuber crops such as taro and yam might have been grown, but there was no primitive agriculture with cereal cultivation. The tropical or subtropical environments favourable to the growth of vegetation must have provided plentiful resources for gathering, fishing and hunting, and the simple and rough stone implements would not have been suitable for exploiting dense forests. Such conditions unavoidably exerted a restrictive influence on the development of primitive agriculture and brought about a Neolithic lacking farming, which did not evolve into a well-developed agricultural culture until later when rice cultivation began to spread here from the middle and lower reaches of the Changjiang river.

Very often there is a wide margin of error in the radiocarbon dates for the specimens found in the south China limestone area, usually causing dates to be attributed to a period more than 10,000 years too early. Samples of different substances even from the same stratum may be separated by a wide margin. The main cause of this is that in the limestone area the ancient carbonate in streams contained almost no carbon-14. Recent laboratory analyses indicate that samples of today's aquatic plants and animals taken from the area are also dated 1,000 to 2,000 years too early. Thus the south China limestone area has been an unusual region (the same is the case with South-East Asia) where carbon-14 examination gives dates obviously earlier than they should be, rendering them useless as a basis for chronology. The point will be reinforced if we take into account the case where, as developments in different areas cannot have occurred at the same rate, some sites display a cultural backwardness but actually belong to a later period. There is a good example, namely the cave site of Baxiandong in Taidong, Taiwan Province, in which all the stone tools were found to be chipped, but its radiocarbon date was as late as about 5,000 years ago.

The cultural primitivity and lack of farming of the early Neolithic in south China was caused by its development, which proceeded at a slow and stagnant rate but was not very old or remote in time. The numerous sites distributed throughout the extensive area may belong to several cultural types. Following their own paths, these types developed as close cultural parallels owing to the same natural environments, ecological system and economic patterns. As for their origin and further development, it remains as an open question calling for further research. For the time being, it can be pointed out that a few cultural elements display some relationship with the Huanghe valley and the reaches of the Changjiang river. For instance, the cord marks and comb marks and the red painting on the surface of pottery must reflect such contact and communication, and, moreover, the emergence and development of rice farming in south China should serve as a still more concrete example to illustrate the point.

CONCLUSIONS

Neolithic China, because of its territorial extent, environmental variety and cultural diversity, presented quite a complex picture; the four-part regionalization discussed above may roughly reflect the basic condition of developments before 5,000 years ago. With respect to the origin of the Neolithic cultures in China, although there remain gaps in the sequence it is beyond any doubt that they were all autochthonous, originating from and developing on Palaeolithic and Mesolithic bases in China herself.

There are also a few gaps in the genetic development of primitive agriculture in China. Nevertheless, it can be said that China was one of the centres of origin of agriculture in the world and that her agriculture was not introduced from outside. As we have seen, such drought-enduring crops as foxtail and broomcorn millet were being grown in the loess zone 8,000 years ago and provided the principal foodstuff for the inhabitants of north China for a long time; and rice cultivation must also have made its appearance as early as 7,000 years ago and has continued up to now. In the northern steppe and southern hilly land, agriculture began later and was closely related to the farming cultures in the Huanghe valley and reaches of the Changjiang river.

The Neolithic cultures of China developed with a clear succession, which was shown especially distinctly in the Huanghe valley. The early complexes represented by the Peiligang, Cishan and Dadiwan cultures are connected closely with the following Yangshao culture and further, through the subsequent Longshan culture, led to historical times represented by the Shang-Zhou civilization; thus a continuous line from remote antiquity can be clearly traced. Of course, mutual influence and communication with other regions in their turn made active contributions to the formation and development of ancient Chinese culture.

BIBLIOGRAPHY

AN ZHIMIN. 1982. *Essays on Neolithic China*. Beijing, Wen Wu Press. (In Chinese.)

ANDERSSON, J. G. 1943. *Researches into the Prehistory of the Chinese*. Stockholm. (Bull., Mus. Far Eastern Antiq., 15.)

CHANG KWANG-CHIH. 1977. *The Archaeology of Ancient China*. 3rd edn. New Haven.

XIA NAI (ed.) 1984a. *Archaeological Discoveries and Researches in New China*. Beijing, Wen Wu Press. (In Chinese.)

—— (ed.) 1984b. *Recent Archaeological Discoveries in the People's Republic of China*. Paris/Tokyo, UNESCO.

47

EUROPE
during the Neolithic

Sigfried J. De Laet

THE IMPORTANCE OF THE EUROPEAN NEOLITHIC

Europe was not part of the 'nuclear zones' in which human beings began, autonomously and without external stimuli, to practise animal husbandry and agriculture (Chapters 36, 37 and 38). In fact, the Neolithic way of life was imported into Europe, and the oldest peasant communities we meet there originated in Asia Minor. It may therefore be wondered why we are paying more attention to the European Neolithic than to the same period in other parts of the world outside the 'nuclear zones'. There are several reasons:

1 research into the Neolithic was begun in Europe much earlier than anywhere else and continues apace, so much so that our documentation on European Neolithic cultures is of unequalled diversity and richness;
2 in many parts of Africa, Asia, America and Oceania, the Neolithic did not begin until after the terminal date chosen for this volume; the Neolithic of these countries will therefore be treated in Volume II;
3 many problems of methodology and interpretation concerning the Neolithic were first posed in Europe, and some continue to be the object of keen debate;
4 finally, the European Neolithic has very special characteristics in various fields (such as megaliths, mining, metallurgy), subjects which will be examined at greater length in Chapters 55 and 56.

THE GRADUAL SPREAD OF NEOLITHIC LIFE IN EUROPE

The end of the Pleistocene and the beginnings of the Holocene profoundly changed the geomorphology of Europe and its inhabitants' way of life. We need merely recall the relatively rapid melting of the ice-cap and of the glaciers covering the higher mountains, the marked rise in sea-level and the submersion of vast lowland tracts, the emergence of the Straits of Dover and of the southern North Sea, the important changes in what was to become the Baltic, the separation of Ireland and Britain from the Continent and the replacement of the periglacial climate by a more temperate one and of tundras and steppes by forests. Humans had to adapt to this new environment. Some groups gradually occupied the northern zones now cleared of the ice; others who stayed where they were had to change their ancestral ways. Hunting big game that roamed in herds through the steppes and the tundra gave way to hunting large forest game which were more difficult to track (the domestication of dogs has been associated with the introduction of these new hunting methods). At the same time, fishing, the gathering of eggs and above all of edible roots, plants and fruits became of much greater importance. These changes have already been discussed at some length (Chapter 21) and we shall not dwell on them here. It must, however, be pointed out that at the end of this Mesolithic period, we encounter, above all in southern Europe, communities of hunter-gatherers that practised selective hunting and systematically harvested certain wild plants (such as leguminous plants). Now, as we stressed earlier (Chapter 36), these are precisely the characteristics one so often meets in cultures which have reached the pre-Neolithic stage. It is therefore possible that these southern European cultures could have attained the Neolithic stage without any external stimulus. But this is clearly a rather daring hypothesis because, as we know, the Neolithic way of life was brought to Europe by immigrants from Anatolia. However, it is worth recalling that at that time Europe already had communities predisposed to this new way of life.

While in western Asia the beginnings of the Neolithic (the PPNA: Pre-pottery Neolithic A) go back to about 11,000 years ago (Chapter 41), the earliest signs of food production did not appear in Europe until nearly two millennia later, primarily in Greece (Crete, Peloponnese, Thessaly). The calibrated radiocarbon dates at these oldest sites oscillate around 9,100 to 9,000 years BP, correponding approximately to the PPNB (Pre-pottery Neolithic B) period of Anatolia. Hence it seems likely that it was immigrants from that region who introduced the domesticated animals and plants we find in the oldest Neolithic sites of Greece (which do not exist there in the wild state).

From the Aegean, the Neolithic life-style spread by various maritime routes (see p. 494) to the central and western Mediterranean. We meet it in Sicily at the end of the ninth millennium BP, in Sardinia and Corsica at the beginning of the eighth millennium BP, in Adriatic Italy during the same millennium and in northern Italy at the end of the eighth millennium BP. The first half of the eighth millennium BP saw the emergence of the Franco-Iberian

Cardial, traces of which can be found in the south of France, in Spain, in Portugal and in the coastal regions of the Maghreb.

Towards the end of the ninth millennium BP, immigrants from Anatolia crossed the Dardanelles and the Bosphorus and introduced the Neolithic into the Balkans. The new way of life spread from there as far as the Carpathians (first half of the eighth millennium BP) but did not cross that barrier until the second half or the end of the eighth millennium BP. It was also during the second half of the eighth millennium that the Neolithic appeared in Ukraine. In Atlantic Europe, agriculture and animal husbandry were introduced fairly late: in western France it was not until the middle or the second half of the eighth millennium BP; in Ireland and Britain it took longer still – until the seventh millennium BP. Northern Europe brought up the rear; here the food production did not begin until the turn of the seventh millennium BP.

This slow spread of the Neolithic way of life from south-eastern Europe to the west and to the north took more than three millennia to be accomplished. Not so very long ago (see for instance Ammerman and Cavalli-Sforza, 1971) it was generally believed that this diffusion had taken place very gradually and at a regular pace, resulting from the slow semi-nomadism of the first farmers, who moved on to new ground every few years when their fields were exhausted; today we have the impression that this spread was very irregular in its timing, with periods of rapid and wide territorial expansion alternating with stages of rest that lasted sometimes for many centuries. Several factors have played a role in this process. Already in Chapter 36 we have mentioned the hypothesis that Mesolithic communities that were perfectly adapted to their natural environment adopted farming only under pressure of certain unforeseen circumstances that plunged them into a state of crisis. In Europe such crises could have resulted from climatic changes (which were rather numerous during the Holocene, with fluctuations from the Preboreal to the Boreal, then to the Atlantic, with many local variations) (Barker, 1985). Among the other factors that could also be taken into account to explain the irregular advance of the Neolithic, we can mention the fact that the first domesticated plants were adapted to the Mediterranean climate and had therefore to undergo some mutations before they could survive in regions with a more rigorous climate, and also the role of the nature of the soil, the rather rudimentary farming methods preventing cultivation of soils which were either not very fertile or too heavy. Views of this subject, however, differ considerably (see the various regional chapters below).

There are many differences, large and small, between archaeologists of different schools about the mode in which the Neolithic life-style spread. The reader should therefore not be surprised to find a number of divergent interpretations in the succeeding chapters. For many years the diffusionist model put forward by V. Gordon Childe enjoyed great vogue: it was argued that every major cultural innovation and all technical progress originated in western Asia and were diffused towards the west by successive waves of immigrants. This model, which still has its champions, has since been challenged. However, the reactions of some anti-diffusionists have been too radical: their model is diametrically opposed to Childe's in that it postulates the completely autochthonous character of nearly every innovation. The truth probably lies halfway between these two extreme theses. It seems very difficult

to deny, for instance, that animal husbandry and agriculture were brought to Europe by two successive waves of immigrants from Anatolia, the first reaching Greece through the Aegean and perhaps also through the Dardanelles, the second reaching the Balkans through the Dardanelles and the Bosphorus several centuries later, and bringing knowledge not only of agriculture and animal husbandry but also of pottery. On the other hand, the question whether there were subsequent waves of Anatolian immigrants and how large they were remains open. Another controversial question is whether or not the diffusion of the Neolithic way of life from Greece and the Balkans to the west and north was the result of migrations of populations already practising the Neolithic way of life (for example for demographic reasons) or whether it was achieved by the acculturation of indigenous Mesolithic populations. It seems impossible to answer this question with a categorical yes or no; the present writer believes the answer varies from case to case, each of which must be examined separately. Some authors minimize the importance of contacts between the first farming communities and Mesolithic groups, which, they believe, were gradually forced back to marginal regions not very propitious to agriculture. Others, by contrast, stress the role of indigenous groups in this process of Neolithic development. For instance, acculturation is alleged to have happened in Ukraine where there is clear cultural continuity between the Mesolithic and the early Neolithic; the introduction of agriculture and animal husbandry there is said to have been the result of contacts with Neolithic populations from the Balkans on the one hand and with western Asia (beyond the Caucasus) on the other. The Neolithic acculturation of northern Europe provides another example: it might well have resulted from contacts between the Mesolithic Ertebølle–Ellerbek population and peasants of the Rössen culture in bordering regions. Another subject on which opinions differ considerably is that of the origins of the Bandkeramik culture in central Europe. Some trace it back to the colonization of the region by groups belonging to the Starčevo–Körös complex, while others consider the Bandkeramik a 'secondary Neolithic', that is, one resulting from the acculturation of autochthonous Mesolithic groups. Good arguments can be advanced in support of either thesis. In any case it would be wrong to minimize the contribution of the Mesolithic population in the development of the Neolithic in Europe. The influence of autochthonous substrata could also have been responsible for the fragmentation of some cultures (for instance the Bandkeramik), which originally exhibited considerable cultural unity over very vast areas into a number of distinct regional groups with smaller territories.

A last remark, linked to the diachronic diffusion of the Neolithic in Europe, concerns the chronological division of that period in that part of the world. In large geographical and cultural areas, we distinguish between an Early Neolithic, a Middle Neolithic, a Late Neolithic and eventually a Chalcolithic. That division is obviously based on the cultural evolution of each of these areas. As a result, the Middle Neolithic in a given region corresponds neither chronologically nor culturally to the Middle Neolithic in another region. As it seems impossible to find a synchronous time-scale for all of Europe, each period of which would correspond to a given cultural stage, the authors of the various chapters have agreed to retain the traditional division for all the regions, while expressly forewarning the reader that such terms as 'Early Neolithic' have no more than a strictly regional value in absolute chronology.

We must finally justify the terminal date chosen for this chapter. The terminal date of this whole volume corresponds to the emergence of the first states in Egypt and western Asia (around 5,000 years ago), but precedes the end of the Neolithic in Europe by several centuries. It was therefore decided not to continue the present chapter until the end of the European Neolithic, but only as far as the archaeological horizon nearest to 5,000 years BP, namely the emergence in large parts of eastern, central, northern and western Europe of the complex of cultures associated with beakers, battle axes and single graves. That (as determined by calibrated radiocarbon dating) happened in the second half of the sixth millennium BP. That complex of cultures will not, however, be treated before Volume II.

THE MEANS OF SUBSISTENCE AND THEIR DEVELOPMENT DURING THE EUROPEAN NEOLITHIC

There is no need to recall that the Neolithic was characterized above all by the production of food with all the consequences that that entailed (Chapter 36). However, during the five or so millennia that the Neolithic lasted in Europe, agriculture and animal husbandry underwent some development. Moreover, hunting, fishing and the gathering of shellfish, eggs and wild plants continued to play some role in the economy of a number of cultures. We shall now proceed to a rapid review of the essential facts connected with agriculture, animal husbandry and other means of subsistence.

Agriculture

The first plants to be cultivated in Europe were imported from Asia Minor in an already domesticated state. They included various cereals (that did not grow wild in Europe) such as cultivated einkorn (*Triticum monococcum*), cultivated emmer (*Triticum dicoccum*), club wheat (*Triticum compactum*), common wheat (*Triticum aestivum*), Durum wheat (*Triticum durum*), bread wheat (*Triticum vulgare*), barley (*Hordeum vulgare*) and leguminous plants (peas, broad beans, lentils). It should be added, however, that some legumes, already harvested systematically in their wild state by Mesolithic groups in southern Europe (see p. 490) might well have been domesticated in Europe. The range of crops was gradually enlarged to include oleaginous plants (flax, papaverous plants), pistachio, fig, almond and grape, but most of these new plants remained confined to the Mediterranean.

The study of the development of agricultural techniques still runs up against a number of problems. At the beginning of our period, these techniques were not yet very advanced, so little so in fact that until the introduction of the scratch plough or ard, agricultural communities were forced to work only with soils that were both fertile and not too difficult to till, for instance loess or marl. That is why the habitats that are associated with the Linear Pottery culture (*Linearbandkeramik*) in central Europe are found almost exclusively on loess. That is also why, in certain regions of northern Europe where such soil is scarce, agriculture could not provide a living, and fishing and hunting and the gathering of shellfish continued to

provide a significant part of human needs (Chapter 54). Good arable land was nearly everywhere covered with forests and an undergrowth of bushes and scrub which had to be cleared to make way for fields and pastures. Trees were felled with flint axes or pediform tools ('adzes') made of hard rock, and the shrub was cleared by burning. After this application of slash-and-burn methods, the soil was prepared with a hoe (an 'adze' probably serving as the blade) or with a spade (Neolithic wooden spades have been found in Denmark), while sowing was sometimes effected with a digging-stick, often weighted with a perforated stone ball for better balance. It is, however, also possible that, as suggested by some ethnographic parallels, the very first sowing following the burning of the scrub was done directly in the ashes without prior tillage of the soil. Cereals were perhaps picked by hand, but more generally reaped with reaping knives or sickles, with wood or bone handles to which flint bladelets had been attached (possibly with resin).

In 1941, J. Iversen, basing himself on pollen analyses, put forward a model of *landnam* (new soil cultivation) that was in vogue for a long time, especially for central and northern Europe: following tree clearing by burning, the fields could not be used for more than a few years because they were quickly exhausted for lack of manure and the absence of crop rotation. The peasants were therefore forced to keep clearing new plots of ground which would have turned them into semi-nomads. This model has since been subjected to severe criticism. Recent excavations have produced indications that rotational cropping was by no means unknown; moreover, the mixed economy of these early peasants makes it unlikely that the improvement of land by the addition of animal manure was unrecognized. The nomadic way of life demanded by the Iversen model would therefore not have been necessary (Rowly-Conwy, 1981). And yet some nomadism there must have been; thus B. Soudsky has found that the Bandkeramik settlement of Bylany in the Czech Republic was abandoned several times, the inhabitants returning after an absence of several years, by which time the soil would have recovered its original fertility by a process of natural regeneration. In general, however, not enough account has been taken of the gradual invasion of the fields by weeds, which must ultimately have formed a thick carpet that could no longer be removed with the tools available at the time. Nor is it impossible that the movement of agricultural populations should have had psychological causes: an irrational desire to go ever further afield in the conquest of new lands, a mentality comparable to that of the nineteenth-century pioneers of the North American West frontier. That sort of mentality would also explain why small groups of peasants should have braved the North Sea to settle in Ireland and Britain.

Very great advances came with the introduction of the ard (Chapter 36). Its use seems to have spread gradually from south-eastern Europe to the west and the north. It had certainly reached Denmark by the period of the Funnel-Beaker culture (*Trichterbecherkultur*), during the sixth millennium BP, and Britain perhaps even earlier. In these regions there are in fact traces of fossilized furrows drawn by a plough and dated by their stratigraphy. The use of the ard certainly facilitated the cultivation of less fertile soils (such as alluvial sand); the resulting extension of cleared land during the Neolithic has been observed in several regions. The cultivation of heavy soils (for instance heavy clay sediment) had to wait until the introduction of the heavy plough with coulter, wheels, ploughshare and mouldboard many centuries later. The cultivation in the Neolithic of less fertile land probably had another cause as well, namely demographic expansion, which is an almost constant corollary of the Neolithic way of life (Chapter 36).

Animal husbandry

We have already referred to the domestication, during the Mesolithic, of dogs, most probably by forest hunters. During the Neolithic, they acquired their traditional role as sheep-dogs and watchdogs. There are few indications, at least in Europe, that dogs were also reared for their meat.

The first domesticated animals we find in the oldest Neolithic sites in Europe, sheep and goats (ovicaprines), were certainly introduced by the first Neolithic immigrants from Asia Minor, since the natural habitat of these animals does not extend as far as Europe (Chapter 38). Pigs and cattle were introduced a little later. Domesticated cattle were found in Thessaly at almost the same time as they appeared in Anatolia (Çatal Hüyük) and it is therefore not impossible that aurochs, the wild ancestors of cattle, should have been domesticated simultaneously and independently in the two regions (Higgs, 1975). Horses were not domesticated until the end of the sixth millennium BP, probably in the Eurasian steppes round the Black Sea, the Caspian Sea and the Aral Sea. They were introduced into Europe at the time of the Beaker cultures: traces of them have been found, *inter alia*, in Hungary, France, the Netherlands and Ireland in association with Bell-Beaker culture remains. The cultural importance of the domestication of horses (which, for instance, made possible a nomadic pastoral life-style) will be examined in Volume II.

The main aim of stock-breeding was the production of meat. However, the breeding of animals also had many other purposes. The importance of rearing sacrifical animals for religious ceremonies should not be overlooked. Very quickly, the milk of sheep, goats and cows began to play a significant role in the diet of peasant communities, and so did cream, butter and cheese. Oxen, donkeys and horses were used to draw the ards and carts. Animal manure was spread over the soil to improve it. Bones and horns were good raw material for the manufacture of many tools. Leather was made from the hides of cattle. Last but not least, the fleece of sheep as well as goat's hair were used to spin wool. Chronologically, this was a somewhat later phenomenon, because the fleece of wild ovicaprines does not lend itself to the production of wool and a mutation was needed for that to happen. We have few precise details about the methods used to rear animals: for the age and the sex of the killed animals, see Chapter 38. In western Asia we have evidence of transhumance in mountainous regions; in Europe this practice was probably not unknown, but we lack precise information. One of the problems the stock farmers must have faced was the provision of winter fodder, especially in regions where the climate demanded stabling during the cold season. It would seem that a number of beasts were slaughtered every autumn, particularly those that no longer served to increase the herd and whose continued existence could therefore not be justified on economic grounds (old females that had grown sterile, surplus males, and so on). Their meat, conserved by drying, smoking or salting, served as winter food. The hypothesis has been put forward more than once that the 'causewayed camps' in several regions of western and north-western Europe (*inter alia* in England, France and Denmark) were used at fixed dates

as *kraals* for herding and slaughtering animals and as fairgrounds and festive sites where religious rites were performed prior to the slaughter. For winter fodder, the stock-breeders probably used the leaves of certain trees; H. Troels-Smith (1960) has attributed the marked reduction of *Ulmus* (elm) pollen in pollen diagrams from the end of the Atlantic climatic epoch, throughout western and north-western Europe, to the large-scale use by Neolithic populations of elm leaves as fodder. This theory however is not generally accepted.

Did Neolithic peasants resort to genetic manipulations in what was of course a purely empirical manner? It would seem that they did so, for instance by selecting breeding stock to improve milk or wool production. It has also been suggested, but without formal proof, that herdsmen sometimes introduced wild animals, such as aurochs or wild boars, into their herds to avoid degeneration.

The castration of bulls was certainly practised, as palaeontological examinations have made clear. This operation was necessary to render these animals less aggressive and more docile, so that they could be used as draught animals and harnessed to carts (introduced into Europe during the Neolithic; see p. 494) and to ards. Rock engravings in southern Scandinavia and in Val Camonica, which are a little later than the period under discussion, often represent pairs of oxen harnessed to ards. Osteological examinations show that certain animals had deformed bones due to their use as draught animals.

Other means of subsistence

With the exception of groups of hunter-gatherers who gradually migrated northwards as the ice-cap melted and who, once settled in the periglacial zones of Scandinavia, Finland and Russia, maintained their way of life as Mesolithic hunters or fisherfolk (Chapter 21), all Europe gradually adopted the Neolithic way of life during the period under discussion. However, some communities, especially those established along the banks and deltas of big rivers, adopted just a few or restricted aspects of the Neolithic life-style, such as a limited form of agriculture and the raising of just a few head of small livestock, and the making of pots; for the rest, they persisted with their ancestral ways and drew their essential means of subsistence from the sea: fish, seals, marine birds, shellfish. Owing to the isostatic movements resulting from the melting of the arctic ice-cap, beaches have risen and many of these coastal sites are found nowadays rather far inland: this happened mainly in Scandinavia. Elsewhere very many of these habitation sites disappeared during the various marine transgressions. Recent excavations at Swifterbant, in the delta region of the 'Big Rivers' in the Netherlands, have yielded many new data on the culture of these communities which continued for many centuries to draw their main subsistence from the rivers and from the sea.

From the inception of the Neolithic, the importance of hunting began to decrease considerably: more than 90 per cent of the bones found in Neolithic habitation sites, even the oldest, generally belong to domestic species. Though hunting still continued on a reduced scale, it probably did so less for the sake of procuring more meat for the table than for obtaining raw materials for the manufacture of artefacts: antlers often were made into axes, axe sheaths, tool handles, awls, chisels, picks, combs to card wool and so on. However, in the sixth millennium BP, some cultures (for instance habitation sites in the foothills of the Alps and the Seine–Oise–Marne culture in France) show an impressive increase in the bony remains of wild animals (from 50 per cent sometimes to as much as 90 per cent). We share J. Lüning's view (Chapter 51) that this was by no means a partial return to the life-style of Palaeolithic and Mesolithic hunter-gatherers; the explanation must rather be sought in the intensification of agriculture at the expense of stock-breeding and in the climatic conditions that led to the clearing of forests, two factors responsible for a rapid multiplication of game which thus forced the peasants to resort to intensive hunting in order to protect their field from the depredations of wild animals.

Finally, repeated deforestation and the use of abandoned fields for pasture often led to the appearance at the edge of the forest of thorn bushes (blackthorns, brambles, wild roses and so on), a semi-natural barrier that stopped the forest from returning to the cleared sites. That barrier also served to keep out intruders and to fence in domestic animals; moreover the fruits it provided (blackberries, raspberries, strawberries, wild apples, hips) helped to vary the menu of Neolithic people most agreeably.

OTHER FACETS OF ECONOMIC LIFE

It seems clear that as far as the production of food was concerned, the great majority of European Neolithic communities were essentially self-sufficient. However, there were probably some exceptions to this rule. Such self-sufficiency was less general, though, when it came to the raw materials needed to fashion tools, weapons, ornaments, some building materials and certain 'prestige objects'. Whenever possible, Neolithic people evidently procured what they needed from near by, but some of these materials or objects came from distant regions. These they almost invariably obtained through barter – maybe often in exchange for food. It is also possible that they gave and received 'prestige objects' as presents or as pledges of friendship and alliance.

Means of transport

Boats

As early as the Upper Palaeolithic, human beings must have been familiar with rafts or small boats, for how else could they have reached Australia? In the Mesolithic, canoes hollowed out from tree-trunks were already in common use, at least for lake and river navigation. But were these canoes reliable enough for the kind of ocean navigation we know to have occurred in the Aegean in the Mesolithic, at the beginning of the trade in obsidian from the island of Melos? It seems much more likely that the migration of the first Neolithic people from Asia Minor to the Peloponnese via the Aegean, involving the transport not only of people but also of domestic animals (in sufficient numbers to ensure their reproduction), called for less primitive craft. These, it has been suggested, must have been made of skins or strips of bark attached to wooden frames, but since no remains or drawings of such vessels have come down to us this remains a speculative idea. The same transport problem is obviously raised by the spread of Neolithic cultures to the central and western Mediterranean (where a number of islands, sometimes at considerable distances from the mainland, were then settled for the first time) and to Britain and Ireland.

But even with less primitive boats the crossing could only be made during calm seasons and always remained dangerous and chancy.

Carts

The oldest wheeled vehicles appeared in western Asia six millennia ago. In Europe, miniature carts (perhaps cult objects) are known from Hungary (the Baden culture), while in the Netherlands a dozen disc-wheels have been dated back to the first half of the fifth millennium BP. It therefore took just a few centuries for the use of carts to spread from Mesopotamia to north-western Europe. However, we cannot tell whether wheeled transport was already known in Europe during the period covered by the present volume, except perhaps at the very end.

All in all, it seems likely that, throughout the greater part of the European Neolithic, the transport of heavy materials was effected on the backs of humans or oxen.

Raw materials

The raw materials Neolithic people used for making their artefacts fall into two categories: those constituting objects of barter over more or less long distances and those that do not.

The latter of these categories consists mainly of wood, bone, antlers, clay, fur and leather and, eventually, textiles.

Wood has only been preserved exceptionally (for example in Swiss lake dwellings or in peatbogs) but it was probably the most common raw material used by Neolithic people. Excavations have brought to light wooden spades, ards, cartwheels, bows, arrow and spear shafts, tool handles, bowls and other vessels, canoes and paddles. It seems very likely that Neolithic people also made some pieces of furniture (not preserved but which must have resembled those made from large slabs of stone discovered in Neolithic villages in the Orkneys, for instance in Skara Brae and Rinyo). We shall be returning to wood in its uses as a building material.

Bone keeps rather better than wood, but acid soils totally destroy it. The items recovered comprise weapons (for example arrowheads), tools (including chisels, potters' gradines, awls and gouges), blades, small plates, buttons, spoons and pendants. The bone was polished, already during the Palaeolithic, by abrasion, and this technique was later adapted for the polishing of stones.

Antlers had many uses, which may partly explain the survival of hunting. In particular, antlers were indispensable for the manufacture of certain tools (such as picks, thousands of which have been found in flint mines).

The clay used to make pots, was, as some analyses have shown, most often of local origin (see Chapter 36 for the importance and significance of pottery from the Neolithic onwards).

Fur and leather have always gone into the making of clothes. They gradually lost their importance with the increasing use of cloth. Leather was also used to make skins for storing liquids before the widespread use of pottery vessels.

Textiles were not used before the Neolithic. The oldest traces of spinning and weaving, apart from spindle-whorls, are textile impressions on pottery from Sitagroi, Greece, around 7,000 years ago. The most ancient European piece of cloth was discovered at Tybring Vig, on the island of Fyn (Denmark), and is dated to around 6,200 years ago. Let us recall that the fleece of sheep and goats did not lend itself to spinning and weaving when these animals were first domesticated, but that they had first to undergo mutations. Nevertheless, wool quickly replaced leather and skins in the manufacture of clothing: by the Bronze Age it was in common use. As for flax, which was first cultivated as an oleaginous plant, it rapidly became a textile plant, as witness the discovery of fragments of linen in Swiss lake dwellings.

The other category of raw materials largely comprises flint, obsidian, various types of hard rock, amber, salt, and, in the course of our period, copper and gold.

Flint, together with wood, constitutes the most important raw material used by prehistoric humans. Flint is found almost everywhere, but is particularly abundant in alluvial river deposits and in places where chalk layers riddled with Cretaceous flint nodules have risen to the surface. In the Neolithic, demand for good-quality flint increased markedly. Moreover, in many parts of Europe – England, France, Belgium, the Netherlands, Denmark and Poland and elsewhere as well – small communities, probably descendants of the autochthonous Mesolithic population, began to specialize in the extraction of flint, first in surface pits but soon afterwards also in underground mines (Chapter 56).

These communities of miners, who probably neither tilled the land nor bred stock, bartered the flint they extracted (in the form of rough nodules or as semi-finished products) for food, clothing, etc. People travelled over long distances to acquire good-quality flint: thus flint from Spiennes (Belgium) has been found in sites associated with the Michelsberg culture near Frankfurt-on-Main, 350 km away from Spiennes as the crow flies; flint from the Krzemionki Opatowksie mines in Poland has been located in Moravia and in Germany; flint from Grand-Pressigny (near Tours, France) was exported to as far away as the mouths of the Weser and Elbe.

Obsidian, a type of lava with a vitreous appearance, has some advantages over flint, sharper edges for instance. Where it was found it was collected and exported from early times. We have already mentioned the obsidian trade in the island of Melos, whence obsidian was exported from about 10,000 years ago to the Peloponnese and Anatolia. Deposits in the Aeolian isles were first exploited at the beginning of the Neolithic and obsidian from Lipari has been found in many parts of peninsular Italy. Hungarian obsidian was exported as far away as Poland.

Hard rocks very often of volcanic origin (basalt, amphibolite, tephrite, trachyte, phthanite, psammitic sandstone, arkose, sandstone, schist) have been used by many Neolithic cultures for the manufacture of various artefacts: millstones, pediform tools ('adzes') and so on. Often these rocks were imported from afar: it has been calculated that 85 per cent of the adzes associated with the Bandkeramik culture in central Belgium were made of rock from the Eifel massif. These artefacts (except for millstones) were polished by abrasion, a method copied from bone workers, and rock polishing preceded flint polishing.

At the end of our period, many regions (France, the west coast of Britain, Belgium, the Netherlands, the Rhineland, Westphalia, Lower Saxony, and others) produced large 'display axes' made from hard green rock (jadeite, chloromelanite, dolerite or nephrite), which were long considered to have been of Breton origin, but some of which must have come from the Rhineland. These axes were some of the earliest 'prestige objects' (see p. 496).

Amber, a transparent fossil resin, owes its importance to its colour and electromagnetic properties. In prehistoric times, only Nordic amber from the coasts of Jutland and the Baltic Sea was used. The export of Nordic amber began in the Neolithic. It was used for beads and magical religious objects.

Salt played a considerable role in the economy of Neolithic people. It is indispensable in human physiological processes. However, during the Palaeolithic and Mesolithic, when humans were still hunter-gatherers living mainly on meat, they had no need for additional salt. By contrast, in the Neolithic when the proportion of carbohydrates in the diet increased appreciably, extra salt was badly needed. Very few vestiges of salt have been brought to light by archaeologists, especially not from the Neolithic. They become more frequent in early Metal Age deposits, by which time salt-making techniques must have been greatly improved. However, there are some indications that the saline springs near Halle (Germany) and the salt mines at Hallein and at Hallstatt (Austria) were exploited as far back as the Neolithic.

Copper. In Chapter 36, we stressed that one of the most spectacular consequences of the dendochronological calibration of radiocarbon dates was the demonstration that copper-working methods were not imported into Europe from western Asia, as had been commonly believed until 1970, but that they were discovered independently in the Balkans at the turn of the eighth millennium BP, long, therefore, before the beginnings of Aegean metallurgy (end of the sixth millennium BP) (Renfrew, 1979). In the Balkans, a very early start was made with the exploitation of several copper mines, for instance at Rudna Glava (former Yugoslavia) and Aibunar (Bulgaria) (see Chapter 50 for the characteristics of the Chalcolithic that developed subsequently in former Yugoslavia, Bulgaria, Romania and Hungary). From that time, the Balkans must have witnessed an intense traffic not only in copper ore but also in weapons and tools made from that metal. Other copper-working centres emerged at the end of the seventh and during the sixth millennium BP in the central and western Mediterranean (Italy and Spain), in all probablility quite independently as well, that is without being affected by south-east European or Aegean influences (Chapter 49).

Gold. The development of gold metallurgy in the Balkans was parallel to that of copper. As early as the second half of the seventh millennium BP, the goldsmith's craft took remarkable strides, something that did not happen in any other region during that period. One sign of this development is the profusion of jewels and prestige objects in gold from the Varna necropolis (Bulgaria).

Building materials

Because we discuss settlements, religious monuments and funerary structures on pp. 497–8, we confine ourselves here to building materials and to some of the technical problems raised by their use.

Sun-dried bricks. Imported from western Asia, the use of sun-dried bricks was confined to part of the Aegean world only.

Wood, wattle and daub. These were used as building materials by a great many Neolithic cultures. Excavations do not generally reveal more than the plan of these buildings, but small clay models give us some idea of the superstructure. One can only marvel at the very advanced methods used by these builders, and this despite their rather primitive tools. Some houses (for instance those associated with the Bandkeramik culture) must have had a heavy timber frame, despite the lack of nails and dowels; the builder did not hesitate to use joists up to 8–9 m long and to keep them in place with the help of ties whose precise nature is not yet clear. Even more arduous problems had to be solved by the builders of lake dwellings in Alpine regions – be they in villages erected on piles over lakes or in villages on marshy ground (shores of lakes, peat bogs): driving long piles into the muddy bottom of lakes or into the marshy soil until they reached solid ground; laying solid floors made of logs, planks and clay that had to be replaced frequently because they kept soaking up water.

In trying to reconstruct these houses, experimental archaeology has demonstrated the exceptional expertise displayed by Neolithic carpenters in overcoming technical difficulties. Even today many problems raised by their crafting have remained unanswered.

Stone was less commonly used in the construction of dwellings except at the end of our period. We know of houses with stone floors and foundations, but the superstructures were made of wood and daub (good examples can be found in the village of Khirokitia in Cyprus). We have mentioned the village of Skara Brae and Rinyo in the Orkneys where, because of the scarcity of wood, the walls of houses were entirely built of flat stones carefully stacked one on top of the other; the furniture (dressers, shelves and so on), too, was made of large, flat slabs. More important was the use of dry-stone methods to build the outside walls of settlements; they were sometimes erected with stones of such large dimensions that we can call them Cyclopean. Megalithic monuments (tombs, sanctuaries, alignments, menhirs) were obviously the most spectacular examples of the use of stones as building material. For the problems raised by the transport, sometimes over long distances, of enormous blocks weighing several tons and also by the construction of these monuments, see Chapters 49, 53 and 55. Calibrated radiocarbon dates have shown that these imposing monuments are older than the great edifices of Egypt and Mesopotamia, from which they were formerly thought to have derived. At the end of our period, towards the turn of the sixth millennium BP, there emerged a new type of funerary building: the *tholos*, a beehive-shaped tomb built in dry-stone or with upright megalithic slabs (Chapters 49, 53, 54).

'Prestige objects'

We can distinguish two categories of 'prestige objects'.

On the one hand there were objects to which supernatural, apotropaic or magical virtues were probably attached; these were mainly 'jewellery' or trinkets – bracelets, collars, pendants and the like – made from various stones, bones, precious material like metals, amber imported from afar, and *Spondylus gaederopus* shells imported from the Aegean and discovered in many Balkan and central European sites.

On the other hand, there were objects made of rare materials that procured prestige for their owners and hence served as status symbols. 'Breton' axes in green rock could not, if only because of their large dimensions, be used as tools and were probably the insignia of civil or military leaders. A similar explanation has been given for the hard-stone battle-axes dating back to the Final Neolithic: the perforation cut into them was often too narrow to hold any but a very thin helve which, even if made of hard wood, would have snapped off at the slightest blow. They, too, were probably status symbols. As for gold objects,

they were evidently reserved for individuals of high rank. Let us note that the Varna (Bulgaria) gold objects included a 'sceptre'.

There remains the problem of the characteristic vessels of a given culture found amongst the remains of another culture. According to some authors, these vessels had no intrinsic value, but were simply used to transport products of commercial importance (perhaps salt) or substances endowed with supernatural, magical virtues (water from a healing source or curative ointments). Such vessels accordingly fall into our first category. Other authors, however, believe that these vessels, and especially the bell-beakers found outside the context of the Bell-Beaker culture, were prestige objects in their own right.

THE HABITATION SITES

Neolithic habitation sites were very varied both in their internal arrangements and also in structural respects. It must be stressed, however, that very few villages have been excavated in their entirety, so that those inferences we can draw must remain, at least for the most part, rather speculative. Nevertheless can the main lines of a general process of development be discerned? We venture here no further than to suggest some tendencies, general rules with numerous exceptions:

At first, the oldest villages comprised few dwellings, sometimes packed into a small area or sometimes consisting of just a few farmsteads so far from one another that the total area of the habitation could cover several hectares (as during the earliest phases of the Bandkeramik culture). As the Neolithic proceeded, agglomerations of larger dimensions are increasingly found, probably reflecting a clear demographic increase.

Then, still very early on, one building began to stand out from the rest by virtue of its larger dimensions and sometimes also by its special architecture – for instance the *megaron* in Greece – and came to occupy a central position in the agglomeration. Was it perhaps the house of the village chief? This is the most common assumption, but there has also been mention of cult buildings or (on the basis of ethnological parallels) of a 'communal house', reserved for adults or the members of a 'confraternity'.

During a later period, these houses became increasingly isolated: they were confined either to high ground, to an acropolis (as in Sesklo and Dimini in Thessaly and elsewhere) or else to some large open space round which all the other houses were ranged (sometimes like the spokes of a wheel as in Kolomiscina in Ukraine). This central building was sometimes separated from the rest of the agglomeration by a wall.

While few of the oldest villages were protected, very soon afterwards they began to be surrounded with one or more ditches or a wall or both; the wall could be an earthwork rampart topped with a palisade or a dry-stone construction of Cyclopean type.

The villages themselves were increasingly built on heights surrounded by steep banks and only accessible from one side. Here there would be a ditch and an earthwork rampart or a defensive wall barring entry. During the last phases of the Neolithic, this wall was sometimes reinforced with semi-circular bastions, for instance at Los Millares (Spain). All these defence works indicate that the Neolithic was not a very pacific period.

Towards the end of the Neolithic we also find that some agglomerations, such as Sesklo and Dimini, were not only protected by one or two solid walls, but had their acropolis (on which the main building stood in isolation) surrounded by yet another thick defensive wall.

A final stage of this development is exemplified by the very elaborate fortifications in some Portuguese sites, such as Vila Nova de São Pedro and Zambujal, where multiple, thick walls with semicircular bastions surround a small central area. Carbon-14 dating seems to refute the old hypothesis that these sites were the trading posts of Aegean prospectors who had come to the Iberian peninsula in search of ores for their own metallurgical workshops; more likely, they were the fortified residences of leaders or chieftains, enriched perhaps by the products of the Iberian metallurgical industry (known to have flourished at the time) and, having grown powerful, turning their backs on the lower orders. This was the final stage of a long social evolution (see pp. 498–9).

FUNERARY CUSTOMS AND STRUCTURES – RELIGION

Throughout prehistory and later, funerary customs and religion were closely linked. Here we shall not list the funerary rites of the various cultures in detail. All of them clearly reflect the eschatological beliefs of Neolithic populations, but we find it impossible to give a precise account of these. At most, we can deduce from the archaeological remains that these people believed in some form of survival after death and that the cult of the dead, in one form or another, played an important role in their communities.

Inhumation was by far the most common form of burial during the Neolithic, but cremation was by no means unknown. In some cultures, for instance the Bandkeramik culture, the two rites coexisted and evidence of them can be found side by side in the same necropolises.

Many cultures were characterized by the presence of single graves of various types. Others used collective tombs that fall into three categories: cave ossuaries, hypogea cut into the rocks, some having a very elaborate structure (for instance in Sardinia and Malta), and finally megalithic tombs (Chapter 55). It is important to stress here that these megalithic tombs (except for the passage graves of the Seine–Oise–Marne culture) were reserved for a small number of privileged people who, because of the prestige they enjoyed in their lifetime, were allowed to take their place in the ranks of ancestors to whom a cult had been dedicated. Mortuary houses discovered in Denmark in association with megalithic tombs, and such ceremonial sites as the one at Alvastra in Sweden also connected with megalithic tombs, bear witness to rites accompanying each new interment in these megaliths.

At the beginning of the Neolithic, grave goods had a fairly egalitarian character, but as social differences grew, the resulting stratification of society was reflected in the grave goods as well. At the end of the period, by which time the leaders had grown richer and more powerful, we find exceptionally lavish tombs, for instance those in the Varna necropolis in Bulgaria or the double tomb in the hypogeum of Ponte San Pietro (of the Rinaldone culture in Italy).

Numerous figurines, cult objects, votive offerings, ritual sites and monuments tell us something about the religious practices of Neolithic people. These differed from one region to the next, and as we cannot possibly hope to present a full list, we must content ourselves with the salient points.

First, a fertility cult related to the one found in different guises in western Asia has left many vestiges in Greece and the Balkans, with offshoots in the central and western Mediterranean and also in central Europe. Most of these vestiges are figurines, often fairly realistic but generally highly stylized representations of women, often fat or pregnant, with accentuated sexual characteristics (thighs, buttocks, pubis), and sometimes seated and suckling an infant. It is generally believed that these figurines represented a fertility goddess, an interpretation that has however been challenged – in our view mistakenly (Chapter 48). They were often found in domestic contexts, which might imply that this cult still had a private character, at least at the beginning. This interpretation seems to be borne out by excavations in Zelenikovo (former Yugoslavia), where the houses had two rooms, one with a hearth and a large altar. In contrast, at Nea Nikomedeia (Greece), a site dating back to the beginning of the Neolithic, a building larger than the rest was found to contain several of these figurines; it is thought to have been a sacred place. It might, however, have been the house of the village chief, who might also have been invested with sacerdotal functions. The large Maltese temples (Chapter 49) might have been dedicated to the fertility goddess as well.

Second, the cult of the dead, in different forms, was of no lesser importance than the fertility cult to which it seems to have been linked very closely. The fertility gods and goddesses, moreover, quite often included the protection of the dead amongst their attributes (Chapter 36). It was thus that the bull god, the fertility god *par excellence*, left his traces as protector of the dead in Sardinian hypogea (De Laet, 1981), and that figurines representing the fertility goddess were found in hypogea in both Sardinia and Malta. We have already mentioned the cult of the dead in connection with funerary structures. Let us recall that megalithic tombs were reserved for a small number of the dead: it has been suggested that these prestigious few had the task of ensuring the perpetuation of the community. The 'mortuary houses' and the sacred places excavated in Scandinavia tell us a little about the ceremonies that were held there during each new interment and perhaps also at fixed periods on the occasion of large communal assemblies. A similar hypothesis has been put forward about the monumental hypogea of Sardinia and Malta, the Maltese temples and some of the big sanctuaries and megalithic tombs in Atlantic Europe.

Third, traces of Neolithic religions are not uncommon in Atlantic Europe either, but their real significance remains uncertain. In Spain, highly schematic female figurines appeared at the beginning of our period, but were later replaced with cylindrical stone idols and carved bone; here we also find the 'two eyes' motif so widespread in all coastal regions of Atlantic Europe as far as southern Scandinavia (where it occurs on ritual vases). This symbol is sexless and it is not even certain whether it really represents two eyes or whether it is of astral significance. The Portuguese schist plaques bearing geometric or anthropomorphic motifs (but without any sexual indications) are no easier to interpret. In western France, Britain and Ireland, the Neolithic was the age of large, open-air sacred sites. Here henge monuments, of which Avebury and above all Stonehenge are the most representative, and stone circles succeeded the causewayed camps from which they seem to have taken over the double role of communal assembly places and sacred sites. As the Stonehenge sanctuary and the imposing megalithic tomb at Newgrange (in Ireland) make clear, the sun played an essential role in the ceremonies that were held there. The solar cult was subsequently to assume increasing importance, especially in the Bronze Age.

Lastly, on several European Neolithic sites, it was believed that traces were found of cannibalism, but the evidence was never entirely convincing. Recent excavations at the Fontbrégoua cave, in south-east France, have, however, provided more reliable data (Villa et al., 1986). Ethnographic parallels suggest that anthropophagy had only very seldom a nutritional function, but was nearly always a magical ceremony.

SOCIAL AND POLITICAL DEVELOPMENTS

The basic social unit during the Neolithic in Europe was unquestionably the nuclear family (the married couple and their children), as the dimensions of the dwellings show. It has sometimes been argued that the extended family (resembling that of the Latin *familia*) has left traces in some cultures, but the evidence is weak and can easily be interpreted differently.

As we saw, the earliest villages were fairly egalitarian: neither the plan of the dwellings nor the grave goods reflect big social differences. No doubt, every village had a chief enjoying a measure of personal prestige and initiating such tasks as had to be performed communally: the erection of houses, the laying-out of the village in accordance with a fixed plan, the building of defensive structures. It has been alleged that these first villages witnessed a division of labour based on sex: the women who, in the Mesolithic, had been responsible for harvesting wild cereals while the men had gone hunting continuing to work in the fields until the introduction of the ard. At this point, agricultural labour is supposed to have become too arduous for them, and so they turned to spinning and weaving, and perhaps also to pottery making. This theory must obviously be treated with reservations. There was certainly some type of specialization in early villages: alongside farmers and shepherds, there would be a specialist in the fashioning of stone implements, a potter, a carpenter under whose direction heavy wooden houses or lake dwellings were put up and finally traders whose task it was to look for raw materials, sometimes in far-away places. Among these raw materials, flint took pride of place, because the procurement of good-quality flint was essential for the running of the Neolithic economy. Mining communities accordingly enjoyed a privileged position, and one that could easily be exploited. Thus communities associated with the Michelsberg culture in the Rhineland procured their flint, *inter alia*, from Spiennes in Belgium. To that end, whole Michelsberg communities apparently migrated to Belgium in the sixth millennium BP, one group settling in Spiennes and reducing the local flint miners to a form of slavery.

By this time, the social stratification of village communities had already been accentuated, as we know from various signs mentioned earlier, for instance from the fact that only some persons, who enjoyed great prestige, had the right of being interred in megalithic tombs and also from the special location of the chief's house in the centre of the agglomeration, sometimes separated from the other dwellings by a wall.

Before we come to the final stage of this development, we must quickly review the political structure of Neolithic villages. At the beginning of our period, the various villages belonging to a single culture were probably linked by ties based on a common technological tradition, a common language and a common religion. It has been assumed, with some probability, that seasonal ceremonies of a religious kind united the inhabitants of different villages in common meeting places such as the causewayed camps and the henge monuments, or in such great sanctuaries as those found in Malta or at Stonehenge. Here people may well have worshipped common mythical ancestors, such ceremonies clearly strengthening solidarity between villages. Gradually, larger political units or 'tribes' emerged, uniting several villages under a common authority. In Ukraine the Chalcolithic saw the grouping of several small agglomerations round a larger settlement, probably the centre of a tribal territory. The appearance of the same phenomenon in western Asia has already been mentioned (Chapter 41).

The crucial factor in this political and social development was the invention of metallurgy first in south-eastern Europe and subsequently in the western Mediterranean (Spain, Italy). Village or tribal chiefs probably succeeded in gaining personal possession of the copper and gold mines, thus increasing their personal wealth, prestige and power. Several facts corroborate this hypothesis: the emergence of such fortified villages as Vila Nova de São Pedro and Zambujal, the proliferation of 'prestige objects' made from rare or precious materials and the appearance of tombs with exceptionally lavish grave goods, for instance at Varna and Ponte San Pietro. It was not only the village chiefs who saw their power growing during the Neolithic: the priests also gained more prestige. The construction of imposing religious monuments (as, for instance, the Maltese temples, the henge monuments at Stonehenge and Avebury, the enormous megalithic tombs, the menhirs, the alignments) indicate very clearly how deep was the influence of religion and the prestige of the priests.

Lastly the development of long-distance trade and the multiplication of 'prestige objects' indicate the privileged position of the traders and of some craftsmen like the metallurgists and the goldsmiths.

Social and political evolution in Europe developed on the same model as in western Asia, but with some chronological delay. However this development in Europe did not reach the stage of the 'urban revolution': it was interrupted, a little earlier than 5,000 years ago, by the arrival of the tribes with beakers, battle axes and single tombs. Some linguists consider these tribes to have been the first Indo-Europeans, but this theory has not convinced everybody.

Further development took place along other lines, but only Crete would during the following centuries reach the urban stage, and this only after the immigration of new populations.

ART AND SCIENTIFIC KNOWLEDGE

Art, in Neolithic Europe, varied considerably from one region to another. In general, however, Neolithic art was much more stylized and abstract than Palaeolithic art had been. The various artistic categories prevalent in that period were rock carvings in the sub-arctic regions; megalithic art; terracotta and stone figurines and statuettes; very beautifully decorated (painted, engraved or excised) pottery; the anthropomorphic steles of Switzerland and northern Italy and so on (see the various regional chapters).

As for scientific knowledge, it was gained by trial and error. First and foremost came astronomical knowledge. Thanks to it, the megalithic monument at Newgrange could be so constructed that, at the winter solstice, the rays of the rising sun fell into the tomb-chamber through a small slit above the entrance passage several metres away. And at Stonehenge, a line drawn from the centre of the monument to the Heel Stone, about thirty metres outside the entrance, marks the rising of the sun at the summer solstice. In the past few years, very bold theories have been put forward about the astronomical knowledge of the builders of megaliths, and Stonehenge has even been alleged to have been a kind of observatory for predicting eclipses and other phenomena. This claim must be treated with reservation, however (Chapter 55). Elementary knowledge of geometry must certainly have gone into the design of some monuments with an oval shape, but here too the extent of that knowledge has been greatly exaggerated. The shifting and erection of heavy slabs of stone during the construction of megalithic monuments also implies familiarity with some of the laws of mechanics.

In quite a different field, that of medicine, which at the time was closely linked to magic, we must mention the performance of daring surgical operations: numerous trepanned skulls have been found in tombs associated with the Seine–Oise–Marne culture and also in central German sites dating back to the same period. The operation was performed *in vivo*, a very painful process with the primitive stone instruments of the time and in quite a few cases the patient survived. The round pieces of bone cut from the skull were later perforated and worn as amulets.

BIBLIOGRAPHY

NB: for more general works on the Neolithic, the reader is referred to the Bibliography of Chapter 43.

AMMERMAN, A. J.; CAVALLI-SFORZA, L. L. 1971. Measuring the Rate of Spread of Early Farming in Europe. *Man* (London), Vol. 6, No. 1, pp. 674–88.

BARKER, G. 1985. *Prehistoric Farming in Europe.* Cambridge.

BLOCH, M. R. 1963. The Social Influence of Salt. *Sci. Am.*, Vol. 209, No. 1, pp. 88–96.

BOGUCKI, P. I. 1988. *Forest Farmers and Stock-herders. Early Agriculture and its Consequences in North-Central Europe.* Cambridge.

BÖKÖNYI, S. 1974. *History of Domestic Mammals in Central and Eastern Europe.* Budapest.

CASE, H. J. 1969. Neolithic Explanations. *Antiquity*, Vol. 43, pp. 176–86.

—— 1976. Acculturation and the Earlier Neolithic in Western Europe. In: DE LAET, S. J. (ed.), *Acculturation and Continuity in Atlantic Europe.* Bruges. pp. 45–58.

CHERNYSH, E. N. 1979. Aibunar, a Balkan Copper Mine of the Fourth Millennium BC. *Proc. Prehist. Soc.*, Vol. 44, pp. 203–17.

CHILDE, V. G. 1929. *The Danube in Prehistory.* Oxford.

—— 1957. *The Dawn of European Civilization.* 6th edn. London.

—— 1958. *Prehistory of the European Society.* Harmondsworth.

CLARK, J. G. D. 1952. *Prehistoric Europe. The Economic Basis.* London.

—— 1965a. Radiocarbon Datings and the Spread of Farming Economy. *Antiquity*, Vol. 39, pp. 45–8.

—— 1965b. Radiocarbon Dating and the Expansion of Farming from the Near East over Europe. *Proc. Prehist. Soc.*, Vol. 21, pp. 58–73.

DE LAET, S. J. (ed.) 1976. *Acculturation and Continuity in Atlantic Europe.* Bruges.

—— 1981. Man and the Bull. *Diogenes* (Fiesole), No. 115, pp. 104–34.

DENNELL, R. 1983. *European Economic Prehistory.* London/New York.

DOLUKHANOV, P. 1989. *Ecology and Economy in Neolithic Eastern Europe.* London.

GIMBUTAS, M. 1974. *The Gods and Goddesses of Old Europe, 6500–3500 BC.* London.

GLOB, P. V. 1951. *Ard og plov i Nordens Oldtid* [Hoe and Plough in Nordic Prehistory]. Aarhus.

GUILAINE, J. 1976. *Premiers Bergers et paysans de l'Occident méditerranéen.* Paris.

HIGGS, E. (ed.) 1975. *Palaeoeconomy.* Cambridge.

HOWELL, J. M. 1983. *Settlement and Economy in Neolithic Northern France.* Oxford.

IVANOV, I. S. 1978. Les Fouilles archéologiques de la nécropole chalcolithique à Varna (1972–1978). *Studia Praehist.* (Sofia), Vol. 1–2, pp. 13–26.

—— 1989. La Nécropole chalcolithique de Varna et les cités lacustres voisines. In: MOHEN, J.-P. (ed.), *Le Premier Or de l'humanité en Bulgarie – 5e millénaire.* Saint-Germain-en-Laye. pp. 49–56. (Catalogue d'exposition, 17 janvier–30 avril 1989.)

IVERSEN, J. 1941. Land Occupation in Denmark's Stone Age. *Dan. Geol. Unders.* (Copenhagen), Vol. 2, pp. 1–68.

—— 1973. The Development of Denmark's Nature since the Last Glacial. *Dan. Geol. Unders.* (Copenhagen), Vol. 5, pp. 7–126.

JARMAN, H. N.; BAY-PETERSEN, J. L. 1976. Agriculture in Prehistoric Europe. The Lowlands. *Phil. Trans. R. Soc. Lond.*, Ser. B, Vol. 175, pp. 175–86.

JARMAN, M. R.; BAILEY, G. N.; JARMAN, H. N. 1982. *Early European Agriculture: Its Foundations and Developments.* Cambridge.

JAVANOVIC, C.; OTTOWAY, B. S. 1976. Copper Mining and Metallurgy in the Vinca Group. *Antiquity*, Vol. 198, pp. 104–13.

KATINCAROV, R. 1989. Le Développement des cultures néolithiques et chalcolithiques et l'apparition de la métallurgie sur les terres bulgares. In: MOHEN, J.-P. (ed.), *Le Premier Or de l'humanité en Bulgarie – 5e millénaire.* Saint-Germain-en-Laye. pp. 16–18. (Catalogue d'exposition, 17 janvier–30 avril 1989.)

MERCER, R. (ed.) 1981. *Farming Practices in British Prehistory.* Edinburgh.

MOHEN, J.-P. (ed.) 1989. *Le Premier Or de l'humanité en Bulgarie – 5e millénaire.* Saint-Germain-en-Laye. (Catalogue d'exposition, 17 janvier–30 avril 1989.)

MULTHAUF, R. P. 1978. *Neptune's Gift: A History of Common Salt.* Baltimore.

MURRAY, J. 1970. *The First European Agriculture, a Study of the Osteological and Botanical Evidence until 2000 BC.* Edinburgh.

NENQUIN, J. A. E. 1961. *Salt: A Study in Economic Prehistory.* Bruges.

PHILLIPS, P. 1975. *Early Farmers of West Mediterranean Europe.* London.

RENFREW, C. 1979. *Problems in European Prehistory.* Edinburgh.

—— 1989. Varna et le contexte social de la première métallurgie. In: MOHEN, J.-P. (ed.), *Le Premier Or de l'humanité en Bulgarie – 5e millénaire.* Saint-Germain-en-Laye. (Catalogue d'exposition, 17 janvier–30 avril 1989.)

ROWLEY-CONWY, P. 1981. Slash and Burn in the Temperate European Neolithic. In: MARCER, R. (ed.), *Farming Practices in British Prehistory.* Edinburgh. pp. 85–96.

SCARRE, C. (ed.) 1983. *Ancient France: Neolithic Societies and their Landscapes, 6000–2000 BC.* Edinburgh.

SCHWABEDISSEN, H. (ed.) 1972–6. *Die Anfänge des Neolithikums vom Orient bis Nordeuropa.* Cologne/Vienna. 4 vols.

TRINGHAM, E. 1971. *Hunters, Fishers and Farmers of Eastern Europe, 6000–3000 BC.* London.

TROELS-SMITH, J. 1960. Ivy, Mistletoe and Elm: Climate Indicators – Fodder Plants. *Dan. Geol. Unders.* (Copenhagen), Vol. 4, pp. 1–32.

VELDE, P. VAN DE. 1979. *On Bandkeramik Social Structure: An Analysis of Pot Decoration and Hut Distribution from the Central European Neolithic Communities of Elsloo and Hienheim.* Leiden. (Analecta Praest. Leidensia, 12.)

VILLA, P. et al. 1986. Cannibalism in the Neolithic. *Science* (Washington), Vol. 233, pp. 431–7.

WAALS, J. D. VAN DER. 1964. *Prehistoric Disc Wheels in the Netherlands.* Groningen.

WHITTLE, A. W. R. 1985. *Neolithic Europe: A Survey.* Cambridge.

WILLMS, C. 1985. Neolithischer Spondylusschmuck. *Germania,* Vol. 63, pp. 331–43.

ZVELEBIL, M. (ed.) 1986. *Hunters in Transition: Mesolithic Societies of Temperate Eurasia and their Transition to Farming.* London.

48

THE AEGEAN

during the Neolithic

Christos Doumas

THE GEOGRAPHICAL SETTING

The morphology of the Aegean territory has strongly influenced cultural developments in all periods. The Aegean Sea which separates yet unites the southernmost tip of eastern Europe, Greece and Asia Minor, scattered with innumerable islands, large and small, comprised a particular environment in which specific activities, such as trade and seafaring, developed. The northern part of Greece, with its extensive plains in Macedonia and Thrace, is directly connected with the central and eastern part of the Balkan peninsula along the valleys of the rivers Axios (Vardar), Strymon (Struma), Nestos (Nesta) and Ebros (Maritsa). Central Greece is bisected longitudinally by the Pindos range into an eastern zone, in close contact with the Aegean Sea, and a western one, with direct access to the Ionian and Adriatic Seas. And last but not least Crete and the remaining Aegean islands form another distintive region. The water barrier both isolated the islanders and protected them from external invasions. Yet as soon as they were able to navigate, the sea became a channel for extraneous influences. In this geographical setting an essentially homogeneous Neolithic culture developed, though it was characterized also by local differences.

HISTORY OF RESEARCH

Systematic research into Aegean prehistory began during the last decade of the nineteenth century with the excavations of Early Bronze Age sites in the Cycladic islands by Christos Tsountas. It was this same indefatigable scholar who, together with Valerios Stais, began excavating the two famous Thessalian sites, Sesklo and Dimini, during the first decade of this century (1908), thus revealing the earliest information about the Neolithic Aegean. At about the same time Sir Arthur Evans brought to light the first Neolithic remains of Knossos in Crete (Evans, 1921–35). The excavations in Thessaly, Crete, and an investigation in Phocis by Soteriadis (1912), constitute almost the only research on Aegean Neolithic before the First World War. More interest was shown in the late 1920s and 1930s when the investigations encompassed a much wider area. Macedonia became the focus of scholarly interest thanks to the work of George Mylonas at Olynthus (1928), mainland Greece with

the research of E. Kunze at Orchomenos (1931), the Athenian Acropolis which was explored by D. Levi (1930–1), the Peloponnese thanks to the investigations of K. Blegen at Nemea (1927), Gonia (1930) and Prosymna (1937) as well as those of N. Valmin in Messenia (1938). In addition to Crete, other islands produced Neolithic material, for Aigina (Welter, 1937) and Samos (Heidenreich, 1935–6) were also investigated during the 1930s. Since the end of the Second World War, research on the Aegean Neolithic has been intensified and from the 1960s onwards has been conducted on a much larger scale. It is impossible to list all the scholars working in this field, but mention should be made of two prehistorians who made an inestimable contribution to post-war Aegean Neolithic studies: the late V. Milojčič and D. Theocharis.

APPEARANCE AND EXPANSION OF THE NEOLITHIC IN THE GREEK MAINLAND AND THE ISLANDS (EIGHTH, SEVENTH AND SIXTH MILLENNIA BP)

Although the existence of the Mesolithic period has not been established stratigraphically, throughout the Hellenic area there is sufficient circumstantial evidence for this phase of transition from a food-gathering to a food-producing economy; from both the Boibe region of Thessaly and Sidari in north-west Corfu there is clear proof of this presence (Theocharis, 1981, p. 27). However, indisputable stratigraphical documentation of the Mesolithic period has come from Franchthi cave on the coast of Hermione in the Peloponnese (Jacobsen, 1981, pp. 303–19). The fourth stage of habitation at this site, which is chronologically coincident with the ninth millennium BP, is characterized by a diversification of food resources and an intensification in the strategies of their exploitation as well as a considerable increase in the number of microlithic tools of Melian obsidian (see also p. 505), testifying to the establishing of marine communication in the Aegean (Jacobsen, 1981, p. 307).

The inception of arable farming and stock raising before the end of the ninth millennium BP is confirmed not only at Franchthi but also in Thessaly (Argissa, Sesklo, Sougli Magoula; Theocharis, 1981, p. 37) and Crete (Knossos; Evans, 1964, p. 136). The first cultivated crops were cereals and legumes (J. Renfrew, 1973, p. 161) and sheep and goat occur for the first time in their domesticated form (Bökönyi, 1973, pp. 166–8). This may be considered as the earliest phase of the Neolithic period and in the previously mentioned sites is characterized by a complete absence of pottery vessels (Pre-pottery Neolithic) and a paucity of architectural remains which are, none the less, clear (Theocharis, 1981, p. 37). From this initial Pre-pottery phase to its end, the following phases may be distinguished in the developmental course of the Neolithic period in the Aegean:

1 Early Neolithic corresponding chronologically to the entire eighth millennium BP;
2 Middle Neolithic, which covers the first half of the seventh millennium BP;
3 Late Neolithic enduring from the middle of the seventh to the end of the sixth millennium BP.

The term Final Neolithic is frequently used in referring to the closing stages of the Late Neolithic.

Despite the fact that research is far from complete – indeed in the islands it has barely begun – a distinct picture of the gradual expansion of the Neolithic way of life throughout the Aegean has emerged from the study of the available material. For some 3,500 years this new way of life, regardless of regional differences, forged the context and created the preconditions for the smooth transition to urbanization characteristic of the Aegean Early Bronze Age.

SETTLEMENT AND ARCHITECTURE

Pre-pottery Neolithic

Permanent settlements are known to have existed during the Pre-pottery stage of the Neolithic. Although, on the basis of information available to date, it is difficult to estimate the size of these early settlements, the evidence from Sesklo in Thessaly suggests that it was rather extensive, since architectural remnants have been located both within and outside the acropolis (Theocharis, 1981, p. 54). A feature evidently common to all these primary settlements was the preference for a coastal, riparian or possibly lacustrine site (Jacobsen, 1981, p. 312). The unusual density of Pre-pottery Neolithic settlements in Thessaly vis-à-vis other regions of Greece may be attributed to an environmental factor: the plain of Thessaly was the area most favourable to the development of the new economy.

In addition to Sesklo, Pre-pottery strata have been identified at other Thessalian sites: Achilleion, Gendiki, Soufli Magoula and Argissa (Theocharis, 1981, p. 37). Outside Thessaly traces of the Pre-pottery Neolithic have been found at Knossos, Crete (Evans, 1964, p. 142) and Franchthi in the Argolid (Jacobsen, 1981), while the evidence from Maroula on Kythnos in the Cyclades is still disputed (Honea, 1975). At Franchthi architectural remains have been observed both inside and outside the cave, consisting of both vestiges of walls and attempted terracing of the area (Jacobsen, 1981, p. 309). But once again it is from Thessaly that we have a more precise picture of the habitations of Neolithic people in the Pre-pottery stage. Timber-and-daub huts of elliptical plan have been found. The floor was dug into the ground and covered with pebbles or beaten earth and there was a hearth (Theocharis, 1981, p. 37). It would seem from the architectural evidence available that there was a distinct regional difference in dwellings between north and south, again probably explicable in terms of the environment.

Those of Thessaly were constructed of more readily perishable material (timber), while the structures at Franchthi were of more durable material (stone).

Early Neolithic

Although architectural remains from the Early Neolithic have not been found throughout the Hellenic area there is little doubt of its geographically wide extent. By the beginning of the Early Neolithic the clusters of dwellings or hamlets of the Pre-pottery stage had evolved into sizeable villages, one of the most thoroughly investigated of which is Sesklo. At this Thessalian site architectural remains have been located over a surface area of about one hectare (Theocharis, 1981, p. 54), while the extent of the Macedonian settlement of Nea Nikomedeia is estimated to have been 2.4 hectares (Rodden, 1962, p. 268). Thus it seems that settlement size in the Greek peninsula conformed to the same norm observed for their western Asian counterparts which vary in size from 1 to 4 hectares (Jacobsen, 1981, p. 313). If one postulates a population density of 100 inhabitants per hectare then these Early Neolithic villages housed between 100 and 400 persons.

Concerning site selection, it is noteworthy that Sesklo and Achilleion in Thessaly, Nea Makri in Attica and Palaia Corinth in the Peloponnese are all located on a natural geological terrace, whereas Nea Nikomedeia in Macedonia is on top of a knoll (Theocharis, 1981, p. 55; Nandris, 1970, pp. 194–5). The architecture of the Early Neolithic is characterized by a diversity of forms, a variety of construction materials and the apparent coexistence of old traditions with conceptual and practical innovations. Thus in addition to buildings of elliptical plan, rectilinear structures appeared, both rectangular and square in outline (Theocharis, 1981, p. 58). With regard to the materials used in their construction, some were of mud in the pisé technique, others had stone foundations, while in Nea Nikomedeia timber posts were driven into the firm ground. An interesting feature of the mud-walled houses is the setting of stone orthostats around the base to protect them from water (Theocharis, 1981, p. 58). The dwellings were quite spacious: in Nea Nikomedeia dimensions of 8 by 11 m have been recorded. At this same site the excavator has distinguished one building as a shrine (Rodden, 1964, p. 114).

Middle Neolithic

During the Middle Neolithic distinct regional differences between northern and southern Greece can be discerned. There is almost no evidence of its existence in Macedonia, which perhaps implies a stagnation or retardation in development, so that it is barely distinguishable from the Early Neolithic. In contrast, its development in southern Greece was rather rapid. So in northern Greece the Middle Neolithic is represented by the flourishing so-called Sesklo culture in Thessaly (Theocharis, 1981, pp. 80, 113), while to the south the so-called Chaironeia culture extended throughout the eastern part of mainland Greece (Theocharis, 1981, p. 113). Further south in the Peloponnese yet another developmental course was followed. All these regional differences are well defined and documented in the pottery techniques and style (Theocharis, 1981, pp. 113–17).

In general there seems to have been an acceleration of

developments in the southern regions during the Middle Neolithic and as a consequence Thessaly ceased to be at the centre of these (Theocharis, 1981, p. 118). It seems that the consolidation of the new economy and way of life effected during the Early Neolithic resulted in a marked population increase. This is reflected not only in the appearance of new settlements, such as Tsangli, Zerelia and Tzani Magoula in Thessaly, but also in the increase in size of those that already existed in the Early Neolithic (Theocharis, 1981, p. 88). Middle Neolithic Sesklo, for instance, has been estimated to have comprised between 500 and 800 dwellings, serving perhaps 3,000 inhabitants (Theocharis, 1981, p. 94).

A number of settlement changes took place during the Middle Neolithic period, none of which seems to have been sudden but rather the crystallization of processes initiated in the preceding stage. With regard to settlements as a whole, two major features appeared in the Middle Neolithic: organization of the buildings according to a rudimentary 'town plan' and, in Thessaly, the construction of successive enclosures around its perimeter (Theocharis, 1981, p. 81). These enclosures, known from Middle Neolithic Sesklo and possibly Magoula Chatzimissiotiki as well as from Late Neolithic Dimini, were originally considered to be defensive walls and the area delimited by them was interpreted as the acropolis of the settlement (Theocharis, 1973, pp. 65–6). Recently, however, G. Chourmouziadis (1979, pp. 92 ff.) has challenged this view, at least for the Dimini enclosures, which he interpreted as being connected with diverse productive activities. This proposition is not particularly convincing, especially as the argument for the protective function of the enclosures has been recently reinforced by the discovery of a V-shaped ditch around the settlement of Soufli Magoula. This particular settlement, lying on the plain with no natural defensive feature and a dearth of stones, could only be protected by a moat, which may have been filled with water (Theocharis, 1973, p. 66; 1981, p. 95). Similar defensive ditches are also known from other sites (for instance Servia; Theocharis, 1973, p. 66, n. 70). However, whatever the purpose of these enclosures and moats, it is an indisputable fact that they are the result of a common effort, communal works requiring a not inconsiderable labour force and some kind of co-ordination.

At Sesklo the plan of the settlement inside the acropolis reveals a primitive grid of narrow streets. The houses, which were small, were built and rebuilt on the same spot and with the same orientation. Those at Otzaki Magoula were densely built and always on the same plot, which suggests that these house plots were predetermined. There was a paved courtyard in front of the building at the epicentre of the acropolis of Sesklo, while small 'squares' were formed at random around it. Outside the acropolis the buildings were well spaced-out, much larger and, although they were free-standing, were aligned contiguously and shared the same orientation. This alignment is probably due to a preconceived plan (Theocharis, 1981, pp. 94–5).

Middle Neolithic architecture is characterized in general by the introduction of stone-built platforms as bases for the houses and the standarization of house plans: the oblong megaron type or the square type with internal buttresses which reduced the space between parallel walls and so facilitated the use of cross-beams. Other technical innovations include the daubing of interior walls and the use of wooden posts in open porticoes. The lining of the outer façades of the foundation platforms with stone orthostats was apparently more frequent too. Both house types have precursors in the Hellenic area and are indigenous developments rather than imported innovations (Theocharis, 1981, p. 102). A rudimentary version of the square house with internal buttresses and a central row of timber posts, common at Sesklo, Tsangli and Otzaki Magoula, is known from Early Neolithic Nea Nikomedeia (Theocharis, 1981, pp. 98–102). Similarly, the megaron type (long and narrow with a portico at the entrance or the rear or both) has as its predecessor the single-roomed Early Neolithic house. It apparently developed by projection of pitched-roof eaves over the front and back of the building to shelter the openings (doors and windows) from the rain, thus creating two open porches (Theocharis, 1981, p. 102). We know for certain that these houses had pitched roofs, both from the discovery of beam impressions on clay and from clay house models that have been found in settlements (Plate 69) (Theocharis, 1973, p. 66, n. 72, 1981, p. 97).

Late Neolithic

In Thessaly the end of the Middle Neolithic is marked by a general and geographically widespread destruction by conflagration as shown by evidence from such sites as Sesklo, Tsangli and Servia (Theocharis, 1981, p. 121). The phase following this devastation is regarded as a brief transitional interlude. Most of the sites were reoccupied, with the exception of Sesklo, which was deserted for some 500 years, after which only its acropolis was reinhabited (Theocharis, 1981, p. 120). The appearance of foreign traits and the introduction of new techniques have been interpreted as indicators of the arrival of new population elements in the area. These newcomers apparently coexisted with those indigenous Middle Neolithic people who had survived the desolation (Theocharis, 1981, p. 123).

With regard to the architecture of the Late Neolithic period, the buildings of the early phases are characterized by lack of standardization, and in the southern areas a preference for habitation in caves is remarked. Such cave sites have been recognized in Attica (Pan's cave near Marathon, Kitsos cave near Lavrion), in the Peloponnese (Alepotrypa in Mani), in south-west mainland Greece (Aghios Nikolaos cave near Astakos) and Leukas (Choirospelia; Nandris, 1970, pp. 194–5; Theocharis, 1981, p. 157). The population evidently continued to rise, for in addition to occupation of those settlements already established during the Middle Neolithic, other areas with no evidence of previous activity emerged in the Late Neolithic and indeed played an important role. These include eastern Macedonia and Aegean Thrace (Sitagroi, Dikili Tash, Paradimi; Bakalakis and Sakellariou, 1981) and some remote islands (for example Saliagos in the Cyclades; Evans and Renfrew, 1968). On examining the geographical distribution of these new settlements a distinct preference for coastal sites is apparent, as well as a marked increase in the importance of the southern regions.

Morphological traits of Late Neolithic settlements include the protective enclosures surrounding the acropolises of Sesklo and Dimini in Thessaly and that uncovered on the islet of Saliagos near Antiparos, which is perhaps the earliest Late Neolithic example (Theocharis, 1973, p. 110; 1981, p. 158). In the Thessalian sites an impressive building, the megaron, stood at the centre of the settlements (Sesklo, Dimini, Magoula Visviki near Velestino). In the latter instance, Magoula Visviki, the megaron was of monumental dimensions, being some 30 m in length, while at Sesklo and Dimini the megaron was virtually the only building within the inner enclosure of the acropolis and was surrounded by spacious open courtyards (recent work by Chourmouziadis has demonstrated that the Dimini megaron resulted from Early Bronze Age architectural alterations; 1979, p. 101). On these two sites there was another unique feature, the porticoes along the inner face of the central enclosures. These impressive edifices or megara have been interpreted as either communal or public buildings or the residence of the ruler of the settlement.

TECHNOLOGY

Pottery

The kiln must have been one of the most important inventions made after the establishment of a sedentary (as opposed to a nomadic) existence. Small schematic figurines of clay have been found in Pre-pottery Neolithic Thessaly, heralding the achievements that were to follow (Nandris, 1970, p. 198; Weinberg, 1965, p. 16). Once the principle of firing clay vessels had been discovered technological developments were astonishingly rapid, both in the choice and preparation of clay and in relating the actual firing process, as is evident from the deliberate red coloration of the surface of the vases.

The earliest pottery forms tend to imitate those either of natural containers (such as gourds), or of vessels made of other materials and in other techniques, often revealed by the decoration applied to the surface of the vase: for instance, wood-carving, basketry, weaving and the like (Theocharis, 1981, p. 51). Monochrome ware is the most ancient pottery throughout the Hellenic peninsula (Theocharis, 1981, p. 51; Weinberg, 1965, p. 27). Despite its uniformity, this pottery in some regions attains a perfection that can only be appraised as the achievement of highly skilled and experienced artisans working in specific centres of production. Such centres have been recognized at Sesklo in Thessaly with its 'all white' vases which have an almost porcelain-like appearance, at Corinth in the north-east Peloponnese with its 'rainbow' or 'variegated' pots (Plate 70) (Theocharis, 1981, p. 52). In addition to monochrome ware other categories of pottery are known from the Early Neolithic. These include vases with painted, plastic, impressed or incised decoration and are all somewhat later developments. The typology of Early Neolithic pottery is mainly confined to various shapes of open bowls, usually provided with a ring base (Theocharis, 1981, p. 66; Weinberg, 1965, p. 27).

Pottery with painted decoration predominates in the Aegean part of Thessaly (Plate 71) and mainland Greece, as well as the Aegean islands (Halinisos, Skyros), and is considered to follow an eastern tradition since it also occurs on the Aegean coast of Asia Minor (Theocharis, 1981, p. 71). The principal decorative elements are either severe linear patterns or solid random motifs. Human and animal figures do exist but are extremely rare (Weinberg, 1965, p. 29).

Pottery with impressed decoration seems to follow a western tradition, since this technique is absent from the Aegean coast of Turkey but is quite widespread along the Adriatic coast and the shores of the western Mediterranean (Theocharis, 1981, p. 70, Weinberg, 1965, p. 29). Impressed Ware has been found in Epirus, Corfu, central Macedonia and western Thessaly. It only appeared in north-east Thessaly towards the end of the Early Neolithic, obviously as a result of contacts with the previously mentioned western regions. Early Neolithic pottery from the Peloponnese (Lerna, Corinth, Franchthi) shows similarities with that of the east Thessalian tradition (Weinberg, 1965, p. 30).

It seems that Nea Marki in Attica (Theocharis, 1956) was the meeting point of the various traditions and techniques, as exemplified by a kind of monochrome ware reminiscent of that of Thessaly and by 'variegated' or 'black-topped' pots indicating an affinity with the northeast Peloponnese. Of particular interest is a special class of pottery from Nea Makri bearing a peculiar impressed decoration, quite different from the normal impressed technique, with white paste infill (Theocharis, 1981, p. 54; Weinberg, 1965, p. 30). Yet another development in Early Neolithic pottery is the category of vases with plastic decoration in the form of either human or animal or anthropomorphic vessels (Theocharis, 1981, p. 54).

During the Middle Neolithic period considerable improvements were made in pottery manufacturing, particularly with regard to firing techniques. There was also a marked increase in the quantity of painted pottery and progress in the evolution of its decoration. As in the Early Neolithic, specific centres of production have been traced from which vessels were exported to other settlements in the country. This implies that skilled specialist artisans produced pottery not only to satisfy the needs of their particular settlement but also to supply the market beyond (Theocharis, 1981, p. 104).

Middle Neolithic pottery falls into two main categories: coarse ware, mainly represented by storage jars from Sesklo, and fine ware, which has been studied in much greater detail and is consequently much better known. Though the Middle Neolithic potters continued the tradition of their forebears, they refined their technique to such a degree that some of the monochrome vases have walls only 2 mm thick. The decorated pottery may also be divided into two classes. The one continues and develops the earlier traditional styles and techniques, while the other is characterized by innovations in both style and syntax. The Thessalian painted pottery of the 'Sesklo culture' may be regarded as the most significant artistic creation of its time and its decoration remains to this day as the most brilliant attainment of prehistoric potters (Theocharis, 1981, p. 105). It consists mainly of red decoration on a whitish ground. White decoration on a dark or red ground also exists but is much rarer. In general there is a tendency for the arrangement of the decoration to be in a spiral round the body of the vase (Theocharis, 1981, p. 104). Three basic styles can be distinguished in the pottery of the 'Sesklo culture':

Solid style (Plate 72)

The decoration comprises solid angular patterns – stepped and denticulated motifs – which are easily wrought in other techniques and materials, such as basketry, weaving and embroidery, and from which they were probably derived. A centre of production probably existed in western Thessaly (Tzani Magoula and Megalo Mazaraki) from where it was distributed to various parts of the country (Theocharis, 1981, p. 104). It has been suggested that the Solid style of Nea Nikomedeia may have been associated with the painted pottery from Anzabegovo, in Bulgarian Macedonia (Nandris, 1970, p. 207).

Linear style

The decoration consists of rectilinear motifs, parallel lines in various combinations, zigzag bands, hatched triangles and lozenges and the like, and seems to have evolved from the solid style where the solid motifs were often outlined (Theocharis, 1981, p. 104).

'Scraped' style

This characterizes the end of the Middle Neolithic period. The linear motifs are executed by scraping the painted surface of the vessel. Although such pottery is found throughout Thessaly, this technique was most probably of southern origin since the finest examples have been found at Lianokladhi (Theocharis, 1981, p. 105). In the southern part of mainland Greece pottery of the Chaironeia culture prevailed. This was contemporary and frequently analogous with its Thessalian counterpart but exhibits motifs of a clear geometric structure disposed in a more severe syntax (Theocharis, 1981, p. 113). Finally, the north-east Peloponnese seems to have been the centre of production of yet another class of Middle Neolithic pottery, that known as Neolithic *Urfirnis*. In fact this technique seems to have been disseminated as far north of Phocis but never actually reached the sphere of influence of the Sesklo and Chaironeia cultures (Theocharis, 1981, p. 114). It has been suggested that *Urfirnis* ware is evidence of the influx of new population elements from the East, but this is somewhat untenable since there are no pictorial themes in its decorative repertoire, whereas these predominate in Halaf pottery with which Greek Neolithic *Urfirnis* has been compared (Weinberg, 1965, p. 39), and also because *Urfirnis* decoration was applied to vase forms indigenous to the Hellenic tradition (Theocharis, 1981, pp. 117–18).

The transitional phase between the Middle and Late Neolithic (second half of the seventh millennium BP) is marked by a gradual change in the pottery. Red scraped ware was gradually transformed into grey scraped ware and at some sites, like Tsangli, Servia and Magoula Tsapocha, pots exhibiting red scraped decoration on one face and grey scraped on the other have been found, testifying to this transmutation. Magoula Tsapocha has also yielded bichrome ware, with black painted decoration on top of the red scraped decoration, which was to gain in popularity during the ensuing period (Theocharis, 1981, pp. 121–2). A general feature of the Late Neolithic is the predominance of dark pottery groups with incised or matt-painted linear decoration. In Thessaly, in the pre-Dimini phases of Tsangli and Arapi (c.6,300 to 5,800 years ago; Milojčić and Hauptman, 1969), polychrome pottery was still abundant, but an appreciable proportion of dark monochrome ware, incised or painted, also existed. Despite its inferior quality, the decoration displays more order and a more disciplined syntax (Theocharis, 1981, p. 126). During these early phases of the Late Neolithic in Thessaly there was a marked orientation towards the southern regions and it is perhaps not without significance that matt-painted pottery is found as far south as Alepotrypa in Mani (Peloponnese; Theocharis, 1981, p. 128). Nevertheless, contacts between the Balkans and the Aegean parts of Macedonia and Thrace appeared to be closer during these phases. Sites like Sitagroi, Dikili Tash and Paradimi have shown affinities with Vinča (Tordos) and Veselinovo (Karanovo III; Theocharis, 1981, pp. 127–8; Bakalakis and Sakellariou, 1981, p. 25; Alexander, 1972, p. 43). The pottery of the Dimini culture (Plate 73) with its dis-tinctive character and somewhat limited geographical distribution (east Thessaly) is an amalgam of earlier forms and diverse extraneous influences. With regard to its decoration, some of the motifs seem to originate from Sesklo (checkered, stepped and so on), but their syntax is entirely new and special care seems to have been taken to underline the different parts of the pot. Another innovation is the arrangement of the decoration in panels, often juxtaposed for contrast (Theocharis, 1981, p. 144). Another feature of the pottery of the Dimini culture is the decided preference for spiral and meander motifs, which were probably derived from incised decoration (Plate 74) and possibly from wood-carving (Theocharis, 1981, p. 148).

As has been stated before, the Late Neolithic in the south is characterized by the predominance of matt-painted pottery (Weinberg, 1965, pp. 45–6). Polychrome ware such as that from Gonia and Prosymna (Peloponnese) is perhaps related to that of Thessaly (Theocharis, 1981, p. 133). In the Cyclades, Saliagos near Antiparos had produced dark pottery which, although displaying affinities with that of mainland Greece and the Peloponnese, constitutes a special insular class of which white decoration dominates (Evans and Renfrew, 1968, p. 36; Theocharis, 1981, p. 158).

The closing phases of the Neolithic era, or Final Neolithic, are represented in Thessaly by the cultures of Larissa and Rachmani (Theocharis, 1981, p. 133; Weinberg, 1965, p. 50). Pottery of the Larissa culture exhibits a variety of forms, without handles and base, widely distributed from Western Macedonia to Attica and Euboia. It belongs to a category of black or dark ware with white linear or burnished and incised decoration. The Rachmani culture is of a rather Chalcolithic character; its distribution in Thessaly is mainly coastal and shows connections with eastern Macedonia. Its pottery shares formal features with that of Larissa but a crusted decorative technique is applied and the motifs include simplified spirals and twisted designs with complementary linear patterns. Since both this technique and mode of decoration are prevalent in the Balkans a northern provenance may be sought for these traits (Theocharis, 1981, p. 133; Weinberg, 1965, p. 50). However, crusted ware is also known from southern regions, such as the Peloponnese (Lerna), Crete (Knossos) and the Cyclades (Saliagos; Theocharis, 1981, p. 152). The motifs seem to continue the Dimini tradition though their syntax is of a more northern appearance (Theocharis, 1981, p. 152). Northern (Balkan) affinities are shown by another class, the graphite ware which is characteristic of Aegean Macedonia and Thrace and may be considered Chalcolithic (Bakalakis and Sakellariou, 1981, pp. 26–8).

Stone and bone industry

The chipped stone tools of the Pre-pottery Neolithic follow the Mesolithic tradition and include microliths of flint and obsidian. The latter material is more common in the southern regions and the islands that are closer to its source, Melos in the Cyclades (p. 508). Blades, the most typical Neolithic tools, made their appearance in the Early Neolithic. Owing to the lack of any published specific and comprehensive study of Neolithic stone tools and implements it is somewhat difficult to trace their typological and morphological development throughout the period. However, it seems that there was a gradual decline in the microlithic industry, so that by the Middle Neolithic period these tools had almost disappeared. An increase in the use of obsidian in Middle Neolithic Thessaly was accompanied by a parallel increase in the production of blades. There was also a wide range of obsidian flakes with one or two worked edges, various types of points (harpoon heads or arrowheads and the like), ovates and other types. The ground-stone tools include pestles and grinders, hammers, axes, chisels, maceheads, waisted weights and so on. Other stone artefacts include lids, mortars and querns, and even sockets for the hinges of doors. The typology of Neolithic bone tools comprises a wide range of points, scoops, needles, awls, spatulae and chisels (Elster, 1977, pp. 45–57).

Basketry and matting

There is only indirect evidence for the existence of basketry deduced from the form and painted decoration of certain pots in form of baskets. Open bowls with straight walls, for instance, probably imitate a basketry container and it is quite plausible that some patterns in the decorative repertoire, as well as their syntax, simply copy the geometric designs in coiled and woven baskets created by the working in of coloured fibres. This effect is obvious on most of the painted Middle Neolithic pottery of Thessaly, in particular that of the Sesklo culture. Indeed, all the angular patterns (stepped, serrated, denticulated, zigzag, checkers and so on) may have been inspired by, if not ultimately derived from, basketry or matting (Theocharis, 1981, pp. 78–9, Figs 30–4). The evidence for matting is more direct, impressions of woven mats having been found on the bottom of vases from several sites both in the north (Nea Nikomedeia, Sitagroi) and south (Saliagos).

Spinning and weaving

Although the technique of weaving was apparently applied for making mats and baskets, its use in the manufacture of textiles was inferred only indirectly until the discovery of cloth impressions in the early strata of Sitagroi (C. Renfrew, 1973, p. 189). The find, dating to about 7,000 years ago, constitutes the earliest direct evidence of textile weaving in Europe. Another impression of material from Kephala on the Cycladic island of Kea is of a later date (5,500 years ago).

Information on textile manufacturing is again supplemented by indirect evidence from the decoration on painted pottery, which seems to copy or echo other techniques. A number of motifs on vases from Aghios Petros in the Northern Sporades (Efstratiou, 1985) and Sesklo were obviously inspired by textile designs.

Direct evidence of spinning and weaving has been obtained in the form of associated artefacts: spindle whorls and loom weights of stone or clay have been found at several sites throughout Greece. In the advanced stages of the Neolithic period (c. 5,500 years ago) they became particularly popular, as the evidence from both northern (Sitagroi) and southern (Knossos) sites has demonstrated. Spindle whorls were either conical in shape, made intentionally for this purpose, or discs of potsherds with a central hole. Sometimes they were embellished with incised patterns, as at Sitagroi (Theocharis, 1973, Fig. 116). Early Neolithic Knossos has produced objects that appear to be more directly associated with cloth weaving. One such assemblage consists of flat, squarish clay tablets with two or four holes which have been interpreted as loom weights. A second group of oblong artefacts, also of clay, have been identified as 'shuttles' by the excavators of the site (Evans, 1964, pp. 233–4). Thus there is

evidence that before the end of the Early Neolithic specialized equipment for both spinning and weaving yarn was made, implying that both processes were known.

Woodcarving

No traces of actual wood have been found in Neolithic contexts: this is certainly due to its perishability. Since timber was used as a building material to a greater or lesser degree throughout the era, carpentry was yet another Neolithic skill (Efstratiou, 1985, p. 52) and so, it may be assumed, was its more artistic manifestation, woodcarving, as it was in Anatolia (Çatal Hüyük). Wood, being a soft material, was easier to work than stone, and wooden vessels were probably made before pottery was invented; indeed, some Neolithic pots with incised decoration could be considered as imitations of wooden prototypes. Two vessels from Knossos, for example, a cylindrical vase decorated with incised zigzag bands and triangles infilled with impressed dots (*pontillé*), and a cylindrical box with incised triangles, could perhaps claim wooden ancestors (Theocharis, 1973, Figs 69, 74).

ART (Plates 75, 76, 77 and 78)

Prehistoric people had already conquered the arts of painting and sculpture in Upper Palaeolithic Europe, as is shown by the remarkable examples of both parietal and plastic art bequeathed to us. Unfortunately nothing is known of painting in the Neolithic Aegean apart from that on the pottery, and sculpture is confined to figurines which were fashioned from such materials as clay, stone, bone and shell.

Clay anthropomorphic figurines are known even from Pre-pottery Neolithic sites, a fact that led some scholars to abandon the term aceramic for this period (Nandris, 1970, p. 193). Some are schematic, others more representational, and they evidently existed side by side throughout the Neolithic era. Although it is difficult to trace their stylistic development, a chronological classification may be possible, in particular for the clay figurines, in connection with technological developments in pottery manufacturing (Chourmouziadis, 1974; Ucko, 1968). One category of clay figurines in which the head is of different material seems to date to the advanced stages of the Neolithic. The commonest schematic anthropomorphic figurine, either in clay or other materials, is the so-called 'fiddle-shaped' type. Others are cruciform or more abstract. Representational types include both male and female figures in various positions: standing, sitting, squatting or reclining, though the majority of these are female. These tend to be obese, and special attention is paid to the breasts and buttocks (speatopygous). Some figures are depicted performing a specific function such as the seated female nursing a child (*kourotrophos*) from Late Neolithic Sesklo (Theocharis, 1973, Fig. 56; 1981, p. 148, Fig. 98). The largest figure known to date (50 cm high) comes from Thessaly (Larissa area) and dates to the Final Neolithic. It depicts a seated male holding his left knee with his left hand while supporting his head with his right (Theocharis, 1973, Fig. 55).

There is a host of speculative literature concerning the function of these figurines, particularly the female ones, but the contextual data are insufficient to support a definitive explanation of their significance (Ucko, 1968, pp. 409–27; Chourmouziadis, 1974, pp. 149–206). Furthermore, not all the figurines of the Neolithic period were anthropomorphic: animals were also fashioned in clay or, more rarely, stone or even other materials. A number of zoomorphic clay figurines, most in fragmentary condition, are known from sites in Thessaly (Prodromos, Platykampos, Nessonis) and Macedonia (Dikili Tash, Sitagroi) and a figurine of green stone portraying a frog was found in Nea Nikomedeia. This variety of forms and their archaeological context led Chourmouziadis (1982, p. 78) to consider Neolithic figurines as means of communication, a kind of 'proto-script'.

In considering art, mention should be made also of a bone tube discovered in Middle Neolithic Sesklo which has been interpreted as a flute (Theocharis, 1973, Fig. 210). If this interpretation is correct then this is tangible proof that Neolithic people also made music; and if they made music then maybe they also danced!

ECONOMY

The economic activities of Neolithic peoples in the Aegean may be examined under two headings: subsistence and trade.

Subsistence

It is axiomatic that where evidence of early farming has been revealed there was Neolithic culture. This evidence is both botanical and zoological: in common parlance, seeds and bones of domesticated species of plants and animals respectively. Seeds found at various sites throughout Greece prove that wheat, barley, millet, oats, peas, lentils, pistachios and plums were already domesticated in Early Neolithic times (J. Renfrew, 1973).

As agriculture developed rather rapidly during the Middle Neolithic period other plants were cultivated, including the vine, the full development of which is documented through the successive levels at Sitagroi, east Macedonia. The population increase reflected in the expansion and proliferation of Middle Neolithic settlements was a corollary of the improved farming methods and the intensification of food production; and the large jars found in Middle Neolithic houses were presumably for storage of the agricultural surplus. During the Late Neolithic the list of crops was further augmented to include figs and almonds. The density of settlement distribution in that period suggests a further population increase and consequent intensification of farming. Palaeo-ethnobotanical analyses of seeds from different Late Neolithic sites have shown that there were regional differences in the cereals cultivated: wheat was mainly grown in Thessaly, wheat and six-row barley in the Drama plain (east Macedonia) while in the Cyclades the staple was barley. Analogous regional preferences have been shown for the legumes or pulses: peas seem to have predominated in the plain of Thessaly, vetch and lentils in east Macedonia and wild peas in the Cyclades. Of the remains of fruits which have been found, figs have the widest distribution. Fig seeds have been found in Thessaly (Sesklo, Dimini, Rachmani), east Macedonia (Olynthus, Dikili Tash) and the Peloponnese (Lerna). Alongside arable farming the gathering of wild fruits continued throughout the Neolithic in the Aegean: grapes, pears, almonds, pistachios, acorns and arbutus berries were evidently collected. In fact many of the species collected by Neolithic people appear in domesticated form in the Early Bronze Age.

Stock-raising in the Aegean appeared at about the same time as arable farming (Bökönyi, 1973). Domesticated sheep and goat remains have been found in the Early Neolithic levels of Franchthi, though there are none of their undomesticated ancestors. It is therefore suggested that sheep and goats were introduced already domesticated from southwest Asia via the Aegean islands. Remains of domesticated bovines have been found in Thessaly (Argissa) and these are contemporary with, if not older than, those of Çatal Hüyük in Anatolia. Around the middle of the ninth millennium BP Thessaly and Macedonia evidently constituted an important centre for bovines in the north-east Mediterranean. These were probably obtained by selective breeding of the species of bison whose natural habitat was the wooded plains of this region. Of the other two domesticated animal species present in the Neolithic Aegean, pig and dog, neither seems to have been domesticated on the Greek mainland. Both were apparently introduced, also from south-west Asia, perhaps together with sheep and goat.

Domesticated animals were the source of food, raw materials and even labour in the case of bovines. Game animals were also hunted, but the scale of this activity suggests that they were not relied on as a major source of food. From coastal and island sites a gradual increase in fish and mollusc consumption is apparent, bearing witness to ever-increasing involvement with the sea.

Trade

The discovery of artefacts or raw materials or both at a distance from their centres of production or sources constitutes conclusive evidence of a system of distribution, in all probability involving an exchange transaction – that is, trade. The archaeological record can furnish only partial evidence of trade in the form of durable items. The nature of the transactions, the networks of exchange and perishable goods involved can be only guessed at, but certainly these reciprocal commercial relations must have been of prime significance in expanding Neolithic people's world view, as well as enriching their material culture.

As has been stated in the section on pottery (pp. 504–5), centres of production have been pinpointed in Thessaly that supplied surrounding settlements with their distinctive wares over a considerable area. Thus there was certainly traffic in goods overland between villages. However, trade for Neolithic people was by no means landlocked, for like their Mesolithic forebears they had contacts with the islands of the Aegean, which were both a source of valuable raw materials and an inducement to maritime adventures. The irrefutable proof of overseas trade is the hard volcanic glass, obsidian, which has been found in Mesolithic levels at Franchthi (c. 10,000 years ago) and in Pre-pottery Neolithic levels in Macedonia (Nea Nikomedeia), Thessaly (Argissa, Soufli Magoula) and Crete (Knossos). Trace element analyses have shown that this obsidian came from the Cycladic island of Melos, where there are two obsidian quarries – Nychia and Demenegaki – which supplied the entire Aegean throughout prehistoric times (C. Renfrew, 1973). This exploitation was initiated as early as the eleventh millennium BP. The fact that obsidian is found so far from its source bears witness also to the early development of seafaring, and its association in Franchthi with bones of tunny – a deep-sea fish – may mean that it was brought by fisherfolk from the Peloponnese who reached Melos. What type of boat they voyaged in and what kind of exchange networks were established for its subsequent distribution are still matters for conjecture: but judging from the available representations of Early Bronze Age Cycladic ships (fifth millennium BP), one can assume that at least towards the end of the Late Neolithic Aegean boats were rowed with oars like their Early Bronze Age derivatives.

It has been suggested that obsidian was exported in the form of cores from which flakes, points and blades were struck as required (C. Renfrew, 1973, p. 186). This may well have been the case in the Early and Middle Neolithic, though there is no evidence of obsidian workshops or wasters from sites of these periods. On the contrary, the scarcity and refinement of the early finds, which undoubtedly required great skill in their production, may be indicative of the trading of ready-made tools, perhaps from Melos, though once again there is no evidence to date of Early or Middle Neolithic habitation on the island. Another possibility is that there was an Early Neolithic work place somewhere outside Melos from which obsidian tools were exported: this, it seems, was the situation in Late Neolithic times when trade in obsidian was conducted on a larger scale. Saliagos near Antiparos (Evans and Renfrew, 1968) was probably a production centre for obsidian tools, since some 24,000 pieces, both tools and wasters, were found in the limited area of the excavated trenches.

Other raw materials evidently traded during the Neolithic in the Aegean include hard stones for the manufacture of tools and vessels. Stones of volcanic origin were used for the manufacture of querns, grinders and mortars, indispensible utensils frequently found in Neolithic settlements (Lambert, 1981, p. 710), and marble, maybe from the Cyclades, was used for fashioning bowls and even figurines. An abrasive was necessary for the finishing process on these latter objects and the ideal substance for this was emery, common on Naxos and Paros. Axes and other tools of Naxian or Parian emery were found on Saliagos, and perhaps mineralogical analysis of similar tools elsewhere may prove that emery was yet another raw material traded far from its source. Imports to the islands, for certainly these transactions were reciprocal, are most likely to have been in commodities of a perishable nature such as timber for boatbuilding, cereals not cultivated locally and so on. There is no doubt that the high concentration of coastal sites in Late Neolithic Thessaly reflects an upsurge in sea trade which seems to have been equally intense in the southern region too. However, coastal Thessaly has provided evidence of contacts with eastern Macedonia and Thrace during the Late Neolithic, again suggesting maritime communication.

Besides quasi-commercial activities within the Aegean region, it seems that Neolithic groups also traded with peoples further north (C. Renfrew, 1973, p. 187). Necklace beads and bracelets of spondylus shell have been found in Late Neolithic sites in Bulgaria and Romania, as well as further north in Bohemia, Moravia and Slovakia as well as in Germany. Oxygen isotope analysis of these shells has shown that they are of Aegean provenance and could only have reached the above regions as a consequence of exchange transactions. Indeed, at Sitagroi in the Drama valley (east Macedonia) considerable quantities of rings and bracelets of spondylus shells have been found. This means that the northern coast of the Aegean was their main export centre and was particularly flourishing around 6,500 years ago, as the main concentration of these shells in the corresponding strata suggests.

RELIGIOUS BELIEFS AND MORTUARY PRACTICES

There is a plethora of theories concerning the religious beliefs of Neolithic peoples in the Aegean area. The majority of these are founded on the fact that anthropomorphic figurines, mainly representing obese, steatopygous females, have been found in many sites of the period. Thus the universal cult of the Mother Goddess in Aegean Neolithic religion has been proposed. Certain features on some of these figurines, such as the possible portrayal of pregnancy, rounded buttocks or placement of the hands beneath the breasts, have been interpreted as being associated with fecundity and thus a fertility cult has been assumed. Similarly, the discovery of figurines has been taken as evidence of cult places, shrines and the like, as at Nea Nikomedeia where figurines were found inside an Early Neolithic building of unusually large dimensions and in a central position in the settlement. However, the site's excavator is not categorical in its interpretation as a shrine and has also expressed the view that it might have been the residence of the leader of the community.

Despite their widespread acceptance, theories on the religious significance of these figurines are largely based on an erroneous methodological approach: the figurines have been studied in isolation, totally divorced from their archaeological context. In this respect the contributions of two scholars – P. J. Ucko (1968) and G. Chourmouziadis (1974) – are of vital importance, for their systematic classification and study of these artefacts has shown that very few come from graves and almost none from a context which could be characterized as having ritual or cult connotations. On the contrary, figurines have been found in domestic contexts in settlements, often in rubbish pits or middens and frequently in association with other objects for which no ritual significance can be assumed (stone tools, food residues and so on). Therefore the multiple function interpretation assigned them by these two scholars invites rather more credence: that they are toys, dolls, initiation figures, vehicles for sympathetic magic and even symbols of ideological communication.

One stands on somewhat firmer ground when seeking evidence of the mortuary practices of Neolithic peoples, but again any suggestions, however tentative, concerning associated rites and beliefs are at best intelligent guesswork, because material evidence can furnish but a partial insight into human cognitive processes.

There is very little evidence of mortuary practices in Neolithic Greece, barely 300 instances, though this may be accidental and future discoveries may change the picture (Chourmouziadis, 1973). Examination of these data reveals that there were no norms for the treatment of the dead and though they were interred there were no systematically organized burial grounds or cemeteries, at least during the Early and Middle Neolithic periods.

Two types of inhumation have been distinguished, primary and secondary. Primary burial was evidently the most common mortuary practice, generally intramural in the early phases either in houses or caves, though simple shallow pits often surrounded with flat stones and even *pithos* burials have also been recorded; however, the latter seem to have been confined to new-born babies and infants rather than adults. There is no consistency in the orientation of the corpse, in its attitude or the position of the arms and legs though a general predilection for flexed or contracted burial is observed. Secondary burials are common for adults, and in some instances there is evidence of cremation as the sites of Magoula Zarkou and Soufli Magoula have demonstrated (Weinberg, 1965, p. 49; Gallis, 1980, pp. 29–100). Grave goods are extremely few and in most cases are utilitarian items (tools, pots and the like). Ritual objects or ornaments which may be characteristic of social status or symbolize authority are extremely rare. Such goods, ochre, beads, pendants or amulets, and figurines, are more commonly found in settlement deposits. Thus grave goods seem to have been personal items rather than objects of religious significance. Finally, there is no evidence that markers of any kind were placed on Neolithic graves, nor were any monumental structures associated with them. As time passed certain burial customs were established: increasing frequency of secondary burials, cremation, furnishing with grave goods, special treatment of the skull, organized cemeteries. All these practices certainly reflect beliefs and attitudes concerning death but what these were we shall probably never know.

The recent discovery of a clay model of a house beneath the floor of a Neolithic house in Thessaly (Gallis, 1985) might be associated with some religious beliefs, if this find is accepted as a foundation offering.

NEOLITHIC SOCIETY

Inevitably it is exceedingly difficult to reconstruct a clear picture of Neolithic society from the indirect evidence of its material remains. With the exception of the rather small dwellings on the Middle Neolithic acropolises of Sesklo and Dimini, Neolithic houses were generally spacious, as is exemplified in Early Neolithic Nea Nikomedeia, and could accomodate quite sizeable households. Whether these were family units, and if so whether they were nuclear or extended, is impossible to tell, and the evidence from the mortuary practices sheds no light on this problem. It seems that the cycle of production, which regulated sedentary life, involved labour co-operation at the household level. However, the manufacture of fine-quality pottery, the working of obsidian, the elaboration of hard shells into ornaments as well as the fashioning of stone vessels and figurines required skill and experience and are indicative of differentiation of labour and possibly of craft specialization (C. Renfrew, 1973, pp. 187–90). Yet it is difficult to assess whether there were full-time artisans, or whether the craftspeople were farmers as well. The same applies to those who were involved in trade. The successive rebuilding of the houses on the same plot might suggest property ownership, though this is speculation. However, some concept of personal property may be inferred from the funerary offerings, since items of communal or domestic use are not included among these. From the mortuary practices there is only negative evidence of the existence of social stratification. However, in certain settlements there is some differentiation between those living inside the acropolises or enclosures and those living outside. This evidence becomes more pronounced during the Late Neolithic, with the appearance of the megaron centrally located inside the acropolises.

Such works as the enclosure, a ditch or even a paved square or street in the Neolithic settlements could be designated as 'public works', since they require communal effort and co-ordination, so we may logically conjecture the existence of a political authority, though its form eludes us.

BIBLIOGRAPHY

ALEXANDER, J. 1972. *Yugoslavia before the Roman Conquest.* London.

BAKALAKIS, G.; SAKELLARIOU, A. 1981. *Paradimi.* Mainz.

BLEGEN, C. W. 1927. Excavations at Nemea. *Am. J. Archaeol.* (New York), Vol. 31, pp. 427–40.

—— 1930. *Gonia.* New York.

—— 1937. *Prosymna: The Helladic Settlement Preceding the Argive Heraeum.* Cambridge. 2 vols.

BÖKÖNYI, S. 1973. Stock Raising. In: THEOCHARIS, D. R. (ed.), *Neolithic Greece.* Athens.

CHOURMOUZIADIS, G. 1973. Burial Customs. In: THEOCHARIS, D. R. (ed.), *Neolithic Greece.* Athens.

—— 1974. *Ta Neolithika Eidolia tes Thessalias* [The Neolithic Figurines of Thessaly]. Athens.

—— 1979. *To neolithiko Dimini* [Neolithic Dimini]. Volos.

—— 1982. *Ancient Magnesia.* Athens.

EFSTRATIOU, N. 1985. *Agios Petros: A Neolithic Site in the Northern Sporades.* Oxford. (BAR, Int. Ser., 241.)

ELSTER, E. 1977. *Neolithic Technology.* Los Angeles. (Unpublished Ph.D. thesis, University of California.)

EVANS, A. 1921–35. *The Palace of Minos at Knossos.* London. 4 vols.

EVANS, J. D. 1964. Excavations in the Neolithic Settlement of Knossos 1957–1960. Part I. *Annu. Br. Sch. Athens* (London), Vol. 59, pp. 132 ff.

EVANS, J. D.; RENFREW, C. 1968. *Excavations at Saliagos near Antiparo.* London. (Br. Sch. Athens, Suppl., 5.)

GALLIS, K. J. 1980. *Kausseis Nekron apo ten archaiotere neolithiké epoché ste Thessalia* [Cremations from the Early Neolithic Period in Thessaly]. Athens.

—— 1985. A Late Neolithic Foundation Offering from Thessaly. *Antiquity,* Vol. 59, pp. 20–4.

HEIDENREICH, R. 1935–6. Vorgeschichtliches in der Stadt Samos. Die Funde. *Athen. Mitt.,* Vol. 60/61.

HONEA, K. 1975. Prehistoric Remains on the Island of Kythnos. *Am. J. Archaeol.* (New York), Vol. 79.

JACOBSEN, T. W. 1981. Franchthi Cave and the Beginning of Settled Village Life in Greece. *Hesperia* (Princeton), Vol. 50.

KUNZE, E. 1931. *Orchomenos. II; Die neolithische Keramik.* Munich.

LAMBERT, N. 1981. La Grotte préhistorique de Kitsos (Attique): missions 1968–1978. Paris, École Française d'Athènes. 2 vols.

LEVI, D. 1930–1. Abitazioni preistoriche sulle pendici meridionali dell' Acropoli. *Annu. R. Scuola Archeol. Atene* (Rome), Vol. 13/14.

MILOJČIĆ, V.; HAUPTMAN, H. 1969. *Die Funde der frühen Diminizeit aus der Arapi-Magula, Thessalien.* Bonn.

MYLONAS, G. 1928. *I neolithiké Epoché en Elladi* [The Neolithic Period in Greece]. Athens.

NANDRIS, J. 1970. The Development and Relationships of the Earlier Greek Neolithic. *Man* (London), Vol. 5, No. 2.

PAPATHANASOPOULOS, G. 1971. Spelaia Derou (1971): ek ton anaskaphon tes Alepotrypas (Diros Caves (1971): from the Excavations of Alepotrypa). *Ann. Archaeol.* (Athens), Vol. 4.

RENFREW, C. 1973. Trade and Craft Specialization. In: THEOCHARIS, D. R. (ed.), *Neolithic Greece.* Athens.

RENFREW, J. 1973. Farming. In: THEOCHARIS, D. R. (ed.), *Neolithic Greece.* Athens.

RODDEN, R. J. 1962. Excavations of the Early Neolithic Site at Nea Nikomedeia, Greek Macedonia (1961 Season). *Proc. Prehist. Soc.,* Vol. 28.

—— 1964. Recent Discoveries from Prehistoric Macedonia: An Interim Report. *Balkan Stud.* (Thessaloniki), Vol. 5.

SOTERIADIS, G. 1912. Fouilles Préhistoriques en Phocide. *Rev. Étud. grecques* (Paris), Vol. 25.

THEOCHARIS, D. R. 1956. Nea Makri. Eine grosse neolithische Siedlung in der Nähe von Marathon. *Athen. Mitt.,* Vol. 71.

—— (ed.) 1973. *Neolithic Greece.* Athens.

—— 1981. *Neolithikos Politismos* [Neolithic Civilization]. Athens.

TSOUNTAS, C. 1908. *Ai Proïstorikai akropoleis Diminiou kai Sesklou* [The Prehistoric Acropolises of Dimini and Sesklo]. Athens.

UCKO, P. J. 1968. *Anthropomorphic Figurines of Predynastic Egypt and Neolithic Crete with Comparative Material from the Prehistoric Near East and Mainland Greece*. London.

VALMIN, N. 1938. *The Swedish Messenia Expedition*. Lund.

WEINBERG, S. S. 1965. The Stone Age in the Aegean. In: *The Cambridge Ancient History*. Rev. edn. Vols 1–2, fasc. 36.

WELTER, G. 1937. Aiginetische Keramik. *Archäol. Anz.* (Berlin).

49

WESTERN MEDITERRANEAN CULTURES

during the Neolithic

Jean Guilaine

The true extent of the indebtedness of central and western Mediterranean countries to south-west Asia and the eastern Mediterranean in their adoption of an agricultural economy continues to be debated and to be the subject of a host of theories: complete diffusion of the Neolithic complex; acculturation by technological gleanings; and finally the autochthonous model based on the prior development of Pre-pottery cultures. We shall content ourselves with a few preliminary remarks.

As far as agriculture is concerned, the absence of self-sown cereals suggests that wheat and barley must have been imported from the east. On the other hand, we must drop the idea that legumes were introduced systematically at the same time – self-sown lentils, peas and chickpeas grew at the Abeurador site in the south of France during and after the eleventh and tenth millennia BP and, together with other wild plants and fruits, were regularly harvested.

As for stock-breeding in the western Mediterranean, palaeontologists have attributed it to the importation of domesticated sheep, goats, cattle and pigs. During a later period, domesticable local species (arouchs, boar) may well have been used to increase the number and quality of the livestock. Because of a lack of data, the origins of the North African domestic sheep remain uncertain.

Does that mean that the Neolithic reached the west as the result of a simple process of diffusion? The answer is more complex than that. Thus an examination of pottery styles shows that there was no morphological and decorative unity in the emergence of the first pottery cultures. The Impressed Ware Neolithic of south-east Italy, parallels for which can be found in Dalmatia, differs markedly from the first Neolithic cultures of Thessaly or the Peloponnese, where the pottery was not decorated. Shapes, methods and arrangements of decorations differed from those found in Apulia even amongst the earliest agricultural communities in central and northern Italy and on the Tyrrhenian islands. Finally, the Adriatic Impressed Ware cannot be typologically likened to the Franco-Iberian Cardial Ware. There was thus a measure of cultural separation from the outset. Moreover, radio-carbon datings reveal a clear chronological shift from the east to the west. Why then did the inhabitants of the western shores of the Mediterranean adopt agriculture at a given stage in their development? To answer that question, we must first try to determine the precise relationship between Epipalaeolithic populations and their plant environment. If we do that, we find that we are dealing with the gradual manipulation of the environment (gathering of local plants, 'exploitation' and storage of these plants) rather than the adoption of cereal agriculture, which can be considered a higher stage in a process with early roots. By contrast, the presence of domestic sheep in certain places shortly before the emergence of pottery and the belated adoption (during the Middle Neolithic) of domestic pigs are examples of regional variations. The irregular emergence of the various elements of the Neolithic complex – a sedentary life-style, stable habitation sites, domesticated animals, pottery, cereal crops – prevents us for the moment from drawing up a standard model for the process of adoption of the Neolithic way of life in the western Mediterranean. Much deeper research is still needed.

SPECIFIC CULTURAL ASPECTS OF THE EARLY NEOLITHIC IN THE WESTERN MEDITERRANEAN (Map 55)

The Early Neolithic in Italy

South-east Italy

This was the first area of the Italian peninsula to see the emergence of an unmistakable Neolithic culture. For lack of information about the last hunter-gatherers in that region, we cannot tell whether the local Mesolithic populations had already prepared the way for forms of behaviour associated with food production. When the first peasant communities appeared in the course of the ninth millennium BP they had all the characteristics of the full-blown Neolithic (domestic animals, cultivated cereals, pottery); not long afterwards they began to settle in habitation sites surrounded by ditches. The idea that life-styles based exclusively on hunting, fishing and gathering could have continued well beyond the emergence of pottery does not seem very convincing. The 'tell' at Coppa Nevigata, near Manfredonia, where pottery was found in association with fine ('Sipontian') flint implements adapted to opening the many shells discarded on the site, was certainly no more than the habitation site of specialists

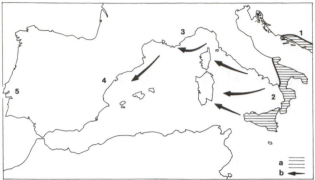

Map 55 The Neolithic in the western Mediterranean *c.*8,500–
8,000 years ago: a, the first impressed-ware groups in Dalmatia,
south-east of Italy and Sicily; b, the Neolithic way of life gaining
westwards: 1, early Neolithic Crvena-Stijena culture (Dalmatia);
2, early Neolithic groups in south-east Italy and Sicily; 3, Provence
(Castelnovian Mesolithic); 4, Catalonia (Cocinian Mesolithic); 5,
Portugal (Muge Mesolithic).

in the exploitation of coastal resources but contemporary
with sites associated with an agricultural economy.

The various species of animal and cultivated plant and
also the methods of raising them were probably of Aegean
origin. By contrast, pottery styles already differed appreciably
from those in the Peloponnese, in Epirus or the Early Neolithic of Thessaly; the most common south Italian ware
comprised flat-bottomed jars, some bottles with a flat base
and slender-footed bowls decorated with irregular
impressions over the whole surface of the vessel – shell
motifs, grooves, coarse marks (the early or so-called Coppa
Nevigata or San Domino de Tremiti phase). During the
next (the Guadone) phase, the pottery had more structured
and more elaborate decorations, and during a third phase,
painted ware of great quality became associated with the
traditional indigenous Impressed Ware tradition (for
instance, the Lagnano da Piede and Masseria–La Quercia
phases in the Tavoliere region). Southern Italy, in fact, was
the scene of the first west Mediterranean Impressed Ware
pottery, a term that may be misleading inasmuch as this vast
complex stretching from the Adriatic to the Atlantic is full
of cultural divisions and chronological differences. Thus the
precocious encirclement of habitations with round or oval
ditches seems to have been a cultural feature specific to this
south Italian region where it proved exceptionally successful.
The oldest sites, mainly on the coast (round Brindisi, Bari
and Salento) do not seem to have been entrenched, but soon
afterwards several hundred moated Neolithic sites appeared
in Apulia: they date from the Guadone phase to the end of
the Middle Neolithic. Discussions about the significance of
these moats are still rife: Did they have a defensive purpose?
Did they delimit inhabited and possibly cultivated areas?
were they animal pens, systems for storing or draining rain
water, a means of irrigating or improving the soil, or were
they external boundaries? Some of these functions, moreover, might have been combined. Inside the moated area,
there was one ditch (or several ditches) of smaller dimensions,
open on one side (the so-called C-ditches). It is thought that
family dwellings were often erected inside them. Towards
the end of the Early Neolithic and the beginnings of the
Middle Neolithic, moated sites seem to have been quite
small (covering less than 2 hectares), several containing just
one C-ditch. Some authors consider this as evidence that
each of these sites sheltered no more than one or two
families, as a farm might. It was not until the beginning of

the eighth millennium BP that larger and better-equipped
dwellings made their appearance. We known very little about
their layout. At Rendina di Melfi, in the Olfanto valley, it
was possible to establish the existence, during the earliest
phase, of a dwelling measuring about 12 by 4 m, and of more
or less rectangular shape (although the northern side bore a
small apse). Posts supported a timber frame round a wattle
and daub lattice. The house was probably divided into two
rooms. The pronounced agricultural character of this Early
Neolithic phase seems borne out by the discovery of wheat
and barley stores (Torre Sabea at Gallipoli). Similarly, animal
husbandry seems already to have played an essential role. S.
Bökönyi estimates that domestic animals constituted 97 per
cent of the fauna (cattle, sheep, goats, pigs, dogs) at Rendina;
at Torre Sabea cattle, sheep and goats held pride of place.

A few baked clay seals, the remains of a horned 'idol' and
a kind of rhyton found at Rendina have affinities with finds
in the Balkans.

Adriatic Italy

The spread of Neolithic techniques to the north of the
Tavoliere region seems to have occurred somewhat later
than it did in the rest of south-east Italy. The first peasant
communities to develop between the Tavoliere and the
mouth of the Po are therefore more recent than those identified in Apulia. No radiocarbon dates obtained here are
earlier than 7,000 years ago. However, the Early Neolithic
was strongly affected by southern influences and the essential
cultural features of the first Neolithic cultures in the Abruzzi,
the Marches and the Romagna came from the south. Here
too the vessels were flower-pots on flat or slightly set-off
bases, together with egg-cups and bottles. The decorations –
impressions and incisions – might be scattered irregularly
over the entire side or be confined to a central area. In
addition to such Impressed Ware we also find vessels of better
quality, few of them decorated (open or carinated bowls,
necked vessels). Sometimes there were also plain vessels made
of refined clay (*figulina*). The most important open-air sites
were Leopardi in Penna di Pescara, Capo d'Acqua in the
Abruzzi, Ripabianca di Monterado and Maddalena di
Muccia in the Marches and Rimola in Romagna. They have
been dated back to the seventh millennium BP. They contain
the remains of domestic animals (cattle, pigs, sheep, goats
and dogs at Leopardi) and of agricultural activities.

Northern Italy

The original character of the Neolithic acculturation of
northern Italy seems due to the vigour of the last groups of
hunter-gatherers on whom external Neolithic influences
were brought to bear. In fact, with the exception of Liguria,
which was mainly exposed to Tyrrhenian influences, the
core of northern Italy (the Po valley and neighbouring
regions) had unique cultural features. A number of cultural
groups, each with a small territory, have been identified
there: Fagnigola in Venezia, Gaban in Trentino, Vhò in the
Cremona and Mantova regions, Isolino in Varese. Briefly
speaking, these groups used stone implements many of
which had preserved Mesolithic characteristics; the pottery
included shapes borrowed from the south Italian stock of
Impressed Ware (such as pedestal vases) but also original
contributions (flagons, decorations involving grooved chevrons or triangles). The economy was only partly food producing. From Venezia to the north of Tuscany, the Fiorano

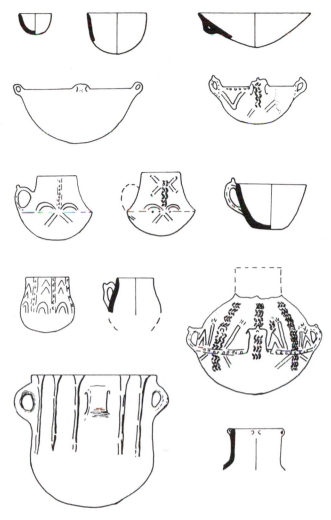

Figure 136 Pottery styles, Fiorano group, seventh millennium BP (northern Italy). (After Barfield, 1971.)

goats, pigs) and agriculture are reported, but hunting and the gathering of molluscs are represented as well.

From the Po valley, Liguria and the Rhodanian axis, the process of Neolithic acculturation spread to the western Alps. A food-producing economy thus gradually took root in the highlands: domestic animals are reported at Balme de Thuy in Haute Savoie towards the end of the eighth millennium BP and at Sion-Planta in Switzerland in the seventh.

The insular domain

Communities of food producers were found in Sicily from the ninth millennium BP. Their remains come mainly from caves (Uzzo, San Calogero, Sperlinga): impressed pottery is associated with remains of sheep, cattle and domestic pigs; einkorn, emmer and lentils were cultivated. Towards the end of the ninth millennium BP, a new phase began with the introduction into eastern Sicily of the Stentinello culture which marked the consolidation of agriculture. Villages ringed with ditches appeared; they comprised quadrangular houses, for instance at Stentinello itself. The pottery, of various shapes, was decorated with sharp impressions and incisions. A comparable facies, the so-called Kronio facies, is known in the western part of Sicily. Obsidian from the Aeolian islands (Lipari) began to be widely circulated and became a spur to primitive barter. Stentinellian groups settled in Calabria (Acconia), in Malta (Skorba) and in the Pelagian islands (Cala Pisana at Lampedusa).

In Sardinia and Corsica the first signs of the Neolithic, at the beginning of the eighth millennium BP, were also associated with groups using an impressed pottery technique; here we identify a Tyrrhenian facies, also found in Tuscany (Pienza). Many of the known sites are shelters (Su Carropu di Sirri, Cagliari), caves (Filiestru, Sassari) and even open-air sites (Basi at Serra di Ferro, Rousse Island, Corsica). The introduction of domestic animals, and of sheep and pigs in particular, led to the emergence of feral species such as island moufflons and boars.

At about the same time, a human presence is recorded for the first time in the Balearic islands (the Muleta cave in Majorca). The absence of pottery together with an economy centred on the hunting of an indigenous gazelle (*Myotragus balearicus*) – which eventually disappeared – seem to indicate the prevalence of a predatory life-style. The evidence suggests that agriculture did not come into its own here before the sixth millennium BP.

Cardial ware

The Cardial culture (Map 56)

By 'Cardial culture' or the 'Franco-Iberian Cardial' we refer to a series of Early Neolithic groups ranging from Provence to Morocco and Portugal. A common feature of all these communities was their method of decorating pottery with the imprint of a cockle shell (*Cardium edule*). While that method was not confined to this particular region, here it became the basis of highly elaborate motifs: finely worked horizontal or vertical bands juxtaposed with undecorated areas, the wealth of motifs producing a thematic exuberance not normally found outside the western Mediterranean. In this quest for motifs, cockle impressions were often accompanied by impressions of combs, plants or fingers, grooves or striations, smooth or cupulate cord impressions and so on. However the cockle-shell motif predominates in

culture, known from open-air sites or shelters, covered a much larger area than did the cultures we have just been describing. Here, too, the implements had a marked Epi-palaeolithic component (backed blades, rhombi, burins of the Ripabianca type). The pottery (Fig. 136) contained original elements (carinated cups with lugs, decoration involving chevrons, lozenges or curvilinear patterns). Radiocarbon dates place this horizon towards the end of the eighth millennium BP or in the first half of the seventh millennium BP.

Liguria

While we still know very little about the Early Neolithic along the Tyrrhenian coast of the Italian peninsula (Latium, Tuscany), we have much better information about Liguria, where several caves have yielded remains from that phase: Arma di Stefanin, Arma di Nasino, Caverna dell'Acqua, Pollera and others, but above all the Arene Candide cave at Finale Ligure, where the chronological superposition of Neolithic cultures in the western Mediterranean was first demonstrated. The pottery styles reflect a Tyrrhenian (flat-bottomed beakers) or western influence (necked vessels, corded mouldings); there were also local decorative variations (impressed groove decorations) that recur at sites in the Côte d'Azur (Caucade), in Corsica and as far afield as Languedoc (Portiragnes). Animal husbandry (cattle, sheep,

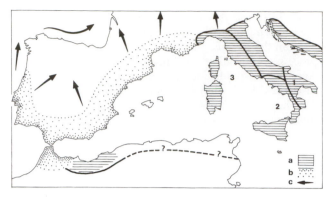

Map 56 The Neolithic in the western Mediterranean *c.*7,800–7,500 years ago: a, impressed pottery groups: 1, Masseria La Quercia and Matera groups; 2, Stentinello group; 3, Tyrrhenian groups; b, maximum development of the Cardial culture from Liguria to Portugal and Morocco; c, partial Neolithization of the more continental regions, such as Aquitaine and the Iberian Meseta.

the early phases. It gradually gave way to groove motifs, which eventually ousted it. The pottery consists almost invariably of spherical vessels with or without necks. The bases are convex or sometimes, particularly in the advanced Iberian phases, conical; flat bases, while not unknown, are extremely rare.

The Cardial was responsible for introducing the cultivation of cereals into the western Mediterranean, and for the rise of stock-farming (mainly sheep and goats which, in many sites, were as much as or more than 50 per cent of the fauna). Some authors consider the Cardial to be the result of a migration, but this view cannot be upheld since we know that in the east of the Tyrrhenian part of the Mediterranean the oldest Neolithic pottery styles differ fundamentally from those found in the west. The alternative hypothesis of the independent emergence of the Cardial from indigenous Mesolithic substrata is no more satisfactory. The Cardial, in fact, seems to have been the upshot of the acculturation of autochthonous populations: in particular they borrowed their method of baking clay from areas that had previously adopted the Neolithic way of life (southern Italy; the Tyrrhenian region), to come up with pottery quite distinct from that of the Italian domain proper. These very contacts allowed the adoption of cereal agriculture and of some domestic animals. Navigation must have played an essential role in the spread of these processes: the dispersion of the Cardial, essentially a coastal and insular phenomenon, shows this well. The resulting rapid economic changes (although hunting continued to play an important role in many parts) no doubt engendered technological changes: the slight or massive advent, depending upon the situation, of agricultural implements (polished axes, weighted digging sticks, sickles), the opening of new routes for the distribution of lithic material, the tendency to standardize blades: this rapid change makes all comparisons with local Mesolithic industries somewhat far-fetched, so much so that persisting with the old 'continuity or break' discussion means continuing to pose a false question.

From that time, the chronological progress of the early Impressed Ware Neolithic in the south of France and the Iberian peninsula is documented by an unusually large number of datings. No doubt one must be slightly sceptical about dates centred on the end of the tenth millennium BP (or on the ninth) because these datings, which would turn the west into a focus of the creation of pottery and of the

domestication of imported wild species, contradict most of the datings for the whole of the Mediterranean. The great thrust of the Cardial came during the first half of the eighth millennium BP, or between 8,000 and 7,300 years ago. Then it quickly made way for more advanced Early Neolithic cultures (Epicardial, 'cultura de las cuevas') which survived until the first centuries of the seventh millennium BP and, locally, even until about 6,300 years ago. This long duration explains why some authors (and Iberian authors in particular) place the Epicardial and Postcardial Neolithic in the Middle Neolithic: this is a matter of terminology. Let us now look at some of the cultural provinces of this Neolithic.

The south of France

Here the early Mediterranean Neolithic is largely known from excavations in caves and shelters. The importance of open-air sites is however being increasingly recognized: coastal sites, sometimes inundated (such as Leucate-Corrège in the Aude), or sites further inland (Courthézon in the Vaucluse). Agriculture took root, while stock-farming was largely confined to sheep and goats and only secondarily to cattle. Pigs were not used until boar hunting declined. It seems likely that caves were used as sheepfolds. Various stratigraphic studies of caves (Châteauneuf in the Bouches-du-Rhône; Fontbrégoua in the Var; Gazel in the Aude) enable us to size up the overall development of that culture and the transformation of the Cardial into derived facies associated with more intense forms of agriculture. In the peri-Mediterranean area (Causses, Aquitaine, Pyrenees) the rapid growth of productive techniques gave rise to groups culturally distinct from the Cardial although more or less contemporary with it. A type of pottery that was often poorly produced, with few if any decorations, characterizes these facies (the Jean Cros shelter in the Aude; the Poujade shelter in the Aveyron; the Roucadour cave in the Lot).

Catalonia and the Valencia region

These constitute the territory richest in remains from the Cardial which extended chiefly to coastal or sub-coastal regions, especially in the mountain massifs close to the sea (Plate 79). Our knowledge of open-air habitation sites is still very sketchy (Guixeres de Vilovi in Penedes). The essential evidence, in fact, comes from caves, doubtless used for occupation (La Sarsa, L'Or) to judge by the number of agricultural implements (sickle elements) found there; the use of these caves as sheepfolds seems equally possible. Four species of wheat and two species of barley have been identified in the Cova de l'Or. From 7,000 years ago onwards, while agriculture became more and more entrenched, the Cardial began to make way for well-identified Epicardial facies in the Les Cendres and Fosca caves. Southern Catalonia also witnessed the emergence of an original culture after 6,800 years ago (El Molinot). The Neolithic acculturation of the central plateaux in the Iberian peninsula is still badly known. Sites containing impressed pottery have been found as far as upper Aragon (Chaves) and in Meseta Norte (La Vaquera).

Andalusia

Here the Cardial is represented in the deeper layers of Cariguela cave near Granada and in some caves in the provinces of Granada, Alhama, Almeria and Malaga in the south-east. In western Andalusia, the early phases are chiefly

known through finds of comb-impressed ware. This Neolithic culture must have emerged about 8,000 years ago
(several ninth millennium BP datings require confirmation). Sheep and goats played a crucial role in the economy
from the outset. In the course of a more advanced phase,
this Early Neolithic culture adopted more original ceramic
forms (amphorae with a pointed base, vessels with spouts,
crested handles) and decorations involving grooves and ochre
paint; at the same time, the making and circulation of prestige
objects (marble bracelets) grew apace. Caves remain the most
thoroughly explored sites (Nerja in Malaga, la Dehessila and
Parralejo at Arcas de la Frontera, Murcielagos de Zuheros at
Cordoba). The last-named cave has provided numerous dates
that place the advanced Early Neolithic between the end of
the eighth and the beginning of the seventh millennium BP;
it also shows that agricultural activity was intense (emmer,
wheat, barley).

Portugal

In Portugal, the Early Neolithic is known mainly from open-
air coastal sites (the Sines and Figueira da Foz regions).
Cockle shell decorations are rare. Some caves and shelters
(Bocas, Alcobaca, Lapo do Fumo, Furninha) have yielded
remains from a more advanced phase characterized by bag-
shaped vessels fitted with lugs and decorated with impressed
or incised herringbone patterns.

Communities using impressed pottery were found as far
afield as Aquitaine (Lède du Gurp) and even in sites between
the Garonne and the Loire, distant offsprings of a rapid and
active form of coastal Neolithic development, possibly with
a Mediterranean influence.

The Maghreb

While we know little about Early Neolithic communities
along much of the north African coast (Tunisia, eastern
Algeria), we have more information about the western
Maghreb. Here, the pottery in the coastal areas (western
Algeria, northern Morocco) is akin to Mediterranean
Impressed Ware. An original Cardial group is known to have
occupied northern Morocco (Car Gahal, Caf That El Gar,
Achakar); it was probably linked to the Iberian sphere. In
western Algeria, Early Neolithic pottery is represented by
vessels with a conical base and impressed, incised or fluted
decorations. The economic aspects of the Early Neolithic
in the western Maghreb need further investigation.

THE CONSOLIDATION OF RURAL LIFE DURING THE MIDDLE AND LATE NEOLITHIC: SEVENTH AND SIXTH MILLENNIA BP (Maps 57 and 58)

The Middle and Late Neolithic are characterized, in the
entire area under consideration, by a consolidation of the
phenomena associated with a sedentary way of life. However,
our knowledge and the cultural characteristics vary strongly
from one region to the next.

Italy and borders

Peninsular Italy

Following those of groups using impressed pottery, horizons
containing engraved or painted pottery appeared at about

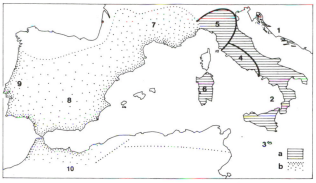

Map 57 The Neolithic in the western Mediterranean c.7,000 years
ago: a, Middle Neolithic groups in Dalmatia and Italy: 1, Danilo
culture in Dalmatia; 2, painted-ware groups; 3, Grey Skorba group
on Malta; 4, Sasso culture; 5, Fiorano culture; 6, Bonu Ighinu
culture on Sardinia; b, Middle Neolithic cultures in southern
France, the Iberian peninsula and the Maghreb; 7, Epicardial
cultures; 8, Las Cuevas culture; 9, Furninha culture; 10, Capsian
tradition in the Maghreb Neolithic.

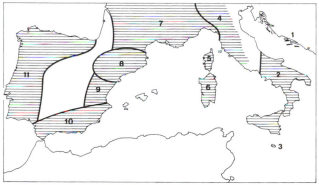

Map 58 The Neolithic in the western Mediterranean c.6,000–
5,500 years ago: 1, Hvar culture, Dalmatia; 2, Diana culture; 3,
Zebbug culture, Malta; 4, Lagozza culture; 5, Basi-group; 6,
Ozieri-group; 7, Chassey culture; 8, Sepulcros de Fosa culture; 9,
Valencian group with incised pottery; 10, Almeria culture; 11,
Portuguese Megalithic groups.

7,800 to 7,600 years ago. South-eastern Italy henceforth
witnessed a marked cultural diversification, reflected in the
development of numerous local facies: the *grafita* or finely
incised pottery of Materano; pottery painted with geometric motifs of Tavoliere–Lagnano da Piede–Masseria–La
Quercia. Not much later, pottery with red bands on a
clear ground appeared over a large area: from the Abruzzi
(Catignano) to the south-east, passing through Tavoliere
(Passo di Corvo). Pottery painted in three colours appeared
at a slightly later stage: Ripoli (mainly in the Abruzzi),
Scaloria (in Tavoliere), Capri (in Campagna), Serra d'Alto
(Plate 80) (throughout the south). Great stress has been laid
on the technical quality of Serra d'Alto pottery with its
zoomorphic handles and painted motifs of lozenges,
meanders, spirals and so on. Many authors have speculated
about the external origins of these horizons, comparing
them to the painted ware of northern Greece or the Peloponnese. In fact, however, it would seem that the agricultural
wealth of southern Italy, very appreciable from the ninth
millennium BP, was all that was needed to foster the emergence of local specialists, the mastery of the firing technique
and the rapid improvement of the potter's art.

We have already mentioned, in our discussion of the Early
Neolithic, the role of ditches, some of them concentric,
round settlements. They continued to be dug throughout the

Middle Neolithic by various south-eastern Italian cultures associated with painted or engraved ware. Some of them lived in fortified camps covering several hectares. Those in the vicinity of Matera (Murgia Timone, Tirlecchia, Murgecchia, Serra d'Alto) are renowned, but remarkable examples can also be found in Tavoliere where the biggest, that of Passo di Corvo, covered some 40 ha and contained about a hundred C-ditches. Ditches can also be found in central Italy, at Ripoli in the Abruzzi and in Sicily, where they are associated with the advanced Impressed Ware of Stentinello. We know more about the dwellings from that time onwards. At Monte Aquilone, a hut measuring about 6 by 3 m had a slightly trapezoidal shape and was marked off by a stone wall. At Casone near San Severo one or two elongated huts about 14 m in length stood inside a C-ditch. At Passo di Corvo a house with a stone foundation had an apsidal end. Rectangular huts or huts with apsidal ends are also characteristic of the Neolithic culture associated with the Murgia Timone site. Similar dwellings with apsidal ends also appeared at Catignano in the Abruzzi: these houses, demarcated by small depressions in the ground, measured 12 to 16 by 6 to 8 metres. On these sites, ditches of various dimensions, their sides strengthened with clay or cob, served as food stores.

Few burial places are known. Most are graves in ditches, for instance those found in the necropolis of Molfetta, associated with the Serra d'Alto culture. The first collective tombs (hypogea) appeared at about that time. Agriculture and stock-raising had begun to take firm root.

The end of the Neolithic, during the sixth millennium BP, saw the replacement of painted ware with the monochrome ware of the Diana culture. The unified character of that horizon found throughout southern Italy (Lipari, Sicily, Calabria, Apulia, the Abruzzi, Umbria and even Romagna) was remarkable. In Malta, there emerged a related facies ('Red Skorba'). The obsidian 'trade' was stepped up and played an obvious role in the expansion of the Diana culture. In Tyrrhenia, the Sasso culture, localized in Latium and Tuscany, is mainly known from excavation in the Fabrizi and Orso caves. In Sardinia, the Bonu Ighinu culture followed by the Ozieri culture occupied many habitation sites that have never been excavated. The many hypogea associated with them are examined (pp. 520–1).

Northern Italy

In northern Italy, the Square-mouthed Pottery culture developed throughout the seventh millennium BP in the Po and Adige valleys (Venice, Trentino, Emilia, Lombardy) and even as far away as Liguria (Finale facies). The pottery often has characteristic square or quadrilobate features. One can, by and large, note a process of decorative development away from engraved ornamentations of the linear geometrical type (bands, criss-crosses, triangles) to engraved or excised meandering or spiral motifs, and finally to incised or impressed decorations. The stone implements comprised end-of-blade scrapers, lozenge-shaped points and, ultimately, fine arrowheads of the Lagozza type. Baked-clay seals (*pintaderas*) were common. This culture definitely implanted the Neolithic economy in northern Italy, at the same time presiding over the decline of hunting and gathering.

The habitation sites were of many types (caves as in Liguria; shelters; plain or hilly occupations as at Rocca di Rivoli Veronese; villages in marshy zones as at Fimon Molino Casarotto. The dead were buried in pits (Chiozza), in cists

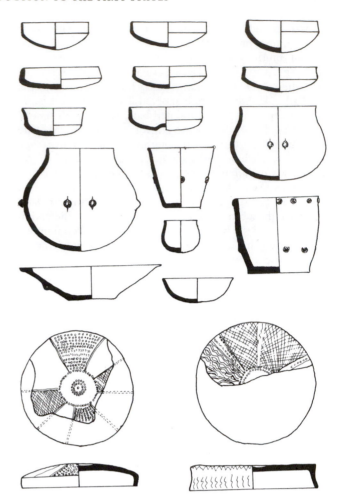

Figure 137 Pottery styles, Lagozza culture, sixth millennium BP, Lagozza di Besnate, Varese (Italy). (After Guerreschi, 1977.)

(Vela di Trento, Arene Candide) or in graves surrounded by stone circles (Vela di Trento).

In the greater part of northern Italy, the Lagozza culture came to supplant the Square-mouth Pottery culture about 6,000 years ago. It is known mainly from the eponymous lake dwelling. Polished axes, blade implements, smooth pottery (Fig. 137) with very few decorations (globular vessels with a convex base, truncated flower-pots with a flat base, plates with a wide rim, lids and above all carinated bowls) make this horizon part of the vast assembly of 'western' pottery cultures (Chassey–Cortaillod–Sepulcros de fosa). At Lagozza, various types of wheat and barley and also lentils were under cultivation.

The Alpine regions

The presence in eastern France (Jura) and western Switzerland of communities with pottery traditions without decorations and meeting certain morphological criteria, suggests that this zone must be attached to the Mediterranean cultural sphere. In the course of the Middle Neolithic (about 6,500–6,000 years ago) there developed a Proto-Cortaillod tradition characterized by bag-shaped vases, embossed decorations, necked vessels and wide-mouthed bowls. Recent excavations at Auvernier-Port and Twann in Switzerland have made it possible to reassess the development of the Cortaillod culture – between about 6,000 and 5,200 years ago - as reflected in the gradual abandonment of carinated shapes in favour of straight and tall vessels (Fig. 138). Subsequently, the emergence of the Horgen culture came to influence the final Swiss Neolithic (the Luschez group round Lakes Neuchâtel, Biel and Murten, followed by the Auvernier group, horizons sometimes combined within the Saône-Rhône complex, also known in the French Alps and along the Rhodanian axis). Although not the only ones, the lakeside dwellings here have attracted most attention because of the variety and quality of the information yielded by the other remains preserved with the pottery. This explains the 'historical' role of Neolithic lake dwellings in our study of the earliest European agricultural communities. To this day, dendrochronology continues to find that these dwellings provide rich pickings. Equipment for agriculture (axes, drilling sticks, picks, sickles), fishing (canoes, nets, floats, weights) and hunting (bows, harpoons, throwing sticks, and so on), not to mention domestic implements, are all widely represented. The remains of edible plants, too, are well preserved: einkorn, wheat, barley, pea, poppy, not to mention numerous wild fruits or textile plants (flax). At Egolzwill 5 (Fig. 139), the village contained several houses measuring 9 by 3.70 m, built parallel to the shore with an enclosure on the landward side. At Twann, a village was rebuilt eight to ten times beside the shore. At Clairvaux, at the end of the Neolithic, the houses had become smaller (measuring 6 to 8 by 3 to 4 m). They stood on piles and had a timber frame of three longitudinal rows of posts; the walls were made of wattle and daub.

From the south of France to Portugal

Mediterranean France

Several facies reflect the transformation in France of the last Impressed Ware cultures into those preferring

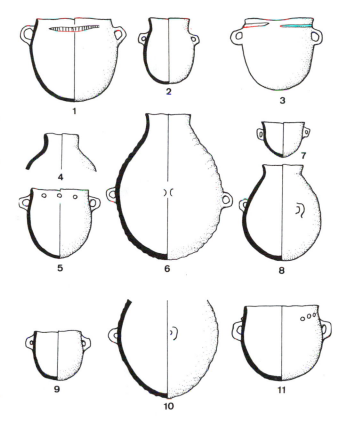

Figure 139 Pottery styles, Egolzwill culture, seventh millennium BP (Switzerland): 1–3, 5–8, Egolzwill 3; 4, 9–11, Schötz. (After Sauter and Gallay, 1969.)

undecorated ware. But it was the Chassean culture that, by its dynamism, would lead to the cultural unification of an area ranging from the eastern half of the Pyrenees to Liguria and even to Tuscany. Across the Rhône valley and the Massif Central, the Chassean, mixed with local influences, is also believed to have manifested itself as far afield as the North of France. In the Mediterranean zone this culture is largely identified as a blade industry (burins, scrapers, truncated blades, borers, arrowheads) associated with heavy implements (polished axes, pounders, grinding-stones and flaked pebbles, or backed knives and halberds as in the Garonne valley). In addition to general shapes, the pottery (Fig. 140) included several characteristic elements (bowls with internal grooves, plates with decorated rims, 'saucers', carinated vessels, 'cartridge pouch' handles). Important distribution networks of lithic material no doubt helped to maintain the strong cultural cohesion of the Chassean by means of constant exchanges: the use of light-coloured flint partly of lower Rhodanian origin, the distribution of south Alpine rock for the manufacture of polished axes as far afield as Provence and Languedoc, the transport of Aveyron tuff to the Toulouse region, to the Quercy region, to Gascony and the Aude. With the Chassean, the first large peasant settlements were established in southern France. These often occupied large sites: St Genès (Tarn-et-Garonne), 30 ha; Villeneuve-Tolosane (Haute-Garonne), 28 ha; St-Michel-du-Touch (Haute-Garonne) 20 ha; all in the immediate vicinity of fertile lands and often entrenched in causewayed camps behind palisades (Toulouse sites). Many structures have been identified inside these settlements (storage pits, paved areas, wells); in particular there were hundreds of hearths

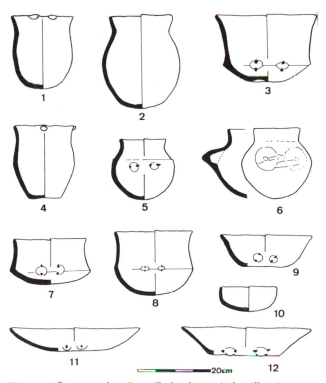

Figure 138 Pottery styles, Cortaillod culture, sixth millennium BP: 1–3, 5–7, 10, 12, Saint Aubin; 4, 8, 9, 11, Onnens. (After Sauter and Gallay, 1969.)

20cm

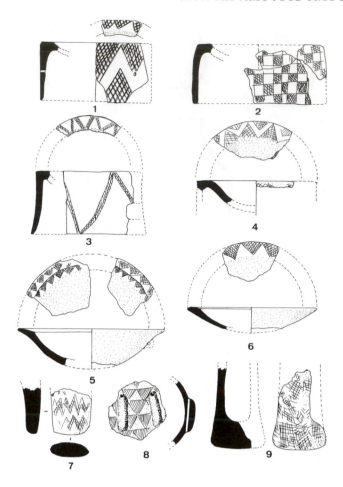

Figure 140 Decorated pottery, Camp de Chassey, seventh to sixth millennium BP, Saône-et-Loire (France): 1–4, 'vases supports'; 5–6, plates; 7, handle; 8, body of a vase; 9, suspension lug. (After Thévenot, 1969.)

filled with heated stones; the function of some measuring 11 by 2 m is not clear.

Mediterranean Spain

In Catalonia, research is not nearly as advanced as it is in the south of France. We know that the Sepulcros de Fosa culture is very close to the Chassean, in respect both of its stone implements and also of its ceramic objects (Fig. 141), but the habitation sites have not yet been thoroughly explored (that of Bovila Madurell is known to have been a causewayed camp). By contrast, unlike the south of France, this region has produced numerous burial sites with the dead in flexed positions, either in ditches (Barcelona region) or in stone cists (Solsona region). High-quality funerary equipment accompanied the dead, especially beads made of variscite, a green secondary mineral consisting of hydrated aluminium. From the Middle Neolithic, this mineral was mined intensively, especially at Can Tintore, near Gava, where recent discoveries include numerous mine shafts, the biggest of which were up to 50 m long. Such constructions have an industrial character and presuppose a highly structured social organization and also a widespread 'market'.

In the Valencia region, the horizons posterior to the Impressed Ware layers are not very distinct. Thanks to material from various caves it has recently been possible to identify an engraved pottery horizon. Smooth ware

(early phase of the Ereta del Pedregal tradition) was to characterize the last phase of the Neolithic in the Levantine region.

Andalusia and Portugal

In the course of the seventh millennium BP, a smooth pottery tradition appeared in the south of the Iberian peninsula. Much the same happened in Portugal at the time that the first megalithic tombs were built there. In the south-east, too, the burial sites have provided much of our knowledge about this advanced Neolithic stage. The study of open-air habitation sites of the Almerian Neolithic has, in fact, not been carried very far and it was not until it came to the study of the next, that is the Chalcolithic, stage that greater attention was paid to an analysis of the various localities. Moreover, as the transition to the Copper Age was a gradual process, the distinction between the Final Neolithic and the Chalcolithic proper (with an efficient metallurgy) often remains a delicate problem. In the Almeria region the sites are often located on hilltops. That of El Garcel undoubtedly represents a Neolithic occupation phase, typified by a type of ovoid jar with a pointed base, vessels with spouts, biconical cups and bowls with a flattened or round base. The associated stone implements are somewhat archaic blade tools, including trapezes, triangles, micro-burins and flint or quartz knives. The site was surrounded by a wall. Tres Cabezos

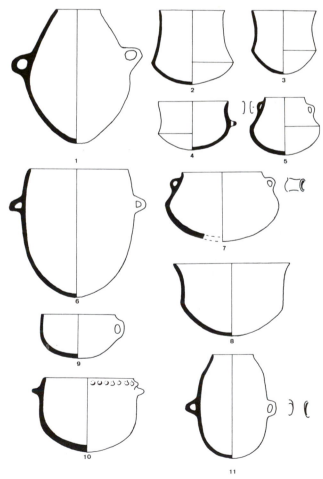

Figure 141 Pottery styles, Sepulcros de Fosa culture, sixth millennium BP, Catalonia (Spain): 1, 5, Aguilar de Segarra; 2–4, Sabassona; 6, Mas d'en Boixas; 7, Castelloli; 8, Masia Nova; 9, Bovila Bellsola; 10, Bovila Fusteret; 11, San Genis de Vilassar. (After Muñoz, 1965.)

contained a hut with a polygonal groundplan 8 m in diameter. At Velez Blanco (Cerro de las Cantaras) small circular or oval huts were divided into two compartments. The presence of oval huts is also mentioned in the lower levels of the Almizaraque site, in the Rio Aguas plain, while the houses there are said to have had a rectangular ground plan. Very interesting results have come from recent excavations at the La Peña de los Gitanos site in Montefrio, near Granada: a stratified habitation site first occupied by populations with an Impressed Ware tradition, followed by Neolithic groups with a smooth pottery tradition of the Almerian style (carinated vases, vessels with spouts). Metallurgy came to the fore during a still later stage, while the pottery developed towards the open shapes (large dishes) known throughout Andalusia and the Algarve; in the last phase, the site was largely occupied by populations with a Bell-Beaker pottery tradition. Montefrio thus provides an example of an open-air site occupied over some two millennia. At Tabernas, the occupation also started in the Neolithic and continued thereafter.

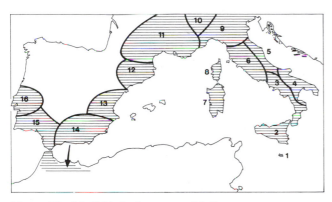

Map 59 The Neolithic in the western Mediterranean c.5,000–4,500 years ago: 1, Tarxien (Malta); 2, Conzo and Piano Conte groups; 3, Gaudo culture; 4, Laterza culture; 5, Conelle culture; 6, Rinaldone culture; 7, Abealazu Filigosa culture; 8, Terrina culture; 9, Remedello culture; 10, Saône–Rhône culture; 11, Early Chalcolithic of southern France; 12, Veraza culture; 13, Ereta del Pedregal culture; 14, Los Millares culture; 15, Algarve culture; 16, Vila Nova de São Pedro culture.

In Portugal Middle to Late Neolithic open-air sites with a smooth pottery tradition have recently been investigated in the Sines region and a regional sequence has been draw up. At Alentejo, prospecting has revealed numerous habitation sites but there have been no excavations. Here, too, most of the work has been concentrated on Copper Age sites.

TOWARDS NEW SOCIETIES (SIXTH MILLENNIUM TO THE BEGINNING OF THE FIFTH MILLENNIUM BP (Maps 58 and 59)

A number of original cultural traits characterized west Mediterranean societies in the second half of the Neolithic: the development of collective burial sites built on the surface (megalithic tombs) or cut into the rock (hypogea); the appearance of sacred places; the important role played by stone in building activities; and finally the beginnings of metallurgy. These manifestations were not necessarily contemporaneous; they appeared at different times in different regions and even within one and the same cultural area. Moreover, they often sprang, at least in the beginning, from

Neolithic cultures in which they marked new stages of development. It was thus that megalithic tombs appeared in Portugal during the seventh millennium BP, that is in the middle of the Middle Neolithic. In the western Mediterranean, the new characteristics appeared mainly during the Final Neolithic and the Chalcolithic. In the central Mediterranean, the first hypogea were built in the seventh millennium BP (Sardinia, southern Italy). After a hesitant appearance in a Neolithic setting (Square-mouthed Pottery culture, Diana, Almeria, Cortaillod, Lagozza) metallurgy was not well established until the end of the sixth millennium BP with the rise of the Italian Chalcolithic cultures (Gaudo, Rinaldone, Remedello) or their Iberian counterparts (Los Milares, Vila Nova de São Pedro). Elsewhere copper began to be worked somewhat later.

Megalithic tombs from the sixth to the fourth millennium BP

Megalithic monuments in the western Mediterranean took various architectural forms. They are most widespread in the insular domain (Malta, Sardinia, Corsica, the Balearic islands), in the south of France, in the Iberian peninsula and in north Africa. Typological diversity goes hand in hand with appreciable time differences. We shall look first at the Iberian peninsula. In fact, its entire western part (Portugal, Galicia, the Basque provinces) was not part of the Mediterranean megalithic phenomenon but was linked directly to its Atlantic counterpart, at least during the earliest phases.

The west of the Iberian peninsula

The Atlantic façade of the Iberian peninsula was a precocious centre of the megalithic phenomenon. An important concentration of megalithic buildings is found in Alentejo. Here, as in the Algarve, small rectangular cists buried in the ground (at Monchique) could have served as prototypes for the first megalithic tombs. The oldest monuments in Alentejo and the Beiras generally had polygonal or circular chambers with massive columns, preceded by a small passage (Anta 1 at Poço de Gateira, Ante 2 at Gorginos, dated back to the middle of the seventh millennium BP by thermoluminescence). Later, while the chambers remained polygonal, the passages became greatly enlarged (Pavia type of megalithic tomb) and the funerary equipment changed. The end of the megalithic cycle in southern Portugal is marked by the appearance of tholoi (Alcalar, Monte de Outeiro, Barro).

A second geographical centre, of great numerical importance, comprises the provinces of northern Portugal (Minho, Douro, Tras-os-Montes), Spanish Galicia and the Asturias. The most common of the megalithic monuments here are polygonal chambers, closed or open, sometimes preceded by short and rather undifferentiated passages. The rectangular chambers here are of rather late provenance. Throughout this region there are also a great many barrows without a clearly defined cella. In the north-east of the Iberian peninsula some pillars of the megalithic tombs were decorated with red or brown geometric patterns or with stylized figures. Several passage graves are known in Alava. Megalithic or submegalithic tombs are also abundant in the Basque provinces: simple, open or closed, and sometimes elongated chambers; cists. Long rectangular monuments are known in Navarra (Artajona).

South-eastern and southern Iberian peninsula

In western Andalusia, megalithic monuments might owe their origin in part to Almerian graves in circular ditches; their walls were sometimes lined with dry-stone or flag-stone. The transformation of such ditches into collective, round or polygonal, graves built of slabs of stone, placed inside a barrow and fitted with a small access passage, was part of the general development of the Almerian Neolithic tradition. Still in the south-east, the rectangular or square cists in the Tabernas, Antas or Nigar regions gradually made way for more massive raised monuments with quadrangular or polygonal chambers, flanked soon after-wards by access vestibules. Similarly, many small megaliths with a short passage or vestibule are scattered over the provinces of Granada and Cordoba in their hundreds. In the Gor region, trapeze-shaped monuments (Los Castellones) often have a short vestibule and doors made of hollowed slabs. In the most elaborate monuments, chamber and passage are one and the final development is a long rectangular or trapezoidal structure with a lowered entrance (la Casilla and la Canada del Carascal in Gandul, Cueva de Menga in Antequera). To the Chalcolithic proper belong the tholoi, round chambers with dry-stone or pillared walls, dome-shaped roofs, segmented passages and circular barrows (Cueve de la Pastora, Seville, Cueva del Romeral at Antequera, Los Millares).

The eastern Pyrenean group

Here, concentrations of megalithic tombs can be found close to the sea (Ampurdan, Albères), but they are much more frequently found in the mountainous regions of Catalonia and the Corbières. A group of burial sites with polygonal chambers preceded by a passage or a vestibule (Font del Roure at Espolla; La Clape 8 at Laroque-de-Fa) seems to be fairly old (perhaps dating to the sixth millennium BP). Rectangular monuments with a lowered and sometimes narrowed entrance are common. Some have quite exceptional dimensions (Pépieux, St Eugène, in the Aude; Cova d'en Daina at Romanya de la Selva; Llanera; Puig ses Lloses at Folgaroles). Monuments with just one quadrangular chamber are the most numerous, and in many cases the most recent.

From the Causses to Provence

Here we meet one of the densest concentrations of megalithic tombs in Europe. Typical are the dolmens of western Languedoc, which occur inside a round mound and containing a quadrangular chamber built of slabs and preceded by an axial passage. Some have an antechamber (Lamalou at Rouet, Hérault) (Plate 81). They are attributed to the Ferrières tradition (Final Neolithic). Some monu-ments are distinguished by lateral walls completely built of dry-stone: these are the lower Rhodanian dolmens, stretching from the Minervois region to the Côte d'Azur. From the Ardèche to Quercy, the Les Causses plateaux are covered with simple monuments, each containing a rectangular chamber, sometimes preceded by an axial or bent passage. Many of these monuments are quite small, though there are also some of respectable size (Ganil at Gréalou, Puench-Gros at Rodelle, Aveyron). This type of megalithic tomb was built mainly in the fifth millennium BP (Final Neolithic and Chalcolithic).

Sardinina, Corsica and the Balearics

In Sardinia and Corsica the most archaic expressions of megalithic tombs are sub-megalithic versions: buried cists sometimes surrounded by stone circles. They are most common in northern Sardinia (Arzachena) and in southern Corsica (Porto-Vecchio region). This type of burial site would continue to be built in these two islands until the Metal Ages. The real megalithic tombs, above ground and of much greater size, came in various forms: rectangular chambers constructed of large slabs (Plate 82) (Mores, Sar-dinia; Cauria, Corsica); polygonal chambers with a passage (Motorra at Dorgali, Sardinia), elongated and narrow passage graves (Pedra Lunga de Austis, Sardinia). These monuments appeared at about the end of the sixth and during the fifth millennium BP. Of more recent, Bronze Age, origin are the Sardinian 'giants' tombs': narrow passage graves preceded by a curved façade sometimes with an archway. The oldest are in the megalithic tradition, that is, constructed of slabs. From the Middle Bronze Age onwards these are replaced with 'Cyclopean' blocks. The Balearic islands can boast no more than about a dozen megalithic tombs; the megalithic origi-nality of these islands lies above all in the Minorcan 'navetas': monuments with a façade of large blocks of stone and with an elongated chamber. They seem to date back to the late fifth millennium and to the fourth millennium BP.

Southern Italy and Malta

By and large, Italy remained resistant to the megalithic phenomenon. Some monuments have been found in the western Alps and in Switzerland (Aosta and Sion), but the only important group of monuments is in the south-east of the peninsula. Near Bari and Taranto there are quadrangular chambers (Accetula) and quite often more spectacular, elon-gated monuments (Bisceglie, Corato, Giovinazzo). Their furniture never dated back further than the Bronze Age. The cap-stones on small walls or on superimposed blocks of stone that can be seen in the vicinity of Giurdignano and in Malta are doubtless from the same period, but there is nothing to indicate that they were tombs.

North Africa

The megalithic phenomenon is particularly well represented in Mediterranean Africa: the biggest concentrations are found in eastern Algeria and western Tunisia, where necrop-olises with several hundreds of monuments are known (Bou Nouara, Roknia). Quite often these were small tombs with the cap-stone resting on vertical supports or on dry-stone walls. A circular footing, sometimes marked by a belt of stones, surrounds the monument. These tombs are pre-Punic and may date back to the fourth millennium BP.

Hypogea

For a long time, burial vaults cut in human-made caves (or hypogea), which are particularly widespread in the central and western Mediterranean, were thought to be derived from eastern or Aegean prototypes. However, recent inves-tigations have thrown fresh light on this point, as on the megalithic phenomenon in general: almost all hypogea were the result of internal developments in the earliest agricultural communities. The great typological diversity of these tombs – often in the same regions - and their chronological spread all bear witness to their autochthonous development, even if some outside interference can be detected here and there.

Proto-hypogea

Among the oldest forms, we must mention the tombs at Su Cucurru S'Arriu in Sardinia, small chambers about 1.5 m in length and reached by a vertical shaft. They held just one individual buried in a flexed position. They are part of the Bonu Ighinu culture, radiocarbon dated back to the first half of the sixth or to the end of the seventh millennium BP. Burial vaults cut in limestone pockets and reached through a shaft were also built in Malta (Ta Trapna) during the first centuries of the sixth millennium BP (Zebbug horizon). In southern Italy, *a forno* tombs also appeared precociously. Finally it is not impossible that some Sepulcros de Fosa in the Barcelona region, attributed to an advanced phase of that culture, might have been hypogea as well (Can Vinyals).

Neolithic hypogea

From these early manifestations there sprang, more or less rapidly, large monuments with features that are typical of certain cultural regions. In southern Italy, consecutive vaults intended for the burial of persons of rank were dug during the seventh millennium BP: for instance in Apulia, at Manfredi de Santa Barbara or at Cala Colombo (Serra d'Alto and Diana cultures, about 6,300 to 5,500 years ago). At the same time there also existed *a forno* tombs built to hold just one body (Arcesano, Lecce). In Malta, the hypogea have an original multifoil layout (Xemxija). However, the most prestigious of these monuments is without question the Hal Safliena hypogeum, a labyrinth with a very complicated layout combining the functions of a vast burial site with that of a sacred building. The sculptures on the walls and ceilings are imitations of contemporary Maltese temple decorations (sixth millennium BP). At the time of the Ozieri culture, which flourished between about 6,300 and 5,000 years ago, Sardinia had several hundred hypogea with various types of layout. Besides tombs with access shafts (San Vero Milis), there were caves with small round porches and horizontal entrances (San Benedetto at Iglesias), monuments with a T-shaped passage, with numerous cells (Anghelu Ruju), and finally very elaborate hypogea with dromos, antechamber and cella surrounded by porches, doors and sculpted walls sometimes with supporting pillars (San Andrea Priu, Santu Pedru). The Iberian peninsula also has numerous hypogea, in the south and in Portugal. Many do not seem to go back further than the Copper Age, but one thermoluminescence dating of the hypogeum at Carenque 2 (Portugal) – around 6,000 years ago – proves the antiquity of a variety of hypogea containing a chamber and a horizontal passage and their contemporaneity with the megalithic tradition. In the south of France pottery of the Ferrières culture (Fig. 142) (Final Neolithic, end of the sixth millennium BP) has been found in one of the hypogea at Arles – large elongated tombs with entrance stairs and a megalithic cap-stone. The hypogea in eastern Languedoc (Serre de Bernon at Laudun) and in the Vaucluse (Roaix) date back to the same time.

Copper Age hypogea

The emergence of cultures familiar with copper metallurgy not only did not put an end to the construction and use of hypogea, but often expanded that process. Tombs with shafts or vestibules as found in Campania (Gaudo), Apulia

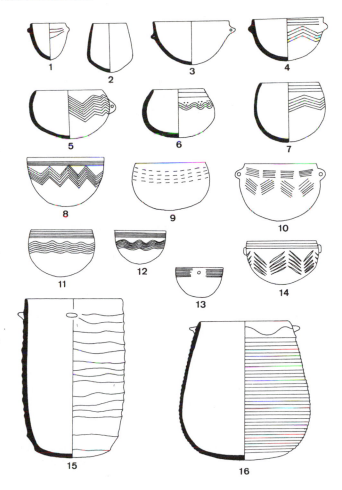

Figure 142 Pottery styles, Ferrières culture, sixth millennium BP, eastern Languedoc (France): 1–3, Ferrières chamber tomb, Hérault; 4, 7, Bois Martin site, Hérault; 5, 6, Grotte de Labeil Hérault; 8, 12, 13, Beaussement, Ardèche; 9, 10, Grotte des Baumelles, Gard; 11, Gaude, Ardèche; 14–16, Grotte des Pins, Gard. (After G.-B. Arnal, 1976.)

(Laterza), at Latium and in Tuscany (Rinaldone) play a decisive role throughout the southern half of the Italian peninsula. In Sicily, hypogea appeared from the time of the horizon of San Cono Piano Notare to give rise to fine monuments (Calaforno) and to a flourishing tradition that would last until the Iron Age. In Sardinia, the fifth millennium BP saw the appearance of elongated tombs (Filigosa) and of tombs with shafts and porches (Monte Claro). In the south of France some hypogea must be attributed to the Fontbouisse culture. The finest hypogea in the south of the Iberian peninsula were built in the Final Neolithic or in the Chalcolithic of Andalusia (Alcaide) or of Portugal (Alapraia, Palmela).

The development of stone architecture

Except in isolated places, stone does not seem to have played a fundamental role in the western Mediterranean during the Neolithic, when wood and clay were the main materials. This remark will doubtless have to be qualified in the wake of more detailed local studies. In the sixth millennium BP at the same time as megalithic tombs made their appearance, there also appeared other buildings, religious or civil, in which stone increasingly took pride of place.

Among the earliest of these buildings were the Maltese temples built of pillars and of Cyclopean appearance. These buildings had a curved façade giving access to small, lobate rooms, the general layout being trifoliate during the earliest phases (Mgarr). It is quite possible that these Maltese temples were the transposition on ground-level of the hypogea mentioned above and that originally they were megalithic tombs before becoming sanctuaries. Later, the buildings grew more complicated, some containing five and others up to seven chambers. Occasionally several temples were combined into a single complex (Ggantija, Tarxien) (Plate 83). These monuments were erected in the sixth millennium BP and were still in use during the fifth millennium BP, after which time they were abandoned.

The use of stone for the construction of houses and of walls that were often built to protect them was greatly stepped up in the sixth millennium BP. This development used to be attributed to Aegean influences, largely because of some architectural similarities (for instance the reinforcement of walls with semicircular bastions). However, in the central Mediterranean the intermediate geographical links are missing, the chronology of these buildings is not strictly concordant as we go from east to west, and finally the cultural contexts are quite dissimilar. It is therefore better to speak of convergence. There is an absence of data on developments in the Italian peninsula, where the Chalcolithic is mainly known through burial structures and cave occupations. The protection of settlements by ditches was still common (Conelle). Stone might be used to build houses (Colombare near Verona in the Remedello context).

The insular part of the Mediterranean seems to have had greater recourse to stone as a building material. Whereas in Sicily the enclosed site of Petraro di Melilli was not built before the Bronze Age, Sardinia has stone houses and stone enclosures of an earlier date. Some may go back to the Old Chalcolithic (for instance the 'Stregone' hut at Monte d'Accodi, Sassari, or the enclosure of San Giuseppe de Padria, Macomer, which can be assigned to the Abealzu and Filigosa cultures). From the Chalcolithic proper (Monte Claro culture) onwards, stone became a common building material (Monte Ossoni enclosure, Biriai huts, Monte Baranta *proto-nuraghe*). It seems likely that in Corsica some sections of the sites generally assigned to the Bronze Age go back to the Final Neolithic or to the Copper Age (Tappa, Pina Canale), stone having been used precociously here. In the south of France, stone walls appeared in the Final Neolithic (Miouvin, La Couronne, Vauvenargues). During the Copper Age, enclosures flanked by circular huts (Le Lébous, Boussargues) and hamlets containing several elongated huts sometimes with apsidal ends (Cambous) were to characterize the Fontbouisse culture. In the south-east of the Iberian peninsula, sites entrenched on hills behind several walls and sometimes flanked by bastions and provided with systems of curvilinear entrances (Los Millares) (Plate 84) went up from about 5,300 years ago. Sometimes small fortresses on the periphery of the main site provided additional defences. In Portugal, at the same period, the *castros*, occupied for a long time, had a central 'fort' with towers and several protective walls (Zambujal).

Art, statuary and prestige objects

In western Mediterranean cultures at the end of the Neolithic and in the Copper Age, there was a marked increase in the number of ornamental objects (bracelets, beads, pendants, trinkets) made from a variety of stones (marble, calcite, steatite, aragonite and so on) or from shells, bone, metal and other materials. Figurines were particularly popular in certain regions. In Malta, where they were made of baked clay or stone, they were often obese (for instance the 'Sleeping Woman'). In Sardinia, a long tradition beginning in the seventh millennium BP (Bonu Ighinu culture) is associated with stout stone statuettes. It made way in the sixth millennium BP for the Ozieri culture which produced even more stylized figures. In Spain, Late Neolithic cruciform figurines were replaced in the Copper Age by cylindrical stone or carved bone idols with an emphasized eye motif (Figs 143 and 144). Schist plaquettes engraved with geometric or anthropomorphic motifs were known in Portugal in association with megalithic buildings. An important collection of statues, believed to represent gods, goddesses or heroes in a highly stylized manner appeared in the south of France (Provence, Languedoc, Rouergue) during the Late Neolithic (Plate 85). The steles at Sion and Aosta, in the Alps, bearing geometric or figurative motifs (daggers, pendants) are older than the Bell-Beaker horizon. Some steles in the Lunigiana district, northern Italy, with an arched top and representations of daggers, seem to go back to the beginning of the Copper Age (Remedello culture).

The beginnings of metallurgy

People still wonder about the conditions in which cultures working copper and to a lesser extent gold, silver and lead could flourish in the western Mediterranean. The premature emergence – at the end of the seventh millennium BP – of metallurgical techniques throughout south-eastern Europe does not seem to have fostered the diffusion of this type of skill to the western Mediterranean. Similarly, the forward march of metalworking techniques in the Aegean does not become obvious until the Early Bronze Age, at about the end of the sixth millennium BP. For a long time, the rise of the Chalcolithic culture in the western Mediterranean was, in fact, attributed to new ties with the Aegean. In reality, however, the problem is more complex. Though the Early Aegean Bronze Age and the central and western Mediterranean Copper Ages were more or less contemporaneous, several characteristics distinguish these two cultural areas: alloys with a tin base remained unknown in the west for some time; the typology of Aegean metal products differs from the weapons and tools of the Italian area, which in turn differ from Iberian artefacts; the use of local mining resources is evident almost everywhere. Moreover the first attempts to melt metals in the west – for instance in Italy – were made earlier than used to be thought. Must we therefore postulate a series of independent local inventions? It is difficult to do so when we remember the role of navigation in the Mediterranean. Still, navigation does not necessarily imply the automatic transfer of techniques to areas in which techno-economic conditions are not such as to demand their rapid adoption and general use. Having for so long given the Aegean credit for the great technical and cultural changes that took place in the western Mediterranean during the fifth millennium BP, archaeological research has radically changed the picture in recent years – little is left of the role of Aegean 'imports' in the west, so often described in literature. Nowadays, the regional characteristics of early Italian metallurgy, though reminiscent of developments in the Iberian peninsula, are no longer assigned to the same vector.

At the end of the seventh millennium BP, some traces of archaic metalwork techniques were found in Italy in the context of the Diana culture (for instance on the acropolis at Lipari or on the Santa Maria in Selva and Fossacesia sites)

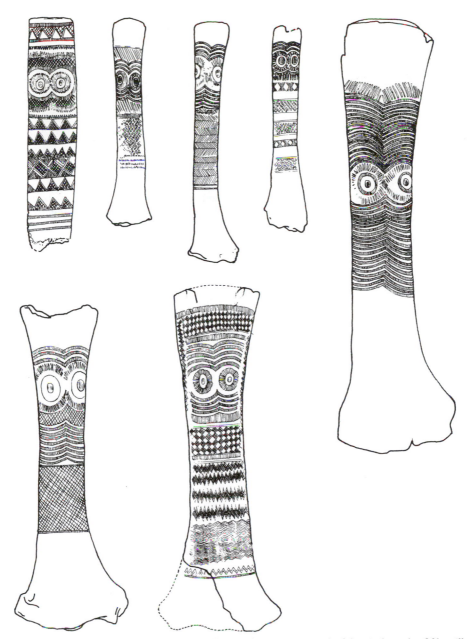

Figure 143 Carved and painted bone idols, Almizaraque, Los Millares culture (Spain), end of the sixth to the fifth millennium BP. (After Leisner and Leisner, 1949–50.)

or in the context of the Square-mouthed Pottery culture (Rivoli). But it was not until the sixth millennium BP that a veritable Copper Age developed there. The choice areas were Campania (Gaudo), Latium and Tuscany (Rinaldone), Emilia and the Po valley (Remedello (Fig. 145), Spilamberto). Elsewhere, for instance in the south-east, on the Adriatic coast, in Calabria and in Sicily, copper tools were not very abundant (Laterza, Sicilian 'Chalcolithic' cultures). This very fact demonstrates, on the geographical plane, the small impact of the alleged links with the Aegean. The Italian Chalcolithic gave rise to daggers with triangular blades, ribbed and having a square or trapezoidal tang (Buccino, Remedello); the blade could have 'horns' (Spilamberto). Other daggers with a pointed or trapezoidal tang and four or five rivets were a Tuscan speciality (Guardistello, Ponte San Pietro). Flat axes occurred in the Rinaldone, Remedello, and Conelle–Ortucchio contexts. More original were some crutch-headed silver pins (Remedello) of which bone replicas are known. Strange, curved daggers have been found at

Laterza, in the south-east, in Sicily (Chiusazza) and as far north as Tuscany (Monte Bradoni).

In Malta, metalwork did not truly appear until the Early Bronze Age, in the second half of the fifth millennium BP. Much the same happened in the Balearic islands. In Corsica, in contrast, traces of a local copper industry dating back to the sixth millennium BP have recently been discovered at Terrina, near Alma. Sardinia, too, probably had a similar industry at about the same time: however, the brilliant Ozieri culture does not seem to have assigned an important place to metallurgy at any time. It was not until the end of the sixth millennium BP, in the context of the Abealzu and Filigosa cultures, that the use of copper began to spread, eventually to take firm root with the Monte Claro culture, about 4,500 years ago.

In the Iberian peninsula, copperwork might have appeared in Neolithic contexts (El Garcel). But here, too, it was not well established until about 5,300 years ago, with the Los Millares and Vila Nova de São Pedro cultures. Its main

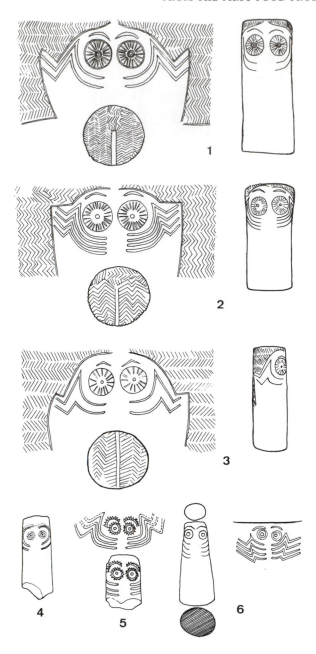

the first manifestations of metalwork in Andalusia are of a later date.

In southern France, finally, metalwork was slow to take root. True, early traces are known from Final Neolithic deposits in the lower Hérault valley (Cabrières, Roquemengarde) and in some parts of the Cévennes and the Causses. The finds include axes, awls, daggers and beads. It was not, however, until about 4,600 years ago that metallurgy became more firmly established: in eastern Languedoc (Fontbouisse), in the Aude–Garonne corridor and, to a smaller extent, in Provence.

At about the same time, the Bell-Beaker culture, which ranged from Sicily to Portugal and Morocco, that is, the entire area covered by this study, presided over the general adoption of metallurgy.

SOCIAL STRUCTURES

With regard to the social structure of these western Mediterranean communities of the ninth to fifth millennium BP, in the absence of written texts and with only culture as a guide, the prehistorian can do little more than put forward

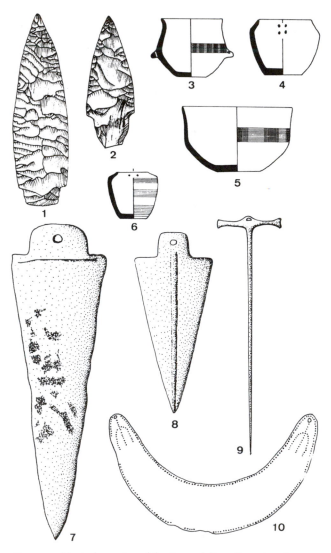

Figure 144 Chalcolithic stone idols, end of the sixth to the fifth millennium BP, south of Iberian peninsula: 1–3, Sierra de Moron, Sevilla (Spain); 4, origin unknown, 5, Olhao, Algarve (Portugal); 6, Sevilla Museum (Spain). (After Leisner and Leisner, 1949–50.)

impact was felt in the south-east (Almeria), Andalusia, the Algarve, and central Portugal. Here there was an obvious link between local mining resources and the emergence of the first metal implements. Early mining operations in the area have recently been investigated (Rio Tinto, Huelva). Despite detailed typological differences, the products are very similar throughout the south of the Iberian peninsula: notched and ribbed daggers (Alcalar, Los Millares), axes with convex or concave cutting edges, gouges, burins, punches, saws (Vila Nova de São Pedro) and double-pointed awls. In the rest of the Iberian peninsula the beginnings of metallurgy seem to be of slightly more recent date and isolated contexts are rare.

Special mention should be made of the recent discovery in a Moroccan site (Kelf el Baroud) of some copper objects in a layer dating back to the first half of the sixth millennium BP. These finds might well have been Iberian imports, but

Figure 145 Typical remains of the Remedello culture (northern Italy), sixth millenium BP: 1, 2, arrowheads; 3–6, pottery; 7, 8, copper daggers; 9, silver pin; 10, silver breastplate. (1–4, 6–9, Remedello; 5, Colombare de Negrar; 10, Villafranca.)

hypotheses based on the analysis of the burial places them-selves (their orientation, plan and content) and on the specific features of certain monuments. It has become almost commonplace that the earliest Neolithic societies – for example those characterized by Impressed Ware or by Cardial pottery – were egalitarian, and thus showed few signs of social hierarchy. As a matter of fact, only a very small number of burials may be safely attributed to the Early Neolithic (in contrast to the larger concentrations that have been dated to slightly earlier periods, for example those associated with the Mesolithic 'middens' at Muge in Portugal). Available literature is far too scanty to permit a convincing demonstration. The few burials attributed to this period are often individual graves, which may be in the open air, under shelter or in caves (for instance those found at Rendina in southern Italy, in the shelter of Castellar, Alpes Maritimes, and in the Gazel cave in the Aude); their grave goods (pottery and sometimes items of personal adornment) tell us little about the social status of the buried person. Grouped burials in specific parts of certain caves may also be attributed to this period. They should not be seen as authentic collective burials of ossuary type, but rather as the result of a deliberate choice of a burial ground where different graves were dug close to each other (examples being the Epicardial burials of La Baume Bourbon, Gard and the Montbolo burials of the Belesta cave in Catalonia). It should also be noted that the use of caves for individual burials was continued during the Middle Neolithic (for instance the Souhait cave at Montagnieu, Ain).

Undoubtedly as a result of increased sedentism and the development of larger agricultural communities, the cultures of the sixth millennium BP created small 'cities of the dead', of which, however, the limited number of graves seems hardly compatible with the size of settlements belonging to the same period. Inhumation may be in box-shaped structures made of stone slabs (as is the case of the Aude-Roussillon and Solsonès cists, and the Chamblandes cists in Switzerland) or in pit-graves (the Sepulcros de Fosa of the region of Barcelona, and the more elaborate Almerian burials) containing a single, or less frequently, two corpses. Here again, the grave goods (knives and arrowheads, pottery, awls or other bone objects, and personal adornments such as the fine calaïs necklaces of Catalonia) are hard to fit into any socially hierarchic pattern. Nevertheless, the excavation of some large ditches which surrounded a number of villages in southern Italy (Passo di Corvo in Tavoliere, or Murgia Timone in Lucania), undoubtedly required the collaboration of a large number of people. From this it may be further deduced that there were chiefs responsible for conceiving and directing the works and for ensuring the cohesion of the community.

It is in these Middle Neolithic societies that collective burials appear for the first time: the hypogea group of Serra d'Alto in Apulia, the first passage graves in Portugal c.6,500 years ago and the hypogea group of Ozieri in Sardinia c.6,200 to 6,000 years ago. What is the exact significance of these tombs? In the first place, the grouping of burials in necropolises (for instance, in the hypogea complex of Ozieri) indicates a population growth. The monumental treatment and the ornamentation of certain large tombs (as at Hal Saflieni, Sant Andrea Priu) suggest that some of them have also been used as sacred sites (perhaps associated with ancestor-worship) and indicate long-term occupation by the community of a given territory. The construction in Malta in Neolithic times (sixth and fifth millennia BP of impressive megalithic temples with rounded façades and forecourts has

suggested that these were places of pilgrimage where the members of several related communities met periodically under the guidance of priests or sorcerers. The large Ozieri tombs give the same impression. Whether or not these religious élites also possessed political authority is uncertain, although it seems that the chiefs of the Tarxian temple complex in Malta had combined spiritual and temporal power.

Nevertheless, with the exception of Malta and certain major western Mediterranean sacred sites, signs of social hierarchization are, at the present stage of research, few and far between. The burial of many corpses in a single collective grave has been used as an argument in claiming that there was no social hierarchy in the Mediterranean societies of the Late Neolithic period. From the grave goods found scattered among the bones it is not possible to relate prestige, for instance, objects to specific individuals, and thus it is difficult to draw social distinctions. The exact significance of the anthropological contents of each tomb also remains undetermined: were the buried persons members of a single family, or of a clan? Were those buried in a collective grave (whether hypogeum or megalithic tomb) selected on the basis of their social status? These questions, which are of capital importance, remain unanswered.

It is noteworthy that the Rinaldone hypogeum of Ponte San Pietro contained the remains of a chief who had been buried with a considerable quantity of ceremonial material: at his side lay his wife (or female slave), her skull crushed, suggesting that at the 'lord and master's' death his companion was brutally dispatched to accompany him into the hereafter.

Another unsolved question concerns settlements that were surrounded by several rings of fortifications, Los Millares in Spain and Zambujal in Portugal being the finest examples. How were they administered? Did they offer shelter to the first skilled metalworkers, precisely at the time when objects in copper and gold were assuming an increasing social significance? This has indeed been suggested. It is possible that these localities, with their elaborate defences, were placed under the protection of potentates who exercised their authority over an agricultural and/or mining region. This, too, is indeed possible. But the fact remains that social hierarchization, which was undoubtedly possible in the fifth millennium BP, is of course something inferred rather than demonstrated.

BIBLIOGRAPHY

ALMAGRO, M.; ARRIBAS, A. 1963. *El poblado y la necrópolis megalíticos de Los Millares (Santa Fé de Mondujar, Almeria)*. Madrid.

ALMAGRO GORBEA, M. J. 1973. *Los ídolos del Bronce I hispano*. Madrid.

ARNAL, G. B. 1976. *La Céramique néolithique dans le Haut-Languedoc*. Lodève.

ARRIBAS, A.; MOLINA, F. 1978. *El poblado de 'Los Castillejos' en Las Penas de los Gitanos (Montefrio, Granado)*. Granada.

ATZENI, E. 1978. *La Dea-Madre nelle culture prenuragiche*. Sassari.

BAGOLINI, B. 1980. *Introduzione al Neolithico dell' Italia settentrionale*. Porderone.

BAILLOUD, G.; MIEG DE BOOFZHEIM, P. 1955. *Les Civilisations néolithiques de la France dans leur contexte européen*. Paris.

BALOUT, L. 1955. *Préhistoire de l'Afrique du Nord: essai de chronologie*. Paris.

BARFIELD, L. 1971. *Northern Italy before Rome*. London.

BATOVIC, S. 1966. *Stariji neolit u Dalmaciji*. Zadar.

BENAC, A. 1973. *Obre*. Sarajevo, Bosnisch-Herzegowinisches Landesmuseum.

BERNABO BREA, L. 1946–56. *Gli scavi nella caverna delle Arene Candide.* Bordighera. 2 vols.

—— 1960. *Sicily before the Greeks.* London.

BERNABO BREA, L.; CAVALIER, M. 1960. *Meligunis Lipara I.* Palermo.

BLANCE, B. 1971. *Die Anfänge der Metallurgie auf der Iberischen Halbinsel.* Mainz.

BOSCH–GIMPERA, P. 1932. *Etnología de la península Ibérica.* Barcelona.

CAMPS, G. 1974. *Les Civilisations préhistoriques de l'Afrique du Nord et du Sahara.* Paris.

CAMPS-FABRER, H. 1966. *Matière et art mobilier dans la préhistoire nord-africaine et saharienne.* Paris.

COLLOQUE DE NARBONNE. 1980. *Actes. Le Groupe de Véreza et la fin des temps néolithiques dans le Sud de la France et la Catalogne.* Paris, CNRS. 2 June 1977.

COLLOQUIO DI PREISTORIA E PROTOSTORIA DELLA DAUNIA. 1975. *Atti. Civiltà preistoriche e protostoriche della Daunia.* Florence. Foggia, 1973.

COLOMINAS, J. 1925. *Prehistoria de Montserrat.* Montserrat.

COURTIN, J. 1974. *Le Néolithique de la Provence.* Paris.

CREMONESI, G. 1976. *La grotta dei Piccioni di Bolognano nel cuadro del neolitico all' età del bronzo in Abruzzo.* Pisa.

DEMOULE, J.-P.; GUILAINE, J. (eds) 1986. *Le Néolithique de la France. Hommage à G. Bailloud.* Paris.

ESCALON DE FONTON, M. 1956. *Préhistoire de la Basse-Provence.* Paris. ('Préhistoire', Vol. 12.)

EVANS, J. D. 1971. *The Prehistoric Antiquities of the Maltese Islands.* London.

FORTEA PEREZ, J. 1973. *Los complejos microlaminares y geométricos del Epipaleolítico mediterráneo español.* Salamanca.

FURGER, A. R. et al. 1981. *Die neolithischen Ufersiedlungen von Twann.* Bern. 2 vols.

GALLAY, A. 1977. *Le Néolithique moyen du Jura et des plaines de la Saône.* Basle.

GEDDES, D. 1980. De la chasse au troupeau en Mediterranée occidentale: les débuts de l'élevage dans le bassin de l'Aude. *Arch. Ecol. préhist.* (Toulouse), Vol. 5.

GUERRESCHI, G. 1967. *La Lagozza di Besnate e il neolitico superiore padano.* Como.

—— 1976–7. *La stratigrafia dell' Isolino di Varese dedotta dall'analisi della ceramica.* Sibrium.

GUIDO, M. 1963. *Sardinia.* London.

GUILAINE, J. 1976. *Premiers Bergers et paysans de l'Occident méditerranéen.* Paris/La Haye.

—— 1980. *La France d'avant la France. Du Néolithique à l'Age du Fer.* Paris.

GUILAINE, J. et al. 1974. *La Balma de Montbolo et le Néolithique de l'Occident méditerranéen.* Toulouse.

—— 1979. *L'Abri Jean Cros. Essai d'approche d'un groupe humain du Néolithique ancien dans son environnement.* Toulouse.

ITTEN, M. 1970. *Die Horgener Kultur.* Basle.

KOROSEC, J. 1958–9. *Neolitiska Naseobina u Danilu-Bitinju.* Zagreb. 2 vols.

LANFRANCHI, F. DE; WEISS, M-C. 1973. *La Civilisation des Corses.* Ajaccio.

LEISNER, G.; LEISNER, V. 1943–59. *Die Megalithgräber der Iberischen Halbinsel.* Berlin. 2 vols.

LILLIU, G. 1967. *La civiltà dei Sardi dal neolitico all' età dei nuraghi.* Torino.

LORIA, R.; TRUMP, D. 1978. *Le scoperte a Sa'Ucca de Su Tintirriolu e il Neolitico sarde.* Rome.

MANFREDINI, A. 1972. *Il villagio trincerato di Monte Aquilone nel cuadro del Neolitico dell' Italia meridionale.* Rome.

MARTI OLIVER, B. et al. 1977–80. *Cova de l'Or (Beniarrès, Alicante).* Valencia. 2 vols.

MESA REDONDA. 1979. *Actas. O Neolítico e o calcolítico em Portugal.* Oporto.

MUÑOZ, A. M. 1965. *La cultura neolítica catalana de los sepulcros de fosa.* Barcelona.

NAVARRETE ENCISO, M. S. 1976. *La cultura de la cuevas con cerámica decorada en Andalucia oriental.* Granada. 2 vols.

PELLICER CATALAN, M. 1964. *El Neolítico y el Bronce de la cueva de la Carigüela de Pinar (Granada).* Madrid.

PERICOT, L. 1972. *The Balearic Islands.* London.

PERICOT GARCIA, L. 1950. *Los sepulcros megalíticos catalanes y la cultura pirenaica.* Barcelona.

PETREQUIN, P. 1984. *Gens de l'eau, gens de la terre.* Paris.

PHILLIPS, P. 1975. *Early Farmers of West Mediterranean Europe.* London.

RADMILLI, A. M. 1962. *Piccola guida della preistoria italiana.* Florence.

RIDLEY, M. 1976. *The Megalithic Art of the Maltese Islands.* London.

RIPOLL PERELLO, E.; LLONGUERAS, M. 1963. *La cultura neolítica de los sepulcros de fosa en Cataluna.* Barcelona.

RIUNIONE SCIENTIFICA. 1974. *Atti.* Florence. 16, Liguria, 3–5 Nov. 1973.

ROUBET, C. 1979. *Économie pastorale préagricole en Algérie orientale: le néolithique de tradition capsienne.* Paris, CNRS.

ROUDIL, J.-L.; ROUDIL, O.; SOULIER, M. 1979. *La Grotte de l'Aigle à Méjannès le Clap (Gard) et le Néolithique ancien du Languedoc oriental.* (Mém. Soc. languedoc. Préhist., I.)

SAN VALERO APARISI, J. 1950. *La cueva de la Sarsa (Bocairente, Valencia).* Valencia.

SAUTER, M.-R.; GALLEY, R. 1969. Les Premières Cultures d'origine méditerranéenne. In: W. DRACK (ed.), *Ur- und frügeschichtliche Archäologie der Schweiz.* Vol. II: *Die jüngere Steinzeit,* pp. 47–66. Basle.

SCHWABEDISSEN, H. (ed.) 1971. *Fundamenta. Die Anfänge des Neolithikums vom Orient bis Nordeuropa.* Cologne. T.6.

THÉVENOT, J.-P. 1969. Eléments chasséens de la céramique de Chassey. *Revue archéologique de l'Est et du Centre-Est,* Vol. XX, pp. 7–95.

TINE, S. 1983. *Passo di Corvo e la civiltà neolitica del Tavoliere.* Genova.

TRUMP, D. 1966a. *Central and Southern Italy before Rome.* London.

—— 1966b. *Skorba.* Oxford, Society of Antiquaries of London.

—— 1983. *La grotti di Filiestru a Bonu Ighinu, Mara (Sassari).* Sassari.

TUSA, S. 1983. *La Sicilia nella preistoria.* Palermo.

WALDREN, W. 1982. *Balearic Prehistoric Ecology and Culture.* Oxford. 3 vols. (BAR Int. Ser., 149.)

50

THE BALKAN PENINSULA AND SOUTH-EAST EUROPE

during the Neolithic

Milutin Garašanin

GEOGRAPHIC SETTING

During the Neolithic, the historical and cultural development of the Balkan peninsula and of the contiguous regions – southern Pannonia and the lower Danubian countries – was rather uneven, mainly for geographical reasons. Thus the centre of the Balkans, roughly speaking the basins of the Vardar (Axios) and Morava rivers, has always been a transitional zone and one of cultural intermingling, thanks to the important role the valleys of these rivers played as a route for communication. Much the same is true of the east of the Balkan peninsula: Thrace proper to the south of the Stara Planina (Haemus), the lower Danube plain and between it and the Carpathians, a region closely linked to the eastern Mediterranean by the valleys of the rivers Marica (Ebros), Nesta (Nestos) and Struma (Strymon) with its tributary, the Strumešnica. Conditions are slightly different in the western part of the peninsula. With the exception of the Adriatic coast, which gives on to the western Mediterranean, this is the mountainous and often inhospitable zone of the Dinaric Alps, a kind of cultural reserve that has always been fairly conservative. We shall be keeping this fact in mind when trying to sketch out the course of the Neolithic and its continuation, the Eneolithic, in these regions.

HISTORY OF RESEARCH

We can distinguish three major stages:

1. an introductory stage comprising the earliest studies made with the scientific methods available at the time. This stage covered the last decades of the nineteenth century and continued until the First World War;
2. a stage of systematic research and some of the first syntheses. This stage covered the inter-war years;
3. a stage of intense, systematic research and of the first interdisciplinary investigations.

At the beginning of the first stage, a project was launched that was destined to become a milestone in European prehistory: the excavations at Butmir in Bosnia by W. Radimsky and F. Fiala (Hörnes and Radimsky, 1895; Hörnes and Fiala, 1898). Most of the work done during that period in Austria-Hungary (Hungary, western Romania-Transylvania, and Yugoslavia: Bosnia-Herzegovina, Croatia, Slovenia and the autonomous region of Voivodina) was contributed by enthusiasts attached to a number of big museums, such as those in Budapest, Cluj (Koloszvar), Sarajevo and Zagreb. Here we shall merely mention the names of F. Milleker, founder of the museum in Vršac, Zs. Torma, the first to conduct excavations at the important site of Turdaş (Tordoś), F. Mora, who organized digs in the Szeged region, and the Transylvanian archaeologist M. Roska. Meanwhile, those south-eastern countries that had already gained their independence (Bulgaria, Romania, Serbia) witnessed the first excavations run by professional archaeologists. It was then (in 1902) that M. M. Vasić, the Serbian archaeologist, began his work at Vinča, a site to which his name has remained coupled, and where excavations were continued with interruptions from 1908 to 1934 (Vasić, 1932, 1936). Vasić was also the first prehistorian to refute older, then prevalent theories and to build the prehistory of the Balkan peninsula on stronger foundations (Vasić, 1907–8). At about the same time, work on tells was begun in Bulgaria, above all by R. Popov and G. Kazarov. In Romania, large-scale excavations were made at Cucuteni under the direction of the German scholar H. Schmidt (Schmidt, 1932).

The second stage was marked above all by a series of excavations, often modest, but leading to the first cultural and chronological classification of Neolithic and Eneolithic cultures. It was as a result of this work that the Hungarian scholars F. Tompa (Tompa, 1935–6) and J. Banner (Banner, 1942) were able to lay the foundations of a chronological and cultural system for these periods. The work of Romanian scholars (H. and V. Dumitrescu, V. Christescu, I. Nestor, G. Stefan, E. and R. Vulpe and, a little later, D. Berciu) on numerous sites in Romania (Boian, Gumelniţa, Câscioarele, Izvoare and others) enabled I. Nestor to present a brilliant synthesis of Romanian prehistory (Nestor, 1933), followed soon afterwards by D. Berciu's prehistory of Oltenia (Berciu, 1939). In Bulgaria, a great deal of work was done on tells, above all by V. Mikov, who also produced the first inventory of prehistoric sites in that country (Mikov, 1933). It is on this work that the first synthetic description of the Bulgarian Neolithic was based (Gaul, 1948). In former Yugoslavia, and more particularly in Serbia and Voivodina, several excavations led by M. Grbić (Botoš, Sremski Karlovci, Pločnik and so on) have made it possible to draw up a first chronological system for these regions (Vulić and Grbić, 1938). A. Orsić-Slavetić's studies at Bubanj are the basis of our knowledge of the Eneolithic in the central Balkans (Orsić-Slavetić, 1940). At that time, a Yugoslav–American team implemented a major prospecting plan in Serbia and Macedonia (see especially Fewkes, 1936). Large-scale excavations, by contrast, are still few and far between; they include, besides continued excavations at Vinča, those at Starčevo (Fewkes et al., 1933) and those in the Grabak cave on the island of Hvar and at Vučedol in Croatia (Novak, 1955; R. R. Schmidt, 1945).

The third stage is marked by a rapid expansion of research throughout south-east Europe, sometimes on a big scale, at numerous Neolithic and Eneolithic sites. Systematic research was also begun in Albania. The research, now pursued along modern and often interdisciplinary lines, did much to enlarge and sometimes to transform our knowledge of the prehistory of certain regions. Previously unknown cultures and their regional variants were defined, among them particularly Anzabegovo-Vršnik, Porodin, Obre I, Smilčić, Danilo, Kakanj, Bubanj-Hum in former Yugoslavia; Gura Baciului, Hamangia, Precucuteni, Černavoda Petreşti in Romania; the Karanovo I–V sequence with numerous regional cultures in Bulgaria. The chronological framework based until then exclusively on the historical scale was adjusted, largely with the help of the radiocarbon method. The results of these studies devoted to particular cultures have been published (see Bibliography).

PRE-NEOLITHIC (LEPENSKI VIR–SCHELA CLADOVEI) (Map 60)

The beginnings of the Neolithic in south-east Europe are not fully known: we have no data on possible links between the Neolithic and the preceding Mesolithic stage. The existence of a Pre-pottery Neolithic in continental Greece (Thessaly) with western Asian links but seemingly also with an autochthonous component, has been responsible for the hypothesis, soon afterwards abandoned, that something similar must have occurred in the Carpathian zone. A special situation existed near the Iron Gates where, between the thirteenth and ninth millennia BP, an Epipalaeolithic culture (Climente, Cuina Turcului) evolved continuously into the Pre-Neolithic culture of Lepenski Vir–Schela Cladovei (Srejović et al., 1969; Srejović and Letica, 1979; Boronant, 1970). The economic life of that group was based on gathering, fishing and hunting, partly selective (50 per cent boar at Schela Cladovei, 53.88 per cent deer at Vlasac). The sedentary habitation sites (perhaps partly base camps) included rows of houses built on a trapezoidal plan. The chipped-stone industry, mainly based on quartz from nearby deposits, and the bone industry, related to the Franco-Cantabrian complex, were well developed. Inhumation in an extended position, side by side with partial inhumations, often of skulls, in and under the dwellings, are signs of well-established funeral rites. One find in particular caused something of a sensation during the first excavations: statues with the heads of fish and of humans made from river pebbles and modelled or carved larger than life (Plate 86). This culture must have been Pre-Neolithic. Some implements made from antlers and believed to have been ploughshares could have been used to dig up edible roots. Traces of gramineous plants 'tending towards the cereals' (Curciumaru

in Srejović and Letica, 1979), examined by coprolite analysis, are not conclusive evidence of an early form of agriculture, nor for that matter is there clear evidence of the domestication of dogs or of stock-breeding. The Lepenski Vir–Schela Cladovei culture certainly paved the way for the introduction of the Neolithic, but did not enter it. It was thanks only to external contributions that the Neolithic emerged in these parts.

Most students of south-east European prehistory distinguish three great Neolithic stages: the Early and Middle Neolithic, covering the whole of the eighth and the beginnings of the seventh millennium BP, and the Late Neolithic in the seventh and in part of the sixth millennium BP. With the exception of Thrace, the Middle Neolithic followed the Early in a continuous process of development, with ever closer contacts between the populations of the various regions. Moreover, an Eneolithic culture emerged in the east of the peninsula during the sixth millennium BP, owing to an upsurge of mining activities and the production of the first copper objects. This process developed in parallel with the advanced phases of the Late Neolithic in the neighbouring regions.

EARLY AND MIDDLE NEOLITHIC (Map 60)

The Early Neolithic in south-east Europe comprises three great cultural complexes, each with a clearly established geographical distribution and a whole series of regional forms (M. Garašanin, 1980).

Balkano-Anatolian complex (Anzabegovo-Vršnik, Karanovo I; Velušina-Porodin)

The Balkano-Anatolian complex, firmly rooted in Anatolia (Çatal Hüyük and partly in Haçilar) and whose development was continued during the Middle Neolithic, includes, apart from Thessaly (Proto-Sesklo and Pre-Sesklo cultures) the entire south of the eastern and central regions of the peninsula, with the cultures of Karanovo I in Thrace (from around 7,300 to around 6,500 years ago) and its local variants, the Anzabegovo-Vršnik I culture (around 7,300 to 6,800 years ago) and the slightly later Velušina–Porodin culture in Pelagonia, and the Veshtemi–Podgoria culture in Albania (M. Garašanin, 1979; Gimbutas et al., 1976; Prendi, 1982). The complex also extends to the north with enclaves in Bulgaria, central Serbia, southern Pannonia and western Romania (Dumitrescu et al., 1983, pp. 66 ff.).

The economy of the complex was based above all on agriculture, with cultivation of wheat (*Triticum dicoccum*, *Triticum monococcum*), barley (*Hordeum vulgare*), lentils and legumes. There was a clear predominance of stock-breeding (the raising of sheep and goats) over hunting (M. Garašanin, 1980). At Anzabegovo, for instance, domestic animals represented 96.16 per cent of all animal species, with the following distribution: sheep and goats 78.30 per cent, cattle 9.60 per cent, pigs 8.26 per cent (see also Chapter 38, Table 14). The types of permanent habitation sites differed in the various regions: tells in the plains of Thrace and Pelagonia; multi-layered sites on river terraces or the slopes of hills in other regions. The surface dwellings at Karanovo I had timbered walls, stamped earth floors and generally two rooms, one with a hearth. Those of the Velušina–Porodin culture were more spacious and solid. The chipped and polished stone industry (various types of axes) was very

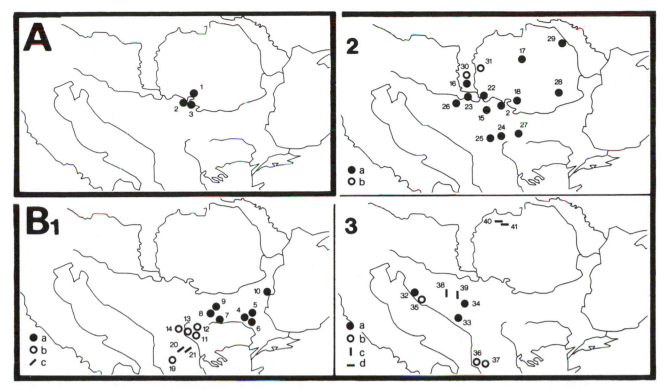

Map 60 Pre-Neolithic, Early and Middle Neolithic in the Balkans. A – Pre-Neolithic: Lepenski Vir–Schela Cladovei culture (1, Schela Cladovei; 2, Lepenski Vir; 3, Vlasac). B1 – Balkano-Anatolian complex: a, Karanovo I–II culture (and regional variants) (4, Karanovo; 5, Azmak; 6, Veselinovo; 7, Banjata; 8, Čavdar; 9, Gradešnica; 10, Conevo); b, Anzabegovo-Vršnik culture (11, Anzabegovo; 12, Vršnik; 13, Zelenikovo; 14, Madžare; 15, Divostin; 16, Donja Branjevina; 17, Gura Baciului; 18, Circea, Lepenski Vir (2); 19, Podgorie); c, Velušina Porodin culture (20, Velušina; 21, Porodin). B2 – Balkano-Carpathian complex: a, Starčevo (Criş) culture (22, Starcevo; 23, Vinkovci; 24, Pavlovac; 25, Gladnica; 26, Gornja Tuzla; 27, Kremimovci; 28, Letz; 29, Valea Lupului; Lepenski Vir (2), Divostin (15); Donja Branjevina (16); Gura Baciului (17); Circea (18)); b, Körös group. 30, Nosa; 31, Hodmezö Vasarhely. B3 – The Western Mediterranean complex: a, Impressed Ware culture (32, Smilčic; 33, Crvena Stijena; 34, Odmut); b, Danilo culture (35, Danilo; 36, Cakran; 37, Dunavec); c, composite cultures (Obre I and Kakanj cultures) (38, Obre I; 39, Kakanj); d, Szatmar (Ciumesti) culture (40, Nagyecsed-Peterzug; 41, Ciumesti).

simple. Sickles with microliths and bone handles are recorded at Karanovo I. The pottery, represented above all by globular or semiglobular vessels with certain local variants (tulip-shaped vessels (Plate 87) at Karanovo I, vessels with several feet at Anzabegovo-Vršnik I), can be classified as light-coloured monochrome fine ware. It often bore decorations painted in white, rarely in red, with the triangle as the basic motif. At Anzabegovo, there were also floral decorations (Plate 88). At Karanovo I, spirals from that period have been recorded. Sculpture is represented above all by standing or sitting female figurines, and sometimes also by zoomorphic vessels (Plate 89) of the type also found in neighbouring Early Neolithic complexes. They bear testimony to a fertility cult. More complex ritual objects are associated with the Velušina–Porodin culture. These are clay models of houses, some of which have roofs with a cylindrical appendage each decorated with a human head – no doubt for apotropaic ends (Plate 90). There were also some miniature altars with the heads of snakes at the corners. The funeral rites are not adequately known. The existence of tombs has been established; some were family graves, with crouched skeletons inside the habitation area. At Anzabegovo, a burial of a new-born child was preserved in a vessel.

In the Balkans, *Triticum dicoccum* and *Hordeum vulgare* did not grow in the wild state, nor did sheep and goats, whose origins must be sought in western Asia. The brightly coloured monochrome pottery must be linked to Anatolia. New economic patterns, too, were brought to that zone of the peninsula from western Asia. The absence of any links

between these and local Mesolithic cultures suggests the intervention of outside groups. We should not, however, dismiss the possibility of the acculturation of earlier populations, especially in the Gura Baciului enclave. Here, the monochrome ware is of considerably poorer quality and the decorations include late motifs from Anzabegovo-Vršnik I. Standard and coarse ware is less fully represented here. Mention should also be made of the fact that the percentage of cattle, particularly those of large size, was greater than that of goats and sheep, whose smaller size suggests the import of domestic animals. At Lepenski Vir IIIa (Gura Baciului culture) hunting still played a dominant role, with 74.50 per cent of the animal remains coming from game as against 15.83 per cent from cattle and an even smaller percentage from goats and sheep. For the rest, close contacts were maintained between this complex and the neighbouring complexes, as we know from the almost ubiquitous, if scattered, appearance of coarse ware decorated with impressions (fingernail marks or fingerprints) or with barbotine.

The development of this complex was continued in the Middle Neolithic, especially in those zones that saw the rise of the Anzabegovo-Vršnik I culture (Anzabegovo-Vršnik II–IV, dated around 6,800 to 6,200 years ago). It is characterized by the gradual increase in coarse and in dark monochrome wares. The decorations are painted on in dark colours; they are geometric motifs accompanied by an old phase of the spiral motif. This is explained by close contacts with the neighbouring Starčevo culture and the Adriatic zone, probably in fairly complex ways: barter, exogamic links, transhumance (M. Garašanin, 1982b). Mention must also be made of some sites from the final stage (Anzabegovo-Vršnik IV), above all of those of Zelenikovo and Madžare in the Skopje plain. Agglomerations built to a careful plan contain dwellings disposed in parallel rows, which facilitated internal communication. The dwellings had two rooms, one usually with a hearth and a large altar, often richly decorated.

Balkano-Carpathian complex (Starčevo, Criş, Körös)

The Balkano-Carpathian complex comprises all central regions of the Balkan peninsula and an important sector of the lower Danubian regions north of the Stara Planina. It also extends into southern Pannonia with the Körös group. This complex comprised the Starčevo culture, which is called Criş or Starčevo-Criş in Romania (not to be confused with the Körös group), and its local variants in the plain of Sofia and in Albania (Arandjelović-Garašanin, 1954; M. Garašanin, 1982b; Dumitrescu et al., 1983; Prendi, 1982). It is dated to around 6,800 to 6,200 years ago.

The economic basis did not differ significantly from that of the previous complex. The same plants were cultivated and the proportion of cattle was approximately equal to that of sheep and goats. At Nosa (Voivodina), game accounted for 78.4 per cent of the animal remains, while cattle and ovicaprids were represented in equal proportions (9.8 per cent) among the domestic animals. However, at Letz (Criş culture), the percentage of sheep and goats was as high as 80 per cent. The settlements, although permanent, rarely comprised more than one habitation level. At Nosa in the Körös group surface dwellings and granaries were found to have their walls coated with a layer of lacustrine clay (D. Garašanin, 1961). All this suggests a rather more seasonal and mobile economy within well-established territories with base camps and temporary dwellings and hence distinct from the cultures of the Balkano-Anatolian complex. Stone implements (polished axes, sometimes microliths) and bone implements are relatively rare. The pottery is of similar shape to that of the preceding complex, but the distribution of the various categories differs appreciably: at Starčevo 73 per cent of the pottery was coarse ware, 15.9 per cent standard ware and 11.03 per cent fine ware. According to Arandjelović and Garašanin (1954) painted ware did not appear before the Starčevo IIa stage. The decoration usually took the form of dark paint, sometimes in two colours. The motifs and their chronological distribution correspond to those of Anzabegovo. Barbotine decoration was predominant in the Starčevo culture, while impressed motifs were the most common in Körös (M. Garašanin, 1980). Anthropomorphic sculptures are rare and related to those of the preceding complex. Crouched inhumations have been found inside the settlements. At Vinča, a collective tomb is reached through a passage (dromos). Similar forms of inhumation have recently been described at Zlatica (Voivodina) and attributed to Starčevo IIb–III (D. Garašanin, 1984).

The general nature of that culture indicates the existence of close links between the Balkano-Carpathian and the Balkano-Anatolian complexes. However, differences in economic and living conditions no less than in the distribution of the various pottery categories demonstrate that this relationship must have been a form of acculturation by contacts emanating from the south. It was within the framework of these contacts that the Szatmar culture, representing a fusion of the Balkano-Carpathian complex and the Bandkeramik complex of central Europe, was established

in Hungary (Kalicz and Makkay, 1977, pp. 18 ff.). The Band-keramik culture, moreover, reached Moldavia and the western Ukraine at a relatively late date (around 6,250 years ago) (Dumitrescu et al., 1983, pp. 95 ff.).

Western Mediterranean complex (Impressed Ware, Danilo, Cakran–Dunavec)

The western Mediterranean complex can be found along the coastline of the Adriatic and on the Adriatic islands (M. Garašanin, 1982b; Batović, 1979). Exceptionally it also extended into the hinterland, especially in Dalmatia and Montenegro (Danilo, Crvena Stijena, Odmut). The Early Neolithic is represented here by the so-called Impressed Ware culture. The economic life of this complex was based, at the beginning, solely on hunting, gathering, fishing and collecting shellfish. Stock-farming, especially of sheep and goats, did not appear until the Early Neolithic, and agriculture came still later. Triticum dicoccum and Triticum monococcum have been found in the Middle Neolithic of Danilo. Sedentary settlements are represented by caves like Markova Špilja on Hvar, Crvena Stijena and Odmut in Montenegro and also by surface agglomerations as at Smilčič and Bribir in the Dalmatian hinterland. These settlements might have been protected by a ditch with the dwellings around its inner perimeter, the central parts of the village being left clear, probably for communal gatherings or for herding livestock. The stone industry was originally based on chipping techniques related to Mesolithic traditions, as we know from specimens found at Crvena Stijena. Pottery, in shapes similar to those of the neighbouring complexes, is mainly represented by standard and coarse ware. The decorations are usually impressed with a bone implement or with a cockle shell (Cardium). Anthropomorphic figures are almost unknown. Inhumations of crouched bodies and of skulls have been recorded on several occasions.

The economy, the stone implements, and the types and decoration of the pottery bear witness to the autochthonous origins of this complex. It is nevertheless undeniable that agriculture, stock-farming and familiarity with pottery were introduced into the complex by a process of acculturation, starting in one of the neighbouring complexes.

This culture was continued during the Middle Neolithic by the emerging Danilo culture in Dalmatia and by its Cakran-Dunavec variant on the Albanian coast as far as the plain of Korce (Batović, 1979; Prendi, 1982). The economic strategies of the previous stage were still employed. The implements, the types of dwelling and settlement and also the funeral rites remained unchanged. These cultures are distinguished above all by their incised (and sometimes excised) ware encrusted with a very profuse range of motifs in red or white (triangles, lozenges, and the like and above all spirals, heralding the Butmir spiral). At Danilo there were also vessels painted on an off-white surface, identical with the pottery found at Ripoli on the Adriatic coast of Italy. A special type of ritual object, a rhyton with several feet, often decorated and provided with a lateral orifice, has been found in the Danilo and Cakran–Dunavec cultures, but is also known in Greece (Elateia, Corinth). It proves the existence of a great Neolithic spiritual Koine parallel to that represented by anthropomorphic idols.

All these observations bear out the local origins of that culture, and its subsequent development partly as a result of close contacts with the neighbouring cultures and of barter: ornaments fashioned from spondylus shells were exported to the interior, and the presence of Ripoli painted pottery confirms the existence of close links with the Apennine coast on the other side of the Adriatic.

Composite cultures (Obre I, Kakanj and others)

A composite culture that appeared in the western Balkans during the Middle Neolithic has been studied particularly at Obre I in Bosnia (Benac, 1979; Gimbutas et al., 1974). Dated around 6,800 to 6,150 years ago, it owes its origin to the fusion of late elements of the Early Adriatic Neolithic (Impressed Ware) with the Starčevo culture. This fusion reflects a chronological shift in the transition from the Early to the Middle Neolithic of the Adriatic and central zones of the Balkan peninsula. In Bosnia, this culture developed into a local form, that of Kakanj, which knew the type of rhyton characteristic of Danilo and Cakran. The economy of Obre I was identical to that of Starčevo.

Close contacts between the different cultures and complexes also existed in the confines of other regions. This was notably so in northern Albania and Kosovo where, as they advanced up the Drim, late Danilo elements made contact with the Vinča culture. An enclave of Middle Neolithic elements from the Adriatic also reached Pelagonia, most probably along the Devoll (Benac, 1979). In southern Albania, we also know of a very late culture, which Albanian archaeologists assign to the Late Neolithic. Its painted ware shows that it is related above all to the classic and late stages of the Dimini culture (Maliq I: Prendi, 1976).

LATE NEOLITHIC (Map 61)

The emergence of the Late Neolithic in eastern and central regions of the Balkan peninsula was marked by many radical innovations which cannot be interpreted as spontaneous developments of earlier forms. The new phase is reflected not only in a number of economic structures, but also in the dark, fine ware which came in a variety of shapes (biconical vessels, bowls, amphorae). The decorations (grooves, and incised and stippled decorations which rapidly spread) are completely different from those of the previous stages. The same is true of the anthropomorphic and zoomorphic figures and also of other ritual objects.

Late Neolithic Balkano-Anatolian Complex (Vinča, Karanovo III–IV and other regional groups)

Most of these innovations have been attributed by the present author to a new complex of Late Neolithic Balkano-Anatolian cultures (M. Garašanin, 1982b; contrary opinion: Chapman, 1981). This complex comprises a whole series of cultures, notably those of Karanovo II with the late stages of Karanovo III–IV (Georgiev, 1961; Todorova, 1979) in Bulgaria, and the Vinča culture, which itself comprises several phases (Vinča A–D according to Milojčić (1949), Vinča-Turdas I–II, intermediate Gradac phase, Vinča-Pločnik I–II according to M. Garašanin) with numerous regional variants in Serbia, southern Pannonia, northern Bosnia, Romania-Transylvania, Oltenia, Banat (M. Garašanin, 1979; Lazarovici, 1980). Several other cultures were confined to more restricted geographical zones: maritime Thrace, Vallachia, south-western Pannonia (Bakalakis and Sakellariou, 1981; Comşa, 1971; Dimitrijević, 1979d). The initial phase of the Boian culture in Muntenia and in neighbouring regions of Romania is also related to this complex, its later phases being more strongly influenced by the South

Danubian Eneolithic. In the Tisza valley in Hungary, in the Romanian Banat and also in Banat there emerged, parallel to the Vinča culture, a mixed culture, the Szakalhat culture, due to the fusion of elements of the Late Bandkeramik culture of central Europe and of the Vinča culture (Comşa, 1974; Kalicz and Makkay, 1977).

According to some observers, *Triticum dicoccum*, *Triticum monococcum* and *Hordeum vulgare* seem to have been introduced independently (Hopf, 1974). In most of the complex we can also detect a slight change in animal husbandry, reflected in a gradual decrease in the proportion of cattle and a fluctuation in the proportion of pigs, that of sheep and goats remaining stable. Thus, at Divostin (Vinča culture) the proportions were cattle 60 per cent, sheep and goats 17 per cent, pigs 9 per cent; later at Rast (an Oltenian variant) the figures were cattle 43.2 per cent, sheep and goats 36.28 per cent, pigs 2.28 per cent. Moreover, at Vadastra it was possible to observe a marked decline in the size of the cattle, possibly owing to their use as beasts of burden. Hunting and fishing at Vinča can be inferred from the presence of hooks and harpoons. Sedentary settlements are represented either by tells (Karanovo II–IV, Sopot, advanced Boian phases) and by multi-layered sites on terraces or the slopes of hills (especially in the case of the Vinča culture). The surface dwellings, often containing several rooms, have a packed–mud floor (or occasionally a timber substructure) and ovens. They are often aligned according to a fixed plan. The chipped stone implements at Vinča have been studied in great detail: at the beginning, 70 per cent of them were made from obsidian of Carpathian origin. Local raw materials predominated in the following stages. The production of stone implements became insignificant during the final stage (Vinča-Pločnik II), no doubt because of the rise of a copper industry. Polished stone implements consisted mainly of shoe-last celts and trapezoidal axes. The pottery, reflecting a single technique and typology, came in a profuse variety of shapes and decorations, especially in the Vinča culture. The same was true of the figurines, most of them anthropomorphic idols, more than a thousand of which were discovered at Vinča in the course of the 1927–34 excavations (Plate 91) (Vasić, 1936, III–IV). Their number and variety are explained by their being used in rites and ceremonies associated with the fertility cult and involving the adoration of a goddess and her male companion (*paredros*). Special mention must also be made of the prosopomorphous lids associated with the Vinča culture; their role was apotropaic (D. Garašanin, 1968; Srejović, 1984, pp. 42 ff.).

This complex appeared first in the south-east of the peninsula, partly during the Middle Neolithic (Karanovo II), later to spread to the north. As a result, the beginnings of Vinča coincide with the end of Karanovo III. This process must have meant a very complex form of acculturation, whose roots have to be sought in Anatolia (possibly at Can Hasan, unfortunately not adequately explored). This shift must certainly have involved human groups in search of arable land in the wake of a population increase, but must also have involved contacts based on barter (the import of obsidian from the Carpathians, of ornaments made from marine shells and the like), on exogamic links, on transhumance (evidenced in one case in the Vinča culture) and finally on the existence of common sacred places. The site of Valač in Kosovo (final Vinča phase) is a good example of such usage, what with its wealth of anthropomorphic figures and the relative scarcity of other cultural remains. A sanctuary has also been discovered in Câscioarele in Muntenia; it dates back to the final (Spantov) phase of the Boian and has its

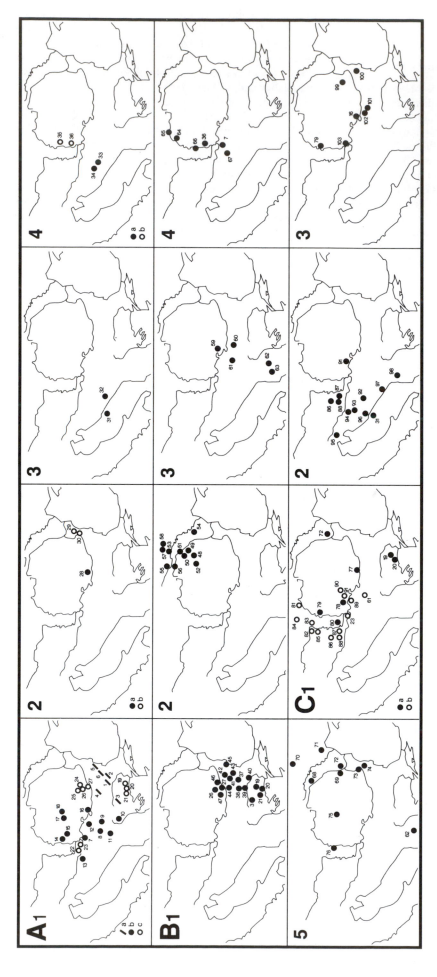

Map 61 Late Neolithic and Eneolithic in the Balkans. A1–Balkano–Anatolian complex: a, Karanovo III–IV culture (and regional variants) (1, Karanovo; 2, Veselinovo; 3, Jasa Tepe; 4, Hotnica; 5, Sava; 6, Ursoe); b, Vinča culture (7, Vinča; 8, Pločnik; 9, Gradac; 10, Anzabegovo; 11, Predionica; 12, Rudna Glava (mining centre); 13, Gornja Tuzla; 14, O Szent Ivan VIII, 15, Parta; 16, Rast; 17, Turdas; 18, Tartaria); c, other regional groups in the Balkano–Anatolian complex (19, Paradimi (culture); 20, Dikili Tash (Paradimi culture); 21, Sitagroi (Paradimi culture); 22, Sopot (Sopot culture); 23, Gomolava (Sopot culture); 24, Bolintineanu (Boian culture); 25, Giulesti (Boian culture); 26, Vidra (Boian culture); 27, Cascioarele (Boian culture)). A2–Other regional cultures: a, Vadastra culture (28, Vadastra); b, Hamangia culture (29, Hamangia; 30, Hirsova) A3–Adriatic zone culture (Lisičići–Hvar culture) (31, Grapčeva Špilja; 32, Lisičići. A4–Composite cultures: a, Butmir culture (33, Butmir; 34, Obre II); b, Szakalhat culture (35, Szakalhat; 36, Crna Bara) B–Early Eneolithic: B1–Kodža–Dermen–Gumelnita–Karanovo VI complex (with introductory Marica phase) (37. Ajbunar (mining centre) (37, Ajbunar (mining centre); 38, Kirilmetodievo; 39, Mečkur; 40, Marica; 41, Poljanica; 42, Ovčarovo; 43, Goljamo Delčevo; 44, Ruse; 45, Varna; 46, Gumelnita; 47, Petru Rares; Jasa Tepe (3); Vidra (26); Cascioarele (27); Paradimi (19); Dikili Tash (20); Sitagroi (21)). B2–Cucuteni–Tripolye (and Pre–Cucuteni) complex (48, Izvoare; 49, Habasçešti; 50, Cucuteni; 51, Trusçešti; 52, Frumusçica; 53, Luka Vrublevečkaja; 54, Karbuna; 55, Bilče Zolote; 56, Šipenci; 57, Tripolye; 58, Veremie. B3–Salcuta–Krivodol–Bubanj complex (59, Salcuta; 60, Krivodol; 61, Bubanj; 62, Šupljevec; 63, Maliç). B4–Tiszapolgar and Bodrogkeresztur cultures (64 Tiszapolgar; 65, Deszk; 66, Deszk; 67, Visešava; Vinča (7); Crna Bara (36)). B5–Pontic intrusions and influences: 68, Horodiştea; 69, Foltesçti; 70, Gorodsk; 71, Usatovo; 72, Černavoda (Cernavoda I culture); 73, Casimcea (sceptre); 74, Resovo (sceptre); 75, Decia Muresului (necropolis); 76, Csongrad (necropolis); Šupljevec (sceptre) (62)). C–Late Aeneolithic (transitional period). C1–Baden complex: a, Černavoda III culture (77, Celei; 78, Kovin, 79, Ketegyhaza, 80, Odžaci; Černavoda (72); Paradimi (19); Dikili Tash (20)); b, Baden culture and related groups (81, Vis; 82, Urry; 83, Pecel; 84, Center; 85, Budakalasz; 86, Zok; 87, Sarvas; 88, Vucedol; 89, Kostolac (Kostolac group); 90, Cotofeni (Cotofeni group); 91, Moldova Veche (Cotofeni group). C2–Vučedol complex (Vučedol culture and regional variants) 92, Debelo Brdo; 93, Hrustovača; 94, Zecovi; 95, Ljubljansko Barje; 96, sources of the Cetina; 97, Tivat; 98, Pazsok; Vučedol (88)) (Cotofeni–Bubanj–Hum II culture), Sitagroi (21) (Cotofeni–Bubanj–Hum II culture). Dikili Tash (20) (Cotofeni–Bubanj–Hum II culture); Grapčeva Špilja (31); Moldova Veche (91); Zok (86). C3–Tumulus tombs with ochre (99, Smeieni; 100, Placidol; 101, Kneza; 102, Trnava; 103, Vojlovica; Rast (16); Ketegyhaza (79)).

walls and two of its pillars decorated with painted motifs (Dumitrescu et al., 1983, p. 78).

Tartaria tablets

A sensational discovery was that of clay tablets at Tartaria (Transylvania): their incised signs resemble Sumerian writing (Vlassa, 1970). Despite the doubts expressed by some archaeologists, for instance by V. Dumitrescu (Dumitrescu et al., 1983, pp. 88 ff.), these tablets must be assigned to the Vinča culture (Vinča-Turdas). A careful analysis of the tablets (Masson, 1984) suggests that they must have been a first step towards the creation of a primitive script, something quite possible in so flourishing a culture as that of Vinča. In such cases, deceptive similarities can appear in distinct geographic and cultural zones. This applies equally to the incised signs found in several Eneolithic sites in Thrace. In fact, radiocarbon dates place the Late Neolithic Balkano-Anatolian complex back at the end of the seventh and the beginning of the sixth millennium BP (Karanovo III around 6,400 to 6,100 years ago; Vinča culture around 6,500 to 5,250 years ago).

Hamangia

A special place must be reserved, in the Late Neolithic, for the Hamangia culture in Dobrudža (around 6,500 to 6,000 years ago) characterized by its fine ware with stippled decorations and its anthropomorphic idols, the most famous being the 'Hamangia Thinker' (Plate 92), whose origins remain uncertain. It is with this culture that the Neolithic began in these regions. This delay is explained by the geological conditions prior to the seventh millennium BP, namely the transgression of the Black Sea and the existence of a maritime gulf at the present mouths of the Danube (Berciu, 1966; Dumitrescu et al., 1983, pp. 97 ff., 140 ff.).

Adriatic zone (Lisičiči–Hvar)

The Late Neolithic of the Adriatic zone is represented by the Lisičiči–Hvar culture (Batović, 1979; Novak, 1955) on the coast, on the islands (Hrabak cave on Hvar) and in the hinterland (Lisičiči on the Neretva). This culture is rooted in the Middle Neolithic and differs from it neither in its economic structures, nor in its settlement patterns and funerary rites. The pottery, of poor typology, has incised or painted decorations (above all in the Hrabak cave) involving geometric motifs (curves, triangles, lozenges), spirals or lunar symbols. The origins of these decorations are believed to lie partly in contacts with the western Mediterranean.

Mixed culture of Obre II–Butmir

Once again, as in the previous stage, a composite culture emerged in the mountainous regions of the west. This was the Butmir culture, studied in detail at Obre II, dated to around 6,200 to 5,800 years ago. It was one of the first Neolithic cultures discovered in Europe (Hörnes and Radimsky, 1895; Hörnes and Fiala, 1898; Benac, 1979; Gimbutas et al., 1974; M. Garašanin, 1982b). Most of the decorations, and especially the admirable spiral motifs (Plate 93), originate from the Middle Adriatic Neolithic (Danilo). By contrast, the monochrome dark ware, the pleated decorations and incised bands and above all the rich and varied anthropomorphic figurines and also the economic structures link it to the Balkano-Anatolian complex. Thus at Obre II, stock-raising predominated over hunting – it accounted for 85 per cent of the animal remains, more than 50 per cent of which came from cattle and the rest from goats and sheep and from pigs in that order (Bökönyi in Gimbutas et al., 1974).

THE ENEOLITHIC (Map 61)

The fundamental economic changes that occurred in the sixth millennium BP in the life of the tribes inhabiting the eastern part of the Balkan peninsula and the lower Danubian plains paved the way for a new stage of historical development: the Eneolithic, the Copper Age of Hungarian scholars (M. Garašanin, 1982a, 1983). It involved, above all, the mining and manufacture of the earliest copper implements, at first of small importance and size but rapidly making way for heavier items, especially axes of various types, the most important of which were axe-hammers and adze-hammers in a series of variations whose distribution and chronology differ (Schubert and Schubert, 1965). Research during the past few years at Aibunar in Thrace and at Rudna Glava in the Bor mining basin (eastern Serbia) confirm the autochthonous beginnings of the exploitation of copper deposits (Chernysh, 1978; Jovanović, 1982). As a result of these activities the Neolithic world, previously very stable, was slightly unbalanced. In particular, the uneven distribution of mining deposits led to hostile confrontations. Moreover, the introduction of new specialized activities (mining, metalworking), coupled with increasing insecurity, wrought marked alterations in the prevailing economic and social structures and led to the creation of a warrior class that gradually assumed a dominant place in tribal society. It should be added that some flourishing cultures managed to keep aloof from this development for some time. Thus the Vinča culture, above all in its Serbian base territory, preserved its Neolithic character during periods contemporary with the first Eneolithic cultures (transition phase, Vinča–Pločnik = Vinča B2). In other cases, the disintegration of the Neolithic world led to the formation of new Eneolithic societies. That is what happened in south-western Pannonia, in the neighbouring Alpine regions and in the Balkan peninsula with the formation of the Lasinja–Balaton culture, the result of a fusion of Vinča and Lengyel elements (Dimitrijević, 1979b). In the Carpathian regions and above all along the Tisza in the Hungarian plain there emerged the Tiszapolgar culture, based on Late Neolithic elements and developing during the Eneolithic into the Bodrogkeresztur culture (Bognar-Kutzian, 1972, particularly pp. 212 ff.). Moreover, in Transylvania, the Vinča culture had its development cut short by the emergence of the Petreşti culture. The apparent similarities between the latter and the Starčevo culture cannot be real in view of the chronological differences (the end of the Starčevo is dated at around 6,200 years ago; the beginning of the Petreşti at around 5,900 years ago). The formation of the Petreşti culture might be attributed to influences from the south and from the Aegean coast, influences also responsible for the formation of Eneolithic complexes using painted ware (Paul, 1981). The transformations that took place in the lower Danubian region in the wake of the emergence of the Eneolithic were followed, from the end of the sixth millennium BP onwards, by migrations of nomadic or semi-nomadic people from the steppes and wooded steppes north of the Black Sea and beyond (the transition period of Romanian scholars). This caused a whole series of population movements into the Balkans and central Europe. The upshot was the regrouping of older cultures, the disintegration of old groups and the emergence of new cultures.

Kodža–Dermen–Karanovo VI–Gumelniţa and Cucuteni–Tripolye complexes

The lower Danubian Eneolithic must be considered above all as part of a great complex of cultures associated with graphite-painted ware (Plate 94) (M. Garašanin, 1982a). It began with the Marića–Karanovo V culture in Thrace (around 5,850 years ago) with its variants in northern Bulgaria.

This culture influenced the formation of the advanced stages of the Boian culture. Its development continued during the Kodža-Dermen–Karanovo VI–Gumelniţa phase (around 5,800 to 5,000 years ago), with as most important elements the Gumelniţa and the Karanovo VI cultures to the north and south of the Stara Planina. These cultures also had a number of local variants of which the most important was undoubtedly the Varna culture in Bulgaria, on the Black Sea (Todorova, 1978, 1979; Dumitrescu et al., 1983, pp. 101 ff.; Ivanov, 1975). Further east, in Moldavia and the Ukraine, we find the great Cucuteni–Tripolye complex with its introductory phase of Precucuteni–Tripolye A (Marinescu-Bîlcu, 1974) and its subsequent phases of Cucuteni A = Tripolye BI, Cucuteni A–B = Tripolye BII and Cucuteni B = Tripolye CI. They are dated from around 5,550 (Precucuteni) or 5,500 to 5,450 (Cucuteni A–Tripolye B) to around 4,900 years ago (Tripolye CI). Unlike Russian scholars, according to whom this complex was formed in the Dnieper and Bug regions and then spread westwards, Romanian archaeologists place the centre of the Precucuteni formation in Moldavia, where it is said to have been based on older cultures (Late Bandkeramik and Boian). Later, the same impulses from the south that led to the emergence of the graphite-painted ware complex were responsible for the rise in Moldavia and Ukraine of the brilliant painted ware of Cucuteni–Tripolye (Plate 95) (Dumitrescu et al., 1983, pp. 108ff.; Chernysh, 1982, pp. 166–252).

The first mining operations in Thrace (Aibunar) were contemporaneous with the Marića culture. In addition to mining and the production of the first copper objects it had other important economic characteristics. Agriculture was represented by *Triticum dicoccum*, *Triticum monococcum* and *Hordeum vulgare*, followed by lentils and other species grown separately, perhaps even selectively. At Goljamo Delčevo (northern Bulgaria), the wheat species accounted for 86.02 per cent of all the crops, the greater part being *Triticum monococcum*. Stock-farming predominated over hunting with domestic animals, accounting for 63.84 per cent of all the animal remains in the same site, which, however, was a smaller percentage than that prevailing during the Neolithic. Here too cattle took the lead. The situation was more or less the same in the Cucuteni–Tripolye complex, though with significant fluctuations, during the Tripolye BI phase, in the percentage of hunted animals (from 15–19 per cent to 37–44 per cent and even to 50 per cent), which reflects the existence of more varied resources. Among domestic species, cattle followed by pigs took pride of place. There were few sheep and goats. We cannot tell whether or not horses had already been domesticated.

The types of settlement associated with graphite-painted ware reflect marked changes in social organization. Thus, at the very beginning of the Eneolithic, Poljanica (Fig. 146) was a proto-urban agglomeration defended by a triple ditch, built on a quadrangular plan with four entrances, one on each side, the dwellings being arranged in an orthogonal system of alleys. Similar agglomerations from the same epoch were discovered at Goljamo-Delčevo (Todorova et al., 1976) and at Ovcarovo (Todorova et al., 1976). Fortified settlements on fluvial terraces protected on their accessible side by ditches were common in the Gumelnita culture. At Câscioarele, the dwellings were scattered rather irregularly inside the agglomeration. In the Cucuteni–Tripolye complex, they were often built with greater care ('ploščadki' – platform dwellings) and to a better plan. In the Habaşeşti agglomeration (Dumitrescu et al., 1954) of the Cucuteni A phase, defended by a double ditch, the houses were built in more or less regular rows. At Kolomiščina in the Ukraine they formed a circle round a central building, the chief's residence or an assembly place. In the Ukraine there were also smaller villages grouped round a large agglomeration, most probably the centre of the tribal territory. In the same region there is also mention of enormous agglomerations in which the dwellings were arranged in several concentric circles, no doubt in accordance with certain rules of tribal organization (Chernysh, 1982).

The transformation of social structures is clearly reflected in the necropolis of Varna, characterized by crouched inhumation and to a lesser extent by cenotaphs. Some tombs containing a host of gold objects (sceptres, ornaments and pendants, some of them zoomorphic) (Plate 96) must have been the graves of persons of high social rank. The use of barter is corroborated by analyses of the Varna gold: nearly 50 per cent of it apparently came from the Caucasus or Armenia (Hartmann, 1978). Despite the expansion, mentioned earlier, of copperwork, stone implements during the Kodža Dermen–Gumelniţa–Karanovo VI phase still took the form of chipped axes of quadrangular section. The pottery was distinguished above all by rich and varied graphite-painted decorations in sumptuous and complicated patterns. This type of ware was well established already in the Marića culture (Plate 94) and its development continued, to the point of decadence, in the subsequent phase. The links between this type of decoration and some categories of pottery associated with the Late Neolithic in Thrace, in maritime Macedonia (Akropotamo, Galepsos) representing late variants of painted Thessalian ware (Dimini), strongly suggest impulses from the south. Anthropomorphic figurines are represented, apart from baked-clay figurines and vases, by flat bone idols (Plate 97) associated above all with the Kodža Dermen–Karanovo VI–Gumelniţa phase (Dumitrescu, 1972; Radunčeva, 1976). In the Cucuteni–Tripolye complex, the same southern influences provoked a veritable explosion of ceramic art. The polychrome paint of the Cucuteni A stage with its sumptuous, mostly spiral, decorations was replaced in the later phases by painted geometric patterns and representations of animals. Apart from the idols, mainly feminine, the altar at Truşeşti (Plate 98) would also seem to represent the great female deity and her male companion. The support of the vase from Frumuşica, with representation of persons dancing around, bears witness to the existence of fertility rites, the details of which unfortunately still escape us (Dumitrescu, 1972).

An important discovery at Karbuna in the Ukraine was a store of metal objects contemporary with an early phase of the Cucuteni–Tripolye complex. The 852 pieces (of which 444 in copper) in it bear witness not only to long-distance commercial contacts but also to the urge to accumulate valuable objects, a tendency that played an important role in

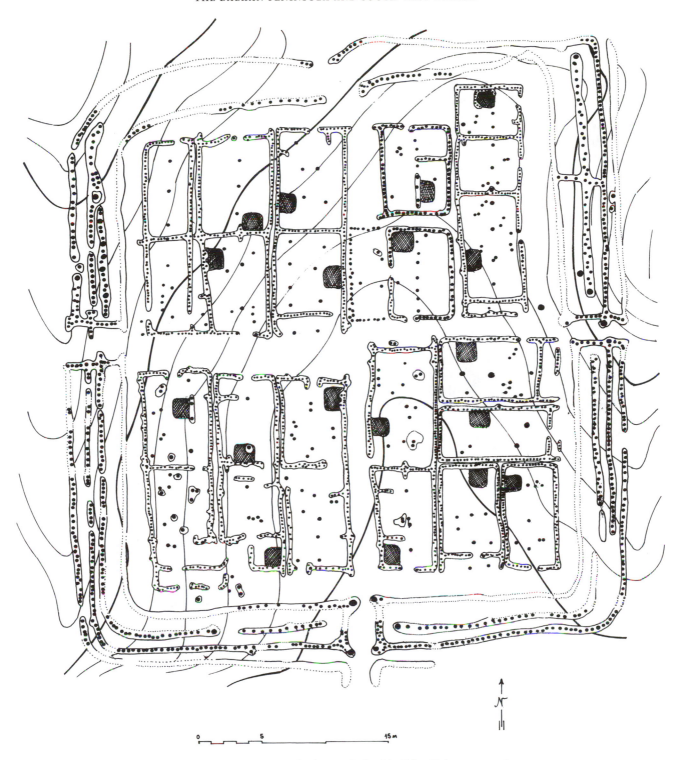

Figure 146 Plan of the Eneolithic proto-urban settlement of Poljanica (Bulgaria). (After Todorova, 1979.)

the transformation of social structures and in the emergence of classes (Chernysh, 1982, p. 235, Pls LVIII, LXIII).

Pontic intrusions

Towards the end of the sixth millennium BP, new Pontic intrusions made themselves felt as early as during the Cucuteni AB stage, with the introduction of a very primitive form of pottery decorated with comb impressions (Cucuteni C pottery of H. Schmidt, 1932), and perhaps a little later with the appearance in the Lower Danubian region of the Černavoda I culture (radiocarbon dated to around 4,500 to

4,250 years ago, though these dates are considered to be very low), whose origins have been rightly sought in the more or less contemporary Sredniy Stog II culture found between the Dnieper and the Don (Roman, 1983; Merpert, 1982, pp. 322 ff.). The primitive pottery, the expansion of big-game hunting (deer, wild boar), the domestication of horses and the preponderance among the domestic animals of cattle, goats, sheep and pigs of large size, clearly reflect a mainly pastoral economy, independent of the Neolithic economy of south-east Europe.

The same process of intrusion by foreign groups and their fusion with the autochthonous populations explains the appearance, on the territory of the old Cucuteni–Tripolye complex, of several related cultures: Horodiştea–Folteşti in Moldavia and Gorodsk–Usatovo in Ukraine. They are distinguished above all by a coarse ware made of clay tempered with cockle shells, similar in this respect to the coarse ware of Cucuteni C and Černadova. Painted decoration from the previous period is not present in significant proportions (5 to 11 per cent at Gorodsk; 21 per cent at Usatovo). The role of stock-breeding, which increased during the Cucuteni–Tripolye epoch, now became dominant. The percentage of domestic animals in the Usatovo culture reached 90 per cent with, in contrast to what happened in the Cucuteni–Tripolye complex, a predominance of ovicaprids (50 per cent) due to the influence of pastoralists from the steppes, and a small number of pigs (Dumitrescu et al., 1983, pp. 183 ff.; Chernysh, 1982, pp. 213 ff.; Merpert, 1982, pp. 322 ff.). These cultures are dated around 4,600 to 4,300 years ago.

The Salcuţa–Krivodol–Bunanj complex

The gradual westward expansion of the Černavoda I culture triggered off a series of other displacements in the partly autochthonous groups. This was particularly so with the Salcuţa group in Oltenia, an impoverished variant of the Gumelniţa culture, whose members, forced to cross the western Danube, formed several regional groups in Bulgaria, central Serbia and even in Pelagonia and in Albania, the whole being known as the Salcuţa–Krivodol–Bunanj complex (M. Garašanin, 1982a; Berciu, 1960; Prendi, 1982). In central Serbia, the Bunanj–Hum Ia group took the place of the final Vinča stage (Vinča-Pločnik IIa = Vinča D). These events are dated to around 5,650 to 5,600 years ago.

In Transylvania, the Banat and eastern Hungary pressure from the Černavoda I culture triggered off amalgamations of local populations leading to the formation of new cultural groups which influenced developments in the central Balkans (Bunanj Ib). The Černavoda I group was certainly not the only newcomer to have moved at that time from north of the Black Sea to the lower Danube and south-east Europe.

Decia Mureşului necropolis and related finds

However, what little we know about other intruders is based on rare finds scattered over a vast territory, a fact that doubtless indicated that they were nomadic pastoralists. An example of this trend is the necropolis at Decia Mureşului (Maros Decse) in Transylvania, where funerary rites were practised and there was a tool set (stone clubs, large flint blades) closely related to the finds in Mariupol on the Sea of Azov. The same is true of the ochre tomb of Casimcea in Dobrudža, which contained a stone sceptre in the shape of a horse's head. Sceptres of that type – an emblem of nomadic chiefs – are known through a series of discoveries from the Kalmuck steppes to Thrace (Resovo) and Pelagonia (Šupljevec). It is the same with the origins of the corded ware in the inventory of a number of cultures (Cucuteni, Horodiştea-Folteşti, Černavoda I, Šupljevec) (M. Garašanin, 1982a; Roman, 1983, Ecsedy, 1983).

Baden and the Vučedol complexes (Plate 99 and Map 61)

This early phase of the confrontation and assimilation of different elements, intrusive and autochthonous, was responsible for other movements and fusions during the fifth mil-

lennium BP, which in turn led to the emergence of new cultures. Thus Romania (Muntenia, Dobrudža, Oltenia and even the Banat) witnessed the emergence, based on a late stage of Černovoda I, of Černovoda III, almost identical with the Boleraz culture in Slovakia. The latter gave rise to the great Baden complex in the Pannonian regions, which comprised several stages and whose spread can be followed as far away as the Alps, Serbia and western parts of the Balkan peninsula (Dimitrijević, 1979a; Banner, 1956; Roman and Nemeti, 1978). The existence of numerous regional variants is explained by the fact that various autochthonous elements were involved in its formation. The Coţofeni culture (Oltenia) and the Kostolac culture (southern Pannonia and Danubian Serbia) are closely related to it (Roman, 1976; Tasić, 1979c). Despite its dynamism, this complex comprised stable settlements in mountainous regions often placed on commanding heights or promontories. Two dwellings with apses dominating the Vučedol agglomeration are thought to have been the residences of chiefs (R. R. Schmidt, 1945), as were the megara which, in the Vučedol culture, later replaced these dwellings on the same site. Familiarity with carts and the domestication of horses as well as inhumation graves known as catacombs at Vučedol reflect Pontic influences. There must also have been some contacts with the Aegean world, as suggested particularly by the anthropomorphic vases from Center, in Hungary, which are identical with those of the early Troadic culture, partly contemporaneous with the Vučedol complex (Kalicz, 1965). The Vučedol complex, which in the last centuries of the fifth millennium BP succeeded the Baden complex in the same regions, and the many variants of it which extended as far as the Alps (Ljubljana culture) and the Adriatic coast, are mainly distinguished by their excised and encrusted decorations reminiscent of wood carving (Dimitrijević, 1979e; R. R. Schmidt, 1945). Here, too, the type of tomb, some of the vessels ('censers') and also the daggers known from the Sarvas moulds bespeak the presence of elements from regions north of the Black Sea (M. Garašanin, 1982a, I, Ch. 3).

Pastoralists from the steppes

Intrusions by these groups can be traced across the Balkan peninsula as far as the northern shore of the Aegean (Dikili Tash, Sitagroi, Paradimi), Thessaly and even the necropolis of the early Helladic II culture at Hagios Kosmas in Attica (M. Garašanin, 1984b). They were caused partly by the last waves of migrations of pastoralists from the steppes. Part of a very primitive culture, but with a strong patriarchal organization, they invaded, in about the middle of the fifth millennium BP (around 4,285 years ago), the Lower Danubian regions between the Carpathians and Stara Planina, as far as Pannonia and the gates of Belgrade (Zirra, 1960; Jovanović, 1979b; Panajotov and Dergamčov, 1984). Their arrival is marked by the appearance of funerary barrows ('kurgans') and pit-graves with a timber framework containing skeletons sprinkled with ochre and sometimes surmounted by a very primitive monumental statue. Their migrations no doubt involved several stages, not all the details of which are known. They once again triggered off a process of fusion with the indigenous population, which is clearly reflected particularly in the barrows of Târnava and Kneza in Bulgaria. Inhumation under barrows became a common practice in south-eastern and central Europe and persisted during the course of the Bronze Age.

Many scholars, including the present author, consider this process of amalgamation and fusion, in which elements from regions north of the Black Sea, between the lower Danube and the Caucasus, played a leading role, to have been the first step in the formation of the Indo-European family (M. Garašanin, 1960–1; Gimbutas, 1970; divergent opinion: I. Ecsedy, 1983).

BIBLIOGRAPHY

ARANDJELOVIĆ-GARAŠANIN, D. 1954. *Starčevačka Kultura* [Starčevo Culture]. Ljubljana.

BAKALAKIS, G.; SAKELLARIOU, A. 1981. *Paradimi*. Mainz.

BANNER, J. 1942. *Das Tisza–Naros–Körös Gebiet bis zur Entwicklung der frühen Bronzezeit*. Szeged/Leipzig.

—— 1956. *Die Peceler Kultur*. Budapest. (Archaeol. hung., 35.)

BATOVIC, Š. 1966. *Stariji neolit u Dalmaciji* [The Early Neolithic in Dalmatia]. Zadar.

—— 1979. Jadranska zona. In: BENAC, A. (ed.), *Praistorija jugoslovenskih zemalja*. Sarajevo. t.2, pp. 473–634.

BENAC, A. 1958. *Neolitsko naselje u Lisičićima*. Sarajevo.

—— 1961. Studien zur Stein- und Kupferzeit im Nordwestbalkan. *Ber. Röm.-Ger. Komm.* (Frankfurt/Main), Vol. 42, pp. 1–170.

—— 1973a. Obre I. A Neolithic Settlement of the Starčevo-Impresso and Kakanj Culture at Raskrsce. *Wiss. Mitt. Bosn.-herzegow. Landesmus.* Sarajevo. t.3A, pp. 327–430.

—— 1973b. Obre II. A Neolithic Settlement of the Butmir Group at Gornje Polje. *Wiss. Mitt. Bosn.-herzegow. Landesmus.* Sarajevo. t.3A, pp. 1–191.

—— 1979. Prelazna zona. In: BENAC, A. (ed.), *Praistorija jugoslovenskih zemalja*. Sarajevo. t.2, pp. 363–470.

BERCIU, D. 1939. *Archeologia preistorica Olteniei* [Prehistoric Archaeology of Oltenia]. Craiova.

—— 1960. *Contribuții la problemele neoliticului in România in lumina noilor cercetari* [Contribution to the Problems of the Neolithic in Romania in the light of recent research]. Bucharest.

—— 1966. *Cultura Hamangia* [The Hamangia Culture]. Bucharest.

BOGNAR-KUTZIAN, I. 1966. Das Neolithikum in Ungarn. *Archaeol. Austriaca* (Vienna), Vol. 60, pp. 249–80.

—— 1972. *The Early Copper Age Tiszapolgar Culture in the Carpathian Basin*. Budapest.

BÖHM, J.; DE LAET, S. J. (eds) 1962. *L'Europe à la fin de l'Age de la Pierre. Actes du Symposium consacré aux problèmes du Néolithique européen, Prague, 1961*. Prague.

BÖKÖNYI, S. 1974. *History of Domestic Mammals in Central and Eastern Europe*. Budapest.

BORONANT, V. 1970. La Période épipaléolithique sur la rive roumaine du Danube. *Prähist. Z.* (Berlin), Vol. 40, pp. 2–25.

BRUKNER, B.; JOVANOVIĆ, B.; TASIĆ, N. 1974. Praistorija Vojvodine [The Prehistory of the Voivodina]. In: GEORGIEV, V. (ed.), *Historia na Bulgaria*. Novi Sad. pp. 54–86.

CHAPMAN, J. 1981. *The Vinča Culture of South-East Europe*. Oxford. (BAR Int. Ser., 119.)

CHERNYSH, E. K. 1978. *Gornoe delo i metallurgia v drevnejsej Bolgarii* [Mining and Metallurgy in Ancient Bulgaria]. Sofia.

—— 1982. Eneolit SSSR, part III [The Eneolithic in the USSR]. In: MASSON, V. I.; MERPERT, N. J. (eds), *Eneolit SSSR*. Moscow. pp. 165–320.

CHILDE, V. G. 1957. *The Dawn of European Civilization*. 6th edn. London.

COMŞA, E. 1971. Données sur la civilisation de Dudești. *Prähist. Z.* (Berlin), Vol. 46, pp. 195–249.

—— 1974. *Istoria comunitatilor culturii Boian*. Bucharest.

DAICOVICIU, C. (ed.) 1960. *Istoria Rominiei, I* [History of Romania, I]. Bucharest.

DESHAYES, J. 1970. Les Fouilles de Dikili Tash et la recherche yougoslave. *Zb. Narod. Muz.* (Beograd), Vol. 6, pp. 21–43.

DIMITRIJEVIĆ, S. 1971. *Sopotsko lengyelska kultura*. Zagreb.

—— 1979a. Badenska kultura [The Baden Culture]. In: BENAC, A. (ed.), *Praistorija jugoslovenskih zemalja*. Sarajevo. t.3, pp. 183–234.

—— 1979b. Lasinjska kultura. In: BENAC, A. (ed.), *Praistorija jugoslovenskih zemalja*. Sarajevo. t.3, pp. 137–82.

—— 1979c. Problem eneolita na istočnojadranskoj obali. In: BENAC, A. (ed.), *Praistorija jugoslovenskih zemalja*. Sarajevo. t.3, pp. 367–80.

—— 1979d. Sjeverna zona. In: BENAC, A. (ed.), *Praistorija jugoslovenskih zemalja*. Sarajevo. t.2, pp. 229–360.

—— 1979e. Vučedolska kultura [The Vučedol Culture]. In: BENAC, A. (ed.), *Praistorija jugoslovenskih zemalja*. Sarajevo. t.3, pp. 267–342.

DUMITRESCU, V. 1959. La Civilisation de Cucuteni. *Ber. Rijksd. Oudheidkd. Bodemonderz.* (Amersfoort), Vol. 9, pp. 6–48.

—— 1972. *Arte preistorica in Romania*. Florence.

—— 1980. *The Neolithic Settlement at Rast, South-West Oltenia, Romania*. Oxford. (BAR Int. Ser., 72.)

—— 1982. The Prehistory of Romania. In: *Cambridge Ancient History*. 2nd edn. Cambridge. Vol. 3, pp. 1–74.

DUMITRESCU, V.; BOLOMAY, M.; MOGOŞANU, P. 1983. *Esquisse d'une préhistoire de la Roumanie*. Bucharest.

DUMITRESCU, V. et al. 1954. *Habașești*. Bucharest.

ECSEDY, I. 1983. Steppeneinflüsse und kulturelle Veränderungen in der Kupferzeit. *God. Centra Balk. Ispit.* (Sarajevo), Vol. 21, pp. 135–64.

ECSEDY, I. et al. 1979. *The People of the Pit Grave Kurgans in Eastern Hungary*. Budapest.

FEWKES, V. J. 1936. Neolithic Sites in the Danubian-Balkan Area. *Bull. Am. Sch. Prehist. Res.*, Vol. 12, pp. 1–8.

FEWKES, V. J.; GOLDMAN, H.; EHRICH, R. 1933. Excavations at Starčevo in the Yugoslav Part of the Danubian-Balkan Area. *Bull. Am. Prehist. Res.*, Vol. 9, pp. 33–52.

GARAŠANIN, D. 1961. Die Siedlung der Starčevo-Kultur in Nosa bei Subotica und das Problem der neolithischen Lehmscheunen. In: INTERNATIONALER KONGRESS FÜR VOR- U. FRÜHGESCHICHTE, 5, Hamburg, 1958. pp. 303–7.

—— 1968. Religija i kult neoliskog čoveka na Centralnom Balkanu, Neolit Centralnog Balkana. *Nar. Muz.* (Beograd), pp. 241–64.

—— 1984. Starčevo-culture. In: SREJOVIC, D. (ed.), *Vinča*. Beograd. pp. 13–21, 191–4. (Catalogue of an exhibition in Beograd.)

GARAŠANIN, D.; GARAŠANIN, M. 1979. *Supska-Stublina, praistorijsko naselje vinčanske grupe*. Beograd. (With German translation.)

GARAŠANIN, M. 1950. Die Theisskultur im jugoslawischen Banat. *Ber. Röm.-Ger. Komm.* (Frankfurt/Main), Vol. 33, pp. 125–32.

—— 1951. *Hronologija vinčanske grupe*. Ljubljana.

—— 1958. Neolithikum und Bronzezeit in Serbien und Makedonien. *Ber. Röm.-Ger. Komm.* (Frankfurt/Main), Vol. 39, pp. 1–130.

—— 1960–1. Pontski i stepski uticaji u Donjem Podunavlju i na Balkanu, na prelazi iz neolita u metalno doba. *Glas. Zemalskog mezeja* (Sarajevo), Vol. 15/16, pp. 5–26.

—— 1973. *Pramstoriia ma tlou SR Srrije*. Beograd.

—— 1978. Zur chronologischen und kulturellen Wertung der Bunbanj-Funde. *Jahrb. Röm.-Ger. Zent.mus.* (Mainz), Vol. 26, pp. 153–66.

—— 1979. Centralnobalkanska regija. In: BENAC, A. (ed.), *Praistorija jugoslovenskih zemalja*. Sarajevo. t.2, pp. 79–212.

—— 1980. Les Origines du néolithique dans le bassin de la Méditerranée et dans le Sud-Est européen. Problèmes de la néolithisation dans certaines régions de l'Europe. *Pr. Kom. Archeol.* (Cracow), pp. 57–72.

—— 1982a. The Eneolithic Period in the Central Balkan Area. In: *Cambridge Ancient History*. 2nd edn. Cambridge. Vol. 3, No. 1, pp. 136–62.

—— 1982b. The Stone Age in the Central Balkan Area. In: *Cambridge Ancient History*. 2nd edn. Cambridge. Vol. 2, No. 1, pp. 75–135.

—— 1983. Considérations sur la transition du néolithique à l'âge du bronze dans les régions centrales de la Péninsule Balkanique. *God. Cent. Balk. Ispit.* (Sarajevo), Vol. 21, pp. 21–6.

—— 1984a. Vinča-culture. In: SREJOVIC, D. (ed.) *Vinča*. Beograd. pp. 57–65, 207–11. (Catalogue of an exhibition in Beograd.)

—— 1984b. Zur chronologischen und historischen Wertung süd-thrakisch-ostmakedonischer Wohnhügelfunde. *Prähist. Z.* (Berlin), Vol. 59, pp. 1–15.

GARAŠANIN, M.; SIMOSKA, D. 1976. Kontrolik iskonuvaia na chou-prieviej K niékoi proliemi na tupata chtupieviej-karavioi gunno. *Maced. Acta Archaeol.* (Prilep), Vol. 2, pp. 9–42.

GARAŠANIN, M.; SPASOVSKA, G. 1976. Iova Iskopuvania vo Iel-lieniskvo kai skonie. *Maced. Acta Archaeol.* (Prilep), Vol. 2, pp. 85–118.

GAUL, J. H. 1948. The Neolithic Period in Bulgaria. *Bull. Am. Sch. Prehist. Res.*, Vol. 16.

GEORGIEV, G. 1961. Kulturgruppen der Jungsteinzeit und der Kup-ferzeit in der Ebene von Thraken. In: BÖHM, J.; DE LAET, S. J. (eds), *L'Europe à la fin de l'Age de la Pierre.* Prague. pp. 41–106.

—— 1967. Beiträge zur Erforschung des Neolithikums und der Bronzezeit in Südbulgarien. *Archaeol. Austriaca* (Vienna), Vol. 42, pp. 155–70.

—— 1973. Die neolithische Kultur in Čavdar und ihre Stellung im Balkanneolithikum. In: CONGRES DE L'UISPP, 8ᵉ, Belgrade, 1971. *Actes.* Beograd. pp. 263–71.

—— 1975. *Stratigrafia i Karakter na kulturata na Praistoriceskoto celiste U.S. kriemikcbtcmi Arheologija.* Sofia.

—— (ed.) 1974. *Historia na Bulgaria* [The History of Bulgaria]. Novi Sad.

GEORGIEV, G. et al. 1979. *Elierc, Ranmobrchzevete – ciea Vtche.* Sofia.

GIMBUTAS, M. 1970. *The Kugan-culture Dating from the Fifth, Fourth and Third Millennia. Indoeuropeans and Indoeuropean.* Philadelphia.

GIMBUTAS, M. et al. 1974. Obre I and Obre II. *Wiss. Mitt. Bon.-Herzegow. Landesmus.* (Sarajevo), Vol. 4.

—— 1976. *Neolithic Macedonia as Reflected by Excavations at Anza.* Los Angeles.

GRBIC, M. et al. 1960. *Porodin, eine spätneolithische Tumba bei Bitolj.* Bitolj.

HARTMANN, A. 1978. Ergebnisse spektralanalytischer Unter-suchungen aeneolithischer Goldfunde aus Bulgarien. *Studi. Praehist.* (Sofia), Vol. 1–2, pp. 27–45.

HOPF, M. 1974. Pflanzenrest aus Siedlungen der Vinča-Kultur in Jugoslawien. *Jahrb. Röm.-Ger. Zent.mus.* (Mainz), Vol. 21, pp. 1–11.

HÖRNES, M.; FIALA, F. 1898. *Die neolithische Station von Butmir bei Sarajevo in Bosnien.* Vienna.

HÖRNES, M.; RADIMSKY, W. 1895. *Die neolithische Station von Butmir bei Sarajevo in Bosnien.* Vienna.

IVANOV, I. S. 1975. Raskopki na Varnenskija eneoliten nekropol prez 1972 g. *Izvest. Narod. Muz. Varna* (Varna), Vol. 11, pp. 1–16.

JOVANOVIĆ, B. 1979a. Rudarstvo i metalurgija eneolitskog perioda Jugoslavije. In: BENAC, A. (ed.), *Praistorija jugoslovenskih zemalja.* Sarajevo. t.3, pp. 27–54.

—— 1979b. Stepska kultura u eneolitskom periodu Jugoslavije. In: BENAC, A. (ed.), *Praistorija jugoslovenskih zemalja.* Sarajevo. t.3, pp. 381–95.

—— 1982. *Rudan Glava.* Beograd.

KALICZ, N. 1965. *Die Peceler (Badener) Kultur und Anatolien.* Budapest.

—— 1980. The Balaton-Lasinja Culture Groups in Western Hungary, Austria and Northwestern Yugoslavia, Concerning their Distribution and Origin. *J. Indo-Eur. Stud.* (Washington), Vol. 8, pp. 245–71.

KALICZ, N.; MAKKAY, J. 1977. *Die Linienbandkeramik in der grossen Ungarischen Tiefebene.* Budapest.

KOROSĔC, J. 1958/9. *Neolitska naselba u Danilu-Bitinju.* 2 vols. Zagreb.

KUTZIAN, I. 1947. *The Körös Culture.* Budapest.

LAZAROVICI, G. 1980. *Neoliticul Banatului.* Cluj-Napoca.

—— 1983. Die Vinča-Kultur und ihre Beziehungen zur Linien-bandkeramik. *Nachr. Niedersachs. Urgesch.* (Hildesheim), Vol. 53, pp. 131–76.

LEKOVIČ, V. 1985. The Mortuary Starčevo Practice. *God. Cent. Balkanol. Ispit.* (Sarajevo), Vol. 23, pp. 157–82.

MARINESCU-BÎLCU, S. 1974. *Culture Precucuteni pe teritoriul Romänei* [The Precucuteni Culture in the Territory of Romania]. Bucharest.

MASSON, E. 1984. L'Écriture dans les civilisations danubiennes néo-lithiques. *Kadmos* (Berlin), Vol. 23, pp. 90–123.

MERPERT, N. J. 1982. Eneolit SSSR part IV [The Eneolithic in the USSR Part IV]. In: MASSONV V. I.; MERPERT, N. J. (eds), *Eneolit SSSR.* Moscow. pp. 321–32.

MIKOV, V. 1933. *Predistoriceski Selista i raskopki v Bulgaria* [Pre-historical Settlements and Excavations in Bulgaria]. Sofia.

MILOJČIĆ, V. 1949. *Chronologie der jüngeren Steinzeit Mittel-und Südo-steuropas.* Berlin.

MORINTZ, S.; ROMAN, P. 1968. Aspekte des Ausgangs des Aene-olithikums und der Übergangszeit zur Bronzezeit im Raum der Niederdonau. *Dacia* (Bucharest), NS, Vol. 12, pp. 45–128.

NESTOR, I. 1933. Der Stand der Vorgeschichtsforschung in Rum-änien. *Ber. Röm.-Ger. Komm.* (Frankfurt/Main), Vol. 22, pp. 11–181.

NESTOR, I.; ZAHARIA, E. 1968. Sur la période de transition du néolithique à l'âge du bronze dans l'aire des civilisations de Cucuteni et de Gumelnitsa. *Dacia* (Bucharest), NS, Vol. 12, pp. 17–44.

NICA, M. 1977. Nouvelles Données sur le néolithique ancien d'Ol-ténie. *Dacia* (Bucharest), NS, Vol. 21, pp. 13–54.

NOVAK, G. 1955. *Prethistoriski Hvar* (Hvar Prehistory). Zagreb.

ORSIĆ-SLAVETIĆ, A. 1940. Bujanj, eine prähistorische Ansiedlung bei Nis. *Mitt. Prähist. Komm. Akad. Wiss.* (Vienna), Vol. 4, No. 1/2, pp. 1–46.

PANAJOTOV, I.; DERGAČOV, V. 1984. Die Ockergrabkultur in Bul-garien (Darstellung des Problems). *Stud. Praehist.* (Sofia), Vol. 7, pp. 99–116.

PASSEK, T. S. 1949. *Periodizacija tripol'skih poselenij* [Dating of Tri-polye Settlements]. Moscow. (Mat. issled. arheol. SSSR.).

—— 1961. *Rannezemledel'ceskie pleumena Podneprovija.* Moscow. (Mat. issled. arheol. SSSR.)

PAUL, I. 1981. Die gegenwärtige Forschung zur Petresti-Kultur. *Prähist. Z.* (Berlin), Vol. 66, pp. 197–324.

PAUNESCU, A. 1970. *Evolutia uneltelor si armelor de piatra cioplite descoperite pe teritoriul Romänici.* Bucharest.

PAVUK, J.; ČORBADŽIEV, M. 1984. Neolithische Tellsiedlung bei Gâlâbnik in Westbulgarien. *Slov. Archeol.* (Nitra), Vol. 32, pp. 195–228.

PRENDI, F. 1976. Neolithi dë eneoliti ne Shgiperi. *Iliria* (Tirana), Vol. 6, pp. 21–101.

—— 1982. The Prehistory of Albania. In: *Cambridge Ancient History.* 3rd edn. Cambridge. Vol. 3, pp. 187–237.

RADUNČEVA, A. 1976. *Prehistoric Art in Bulgaria.* Oxford. (BAR Int. Ser., 13.)

RENFREW, C. 1970. The Place of the Vinča-Culture in European Prehistory. *Zb. Narod. Muz.* (Beograd), Vol. 6, pp. 45–57.

ROMAN, P. 1974. Das Problem der 'schnurverzierten' Keramik in Siebenbürgen. *Jahrb. Mitteldtsch. Vorgesch.* (Halle), Vol. 58, pp. 157–74.

—— 1976. *Cultura Cotofeni* (Cotofeni Culture). Bucharest.

—— 1983. Der Übergang vom Neolithikum zur Bronzezeit auf dem Gebiet Rumäniens. *God. Cent. balkanol. Ispit.* (Sarajevo), Vol. 21, pp. 115–34.

ROMAN, P.; NEMETI, J. 1978. *Cultura Baden in Romänia* [The Baden Culture in Romania]. Bucharest.

ROSKA, M. 1941. *A Torma Zsofia-Gyüjtemény az Erdélyi Nemzeti Museum érem es régiségtaraban.* Kolszvar. (With German translation.)

SANEV, V. 1975. Neolitichka nazielia rumania kaj c gorubinii. *Ietiernik chtinskist Nargdien Mus.* (Stip), Vol. 4–5, pp. 203–22.

SCHMIDT, H. 1932. *Cucuteni in der Oberen-Moldau, Rumänien.* Berlin/Leipzig.

SCHMIDT, R. R. 1945. *Die Burg Vučedol.* Zagreb.

SCHUBERT, F.; SCHUBERT, E. 1965. Zu den osteuropäischen Kup-feräxten. *Germania* (Frankfurt/Main), Vol. 23, pp. 274–95.

SEFERIADIS, A. 1983. Introduction à la préhistoire de la Macédoine orientale. *Bull. Corresp. hell.* (Paris), Vol. 107, pp. 635–77.

SIMOSKA, D.; SANEV, V. 1975. Neolitichka Naselba Vieluska Tumba kaj Vitona. *Maced. Acta Archaeol.* (Prilep), Vol. 1, pp. 25–88.

SREJOVIĆ, D. 1979. Protoneolitske kulture [Protoneolithic Culture].

In: BENAC, A. (ed.), *Praistorija jugoslovenskih zemalja*. Sarajevo. t.2, pp. 33–76.

—— (ed.) 1984. *Vinča*. Beograd. (Catalogue of an exhibition in Beograd.)

SREJOVIĆ, D.; LETICA, Z. 1979. *Vlassač I–II*. Beograd.

SREJOVIĆ, D. et al. 1969. *Lepenski Vir*. Beograd.

STALIO, B. 1984. Houses and Settlements. In: SREJOVIČ, D. (ed.), *Vinča*. Beograd. pp. 34–41, 199–203. (Catalogue of an exhibition in Beograd.)

TASIČ, N. 1979a. Bujanj-Salcuţa-Krivodol kompleks [The Bubanj-Salcuta-Krivodol Complex]. In: BENAC, A. (ed.), *Praistorija jugoslovenskih semalja*. Sarajevo. t.3, pp. 87–114.

—— 1979b. Coţofeni kultura [Cotofeni Culture]. In: BENAC, A. (ed.), *Praistorija jugoslovenskih zemalja*. Sarajevo. t.3, pp. 115–28.

—— 1979c. Kostolacka kultura [Kostolac Culture]. In: BENAC, A. (ed.), *Praistorija jugoslovenskih semalja*. Sarajevo. t.3, pp. 235–66.

THEOCHARIS, D. et al. 1973. *Neolithic Greece*. Athens.

TODOROVA, H. 1976. *Sostarovo*. Sofia.

—— 1978. *The Eneolithic Period in Bulgaria*. Oxford. (BAR Int. Ser., 49.)

—— 1979. *Eneolit Bulgarii* [The Eneolithic in Bulgaria]. Sofia.

TODOROVA, H. et al. 1976. *Selistnata mogila pri golmio Dielzevo. Raskopki i Porucvanija V.* Sofia.

TOMPA, F. 1935–6. Fünfundzwanzig Jahre Urgeschichtsforschung in Ungarn. *Ber. Röm.-Ger. Komm.* (Frankfurt/Main), Vol. 14/15, pp. 27–128.

THRINGHAM, R. 1971. *Hunters, Fishers and Farmers in Eastern Europe, 6000–3000 BC*. London.

VAJSOVA, H. 1966. Der Stand der Jungsteinzeitforchung in Bulgarien. *Slov. Arheol.* (Bratislava), Vol. 14, pp. 5–48.

VASIĆ, M. M. 1907–8. South-Eastern Elements in the Prehistoric Culture of Serbia. *Ann. Br. Sch. Athens* (London), pp. 319–42.

—— 1932. *Preistorijska Vinča I* [Prehistoric Vinča I]. Beograd.

—— 1936. *Preistorijska Vinča II-IV* [Prehistoric Vinča II–IV]. Beograd.

VLASSA, N. 1970. Kulturelle Beziehungen des Neolithikums Siebenbürgens zum Vorderen Orient. *Acta Mus. Napocensis* (Cluj), Vol. 8, pp. 3–39.

—— 1972. Eine frühneolithische Kultur mit bemalter Keramik der Vor-Starčevo-Körös-Zeit in Cluj-Gura Baciului. *Prähist. Z.* (Berlin), Vol. 47, pp. 174–97.

VULIĆ, N.; GRBIĆ, M. 1938. *Corpus Vasorum Antiquorum. Yougoslavie*. Beograd, Musée du Prince Paul. Fasc. 3.

VULPE, R. 1957. *Izvoare, sapaturile din 1936–1949*. Bucharest.

ZIRRA, V. 1960. Kult'ura Progrebenij s scroi v zakapatskih obeasthah rir. In: *Materialy i isledovanija po arheologii yugo-zlapada SSSR i Rumynskoj Narodnoj Respubliki*. Kishinev. pp. 97–128.

51

CENTRAL EUROPE

during the Neolithic

Jens Lüning

HISTORY OF RESEARCH

Modern scientific research into the Neolithic cultures in central Europe (Müller-Karpe, 1968, pp. 1–17, 1979, pp. 188–265; Jazdzewski, 1984, pp. 13–44) began with the spectacular discovery of the Swiss 'lake dwellings' by Ferdinand Keller in 1853–4. This made it suddenly clear that in this area there was once a Stone Age people complete with crop farming, animal husbandry and well-developed architecture. Equally significant was the fact that from the outset specialists in the natural sciences and in particular zoologists and botanists played an important part in the investigations of these wetland settlements and the organic remains they preserved so well (Kimmig, 1981; Smolla, 1981). Since that time co-operation between archaeologists and natural scientists has continued to be one of the most important features of research into the central European Neolithic. Apart from economic questions, the main concern has been with reconstructing the Neolithic environment: climate, soil, flora and fauna.

In the second half of the nineteenth century there was a big increase in the volume of discoveries. Wetland settlements were brought to light throughout the region around the Alps as in Switzerland (Willvonseder, 1968). From the most important regions where finds have been made in central Europe, that is the loess-covered plains and river basins of the highlands, mention should be made of the burial site of Hinkelstein near Worms (Germany), which was found in 1866 and after which a culture has been named (Meier-Arendt, 1975). By the end of the century the time was ripe for systematizing the knowledge that had been gained and for the first time all the major central European cultural groups were defined (Bandkeramik, Grossgartach, Rössen, Michelsberg, Corded Ware, Bell-Beaker). It took another thirty years and intensive discussion by many authors before these groups were put into their correct chronological order, and work on refining the system is still going on.

In the period between the two World Wars, settlement archaeology questions held the stage. It was already known by the turn of the century that Neolithic people had built huge earthworks consisting of ditches, banks and palisades (Lehner, 1910). But it was not until later that the first outlines of dwellings and, indeed, complete settlements were discovered in Aichbühl (Germany) (Schmidt, 1937), Köln-Lindenthal (Germany) (Buttler and Haberey, 1936) and Brześć Kujawski (Poland) (Jazdzewski, 1938). After the interruption of the Second World War, settlement archaeology developed with considerable vigour and the study of economic and ecological aspects has been added. Particularly large-scale excavations have been undertaken at Bylany in the Czech Republic (Soudský, 1966; Pavlů, 1982), the southern part of the Netherlands (Modderman, 1970; Bakels, 1978), the Aldenhoven plateau in western Germany (Lüning, 1982a) and the Aisne valley in France (Ilett et al., 1982).

A novel methodological approach is observable in recent years. Because of the extensive nature of the excavations, interest has widened from the individual settlement to complete settlement units and micro-regions, and the settlement structures, ecology, economic functions and social organization of these limited geographic areas have been studied in their systematic interrelationships (Kruk, 1980; Bakels, 1982, Lüning 1982b; Milisauskas and Kruk, 1984).

Investigation of the wetland settlements of the northern Alps continued after the nineteenth century with varying intensity. More recently, modern excavations have been carried out particularly in Switzerland (Stöckli, 1981) and the Lake Constance area in southern Germany (Schlichtherle, 1985). As a result of the many stratigraphic studies and because of the remarkable preservation of organic material the picture of the cultures has changed at a rapid pace. Dendrochronological findings have been particularly important for absolute dating purposes (Ruoff, 1978).

Other aspects of Neolithic culture have been less intensively studied. Thirty years ago Ulrich Fischer developed new methods of analysing graves and burial places (Fischer, 1956). A. Häusler is responsible for some remarkable interpretations (Häusler, 1966). Since then, however, the quantity of material produced has increased only very slowly and it was not until the 1970s that new major burial sites were found (Pavúk, 1972), though information about most of them has not yet been published.

The Neolithic period is subdivided differently in the various European countries. The later part is called the Copper Age in Hungary, the Eneolithic in former Czechoslovakia and the Young Neolithic in southern Germany, the terms for the earlier periods differing in similar ways (Behrens, 1973, p. 15, Fig. 2). These differences reflect the fact that the use of copper originated in the Balkans and spread into central Europe and in that area was more intensive in the east than the west. In this chapter the neutral terms Lower, Middle and Upper Neolithic are used (Driehaus, 1960, pp. 1–11). The archaeological cultures and groups of the Neolithic are defined with the help of pottery and primarily represent a space–time scheme of pottery styles. They provide a convenient framework for dating all other Neolithic cultural phenomena (Eggert, 1978; Klejn, 1982).

Absolute dating has evolved from a traditional short chronology, allowing only about 1,000 years for the whole of the Neolithic to the present-day long chronology. Based on radiocarbon dating and calibration, this postulates that there were about 3,000 years from the beginning of the Bandkeramik to the beginnings of the Beaker cultures (Table 18) but this 'long' chronology has only been current for a few years and its implications for cultural history have not yet been fully elucidated (Neustupný, 1969; Quitta, 1971).

Table 18 Chronology of the most important Neolithic cultures in central Europe. BP: years before present (calibrated); b.p.: radio-carbon-dated years before present (uncalibrated).

BP	Neolithic periods	Cultures			b.p.
		West	Middle	East	
4,900					4,300
	Upper	Horgen, Cham	Řivnáč		
				Baden	
		Michelsberg	Trichter-becher		
				Lengyel (unpainted)	
6,400					5,500
	Middle	Bischheim Rössen	Stich band keramik	Lengyel (painted)	
		Großgartach			
6,800					6,000
	Lower	Bandkeramik			
7,800					7,000

ORIGINS OF NEOLITHIC CULTURE

The Neolithic period began in central Europe 7,800 years ago with, from the outset, fully developed agriculture based on crop and animal farming. These early farmers were sedentary and, for the first time in Europe, built big and permanent wooden dwellings. They also began the production of pottery described as Bandkeramik because of its banded decoration (Müller-Karpe, 1968, pp. 113–39).

The sedentary life-style was necessary and possible because the fields needed attention over a long period and produced a considerable yield. Grain was probably the most important source of plant food, so that relatively large amounts had to be stored each year against future food and sowing requirements. Winter feed for the cattle was another bulky requirement that could not be transported and made sedentism a necessity.

The Bandkeramik was the most widespread of all the Neolithic cultures in central Europe. In its earliest phase it stretched over 1,000 km from eastern Hungary to western Germany. Its latest forms, between Normandy and the Ukraine, were some 2,000 km apart (Map 62). It preferred the best European arable land – the loess lands – and therefore ranged, as did the loess, between the Alps and the northern

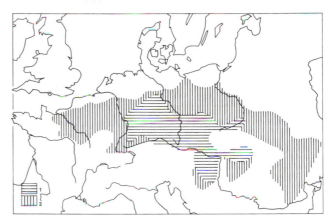

Map 62 Expansion of the Bandkeramik culture: 1, oldest phase (7,800 to 7,300 years ago); 2, later expansion (7,300 to 6,800 years ago).

edge of the highland area of Europe. In the northern European lowlands the Bandkeramik penetrated only where loess or similar soils were available, in the lower reaches of the Oder and the Vistula.

The Bandkeramik began in the middle Atlantic period with a mild oceanic climate featuring relatively high summer moisture levels (Frenzel, 1977, p. 308). Temperatures were probably some 2 °C higher and the climate wetter than today (Bakels, 1978, pp. 11–17). The whole area was wooded. Research based on pollen analysis suggests that the trees were deciduous and consisted of oak, lime, ash, maple and elm. In the west, more affected by maritime climate, lime trees were the dominant species so that the forest is assumed to have been dark and closed in with little undergrowth, grass or herbage and very little game (Bakels, 1978, pp. 28–43). In the more continental eastern part of central Europe more pine trees and other conifers grew, particularly in the medium-altitude mountain areas (Firbach, 1949).

The prevailing view in present-day cultural history research is that the earliest Bandkeramik farmers were immigrants into central Europe. Their animals, including goats and sheep, which must have been imported because there were no indigenous forms of these species, were domesticated from the outset. The same applies to most of the plants that were farmed and especially cereals. Since the earliest pottery (Fig. 147) shows considerable similarity to the ceramics of the Starčevo–Körös culture in the Carpathian basin, the whole of the early Neolithic culture complex was probably brought into existence by stimuli from south-eastern Europe (Quitta, 1964) and, given the many alien elements, immigration must presumably have played a major role in the process. On the anthropological side, however, opinions vary and recently there has, instead, been emphasis on the significant contribution made by the indigenous population (Bernhard, 1978).

In fact, the Neolithic began in south-eastern Europe at an earlier date (Quitta, 1960, 1971; Pavúk, 1980; Kalicz, 1983).

Certainly there were clear differences from the start from Starčevo–Körös pottery, particularly in the case of the scratched ornamentation which only occurs in the Bandkeramik. This suggests that the earliest Bandkeramik arose in direct contact with but outside the Starčevo-Körös area, in western and northern Hungary, former Czechoslovakia and eastern Austria. This is where the economic and technical equipment of the new agriculture-orientated culture adapted to central European climate and soil conditions must have originated and developed. A particular feature was the development of a new type of house which, to suit the higher rainfall of central Europe, was protected by its walls and roof and had a larger interior capacity than the small houses of the south-eastern European Neolithic. This new, larger, dwelling proved so successful that the type was adopted more or less generally and is rightly regarded as one of the most important characteristics of the Bandkeramik culture.

The appearance of the Neolithic in central Europe is therefore to be regarded as a colonizing process in which, after the first wave of immigrants had arrived from outside, the surplus population was produced by the Bandkeramik culture itself (Quitta, 1964). It must have come into contact with an indigenous hunting and gathering society, too, alien to the colonizing farmers. In a historical situation like this the relations between the two sides frequently pursue a hostile course, ending with the expulsion of the hunters and gatherers; assimilation is likely to have been the exception (Vencl, 1982). Unfortunately there is a lack of informative Late Mesolithic settlements and burial sites in central Europe, so that for the time being there is very little, archaeologically speaking, to be said about this problem (Taute, 1980). Neither are there any indications pointing to contact with the indigenous population in the earliest Bandkeramik settlements.

SPACE–TIME STRUCTURE OF NEOLITHIC CULTURES

Lower Neolithic

Even during the middle Lower Neolithic, the uniform Bandkeramik culture split up into large regional blocs. First, in the eastern area, there was the '*Notenkopfkeramik*' in which, with increasing frequency, pits were punched on the lines of the decoration themselves, resembling musical notation (Fig. 147), whereas, in the west, pit-filled bands came to the fore so that two major style provinces were formed whose boundary ran roughly between Bohemia and Moravia (Tichy, 1962; Pavúk and Šiška, 1971, p. 360; Pavlů, 1978).

By about 6,800 years ago this regionalization had developed further. In eastern Hungary later groups of the *Alföld Linienbandkeramik* had arisen that could no longer be placed within the overall context of the Bandkeramik culture (Kalicz and Makkay, 1977). The Želiezovce group had its centre in western Slovakia (Pavúk, 1969). In Bohemia and central Germany the first beginnings of the Stichbandkeramik culture were becoming manifest (Steklá, 1959; Zápotocká, 1967). In the Rhine area several decorative styles had developed with varying regional focuses (Meier-Arendt, 1972). Here very late Bandkeramik groups like Hinkelstein and Gehring (Meier-Arendt, 1975; Dohrn-Immig, 1974) extended into the Middle Neolithic. The same applies to the Bandkeramik in western Belgium (De Laet, 1972) and in northern France (Bailloud, 1976). As in eastern Hungary, material on the western periphery, in Normandy, has only loose connections with the Bandkeramik tradition.

This process of intensifying regionalization was evidently the result of diminishing contacts between the major settlement centres in central Europe. The mobility that had existed during the earliest part of the Neolithic (stage I) had declined. So long as the agricultural boundary was moving west during the colonization phase, the surplus population it needed probably came from throughout the hinterland, so

that a gigantic and unified cultural area came into being through the many contacts that occurred (Map 62). During the consolidation in phase II as well (Flomborn and Ackovy pottery styles) there must have been intensive internal migration because the pottery style remained uniform.

As research in the Rhineland (Dohrn-Immig, 1979, p. 297; Lüning, 1982a, p. 23) and in the Rhein–Main area (Sielmann, 1972, pp. 46–51) has shown, population density rose vigourously in the Middle and Upper Bandkeramik and then declined again steeply. This has to be regarded as the greatest reason for the regionalization process. Agriculture brought about the development of mother and daughter settlements with local dependencies and traditions. As resources became scarcer they had to be distributed fairly by means of supra-local organization so that it may be assumed that social institutions developed drawing small and large settlements together and that a regional system of exchange built up as well. Together they could well have brought about the development of regional traditions. The archaeological expression of this process has so far been found in pottery style characteristics, but it ought to be possible to find other proofs – in the more intensive use of regional stone as a raw material, for example. In anthropology, authors have already been referring for some time to regional differences between population groups within the Bandkeramik (Bernhard, 1978).

Middle Neolithic

Between about 6,800 and 6,300 years ago three great pottery style provinces arose centred on the Danube, Elbe and Rhine basins (Map 63). Bandkeramik was everywhere the ethnic and cultural basis, but in every case underwent a fundamental transformation. This happened most intensively in the east, where the Lengyel culture with its richly coloured pottery (stages I and II) developed between western Hungary and Moravia (Pavúk, 1981). Influences from the Balkan area were no doubt involved. During the course of its development, the Lengyel culture spread increasingly towards the north and west and influenced neighbouring cultures (Map 63).

In the middle Elbe, that is in Bohemia and Saxo-Thuringia, the Stichbandkeramik culture had formed (Steklá, 1959; Kaufmann, 1976), its border areas including lower Bavaria, northern Moravia and Silesia. The later Lengyel culture, whose unpainted phases (III, IV) already

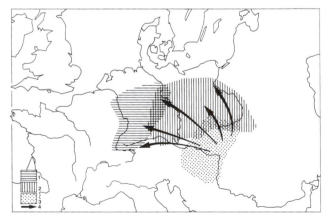

Map 63 Three important Middle Neolithic cultures centred around the Rhine, the Elbe and the middle Danube: 1, Rössen culture; 2, Stichbandkeramik culture; 3, Lengyel culture; 4, expansion of the Lengyel culture.

Upper Neolithic

Cham

Rivnáč

Baden

Bernburg

Michelsberg
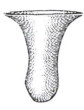

Trichterbecher
Baalberg

Lengyel
unpainted

Middle Neolithic

Rössen

Stichbandkeramik

Lengyel
painted

Großgartach

Lower Neolithic

Bandkeramik

Figure 147 Some main pottery types of the central European Neolithic.

fall within the Upper Neolithic (Fig. 147) developed at the expense of the Stichbandkeramik culture, which was first ousted from the border areas, transformed in the heartland and finally completely supplanted by the latest Lengyel groups (Aichbühl, Münchshöfen, Gatersleben, Kolín, Ottitz, Modlnica–Zlotniki–Wyciaze, Jordansmühl–Jordanów, Brześć-Kujawski) (Lüning, 1971; Lichardus, 1976a).

At the same time, in the Rhine area, the Middle Neolithic Grossgartach had developed out of the Hinkelstein group, and the Rössen out of the Grossgartach (Meier-Arendt, 1969). With the Rössen pottery an extensive style province once again arose, for a short time, in the west, stretching from the Alpine foothills to the lower Rhine and towards central Germany. Under the influence of the expansive late Lengyel culture in the late Rössen horizon, this unit broke up into a large number of small regional groups, the most important in terms of future development being the Bischheim group in the Rhine valley, the Schwieberdingen group in the Neckar province and the Wauwil group in eastern Switzerland (Lüning, 1971). During all this time it was in the west, screened by the Stichbandkeramik culture so that the Lengyel influences would only penetrate this far in a weakened form, that indigenous traditions were kept alive most strongly.

Research on the Middle Neolithic between the Rhine and the Seine is so far insufficient. Here the Cerny group arose from a late Bandkeramik base, extending into the Middle Neolithic, but too little is yet known about the inventory of its culture (Bailloud, 1976). The recently discovered Blicquy group also belongs to this period (Constantin, 1985).

Not long ago a range of typical Bischheim artefacts was found in the valley of the Aisne, north-east of Paris (Demoule and Ilett, 1978; Duboulez et al., 1984). Together with material discovered earlier in west Belgium (Moisin and Joris, 1972), this points to a common late Middle Neolithic cultural horizon embracing the area between the Rhine and the Seine. It would also mean that, as in the late Bandkeramik, a strong cultural impulse was once again transmitted westwards from the Rhine.

Earlier researchers felt the traditional connection between the Bandkeramik and the Middle Neolithic to be so strong that the term 'Danubian province' or 'Donauländischen Kreis' was used (Childe, 1929; Buttler, 1938). It has since become clear that the Bandkeramik traditions in central Europe were handed down to a variable extent. The strongest upheavals were in the east, where Lengyel Keramik represented a radically new beginning which, stage by stage, transformed and finally supplanted the Stichbandkeramik culture and whose effects were to be traced even as far as the Rhine. The picture is therefore one of a wave of innovation that weakened as it moved from east to west, so that Bandkeramik traditions were preserved longest in the west.

Upper Neolithic

Early Upper Neolithic

During the westward spread of the Lengyel culture (stages III and IV) two completely new factors entered the arena of central European cultural development: the Funnel-Beaker culture in the north and the Western Neolithic (Map 64). The Neolithic peasant culture first halted for a long time at the northern boundary of the loess which to some extent coincided with the northern boundary of the highlands. In the later Middle Neolithic the Rössen and Stichbandkeramik

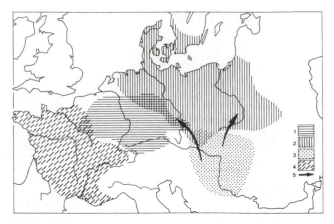

Map 64 The most important Upper Neolithic cultures in central, western and northern Europe: 1, Michelsberg culture; 2, Funnel Beaker culture; 3, Late Lengyel and Baden cultures; 4, Chassey culture; 5, expansion of the Baden culture.

cultures began to advance into the north European Lowlands (Kulczycka-Leciejewiczowa, 1970; Schwabedissen, 1979). In the Baltic area they encountered an intact hunting–gathering culture (the Ertebølle–Ellerbek) and developed active relations as far as south Scandinavia. Out of these influences a new Neolithic culture developed in the northern highlands, the northern lowlands and southern Scandinavia known as the Funnel-Beaker culture. Here only its southern area, where it coincided with part of the Lower Neolithic settlement area, is dealt with (Chapter 54).

The so-called 'A/B Keramik' is described as the oldest phase of the Funnel-Beaker culture (Becker, 1947, 1954; Steinmetz, 1982). Material of this kind comes from the Kujawy black earth area on the lower Vistula, settled since Bandkeramik times (Sarnowo: Kowalszyk, 1970, p. 167), from Bohemia (Božice: Lichardus, 1976b) and from the Rhine valley. Here the early Funnel-Beaker culture occurs among some groups of the late Rössen horizon (Bischheim, Strasbourg, Schwieberdingen) and represents the origins of Upper Neolithic cultural development (Lüning, 1971).

From these roots there arose the Michelsberg culture, the most important product of the northern influences in the Rhine area (Lüning, 1968). In the older literature, however, it is attributed to a 'western cultural area' (Buttler, 1938), and with good reason because it is at this time that the Western Neolithic first appears as an independent factor on an equal footing with the Danubian central European cultural tradition. The Neolithic had, it is true, already begun much earlier in southern France but in the early stages it was limited to that region (Chapter 49). The western European cultural province did not reach northern France, which was previously Bandkeramik territory, the foothills of the Swiss Alps (Sauter and Gallay, 1969; Winiger, 1981) and as far as the Rhine until some time in the later Middle Neolithic. It was as the Upper Neolithic began that it first took an active part in central European cultural development.

The strongest evidence for this is the Michelsberg culture, which from the outset showed strong western features in its pottery (Lüning, 1968; Eckert, 1979). Its independence of the northern Funnel-Beaker culture is based not only on indigenous tradition but primarily on these western European influences. Early Michelsberg finds have recently been made in the Paris area (Mordant and Mordant, 1978; Le Bolloch, 1984). This has widened the area of origin of the Michelsberg culture, as already indicated by the Bischheim finds, to the broad zone between the Rhine and the Seine, enabling the western influences to be correctly understood for the first time.

These influences stemmed from the Chassey culture that was in direct contact with the Michelsberg culture in the Paris region (Bailloud, 1976; Mordant, 1980). Together with the Cortaillod culture in western Switzerland the Chassey culture formed the eastern edge of the Western Neolithic (Chapter 49).

In eastern Switzerland, on the other hand, it was the Michelsberg-related Pfyn culture that prevailed and formed the boundary of the central European cultural zone (Winiger, 1981; Kustermann, 1984). It is also related to a series of regional pottery groups which J. Driehaus lumps together in a 'north-Alpine province' (Driehaus, 1960, p. 209). They include the Altheim culture in lower Bavaria and the Baalberge culture in central Germany (Preuss, 1966) and Bohemian and Moravian sub-groups of the Funnel-Beaker culture (Houštová, 1960). Closely related are four groups with decorated pottery: the Schussenried in Würt-temberg (Lüning, 1971, p. 41), the Mondsee group in Upper Austria (Ruttkay, 1981, 1983), the Balaton group in western Hungary (Kalicz, 1973) and the Jordansmühl–Jordanów culture in Silesia, Bohemia and Moravia (Lüning, 1976).

It is difficult, in this complex of cultures, to reconstruct the spatial structure of the Middle Neolithic. Direct heirs of the Rössen culture were the Michelsberg (via Bischheim) and the Schussenried group (via Schwieberdingen). The Pfyn group must have developed out of the late Rössen group, Wauwil. What is more, both groups reveal an important stage in settlement history: the very first appearance of Neolithic cultures in the Alpine foreland. This also involved the Upper Austrian Mondsee culture, which came into being without any regional precursors. As stated, it lay on the edge of the north Alpine province which mainly developed in the area of what was once the Stich-bandkeramik culture and of the late Lengyel culture, which had, as described, finally ousted the Stichbandkeramik culture. That is how the Altheim culture came to follow the Münchshöfen Lengyel group in lower Bavaria. Further to the north-east, the southern groups of the Funnel-Beaker culture developed out of the late Lengyel groups in Saxo-Thuringia, Bohemia, Moravia and to some extent lower Austria.

To the east, the Lengyel culture was also inherited by the Funnel-Beaker culture (eastern group) which developed in Silesia and Great and Little Poland (Kowalszyk, 1970). The Balaton group in the north-west Carpathian area also stemmed from the Lengyel culture and, with its decorated pottery, was closely related to the other decorated pottery groups.

As a whole, central Europe was extremely closely related at this time to the north European Funnel-Beaker culture, whose essential characteristics are to be perceived through-out the area between the edge of the Alps and southern Scandinavia. Middle Neolithic elements were more mark-edly handed down in the interspersed decorated pottery groups. On the western edge of central Europe influences of the Western Neolithic made themselves felt as did those of the Copper Age cultures of the Carpathian basin on the eastern edge. Here the east Hungarian area was of particular importance for it is there that the intensive production and working of copper began with the Tiszapolgar followed by the Bodrogkeresztur culture (Bognár-Kutzian, 1969, 1972). So it is from here that the stimuli came that resulted in independent copper production in central Europe (see p. 547).

Late Upper Neolithic

In this last phase of the central European Neolithic prior to the emergence of the Beaker cultures which once again reunited the whole area, central Europe featured a het-erogeneous miscellany of forms. The strongest radiation came from the Baden culture, a new cultural power centre in the eastern part of central Europe (Neustupný, 1973). The area where it originated lay between the north-western Carpathian basin and Moravia, in other words precisely where the Lengyel culture had also been born. In fact the Baden culture showed very similar tendencies in the way it spread, but its overall influence was less (Map 64). With marginal groups it reached the areas of Bohemia and Little Poland where it was the successor to the Funnel-Beaker culture. Lower Austria was also part of the area to which the Baden culture extended and so was the whole of the Carpathian basin (Petrasch, 1984).

Later Funnel-Beaker culture groups developed to the north of the Baden culture (Great Poland, central Germany). In the west the situation is not altogether clear. Though successor groups can be given for the cultures in the area of the northern Alps (southern Germany – Wartberg and Goldberg III: see Schwellnus, 1979; Spennemann, 1984; lower Bavaria – Chamer group, see Vriezen, 1977; Uenze, 1987; eastern Switzerland – Horgen culture: see Itten, 1970), conclusive finds are lacking in the area over which the Michelsberg culture extended, at any rate in the Rhine valley (Pape, 1978). It is only in the Paris basin and in Belgium that there is a proven successor to the Michelsberg, namely the Seine–Oise–Marne culture (Bailloud, 1976).

In general terms, the central European area at this time lay in the field of tension between the Baden culture in the east, the Funnel-Beaker culture in the north and the Seine–Oise–Marne culture in the west. The constellation that had developed in the early Upper Neolithic thus continued in existence. Central Europe was no uniform and enclosed cultural area but instead was covered by a mosaic of small cultural territories exposed to manifold external influences.

ECONOMY AND TECHNOLOGY

Agriculture

The Bandkeramik culture was based, from its beginnings, on a fully developed agriculture-oriented economic system which included both crop growing and animal husbandry. These components remained closely associated throughout the Neolithic age that followed. There was no specialization in animal husbandry (the nomadic system), for example, in central Europe during this period. All the same, there will have been variations in the relative importance of one or the other aspect – an indirect inference from the fact that some of the settlements lay in the higher and wetter areas, which were more suitable for animal farming (Sielmann, 1971a, 1971b).

The Bandkeramik culture occupied the loess areas of central Europe. In many regions – the Rhineland for example – practically all settlements were located on loess (Dohrn-Ihmig, 1979, p. 215). Elsewhere, however, the rule did not apply, the proportion of settlements on loess in Bohemia being only 51 per cent (Rulf, 1982, p. 251). B. Sielmann (1972, p. 35) has looked into this question in western central Europe more closely. The unfavourable lands in what he describes as 'ecology area A' were chosen because the climate there was more favourable than in 'ecology area B'.

There were variations in time as well as space. Bandkeramik settlement increasingly included zones that were unfavourable and marginal in terms of both soil and climate and did not revert to the favourable territories occupied by the first settlers until the last phase (Sielmann, 1971a, p. 102; Dohrn-Ihmig, 1979, p. 227). Since the trend was accompanied by an increase and then a decrease in population, demographic growth and decline must have been one of the main reasons for the phenomenon. Later shifts in Middle and Late Neolithic settlement centres may have had other causes. In any case such processes must have brought about greater differentiation in agricultural production.

In general the Bandkeramik and most later settlements lay on the border between two biotopes, between the floodplains of the rivers and the higher terraces, reflecting the fact that farming settlements had to be built near water but at the same time protected against flooding. It is also generally assumed that floodplains were particularly good for grazing cattle and yet the relatively small areas they covered could have had only minor significance for this purpose since, in the densely settled loess areas, even the higher land between the rivers did not provide enough forest pasture (Bakels, 1982, p. 38).

The importance of animal husbandry seems generally to have increased during the 3,000 years of the Neolithic. For western central Europe, this is shown, for one thing, by the growth (Upper compared with Lower Neolithic) in the relative frequency of animal bones (Sielmann, 1971b). Throughout central Europe, settlement sites occur with increasing frequency in the Middle Neolithic and particularly in the Upper Neolithic which, on topographic and ecological grounds (altitude, rainfall, soil quality), must have been more suitable for animal than arable farming.

Since Lower Neolithic times the domestic animals included cattle, pigs, goats, sheep and dogs, with cattle generally predominating, though in the Upper Neolithic there were settlements of the Horgen and other cultures in the Alpine foothills where pigs were most numerous (Murray, 1970; Bökönyi, 1974). Whether the horse, evidence for which on an individual basis is repeatedly found from the Bandkeramik onwards, was already domesticated in the Upper Neolithic is not clear, but quite certainly this did happen in the Late Neolithic (Boessneck, 1958; Lichardus, 1980).

The general preference for the loess territories in the central European Neolithic shows that crop growing must have played a significant role. Grain (wheat, barley, millet), legumes (peas, lentils, beans), flax and poppy were used as crops. The oldest grain types were the einkorn and emmer wheats (*Triticum monococcum* and *T. dicoccum*) and the naked barley (*Hordeum vulgare*, var. *nudum*). Later other types of grain were added like rye (*Secale cereale*) and seed wheat (*Triticum sativum*) (Klichowska, 1976; Heitz et al., 1981). In line with the increasing continentality, from west to east, of the European climate, the combination of species cultivated changed as has recently been shown for the Lower Neolithic (Willerding, 1980).

Grain evidently served as the basic plant foodstuff. When one thinks of the lengthy process of labour from sowing the seed to using the produce (Hillman, 1984) and the fact that a full range of tools for cereal cultivation and processing was in existence – and in plenty – from the Bandkeramik onwards (sickles, millstones, ovens) it has to be assumed that cereals were cultivated intensively on a relatively large scale (Behm-

Blanke, 1962–63; Soudský, 1966). The first evidence of a primitive plough, the ard, dates from the Upper Neolithic, and some authors see this as an argument for a revolutionary transformation of agriculture (Sherratt, 1981). But the grave mounds under which the plough marks were preserved existed only from the Upper Neolithic so that, given the likely intensity of crop cultivation, ploughs could well have been in use from Bandkeramik times (Lüning, 1979–80). A positive pointer to this is the castration of oxen, which dated from the Bandkeramik (H. H. Müller, 1964). The more general assumption, however, failing further evidence, is that the land was tilled by hoe and spade.

Hunting and gathering

Wild animals were hunted throughout the Neolithic, but their share in the Lower Neolithic was generally well below 10 per cent. It was not until the Upper Neolithic that, in some areas and particularly the foothills of the Alps, it rose to 50 to 90 per cent (Boessneck et al., 1963). This is not interpreted as a return to a pre-Neolithic hunting economy but, on the contrary, as evidence of intensive arable farming. For one thing, the low proportion of domesticated animals shows that stock-farming played only a secondary role compared with crops and for another the forest was already allowing more light through in the Upper Neolithic, giving better conditions for game to survive in and therefore to reproduce. So, to protect their fields, the Neolithic farmer had to spend more time hunting (Uerpmann, 1977).

Little is known about the significance of fishing, the main reason probably being the poor chances of survival of fishbones but another being inadequate excavation techniques. Recently, however, a large quantity of fish remains was found in Liège (Belgium) in a late Bandkeramik settlement (Desse, 1984). The Bandkeramik is also represented in a specialized fish catching station at Lauterach on the upper Danube, which also continued to be used in the Middle and Upper Neolithic (Taute, 1967), so in general terms, it would be wrong to underestimate fishing as a means of obtaining food. Evidence of freshwater mussels and turtles is fairly frequent. The produce of wild plant-life, such as hazelnuts, wild fruit (apples, pears) and wild berries (blackberries, raspberries), was also gathered throughout the Neolithic but, given the nature of middle European flora, could never have represented more than a supplement of minor quantitative importance.

Raw materials, transport, technology

From the Upper Neolithic on, at the latest, there were ox-drawn carts with four wheels (Häusler, 1985). Nothing is known about any roads or bridges before the end of the Neolithic and vehicles must have been used primarily for local transport. Neolithic settlements were largely autonomous and obtained most of their food and building and other materials from the immediate environment (Bakels, 1978).

The long-distance transport of heavy loads could well have been carried out by river boat (dug-out) (Deichmüller, 1965). Spondylus shells, which were used as ornaments, represent classic evidence of economic relations, even in the Lower Neolithic, ranging right across the European continent (Willms, 1985) as does the amphibolite rock used for making hatchets and axes (Schwarz-Mackensen and Schneider, 1983). Flint (silex), which occurs only in certain regions and had been transported over long distances (up to

200 km) since Bandkeramik times, was particularly important. In the Upper Neolithic the flint quarries were supplying places up to 400 or 600 km away (Willms, 1982). (Chapter 56.)

Many mines in the late Upper Neolithic specialized in the production of a particular type of implement such as axeheads (for instance at Lousberg near Aachen). The axeheads were then finished, that is, ground and hafted, which took at least as long as quarrying the stone and producing the blanks, away from the mine. This suggests that the distribution of the finished tools was also carried out by specialist 'traders', although the question of whether the exchange of goods was organized as barter or with the help of a form of money is still a matter of debate (Pittioni, 1985). Much of the exchange procedure could well have had ritual and social aspects, though some bulk goods may have been traded on an economic basis.

Special craft knowledge was undoubtedly also necessary for the manufacture of copper articles. The use of copper for ornamental items began at the end of the Middle Neolithic (Lüning, 1981, p. 141) as a result of influences arriving from the Carpathian basin (Ottaway, 1973). During the Upper Neolithic, tools and weapons, like axes and daggers, were made mainly in the northern part of the Carpathian basin (Bognár-Kutzian, 1972; Pleslová-Štícková, 1977).

These examples clearly show that the Neolithic economy produced a large range of implements and goods, many of them in considerable quantity. For this to be so, specialized craftsmen must have existed since the Upper Neolithic. Their technical equipment was obviously relatively simple, because evidence of any complicated 'machinery' is lacking. But some rationalization of work processes was probable, in other words the use of simple machines, such as drilling tools for making beads (d'Aujourd'hui, 1977).

HOUSES, SETTLEMENTS AND SETTLEMENT AREAS

Lower Neolithic

Houses

Strangely enough, it is precisely the early part of Neolithic settlement history in central Europe about which most, so far, is known. One reason for this is that excavations have taken place in many countries over the wide area across which the Bandkeramik extended, so information is now available covering over 1,000 floor plans from this period. Another is that Lower Neolithic dwellings were particularly large and solidly constructed and above all built of deeply embedded posts, so that their ground plan has been particularly well preserved.

Even so, one should have no illusions about the great extent of destruction (Modderman, 1976). In every case the Bandkeramik settlements were located on the best arable land that has been tilled often continuously for 8,000 years; this explains why no house floors have been preserved in any part of central Europe, with the result that no direct observations regarding internal arrangements (fireplaces, working places, partition walling) have ever been possible. As a rule the excavation level is some 100 cm below the Neolithic surface, so that only postholes and traces of walls that were particularly deeply laid are left, mostly discernible for a depth of a further 20 to 40 cm. This means that posts and walls were, originally, sunk to a depth of 1.5 m and in

fact there are a few well-preserved buildings going down to that depth.

The houses of the earliest Bandkeramik period are also those with the most complex ground plan (Fig. 148). Four chambers can be discerned lengthwise and six naves in the transverse direction (Pavlů, 1982; Lüning and Modderman, 1982). In the middle of the dwelling there was a space relatively free of posts that was probably the living and working area. To the north-west there was another chamber with particularly strongly built walls, presumably for sleeping and storage of special items.

South-east of the central chamber there followed a part of the dwelling with double posts, one set probably supporting the roof and the other a storage loft. Here it may be assumed that stocks were stored which needed a particularly large area, like grain, winter feed for the animals or possibly straw. This southerly section was the end of the dwellings of the middle and later Bandkeramik; those of the earliest stages of the culture had an additional anteroom.

In the crosswise direction, between the walls, Bandkeramik houses had frames of three posts supporting the roof so that there were four naves. The centre row probably carried the ridge at the top of a gable roof. In the dwellings of the earliest stage the roof was brought down at the side almost to ground-level to give even more space for provisions – perhaps winter feed or firewood. To begin with there was just this type of dwelling with no ancillary buildings, so that all the functions of agricultural life had to be housed under the one roof. It is clear from this that these dwellings must have been very well adapted to the damp climate and long winter of central Europe. Parallel to the lengthwise walls ran narrow ditches evidently serving to drain away the rainwater running off the roof. From this, too, can be seen how necessary it was for the early farmers to have a large dry area. In contrast with southern Europe and the Mediterranean area, here life was clearly carried on more inside the dwellings than in the open.

Because of the large size of these 20 to 30 m-long dwellings, it has been assumed, e.g. by B. Soudský (1969), that they accommodated twenty to forty people at a time – a whole lineage in fact – but it is certain, from the typical distribution of internal space that the different chambers were intended to serve specific purposes so that it may well be imagined that a farming nuclear family of five to seven persons lived and worked in such a building.

The three-way division into north-west, central and south-eastern parts was retained throughout the Bandkeramik and it is interesting to note that in the middle and late Bandkeramik there were smaller-scale forms, structures that had only the north-west and central parts and even smaller buildings that had only the central part. A first conclusion is that the central part was the most important and must definitely, therefore, have served as accommodation. Secondly, a differentiation in the farming population also comes to light. It has been possible to show, at the Aldenhoven plateau site in the Rhineland, that the smaller dwellings, those in which there was no storage area, certainly used and processed grain but that no grain was cleaned (threshed and winnowed) in them. Conversely, in the excavations of dwellings with a south-eastern storage space, large quantities of refuse from the cleaning of harvested grain were found (Boelicke, 1982). On this basis a distinction is discernible between grain producers and consumers.

During the course of the Lower Neolithic a change is perceivable in the shape of the ground plan (Modderman, 1970). In the earliest stage of the Bandkeramik, the central

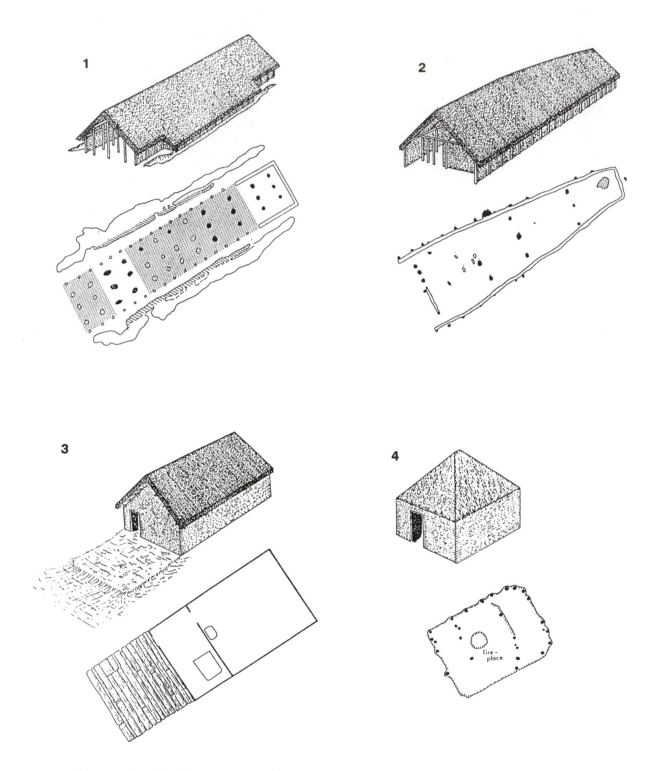

Figure 148 Development of Neolithic house-types, central Europe: 1, Lower Neolithic, Schwanfeld; 2, Middle Neolithic, Inden 1; 3, Early Upper Neolithic, Ehrenstein; 4, Late Upper Neolithic, Goldburghausen (Golberg), all Germany. (After Bersu, Kuper, Lüning, Zürn.)

part was practically free of posts. In the second stage (Flomborn) there was a post structure in the form of a 'Y' (though this was in the western part of the Bandkeramik area) whose purpose is unknown. In the later Bandkeramik the Y-shape is replace by two 3-post yokes.

Settlements and settlement areas

Because of the large settlement areas, often covered with numerous house outlines and pits, the tendency at one time was to refer to Bandkeramik 'villages', but careful analysis shows that only a few dwellings were standing at any given time and that the settlements often had a long and more or less continous history, for instance Bylany in Bohemia (Pavlů, 1977, 1982) and Elsloo in the Netherlands (van de Velde, 1979).

The biggest Bandkeramik settlement so far known consisted of eleven houses (Langweiler 8, Phase VII, Rhineland). They were an average of 74 m apart and spread over an area of 7 ha. There were no buildings of special prominence. Also to be found in the Rhineland were smaller settlements with two or three dwellings and finally some isolated individual houses (Lüning, 1982b). This distribution may be described as a loose, scattered settlement system including small and medium-size group settlements. Evidence of central and communal institutions is lacking so there can be no thought of organized villages. Rather it is a matter of independent, and in principle equal-ranking, farming enterprises.

These farms ranged along the, in most cases, smaller watercourses and were rarely more than 200 to 400 m away from their source of water. In this way they formed narrow settlement strips (corridors) at about 3 km intervals. Within the settlement corridors too there were breaks so that even in times of densest settlement there were at least 15 ha available to each farm for crop growing and animal farming.

As large-scale investigations in the Rhine–Main area (Sielmann, 1972) and the lower Rhine (Dohrn-Ihmig, 1979) have shown, the density of Bandkeramik settlement was at first relatively low. Then it increased steeply and, at the end, declined drastically again. This process has been proven even at the chronologically very finely divided Langweiler 8 settlement (Lüning, 1982a). At the time of its greatest development there were probably 1.45 inhabitants per square kilometre in the western Bandkeramik. Calculated only for the intensive settlement areas, the loess lands, the figure was 16.7 inhabitants per square kilometre (Lüning, 1982a, p. 26).

In the later western Bandkeramik, oval to trapeze-shaped earthworks were built in the broad territory between the Rhineland and southern Bavaria. Generally they consisted of V-section ditches and must at the time have possessed ramparts; several gates gave access within (Dohrn-Ihmig, 1971; Höckmann, 1975; Schwellnus, 1983, Fig. 15). More recent research has shown that some of these emplacements were empty, that is they contained no dwellings (Langweiler 9, Rhineland: Lüning, 1982a, pp. 18–21). In one case it has been reliably shown that four associated dwellings were located outside the ditch system (Langweiler 8, Rhineland: Lüning, 1982b, Fig. 15) (Fig. 149). There are arguments for considering these to have been religious sites (Lüning, 1983–4, p. 17) but it is more generally assumed that they were protective enclosures for cattle.

Broadly speaking, the Bandkeramik settled the loess basins of central Europe. The highlands were not occupied, but were doubtless crossed by traffic routes and were possibly used for grazing as well, at least in the marginal areas (D.

Müller, 1985). Within the major regions there were smaller settlement areas which it has already been possible to define with some precision, as in Bohemia (Pavlů and Zápotocká, 1979). These settlement areas consisted of yet smaller geographical units, settlement sub-areas, in which the individual sites where finds have been made were grouped together in small concentrations (Kruk, 1980).

Middle Neolithic

Houses

In the Middle Neolithic, two major dwelling provinces can be distinguished. In the area of the Grossgartach culture, perhaps still in the Stichbandkeramik culture, house plans were developed with outward-bowed walls, like the sides of a ship (Günther, 1973). From these, in the Rössen culture, trapeze-shaped dwellings (Fig. 148) developed whose area of use ranged from the Paris basin via Bohemia to south-eastern Poland (Soudský, 1969). Thus the same type of dwelling was being built across central Europe in at least three archaeological cultures (Rössen, Stichbandkeramik, northern Lengyel).

The trapeze-shaped houses go back to the Bandkeramik but reflect the changed social conditions. There were both small buildings only 12 m long and large ones up to 56 m in length. Houses often had an outhouse and an open porch. In the living area itself there is often evidence of dividing walls, but this does not correspond to any difference in house plan. It may therefore be assumed that all these rooms were used for living purposes. Depending on its size, therefore, from one to four 'families' occupied each dwelling. Provisions were partly stored in the outhouse (Lüning, 1982b).

To the south of the big area with trapeze-shaped dwellings was an area of two-roomed rectangular dwellings. Not enough is yet known about their origins in the older painted Lengyel culture (Podborský, 1984). In the later Lengyel culture the house plan in many districts was sunk about 1 m into the ground and for that reason the internal arrangement of the dwellings with their hearths, ovens and working and living areas has been excellently preserved (Vladar and Lichardus, 1968; Lüning; 1981). The two rooms were intended for different purposes. In the first the oven was frequently placed and craftwork also took place there, whereas the other contained the fireplace and was therefore used primarily for living and sleeping. Reconstruction of the dwellings was greatly facilitated by several clay models of houses. This type of dwelling advanced far into the north and west and supplanted the trapeze-shaped forms. Compared with the 'multi-family units' of the early Middle Neolithic it was distinctly smaller and thus served as a 'one-family' dwelling.

Settlements and settlement areas

Completely excavated settlements, particularly in the early Middle Neolithic, are still rare. The best example is the Rössen settlement at Inden, in the Düren district in the Rhineland (Kuper, 1975). Here, at the start, four homesteads, that is dwellings with their outhouses, stood on 2.5 ha of land. In the middle they left room for a special group of buildings, and the whole settlement was encircled by a fence. Later it was enlarged to the north and its area practically doubled (Lüning, 1982a). All this is evidence of the first villages with their central buildings and palisade fence as communal structures; they consisted of independent farm

1.

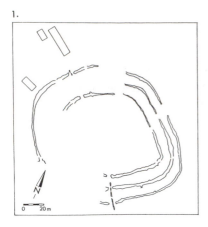

2.

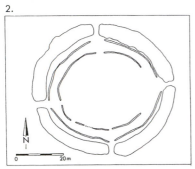

3.

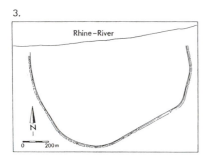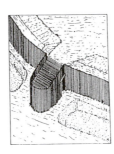

Figure 149 Development of Neolithic earthworks, central Europe: 1, Lower Neolithic, Langweiler 8, Germany; 2, Middle Neolithic, Těsetice-Kyjovice, former Czechoslovakia; 3, Upper Neolithic, Urmitz, Germany, with detail (bastioned gate).

enterprises which were no longer scattered over the countryside as in the Bandkeramik but grouped together in community settlements. There was therefore a concentration of population and dwellings in small villages that were inhabited for several generations. The central buildings were farmsteads like all the others but in addition they had a big rectangular hall.

Throughout central Europe the Bandkeramik settlement sites were also used in the Middle Neolithic, but in addition the villages also advanced into previously unoccupied areas that were farther away from water, for instance on the high plateaux between the river basins, as in Little Poland (Kruk, 1980), Bohemia (Rulf, 1983) and the Rhineland (Lüning, 1982b). In total, however, the number of settlements fell, as in central Germany (Starling, 1983); in southern Bohemia whole regions were abandoned (Zápotocká, 1982). Both were the result of the process of concentration mentioned above.

With the beginning of the Middle Neolithic appeared the first indubitable religious sites. They were circular systems of ditches some 50 to 100 m in diameter, their entrances often corresponding with the cardinal points (Fig. 149).

There were also square sites. It is primarily the pronounced geometry of these structures that prompts the idea of religious and social centres. These geometric sites were widespread in the three main Middle Neolithic cultures, Grossgartach–Rössen, Stichbandkeramik and Lengyel. Whether there were also earthworks for non-religious purposes is not clear, except for the Lengyel culture, where they exist.

Upper Neolithic

Houses

In this period a radical change in house-building technique seems to have appeared, namely the switch from post-based structures to dwellings with floor joists. The supporting posts and walls were no longer sunk into the earth but placed on horizontal beams level with the surface. This is the only explanation there can be for the fact that in the old settlement areas, ranging from the Chassey and Michelsberg to the Baden culture, practically no house outlines have been brought to light.

It was only in the foothills of the Alps newly settled by the Upper Neolithic that the technique of building post-based houses endured. Here the remains of dwellings have been excellently preserved in what today is marshland and under the surface of the water on the shores of lakes, often with wooden floors still intact and the lower portions of walls. Through them we are excellently informed about the carpentry methods of the time which show that floor joints and mortise and tenon joints definitely existed (Billamboz and Schlichtherle, 1985). This made possible the complicated wood joints that have to be provided in the upper parts of dwellings when building level with the ground. The wooden remains have been described since the nineteenth century as pile dwellings and this is still an acceptable description, although it has also been proved that many of the dwellings were originally built on dry land and only later submerged or overtaken by marsh (Strahm, 1983).

In plan, the dwellings in the Alpine foothills carried on the tradition of the late Middle Neolithic. They consisted of one- or two-roomed buildings with a fireplace and an oven measuring 4.5 to 9 m long by 4.5 to 5 m wide, as shown by the Schussenried settlement at Ehrenstein near Ulm in southern Germany (Zürn, 1965, p. 52) (Fig. 148).

In the loess areas of central Europe no recognizable floor plans of dwellings exist prior to the later part of the Upper Neolithic. Sunken square to rectangular floor plans with a wall length of 3 to 7 m have been found on the Goldberg in southern Germany (Bersu, 1937) in the Řivnáč culture in Bohemia (Ehrich and Pleslová-Šticková, 1968, p. 47) and in the central German Bernburg culture (Behrens and Schröter, 1980, p. 35). The walls consisted of rows of posts. Inside there were supporting posts for the roof and fireplaces (Fig. 148).

The one- and two-roomed houses of the early and the sunken houses of the late Upper Neolithic had a relatively small floor area, suggesting they were occupied by family nuclei of no more than five to seven persons.

Settlements and settlement areas

Typical of the central European Upper Neolithic are relatively small but densely built enclosed village patterns. Frequently they were encircled with fences and palisades which are certainly not sophisticated fortifications but clearly served as a protection for the inhabitants. The settlement layout is structured, for the buildings run in rows along streets and narrow alleys. The settlement type originated in the late Middle Neolithic with the well-known village of Aichbühl in southern Germany (Schmidt, 1930–37). So far this is the only place where a central, open area with a community building (large hall) has been found. At the other settlements only parts of the outline have been brought to light, except for the small lakeside settlement of Egolzwil 5 in Switzerland, which does not have this central arrangement (Wyss, 1976). The relatively small dwellings were only used for living and working so, strangely enough, rooms for agricultural activities and storage buildings are lacking. Exceptionally it has been possible to demonstrate the existence of open areas between the dwellings for goats and sheep to be kept in, recently described as stabling, and the possibility of ox-stables is discussed (Guyan, 1976).

The above description relates to the wetland settlements of the Alpine foothills. As mentioned, there are no houses, and therefore no settlement plans, in the central European loess lands. It is only the fact that sunken dwellings were usual in the Bohemian Řivnáč culture that showed, witness the Homolka settlement in central Bohemia, that the densely built village type was also known further north and was probably widespread (Ehrich and Pleslová-Štícková, 1968).

Perhaps, however, there were also bigger settlements here, for large-scale wall and ditch structures from the Upper Neolithic have long been known. These structures reach mighty proportions, particularly in the Michelsberg culture (Boelicke, 1977). That of Urmitz in the Rhineland lay semicircular to the Rhine and was 1.2 km in size. Its bastioned gates remind one vividly of fortified 'cities', but very little is known about the use to which the interior was put (Fig. 149) (Müller-Karpe, 1974; Boelicke, 1979).

In the European highlands, heights were for the first time systematically occupied and frequently fortified. It was then, in fact, that the opening up of the highland regions was completed, thus continuing the trend already described, that began in the Middle Neolithic, for the Neolithic economic and settlement system to be extended to all regions with the exception of the Alps.

All in all, the Neolithic settlement style went through radical changes in 3,000 years. The Bandkeramik dwelling/ storage houses were autonomous farmsteads relatively independent of their neighbours and therefore built in isolation or loosely scattered over the countryside. In the Middle Neolithic, villages were formed with communal facilities, but these arose purely from the practice of locating the individual farms together to safeguard their economic independence. It was only in the Upper Neolithic that the dwellings and villages lost their 'agricultural' look. In the narrowly built lines of streets there was no room for gardens or farm installations. The settlement was primarily intended for living and working and agricultural equipment must, for the most part, have been accommodated elsewhere. In settlement concentrations the need for protection always comes to the surface. This is obvious from the densely built, high-altitude settlements of the late Upper Neolithic. At the same time the Neolithic settlement area was continuously expanding so that, in general, it may be assumed that there was a relatively continuous increase in the population.

BURIAL PRACTICE AND RELIGION

It is often supposed that burial customs are a particularly conservative sector of human culture, but Ulrich Fischer's research into the Neolithic proves the opposite (Fischer, 1956, p. 254). Grave design, burial offerings and the position of the body and differentiation by sex and social categories all betray an extraordinary variety. Many cultures have their own particular features (Häusler, 1971).

Mostly inhumation graves have been found from the Neolithic, so burial of the complete body seems to have been the prevailing custom. Even so there are cremation graves, from Bandkeramik times onwards, which, in general, were only shallow, so that there has been much destruction by the plough. In some cemeteries inhumation and cremation burials occur side by side. It may therefore be assumed that cremation was originally far more frequent in the Band-keramik than it appears today and that it may even have predominated. This may also apply to other periods of the Neolithic because the partial or dominating practice of cremation has been substantiated. In general, far too few graves from the Neolithic have been found, so that we have to postulate the existence of many practices, such as ground-level or above-ground-level burial, which have left no trace behind them in the ground.

A fully developed and characterized burial system was already in existence in the Lower Neolithic. In the Band-keramik, the dead were buried in cemeteries a few hundred metres away from the settlements (Modderman, 1970). These were flat graves, most of them orientated in the east–west direction. The bodies were placed on their side in the sleeping position, not facing predominantly in one particular direction. The vessels, tools and weapons placed with the bodies were found in the region of the head and the upper part of the body. Women's graves can frequently be recognized by ornaments and milling stones and men's more particularly by weapons (stone axes, arrowheads). Social distinctions are not demonstrable. In Nitra (Slovakia) and many other cemeteries the men's graves seem more richly furnished than the women's (Pavúk, 1972, p. 73). In Elsloo (the Netherlands) the frequent combination of one man's with one woman's grave is evidence of monogamy (van de Velde, 1979, p. 111).

The Bandkeramik burial customs continued into the Middle Neolithic, though regional particularities came more frequently to the fore. In the southern Rhine area the dead were generally buried lying on their backs (Meier-Arendt, 1975, p. 69). In the Rössen cemetery (central Germany) the traditional crouched position was retained and stricter rules were applied because practically all skeletons were found lying on their right side (Fischer, 1956, p. 32). In Bréšc Kujawski on the Vistula (Poland) the north–south orientation for the crouched position dominated, but men lay on their right and women on their left sides (Jaźdźewski, 1938).

Bigger changes came in with the Upper Neolithic. In the east, it is true, the cemetery tradition was carried on, for example in Hungary with the Bodrogkeresztúr and the Baden culture (Banner, 1956, p. 184; Patay, 1973), but in the west cultures arose in which graves were almost completely absent, such as Michelsberg, Pfyn, Chassey.

Influences from the northern Funnel-Beaker culture were involved in the origin of the first big collective graves in the Elbe-Saale region. To some extent these were monumental megalithic graves from which it is clear that the grave and the cult at the graveside had become important for the living. In this way the collective graves stressed the continuity of the family, something for which there is also anthropological evidence (Ullrich, 1965, 1969). The memory of individuals, too, was kept alive to a similar extent because individual graves occurred for the first time in the Baalberge and

Salzmünde Funnel-Beaker cultures under monumental grave mounds (Fischer, 1956, pp. 48–55; Preuss, 1966, p. 34).

H. Müller-Karpe has written in detail about the religion of the Neolithic (1968, pp. 333 ff., 1979, pp. 605 ff.). In his view, the Lower and Middle Neolithic treatment of the dead was testimony to the loving relationship between living and dead, which reached beyond the grave, and the survival of the social community, but belief in the continuance of a person's life after death in another world was not connected with it. This idea first arose with the Upper Neolithic when the individual, as the large grave mounds show, was believed to live beyond death for all eternity. Logically the earliest evidence of a sepulchral cult establishing a link with the ever-living dead dates from this time.

Quite apart from this, religious practices and sacrifices forging links with the powers of the other world are known to go back as far as the Lower Neolithic. A very well-known site is the Jungfern cave at Tiefenellern in southern Germany which was used as a place of sacrifice from Bandkeramik times onwards (Kunkel, 1955). One particular group of sacrifices consists of human skeletons or parts of skeletons found in the refuse pits of settlements. A few of them are rightly interpreted as coming from settlement burials, but most are very probably the remains of religious practices and magical rites. In the Lower and Middle Neolithic finds of this kind are few and far between but in the Upper Neolithic there are pits (*bothroi*) containing human and animal skeletons in many cultures, such as the Michelsberg culture (Lüning, 1968, p. 125), the Baalberge and Salzmünde cultures (Fischer, 1956, pp. 53–63) and the Baden culture (Makkay, 1975, 1978). Animal burials (Behrens, 1964) and foundation sacrifices under house footings (Soudský, 1969) also belong under this heading.

Lastly, the geometric earthworks of the Middle Neolithic are evidence of religious practices carried on by large cult communities, probably combining several settlements. This tradition of ritual ceremonies by large communities, which must have been related to the agricultural cycle of the seasons, continued unchanged into the Upper Neolithic. Probably most earthworks of this period had a religious character, the decisive importance of religion in the Neolithic being reflected in the most impressive monuments of the age (Maier, 1962).

SOCIAL AND POLITICAL DEVELOPMENT

The graves and settlements of the Lower Neolithic reveal an egalitarian society with no social stratification or institutionalized rule. Ethnographic parallels suggest that relationship and common lineage formed the basis of internal organization. The family, as the smallest social unit, clearly had considerable economic importance, as the system of individual farmstead settlements in the Bandkeramik indicates. On the other hand, the cemeteries point to the existence of larger communities, probably associations of settlements; they may have built up 'tribes'. There is no way of knowing how large was the territory belonging to these 'tribes'.

In the Middle Neolithic the significance of the territorial and regional concept clearly increased. The individual family gave up part of its economic independence to the village. Communal institutions developed together with a village 'higher echelon'. Society, however, remained 'democratic', because no political or social distinctions can be discerned in the graves. The central buildings in the settlements must have been institutions for the whole village community.

In the Lower and Middle Neolithic there is no evidence of any craft specialization on the part of individuals or families. Signs of economic distinctions between producers and consumers are confined to some rare raw materials such as spondylus shells, flint and amphibolite axes. How production and distribution were organized is not yet clear.

The Upper Neolithic ushered in some noteworthy changes. In the new type of settlement – the enclosed street-village – the communal element came even more to the fore and possibly a ruling class developed. The grave mounds of the central German Funnel-Beaker culture (Baalberge, Salzmünde) were interpreted by Ulrich Fischer (1956, pp. 54–67) as evidence of the existence of a higher social stratum, to which, however, nothing in the settlement architecture corresponds. Possibly the craft specialization of the later Upper Neolithic is also related to this political differentiation.

ART AND SCIENCE

Mobiliary and domestic art account for most of the works that have come down to us from the central European Neolithic. Pride of place here goes to the plastic idol figures, a genre that had a rich development in some periods, particularly in the early Lengyel culture. From the same culture comes the highest quality pottery, featuring an extraordinary variety of geometric painting. Varied artistic activity was also manifest in other media, particularly in the shape and decoration of pottery. 'Architecture' is hardly a term that can be used in relation to the primarily functional dwelling and work buildings. Even so, the earthworks consisting of ditches, walls, palisades and bastions must often have possessed a monumental character. The wood and textile art of which there must surely have been an abundance is practically all lost. Compared with other regions of Europe the art of the central European Neolithic makes a modest showing.

Scientific thought in the modern sense certainly cannot have existed; for one thing, religious ideas are everywhere likely to have had considerable influence. But it is also just as self-evident that life was based on a quantity of rational concepts and practices. The primary evidence of this is provided by the craftsmanship that required long experience, in pottery and copperware for example, and also the daily tasks of farming and house-building. The basics of geometry were necessary for measurement purposes when laying out building plans but even more indispensable for constructing the Middle Neolithic earthworks with their perfectly circular and rectangular designs. They were often oriented on the basis of the cardinal points, a fact that brings in another area, astronomy, where systematic observation and scientific surveying would have had to be applied. The margin of error in grave orientation lies within 5 per cent. Even the simplest possible instrument necessary for that kind of accuracy, the Indian circle, calls for at least partial knowledge of the geometry of circles and the overriding significance of the right angle (Schlosser et al., 1981).

For astronomy and farming routine a calendar is needed, no details of which are known, however. All in all, the available evidence of 'art and science' in the central European Neolithic suggests a relatively sober age marked by functional agricultural thinking and agricultural religiosity.

BIBLIOGRAPHY

AUJOURD'HUI, R. D'. 1977. Bedeutung und Funktion der Dickenbännlispitzen. Mikroskopische Untersuchungen zur Funktionsdeutung von Silexgeräten. *Verh. nat.forsch. Ges. Basel*, Vol. 86, pp. 237–56.

BAILLOUD, G. 1976. Les Civilisations néolithiques du Bassin Parisien et du Nord de la France. In: GUILAINE, J. (ed.), *La Préhistoire française*. Paris. Vol. 2, pp. 375–86.

BAKELS, C. C. 1978. *Four Linearbandkeramik Settlements and their Environment: A Palaeoecological Study of Sittard, Stein, Elsloo and Hienheim*. Leiden. (Analecta Praehist. Leidensia, 11.)

—— 1982. The Settlement System of the Dutch Linearbandkeramik. In: *Prehistoric Settlement Patterns around the North Sea*. Leiden. pp. 31–44. (Analecta Praehist. Leidensia, 15.)

BANNER, J. 1956. *The Peceler Kultur*. Budapest. (Archaeol. Hung., 35.)

BECKER, C. J. 1947. Mosefunde Lerkar fra yngre Stenalder [Neolithic Pottery in Danish Bogs]. *Aarb. nord. Oldkynd. hist.* (Copenhagen), pp. 1–318.

—— 1954. Stenalderbebyggelsen ved Store Valby i Vestsjaelland [Stone Age Settlements at Store Valby in Western Sjaelland]. *Aarb. nord. Oldkynd. hist.* (Copenhagen), pp. 127–97.

BEHM-BLANKE, G. 1962–3. Bandkeramische Erntegeräte. Zur Typologie der ältesten Sicheln und Erntemesser. *Alt-Thüring.* (Weimar), Vol. 6, pp. 104–75.

BEHRENS, H. 1964. *Die neolithisch-frühmetallzeitlichen Tierskelettfunde der Alten Welt*. Berlin. (Veröff. Landesmus. Vorgesch. Halle, 19.)

—— 1973. *Die Jungsteinzeit im Mittelelbe-Saale-Gebiet*. Berlin. (Veröff. Landesmus. Vorgesch. Halle, 27.)

BEHRENS, H.; SCHRÖTER, E. 1980. *Siedlungen und Gräber der Trichterbecherkultur und Schnurkeramik bei Halle (Saale)*. Berlin. (Veröffentlichungen des Landesmuseums für Vorgeschichte in Halle, 34.)

BERNHARD, W. 1978. Anthropologie der Bandkeramik. In: SCHWABEDISSEN, H. (ed.), *Die Anfänge des Neolithikums vom Orient bis Nordeuropa; Anthropologie*. Cologne/Vienna. pp. 128–63. (Fundamenta Reihe B, Vol. 3, p. VIIIb.)

BERSU, G. 1937. Altheimer Wohnhäuser von Goldberg, OA. Neresheim, Württemberg. *Germania* (Berlin), Vol. 21, pp. 149–58.

BILLAMOZ, A.; SCHLICHTHERLE, H. 1985. Pfahlbauten – Häuser in Seen und Mooren. In: *Der Keltenfürst van Hochdorf. Methoden und Ergebnisse der Landesarchäologie. Katalog zur Ausstellung 1985*. Stuttgart. pp. 249–66.

BOELICKE, U. 1977. Das neolithische Erdwerk Urmitz. *Acta Praehist. Archaeol.* (Berlin), Vol. 7/8, pp. 21–34.

—— 1979. Überlegungen zur Rekonstruktion der Umfassungsanlage des Erdwerks Urmitz. *Köln. Jahrb. Vor-Frühgesch.* (Berlin), Vol. 16, pp. 21–34.

—— 1982. Gruben und Häuser: Untersuchungen zur Struktur bandkeramische Hofplätze. In: INTERNATIONALES KOLLOQUIUM NOVE VOZOKANY, 1981. *Siedlungen der Kultur mit Linearkeramik in Europa*. Nitra. pp. 17–28.

BOESSNECK, J. 1958. *Studien an vor- und frühgeschichtlichen Tierresten Bayerns*. Munich.

BOESSNECK, J.; JEQUIER, J.-P.; STAMPFLI, H. R. 1963. *Seeberg, Burgaschisee-Süd. Die Tierreste*. Bern. (Acta Bernens., Vol. II, t.3.)

BOGNAR-KUTZIAN, I. 1969. Probleme der mittleren Kupferzeit im Karpathenbecken. In: SYMPOSIUM ÜBER DEN LENGYEL-KOMPLEX UND BENACHBARTE KULTUREN, Nitra, 1967. [*Materialien.*]

—— 1972. *The Early Copper Age Tiszapolgar Culture in the Capathian Basin*. Budapest. (Archaeol. Hung., 48.)

BÖKÖNYI, S. 1974. *History of Domestic Mammals in Central and Eastern Europe*. Budapest.

BUTTLER, W. 1938. *Der donauländische und der westliche Kulturkreis der jüngeren Steinzeit*. Berlin/Leipzig. (Handb. Urgesch. Dtschl., 2.)

BUTTLER, W.; HABEREY, W. 1936. *Die bandkeramische Ansiedlung bei Köln-Lindenthal*. Berlin/Leipzig. (Römi.-Ger. Forsch., 11.)

CHILDE, V. G. 1929. *The Danube in Prehistory*. London.

CLARK, J. G. R. 1952. *Prehistoric Europe: The Economic Basis*. London.

CONSTANTIN, C. 1985. *Fin du Rubané, céramique du Limbourg et Post-Rubané: le néolithique le plus ancien en Bassin Parisien et en Hainaut*. Oxford. (BAR Int. Ser., 273.)

DEICHMÜLLER, J. 1965. Die neolithische Moorsiedlung Hüde I am Dümmer, Kreis Grafschaft Diepholz. *Neue Ausgrab. Forsch. Niedersachs.* (Hildesheim), Vol. 2, pp. 1–18.

DE LAET, S. J. 1972. Das ältere und mittlere Neolithikum in Belgien (von etwa 4300 bis etwa 2000 v.d.Z.). In: SCHWABEDISSEN, H. (ed.), *Die Anfänge des Neolithikums vom Orient bis Nordeuropa*. Cologne. pp. 185–230. (Fundamenta Reihe A3, p. Va.)

DEMOULE, J.-P.; ILETT, M. 1978. Le site de Berry-au-Bac: La Croix Maigret. In: UNIVERSITÉ DE PARIS I. Centre de Recherches Protohistoriques. *Les Fouilles protohistoriques dans la vallée de l'Aisne, 6, Raport d'Activité: Campagne de fouille 1978*. Paris. pp. 51–77.

DESSE, J. 1984. Les Restes de poissons dans les fosses omaliennes. In: OTTE, M. (ed.), *Les Fouilles de la Place Saint-Lambert à Liège*. Liège. Vol. 1, pp. 239–40.

DOHRN-IHMIG, M. 1971. Ein bandkeramischer Graben mit Einbau bei Langweiler, Kr. Jülich, und die zeitliche Stellung bandkeramischer Gräben im westlichen Verbreitungsgebiet. *Archäol. Korresp.bl.* (Mainz), Vol. 1, pp. 23–30.

—— 1974. Die Geringer Gruppe der späten Linienbandkeramik im Mittelrheintal. *Archäol. Korresp. bl.* (Mainz), Vol. 4, pp. 301–6.

—— 1979. Bandkeramik an Mittel- und Niederrhein. In: *Beiträge zur Urgeschichte des Rheinlandes*. Cologne/Bonn. Vol. 3, pp. 191–362. (Rhein. Ausgrab., 19.)

DRIEHAUS, J. 1960. *Die Altheimer Gruppe und das Jungneolithikum in Mitteleuropa*. Bonn.

DUBOULEZ, J.; LASSERRE, M.; LE BOLLOCH, M. A. 1984. Eléments pour une chronologie relative des ensembles Roessen, Post-Roessen, Michelsberg et Chasséen dans la vallée de l'Aisne, le Bassin Parisien. *Rev. Archéol. Picardie* (Amiens), Vol. 1/2, pp. 11–23.

ECKERT, J. 1979. Koslar 10. Untersuchungen zur neolithischen Besiedlung der Aldenhovener Platte VIII. *Bonn. Jahrb. Rhein. Landesmus.* (Bonn), Vol. 179, pp. 313–21.

EGGERT, M. K. H. 1978. Zum Kulturkonzept in der prähistorischen Archaeologie. *Bonn. Jahrb. Rhein. Landesmus.* (Bonn), Vol. 178, pp. 1–20.

EHRICH, R. W.; PLESLOVÁ-ŠTICKOVÁ, E. 1968. *Homolka, an Eneolithic Site in Bohemia*. Prague/Cambridge, Mass.

FIRBACH, F. 1949. *Spät- und nacheisenzeitliche Waldgeschichte Mitteleuropas nördlich der Alpen. Allgemeine Waldgeschichte I*. Jena. 2 vols.

FISCHER, U. 1956. *Die Gräber der Steinzeit im Saalgebiet*. Berlin.

FRENZEL, B. 1977. Postglaziale Klimaschwankungen im südwestlichen Mitteleuropa. In: FRENZEL, B. (ed.), *Dendrochronologie und postglaziale Klimaschwankungen in Europa*. Wiesbaden. pp. 297–322.

GÜNTHER, K. 1973. Eine neue Variante des mittelneolithischen Trapezhauses. *Germania* (Mainz), Vol. 51, pp. 41–53.

GUYAN, W. U. 1976. Jungsteinzeitliche Urwald-Wirtschaft am Einzelbeispiel von Thaygen 'Weier'. *Jahrb. Schweiz. Ges. Ur-Frühgesch.* (Frauenfeld), Vol. 59, pp. 93–117.

HÄUSLER, A. 1966. Zur Verhältnis von Männern, Frauen und Kindern in Gräbern der Steinzeit. *Arb.-Forsch. ber. sächs. Bodendenkmalpfl.* (Dresden), Vol. 14/15, pp. 25–73.

—— 1971. Die Bestattungssitten des Früh- und Mittelneolithikums und ihre Interpretation. In: SCHLETTE, F. (ed.), *Evolution und Revolution im Alten Orient und in Europa*. Berlin. pp. 101–19.

—— 1985. Die Anfänge von Rad und Wagen in der Kulturgeschichte Europas. In: HORST, F.; KRÜGER, B. (eds), *Produktivkräfte und Produktionsverhältnisse in ur- und frühgeschichtlicher Zeit*. Berlin. pp. 121–33.

HEITZ, A.; JACOMET, S.; ZOLLER, H. 1981. Vegetation, Sammelwirtschaft und Ackerbau im Zürichseegebiet zur Zeit der neolitischen und spätbronzezeitlichen Ufersiedlungen. *Helvetia archaeol.* (Basle), Vol. 12, pp. 139–52.

HILLMAN, G. 1984. Traditional Husbandry and Processing of Archaic Cereals in Recent Times: The Operations, Products and Equipment which might Feature in Sumerian Texts. *Bull. Sumer. Agric.* (Cambridge), Vol. 1, pp. 114–52.

HÖCKMANN, O. 1975. Wehranlagen der jüngeren Steinzeit. In: BÖHME, H. W. (ed.), *Ausgrabungen in Deutschland*. Mainz. Vol. 3, pp. 277–96.

HOUŠTOVÁ, A. 1960. *Kultura nalevkovitych poharu na Morave* [The Funnel-Beaker Culture in Moravia]. Prague. (Font. Archaeol. Prag., 3.)

ILETT, M. et al. 1982. The Late Bandkeramik of the Aisne Valley: Environment and Spatial Organisation. In: *Prehistoric Settlement Patterns around the Southern North Sea*. Leiden. pp. 45–61. (Analecta Praehist. Leidensia, 15.)

ITTEN, M. 1970. *Die Horgener Kultur*. Basle.

JAŻDŻEWSKI, K. 1938. Cmentarzyska kultury ceramiki wstegowej i zwiazane z nimi slady osadnictwa w Brzesciu Kujawskim [Grave-fields of the Bandkeramik Culture and the Related Settlements in Bresc Kujawski]. *Wiad. Archeol.* (Warsaw), Vol. 15, pp. 1–105.

—— 1984. *Urgeschichte Mitteleuropas*. Wroclaw.

KALICZ, N. 1973. Über die chronologische Stellung der Balaton-Gruppe in Ungarn. In: SYMPOSIUM ÜBER DIE ENTSTEHUNG UND CHRONOLOGIE DER BADENER KULTUR, Male Vozokany, 1969. [*Materialien*]. Bratislava. pp. 131–65.

—— 1983. Die Körös-Starčevo-Kulturen und ihre Beziehungen zur Linearbandkeramik. *Nachr. Niedersachs. Urgesch.* (Hildesheim), Vol. 52, pp. 91–130.

KALICZ, N.; MAKKAY, J. 1977. *Die Linienbandkeramik in der grossen ungarischen Tiefebene*. Budapest.

KAUFMANN, D. 1976. *Wirtschaft und Kultur der Stichbandkeramiker in Saalegebiet*. (Veröff. Landesmus. Vorgesch. Halle, 30.)

KIMMIG, W. 1981. Feuchtbodensiedlungen in Mitteleuropa. *Archäol. Korresp.bl.* (Mainz), Vol. 11, pp. 1–14.

KLEJN, L. S. 1982. *Archaeological Typology*. Oxford. (BAR, Int. Ser., 153.)

KLICHOWSKA, M. 1976. Aus paläoethnobotanische Studie über Pflanzenfunde aus dem Neolithikum und der Bronzezeit auf polnischem Boden. *Archaeol. Polona* (Wroclaw), Vol. 17, pp. 27–67.

KOWALSZYK, J. 1970. The Funnel Beaker Culture. In: WISLANSKI, T. (ed.), *The Neolithic in Poland*. Warsaw. pp. 144–77.

KRUK, J. 1980. *The Neolithic Settlement of Southern Poland*. Oxford. (BAR Int. Ser., 93.)

KULCZYCKA-LECIEJEWICZOWA, A. 1970. The Linear and Stroked Pottery Cultures. In: WISLANSKI, T. (ed.), *The Neolithic in Poland*. Warsaw. pp. 14–75.

KUNKEL, O. 1955. *Die Jungfernhöhle bei Tiefenellern, eine neolithische Kultstätte auf dem Fränkischen Jura bei Bamberg*. Munich.

KUPER, R. 1975. Die rössener Siedlung Inden 1. In: BÖHME, H. W. (ed.), *Ausgrabungen in Deutschland*. Mainz.

KUSTERMANN, A.-C. 1984. Die jungneolithische Pfynergruppe im unteren Zürichsee-Becken. *Zür. Stud. Archäol.* (Zurich), Vol. 2, pp. 9–92.

LE BOLLOCH, M. 1984. La Culture de Michelsberg dans la vallée de l'Aisne. *Rev. Archéol. Picardie* (Amiens), Vol. 1/2, pp. 133–45.

LEHNER, H. 1910. Der Festungsbau der jüngeren Steinzeit. *Prähist. Z.* (Berlin), Vol. 2, pp. 1–23.

LICHARDUS, J. 1976a. *Rössen-Gatersleben-Baalberge. Ein Beitrag zur Chronologie des mitteldeutschen Neolithikums and zur Entstehung der Trichter Becher-Kulturen*. Bonn. (Saarbr. Beitr. Altertumskd.)

—— 1976b. Das Keramikdepot von Bozice und seine chronologische Stellung innerhalb des frühen Äneolithikums in Mitteleuropa. *Jahresschr. mitteldtsch. Vorgesch.* (Halle), Vol. 60, pp. 161–74.

—— 1980. Zur Funktion der Geweihspitzen des Types Ostorf. Überlegungen zu einer vorbronzezeitlichen Pferdeschirrung. *Germania* (Mainz), Vol. 57, pp. 1–24.

LÜNING, J. 1968. Die Michelsberger Kultur. Ihre Funde in zeitlicher und räumlicher Gliederung. *Ber. Röm.-Ger. Komm.* (Mainz), Vol. 48, pp. 1–350.

—— 1971. Die Entwicklung der Keramik beim Übergang vom Mittel- zum Jungneolithikum im süddeutschen Raum. *Ber. Röm.-Ger. Komm.* (Mainz), Vol. 50, pp. 1–95.

—— 1976. Schussenried und Jordansmühl. In: SCHWABEDISSEN, H. (ed.), *Die Anfänge des Neolithikums vom Orient bis Nordeuropa*. Cologne/Vienna. pp. 122–87. (Fundamenta, Reihe A, Vol. 3, p. Vb.)

—— 1979–80. Bandkeramische Pflüge? *Fundber. Hess.* (Bonn), Vol. 19/20, pp. 55–68.

—— 1981. *Eine Siedlung der mittelneolithischen Gruppe Bischheim in Schernau, Ldkr. Kitzingen*. Kallmünz. (Mater. hefte Bayer. Vorgesch., 44.)

—— 1982a. Research into the Bandkeramik Settlement of the Aldenhovener Platte in the Rhineland. In: *Prehistoric Settlement Patterns around the South North Sea*. Leiden. (Analecta Praehist. Leidensia, 15.)

—— 1982b. Siedlung und Siedlungslandschaft in bandkeramischer und rössener Zeit. *Offa* (Neumünster), Vol. 39, pp. 9–33.

—— 1983–4. Mittelneolithische Grabenanlagen im Rheinland und in Westfalen. *Mitt. österr. Arb.gem. Ur-Frühgesch.* (Bern), Vol. 33/34, pp. 9–25.

LÜNING, J.; MODDERMAN, P. J. R. 1982. Hausgrundrisse der ältesten Bandkermik aus Schwanfeld, Landkreis Schweinfurt, Unterfranken. In: CHRISTLEIN, R. (ed.), *Das archäologische Jahr in Bayern*. Stuttgart. p. 66.

MAIER, R. A. 1962. Fragen zu neolithischen Erdwerken Südbayerns. *Jahresber. bayer. Bodendenkmalpfl.* (Munich), pp. 5–21.

MAKKAY, J. 1975. Über neolithische Opferformen. In: ANATI, E. (ed.), *Valcamonica Symposium 72. Les Religions de la préhistoire*. Capo di Ponte. pp. 161–73.

—— 1978. Mahlstein und das rituale Mahlen in den prähistorischen Opferzeremonien. *Acta Archaeol. Acad. Sci. Hung.* (Budapest), Vol. 30, pp. 13–36.

MEIER-ARENDT, W. 1969. Zur relativen Chronologie der Gruppen Hinkelstein und Grossgartach sowie der Rössener Kultur. *Kölner Jahrb. Vor-Frühgesch.* (Berlin), Vol. 10, pp. 24–36.

—— 1972. Zur Frage der jüngerlinienbandkeramischen Gruppenbildung: Omalien, 'Plaidter', 'Kölner', 'Wetterauer' und 'Wormser' Typ; Hinkelstein. In: SCHWABEDISSEN, H. (ed.), *Die Anfänge des Neolithikums vom Orient bis Nordeuropa*. Cologne/Vienna. pp. 85–152. (Fundamenta Reihe A, Vol. 3, p. Va.)

—— 1975. *Die Hinkelstein-Gruppe. Der Übergang vom Früh- zum Mittelneolithikum in Südwestdeutschland*. Berlin. (Röm.- Ger. Forsch., 3.)

MILISAUSKAS, S.; KRUK, J. 1984. Settlement Organisation and the Appearance of Low Level Hierarchical Societies during the Neolithic in the Bronocice Microregion, Southeastern Poland. *Germania* (Mainz), Vol. 62, pp. 1–30.

MODDERMAN, P. J. R. 1970. *Linearbandkeramik aus Elsloo und Stein*. 's-Gravenhage. (Analecta Praehist. Leidensia, 3.)

—— 1976. Abschwemmung und neolithische Siedlungsplätze in Niederbayern. *Archäol. Korresp.bl.* (Mainz), Vol. 6, pp. 105–8.

MOISIN, P. H.; JORIS, J. 1972. Rössener Einflüsse in der Gegend von Mons (Hennegau, Belgien) und die C14-Datierung aus Givry (GrN 6021). *Archäol. Korresp.bl.* (Mainz), Vol. 2, pp. 243–8.

MORDANT, C.; MORDANT, D. 1978. Les Sépultures néolithiques de Noyen-sur-Seine (Seine-et-Marne). *Bull. Soc. préhist. Fr.* (Paris), Vol. 75, pp. 559–78.

MORDANT, D. 1980. Noyen et les enceintes de La Bassée. In: COLLOQUE DE SENS, 1980. *Approche des questions culturelles. Le Néolithique dans l'Est de la France*. pp. 119–27.

MÜLLER, D. W. 1985. Besiedlung und wirtschaftliche Nutzung von Mittelgebirgsregionen in neolithischer und nachneolithischer Zeit. In: HORST, F.; KRÜGER, B. (eds), *Produktivkräfte und Produktionsverhältnisse in ur- und frühgeschichtlicher Zeit*. Berlin. pp. 51–61.

MÜLLER, H.-H. 1964. *Die Haustiere der mitteldeutschen Bandkeramik*. Berlin.

MÜLLER-KARPE, H. 1968. *Handbuch der Vorgeschichte. Jungsteinzeit*. Munich. Vol. 2.

—— 1974. Zur kupferzeitlichen Kultur in Hessen. *Fundber. Hess.* (Bonn), Vol. 14, pp. 215–226.

—— 1979. *Handbuch der Vorgeschichte*, Vol. 3: *Kupferzeit*. Munich.

MURRAY, J. 1970. *The First European Agriculture, a Study of the Osteological and Botanical Evidence until 2000 BC*. Edinburgh.

NEUSTUPNÝ, E. 1969. Absolute Chronology of the Neolithic and Aeneolithic Periods in Central and South-East Europe. *Archeol. rozhl.* (Prague), Vol. 21, pp. 783–809.

—— 1973. Die Badener Kultur. In: SYMPOSIUM ÜBER DIE ENT-

STEHUNG UND CHRONOLOGIE DER BADENER KULTUR, Male Vozokany, 1969. (*Materialien*) Bratislava. pp. 317–52.

—— 1978. Prehistoric Migrations by Infiltration. *Archaeol. rozhl.* (Prague), Vol. 34, pp. 278–93.

OTTAWAY, B. 1973. The Earliest Copper Ornaments in Northern Europe. *Proc. Prehist. Soc.*, Vol. 39, pp. 294–331.

PAPE, W. 1978. *Bemerkungen zur relativen Chronologie des Endneolithikums am Beispiel Südwestdeutschlands und der Schweiz.* Tübingen. (Tüb. Monogr. Urgesch., 3.)

PATAY, P. 1973. Probleme der Beziehungen der Bodrogkereszturer und der Badener Kultur. In: SYMPOSIUM ÜBER DIE ENTSTEHUNG UND CHRONOLOGIE DER BADENER KULTUR, Male Vozokany, 1969. (*Materialien*) Bratislava. pp. 353–65.

PAVLŮ, I. 1977. To the Methods of Linear Pottery Settlements Analysis. *Pamat. archaeol.* (Prague), Vol. 68, pp. 5–55.

—— 1978. Das linienbandkeramische Ornament und seine Westausbreitung. *Arbeits-Forsch. Sächs. Bodendenkmalpfl.* (Dresden), Vol. 22, pp. 205–18.

—— 1981. Altneolithische Häuser in Böhmen. *Archeol. rozh.* (Prague), Vol. 33, pp. 534–43.

—— 1982. Die Entwicklung des Siedlungsareals Bylany 1. In: INTERNATIONALES KOLLOQUIUM, Nové Vozokany, 1981. *Siedlungen der Kultur mit Linearkeramik in Europa.* Nitra. pp. 193–206.

PAVLŮ, I.; ZÁPOTOCKÁ, M. 1979. The Current State and Future Aims of the Study of the Bohemian Neolithic Cultures. *Pamat. Archaeol.* (Prague), Vol. 70, pp. 281–318.

PAVÚK, J. 1969. Chronologie der Želiezovce-Gruppe. *Slov. Archaeol.* (Bratislava), Vol. 17, pp. 265–367.

—— 1972. Neolithisches Gräberfeld in Nitra. *Slov. Archaeol.* (Bratislava), Vol. 20, pp. 5–105.

—— 1980. Ältere Linearkeramik in der Slowakei. *Slov. Archaeol.* (Bratislava), Vol. 28, pp. 7–90.

—— 1981. Sucasny stav studia Lengyelskej kultury na Slovensku [The Present State of Knowledge of the Lengyel Culture in Slovakia]. *Pamat. Archeol.* (Prague), Vol. 72, pp. 255–99.

PAVÚK, J.; ŠIŠKA, S. 1971. Neoliticke a eneoliticke osidlenie Slovenska [The Neolithic and Aeneolithic Settlement of Slovakia). *Slov. Archaeol.* (Bratislava), Vol. 19, pp. 319–64.

PETRASCH, J. 1984. Die absolute Datierung der Badener Kultur aus der Sicht des süddeutschen Jungeneolithikums. *Germania* (Mainz), Vol. 62, pp. 269–87.

PITTIONI, R. 1985. Über Handel im Neolithikum und der Bronzezeit Europas. In: DÜVEL, K. et al. (eds), *Untersuchungen zu Handel und Verkehr der vor- und frühgeschichtlichen Zeit in Mittel- und Nordeuropa.* Göttingen. pp. 127–80.

PLESLOVÁ-ŠTICKOVÁ, E. 1977. Die Entstehung der Metallurgie auf dem Balkan, im Karpathenbecken und in Mitteleuropa, unter besonderer Berücksichtigung der Kupferproduktion im ostalpenländischen Zentrum. *Pamat. Archaeol.* (Prague), Vol. 68, pp. 56–73.

PODBORSKY, V. 1984. Domy lidu s Moravskou Malovanou Keramikou [Houses with Moravian Ceramic Painting]. *Sb. pr. filos. fak. Brnenske Univ.* (Brno), Vol. 33, pp. 25–66.

PREUSS, J. 1966. *Die Baalberger Gruppe in Mitteldeutschland.* Berlin. (Veröff. Landesmus. Vorgesch. Halle, 21.)

QUITTA, H. 1960. Zur Frage der ältesten Bandkeramik in Mitteleuropa. *Prähist. Z.* (Berlin), Vol. 38, pp. 153–88.

—— 1964. Zur Herkunft des frühen Neolithikums in Mitteleuropa. In: GRIMM, P. (ed.), *Varia Archaeologica.* Berlin. pp. 14 ff.

—— 1971. Der Balkan als Mittler zwischen Vorderem Orient und Europa. In: SCHLETTE, F. (ed.), *Evolution und Revolution im Alten Orient und in Europa.* Berlin. pp. 38–76.

RULF, J. 1982. Die Linienbandkeramik in Böhmen und die geographische Umwelt. In: INTERNATIONALES KOLLOQUIUM, Nové Vozokany, 1981. *Siedlungen der Kultur mit Linearkeramik in Europa.* Nitra. pp. 247–60.

—— 1983. Prirodni prostředi a kultury českeho neolitu a eneolitu [Environment and Cultures of Bohemian Neolithic and Aeneolithic]. *Pamat. Archeol.* (Prague), Vol. 54, pp. 35–95.

RUOFF, U. 1978. Die schnurkeramischen Räder von Zürich-'Pressehaus'. *Archäol. Korresp. bl.* (Mainz), Vol. 8, pp. 275–83.

—— 1981. Alterbestimmung mit Hilfe der Dendrochronologie. *Helvetia Archaeol.* (Basle), Vol. 12, pp. 89–97.

RUTTKAY, E. 1981. Typologie und Chronologie der Mondsee-Gruppe. In: *Das Mondseeland. Geschichte und Kultur. Katalog zur Ausstellung des Landes Oberösterreich in Mondsee 1981.* Linz. pp. 269–94.

—— 1983. *Das Neolithikum in Niederösterreich.* Vienna. (Forsch. ber. Ur-Frühgesch., 12.)

SAUTER, M.-R. AND GALLAY, A. 1969. Les Premières Cultures d'origine méditerranéenne. In: DRACK, W. (ed.), *Ur- und frühgeschichtliche Archäologie der Schweiz*, Vol. 2: *Die jüngere Steinzeit.* Basle. pp. 47–66.

SCHLICHTHERLE, H. 1985. Prähistorische Ufersiedlungen am Bodensee. Eine Einführung in naturräumliche Gegebenheiten und archäologische Quellen. In: BECKER, B. et al. (eds), *Bericht zu Ufer- und Moorsiedlungen Südwestdeutschlands.* Stuttgart. Vol. 2, pp. 9–42. (Mater. h. Vor-Frühgesch. Baden-Wüttembg., 4.)

SCHLOSSER, W.; CIERNY, J.; MILDENBERGER, G. 1981. *Astronomische Ausrichtungen im Neolithikum II.* Bochum.

SCHMIDT, R. R. 1930–7. *Jungsteinzeit-Siedlungen im Federseemoor.* Stuttgart. 3 vols. (Vol. 1, 1930; Vol. 2, 1936; Vol. 3, 1937.)

SCHWABEDISSEN, H. 1979. Der Beginn des Neolithikums im nordwestlichen Deutschland. In: SCHIRNIG, H. (ed.), *Grossteingräber in Niedersachsen.* Hildesheim. pp. 203–22. (Veröff. urgesch. Samml. Landesmus. Hannover, 24.)

SCHWARZ-MACKENSEN, G.; SCHNEIDER, W. 1983. Wo liegen die Hauptliefergebiete für das Rohmaterial donauländischer Steinbeile und -äxte in Mitteleuropa? *Archäol. Korresp.bl.* (Mainz), Vol. 13, pp. 305–14.

SCHWELLNUS, W. 1979. *Wartburg-Gruppe und hessische Megalithik.* Wiesbaden. (Mater. Vor-Frühgesch. Hesse, 4.)

—— 1983. Archäologische Untersuchungen im rheinischen Braunkohlegebiet. In: *Archäologie in den Rheinischen Lössbörden.* Cologne/Bonn. pp. 1–31. (Reinische Ausgrab., 24.)

SHERRATT, A. 1981. Plough and Pastoralism: Aspects of the Secondary Products Revolution. In: HODDER, I.; ISAAC, G.; HAMMOND, N. (eds), *Pattern of the Past: Studies in Honour of David Clarke.* Cambridge. pp. 261–305.

SIELMANN, B. 1971a. Der Einfluss der Umwelt auf die neolithische Besiedlung Südwestdeutschlands unter besonderer Berücksichtigung der Verhältnisse am nördlichen Oberrhein. *Acta Praehist. Archaeol.* (Berlin), Vol. 2, pp. 65–197.

—— 1971b. Zum Verhältnis von Ackerbau und Viehzucht im Neolithikum Südwestdeutschlands. *Archäologisches Korresp. bl.* (Mainz), Vol. 1, pp. 65–77.

—— 1972. Die frühneolithische Besiedlung Mitteleuropas. In: SCHWABEDISSEN, H. (ed.), *Die Anfänge des Neolithikums vom Orient bis Nordeuropa.* Cologne/Vienna. pp. 1–65. (Fundamenta, Reihe A, Vol. 3, p. Va.)

SMOLLA, G. 1981. Umweltprobleme der 'Pfahlbauforschung'. *Archäol. Korresp. bl.* (Mainz), Vol. 11, pp. 15–19.

SOUDSKÝ, B. 1966. *Bylany.* Prague.

—— 1969. Étude de la maison néolithique. *Slov. Archaeol.* (Bratislava), Vol. 17, pp. 5–96.

SPENNEMANN, D. R. 1984. *Burgerroth. Eine spätneolithische Höhensiedlung in Unterfranken.* Oxford. (BAR Int. Ser., 219.)

STARLING, N. J. 1983. Neolithic Settlement Patterns in Central Germany. *Oxf. J. Archaeol.*, Vol. 2, pp. 1–11.

STEINMETZ, W.-D. 1982. Anmerkungen zum Nordischen Frühneolithikum. *Neue Ausgrab. Forsch. Niedersachs.* (Hildesheim), Vol. 15, pp. 13–52.

STEKLÁ, M. 1959. Třiděni vypichane keramiky. *Archeol. rozhl.* (Prague), Vol. 11, pp. 211–60.

STÖCKLI, W. E. 1981. *Die Keramik der Cortaillod-Schichten.* Bern. (Die neolithische Ufersiedlung von Twann, 20.)

STRAHM, C. 1983. Das Pfahlbauproblem. Eine wissenschaftliche Kontroverse als Folge falscher Fragestellung. *Germania* (Mainz), Vol. 61, pp. 353–60.

TAUTE, W. 1967. Das Felsdach Lautereck, eine mesolitisch-neolithisch-bronzezeitliche Stratigraphie an den Oberen Donau. *Palaeohist.* (Groningen), Vol. 12, pp. 483–504.

—— 1980. *Mesolithikum in Süddeutschland. 2: Naturwissenschaftliche Untersuchungen.* Tübingen. (Tübing. Monog. Urgesch., 5/2.)

TICHY, R. 1962. Osidleny s volutovou keralikou na Morave. *Pamat. Archeol.* (Prague), Vol. 53, pp. 245–301.

UENZE, H.-P. 1987. Die endneolithische befestigte Siedlung von Dobl, Ldkr. Rosenheim. *Bayer. Vorgesch.bl.* (Munich), Vol. 46, pp. 1–36.

UERPMANN, H.-P. 1977. Betrachtungen zur Wirtschaftsform neolithischer Gruppen in Südwestdeutschland. *Fundber. Baden-Württemb.* (Stuttgart), Vol. 3, pp. 144–61.

ULLRICH, H. 1965. Zur Anthropologie der Walternienburger Bevölkerung. *Alt-Thüring.* (Weimar), Vol. 7, pp. 130–202.

—— 1969. Interpretation morphologisch-metrischer Ühnlichkeiten an ur- und frühgeschichtlichen Skeletten in verwandtschaftlicher Hinsicht. *Z. Archäol.* (Berlin), Vol. 3, pp. 48–88.

VELDE, P. VAN DE. 1979. *On Bandkeramik Social Structure: An Analysis of Pot Decoration and Hut Distribution from the Central European Neolithic Communities of Elsloo and Hildesheim.* Leiden. (Analecta Praehist. Leidensia, 12.)

VENCL, S. 1982. K otazce zaniku sberačko-loveckych kultur. *Archeol. rozhl.* (Prague), Vol. 34, pp. 648–94.

VLADAR, J.; LICHARDUS, J. 1968. Erforschung der frühäneolithischen Siedlungen in Branc. *Slov. Archaeol.* (Bratislava), Vol. 16, pp. 263–52.

VRIEZEN, K. J. H. 1977. Die Gefässe der Chamer Gruppe. In: MODDERMAN, P. J. R. (ed.), *Die neolithische Besiedlung bei Hienheim,*

Ldkr. Kelheim. Leiden. (Analecta Archaeol. Leidensia, 10.)

WILLERDING, U. 1980. Zum Ackerbau der Bandkeramiker. In: *Beiträge zur Archäologie Nordwestdeutschlands und Mitteleuropas. Festschrift K. Raddatz.* Hildesheim. pp. 421–56. (Mater. hefte Ur-Frühgesch. Niedersachs., 16.)

WILLMS, C. 1982. *Zwei Fundplätze der Michelsberger Kultur aus dem westlichen Münsterland, gleichzeitig ein Beitrag zum neolithischen Silexhandel in Mitteleuropa.* Hildesheim. (Münst. Beit. Ur- Frühgesch., 12.)

—— 1985. Neolithischer Spondylusschmuck. *Germania* (Mainz), Vol. 63, pp. 331–43.

WILLVONSEDER, K. 1968. *Die jungsteinzeitlichen und bronzezeitlichen Pfahlbauten des Attersees in Oberösterreich.* Graz/Vienna. (Mitt. Prähist. Komm. österr. Akad. Wiss., 11/12.)

WINIGER, J. 1981. *Das Neolithikum der Schweiz.* Basle.

WYSS, R. 1976. *Das jungsteinzeitliche Jäger-Bauerndorf von Egolzwil 5 im Wauwilermoos.* Zurich.

ZÁPOTOCKÁ, M. 1967. Das Skelettgrab von Praha-Dejvice. Beitrag zum chronologischen Verhältnis der Stichbandkeramik zu der Lengyelkultur. *Archeol. rozhl.* (Prague), Vol. 19, pp. 64–87.

—— 1982. Zur Auswahl der Siedlungsregionen der Stichbandkeramik. In: INTERNATIONALES KOLLOQUIM, Nové Vozokany, 1981. *Siedlungen der Kultur mit Linearkeramik in Europa.* Nitra. pp. 305–17.

ZÜRN, H. 1965. *Das jungsteinzeitliche Dorf Ehrenstein (Kreis Ulm). Teil A: Die Baugeschichte.* Stuttgart. (Veröff. Staatl. Amt. Denkmalpfl. Stuttgart, 10/1.)

52

THE EUROPEAN PART OF THE FORMER USSR

during the Neolithic and the Chalcolithic

Nikolai J. Merpert

NEOLITHIC PERIOD

In face of all the limitless variety of natural and historical conditions of development in the different regions of the former USSR, the most acceptable and general indicator of the beginning of the Neolithic over the greater part of the territory is the appearance of pottery. This feature is valid for the entire Neolithic ecumene within the borders of the post-Soviet republics, irrespective of differences in economic systems and the presence or absence of polished and perforated tools and implements. It is equally indicative of the start of the Neolithic in the oldest southern centres of agricultural and livestock-rearing cultures within this territory, in the still sparsely settled steppes where the transition to livestock-rearing had barely begun and in the giant forest and circumpolar regions where the hunting, fishing and gathering type of economy was still completely dominant. Everywhere it indicates extremely important changes in people's lives, particularly in their system of nutrition.

At the same time it must be noted that, in settlements in some areas among the oldest centres of productive economy in the post-Soviet south, the lower layers, although already marked by evidence of the beginning of livestock-rearing and agriculture, still contain no pottery. Some authors assign such remains to the end of the Mesolithic, while others prefer to speak of the Pre-pottery Neolithic (Markevich, 1974).

As a result of the uneven development among specific population groups in different areas, particularly in the different landscape and climatic zones of the former USSR, the chronological boundaries of the Neolithic vary sharply. In southern central Asia, the Caucasus, Crimea and the northern Black Sea coastal region the Neolithic developed from the eighth (possibly from the end of the ninth) millennium BP to the first centuries of the sixth millennium BP, whereas the cultures of that chronological period in the forest zone were still entirely Mesolithic in character. It was only at the turn from the sixth to the fifth millennium BP that they were replaced by specific forest-zone Neolithic cultures that coexisted with the developed Chalcolithic and Early Bronze Age in the southern areas mentioned. On the whole, the beginning of the Neolithic in post-Soviet territory of the USSR ranges from the eighth (or the end of

the ninth) to the end of the sixth millennium BP and the end of the Neolithic from the beginning of the sixth to the beginning of the fourth millennium BP; in a number of forest and circumpolar areas, Neolithic cultures are known to have survived to an even later period.

Towards the end of the Mesolithic, the territory of the former USSR was already quite densely settled. This applies particularly to the European part of the country where numerous and varied Mesolithic remains are now known from the Caucasus in the south to the Rybachii peninsula and the basin of the Pechora in the north, from the Dniester and the Neman in the west to the Urals in the east. The internal development of the Mesolithic population and its descendants was, naturally, a most important factor in the formation of the earliest Neolithic culture. It is demonstrated by many even now quite clearly stratified site deposits whose lower layers are entirely Mesolithic in character and precede both the appearance of pottery and the beginnings of a productive economy; whereas their upper layers show evidence of both those features of the Neolithic, together with all the traditional elements that marked the preceding period, particularly flint and stone items, and further developments thereof. Such sites are known in the Dniester area (Soroki 1 and 2: Markevich, 1974), and on the southern Bug (Bazkov Ostrov, Mitkov Ostrov, Sokoltsy: Danilenko, 1969), in the coastal area of the Sea of Azov and on the northern Donets (Kamennaya Mogila and so on: Danilenko, 1969, 1974; Telegin, 1968), in Crimea (Tash-Air 1, Zamil'-Koba II and the rest: Krainov, 1960) and in the Caucasus (the cave at Kamenny Most in the Kuban valley, Samele-klde in Imeretiya and so on: Formozov, 1977, pp. 46–7). The development of the Mesolithic into the Neolithic may be traced directly at the above-mentioned sites and at many others (Formozov, 1977, p. 63).

But, in addition to this undoubted continuity, a second essential factor in the formation of Neolithic cultures in post-Soviet territory must be taken into account: the links with and influence of adjoining areas, particularly the earliest centres of a food-producing economy in western Asia and the Balkan–Danube region, which sharply increased in the course of economic and cultural development. To a considerable extent, this influence determined the formation of the first independent Neolithic centres with a food-producing economy in the territory of the former USSR. Of course, these centres appeared mainly in the southern areas of the country, where natural conditions were suitable and which were in direct contact with the above-mentioned centres. Among these areas were the north-west coastal area of the Black Sea, the Caucasus and southern central Asia. Here the actual transition to the Neolithic is connected with the appearance and, subsequently, the dominance of the agricultural and livestock-raising economy. Somewhat later, both branches of this economy, but particularly livestock-rearing, appear further north in the steppe and the forest steppe, although hunting and fishing still retain a dominant position in the Neolithic economy of these regions.

Further north still, in the forest zone, under different ecological conditions far from the agricultural and livestock-rearing centres of the south and their decisive influence, Neolithic cultures were based on traditional forms of the gathering economy, which was entirely dominant until the end of the Neolithic and even considerably later in a number of regions. Here again, however, the beginning of the Neolithic was marked by a series of progressive changes both in the production of flint and stone artefacts and in the level of development of the forms of economy mentioned, their productivity, and the scale, nature and intensity of interchanges during the formation of ethnocultural complexes (Gurina, 1970, p. 134). Also in this region features of undoubted continuity between the Mesolithic and the Neolithic cultures accompany a number of important changes, produced by internal development and by external factors such as migrations, the diffusion of cultural achievements and so on.

The picture of the development of the Neolithic in the European post-Soviet republics, central Asia and the Caucasus is generally extremely complex and varied. Here, it is only possible to give a rather sketchy description of two zones, a northern and a southern, where specific natural and historical conditions determined the features of the Neolithic cultures that developed within their limits. This division is justified by the presence of several specific features within each zone common to all its Neolithic cultures. In the European part of the former USSR the Neolithic cultures of Karelia, the Urals, the basin of the Oka and upper Volga, Belarus, the Baltic coast and northern Ukraine, have been assigned to the northern zone, and the cultures of the larger part of Ukraine, Moldavia, Crimea and the Caucasus to the southern zone (Formozov, 1977, pp. 73–4). The cultures of the Caspian and Black Sea steppes and the southern part of the forest steppe should also be included in the southern zone: these territories constituted a transitional area between the two major zones and were influenced by both, although the influence of the southern zone was determinant.

Neolithic cultures will be considered here in an order corresponding to the division indicated, beginning with the southern zone and, in particular, the earliest centres of the food-producing economy in the former Soviet republics.

NORTHERN BLACK SEA AND AZOV SEA COASTAL REGIONS AND THE VOLGA REGION DURING THE NEOLITHIC PERIOD (Fig. 150)

The area between the Bug and Dniester and Transcarpathia

The area of the north-western Black Sea coast and, particularly, the area between the Dniester and the Bug, borders directly on the Balkan–Danube region. This played an important part in the formation of the specific Neolithic cultures of this area, particularly in the spread of the rudiments of productive forms of economy. The influence concerned can be traced here from a very early period, which is represented in the Balkans and the Danube basin by a grouping of agricultural cultures – Starčevo–Criş–Körös – which are the earliest in the region (and in Europe as a whole). As already stated, these influences were combined on the Dniester and the Bug with the direct continuation of local Mesolithic traditions, testifying to a degree of continuity in development. By the beginning of the Neolithic period, this development had reached quite a high level and led to the formation of local cultures whose founders had already assimilated the elementary skills of agriculture and livestock-rearing.

The earliest culture chronologically in this area was the Bug–Dniester culture, which developed in the second half of the eighth to the seventh millennium BP on the boundary between the forest-steppe and steppe zones between the Dniester and the southern Bug, particularly in the basins of the rivers themselves. Over sixty settlements have been discovered there, a number of which have been extensively excavated. On the basis of stratigraphic and horizontal observations and a comparison of the principal categories of finds, it has proved possible to distinguish a number of phases in the development of the culture (Danilenko, 1969; Markevich, 1974).

The earliest phase is represented by the remains of settlements with oval, semi-subterranean dwellings or light surface structures. There is as yet no pottery. The flint artefacts are extremely archaic and largely keep to Mesolithic traditions. The microlithic nature of the items found, consisting of a large number of blade artefacts, is particularly characteristic. Alongside forms already familiar in the Mesolithic period – trapezes, cutters, end-scrapers and borers – occasional tanged blades for sickles with a characteristic longitudinal gloss make their appearance. Tips for digging-sticks and hoes with longitudinal blades are found among the many artefacts made of bone and horn as well as arrow-heads, awls and flakers. The main roles in the economy of the settlements were played by hunting and fishing, but occasional finds of bones testify to the presence of domestic animals, pigs (*Sus scrofa domestica*), cattle (*Bos taurus* L.) and dogs (*Canis familiaris* L.), while finds of the characteristic tools already mentioned also suggest that the rudiments of agriculture were practised. The earliest stage is represented most clearly on the southern Bug (Soroki, settlements 1 and 2). There are two radiocarbon dates for samples from these settlements: around 7,500 and 7,400 years ago. When a correction factor is applied these dates are pushed back to the end of the ninth or the beginning of the eighth millennium BP. The early stage of the Bug-Dniester culture contains the earliest evidence of a food-producing economy in the south-west European part of the former USSR and indicates the start of the transition to the Neolithic in this region.

Pottery appears during the next stage, during which the earlier traditions in house building and the working of flint and bone were maintained. The earliest vessels are deep, straight-sided pots with round or pointed bases, decorated with smooth bands forming complex voluted and scalloped designs, with comb ornament, incised net motifs and finger indentations. During the third stage, vessels with flat bases and oval sides, ornamented by straight or wavy smooth bands, outlined by pin-pricks, became widespread alongside the round-based vessels. Hunting and fishing continue to

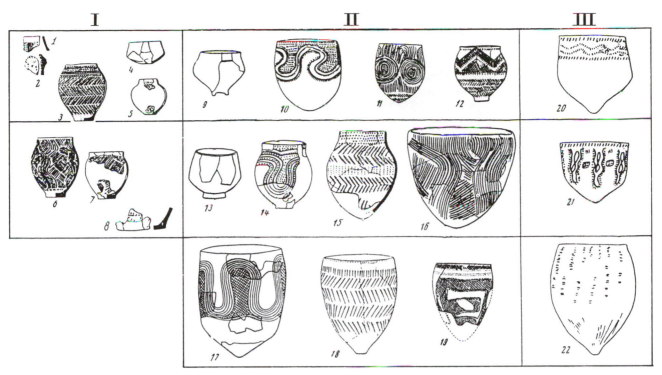

Figure 150 Comparative table of the pottery of the Neolithic cultures of the region north of the Black Sea: I, Bug–Dniester culture – the Dniester variant: 1–5, Soroki I; 6–8, Soroki II. (After Markevich, 1974) II, Bug–Dniester culture – the southern Bug variant: 9, Glinskoe; 10, Gaivoron; 11, Chimanosvkoe; 12, Zankovtsy; 13–16, Sokoltsy II; 17–18, Bazkov Ostrov; 19, Mitkov Ostrov. III, Dnieper–Donets culture: 20, Grini; 21, Zavalovka; 22, Strumel. (After Passek, 1949, 1961.)

dominate the economy, but bones from pigs, cattle and dogs are more common, while direct evidence of agriculture appears in the third stage – impression of einkorn and emmer grains. The second and third stages date from the end of the eighth to the beginning of the seventh millennium BP, and this is confirmed by the appearance of chronologically equivalent examples of pottery of the Starčevo–Criş type.

During the following three stages, which lasted until the beginning of the sixth millennium BP, the Bug–Dniester culture continued to develop and progress, while maintaining a common tradition in the main branches of productive activity. The predominant type of dwelling became the rectangular, ground-level house with stone foundations and a wattle and daub frame. The number of microlithic forms declined and ground tools and quadrangular grain graters became common along with hoes with transverse blades among the items made of bone. In pottery, the Criş element lost and gained importance by turns; flat-based vessels with deep wavy and linear ornament are characteristic of the last stage. Hunting and fishing held their own, but productive types of economy continued to develop: the evidence of agriculture noted above is supplemented by impressions of barley grains.

New features in flintworking techniques and pottery that appeared in the final stage developed further in the subsequent Eneolithic Tripolye culture, of which the Bug–Dniester Neolithic period must be considered a component. It must again be emphasized that the Bug–Dniester Neolithic took shape mainly on the basis of the local Mesolithic, but was considerably, and from the economic viewpoint decisively, influenced during its development by the early centre of agriculture in the Balkans.

There is also evidence that central European early agricultural cultures without local roots advanced directly into the north-western Black Sea coastal area. Archaeological

remains from the first half of the seventh millennium BP are connected with the previously mentioned Starčevo–Criş–Kórôs group of cultures and are similar to what is designated in Hungary as the Mekhtelek type of settlement (Potushnyak, 1978; Titov, 1980). They are found throughout ex-Soviet Transcarpathia. Typical of these remains are dugout structures with stoves and open hearths, flint blade artefacts, ground-stone tools, assorted vessels (including vessels with legs and bases) with incised and stamped decoration and sometimes black linear and geometric painting, female clay figurines and models of dwellings. Evidence of the agriculture is provided by grains of einkorn, emmer, barley and millet, and livestock-rearing is indicated by the bones of domestic cattle, pigs, sheep and goats. During the third quarter of the seventh millennium BP, tribes of the Bükk culture moved from north-eastern Hungary into the Transcarpathian area: this facilitated the formation there of a specific Dyakovo painted ware – one of a number of groups identified among the large number of related cultures of Alföld painted ware (Titov, 1980). In this area, agriculture and livestock-rearing already formed the basis of the economy, but hunting, fishing and gathering retained a significant role.

During the same period – at the end of the seventh millennium BP – there appeared in the valleys of the Upper Dniester and Prut traces of the central European Bandkeramik culture, which had spread there during the middle stage of its development. Some thirty settlements have been discovered of which Floresty and Nezvisko have been most thoroughly examined. Subterranean and semi-subterranean dwellings and, less commonly, ground-level houses are the forms of dwelling found. The most characteristic pottery consists of spherical, flat-based vessels decorated with various combinations of lines and pits ('musical notations'). The flint, stone and bone artefacts include many implements connected with agriculture, such as hoes, sickle blades and grain graters. There is also direct evidence that the inhabitants of these settlements engaged in agriculture and animal husbandry: grains of common wheat (*Triticum aestivum* L.) (including grain stored in jars), durum wheat (*Triticum durum* Desf.), emmer (*Triticum dicoccum* Schrank), peas (*Pisum arvense* L.) and the bones of domestic cows, pigs, sheep and goats. Inhumation was characteristic of the culture's funerary rites, although during the later period the body was cremated.

All of the cultures mentioned, both those that developed locally and those that moved in from south-east and central Europe, played a decisive role in the formation of the northern Black Sea centre of productive economy, which achieved an impressive level of prosperity in the Eneolithic age that followed. Even during the Neolithic, however, this centre exerted an appreciable influence on the development of large areas to the east and north and on the transition to the Neolithic of the entire steppe and forest-steppe area of the Black and the Caspian Sea regions.

The steppe zone and southern forest-steppe

The steppe to the east of the area between the Bug and Dniester was still settled very unevenly. The population was mainly concentrated in the river valleys. Settlement of the open steppe had just begun: this was brought about by the first appearance in the steppe of various forms of food-producing economy, primarily livestock-rearing, which determined the particular course of the transition to the Neolithic in this area. The question of the main forces behind this process is controversial. Some scholars connect the appearance of domestic livestock in the steppes with the influence of the Balkan–Danube centre of productive economy (Formozov, 1977), while others perceive an impetus from areas further to the east – as far away as the Transcaspian area (Danilenko, 1969). Later, during the Chalcolithic, the specific nomadic forms of stock-rearing developed that were to be so characteristic of the entire subsequent history of the Eurasian steppe. It is only the first signs of livestock-rearing that date back to the Neolithic period; they appeared quite early.

The Sura–Dnieper culture, represented by a series of small settlements with light ground-level structures (lath-framed huts), developed from the end of the eighth to the middle of the sixth millennium BP, beside the rapids of the lower Dnieper. Some of these settlements have left stratified deposits, enabling a number of stages in the development of the culture to be distinguished. At the very earliest stage there is not yet any pottery; pointed-based stone vessels are widespread. The items found are characteristic of a hunting and fishing economy; flint artefacts retain their Mesolithic forms (particularly geometric microliths). However, occasionally bones from domesticated cattle and pigs are already found in addition to numerous bones of wild animals. Their number increases appreciably during the subsequent stages, until they account for as much as 50 per cent of the bone material. Hoes made of horn and flint blades from reaping knives suggest that the rudiments of agriculture were also practised. Pointed or spike-based earthenware vessels with an S-shaped profile and, in rare cases, ornamented with smooth lines (of a linear-geometrical pattern) make their appearance during the second stage and flat-based vessels during the final stage. The culture was one of the complex of cultures adapted to the steppe that flourished in the Chalcolithic and Early Bronze Age, whose economies were primarily based on livestock-rearing.

Neolithic remains in Crimea, where there is also very early evidence of livestock-rearing, also belong to the same period – from the end of the eighth to the beginning of the sixth millennium BP. The bones of domesticated pigs were found even in the Mesolithic levels, preceding the appearance of pottery (Fatma-Koba, Tash-Air, levels 8 and 7: Kraĭnov, 1960; Stolyar, 1959). The bones of cattle, sheep and goats are found in addition to these in the Neolithic levels. The clay vessels are initially thick-walled with thick, pointed bases and little shaping; thin-walled, flat-based pots later appear alongside the others, their surfaces smoothed with a comb-like implement and decorated with line and pit designs. The flint implements in the early stage preserve the forms of Mesolithic geometric microliths, whereas during the second stage very common types also include segments with the point worked by flat retouching, trapeze microliths with their backs smoothed with a plane scraper and the blades of reaping implements, suggesting the collection of wild cereals or the beginnings of agriculture in this area.

In the Azov Sea region, the bones of domesticated cattle, sheep and pigs have been found in the very early Neolithic layer of the Kamennaya Mogila settlement on the river Molochnaya alongside archaic, spike-based unornamented vessels and flint microliths. Underlying this layer is a Mesolithic layer; it is noteworthy that in this same Azov Sea region on the river Mius, the Matveev-Kurgan settlement, which has also been investigated (Krizhevskaya, 1973a), contains one layer in which a typical Mesolithic flint industry (microliths of specific forms) is combined with items showing a typically Neolithic technique for the working of stone implements (ground-stone axes and adzes). This transitional layer dated from the second half of the eighth millennium BP.

An extremely interesting multilayer settlement, Raku-shechnyĭ Yar, has been discovered on the lower Don (Belanovskaya, 1973). The lower four of its six layers (with an overall thickness of more than 5 m) have been classified as Neolithic. The gaps in the life of the settlement are obviously due to the river overflowing. The clearly artificial shell-middens (up to 60 cm thick) are characteristic. The remains of rectangular wattle and daub dwellings have been found in these and other layers. The genetic continuity between the layers is indisputable. Layers 6 to 4 have been assigned to the Early Neolithic period. In them the microlithic traditions have been preserved in the flint items; stone vessels are found along with thick-walled, pointed-based and round-based earthenware vessels (the round-based type subsequently predominated), and drawn and stamped ornament also appears. This was particularly developed in the third (Late Neolithic) layer, where the microlithic traditions disappear and large-blade implements become common. The economy of the settlement was based on hunting and fishing, with livestock-rearing (cattle, sheep, pigs, dogs) occupying a definite place. Its lower layers date from the seventh and the upper layers from the beginning of the sixth millennium BP.

The important and complex Dnieper–Donets culture, whose development spanned both the Neolithic period and the beginning of the Chalcolithic (Telegin, 1968), took shape further north in the forest-steppe zone between the Dnieper and the Don and in adjacent areas. Its characteristic features are the coexistence of microlithic, macrolithic and grinding techniques for the production of implements and the presence of particular thick-walled clay vessels, with combed and pricked ornamentation, which had pointed bases and little shaping during the earlier stage, becoming round-based and distinctively shaped during the later stage. As many as 150 settlements are now known from this culture. The ground-level dwellings are primitive in construction, made of wood, rushes and clay, and are sometimes slightly recessed below ground-level. Hunting and fishing accounted for an important part of the economy, but livestock-rearing played a definite role of clearly increasing importance: the bones of cattle and pigs have been found in settlements belonging to the culture's early stage of development (Igren 8, Buzki), while the bones of domesticated animals constitute 80 per cent of the osteological material in the later stage (Sobachki, Srednyi Stog I). The presence of primitive agriculture may also be inferred from impressions of barley grains. Developing from the end of the seventh to the middle of the fifth millennium BP (when copper artefacts appear), the Dnieper-Donets culture played an important role in the transition to the Neolithic of both the southernmost areas of the forest-steppe and the vast adjacent territories to the north as far as the Baltic coast and central Russia.

A particular problem is posed by the funerary remains of the steppe and forest-steppe zones between the Dnieper and Don, the so-called Mariupol-type burial grounds (Telegin, 1968; Stolyar, 1953). They number about twenty and over 700 burials have been examined there, in large collective pits or trenches marked on the surface by wooden structures. The bodies lie fully extended on their backs and are covered with red ochre. Heaps of skulls have been found in some burial grounds. Pottery is either absent from the burial grounds or is found above the burials and is connected with funeral feasts. The rest of the items found are varied and include stone implements (wedge-shaped axes, blade knives) and weapons (polished maces), large numbers of ornaments made of stone, bone, animal and fish teeth, shells (beads, pendants, bracelets, zoomorphic figurines) and, lastly, copper and gold (pendants); particularly typical are blades made from wild boar tusk. Anthropologically, the bodies belong to the late Cro-Magnon type (tall, broad-faced, dolichocephalic). Most of these cemeteries are located in the Dnieper steppe region (Lysogorskiï, Nikolskiï, Vilnyanskiï and so on), with isolated examples on the northern Donets and in the Sea of Azov region (Dereivka, Aleksandriya, Mariupol and so on). It is important to stress, however, that similar cemeteries have also been discovered on the lower Don (on the river Chir) and in Crimea (Dolinka), while remains that are distinct but have similar rites, and similar sets of items have been found in areas further to the east and the south. A remarkable cemetery containing extended burials covered with ochre and with a rich collection of items that include boar tusk pendants, animal figurines made of bone and a large number of ornaments of the Mariupol type has been discovered near the village of Syezzheye on the left bank of the Middle Volga (Vassilyev and Matveeva, 1979). Pottery similar to that in this cemetery is found both in the Volga area and in the northern Caspian region (Vassilyev, 1981).

These facts indicate that the cultural development of a number of groups in the vast area of the Black Sea and Caspian steppe was marked by certain common features, even in the Neolithic period, including the important ethnographic feature of burial rites. This similarity was due to identical paths of development under similar ecological conditions and to real links between and the dispersal of culturally similar groups. These links extend considerably further east: the cemetery of Tumek-Kichidzhik, which is also very similar to that described above (Vinogradov, 1981) in a number of features of the rites and the items found

(including boar's tusk blades), was discovered in the desert zone of the southern Aral Sea area on the lower reaches of the Amu Daria.

The most important similar site in the south is the cemetery in the town of Nalchik (Kruglov et al., 1941). The similarity in the items found is particularly significant here (the same boar tusk blades, beads of a specific kind of stone (geshir), shell and animal-tooth pendants), the more so in that a number of artefacts (maces, metal ornaments) in burial grounds of the Mariupol type are Caucasian in origin. These are definite indications of interaction between the Neolithic cultures of the steppe and the Caucasus – the second Neolithic centre of food-producing economy in former Soviet territory.

THE CAUCASUS DURING THE NEOLITHIC PERIOD

Adjoining the oldest cultural centres in western Asia, the Caucasus interacted with them, adopting their achievements and spreading them over vast areas of Eurasia. At the same time, however, the Caucasus itself was the site of major economic changes and the formation of highly developed and original cultures. The particular wealth and variety of its natural conditions contributed to this, particularly the biological background necessary if a food-producing economy was to arise and develop. An impressive variety of wild cereals has been recorded here (particularly types of wheat and barley), in addition to a number of species of subsequently domesticated animals (mountain goats, wild sheep, goats and pigs). It is therefore quite natural that one of the oldest centres of productive economy should have taken shape here, although the nature of this process (local or due to western Asian influences) still remains controversial.

The genetic link between the Caucasian Neolithic and the local Mesolithic cultures is undisputed. The earliest Neolithic remains testify to the continuing dominance of foraging forms of economy: mainly hunting and gathering. However, extremely long-lived permanent settlements spread throughout Transcaucasia as early as the eighth millennium BP, with a fully developed agricultural and livestock-rearing economy. Their founders cultivated five species of wheat, four species of barley, millet, rye, peas, lentils and grapes, and it is very likely that the cereals were locally domesticated (Lissitzyna and Prishchepenko, 1977); they were also familiar with all types of domesticated animals, with the exception of the horse (Munchaev, 1982). The first links in the formation of this culture (or group of related cultures) have still not been discovered. Much of the period in which the settlements developed and which continued until the middle of the eighth millennium BP, belongs to the Eneolithic (in the Caucasus, as in western Asia, occasional metal artefacts appeared at a very early date). The earliest settlements, however, were founded no later than the late Neolithic (Munchaev, 1982). Here the lower (ninth to fourth) construction levels in the settlement of Chulaverisgor in the Kvemo-Kartliiskiï group of settlements in Georgia are quite typical (Kiguradze, 1976). The houses on these levels are circular in plan, domed or cylindrical, one-roomed, with doors, window openings, and hearths dug into the ground. They are built of plano-convex adobe bricks. There are numerous and varied flint and obsidian artefacts. The blade industry is predominant. An impressive series of blades for reaping knives of the primitive straight type have been found alongside knives, cutters, scrapers, borers and occasional microliths. Oval perforated stones (weights for digging-sticks), grain graters and hoes made of deer antler must be included among the implements with an undoubtedly agricultural function. The pottery is crude and poorly fired. The vessels are flat-bottomed and egg-shaped on massive bases; ornamentation is limited to single- or double-adhesion studding along the rim of the vessel. The palaeobotanical material includes grains of common wheat (*Triticum aestivum* L.), einkorn (*Triticum monococcum* L.), emmer (*Triticum dicoccum* Schrank), club wheat (*Triticum compactum* Host.), spelt (*Triticum spelta*), two-row barley, millet and so on (Lissitzyna and Prishchepenko, 1977). The bones of domesticated animals – cattle, sheep, goats and pigs – predominate in the osteological material. Thus, it is indisputable that the Neolithic inhabitants of the settlements in the Kvemo-Kartliĭskiĭ group engaged in agriculture and livestock-rearing. The radiocarbon dates for items from Shulaverisgor range from the turn of the eighth and seventh millennium to the turn of the seventh and sixth millennium BP; application of correction factors limits the period to between the mid-eighth and mid-seventh millennia BP.

Of extreme importance is the discovery of undoubtedly Neolithic remains, including evidence of a food-producing economy on the other side of the Caucasus, in Dagestan, which is characterized by a particular wealth of botanical resources. First and foremost is the multi-layer Chokhskoye settlement situated at a height of 1,700 to 1,800 metres (Amirkhanov, 1983). Its lower layers date to the Upper Palaeolithic and the top layer to the Neolithic. The remains of semi-circular dwellings built against the rock, with entrances in the form of broad corridors, have been discovered in the upper layer. The foundations of the walls are composed of undressed blocks of limestone, while their upper part is made of wood and clay. This is a special line of development in house architecture, which differs markedly from the Transcaucasian type. The flint and stone finds, while preserving Mesolithic and even Upper Palaeolithic traditions (geometric microliths, scrapers, cutters, blade and flake knives), include a number of new forms, particularly grain graters and sickle blades or reaping knives, the bone frames for which have been discovered in the settlement. Extremely primitive pottery is already present: kettle-shaped vessels and bowls are flat-based, thick-walled and poorly fired, with ornamentation limited to occasional conical clay studs. Grains of a number of species of domesticated wheat and barley testify to the development of a very specific form of agriculture: terrace cultivation, which is markedly different from the valley agriculture of the Transcaucasus and western Asia. The settlement dates from the first half of the eighth millennium BP.

The Chokhskoye settlement appreciably extends the known early agricultural area in the Caucasus, which comprised independent centres in the plains and the mountains and exercised a decisive influence on large adjacent areas.

In neither the western nor the Black Sea areas of the Caucasus is there any evidence of agriculture and livestock-rearing in the Early Neolithic settlements (Anaseuli I, Verkhnyaya Lemsa and the rest), and Mesolithic forms dominate among the finds alongside ground-stone tools and occasional items of pottery (Formozov, 1962; Munchaev, 1975; Nibieridze, 1972). During the late stage the number of settlements increased appreciably (Samele-Klde, Anaseuli II, Odishi, Nizhnyaya Shilovka, Kistrik and others) with a continuation of the microlithic traditions side by side with a marked increase in the number of ground-stone axes, hammers and adzes, and the appearance of reaping knife

blades, grain graters and hoes, suggesting the presence of a certain, although not a major, agricultural component in the economy. The same may be said of livestock-rearing, for which there is evidence in the osteological material from the Kamenny Most cave in the Kuban. Pottery is already common and is represented by flat-based jars, sometimes with incised and raised decoration.

In the development of the Neolithic cultures of the western Caucasus from the end of the eighth to the beginning of the sixth millennium BP, a definite link can be seen both with the previously mentioned main Caucasian area of early agriculture and with regions further west: the Crimea and the Black Sea steppe areas, in whose transition to the Neolithic the Caucasus played a definite role.

Several groups of Neolithic remains are known in the eastern Transcaucasus. First and foremost are two sites in Kobystan close to a large group of petroglyphs, some of which – the outlines of people and animals – may be dated to the Neolithic (Formozov, 1969). A Mesolithic complex is preserved at the sites where microlithic artefacts predominate alongside crude pebble-tools, stone dishes and clay pots with pointed bases. There is no direct evidence of agriculture, although livestock-rearing may have begun. The date is the end of the eighth millennium BP. There is evidence of links with the northern Caspian area and through it with areas of the steppe belt further to the east. It should again be stressed that interaction with the steppe belt played an important role in the transition to the Neolithic and in all the subsequent development of the areas directly adjoining the Caucasus and the vast areas of Eurasia further away from it.

THE FOREST ZONE AND NORTHERN FOREST-STEPPE DURING THE NEOLITHIC PERIOD (Fig. 151)

In the severe climatic conditions of the northern half of the European part of the former Soviet republics, the development of the Neolithic population differed markedly from that in the southern zone considered above. Here, the transition to various food-producing economies cannot be related to traces of the Neolithic or the phenomena that led to its appearance. The ecological conditions necessary for such a transition were absent here. The southern centres of food production were quite remote from this area: their influence rarely reached this far and was very attenuated (Formozov, 1977, p. 101). Economies based on hunting, fishing and gathering prevailed here until the beginning of the Metal Age and even longer in some areas.

However, here too the Neolithic is marked by progress in all domains of human life, beginning with an improvement in tools and an increase in the range of tools used, thus increasing humans' productive potential and enabling them to go over to more productive forms of hunting, fishing and gathering. The climatic conditions of the Holocene also contributed to this: the Neolithic developed in the northern zone in the conditions of the comparatively warm and humid Atlantic period (from the eighth to the fifth millennium BP) and also, partly, the Sub-Boreal period (from the fifth to the fourth millennium BP) (Gurina, 1970) in which the plant and animal life were richer than now. Raw material resources began to be used much more extensively for the production of working implements and weapons: the appearance of the oldest galleries and shafts for the extraction of high-grade types of stone dates from the Neolithic (Gurina, 1976). Progress in hunting and fishing was based on improvements

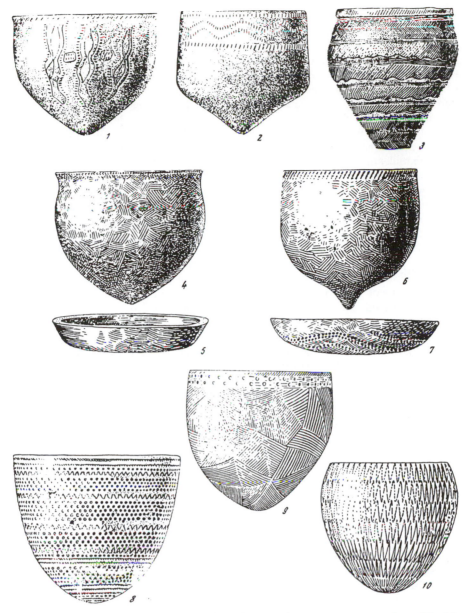

Figure 151 Types of Neolithic pottery (former USSR): 1–3, Dnieper–Donets culture; 4–5, western variant of the Narva culture; 6–7, eastern variant of the Narva culture; 8, Lyalova culture; 9, Sperrings culture; 10, Volga–Kama culture. (After Gurina, 1970.)

in the corresponding implements (bows, spears, darts, daggers, harpoons, fish-hooks and nets) and methods (from individual hunting to the mass use of beaters) and on the appearance of the most important types of transport: sledges, skis and many sizes and types of boat.

The gradual improvements in the gathering economy in turn produced a relatively settled way of life in certain primarily coastal regions and a comparatively regular population distribution and the establishment of large cultural complexes in large areas of the forest and forest-steppe. The archaeological evidence consists mainly of large numbers of settlements and temporary camps, plus a much smaller number of burial grounds and a small number of extremely important petroglyphs.

It is mainly the link with specific groups of the local Mesolithic period that can be traced in the process of the formation and development of Neolithic cultural complexes in the northern zone. In a number of cases, it is possible to distinguish transitional layers linking these two periods. The influence of neighbouring forest-steppe cultures, expressed in various forms, can also be traced; particularly that of the

Dnieper–Donets culture to which reference has already been made.

Thus, in the Baltic area, the boundary between the Mesolithic and the Neolithic is marked by settlements of the Kunda type which are rich in bone and stone items related to hunting and fishing. The type of culture represented by these settlements developed from the tenth to the beginning of the eighth millennium BP. The micro-macrolithic complex which developed in its final phase formed the basis for the oldest Neolithic pottery industry in this region. The pottery, represented by round-based vessels with pricked decoration, resembles that of the Dnieper–Donets cultures (Rimantene, 1973; Formozov, 1977). This suggests the mutual assimilation of the descendants of the local Mesolithic population and groups which had reached there from the south. The related Early Neolithic Narva and Neman cultures, which covered the entire Baltic region, the south of lake Ladoga and northern Belarus, were formed in this way (Gurina, 1961, 1973, Yanits, 1973; Vankina et al., 1973; Issaenko and Chernyavskii, 1970). Round semi-subterranean dwellings, a great abundance and variety of horn and bone objects side by side with a relative paucity of flint artefacts, and pots with pointed bases decorated with combed, incised and pitted ornamentation are typical of both cultures, although there are a number of local differences. Amber ornaments are common in western regions, including figurines of people and animals. These cultures may be dated through a series of radiocarbon assays to the sixth and beginning of the fifth millennium BP (Dolukhanov and Timofeev, 1972, p. 59). Marked changes occurred throughout the entire area in question at the end of the first half of the fifth millennium BP, as a result of the arrival from the Volga–Oka region and the area of Lake Ladoga of population groups with different cultural traditions. These traditions are expressed mainly in pottery with a characteristic pit-comb ornamentation. A new cycle of interaction between the local population and the newcomers led to the formation of the Baltic culture of the Middle and Late Neolithic period (second half of the fifth millennium BP). Its typical features are the preservation of the previous traditions in the case of bone and stone artefacts and the diffusion of kettle-shaped vessels with combed, pricked or pitted decoration. New population groups arrived in the Baltic area at the end of the fifth millennium BP with a culture of corded ware and boat-axes. In this case also a process of mutual assimilation occurred between the local and the newly introduced cultures (Lozé, 1979). Food-producing economies began to spread in the Baltic area during the Late Neolithic period.

The course of development of the Neolithic in Karelia and the area to the west of Lake Ladoga is similar in many respects. The Sperrings culture developed there in parallel to the Narva and Neman cultures (Pankrushev, 1964, 1973). Log houses at or slightly below ground level have been discovered in its settlements. There are also cemeteries containing bodies covered with ochre, a varied set of stone and bone items (including sculpted anthropomorphic and zoomorphic images) (Plates 100 and 101) and a very small quantity of pottery. The stone and bone artefacts of the Sperrings culture are similar to the Baltic artefacts. The pottery consists of round-based and pointed-based vessels with an original form of drawn, pricked and stamped ornament. Here too, the arrival of Volga–Oka groups whose pottery had ornamentation of a pit-comb type resulted in appreciable changes and the formation of a hybrid Late Neolithic Karelian culture (second half of the fifth millennium BP). This culture had vessels covered with pitted, combed and incised ornament, flint and clay figurines of people and animals, and remarkable petroglyphs (Plates 102 and 103) combining pictures of cult ceremonies with hunting and fishing scenes, representations of animals, birds, fish, goats, skis, traps, spears, bows, harpoons and so on (Ravdonikas, 1936, 1938; Savvateev, 1966; Formozov, 1969). There is undoubted continuity between the Karelian culture and the subsequent development of this region, where metal began to be used from the middle of the fourth millennium BP.

The pattern of Neolithic development in the central part of the northern zone between the Oka and the Volga is extremely interesting. The Upper Volga Neolithic culture, which covered a large part of this region, is the oldest one here (Krainov et al., 1973). It developed in the second half of the seventh to the first half of the sixth millennium BP and is represented by settlements, some of which are multilayered. During the early stage the flint items still include Mesolithic forms of blade tools and the round-based vessels mainly have a form of pricked decoration. The number of

flake-tools increases during the middle stage and combed ornament appears alongside pricked ornament. During the late stage Mesolithic tools are already in a minority: combed ornament is much more common than pricked ornament and flat-based vessels occur alongside round-based ones. In general the pottery of the Upper Volga culture is marked by western Dnieper–Donets traditions.

A different tradition in the development of pottery is represented in the Lyalovo culture, the oldest culture in a large cultural area with pit-comb pottery. Nevertheless, the Lyalovo culture developed from the same Mesolithic base as the Upper Volga culture, by which it was influenced to a certain degree during its formation.

The Lyalovo culture occupied a large area from the upper reaches of the Volga to the Don in the south and from the Oka to the upper Dnieper in the west. Its general features and the stages in its development may be established from its many settlements and temporary camps (Rauschenbach, 1973). Three stages of development have been distinguished within a common time frame: the beginning of the sixth to middle of the fifth millennium BP (Dolukhanov et al., 1973). The pottery is typified by round-based vessels decorated by a chessboard pattern of conical pits in areas divided by lines produced by a comb-type stamp. There are few traces of this last type of ornamentation during the early period, but the quantity increases during the middle period while the ornamentation generally becomes more complex; during the late period the ornamentation becomes slipshod. Blade artefacts predominate among the flint items from the early period, then during the middle period they exist alongside flake-tools, which become predominant in the late period. The number of ground-stone implements also rises sharply during the later two periods.

The Upper Volga and Lyalovo cultures exerted a decisive influence on the development of the Neolithic, both in the region between the Volga and the Oka and widely over adjacent areas. In the actual territory of the Lyalovo culture mentioned above, its traditions provided a basis for the formation of local Late Neolithic cultures during the fifth millennium BP, the Balakhna, Ryazan', Belev and Desna-Sozh cultures (Gurina, 1970; Tsvetkova, 1973; Tretyakov, 1972). These cultures are all associated with the pit-comb pottery already mentioned. Their distinctive features as expressed in the flint artefacts and the pottery are due to the specific features of local development in particular areas and their interaction with the Neolithic cultures of adjacent areas. A particular place is occupied by the Volosovo culture, which marks the final period of the Neolithic and the transition to the Metal Age: it includes a number of new elements related to the Volga–Kama areas further to the east, but the Lyalovo traditions also played a certain role in its formation. The Lyalovo traditions are also evident further north in the Vologda area, where the Kargopol Neolithic culture took shape in the fifth millennium BP. The influence of the upper Volga culture (along with the Dnieper–Donets culture) also determined to a significant extent the nature of the Neolithic period in the Valdai hills, with its round- and pointed-based vessels covered by combed, incised and pricked ornament (Gurina, 1973a).

The Volga–Kama cultural area took shape in the Neolithic period to the east of the area between the Volga and the Oka (Bader, 1973; Khalikov, 1973). It stretched from the middle Volga to the Urals in the east and the Pechora in the north. Its cultures developed from the end of the sixth to the end of the fifth millennium BP. Their remains are extremely varied. These include settlements with rectangular, semi-subterranean dwellings, which at surface level consisted of pillared or framed structures, temporary camps with light structures and, finally, individual burials in an extended position on the settlement sites, with an abundance of ochre and very occasionally stone tools and ornaments. Both blade and flake implements are common among the flint finds, including large biface spear, dart and arrow tips. Stone axes and adzes are common. The vessels are egg-shaped with sharp, round and sometimes flattened bases. The ornament covering their entire surface consists of impressions made by a comb-type stamp supplemented by pinpricks which form geometrical shapes (rhombi, triangles, zigzags and the like). The continuous movement of the stamp at a specific angle (the so-called 'walking comb' technique) is particularly characteristic.

In resolving the problem of the formation of Neolithic cultures in the Volga–Kama area, account must be taken both of the continuity with the local Mesolithic in the flint industry and of the borrowing of pottery from areas further to the west and south (including the Kelteminar culture of central Asia).

The cultural areas discussed also played a significant role in spreading the Neolithic to the more northerly regions of the European part of the former USSR: the Vychegod area, the lower reaches of the Pechora, the Arctic coast and the Kola peninsula. The facts that they were settled as early as the ninth to eighth millennium BP and that hybrid cultures with elements of the Volga–Oka, Volga–Kama and Karelian Neolithic were established there have now been demonstrated (Khlobystin, 1973; Gurina, 1970, 1973b).

The eastern limits of the Neolithic cultures in the areas considered are connected with the Urals (Bader, 1970; Krizhevskaya, 1968). One of the cultural areas in this vast region, which is extremely varied in its natural and historical conditions, has already been considered: the Volga–Kama area. A second, the eastern Ural area, which extends to the basins of the Ob, the Irtysh and the Tobol, is similar to the first and developed from the end of the eighth to the fifth millennium BP, in close relationship with it, and also experienced considerable influences from the regions of the southern and eastern Caspian. This resulted in the appearance of pottery in the eastern Ural area (characteristic egg-shaped vessels with stamped, drawn and raised ornament). The working of wood reached a remarkable level of development: wooden idols, oars, sleigh runners, skis, buckets with handles shaped like birds' heads, vessels with elk figures on them and so on have been found in the famous Gorbunov peat bog and at the Strelka site near Nizhnii Tagil (Eding, 1940). The petroglyphs in this area, with outlines mainly of solar signs and animal figures, date to the end of the Neolithic period. The third Neolithic area, the southern Ural region, extended to the south-east as far as the borders of northern Kazakhstan (Krizhevskaya, 1973b). The characteristic features of the Neolithic period in Asia can be seen clearly here as in the previous area, which is entirely natural: both areas extend far beyond the eastern limits of the European part of the former USSR.

CHALCOLITHIC PERIOD

One of the most important characteristics of the Chalcolithic period is the spread of productive types of economy that were far superior to the corresponding features of the Neolithic. Chalcolithic cultures took in a significant part of eastern Europe, within the limits of the entire southern zone and part of the northern as well: these cultures occupied not only the advanced cultural centres of the southern area, but a much larger region. The general progress of productive activity brought on the scene vast new population masses and led to their consolidation, contacts, collaboration and cultural integration. Together with the productive economy, an enormous role was played in this progressive process by the appearance of metallurgy and metalworking within the territory of eastern Europe. These new and highly important aspects of human activity became one of the decisive factors in technical, general economic and cultural development, in the promotion and direction of contacts and in the organization of production and the general structure of society. Metallurgy significantly widened not only people's productive capabilities but also their knowledge, leading to the use of vast natural resources, which till then had remained only potentially useful. This knowledge extended both to the nature and to the properties of the new materials being used and to the chemical, physical and technological processes associated with them. The establishment of mining centres and of metalworking centres had a marked influence on the general level and pace of development in specific regions and on the relationship between them. On the one hand, this exacerbated inequalities in social development and, on the other, sharply increased the capabilities and importance of a number of regions, leading to a kind of 'redistribution' of their historical roles. This also led to considerable changes in the historical geography and general nature of development of Eastern Europe at the beginning of the metal age.

These changes did not occur all at once, however. The traditional centres of productive economy, the Balkan–Danubian and the Caucasian, which had emerged in the Neolithic era, maintained their characteristic importance in the early stage (the Chalcolithic) of the establishment of metallurgy in eastern Europe, where they were the first metallurgical centres. At the same time, the traditional kinds of influence and the corresponding systems of communication persisted. Only later (during the Bronze Age; see Volume II) were new sources of metal developed and did new centres of metallurgy emerge; metalworking spread over vast areas, which led to considerable changes both in the system of communication and in the nature of the interaction between various regions.

CHALCOLITHIC PERIOD IN THE BALKAN–CARPATHIAN REGION

The first stage of the early metal age in Eastern Europe takes in mainly the sixth millennium BP and is distinguished by the formation and operation of two metallurgical provinces – the Balkan–Carpathian in the west and the Caucasian in the east. From the point of view of the development of metallurgy, this whole stage is related to the Chalcolithic. Characteristic of this is the use of only 'pure' native or metallurgical copper, without deliberate additives to form alloys. In metalworking, hammering was combined with increasingly sophisticated casting techniques, going as far as casting in built-up and compound moulds.

In the Chalcolithic period individual population groups from the Balkan and central European early agricultural cultures such as the Gumelnita, the Tiszapolgár, the Lengyel, the Funnel-Beaker and the like spread into the north-west Black Sea area and the south-west European part of what was the USSR. However, the main early agricultural event in this territory in the Chalcolithic period was the Cucuteni–Tripolye culture. It emerged as the result of an intrusion at the end of the seventh millennium BP into the Moldova and into Transylvania by tribes of the Boian culture (in the Juleşti phase), who came into contact with the tribes of the late Bandkeramik culture, with definite influences from the Criş and Vinča–Tordos cultures and with some local components also playing a part (Dumitrescu, 1963a, 1973; Marinescu-Bilcu, 1974; Zbenovich, 1982, 1985). The Cucuteni–Tripolye culture developed from the end of the seventh and the beginning of the sixth millennium up to the third quarter of the fifth millennium BP. Within this chronological period, three main consecutive periods have been distinguished (Passek, 1949, 1961, 1962; Dumitrescu, 1963a).

The early period: Tripolye A (Pre-Cucuteni II–III)

This is dated to between 6,000 and 5,500 years ago. This is the culture of the tribes that settled on the Moldova and in the region between the Prut and the Dniester, with an extension to the southern Bug. The settlements of that period are small (1 or 2 ha), with rectangular houses made of pisé and oval dwellings dug into the ground. No burial grounds have been discovered. Copper ornaments and small tools are widespread, together with a developed flint industry. The metal came from deposits in the northern Balkan (Chernysh, 1978). Vessels were decorated by the use of incisions, pin marks and appliqué, and were stamped. There are many clay statuettes of female figures.

The Tripolye B period

In the second half of the sixth millennium BP the culture spread eastwards up to the middle reaches of the Dnieper and northwards to the upper Dniester. The size of the settlements increased to 50 and even 100 ha and the houses to 200 m². Making their appearance are large copper tools such as celts, chisels and axes. Monochrome and polychrome decoration of vessels became widespread, with geometrical, animal and anthropomorphic motifs. Statuettes of male figures make their appearance, together with those of female figures. Distinct local groups began to emerge within the culture.

The Tripolye C period

This takes in the first three-quarters of the fifth millennium BP; in it the area of the culture extended still further as far as Volynia and the left bank of the Dnieper; differences between local groups became much sharper. The settlements, which are occasionally very large (up to 200 ha), were on high ground difficult of access and were frequently fortified. Necropolises have been found with individual crouched burials. Vessels have monochrome decoration. Typical are black-glazed vessels with incised, corded and stamped decoration. Copper daggers made their appearance. Statuary took on a very stylized nature. This stage marks the transition to the early Bronze Age. Internal centrifugal phenomena and the ever increasing influence of the steppe cattle-breeders of the shaft-and-chamber culture from the east and the tribes of the globular amphora and corded ware cultures from the west led to the end of the Tripolye culture. That culture, however, exercised a decisive influence on the spread of the productive economy and metallurgy in the European part of the former USSR.

CHALCOLITHIC PERIOD IN THE CAUCASUS

The second most important Chalcolithic centre in the territory under consideration was the Caucasus.

Here, and primarily in the southern and north-eastern Caucasus, the early agricultural cultures, which had begun to emerge even in Neolithic times, continued to develop. In the southern Caucasus, the principal kinds of remains are the permanent, many-layered settlements with cultural layers up to 8 and even 9 m thick. They form two groups (Munchaev, 1982). The first one is located in central Transcaucasia, and primarily the middle reaches of the river Kura. Its most significant remains are to be found at Shulaverisgora, Khramis-Didigora, Shomutepe and Arukhlo. The second group is found in southern Transcaucasia (Kyultepe I at Nakhichevan, Tekhut and so on). The main period of development of these cultures was in the seventh and early sixth millennium BP. In both groups, buildings were mostly round, domed constructions or cylindrical houses with a single room, made out of sun-dried brick or, more rarely, stone. The clay-covered floors and walls were sometimes decorated. Burials were within the settlements (crouched skeletons lying on their backs or sides). By far the greatest number of tools were made from obsidian, flint and stone (sickle blades, scrapers, hoes, millstones, pins and the like), but artefacts made of copper and copper–arsenic alloys are also found (pendants, beads, knives, awls and so on). The pottery was rough and simple in shape with relief, stamped or incised ornamentation. However, side by side with this, in the southern group, has been found imported, decorated Halaf ware and also local ware with decoration which imitated Mesopotamian and northern Iranian patterns (Munchaev, 1982, pp. 111–12, 116–22). On the whole, the culture is clearly of an early agricultural kind.

The same thing must also be said about a number of remains in the north-east Caucasus. The most outstanding of these is the settlement of Ginchin in Dagestan. It is surrounded by a stone wall and the walls of the rectangular and circular houses are likewise of stone (Munchaev, 1982, pp. 124–6). Together with the rough local pottery are found vessels akin to trans-Caucasian and northern Iranian ones. The stone implements are also akin to the trans-Caucasian ones, although they have their own definite characteristics (Gadshiev, 1978). At the same time, there is also incontrovertible evidence of a knowledge of metal. Here, as early as the Chalcolithic Age, the foundations were being laid for the powerful metallurgical centre that emerged in the following period.

CHALCOLITHIC PERIOD IN THE STEPPE AND IN THE SOUTHERN PART OF THE FOREST-STEPPE REGIONS

The Chalcolithic centres of the north-west Black Sea area and the Caucasus exercised a decisive influence on the Black Sea – Caspian steppe region which directly adjoined them, and on the more northerly regions. Here, too, the Chalcolithic period was marked by the spread of productive economic forms on a far wider scale than in Neolithic times. Conditions for the development of early agriculture were extremely limited here, since agriculture could be practised only in the isolated river valleys and there was a virtually unlimited supply of food for cattle-raising on the feather grass and wormwood steppes. However, to exploit the potential resources of the open steppes required the development of specific migratory forms of cattle-raising. The earliest stages of this prolonged and complex process, which finished towards the end of the Bronze Age with the emergence of 'traditional' forms of nomadism, can now be linked with the Chalcolithic. It was precisely the migratory forms of stock raising, primarily of sheep and horses, that were responsible for the extent and efficiency of the spread into the steppe of the technical and cultural achievements of the southern centres, and especially of metallurgy and metal-working. Already throughout the sixth millennium BP, copper was becoming widespread in the steppes and forest-steppe regions of eastern Europe and became quite abundant, represented by complicated and bulky artefacts. Chemical analysis has shown that the metal came from the steppe region – as far as the Volga in the east – of the Balkan–Carpathian metallurgical province, the metal deposits of which, mostly situated in the mining area of northern Thrace, provided the whole of this vast area with copper (Chernysh, 1978, pp. 119 ff., 263 ff.). In the process of the spread of the production economy, from the general cultural point of view and as regards the appearance of metal, the dominant influence in the steppe areas at this stage was exercised by the Balkan–Danube centres and their very important north-east outpost, the Tripolye culture.

However, the influences quite quickly became two-way. Beginning with the middle period of the Tripolye, and to the east of the territory of that culture, on the boundary between the forest-steppe and the true steppe, there emerged a number of cultures in whose economies the importance of stock raising grew quickly alongside the traditional hunting and fishing activities, while in the spread of cultures there were ever more pronounced intrusions into the open steppe (Merpert, 1980). At the same time, the originators of these cultures intruded actively into the territory of the Cucuteni–Tripolye culture itself as far as the Balkan–Danube region, exercising an ever more active influence on the early agricultural population (Movsha, 1981; Kósko, 1985).

Thus in the forest-steppe regions and partly also in the steppe regions of the Dnieper and Ukraine on the left bank, right up to the middle and lower reaches of the Don, from the middle of the sixth to the first quarter of the fifth millennium BP, there developed the middle Serednij Stog II culture (Telegin, 1972–3, 1985), with which is associated one of the most ancient centres of the domestication of the horse (Tsalkin, 1970). In the purely steppe regions of the area between the Dnieper and the Don, dating from the sixth millennium BP, there are widespread remains of the neo-Danilo type (Telegin, 1985, p. 318) such as stone graves, crouched corpses decorated with ochre, lying on their backs, and, among the grave goods, Balkan–Danube objects (copper ornaments), objects characteristic of the steppes (flints) and possibly also Caucasian items (ceramics). Further east, in the middle reaches of the Don, a Chalcolithic culture (Repinsk) has been discovered and in the Volga region and the territory between the Volga and the Urals occurs the particularly expressive Khvalynsk culture with conclusive evidence of stock raising, crouched corpses decorated with ochre and laid on their backs, many stone artefacts (knife-shaped blades, arrow-heads, socketed axe-heads, a sceptre and bracelets) and copper artefacts (spiral bracelets, and so on), together with typical steppe pottery, found later in the shaft-and-chamber culture (Vassilyev, 1981; Malov, 1982; Pestrikova, 1987). Here too the metal is of northern Balkan origin (Chernysh, 1980, p. 323). Recently very similar cul-tural objects have also been discovered in the northern Caspian region (Vassilyev et al., 1986).

As a whole, in the steppe zone and in the south of the forest steppe, a definite stage can be identified, seen in the interaction of a number of Chalcolithic cultures that were independent but were nevertheless drawing closer to each other. This was brought about by the similarity of ecological conditions and forms of adaptation, by links in many directions, which were particularly active in the conditions prevailing in the open steppe areas, by mutual assimilation and by the diffusion of productive skills and cultural traditions. The growth of integrationist trends led to the establishment of gigantic cultural communities in the steppes, pointing already to the following stages of the Bronze Age.

Only individual parts of the north of the forest steppe and the forest zone were affected by the spread of Chalcolithic cultures. Large areas remained at the Neolithic stage of development and did not in general reach the Chalcolithic stage.

BIBLIOGRAPHY

AMIRKHANOV, K. A. 1983. Načalo zemledelija v Dagestane [The Beginnings of Agriculture in Dagestan]. *Priroda* (Moscow), Vol. 2.

BADER, O. N. 1970. Ural'skij neolit [The Neolithic in the Urals]. In: *Kamennyj vek na territorii SSSR* [The Stone Age in the Territory of the USSR]. Moscow, Nauka.

—— 1973. *Volga-Kamskaja ètnokul'turnaja oblast' epohi neolita* [The Ethno-cultural Volga-Kama Region during the Neolithic]. Leningrad, Nauka. (Mat. issled. arheol. SSSR, 172.)

BELANOVSKAYA, T. D. 1973. Hozjajstvo obitatelej neolitičeskogo poselenija Rakušečnyj Yar [The Economy of the Neolithic Village of Rakushechny Yar]. In: *Arheologičeskie raskoki na Donu* [Archaeological Excavations on the Banks of the Don]. Rostov-on-Don.

CHERNYSH, E. N. 1978. Metallurgičeskie provincii i periodizacija epohi rannego metalla na territorii SSSR [Metallurgical Provinces and Dating of the Early Metal Age in the Territory of the USSR]. *Sov. arheol.* (Moscow), Vol. 4.

—— 1980. Metallurgical Provinces of the 5th–2nd Millennia BC in Eastern Europe in Relation to the Process of Indo-Europeanization. *J. Indo-Eur. Stud.* (Washington), Vol. 8, No. 3/4.

DANILENKO, V. N. 1969. *Neolit Ukraïny* [The Neolithic of the Ukraine]. Kiev.

—— 1974. *Èneolit Ukraïny* [The Chalcolithic of the Ukraine]. Kiev.

DOLUKHANOV, P. M.; TIMOFEEV, V. I. 1972. Absoljutnaja hronologija neolita Evrazii [Absolute Chronology of the Eurasian Neolithic]. In: *Problemy absoljutnogo datirovanija v arheologii* [The Problems of Absolute Chronology in Archaeology]. Moscow, Nauka.

DOLUKHANOV, P. M.; ROMANOVA, V. N.; SEMENTSOV, A. A. 1973. *Absoljutnaja hronologija evropejskogo neolita* [Absolute Chronology of the European Neolithic]. Leningrad, Nauka. (Mater. issled. arheol. SSSR, 172.)

DUMITRESCU, V. 1963a. *Originea si evolutia culturii Cucuteni-Tripolie.* SVIV, No. 1.

—— 1963b. The Date of the Earliest Western Expansion of the Kurgan Tribes. *Dacia*, NS, Vol. 7.

—— 1973. À propos d'une nouvelle synthèse concernant l'époque néo-énéolithique du Sud-Est et Centre-Est de l'Europe. *Dacia*, NS, Vol. 17.

EDING, D. N. 1940. *Reznaja skul'ptura Urala* [Wood Carvings in the Urals]. Moscow. (Tr. Gos. Istor. Muz., 10.)

FORMOZOV, A. A. 1962. *Neolit Kryma i černomorskogo poberež'ja Kavkaza* [The Neolithic in the Crimea and the Caucasian Shores of the Black Sea]. Moscow. (Mater. issled. arheol. SSSR, 102.)

—— 1969. *Očerki po pervobytnomu is kusstvu* [Essays on Primitive Art]. Moscow, Nauka.

—— 1977. *Problemy ětnokul'turnoj istorii kamennogo veka na territorii Evropejskoj časti SSSR* [Ethno-cultural History of the Stone Age in the Territory of the European Part of the USSR]. Moscow, Nauka.

GADZHIEV, M. G. 1978. K vydeleniju severovostočnokavkazskogo očaga kamennoj industrii [Identification of Centres of Stone Age Industries in the North-Eastern Caucasus]. In: *Pamjatniki epohi bronzy i rannego zeleza v Dagestane* [Monuments of the Bronze Age and Early Iron Age in Dagestan]. Makhachkala.

GURINA, N. N. 1955. *Oleneostrovskij mogil'nik* [The Graves of Oleny Ostrov]. Leningrad. (Mater. issled. arheol. SSSR, 47.)

—— 1961. *Drevnjaja istorija Severo-Zapada Evropejskoj časti SSSR* [The Ancient History of the North-Western European Part of the USSR]. Moscow. (Mater. issled. arheol. SSSR, 87.)

—— 1970. Neolit lesnoj i leso-stepnoj zon evropejskoj časti SSSR [The Neolithic in the Forest and Forest-steppe Zones of the European Part of the USSR]. In: *Kamennyj vek na territorii SSSR* [The Stone Age in the Territory of the USSR]. Moscow.

—— 1973. Nekotorye obščie voprosy izučenija neolita lesnoj i leso-stepnoj zony Evropejskoj časti SSSR [Some General Problems Concerning the Study of the Neolithic in the Forest and Forest-steppe Zone of the European Part of the USSR]. Leningrad, Nauka. (Mater. issled. arheol. SSSR, 172.)

—— 1973a. *Neolitičeskie plemena Valdajskoj vozvyšennosti* [The Neolithic Tribes of the Valdai Plateau]. Leningrad, Nauka. (Mater. issled. arheol. SSSR, 172.)

—— 1973b. *Drevnie pamjatniki Kol'skogo poluostrova* [Ancient Monuments of the Kola Peninsula]. Leningrad, Nauka. (Mater. issled. arheol. SSSR, 172.)

—— 1976. *Drevnie kamnedobyvajuščie šahty* [Ancient Quarries]. Leningrad, Nauka.

ISSAENKO, V. F.; CHERNYAVSKII, M. M. 1970. Neolit [The Neolithic]. In: *Očerki po arheologii Belorussii* [Essays on the Archaeology of Belorussia]. Minsk.

KHALIKOV, A. K. 1973. *Neolitičeskie plemena Srednego Povolž'ja* [The Neolithic Populations of the Middle Volga]. Leningrad, Nauka. (Mater. issled. arheol. SSSR, 172.)

KHLOBYSTIN, L. P. 1973. *Krajnij Severo-Vostok Evropejskoj časti SSSR v epohu neolita i rannej bronzy* [The Most North-Eastern Limits of the European Part of the USSR during the Neolithic and the Beginning of the Bronze Age]. Leningrad, Nauka. (Mater. issled. arheol. SSSR, 172.)

KIGURADZE, T. V. 1976. *Periodizacija rannezemledel' českoj kul'tury Vostočnogo Zakavkaz'ja* [Dating of the First Land Husbandry Cultures in Eastern Transcaucasia]. Tbilisi. (In Georgian, with a summary in Russian.)

KÓSKO, A. 1985. Influence of the 'Pre-Yamnaya' (Pre-Pitgarve) Communities from the Black Sea Steppe Area in Western European Cultures. In: *L'Énéolithique et le début de l'âge du bronze dans certaines régions de l'Europe*. Cracow.

KRAINOV, D. A. 1960. *Peščernaja stojanka Tac-Air kak osnova dlja periodizacii poslepaleolitičeskih kul'tur Kryma* [The Caves of Tach-Air as a Basis for the Dating of the Post-palaeolithic Cultures of Crimea]. Moscow. (Mater. issled. arheol. SSSR, 91.)

KRAINOV, D. A. et al. 1973. Drevnejšaja neolitičeskaja kul'tura Verhnego Povolž'ja [The First Neolithic Culture of the Upper Volga]. *Vest. Akad. Nauk SSSR* (Moscow), Vol. 5.

KRIZHEVSKAYA, L. Y. 1968. *Neolit Južnogo Urala* [The Neolithic in the Southern Urals]. Leningrad. (Mater. issled. arheol. SSSR, 141.)

—— 1973a. K voprosu o neolite Severo-Vostočnogo Prikaspija [The Neolithic on the North-Eastern Shores of the Caspian Sea]. Moscow, Nauka. (Mater. issled. arheol. SSSR, 185.)

—— 1973b. *Neolitičeskie plemena Južnogo Priural'ja* [The Neolithic Populations of the Southern Urals]. Leningrad, Nauka. (Mater. issled. arheol. SSSR, 172.)

KRUGLOV, A. P.; PIOTROVSKI, B. B.; PODGAETSKI, G. V. 1941. *Mogil'nik v gorode Nal'cike* [The Graves of Nalchik]. Moscow/Leningrad. (Mater. issled. arheol. SSSR, 3.)

LINEVSKI, A. M. 1949. *Petroglify Karelii* [Rock-engravings of Karelia]. Petrozavodsk.

LISSITSYNA, G. N.; PRISHCHEPENKO, L. V. 1977. *Paleoetnobotaničeskie nahodki Kavkaza i Bližnego Vostoka* [Palaeoethnobotanic Discoveries in the Caucasus and the Near East]. Moscow, Nauka.

LOZE, I. A. 1979. *Pozdnij neolit i rannjaja bronza Lubanskoj doliny* [The Late Neolithic and the Beginning of the Bronze Age in the Lubana Valley]. Riga.

MALOV, N. M. 1982. Slopovskij mogil'nik i ego mesto v ěneolite Povolž'ja [The Slopov Graves and their Place in the Chalcolithic of the Middle Volga]. In: *Volgo-Ural'skaja step' i lesotep' epohu rannego metalla* [The Steppe and Forest-steppe of the Volga and Urals in the Early Metal Age]. Kuibyshev.

MARINESCU-BILCU, S. 1974. *Cultura Precucuteni pe teritoriul României*. Bucharest.

MARKEVICH, V. I. 1974. *Bugo-dnestrovskaja kul'tura na territorii Moldavii* [The Bug–Dniester Culture in Moldavia]. Kishinev.

MERPERT, N. J. 1980. Problemy ěneolita stepi i lesostepnoj zony Vostočnoj Evropy [Problems in the Chalcolithic of the Steppe and Steppe-forest Zone in Eastern Europe]. In: *Ěneolit Vostočnoj Evropy* [The Chalcolithic in Eastern Europe]. Moscow, Nauka.

MOVSHA, T. G. 1981. Problemy svjazei Tripol'ja-Kukuteni s plenenami kul'tur stepnogo areala [The Problem of the Links of Tripolye-Kukuteni with the Populations of the Steppe Habitat Cultures]. *Studia Praehist.* (Sofia), Vol. 5/6.

MUNCHAEV, R. M. 1975. *Kavkaz na zare bronzovogo veka* [The Caucasus at the Dawn of the Bronze Age]. Moscow, Nauka.

—— 1982. Ěneolit Kavkaza [The Caucasian Chalcolithic]. In: *Ěneolit SSSR* [The Chalcolithic in the USSR]. Moscow, Nauka.

NIBIERIDZE, L. D. 1972. *Neolit Zapadnogo Zakavkaz'ja* [The Neolithic in Western Transcaucasia]. Tbilisi. (In Georgian.)

PANKRUSHEV, G. A. 1964. *Plemena Karelii v epohu neolita i rannego metalla* [The Tribes of Karelia in the Neolithic and Early Metal Age]. Moscow.

—— 1973. *Neolitičeskie plemena Karelii* [The Neolithic Tribes of Karelia]. Leningrad, Nauka. (Mater. issled. arheol. SSSR, 172.)

PASSEK, T. S. 1949. *Periodizacija tripol'skih poselenij* [Dating of Tripolye Settlements]. Moscow. (Mater. issled. arheol. SSSR, 10.)

—— 1961. *Rannezemledelčeskie (tripol'skie) plemena Podnestrov'ja* [Early Agricultural Populations [Tripolye] of the Dniester Region]. Moscow. (Mater. issled. arheol. SSSR, 84.)

—— 1962. Relations entre l'Europe occidentale et l'Europe orientale à l'époque néolithique. In: CONGRÈS INTERNATIONAL DES SCIENCES PRÉHISTORIQUES ET PROTOHISTORIQUES, 6ᵉ, Moscow. *Les Rapports et les informations des archéologues de l'URSS*. Moscow.

PESTRIKOVA, V. I. 1987. *Svalinskij ěneolitičeskij mogil'nik kak istoričeskij istočnik* [The Chalcolithic Graves of Svalin as a Historical Source]. Moscow.

POTUSHNYAK, M. F. 1978. Rezul'taty issledovanija pamjatnikov neolita-eneolita v Zakarpat'e [Results of the Study of Neolithic and Chalcolithic Remains in Sub-Carpathia]. In: *Arheologičeskie issledovanija na Ukraine v 1976–1978* [Archaeological Investigations in the Ukraine in 1976–1978]. Uzhgorod.

RAUSCHENBACH, V. M. 1973. *Neolitičeskie plemena bassejna Verhnego Povolžja i Volgo-Okskogo meždurečja* [The Neolithic Populations of the Upper Volga Basin and of the Region between the Volga and the Oka]. Leningrad, Nauka. (Mater. issled. arheol. SSSR, 172.)

RAVDONIKAS, V. I. 1936. *Naskalnye izobraženija Onežskogo ozera* [Rock Engravings of Lake Onega]. Moscow/Leningrad.

—— 1938. *Naskalnye izobraženija Belogo morja* [Rock Engravings of the White Sea]. Moscow/Leningrad.

RIMANTENE, R. K. 1973. *Neolit Litvy i Kaliningradskoj oblasti* [The Neolithic in Lithuania and in the Kaliningrad Region]. Leningrad, Nauka. (Mater. issled. arheol. SSSR, 172.)

SAVVATEEV, Y. A. 1966. Nekotorye voprosy izučenija naskal'nyh izobraženij Karelii [Some Problems Concerning the Study of the Rock Engravings of Karelia]. In: *Novye pamjatniki istorii drevnej Karelii* [New Documents Illustrating the History of Ancient Karelia]. Moscow/Leningrad.

STOLYAR, A. D. 1953. *Mariupol'skij mogil'nik kak istoričeskij istočnik* [The Mariupol Necropolis Considered as a Historical Source]. Leningrad.

—— 1959. Ob odnom centre odomašnivanija svin'i [A Centre for the Domestication of Pigs]. *Sov. arheol.* (Moscow), No. 3.

TELEGIN, D. J. 1968. *Dnipro-donec'ka kul'tura* [The Dnieper–Donets Culture]. Kiev.

—— 1972–3. *Srednestogivs'ka kul'tura epohy midi* [Middle Stogov Culture of the Copper Period]. Kiev.

—— 1985. Srednestogovskaja kultura i pamjatniki nov-odanilovskogo tipa v Podneprov'e i stepnom levoberež'e Ukrainy [Middle Stogov Culture and Neodanilov-type Monuments in the Dnieper Region and the Left-bank Steppe of Ukraine]. *Arheol. Ukrain.* (Kiev), Vol. 1.

TITOV, V. S. 1980. Neolit [The Neolithic]. In: *Arheologija Vengrii* [The Archaeology of Hungary]. Moscow.

TRETYAKOV, V. P. 1972. *Kul'tura jamočno-grebenčatoj keramiki v lesnoj polose evropejskoj časti SSSR* [The Bandkeramik Culture in the Forest Zone of the European Part of the USSR]. Leningrad, Nauka.

TSALKIN, V. I. 1970. *Drevnejšie domašnie životnye Vostočnoj Evropy* [Early Domestic Animals in Western Europe]. Moscow.

TSVETKOVA, I. K. 1973. *Neolitičeskie plemena rjazanskogo tečenija reki Oki* [The Neolithic Tribes of the Oka Valley in the Ryazan Region]. Leningrad, Nauka. (Mater. issled. arheol. SSSR, 172.)

VANKINA, I. B.; ZAGORSKIS, F. A.; LOZE, I. A. 1973. *Neolitičeskie poselenija Latvii* [Neolithic Villages in Latvia]. Leningrad. (Mater. issled. arheol. SSSR, 172.)

VASSILYEV, I. B. 1981. *Ěneolit Povolžja. Step' i lesostep'* [The Chalcolithic in the Volga Region. Steppe and Forest-steppe]. Kuibyshev.

VASSILYEV, I. B.; MATVEEVA, G. I. 1979. Mogil'nik u sela S'ezzee na reke Samare [Graves of the Village of Syezzhee on the River Samara]. *Sov. arheol.* (Moscow), Vol. 4.

VASSILYEV, I. B.; VIBORNOV, A. A.; KOZIN, E. B. 1986. Pozdneneolitičeskaja stojanka Tenteksor v Severnom Prikaspii [The Late Neolithic Site of Tenteksor in the Northern Caspian]. In: *Drevnie Kul'tury Severnogo Prikaspija* [Ancient Cultures of the Northern Caspian]. Kuibyshev.

VINOGRADOV, A. V. 1981. *Drevnie ohotniki i rybolovy Sredneaziatskogo mezdurec'ja* [Ancient Hunters and Fishermen of Central Asia]. Moscow, Nauka.

YANITS, L. Y. 1973. *Neolit Ěstonii* [The Estonian Neolithic]. Leningrad, Nauka. (Mater. issled. arheol. SSSR, 172.)

ZBENOVICH, V. G. 1982. Složenie tripol'skoj kul'tury na territorii SSSR [The Formation of the Culture of Tripolye on the Territory of the USSR]. *Thracia Praeist.*, Suppl. Polpudeva (Sofia), Vol. 3.

—— 1985. *Rannetripol'skie plemena na territorii Ukrainy* [Early Tripolye Tribes in the Ukraine]. Kiev.

53

ATLANTIC EUROPE
during the Neolithic

Pierre-Roland Giot

ATLANTIC FRANCE DURING THE NEOLITHIC

Here we shall be dealing with the Early and Middle Neolithic in France west of the Massif Central and the Paris basin: the Armorican plateau and its sedimentary surroundings from Normandy to Poitou, and the northern parts of Aquitaine. In order to give a balanced account, our discussion of the Late Neolithic extends to the entire Paris basin, and includes examples of that Neolithic culture as far afield as Belgium and Switzerland.

Most of the areas concerned are plains or low plateaux at an average altitude of less than 200 m, where the climate is oceanic and where in any case the influence of the ocean is powerful. What differentiates these regions, apart from their proximity to or distance from the waters of the Atlantic or the English Channel, is the ancient platform of the Armorican plateau, which contrasts with the post-Palaeozoic sedimentary basins of the other territories. Natural conditions, and especially soils, varied considerably at the local level, although a layer of Pleistocene alluvia covered the regions bordering the Channel. The level of the sea obviously rose during the Postglacial period, reaching approximately the present level at the end of what is known as the Atlantic period just after the climate optimum.

The two main streams of Neolithic culture converge in this part of western Europe: the Mediterranean culture (impressed, cardial and Epicardial ceramics) and the later forms of the Bandkeramik culture. They arrived either with the influx of migrant populations or, more probably, mainly through gradual diffusion of the various techniques and styles of the new way of life.

We are faced with the task of discovering which of the two streams was first to arrive in Atlantic France, and what were the effects of their convergence and subsequent meeting, in the Early Neolithic, and also in the Middle Neolithic. The Mediterranean Neolithic is manifest from south to north, from the eastern border of France along the Rhône–Saône corridor to the west coast, right along the Atlantic seaboard.

It follows that in addition to the regional cultural variations there may be differences in the degree of influence. There has been an unfortunate tendency to give these variations unnecessary individual labels. We must beware also of chronological assimilations that are based solely on typological and stylistic similarities (Bailloud, 1973, 1974, 1985; Guilaine, 1976, 1980; Scarre, 1983; Giot, 1983; Burnez, 1976; Joussaume, 1981; Giot et al., 1979; Verron, 1980; Whittle, 1985).

Early Neolithic

The southern type of Early Neolithic

Early Neolithic with impressed pottery of the Epicardial type is well attested in Aquitaine as far as Guyenne, where it takes on an unusual appearance in the interior, at Roucadour. Further to the north indications are more sporadic and tenuous. In the cave of Bellefonds (Vienne), a level lying upon a purely Mesolithic level contained sherds of pottery associated with microliths; the decoration of the pottery showed both Bandkeramik and Epicardial affinities, which gives an idea of the difficulty of the problem. Yet at Gouillauds, in the Île de Ré (Charente-Maritime), a sherd with the imprint of a shell was found beside a group of fragments in a trench whose radiocarbon dating is around 6,800 years ago.

In Vendée there are several sites, mainly at the Pointe du Grouin du Cou near La-Tranche-sur-Mer, that contained complete groups of thin fragments of round-bottomed vessels along with others that were thicker, coarser and decorated with fingerprints (Joussaume, 1981). The oldest dating obtained was around 7,400 years ago.

Almost all those sites – the exception being Grouin du Cou – showed a conjunction of this very early pottery with a preponderance of domestic animal bones (of small ox, sheep or goats, pigs) over the bones of wild animals, with millstones (north of the Loire the site of Dissignac in Saint-Nazaire contained calcined seeds of wheat and vetch), and with a microlithic industry typical of the end of the Mesolithic in the area concerned. Sites dating from the close of the Mesolithic in Brittany testify to settlements at least of a seasonal nature, and to the practice of collective and family burials (in Téviec and Hoëdic), with even the erection of a small pile of stones over the multiple tomb; the sites also yielded piles of shells and some domestic animal bones among a preponderance of game (at Téviec, Hoëdic and La Torche), at comparable dates.

Finally, there are many signs that the distinction between 'Mesolithic' and 'Neolithic' life is somewhat artificial, although there is no way of telling whether this is due to the contacts between neighbouring populations whose ways of life were initially different, one autochthonous and the other from elsewhere, or to a gradual transformation of the way of life of the autochthonous population by slow acculturation. Palynological data would seem to indicate that deforestation would have commenced in the Mesolithic.

The Bandkeramik type of Early Neolithic

Flourishing in the Paris basin, the influence of the latest forms of the Bandkeramik culture are detectable along the Loire as far as Anjou (in sherds belonging to the Augy–Sainte-Pallaye group at La Bajoulière), and along the Channel coast as far as Basse-Normandie and the Channel Isles (with fragments of an epi-Bandkeramik of the Cerny group under the tumulus of La Hoguette at Fontenay-le-Marmion, Calvados, or associated with the first phase of the earthen long barrow at Fouaillages in Guernsey). Some fragments that are possibly related were found at Carnac in long cairns (Caillaud and Lagnel, 1972; Kinnes, 1982).

This gives us an indication of the antiquity of the barrows, often trapezoidal in shape, which would seem to be linked with a north-east European tradition (flourishing in Poland for instance) that featured wooden structures on the inside reminiscent of houses; these fragile structures are a form of para-megalithic architecture, the start of a succession of monuments that developed in a variety of local forms throughout the Neolithic in western France, and which tend to be neglected. Because of their relatively poor state of preservation and the absence of furnishing, it may be that an essential aspect of these cultures is overlooked. The monuments are made of small stones rather than earth and the para-megalithic cairns may contain small cists and cells, whose function was not necessarily always related to burial. The burial mounds of southern Brittany (Loire-Atlantique, Ille-et-Vilaine and Morbihan) are often associated topographically with configurations of standing stones, which they sometimes precede. Other barrows contain cists with individual graves related to those of the Bronze Age.

Middle Neolithic

Megalithic monuments

The oldest megalithic cairns It is remarkable that of the monuments known as 'megalithic tombs' – for lack of a term to cover all their different features - the oldest in Europe that have been discovered to date are situated in Armorica and on the Armorican Jurassic fringes of Poitou and Basse-Normandie (where the calcareous nature of the building materials is more conducive to the preservation of bones), and that in those three regions the extreme dates are identical: for monuments such as Bougon Fo (Deux-Sèvres) (Plate 104), Barnenez G, Guennoc IIIC and Roc'h-Avel (Finistère) around 7,200 to 6,400 years ago, and for sites such as Carn (Fig. 152); Saint-Thois 2 N (Finistère) and La Hoguette VI (Calvados) (Fig. 153) around 6,700 to 5,900 years ago. It is equally remarkable that these monuments, far from being among the simplest we know of, are highly elaborate structures in prestigious groups, either arranged like cemeteries or clustered under large cairns or barrows of various shapes, often testifying to a very complex history with many alterations and successive additions (L'Helgouach, 1965, 1971, 1973, 1976; Giot, 1982; Mohen, 1984).

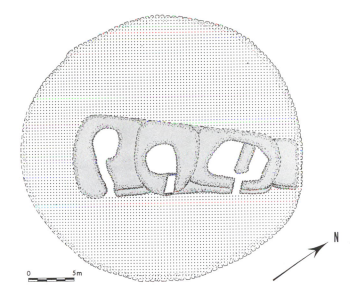

Figure 152 Plan of the Carn Island cairn, Ploudalmézeau, Finistère (France). Dark stippling: primary cairn, wedge-shaped, comprising three chamber and passage graves with dry-stone walls. The centre grave still had its closing walls at the entrance to the chamber and the entrance to the passage. Lighter stippling: the secondary cairn, a huge circular mound, preventing further use of the graves. The primary cairn dates back to the Middle Neolithic; the second cairn corresponds to the Terminal Neolithic. (Documents by Giot.)

The basic monuments are essentially of the passage grave type with many variants that derive from local materials and the resultant traditions – for the construction methods used with limestone slabs cannot be used with blocks or slabs of gneissose granite, or unshaped granite boulders. The result is a plethora of local styles that defy description. The oldest structures are the circular chamber tombs, which usually have dry-stone walls and corbelled vaults, but which may have vertical slabs, and are always covered with megalithic capstones. When these tombs stand alone they are covered by a cairn with low facing walls, rectangular in form, or sometimes circular. Where the original monuments have others added to them, they are covered with large cairns and their passages can be considerably extended, as is the case at Barnenez in Plouézoc'h (Finistère). These cairns vary in shape from roughly trapezoidal or rectangular, when the tombs are side by side, to rounded when they radiate from a point (as in the cairns of Normandy). The low, concentric facing walls are tiered and in some cases there are several of them. The layout of the burial chambers is reminiscent both of a grotto and of a wooden house. In the cairns, too, we find aspects of the houses of the dead seen in other cultures.

In the limestone tombs where the bones are relatively well preserved (in Poitou and in Normandy), as many as fifteen bodies are to be found, laid flexed on their sides.

The development of passage graves ('dolmens') (Fig. 154) Some geographical areas continued to favour polygonal chambers, while others produced their own variants. In west central France there are monuments of the Angoumoisin type with a rectangular chamber, the position of the passage forming 'P', 'q' or 'T' plans. In the south of Brittany from the Loire to Morbihan, chambers with lateral cells were succeeded by chambers with transepts, while in the south of Finistère there were many chambers divided into compartments. In the Channel Isles there are rectangular chambers around

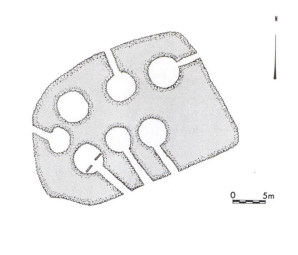

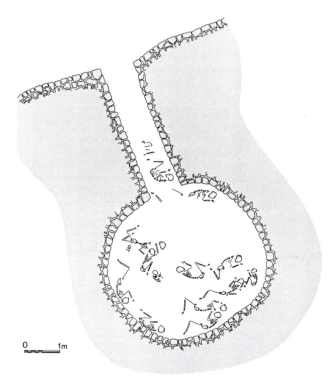

Figure 153 Plan of La Hoguette cairn, Fontenay-le-Marmion, Calvados (France) and detail of burial I, with the positions of the skeletons. The cairn, from the Middle Neolithic, is of limestone. (Diagram after Caillaud and Lagnel, 1972.)

which cells or stalls were added; in this way La Hougue Bie and Faldouet (Plate 105) in Jersey acquired a cruciform plan.

Modern excavations confirm here again that large monuments, especially when grouped together, show signs of restructuring. A number of tombs were in use only for a short time and were then sealed and blocked up, whereas others were used repeatedly for a very long time, two millennia in some cases, as can be deduced from their contents, particularly the pottery. The fact that a tomb continued to be used does not imply that it was still considered as a grave or an ossuary, for it is certain that the socio-religious function of these monuments was much more complex and comprehensive than a simple cult of the dead.

The large (and occasionally gigantic) barrows are a very curious phenomenon. Poitou contains some large remnants of non-megalithic barrows, with no clearly defined internal structure. Yet it is in the region around the mouth of the

Gulf of Morbihan, Arzon, Locmariaquer and Carnac that we find a series of monuments that have certain points in common with some of the barrows in the necropolis of Bougon, Poitou. No two of these monuments are alike. Almost all of them seem to have begun as passage graves, and in some this earlier part is at one end, functioning in the normal way as entrance and exit (as in Petit-Mont, Mané-Lud and Moustoir), while in others it has been incorporated and sealed up in the later barrow (as at Saint-Michel); the remainder of the barrow contains one or more sealed chambers or cells, which may have served as individual tombs. In other cases (Tumiac and Mané-er-Hroëck) the barrow is roughly circular and seems to contain a single, closed chamber. These chambers are of megalithic construction with slabs and dry-stone work in the walls.

These tombs, which are presumed to have been individual and which in any case were used only once, at the time of building, yielded sumptuous funerary treasures and ceremonial objects when they were excavated in the middle of the last century. The most extraordinary was the site of Mané-er-Hroëck, which contained 106 polished axes of rare materials (fibrolite and jadeite), 49 variscite beads and pendants, and an annular serpentine disc. On occasion the associated passage graves also contained many variscite beads and pendants.

The barrows are constructed partly of loose stone and partly of earth, sometimes with evidence of gradual accumulation.

Menhirs and decorated stelae One of the most remarkable features of the regions of Atlantic France is the wealth of standing stones or 'menhirs' (Plate 106). Even if we disregard the alignments, we find the greatest profusion of isolated stones or small groups. Most of them date from the Late Neolithic, or at least such is the general opinion, since very few of the stones have datable elements; the excavations of the last century, which often completely destabilized them, at least succeeded in demonstrating from the objects laid in the foundations of the menhirs with the stones that wedge their base, that this type of monument goes back to the Neolithic.

There are also menhirs with decorative motifs, incised or, more often, in bas-relief, which are also found on the slabs of passage graves, the most common being crooks and hafted axes. Erosion and deterioration of the stone has effaced much of this art, which was in any case possible only on some of the monuments. The most outstanding example – the menhir of Saint–Samson-sur–Rance (Côtes-du-Nord), stands 7 m high and is completely covered with designs on the front and also decorated on both sides.

Recent discoveries enable us to affirm that very large menhirs or decorated stelae were present at the beginning of the Middle Neolithic at Locmariaquer (Fig. 155), that they were later deliberately demolished and cut up, and that fragments of some of them were used as capstones for the chambers of the most prestigious of the megalithic tombs in the region. The broken pieces of the Great Menhir of Locmariaquer, which had been 20.5 m in length, remained on site; despite the work of erosion we can distinguish on it the image of a hafted axe. There must have been another decorated stele nearby, whose fragments were used to cover the 'dolmen' of the 'Table des Marchands' and the Er Vinglé tomb next to it, as well as the chamber of the prestigious tomb on the island of Gavrinis. Precise chronological information therefore exists; and the designs on the underside of the Table des Marchands match the top of the Gavrinis slab

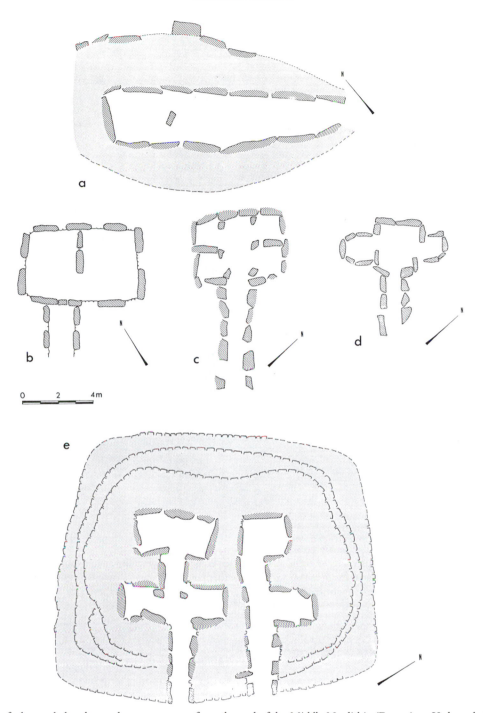

Figure 154 Plans of advanced chamber and passage graves, from the end of the Middle Neolithic (France): a, V-shaped chamber grave of Ty-ar-Boudiget, Brennilis, Finistère, with oval tumulus and remains of its megalithic enclosure (after L'Helgouach, 1965); b, 'Angoumoisin'-type grave from Tumulus A at Bougon, Deux-Sèvres, which is contained in a round cairn (after Mohen, 1973); c, Mané-Groh partitioned chamber grave at Erdeven, Morbihan, which is contained in an elongated mound (after L'Helgouach, 1965); d, Grave with side chambers opening from the square chamber, at Locqueltas, Locoal-Mendon, Morbihan (after L'Helgouach, 1965); e, Les Mousseaux cairn at Pornic, Loire-Atlantique, with two transept graves and concentric rings of kerbstones (after L'Helgouach and Poulain, 1984).

perfectly: the complete pattern features two quadrupeds with upright horns between two hafted axes of different sizes and a number of crooks (L'Helgouach, 1983; Le Roux, 1984).

This means that not only were there menhirs already standing in the Middle Neolithic, but that at least some of the most massive of them were erected very early, given the typological sequences of the passage tombs.

Megalithic construction techniques Many of the most spectacular feats of engineering, as regards both cairns and stand-ing stones, are also among the earliest. The Bougon excavations have shed light on how the limestone slabs were quarried. A number of marks made in the cutting up of natural blocks of granite have been noted. In addition to comparative study of ethnological data and what is known of ancient technology, experimental archaeology has confirmed the most likely methods of transport and construction used. In Brittany the geological origin of material shows that it was not uncommon for stones to be transported 4 km. The large menhir of Plouarzel (Finistère), which stands 10 m high and weighs some 150 tonnes, must have been shifted

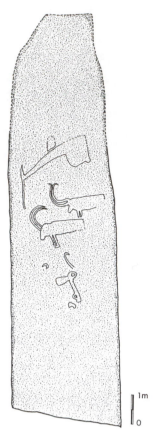

1m
0

Figure 155 Reconstitution of a large decorated stele from Locmariaquer (France). The lower part of the decorated area is actually underneath the capstone of the 'Table des Marchands' dolmen at Locmariaquer. The upper part of this decorated area is to be found on the top of the capstone of the Gavrinis dolmen. (After Le Roux, 1984.)

at least 2.5 km from the spot 100 m below its present site. While such operations required a great many people, many others must have taken small teams a long time. It has been estimated on the basis of many examples that the construction of an average megalithic tomb was quite within the 'leisure time' available to a population of a few hundred in a few months.

These immense monuments which seem destined to outlast time, in contrast to the dwellings of the living, were for the most part built over a considerable period, often refashioned and recommenced, re-using materials taken from earlier structures; they must be considered in a very long perspective.

Megalithic art There is an architectural art that, notwithstanding the coarser execution of certain monuments in comparison to the careful finishing of others, is to be seen in the disposition of three-dimensional space and the organization of groups. Wall decoration, which usually involves pecking rather than carving, depends on the materials. It includes the rather narrow range of geometric motifs that are to be seen on some of the pottery of the period, especially shield motifs, which might be stylized depictions of an anthropomorphic idol, U-shapes, snakes and zigzags set either in no discernible order or, as at Gavrinis, in a highly organized way. The most easily recognizable object is the axe and its variants, either the head alone or the hafted tool, which was either an object of reverence or an emblem of prestige and a symbol (Shee Twohig, 1981; Pequart et al., 1927).

Regional variants are to be found: in Poitou the limestone slabs lend themselves to squaring and jointing, the cutting of rabbets, the fashioning of a monolithic door at Sainte-Soline. In Brittany there is a trend towards anthropomorphism in a number of slabs acting as supports or as vertical stelae, which is expressed in the outline of the stone.

Middle Neolithic society

Social organization We lack precise data on the habitation sites of these regions, partly because soil erosion has removed traces of them. Concentrations of flint and polished axes in arable land occasionally allow us to guess where settlements were. There is a lack of storage pits, either because shelters were used or because of the difficulty of digging ditches. Dwellings must have been wooden, but the few postholes detected tell us nothing of their size and arrangement. A number of hearths were embedded in the old coastal soils.

This means that our information on population distribution comes only indirectly from the location of objects discovered and from the siting of megalithic tombs and other structures. There are no sound bases on which to build theories.

As regards society, all we can infer derives from what we can guess about the funerary sites and the relative importance of the different types of monument. It is now certain that while much manpower went into their construction, few bodies were buried there or had their bones placed in such tombs. There was therefore some selection, and we do not know on what criteria, although judging by the sites where remains were preserved we can say that the criteria did not exclude either sex, nor did they debar very young children. The tombs, whether individual or collective, which certainly contained objects of prestige, more refined jewellery or tools, and which were built on a grand scale, cannot but make us think of a hierarchy, and considerable differences in relative 'wealth'.

We should note that the funerary objects of the tombs of north Brittany seem more simple and less sumptuous than those of the more southerly regions, and that the polished axe, as an object, does not seem to appear before an advanced phase of the Middle Neolithic, some centuries after its appearance in dated sites.

The agricultural economy The palynological sequences of the peat beds point to a fairly early human impact on the flora, from about 7000 years ago. Burned hexaploid wheat grain has been identified at Dissignac, confirming the transient evidence of scattered pollen. Vetch, too, was gathered. However, there are not sufficient data to enable us to assess the relative importance of the crops.

The usual domestic animals for the time were kept – sheep and cattle – although hunting still played an important role.

Mineral extraction Open-cast mining of flint must have begun early, when outcrops were not available. In the plain of Caen in Normandy, extraction from shafts and tunnels may have begun towards the end of the Middle Neolithic. The absence of flint in the ancient massif, apart from small amounts in beach pebbles, prompted the search for substitutes, especially for the manufacture of polished stone axes.

Half the polished stone axes of Brittany are made of a distinctive dolerite from Plussulien (Côtes-du-Nord) where quarries and cutting workshops occupied a vast area round a rock. Fires were used to heat the rock till it cracked, after which the splinters were cut to shape. The oldest date obtained for the workshop corresponds to the Middle Neolithic towards 6,000 years ago, although extraction continued until the end of the Neolithic. Exported in quantity throughout the Armorican Plateau from Normandy to Poitou, these axes were to be found almost everywhere in France, as well as in Britain and Belgium.

The use of natural blocks of fibrolite, which can be fashioned only by sawing and polishing, began earlier; it is to be found in several parts of the Armorican plateau, which also provided eclogite, although some of the beautiful jadeite axes must have come from the Alps, which implies a long chain of exchange.

The origin of the callaïs (variscite) jewellery was a puzzle for a long time. It is known that callaïs was to be found in Neolithic mines in Catalonia, but a deposit of the mineral has been located in south-east Brittany, which means that a regional origin is possible.

All the resources of the mineral environment were therefore exploited very early on to meet specific needs.

The development of pottery and its styles   Pottery, whose development was at times very rapid and which is easily divided into regional styles, is a very useful tool for distinguishing cultural groups, although its nomenclature and typology are too easily encumbered with excessive distinctions.

If we leave aside the late epi-Rössen influences that are detectable as far off as the Channel Isles, the regional pottery of the Middle Neolithic tends to be very simple in shape, round-bottomed, with a uniform, smooth surface. There are some very carefully made pieces, at times astonishing in their regularity, comparable to the best products of the Carn style in Brittany, despite their low firing. These forms are so simple and ubiquitous that it is easy to see in them affinities with both currents of Neolithic culture, which ultimately renders the question of their affinities meaningless. There are also less successful pieces, depending on the quality of the clay and of the temper.

At a more advanced stage of the Middle Neolithic, the problems become more complicated. There are on the one hand more developed forms of various local styles, with the appearance of reinforcement, handles and knobs for hanging the vessels, and occasional decoration. On the other hand there is the infiltration up to the Atlantic shore of the great ceramic tradition of the south and centre of France producing what might be termed the Atlantic Chassey culture, with interactions seen in local products. The most typical form is that of cups on bases, hollow cylinders or tubes with a small cup used as a lid, decorated with incised or pecked geometrical motifs such as triangles. An Armorican speciality, the hollow-based vase, smooth or decorated, seems to have been used for libations and was often found in front of the façade of the large megalithic tombs, at a precise spot where certain ceremonies seem to have taken place.

In Poitou, on the isolated spur of Les Châtelliers-du-Vieil-Auzay (Vendée), a hoard of Atlantic Chassey pottery of various forms was discovered, showing the appearance of defended settlements. In Brittany, on the islet of Er-Lannic at the mouth of the Gulf of Morbihan, an incredible quantity of cups on bases in a strange type of local ceramic was discovered along with a variety of objects that mark a site whose purpose is still a mystery, since it became the place at which two tangent semicircles of menhirs were set up (L'Helgouach, 1971).

Late Neolithic

From approximately 6,000 years ago a number of innovations and gradual cultural changes are to be observed. Some are strictly local, while others extend beyond the bounds of our chosen region, which is why we must consider a larger zone, covering all of northern France and beyond.

The tombs

Later types of megalithic tombs (Fig. 156)   Passage graves continued to diversify. A fairly widespread type is the 'dolmen' of Anjou with a portalled entrance, which in fact is to be found on both sides of the mid-Loire valley, and as far afield as eastern Brittany (La Roche aux Fées d'Essé), Poitou and Vendée. Some of these monuments are of considerable size, with the chamber subdivided into stalls. The cairn or barrow is trapezoidal.

The angled or right-angled graves are found only on the southern coast of Brittany, an obtuse or right angle marking the meeting of the passage with the chamber, which is extended, and can be subdivided into stalls. The tomb at Gâvres, recently excavated, is remarkable for the large slab that acts as a 'door' between chamber and passage. Such angled graves as those at Gâvres and Luffang-en-Crac'h (Plate 107) have a different style of wall decoration which features especially frames or shields filled with decorations (L'Helgouach, 1970; Le Roux, 1984).

Another category of monuments, scattered throughout Brittany and the Channel Isles, reduces the distinction between chamber and passage, tending to form a long, wedge-shaped chamber. The date of the monument of Liscuis I at Lanniscat (Côtes-du-Nord) is interesting in that it is contemporary with the opening of the nearby Plussulien dolerite workshop, around 6,000 years ago.

It should not be forgotten that, except in cases where the tombs were sealed and not reopened, it often happened that Middle Neolithic tombs continued to be used for burials and the deposition of funerary objects. Some were finally sealed up with massive obstructions in the Late Neolithic, examples being Carn Island and Gavrinis.

Non-megalithic graves   In the long barrows we find additional cells or cists with more recent contents; the same is true of the barrows surrounding some megalithic tombs. In Brittany there are also a number of earthen round barrows without well-defined internal structure, which seem to have covered central tombs. The barrow at Penvenan (Côtes-du-Nord) was built on top of an oval ring of vertical stones that were almost joined together. The Guidel barrow in Morbihan seems to have been crowned with a statue menhir representing a woman, some pieces of which have been rediscovered (Briard and Giot, 1968). Statue menhirs are to be found also in Brittany (Le Trévoux, Finistère) and in Guernsey; the head is reduced to a cone, but the breasts are well sculpted.

Gallery graves and hypogea (Fig. 157)   Megalithic graves of the Late Neolithic, which are the most common, are traditionally known as 'gallery graves'. By this stage there is only a long chamber, although opposite the entrance there may be a cell or *cella* that is cut off from the chamber.

In contrast to the passage graves there is no distinction at all between passage and chamber, although this arrangement is reached by different, converging routes. In Armorica it would seem to be mainly an extension of the wedge-shaped

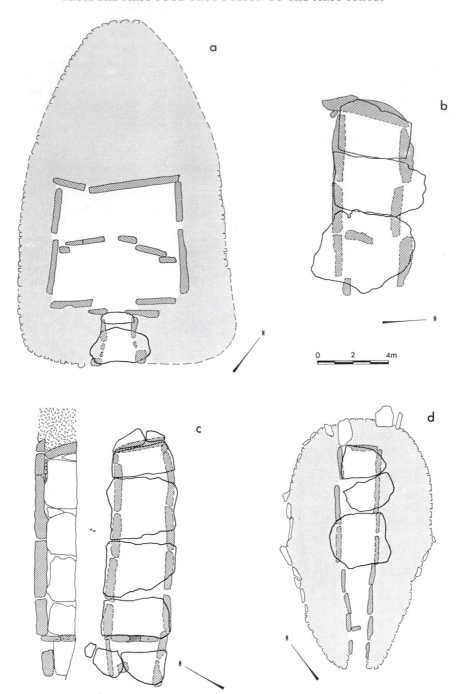

Figure 156 Plan of megalithic tombs, Late Neolithic (France): a, 'Angevin' tomb with portal slabs, at La Bajoulière, Saint-Rémy-la-Varenne, Maine-et-Loire, in its wedge-shaped cairn (after Gruet, 1967); b, the 'Grotte des Fées', or dolmen de Mettray, at Saint-Antoine-du-Rocher, Indre-et-Loire, another Angevin portal dolmen (after Cordier, 1963); c, half-buried gallery grave, 'La Pierre Turquaise', Saint-Martin-du-Tertre, Val d'Oise (after Peek, 1975); d, V-shaped Liscuis I tomb at Laniscat, Côtes-du-Nord, an intermediate form preparatory to that of the gallery grave – its mound is marked out by a few small standing slabs (after Le Roux, 1984).

graves; the interior of the tombs is paved. It is covered with a long burial mound and decorated with small vertical slabs that form a rectangular border, very similar to that of the para-megalithic earthen long barrows.

Another Armorican variant is the tomb with side entrance, which may derive from the T-shaped tombs. The latter are very similar to certain dolmens that have a long chamber at right angles to a short corridor, and are to be found in northern Germany and Scandinavia. These monuments often have port-holes, with two indented slabs between chamber and entrance (L'Helgouach, 1965).

It is not beyond the bounds of possibility that portal graves, in losing this last feature, should have acquired short galleries. All manner of simplified graves inland as far as the Massif Central seem to derive from gallery graves.

The gallery graves of the Paris basin are usually sunk in a trench instead of being built above ground like most megalithic tombs. Since conditions often favour the preservation of bones, it has been ascertained that these graves, which were used as ossuaries in the proper sense, could contain the remains of several hundred individuals. The meticulous excavation of the gallery grave at La Chaussée-Tirancourt (Somme), which accommodated the remains of 350 people, showed that the first burials were set in compartments separated by stones or planks; subsequent burials shifted most of the original ones. At first bodies were placed flexed on

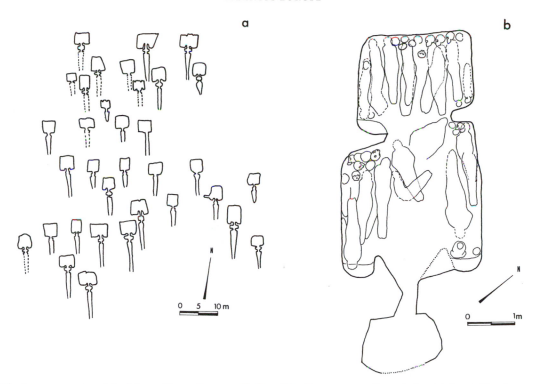

Figure 157 The hypogea tombs of the Marne (France): a, overall plan of the Razet necropolis at Coizard (after Bailloud, 1974); b, plan of the Les Mournouards hypogeum at Mesnil-sur-Oger with site of the last burials in the forecourt and the chamber (after Leroi-Gourhan et al., 1962).

the side, and at a later stage they were laid supine (Masset, 1972; Bailloud, 1974; Masset and Leclerc, 1979).

Five monuments related to the gallery graves are known in south-west Belgium. The *Steinkisten* of western Germany, especially in Hessen and Westphalia, show striking similarities to the Parisian gallery graves, and the Etteln grave even has stones surrounding the burial mound, as in the Armorican examples. The mobiliary objects, however, are related to the cultures of Central Europe.

In the chalky regions of Champagne, especially the Marne and as far as the limestone of the Oise, we find graves cut into the rock. These are substitutes, since building materials are lacking. A trench leads to a rectangular chamber with a reduced entrance, often through an antechamber. This plan results from the transposition of domestic architecture (such as we encounter in Late Neolithic villages in central Europe) to the realm of the dead. The careful excavation at Les Mournouards has shown that about sixty bodies were buried there successively, sewn up in sacks, the last ones shifting the bones of the first against the walls (Leroi-Gourhan et al., 1962).

Where there are 'doors' instead of the Armorican indented slabs, we find 'porthole' windows in the Parisian gallery graves, a kind of manhole between the vestibule and the chamber proper, very similar to the reduced entrance to the hypogea.

The construction and use of such monuments continues beyond the Late Neolithic throughout the Chalcolithic. Other megalithic monuments are to be found around the mid-Rhine, in Bavaria, Switzerland and Franche-Comté. Beginning with square chambers with porthole slabs and very low cairns, or podia, the series ends with chambers and antechambers that are very similar to the wooden houses of the era, having very long trapezoidal podia bordered with slabs set on edge, or low walls (Petrequin, 1985).

The simple pseudo-dolmens that appear here and there

in various forms and are little more than large boxes, must be ranged with other manifestations of megalithic graves.

The mural art of the Armorican and Parisian gallery graves and of the hypogea consists in the main of depictions of a feminine idol, usually stylized with simple pairs of breasts in bas-relief, sometimes adorned with a 'necklace'. This, unlike the asexual art of the passage graves, evokes the great goddess of death.

Menhirs and alignments As well as isolated menhirs we find very complex monuments comprising lines of menhirs more or less regularly spaced in parallel lines, isolated lines and enclosures. Since it is unusual to find these monuments in a complete state, given that they were easy quarries, we do not have a good idea of their original and complete appearance. It must be assumed that little lines of menhirs that are to be found all over western France were the most common type of monument, and that the great fields of menhirs in Brittany (which were not to be found in the Carnac region alone) (Plate 108) represented a more specific development. The principal features of the latter are multiple sub-parallel lines and roughly circular or ovoid enclosures of joined menhirs (often improperly referred to as 'cromlec'h'). Over the last hundred years there has been much speculation on the significance of these groups, especially in terms of archaeo-astronomy, although no really convincing conclusion has been reached (Giot, 1979).

Late Neolithic society

Demography The fact that many more bodies were buried in the collective graves does not mean that the entire population had access to such burial. Rituals must have changed down the centuries as much as the architecture of the mega-liths, and in different ways in the different regions. A common feature is the considerable increase in graves and in settlements of objects that can be interpreted as weapons, and in fact lesions are found on bones, such as might result from stab wounds inflicted by arrowheads, suggesting that populations were unstable or warring, perhaps because they had become more numerous.

It is from this period also that we find evidence of such surgical skills as trepanation.

Settlements and fortified camps In many regions habitation sites are still little known. There was a tendency to occupy spurs between rivers or coastal promontories (which were often fortified subsequently), at least in Armorica, in contrast to the Paris basin where there is a marked dispersal. In west-central France, the Charentes and adjoining regions, some sixty fortified sites on limestone plateaux bordering low and marshy areas are now known. They were encircled by a ditch that at first had a single gap for an entrance, and in later examples had an entrance shaped like crab pincers protected by a small external construction. There were as many as three concentric ditches. At Champ-Duran in Nieul-sur-Autize (Vendée) (Fig. 158) it was possible to demonstrate that the entrances, which correspond to gaps in the ditches, were always protected with thick, dry-stone walls, and even had towers to protect the inner entrance. Thus there already existed highly elaborate fortifications on this site. Graves were discovered in niches dug in the walls. The ditches contained many relics of occupation (Joussaume, 1981).

Nearer the Loire, the recent discovery of the camp of Machecoul (Loire-Atlantique) with its interrupted ditches showed traces of palisades within a defence consisting of two banks and three ditches. Within the camp, the houses were large wooden buildings.

The economy The palynological sequences and the wider diffusion of isolated objects show that clearings were extended. The fauna discovered in the ditches of the Machecoul camp, for example, show that hunting still played an important role in providing food, alongside arable farming. The antler industry developed considerably in most regions as a by-product of hunting.

The Late Neolithic saw a general expansion of flint mining, affecting Normandy in the region under consideration, and massive exploitation of flint mines and quarries in other places: the blond flint of Le Grand Pressigny in Touraine, and the ribbon flint of Taillebourg in the Charentes. Large workshops came into existence for the cutting of flint. At the same time the extraction of the Plussulien dolerite reached its apogee. All these products, in rough or finished form, were sent far from their sources in large quantities, by whatever systems of exchange were in operation. Laboratory examination of the raw materials tells us much about this matter. The most successful workshops, which used the best raw materials, were still flourishing in the Chalcolithic. Thus, for example, a very limited deposit of hornblendite at Pleuven (Finistère), which produced battle-axes almost exclusively, had its artefacts distributed widely in the valleys of the Loire, the Seine and the Somme.

Late Neolithic ceramic styles and regional cultures Laying aside regional variation, we can discern a trend towards utilitarian artefacts made with coarser clay and less concern for formal perfection, as well as the diffusion of flat-bottomed vases. Archaeologists who specialize in typology distinguish many varieties and styles, striving to establish them as the principal relics of cultures they recognize through their association with other cultural traits. In northern Aquitaine as far as Poitou we see the appearance of ceramic styles influenced by southern France, with plastic decoration in the Matignons style, and exuberantly incised or grooved in the Peu-Richard style. In Brittany we find much more simple pottery, in which round-bottomed vessels are succeeded by the first flat-bottomed bowls, while in the south, from the Machecoul Camp to Finistère, the Kerugou style is expressed notably in bowls decorated with vertical ribs in relief extending between the lip and the top of the belly.

The Seine-Oise-Marne (SOM) culture was defined in 1926 by the conjunction of gallery graves of the Paris basin, hypogea and a ceramic style whose most prominent element is a coarsely made 'flowerpot' vase (Bailloud, 1974).

This style is found in all the neighbouring regions, from Normandy to Brittany, where it is associated with collared bottles of similarly crude fabrication, which have perhaps affinities with the collared flasks of the Funnel-Beaker culture of northern Europe. To the east and south-east this ceramic style is diffused as far as Switzerland, where it is reflected in the so-called Horgen culture. Thanks to the marvellous conditions for preservation among the lakes, the ceramic, stone and bone industries were found associated with all the wealth of wooden objects. Recent advances in dendrochronology enable the extreme dates of the Horgen culture, as shown by the stages at which oaks were cut down in nine villages by the lakes of Neuchâtel, Bienne and Morat, to be set in truly absolute chronology at 3391 and 2958 BC (Lichardus and Lichardus-Itten, 1985).

Such precise dating is the envy of prehistorians, who at best have only the wide margins provided by radiocarbon dating. In so far as the equivalence between the Horgen and SOM cultures is assured, as well as between the latter and the Armorican gallery graves, that dating can be applied to the Atlantic regions. After this episode, whose mature phase is relatively brief, there is a transition to the Saône–Rhône culture in the east, the Gord culture of the Paris basin, and to the Artenac culture in Aquitaine and Poitou. What takes over in Armorica is less easily summarized.

GREAT BRITAIN AND IRELAND DURING THE NEOLITHIC

The land bridge linking Britain to the European continent was finally submerged during the Mesolithic around 8,500 to 9,000 years ago. The regional Mesolithic cultures of the islands continued to evolve towards societies with distinct territories, but in south-east Britain microlithic industries seem to have disappeared around 7,000 years ago, while the Neolithic is not known there before 6,000 years ago – despite the fact that the cliffs across the Straits of Dover were clearly visible.

However, these insular and largely coastal Mesolithic populations seem to have developed nautical skills, braving the sea constantly in frail boats, coming and going, the sea having become a link rather than a barrier for them. The classic scheme of a process of colonization by dominating immigrants from the continent has made way for one of convergence and acculturation, the exchanges being confined to the transport of grain and livestock by a few members of independent and equal societies. The wild ancestors of the plants and animals reared in Neolithic Britain were not native to the islands and had to be imported; various aspects of the material culture had affinities with

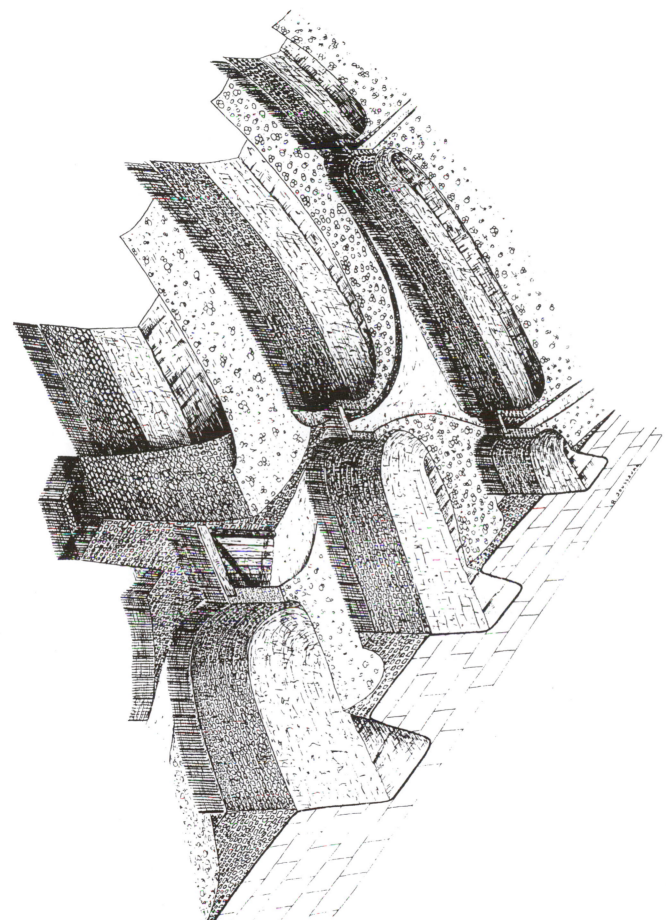

Figure 158   Theoretical reconstruction of an entrance to the village of Champ-Duran at Nieul-sur-Autize, Vendée (France). Causewayed camp of the Late Neolithic. (After Joussaume, 1981.)

elements found from Brittany to Denmark. No continental economic and cultural system was introduced complete, and the various facets of the British Neolithic were derived from different sources, at different times and in different socio-cultural contexts, the result being an eclectic amalgam. Along with their insularity, this explains the specific features of these cultures.

The earliest radiocarbon dates for Neolithic sites, no less than the relevant palaeobotanical records, come mainly from Ireland, around 6,700 years ago, while evidence of defor-estation at about the same time has been discovered in southern England. The introduction of domestic animals, even in small numbers, implies short maritime crossings during the summer months in small boats made of skin or bark on a wooden frame, which were more manoeuvrable than rafts. At the start, a small number of colonists came in search of fertile, virgin land, a process seemingly not very different from the spread of the new life-style on the con-tinent (Piggott, 1954; Smith, 1974; Megaw and Simpson, 1979; Whittle, 1977; Bradley, 1978, 1984).

Middle Neolithic

The beginnings of the Neolithic life-style

The Neolithic life-style thus reached these islands later than it did the continent – during the Middle Neolithic of the traditional chronological scheme. Chalky soil, which covers a good part of England, along with light soils that were easier to work with primitive implements, although they were still largely covered with oak groves, have yielded a wealth of information. This is because they are also very propitious to archaeological excavations and the preservation of bones. The name 'Windmill Hill culture' is used for the whole Middle Neolithic in southern and south-eastern England. Somewhat like the Chassean in France, this term, the moment one leaves the original region typical for this culture, becomes rather inadequate and misleading.

Settlements, defended camps, walls and enclosures

The most characteristic structural remains of occupation consist of walls or oval enclosures such as were found at Windmill Hill (Wiltshire) (Fig. 159), each covering between 1 and 70 ha, bounded by banks and fronted by ditches from which the earth for the banks was taken. At several points, the ditches are interrupted to accommodate causeways. They may be single or there may be up to five concentric circles. Some include the remains of palisades and a host of animal bones and portable objects. The inside of these enclosures rarely contains identifiable structures other than waste-disposal ditches. Their location, more often on the slopes of hills than on terraces, is not specifically defensive. They are believed to have been *kraals* for herding cattle prior to feasts, or perhaps fairgrounds where propitiatory ceremonies involving the sacrifice and burial of whole animals took place.

More rarely there were defensive structures – gateways, banks studded with stone revetments or palisades – the majority of them located to the west or north-west of the chalklands. Perhaps the best-known example, thanks to recent excavations, is Hambledon Hill (Dorset), with two enclosures. The first was possibly used for stripping the flesh off corpses, the bones of a small number being selected for burial in two nearby long barrows, the rest being buried in the ditches together with a large number of funerary offer-ings: quality pottery and stone axes, often imported from distant lands. A secondary, smaller, enclosure contained dwellings and its ditches were filled with the waste of dom-estic activities (flint and antler chippings) and banqueting scraps. Finally, the whole system of hills surrounding these enclosures – covering 60 ha – was fortified in an impressive way, the old enclosure having become dilapidated. There must have been three ramparts on one face of the hill, fronted by discontinuous ditches, covered by wooden palisades, the second and third reinforced with oak beams; the inner rampart must have contained up to 10,000 oak beams. The

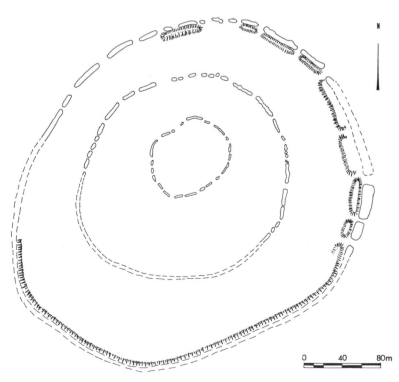

Figure 159 Windmill Hill causewayed camp, Winterborne Monkton, Wiltshire (United Kingdom). (Plan modified after Keiller, 1965.)

three entrances had swing doors closing on a central post. It would seem that the site was abandoned after a raid followed by fire, many of the dead being buried in the ditches (Mercer, 1980; Keiller, 1965).

This example shows how much caution is needed in the interpretation of causewayed camps, whose functions might well have changed in the course of time. At Crickley Hill (Gloucestershire) the defences included stone walls and palisades, and, as at Hambledon Hill, many flint arrowheads were discovered near the doorway; there were dwellings here, as well. Finally at Carn Brea, in Cornwall, and hence outside the immediate sphere of the Windmill Hill culture, a rocky hilltop was defended with massive stone parapets; hundreds of leaf-shaped arrowheads suggest a raid. Inside, wooden huts had been raised on platforms, and there was a great deal of pottery.

However, not all settlements were fortified or built on impressive sites. Small, rectangular houses have been identified in the west and north of Britain, with broken stones round posts or with two rows of four postholes each. In Northern Ireland, at Ballynagilly (Co. Tyrone) an almost square building had walls made of planks placed in trenches and wedged in with stones. Traces of cultivated fields surrounded by dry-stone walls have been discovered nearby. At Ballyglass (Co. Mayo) a larger, two-roomed, rectangular house was defined by trenches and postholes. All these houses had hearths, but were not nearly as grand as the much bigger houses of central Europe (Apsimon, 1976).

Funerary monuments

The reader will have noticed that funerary structures are often associated with large enclosures. There are close links between the dwellings of the living and those of the dead.

Long barrows (Fig. 160) Within the Windmill Hill culture, we know of 200 earthen long barrows, most in the ancient kingdom of Wessex, but a few in eastern and south-eastern England and some thirty in Lincolnshire and Yorkshire. These are elongated, trapezoidal or (only in the south) rectangular mounds flanked by lateral ditches, the spoil from which was used to build the barrows. Such barrows may be associated with rectangular enclosures sometimes without any superstructure. The average long barrow is between 30 and 60 m in length; the mounds might have been encased in wood or stone to retain the earth (or the chalk); some were made of piled-up sods of earth, occasionally with wood at either end. Recent excavations have revealed the existence of wooden 'mortuary houses', large funerary chambers either tent-shaped and between two axial posts carrying a ridge pole, or rectangular; the second type might be built with wooden stakes or with sods.

Inhumation involved the burial of complete skeletons in a contracted position or of dismembered skeletons or both. Some barrows, particularly in Yorkshire, also contain burnt bones, generally dismembered, possibly as a result of accidental fire of the mortuary house. Funeral grave goods (pottery, flint, animal bones) might be included as well, but not very often – such material is more generally scattered over the earthwork of the ditch fillings.

The construction of these collective tombs and their internal structure implies the existence of a social organization similar to that associated with the builders of megalithic monuments. All the long barrows in northern Europe, from Poland to the North Sea, have clear similarities, which does not mean that all were identical responses to similar needs. Their external appearance was similar to that of the long, rectangular or trapezoidal houses of the Bandkeramik cultures, but their function and method of use, as reliquaries rather than tombs, do not seem to be distinct from those of the great stone monuments (Ashbee, 1984).

Megalithic tombs of the Cotswolds–Severn type (Plate 109) The megalithic tombs of the Cotswolds–Severn type do not differ fundamentally from long barrows, except that stone has taken the place of timber. Numbering nearly 200, they are found in the west of central England and in south Wales. Their trapezoidal barrows or cairns contain simple end-chambers, transepted chambers, or lateral chambers. On either side of them are ditches from which their material was taken. The walls of the chambers might be purely megalithic or a mixture of stone slabs and dry-stone. The multichambered monuments show clearly that they were built in several stages. Some barrows have blind façades, without access to the chambers. These are collective tombs for the inhumation of from three to fifty individuals; some of the bones in them might have been burnt by ritual fire. The best-known of these monuments is that of West Kennet. We know that bones were taken out of the chambers and that only some were later replaced. This suggests that particular bones were used for ritual purposes elsewhere (Piggott, 1962).

Portal dolmens The portal dolmens in north Wales form a small group of tombs consisting of one chamber with four slabs supporting a chamber sloping backwards, while the two front uprights framed an entrance or 'porch', sometimes with a façade. The portal dolmen of Dyffryn Ardudwy contains two monuments built one behind the other in a rectangular cairn. The Cornish portal dolmens and the many in Ireland (160, mainly in the north-east) are generally considered latecomers, but those in Ireland contain grave goods identical with those found in court tombs.

The Clyde group In south-eastern Scotland can be found a series of 80 to 100 cairns, the Clyde group, mounds of trapezoidal, rectangular or oval shape, containing a rectangular chamber that might be subdivided by septal slabs. Multi-chambered monuments in this group were built in several stages. The Lochill one first comprised a structure combining a wooden frame with rubble, fired before being incorporated into a long trapezoidal cairn with an outer, rectangular megalithic chamber. A distinction is sometimes made between long barrows and long cairns and Scottish megalithic chambers (Henshall, 1963, 1972).

Court cairns (Fig. 161) The 'court cairns' or 'court tombs' in the centre of northern Ireland, numbering about 330, consist of trapezoidal cairns enclosing megalithic chambers, sometimes subdivided, giving on to a large, semicircular forecourt, which occasionally became a veritable courtyard, with a passage to the façade. Many of these complex monuments were clearly built in stages, the initial structure possibly being of timber. Cremation seems to have been a fairly common practice (Herity and Eogan, 1977).

Economy and technology

The bones of domestic animals found in the ditches surrounding enclosures show the importance of stock-farming. Burnt cereals have also been found in certain pits, which clearly served as storage pits. The use of primitive ploughs

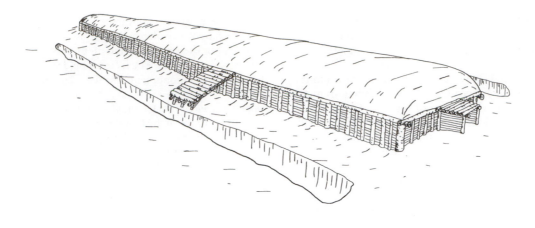

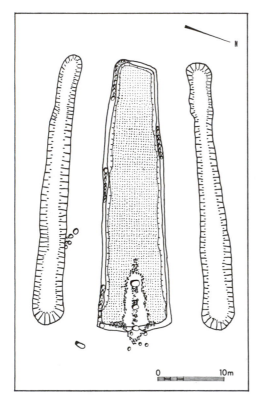

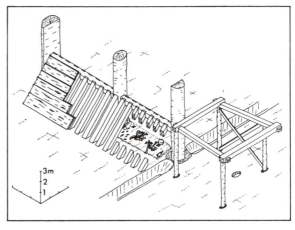

Figure 160 Reconstitution and plan of Fussell's Lodge long barrow, Clarendon Park, Wiltshire (United Kingdom). Ditches and earthen mound supported by wooden structures. (Simplified diagram after Ashbee, 1984.)

is evidenced by the (exceptional) observation of crisscross furrow marks in the chalky soil under a Wiltshire long barrow (Piggott, 1981).

Flint was being mined, especially in Norfolk and Sussex, which shows a degree of parallelism with continental activities at the time (see Chapter 56). In Sussex, few of the mines were very deep, whereas the famous Grimes Graves in Norfolk (Mercer, 1981) boasts shafts down to 15 m with numerous horizontal galleries; the remains of wooden ladders have been discovered here. Nearby there were workshops for chipping flint. A by-product of flint mining was the creation of ritual chalk sculptures, mostly of very obese women and phalluses, two fertility symbols. Flint was transported over long distances. Without entering into typological details, we must make special mention of the British predilection for leaf-shaped arrowheads.

Polished flint axes were rivalled by crystalline rock implements, the oldest of which came from Cornwall. But it was the great workshops of Graig Llwyd in Gwynedd, Wales, Great Langdale in Cumbria, England and Tievebulliagh in Co. Antrim, Ireland, each with petrographic characteristics of its own which, while preferably distributing their products among their immediate neighbours, eventually spread them over the whole of Britain (Clough and Cummins, 1979). Apart from their practical importance, these axes may also have served as ritual objects or status symbols. This might explain the importation from the continent of some Breton axes made of fibrolite or dolerite and above all of the hundred or so Alpine jadeite ceremonial axes, most having the continental shapes whose diffusion can be followed along the Rhine valley.

The state of preservation of bone implements is a crucial factor in their identification; apart from picks made of antlers, used for digging ditches and mine shafts, bones were made into ornaments, combs and pins. Recent excavations in the humid environment of the Somerset Levels have

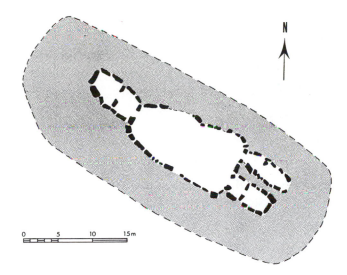

Figure 161 Deerpark court cairn in Co. Sligo (Ireland). The central court here does not appear to communicate with the outside. (After Hemp, 1931.)

brought to light a host of wooden implements: tools, handles, bows and crooks. Log-built paths across the peatbogs are evidence of the continued attraction of fowling, game hunting, fishing and particular plants (Coles, 1975).

The fine Devon pottery known as Hembury ware was invariably made from clay originating in an outcrop of gabbro rock on the Lizard Head peninsula in Cornwall, and distributed over a distance of up to 300 km.

The basic variants of the pottery styles of the time constitute a tradition of well-made, bag-shaped or carinated vessels with a round base. In south-eastern England and in Scotland, that tradition is associated with vessels richly decorated on the neck and rim with incisions and punctations.

The Insular Late Neolithic

The technical and economic aspects of the first Neolithic were significantly perfected and diversified: above all, a host of new cultural or religious preoccupations specific to the islands emerged, no doubt associated with transformations of socio-political structures. British archaeologists believe this was the expression of a loosening of continental ties rather than of 'splendid isolation'. In any case, it was in a very advanced stage that Bell-Beakers, of a shape that has a Rhenish origin, and their associated objects were to make their appearance in Britain.

Dwellings

In southern and eastern England archaeologists have found no signs of human habitation other than ditches or silos, together with a few enclosures ringed with circular or sub-rectangular ditches and some postholes. It is possible that some population groups were less sedentary than others and hence took little care of their dwellings.

By contrast, houses are known in the west and the north of England. In Wales and on the Isle of Man these were detached, small and rectangular and had a foundation of stone walls, the postholes suggesting that there was a timber framework superstructure.

To the north of the Scottish mainland, the dunes of the

Orkneys cover marvellous settlements of villages built of thin sandstone slabs (Knap of Howar on Papa Westray, the oldest; Skara Brae (Plate 110) on Mainland Orkney; Links of Noltland on Westray, and Rinyo on Rousay). Every house is sub-rectangular, linked to the rest by passages having the same kind of walls as the rooms. Most houses had a central hearth, stone benches, two beds with stone 'boards', a dresser and wall 'cupboards' (Fig. 162). Between house and passage was a midden-and-earth infill (containing particularly the bones of sheep and marine mammals). The comfort provided by these structures is remarkable, though the use of wood no doubt allowed equally satisfactory arrangements elsewhere (Renfrew, 1985).

In the Shetlands, even further north, we also find prehistoric houses, the oldest of which date back to the Final Neolithic. They were associated with barley fields surrounded by low dry-stone walls.

Megalithic tombs

Megalithic chambers and passage graves In comparison with continental Europe, this type of megalithic tomb appeared very late in the British Isles, so much so that it might have been an independent re-invention. Groups of such tombs are found in western Scotland, in the Hebrides, in the Orkneys and a late group even in the remote Shetlands. There is also the Clava group in north-eastern Scotland. Each regional group has its own groundplan, building method and cairn shape. In the Orkneys, there are sixty graves of the Orkney–Cromarty type, as exemplified by those of Ibsister, which were recently excavated, all with transverse slabs subdividing long chambers into compartments. There are also the ten tombs of the Maes Howe group, which owe their spectacular appearance to the exceptional characteristics of the stone from which they were built. The chamber at Maes Howe, one of the most magnificent passage graves in Europe, is built on a cruciform plan, that is, it is square and corbelled and has three small cells. The Quanterness tomb, recently excavated, has a T-shaped chamber with six cells. The Holm on Papa Westray has an elongated and compartmented chamber (Henshall, 1963, 1972; Hedges, 1984; Renfrew, 1979, 1985).

In Ireland there are four large groups of passage graves: those in the valley of the Boyne, in Loughcrew, in Carrowkeel and in Carrowmore (Herity, 1974; Herity and Eogan, 1977; O'Kelly, 1982; Eogan, 1984; Burenhult, 1980; Shee Twohig, 1981). The last, which still contained some hundred graves during the last century, has recently yielded very early carbon-14 dates for two very simple tombs, dates that most prehistorians prefer to attach to the Mesolithic and pre-megalithic substrate and not to the tombs themselves. These monuments are built of irregular blocks and, like those of Carrowkeel, have no ornamentation; however, those at Carrowkeel are built of limestone slabs and have the most characteristic plan of Irish passage graves: a cruciform chamber and a long passage. Many of the mounds have a retaining kerb.

Several of the splendid monuments in the Boyne valley have recently been re-excavated. Newgrange (Fig. 163) is particularly renowned; radiocarbon dates put its construction at approximately 5,200 years ago. The mean diameter of the mound is approximately 80 m; it holds just one vast cruciform tomb. Dowth has two tombs, one cruciform with a strange appendage, the other with a polygonal chamber and a small lateral recess, the whole under a mound 85 m in diameter. Knowth has two large tombs placed back-to-back.

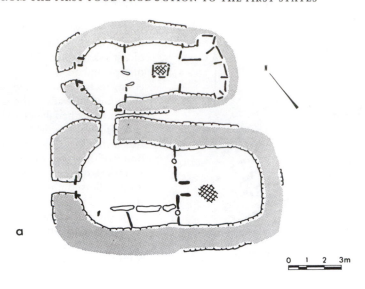

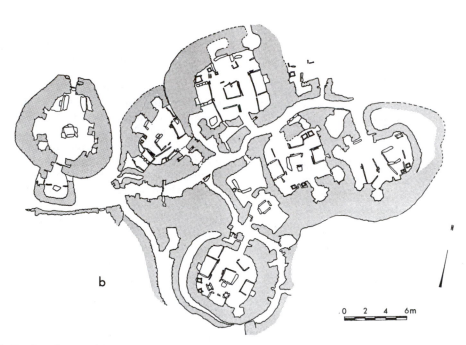

Figure 162 Houses built of small stone slabs, Orkney Islands (United Kingdom): a, houses of the earliest type at Knap of Howar, Papa Westray; note the fireplaces in the middle of the rooms (after Ritchie, 1984); b, village of Skara Brae (Mainland), of a more advanced type; the internal furnishings of the houses have increased (after Childe, 1931; Clarke, 1976).

One has a cruciform chamber, the other a trapezoidal one running from east to west, also under a mound measuring 85 m in diameter. The dead were cremated here and large stone basins served to hold the bones. The decorations, on the supports as well as on the outside of the kerbstones, are very exuberant; they were made by incision and punctation. The many motifs include zigzags, lozenges and spirals.

The principal cemeteries are surrounded by small satellite mounds. Round Knowth, for example, there are eighteen of these, with simpler chambers and passages.

Wedge tombs   In Ireland, and especially in the west, we also meet other, still later, megalithic tombs under trapezoidal mounds. These are the so-called wedge tombs; they contain just one elongated chamber, which Irish archaeologists liken to continental passage graves, an interpretation that remains open to discussion. There are between 400 and 500 of these

tombs, but few have been excavated, yielding mainly Bell-Beaker material.

Ritual monuments

Henges (Fig. 164)   Britain is characterized by the presence of several types of circular monuments not found elsewhere. They must all be related to one another and are sometimes found together. These are the henges, circular areas often containing a ring of stones or wooden posts. Henges were in use throughout the Final Neolithic and into the Middle Bronze Age, that is, for more than a thousand years. Here we merely examine the oldest forms and phases (Burl, 1976, 1979a, 1979b, 1981).

Henges are generally surrounded by a ditch, with the earthworks placed on the outside (unlike the earthworks in fortified sites).

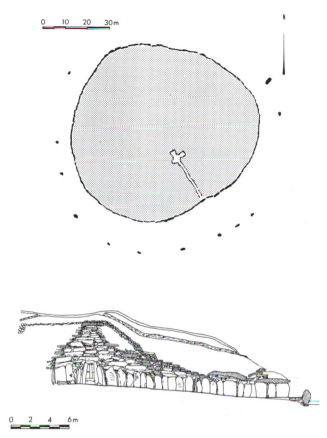

Figure 163 Newgrange, large megalithic cairn, Boyne valley, Co. Meath (Ireland). The plan (top) shows the slabs surrounding the cairn and the outer circle of stones. There is a cruciform chamber with a corbelled roof, the latter clearly depicted in the vertical section (bottom), which also shows the elevation of the north-east side of the passage. The upper mass of the cairn consists of loose stones interspersed with turf as a coating. The decoration of the surrounding K 67 stone consists of the diamonds and spirals typical of Newgrange art. (After O'Kelly, 1982.)

The oldest (Class I), about forty in number, have a single entrance and an average diameter of 70 m. Most are situated near valleys.

Class II henges are larger (mean diameter 140 m) and comprise the most famous monuments in Wessex: Stonehenge (Plate 111), Avebury, Woodhenge, Durringon Walls, Marden and Mount Pleasant. Most contained internal traces of major wooden structures, which differed markedly from one site to the next.

Stonehenge I comprised, as we go from the outside to the inside, a ditch, a bank (an unusual feature in a henge where the bank is usually outside the ditch) and a circle of thirty-six holes (the Aubrey holes), no doubt for wooden posts; and finally, 30 m to the north-east of the entrance, and marking the rising of the sun at the winter solstice, a single upright, the Heel Stone. In the Neolithic, therefore, this prefiguration of a famous monument has none of the monumental stone structures that impress the visitor today.

Avebury, by contrast, must have looked much as it does today, damage excepted. It has a diameter of 450 m, contained a village, had four entrances across the bank and ditch and a circle of upright stones of imposing dimensions; inside were two circles of menhirs about 80 and 100 m in diameter. So far no excavations have been made to look for signs of wooden structures.

Woodhenge owes its name to the result of excavations. It

has an external diameter of 80 m, comprises a bank, a ditch and an inner area completely covered by a circular wooden building with six concentric rings of timber posts, and has a single entrance.

Mount Pleasant is a more irregular structure (Wainwright, 1979; Wainwright and Longworth, 1971). It is about 350 m in diameter with (starting from the outside): bank, ditch (with four causeways) and a trench that once held a palisade. In the inner area, a structure measuring almost 50 m in diameter contained, within a ditch with a single entry, a circular wooden building with four concentric circles of posts.

Durrington Walls, with a diameter of more than 450 m, a bank and ditch with two opposite entrances, contained in its interior, which has not yet been fully excavated, two circular structures with concentric wooden posts, the main one 35 m in diameter and six other circles, but there was room enough for many other structures of the same type (Wainwright and Longworth, 1971).

The material associated with the first phases of construction of these henges invariably dates back to the Final Neolithic.

Stone circles   Stone circles are particularly widespread in northern and western parts of Great Britain and also in Ireland in regions with subsoil difficult to dig: where they are found, banks and ditches are of modest size and appearance. More than 1,000 such circles have survived, the average being from 20 to 30 m in diameter – the 400 m-diameter Avebury circle is linked with the henge. The stones, their number proportionate to their dimensions, vary from small uprights to splendid menhirs 5 to 6 m high. In one part of Scotland there are also circles with recumbent stones. Often an adventitious tomb, generally from the Bell-Beaker period, has been added to the centre of the structure. In any case, a large proportion of these monuments must be post-Neolithic.

These monuments are often associated with avenues – double, and occasionally single, files of upright stones – or, in the case of henges, with double banks each with its own ditch. Finally, although British archaeologists have not taken a great deal of interest in them, we must mention the existence of isolated standing stones, for example in Yorkshire, where the largest measures 8 m.

Function and significance   All sorts of theories have been advanced over more than three centuries to account for this somewhat heterogeneous group of often very impressive structures. Determining their function and significance is a thankless task. The problem of their orientation, which in some cases obviously serves to mark solar, lunar or stellar events, has given rise to a spate of papers that are hard to summarize and to evaluate, the more so as, in the guise of scientific discussion, there have been numerous rash statements and false conclusions: much the same is true in the metrological sphere. Quite possibly, the builders did have recourse to units of measurement, but mathematicians are very divided about the validity of the methods used to reconstruct them. All in all, we may take it that there probably was a link between the motion of the stars and these monuments, which would suggest that the latter had some sort of calendrical significance, but to suppose that the builders of these megaliths had access to an extremely elaborate body of knowledge, as has been suggested so often, is dealing in myths rather than in reality. There is a limit to the empirical observations that can be handed down from

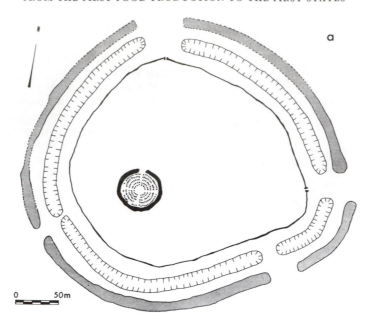

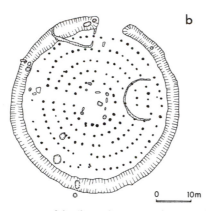
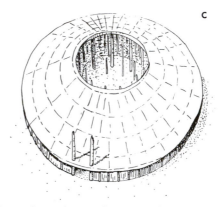

Figure 164 Ritual monuments of the 'henge' type, southern England (United Kingdom). a, b, Mount Pleasant, Dorset. The overall plan (a) shows, from the outside towards the inside, the bank and ditch broken by four entrances, a fenced ditch and a circular building. The detailed plan of the building (b), which is wooden and made up of five concentric circles of stakes, surrounded by a ditch and intersecting earlier holes and small pits. (After Wainwright, 1979.) c, Durrington Walls, Wiltshire: reconstitution of the circular building in wood. (After Wainwright and Longworth, 1971.)

one generation to the next (Thom, 1967, 1971; Thom and Thom, 1978; Heggie, 1981).

In any case, with the building, decoration and elaboration of the stone monuments, lumped together rather artificially as megalithic or para-megalithic tombs, and also with the movement of large masses of earth, quantities of logs and large stone slabs for other monuments assumed to be less connected with funerary rites than with communal worship, the inhabitants of Britain and of Ireland have left us one of the most remarkable achievements of the European Neolithic.

Economy and technology

There was nothing fundamentally new in the agricultural economy that developed in Britain and Ireland during the Late Neolithic.

The extraction of flint and other rocks for polished axes was intensified, as was barter.

Pottery was divided into two groups. The first, the so-called Peterborough style, was confined to southern Britain and continued the earlier ornamental ware tradition with several almost successive variations. The decorations were impressed (by fingernail pressure or with cords) or incised; the rim became more complicated but the base remained round. The other group, the so-called grooved ware (though it was not really grooved) has been identified more recently; it was more innovative and more homogeneous. The basic vessel form was bucket-shaped with a flat base; the most common decorations involved fluted or incised chevrons or lozenges, but some of the vessels were also decorated by the pressure of cords or buttons. There were several regional styles.

In Ireland, vessels remained essentially round-based, with a variety of shapes and decorations. Special mention must be made of the Carrowkeel style pottery found in the passage graves and decorated with punched motifs.

There was also a tendency to make purely decorative or prestige objects, many of which have been found in graves in association with ornamental clothing, and also in settlements and ritual sites. Their motifs have been used on pottery, or in the representations on megalithic slabs and blocks.

Thus chalk was used to make imitation polished axes (Stonehenge and Woodhenge) and above all the three famous carved cylinders from Folkton, Yorkshire, with their regular curvilinear and geometrical motifs, and stylized representations of human beings with eyebrows over a pair of eyes and a vertical stroke for the nose. Chalk balls have been found in some Irish tombs; the tombs associated with the large stone basins of the Boyne contain superbly polished balls in serpentine, marble or other hard stone, with a diameter of from 6 to 8 cm. In Scotland, close on four hundred carved stone balls have been found, many engraved with spirals or concentric circles; some were discovered *in situ* in the village of Skara Brae in the Orkneys. The manufacture of these spectacular objects continued until the Bronze Age. Skara Brae has also yielded a double-pointed stone macehead decorated with geometric motifs. Less spectacular maces made of stone and sometimes of antler were quite common. More recently the western tomb at Knowth in Ireland has yielded a perfectly splendid perforated macehead decorated with spiral motifs. This mace is related to a group of ovoid maceheads from the Final British Neolithic, fashioned from flint or hard rock from the polished stone axe workshops at Graig Llwyd and Great Langdale. More than 100 of them have been found scattered between southern England and the northernmost Scottish islands.

Compared with these objects, the small stone pendants and bone pins made at the time are modest trinkets. It should be stressed that much greater importance was attached to prestige objects or status symbols in Britain and Ireland than on the continent (Clarke et al., 1985).

BIBLIOGRAPHY

APSIMON, A. M. 1976. Ballynagilly and the Beginning and End of the Irish Neolithic. In: DE LAET, S. J. (ed.), *Acculturation and Continuity in Atlantic Europe*. Bruges. pp. 15–30.

ASHBEE, P. 1984. *The Earthen Long Barrow in Britain*. 2nd edn. Norwich.

BAILLOUD, G. 1973. The First Agriculturalists: 4000–1800 BC. In: PIGGOTT, S.; DANIEL, G.; MCBURNEY, C. (eds), *France before the Romans*. London. pp. 102–30.

—— 1974. *Le Néolithique dans le Bassin Parisien*. 2nd edn. Paris.

—— 1985. Le Néolithique et le Chalcolithique en France. In: LICHARDUS, J.; LICHARDUS-ITTEN, M. (eds), *La Protohistoire de l'Europe; Le Néolithique et le Chalcolithique*. Paris, pp. 516–68.

BRADLEY, R. 1978. *The Prehistoric Settlement of Britain*. London.

—— 1984. *The Social Foundations of Prehistoric Britain*. London.

BRIARD, J.; GIOT, P.-R. 1968. Le Tumulus de Tossem-Keler en Penvenan. *Anthropologie* (Paris), Vol. 72, pp. 5–40.

BURENHULT, G. 1980. *The Archaeological Excavations at Carrowmore*. Stockholm.

BURL, A. 1976. *The Stone Circles of the British Isles*. London.

—— 1979a. *Prehistoric Avebury*. London.

—— 1979b. *Rings of Stone*. London.

—— 1981. *Rites of the Gods*. London.

BURNEZ, C. 1976. *Le Néolithique et le Chalcolithique dans le Centre-Ouest de la France*. Paris.

CAILLAUD, R.; LAGNEL, S. 1972. Le Cairn et le crématoire néolithiques de La Hoguette à Fontenay-le-Marmion (Calvados). *Gallia, Préhist.* (Paris), Vol. 15, pp. 137–97.

CHILDE, V. G. 1931. *Skara Brae*. London.

CLARKE, D. V.; COWIE, T. G.; FOXON, A. (eds) 1985. *Symbols of Power at the Time of Stonehenge*. Edinburgh.

CLOUGH, T. H. M.; CUMMINS, W. A. (eds) 1979. *Stone Axe Studies*. London.

COLES, J. M. (ed.) 1975 ff. *Somerset Lev. Pap.* (Cambridge), No. 1 ff.

CORDIER, G. 1963. *Inventaire des mégalithes de la France*, Vol. I: *Indre et Loire*. Paris.

EOGAN, G. 1984. *Excavations at Knowth, 1*. Dublin.

GIOT, P.-R. 1979. La Vie spirituelle au Néolithique. In: GIOT, P.-R.; L'HELGOUACH, J.; MONNIER, J. L. *La Préhistoire de la Bretagne*. Rennes. pp. 375–440.

—— 1982. *Barnenez, un grand cairn mégalithique*. Châteaulin.

—— 1983. The Megaliths of France. In: RENFREW, C. (ed.), *The Megalithic Monuments of Western Europe*. London. pp. 18–29.

GIOT, P.-R.; L'HELGOUACH, J.; MONNIER, J. L. 1979. *La Préhistoire de la Bretagne*. Rennes.

GRUET, M. 1967. *Inventaire des mégalithes de la France*, Vol. II: *Maine et Loire*. Paris.

GUILAINE, J. (ed.), 1976. *La Préhistoire française*. Vol. II: *Les Civilisations néolithiques et prothistoriques*. Paris.

—— 1980. *La France d'avant la France*. Paris.

HEDGES, J. W. 1984. *Tomb of the Eagles, a Window on Stone Age Tribal Britain*. London.

HEGGIE, D. C. 1981. *Megalithic Science*. London.

HENSHALL, A. S. 1963. *The Chambered Tombs of Scotland*. Edinburgh. Vol. 1.

—— 1972. *The Chambered Tombs of Scotland*. Edinburgh. Vol. 2.

HERITY, M. 1974. *Irish Passage Graves*. Dublin.

HERITY, M.; EOGAN, G. 1977. *Ireland in Prehistory*. London.

JOUSSAUME, R. 1981. *Le Néolithique de l'Aunis et du Poitou occidental, dans son cadre atlantique*. Rennes.

—— 1985. *Des dolmens pour les morts. Les mégalithes à travers le monde*. Paris.

KEILLER, A. 1965. *Windmill Hill and Avebury*. Oxford.

—— 1985. *Des dolmens pour les morts. Les Mégalithes à travers le monde*. Paris.

KINNES, I. 1982. Les Fouaillages and Megalithic Origins. *Antiquity*, Vol. 56, pp. 24–30.

LEROI-GOURHAN, A.; BAILLOUD, G.; BREZILLON, M. 1962. L'Hypogée II des Mournouards, Mesnil-sur-Oger, Marne. *Gallia, Préhist.* (Paris), Vol. 5, pp. 23–133.

LE ROUX, C. T. 1984. L'Implantation néolithique en Bretagne centrale. *Rev. archéol. Ouest* (Rennes), Vol. 1, pp. 33–54.

—— 1984. À propos des Fouilles de Gavrinis (Morbihan): nouvelles données sur l'art mégalithique armoricain. *Bull. Soc. préhist. fr.* (Paris), Vol. 81, pp. 240–5.

L'HELGOUACH, J. 1965. *Les Sépultures mégalithiques en Armorique; dolmens à couloir et allées couvertes*. Rennes.

—— 1970. Le Monument mégalithique du Goëren à Gâvres, Morbihan. *Gallia, Préhist.* (Paris), Vol. 13, pp. 217–61.

—— 1971. Les Débuts du Néolithique en Armorique. *Fundamenta*, A (Cologne/Vienna), Vol. 3, pp. 178–200.

—— 1973. Les Mégalithes de l'Ouest de la France. In: DANIEL, G.; KJAERUM, P. (eds), *Megalithic Graves and Ritual*. Aarhus. pp. 203–19. (Jutland Archaeol. Soc., 11.)

—— 1976. Les Tumulus de Dissignac à St-Nazaire, Loire-Atlantique. In: DE LAET, S. J. (ed.), *Acculturation and Continuity in Atlantic Europe*. Bruges. pp. 142–9.

—— 1983. Les Idoles qu'on abat ... (ou les vicissitudes des grandes stèles de Locmariaquer). *Bull. Soc. Polymath. Morbihan* (Vannes), Vol. 110, pp. 57–68.

L'HELGOUACH, J.; POULAIN, M. 1984. Le Cairn des Mousseaux à Pornic et les tombes mégalithiques transeptées de l'estuaire de la Loire. *Rev. Archéol. Ouest* (Rennes), Vol. 1, pp. 15–32.

LICHARDUS, J.; LICHARDUS-ITTEN, M. 1985. *La Protohistoire de l'Europe, le Néolithique et le Chalcolithique*. Paris.

MASSET, C. 1972. The Megalithic Tomb of La Chaussée-Tirancourt. *Antiquity*, Vol. 47, pp. 297–300.

MASSET, C.; LECLERC, J. 1979. Construction, remaniements et condamnation d'une sépulture collective néolithique: La Chaussée-Tirancourt, Somme. *Bull. Soc. préhist. fr.* (Paris), Vol. 77, pp. 57–64.

MEGAW, J. V. S.; SIMPSON, D. D. A. 1979. *Introduction to British Prehistory*. Leicester.

MERCER, R. 1980. *Hambledon Hill, a Neolithic Landscape*. Edinburgh.

—— 1981. *Grimes Graves, Norfolk, Excavations*. London.

MOHEN, J. P. 1973, 1977. Les Tumulus de Bougon. *Bull. Soc. hist. et scien. des Deux-Sèvres*, 1973, Nos. 2–3, 55 pp.; 1977, Nos. 2–3, 42 pp.

—— 1984. *Les Architectures mégalithiques*. *Recherche* (Paris), Vol. 15, No. 161, pp. 1528–38.

O'KELLY, M. J. 1982. *Newgrange, Archaeology, Art and Legend*. London.

PEEK, J. 1985. *Inventaire de mégalithes de la France*. Vol. IV: *Region parisienne*. Paris.

PEQUART, M.; PEQUART, S. J.; LE ROUZIC, Z. 1927. *Corpus des signes gravés des monuments mégalithiques du Morbihan*. Paris.

PETREQUIN, P. 1985. Les Sépultures collectives de la fin du Néolithique en Haute-Saône. *Rev. archéol. Est Cent.-Est* (Dijon), Vol. 36, pp. 13–32.

PIGGOTT, S. 1954. *Neolithic Cultures of the British Isles*. Cambridge.

—— 1962. *The West Kennet Long Barrow: Excavations 1955–56*. London.

—— (ed.) 1981. Prehistory. In: *The Agrarian History of England and Wales*. Cambridge. Vol. 1.

POWELL, T. G. E. (ed.) 1969. *Megalithic Enquiries in the West of Britain*. Liverpool.

RENFREW, C. 1979. *Investigations in Orkney*. London.

—— (ed.) 1983. *The Megalithic Monuments of Western Europe*. London.

—— (ed.) 1985. *The Prehistory of Orkney*. Edinburgh.

SCARRE, C. (ed.) 1983. *Ancient France, Neolithic Societies and their Landscapes*. Edinburgh.

SHEE TWOHIG, E. 1981. *The Megalithic Art of Western Europe*. Oxford.

SMITH, I. F. 1974. The Neolithic. In: RENFREW, C. (ed.) *British Prehistory, a New Outline*. London. pp. 100–36.

THOM, A. 1967. *Megalithic Sites in Britain*. Oxford.

—— 1971. *Megalithic Lunar Observatories*. Oxford.

THOM, A.; THOM, A. S. 1978. *Megalithic Remains in Britain and Brittany*. Oxford.

VERRON, G. (ed.) 1980. *Préhistoire de la Normandie*. Caen.

WAINWRIGHT, G. J. 1979. *Mount Pleasant, Dorset: Excavations 1970–1971*. London.

WAINWRIGHT, G. J.; LONGWORTH, I. H. 1971. *Durrington Walls: Excavations 1966–1968*. London.

WHITTLE, A. W. R. 1977. *The Earlier Neolithic of Southern England and its Continental Background*. Oxford.

—— 1985. *Neolithic Europe, a Survey*. Cambridge.

54

THE NORTH EUROPEAN LOWLANDS

Neolithic acculturation

Lili Kaelas

THE LANDSCAPE

In the north European lowlands the first traces of cereal cultivation and animal husbandry are dated to the end of the seventh millennium BP. Knowledge of these techniques came from the central European loesslands, where they were developed in an ecological environment completely different from that of northern Europe. It is therefore appropriate to give a short survey of the characteristics of northern European landscapes.

The north European lowlands encompass an area south of the North Sea and the Baltic from the Netherlands to Poland, and further to the north Denmark, south Sweden and south Norway. This region is not in its entirety flat plain, since it includes some low mountainous areas as well as undulating landscapes. Around 12,000 years ago most of the area was covered by ice as is Greenland today.

The heavy ice-sheet eroded the ground beneath it and remodelled the landscape. Till (the type of soil predominantly produced beneath the ice-sheet) was carried by the moving ice and dumped in valleys and flowland areas in Scandinavia and brought as far south as north Poland and north Germany, where it formed a morainic landscape, the so-called 'Baltic moraine-ridge'.

The weight of the ice-sheet depressed the earth's crust so that much of what now is land was then below sea-level. Melt-water streams carried fine silt and clay material into the sea, where it was deposited as clay. Coarse particles were laid down nearer the mouth of melt-water streams, for example in delta formations of glacifluvial ridges of sand and gravel.

When the ice-sheet melted, the earth's crust rose (isostatic recovery) but later sank and after thousands of years some areas were again covered by sea. This phenomenon is still operating, thus in Scandinavia isostatic recovery continues but in Denmark in parts south of the Baltic and the Netherlands land is still being lost to the sea.

The result of the effects of the ice-sheet is a special Nordic landscape of bare, infertile mountain areas, valleys and lowland areas of light gravel and sandy soil, alternating with areas of heavy marine clay – a landscape dissected by bare mountains, hills of morainic material and valleys with lakes and streams. As a result, not for nothing is Finland called 'the land of a thousand lakes'. Within the southern part of Fennoskandia there are some impressive tectonic depressions, which have now become large lakes, for example Lakes Ladoga (Russia), Mälar, Väner and Vettern (Sweden), but the most characteristic features of the glacial landscape are the numerous small lakes and bogs. Immediately south of the Baltic moraine-ridge, for example between the middle Elbe and the Saale, we meet a landscape of a different type, with black earth and ecological conditions more similar to the loesslands.

This complicated landscape history has necessitated close collaboration between archaeologists and geologists. The system of dating using varves is well known. This comprises a study of the period when the ice-sheets were melting by measuring annual differences in the thickness of layers of varved clay. In summer they were thicker and more coarse-grained than in winter. Botanical remains in peatbogs were also studied to determine changes in the postglacial climate. In addition pollen analysis and dendrochronology have been used for investigating environmental change. In the last decades drillings in the Greenland ice-cap (c.1,400 m thick) have enabled the sequence of climatic changes in the northern hemisphere during the last 8,300 years to be established. Such studies provide a better appreciation of the history of the Nordic landscape, especially that of Scandinavia, Denmark and adjacent areas.

The Greenland type of Arctic climate, prevalent during the melting period of the ice-sheet, changed over millennia and became the Atlantic type, i.e. warm and humid. Around 6,000 years ago the climate was about the same as in south-west France today, with summer temperatures from 2 to 3 °C higher than at present. Today coniferous trees dominate the forests of northern Europe, but in the period referred to there were forests of deciduous trees dominated by oak, lime, elm and ash, which reached as far north as central Sweden and the southern parts of Norway and Finland. Indicative of the mild climate are the abundant occurrences of holmoak (*Ilex*), holly, ivy (*Hedera*) and hazel (*Corylus avellana*) in southern Scandinavia. In the continental forests, however, broadleafed trees tended to be slightly more abundant.

Of the world's seas, the North Sea and the north Atlantic, including the neighbouring Sound and the Baltic Sea are among those richest in fish. Fish, shellfish and freshwater molluscs were abundant in the sea, lakes, rivers and streams. Some rivers in Scandinavia are still the richest in salmon in the world, and sturgeon, for instance, lived in these rivers until medieval times. Game was plentiful in the forests. Along the coasts and in the interior hundreds of species of edible plants were available. This was an ideal area for fishing, hunting and gathering. Several Mesolithic cultures developed an affluent life on the north European sea-coasts, in estuaries and on lake shores. However, as a whole it was a sparsely populated area.

Given the technological limitations of Neolithic farming, only small areas in northern Europe could be used for cultivation. The wide areas of heavy marine clays, which today are the most fertile, were unsuitable for tilling until modern steel ploughs became available.

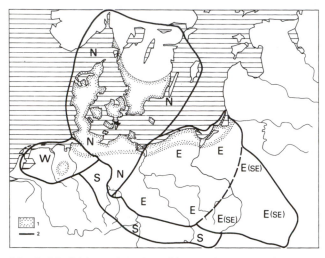

Map 65 Neolithic acculturation of the North European lowlands. 1, Zone of occurrence of the Ertebølle–Ellerbek settlement with evidence of incipient food production; 2, Funnel-Beaker culture area: N, northern province, W, western province, E, eastern province, E(SE), south-eastern part of the eastern province, S, southern province.

THE DAWN OF THE NEW MODE OF SUBSISTENCE

Transition from the Mesolithic to the Neolithic (Map 65)

The transition of Mesolithic food-gathering societies in the North European Lowlands to food production by means of cultivation and stock-rearing has always interested scholars. In particular they have tried to solve the problem of how the new technology, including foreign kinds of cereals and livestock, came to northern Europe and how the relevant knowledge and expertise was transmitted. Earlier research always pre-supposed that farming was in all circumstances superior to food-gathering, which is a product of our traditional evolutionary ideas. Actual experiments have produced results that to some extent conflict with this viewpoint.

Because of the lack of empirical evidence, discussion has always been along highly theoretical lines and there are considerable differences between the views of archaeologists of different schools. Earlier the prevailing opinion was that the new technological ideas were introduced by wandering ethnic groups from somewhere in south-eastern central Europe, who had occupied plots of ground suitable for the new economy, and established communities next to the sites of the earlier Mesolithic inhabitants. The latter were supposed to have been gradually converted to the new ideas of food production. This hypothesis was based on an analogy

with medieval migrations formerly understood to have been the wandering of whole tribes, an idea which is now being questioned.

According to another theory there was an infiltration of small groups of people from central Europe to the North, a kind of individual immigration. In other words, this theory presupposes individual migration of the modern type, a mode of behaviour scarcely known from early societies.

A theory current since the early 1970s explains the transition as being caused by growing population pressure. This was supposed to be the effect of sedentary life on late Mesolithic communities. Simultaneously it was understood that the food supplies around the sedentary sites had become reduced because of population growth. Thus they were compelled to adopt the more labour-intensive mode of production that cultivation and animal husbandry were considered to have been. The theory is based on analogies with observations made by the Danish sociologist Ester Boserup (1965) when studying actual processes in developing countries. The weakness of this theory, however, is that it does not explain the decision processes of the prehistoric societies in question. It seems to hide analogies with laws valid in the natural sciences but not applicable to human societies, or perhaps the model of applying new know-how in modern society by decisions of enterprising individuals.

In the evolutionary scheme Mesolithic societies are usually characterized as egalitarian societies living in bands (Chapter 55). A French anthropologist, Alain Testart (1983), has attempted to show that the sedentary societies of the late Mesolithic stored food and were redistributive and thus hierarchical societies. Only nomadic Mesolithic societies are egalitarian, according to this theory. He is well aware that archaeological research on late Mesolithic societies, as for example the Ertebølle–Ellerbek societies (in Denmark and Schlewig-Holstein, Germany) referred to, show only vague evidence of hierarchies, perhaps due to lack of archaeological observation of such evidence. This theory is mostly based on anthropological observations, which indicate a connection between an economy practising food storage and redistribution, which implies hierarchy.

It is easier to explain the transition of a redistributive society, with central resources for investment, into a more labour-intensive system of food-production and production processes than to explain the transition of a band society to this system. A hierarchical system with its use of gifts and barter between the élites of the communities and the acquisition of slaves is a more open society than a band society. With this theory it is more convenient to explain differences in the adoption of new ideas between neighbouring societies. In addition a communicative élite as a means of transmitting new ideas from society to society with the barter of food and slaves can explain the needed dynamic decision process.

The oldest traces of cereal cultivation – grain impressions in pottery and cereal pollen from nearby bogs – and bones of domesticated animals in northern Europe are found in the uppermost layers of the settlements of the Ertebølle–Ellerbek culture in Denmark and Schleswig-Holstein and sometimes also in southernmost Sweden. The sedentary phase of this Mesolithic culture is calculated to have developed between the mid-seventh and the beginning of the sixth millennium BP. Its settlements were located along sea-coasts, lake-shores or river-mouths. In Denmark they are characterized by enormous refuse heaps of mussel and oyster shells and other types of food waste, which in archaeological literature are often referred to by the Danish word *kjøkkenmøddinger* (kitchen middens). In these heaps tools and implements of horn, bone and wood are also frequently found. Finds reveal that the communities depended on fishing, seal-hunting and hunting wild animals, especially small game, in the nearby forest. Gathering edible plants, roots, berries, larvae and so forth, according to the season, played an important nutritional role.

In the late Ertebølle–Ellerbek period appears an important novelty in northern Europe, pottery – coarse vessels in several variants with a pointed base (Plate 112) and oval, flat blubber lamps. Breakable pottery, unpractical in nomadic life, is usually considered as a sign of a more sedentary way of life. Pots were used for the storage of food, for example seal fat, and are regarded as the equipment of an economy reliant on storage. The big coastal settlements of the Ertebølle–Ellerbek culture were situated in an environment rich in sources of food. Typical of the fishing industry is its seasonal character and consequent need for methods of preservation. The settlements have therefore been understood to be permanently based. Besides these main settlements, we may reckon with temporary camps for small groups of people from the main habitation, for seasonal salmon fishing or for hunting some particular game.

The pottery and T-shaped antler axes in Ertebølle–Ellerbek dwelling places are regarded as evidence of contacts with the contemporary Rössen culture of the loesslands in north-west Germany (Chapter 51).

The discoveries of small cemeteries also indicate ideas from outside. The corpses of the deceased are often buried there with many objects (ornaments and tools). Several graves were coloured with ochre and other red minerals (Plate 113). Though differences in grave equipment are small, they may be a sign of a hierarchical system in society. However, to prove this hypothesis more research is needed.

Evidence of cereals and bones of domesticated animals, though scanty, indicates the adoption of new techniques. This late stage of the culture is often termed the 'classic Ertebølle' and its economy is seen as semi-agrarian. Its advent is radiocarbon dated to the end of the seventh millennium BP.

It seems plausible that these late Mesolithic groups, living in a favourable ecological milieu, had developed a storage economy and probably also hierarchism, both signs of a redistributive society, and had to a very restricted extent adopted cereal cultivation and stock raising, though only as a sort of luxury production of very little importance for daily calorific requirements. The innovation was a result of communication with neighbouring agricultural communities on the Lower Elbe.

The Funnel-Beaker culture (TRB)

About the beginning of the sixth millennium BP in the countries around the South Baltic and the Sound, there are traces of a new tool assemblage, in which polished flint axes with a sharp cutting edge have a central role (Plate 114). These were designed for woodworking as well as for felling trees. Fine, thin-walled pottery shows that a new ceramic technology with tempered clay and with higher firing temperatures (up to 600 °C) than used for Ertebølle–Ellerbek pottery had been adopted (Plate 115). By pollen analysis it has been shown that the forest in the neighbourhood of settlements has become more open. The diagrams show more grass and herb as well as grain pollen than before. Plausibly, this implies that the communities have started to burn woodlands for swidden cultivation (also known in archaeological literature as slash-and-burn agriculture). But the location of settlements has much the same character as the settlements of the Ertebølle–Ellerbek culture, that is near coasts, lakes and rivers. Fishing was still dominating food supply. But there is well-proved evidence of incipient food production by animal husbandry and cereal cultivation, that is, of the Neolithic system of production. Other characteristic features are new pottery forms, among which a type with a funnel-shaped neck has given this culture its name – the Funnel-Beaker culture. A new form of offerings also appeared: pots, originally filled with food-stuffs, and polished flint axes in watercourses and bogs. The pottery assemblage, polished flint axes and offerings give this culture an appearance different from that of the Ertebølle–Ellerbek. However, many of the tool forms of the latter continue. The Funnel-Beaker culture is widely spread in north and central Europe.

Before the invention of carbon-14 dating, pottery was the most important type of artefact for building chronologies as well as for tracing regional similarities and differences. Since that time forms and styles of decoration of pottery have given their names to whole production and social systems. Where carbon-14 dates are lacking pottery styles still have a function for archaeological systematization and taxonomy. It was pottery, found in bogs, upon which the Danish scholar Becker (1947) based his study of the chronology and origins of the Funnel-Beaker culture with special regard to Denmark.

On the basis of pottery styles Becker included a far wider area of central Europe than did the Polish scholar Jazdzewski (1936), who first gathered the various groups in the north European lowlands under the heading of the 'Funnel-Beaker culture'. Becker also considered groups in the Saale–Middle Elbe area (for example, the Baalberge groups) to be part of this culture. With regard to the introduction of the Neolithic over this vast area, he adopted the theory of immigration. In the beginning (Early Neolithic according to northern European chronology) the culture was by and large similar over the whole north European lowlands. Once the immigrant groups had settled down, they developed in different regions different culture forms. With regard to Denmark in particular he distinguished two immigrant waves: the earliest one mainly with cereal cultivation, the second one of pastoral groups with stock-rearing as the main agricultural activity. The 'homeland' of these groups was according to Becker in south-eastern Europe, Ukraine or beyond, where their culture had developed.

An early opponent of Becker's theories, Troels-Smith (1953, 1982), basing his investigations on palaeobotanical studies in a bog (Aasmosen) on Zealand, considered the earliest phase of the Funnel-Beaker culture as an integrated part of the late Ertebølle–Ellerbek culture because potsherds typical of both cultures were found together in the uppermost layers of the Ertebølle–Ellerbek settlements (Schwabedissen, 1968, 1982). These observations are only made in the western Ertebølle–Ellerbek sites (in Jutland and Schleswig-Holstein), but not in the eastern ones (in Mecklenburg and Rügen, Germany). Troels-Smith considered, however, that animal husbandry was introduced by immigrant groups from an unspecified southern area of central Europe contemporary with the late Ertebølle–Ellerbek culture.

Becker's chronological system for the Early Neolithic was applied widely into the 1970s, and his theory of the origin of the Funnel-Beaker culture is called into question by scholars of the younger generation, such as Skaarup (1973),

Madsen (1982), Jensen (1982) and Preuss (1966, 1980), who reject the theory that the emergence of the Funnel-Beaker culture, including the groups that Becker termed pastoral bands, was due to immigrant ethnic elements. Instead this culture is explained as being based on the local late Mesolithic population (Ertebølle–Ellerbek), the nature of whose culture changed gradually because of strong influences brought about by contacts with continental agricultural groups. The result was a new production system and a new cultural image.

Modern investigations into the early Funnel-Beaker culture in central Europe (named the Baalberge groups after a find spot) also point in the same direction. There was a local Mesolithic population that developed a new culture under strong influence from the south-east (Moravia, Czech Republic, where the Neolithic way of life had long since been adopted) (Preuss, 1966, 1980) (Plates 116 and 117). The same is valid for groups in Bohemia (Czech Republic) and Saxony (Germany): Walternienburg group (Plate 118), Salzmünde group (Plate 119). The Neolithic acculturation of the Baalberge groups coincides approximately with that of the northern Funnel-Beaker culture, but is probably somewhat earlier.

The Neolithic acculturation of northerly Mesolithic communities is thus due to influences from two different directions: one from the west along the lower Elbe to Schleswig-Holstein and Denmark (including Scania, Sweden), the other along the Oder to the Baltic area (including the Mälar valley in middle Sweden).

Notwithstanding a series of new investigations and criticism, Becker in a series of successive works has still maintained his chronological scheme for the Early Neolithic and the immigration theory for the origin of the Funnel-Beaker culture. Consequently he does not approve the dating of the western late Ertebølle–Ellerbek dwelling layers prior to the Funnel-Beaker culture, but considers them to be contemporary. The finds of the latter culture there are interpreted as evidence of contacts between these two different ethnic groups.

With regard to the different hypotheses propounded by various scholars concerning the Neolithic acculturation of the north European lowlands, one may ask why there are so many divergent theories (only a selection of which is referred to), all based on the same archaeological data. The reason is that the chronology is still widely based on pottery styles and is not confirmed for the entire Funnel-Beaker culture area by carbon-14 dates.

Since carbon-14 dating and other natural-scientific methods have come to form the basis of the chronology, the interest of scholars has changed from the study of elements of style to that of settlements and their relationship to the environment and to geomorphological, geographical and ecological matters. The results of this research demonstrate that, besides the common features such as certain pottery types and bog offerings, the settlement pattern, of the early phase in particular, also seems to be similar throughout the whole Funnel-Beaker culture area. Apart from a broad preference for coastal and riverine locations, the main settlements show a specific preference for dry and sandy areas or ridges in a damp environment. Besides the main settlements, there occur special seasonal camps for hunting and trapping as an important part in the subsistence system as evidenced in many regions. This description is especially true of the vast, once glaciated areas north of the Baltic moraine-ridge.

The source material obtained from the huge Funnel-

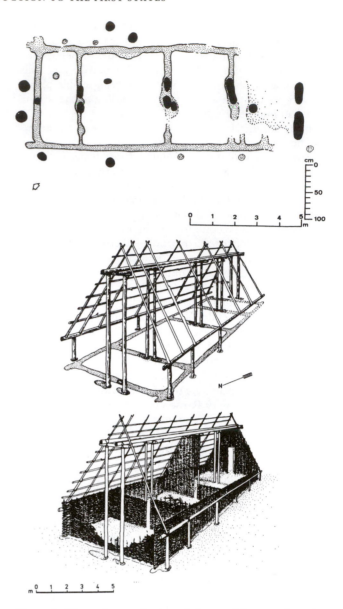

Figure 165 Plan and reconstitution of a house of the Funnel-Beaker culture, Flögeln-Eekhölten (Germany).

Beaker culture area, however, varies substantially in value. Some areas, for instance south Scandinavia and the adjacent areas immediately to the south, have provided rich material of various types both from settlements and as votive offerings from bogs (Plate 120), frequently accompanied by information and data about environment, as a result of multidisciplinary co-operation on excavations in places favourable for such collaboration. Other areas, on the contrary, have yielded less significant and more biased finds and information, derived mainly from graves. From settlement finds it is possible to determine more precisely in which types of terrain the Funnel-Beaker people lived. Nevertheless, traces of their houses are few and difficult to assess. Some seem to have been rectangular and of varying length, some in the central European tradition (Fig. 165) (Chapter 51). But there are also traces of horseshoe-shaped, hut-like structures in some settlements, used for habitation. How many buildings there were at the same time in a settlement is even more difficult to establish. To answer these and allied questions, more refined methods of archaeological prospection and excavation badly need to be employed.

Regional groups of the Funnel-Beaker culture

The Neolithic groups spread over the very great area of the north European lowlands have so many common features that each of these groups can be defined as part of one and the same culture – the Funnel-Beaker culture. That indicates a capacity for communication between communities over the whole area. It must be emphasized, however, that in the course of time regional and local differences also developed and became more and more evident. These regional differences in pottery styles (Plate 121), stone tools and so on depend on contacts with other cultures in neighbouring areas. On the basis of these differences, Jazdzewski (1936) divided the wide Funnel-Beaker area into provinces: northern, western, southern and eastern provinces (Map 65).

These 'provinces' show for example different changes in burial customs. During the early stage of Neolithic acculturation the deceased were buried in simple earth graves (Plate 122), but in the late part of the Early Neolithic a shift in grave conventions took place. In the northern and western provinces construction of megalithic tombs began documenting communications along the coasts of the Atlantic, the Channel and the North Sea (Chapter 55). In the eastern province, in Kujavia (Poland), long barrows, surrounded by boulders but without stone chambers, are the monumental graves of the region. In the southern province the prevailing grave type is a modest cist, but towards the end of the Early Neolithic large, round mounds placed in conspicuous locations appear in the Saale–middle Elbe area – tombs for selected people.

Besides the more noticeable graves, simple earth graves below ground-level – and thus difficult to detect – continued in all areas throughout the period. In some areas the deceased were buried in earth graves in a crouched (sleeping) position on their side and with strict orientation (for example the Baalberge group in the Saale–Elbe area). In other areas there is more variation, while in others detailed knowledge is yet scanty, with the result that a more general statement is not possible. Variations occur even within limited geographical areas.

Pottery decoration also reflects influence from other cultural domains. In the western and northern parts of the Funnel-Beaker cultural area some style elements in the decoration - eye or sun motifs (Plate 123), designs resembling the human face and wild animals (perhaps deer) – can be derived from the Iberian peninsula (Chapter 55). But there are also parallels in design and motifs that reveal contacts with the central European area and also in course of time a flow of influences from the affluent communities in the north towards Funnel-Beaker cultural groups in central Europe.

Common to the whole area of the Funnel-Beaker culture are central or regional cult places, which are signs of regional co-ordination. In the transition period between Early and Middle Neolithic, so-called 'causewayed camps' were built centrally in settled regions. These consist of a central area enclosed by a ditch and wooden palisade of which only traces are left in the ground with narrow causewayed paths forming entrances. Investigations reveal that they are not dwelling places or kraals for cattle but were intended for ceremonial use. The causewayed camps seem to have served as festive sites for gathering together the scattered population of a wider surrounding area, that is for manifestations of social and cultural unity. However, there are parallels known also from other Neolithic cultures, for instance in the Rhine valley, France and England.

Some of the causewayed camps are of considerable size. At Sarup on the south-west of Fyn (Denmark) there are two camp constructions, one overlying the other. The older dates from the transition of Early to Middle Neolithic (second half of the sixth millennium BP) and comprises an area of about 90,000 m². The second foundation is somewhat younger and covers an area of c.30,000 m². In the region of Sarup three settlements are known and 108 dolmens (estimated to be contemporary with the older structure). From the time of the second foundation five settlements and twelve passage graves are known. Many dolmens of the first period were also re-used during the period of the second structure.

To give an idea of what a central cult place could look like, the site at Alvastra, near Lake Vättern (Sweden), is now described in greater detail. This site was formerly considered to be a pile or lake dwelling, because of its location in the middle of a bog. A recent re-excavation has revealed attributes that were previously unsuspected. The pile-works contain some one thousand vertical piles and a floor of logs and narrow footbridges or causeways leading to dry land. Upon the first-built floor was a second of somewhat later date. On these floors were found about a hundred hearths of limestone, surrounded by the bones of wild and domesticated animals. Nearly all the marrow-bones were broken. Other foodstuffs included large quantities of charred cereals, nuts and wild apple. Among the artefact finds of particular interest were flint implements, found sorted into categories and placed in small heaps, numerous battle-axes (mostly unfinished) and miniatures of these axes in amber and bone. It is noteworthy that flint waste, usual in all dwelling sites, was almost absent. Pottery and tools were scanty compared with what is generally found in habitation sites.

On the upper floor scattered human bones were found. No traces of cannibalism have been observed.

By means of dendrochronological studies of the oak poles it has been possible to determine the construction time of the site. According to a preliminary report the first phase of the pile-works was accomplished in seventeen years, followed by an interval of about twenty-two years. Thereafter began a new construction phase of two to three years. The construction is radiocarbon dated to the second half of the sixth millennium BP. The first use of it can on the basis of the finds be attributed to the Funnel-Beaker culture. Later the site was visited by another cultural group, named the Pitted-Ware culture (because of its characteristic pit-decorated pottery).

In the neighbourhood of the Alvastra pile-works, at a distance of about 2 km, a previously unknown megalithic tomb – the remains of a dolmen or passage grave – was discovered. It is not improbable that there are more megalithic graves in the vicinity, and there are indications of settlements in the area as well. Further, it is worth mentioning that on the other side of Lake Vättern, at a distance of 60 km as the crow flies, there is the largest concentration of passage graves – some 300 are documented – in the whole of southern Scandinavia.

Subsistence economy

Evidence – though scanty – of cultivation and stock raising is found in many settlements of late Ertebølle–Ellerbek culture in Denmark and adjacent areas (Schleswig-Holstein, southernmost Sweden). Other observations, as mentioned before, have indicated that these communities were sedentary, with the products of fishing, gathering and hunting providing basic sustenance. Agricultural production was marginal, perhaps a luxury. Cultivation and stock-rearing were adopted due to contacts with agricultural neighbours on the Lower Elbe. Initially seed and domesticated animals were 'imported'. Communities on the Lower Elbe are considered to have practised continuous cultivation of small plots and leaf feeding of lifestock, the cattle being mainly stalled. It is assumed that the same type of agriculture was practised also by the Ertebølle–Ellerbek people (Troels-Smith, 1982).

The techniques to cultivate these small plots are not known, but according to current ideas it can be imagined to have been horticulture. There are finds of spades or spade-like implements of ashwood from this early period. However, 'horticulture' is not known among Ertebølle communities south of the Baltic, for instance in Mecklenburg.

The first cereals cultivated in such 'horticulture' were two varieties of wheat, emmer (*Triticum dicoccum*) and einkorn (*Triticum monococcum*) and naked barley (*Hordeum vulgare*). The domesticated animals kept were cattle, pigs, sheep and goats.

Domesticated animals were a meat reserve. In addition sheep, goats and cows provided a new foodstuff – milk. Though milk production probably was small, it was soon used for making cheese. Sheep provided wool and it is not unlikely that the weaving of woollen textiles for cloth started about the same time as stock-rearing.

Apart from the horticulture of the Ertebølle–Ellerbek communities, swidden cultivation was probably the form in which the agrarian production system was introduced and spread over the whole north European lowlands. During the initial period, around 6,000 years ago, it was spread to Mesolithic groups there, together with domesticated animals and seed, from loessland areas to the south in central Europe, where it had become established long before. This process is probably better known in Denmark than in other regions of the Funnel-Beaker culture, where dwelling sites either are difficult to trace or have not been examined thoroughly enough. In swidden agriculture, fire and the axe were the pre-requisites for clearing the forests and creating pastures and fields for sowing. The appreciation of the importance of the flint axe is also evident from offerings made from the very beginning (Plate 114). Probably the major investment of energy in swiddening was cattle-breeding. But during the first and second years after burning, cereals were sown.

To test the yield of primitive swidden agriculture practical experiments have been carried out in Denmark in deciduous forest, closely similar to the Early Neolithic forest. The work was done throughout with assumed prehistoric methods and implements. The average yield was three times the seed the first year, but taking into consideration the better climate of the Neolithic, it could have been greater then. Already in the second year the output from the cereal cultivation was reduced to below the weight of the seed sown (Steensberg, 1980). From the experiments it can be concluded that cereals could have played only a marginal role in the diet.

The type of cereal, finds of charred grain in rather large quantities (occasionally more than a litre from one site) and pollen analyses all testify that the species that had been cultivated by Ertebølle–Ellerbek communities continued in use. Which of the two species of wheat, emmer or einkorn, was preferred, is not known. In general it can be stated that wheat was the main cereal.

Apart from extensive swidden agriculture there is in a later phase (Middle Neolithic) also some evidence of cultivation based on ard ploughing. From Denmark alone as many as ten localities with plough marks under Funnel-Beaker graves are known (the oldest from the end of the sixth millennium BP). Light ard-ploughing cultivation was practicable on plots with very light soil, whereas swidden cultivation – which strictly speaking is sowing in ashes – could be used to work heavier soils. Experiments made in ard ploughing have revealed a number of negative effects that led inevitably to soil exhaustion. These effects were not eliminated until manuring was introduced.

Of the two branches – cereal cultivation and stock raising – the latter was certainly predominant. The potential for increase in productivity therefore depended upon the expansion of stock-breeding. With regard to input of labour per unit of food gained compared with the yield of fishing and hunting, it is not surprising to find a lot of bones of game and fish among the remains on settlements. For example, one adult elk or 100 codfish provided enough food for a group of twenty-five persons (three to four families, each with two adults, two children of 10–12 and two of 5–8 years old) for a week. So incipient food production played a subordinate role in the provision of daily food. The significance of the agricultural economy lies on a different level in the history of food production. It implied long-term invest of labour, of a different order from that invested in fishing and hunting, as well as employing another type of working organization.

There is a good reason to assume that swidden agriculture in some areas destroyed the forest, as fields and pastures were short-lived and abandoned after a brief period of use. The practice of swidden is in some areas of northern Europe evidenced by soil destruction and soil erosion. The development of heath in Jutland, for example, stems from this period. Nevertheless, it must be emphasized that early agriculture was practised on a restricted scale, as numerous pollen analyses from different regions show. The total effect on the virgin forest was thus limited.

It is further assumed that households practising swidden agriculture moved at regular intervals. When the distance between the new fields and pastures and the habitation site grew too great, the household moved. Of whether the moving of fields and habitation took place within a given territory or to any area in the course of time practically nothing is known. Somewhat later the megalithic monuments in certain regions, permanent symbols of individual communities, indicate settlement territories.

As regards the once glaciated area, investigations of settlement distribution indicate a clear preference for high-lying, well-drained sandy places or low ridges. The preference was for sandy soil and a damp or marshy environment combined. This preference is well documented for the whole Funnel-Beaker culture area. With regard to the northern regions, the settlements of the early communities, in particular, were frequently located in archipelago-like regions. The reason for land selection was essentially ecological, the zone between forest and water, especially near the sea coast, being the most productive source area, consisting of a multitude of biological zones for fishing, hunting and gathering. This observation is emphasized by the location of megalithic tombs in coastal regions, which also gives a hint that the rich marine and other aquatic resources were decisive factors in the choice of settlement areas. Even Funnel-Beaker culture settlements in the black earth areas between the Saale and the Middle Elbe were in a damp general environment.

Forests on sandy soil were composed of oak, lime, ash and hazel and light ground vegetation. Such woods produced acorns, bracken, hazelnuts, apples and herbs. This environment facilitated the keeping of livestock. Pigs adapt to a forest environment because they feed on acorns and no forest clearance was needed. But even more important, boars also dwelt in these woods, and bones in settlement layers bear witness that boar was appreciated as a food resource. In open woodlands, where grass was well developed, cattle would find enough food and clearance by fire was unnecessary. This seems to have been the case in many regions in the Netherlands and north-western Germany, as demonstrated by pollen diagrams. These examples show the existence of local variations and changes in the course of time all over the north European lowlands. The composition of the livestock was therefore dependent upon ecological conditions in the environment.

Specialized production

Abundant resources of flint and amber have given a special significance to regions around the Sound and Baltic. These sources of raw material gave this area articles highly prized for barter and stimulated a specialized production of flint, flint products, amber and amber products.

Flint was an important material for edged tools, but high-quality flint was not available everywhere. This occurs only in parts of northern Europe: on the island Rügen (Germany), northern Jutland, eastern Zealand (Denmark), Scania (Sweden) and in an area north-east of Krakow (Poland) where there is striped or banded flint. In some parts of these Funnel-Beaker areas the mining of flint was already developed in the Early Neolithic period. The best-studied mines are in the hilly region of northern Jutland. There the cretaceous limestone, and with it the coveted Senon flint, is found close to the surface. Numerous early flint mines are located in this region, north of Thisted. The shafts resemble inverted cones, about 4 to 5 m wide at the surface. The flint lies in horizontal deposits 3 to 4 m deep in the limestone. The mining took place from galleries 3 to 5 m long, hewn outwards from the bottom of the shaft with deer-antler picks. When a shaft was exhausted, it was filled up with chalk from the functioning mine next to it. Between the shafts were sites for flint knappers, who executed the initial shaping of the fresh flint, before the half-finished products were transported elsewhere for final fashioning. So far as is known, only thin-butted axes were produced on an industrial scale (Plate 114). At least two mines of the Thisted region can be dated to the late part of the Early Neolithic, that is the second half of the sixth millennium BP. No permanent settlements have been found near any of these mines. This indicates work by gangs of workmen stationed seasonally at the mines with tools and food provided by those who had commissioned the mining.

Flint as either raw material or finished products found a wide distribution in northern areas, to some extent even beyond. Special prestige objects, such as over-sized ceremonial thin-butted axes, up to nearly half a metre long, deposited as offerings in bogs and waters, singly or several together, were distributed over great distances, for example as far away as the island of Gotland in the Baltic. Objects of that size could be hewn only from freshly mined flint and were usually made in the quarries. Flint thus had, besides its great utilitarian importance for tools, a value for cult and prestige objects.

In the eastern settlement area of Funnel-Beaker groups the best-investigated mines are situated in the province of Kielce at Krzemionki (Opatów district, Poland). The typical striped flint there, easily recognizable, was mined on about

the same industrial scale as in Denmark, and distributed through central Europe.

The 'gold' of northern Europe was amber (Plate 120). The source areas were and still are the North Sea coast of Jutland and the Baltic coasts of Latvia, Lithuania and Poland. Amber (fossilized resin) was collected and traded for its beauty, but primarily for its assumed apotropaic and protective, magical qualities (in reality for its electromagnetic properties, some of which were known in prehistoric times but of course not understood). Amber was therefore a very precious material. For its beauty it was used as a material for ornaments such as beads and pendants. As well as beads, pendants in the shape of miniature Amazon axes are found in graves and as offerings. These miniature axes and related forms, characteristic ornament types of the Middle Neolithic, seem to have been highly prized for gifts and barter, not least in the rich communities who built big megalithic chamber tombs intended for a special category of people.

In the area of the Funnel-Beaker culture, Jutland was the major source area. During the Early Neolithic (the first half of the sixth millennium BP) amber finds are most frequent within the area near to rich natural sources in western Denmark. From the later part of the sixth millennium BP onwards rich amber finds stem largely from eastern Denmark, where megalithic monuments and large settlements give evidence of populous communities. This change to eastern Denmark seems to be connected with the period of passage grave building.

However, amber finds are also characteristic of regions with megaliths in south Sweden and in north-west Germany. Not infrequently the poor state of preservation of amber in tombs (only in tiny fragments and resembling kibbled corn) has meant that the beads and other objects have not been recognized from old excavations. Their occurrence in tombs was originally far more frequent than the finds made would suggest. Nevertheless, this does not change the general picture – amber is most frequent in graves of the northern regions with an affluent economy.

However, amber is also found in central Europe. A unique find, a deposit of 4 to 500 kg of raw amber, came to light at Rospond (formerly known as Harlieb), near Wroclaw (Poland). It has usually been considered as proof of amber circulation within the Funnel-Beaker culture. As the provenance of amber can be established only by means of the typology of the objects, it cannot be determined from which source the deposit derived.

The production of grave pottery also seems to have been to a certain extent a specialized industry. A study of funerary pottery (Plate 124), from megalithic tombs in particular, reveals that beakers and bowls of various forms show such close similarities in shape, finish, decoration and the technique of executing motifs that it is likely that they were produced in the same workshop. Funerary pottery is the product of skilled craftsmanship, showing strong feeling for form and for ornamental effects. (As a matter of fact the deeply incised decoration was originally filled with a white paste, now only occasionally preserved.) Pottery has often been considered as a handicraft produced by women, but this is only an assumption. Anthropological experience based on existing preliterate societies shows that there are potters who are women as well as those who are men, while trading pots is a job for men.

What did the 'export' of flint, flint products and amber bring in exchange? What the people or communities in areas where flint was lacking or of poor quality gave in exchange for the exquisite 'Danish' flint axes is not known. It must have been perishable barter material, perhaps furs, or slaves for the mining industry. The only objects preserved that can have been used as payment both for flint and for amber are high-quality grave pottery and copper objects. Copper ornaments, weapons, axe blades, bars in the form of spirals and rolls are found both in the graves of persons of rank and as offerings. From the type and form of these copper objects, supported by metal analysis, it has been possible to determine their origin. Many forms have their parallels in central European cultures, for instance in the Jordanów and Brzesz groups in Poland and in Hábáşeşti in Romania. From there the route to Jutland was probably along the river Oder, whereas to north-west Germany it may have been along the rivers Saale and Elbe. The evidence of find circumstances and their association with datable Funnel-Beaker culture objects show that the exchange of copper objects started already at the end of the Early Neolithic and increased in the beginning of the Middle Neolithic period. From that time copper was known as luxury and prestige objects available to only a few in the northern and western Funnel-Beaker communities.

Compared with copper artefacts, gold is rare at this early stage in the North European Lowlands. So far only one gold object - a bracelet - has been found. It was discovered in an earth grave, together with a thin-butted flint axe and a typical ceramic bottle from the Early Neolithic period, near Stade at the mouth of the Elbe. The bracelet could have come from south-eastern Europe (Transylvania) or from Ireland.

How the circulation of goods was organized is not known. It could be an exchange from community to community in a chain, as gifts between the élite, or as barter trade. From finds of prestige and luxury items it can be seen that contacts were established in more than one direction. In the beginning they went predominantly towards the south and south-eastern regions of central Europe, but this changed in the course of time towards the west. It is evident that communications and the transport of items were carried out by boats and rafts following the coasts and along rivers.

Society

How prehistoric societies were organized is the most difficult task to reconstruct. People's mutual relations leave fewer traces than the production of tools and food. In order to get an idea of how Neolithic societies could function, archaeology studies the social organization of present-day preliterate societies still living on a Stone Age level. Such societies exist, for example in the tropics – Papua-New Guinea and the islands of the Solomon Sea in the South Pacific. If it is possible to see a connection between the social system and different types of graves, implements and prestige items in these societies, this would give guidance for the interpretation of equivalent archaeological finds. Observations provide evidence that there are items that can indicate hierarchies. But studies also show how complex these systems are and thus how difficult it is to make analogies.

With regard to Neolithic acculturation the problem is whether the sedentary Mesolithic societies were egalitarian or hierarchical. Testart's hypothesis, that the late or classic Ertebølle–Ellerbek society was already a hierarchical society, has been briefly discussed (see p. 591).

In the Funnel-Beaker culture the signs of hierarchy are more obvious than in the Ertebølle–Ellerbek culture. In the initial phase there were few well-finished graves, but quite soon the situation changed. In the late Early Neolithic began the raising of monumental grave mounds for a few of the population. Some mounds were of enormous size. The mounds were shaped differently in different areas, with stone chambers in some areas and with earth graves and wooden structures in others (see p. 594). Parallel with these impressive grave monuments, simple earth graves beneath the ground continued, which have been discovered only by chance.

Further signs of stratification in the society are the regional cult-places of considerable size, placed centrally in settled areas. All these large constructions, as well as the working of flint mines, suggest the existence of a labour force greatly in excess of the number of individuals found in monumental graves. These societies had in the course of the late sixth millennium BP a capacity for an increasing production of non-utilitarian objects, for example oversized flint axes in offerings, amber in offerings and tombs. Even cereals – a commodity produced in small quantities with much effort – were offered in pots or otherwise. The seed was sacred. The growing complexity of ceremonies reduced the labour force available for food production.

All these factors suggest a complicated structure of society with a division of labour and a small élite – hierarchy – and a capacity to organize a workforce for large-scale construction and other non-utilitarian activities.

In recent decades there has been a strong desire among archaeologists to determine the territories of communities from the distribution of graves, settlements and regional cult-places and thence the principles of territorial division. Many hypotheses have been suggested, but all are of course conjectural. However, it is certain that cult-places suggest a regional gathering area with a form of regional authority for activities of common interest to scattered groups.

In the regions around large flint and amber sources the finds of tools, implements and luxury items are more abundant than on their peripheries. Although their frequency can in part result from a different intensity of investigations in various areas, this tendency for finds to be concentrated around source areas seems to be clear. This implies, as is to be expected, that abundant sources of raw material of extraordinary importance for the equipment of the period, a well as an abundance of luxurious amber, constituted a factor for promoting the wealth of the region. The areas around the south Baltic and the Sound seem to have been a centre of wealth and luxury in the Funnel-Beaker world. Already in this early culture it is possible to distinguish a centre–periphery relationship, a phenomenon that historians have observed for many later cultures.

CONCLUSION

As fishing, hunting and gathering continued to be the backbone of the economy of the Funnel-Beaker culture in the north European lowlands, it can thus be concluded that agricultural food production did not imply a revolution for subsistence, as the late V. Gordon Childe had assumed. There are changes in economic and social practice and attitudes, which are very slow and which nowadays are termed 'longues durées'. Neolithic acculturation is one of them. Thousands of years passed before an agricultural economy became the principal method of food production. Neolithic acculturation of the north European lowlands thus had no immediate dramatic effects but far-reaching consequences in the long term – it opened up a new area.

In the fifth millennium BP, during the time of the late

Funnel-Beaker culture, new forms of implements and axes (battle axes in particular), pottery and pottery technology, and graves came into use in this area.

BIBLIOGRAPHY

AABY, S. 1974. Cykliske klimavariationer i de sidste 7,500 år ved undersøgelser av højmoser or marine transgressioner [Cyclic Climate Variations During the Last 7,500 Years]. *Dan. Geol. Unders.* (Arbøg), pp. 91–107.

BAKKER, J. A.; VOGEL, J. C.; WISLANSKI, T. 1969. TRB and other C^{14} Dates from Poland. *Helinium* (Wetteren), Vol. 9, pp. 3–27, 209–38.

BECKER, C. J. 1947. Mosefunde Lerkar fra yngre Stenalder [Neolithic Pottery in Danish Bogs]. *Aarb. Nord. Oldynd. hist.* (Copenhagen), pp. 1–318.

—— 1955. The Introduction of Farming into Northern Europe. *J. World Hist.* (Honolulu), Vol. 2, No. 4, pp. 749–66.

—— 1984. Dänemark, III: Archäologisches. In: HOOPS, J. (ed.), *Reallexikon der germanischen Altertumskunde.* 2nd edn. Berlin/New York. Vol. 5, pp. 155–74.

BEHRENS, H. 1973. *Die Jungsteinzeit im Mittelelbe-Saale-Gebiet.* Halle. (Veröff. Landesmus. Vorgesch. Halle, 27.)

BOGUCKI, P. J. 1981. *Early Neolithic Subsistence and Settlement in the Polish Lowlands.* Oxford. (BAR Int. Ser., 150.)

BRØNDSTED, J. 1960. *Nordische Vorzeit I. Steinzeit.* Neumünster.

CHILDE, V. G. 1957. *The Dawn of European Civilization.* 6th edn. London.

GRAMSCH, B. 1971. Zum Problem des Übergangs vom Mesolithikum zum Neolithikum im Flachland zwischen Elbe und Oder. In: SCHLETTE, F. (ed.), *Evolution und Revolution im Alten Orient und in Europa.* Berlin. pp. 127–44.

—— 1973. *Das Mesolithikum im Flachland zwischen Elbe und Oder.* Potsdam. (Veröff. Mus. Ur-Frühgesch. Potsdam, 7.)

HERRMANN, J. (ed.) 1986. *Ralswiek und Rügen. Landschaftsentwicklung und Siedlungsgeschichte der Ostseeinsel. I, Die Landschaftsgeschichte der Insel Rügen seit dem Spätglazial.* Berlin.

JAŹDŹEWSKI, K. 1936. *Kultura Pucharow Lejkowstych w Polsce. Die Trichterbecherkultur in West- und Mittelpolen.* Poznań.

—— 1961. Kultura Pucharow Lejkowstych [The Funnel-Beaker Culture. Notes on its Origin and Systematization]. *Pr. Mater. Mus. Archaeol. Etnogr. Łódzi* (Łódź), Vol. 6, pp. 73–100.

JENSEN, J. 1982. *The Prehistory of Denmark.* London.

LICHARDUS, J. 1976. *Rössen-Gatersleben-Baalberge. Ein Beitrag zur Chronologie des mitteldeutschen Neolithikums und zur Entstehung der Trichterbecher Kulturen.* Bonn. (Saarbr. Beitr. Altertumskd., 17.)

MADSEN, T. 1982. Settlement Systems of Early Agricultural Societies in East Jutland, Denmark. A Regional Study of Change. *J. Anthropol. Archaeol.* (San Diego), Vol. 1, pp. 197–236.

MALMER, M. P. 1986. Aspects of Neolithic Ritual Sites. In: STEINSLAND, G. (ed.), *Words and Objects. Towards a Dialogue between Archaeology and History of Religion.* Oslo. pp. 91–110.

MEURERS-BALKE, J. 1983. *Siggeneben-Süd. Ein Fundplatz der frühen Trichterbecherkultur an der holsteinischen Ostseeküste.* Neumünster. (Offa-Bücher, 50.)

PREUSS, J. 1966. *Die Baalberger Gruppe in Mitteldeutschland.* Berlin. (Veröff. Landesmus. Vorgesch. Halle, 21.)

—— 1980. *Die altmärkische Gruppe der Tiefstichkeramik.* Berlin. (Veröff. Landesmus. Vorgesch. Halle, 33.)

SCHWABEDISSEN, H. 1967. Ein horizontierter Breitkeil aus Sarup und die mannigfachen Kulturbeziehungen des beginnenden Neolithikums im Norden und Nordwesten. *Palaeohistoria* (Groningen), Vol. 12, pp. 409–68.

—— 1968. *Übergang vom Mesolithikum zur Neolithikum in Schleswig-Holstein.* Schleswig. (Führer zu vor-frühgesch. Denkmälern, 9.)

—— 1982. *Vom Jäger zum Bauern der Steinzeit.* Neumünster. (Schlesw.-Holst. Landesmus. Wegweiser, 10.)

SJØVOLD, T. (ed.), 1982. *Introduksjonen av Jordbruk i Norden* [Introduction of Agriculture to Northern Europe]. Oslo/Bergen/Trondheim. (With English summaries.)

SKAARUP, J. 1973. *Hesselø-Sølager. Jagdstationen der südskandinavischen Trichterbecherkultur.* Copenhagen.

STEENSBERG, A. 1980. *Draved: An Experiment in Stone Age Agriculture; Burning, Sowing and Harvesting.* Copenhagen.

TESTART, A. 1983. *Les Chasseurs-cueilleurs ou l'origine des inégalités.* Paris.

TROELS-SMITH, J. 1953. Ertebøllekultur-Bondekultur [Ertebølle Culture–Peasant Culture]. *Aarb. nord. olkynd. hist.* (Copenhagen), pp. 15–62.

—— 1967. The Ertebølle Culture and its Background. *Palaeohistoria* (Groningen), Vol. 12, pp. 505–28.

—— 1982. Vegetationshistoriske vidnesbyrd om skovrydninger, planteavl og husdyrhold i Europa, specielt Skandinavien [Forest Clearing, Plant Cultivation and Animal Husbandry in Europe as Shown by Evidence from Vegetation History, with Special Reference to Scandinavia. In: SJØVELD, T. (ed.), *Introduksjonen av Jordbruk i Norden.* Oslo/Bergen/Trondheim. pp. 39–62.

WISLANSKI, T. (ed.), 1970. *The Neolithic in Poland.* Wroclaw/Warsaw/Cracow.

WITTLE, A. 1985. *Neolithic Europe: A Survey.* Cambridge.

55

MEGALITHIC MONUMENTS OF EUROPE

Lili Kaelas

The term megalithic (derived from Greek: *mega* big + *lithos* stone) is in European archaeological research restricted to certain specific types of prehistoric monuments,[1] distributed over large parts of Atlantic Europe from the western Mediterranean to Scandinavia. The term is appropriate because it emphasizes the most striking feature of such monuments, namely the use of large, usually undressed or roughly dressed, stone blocks. The blocks can be placed upright on their narrow ends, either singly in rows or rings, or as walls and roofs in order to form rooms. The monuments were constructed between the seventh and fourth millennia BP. There are today around 50,000 monuments of all kinds remaining in Europe. This type of architecture and construction technique, when dated to the Stone and Bronze Ages, is named 'megalithism'. For later monuments of large stones in Europe, for example those from the Iron Age, the term is not used.

Owing to their massive size, though many of them have suffered damage over the ages, the monuments awake a sense of wonderment at the achievements of prehistoric people who might otherwise be regarded as primitive. Many of the monuments have a commanding position in the landscape and attract thousands of visitors. Others, once visible in an open pastoral environment, are overgrown by scrub and wood, which is the result of the modern farming practice of pasture reduction.

Because of the dimensions of the stones, megaliths are described in folklore as constructions by giants or the devil. This is also reflected in their popular names: giants' graves, giant's castle, giant's bed (the barrow), devil's stones and so on.

The words megalith and megalithic are scholarly terms. The adjective was used first, in 1830, by the Reverend Algernon Herbert, Dean of Merton College in Oxford, in his paper on monuments in England and Brittany (France). The substantive was used first by Dr F. C. Lukis of Guernsey in 1853. Since the term was accepted by the Congrès International d'Anthropologie et d'Archéologie préhistoriques in Paris in 1867, it has come into general use with reference to prehistoric monuments built of large stones.

Monuments of big stones, which were first studied scientifically in Europe, have a worldwide distribution. Apart from Europe, constructions of large stones occur in Africa (mainly in the north, in Ethiopia and in central Africa), in the Arabian peninsula and in Madagascar. There are megaliths in western Asia, in the Caucasus, in India, in Indonesia (Sumatra) and even in Melanesia (Malikula in the New Hebrides) and in South America (Colombia). Within this wide area types, forms and ages vary greatly, the most recent ones being built just prior to our era. However, it is a terminological question whether these latter may be referred to as megaliths.

The present survey is devoted exclusively to the megaliths of Europe. In order to ensure a reasonable scientific classification, megaliths are customarily grouped into five types:

1 chamber tombs, walled and roofed by megalithic stones or by vaulted construction;
2 the absidial buildings, named 'temples', of Malta (and Gozo). Because of their limited regional distribution, these temples will not be discussed in this chapter (see Chapter 49);
3 single standing stones or 'menhirs' (from the Breton words *mean* (stone) and *hir* (long));
4 groups of standing stones set in rows, of which the stone alleys or alignments, as they are often called in the archaeological literature, at Carnac in Brittany (France) are the best known;
5 circular arrangements of large stones, consisting only of a paced circle or forming an integral part of a monument with bank and ditch, like the well-known Stonehenge, near Salisbury in southern England.

This classification, made against the background of the European types of megaliths, involves, as do all classifications, some simplification, but has been of practical value for scientific discussion. The main types are illustrated in plates and figures by type examples, chosen from well-known and easily accessible monuments in various areas.

It is possible to estimate only roughly the numbers of such monuments. Modern, complete surveys registering all megaliths or traces of them are not available for all areas.

An estimate of numbers of tombs is as follows: Denmark, 5,500 to 6,000; Sweden, 700 to 800; Norway, a few; Germany, 1,300 to 1,400; the Netherlands, 55 (plus about 30 destroyed sites); Belgium and Switzerland, a few in both countries; France, 6,000 to 6,500; Ireland, 1,220 to 1,500; Britain, including the Channel Isles, 1,500 to 2,000; Iberia (Portugal, Spain, the Balearics), 6,000 to 7,000; Italy and the west Mediterranean islands, 1,000.

Estimates for other categories of monuments, such as

single standing stones (menhirs), stone rows (alignments) and circular monuments (open circles of various forms and henges, that is circles surrounded by a bank and a ditch), are even more approximate than for tombs. Only for central Europe (Germany, Switzerland, former Czechoslovakia) is the number of menhirs better known (Kirchner, 1955). There are about eighty remaining menhirs (thirty having disappeared). According to older references, about forty plausible ones can be added. Thus there is some information on 150 menhirs. In Switzerland there are ten, and from Bohemia (Czech Republic) three are reported. There are a few stone rows but no stone circles known in central Europe.

In Atlantic Europe the number of menhirs, alignments and circles can be estimated at some thousands. In France, in Brittany alone more than 100 alignments containing more than 3,000 stones are known, and of preserved menhirs the total is estimated from 1,000 to 1,200, some 180 of which are under government protection by the Monument Law. But alignments occur also in other parts of France, and menhirs in practically all departments. In Belgium about fifteen menhirs are known. In Portugal, menhirs are estimated at nearly 150, while in Spain there are far more and in both countries new menhirs are continually being discovered. Stone circles, so far as is known, are rare in these countries. Alignments also occur, the total of which is not recorded in publications.

Stone circles and henges occur mainly in Britain and Ireland, but figures are available only for some areas. In counties Cork and Kerry in south-eastern Ireland and in mid-Ulster in the north there is a remarkable concentration of free-standing monuments. According to information given by the Irish scholar Sean O'Nuallain there are more than 600 menhirs, some 150 stone rows of two to six stones and almost 100 stone circles, but only a few henges. In Britain all these monuments are abundant, the total being estimated at about 1,000 (of which some 800 are stone circles and 80 to 90 henges). Menhirs and alignments are frequent in the southern and western parts of the country and stone circles in the western and northern parts (with concentration of circles in north-east Scotland, in the outer Hebrides, the Lake District and Cornwall). Henges may be found all over Britain but are most frequent in the eastern lowland zone. In northern Europe, rich in megalithic tombs, free-standing monuments of the above types are unknown. Stone circles in northern Europe belong to later times (Late Bronze Age and Iron Age) and are not considered as megaliths.

The frequency of megalithic monuments is not the same in all the areas involved. Nuclear or central zones can be distinguished in contrast to marginal areas with few monuments. Is such a picture representative of prehistory? This is one of the questions archaeologists must face when dealing with prehistoric remains as sources for habitation history. Three examples may illustrate the general problem. In northern Germany, in Landkreis Ülzen, there are today thirteen megalithic tombs remaining. Around the middle of the nineteenth century the number of registered tombs was 250. On the island of Rügen in the Baltic Sea there were 38 tombs in 1938, but in 1827 they numbered 229. Of the 5,000 recorded dolmens in Denmark, only 1,800 are now preserved (often in wooded areas). These examples are typical. They indicate that present-day figures do not enable us to draw reliable conclusions about the initial prehistoric numerical distribution of megalithic monuments. Disappearence in many areas is a result of agrarian disturbances, including agrarian reforms in the last century. In the present century

many areas with megaliths have been devastated not only by agricultural mechanization, but also by quarrying, building, road construction, and so on. Urbanized regions, densely populated over a long period of time, that today have a few scattered megaliths left, may in prehistoric times have had just as many as in those areas with sparse modern population. This is evidenced by detailed studies in toponymy in some areas, where formerly existing monuments have given their names to villages and fields. Thus menhirs in France have given a place-name Pierrefitte (from *petra ficta*) of which there are at least fourteen examples. Near Magdeburg (Germany) there is a village, named Langenstein, known since the year 1223, after a menhir which has now disappeared. These examples suffice to show how megaliths can be traced, when different disciplines co-operate.

In and near the tombs, artefacts (pottery, tools, idols and ornaments) are often found. During research they have played an important role in determining the age of the monuments, specially before the invention of radiocarbon dating. Problems concerning artefacts are not considered in this chapter. There are problems, indeed, regarding the relationship between the megalithic monuments and the associated artefact material. For example, even if megalithic constructions in two areas show similar features, the objects found can be quite different. This is the case if the artefacts in the Scandinavian area are compared with the assemblages associated with megaliths in Spain and Portugal or in France: these are quite different, yet the tombs are constructed on the same principles.

Archaeologists are usually aware of the risk of dealing separately with one kind of cultural remains without considering the whole ensemble of which it is a constituent. However, the megaliths present specific problems of their own. As in the case of Romanesque churches, megaliths can also be studied as architectural achievements, cult places and symbols of prestige.

It is natural that national and regional studies of megalithic monuments cover all varieties of monuments in the area involved. But in this survey, which covers the whole of Europe, a study will be made of the basic construction principles and those features that are common to various areas. However, it must be added that owing to the variety, especially among the tomb forms, local groups and developments make it possible to define regional megalithic provinces, each with its own particular characteristics (Chapter 53). Nevertheless, there are basic types too, which have a wide distribution, even if geographically very distant from one another.

MEGALITHIC MONUMENTS: MAIN TYPES, ARCHITECTURE, CONSTRUCTION PRINCIPLES AND METHODS

Tombs

Typology

Among the megaliths, chamber tombs are the most numerous and best-studied major category of monument. Since the time of Oscar Montelius, a leading Swedish archaeologist (1843–1921), it has been customary to classify megalithic tombs normally into three types: (a) dolmens (Fig. 166), (b) passage graves (Fig. 167), (c) gallery graves (Fig. 168).

According to this theory, which adopted the evolution theory of natural history and applied it methodically to

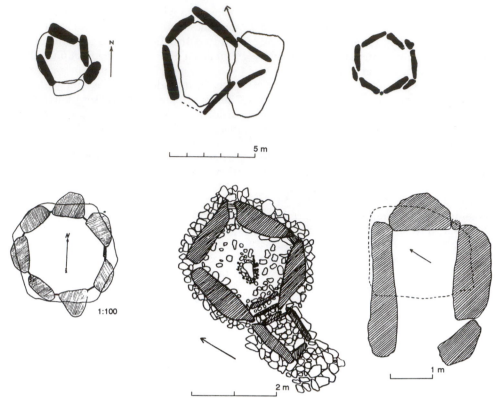

Figure 166 Types of megalithic chamber tombs (dolmens) in Europe.

archaeological material in order to build up chronological systems, the course of development was from the simplest to the more complicated forms and constructions. This classification of tombs implied an evolutionary succession and was also understood to be a chronological series. Montelius's works were translated into other languages and his ideas spread and were at one time accepted internationally. The theory that the three tomb types were developed in typological succession, the second from the first and the third from the second, has now been abandoned, however, but the division into three types has in general been retained and is followed in the present study.

As has already been said, the monuments differ from area to area. In addition to local developments, differences are produced by variations in the type of stone locally available. A structure of erratic boulders has a different character from that constructed of sandstone or limestone slabs. The variations can create confusion and therefore the classification is not always simple. However, classifications are taxonomic conveniences with distributional reality. In order to give a general view, simplification is necessary.

In order to make the discussion of the megalithic phenomenon in Europe easier to follow, a short description of the three categories of tombs according to the classification of Montelius will be made. The description is only concerned with widespread types. Interested readers will find descriptions of local varieties in regional studies listed in the bibliography.

Dolmens (Fig. 166 and Map 66)

The term 'dolmen' (in French 'dolmen simple') is a Breton word, dol-men, meaning 'stone-table'. Dolmens are found from Iberia (Plate 125) to Scandinavia, mostly in coastal areas, with inland examples being found near rivers and lakes.

A dolmen is a closed stone chamber of moderate height (up to 2 m), with a groundplan that is polygonal (Plate 126) (including square) or rectangular, and roofed by one or two cap stones, which often project beyond the walls like a table-top. The walls themselves consist of stone blocks set on edge – 'orthostats' to archaeologists – and embedded in pits. Interstices between two boulders can be filled by dry-stone walling of small slabs.

Each small dolmen chamber measures about 0.8 by 1.5 to 1.8 m or 1.5 to 2 m in diameter and 0.8 to 2 m in height. Such a dolmen is regarded as a tomb for single burial. The bigger dolmens measure about twice the size (except in height, which is about 1.5 to 2 m) and have space for more than one corpse. If there is a special entrance to the chamber, it can be marked by one or two pairs of stones, normally lower than those of the chamber. Dolmens are generally isolated, but are occasionally also found in groups and in passage grave cemeteries.

Today a large proportion of dolmens remain as 'nude' stone constructions in the landscape. The romantic view of their boulders has made them attractive to present-day tourists, artists and photographers. But actually their contemporaries never saw this view except during construction. Dolmens were covered by mounds (those of earth are called barrows and those of stones cairns). Only the upper part of the capstone was visible. The mound, if present or traceable, is round or oblong (more or less rectangular or trapezoid) (Plate 127). The latter form is the prevailing type in Denmark. Outside the Nordic area, round barrows or cairns predominate.

Of the two barrow types, the long barrow is by far the more impressive. The usual size is 20 to 30 m by 6 to 8 m, but many are more than 100 m and about 10 m wide – for example, the longest in Denmark is 170 m. The height is moderate. The monumentality is emphasized by a surrounding kerb of boulders, often highest at the short ends.

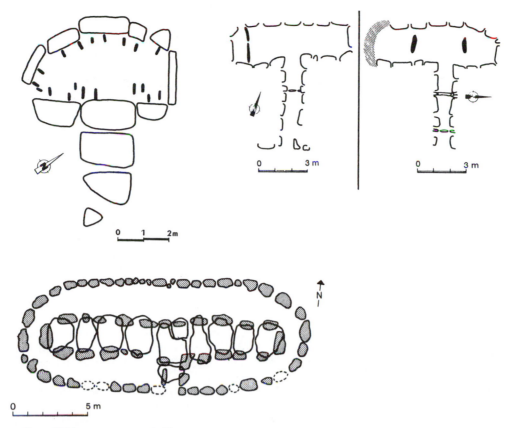

Figure 167 Types of megalithic passage graves in Europe.

The round mounds normally contain one dolmen, long ones more than one and occasionally up to five.

The size of the mounds exceeds that of the stone chambers many times over, in extreme cases being perhaps a thousand times greater, as can be seen when the mound is preserved. The architectonic idea, therefore, was a large mound with, in its interior, a hidden, carefully built megalithic chamber, the house of the dead.

Passage graves (Fig. 167 and Map 66)

The term 'passage grave' (in French '*dolmen à couloir*') is used for stone chambers which have a long passage, 3 to 10 m or occasionally longer, usually oriented south to east. The location of passage graves is the same as that of dolmens (Plates 128 and 129).

Passage graves are solid and heavy megalithic constructions, and like dolmens constructed to withstand the pressure of mounds. The predominant form of mound is round. In some regions more or less rectangular forms also occur. Round mounds contain as a rule only one tomb, not centrally placed. Rectangular ones have mostly two or more, and in Normandy and Brittany (France) up to twelve. The form of the chamber can be polygonal or square, oval or rectangular, with a clearly demarcated passage (Plates 130 and 131). As regards the oblong chamber, the passage joins it either in the middle or near one of the sides, forming thus a letter 'T', 'P', or 'q'. There is also a completely different type, in which the chamber appears as an enlargement of the passage without clear demarcation, resembling the letter 'V'. All the forms are widespread, from the Iberian peninsula to Scandinavia.

The floor space of passage grave chambers is usually bigger than that of dolmens. The smaller polygonal chambers measure 1.5 to 2.5 m in diameter, the oblong ones 3 to

4 m by 2 m, but there are numerous considerably bigger chambers. In north-west Germany and the Netherlands the rectangular chamber can be extremely long, up to 40 m but only about 2 m wide and with a short passage. As a rule the height of the chambers does not exceed 2.2 m.

The interest of the passage grave communities in developing various types and forms of graves, often in the same region, has presented archaeologists with many problems. Are different types contemporary or have they succeeded each other in time? The builders varied the standard types in many ways. In some regions they divided the chambers with transverse walls into sections or compartments, sometimes with different flooring (Plate 132). In other regions they built side-chambers or cells to the main chamber or to the passage, as medieval church builders constructed transepts or aisle chapels to the nave. Thus the result might be a cross-shaped or even double cross-shaped tomb, found from western Iberia to France, eastern Ireland and south-western Britain.

The problem of preventing earth being pressed into the chamber by the weight of the mass of the mound was solved by dry-stone walling between the interstices of the wall stones. This is also true of dolmens. In the passage grave cairns dry-stone walls are sometimes constructed as a system of support-terraces, whose object seems not only functional but also architectural and one of prestige.

The roofing of chambers and passages varies. They can be covered by large stones resting on the orthostats. Sometimes, when the latter are supported by dry walls, the cap-stones rest on the wall, which is higher than the orthostats. The roofing can also be formed as a primitive vault by corbelling. This implies that more or less flat stones are placed one above the other, in such a way that each succeeding course overlaps the one below. The top opening is covered by one slab.

Today it is usually easy to enter the chamber through the

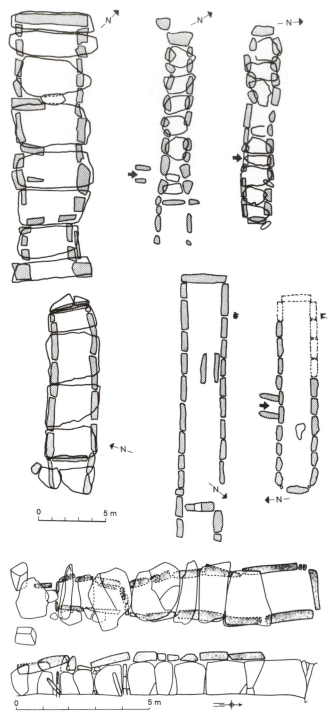

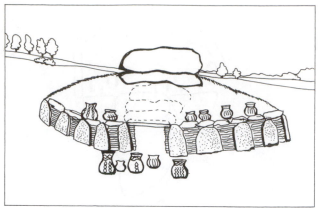

Figure 169 Reconstitution of a megalithic grave, Scandinavia, with vases of offerings in front of the grave.

did prestige and status, the mound was the determining element.

The mounds, held in respect, could be extended and enlarged in volume and provided with additional chambers like medieval churches, which were extended and never definitively completed. In some areas the passage graves are dispersed, while in others they are concentrated in cemeteries.

In order to give a picture of the great monuments of which quite a number still exist, two different types are here described. One is the impressive cairn, now carefully restored, of Barnenez, on the highest point of the Kernelehen peninsula, Finistère (Brittany), which is 75 m long, 20 to 25 m wide and 6 to 8 m high, and encircled by several terraced walls. In the cairn there are eleven passage graves with long passages side by side, each tomb being slightly different from the one next to it. Nine of the chambers are built of dry-stone walling and are provided with a corbelled 'dome', some resting on uprights and others not.

Figure 168 Types of megalithic gallery graves in Europe.

passage. Once the chamber and passage were closed with well-fixed doorstones and covered by a mound, access must have been practically impossible without demolishing the entrance. The entrance side of the mound is always carefully shaped. Finds made in front of the passage end are evidence that cult ceremonies took place there (Fig. 169). Sometimes in western Europe the passage grave mound, as well as the surrounding kerb for keeping the mound in place, is surrounded by a free-standing circle of big stones, a peristalith. The most magnificent example is at Newgrange (Ireland) (Fig. 163; Plates 133 and 134).

This description of passage graves has dwelt mainly on the construction of the chambers and passages, as do the observations and the taxonomy of archaeologists. But in the architectural conception of the monument, bestowing as it

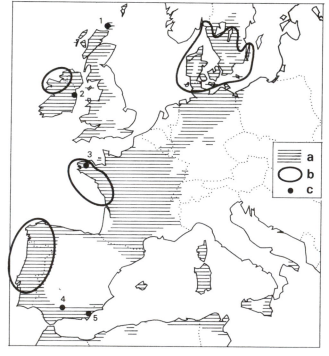

Map 66 Megalithic graves in Europe: a, distribution of megalithic graves; b, areas of polygonal dolmens and passage graves with similar plan and construction; c, important sites – 1, Maes Howe; 2, Newgrange, Knowth and Dowth; 3, Barnenez; 4, Antequera; 5, Los Millares.

The passages to these chambers have walls of flat slabs or dry-stone walling, but are always roofed with capstones. The two others are of a different construction. One is built entirely of flat stones. The other has, between the chamber and the passage, which are both constructed of slabs, an antechamber with a corbelled roof resting on uprights. This chamber is the biggest in the cairn and has parietal decoration of zigzag lines, axes, arcs and so on.

The cairn is an example of a two-stage construction, raised over a period of 200 to 300 years (Chapter 53). It also illustrates that two building techniques – megalithic and dry-stone walling – were in vogue simultaneously.

The other magnificent monument is the passage grave at Newgrange in the Boyne valley in eastern Ireland, dominating the cemetery and the valley. Newgrange is one of the greatest achievements of prehistoric Europe (Fig. 163; Plates 133 and 134).

The monument consists of a round cairn 78 to 85 m in diameter, and 11 to 13 m high. Its base is surrounded by a kerb of orthostats, many of which are decorated with various motifs and designs (Plate 134). Behind the kerb is a retaining wall, the original height of which is estimated to have been 3 m above the kerb. The cairn covers a cross-shaped passage grave, built of orthostats. The main chamber rises up to 6 m above the floor and has a corbelled vault, closed by one capstone. The passage opens towards the south-east. Above the roof of the passage entrance is a roof-box, oriented towards the winter solstice. On the roof slabs is a series of grooves, cut to enable rainwater percolating through the cairn to be led off outside the confines of the passage. The monument is also richly ornamented inside. The cairn is surrounded by a peristalith 104 m in diameter, enclosing an area of one hectare.

Gallery graves (Fig. 168 and Map 67)

Gallery graves are rectangular megalithic chambers with straight, parallel walls, forming rectangular narrow rooms (galleries). The size of the chambers varies from 3 to 30 m in length, is from 1.5 to 5 m wide and up to 2 m in height throughout. Compared with passage graves, gallery graves are more uniform in design. But they represent quite a different 'architectural' idea altogether. With dolmens and passage graves the mound is the leading element, often situated on a commanding point in the landscape, the chambers being totally hidden within the mounds. The gallery grave mound (oblong or round), however, is a light 'dressing' added to the chamber. Consequently, these mounds do not dominate the environment. A light mound does not present the same problem for the chamber construction as a heavy one. Therefore the chamber wall could be constructed of comparatively slender slabs. There are even gallery graves about which there is no certainty that they were ever enclosed in mounds. This is true especially of the gallery graves of the Saumur and Anjou region (France), the megaliths of so-called 'Angevin type', also known in archaeological literature as 'gallery graves of Loire type'. Among those monuments are several that are ranked as the most impressive megalithic chambers in France, for instance that at Bagneux, near Saumur, which is 17 m long and 4 to 5 m wide. This gives an interior floor area of some 85 m² – the size of a modern apartment with three to four rooms. Another is the 'La Roche aux Fées' at Essé, south-east of Rennes, measuring 14 by 4 m inside and over 2 m high.

The chamber of a gallery grave is often divided into two or more rooms by transverse slabs. The entrance in most

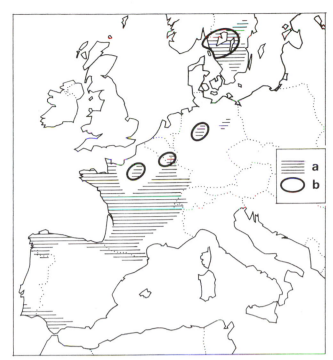

Map 67 Megalithic gallery graves in Europe: a, areas of occurrence of gallery graves; b, distribution of gallery-graves of Seine-Oise-Marne type.

types is in the short side, preceded by an antechamber or entrance porch, usually narrower and lower than the 'gallery'. In some groups the graves are provided with portholes, round or square, in the transverse slab or slabs between the porch and the chamber, and sometimes also in the transverse slabs dividing the chamber. However, portholes occur occasionally even in other categories of chamber tombs in various areas.

In northern France, in the valleys of the Seine, Oise and Marne (Paris region), there were societies that used to dig their gallery graves in the ground, often on a slope. Surprisingly enough this type of grave occurs also in two distant regions: Westphalen–Hesse (Germany) and south-western Sweden (with a concentration between Lakes Vänern and Vättern). The Swedish gallery graves, however, are as a rule shorter (mostly 4 to 8 m) than the west European forms. The assumed connection between these localized occurrences is much discusssed among scholars.

Besides the forms described above, there are also gallery graves consisting only of one room, with access either laterally (an opening between two wall stones) or through the short end. They appear in the same environment as the more sophisticated types.

The compass orientation of the gallery graves is generally south to north, but it is in certain areas almost regularly east to west. This latter probably indicates new cosmological ideas among those who decided on the orientation of tombs.

Gallery graves occur both on the coast and inland, but in contrast to dolmens and passage graves they are more frequently found inland – generally in river landscapes. The main areas are the Iberian peninsula, France, Germany and western Sweden. There are few in Belgium and Switzerland.

Gallery graves represent an innovation both in architectural conception and building technique, thus forming a discontinuity with dolmens and passage graves, not an 'evolution' as Montelius thought.

Other types of contemporary tombs

There is a type of long barrow of similar appearance to those covering dolmens, but without a stone chamber. These barrows, too, are often considered as megalithic monuments because of their kerb of boulders.

In France and some other parts of the western Mediterranean there occurs a type of tomb that is a kind of artificial cave (hypogeum) cut into soft rock. These are also regarded by many scholars as megalithic constructions, but their construction did not require the handling of large stone blocks and so they are not reviewed here (see Chapters 49 and 53).

How old are the tombs?

Megalithic tombs like any other type of tombs can be dated either by artefacts found in them or by applying the C^{14} method to samples related to tomb construction. The first radiocarbon dates published at the end of the 1950s caused a considerable sensation, because the tombs suddenly became a thousand years older than had previously been thought.

By now there are many radiocarbon dates related to megaliths. The dates are, however, not equally distributed all over the megalithic provinces. At present there are more dates from France than from elsewhere. According to these, dolmens and passage graves with a polygonal chamber and a littoral spread – a category with a wide distribution – are the oldest, having already been constructed in France some 7,000 years ago.

Such early megaliths were raised from Normandy to Charente, both types in cairns containing one or many chambers. But there is no time difference between the early dolmens and the early passage graves. This contradicts the old idea of Montelius, that passage graves were developed from dolmens.

The heyday of megalithic constructions falls within the late seventh and the sixth millennium BP, that is within a period of about 1,000 years. During this time passage graves with rectangular and square chambers as well as forms with side-chambers or cells were built widely. The construction of passage graves continued into the fifth millennium BP.

In Ireland, carbon-14 dates related to megalithic tombs are few. The earliest tombs there are the simple structures of the Carrowmore cemetery on the west coast, near the town of Sligo. A chamber (code No. 7) with a hint of a passage belongs according to carbon-14 dating to the beginning of the sixth millennium BP and is thus more recent than the oldest megaliths in France. Some centuries later, sophisticated forms, for example with a cross-shaped groundplan, were built. One of these, the magnificent monument of Newgrange (Plates 133 and 134; Fig. 163) dates to the second half of the sixth millennium BP. But the simple type of passage grave continued to be raised contemporaneously. This is evidenced for instance by tombs in the cemetery of the Boyne valley, where the sites of Newgrange and Knowth were recently excavated. Thus there is apparently a hierarchy of the graves on these sites.

The rare carbon-14 dates relating to the passage grave category of chamber tombs in Britain correspond closely to the Irish series.

According to radiocarbon dates, dolmens and passage graves in Portugal and Spain were built nearly a thousand years later than those in France. Published dates show that the earliest tombs are those of northern Portugal, in Beira Alta (Orca dos Castenairos, Carapito I, Orca de Seixas),

constructed around the end of the seventh millennium BP. The few dates related to megaliths in Spain tally with the Portugese ones. These Iberian dates have been challenged, however (Kalb, 1981); according to archaeological dating, based on the comparison of artefacts and parietal art, the Iberian tombs seem to be contemporary with the French monuments. Recent radiocarbon dates from Portugal, though few in number, indicate the same.

What is the situation in northern Europe? All radiocarbon datings of dolmens and passage graves show that these are more recent than the oldest megalithic tombs in France. Datings of megalithic tombs in Mecklenburg demonstrate that these were raised from the late sixth millennium BP onwards. In Scandinavia, for which there are quite a few C^{14} dates, certainly the earliest dolmens were built slightly earlier than in Mecklenburg, that is some time after the mid-sixth millennium BP. In northern Europe the earliest dolmens are older than the oldest passage graves, which began in the early Nordic Middle Neolithic (some centuries before 5,000 years ago). Nevertheless, both forms were for a time raised concurrently. In Scandinavia there is no time difference established for passage graves with T-, P-, q- and V-shaped groundplans. There, the finds associated with tombs indicate that the difference is spatial rather than temporal.

For how long the passage graves were built in northern Europe is not established by radiocarbon dates. According to finds made there, the period is estimated to have lasted for about two centuries. The re-use of megalithic tombs – dolmens as well – continued there, as in other regions, far beyond the Neolithic.

Gallery graves are later than dolmens and passage graves, and belong culturally to the Late Neolithic. This is confirmed by radiocarbon dating, though direct evidence is only available from France. In western France gallery graves at Liscuis, Laniscat and at Kerivaelen, Plelauff (Brittany) have been dated to the first half of the fifth millennium BP.

The Nordic gallery graves are dated only by associated artefact assemblages, according to which they were built between 3,800 and 3,500 years ago, that is the Nordic Late Neolithic. They are contemporary with a group of similar type (sunk into the ground and with a porthole) in the Seine–Oise–Marne region (France). The latter are, however, not dated by the radiocarbon method, but contain finds of artefacts similar to those from the rock-cut tomb at Mesnil-sur-Oger, which is radiocarbon dated to the beginning of the fourth millennium BP.

Here the question arises as to whether the construction of passage graves in western Europe had stopped before the emergence of gallery graves. Or were they constructed for a time concurrently? The evidence of radiocarbon dating is not conclusive in the matter. In western Europe there seems to be an overlap in time. It has been assumed that in France grave architects built the gallery graves using the V-shaped passage graves as their model (Chapter 53). The archaeological evidence in Scandinavia shows clearly that there is a hiatus between passage grave construction and the appearance of gallery graves. The cultural picture of Middle Neolithic and Late Neolithic in northern Europe is quite different.

From the above it can be inferred that the megalithic technique was used for burial and cult buildings in Europe for around 2,500–3,000 years, which is indeed a surprisingly long period of time. The time range is not equally long everywhere, but the architectural succession of tombs is broadly the same. How to explain this is a continuing challenge. In the Bronze Age megalithic structures were replaced in most regions by single graves under barrows.

Free-standing monuments (Map 68)

Free-standing monuments – menhirs, alignments, stone circles and henge monuments – are abundant, as already mentioned, mainly in western Europe, that is France, Portugal and Spain, Ireland and Britain. Quite a number of menhirs and a few alignments are also known from central Europe. Owing to the lack of detailed studies (except in a few regions) the character of these monuments is obscure and so is their purpose. Exposed as they have been in the open, the free-standing monuments have suffered by being exploited as stone quarries. Owing to such destruction, ancient and recent, only a small proportion of these probably complex monuments has survived. Because of their appearance as free-standing megaliths, they are grouped together.

Menhirs (Plate 106)

As already pointed out, menhirs are frequent in Brittany, and archaeologists have used this Brythonic word since the end of eighteenth century. Some scholars employ it to refer both to isolated monoliths and to ensembles of free-standing stones, grouped in rows or crossing lines, and so on, but here it is used exclusively for single standing stones. It must be noted, however, that a menhir can be the remainder of what once was an ensemble, as has been discovered repeatedly in excavations. Furthermore, many observations tend to indicate that menhirs stood in a relationship to other megalithic monuments, as for example gallery graves and stone circles.

Both naturally occurring blocks and blocks quarried from the parent rock are used for menhirs. In the latter case the fresh break can be seen. The majority of menhirs seem to be rough or only slightly dressed. The size varies widely in height and in weight. Menhirs can measure from about 1 to 12 m and weigh up to 100 tons. Usually one-fifth of the total height is below the ground. A unique menhir, now broken, at Locmariaquer in Brittany is 20 m high and weighs 350 tons.

As examples of some impressive and easily accessible menhirs, the well-known stone of Kerloas in Plouarzel (Finistère) and the one at Champ Dolent near Dol (Ille-et-Vilaine) (Plate 106) in Brittany may be mentioned.

In general the menhirs are of local stone, but it is geologically proved that they may have been transported over a distance of 1 km. The efforts needed for quarrying, transporting and erecting the blocks are evidence of the importance attached to menhirs. They too are part of megalithism, that is cultural ambition expressed by using large blocks. They are found in the same parts of Atlantic and central Europe as megalithic tombs, except for northern Europe. But they have a wider spread and are found mostly in places where there are no chamber tombs. The distribution of menhirs thus gives a hint that they differ in nature from the tombs, though in Brittany an association with gallery graves is not unusual. There they seem to serve as markers for gallery graves. They are found more often on gentle slopes than on hills or in the bottoms of valleys.

Without knowledge of the function of menhirs their purpose can only be conjectured. Were they funeral monuments or did they commemorate something? Or were they associated with a fertility cult? (Some scholars see a phallic

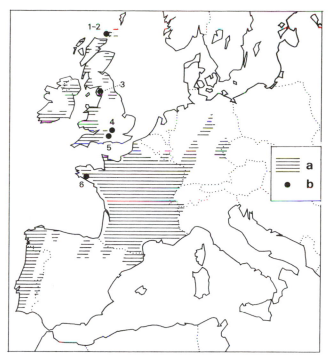

Map 68 Megalithic monuments in Europe. a, areas of occurrence of menhirs and alignments; b, as stone circles and henge monuments occur mainly in Britain and Ireland, only a few important sites are indicated – 1, Ring of Brodgar; 2, Stones of Stenness; 3, Castlerigg, Keswick; 4, Avebury; 5, Stonehenge; 6, the great alignments at Carnac.

form in a number of dressed monoliths.) Or did they mark the centre of the territory of the community?

Finds excavated at the base of menhirs, that is artefacts, contain not prestige objects, but everyday ones characteristically associated with habitation sites, belonging to the Neolithic or the Early Bronze Age. Their association with the monuments is, however, not always indubitable, as a menhir can have been erected upon an abandoned habitation site.

Alignments (Plate 108)

Monuments composed of standing stones in rows – single, double, treble or multiple lines, parallel lines or lines set at right angles, or even more complex forms, such as fan-shaped lines – are usually named alignments in archaeological literature.

The surviving alignments have a variety of length, owing partly to differential destruction. Usually it is not possible without excavation to determine the original row length. Also, the size of stones varies from small (0.5 to 1 m) to megalithic proportions (2 to 4 m) and the orientation of rows also varies. What was said about the origin of stone for menhirs is valid also for alignments. From excavation it has been learned that as well as stone, wooden poles were used also for the monuments. It is difficult to assess the significance of the differential number of rows in these monuments, as the function of alignments is unknown. One explanation may be that a single-row alignment was a single-phase structure, whereas the double, treble and so on rows were built in stages and the number of rows and their length thus indicate the duration of activity of each site. Apart from the variety of forms, the unifying trait for alignments is the straightness of the rows.

The lack of detailed studies of geographical groups, except in a few areas, makes it almost impossible to consider extant regional characteristics, including preferences in siting and their association with other 'ritual' structures.

In general it can be pointed out that wherever there are menhirs, alignments also occur. As menhirs are sited in different types of landscape, so also are alignments. However, it should be emphasized that particularly in Ireland and Britain alignments are often found on fenland, even today covered by peat.

In some areas alignments are obviously part of multi-phase complexes and associated with other 'ritual' structures, such as stone circles and henges, for example at Carnac (Brittany) and Avebury (Wiltshire), whereas in other areas such a relationship does not occur consistently. The alignments near Carnac (Plate 108) in Brittany are outstanding and have a special public appeal. At Menec the best preserved alignment contains 1,169 stones, 1,099 of which form twelve lines, 100 m wide and 1.167 m long. The rows move off to an oval of uprights placed edge to edge (incorrectly named a 'cromlech', a Brythonic word). At Kermario 1,029 stones are grouped in ten lines, the width about the same as at Menec and the length 1.120 m. The 'cromlech' here has disappeared, but the empty site indicates its position. At Kerlescan 594 stones remain, 555 of which are in thirteen lines, 880 m long, and 39 in an oval. These three fields of alignments follow on from each other with gaps of about 250 and 400 m, but with a change in direction. Most alignments, however, consist of short lines of stones.

The best-studied alignments in Great Britain are those on Dartmoor (Devon). Of the many fan-shaped alignments in Scotland the one at Mid Clyth is well known and often discussed in archaeological and astronomical literature.

Henges and stone circles

The term 'henge' is derived from the great English megalithic monument of Stonehenge, near Salisbury (Wiltshire), known over the whole world. The term is used by archaeologists to denote a circle of upright stones with a circular ditch and an external bank (Fig. 164), and is also applied to big circular earthworks consisting of a ditch and external bank but lacking stones. Instead of stones in many sites wooden posts have been used for the circular structure, as shown by pits discovered in excavations both in Britain and in central Europe. The principal and best-studied area of henges is Britain.

Among the henge monuments, Stonehenge (Plate 111) occupies the most outstanding place. As already mentioned by P.-R. Giot (Chapter 53), the first building period, dating back to about the middle of the fifth millennium BP, consisted of an outside ditch (with a diameter of about 115 m), a bank, a circle of about thirty-six holes (very probably for wooden posts) and finally a single upright, the 'Heel Stone', 30 m to the north-east of the entrance and marking the rising of the sun at the winter solstice. Later, during the Bronze Age, the erection of a double circle of bluestones had been started but this work never saw completion, as it was overtaken by an impressive sarsen monument which consists of an outer circle (diameter 31 m) of thirty massive sarsen blocks, each nearly 4 m high and capped with lintels, set around a still more impressive setting of five free-standing sarsen trilithons. All the stones were dressed to shape and joined together by tongue-and-groove and mortise-and-tenon joints. The bluestones were rearranged and placed as a free-standing circle between the sarsen ring and the tri-

lithons, with a further bluestone horsehoe placed at the centre of the monument around the 'altar stone'. The latter and the Heel Stone remained in use to mark the rising of the sun at the winter solstice.

Monuments consisting only of stone circles are abundant, mainly in western France, Ireland and Britain. Like alignments, they too show a variety of forms (round or oval, of upright or recumbent stones). Most of them consist of an uneven number of stones. Medium-sized circles contain from nine to nineteen stones and measure 20 to 30 m in diameter. The large ones measure more than 100 m in diameter and contain blocks 5 to 6 m in height, as for example in Cumbria, especially those of the Lake District (England), where there is a striking concentration of stone circles. One of the finest is the Castlerigg, Keswick.

How old are menhirs, alignments, henges and stone circles?

With regard to the dating of menhirs, alignments, henges and stone circles, it has to be emphasized that the initial phase of construction is difficult to assess. Systematic modern excavations are few.

According to finds made in France, some menhirs date back to quite an early phase of passage grave construction, as evidenced by a menhir the parts of which were used as cap-stones for three tombs (Chapter 53). However, finds made at the base of some menhirs indicate that a proportion of them date from the Late Neolithic or the Early Bronze Age.

This dating is valid also for some of the alignments. A recent discovery at the town of Lubry (Switzerland) assures an Early Bronze Age date for one such monument. The pottery from this period found there was certainly associated with the monument.

Some henge monuments in Britain were constructed during the Late Neolithic or Early Bronze Age. For example, Stonehenge owes its present appearance to two major building phases: in the Late Neolithic, c.4,500 years ago and in the Bronze Age. The latter estimate is based on carved designs of thirty bronze axes and a dagger of Early Bronze Age type.

Some stone circles excavated in Ireland (County Cork) have also yielded a few datable finds from these two periods. They indicate too that some circles were intended for cremation burials. The circles of north-west Scotland also contain cremation burials, whereas those of western and southern England usually do not (the Dartmoor area being an exception). The big stone circles of Cumbria, however, are considered amongst the earliest in Britain and Ireland and may date back as far as 5,500 years.

In many areas there is a general coincidence in the distribution of stone circles and alignments, sometimes forming complexes with cairns or barrows, menhirs and burials.

Summary

There are thus two categories of megalithic monuments: on the one hand the stone chambers, the so-called tombs, and on the other the free-standing monuments – menhirs, alignments, and so forth. There is a big difference in the distribution of these two categories.

The chamber tombs of related forms were built from the Iberian peninsula along the coasts of the Atlantic, North Sea and South Baltic as far north as the Scandinavian peninsula. The free-standing monuments, however, were not raised further north than in central Europe. These are thus a western European phenomenon.

This distribution pattern creates a problem. Why did the ideas and construction techniques of chamber tombs spread to northern Europe and not those of free-standing monuments? The question has not been answered. Is it a problem of dating or of different social and ceremonial systems?

Logistics and construction

As already emphasized, megalithic monuments have awakened people's wonder regarding the acquisition and handling of large stones. It is likely that most stones used in their construction were found locally. Many monuments are built of glacial erratic boulders obtained nearby, at least on the great Baltic plain including Scandinavia. Others are of local rock outcropping close to the site chosen for the monument. Evidently the megalith builders were acquainted with techniques for quarrying blocks and slabs from massive rock, especially the very large, thin slabs often used by the gallery grave builders, which would have required considerable knowledge of the properties of rocks and of quarrying techniques.

Not everywhere was the stone available *in situ*. Apart from the short-distance transport, say 1 to 4 km, long-distance transport also occurred. Sometimes the stones had to be brought uphill to the site. A few examples will illustrate the problems. The stones of the chamber tomb of Moulin, near Châteauroux in central France, were transported from a distance of nearly 30 km. The most remarkable transport achievements so far were at Stonehenge. Here the architects used different kinds of stones in the monument: the blue-stones used in the smaller circle and the smaller 'horseshoe' within the monument were quarried from the rock at the east end of the Presceli mountains in Dyfed (Wales), 225 km from Stonehenge as the crow flies. The 'altar stone' was brought either from Glamorgan or from Milford Haven, that is about the same distance, while the other stones (including all the very big ones) were found nearer in north Wiltshire. Whatever routes were used, the transport of these stones was a remarkable achievement. Apart from the distance, the technique employed to move them must have been the same: inclined planes, levers, split tree-trunks, ropes of hide and perhaps draught animals (oxen). Such techniques have continued to be in use up to our own times in parts of the world where monuments of large stones were built without modern facilities, as for instance in Asia and Africa. Experiments have confirmed that it works even if only human labour is used. Additional problems to solve were how the boulders to build chamber walls were raised, how the cap-stone was placed on top of the walls, how many labourers were needed, and for how long a period, to complete a monument.

In 1979 an experiment was filmed at Bougon, Deux-Sévres, in France. A cap-stone of 32 tons was copied in concrete. Over two days a rope of flax was tied around the block, the smooth face of which was turned to the underside and four ropes each of 100 m were attached. The cap-stone was dragged along a rail of tree-trunks. Two hundred people provided the draught force for removal: 170 for draught and 30 on the levers. In a single morning the megalith was moved 40 m. To remove a stone of that size from its original site 4 km away, the time needed was estimated to be a month and a half (Chapter 53). To be able to release for transport work from the provision of food and other necessities as many individuals as the French experiment required, a total population estimated at 2,000–3,000 people, including children, would have been required. This was about the number of inhabitants in a medieval town. Consequently the population involved in the construction of the biggest monuments must have comprised many groups from a large region, all gathering around an edifice of common interest for veneration.

A great monument, however, consists of many big stones. The great alignments at Carnac (Plate 108), for instance, are constructed of 3,000 stones! The kerb of Newgrange consists of ninety-seven slabs, none weighing less than a ton and some considerably more. In the tomb structure itself there are 450 stones, orthostats and roof-corbels. None of the stones was quarried, all showing geologically weathered surfaces except where slabs have been deliberately pick-dressed. This suggests that they had been found where they had been lying since the end of the last glaciation. They were collected near or at a distance from the tomb site. The stones had to be brought uphill as the monument is on the ridge. Furthermore, the cairn material also, calculated to about 200,000 tons of stones, had to be collected and transported uphill (O'Kelly, 1982). Whatever estimates are made, it is clear that purely from a logistic point of view, simply amassing the materials demanded great human resources in order to provide the work-force.

In the light of today's mechanization, and the ready availability of bulldozers, cranes, scaffolds and other modern equipment, it seems difficult to understand the construction of megalithic monuments and the raising of huge stones without modern technical equipment. Archaeologists, however, have made many experiments in construction, especially in recent years, working with the methods and techniques available to prehistoric people, and this has been shown to be a most fruitful approach to understanding prehistoric know-how.

In Sweden an experiment filmed in 1983 involved the reconstruction of an excavated dolmen in a museum park. The monument was one of moderate size, and before the reconstruction began all the stone material was made available at a distance of 50 m. The chamber, containing six wall-stones, weighing 3 to 5 tons each, and a cap-stone weighing 5 to 8 tons, was in a rectangular barrow, surrounded by twenty-six blocks, 1 to 1.3 m high and weighing 1.7 to 3 tons each. The stone layer at the bottom of the barrow contained about 50 m³ of stone and above this the barrow material was about 170 m³. All work was carried out by a human labour force and took about 620 person-hours, except for the mound, which was not rebuilt. The work force comprised about ten people. Works of that size could be accomplished by a community of fifteen to twenty-five adults.

Megaliths of moderate size could thus be completed in one season, but large monumental tasks demanded more human resources and were carried out in stages over a longer period of time.

Quite apart from the work force needed for construction, the building of megaliths is greatly dependent upon know-how and co-ordinated work, planned in advance. This presupposes also a certain general technical level. In every society any branch of technical know-how is only a part of a complex body of knowledge and technical skill.

MEGALITHIC ART

Art in this context implies ornaments pecked, carved or painted on stones of megalithic tombs and on menhirs. Ornaments are not understood as mere aestheticism but as expressions of the Neolithic people's spiritual life.

Only a small fraction of the many thousands of megaliths have decoration. They are known from fifty sites in Iberia (northern Portugal and north-west Spain), sixty-two sites in Brittany, nineteen in central-west France, the Paris basin and the Channel Isles, six sites in Britain and eighty-one in eastern Ireland and only a few in central Germany (only in gallery graves). Apart from these, a few paintings, in red or black, are preserved in Portugal (Visu region, Beira Alta). Some traces of paint have also been discovered in the rock-cut tombs of the Paris basin, contemporary with gallery graves. Decorations do not occur in the megaliths north of central Europe. Despite the small number of decorated monuments, they have attracted a great deal of attention from archaeologists and historians of religion. Most of the art is found within passage graves, both large and small. In general the big monuments are more richly decorated. The important sociological question of the numerical relation of ornamented tombs to undecorated ones in the vicinity, has not yet been studied. Were the decorated tombs designated for a special cult, or for special individuals or selected persons in the society? Both hypotheses are plausible.

As to the motifs, there are two major groups of designs, the abstract (or geometrical) and the representational. The geometric ornaments consist of circles with or without dots, zigzags, lozenges, spirals, arches, U-forms, radials and so on, singly or in groups. They appear throughout the Atlantic zone, but are in particular characteristic of Irish grave art, also including Wales, Anglesey and Orkney. The selection of motifs varies from tomb to tomb and each tomb seems to have had its own stonemaster. Masterpieces of geometric art are found in the passage graves at Newgrange (Plate 134), Knowth (Plate 135) and Dowth (Plate 136) and on the isle of Gravrinis (on the southern coast of Brittany).

Representational decoration is the special feature of the parietal art style in Iberia and France. In Iberian art typical motifs are stylized human faces (oculus designs or owl-faces). The oculus motif extends also to southern France. The motif appears twice in eastern Ireland and once in Orkney (the island of Papa Westray). In southern Spain oculus designs occur on pottery and portable objects found in the chamber tombs (Figs. 143 and 144) but there is no decoration on the walls. A similar design appears also on Funnel-Beaker pottery in passage graves in the Netherlands, north-west Germany and southern Scandinavia (Plate 123). Here too there is no parietal art in the tombs.

In western France, where passage grave art occurs from Brittany to Charente, the richest area being south Morbihan, the central element in the art is the stylized human figure – often a pot-shaped head, with hair standing on end and ears in the form of handles.

In gallery graves too the walls are decorated. They represent a 'school of art' different from that of the passage graves. It is, with few exceptions, thoroughly representational. The most striking feature is its clearly female, sexual character, which contrasts with the older, sexless art. The central motif is a pair of breasts in relief in an extremely stylized form. They can appear as a single pair or in two scrolls, each comprising two pairs of breasts, or repeated on three wall stones next to each other or nine pairs side by side, some of which have a necklace engraved below. There are also designs of weapons, metal daggers or axes, as well as rectangular shields (Plate 107) and pots. All these motifs are typical of gallery graves in Brittany and the Paris basin.

Similar art occurs in the gallery graves of Westphalen–Hessen (Germany), but in addition to this zoomorphic motifs (oxen, oxen with a two-wheeled cart) and geometrical motifs (zigzag lines) are found.

It has already been demonstrated that gallery graves represent a new architectural concept in relation to dolmens and passage graves. Even the art is new, with its sexual and zoomorphic symbols. Recently it has been suggested that eastern influences in central Europe deriving from the western Caucasus had introduced both gallery graves and zoomorphic motifs (Dehn, 1980). That means that cultural ideas from the south-east affected the architects, builders and stone-masons in the west. This idea conflicts with the conventional theory, according to which gallery graves have a western origin. Though the indications of eastern influence seem vague, they deserve further study.

There is a lively debate among scholars about the meaning of decoration. All decorations are a means of communication, ideological or of another kind. Were the decorations only signals to the living persons and society, or were they signals to the dead or to magical forces, for example signs of sorcery? Excavations have revealed, for instance at Newgrange, that there are designs on the sides of stones that are not visible in the completed structure, and this indeed seems to favour the idea of magic signs.

There are examples of hidden carvings in passage graves, too, which apparently do not belong originally to these monuments. For instance, one such carving was discovered on a cap-stone of a passage grave on the island of Gavrinis, during restoration of the monument. On the upper surface of the cap-stone, covered by the cairn, there were representations of two bovine animals with very long horns. Part of the carving was missing. This missing part was found on the cap-stone of another passage grave chamber, that of the 'Table des Marchands' at Locmariaquer in Morbihan, at a distance of 4 km. It turned out that the two enormous cap-stones were part of a menhir, the original height of which is estimated at 14 m, and which had been broken (perhaps deliberately) into at least three pieces (the third piece served as the cover to the tomb of Er Vinglé in the immediate vicinity of the latter) (Fig. 155). This and other examples demonstrate that not all hidden carvings are intentionally hidden but derive from destroyed monuments, the stones of which have been reused. This is a new aspect to reckon with in the study of so-called megalithic art.

ASPECTS OF MATHEMATICS AND ASTRONOMY

Certain regularities in the megalithic structures and their orientation with regard to the points of the compass have for a hundred years caused debates about the megalith builders' knowledge of mensuration, geometry and astronomy. The observed general orientation of entrances to passage graves between south and east has initiated a discussion on the importance of sunrise, particularly at the winter solstice.

As regards mensuration, the late Alexander Thom, who measured a great many stone circles of Scotland and England, attempted to establish that their diameters were a multiplier of a precise measure unit 2.72 ft (0.829 m), which he named 'the megalithic yard' (MY). Through his energetic research he thought he was able to prove that the MY was used as a standard measure, not only in Britain but also at Carnac for setting out the great alignments.

His theory has been met with much criticism from other scientists. It is obvious that accurate units of measurement were used when setting out stone circles, henges and alignments. But the statistical examinations indicate that these were different in different regions. It is likely that measures related to the human body were used, such as for instance pacing, a man's height and so forth. Probably a unit of 2.72 ft was used in Scotland, where Thom first carried out his measurements. The variation of the units of measurement from region to region agrees better with the historical experience that measures have varied up to our time from area to area.

The idea of the megalith builders' inclination to precision received, however, new stimulation by a dramatic observation in 1969 by the late Michael O'Kelly at Newgrange (1982). In the neighbourhood of the big monument, which in Irish folklore was the mansion of a god, existed a tradition that the rising sun, at some unspecified time, used to light up a stone decorated with three carved spirals in the main chamber. None of those who claimed this had, however, witnessed this phenomenon. It was decided to investigate the orientation of the passage in relation to the sunrise at the winter solstice. And to the surprise of the excavator, on 21 December 1969 it was actually recorded that during 17 minutes at sunrise direct sunlight entered the passage through a specially contrived slit, (0.9 m high, 1 m wide and 1.2 m long) towards the outer end of the passage, which the excavator had earlier called a 'roof-box' without understanding its function. As a thin line of light widened to a 17 cm band and swung across the chamber floor, the tomb and the two sidechambers were dramatically illuminated. Observations repeated since then have confirmed that direct sunlight penetrates the chamber for about a week before and a week after the winter solstice. Here was incontestable evidence that the tomb was orientated intentionally to the position of the winter solstice. What the precise meaning of it was is not known. In the cosmology of megalith builders the sun has certainly played a prominent role, as various signs seem to indicate.

The question now arises of how the builders of the tomb could have set up this orientation. As far as can be judged, no particular scientific knowledge was required. The excavator held that observations before the building started would have been enough. One or more observers would have needed to be on the proposed site for a time before the solstice to watch for the point of sunrise on the local horizon and to note its southward movement until the point was reached when the sun began to move back again. Having determined the southernmost point of sunrise, the observer must have put a line of stones into the ground, to mark the axis of the future passage and chamber, about which the builders had to work.

Since the 1960s there has been a flow of books and papers on astronomical subjects, both serious works (e.g. Heggie, 1981) and disputable ones, where the evidence is confounded with fanciful theories. All these theories presuppose that the Neolithic cultures needed and possessed a knowledge of the geodesic and astronomical sciences for determining orientations and making surveys. Such ideas seem very reasonable to scientists of our time. Ethnological observations, however, show that such problems can be solved without logical scientific theories.

A theory that has not evoked much enthusiasm from archaeologists concerns solar, lunar and stellar orientations of the alignments of Brittany. Unfortunately, not much is known about the original position of the stones. Records since the last century give information about the large number of fallen stones in these structures, and many monuments have been roughly restored.

Consequently, the base for sophisticated mathematics, equations and astronomical orientations is weak. They cannot be used as evidence that the megalith builders had an astronomical theory. The data produced by so-called archaeo-astronomers to date have not given any clues that explain the alignments as astronomical agencies. Similar theories have been built up about Stonehenge, which has been given the rank of an astronomical observatory. According to the views of archaeologists they are ceremonial monuments, constructed on the basis of observations and not of theoretical science.

MEGALITHIC MONUMENTS AND SOCIETY

The use of tombs and burial conventions

With the help of the structure of the tombs and finds made in them, archaeologists have tried to form ideas about megalithic burial rites and from them to widen the perspective to the religious and ideological concepts of relevant cultures.

Here some of the conclusions about burial rites are now discussed. In accordance with the principal aim of considering features common throughout western Europe including Scandinavia, discussion of regional and local differences (so natural when communications between separate regions were not as lively as in later times) is omitted.

Archaeologists have for a long time considered dolmens, passage graves and gallery graves as graves in the European sense of the word. The ideas of archaeologists about these megaliths have, as is natural, been influenced by the funerary conventions of our own time. The structures have been understood as crypts or sepulchral chambers, where corpses of the deceased were placed. The discussion has often been concerned with the posture in which the corpse was committed to the chamber: extended as in our own time in a coffin, or sitting, squatting or in a foetal position.

Because of the limited space in small dolmens they have been considered, as already mentioned, to be intended for one individual. But this is evidenced in only a few cases. As a rule skeletal remains represent more than one individual as often in dolmens as in passage graves.

Bones found in the chambers are as a rule unburnt. Traces of cremation are rare except in Ireland and Scotland, where cremation seems to have been current.

A problem that has caused much discussion is the observation that skeletons (mostly very fragmentary) in chambers are usually found in disorder, higgledy-piggledy. Only skulls are sometimes lying gathered separately. This is true even of well-preserved monuments not damaged by treasure-hunters. In other words, disorder is a normal condition in the interior of a chamber tomb. This is in striking contrast to the carefully planned and built monuments.

The disarray of skeletal remains has been explained mainly in two ways. According to one theory the tombs were used for several successive interments by the society of the megalith builders. Bones from earlier burials have therefore been stowed away in order to make room for new corpses. When for instance at Los Millares in southern Spain in a passage grave twenty skulls were found gathered in a heap (a common occurrence in many regions) this was interpreted as evidence of successive interments. This theory was considered to be supported also by finds of potsherds located in front of the passage entrance and thus thought to have been cleaned out from the chamber.

The other theory, put forward already more than a hundred years ago, implied that complete corpses were never placed in the chambers but only skeletons after the flesh had decomposed. The corpses may first have been deposited in a temporary place, in a repository or in the open, or alternatively cremated. A flood of observations, even from recent excavations, indicate that the skeletons are never complete, but that the bones were already disarticulated when they were placed in the tomb. This thus seems to support the latter theory, namely that the tombs are ossuaries or charnel houses.

However, one question to be answered is whether the bones found in the chambers were deposited there on one occasion or successively. The successive use of chamber tombs has been questioned because of the difficulty of entering there, when they were closed and covered by mounds. There are quite a number of examples from different regions that support single use.

Newgrange is one such monument, which had not been reopened since it was first closed. In the tomb were found burnt and unburnt human bones and faunal remains (including dog). The unburnt human bones were predominant. The examination suggests that they may represent a pair of incomplete skeletons (large parts were missing), broken into small pieces. The burnt material may have derived from at least three humans. The greater part of the skeletal material, mixed with faunal remains, was widely scattered over the main chamber and three side-chambers, intermingled with one another. No later interference was discovered, not even in the mound (O'Kelly, 1982). They must have been deposited there on one occasion.

In one of the chamber tombs at Fourknocks, a cross-shaped passage grave in eastern Ireland not far from Newgrange, bones of a total of twenty-four individuals, most of them cremated, were found in three side-chambers. The find circumstances suggest that they were put in each side-chamber as a single collective burial and sealed afterwards with slabs over each deposit. No further access to the chambers was possible because the roof had collapsed after the third burial and cut off access (O'Kelly, 1982).

However, at Knowth in the Boyne Valley, in the neighbourhood of Newgrange, where a huge mound is surrounded by seventeen small ones, some of the latter have had successive depositions, others just one (Eogan, 1984).

As already mentioned, the floor space of passage grave chambers in some regions is divided into sections or compartments, six to ten per tomb, and exceptionally up to twenty (Plate 132). Such compartments are frequent in northern Europe, especially in Sweden and Mecklenburg (Germany), and are also known elsewhere. They are constructed of low, vertical slabs or small stones. The size varies from just under a man's length to small ones (0.5 by 0.5 m). In northern Europe compartments appear also in big dolmens.

According to old publications from Scandinavia and Germany, corpses of the deceased were placed in the compartments in a sitting or squatting position. Finds of bone heaps with a skull placed carefully on top, found in modern excavations, have also been interpreted in the same way. However, observations made in investigations at Mecklenburg in the 1960s, when numerous finds from more than a hundred dolmens and passage graves were studied, show that burials of complete corpses in an extended or crouched position had never taken place. Bones from fragmentary skeletons in a compartment often derive from more than one individual (though never more than twenty). Now and then they have been found in a bone heap, sometimes with a skull on top, the bones deriving from one or more individuals. This implies that they had been placed like this. The large number of observations in Mecklenburg, which included quite a number of undisturbed tombs, give a solid statistical base to the evidence of ossuaries. From this it can be confirmed that the dolmens and passage graves even in northern Europe had been used as charnel-houses, left open for a time for successive depositions as, for example at Knowth.

When the time arrived to close the chamber, it was also filled up. After this there was no access, except when it was broken into, which also happened as is evidenced by finds of interments belonging to other culture groups.

What happened to the corpses before the skeletons were deposited in these charnel-houses? As mentioned, in some regions the flesh had been destroyed by cremation, in others by decomposition. The corpses may have been exposed to weather and wind, to birds and insects. There must have been some place to collect or store them before the deposition in the chamber. About this we do not have any knowledge. But in Jutland, at least seven mortuary houses near or not far from dolmens and passage graves have been discovered. In at least one of them there was an empty cist of a man's length (at Tustrup) (Plate 137). The earliest mortuary houses are contemporary with the introduction of passage grave building. In none of them have skeletal remains been found, though they have been found to contain a special type of pottery for ritual use (Plate 124). Besides these, at Vroue Hede (Jutland) in front of passage graves, traces of puzzling structures from the Nordic Middle Neolithic, perhaps serving as repositories, have been discovered.

Dolmens and passage graves were not only ossuaries but also reliquaries, cult places and real sanctuaries, as is evidenced by finds of pottery (often of high quality) in front of the passage entrance (from the Iberian peninsula to Scandinavia). Though some of the finds may derive from a cleaning out of the chamber, the majority are offerings outside (Fig. 169). Pots containing some provisions were put on shelves of slabs, placed on the kerb edge and on the ground in front of the passage. In flint areas it is also usual to find flint deposits of various sizes (raw material, blades, and even burnt flint, which also often covers the chamber floor) as offerings outside the monument. Fire traces bear witness to ritual activity.

The deposition of bones in chamber tombs was therefore not an act of inhumation but a translation of relics. By and large, the use of tombs follows the same basic pattern all over the Atlantic area and bears witness to communications over long distances, even in the early period of megalithic construction.

But in the gallery graves, it seems, real inhumations are encountered. It has already been shown that gallery graves mark a striking discontinuity in construction, decoration and art in relation to passage graves. They also represent new burial customs and rites. There are no traces of cult activities in front of the porch of the gallery graves of standard types. Observations made during excavations give a hint, though vague, that gallery graves were used for successive burials. The number of individuals in each gallery grave varies strongly from a few to more than a hundred. The meticulously excavated tomb at La Chaussée-Tirancourt, Somme

(France), contained 350. The problem is whether all the remains from this tomb belong to the gallery grave society. With regard to the floor size, such numbers at least imply that skeletons must have been stowed away at the back of the gallery, and even 'cleaning out' has to be considered. The old records, however, are unclear as regards the number of individuals found. A new examination of old skeletal material is needed.

The funerary art in gallery graves reminds one of the theory of oriental influence in art and the concept of life. In any case, new ideas were introduced and the old tradition of the sacred mound with passage graves had disappeared or was just leaving the stage.

The megalithic phenomenon

The origin of chamber tombs

The question of the origin of the megalithic idea has kept archaeological discussion alive for more than a hundred years. At first, when it was an axiom that the megalithic techniques went back to an original design, the debate was concerned with establishing the region or country in which the innovation was made. Today theoretical debate is concerned with the problem of whether the megalithic technique in Europe has a single or multiple origin.

Oscar Montelius (1899) suggested that the emergence of dolmens and passage graves was a result of a flow of oriental influences. This was in line with the common trend in European prehistory that explains culture changes by influences from the higher cultures of western Asia to those of a lower level in Europe – 'ex oriente lux'. According to this theory the Iberian peninsula was the gateway from the Mediterranean to Atlantic Europe and therefore invited a strong interest in megalithic research.

Already from the 1920s onwards some archaeologists working in Iberia abandoned the idea of an oriental origin and considered megalithic monuments there as indigenous. According to one view all Iberian megaliths were derived from the simple dolmens of Galicia (Spain) and north Portugal, and developed in the course of time into passage graves and further into corbelled passage graves. According to another theory (1940s and 1950s) the latter were developed in south-east Spain from the round dolmens, whereas the megalithic passage graves, built of big stones, had their roots in a type of stone cist frequent in north-west and central Spain (Leisner and Leisner, 1943, 1956). The idea of an Iberian origin of megalithism received new support at the end of the 1950s from carbon-14 dating, which showed that megalithic structures in the west were older than their assumed oriental ancestors.

The French tombs have been considered as introduced by settlers coming from the Iberian peninsula and bringing with them the knowledge of both dry-walled tombs with a corbelled roof and the megalithic forms (Daniel, 1960). The same origin has been approved for Irish and British monuments. Megalithic constructions in Scandinavia, Germany and the Netherlands were supposed to have been introduced from the west. Megalithic structures were thus regarded as originating in Iberia, from where they spread all over Atlantic Europe.

However, claims of the independent origin of Nordic megaliths have not been lacking either. But it was not until the Danish scholar Becker (1947) propounded the thesis that the rectangular dolmens of a human's length in Denmark were the local translation of stone cists into megalithic form

that learned society responded positively. He argued that this type of dolmen spread from its 'homeland', the island of Zealand, to other parts of Denmark and to the neighbouring areas in present-day Sweden and as far as central Europe. This thesis was based on a study of pottery styles, but is today, over forty years later, questioned because of the uncertainty of the chronological value of pottery styles (Chapter 54). On the other hand, polygonal dolmens and passage graves have always been regarded by Scandinavian scholars (including Becker) as due to the impact of west European influences. This view is supported even by the distribution pattern of the polygonal dolmens, which differs from that of the rectangular forms.

Probably inspired by the theory of Becker, a new hypothesis was launched. The megalithic tombs did not have a unique origin. They were now regarded as having been invented in several areas more or less synchronously. The idea was propounded by a British archaeologist, Glyn Daniel (1960) when discussing the impact of C^{14} dates on prehistory, which changed earlier datings. This idea was developed by another British scholar, Colin Renfrew (1976), who dealt with the structure of megalithic society. These and other authors have in various works emphasized the fact that there is very little evidence in the artefactual material of everyday life of the assumed communication between the megalithic provinces. Anthropological experience, too, shows that formal similarities of traits do not necessarily indicate common roots. Humanity's nature and needs conspire to make repeated inventions possible.

The reaction against the diffusionist views had thus grown in course of time. Both theories, the diffusionist and the 'isolationist' (multiple origins), bear on questions which have not been empirically supported. Many of the arguments are logical, analogical and hypothetical. In fact the theories of the origins of the megaliths are part of wide-ranging anthropological theories.

In megalithic construction there are not only technical problems, which have received similar or even the same solution in various regions, but also architectural and artistic style elements that are closely related. Also associated with the architecture are cult conventions such as offerings, for instance in front of passages, all the way from Iberia to Scandinavia. Thus raising a tomb was not only a question of techniques and architecture; it was also embedded in a system of cultural behaviour, funerary customs and special cults, a question of slow-flowing systems, so-called attitudes of 'longue durée'. To find empirical evidence for the emergence of such 'software' phenomena at different places without communication is difficult. Changes in architecture cannot thus be explained merely as technical developments.

The problem for the diffusionists, on the other hand, is to explain how the idea and execution of the architecture of sacred building could be transferred from the region generating the pattern to one adopting it without a parallel process for everyday objects, such as pottery, axes and other implements.

The hypothesis of V. Gordon Childe, according to which the spread of megaliths was a work of an active missionary force of a powerful religion, is an idea based on too vague an analogy. A possible explanation could be that Europe at that time had a stratified social structure, for which there is some evidence, with a communicative cultural élite which could take over the ideology and know-how of such prestige-creating institutions as mounds with chamber constructions of stone from certain centres and have them executed, while food, houses and other implements were still produced in the traditional manner of the broader indigenous strata. A parallel phenomenon is the spread of Romanesque church architecture during the medieval period over half of Europe from the Mediterranean to Scandinavia, while the everyday utensils used by the broader mass of population retained different local characters.

The prestigious mounds with stone chambers were raised for a few in social milieux where probably most people were buried in earth graves, hence the disproportion between the number of individuals in the work teams to have been needed for the construction, and the number of individuals in the chamber tombs. To produce more evidence on these social strata relationships is an important task for further investigations.

Megalithic architecture is an Atlantic phenomenon, the greater part of the monuments belonging to the landscape facing the Atlantic and the North Sea, the Sound and the western Baltic Sea. The economic system must have been to a great degree seaborne, with boats of basic importance both for food production and communication. This facilitated the diffusion of knowledge about the building of stone chambers along the western and northern coasts of Europe, including the exchange of stonemasons and builders in the service of the cultural élite. With regard to northern Europe, we may be fairly certain that the direction has been from south to north and not the reverse.

According to diffusionist theory the Iberian peninsula is the cradle area. However, as already pointed out, the radiocarbon datings have created problems, as the Iberian dates are more recent than the French ones. As the sampling methods at Iberian excavations have been criticized, we have to wait for the results of new datings.

Most of this discussion so far applies to dolmens and passage graves. The origin and distribution of gallery graves does not lack problems either. As mentioned already, these monuments were built by societies that preferred to live in riverine landscapes. That implies that boats were still required for communications, but that sea fishing was not the basic means of obtaining food.

In addition, gallery grave architecture, art and cult conventions imply a rupture with the mound–stone-chamber tradition.

According to a previous generally accepted but now abandoned view, the gallery graves of the classical type of the Paris region developed under the influence of ideas originating in the Mediterranean, from where they spread via the Rhône valley to the Paris Basin. From there the new grave architecture spread to Westphalen–Hessen (Germany) (Sprockhoff, 1938).

Later, however, it was established that the gallery graves of this latter area are older than those of the Paris region. On the basis of this chronological situation the Belgian scholar De Laet (1976b, 1981) concluded that the gallery graves developed autochthonously in Westphalen–Hessen. He explains this development as an evolutionary process from the local small to the long galleries dug in the ground and finally to the classical type with a transversal slab with a porthole dividing the tomb into a burial chamber and an antechamber. Hence the new tomb form is considered to have spread from Westphalen–Hessen through Belgium to the Seine–Oise–Marne area and further south-west to Brittany, Charente and so on by the valleys of the Meuse and the Sambre, and by the Rhine to Switzerland.

With regard to this suggested evolution in Westphalen–Hessen, however, it is not possible to indicate a clear time difference between the three different tomb forms. They may have been built simultaneously. Consequently, the different tomb-forms may indicate social levels rather than development along the time-axis.

Recently a new theory has been added to the debate. According to this hypothesis the origin of the new ideas should be sought in the Caucasus (Dehn, 1980). This view has some support in the tomb art, but is on weak ground with regard to the characteristics of the tombs.

How were the new ideas brought from one area to another? Neither in central Europe nor in the Paris region does the archaeological picture offer any proof of emigration or immigration. So far the archaeological remains indicate contacts of another kind. It is of interest in this context to remember that the characteristic Paris basin type of gallery grave was also constructed by Late Neolithic societies (according to Nordic chronology) living in west Sweden. Has there been a seaborne communication from the Paris region, or have contacts been with central European communities? We cannot make a clear distinction in this respect. A local origin in the west of Sweden, however, is difficult to conceive. The Swedish gallery graves date as far as is known, from the beginning of the fourth millennium BP. From the chronological point of view they stay closer to the French forms, but this is not a decisive criterion. The construction of these tombs in central Europe continued simultaneously.

Megalithism and society

The megalithic monuments are manifestations of the capabilities of their societies. The construction work required labour, at least in the bigger monuments, but was an unproductive investment. What were the economic prerequisites for the erection of these monuments? A precondition of such work, connected with time-consuming ceremonies, would be a surplus of food supplies for the labour force involved. What did their subsistence economy rely upon?

The megaliths, like gravefields of later periods, give an indication of where people lived. When habitation sites are discovered they are located at a distance of 1 to 5 km from the tombs. The older category of megaliths, dolmens and passage graves, are in a coastal environment. As an example elucidating this, are the big 'køkkenmøddinger' (an internationally used Danish term) or 'kitchen middens', composed mainly of oyster and blue-mussel shells along Sligo Bay in north-west Ireland. House remains, hearths and animal bones bear witness of long-term use of these marine food resources. At half a day's distance, located centrally on the Knocknarea peninsula, there is an assemblage of dolmens and passage graves. According to radiocarbon datings these megaliths are older than the incipient agricultural food production and are thus connected with a food-gathering society.

When dolmens and passage graves appear inland, they are sited on rivers, lakes and moors. This is also typical of gallery graves. With regard to this location it should be kept in mind that in the prehistoric environment there was always more water than today. Brooks and wells have, due to cultivation and urbanization, diminished considerably in most regions.

The river estuaries with Atlantic tidal waters (Portugal, western France, Ireland, Britain) are very productive ecological zones. The location near the coast and river mouths of dolmens and passage graves gives a clear hint that rich resources (abundant fish and shell-fish, aquatic birds and eggs) were the decisive factor for settlements of megalithic communities. For some regions the pursuit of fish has been considered a reason for the spread of chamber tombs along the coast. In the valleys of the interior, along the rivers and tributaries, angling, hunting and the gathering of edible plants certainly remained an important source of sustenance long after the knowledge of animal husbandry and grain production was introduced. A society based mainly on an agrarian economy with heavy labour requirements could hardly have had the reserves in manpower sufficient for raising large monuments. In the seasonal work-rhythm of rich fishing and hunting societies it was easier to reserve work periods for building megaliths.

Generally the majority of megalithic habitations are considered to be small units, that is villages or farmsteads, now and then grouped together in an area. Only in southern Spain were there township-like settlements, as exemplified by Los Millares.

According to one theory, passage graves have been characterized as a kind of clan or family group grave, where the members were buried. The small unit has been understood as a co-ordinated part of an egalitarian segmentary society; that is, one where no hierarchical character can be recognized. In a segmented society the unit is a family or village that is a self-sustaining body exercising social control over its productive resources. According to a general anthropological definition the parts of segmentary society are not subordinated to an effective and larger political or economic entity, whose hierarchical control diminishes the autonomy of its constituent parts. Further, it has been suggested that the mound also functioned as a landmark for the territory of the unit. On maps, where dispersed mounds are pointed out, some archaeologists have tried to mark the borders of territories with circles or polygons (so-called Thiessen polygons), but it is naturally only a theoretical demonstration of such segmentary societies (see for instance Renfrew, 1976). The weakness of this theory is that we do not know if the bones in a chamber tomb are a sure measure of the number of individuals in habitations. It is necessary to know whether or not other individuals were buried in earth graves, which are difficult to discover.

According to another view the passage graves are regarded as graves for the élite in a stratified society. This is proved by the impressive monumental megalithic tombs like the three passage graves at Antequera (Spain), Gavrinis, Bougon, Barnenez (the latter with terraced dry walling in the cairn) and Newgrange. Already the calculated input of manpower needed for transport and construction work, including the mound, suggests they must be the work of rather large and already stratified societies. Emergence of stratification created a need for symbols of prestige to distinguish hierarchies in the group. Also, there are arrangements where the deliberate monumentality of one construction in relation to surrounding ones reflects a stratified society, for example Maes Howe on Mainland Orkney, Dowth, Newgrange and Knowth, which are all surrounded by smaller mounds. The great mounds there have been given a dominating position. Newgrange dominates the entire Boyne valley (Knowth and Dowth are subordinate to Newgrange in this respect), and Maes Howe dominates the entire island of Mainland Orkney. These big monuments manifest a wider ritual organization. They played a role in the social life of a population far larger than that of the immediate area. The huge monument of Maes Howe had a central role for the whole Orkney archipelago, Newgrange for an area far beyond the Boyne valley.

The site of Bougon, Deux-Sèvres, represents a different example of a cult place. In a zone of 10 km diameter, delimited by a valley both to the north and to the south,

there is a centrally situated cemetery of six big mounds with eight megalithic tombs. Within this area traces of contemporary settlements have come to light. The periphery of this territory is further 'staked out' by a series of chamber tombs, mostly in an isolated position. Excavation and research of the complex show, according to the excavator J. P. Mohen, that the area had been used from the seventh to the late fifth millennium BP, that is for around 2,500 years, from the Middle Neolithic to the Early Bronze Age. Sealed skeletal remains and other finds of the tomb builders' society have been distinguished. The number of individuals has been estimated at ten to a tomb (the total being 100 in the six monuments). Compared with the impressive volumes of the mounds, this suggests that the tombs were reserved for selected members of society, who were special in some respect and few in relation to those who came to worship there. Finds discovered outside the tombs support the view that the area with the mounds was a cult place for communities around. Not all have been raised contemporaneously, and there was some time difference. This may imply that they were built by successive generations. The tombs were used even in later times – Late Neolithic and Early Bronze Age, about 4,500 to 4,000 years ago – but the rites and cult ceremonies changed. Nevertheless, the site kept its role as a cult place for eighty generations.

Bougon is not a unique site in its long use. The re-use of megalithic tombs was continued practically everywhere by succeeding culture groups. This argues for a certain degree of continuity in the settlement pattern, though this is not synonymous with permanent occupation of one and the same site for centuries. Settlement relocation occurred, but within the area 'legitimized' by the monuments.

The examples above illustrate societies in the development of which dolmens and passage graves had a given role. These are monuments whose construction implies some kind of central command for co-ordinating labour for large-scale undertakings and accumulating food resources for the individuals who were occupied with unproductive work. It must have been some sort of hierarchical society, in which the sanctuary had a consensus-creating function, perhaps some kind of religious chiefdom. The hierarchy among monuments was probably also marked by parietal art.

In northern Europe, too, there are impressive monuments distinguishable in several areas – but none that can be paralleled in size to the most outstanding ones dealt with above. Nevertheless, the differentiation is clear, particularly in eastern Jutland and the south Danish islands, which were comparatively densely populated and a nuclear area for megalith building. But in northern Europe there is also another type of cult place located centrally near to or at a distance from megalithic tombs, intended for gathering together larger groups than those inhabiting the vicinity (Chapter 54).

Within the gallery grave society the hierarchy among tombs is distinguishable first of all by their decoration. Even if there is some apparent difference in the size of the tombs, it is not as clearly manifested as before.

It is possible that menhirs, alignments and monumental stone circles, which were by and large contemporary with gallery graves, had taken over the role of demonstrating stratification in society. The big monuments of this category indicate not only changes in ceremonial systems. The concentrations of alignments in impressive fields, such as those in the Carnac region, and the henge monuments, for example Stonehenge, show also where important power centres were situated. They mark festival places where people gathered for ceremonies different from those for the veneration of the dead, perhaps for manifesting the power of the priesthood or another kind of chiefdom.

From the above it can therefore be inferred that megalithic monuments were intended for selected individuals, people who in some way were special – but we have no way of knowing in what way. Investigation of settlements has not yet given indications in this respect. But the megalithic monuments show that the societies developed in a hierarchical direction. Power and religion seem to have lived in symbiosis. Chiefdom and priesthood merged into each other. Hierarchy was related to the control of ritual. The emergence of central cult places also expresses the evolution towards increasing social differentiation in the richest societies of the western Atlantic regions.

CONCLUDING REMARKS

The megaliths represent the oldest monumental architecture in Europe. In relation to other contemporary constructions of which we can find traces, there are quite a number of graves and free-standing monuments that embody an overwhelming, not to say a crushing, volume and powerfulness. Their formation and their meaning, the impression that they were intended to make on their contemporaries, can be understood by us only if we see them in relation to their physical environment of fragile dwellings for daily life and to what we assume to be the type of society and the ideological milieu in which they were built.

To develop more concrete theses for the problems touched upon, however, much research remains to be done in every area where megalithic monuments are found. Certainly, meticulous excavations of well-preserved monuments are desirable, but the re-examination of earlier excavated megaliths is also essential because the old records preserved in archaeological literature may be misleading. However, it is now high time to concentrate research on dwelling sites and habitation areas, and the physical environment of the monuments. This indeed presupposes close co-operation between archaeologists and scientists of different disciplines, such as geography and osteology. Also, macrostatistics are badly needed for comparative studies region by region. But the formulation of problems to be studied will increasingly be dependent not only on archaeological concepts but also on the general aims and methods of the social sciences.

NOTE

1 Megalithic monuments are one of the most characteristic features of the Neolithic period in large parts of southern, western, central and northern Europe and the problems they raise can only be treated on a pan-European basis. Therefore it seemed suitable to devote a special chapter to this topic. However, some megaliths have already been mentioned in previous regional chapters (49 and 53); some overlapping and some divergences in the interpretation of these monuments were therefore unavoidable. Each author has, of course, been left free to put forward his or her own ideas. As megalithic monuments were still in use or built during the Early Bronze Age, we have asked Dr Kaelas to treat the subject in its entirety and to encroach slightly on the chronological period covered by Volume II – Ed.

BIBLIOGRAPHY

ALMAGRO, M.; ARRIBAS, A. 1963. *El poblado y las necrópolis megalíticas de los Millares (Santa Fe de Mondujar, Almeria)*. Madrid.

BECKER, C. J. 1947. Mosefunde lerkar fra yngre stenalder [Neolithic Pottery in Danish Bogs]. *Aarb. nord. oldkynd. hist.* (Copenhagen), pp. 1–138.

BURL, A. 1976. *The Stone Circles of the British Isles*. London.

CLARK, D. V.; COWIE, T. G.; FOXON, A. 1985. *Symbols of Power in the Time of Stonehenge*. Edinburgh.

DANIEL, G. E. 1958. *The Megalith Builders of Western Europe*. London.

—— 1960. *The Prehistoric Chamber Tombs of France: A Geographical, Morphological and Chronological Survey*. London.

DANIEL, G. E.; KJAERUM, P. (eds) 1973. *Megalithic Graves and Ritual*. Aarhus. (Papers presented at the 3rd Atlantic Colloquium, Moesgaard, 1969.)

DEHN, W. 1980. Hessische Steinkisten und frühes Metall. *Fundber. Hess.*, Vol. 19/20, pp. 162–76.

DE LAET, S. J. (ed.) 1976a. *Acculturation and Continuity in Atlantic Europe, Mainly during the Neolithic and the Bronze Age*. Bruges.

—— 1976b. L'Explication des changements culturels: modèles théoriques et applications concrètes. Le cas du S. O. M. In: DE LAET, S. J. (ed.), *Acculturation and Continuity in Atlantic Europe, Mainly during the Neolithic and the Bronze Age*. Bruges. pp. 67–76.

—— 1981. Megalithic Graves in Belgium. A Status Quaestionis. In: EVANS, J. D.; CUNLIFFE, B.; RENFREW, C. (eds), *Antiquity and Man. Essays in Honour of Glyn Daniel*. London. pp. 155–60. (Reprint in: RENFREW, C. (ed.), 1983, *The Megalithic Monuments of Western Europe*. London. pp. 91–6.)

EMMETT, D. D. 1979. Stone Rows: The Traditional View Reconsidered. *Devon Archaeol. Soc.*, pp. 94–114.

EOGAN, G. 1984. *Excavations at Knowth*. Dublin.

EVANS, J. D.; CUNLIFFE, B.; RENFREW, C. (eds) 1981. *Antiquity and Man. Essays in Honour of Glyn Daniel*. London.

GIOT, P.-R.; L'HELGOUAC'H, J.; MONNIER, J. L. 1987. *Préhistoire de la Bretagne*. 3rd edn. Rennes.

GUILAINE, J. 1976. *Premiers Bergers et paysans de l'Ouest méditerranéen*. Paris.

HEGGIE, D. C. 1981. *Megalithic Science*. London.

HENSHALL, A. S. 1963–1972. *The Chambered Tombs of Scotland*. Edinburgh. 2 vols.

HERITY, M. 1974. *Irish Passage Graves*. Dublin.

JOUSSEAUME, R. 1988. *Dolmens for the Dead. Megalithic Building throughout the World*. London.

KAELAS, L. 1955. Wann sind die ersten Megalithgräber in Holland entstanden? *Palaeohistoria* (Groningen), Vol. 4, pp. 47–79.

—— 1956. Dolmen und Ganggräber in Schweden. *Offa*, Vol. 15, pp. 5–24.

—— 1966–7. The Megalithic Tombs in South Scandinavia. Migration of Cultural Influence? *Palaeohistoria* (Groningen), Vol. 12, pp. 287–321.

—— 1981. Megaliths of the Funnel Beaker Culture in Germany and Scandinavia. In: EVANS, J. D.; CUNLIFFE, B.; RENFREW, C. (eds), *Antiquity and Man. Essays in Honour of Glyn Daniel*. London. pp. 77–91. (Reprint in: RENFREW, C. (ed.), 1983, *The Megalithic Monuments of Western Europe*. London. pp. 77–91.)

KALB, P. 1981. Zur relativen Chronologie portugiesischer Megalithgräber. *Madrider Mitt.*, Vol. 22, pp. 56–77.

KIRCHNER, H. 1955. Die Menhire in Mitteleuropa und der Menhirgedanke. Wiesbaden.

LEISNER, G.; LEISNER, V. 1943. *Die Megalithgräber der Iberischen Halbinsel. Der Süden*. Berlin. (Reprint 1959.)

—— 1956–65. *Die Megalithgräber der Iberischen Halbinsel. Der Westen*. Berlin. 2 vols.

L'HELGOUAC'H, J. 1968. *Les Sépultures mégalithiques en Armorique: dolmens à couloir et allées couvertes*. Rennes.

MACKIE, E. 1977. *The Megalith Builders*. Oxford.

MARCOTIC, V. (ed.) 1977. *Ancient Europe and the Mediterranean*. Warminster.

MEGAW, J. V. S.; SIMPSON, D. D. A. 1979. *Introduction to British Prehistory.* Leicester.

MOHEN, J. P. 1973. Les Tumulus de Bougon. *Bull. Soc. hist. sci. Deux-Sèvres,* No. 2/3.

—— 1977. Les Tumulus de Bougon. *Bull. Soc. hist. sci. Deux-Sèvres,* No. 2.

MONTELIUS, O. 1899. *Das Orient und Europa.* Stockholm.

NORDMAN, C. A. 1935. The Megalithic Culture of Northern Europe. *Fin. Fornm.fören. Tidskr.,* Vol. 39, pp. 1–137.

O'KELLY, M. 1982. *Newgrange.* London.

O'NUALLAIN, S. 1984. A Survey of Stone Circles in Cork and Kerry. *Proc. R. Irish Acad.,* Vol. 84C, No. 1, pp. 1–77.

PIGGOTT, S. 1962. *The West Kennet Long Barrow.* London.

POWELL, T. G. E. (ed.) 1969. *Megalithic Enquiries in the West of Britain.* Liverpool.

RANDSBORG, K. 1975. Social Dimensions of Early Neolithic. *Proc. Prehist. Soc.,* Vol. 45.

RENFREW, C. (ed.) 1973. *The Explanation of Culture Change: Models in Prehistory.* London.

—— 1976. Megaliths, Territories and Populations. In: DE LAET, S. J. (ed.), *Acculturation and Continuity in Atlantic Europe, Mainly during the Neolithic and Bronze Age.* Bruges. pp. 128–220.

—— 1979. *Investigations in Orkney.* London.

—— 1981. Introduction: The Megalith Builders of Western Europe. In: EVANS, J. D.; CUNLIFFE, B.; RENFREW, C. (eds), *Antiquity and Man. Essays in Honour of Glyn Daniel.* London. pp. 72–81. (Reprint in: RENFREW, C. (ed.), 1983, *The Megalithic Monuments of Western Europe.* London. pp. 8–17.)

—— (ed.) 1983. *The Megalithic Monuments of Western Europe.* London.

SCHIRNIG, H. (ed.) 1979. *Grosssteingräber in Niedersachsen.* Hildesheim.

SCHULDT, E. 1972. *Die mecklenburgischen Megalithgräber.* Berlin.

SHEE TWOHIG, E. 1981. *The Megalithic Art of Western Europe.* Oxford.

SPROCKHOFF, E. 1938. *Die Nordische Megalithkultur.* Berlin.

—— 1966–75. *Atlas der Megalithgräber Deutschlands.* Bonn. 3 vols.

STRÖMBERG, M. 1971. *Die Megalithgräber von Hagestad.* Lund/Bonn.

VALERA, R. DE; O'NUALLAIN, S. 1961–72. *Survey of the Megalithic Tombs of Ireland.* Dublin. 3 vols.

WAALS, J. D. VAN DER (ed.) 1966–7. *Neolithic Studies in Atlantic Europe.* Groningen. (Palaeohistoria, 12.)

56

MINING IN EUROPE

during the Neolithic and the Chalcolithic

Robert Shepherd

Mining in the Neolithic era is the subject of the present chapter, but it is first necessary to consider what mining implies, since the date of its inception depends on how it is defined. Basically mining is the industry involved in extracting minerals and rocks from the earth's crust. It may therefore include 'grubbing', collection from screes, the working of placers, pits, open pits, trenches and quarries, and underground mining. If, however, it is regarded as being restricted to underground work with galleries, leading from adits or shafts, there is little evidence that such mining took place before the Neolithic era. The other operations on the surface were in train long before Neolithic times, in the Palaeolithic. These considerations therefore govern the determination of the age of mining. Mining can then be accepted as the very oldest industry, despite the generally held view that it was preceded by that of agriculture. This latter assumption is based on the premise that the evolution of agriculture emphasized the need for better raw materials from which to manufacture the essential tools for tilling the ground. At the same time the establishment of settled habitation sites also introduced a need for better weapons for defence and implements with which to prepare the ground.

Prior to the Neolithic age, going back over a period of many thousands of years, the main requirement was weapons for hunting and fishing. Tools and weapons were first made from wood and later from stone, bone and flint. Weathered stone, flint, obsidian and so on were collected from the surface and from very shallow deposits. The disappearance of the ice-sheets northwards, including the removal of the land bridge connecting Britain with the continent of Europe, brought warmer conditions and new settlers from the south and heralded the dawn of agriculture. Weathered rocks and flints were no longer suitable for the new needs and it was eventually discovered that by digging deeper into the earth more durable and more efficiently worked flints and cherts could be obtained. Thus the very first actual underground mines were sunk.

Preceding chapters of this work have covered the main divisions and subdivisions of prehistory in sufficient detail, but it might be useful at this stage to consider these briefly in the context of actual mining. Evidence of actual excavation sites of Pre-Neolithic age in Europe is sparse. However, mention can be made, for instance, of a possible Palaeolithic flint quarry at Findesbury in Kent, in southern England, and the Mesolithic mines of the Holy Cross mountains in Poland.

The Linear Bandkeramik culture, the Danubian I phase postulated by Childe (1957, pp. 105–19), and extending over the period from about 7,300 to about 6,900 years ago, from central Europe spread into Poland, the Rhine valley, the Low Countries and northern France. Little is known of any actual mining by these peoples although the area of Olszanica in Poland is often referred to as a Bandkeramik mining site. The Mayen basalt quarries in western Germany were also probably worked at this time and their products traded far and wide for use particularly in the manufacture of querns. Mines at Kleinkems in the Rhine valley, in the Isteiner Klotz, the Jurassic limestone range, worked jasper and it is thought that these were possibly of a Bandkeramik date or from even later in the Neolithic, but no radiocarbon dates are yet available. When the migration reached northern Europe it fanned out and a form of regionalization developed. New cultures came into being and included the Lengyel of Austria, the Funnel-Beaker culture (TRB) of Scandinavia, the Michelsberg culture of the Rhineland and of Belgium and the Windmill Hill culture of southern Britain. Examples of extraction by the Lengyel peoples include the chert mining site at Mauer (about 6,100 years ago) in Austria and Saspow in Poland (about 5,500 years ago). At Kvarnby in Sweden, the Gallerup and Tullstorp mines and flint quarries date from about 5,100 years ago and relate to the Funnel-Beaker culture. Dolerite quarries at Sélédin in northern France were worked by the Chassey culture between about 5,800 and 4,500 years ago. In Switzerland the chert mining site of Löwenberg was developed by the Cortaillod culture about 5,300 years ago, according to Schmid (1975, pp. 78–80). The Michelsberg peoples worked many flint mining sites in Belgium and Holland and northern France around 6,100 to 5,500 years ago and these together with those of the Windmill Hill culture in Britain are briefly described on p. 623 ff. There is a strong possibility that the Windmill Hill culture was derived from a cross-channel migration by the Michelsberg peoples: the mining techniques used in the later Michelsberg flint mines in northern Europe bear a strong resemblance to those in the British counties of Sussex, Wiltshire, Hampshire, Surrey and Norfolk.

TYPES OF MATERIALS USED IN THE NEOLITHIC PERIOD

Before the later use of native copper and the extraction of copper ores the pre-Bronze Age cultures depended on rocks, flints, chert, jasper and obsidian for making weapons and tools. Of these, rock was the most easily obtained, but even the most suitable varieties of rocks were inferior to such materials as, for example, silex and obsidian. Before the advent of underground mining of flint and chert, the use of rocks was predominant and even in later times rock was still extracted in those places which were at a great distance from the exposed chalk areas which usually contained seams or deposits of workable flint. Conversely, artefacts of flint, chert, jasper and obsidian have often been found far from the source of the raw materials, thus indicating the existence of some form of trade routes in prehistoric times.

There is little evidence on the ground for the extraction of igneous rocks by quarrying, and the reason must be that it has been destroyed by later developments. Axes made from various types of igneous rock, such as greenstone, volcanic tuff or dolerite, and sedimentary grit have been found all over Europe. By making petrographical analyses of the rock from which an artefact has been made and comparing the result with those of similar analyses of rocks from known exposures in existing quarries, cliffs, screes and the like it has been possible to suggest possible sources of production (Keiller et al., 1941).

Flint is a highly siliceous material containing up to 98 per cent pure silica and is therefore very abrasive and also of a brittle nature. In the pure state it is normally black in colour, but may be pink, yellow, blue or various shades of red, depending on the conditions under which it was laid down. Normally it is covered by a white cortex. One of the features of flint is that it breaks with a conchoidal fracture, and this property tends to enhance its appearance when trimmed into axes, spearheads, arrowheads and other objects, especially when the final product is polished. Normally it is found as nodular lumps in the sedimentary rock, chalk, either sporadically or in masses, but usually in stratified seams that consist of nodules in close contact, each maybe more than 30 cm in thickness.

There is some divergence of opinion on the terminology of the three materials flint, chert and jasper. In German a general term 'silex' is often used: this embraces all three, that is, *feuerstein*, *hornstein* and *jaspis*. In French, according to Jung (1963, pp. 126, 319), silex is often used for what in Britain is termed flint. Chert is often referred to as an impure form of flint, but in America and Australia flint is understood to represent a kind of chert. The salient difference is that when the material is found in chalk it is labelled flint, but when it occurs in limestone or sandstone it is regarded as chert. Flint and chert look very much alike and can often be found together in screes formed from the weathering of two or more rock types.

Jasper is another highly siliceous material and is found often in the Jurassic rocks of central Europe. It is of a red colour resulting from the effects of oxidization.

Obsidian contains over 66 per cent silica and is a product of acid igneous lavas. It has a glassy lustre and a conchoidal fracture and had a variety of uses for the manufacture of decorative objects such as jars and boxes, as well as for axes and arrow-heads. In prehistoric times it was traded far and wide.

METHODS OF MINING

Extraction methods

Fig. 170 provides an approximate indication of the variety of methods used for the extraction of the chief materials from the earth throughout the ages in northern Europe.

As indicated already, the early methods of mining were crude and non-selective in the type of material extracted. Grubbing consisted essentially of removing lumps of rock from the surface of the ground and from screes and cliff faces. These were often in the form of boulders and pebbles and were sometimes used in their unshaped form as hammers to extract other pieces or to shape them roughly. They could be used as crude hand-held tools, to be hurled at animals by hand or later from catapults or slings, or were employed in the rough cutting up and preparation of food. Nodular lumps of flint were often removed in the same way and often the weathered state of such materials, which had been exposed to frost and other weathering agents, made them unsuitable for precise or elaborate tool manufacture; they were therefore used in their original form.

From these rudimentary beginnings a form of quarrying developed. An outcrop of stone on a hillside would attract attention and portions would be prised out of the solid rock with crude stone tools. In the early stages no attempt was made to go deeper, but the workings followed the outcrop as far as possible. This was also the case for outcrops of flint and chert, lumps of these materials being removed with comparative ease from the parent chalk, limestone or soft sandstone. Sometimes work was not confined to one level and with massive outcrops of igneous rock, such as dolerite and basalt, the weathered rock was extracted by benches. As soon as the rock was no longer broken sufficiently to be eased out, a bench or step was formed and a higher portion of the cliff was attacked. An example of early benching is seen at Sélédin in northern France where dolerite was extracted as early as around 5,800 years ago. Several bands or seams of weathered flint were extracted elsewhere by similar methods.

Concurrently, where an outcrop of flint or chert was noticed on level or slightly rising ground, the soil or subsoil being absent, crude pits were dug to a depth of barely a metre and a series of them made along the outcrop. Later it was discovered that a larger quantity of material could be won from a given area by following the outcrop with a trench again no more than a metre in depth. Where the seam of flint had a very slight dip, or was moderately level, another long trench parallel to the first was dug at a distance of a metre away. As trenches became deeper, with the corresponding and increasing depth of the seam, small galleries or tunnels were made to connect two trenches in order to extract the maximum quantity of flint. Examples of the trenching method have been found at Obourg (De Munck, 1886–87) and Strépy in Belgium (Marien, 1952, p. 87, Fig. 86) and at Durrington Walls in England (*Antiquaries Journal*, 1975, p. 5).

The crude methods of extraction were the early stages in the progressive development of mining, a process which has continued right down through the ages. Such mining, following on from the mere collection of loose pieces of material, has been termed open-cast by some non-mining observers. It was, however, really a form of open pit extraction, whereas true open-cast is a much more sophisticated method involving full extraction by following the seam deeper and deeper until the depth of overburden is so great that it becomes no longer economic to remove. The area from which the material has been removed is filled with overburden cleared off to expose the deposit, leaving sufficient room between the backfill and the working face to allow extraction to continue. Such a method was not

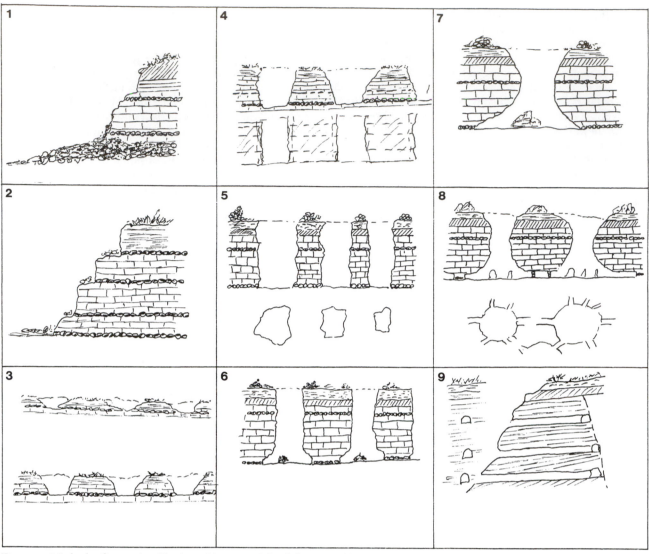

Figure 170 Methods of extracting flint in prehistory. 1, Palaeolithic – 'grubbing' stones, flints, cherts from cliffs and screes; 2, Palaeolithic and Early Neolithic – 'benching' stones, flints, cherts; 3, Palaeolithic and Early Neolithic – digging crude shallow pits, and later shallow trenches for flints, cherts, possibly coal; 4, Neolithic – deep trenches (with galleries) for flint, chert; 5, Neolithic – vertical shafts for flint, chert; 6, Neolithic – shafts with basal undercutting, for flint, chert; 7, Neolithic – bell pits for flint, chert (later: thick ironstone and coal); 8, Neolithic – shafts and galleries for flint and chert; 9, Eneolithic, Bronze Age and later – adits for copper, gold, lead, salt.

even possible until suitable machinery had been developed during the last hundred or so years.

It was soon realized from the methods used that as workings went deeper the quality of the flint tended to improve. There are many prehistoric flint mining sites with shafts sunk through several seams of flint, where only the bottom one was worked. After testing samples from the upper levels the miners would decide to go deeper to investigate the possibility of the presence of more suitable flint deposits further down. By making holes in the ground, trenches and so on, the prehistoric miner had inadvertently stumbled upon some of the basic elements of sedimentary geology. First it was noticed that rocks and seams were bedded in layers and that seams of flint occurred in succession in more or less parallel layers. It would not, of course, have been appreciated that older beds would be lower in the succession, or conversely that each bed was more recent than the one immediately underneath, that is of course in normal undisturbed strata. These facts were not recognized until the nineteenth century. This, however, was irrelevant, but what the prehistoric miner did realize was that if a seam became too deep to extract, the extraction of a lower seam at the

outcrop could immediately be commenced. The recognition of the fact that the better seams lay deeper was very significant for the miner in the Neolithic era, for farming communities required tools suitable to withstand the arduous tasks involved in tilling the ground and preparing raw materials.

All these considerations led to the sinking or making of the earliest shafts for the extraction of flint. At first such shafts were shallow and of small diameter. Most flint mining shafts were of a circular shape, which is much stronger than other forms and less likely to require any form of support for the sides, especially in homogeneous strata, rather than the rectangular version which was also widely used in later metal mining. There are other reasons, of course, but it is somewhat strange to realize that early miners understood and appreciated the advantages of the circular shape.

The earliest shafts simply went down to the shallow seams or seams from which the flint was to be extracted. The prehistoric miner was able to determine at what depth the seam would be present, as he had probably extracted it already, possibly as far as he could, with trenches or open pits. The earliest shafts were really more sophisticated versions of the open pit or trench, but there was at first no connection between vertical shafts, although they were sunk in lines at the same depth and following the strike of the seams. The miner only extracted the flint necessary to make the shaft. The next development was the undercutting of the base, widening out the bottom as far as it was safe to do so in order to extract more flint. This was only possible with any degree of safety when the chalk was reasonably strong and probably self-supporting, or in mining terms competent.

Undercutting of the base of the shaft, especially where the flint was present in a thick section, increased the yield of flint per unit of debris removed. Further intensification of undercutting led ultimately to the development of what is known as the bell pit. With this method the final shape of the shaft resembled that of a bell, being narrower in the centre and wider at the top and bottom. The method had its widest development in thicker seams of ironstone and coal in much later times, but was also used in prehistoric mining, especially in flint working, before mining with galleries came into vogue. The procedure was to extract flint by widening out the base of the shaft, but, unlike in the undercutting method, chalk was removed as well as the flint. When it became virtually impossible to support the overhanging chalk strata the shaft was abandoned and a new one sunk. Accidents from the use of this method must have been very numerous compared to those arising during the making of simple pits or holes in the ground.

The ultimate logical development of flint mining was actual underground mining. This was the method which produced the greatest return in the form of weight of flint produced per unit of dead work, that is, of chalk debris removed. Basically the method consisted of sinking a shaft down to the seam to be worked and driving galleries radially from the base of the shaft. The flint was thus extracted at floor level. There are, however, numerous examples of the flint seam being extracted at other horizons, in the middle of the seam section or even at roof level. The advantage of extraction at floor level was that an area of flint could be more easily exposed before it was extracted thereby ensuring a cleaner product. When the approximately square galleries, 1 m high by 1 m wide, became too long for easy transport to the shaft bottom another shaft was sunk and the operation repeated, connections often being made between shafts spaced about 10 m apart. The worked-out shaft was mostly filled in with chalk debris from a shaft in the course of being sunk. By careful planning it was possible to maintain production by having several shafts in the course of operation and several in the process of being sunk or backfilled. Some major Neolithic mining sites such as Grimes Graves (Plates 138 and 139) have been preserved and investigated and show evidence of over 600 shafts in the form of depressions in the ground. A series of depressions in any area of chalk could indicate the presence of old flint mines, although these would not necessarily be advanced workings with underground galleries.

Many old flint mining sites have been investigated intensively, although much remains still to be done and many are left for posterity. The similarity of the methods used in prehistoric mining is striking even at sites many hundreds of kilometres apart. Studies of plans of such prehistoric workings reveal that the system can be simplified to give a basic layout common to all, a typical example of which is the plan of the workings at Cissbury (Fig. 171). The basic procedure was to drive out galleries radially from the base of the shaft, which was about 10 m in diameter in Britain, but often no more than 10 to 15 m deep. The top of the shaft and the bottom were often enlarged probably to reduce the risks of cave-ins, but the extent of the widening was considerably less than in the case of bell pits. Often six to eight galleries were excavated, the number appearing to depend on the degree to which the chalk needed to be supported. The floor was formed immediately at the base of the seam. The chalk between the galleries was not normally extracted, but left to provide support not only for the galleries, but also for the shaft. Sometimes the entrance to the galleries was narrow and the width was increased as the work progressed. The flint was extracted in the galleries; although an attempt was made to conform to a basic layout, this was rarely successful: the reasons for the modification of this layout are considered later in this chapter.

Tools

The oldest types of tools used were hand-held axes, picks, wedges and hammers, shaped roughly from pieces of igneous rock. Strangely, the use of actual flint tools was very rare and appears to have been adopted only for the working of the hardest chalk and limestone, as for example at Spiennes in Belgium and at Rijckholt in the Netherlands. Flint axes were later mounted in antler or had wooden handles to which they were fastened with thongs made from hide. In Britain, as in many flint mines on the continent of Europe, the basic tool in its many forms was derived from the antlers of red deer. An attempt was made to use every part of the antler economically. Normally all the tines were removed except one, which provided the working end of the tool. The parts removed were modified and used as piercing tools, hammers, wedges, gouges and so on. The most common type of tool was the pick, which was not, however, normally used as one might have imagined for hacking out a groove in the solid rock or for the making of an undercut to free the chalk. It was in fact inefficient as a slot-making tool and would appear to have been used as a kind of lever to remove cracked blocks of chalk and to ease out nodules of flint. Sanders (1910, pp. 101-24) notes that by severing the cup end and removing the bez and trez tines a beam, forming the haft, and brow tines were left, giving the pick strength at its weakest point, i.e. the angle of intersection between the handle and blade; they would also add weight to the blow required to insert the tool into a hole that had been made or a break in the strata. Such a break was made with a pointed wedge driven in by a hammer both made from antler. The pointed wedge or hammer was sometimes mounted on an antler or wooden shaft. Occasionally double-headed antler picks have been found and these were essentially used as rakes. Andree (1922, pp. 1-72) refers to these as picks. A very large number of such antler tools have been recovered from flint mines and they can be radiocarbon dated. Plate 140 shows part of an antler used as a support for the roof at Grimes Graves.

Shovels made from the scapulae of oxen have been found on some prehistoric mining sites. Tests have shown that this type of tool represents a very inefficient way of lifting heavy broken material, especially lumps of chalk and flint nodules, and in fact is suitable only for moving quantities of fine powdered material.

In prehistoric and ancient mines a method known as fire-setting has been used to break out very hard rock that cannot be excavated efficiently with the tools already mentioned (Collins, 1893, pp. 83-92). It was widely used in Europe before the introduction of explosives. No evidence has been found for the use of fire-setting in British flint mines, but possible traces of its application have been found at Mur-

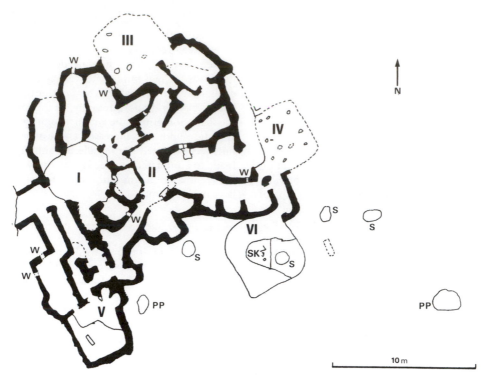

Figure 171 Cissbury flint mine (United Kingdom). Shafts I to VI: excavations of 1876 and 1877: W, windows; s, small oval pits; SK, skeleton found; pp, pottery sherds found. (After Harrison, 1878.)

de-Barrez in France and at Kleinkems in Germany, amongst others, as well as in the prehistoric dolerite quarry at Sélédin in northern France. The method consists in making a fire of material easy to ignite, such as brushwood and logs, close to the face of the rock to be broken, and, after the rock has been heated sufficiently, throwing water on to the rock, thus, if the attempt is successful, initiating the formation of cracks that enable the rock to be broken out with hand-held tools. Basically the technique operates on the principle that the constituent materials in the rock have different properties of thermal expansion or contraction. The hot rock when subjected to the shock of rapid cooling splits or breaks with a noisy reaction.

There are a few serious disadvantages to the method, the most important being that the two interrelated processes of heating and cooling produce heat, smoke and steam, and miners must, for their own safety, work on the incoming side of the ventilation, which must be sufficient to carry away the products of combustion and cooling. Dead ends and badly ventilated workings create insurmountable problems. Paradoxically, under suitable conditions the use of fires assists the ventilation as the less-dense warm air creates a vacuum and so promotes the circulation of air. Water also creates messy conditions, especially in chalk strata, and it is an advantage if the water can be channelled away into old workings. In the later Bronze Age this was used at the Mitterberg copper sulphide mines in the Austrian Tyrol with a great deal of success, the workings having been planned for the suitable application of the process (Pittioni, 1950, 23–4).

Support

Flint mine workings of the Neolithic were not subject, by virtue of their shallow depth, to excessive strata pressures compared with the moderately deep mines of more modern times. The chief problem in the context of support was the occurrence of falls of chalk from the underside of the roof when the workings were too wide and where joint planes were prevalent. Skeletons of prehistoric miners killed and buried by such falls have often been found by modern excavators. There is hardly any evidence for the use of wooden supports in the chalk of flint mines, although at Spiennes props were used in the early inclined shafts where these passed through newer Tertiary or Pleistocene rocks. Chalk is a near-competent rock provided the shape of opening is correct and the roadways are not excessively wide. It is, surprising however, that in view of the amount of forests in Neolithic times, wood was not apparently used, so far as evidence suggests, for the support of workings. Recesses have been found in some flint mining shafts and this possibly indicates that chordal or diagonally placed struts were used, as at Grimes Graves in England, but they could have represented anchorage points for staging or ladderways to provide easier access to the mine. There are numerous instances where miners robbed out the supporting pillars: this provided easily won flint, but often had disastrous results. When workings became too wide, chalk packs were often built. Old workings were often backfilled with packed debris and removal of this during investigation has occasionally resulted in cave-ins.

Transport

After the flint was broken out from the seam and separated from the chalk it was probably loaded into leather bags or baskets and taken to the shaft bottom, being hauled from there to the surface by ropes made from hide. It seems possible that a tree-trunk was placed across the shaft mouth, mounted on forked boughs to facilitate rotation or simply placed across the circular shaft resting on the ground on either side. In the latter case the rope would be attached to the bag or basket, passed over the trunk and fed down to the miner standing at the base of the shaft who, by pulling on it, would hoist the material to the surface. In the former case the operation of lifting the full basket and lowering the empty one could have been carried out by an assistant standing on the surface. Chalk debris also had to be transported, but whenever possible it was used to infill old discarded galleries or to build packs or chocks to support weak strata. This to some extent obviated the arduous work of sending it out to the surface, although moving lumps of chalk, even over short distances, must have been a very laborious task, especially in such a restricted space, and the use of rakes could hardly have compensated for the absence of efficient shovelling equipment. The procedure appears to have been that when a new shaft was completed, a connection was made to the existing workings, so that the old workings could be infilled.

Lighting

The sinking of shallow shafts could be carried out without any form of artificial light and it is unlikely that the work continued into the hours of darkness. Once gallery work was undertaken, lighting was by lamps constructed out of chalk lumps, burning animal fats or oil; such lamps had been in use some thousands of years earlier in the Palaeolithic period. There is some controversy over the reason for making small orifices through chalk pillars. Some observers suggest that they were to ascertain the width of a pillar (Harrison, 1878, Plate X) but this is extremely unlikely as the tunnels were driven only short distances and although surveying by the standards of today was obviously non-existent, the miners must have had some kind of guideline which would enable them to lay out the mine. Windows, however, could have been made to allow as much light as possible to penetrate from the bottom of shafts.

Ventilation

There was no problem in supplying sufficient air to ventilate prehistoric flint mines, especially in the very shallow workings with shafts very close together. Where the shafts were some distance apart and the communicating tunnels were therefore of great length, there could have been some danger of lack of oxygen resulting from stagnant air, the miners' breathing and the burning of oil and fats in the lamps. This would result in an excess of carbon dioxide in the atmosphere of the mine and possibly what miners refer to as 'blackdamp'. Actually in practice there were numerous connections between galleries as mentioned, to extract the maximum amount of flint. Wafting of leather skins, an undesirable practice, must have been used to create some air movement. Where shafts were connected by galleries, natural ventilation could have been induced, especially where the base of one shaft was at a slightly higher level than that of another. The warm air would tend to flow upwards thereby creating a movement of warmer and less dense air in one shaft.

The movement of air can be induced by what is termed furnace ventilation, that is, lighting a fire at the base of what could have been the upcast or return shaft. Some observers have suggested its use, from the evidence of soot marks on the roof, as, for example, at Champignolles and Mur de Barrez in France; however, such signs might indicate not the use of furnace ventilation, but that of a fire for warmth or even for cooking. However, with an open circuit these

could assist ventilation, but the dead ends of galleries could prove an additional hazard.

Water

One of the most serious dangers in mining is from possible flooding of the workings. This may be caused by the tapping of accumulations of water stored in old workings which have been abandoned, by shallow mining under rivers, lakes and the sea and by the passage of rain water into shallow workings. The chief problem in chalk workings is a slow, but nevertheless continuous, dissolving of the rock by water. This increases the dangers from rock which has become loosened, especially in shafts. Apart from this, mining in chalk during rainy seasons must have been a very unpleasant operation, because the floors of shafts and galleries would become coated with a thick covering of white mud, thereby adding difficulties to the handling and transporting of flints. There is of course no evidence of the flooding of flint mine workings, but such a situation was highly possible.

Preparation

Only very rarely were the extracted flint nodules broken or knapped to the requisite shape and then polished in the mine itself. Mostly the lumps were taken to a workshop site either at the base of the shaft or on the surface near to the mine entrance. Where there was a multiplicity of shafts there was often one central workshop floor or one central collecting point. At these places only rough breakage was carried out and the products were then transported to a village workshop for final preparation. This procedure reduced the weight of the material to be transported. Flint knapping is a skilled craft and it is possible that expert knappers were located in the villages and employed to produce finished axes, chisels, knives, arrowheads and the like. Many workshop floors, used for the preliminary roughing out process, have been discovered in mines, but most have been found on the surface.

TYPICAL PREHISTORIC MINING SITES (Map 69)

The approximate geographical locations of prehistoric mine sites in Europe are given on Map 69. The best-known sites in Britain are Cissbury and Grimes Graves, in Belgium Spiennes, in France Champignolles, in the Netherlands Rijckholt, Hov in Denmark, Kleinkems in Germany, in Sicily Monte Tabuto, in Poland Krzemionki Opatowskie and in Austria Mauer, but these are only a few of the vast number found. It is not possible in the space of the present chapter to attempt to summarize the main features of more than a few of these (Shepherd, 1980, pp. 23–107).

Until the nineteenth century many of the sites mentioned were not regarded as flint mines and it is surprising that such a long period elapsed before investigations were carried out. A large number of sites were discovered by accident when newer excavations took place during quarrying or for railway construction and housing developments. Many visible depressions and hillocks had been interpreted as being of religious significance, as burial sites or as store pits and often were associated with nearby later structures such as Iron Age forts or the remains of Roman buildings and burial grounds. Many of the known sites, especially in Britain, were shown to be prehistoric sites indeed as a result of work arduously

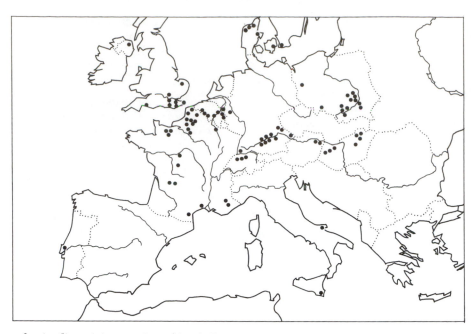

Map 69 Distribution of major flint-mining areas in prehistoric Europe.

conducted and later reported on by amateur archaeologists. Typical examples are Grimes Graves and Harrow Hill in Britain. Although professional archaeologists, who carried out much later investigations, are often critical of the early methods employed, most of the original findings cannot be disputed. What is unfortunate is that often the speed of the early investigations possibly destroyed useful evidence of many facets of operation of the mines that could well have been useful in assessing the chronology and methods of working. This may partly be excused, however, by the fact that modern scientific methods such as those of dating, pollen analysis, bone identification, etc., were not then available.

Britain

The chief British flint mines are located principally on the South Downs in West Sussex and Wiltshire. The chalk belt stretches from here northwards through the Chilterns up to Norfolk where the famous large flint mining complex of Grimes Graves is found. North of Worthing, in the Findon area, are located Cissbury (Lane Fox, 1876, pp. 357–90), Harrow Hill (Curwen and Curwen, 1924, pp. 102–38), Blackpatch (Pull, 1932), Church Hill (Law, 1927, pp. 222–4), Bow Hill, Stoke Down (Wade, 1922, pp. 82–91) and Lavant Caves (Allcroft, 1916, pp. 68–74).

Cissbury (Fig. 171) lies about 6.5 km north of Worthing and is famous for its Iron Age hillfort; on the periphery of the large earthworks are found the remains of the flint mines, consisting of up to 200 old shafts. One excavated shaft was 13 m deep and cut through six seams of flint of which only the bottom one was worked. Here again the ancient miner was able to determine that the best flint could often be found deeper down. Unlike on many sites in continental Europe, the miner in Britain had no guidance in the form of outcrops of the flint to help to locate that of the best quality. The most recent radiocarbon dates for this site include one giving a date of around 5,500 years ago. This confirmed the original conjecture that the site was of Neolithic origin, which had been based on the find of a fragment of a typical shouldered Neolithic pot.

An extensive investigation was carried out at Harrow Hill flint mine in 1924–25.

The Grimes Graves prehistoric flint mining site (Plates 138, 139 and 140) is situated about 12 km north-west of Thetford in Norfolk and contains about 366 known shafts over an area of about 14 ha. It was not until 1870 that it was accepted as representing an extensive flint mining area and not, as previously thought, an early medieval encampment. This was the result of excavations made to open up a pit measuring 12 m in depth and 8.5 m in diameter; it is known as Greenwell's and was named after an amateur archaeologist, Canon Greenwell, who did excellent work. Extraction of the debris that filled the pit disclosed three seams of flint: an inferior one at a depth of 3 m; a better one termed the 'wallstone', but still not considered of sufficient quality for the manufacture of implements; and the worked 'floorstone' at the base of the shaft. Radiating galleries had been driven from the bottom of the shaft and these averaged 1.75 m in width and were approximately 1.25 m high. Greenwell, after he had cleared one of the galleries, found antler picks still bearing the imprints in chalk of miners' hands. A total of seventy-nine such picks as well as a basalt hammer were found. Several more pits have since been cleared of debris and one has been kept open for inspection by the public. Recent investigations in one shaft have revealed notches in the side walls, evidently to support ladders or staging for access and egress.

The whole range of working consisted of shallow pits 2 by 1 m and 3 to 4 m deep, intermediate pits 6 m deep and the deep pits with galleries which are just over 12 m deep. Radiocarbon tests date the mines to a period from around 5,000 to 3,600 years ago.

Radiocarbon dates for the Findon group of flint mines and those for Grimes Graves, as well as those in the area north of Sussex, show that the oldest flint mines are in the south of the country, with the newer ones such as Grimes Graves to the north and much later. This would appear from the few dates so far available to indicate a trend northwards by the flint mining communities.

Belgium

The flint mines that have been recognized in this country have been found in the Cretaceous belt that runs north-east to south-west across the central part of the country, north of the river Meuse, from Liège to Mons. Near Mons are the sites of Spiennes, Flénu, Obourg and Strépy. In the north-east are Orp le Grand, Meeffe, Avennes, Latinne, Wansin and Jandrain-Jandrenouille north of the Meuse and Rullen Bas south of the river (Hubert, 1980, pp. 412–33).

It is now strongly believed that the Belgian flint mines were not exploited solely by the Michelsberg culture, with which, nevertheless, there are strong connections. De Laet more recently has studied the subject of the dating of these mines in greater depth and says:

> some years ago the exploitation of the Belgian flint mines was attributed to groups of the Michelsberg culture, but that it seems now increasingly clear that the first people specialized in extracting the flint were the acculturated Neolithic descendants of the Mesolithic populations.
>
> (De Laet, 1982, p. 246)

There was wide trading in flint, as evidenced by artefacts from Belgian flint mines and preparation sites found over a distance of 270 km from the working areas.

The large and important prehistoric mining site of Spiennes lies on a chalk plateau covered with loess and flanked on the south and west by the river Trouille. The beds of workable flint outcrop on the eastern and western slopes of the river valley and were worked over a long period from around 6,100 to 4,100 years ago. The earliest workings were in the shallow deposits of the east; they were first exploited by open pit methods and later had sloping and vertical shafts. The earliest known shafts crossed several beds of inferior flint before tapping the flint to be worked at a depth of 5 to 6 m. Unlike the shafts in Britain all were small in cross-section. The reason for this is that the rock at Spiennes is harder than the corresponding material associated with the British flint mines. One excavated shaft was 2.4 m in diameter at the surface, but at 1.7 m deep was approximately elliptical in shape and measured 1.3 by 1.1 m. At the bottom the shaft was widened to 3 m. Another difference from the British design was that the worked flint was in the roof of the galleries instead of at floor level.

As workings moved across the plateau westwards they became deeper. Extensive investigations have been carried out, with intermissions, from 1886 onwards, but it was not until 1928 that the deepest shafts were discovered. One of these was 16 m deep and 1 m in diameter and had been enlarged at the top and bottom. These deeper shafts crossed as many as twelve seams of flint and were 12 to 15 m apart. Galleries were driven out from the base and each shaft when no longer required was filled with chalk debris from the one in the process of being sunk. Chalk pillars were left to support the roof of the workings. The layout of the mines appears to have been very systematic, despite the fact that they date back some 6,000 years. In fact the method used represented a rudimentary form of partial extraction by the bord and pillar system similar to that used in more recent times in coal mining. The only artificial support was in the adits or sloping shafts, as already mentioned, and consisted of wood props and roof bars. Notches cut in the vertical shafts could have been for anchoring cross-beams to support a staircase for the miners. As already mentioned, the chalk was very hard and although antler picks were used to trim the galleries and shafts, use was made of flint picks, often set

in shafts of wood, to attack the chalk for flint extraction. Numerous marks on blocks of chalk made by such tools have been found.

France

About forty-nine flint and chert mining sites and quarries stretching over a wide area have been found and investigated in this country (Deutches Bergbaumuseum, 1980, pp. 474–508). Nineteen, including Champignolles, are located in the triangle north of Paris formed by the rivers Seine and Oise. The remainder are scattered: three lie near Caen and La Petite Garonne and Les Martins in the east-central part of the country south of Limoges. The famous flint or chert quarry of Le Grand Pressigny is rather isolated at a distance of 50 km south of Tours. Likewise Mur-de-Barrez is some distance away from the other sites in the Massif Central. Others are located in Provence and in the area south-west, south and south-east of Paris and include Petit Martin and others. South of this near the Upper Yonne and Upper Seine valleys are Portonville and Doxmont respectively. There are two more sites about 40 km south-west of Metz and two in the Pas de Calais region.

Campignolles is one of the best known prehistoric flint mines in France (Sanders, 1910, pp. 101–24). It is situated near Serifontaine (Oise). Workings were discovered in a chalk pit in 1890. Eleven shafts with radiating galleries have been found with old workings in the lowest of three seams. Shafts were bottle-shaped and 4 m deep, just over 1 m wide at the top and 1.5 m at the bottom.

One of the very few prehistoric chert quarries known is Le Grand Pressigny in Indre-et-Loire. It was worked extensively from Palaeolithic to Bronze Age times, but the period of highest production was from the fifth to the fourth millennium BP. The material mined is of a honey-brown colour and occurs in sandstone. The most famous feature of the workings is that the chert was traded over large areas of France, Belgium and Switzerland and even to the island of Jersey (Jahn, 1956, pp. 5–40).

Mines were found near Mur de Barrez in the department of Aveyron during the working of a limestone quarry in the 1880s, an old shaft and communicating gallery being exposed. Later, ten more shafts were discovered. These were 80 cm in diameter and from 3 to 6 m deep.

Germany

An important prehistoric mining site has been found near Aachen and another at Kleinkems in Baden-Württemberg. In addition twenty-three important finds of flint and chert implements in various stages of manufacture have been made in the Danube valley and north of it, stretching over a distance of more than 200 km, indicating the presence of a mining activity which is now probably concealed.

At the Lousberg, near Aachen, flint tools together with deer antlers had been found as long ago as 1808 and the area has been well known for its geological interest for many years. Extensive investigations, carried out from 1978 to 1980, revealed not only further evidence of flint preparation sites, but actual mine shafts. Bone tools have also been found. The flint from the site has also been exported over a wide area.

The prehistoric jasper mine near Kleinkems in the Jurassic limestone of the Isteiner Klotz in the extreme south-west of the country, near the border with Switzerland, was discovered during the making of a railway over 125 years ago.

There are four seams of jasper and these were exposed when a cement works was built on the site. Unfortunately the site is now mostly concealed by new developments. Although the limestone is very hard it was worked with antler picks as well as flint tools. Fire-setting is presumed to have been used, as is evidenced by the presence of baked limestone and charcoal. Schmid (1969, pp. 4–13) estimates that the site dates back to around 4,000 years ago at least.

The Netherlands

Two mining sites have been found in the south of the country to the south-east near Maastricht. Although Rijckolt Sint-Geertruid was presumed to be a flint preparation area as long ago as 1881 and a mine in 1910, and various investigations had been carried out up to 1964, it was not until some time later that a thorough examination of the underground working was made (Engelen, 1969, pp. 15–22). This was completed in 1970. Sixty-six shafts of diameter 1 to 1.4 m and from 6 to 16 m deep have been found during extensive excavation of exploratory tunnels across the site. Radiocarbon dates indicate that the workings date back at least to 5,800 years ago. One interesting feature is that the rock, which is chalk, is much harder than that encountered in many other flint mines and this virtually prohibited the use of antler tools. Instead, flint tools were used and about 7,000 such implements have been recovered in various stages of manufacture and use.

Denmark

Five flint mining and preparation sites have been found in Jutland: Hov, Bjerre, Aalborg, Hillerslev and Fornaes and one, Steves Klint, in Sjaelland (Zealand). Hov and Aalborg are the best-known sites in the country. Shafts had been sunk at Hov to a depth of 7 m to a flint seam, but one at 4 m depth had been worked. The shafts were 4.5 m in diameter with galleries driven off to a distance of 4 m. The workings date to around 5,200 years ago according to Becker (1959, pp. 87–92; 1976, pp. 3–12). Thirty-six shafts were discovered around 1957, but were not investigated until 1967. The workings at Aalborg, found in 1950–52, consist of shafts 1 to 4.7 m deep and 1 to 1.5 m in diameter, which were widened out at the base, but had no galleries. The workings date to around the middle of the fourth millennium BP.

Sweden

The flint mines near Malmö in the extreme south of the country are the only ones known in Sweden. For many years they were thought to be merely chalk pits, but investigations carried out since 1951 have confirmed that a deeper seam of flint had been worked with antler picks and that the mines were dated to around the end of the sixth millennium BP.

Other areas

Other important prehistoric flint mining sites worth mentioning are Löwenbürg in Switzerland, Mauer in Austria, Sumag in Hungary, Krzemionki Opatowskie in Poland and Monte Tabuto in Sicily. Probably the largest flint mine complex in Europe is to be found in Poland, where nineteen

sites have so far been recognized. According to Jazdzewski some of the oldest flint mines, dating back to the Mesolithic, have been found in Poland. The majority of the mines are located in two groups, one near and to the south-east of Radom, the other north and south of Krakow. The largest prehistoric flint mine has been found at Krzemionki Opatowskie at the east end of the Lysa Gora. This major site, with over 1,000 shafts of depths from 9 to 11 m, worked a strongly banded chert or jasper which produced an attractive raw material for the manufacture of axes. The conventional dating for Krzemionki Opatowskie is given in *5000 Jahre Feuersteinbergbau* (Deutsches Bergbaumuseum, 1980, pp. 474–508) as around 6,200 to 5,200 years ago. Space does not allow even a brief mention of all the 150 or so sites at present known to investigators in Europe.

Significant features of a few sites have been given, and these show some diversity in the methods used in planning and extraction, but in general basic common features predominate: narrow shallow shafts sunk to a selected seam and galleries driven out from the base. Antler picks have been found to have been used widely in mines often hundreds of kilometres apart, and where the chalk or limestone was hard, flint picks or even fire-setting were employed.

In addition to flint and chert extraction there are several examples of quarries for igneous rocks as at Sélédin in France and the well-known basalt quarries of Mayen in the Eifel region of Germany. The latter were worked in the Neolithic era and through to Roman times. The basalt was used chiefly to make querns for the grinding of corn and the like, and was widely exported.

With modern methods of identification and the dating of material found in excavations there is now less doubt about the age of a worked-out prehistoric mining site. Before the advent of radiocarbon dating the only means of assessing the probable chronology was from finds of fragments of pottery. This, as with coin recovery from possible later though still ancient mines, is fraught with problems. Pottery, for example, could have been deposited with debris in an old pit or hollow long after working had ceased, and can only under the best conditions indicate a rough period of working within many hundreds of years. Even with radiocarbon dating the same problem may arise and this method cannot be used if fragments of wood, antler picks, charcoal and other datable material are absent from the site.

Some writers have drawn attention to the diverse markings and scratches found on the chalk walls in many prehistoric flint mines. As the dates of these are not known and, in many cases of course cannot be deciphered, they have mostly been dismissed as being of little or no significance. As far as is known many mines where such markings have been found were filled in immediately the workings ceased and another shaft was excavated, the backfilled shaft being left undisturbed. If this is true then the marks could not have been made in more modern times. Some consist of straight lines forming a chequerboard pattern. Others present a series of angled lines and circles. As such they could have been the result of doodling or even tally marks to indicate amounts of flint removed from the mine. The basic features of many mines indicate that some rudimentary form of surveying was required to locate the radial galleries and to give direction and connections between shafts. Some marking might well be a visual aid to discussion between miners on the matter of layout. It is almost impossible to assign, with the slightest degree of certainty, any meaning to the symbols.

SOCIAL AND TECHNOLOGICAL CONSIDERATIONS

Reference is often made to the 'Neolithic revolution'. If all developments in the era are considered there can be no doubt, based on a comparison with preceding and succeeding cultural epochs, that there was a major revolution rivalling that of the industrial revolution of the nineteenth century in Europe. Changes taking place in the Neolithic era were of fundamental significance, whereas events over a hundred years ago were those of application, being mainly the introduction of motive power to already accepted procedures. Thus the Neolithic revolution signified a greater change, involving as it did settlement patterns, change of diet, agriculture and the production of raw materials. As indicated already, a crude form of mining already existed in pre-Neolithic times, but extensive patterns of migration with regional settlement and fixed habitation sites based on agriculture led to more sophisticated means of production of tools and implements required by a subsistence food-producing economy.

An impressive feature of Neolithic times is the extensive number of known flint mines in Europe alone. It is possible that a far greater number than those already discovered are still awaiting excavation and recognition. The massive quantity of flint instruments manufactured in the Neolithic point to an extensive and thriving society and accordingly a very large population. So great was production that wide trading in rock and flint products developed. It was quite likely that all this was conducted on a barter basis: there can be no evidence to refute this. It is not uncommon for flint tools and those made from igneous rocks to be found hundreds of kilometres from their presumed place of origin, examples being products of the Lake District quarries in England was well as those of Le Grand Pressigny in France, Spiennes in Belgium, the Holy Cross Mountains in Poland, Mayen in Germany and many more.

Childe (1954, p. 66) estimates that Neolithic villages or hamlets covered an area of between approximately 0.5 and 2.5 ha and contained small communities of twenty-five to thirty-five households. If such habitation sites were very close to chalk deposits, mining was carried out, but there is some controversy concerning the people who actually mined the flint. Did the farmers work the chalk for flint, or alternatively were skilled miners available on a full-time basis? Or did the farmers work the soil in summer and mine the flint in winter, indicating, if so, an organized round of seasonal activity? Childe suggests that the miners were skilled specialists, and if this is true mining then could already have been a highly specialized occupation and therefore an activity undertaken all year round.

If the basic layout of a flint mine is again examined it is apparent that there can be no doubt concerning the know-how of the prehistoric miners. They followed a basic pattern and had the ability to recognize that the flint tended normally to improve in quality with depth. It might be said, however, that miners did not sink shafts deeper than 15 to 20 m, but this was unnecessary. Flint seams are usually level or at least only slightly dipping, and therefore vast areas could be worked with no significant increase in depth. There are some exceptions, however, such as where seams outcrop on the flanks of a plateau. This is the case at Spiennes, as already indicated, but few sites in this category have so far been found. If seams had been steeply inclined then there is no doubt that prehistoric miners would have gone deeper to extract the precious flint. They might well have followed

steep seams with galleries or adits driven in from the hillsides as the later Bronze Age copper miners did at Mitterberg in the Austrian Tyrol. They had the ability to make stable shafts, but all this was unnecessary. If copper, bronze and later iron had not replaced flint as the essential raw material, workings would have covered an even larger area and eventually they would have been very much deeper. The overall position is that no reflection can be cast on the prehistoric miners for the layout of their workings which are so often found today. When the shaft struck a workable seam they soon found that it was better to drive galleries than to cut at random into the base of the shaft. They learned to protect the shaft from collapse by correctly spacing their galleries and inadvertently initiated the concept of the shaft pillar. Where the ground was broken they left pillars of chalk or built packs with the debris, and so avoided transporting it out of the mine. All this points to highly experienced operators, and would appear to substantiate the suggestion made by Childe. Other facets include the miners' development of fire-setting when this was necessitated by the presence of very hard rock, their use of wedges, picks, crow-bars and shovels and their grasp of the basic skill of flint knapping.

Why did flint mines, therefore, appear to develop, to judge from actual plans of workings made by modern investigators, into apparently random exploitation away from the shafts? Plans show the robbing of pillars, extensive cave-ins and galleries going nowhere but finishing in dead ends. This conflicts with the hypothesis that the workings were executed by highly efficient mining specialists. It is known that the final preparation of flint was rarely carried out on site, but only the rough-outs were made here, that is the blanks for later treatment in the villages. This would reduce considerably the weight of material to be carried. At many sites the only finished tools found were those apparently used for the preparation of food. It is highly likely, therefore, that the villagers came to the mine, camped in the vicinity and extracted as much flint as they could carry back to the village, where it was made into implements and tools that would be used locally or traded over long distances to other habitation sites. It seems highly probable that once the mine shafts had been sunk and the portals made for the branching of galleries, work that would be done by miners, the mines were left open for any person to come along and take whatever flint they required and at any cost to their personal safety. This is of course pure hypothesis, but the random development in level and mostly unfaulted conditions lead to no other possible conclusion.

At Obourg a skeleton of a miner holding an antler pick and in the apparent process of hacking at the face of the tunnel was found. A gallery had been driven out from a disused trench and a seam of flint worked under older, filled-in trenches. It appears that the workman had been killed by a roof fall while breaking out chalk which actually supported old workings. This find lends credence to the concept of possibly unskilled workers going into existing mines alone to remove what flint they could hack out of the solid face. Probably the man had gone into the mine without the knowledge of his fellow villagers and was given up for lost. The Neolithic peoples practised inhumation and could have regarded the death of a person underground as constituting a burial and therefore left the body there for all time. Many interpretations can be put on this belated find, but what it does not suggest is the presence of a group of skilled specialist miners familiar with the working of deposits under difficult ground conditions.

Nothing is known about the life-style of the Neolithic

miners as regards their religion and the way they dressed and spoke, but a certain amount of information can rightly be deduced about their diet from the data collected from contemporary habitation sites. Whether the miners worked naked or not has never been verified and can never be so. Possibly they developed cult and religious symbols, for in one shaft at Grimes Graves a small chalk statuette of possibly a goddess was found at the level of the 'wallstone' seam of flint which was not worked. Near the figure was an altar of stones and a phallic-shaped object. This cult figure, presumed to represent a goddess of fertility, is regarded as of suspect validity and could have been placed in position at any time from, say, 3,500 years ago to the nineteenth century, when the pit was cleared out for some purpose. It is always possible to find some apparently plausible interpretation for such finds, and one is that the figure was placed in the position in which it was discovered when the wallstone seam was found to be inferior, with the fervent hope that by so doing the deepening of the shaft would result in the finding of a better seam of flint.

From what has been said it is clear that any survey of prehistoric mining in the Neolithic era reveals a major revolution in mining, which came in as a result of the changes in the social and subsistence environment. This revolution actually marked the ancestry of underground mining as it is known today. While all this activity was in progress around the sixth millennium BP in western and central Europe, other changes were taking place much further south in the Balkans and Mediterranean area: the arrival of the age of metals. Non-sulphide copper ores, for example, were being mined in crude pits in the Eneolithic or Copper Age, which is the traditional phase between the Neolithic and the Bronze Age. In former Yugoslavia and Bulgaria examples of such workings are known, at Rudna Glava and Aibunar respectively.

The method of working copper ore at Rudna Glava by the Vinča culture was somewhat different from that employed by the Neolithic miners. The reason was that the outcropping veins of ore, consisting of magnetite and chalcopyrite, were steep and had a variable dip. The deep ore was malachite. Crude shafts were sunk and these followed the vein downwards to a depth of 20 to 25 m, according to Renfrew (1973, p. 209). So far as is known the early cultures responsible for such mining had no experience of the metallurgical treatment of pyritic (sulphide) ores. Jovanovic and Ottaway (1976, p. 107), however, mention the effect of oxidation down to a depth of 20 to 25 m, which led to the accumulation of rich concentrations of copper carbonate in the form of malachite. The mines have been dated several centuries before 6,000 years ago on the basis of extensive finds of Vinča pottery. Chernysh (1978, pp. 203–17) describes investigations at the contemporary site of Aibunar in Bulgaria. At this site eleven old mining projects have been investigated consisting of open pits and one small shaft. Lengths of workings averaged 10 to 50 m, with average widths of 3 to 10 m and depths from 1 to as much as 20 m.

It is highly likely that many more Neolithic flint mines will be found in western Europe and elsewhere. Flint is now no longer of any economic value as a raw material for the manufacture of tools and weapons, and its use gave way to that of copper, bronze and later iron and steel. Metals have been mined continuously throughout the centuries, so that old flint workings are more likely to be found than early metal mines, which have mostly been destroyed by later workings such as those of the Romans and their successors.

BIBLIOGRAPHY

ALLCROFT, A. H. 1916. Some Earthworks of East Sussex, Lavant Caves. *Sussex Archaeol. Collect.* (Sussex), Vol. 56, pp. 68–74.

ANDREE, J. 1922. *Bergbau in der Vorzeit.* Leipzig.

BECKER, C. J. 1959. Flint Mining in Neolithic Denmark. *Antiquity,* Vol. 33, pp. 87–92.

—— 1976. Flint Mining in Neolithic Denmark. In: *Festschrift für Richard Pittioni zum siebzigsten Geburtstag.* Vienna. pp. 3–12.

CHERNYSH, E. N. 1978. Aibunar, a Balkan Copper Mine of the Fourth Millennium BC. *Proc. Prehist. Soc.,* Vol. 44, pp. 203–7.

CHILDE, V. G. 1954. *What Happened in History.* London.

—— 1957. *The Dawn of European Civilization.* London.

COLLINS, A. L. 1893. Fire-setting. *Trans. Inst. Min. Engin.* (London), Vol. 3, pp. 83–92.

CURWEN, E.; CURWEN, E. C. 1924. Harrow Flint Mining Excavation. *Sussex Archaeol. Collect.* (Sussex), Vol. 67, pp. 102–38.

DE LAET, S. J. 1982. *La Belgique d'avant les Romains.* Wetteren.

DE MUNCK, E. 1986–87. Exposé des principales découvertes archéologiques faites à Obourg. *Bull. Soc. Anthropol. Brux.,* Vol. 5, pp. 298–300.

DEUTSCHES BERGBAUMUSEUM. 1980. *5000 Jahre Feuersteinbergbau.* Bochum.

ENGELEN, F. 1969. 5000 Jahre Feuersteinbergbau in den Niederlanden. *Der Anschnitt* (Bochum), Vol. 21, pp. 15–22.

HARRISON, J. P. 1878. Additional Discoveries at Cissbury. *J. R. Anthropol. Inst. G.B. Irel.* (London), Vol. 7.

HUBERT, F. 1980. Silexabbau und -gewinnung in Belgien. In: DEUTSCHES BERGBAUMUSEUM. *5000 Jahre Feuersteinbergbau.* Bochum. pp. 412–33.

JAHN, M. 1956. Gab es in der vorgeschichteichen Zeit bereits einen Handel? *Abh. sächs. Akad. Wiss. Leipz.,* Vol. 48, pp. 5–40.

JOVANOVIC, B.; OTTAWAY, B. S. 1976. Copper Mining and Metallurgy in the Vinča Group. *Antiquity,* Vol. 50, pp. 107 ff.

JUNG, J. 1963. *Précis de Pétrographie.* Paris.

KEILLER, A.; PIGGOTT, S.; WALLIS, F. S. 1941. First Report of the Sub-Committee of the South Western Group of Museums and Art Galleries on the Petrological Identification of Stone Axes. *Proc. Prehist. Soc.,* Vol. 7, pp. 50–72.

LANE FOX, A. J. 1876. Excavations in Cissbury Camp, Sussex. *J. R. Anthropol. Inst. G.B. Irel.* (London), Vol. 5, pp. 357–90.

LAW, W. 1927. Flint Mines on Church Hill, Findon. *Sussex Notes Queries* (Sussex), Vol. 1, pp. 222–4.

MARIEN, M. E. 1952. *Oud-België* (Ancient Belgium). Antwerpen.

PITTIONI, R. 1950. Prehistoric Copper Mining in Austria, Problems and Facts. *Annu. Rep. Inst. Archaeol.* (London), pp. 23–4.

PULL, J. R. 1932. *Flint Mines of Black Patch.* London.

RENFREW, C. 1973. *Before Civilization.* Harmondsworth.

SANDERS, H. W. 1910. The Deer Horn Pick in the Mining of the Ancients. *Archaeologia* (London), Vol. 62, pp. 101–24.

SCHMID, E. 1969. Jungsteinzeitliches Jasper-Bergwerk am Istainer Klotz. *Der Anschnitt* (Bochum), Vol. 21, pp. 4–13.

—— 1975. Der Silex Abbau der Löwenberg im Schweizer Jura. *Staringia* (Sittard), No. 3, pp. 78–80. (2nd International Symposium on Flint, Maastricht, 1975.)

SHEPHERD, R. 1980. *Prehistoric Mining and Allied Industries.* London.

WADE, A. G. 1922. Ancient Flint Mines at Stoke Down, Sussex. *Proc. Prehist. Soc.,* Vol. 4, pp. 82–91.

57

MEXICO AND CENTRAL AMERICA

Incipient food production

José L. Lorenzo

The Proto-Neolithic (Map 70), a name rescued from oblivion but, none the less, wholly appropriate for the subject in hand, which is the last phase of the Lithic Period, lasted in Mexico and Central America from *c.*7,000 to *c.*4,500 years ago. It should be regarded as being of considerable significance, since it marks the beginning of agriculture and hence of sedentary life; selective gathering would appear to have been superseded by the selection of certain specific crops, resulting in greater productivity through increasingly refined processes and methods. This period, in certain instances and regions, is the threshold of a new mode of production, the foundation for the most refined forms of cultural expression in Central America; but in others, excluded from this trend for various reasons, it represents a final phase, a way of life that persisted until contact occurred with European civilization.

A salient feature of the Lithic Period was the general diminution in the size of tools and the greater care taken over the way they were finished. The trend towards an improvement in shapes can be found not merely in artefacts of chipped stone but also in those of polished stone, showing signs of endeavours to improve the functioning of tools *pari passu* with their appearance and the harmony of their proportions. There are beads for necklaces and bracelets, pipes, axes, tiles, chisels, mortars and querns, these with their respective handstones, all made with great care and highly finished. The large number of different stone artefacts of a functional nature points to the variety of tasks for which they were used. There is a great variety of ropes, nets, baskets, textiles and various receptacles made of vegetable matter, as well as some examples of fabrics coloured with vegetable dyes. Wooden tools are also found, such as frames for bags and the components of waist looms. There are also various objects made of antler, horn and shell, which suggest an increase in body adornment, over and above practical considerations.

There is evidence of primary and secondary burials in various positions. The presence of offerings suggests the existence of a particular ideology surrounding death. There is also some evidence of cannibalism, but it is not possible to detect whether this was of a ritual nature or the consequence of famine.

The Proto-Neolithic was marked by the establishment of the cultivation of maize, beans and gourds that had begun in the Upper Cenolithic when these plant species were gathered in preference to others; the cultivation of other species began, but these did not acquire the same status as staple foods, and there were some that, as time went on, lost some of their initial relative importance. However, these incipient farming practices were limited in scale, and the human diet was largely composed of the fruits of hunting and gathering. Nevertheless, the need to tend the planted fields, in order to ensure the growth of the crops, for at least a few months must have led to fixed settlements and the formation of groups of dwellings or hamlets that were occupied all year round, since besides tending the plantation it was necessary to store part of the crop harvested for subsequent sowing; part of the community was free to migrate to outlying encampments from which it was possible to provide the sedentary community with sufficient food to sustain it between harvests.

There is also a very interesting example of a hamlet on an oval plan, composed of semi-underground dwellings, in the valley of Tehuacan, in Chilac, Puebla (MacNeish, 1972).

This period closes with total sedentism, stable farming practices, fruit cultivation and the domestication of the *guajolote* or turkey, while the dog seems to have been associated with human beings since the previous period. It is possible that land ownership began as early as this, perhaps of land belonging to the tribe, or at least of land immediately adjacent to human settlements. The presence of pottery marks the beginning of the subsequent phase and is the element that, better than any other, provides ready identification of when the phase actually began. In this particular field of study, no primitive pottery has been found, and the earliest known specimens display considerable technical and aesthetic qualities. It may well be that once the process for the physico-chemical conversion of clay into pottery had been mastered, the ready availability of raw materials and firewood and the tractability of the material led to very rapid progress.

Special attention should be paid to the species of plants cultivated and their origin. According to Pickersgill (1977), America can be divided into four areas of plant cultivation: Central America, the Andean zone, the eastern part of North America and the low-lying humid, tropical areas. Two of these stand out: Central America and the Andean zone; the other two are of secondary importance for our purposes. We shall confine our investigations to Central America and leave to others the task of dealing with the Andean region.

In Central America, *Phaseolus coccineus* (scarlet runner) has

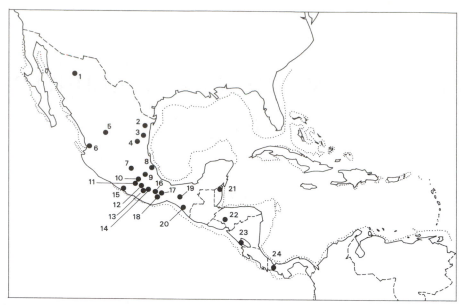

Map 70 Mexico and Central America in the Proto-Neolithic. ..... isobarth of −100 m. ★, Radiocarbon-dated sites. 1, Cueva de la Golondrina (Chihuahua); 2, Repelo complex★ (Tamaulipas); 3, Nogales complex★ (Tamaulipas); 4, La Perra complex★ (Tamaulipas); 5, Guadiana★ (Durango); 6, Matanchel★ (Nayarit); 7, San. Nicolas (Querétaro); 8, Veracruz centre★ (Veracruz); 9, El Tecxolote (Hidalgo); 10, Chicoloapan (Estado de Mexico); 11, Tlapacoya II, IV and XVIII★ (Estado de Mexico); 12, Texcal★ (Puebla); 13, Coxcatlan★ (Puebla); 14, Abejas★ (Puebla); 15, Tecpan★ (Guerrero); 16, Yanhuitlan★ (Oaxaca); 17, Cueva Blanca★ (Oaxaca); 18, Guila Naquitz★ (Oaxaca); 19, Santa Marta★ (Chiapas); 20, Chantuto★ (Chiapas); 21, Northern Belize★; 22, La Esperanza (Honduras); 23, Acahualican★ (Nicaragua); 24, Chiriqui★ (Panama).

been used by human beings for some 11,000 years, while its cultivation can be traced back with certainty to 2,200 years ago. *Cucurbita pepo* (pumpkin, summer squash) has been a source of food for some 10,000 years and has been cultivated for 7,000 years. *Setaria* (foxtail millet) can be traced back some 9,000 years, but is considered to have been cultivated for 5,000 years. There has been evidence of *Persea americana* (avocado pear) for 9,000 years, but it is difficult to establish exactly when it became a cultivated crop, as the size of the fruit, which is usually a guide, does not indicate whether it is of wild or cultivated origin. As far as fruit-growing is concerned, it was probably not until the communities had become fully sedentary that fruit was actually cultivated.

Lagenaria siceraria (bottle gourd) has been in use for 9,000 years, but there are no apparent traces of cultivation. It can safely be said that, in Central America, such species as *Phaseolus acutifolius* (tepary bean), some of the Amaranthaceae family and *Capsicum annuum* (sweet pepper) have been cultivated for 6,000 years, and *Phaseolus vulgaris* (kidney bean), *Cucurbita mixta* (cushaw pumpkin) and *Gossypium hirsutum* (cotton) for 5,000 years (Lorenzo, 1977b).

Although no precise date can be determined, analysis of human faeces found in dry places and more specifically in the valley of Tehuacán has revealed that *Setaria* and *Amaranthus leucocarpus*, which were used until the early years of the colonial period and subsequently banned because of their religious connotations, date back earlier than most other plants and must have been eaten from very early times. Moreover, in Mexico, there grew in abundance a species of wild potato, *Solanum cardyophyllum*, that was always gathered and sold at local markets, together with the fruit of *Brosimum alicastrum*, the ramón or breadnut tree, used as food in time of famine.

Maize, *Zea mays*, poses a more complex problem on account of its importance. Evidence, if not proof, has been produced of the existence of maize since times that vary from 80,000 to 40,000 years ago (Baghoorn et al., 1954) but it was observed much later (Banerjee and Baghoorn, 1972)

that the size and peculiarities of maize pollen grains and teosinte made the two virtually indistinguishable.

For some time Beadle (1977, 1980) maintained that there was a close link between maize and teosinte, while Galinat (1975, 1977), for want of any archaeological proof that teosinte had evolved into maize, apart from the experimental work of Beadle (1977, 1980), supported the thesis that maize was a mutant of teosinte.

It is thought today that there is a distinct ancestral link between maize and teosinte and that certain mutants of the latter, the older and original species, may have been used by human beings, easily consumed, gathered, stored and planted until, through a process of selection, maize as we know it came to be an established crop.

It is interesting to observe that teosinte is to be found within a limited area of Central America, ranging from south-western Chihuahua to southern Honduras and covering the western and central regions of Mexico and the western and eastern parts of Guatemala, at altitudes varying between 2,350 and 650 m above sea-level and in climates ranging from those of grasslands to those of temperate zones (Wilkes, 1967). (Incidentally, the plant is often referred to in English writings as 'teosinte', which is erroneous, as the word originates from the Nahuatl term 'teotl', a deity or god, and 'centli', maize: hence 'divine maize'.)

The most important sites attributable to this period, some of which are also typical of earlier or later periods, are not very numerous, but are those that have been most closely studied, probably on account of the abundant material found there. These include the cave of Golondrina in Chihuahua; the Nogales, La Perra and Ocampo complexes in Tamaulipas; the valley of the Guadiana in Durango; the coastline of Matanchel in Nayarit; the cave of San Nicolás in Querétaro; that of El Tecolote in Hidalgo; the site of Chicolapan in the province of Mexico; the sites of Tlapacoya II, IV (Zohapilco) and XVIII; the centre of Veracruz; in Puebla, Texcal, Coxcatlán and Abejas; the coastline at Tecpan, Guerrero; Yanhuitlan in Oaxaca; certain conchiferous deposits on the coast at Chiapas and the cave Santa Marta; and also a few sites in northern Belize.

Apart from Mexico, there are La Esperanza in Honduras and Acahualican in Nicaragua, with the only evidence being some human footprints in a layer of ash, and the sites of Chiriquí in Panama. In Panama the presence of maize seeds has been reported in certain pollen studies, but there is no established chronology.

We end this chapter by referring to the few places where, from very early on, the first fragments of pottery were found. First there is the very special case of Tlapacoya IV (Zohapilco) in the province of Mexico, where in a layer of soil dated around 4,250 years ago a terracotta statuette was found, representing a female human figure; there were no other traces of pottery to be found in the same layer. Also, in Yanhuitlan, Oaxaca, two fragments of pottery were found associated with a dwelling dated about 4,000 years ago. Further, in Puerto Marqués, adjacent to Acapulco, Guerrero, a type of pottery called 'Pox', was found, dated about 4,200 years ago; finally, in the cave at Purrón, Puebla, two types of pottery were found dated about 3,400 years ago. A new era had begun.

BIBLIOGRAPHY

ALVÁREZ, T.; CASAMIQUELA, R.; POLACO, O. 1977. *Informe de la 1er temporada de excavaciones realizadas en El Cedral, SLP.* México, DF, INAH.

ARNOLD, B. A. 1957. Late Pleistocene and Recent Changes in Land Form, Climate and Archaeology in Central Baja California. *Univ. Calif. Pub. Geogr.* (Berkeley), Vol. 10, No. 4, pp. 201–318.

BANERJEE, U. C.; BARGHOORN, E. S. 1972. Fine Structure of Pollen Grain Ektextine of Maize, Teosinte and Tripsacum. In: *Thirtieth Annual Proceedings of the Electro-Microscopy Society of America.* Los Angeles. pp. 226–7.

BARGHOORN, E. S.; WOLFE, M. K.; CLISBY, K. H. 1954. Fossil Maize from the Valley of Mexico. *Bot. Mus. Leafl., Harv. Univ.* (Cambridge, Mass.), Vol. 16, pp. 229–40.

BEADLE, G. W. 1977. The Origin of *Zea mays*. In: REED, C. A. (ed.), *Origins of Agriculture.* The Hague. pp. 615–35.

—— 1980. The Ancestry of Corn. *Sci. Am.*, Vol. 242, pp. 96–103.

DANIEL, G. E. 1981. *A Short History of Archaeology.* London.

ESPINOSA ESTRADA, J. 1976. *Excavaciones arqueológicas en 'El Bosque'.* Managua.

GALINAT, W. C. 1975. The Evolutionary Emergence of Maize. *Bull. Torrey Bot. Club*, Vol. 102, No. 5, pp. 313–24.

—— 1977. The Origin of Corn. In: SPRAGUE, F. (ed.), *Corn and Corn Improvement.* Madison. pp. 1–47.

GARCÍA-BÁRCENA, J. 1979. *Una Punta Acanalada de la Cueva Los Grifos, Ocozocoautla, Chiapas.* Mexico, DF, INAH.

—— 1982. *El Precerámico de Aguacatenango, Chiapas, México.* Mexico.

GUEVARA SÁNCHEZ, A. 1981. *Los Talleres líticos de Aguatenango, Chiapas.* Mexico.

LORENZO, J. L. 1972. Problèmes du peuplement de l'Amérique à la lumière des découvertes de Tlapacoya. In: UNESCO. *Proceedings of the Colloquium on the* Homo sapiens *Origins.* Paris. pp. 261–4.

—— 1977a. *Un conjunto lítico de Teopisca, Chiapas.* Mexico, DF, INAH.

—— 1977b. Agroecosistemas prehistóricos. In: HERNANDEZ XOCOLOTZI, E. (ed.), *Agrocistemas de México: contribuciones a la enseñanza, investigación y divulgación agrícola.* Chapingo, Collegio de Postgraduados.

—— 1986. Conclusiones. In: LORENZO, J. L.; MIRAMBELL, L. (eds), *Treintaicinco mil años del Lago de Chalco.* Mexico, DF, INAH. pp. 225–87.

LORENZO, J. L.; ALVAREZ, T. 1979. Presencia del Hombre en México hace mas de 30,000 años. *Cienc. Desarrolo.* Mexico, Vol. 26, pp. 114–15.

LORENZO, J. L.; MIRAMBELL, L. 1978. *Informe de 2a. temporada de excavaciones realizadas en El Cedral, San Luis Potosí.* Mexico.

—— 1979. *Informe de la 3a. temporada de excavaciones realizadas en El Cedral, San Luis Potosí.* Mexico.

—— 1980. *Informe de la 4a. temporada de excavaciones realizadas en El Cedral, San Luis Potosí.* Mexico.

—— 1982. *Informe de la 5a. temporada de excavaciones realizadas en El Cedral, San Luis Potosí.* Mexico.

—— 1983. *Informe de la 6a. temporada de excavaciones realizadas en El Cedral, San Luis Potosí.* Mexico.

—— 1984. *Informe de la 7a. temporada de excavaciones realizadas en El Cedral, San Luis Potosí.* Mexico.

MACNEISH, R. S. (ed.) 1972. *The Prehistory of the Tehuacan Valley. 4. Chronology and Irrigation.* Austin.

MACNEISH, R. S.; WILKERSON, S. J.; NELKEN, A. 1980. *First Annual Report on the Belize Archaeological Reconnaisance.* Andover.

MIRAMBELL, L. 1978. Tlapacoya: A Late Pleistocene Site in Central Mexico. In: BRYAN, A. L. (ed.), *Early Man in America from a Circum-Pacific Perspective.* Edmonton. pp. 221–30.

MORGAN, J. DE. 1947. *La humanidad prehistórica.* Barcelona. (Trad. 2nd French edn.)

OBERMAIER, H. 1925. *El hombre fosil.* 2nd edn. Madrid.

PICKERSGILL, B. 1977. Taxonomy and the Origin and Evolution of Cultivated Plants in the New World. *Nature* (London), Vol. 268, No. 5621, pp. 591–5.

PULESTON, D. E. 1975. Richmond Hill, a Probable Early Man Site in the Maya Lowlands. In: *Acts XLI Congr. Intern. Americas.* Mexico, DF. Vol. 1, pp. 522–33.

RITTER, E. W. 1976. The Antiquity of Man in the Laguna Seca Chapala Basin of Baja California. *Pacific Coast Archaeol. Soc. Quart.*, Vol. 12, No. 1, pp. 39–46.

SCHOBINGER, J. 1973. Nuevos hallazgos de puntas 'Cola de Pescado' y consideraciones en torno al origen y dispersión de la cultura de los cazadores superiores toldense (Fell II) en Sudamérica. In: *Atti XL Congr. Intern. Americ.* Rome. Vol. 1, pp. 33–50.

SHOOK, E. M. 1961. The Present Status of Research in the Preclassic Horizons of Guatemala. In: TAX, S. (ed.), *The Civilizations of Ancient America.* Chicago. pp. 93–100. (Selected papers XXIX Int. Congr. Americanists.)

SNARKIS, M. J. 1979. Turrialba: A Paleoindian Quarry and Workshop Site in Eastern Costa Rica. *Amer. Antiq.*, Vol. 44, No. 1, pp. 125–38.

SOLÓRZANO, F. A. 1962. *Reporte preliminar sobre el estudio de artefactos y huesos humanos fosilizados procedentes dela zona de Chapala.* Guadalajara.

—— 1976. *Artefactos prehistóricos de huseco del Occidente de México.* Guadalajara.

SZABO, B. J.; MALDE, H.; IRWIN-WILLIAMS, C. 1969. Dilemma Posed by Uranium Series Dates of Archaeological Significant Bones from Valsequillo, Puebla, Mexico. *Earth and Planetary Science Letters*, Amsterdam, Vol. 6, pp. 237–44.

WEST, R. C. 1964. The Natural Regions of Middle America. In: WAUCHOPE, R. (ed.), *Handbook of Middle American Indians.* Vol. 1, pp. 363–83.

WILKES, M. G. 1967. *Teosinte: The Closest Relative to Maize.* Cambridge.

WILLEY, G. R.; PHILLIPS, P. 1958. *Methods and Theory in American Archaeology.* Chicago.

CENTRAL AMERICA, THE CARIBBEAN, NORTHERN SOUTH AMERICA AND THE AMAZON

The beginnings of food production

Mario Sanoja Obediente

From the investigations of Correal and Van der Hammen in Colombia (1977), the hunting and gathering peoples whose traces were discovered in various small caves in the Bogotá savannah (Correal, 1979) also seem to have spread towards the low regions of west Colombia, particularly the valleys between mountains, such as the Magdalena and the Cauca valleys, finally reaching the Caribbean coastal area. This process of expansion by the groups associated with the hunting and gathering way of life appears to have been stimulated or accelerated by the advent of a dry period that is thought to have occurred about 5,300 years ago. The reduced quantity and quality of the prey hunted by those communities on the Andean plateaux most probably forced them to seek more reliable sources of food. Some of them found such resources in the areas bordering the mouth of the river Magdalena, where a diverse population of gatherers, fishermen, sea and coastal hunters, who developed at the same early date, began to manufacture hoes and axes made of the shell of *Strombus gigas* (a type of marine snail), stone pestles and grinding stones, clay pots or dishes for baking cassava flour and containers decorated with engraved rural designs, broad and curved, made by shaping and incision, as attested by the sites at Monsú, Puerto Hormiga and Rotinet.

The fluctuations in climate, in particular the drought and heat which were characteristic of that period in history, led to a reorientation of the economic activity of the hunter-gatherer-fisher folk, who on arrival in the region of the lower Magdalena found a concentration of vegetation belonging to the two species of sweet and bitter (poisonous) cassava (*Manihot esculenta*) (Sanoja, 1982b). The latter species can be processed to remove the poison, and there are signs that this actually happened, and cassava can be included in the list of edible plants eaten by the hunter-gatherer-fisher folk of the sea and coastal regions of the lower Magdalena. Although there is still no direct evidence of its early use, there appear to be indications of a possible original centre for the domestic use of *Manihot esculenta* in this region of Colombia, where the non-poisonous species was cultivated to the west of the Magdalena, and on the east of the river both the poisonous and non-poisonous species were cultivated. Other authors such as Sanoja (1982b) are in agreement in noting the north-west of Colombia as one of the possible original centres of tropical plant cultivation, a view which has now been reinforced by the presence in Monsú of two types of hoe: a large, heavy one with a thick rim which shows signs of erosion caused by chipping, and which could possibly have been used to till the soil, and another type, lighter and narrower with a curved blade, which could have been used for woodwork.

The previous dates would indicate that the lower Magdalena could be considered as one of the early examples of the change-over to the Neolithic way of life that marked the break-up of the hunting and gathering community and the beginning of tribal society in the north of South America. This process appears to have reached its height in Colombia with the Malambo phase, dated at about 3,100 years ago, when there was a very significant qualitative and quantitative change in the subsistence techniques of the aboriginal communities that are noted for having spread the method for processing the toxic variety of cassava. This change appears to have been the result of a progressive accumulation of experience in horticulture, which dates from about 5,000 years ago in Monsú and Rotinet. In Rotinet there are actually fragments of flat earthenware pans, artefacts that become widely used in Malambo. This new technology had a surprisingly rapid effect on the aboriginal societies in northern South America. On the one hand, the sweet variety of cassava could be cooked in a shorter time and was less risky to eat, while the poisonous variety needed to undergo a series of technical processes to make it safe for consumption. With regard to productivity and yield, the bitter cassava does better than the sweet or non-poisonous variety. On the other hand, if the growing of cassava was a compromise between gathering and a type of farming where reserves were kept naturally underground until the primitive farmer decided to pull up the plant, then, with the invention of methods for processing poisonous cassava, food reserves in the form of flour or tapioca and cassava could be stored within the farmer's own house, thus dispensing with daily dependence on the kitchen garden or 'small-holding' for carbohydrate foodstuffs. These reserves, or the accumulated work surplus, would act as an investment that could be transferred or bartered for other stored surplus products or materials; this appears to have introduced a significant change in social relations both within and between communities, that is to say, in the processes of exchange and population mobility. This explains why, within a short space of time, the technology for refining bitter cassava spread throughout the north of South America, Central America and the West Indies, serving as a basis for the subsistence of the crop-growing village society that developed very early on in that vast region (Sanoja, 1982a, 1982b).

As we have seen, the development of horticulture in various regions of South America seems to have marked the beginning of the changeover to a sedentary and Neolithic way of life of the societies previously associated with the land and coastal hunter-gatherer way of life, showing that there were perhaps not one, but several processes of local evolution leading to the development of food production. This is possibly true for the Las Varas site in the north-west of Venezuela, and perhaps also for the coastal hunters and gatherers who from very early on occupied the coastal region State of Para in an area known as Salagado, bathed by brackish waters, which stretches from the bay of Marajó at the mouth of the Amazon to the mouth of the river Gurupí.

Various radiocarbon datings of scoured potsherds indicate a timescale extending from 5,000 to 3,600 years ago for this site. The archaeological remains show signs of subsistence practices based on the gathering of sea-shells, territorial hunting and the consumption of plant species, possibly seeds, roots and fruits, which were prepared for eating by using grinding pestles, hammerstones, scrapers and choppers. The pottery of this archaeological period, called Mina, is scoured with sea-shells and decorated with red paint, incised or painted, suggesting similarities with Puerto Hormiga, Valdivia and Machalilla, in the north-west of South America (Sanoja, 1982b). This poses the question whether the appearance of horticulture and village life on the northern coast of Brazil resulted from local evolution or, on the contrary, was induced by migrations from the western Amazon, where there were the cultures of the Grazing period dated around 4,000 years ago, located on the eastern slopes of the Ecuadorian Andes, and Early Tutishcayno, located on the eastern slope of the Peruvian Andes and stylistically related to Kotosh, whose date has been estimated at between 3,800 and 3,000 years ago. In both locations, the basis of horticultural subsistence appears to have been the cultivation of plants, while, on the coast of the Amazon, grinding implements were used that were associated with the gathering of sea-shells by pottery-making groups that were already clearly horticultural, as in the Ananatuba period, continuing up until the beginning of the third millennium BP.

There is evidence in Panama of the presence of woodland hunter-gatherers in the river Chiriqui area (Talamanca phase) at a date estimated at between 7,000 and 5,000 years ago, who, up to 5,000 years ago, appear to have developed a form of subsistence based on the gathering of wild fruits and possibly a form of plant growing associated with the practice of clearing and burning, which would seem to be supported by the presence of polished axes and a collection of chipped stone artefacts such as chisels, knives, drills, awls and scrapers, possibly used for woodwork. This period, termed the Boquete phase, saw a gradual process of stabilization in food production, which reached its height around 4,000 years ago with the appearance of pottery and a diversified form of subsistence that included vegetable growing and possibly also maize cultivation. It is possible that in this process of transition towards forms of food production in Panama, the hunter-gatherer peoples may have taken advantage of the rare opportunity of being able to exploit simultaneously the coastal ecosystem and the bordering woodland area of the interior in an area as narrow as the isthmus between the Caribbean Sea on the east and the Pacific Ocean on the west.

Summing up the historical and cultural contents of the region for the period studied, we can see that, much as elsewhere on the continent, the way of life of the old hunters begins to decline towards the eighth millennium BP. There could have been various causes for this process: the sequence of postglacial climatic changes that affected a way of life so dependent upon the possibilities offered by the environment, the gradual disappearance of the megafauna, changes in sea-level, changes in temperature and general modifications to the available fauna and flora, and so on.

Environmental modifications also appear to have had an influence on the bases for subsistence and the social structure of those human groups. The abandonment of predatory forms of existence and the search for increasingly abundant and stable sources of food appear to have given rise to an increasingly greater territorial stability of human groupings, as well as an increased interest in the search for and consumption of plant food, the production or adoption of a complex of techniques and artefacts for specialized gathering, and the initial steps towards cultivation of certain plants.

The majority of works published up to the present time concerning the hunting and gathering societies of the coastal areas or interior of continents tend to admit the existence of an intermediate stage (Mesolithic, Archaic, Mesoindian and so on) that bridged the gap between the old hunting societies (Palaeolithic, Lithic, Palaeoindian and so on) and the agricultural societies (Neolithic, Formative, Neoindian and the like); alternatively they see it as a continuation of the Palaeolithic (Epipalaeolithic) age or as preceding the Neolithic age (Proto-Neolithic). However, the dates provided by recent studies show that the gathering, or transitional, societies succeeded in making advances in various fields of food production technology and in the organization of society for production, both of which were crucial for the subsequent development and expansion of agricultural societies, and that it was in these societies that the bases of knowledge were laid that probably led to a predominantly agricultural way of life of farmers and potters.

The appearance of agriculture does not appear to have been a sudden and original invention of one society in particular. On the contrary, one might see it as a logical consequence of the processes of intensification of the relations between humans and plants that took place in several locations on the various continents.

The beginning of pottery-making is not the result of pure chance. It appears at the precise time when cultivated plants begin to predominate over wild ones. It might be added that the introduction of instruments of production such as containers is a consequence of the development of the productive forces that began to appear in societies with a gathering way of life. This reflected a conception of the soil not as an object but as a medium for human labour; this meant a reformulation of the social organization in order to produce the radical changes that were necessary to consolidate the new agricultural tribal society.

BIBLIOGRAPHY

ABSY, M. L. 1982. Quaternary Palynological Studies in the Amazon Basin. In: PRANCE, G. T. (ed.), *Biological Diversification in the Tropics.* New York. pp. 67–73.

ANDERSON, D. 1974. A Stone Campsite at the Gateway to America. In: ZUBROW, E. et al. (eds), *New World Archaeology: Readings from Scientific American.* San Francisco.

AVELEYRA DE ANDA, L. 1964. The Primitive Hunters. In: WAUCHOPE, R. (ed.), *Handbook of Middle American Indians.* Dallas. Vol. I, pp. 384–412.

BATE, L. P. 1983. Comunidades primitivas de cazadores recolectores en Sudamérica. In: *História General de América.* Caracas. Vol. 2–1–2–II.

BEARDSLEY, R. et al. 1955. In: WAUCHOPE, R. (ed.), *Seminars in Archaeology: 1955.* Salt Lake City. (Mem. Soc. Am. Archaeol., No. 11, Vol. 22, No. 2, Part 2.)

BELL, R. E. 1965. *Investigaciones arqueológicas en el sitio El Inga, Ecuador.* Quito.

BIGARELLA, J. J.; ANDRADE LIMA, D. DE. 1982. The Paleoclimate and Palaeoecology of Brazilian Amazonia. In: PRANCE, G. T. (ed.), *Biological Diversification in the Tropics.* New York. pp. 27–40.

BIRD, J. 1938. Antiquity and Migration of the Early Inhabitants of Patagonia. *Geogr. J.* (New York), Vol. 28, pp. 250–75.

—— 1946. The Cultural Sequence in the North Chilean Coast. In: *Handbook of South American Indians.* Vol. I, pp. 17–24.

BIRD, J.; COOKE, R. 1977. Los artefactos mas antiguos de Panamá. *Rev. Nac. Cult.* (Panama), No. 6.

—— 1978. The Occurrence in Panama of Two Types of Palaeo-indian Projectile Points. In: BRYAN, A. L. (ed.), *Early Man in America from a Circum-Pacific Perspective.* Edmonton.

BRYAN, A. L. 1973. New Light on Ancient Nicaraguan Footprints. *Archeology* (New York), Vol. 26.

—— 1978. An Overview of Palaeoamerican Prehistory from a Circum-Pacific Perspective. In: BRYAN, A. L. (ed.), *Early Man in America from a Circum-Pacific Perspective.* Edmonton. pp. 306–27.

BRYAN, A. L. et al. 1978. *An 'El Jobo' Mastodon Kill Site at Taima-Taima, Northern Venezuela.*

COLLINS, M. B. 1981. The Implications of the Lithic Assemblage from Monte Verde, Chile, for Early Man Studies. In: CONGRESO DE LA UISPP, 10, Mexico. *Actas.* Mexico.

CORREAL, G. 1979. *Investigaciones en Abrigos Rocosos de Nemocon y Sueva.* Bogota.

—— 1981. *Evidencias culturales y megafauna Pleistocenica en Colombia.* Bogota.

CORREAL, G.; HAMMEN, T. VAN DER. 1977. *Artefactos líticos de las Abrigos Rocosos del Tequendama.* Bogota.

COURSEY, D. G. 1976. The Origins and Domestication of Yams in Africa. In: HARLAN, J.; QET, A. M. J. DE; STEMMLER, A. B. L. (eds), *Origins of African Plant Domestication.* The Hague. pp. 383–408.

CRAWFORD, 1891. Neolithic Man in Nicaragua. *Am. Geol.* (Minneapolis), Vol. 8, pp. 160–6.

CRUXENT, J. M. 1961. Huesos quemados en el yacimiento pre-histórico de Muaco, Estade Falcon. *Inst. Venez. Invest. Cient., Dep. Antropol. Bol. Inf.* (Caracas), No. 2, pp. 20–1.

—— 1962. Artifacts of Paleoindian Type, Maracaibo, Zulia, Venezuela. *Ame. Antiq.,* Vol. 27, pp. 576–9.

—— 1970. Projectile Points with Pleistocene Mammals in Venezuela. *Antiquity,* Vol. 175, pp. 223–6.

—— 1971. Apuntes sovre arqueología Venezolana. In: *Arte Prehispanico de Venezuela.* Caracas.

CRUXENT, J. M.; ROUSE, I. 1961. *Arqueolgía chronológica de Venezuela.* Washington, Unión Panamericana.

—— 1963. *Venezuelan Archaeology.* New Haven/London.

DEREVIANKO, A. P. 1979. On the Immigration of Ancient Man from the Asian Pleistocene. In: BRYAN, A. L. (ed.), *Early Man in America from a Circum-Pacific Perspective.* Edmonton.

DIKOV, N. N. 1978. Ancestors of Paleoindians and Proto-Eskimos Aleuts in the Palaeolithic of Kamchatka. In: BRYAN, A. L. (ed.), *Early Man in America from a Circum-Pacific Perspective.* Edmonton.

DILLEHAY, T. 1981. Early Man in South Central Andes, Monte Verde. In: CONGRESO DE LA UISPP, 10, Mexico. *Actas.* Mexico.

ESPINOZA, E. J. 1976. *Excavaciones en El Bosque: informe no. 1.* Managua.

EVANS, C.; MEGGERS, B. 1960. *Archaeological Investigations in British Guiana.* Washington. (Smithson. Inst., Bull., 177.)

FLINT, E. 1885. Human Footprints in Nicaragua. *Am. Antiq.* (Chicago), Vol. 7, pp. 112–4.

GONZÁLES, A. R. 1952. Antiguo horizonte preceráamica en las Sierras Centrales de la Argentina. *Runa* (Buenos Aires), Vol. 5, pp. 110–33.

—— 1960. La Estratigrafia de la Gruta de Itihuasi (Provincia de San Luis, RA) y sus relaciones con otros sitios precerámicos de Sudamérica. *Rev. Inst. Anthropol., Univ. Nac. Cordoba,* Vol. I.

GRUHN, R. 1976. A Note on Excavations at El Bosque, Nicaragua, in 1975. In: BRYAN, A. L. (ed.), *Early Man in America from a Circum-Pacific Perspective.* Edmonton.

GRUHN, R.; BRYAN, A. 1981. A Summary and Implications of the Taima-Taima Mastodon Kill Site, Northern Venezuela. In: CONGRESO DE LA UISPP, 10, Mexico. *Actas.* Mexico.

HAMMEN, T. VAN DER. 1972. Changes in Vegetation and Climate in the Amazon Basin and Surrounding Areas during the Pleistocene. *Geol. Mijnb.* (Dordrecht), Vol. 51, pp. 641–3.

—— 1974. The Pleistocene Changes of Vegetation and Climate in Tropical South America. *J. Biogeog.* (Oxford), Vol. I, pp. 3–26.

—— 1982. Palaeoecology of Tropical South America. In: PRANCE, G. T. (ed.), *Biological Differentiation in the Tropics.* New York. pp. 60–6.

HURT, W. R.; BLASI, O. 1969. *O projeto arqueológico Lagoa Santa, Minas Gerais, Brasil.* Curitiba. (Arq. Mus. Paranaense, 4.)

HURT, W. R.; HAMMEN, T. VAN DER; CORREAL, G. 1972. Preceramic Sequences in the El Abra Rock, Colombia. *Science* (Washington), Vol. 175, pp. 1106–8.

KRIEGER, A. 1962. The Earliest Cultures in the Western United States. *Am. Antiq.,* Vol. 28, No. 2, pp. 138–43.

—— 1964. Early Man in the New World. In: JENNINGS, J.; NORBECK, E. (eds), *Prehistoric Man in the New World.* Chicago.

LEROI-GOURHAN, A. 1946. *Archéologie du Pacifique Nord.* Paris, Musée de l'Homme.

LYNCH, T. 1978. The South American Palaeoindians. In: JENNINGS, J.; FREEMAN, W. H. (eds), *Ancient Native Americans.* San Francisco.

MATILLO, V. J. 1977. *Acahualinca en el panorama arqueológico de Nicaragua.* Managua.

MEGGERS, B. J. 1982. Archaeological and Ethnographic Evidences Compatible with the Model of Forest Fragmentation. In: PRANCE, G. T. (ed.), *Biological Differentiation in the Tropics.* New York. pp. 483–96.

MÉNDEZ GUTIÉRREZ, M. 1984. *Puntas de proyectil de Cajibio, Cauca, Colombia.* Popayan.

MEYER-OAKES, W. 1974. Early Man in the Andes. In: SUBROW, E. et al. (ed.), *New World Archaeology: Theoretical and Cultural Transformation.* San Francisco.

—— 1981. Early Man Projectile Points and Lithic Technology in the Ecuadorian Sierra. In: CONGRESO DE LA UISPP, 10, Mexico. *Actas.* Mexico.

MILLER, W.; LUNDELIUS, E. 1976. The Fossils from El Bosque: A Preliminary Report to Jorge Espinoza. In: ESPINOZA, E. J. *Excavaciones en El Bosque: informe no. 1.* Managua. pp. 22–9.

MOCHANOV, Y. A. 1978. Stratigraphy and Absolute Chronology of the Palaeolithic of Northeastern Asia According to the Work of 1963–1973. In: BRYAN, A. (ed.), *Early Man in America from a Circum-Pacific Perspective.* Edmonton. pp. 54–66.

MOLINA, L. 1985. *Wachakaresai: la história que duerme bajo tierra.* Caracas.

MORGANTI, A.; RODRÍGUEZ, M. H. 1983. *Cazadores recolectores de Monte Cano, Paraguana, Venezuela.*

MÜLLER-BECK, H. 1966. Palaeohunters in America: Origins and Diffusion. *Science* (Washington), Vol. 52, pp. 1191–210.

—— 1967. On Migrations of Hunters across the Behring Land Bridge in the Upper Pleistocene. In: HOPKINS, D. M. (ed.), *The Behring Landbridge.* Stanford. pp. 373–408.

PAGE, W. 1978. Geology of El Bosque Archaeological Site. In:

BRYAN, A. L. (ed.), *Early Man in America from a Circum-Pacific Perspective*. Edmonton.

PANTEL, A. 1983. *La Hundición, Estado Lara, Venezuela: Draft Field and Labor, Report*. San Juan, MS. Fundación Arqueo. Puerto Rico.

PATTERSON, T.; LANNING, E. P. 1974. Early Man in South America. In: ZUBROW, E. et al. (eds), *New World Archaeology: Readings from Scientific American*. San Francisco. pp. 44–50.

RODRÍGUEZ, M. E. 1985. Grupos precerámicos del Noroccidente de Venezuela y su relación con la Cuenca del Lago de Maracaibo. *Rev. GENS*, Vol. 1, No. 2, pp. 38–53.

ROYO Y GÓMEZ, J. 1956. El Cuaternario en Venezuela. *Bol. Geol. Publ. Espec. No. 1, Lexico Estratigráfico de Venezuela* (Caracas), pp. 199–204.

—— 1960a. Características Paleontológicas y Geológicas del yacimiento de vertebrados de Muaco, Estado Falcon, con industria lítica humana. *Boletín de Geología Publ. Espec. No. 3: Memórias III. Congreso Geológico Venezolano II* (Caracas) pp. 501–5.

—— 1960b. El Yacimiento de vertebrados Pleistocenos de Muaco, Estado Falcon, Venezuela, con industria humana lítica. In: INTERNATIONAL CONGRESS OF GEOLOGY, 21, Copenhagen. *Report*. Copenhagen. Vol. 14, pp. 154–7.

SALGADO-LABORIU, M. L. 1982. Climatic Change at the Pleistocene Holocene Boundary. In: PRANCE, G. T. (ed.), *Biological Differentiation in the Tropics*. New York.

SANOJA, M. 1980. Los recolectores tempranos del Golfo de Paria, Estado Sucre, Venezuela. In: CIPECPAN, 8, St Kitts. *Actas*. pp. 139–51.

—— 1982a. *Los hombres de la yaca y del maïz*. Caracas.

—— 1982b. De la recolección a la agricultura. In: *Historia General de América*. Caracas. Vol. 3.

—— 1984. Problemas de la Arqueología del Noreste de Venezuela. In: *Los Problemas de la Arqueología de América Latina*. (Inst. Arqueol., Acad. Cienc. URSS.)

—— 1985. Preceramic Sites in Eastern Venezuela. *Nat. Geogr. Res. Rep.* (Washington, DC), Vol. 18, pp. 663–8.

SANOJA, M.; ROMERO, L.; RONDON, J. 1982. Investigaciones arqueológicas en los Concheros, Guayana, El Bajo y Las Varas, Estado Sucre, Venezuela. *Acta Cient. Venez.* (Caracas), Vol. 33, suppl.

SANOJA, M.; VARGAS, I. 1979. *Antiguas formaciones y modos de produción venezolanos*. 2nd edn. Caracas.

—— 1983. New Light on the Prehistory of Eastern Venezuela. In: WENDORF, F.; CLOSE, A. (eds), *Advances in World Archaeology*. New York. Vol. 2, pp. 205–44.

SCHOBINGER, J. 1973. Nuevos hallazgos de puntas 'Cola de Pescado' y consideraciones en torno al origen y dispersión de la cultura de los cazadores superiores Toldenses (Fell I) en Sudamérica. In: CONGRESSO INTERNATIONAL DEGLI AMERICANISTI, 40, Rome, Genova. *Atti*. Vol. 1, pp. 33–50.

SIMPSON-VUILLEMIER, B. 1971. Pleistocene Changes in the Fauna and Flora of South-America. *Science* (Washington), Vol. 173, pp. 771–80.

SNARKIS, M. 1984. Central America: The Lower Caribbean. In: LANGE, F. W.; STONE, D. Z. (eds), *The Archaeology of Lower Central America*. Albuquerque.

STEWARD, T.; NEWMAN, M. 1950. Anthropometry of South-american Indians: Skeletal Remains. In: STEWARD, T. (ed.), *Handbook of South American Indians*. Washington. (Smithson. Inst., Bull., 6).

VELOZ MAGGIOLO, M. et al. 1982. Las Técnicas Unifaciales de los yacimientos de El Jobo y sus similitudes con el Paleoarcaico Antillano. *Bol. Mus. Hombre Dominicano* (Santo Domingo), Vol. 18.

WILLEY, G. 1966. *An Introduction to American Archaeology*. Vol. I: *North and Middle America*. New Jersey.

—— 1971. *An Introduction to American Archaeology*. Vol. II: *South America*. New Jersey.

WILSEM, E. 1964. Flake Tools in the American Arctic: Some Speculations. *Am. Antiq.*, Vol. 29, pp. 338–44.

WORMINGTON, H. M. 1961. Prehistoric Cultural Stages of Alberta, Canada. In: *Homenajes a Pablo Martinez del Rio; 25. Aniversario de la Edición de los Origines*. Mexico, DF. pp. 163–71.

THE EQUATORIAL AND TROPICAL ANDES

from the beginnings of food production up to 5,000 years ago

Luis G. Lumbreras Salcedo

The millennia between 9,000 and 7,000 years ago were a period of major climatic change, temperatures gradually rising and producing the conditions now prevailing in the Andean territory as a whole.

It is estimated that the highest temperatures were reached around 7,000 years ago, when the climate was hot and humid, but began to fall thereafter, reaching today's levels by 5,000 years ago.

It should be noted that all these general statements are only very broadly applicable to the Andean world, which can on no account be described as uniform. Each landscape reacted in its own way to these changes; furthermore, the factors conditioning climate in the Andes – the cordillera and ocean currents – operate differently in each of the geographical areas, and their corresponding climates are more strongly influenced by these individual factors than by large-scale general changes.

Running down the west of South America from north to south, the Andes cross the Equator and the tropic of Capricorn and fade out in the vicinity of the Antarctic. The cordillera actually begins in the Caribbean, the islands of the West Indies and the southern part of Central America; its structure throughout this area as far as the Nudo de Pasto in southern Colombia is dispersed and irregular, like an archipelago, with three main branches in Colombia separated by the Magdalena, Cauca and Patía rivers. In this region the mountains are relatively low. Very few rise above 3,200 metres, so that the effects of the cordillera are insignificant and the environment tends towards tropical features, with heavy plant cover, high forests and at the highest altitudes a very damp and barren plateau.

The Andean Equatorial region, consisting basically of the Republic of Ecuador, extends from latitude 4° N, the Colombian massif, to latitude 5° S, the deserts of Piura in Peru. Here the Andes are much more compact, although they are relatively narrow (150 to 250 km wide). In the north there are valleys flanked by volcanoes rising to more than 5,000 m, with plateaux of damp scrubland in the highest areas. Towards the south, by contrast, the valleys are drier and a distinction begins to be discernible between the humid and tropical east and the dry and increasingly desert-like

west, a feature of the tropical Andes to the south of latitude 5°. The effects of the cordillera on the physical features of the region are marked but not overwhelming, so that in the narrow mountainous strip the changes range from savannah to bleak plateaux, tundra and permanent snow. In the west, as far as the ocean, there are evergreen forests and on the coast one even finds mangrove-type outcrops with their characteristically lush plant cover.

The drastic effects of the altitude of the Andes and their interaction with very cold ocean currents off the coasts of Peru begin to be felt to the south of latitude 5° in the central and south-central Andes in the tropical zone running as far as the tropic of Capricorn. In the central Andes within Peru the cordillera is broader, with peaks rising to more than 5,000 and up to 6,000 metres, damp and forest-clad to the east and entirely desertified to the west. The whole of the cordillera system drains into the basin of the great river Amazon and consists of a wide variety of geological configurations depending on the altitude and longitude of their location. The western section of the cordillera, on the other hand, produces rivers that flow steadily down to the sea, crossing the desert and forming fertile alluvial fans that are replenished each year. This conglomerate of land forms includes a new type of dry desolate plateau known as a puna, which is the most characteristic feature of the south-central Andes in the southern part of the tropical belt. In the south-central Andes the cordillera is at its widest (up to 500 km), with broad high plateaux, rivers with narrow basins and little water, and streams that get deeper as they flow towards the ocean and do not form alluvial fans because the cordillera drops abruptly into the ocean. The predominant land forms are puna and desert, although there are many fertile oases scattered throughout the territory. It is thus basically pastureland, the most characteristic habitat of the wild and domesticated Andean camelids.

To the south of the tropic of Capricorn, the Andean cordillera becomes narrow again, while remaining a dry region with high peaks rising to about 7,000 metres, as in the case of the Aconcagua. But here the cordillera itself is no longer important, to the extent that it is actually uninhabited. Only its western (Chile) and eastern

(Argentina) slopes are of any human significance and the cordillera becomes no more than an obstacle to be surmounted. Further to the south, the Andes gradually disintegrate and in the extreme south of the continent they crumble into the ocean.

It was in these environmental conditions that human life evolved in the Andes, having a great variety of different circumstances to contend with. In the Equatorial and tropical Andes, it was this context of confrontation that generated the great civilizations that culminated in that of the Inca or Tawantinsuyo empire. The process of civilization in the Andes was actually the result of a cross-fertilization of human experience in the Equatorial and in the tropical areas, which were the scene of the most significant historical events, from the discovery of agriculture to the development of urban society.

From the end of the Pleistocene up to 9,000 years ago, a 'wave' of hunters spread over the entire Andean world. They are best known as the producers of leaf-shaped projectile points and for their successful exploitation of the varied resources of the highly diverse territory of the Andes.

Very roughly speaking, there were at least three basic types of economic organization among these hunters of the early Holocene. One was that of the high Andean hunters of camelids. They lived on the bleak plateaux and punas that were the habitat of the guanaco (*Lama guanicoe*) and the vicuña (*Vicugna vicugna*). Another form of economic organization was that of the nomadic hunter-gatherers who roamed the sparse inter-Andean woods and the valleys, ravines and thickets in search of fruit and small animals including deer, viscachas (*Lagidium* sp.) and other rodents and birds. A third was that of the coast dwellers, who tended to specialize in activities based on fish and shellfish and the collection of plants from areas close to the sea-shore.

John W. Rick (1980, 1983) has carried out studies of the puna hunters. He has shown that in the region of the puna of Junín in the central mountain ranges of Peru conditions were favourable to the formation of settled communities of hunters because, according to him (Rick, 1983, p. 192), one of the puna's resources, the camelids, could be exploited throughout the year and their population density was sufficiently high to make migration unnecessary. He added that sedentism in the puna had not led to rapid change in the direction of more complex organization, nor had it stimulated population growth. It was a type of sedentism associated with a state of stable equilibrium between the animal resources available for hunting and the groups of hunters living in caves and rock shelters on the Andean high plateau.

It was probably these same conditions that led to the domestication of the camelids. Thanks to the work of Danièle Lavallée and Michèle Julian (1975) in the same region of Junín, we know that it is possible that this kind of domestication occurred there around 6,000 years ago. In the cave of Telarmachay, where they found a long sequence of strata dating from 9,000 years ago, according to various carbon-14 dates, to pottery-making periods within our own era, they observed a gradual decline in the quantity of remains of obviously wild animals such as Cervidae and an increase in the remains of camelids; there was also an increase in the remains of young camelids from the fifth phase of the sequence and changes in the dental morphology of the camelids during the same period, with the emergence of the incisor-type teeth characteristic of the alpaca (*Lama pacos*) which, together with the llama (*Lama glama*), is one of the domestic camelids. They add that the presence of a considerable quantity of remains of young camelids in the cave would seem to indicate that the animals were being held in captivity, a process of confinement that seemed to have led to the death by heterotoxaemia of newly born camelids.

Between 9,000 and 7,000 years ago all the punas and the barren plateaux were occupied by groups of hunters familiar with the camelids and Cervidae of the Andean high plateaux; many of them probably lived in permanent settlements.

The hunters who used leaf-shaped spearheads, on the other hand, were more familiar with other kinds of resources in the bushy valleys and ravines. In 1981 Lynch and Pollock excavated the cave of Chobshi in southern Ecuador, which contained a sequence beginning around 8,700 years ago in a low cordillera environment (about 2,400 m above sea-level), in which deer were the animals hunted most frequently, although there were also remains of rabbits, partridges and other small animals. It was not possible to obtain information in Chobshi on what might have been happening in the Equatorial Andes at the time, mainly because of the difficulties encountered in studying the cave, but the area was probably the scene of major discoveries leading to the domestication of macrothermal tropical plants. However, thanks to excavations, also by Thomas Lynch (1980), in the cave of Guitarrero in the Callejón de Huaylas at a height of 2,580 m, we know that in this part of the Andes the hunters with leaf-shaped spearheads were engaged in plant domestication around 8,000 years ago. When we refer to 'leaf-shaped spearheads', we do not imply that these were the only form of projectile point used by these various groups; indeed the tradition of adding a stem to the heads continued in most places and in each of them or in each region one finds particular forms and styles and different materials used in making them.

Significant events occur in the cave of Guitarrero after phase I, that is to say around 10,000 to 8,000 years ago. Complex II has a set of radiocarbon dates that enable the remains to be divided into two phases, an earlier one running from 10,500 to 9,500 years ago, and the other beginning with complex IIC, running from 9,000 to 7,000 years ago. The changes that occurred during this period, however, seem to relate exclusively to human intervention, since the data indicate that there have been no significant natural changes in the area since that time. The inhabitants of Guitarrero were active plant gatherers – there is evidence of large-scale consumption of tubers and rhizomes such as the oca (*Oxalis* sp.) and the ullucu (*Ullucus tuberosus*) – and also cultivators of Leguminosae such as the dry, or kidney, bean (*Phaseolus vulgaris*) and the lima bean or pallar (*Phaseolus lunatus*) from 9400 years ago according to data provided by T. F. Lynch (1980), C. E. Smith (1980) and L. Kaplan (1980). The plant diet included fruit such as the pepper (*Capsicum chilense*), gourds, eggfruit (*Pouteria lucuma*), pacay (*Inga* sp.) and so on.

In addition, of course, as Elizabeth Wing points out (1977, 1980), the animal bones bear witness to a process of domestication similar to that in the puna caves, but with major quantitative differences; at the lowest levels, deer are predominant among the larger animals, and bones of camelids only begin to occur in significant numbers from phase II, although they never attain the significance of these animals in the higher regions. Their domestication must therefore have 'filtered down' to the gorges and valleys from the puna. On the other hand, the consumption of rabbits (*Sylvilagus brasiliense*) and viscachas (*Lagidium peruvianum*), both rodents which are at the limit of their geographical coverage in this region (the southern limit for rabbits and the northern limit for viscachas), was much more significant.

The Guitarrero finds are even more informative, since they include wooden and bone implements in a good state of preservation: knives, punches and even tree-stumps used to produce fire. Lastly, the cave contained the remains of cords, baskets and fabrics that can be used to reconstruct the development of those techniques from at least 10,500 years ago until their formal existence: the first to appear are cords made of plant fibres, at the beginning of phase II; later on in phase II, concurrently with the advent of agriculture, they become more complex. There is no evidence of the use of cotton, which was very late to appear in this region. The development of cords was accompanied by that of twining.

The textiles found in the Guitarrero cave are certainly the oldest hitherto discovered in America; from the beginning of phase II there are examples of both loose and rigid twining, the precursor of textile making proper and basket making. In view of the fact that the fabrics found represent the simplest form of twining, it may be assumed that they represent a stage in their technological discovery, as noted by Adovasio and Maslowski (1980, p. 288): 'The fabrics of Complex II in Guitarrero are, on the whole, much more simple and represent a more rudimentary stage of technological development than those discovered in any other pre-ceramic site.' Furthermore, the bases for subsequent development are discernible in the fabrics of Guitarrero II, including primitive looping work and other basic techniques. It is also interesting to note that the pieces of textile found are used to make baskets or bags and do not seem to be materials that could be used for clothing. F. Engel (1966, p. 31) suggests that a similar situation occurred on the coast of central Peru, where even before the discovery of the use of cotton, nets and bags were being made from plant fibres, while camelid skins were being used to cover the body, as may be inferred from the graves of hunters who were presumably contemporaneous with Guitarrero II, around 9,000 years ago.

The finds of Lynch and his associates indicate that the process of plant domestication began very early in the tropical Andes, not long after the climatic revolution of the Pleistocene and in association with a rise in general temperatures. The Guitarrero evidence points to an independent process, with the participation of the hunters of the early neothermal period, adapted to inter-Andean environmental conditions and probably, as Lynch surmises, associated with a nomadic way of life, familiar with several different ecological zones and hence tending towards diversification in the use of plant and animal resources.

The evidence in the area is that the peoples of that time had a form of social organization fully consonant with the nomadic 'band' pattern, living in caves, shelters or small seasonal encampments; there is not the slightest indication of the existence of villages or farming settlements. Moreover, everything seems to indicate that farming was not general, although the existence of mortars and pestles in various sites of that period, on the coast and in the mountains (Arenal, Quiqché and the like), would seem to indicate that plant gathering and processing were technologically well developed.

In any case, between 10,500 and 7,000 years ago the predominant activity was hunting, backed up by plant gathering and with additional selective or agricultural harvesting of tubers, rhizomes, Leguminosae and fruits, that is to say a relatively well-balanced diet in terms of protein and carbohydrate consumption. Simultaneously, at the higher levels,

on the puna and bleak plateaux, animal domestication and rudimentary pastoral farming are the characteristic features of the age. Unfortunately, there is very little information available on the guinea-pig (Cavia porcellus) and very much less on the duck (Cairina moschata), which were the other domestic animals, but it seems that the former was domesticated some time before the fourth millennium BP. The dog (Canis familiaris) seems to have arrived with the migrant Pleistocene hunters, although we still lack empirical evidence for this.

Speculations about the origins of Andean agriculture in the tropical forests must therefore be revised in the light of these discoveries. The Callejón de Huaylas, the location of Guitarrero, is in a temperate, relatively fertile valley surrounded by very high mountains at the foot of the snow-capped Huascarán (6,768 m); it is therefore in a very favourable area for combining within short distances resources from various ecological levels. It is also on the route linking the desert coastline and the tropical Amazon forest, closer to the latter than to the coast. It was by no means difficult to establish and maintain contact with the forest-clad eastern Andes, which are not more than two or three days distant on foot, and with the coast which is about the same distance away. This closeness to the Andes and the position of staging post have always been characteristic features of Callejón de Huaylas, which is still the point of departure of the best route into the forest. The Leguminosae of the genus Phaseolus, which were certainly cultivated or in the process of being domesticated, do not need extreme temperature conditions and can be quite at home in a mesothermal environment, but the possibility that they were first found in a forest environment cannot be ruled out. The Guitarrero evidence indicates that these Leguminosae were already domesticated around 8,000 years ago.

Likewise, rhizomes and tubers such as the oca (Oxalis tuberosa) and the ullucu (Ullucus tuberosus) could easily have originated in the cordillera, although some people tend to think that a macrothermal forest origin is more likely. It is quite possible, moreover, that the same thing was happening elsewhere with such basic Andean products as the papa, or potato (Solanum tuberosum), another cordillero tuber that is much more adaptable to different ecosystems. In Ayacucho there is no evidence of the potato until 5,000 years ago, although it seems that events similar to those of Guitarrero were taking place there from the Jaywa phase (6,500 to 5,000 years ago). In the Tres Ventanas site (Engel, 1972) there were other tubers estimated to date from 10,000 years ago, but most specialists have doubts about the associations excavated there and also about the systematic identifications, which were carried out in a very haphazard way. J. G. Hawkes (1967) and other researchers believe that the domestication of the potato and of other high Andean products such as the quinoa (Chenopodium quinoa) and the cañiwa (Chenopodium pellidicaule) must have occurred in the region around Titicaca in the south, between Peru and Bolivia. MacNeish identified traces of quinoa grains in the Piki phase (about 7,000 to 5,000 years ago) in Ayacucho.

In any case, the evidence available at the moment seems to indicate that in the tropical Andes, and especially in the central region, the domestication of plants and animals took place broadly between 10,000 and 8,000 years ago and that the discovery of this possibility did not substantially affect social life, although it appears that it did lead to a population increase, reflected in extensive occupation of the territory by bands of various types of hunter-gatherers.

These groups of human beings included those associated

with the sea. Close to them were other nomadic hunter-gatherers living in areas of typical desert vegetation known locally as 'lomas', which have a plant cover in the winter (June–October) and turn into deserts in the spring. The temporary inhabitants of the lomas must have belonged to a nomadic circuit of coastal origin, in view of the great quantity of shellfish associated with their remains (Engel, 1972); it is also possible that some of them came from the valleys and gorges of the western slopes of the cordillera, which have a very dry winter with little rain where there would have been some difficulty in finding food.

The coastal communities living in coves and on sheltered beaches lived mainly on fish and shellfish, although the records indicate that they supplemented their diet with plant products from the lomas or from the valleys and oases crossing the desert. However, most of the oldest coastal human settlements are now beneath the sea because the level of the sea rose by several metres after the Pleistocene and many beaches were submerged.

So when we reach the seventh millennium BP we find that the inhabitants of the Andean region were already quite skilled in adapting to the environment, making very wide use of various ecological systems and their respective subsistence resources. All this was accomplished with a technology, population and form of social organization that differed little from those of their Stone Age predecessors, although we are dealing with people who had domesticated plants and knew how to make cords, baskets and cloth bags, which represent a major advance in the direction of a more complex life.

Between 7,000 and 5,000 years ago this way of life was consolidated and became general; in addition, marked changes occurred in the organization of the family, which began to live in more stable farming settlements and villages with a larger number of individuals, which probably means an extension of the basic unit of close kin constituting the 'band' to more complex or simply larger communal forms typical of the 'clan' or 'tribe'. If this era is to be given a name, perhaps the most appropriate would be the age of 'Neolithization'.

More of our data come from the coast, where we find that agriculture continues to be based on Leguminosae, in particular the lima bean (Phaseolus lunatus), supplemented basically by gathering fruit and, of course, shellfish and fish. The fisherfolk and shellfish gatherers supplemented their diet with carbohydrates from crops grown in the valleys close to their farms or villages. In the Ancon (Encanto phase) and Chilca zones a number of settlements from this period have been found.

Encanto to the north of Lima is represented by a group of thirteen sites studied by the archaeologist Edward Lanning (1967) and his team. Lanning maintains that the livelihood of these settlements was based mainly on loma products, supplemented by fish caught with nets and hooks made of shell or cactus needles. They also hunted seals (Otaria sp.) and some land animals. The main economic activities certainly continued to be hunting and above all gathering. A significant feature in this context is the abundance of squashes and pumpkins (Lagenaria siceraria and Cucurbita moschata), which were already well known from finds in the Equatorial Andes (they are found in the Siches phase of Piura) down to southern Peru.

The peoples of Chilca lived in small circular houses dug out of heaps of garbage. The village of Chilca may perhaps have contained up to a hundred families; in Encanto, on the other hand, although the houses were larger than those of previous hunting groups, the camps were still seasonal with a more scattered distribution of population.

Engel (1966) mentions another place, about 400 km south of Chilca on the banks of the Rio Grande de Nazca, where there was built on a slope a group of houses made from willow or acacia poles supporting roofs made of the same material.

This type of dwelling also existed in Chilca, but there it was made from reeds tied together with rush cords. Twenty or more houses were found there. Christopher Donnan (1964) gives a detailed description of house no. 12, estimated according to the C¹⁴ dating to be about 5,400 years old. The house is conical with a diameter of 2.4 m, built in a circular hole about 35 cm deep. It is made basically of intertwined reeds (Gynerium sagitarum) with poles joined together in the upper part, the entire construction being covered with rush fibres (Cyperus sp.). There were several graves in the interior and the size of the house indicated that it was a family home; although Engel's calculation seems exaggerated, the settlement is quite a large one and confirms the village-type dwelling pattern of that period.

The Rio Grande de Nazca group, although slightly later, has small, low walls made of pebbles held together with mud and apparently covered with earth.

A further symptomatic change may have occurred in the treatment of the dead. Although the method of burial was relatively simple, the grave furnishings were quite distinctive, for example rush matting and sometimes nets with long fringes and knots on the end. Something that might be related to particular funerary rites is the find in Chilca of eight heaps of corpses, in which the bones were partly burnt and mixed with numerous bones of human beings or sea-mammals beneath a layer of ashes. This is not, of course, necessarily a sign of cannibalism, although the possibility cannot be ruled out. In Rio Grande archaeologists have found ossuaries of individuals who had been thrown into pits dug in sandy ground. They were clothed and accompanied by implements used for everyday tasks. This same type of burial was found near Paracas on the Cabeza Larga site and since it is of the same age it must correspond to the same level of development.

The grave furnishings are a good indicator of the formal development of textile technology. Plant fibres, especially rushes, were used to make twined fabrics, a technique that does not require weaving equipment. It consists of two active fibres crossing each other around one or two passive fibres (warp). At this stage, the woven material was already being used to make cloth capable of covering the body, alongside the possible use of skins; small baskets, bags and other containers were also being made. In Cabeza Larga archaeologists found a short rush skirt believed to be the direct antecedent of later similar garments known as 'waras' to the peoples of the Andes.

The discovery of cloth-making by fibre combination actually occurred around 10,000 years ago, when 'twining' of fibres first began; from then on, the favourite materials were rushes (Juncos sp.), maguey or cabuya (Fourcraea andina) and bulrushes (Typha angustifolia).

The Chilca materials also give us an indication of the possible impact of the new mixed farming-gathering-hunting economy on the population. According to Engel (1966), only one of the corpses in Chilca had reached a relatively advanced age, of around 50 or 60 years. Most died between the ages of 20 and 30 and many in early childhood. Living conditions in previous periods were probably therefore much harsher still and life expectation much shorter, since by contrast with the earlier period an increase in population is discernible between 7,000 and 5,000 years ago.

Materials are scanty in the mountains and even in the Guitarrero cave – phase III – they are inadequate. On the puna and the highlands in general, the changes are not significant, although there appears to have been some growth in population, associated perhaps with pastoral farming. In Ayacucho, MacNeish (1969) notes that the crucial period, represented by the Piki phase, corresponding to this era, provides indications that previous nomadic habits had not died out. There was camelid-hunting on the puna, while in the gorges and medium-altitude valleys, such as that containing the cave of Pikimachay, there are remains of what were probably domesticated guinea-pigs (*Cavia* sp.), birds and a very small number of deer, together with squash and pumpkins which, according to MacNeish, means that these peoples of the lower levels basically gathered plants and small animals (rodents and birds), grew a small number of plants and hunted very seldom, although the same peoples did hunt on the puna.

We must assume that something similar was happening throughout the northern and central Andes, where the system included intensive exchanges among hunters. For the time being, this might account for the spread of farming based on Leguminosae and Cucurbitaceae both in the mountains and on the coast, although some mountain products such as the oca and ullucu could not be grown on the coast.

At the dawn of the fifth millennium BP, we find a territory occupied basically by Neolithic communities engaging to varying degrees in agricultural activities and animal husbandry. Products as important as cotton and maize had not yet been or were still in the process of being domesticated, in and beyond the Andes region. We have recently found evidence that they appeared around 5,000 years ago or shortly afterwards. These products, together with effective interregional exchanges of products of macrothermal origin such as the peanut (*Arachis hypogaea*), the sweet potato (*Ipomoea batatas*), the yucca or bitter cassava (*Manihot utilissima*) and so on, with microthermal products such as the potato, the quinoa and the oca, and mesothermal products such as the lima bean, the kidney bean and so on, are part of a substantial enrichment of the Neolithic that generated revolutionary social change between the fifth and fourth millennia BP.

BIBLIOGRAPHY

ADOVASIO, J. M.; MASLOWSKI, R. 1980. Cordage, Basketry and Textiles. In: LYNCH, T. (ed.), *Guitarrero Cave*. Ann Arbor.

BELL, R. E. 1965. *Investigaciones arqueológicas en el Sitio de El Inga, Ecuador*. Quito.

CARDICH, A. 1958. Los yacimientos de Lauricocha y la nueva interpretación de la prehistoria Peruana. *Stud. Praehist.* (Buenos Aires), No. 1.

—— 1964. Lauricocha: fundamentos para una prehistoria de los Andes Centrales. *Stud. Praehist.* (Buenos Aires), No. 3.

CHAUCHAT, C. 1975. The Paijan Complex, Pampa de Cupisnique, Peru. *Nawpa Pacha* (Berkeley), No. 13, pp. 85–96.

CHAUCHAT, C.; LACOMBE, J. P. 1984. El hombre de Paijan? El más antiguo Peruano? *Gac. Arqueol. Andina* (Lima), Vol. 11, pp. 4–6, 12.

CHAUCHAT, C.; ZEVALLOS, J. 1979. Una punta en cola de pescado procedente de la Costa Norte del Perú. *Nawpa Pacha* (Berkeley), No. 17, pp. 143–6.

COHEN, M. N. 1981. *La Crisis alimentaria de la prehistoria*. Madrid.

CRAIG, A. K.; PSUTY, N. P. 1968. *The Paracos Papers: Studies in Marine Desert-Ecology I, Reconnaissance Report*. Boca Raton. (Dep. Geogr., Fla. Atl. Univ., Occasi. Publ., 1.)

DOLLFUS, O. 1981. *El reto del Espacio Andino*. Lima.

DONNAN, C. B. 1964. An Early House from Chilca, Peru. *Am. Antiq.*, Vol. 30, pp. 137–44.

ENGEL, F. 1966. *Paracos: cien siglos de historia Peruana*. Lima.

—— 1972. New Facts about Pre-Columbian Life in the Andean Lomas. *Curr. Anthropol.*, Vol. 14, pp. 271–80.

FUNG, P.; CENZANO, C. F.; ZAVALETA, A. 1972. El taller lítico de Chivateros, Valle de Chillon. *Rev. Mus. Nac.* (Lima), Vol. 38, pp. 61–72.

HAWKES, J. G. 1967. The History of the Potato. *J. R. Hortic. Soc.* (London), Vol. 92, pp. 207–24, 249–62, 288–302, 364–5.

HESTER, J. J. 1973. Late Pleistocene Environments and Early Man in South America. In: GROSS, D. (ed.), *Peoples and Cultures of Native South America*. New York. pp. 4–18.

KAPLAN, L. 1965. Archaeology and Domestication of American Phaseolus (Beans). *Econ. Bot.*, Vol. 19, pp. 358–68.

—— 1980. Variation in the Cultivated Beans. In: LYNCH, T. (ed.), *Guitarrero Cave*. Ann Arbor.

LANNING, E. P. 1963. A Pre-agricultural Occupation of the Central Coast of Peru. *Am. Antiq.*, Vol. 28, pp. 360–71.

—— 1965. Early Man in Peru. *Sci. Am.*, Vol. 213, pp. 68–76.

—— 1967. *Peru before the Incas*. New Jersey.

—— 1970. Pleistocene Man in South America. *World Archaeol.*, Vol. 2, pp. 90–111.

LANNING, E. P.; HAMMEL, E. 1961. Early Lithic Industries in Western South America. *Am. Antiq.*, Vol. 27, pp. 139–54.

LANNING, E. P.; PATTERSON, T. C. 1967. Early Man in South America. *Sci. Am.*, Vol. 217, pp. 44–50.

LAVALLÉE, D.; JULIAN, M. 1975. El habitat prehistórico en la zona de San Pedro de Cajas, Junín. *Rev. Mus. Nac.* (Lima), Vol. 41, pp. 81–127.

LEMON, R. H.; CHURCHER, C. S. 1961. Pleistocene Geology and Palaeontology of the Talara Region, North West Peru. *Am. J. Sci.* (New Haven), Vol. 259, pp. 410–29.

LUMBRERAS, L. G. 1974. La evidencia etnobotánica en el tránsito de la economía recolectora a la producción de alimentos. In: *La Arqueología como Ciencia Social*. Lima. pp. 177–209.

—— 1976. *The Peoples and Cultures of Ancient Peru*. Washington, DC.

LYNCH, T. F. 1967. *The Nature of the Andean Preceramic*. Pocatello. (Idaho State Univ. Mus., Occas. Pap., 21.)

—— 1970. *Excavation at Quishqui Puncu in the Callejon de Huaylas, Peru*. Pocatello. (Idaho State Univ. Mus., Occas. Pap., 26.)

—— 1971. Preceramic Transhumance in the Callejon de Huaylas, Peru. *Am. Antiq.*, Vol. 36, pp. 139–48.

—— 1974. The Antiquity of Man in South America. *Quat. Res.*, Vol. 4, pp. 356–77.

—— (ed.) 1980. *Guitarrero Cave: Early Man in the Andes*. New York.

MACNEISH, R. S. 1969. *First Report of the Ayacucho Archaeological-Botanical Project*. Andover.

—— 1971. Early Man in the Andes. *Sci. Am.*, Vol. 224, pp. 36–46.

—— 1979. The Early Man Remains from Pikimachay Cave. In: HUMPHREY, R. L.; STANFORD, D. (eds), *Pre-llano Cultures of the Americas*. Washington, DC.

MACNEISH, R. S.; NELKEN-TERNER, A.; GARCIA COOK, A. 1970. *Second Annual Report of the Ayacucho Archaeological Project*. Andover.

MACNEISH, R. S.; PATTERSON, T. C.; BROWMAN, D. L. 1975. *The Central Peruvian Interaction Sphere*. Andover.

MACNEISH, R. S. et al. 1980. *Prehistory of the Ayacucho Basin, Peru*. Ann Arbor. Vol. 3.

—— 1981. *Prehistory of the Ayacucho Basin, Peru*. Ann Arbor. Vol. 2.

MATOS, M. R.; RICK, J. W. 1980. Los recursos naturales y el poblamiento precerámico de la Puna de Junín. *Rev. Mus. Nac.* (Lima), Vol. 44, pp. 23–64.

MAYER-OAKES, W. J. 1966. El Inga Projectile Points: Surface Collections. *Am. Antiq.*, Vol. 31, pp. 644–61.

OSSA, P. 1975. Fluted 'Fishtail' Projectile Point from La Cumbre, Peru. *Nawpa Pacha* (Berkeley), Vol. 13, pp. 97–8.

OSSA, P.; MOSELEY, M. E. 1971. La Cumbre: A Preliminary Report on Research into the Early Lithic Occupation of the Moche Valley, Peru. *Nawpa Pacha* (Berkeley), Vol. 9, pp. 1–16.

PATTERSON, T. C. 1966. Early Cultural Remains on the Central Coast of Peru. *Nawpa Pacha* (Berkeley), Vol. 4, pp. 145–53.

—— 1971. Central Peru: Its Population and Economy. *Archaeology* (New York), Vol. 24, pp. 316–21.

PICKERSGILL, B. 1969. The Archaeological Record of Chili Peppers (*Capsicum* sp.) and the Sequence of Plant Domestication in Peru. *Am. Antiq.*, Vol. 34, pp. 54–66.

RICHARDSON, J. B., III. 1972. The Preceramic Sequence and the Pleistocene and Post-Pleistocene Climate of Northwest Peru. In: LATHRAP, D.; DOUGLAS, J. (eds), *Variation in Anthropology.* Urbana.

RICK, J. W. 1980. *Prehistoric Hunters of the High Andes.* New York.

—— 1983. *Cronología, clima y subsistencia en el precerámico Peruano.* Lima.

SCHOBINGER, J. 1969. *Prehistoria de Sudamérica.* Madrid.

SMITH, C. E. 1980. Plant Remains from Guitarrero Cave. In: LYNCH, T. H. (ed.), *Guitarrero Cave.* Ann Arbor. pp. 87–120.

STEINMANN, H. 1930. *Geología del Perú.* Lima.

TOSI, J. A. 1960. *Zonas de vida natural en el Perú.* Lima. (Inst. Interam. Cienc. Agríc., Zona Andina, Bol. Téc., 15.)

TOWLE, M. A. 1961. *The Ethnobotany of Pre-Columbian Peru.* Chicago.

WILLEY, G. R. 1971. *An Introduction to American Archaeology: South America.* New Jersey. Vol. 2.

WING, E. 1977. Animal Domestication in the Andes. In: REED, C. A. (ed.), *The Origins of Agriculture.* The Hague. pp. 837–60.

—— 1980. Faunal Remains. In: LYNCH, T. H. (ed.), *Guitarrero Cave.* Ann Arbor. pp. 149–71.

WRIGHT, H. A.; BRADBURY, J. P. 1975. Historia ambiental del Cuaternario tardio en el area de la Planicie de Junín, Perú. *Rev. Mus. Nac.* (Lima), Vol. 41, pp. 75–6.

AFTERWORD

Sigfried J. De Laet

The first volume of the *History of Humanity* has taken the reader from anthropogenesis – the period which witnessed, some 2 to 2.5 million years ago, the emergence in the midst of the primates of the first being who, as a result of increased brain capacity and the ability to make tools must be considered as representative of the genus *Homo* – to the birth of the first city-states and the invention of writing, about 5,000 years ago. This period covers more than 99.5 per cent of the history of humankind. However, this enormous period remained practically unknown until the end of the eighteenth century or the beginning of the nineteenth century and its scarce remains were dated and interpreted in a rather fanciful way (see Introduction).

This ignorance of the most ancient past of humanity may seem, at first sight, rather strange, as all people, from the humblest to the most cultivated, feel in their innermost selves an innate desire to be informed about their past – not just on an individual level but first and foremost on a collective one – and to know more about the roots of the group to which they belong, whether it is their family, clan, village, community, tribe, town, ethnic group, people or nation. It was during this collective past that their customs, traditions and beliefs were in fact formed.

Today, when knowledge of writing has become virtually universal, the memory of the past is preserved in written documents and history books. However, writing is a relatively recent invention: in particularly favoured regions it goes back some 5000 years. Elsewhere, writing did not appear until quite recently.

Among peoples of the period before writing, the group's collective memory was conserved by 'oral tradition', passed on from generation to generation by specialized storytellers who were, in a way, the guardians of the group's past. They often memorized their stories by mnemonic techniques such as song and verse. One need think only of the rhapsodes of ancient Greece, the griots of Black Africa or the Celtic bards.

Today, it is recognized that there is a basis of historical truth in these oral traditions, at least if the events related do not date back more than 400 or 500 years. For more ancient periods, however, oral traditions are less and less trustworthy. Not only have an increasing number of anachronisms been unconsciously introduced into the stories, but many exaggerations and legendary, supernatural or mythical elements have also been included: monsters, supernatural creatures and even gods intervened. Some stories were of an essentially religious nature, for instance, the theogonies, mythologies, and tales of creation of the world and of humanity.

After the introduction of writing, many of these oral traditions were very soon written down. The most ancient books of the Bible, the *Iliad*, the *Odyssey*, the *Mahabharata*, the heroic Celtic myths, the Scandinavian Sagas, the Legend of Sundiata, founder of the Mali Empire, and many other stories, come from such oral traditions. These, we repeat, almost always have some element of truth in them. They have given rise not only to epics and legends but also to the sacred books of many religions and to history.

Nevertheless, even if all the supernatural elements they contain were ignored, oral traditions have, in the eyes of the historian, one major weakness, which is their lack of chronological perspective. As the events related go further back in time, they are put in a vague and cloudy past, expressed in stereotyped phrases such as 'quite a long time ago', or 'at the dawn of time'. Only in exceptional cases do some traditions seem, at first sight, to allow a more precise chronology, but when this is subjected to strict historical criticism it nevertheless nearly always proves disappointing. The Bible provides a striking example of this, since it contains many elements that give the impression that they can be used to establish an accurate chronology. The oldest reference to a biblical chronology goes back to the third century AD; it is mentioned by Rabbi Hanina in the Babylonian Talmud. It dates the second destruction of the Temple of Jerusalem (AD 70) to 3828 years after the Creation (which would thus date from 3758 before the Christian era). At the beginning of the fourth century AD the historian Eusebius of Caesarea made similar calculations. His biblical chronology was revised and added to a few years later by Hieronymus (St Jerome), one of the Fathers of the Church, to whom we owe the Vulgate – the first Latin translation of the Bible – as well as the Latin translation of the works of Eusebius. According to this chronology, the Creation of the world is supposed to have taken place about 4,000 years before the birth of Jesus. As St Jerome was one of the Church Fathers, his biblical chronology nearly became a dogma and remained generally accepted in the Christian world with slight modifications up to the end of the nineteenth century.

The same lack of chronological and historical perspective is also reflected in the fact that although many oral traditions say that the manufacture of iron objects was preceded by the manufacture of bronze weapons and tools, they do not, on the other hand, make any mention of the Stone Ages. A remarkable exception is the tradition preserved in the *De rerum Natura* by the Latin poet, Lucretius (first century BC), in which we read (lines 1285–9):

The first weapons were hands, nails and teeth
and also stones, branches broken from trees,
then flame and fire as soon as they were known.
Later the properties of iron and bronze were discovered,
and the use of bronze preceded that of iron.

This tradition is all the more remarkable because it places

mastery of fire after the beginning of the use of the stone, but before the Bronze Age. In many other traditions, the Bronze Age is preceded by a mythical Golden Age or the period of paradise on earth.

We should add that in many of these traditions, human beings, from the moment of their creation, were producers of food. According to Genesis, the two sons of Adam, Cain and Abel, were a farmer and a shepherd respectively. We find another example of the image of the first people as farmers in the mythology of the Mayas, according to which the gods created the first human from an ear of maize, the staple food of the inhabitants of Central America as soon as it was domesticated.

In practically all the cosmogonies, people were created by one or more gods. However, divine intervention was not limited to the Creation. Although the Stone Ages seem to be virtually absent from oral traditions, collective memory has, however, certainly preserved the memory of some of the most important stages of human progress, while attributing them to the intervention of one divinity or another. Here we give just two examples: the mastery of fire and the beginnings of agricultural life. One of the best-known myths of Ancient Greece is that of Prometheus, that Titan who is said not only to have created human beings (at least according to some versions of the myth), but also to have brought them fire stolen from the Olympian gods. As far as farming is concerned, humans are supposed to owe it to a kind divinity, according to the traditions of Egypt, Mesopotamia, Greece and Rome, as well as those of China, the Aztecs, the Incas and so on (see Chapter 37).

To conclude, oral traditions can provide valid information on the few centuries that preceded their transcription, provided that the anachronisms, exaggerations and errors that crept into them, as well as their mythical and fabulous elements, are discarded. The lively description of Mycenaean society and civilization that we find in the *Iliad* and *Odyssey* provides us with a good example. On the other hand, these traditions throw only faint light on a more distant past. The whole of that vast period that humanity must have lived through before the great cultural break that occurred when food production began (the subject of the first part of this volume) has been wiped from the collective memory; and the Neolithic has left only slight traces.

This nearly complete ignorance of prehistoric times lasted until the end of the eighteenth century, not only among the general public, but also among scientists. However, during the last years of the eighteenth century, and especially in the first half of the nineteenth, some truth began to come to light, thanks to the increasing progress of geology and palaeontology, though not without a fight against many preconceived notions and dogmas. It was only after violent controversies that around 1859 prehistoric research, especially that concerning the most ancient periods, was accepted as a scientific discipline (see Introduction). However, these discussions and controversies were limited to the world of researchers and scientists. As is shown by French and English literature, the general public began to show some interest in 'primitive times' only towards the end of the nineteenth century.

The picture offered by this volume is in stark contrast to the almost complete ignorance in which the oral tradition left us concerning the origins and first achievements of humanity. It is also profoundly different from the idea that the geologists and palaeontologists of the early nineteenth century had of early human times. Today, we find ourselves with such an accumulation of data of all kinds that it has become practically impossible for a single scientist to master them all and make a valid synopsis of them. And yet we feel that we are still only at the beginning of this prodigious voyage of exploration in search of our deepest roots since, every year, new discoveries are made that constantly modify and add to our knowledge of this distant past. Indeed, between the time these very words are written and the day the book is published new data may already have made several pages of it obsolete.

In this context, it is not superfluous to emphasize here two areas that seem to be of very great importance but have perhaps, in the book itself, occasionally been somewhat lost to sight. The first concerns some recent important upheavals in the state of our knowledge and also some substantial shortcomings and uncertainties in our documentation, that are often the reason for divergent and even contradictory interpretations. The second relates to the elucidation of the main stages which seem to us to have marked humanity's long trek from the animal state to civilization.

Where the first of these areas is concerned, the greatest upheaval in recent years has been the introduction of genetics and molecular biochemistry into the sciences of prehistory. Study of the modifications of DNA (the deoxyribonucleic acids present in cell nuclei and carrying the genetic characteristics) has in fact shown that the separation between the Panidae (chimpanzee and gorilla) and the hominians (*Australopithecus* and *Homo*) occurred only 5 to 6 million years ago, instead of 14 to 15 million years ago as previously accepted, whereas the gorilla and the chimpanzee appear to have become distinct from each other only about 3 million years ago. Another theory advanced by some biogeneticists, also based on cellular biochemistry and more especially on the study of the DNA of mitochondria, is still giving rise to considerable discussion because it seems almost incompatible with the data of palaeontology. It is generally held that Modern humans (*Homo sapiens sapiens*) are descendants of *Homo erectus* following different but parallel genetic lines; however, according to this new theory, Modern humans descend from a unique genetic line. In effect, the similarities which exist between small segments of the DNA in the genes of haemoglobin β in four contemporary populations of the world would indicate a very rapid diffusion of Modern humans from one unique source, supposedly situated in Africa. Moreover, the very slow changes (2 to 4 per cent every million years) that took place in the DNA of human mitochondria over the millennia, and are transmitted only through the female line, would suggest that *all* Modern human beings are from a single common female ancestor (or from a very small group) who lived between 280,000 and 140,000 years ago, probably in Africa (these dates are based on the frequency of change in the DNA and not on radiometric or other physical dating methods) (see J. D. Clark, Chapter 20). One understands that this 'Black Eve' theory has met with many reservations, from palaeontobiologists as well as from archaeologists.

There is another essential problem. Although we know today *how* life evolved from the time of the first living organisms, namely blue-green algae that appeared about 3,000 million years ago (the earth itself having then already been in existence for about 2,000 or 3,000 million years), up to the birth, 2 or 3 million years ago, after endless changes and dichotomies, of the first beings who could be classified in the genus *Homo*, we know virtually nothing about the *reasons* for this evolution. Climatic and environmental changes as well as geomorphological upheavals certainly contributed to it, but do not explain why the DNA changes at a more or less constant pace (geneticists speak of a 'molecular clock').

We can list more briefly some questions that still need a satisfactory answer, such as those concerning the genetic filiation between the proto-australopithecines and those who succeeded them, the australopithecines and humans, and the relationship between *Australopithecus africanus* (or *gracilis*), *Australopithecus robustus* (or *A. boisei*) and *Homo habilis*. At least six or seven models of human phylogeny have been presented with more or less convincing arguments, but each new discovery of fossil bones of Hominidae brings modifications to these models of the genealogy of the human family.

Another problem, clearly linked, concerns the possible manufacture of tools by the australopithicines.

Two other problems, of an archaeological nature, concern the transition from the Lower to the Middle Palaeolithic and the transition from the Middle to the Upper Palaeolithic. Although only a few decades ago these problems had not arisen, they appeared when it was realized that the great changes in the technique of manufacturing stone artefacts did not, as was previously maintained, match the morphological evolution of humankind. The equations Neanderthaler = Mousterian and *Homo sapiens sapiens* = blade cultures are no longer valid. This explains the overlappings, or contradictions, even, that the reader has doubtless noted in the different chapters on the period of the Neanderthalers and their contemporaries.

As far as the Middle and Upper Palaeolithic are concerned, it is becoming vital to abandon the traditional phylogenetic pattern of lithic industries. This pattern, devised over half a century ago and modified on several occasions since, had originally been drawn up for south-west France but had been extended to the whole of western and central Europe. It is increasingly criticized today because it contains errors and internal contradictions and does not provide consistent answers to questions raised by the great variation found in the typological composition of assemblages. A thorough revision is necessary to escape from the present impasse. This observation also holds good for all regions where remains from these periods have been found.

Despite the increasingly intense research of the past few years, there are still no answers to many questions concerning the Neolithic, such as the domestication of plants and animals as well as others related to the way in which the change was made from an economy based on hunting, fishing and gathering to a food-producing economy. In addition, in many regions, research on this subject has only just started.

Finally, we looked earlier (see Chapter 36) at the problems relating to the period from the beginning of food production to the beginning of civilized urban life. We need not repeat what was said except to emphasize, once again, that the model followed is based essentially on data provided by research in western Asia and Egypt. These data are nevertheless still very incomplete. More than anything else we need the complete excavation of one or more of the sites that were occupied throughout the whole period being considered here. We must not forget that only a very small part of one of the main sites, Çatal Hüyük, has been excavated, and that the lower levels have not yet been examined. In addition, we know virtually nothing about the beginning of urban life in Egypt, where the 'Historic' Age started a century earlier than in western Asia, since no pre-urban site of the Predynastic period has yet been excavated.

After this survey of some important problems that remain unsolved, it is not superfluous to give a general portrayal of the physical, cultural and social development of humanity during the period covered by this first volume.

When human beings first appeared, they were physically relatively weak, without fangs or claws to attack prey or fur to protect themselves from the cold. Most animals, on the contrary, during their evolution, acquired bodily features that linked them to a particular climate, environment or mode of life, such that a polar bear or a mammoth would not be able to live in the tropics, an elephant is associated with plant food and so on. Humans, on the contrary, precisely because they have no special physical characteristics which necessarily link them to one particular region, climate or diet, were able to adapt quite quickly to living more or less anywhere (except in regions with extreme climates) and to seek the most varied means of subsistence. They also had other assets apart from this adaptability. It will not be irrelevant to describe again, in brief outline, the main stages of the being whom Desmond Morris, in a highly successful book, called *The Naked Ape*.

The first steps in the evolution that led humans to the top of the hierarchy of living beings were made during the 60 million years during which our ancestors belonged to the order of primates. Some of them then acquired important characteristics that were to be found later in humans. Thus, more than 55 million years ago, adapiformes already had an opposable thumb, an adaptation to arboreal locomotion from which our hands originate. Adapiformes were succeeded by haplorhines whose eye sockets, arranged frontally, meant that stereoscopic vision had been acquired. Later still, between 25 to 30 million years ago, some catarrhines (or Old World simians) had a dentition similar to ours; about the same time, a Fayum primate, *Aegyptopithecus*, by the transformation of the encephal structure, marks the transition between catarrhines and hominoids.

The next stage was cultural. During his excavations at Fort Ternan, in Kenya, in 1960, Louis Leakey discovered, in a site with kenyapithecine remains 14 million years old, natural stones with crushed edges and long splintered bones. He claimed that these stones could have been used by *Kenyapithecus* to crack nuts or to break bones to extract their marrow. A similar method is still used today by chimpanzees. They could be the oldest known *tools*, but they are rough, not intentionally made tools. *Kenyapithecus* must then have been the first *tool-user*, but not yet a *toolmaker*. The making of artefacts is peculiar to humans and to them alone.

Shortly afterwards, the hominoid primates divided into two families, that of the Pongidae (comprising amongst others *Sivapithecus/Ramapithecus*, ancestors of the orangutan) and that of Hominini (comprising the ancestors of the big African apes – gorilla and chimpanzee, and the hominians).

Finally, according to recent biogenetic data it was not until relatively recently (about 5 or 6 million years ago) that the hominian branch (*Australopithecus* and *Homo*) separated from that of the Panidae (chimpanzee and gorilla). Opinions vary. According to the rather attractive ecologeographic hypothesis advanced by Yves Coppens, the collapse of the Rift Valley, separating east and south Africa from central and west Africa, was the cause of this dichotomy. Western and central Africa remained a very humid zone with intertropical rain forests, where the Panidae remained and where their descendants (gorillas and chimpanzees) still live today. On the contrary, east and austral Africa became a region with large, open environments; the hominians whose remains are found exclusively in that region were forced to adapt themselves to their new surroundings. This adaptation to the prairie and the savannah is the reason why hominians about 3.5 to 4 million years ago became bipeds. The oldest traces of this phenomenon are the famous footprints of Laetoli.

It was one of the most important stages in the process of hominization. The standing position deeply affected the anatomy of our ancestors of this period (see Chapter 2). The foot (where the big toe had lost its opposability) became the main organ of propulsion, whereas the hand, freed from this task, was entirely used for prehension. Its increased dexterity (thanks to the development of the brain) was a necessary prerequisite for the making of tools. Finally, the skull was also deeply modified and, because of the displacement of the occipital foramen to beneath the skull, the brain was able to grow in volume. The volume of the brain, about 400 cc in *Australopithecus afarensis* and about 500 cc in *Australopithecus africanus* (or *gracilis*) and *Australopithecus robustus*, increased to about 700 cc in *Homo habilis*, to between 900 and 1,100 cc in *Homo erectus* and, finally, to between 1,250 and 1,450 cc in *Homo sapiens*.

The period extending from 3.5 to 1.5 million years ago saw the dichotomy between australopithicines and *Homo*. But it still poses quite a few problems. Nearly every year over the last thirty years, excavations have brought to light new fossils that raise new questions, mostly concerning phylethic relations between the different sub-families of the Hominidae. No one believes any longer that there was unilinear development, and the idea of a complex ramification, of which *Homo habilis* would have been only one branch, seems to be increasingly gaining ground. We can recall here the sensation caused by the discovery, at Hadar in 1974, of the oldest Hominidae skeleton (40 per cent intact), called Lucy and about 3 million years old. One year later, at Hadar, bones of at least thirteen different *Australopithecus afarensis*, all of them probably having died at the same time, and which were even older than Lucy, were also found at the same site (333), lying together ('the First Family'). This was the first direct proof that Hominini lived in groups, a fact that had, however, already been extrapolated from ethological data on the social behaviour of gorillas and chimpanzees. This organization in hierarchical groups, headed by a 'chief', probably goes back much further than the Hominini, perhaps, even to the hominoid primates.

We have finally arrived at *Homo*. The most ancient representative of this genus known at present is *Homo habilis*, whose bones are thought to date back to about 2 million years ago, but whose most ancient cultural remains could date back to 2.6 million years ago: these are small fragments of quartzite found by J. Chavaillon in the Omo Valley, which are supposed to prove that *Homo* (since it seems an established fact that only humans *make* tools) already existed then.

Compared with the australopithecines, *Homo habilis* not only had a bigger brain but also had a qualitatively more developed one. The internal surface of the cranium indeed bears traces of the encephalon, and indicates a marked development of the endocranial morphology. Broca's area (the speech centre) was thus already quite developed, which would indicate that *Homo habilis* had the intellectual aptitude to develop a certain form of complex language. Nevertheless, the buccopharyngeal cavity was still not large enough to enable truly articulate sounds to be made. Articulate speech was, however, an established fact as far as *Homo erectus* was concerned. We know the essential role that language has played in the cultural development of humanity, for instance in the communication of experience acquired by an individual member of a group to the members of that group, and also in the education of children.

Homo habilis was the first tool-*maker*. The lithic industry of those first people is well known (Oldowan, based on pebble tools, *choppers* and *chopping tools*), but it is obvious that they also made tools from wood and bone, which the soil, however, did not preserve.

Unlike the Panidae, humans, apart from temporary encampments occupied for only a few days, set up more or less permanent 'base camps', which permitted a division of labour between members of the groups and did not compel the sick, the disabled or children to follow the group on its daily peregrinations. Some camps consisted of light huts, as indicated, for example, by the circle of large stones at Site DK I at Olduvai or the raised site of Gomboré I at Melka Kunturé. Unlike the australopithecines, *Homo habilis* was an omnivore and was no longer satisfied with a diet exclusively of vegetables, bones in the settlements indicating the importance of meat. Humans hunted small animals but were still too weak and had too few weapons to hunt the big game whose remains are found in their encampments. These bones and teeth are more than likely from carcasses that humans had fought the vultures for, or from prey killed and then abandoned by carnivores.

There is no doubt that *Homo erectus* is descended from *Homo habilis*. As this evolution was a gradual one, it is not easy to distinguish clearly between the two during the transition period. *Homo erectus*, taller and heavier than *Homo habilis*, with bigger bones and a bigger brain, appeared in Africa around 1.6 million years ago. *Homo habilis* had remained within the confines of Africa, but *Homo erectus*, for reasons still obscure, gradually spread to vast territories where humans had not yet ventured. Remains of *Homo erectus* are found not only in eastern and southern Africa but also in the Maghreb (Ternifine, Algeria, around 700,000 years ago; Salé, Morocco, around 350,000 years ago). They occur in western Asia, dating to shortly after 1 million years ago. The only human remains found at Zuttiyeh, in connection with a Jabrudian industry, are those of an evolved *Homo erectus*, sometimes considered a pre-*sapiens*, who lived about 150,000 years ago. From there – most probably passing through the Dardanelles and the Bosphorus –*Homo erectus* went to Europe, where the oldest site, at Solheihac, in France, dates back to between 970,000 and 900,000 years ago. The oldest European sites are all in southern Europe, but from around 500,000 years ago *Homo erectus* also occupied temperate Europe (up to around 51° to 54° N). We also find traces in south Asia (India, Narmada skull), China (where the lower level of Zhoukoudian is dated to around 700,000 years ago), and finally, in Java, apparently posterior to 700,000 years ago. The length of the *Homo erectus* period and the lack of communication between the different regional groups resulted in certain biological divergences. Thus, *Homo erectus* of China (the *Sinanthropus* or *Homo pekinensis*) already had certain Mongoloid features which were transmitted to the first *Homo sapiens* in the region. Those in Java (the *Pithecanthropus*) had Australoid features, which, through the later *Homo erectus* of Ngandong and the *Homo sapiens* of Wajak (Wadjack) (Java) and Kow Swamp (Australia), would be transmitted to the Australian aborigines. In eastern and southern Africa, *Homo erectus* is the ancestor of the *Homo sapiens* of these regions. Finally, in Europe, *Homo erectus* was the ancestor, through the pre-Neanderthalers, of *Homo sapiens neanderthalensis*, but the latter died out without leaving any descendants. Data from biological anthropology would seem to indicate, therefore, that after leaving Africa *Homo erectus* probably engendered a series of regional lineages, each with its particular features which can be found among the present populations of certain major regions. This generally accepted theory is now being challenged by the recent thesis of some geneticists, according to which *all* present-day people have descended from the African *Homo sapiens*.

The stone tools of *Homo erectus* derive from those of *Homo habilis* and, in Africa, it has been possible to trace their evolution from the Oldowan to the Acheulean. Archaic items such as pebble-tools and choppers are found there, as well as new tools such as bifaces, hatchets, polyhedrons and spherical bola stones. In addition, these tools gradually took on more regular and repetitive forms. Outside Africa, considerable regional differences can be seen. In China, the survival of choppers is more marked than elsewhere. The prevalence of bifaces is generally considered a characteristic of the Acheulean industry, but within this Acheulean is a very great variety of assemblages and the term 'Acheulean' refers to quite dissimilar industries whose divergences can have very different causes such as chronological evolution, the difference in environment, the activities of which these assemblages are a reflection and so on. Wooden and bone industries have left only few traces, but their importance must have been considerable. Settlement structures evolved. However, quite divergent interpretations have been given of the remains of encampments. These on occasion seem to be divided into distinct areas, sometimes set aside for a specific occupation (such as a toolmaker's workshop). In Europe, and in China (Zhoukoudian) we find the first inhabited caves.

Social organization must have remained more or less similar to the social organization of *Homo habilis*. *Homo erectus* continued to live mainly on dead animals, but hunting became increasingly important as shown, for example, by the great abundance of Cervidae remains at Zhoukoudian. The beginning of big-game hunting, mainly through the use of natural traps, can be noted. At La Cotte de Saint-Brelade (Jersey) a ravine under a rocky spur has yielded the dismembered bones of a large number of mammoths and rhinoceroses.

The most important contribution of *Homo erectus* to the cultural development of humanity was without any doubt the mastery of fire. In Africa, traces of fire attributable to *Homo erectus* are rare and could be due to brush fires. On the other hand, undoubted remains of hearths have been found in Europe and China. In Europe, they are still few and far between in the Mediterranean zone, but they increase above all from 0.5 million years onwards, particularly in the non-Mediterranean temperate zone into which *Homo erectus* started to move around this period. This advance northwards would hardly have been possible without the mastery of fire, for fire was absolutely vital as a protection against the rigours of winter. The increase in cave dwellings was also due to the same cause. It was also around the same period that people started to wear fur to protect themselves from the cold. Fire must also have protected open-air encampments and cave entrances against attacks by predators. It was also used to harden the tips of wooden hunting-spears and possibly to roast meat.

The problems posed by the passage from the Lower to the Middle Palaeolithic have already been examined. After a long existence of nearly 1.5 million years, *Homo erectus* gradually engendered *Homo sapiens*. The date of the latter's appearance varies from region to region. The different phyletic lines of descent have been considered above, and the morphological features present regional differences. *Homo sapiens* is primarily characterized by an increase in the volume of the brain (which reached a capacity of 1,450 cc). The first *Homo sapiens*, prior to the appearance of *Homo sapiens sapiens*, are often designated as 'Palaeoanthropians', whereas *Homo sapiens sapiens* are referred to as 'Modern' humans.

In eastern and southern Africa, a few skulls, such as those at Broken Hill (Zambia), dated to around 130,000 years ago, and at Ngaloba (Tanzania), mark the transition from *Homo erectus* to *Homo sapiens*. But the evolution continued at a very quick pace in this region, where one finds archaic *Homo sapiens*, such as at Bodo (Ethiopia) and Lake Eyasi (Tanzania), soon replaced by Modern people, notably at Kibbish 2 in the Omo Valley in Ethiopia (from around 130,000), Border Cave (Province of Natal) (from around 115,000) and Klasies River Mouth (near Capetown) (from around 100,000). The finds from those sites are at present the most ancient Modern remains known. From certain characteristics, they could be the ancestors of some present populations of the region.

Another line developed in the Maghreb, starting with the *Homo erectus* of this region (Salé, Ternifine), through the ancient *Homo sapiens* (Rabat, Sidi Abderrahman) and the more recent *Homo sapiens* (Haua Fteah, Mugharet el 'Aliya, Jebel Irhoud) – until quite recently erroneously considered to be Neanderthalers – and ending with the Iberomaurusian Modern human (Dar es-Soltan).

In China, the evolution goes from *Sinanthropus*, through the Dali Man, who existed at the end of the Middle Pleistocene, and the Xujiayao Man, who were at the point of transition between *Homo erectus* and *Homo sapiens*, around 100,000, and ends with the Maba Man, a Palaeanthropian. This line led to the Mongoloid populations.

In Java, another line went from *Pithecanthropus* to *Homo erectus soloensis* of Ngandong, who was more evolved than *Pithecanthropus* (around 125,000 to 100,000 years ago), and ended with the *Homo sapiens* of Wajak (Java) and of Kow Swamp (Australia) around 20,000, who had very distinct Australoid features.

The situation is less clear in western Asia and one does not know if the evolved *Homo erectus* of Zuttiyeh has left any descendants. Neanderthalers immigrated from Europe (around 100,000 years ago according to B. Vandermeerch (Chapter 9) or around 75,000 years ago according to O. Bar-Yosef (Chapter 24), then co-habitated there for several millennia with Modern humans (whose origin – most likely Africa (?) – remains uncertain), the latter having arrived there at an uncertain date (around 100,000 to 90,000 years ago according to some palaeontologists, or around 50,000 years ago according to others). These Modern people (Qafzeh, Skhul) seem to be ancestors of the Cro-Magnons of the European Aurignacian. It is noteworthy that both these Neanderthalers and these Modern people produced the same Mousterian industry.

Finally, in Europe, pre-Neanderthalers originated from *Homo erectus*, the most ancient of whom (Tautavel, Steinheim, Petralona) are still very close to *Homo erectus* (350,000 to 250,000 years ago). Among the first Palaeanthropians we should mention those of Biache-Saint-Vaast, Swanscombe, La Chaise, Salzgitter-Lebenstedt, Ehringsdorf and Saccopastore. Then come the 'classical' Neanderthalers themselves (from c.100,000 to c.35,000 years ago). Around 100,000 years BP, the Neanderthalers spread over western and central Asia (Teshik-Tash, in Uzbekistan). In western Asia they lived together (from at least 50,000 years ago) with *Homo sapiens sapiens*. It is probable that this coexistence was peaceful for, according to some anthropologists, there was interbreeding between the two subspecies. The Neanderthaler line is the only one to have disappeared without leaving any descendants. We do not know whether the Neanderthalers met with a brutal end, exterminated by the *Homo sapiens sapiens* of the early Upper Palaeolithic in Europe. The discovery of the Saint-Césaire skull, in a Châtelperronian context, indicates, however, that for a few thousand years, Neanderthalers and the first European *Homo sapiens sapiens* (the Aurignacians, coming probably from western Asia) lived side by side in Europe. Whatever happened, the Neanderthalers disappeared for good around 35,000 years ago.

Despite these numerous anthropological differences, the people of the Middle Palaeolithic, scattered over the Ancient World, had very many cultural characteristics in common, which marked a new development in human culture. There are many more archaeological sites attributable to the first Palaeoanthropians than sites with remains of *Homo erectus*, and it can probably be deduced that the density of the human population was increasing. The area occupied by human beings extended and now included the northern periglacial zones. Material culture obviously made some progress, with, in the different industries, more specialized artefacts of stone, bone and wood and increasingly standardized forms. We should recall here that the equation Neanderthaler = Mousterian (applying, obviously, to Europe and western Asia) is no longer accepted today, since it is established that the Palaeo-anthropians participated in the last phases of the Acheulean and also in the first phases of the Upper Palaeolithic. In addition, the main complexes such as the Mousterian, the African Middle Stone Age and so on, vary a great deal; these terms probably refer to rather different cultures (see p. 642).

The way of life also evolved. The first Palaeo-anthropians, without giving up their tradition of feeding on dead animals, increasingly hunted less dangerous animals, but were not reluctant to attack big game. The exploitation of marine resources (fish, seals, whales washed ashore and so on) also became an important source of subsistence, both in Europe and in Africa. There were many cave dwellings, but we also know of many open-air sites, with small huts (or tents), one for each natural family. However, remains of bigger dwellings (10 by 7 m) have also been found on certain sites such as Molodova I (on the Dnieper) and Ripiceni-Izvor (Romania). These had wooden or mammoth bone frameworks on which skins were hung, and contained several families. The theory has been put forward that if the natural family was the basic unit, there was a larger social unit of between twenty-five and thirty individuals. Raw materials (stones and pigments) sometimes came from more than 100 km away. In addition, we know in Africa of two sites – the oldest so far – where mining was carried out. These are the chert pebble pits at Qena in Upper Egypt (Middle Palaeolithic) and the site for the extraction of specular iron ore (used as a pigment) at Lion Cavern in Swaziland. Here can be seen not only the beginning of mining but also, in embryo, a very primitive barter system.

Although great progress was therefore made in material culture, the great importance of the period resides in the fact that, for the first time, very clear traces of spiritual culture are found. Whereas it seems quite clear that *Homo habilis* and *Homo erectus*, like the hominoid primates, were not concerned about the corpses of their fellow beings, among Palaeo-anthropians one finds tombs that had been deliberately made and, in some cases, traces even of the dead having been buried with some ritual. On occasion tools, and even, in one case, at Shanidar, flowers, were put next to the body. We do not know, however, if all the dead were entitled to such funerary rites. However that might be, Palaeoanthropians – in Europe, as well as in western Asia and southern Africa – thus already had some eschatological ideas. They also already had the capability of forming abstract notions. Thus bones and stones have been found on which series of parallel grooves had been made, and these are thought to have been either a primitive calculating system or a rudimentary calendar. The use of colouring materials (such as ochre, haematite, specular iron) for burials, body paint or colouring objects of wood, bone, stone or skin, almost certainly had a symbolical or magical significance. The Neanderthal skull of Monte Circeo (Italy), the occipital foramen of which had been purposely widened – perhaps to remove the brain – could indicate the existence of cannibalism (possibly of a magical nature). The existence of bear worship by the Neanderthalers is still the subject of lively controversy (see, for example, Chapter 12, where K. Valoch opposes this theory, and Chapter 13, where V. P. Alexeev is, on the contrary, in favour of it). Finally, objects of bone and stone dating from the end of the Palaeolithic, engraved with abstract decorations and even, in one case, a stylized animal, have been found at several Neanderthal sites in France, former Czechoslovakia and the former USSR. It seems, then, that the beginnings of art go back not to the Upper Palaeolithic, as accepted until very recently, but to the Neanderthal period. Neanderthalers, for a long time represented as too primitive to have a spiritual culture, were then at the very least as advanced as the Modern humans of Africa and western Asia who were their contemporaries.

We have already mentioned above some of the problems posed by the transition from the Middle to the Upper Palaeolithic. As long as prehistoric research was concentrated in Europe, a distinction was made between the two, both from the point of view of anthropology (appearance of *Homo sapiens sapiens* and disappearance of Neanderthalers) and from that of archaeology (appearance of blade industries, beginnings of spiritual culture). However, we know that Modern humans were living in southern Africa already 100,000 years ago and that they had developed there an early blade industry in the Middle Stone Age; that in western Asia, they lived together with the Neanderthalers from around 50,000 years ago; that, in Europe, at the beginning of the Palaeolithic, Neanderthalers were living side by side with *Homo sapiens sapiens* for a few thousand years before disappearing around 35,000 years ago, and finally, that Neanderthalers were in no way the brutish louts that they were once thought to be but had developed a spiritual culture in the Middle Palaeolithic, which contained in embryo most of the facets of the culture that would flourish in the Upper Palaeolithic. The passage from the Middle to the Upper Palaeolithic was, therefore, even in Europe, a very gradual one.

Around 40,000 years ago, human beings considerably extended their territory. Australoid populations (perhaps the descendants of the *Pithecanthropus* of Java) occupied New Guinea, Australia and Tasmania, which they could not have done without some means of sailing (perhaps rafts or canoes or both – see Chapter 28). On the other hand, populations with Mongoloid features (possibly descendants of the *Sinanthropus* of China) occupied Japan and arrived in Alaska via Beringia and progressively occupied the American continent down to Tierra del Fuego. From this period, human beings occupied most of the world's landmass apart from the part covered by ice-caps (northern and southern) and most of the Pacific islands (the most important being those of New Zealand), which were not inhabited until much later.

The later Palaeolithic occurred entirely within the last glaciation, when large parts of Europe, Asia and North America were covered by tundra and periglacial steppe and the more southern zones, less warm and rainier than today, had vast stretches of savannah. Men had now become mainly hunters while women collected edible plants. Their tools and weapons had become much more efficient because of different factors such as improved stone-cutting techniques, use of more diversified raw materials (bone, ivory, horn, reindeer and red-deer antlers) and the invention of new weapons. The weapons were mainly projectiles (which implies empirical knowledge of some of the laws of mechanics) such as much more manageable assegais than the heavy hunting-spears of the past, spear-throwers, harpoons and, especially at the end of the period, bows and arrows – all weapons which made it possible to attack game from a distance, very often after driving it, with great shouts and the waving of burning torches, to swamps or sheer cliffs.

Animals living in herds were the ones chiefly hunted. This implies the collaboration of a number of hunters from outside the immediate family, which could indicate that the basic social unit comprised several families. In addition, it is probable that each group had its own hunting ground and that it was guided by a 'chief'.

We saw, in the previous period, the appearance of supernatural beliefs. These beliefs and magic or religious practices had become extremely important, as shown by funerary rites, anthropomorphic and animal statuettes and cave art. Another person, apart from the chief, dominated the social group, namely the 'witch doctor' or 'shaman', to whom was attributed the power of communicating with spirits. This individual had to secure the group's survival through magical practices, by ensuring the success of the hunt, for example. It is at this time that myths appeared, handed down from generation to generation by the witch doctor. We should mention here the theory that caves where parietal art flourished might have been communal sanctuaries where different groups – related to each other by blood ties and through exogamy – met on some days to take part in magical ceremonies. Whatever the truth of the matter, the social organization of the Upper Palaeolithic hunters remained relatively simple.

At that period already, many groups were specialist hunters and preferred only one kind of quarry, such as mammoths (in Moravia), wild horses (for instance at Solutré), reindeer (the Magdalenians, the Hamburgians and so on) or aurochs (in Egypt). The women gathered fruits and edible plants and also selectively gathered the tastiest and most nourishing plants. This implies the beginning of an empirical knowledge of plant and animal biology, which was going to be of great importance after the end of the Ice Age.

We have examined at length above the consequences, for the hunter-gatherers of the Upper Palaeolithic, of the climatic and environmental changes caused by the end of the Ice Age (see Chapter 36). After a period of confusion and crisis, people progressively adapted to these new conditions of life, with new hunting methods, better adapted to the pursuit of forest game, and with gathering and the exploitation of marine resources becoming more important in their diet. It is possible to see that a large number of these Epipalaeolithic or Pre-Neolithic groups exploited their biotope rationally so as to obtain from it the highest possible yield.

The practice of selective hunting and the selective gathering of plants contained in embryo the essential elements of the Neolithic way of life based on food production by agriculture and animal husbandry. We have already dealt at length (see Chapters 36 to 38) with the reasons that made communities rear certain animals and cultivate certain plants (what was called – not altogether correctly – the 'Neolithic revolution'). We will not return to that here. Similarly, we will not dwell on how the Neolithic way of life progressively spread from a few 'nuclear' regions (such as western Asia, Upper Egypt, China, South-East Asia, Central America, the high Andean plateaux).

On the other hand, it will not be irrelevant to take another brief look at the consequences of the passage to food production, since this was one of the most important stages in the history of humankind. From the technical point of view, stress can be laid on the importance of making pots and the invention of weaving. The Neolithic way of life led to a profound modification in the diet. In the Upper Palaeolithic it was still mainly a meat diet but had become more diversified in the Mesolithic. In the Neolithic, however, it was based mainly on cereals (wheat in Western Asia and Europe, rice in southern and eastern Asia, sorghum and millet in Africa, maize in America). In addition, animal husbandry added an entirely new and important item to the daily diet – milk and its by-products (butter and cheese).

Finally, the invention of pottery led to the preparation of food by cooking or boiling becoming widespread. The replacement of a meat diet by a mainly vegetable one necessitated the use of salt (for which salt gathering and mining duly took place, and which became a keenly traded item). The Neolithic way of life also caused an unprecedented population increase. The transition to food production had the most profound consequences, however, as regards society and the economy. The first peasants, who were tied to their fields, settled down and lived in villages, where they put up strong timber and mud buildings and sometimes even dry-stone ones – dwellings, barns and cowsheds – which replaced the previous cave dwellings and primitive huts. In those villages there was a growing distinction between the different social categories. There was, on the one hand, greater specialization of activities (farmers, stock-breeders and shepherds, potters, weavers, stonecutters, carpenters and the like) and, on the other, increasingly complex social stratification.

We have already encountered the 'chief' and the 'witch doctor' of the Upper Palaeolithic communities, but their role changed profoundly in the Neolithic. The 'chief' became the 'king', whose powers were increasingly of a military nature and whose functions became hereditary. The 'witch doctor's' power became gradually coupled with secular, economic and political power. Whereas the Palaeolithic and Mesolithic groups of hunter-gatherers probably made a practice of sharing equally the produce of hunting and gathering, the transition to food production put an end to this interdependence and reciprocity, which were replaced by competition for possession of the greatest possible quantity of resources. Here we see the advent of 'property', which also brought its concomitants – theft, plunder and war. Wars for possession of a neighbouring community's property were relatively frequent, as borne out by the fact that the great majority of Neolithic villages were fortified.

A Neolithic village, with its highly diversified activities, the problem of relations between the peasants and the first specialized workers who had to be paid in kind for their labour, and the need to undertake certain major works in common (such as the construction of fortifications), required set customs, accepted by all, for the harmonious government of relations between the inhabitants. It is in this *mos maiorum*, these unwritten laws, that the laws of the historical period have their deepest roots.

Religious beliefs were also affected by the new way of life. These beliefs, which are also reflected in funerary rites, vary from region to region but nevertheless have a few main features in common. Neolithic religions are clearly fertility cults, with the duality of two opposite and complementary principles, the female principle (the Chinese 'Yin') represented by the earth, the moon and chthonic or moon goddesses of fertility, and the male principle (the 'Yang') represented by the sun, the sky, rain, sun gods, bull-gods and phallic representations. At the beginning of the period, when farming and the rearing of smaller livestock were still mainly female work, the female principle dominated, but when the domestication of the aurochs and the invention of the ard made field work too heavy for women, the male principle progressively grew in importance. The growing importance of religion and religious practices in daily life increased social distinctions to the advantage of the priests, successors of the former Shamans, who represented the deities on earth.

All the inventions that mark the beginning of the Neolithic indicate that human sense of observation had greatly developed. People began to ask themselves questions about the phenomena they noticed around them, and even if the answers to these were still often irrational, they were, nevertheless, the first seeds of the scientific outlook. To recapitulate what we said in Chapter 36, social and political institutions, the first elements of law, the spirit of observation and the germ of scientific thought are linked directly with the introduction of the Neolithic way of life, as are war and social stratification, characterized from then on – and for thousands of years – by the domination of the military and priestly castes. Also, whereas before, humans were subject, like other living beings, to the opportunities and limitations imposed on them by their environment, they now intervened to modify that environment and adapt it to their own needs, thus upsetting the biological equilibrium – which, as time went by, they were to do with increasing violence and increasing intensity, the serious consequences of which we are only just beginning to understand.

Once the Neolithic way of life had come into being, material progress simply increased and accelerated. More than 2 million years have passed from the beginnings of humanity to the present time, but only 8,000 years went by between the appearance of the first peasant communities and that of the first city-states, and only 5,000 years separate the city-states from us.

It only remains to sum up the evolution of human civilization during the 8,000 years that separate the first villages from the first civilized states. It should be remembered that the model used here is based on data relating to western Asia, Egypt and China. In the other regions the transition to urban life took place later and falls outside the chronological limits of this volume.

Three factors played a decisive role. First, account must be taken of a series of inventions and technical improvements both in animal husbandry (where the domestication of the dog, the goat and the sheep was followed by that of the pig and then of cattle about 9,000 to 8,000 years ago, and of the donkey and the horse about 6,000 to 5,000 years ago) and in farming. Here, in addition to the domestication of new plants for food and for fibre, the importance must be emphasized of the invention of the ard and of irrigation and

drainage, from about 9,000 to 8,000 years ago. These made possible the cultivation of soils that were otherwise either too dry or too wet, but called for major collective works such as the digging of ditches and the construction of dykes. The valleys of the Nile, the Tigris, the Euphrates, the Indus, the Huanghe and the Changjiang, too swampy for primitive farming, now became very fertile regions where the first urban civilizations appeared. This progress made it possible to produce a surplus of food which formed the vital economic basis for the birth of the first towns.

The invention of the wheel led to that of the cart, and the invention of the sail was the foundation of seafaring. Long-distance transport became possible. Another major invention was that of metallurgy. The first traces of metalwork in western Asia are to be found between 9,000 and 8,000 years ago, but metallurgy was also separately discovered in the Balkans a little more than 7,000 years ago, and about a thousand years later in Italy and the Iberian peninsula.

Second, the self-sufficiency of Neolithic villages, whose economies had been essentially self-contained, gradually broke down following the inventions just mentioned. Surplus production enabled exchanges to be established between different communities so that consumer goods, raw materials and, soon afterwards, luxury and prestige items as well, could be obtained. By seizing this surplus, military and religious heads were able to organize or finance trade expeditions to acquire, often from far away, certain raw materials or luxury products that would enhance their social prestige. This increase in trade is very characteristic of the period in question here. Certain urban areas of this period owed their prosperity to it.

Third and finally, there was a considerable increase in the social stratification that had started in the Early Neolithic. The rulers and priests in close alliance concentrated all economic and political power in their own hands. The peasants were deprived of their fields and cattle, which were often declared the property of the gods. Myths that explained farming as having been revealed to people by a kind deity obviously contributed to this situation since priests were the intermediaries between the gods and people, and rulers were considered as the representative of the gods on earth or even as gods incarnate (for instance in Egypt).

The peasants were reduced to the level of ordinary farmers, obliged to deliver a portion of their harvests or cattle to the Palace or Temple every year. The submission of the great majority of the population to a small minority and the emergence of a strong central authority were fraught with consequences. Only a strong authority could have major works undertaken such as irrigation, drainage and fortifications, already mentioned, or organize the construction of 'prestigious' monuments like temples, palaces and monumental tombs, of no direct economic benefit. The central authority forced the peasant masses to overproduce and the surplus (further increased by the cultivation of excessively swampy land, through irrigation and drainage) went to the ruling classes as farm rent. The great majority of craftsmen now worked for these rulers and priests, as they were the only ones who could acquire 'expensive' objects, especially those made of metal. Craftsmen, who were paid in kind, were of a higher social standing than peasants. Among them, metalworkers and jewellers were in a privileged position. On a higher level still were the soldiers, paid by the ruler, in whose exclusive service they were, and civil servants, vital for administration, such as the collection of taxes in kind, drawing up tax farming contracts and so on. It was to meet the needs of this bureaucracy that arithmetical and writing systems were developed. Only one social class, the traders, had been able to preserve some degree of independence. The ruling classes needed them for the import of both raw materials and luxury and prestige goods.

We have already pointed out that war was one of the adverse consequences of the Neolithic way of life, and here is where we must look for the origin of the warrior class and its power. As the military power of rulers grew, they strove to increase their wealth and power still further. They often set about conquering the territories of neighbouring communities to lay hands on their natural resources and the surpluses produced there. The most striking example of such imperialism comes from Egypt, which, at the end of the Predynastic period, was unified after a war of conquest of this kind.

This unification of Egypt also marks the chronological limits of the first volume of the *History of Humanity*. At that time a few scattered regions had just reached the threshold of what is conventionally called the 'historical' period. Others were still rapidly evolving towards this urban stage and reached it a few centuries later. Yet others had hardly reached the Neolithic stage, and various circumstances would stop or slow down their subsequent development. Again, certain groups of hunter-gatherers, still occupying extremely vast areas, were so well adapted to their natural environment that they had not yet felt the need to adopt the Neolithic way of life. In succeeding volumes, the authors will obviously have to take into account this diachronic development of civilizations.

A last remark must be made. It has often been written that the period characterized by the birth of the first towns marks not only the beginning of the 'historical' period but also the *beginnings of civilization*. This is, for instance, the title of the second part of Volume I of the first editon of this work, published under the title of the *History of Mankind*, more than a quarter of a century ago, at a time when, for the majority of historians, history could not be conceived without written sources and when many of them ignored the contributions of prehistoric archaeology and anthropology to the knowledge of the periods before the invention of writing.

Therefore, it is not at all suprising that these 'traditional' historians, observing that the beginnings of writing coincided with the appearance of the prestigious civilizations of Egypt and western Asia, saw a relationship of cause and effect between the two.

It would, of course, be erroneous to minimize the importance of the invention of the first system of writing, but this is only one of the cultural aspects that characterize these civilizations; other aspects are at least as important, or even more so, than the first texts. In fact, the great majority of these other aspects originated during the 8,000 years or so which elapsed from the beginnings of food production to the beginnings of the Dynastic period in Egypt and the first kingdoms of Mesopotamia.

Without going into the problems raised by the exact meaning of the concept of 'civilization', we will mention here some of the material, social and economic aspects of civilization revealed by prehistoric archaeology. The progress in agriculture and especially the techniques of irrigation and drainage made it possible to cultivate the wide river valleys where the 'first civilizations' were to develop. The construction of the Maltese temples and large Megalithic monuments necessitated finding solutions to enormous technical and transport problems, without which the construction of the impressive monuments of Egypt and Mesopotamia (pyramids, ziggurats, temples) would not have been possible. The first states were developed during the preceding millennia. The plastic arts, both figurative and abstract, have produced remarkable works that are much older than those of the Nile, Tigris and Euphrates valleys.

To be objective, it must be said that the 'first civilizations' also had some negative aspects, especially in the field of 'moral civilization', which have their roots in the Neolithic and pre-urban period. One striking example will suffice: the 'imperialistic' policies of the first states and the practically uninterrupted existence of wars and armed conflicts: this is a heritage of the prehistoric period.

In short, the beginnings of civilization do not at all coincide with the invention of writing, but they go back practically, in nearly all their facets, to the last millennia of the prehistoric period.

INDEX

Bold page numbers refer to figures and maps; plate numbers are in **bold** and are prefixed by **Pl.** or **Pls**

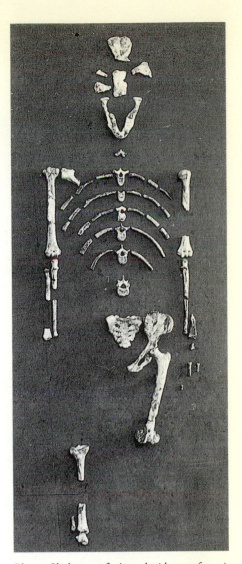

Plate 1 Fossilized imprint of the skeleton of an *Oreopithecus* on a sheet of lignite, Baccinello, Province of Grossetto (Italy). (Courtesy Musée de l'Homme, Paris, France.)

Plate 2 Skeleton of *Australopithecus afarensis* ('Lucy'), about 3 million years old, discovered in 1974 at Hadar, in the Afar depression (Ethiopia). (National Museum, Addis-Ababa, Ethiopia.)

Plate 3 Skulls of *Australopithecus boisei* (or *robustus*), left, and *Australopithecus africanus* (or *gracilis*), right. (Photo D. Geraads.)

Plate 4 Artefacts of *Homo erectus*. (Photo D. Geraads.)

Plate 5 Melka Kunturé. The Developed Oldowan site of Gomboré I (1.6 million years ago). Detail of the living-floor, with stone artefacts, hippopotamus tooth and other bones. (Photo J. Chavaillon.)

Plate 6 Melka Kunturé. The Developed Oldowan site of Garba IV (1.4 million years ago). Detail of the living-floor, with stones serving as chopping blocks, pelvis of an elephant and hippopotamus ribs. (Photo J. Chavaillon.)

Plate 7 Melka Kunturé. Upper Acheulean site of Garba I (about 500,000 years old). Detail: cleaver and bifaces. (Photo J. Chavaillon.)

Plate 8 Melka Kunturé. Upper Acheulean site of Garba I. Cleaver (scale in cm). (Photo J. Chavaillon.)

Plate 9 Melka Kunturé. Early Acheulean site of Garba XII – limits of a structure (constructed shelter?). (Photo J. Chavaillon.)

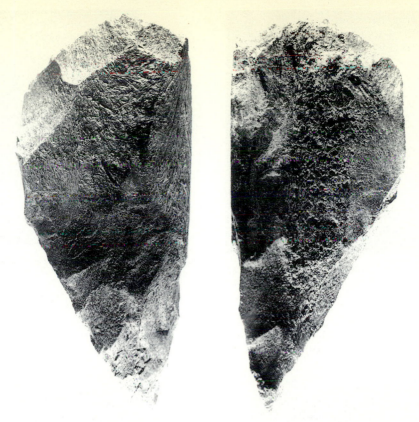

Plate 10 Castel di Guido (Italy). Bone biface. (Courtesy A. M. Radmilli.)

Plate 11 Partly reconstructed skull of 'Peking Man' (*Sinanthropus, Homo erectus*). The original anterior and posterior parts were found in Zhoukoudian locus H (China) in 1966. (Photo Wu Rukang.)

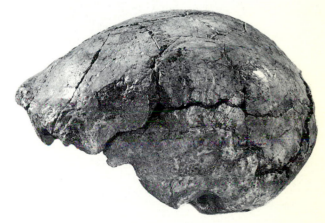

Plate 12 Skull-cap (lateral view) of *Homo erectus* cranium found in Hexian County, Province of Anhui (China) in 1980. (Photo Wu Rukang.)

Plate 13 Skull-cap of *Pithecanthropus* (*Homo erectus javensis*) found in 1891 by E. Dubois in Trinil, Java (Indonesia). (Courtesy National Museum of Natural History, Leiden, the Netherlands.)

Plate 14 Neanderthal brain-pan (Germany), the first Neanderthal fossil, discovered in 1856. (Courtesy Musée de l'Homme, Paris, France.)

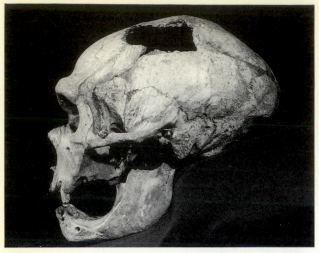

Plate 15 The Chapelle-aux-Saints skull. The Chapelle-aux-Saints (France) skeleton was discovered in 1909. It served as a basis for the first description of the Neanderthal type: low-vaulted receding skull, strong brow ridges, powerful face, etc. Despite their very specific features, the Neanderthalers are now classified in the same species as present-day humans (*Homo sapiens neanderthalensis*). (Courtesy Musée de l'Homme, Paris, France.)

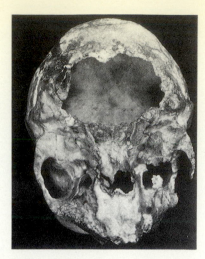

Plate 16 The Monte Circeo skull (Italy). (Courtesy Bouvier Verlag, Bonn, Germany.)

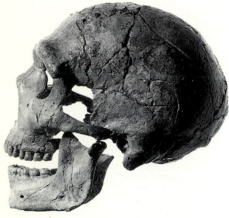

Plate 17 The Amud skull (Israel). The Amud skeleton is a good example of Neanderthalers of Western Asia. The skull, compared with that of Chapelle-aux-Saints (see Plate 15) is higher, more rounded at the back, and the face is less voluminous. The Neanderthal features are attenuated as compared to those of the European population. (Israel Antiquities Authority, Jerusalem.)

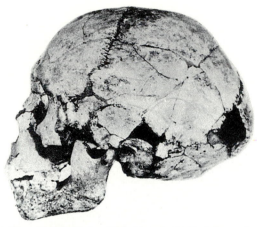

Plate 18 The Teshik-Tash (Uzbekistan) skull belonged to a Neanderthal child of about 9 years of age. According to some anthropologists it shows some progressive features, but this is not generally accepted. (Institute of Archaeology of the All-Russian Academy of Sciences, Moscow.)

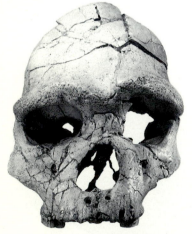

Plate 19 The Caume de l'Arago at Tautavel skull (France) ('Tautavel skull' or 'Arago skull') dates back more than 300,000 years. Although the morphology is still very archaic, it already has some Neanderthal features, which allow its placement in this phyletic line. The Neanderthalers began to differentiate in Europe between 400,000 and 300,000 years ago. (Courtesy Musée de l'Homme, Paris.)

Plate 20 Skull-back from Swanscombe (United Kingdom). The back of this skull is also a very early example of the Neanderthal phyletic line, but the morphology of the occipital bone is already characteristic. (National History Museum, London, United Kingdom.)

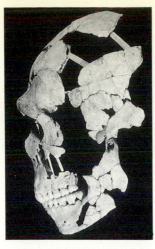

Plate 21 The Saint-Césaire skull (France) is the last Neander-thaler known to date. It was found in a level of the beginning of the Upper Palaeolithic (Châtelperronian) and was contemporaneous with the first European Modern humans. Its age can be estimated at about 32,000 years. (Photo B. Vandermeersch.)

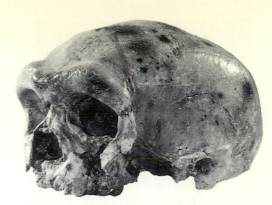

Plate 22 Skull of early *Homo sapiens* found in Dali County, Shaanxi (China), in 1978. (Photo Wu Rukang. Institute of Vertebrate Palaeontology and Paleoanthropology, Beijing.)

Plate 23 Skull of an early *Homo sapiens* found in Maba village, Shaoguan County, Guangdong Province (China), in 1958. (Photo Wu Rukang.)

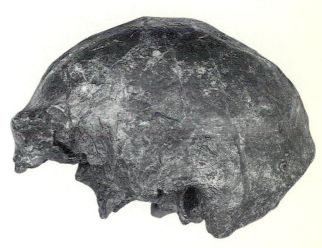

Plate 24 Brain-pan no. 6 from Ngandong, Java (Indonesia). Eleven brain-pans were found in 1931 at Ngandong, a village in central Java, on the Solo river. *Homo soloensis* is more advanced than *Homo erectus javensis* (see Plate 13), but still belongs to the species *Homo erectus.* (Senckenberg Museum and Research Institute, Frankfurt on Main, Germany.)

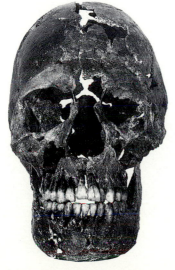

Plate 25 The Qafzeh 9 skull (Israel), although contemporaneous with the Neanderthalers, shows many similarities to Cro-Magnon skulls and is considered to belong to a *Homo sapiens sapiens.* (Photo B. Vandermeersch.)

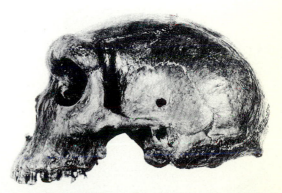

Plate 26 The Kabwe (Broken Hill) skull probably goes back to more than 130,000 years ago. It still shows many *Homo erectus* features, but its cranial capacity and some other features are of the Modern type. The Broken Hill skull is considered to be that of an archaic *Homo sapiens.* (National History Museum, London, United Kingdom.)

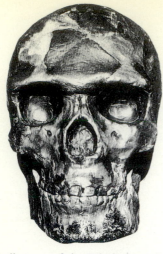

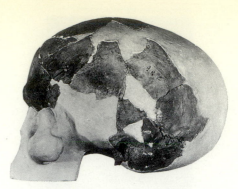

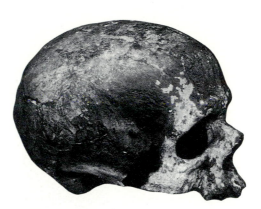

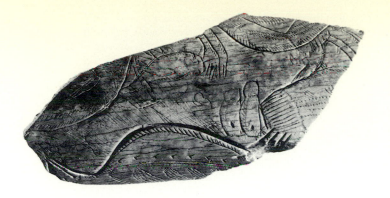

Plate 33 Grasshopper carved on a fragment of bone (length 3 cm), Grotte des Trois Frères, Ariège (France), Magdalenian. (Musée de l'Homme, Paris, France.)

Plate 34 Horses and aurochs in Lascaux cave, Dordogne (France). (Photo N. Aujoulat. Centre National de Préhistoire, Périgueux, France.)

Plate 36 Fragment of a *bâton de commandement* representing a bison's head, Grotte d'Isturiz, Basses-Pyrénées (France), Magdalenian. (Courtesy Musée des Antiquités Nationales, Saint-Germain-en-Laye, France.)

Plate 35 *La Dame à la capuche* – Venus head in mammoth ivory (height 3.65 cm), Grotte du Pape, Brassempouy, Département des Landes (France), Gravettian. (Courtesy Musée des Antiquités Nationales, Saint-Germain-en-Laye, France.)

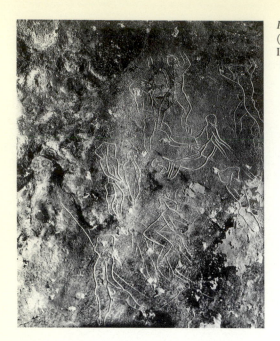

Plate 37 Group of dancing(?) figures, Addaura cave, Palermo, Sicily (Italy), Epigravettian. (Courtesy Museo Archaeologico Palermo, Italy.)

Plate 38 Wall figures from the Kapova (or Shulgantash) cave, southern Urals (Russian Federation). (Institute of Archaeology of the All-Russian Academy of Sciences, Moscow.)

Plate 39 Female statuette from Malta, Siberia (Russian Federation). (Institute of Archaeology of the All-Russian Academy of Sciences, Moscow.)

Plate 40 Decorated piece of bone (length 11 cm), Abri Blanchard-des-Roches, Dordogne (France). Aurignacian. The dotted lines on the right half are sometimes interpreted as a lunar calendar (by A. Marshack *inter alia*). (Courtesy Musée des Antiquités Nationales, Saint-Germain-en-Laye, France.)

Plate 41 Large engraved slab with an animal figure, Abri du Renne, Belcayre, Dordogne (France), Aurignacian. (Musée National de Préhistoire, Les Eyzies-de-Tayac, France.)

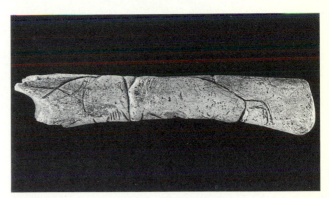

Plate 42 Engraved bison (length 60 cm), Grotte de la Grèze, Dordogne (France), Gravettian. (Photo N. Aujoulat. Centre National de Préhistoire, Périgueux, France.)

Plate 43 Fragment of a *bâton de commandement* made of reindeer antler, representing two mammoths face to face, Abri de Laugerie-Haute, Dordogne (France), Gravettian or Solutrean. (Musée National de Préhistoire, Les Eyzies de Tayac, France.)

Plate 44 Carving of a hare (length 23 cm), Grotte du Gabillou, Dordogne (France), Magdalenian. (Photo N. Aujoulat. Centre National de Préhistoire, Périgueux, France.)

Plate 45 Painting in black of a bull (length 3 m) superimposed on earlier paintings, Lascaux cave, Dordogne (France), Magdalenian. (Photo N. Aujoulat. Centre National de Préhistoire, Périgueux, France.)

Plate 46 Large dwelling structure at Eynan, Mallaha. Note the post holes. (Photo O. Bar-Yosef.)

Plate 47 Burial of a woman with a puppy at Eynan, Mallaha. (Photo O. Bar-Yosef.)

Plate 48 Upper Palaeolithic artefacts from Renigunta (south India), burins and retouched blades. (Courtesy M. L. K. Murty.)

Plate 49 Waisted stone axe from Papua New Guinea. It is at least 37,000 years old. Wear marks are visible between the lateral notches, indicating that a binding was used to haft the axehead to a handle. (Courtesy L. Groube.)

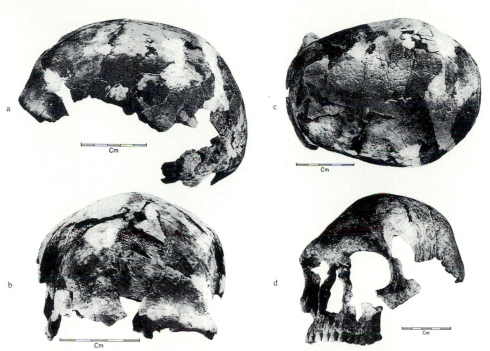

Plate 50 Gracile skull from Lake Mungo, New South Wales, compared with Kow Swamp I. The three views of Lake Mungo I cranium are: a, left lateral; b, frontal; c, vertical. Kow Swamp, d. The thin bone, rounded forehead and lack of brow ridges of Mungo I are characteristic of gracile early Australians. (Photo D. Markovic; after Thorne and Macumber, 1972.)

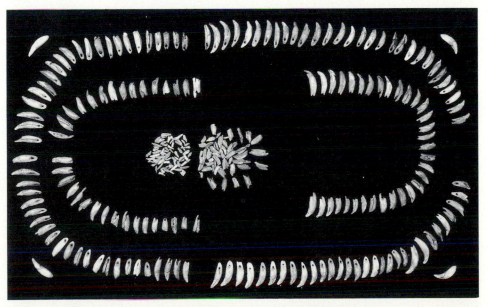

Plate 51 Necklace from the Lake Nitchie burial, New South Wales. The Lake Nitchie man wore a unique necklace of 178 pierced Tasmanian devil teeth, taken from at least forty-seven different animals. Each tooth is pierced by a hole that was ground and gouged out. (The Australian Museum.)

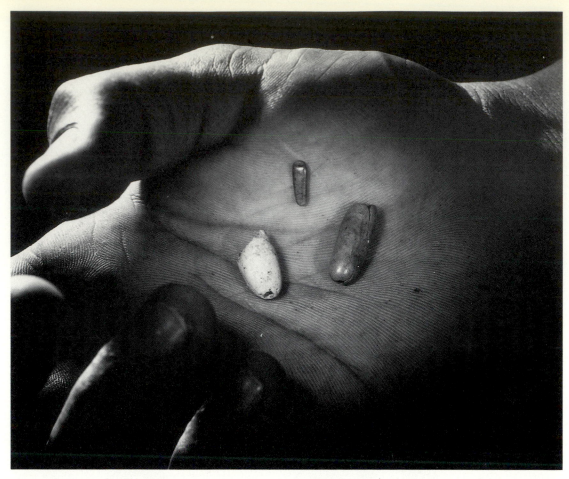

Plate 52 Bone beads, 15,000 years old, excavated from the cave of Devil's Lair (Western Australia). The right-hand bead is 21 mm long. (Courtesy C. Dortch.)

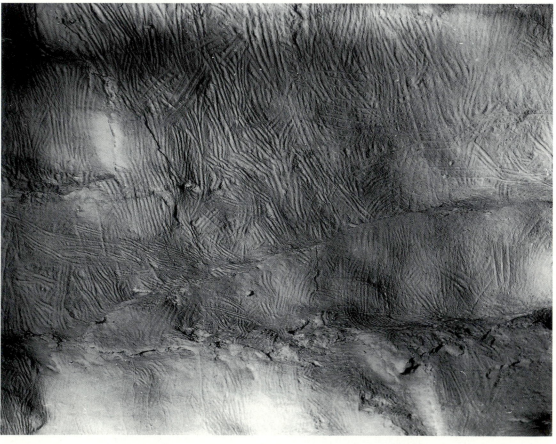

Plate 53 Wall markings in Koonalda cave (South Australia). (Courtesy R. Edwards.)

Plate 54 Prehistoric pecked engravings of emu, bird and kangaroo tracks at Mootwingee in western New South Wales. (Courtesy R. Edwards.)

Plate 55 Boomerang, 10,000 years old, being excavated from Wyrie Swamp (South Australia). (Courtesy R. Luebbers.)

Plate 56 Artefacts of the Archaeolithic. (Photo INAH, Mexico.)

Plate 57 Artefacts of the Lower Cenolithic. (Photo INAH, Mexico.)

Plate 58 Points of the Upper Cenolithic. (Photo INAH, Mexico.)

Plate 59 Rock drawings of Neolithic hunting scenes in the Western Desert (Egypt) ('Earliest Hunters' style). (Courtesy Archaeological Museum, Poznań, Poland.)

Plate 60 Rock paintings of Neolithic cattle husbandry at Jebel Uweinat (Libya) ('Uweinat Cattle-Breeders' style). (Photo F. van Noten.)

Plate 61 Anthropomorphic Neolithic figurine from Merimde (Egypt). (Courtesy German Archaeological Institute, Cairo Branch, Egypt.)

Plate 62 Rock figure with 'ritual boat', Gerzean (Egypt). (Courtesy Archaeological Museum, Poznań, Poland.)

Plate 63 Grave goods from Minshat Abu Omar, eastern Delta (Egypt). (Courtesy D. Wildung.)

Plate 64 Typical Neolithic rock art with cattle and human figures from Jubbah (Saudi Arabia), depicted in low relief. (Photo Department of Antiquities and Museums, Riyadh, Saudi Arabia.)

Plate 65 Human figure with distinctive long hair and a dagger from Bi'r Hima (Saudi Arabia). Possibly dated to Late Chalcolithic or Early Bronze Age. (Photo Department of Antiquities and Museums, Riyadh, Saudi Arabia.)

Plate 66 Polychrome vase from Mehrgarh (Pakistan). (Department of Archaeology, Pakistan.)

Plate 67 Anthropomorphic figurines from Mehrgarh (Pakistan). (Department of Archaeology, Pakistan.)

Plate 68 Sherds of two face urns (Final Neolithic), Voznesenska culture, Lower Amur (Russian Federation). (Courtesy Institute of History, Philology and Philosophy, Novosibirsk, Russian Federation.)

Plate 69 Clay model of a Middle Neolithic house from Krannon, Thessaly (Greece). (Courtesy Volos Museum, Greece.)

Plate 70 Early Neolithic monochrome ware from Corinth (Greece). (Courtesy Corinth Museum, Greece.)

Plate 71 Early Neolithic 'Early painted' ware from Sesklo, Thessaly (Greece). (Courtesy Volos Museum, Greece.)

Plate 72 Middle Neolithic painted cup of the 'Solid style' from Tzani Magoula, Thessaly (Greece). (Courtesy Volos Museum, Greece.)

Plate 73 Late Neolithic polychrome ware from Dimini, Thessaly (Greece). (Courtesy National Archaeological Museum, Athens, Greece.)

Plate 74 Late Neolithic incised ware from Dimini, Thessaly (Greece). (National Archaeological Museum, Athens, Greece.)

Plate 75 Early Neolithic marble figurine from Knossos, Crete (Greece). (Courtesy Herakleion Museum, Crete, Greece.)

Plate 76 Crouched figure carved on a flat pebble from Karamourlar Magoula, Thessaly (Greece). (Courtesy Volos Museum, Greece.)

Plate 77 Early Neolithic marble female figurine from Sparta (Greece). (Courtesy National Archaeological Museum, Athens, Greece.)

Plate 78 Middle Neolithic clay figurine of a female seated figure from the Pharsala region, Thessaly (Greece). (Courtesy Volos Museum, Greece.)

Plate 80 Vase of Serra d'Alto type with handle in form of a stylized bull's head, Sette Ponti, Matera (Italy). (Courtesy Museum D. Ridola, Matera, Italy.)

Plate 79 Cardial ware from Montserrat, Catalonia (Spain). (Courtesy Montserrat Abbey, Spain.)

Plate 81 Lamalou passage grave, Rouet, Hérault (France). (Courtesy A. Colomer.)

Plate 82 Sa Coveccada chamber tomb with entrance in form of door and rectangular chamber, Sardinia (Italy). (Photo J. Guilaine.)

Plate 83 Tarxien temples: general view of the architectural complex (Malta). (Photo J. Guilaine.)

Plate 84 Walls and barbican of Los Millares, Santa Fe de Mondujar (Spain). (Photo J. Guilaine.)

Plate 85 'Statue-menhir' (height 1.22 m) from Rosseironne, Gard (France). (Photo J. Guilaine.)

Plate 86 Head carved on a river pebble (known as 'Danubius'), Lepenski Vir (Serbia). (Courtesy Lepenski Vir Museum, Serbia.)

Plate 87 Tulip-shaped vase from Azmasuka Moguila, region of Stara Zagora (Bulgaria), Karanovo I culture. Red ground decorated with a geometrical pattern in white (height 16.5 cm). (Courtesy Regional Historical Museum, Stara Zagora, Bulgaria.)

Plate 88 Vase with floral decoration, Anzabegovo. (Courtesy Macedonian Museum, Skopje.)

Plate 89 Zoomorphic vase from Mouldava, region of Plovdiv (Bulgaria), Karanovo I civilization. Red ground with white decoration. (Courtesy Archaeological Museum, Plovdiv, Bulgaria.)

Plate 90 Model of house, Porodin. (Courtesy National Museum, Bitolj.)

Plate 91 Statuette known as 'Vidov-danka' Vinča (Serbia). (Courtesy Belgrade National Museum, Serbia.)

Plate 92 Figurines: male (the 'Thinker') and female, Hamangia (Romania). (Courtesy Archaeological Museum, Bucharest, Romania.)

Plate 93 Vase with spiral meander from Butmir (Bosnia). (Courtesy National Museum, Sarajevo, Bosnia.)

Plate 94 Vessel painted with graphite, Azmasuka Moguila, region of Stara Zagora (Bulgaria), Marića civilization. (Courtesy Regional Historical Museum, Stara Zagora, Bulgaria.)

Plate 95 Cucuteni-A vase, Cucuteni (Romania). (Courtesy Archaeological Museum, Bucharest, Romania.)

Plate 96 Zoomorphic gold pendants, Varna necropolis, Varna (Bulgaria). (Courtesy Historical Museum, Varna, Bulgaria.)

Plate 97 Bone idol, Cascioarele (Romania). (Courtesy Archae-ological Museum, Bucharest, Romania.)

Plate 98 Altar, Truşeşti (Romania). (Courtesy Archaeological Museum, Bucharest, Romania.)

Plate 99 Vase in the form of a bird, from Vučedol (Croatia). (Courtesy Archaeological Museum, Zagreb, Croatia.)

Plate 100 Statuette of an elk, Sperrings culture, Karelia (Russian Federation). (Photo N. Merpert.)

Plate 101 Spoon in the form of a goose, Sperrings culture, Karelia (Russian Federation). (Photo N. Merpert.)

Plate 102 Petroglyphs, Late Neolithic Karelian culture (Russian Federation). (After V. Ravdonikas, 1936–8.)

Plate 103 Petroglyphs, Late Neolithic Karelian culture (Russian Federation). (After V. Ravdonikas, 1936–8.)

Plate 104 Middle Neolithic megalithic cairn, Bougon-Fo, Deux-Sèvres (France). (Courtesy Musée des Antiquités Nationales, Saint-Germain-en-Laye, France.)

Plate 105 Passage grave with cruciform plan at Faldouet, Jersey (United Kingdom). (Jersey Museum Service, Jersey, Channel Islands, United Kingdom.)

Plate 106 Menhir du Champ Dolent, Dol-de-Bretagne, Ille-et-Vilaine (France). (Photo Jos le Doaré.)

Plate 107 Ornamented stone of a Late Neolithic megalithic angled grave, Luffang-en-Crac'h, Morbihan (France). (Photo Jos le Doaré.)

Plate 108 Alignments of Menec, Carnac, Morbihan (France). (Photo Jos le Doaré.)

Plate 109 Megalithic tomb of the Cotswolds–Severn type with cruciform plan, under a long barrow, lateral view, Wayland's Smithy, Berkshire (United Kingdom). (Photo Richard Muir.)

Plate 110 Late Neolithic village, Skara Brae, Mainland Orkney (United Kingdom). (Photo Richard Muir.)

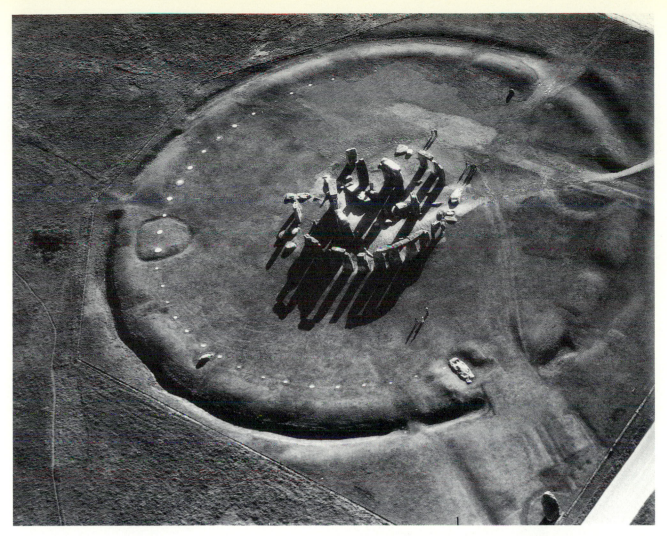

Plate 111 Stonehenge, Wiltshire (United Kingdom), from the air. (Cambridge University, Collection of Air Photographs, United Kingdom.)

Plate 112 Pot of the Ertebølle-Ellerbek culture. (National Museum, Copenhagen, Denmark.)

Plate 113 Typical Early Neolithic grave, Esbjerg (Denmark). (National Museum, Copenhagen, Denmark.)

Plate 114 Thin-butted flint axe, with its handle. (National Museum, Copenhagen, Denmark.)

Plate 115 Vase of the Funnel–Beaker civilization of Asmåsa, Sövde parish, Färs härad (Sweden). (Courtesy Lunds Universitets Historiska Museum, Sweden.)

Plate 116 Pottery of the Baalberge group, Dölauer Heide (Germany). (Courtesy Halle Museum, Germany.)

Plate 117 Middle Neolithic pottery, Baalberge group (Germany). (Courtesy Halle Museum, Germany.)

Plate 118 Pottery and battle-axe, Walternienburg group (Germany). (Courtesy Halle Museum, Germany.)

Plate 119 Pottery of the Salzmünde group, Rössen, Kreis Merseburg (Germany). (Courtesy Halle Museum, Germany.)

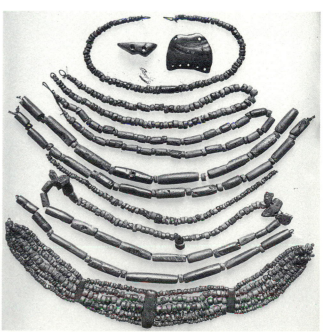

Plate 120 Vase with amber beads found in a peatbog, Sortekaer Ringköbing (Denmark). (National Museum, Copenhagen, Denmark.)

Plate 137 Foundations of a 'mortuary' or 'cult house', Tustrup, Jutland (Denmark). (Photo Poul Kjaerum. Forhistorisk Museum, Moesgård, Höjbjerg, Denmark.)

Plate 138 Opening of shaft, Grimes Graves, Norfolk (United Kingdom). (Courtesy British Museum, London, United Kingdom.)

Plate 139 Base of shaft No. 1 showing gallery entrances, Grimes Graves, Norfolk (United Kingdom). (English Heritage, London, United Kingdom.)

Plate 140 Part of an antler being used to support the roof of a mine gallery, Grimes Graves, Norfolk (United Kingdom). (Courtesy British Museum, London, United Kingdom.)